# The Complete Directory for People with Disabilities

# 2013
## Twenty-First Edition

# The Complete Directory for People with Disabilities

## A Comprehensive Source Book for Individuals and Professionals

A SEDGWICK PRESS Book

Grey House Publishing

PUBLISHER: Leslie Mackenzie
EDITORIAL DIRECTOR: Laura Mars

PRODUCTION MANAGER: Kristen Thatcher
PRODUCTION ASSISTANT: Dawn Jenkins
COMPOSITION: David Garoogian
MARKETING DIRECTOR: Jessica Moody

A Sedgewick Press Book
Grey House Publishing, Inc.
4919 Route 22
Amenia, NY 12501
518.789.8700
FAX 845.373.6390
www.greyhouse.com
e-mail: books @greyhouse.com



First edition published 1991
Twenty-first edition published 2012

The complete directory for people with disabilities : products, resources, books, services.-1992-2012

1. People with disabilities-Services for-United States-Directories. 2. People with disabilities-Services for-United States-Periodicals. 3. Disabled Persons-United States-Bibliography. 4. Disabled Persons-United States-Directory. 5. Information Services-United States-Bibliography. 6. Information Services-United States-Directory. 7. Mental Retardation-Rehabilitation-United States-Bibliography. 8. Mental Retardation-Rehabilitation-United States-Directory. 9. Rehabilitation-United States-Bibliography. 10. Rehabilitation-United States-Directory. I. Title: Directory for people with disabilities.

HV1553.C58
362.4/048/02573 92-658843

Printed in Canada
ISBN 13: 1-59237-872-2 Softcover

# Table of Contents



## SECTION 1: General Resources for People with Disabilities

## SECTION 2:
## Resources for People with Specific Disabilities

# Introduction

This 21st edition of the award-winning *Complete Directory for People with Disabilities* is an invaluable resource for all those living with a disability and all those committed to empowering these individuals. It offers thousands of ways for people with disabilities to succeed at work, in school, and in their community. Coverage includes Associations, Products, Camps, Living Facilities, Print and Electronic Resources and much more. The comprehensive Table of Contents guides you through the 27 chapters and more than 100 subchapters contained in this rich resource.

Careful research and compilation of the best data available maintains the reputation of *The Complete Directory for People with Disabilities* among educators, librarians and the disability community. This resource is a repeat recipient of the **National Mature Media Award** and the **National Health Information Award**.

Sure to save hours of Internet research time, *The Complete Directory for People with Disabilities* provides comprehensive, critical and immediate information in one source that can be accessed quickly and easily. This edition provides 9,009 descriptive listings, and numbers are up for specific data points: 18,934 key contacts; 8,208 fax numbers; 6,583 e-mail addresses; 8,283 web sites. In addition, a Disability-related Glossary follows this Introduction.

Following the listings are three indexes to provide quick, easy access to the data:

- **Entry Index**: Lists all directory listings alphabetically.
- **Geographic Index**: Organizes listings alphabetically by state.
- **Subject Index**: Organizes directory listings by relevant alphabetical topics, i.e. autism , language disorders.

In addition to the print directory, *The Complete Directory for People with Disabilities* is available for subscription on G.O.L.D., Grey House OnLine Databases. This gives you immediate access to the most valuable disability industry contacts in the United States, plus offers easy-to-use keyword searches, organization type and subject searches, hotlinks to web sites and emails, and so much more. Call 800-562-2139 for a free trial or visit http://gold.greyhouse.com for more information.

We welcome your comments, and look forward to another year of serving the disability community.

**Praise for previous editions**:

> *"Recommended [for] all levels."*
>
> —CHOICE

> *"...thousands of resources...covering a diverse range of services...separate section for specific disabilities...from aging to mobility and from the blind and deaf to speech and language disorders. Libraries...will want to consider..."*
>
> —Against the Grain

> *"...will definitely help you answer the 'where can I find' questions about disabilities."*
>
> —Doody's Book Reviews

> *"...massive guide...three extensive indexes...valuable resource for public and academic libraries [and] social service professionals in related fields."*
>
> —ARBA

# Bullying and Students with Disabilities

*A Briefing Paper from the National Council on Disability*

Authors[1]:
*Dr. Jonathan Young*
Chairman, National Council on Disability
*Ari Ne'eman*
Vice Chair for Engagement, National Council on Disability
*Sara Gelser,*
Member, National Council on Disability

Like bullying in general, bullying of students with disabilities represents both a civil rights and public health challenge. Amongst the possible effects of bullying the U.S. Department of Education (DOE, 2010) includes lowered academic achievement and aspirations, increased anxiety, loss of self-esteem and confidence, depression and post-traumatic stress, deterioration in physical health, self-harm and suicidal thinking, suicide, feelings of alienation, absenteeism and other negative impacts, both educational and health related. While both students with and without disabilities face significant negative emotional, educational and physical results from bullying, students with disabilities are both uniquely vulnerable and disproportionately impacted by the bullying phenomena. Despite this, there exists a dearth of both research and policy focusing on eliminating the bullying of students with disabilities. Furthermore, evidence suggests that existing legal and policy tools available to address bullying against students with disabilities remain significantly under-utilized. Additional focus is needed on the bullying of students with disabilities, both as part of a general strategy of bullying prevention efforts and as a specific area of focus in policy and practice.

**Background**

In 1970, only one in every five children with disabilities received a public education and many states had laws specifically excluding particular disability categories (i.e., children who were deaf, blind, with intellectual disabilities, or emotional disturbance) from public education (DOE). As a result of landmark court cases such as *PARC v. Pennsylvania (1971),* it was established that the 14$^{th}$ Amendment's equal protection clause required that students with disabilities have the same opportunity to receive a free and appropriate public education as students without disabilities and that, wherever possible, placement in a regular public school class should be the preference. Public Law 94-142 (1975), known then as the Education for All Handicapped Children Act and today Public Law 108-446, the Individuals with Disabilities Education Improvement Act (IDEA) of 2004, created both a legal and funding infrastructure to help ensure that students with disabilities would enjoy the right to a "free and appropriate public education" in the "least restrictive environment." As a result, many more students with disabilities began to attend and be educated in general education schools and classrooms and thus interacted more with students without disabilities.

[1] With thanks to Dr. Gerrie Hawkins of the National Council on Disability Staff for support and assistance in research and drafting

Research confirms that students with disabilities benefit from being included in the same school settings as their non-disabled peers and that segregated programs fail to demonstrate greater effectiveness (Lipsky, 1997; Buckley, 2000; and Sailor, 2002). Furthermore, research suggests that students without disabilities may also benefit from inclusion and that, when properly implemented, inclusion of students with disabilities does not negatively impact student test scores, grades, the amount of allocated and engaged instructional time or the rate of interruption to planned activities (York, Vandercook, MacDonald, Heise-Neff, and Caughey, 1992). Despite this, the increased inclusion of students with disabilities, while the right policy and legal decision, necessitates additional efforts to ensure welcoming school environments for students with disabilities. As demonstrated by both the all too frequent bullying experiences students with disabilities continue to face and the slow progress in fully integrating students with disabilities in public schools (NCD, 2008) across the country, such welcoming environments have not always been forthcoming.

**Literature Review**

Studies show that students with visible and non-visible disabilities are subject to more bullying than non-disabled peers (Carter and Spencer, 2006). Bullying is frequently a direct result of a student's disability (Whitney, Smith & Thompson, 1994). Students with disabilities are disproportionately likely to face peer rejection, a significant risk factor for victimization (Martlew & Hodson, 1991; Whitney, et al, 1994; and Hodges and Perry, 1996). Many students with disabilities have significant social skills challenges, either as a core trait of their disability or as a result of social isolation due to segregated environments and/or peer rejection. Such students may be at particular risk for bullying and victimization. For example, Little's (2002) study of U.S. mothers found that 94% of children with a diagnosis of Asperger's Syndrome faced peer victimization, with a broad swatch of different types of victimization including emotional bullying (75%), gang attacks (10%) and nonsexual assaults to the genitals (15%).

Other research (Siebeker, Swearer, and Lieske, 2005; and Regional Education Laboratory, 2010) has indicated that students with a wide range of disabilities face increased bullying victimization, including students with visible and invisible disabilities, students with physical, developmental, intellectual, emotional and sensory disabilities and others. A 2003 study found that 34% of students who report taking medication for ADHD face bullying victimization at least 2-3 times a month, a substantial increase over the rate of bullying victimization from other students surveyed (Unnever and Cornell, 2003). Wiener and Mak (2009) also found high rates of victims among girls with Attention Deficit and Hypertension Disabilities. Langevin, Bortnick, Hammer and Wiebe's (1998), a Canadian study examining the relationship between stuttering and selection as a target for bullying, found that at least 59% of students studied were bullied about their stuttering, 69% of students who stutter were also bullied about other things and that said bullying very frequently takes place on at least a weekly basis.

Evidence suggests that the response of policymakers, educators and researchers to the bullying of students with disabilities has not been nearly sufficient to address the breadth or gravity of the problem. For example, Massachusetts Advocates for Children's (2009) survey of families of children on the autism spectrum found that almost 40% of said children experienced bullying for in excess of a year and that while 92% of parents discussed the bullying with school officials, 68% of families found the response of the school district to be inadequate. Only 21.5% of parents surveyed heard about the bullying from the school, with 80.6% hearing from the student him or herself. Given that many students with disabilities face significant communication barriers and are thus unable to report bullying and victimization themselves, protecting the rights of parents to be informed when their children face incidents of bullying or victimization may be a critical area for future law and practice around bullying. Increased research in this area is also necessary. While the existing literature has clearly established that students with disabilities face higher rates of bullying and victimization than the general student population, very little research on bullying prevention has focused on students with disabilities either in isolation or as an identified sub-category in broader bullying prevention initiatives.

**Who Qualifies as a Student with a Disability?**

One of the first and most important legal questions with respect to bullying and students with disabilities is: who qualifies as a student with a disability? The answer to this question varies depending on the law under question. There are two major definitions of disability that are relevant in the educational context: students with disabilities under Section 504 of the Rehabilitation Act and students with disabilities under IDEA. To be a student with a disability under Section 504, a student must, (1) have a physical or mental impairment that substantially limits one or more major life activities; (2) have a record of such an impairment; or (3) be regarded as having such an impairment (DOE, 2010)." While there does not exist a comprehensive list of what constitutes a physical or mental impairment, the term is intended to be construed broadly. Recently, in the ADA Amendments Act of 2008, Congress provided a non-exhaustive list of major life activities, including but not limited to, "caring for oneself, performing manual tasks, seeing, hearing, eating, sleeping, walking, standing, lifting, bending, speaking, breathing, learning, reading, concentrating, thinking, communicating, and working (ADA, 2008). The ADA Amendments Act makes clear that the ADA's, and as a result Section 504's, definition of disability is intended to be construed very broadly. IDEA's definition of a child with a disability is narrower, in part because of the broader legal rights and educational entitlements available to eligible students under IDEA. Under IDEA, a child with a disability must be evaluated and determined to fall within one of a series of specific, defined disability categories, such as intellectual disability, deafness, blindness, emotional disturbance, autism, specific learning disability and others, and need special education and related services by reason thereof (ADA, 2008).

**Bullying and Existing Disability and Special Education Laws**

Bullying prevention efforts interact in various ways with disability non-discrimination laws, some of which are similar to dynamics around laws protecting other minority groups while others remain unique. In 2000, the Department of Education's Office of Special Education and Rehabilitative Services and Office on Civil Rights issued a joint, "Dear Colleague" letter highlighting the issue of disability harassment, a category within which bullying of students with disabilities is included (DOE, 2000). The letter noted that several laws were relevant to the issue of disability harassment. It notes that educational institutions, including both K-12 schools and institutions of higher education, have a responsibility to ensure equal educational opportunity for all students and that disability harassment denies that right and as a result is a form of discrimination prohibited by Section 504 of the Rehabilitation Act and Title II of the Americans with Disabilities Act. The DOE (2000) letter defines disability harassment as "intimidation or abusive behavior toward a student based on disability that creates a hostile environment by interfering with or denying a student's participation in or receipt of benefits, services, or opportunities in the institution's program…When harassing conduct is sufficiently severe, persistent, or pervasive that it creates a hostile environment, it can violate a student's rights under the Section 504 and Title II regulations…even if there are no tangible effects on the student (DOE, 2000, p. 3)." The letter also notes that failure to address disability harassment may constitute a violation of the Individuals with Disabilities Education Act's (IDEA) guarantee of a Free and Appropriate Public Education (FAPE) for students with disabilities when harassment prevents or diminishes the ability of a student to benefit from his or her education (DOE, 2000. p.4). Although the letter does not say so specifically, bullying of students with disabilities may also constitute a violation of IDEA when it forces a student with a disability into a more restrictive educational setting such as a self-contained classroom or out of district placement in order to benefit from their educational experience, given IDEA's legal right for students with disabilities to receive a Free and Appropriate Public Education (FAPE) in the Least Restrictive Environment (LRE).

More recently, the DOE's (2010) "Dear Colleague" letter included disability in a list of protected classes (e.g., race, gender, disability) from which schools must respond to bullying and harassment on the basis of. The DOE (2010) letter spelled out the legal obligations schools possess under existing civil rights laws, including Section 504 of the Rehabilitation Act and Title II of the Americans with Disabilities Act and provided examples of various types of harassment and bullying against protected classes as well as potential school responses. Among the responses mentioned in the context of disability include "disciplinary action against the harassers, consultation with the district's Section 504/Title II coordinator to ensure a comprehensive and effective response, special training for staff on recognizing and effectively responding to harassment of students with disabilities, and monitoring to ensure that the harassment did not resume (DOE, 2010)."

It should be noted that while DOE 2010 speaks primarily of harassment on the basis of protected class status, IDEA's FAPE and LRE provisions may impose upon school districts a legal responsibility to act to protect students with disabilities eligible under IDEA from more general bullying and harassment as well. IDEA does not simply require districts to protect students with disabilities from bullying, harassment and overt discrimination on the basis of disability, but also creates an entitlement to a "free and appropriate public education in the least restrictive environment" which frequently requires funding related services, making educational accommodations and modifications as well as working to address issues such as school climate, access needs and other factors that might hinder a student's ability to fully benefit from their education in the least restrictive environment possible. For example, when bullying of a student with a disability results in a student being transferred into a self-contained classroom or a special education school serving only students with disabilities as opposed to receiving an education in a general classroom setting, a student's IDEA LRE rights may have been violated regardless of the type of bullying that precipitated the change in placement. As research shows that students with disabilities are not only subject to bullying and harassment on the basis of disability, but also are frequently more vulnerable to bullying and harassment of a more general nature as well, it is important that the potentially broader protections of IDEA are made use of for this population.

IDEA is relevant to the issue of bullying of students with disabilities in at least two additional respects. First, the Individualized Education Plan process represents a potentially useful avenue to address bullying through both pro-active and reactive measures. Under IDEA, students with disabilities receive an Individualized Education Plan (IEP) as a result of a deliberative process involving educators, administrators, child study team members, parents and, where appropriate, the student. The IEP outlines the student's educational plan, accommodations, related services and goals for the year. The IEP can be useful both for helping students develop useful self-advocacy skills to avoid or effectively respond to bullying and harassment from peers or adults. It can also be a useful way of planning for how educators can intervene in the classroom, during extracurricular activities or in other school settings to help protect students from bullying behaviors. The utility of the IEP as a tool to address bullying has been recognized at the state level. Massachusetts (2010) recently passed into law a requirement that IEPs "address the skills and proficiencies needed to avoid and respond to bullying, harassment or teasing" for students with social skills related disabilities and whenever a student with a disability is vulnerable to disability-based bullying, harassment or teasing.

Secondly, IDEA's provisions around discipline state that a student with a disability may not have their educational placement changed in response to behavior that was a manifestation of a student's disability or the result of a school's failure to implement the student's IEP (34 C.F.R. § 300.530). In an instance in which a child with a disability under IDEA is engaged in bullying behavior, it is important that anti-bullying measures not come into conflict with or serve to restrict existing rights under IDEA. State anti-bullying laws have in many instances attempted to address this with language indicating that anti-bullying laws are not intended to infringe upon IDEA rights. Such language must be carefully constructed to ensure that it does not serve to exclude students with disabilities from anti-bullying efforts and protections. For example, an early proposed draft of a New Jersey (2010) anti-bullying law had attempted to address the potential conflict with IDEA by excluding bullying and harassment which occurred "exclusively among or between special education students or students with developmental disabilities". Such an approach would have deprived students with disabilities of the same civil rights protections other groups would benefit from in the anti-bullying legislation, and would have been extremely inadvisable. Instead, the legislation was modified before it passed the legislature to simply clarify that, "nothing contained in the "Anti-Bullying Bill of Rights Act," shall alter or reduce the rights of a student with a disability with regard to disciplinary actions or to general or special educational services and supports

**Policy Recommendations**

Effectively addressing bullying of students with disabilities will require undertaking action as part of both general and special education policy. Students with disabilities must be included on an equal basis with other protected classes in bullying prevention efforts undertaken as part of general education laws and policy initiatives such as the upcoming re-authorization of the Elementary and Secondary Education Act and bullying prevention efforts from the Health Resources and Services Administration (HRSA) and the Department of Education Office for Civil Rights. In addition, it is also necessary to strengthen and increase the use of anti-bullying tools unique to students with disabilities, such as IEP process and IDEA's guarantee of a Free and Appropriate Public Education (FAPE) in the Least Restrictive Environment (LRE). We recommend the following policy actions:

1. **Collaborating in Federal Research Program on Bullying Prevention:** Given that bullying prevention has implications for educational practice, civil rights and public health, research will play a crucial role in shaping anti-bullying efforts in the coming years. The executive branch should ensure that disability is included in federal research efforts on bullying through encouraging the involvement of disability-oriented agencies with mandated broad research and policy missions, like the National Institute for Disability and Rehabilitation Research (NIDRR) and the National Council on Disability (NCD), in broader federal bullying prevention efforts such as the Federal Partners in Bullying Prevention Task Force.
2. **Requiring Parental Notification:** Families frequently learn of incidents of bullying and harassment only well after they occur, if at all. As Congress considers means by which to incorporate bullying prevention into the re-authorization of the Elementary and Secondary Education Act (ESEA) and other relevant education policy laws, a requirement that parents be notified when their child is involved as either victim or perpetrator in an incident of bullying or harassment may be a useful tool to consider. This may be particularly important for students with communication related disabilities whose families may not otherwise become aware of incidents.
3. **Expanding the Role of the IEP:** For students with disabilities, the IEP is a natural tool for bullying prevention and elimination. The DOE Office on Special Education and Rehabilitation Services should expand technical assistance on how to utilize the IEP to protect students with disabilities from bullying and harassment and effective ways to address bullying behaviors that may be linked to a disability. Consideration should be given to incorporating bullying prevention as a priority within the IEP in the next re-authorization of the Individuals with Disabilities Education Act (IDEA).
4. **Broadening Data Collection:** Disability must be included in all federal data collection around bullying, victimization, violence, harassment and hate crimes.
5. **Eliminating Workplace Bullying:** Bullying is not limited to educational settings. Many youth and adults continue to face bullying, harassment and other forms of victimization during transition and within the workplace. The Employment Equal Opportunity Commission (EEOC) should be recognized and invited as a critical stakeholder in federal bullying prevention efforts and issues surrounding workplace bullying should be incorporated into our evolving national conversation on bullying.
6. **Fighting Hate Crimes:** The Department of Justice and the Federal Bureau of Investigation should work collaboratively with civil rights and community groups, including those in the disability community, to ensure effective and comprehensive implementation and enforcement of the Matthew Shepard and James Byrd, Jr. Hate Crimes Prevention Act for both adults and youth.
7. **Private Right of Action:** Congress should consider supplementing existing non-discrimination laws such as the Americans with Disabilities Act, Title IX, the Civil Rights Act of 1964 and others, with an explicit private right of action aimed at holding schools accountable for severe, persistent and pervasive bullying and harassment.

**References:**


Authority of school personnel, 34 C.F.R. § 300.530 (2010)

Buckley, S. J., Bird, G., Sacks, B. I., & Archer, T. (2000). The development of teenagers with Down syndrome in 1987 and 1999: Implications for families and schools. Down Syndrome News and Update, 2(2), 3.

Carter, B. B. and Spencer, V. G. (2006) The Fear Factor: Bullying and Students with Disabilities. George Mason University. International Journal of Special Education Vol 21 No.1 Retrieved December 18, 2010 http://www.forockids.org/PDF Docs/Bullying.pdf

Hodges, E.V.E. & Perry, D.G. (1996). Victims of peer abuse: An overview. *Journal of Emotional and Behavioral Problems, 5,* 23-28.

Langevin, M., Bortnick, K., Hammer, T., & Wiebe, E. (1998). Teasing/bullying experienced by children who stutter: Toward development of a questionnaire. *Contemporary Issues in Communication Science and Disorders, 25*, 12-24.

Lipsky, D.K. & Gartner, A. (1997). Inclusion and school reform: Transforming America's classrooms. Baltimore, MD: Paul H. Brooke

Little, L. (2002). Middle class Mothers' perceptions of peer and sibling victimization among children with Asperger's Syndrome and nonverbal learning disorders. *Issues in Comprehensive Pediatric Nursing, 25(1),* 43-54. http://www.ncbi.nlm.nih.gov/pubmed/11934121

Martlew, M., & Hodson, J. (1991). Children with mild learning difficulties in an integrated and in a special school: Comparisons of behaviour, teasing and teachers' attitudes. *British Journal of Educational Psychology, 61*, 355-372.

Massachusetts Advocates for Children. Targeted, Taunted, Tormented: the Bullying of Children with Autism Spectrum Disorder." (2009). Boston, MA. Retrieved December 29, 2010 http://www.massadovates.org/documents/Bullying-Report_000.pdf

Massachusetts Legislature 2010, CHAPTER 92. An Act Relative to Bulling in Schools (see Senate, No. 2404) Approved by the Governor, May 3, 2010. Retrieved December 28, 2010 http://www.malegislature.gov/Laws/SessionLaws/Acts/2010/Chapter92

Nabuzoka, D. (2003). Teacher ratings and peer nominations of bullying and other behavior of children with and without learning difficulties. *Educational Psychology, 23*(3), 307-321.

National Council on Disability (2008) No Child Left Behind and the Individuals with Disabilities education act: A Progress Report. Retrieved December 29, 2010 http://www.ncd.gov/newsroom/publications/2008/NoChildLeftBehind_IDEA_Progress_Report.html

New Jersey, Assembly, No. 3466. 214th Legislature, Reported on November 15, 2010 *With Amendments. Anti-Bullying Bill of Rights Act. Retrieved December 28, 2010* http://www.njleg.state.nj.us/2010/Bills/A3500/3466_R1.HTM.

Pennsylvania Association for Retarded Children (PARC) v. Pennsylvania, 334 F. Supp.1257 (E.D. PA 1971)

Public Law 94-142. Education for All Handicapped Children Act

Public Law 108-446. Individuals with Disabilities Education Improvement Act of 2004. 20 U.S.C. 1400 December 3, 2004 Retrieved December 29, 2010 http://www.copyright.gov/legislation/pl108-446.html

Public Law 110-325. Americans with Disabilities Amendments Act of 2008, 42 U.S.C. 12102 September 25, 2008 Retrieved December 29, 2010 http://www.access-board.gov/about/laws/ada-amendments.htm

Regional Education Laboratory, Northeast and Islands: National Crime Victimization Survey Crime Supplement "What characteristics of bullying, bullying victims, and schools are associated with increased reporting of bullying to school officials?" Retrieved December 19, 2010 http://ies.ed.gov/ncee/edlabs/regions/northeast/pdf/REL_2010092.pdf

Sailor, W. (ED.), (2002) Whole school success and inclusive education, New York. Teachers College Press. http://www.beachcenter.org/Books/FullPublications/PDF/PresidentReport.pdf

Siebecker, A., Swearer, S., and Lieske, J. National Association of School Psychologists, Atlanta, GA, March 2005. Poster Session Risky Business: Bullying and Students with Disabilities. Retrieved December 21, 2010 www.targetbully.com/uploads/NASP2005.Siebecker.ppt

Unnever, J.D. & Cornell, D.G. (2003). Bullying, Self-Control, and ADHD. *Journal of Interpersonal Violence, 81*(2), 129-147.

U.S. Department of Education, Office for Civil Rights. Dear Colleague Letter: Prohibited Disability Harassment (July 25, 2000), http://www2.ed.gov/about/offices/list/ocr/docs/disabharassltr.html.

U.S. Department of Education, Office for Civil Rights (Last Modified March 27, 2009) *Protecting students with Disabilities: Frequently Asked Questions About Section 504 and the Education of Children with Disabilities* Retrieved December 28, 2010 http://www2.ed.gov/about/offices/list/ocr/504faq.html

U.S. Department of Education, Office for Civil Rights. Dear Colleague Letter: Harassment and Bullying, Background, Summary, and Fast Facts (October 26, 2010). http://www2.ed.gov/about/offices/list/ocr/docs/dcl-factsheet-201010.pdf

U.S. Department of Education, Office of Special Education and Rehabilitative Services. Archived: Twenty-Five Years of Progress in Educating Children with Disabilities Through IDEA (http://www2.ed.gov/policy/speced/leg/idea/history.html).

Wiener, J., & Mak, M. (2009). Peer victimization in children with Attention-Deficit/Hyperactivity Disorder. *Psychology in the Schools*, *46*(2), 116-131.

Whitney, I., Smith, P.K., & Thompson, D. (1994). Bullying and children with special educational needs. In P.K. Smith & S. Sharp (Eds.), *School bullying: Insights and perspectives.* London: Routledge.

York, J., Vandercook, T., Macdonald, C., Heise-Neff, C., & Caughey, E. (1992). Feedback about integrating middle-school students with severe disabilities in general education classes. *Exceptional Children*, *58(3),* 260-269.

Gelser, Sara, Ari Ne'eman, Dr. Johnathan Young. "Bullying and Students with Disabilities." *National Council on Disability*. 8/17/2011. http://www.ncd.gov/NCD/publications/2011/March92011#69ac0c5f_bce0_4302_9de6_2838a1e66071.

# How Do You Talk About People with Disabilities?

| Use People First Language... | ...Instead of Labels that Stereotype and Devalue |
|---|---|
| • people/individuals with disabilities<br>• an adult who has a disability<br>• a child with a disability<br>• a person | • the handicapped<br>• the disabled |
| • people/individuals without disabilities<br>• typical kids | • normal people/healthy individuals<br>• atypical kids |
| • people with intellectual and developmental disabilities<br>• he/she has a cognitive impairment<br>• a person who has Down syndrome | • the mentally retarded; retarded people<br>• he/she is retarded; the retarded<br>• moron, idiot, imbecile<br>• he/she's a Downs kid; a Mongoloit; a Mongol |
| • a person who has autism | • autistic |
| • people with a mental illness<br>• a person who has an emotional disability<br>• a person with a psychiatric illness/disability | • the mentally ill; the emotionally disturbed<br>• he/she is insane; crazy; demented; psycho; a maniac; a lunatic |
| • a person who has a learning disability | • he/she is learning disabled |
| • a person who is deaf<br>• he/she has a hearing impairment/loss<br>• a man/woman who is hard of hearing | • the deaf |
| • a person who is deaf and cannot speak<br>• a person who has a speech disorder<br>• he/she uses a communication device<br>• he/she uses synthetic speech | • he/she is deaf and dumb<br>• a mute |
| • a person who is blind<br>• a person who has a visual impairment<br>• a man/woman who has low vision | • the blind |
| • a person who has epilepsy<br>• people with a seizure disorder | • an epileptic<br>• a victim of epilepsy<br>• a spaz |
| • a person who uses a wheelchair<br>• people who have a mobility impairment<br>• a person who walks with crutches | • he/she is wheelchair bound<br>• he/she is confined to a wheelchair<br>• a cripple |
| • a person who has quadriplegia<br>• people with paraplegia | • a quadriplegic; a quad<br>• a paraplegic |
| • he/she is of small or short stature | • a dwarf<br>• a midget |
| • he/she has a congenital disability | • he/she has a birth defect |
| • accesible buses, bathrooms, etc<br>• reserved parking for people with disabilities | • handicapped buses, bathrooms, etc handicapped parking |

**Source:** www.aucd.org

# Glossary of Disability-Related Terms

**Accessible:** In the case of a facility, readily usable by a particular individual; in the case of a program or activity, presented or provided in such a way that a particular individual can participate, with or without auxiliary aids(s); in the case of electronic resources, accessible with or without the use of adaptive computer technology.

**Access barrier:** Any obstruction that prevents people with disabilities from using standard facilities, equipment and resources.

**Accessible Web design:** Creating World Wide Web pages according to universal design principles to eliminate or reduce barriers, including those that affect people with disabilities.

**Accommodation:** An adjustment to make a workstation, job, program, facility, or resource accessible to a person with a disability.

**Adaptive technology:** Hardware or software products that provide access to a computer that is otherwise inaccessible to an individual with a disability.

**ALT attribute:** HTML code that works in combination with graphical tags to provide alternative text for graphical elements.

**Americans with Disabilities Act of 1990 (ADA):** A comprehensive Federal law that prohibits discrimination on the basis of disability in employment, telecommunications, public services, public accommodations and services.

**American Standard Code for Information Interchange (ASCII):** Standard for unformatted text which enables transfer of data between platforms and computer systems.

**Assistive technology:** Technology used to assist a person with a disability (e.g., a handsplint or computer-related equipment).

**Auxiliary aids and services:** May include qualified interpreters or other effective methods of making aurally delivered materials available to individuals with hearing impairments; qualified readers, taped texts, or other effective methods of making visually delivered materials available to individuals with visual impairments; acquisition or modification of equipment or devices; and other similar services and actions.

**Braille:** A system of embossed characters formed by using a Braille cell, a combination of six dots consisting of two vertical columns of three dots each. Each simple Braille character is formed by one or more of these dots and occupies a full cell or space.

**Browser:** A program that runs on an Internet-connected computer and provides access to the World Wide Web. Web browsers may be text-only, such as Lynx, or graphical, such as Internet Explorer and Netscape Navigator.

**Captioned film or videos:** Transcription of the verbal portion of films or videos is displayed to make them accessible to people who have hearing impairments.

**Closed Circuit TV Magnifier (CCTV):** A camera used to magnify books or other materials on a monitor.

**Cooperative education:** Programs that work with students, faculty, staff, and employers to help students clarify career and academic goals, and expand classroom study by allowing students to participate in paid, practical work experiences.

**Compensatory tools:** Adaptive computing systems that allow people with disabilities to use computers to complete tasks that would be difficult without a computer (e.g., reading, writing, communicating, accessing information).

**Disability:** A physical or mental impairment that substantially limits one or more major life activities; a record of such an impairment; or being regarded as having such an impairment (Americans with Disabilities Act of 1990).

**Discrimination:** The act of treating a person differently in a negative manner based on factors other than individual merit.

**Dymo Labeller:** A device used to create raised print or Braille labels.

**Electronic information:** Any digital data for use with computers or computer networks, including disks, CD-ROMs, and World Wide Web resources.

**Essential job functions:** Those functions of a job or task which must be completed with or without an accommodation.

**Facility:** All or any portion of a physical complex, including buildings, structures, equipment, grounds, roads, and parking lots.

**FM sound amplification system:** An electronic amplification system consisting of three components: a microphone/transmitter, monaural FM receiver and a combination charger/carrying case. It provides wireless FM broadcasts from a speaker to a listener who has a hearing impairment.

**Frame tags:** A means of displaying Web pages. The browser reads the frame tags and produces an output that subdivides output within a browser into discrete windows.

**Graphical user interface (GUI):** Program interface that presents digital information and software programs in an image-based format as compared to a character-based format.

**Hardware:** Physical equipment related to computers.

**Hearing impairment:** Complete or partial loss of the ability to hear, caused by a variety of injuries or diseases, including congenital causes. Limitations, including difficulties in understanding language or other auditory messages and/or in production of understandable speech, are possible.

**Independent study:** A student works one-on-one with individual faculty members to develop projects for credit.

**Informational interview:** An activity where students meet with people working in careers to ask questions about their jobs and companies, allowing students to gain personal perspectives on career interests.

**Input:** Any method by which information is entered into a computer.

**Internet:** Computer network connecting governmental, educational, commercial, other organizations, and individual computer systems.

**Internship:** A time-limited, intensive learning experience outside of the typical classroom.

**Interpreter:** Professional person who assists a person who is deaf in communicating with hearing people.

**Job shadowing:** A short work-based learning experience where students visit businesses to observe one or more specific jobs to provide them with a realistic view of occupations in a variety of settings.

**Keyboard emulation:** Uses hardware and/or software in place of a standard keyboard.

**Kinesthetic:** Refers to touch-based feedback.

**Large-print:** Most ordinary print is six to ten points in height (about 1/16 to 1/8 of an inch). Large-print type is fourteen to eighteen points (about 1/8 to 1/4 of an inch) and sometimes larger.

**Link:** a connection between two electronic files or data items.

**Lynx:** A text-based World Wide Web browser.

**Macro:** A mini-program that, when run within an application, executes a series of predetermined keystrokes and commands to accomplish a specific task. Macros can automate tedious and often-repeated tasks or create special menus to speed data entry.

**Mainstreaming:** The inclusion of people with disabilities, with or without special accommodations, in programs, activities, and facilities with non-disabled people.

**Major life activities:** Functions such as caring for oneself, performing manual tasks, walking, seeing, hearing, speaking, breathing, learning, working, and participating in community activities (Americans with Disabilities Act of 1990).

**Multimedia:** A computer-based method of presenting information by using more than one medium of communication, such as text, graphics, and sound.

**Optical Character Recognition (OCR):** Machine recognition of printed or typed text. Using OCR software with a scanner, a printed page can be scanned and the characters converted into text in an electronic format.

**Output:** Any method of displaying or presenting electronic information to the user through a computer monitor or other device (e.g., speech synthesizer).

**Portable Document Format (PDF):** The file format for representing documents in a manner that is independent of the original application software, hardware and operating system used to create the documents.

**Physical or mental impairment:** Any physiological disorder or condition, cosmetic disfigurement, or anatomical loss affecting one or more, but not necessarily limited to, the following body systems: neurological; musculoskeletal; special sense organs; respiratory, including speech organs; cardiovascular; reproductive; digestive; genitourinary; hemic and lymphatic; skin and endocrine; or any mental or psychological disorder, such as mental retardation, organic brain syndrome, emotional or mental illness, and specific learning disabilities (Americans with Disabilities Act of 1990).

**Plug-ins:** Programs that work within a browser to alter, enhance, or extend the browser,s operation. They are often used for viewing video, animation or listening to audio files.

**Proprietary software:** Privately owned software based on trade secrets, privately developed technology, or specifications that the owner refuses to divulge, thus preventing others from duplicating a product or program unless an explicit license is purchased. The opposite of proprietary is open (publicly published and available for emulation by others).

**Qualified individual with a disability:** An individual with a disability who, with or without reasonable modification to rules, policies or practices, the removal of architectural, communication, or transportation barriers, or the provision of auxiliary aids and services, meets the essential eligibility requirements for the receipt of services or participation in programs or activities provided by a public entity (Americans with Disabilities Act of 1990).

**Reader:** Volunteer or employee of a blind or partially sighted individual who reads printed material in person or records to audiotape.

**Relay service:** A third-party service (usually free) that allows a hearing person without a TTY/TDD device to communicate over the telephone with a person who has a hearing impairment. The system also allows a person with a hearing impairment who has a TTY/TDD to communicate in voice through a third party, with a hearing person or business.

**Screen reader:** A text-to-speech system intended for use by computer users who are blind or have low vision that speaks the text content of a computer display using a speech synthesizer.

**Service learning:** A structured, volunteer work experience where students provide community service in non-paid, volunteer positions to give them opportunities to apply knowledge and skills learned in school while making a contribution to local communities.

**Sign language:** Manual communication commonly used by people who are deaf. Sign language is not universal; deaf people from different countries speak different sign languages. The gestures or symbols in sign language are organized in a linguistic way. Each individual gesture is called a sign. Each sign has three distinct parts: the hand shape, the position of the hands, and the movement of the hands. American Sign Language (ASL) is the most commonly used sign language in the United States.

**Specific learning disability (SLD):** A disorder of one or more of the basic psychological processes involved in understanding or in using language, spoken or written, which may manifest itself in difficulties listening, thinking, speaking, reading, writing, spelling, or doing mathematical calculations. Limitations may include hyperactivity, distractibility, emotional instability, visual and/or auditory perception difficulties and/or motor limitations, depending on the type(s) of learning disability.

**Speech output system:** A system that provides the user with a voice alternative to the text presented on the computer screen.

**Speech impairment:** A problem in communication and related areas, such as oral motor function, ranging from simple sound substitutions to the inability to understand or use language or use the oral-motor mechanism for functional speech and feeding. Some causes of speech and language disorders include hearing loss; neurological disorders; brain injury; mental retardation; drug abuse; physical impairments, such as cleft lip or palate; and vocal abuse or misuse.

**Speech input system:** A computer-based system that allows the operator to control the system using his/her voice.

**Sticky keys:** Enables a computer user to do multiple key combinations on a keyboard using only one finger at a time. The sticky keys function is usually used with the Ctrl, Alt, and Shift keys. Simultaneous keystrokes can be entered sequentially.

**Telecommunications Device for the Deaf (TDD) or Teletypewriter (TTY):** A device which enables someone who has a speech or hearing impairment to use a telephone when communicating with someone else who has a TDD/TTY. TDD/TTYs can be used with any telephone, and one needs only a basic typing ability to use them.

**Trackball:** A pointing device consisting of a ball housed in a socket containing sensors to detect the rotation of the ball " like an upside down mouse. The user rolls the ball with his thumb or the palm of his hand to move the pointer.

**Traumatic Brain Injury (TBI):** An open or closed head injury resulting in impairments in one or more areas, such as cognition; language; memory; attention; reasoning; abstract thinking; judgment; problem-solving; sensory, perceptual, and motor abilities; psychosocial behavior; physical functions; information processing; and speech. The term does not apply to brain injuries that are congenital or degenerative, or brain injuries induced by birth trauma.

**Undue hardship:** An action that requires significant difficulty or expense in relation to the size of the employer, the resources available, and the nature of the operation (Americans with Disabilities Act of 1990).

**Universal design:** Designing programs, services, tools, and facilities so that they are usable, without additional modification, by the widest range of users possible, taking into account a variety of abilities and disabilities.

**Vocational Rehabilitation Act of 1973:** An act prohibiting discrimination on the basis of disability which applies to any program that receives federal financial assistance. Section 504 of the act is aimed at making educational programs and facilities accessible to all people with disabilities. Section 508 of the act requires that electronic office equipment purchased through federal procurement meets disability access guidelines.

**Voice input system:** A computer-based system that allows the operator to control the system using his/her voice.

**Vision impairments:** A complete or partial loss of the ability to see, caused by a variety of injuries or diseases including congenital causes. Legal blindness is defined as visual acuity of 20/200 or less in the better eye with correcting lenses, on the widest diameter of the visual field subtending an angular distance no greater than 20 degrees.

**World Wide Web (WWW, W3, or Web):** Hypertext and multimedia gateway to the Internet.

DO-IT
University of Washington
Box 354842
Seattle, WA 98195-4842
doit@uw.edu
http://www.washington.edu/doit/
206-685-DOIT (3648) (voice/TTY)
888-972-DOIT (3648) (toll free voice/TTY)
206-221-4171 (FAX)
509-328-9331 (voice/TTY) Spokane

Director: Sheryl Burgstahler, Ph.D.

# User Guide

Descriptive listings in *The Complete Directory for People with Disabilities* are organized into 24 chapters, by either resource type or disability category type. You will find the following types of listings throughout the book:

- National Agencies & Associations
- State Agencies & Associations
- Camps & Exchanges Programs
- Manufacturers of Assistive Devices, Clothing, Computer Equipment & Supplies
- Print & Electronic Media
- Living Centers & Facilities
- Libraries & Research Centers
- Conferences & Trade Shows

Below is a sample listing illustrating the kind of information that is or might be included in an Association entry. Each numbered item of information is described in the paragraphs on the following page.

---

1 → 1234
2 → **Advocacy Center for Seniors with Disabilities**
3 → 1762 South Major Drive
New Orleans, LA 98087

4 → **800-000-0000**

5 → **058-884-0709**

6 → **Fax: 058-884-0568**

7 → **TDD: 800-000-0001**

8 → **email: info@sadvoc.com**

9 → **www.sadvoc.com**

10 → Barbara Pierce, Executive Director
Diane Watkins, Marketing Director
Robert Goldfarb, Administrative Assistant

11 → The mission of the Center is to advance the dignity, equality, self-determination and choices of senior citizens with disabilities. It provides referrals, publishes information, including a monthly newsletter, offers workshops and consultation on legal, social, travel, and medical issues. The Center works with various local organizations to help seniors with disabilities stay active in their community.

12 → Founded 1964

13 → 18 pages

14 → Monthly

# User Key

1 → **Record Number**: Entries are listed alphabetically within each category and numbered sequentially. The entry numbers, rather than page numbers, are used in the indexes to refer to listings.

2 → **Organization Name**: Formal name of company or organization. Where organization names are completely capitalized, the listing will appear at the beginning of the alphabetized section. In the case of publications, the title of the publication will appear first, followed by the publisher.

3 → **Address**: Location or permanent address of the organization.

4 → **Toll Free Number**: This is listed when provided by the organization.

5 → **Phone Number**: The listed phone number is usually for the main office of the organization, but may also be for the sales, marketing, or public relations office as provided by the organization.

6 → **Fax Number**: This is listed when provided by the organization.

7 → **TDD Number**: This is listed when provided. It refers to Telephone Device for the Deaf.

8 → **E-Mail**: This is listed when provided by the organization and is generally the main office e-mail.

9 → **Web Site**: This is also referred to as an URL address. These web sites are accessed through the Internet by typing *http://* before the URL address.

10 → **Key Personnel**: Name and titles of department heads of the organization.

11 → **Organization Description**: This paragraph contains a brief description of the organization and their services.

12 → **Year Founded:** The year in which the organization was established or founded. If the organization has changed its name, the founding date is usually for the earliest name under which it was known.

13 → **Number of Pages**: Number of pages if the listing is a publication.

14 → **Frequency:** The frequency of the listing if it is a publication.

# Arts & Entertainment

## Resources for the Disabled

1 **American Art Therapy Association (AATA)**
225 North Fairfax Street
Alexandria, VA 22314
703-548-5861
888-290-0878
FAX: 703-783-8468
e-mail: info@arttherapy.org
www.americanarttherapyassociation.org

*Susan Corrigan, Exec. Dir.*
*Michele Basham, Dir., Membership Information*
*Mary Ann Kibler, CFO*
*Julia Connell, Communications Mgr*
Organization of professionals who believe the art process is a beneficial and healing process.

2 **American Council of the Blind**
2200 Wilson Boulevard
Ste 650
Arlington, VA 22201-3354
202-467-5081
800-424-8666
FAX: 703-465-5085
e-mail: info@acb.org
www.acb.org

*Mitch Pomerantz, President*
*Kim Charlson, First Vice President*
*Brenda Dillon, Second Vice President*
*Marlaina Lieberg, Secretary*
Aims to enlarge the art experience of blind people, encourages blind people to visit museums, galleries, concerts, the theater and other enjoyable public places, offers consultation to program planners in establishing accessible art and museum exhibits and presents Performing Arts Showcases at the American Council of the Blind's national convention.

3 **American Dance Therapy Association (ADTA)**
10632 Little Patuxent Pkwy
Ste 108
Columbia, MD 21044- 6258
410-997-4040
FAX: 410-997-4048
e-mail: info@adta.org
www.adta.org/

*Sharon Goodill, President*
*Jody Wager, Vice President*
*Ty Tedmon-Jones, Secretary*
*Meghan Dempsey, Treasurer*
Dance-movement therapy is a psychotherapeutic use of movement as a process which furthers the emotional, cognitive and physical integration of the individual.

4 **American Music Therapy Association(AMTA)**
Ste 1000
8455 Colesville Rd
Silver Spring, MD 20910-3392
301-589-3300
FAX: 301-589-5175
e-mail: info@musictherapy.org
musictherapy.org

*Andrea Farbman, Exec. Dir.*
*Mary Ellen Wylie, President*
*Al Bumanis, Dir. of Communications*
*Jane P. Creagan, Dir. of Professional Programs*
AMTA's purpose is the progressive development of the therapeutic use of music in rehabilitation, special education and community settings. Predecessors to the American Music Therapy Association included the National Association for Music Therapy founded in 1950 and the American Association for Music Therapy founded in 1971. AMTA is committed to the advancement of education, training, professional standards, credentials and research in support of the music therapy profession.

5 **Art Therapy SourceBook**
McGraw-Hill Company
2 Penn Plaza
New York, NY 10121-101
212-904-2000
www.mhhe.com/hper/physed

*Cathy Malchiodi, Author*
An overview of the uses of art as a mentally therapeutic tool.
*$18.00*
*272 pages*
*ISBN 1-565658-84-1*

6 **Art and Disabilities**
Brookline Books
8 Trumbull Rd
Suite B-001
Northampton, MA 01060
413-584-0184
800-666-2665
FAX: 413-584-6184
e-mail: brbooks@yahoo.com
www.brooklinebooks.com

*Florence Ludins-Katz, Author*
A step-by-step guide to establishing creative arts centers for people with disabilities. Includes philosophy and making creative arts centers happen.

7 **Art and Healing: Using Expressive Art to Heal Your Body, Mind, and Soul**
Three Rivers Press/Crown Publishing-Random House
1745 Broadway
New York, NY 10019
212-782-9000
e-mail: crownpublicity@randomhouse.com
www.randomhouse.com/crown/trp.html

*Barbara Ganim, Author*
*Markus Dohle, Chairman & CEO*
*Melanie Fallon-Houska, Dir., Corporate Contributions*
The author believes creating a visual image through any medium can produce physical and emotional benefits for both the creator as well as those who view it. *$17.00*
*256 pages*
*ISBN 0-609803-16-6*

8 **Art for All the Children: Approaches to Art Therapy for Children with Disabilities**
Charles C. Thomas
2600 S 1st St
Springfield, IL 62704-4730
217-789-8980
800-258-8980
FAX: 217-789-9130
e-mail: books@ccthomas.com
ccthomas.com

*Frances E Anderson, Author*
*Sharon Moorman, Editorial Assistant*
This second edition is for art therapists in training and for in-service professionals in art therapy, art education and special education who have children with disabilities as a part of their case/class load. *$56.95*
*398 pages Paperback*
*ISBN 0-398060-07-7*

9 **Arts Unbound**
542/544 Freeman Street
Orange, NJ 07050
973-675-2787
FAX: 973-678-4408
e-mail: info@artsunbound.org
www.artsunbound.org

*Louis Copeland, Executive Director*
*Catherine Lazen, Founder and Board Member*
*Robert Ramos, Gallery Director*
*Tashea Patterson Carless, Director of Agency Operations*
Arts Unbound is a nonprofit organization dedicated to the artistic achievement of youth, adults, and senior citizens with disabilities.

10 **Association of Mouth and Foot Painting Artists (AMPFA)**
2070 Peachtree Court
Suite 101
Atlanta, GA 30341
770-986-7764
FAX: 770-986-8563
e-mail: mfpausa@bellsouth.net
www.mfpausa.com

*Erich Stegmann, Founder*

The AMPF is an international, for-profit association wholly owned and run by disabled artists to help them meet their financial needs. Members paint with brushes held in their mouths or feet as a result of a disability sustained at birth or through an accident or illness that prohibits them from using their hands.

11 **Brookline Books**
8 Trumbull Rd
Suite B-001
Northampton, MA 01060
413-584-0184
800-666-2665
FAX: 413-584-6184
e-mail: brbooks@yahoo.com
www.brooklinebooks.com

Brookline Books has been publishing reader-friendly and informative edutation literature for more than 20 years, with a mission to reach both a specialized and non-specialized audience. They have a strong list of books for people with disabilities, including general information on advocacy, assistive technology, parent involvement, professional resources, early childhood intervention, as well as on specific disabilities.

12 **Clinical Applications of Music Therapy in Developmental Disability, Pediatrics and Neurolog**
Taylor & Francis
400 Market Street
Ste 400
Philadelphia, PA 19106-4738
215-922-1161
866-416-1078
FAX: 215-922-1474
e-mail: orders@jkp.com
www.jkp.com

*Tony Wigram, Editor*
*Jessica Kingsley, Chairman, Managing Director*
*Jemima Kingsley, Director*
*Dee Brigham, Company Secretary and Director*

More and more, music therapy is being practiced as an intervention in medical and special educational settings. This book describes and explains the planning and evaluation of music therapy intervention and how it can be used for assessing complex organic and emotional disabilities. *$34.95*
*312 pages*
*ISBN 1-853027-34-0*

13 **Contemporary Art Therapy with Adolescents**
Taylor & Francis
400 Market Street
Ste 400
Philadelphia, PA 19106-4738
215-922-1161
866-416-1078
FAX: 215-922-1474
e-mail: orders@jkp.com
www.jkp.com

*Shirley Riley, Author*
*Jessica Kingsley, Chairman, Managing Director*
*Jemima Kingsley, Director*
*Dee Brigham, Company Secretary and Director*

Reviews contemporary theories on adolescent development and therapy and offers solutions to the treatment of young people. *$ 26.95*
*285 pages*
*ISBN 1-853026-37-9*

14 **Creative Arts Resources Catalog**
MMB Music
9051 Watson Road
Ste 161
St. Louis, MO 63126
314-531-9635
80- 54- 377
FAX: 314-531-8384
e-mail: info@mmbmusic.com
www.mmbmusic.com

*Norm Goldberg, Founder & Chair*

Publisher and distributor of creative arts therapy materials in the areas of music, dance, art, drama, and poetry. Free catalog contains hundreds of books, recordings, and videos.

15 **Creativity Explored**
3245 16th Street
San Francisco, CA 94103
415-863-2108
FAX: 415-863-1655
e-mail: store@creativityexplored.org
www.creativityexplored.org

*Amy Taub, Executive Director*
*Matthew Verscheure, Associate Director*
*Sara Davis, President*
*Kim Malhotra, Development Director*

Creativity Explored is a nonprofit visual arts center for artists with developmental disabilities.

16 **Dancing from the Inside Out**
Fanlight Productions
c/o Icarus Films
32 Court Street
Brooklyn, NY 11201
718-488-8900
800-876-1710
FAX: 718-488-8642
e-mail: info@fanlight.com
www.fanlight.com

*Ben Achtenberg, Founder*

This eloquent video looks at the lives and work of three talented dancers who dance professionally with the acclaimed AXIS Dance Troupe, which includes both disabled and non-disabled dancers. They discuss the process they went through in adapting to their disability and how they came to re-discover physical expression through dance.

17 **Disability and Social Performance: Using Drama to Achieve Successful Acts**
Brookline Books
8 Trumbull Rd
Suite B-001
Northampton, MA 01060
413-584-0184
800-666-2665
FAX: 413-584-6184
e-mail: brbooks@yahoo.com
www.brooklinebooks.com

*Ernie Warren, Author*

This book makes a major contribution to the understanding of disability, people with disabilities and the creative power they possess which can be unleashed through performance. The books name is Disability and Social Performance: Using Drama to Achieve Successful ""Acts of Being"" *$17.95*

18 **Expressive Arts for the Very Disabled and Handicapped of All Ages**
Charles C. Thomas
2600 S First Street
Springfield, IL 62704-4730
217-789-8980
800-258-8980
FAX: 217-789-9130
e-mail: books@ccthomas.com
www.ccthomas.com

*Marilyn Wannamaker, Author*
*Jane G. Cohen, Author*

The ideas presented are not only designed to hold the interest of the children and adults, but to meet the needs of professionals and volunteers working with the disabled artists. All crafts are rated on a sliding scale, are of a low difficulty rating, use inexpensive and safe materials, and include explicit instructions. *$ 49.95*

*236 pages Spiral-Paper 1996*

*ISBN 0-398067-04-5*

19 **Fanlight Productions**

c/o Icarus Films
32 Court Street
Brooklyn, NY 11201
718-488-8900
800-876-1710
FAX: 718-488-8642
e-mail: info@fanlight.com
www.fanlight.com

*Ben Achtenberg, Founder*

Fanlight Productions is a leading distributor of innovative film and video works on the social issues of our time, with a special focus on healthcare, mental health, professional ethics, aging and gerontology, disabilities, the workplace, and gender and family issues. Select titles include Acting Blind, Autism: A World Apart, Dancing from the Inside Out, and Able to Laugh.

20 **Friends In Art (FIA)**

4317 Vermont Court
Columbia, MO 65203
573-445-5564
e-mail: paltschul@centurytel.net
www.friendsinart.com

*Peter Altschul, President*
*Lynn Hedl, Vice President*
*Don Horn, Corresponding Secretary*
*Arlo Monthei, Treasurer*

Friends in Art is a national organization for blind, visually impaired, and deaf-blind artists, musicians and writers, and art enthusiasts. The organization is dedicated to enhancing the skills and broadening the opportunities of the individuals involved with the organization.

21 **Future Horizons**

721 West Abram Street
Arlington, TX 76013-6995
817-277-0727
800-489-0727
FAX: 817-277-2270
www.fhautism.com

*R. Wayne Gilpin, President*
*Jennifer Gilpin, VP, Foreign Translations*
*Kelly Gilpin, Editorial Dir.*
*Teresa Corey, Conference Administration*

Founded in 1996, Future Horizons is devoted to supporting and fostering works and programs for those who live and work with autism and asperger's syndrome.

22 **Guide to the Selection of Musical Instruments**

MMB Music
9051 Watson Road
Ste 161
St. Louis, MO 63126
314-531-9635
800-543-3771
FAX: 314-531-8384
e-mail: info@mmbmusic.com
www.mmbmusic.com

*Norm Goldberg, Founder & Chair*

A marvelous resource book to aid therapists teaching those who are disabled to play musical instruments. *$7.75*

23 **In-Definite Arts Society**

8038 Fairmount Drive SE
Calgary, AB T2H0Y
403-253-3174
FAX: 403-255-2234
e-mail: ida@indefinitearts.com
www.indefinitearts.com

*Darlene Murphy, Executive Director*
*Dijana Andric, Client Services Manager*
*Peter Kelsch, Accountant*
*Bernice Webb, Facility Coordinator*

Promotes opportunities for people with developmental disabilities to express themselves and to grow and develop through their involvement in art.

24 **Instrumental Music for Dyslexics: A Teaching Handbook**

Wiley & Sons
111 River Street
Hoboken, NJ 07030-5774
201-748-6000
FAX: 201-748-6088
e-mail: info@wiley.com
www.wiley.com

*Sheila Oglethorpe, Author*
*Stephen M. Smith, President and CEO*
*Ellis E. Cousens, Exec VP*
*William J. Arlington, Senior VP, Human Resources*

Describes dyslexia in layman's terms and explains how the various problems that a dyslexic may have can affect all aspects of learning to play a musical instrument. It alerts the music teacher with a problem pupil to the possibilities of that pupil having some form of dyslexia. It offers suggestions as to how to teach dyslexics, with particular reference to piano teaching, and it suggests ways in which the music teacher may contribute to the welfare of a dyslexic pupil. *$ 34.95*

*200 pages*

*ISBN 1-861562-91-8*

25 **Kaleidoscope: Exploring the Experience of Disability through Literature & the Fine Arts**

United Disability Services
701 S Main St
Akron, OH 44311-1019
330-762-9755
FAX: 330-379-3342
e-mail: kaleidoscope@udsakron.org
www.udsakron.org/services/kaleidoscope

*Gail Willmott, Editor in Chief*

This magazine explores the experiences of disability through the lens of creative arts. Unlike rehabilitation, advocacy or independent living journals, this journal challenges and transcends stereotypical, patronizing and sentimental attitudes about disability. It offers a variety of articles, fiction, art and poetry relating to issues of disability, literature and the fine arts. *$10.00*

*64 pages BiAnnually*

26 **Learning Disabilities Sourcebook, 3rd Ed.**

Omnigraphics
Order Department
PO Box 8002
Aston, PA 19014-8002
610-461-3548
800-234-1340
FAX: 800-875-1340
e-mail: info@omnigraphics.com
www.omnigraphics.com

*Joyce Brennfleck Shannon, Editor*
*Fred Ruffner, Founder*
*Peter Ruffner, Co-Founder*

Learning Disabilities Sourcebook, Third Edition provides updated information about specific learning disabilities and other conditions that make learning difficult. These include dyscalculia, dysgraphia, dyslexia, auditory and visual processing, communication disorders, autism spectrum disorders, attention deficit/hyperactivity disorder, hearing and visual impairments, and brain injury. *$84.00*

*600 pages Hard cover*

*ISBN 0-780810-39-6*

27 **Manual of Sequential Art Activities for Classified Children and Adolescents**
Charles C. Thomas
2600 S 1st St
Springfield, IL 62704-4730
217-789-8980
800-258-8980
FAX: 217-789-9130
e-mail: books@ccthomas.com
ccthomas.com

*Rocco A L Fugard, Author*
Offers information to the special education professional on art therapy and management. *$41.95*
*246 pages Softcover*
*ISBN 0-39805 -85-6*

28 **Mozart Effect: Tapping the Power of Music to Heal the Body, Strengthen the Mind**
Harper Collins Publishers
10 E 53rd St
New York, NY 10022-5244
212-207-7000
www.harpercollins.com

*Don Campbell, Author*
Offers dramatic accounts of how doctors, shamans, musicians, and others use music to deal with everything from anxiety, cancer, and chronic pain, to dyslexia and mental illness. *$14.95*
*352 pages*
*ISBN 0-060937-20-3*

29 **Music Therapy**
Future Horizons, Inc.
721 West Abram St
Arlington, TX 76013-6995
817-277-0727
800-489-0727
FAX: 817-277-2270
www.fhautism.com

*Betsey King Brunk, Author*
*R. Wayne Gilpin, President*
*Jennifer Gilpin, VP, Foreign Translations*
*Kelly Gilpin, Editorial Dir.*
Music therapy is the use of music to address non-musical goals. Parents and professionals are finding that music can break down barriers for children with autism in areas such as cognition, socialization, and communication. *$19.95*
*123 pages*
*ISBN 1-885477-53-8*

30 **Music Therapy and Leisure for Persons with Disabilities**
Sagamore Publishing
1807 N Federal Drive
Urbana, IL 61801
217-359-5940
800-327-5557
FAX: 217-359-5975
e-mail: books@sagamorepub.com
www.sagamorepub.com

*Alicia L. Barksdale, Author*
*Joseph J. Bannon, Publisher & CEO*
*Peter L. Bannon, President*
*William Anderson, Director of Sales and Marketing*
Explores the use of musical therapy in order to enhance the development of independent leisure skills with a variety of special populations. Suggestions are provided for alternative avenues through musical experiences enabling individuals to achieve their greatest potential for independence and a high quality of life. *$19.95*

*ISBN 1-571675-11-6*

31 **Music Therapy for the Developmentally Disabled**
Sage Publications
2455 Teller Road
Thousand Oaks, CA 91320
805-499-9774
800-818-7243
FAX: 800-583-2665
e-mail: info@sagepub.com
www.sagepub.com

*S. Venkatesan, Author*
Included are practical guidelines, case samples and step-by-step instructions that enable a music therapist to bring about dramatic improvements in developmentally disabled adults and children. *$40.00*
*269 pages Hardcover*
*ISBN 0-890791-90-2*

32 **Music Therapy in Dementia Care**
Jessica Kingsley Publishers
400 Market Street
Suite 400
Philadelphia, PA 19106-4738
215-922-1161
866-416-1078
FAX: 215-922-1474
e-mail: orders@jkp.com
www.jkp.com

*David Aldridge, Editor*
*Jessica Kingsley, Chairman, Managing Director*
*Jemima Kingsley, Director*
*Dee Brigham, Company Secretary and Director*
A comprehensive look at music therapy as a means of improving memory, health, and identity in those suffering from dementia, particularly Alzheimer's. For music therapists and those involved in psychogeriatry. *$29.95*
*256 pages*
*ISBN 1-853027-76-6*

33 **Music Therapy, Sensory Integration and the Autistic Child**
Jessica Kingsley Publishers
400 Market Street
Suite 400
Philadelphia, PA 19106-4738
215-922-1161
866-416-1078
FAX: 215-922-1474
e-mail: orders@jkp.com
www.jkp.com

*Dorita S. Berger, Author*
*Jessica Kingsley, Chairman, Managing Director*
*Jemima Kingsley, Director*
*Dee Brigham, Company Secretary and Director*
Examines the human physiologic function, the brain, information processing, functional adaption, and how that might be affected by music interventions in persons with sensory integration difficulties. *$23.95*
*256 pages*
*ISBN 1-843107-00-7*

34 **Music and Dyslexia: A Positive Approach**
Wiley & Sons
111 River Street
Hoboken, NJ 07030-5774
201-748-6000
FAX: 201-748-6088
e-mail: info@wiley.com
www.wiley.com

*John Westcombe, Editor*
*Stephen M. Smith, President and CEO*
*Ellis E. Cousens, Exec VP*
*William J. Arlington, Senior VP, Human Resources*
This book shows how some people who have Dyslexia can be gifted musicians. The main point this books makes is that Dyslexic musicians can succeed provided only that they are given sufficient encouragement and understanding. *$34.95*
*200 pages*
*ISBN 1-861562-05-5*

35 **Music for the Hearing Impaired**
MMB Music
9051 Watson Road
Ste 161
St. Louis, MO 63126
314-531-9635
800-543-3771
FAX: 314-531-8384
e-mail: info@mmbmusic.com
www.mmbmusic.com

*Norm Goldberg, Founder & Chair*
A resource manual and curriculum guide. It is the product of a four-year developmental music program, placing emphasis on the needs of those with severe and profound losses. *$29.95*

36 **Music: Physician for Times to Come**
Quest Books
P.O.Box 270
Wheaton, IL 60187-270
630-665-0130
800-669-9425
FAX: 630-665-8791
e-mail: customerservice@questbooks.net
www.questbooks.net

*Don Campbell, Author*
A resource guide for various types of music and their theraputic oputcome.
*365 pages*
*ISBN 0-835607-88-7*

37 **National Arts and Disability Center (NADC)**
Tarjan Center at UCLA
760 Westwood Plaza
Los Angeles, CA 90095-8346
310-825-2631
800-825-2631
FAX: 310-794-1143
e-mail: oraynor@mednet.ucla.edu
www.semel.ucla.edu/nadc

*Peter Whybrow, Director*
*Fawzy Fawzy, Associate Director*
*Alan Han, Director of Development*
*Monica Rodriguez, Director of Human Resources*
NADC has a database and website which deals with access to and participation in the arts by people with disabilities.

38 **National Association for Drama Therapy**
Ste 220
44365 Premier Plz
Ashburn, VA 20147-5058
571-223-6440
888-416-7167
FAX: 571-223-6440
e-mail: answers@nadt.org
www.nadt.org

*Nisha Sajnani, President*
*Lisa Merrell, Vice President*
*Nadya Trytan, President-Elect*
*Gary Raucher, Secretary*
The National Association for Drama Therapy (NADT) was incorporated in 1979 to establish and uphold rigorous standards of professional competence for drama therapists. The NADT promotes drama therapy through information and advocacy.

39 **National Endowment for the Arts: Office for AccessAbility**
1100 Pennsylvania Ave NW
Washington, DC 20506-1006
202-682-5400
FAX: 202-682-5666
TTY:202-682-5496
e-mail: webmgr@arts.gov
www.arts.gov/

*Rocco Landesman, Chairman*
*Joan Shigekawa, Senior Deputy Chairman*
*Jamie Bennett, Chief of Staff*
*John Sotelo, Budget Officer (Director)*
The National Endowment for the Arts Office for AccessAbility is the advocacy-technical assistance arm of the Arts Endowment to make the arts accessible for people with disabilities, older adults, veterans, and people living in institutions.

40 **National Institute of Art and Disabilities**
551 23rd St
Richmond, CA 94804-1626
510-620-0290
FAX: 510-620-0326
e-mail: admin@niadart.org
www.niadart.org

*Deborah Dyer, Exec. Dir.*
*Brian Stechschulte, Dir. of Art Sales & Exhibitions*
*Belinda Sifford, Client Svcs*
*Judith Zoon, Administrative Coordinator*
The National Institute of Art & Disabilities (NIAD) provides an art program that promotes creativity, independence, dignity, and community integration for people with developmental and other disabilities.

41 **National Library Service for the Blind And Physically Handicapped**
1291 Taylor St NW
Washington, DC 20011
202-707-5100
FAX: 202-707-0712
TTY:202-707-0744
e-mail: nls@loc.gov
www.loc.gov/nls

*Karen Keninger, Dir.*
*Erica Vaughns, Exec. Assistant to the Dir.*
*Michael Martys, Automation Officer*
*Neil Bernstein, R & D Officer*
Administers a national library service that provides braille and recorded books and magazines on free loan to anyone who cannot read standard print because of visual or physical disabilities.
*Annual*

42 **National Theatre Workshop of the Handicapped (NTWH)**
535 Greenwich Street
New York, NY 10013-1004
212-206-7789
FAX: 212-206-0200
e-mail: admissions@ntwh.org
www.ntwh.org

*Jason Matthews, Director of Admissions*
*Rick Curry, President & CEO*
*John Spalla, General Manager*
A non-profit organization that provides individuals within the disabled community with the communication skills and the artistic discipline necessary to pursue a life in professional theatre.

43 **National Theatre of the Deaf**
139 N Main St
West Hartford, CT 06107-1264
860-236-4193
FAX: 860-236-4163
e-mail: Info@NTD.org
www.ntd.org

*Betty Beekman, Executive Director*
*William C. Martin, Marketing/PR Director*
*George Ghista, Accountant*
*Kathy Strauss, Company Interpreter*
The mission of the National Theatre of the Deaf is to produce theatrically challenging work of the highest quality, drawing from as wide a range of the world's literature as possible and to perfrom these original works in a style that links American Sign Language with the spoken word.

44 **New Music Therapist's Handbook, 2nd Ed. Berklee School of Music**
Berklee Press Publications
1140 Boylston Street
Boston, MA 02215
617-747-2146
866-237-5533
www.berkleepress.com

*Suzanne B. Hanser, Author*

Dr. Hanser's well-respected Music Therapist's Handbook has been revised and thoroughly updated to reflect the latest developments in the field of music therapy. *$29.95*
*256 pages*
*ISBN 0-634006-45-2*

**45 Non-Traditional Casting Project**
Ste 1600
1560 Broadway
New York, NY 10036-1518
212-730-4750
FAX: 212-730-4820
TTY:212-730-4913
e-mail: info@ntcp.org
www.ntcp.org/

*Nancy Kim, Manager*
The Non-Traditional Casting Project (NTCP) is a not-for-profit advocacy organization whose purpose is to address and seek solutions to the problems of racism and exclusion in theatre, film and television. NTCP's principal concerns are those of artists of color, female artists, Deaf and hard of hearing artists, and artists with disabilities.

**46 Nuvisions For Disabled Artists, Inc.**
C/O Rose Marcus
1319 Magee Street
Philadelphia, PA 19111
e-mail: hbedelstein@att.net
hbedelstein.home.att.net

*Kaye E Schonbach, Executive Director*
Nivisions was established to enable physically challenged artists to pursue professional and semi-professional artistic opportunities. Nuvisions supports these these artists by sponsoring accessible exhibitions, special projects and educational opportunities in Southeastern Pennsylvania and Southern New Jersey.

**47 Pied Piper: Musical Activities to Develop Basic Skills**
Jessica Kingsley Publishers
400 Market Street
Suite 400
Philadelphia, PA 19106-4738
215-922-1161
866-416-1078
FAX: 215-922-1474
e-mail: orders@jkp.com
www.jkp.com

*John Bean, Author*
*Jessica Kingsley, Chairman, Managing Director*
*Jemima Kingsley, Director*
*Dee Brigham, Company Secretary and Director*
Describes 78 enjoyable music activities for groups of children or adults who may have learning difficulties. The emphasis is on using music, rather than learning songs or rhythms, so group members do not need any special skills to be able to participate. Full details are given about any equipment required for the games, as well as suggestions for variations or modifications. *$21.95*
*96 pages*
*ISBN 1-853029-94-*

**48 Reaching the Child with Autism Through Art**
Future Horizons, Inc.
721 W Abram St
Arlington, TX 76013-6995
817-277-0727
800-489-0727
FAX: 817-277-2270
www.fhautism.com

*Toni Flowers, Author*
*R. Wayne Gilpin, President*
*Jennifer Gilpin, VP, Foreign Translations*
*Kelly Gilpin, Editorial Dir.*
This book uncovers how art encourages communication, positive self-image, concept development, spatial relationships, fine-motor skills, and many more facets of health child development. *$19.95*
*130 pages*

**49 Survivors Art Foundation**
PO Box 383
Westhampton, NY 11977
e-mail: safe@survivorsartfoundation.com
www.survivorsartfoundation.org

*Michael Herships, Project Leader & Board President*
*Candyce Brokaw, Art Director*
Dedicated to encourage healing through the arts, committed to empowering Trauma-Survivors with Effective Expressive Outlets via Internet Art Gallery, Outreach Programs, National Exhibitions, Publications and Development of Employment Skills.

**50 Teaching Asperger's Students Social Skills Through Acting**
Future Horizons, Inc.
721 W Abram St
Arlington, TX 76013-6995
817-277-0727
800-489-0727
FAX: 817-277-2270
www.fhautism.com

*Amelia Davies, Author*
*R. Wayne Gilpin, President*
*Jennifer Gilpin, VP, Foreign Translations*
*Kelly Gilpin, Editorial Dir.*
This book provides the theories and activities needed for setting up acting classes that double as social skills groups for individuals with Asperger's or high-functioning autism. Using these skills, students will be able to develop social understanding through repetition and generalization. *$19.95*
*211 pages*

**51 Teaching Basic Guitar Skills to Special Learners**
MMB Music
9051 Watson Road
Ste 161
St. Louis, MO 63126
314-531-9635
800-543-3771
FAX: 314-531-8384
e-mail: info@mmbmusic.com
www.mmbmusic.com

*Norm Goldberg, Founder & Chair*
The first-of-its-kind guitar book for use with persons who have difficulty learning to play via traditional methods. *$16.00*

**52 The Awakenings Project**
PO Box 177
Wheaton, IL 60187
www.awakeningsproject.org

*Robert Lundin, Co-Director*
*Irene O'Neill, President and Co-Director*
*Mary Lou Lowry, Secretary*
*John Rakow, Vice President*
The Awakenings Project is an organization whose mission is to assist those artists with psychiatric illnesses in developing their talent and finding an outlet for their creative abilities through art in all forms.

**53 Theatre Without Limits**
P.O.Box 4002
Portland, ME 04101
207-607-4016
FAX: 207-761-4740
www.vsartsmaine.org

*Kippy Rudy, Executive Director*
VSA Maine is a 501(c)(3) non-profit organization providing educational, arts, and cultural opportunities to children and adults with disabilities in Maine.

**54 VSA - The International Organization on Arts and Disability**
2700 F Street, NW
Washington, DC 20566
202-467-4600
800-933-8721
FAX: 202-429-0868
TTY: 202-737-0645
e-mail: info@vsarts.org
www.kennedy-center.org/education/vsa/

*Ambassador J Kennedy Smith, Founder*
*David M. Rubenstein, Chair*
*Michael M. Kaiser, President*
*Christoph Eschenbach, Music Dir., NSO and Kennedy Ctr*

VSA offers a large selection of guides, publications, and other resources dealing with a wide variety of subject matter in education, arts, and disabilities.

**55 VSA arts**
2700 F Street, NW
Washington, DC 20566
202-467-4600
800-933-8721
FAX: 202-429-0868
TTY: 202-737-0645
e-mail: info@vsarts.org
www.kennedy-center.org/education/vsa/

*Ambassador J Kennedy Smith, Founder*
*David M. Rubenstein, Chair*
*Michael M. Kaiser, President*
*Christoph Eschenbach, Music Dir., NSO and Kennedy Ctr*

VSA arts is an international, nonprofit organization founded in 1974 by Ambassador Jean Kennedy Smith whose mission is to create a society where all people with disabilities learn through, participate in, and enjoy the arts. Most states offer local programs, such as Arts in Action, that showcases the accomplishments of artists with disabilities and promotes increased access to the arts for people with disabilities.

**56 We Are PHAMALY**
Fanlight Productions
c/o Icarus Films
32 Court Street
Brooklyn, NY 11201
718-488-8900
800-876-1710
FAX: 718-488-8642
e-mail: info@fanlight.com
www.fanlight.com

*Ben Achtenberg, Owner*

Stands for Physically Handicapped Musical Actors League. This dynamic troupe doesn't cut any corners or make any comprmises. The musicals they perform are chosen for their appeal to the audience, not because they are easy for the performers, who have a variety of sensory and mobility handicaps. *$199.00*

*ISBN 1-572954-08-6*

# Assistive Devices

## Automobile

57 **Ability Center**
Contact Technologies
11600 Western Ave
Stanton, CA 90680-3436
866-405-6806
FAX: 714-901-1492
e-mail: info@abilitycenter.com
www.abilitycenter.com

*Darrell Heath, CEO*
*Dan Monahan, Manager*
Offers rear or side entry designed with painstaking craftsmanship using steel.

58 **Acc-u-trol**
Ahnafield Corporation
9850 E. 30th Street
Indianapolis, IN 46229
877-223-5301
e-mail: info@acemobility.us
www.acemobility.us
Computer-controlled device that operates all secondary accessory functions. These functions may include ignition, lift and door operation, windows, wipers, lights and flashers.

59 **All View Mirror**
4335 S Santa Fe Dr
Englewood, CO 80110-5417
303-781-2062
800-782-4335
FAX: 303-761-6811
e-mail: info@handicapsinc.com
www.handicapsinc.com
Manufacturers of hand driving devices for disabled persons.

60 **Arcola Mobility**
51 Kero Rd
Carlstadt, NJ 07072-2601
201-507-8500
800-272-6521
FAX: 201-507-5372
e-mail: info@arcolasales.com
www.arcolasales.com

*Andrew Rolfe, President*
*Jeff Krane, Sales Mgr/Nat'l Accounts*
*John Akerlind, Controller*
*Debbie Britt, Comml Bus Sales Coord*
Arcola sells new and used accessible vehicles and adaptive driving equipment including hand controls, wheelchair lifts and securement systems. Daily, weekly and monthly vehicle rentals available. Stairway lift, porch elevators and ramps for the home sold and rented.

61 **Automobile Lifts for Scooters, Wheelchairs and Powerchairs**
Bruno Independent Living Aids
P.O.Box 84
Oconomowoc, WI 53066
262-567-4990
800-882-8183
FAX: 262-953-5501
www.bruno.com

*Michael R. Bruno, Owner*
*Mike Krawczyk, Marketing Manager*
*Andrew Bayer, Product Manager*
Over 18 different styles of automobile lifts for scooters, wheelchairs and powerchairs for nearly any car, van, truck or sport utility vehicle that can raise most scooters or wheelchiars under 200 pounds and powerchairs up to 300 pounds. All Bruno lifts are eligible for reimbursement of up to $1000.00 from GM, Saturn, Ford, and Chrysler under the terms of their Mobility Programs.

62 **Blinker Buddy II Electronic Turn Signal**
HARC Mercantile
1111 W Centre Ave
Portage, MI 49024-5317
269-324-1615
800-445-9968
FAX: 269-324-2387
TTY: 800-445-9968
e-mail: info@harc.com
www.harc.com
Sounds a loud tone and flashes a light when the turn signal is on.
*$79.95*

63 **Braun Corporation**
574-946-6153
800-THE-LIFT
e-mail: mediaquestions@braunlift.com
www.braunability.com

*Ralph Braun, Founder*
Manufactures wheelchair lifts and lowered floor minivans as well as many other mobility products.

64 **Chevy Lowered Floor**
Ahnafield Corporation
9850 E. 30th Street
Indianapolis, IN 46229
877-223-5301
e-mail: info@acemobility.us
www.acemobility.us
Full size Chevy van lowered floor from 4 to 12 depths.

65 **Classic**
Ricon
7900 Nelson Rd
Panorama City, CA 91402-6090
818-267-3000
800-322-2884
FAX: 818-267-3001
e-mail: sales@riconcorp.com
www.riconcorp.com
Deluxe van conversion with equipment and accessories to offer freedom to the physically challenged.

66 **DW Auto & Home Mobility**
1208 N Garth Ave
Columbia, MO 65203-4056
573-449-3859
800-568-2271
FAX: 573-449-4187
e-mail: contactus@dwauto.com
dwauto.com

*Shawn Bright, Owner*
*Don Rothwell, General Manager*
*Brian Lutz, Service Manager*
Paratransit conversions and personalized conversions for the physically challenged. Home elevators and lifts. Scooter, wheelchairs and DME.

67 **Dodge Lowered Floor**
Ahnafield Corporation
9850 E. 30th Street
Indianapolis, IN 46229
877-223-5301
e-mail: info@acemobility.us
www.acemobility.us
Full size Dodge van lowered floor from 4 to 12 depths.

68 **Drive Master Company**
37 Daniel Rd West
Fairfield, NJ 07004-2521
973-808-9709
FAX: 973-808-9713
e-mail: sales@drivemaster.net
www.drive-master.com

*Peter B. Ruprecht, President*
*Adrienne Ruprecht, Bookkeeping*
*Christina M. Knapik, General Office Manager*
*Vinnie Dalli-Cardillo, Dealer Relations*
Full service mobility center, raised tops/doors, drop floors, custom driving equipment, distributor of name brand devices and

systems for full sized and mini vans. Sister company Van Master rents mobility equipped vans.

69 **Dual Brake Control**
Kroepke Kontrols
104 Hawkins Street
Bronx, NY 10464
718-885-2100
FAX: 337-235-4181
e-mail: kroepke@mail.idt.net

One lever fingertip brake controls, precision machines of the finest quality steel, are inconspicuous and do not take up lots of leg room. *$105.00*

70 **Entervan**
Braun Corporation
574-946-6153
800-THE-LIFT
e-mail: mediaquestions@braunlift.com
www.braunability.com

*Ralph Braun, Founder*
The Entervan accessible features are designed to blend seamlessly into the original design of the Chrysler minivan. In fact, you'll find the Entervan to be virtually indistinguishable from other minivans on the road, with the only differences being the easily accessible qualities of the van.

71 **Escort II XL**
Worldwide Mobility Products
Mesa, AZ
480-497-4692
800-848-3433
FAX: 480-497-3834
e-mail: service@worldwide-mobility.com
www.worldwide-mobility.com

Automatically lifts and secures for transportation a fully assembled, three-wheel, electric scooter. *$1625.00*

72 **Foot Pedal Extensions**
4335 S Santa Fe Dr
Englewood, CO 80110-5417
303-781-2062
800-782-4335
FAX: 303-761-6811
e-mail: info@handicapsinc.com
www.handicapsinc.com

Manufacturers of hand driving devices for disabled persons.

73 **Foot Steering**
Drive Master Company
37 Daniel Rd West
Fairfield, NJ 07004-2521
973-808-9709
FAX: 973-808-9713
e-mail: sales@drivemaster.net
www.drive-master.com

*Peter B. Ruprecht, President*
*Adrienne Ruprecht, Bookkeeping*
*Christina M. Knapik, General Office Manager*
*Vinnie Dalli-Cardillo, Dealer Relations*
Custom installed system to steer a vehicle with your foot.

74 **Foot Steering System**
Ahnafield Corporation
9850 E. 30th Street
Indianapolis, IN 46229
877-223-5301
e-mail: info@acemobility.us
www.acemobility.us

Computer-controlled device that operates all secondary accessory functions. These functions may include ignition, lift and door operation, windows, wipers, lights and flashers.

75 **Ford Lowered Floor**
Ahnafield Corporation
9850 E. 30th Street
Indianapolis, IN 46229
877-223-5301
e-mail: info@acemobility.us
www.acemobility.us

Full size Ford van lowered floor from 4 to 12 depths.

76 **Gear Shift Adaptor By Handicaps, Inc.**
4335 S Santa Fe Dr
Englewood, CO 80110-5417
303-781-2062
800-782-4335
FAX: 303-761-6811
e-mail: info@handicapsinc.com
www.handicapsinc.com

*Jeanenne Phillips, Executive Director*
Allows column mounted gear shift to be used with the left hand. *$90.00*

77 **Gresham Driving Aids**
30800 S Wixom Rd
Wixom, MI 48393-2418
248-624-1533
800-521-8930
FAX: 248-624-6358
e-mail: dave@greshamdrivingaids.com
www.greshamdrivingaids.com

*David Ohrt, General Manager*
*Craig Wigginton, Sales Consultant*
*Dexter Jackson, Service Manager*
*Joyce Martell, Customer Service*
Offers a full-service package to physically challenged individuals including lowered floors, raised roofs and doors and high-quad driver control systems. Dealer for Braun, Ricon, Crow River and Bruno wheelchair lifts.

78 **Hand Brake Control Only**
Kroepke Kontrols
104 Hawkins Street
Bronx, NY 10464
718-885-2100
FAX: 337-235-4181
e-mail: kroepke@mail.idt.net

One lever, fingertip brake controls that are custom designed to fit each car, completely adjustable and offer positioning operation at your fingertips. *$130.00*

79 **Hand Dimmer Switch**
Gresham Driving Aids
30800 S Wixom Rd
Wixom, MI 48393-2418
248-624-1533
800-521-8930
FAX: 248-624-6358
e-mail: dave@greshamdrivingaids.com
www.greshamdrivingaids.com

*David Ohrt, General Manager*
*Craig Wigginton, Sales Consultant*
*Dexter Jackson, Service Manager*
*Joyce Martell, Customer Service*
This switch is recommended for left leg handicaps or when a right leg handicap uses a left foot throttle. *$36.25*

80 **Hand Dimmer Switch with Horn Button**
Gresham Driving Aids
30800 S Wixom Rd
Wixom, MI 48393-2418
248-624-1533
800-521-8930
FAX: 248-624-6358
e-mail: dave@greshamdrivingaids.com
www.greshamdrivingaids.com

*David Ohrt, General Manager*
*Craig Wigginton, Sales Consultant*
*Dexter Jackson, Service Manager*
*Joyce Martell, Customer Service*
Attaches to the handle of control with a chrome plated steel insulated switch box, giving an instant warning without removing your hand from the steering wheel. *$28.75*

81 **Hand Gas & Brake Control**
Kroepke Kontrols
104 Hawkins Street
Bronx, NY 10464-288
718-885-2100
FAX: 337-235-4181
e-mail: kroepke@mail.idt.net
www.kroepkekontrols.com

Driving controls that are attached by a control level right on to the gas and brake pedals for easy maneuvering and convenience. *$220.00*

82 **Hand Operated Parking Brake**
Gresham Driving Aids
30800 S Wixom Rd
Wixom, MI 48393-2418
248-624-1533
800-521-8930
FAX: 248-624-6358
e-mail: dave@greshamdrivingaids.com
www.greshamdrivingaids.com

*David Ohrt, General Manager*
*Craig Wigginton, Sales Consultant*
*Dexter Jackson, Service Manager*
*Joyce Martell, Customer Service*

Converts foot parking brake to a hand operation for easy access and maneuverability. *$30.20*

83 **Hand Parking Brake**
Kroepke Kontrols
104 Hawkins Street
Bronx, NY 10464-288
718-885-2100
FAX: 337-235-4181
e-mail: kroepke@mail.itd.net
www.kroepkekontrols.com

One lever fingertip brake controls for your car that offer easy installment, complete adjustability, complete independence and more. *$25.00*

84 **Handicapped Driving Aids**
Handicapped Driving Aids of Michigan
3990 2nd Street
Wayne, MI 48184-1715
734-728-8808
FAX: 734-595-4520

*Jim Bishop, President*

Automobiles and vans customized, modified and equipped with industry approved handicapped equipment for ease of operation.

85 **Handicaps, Inc.**
4335 S Santa Fe Dr
Englewood, CO 80110-5417
303-781-2062
800-782-4335
FAX: 303-761-6811
e-mail: info@handicapsinc.com
www.handicapsinc.com

*Jeanenne Phillips, Executive Director*

Manufacturer of 'Superarm' wheelchair lifts, hand driving controls, and left foot gas pedals for vans & motorhomes. *$120.00*

86 **Headlight Dimmer Switch**
Kroepke Kontrols
P.O.Box 288
Bronx, NY 10464-288
718-885-2100
FAX: 337-235-4181
e-mail: kroepke@mail.idt.net
www.kroepkekontrols.com

One lever, fingertip controls for the disabled driver. *$23.00*

87 **Horizontal Steering**
Drive Master Company
37 Daniel Rd West
Fairfield, NJ 07004-2521
973-808-9709
FAX: 973-808-9713
e-mail: sales@drivemaster.net
www.drive-master.com

*Peter B. Ruprecht, President*
*Adrienne Ruprecht, Bookkeeping*
*Christina M. Knapik, General Office Manager*
*Vinnie Dalli-Cardillo, Dealer Relations*

Horizontal steering system is customized to meet the needs of the high-level, spinally injured and all others who experience limited arm strength and range of motion.

88 **Horn Control Switch**
Kroepke Kontrols
P.O.Box 288
Bronx, NY 10464-288
718-885-2100
FAX: 337-235-4181
e-mail: kroepke@mail.idt.net
www.kroepkekontrols.com

One lever, fingertip controls that do not interfere with the normal operation of your car. *$23.00*

89 **Joystick Driving Control**
Ahnafield Corporation
9850 E. 30th Street
Indianapolis, IN 46229
877-223-5301
e-mail: info@acemobility.us
www.acemobility.us

Single lever, two axis, remote control system for steering, brakes, and accelerator.

90 **Kessler Institute for Rehabilitation**
1199 Pleasant Vallely Way
West Orange, NJ 07052
973-731-3600
888-KES-SLER
FAX: 973-243-6819
www.kessler-rehab.com

*Bonnie A. Evans, CEO*
*Steve Kirshblum, MD, Medical Director*
*Karen Liszner, Chief Nurse Executive*
*Kim Ratner, AVP, Rehabilation Services*

Driver evaluation training for the physically/mentally challenged offering state certified driving instructors. Door-to-door pickup at home, work or rehab centers.

91 **Key Holders, Ignition & Door Keys**
Gresham Driving Aids
30800 S Wixom Rd
Wixom, MI 48393-2418
248-624-1533
800-521-8930
FAX: 248-624-6358
e-mail: dave@greshamdrivingaids.com
www.greshamdrivingaids.com

*David Ohrt, General Manager*
*Craig Wigginton, Sales Consultant*
*Dexter Jackson, Service Manager*
*Joyce Martell, Customer Service*

Easy for arthritic hands to handle. Easily installed. *$18.70*

92 **Kneelkar**
Mednet
923 E. Michigan Avenue
Battle Creek, MI 49014
269-660-1002
888-625-6335
FAX: 269-660-1296
e-mail: kneelvan@fminow.com
http://www.freedommotors.com

*Mike Thompson, Vice President*
*Chet Baranski, Mobility Specialist-Midwest Vans*
*Danielle Baughman, Product Manager*

Offers the ultimate van conversions with equipment that is easily installed and accessible for the physically challenged.

**93 Latchloc Automatic Wheelchair Tiedown**
Ahnafield Corporation
9850 E. 30th Street
Indianapolis, IN 46229
877-223-5301
e-mail: info@acemobility.us
www.acemobility.us

An independent wheelchair tiedown system utilized primarily by individuals who drive from their wheelchairs.

**94 Left Foot Accelerator**
Gresham Driving Aids
30800 S Wixom Rd
Wixom, MI 48393-2418
248-624-1533
800-521-8930
FAX: 248-624-6358
e-mail: dave@greshamdrivingaids.com
www.greshamdrivingaids.com

*David Ohrt, General Manager*
*Craig Wigginton, Sales Consultant*
*Dexter Jackson, Service Manager*
*Joyce Martell, Customer Service*

A custom pedal designed for left-foot usage. Stainless steel cross bar attaches above the throttle pedal and leaves right pedal free for right foot use. *$80.50*

**95 Left Foot Gas Pedal**
Kroepke Kontrols
P.O.Box 288
Bronx, NY 10464-288
718-885-2100
FAX: 337-235-4181
e-mail: kroepke@mail.itd.net
www.kroepkekontrols.com

One lever, fingertip controls that offer custom design, easy installment and complete freedom for the disabled driver. *$90.00*

**96 Left Foot Gas Pedal by Handicaps, Inc.**
4335 S Santa Fe Dr
Englewood, CO 80110-5417
303-781-2062
800-782-4335
FAX: 303-761-6811
e-mail: info@handicapsinc.com
www.handicapsinc.com

Necessary when right foot use is impossible or limited. Can be replaced with #103 accelerator shield. *$280.00*

**97 Left Hand Shift Lever**
Gresham Driving Aids
30800 S Wixom Rd
Wixom, MI 48393-2418
248-624-1533
800-521-8930
FAX: 248-624-6358
e-mail: info@handicapsinc.com
www.greshamdrivingaids.com

*David Ohrt, General Manager*
*Craig Wigginton, Sales Consultant*
*Dexter Jackson, Service Manager*
*Joyce Martell, Customer Service*

Converts steering wheel lever or automatic transmission selector lever to left hand usage for right arm handicaps. *$34.50*

**98 Low Effort and No Effort Steering**
Drive Master Company
37 Daniel Rd West
Fairfield, NJ 07004-2521
973-808-9709
FAX: 973-808-9713
e-mail: sales@drivemaster.net
www.drive-master.com

*Peter B. Ruprecht, President*
*Adrienne Ruprecht, Bookkeeping*
*Christina M. Knapik, General Office Manager*
*Vinnie Dalli-Cardillo, Dealer Relations*

Reduced effort steering modifications available for nearly all vehicles. Additional products are pedal extensions which are 1 inch to 4 inch clamp-on aluminum blocks and 6 inch to 12 inch adjustable fold-down pedals.

**99 Mini-Bus and Mini-Vans**
Arcola Bus Sales
51 Kero Rd
Carlstadt, NJ 07072-2604
201-507-8500
800-ARC-OLA1
FAX: 201-507-5372
e-mail: info@arcolasales.com
www.arcolamobility.com

*Andrew Rolfe, President*
*Jeff Krane, Sales Mgr/Nat'l Accounts*
*John Akerlind, Controller*
*Debbie Britt, Comml Bus Sales Coord*

Offers a virtually unlimited choice of chassis size, body style, floor plan and optional features. We provide transporters for almost every use, including school buses, vans, mini-coaches, medium-duty buses and personalized vans for the disabled.

**100 Mini-Rider**
Ricon
7900 Nelson Rd
Panorama City, CA 91402-6090
818-267-3000
800-322-2884
FAX: 818-267-3001
e-mail: sales@riconcorp.com
www.riconcorp.com

Deluxe van conversions.

**101 Mobility Vehicle Stairlifts and Ramps**
Arcola Bus Sales
51 Kero Rd
Carlstadt, NJ 07072-2604
201-507-8500
800-ARC-OLA1
FAX: 201-507-5372
e-mail: info@arcolasales.com
www.arcolamobility.com

*Andrew Rolfe, President*
*Jeff Krane, Sales Mgr/Nat'l Accounts*
*John Akerlind, Controller*
*Debbie Britt, Comml Bus Sales Coord*

Arcola Mobility is a leading dealer of personal, accessible mini and full-size vans with custom conversions and modifications available. We offer a complete line of adaptive driving equipment, including wheelchair lifts, ramps, hand controls, steering devices, scooter lifters, car top wheelchair carriers and power transfer seats. In addition to new custom vehicles, we also have an extensive selection of used vehicles for the physically challenged.

**102 Monarch Mark 1-A**
Access Mobility Systems
7202 Evergreen Way
Everett, WA 98203
425-353-6563
800-854-4176
FAX: 425-355-6159
e-mail: info@accessams.com
www.accessams.com

System of hand controls which incorporates a popular method of operation by pushing the control handles directly toward the brakes.

**103 Monmouth Vans, Access and Mobility**
5105 New Jersey 33
Farmingdale, NJ 07727-4003
877-275-4930
e-mail: ask@mobilityworks
www.mobilityworks.com/

*Gene Morton, President*
*Ray Morton, General Manager*
*Don Dufty, Certified Mobility Consultant*
*Craig Phillips, Service Manager*

Full vehicle modifications for driving and for transport of people with disabilities. Access equipment for buildings, e.g. ramps, stair lifts, pool lifts, automatic door openers and patient transfer lifts, pride jazzy portable and modular wheelchairs and scooters. Large selection of modified vans in stock.

**104 New Quad Grip**
Gresham Driving Aids
30800 S Wixom Rd
Wixom, MI 48393-2418
248-624-1533
800-521-8930
FAX: 248-624-6358
e-mail: dave@greshamdrivingaids.com
www.greshamdrivingaids.com

*David Ohrt, General Manager*
*Craig Wigginton, Sales Consultant*
*Dexter Jackson, Service Manager*
*Joyce Martell, Customer Service*
Automobile aids for the disabled. *$40.25*

**105 PAC Unit**
Ahnafield Corporation
9850 E. 30th Street
Indianapolis, IN 46229
877-223-5301
e-mail: info@acemobility.us
www.acemobility.us
Low effort accelerator and brake remote serves hand control.

**106 Park Brake Extension By Handicaps, Inc.**
4335 S Santa Fe Dr
Englewood, CO 80110-5417
303-781-2062
800-782-4335
FAX: 303-761-6811
e-mail: info@handicapsinc.com
www.handicapsinc.com
For cars with foot operated parking brake, to operate with hand. *$90.00*

**107 Pedal Ease**
Ahnafield Corporation
9850 E. 30th Street
Indianapolis, IN 46229
877-223-5301
e-mail: info@acemobility.us
www.acemobility.us
Low effort accelerator and brake remote serves foot control.

**108 Portable Hand Controls**
Ahnafield Corporation
9850 E. 30th Street
Indianapolis, IN 46229
877-223-5301
e-mail: info@acemobility.us
www.acemobility.us
Low effort accelerator and brake remote serves foot control.

**109 Portable Hand Controls By Handicaps, Inc.**
4335 S Santa Fe Dr
Englewood, CO 80110-5417
303-781-2062
800-782-4335
FAX: 303-761-6811
e-mail: info@handicapsinc.com
www.handicapsinc.com
Great for those who travel or use multiple vehicles. To be used on a temporary basis only. Must be used on vehicles with automatic transmission, power brakes, and power steering. Kn-Impaired hand use is required. *$392.00*

**110 Portable Vehicle Controls**
Contact Technologies
1033 Business Center Cir
Newbury Park, CA 91320-1128
805-498-8157
FAX: 805-498-2747
Fully portable, integrated, automotive hand control unit.

**111 Power Seat Base (6-Way)**
Ricon
7900 Nelson Rd
Panorama City, CA 91402-6090
818-267-3000
800-322-2884
FAX: 818-267-3001
e-mail: sales@riconcorp.com
www.riconcorp.com
Facilitates a driver's self-transfer from a wheelchair to the driving seat and allows optimal driving positioning.

**112 Quad Grip with Pin**
Gresham Driving Aids
30800 S Wixom Rd
Wixom, MI 48393-2418
248-624-1533
800-521-8930
FAX: 248-624-6358
e-mail: dave@greshamdrivingaids.com
www.greshamdrivingaids.com

*David Ohrt, General Manager*
*Craig Wigginton, Sales Consultant*
*Dexter Jackson, Service Manager*
*Joyce Martell, Customer Service*
Automobile aids for the disabled. *$40.25*

**113 Rampvan**
Independent Mobility Systems
574-946-6153
800-THE-LIFT
e-mail: mediaquestions@braunlift.com
www.braunability.com

*Ralph Braun, Founder*
Fully accessible minivan conversions with automatic doors and ramps, manufactured by Toyota, Chrysler, Dodge and Ford minivans.

**114 Recreation Vehicles**
Lazy Days RV Center
6130 Lazy Days Blvd
Seffner, FL 33584-2968
800-350-672
www.lazydays.com
Customized recreational vehicles for people with disabilities. Specializing in wheelchair accessible bathrooms.

**115 Reduced Effort Steering**
Ahnafield Corporation
9850 E. 30th Street
Indianapolis, IN 46229
877-223-5301
e-mail: info@acemobility.us
www.acemobility.us
Low effort accelerator and brake remote serves foot control.

**116 Right Hand Turn Signal Switch Lever**
Gresham Driving Aids
30800 S Wixom Rd
Wixom, MI 48393-2418
248-624-1533
800-521-8930
FAX: 248-624-6358
e-mail: dave@greshamdrivingaids.com
www.greshamdrivingaids.com

*David Ohrt, General Manager*
*Craig Wigginton, Sales Consultant*
*Dexter Jackson, Service Manager*
*Joyce Martell, Customer Service*
Converts signal switch to right hand usage for left arm handicaps. *$34.50*

**117 Slim Line Brake Only**
Gresham Driving Aids
30800 S Wixom Rd
Wixom, MI 48393-2418
248-624-1533
800-521-8930
FAX: 248-624-6358
e-mail: dave@greshamdrivingaids.com
www.greshamdrivingaids.com

*David Ohrt, General Manager*
*Craig Wigginton, Sales Consultant*
*Dexter Jackson, Service Manager*
*Joyce Martell, Customer Service*
A chrome plated steel handle, contour shaped, with a left hand or right hand unit available. *$155.25*

**118 Slim Line Control**
Gresham Driving Aids
30800 S Wixom Rd
Wixom, MI 48393-2418
248-624-1533
800-521-8930
FAX: 248-624-6358
e-mail: dave@greshamdrivingaids.com
www.greshamdrivingaids.com

*David Ohrt, General Manager*
*Craig Wigginton, Sales Consultant*
*Dexter Jackson, Service Manager*
*Joyce Martell, Customer Service*
A plated, strong, compact unit designed to be easily transferred from car to car. Built of heavy steel tubing, welded and chrome plated and contour-shaped for maximum driving room. *$201.25*

**119 Slim Line Control: Brake and Throttle**
Gresham Driving Aids
30800 S Wixom Rd
Wixom, MI 48393-2418
248-624-1533
800-521-8930
FAX: 248-624-6358
e-mail: dave@greshamdrivingaids.com
www.greshamdrivingaids.com

*David Ohrt, General Manager*
*Craig Wigginton, Sales Consultant*
*Dexter Jackson, Service Manager*
*Joyce Martell, Customer Service*
Brake is actuated by pushing the control lever directly towards the brake. Throttle is actuated by moving the lever at right angles to the brake movement, toward the seat. The weight of the operator's hand is sufficient to hold the throttle at any designed speed. *$300.00*

**120 Steering Backup System**
Ahnafield Corporation
9850 E. 30th Street
Indianapolis, IN 46229
877-223-5301
e-mail: info@acemobility.us
www.acemobility.us

Low effort accelerator and brake remote serves foot control.

**121 Steering Device By Handicaps, Inc.**
4335 S Santa Fe Dr
Englewood, CO 80110-5417
303-781-2062
800-782-4335
FAX: 303-761-6811
e-mail: info@handicapsinc.com
www.handicapsinc.com

Mounts to one side of steering wheel. Allows for easier steering using only one hand. *$26.00*

**122 Super Grade 4 Hand Controls By Handicaps, Inc.**
4335 S Santa Fe Dr
Englewood, CO 80110-5417
303-781-2062
800-782-4335
FAX: 303-761-6811
e-mail: info@handicapsinc.com
www.handicapsinc.com

Hand controls the operation of accelerator and brakes. VA tested. Right angle style. *$680.00*

**123 Super Grade IV Hand Controls**
4335 S Santa Fe Dr
Englewood, CO 80110-5417
303-781-2062
800-782-4335
FAX: 303-761-6811
e-mail: info@handicapsinc.com
www.handicapsinc.com

Manufacturers of hand driving devices for disabled persons.

**124 The HANDYBAR**
Maxi Aids
42 Executive Blvd
Farmingdale, NY 11735-4710
631-752-0521
800-522-6294
FAX: 631-752-0689
TTY: 800-281-3555
e-mail: sales@maxiaids.com
www.maxiaids.com

*Elliot Zaretsky, Founder & President*
For those who have trouble getting in and out of a car. Sturdy bar slides into door striker and allows you better support to lift yourself out of the car. Stores easily under car seat. *$39.95*

**125 Tim's Trim**
25 Bermar Park
Rochester, NY 14624-1542
585-429-6270
888-468-6784
FAX: 585-429-6355
e-mail: timstriminc@yahoo.com
www.timstrim.com/

Offers vehicle modifications, drop floors, raised tops/doors, driving equipment, touch pads and lifts. Also is a member of NEMDA and QAP certified

**126 Transportation Equipment for People with Disabilities**
Drive Master Company
30800 S Wixom Rd
Wixom, MI 48393-2418
248-624-1533
800-521-8930
FAX: 248-624-6358
e-mail: dave@greshamdrivingaids.com
www.greshamdrivingaids.com

*David Ohrt, General Manager*
*Craig Wigginton, Sales Consultant*
*Dexter Jackson, Service Manager*
*Joyce Martell, Customer Service*
Wheelchair lifts and ramps, hand and foot controls, steering and braking modifications, complete van conversions, home modifications, wheelchairs and scooters and wheelchair accessible van rentals.

**127 Tri-Post Steering Wheel Spinner**
Gresham Driving Aids
37 Daniel Rd West
Fairfield, NJ 07004-2521
973-808-9709
FAX: 973-808-9713
e-mail: sales@drivemaster.net
www.drive-master.com

*Peter B. Ruprecht, President*
*Adrienne Ruprecht, Bookkeeping*
*Christina M. Knapik, General Office Manager*
*Vinnie Dalli-Cardillo, Dealer Relations*
Three nylon posts, adjustable for proper fit to drivers hand, to control the wheel, for use by persons with weak or limp wrists. *$40.25*

**128 Turn Signal Adapter By Handicaps, Inc.**
Handicaps
4335 S Santa Fe Dr
Englewood, CO 80110-5417
303-781-2062
800-782-4335
FAX: 303-761-6811
e-mail: info@handicapsinc.com
www.handicapsinc.com
Allows turn signals to be used with the right hand. *$ 80.00*

**129 Ultra-Lite XL Hand Control**
Drive Master Company
30800 S Wixom Rd
Wixom, MI 48393-2418
248-624-1533
800-521-8930
FAX: 248-624-6358
e-mail: dave@greshamdrivingaids.com
www.greshamdrivingaids.com

*David Ohrt, General Manager*
*Craig Wigginton, Sales Consultant*
*Dexter Jackson, Service Manager*
*Joyce Martell, Customer Service*
Allows the driver to operate gas and brake by hand- push for brake- pull for gas. Can be installed in nearly every vehicle.

**130 United Access**
Wright-Way
175 E Interstate 30
Garland, TX 75043-4021
972-240-8839
877-503-9399
888-939-1010
FAX: 972-240-0412
e-mail: info@unitedaccess.com
www.unitedaccess.com
Various automobile control systems that use hand, foot and steering aids for the disabled, including complete vehicle modifications.

**131 Vantage Mini-Vans**
Vantage Mini-Vans
5202 S 28th Pl
Phoenix, AZ 85040-3799
602-243-2700
800-348-VANS
FAX: 602-304-3290
www.vantagemobility.com
Personalized vehicles with lowered floors and swing-away ramps.

**132 Velcro Peel-Off Shoes**
4335 S Santa Fe Dr
Englewood, CO 80110-5417
303-781-2062
800-782-4335
FAX: 303-761-6811
e-mail: info@handicapsinc.com
www.handicapsinc.com
Manufacturers of hand driving devices for disabled persons.

**133 Voice Choice**
Ahnafield Corporation
9850 E. 30th Street
Indianapolis, IN 46229
877-223-5301
e-mail: info@acemobility.us
www.acemobility.us

**134 Voice Scan**
Ahnafield Corporation
9850 E. 30th Street
Indianapolis, IN 46229
877-223-5301
e-mail: info@acemobility.us
www.acemobility.us

**135 Warp Drive**
Ahnafield Corporation
9850 E. 30th Street
Indianapolis, IN 46229
877-223-5301
e-mail: info@acemobility.us
www.acemobility.us

**136 Wheelers Accessible Van Rentals**
Wheelers Accessible Van Rental
6614 West Sweetwater
Glendale, AZ 85304
623-776-8830
800-456-1371
FAX: 623-412-9920
e-mail: info@WheelersVanRentals.com
www.WheelersVanRentals.com
Daily, weekly and monthly rentals. Locations throughout the US.

**137 XL Steering**
Ahnafield Corporation
9850 E. 30th Street
Indianapolis, IN 46229
877-223-5301
e-mail: info@acemobility.us
www.acemobility.us
Extra light, small diameter, remote steering system.

## Bath

**138 ARJO Inc.**
2349 West Lake Street
Suite 250
Addison, IL 60101
630-785-4490
800-323-1245
FAX: 630-576-5020
e-mail: usa.info@ArjoHuntleigh.com
www.arjohuntleigh.com
ARJO offers a complete line of patient bathing, showering and lift/transport systems, bariatric solutions, and accompanying skin care products for long-term and acute care facilities.The name of the company is ArjoHuntleigh.

**139 Adjustable Bath Seat**
Arista Surgical Supply Company/AliMed
297 High St
Dedham, MA 02026-2852
781-329-2900
800-225-2610
FAX: 781-329-8392
e-mail: info@alimed.com
www.alimed.com

*Julian Cherubini, President*
Bath seat that fits easily in any size tub. Easily adjustable to any height for easier maneuverability. *$44.00*

**140 Adjustable Raised Toilet Seat & Guard**
Frohock-Stewart
1 Invacare Way
Elyria, OH 44035-4190
440-329-6000
800-333-6900
FAX: 877-619-7996
www.invacare.com

*A Malachi Mixon III, Chairman*
*Gerald B. Blouch, President & CEO*
*Joseph B. Richey III, President, Invacare Technologies*
*Dan T. Moore, III, Founder and President*
The seat features an exclusive pivot locking system so it won't slip or tip and the adjustable guard rail fits all toilets.

**141 Bath Fixtures**
Crane Plumbing/Fiat Products
1000 Industrial Dr
Ste 2A
Bensenville, IL 60106-1260
630-350-7575
FAX: 630-350-7775
www.deery-pardue.com

*Dave Pardue, Chairman Emeritus*
*Greg Pardue, Sales*
*Mark Nasuta, Sales*
*Matt Pardue, Sales*
Manufacturers plumbing fixtures for the disabled. Products include toilets, lavatories, showers and tub/shower units.

**142 Bath Products**
Snug Seat
P.O.Box 1739
Matthews, NC 28106-1739
800-336-7684
FAX: 704-882-0751
e-mail: information@snugseat.com
www.snugseat.com

*Steve Scribner, VP Sales*
*Kirk MacKenzie, President*
*Matt Abrahams, Territory Sales Representative*
*Steve Ricker, Territory Sales Representative*
Offers a wide range of products to meet the transportation, mobility, seating and bath aid needs for people of all ages. From car seats and standers for children with special needs to versatile wheelchairs that offer adults customized options and the freedom to go anywhere with confidence.

**143 Bath Shower & Commode Chair**
1003 International Dr
Oakdale, PA 15071-9226
724-695-2122
888-347-4537
FAX: 724-695-2922
e-mail: info@clarkehealthcare.com
www.clarkehealthcare.com

Aquatic Stainless steel shower/commode chairs and powered bathlifts. Mobeli portable grab bars, Dolomite rollators, Arco bed rails, Care bags for hygiene collection, DecPac portable ramps, Ableware eating, hygiene and dressing aids.

**144 Bath and Shower Bench 3301B**
Mada Medical Products
625 Washington Ave
Carlstadt, NJ 07072-2901
201-460-0454
800-526-6370
FAX: 201-460-3509
e-mail: dianelind@mail.madamedical.com
www.madainternational.com

*Jeffrey Adam, President*
The bath and shower bench is corrosion resistent, has a cross brace design and angled legs to prevent tipping, and seat height adjustments.

**145 BathEase**
3815 Darston St
Palm Harbor, FL 34685-3119
727-786-2604
888-747-7845
FAX: 727-786-2604
e-mail: bathease@aol.com
www.bathease.com

*Alison , President*
*Terry , Director of Design & Development*
*Gerry , Supervisor of Manufacturing*
*Bill , Supervisor of Operations*
BathEase is the original, standard size, residential style, acrylic bathtub with a door. Ideal for use in private homes by all who are ambulatory, the award winning design was specially created as an aid to daily living for the elderly and physically challenged. *$ 1897.00*

**146 Bathroom Transfer Systems**
Columbia Medical Manufacturing
11724 Willake Street
Santa Fe Springs, CA 90670-5032
562-282-0244
800-454-6612
FAX: 310-305-1718
e-mail: info@columbiamedical.com
www.columbiamedical.com

*Gary Werschmidt, CEO*
*Keith Wright, Dir. of Sales & Mktg*
*Sue Johnson, Dir. of Finance*
*Reese Regan, Dir. of Engineering*
Offers a complete line of bathroom transfer systems, bath lifts, reclining bath chairs, bath/shower/commode chairs, wrap-around bath supports, toilet supports, positioning commodes, premium air, foam and gel seat cushions, giat trainers and positioning restraint car seats that accommodate individuals from 20-130 pounds.

**147 Bathtub Safety Rail**
Arista Surgical Supply Company/AliMed
297 High St
Dedham, MA 02026-2852
781-329-2900
800-225-2610
FAX: 781-329-8392
e-mail: info@alimed.com
www.alimed.com

*Julian Cherubini, President*
Made of stainless steel, this safety rail fits in any size bathtub and offers safety and independence at bathing time. *$55.00*

**148 Braun Corporation**
Braun Corporation
574-946-6153
800-843-5438
e-mail: mediaquestions@braunlift.com
www.braunability.com

*Ralph Braun, Founder*
Offers a variety of assistive devices for the bath and surrounding environment.

**149 Can-Do Products Catalog**
Independent Living Aids
200 Robbins Lane
Jericho, NY 11753-9022
516-937-1848
800-537-2118
FAX: 516-937-3906
e-mail: can-do@independentliving.com
www.independentliving.com

*Irwin Schneidmill, President*
*Fran Hennelly, Sales Director*
*Russell Pennington, Marketing Director*
Provide essential aids and products for the blind and visually impaired.
*84 pages Quarterly*

**150 Clarke Healthcare Products, Inc.**
Clarke Health Care Products
1003 International Dr
Oakdale, PA 15071-9226
724-695-2122
888-347-4537
FAX: 724-695-2922
e-mail: info@clarkehealthcare.com
www.clarkehealthcare.com

Aquatic Stainless steel shower/commode chairs and powered bathlifts. Mobeli portable grab bars, Dolomite rollators, Arco bed rails, Care bags for hygiene collection, DecPac portable ramps, clarke aluminum ramps.

**151 Commode**
Maxi Aids
42 Executive Blvd
Farmingdale, NY 11735-4710
631-752-0521
800-522-6294
FAX: 631-752-0689
TTY: 800-281-3555
e-mail: sales@maxiaids.com
www.maxiaids.com

*Elliot Zaretsky, Founder & President*
Adjustable seat height for patient comfort. *$65.95*

**152 Deluxe Bath Bench with Adjustable Legs**
Maxi Aids
42 Executive Blvd
Farmingdale, NY 11735-4710
631-752-0521
800-522-6294
FAX: 631-752-0689
TTY: 800-281-3555
e-mail: sales@maxiaids.com
www.maxiaids.com

*Elliot Zaretsky, Founder & President*
Bath bench with back support and adjustable legs. *$ 49.95*

**153 Driving Systems**
16141 Runnymede St
Van Nuys, CA 91406-2913
818-782-6793
FAX: 818-782-6485
e-mail: info@drivingsystems.com
www.drivingsystems.com

*Rudolf Schinz, President*
*William C Butt, VP*
DSI is the manufacturer of the Scott Driving Controls for the severely disabled driver. Also manufacturers of the 'Wave Grip' grab rails and bathroom accessories for the disabled and elderly. DSI is also the importers of the Carospeed Menox Hand Controls, Left Foot Pedals and other handicapped driving aids.

**154 Electric Leg Bag Emptier and Tub Slide Shower Chair**
RD Equipment
230 Percival Dr
West Barnstable, MA 02668-1244
508-362-7498
FAX: 508-362-7498
e-mail: info@rdequipment.com
www.rdequipment.com

*Richard Dagostino, Owner*
Designed for independence, this small, lightweight, battery-operated valve attaches to the bottom of the leg bag. A simple flip of the switch empties the leg bag, allowing the user to take in unlimited amounts of fluids. Tub Slide Shower Chair is a complete bathroom care system, with no need of costly renovations. Eliminates all transfers in the bathroom. *$200.00*

**155 Freedom Bath**
Arjo Inc
2349 West Lake Street
Suite 250
Addison, IL 60101
630-785-4490
800-323-1245
FAX: 630-576-5020
e-mail: usa.info@ArjoHuntleigh.com
www.arjohuntleigh.com

Residents can relax on a semi-reclining seat and enjoy the soothing deluxe whirlpool system. Freedom Bath offers a revolutionary solution with its unique Roll-Door.The name of the company is ArjoHuntleigh.

**156 Great Big Safety Tub Mat**
Maxi Aids
42 Executive Blvd
Farmingdale, NY 11735-4710
631-752-0521
800-522-6294
FAX: 631-752-0689
TTY: 800-281-3555
e-mail: sales@maxiaids.com
www.maxiaids.com

*Elliot Zaretsky, Founder & President*
Tub mat provides security against falls in the bath and shower. *$16.95*

**157 Long Handled Bath Sponges**
Therapro, Inc.
225 Arlington St
Framingham, MA 01702-8723
508-872-9494
800-257-5376
FAX: 508-875-2062
e-mail: info@therapro.com
www.therapro.com

*Karen Conrad, Owner*
Plastic-handled, 18-inch bath sponge. Handle may be heated and bent for easy reach. *$2.50*

**158 Mariner Shower and Commode Chair**
Maxi Aids
42 Executive Blvd
Farmingdale, NY 11735-4710
631-752-0521
800-522-6294
FAX: 631-752-0689
TTY: 800-281-3555
e-mail: sales@maxiaids.com
www.maxiaids.com

*Elliot Zaretsky, Founder & President*
The all aluminum frame and stainless steel hardware provides optimum rust resistance making it ideal for use in the shower. Lightweight; folds easily for transport or storage. Padded 4-position seat with easy access, swing-away front riggings with tool-less adjustable height footrests. *$699.95*

**159 Modular Wall Grab Bars**
Frohock-Stewart
1 Invacare Way
Elyria, OH 44035-4190
440-329-6000
800-333-6900
FAX: 877-619-7996
www.invacare.com

*A Malachi Mixon III, Chairman*
*Gerald B. Blouch, President & CEO*
*Joseph B. Richey II, President, Invacare Technologies*
*Robert K. Gudbranson, Senior VP/CFO*
Engineered for strength and beauty, these bars can be assembled in various combinations to fit any bath or shower.

**160 Portable Shampoo Bowl**
Ambulatory Cosmetology Technicians
JK Designs
4004 NE 4th Street suite #107-456
Renton, WA 98059
206-999-8226
e-mail: info@portableshampoobowl.com
www.portableshampoobowl.com

A bowl designed to allow a person who is in a wheelchair or sitting on a regular chair to shampoo hair.

**161 Prelude**
Arjo Inc
2349 West Lake Street
Suite 250
Addison, IL 60101
630-785-4490
800-323-1245
FAX: 630-576-5020
e-mail: usa.info@ArjoHuntleigh.com
www.arjohuntleigh.com

Prelude shower cabinet allows patients to be showered in comfort and privacy, at the same time as protecting staff from excessive splashing. The name of the company is ArjoHuntleigh.

**162 SLIDER Bathing System**
Assistive Technology
21279 Protecta Dr
Elkhart, IN 46516-9539
574-522-7201
800-478-2363
FAX: 574-293-0202
e-mail: info@pvcdme.com
www.pvcdme.com

The SLIDER bathing system eliminates costly roll-in shower renovations, bathroom transfers and other family members don't lose access to a bathtub. The SLIDER works with any standard built-in tub and rolls directly over any commode. The SLIDER utilizes 5 inch lock casters and has two swing-away arm rests for lateral transfers. Sliding gear functions in either direction. The SLIDER bathing system...a cost effective alternative to bathroom renovation.

**163 Suregrip Bathtub Rail**
Frohock-Stewart
1 Invacare Way
Elyria, OH 44035-4190
440-329-6000
800-333-6900
FAX: 877-619-7996
www.invacare.com

*A Malachi Mixon III, Chairman*
*Gerald B. Blouch, President & CEO*
*Joseph B. Richey II, President, Invacare Technologies*
*Robert K. Gudbranson, Senior VP/CFO*
Compact and versatile, the bars have a soft-touch, contoured, white vinyl gripping area for added safety.

**164 Talking Bathroom Scale**
Independent Living Aids
200 Robbins Lane
Jericho, NY 11753-9022
516-937-1848
800-537-2118
FAX: 516-937-3906
e-mail: can-do@independentliving.com
www.independentliving.com

*Irwin Schneidmill, President*
*Fran Hennelly, Sales Director*
*Russell Pennington, Marketing Director*
Talking scale. *$59.95*

**165 Terry-Wash Mitt: Medium Size**
Therapro, Inc.
225 Arlington St
Framingham, MA 01702-8723
508-872-9494
800-257-5376
FAX: 508-875-2062
e-mail: info@therapro.com
www.therapro.com

*Karen Conrad, Owner*
Includes a thumb socket and a palm pocket to hold a bar of soap. *$8.00*

**166 Toilet Guard Rail**
Maxi Aids
42 Executive Blvd
Farmingdale, NY 11735-4710
631-752-0521
800-522-6294
FAX: 631-752-0689
TTY: 800-281-3555
e-mail: sales@maxiaids.com
www.maxiaids.com

*Elliot Zaretsky, Founder & President*
Made of chrome-plated, heavy gauge steel. Fits securely to the toilet for maximum sturdiness. *$43.95*

**167 Transfer Tub Bench**
Arista Surgical Supply Company/AliMed
297 High St
Dedham, MA 02026-2852
781-329-2900
800-225-2610
FAX: 781-329-8392
e-mail: info@alimed.com
www.alimed.com

*Julian Cherubini, President*
Curved padded backrest for comfortable support. Backrest also assists patient during lateral transfer. *$64.00*

**168 Tri-Grip Bathtub Rail**
Maxi Aids
42 Executive Blvd
Farmingdale, NY 11735-4710
631-752-0521
800-522-6294
FAX: 631-752-0689
TTY: 800-281-3555
e-mail: sales@maxiaids.com
www.maxiaids.com

*Elliot Zaretsky, Founder & President*
Two gripping heights for easy bathtub entrance or exit. *$36.95*

**169 Tub Slide Shower Chair**
RD Equipment
230 Percival Dr
West Barnstable, MA 02668-1244
508-362-7498
FAX: 508-362-7498
e-mail: info@rdequipment.com
www.rdequipment.com

*Richard Dagostino, Owner*
The tub slide shower chair was designed for the elderly and disabled to make any bathroom (at home or when travelling) accessible with little or no renovations. Go from the bed, to the commode and over to the bathtub for a shower using one product. No transfers in the bathroom whatsoever. *$2000.00*

## Bed

**170 ASSISTECH Special Needs**
4801 W Calle Don Miguel
Tucson, AZ 85757-1400
520-883-8600
866-674-3549
FAX: 520-883-5926
www.assistech.com

*Oliver Simoes, Owner*
Sells hearing, visual and mobility aid devices. *$39.00*

**171 Adjustable Bed**
Golden Technologies
401 Bridge St
Old Forge, PA 18518-2323
570-451-7477
800-624-6374
FAX: 800-628-5165
www.goldentech.com

*Richard Golden, CEO*
*Robert Golden, Co-Founder and Chairman*
*Fred Kiwak, Co-Founder and VP*
Trouble-free gear motor, safety features, dual massage, variable speed timer and more, for the ultimate sleep experience.

172 **Bye-Bye Decubiti Air Mattress Overlay**
Ken McRight Supplies
401 Linden Center Drive
Fort Collins, CO 80524
970-484-7967
800-467-7967
FAX: 970-484-3800
e-mail: info@randscot.com
www.randscot.com

*Joel Lerich, Co-Founder*
*Barbara , Co-Founder*
Originally designed for hospital beds, converts any bed into an exceptionally therapeutic, flotation unit when used between the conventional mattress and pad. The complete overlay is comprised of five individually inflatable, 100 percent natural rubber, ventilated sections enclosed within separate pockets of a soft fleece cover. Conforms to any configuration of electric or manual beds. *$731.50*

173 **Cervical Support Pillow**
Wise Enterprises
5017 El Don Dr
Rocklin, CA 95677-4417
916-624-3848
888-947-3368
e-mail: sales@winsent.com
www.wisent.com

*Tom Wise, Owner*
These hypoallergenic, antimicrobial fiber pillows support the neck in a natural position. Standard, midsize and petite pillows support the neck while sleeping on the back or side. The compact travel pillow offers support while sitting or lying down. The cervical roll has a gentle center and firm ends to ensure maximum comfort and proper support. Position the roll under the neck, back or knees. Standard and midsize fits adults, petite fits children and small adults.

174 **Dual Security Bed Rail**
Maxi Aids
42 Executive Blvd
Farmingdale, NY 11735-4710
631-752-0521
800-522-6294
FAX: 631-752-0689
TTY: 800-281-3555
e-mail: sales@maxiaids.com
www.maxiaids.com

*Elliot Zaretsky, Founder & President*
Sleep without worry! Dual rails for double the safety. Steel with Powder Coat. Rails adjust up and down.

175 **Foam Decubitus Bed Pads**
Profex Medical Products
P.O.Box 140188
Memphis, TN 38114
800-325-0196
FAX: 901-454-9850
e-mail: customercare@ProfexMed.com
www.profexmed.com

*Robert Gates Watel, Founder*
Convoluted foam provides extra back support and comfort for wheelchair users.

176 **Global Assistive Devices, Inc.**
1121 East Commercial Blvd. #39
Oakland Park, FL 33334-3920
954-776-1373
888-778-4237
FAX: 954-776-8136
TTY:954-776-1373
e-mail: sales@GlobalAssistive.com
www.GlobalAssistive.com

*Jason , General Manager*
Manufacturer of assistive devices designed to make life easier. Products include: vibrating watches/countdown timers, extra loud alarm clocks with adjustable tone and bed shaker option, door signalers, telephone ring signaler and caller identification for the television.

177 **Hard Manufacturing Company**
230 Grider St
Buffalo, NY 14215-3797
800-873-4273
www.hardmfg.com
Manufacturer of pediatric cribs and age appropriate youth beds. Free catalog.

178 **Jackson Cervipillo**
Wise Enterprises
5017 El Don Dr
Rocklin, CA 95677-4417
916-624-3848
888-947-3368
e-mail: sales@winsent.com
www.wisent.com

*Tom Wise, Owner*
The Jackson Cervipillo confortably supports the neck vertebrae when sleeping on the side or on the back. Pillow measures 7 in diameter and is 17 long. A machine-washable cover is available separately.

179 **NeckEase**
Wise Enterprises
5017 El Don Dr
Rocklin, CA 95677-4417
916-624-3848
888-947-3368
e-mail: sales@winsent.com
www.wisent.com

*Tom Wise, Owner*
Microwave NeckEase for penetrating heat that sooths stiff necks and shoulders, easing tension. NeckEase features a unique filling of organic, long grain rice and aromatic herbs and spices. When heated, this filling provides soothing, moist aromatherapy. Heat lasts about 30-45 minutes. Available in two sizes: small fits snugly around the neck, applying gentle pressure at the base of the skull; Large may be worn for a snug fit, or loosely for application on the shoulder and upper back.

180 **Permaflex Home Care Mattress**
BG Industries
8550 Balboa Blvd
Ste 214
Northridge, CA 91325-3564
818-894-0744
FAX: 818-894-7972
e-mail: maxifloat@bgind.com
www.bgind.com

*Larry Lankard, Director*
*Arnie Balonick, CEO/Director*
Mattress with flame retardant upholstery material, water-repellant, anti-microbial and tear-resistant cover, for extra comfort.

181 **SleepSafe Beds**
3629 Reed Creek Drive
Bassett, VA 24055
276-627-0088
866-852-2337
FAX: 276-627-0234
e-mail: SleepSafeBed@SleepSafeBed.com
www.sleepsafebed.com

*Joe Hallock, CEO*
*Gregg Weinschreider, President*
*Casey Collins, Office Manager*
*Al Flora, Sales*
Perfect for adult home or home care use. Offering twin or full size bed frames in classic style, these beds offer an attractive alternative to a hospital bed. Keeps the user safe during rest and electrically adjusts smoothly for user comfort and caregiver ease of use.

**182 Sonic Alert Bed Shaker**
ASSISTECH
4801 W Calle Don Miguel
Tucson, AZ 85757-1400
520-883-8600
866-674-3549
FAX: 520-883-5926
www.assistech.com

*Oliver Simoes, Owner*
Sells hearing, visual and mobility aid devices. *$49.00*

**183 Vibes Bed Shaker**
ASSISTECH
4801 W Calle Don Miguel
Tucson, AZ 85757-1400
520-883-8600
866-674-3549
FAX: 520-883-5926
www.assistech.com

*Oliver Simoes, Owner*
Sells hearing, visual and mobility aid devices.

**184 Waterproof Sheet-Topper Mattress and Chair Pad**
Pillow Talk
260 Madison Avenue
New York, NY 10016
732-780-9483
FAX: 732-780-0279
e-mail: info@PTIproductmarketing.com
www.pillowtalkusa.com

*Dorothy Fajerman, President*
*Jack Fajerman, Marketing Director*
This soft pad lies on the top sheet, absorbing accidents from incontinence, pregnancy or medical problems. Waterproof barrier locks out moisture, soiling and stains and eliminates midnight linen changes and the resulting laundry. Available in bed sizes W/4 Anchor, twin, full, queen, king, and crib.

## Communication

**185 ADA Hotel Built-In Alerting System**
HARC Mercantile
1111 W Centre Ave
Portage, MI 49024-5317
269-324-1615
800-445-9968
FAX: 269-324-2387
TTY: 800-445-9968
e-mail: info@harc.com
www.harc.com

Visual alerting system for ADA compliance for multihousing/rooms facilities, like hospitals, dorms, senior housing for persons who are hard of hearing or deaf. Alerts to five conditions: smoke, door bell, telephone ring, wake up and House central alarm.

**186 Access Control Systems: NHX Nurse Call System**
Aiphone Corporation
1700 130th Ave NE
Bellevue, WA 98005-2203
425-455-0510
800-692-0200
FAX: 425-455-0071
e-mail: info@aiphone.com
www.aiphone.com

*Futoshi Tanaka, President/CEO*
AIPHONE manufactures audio and video intercom systems for home or business to help the physically disabled answer doors and communicate through physical barriers; also ADA-compliant emergency call intercom stations for use in public facilities and an Environmental Control System for persons with limited mobility.

**187 Adaptek Systems**
14224 Plank Street
Fort Wayne, IN 46818
260-637-8660
FAX: 260-637-8597
e-mail: info@adapteksystems.com
www.adapteksystems.com

Developers of a voice output module designed to work with the Kurzweil voice-recognition system. The device provides voice output of what the computer hears for persons with visual impairments.

**188 Akron Resources**
20 La Porte St
Arcadia, CA 91006-2827
626-254-9005
800-841-0884
FAX: 626-254-9266
www.arkon.com

*Paul Brassard, Owner*
*Aaron Roth, VP, Marketing & Sales*
*Benjamin Arana, Sr. Account Manager*
*Cleber Gandra, Account Manager*
Manufacturers of infrared amplification systems for televisions or stereos. $29-$69.00. The company name is Arkon Resources.

**189 Amplified Handsets**
HARC Mercantile
1111 W Centre Ave
Portage, MI 49024-5317
269-324-1615
800-445-9968
FAX: 269-324-2387
TTY: 800-445-9968
e-mail: info@harc.com
www.harc.com

Choices of touch activated, electronic control, rotary (thumb wheel) volume control, that can directly replace old handset, stocked in round and square styles. This also includes an electric transmitter with variable settings. *$39.95*

**190 Amplified Phones**
HARC Mercantile
1111 W Centre Ave
Portage, MI 49024-5317
269-324-1615
800-445-9968
FAX: 269-324-2387
TTY: 800-445-9968
e-mail: info@harc.com
www.harc.com

Low frequency ringer, indicator light, enhances or amplifies sound, some that automatically return to normal dial tone when phone receiver is hung up, lighted easy to read dial pad and volume control boosts incoming sound. *$95.00*

**191 Amplified Portable Phone**
HARC Mercantile
1111 W Centre Ave
Portage, MI 49024-5317
269-324-1615
800-445-9968
FAX: 269-324-2387
TTY: 800-445-9968
e-mail: info@harc.com
www.harc.com

Portable amplified phones. *$199.00*

**192 Artificial Larynx**
HARC Mercantile
1111 W Centre Ave
Portage, MI 49024-5317
269-324-1615
800-445-9968
FAX: 269-324-2387
TTY: 800-445-9968
e-mail: info@harc.com
www.harc.com

For people unable to use their larynx, a hand-held speaking aid that simulates the natural vibrations of voice. *$220.00*

**193 Assistive Technology**
333 Elm St
Dedham, MA 02026-4530
781-461-8200
800-793-9227
FAX: 781-461-8213
e-mail: sales@tobiiATI.com
www.tobii.com/

*Henrik Eskilsson, CEO*
*John Elvesjo, Executive Vice President and CTO*
*Mårten Skogö, Chief Science Officer*
*Oscar Werner, Executive Vice President*

A premiere developer of innovative technology solutions for people with physical and learning disabilities. Breakthrough products enable people of all ages and abilities to live and learn independently. Supportive material for teachers, clinicians and those with disabilities.

**194 Big Red Switch**
AbleNet
2625 Patton Road
Roseville, MN 55113-1308
651-294-2200
800-322-0956
FAX: 651-294-2222
e-mail: customerservice@ablenetinc.com
www.ablenetinc.com

*Bill Sproull, Chairman*
*Jennifer Thalhuber, CEO/President*
*Cheryl Volkman, Board of Directors*
*William Mills, Board of Directors*

Five inches across the top and activates no matter where on its surface it is touched. It is made of shatterproof plastic and contains a cord storage compartment. Also available in green, yellow and blue. *$42.00*

**195 Cornell Communications**
7915 N 81st St
Milwaukee, WI 53223-3830
414-351-4660
800-558-8957
FAX: 414-351-4657
e-mail: sales@cornell.com
www.cornell.com

Cornell's Rescue Assistance Systems allow personnel to request emergency assistance. Applications include handicapped evacuations, parking garages and elevators. Voice, intercom and visual only signaling systems are available.

**196 Davis Center**
19 State Rte 10 E
Ste 25
Succasunna, NJ 07876
862-251-4637
FAX: 862-251-4642
e-mail: info@thedaviscenter.com
www.thedaviscenter.com

*Dorinne S Davis MA CCC-A FAAA RC, President*

Offers sound-based therapies supporting positive change in learning, development and wellness. All ages/all disabilities. The Davis Model of Sound Intervention-an alernative approach. The company name is The Davis Center.

**197 Flashing Lamp Telephone Ring Alerter**
Independent Living Aids
200 Robbins Lane
Jericho, NY 11753-9022
516-937-1848
800-537-2118
FAX: 516-937-3906
e-mail: can-do@independentliving.com
www.independentliving.com

*Irwin Schneidmill, President*
*Fran Hennelly, Sales Director*
*Russell Pennington, Marketing Director*

Once your phone is plugged into the Telephone Ring Alerter, the lamp light will flash with each ring, alerting you that there is a phone call. *$62.00*

**198 Harc Mercantile Ltd**
HARC Mercantile
1111 W Centre Ave
Portage, MI 49024-5317
269-324-1615
800-445-9968
FAX: 269-324-2387
TTY: 800-445-9968
e-mail: info@harc.com
www.harc.com

HARC sells assistive devices for the hard of hearing and deaf. amplified telephones, personal amplifiers, personal and large area fm systems, induction hearing loops, signaling systems for wake-up,smoke/fire door and telephone, haering aid batteries and supplies. *$39.95*

**199 Ideal-Phone**
IDEAMATICS
1364 Beverly Road
McLean, VA 22101-3617
703-903-4972
800-247-IDEA
FAX: 703-903-8949
e-mail: ideamatics@ideamatics.net
www.ideamatics.com

*David L Danner, President*
*Michael A. Schwartz, Vice President*
*Mark A. Moore, Vice President of Operations*

Integrates the personal computer and the telephone into a single, efficient workstation. It is ideal for mobility-impaired persons and others who need a hands-free operation of the phone. The Ideal-Phone includes one PC Board, a Plantronics headset, software for access and logging and complete documentation. It can be integrated into programs or pops-up over any application. MS-DOS based, version 3.0 or higher are available. *$195.00*

**200 IntelliKeys**
IntelliTools
24 Prime Parkway
Natick, MA 01760
303-651-2829
800-547-6747
FAX: 720-382-7438
e-mail: customerservice@cambiumlearning.com
www.intellitools.com

*Arjan Khalsa, CEO*

Card and cable to create keyboard port on Apple IIe computer to allow use of IntelliKeys alternative keyboard.

**201 LPB Communications**
960 Brook Rd
Norristown, PA 19401
856-365-8080
FAX: 856-365-8999
e-mail: info@LPBInc.om
www.lpbinc.com

*John Devecka, VP Sales*

Limited area AM and FM broadcast systems for hearing assistance and language translation manufacturing since 1960. Systems for small conference halls, churches and Olympic stadiums. Components or complete system. *$400.00*

**202 Language, Learning & Living**
Prentke Romich Company
1022 Heyl Rd
Wooster, OH 44691-9786
330-262-1984
800-262-1984
FAX: 330-263-4829
e-mail: info@prentrom.com
www.prentrom.com

*David L Moffatt, President*
*Barry Romich, Co-Founder*
*Dave Moffatt, President & COO*

A Minspeak application program designed for adolescent and adult individuals with developmental disabilities and associated learning difficulties. The software is used with Prentke Romich Company augmentative communication devices. *$355.00*

**203 Large Button Speaker Phone**
HARC Mercantile
1111 W Centre Ave
Portage, MI 49024-5317
269-324-1615
800-445-9968
FAX: 269-324-2387
TTY: 800-445-9968
e-mail: info@harc.com
www.harc.com

Speakerphone with or without remote control. *$395.00*

**204 Large Print Telephone Dial**
Maxi Aids
42 Executive Blvd
Farmingdale, NY 11735-4710
631-752-0521
800-522-6294
FAX: 631-752-0689
TTY: 800-281-3555
e-mail: sales@maxiaids.com
www.maxiaids.com

*Elliot Zaretsky, Founder & President*
Pressure sensitive dial with numbers that are easy to see for the disabled. *$69.00*

**205 Large Print Touch-Telephone Overlays**
Maxi Aids
42 Executive Blvd
Farmingdale, NY 11735-4710
631-752-0521
800-522-6294
FAX: 631-752-0689
TTY: 800-281-3555
e-mail: sales@maxiaids.com
www.maxiaids.com

*Elliot Zaretsky, Founder & President*
Pressure-sensitive and easy to apply overlays that make everyday phones accessible. *$49.00*

**206 Liberator**
Prentke Romich Company
1022 Heyl Rd
Wooster, OH 44691-9786
330-262-1984
800-262-1984
FAX: 330-263-4829
e-mail: info@prentrom.com
www.prentrom.com

*David L Moffatt, President*
*Barry Romich, Co-Founder*
*Dave Moffatt, President & COO*
A portable electronic communication device that uses Minspeak so that symbols are used to represent words, sentences or phrases. Liberator can be accessed by pressing keys, optical headpointing and a wide variety of switch activated scans. It can be configured with 8, 32 or 128 locations. It offers a variety of unique features to permit the most effective communication possible. $7,345-$8,575.

**207 Metropolitan Washington Ear**
12061 Tech Road
Silver Spring, MD 20904-7826
301-681-6636
FAX: 301-625-1986
e-mail: information@washear.org
www.washear.org

*Brother Hilary Mettes, Chairman*
*Freddie L Peaco, President Pro Tem*
*Dr. George Long, Vice President*
*Neely Oplinger, Executive Director*
Multi-media reading service for blind and visually impaired. Offering 24 hour audio radio reading, dial-in newspapers and web casting, as well as audio description at theaters, museums and films. The name of the company is THE METROPOLITAN WASHINGTON EAR, INC..

**208 Mini Teleloop**
HARC Mercantile
1111 W Centre Ave
Portage, MI 49024-5317
269-324-1615
800-445-9968
FAX: 269-324-2387
TTY: 800-445-9968
e-mail: info@harc.com
www.harc.com

Home induction loop amplifier for use with hearing aids equipped with T-Coil. *$159.95*

**209 Multiple Phone/Device Switch**
HARC Mercantile
1111 W Centre Ave
Portage, MI 49024-5317
269-324-1615
800-445-9968
FAX: 269-324-2387
TTY: 800-445-9968
e-mail: info@harc.com
www.harc.com

Used to switch phone lines between two devices. *$34.95*

**210 Personal FM Systems**
HARC Mercantile
1111 W Centre Ave
Portage, MI 49024-5317
269-324-1615
800-445-9968
FAX: 269-324-2387
TTY: 800-445-9968
e-mail: info@harc.com
www.harc.com

Wireless FM systems transmit sound via a radio carrier wave. *$599.95*

**211 Personal Infrared Listening System**
HARC Mercantile
1111 W Centre Ave
Portage, MI 49024-5317
269-324-0301
800-445-9968
FAX: 269-324-2387
TTY: 269-324-1615
e-mail: info@harc.com
www.harc.com

Wireless method of listening to TV and radio with individually controlled amplification. *$199.00*

**212 Prentke Romich Company**
1022 Heyl Rd
Wooster, OH 44691-9786
330-262-1984
800-262-1984
FAX: 330-263-4829
e-mail: info@prentrom.com
www.prentrom.com

*David L Moffatt, President*
*Barry Romich, Co-Founder*
*Dave Moffatt, President / COO*
The Prentke Romich Company is a full service company offering easy, yet powerful communication aids. The company believes in supporting customers before and after the sale by offering funding assistance, distance learning training, extended warranty, service assistance and much more. Visit our website to view our full line catalog, read about our success stories and to sign up for our online newsletter.

**213 Push to Talk Amplified Handset**
HARC Mercantile
1111 W Centre Ave
Portage, MI 49024-5317
269-324-0301
800-445-9968
FAX: 269-324-2387
TTY: 269-324-1615
e-mail: info@harc.com
www.harc.com

Replacement receiver which is hearing aid compatible and is designed for high noise conditions. *$79.95*

**214 Room Valet Visual-Tactile Alerting System**
HARC Mercantile
1111 W Centre Ave
Portage, MI 49024-5317
269-324-0301
800-445-9968
FAX: 269-324-2387
TTY: 269-324-1615
e-mail: info@harc.com
www.harc.com

ADA compliant built-in visual-tactile alerting system. The Room Valet is fully supervised and has power failure back up. Alerts to in-room smoke, building alarm, door, phone and alarm clock. Designed for permanent installation.

**215 Silent Call Communications**
5095 Williams Lake Rd
Waterford, MI 48329-3553
248-673-7353
800-572-5227
FAX: 248-673-7360
e-mail: customerservice@silentcall.com
www.silentcall.com

*George Elwell, President*
*Diana Elwell, President*
*Lisa DeLeuil, Director of Sales & Marketing*
Alerting devices such as paging systems and smoke detectors for deaf and deaf-blind people.

**216 Sonic Alert**
Harris Communications
15155 Technology Dr
Eden Prairie, MN 55344-2273
952-906-1180
800-825-6758
FAX: 952-906-1099
TTY: 800-825-9187
e-mail: info@harriscomm.com
www.harriscomm.com

*Dr.Robert Harris, Owner*
*Lori Foss, Marketing Director*
Offers visual alerting devices that provide safety and convenience by turning vital sound into flashing light: telephone ring signalers, doorbell signalers, baby cry signalers and wake up alarms. Free catalog available.

**217 Sound Induction Receiver**
HARC Mercantile
1111 W Centre Ave
Portage, MI 49024-5317
269-324-0301
800-445-9968
FAX: 269-324-2387
TTY: 269-324-1615
e-mail: info@harc.com
www.harc.com
Sound induction receiver to be used with any loop system. *$67.00*

**218 SpeakEasy Communication Aid**
AbleNet
2808 Fairview Ave N
Saint Paul, MN 55113-1308
612-379-0956
800-322-0956
FAX: 612-379-9143
e-mail: customerservice@ablenetinc.com
www.ablenetinc.com

*Jennifer Thalhuber, President / CEO*
SpeakEasy is a digitalized voice output communication Aid that is ideal for anyone who is beginning to develop communication skills such as making choices and identifying symbols. It holds 12 messages totaling four minutes and 20 seconds of recording time. It measures 7 1/2 inch by 1 3/4 inch and weighs only one pound. Activate messages using the built-in keyboard or via external switch. *$399.00*

**219 Speech Discrimination Unit**
HARC Mercantile
1111 W Centre Ave
Portage, MI 49024-5317
269-324-0301
800-445-9968
FAX: 269-324-2387
TTY: 269-324-1615
e-mail: info@harc.com
www.harc.com

Speech Adjust-A-Tone improves speech discrimination for use with telephone and/or TV and radio. *$189.95*

**220 Speechmaker-Personal Speech Amplifier**
HARC Mercantile
1111 W Centre Ave
Portage, MI 49024-5317
269-324-0301
800-445-9968
FAX: 269-324-2387
TTY: 269-324-1615
e-mail: info@harc.com
www.harc.com

Portable, body worn, personal speech amplifier for people with a weak voice. *$316.00*

**221 Standard Touch Turner Sip & Puff Switch**
Access to Recreation
8 Sandra Ct
Newbury Park, CA 91320-4302
805-498-7535
800-634-4351
FAX: 805-498-8186
e-mail: customerservice@accesstr.com
www.accesstr.com

*Don Krebs, President /Founder*
A page turning device.

**222 Step-by-Step Communicator**
AbleNet
2808 Fairview Ave N
Saint Paul, MN 55113-1308
612-379-0956
800-322-0956
FAX: 612-379-9143
e-mail: customerservice@ablenetinc.com
www.ablenetinc.com

*Jennifer Thalhuber, President / CEO*
Allows you to record a series of messages (as many as you want up to the 75 second limit). It has a 2 1/2 inches diameter switch surface and is 3 inches at its tallest point. Angled switch surface makes it easy to see and access. *$129.00*

**223 Strobe Light Signalers**
1111 W Centre Ave
Portage, MI 49024-5317
269-324-0301
800-445-9968
FAX: 269-324-2387
TTY: 269-324-1615
e-mail: info@harc.com
www.harc.com

Strobe alerts. Plugs into receivers for signaling systems.

**224 TTY's: Telephone Device for the Deaf**
HARC Mercantile
1111 W Centre Ave
Portage, MI 49024-5317
269-324-0301
800-445-9968
FAX: 269-324-2387
TTY: 269-324-1615
e-mail: info@harc.com
www.harc.com

With or without printer. *$239.00*

**225 TalkTrac Wearable Communicator**
Ablenet
2808 Fairview Ave N
Saint Paul, MN 55113-1308
612-379-0956
800-322-0956
FAX: 612-379-9143
e-mail: customerservice@ablenetinc.com
www.ablenetinc.com

*Jennifer Thalhuber, President / CEO*
The TalkTrac Wearable Communicator is a personal, portable communication aid that is wearable on the wrist. TalkTrac features: simple to use, 75 seconds of recording time, four 3/4 x 1/2 message locations, rechargeable, water resistant, adjustable 9 inch band, Boardmaker compatible.

**226 Talking Calculators**
ASSISTECH
4801 W Calle Don Miguel
Tucson, AZ 85757-1400
520-883-8600
866-674-3549
FAX: 520-883-5926
www.assistech.com

*Oliver Simoes, Owner*
*Marsha Neilson, Sales Representative*
Carries a complete line of assistive products for the deaf and ahrd of hearing, blind and visually impaired, speech impaired, and physically challenged . They also feature products for everyone such as medicine reminder watches and electronic language translators.

**227 Talking Clocks**
HARC Mercantile
1111 W Centre Ave
Portage, MI 49024-5317
269-324-0301
800-445-9968
FAX: 269-324-2387
TTY: 269-324-1615
e-mail: info@harc.com
www.harc.com

Talking clocks with loud alarms, high and low volume control, choices of sound effects, hourly report options. Other languages are available. *$20.50*

**228 Talking Watches**
HARC Mercantile
1111 W Centre Ave
Portage, MI 49024-5317
269-324-0301
800-445-9968
FAX: 269-324-2387
TTY: 269-324-1615
e-mail: info@harc.com
www.harc.com

Digital display, hourly reports, alarm with rooster crow, in English or Spanish. *$20.25*

**229 Telecaption Adapter**
HARC Mercantile
1111 W Centre Ave
Portage, MI 49024-5317
269-324-0301
800-445-9968
FAX: 269-324-2387
TTY: 269-324-1615
e-mail: info@harc.com
www.harc.com

Caption opens up the world of television to hearing impaired people. Viewers can read on the screen what they may not be able to hear. Closed captions are the dialogue and sound effects of a TV program or home video printed on the screen, similar to subtitles. *$ 159.95*

**230 Touch Turner-Page Turning Devices**
Touch Turner Company
13621 103rd Ave NE
Arlington, WA 98223-8827
360-651-1962
888-811-1962
FAX: 360-658-9380
e-mail: touchturner@worldnet.att.net
www.touchturner.com

Turns pages in either direction powered by flashlight batteries or AC Adapter. Works with soft or hard bound books and magazines.

**231 Unity**
Prentke Romich Company
1022 Heyl Rd
Wooster, OH 44691-9786
330-262-1984
800-262-1984
FAX: 330-263-4829
e-mail: info@prentrom.com
www.prentrom.com

*David L Moffatt, President*
*Barry Romich, Co-Founder*
*Dave Moffatt, President / COO*
A Minspeak application program available for the Liberator and Delta Talker communication devices. Provides single word vocabulary to people of all ages at varying stages of language development, who may be either cognitively intact or challenged. *$355.00*

**232 Vantage**
Prentke Romich Company
1022 Heyl Rd
Wooster, OH 44691-9786
330-262-1984
800-262-1984
FAX: 330-263-4829
e-mail: info@prentrom.com
www.prentrom.com

*David L Moffatt, President*
*Barry Romich, Co-Founder*
*Dave Moffatt, President / COO*
Vantage is a portable communication aid that features the Unity Enhanced vocabulary software and a large high quality dynamic display. Vantage also employs the recently upgraded 4.0 operating system that makes system settings quick and easy. Vantage has synthesized speech powered by DECtalk Software, Spelling and Word Protection software, built-in visor (flip-up protective cover), digitized speech capability and built-in computer access and ECU controls. 15 and 45 location keyguards available. *$6295.00*

**233 Vibrotactile Personal Alerting System**
HARC Mercantile
1111 W Centre Ave
Portage, MI 49024-5317
269-324-0301
800-445-9968
FAX: 269-324-2387
TTY: 269-324-1615
e-mail: info@harc.com
www.harc.com

Composed of a small wireless personal device that receives coded signals and a group of transmitters that send them. *$195.95*

**234 Voice Amplified Handsets**
HARC Mercantile
1111 W Centre Ave
Portage, MI 49024-5317
269-324-0301
800-445-9968
FAX: 269-324-2387
TTY: 269-324-1615
e-mail: info@harc.com
www.harc.com

Designed for the person who has a weak speaking voice. Control increases the level of the user's voice and can increase as much as 30%. *$65.00*

235 **WalkerTalker**
Prentke Romich Company
1022 Heyl Rd
Wooster, OH 44691-9786
330-262-1984
800-262-1984
FAX: 330-263-4829
e-mail: info@prentrom.com
www.prentrom.com

*David L Moffatt, President*
*Barry Romich, Co-Founder*
*Dave Moffatt, President / COO*
A portable direct selection communication device for active persons. The 16 location keyboard and speakers are carried in a belt that straps comfortably around the waist. The keyboard can be removed from its pouch to use by activating keys. Two versions are available, standard memory and expanded memory. *$1195.00*

## Chairs

236 **Adjustable Chair**
Bailey Manufacturing Company
P.O.Box 130
Lodi, OH 44254-130
330-948-2655
800-321-8372
FAX: 800-224-5390
e-mail: baileymfg@baileymfg.com
www.baileymfg.com

*Larry Strimple, President*
*Sandy Mooney, Customer Service*
*Judie Butler, Dealer Contact*
The seat and footboard of this versatile chair can be adjusted to accommodate children of various sizes. A classroom-suitable variation of this model is also available.

237 **Adjustable Clear Acrylic Tray**
Bailey Manufacturing Company
P.O.Box 130
Lodi, OH 44254-130
330-948-2655
800-321-8372
FAX: 800-224-5390
e-mail: baileymfg@baileymfg.com
www.baileymfg.com

*Larry Strimple, President*
*Sandy Mooney, Customer Service*
*Judie Butler, Dealer Contact*
Adjusts for height and depth and is equipped with a spill rim for easy to clean edges.

238 **Adjustable Rigid Chair**
Kuschall North America
1811 Lefthand Cir
Ste B
Longmont, CO 80501-6785
303-682-2571
888-682-2571
FAX: 866-651-6973
www.kuschallna.com

*Terry Mulkey, Owner*
The Champion 3000 is a fully adjustable rigid frame chair weighing only 21 pounds with a new clamping system that adjusts seat height and angle without tools.

239 **Adjustable Tee Stool**
Bailey Manufacturing Company
P.O.Box 130
Lodi, OH 44254-130
330-948-2655
800-321-8372
FAX: 800-224-5390
e-mail: baileymfg@baileymfg.com
www.baileymfg.com

*Larry Strimple, President*
*Sandy Mooney, Customer Service*
*Judie Butler, Dealer Contact*
May be used to encourage balance as well as develop integrative and perceptual motor skills.

240 **BackSaver**
BackSaver Products Company
53 Jeffrey Ave
Holliston, MA 01746-2084
508-893-6990
800-251-2225
FAX: 508-429-8698
e-mail: stevek@backsaver.com
www.backsavercorp.com

*Ed Foye, Owner*
Eliminates slouching and extra pressure on your back and thighs which impairs circulation.

241 **Better Back**
Orthopedic Products Corporation
4100 1/2 Glencoe Ave
Marina Del Rey, CA 90292
323-584-6977
FAX: 310-306-0177

An orthopedic multi-purpose seat.

242 **Carendo**
Arjo Inc
2349 West Lake Street
Suite 250
Addison, IL 60101
630-785-4490
800-323-1245
FAX: 630-576-5020
e-mail: usa.info@ArjoHuntleigh.com
www.arjo.com

*Philip M. Croxford, President/ CEO*
The Carendo hygiene chair has been designed for caregivers.

243 **Century 50/60XR Sit**
Arjo Inc
2349 West Lake Street
Suite 250
Addison, IL 60101
630-785-4490
800-323-1245
FAX: 630-576-5020
e-mail: usa.info@ArjoHuntleigh.com
www.arjo.com

*Philip M. Croxford, President/ CEO*
This bathing system has a built-in cleaning/disinfectant injection system with adjustable flowmeter. The incorporation of an automatic hot water alarm/shut-off system, and digital temperature monitors, helps to assure resident safety and comfort.

244 **Convert-Able Table**
REAL Design
187 S Main St
Dolgeville, NY 13329-1455
315-429-3071
800-696-7041
FAX: 315-429-3071
e-mail: rdesign@twcny.rr.com
www.realdesigninc.com

*Sam Camardello, Owner*
This table has push button height adjustment and interchangeable tops so it can become a desk, art easel or a sensory stimulation bowl.

**245 Evac + Chair Emergency Evacuation Chair**
Evac + Chair North America LLC
3000 Marcus Ave
Ste 3E6
Lake Success, NY 11042-1012
516-502-4240
FAX: 516-327-8220
e-mail: sales@evac-chair.com
www.evac-chair.com

*Richard Perl, VP Business Dev.*
*David Egen, Founder*
Gravity driven evaluation chair allows one nondisabled person to smoothly glide a seated passenger down fire stairs and across landings to exit on a combination of wheels and track belts. Pivots in own width for tight landing turns. Aluminum; weight 19 pounds. Compactly stores on wall mount, 38 by 20 by 9 inches. Maximum capacity 330 pounds. Self braking features. No installation, works on all fire exit stairs. *$950.00*

**246 Golden Technologies**
401 Bridge St
Old Forge, PA 18518-2323
570-451-7477
800-624-6374
FAX: 800-628-5165
e-mail: johngcei@excite.com
www.goldentech.com

*Richard Golden, CEO*
*Robert Golden, Chairman of the Board*
*Fred Kiwak, VP of R & D*
The largest facility in the world dedicated solely to the manufacture of lift chairs.

**247 High-Low Chair**
Rehab and Educational Aids for Living
NY
800-696-7041
e-mail: rdesign@twcny.rr.com
www.realdesigninc.com/

*Sam Camardello, President*
*Kris Wohnsen, Vice President*
A high chair and mobile floor sitter in one. The high-low chair comes with colorful upholstered wipe clean seat and height adjustable tray. The chair has a single lever adjustment to change the seat height. Lateral and head supports are available as options. *$ 1199.00*

**248 Ladybug Corner Chair**
Rehab and Educational Aids for Living
NY
800-696-7041
e-mail: rdesign@twcny.rr.com
www.realdesigninc.com/

*Sam Camardello, President*
*Kris Wohnsen, Vice President*
For children 0-3 years. This chair is adjustable for long legs for conventional sitting.

**249 Lumex Recliner**
Graham-Field Health Products
2935 Northeast Pkwy
Atlanta, GA 30360-2808
770-368-4700
800-347-5678
FAX: 770-368-4702
e-mail: cs@grahamfield.com
www.grahamfield.com

*Ken Spett, CEO*
Combines therapeutic benefits of position change with attractive appearance.

**250 Modular QuadDesk**
Gpk
535 Floyd Smith Dr
El Cajon, CA 92020-1228
619-593-7381
800-468-8679
FAX: 888-755-5603
e-mail: sales@gpk.com
www.gpk.com
Worktable specially dsigned for people in wheelchairs who lack grip strength, or cannot learn or reach. Small or medium.

**251 Mulholland Positioning Systems**
P.O.Box 70
839 Albion Avenue
Burley, ID 83318
208-878-3840
800-543-4769
FAX: 208-878-3841
e-mail: info@mulhollandinc.com
www.mulhollandinc.com

*Larry Mulholland, Owner*
*Dick Stepan, Sales Manager*
Provides a full line of standing aids, seating systems, adaptive components and bath aids.

**252 Prime Engineering**
Prime Engineering
4202 W Sierra Madre Ave
Fresno, CA 93722-3932
559-276-0991
800-827-8263
FAX: 800-800-3355
e-mail: info@primeengineering.com
www.primeengineering.com

*Bruce Boegel, CFO*
*Mary Wilson Boegel, President*
*Mark Allen, Vice President*
*Dawn Perez, Customer Service Manager*
Prime Engineering is a leading manufacturer of adult and pediatric standing devices and patient transfer equipment. Products include the all-new Support Standing System, Granstand III MSS Standing System Kidstand III MSS Standing System Superstand Multi-Position Pediatric Stander, the Lift, the CindyLift and the Original Lift Walker.

**253 Roll Chair**
Bailey Manufacturing Company
P.O. Box 130
Lodi, OH 44254-130
330-948-2655
800-321-8372
FAX: 800-224-5390
e-mail: baileymfg@baileymfg.com
www.baileymfg.com

*Larry Strimple, President*
*Sandy Mooney, Customer Service*
*Judie Butler, Dealer Contact*
The padded roll helps maintain proper hip abduction and prevents scissoring of the legs.

**254 Safari Tilt**
Convaid Products
2830 California Street
Torrance, CA 90503
310-618-0111
888-266-8243
FAX: 310-618-2166
www.convaid.com

*Chris Braun, President*
A semi-contour seat provides positioning with 5-45 degree tilt adjustment. One step design folds compactly into a lightweight chair.

**255 Spatial Tilt Custom Chair**
Redman Powerchair
Suite 107
1601 S Pantano Road
Tucson, AZ 85710-6791
520-546-6002
800-727-6684
FAX: 520-546-5530
e-mail: info@redmanpowerchair.com
www.redmanpowerchair.com

*Don Redman, CEO*
*Paula Redman, CFO*
*Scott Evans, Regulatory affairs*
*Samuel Redman, Sales manager*
Custom chair designed for comfort with a solid seat and back with modifications available for seat depth, height or width.

**256 Transfer Bench with Back**
Frohock-Stewart
39400 Taylor Parkway
North Ridgeville, OH 44035-6263
440-329-6000
FAX: 440-366-1803
www.invacare.com

*A. Malachi Mixon III, Chairman of the Board*
*Mark Sullivan, VP & Category Mgr*
*Mal Mixon, CEO*
This bench with air-cushioned seat sections has a full, reversible backrest for safety and comfort.

## Cushions & Wedges

**257 Action Products**
954 Sweeney Drive
Hagerstown, MD 21740-4910
301-797-1414
800-228-7763
FAX: 301-733-2073
e-mail: service@actionproducts.com
www.actionproducts.com

*Mistie Witt, President*
*Janet Kaplan, Marketing Director*
Wheelchair pads, mattress pads, positioning cushions and insoles that aid in the prevention and cure of pressure sores by reducing pressure. All products are made of Akton viscoelastic polymer that does not leak, flow or bottom out. Manufacturer of the Xact line of positioning cushions for patients with high risk of skin breakdown.

**258 Adjustable Wedge**
Bailey Manufacturing Company
P.O. Box 130
Lodi, OH 44254-130
800-321-8372
FAX: 800-224-5390
baileymfg.com
Orthopedically and neurologically disabled children can freely move arms and hands while lying on this adjustable wedge.

**259 Back-Huggar Pillow**
Bodyline Comfort Systems
3730 Kori Rd
Jacksonville, FL 32257-6036
904-262-4068
800-874-7715
FAX: 904-262-2225
e-mail: info@bodyline.com
www.bodyline.com

*Dr.John W. Fiore, Owner*
Exclusive design makes almost any seat more comfortable by exerting soothing pressure against back muscles and discs.

**260 Bye-Bye Decubiti (BBD)**
Ken McRight Supplies
7456 S Oswego Ave
Tulsa, OK 74136-5903
918-492-9657
FAX: 918-492-9694

*Ken McRight, President*
The BBD therapeutic wheelchair cushions have been market-proven since 1951 - in the prevention and cure of pressure sores (decubiti). These natural rubber inflatable products have recently been expanded to include pediatric, sports and double-valve models. Moderately priced, they offer a viable and cost-effective alternative in the market. $84.00-$112.00.

**261 Dynamic Systems**
104 Morrow Branch Rd
Leicester, NC 28748-9635
828-683-3523
855-786-6283
FAX: 828-683-3511
e-mail: dsi@sunmatecushions.com
www.sunmatecushions.com

*Charles A Yost, CEO*
*Lewis McCrain, General Manager*
SunMate orthopedic foam sheets and cushions, pudgee pads for pressure relief and skin breakdown prevention, laminar wheelchair cushions and Foam-in-Place Seating for custom molding seat inserts. Sample packs and literature available upon request.

**262 Econo-Float Water Flotation Cushion**
Jefferson Industries
1985 Rutgers Blvd
Lakewood, NJ 08701-4569
732-905-9001
800-257-5145
FAX: 732-905-9899

*Charles Landa, General Manager*
An inexpensive, yet effective approach to the problem of pressure ulcers for patients confined to wheelchairs, geriatric chairs, etc. *$15.00*

**263 Econo-Float Water Flotation Mattress**
Jefferson Industries
1985 Rutgers Blvd
Lakewood, NJ 08701-4569
732-905-9001
800-257-5145
FAX: 732-905-9899

*Charles Landa, General Manager*
Helps prevent and treat pressure ulcers by reducing and distributing pressure over the patient's bony prominences while supporting the body evenly over a greater surface area. *$39.00*

**264 Enhancer Cushion**
ROHO Group
100 N Florida Ave
Belleville, IL 62221-5429
618-277-9173
800-851-3449
FAX: 618-277-9561
e-mail: tomb@therohogroup.com
www.therohogroup.com

*Tom Borcherding, President*
*Bobby Graebe, CEO*
*Jeff Baker, CFO/Sr. VP*
*Dave McCausland, Sr. VP of Planning*
Uses AIR IN PLACE progressive positioning for enhanced midline channeling of the femurs, lateral stability and tissue protection.

**265 Functional Forms**
Consumer Care Products
1446 Pilgrim Rd
Plymouth, WI 53073-4969
920-893-4614
FAX: 800-977-2256
e-mail: ccpi@consumercareinc.com
www.consumercareinc.com

*Terry Grall, Owner*
These blocks, wedges, rolls, cervical pillows, head and leg supports and barrel rolls in resilient high density foam covered with durable antibacterial, antistatic, flame resistant, nonabsorbent vinyl are used to attain individualized support for the most difficult positioning needs for children and adults. Unique sizes allow fitting for almost any person. Use during exercise, feeding, therapy, recreation and rest at home, school and health care facilities. Packages available.

**266 Gaymar Industries**
Gaymar Industries
10 Centre Dr
Orchard Park, NY 14127-2295
716-662-2551
800-828-7341
FAX: 716-662-0748
e-mail: webmaster@gaymar.com
gaymar.com

*Dan Kormowicz, International Sales & Mktg*
*Cindy Sylvia, Educational Svcs Administrator*
*Heather Lindstrom, Medical Res*
*Brian McLaughlin, International Order Coordinator*
Gaymar offers a complete line of support surfaces, including low-air-loss mattresses, specialty foam mattresses, turning mattresses, air overlays and fluid therapy beds. These products economically prevent and treat bedsores. Clinical and reimbursement professionals are available to answer any question related to bedsores (decubitus ulcers). Also offers a complete line of temperature control devices. The T-Pump delivers warm therapy to effectively dilate vessels and increase blood flow.

**267 Geo-Matt for High Risk Patients**
Span-America Medical Systems
70 Commerce Ctr
Greenville, SC 29615-5814
864-288-8877
800-888-6752
FAX: 864-288-8692
spanamerica.com

*James D Ferguson, CEO*
Helps prevent pressure sores in high risk patients.

**268 High Profile Single Compartment Cushion**
ROHO Group
100 N Florida Ave
Belleville, IL 62221-5429
618-277-9173
800-851-3449
FAX: 618-277-9561
e-mail: tomb@therohogroup.com
www.therohogroup.com

*Tom Borcherding, President*
*Bobby Graebe, CEO*
*Jeff Baker, CFO/Sr. VP*
*Dave McCausland, Sr. VP of Planning*
With 4 inch cells, the HIGH PROFILE is the cushion of choice for individuals who suffer from ischemic ulcers (pressure sores) or who have a history of tissue breakdown.

**269 Inflatable Back Pillow**
Corflex
669 East Industrial Park Dr
Manchester, NH 03109-5625
603-623-3344
800-426-7353
FAX: 603-623-4111
e-mail: sales@corflex.com
corflex.com

*Paul Lorenzetti, CEO*
Folds flat to fit into its own carrying case, this inflatable back pillow ensures comfort while at home or traveling.

**270 Jobri**
520 N Division St
Konawa, OK 74849-2223
580-925-3500
800-432-2225
FAX: 580-925-3501
e-mail: support@jobri.com
jobri.com

*Brian Gourley, CEO*
Jobri manufactures ergonomic back supports, ergonomic chairs, orthopedic soft goods and sleep products.

**271 Lumex Cushions and Mattresses**
Graham-Field Health Products
2935 Northeast Pkwy
Atlanta, GA 30360-2808
770-368-4700
800-347-5678
FAX: 770-368-4702
www.grahamfield.com

*Ken Spett, CEO*
Line of cushions and pillows give comfort and independence to the physically challenged.

**272 Medpro Static Air Chair Cushion**
Medpro
1950 Rutgers Blvd
Lakewood, NJ 08701-4537
800-257-5145
FAX: 732-905-9899

*Jody Gorran, President*
Provides a protective layer of air beneath the patient helping prevent and treat pressure ulcers. *$94.95*

**273 Medpro Static Air Mattress Overlay**
Medpro
1950 Rutgers Blvd
Lakewood, NJ 08701-4537
800-257-5145
FAX: 732-905-9899

*Jody Gorran, President*
Supports the patient on a cushioned network of air designed to redistribute the patient's weight reducing tissue interface pressure. Medpro's design incorporates a series of 65 air-breather vents that maintain air circulation. Medpro effectively reduces pressure and helps prevent and treat pressure ulcers. *$164.95*

**274 Mini-Max Cushion**
ROHO
100 N Florida Ave
Belleville, IL 62221-5429
618-277-9173
800-851-3449
FAX: 618-277-9561
e-mail: tomb@therohogroup.com
www.therohogroup.com

*Tom Borcherding, President*
*Bobby Graebe*
*Jeff Baker, CFO/Sr. VP*
*Dave McCausland, Sr. VP of Planning*
Designed for the active individual with low risk of skin breakdown. The unique air cells of the MINI-MAX provide significant shock and impact absorption, skin protection and stability.

275 **NEXUS Wheelchair Cushioning System**
ROHO
100 N Florida Ave
Belleville, IL 62221-5429
618-277-9173
800-850-7646
FAX: 618-277-9561
e-mail: tomb@therohogroup.com
www.therohogroup.com

*Tom Borcherding, President*
*Bobby Graebe, CEO*
*Jeff Baker, CFO/Sr. VP*
*Dave McCausland, Sr. VP of Planning*
A unique modular cushion that mates a contoured polyurethane foam base with a dry flotation support pad. It is designed to give the user positioning and stability, while offering maximum protection to the ischia, sacrum and coccyx.

276 **Pediatric Seating System**
ROHO
100 N Florida Ave
Belleville, IL 62221-5429
618-277-9173
800-850-7646
FAX: 618-277-9561
e-mail: tomb@therohogroup.com
www.rohoinc.com

*Tom Borcherding, President*
*Bobby Graebe, CEO*
*Jeff Baker, CFO/Sr. VP*
*Dave McCausland, Sr. VP of Planning*
ROHO Cushions for kids use individual air cells, creating the most versatile and dynamic cushioning products available. These cushions are designed to specifically fit pediatric wheelchairs.

277 **Quadtro Cushion**
ROHO
100 N Florida Ave
Belleville, IL 62221-5429
618-277-9173
800-851-3499
FAX: 618-277-9561
e-mail: tomb@therohogroup.com
therohogroup.com

*Tom Borcherding, President*
*Bobby Graebe, CEO*
*Jeff Baker, CFO/Sr. VP*
*Dave McCausland, Sr. VP of Planning*
For individuals who require special positioning of the pelvis or thighs and are at risk of skin breakdown, the Quadtro, with 4 inch cell height and air in place, progressive positioning is the cushion of choice.

278 **Silicone Padding**
Spenco Medical Group
P.O.Box 2501
Waco, TX 76702-2501
254-772-6000
800-877-3626
e-mail: spenco@spenco.com
spenco.com

*Jeff Antonioli, VP Sales*
*Ryan Cruthirds, Vice President*
For the management of pressure sores, this padding provides a special support system which allows even distribution of pressure and cool, comfortable, well-ventilated support.

279 **Soft-Touch Convertible Flotation Mattress**
Medpro
1950 Rutgers Blvd
Lakewood, NJ 08701-4537
800-257-5145
FAX: 732-905-9899

*Jody Gorran, President*
Gives the patient the option to choose between water and gel flotation depending on the needs of the patient. The mattress helps prevent and treat pressure ulcers by spreading the patient's weight over a greater surface area. $164.95-$239.95.

280 **Soft-Touch Gel Flotation Cushion**
Medpro
1940 Rutgers Blvd
Lakewood, NJ 08701-4537
732-905-9001
800-257-5145
FAX: 732-905-9899

*Jody Gorran, President*
Acts like an additional layer of fatty tissue beneath the patient to help prevent and treat pressure sores. *$99.95*

281 **Spenco Medical Group**
P.O.Box 2501
Waco, TX 76702-2501
254-772-6000
800-877-3626
e-mail: spenco@spenco.com
spenco.com

*Jeff Antonioli, VP Sales*
*Ryan Cruthirds, Vice President*
Wheel chair cushions, silicore mattress pads, wound dressings, second skin blister and burn pads, polysorb insoles, elbow, knee and wrist supports and walking shoes.

282 **Stop-Leak Gel Flotation Mattress**
Jefferson Industries
1989 Rutgers Blvd
Lakewood, NJ 08701-4538
732-905-9001
800-257-5145
FAX: 732-905-9899

*Charles Landa, General Manager*
Protects persons from messy leaks while it protects from pressure ulcers. *$54.00*

283 **Sun-Mate Seat Cushions**
Dynamic Systems
235 Sunlight Dr
Leicester, NC 28748-5710
828-683-3523
855-786-6283
FAX: 828-683-3511
e-mail: dsi@sunmatecushions.com
www.sunmatecushions.com

*Charles A Yost, CEO*
*Lewis McCrain, General Manager*
Line of cushions, pads and accessory items for personal comfort of the disabled. SunMate Orthopedic foam cushions and sheets that contours slowly to give uniform pressure distribution and soft spring back. Liquid SunMate for Foam-in-Place Seating (FIPS) to make custom molded seat inserts.

284 **Twin-Rest Seat Cushion & Glamour Pillow**
Better Sleep
57 Industrial Rd
Berkeley Heights, NJ 07922-1501
908-464-6568
FAX: 908-464-0058

*William Emery Jr, President*
Makes any seat more comfortable because it is ingeniously designed to soothe sensitive areas while at work, in the car or at home.

## Dressing Aids

285 **Button Aid**
Maxi Aids
42 Executive Blvd
Farmingdale, NY 11735-4710
631-752-0521
800-522-6294
FAX: 631-752-0689
TTY: 800-281-3555
e-mail: sales@maxiaids.com
www.maxiaids.com

*Elliot Zaretsky, Founder / President*

Makes buttoning possible with the use of only one hand. *$9.95*

**286 Deluxe Sock and Stocking Aid**
Therapro, Inc.
225 Arlington St
Framingham, MA 01702-8723
508-872-9494
800-257-5376
FAX: 508-875-2062
e-mail: info@therapro.com
www.therapro.com

*Karen Conrad, ScD, OTR/L, Owner*
Flexible plastic, lined with blue nylon to reduce friction and outside with beige terry cloth to hold sock firmly until it is on the foot. *$12.95*

**287 Dressing Stick**
Maxi Aids
42 Executive Blvd
Farmingdale, NY 11735-4710
631-752-0521
800-522-6294
FAX: 631-752-0689
TTY: 800-281-3555
www.maxiaids.com

*Elliot Zaretsky, Founder / President*
Helps put on coats, sweaters and garments even when arm and shoulder movement is limited. *$7.95*

**288 Elastic Shoelaces**
Therapro, Inc.
225 Arlington St
Framingham, MA 01702-8723
508-872-9494
800-257-5376
FAX: 508-875-2062
e-mail: info@therapro.com
www.therapro.com

*Karen Conrad, ScD, OTR/L, Owner*
The elastic laces allow the wearer to slip tied shoes on and off. *$4.25*

**289 Featherweight Reachers**
Therapro, Inc.
225 Arlington St
Framingham, MA 01702-8723
508-872-9494
800-257-5376
FAX: 508-875-2062
e-mail: info@therapro.com
www.therapro.com

*Karen Conrad, ScD, OTR/L, Owner*
Useful in dressing or retrieving objects. *$17.95*

**290 Mirror Go Lightly**
AbleNet
2808 Fairview Ave N
Saint Paul, MN 55113-1308
612-379-0956
800-322-0956
FAX: 612-379-9143
e-mail: customerservice@ablenetinc.com
www.ablenetinc.com

*Jennifer Thalhuber, President / CEO*
Framed in plastic, the mirror can be tilted to provide either a normal or magnified image or to direct its lights at, or away from, the user. *$22.00*

**291 Molded Sock and Stocking Aid**
Therapro, Inc.
225 Arlington St
Framingham, MA 01702-8723
508-872-9494
800-257-5376
FAX: 508-875-2062
e-mail: info@therapro.com
www.therapro.com

*Karen Conrad, ScD, OTR/L, Owner*
Sock or stocking is pulled over the molded plastic and then can be put on more easily. *$13.25*

**292 Say What**
Maxi Aids
42 Executive Blvd
Farmingdale, NY 11735-4710
631-752-0521
800-522-6294
FAX: 631-752-0689
TTY: 800-281-3555
www.maxiaids.com

*Elliot Zaretsky, Founder / President*
Braille the tag with information that the wearer wants on the tag and place the tag on a hanger. The custom-identification program makes it easier for the user to remember and identify just the right clothes. *$4.95*

**293 Shoe and Boot Valet: Decreased Mobility Aid**
Maxi Aids
42 Executive Blvd
Farmingdale, NY 11735-4710
631-752-0521
800-522-6294
FAX: 631-752-0689
TTY: 631-752-0738
maxiaids.com

*Elliot Zaretsky, Founder / President*
This is the perfect device to alleviate and in many cases eliminate the pain and embarrassment for millions of people who have a problem doing the simple everyday task of putting on and taking off their footwear. It works perfectly with shoes, boots, galoshes and slippers. *$49.95*

## Health Aids

**294 AMI**
P.O.Box 808
Groton, CT 06340-808
860-536-3735
800-248-4031
FAX: 860-536-4362
e-mail: sales@aquamassage.com
aquamassage.com

*David Cote, President*
*Dow Cote, Vice President Sales*
*Hilaire Cote, Senior Vice President*
*Scott Gilbert, Customer Service Manager*
The Aqua PT provides the major benefits of Hydrotherapy, Massage Therapy and Dry Heat Therapy. 36 water jets provide continuous full body or localized massage while the client remains CLOTHED AND DRY! Adjustable water pressure, temperature and pulsation frequency can massage in either a two direction travel mode for musculoskeletal pain management or a one direction mode, flowing water from head to foot for a contrast massage-relax therapy. $25,000 to $30,000.

**295 American Medical Industries**
Ste 2
330 E 3rd St
Dell Rapids, SD 57022-1918
605-428-5501
FAX: 605-428-5502
e-mail: info@pillcrusherguys.com
www.ezhealthcare.com

*Dan Anderson, CEO*

EZ-Swallow, EZ-Health, EZ-Home Care, Kleen-Handz, Kleen-Scent, EZ-Irrigator, EZ-VU, Pureshark, Gobot and AMI are all trademarks of American Medical Industries. Healthcare products made easy.

296 **BIPAP S/T Ventilatory Support System**
Respironics
1010 Murry Ridge Ln
Murrysville, PA 15668-8517
724-387-5200
FAX: 724-387-5010
e-mail: customerservice@respironics.com
respironics.com

*John L Miclot, CEO*
*Gerald McGinnis, Chairman*
*Daniel Bevevino, VP/CFO*
*Craig Reynolds, Executive VP/COO*
Respironics, a recognized resource in the medical device market, provides innovative products and unique designs to the health care provider while helping them to grow and manage their business efficiently.

297 **Bed Rails**
Mada Medical Products
625 Washington Ave
Carlstadt, NJ 07072-2901
201-460-0454
800-526-6370
FAX: 201-460-3509
e-mail: dianelind@mail.madamedical.com
www.madainternational.com

*Jeffrey Adam, President*
Chrome plated steel rails and crossbars, all welded construction, telescopic side rail length adjustable, and a standard rail height of 16 inches.

298 **Coast to Coast Home Medical**
Ste 4d
3381 Fairlane Farms Rd
Wellington, FL 33414-8711
561-792-4009
800-330-6316

*Keri Suess, Owner*
Home-delivered medical supplies for diabetes, respiratory, arthritis and impotence supplies.

299 **Drew Karol Industries**
P.O.Box 1066
Greenville, MS 38702-1066
662-378-2188
FAX: 601-378-3188
e-mail: dki@techinfo.com

*Andrew K Hoszowski, Owner*
Orally operated toothbrush and dental care system for persons with limited or complete loss of hand or arm use - wheelchair accessible. *$600.00*

300 **Duraline Medical Products Inc.**
P.O.Box 67
324 Werner Street
Leipsic, OH 45856-1039
419-943-2044
800-654-3376
FAX: 419-943-3637
e-mail: duraline@fairpoint.net
dmponline.com

*Kathy Peck, General Manager*
An assortment of quality incontinence products for adults and children.

301 **Duro-Med Industries**
1931 Norman Drive
Waukegan, IL 60085
800-526-4753
800-622-4714
FAX: 800-479-7968
www.mabisdmi.com

*Mike Mazza, President*
*Tony D'Antonio, Senior VP of Sales*
*Alan Yefsky, Exec VP, Sales & Mktg*
Manufacturers of a complete line of home health care products. Featured products are patient gowns, back and seat cushions, pillows and a complete line of aids for daily living.

302 **Easy Ply**
BioMedical Life Systems
P.O.Box 1360
Vista, CA 92085-1360
800-726-8367
FAX: 760-727-4220
e-mail: information@bmls.com
www.bmls.com

This disposable electrode has a cloth backing of a super-breathable medical tape that allows for comfort and a longer life.

303 **Electronic Stethoscopes**
HARC Mercantile
1111 W Centre Ave
Portage, MI 49024-5317
269-324-0301
800-445-9968
FAX: 269-324-2387
TTY: 269-324-1615
e-mail: info@harc.com
harc.com

High production fidelity with a number volume control wheels. *$454.95*

304 **Fold-Down 3-in-1 Commode**
Mada Medical Products
625 Washington Ave
Carlstadt, NJ 07072-2901
201-460-0454
800-526-6370
FAX: 201-460-3509
e-mail: dianelind@mail.madamedical.com
www.madainternational.com

*Jeffrey Adam, President*
The Fold-Down commode is constructed of heavy duty, 1 inch diameter, steel tubing with X frame, has folding features convenient for storage and transport, easily removable back rest, and full length armrests.

305 **Healing Dressing for Pressure Sores**
Baxter Healthcare Corporation
1 Baxter Pkwy
Deerfield, IL 60015-4625
800-422-9837
FAX: 80- 56- 502
baxter.com

*Robert L Parkinson Jr, Chairman of the Board/CEO*
*Phillip L. Batchelor, Corporate VP - Quality*
*Robert M. Davis, Corporate VP*
*Robert J. Hombach, Corporate VP/CFO*
A dressing specifically designed to promote healing of pressure sores and other dermal ulcers.

306 **Invacare Corporation**
1 Invacare Way
Elyria, OH 44035-4196
440-329-6000
800-333-6900
FAX: 440-366-1803
e-mail: info@invacare.com
invacare.com

*A Malachi Mixon Iii, CEO*
The world's leading manufacturer and distributor of innovative home and long-term care medical products which promote recovery and active lifestyles.

**307 MADAMIST 50/50 PSI Air Compressor**
Mada Medical Products
625 Washington Ave
Carlstadt, NJ 07072-2901
201-460-0454
800-526-6370
FAX: 201-460-3509
e-mail: dianelind@mail.madamedical.com
www.madainternational.com

*Jeffrey Adam, President*
The new compressor rated at 50 PSI is designed to drive humidifiers, nebulizers, mist tents and is ideal to administer pentamidine aerosol therapy.

**308 MedDev Corporation**
730 N Pastoria Ave
Sunnyvale, CA 94085-3522
408-730-9702
800-543-2789
FAX: 408-730-9732
e-mail: info@meddev-corp.com
meddev-corp.com

Aids to rehabilitate hands following injury or illness, including patented complementary FingerHelper, ThumbHelper and Iso HandHelper models. Med Dev also manufactures Soft Touch foam exercisers and the FiddlLink exerciser for digital dexterity. The Ultimate Hand Helper, an ergonomically designed hand excerciser, is curved to conform to the shape of the hand.

**309 Medi-Grip**
Therapro, Inc.
225 Arlington St
Framingham, MA 01702-8723
508-872-9494
800-257-5376
FAX: 508-875-2062
e-mail: info@therapro.com
www.therapro.com

*Karen Conrad, ScD, OTR/L, Owner*
Reasonably priced, nonskid material. This nonslip material is available in marine blue, desert sand and burgundy rolls 12 inches x 144 inches. *$11.95*

**310 Pocket Otoscope**
HARC Mercantile
1111 W Centre Ave
Portage, MI 49024-5317
269-324-0301
800-445-9968
FAX: 269-324-2387
TTY: 269-324-1615
e-mail: info@harc.com
harc.com

Simple, durable and dependable pocket otoscope uses standard replaceable parts. *$24.00*

**311 Standard 3-in-1 Commode**
Mada Medical Products
625 Washington Ave
Carlstadt, NJ 07072-2901
201-460-0454
800-526-6370
FAX: 201-460-3509
e-mail: dianelind@mail.madamedical.com
www.madainternational.com

*Jeffrey Adam, President*
The standard commode is constructed of a heavy duty anodized aluminum frame, seat adjustment and an easily removable back rest.

**312 Strider**
Osborn Medical Corporation
P.O.Box 324
100 West Main St.
Utica, MN 55979-324
507-287-6554
800-535-5865
FAX: 507-932-5044
e-mail: info@osbornmedical.com
osbornmedical.com

Strider allows you to exercise in most chairs found in your home. No more small, uncomfortable bicycle seats to sit on while exercising. With Strider, your hands are free to read the paper or your favorite book while you exercise.

**313 Talking Clinical Thermometer**
Maxi Aids
42 Executive Blvd
Farmingdale, NY 11735-4710
631-752-0521
800-522-6294
FAX: 631-752-0689
TTY: 800-281-3555
www.maxiaids.com

*Elliot Zaretsky, Founder / President*
Audible clinical thermometer. *$199.95*

**314 Talking Thermometers**
Maxi Aids
42 Executive Blvd
Farmingdale, NY 11735-4710
631-752-0521
800-522-6294
FAX: 631-752-0689
TTY: 800-281-3555
www.maxiaids.com

*Elliot Zaretsky, Founder / President*
Clearly announces temperature in Fahrenheit or Celcius. *$17.95*

**315 Transfer Bench**
Mada Medical Products
625 Washington Ave
Carlstadt, NJ 07072-2901
201-460-0454
800-526-6370
FAX: 201-460-3509
e-mail: dianelind@mail.madamedical.com
www.madainternational.com

*Jeffrey Adam, President*
The transfer bench is a one piece bench with a wide base for stability, 1 inch diameter aluminum framework, corrosion resistant, and an adjustable seat.

## Hearing Aids

**316 Auditech: Personal PA Value Pack System**
P.O.Box 821105
Vicksburg, MS 39182-1105
800-229-8293
FAX: 800-221-8639
e-mail: info@auditechusa.com
www.auditechusa.com

Reliable hearing assistance. This wireless FM system broadcasts to listeners with a hearing assistance system, helping them overcome background noise at a distance from the sound source. *$899.00*

**317 Auditech: Pocketalker Pro**
P.O.Box 821105
Vicksburg, MS 39182-1105
800-229-8293
FAX: 800-221-8639
e-mail: info@auditechusa.com
www.auditechusa.com

Pocketalker Pro can help you hear virtually anywhere whether in a car, crowded restaurant or at a noisy gathering. It can work to reduce background noise and easily converts to the Telelink. *$ 140.00*

**318 Battery Device Adapter**
AbleNet
2808 Fairview Ave N
Roseville, MN 55113-1308
612-379-0956
800-322-0956
FAX: 651-294-2259
e-mail: customerservice@ablenetinc.com
www.ablenetinc.com

*Jennifer Thalhuber, President / CEO*
A cable which connects to and adapts battery-operated devices for external switch control. Two sizes are available to adapt devices with either AA or C and D size batteries. *$8.00*

**319 Custom Earmolds**
Lloyd Hearing Aid Corporation
P.O.Box 1645
4435 Manchester Dr
Rockford, IL 61109-1645
815-964-4191
800-323-4212
FAX: 815-964-8378
e-mail: info@lloydshearingaid.com
lloydhearingaid.com

*Andy PalmQuist, President*
Hearing aid molds, custom built to the exact fit of the customer. *$29.95*

**320 Digital Hearing Aids**
Lloyd Hearing Aid Corporation
P.O.Box 1645
4435 Manchester Dr
Rockford, IL 61109-1645
815-964-4191
800-323-4212
FAX: 815-964-8378
e-mail: info@lloydshearingaid.com
lloydhearingaid.com

*Andy PalmQuist, President*
Latest hearing technology. Huge discounts on most makes. *$7.50*

**321 Doorbell Signalers**
HARC Mercantile
1111 W Centre Ave
Portage, MI 49024-5317
269-324-0301
800-445-9968
FAX: 269-324-2387
TTY: 269-324-1615
e-mail: info@harc.com
harc.com

Doorbell signalers to alert with either louder chime or flashing light. *$29.99*

**322 Double Gong Indoor/Outdoor Ringer**
HARC Mercantile
1111 W Centre Ave
Portage, MI 49024-5317
269-324-0301
800-445-9968
FAX: 269-324-2387
TTY: 269-324-1615
e-mail: info@harc.com
harc.com

Loud outdoor ringer that attaches to the wall for outside applications. *$50.00*

**323 Duracell & Rayovac Hearing Aid Batteries**
Lloyd Hearing Aid Corporation
P.O.Box 1645
4435 Manchester Dr
Rockford, IL 61109-1645
815-964-4191
800-323-4212
FAX: 815-964-8378
e-mail: info@lloydhearingaid.com
lloydhearingaid.com

*Andy PalmQuist, President*
Batteries for hearing aids at discounted prices. As low as 45 cents each.

**324 Harris Communications**
Harris Communications
15155 Technology Dr
Eden Prairie, MN 55344-2273
800-825-6758
FAX: 952-906-1099
TTY:800-825-9187
e-mail: info@harriscomm.com
harriscomm.com

*Dr.Robert Harris, Owner*
A national distributor of assistive devices for the deaf and hard-of-hearing with many manufacturers represented. Catalog includes a wide range of assistive devices as well as a variety of books and video tapes related to deaf and hard-of-hearing issues. Products available for children, teachers, hearing professionals, interpreters and anyone interested in deaf culture, hearing loss and sign language.
*180 pages Yearly*

**325 Hearing Aid Batteries**
HARC Mercantile
1111 W Centre Ave
Portage, MI 49024-5317
269-324-0301
800-445-9968
FAX: 269-324-2387
TTY: 269-324-1615
e-mail: info@harc.com
harc.com

Hearing aid batteries in all popular sizes in mercury, zinc air, silver as well as Nicad and Varta and batteries for electrolarynx and infrared systems. $3.95-$25.00.

**326 Hearing Aid Battery Testers**
HARC Mercantile
1111 W Centre Ave
Portage, MI 49024-5317
269-324-0301
800-445-9968
FAX: 269-324-2387
TTY: 269-324-1615
e-mail: info@harc.com
harc.com

From pocket size to professional type battery testers which test mercury, zinc air, silver, specialty and general usage batteries. *$11.95*

**327 Hearing Aid Dehumidifier**
HARC Mercantile
1111 W Centre Ave
Portage, MI 49024-5317
269-324-0301
800-445-9968
FAX: 269-324-2387
TTY: 269-324-1615
e-mail: info@harc.com
harc.com

Removes moisture from hearing aids and valuables. Contains desiccant pack and humidity guide, all in a rugged, vinyl case which provides protection and is water resistant. *$6.00*

**328 In the Ear Hearing Aid Battery Extractor**
HARC Mercantile
1111 W Centre Ave
Portage, MI 49024-5317
269-324-0301
800-445-9968
FAX: 269-324-2387
TTY: 269-324-1615
e-mail: info@harc.com
harc.com

Ideal tool to use when battery is stuck in battery compartment in ITE and canal hearing aids. *$3.00*

**329 Micro Audiometrics Corporation**
655 Keller Rd
Murphy, NC 28906-5890
828-644-0771
800-729-9509
866-327-7226
FAX: 866-683-4447
e-mail: sales@microaud.com
microaud.com

*Jason Keller, President*
Manufacturer and distributor of hearing testing instruments, including the complete line of Earscan.

**330 Mushroom Inserts**
Lloyd Hearing Aid Corporation
P.O.Box 1645
4435 Manchester Drive
Rockford, IL 61109- 1645
815-964-4191
800-323-4212
FAX: 815-964-8378
e-mail: info@lloydhearingaid.com
www.lloydhearingaid.com

*Andy PalmQuist, President*
A universal earplug useful in wearing behind the ear type hearing instruments. *$2.50*

**331 Oval Window Audio**
33 Wildflower Ct
Nederland, CO 80466-9638
303-447-3607
FAX: 303-447-3607
TTY:303-447-3607
e-mail: info@ovalwindowaudio.com
ovalwindowaudio.com

*Norman Lederman, Dir. of R & D*
*Paula Hendricks, Educational Dir.*
Manufacturer of induction loop hearing assistance technologies compatible with hearing aids already used by many hard of hearing people. Also multisensory sound systems for use in speech and music therapy and science classes.

## Kitchen & Eating Aids

**332 Bagel Holder**
Maxi Aids
42 Executive Blvd
Farmingdale, NY 11735-4710
631-752-0521
800-522-6294
FAX: 631-752-0689
TTY: 800-281-3555
www.maxiaids.com

*Elliot Zaretsky, Founder / President*
Holds bagels in place for easy slicing. *$3.95*

**333 Big Bold Timer Low Vision**
Maxi Aids
42 Executive Blvd
Farmingdale, NY 11735-4710
631-752-0521
800-522-6294
FAX: 631-752-0689
TTY: 800-281-3555
www.maxiaids.com

*Elliot Zaretsky, Founder / President*
Sixty-minute mechanical timer with large, easy-to-read numbers for the vision impaired. *$9.95*

**334 Box Top Opener**
Sammons Preston Rolyan
Suite 210
1000 Remington Blvd
Cedarburg, WI 60440-5117
630-378-6000
800-323-5547
FAX: 630-378-6010
e-mail: sp@pattersonmedical.com
www.pattersonmedical.com

*David P Sproat, President*
*Bruce Curtis, Sales Representative*
This handy device exerts the pressure on those hard-to-open boxes of laundry/dishwasher soap, rice and prepared dinners. *$2.95*

**335 Capscrew**
Access with Ease
P.O.Box 1150
Chino Valley, AZ 86323-1150
928-636-9469
800-531-9479
FAX: 928-636-0292
e-mail: KMJC@northlink.com
Remove lids and caps easily. Can be mounted on walls or cupboards. Non-slip surface grips small and large jars. *$7.95*

**336 Cool Handle**
Maxi Aids
42 Executive Blvd
Farmingdale, NY 11735-4710
631-752-0521
800-522-6294
FAX: 631-752-0689
TTY: 800-281-3555
www.maxiaids.com

*Elliot Zaretsky, Founder / President*
A specially designed, heat-resistant handle, available in three sizes which can be affixed to the handles of most fry, sauce and saute pans. *$7.95*

**337 Cordless Receiver**
AbleNet
2808 Fairview Ave N
Saint Paul, MN 55113-1308
612-379-0956
800-322-0956
FAX: 651-294-2259
e-mail: customerservice@ablenetinc.com
www.ablenetinc.com

*Jennifer Thalhuber, President / CEO*
The Cordless Receiver in conjunction with the Cordless Big Red Switch, can be used anywhere a switch is currently used to control battery or electrically-operated toys, games or appliances; augmentative communication systems; and computers (through a computer switch interface). *$79.00*

**338 Deluxe Long Ring Low Vision Timer**
Maxi Aids
42 Executive Blvd
Farmingdale, NY 11735-4710
631-752-0521
800-522-6294
FAX: 631-752-0689
TTY: 800-281-3555
www.maxiaids.com

*Elliot Zaretsky, Founder / President*
Bold black numerals on white background allows for easy reading at any distance. *$17.95*

339 **Deluxe Roller Knife**
Sammons Preston Rolyan
Suite 210
1000 Remington Blvd
Bolingbrook, IL 60440-5117
630-378-6000
800-323-5547
FAX: 630-378-6010
e-mail: sp@pattersonmedical.com
www.pattersonmedical.com

*David P Sproat, President*
*Bruce Curtis, Sales Representative*
Stainless steel blade rolls smoothly, cutting food cleanly. *$10.95*

340 **Dual Brush with Suction Base**
Sammons Preston Rolyan
Suite 210
1000 Remington Blvd
Bolingbrook, IL 60440-5117
630-378-6000
800-323-5547
FAX: 630-378-6010
e-mail: sp@pattersonmedical.com
www.pattersonmedical.com

*David P Sproat, President*
*Bruce Curtis, Sales Representative*
Two brushes clean the inside and outside of bottles and glasses at the same time using just one hand. *$14.50*

341 **Easy Pour Locking Lid Pot**
Maxi Aids
42 Executive Blvd
Farmingdale, NY 11735-4710
631-752-0521
800-522-6294
FAX: 631-752-0689
TTY: 800-281-3555
www.maxiaids.com

*Elliot Zaretsky, Founder / President*
Baked enamel and dishwasher safe, the pot comes with an easy lid that locks in place for extra safety. *$24.95*

342 **Electric Can Opener & Knife Sharpener**
Maxi Aids
42 Executive Blvd
Farmingdale, NY 11735-4710
631-752-0521
800-522-6294
FAX: 631-752-0689
TTY: 800-281-3555
www.maxiaids.com

*Elliot Zaretsky, Founder / President*
Features include a powerful magnetic lid holder, the ability to open odd-shaped cans, and easy operation for the physically challenged. *$19.95*

343 **Evio Plastics**
P.O.Box 2295
Sandusky, OH 44871-2295
419-621-1105
FAX: 419-626-2183

*Doug Didion, Admininstrator Director*
*Danny Thomas, Owner*
Handi Holder is a plastic holder for 1/2 gallon paper cartons of milk or juice. It is used to pour milk or juice without spills by using the handle.

344 **Food Markers/Rubberbands**
Maxi Aids
42 Executive Blvd
Farmingdale, NY 11735-4710
631-752-0521
800-522-6294
FAX: 631-752-0689
TTY: 800-281-3555
www.maxiaids.com

*Elliot Zaretsky, Founder / President*
These are durable plastic markers, easily identified by touch, texture, shape and form which help the visually impaired orient themselves to food location on the plate. *$11.95*

345 **Good Grips Cutlery**
Therapro, Inc.
225 Arlington St
Framingham, MA 01702-8723
508-872-9494
800-257-5376
FAX: 508-875-2062
e-mail: info@therapro.com
www.therapro.com

*Karen Conrad, ScD, OTR/L, Owner*
Stainless steel utensils have a special twist built into the metal to facilitate bending of a spoon or fork at any angle for right or left handed people. *$7.50*

346 **H.E.L.P. Knife**
Maxi Aids
42 Executive Blvd
Farmingdale, NY 11735-4710
631-752-0521
800-522-6294
FAX: 631-752-0689
TTY: 800-281-3555
www.maxiaids.com

*Elliot Zaretsky, Founder / President*
Adjustable food slicing system guides the knife for even, uniform slices while protecting the user. *$11.95*

347 **Handy-Helper Cutting Board**
Maxi Aids
42 Executive Blvd
Farmingdale, NY 11735-4710
631-752-0521
800-522-6294
FAX: 631-752-0689
TTY: 800-281-3555
www.maxiaids.com

*Elliot Zaretsky, Founder / President*
Laminated cutting board with unique features to hold food in place with corner ledge for cutting and spreading. *$19.95*

348 **Innerlip Plates**
Therapro, Inc.
225 Arlington St
Framingham, MA 01702-8723
508-872-9494
800-257-5376
FAX: 508-875-2062
e-mail: info@therapro.com
www.therapro.com

*Karen Conrad, ScD, OTR/L, Owner*
Food may be pushed to the side of the plate, then scooped up with a fork and spoon. Available in beige or blue. *$5.00*

349 **Long Oven Mitts**
Sammons Preston Rolyan
Suite 210
1000 Remington Blvd
Bolingbrook, IL 60440-5117
630-378-6000
800-323-5547
FAX: 630-378-6010
e-mail: sp@pattersonmedical.com
www.pattersonmedical.com

*David P Sproat, President*
*Bruce Curtis, Sales Representative*
Protect hands and forearms from heat, flames and oven grates with these practical mitts that allow a longer reach and less bending. *$8.95*

**350 Magnetic Card Reader**
Maxi Aids
42 Executive Blvd
Farmingdale, NY 11735-4710
631-752-0521
800-522-6294
FAX: 631-752-0689
TTY: 800-281-3555
www.maxiaids.com

*Elliot Zaretsky, Founder / President*
Produces audible labels so a recorded card can be taped on cans of food or a box of cake mix; even adding instructions for baking. *$159.95*

**351 Maxi-Aids Braille Timer**
Maxi Aids
42 Executive Blvd
Farmingdale, NY 11735-4710
631-752-0521
800-522-6294
FAX: 631-752-0689
TTY: 631-752-0738
maxiaids.com

*Elliot Zaretsky, Founder / President*
Three raised dots at 15, 30 and 45, two raised dots at remaining five minute intervals and one raised dot at remaining two and a half minute intervals, offers ease of operation to make this a helpful aid for the visually impaired. *$12.95*

**352 Nosey Cup**
Therapro, Inc.
225 Arlington St
Framingham, MA 01702-8723
508-872-9494
800-257-5376
FAX: 508-875-2062
e-mail: info@therapro.com
www.therapro.com

*Karen Conrad, ScD, OTR/L, Owner*
For those with a stiff neck or persons who can't tip their head back while drinking. *$6.00*

**353 Paring Boards**
Therapro, Inc.
225 Arlington St
Framingham, MA 01702-8723
508-872-9494
800-257-5376
FAX: 508-875-2062
e-mail: info@therapro.com
www.therapro.com

*Karen Conrad, ScD, OTR/L, Owner*
Suction feet stabilize board and stainless steel prongs hold food in place for easy, one-handed cutting. *$32.50*

**354 PowerLink 2 Control Unit**
AbleNet
2808 Fairview Ave N
Saint Paul, MN 55113-1308
612-379-0956
800-322-0956
FAX: 651-294-2259
e-mail: customerservice@ablenetinc.com
www.ablenetinc.com

*Jennifer Thalhuber, President / CEO*
The PowerLink 2 Control Unit allows switch operation of electrical appliances. It can be used to activate 1 or 2 appliances (up to 1700 watts combined). If 2 appliances are used, they will activate simultaneously. There are four modes of control on the PowerLink 2; direct mode, timed (seconds) mode, timed (minutes) mode and latch mode. Meets safety standards from Underwriters Laboratory (UL) and Canadian Standards Association (CSA) for electrical appliances. *$159.00*

**355 Sammons Preston Rolyan**
Suite 210
1000 Remington Blvd
Bolingbrook, IL 60440-5117
630-378-6000
800-323-5547
FAX: 630-378-6010
e-mail: sp@pattersonmedical.com
www.pattersonmedical.com

*David P Sproat, President*
*Bruce Curtis, Sales Representative*
Sammons Preston Rolyan is a leading provider of rehabilitation and assistive devices to help those with disabilities meet daily physical challenges and achieve their greatest level of independence. With one of the industry's largest catalogs, Sammons Preston Rolyan offers a wide range of products available.
*Annually*

**356 Slicing Aid**
Snug Seat
P.O.Box 1739
Matthews, NC 28106-1739
704-882-0666
800-336-7684
FAX: 704-882-0751
e-mail: sales@snugseat.com
www.snugseat.com

*Steve Scribner, VP Sales*
*Kirk Mackenzie, President*
*Matt Abrahams, Territory Sales Representative*
*John MacIntosh, Territory Sales Representative*
The design of these knives allows a better working posture and makes optimal use of strength in the arms and hands.

**357 Small Appliance Receiver**
AbleNet
2808 Fairview Ave N
Saint Paul, MN 55113-1308
612-379-0956
800-322-0956
FAX: 651-294-2259
e-mail: customerservice@ablenetinc.com
www.ablenetinc.com

*Jennifer Thalhuber, President / CEO*
The Small Appliance Receiver, in conjunction with the Cordless Big Red Switch, allows you to control small electrical appliances in the environment without a cord. It should only be used with low-wattage appliances (under 500 watts) which have two prong plugs (ie, radios, fans, lamps, blenders, etc.). It should not be used with heat generating appliances. *$32.00*

**358 Steel Food Guard**
Maxi Aids
42 Executive Blvd
Farmingdale, NY 11735-4710
631-752-0521
800-522-6294
FAX: 631-752-0689
TTY: 800-281-3555
www.maxiaids.com

*Elliot Zaretsky, Founder / President*
Provides stable area to push against while eating. *$ 10.95*

**359 Thick-n-Easy**
Therapro, Inc.
225 Arlington St
Framingham, MA 01702-8723
508-872-9494
800-257-5376
FAX: 508-875-2062
e-mail: info@therapro.com
www.therapro.com

*Karen Conrad, ScD, OTR/L, Owner*
Instant food thickener that sets in 30 seconds and will not become thicker even after refrigeration. *$6.50*

**360 Thumbs Up Cup**
Therapro, Inc.
225 Arlington St
Framingham, MA 01702-8723
508-872-9494
800-257-5376
FAX: 508-875-2062
e-mail: info@therapro.com
www.therapro.com

*Karen Conrad, ScD, OTR/L, Owner*

This cup is designed for those with limited strength or coordination or arthritis. The two backward-tilt handles and thumb rests allow finger joints to be used to their greatest mechanical advantage. *$9.50*

**361 Undercounter Lid Opener**
Sammons Preston Rolyan
Suite 210
1000 Remington Blvd
Bolingbrook, IL 60440-5117
630-378-6000
800-323-5547
FAX: 630-378-6010
e-mail: sp@pattersonmedical.com
www.pattersonmedical.com

*David P Sproat, President*
*Bruce Curtis, Sales Representative*

The gripper of this unit which installs under the counter can help unscrew any cap. *$5.75*

**362 Uni-Turner**
Sammons Preston Rolyan
Suite 210
1000 Remington Blvd
Bolingbrook, IL 60440-5117
630-378-6000
800-323-5547
FAX: 630-378-6010
e-mail: sp@pattersonmedical.com
www.pattersonmedical.com

*David P Sproat, President*
*Bruce Curtis, Sales Representative*

Odd shaped handles can be turned easily with one-handed, L-shaped Uni-Turner. *$16.50*

**363 Universal Hand Cuff**
Therapro, Inc.
225 Arlington St
Framingham, MA 01702-8723
508-872-9494
800-257-5376
FAX: 508-875-2062
e-mail: info@therapro.com
www.therapro.com

*Karen Conrad, ScD, OTR/L, Owner*

Comfortable cuff with Velcro strap holds utensils, toothbrushes, etc. *$9.95*

## Lifts, Ramps & Elevators

**364 Accessibility Lift**
Inclinator Company of America
601 Gibson Blvd
Harrisburg, PA 17104-3215
717-939-8420
800-343-9007
FAX: 717-234-0941
e-mail: isaks@inclinator.com
www.inclinator.com

*Stephen Nock, President*

An economical lift for restricted usage that provides barrier-free access that can be used by churches, schools, lodging halls and meeting halls to meet compliance requirements, with the dignified convenience and freedom they deserve.

**365 Adjustable Incline Board**
Bailey Manufacturing Company
P.O. Box 130
Lodi, OH 44254-130
800-321-8372
FAX: 800-224-5390
baileymfg.com

Incline board for the physically challenged with a foot board with non-slip tread.

**366 AlumiRamp**
855 E Chicago Rd
Quincy, MI 49082-9450
800-800-3864
FAX: 517-639-4314
e-mail: sales@alumiramp.com
alumiramp.com

*Doug Cannon, General Manager*

Complete line of modular, aluminum and portable ramps for both home and vehicle use. Welded construction and non-skid extruded surfaces are featured on all our ramps.

**367 Area Access**
7131 Gateway Court
Manassas, VA 20109-1015
703-396-4949
800-333-2732
FAX: 703-207-0446
areaaccess.com

Serving the entire Mid-Atlantic with scooters, stairway lifts and elevators. Large inventory and fully stocked showrooms.

**368 Basement Motorhome Lift By Handicaps, Inc.**
4335 S Santa Fe Dr
Englewood, CO 80110
303-781-2062
800-782-4335
FAX: 303-761-6811
e-mail: info@handicapsinc.com
www.handicapsinc.com

Wheelchair lifts made for vans and motor homes. The only lift on the market made without a platform so no doorways are blocked. Also make hand driving controls and other driving equipment. Quiet, quick and transferable. Saves on vehicle resale value. *$7200.00*

**369 Bruno Independent Living Aids**
P.O.Box 84
1780 Executive Drive
Oconomowoc, WI 53066
262-567-4990
800-882-8183
FAX: 262-953-5510
bruno.com

*Michael R. Bruno, II, President/CEO*
*Andrew Bayer, Product Mgr, Automotive Div.*
*Mike Krawczyk, Mktg Svcs Mgr*

An ISO 9001 Certified Manufacturer of automotive lifts for scooter, wheelchairs, and powerchairs, three and four wheel scooters, and straight and custom curve stairlifts.

**370 Butlers Wheelchair Lifts**
Flinchbaugh Company
629 Lowther Road #C
Lewisberry, PA 17339
717-938-4253
888-847-0804
FAX: 717-938-4238
e-mail: hal@butlermobility.com
butlermobility.com

*Hal Feinstein, VP Sales / Marketing*

This wheelchair lift can be equipped with an end ramp and guard. Automatically retractable, it locks firmly into place when the lift is in operation.

**371 Classique**
Handi-Lift
730 Garden St
Carlstadt, NJ 07072-1625
201-933-0111
800-432-5438
FAX: 201-933-0050
e-mail: sales@handi-lift.com
handi-lift.com

*Douglas Boydston, President*
The Classique elevator answers access problems in churches, schools and small offices.

**372 Columbus McKinnon Corporation**
140 John James Audubon Pkwy
Amherst, NY 14228-1197
716-689-5400
800-888-0985
FAX: 716-689-5644
cmworks.com

*Timothy T. Tevens, President/CEO*
*Gregory P. Rustowicz, VP/CFO*
*Charles R. Giesige, VP, Corporate Dev.*
*Richard A. Steinberg, VP, Human Resources*
Supplies various lift and transfer systems for independent or attended applications including ceiling mounted or freestanding overhead track lifts and mobile floorbase units for homes, schools and healthcare facilities. Lift Systems for transferring between bed, chair, commode or bath are available with a variety of slings, scales and accessories.

**373 Curb-Sider**
Bruno Independent Living Aids
PO Box 84
1780 Executive Drive
Oconomowoc, WI 53066
262-567-4990
800-882-8183
FAX: 262-953-5501
www.bruno.com

*Michael R. Bruno, II, President/CEO*
*Andrew Bayer, Product Mgr, Automotive Div.*
*Mike Krawczyk, Mktg Svcs Mgr*
The lift of choice for storing your fully or partially assembled scooter or power chair weighing up to 400 pounds in the rear of your van or minivan, SUV, pickup truck or some station wagon applications.

**374 Curb-Sider Super XL**
P.O.Box 84
1780 Executive Drive
Oconomowoc, WI 53066
262-567-4990
800-882-8183
FAX: 262-953-5510
bruno.com

*Michael R. Bruno, II, President/CEO*
*Andrew Bayer, Product Mgr, Automotive Div.*
*Mike Krawczyk, Mktg Svcs Mgr*

**375 Custom Lift Residential Elevators**
Waupaca Elevator Company
1726 N Ballard Rd
Appleton, WI 54911-2444
920-991-9082
800-238-8739
FAX: 920-991-9087
e-mail: csr@waupacaelevator.com
waupacaelevator.com

*Bill Mc Michael, Owner*
Waupaca Elevator residential elevators and dumbwaiters add value, convenience and reliability to today's homes.

**376 Deluxe Convertible Exercise Staircase**
Sammons Preston Rolyan
Suite 210
1000 Remington Blvd
Bolingbrook, IL 60440-5117
630-378-6000
800-323-5547
FAX: 630-378-6010
e-mail: sp@pattersonmedical.com
www.pattersonmedical.com

*David P Sproat, President*
*Bruce Curtis, Sales Representative*
Here's an exercise staircase to fit any department configuration. Just reposition a few nuts and bolts to change from a straight to a corner type staircase.

**377 E-Z Access Van Ramp**
Maxi Aids
42 Executive Blvd
Farmingdale, NY 11735-4710
631-752-0521
800-522-6294
FAX: 631-752-0689
TTY: 631-752-0738
maxiaids.com

*Elliot Zaretsky, Founder / President*
Telescopic ramps for manual and electric wheel chairs. Bridges gaps over steps and curbs and makes vans more accessible. Extends 7'ft. in length, locking securely in place with snap-button catches. Easy to store.Holds up to 600lbs. *$299.95*

**378 Easy Pivot Transfer Machine**
Rand-Scot
401 Linden Center Dr
Fort Collins, CO 80524-2429
970-484-7967
800-467-7967
FAX: 970-484-3800
e-mail: info@randscot.com
randscot.com

*Joel Lerich, President*
The Easy Pivot Patient Lifting System allows for strain-free, one-caregiver transfers of the disabled individual.

**379 Easy Stand**
Altimate Medical
P.O.Box 180
262 W. 1st St.
Morton, MN 56270-180
507-697-6393
800-342-8968
FAX: 507-697-6900
e-mail: info@easystand.com
www.easystand.com

*Andrew Gardeen, International Sales Manager*
Designed to make standing fast and simple. The easy to operate, hydraulic lift system provides a controlled lifting and lowering. With the convenience of simply transferring to the chair and reaching a standing position in seconds with no straps to struggle with.

**380 Economical Liberty**
Handi-Lift
730 Garden St
Carlstadt, NJ 07072-1625
201-933-0111
800-432-5438
FAX: 201-933-0050
e-mail: sales@handi-lift.com
handi-lift.com

*Douglas Boydston, President*
Installs quickly and easily on most straight stairways. It uses regular household current and mounts over the carpet or directly to the stairs without marring.

**381 Electra-Ride**
Bruno Independent Living Aids
PO Box 84
1780 Executive Drive
Oconomowoc, WI 53066
262-567-4990
800-882-8183
FAX: 262-953-5501
www.bruno.com

*Michael R. Bruno, II, President/CEO*
*Andrew Bayer, Product Mgr, Automotive Div.*
*Mike Krawczyk, Mktg Svcs Mgr*
Bruno stairlifts can fit almost any custom curve or straight rail application and require no structural modification to the stairway. Plus, battery power allows for uninterrupted operation even during a power outage.

**382 Electra-Ride Elite**
Bruno Independent Living Aids
P.O.Box 84
1780 Executive Drive
Oconomowoc, WI 53066
262-567-4990
800-882-8183
FAX: 262-953-5510
bruno.com

*Michael R. Bruno, II, President/CEO*
*Andrew Bayer, Product Mgr, Automotive Div.*
*Mike Krawczyk, Mktg Svcs Mgr*
The new Electra-Ride Elite installs to within 5 inches of the wall and has a 350 pound weight capacity. Bruno stairlifts can fit almost any custom curve or straight rail application and require no structural modification to the stairway. Plus, battery power allows for uninterupted operation even during a power outage.

**383 Electra-Ride III**
P.O.Box 84
1780 Executive Drive
Oconomowoc, WI 53066
262-567-4990
800-882-8183
FAX: 262-953-5510
bruno.com

*Michael R. Bruno, II, President/CEO*
*Andrew Bayer, Product Mgr, Automotive Div.*
*Mike Krawczyk, Mktg Svcs Mgr*

**384 Freedom Wheels**
580 Tc Jester Blvd
Houston, TX 77007
713-864-1460
888-422-5337
FAX: 713-864-1469
e-mail: info@freedomwheels.com
freedomwheels.com

*Carlos Saez, Owner*
An assistive technology and mobility equipment provider and is committed to people with disabilities and personal transportation options for an independent lifestyle.

**385 Handi Home Lift**
Handi-Lift
730 Garden St
Carlstadt, NJ 07072-1625
201-933-0111
800-432-5438
FAX: 201-933-0050
e-mail: sales@handi-lift.com
handi-lift.com

*Douglas Boydston, President*
An outdoor lift designed to provide access over porch stairs or other steps that impede movement.

**386 Handi Lift**
730 Garden St
Carlstadt, NJ 07072-1625
201-933-0111
800-432-5438
FAX: 201-933-0050
e-mail: sales@handi-lift.com
handi-lift.com

*Douglas Boydston, President*
Accessibility with Dignity. We create solutions that enable people with mobility impairments to live freely with products like wheelchair lifts and home elevators.

**387 Handi Prolift**
Handi-Lift
730 Garden St
Carlstadt, NJ 07072-1625
201-933-0111
800-432-5438
FAX: 201-933-0050
e-mail: sales@handi-lift.com
handi-lift.com

*Douglas Boydston, President*
Provides dependable vertical transportation for multi-level buildings.

**388 Handi-Ramp**
Handi-Ramp
510 North Ave
Libertyville, IL 60048-2025
847-680-7700
800-876-7267
FAX: 847-816-7689
e-mail: info@handiramp.com
handiramp.com

*Thomas Disch, President/ CEO*
*Alicia C. Johns, Program Manager*
Provides a complete line of economical, ADA Compliant access ramping products. Line includes van attachable and wheelchair tie downs; aluminum or expanded metal folding portables; aluminum channels; portable, sectional ramp systems; semi-permanent ramps, platforms and systems. All ramp series are available in varied lengths and widths in combination with platforms and optional hand railing, single or double bar construction with return ends. Special Order ramps and ramp systems.

**389 Homewaiter**
Inclinator Company of America
601 Gibson Blvd
Harrisburg, PA 17104-3215
717-939-8420
800-343-9007
FAX: 717-234-0941
e-mail: isaks@inclinator.com
www.inclinator.com

*Stephen Nock, President*
With its roller truck riding in a specially formed monorail, it is easy to install and highly adaptable to existing conditions. It can travel up to 35 feet, opening on any or all three sides at different stations, whether at counter level or floor level.

**390 Horcher Lifting Systems**
324 Cypress Rd
Ocala, FL 34472-3102
352-687-8020
800-582-8732
FAX: 866-378-3318
e-mail: us-office@horcher.com
www.horcher.com

*David Schultz, General Manager*
*Sharon Harbert, Administrative Assistant*
Barrier Free Lifts by Horcher leads the industry for excellence in patient transfers and technology for over 18 years. They offer state of the art ceiling track systems, floor base lifts and bathing systems such as the Unilift, PC-2, Diana, Lexa, and Raisa to achieve greater mobility.

**391 Inclinette**
Inclinator Company of America
601 Gibson Blvd
Harrisburg, PA 17104-3215
717-939-8420
800-343-9007
FAX: 717-234-0941
e-mail: isaks@inclinator.com
www.inclinator.com

*Stephen Nock, President*
Inclinette provides comfort and convenience in providing multi-floor access to persons who have difficulty climbing stairs.

**392 Independent Driving Systems**
580 Tc Jester Blvd
Houston, TX 77007
713-864-1460
FAX: 713-864-1469
e-mail: info@independentdrivingssytems.com
www.independentdrivingsystems.com

*Chad Donnelly, Owner*
Provides adaptive driving systems for individuals with disabilities with more severe higher levels of injury that require more sophisticated types of assistive technology to enable them to drive safely.

**393 Joey Interior Platform Lift**
Bruno Independent Living Aids
PO Box 84
1780 Executive Drive
Oconomowoc, WI 53066
262-567-4990
800-882-8183
FAX: 262-953-5501
www.bruno.com

*Michael R. Bruno, II, President/CEO*
*Andrew Bayer, Product Mgr, Automotive Div.*
*Mike Krawczyk, Mktg Svcs Mgr*
Lifts and stores your unoccupied scooter or powerchair in the back of your minivan at the touch of a button.

**394 Lectra-Lift**
La-Z-Boy
1284 N Telegraph Rd
Monroe, MI 48162-5138
734-242-1444
FAX: 734-457-2005
www.lazboy.com

*Kurt L Darrow, CEO*
*David M Risley, SVP/CFO*
*Patrick H Norton, Chairman*
*Kurt Darrow, CEO*
This power recliner has a single motor drive that operates three distinct cycles: lifting, leg elevation and full power recline.

**395 Liberty LT**
Handi-Lift
730 Garden St
Carlstadt, NJ 07072-1625
201-933-0111
800-432-5438
FAX: 201-933-0050
e-mail: sales@handi-lift.com
handi-lift.com

*Douglas Boydston, President*
Stair lift with dual armrests that lock into position. The comfortable, contoured seat is designed to swivel and move forward at the bottom or top landings to facilitate transfer.

**396 Lift-All**
Amigo Mobility International
6693 Dixie Highway
Bridgeport, MI 48722-9725
989-777-0910
800-692-6446
FAX: 989-777-8184
e-mail: info@myamigo.com
www.myamigo.com

*Dietrich Mackel, VP Of Sales*
*Shirley Beebe, International & Gov't Sales Mgr*
*Heather Cross, Sales Rep*
*Sandy Humpert, Sales Rep*
Leading manufacturer of electric mobility; Amigo's Lift-All transports your wheelchair easily into the trunk of an automobile and neatly stores it for easy access. Also available is the Lift-It. *$965.00*

**397 Lifts for Swimming Pools and Spas**
Aquatic Access
1921 Production Dr
Louisville, KY 40299-2110
502-425-5817
800-325-5438
FAX: 502-425-9607
e-mail: info@AquaticAccess.com
aquaticaccess.com

*Linda Nolan, President*
*David Nolan, Vice President*
Aquatic Access manufacturers and sells water-powered lifts providing access to in-ground and above-ground swimming pools, spas, boats and docks. *$2310.00*

**398 Mac's Lift Gate**
2715 Seaboard Ln
Long Beach, CA 90805-3751
562-634-5962
800-795-6227
FAX: 562-634-4291
e-mail: rpearce@macslift.com
macsliftgate.com

*Randy Maner, Training Mgr*
Sales and service of van and truck lifts. Sales and service of wheel chair lifts for vans and automobiles. Sales, installation and service of vertical home lifts, scooter lifts and pool lifts. Sales of scooters.

**399 Mecalift Sling Lifter**
Arjo Inc
Ste A
50 Gary Ave
Roselle, IL 60172-1605
630-785-4490
800-323-1245
FAX: 63- 57- 502
e-mail: info@arjousa.com
www.arjo.com

*Philip M. Croxford, President/ CEO*

**400 Motorhome Lift By Handicaps, Inc.**
4335 S Santa Fe Dr
Englewood, CO 80110
303-781-2062
800-782-4335
FAX: 303-761-6811
e-mail: info@handicapsinc.com
www.handicapsinc.com

Wheelchair lifts made for vans and motor homes. The only lift on the market made without a platform so no doorways are blocked. Also make hand driving controls and other driving equipment. Quiet, quick and transferable. Saves on vehicle resale value. *$5950.00*

401 **One for All Lift All**
6693 Dixie Hwy
Bridgeport, MI 48722-9725
800-248-9131
800-692-6446
FAX: 800-334-7274
e-mail: info@myamigo.com
myamigo.com

*Allan R. Thieme, Founder*
*Beth Thieme, Founder*
Amigo Mobility designs and manufactures a complete line of power operated vehicles/mobility scooters and accessories in Bridgeport, Mich.

402 **Out-Sider III**
P.O.Box 84
1780 Executive Drive
Oconomowoc, WI 53066
262-567-4990
800-882-8183
FAX: 262-953-5510
bruno.com

*Michael R. Bruno, II, President/CEO*
*Andrew Bayer, Product Mgr, Automotive Div.*
*Mike Krawczyk, Mktg Svcs Mgr*

403 **Out-Sider Meridian**
Bruno Independent Living Aids
P.O. Box 84
1780 Executive Drive
Oconomowoc, WI 53066
262-567-4990
800-882-8183
FAX: 262-953-5501
www.bruno.com

*Michael R. Bruno, II, President/CEO*
*Andrew Bayer, Product Mgr, Automotive Div.*
*Mike Krawczyk, Mktg Svcs Mgr*
Lets you carry your scooter fully assembled and keeps your trunk space available for other things.

404 **Parker Bath**
Arjo Inc
Ste A
50 Gary Ave
Roselle, IL 60172-1605
630-785-4490
800-323-1245
FAX: 63- 57- 502
e-mail: info@arjousa.com
www.arjo.com

*Philip M. Croxford, President/ CEO*
*Ross Scavuzzo, President*
This involves no manual lifting, strain or stress for the caregiver.

405 **Patient Lifting & Injury Prevention**
Arjo Inc
Ste A
50 Gary Ave
Roselle, IL 60172-1605
630-785-4490
800-323-1245
FAX: 63-57- 502
e-mail: info@arjousa.com
www.arjo.com

*Philip M. Croxford, President/ CEO*
Aids in patient lifting while protecting the caregiver from the risk of backstrain.

406 **Ramplette Telescoping Ramp**
Graham-Field Health Products
2935 Northeast Pkwy
Atlanta, GA 30360-2808
770-368-4700
800-347-5678
FAX: 770-368-4702
www.grahamfield.com

*Irwin Selenger, Owner*
A multi-functional, easily moved, economical ramp weighing 25 pounds.

407 **Rickshaw Exerciser**
Access to Recreation
8 Sandra Ct
Newbury Park, CA 91320-4302
805-498-7535
800-634-4351
FAX: 805-498-8186
e-mail: customerservice@accesstr.com
www.accesstr.com

*Don Krebs, President/ Founder*
This Exerciser develops the muscle used most by those in wheelchairs. It develops the strength you need to lift yourself for pressure relief, doing transfers and pushing your wheelchair.

408 **Ricon Corporation**
7900 Nelson Rd
Panorama City, CA 91402-6090
818-267-3000
800-322-2884
FAX: 818-267-3001
e-mail: sales@riconcorp.com
riconcorp.com

*John Condon, National Sales Manager*
*Mike O'Neill, Eastern Saler Manager*
*Peter Buckley, Central Area Sales Manager*
Ricon corporation is a world leader in the manufacture of lifts and other mobility products for people with disabilities. The Ricon product line features the Activan(R) a lowered floor minivan conversion, wheelchair lifts power seat base and automatic door openers.

409 **Smart Leg**
Invacare Corporation
899 Cleveland St
Elyria, OH 44035-4107
440-329-6000
FAX: 440-366-1803
e-mail: info@invacare.com
www.invacare.com

*A Malachi Mixon Iii, CEO*
*Gerald B Blouch, President/COO*
*Thomas R Miklich, CFO*
*Joseph B Richey II, President Technical Division*
An ingenious elevating leg rest that automatically extends to correctly fit every outstretched leg.

410 **Smooth Mover**
Dixie EMS
385 Union Ave
Brooklyn, NY 11211-3425
718-387-9305
800-347-3494
FAX: 718-387-9310
e-mail: customerSVC@dixieems.com
www.dixieems.com

*Eva Silverstein, President*
Patient mover is a board designed to transfer patients from bed to stretcher or table with one or two people. *$199.95*

411 **SpectraLift**
Inclinator Company of America
601 Gibson Blvd
Harrisburg, PA 17104-3215
717-939-8420
800-343-9007
FAX: 717-234-0941
e-mail: isaks@inclinator.com
www.inclinator.com

*Stephen Nock, President*
A newly designed hydraulic wheelchair lift made of fiberglass construction suitable for commercial and residential use.

412 **Spectrum Aquatics**
7100 Spectrum Ln
Missoula, MT 59808-8416
406-543-6823
FAX: 406-543-6823

*Dave Murray, Owner*

413 **Spectrum Products Catalog**
Spectrum Products
7100 Spectrum Ln
Missoula, MT 59808-8416
406-542-9781
800-791-8056
FAX: 800-791-8057
e-mail: info@spectrumproducts.com
spectrumproducts.com

*Nabil Khaled, Dir. of Sales*
*Chris Rhyne, Business Dev. Specialist*
*Rob Nelson, Mgr of Logistics*
Manufacturers of swimming pool disabled access products such as lifts, ramps, railings, ladders, and stainless steel hydrotherapy tanks for the swimming pool and medical therapy markets.

414 **StairLIFT SC & SL**
Inclinator Company of America
601 Gibson Blvd
Harrisburg, PA 17104-3215
717-939-8420
800-343-9007
FAX: 717-234-0941
e-mail: isaks@inclinator.com
www.inclinator.com

*Stephen Nock, President*
Simple, self-contained and efficient stair units.

415 **Stairway Elevators**
Bruno Independent Living Aids
P.O. Box 84
1780 Executive Drive
Oconomowoc, WI 53066
262-567-4990
800-882-8183
FAX: 262-953-5510
bruno.com

*Michael R. Bruno, II, President/CEO*
*Andrew Bayer, Product Mgr, Automotive Div.*
*Mike Krawczyk, Mktg Svcs Mgr*
Bruno offers a full line of stairway elevators, including the Electra-Ride II featuring access during power interruptions, convenient installation, comfort and a powerful drive system. The Electra-Ride which features battery-powered technology, a rail width of 25 inches and seat rotation for easy transfers. The Comfort-Ride AC stair lift which is battery operated, has a rail width of 7.25 inches and folded width of less than 14.5 inches.

416 **Straight and Custom Curved Stairlifts**
Bruno Independent Living Aids
P.O.Box 84
1780 Executive Drive
Oconomowoc, WI 53066
262-567-4990
800-882-8183
FAX: 262-953-5501
bruno.com

*Michael R. Bruno, II, President/CEO*
*Andrew Bayer, Product Mgr, Automotive Div.*
*Mike Krawczyk, Mktg Svcs Mgr*
Bruno stairlifts can fit almost any curve or straight rail application and requires little or no structural modification to the stairway. Normal rail position for a Bruno inside turn is 7 to 8 inches from the wall or obstruction which is the tightest radius of any stairlift manufacturing company in the world. The Bruno inside turn is ideal for bi-level homes or staircases with mid-level doors. Bruno's unique battery power allows for uninterrupted operation even during a power outage.

417 **Superarm Lift for Vans By Handicaps, Inc.**
4335 S Santa Fe Dr
Englewood, CO 80110
303-781-2062
800-782-4335
FAX: 303-761-6811
e-mail: info@handicapsinc.com
www.handicapsinc.com

Wheelchair lifts made for vans and motor homes. The only lift on the market made without a platform so no doorways are blocked. Also make hand driving controls and other driving equipment. Quiet, quick and transferable. Saves on vehicle resale value.
*$5950.00*

418 **SureHands Lift & Care Systems**
982 County Route 1
Pine Island, NY 10969-1205
845-258-6500
800-724-5305
FAX: 845-258-6634
e-mail: info@surehands.com
www.surehands.com

*Thomas F Herceg, President*
*Joyce Moraczewski, Marketing Coordinator*
SureHands specializes in lift & care systems for both homecare and professional settings where the user's safety is most important. Offering a variety of lift and transfer options, SureHands provides the necessary tools to overcome physical and architectural barriers to deliver a system designed to meet the specific needs of the user.

419 **The Braun Corporation**
631 West 11th Street
Winamac, IN 46996-310
574-946-6153
800-843-5438
FAX: 574-946-4670
e-mail: mediaquestions@braunlift.com
www.braunability.com

*Nick Gutwein, President*
*Greg Cook, Vice President Sales & Marketing*
*Joe Garnett, Director Of Marketing*
*Ralph Braun, Founder/ CEO*
The Braun Corporation is the world's largest manufacturer of wheelchair-accessible vans, ramps and wheelchair lifts. Our products enable people with physical disabilities to regain thier mobility and to lead active and independent lives. Our companies broad product line includes the Chrysler/Dodge Entervan, the Honda Odyssey Entervan, and the Toyota Sienna Rampvan.

420 **Thyssen Krupp Access**
4001 E 138th St
Grandview, MO 64030-2837
816-200-1954
800-820-0537
FAX: 816-763-4467
e-mail: dealerinfo@tkaccess.com
tkaccess.com

*Jurrien van Akker, CEO*
*Scott Zoetewey, Vice President of Operations*
*Thomas Hance, President*
Whether you want to open your facility or stay in the home you love, Thyssen Krupp Access has the perfect wheelchair lift, stair lift or elevator to suit your budget and needs. Our lifts have the best warranties. Our nationwide network of dealers are close by and ready to help.

421 **Turning Automotive Seating (TAS)**
Bruno Independent Living Aids
P.O.Box 84
Oconomowoc, WI 53066-84
262-567-4990
800-882-8183
FAX: 262- 95- 550
e-mail: info@bruno.com
bruno.com

*Michael Bruno, II, President*
*Cindy Schmidt, Customer Relations*
*Steve Nelson, Service Manager*
*Thomas Jacobson, Senior Vice President*

Transfer in and out of a car, minivan, pickup truck and full size van without any lifting!

422 **Vangater, Vangater II, Mini-Vangater**
P.O.Box 310
Winamac, IN 46996-310
800-THE-LIFT
FAX: 574-946-7935
e-mail: mediaquestions@braunlift.com
www.braunlift.com

*ralph Braun, CEO*

Tri-fold and fold-in-half lifts represent a major innovation in the field of adapted van transportation.

423 **Versatrainer**
Pro- Max/ Division Of Bow- Flex Of America
2200 NE 65th Ave
Vancouver, WA 98661-6978
800-605-3369
800-952-7205
FAX: 360-993-3610
e-mail: customerservice@bowflex.com.
www.bowflex.com

One exercise system for the disabled person that does everything. Incorporates full body strength, muscle development, cardiovascular conditioning, gives full muscle movement and balanced muscle development.

424 **Vestibular Board**
Bailey Manufacturing Company
Ste 130
118 Lee St
Lodi, OH 44254-1056
800-321-8372
FAX: 800-224-5390
e-mail: baileymfg@attmail.com
baileymfg.com

Creates tilting in a rolling motion for reclining patients who need help developing balance.

425 **Wheelchair Carrier**
203 Matzinger Rd
7325 Douglas Road
Lambertville, MI 48144-2624
734-568-6083
800-541-3213
FAX: 734-568-6705
e-mail: admin@WheelChairCarrier.com
wheelchaircarrier.com

*David Makulinsky, President*
*Mike Siler, Engineer*
*Christina Makulinski , Office Manager*

Wheelchair, scooter and powerchair carriers for hitch mount on vehicles, priced from $199 to $999.

## Major Catalogs

426 **Access Store Products for Barrier Free Environments**
Access Store.Com
820 W 7th St
Chico, CA 95928-5011
530-893-1596
800-497-2003
FAX: 530-893-1560
e-mail: sales@accessstore.com
www.accessstore.com

*Tim Vander Heiden, Owner*
*Lisa Bantum, Sales Administrator*

One of the largest online ADA Compliance Catalogs available. Offers everything from innovative barrier removal products to survey equipment, to unique specialty products.

427 **Access to Recreation**
8 Sandra Ct
Newbury Park, CA 91320-4302
805-498-7535
800-634-4351
FAX: 805-498-8186
e-mail: customerservice@accesstr.com
www.accesstr.com

*Don Krebs, President*

The Access to Recreation catalog is full of recreation and exercise equipment. One can find items such as electric fishing reels and other fishing and hunting equipment for the disabled sportsman. There are also adapted golf clubs, swimming pool lifts, wheelchair gloves and cuffs and bowling equipment. There are devices to help with embroidery, knitting and card playing, videos, books and practical aides such as wheelchair ramps and book.

*64 pages Bi-Annually*

428 **Achievement Products**
P.O. Box 6013
Carol Stream, I 60197-6013
800-373-4699
FAX: 800-766-4303
e-mail: Bids@achievement-products.com
www.specialkidszone.com

*Teresa Cardon, VP*

Offer a wide range of pediatric rehabilitation equipment and special education products including handwriting aids, weighted vests, positioning equipment, sensory integration products and adaptive furniture. Call for your free catalog.

429 **Adaptive Clothing: Adults**
Special Clothes
P.O.Box 333
E Harwich, MA 02645-333
508-430-2410
FAX: 508-430-2410
TTY:508-430-2410
e-mail: SPECIALCLO@aol.com
www.special-clothes.com

*Judith Sweeney, President*

Special Clothes produces a catalogue of garments for adults with disabilities and/or incontinence. Offerings include: undergarments, snap-crotch tee shirts, sleepwear, jumpsuits, bibs and some footwear. The catalogue is available without charge. Comparable to department store prices. Special Clothes produces a catalog of adaptive clothing for children in sizes from toddler through young adults. A full line of clothing is included from undergarments through wheelchair jackets and ponchos.

**430 Adaptive Technology Catalog**
Synapse Adaptive
14 Lynn Ct
San Rafael, CA 94901-5114
415-455-9700
800-317-9611
FAX: 415-455-9801
e-mail: info@synapse-ada.com
synapseadaptive.com

*Martin Tibor, President*
Adaptive technology for individuals with disabilities, ADA compliant workstations, and ergonomic furniture. Products accommodate blindness, low vision, mobility impairments or learning differences.

**431 Adult Long Jumpsuit with Feet**
Special Clothes
P.O.Box 333
E Harwich, MA 02645-333
508-896-7939
FAX: 508-896-7939
e-mail: specialclo@aol.com
www.special-clothes.com

*Judith Sweeney, President*
Line of clothing for people with disabilities. Child and adult catalog available.

**432 Adult Short Jumpsuit**
Special Clothes
P.O.Box 333
E Harwich, MA 02645-333
508-896-7939
FAX: 508-896-7939
e-mail: specialclo@aol.com
www.special-clothes.com

*Judith Sweeney, President*
This pull-on jumpsuit provides comfort and full coverage without bulk. Wide leg ribbing ends at mid-thigh, with snaps at the crotch. We use fine quality, comfortable cotton knit. 100% cotton knit. Made in USA. Option: long sleeves - add $3.00. Colors: white, navy, teal, light blue, light pink, red, burgundy, royal blue and black. Sm & Med: $36.50/3 for $104.00; L & XL: $39.00/3 for $111.25; and XXL: $42.00/3 for $119.25.

**433 American Discount Medical**
459 Main St
Ste 101-417
Trussville, AL 35173
205-467-6995
800-877-9100
FAX: 205-467-7095
e-mail: Sales@AmericanDiscountMed.com
americandiscountmed.com

*Tom Ruf, President*
Deeply discounts every major brand medical product available.

**434 Apria Healthcare**
26220 Enterprise Ct
Lake Forest, CA 92630-8405
949-639-2000
800-277-4288
e-mail: contact_us@apria.com
apria.com

*Lawrence M Higby, CEO*
Lifts, chairs, bathroom aids, bedroom aids, eating utensils and independent living aids for the physically challenged.

**435 Armstrong Medical**
575 Knightsbridge Pkwy
Parkway
Lincolnshire, IL 60069- 700
847-913-0101
800-323-4220
FAX: 847-913-0138
e-mail: djoseph@armstrongmedical.com
armstrongmedical.com

*Armstrong, CEO*
*Diane Joseph, customer representative*
Training aids, anatomical models, medical equipment, pediatrics equipment and rehabilitation equipment.

**436 Assistive Technology Journal**
1700 N Moore St
Suite 1905
Rosslyn, VA 22209-1905
703-243-1975
FAX: 703-524-6630
e-mail: info@technologistsinc.com
technologistsinc.com

*$32.50*
*Bi-Annually*

**437 Assistive Technology Sourcebook**
Special Needs Project
Ste H
324 State St
Santa Barbara, CA 93101-2364
805-962-8087
800-333-6867
FAX: 805-962-5087
e-mail: editor@specialneeds.com
www.specialneeds.com

*Hod Gray, Owner*
*Marian Hall, Editor*
Provides you with 18 chapters of practical information on all aspects of assistive technology for individuals with functional limitations. *$60.00*
*576 pages*

**438 Bailey**
Bailey Manufacturing
P.O.Box 130
Lodi, OH 44254-130
800-321-8372
FAX: 800-224-5390
e-mail: baileymfg@baileymfg.com
baileymfg.com

Ambulation aids, balance aids, benches, chairs, exercise devices, tables, stools, rehabilitation and physical therapy equipment for the physically challenged.
*70 pages*

**439 Best 25 Catalog Resources for Making Life Easier**
Meeting Life's Challenges
9042 Aspen Grove Ln
Madison, WI 53717-2700
608-824-0402
FAX: 608-824-0403
e-mail: help@meetinglifeschallenges.com
www.meetinglifeschallenges.com

*Shelley Peterman Schwarz, President*
*Deborah , Dir. of Mktg & Dev.*
Unique reference guide to locate thousands of useful and hard-to-find adaptive devices to make dressing, eating, cooking, grooming, communicating, playing, exercising, etc. easier, safer and less frustrating for people of all ages and disabilities. A comprehensive, up-do-date reference for people with disabilities, caregivers and healthcare professionals. *$8.95*
*36 pages*
*ISBN 1-891854-03-8*

**440 Body Suits**
Special Clothes
P.O.Box 333
E Harwich, MA 02645-333
508-430-2410
FAX: 508-430-2410
e-mail: specialclo@aol.com
www.special-clothes.com

*Judith Bari, President*
Bodysuits, Jumpsuits, back opening garments, incontinence wear, bibs. Features include snap crotches and g-tube pockets.

441 **Cambridge Career Products Catalog**
Cambridge Educational
132 West 31st Street
17th Floor
New York, NY 10001
800-322-8755
800-468-4227
FAX: 609-679-0266
e-mail: custserv@films.com
www.cambridge.films.com/

*Lisa Schmuclei, Marketing Director*
A full color catalog featuring hundreds of products designed to aid people in career exploration, selecting specific occupations and obtaining these jobs through resume and interview preparation.
*64 pages BiAnnual*

442 **Carolyn's Low Vision Products**
3938 S Tamiami Trl
Sarasota, FL 34231-3622
941-373-9100
800-648-2266
FAX: 941-739-5503
e-mail: support@carolynscatalog.com.
carolynscatalog.com

*John Colton, Owner*
Free mail-order catalog of items for visually impaired people. We also have a retail store.

443 **Communication Aids for Children and Adults**
Crestwood Communication Aids
6589 N
Crestwood Drive
Milwaukee, WI 53209
414-351-0311
FAX: 414-351-0311
e-mail: crestcomm@aol.com
www.communicationaids.com

*Ruth B Leff, President*
A free catalog of communication aids for children and adults with disabilities. Over 300 light and high tech switches and aids, and a large selection of adapted and voice-activated toys. Talking Pictures and Passports communication boards, easy to use and moderately priced talking aids.
*32 pages Yearly*

444 **Danmar Products**
221 Jackson Industrial Drive
Ann Arbor, MI 48103-9104
734-761-1990
800-783-1998
FAX: 734-761-8977
e-mail: sales@danmarproducts.com
danmarproducts.com

*Dan Russo, President*
*Karen Green, Sales*
*Hidie Bowman, Sales*
Manufactures adaptive equipment for persons with physical and mental disabilities, from seating and positioning equipment, flotation devices, toileting aids to hard and soft shell helmets.

445 **Dayspring Associates**
2111 Foley Rd
Havre De Grace, MD 21078-1703
410-939-5900
FAX: 410-939-6252

*Benedict Schwartz, Manager*
This publisher provides a directory of 1,000 rehabilitation aids.

446 **Disabilities Sourcebook**
Omnigraphics
PO Box 31-1640
Detroit, MI 4823-1640
610-461-3548
800-234-1340
FAX: 800-875-1340
e-mail: info@omnigraphics.com
www.omnigraphics.com

*Paul Rogers, Publicity Associate*
*Georgiann Fratoni, Customer Service Manager*
*Peter Ruffner*
*$78.00*
*616 pages*
*ISBN 0-780803-89-2*

447 **Disability Bookshop Catalog**
P.O.Box 129
Vancouver, WA 98666-129
360-694-2462
800-637-2256
FAX: 360-696-3210
e-mail: twinpeak@pacifier.com
disabilitybookshop.virtualave.net/

Offers more than 400 hard-to-find titles covering a wide range of health topics for the general public, and matters of interest to people with disabilities. Catalog. *$4.00*
*40 pages*

448 **Dressing Tips and Clothing Resources for Making Life Easier**
Attainment Company
P.O.Box 930160
Verona, WI 53593-160
608-845-7880
800-327-4269
FAX: 608-845-8040
e-mail: info@attainmentcompany.com
attainmentcompany.com

*Don Bastian, President*
*Brent Denu, Marketing Manager*
*Sherri Erickson, Dealer Services*
Learn hundreds of simple tips and techniques to make dressing easier. Learn how to adapt/modify ready-to-wear garments to accommodate your special dressing needs. Find out how to locate more than 100 resources offering specially designed or easy-on/easy-off clothing for men, women, children and/or wheelchair users. You'll find everything you need to look your best. An invaluable resource for people with special dressing needs, people with disabilities, caregivers and healthcare professionals. *$19.00*
*144 pages 2000*
*ISBN 1-578611-19-9*

449 **Enrichments Catalog**
Sammons Preston Rolyan
1000 remmington blvd
suite 210
Bolingbrook, IL 60440- 5117
630-378-6000
800-323-5547
FAX: 630-378-6010
e-mail: sp@pattersonmedical.com
www.pattersonmedical.com

*David P Sproat, President*
*Bruce Curtis, Sales Representative*
Provides people with physical challenges with the products they need to help live their lives to the fullest. Includes items for everyday tasks and personal care; assistive products for home use; toileting and bathing aids; grooming and dressing devices; kitchen and dining aids. Also items for range of motion, mobility and exercise such as weights, therapy putty and exercise equipment; ergonomic gloves and supports; canes, crutches, walkers and wheelchair accessories. 36-page catalog.

**450 Equipment Shop**
34 Hartford Street
Bedford, MA 01730-33
781-275-7681
800-525-7681
FAX: 781-275-4094
e-mail: info@equipmentshop.com
equipmentshop.com

*Ken Larson, Owner*
*Barbara Johnston, General Manager*
Specializing in oral motor therapy equipment including flexi cut cups, maroon spoons, chewy tubes, ARK grabbers and z-vibes. Also tricycle foot peal attachments and trike back supports as well as fat wheels.

**451 Everest & Jennings**
Division of Graham-Field
2935 Northeast Parkway
Atlanta, GA 30360
678-291-3207
800-347-5678
FAX: 770-368-2386
e-mail: cs@grahamfield.com
www.grahamfield.com

*KENNETH SPETT, President*
*Beatrice Scherer , Board Member*
Manufactures more than 200 items for persons with physical disabilities, including wheelchairs, seat cushions, shower chairs, grab bars and more.

**452 Express Medical Supply**
28 Seebold Spur
Fenton, MO 63026
636-349-8448
800-633-2139
FAX: 800-633-9188
e-mail: sales@exmed.net
exmed.net

*Bill Nahm, President*
Offers a full line of medical and ostomy supplies at discounted prices. Order by phone or online.

**453 FlagHouse Rehab Resources**
601 FLAGHOUSE DRIVE
Hasbrouck Heights, NJ 07604-3116
201-288-7600
800-793-7900
FAX: 800-793-7922
www.flaghouse.com

*George Carmel, President*

**454 FlagHouse Special Populations**
601 FLAGHOUSE DRIVE
Hasbrouck Heights, NJ 07604-3116
201-288-7600
800-793-7900
FAX: 800-793-7922
e-mail: sales@flaghouse.com
www.flaghouse.com

*Brigid de Lime, Sr Brand Manager*
*Diana Hohman, Brand Manager*
Contains over 2,000 products of interest to therapy professionals.
*Bi-Annually*

**455 Freedom Rider**
Freedom Rider
P.O.Box 4187
Manchester, NH 03108-4187
603-645-1811
888-253-8811
FAX: 888-253-8811
e-mail: info@freedomrider.com
freedomrider.com

*Victoria Surr, President*
A catalog of equipment for people with disabilities who ride and drive horses which includes instructional aids, vaulting equipment, and lots of hard to find items.

**456 HAC Hearing Aid Centers of America: HARC Mercantile**
Hearing Center
1111 W Centre Ave
Portage, MI 49024
269-324-0301
800-445-9968
FAX: 269-324-2387
e-mail: info@harc.com
hacofamerica.com

Specializes in products for the hard of hearing and deaf as required under ADA including visual alerting products for fire, phone, door, wake up, phone amplification, TTY, FM and infrared listening systems.

**457 Health and Rehabilitation Products**
Luminaud
8688 Tyler Blvd
Mentor, OH 44060
440-255-9082
800-255-3408
FAX: 440-255-2250
e-mail: info@luminaud.com
luminaud.com

*Thomas M Lennox, President*
*Dorothy Lennox, VP*
Switches for limited capability, stoma and trach covers, shower protectors and thermo-stim oral motor stimulator. Personal voice amplifiers for people with weak voices. Artificial larynges for people with no voices. Small electronic communication boards. Books for laryngectomies and speech pathologists.

**458 HealthCare Solutions**
Blue Chip II
3478 Hauck Rd
Cincinnati, OH 45241
513-271-5115
800-417-5115
FAX: 513-527-3686

*Michael Leabhart, Manager*
Quality rehabilitation equipment sales and rental. Available equipment includes manual and powered mobility, positioning/seating equipment, vehicle modification, environmental controls, augmentative and alternative communication devices, adaptive computer access, ambulance aids and aids for daily living. Equipment provision is carried out through a total team approach. .

**459 Hear You Are**
98 Us Highway 46
Budd Lake, NJ 07828-1818
973-347-7662
FAX: 973-691-0611

*Dorinne S Davis, President*
A large catalog of various assistive and communication devices for people who are hearing impaired. *$3.00*
*42 pages*

**460 Hig's Manufacturing**
8375 Sunset Rd Ne
Minneapolis, MN 55418-3238
763-795-9478
FAX: 612-788-1926

*Jim Murphy, Owner*
Factory direct, lightweight aluminum, portable, 2 & 4-way folding, telescoping tracks, threshold, van, scooter and approach ramps.

**461 Huntleigh Healthcare**
2349, W Lake Street
Suite 250
Addison, IL 60101
630-785-4490
800-323-1245
FAX: 630-576-5020
e-mail: us.info@ArjoHuntleigh.com
www.huntleigh-healthcare.com

Offers quality products including support surfaces, seating surfaces and intermittent pneumatic compression devices.

**462 Kleinert's**
433 Newton Street
Elba, AL 36323
800-498-7051
FAX: 305-937-0825
e-mail: customercare@kleinerts.com
hygienics.com

*Michael Brier, President*
Offers a complete line of incontinence products and skin care products consisting of disposable and reuseable panties for women and pants for men. Also disposable liners, diapers and underpads.
*16 pages Bi-Annual*

**463 LS&S**
145 River Rock Drive
Buffalo, NY 14207
716-348-3500
800-468-4789
FAX: 847-498-1482
TTY: 800-317-8533
www.LSSproducts.com

*Melissa Balbach, President*
*John K Bace, Executive Vice President.*
Specializes in products for the blind, visually impaired, hearing impaired, and deaf. Free catalog upon request.

**464 Lighthouse Low Vision Products**
Lighthouse International
111 E 59th St
New York, NY 10022-1202
212-821-9200
800-829-0500
FAX: 212-821-9707
e-mail: info@lighthouse.org
lighthouse.org

*Mark Ackermann, Chief Executive Officer*
*Joseph A Ripp, Chairman*
*Sarah Smith, Treasurer*
This organization provides health care services related to vision loss; Career and academic services for people with vision loss; Music instruction and pre K curriculum for visually impaired students.

**465 Luminaud**
8688 Tyler Blvd
Mentor, OH 44060-4348
440-255-9082
800-255-3408
FAX: 440-255-2250
e-mail: info@luminaud.com
luminaud.com

*Thomas M Lennox, President*
*Dorothy Lennox, VP*
Offers a line of artificial larynx, personal voice amplifiers, special switches, stoma covers and other communication, health and safety items.

**466 MOMS Catalog**
9385 Dielman Ind Dr
Saint Louis, MO 63132-2214
31- 9-7 87
800-232-7443
FAX: 314-997-0047
e-mail: custcare@hdis.com
www.momscatalog.com

*Bruce Grench, President*
MOMS catalog features high quality, incontinence supplies, mobility products, bath safety products urological products, aids for daily living products, ostomy supplies and many other adpative items. MOMS offers low prices, excellent customer service and convenient home delivery to your doorstep.
*52 pages*

**467 Maxi Aids**
42 Executive Blvd
Farmingdale, NY 11735-4710
631-752-0521
800-522-6294
FAX: 631-752-0689
TTY: 800-281-3555
e-mail: sales@maxiaids.com
www.maxiaids.com

*Elliot Zaretsky, Founder/ President*
Products specially designed for the blind, low vision, visually impaired, deaf, deaf-blind, hard of hearing, arthritic, diabetic and individuals with special needs.

**468 New Vision Store**
919 Walnut St
Philadelphia, PA 19107
215-627-0600
FAX: 215-922-0692
e-mail: asbinfo@asb.org
asb.org

*Dolores Fabianski, Director*
*Rick Forsythe, PC Instructor*
*Linda Gaffney, Coordinator*
Catalog for individuals with visual impairments, listing visual aids, magnifiers, large print books and more.
*30 pages*

**469 Pearson Performance Solutions**
1 North Dearborn Street
Chicago, IL 60602
800-922-7343
FAX: 312-242-4403
e-mail: HCM.info@vangent.com
www.vangent-hcm.com

*David Fabianski, Senior VP and General Mgr*
*Cindy Hotsky, finance Dir.*
*Julia McClung, VP, Talent Management Solutions*
Publishes human resource assessment instruments for employment settings. The instruments include job analysis procedures to identify important characteristics for job success and objective assessment procedures to evaluate applicants and employees on these characteristics.

**470 Pearson Reid London House**
1 North Dearborn Street
Chicago, IL 60602-4335
FAX: 312-242-4403
e-mail: HCM.info@vangent.com
www.pearsonreidlondonhouse.com/index.htm

*David Fabianski, Senior VP and General Mgr*
*Cindy Hotsky, finance Dir.*
*Julia McClung, VP, Talent Management Solutions*

**471 Potomac Technology**
1500 Olympic Boulevard
Santa Monica, CA 90404
310-656-4924
800-233-9130
FAX: 310-450-9918
TTY: 800-233-9130
www.weitbrecht.com/
This catalog offers a variety of products for the deaf and hard of hearing, such as: wake-up devices, alarm clocks, alerting systems, assistive listening devices, signalers, smoke detectors, TTY, telephones and telephone amplifiers. We also carry novelties, and educational books and videos.
*24 pages*

**472 Prentke Romich Company Product Catalog**
1022 Heyl Rd
Wooster, OH 44691-9786
330-262-1984
800-262-1984
FAX: 330-263-4829
e-mail: info@prentrom.com
prentrom.com

*David L Moffatt, President*
*Dave Moffatt, President/ COO*
*Barry Romich, Co-Founder*
A full line, product catalog containing information on speech-output communication devices, environmental controls and computer access products.

**473 Products for People with Disabilities**
LS&S
145 River Rock Drive
Buffalo, NY 14207
716-348-3500
800-468-4789
FAX: 877-498-1482
TTY:(866) 317-85
e-mail: info@LSSproducts.com
www.LSSproducts.com

*John K Bace, Executive Vice President*
LS&S, LLC has a free catalog of products for the blind, deaf, visually and hearing impaired including: TTYs, computer adaptive devices, CCTVs, talking blood pressure, blood glucose and talking scales.

**474 Rehabilitation Engineering and Assistive Technology Society of North America (RESNA)**
1700 N. Moore Street,
Suite 1540
Arlington, VA 22209- 1903
703-524-6686
FAX: 703-524-6630
TTY:703-524-6639
e-mail: info@resna.org
resna.org

*Heidi Horstmann Koester, Treasurer*
*Jerry Weisman, President*
*Ray Grott, Secretary*
RESNA improves the potential of people with disabilities to achieve their goals through the use of technology. RESNA promotes research, development, education, advocacy and provision of technology; and by supporting the people engaged in these activities.

**475 Sammons Preston Enrichments Catalog**
Sammons Preston Rolyan
1000 remmington blvd
suite 210
Bolingbrook, IL 60440- 5117
630-378-6000
800-323-5547
FAX: 630-378-6010
e-mail: sp@pattersonmedical.com
www.pattersonmedical.com

*David P Sproat, President*
*Bruce Curtis, Sales Representative*
Our Enrichments Catalog offers products that make the tasks and challenges of living at home- bathing, getting dressed, getting around- a little easier. Choose from personal care items to kitchen and dining aids, household helpers to mobility devices, plus a complete selection of pain-reducing products, exercise items, health monitoring equipment and more.
*40 pages Yearly*

**476 Sportaid**
78 Bay Creek Rd
Loganville, GA 30052
770-554-5130
800-743-7203
FAX: 770-554-5944
e-mail: stuff@sportaid.com
www.sportaid.com

*Stacy Green, Owner*
*jimmy green, Owner*
Offers an assortment of wheelchairs (everyday and racing), wheelchair sports equipment, replacement tires, hubs, spokes, pushrims, cushions and more. Call for free catalog.
*68 pages Yearly*

**477 Store @ HDSC Product Catalog**
Hearing, Speech & Deafness Center (HDSC)
1625 19th Ave
Seattle, WA 98122-2848
206-323-5770
1 8-8 2-2 50
800-761-2821
FAX: 206-328-6871
TTY:206.388.1275
e-mail: seattle@hsdc.org
hsdc.org

*Susie Burdick, Executive Director*
*32 pages Yearly*

**478 Ultratec**
450 Science Dr
Madison, WI 53711-1166
608-238-5400
800-482-2424
FAX: 608-238-3008
TTY: 800-482-2424
e-mail: service@ultratec.com
ultratec.com

*Jackie Morgan, Marketing Director*
*Robert M Engelke, CEO*
Works to make telephone access more convenient and reliable for people with hearing loss.
*Yearly*

**479 WCI/Weitbrecht Communications**
1500 Olympic Boulevard
Santa Monica, CA 90405
31- 9-7 87
800-233-9130
FAX: 310-450-9918
TTY: 800-233-9130
www.weitbrecht.com

Catalog featuring a wide range of assistive devices for the deaf, hard of hearing, mobility and speech impaired.
*24 pages*

**480 Walgreens Home Medical Center**
7173 Cermak Rd
Berwyn, IL 60402-2103
708-795-1295
800-323-2828
FAX: 708-795-1308

*Stan Kozlowski, Manager*
Hospital supplies and home medical equipment with nationwide direct mail delivery. .

**481 Walton Way Medical**
1225 Walton Way
Augusta, GA 30901-2141
706-722-0276
FAX: 706-722-0279

*Michael Bower, President*
Offers medical, therapeutic, urological, hygiene and skin care products for disabled persons.

## Miscellaneous

**482 Access-USA**
242 James St
PO Box 160
Clayton, NY 13624-160
800-263-2750
FAX: 800-563-1687
e-mail: info@access-usa.com
www.access-usa.com

*Deborah Haight, PICOE*

Access-USA provides one-stop alternate format transcription services for almost any type of document-reports, schedules, menus, monthly statements, brochures, reports, etc. Items may be submitted on computer disk, hard copy or email. Alternate formats include Braille, large print, Braille and print, audio recordings, adapted disks as well as video services-open/closed captioning and video descriptions. Accessible products also include Braille Business Cards and ADA signage.

**483 Access-USA: Transcription Services**
242 James St
PO Box 160
Clayton, NY 13624-160
800-263-2750
FAX: 800-563-1687
e-mail: info@access-usa.com
www.access-usa.com

*Deborah Haight, PICOE*

Access-USA produces braille business cards as well as offering alternate format services and products to enhance accessibility. Braille, large print, captioning, audio-descriptive forms are available. We help business, government, education, corporations by providing brochures, menus, manuals, books, collateral materials, videos, specialties and promotion items that can be more accessible to more people.

**484 BeOK Key Lever**
Sammons Preston Rolyan
1000 remmington blvd
suite 210
Bolingbrook, IL 60440- 5117
630-378-6000
800-323-5547
FAX: 630-378-6010
e-mail: sp@pattersonmedical.com
www.pattersonmedical.com

*David P Sproat, President*
*Bruce Curtis, Sales Representative*

Handy accessory helps position key to provide maximum leverage enabling the user to work the most stubborn lock. *$11.50*

**485 Big Lamp Switch**
Maxi Aids
42 Executive Blvd
Farmingdale, NY 11735-4710
631-752-0521
800-522-6294
FAX: 631-752-0689
TTY: 800-281-3555
e-mail: sales@maxiaids.com
www.maxiaids.com

*Elliot Zaretsky, President*

This big, three-spoked knob replaces small rotating knobs which are a problem for those with arthritis or other limitations of the fingers. *$6.75*

**486 Bookholder: Roberts**
Therapro, Inc.
225 Arlington St
Framingham, MA 01702-8723
508-872-9494
800-257-5376
FAX: 508-875-2062
e-mail: info@therapro.com
www.therapro.com

*Karen Conrad , ScD, OTR/L, Owner*

Gray plastic, ideal for hand free reading, adjusts to all sizes of books and prevents pages from flipping for the physically challenged. *$27.50*

**487 Brandt Industries**
4461 Bronx Blvd
Bronx, NY 10470-1496
718-994-0800
800-221-8031
FAX: 718-325-7995
e-mail: brandtequip@yahoo.com
brandtind.com

**488 Bus and Taxi Sign**
Maxi Aids
42 Executive Blvd
Farmingdale, NY 11735-4710
631-752-0521
800-522-6294
FAX: 631-752-0689
TTY: 800-281-3555
e-mail: sales@maxiaids.com
www.maxiaids.com

Signs that the individual with a disability can use to attract the attention of bus or taxi drivers. *$3.75*

**489 Care Electronics**
Ste D
4700 Sterling Dr
Boulder, CO 80301-2305
303-444-2273
888-444-8284
FAX: 303-447-3502
e-mail: donna@medicalshoponline.com
medicalshoponline.com

*Tom Moody, President*

Care Electronics manufactures safety monitoring systems for caregivers, home-health care, and nursing homes. WanderCARE monitors loved ones who tend to wander away from home. Care Deluxe Occupancy systems monitor patients in bed and in wheelchairs to help prevent falls. WetSENSE provides incontinence monitors.

**490 Child Convertible Balance Beam Set**
Bailey Manufacturing Company
P.O. Box 130
Lodi, OH 44254-130
800-321-8372
FAX: 800-224-5390
e-mail: baileymfg@baileymfg.com
baileymfg.com

This convertible set is used to develop balance in two stages.

**491 Child Variable Balance Beam**
Bailey Manufacturing Company
P.O. Box 130
Lodi, OH 44254-130
330-948-1080
800-321-8372
FAX: 330-948-4439
e-mail: baileymfg@baileymfg.com
www.baileymfg.com

The four walking beams can be arranged in several different ways for variable balance training.

**492 Child's Mobility Crawler**
Bailey Manufacturing Company
P.O. Box 130
Lodi, OH 44254-130
800-321-8372
FAX: 800-224-5390
e-mail: baileymfg@baileymfg.com
baileymfg.com

Neurologically delayed or orthopedically impaired small children can perform crawling and coordination exercises while being comfortably supported by the crawler.

**493 Choice Switch Latch and Timer**
AbleNet
2625 Patton Road
Roseville, MN 55113-1308
651-294-2200
800-322-0956
FAX: 651-294-2259
e-mail: customerservice@ablenetinc.com
www.ablenetinc.com

*Jen Thalhuber, CEO*
*Joe Volp, Marketing Manager*
A Choice Switch Latch and Timer allows one user to learn to make choices. It has two switch inputs and can control two devices. Once one device has been activated, the other will not function until the first one is turned off or completes its timed cycle. *$83.00*

**494 Cordless Big Red Switch**
AbleNet
2625 Patton Road
Roseville, MN 55113-1308
651-294-2200
800-322-0956
FAX: 651-294-2259
e-mail: customerservice@ablenetinc.com
www.ablenetinc.com

*Jen Thalhuber, CEO*
*Joe Volp, Marketing Manager*
The Cordless Big Red Switch, when used in conjunction with either the Cordless Receiver or the Small Appliance Receiver, gives you cordless control of toys, games, and appliances in your environment. *$89.00*

**495 DEUCE Environmental Control Unit**
APT Technology
236a N Main St
Shreve, OH 44676
330-567-2001
888-549-2001
FAX: 330-567-3073
e-mail: sales@apt-technology.com
www.apt-technology.com

*Grace Miller, Office Manager*
Allows a severely disabled person to control a variety of useful devices via a dual switch. DEUCE controls phone, 4 AC powered devices such as a radio, 4 switch controlled devices such as a page turner and up to 16 lights and or appliances distributed around the environment. Starts at $1,500. .

**496 Dazor Manufacturing Corporation**
2079 Congressiona
Saint Louis, MO 63146
314-652-2400
800-345-9103
FAX: 314-652-2069
e-mail: info@dazor.com
www.dazor.com

*Kirk Cressey, Marketing Director*
*Bob Smith, National Sales Manager*
*Mark Hogrebe, President*
Dazor is a US manufacturer of quality task lighting. Products include fluorescent, incandescent and halogen lighting fixtures. Illuminated magnifiers combine light and magnification to greatly enhance activities such as reading and make hobbies more enjoyable. All lamps come in a variety of mounting options to include desk bases, clamp on, floor stands and wall tracks. $95 - $450.

**497 Digi-Flex**
Therapro, Inc.
225 Arlington St
Framingham, MA 01702-8723
508-872-9494
800-257-5376
FAX: 508-875-2062
e-mail: info@therapro.com
www.therapro.com

*Karen Conrad , ScD, OTR/L, Owner*
This is a unique hand and finger exercise unit. Recommended for use of individuation of fingers, web space and general strengthening of work hands. Available in a variety of resistances. *$ 17.50*

**498 Dorma Architectural Hardware**
DORMA Drive, Drawer AC
Reamstown, PA 17567-411
717-336-3881
800-523-8483
FAX: 717-336-2106
e-mail: archdw@dorma-usa.com
www.dorma-usa.com

*Larry O'Toole, CEO*
*Gary Phillips AHC, VP Regional Sales, East*
*Ken Theaker, VP Regional Sales West*
DORMA provides a complete line of door controls, including barrier-free units that comply with the Americans with Disabilities Act. A wide variety of surface applied and concealed closers, low energy operators, exit devices and electronic access control systems are available to address these equipments.

**499 Dual Switch Latch and Timer**
AbleNet
2625 Patton Road
Roseville, MN 55113-1308
651-294-2200
800-322-0956
FAX: 651-294-2259
e-mail: customerservice@ablenetinc.com
www.ablenetinc.com

*Jen Thalhuber, CEO*
A Dual Switch Latch and Timer allows two users to activate two devices at a time in the latch. Timed seconds or timed minutes mode of control. *$88.00*

**500 Enabling Devices**
50 Broadway
Hawthorne, N 10532
914-747-3070
800-832-8697
FAX: 914-747-3480
e-mail: customer_support@enablingdevices.com
www.enablingdevices.com

*Elizabeth Bell, Marketing Manager*
*Karen O'Connor, VP Operations*
*Steven Kanor, Owner*
For more than 25 years, Enabling Devices has been dedicated to providing affordable learning and assistive devices for the physically challenged. Products include augmentative communicators, adapted toys, capability switches, training and sensory devices and activity centers. Call for a free catalog.

**501 Foot Inversion Tread**
Bailey Manufacturing Company
P.O. Box 130
Lodi, OH 44254-130
800-321-8372
FAX: 800-224-5390
e-mail: baileymfg@baileymfg.com
baileymfg.com

Effective for correcting flat feet. These angled boards require the patient to walk on the outside of the foot instead of the arch.

**502 Foot Placement Ladder**
Bailey Manufacturing Company
P.O. Box 130
Lodi, OH 44254-130
800-321-8372
FAX: 800-224-5390
e-mail: baileymfg@baileymfg.com
baileymfg.com

Adjustable cross bars for different length steps. Reinforced metal crosses for easier climbing for the physically-disabled.

**503 HealthCraft SuperPole Traveller**
Maxi Aids
42 Executive Blvd
Farmingdale, NY 11735-4710
631-752-0521
800-522-6294
FAX: 631-752-0689
TTY: 800-281-3555
e-mail: sales@maxiaids.com
maxiaids.com

*Elliot Zaretsky, President*
Central to the system is a stylish floor-to-ceiling grab bar, which provides a secure structure that can be installed in minutes between a floor and ceiling. Use it beside a bed, bath, toilet or chair. *$193.00*

**504 Home Bed Side Helper**
Maxi Aids
42 Executive Blvd
Farmingdale, NY 11735-4710
631-752-0521
800-522-6294
FAX: 631-752-0689
TTY: 800-281-3555
e-mail: sales@maxiaids.com
maxiaids.com

*Elliot Zaretsky, President*
The extra support you need getting in and out of bed is within your grasp with this easy to install Home Bed Side Helper. The rail itself features four easily accessible grasping points for the secure support you need when getting in or out of bed. *$126.75*

**505 Hospital Environmental Control System**
Prentke Romich Company
1022 Heyl Rd
Wooster, OH 44691-9786
330-262-1984
800-848-8008
800-262-1933
FAX: 330-263-4829
e-mail: sales@prentrom.com
prentrom.com

*David L Moffatt, President*
Permits the non-ambulatory patient to operate a variety of electrical items in a single room. A large liquid crystal display is mounted in front of the user and they scan through the menu of operations and make a selection using a sip-puff switch. Options include nurse call, standard telephone functions, electric bed control, hospital television operation and electrical appliance on and off. *$3860.00*

**506 Knock Light**
HARC Mercantile
1111 W Centre Ave
Portage, MI 49024-5317
269-324-0301
800-445-9968
FAX: 269-324-2387
TTY: 269-324-1615
e-mail: info@harc.com
harc.com

Easily attaches to a door with velcro, portable. *$ 29.95*

**507 Leg Elevation Board**
Bailey Manufacturing Company
P.O. Box 130
Lodi, OH 44254-130
800-321-8372
FAX: 800-224-5390
e-mail: baileymfg@baileymfg.com
baileymfg.com

Includes seven positions to a 30 degree incline, three pillows with Velcro, easy carry hand slot and a natural finish.

**508 Leveron**
Lindustries
21 Shady Hill Rd
Weston, MA 02193-1407
781-237-8177
877-794-9511
FAX: 651-989-2131
www.trademarkia.com/leveron-73486756.html

*Willard H Lind, Owner*
*Louise T Lind, VP*
Leveron is a doorknob lever handle for ease of operation. Leveron converts standard doorknobs to lever action without removing existing hardware. No gripping, twisting or pinching when hands are wet, arthritic or arms are full. Leveron provides convenience. Available in five colors: almond, satin brass, silver metallic, dark bronze and Hi-Glow (glows in the dark) at low cost to comply with ADA access requirements in public and private places. *$16.95*

**509 Longreach Reacher**
Therapro, Inc.
225 Arlington St
Framingham, MA 01702-8723
508-872-9494
800-257-5376
FAX: 508-875-2062
e-mail: info@therapro.com
www.therapro.com

*Karen Conrad , ScD, OTR/L, Owner*
Reacher is useful when reaching, sitting or when standing. *$18.95*

**510 Loop Scissors**
Therapro, Inc.
225 Arlington St
Framingham, MA 01702-8723
508-872-9494
800-257-5376
FAX: 508-875-2062
e-mail: info@therapro.com
www.therapro.com

*Karen Conrad , ScD, OTR/L, Owner*
Pliable, plastic handles that allow for easy and controlled cutting. *$14.25*

**511 Pedal-in-Place Exerciser**
Thoele Manufacturing
475 County Road 100 N
Montrose, IL 62445-3019
217-924-4553
FAX: 217-924-4553
www.axistive.com/thoele-manufacturing.html

A great in-home exerciser that can benefit quadraplegics, paraplegics, stroke patients or anyone with limited use of their arms and legs.

**512 Plastic Card Holder**
Therapro, Inc.
225 Arlington St
Framingham, MA 01702-8723
508-872-9494
800-257-5376
FAX: 508-875-2062
e-mail: info@therapro.com
www.therapro.com

*Karen Conrad , ScD, OTR/L, Owner*
For those with reduced finger control. *$4.00*

**513 Power Door**
11240 Gemini Ln
Dallas, TX 75229-4710
800-688-1758
FAX: 972-620-9875
e-mail: info@powerdoor.com
www.powerdoor.com

*Jim Goldthwaite, National Sales Manager*
Power door, low energy door operators.

**514 ProtectaCap, ProtectaCap+PLUS, ProtectaChin Guard and ProtectaHip**
Plum Enterprises
P.O.Box 85
Valley Forge, PA 19481-85
610-783-7377
800-321-PLUM
FAX: 610-783-7577
e-mail: info@PlumEnt.com
www.plument.com

*Janice Carrington, CEO*
Plum Enterprises award winning, exquiste, ergonomic protective wear keeps you safe from the dangers of falls. ProtectCap+Plus and ProtectHips are engineered for superior shock-absorption and designed for exquiste simplicity and amazing lightweight comfort. The perfect blend of style and function.

**515 Quad Commander**
Gpk
535 Floyd Smith Dr
El Cajon, CA 92020-1228
619-593-7381
800-468-8679
FAX: 888-755-5603
e-mail: info@gpk.com
www.gpk.com

Joystick for people with quadriplegia.

**516 Rocker Balance Square**
Bailey Manufacturing Company
P.O. Box 130
Lodi, OH 44254-130
800-321-8372
FAX: 800-224-5390
e-mail: baileymfg@baileymfg.com
baileymfg.com

The rocker is used in developing activity, balance control and coordination.

**517 Scott Sign Systems**
7525 Pennsylvania Ave
Suite 101
Sarasota, FL 34243
941-355-5171
800-237-9447
FAX: 941-351-1787
e-mail: mail@scottsigns.com
www.scottsigns.com

*Kathy Hannon, VP*
*Evelyn Brown, Sales*
Call for a brochure.

**518 Series Adapter**
AbleNet
2625 Patton Road
Roseville, MN 55113
651-294-2200
800-322-0956
FAX: 651-294-2259
e-mail: customerservice@ablenetinc.com
www.ablenetinc.com

*Jen Thalhuber, CEO*
Allows two-switch operation of any battery-operated device or electrical devices. *$13.00*

**519 Signaling Wake-Up Devices**
HARC Mercantile
1111 W Centre Ave
Portage, MI 49024-5317
269-324-1615
800-445-9968
FAX: 269-324-2387
TTY: 269-324-1615
e-mail: info@harc.com
harc.com

*Ron Slager, Owner*
Wake up devices. Vibrating alarm clocks, available with flashing lights, louder alarm noises and more. *$29.50*

**520 Smoke Detector with Strobe**
HARC Mercantile
1111 W Centre Ave
Portage, MI 49024-5317
269-324-1615
800-445-9968
FAX: 269-324-2387
TTY: 269-324-1615
e-mail: info@harc.com
harc.com

*Ron Slager, Owner*
Most of the smoke alarms are twice as loud, and have a 120+ candela strobe that will wake a person from a sound sleep. Mounting hardware for ceiling or wall. *$165.95*

**521 Spinal Network: The Total Wheelchair Resource Book**
No Limits Communications & New Mobility
75-20 Astoria Blvd.
East Elmhurst, NY 11370
800-404-2898
888-850-0344
www.newmobility.com

*amy B+T500lackmore, Vice President Sales*
*Jean Dobbs, Editorial Director*
*Tim Gilmer, Senior Correspondent*
Nearly 600 pages of profiles, articles and resources on every topic of interest to wheelchair users. Subjects include health, coping, relationships, sexuality, parenthood, computers, sports, recreation, travel, personal assistance services, legal rights, financial strategies, employment, and media images. *$34.95*
*400 pages*

**522 SteeleVest**
Steele
P.O.Box 7304
Kingston, WA 98346-7304
360-297-4555
888-783-3538
FAX: 360-297-2816
steelevest.com

*Sandra Steele, President*
Vest developed by NASA provides an external cooling system.

**523 TV & VCR Remote**
AbleNet
2625 Patton Road
Roseville, MN 55113
651-294-2200
800-322-0956
FAX: 651-294-2259
e-mail: customerservice@ablenetinc.com
www.ablenetinc.com

*Jen Thalhuber, CEO*
Controls a TV, a VCR or a TV that is connected through a VCR tuner. It may be programmed to control functions such as on and off, channel up, preprogrammed TV channels and, if desired, other TV functions such as mute and pause. *$82.00*

**524 Tactile Thermostat**
Sense-Sations
919 Walnut St
Philadelphia, PA 19107-5237
215-627-0600
FAX: 215-922-0692
e-mail: asbinfo@asb.org
asb.org

*Patricia Johnson, CEO*
*Derby Ewing, Dir., Human Svcs*
*Patricia Cautilli, Certified Psychologist*
*Dolores Ferrara-Godzieba, Dir., Braille Div.*
Large embossed numbers on cover ring and raised temperature setting knob. *$31.50*

525 **Therapy Putty**
Therapro, Inc.
225 Arlington St
Framingham, MA 01702-8723
508-872-9494
800-257-5376
FAX: 508-875-2062
e-mail: info@therapro.com
www.therapro.com

*Karen Conrad , ScD, OTR/L, Owner*
Designed to exercise and strengthen hands, ranging from soft to firm for developing a stronger grasp. Available in two, four and six ounce sizes. Three ounce putty in unique clear fist shaped container.

526 **Uppertone**
535 Floyd Smith Dr
El Cajon, CA 92020-1228
619-593-7381
800-468-8679
FAX: 888-755-5603
e-mail: sales@gpk.com
www.gpk.com

Unassisted muscle strengthening and conditioning system for quads. *$2495.00*

527 **Visual Alerting Guest Room Kit**
HARC Mercantile
1111 W Centre Ave
Portage, MI 49024-5317
269-324-1615
800-445-9968
FAX: 269-324-2387
TTY: 269-324-1615
e-mail: info@harc.com
harc.com

*Ron Slager, Owner*
ADA compliant visual alerting guest room kit for the hard of hearing and deaf. Includes visual smoke detector, phone alert, door knock sensor, tactile alarm clock and telephone amplifier. Variations include TTY.

528 **Window-Ease**
A-Solution
1332 Cobo Pl NE
Albuquerque, NM 87111
505-856-6632
FAX: 505-856-6652
e-mail: info@windowease.com
www.windowease.com

*Robert Gorrell, President*
*Jeff Dodd, Sales*
Device adapts horizontally and vertically sliding windows to ANSI A117.1 standards. 10:1 mechanical advantage at the crank arm opens a 50lb window with 5lbs force. Price ranges from $350.00-$450.00.

## Office Devices & Workstations

529 **Combination File/Reference Carousel**
Center for Rehabilitation Technology
Ste 118
490 10th St NW
Atlanta, GA 30318-5754
404-712-5667
800-457-9555
FAX: 404-875-9409
e-mail: rerc-br@scsn.net

*TW Gannaway, Executive VP*
*Anthony Stringer PhD*
Offers two reading platforms and file holders joined on one easily rotated carousel. The carousel is easily rotated by head, mouth or handstick. Page retainer adjusts to hold open a variety of books and magazines. *$299.00*

530 **Don Johnston**
26799 W Commerce Dr
Volo, IL 60073-9675
847-740-0749
800-999-4660
800-889-5242
FAX: 847-740-7326
e-mail: info@donjohnston.com
www.donjohnston.com

*Don Johnston, President*
A provider of quality products and services that enable people with special needs to discover their potential and experience success. Products are developed for the areas of Physical Access, Augmentative Communication and for those who struggle with reading and writing.

531 **Extensions for Independence**
6100 Center Drive
Suite 1190
Los Angeles, CA 90045
757-416-6575
888-321-4678
FAX: 866-632-7149
e-mail: support@inmotionhosting.com
www.mouthstick.net

*Ted Sakis , Director of Operations*
Develops, manufactures and markets special vocational equipment for the physically handicapped. Products: mouthsticks, computer mechanical aids: key locks and diskette loaders. Also, turntable desks, wheelchair portable desks, filing trays with slanted sides, telephone adapters, and motorized artist easel. All these products have been designed to solve the functional limitations of people with little or no use of hands and/or arms.

532 **Fairway Spirit Adaptive Golf Car: Model4852**
Fairway Golf Cars
Ste 300
3225 Gateway Rd
Brookfield, WI 53045-5139
262-790-9363
888-320-4850
888-320-4850
FAX: 262-790-9396
e-mail: bob_hansen@fairwaygolfcars.com
www.fairwaygolfcars.com
Fairway Spirit is designed to allow access to all aspects of the game of golf- even greens and tee. Spirit 4850 features a 48 volt electronic system to provide unsurpassed power, range and speed. Couple the drive system performance with ergonomic features like an adjustable seat with flip up arm rests, 360 degree swivel and an adjustable tilter position.

533 **Freedom Ryder Handcycles**
Brike International
20589 SW Elk Horn Ct
Tualatin, OR 97062-9518
503-692-1029
800-800-5828
FAX: 970-221-4308
e-mail: Mike @ Freedomryder.com
freedomryder.com

*Mike Lofgren, Owner*
*Brian Stewart, VP*
The finest handcycle in the world. The cycles incorporate body, lean steering and the finest bicycle components to make this a three-wheeled vehicle without equal. Suitable for both recreation and competition. *$1995.00*

534 **Golf Xpress**
Emotorsports
4400 West M-61
Standish, MI 48658
989-846-6255
FAX: 989-846-6255
e-mail: mitch@golfxpress.com
www.golfxpress.com

Patented single-rider adaptive golf cart allows you to play golf seated or supported. Hit woods, irons, and putt from the car. Drives onto tees and greens and into traps without damaging the course.

**535 Infogrip: AdjustaCart**
1794 E Main St
Ventura, CA 93001-3411
805-652-0770
FAX: 805-652-0880
e-mail: tech@infogrip.com
www.infogrip.com

Sit or stand while working with this easily adjustable desk. With a simple squeeze of a paddle the front surface travel range of 12 3/4. The front surface tilts 9 degrees toward and 15 degrees away from you. Anthro carts are made of 1in thick industrial grade particleboard shelves with high-pressure laminated 16 gauge steel tube legs that safely hold 150 pounds. Spring assisted mechanism. There are holes in 1: increment in the legs so that you can put the shelves and accessories where needed. *$629.00*

**536 Infogrip: BAT Personal Keyboard**
1794 E Main St
Ventura, CA 93001-3411
805-652-0770
800-397-0921
FAX: 805-652-0880
e-mail: tech@infogrip.com
www.infogrip.com

Infogrip has creative computer access solutions for people with all types of disabilities. Alternative keyboards and mice, switches, screen readers, magnifiers and educational software. We also have a retail store, Your Low Vision Store. We have three locations in Southern California offering the best selection of video magnifiers in the industry. *$200.00*

**537 Maxi Marks**
Maxi Aids
42 Executive Blvd
Farmingdale, NY 11735-4710
631-752-0521
800-522-6294
FAX: 631-752-0689
TTY: 800-281-3555
e-mail: sales@maxiaids.com
www.maxiaids.com

*Elliot Zaretsky, President*
Braille writing and identification products. *$2.50*

**538 Pencil/Pen Weighted Holders**
Therapro, Inc.
225 Arlington St
Framingham, MA 01702-8723
508-872-9494
800-257-5376
FAX: 508-875-2062
e-mail: info@therapro.com
www.therapro.com

*Karen Conrad , ScD, OTR/L, Owner*
Securely hold any pencil or pen. These weighted holders allow for more control along with proprioceptive feedback to encourage better writing skills.

**539 Perkins Brailler**
Maxi Aids
42 Executive Blvd
Farmingdale, NY 11735-4710
631-752-0521
800-522-6294
FAX: 631-752-0689
TTY: 800-281-3555
e-mail: sales@maxiaids.com
www.maxiaids.com

*Elliot Zaretsky, President*
Can emboss 25 lines with 42 cells on an 11 x 11 1/2 sheet. *$495.00*

**540 PhoneMax Amplified Telephone**
Assistech
2738 N Campbell Ave
Tucson, AZ 85719-3141
520-883-8600
866-674-3549
FAX: 520-883-3172
assistivedevices.net

*Oliver Simoes, Owner*

**541 Raised Line Drawing Kit**
Maxi Aids
42 Executive Blvd
Farmingdale, NY 11735-4710
631-752-0521
800-522-6294
FAX: 631-752-0689
TTY: 800-281-3555
e-mail: sales@maxiaids.com
www.maxiaids.com

*Elliot Zaretsky, President*
For writing script or drawing graphs by the use of special plastic paper. *$24.45*

**542 Reizen Braille Labeler**
Maxi Aids
42 Executive Blvd
Farmingdale, NY 11735-4710
631-752-0521
800-522-6294
FAX: 631-752-0689
TTY: 800-281-3555
e-mail: sales@maxiaids.com
www.maxiaids.com

*Elliot Zaretsky, President*
Label everything in Braille with 3/8 or 1/2 wide labeling tape. *$47.95*

**543 Sharp Calculator with Illuminated Numbers**
Independent Living Aids
P.O.Box 9022
Hicksville, NY 11802-9022
516-937-1848
800-537-2118
855-746-7452
FAX: 516-937-3906
e-mail: can-do@independentliving.com
independentliving.com

*Irwin Schneidmill, President*
A trim desktop calculator with large illuminated numbers that can be carried anywhere. *$34.95*

**544 Signature and Address Self-Inking Stamps**
Independent Living Aids
P.O.Box 9022
Hicksville, NY 11802-9022
516-937-1848
800-537-2118
855-746-7452
FAX: 516-937-3906
e-mail: can-do@independentliving.com
independentliving.com

*Irwin Schneidmill, President*
Gives thousands of impressions before requiring re-inking. *$11.95*

**545 Steady Write**
Maxi Aids
42 Executive Blvd
Farmingdale, NY 11735-4710
631-752-0521
800-522-6294
FAX: 631-752-0689
TTY: 800-281-3555
e-mail: sales@maxiaids.com
www.maxiaids.com

*Elliot Zaretsky, President*
Furnishes the writer with increased holding capacity and stabilizes the hand. *$6.95*

**546 Talking Desktop Calculators**
Maxi Aids
42 Executive Blvd
Farmingdale, NY 11735-4710
631-752-0521
800-522-6294
FAX: 631-752-0689
TTY: 800-281-3555
e-mail: sales@maxiaids.com
www.maxiaids.com

*Elliot Zaretsky, President*
Unique voice synthesizers call out numerals and functions as they are keyed in or read out data stored in memory. *$467.95*

**547 Talking Electronic Organizers**
Independent Living Aids
P.O.Box 9022
Hicksville, NY 11802-9022
516-937-1848
800-537-2118
855-746-7452
FAX: 516-937-3906
e-mail: can-do@independentliving.com
independentliving.com

*Irwin Schneidmill, President*
Electronic, portable, personal organizers that talk the user through all the functions and are totally voice interactive. $199.95 and up.

**548 Television Remote Controls with Large Numbers**
Independent Living Aids
P.O.Box 9022
Hicksville, NY 11802-9022
516-937-1848
800-537-2118
855-746-7452
FAX: 516-937-3906
e-mail: can-do@independentliving.com
independentliving.com

*Irwin Schneidmill, President*
Large 5 1/2 inch x 8 1/2 inch unit that has easy to see and use buttons. Can be used on nearly every TV, VCR and cable boxes. *$39.95*

**549 Wheelchair Activity/Computer Table**
Maxi Aids
42 Executive Blvd
Farmingdale, NY 11735-4710
631-752-0521
800-522-6294
FAX: 631-752-0689
TTY: 800-281-3555
e-mail: sales@maxiaids.com
www.maxiaids.com

*Elliot Zaretsky, President*
This powered height-adjustable table is a wheelchair accessible activity table or computer workstation that's as stylish as it is functional. Adjusts with the push of a button from 27-39 inches, powered by an extremely quiet motor. ADA compliant computer workstation for assistive technology and school computer labs.

## Scooters

**550 Aerospace Compadre**
Aerospace America
Ste 189
900 Harry S Truman Pkwy
Bay City, MI 48706-4171
989-684-2121
800-237-6414
FAX: 989-684-4486
aerospaceamerica.com

*Mike Alley, President*
Fully customized golf cart type vehicle for the physically impaired person. Fully equipped with hand controls, wheelchair rack, storage racks, head and tail lights and full safety belts. *$2500.00*

**551 Alante**
Golden Technologies
401 Bridge St
Old Forge, PA 18518-2323
800-624-6374
FAX: 800-628-5165
www.goldentech.com

*Robert Golden, Chairman*
*Richard Golden, CEO*
*Fred Kiwak, President*
Rear-wheel-drive vehicle that represents the best in powered mobility.

**552 Amigo Mobility International**
Amigo Mobility International
6693 Dixie Hwy
Bridgeport, MI 48722
989-777-0910
800-248-9131
FAX: 800-334-7274
e-mail: info@myamigo.com
myamigo.com

*Allan R Thieme, President*
*Sandy Humpert, Sales Rep*
*Allan Thieme, CEO*
An industry leader in power operated vehicles/scooters, Amigo provides innovative, durable, and customized mobility solutions for the disabled, injured, and seniors worldwide. Other services include healthcare, travel and transportation services. *$1295.00*

**553 Amphibious ATV Distributors**
Amphibious ATV Distributors
2760 Greendale Dr
Sarasota, FL 34232-3702
941-379-6186
800-843-2811
FAX: 941-377-8979
e-mail: CBeach1419@aol.com
www.maxsixwheel.com

*Clay Beach, Owner*
A two and four passenger, all-terrain vehicle that can provide you with year round activities the whole family can enjoy. Accessible and drivable for the physically disabled. Used in hunting, fishing and outdoor activities on land and in the water. Many options and accessories available. Delivery anwyhere in the US and worldwide. $5,000-$9,000.

**554 Bravo! + Three-Wheel Scooter**
EZ-International
W194 N11301
McCormick Drive
Germantown, WI 53022
262-250-7740
800-824-1068
FAX: 262-250-7741
e-mail: sales@ek-tech.com
www.ek-tech.com

Designed to increase your mobility indoors. The Bravo! plus has extendible rear wheels for outdoor use and comes with easy to use finger tip controls and a maintenance free gel-cell battery. Available in red, blue, green or light sand gray with an optional power seat lift. Call for complete line of 3 and 4-wheel electronic vehicles.

**555 Cruiser Bus Buggy 4MB**
Convaid Products
2830 California Street
Torrance, CA 90503
310-618-0111
888-266-8243
FAX: 310-618-2166
www.convaid.com

*Linda , product specialist*
*rocio , Inside Sales Manager*
In sizes from infant through young adult, this positioning buggy is crash-tested.

**556 Cub, SuperCub and Special Edition Scooters**
1780 Executive Dr
Oconomowoc, WI 53066
262-567-4990
FAX: 262-953-5502
bruno.com

*Thomas Jacobson , Vice President*
*Michael R Bruno II, President/CEO*
*Steve Nelson, Service Manager*

**557 Electric Mobility Corporation**
P.O.Box 156
Sewell, NJ 08080-156
856-468-0083
800-257-7955
FAX: 856-468-3426
rascalscooters.com

*Linda Autore, CEO*
Manufactures Rascal Scooters. SITE IS UNDER CONSRTUCTION

**558 Explorer+ 4-Wheel Scooter**
EZ-International
W194 N11301
McCormick Drive
Germantown, WI 53022
262-250-7740
800-824-1068
FAX: 26-25- 774
e-mail: sales@ek-tech.com
www.ek-tech.com/

A tough and rugged 4-wheel, rear-wheel drive, transaxle scooter designed to take you just about anywhere you want to go. Easy to use finger-tip controls and maintenance free gel-cell batteries and an extendible, take-apart frame, make the Explorer+ a perfect fit for people seeking greater mobility. Available in red, blue, green and gray, with an optional power seat lift. $3,499-$3,999.

**559 Featherlite**
No Boundaries
550 Monica Circle Suite 201
Corona, , CA 92880
714-891-5899
800-426-7367
FAX: 714-891-0658
e-mail: info@hansens.com
hansens.com

*Hubert Hansen , Founder*
Lightweight scooter folds in seconds without tools or bending down for hassle free travel on airplanes, cruise ships, trains, RVs, buses and more! Heaviest component weighs 27 pounds. Fits easily in almost any vehicle trunk.

**560 Invacare Fulfillment Center**
Invacare Corporation
1 Invacare Way
Elyria, OH 44035-4190
440-329-6000
800-333-6900
FAX: 87- 6-9 79
invacare.com

*A Malachi Mixon Iii, Chairman*
*Gerald B. Blouch, President*
*Robert K. Gudbranson, Senior Vice President*
Invacare Corporation is the world's leading manufacturer and distributor of non-acute medical products which promote recovery and active lifestyles for people requiring home and other non-acute health care.

**561 Invacare Lynx L-3 Scooter**
Maxi Aids
42 Executive Blvd
Farmingdale, NY 11735-4710
631-752-0521
800-522-6294
FAX: 631-752-0689
TTY: 800-281-3555
e-mail: sales@maxiaids.com
maxiaids.com

*Elliot Zaretsky, President*
The L-3 model conveniently disassembles into four compact pieces for easy transport. With an estimated seven miles of range, a plug-in battery charger and flat-free tires, consumers can plan their schedule around what they want to do, not around the limitations of their scooter. *$795.00*

**562 Leisure Lift**
Leisure Lift
1800 Merriam Ln
Kansas City, KS 66106-4714
913-722-5658
800-255-0285
FAX: 913-722-2614
e-mail: Leisure-Lift@Leisure-Lift.com
pacesaver.com

*Bill Burke, Founder*
Leisure Lift offers light three wheel scooter models and seven power wheelchair models. *$2695.00*

**563 MVP+ 3-Wheel Scooter**
EZ-International
W194 N11301
McCormick Drive
Germantown, WI 53022
262-250-7740
800-824-1068
FAX: 26- 25- 774
e-mail: sales@ek-tech.com
www.ek-tech.com/contact.php

The MVP+ is the rugged 3-wheel rear-wheel drive, transaxle scooter with finger tip controls, and featuring an extendible, take-apart frame for a perfect fit. The MVP+ comes with maintenance free gel-cell batteries and is available in red, blue, green or light sand gray, with an optional power seat lift. $2,599-$3,099.

**564 Moxie**
No Boundaries
550 Monica Circle Suite 201
Corona, , CA 92880
714-891-5899
800-824-1068
FAX: 714-891-0658
e-mail: info@hansens.com
hansens.com

*Hubert Hansen , Founder*
Disassembles into three parts in less than a minute. Heaviest component weighs 41 pounds. Portable, affordable and downright snazzy!

**565 Outdoor Independence**
Palmer Industries
P.O.Box 5707
Endicott, NY 13763-5707
607-754-2957
800-847-1304
FAX: 607-754-1954
e-mail: palmer@palmerind.com
www.palmerind.com

*Jack Palmer, President*
The futuristic, one, two and three seater, electric three-wheeler designed to take you almost anywhere.

566 **Pace Saver Plus II**
Leisure-Lift
1800 Merriam Ln
Kansas City, KS 66106-4714
913-722-5658
800-255-0285
FAX: 913-722-2614
e-mail: Leisure-Lift@Leisure-Lift.com
www.pacesaver.com

*Bill Burke, Founder*

The scooter combines outdoor ruggedness with indoor maneuverability at a low price.

567 **Palmer Independence**
Palmer Industries
P.O.Box 5707
Endicott, NY 13763-5707
607-754-2957
800-847-1304
FAX: 607-754-1954
e-mail: palmer@palmerind.com
palmerind.com

*Jack Palmer, President*

Futuristic electric outdoor three wheeler designed to take the rider almost anywhere.

568 **Palmer Twosome**
Palmer Industries
P.O.Box 5707
Endicott, NY 13763-5707
607-754-2957
800-847-1304
FAX: 607-754-1954
e-mail: palmer@palmerind.com
www.palmerind.com

*Jack Palmer, President*

All electric two seat vehicle for those who can't pedal.

569 **Phantom Compact Size Scooter**
Maxi Aids
42 Executive Blvd
Farmingdale, NY 11735-4710
631-752-0521
800-522-6294
FAX: 631-752-0689
TTY: 800-281-3555
e-mail: sales@maxiaids.com
www.maxiaids.com

*Elliot Zaretsky, President*

Travel in style-ideal/affordable compact scooter. Great for both indoor and outdoor use. Three wheel design allows for small 32.3 turning radius. Top speed 4 miles per hour and a cruising range of 15 miles. Large carry basket.

570 **Polaris Trail Blazer**
Polaris Industries
2100 Highway 55
Medina, MN 55340-9770
888-704-5290
FAX: 763-542-0599
polarisindustries.com

*Scott Wine, CEO*
*Bennett J. Morgan, President*
*Michael Malone, VP*
*James Williams, VP (HR)*

A four-wheeler that has many engineered innovations, features such as: full floorboards for full comfort, single lever breaking with auxiliary foot brake, electronic throttle control, parking brake and adjustable handlebars.

571 **Quickie 2**
Sunrise Medical/Quickie Designs
2842 Business Park Avenue
Fresno, CA 93727
800-333-4000
800-300-7502
www.sunrisemedical.com

*Pete Coburn, President*
*Randi Binstock, VP- Business Dev.*
*Peter Riley, Senior VP - Corporate CFO*
*Kevin Marshman, North American Controller*

This custom, ultralight, folding, everyday scooter offers portability and performance plus modular flexibility.

572 **Rascal 3-Wheeler**
Electric Mobility Corporation
P.O.Box 156
Sewell, NJ 08080-156
856-468-1000
800-257-7955
FAX: 856-468-3426
www.emobility.com

*Scott Patrick, Manager*

For primarily outdoor use, this three wheeler provides extra strength, durability and reliability.

573 **Rascal ConvertAble**
Electric Mobility Corporation
P.O.Box 156
Sewell, NJ 08080-156
856-468-1000
800-257-7955
FAX: 856-468-3426
www.emobility.com

*Scott Patrick, Manager*

An electric vehicle that's a compact mobile chair one minute and a rugged outdoor scooter the next. Use both indoors and outdoors. Also available with joystick controls.

574 **Regal Scooters**
Bruno Independent Living Aids
Ste 84
1780 Executive Dr
Oconomowoc, WI 53066-4830
262-567-4990
800-882-8183
FAX: 262-953-5510
e-mail: webmaster@bruno.com
bruno.com

*Michael Bruno II, President & CEO*

This line includes the Regal Standard, the Regal Large Adult, the Regal Small Adult, the Regal Pediatric, The Regal Ten models 65 and 75, and The Regal Four. These scooters offer adjustable flip-up armrests, pneumatic tires front and rear, and more.

575 **Regent**
Golden Technologies
401 Bridge St
Old Forge, PA 18518-2323
570-451-7477
800-624-6374
FAX: 800-628-5165
e-mail: info@goldentech.com
www.goldentech.com

*Richard Golden, CEO*
*Lisa Miller, Senior Customer Service*

Top-rated performance scooter, with extra features and economically priced.

**576 Roadster 20**
ATV Solutions
Unit 4
4700 W 60th Ave
Arvada, CO 80003-6928
303-450-2881
866-777-9727
888-867-1159
FAX: 303-450-2880
e-mail: sales@atvsolutions.com
www.atvsolutions.com

*Andrew Miro, Owner*
Great for indoor or outdoor use. The powerful, quiet drive system, independent front suspension and fully reclining high-back seat make for a smooth, quiet ride. The Roadster is loaded with great features at a bargain price.

**577 Safari Scooter**
Ranger All Seasons Corporation
P.O.Box 132
George, IA 51237-132
712-475-2811
800-225-3811
FAX: 712-475-2810
rangerallseason.com

Ranger all season Corporation is proud to introduce the 'new' auto plug design. Incorporated with our patented take-apart design, it will revolutionize the scooter industry. Ranger is the first company to have this feature on scooters rated with a rider capacity up to 450 lbs. For more information, call toll free 800-225-3811.

**578 Scoota Bug**
Golden Technologies
401 Bridge St
Old Forge, PA 18518-2323
570-451-7477
800-624-6324
FAX: 800-628-5165
e-mail: info@goldentech.com
www.goldentech.com

*Richard Golden, CEO*
A lightweight, completely modular scooter, that disassembles and fits into most auto trunks.

**579 Sierra 3000/4000**
EZ-International
W194 N11301 McCormick Drive
Germantown, WI 53022
262-250-7740
FAX: 262-250-7741
e-mail: Sales@EK-Tech.com
www.ek-tech.com/

Look to the Sierra 3000/4000 series vehicles for comfort, convenience and performance. Increased leg and foot room, adjustable seat height and arm width, as well as adjustable tiller angle provide maximum comfort. For convenience, the Sierra is equipped with integrated cargo and cup holders and thumb/finger controls with built in wrist rest. Advanced safety features such as stall and free-wheeling situation identification and correction, anti roll-back sensory device and audio/visual feedback.

**580 Solo Scooter**
Ranger All Seasons Corporation
P.O.Box 132
George, IA 51237-132
712-475-2811
800-225-3811
FAX: 712-475-2810
e-mail: sales@rangerallseason.com
rangerallseason.com

The SOLO is Ranger's flagship model. Introduction of the SOLO 1991 set the standard for easy disassembly of a scooter. The SOLO has a long list of user friendly features including patented take-apart and tiller adjustment mechanisms, non-rusting aluminum frame, comfortable contoured seats as standard, color impregnated-not painted-ABS plastic bodies, charger plug conveniently located on the Accelerator box and many more. Available in ultra-quiet drive and four wheel models.

**581 SoloRider Industries**
Regal Research & Manufacturing Company
1200 East Plano Parkway
Plano, TX 75074
972-422-5324
800-898-3353
FAX: 972-422-8010
e-mail: info@solorider.com
solorider.com

*Roger Pretekin, Founder*
Manufacturer and distributor of the Solorider Golf Cart. This revolutionary single rider adaptive cart is specifically designed to meet the needs of individuals with mobility impairements.

**582 Sportster 10**
ATV Solutions
Unit 4
4700 W 60th Ave
Arvada, CO 80003-6928
303-450-2881
866-777-9727
888-867-1159
FAX: 303-450-2880
e-mail: sales@atvsolutions.com
www.atvsolutions.com

*Andrew Miro, Owner*
Sportster 10 is our most maneuverable scooter, ideal for riders who must operate in tight spaces. Equipped with all of the great features of the Roadster 20, this three-wheeler is an exceptional buy.

**583 Systems 2000**
BioMedical Life Systems
P.O.Box 1360
Vista, CA 92085-1360
760-727-5600
800-726-8367
FAX: 760-727-4220
e-mail: information@bmls.com
bmls.com

This five-mode TENS device has four adjustable modulations, plus conventional settings and comes with a five-year warranty.

**584 Terra-Jet: Utility Vehicle**
TERRA-JET USA
P.O.Box 918
Innis, LA 70747-918
225-492-2249
800-864-5000
FAX: 225-492-2226
e-mail: Terra-Jet@Terra-Jet.Com
terra-jet.com

*Larry Rabalais, President*
*Shawn Oubre, Sales*
TERRA-JET utility vehicles are unique in their ability to traverse many different types of terrain in remote areas otherwise inaccessible. It has a multitude of uses for industry, sportsmen or the whole family. Uniquely designed, industrial duty construction of low maintenance and low fuel consumption. $8,675-$21,995.

**585 Terrier Tricycle**
TRIAID
P.O.Box 1364
Cumberland, MD 21501-1364
301-759-3525
800-306-6777
FAX: 301-759-3525
e-mail: sales@triaid.com
www.triaid.com

Provides fun therapy and actively encourages participation, awareness and the building of self confidence. Designed for children from about five years it features ATB styling, 16 inch wheels, adjustable steering stop and a supportive saddle. Handlebar and seat adjustments combine with a broad wheelbase to ensure the rider is in the optimum position to pedal and the tricycle gives good stability and confident handling. Support accessories are available.

**586 Trekker 40**
ATV Solutions
Unit 4
4700 W 60th Ave
Arvada, CO 80003-6928
303-450-2881
866-777-9727
888-867-1159
FAX: 303-450-2880
e-mail: sales@atvsolutions.com
www.atvsolutions.com

*Andrew Miro, Owner*
Our biggest, toughest scooter. With a huge 450 pound capacity and five inches of ground clearance, this machine is ideal for the daily outdoor user. The high top speed means you get there fast and the four-wheel suspension makes the ride smooth and comfortable.

**587 Tri-Lo's**
TRIAID
P.O.Box 1364
Cumberland, MD 21501-1364
301-759-3525
800-306-6777
FAX: 301-759-3525
e-mail: sales@triaid.com
www.triaid.com
Available in three sizes, these tricycles provide fun therapy for children from 2-15 years. Propelled by hand cranks, the Tri-Lo's are highly recommended by therapists for spina bifida children and any other child where the use of the lower limbs is restricted. The Tri-Lo's feature a robust frame with allowance for growth, low foot platform for ease of transfer, padded seat and back cushion, padded armrests, two forms of braking and an anti-tipping device. *$740.00*

**588 Triumph 3000/4000**
EZ-International
W194 N11301 McCormick Drive
Germantown, WI 53022
262-250-7740
FAX: 262-250-7741
e-mail: Sales@EK-Tech.com
www.ek-tech.com/
The Triumph 3000/4000 series vehicles provide unique comfort and convenience features found nowhere else. Digital Dash with soft touch keypad, deluxe seat with suspension and integral cargo and cup holders are just a few of these features. Equipped with TOPS 24 (Total Ortho Power System) ensuring maximum power, performance and reliability. Luxurious options such as velour or allante seat fabrics, stylized wheels, metallic or pearl color options and digital controls are all standard. $2,899-$3,39

**589 Triumph Scooter**
EZ-International
W194 N11301 McCormick Drive
Germantown, WI 53022
262-250-7740
FAX: 262-250-7741
e-mail: Sales@EK-Tech.com
www.ek-tech.com/
The sleek, rugged, three-wheel, rear-wheel drive, transaxle scooter with up-top controls, designed to help increase mobility and become more active. The Triumph is designed for both indoor and outdoor use. Available in red, blue, green or gray, with an optional power seat lift. $2,899-$3,399.

## Stationery

**590 Access-USA**
PO Box 160
Clayton, NY 13624-160
800-263-2750
FAX: 800-563-1687
e-mail: info@access-usa.com
www.access-usa.com

*Deborah Webster, PICOE*
Access-USA provides one-stop alternate format transcription services for almost any type of document-reports, schedules, menus, monthly statements, brochures, reports, etc. Items may be submitted on computer disk, hard copy or email. Alternate formats include Braille, large print, Braille and print, audio recordings, adapted disks as well as video services-open/closed captioning and video descriptions. Accessible products also include Braille Business Cards and ADA signage.

**591 Address Book**
Sense-Sations
919 Walnut St
Philadelphia, PA 19107-5237
215-627-0600
FAX: 215-922-0692
e-mail: asbinfo@asb.org
asb.org

*Patricia Johnson, CEO*
*Derby Ewing, Director, Human Services*
*Brian Rusk, Public Relations Officer*
*Dolores Ferrara-Godzieba, Director, Braille Division*
The big print address book is the first personal book to provide enlarged writing spaces, making it easier to write down and retrieve information. *$12.50*

**592 Big Print Address Book**
Access with Ease
42 Executive Blvd
Farmingdale, NY 11735-4710
631-752-0521
800-522-6294
FAX: 631-752-0689
TTY: 800-281-3555
e-mail: sales@maxiaids.com
www.maxiaids.com

*Elliott Zaretsky, Founder and President*
Rods supported by two rubber blocks facilitate writing. *$16.95*

**593 Bold Line Paper**
Sense-Sations
919 Walnut St
Philadelphia, PA 19107-5237
215-627-0600
FAX: 215-922-0692
e-mail: asbinfo@asb.org
asb.org

*Patricia Johnson, CEO*
*Derby Ewing, Director, Human Services*
*Brian Rusk, Public Relations Officer*
*Dolores Ferrara-Godzieba, Director, Braille Division*
This pad consists of 100 sheets of paper with bold lines to help guide the writing of an individual with limited vision. *$2.50*

**594 Braille Notebook**
Maxi Aids
42 Executive Blvd
Farmingdale, NY 11735-4710
631-752-0521
800-522-6294
FAX: 631-752-0689
TTY: 800-281-3555
e-mail: sales@maxiaids.com
www.maxiaids.com

*Elliott Zaretsky, Founder and President*
Made of heavy-duty board, covered with waterproof imitation leather and three rings for binding, including braille paper and titles. *$12.95*

**595 Braille: Desk Calendar**
Maxi Aids
42 Executive Blvd
Farmingdale, NY 11735-4710
631-752-0521
800-522-6294
FAX: 631-752-0689
TTY: 800-281-3555
e-mail: sales@maxiaids.com
www.maxiaids.com
*Elliott Zaretsky, Founder and President*

Schedule appointments, remember birthdays or write messages for a particular day. *$39.95*

596 **Braille: Greeting Cards**
Sense-Sations
919 Walnut St
Philadelphia, PA 19107-5237
215-829-9997
FAX: 215-922-0692
e-mail: asbinfo@asb.org
asb.org

*Patricia Johnson, CEO*
*Derby Ewing, Director, Human Services*
*Brian Rusk, Public Relations Officer*
*Dolores Ferrara-Godzieba, Director, Braille Division*
Birthday, anniversary, get well, sympathy and Christmas cards offering braille print for the blind. *$.95*

597 **Clip Board Notebook**
Sense-Sations
919 Walnut St
Philadelphia, PA 19107-5237
215-627-0600
FAX: 215-922-0692
e-mail: asbinfo@asb.org
asb.org

*Patricia Johnson, CEO*
*Derby Ewing, Director, Human Services*
*Brian Rusk, Public Relations Officer*
*Dolores Ferrara-Godzieba, Director, Braille Division*
Kit includes a pack of Bold Line paper and black ink pen. *$5.95*

598 **Deluxe Signature Guide**
Maxi Aids
42 Executive Blvd
Farmingdale, NY 11735-4710
631-752-0521
800-522-6294
FAX: 631-752-0689
TTY: 800-281-3555
e-mail: sales@maxiaids.com
www.maxiaids.com

*Elliott Zaretsky, Founder and President*
Rods supported by two rubber blocks facilitate writing. *$1.25*

599 **Highlighter and Note Tape**
Therapro, Inc.
225 Arlington St
Framingham, MA 01702-8723
508-872-9494
800-257-5376
FAX: 508-875-2062
e-mail: info@therapro.com
www.therapro.com

*Karen Conrad, Owner*
A great way to highlight and draw attention to words without damaging original. Price ranges from $4.00-$7.00.

600 **Letter Writing Guide**
Independent Living Aids
P.O.Box 9022
Hicksville, NY 11802-9022
800-537-2118
855-746-7452
FAX: 516-937-3906
independentliving.com

*Marvin Sandler, President*
Sturdy plastic sheet with 13 apertures corresponding to standard line spacing. *$3.49*

601 **Lettering Guide Value Pack**
Independent Living Aids
P.O.Box 9022
Hicksville, NY 11802-9022
800-537-2118
855-746-7452
FAX: 516-937-3906
independentliving.com

*Marvin Sandler, President*
Included in this useful pack are four durable plastic lettering and number guides for tracing letters when the individual is unable to write letters unassisted. *$6.29*

## Visual Aids

602 **Aluminum Adjustable Support Canes for the Blind**
Maxi Aids
42 Executive Blvd
Farmingdale, NY 11735-4710
631-752-0521
800-522-6294
FAX: 631-752-0689
TTY: 800-281-3555
e-mail: sales@maxiaids.com
www.maxiaids.com

*Elliott Zaretsky, Founder and President*
Adjustable canes for the visually impaired. *$17.95*

603 **Audio Book Contractors**
P.O. Box 96
Riverdale, MD 20738-96
301-439-5830
FAX: 301-439-5830
e-mail: info@audiobookcontractors.com
www.audiobookcontractors.com

*Flo Gibson, President*
Over 950 titles of unabridged classic books on audio cassettes in sturdy vinyl covers with picture and spine windows. Discounted prices for disabled patrons.

604 **Beyond Sight**
5650 S Windermere St
Littleton, CO 80120-1240
303-795-6455
FAX: 303-795-6425
e-mail: jim@beyondsight.com
beyondsight.com

*Jim Misener, Owner*
*Scott Chaplick, Owner & President*
*Peter Kane, Low Vision Consultant*
*Gina Whetzel, Sales & Merchandise Specialist*
Products for the blind and visually impaired including talking clocks, watches and calculators, also carry a large selection of braille products, magnifiers, reading machines and computer equipment.

605 **Big Number Pocket Sized Calculator**
Independent Living Aids
P.O.Box 9022
Hicksville, NY 11802-9022
516-937-1848
800-537-2118
855-746-7452
FAX: 516-937-3906
e-mail: can-do@independentliving.com
independentliving.com

*Marvin Sandler, President*
A handy pocket size calculator with big numbers that fits easily into purse or pocket. *$14.95*

606 **Braille Compass**
Maxi Aids
42 Executive Blvd
Farmingdale, NY 11735-4710
631-752-0521
800-522-6294
FAX: 631-752-0689
TTY: 800-281-3555
e-mail: sales@maxiaids.com
www.maxiaids.com

*Elliott Zaretsky, Founder and President*
The visually impaired can tell the direction by using this compass. *$42.95*

607 **Braille Plates for Elevator**
Maxi Aids
42 Executive Blvd
Farmingdale, NY 11735-4710
631-752-0521
800-522-6294
FAX: 631-752-0689
TTY: 800-281-3555
e-mail: sales@maxiaids.com
www.maxiaids.com

*Elliott Zaretsky, Founder and President*
The plates have curing type pressure sensitive material applied for metal to metal bonding. *$79.95*

608 **Braille Touch-Time Watches**
Independent Living Aids
P.O.Box 9022
Hicksville, NY 11802-9022
516-937-1848
800-537-2118
855-746-7452
FAX: 516-937-3906
e-mail: can-do@independentliving.com
independentliving.com

*Marvin Sandler, President*
White dial with black numerals and hands makes telling time possible quickly and easily for the visually impaired. *$44.95*

609 **Circline Illuminated Magnifer**
Dazor Manufacturing Corporation
2079 Congressional
St. Louis, MO 63146
314-652-2400
800-345-9103
FAX: 314-652-2069
e-mail: info@dazor.com
www.dazor.com

*Mark Hogrebe,Ph.D, Past President*
Provides even, shadow free light under the magnifying lens with a 22-watt circline fluorescent. The magnifier is mounted on a floating arm that allows you to position the light source and lens with the touch of a finger.

610 **Extra Loud Alarm with Lighter Plug**
HARC Mercantile
1111 W Centre Ave
Portage, MI 49024-5317
800-445-9968
FAX: 269-324-1615
TTY:269-324-1615
e-mail: info@harc.com
harc.com

*Ron Slager, Owner*
Battery operated, easy to read, digital clock with extra loud alarm. *$45.00*

611 **Low Vision Telephones**
2738 N Campbell Ave
Tucson, AZ 85719-3141
520-883-8600
866-674-3549
FAX: 520-883-3172
e-mail: info@assistivedevices.net
assistivedevices.net

*Oliver Simoes, Owner*

612 **Magni-Cam & Primer**
Innoventions
9593 Corsair Dr
Conifer, CO 80433-9317
303-797-6554
800-854-6554
FAX: 303-727-4940
e-mail: magnicam@magnicam.com
magnicam.com

*Mark Freeman, President*
Magni-Cam and Primer are hand-held, light weight, inexpensive auto-focus electronic magnification systems designed to meet the reading and writing needs of those with low vision. The systems present the image in black and white or in color with three different view modes. Connects to any TV monitor in minutes. Systems read any surface with no distortion. A battery powered system is available, providing total portability and flexibility.

613 **Magnifier Bookweight**
Levenger
420 S Congress Ave
Delray Beach, FL 33445-4693
561-276-4141
800-667-8034
FAX: 561-274-0263
e-mail: cservice@levenger.com
www.levenger.com

*Steve Leveen, CEO*
The Magnifier Bookweight features an optical quality magnifier and is long enough to enlarge the full width of most book pages while holing the pages open. This magnifier is encased in embossed leather and enlarges approximately four lines of text at a time to twice the original size.

614 **Man's Low-Vision Quartz Watches**
Independent Living Aids
P.O.Box 9022
Hicksville, NY 11802-9022
516-937-1848
800-537-2118
855-746-7452
FAX: 516-937-3906
e-mail: can-do@independentliving.com
independentliving.com

*Marvin Sandler, President*
An inexpensive, easy-to-read watch with chrome case. *$27.95*

615 **Men's/Women's Low Vision Watches & Clocks**
Maxi Aids
42 Executive Blvd
Farmingdale, NY 11735-4710
631-752-0521
800-522-6294
FAX: 631-752-0689
TTY: 800-281-3555
e-mail: sales@maxiaids.com
www.maxiaids.com

*Elliott Zaretsky, Founder and President*
Choose from a wide range of watches from braille automatic to quartz pocket watches.

**616 MonoMouse Electronic Magnifiers**
Maxi Aids
42 Executive Blvd
Farmingdale, NY 11735-4710
631-752-0521
800-522-6294
FAX: 631-752-0689
TTY: 800-281-3555
e-mail: sales@maxiaids.com
www.maxiaids.com

*Elliott Zaretsky, Founder and President*

Simple and affordable magnifier for people with Low Vision. Just about the size of a standard computer mouse. Allows you to read books, newspapers, product labels, etc. on either a computer or TV screen.

**617 Rigid Aluminum Cane with Golf Grip**
Maxi Aids
42 Executive Blvd
Farmingdale, NY 11735-4710
631-752-0521
800-522-6294
FAX: 631-752-0689
TTY: 800-281-3555
e-mail: sales@maxiaids.com
www.maxiaids.com

*Elliott Zaretsky, Founder and President*

A straight, tubular, heavy gauge aluminum rigid cane for blind and visually impaired persons. *$12.95*

**618 Stretch-View Wide-View Rectangular Illuminated Magnifier**
Dazor Manufacturing Corporation
2079 Congressional
St. Louis, MO 63146
314-652-2400
800-345-9103
FAX: 314-652-2069
e-mail: info@dazor.com
www.dazor.com

*Mark Hogrebe,Ph.D, Past President*

Provides even, shadow free light under the magnifying lens with a 22-watt circline fluorescent. The magnifier is mounted on a floating arm that allows you to position the light source and lens with the touch of a finger.

**619 Timex Easy Reader**
Independent Living Aids
P.O.Box 9022
Hicksville, NY 11802-9022
516-937-1848
800-537-2118
855-746-7452
FAX: 516-937-3906
e-mail: can-do@independentliving.com
independentliving.com

*Marvin Sandler, President*

An easy-to-read large face watch that's water resistant. *$29.95*

**620 Unisex Low Vision Watch**
Independent Living Aids
P.O.Box 9022
Hicksville, NY 11802-9022
516-937-1848
800-537-2118
855-746-7452
FAX: 516-937-3906
e-mail: can-do@independentliving.com
independentliving.com

*Marvin Sandler, President*

Unisex watch with large numbers and wide hands. Gold-toned case with either expansion or leather band. *$31.95*

## Walking Aids: Canes, Crutches & Walkers

**621 Air Lift Oxygen Carriers**
Air Lift Unlimited
1212 Kerr Gulch Rd
Evergreen, CO 80439-6397
800-776-6771
FAX: 303-526-4700
e-mail: info@airlift.com
www.meridianmedicalusa.com

Air Lift together with CareFore Medical offers the broadest selection of Respiratory Accessories available including Air Lift's innovative and versatile portfolio of soft-sided portable oxygen carriers. The CareFore medical line offers an unmatched array of quality and brand name respiratory accessories and supplies.

**622 Aluminum Crutches**
Arista Surgical Supply Company
297 High St
Dedham, MA 02026-2852
781-329-2900
800-225-2610
FAX: 781-329-8392
e-mail: info@alimed.com
www.alimed.com

*Julian Cherubini, President*

Lightweight aluminum crutches with wood underarms and handgrips. *$25.00*

**623 Aluminum Walking Canes**
Maxi Aids
42 Executive Blvd
Farmingdale, NY 11735-4710
631-752-0521
800-522-6294
FAX: 631-752-0689
TTY: 800-281-3555
e-mail: sales@maxiaids.com
www.maxiaids.com

*Elliott Zaretsky, Founder and President*

Lightweight but strong, these walking canes are made of a heavy gauge aluminum tube with safety locknuts and heavy-duty rubber tips. *$10.75*

**624 Compact Folding Travel Rollator**
Maxi Aids
42 Executive Blvd
Farmingdale, NY 11735-4710
631-752-0521
800-522-6294
FAX: 631-752-0689
TTY: 631-752-0738
e-mail: sales@maxiaids.com
maxiaids.com

*Elliott Zaretsky, Founder and President*

Is perfect for someone on the go. Pull strap for quick folding and disassembly. Folds down to half its assembled size in seconds, to a manageable 26 inch L x 22 inch W x 8 inch D for easy storage. *$ 149.95*

**625 Crutches**
Mada Medical Products
625 Washington Ave
Carlstadt, NJ 07072-2901
201-460-0454
800-526-6370
FAX: 201-460-3509
e-mail: dianelind@mail.madamedical.com
www.madainternational.com

*Jeffrey Adam, President*

All aluminum construction, underarm crutch with double pushbutton height adjustment.

626 **Dapper Folding Adustable Cane**
Maxi Aids
42 Executive Blvd
Farmingdale, NY 11735-4710
631-752-0521
800-522-6294
FAX: 631-752-0689
TTY: 631-752-0738
e-mail: sales@maxiaids.com
maxiaids.com

*Elliott Zaretsky, Founder and President*
The Dapper walking stick can be folded and unfolded with only one hand and with minimum effort. The durable lanyard attached prevents loss and allows trailing of staff. Features a non-slip handle, non-skid rubber tip and is made of high quality sturdy aluminum. *$ 34.95*

627 **Dapper Walking Stick**
Maxi Aids
42 Executive Blvd
Farmingdale, NY 11735-4710
631-752-0521
800-522-6294
FAX: 631-752-0689
TTY: 631-752-0738
e-mail: sales@maxiaids.com
maxiaids.com

*Elliott Zaretsky, Founder and President*
The Dapper walking stick is safe durable and sturdy allowing the user to conveniently store it when not in use. It can be folded and unfolded with only one hand and with minimum effort. The durable lanyard attached prevents loss and allows trailing of staff. Features a non-slip handle, non-skid rubber tip and is made of high quality sturdy aluminum construction. *$34.95*

628 **Deluxe Nova Wheeled Walker & Avant Wheeled Walker**
Sammons Preston Rolyan
W68n158 Evergreen Blvd
Cedarburg, WI 53012-2637
262-387-8720
800-323-5547
FAX: 262-387-8748
e-mail: CustomerSupport@PattersonMedical.com
www.pattersonmedical.com/

*Bruce Curtis, Sales Representative*
*David.P Sproat, President*
Lightweight and simple to handle with an easy-to-operate braking system. *$425.40*

629 **Deluxe Standard Wood Cane**
Arista Surgical Supply Company/AliMed
297 High St
Dedham, MA 02026-2852
781-329-2900
800-225-2610
FAX: 781-329-8392
e-mail: info@alimed.com
www.alimed.com

*Julian Cherubini, President*
A standard old-fashioned wooden cane for the physically challenged. *$10.00*

630 **EasyStand 6000 Glider**
Access To Recreation
8 Sandra Ct
Newbury Park, CA 91320-4302
800-634-4351
FAX: 805-498-8186
e-mail: customerservice@accesstr.com
www.accesstr.com

*Don Krebs, President*
Provides dynamic leg motion for individuals who are unable to stand upright or walk on their own.

631 **Freedom Three Wheel Walker**
Mada Medical Products
625 Washington Ave
Carlstadt, NJ 07072-2901
201-460-0454
800-526-6370
FAX: 201-460-3509
e-mail: dianelind@mail.madamedical.com
www.madainternational.com

*Jeffrey Adam, President*
The freedom walker has ultra light touch, locking loop brakes and sure grip hand grips.

632 **Liberty Lightweight Aluminum Stroll Walker**
Mada Medical Products
625 Washington Ave
Carlstadt, NJ 07072-2901
201-460-0454
800-526-6370
FAX: 201-460-3509
e-mail: dianelind@mail.madamedical.com
www.madainternational.com

*Jeffrey Adam, President*
The Liberty walker has a spring loaded push down braking system, adjustable handle height with locking system, a 12in wide fully padded seat, and a removable shopping basket.

633 **Maxi Superior Cane**
Maxi Aids
42 Executive Blvd
Farmingdale, NY 11735-4710
631-752-0521
800-522-6294
FAX: 631-752-0689
TTY: 800-281-3555
e-mail: sales@maxiaids.com
www.maxiaids.com

*Elliott Zaretsky, Founder and President*
Convenient folding cane designed for optimum balance. Tapered joints provide rigidity when open, and are made of heavy gauge aluminum. *$17.50*

634 **Out-N-About American Walker**
742 Market St
Oregon, WI 53575-1059
608-835-9255
FAX: 608-835-5234

*Luann Smith, President*
The lightweight Out-N-About is easy to handle. The four wheel design provides greater support and stability than any other walking aids. Its large rubber tires move effortlessly over most surfaces, indoors and out. The small turning radius makes it ideal for getting through confined spaces and narrow doorways. The attractive, burgundy colored, tubular steel frame is extremely durable. The Out-N-About folds flat and stands alone for easy storage. Made in USA.

635 **Patriot Extra Wide Folding Walkers**
Mada Medical Products
625 Washington Ave
Carlstadt, NJ 07072-2901
201-460-0454
800-526-6370
FAX: 201-460-3509
e-mail: dianelind@mail.madamedical.com
www.madainternational.com

*Jeffrey Adam, President*
The extra wide walkers have padded foam hand grips, two-stage push button folding mechanism, dual width adjustment, height adjustment, and nonskid tips.

**636 Patriot Folding Walker Series**
Mada Medical Products
625 Washington Ave
Carlstadt, NJ 07072-2901
201-460-0454
800-526-6370
FAX: 201-460-3509
e-mail: dianelind@mail.madamedical.com
www.madainternational.com

*Jeffrey Adam, President*

The patriot walker has high density, padded foam hand grips, high strength 1in lightweight, anodized, dull silver aluminum tube construction, adjustable height with push-button lock security, nonskid tips, and a single button folding mechanism.

**637 Patriot Reciprocal Folding Walkers**
Mada Medical Products
625 Washington Ave
Carlstadt, NJ 07072-2901
201-460-0454
800-526-6370
FAX: 201-460-3509
e-mail: dianelind@mail.madamedical.com
www.madainternational.com

*Jeffrey Adam, President*

The reciprocal folding walkers have padded foam hand grips, adjustable height with snap-in security, double front cross brace, and nonskid tips.

**638 Prone Support Walker**
Consumer Care Products
W222 N5739 Miller Way
Sussex, WI 53089-684
262-820-2300
e-mail: info@consumercarellc.com
www.consumercarellc.com

This walker, in five sizes for children to adults, facilitates semi-prone to full upright mobility and dynamic weight bearing. The walker requires the user to push off the floor teaching the user to work with the floor and achieving a more efficient gait. Options such as tray, back support, and hip pads allow adaptation to most needs. $750-$1,300.

**639 Push-Button Quad Cane**
Arista Surgical Supply Company/AliMed
297 High St
Dedham, MA 02026-2852
781-329-2900
800-225-2610
FAX: 781-329-8392
e-mail: info@alimed.com
www.alimed.com

*Julian Cherubini, President*

A reliable walking cane offering independence to the physically challenged user. *$25.00*

**640 Quad Canes**
Mada Medical Products
625 Washington Ave
Carlstadt, NJ 07072-2901
201-460-0454
800-526-6370
FAX: 201-460-3509
e-mail: dianelind@mail.madamedical.com
www.madainternational.com

*Jeffrey Adam, President*

There are large and small base quad canes with high density foam grips.

**641 Rand-Scot**
401 Linden Center Dr
Fort Collins, CO 80524-2429
970-484-7967
800-467-7967
FAX: 970-484-3800
TTY: 800-467-7967
e-mail: info@randscot.com
randscot.com

*Joel Lerich, President*
*Barbara Hoehn, President*

Manufactures the Easy Pivot patient lift, the BBD wheelchair cushion line and Saratoga Exercise products for the disabled. Offers a line of patient lifts and standers for the disabled. Rand-scot products are designed to help the disabled acheive independence, comfort, and stamina. A video or dvd is available at no charge for potential users, $800-$3,000.

**642 Secret Agent Walking Stick**
Gold Violin
PO BOX 147
Jessup, PA 18434
877-648-8400
FAX: 800-821-1282
www.goldviolin

*Connie Hallquist, CEO*

The Secret Agent Walking Stick features a built-in flashlight, a red reflector and a built-in secret pill compartment. this folding aluminum cane is height adjustable and has a derby-style handle and a non-skid rubber tip. A nylon carrying case is included. The walking stick comes in a choich of gold, bronze, or black shaft with a faux burled walnut handle. . It has been taken over by Orchard Brands.

**643 StairClimber**
Martin Technology
29 N Main St
Gloversville, NY 12078-3006
518-725-1837
800-800-1410
FAX: 518-725-9522

*Michael Lewy, Owner*

A walker-capable person can climb and descend stairs with this walker-designed StairClimber.

**644 Standing Aid Frame with Rear Entry**
Consumer Care Products
W222 N5739 Miller Way
Sussex, WI 53089-684
262-820-2300
FAX: 920-459-9070
www.consumercarellc.com

This rugged stander, made of natural hardwood in sizes for one to twelve year olds, allows weight bearing in an upright position. Table, upper trunk and/or head support, hip pads and casters allow individualized fitting. The new hinged rear entry option makes entry into this stander easy and quick for parents, teachers and therapists. $572-$1,800.

**645 Stick Canes**
Mada Medical Products
625 Washington Ave
Carlstadt, NJ 07072-2901
201-460-0454
800-526-6370
FAX: 201-460-3509
e-mail: dianelind@mail.madamedical.com
www.madainternational.com

*Jeffrey Adam, President*

Mada's stick canes are adjustable with a locking security system.

646 **Torso Support**
Grandmar
5635 Peck Rd.
Arcadia, CA 91006-20
626-443-3143
1 8-0 4-7 67
FAX: 800-767-3933
e-mail: info@posey.com
www.posey.com

*Ernest Posey, CEO*
*Bob Kelleher, Senior VP Finance & Operations*
*Tracey Bertolina, CFO*
*Gary Platzman, VP of Sales & Mktg*
An aid for people who are unable to maintain an upright position in an automobile or a wheelchair.

647 **U-Step Walking Stabilizer: Walker**
Maxi Aids
42 Executive Blvd
Farmingdale, NY 11735-4710
631-752-0521
800-522-6294
FAX: 631-752-0689
TTY: 631-752-0738
e-mail: sales@maxiaids.com
maxiaids.com

*Elliott Zaretsky, Founder and President*
If you want to feel as stable as you would while holding onto another person's arm, the U-Step Walking Stabilizer is for you. The innovative braking system is easy to use and puts you in complete control; roll only when you want to. Plus, it easily folds for transport. *$ 539.95*

648 **Ventura Enterprises**
35 Lawton Ave
Danville, IN 46122-1217
317-745-2989
FAX: 317-745-3179
www.venturaenterprises.com

*Linda Plunkett, Owner*
Manufacturer of everyday living mobility aids. Products include carrying aids for walkers and wheelchairs and also wheelchair cushions.

649 **WCIB Heavy-Duty Folding Cane**
Maxi Aids
42 Executive Blvd
Farmingdale, NY 11735-4710
631-752-0521
800-522-6294
FAX: 631-752-0689
TTY: 800-281-3555
e-mail: sales@maxiaids.com
www.maxiaids.com

*Elliott Zaretsky, Founder and President*
A four section aluminum folding cane with a golf-type grip handle and flexible wrist loop. Available in 34-60 lengths. *$17.95*

650 **Walker Leg Support**
Sammons Preston Rolyan
W68n158 Evergreen Blvd
Cedarburg, WI 53012-2637
262-387-8720
800-228-3693
FAX: 262-387-8748
e-mail: CustomerSupport@PattersonMedical.com
www.pattersonmedical.com/

*Bruce Curtis, Sales Representative*
*David.P Sproat, President*
For lower extremity trauma. An alternative to crutches that allows safe, stable ambulation and frees hands and arms for daily tasks. *$11.50*

## Wheelchairs: Accessories

651 **Advantage Wheelchair & Walker Bags**
Laurel Designs
TORRANCE, CA 90505
800-556-6307
FAX: 310-316-2561
e-mail: advantagebag@verizon.net
www.advantagebag.com/
Wheelchairs with and without push handles.Pac slips over back of almost any wheelchair.

652 **Automatic Wheelchair Anti-Rollback Device**
Alzheimer's Store
3197 Trout Place Rd
Cumming, GA 30041-8260
678-947-4001
800-752-3238
FAX: 678-947-8411
e-mail: cs@alzstore.com
www.alzstore.com

*Ellen Warner, President*
As a wheelchair user transfers to and from the chair, a pair of brake arms grabs the tires to prevent the chair from rolling backwards. Once the individual is seated, the device switches to stand-by modeand the wheelchair returns to standard funcion.

653 **Battery Operated Cushion**
DA Schulman
3827 Creekside Lane
Holmen, WI 54636
608-782-0031
866-782-9658
FAX: 608-782-0488
e-mail: aquila@aquilacorp.com
www.aquilacorp.com
Battery-operated, dynamic cushion for wheelchairs. The Airpulse PK wheelchair cushion system is Aquila Corporation's most dynamic cushion system. It was designed to be the most advanced solution to help prevent and heal pressure ulcers.

654 **Dual-Mode Charger**
Lester Electrical
625 W a St
Lincoln, NE 68522-1794
402-477-8988
FAX: 402-474-1769
e-mail: sales@lesterelectrical.com
www.lesterelectrical.com
Fully automatic battery charger.

655 **Equalizer 1000 Series**
Helm Distributing
P.O Box 25105 Deer Park P.O, Rd Dee
Alberta, CA 45418-2713
403-309-5551
FAX: 403-342-5509
e-mail: info@equalizerexercise.com
www.equalizerexercise.com

*$7050.00*

656 **Equalizer 5000 Home Gym**
Helm Distributing
P.O Box 25105 Deer Park P.O, Rd Dee
Alberta, CA 45418-2713
403-309-5551
FAX: 403-342-5509
e-mail: info@equalizerexercise.com
www.equalizerexercise.com

Exercise machine for the able-bodied and the disabled, but specifically designed with a wheelchair user in mind. *$4250.00*

657 **Featherspring**
105 W Lincoln Hwy
DeKalb, IL 60115
1 8-0 6-8 46
FAX: 800-261-1164
e-mail: customerservice@luxis.com
www.luxis.com
Foot supports for wheelchair users to prevent and treat cold feet, sore heels, swollen feet and weak ankles. The name of the company has been changed to ""Luxis International Inc."" *$199.95*

658 **Gem Wheelchair & Scooter Service: Mobility & Homecare**
17639 Union Tpke
Flushing, NY 11366-1515 718-969-8600
800-943-3578
e-mail: help@gemwheelchairservice.com
www.gemwheelchairservice.com/

GEM sells, repairs and rents all makes and models of manual and motorized wheelchairs, power scooters, ramps, stairway lifts, and homecare products including diapers, chux, and bathroom safety equipment. Clients are in all five New York City Boroughs and Nassau County. Medicare and Medicaid accepted, pick-up and delivery, loaner equipment, and while-u-wait repair services available. Gem also buys and sells used equipment. Wholesale and retail services available.

659 **Lifestand**
Frank Mobility Systems
300 Duke Drive
Lebanon, TN 37090 800-736-0925
FAX: 800-231-3256
e-mail: info@permobil.com
www.lifestandusa.com

*Jon Sintorn, President and CEO*
*James (Buck) Taylor, Sales Manager*
*Jason Strawser , Sales Manager*
*John Richards, National Sales Manager*

Lifestand offers a full line of standing wheelchairs for manual operation. Power assisted are fully motorized. *$7000.00*

660 **Mat Factory**
6726 North Figueroa Street
Los Angeles, CA 90042 800-628-7626
FAX: 323-254-4545
www.matfactoryinc.com

Wheelchair access mats for pathways, walkways, trails and playgrounds. Mats also allow for natural grass to grow up through them.

661 **One Thousand FS**
Fortress
P.O.Box 489
Clovis, CA 93613-489 559-322-5437
FAX: 559-323-0299

Add-on power system installs in minutes, enabling the driver to relax and drive anywhere with smooth, silent electric power.

662 **Pac-All Wheelchair Carrier**
Pac-All Carriers
2321 Carolton Rd
Maitland, FL 32751-3624 407-830-6604
800-628-6672
FAX: 407-339-2847

*LE Angel*

No more lifting and no more pain wheelchair carrier. VA approved. Made in USA.
*$158 - $226.40*

663 **Safety Deck II**
Mat Factory
6726 North Figueroa Street
Los Angeles, CA 90042 800-628-7626
FAX: 323-254-4545
www.matfactoryinc.com

The Safety Deck II is an interlocking grid system made from recycled rubber tires and recycled PVC. The tiles are set directly on top of the ground and permit grass to grow through the holes and cover the surface. The system provides safe, non-barrier access for wheelchairs over grass. Once the grass has covered the tiles the only maintenance required is watering and mowing. Safety Deck II also allows for beach and sand access. Priced per square foot with volume discounts. *$7.80*

664 **Scooter & Wheelchair Battery Fuel Gauges and Motor Speed Controllers**
Curtis Instruments, Inc.
200 Kisco Ave
Mount Kisco, NY 10549-1407 914-666-2971
FAX: 914-666-2188
e-mail: gomezj@curtisinst.com
curtisinst.com

*Stuart E Marwell, President and CEO*
*David Matthews, VP Sales Americas*
*Cheryl Leonaggeo, Customer Service Manager*
*Richard McFarlane, Customer Support Engineer*

Provides a readable, accurate indication of battery in easy to read type of display. Innovative, efficient motor speed controllers for single or dual PM motor vehicles.

665 **Softfoot Ergomatta**
Mat Factory
6726 North Figueroa Street
Los Angelesa, CA 90042 949-645-3122
800-628-7626
FAX: 323-254-4545
www.matfactoryinc.com

Interlocking roll-up mat system with antimicrobial additive. Allows wheelchairs and walkers to move easily and safely along wet and potentially hazardous surfaces. Priced per tile with volume discounts. *$9.90*

666 **Tilt-N-Table**
Osterguard Enterprises c/o Jim's Shop
3228 W Olive Ave
Fresno, CA 93722-5733 559-275-4695

*Jim Ostergaard Ii, Owner*

These are lightweight tables for wheelchairs that are angle and height adjustable to your changing needs.

667 **Wheel Life News**
University of Virginia, Rehab Engineering Centers
3363 University Sta
Charlottesville, VA 22903 434-924-5118
www.medicine.virginia.edu

*Kristine M. Garza, Ph.D., Executive Director of SACNAS*
*Steven T. DeKosky, Dean*

Features tie downs and other adaptive technology for persons with disabilities.

668 **Wheelchair Accessories**
Diestco Manufacturing Company
P.O.Box 6504
Chico, CA 95927-6504 800-795-2392
e-mail: info@diestco.com
diestco.com

Diestco makes innovative accessories for wheelchairs, scooters and walkers. Products include canopies, backpacks, cupholders, pouches, threshhold ramps, laptrays and others.

669 **Wheelchair Aide**
Graham-Field
400 Rabro Dr
Hauppauge, NY 11788-4258 631-348-1364

This is a heavy-duty wheelchair comfort tray which surrounds the wheelchair user and provides a large, smooth surface for dining, writing, hobbies or work. The heavy gauge plastic tray is easy to clean and attaches with two Velcro straps.

670 **Wheelchair Back Pack and Tote Bag**
Med Covers
320 Roebling Street, Suite 515
Brooklyn, NY 11211 718-302-1923
e-mail: info@1800wheelchair.com
www.1800wheelchair.com

Accessories are specifically designed with the wheelchair user in mind. The Back Pack has a main roomy pouch for larger items and has a full length zipper with four sliders for convenient access.

**671 Wheelchair Roller**
Access To Recreation
8 Sandra Ct
Newbury Park, CA 91320-4302
800-634-4351
FAX: 805-498-8186
e-mail: customerservice@accesstr.com
www.accesstr.com

*Don Krebs, President*
The McClain Wheelchair Roller allows you to build strength and stamina in the comfort of your own home.

**672 Wheelchair Work Table**
Bailey Manufacturing Company
118 Lee St
Lodi, OH 44254-130
800-321-8372
FAX: 800-224-5390
e-mail: baileymfg@attmail.com
baileymfg.com

An adjustable height, functional, individual cut-out work table featuring a wood-grain laminate, scratch resistant top with chrome plated steel legs.

## Wheelchairs: General

**673 21st Century Scientific, Inc.Bounder Power Wheelchair**
4931 N Manufacturing Way
Coeur D Alene, ID 83815-8931
208-667-8800
800-448-3680
FAX: 208-667-6600
e-mail: 21st@wheelchairs.com
wheelchairs.com

*Ronald E. Prior, Ph.D., CEO*
*RD Davidson, Sales/Marketing Director*
*Susan Harris, CFO*
High performance power chairs for active individuals. Very fast (11+ MPH), OFF-ROAD and Bariatric options available. Power seating options include tilt, recline, 13-inch seat elevator, reverse tilt, legrests, standing and front load (latitude). 6-drive prgrammable electronics standard; lights,horn,electric leg bag emptier and many other options available. Customization is our specialty.

**674 Arcoa Travel Chair**
Maxi Aids
42 Executive Blvd
Farmingdale, NY 11735-4710
631-752-0521
800-522-6294
FAX: 631-752-0689
TTY: 631-752-0738
e-mail: sales@maxiaids.com
maxiaids.com

*Elliott Zaretsky, Founder and President*
The unique Comfort Travel Chair collapses into an easy to manage 25in x 26in x 11in and includes a strap for easy carrying. It weighs just 16 lbs. but can hold up to 200 lbs., making it the perfect travel companion. You can rest assured that it will 'stay put' with a dual wheel lock, while you enjoy the comfort and support of the padded swing-back armrests and 16in seat. *$197.00*

**675 Bariatric Wheelchairs Regency FL**
Gendron
520 W. Mulberry St. Suite 100
Bryan, OH 43506
800-537-2521
FAX: 419-636-9261
www.gendroninc.com

*Steven Cotter, VP Sales/President*
Bariatric wheelchairs, for users weighing up to seven hundred pounds. Manual and power styles built to order for specific needs.

**676 Breezy**
Sunrise Medical/Quickie Designs
2842 Business Park Avenue
Fresno, CA 93727
800-333-4000
800-300-7502
www.sunrisemedical.com

*Pete Coburn, President*
*Randi Binstock, VP, Business Dev.*
*Peter Riley, Senior VP/Corporate CFO*
*Kevin Marshman, North American Controller*
This lightweight chair is durable, comfortable and flexible enough to meet the needs of a wide range of wheelchair users.

**677 Champion 1000**
Kuschall of America
3601 Rider Trl S
Earth City, MO 63045-1116
314-512-7000
800-654-4768
FAX: 800-542-3567

Ultralight wheelchair designed to improve mobility. $1,689

**678 Champion 2000**
Kuschall of America
3601 Rider Trl S
Earth City, MO 63045-1116
314-512-7000
800-654-4768
FAX: 800-542-3567

Rigid chair that folds side-to-side. $1,765

**679 Champion 3000**
Kuschall of America
3601 Rider Trl S
Earth City, MO 63045-1116
314-512-7000
800-654-4768
FAX: 800-542-3567

The high-performance chair built for perfectionists. $1,695

**680 Choosing a Wheelchair: A Guide for Optimal Independence**
Patient-Centered Guides
1005 Gravenstein Hwy N
Sebastopol, CA 95472-3836
707-829-0515
800-889-8969
FAX: 707-824-8268
e-mail: order@oreilly.com
www.patientcenters.com

*Linda Lamb, Editor*
*Shawnde Paull, Marketing*
*Tim O'Reilly, Publisher*
*Gary Karp, Author*
With the right wheelchair, quality of life increases dramatically and even people with severe disabilities can have a considerable degree of independence and activity. Choosing the wrong chair can indeed the tantamount to confinement. This book describes technology, options, and the selection process to help you identify the chair than can provide you with optimal independence.
*$9.95*
*186 pages Paperback*
*ISBN 1-565924-11-8*

**681 Convaid**
2830 California Street
Torrance, CA 90503
310-618-0111
888-266-8243
FAX: 310-618-2166
e-mail: convaid@convaid.com
www.convaid.com

Five different styles of wheelchairs.

**682 Custom**
Fortress
P.O.Box 489
Clovis, CA 93613-489
559-322-5437
FAX: 559-323-0299

Ultralight aluminum wheelchair that can be customized to customer's requests. Fifteen frame colors, eight seat widths and depths, along with thirteen rear wheel combinations are just a few of the features offered at the standard package price.

683 **Custom Durable**
21279 Protecta Dr
Elkhart, IN 46516-9539
574-522-7209
800-478-2363
FAX: 574-293-0202
e-mail: info@pvcdme.com
pvcdme.com

Wheelchairs; accessories.

684 **Edge**
Fortress
P.O.Box 489
Clovis, CA 93613-489
559-322-5437
FAX: 559-323-0299

An ultra lightweight aircraft aluminum wheelchair that is suitable for sports, school or the workplace.

685 **Etac USA: F3 Wheelchair**
Ste J
2325 Parklawn Dr
Waukesha, WI 53186-2938
262-717-9910
800-678-3822
FAX: 262-796-4605
e-mail: etac1usa@execpc.com
www.execpc.com/~etac1usa

*Mark Samolyk, Manager*
A swedish wheelchair designed to provide function, comfort and flexibility. Seat frame and upholstery are adjustable to fit each individual. Swing away, detachable footrests are standard. Available in frame widths from 14, 18 and 20 inch. Numerous accessories are available in order to individualize each chair. Lifetime warranty on frame for original user.

686 **Evacu-Trac**
Garaventa Canada
7505 - 134 A Street, Surrey, BC V3W
Blaine, WA 98231-1769
800-663-6556
e-mail: customerrelations@garaventalift.com

This emergency evacuation chair is designed for safety and fast operation.

687 **Folding Chair with a Rigid Feel**
Kuschall of America
3601 Rider Trl S
Earth City, MO 63045-1116
314-512-7000
800-654-4768
FAX: 800-542-3567

The Champion 1000 is a new concept in folding chairs. Even though it's ultra light, it has the feel and performance of a rigid chair.

688 **Formula Series Active Mobility Wheelchairs**
Everest & Jennings
3233 Mission Oaks Blvd
Camarillo, CA 93012-5047
805-389-7450

This is a new series of lightweight wheelchairs designed for the active user.

689 **Freestyle II**
Fortress
P.O.Box 489
Clovis, CA 93613-489
559-322-5437
FAX: 559-323-0299

Effort-sparing, ultra-lightweight aircraft aluminum construction and design allow for easy propelling over various rolling surfaces.

690 **Gadabout Wheelchairs**
Gadabout Wheelchairs
1165 Portland Ave
Rochester, NY 14621-3945
585-338-2110
800-828-4242
FAX: 585-338-2696

*Michael Fonte, Owner*
Enjoy independence with the wheelchair that is lightweight, portable, convenient, comfortable and sturdy.

691 **Gem Wheelchair & Scooter Service: Mobility & Homecare**
17639 Union Tpke
Flushing, NY 11366-1515
718-463-3800
800-943-3578
FAX: 718-969-8300
e-mail: help@gemwheelchairservice.com
www.gemwheelchairservice.com/

GEM sells, repairs and rents all makes and models of manual and motorized wheelchairs, power scooters, ramps, stairway lifts, and homecare products including diapers, chux, and bathroom safety equipment. Clients are in all five New York City Boroughs and Nassau County. Medicare and Medicaid accepted, pick-up and delivery, loaner equipment, and while-u-wait repair services available. Gem also buys and sells used equipment. Wholesale and retail services available.

692 **Gendron**
520 W. Mulberry St. Suite 100
Bryan, OH 43506
419-445-6060
800-537-2521
FAX: 419-636-9261
www.gendroninc.com

*Steven Cotter, VP Sales/President*
Manufacturer of wheelchairs for a variety of other applications, specializing in bariatric mobility products.

693 **HiRider**
Gaymar Industries
10 Centre Dr
Orchard Park, NY 14127-2280
716-662-2551
800-828-7341
FAX: 800-993-7890
gaymar.com

*Frank L Lumbar, CEO*
*John.K Whitney, Founder*
*Cindy Sylvia, Educational Svcs Administrator*
*Dan Kormowicz, International Sales Coordinator*
A wheelchair that provides mobility in both sitting and standing positions.

694 **Innovative Products**
4351 W College Ave
Appleton, WI 54914-3928
920-738-9090
800-424-3369
FAX: 920-738-9050
att.com

*Fritz H Heerdt, President*
Wheelchairs; accessories.

695 **Liberty**
Fortress
P.O.Box 489
Clovis, CA 93613-489
559-322-5437
FAX: 559-323-0299

Ultra lightweight wheelchair provides a comfortable fit and leaves people able to function as normally as possible in daily activities.

**696 Lightweight Breezy**
Motion Design
2842 Business Park Avenue
Fresno, CA 93727
800-333-4000
800-300-7502
www.sunrisemedical.com

*Pete Coburn, President*
*Randi Binstock, VP, Business Dev.*
*Peter Riley, Senior VP/Corporate CFO*
*Kevin Marshman, North American Controller*
A lightweight wheelchair. *$750.00*

**697 Majors Medical Equipment**
415 W Wilshire Blvd., Suite A
Oklahoma City, OK 73116
405-840-5272
1 8-8 4-4 01
FAX: 405-840-5274
e-mail: help@mmedsupply.com
www.majorsmedicalequipment.com

*Pat Metz, Owner*
America's largest selection of wheelchairs and homecare equipment.

**698 Natural Access**
PO Box 5729
Santa Monica, CA 90409
310-392-9864
800-411-7789
FAX: 310-392-3874
e-mail: john_egan_2000@yahoo.com
www.landeez.com

*John Egan, Owner*
Provides the Landeez all-terrain wheelchair, that can roll easily on sand, gravel and snow for outdoor fun. The entire chair can fit inside a travel bag!

**699 Patient Transport Chair**
Mada Medical Products
625 Washington Ave
Carlstadt, NJ 07072-2901
201-460-0454
800-526-6370
FAX: 201-460-3509
e-mail: dianelind@mail.madamedical.com
www.madainternational.com

*Jeffrey Adam, President*
Mada's lightweight design transport chair is constructed of heavy gauge chrome-plated, steel tubing with reinforced cross braces.

**700 Posture-Glide Lounger**
Graham-Field Health Products
2935 Northeast Pkwy
Atlanta, GA 30360-2808
678-291-3207
FAX: 770-368-2386
e-mail: cs@grahamfield.com
www.grahamfield.com

*Beatrice Scherer, Board Member*
*Kenneth Spett, President & CEO*
*Cherie Antoniazzi, Senior Vice President*
*Ivan Bielik, Senior Vice President*
Provides all day comfort and safe, independent mobilization with feet or hands. The ergonomically engineered seat back provides correct support.

**701 Prairie Cruiser**
Wheelchairs of Kansas
204 West 2nd Street P.O.Box 32
Ellis, KS 67637-32
785-726-4885
800-537-6454
FAX: 800-337-2447
e-mail: workinfo@go2wok.com
www.wheelchairsofkansas.com
A large-frame powerchair constructed of high quality, stress tested stainless steel to insure durability and peak performance.

**702 Redman Apache**
Redman Powerchair
601 S Pantano Road Suite 107
Tucson, AZ 85710
520-546-6002
800-727-6684
FAX: 520-546-5530
e-mail: info@redmanpowerchair.com
www.redmanpowerchair.com

*Don Redman, CEO*
*Paula Redman, CFO*
*Scott Evans, Regulatory affairs*
*Samuel Redman, Sales manager*
These ultralight, active use wheelchairs offer quick release rear wheels, adjustable arm height and detachable arm swing-away.

**703 Redman Crow Line**
Redman Powerchair
601 S Pantano Road Suite 107
Tucson, AZ 85710
520-546-6002
800-727-6684
FAX: 520-546-5530
e-mail: info@redmanpowerchair.com
www.redmanpowerchair.com

*Don Redman, CEO*
*Paula Redman, CFO*
*Scott Evans, Regulatory affairs*
*Samuel Redman, Sales manager*
Reclining wheelchair that reclines a full 90 degrees to flat and can be stopped anywhere on the axis.

**704 Rolls 2000 Series**
Invacare Corporation
1 Invacare Way
Elyria, OH 44035-4107
440-329-6000
800-333-6900
FAX: 877- 61- 799
e-mail: info@invacare.com
www.invacare.com

*Mal Mixon, CEO*
*Joe Lewarski, VP of Clinical Affairs*
*Bob Messenger, Clinical Respiratory Specialist*
These wheelchairs are the first light-weight wheelchairs designed for rental use.

**705 Skyway**
Skyway Machine
4451 Caterpillar Rd
Redding, CA 96003-1496
530-243-5151
800-332-3357
FAX: 530-243-5104
e-mail: sales@skywaywheels.com
skywaytuffwheels.com

*Ken Coster, Sales Department*
*Bart Weems, Sales Department*
*Rein Stolz, Engineering Department*
*Patrick McEachen, ustomer Service*
For over 20 years Skyway has been the world leader in composite wheels. Supplying over 650 different wheel combinations for wheelchairs, lawn and garden products, bicycles and a large assortment of wheeled devices. Wheel sizes range from 4 inch to 24 inch diameter.

**706 Stand-Up Wheelchairs**
Lifestand
P.O.Box 232171
Encinitas, CA 92023-2171
800-782-6324
FAX: 610-586-0847
e-mail: dallery@msn.com

*Jacques A Dallery, President*
Offers a complete line of manual, electric and stand-up wheelchairs for the disabled.

**707 Standard Wheelchair**
Mada Medical Products
625 Washington Ave
Carlstadt, NJ 07072-2901 201-460-0454
800-526-6370
FAX: 201-460-3509
e-mail: dianelind@mail.madamedical.com
www.madainternational.com

*Jeffrey Adam, President*
Mada's standard wheelchairs are designed and built for long-lasting, reliable operation. Each wheelchair is constructed of heavy gauge, chrome plated, steel framework and tube in tube construction at stress points. Mada's state-of-the art engineering uses the most modern components to provide the strength needed while keeping the chair's weight down.

**708 Super Light Folding Transport Chair with Carry Bag**
Maxi Aids
42 Executive Blvd
Farmingdale, NY 11735-4710 631-752-0521
800-522-6294
FAX: 631-752-0689
TTY: 631-752-0738
e-mail: sales@maxiaids.com
maxiaids.com

*Elliott Zaretsky, Founder and President*
Folds like a conventional folding chair for added convenience and includes carry bag, fold-down footrests, padded flip back armrests, standard rear wheel locks and an attractive frame with durable lightweight nylon upholstery and limited lifetime warranty. Weighs only 18 pounds. Easy to push or transport. *$319.95*

**709 Surf Chair**
2052 S Peninsula Dr
Daytona Beach, FL 32118-5237 386-253-0986
800-841-6610
FAX: 386-253-7600

Wheelchairs; accessories.

**710 Vista Wheelchair**
Arista Surgical Supply Company/AliMed
297 High St
Dedham, MA 02026-2852 781-329-2900
800-223-1984
FAX: 781-329-8392
e-mail: cust_serv@alimed.com
www.alimed.com

Vista has a rugged cold-rolled steel frame, durable vinyl upholstery and steel bearings to assure a smooth ride. *$220.00*

**711 Wheelchair with Shock Absorbers**
Iron Horse Productions
3114 Strawberry Ln
Port Huron, MI 48060-1727 810-987-6700
800-426-0354

The Iron Horse is a revolutionary concept in wheelchair design that offers comfort, indoors and outdoors. *$2375.00*

## Wheelchairs: Pediatric

**712 Commuter & Kid's Commuter**
Fortress
P.O.Box 489
Clovis, CA 93613-489 559-322-5437
FAX: 559-323-0299

The first of a new generation of power wheelchairs. These chairs feature direct drive power yet are foldable, transportable and affordable.

**713 Convaid**
2830 California St
Torrance, CA 90503-3908 310-618-0111
888-266-8243
FAX: 310-618-2166
e-mail: convaid@earthlink.net
www.convaid.com

Convaid manufactures Mobile Positioning Systems for children. The Expedition, Safari Tilt, Cruiser, EZ Rider and Metro offer a noninstitutional styling and are lightweight and compact-folding. The steel/aluminum structure is engineered for maximum comfort and durability. The mobile positioning lines come with more than 20 positioning features and a full range of positioning adaptations. All chairs have been successfully crash-tested and offer a limited lifetime warranty (except the Metro).

**714 Imp Tricycle**
TRIAID
P.O.Box 1364
Cumberland, MD 21501-1364 301-759-3525
800-306-6777
FAX: 301-759-3525
e-mail: sales@triaid.com
www.triaid.com

Provides fun therapy and actively encourages participation, awareness and the building of self confidence. Designed for children from about 3 years, it features ATB styling, 12 inch wheels, adjustable steering stop and a supportive saddle. Handlebar and seat adjustments combine with a broad wheelbase to ensure the rider is in the optimum position to pedal and the tricycle gives good stability and confident handling. Support accessories are available. *$590.00*

**715 Kid's Custom**
Fortress
P.O.Box 489
Clovis, CA 93613-489 559-322-5437
FAX: 559-323-0299

Custom pediatric mobility needs. This ultra light-weight chair is tailored fit to each child, to make wheeling fun and encourages kids to be active because they feel free, safe and secure.

**716 Kid's Edge**
Fortress
P.O.Box 489
Clovis, CA 93613-489 559-322-5437
FAX: 559-323-0299

This wheelchair offers multiple options, features and modifications at no upcharge.

**717 Kid's Liberty**
Fortress
P.O.Box 489
Clovis, CA 93613-489 559-322-5437
FAX: 559-323-0299

Offers a broad range of seat heights, widths and depths, back heights and numerous other modifications to accommodate the specific and unique requirements of children.

**718 Kid-Friendly Chairs**
Vector Mobility
5030 E Jensen Ave
Fresno, CA 93725-4010 559-431-3334
800-441-0358
FAX: 559-431-5535

*Dave Deatherage, Owner*
Manual base offers the lowest available floor to seat height, growth capability, one-third the parts of a conventional chair and no welds to break. The power unit features standard shapes and personality designs from elephants to inch worms and autos to rainbows, lowest seat height, and smallest turning radius on the market.

719 **Seven Fifty-Five FS**
Fortress
P.O.Box 489
Clovis, CA 93613-489
559-322-5437
FAX: 559-323-0299

Unharness the curiosity of childhood with the modular power/base seating system that sets kids free. This device is engineered and built especially for children.

720 **TMX Tricycle**
TRIAID
P.O.Box 1364
Cumberland, MD 21501-1364
301-759-3525
800-306-6777
FAX: 301-759-3525
e-mail: sales@triaid.com
www.triaid.com

Provides fun therapy and actively encourages participation, awareness and the building of self confidence. Designed for children from about eight years, it features ATB styling, 20 inch wheels, adjustable steering stop and a supportive saddle. Handlebar and seat adjustments combine with a broad wheelbase to ensure the rider is in the optimum position to pedal and the tricycle gives good stability and confident handling. Support accessories are available. *$795.00*

## Wheelchairs: Powered

721 **Bounder Plus Power Wheelchair**
21st Century Scientific
4915 N Industrial Way
Coeur D Alene, ID 83815-8931
208-667-8800
800-448-3680
FAX: 208-667-6600
e-mail: 21st@wheelchairs.com
wheelchairs.com

*Ronald E. Prior, Ph.D., CEO*
*RD Davidson, Sales/Marketing Director*
*Susan Harris, CFO*

Available in widths of 16 to 20 inches for users up to 500 pounds with a 2 year warranty on the entire chair. It offers all the standard features of a BOUNDER, plus reinforced rear wheel mounts, reinforced caster barrels, and super duty upholstery (with double liner and web straps under every screw). The BOUNDER Plus also features tandem cross struts, middle vertical support strut, seat rails supported at five points and back upholstery attached with machine screws.

722 **Bounder Power Wheelchair**
21st Century Scientific
4915 N Industrial Way
Coeur D Alene, ID 83815-8931
208-667-8800
800-448-3680
FAX: 208-667-6600
e-mail: 21st@wheelchairs.com
wheelchairs.com

*Ronald E. Prior, Ph.D., CEO*
*RD Davidson, Sales/Marketing Director*
*Susan Harris, CFO*

Available in a variety of widths from 16 to 18 inches for users up to 250 pounds. The rugged frame is constructed with steel tubing. The standard 12 position Adjustable Front Forks, made of 1/4 inch thick steel, provides impact dampening and seat tilt adjustment. A Dual Group 27 Sliding Battery Box provides extended range and easy battery maintenance. *$8695.00*

723 **Damaco D90**
Damaco
28918 Hancock Parkway
Valencia, CA 91355
661-775-2020
87- 52- 228
FAX: 661-775-2025
www.atbatt.com

Damaco D90 Wheelchairs use Sealed Lead Acid batteries (SLA). SLA batteries do not charge quickly. Typical charge time is 8-16 hours. If you depend on your Damaco D90 wheelchair to be fully operational at all times, we recommend that you invest in two batteries and one of our Battery Tender chargers so you will always have a spare. *$2495.00*

724 **Gem Wheelchair & Scooter Service: Mobility & Homecare**
17639 Union Tpke
Flushing, NY 11366-1515
718-969-8600
800-943-3578
FAX: 718-969-8300
e-mail: help@gemwheelchairservice.com
www.gemwheelchairservice.com/

GEM sells, repairs and rents all makes and models of manual and motorized wheelchairs, power scooters, ramps, stairway lifts, and homecare products including diapers, chux, and bathroom safety equipment. Clients are in all five New York City Boroughs and Nassau County. Medicare and Medicaid accepted, pick-up and delivery, loaner equipment, and while-u-wait repair services available. Gem also buys and sells used equipment. Wholesale and retail services available.

725 **Geronimo**
Redman Powerchair
Ste 202
3840 S Palo Verde Rd
Tucson, AZ 85714-2076
520-294-1466
800-727-6684
FAX: 520-294-1460

*Arnie Johnson, Owner*

Wheelchair offering direct drive, two year electronic guarantee and micro controls.

726 **Invacare IVC Tracer EX2 Wheelchair with Legrest**
Maxi Aids
42 Executive Blvd
Farmingdale, NY 11735-4710
631-752-0521
800-522-6294
FAX: 631-752-0689
TTY: 631-752-0738
e-mail: sales@maxiaids.com
maxiaids.com

*Elliott Zaretsky, Founder and President*
*Bob Messenger, Clinical Respiratory Specialist*

The Tracer EX2 combines the design and technology of the Invacare 9000 A true dual axle position allows for repositioning the 24 inch rear wheels and 8 inch casters for adult and hemi seat-to-floor heights. The new design also makes it possible to interchange components with the 9000 series chairs. *$189.95*

727 **Jet 3 Ultra Power Wheelchair**
Maxi Aids
42 Executive Blvd
Farmingdale, NY 11735-4710
631-752-0521
800-522-6294
FAX: 631-752-0689
TTY: 800-281-3555
e-mail: sales@maxiaids.com
www.maxiaids.com

*Elliott Zaretsky, Founder and President*

Delivers a broad range of standard performance features like Active-Trac Suspension and a powerful 50 amp PG VSI controller on a very compact and maneuverable frame.

728 **One Thousand FS**
Fortress
P.O.Box 489
Clovis, CA 93613-489
559-322-5437
FAX: 559-323-0299

Add-on power system installs in minutes, enabling the driver to relax and drive anywhere with smooth, silent electric power.

729 **Permobil Max 90**
Permobil
4020 Christopher Way
Plano, TX 75024
877-394-3941
e-mail: mumu.moorthi@sigmabatteries.com
www.sigmabatteries.com
The power wheelchair for those needing an easily maneuverable and quiet indoor chair but who also need to use their chair outdoors.

730 **Permobil Super 90**
Permobil
4020 Christopher Way
Plano, TX 75024
877-394-3941
e-mail: mumu.moorthi@sigmabatteries.com
www.sigmabatteries.com
The power wheelchair is designed for travel over uneven and hilly terrain outdoors and indoors.

731 **Power Wheelchairs**
LaBac Systems
3845 Forest St
Denver, CO 80207-2516
800-370-6808
www.falconrehab.net
*Daniel*
Power tilt and recline seating systems for wheelchairs, offering more comfort and dependability for the physically challenged.

732 **Power for Off-Pavement**
Redman Powerchair
601 S Pantano Road Suite 107
3840 S Palo Verde Rd
Tucson, AZ 85710-2076
520-546-6002
800-727-6684
FAX: 520-546-5530
e-mail: info@redmanpowerchair.com
www.redmanpowerchair.com
*Don Redman, CEO*
*Paula Redman, CFO*
*Scott Evans, Regulatory Affairs*
*Samuel Redman, Sales manager*
Power-drive wheelchair has a solid seat and can handle safely and securely knolls and off-pavement terrain.

## Wheelchairs: Racing

733 **Eagle Sportschairs, LLC**
2351 Parkwood Rd
Snellville, GA 30039-4003
770-972-0763
800-932-9380
FAX: 770-985-4885
e-mail: eaglesportschairs@gmail.com
www.eaglesportschairs.com
*Barry Ewing, Owner*
The Eagle line of custom lightweight performance chairs includes a range of options to fit all racing and sport needs including; track, baseball, quad-rugby, tennis, field events and waterskiing. Also popular for daily use. We are able to customize any chair to accommodate size and disability and all frames have a full five year warranty.

734 **East Penn Manufacturing Company**
East Penn Manufacturing Company
Deka Road P.O.Box 147
Lyon Station, PA 19536-147
610-682-6361
FAX: 610-682-4781
e-mail: eastpenn@eastpenn-delu.com
eastpenn-deka.com
*Harold DeLight, Breidegam*
*Chairman*
Specially engineered for demanding deep-cycle applications Gelled electrolyte Deka Dominator Batteries provides maintenance-free operation, longer battery life and hours of reliable performance. Their excellent recharge characteristics provide quick turn around time.

735 **Invacare Top End**
1 Invacare Way
Elyria, OH 44035-4107
440-329-6000
800-333-6900
FAX: 877- 61- 799
e-mail: info@invacare.com
invacare.com
*Mal Mixon, CEO*
*Joe Lewarski, VP of Clinical Affairs*
*Bob Messenger, Clinical Respiratory Specialist*
Manufacturers of light weight, rigid, sport-specific wheelchairs such as the Eliminator line of racing chairs,T-3 tennis and softball chairs, and the Terminator for quad rugby and basketball. The Excelerator, XLT three-wheel hand cycle for adults and juniors. Check out our full line of wheelchairs to fit every need. $1,895-$2,495

736 **Invacare Top End Excelerator XLT Gold Handcyle**
Maxi Aids
42 Executive Blvd
Farmingdale, NY 11735-4710
631-752-0521
800-522-6294
FAX: 631-752-0689
TTY: 631-752-0738
e-mail: sales@maxiaids.com
maxiaids.com
*Elliott Zaretsky, Founder and President*
It's been completely re-designed to be light and faster with more control than ever before. The 27 speeds operated by Shimano Rapid fire hands-on-shifter/brake delivers smooth, responsive shifting and braking right at your fingertips. No foot pedaling! *$3036.00*

# Associations

## General Disabilities

**737 ACS Federal Healthcare**
5270 Shawnee Rd
Alexandria, VA 22312-2310
703-941-4387
FAX: 703-310-0126

*Helene Fisher, VP*
Project RSVP supports the SSA's initiative to expand operations vocational rehabilitation services through a national network of private providers. Rehabilitation companies interested in gaining access to a new client base, acquiring a new funding stream, and developing creative service delivery and entrepreneurial partnerships, may benefit from such a program.

**738 AHEAD Association**
107 Commerce Centre Drive
Suite 204
Huntersville, NC 28078-5870
704-947-7779
FAX: 704-948-7779
e-mail: ahead@ahead.org
www.ahead.org

*Stephan J Smith, Exec. Dir.*
*Richard Allegra, Professional Dev. Dir.*
*Scott Lissner, President-Elect*
*Jean Ashmore, President*
The premiere professional association committed to full participation of persons with disabilities in postsecondary education. AHEAD values diversity, personal growth and development and creativity. Promotes leadership and exemplary practices. Provides professional development and disseminates information. Orchestrates resources through partnership and collaboration. AHEAD dynamically addresses current and emerging issues with respect to disability, and education to achieve universal access.

**739 Abilities!**
201 I U Willets Rd
Albertson, NY 11507-1516
516-465-1400
FAX: 516-465-3358
e-mail: info@abilitiesonline.org
www.abilitiesonline.org

*John.D. Kemp, President/CEO*
*Sheryl P Buchel, SVP/CFO*
*Jessica Swirsky-Gerschitz, President*
*Patrice McCarthy Kuntzler, Exec. Dir.*
Dedicated to creating a world in which people with disabilities will live simply as people.

**740 Acupressure Institute**
1533 Shattuck Ave
Berkeley, CA 94709-1516
510-845-1059
800-442-2232
e-mail: info@acupressure.com
acupressure.com

*Michael Gach, Ph. D., Exec. Dir.*
*Joseph Carter, B.S., L.Ac., Dir. of Acupressure Institute*
*Kathleen Davis, B.A., C.M.T. Di, Teacher*
*Katie Carrin, Instructor*
Since 1976 the Acupressure institute has offered comprehensive acupressure trainings in the traditional Asian Bodywork Therapy (ABT)such as Thai massage and Shiatsu massage to students from around the world. In comparing other Acupressure schools, our trainings provide high quality education to support each student'sprofessional and personal goals, in a setting that encourages communication, respect, and confidentiality and safety for everyone.

**741 Advocacy Center**
590 South Ave
Rochester, NY 14620-1371
585-546-1700
800-650-4967
FAX: 585-546-7069
TTY: 585-546-1700
e-mail: info@advocacycenter.com
advocacycenter.com

*Paul Shew, Executive Director*
*Joyce Steel, Director*
Is a non profit organization located in New York State that educates, supports, and advocates with people who have disabilities, their families and circles of support. A diverse consumer-driven organization leading New York State in shaping the future through the development of innovative, outcome-oriented, and quality initiatives for people with disabilities, their families, and circle of support.

**742 Advocacy Center for Persons with Disabilitites**
2728 Centerview Dr
Ste 102
Tallahassee, FL 32301-6298
800-342-0823
FAX: 850-488-8640
TTY:800-346-4127
e-mail: info@advocacycenter.org
www.advocacycenter.org

*Bob Whitney, Executive Director*
*Paige Morgan, Executive Assistant*
A non-profit organization providing protection and advocacy services in the State of Florida. The Center's mission is to advance the dignity, equality, self-determination and expressed choices of individuals with disabilities.

**743 Advocates for Children of New York**
151 W 30th St
5th Fl
New York, NY 10001
212-947-9779
FAX: 212-947-9790
e-mail: info@advocatesforchildren.org
advocatesforchildren.org

*Kim Sweet, Executive Director*
*Jamie A Levitt, President*
*Barry Ford, Treasurer*
*Harriet Chan King, Secretary*
AFC works on behalf of children from infancy to age 21 who are at greatest risk for school-based discrimination and/or academic failure. These include children with disabilities, ethnic minorities, immigrants, homeless children, foster care children, limited English proficient children and those living in poverty.

**744 Alliance for Technology Access**
1119 Old Humboldt Rd
Jackson, TN 38305
731-554-5282
800-914-3017
FAX: 731-554-5283
TTY: 731-554-5284
e-mail: atainfo@ataccess.org
www.ataccess.org

*Margaret Doumitt, Executive Director*
*James Allison, President*
The ATA is a growing national network of technology resource centers, organizations, individuals and companies. ATA encourages and facilitates the empowerment of people with disabilities to participate fully in their communities. Through public education, information and referral, capacity building in community organizations, and advocacy/policy efforts, the ATA enables millions of people to live, learn, work, define their futures, and achieve their dreams.

745 **American Academy of Environmental Medicine**
6505 E Central Ave #296
Wichita, KS 67206-1924 316-684-5500
FAX: 316-684-5709
e-mail: administrator@aaemonline.org
www.aaemonline.org

*De Rogers Fox, Executive Director*
*Robin Bernhoft, M.D., President*
*Amy Dean D.O., President-Elect*
*Charles L. Crist, M.D., Secretary*

Environmental Medicine is the comprehensive, proactive and preventive strategic approach to medical care dedicated to the evaluation, management, and prevention of the adverse consequences resulting from Environmentally Triggered Illnesses.

746 **American Academy of Pediatrics**
141 NW Point Blvd
Elk Grove Village, IL 60007-1098 847-434-4000
800-433-9016
FAX: 847-434-8000
e-mail: kidsdocs@aap.org
www.aap.org

*Rober.W. Block,MD,FAAP, President*
*Thomas K. McInerny, MD, FAAP, President-Elect*
*Errol Alden, MD, Executive Director/CEO*
*O. Marion Burton, MD, FAAP, Immediate Past President*

Organization of 60,000 pediatricians committed to the attainment of optimal physical, mental, and social health and well-being for all infants, children, adolescents and young adults.

747 **American Association of Children's Residential Centers**
11700 W Lake Park Dr
Milwaukee, WI 53224-3021 877-332-2272
FAX: 877-362-2272
e-mail: info@aacrc-dc.org
www.aacrc-dc.org

*Kari Sisson, National Dir.*
*Margaret Vimont LCSW, President*
*Okpara Rice, Secretary*
*William P. Martone, MS, President*

The American Association of Children's Residential Centers believes that children and adolescents, and their families, are entitled to treatment which offers the maximum opportunity for growth and change. AACRC believes that clinically crafted residential treatment options, ranging from community based homes through institutional environments, are essential components in a comprehensive system of behavioral health care.

748 **American Association of Oriental Medicine**
9650 Rockville Pike
Bethesda, MD 20814 866-455-7999
FAX: 301-634-7099
www.aaaomonline.org

*Michael Jabbour, MS, LAc, President*
*Kimberley Benjamin, LAc, VP*
*Jane Yu, LAc, Secretary*
*John B. Barrett, CPA, LAc, Treasurer*

Dedicated to the promotion and advancement of high ethical, educational, and professional standards in the practice of acupuncture and Oriental medicine (AOM) in the U.S. The name of the company is ""American Association of Acupuncture and Oriental Medicine""

749 **American Association of People with Disabilities**
2013 H Street, NW, 5th Floor
Washington, DC 20006-1675 202-457-0046
800-840-8844
FAX: 202-457-0473
TTY: 800-840-8844
e-mail: referrals@aapd.com
www.aapd.com

*Mark Perriello, President/CEO*
*Helena Berger, Exec VP & COO*
*Jason Mida, VP of Dev.*
*Lara Schwartz, VP of External Affairs*

The largest national nonprofit cross-disability member organization in the United States, dedicated to ensuring economic self-sufficiency and political empowerment for the more than 56 million Americans with disabilities. AAPD works in coalition with other disability organizations for the full implimentation and enforcement of disability nondiscrimination laws, particularly the Americans With Disabilities Act (ADA) of 1990 and the Rehabilitation Act of 1973.

750 **American Board of Clinical Metal Toxicology**
4889 Smith Rd
West Chester, OH 45069 513-863-6277
80- 35- 222
FAX: 513-942-3934
e-mail: treasurer@abcmt.org
www.abcmt.org

*Rashid A Buttar, Chairman*
*James M. Holbert, MD, PhD, Vice Chairman*
*James Smith, DO, Treasurer*
*J Joseph Holliday, MD, Director*

Dedicated to establishing and maintaining guidelines and standards for the practice of Clinical Metal Toxicology and to the assurance of a superior level of competence on the part of physicians treating patients with this psectrum of expanding global afflictions.

751 **American Board of Professional Disability Consultants**
Belle Meade Office Park. 4525 Hardi
3rd Fl
Nashville, TN 37205 615-327-2984
FAX: 615-327-9235
e-mail: americanbd@aol.com
www.americandisability.org

Certifies physicians, psychologists, attorneys, and counselors as specialists in disability and personal injury. The name of the company is ""American Board of Disability Analysts (ABDA)""

752 **American Botanical Council**
6200 Manor Rd
Austin, TX 78723-3754 512-926-4900
FAX: 512-926-2345
e-mail: abc@herbalgram.org
www.herbalgram.org

*Mark Blumenthal, Executive Director/Founder*
*Lucy Bruno, Executive Assistant*
*Gayle Engels, Special Projects Director*

The American Botanical Council (ABC) is the leading independent, nonprofit, international member-based organization providing education using science-based ad traditional information to promote the responsible use of herbal medicine.

753 **American Camping Association**
5000 State Road 67 N
Martinsville, IN 46151-7902 765-342-8456
800-428-2267
FAX: 765-342-2065
acacamps.org

*Tisha Bolger, President*
*Peg Smith, CEO*
*Scott Brody, VP*
*Dayna Hardine, VP*

The American Camp Association is a community of camp professionals who, for nearly 100 years, have joined together to share our knowledge and experience and to ensure the quality of camp programs. Because of our diverse 7,000 plus emmbership and exceptional programs, children and adults have the opportunity to learn powerful lessons in cmmunity, character-building, skill development, and healthy-living—lessons that can be learned nowhere else.

**754 American Chiropractic Association**
1701 Clarendon Blvd
Arlington, VA 22209-2721
703-276-8800
FAX: 703-243-2593
e-mail: memberinfo@acatoday.org
www.acatoday.org

*Keith S. Overland, DC, President*
*Bill O'Connelll, VP*
*Janet Ridgely, Deputy Exec VP*
*Dean Millard, Information Systems Senior Dir.*

The ACA is a professional organization representing Doctors of Chiropratic. Its mission is to preserve, protect, improve, and promote the chiropractic profession and the services of Doctors of Chiropratic for the benefit of the patients they serve. The purpose of the ACA is to provide leadership in health care and a positive vision for the chiropractic profession and its natural approach to health and wellness.

**755 American College of Advancement in Medicine**
8001 Irvine Center Dr
Ste 825
Irvine, CA 92618-2967
949-309-3520
800-532-3688
FAX: 949-309-3538
e-mail: info@acam.org
www.acam.org

*Mark O'Neal Speight, MD, President/CEO*
*Jeffrey Morrison, MD, Executive VP*
*Allen Green, MD, Treasurer and CFO*
*Dana Cohen, MD, Director*

The American College for Advancement in Medicine (ACAM)is a not-for-profit society dedicated to educating physicians and other health care professionals on the latest findings and emerging procedures in preventive/nutritional medicine. ACAM's goals are to improve skills, knowledge and diagnostic procedures as they relate to complimentary and alternative medicine; to support research; and to develop awareness of alternative methods of medical treatment.

**756 American College of Nurse Midwives**
8403 Colesville Rd
Ste 1550
Silver Spring, MD 20910-6374
240-485-1800
FAX: 240-485-1818
e-mail: info@acnm.org
midwife.org

*Lorrie Kaplan, Exec. Dir.*
*Kathleen Przybylaski, Mgr of Administration*
*Melinda Bush, Program Coordinator*
*Holly Burns, Financial Specialist*

The American College of Nurse-Midwives (ACNM) is the oldest women's health care organization in the U.S. ACNM provides research, accredits midwifery education programs, administers and promotes continuing education programs, establishes clinical practice standards, creates liasons with state and federal agencies and members of Congress.

**757 American Counseling Association**
5999 Stevenson Ave
Alexandria, VA 22304-3304
703-823-0252
800-347-6647
FAX: 800-473-2329
TTY: 703-823-6862
e-mail: webmaster@counseling.org
counseling.org

*Richard Yep, Executive Director*
*Marcheta Evans, Immediate Past President*
*Stacy Shaver, Executive Office*
*Brad Erford, President*

The American Counseling Association is a not-for-profit, professional and educational organization that is dedicated to the growth and enhancement of the counseling profession.

**758 American Herbalists Guild**
PO Box 230741
Boston, M 02123
857-350-3128
e-mail: ahgoffice@earthlink.net
www.americanherbalistsguild.com

*Bevin Clare, M.S., R.H., CN, VP*
*Roy Upton RH(AHG), Board of Advisors*
*KP Khalsa, RH(AHG), President*
*David N. Harder, RH (AHG) , Treasurer*

Founded in 1989 as a non-profit, educational organization to represent the goals and voices of herbalists specializing in the medicinal use of plants. Our primary goal is to promote a high level of professionalism and education in the study and practice of theraputic herbalism.

**759 American Holistic Medical Association**
27629 Chagrin Blvd. Suite 213
Woodmere, OH 44122
216-292-6644
FAX: 216-292-6688
e-mail: info@holisticmedicine.org
www.holisticmedicine.org

*Molly Roberts, M.D., M.S, President*
*David Riley MD, Member at Large*
*Natalie Talis, BA, Marketing Manager*
*Steve.L Caldwell, Executive Director/CEO*

The mission of the AMHA is to support practitioners in their evolving personal and professional development as healers and to educate physicians about holistic medicine.

**760 American Massage Therapy Association**
500 Davis St
Ste 900
Evanston, IL 60201-4695
847-864-0123
877-905-2700
FAX: 847-864-5196
e-mail: info@amtamassage.org
amtamassage.org

*Cynthia Ribeiro, President*
*Rachel Mann, VP*
*Nancy M. Porambo, VP*
*Jeff Smoot, VP*

AMTA works to establish massage therapy as integral to the maintenance of good health and complementary to other therapeudic processes; to advance the profession through ethics and standards, certification, school accreditation, continuing education, professional publications, legislative efforts, public education, and fostering the development of members.

**761 American Occupational Therapy Association**
4720 Montgomery Lane
Suite 600
Bethesda, MD 20824-1220
301-652-2682
800-789-2682
FAX: 301-652-7711
TTY: 800-377-8555
e-mail: praota@aota.org
aota.org

*Florence Clark, President*
*Virginia Stoffel, VP*
Advances the quality, availability, use and support of occupational therapy through standard setting, advocacy, education, and research on behalf of its members.

**762 American Organization for Bodywork Therapies of Asia**
1010 Haddonfield Berlin Rd
Ste 408
Voorhees, NJ 08043- 3514
856-782-1616
FAX: 856-782-1653
e-mail: office@aobta.org
www.aobta.org

*Wayne Mylin, President*
*Beverly Sonen, VP*
*Stuart Watts, Treasure/Secretary*
*Angela.H. McConnell, Director of Membership*
The American Organization for Bodywork Therapies of Asia (AOBTA) is a professional membership organizaton which promotes Asian Bodywork Therapy and its practitioners while honoring a diversity of disciplines. AOBTA serves its community of members by supporting appropriate credentialing; defining scope of practice and educational standards; and providing resources for training, professional development and networking. AOBTA advocates public policy to protect its members.

**763 American Public Health Association**
800 I St NW
Washington, DC 20001-3710
202-777-2742
FAX: 202-777-2534
TTY:202-777-2500
e-mail: comments@apha.org
apha.org

*George Benjamin, Executive Director*
*Melvin D. Shipp, OD, MPH, DrPH, President*
*Adewale Troutman, MD, MPH, MA, President-Elect*
*Richard J. Cohen, PhD, FACHE, Treasurer*
Founded in 1872, APHA is the oldest, largest and most diverse organization of public health professionals in the world. The association works to protect all Americans and their communities from preventable, seruious health threats. APHA represents a broad array of health officials, educators, environmentalists, policy-makers and health providers at all levels working both within and outside governmental organizations and educational institutions.

**764 American Red Cross**
33 Everett Rd
Albany, NY 12205-6434
518-458-8111
FAX: 518-459-8268
e-mail: news@redcrossneny.org
redcrossneny.org

*Gary Striar, CEO*
*Susan Rounds, COO*
*Gary Ferris, Executive Director*
*Lynn Gilbert, Executive Director*
Today, in addition to domestic disaster relief, the American Red Cross offers compassionate services in five other areas: community services that help the needy; support and comfort for military members and their families; the collection, processing and distribution of lifesaving blood and blood products; educational programs that promote health and safety; and international relief and development programs.

**765 American Self-Help Clearinghouse**
50 Morris Avenue
St Clares Health Services
Denville, NJ 07834
973-625-7107
800-367-6274
FAX: 973-326-9467
e-mail: info@selfhelpgroups.org
www.selfhelpgroups.org

*Edward J Madara MS, Director*
Provides information on national self-help groups and offers training and technical assistance to exisiting and new self-help groups and clearinghouses. It has compiled a national database of over 800 of these model groups. Provides information on resource groups such as Violence Anonymous, Batterers Anonymous, and Stalkers' Victims Support Groups.

**766 American Society for the Alexander Technique**
PO Box 2307
Dayton, OH 45401-2307
937-586-3732
800-473-0620
FAX: 937-586-3699
e-mail: info@AmSATonline.org
www.amsat.ws

*Kathryn Miranda, Chair*
*Ann Rodiger, Treasurer*
*Rebecca Nettl-Fiol, Member at Large*
*Meg Jolley, Member at Large*
The Alexander Technique is a proven, effective self help method for improving balance and coordination and increasing movement awareness by eliminating habitual reactions of misuse in every day activities. AmSats mission is to define, maintain and promote the Alexander Technique at its highest standard of professional practice and conduct.

**767 American Society of Bariatric Physicians**
2821 S Parker Rd
Ste 625
Aurora, CO 80014-2711
303-770-2526
FAX: 303-779-4834
e-mail: laurie@asbp.org
asbp.org

*Laurie Traetow,CPA, Executive Director*
*Stacy Schmidt,PhD, Health Director*
*David Bryman, DO, President*
*Deborah Bade Horn DO, MPH, MS, Vice President*
The American Society of Bariatric Physicians is an international association and allied health care professionals with special interest and experience in the comprehensive treatment of overweight, obesity and related disorders.

**768 American Society of Clinical Hypnosis**
140 N Bloomingdale Rd
Bloomingdale, IL 60108-1017
630-980-4740
FAX: 630-351-8490
e-mail: info@asch.net
www.asch.net

*Michael White, Communication/Marketing Director*
*Erickson, MD Founder*
To provide and encourage education programs to further, in every ethical way, the knowledge, understanding, and application of hypnosis in health care; to encourage research and scientific publication in the field of hypnosis; to promote the further recognition and acceptance of hypnosis as an important tool in clinical health care and focus for scientific research; to cooperate with other professional societies that share mutual goals, ethics, and interests

**769 Association for Applied Psychophysiology and Biofeedback**
10200 W 44th Ave
Ste 304
Wheat Ridge, CO 80033-2840
303-422-8436
800-477-8892
e-mail: info@aapb.org
www.aapb.org

*Francine Butler, Executive Director*
*Jeffrey Bolek, PhD, President*
*Richard Harvey, PhD, Treasurer*
*Richard Sherman, President-Elect*
Provides names and phone numbers of local chapters. Mission is to advance the development, dissemination and utilization of knowledge about applied psychophysiology and biofeedback to improve health and the quality of life through research, education, and practice.

**770 Association for Persons in Supported Employment**
PO Box 1280
Rockville, MD 20849
301-279-0060
FAX: 301-251-3762
e-mail: jenny@apse.org
www.apse.org

*David Hoff, President*
*Susan Rinne, VP*
*Laura.A. Owens,PhD, Executive Director*
*Vic Gable, Treasurer*
Supported employment enables people with disabilities who have not been successfully employed to work and contribute to society. Focuses on a person's abiliities and provides the supports the individual needs to be successful on a long-term basis.

**771 Association for Persons with Severe Handicaps (TASH)**
1001 Connecticut Avenue, NW
Ste 285
Washington, DC 20036
202-540-9020
FAX: 202-540-9019
e-mail: info@tash.org
www.tash.org

*David Westlin, President*
*Barbara Trader, Executive Director*
*Jean Trainor, VP*
*Jonathan Riethmaier, Advocacy Communications Manager*
International association of people with disabilities, their family members, other advocates and professionals, fighting for a society in which inclusion of all people in all aspects of society is the norm.

**772 Association of Educational Therapists**
7044 S. 13th St.
Oak Creek, WI 90064-5315
414-908-4949
FAX: 41- 76- 800
e-mail: aet_membership@aetonline.org
www.aetonline.org

*Daniel Franklin, PhD, BCET, Treasurer*
*Marcy Dann, MA, BCET, President*
*Jeanette Rivera, MA, BCET, Secretary*
*Vicki Bergoff, JD, ET/P, Director*
Educational Therapy offers children and adults with learning disabilities and other learning challenges a wide range of intensive, individualized interventions designed to remediate learning problems.

**773 Association of University Centers on Disabilities**
AUCD
1010 Wayne Ave
Ste 920
Silver Spring, MD 20910-5646
301-588-8252
FAX: 301-588-2842
e-mail: aucdinfo@aucd.org
www.aucd.org

*George Jesien, Executive Director*
*A. Anthony Antosh, EdD, President*
*Leslie Cohen, JD, Treasurer*
*Karen Edwards, MD, MPH, Secretary*
The central office for the 61 University Centers for Excellence programs and 21 Mental Retardation and Developmental Disabilities Research Centers and is their representative to the federal government. UCEDD's are located at major universities and teaching hospitals in all 50 states, the District of Columbia and many US territories. UCCED's target their activities to support the independence, productivity and integration into the community of individuals with developmental disabilities.

**774 Association on Higher Education and Disability (AHEAD)**
107 Commerce Centre Dr
Ste 204
Huntersville, NC 28078- 5870
704-947-7779
FAX: 704-948-7779
e-mail: ahead@ahead.org
www.ahead.org

*Richard Allegra, Director of Professional Dev.*
*Jean Ashmore, President*
*Michael Johnson, Treasurer*
*Scott Lissner, President-Elect*
International, multicultural organization of proessionals committed to full participation in higher education for persons with disabilities. Plans and develops training programs, workshops, publications and conferences. Founded in 1977 to address the need and concern for upgrading the quality of services and support available to persons with disabilities in higher education.

**775 Bastyr University Natural Health Clinic**
3670 Stone Way N
Seattle, WA 98103-8004
206-834-4110
FAX: 206-834-4107
bastyrcenter.org

Bastyr Center is the teaching clinic of Bastyr University, which is a leading expert in natural medicine. We provide a team care approach that involves one licensed, experienced practicioner and two or three students, all invested in the outcome of your care. Working together with you to discover your own unique route to wellness. By offering the latest scientific information as well as the wisdom of ancient healing we can safeguard the health of the whole family.

**776 Beach Center on Families and Disability**
University of Kansas
1200 Sunnyside Ave
Rm 3136
Lawrence, KS 66045-7600
785-864-7600
FAX: 785-864-7605
TTY:785-864-3434
e-mail: beachcenter@ku.edu
www.beachcenter.org

*Ann Turnbull, Co-Founder, Co-Director*
*Rud Turnbull, Co-Founder, Co-Director*
*Victoria Cotsworth, Project Coordinator*
*Peter Griggs, Evaluation Coordinator*
A federally funded center that conducts research and training in the factors that contribute to the successful functioning of families with members who have disabilities.

**777 Birth Defect Research for Children**
976 Lake Baldwin Lane, Suite 104
Orlando, FL 3281
407-566-8304
e-mail: staff@birthdefects.org
www.birthdefects.org

*Betty Mekdeci, Manager/Founder*
A nonprofit organization that provides information about birth defects of all kinds to parents and professionals. Offers a library of medical books and files of information on less common categories of birth defects and is involved in research to discover possible links between environmental exposures and birth defects.

**778 Bonnie Prudden Myotherapy**
4330 E. Havasu Road PO Box 65240
Tucson, AZ 85718
520-529-3979
800-221-4634
FAX: 520-529-6679
e-mail: info@bonnieprudden.com
bonnieprudden.com

*Enid Whittaker, Associate Director*
Myotherapy is a method for relaxing muscle spasm, improving circulation and alleviating pain. Pressure is applied using elbows, knuckled or fingers, and held for several seconds to defuse trigger points. The success of this method depends upon the use of specific corrective exercises of the freed muscles.

**779 Brain Injury Association of America**
1608 Spring Hill Rd
Ste 110
Vienna, VA 22812
703-761-0750
800-444-6443
FAX: 703-761-0755
e-mail: shconnors@biausa.org
www.biausa.org

*Susan H Connors, President/CEO*
*Mary Ritter, Exec VP/COO*
*Marianna Abashian, Dir. of Professional Svcs*
*Amy C. Colberg, Dir. of Govt Affairs*
Founded in 1980, the Brain Injury Association of America (BIAA) is the leading national organization serving and representing individuals, families and professionals who are touched by a life-altering, often devistating, traumatic brain injury (TBI) Together with its network of more then 40 charted state affiliates, as well as hundreds of local chapters and support groups across the country, the BIAA provides information, education and support to assist the 5.3 million living with brain injuries

**780 CAPP National Parent Resource Center Federation for Children with Special Needs**
45 Bromfield St
10th Fl
Boston, MA 02108
866-815-8122
FAX: 617-542-7832
e-mail: info@ppal.net
www.ppal.net

*Lisa Lambert, Executive Director*
*Chip Wilder, Chair*
*Joanna Allison, Vice Chair*
*Anne Silver, Treasurer*
A parent-run resource system designed to further the needs and goals of family-centered, community-based coordinated care for children with special health needs and their families. Offers written materials, training packages, workshops and presentations for parents and professionals on special education, health care financing and other topics.

**781 CARF Rehabilitation Accreditation Commission**
6951 E Southpoint Rd
Tucson, AZ 85756
520-325-1044
888-281-6531
FAX: 520-318-1129
TTY: 888-281-6531
e-mail: info@carf.org
carf.org

*Brian J Boon, Ph.D., President/CEO*
*Amanda E Birch, Administrator of Operations*
*Cindy L. Johnson, CPA, Chief Resource*
*Darren M. Lehrfeld, Chief Accreditation Officer*
CARF serves as the standards-setting and accrediting body for rehabilitation and life enhancement programs and services. The independent, not-for-profit commission provides accrediation of human service providers in the areas of aging services, behavioral health, child and youth services, DMEPOS, employment and community services, medical rehabilitation, and opioid treatment programs.

**782 Canine Companions for Independence**
National Offices
P.O.Box 446
Santa Rosa, CA 95402-446
707-577-1700
800-572-2275
TTY:707-577-1756
e-mail: info@cci.org
www.cci.org

*Alan Feinne, CFO*
*Corey Hudson, CEO*
*Paul Mundell, National Dir. of Canine Programs*
*Anne Gittinger, Chair of Board of Officers*
A nonprofit organization that enhances the lives of people with disabilities by providing highly trained assistance dogs and ongoing support to ensure quality partnerships.

**783 Canine Helpers for the Handicapped**
5699 Ridge Rd
Lockport, NY 14094-9408
716-433-4035
FAX: 716-439-0822
e-mail: chhdogs@aol.com
www.caninehelpers.org

*Beverly D. Underwood, Executive Director*
A nonprofit organization devoted to custom training Assistance Dogs to assist people with disabilities to lead more independent, secure lives.

**784 Cape Organization for Rights of the Disabled (CORD)**
106 Bassett Ln
Hyannis, MA 02601-3800
508-775-8300
800-541-0282
FAX: 508-775-7022
TTY: 800-541-0282
e-mail: cordinfo@cilcapecod.org
cilcapecod.org

*Cathy Taylor, ADA Specialist*
The Cape Organization for the Rights of the Disabled (CORD) has been aggresively working since 1984 to advance the independence, productivity, and integration of people with disabilities into mainstream society. CORD is the Center for Independent Living (CIL) and is a member of the Aging and Disability Resources Consortium (ADRC) serving Cape Cod and the Islands.

785 **Case Management Society of America**
6301 Ranch Dr
Little Rock, AR 72223-4623
501-225-2229
800-216-2672
FAX: 501-221-9068
e-mail: cmsa@cmsa.org
cmsa.org

*Mary Beth Newman, MSN, RN-B, President*
*Nancy Skinner, RN-BC, CCM, President Elect*
*Betty Overbey, RN-BC, CRRN,, Secretary*
*Jose Alejandro, RN-BC, MSN,, Treasurer*

The Case Management Society of America is an international, non-profit organization founded in 1990 dedicated to the support and development of the profession of case management through educational forums, networking opportunities and legislative involvement.

786 **Center for Assistive Technology and Environmental Access**
490 Tenth St NW
Atlanta, GA 30332-156
404-894-4960
800-726-9119
FAX: 404-894-9320
TTY: 404-894-4960
e-mail: catea@coa.gatech.edu
www.catea.org

*Carrie Bruce, Research Scientist*
*Karen Milchus, Research Engineer*
*Charlie Drummond, Administrative Assistant*
*Sarah Endicott, Research Scientist*

CATEA supports individuals with disabilities of any age within the State of Georgia and beyond through expert services, research, design and technological development, information dissemination, and educational programs.

787 **Center for Disability Resources**
Pediatrics, School Of Medicine,Univ Of S. Carolina
8301 Farrow Rd
Columbia, SC 29208-1
803-935-5231
FAX: 803-935-5059
e-mail: steve.wilson@uscmed.sc.edu
uscm.med.sc.edu/cdrhome/

*Jerome D. Odom Ph.D., Exec. Dir.*
*Susan Greer, Fiscal/Foundation Coordinator*
*Mechelle English, Senior Dev. Dir.*
*Kim E. Creek, PhD., Dir.*

A University Affiliated Program which develops model programs designed to serve persons with disabilities and to train students in fields related to disabilities.

788 **Center for Mind/Body Studies**
5525 Connecticut Ave NW
Suite 415
Washington, DC 20015- 1813
202-966-7338
FAX: 202-966-2589
e-mail: center@cmbm.org
www.cmbm.org

*Jim S. Gordon, MD, Founder & Dir.*
*Jo Cooper, Dir. of Nutrition Programs*
*Rosemary Murrain, Dir. of Administration & Finance*
*Amy Shinal, Clinical Dir.*

The Center for Mind-Body Medicine is a non-profit educational organization dedicated to reviving the spirit and transforming the practice of medicine. The Center is working to create a more effective, comprehensive and compassionate model of healthcare and education. The Center's model combines the precision of modern science with the best of the world's healing traditions.

789 **Center for Universal Design**
NC State University
PO Box 8613
Raleigh, NC 27695-8613
919-515-3082
800-647-6777
FAX: 919-515-8951
e-mail: cud@ncsu.edu
www.design.ncsu.edu/cud

*Sean Vance, Acting Director*
*Richard C Duncan, MRP:, Director of Training*
*Leslie Young, M.S.,, Director of Design*
*Angela Brockelsby, Director of Communications*

A federally funded resource center that works toward improving housing for people with disabilities. Provides technical assistance, training and publications on accessible housing and universal design.

790 **Change**
1413 Park Rd NW
Washington, DC 20010-2801
202-387-3725
FAX: 202-387-3729
e-mail: changeinc@hotmail.com

*Gracie Rolling, Executive Director*
*Therman Walker, President*
*Preston Hursey Jr., VP*

Offers counseling/assessment, emergency food and clothing referrals, rental assistance and job assistance to disabled persons in the District of Columbia area.

791 **Child and Parent Resource Institute**
600 Sanatorium Road
London, ON, ON N6H-3W7
519-858-2774
877-494-2774
FAX: 519-858-3913
TTY: 519-858-0257
e-mail: Gillian.Kriter@ontario.ca
www.cpri.ca

*Dr. Shannon Stewart, Program Manager*
*Laura Theall-Honey, Research Coordinator*
*Liz Willits, Research Project Assistant*
*Melissa Currie, Manager (A)*

Provides highly specialized services to children and youth from 0-18 years of age with complex mental health and/or developmental challenges on a short term inpatient and community basis.

792 **Children's Alliance**
420 Capitol Ave
Frankfort, KY 40601-2837
502-875-3399
FAX: 502-223-4200
e-mail: michelle@childrensallianceky.org
www.childrensallianceky.org

*Michelle Sanborn, President*
*Mary Smither, Office Assistant*
*Melissa Muse, Member Services Director*
*Kathy Adams, Director of Public Policy*

An association of individuals and human services organizations committed to being a voice for at-risk children and families. Interacts with the legislative and executive branches of government and assists members in developing services that most effectively meet the needs of at-risk children and families.

793 **Children's National Medical Center**
111 Michigan Ave NW
Washington, DC 20010-2916
202-476-2327
888-884-2327
FAX: 202-476-2270
e-mail: tbear@childrensnational.org
www.cnmc.org

*Kurt Newman, MD, President/CEO*
*Raymond S. Sczudlo, Esq, Exec VP, Chief Legal Officer*
*Douglas Myers, Exec VP, CFO*
*Mark Batshaw, MD, Exec VP/CAO*

Our mission is to be preeminent in providing health care services that enhance the health and well-being of children regionally, nationally and internationally. Through leadership and innovation, Children's will create solutions to pediatric health care problems. To meet the unique health care needs of children, adolescents and their families, Children's will excel in Care, Advocacy, Research and Education.

**794 Clay Tree Society**
838 Old Victoria Road
Nanaimo, BC V9R-6A1
250-753-5322
FAX: 250-753-2749
e-mail: claytree@shaw.ca
www.claytree.org

*Patty Buttimer, Vice President*
*Juli Stevenson, Executive Director*
*Peter Jochumsen, President*
*Kim Chadwick, Treasurer*

Non-profit society providing day programming for 75 adults with various developmental disabilities governed by an elected Board of Directors and funded by Community Living British Columbia and BC Gaming.

**795 Community Enterprises**
441 Pleasant Street
Northampton, MA 01061-598
413-584-1460
FAX: 413-586-1121
TTY:413-584-1460
www.communityenterprises.com

*Dick Venne, President/CEO*
*William D. Donahue, Vice-Chair*
*Joanne Carlisle, Secretary/Clerk*
*Kate LaMay-Miller, Chair*

Provide supported education services in a community college setting; supported employment including job training, placement and follow-up; transitional services from group homes and other settings to supported living within the community.

**796 DB-Link**
National Consortium on Deaf-Blindness
345 N. Monmouth Ave.
Monmouth, OR 97361-1329
503-838-8391
800-438-9376
FAX: 503-838-8150
TTY: 800-854-7013
e-mail: info@nationaldb.org
www.nationaldb.org

*Kathy McNulty, Associate Director*
*D Jay Gense, Director*
*John W. Reiman, PhD., Associate Director*
*Joe McNulty, Co-Principal Investigator*

Found at the National Consortium of Deaf-Blindness, DB-LINK is the largest collection of information related to deaf-blindness worldwide. A team of information specialists makes this extensive resource available in response to direct requests, via the NCDB website, through conferences, and via a variety of electronic medium.

**797 Department of Physical Medicine & Rehabilitation at Sinai Hospital**
2401 W Belvedere Ave
Baltimore, MD 21215-5271
410-601-9000
FAX: 410-601-9692
lifebridgehealth.org

*Scott E. Brown, Department Chief*
*Neil Meltzer, President*
*Melanie C. Brown, M.D., Residency Program Dir.*
*Michael Anderson, Core Teaching Faculty*

As one of largest, most comprehensive and most highly respected providers of health-related services to the people of the Northwest Baltimore region, LifeBridge heath advocates preventive services, wellness and fitness services and programs to educate and support the communities it serves. LifeBridge is dedicated to advancing the health of the community through a variety of health and wellness programs and services.

**798 DisAbility LINK**
755 Commerce Drive
Suite 105
Decatur, GA 30030-2613
404-687-8890
800-239-2507
FAX: 404-687-8298
TTY:711
e-mail: info@disabilitylink.org
www.disabilitylink.org

*Larry Brown, Finance Director*
*Linda Pogue, Advocacy Director*
*Danny Housley, Social Media/I&R Coordinator*
*Rashidah Shariff, Youth Advocacy Coordinator*

This center for rights and resources is committed to promoting the rights of all people with disabilities in allowing them to be independent, achieve goals, have access to their community and make decisions for themselves.

**799 Disabled Children's Relief Fund**
PO Box 89
Freeport, NY 11520-89
516-377-1605
FAX: 516-377-3978
www.dcrf.com

National not-for-profit organization that provides modest grants for disabled children with preference given to those with no health insurance. Grants are provided for assistive devices, equipment and rehabilitative services.

**800 Disabled and Alone/Life Services for the Handicapped**
61 Broadway
Suite 510
New York, NY 10006
212-532-6740
800-995-0066
FAX: 212-532-3588
e-mail: info@disabledandalone.org
disabledandalone.org

*Lee Ackerman, Executive Director*
*Leslie D. Park, Chairman*
*Rex L. Davidson, Vice President*
*William G. Shannon, J.D., Treasurer*

A national nonprofit humanitarian organization whose primary concern is the well-being of handicapped persons, particularly when their families can no longer care for them. Disabled and Alone 1) Helps families do sensible planning for and with their disabled children; 2) Provides advocacy and oversight when the parents cannot do so; 3) Advises families, attorneys and financial planners about life planning for a family member with a disability.

**801 Educational Accessibility Services**
Wayne State University
5155 Gullen Mall
1600 UGL
Detroit, MI 48202
313-577-1851
FAX: 313-577-4898
TTY:313-577-3365
e-mail: studentdisability@wayne.edu
www.eas.wayne.edu

*Jane DePriester-Morandini,, Interim Dir.*
*Randie Kruman, M.A., University Counselor II*
*Kimberly Werth, M.A., LLPC, Professional Technician*
*Fran Marlowe, Program Specialist*

To ensure a university experience in which individuals with disabilities have equitable access to programs and to empower students to self advocate i norder to fulfill their academic goals.

802 **Esalen Institute**
55000 Highway 1
Big Sur, CA 93920-9546
831-667-3000
888-837-2536
FAX: 831-667-2724
e-mail: info@esalen.org
www.esalen.org

*Gordon Wheeler, President/CEO*
*Michael Murphy, Founder*
*Dick Price, Founder*
*Tricia McEntee, CFO & CEO-elect*

Founded in 1962 as an alternative education center devoted to the exploration of the world of unrealized human capacities that lies beyond the imagination. Blends East/West philosophies, experiential/didactic workshops, and a steady influx of philosophers, psychologists, artists, and religious thinkers.

803 **Family Resource Center on Disabilities**
20 E. Jackson Blvd.
Suite 300
Chicago, IL 60604-2265
312-939-3513
800-952-4199
FAX: 312-939-7297
TTY: 312-939-3519
e-mail: info@frcd.org
www.frcd.org

Not-for-profit advocacy organization dedicated to improving services for all children with disabilities by providing support and services to affected families, informing parents of their rights, and helping parents become advocates for their children. Offers family support services, training, seminars and information and referral services. Publishes monthly newsletter.

804 **Family Voices**
3701 SAN MATEO BLVD NE
Suite 103
Albuquerque, NM 87110
505-872-4774
888-835-5669
FAX: 505-872-4780
e-mail: lkeene@familyvoices.org
familyvoices.org

*Sophie Arao-Nguyen, Ph.D, Interim Exec. Director*
*Lacey Keene, Dir. of Finance & Administration*
*Adelita Martinez, National Office Mgr*
*Melanie Rubin, Dir. of Communications*

Not-for-profit voluntary organization dedicated to ensuring that children's health issues are addressed as public and private healthcare systems undergo change in communities, states and the nation. National grassroots clearinghouse for information and education in ways to assure and improve health care for children with disabilities and chronic conditions. Provides materials including pamphlets, a newsletter and one-page papers on important topics.

805 **Favarh/Farmington Valley ARC**
225 Commerce Dr
PO Box 1099
Canton, CT 06019-1099
860-693-6662
FAX: 860-693-8662
e-mail: favarh@favarh.org
favarh.org

*Rick Stanton, Creative Arts Coordinator*
*Stephen E. Morris MPA, Business Relations Manager*
*Annie George, Human Resources Director*
*Tim Hennessey, Recreation Director*

Provides a variety of programs and services to adults with developmental, physical or mental disabilities and their families throughout the Farmington Valley communities of Avon, Burlington and more. Favarh's programs are designed to enhance the personal, social, emotional, vocational and living capabilities of persons with disabilities.

806 **Fedcap Rehabilitation Services**
211 W 14th St
New York, NY 10011-7157
212-727-4200
FAX: 212-727-4374
TTY:212-727-4384
e-mail: info@fedcap.org
fedcap.org

*Christine McMahon, President and CEO*
*Michael Kurtz, Chief Financial Officer*
*Joseph Giannetto, Chief Operating Officer*
*Lorrie Lutz, Chief Strategy Officer*

Fedcap helps people with barriers achieve economic independence through employment. Through evaluation, vocational and soft-skills training, job placement, job creation and support programs, each year Fedcap helps thousands of Americans overcome obstacles, rebuild their lives, and find and keep meaningful employment.

807 **Federation for Children with Special Needs**
529 Main Street
Suite 1102
Boston, MA 02129
617-236-7210
800-331-0688
FAX: 617-241-0330
e-mail: fcsninfo@fcsn.org
www.fcsn.org

*Rich Robison, Exec. Dir.*
*Mary Summers, Project Dir.*
*John Sullivan, Dir. of Information Technology*
*Mary Thompson, Dir. of Finance*

The Federation for Children with Special Needs provides information, support, and assistance to parents of children with disabilities, their professional partners, and their communities. We are committed to listening to and learning from families, and encouraging full participation in community life by all people, especially those with disabilities.

808 **Federation of Families for Children's Mental Health**
Ste 280
9605 Medical Center Dr
Rockville, MD 20850-6390
240-403-1901
FAX: 240-403-1909
e-mail: ffcmh@ffcmh.org
www.ffcmh.org

*Sandra Spencer, Executive Director*
*Sue Smith, President*
*Peggy Nikkel, Vice President*
*Sherri Luthe, Secretary*

The FFCMH, a nationally family-run organization serves to provide advocacy at the national level for the rights of children and youth with emotional, behavioral and mental health challenges and their families. Provide leadership and technical assistance to a nation-wide network of family run organizations. Collaborate with family run and other child serving organizations to transform mental health care in America. The correct name is ""National Federation of Families for Children's Mental Health

809 **Feingold Association of the US**
11849 Suncatcher Drive
Fishers, IN 46037
631-369-9340
800-321-3287
FAX: 631-369-2988
e-mail: help@feingold.org
www.feingold.org

*Annette Miller, President*
*Kathleen Bratby MSN, RN, Secretary*
*Larisa Scarbrough, Vice President*
*Gail Wachsmuth, Treasurer*

An organization of families and professionals, the Feingold Association of the United States is dedicated to helping children and adults apply proven dietary techniques for better behavior, learning and health.

**810 Feldenkrais Guild of North America (FGNA)**
5436 N Albina Ave
Portland, OR 97217
503-221-6612
800-775-2118
FAX: 503-221-6616
e-mail: executivedirector@feldenkrais.com
www.feldenkrais.com

*Susan Marshall, Executive Director*
*Robert Black, BA, MSc, President*
*Jaclyn Boone, Vice President*
*Tom Bode, Treasurer*

This is the organization which sets the standards for and certifies all FELDENKRAIS practitioners in North America. In order to practice, a practitioner must be a graduate of an FGNA accredited program (a minimum of 800 instruction hours over a three to four year period), and agree to follow both the Code of Professional Conduct and the Standards of Practice. FGNA may be contacted for further information about the FELDENKRAIS METHOD or for a list of FELDENKRAIS practitioners sorted by region.

**811 Focus Alternative Learning Center**
126 Dowd Avenue
PO Box 452
Canton, CT 06019
860-693-8809
FAX: 860-693-0141
e-mail: info@focuscenterforautism.org
www.focuscenterforautism.org

*Donna Swanson, Exec. Dir.*
*Susan Daly, Finance & Human Resources Dir.*
*Sandy Kissel RN, BSN, MSN, Program Dir.*
*Carol Doiron, LCSW, Dir. of Education Svcs*

A private non profit, licensed clinical and learning center specialized in the treatment of creatively wired and socially challenged kids. We treat kids on the autism spectrum who suffer from high anxiety, experience processing difficulties and learning problems. The name has been changed to ""FOCUS Center for Autism""

**812 George Washington University Health Resource Center**
2134 G St NW
Washington, DC 20052-1
e-mail: askheath@gwu.edu
www.heath.gwu.edu

*Stephen J Trachtenberg, CEO*
*Timothy W. Tong, Ph.D., Dean-School of Engineering*
*Rachelle Heller, Ph.D., Assoc. Dean, Academic Affairs*
*William Roper, Ph.D., Civil & Env Engineer*

National clearinghouse for information about education after high school for people with disabilities. Also serves as an information exchange about educational support services, policies, procedures, adaptations and opportunities on American campuses, vocational-technical schools, adult education programs, independent living centers and other training entities after high school.

**813 Goodwill Industries International**
15810 Indianola Dr
Rockville, MD 20855-2674
301-530-6500
800-741-0186
FAX: 301-530-1516
TTY: 301-530-9759
e-mail: Contactus@goodwill.org
goodwill.org

*Jim Gibbons, President/CEO*
*Lauren Lawson, Public Relations Director*
*Pat Boelter, Vice President of Marketing*
*Paul Spears, SCSEP Program Manager*

Strives to achieve the full participation in society of disabled persons and other individuals with special needs by expanding their opportunities and occupational capabilities through a network of autonomous, nonproft, community-based organizations providing services throughout the world in response to local needs.

**814 HRSA Information Center**
PO Box 2910
Merrifield, VA 22116-2910
888-275-4772
FAX: 703-821-2098
TTY:877-489-4772
e-mail: ask@hrsa.gov
www.ask.hrsa.gov

Provides publications, information, resources, and referrals about health care services for medically underserved individuals and populations.

**815 Haldimand-Norfolk Resource Education and Counseling**
101 Nanticoke Creek Parkway
Townsend, ON, ON N0A-1S0
519-587-2441
800-265-8087
FAX: 519-587-4798
e-mail: info@hnreach.on.ca
www.hnreach.on.ca

*Leo Massi, Exec. Dir.*
*Denise Butt, Exec. Assistant*
*Deb Young, Dir. of Child Services*
*Wendy Carron, Dir. of Svcs, Early Childhood*

Promote and support community well-being by providing co-ordinated access, planning, programs and services for individuals and families.

**816 Health Action**
5276 Hollister Ave
Ste 257
Santa Barbara, CA 93111
805-617-3390
FAX: 805-685-4710
e-mail: ha@healthaction.net.
www.healthaction.net

*Dr. Roger Jahnke, Co Founder and CEO*
*Rebecca Mclean, Co Founder*

Our mission is to foster innovation in health care that will increase health status, increase customer satisfaction, increase profitability, increase clinical efficacy and eliminate error, support provider efficiency and enhance clinical outcomes, and empower consumer self-managed care.

**817 Health Resource Center for Women with Disabilities**
Rehabilitation Institute of Chicago
345 E Superior St
Chicago, IL 60611-2654
312-238-1000
800-354-7342
FAX: 312-238-2208
e-mail: webmaster@ric.org
ric.org

*Joanne C. Smith, MD, MBA, President/CEO*
*Edward B. Case, Exec VP/CFO*
*Nancy E. Paridy, JD, Senior VP, General Counsel*
*Dennis M. Cary, Senior VP*

RIC has earned a worldwide reputation as being a leader in patient health care, advocacy, research and educating health professionals in physical medicine and rehabilitation. People from around the globe choose RIC because of our expertise in treating a range of conditions, from the most complex conditions including cerebral palsy, spinal cord injury, stroke and traumatic brain injury, to the more common, such as arthritis, chronic pain, and sports injuries.

**818 Homeopathic Educational Services**
2124b Kittredge St
Berkeley, CA 94704
510-649-0294
800-359-9051
FAX: 510-649-1955
e-mail: email@homeopathic.com
homeopathic.com

*Dana Ulman, MPH, Owner*

Resource center for homeopathic products and services including books, tapes, research, medicines, medicine kits, software for the general public and the health professional and correspondence courses.

**819 Human Ecology Action League (HEAL)**
PO Box 509
Stockbridge, GA 30281-509 770-389-4519
FAX: 770-389-4520
e-mail: HEALNatnl @aol.com / HEAL3@aol.com
www.healnatl.org

HEAL is a national non-profit education and information organization, founded in 1977 by physicians and citizens concerned about the health effects of environmental exposures. HEAL is a member-service organization funded solely by memberships, advertising and donations. Our purpose is to serve those whose health has been adversely affected by environmental exposures, provide information to those concerned about the health effects of chemicals and to alert the public about chemical dangers.

**820 Institute for Scientific Research**
1000 Technology Dr
Ste 1000
Fairmont, WV 26554-8827 304-366-2577
877-363-5482
FAX: 304-366-2699
e-mail: info@wvhtf.org
wvhtf.org

*James L. Estep, President/CEO*
*Dr Brian Lemoff, VP Advanced Technology*
*Brian Stolarik, VP, Mission Systems*
*Nancy E. Trudel, Esquire, General Counsel*

Institute for Scientific Research, Inc. performs cutting-edge research across a variety of scientific and engineering disciplines. Our people participate in world-class projects from concept through development, in some of today's most fascinating scientific fields.

**821 Institute of Transpersonal Psychology**
1069 E Meadow Cir
Palo Alto, CA 94303-4231 650-493-4430
FAX: 650-493-6835
e-mail: itpinfo@itp.edu
itp.edu

*Neal King, President*
*Brigitte Lindsey, Exec Assistant to President*
*Roger Ono, CFO*
*Paul Roy, Provost & VP*

The Institute of Transpersonal Psychology is a private, non-sectarian graduate school accredited by the Western Association of Schools and Colleges. For over twenty-five years the Institute has remained a leader at the forefront of psychological research and education, probing the mind, body, spirit connection. The Institute's challenging and transformative educational paradigm has attracted students from all over the world.

**822 International Association of Machinists**
9000 Machinists Pl
Upper Marlboro, MD 20772-2687 301-967-4500
FAX: 301-967-4588
e-mail: websteward@iamaw.org
goiam.org

*R Thomas Buffenbarger, President/CEO*
*Robert Roach, Jr., General Secretary-Treasurer*
*Dave Ritchie, General VP, Canada*
*Lynn D. Tucker, Jr., General VP, Eastern Territory*

Placement programs for persons with disabilities.

**823 International Association of Yoga Therapists**
PO Box 12890
Prescott, AZ 86304 928-541-0004
FAX: 928-541-0182
e-mail: mail@iayt.org
www.iayt.org

*John Kepner, MA, MBA, Executive Director*
*Eleanor Criswell Ed.D, President*
*Matra Raj,OTR, TYC,, Treasurer*
*Molly Lannon Kenny, Vice President*

IAYT supports research and education in Yoga and serves Yoga practitioners, Yoga teachers, Yoga therapists, health care professionals, and researchers worldwide. Our mission is to establish Yoga as a recognised and respected therapy in the Western world. IAYT also serves members, the media, and the general public as a comprehensive source of information about contemporary Yoga education, research, and statistics.

**824 International Chiropractors Association**
6400 Arlington Blvd
Ste. 800
Falls Church, VA 22042 703-528-5000
800-423-4690
FAX: 703-528-5023
e-mail: chiro@chiropractic.org
chiropractic.org

*Gary Walsemann, DC, President*
*W. Gene Cretsinger, DC, Â LCP,, Vice President*
*Stephen P. Welsh, DC, Secretary-Treasurer*
*Corey B. Rodnick, DC, Central Regional Director*

Established in 1926 to empower humanity in the expression of maximum health, wellness and human potential through the universal chiropractic expression and utilization. Strives to advance chiropractics throughout the world as a distinct health care profession predicated upon its unique philosophy, science and art.

**825 International Clinic of Biological Regeneration**
PO Box 509
Florissant, MO 63032-509 314-921-3997
800-826-5366
FAX: 314-921-8485
e-mail: icbr@aol.com
icbr.com

*Dr. C. Tom Smith MD, HMD, D Hom (, Medical Director*

The International Clinic of Biological Regeneration (ICBR) is a leading international cell therapy center that has been in continuous operation since 1981. During this time, Dr. Smith has constantly improved theraputic results of the treatment by selecting newer, safer and more effective formulations as delveloped by leading European research centers.

**826 International Women's Health Coalition**
333 7th Ave
6th Fl
New York, NY 10001-5004 212-979-8500
FAX: 212-979-9009
e-mail: info@iwhc.org
www.iwhc.org

*Francoise Girard, President*
*Debora Diniz, Vice Chair*
*Ann Unterberg, Vice Chair*
*Brian A. Brink, MD, Chair*

Information and pamphlets on sexually transmitted diseases and other health concerns. IWHC works to generate health and population policies, programs, and funding that promote and protect the rights and health of girls and women worldwide.

**827 Job Accommodation Network**
PO Box 6080
Morgantown, WV 26506-6080 304-293-7186
800-526-7234
FAX: 304-293-5407
TTY: 877-781-9403
e-mail: jan@askjan.org
www.jan.wvu.edu

*Anne Hirsh, Co-Director*
*Louis Orslene, Co-Director*
*Linda Carter Batiste, Principal Consultants*
*Beth Loy, Principal Consultants*

JAN's mission is to facilitate the employment and retention of workers with disabilities by providing employers, employment providers, people with disabilities, their family members and other interested parties with information on job accomodations, self-employment and small business opportunities and related subjects. JAN's efforts are in support of the employment, including self-employment and small business ownership, of people with disabilities.

**828 Joni and Friends**
PO Box 3333
Agoura Hills, CA 91376-3333
818-707-5664
800-736-4177
FAX: 818-707-2391
TTY: 818-707-9707
e-mail: jafmin@joniandfriends.org
joniandfriends.org

*Joni Eareckson-Tada, Founder and CEO*
*Doug Mazza, President & COO*
*Billy C. Burnett, VP/CFO*
*Steve Bundy, VP*

A nonprofit organization seeking to accelerate Christian ministry with people affected by disabilities. JAF educates churches and the community worldwide concerning the needs of the disabled and how those needs can be met. We sponsor family retreats for families with disabled members. Wheels for the World collects, restores and distributes used wheelchairs to disadvantaged populations around the world.

**829 Juvenile Diabetes Research Foundation International**
26 Broadway
14th Fl
New York, NY 10004
212-785-9500
800-533-2873
FAX: 212-785-9595
e-mail: info@jdrf.org
jdrf.org

*Jeffrey Brewer, President/CEO*
*Gil King, VP, Internal Audit*
*Michael Malekoff, VP, Business Dev.*
*Cynthia Rice, VP, Govt Relations*

The world's leading nonprofit, nongovernmental funder of diabetes research. It was founded in 1970 by parents of children with diabetes. JDF's mission is to find a cure for diabetes and its complications through the support of research. JDF also sponsors international workshops and conferences for biomedical researchers, individual chapters offer support groups and other activities for families affected by diabetes. JDF has more than 110 chapters and affiliates worldwide. Quarterly newsletter.

**830 Lambton County Developmental Services**
339 Centre St
PO Box 1210
Petrolia, ON N0N-1R0
519-882-0933
FAX: 519-882-3386
e-mail: administration@lcds.on.ca
www.lcds.on.ca

*Frank Huybers, President*
*Tony Hogervorst, 1st Vice-President*
*Kari Lupton, 2nd Vice-President*
*Frank Back, Treasurer*

A network of caring people, working together to provide services for people with developmental disabilities to facilitate the achievement of their life dreams.

**831 LoSeCa Foundation**
215-1 Carnegie Drive
St Albert, AB T8N-5B1
780-460-1400
FAX: 780-459-1380
e-mail: rbourret@telus.net
www.loseca.ca

*Ron Bourret, Program Manager*
*Raymond Nkorimana, Program Manager*
*Francois Busque, Program Manager*
*Jules Lefebvre, Human Resources Manager*

A non-profit organization that provides support services to adults with developmental disabilities

**832 MCC Supportive Care Services**
103-2776 Bourquin Circle W
Abbotsford, BC V2S-6A4
604-850-6608
800-622-5455
FAX: 604-850-2634
e-mail: office@communitascare.com
www.communitascare.com/

*Steve Thiessen, CEO*

A service provider, advocate and resource for persons living and dealing with mental, physical and/or emotional disabilities. The correct name is ""Communitas Supportive Care Society""

**833 Mainstream**
300 S Rodney Parham Rd
Ste 5
Little Rock, AR 72205-4774
501-280-0012
800-371-9026
FAX: 501-280-9267
TTY: 501-280-9262
mainstreamilrc.com

A non-residential, consumer driven independent living resource center for persons with disabilities. Mainstream operates with the conviction that people with disabilities have the right and responsibility to make choices, to control their lives and to participate fully and equally in the community. Mainstream, in order to accomplish this concept, offers the following services free of charge: Advocacy, Peer Support, Training and Education, Information and Referral, Ramp program, and more.

**834 March of Dimes Birth Defects Foundation**
1275 Mamaroneck Ave
White Plains, NY 10605-5201
914-997-4488
FAX: 914-428-8203
e-mail: nbrown@marchofdimes.com
www.marchofdimes.com/

*Dr. Jennifer Howse, President*
*Richard Mulligan, Exec VP*
*Lisa Bellsey, Esq., SVP & General Counsel*

The mission of the March of Dimes is to improve the health of babies by preventing birth defects and infant mortality.

**835 Mental Health America**
2000 N Beauregard St
6th Fl
Alexandria, VA 22311
703-684-7722
800-969-6642
FAX: 703-684-5968
e-mail: dshern@mentalhealthamerica.net
mentalhealthamerica.net

*David Shern, Ph.D., President and CEO*
*Dianne Felton, Senior VP of Operations*
*Julie Nicholson Burke, VP of Finance*
*Mike Turner, VP of Dev*

Nonprofit organization addressing all issues related to mental health and mental illness. With more than 340 affiliates nationwide, NMHA works to improve the mental health of all Americans, especially the 54 million individuals with mental disorders, through advocacy, education, research and service.

**836 Metametrix Clinical Laboratory**
3425 Corporate Way
Duluth, GA 30096-2552
770-446-5483
800-221-4640
FAX: 770-441-2237
e-mail: inquiries@metametrix.com
www.metametrix.com

*J Alexander Bralley PhD, CEO*
*Robert M David PhD, Laboratory Director*
*Richard S Lord PhD, Chief Science Officer*
*Carolyn Bralley, President*

Metametrix Clinical Laboratory has been a pioneer and leader in the development of nutritional, metabolic, and toxicant analyses since 1984. Metametrix is committed to helping health care professionals identify nutritional influences on health and disease, and is recognized internationally for its laboratory procedures in nutritional and biochemical testing.

**837 Mind, Body, Health Sciences**
393 Dixon Rd
Boulder, CO 80302-9769
303-440-8460
FAX: 303-440-7580
e-mail: luzie@joanborysenko.com
www.joanborysenko.com

*Joan Borysenko, Founder*
publish free annual newsletter/catalogue:Circle of Healing. Information about the works of Joan Borysenko.

**838 Muscular Dystrophy Association - USA**
3300 E Sunrise Dr
Tucson, AZ 85718-3299
520-529-2000
800-572-1717
FAX: 520-529-5454
e-mail: mda@mdausa.org
www.mdausa.org

*Robert Ross, CEO*
*Valerie Cwik, M.D., Interim President*
MDA provides comprehensive medical services to tens of thousands of people with neuromuscular diseases at some 230 hospital-affiliated clinics across the country. The Association's worldwide research program, which funds over 400 individual scientific investigations annually, represents the largest single effort to advance knowledge of neuromuscular diseases and to find cures and treatments for them. In addition, MDA conducts far-reaching educational programs for the public and professionals.

**839 National Association for Holistic Aromatherapy**
PO Box 1868
Banner Elk, NC 28604
828-898-6161
FAX: 828-898-1965
e-mail: info@naha.org
www.naha.org

*Kelly Holland Azzaro, RA CCA, Vice President*
*Michele A. Miller, President*
*Shellie Enteen, BA, LMBT, Director Coordinator*
*Cheryl Hoard, Chairperson-Advisory Committee*
The NAHA is an educational, nonprofit organization dedicated to enhancing public awareness of the benefits of true aromatherapy. It offers aromatherapy Tele-classes & membership benefits, and acts as a referral service.

**840 National Association of Blind Merchants**
1837 S Nevada Ave
PMB #243
Colorado Springs, CO 80905
719-527-0488
866-543-6808
e-mail: kevanwirkey@blindmerchants.org
www.blindmerchants.org

*Nicky Gacos, President*
Membership organization of blind persons employed in either self-employment work or the Randolph-Sheppard vending program. Provides information regarding rehabilitation, social security, tax and other issues which directly affect blind merchants. Serves as advocacy and support group.

**841 National Association of Developmental Disabilities Councils**
1825 K Street, NW
Suite 600
Washington, DC 20006
202-506-5813
FAX: 202-506-5846
e-mail: info@nacdd.org
www.nacdd.org

*Wanda Willis, President, Exec. Dir.*
*Michael Brogioli, CEO*
*Dan Shannon, Treasurer, Exec. Dir.*
*Sheryl Matney, Senior Mgr, Council Svcs*
The National Association of Councils on Developmental Disabilities (NACDD) is a national, member-driven organization consisting of 55 State and Territorial Councils. NACDD places high value on meaningful participation and contribution by Council members.The correct name of the organization is ""National Association of Councils on Developmental Disabilities""

**842 National Association of State Directors of Developmental Disabilities Services (NASDDDS)**
113 Oronoco St
Alexandria, VA 22314-2015
703-683-4202
FAX: 703-684-1395
e-mail: cmosely@nasddds.org
www.nasddds.org

*Nancy Thaler, Executive Director*
*Charles R Moseley, Ed.D., Associate Executive Director*
*Robin Cooper, Director of Technical Assistance*
*Barbara Brent, Director of State Policy*
The association's goal is to promote and assist state agencies in developing effective, efficient service delivery systems that furnish high-quality supports to people with developmental disabilities.

**843 National Business & Disability Council**
201 I U Willets Rd
Albertson, NY 11507-1516
516-465-1516
FAX: 516-465-3730
e-mail: jtowles@abilitiesonline.org
www.nbdc.com

*John D. Kemp, President/CEO*
*Michael C. Pascucci, Exec. Leadership Team*
*Jennifer Towles, Membership Specialist*
*Sheryl P. Buchel, Senior VP*
The NBDC is the leading resource for employers seeking to integrate people with disabilities into the workplace and companies seeking to reach them in the consumer marketplace.

**844 National Center for Education in Maternal and Child Health**
Georgetown University
PO Box 571272
Washington, DC 20057-1272
202-784-9770
877-624-1935
FAX: 202-784-9777
e-mail: mchlibrary@ncemch.org
www.ncemch.org

*Rochelle Mayer, Research Professor and Director*
Provides information on children with special health needs, child health and development, adolescent health, nutrition, violence and injury prevention and other issues of maternal and child health for health professionals and the public.

**845 National College of Naturopathic Medicine**
049 SW Porter St
Portland, OR 97201-4848
503-552-1555
FAX: 503-226-8133
e-mail: jstanard@ncnm.edu
www.ncnm.edu

*David J. Schleich, President*
*Nancy W. Garbett, Board Chair*
*Richard Jones, Vice Chair of the Board*
*Don Drake, Chair Strategic Pathways Comm*
NCNM offers two graduate professional degrees in accredited and recognized programs that prepare you for licensed practice in many states and provinces: Doctor of Naturopathic Medicine, a four-year program of clinical sciences and holistic methods of heal

**846 National Council on Disability**
1331 F Street Northwest
Suite 850
Washington, DC 20004- 1138 202-272-2004
FAX: 202-272-2022
TTY:202-272-2074
e-mail: ncd@ncd.gov
www.ncd.gov

*Aaron Bishop, Exec. Dir.*
*Anne Sommers, Dir. of Legislative Affairs*
*Joan M. Durocher, General Counsel & Dir. of Policy*
*Sylvia Menifee, Dir. of Administration*
NCD is a small, independent federal agency charged with advising the President, Congress, and other federal agencies regarding policies, programs, practices, and procedures that affect people with disabilities.

**847 National Council on Independent Living**
1710 Rhode Island Ave NW
5th Fl
Washington, DC 20036 202-207-0334
877-525-3400
FAX: 202-207-0341
TTY: 202-207-0340
e-mail: ncil@ncil.org
www.ncil.org

*Kelly Buckland, Executive Director*
*Dan Kessler, President*
*Phil Pangrazio, Treasurer*
*Lou Ann Kibbee, Vice President*
NCIL advances independent living and the rights of people with disabilities through consumer-driven advocacy.

**848 National Deaf Education Network and Clearinghouse/Info To Go**
Deaf Education Center/Gallaudet University
800 Florida Ave NE
Washington, DC 20002-3695 202-651-5051
FAX: 202-651-5704
TTY:202-651-5052
e-mail: clerc.center@gallaudet.edu.
www.gallaudet.edu/clerc_center

*Dr T Alan Hurwitz, President*
*Edward Bosso, VP, National Deaf Education*
*Dr. Lynne Murray, VP for Dev. and Alumni Relations*
*Dr. Cynthia King, Chief Information Officer*
Info to Go, from the Laurent Clerc National Deaf Education Center, provides information on topics dealing with deafness and hearing loss in children and young people under 21 years of age.

**849 National Disability Rights Network**
Ste 211
900 2nd St NE
Washington, DC 20002-3560 202-408-9514
FAX: 202-408-9520
TTY:202-408-9521
e-mail: info@ndrn.org
www.ndrn.org

*Curtis L. Decker, JD, Exec. Dir.*
*Judith Stickle, Deputy Exec. Dir. for Finance*
*Janice K. Johnson Hunter, Deputy Exec. Dir.*
*Eric Buehlmann, Dir. of Public Policy*
Voluntary national membership association of protection and advocacy systems and client assistance programs. Promoting and strengthening the role and performance of its members in providing quality legally based advocacy services.

**850 National Dissemination Center for Children and Youth with Disabilities (NICHCY)**
1825 Connecticut Ave NW
Ste 700
Washington, DC 20009 202-884-8200
800-695-0285
FAX: 202-884-8441
TTY: 800-695-0285
e-mail: nichcy@aed.org
www.nichcy.org

*Suzanne Ripley, Director*
*Carol Valdivieso, Principal Investigator*
*Theresa Rebhorn, Writer / Designer*
*Lisa Kupper, Writer / Designer*
NICHCY is the center that provides information to the nation on disabilities in children and youth; programs and services for infants, children, and youth with disabilities; IDEA, the nation's special education law; and research-based information on effective practices for children with disabilities. The correct name of the organzation is ""National Dissemination Center for Children with Disabilities"".

**851 National Early Childhood Technical Assistance Center**
8040 Unc-Ch
Chapel Hill, NC 27599-8040 919-962-2001
FAX: 919-966-7463
e-mail: nectac@unc.edu
www.nectac.org

*Lynne Kahn, Dir. & Principal Investigator*
*Joan Danaher, Associate Dir. Information*
*Christina Kasprzak, Associate Dir. Evaluation*
*Martha Diefendorfer, Associate Director*
Assists states and other designated governing jurisdictions as they develop multidisciplinary, coordinated and comprehensive services for children with special needs.

**852 National Easter Seal Society**
233 S Wacker Drive
Ste 2400
Chicago, IL 60606-4851 312-726-6200
800-221-6827
FAX: 312-726-1494
TTY: 312-726-4258
easterseals.com

*Alison A. Coady, Secretary*
*James E. Williams Jr, Assistant Secretary*
*Stephen F. Rossman, Chairman*
*Richard F. Vincent, Treasurer*
Easter Seals provides exceptional services, education, outreach, and advocacy so that people living with autism and other disabilities can live, learn, work and play in our communities. The name of the company is ""Easter Seals Society"".

**853 National Guild of Hypnotists**
PO Box 308
Merrimack, NH 03054-308 603-429-9438
FAX: 603-424-8066
e-mail: ngh@ngh.net
www.ngh.net

*Dr. Dwight F Damon, DC, DNGH, OB, President*
*Don Mottin, NGH VP, CMI, D, Vice President*
*Melody Damon-Bachand, BCH, Executive Director*
*Dawn Huard, CH, Membership / Member Services*
The National Guild of Hypnotists, Inc.is a not-for-profit, educational corporation in the State of New Hampshire. Officially founded in Boston, Massachusetts in 1950 the Guild is a professional organization comprised of dedicated individuals committed to advancing the field of hypnotism.

**854 National Information Center for Children**
1825 Connecticut Ave NW
Ste 700
Washington, DC 20009
202-884-8200
800-695-0285
FAX: 202-884-8441
TTY: 800-695-0285
e-mail: nichcy@fhi360.org
www.nichcy.org

*Suzanne Ripley, Director*
*Carol Valdivieso, Principal Investigator*
*Theresa Rebhorn, Writer / Designer*
*Lisa Kupper, Writer / Designer*
Information on disabilities and disibility-related issues for family, educators and professionals related to children and youth. The correct name of the organozation is ""National Dissemination Center for Children with Disabilities"".

**855 National Institute on Disability and Rehabilitation Research**
Potomac Center Building
550 12 St., SW
Washington, DC 20202-7100
202-245-7640
800-872-5327
FAX: 202-245-7643
TTY: 800-437-0833
e-mail: nidrr-mailbox@ed.gov
www.ed.gov

*Charlie Lakin, Dir.*
*Ruth Brannon, Acting Deputy Dir.*
*Tim Muzzio, Dir. Program Budget*
Conducts comprehensive and coordinated programs of research and related activities to maximize the full inclusion, social integration, employment and independent living of individuals of all ages with disabilities. NIDRR's focus includes research in areas such as employment, health and function, technology for access and function, independent living and community integration, and other associated disability research areas.

**856 National Organization on Disability**
5 East 86th Street
New York, NY 10028
646-505-1191
e-mail: info@nod.org
nod.org

*Carol Glazer, President*
*Kate Brady, Dir. of Res*
*Anne Fitzsimmons, Project & Business Associate*
*Howard Green, Deputy Director*
The National Organization on Disability promotes the full and equal participation of men, women and children with disabilities in all aspects of American life. Founded in 1982, NOD is the leading national disability organization concerned with all disabil

**857 National Rehabilitation Association (NRA)**
633 S Washington St
Alexandria, VA 22314-4109
703-836-0850
FAX: 703-836-0848
TTY:703-836-0849
e-mail: info@nationalrehab.org
www.nationalrehab.org

*Beverlee Stafford, Executive Director*
*Sandra Mulliner, Administrative Assistant*
*Patricia Leahy, Governmental Affairs Director*
*Brian Coupe, Membership Director*
NRA members work to eliminate barriers and increase employment opportunities for people with disabilities. We provide our members opportunities for advocacy and increased awareness of issues through professional development and access to current research topics.

**858 National Rehabilitation Information Center(NARIC)**
8400 Corporate Drive
Suite 500
Landover, MD 20785-2245
301-459-5900
800-346-2742
FAX: 301-459-4263
e-mail: naricinfo@heitechservices.com
www.naric.com

*Mark Odum, Director*
NARIC is a federally-funded library and information center that focuses on disability and rehabilitation information.

**859 National Vaccine Information Center**
407 Church St. NE
Ste H
Vienna, VA 22180-4737
703-938-3783
FAX: 703-938-5768
e-mail: contactnvic@gmail.com
www.nvic.org

*Barbara Loe Fisher, Co-Founder/President*
*Kathi Williams, Co-Founder/VP*
*Theresa Wrangham, Executive Director*
*Paul Arthur, Director of Operations*
A national nonprofit educational organization dedicated to preventing, through public education, vaccine injuries and deaths. NVIC represents vaccine consumers and health care providers, including parents whose children suffered illness or died following vaccination. NVIC supports the right of vaccine consumers to have access to the safest and most effective vaccine as well as the right to make informed, independent vaccination decisions.

**860 National Women's Health Network**
1413 K St NW
4th Fl
Washington, DC 20005-3459
202-682-2640
FAX: 202-682-2648
e-mail: nwhn@nwhn.org
www.nwhn.org

*Cynthia Pearson, Executive Director*
*Heidi Gider, Director of Advancement*
*Amy Allina, Program & Policy Director*
*Latasha Jackson, Office Coordinator*
The National Women's Health Network improves the health of all women by developing and promoting a critical analysis of health issues in order to affect policy and support consumer decision-making. The Network aspires to a health care system that is guided by social justice and reflects the needs of diverse women.

**861 Native American Protection and Advocacy**
PO Box 306
Window Rock, AZ 86515
928-871-4151
800-789-7287
FAX: 928-871-5036
www.nativelegalnet.org

*Levon Henry, Executive Director*
*Sylvia Struss, Administrative Director*
*Kathy Gallagher, Development Director*
*Victoria Lee, Executive Assistant .*
The Native American Protection & Advocacy which helps protect, promote, and expand the legal and human rights of Native Americans with disabilities. There are several goals for this organization, including quality legal representation for individuals with disabilities in various areas such as abuse and neglect, special education, civil rights and discrimination and employment.

862 **New York Therapeutic Riding Center-Equestria**
212-535-3917
FAX: 212-535-3917
e-mail: info@equestria.org
www.equestria.org

*Richard Brodie, Board Of Director*
*Patricia Neal, Board Of Director*
*Karen Nielsen Esq., Board Of Director*
*Peter Rajsingh Esq., Board Of Director*

The Therapeutic Riding Center has been conducting therapeutic horseback riding progams for children and adults with disabilites living in New York City for 11 years. Its riding facility is located at the well-equipped Chateau Stables, and staffed by volunteers with experience in physical therapy, osteopathy, art therapy and other areas designed to deal with various aspects of disabled individuals.

863 **North America Riding for the Handicapped Association**
PO Box 33150
Denver, CO 80233-150
303-452-1212
800-369-7433
FAX: 303-252-4610
e-mail: pathintl@pathintl.org
www.narha.org

*Kay Green, CEO*
*Kaye Marks, Dir. of Mktg*
*Carolyn Malcheski, Finance/Human Resources Dir.*
*Megan Ream, Sponsorship/Dev. Mgr*

National nonprofit equestrian organization dedicated to serving individuals with disability by giving disabled individuals the opportunity to ride horses. Establishes safety standards, provides continuing education and offers networking opportunities for both its individuals and center members. Produces educational materials including fact sheets, brochures, booklets, audio-visual tapes, a directory and NARHA's magazine Strides. The name has been changed to “"Professional Association of Therapeu

864 **North Hastings Community Integration Association**
2 Alice Street
Box 1508
Bancroft, ON K0L-1C0
613-332-2090
FAX: 613-332-4762
e-mail: communityliving@nhcia.ca
www.nhcia.ca

*John Muro, President*
*Cathy Fulford, Vice President*
*Peter Stone, Treasurer*
*Barb Millar, Secretary*

Supports people with an intellectual disability and their families.

865 **Nurse Healers: Professional Associates International**
PO Box 419
Craryville, NY 12521-419
518-325-1185
FAX: 509-693-3537
e-mail: info@therapeutic-touch.org
www.therapeutic-touch.org

*Sue Conlin, QTTT, President*
*Lin Beilly, Communications*
*Cheri Brady, Education*
*David Shields, Membership*

Cooperative among health professionals interested in healing. Sets the standards for the practice and teaching of Therapeutic Touch. Voluntary, not-for-profit organization.

866 **PACER Center (Parent Advocacy Coalition for Educational Rights)**
8161 Normandale Blvd
Bloomington, MN 55437-1044
952-838-9000
800-537-2237
FAX: 952-838-0199
TTY: 952-838-0190
e-mail: pacer@pacer.org
pacer.org

*Paula F. Goldberg, Executive Director*
*Mary Schrock, Chief Operating/Development Off*
*Alicia Kunin-Batson, Board President*
*Alison Bakken, Board Treasurer*

Mission is to expand opportunities and enhance the quality of life of children and young adults with disabilities and their families based on the concept of parents helping parents. Offers workshops, individual assistance and written information. Provides programs and materials that assist multicultural families, programs for students, schools and professionals with disability awareness puppet and child abuse prevention programs. Computer Resource Center/Software Lending Library available.

867 **PEAK Parent Center**
Ste 200
611 N Weber St
Colorado Springs, CO 80903-1072
719-531-9400
800-284-0251
FAX: 719-531-9452
e-mail: info@peakparent.org
www.peakparent.org

*Barbara Buswell, Executive Director*
*Kent Willis, President Attorney*
*Sarah Billerbeck, Vice President*
*Delois Meyer, Secretary*

PEAK Parent Center is Colorado's federally-designated Parent Training and Information Center (PTI). As a PTI, PEAK supports and empowers parents, providing them with information and strategies to use when advocating for their children with disabilities. PEAK works one-on-one with families and educators helping them realize new possibilities for children with disabilities by expanding knowledge of special education and offering new strategies for success.

868 **Pacific Institute of Aromatherapy**
PO Box 6723
San Rafael, CA 94903
415-479-9120
FAX: 415-479-0614
e-mail: contact@osapia.com
www.pacificinstituteofaromatherapy.com

To elevate the status of aromatherapy toward a classic discipline of learning and to present substance not currently availiable. Understanding the chemical composition and pharmacology of essential oils will lead to the most successfull aromatherapy treatments today. Insight into the biology of essential oils transcends the chemical worldview and will become the tool to design superior healing strategies.

869 **Parent Professional Advocacy League**
45 Bromfield St
10th Fl
Boston, MA 02108
617-542-7860
866-815-8122
FAX: 617-542-7832
e-mail: info@ppal.net
www.ppal.net

*Lisa Lambert, Executive Director*
*Deborah A. Fauntleroy, MSW, Associate Director*
*Meri Viano, Senior Regional Manager*
*Chantell Albert, Outreach Coordinator*

An organization that promotes a strong voice for families of children and adolescents with mental health needs. PAL advocates for supports, treatment and policies that enable families to live in their communities in an environment of stability and respect.

870 **Parents Helping Parents (PHP)**
1400 Parkmoor Ave
Ste 100
San Jose, CA 95126-3797
408-727-5775
855-727-5775
FAX: 408-286-1116
e-mail: info@php.com
www.php.com

*Mary Ellen Peterson, M.A., CEO/Executive Director*
*Suzanne Cistulli, Board Chair*
*James Quaranta, Board Treasurer*
*Joyce Uggla, Board Secretary*

Dedicated to assisting children with any type of special need: mental, physical, emotional, or learning disability. Mission is to help children with special needs receive love, hope, respect, and services needed to achieve their full potential by strengthening their families and the professionals who serve them. Developed and implemented numerous programs; produce a variety of educational and support materials, including information packets, brochures, database and a quarterly newletter.

871 **People First of Canada**
120 Maryland St
Suite 5
Winnipeg, MB R3G-1L1
204-784-7362
866-854-8915
FAX: 204-784-7364
e-mail: info@peoplefirstofcanada.ca
www.peoplefirstofcanada.ca

*Shelley Rattai, Exec. Dir.*
*Catherine Rodgers, Community Inclusion*
*Shane Haddad, President*
*Patty Ward, Treasurer*

People First of Canada is the national voice for people who have been labeled with an intellectual disability. People First is a movement of people who want all citizens to live equally in the country.

872 **People First of Oregon**
PO Box 12642
Salem, OR 97309-642
503-362-0336
FAX: 503-585-0287
e-mail: people1@people1.org
www.people1.org

*Steven Kramer, President*

Self-advocacy organization of developmentally disabled people who have joined together to learn how to speak for themselves. People first offers support, a united voice and advocacy to its members. Offers information and helps develop service projects in the communities they live in. Offers information and assistance to countries around the world in starting new chapters. Offers participation on DD boards, ARC boards, Transit Boards, and other boards in the community. .

873 **People-to-People Committee on Disability**
911 Main St
Ste 2110
Kansas City, MO 64105
816-531-4701
800-676-7874
FAX: 816-561-7502
e-mail: execadmin@ptpi.org
www.ptpi.org/programs/disability.jsp

*Mary Eisenhower, President and CEO*
*Mark Stansberry, Chairman*
*Anita Manuel, Vice Chairman*
*Piya Radia, Secretary*

Individuals concerned about the circumstances of handicapped people throughout the world. Disseminates information, acts as a consultant in promoting exchange activities, coordinates special assistance projects in developing countries and more.

874 **People-to-People International: Committee for the Handicapped**
911 Maint St
Ste 2110
Kansas City, MO 64105
816-531-4701
800-676-7874
FAX: 816-561-7502
e-mail: ptpi@ptpi.org
www.ptpi.org

*Mary Eisenhower, President and CEO*
*Mark Stansberry, Chairman*
*Anita Manuel, Vice Chairman*
*Piya Radia, Secretary*

Goals of this committee include: betterment of the handicapped through international unity; educating those with and without handicaps through technical assistance; opening access doors through sensory aids, prosthetic devices and travel tips; and coordination of major international cultural exchanges.

875 **Quan Yin Healing Arts Center**
965 Mission St
Ste 405
San Francisco, CA 94103-3416
415-861-4964
FAX: 415-644-0614
e-mail: info@qyhac.org
www.quanyinhealingarts.com

*Carla Wilson, Exec. Dir.*
*Colin Howard, President*
*Hulda Brown, VP*
*Misha Cohen, Chair, Res & Education*

The mission of Quan Yin Healing Arts Center is to provide accessable high quality, affordable acupuncture and Chinese medicine regardless of income. Collaborating with other healthcare providers, we support a holistic philosophy, empowering the individual to take responsibility for their health and well being.

876 **Rehabilitation International**
25 E. 21st Street
4th Floor
New York, NY 10010-6207
212-420-1500
FAX: 212-505-0871
e-mail: RI@riglobal.org
riglobal.org

*Venus Ilagan, Secretary General*
*Iris Reiss, Rehabilitation Expert*
*Anne President*

RI and its members develop and promote initiatives to protect the rights of people with disabilities and improve rehabilitation and other crucial services for disabled people and their families. RI also works toward increasing international collaboration and advocates for policies and legislation recognizing the rights of people with disabilities and their families, including the establishment of a UN Convention on the Rights and Dignity of Persons with Disabilities.

877 **Rehabilitation Services**
3075 Orchard Vista Drive SE
Grand Rapids, MI 49546
616-301-8000
800-695-7273
FAX: 616-301-8010
TTY: 800-649-3777
e-mail: mtanis@hopenetwork.org
hopenetwork.org

*Dana DeVos, Chair*
*Joanne Voorhees, Vice Chair*
*Patrick A. Miles, jr., Secretary/Treasurer*
*Wilbur Lettinga, Ex Offico*

An office of Hope Netowrk, one of the largest, private, nonprofit organization of its kind in Michigan. The purpose is to assist people with brain injuries and/or physical disabilities in achieving an optimal level of self determinations, dignity, and independence as they develop and attain goals to overcome environmental barriers and mobilize adaptive skills.

**878 Rolf Institute**
5055 Chaparral Ct
Ste 103
Boulder, CO 80301-3326
303-449-5903
800-530-8875
FAX: 303-449-5978
rolf.org

*Ida P Rolf, Founder*
*Diana Yourell, Executive Director*
*Heidi Hauge, Membership Services Coordinator*
*Jim Jones, Director of Education*

Established in 1971, The Rolf Institute is a nonprofit corporation, organized and existing under the laws of California and Colorado. It is recognized by the US Government as a tax-exempt educational and scientific research organization.

**879 Ronald McDonald House**
1500 17th St
Huntington, WV 25701-3956
304-529-1122
FAX: 304-529-2970
e-mail: margaret@mchouse.org
mchouse.org

*Daniel Yon, Board Treasurer*
*Susan Barnes, Board President*
*Paul E. Smith, Board Vice President*
*Robert E. Yost, Board Secretary*

A home-away-from-home, a temporary lodging facility for the families of seriously ill children being treated at nearby hospitals. Each house is run by a local nonprofit agency comprised of members of the medical community, McDonald's owners, businesses and civic organizations and parent volunteers.

**880 St. Paul Abilities Network**
4637-45 Avenue
St Paul, AB T0A-3A3
780-645-3441
866-645-3900
FAX: 780-645-1885
e-mail: mail@spanet.ab.ca
www.stpaulabilitiesnetwork.ca

*Tim Bear, Exec. Dir.*
*Sam Chang, Finance Controller*
*Eugene McCafferty, Human Resources*
*Daina Foerster, Dir. of Residential Svcs*

Provides support and opportunities to encourage the development of an individual's full potential through education, advocacy and community partnerships.

**881 Student Disability Services**
Wayne State University
5155 Gullen Mall
1600 UGL
Detroit, MI 48202-3919
313-577-1851
877-978-4636
FAX: 313-577-4898
TTY: 313-577-3365
e-mail: studentdisability@wayne.edu
www.studentdisability.wayne.edu

*Jane DePriester-Morandini,, Interim Dir.*
*Randie Kruman, M.A., University Counselor II*
*Fran Marlowe, Program Specialist*
*Claressa Adams, M. A., Administrative Assistant II*

Their mission is to ensure a university experience in which individuals with disabilities have equitable access to programs and to empower students to self-advocate in order to fulfill their academic goals.

**882 Teacher Preparation and Special Education**
2134 G St NW
Ste 416
Washington, DC 20052
202-994-8860
800-449-7343
FAX: 202-994-8613
e-mail: gsehdcom@gwu.edu
gsehd.gwu.edu

*Michael J. Feuer, Dean*
*Carol Kochhar-Bryant, Senior Associate Dean*
*Maxine Freund, Associate Dean for Research*
*Phoebe Stevenson, Administrative Dean*

Administers the Education of the Handicapped Act and related programs for the education of handicapped children, including grants to institutions of higher learning and fellowships to train educational personnel. Grants to states for the education of handicapped children, research and demonstration.

**883 Technology and Media Division**
Council For Exceptional Children
2900 Crystal Drive
Suite 1000
Arlington, VA 22202-3557
866-509-0218
888-232-7733
FAX: 703-264-9454
TTY: 866-915-5000
e-mail: service@cec.sped.org
www.cec.sped.org

*Bruce Ramirez, Exec. Dir.*
*Margaret J. McLaughlin, President*
*James P. Heiden, Treasurer*
*Ken Dickson, Coordinator Gifted & Talented*

To support educational participation and improved results for individuals with disabilities and diverse learning needs through the selection, acquisition, and use of technology. The secondary purpose is to provide services to members and other units of CEC, to federal, state and local education agencies, and to business and industry regarding the current and future uses if technology and media with individuals with exceptionalities

**884 The Davis Center**
19 State Route 10 E
Ste 25
Succasunna, NJ 07876
862-251-4637
FAX: 862-251-4642
e-mail: npdunn@thedaviscenter.com
www.thedaviscenter.com

*Dorinne S Davis MA CCC-A FAAA, Director*
*Elizabeth Meade, Head Sound Therapist*
*Nancy Puckett-Dunn, Office Manger*
*Laura Darby, Part Time Sound Therapist*

Offers sound-based therapies supporting positive change in learning, development, and wellness. All ages/all disabilities. The Davis Model of Sound Intervention-an alternative approach.

**885 Thresholds Psychiatric Rehabilitation Centers**
4101 N Ravenswood Ave
Chicago, IL 60613-2196
773-572-5500
888-997-3422
FAX: 773-880-6279
TTY: 773-880-6263
e-mail: thresholds@thresholds.org
www.thresholds.org

*Gregory Hedges, Vice President*
*Michael Szkatulski, President*
*Jeffrey M. Josephs, Treasurer*
*Rand E. Arons, Secretary*

A nationally-recognized psychosocial rehabilitation agency serving persons with severe and persistent mental illness. The agency offers its programming at 22 service locations and more than 40 residential facilities throughout Chicago and Northern Illinois. Also offers specialized programming for older adults,

young adults, parents, the homeless and the hearing impaired and mentally ill.
*Sliding scale*

**886 United States Trager Association**
13801 W Center St
Ste C, P.O. Box 1009
Burton, OH 44021-9005
440-834-0308
FAX: 440-834-0365
e-mail: info@tragerus.org
www.tragerus.org

*Anna Marie Bowers, Executive Director*
*Sharon Johnson, President*
*Sharon King Green, Vice President*
*Shelley Parker, Treasurer*
The Trager approach is a pleasurable, gentle and effective approach to movement education and mind/body integration. The Trager approach helps release deep-seated physical and mental patterns and facilitates deep relaxation, increased physical mobility, and mental clarity. The benefits of a Trager session are long-lasting and cumulative, with subsequent sessions allowing for deeper and longer lasting changes.

**887 Universal Pediatric Services**
6750 Westown Parkway
Suite 115A
West Des Moines, IA 50266
800-383-0303
upsi.net

*Tucker Anderson, President*
Universal Pediatric Services, provides high tech care to medically fragile children and adults in the home setting. Emphasis is placed on the provision of services in the rural areas, the ability to service high tech needs and the promotion of primary nurse concept.

**888 Upledger Institute**
11211 Prosperity Farms Rd
Ste D-325
Palm Beach Gardens, FL 33410
561-622-4334
800-233-5880
FAX: 561-622-4771
e-mail: upledger@upledger.com
www.upledger.com

*John M Upledger, CEO*
*Roy Desjarlais, VP*
*Alex Jozefyk, Director of Accounting*
*Steve Keller, Director of Distributions*
A healthcare resource center recognized worldwide for its comprehensive education programs, advanced treatment options and unique outreach initiatives. The Institute has trained more than 100,000 healthcare professionals throughout the globe in the therapeutic approach.

**889 Women to Women**
PO Box 306
Portland, ME 04112-306
800-798-7902
FAX: 207-846-6167
e-mail: personalprogram@womentowomen.com
www.womentowomen.com

*Marcelle Pick OB/GYN, NP, Co Founder/Director*
Combination of alternative and conventional medicine in women's health, bring science and disipline to natural and preventative methods. Publishes the Creating Health Guide, a quarterly collection of articles written by the health care professionals at Women to Women.

**890 World Institute on Disability**
3075 Adeline Street
Suite 280
Berkeley, CA 94703
510-225-6400
FAX: 510-225-0477
TTY:510-225-0478
e-mail: wid@wid.org
www.wid.org

*Anita Shafer Aaron, Exec. Dir.*
*Thomas Foley, Deputy Dir/Access to Assets*
*Julia Day, Content Production Mgr*
*Bruce Curtis, Dir. of International Programs*
The mission of the World Institute on Disability (WID) in communities and nations worldwide is to eliminate barriers to full social integration and increase employment, economic security and health care for persons with disabilities. WID creates innovative programs and tools; conducts research, public education, training and advocacy campaigns; and provides technical assistance.

**891 YAI: National Institute for People with Disabilities**
460 W 34th St
New York, NY 10001-2382
212-273-6100
FAX: 212-273-6200
www.yai.org

*Stephen E. Freeman, L.C.S.W., CEO*
*Stephen Freeman, President/COO*
*Marco Damiani, M.A., Senior Dir.*
*Thomas A. Dern, L.C.S.W., Chief Operating Officer*
Mission is to build brighter futures for people with developmental and learning disabilities and thier families. Every person, at every age and level of disability, has the potential for growth. Each individual is entitled to the same dignity, respect, and opportunities as all other members of society. Firmly committed to helping the people we serve to achieve their potential for independence, individuality, productivity, and inclusion in their communities.

# Camps

## Alabama

**892 ASCCA**
Alabama Easter Seal Society
520 N. Northwest Highway
Park Ridge, IL 60068-847-
FAX: 847-825-5658
socca.org/

*Michael F. O'Connor, M.D., FCCM, President*
*Brenda G. Fahy, M.D., FCCM, President-elect*
*Aryeh Shander, M.D. FCCM, FC, Treasurer*
*Avery Tung, M.D., Secretary*
The Society of Critical Care Anesthesiologists (SOCCA) formerly ASCCA, was founded in 1986 to address the unique concerns of intensivists before the American Society of nesthesiologists (ASA). The founding members of SOCCA believed and continue to believe that multidisciplinary critical care medicine is a desirable goal.

**893 Camp Merrimack**
Merrimack Hall Performing Arts Center
3320 Triana Blvd.
Huntsville, AL 35805
256-534-6455
FAX: 212-397-4684
www.merrimackhall.com

*Debra Jenkins, President*
*Alan Jenkins, Vice President*
*Joe Ritch, Secretary / Treasurer*
*Kay Harrington, Financial Advisor*
For children ages 3-12 with special needs including Down Syndrome, Cerebral Palsy, Autism and others. Camp includes theatre, visual arts and dance.

**894 Camp Rap-A-Hope**
2701 Airport Blvd
Mobile, AL 36606-2319
251-476-9880
FAX: 251-476-9495
e-mail: info@camprapahope.org
www.camprapahope.org

*Melissa McNichol, Exec. Dir.*
*Roz Dorsett, Assistant Dir.*
*Nell Gustavson, Financial Secretary*
*West Sanders, Special Events*
Camp Rap-A-Hope is a one-week summer camp for children and teenagers who are battling cancer or have ever been diagnosed with cancer and are 7 to 17 years of age. It is free of charge. Camp Rap-A-Hope strives to make sure every camper gets the opportunity to develop new skills and self-confidence. Camp activities are appropriate for our campers' ages and abilities and include, but are not limited to: swimming, music, arts and crafts, archery, fishing, canoeing and horseback riding.

**895 Camp Seale Harris**
Southeastern Diabetes Education Services
500 Chase Park South
Suite 104
Hoover, AL 35244-1869
205-402-0415
FAX: 205-402-0416
e-mail: info@southeasterndiabetes.org
www.southeasterndiabetes.org

*Gordon Gary, Chair*
*Vickie Adkins, Secretary*
*Stacy Schneider, Vice-Chair*
*Rhonda McDavid, Executive Director*
A summer residential program that is located at Camp ASCCA (Alabama's Special Camp for Children and Adults), that encourages and motivates youth to reach their full potential despite diabetes, and teaches families how to serve as the primary educators and supporters for children and adolescents living with this illness. Fpur programs are offered: Senior Camp; Junior Camp; Family Camp; and Adventure Camps.

**896 Camp Shocco For The Deaf**
P.O. Box 6569
Talledega, AL 35161
256-761-1100
800-280-1105
FAX: 256-761-1270
TTY: 256-474-0109
e-mail: campshocco@albcdeaf.org
www.campshocco.org

*Chad Fleming, Dir.*
*Linnea Elliott, Assistant Dir. - Youth Camp*
*Mathew Dixon, Assistant Dir. - Children Camp*
*Adam Schrimsher, Dir. of Recreational Activities*
One week camp of fun, games and spiritual growth for deaf children and teens.

**897 Camp Shocco for the Deaf**
AL Baptist State Board of Missions
P.O. Box 6569
Talladega, AL 35161
256-761-1100
TTY:256-474-0109
e-mail: campshocco@albcdeaf.org
www.campshocco.org

*Chad Fleming, Dir.*
*Linnea Elliott, Assistant Dir. - Youth Camp*
*Mathew Dixon, Assistant Dir. - Children Camp*
*Adam Schrimsher, Dir. of Recreational Activities*
Camp Shocco gives each child and teenager attending camp the opportunity opportunity to have an unforgettable one week of fun, games, and spiritual growth. Campers also learn the essence of teamwork, while developing their own unique abilities and talents that can often be overlooked.

**898 Camp Smile-A-Mile**
P.O.Box 550155
Birmingham, AL 35255-155
205-323-8427
888-500-7920
FAX: 205-323-6220
e-mail: info@campsam.org
www.campsam.org

*C. Dennis Hughes, President*
*Meredith McLaughlin, Vice President*
*John Redmond, Vice President*
*Daniel M. Sims, Jr., Secretary*
Camp Smile-A-Mile is a non-profit organization for children who have or had cancer in Alabama. Camp Smile-A-Mile's mission is to provide challenging, unforgettable recreational and educational experiences for young cancer patients from across Alabama at no cost to their families. Our purpose is to provide these children with avenues for fellowship, to help them cope with their disease, and to prepare them for life.

**899 Camp WheezeAway**
American Lung Association Of Alabama
P. O. Box 2336
Bessemer, AL 36102
334-229-0035
e-mail: campchandler@ymcamontgomery.org
www.campchandler.org

*Jeff Reynolds, Executive Director*
*Justin Castanza, Associate Camp Director*
*Art Mason, Operations Director*
Camp WheezeAway is a 5 day overnight camp for children ages 8-12 with moderate to severe asthma, and is sponsored by the American Lung Association. Children are monitered while enjoying all the normal camp activities including ropes courses, canoeing, swimming, arts & crafts, horseback riding, fishing, tubing & more and above all learn to manage their asthma.

## Alaska

**900 ADA Camp Kushtaka**
American Diabetes Association
201 West Fireweed Lane
Suite 103
Anchorage, AK 99503- 1893
907-272-1424
800-342-2383
FAX: 907-272-1428
e-mail: askada@diabetes.org
www.childrenwithdiabetes.org

*Michelle Cassano, Executive Director*
*Pam Bell, Organizer*
ADA Camp Kushtaka is a five day camp for children & teens age 7-17 and their families (space permitting) and is held on the shores of Kenai Lake on the Kenai Peninsula in Cooper Landing. The camp combines ongoing and informal diabetes management and education along with the fun of outdoor activities such as hiking, canoeing, crafts and swimming.

**901 Camp Alpine**
Alpine Alternatives
2518 E. Tudor Road
Suite 105
Anchorage, AK 99507-1105
907-561-6655
800-361-4174
FAX: 907-563-9232
e-mail: info@alpinealternatives.org
www.alpinealternatives.org

*Margaret Webber, Executive Director*
Our programs are designed to help people expand their horizons, master new skills, make new friends, and increase motor coordination. Most importantly, participants experience growth in self-confidence and independence that affects all aspects of an individual's life. Our services are open to all, regardless of type of disability or age. Activities include canoeing, hiking, swimming, outdoor games, sports, nature identification and much more.

**902 Camp Birchwood**
Muscular Dystrophy Association
17161 David Blackburn Drive
Chugiak, AK 99567-49
907-688-2734
FAX: 907-688-2734
e-mail: info@birchwoodcamp.org
www.birchwoodcamp.org

*Von Cawvey, President*
*Rev. Dan Lush, Vice President*
*Benee Braden, Treasurer*
*Nathan Woods, Secretary*
A summer camp at Birchwood Camp in Chugiak, Alaska for individuals ages 6-21 who are affected by any of the 40-plus neuromuscular diseases in MDA's program. Common activities include: swimming, hockey, baseball, soccer, football, boating, horseback riding, fishing, music, cooking, arts and crafts, movies, dancing, talent shows, Harley-Davidson motorcycle sidecar or three-wheeled cycle rides, a visit from fire fighters and time for socializing and laughing.

**903 Champ Camp**
American Lung Association In Alaska
500 West International Airport Rd.
Suite A
Anchorage, AK 99518-1175
907-276-5864
800-586-4872
FAX: 907-565-5587
e-mail: champcamp@lungcolorado.org
www.lung.org/

*Charles D. Connor, President and CEO*
*George Walker, Regional Director*
*Cindy Liverance, VP of Programs*
*Liz Toohey, Director of Development*
Champ Camp is a week long summer recreation and asthma education program at Camp Kushtaka on the beautiful shores of Kenai Lake. Campers are able to explore their skills in outdoor activities including canoeing, hiking, swimming, archery, and arts and crafts. More importantly, Champ Camp boosts self-confidence and instills a sense of responsibility. It teaches preventive measures to improve asthma management, and avoid asthmatic episodes as well as increases a camper's sense of independence.

**904 Muscular Dystrophy Association Free Camp**
3300 E. Sunrise Dr.
Tucson, AZ 85718-3208
800-344-4863
e-mail: mda@mdausa.org
www.mda.org

*Valerie A. Cwik, M..D., Interim President*
*Irwin M. Siegel, M.D., National VP and Clinic Co-Dir.*
*Catherine Lomen-Hoerth, Clinic Dir.*
*Jean-Pierre Julien, Clinic Dir.*
MDA Camp provides a wide range of activities for those with limited mobility or are in wheelchairs. The camp offers many outdoor sporting events, arts & crafts and talent shows.

## Arizona

**905 Arizona Camp Sunrise**
American Cancer Society
4550 E. Bell Road
Suite 126
Phoenix, AZ 85032-9344
602-952-7550
FAX: 602-404-1118
e-mail: barb.nicholas@cancer.org
www.azcampsunrise.org

*Barbara Nicholas, Dir.*
*Leigh Ansley, Mgr of Childhood Cancer Support*
*Melissa Lee, Camp Dir.*
*Jason Poulter, Technical Media Dir.*
Provides one-week summer camping sessions to children aged 8-16 who have had, or currently have, cancer. The classes range from sports and outdoor games to dance and drama, arts, crafts, and cooking. Other activities planned for the campers include horseback riding, a trip to a lake, a dance, and learning to make friendship bracelets.

**906 Camp Abilities Tucson**
P.O. Box 86838
Tucson, AZ 85754
e-mail: campabilitiestucson@gmail.com
www.campabilitiestucson.org

*Jeanine Fittipaldi-Wert, Camp Director*
One week camp offering comprehensive developmental sports for children in middle and high school who are blind, deaf-blind or multiply disabled.

**907 Camp Civitan**
Civitan Foundation
3519 East Shea Blvd. #133
Phoenix, AZ 85028-3339
602-953-2944
FAX: 602-953-2946
e-mail: info@campcivitan.org
www.campcivitan.org

*Mike Horne, Director, Partner & COO*
*John W Day, DMD, MS, Director Orthodontist*
*Kathy Spude, Director Credit Analyst*
*Gary Holliday, Director Pharmacy Director*
We are the premier camp for developmentally disabled individuals of all ages. People from around Arizona and neighboring states come to Camp Civitan to enhance their quality of life, enjoy the multitude of outdoor experiences we offer and make lifelong friends.

908 **Camp Honor**
Hemophilia Association
826 North 5th Avenue
Phoenix, AZ 85003
602-955-3947
888-754-7017
e-mail: cindy@hemophiliaz.org
www.hemophiliaz.org

*Steven Helm, President*
*Jim Durr, Vice President*
*Victor Alonzo, Treasurer*
*Sarah Fey, Secretary*
Camp is located in Payson, Arizona at the Whispering Hope Ranch. One-week sessions for children with hemophilia or HIV and their siblings, as well as children of hemophiliacs. Coed, ages 7-17. Activities include swimming, canoeing, sports, archery and arts and crafts (to name a few fun things).

909 **Camp Not-A-Wheeze**
American Lung Association In Arizona
102 W McDowell Rd
Phoenix, AZ 85003-1213
602-258-7505
800-586-4872
FAX: 602-258-7507
e-mail: notawheeze@lungarizona.org.
www.lung.org/

*Charles D. Connor, President and CEO*
*George Walker, Regional Dir.*
*Cindy Liverance, VP of Programs*
*Liz Toohey, Dir. of Dev*
Camp Not-A-Wheeze is designed especially for kids ages 7-14 with moderate to severe asthma and was created to provide a traditional residential camp experience and teach children how to manage their asthma.

910 **Camp Rainbow**
Phoenix Childrens Hospital
1919 East Thomas Road
Phoenix, AZ 85016-7710
602-933-1000
888-908-5437
e-mail: cnelson1@phoenixchildrens.com
www.phoenixchildrens.com/

*Robert Meyer, President and CEO*
*David Cavazos, Chairman of the Board*
*Larry Clemmensen, Chairman of the Board*
*Steven S. Schnall, Senior VP*
Camp is located in Prescott, Arizona. Offers one-week sessions for children who have had, or currently have, cancer. Boys and girls ages 7-17. Camp activities include swimming, horseback riding, arts and crafts, canoeing, performing arts, archery, rollerskating, fishing, an overnight camping trip and much more! It's a week filled with laughter, new experiences and new friends.

911 **Dream Street Camp**
Dream Street Foundation
433 North Camden Avenue
Suite 600
Beverly Hills, CA 90210
424-248-0696
FAX: 310-496-0439
e-mail: Dreamstreet9536@aol.com
www.dreamstreetfoundation.org

*Patty Grubman, Director*
*Louise Gonzales, Office Manager*
*Tiffany Alfaro, Director*
For children and young adults with life threatening and chronic illnesses.

912 **Lions Camp Tatiyee**
Arizona Lions Clubs Multiple District 21
P.O.Box 6910
Mesa, AZ 85216-6910
480-380-4254
800-246-9771
FAX: 602-244-8667
e-mail: arizonalionscamp@cox.net
www.arizonalionscamp.com

*Pamela Swanson, Executive Director*
*Desirae Bender, RN BSN, Lead Nurse*
*Megan Anderson, Assistant Program Director*
Camp is located in Lakeside, Arizona. Sessions are provided for campers of all ages, with a wide variety of disabilities/special needs and are divided by age and disability. Featured activities include arts and crafts, ceramics/pottery, climbing/rappelling, counselor training (CIT), drama, fishing, football, hiking, nature/environmental studies and team building.

913 **Summer Camp for Children with Muscular Dystrophy**
Muscular Dystrophy Association - USA
3300 E Sunrise Dr
Tucson, AZ 85718-3208
520-529-2000
800-344-4863
FAX: 520-529-5300
e-mail: mda@mdausa.org
www.mda.org

*Irwin M. Siegel, M.D., National VP and Clinic Co-Dir.*
*Catherine Lomen-Hoerth, Clinic Dir.*
*Jean-Pierre Julien, Clinic Dir.*
*Valerie A Cwik MD, Interim President*
The MDA Summer Camp offers a wide range of activities specifically designed for young people with limitted mobility or who use a wheelchair. Some of the activities include boating and canoeing, swimming, adaptive sports, fishing, archery, karaoke, scavenger hunts, arts & crafts, dances, talent shows and campfires.

## Arkansas

914 **Camp Aldersgate**
Camp Aldersgate, Inc.
2000 Aldersgate Road
Little Rock, AR 72205
501-225-1444
FAX: 501-225-2019
www.campaldersgate.net

*Sarah C. Wacaster, CEO*
*Bill Faggard, Chief Operating Officer*
*Amy Frank, Dir. of Programs*
*Regina Riehl, Dir. of Human Resources*
A non-profit camp for children and young adults with medical or physical conditions such as cerebral palsy, diabetes, arthritis, asthma, kidney disorders.

915 **Camp Kota**
Junior League Of Little Rock
401 South Scott Street
Little Rock, AR 72201
501-375-5557
FAX: 501-907-5296
www.jllr.org

*Tisha Gribble, President*
*Maggie Young, President Elect*
*Brooke Hicks, Community Vice President*
*Jamie Jones, Membership Vice President*
Camp Kota is for disabled and non-disabled children ages 6-16. Some of the activities include fishing, canoeing, swimming, archery, music and arts & crafts.

**916 Camp Quality Arkansas**
1444 Mockingbird Circle
Stow, OH 44224
870-931-2844
FAX: 866-285-5208
e-mail: chris.jennings@campqualityusa.org
www.campqualityusa.com

*Myron Scafe, Vice-President*
*Patricia Harris, Executive Director*
*Lois Hartje, President*
*Dennis Hart, Secretary/Treasurer*
Camp Quality is for children with cancer and their siblings. The camp allows for children to be children again and strives to create a stress-free environment that offers exciting activities, fosters new friendships and helps in giving the children courage, motivation and emotional strength.

## California

**917 Bearskin Meadow Camp**
Diabetic Youth Foundation
5167 Clayton Road
Suite F
Concord, CA 94521-3163
925-680-4994
FAX: 925-680-4863
e-mail: info@dyf.org
www.dyf.org

*Mats Wallin, Executive Director*
*Paula Gogin, Director of Development*
*Janet Kramschuster, Director of Programs*
*Dr. Mary Simon, Medical Director*
Bear Skin Meadow Camp is for children, teens and families who are affected by diabetes. The Camp also teaches the children and teens diabetes management and education, skills for blood glucose checking and techniques for adjusting insulin, as well as food choices and how to have a fun, active life while living with diabetes.

**918 Camp Beyond The Scars**
Burn Institute
8825 Aero Drive
Suite 200
San Diego, CA 92123-2269
858-541-2277
FAX: 858-541-7179
www.burninstitute.org

*Chief David Ott, President*
*Chief Bob Pfohl, VP Chief Financial Officer*
*Dale Ganzow, VP Dev.*
*Michael D. Pierschbacher, Ph.D., VP Program*
Summer camp for children who have suffered burns. The camp provides a relaxed social setting and helps to enhance the children's self esteem.

**919 Camp Bloomfield**
Junior Blind
35375 Mulholland Highway
Malibu, CA 90265
310-457-5330
FAX: 310-457-3952
e-mail: info@juniorblind.org
www.juniorblind.org

*Miki Jordan, President and CEO*
*Jay Allen, Exec VP*
*Laura M. Hardy, Senior VP of Dev. and Mktg*
*Kami Mann, Senior VP, Finance*
Offers children and youth's who are blind, visually impaired or multi-disabled with a safe and natural environment where they can develop self esteem and build independence. The camp offers swimming, horseback riding, fishing, hiking, track and field, arts and crafts and more.

**920 Camp Christian Berets**
Christian Berets, Inc.
1317 Oakdale Road
Suite 340
Modesto, CA 95355
209-524-7993
FAX: 209-524-7979
www.christianberets.org

*Brian Robison, Retreat Director*
*Karen Gwynn, Office Mgr*
*Brice Ringsby, Ministry Volunteer*
Camp for children, students and adults with special needs.

**921 Camp Coelho**
The Epilepsy Foundation Of Northern California
155 Montgomery Street
Suite 309
San Francisco, CA 94104
416-677-4011
800-632-3532
FAX: 416-677-4190
www.epilepsynorcal.org

*Michael A. Scott, Executive Director*
*Joseph McGrath, President*
*D. Andrew Neff, Vice President*
*Lane Auten, Treasurer*
Camp for children and young adults ages 5-15 with epilepsy and seizure disorders.

**922 Camp Conrad-Chinnock**
Diabetic Youth Services
12045 E. Waterfront Drive
Playa Vista, CA 90094
310-751-3057
FAX: 888-800-4010
e-mail: rocky.wilson@dys.org
campconradchinnock.weebly.com/

*Rocky Wilson, Ph.D., Executive And Camp Director*
*Dale Lissy, Camp Manager*
*Ryan Martz, Program Director*
*Tom Jenkins, Chief Operating Officer*
Camp conrad-chinnock offers social, recreational and educational opportunities for youth and families with diabetes. Campers are taught diabetes self-management skills in an interactive, fun & safe environment.

**923 Camp Costanoan**
VIA Services West
2851 Park Avenue
Santa Clara, CA 95050
408-243-7861
e-mail: info@viaservices.org
www.viaservices.org

*Kay R. Walker, Ed.D., President and CEO*
*Dean Munro, Director of Advancement*
*Leslie Leger, Vice President of Administration*
*Jennifer Kam, Business Development Officer*
Camp Costanoan is a residential, outdoor education, and recreational camp for children and adults, ages 5 and older, with physical and/or developmental disabilities and special needs. Camp Costanoan enhances camper self-esteem, improves socialization skills and provides hands-on learning and therapeutic recreation opportunities.

**924 Camp Del Corazon**
11615 Hesby St
North Hollywood, CA 91601-3620
818-754-0312
888-621-4800
FAX: 818-754-0842
e-mail: information@campdelcorazon.org
www.campdelcorazon.org

*Lisa Knight, RN, Exec. Dir. and Co-Founder*
*Kevin Shannon, MD, Medical Dir. & Co-Founder*
*Tom Klitzner, MD, Exec. Board Member*
*Carl Schuster, Exec. Board Member*
Active program for campers with heart disease, Camp del Corazon provides summer activities free of charge that include

hiking and archery, arts and crafts, court and field games, waterfront activities and a beach barbecue.

**925 Camp Esperanza**
Southern California Chapter
800 West 6th Street
Suite 1250
Los Angeles, CA 90017 323-954-5750
800-954-2873
FAX: 323-954-5790
e-mail: info.sca@arthritis.org
www.arthritis.org

*Manuel Loya, CEO*
*Richard Klein, COO*
*Amy Daugherty, Chief Development Officer*
*Angele Price, VP, Development*
A one-week camp in August that allows children with arthritis to participate in such activities as horseback riding, swimming, etc. in a fun-filled environment.

**926 Camp Firefly**
The Firefly Foundation
5737 Kanan Road
Suite 180
Agoura Hills, CA 91301 e-mail: mail@campfirefly.com
www.campfirefly.com

Free week-long camp for terminally and seriously ill children and their families.

**927 Camp Forrest**
Angel View Crippled Children's Foundation
12379 Miracle Hill Rd
Desert Hot Springs, CA 92240-4010 760-329-6471
FAX: 760-329-9024
e-mail: angelview44@aol.com
www.angelview.org

*David Thorton, Executive Director*
*Mary Meze, CFO*
*Catherine Rips, Director of Development*
*DeAnn Lubell, Director of Public Relations*
Camp is located in Joshua Tree, California. Offers to one-week sessions June-August to both able-bodied campers and those with a wide variety of disabilities. Coed, ages 10-25. Activities include archery, arts and crafts, cookouts, swimming, sports and games, hiking and star study.

**928 Camp Grizzly**
NorCal Services For Deaf & Hard Of Hearing, Inc.
4708 Roseville Road
Suite 112
North Highlands, CA 95660-5172 916-349-7500
FAX: 916-474-1570
e-mail: info@nocalcenter.org
www.norcalcenter.org/

*Sheri Farinah, CEO*
*Cheryl Bella, Chair*
*Molly Senecal, Vice Chair*
*Yim Orsi, Secretary*
This camp is designed the deaf and hard of hearing youth or hearing youth with deaf or hard of hearing parent. The camp helps with social interaction, building self esteem, leadership skills while enriching the lives of the deaf and hard of hearing.

**929 Camp Krem**
Camping Unlimited
4610 Whitesands Court
El Sobrante, CA 94803 510-222-6662
e-mail: info@campingunlimited.org
www.campingunlimited.com

*Mary Farfaglia, Executive Director*
Year-round camp offering recreational activities and camping for children and adults with developmental disabilities.

**930 Camp Okizu**
Okizu Foundation
16 Digital Dr
Novato, CA 94949-5755 415-382-9083
FAX: 415-382-8384
e-mail: info@okizu.org
www.okizu.org

*Suzanne Randall, Exec. Dir. and Camp Dir.*
*Heather Ferrier, Assistant Exec. Dir.*
*John H. Bell, Chairman*
*Michael D. Amylon, M.D., Vice-Chairman*
Camp Okizu is located in Berry Creek, California, and offers children who are struggling with life threatening illnesses and their families a place to go and exlore and enjoy a normal life experience. The camp also offers peer support, respite, mentoring as well as other programs designed to meet the needs of all members of families whom are affected by childhood cancer. The camp is open from April through October.

**931 Camp Pacifica, Inc.**
California Lions Camp
Mail Box 110
257 Belle Vue Rd
Atwater, CA 95301-209- e-mail: ilybrookeb@yahoo.com
www.californialionscamp.org

*Russ Custer, President*
*Jill Loving, Secretary*
*Ted Allan, Treasurer*
*Dee Heller, Vice President*
Camp Pacifica has been developed to provide a unique environment where special needs children have opportunites to grow and understand themselves. The camp is open to special needs children ages 7-17 years old, and strives to promote greater independence and self confidence and provides opportunities for social interaction, further development of social skills and the opportunity to develop friendships.

**932 Camp Paivika**
AbilityFirst
1300 E Green St
Pasadena, CA 91106-2606 626-639-1731
877-768-4600
FAX: 626-396-1021
e-mail: info@abilityfirst.org
www.abilityfirst.org

*Lori Gangemi, President and CEO*
*Steven Schultz, CFO*
*Richard R. Frank, Chair*
*Steve Brockmeyer, Vice Chair*
AbilityFirst has 24 locations throughout So. California, including a camp, serving children and adults with disabilities.

**933 Camp Quest**
The Epilepsy Foundation Of Northern California
155 Montgomery Street
Suite 309
San Francisco, CA 94104 416-677-4011
800-632-3532
FAX: 416-677-4190
www.epilepsynorcal.org

*Michael A. Scott, Executive Director*
*Joseph McGrath, President*
*D. Andrew Neff, Vice President*
*Lane Auten, Treasurer*
Summer camp for children and young adults ages 5-15 with epilepsy and seizure disorders.

**934 Camp Ramah In California**
17525 Ventura Blvd. #201
Encino, CA 91316
310-476-8571
888-226-7726
FAX: 310-472-3810
e-mail: info@ramah.org
www.ramah.org

*Rabbi Joe Menashe, Exec. Dir.*
*Randy Michaels, Dir. of Finance & Administration*
*Elie Mechaly, Dir. of Operations*
*Ilana Ormond, Dir. of Dev*
Camp for young adults ages 11-18 with learning, emotional and developmental disabilities.

**935 Camp ReCreation**
2110 Broadway
Sacramento, CA 95818
916-733-0136
FAX: 916-733-0195
e-mail: CampRec@scd.org
camprecreation.org

*Kathy Barber, Administrator*
A residential summer camp program for adults and children with developmental disabilities.

**936 Camp Reach for the Sky**
American Cancer Society c/o CR4TS
Ste 100
2655 Camino Del Rio N
San Diego, CA 92108-1633
619-682-7427
800-227-2345
FAX: 404-417-5974
TTY: 866-228-4327
www.cancer.org

*Kimberly Wright, Dir., Mission Solutions & Tools*
*Kristina Thomson, LCSW, Division Director*
*Sheila G. Williamson, Regional VP*
*Tawana Thomas Johnson, Dir., Health Disparities*
One-week sessions for children who have had, or currently have, cancer, and are residents of San Diego and Imperial counties. Coed, ages 4-18. Siblings are also invited to participate in activities.

**937 Camp Ronald McDonald for Good Times**
Ronald McDonald House Charities - Southern Calif.
1954 Cotner Ave
Los Angeles, CA 90025-5602
310-268-8488
800-625-7295
FAX: 310-473-3338
e-mail: info@campronaldmcdonald.org
www.campronaldmcdonald.org

*Laurie Dubchansky, Executive Director*
*Brad Baillie, Facility Supervisor*
*Brian Crater, Associate Executive Director*
*Chad Edwards, Program Director*
Free year-round residential camping for children with cancer and their families.

**938 Camp Ronald McDonald(r) at Eagle Lake**
P.O. Box 172
Susanville, CA 96130
530-825-3158
FAX: 530-825-3158
e-mail: vicky@campronald.org
www.campronald.org

*Vicky Flaig, MEd, RD, Manager*
Supported by Ronald McDonald House Charities(r) Northern California-a fully accessible residential camp for kids with special needs. The goal of the camp is to provide confidence building experiences to children who are at risk, disadvantaged and/or living with physical, developmental or emotional disabilities. The correct name is ""Camp Ronald McDonald at Eagle Lake""

**939 Camp Rubber Soul**
325A East Redwood Avenue
Fort Bragg, CA 95437
707-962-0906
e-mail: camp@camprubbersoul.org
www.camprubbersoul.org

*Rachel Miller, Camp contact person*
*Sayre Statham, Camp contact person*
The camp offers five one-week camping stays for children and young adults with special needs. Some of the activities include sports, wood working, painting, theatre, music and arts and crafts.

**940 Camp Sunshine Dreams**
P.O. Box 28232
Fresno, CA 93729-8232
559-301-5419
www.campsunshinedreams.com

*Bryan Wood, Camp contact person*
*Anthony Aiello, Camp contact person*
Camp Sunshine Dreams is open for children and young adults ages 8-15 years and their siblings. The camp focuses on providing an enjoyable, stimulating and supportive camping experience while also providing for each childs special emotional and physical needs.

**941 Camp Taylor, Inc.**
5424 Pirrone Road
Salida, CA 95368-9094
209-545-4715
FAX: 209-543-1861
e-mail: kimberlie@kidsheartcamp.org
www.kidsheartcamp.org

*Kimberlie Gamino, Executive Director and Founder*
*Rollin A. Podwys, Camp Director*
*Steven Barbieri, Camp Counselor*
*Charlie Liamos, Venture Capitalist*
Camp Taylor is open to children and young adults and thier families who have heart disease and offers many recreational activities.

**942 Camp Trinity**
Bar 717 Ranch
Hayfork, CA 96041
530-628-5992
FAX: 530-628-9392
e-mail: camptrinity@bar717.com
www.bar717.com/

*Pen Perry, Executive Director*
*Mary Beth Gay, Director*
*Stephanie Rudolph, Registrar*
Offers two, three and four-week camping sessions May-September. Accepts campers with diabetes and mobility limitation. Coed, ages 8-16. Also families, single adults and seniors.

**943 Camp-A-Lot And Leisure Express (PALS Program)**
Arc of San Diego
3030 Market Street
San Diego, CA 92102
619-685-1175
FAX: 619-234-3759
e-mail: info@arc-sd.com
www.arc-sd.com

*David W. Schneider, President and CEO*
*Anthony J. DeSalis, Esq, Exec VP & COO*
*Rich Coppa, VP of Infrastructure*
*Chad Lyle, VP of Finance/CFO*
Recreatonal opportunities for children, teens and adults with developmental and intellectual disabilities. Programs include summer resident camp, San Diego local activities and trip/travel vacations.

**944 Camping Unlimited-Camp Krem**
Camping Unlimited for Children & Adults
102 Brook Ln
Boulder Creek, CA 95006-9320 831-338-3210
e-mail: campkrem@campingunlimited.com
campingunlimited.com

*Mary Farfaglia, Executive Director*
Camp is located in Boulder Creek, California in the Santa Cruz mountains. Offers one and two-week sessions June-August to campers with a variety of disabilities. Coed, ages 5-50. Camping unlimited also offers weekend programs and travel camps, year round progams and recreation. Boulder Creek is located 15 minutes from Santa Cruz, CA, and Pacific Ocean Beach.

**945 Camps for Children & Teens with Diabetes**
Diabetes Society
1165 Lincoln Ave
Ste 300
San Jose, CA 95125-3052 408-287-3785
800-989-1165
FAX: 408-287-2701
e-mail: camp@diabetessociety.org
www.diabetessociety.org

*Carol Kassouf, Executive Director*
*Kat Carpenter, Director*
Since 1974, sponsors up to 20 day camps, family camps and resident camps for children 4 through 17. These camps provide an opportunity for children with diabetes to go to camp, meet other children and gain a better understanding of their diabetes. The total experience can help campers develop more confidence in their abilities to control their diabetes effectively while enjoying the traditional camp experience. Camps are located throughout CA and parts of Nevada.

**946 Deaf Kid's Kamp**
Sproul Ranch, Inc.
42263 50th Street West
Suite 610
Quartz Hill, CA 93536- 3500 661-675-3323
e-mail: deafkidskamp@earthlink.net
www.deafkidskamp.com

*Buffy Sproul, Executive Director*
Our purpose is to meet the needs of deaf children outside of the classroom setting. These needs, as we have defined them, would include but are not limited to: social contact with peers; contact with the culture of the Deaf Community; educational and recreational programs not available in most school settings.

**947 Easter Seals Camp Harmon**
Easter Seals Central California
16403 Highway 9
Boulder Creek, CA 95006-9696 831-338-3383
800-400-0671
FAX: 831-684-1018
e-mail: campharmon@es-cc.org
www.centralcal.easterseals.com

*Bruce Hinman, President and CEO*
*Ruth Hutchison, Board Chair*
*Robert Guerin, Board Vice Chair*
*Judy Anderson, Secretary / Treasurer*
Camp is located in Boulder Creek, California. 6-10 day sessions for children and adults with physical and developmental disabilities. Coed, ages 8-65.

**948 Enchanted Hills Camp for the Blind**
Lighthouse for the Blind
214 Van Ness Ave
San Francisco, CA 94102-4508 415-431-1481
888-400-8933
FAX: 415-863-7568
TTY: 415-431-4572
e-mail: info@lighthouse-sf.org
lighthouse-sf.org

*Joshua A. Miele, Ph.D., President*
*Stephen Dobbs, 1st Vice President*
*Chris Downey, 2nd Vice President*
*Kathleen Knox, 3rd Vice President*
Camp is located in Napa, California. Half-week, one and two-week sessions for blind, deaf/blind children and adults, ages 5 and up. This program offers a basic camping experience. Activities include music, art, dance, hiking and riding. Camperships are available to California residents.

**949 Firefighters Kids Camp**
Firefighters Burn Institute
3101 Stockton Blvd.
Sacramento, CA 95820 916-739-8525
FAX: 916-455-4376
e-mail: website@ffburn.org
www.ffburn.org

*Brian Rice, President*
*Pat Cook, Secretary-Treasurer*
*Ty Bailey, Metro Vice President*
*Svend Nance, Director of Membership Services*
Provides children and young adults ages 6-17 who have had serious burn injuries the opportunity to continue their rehabilitation and recovery in an outdoor environment where they are safe and can have fun.

**950 Lions Wilderness Camp for Deaf Children, Inc.**
Lions Clubs of California and Nevada
P.O.Box 195
Knightsen, CA 94548-195 925-625-4874
e-mail: campdirector@lionswildcamp.org
www.lionswildcamp.org

*William L. Arnold, Jr., President*
*Benjamin Fregoso, Vice President*
*Denise Arnold, Secretary*
*Danny Raymond, Treasurer*
A camp experience where a deaf child age 7 to 15 can learn outdoor skills and enjoy the wonder and beauty of nature to the fullest extent.

**951 New Horizons Summer Day Camp**
YMCA
13821 Newport Avenue
Suite 200
Tustin, CA 92780-7803 714-549-9622
FAX: 714-838-5976
www.ymcaoc.org

*Jeff Black, Board Of Director*
*Tom Reyes, Board Of Director*
*John Rochford, Board Of Director*
*Hugh Helm, Board Of Director*
One-week sessions for children with ADD and speech/communication impairment. Coed, ages 5-14.

**952 Pilgrim Pines Camp & Conference Center**
United Church of Christ
39570 Glen Road
Yucaipa, CA 92399 909-797-1821
800-616-6612
800-678-5102
FAX: 909-797-2691
e-mail: info@pilgrimpinescamp.org
www.pilgrimpinescamp.org

*June Boutwell, Executive Director*

Christian camp offering one-week sessions for campers with developmental disabilities. Coed, ages 10-Adult. Also families.

953 **Quest Camp**
2333 San Ramon Valley Blvd.
Suite 125
San Ramon, CA 94583-1763
925-743-2900
800-313-9733
FAX: 925-820-9761
e-mail: questcamps@mac.com
questcamps.com

*Dr. Robert B Field, PhD., Founder/Executive Director*
*Debra Forrester-Field, M.A., Administrative Director*
*Aimee Coonerty-Femiano, Ph.D, Director*
*Jodie Knott, Ph.D., Director*
Camp is located in Alamo, California. Day camp offering three to eight-week sessions including psychological treatment for children with ADD and other mild to moderate psychological disorders. Coed, ages 6-15.

954 **Special Camp For Special Kids**
31641 La Novia Avenue
San Juan Capistrano, CA 92675
949-661-0108
FAX: 949-661-8637
e-mail: lindsay.eres@smes.org
www.specialcamp.org

*Lindsay Eres, Executive Director*
*Stefani Baker, Camp Operations Director*
*Patty Canright, RN, Nursing Director*
*Katie MacNair, LVN, Asst. to the Directors*
Day camp for youths with disabilities offering arts & crafts, games, reading, and entertainment.

955 **The Painted Turtle**
1300 4th Street
Suite 300
Santa Monica, CA 90401
310-451-1353
866-451-5367
FAX: 310-451-1357
e-mail: info@thepaintedturtle.com
www.thepaintedturtle.com

*Blake Maher, Exec. Dir.*
*Chris Butler, Dir. of Finance & Administration*
*Gina Jansheski, M.D., Medical Dir.*
*Allen McBroom, Operations Dir.*
This camp is the sixth edition to the 'Hole in the Wall' camps and is for seriously ill children in the California area. The Painted Turtle offers swimming, boating, fishing, horseback riding, art and crafts, and nature activities.

## Colorado

956 **Adam's Camp**
6767 South Spruce Street
Suite 102
Centennial, CO 80112
303-563-8290
FAX: 303-563-8291
e-mail: laura@adamscamp.org
www.adamscamp.org/

*Karel Horney, Exec. Dir.*
*Lisa Townsend, Program Dir.*
*Laura Johnson, Billing and Finance Dir.*
*Sarah Hartway, Dir. of Dev. and Communications*
Adam's camp is designed for infants and children with special needs and their families, as well as young adults with mild to moderate developmental disabilities. The camp offers a variety of intensive, therapeutic programs and recreational programs.

957 **Aspen Camp of the Deaf & Hard of Hearing**
PO Box 1494
Aspen, CO 81612
970-923-2511
FAX: 970-923-0643
TTY:970-315-0513
e-mail: office@aspencamp.org
www.aspencamp.org

*Lesa V. Thompson, Camp Director*
*Ryan Thomason, Executive Assistant*
*Katie Murch, Outreach*
*Gloria Edwards, Grants*
Provide enriching experiential educational and recreational experiences for Deaf and Hard of Hearing individuals.

958 **Breckenridge Outdoor Education Center**
P.O.Box 697
Breckenridge, CO 80424-697
970-453-6422
FAX: 970-453-4676
e-mail: boec@boec.org
www.boec.org

*Bruce Fitch, Executive Director*
*Tim Casey, Chair*
*John Ebright, Treasurer*
*Raule Nemer, Vice Chair*
Provides year-round adventure based wilderness and adaptive ski programs for people with disabilities. The Center excels in offering challenging, rewarding outdoor experiences individually designed to the abilities and needs of participants.

959 **CNI Cochlear Kids Camp**
Colorado Neurological Institute
701 East Hampden Avenue
Suite 415
Englewood, CO 80113- 2059
303-783-9220
855-463-6264
FAX: 303-788-4010
e-mail: info@TheCNI.org
www.thecni.org

*Tami Lack, MA, CFRE, Executive Director*
*Ellen Belle, MA-PT, Director, CNI NeuroHealth Center*
*Luci Draayer, LCSW, CMC, Director of Patient Care*
*Amy Evans, Director of Operations*
Designed to bring together children ages 1-18 with cochlear implants and their families. Campers enjoy both indoor and outdoor recreational and educational programs.

960 **Camp Paha Rise Above**
City of Lakewood
13198 W. Green Mountain Drive
Lakewood, CO 80228-2803
303-987-4866
FAX: 303-987-7832
TTY:303-987-4862
e-mail: marsno@lakewood.org
www.lakewood.org

*Shane Wright, Camp Director*
*Mark Snow, Camp Director*
*April Rosenthal, RISE Program Coordinator*
*Mark Snow, RISE Program Specialist*
Camp Paha is a City of Lakewood day camp for children ages 6-17 and young adults ages 18-25 with disabilities. We provide programs for campers with all disability types: developmental, physical, emotional, behavioral, and learning. Camp Paha offers safe, quality, fun and challenging activities. Camp provides campers an opportunity to participate in aquatics, sports, games, nature, music, drama, hiking, arts and crafts, and field trips into the community.

**961 Camp Rocky Mountain Village**
Easter Seals Colorado
P.O. Box 115
Empire, CO 80438
303-569-2333
FAX: 303-569-3857
e-mail: campinfo@eastersealscolorado.org
www.co.easterseals.com

*Chris Whitley, Chair*
*Bill Evert, Co-Treasurer*
*Nancy Hanson, Corporate Secretary*
*Lynn Robinson, President/CEO*
For children and adults with disabilities. Campers enjoy swimming, fishing, day trips, sports and recreation, arts and crafts.

**962 Camp Wapiyapi**
910 16th Street
Suite 226
Denver, CO 80202
303-534-0883
FAX: 303-534-0874
e-mail: lindsay@wapiyapi.org
www.wapiyapi.org

*Stephanie Hearn, Executive Director*
*Kristin Schmitt, Staff Assistant*
*Lindsay Graveley, Program and Volunteer Cordinator*
A no-cost respite for children with cancer and their families. The camp offers a wide variety of group and individual activities

**963 Challenge Aspen**
P.O.Box 6639
Snowmass Village, CO 81615
970-923-0578
FAX: 970-923-7338
e-mail: possibilities@challengeaspen.com
challengeaspen.org

*Houston Cowan, CEO*
*Stacey Wooley, Recreational Program Director*
*Nikki Malcolm, Groups/Camps Coordinator*
Challenge Aspen provides recreational and cultural experiences for individuals who have cognitive or physical challenges. Challenge Aspen offers a variety of recreational programs to fit a diversity of needs and interests. We offer both summer, winter and special events for both adults and children.

**964 Cheley/Children's Hospital Burn Camps Program**
The Children's Hospital
Anschultz Medical Campus
13123 East 16th Avenue
Aurora, CO 80045
720-777-1234
800-624-6553
TTY:770-777-6050
e-mail: boulter.trudy@tchden.org
www.thechildrenshospital.org

*Jim Shmerling, DHA, FACHE, President and CEO*
Camp is open for children ages 8 to 18 who have been hospitalized at The Children's Hospital or other burn units across the country. Campers gain life skills and confidence whether they are on a challenge course, catching a fish or climbing onto a horse.

**965 Colorado Lions Camp**
P.O.Box 9043
Woodland Park, CO 80866-9043
719-687-2087
FAX: 719-687-7435
e-mail: jpierie@coloradolionscamp.org
www.coloradolionscamp.org

*Mike Schmeeckle, President*
*Leo Kuntz, VP*
*Jim Pierie, Executive Director*
*Michelle Werner, Executive Assistant Camp Office*
Outdoor recreational camping for the visually and hearing impaired and developmentally delayed. All normal camp activities are offered at the year-round facility. Summer and winter programs. 1 to 4 staff supervision with a nurse or doctor in attendance.

**966 Rocky Mountain Village**
Easter Seals Colorado
PO Box 115
Empire, CO 80438-115
303-569-2333
FAX: 303-569-3857
e-mail: campinfo@eastersealscolorado.org
www.co.easterseals.com

*Chris Whitley, Chair*
*Bill Evert, Co-Treasurer*
*Nancy Hanson, Corporate Secretary*
*Lynn Robinson, President/CEO*
An 11 week summer camp for people with disabilities. After the summer season there is repsite weekends for people with disabilities - once a month.

**967 YMCA Camp Shady Brook**
YMCA of the Pikes Peak Region (PPYMCA)
8716 South Y Camp Road
Sedalia, CO 80135
303-647-2313
FAX: 303-647-0513
e-mail: campinfo@ppymca.org
www.campshadybrook.org

*Joanna Stark, Executive Director*
*Pat Soldan, Program Director*
*Patrick A. Casey, Facility Director*
*Michaela Eddleston, Conference & Retreat Director*
Camp is located in Sedalia, Colorado. One-week sessions for campers with HIV. Boys and girls 7-16. Also families, seniors and single adults.

## Connecticut

**968 Arthur C. Luf Children's Burn Camp**
Connecticut Burns Care Foundation
601 Boston Post Road
Milford, CT 06460
203-878-6744
FAX: 203-878-4044
e-mail: ctburnscare@optonline.net
www.ctburnsfoundation.org

*Frank Szivos, Executive Director*
*Susan M. Howard, Foundation Secretary*
A safe outdoor environment for children ages 8-18 from around the world who have survived life altering burn injuries. Children learn to build self-confidence and self-esteem.

**969 Camp Harkness**
Arc of New London County
P.O. Box 2545
Hartford, CT 06146-2545
sbacct.tripod.com/
In 1991 a group of parents and adults with spina bifida, were brought together with the mission to educate the public about spina bifida and issues affecting people who have this disability in addition To providing support and information and promoting programs that will help people with spina bifida. Since then SBAC has worked hard to support parents, adults with spina bifida and families

**970 Camp Hemlocks**
Easter Seals: Connecticut
85 Jones Street
P.O. Box 198
Amston, CT 06231
860-228-9496
800-832-4409
FAX: 860-228-2091
e-mail: campinfo@eastersealsct.org
www.eastersealscamphemlocks.org

*Chris Whitley, Chair*
*Bill Evert, Co-Treasurer*
*Nancy Hanson, Corporate Secretary*
*Lynn Robinson, President/CEO*
Camp is located in Hebron, Connecticut. One and two-week sessions June-August for campers with a variety of disabilities.

Coed, ages 6 and up. Families, seniors, single adults. Campers can enjoy nature walks, swimming, boating arts & crafts and sing-a-longs around the campfire.

**971 Camp Horizons**
127 Babcock Hill Rd
PO Box 323
South Windham, CT 06266
860-456-1032
FAX: 860-456-4721
e-mail: scott.lambeck@camphorizons.org
www.camphorizons.org

*Adam Milne, Board Chairperson*
*L. Sanford (Sandy) Rice, Board Treasurer*
*Deirdhre (Dede) Delaney, Board Secretary*
*Kathleen McNaboe, Board Vice President*

Bordering Lake Probus, the facilities at the camp are equipped to accomodate a wide range of activities and programs for campers with developmental disabilities, or other challenging emotional and social needs. There is a 5:1 camper-counselor ratio with a schedule of three programs in the morning and four in the afternoon.

**972 Camp Isola Bella**
American School for the Deaf
139 N Main St
West Hartford, CT 06107-1264
860-570-2300
TTY:860-570-2222
e-mail: Steve.Borsotti@asd-1817.org
www.asd-1817.org

*Steve Borsotti, Reunion Chairperson*

Hearing-impaired children, ages 6-19, blend educational instruction in communications with recreational activities. Qualified deaf and hearing staff members with experience in education, child care and counseling are employed at the camp.

**973 Hole in the Wall Gang Camp**
565 Ashford Center Rd
Ashford, CT 06278-1720
860-429-3444
FAX: 860-429-7295
e-mail: ashford@holeinthewallgang.org
www.holeinthewallgang.org

*James H. Canton, CEO*
*Kevin M. Magee, CFO*
*Rebecca Allen, LCSW, Chief Program Officer*
*Ken Alberti, Director of Development*

Low-cost eight-week sessions June-August for children with cancer and HIV. Coed, ages 7-15.

**974 Marvelwood Summer**
Marvelwood School
476 Skiff Mountain Road
P.O. Box 3001
Kent, CT 06757- 3001
860-927-0047
FAX: 860-927-0021
e-mail: summerschool@marvelwood.org
www.marvelwood.org

*James R. Samartini, President, Chair*
*Mary Bainbridge, Vice Co-Chair*
*Ted Bohnen, Vice Co-Chair*
*Mark Esposito, Dev. Committee Chair*

The emphasis in this summer program is on diagnosis and remediation of individual reading, spelling, writing, mathematics and study problems. Offered to ages 12-16.

**975 TSA CT Kid's Summer Event**
Tourette Syndrome Association of Connecticut (TSA)
PO Box 185883
Hamden, CT 06518
203-980-4215
e-mail: joytavo@tsact.org
www.tsact.org

*Peter Tavolacci, Vice Chairman*
*Paul Nazario, Treasurer*
*Jeanette Nazario, Board Member*
*Mike Tavolacci, Board Member*

TSA of Connecticut sponsors summer events for children with TS/Tourette Syndrome activities of which include minature golf in addition to an Annual Conference. The kids' program at this annual conference provides children who have TS a unique opportunity to meet other children like them who also struggle with TS. Entertainment includes puppeteers, magicians, learning karate from the experts, getting face paintings and more.

*uniqu pages*

**976 YMCA Camp Jewell**
YMCA of Greater Hartford
6 Prock Hill Road
P.O. Box 8
Colebrook, CT 06021-8
860-379-2782
888-412-2267
FAX: 860-379-8715
TTY: 888-412-2267
e-mail: camp.jewell@ghymca.org
www.ghymca.org

*Eric Tucker, Executive Director*
*Ray Zetye, Director*
*Marilyn Ducor, Camp Registrar*
*Kathie Reese, Office Manager*

Camp is located in Colebrook, Connecticut. Two-week sessions for children with cancer. Coed, ages 8-16. Also families.

## Delaware

**977 Camp Fairlee Manor**
Easter Seals Of Delaware
22242 Bay Shore Road
Chestertown, MD 21620
410-778-0566
FAX: 410-778-0567
de.easterseals.com

*Amy Walls, Advisory Council Member*

For children and adults with physical disabilities and/or cognitive impairements. Activities include arts and crafts, sports and games, nature walks, swimming, and fishing

**978 Camp Manito/Camp Lenape**
United Cerebral Palsy Of Delaware
UCP Center
700 A River Road
Wilmington, DE 19809
302-764-2400
FAX: 302-764-8713
www.ucpde.org

*William J. McCool, III, Executive Director*
*Donna M. Hopkins, President*
*D. Bruce McClenathan, Vice President*
*Daniel Edgar, Treasurer*

For children & young adults aged 3-21 with orthopedic disabilities. Campers find a structured program of arts, crafts, sports, swimming, music and nature studies.

979 **Childrens Beach House**
100 West 10th Street
Suite 411
Wilmington, DE 19801-1674
302-655-4288
FAX: 302-655-4216
www.cbhinc.org

*Richard T Garrett, Exec. Dir.*
*Steven T. Martinenza, Dir. of Youth Dev. Program*
*Amanda Ryan, Dir. of Dev.*
*Jennifer A. Clement, Dir., Delaware Center*
Camp is located in Lewes, Delaware. Four-week sessions June-August for Delaware children with hearing impairment or speech/communication impairment,also fine or gross motor delays. Coed, ages 7-18. Also, serves children year round on weekends only.

980 **Sandcastle Day Camp**
Children's Beach House
1800 Bay Ave
Lewes, DE 19958-1859
302-645-9184
FAX: 302-655-4216
www.cbhinc.org

*Richard Garrett, Exec. Dir.*
*Steven T. Martinenza, Dir. of Youth Dev. Program*
*Amanda Ryan, Dir. of Dev.*
*Jennifer A. Clement, Dir., Delaware Center*
Camp is located in Lewes, Delaware. Four-week sessions June-August for Delaware children with hearing impairment or speech/communication impairment. Coed, ages 6-12.

## District of Columbia

981 **Columbia Lighthouse for the Blind Summer Camp**
Columbia Lighthouse for the Blind
Ste 1103
1825 K St NW
Washington, DC 20006-1261
202-454-6400
FAX: 202-454-6401
e-mail: info@clb.org
clb.org

*Tony Cancelosi, K.M.,, President and CEO*
*Jocelyn Hunter, Director of Communications*
*Cathy Miller, Director of Development*
Helps enable the blind or visually impaired to obtain and maintain independence at home, school, work and in the community. Programs and services include early intervention services, training and consultation in assistive technology, career placement services, comprehensive low vision care and a wide range of rehabilitation services. Highly acclaimed summer camp, picnics and holiday activities encourage blind and visualy impaired children to make new friends and experience the joys of childhood.

982 **Lab School of Washington**
4759 Reservoir Rd NW
Washington, DC 20007-1921
202-965-6600
e-mail: labschool@webmail.org
labschool.org

*Sally Seawright, Interim Dir.*
*Robert Mathias, Chair*
*Mimi Dawson, Vice-Chair*
*Bill Tennis, Vice-Chair*
The Lab School six week summer session includes individualized reading, spelling, writing, study skills and math programs. A multisensory approach addresses the needs of bright learning disabled children. Related services such as speech/language therapy and occupational therapy are integrated into the curriculum. Elementary/Intermediate; Junior High/High School.

## Florida

983 **Camp Amigo Burn Camp**
Children's Burn Camp Of North Florida, Inc.
P.O. Box 368
Tallahassee, FL 32302
850-509-6200
www.campamigo.com

*Rusty Roberts, President*
*Stephanie Powell, Treasurer*
Camp Amigo is open to burn suvivors ages 6-18 living in North or Central Florida. The camp is free of charge and provides children who have physical and emotional scarring a place to be themselves and build a network of support.

984 **Camp Boggy Creek**
30500 Brantley Branch Rd
Eustis, FL 32736-9596
352-483-4200
866-468-6449
FAX: 352-483-0589
e-mail: info@BoggyCreek.org
www.boggycreek.org

Year-round sessions for children with a variety of chronic or life-threatening illnesses including cancer, hemophila, epilepsy, heart defects, HIV, spina bifida and asthma/respiratory ailments. Coed, ages 7-16.

985 **Camp Challenge**
Easter Seals Of Florida
31600 Camp Challenge Road
Sorrento, FL 32776
352-383-4711
e-mail: camp@fl.easterseals.com
www.fleasterseals.com
Recreational and social activities for individuals with disabilities.

986 **Camp Thunderbird**
Quest, Inc.
P.O.Box 531125
Orlando, FL 32853-1125
407-218-4300
888-807-8378
FAX: 407-218-4301
e-mail: webadmin@questinc.org
www.questinc.org

*Katie Porta, President*
*Vicki Bauer, VP Residential Program*
*Michelle Bellamy, VP Employment Svcs*
*Robert E. Cage, Dir. Quest's Camp Thunderbird*
Residential summer camping program for children and adults with a developmental disability. Located on 19-acres of Wekiwa Springs State Park. Campers enjoy swimming, sports, nature hikes, an outdoor amphitheater, etc. One and two-week sessions June-August. Coed, ages 8-80.

987 **Center Academy at Pinellas Park**
6710 86th Ave
Pinellas Park, FL 33782-4502
727-541-5716
FAX: 727-544-8186
e-mail: infopp@centeracademy.com
www.centeracademy.com

*Eric V. Larson, Ph. D.,, President*
*Mack R Hicks PhD, Founder/Chairman of the Board*
*Andrew P Hicks PhD, CEO/Clinical Dir.*
*Lisa Hartmann, Dir. Education*
Specifically designed for the learning disabled child and other children with difficulties in concentration, strategy, social skills, impulsivity, distractibility and study strategies. Programs offered include: attention training, visual-motor remediation, socialization skills training, relaxation training, horseback riding and more. The day camp meets weekdays from 9-3 for 3,4 or 5 week sessions.

988 **Dream Oaks Camp**
Foundation For Dreams, Inc.
16110 Dream Oaks Place
Bradenton, FL 34212
941-746-5659
FAX: 941-745-1409
e-mail: jfranke@foundationfordreams.org
www.foundationfordreams.org

*Jodi Franke, Executive Director*
*Elena Cassella, Director of Development*
*Gilda Poe, Administrative Assistant*
Weekend camps and day residential programs open to children with physical and developmental disabililties and serious illnesses. Activities include horseback riding, nature programs, sports, game, swimming, talent shows, and arts and crafts.

989 **Florida Diabetes Camp**
P.O.Box 14136
Gainesville, FL 32604-2136
352-334-1321
FAX: 352-334-1326
e-mail: fccyd@floridadiabetescamp.org
www.floridadiabetescamp.org
*Helene , Director*
*Tim , Camp Director*
*Karen , Camp Director*
*Gary , Camp Director*
Camp is located in Florida. One and two-week sessions June-August for children with diabetes. Coed, ages 6-18 and families. Camps throughout the year.

990 **Florida Lions Camp**
Lions of Multiple District 35
2819 Tiger Lake Rd
Lake Wales, FL 33898-9465
863-696-1948
FAX: 863-696-2398
e-mail: jrv113@gmail.com
www.lionscampfl.org

*Barbara Cage, Executive Director*
*Liz Cage, Program Director*
One-week sessions June-August for youths and adults with visual impairments and other challenging disabilities. Coed, ages 5 and up. A variety of traditional summer camp activities which include: swimming, canoeing, fishing, hiking, camping out and cooking over a fire, games, arts & crafts, singing & dancing, hay-wagon rides, challenge course and much more. Activities are adapted to the age and ability of each camper to ensure maximum participation, safety and fun.

991 **Florida Sheriffs Caruth Camp**
Florida Sheriffs Youth Ranches
2486 Cecil Webb Place
Live Oak, FL 32060
386-842-5501
FAX: 386-842-2429
youthranches.org

*Roger Bouchard, President*
*Bill Frye, Vice President of Programs*
*Janet Bass, Vice President of Operations*
*Wayne Walden, Vice President of Finance*
Camp is located in Inglis, Florida. One-week sessions for children with ADD. Coed, ages 10-15.

992 **Sertoma Camp Endeavor**
Sertoma Camp Endeavor
P.O.Box 910
Dundee, FL 33838-0910
863-439-1300
e-mail: info@sertomacampendeavor.com
www.sertomacampendeavor.org
The intergration of deaf, hard of hearing and hearing youngsters is a unique characteristic of our camping program. Both hearing, deaf and hard of hearing children have the opportunity to learn about themselves and each other in an informal and empowering setting.

993 **VACC Camp**
Miami Childrens Hospital
3200 S.W. 60 Ct.
Suite 203
Miami, FL 33155-4076
305-662-8222
FAX: 305-663-8417
e-mail: bela.florentin@mch.com
www.vacccamp.com

*Bela Florentin, Camp Coordinator*
Free week-long overnight camp for ventilation assisted children and their families.

## Georgia

994 **Camp Breathe Easy**
American Lung Association
2452 Spring Rd
Smyrna, GA 30080-3828
404-231-9887
e-mail: annie@camptwinlakes.org
campbreatheeasy.com/

*Annie Garrett, Camp Director*
Camp Breathe Easy is a seven-day, six-night overnight camp for children, ages 7-13, with asthma who need medication and are limited in summer camping opportunities. The children learn asthma self-management techniques and coping strategies to better handle their illness. Campers swim, repel off trees, fish, canoe, play soccer, basketball and miniature golf, and participate in ceramics and arts and crafts.

995 **Camp Caglewood**
Caglewood, Inc.
P.O. Box 158
Flowery Branch, GA 30542
678-405-9000
FAX: 770-441-3406
e-mail: info@caglewood.org
www.caglewood.org
Camp Caglewood is for children and adults with developmental disabililties in which campers learn life skills which will in turn help them to become socially involved in their communities and be capable of living independently in the future.

996 **Camp Dream**
Camp Dream Foundation
4355 Cobb Parkway
Suite J117
Atlanta, GA 30339
www.campdreamga.org

*JR Clark, President*
*Jerry Cochran, Vice President*
*Rich Little, Treasurer*
*Clete Taylor, Secretary*
Camp Dream is a free camp where special needs children can camp and have fun regarless of their physical and/or mental condition. The camp offers many recreational activities and programs.

997 **Camp Hawkins**
GA Baptist Childrens Homes & Family Ministries,Inc
P.O. Box 329
Palmetto, GA 30268
770-463-3800
e-mail: ksewell@gbchfm.org
www.gbchfm.org

*James Harper, D.Min, President/CEO*
*Kendra Sewell, Contact Person*
Residential summer camp for youth's ages 8-12 coping with varying developmental disabilities such as down's syndrome, traumatic brain injuries, cerebral palsy, and learning disorders and/or developmental delays. Staff works one-on-one with each camper.

998 **Camp Independence**
National Kidney Foundation
2951 Flowers Road South
Suite 211
Atlanta, GA 30341-5533
770-452-1539
800-633-2339
FAX: 770-452-7564
e-mail: tracy@kidneyga.org
www.kidney.org

Camp Independence is Georgia's a overnight, week-long summer camp providing essential medical care, treatment & fun for kids with kidney disease and transplants. Camp Independence recognizes that campers are normal children but have special needs providing these children with opportunities for development & individual growth, peer support & normal life experiences. Activities include swimming, arts & crafts, fishing and horsebackriding, in addition to archery, games and sports, and ceramics.

999 **Camp Juliena**
Georgia Council for the Hearing Impaired
4151 Memorial Drive
Suite 103B
Decatur, GA 30032-1511
404-292-5312
800-541-0710
FAX: 404-299-3642
e-mail: campjuliena@gmail.com
http://www.fullcirclegrp1.com

*Thomas Galey, Executive Director*
*Bonna Lenyszyn, Camp Director*
*Ron Vickery, President*
*Deborah Douglin, Treasurer*

A weeklong residential summer camp for youths and teens who are deaf or hard of hearing. Through challenging, team-oriented activities, campers form lasting friendships and acquire valuable leadership, social and communication skills.

1000 **Camp Kudzu**
Camp Kudzu, Inc.
5885 Glenridge Drive
Suite 160
Atlanta, GA 30328
404-250-1811
FAX: 404-250-1812
e-mail: info@campkudzu.org
www.campkudzu.org

*Alex Allen, Executive Director*
*Sarah Hersh, Development Coordinator*
*Bethany Kinsey, RN, BSN, CDE, Medical Director*
*Cyndy McCoy Oastler, Camper Services Administrator*

Camp for children, teens and families with type 1 diabetes. Besides teaching diabetes management, campers learn that they are not alone in their struggles and enjoy climbing, swimming and many other outdoor activities.

1001 **Camp Sunshine**
1850 Clairmont Road
Decatur, GA 30033-3405
404-325-7979
866-786-2267
FAX: 404-325-7929
www.mycampsunshine.com

*Dorothy H. Jordan, Founder*
*Mindy Shoulberg, Secretary*
*Mo Thrash, Chair*
*Eric Newberg, Treasurer*

Camp sunshine gives children with cancer the opportunity to enjoy normal activities such as horseback riding, swimming, and arts & crafts.

1002 **Camp Twin Lakes**
1391 Keencheefoonee Rd
Rutledge, GA 30663-2818
706-557-9070
FAX: 706-557-9147
e-mail: contact@camptwinlakes.org
www.camptwinlakes.org

*Eric Robbins, Executive Director*
*Daniel C. Mathews, M.Ed., CTR, Director of Camping Services*
*Jessie Rosenberg, Director of Development*
*Leena Sidhu, Annual Campaign Manager*

One-week sessions June-August for children with serious illnesses and life challenges. Works with over 40 different special needs organizations. Coed, ages 8-18. Two locations: Rutledge and Will-A-Way in Winder, GA.

1003 **Paddy Rossbach Youth Camp**
Amputee Coalition Of America
900 East Hill Avenue
Suite 205
Knoxville, TN 37915-2566
888-267-5669
TTY:865-525-4512
www.amputee-coalition.org

*Matt Brunger, Resource Specialist*
*Kendra Calhoun, President & Chief Executive Officer*
*Dawn Draayer, Director of Development*
*Andrea Crabtree-Coin, Office Manager*

Georgia camp for youths ages 10-17 years of age who have limb loss or limb difference. Activities include sports, swimming, fishing, arts and crafts.

1004 **Squirrel Hollow Summer Camp**
The Bedford School
5665 Milam Rd
Fairburn, GA 30213-2851
770-774-8001
FAX: 770-774-8005
e-mail: bbox@thebedfordschool.org
www.thebedfordschool.org

*Betsy Box, Executive Director*
*James Jeff, Headmaster/Athletic Director./MS Math*
*Day Allison, Asst. Headmaster/MS Admin./MS English*
*Shipmon Kendra, LS Admin./LS Math*

A remedial summer program for children with academic needs held on the campus of The Bedford School in Fairburn, Georgia. It is a five week day camp held from June 19 to July 21 and serves ages 6-16. For mor information contact Betsy Box at (770) 774-8001.

## Hawaii

1005 **Camp Anuenue**
American Cancer Society
Waialua, HI 96791
808-595-7500
FAX: 808-595-7502
e-mail: dglowik@cancer.org
www.specialneeds.com/directory/camp/cancer/hi

*Debra Glowik, Director*

Camp Anuenue is for children ages 7-17 who have or have had cancer.

1006 **YMCA Camp Erdman**
YMCA Of Honolulu
69-385 Farrington Hwy
Waialua, HI 96791-9383
808-637-4615
FAX: 808-637-8874
e-mail: camperdman@ymcahonolulu.org
www.ymcahonolulu.org

*Josh Heimowitz, Executive Director*
*Tom Rapine, Executive Director*
*Edd Fishlock, Program Director*
*Sarah Miller, Associate Program Director*

Traditional Resident Camp program is five nights and six days of fun-filled activities that will create positive lifetime memories. Camp activitiesinclude: arts & crafts, swimming, kayaking, hiking, challenge course, snorkeling, athletics, nature, dance & drama, beach writing and archery . Traditional Resident Camp Experience (Ages 6-17) serving the needs of the disabled.

## Idaho

**1007 Camp Hodia**
1701 N 12th St
Boise, ID 83702
208-891-1023
FAX: 208-891-1023
e-mail: lisa1@hodia.org
http://www.hodia.org

*Lisa Gier, Executive Director*
*Alan Bean, MD, Director, Hodia Teen Camp*
*Kathlynn Ireland, Director, Hodia Shooting Stars Camp*
*Vicki Cutshall, R.N., Director, Hodia Kids Camp*
Camp is located in Alturas Lake, Idaho. One-week sessions for children with diabetes. Coed, ages 8-18. Ski Camp in Sun Valley in January, ages 12-18.

**1008 Camp Sawtooth**
Oregon-Idaho Conference Center
HC 64 BOX 8290
Ketchum
ID 83340
208-726-1155
e-mail: directorscampsawtooth@yahoo.com
www.campsawtooth.org/

## Illinois

**1009 ADA Camp Grenada**
American Diabetes Association
2501 Chatham Rd
Suite 210
Springfield, IL 62704
217-875-9011
888-342-2383
e-mail: wwallace@diabetes.org
diabetes.org

*Donna Scott, Executive Director*
*Wendy Wallace, Contact Person*
Camp Granada is an American Diabetes Association resident Camp located in Monticello, Illinois at the 4H Memorial Camp owned by the University of Illinois. For children with diabetes, ages 8-16. Activities include swimming, canoeing, wall climbing, tie-dying shirts, arts & crafts and fun filled evening programs. The name of the company is ""ADA Camp Granada""

**1010 ADA Teen Adventure Camp**
American Diabetes Association
32405 N
Highway 12
Ingleside, IL 60041
312-346-1805
888-342-2383
FAX: 312-346-5342
e-mail: sapsey@diabetes.org
http://www.ncpad.org

*Sue Apsey, Program Director*
Camping for teenagers with diabetes. Coed, ages 14 to 18. Camp dates are early in August. Located at the YMCA Camp Duncan in Ingleside, Illinois. Featured activities include archery and crafts, singing, outdoor movie night, and roller skating.

**1011 ADA Triangle D Camp**
American Diabetes Association
32405 N
Highway 12
Ingleside, IL 60041
312-346-1805
888-342-2383
e-mail: sapsey@diabetes.org
http://www.ncpad.org

*Sue Apsey, Program Director*
Triangle D Camp is a resident camp program located at the YMCA Camp Duncan in Ingleside, Illinois. Activities include swimming, row boating, canoeing, high ropes (11-13 yr. olds), climbing tower (9-10 yr. olds), Camp games, singing, archery, campfires, soccer, basketball, volleyball and diabetes education.

**1012 Bright Horizons Summer Camp**
Sickle Cell Disease Association of Illinois
200 Talcott Avenue South
Watertown
MA 02472
617-673-8000
e-mail: parents@brighthorizons.com
http://www.brighthorizons.com

*David Lissy, CEO*
*Linda Mason, Chairman and Founder*
*Mary Ann Tocio, President and COO*
*Elizabeth Boland, CFO*
Camping for children with blood disorders, ages 7-13. The joys of learning include instruction in first aid, swimming and water safety, boating, horseback riding and bowling plus arts and crafts. In addition, there is a traditional menu of camp pleasures, like hayrides, cookouts, nature hikes and sing-a-longs.

**1013 Camp Callahan**
Camp Callahan, Inc.
P.O. Box 5253
Quincy, IL 62305
217-833-2377
www.campcallahan.com

Dedicated to serving youth's with wide-ranging disabilities.

**1014 Camp Hug The Bear**
Northern Suburban Special Recreation Association
3105 MacArthur Blvd.
Northbrook, IL 60062
847-509-9400
FAX: 847-509-1177
e-mail: info@nssra.org
www.nssra.org

*Maggie Richey MSW, LSW, Manager of ELA and Operations*
*Craig Culp, Executive Director*
*Katie Koske, CPRP, Manager of Cooperative Programs*
*Jerry Barton, CTRS, Manager of Programs*
For children who have sensory integration disorder or children who are on the austism spectrum. Children have the opportunity to take part in a unique camp experience which is vital in their growth and development. Recreation based programs include sports, arts and crafts, swimming, and games.

**1015 Camp I Am Me**
Illinois Fire Safety Alliance
P.O. Box 911
Mount Prospect, IL 60056
847-390-0911
800-634-0911
www.ifsa.org

Camp is held during the third week of June for children who are burn survivors. The children are able to share their common experiences, have fun and not feel self conscious about what others think. Some of the activities include swimming, boating, fishing, archery, basketball and volleyball.

**1016 Camp Little Giant**
SIU:Carbondale Therapeutic Recreation Prgm
1206 Touch of Nature Rd
Makanda, IL 62958
618-453-1121
e-mail: tonec@siu.edu
www.ton.siu.edu

*Mary Anne Cunningham, Manager*
Camp Little Giant is a summer program but the Therapeutic Program runs all year round. One and two week sessions for campers with a variety of disabilities. Coed, ages 8-80.

**1017 Camp New Hope**
P.O.Box 764
Mattoon, IL 61938-764
217-895-2341
FAX: 217-895-3658
e-mail: cnhinc@rr1.net
www.myfavoritecamp.org

*Kim Carmack, Executive Director*
*Terri Taylor, Camp Director*
Weekend Respite, advocacy services, social and recreational services and a summer camp for the disabled. The camp accommodates people of widely diverse needs and abilities including access for wheelchair users. Co-ed, for those 8 years and older, including adults. Facilities include a mini golf area; pontoon boat; fishing deck; playground; trails; swimmming pool; and sleeping cabins with air conditioning.

**1018 Camp Roehr**
Epilepsy Foundation Greater Southern Illinois
140 Iowa Avenue #A
Belleville, IL 62220
618-236-2181
866-848-0472
FAX: 618-236-3654
e-mail: ellen.epilepsy@gmail.com
www.epilepsyfoundation.org

*Ellen Becker, Executive Director*
*Trudy Baxter, Director of Programs*
*Mike Buehlhorn, President*
*Dr. Rosella Wamser, PhD, Vice-President*
A seven day residential camp for children diagnosed with epilepsy. The camp is held at the Pere Marquette State Park where children enjoy swimming, horseback riding, arts and crafts, nightly entertainment and the comaraderie of other children with epilepsy.

**1019 JCYS Camp Red Leaf**
Jewish Council for Youth Services
180 W Washington St.,
Suite 1100
Chicago, IL 60602
312-726-8891
FAX: 312-726-7920
www.jcys.org

*Martin Oliff, Ph.D., Executive Director*
*Susan E Rochlis, Associate Executive Director*
*Barbara Uher Vijuk, Assistant Executive Director*
*Kevin Faulkner, Director of Property Management*
Our special needs camp, serves adults and children with developmental disabilities in 8- one week sessions during the summer, several travel adventures for adults and ten respite weekends during the year for children and young adults.

**1020 Rimland Services for Autistic Citizens**
1265 Hartrey Ave
Evanston, IL 60202-1056
FAX: 847-328-8364
TTY:847-328-4090
e-mail: dwork@rimland.org
www.rimland.org

*Pamela Watson, CEO*
*Dave Work, Assoc Executive Director Program*
*Brendy Sims, Chief Operating Officer*
*Terrance Wimberly, Associate Executive Director of Client Services*
An accessible camp facility that can be utilized by groups for day use or overnight camping experiences. Six winterized cabins, a meeting facility, indoor pool, full food service, and an excellent staff are available. Educational programs can be arranged or you can utilize the facility to manage your own programs.

**1021 Shady Oaks Camp**
16300 Parker Rd
Homer Glen, IL 60491
708-301-0816
FAX: 708-301-5091
e-mail: soc16300@sbcglobal.net
shadyoakscamp.org

*Mary Pisano, Camp Treasurer*
Shady Oaks Camp provides outdoor fun and recreation for children and adults with cerebral palsy and similar disabilities. Our camp is organized with the goal of providing stimulating life experiences that our campers may not have the opportunity to engage in elsewhere.

**1022 Summer Wheelchair Sport Camps**
University of Illinois
1207 S Oak St
Champaign, IL 61820-6901
217-333-4607
FAX: 212-333-0248
e-mail: sportscamp@illinois.edu
www.illinoiswheelchairathletics.com

*Maureen Gilbert, Camp Director*
Rigorous camps designed for individuals with lower extremity physical disabilities. Camp attendees will spend an average of 8-9 hours a day, focusing on development and refinement of fitness, techniques and strategies. Strength training, nutrition and mental training sessions will also be included in all camps. The camp staff is comprised of athletic staff and local wheelchair athletes with coaching experience from the University of Illinois Wheelchair Athletics Program.

**1023 Timber Pointe Outdoor Center**
Easter Seals UCP
507 East Armstrong Avenue
Peoria, IL 61603
309-686-1177
FAX: 309-686-7722
www.ci.easterseals.com

*Steve Thompson, President & CEO*
*David Bateman, Community President*
*Kory Kaeb, Executive Vice President Operations*
*Joette Blakesley, Chief Development Officer*
One and two-week sessions for campers with a wide variety of disabilities. Coed, ages 6-99. Campers experience different activities each day such as arts and crafts, music, horses, field sports, outdoor nature, swimming, canoeingand fishing. Every night there is a different activity: skit night, casino night, boat night (campers go out on the lake on pontoon boats), night swim, camp fires, and of course, everyone's favorite - a dance on the last night.

**1024 Triangle D Camp**
American Diabetes Association
30 N. Michigan
Suite 2015
Chicago, IL 60602
312-346-1805
888-342-2383
e-mail: JRoss@diabetes.org
www.childrenwithdiabetes.com

Summer camp for children and young adults with diabetes. Along with diabetes education and support, campers get to enjoy swimming, archery, sailing, canoeing, nature hikes, games and crafts.

**1025 YMCA Camp Duncan**
32405 N Highway 12
Ingleside, IL 60041-9312
847-546-8086
FAX: 847-546-3550
www.ymcacampduncan.org

*Kim Kiser, Executive Director*
*Rona Roffey, Camp Director*
*Addie Smits, Director of Group Services*
*Danielle Kiessel, Day Camp Director*

The Tourette Syndrome/TS Camp USA, founded in 1994, is a residential camping program designed for girls and boys ages 8 - 16+ whose primary diagnosis is TS, and to a lesser degree, OCD and ADD/ADHD. The TS Camp is held at YMCA Camp Duncan which is located 30 miles north of Chicago. The goal of the camp is to allow children with TS an opportunity to meet other children, share similar experiences and coping mechanisms in a fun, safe and positive environment.

## Indiana

**1026 Anderson Woods**
P.O. Box 498
Henderson, KY 42419
812-357-2325
e-mail: andersonwoodspsci.net
www.andersonwoods.org

*Judy Colby, Administrative Office*

Provides camping experience and residential services to persons with mental and/or physical disabilities. Campers learn self confidence, trust and responsibilities through working together, tending gardens, feeding animals all while enjoying natures beauty.

**1027 Autism Day Camp**
Hillcroft Services: Isanogel
114 East Streeter Avenue
Muncie, IN 47303
765-284-4166
e-mail: bwilliamson@hillcroft.org
www.hillcroft.org

*Brenda Williamson, Vice President of Development at Marketing*
*Debbie Bennett, Chief Executive Officer*

The camp is designed to improve the academic, social skills, and behaviors of children with autism spectrum disorders. The day camp is an 8-week intensive experience for children classified with autism spectrum disorders.

**1028 Bradford Woods: Camp Riley**
Indiana University
5040 State Road 67 N
Martinsville, IN 46151-8995
765-342-2915
FAX: 765-349-1086
TTY:765-349-5117
e-mail: bradwood@indiana.edu
www.bradwoods.org

*Shay Dawson, CTRS, Dawson, CTRS*
*Melanie Wills, Adventure Education Director*
*Anne Lucas, Environmental Education Director*
*Tim Street, MPA, Director of Marketing, Retreats, and Special Events*

One and two-week sessions for children with a variety of disabilities. Coed, ages 8-18.

**1029 Brave Heart's Camp**
The People's Burn Foundation
6337 Hollister Drive
Suite 2H
Indianapolis, IN 46224
317-803-2876
FAX: 317-692-0876
www.peoplesburnfoundation.org

*Cindy Allison, Camp Director*
*Lora Hays, Adult, Child & Family Counselor*
*Susan Cline, President*
*Daryl Mickens, Vice President*

Specialized residential summer camp for burn survivor children. The camp gives the children an opportunity to heal from the physical and emotional scars by giving them the opportunity to just be kids.

**1030 CHAMP Camp**
212 W 10th St
Suite B-210
Indianapolis, IN 46202
317-679-1860
FAX: 317-245-2291
e-mail: admin@champcamp.org
www.champcamp.org

*Dave Carter, Camp Director*
*Jamie Mitchell, Camp Director*
*Jennifer Kobylarz, Executive Director*
*Donna Guider RN, Lead Nurse*

**1031 Camp About Face**
The Head's Up Foundation
Camp Cood., Craniofacial Program
Riley Hosp #2514, 702 Barnhill Dr.
Indianapolis, IN 46202
317-274-2489
e-mail: headsupfoundation@rocketmail.com
http://www.headsupfoundation.org

Designed to benefit youth's ages 8-18 with craniofacial anomalies. Camping activities include swimming, nature projects and camp outs that are supplemented by social work, medical support and educational sessions which helps to build self-esteem and self confidence.

**1032 Camp Alexander Mack**
Indiana Deaf Camps Foundation
1113 E. Camp Mack Rd.
Milford, IN 46542
574-658-4831
www.campmack.org

*Rex M Miller, CCCP, Executive Director*
*Mike Kauffman,, Guest Services Director*
*Phyllis Leininger, Administrative Assistant*
*Norma Miller, Spiritual Director*

Our program is intentionally designed to provide campers with life changing experiences that lead to a formation of personal faith within a safe faith community.

**1033 Camp Brave Eagle**
Indiana Hemophilia And Thrombosis Center
8402 Harcourt Road
Suite 500
Indianapolis, IN 46260
317-570-0039
800-241-2873
www.campbraveeagle.org/

*Briana Vieke, Program Director*
*Jennifer Maahs, Pediatric Nurse Practitioner*

Summer camp for children with bleeding disorders and their siblings. Campers participate in a traditional summer camp experience with swimming, canoeing, fishing, and nature education. The goal is to encourage the children to have fun while learning to be self-sufficient, building their self confidence and self-esteem and promoting a positive outlook.

**1034 Camp Catch-a-Rainbow**
American Cancer Society
1755 Abbey Road
East Lansing, MI 48823
517-332-2222
800-227-2345
FAX: 517-664-1349
e-mail: kathleen.wilson@cancer.org
www.cancer.org

*Katie Wilson, Director*

Camp Catch-a-Rainbow's programs are available completely free to any child in MI or IN who has or has had cancer, between the ages of 4 and 20, with their doctor's approval. Family Camp is reserved for those campers who have attended camp during that year's summer sessions and their families. Day, week, adult retreat, and family camp are available options.

**1035 Camp Challenge**
8914 Us Highway 50 East
Bedford, IN 47421-8704
812-834-5159
e-mail: info@gocampchallenge.com
www.gocampchallenge.com

*Ralph Price, Executive Director*
*Camp Registr*
One and two-week sessions for campers with developmental and or physical disabilities, hearing impairment and the blind/visually impaired. Ages 6-99 and families.

**1036 Camp Crosley YMCA**
165 Ems T2 Ln
North Webster, IN 46555-9378
574-834-2331
877-811-6189
FAX: 574-834-3313
e-mail: info@campcrosley.org
www.campcrosley.org

*Richard Armstrong, Executive Director*
*Mark Battig, Senior Program Director*
*Eric Hindmon, Groups Program Director*
*Andrea Hindmon, Office Manager*
Camp is located in North Webster, Indiana. Half-week, one, two and three-week sessions for campers with asthma/respiratory ailments and diabetes. Coed, ages 7-17. Also families and seniors.

**1037 Camp John Warvel**
American Diabetes Association
6415 Castleway West Drive
Suite 114
Indianapolis, IN 46250-1939
317-352-9226
888-342-2383
e-mail: cdixon@diabetes.org
www.diabetes.org

*Carol Dixon, Contact Person*
Camp is located in North Webster, Indiana. Provides an enjoyable, safe and educational out-of-doors experience for children with insulin-dependent diabetes. A unique learning atmosphere for children to acquire new skills in caring for their disease. The camp experience instills confidence for the child's self-management of diabetes. Offers one-week sessions and can accommodate 200 campers, boys and girls aged 7-16.

**1038 Camp Little Red Door**
Little Red Door Cancer Agency
1801 North Merideian Street
Indianapolis, IN 46202
317-925-5595
FAX: 317-925-5597
www.littlereddoor.org

*Shaun Forkin, President*
*Bob Braun, VP*
*Tim Harvey, Treasurer*
*Dr.Robert Boeglin, Secretary*
Camp for pediatric cancer patients ages 8-19. The program is open to children diagnosed with or receiving treatment for cancer in the state of Indiana. Activities include swimming, fishing, canoeing, nature hikes, astronomy, arts and crafts.

**1039 Camp Millhouse**
25600 Kelly Rd
South Bend, IN 46614-9390
574-233-2202
FAX: 574-233-2511
e-mail: leabee37@comcast.net
www.campmillhouse.org

*Lea Anne Pitcher, Director*
Nestled in a rustic clearing surrounded by 45 acres of woods, Camp Millhouse is a retreat for children and young adults with mental and physical disabilities. Hiking trails, nature studies, crafts, swimming, and stories around the bonfire make up activities campers long remember. One-week session. Co-ed, ages 4 to 30.

**1040 Camp Red Cedar**
3900 Hursh Road
Fort Wayne, IN 46845
260-637-3608
e-mail: redcedar@awsusa.com
http://www.awsredcedar.com
Camp Red Cedar is open for children and adults with or without disabilities. Activities include, fishing, hiking, swimming and arts and crafts.

**1041 Camp Riley**
Camp Riley/Riley's Children Foundation
Attn: Camp Coordinator
30 S. Meridian Street, Suite 200
Indianapolis, IN 46204-3509
317-759-6949
877-867-4539
FAX: 317-634-4478
e-mail: campriley@rileykids.org
www.rileykids.org/camp
Camp Riley is for youth's ages 8-18 with physical disabilities. The camp helps them to realize their potential as they become increasingly independent. Some of the activities that the camp offers is horseback riding and swimming.

**1042 Englishton Park Academic Remediation**
Englishton Park Presbyterian
P.O.Box 228
Lexington, IN 47138-228
812-889-2046
FAX: 812-934-4322
e-mail: ThomasLisaBarnett@etczone.com
www.englishtonpark.org

*Thomas Barnett, Co-Directors*
*Thomas Barnett, Co-Director*
Camp is located in Lexington, Indiana. Two-week sessions for children with ADD. Boys and girls, ages 7-12.

**1043 Happiness Bag**
3833 Union Rd
Terre Haute, IN 47802-5516
812-234-8867
FAX: 812-238-0728
e-mail: jmexdir@aol.com
www.happinessbag.org/

*Jodi Moan, Executive Director*
*Anita Bryant, Program Director*
*Lisa Bennett, ResHab Director*
Serves developmentally disabled age 5-adult; day and residential camp program; after school program; scouting; Special Olympic anticipation (basketball, athletics, bowling, softball and aquatics); and a bowling league.

**1044 Hoosier Burn Camp**
P.O. BOX 233
Battle ground
IN 47920
765-567-0115
FAX: 765-567-0195
e-mail: markkoopman@hoosierburncamp.org
www.hoosierburncamp.org

*Mark Koopman, Director*
*Kim Jones, Contact Person*
Held at Camp Tecumseh in Brookston, IN., the camp is for burn survivors ages 8-18. Campers learn how to have fun and just be kids, while building their self-esteem and self confidence, learning independence and the life skills they need to fully recover from burn injuries.

**1045 Indiana Children's Deaf Camp**
The Indiana Deaf Camps Foundation, Inc.
100 West 86th Street
Indianapolis, IN 46260
317-846-3404
FAX: 317-844-1034
e-mail: deafcamp@hotmail.com
www.deafcamps.org
Camp is open to all children ages 5-16 who are deaf or hard-of-hearing. Activities include swimming, skating, crafts, volleyball, basketball, fishing and hiking.

**1046 Residential Camp**
Hillcroft Services: Isanogel
114 East Streeter Avenue
Muncie, IN 47303
765-284-4166
TTY:765-288-1073
e-mail: bwilliamson@hillcroft.org.
www.hillcroft.org

*Brenda Williamson, Vice President of Development*
Programming at Isanogel includes creative arts, nature, recreation and aquatics. Individuals age 8 and older participate in one and two week programs.

**1047 Twin Lakes Camp**
1451 E Twin Lakes Rd
Hillsboro, IN 47949-8004
765-798-4000
FAX: 765-798-4010
e-mail: outdoors@twinlakescamp.com
www.twinlakescamp.com

*Jon Beight, Executive Director*
*Brad Carter, Director*
*Walter Payne, Director*
Provides a summer camp program for special needs children and young adults. Campers suffer from a wide range of maladies including crippling accidents, Spina Bifida, epilepsy, Cerebral Palsy, Muscular Dystrophy, Quadriplegia, Paraplegia, and other disabling diseases. Campers range in age from 8 to 27.

## Iowa

**1048 Camp Albrecht Acres**
14837 Sherrill Rd
Sherrill, IA 52073
563-552-1771
FAX: 563-552-2732
e-mail: info@albrechtacres.org
www.albrechtacres.org

*Dick McGrane, President*
*Randy Judge, VP*
*Jeff Streinz, Treasurer*
*Terry Mozena, Secretary*
For children and adults with special needs. Campers enjoy swimming, fishing, nature studies, cookouts and dances.

**1049 Camp Comeca & Retreat Center**
United Methodist Church
75670 Road 417
Cozad, NE 69130-4117
308-784-2808
e-mail: comeca@cozadtel.net
www.campcomeca.com

*John Butler, Site Director*
Camp is located in Cozad, Nebraska. Summer sessions for campers with diabetes and hearing impairment. Coed, ages 6-19, families, seniors, single adults.

**1050 Camp Courageous of Iowa**
P.O.Box 418
Monticello, IA 52310-418
319-465-5916
FAX: 319-465-5919
e-mail: info@campcourageous.org
www.campcourageous.org

*Jeanne Muellerleile, Camp Director*
*Charlie Becker, Executive Director*
*Shannon Poe, Respite Care/Volunteers Director*
A year round residential and respite care facility for individuals with special needs and their families. Campers range in age from 1-99 years old. Activities include traditional activities like canoeing, hiking, swimming, nature and crafts plus adventure activities like caving, rock climbing, etc. Campers with disabilities have opportunities to succeed at challenging activities. This feeling of self-worth can transfer to home, work or school environments.

**1051 Camp Hertko Hollow**
101 Locust St
Des Moines, IA 50309-1720
515-471-8523
FAX: 515-288-2531
e-mail: a.wolf@camphertkohollow.com
www.camphertkohollow.com

*Ann Wolf, Executive Director*
*Vivian Murray, Camp Director*
*Deb Holwegner, Director of Development*
Camp Hertko Hollow is a resident camp held at the Des Moines YMCA Camp site, located along the Des Moines River north of Boone, Iowa. Activities include horseback riding, swimming, canoeing, rappelling, crafts, ropes course, archery and riflery to name a few, plus special activities for different ages. Half-week and one-week sessions for children with diabetes. Coed, ages 6-16.

**1052 Camp L-Kee-Ta**
1308 Broadway Street
P.O. Box 190
West Burlington, IA 52655-190
319-752-3639
FAX: 319-753-1410
www.gseiwi.org

*Haley Scott, Director*
Camp is located in Danville, Iowa. Half-week and one-week sessions June-August for children with asthma/respiratory ailments. Girls, ages 7-18 and families.

**1053 Camp Sunnyside**
Easter Seals Of Iowa
401 N.E. 66th Avenue
Des Moines, IA 50313
515-289-1933
e-mail: krumpf@easterseals.org
www.easterseals.org

*Claire LeCroy, Director, Camping & Respite Svcs*
*Kelsey Rumpf, Program Assistant*
The camp is open year-round and is a place for children and adults with or without disabilities to gather and enjoy themselves while exploring their potentials. Activities include swimming, boating arts and crafts and games.

**1054 Camp Tanager**
Tanager Place
1614 W Mount Vernon Rd
Mount Vernon, IA 52314-9533
319-363-0681
FAX: 319-365-6411
e-mail: dpirrie@tanagerplace.org
www.camptanager.org

*Donald Pirrie, Executive Director*
Offers camp experiences for children 7 to 11 whose special social, economic or medical needs might not otherwise allow them to enjoy a summer camp experience. This private, non-profit camp serves over 600 children each summer with the staff-camper ratio being 1:6.

**1055 Camp Wyoming**
Presbyterian Church USA
9106 42nd Ave
Wyoming, IA 52362-7647
563-488-3893
FAX: 563-488-3895
e-mail: campwyo@netins.net
www.campwyoming.net

*Kevin Cullum, Camp Director*
Youth and adults, ages 16 and up, with mild to moderate mental and physical disabilities can take part in a one week experience of fun and fellowship in early July.

**1056 Diabetes Camp**
Tanager Place
1614 W Mount Vernon Rd
Mount Vernon, IA 52314-9533
319-363-0681
FAX: 319-365-6411
e-mail: dpirrie@tanagerplace.org
www.camptanager.org

*Donald Pirrie, Executive Director*
Provides children and adolescents with Diabetes a safe and healthy environment and healthy environment to enjoy a variety of recreational activities designed for fun and fitness. The camp held each July has an on-site 24-hour physician and nursing staff. Ages 6-13.

**1057 Easter Seals Camp Sunnyside**
Easter Seals Iowa
401 N.E. 66th Avenue
Des Moines, IA 50313
515-289-1933
FAX: 515-289-1281
TTY:515-289-4069
e-mail: krumpf@eastersealsia.org
www.easterseals.com

*Sherri Nielsen, President*
*Kelsey Rumpf, Program Assistant*
Each summer from June through August, campers with disabilities ages five and up, take part in one week camping sessions, gaining skills and independence by participating in activities like swimming, horseback riding, canoeing, fishing, camping and more. Coed, ages 4-95. Accepts seniors and single adults. Financial assistance available.

**1058 Hemophilia Camp**
Tanager Place
116 West 32nd Street, 11th Floor
New York, N 10001-9533
212-328-3700
FAX: 212-328-3777
e-mail: dpirrie@tanagerplace.org
www.hemaware.org/story/hemophilia-summer-camp

*Donald Pirrie, Executive Director*
During the six-day camp children with Hemophilia and their siblings participate in individual and group activities designed for fun and fitness. The camp held each year in mid-June has a 24-hour physician and nursing staff. Ages 5-16.

**1059 Wendell Johnson Speech And Hearing Clinic**
University Of Iowa
250 Hawkins Dr
Iowa City, IA 52242-1025
319-335-8736
FAX: 319-335-8851
e-mail: kathy-miller@uiowa.edu
www.uiowa.edu/~comsci/

*Linda Souke, Clinic Director*
*Kathy Miller, Clinic Assistant*
The clinic offers assessment and remediation for communication disorders in adults and children. The clinic also offers services during the Summer for school age children needing intervention services because of speech, language, hearing and/or reading problems.

**1060 Wesley Woods Camp and Retreat Center**
Iowa Conference United Methodist
10896 Nixon St
Indianola, IA 50125-7301
515-961-4523
866-684-7753
FAX: 515-961-4162
e-mail: wesleywoods.camp@iaumc.org
www.wesleywoodsiowa.org

*Deke Rider, Executive Director*
*Suzanne Rider, Equestrian Coordinator*
Camp is located in Indianola, Iowa. Half-week and one-week sessions June-August for campers with developmental disabilities. Coed, ages 18-99. Horses Helping People program is also available for developmentally and physically challenged persons age 4 and older.

**1061 Y Camp**
YMCA of Greater Des Moines
1192 166th Drive
Boone, IA 50036-1720
515-432-7558
FAX: 515-432-5414
e-mail: ycamp@dmymca.org
www.y-camp.org

*Mike Havlik, Program Director- Environmental Education*
*David Sherry, Executive Director*
*BJ Murray, Program Director- Summer Camp*
*Cole Bowermaster, Program Director - Groups and Retreats*
Camp is located in Boone, Iowa. Year-round one and two-week sessions for boys and girls with cancer, diabetes, asthma, cystic fibrosis, hearing impaired and other disabilities. Coed, ages 6-16 and families.

## Kansas

**1062 Camp Discovery**
American Diabetes Association
837 S Hillside St
Wichita, KS 67211-3005
316-684-6091
800-362-1355
888-342-2838
FAX: 316-684-5675
e-mail: lthomas@diabetes.org
www.diabetescamps.org

*Bill Dyar, Manager*
*Bridget Kroner, Associate Director*
Camp is located in Junction City, Kansas. Offers young people with diabetes a week of fun at rock springs 4-H Center. Special attention to diabetes makes Camp Discovery a safe environment for active youth while providing valuable diabetes managment education. Call the American Diabetes Association Kansas area office for more information. Coed, ages 8-17.

**1063 Camp Ka-Di-Da-Ca**
American Diabetes Association
608 West Douglas, Suite 100
Wichita, KS 67211
316-684-6091
FAX: 316-684-5675
http://www.diabetes.org

*RaeAnn Moreno, Contact Person*
Day camp for young adults ages 9-12 with diabetes.

**1064 Camp Quality Kansas**
2617 N. 75th Street
Kansas City, MO 66109
913-424-8355
FAX: 913-334-2802
e-mail: susie.mooney@campqualityusa.org
www.campqualityusa.org

*Susie Mooney, Assistant Director*
*Ben Broxterman, Assistant Director*
*Sara Jolliff, Secretary*
*Michelle Fields, Treasurer*
For children with cancer and their siblings. Camp Quality allows children to be children again by offering a stress-free environment that is filled with exciting activities, fosters new friendships and helps to give the children courage, motivation and emotional strength.

**1065 Summer Camp for Physically & Mentally Challenged Children & Adults**
Kansas Jaycees' Cerebral Palsy Foundation
P.O.Box 267
Augusta, KS 67207-267 316-775-2421
e-mail: execdirector@cpranch.org
http://cpranch.cfsites.org

*Cheryl Schmeidler, Executive Director*
*Camp Directo*
Our mission is to provide a program which will allow individuals to enjoy their highest level of functioning and independence, consistant with their abilities, in a summer camp setting.

## Kentucky

**1066 Bethel Mennonite Camp**
2773 Bethel Church Rd
Clayhole, KY 41317-9028 606-666-4911
FAX: 606-666-4216
e-mail: grow@bethelcamp.org
bethelcamp.org

*Mark & Mary Driskill, Summer Camp Pastors*
*Roger Voth, Camp Director*
A Christ-centered ministry with an emphasis on Bible study and personal commitment to Christ. We offer a week long Special Needs Camp in June, with lodging for caregivers.

**1067 Cedar Ridge Camp**
57 Cemetery Road
McArthurs Mills,
Ontario
e-mail: info@cedarridgecamp.com
www.cedarridgecamp.com

*Peter Ruys de Perez, Owner & Executive Director*
*Grayson Burke, Director*
*Jodie Campbell, Assistant Director*
*Alexandra Campbell, Director of Operations*
Half-week, one and two-week sessions for children with diabetes, developmental disabilities and muscular dystrophy. Coed, ages 6-17.

**1068 Indian Summer Camp**
P.O. Box 24337
Louisville, KY 40224 502-794-7103
e-mail: Shelby.Dehner@gmail.com
www.iscamp.org

*Shelby Dehner, Executive Director*
*Amy Steinkuh, Camp Director*
*Jon Dubins, Board Director*
*David Power, VP*
Indian Summer Camp is open to boys and girls aged 6-18 years old who have had or are currently receiving treatment for cancer. Children can come to have fun, while having the opportunity to grow, learn and build self reliance.

**1069 Lions Camp Crescendo, Inc.**
1480 Pine Tavern Road
P.O. Box 607
Lebanon Junction, KY 40150-0607 502-833-3554
888-879-8884
e-mail: bjflannery@lions-campcrescendo.org
www.lions-campcrescendo.org

*Billie Flannery, Administrator*
*Kevin Patton, Resident Manager*
*Lion Paul Witten, Chairperson*
*Lion Cebert Gilbert, Vice-Chairperson*
The enhancement of the quality of life for youth, especially those with disabilities, through the delivery of a traditional camp experience by caring individuals and to enable others to use our camping and retreat facilities to serve the larger communities humanitarian needs.

**1070 Medical Camping**
The Center For Courageouos Kids
1501 Burnley Road
Scottsville, KY 42164 270-618-2900
FAX: 270-618-2901
e-mail: info@courageouskids.org
www.courageouskids.org

*Ed Collins, Camp Director*
*Roger Murtie, President/Executive Director/CEO*
*Croley Graham, Secretary*
*Stockton Clark, Director*
A year-round, fun, safe camping experience for seriously ill and disabled children and their families.

## Louisiana

**1071 Camp Bon Coeur**
Bon Coeur, Inc.
P.O.Box 53765
Lafayette, LA 70505-3765 337-233-8437
FAX: 337-233-4160
e-mail: info@heartcamp.com
www.heartcamp.com

*Susannah Craig, Executive Director*
Two-week sessions June-July for children with heart defects. Coed, ages 8-16.

**1072 Camp Challenge**
P.O.Box 10591
New Orleans, LA 504-347-2267
e-mail: campdirector@campchallenge.org
www.campchallenge.org

*Cathy Allain, Camp Director*
*Alaina Wertz, Public Relations*
Camp Challenge is a grass roots non-profit organization dedicated to giving ill children and their siblings ages 6 through 18 a summer camp experience. Camp is open to all children who reside in Louisiana and have a form of cancer and chronic hematological disorders. These children do not have to pay for camp, it is free for all campers.

**1073 Camp Pelican**
Louisiana Lions Camp
P.O.Box 10235
New Orleans, LA 70181 504-466-7124
FAX: 866-295-3803
e-mail: Camppelican@Gmail.com
www.lionscamp.org

*Ray Cecil, Executive Director*
*R Tony Richard, Director*
Camp Pelican is an overnight residential camp for children with moderate to severe asthma or other pulmonary problems. Founded in 1977, Camp Pelican is jointly sponsored by the Louisiana Pulmonary Disease Camp Inc and the Louisiana Lions Camp. Over 100 children attend annually and participate in education, sports, arts and crafts, swimming and other camping activities. Medical staff including physicians, nurses, respiratory therapists and social workers participate in camp. Coed, ages 5-17.

**1074 Camp Victory**
Lions Club And American Diabetes Association
2644 S. Sherwood Forest Blvd.
Suite 122
Baton Rouge, LA 70816 www.lionscamp.org

*Lori Koonce, Manager*
*Treva Lincoln, Contact Person*
Camp is for children with diabetes age 6-14 years old. The camp offers many outdoor activities as well as daily diabetes education classes.

**1075 Louisiana Lions Camp**
LA Lions League for Crippled Children
292 L. Beauford Drive
Anacoco, LA 71403
800-348-6567
FAX: 337-239-9975
e-mail: lalions@lionscamp.org
www.lionscamp.org

*Raymond E Cecil III, Camp Director*
*Susan Todd, President*
Free camp for boys and girls with mental and physical challenges, diabetes and pulmonary disorders.

**1076 Louisiana Lions Camp - Camp Pelican**
Lions Club Of Louisiana
292 L. Beauford Drive
Anacoco, LA 71403
800-348-6567
FAX: 337-239-9975
www.lionscamp.org

*Jerry Adams, President*
Free, residential summer camp for children with special needs, diabetes and pulmonary disorders.

**1077 Med-Camps of Louisiana**
102 Thomas Road
Suite 615
West Monroe, LA 71291
318-329-8405
e-mail: info@medcamps.com
www.medcamps.com

*Caleb Seney, Executive Director*
*Wes Cavin, Camp Director*
*Cindy Lillo, Administrative Assistant*
Serves children with severe asthma and allergies and many more.

## Maine

**1078 Camp Waban**
Waban Projects, Inc.
5 Dunaway Drive
Sanford, ME 04073
207-324-7955
FAX: 207-324-6050
www.waban.org

*Dorinda Vezina, Assistant Residential Director*
*Jon Stimmel, Program Assistant*
*Sandra Clark, Direct Support Professional*
Recreational opportunities in fully handicapped accessible waterfront facilities for children and adults with developmental disabilities. Activities include swimming, kayaking, pontoon boat rides, fishing and nightly camp fires.

**1079 Camp Bishopswood**
Diocese of Maine Episcopal
143 State St
Portland, ME 4101-3701
207-772-1953
800-244-6062
e-mail: georgia@bishopswood.org
www.bishopswood.org

*Georgia Koch, Director*
*Sara Foster, Assistant Director*
*Lisa Sholudko, Health Care Manager*
Camp is located in Hope, Maine. One to seven-week sessions for hearing impaired children June-August. Coed, ages 7-16.

**1080 Camp Capella**
8 Pearl Point Road
P. O. Box 552
Holden, ME 04429
207-843-5104
e-mail: dana@campcabella.org
www.campcapella.org

*Dana Mosher, Religious Leader*
Provides an opportunity for children with disabilities to engage in various recreational and social experiences.

**1081 Camp Jabberwocky**
200 Greenwood Avenue Ext.
P.O. Box 1357
Vineyard Haven, MA 02568
508-693-2339
e-mail: info@campjabberwocky.org
www.campjabberwocky.org

*Lynne Wolf, Chair*
*Jane Price, Vice Chair*
*Corby Reese, Treasurer*
*Melissa Mueller, Secretary*
Residential vacation camp for people with disabilities.

**1082 Camp Lawroweld**
Northern New England Conference
228 West Side Road
Weld, ME 04285
207-585-2984
www.lawroweld.org

*Harry Sabnani, Executive Director*
Camp is located in Weld, Maine. Week sessions July for campers who are blind or visually impaired, all ages. Other camps coed, ages 9-16 and families, single adults, June - September.

**1083 Camp No Limits**
No Limits Limb Loss Foundation
265 Centre Road
Wales, ME 04280
207-240-5762
e-mail: info@NoLimitsFoundation.org
www.nolimitsfoundation.org

*Mary Leighton, OTR/L, Executive Director*
*Michelle Buckley, Secretary*
*Jason Melanson, Treasurer*
*Marq Paquette, President*
Camp No Limits is the leading camp for young people with limb loss and their families. The camp also has several other locations in California, Florida, Idaho, Maryland and Missouri.

**1084 Camp Pinecone**
Pine Tree Society
149 Front Street
P.O. Box 518
Bath, ME 04530-518
207-443-3341
FAX: 207-443-1070
e-mail: ptcamp@pinetreesociety.org
www.pinetreesociety.org

*Emily Hawkins, President*
*Gerard Queally, 1st Vice President*
*Paul Jacques, 2nd Vice President:*
*Diane Gilbert, Treasurer*
A day camp for children with physical and/or developmental disabilities, ages 5 to 12. May through September.

**1085 Camp Sunshine**
35 Acadia Road
Casco, ME 04015
207-655-3800
FAX: 207-655-3825
e-mail: info@campsunshine.org
www.campsunshine.org

*Matt Hoidal, Esq., Executive Director*
*Michael Katz, Campus Director*
*Michael Smith, Director of Special Events*
*Rob Butcher, Business Manager*
This year round program provides respite, support, hope & joy to children with life threatening illnesses and their immediate families. The camp is open to families of children diagnosed with kidney disease, cancer, lupus, solid organ transplants and other life threatening illnesses. The camp is free of charge and includes onsite medical and psychosocial support, and bereavement groups.

**1086 Camp Waziyatah**
530 Mill Hill Rd
Waterford, ME 04088
207-583-2267
FAX: 509-357-2267
e-mail: info@wazi.com
www.wazi.com

*Gregg Parker, Owner/Director*
*Mitch Parker, Owner/Director*
Camp is located in Waterford, Massachusetts. Three, four and seven-week sessions June-August for campers with cancer and diabetes. Coed, ages 8-15 and families, single adults.

**1087 Indian Acres Camp for Boys**
1712 Main St
Fryeburg, ME 04037-4327
207-935-2300
e-mail: geoff@indianacres.com
www.indianacres.com

*Michael Burness, Assistant Director*
*Lisa Newman, Director*
*Geoff Newman, Director*
*Mary Wiig, Head Counselor*
Camp is located in Fryeburg, Florida. Four and seven-week sessions June-August for boys with ADD ages 7-16.

**1088 Pine Tree Camp**
Pine Tree Society
149 Front Street
P.O. Box 518
Bath, ME 04530
207-443-3341
FAX: 207-397-5324
e-mail: ptcamp@pinetreesociety.org
www.pinetreesociety.org

*Harvey Chesley, Manager*
*Emily Fuller Hawkins, President*
*Diane Gilbert, Treasurer*
*Cheryl Timberlake, Secretary*
Offers Maine children and adults with disabilities an extraordinary summer camp experience. The barrier-free setting and commitment of our staff allow campers to fully participate in activities that normally aren't available to them including swimming, fishing, boating, outdoor games, kayaking, arts and crafts and even camping in a tent under the stars. May through September.

**1089 YMCA Camp of Maine**
305 Winthrop Center Rd
P.O. Box 446
Winthrop, ME 04364
207-395-4200
FAX: 207-395-7230
e-mail: info@maineycamp.org
www.maineycamp.org

*Barry W Costa, Executive Director*
Activities include arts and crafts, nature study, hiking, and overnight camping, dancing, and singing. Summer session dates run from June through August; for ages 8-16.

## Maryland

**1090 Camp Fairlee Manor**
Easter Seals DE/MD Eastern Shore
61 Corporate Circle
New Castle, DE 19720
302-324-4444
800-677-3800
FAX: 302-324-4441
e-mail: contact@esdel.org
www.de.easterseals.com

*Steve Nkurlu, Manager*
Residential camp at Fairlee Manor serves an average of 50 to 75 children and adults each week with physical disabilities and/or cognitive, behavioral impairments throughout the summer and on select weekends year-round.

**1091 Camp Glyndon**
American Diabetes Association
PO Box 56
Nanjemoy, MD 20662
301-870-5858
FAX: 301-246-9108
e-mail: CampOfficeLCM@aol.com
www.lionscampmerrick.org

*Donna Wadsworth, Camp Administrator*
Camp is located in Nanjemoy, Maryland. One and two-week sessions July-August for children with diabetes and their families. Coed, ages 8-16.

**1092 Camp JCC**
Jewish Community Center of Greater Washington
6125 Montrose Rd
Rockville, MD 20852-4860
301-881-0100
FAX: 301-881-6549
e-mail: fgold@jccgw.org
www.jccgw.org

*Scott Cohen, President*
*Bradley Stillman, Vice President for Administration/Treasurer*
*Mindy Berger, Vice President for Development*
*Heidi Brodsky, Vice President for Member & Guest Services*
Camp JCC serves children with disabilities alongside their neighbors and friends. The American Camping Association has presented a National award to Camp JCC for its extraordinary model inclusion program. We also offer a program designed especially for 13-21 year olds with severe to profound disabilities. In order for us to afford to do these things, we count on contributions to our Inclusion Fund. Four and eight-week sessions general day camp program offering June-August for children.

**1093 Camp Milldale**
Jewish Community Center
3506 Gwynnbrook Avenue
Owings Mills, MD 21117
410-356-5200
e-mail: info@campmilldale.org
www.campmilldale.org

*Dori Zvili, Camp Director*
*Dianne Newborn, Office Administrator*
Camp is located in Reisterstown, MD. Four and eight week sessions, June - August. Inclusion program for children entering grades 5-13 with learning, developmental, social, emotional and physical disabilities. Self-contained program for teenagers with disabilities ages 14-21 focusing on recreational and vocational activities, including weekly field trips.

**1094 Camp Sunrise**
John Hopkins Hospital
One Charles Center
100 North Charle
Baltimore, MD 21201
410-516-2385
e-mail: mscalf19@yahoo.com
www.hopkinsmedicine.org

*Jaclyn Young, Staff*
*Stephanie Davis, Staff*
*Gloria Jetter, Regional Executive Director*
*Jack Shipkoski, CEO*
Camp Sunrise is open to children ages 6-18 who have or have had cancer. The camp also has a 'day camp' program for children ages 4-5 years old. Some of the camps activities include swimming, arts & crafts, nature walks, sports and games.

**1095 Camp Superkids**
John Hopkins Bayview Medical Center
P.O. Box 96
Maryland Line, MD 21105
410-550-0374
e-mail: campsuperkids@gmail.com
www.hopkinsbayview.org/campsuperkids

*Ceal Curry, Camp Director*
*Heather Dougherty, Camp Administrator*
Camp Superkids is an overnight camp for children between the ages of 8-14 with asthma.

**1096 Kamp A-Komp-Plish**
9035 Ironsides Rd
Nanjemoy, MD 20662-3432
301-870-3226
301-934-3590
FAX: 301-870-2620
e-mail: recreation@melwood.org
http://www.melwoodrecreation.org

*Marisa Cucuzzella, Assistant Director*
*Jonathan Rondeau, Chief Program officer*
*Bekah Carmichael, Director*
*Doria Fleisher, Associate Director*
Camp is located in Nanjemoy, Maryland. Half-week, one-week and two-week sessions for blind/visually impaired children and those with developmental disabilities and mobility limitation. Coed, ages 8-16.

**1097 League at Camp Greentop**
The League for People with Disabilities
1111 E. Cold Spring Lane
Baltimore, MD 21239
410-323-0500
FAX: 410-323-3298
TTY:410-435-4298
e-mail: vfoster@leagueforpeople.org
www.leagueforpeople.org

*Bill Morgan, VP,Camping & Therapeutic Recreation*
*David Greenberg, President*
*Stephen Freeman, VP, Employment, Wellness & Day Habilitation*
*Jill Rosato Huey, VP,Development & Marketing*
Camp is located in Thurmont, Maryland. Summer residential camp located in the Catoctin Mountain National Park. Since 1937, Greentop has been serving children and adults with physical and multiple disabilities in a completely accessible camp setting. Campers enjoy a traditional camping program. Medical facilities staffed 24 hours a day. Half-week/one/two-week sessions June-August. ACA/MD Youth Camp.

**1098 Lions Camp Merrick**
Lions Clubs of District 22-C
3650 Rick Hamilton Place
P.O. Box 56
Nanjemoy, MD 20662-56
301-870-5858
FAX: 301-246-9108
e-mail: cmpmerrick@aol.com
lionscampmerrick.org

*Wayne Magoon, President*
*Ray Shumaker, Vice President*
*Heather Zeolla, Secretary*
*Frank Culhan Treasurer*
This recreational camp for special needs children offers a complete waterfront program including swimming, canoeing and fishing for ages 6-16. Designed for children who are deaf and hard of hearing, children of deaf parents, and children with diabetes. Also helps children to learn to deal with their special conditions.

**1099 Raven Rock Lutheran Camp**
17912 Harbaugh Valley Road
P.O.Box 136
Sabillasville, MD 21780-136
800-321-5824
e-mail: ravenrock@innernet.net
Christ-centered program for youth and mentally retarded adults.

**1100 TLC's Summer Programs**
9975 Medical Center Drive
Rockville, MD 20850
301-738-9691
FAX: 301-738-8897
www.tlc.org

*Debra Piccirillo,, Director of Speech-Language Services*
*Brigid Baker,, Director of Outpatient Occupational Therapy*
*Cathleen Burgess,, Director, Katherine Thomas Lower/Middle School Program*
*Rhona Schwartz,, Director, Katherine Thomas High School Program*
For children ages 3-13 and high school students in grades 9-12, who have special needs in the areas of speech, language, perceptual motor, sensory processing, academic development, and/or skill maintenance. Some programs also fulfill the requirements for Extended School Year Services (ESY). Extended Day is available for children 5 years or older in all programs (excluding the high school program). Extended day hours are 8:00 am to 9:00 am and 3:00 pm to 5:00 pm.

**1101 Youth Leadership Camp**
National Association of the Deaf
8630 Fenton Street
Suite 820
Silver Spring, MD 20910- 3819
301-587-1788
FAX: 301-587-1791
TTY:301-587-1789
e-mail: infor@nad.org
www.nad.org

*Howard Rosenblum, Chief Executive Officer*
*Shane Feldman, Chief Operating Officer*
Sponsored by the National Association of the Deaf, this camp emphasizes leadership training for deaf teenagers and young adults. In addition to many recreational activities and sports, there are academic offerings and camp projects.

## Massachusetts

**1102 Agassiz Village Camp**
Easter Seals: Massachusetts
484 Main St
Worcester, MA 01608
800-244-2756
FAX: 508-831-9768
TTY:800-564-9700
e-mail: info@eastersealsma.org
www.eastersealsma.org

*Harry Salerno, Chairman*
*David Hoffman, Vice Chair*
*Anthony Tambone, Treasurer*
*Cheryl.E Mongell, Secretary*
Operates a full inclusion residential summer camp that serves campers with disabilities (ages 8-13). Camp activities are facilitated with consideration to the needs of youth with disabilities.

**1103 Becket Chimney Corners YMCA Camps and Outdoor Center**
748 Hamilton Rd
Becket, MA 1223-9686
413-623-8991
FAX: 413-623-5890
e-mail: cburke@bccymca.org
www.bccymca.org

*Phil Connor, CEO*
*Jim Brown, Chief Operations Officer*
*Christine Kalakay, Chief Financial Officer*
*Steve Turner, Director of Property & Maintenance*
Half-week and one-week sessions for campers with asthma/respiratory ailments. Coed, ages 3 and up, families, seniors, single adults.

**1104 Camp Howe**
P.O.Box 326
Goshen, MA 01032
413-549-3969
e-mail: office@camphowe.com
www.camphowe.com

*Heidi Gutekenst, Camp Director*
*Heather.B Baylis, President*
*David Duffie, VP*
*Ramon Jon Black, Secretary/Treasurer*
One and two-week sessions June-August for children with a variety of disabilities. Coed, ages 7-17.

**1105 Camp Joslin**
Barton Center for Diabetes Education
P.O. Box 356
North Oxford, MA 01537-0356 508-987-2056
FAX: 508-987-2002
e-mail: info@bartoncenter.org
www.bartoncenter.org

*John Latimer, Manager*
*Thomas.C Lynch, President*
*Carol.B Lawrence, Treasurer*
*Robert.L Macdonald, Vice Chair*

Camp is located in Charlton, Massachusetts. For boys, ages 7-16, with diabetes. This program offers active summer sports and activities, supplemented by medical treatment and diabetes education. Coed Winter Camp and Coed Weekend Retreats are offered during the school year.

**1106 Camp New Connections**
McLean Hospital
115 Mill Street
Belmont, MA 02478 617-855-2000
e-mail: kamadden@partners.org
www.mclean.harvard.edu/

*Scott Rauch, MD, President and Psychiatrist in Chief*

A four-week, summer day camp for children ages 7-17 who have Asperger's Syndrome, autism spectrum disorders, pervasive developmental disorders and non-verbal learning disabilities. Recreational activities include arts & crafts, swimming, field trips and communication games.

**1107 Camp Ramah in New England**
39 Bennett St
Palmer, MA 01069-9514 413-283-9771
FAX: 413-283-6661
www.campramahNE.org

*Rabbi Ed Geld, Executive Director*
*Davey Rosen, Assistant Director*

8 week sleep-away camp for Jewish adolescents with developmental disabilities. Full camping program includes swimming, Hebrew singing and dancing, sports, arts and crafts, daily services, Kosher food and Jewish studies classes. Some mainstreaming and vocational opportunities.

**1108 Camp Starfish**
1121 Main Street
Lancaster, MA 01523 978-368-6580
FAX: 978-368-6578
e-mail: campers@campstarfish.org
www.campstarfish.org

*Emily Golinsky, Executive Director*
*Michele Cyr, MSW, Associate Director*
*Jill Connell, Administrative & Development Assistant*

Fosters the growth and success of children with emotional, behavioral and learning problems.

**1109 Camp Wee-Kan-Tu**
127 Worcester Street
Watertown, MA 02472 e-mail: info@campweekantu.org
www.campweekantu.org

*Leslie G Brody, Ph.D, President and CEO*
*Charlene Sturgis, Director of Operations*
*Susan Welby, Director of Programs*
*Kristine Binette, Maine Field Service Coordinator*

The camp offers children and teenagers aged 8-17 with epilepsy an overnight camping program full of fun and adventure. The camp strives to enhance the child's self esteem, confidence and independence.

**1110 Carroll School Summer Programs**
25 Baker Bridge Rd
Lincoln, MA 01773-3199 781-259-8342
FAX: 781-259-8842
e-mail: info@carrollscholl.org
carrollschool.org

*Steve Wilkins, Head of the school*

Academic and recreational programs designed to improve learning skills and build self-confidence. The school is a tutorial program for students not achieving their potential due to poor skills in reading, writing and math. The summer camp complements the summer school offering outdoor activities in a supportive, non-competitive environment.

**1111 Clara Barton Diabetes Camp**
Clara Barton for Girls with Diabetes
30 Ennis Road
PO Box 356
North Oxford, MA 01537-0356 508-987-2056
FAX: 508-987-2002
e-mail: info@bartoncenter.org
www.bartoncenter.org

*Mark Bissell, Camp Joslin Director*
*Lynn Butler, Associate Executive Director & Director of Development*
*Sadie Vivenzio, Finance Director*
*Kevin Wilcoxen, Executive Director*

Girls, ages 3-17, with diabetes participate in a well-rounded camp program with special education in diabetes, health and safety. Activities include swimming, boating, sports, dance, music and arts and crafts. Two week adventure camp for high school girls offering camping, hiking, canoeing, etc. Also a minicamp (one week) for girls 6-12. Day camps are offered in Worcester, Boston, and New York City.

**1112 Eagle Hill School: Summer Program**
242 Old Petersham Road
P.O. Box 116
Hardwick, MA 01037- 0116 413-477-6000
FAX: 413-477-6837
e-mail: admission@ehs1.org
www.ehs1.org

*Robert M Breakell, B.A., M.A, Assistant Headmaster*
*Marjorie E Castro, B.S., M.A., Ed, Head of School*
*Wendy G Salisbury, B.A., M.A, Director of Education*
*Tom Cone, B.A., M.A, Director of Admissions*

For children ages 9-19 with specific learning (dis)abilities and/or Attention Deficit Disorder, this summer program is designed to remediate academic and social deficits while maintaining progress achieved during the school year. Electives and sports activities are combined with the academic courses to address the needs of the whole person in a camp-like atmosphere.

**1113 Handi Kids**
The Bridge Center
470 Pine St
Bridgewater, MA 02324-2112 508-697-7557
FAX: 508-697-1529
e-mail: info@TheBridgeCtr.org
www.bridgectr.com

*Anita Howards, Director of Administration*
*Karen Ellis, Office Manager*
*Spencer Nichols, Program Director*
*Sarah Norris, Riding Programs Coordinator*

A therapeutic recreational facility in Bridgewater, Massachusetts offering after-school programs, special events, school vacation full-week and summer day camp programs. Every individual is welcome. Two-week sessions July-August.

**1114 Kamp for Kids: Camp Togowauk**
Abilities Unlimited of Western New England
754 Russell Road
Westfield, MA 01085
413-562-5678
TTY:800-764-0200
e-mail: info@disabilityinfo.com
www.disabilityinfo.org

*Anne Benoit, Director*
Two-week sessions July-August for children and young adults with a variety of disabilities. Coed, ages 3-22.

**1115 PKU Camp**
YMCA Camp Burgess & Hayward
75 Stowe Road
Sandwich, MA 02563
508-428-2571
FAX: 508-420-3545
e-mail: pgorman@ssymca.org
www.ssymca.org

*Paul Gorman, President*
*John Ireland, Executive Vice President*
*Jim Jarosz, Vice President of Finance and Systems*
*Andy Levin, IT Director*
Coed camp in August where children with PKU join other campers with or without PKU. This opportunity allows children to meet other children facing the same issues. Recreational activities include tennis, sailing, horseback riding and performing arts.

**1116 Tower Program at Regis College**
Regis College
235 Wellesley St
Weston, MA 2493-1545
781-768-7000
FAX: 781-899-7209
e-mail: admission@regiscollege.edu
regiscollege.edu

*Antoinette M Hays, PhD, RN, President*
Helps average and above average college-bound students, ages 16-17, having a diagnosed dyslexic learning disability, to adjust to a college setting. Emphasis is on instruction and academic reinforcement, affective support, awareness of support services available on most college campuses and strategy training.

## Michigan

**1117 Camp Barakel**
P.O. Box 159
Fairview, MI 48621-0159
989-848-2279
FAX: 989-848-2280
e-mail: info@campbarakel.org
www.campbarakel.org

*Paul Gardner, Camp Director*
Five-day Christian camp experience in mid-August for campers ages 18-55 who are physically disabled, visually impaired, upper trainable mentally impaired or educable mentally impaired, bus transportation provided from locations in Lansing, Flint and Bay City, Michigan.

**1118 Camp Barefoot**
The Fowler Center For Outdoor Learning
2315 Harmon Lake Rd
Mayville, MI 48744-9737
989-673-2050
FAX: 989-673-6355
e-mail: info@thefowlercenter.org
www.thefowlercenter.org

*Kyle L Middleton, CTRS, Executive Director*
*Lynn M Seeloff, CTRS, Assistant Director*
*Pat Jordan, Office Manager/Program Registrar*
*Kyle.L Middleton, Executive Director*
Offered to adults with traumatic brain injuries/closed head injuries. A wide variety of activities are offered. The participants in Camp Barefoot request their week's activities, allowing each participant to design their own activity schedule.

**1119 Camp Catch-a-Rainbow**
American Cancer Society
1755 Abbey Road
East Lansing, MI 48823
517-332-2222
800-ACS-2345
FAX: 517-664-1497
e-mail: kathleen.wilson@cancer.org
www.cancer.org

*Katie Wilson, Director*
Camp Catch-a-Rainbow's programs are available completely free to any child in MI or IN who has or has had cancer, between the ages of 4 and 20, with their doctor's approval. Family Camp is reserved for those campers who have attended camp during that year's summer sessions and their families. Day, week, adult retreat, and family camp are available options.

**1120 Camp Chris Williams**
Lions 11 B-2 and MADHH
5236 Dumond Court
Suite C
Lansing, MI 48917-6001
517-487-0066
800-968-7327
e-mail: info@madhh.org
www.madhh.org

*Nancy Asher, Executive Director*
*Office Manag*
An exciting summer camp experience for deaf and hard of hearing youth and their siblings ages 8-14.

**1121 Camp Nissokone**
YMCA Camping Services
7300 Hickory Ridge Rd
Holly, MI 48442-8929
248-887-4533
FAX: 248-887-5203
e-mail: office@ycampingservices.org
miymcacamps.org

*Doug Grimm, Vice President Camping Services*
*David Marks, Director*
A six week summer resident camp program for boys and girls whose learning and behavior styles have made successful participation in the traditional camp program difficult. All camp activities have a special emphasis on building self-esteem and peer relationships. Strong in waterfront, nature, campcrafts and a special arts program.

**1122 Camp Roger**
8356 Belding Road
Rockford, MI 49341-9628
616-874-7286
FAX: 616-874-5734
e-mail: doug@camproger.org
www.camproger.org

*Doug Vanderwell, Executive Director*
*Phil Warners, Director of Outdoor Education*
*Matt Zwiep, Director of Operations*
*Jack Heyboer, Director of Development*
Camp Roger provides a fun top-notch summer program for disabled campers. Campers learn to love the woods, the water and the trails, getting to enjoy a wide variety of activities all designed to be fun, to build friendships, and develop self confidence.

**1123 Camp Tall Turf**
816 Madison SE
Grand Rapids, MI 49507
616-452-7906
FAX: 616-988-4596
e-mail: info@turf.org
tallturf.org

*Jack Kooyman, President*
Camp is located in Walkerville, Michigan. Summer camping sessions for youth with asthma/respiratory ailments and ADD. Coed, ages 8-16.

**1124 Echo Grove Camp**
Salvation Army
1101 Camp Rd
Leonard, MI 48367-2812
248-628-3108
FAX: 248-628-7055
e-mail: info@echogrove.org
echogrove.org

*Mark Mc Clenaghan, Executive Director*
*Sharon McClenaghan, Associate Camp Director*
Since 1921, the Army's Echo Grove Camp has offered a structured camping program for children, adults and seniors referred through Corps Community Centers. During the course of Echo Grove's 12 week season, the camp includes programs geared for every need and interest. In addition to outdoor recreation, camps may include religious, musical and skill-building instruction.

**1125 Indian Trails Camp**
0-1859 Lake Michigan Drive
Grandville, MI 49534
616-677-5251
FAX: 616-677-2955
e-mail: info@indiantrailscamp.org
www.indiantrailscamp.org

*Betsy Buist, Director of Camp Services*
*Karen Bultsma, Admin & Food Svc Director*
Year round residential camping program for children and adults with physical disabilities. One and two-week sessions. Coed, ages 6-70.

**1126 Sherman Lake YMCA Outdoor Center**
6225 N 39th St
Augusta, MI 49012-9722
269-731-3000
FAX: 269-731-3020
e-mail: shermanlakeymca@ymcasl.org
shermanlakeymca.org

*Luke Austenfeld, Executive Director*
Summer camping sessions for campers with ADD and spina bifida. Coed, ages 6-15 and families, seniors.

**1127 St. Francis Camp On The Lake**
10120 Murrey
Jerome, MI 49249
517-688-9212
e-mail: mike_carp@sbcglobal.net
www.saintfranciscamp.org

The camp runs one-week sessions from June through August for cognitively impaired children and adults and is staffed with a 3-to-1 camper ratio. Campers are encouraged to plan their own activities and can partake in swimming, hiking, volleyball, and basketball. Camp staff also helps to emphasize the importance of daily living and socialization skills, and other activities such as helping in the kitchen, and making beds.

**1128 Trail's Edge Camp**
Mott Respiratory Care
1500 E. Medical Center Drive
Ann Arbor, MI 48109-0208
734-936-4000
e-mail: mdekeon@umich.edu
www.med.umich.edu

*Mary Dekeon*
Summer camp for children and young adults between the ages of 3-18 with special medical needs. Campers have tracheostomies or need ventilator assistance. Some of the camp activities include fishing, hiking, horseback riding, boating, swimming, nature & outdoor living skills.

**1129 YMCA Camp Copneconic**
10407 North Fenton Road
Fenton, MI 48430
810-629-9622
FAX: 810-629-2128
e-mail: request@campcopneconic.org
www.campcopneconic.org

*John Carlson, Executive Director*
Camp is located in Fenton, Michigan. Summer sessions for campers with diabetes. Coed, ages 3-16 and seniors.

## Minnesota

**1130 ADA Camp Needlepoint**
American Diabetes Association
5100 Gamble Dr
St Louis Park, MN 55437-1521
763-593-5333
800-676-4065
e-mail: rmartin@diabetes.org
www.diabetescamps.org

*Becky Barnett, Camp Director*
*Carol Holten, Coordinator*
Camping for children who have type 1 diabetes. Coed, ages 5-16.

**1131 Camp Buckskin**
PO Box 389
Ely, MN 55731
218-365-2121
FAX: 218-365-2880
e-mail: info@campbuckskin.com
www.campbuckskin.com

*Thomas R Bauer CCD, Camp Director*
*Mary Bauer, Co-Director*
*Jared Griffin, Program Director*
Camp is located in Ely, Minnesota. Buckskin assists LD, AD/HD, Asperger's, and adopted individuals to realize and develop the potentials and abilities which they possess. Teaches a combination of traditional camp, academic activities and social skills so the campers experience success in many areas. Ages 6-18.

**1132 Camp Courage North**
Courage Center
3915 Golden Valley Rd
Golden Valley, MN 55422-4249
763-520-0504
866-520-0504
e-mail: camping@courage.org
www.couragecenter.org

*Jan Malcolm, CEO*
Camp is located in Lake George, Minnesota. Summer sessions for campers who have blood disorders, hearing impairment, mobility limitation or are blind/visually impaired. Coed, ages 7-70.

**1133 Camp Discovery**
American Academy Of Dermatology
930 E. Woodfield Road
Schaumburg, IL 60173
847-240-1737
FAX: 847-330-8907
e-mail: jmueller@aad.org
www.campdiscovery.org

Free camp for ages 8-16 with chronic skin conditions such as psoriasis, eczema, scleroderma, epidermolysis bullosa, alopecia, Vitiligo, congenital nevus. Campers can enjoy boating, fishing, water skiing, swimming, arts and crafts.

**1134 Camp Eden Wood**
Friendship Ventures
8707 Dufferin St. Unit 1
Thornhill, ON L4J 0
905-882-1679
FAX: 905-248-3340
e-mail: info@campedenwoods.com
www.campedenwoods.com/

*Sharon Gluzberg, Owner and Director*
*Lior Gluzberg, Owner and Director*
Camp Eden and Eden Art Classes are dedicated to maintaining a friendly and nurturing environment where all our students and campers can unleash their creativity. Opening Camp Eden Woods the residential camp was a natural progression to our growing camp family.

**1135 Camp Friendship**
Friendship Ventures
10509 108th St NW
Annandale, MN 55302
952-852-0102
800-450-8376
FAX: 320-852-0123
e-mail: fv@friendshipventures.org
www.friendshipventures.org

*Georgann Rumsey, CEO*
Camp Friendship offers resident camp programs for children, teenagers and adults with developmental, physical or multiple disabilities, special medical conditions, Down Syndrome, Williams Syndrome, autism or other conditions. Summer camp offers archery, sailing, horseback riding, biking, fishing, creative arts, adventure challenge programs and other activities. Weekend camps and longer available. Other services available throughout the year. Coed, ages 5-90, families, seniors.

**1136 Camp Heartland**
One Heartland
2101 Hennepin Avenue
Suite 107
Minneapolis, MN 55405
1 8-8 2-6 20
FAX: 612-824-6303
e-mail: helpkids@oneheartland.org
www.oneheartland.org

*Patrick Kindler, Executive Director*
Non-profit organization committed to improving the lives of children, youth and their families who have been impacted by HIV/AIDS.

**1137 Camp Knutson**
Camp Knutson And Knutson Point Retreat Center
11169 Whitefish Avenue
Crosslake, MN 56442
218-543-4232
www.lssmn.org/camp/

*Rob Larson, Camp Director*
*Mary (Kate) Williams, Assistant Director*
Camp for children with autism, down syndrome, heart disease and skin disease. Activities include boating, swimming and other water actvities.

**1138 Camp New Hope**
FriendshipVentures
4805 N Carolina 86
Chapel Hill, NC 27514
919-942-4716
FAX: 919-942-3266
e-mail: info@newhopeccc.org
www.newhopeccc.org

*Richard Stevens, Executive Director*
*Bruce Aycock, Program Director*
*Gerald Singleton, Facilities Manager:*
*Minnilue Braverman, Administrative Assistant*
A place for children, teens and adults to have the time of their lives. The program focuses on building self esteem, independence and provides opportunities to practice social skills specifically designed for persons with developmental, physical and multiple disabilities, special medical needs, Down Syndrome, autism, or other conditions.

**1139 Camp Sertoma**
1105 Camp Sertoma Dr
Westfield, NC 27053
336-593-8057
www.campsertoma.org

*Keith Russell, Center Director*
*Mike Bowman, Property Director*
Camp Sartoma is a place where deaf and hard of hearing children can come to meet people just like them, with out communication barriers. Activities include swimming, canoeing, fishing, hiking, hayrides, campfires, games, astronomy, and nature crafts.

**1140 Camp Winnebago**
131 Ocean Street
South Portland, ME 04106
800-932-1646
FAX: 207-767-1018
e-mail: andy@campwinnebago.com
www.campwinnebago.org

A non profit organization specializing in the recreational needs of adults and children with developmental disabilities.

**1141 Confidence Learning Center**
Confidence Learning Center
1620 Mary Fawcett Memorial Drive
East Gull Lake, MN 56401
218-828-2344
FAX: 218-828-2618
e-mail: jeffs@campconfidence.com
www.campconfidence.com/

*Jeff Olson, Executive Director*
*Bob Slaybaugh, Program Director*
*Mary Harder, Volunteer Director*
*Jenni Bailey, Camp Sertoma Director*
A year-round outdoor center for persons with developmental disabilities. Some of the summer activities include fishing, archery, beach activities, water volleyball and basketball. Also a specialty camps for deaf and hearing impaired campers.

**1142 Courage Center Camps**
Courage Center
8046 83rd St NW
Maple Lake, MN 55358-2454
320-963-3121
866-520-0504
FAX: 320-963-3698
e-mail: couragecamps@couragecenter.org
www.couragecenter.org/camps

*Jan Malcolm, CEO*
*Pamela J. Lindemoen, Exec VP of Operations*
*Stephen Bariteau, Chief Dev. Officer*
*Alice Johnson, Chief Financial Officer*
Camp is located in Maple Lake, Minnesota. Summer sessions for campers with a variety of disabilities. Coed, ages 6-99, families, seniors.

**1143 YMCA Camp Ihduhapi**
Minneapolis YMCA Camping Services
3425 Ihduhapi Rd
Loretto, MN 55357-9512
763-479-1146
FAX: 612-823-2482
e-mail: info@campihduhapi.org
www.ymcatwincities.org/camps/camp_ihduhapi/

*Kerry Pioske, Camp Executive*
*Joey Cottew, Camp Program Director*
*Devin Hanson, Day Camp Director*
*Josh Cobb, Overnight Camp Director*
Camp is located in Loretto, Minnesota. Summer sessions for campers with asthma/respiratory ailments and epilepsy. Coed, ages 7-16.

## Mississippi

**1144 Camp Dream Street**
Camp Dream Street, MS
3863 Morrison Road
Utica, MS 39175
601-885-6042
e-mail: info@dreamstreetms.org
www.dreamstreetms.org

*Kimberly Evans, Program Director*
*Mike Kaiser, Assistant Program Director*
*Scott Levy, Chairman*
*Henry S. Jacobs, Camp Director*
For children with physical disabilities. The camp is full of fun and excitement and offers activities such as swimming, art's and crafts, horseback riding and more.

**1145 Sequanota Lutheran Conference Center and Camp**
P.O. Box 245
Jennerstown, PA 15547 814-629-6627
FAX: 814-629-0128
e-mail: contact@sequanota.com
www.sequanota.com/

*Rev. George Mason, Exec. Dir.*
*Ang Illar, Program Dir.*
*Dawna Horner, Food Service/House Keeping Dir.*
*Mike Pluta, Maintenance Dir.*
Summer sessions for adults with developmental disabilities and speech/communication impairment. The name of the company is ""Sequanota Lutheran Camp and Conference Center""

## Missouri

**1146 Camp Barnabas**
901 Private Road 2060
Purdy, MO 65734 417-476-2565
FAX: 417-486-2980
e-mail: info@campbarnabas.org
www.campbarnabas.org

*Paul Teas, Exec. Dir. and Co-Founder*
*Cyndy Teas, R.N., BSN, Dir. of Dev. and Co-Founder*
*Jason Brawner, Dir. of Operations*
*Keri McKee, Dev. Officer*
Camp for people with developmental challenges, post traumatic burns, blood disorders, cancer, low vision/blindness, and physical challenges. The camp runs from June to August and provides activities such as canoeing, horseback riding and swimming.

**1147 Camp Encourage**
P.O. Box 10433
Kansas City, MO 64171 816-830-7171
e-mail: camp.encourage@sbcglobal.net
www.campencourage.org

*Eric Lanham, J.D., President*
*Kelly Lee, Executive Director*
*Michelle Long, CPA, Treasurer*
*Marita Burrow, Ph.D., Secretary*
Encourages social growth, independence and self esteem in children and young adults with autism spectrum disorders.

**1148 Camp Funshine**
Camp Funshine Foundation, Inc.
P.O. Box 576
Pea Ridge, AR 72751 www.campfunshine.com

*Jeff Brown, President*
*Aimee Albright, Vice President*
*Holly Floyd, Treasurer*
*Rain Sheppard, Secretary*
A free camp for children ages 7 and up who have cystic fibrosis. The mission of the camp is to provide a fun, safe enviroment in which the kids can talk openly about themselves or their disease.

**1149 Camp Hickory Hill**
Central Missouri Diabetic Childrens Camp
P.O.Box 1942
Columbia, MO 65205-1942 573-445-9146
e-mail: camphickoryhill@yahoo.com
www.camphickoryhill.com

*David Bernhardt, President*
*Doug Phillips, Vice-President*
*Jessica La Mantia Bernhardt, Camp Director*
*Michael Gardner MD, Medical Director*
Educates diabetic children concerning diabetes and its care. In addition to daily educational sessions on some aspects of diabetes, campers participate in swimming, sailing, arts and crafts and overnight camping. Coed, ages 7-17.

**1150 Camp MITIOG**
Share, Inc
7615 N. Platte Purchase Drive
Suite 116
Kansas City, MO 64118 913-522-9516
877-221-4450
FAX: 816-221-1420
e-mail: midlands@midlandsmc.org
www.campmitiog.org
Camp is located in Excelsior Springs, Missouri. One-week summer sessions for children with spina bifida. Coed, ages 6-16.

**1151 Concerned Care Recreation Day Camp**
Concerned Care, Inc.
320 Armour Rd
North Kansas City, MO 64116-3506 816-474-3026
FAX: 816-474-3029
www.concernedcarekc.org

*Barbara Griggs, Executive Director*
*Gayle Bennett-Grant, Director of Residential Services*
*Jim Huffman, Director of Community Services*
*Carolyn Henry, Director of Development*
Summer sessions for campers with developmental disabilities. Coed, ages 7-16.

**1152 Kiwanis Camp Wyman**
Wyman Center
600 Kiwanis Dr
St. Louis, MO 63025-2212 636-938-5245
FAX: 636-938-5289
e-mail: info@wymancenter.org
www.wymancenter.org

*Dave Hilliard, President/CEO*
*Kristine Ramsey, Sr. VP, Dev.*
*Claire Wyneken, Senior VP & Dir. of Partner Svcs*
*Tom Etzkorn, VP, Special Projects*
Summer sessions for youth with diabetes. Coed, ages 8-16, run in conjunction with the American Diabetes Association. Call for program description.

**1153 Lions Den Outdoor Learning Center**
600 Kiwanis Dr
St. Louis, MO 63025-2212 636-938-5245
FAX: 636-938-5289
e-mail: info@wymancenter.org
wymancenter.org

*Dave Hilliard, President/CEO*
*Kristine Ramsey, Sr. VP, Dev.*
*Claire Wyneken, Senior VP & Dir. of Partner Svcs*
*Tom Etzkorn, VP, Special Projects*
Varied programs for mentally retarded children, ages 6 and up, includes daily living, socialization and language skills. Sports, tent camping, crafts, and nature study are also offered. Sliding scale tuition for 2 weeks.

**1154 Sunnyhill Adventure Center**
Council for Extended Care
6555 Sunlit Way
Dittmer, MO 63023-3306 636-274-9044
FAX: 636-285-1305
e-mail: dropin4fun@aol.com
sunnyhilladventures.org

*Victoria James, President/CEO*
*Jessica Erfling, Vice President of Operations*
*Donald Mitchell, Director of ISLA*
*Rob Darroch, Director*
Camp is located in Dittmer, Missouri. Summer sessions for campers with developmental disabilities and autism. Coed, ages 8-99. Sunnyhill Adventures is program that offers campers fun, exciting, educational experiences in a beautiful outdoor setting. Our residential summer camp combines traditional camping activities plus specially selected and adapted events to meet the needs of each camper group.

**1155 Wonderland Camp Foundation**
18591 Miller Circle
Rocky Mount, MO 65072-2400 573-392-1000
e-mail: info@wonderlandcamp.org
www.wonderlandcamp.org

*Allen Moore, CEO*
*Gerald Moore, President*
*Don Borchelt, Vice President*
*Dan Volmert, Vice President*
A residential camp for children and adults with mental and physical disabilities. 12 one week sessions. Coed. All Ages starting at age 6 through adult.

## Montana

**1156 Big Sky Kids Cancer Camps**
Eagle Mount-Bozeman
6901 Goldenstein Lane
Bozeman, MT 59715 406-586-1781
FAX: 406-586-5794
e-mail: eaglemount@eaglemount.org
www.eaglemount.org

*Mary Peterson, Executive Director*
*Lisa Batzler, Big Sky Kids Director*
*Chad Biggerstaff, Big Sky Program Director*
*Heather Collins, Development Coordinator*
Provides recreational opportunities for people of all ages with disabilities and children with cancer. Big Sky offers skiing, swimming, fishing, ice-skating, golf, cycling, and so much more.

**1157 Camp Kindle**
Project Kindle/Camp Kindle
201 North 8th Street
Suite 220
Lincoln, NE 68508 661-257-1901
877-800-2267
FAX: 702-995-9186
e-mail: info@projectkindle.org
www.campkindle.org

*Eva Payne, Founder and Executive Director*
*Alison Boring, Co-Camp Director*
*Erin FitzGerald, Co-Camp Director*
*Nikki Wiener, Medical Director*
The camp offers children with HIV and AIDS a safe environment where they can go to strengthen their self esteem through interactive participation in educational and recreational programming.

**1158 Camp Mak-A-Dream**
P.O. Box 1450
Missoula, MT 59806 406-549-5987
FAX: 406-549-5933
e-mail: info@campdream.org
www.campdream.org

*Stuart J. Kaplan, MD, Medical Dir. and CEO*
*Beth Jones, Camp Dir.*
*Jennifer Benton, Dir. of Mktg & Special Events*
*Shirley Hummer, Campus Dir.*
A unique experience for young children in various stages of cancer therapy. The camp gives the children a chance to make new friends, try new things and experience how fun camp can be. Some of the activities include art projects, swimming, archery and campouts.

**1159 Charles Campbell Childrens Camp**
The Billings Lions Club
PO Box 23342
Billings, MT 59104 406-670-2496
e-mail: campbellcamp@msn.com
www.billingslions.org/ccc.htm

*Doug Hanson, Director*
*Sue Hanson, Director*
Camp is open to young adults with physical disabilities that include sight or hearing impairement, spina bifida, cerebral palsy, gross motor skill impairements and other disabilities. Campers enjoy hiking, swimming, fishing, dances, campfires and much more.

## Nebraska

**1160 Camp Floyd Rogers**
Floyd Rogers Foundation
P.O. Box 31536
Omaha, NE 68131-536 402-341-0866
e-mail: campers@campfloydrogers.com
www.campfloydrogers.com
A camp for diabetic children. Coed, ages 8-18. 100 children come to Camp Floyd Rogers each summer. They come to enjoy activities, participate in special events, engage in innovative evening programs, and they meet other children their own age with diabetes. Camp Floyd Rogers offers young people an opportunity to share some of life's adventures with others who also happen to have diabetes.

**1161 Camp Quality Heartland**
P.O. Box 402
Council Bluffs, IA 51502 712-484-3625
e-mail: heartland@campqualityusa.org
www.campqualityusa.com

*Missy Schreiber, Camp Director*
*Sandy Ludwig, Director Elect*
*Michele Martindale, Camper Registrar*
*Marcia Hopkins, Volunteer to be a Companion*
Camp Quality is for children with cancer and their siblings. The camp offers a stress-free environment that offers exciting activities and fosters new friendships, while helping to give the children courage, motivation and emotional strength.

**1162 Easter Seals Nebraska**
Easter Seals Nebraska
638 N 109th Plz
Omaha, NE 68154-1722 402-345-2200
800-650-9880
FAX: 402-345-2500
www.ne.easterseals.com

*Karen C. Carlson, President & CEO*
Offers a variety of services to help people with disabilities address life's challenges and achieve personal goals. Terrific fun for campers and a much needed respite for families and caregivers from the daily challenges of caring for special needs individuals.

**1163 Kamp Kaleo**
46872 Willow Springs Rd
Burwell, NE 68823-8805 308-730-0333
FAX: 308-346-5083
e-mail: kampkaleo@nctc.net
www.kampkaleo.com

*Gaylene O'Brien, Facilities Administrator*
*Sandy Denton, Minister of Faith Dev.*
*Jim Becker, Chairperson*
Camp is located in Burwell, Nebraska. Summer sessions for campers who are blind/visually impaired or have developmental disabilities. Coed, ages 9-18 and families, seniors, single adults.

1164 **National Camps for Blind Children**
Christian Record Services
4444 S 52nd Street
Lincoln, NE 68516-1302 402-488-0981
FAX: 402-488-7582
e-mail: info@christianrecord.org
www.christianrecord.org

*Larry Pitcher, President*
*Matthew Orian, VP for Finance*
*Dan Jackson, Chair*
*Tom Lemon, Vice Chair*
Provides free Christian publications and programs, as well as new opportunities for people with visual impairments. Free services include subscription magazines available in braille, large print and audio cassette, full-vision books combining braille and print, lending library, gift bibles and study guides in braille, large print and audio cassette, national camps for blind children and scholarship assistance for blind young people trying to obtain a college education.

1165 **YMCA Camp Kitaki**
Lincoln YMCA
570 Fallbrook Blvd.
Suite 210
Lincoln, NE 68521-3110 402-434-9222
FAX: 402-434-9226
e-mail: CampKitaki@ymcalincoln.org
www.ymcalincoln.org

*Jason Smith, Executive Director*
*John Senser, Property Director*
*Natalie Roberts-Day, Program Director*
*Jodi Wallace, Program Director*
Camp is located in Louisville, Nebraska. Summer sessions for children with cystic fibrosis. Coed, ages 7-17 and families.

## Nevada

1166 **Camp Buck**
Nevada Diabetes Association
1005 Terminal Way #170
Reno, NV 89502 775-856-3839
800-379-3839
FAX: 775-348-7591
e-mail: camp@diabetesnv.org
www.diabetesnv.org

*Sarah Gleich, Associate State Exec. Dir.*
*Mylan Hawkins, State Exec. Dir.*
*Diana Kern, State Dir. of Dev.*
*Celeste Ochal, Southern Nevada Exec. Dir.*
Co-ed summer camp for children with diabetes ages 8-17. While at the camp, the children develop a better understanding of their diabetes while enjoying a week filled with recreational and athletic activities such as swimming, kayaking, fishing and arts & crafts.

1167 **Camp Lotsafun**
3660 Baker Lane
Suite 103
Reno, NV 89509 775-827-3866
FAX: 775-827-0334
e-mail: camp@camplotsafun.com
www.camplotsafun.com

*Bill Wagner, Director*
*Chuck Marks, Director*
*Cindy Anderson, Advisory Director*
*Jill Gabel, Program Director*
Provides therapeutic, educational, and recreational opportunities for individuals with developmental disabilities, while providing respite care for thier families. Children, teens and adults with autism, down syndrome, traumatic brain injury, cerebral palsy and attention deficit hyperactive disorder are among some of the individuals who attend camp for fun and recreational activities such as swimming, kayaking, pet therapy, arts & crafts, drama and music.

1168 **Camp SignShine**
DHHARC
999 Pyramid Way
Sparks, NV 89431 775-434-0290
FAX: 775-355-8996
TTY:775-355-8994
www.dhharc.org
Week long camp for children ages 7-19 who are deaf or hard of hearing and their siblings. Campers enjoy recreational and educational activities in a safe and comfortable environment.

1169 **CampCare**
P.O. Box 12155
Reno, NV 89510-2155 775-323-3737
FAX: 775-323-1019
e-mail: cmoore@campcarenevada.org
www.campcarenevada.org
The camp provides a special time for individuals with special needs by helping them make friends, have fun and explore their gifts and talents.

## New Hampshire

1170 **Camp Allen**
56 Camp Road
Bedford, NH 03110-6606 603-622-8471
FAX: 603-626-4295
e-mail: mary@campallennh.org
www.campallennh.org

*Mary Constance, Executive Director*
*Michael Constance, Summer Camp Director*
*John Cronin, Director*
*Jean Lemire, Director*
A residential summer camp for individuals with disabilities. All of the activities are conducted by individual coordinators under the supervision of Program Director. Some of the activities include, aquatics, arts, crafts, games and nature programs. All camp events, special events, evening programs, and field trips are scheduled throughout the summer and are structured to meet the individual abilities and needs of each camper.

1171 **Camp Sno Mo**
Easter Seals: New Hampshire
555 Auburn St
Manchester, NH 03103-4803 603-623-8863
800-870-8728
FAX: 603-625-1148
e-mail: rkelly@eastersealsnh.org
www.nh.easterseals.com

*Larry J. Gammon, President & CEO*
*Elin A. Treanor, Senior VP and CFO*
*Tina Sharby, Senior VP Human Resources*
*Robert Kelly, Camp Dir.*
Mission is to create solutions that change the lives of children and adults with disabilities or special needs or their families. From campfire sing-a-longs and late night ghost stories, to boating, nature walks, swimming, and arts and crafts, Easter Seals camps provide the same excitement and activity available at other summer camp programs. Easter Seals campers experience the joys and challenges of camp in a fully-accessible setting.

**1172 Windsor Mountain American Sign Language Camp Program**
Windsor Mountain International
One World Way
Windsor, NH 03244 603-478-3166
800-862-7760
FAX: 603-478-5260
e-mail: Jake@WindsorMountain.org
www.windsormountain.org

*Jake Labovitz, Director*
*Kerry Labovitz, Director*
*Pam Butler, Administrative Assistant*
*Richard Herman*
Camp Windsor is for children from around the world who are deaf or hard of hearing.

## New Jersey

**1173 Camp Carefree**
American Diabetes Association
275 Carefree Lane
Stokesdale, NC 27357 336-427-0966
e-mail: carefreedirectors@gmail.com
www.campcarefree.org/

*Anne Jones, Founder & Executive Director*
*Tony McCallum, Program Director*
*David Sugg, Program Director*
*Jordan Harrell, Program Director*
Since 1986, Camp Carefree has provided a FREE, one week camping experience for kids with chronic illnesses. Our program also includes camps for well siblings of ill children, and a week for children with a sick parent.

**1174 Camp Chatterbox**
P.O. Box 8310
Red Bank, NJ 07701-2015 908-301-5451
e-mail: Campchatterbox@gmail.com
www.campchatterbox.org

*Joan Bruno, Ph.D., Director*
Camp Chatterbox is an overnight camp for children who use augmentative communication devices. The camp offers recreational activities such as swimming, boating, sports and being with nature, and the camp activities programs are designed to facilitate device use throughout the day.

**1175 Camp Dream Street**
Kaplen JCC On The Palisades
411 East Clinton Avenue
Tenafly, NJ 07670 201-569-7900
FAX: 201-569-7448
e-mail: info@jccotp.org
www.jccotp.org

*Danny Rocke, CFO*
*Avi A. Lewinson, Exec. Director*
*Deann Forman, COO*
*Lisa Robbins, Director*
A one-week camp for children ages 4-14 who have cancer and other blood disorders. Campers and their siblings can enjoy a wide variety of activities such as arts and crafts, sports, nature, swimming, entertainement and music.

**1176 Camp Jotoni**
ARC of Somerset County
141 S Main St
Manville, NJ 08835-1803 908-725-8544
e-mail: taraa@thearcofsomerset.org
www.thearcofsomerset.org

*Eric Mandelbaum, President/Secretary*
*Edmond Brown, Treasurer*
*Lauren Panarella, Executive Director*
*Christopher Corvino, Associate Executive Director*
Sponsored by the Arc of Somerset County, Camp Jotoni is a day and residential camp for children and adults with developmental disabilities. Campers are ages five to adult. Set on 15 acres in Somerset County, the camp features a junior Olympic size pool, cabins, dining hall, playgrounds, open air pavilions, unspoiled woods, and wildlife. Coed, ages 5-99.

**1177 Camp Lou Henry Hoover**
Girl Scouts of Washington Rock Council
201 E Grove St
Westfield, NJ 07090-5614 908-518-4403
FAX: 908-232-2140
e-mail: chay@gshnj.org
www.gshnj.org

*Susan M. Brooks, CEO*
*Nancy Faulks, Chair*
*Michael Kzirian, Secretary*
*Lori Grier, Treasurer*
Camp is located in Middleville, New Jersey. Sessions for girls who are blind/visually impaired, ages 7-18.

**1178 Camp Merry Heart**
Easter Seals: New Jersey
21 O'Brien Road
Hackettstown, NJ 07840 908-852-3896
FAX: 908-852-9263
e-mail: camp@nj.easterseals.com
nj.easterseals.com

*Todd Thompson, Director*
*Samantha Maina, Camp Specialist*
*Mary Simpson, Registrar*
*Michelle Marzigliano, Admin Asst*
An organized program of swimming, arts and crafts, boating, nature study and travel offered to campers with a variety of disabilities. Coed, ages 5-80, families, seniors. Fall and spring travel programs for adults.

**1179 Camp Nejeda**
Camp Nejeda Foundation
910 Saddlebrook Road
P.O. Box 156
Stillwater, NJ 07875- 156 973-383-2611
FAX: 973-383-9891
e-mail: information@campnejeda.org
nejeda.convio.net

*Philip E. De Rea, Executive Director*
*Jim Daschbach, Camp Director*
*Rich Ramage, Maintenance Director*
*Jennifer Passerini, Development Director*
For children with diabetes, ages 7-15. Provides an active and safe camping experience which enables the children to learn about and understand diabetes. Activities include boating, swimming, fishing, archery, as well as camping skills.

**1180 Camp Oakhurst**
New York Service for the Handicapped
111 Monmouth Rd
Oakhurst, NJ 07755-1514 732-531-0215
FAX: 732-531-0292
e-mail: info@nysh.org
www.nysh.org/

*Charles Sutherland, Camp Director*
*Robert Pacenza, Executive Director*
*Andy Arno, Board of Director*
*Julian Bach, Board of Director*
Camp is located in Oakhurst, New Jersey. Summer sessions for campers with cerebral palsy, mobility limitation and spina bifida. Coed, age 8-18.

**1181 Camp Sun'N Fun**
ARC of Gloucester
1036 N Tuckahoe Rd
Williamstown, NJ 08094-3486 856-629-4502
FAX: 856-875-1499
e-mail: camp@thearcgloucester.org
www.thearcgloucester.org

*Robert H. Weir, Charter President*
*Dottie Weir, Charter President*
*Charles Funk, Vice President*
*Terri Wilson, Camp Director*
Camp is located in Williamstown, New Jersey. Summer sessions for campers with developmental disabilities. Coed, ages 8-88. Activities include swimming, arts & crafts, nature, sports, games, music, dance and drama.

**1182 Camp Vacamas**
256 Macopin Rd
West Milford, NJ 07480-3718 973-838-0942
877-428-8222
e-mail: info@vacamas.org
www.vacamas.org

*Michael Friedman, Executive Director*
*Ely Connelly Newberry, Director*
*Sandra I. Friedman, Associate Executive Director*
*Gail Gailbraith, Director*
Disadvantaged children with asthma or sickle cell anemia, ages 8-16, are offered special programs in canoeing, backpacking, camping, music and leadership training. Sliding scale tuition. Year round programs for youth at risk groups. Conference center facility open for group rentals.

**1183 New Jersey Camp Jaycee**
The Arc of New Jersey
985 Livingston Ave
North Brunswick, NJ 08902-1843 732-246-2525
FAX: 732-214-1834
e-mail: info@campjaycee.org
www.campjaycee.org

*Frank Pirrello, President*
*John O'Brien, Vice President*
*Patricia Rhein, Secretary*
*Jason Brakeman, Camp Director*
Camp Jaycee is located on 185 acres of forests, fields and streams located in the lovely Pocono Mountains, a short distance from the New Jersey border. Sessions for children and adults with autism and developmental disabilities. Goals of Camp Jaycee are centered around developing social skills, improving self esteem, increasing confidence, learning in a fun environment, developing physical fitness, and establishing meaningful relationships with new friends. Coed, ages 7-85.

**1184 New Jersey YMHA/YWHA Camps Milford**
21 Plymouth St
Fairfield, NJ 07004-1686 973-575-3333
800-776-5657
FAX: 973-575-4188
e-mail: info@njycamps.org
www.njycamps.org

*Bruce L. Nussman, President*
*Silvio Berlfein, Assistant Director*
*Leonard Robinson, Executive Director*
*Hylton Wener, Director*
Camp is located in Milford, Pennsylvania. Summer sessions for children with ADD. Coed, ages 6-17 and families.

**1185 Rolling Hills Country Day Camp**
P.O.Box 172
Marlboro, NJ 07746 732-308-0405
FAX: 732-780-4726
e-mail: info@rollinghillsdaycamp.com
www.rollinghillsdaycamp.com

*Billy Breitner*
Summer sessions for children with ADD. Coed, ages 3-12.

**1186 Round Lake Camp**
21 Plymouth Street
Fairfield, NJ 07004 973-575-3333
e-mail: rlc@njycamps.org
www.roundlakecamp.org
Round Lake Camp is for children with learning differences and social communication disorders. Campers can enjoy swimming, boating, sailing, mountain biking, and arts and crafts.

## New Mexico

**1187 ADA Camp for Kids**
American Diabetes Association
2625 Pennsylvania NE
Suite 225
Albuquerque, NM 87110- 3649 888-342-2383
e-mail: lbrown@diabetes.org
www.diabetes.org/living-with-diabetes/parents

*Larry Hausner, MBA, CEO*
*Shereen Arent, Exec VP*
*Mary Vaneeda Bennett, Chief Revenue Officer*
*Greg Elfers, Chief Field Dev. Officer*
One-week camping session for children with diabetes. Coed, ages 8-13. Camp will be held at Manzano Mountain Retreat, one hour from Albuquerque, New Mexico. Please call for exact dates.

## New York

**1188 ADA Camp Sunshine**
American Diabetes Association
160 Allens Creek Rd
Rochester, NY 14618-3309 FAX: 585-458-3810
e-mail: dhumphreys@diabetes.org
www.diabetescamp.org

*Terry Ackley, Exec. Dir.*
*Lorne Abramson, Consultant*
*Shelley Yeager, Dir. of Outreach & Dev.*
*Kathy Latimer, Administrative Assistant*
The American Diabetes Association New York Area's Camp is a residential camp for children with diabetes. The program is held on the Rotary Sunshine Campus in Rush, only 15 miles from Rochester. The camp is located on 133 acres of land in a rural setting including modern year round cabins, an Olympic-sized swimming pool, nature trails, athletic fields and a fishing pond. Ages 8-16; held during July.

**1189 Camp Abilities Brockport**
The College At Brockport, State Univ Of New York
350 New Campus Drive
Brockport, NY 14420 585-395-5361
FAX: 585-395-2771
e-mail: llieberm@brockport.edu
www.campabilitiesbrockport.org

*Dr. Lauren Lieberman, PhD, Camp Director*
*Haley Schedlin, Assistant Director*
*Amanda Tepfer, Aquatic and Boating Director*
*Jeff Yellen, Graduate Assistant*
A one-week sports camp for children who are visually impaired, blind or deafblind. Children learn to be more physically active, which in turn improves their health and well being.

**1190 Camp Glengarra**
Girl Scouts - Foothills Council
33 Jewett Pl
Utica, NY 13501-4715 e-mail: nbrown@girlscoutsfoothills.org

*Karen Lubecki, Director*
Camp Glengarra is located on 500+ acres of fields and forests, about eight miles west of Camden. This Girl Scout Camp hosts a

myriad of programs throughout the year as well as summer day and resident camp. Summer sessions for girls 5-17 with ADD or asthma/respiratory ailments.

**1191 Camp Good Days and Special Times**
1332 Pitsford-Mendon Rd
PO Box 665
Mendon, NY 14506
585-624-5555
800-785-2135
FAX: 585-624-5799
www.campgooddays.org

*Gary Mervis, Chairman and Founder*
*Wendy Bleier-Mervis, Exec. Dir.*
*Lisa Donato, Western New York Regional Dir.*
*Renee Devesty, Central New York Regional Dir.*
The camp is dedicated to improving the quality of life for children, adults and their families whose lives have been touched by cancer and/or other life challenges.

**1192 Camp Huntington**
P.O. Box 37
High Falls, NY 12440
845-687-7840
866-514-5281
FAX: 845-213-4313
e-mail: mbednarz@camphuntington.com
www.camphuntington.com

*Michael Bednarz, Executive Director*
*Amber Allen-Latham, Camp Director*
*Nicole Nevin, Administrative Assistant*
*Cathy Crowley, Program Consultant*
A co-ed residential summer camp specifically designed to focus on Adaptive and Therapeutic Recreation. Campers include those with learning and developmental disabilities, ADD/HD, Autism Spectrum Disorders, Asperger's, PDD, and other special needs. Three programs are offered that focus on: recreation and social skills; independence; and participation. Campers may attend for a week at a time with a full summer lasting nine weeks.

**1193 Camp Jened**
United Cerebral Palsy Association New York
P.O.Box 483
Rock Hill, NY 12775-483
845-434-2220
FAX: 845-434-2253
www.campjened.org
Camp is located in Rock Hill, New York. Sessions for adults with severe developmental and physical disabilities. Coed, ages 18-99.

**1194 Camp Mark Seven**
Mark Seven Deaf Foundation
144 Mohawk Hotel Rd
Old Forge, NY 13420-4010
315-357-6089
e-mail: execdir@campmark7.org.
www.campmark7.org

*Andrew Brinks, Ph.D., Executive Director*
*Vicki Liggera, Registrar*
*Gregoire Youbara, Office Manager*
*JJ Bechhold, Deaf Programs Director*
Adirondack Mountain camp for hard-of-hearing, deaf and hearing people. Coed, ages 1-99, families, seniors and single adults.

**1195 Camp Northwood**
132 State Route 365
Remsen, NY 13438-5700
315-831-3621
FAX: 315-831-5867
e-mail: northwoodprograms@hotmail.com
www.nwood.com

*Gordon W Felt, Director*
*Donna Felt, Director*
Summer sessions for children with ADD. Coed, ages 8-18.

**1196 Camp Ramapo**
Route 52 Salisbury Turnpike
PO Box 266
Rt. 52 / Salisbury Turnpike
Rhinebeck, NY 12572
845-876-8403
FAX: 845-876-8414
e-mail: office@ramapoforchildren.org
www.ramapoforchildren.org

*Adam Weiss, CEO*
*Bruce Kuziola, Chief Financial Officer*
*Mike Kunin, Exec. Dir.*
*Jennifer Buri da Cunha, Associate Exec. Dir.*
Ramapo's specific focus is adventure-based, experiential learning programs that promote positive character values in children and teens with special needs.

**1197 Camp Sisol**
Jewish Community Center of Greater Rochester/JCC
1200 Edgewood Ave
Rochester, NY 14618-5408
585-461-2000
e-mail: rrosner@jccrochester.org
www.jccrochester.org

*Leslie Berkowitz, Exec. Dir.*
*Dan Iriving, Children's Programs*
*Hanna Bergwal, Assistant Aquatics Dir.*
*Bill Blodgett, Facilities Dir.*
Camp is located in Honeoye Falls, New York. Summer sessions for children with autism. Coed, ages 5-16.

**1198 Camp Tova**
92nd Street Y
1395 Lexington Ave
New York, NY 10128-1612
212-415-5500
www.92y.org

*Stuart J. Ellman, President*
*Sol Adler, Executive Director*
*Laurence D. Belfer, Vice President*
*Cheryl Minikes, Vice President*
Children with learning and developmental disabilities thrive in Camp Tova's small group setting. Making friends and developing a wide variety of creative, social, and physical skills are the goals for Tova campers.

**1199 Camp Venture, Inc.**
25 Smith Street
Suite 510
Nanuet, NY 10954-2970
845-624-3860
www.campventure.org

*Meagen Ryan, President*
*Daniel Lukens, Exec. Dir.*
*Dorothy Cox, Deputy Exec. Dir.*
*Lisa Nolte, Associate Exec. Dir.*
In more than a dozen Rockland neighborhoods, residential, employment, rehabilitation or recreation programs have arisen to help people with disabilities contribute to the life of the community. There are, for instance, more than a dozen Community Residential Facilities, Venture Industries, Venture Day Treatment, Day Habilitation, Venture Chorus, after school programs and more.

**1200 Camp Whitman on Seneca Lake**
Presbyterian Church USA
150 Whitman Road
Penn Yan, NY 14527-278
315-536-7753
FAX: 315-536-2128
e-mail: camp@campwhitman.org
www.campwhitman.org

*Idelle Dillon, Camp Director*
*Rev. Joelle Davis, Executive Presbyter*
*Chris Ruthven, Property Manager*
*Karen Jensen, Registrar*
To give the developmentally disabled youth/adult, ages 10-60, the opportunity to enjoy him/herself in a camping program.

Campers are encouraged to participate in a full range of activities including games, sports, swimming, singing, and dancing. Because the camps are fairly small, we have a low camper to counselor ratio, and all have a chance to know one another and form close friendships.

**1201 Casowasco Camp, Conference and Retreat Center**
158 Casowasco Dr
Moravia, NY 13118-3498
315-364-8756
FAX: 315-364-7636
e-mail: info@casowasco.org
www.campsandretreats.org/index.php/casowasco/

*Mike Huber, Executive Director, CRM*
*Shelby Wilson, Program Director, Casowasco*
*Joan Newlon, Executive Assistant, CRM*
*Shelley Sherboneau, Coordinating Registrar, CRM*
Camp is located in Moravia, New York. Summer sessions for children with ADD. Coed, ages 6-18 and families.

**1202 Clover Patch Camp**
Center for Disability Services
55 Helping Hand Ln
Glenville, NY 12302-5801
518-384-3080
FAX: 518-384-3001
e-mail: cloverpatchcamp@cfdsny.org
www.cloverpatchcamp.org

*Laura Taylor, Camp Director*
*Christopher Schelin, Program Administrator*
Camp is located in Scotia, NY. Summer sessions for campers with a variety of disabilities. Coed, ages 5-85.

**1203 Double H Ranch**
A Hole In The Wall Camp
97 Hidden Valley Road
Lake Luzerne, NY 12846
518-696-5676
FAX: 518-696-4528
e-mail: myurenda@doublehranch.org
www.doublehranch.org

*Max Yurenda, CEO/Executive Director*
*Jacqui Royael, Director Of Operations*
*Kim Adams, Program Associate-Barn Manager*
*Tara Bogucki, Admissions Director*
Summer residential camp and winter sports programs for children and young adults ages 6-16 who have cancer and other life threatening illnesses. The programs are free of charge and some of the recreational activities include bead making, arts & crafts, kickball, tennis, soccer, and volleyball.

**1204 Father Drumgoole Connelly Summer Camp**
MIV Mount Loretto
6581 Hylan Blvd
Staten Island, NY 10309-3830
718-317-2803
e-mail: srynn@mountloretto.org
www.mountloretto.org

*Stephen Rynn, Exec. Dir.*
*Gerri Gatto, Exec. Assistant*
*William D'Ambrosio, Assistant Exec. Dir.*
*Loretta Polanish, Exec. Secretary*
Summer sessions for children with epilepsy, hearing impairment and developmental disabilities. Coed, ages 5-13.

**1205 Friends Academy Summer Camps**
Duck Pond Rd
Locust Valley, NY 11560
516-393-4207
FAX: 516-465-1720
e-mail: camp@fa.org
www.fasummercamp.org

*Richard Mack, Camp Director*
Summer sessions for children with diabetes. Coed, ages 3-14, families.

**1206 Gow School Summer Programs**
2491 Emery Road
P.O. Box 85
South Wales, NY 14139-85
716-652-3450
FAX: 716-652-3457
e-mail: summer@gow.org
www.gow.org

*Robert Garcia, Director of Admissions*
*Gayle Hutton, Director of Development*
*Eric Bray, Summer Program Director*
*Rosemary Shields, CPA, Director of Finance*
Co-ed summer programs for students ages 8-16 with dyslexia or similar learning disabilities offer a balanced blend of morning academics, afternoon/evening traditional camp activities and weekend overnights. The primary purpose of these programs is to provide a positive experience while balancing these three elements. Committed to the creation of a positive and enjoyable experience for each participant by defining and merging the goals of the camp and the school with those of camper students.

**1207 Happiness Is Camping**
2169 Grand Concourse
Bronx, NY 10453-2201
718-295-3100
FAX: 908-362-6733
e-mail: hicoffice@happinessiscamping.org
www.happinessiscamping.org

*Kurt Struver, Executive Director*
*Louis D'Agostino, President of the Board*
*Antonio Dominguez, Secretary/Treasurer*
*Martin Elson, Esq., Counsel*
Camp is located in Blairstown, New Jersey. Free camping sessions for children with cancer. Coed, ages 6-15. June 30 - July 31, 2008.

**1208 Kamp Kiwanis**
New York District Kiwanis Foundation
9020 Kiwanis Rd
Taberg, NY 13471-2727
315-336-4568
FAX: 315-336-3845
e-mail: kamp@kampkiwanis.org
www.kamp-kiwanis.org

*Rebecca O. Lopez, Executive Director*
Kamp Kiwanis is a mainstream camp for underprivileged youth with and without special needs. 20 campers with disabilities are integrated into weekly sessions. Coed, ages 8-14, seniors and single adults.

**1209 Maplebrook School**
5142 Route 22
Amenia, NY 12501-5357
845-373-9511
FAX: 845-373-7029
e-mail: jscully@maplebrookschool.org
www.maplebrookschool.org

*Dr. Roger Fazzone, Administration President*
*Donna Konkolics, Head of School/CEO*
*Lori Hale, Dir. of Dev. & Alumni Relations*
*Ann Thomas, Daycare Director*
A coeducational boarding school which offers a six week camp for children with learning differences and ADD.

**1210 Marist Brothers Mid-Hudson Valley Camp**
P.O.Box 197
Esopus, NY 12429-197
845-384-6620
e-mail: maristreathouse@gmail.com
www.maristretreathouse.net

*Michelle Flemen-Tung, Camp Director, Special Children*
*Kerry McCormack, Camp Director, Special Children*
*Amy Reinwald, Director Special Children*
*Derek Zaphire, Director Special Children*
Serves special people: children who have cancer or who are HIV positive, deaf or mentally retarded.

**1211 Summit Camp**
322 Route 46 West
Suite 210
Parisppany, NJ 07054
973-732-3230
800-323-9908
FAX: 973-732-3226
e-mail: info@summitcamp.com
www.summitcamp.com

*Eugene Bell, Senior Director*
*Debs Hugill, Head, Counselor & Program Director*
*Abbey-Layne Ball, Assistant Director*
Camp is located in Honesdale, Pennsylvania. Summer sessions for children with ADD. Coed, ages 8-17.

**1212 Sunshine Campus**
Rochester Rotary Club
180 Linden Oaks
Suite 200
Rochester, NY 14625
585-546-7435
e-mail: tdreisbach@rochesterrotary.org
www.sunshinecampus.org

*Tracey Dreisbach, Executive Director*
*Brandi Koch, Sunshine Campus Partner Director*
*Amy Nicolis*
Camp is located in Rush, New York. Camping sessions for children and young adults with a variety of disabilities. Ages 7-21.

**1213 VISIONS Vacation Camp for the Blind**
VISIONS Center on Blindness
111 Summit Park Rd
Spring Valley, NY 10977-1221
212-625-1616
FAX: 888-245-8333
e-mail: info@visionsvcb.org
www.visionsvcb.org

*Nancy T. Jones, President*
*Richard P. Simon, Vice President*
*Burton M. Strauss, Jr., Treasurer*
*Carol Spawn Desmond, Secretary*
Is a non profit agency that promotes the independence of people of all ages who are blind or visually impaired. Camp offers braille classes, computers with large print and voice output, support groups, discussions, mobility lessions, cooking classes, personal and home management training, large print and Braille books.

**1214 Wagon Road Camp**
Children's Aid Society
431 Quaker Rd
Chappaqua, NY 10514-2000
914-238-4761
FAX: 914-238-0714
e-mail: webmaster@childrensaidsociety.org
www.childrensaidsociety.org

*Richard R. Buery, Jr., President and CEO*
*William D. Weisberg, Ph.D., Exec VP*
*Dan Lehman, VP and Chief Financial Officer*
*Valerie Russo, VP of Strategy and Excellence*
Wagon Road Day Camp is a co-ed program for children ages 6-13 with a variety of disabilities held within Chappaqua, New York. Uniquely qualified specialists in Project Adventure activities, athletics, horsemanship, theater arts, nature/ecology studies and arts/crafts complement the day camp staff. Special events including Carnival, Olympics, Crazy Hat Day, Western Day, and optional sleepovers add to the summer excitement providing children with an enriching multicultural experience.

**1215 YMCA Camp Chingachgook on Lake George**
Capital District YMCA
1872 Pilot Knob Rd
Kattskill Bay, NY 12844-1802
518-656-9462
FAX: 518-656-9362
e-mail: chingachgook@cdymca.org
www.cdymca.org

*George Painter, Executive Director*
*Billy Rankin, Senior Program Director*
*Lesley Munshower, Summer Camp Program Director*
*Heather Siegel-Sawma, Groups Director*
Sailing programs for people with disabilities. Sessions for campers who are blind/visually impaired. Coed, ages 7-16, families, seniors and single adults.

**1216 YMCA Camp Weona**
YMCA of Greater Buffalo
301 Cayuga Rd
Suite 100
Buffalo, NY 14225-1912
716-565-6008
FAX: 716-565-6007
e-mail: jczochara@ymcabuffaloniagara.org
www.ymcabuffaloniagara.org

*Jeff Burghardt, Finance/Financial Dev. Chair*
*A.L. Ferreira, Camp Exec. Dir.*
*Tim Marble, Camp Ranger*
*Julie Czochara, Business and Sales Coordinator*
Camp is located in Gainesville, New York. Camping sessions for children and adults with epilepsy. Coed, ages 7-16, families and single adults. Nestled in 1,000 acres of hardwood and pine forests, Weona has miles of picturesque hiking trails, brooks, a heated outdoor pool and a world class adventure ropes course. Our indoor facilities include arts and crafts studios, environmental classrooms and a challenging rock climbing wall. It is the ideal setting for hands-on fun, adventure and learning.

## North Carolina

**1217 Adventure Camp**
Amputee Coalition Of America
P.O. Box 485
Lovingston, VA 22949
434-263-5432
e-mail: meh8f@virginia.edu
www.adventurecampinc.org

*Ed Hicks, Treasurer*
*Mary Grant, President*
*Karen Johnson, Vice President*
*Jennifer Puskaric, Secertary*
Adventure Camp is held each summer for children and adolescents with limb loss. Activities include swimming, ropes course, canoeing, fishing, golf , scavenger hunts, karaoke and much more.

**1218 Camp Carefree**
275 Carefree Lane
Stokesdale, NC 27357
336-427-0966
e-mail: carefreedirectors@gmail.com
www.campcarefree.org

*Anne Jones, Founder & Executive Director*
*Tony McCallum, Program Director*
*David Sugg, Program Director*
*Jordan Harrell, Program Director*
A free, one-week camp for youngsters with serious health problems. The camp gives the children a chance to have the freedom to play, learn and enjoy all the recreational and craft activities the camp has to offer.

1219 **Camp Carolina Trails**
American Diabetes Association
2418 Blue Ridge Rd
Suite 206
Raleigh, NC 27607
743-540-3217
888-342-2383
FAX: 704-373-9113
e-mail: jthomas@diabetes.org
www.diabetes.org

*Larry Hausner, MBA, CEO*
*Shereen Arent, Exec VP, Govt Affairs*
*Mary Vaneeda Bennett, Chief Revenue Officer*
*Greg Elfers, Chief Field Dev. Officer*
The American Diabetes Association is the nation's leading nonprofit health organization providing diabetes research, information, advocacy and year round programs for children with diabetes.

1220 **Camp Royall**
Autism Society of North Carolina
250 Bill Ash Road
Moncure, NC 27559
919-542-1033
e-mail: sgage@autismsociety-nc.org
www.autismsociety-nc.org

*Tracey Sheriff, Chief Executive Officer*
*Paul Wendler, Chief Financial Officer*
*Sara Gage, Program Director*
*David Yell, Property Director*
The best source in North Carolina for connecting people who live with autism (and those who care about them) with resources, support, advocacy and informantion tailored to thier unique needs.

1221 **Camp Sky Ranch**
634 Sky Ranch Rd
Blowing Rock, NC 28605-8231
828-264-8600
FAX: 828-265-2339
e-mail: jsharp1@triad.rr.com
www.campskyranch.com

*Jack Sharp, Owner*
A private, residential camp for the developmentally delayed. This season is the camp's 56th year of providing a real camping experience for the handicapped. Camp Sky Ranch was the first private camp for the handicapped in the Southeast. Activities include: swimming, boating, horseback riding, and more. Campers must be able to walk, dress and feed themselves, and toilet trained.

1222 **Camp Tekoa UMC**
Western NC Conference/United Methodist Church
P.O. Box 160
Hendersonville, NC 28793-160
828-692-6516
FAX: 828-697-3288
e-mail: ecampbell@camptekoa.org
www.camptekoa.org

*James Johnson, Exec. Dir.*
*Mike Pruett, Program Dir.*
*Karen Rohrer, Business Mgr*
*Melisa Coates, Administrative Assistant*
Camping for children with asthma/respiratory ailments, hearing impairment and developmental disabilities. Coed, ages 6-17.

1223 **Edward J Madden Open Hearts Camp**
250 Monument Valley Road
Great Barrington, MA 01230
413-528-2229
888-611-1113
e-mail: hearts@openheartscamp.org
www.openheartscamp.org

*David Zaleon, Executive Director*
*Jill Helme, Assistant Director*
*Jacqueline Reasor, Counselor*
*David Andrew, Counselor*
Eight week program for children who have had and are fully recovered from open heart surgery or a heart transplant. Four two week sessions by age group. Small camp - 25 campers per session.

1224 **SOAR Summer Adventures**
NC Base Camp
P.O.Box 388
Balsam, NC 28707-388
828-456-3435
FAX: 828-456-3449
e-mail: admissions@soarnc.org
www.soarnc.org

*Jonathan Jones, Dir. Emeritus*
*Wandajean Jones, Dir. Emeritus*
*John Willson, M.S., LRT/CTR, Exec. Dir.*
*Laura Pate, Dir. of North Carolina Programs*
A nonprofit adventure program working with disadvantaged youth diagnosed with learning disabilities in an outdoor, challenge based environment. Focuses on esteem building and social skills development through rock climbing, backpacking, whitewater rafting, mountaineering, sailing, snorkeling, and much more. Offers two week, one month, and semester programs available. SOAR programs utilize North Carolina, Florida, Colorado, American Southwest, Alaska, and Jamaica as program areas.

1225 **Talisman Summer Camp**
64 Gap Creek Rd
Zirconia, NC 28790-8791
828-697-6313
855-588-8254
FAX: 828-697-6249
e-mail: info@talismancamps.com
talismancamps.crchealth.com/

*Linda Tatsapaugh, Executive Director*
*Amy Allen, Admission Counsellor*
*Doug Smathers, Summer Camp Director*
Camp is located in Black Mountain, North Carolina. Offers a program of hiking, rafting, climbing, and caving for learning disabled ADD/ADHD and autistic young people. Coed, ages 9-18.

1226 **Victory Junction Gang Camp**
4500 Adam's Way
Randleman, NC 27317
336-498-9055
877-854-2268
www.victoryjunction.org

*Pattie Petty, Founder, Chairman & CEO*
*Kyle Petty, Founder; Vice-Chairman*
*Brian Flynn, Director*
*Diane Hough, Director*
The camp serves children with Autism, cancer, Craniofacial Anomalies, Diabetes, Sickle Cell and Spina Bifida.

## North Dakota

1227 **Camp Sioux**
American Diabetes Association
5100 Gamble Drive
Suite 394
Minneapolis, MN 55416
763-593-5333
FAX: 952-582-9000
e-mail: rbarnett@diabetes.org
www.diabetes.org

*Larry Hausner, MBA, CEO*
*Shereen Arent, Exec VP, Govt Affairs*
*Mary Vaneeda Bennett, Chief Revenue Officer*
*Becky Barnett, Camp Dir.*
Camp Sioux, located in Park River, ND, is a week-long residential summer camp for children ages 8-14 who are living with diabetes. Programs encourage independence and self management with appropriate medical supervision to ensure the best possible experience for every camper. Nutrition activities, blood glucose monitoring, and injections/medications are integrated into the camp program.

## Ohio

**1228 CYO Day Camp: Wickliffe**
Catholic Charities Health and Human Services
7911 Detroit Avenue
Cleveland, OH 44102-2815 216-334-2963
e-mail: kbildstein@clevelandcatholiccharities.org
www.clevelandcatholiccharities .org

*Marilyn Scott, Program Administrator*
Welcomes children and young adults ages 6-21 with cognitive (mr/dd) and other developmental disabilities, regardless of race, religion, culture or economic background.

**1229 Camp Allyn**
Stepping Stones Center
5650 Given Rd
Cincinnati, OH 45243-3426 513-831-4660
FAX: 513-831-5918
e-mail: info@steppingstonescenter.org
www.steppingstonescenter.org

*Chris Adams, Exec. Dir.*
*Sam Browne Allen, Programs/Operations Dir.*
*Tim Stitzer, Dev. Dir.*
*CAS Brockman, Facilities/Support Svcs Dir.*
A residential camp in Batavia, Ohio for children and adults with disabilities. Coed, ages 7-60. Campers participate in crafts, swimming, hiking, nature, sports and motor activities. Camp sessions range from 3 to 10 days, are theme oriented, and geared to individual abilities and interests. Also offers day camps for children ages 5-22.

**1230 Camp Cheerful**
Achievement Centers For Children
15000 Cheerful Ln
Strongsville, OH 44136-5420 440-238-6200
FAX: 440-238-1858
e-mail: barb.fields@achievementctrs.org
www.achievementcenters.org

*Connie Boros, VP Of Rec & Sports*
*Patricia W. Nobili, MSSA, President and CEO*
*Bonnie Boenig, OTR/L, Dir. Therapy Services*
*Sally Farwell, M.Ed., VP of Programs*
Sessions for campers with developmental disabilities, mobility limitation and speech/communication impairment. Coed, ages 7-99.

**1231 Camp Courageous**
12701 Waterville-Swanton Rd
Whitehouse, OH 43571-9551 419-875-6828
e-mail: stevek@campcourageous.com
www.campcourageous.com

*Steve Kiessling, Executive Director*
*Chelsea Banas*
Camp Courageous provides residential camping services for people with developmental disabilities from ages 7-75 years old. Our six day, 5 night programs give campers a chance to experience activities such as: aquatics, arts and crafts, animal programs, sports skills, hiking, recreational and leisure education programs, nature studies, drama, cookouts and campfires.

**1232 Camp Emanuel**
P.O. Box 752343
Dayton, OH 45475 937-477-5504
e-mail: nan33@sbcglobal.net
campemanuel.weebly.com

*George Punter, President*
*Nan Crawford, Executive Director*
*Dan Trunk, Vice President*
*Mary Foreman, Secretary*
Camp for hearing impaired and normal hearing youth.

**1233 Camp Happiness**
Catholic Charities Health & Human Services
7911 Detroit Road
Cleveland, OH 44102-2815 216-334-2963
e-mail: mjscott@clevelandcatholiccharities.org
www.clevelandcatholiccharities.or g

*Marilyn Scott, Program Administrator*
Offers a summer camp program for persons with developmental disabilities. Camp Happiness is a six-week day camp at several sites throughout the Diocese for individuals six years of age to 21 years of age.

**1234 Camp Ho Mita Koda**
Diabetes Association Of Greater Cleveland
3601 South Green Road
Suite 100
Cleveland, OH 44122-5719 216-591-0800
FAX: 216-591-0320
e-mail: information@diabetespartnership.org
www.dagc.org

*Jackquie Dickinson, President*
Camp is located in Newbury, Ohio. Summer sessions for children with type 1 diabetes. Coed, ages 6-15. Type 2 diabetes, coed, ages 12-17. Bicycle adventure, coed, ages 13-19. Mini-day camp, ages 4-7, coed.

**1235 Camp Ko-Man-She**
American Diabetes Association
2555 S Dixie Drive
Suite 112
Dayton, OH 45409 937-220-6611
FAX: 937-224-0240
e-mail: dada@diabetesdayton.org
www.diabetesdayton.org

*Susan Mc Govern, Executive Director*
*Carol Clark, President*
*Rafat Fields, President-elect*
*Terry Fague, Secretary, Legal Advisor*
Camp is located in Bellefontaine, Ohio. Summer sessions for children with diabetes. Coed, ages 8-17. Held in July.

**1236 Camp Libbey**
Maumee Valley Girl Scout Center
2244 Collingwood Blvd
Toledo, OH 43620-1147 419-243-8216
800-860-4516
FAX: 419-245-5357
e-mail: roniluckenbill@girlscoutsofwesternohio.org
girlscoutsofwesternohio.org

*Roni Luckenbill, Chief Executive Officer*
*Susan Osborn, Chief Strategy Officer*
*Linda Odenbeck, Finance Director*
*Chris Salley Davis, Director of Program Services*
Camp for girls 7-18 with asthma/respiratory ailments, diabetes, epilepsy and muscular dystrophy is located in Defiance, Ohio.

**1237 Camp Nuhop**
404 Hillcrest Dr
Ashland, OH 44805-4152 419-289-2227
e-mail: info@campnuhop.org
www.campnuhop.org

*Trevor Dunlap, CEO*
*Jason Picking, Dir.*
*Jim Machin, Dir. of Facilities*
*Terri Pringle, Dir. of Dining Svcs*
A summer residential program for any youngster from 6 to 18 with a learning disability, behavior disorder or Attention Deficit Disorder. 84 campers and 41 staff members live on site in groups of to seven campers to every three counselors. Activities focus on positive self-concept and behaviors and teaches children to learn how to find their strengths, abilities and talents from a positive, yet realistic viewpoint.

**1238 Camp Stepping Stone**
Stepping Stones Center
5650 Given Rd
Cincinnati, OH 45243-3499 513-831-4660
FAX: 513-831-5918
steppingstonescenter.org

*Chris Adams, Executive Director*
*Sam Browne Allen, Programs/Operations Director*
*Marcie Brooks, VP Client Services*
*Tim Stitzer, Development Director*
Day camp for children ages 5-22, serving persons with autism, cognitive deficits, Down Syndrome, cerebral palsy, brain injury, and multiple disabilities.

**1239 Echoing Hills**
36272 County Road 79
Warsaw, OH 43844-9770 800-419-6513
FAX: 740-327-6371
e-mail: info@echoinghillsvillage.org
www.echoinghillsvillage.org/

*Buddy Busch, President*
*Larry Armentrout, Board of Director*
*Charles Bethel, Board of Director*
*Todd Imhoff, Board of Director*
Summer camp for children and adults with cerebral palsy. Coed, ages 7-70.

**1240 Highbrook Lodge**
Cleveland Sight Center
P.O.Box 1988
Cleveland, OH 44106-188 216-791-8118
877-776-9563
e-mail: camp@clevelandsightcenter.org
www.clevelandsightcenter.org

*Steven M. Friedman, Ph.D., Executive Director*
*Gary W. Poth, Treasurer*
*David E. Cook, Assistant Treasurer*
*Sheryl King Benford, Secretary*
Camp is located in Chardon, Ohio. Summer sessions for children, adults and familieswho are blind or have low vision. There are seven sessions held annually through June, July and August with an wide range of outdoor camp activities. Camp activities focus on gaining independent skills, mobility, orientation and self confidence in an accessable and traditional camp setting.
*220-660/session*

**1241 Leo Yassenoff JCC Specialty Day Camp**
Jewish Community Center of Greater Columbus
1125 College Ave
Columbus, OH 43209-7802 614-231-2731
FAX: 614-231-8222
e-mail: cfolkerth@columbusjcc.org
www.columbusjcc.org

*Carol Folkerth, Executive Director*
*Mike Klapper, Assistant Executive Director*
*Louise Young, Finance Director*
*Melanie Butter, Program Director*
Summer camping sessions for children and young adults with developmental, physical, emotional, mental and learning disabilities. Coed, ages 3-25.

**1242 Recreation Unlimited: Day Camp**
Recreation Unlimited Foundation
7700 Piper Rd
Ashley, OH 43003-9741 740-548-7006
FAX: 740-747-2640
e-mail: info@recreationunlimited.org
recreationunlimited.org

*Paul L. Huttlin, Executive Director & CEO*
*Chris Link, Operations Manager*
*David D. Hudler, Business Development Manager*
*Michelle Higgins, Billing Coordinator*
Camping sessions for children and adults with a variety of disabilities. Coed, ages 5-99, families, seniors and single adults.

**1243 Recreation Unlimited: Residential Camp**
Recreation Unlimited Foundation
7700 Piper Rd
Ashley, OH 43003-9741 740-548-7006
FAX: 740-747-2640
e-mail: info@recreationunlimited.org
recreationunlimited.org

*Paul L. Huttlin, Executive Director & CEO*
*Chris Link, Operations Manager*
*David D. Hudler, Business Development Manager*
*Michelle Higgins, Billing Coordinator*
Camping sessions for children and adults with a variety of disabilities. Coed, ages 5-99, families, seniors and single adults.

**1244 Recreation Unlimited: Respite Weekend Camp**
Recreation Unlimited Foundation
7700 Piper Rd
Ashley, OH 43003-9741 740-548-7006
FAX: 740-747-2640
e-mail: info@recreationunlimited.org
recreationunlimited.org

*Paul L. Huttlin, Executive Director & CEO*
*Chris Link, Operations Manager*
*David D. Hudler, Business Development Manager*
*Michelle Higgins, Billing Coordinator*
Camping sessions for children and adults with a variety of disabilities. Coed, ages 5-99, families, seniors and single adults.

**1245 Recreation Unlimited: Specialty Camp**
Recreation Unlimited Foundation
7700 Piper Rd
Ashley, OH 43003-9741 740-548-7006
FAX: 740-747-2640
e-mail: info@recreationunlimited.org
recreationunlimited.org

*Paul L. Huttlin, Executive Director & CEO*
*Chris Link, Operations Manager*
*David D. Hudler, Business Development Manager*
*Michelle Higgins, Billing Coordinator*
Camping sessions for children and adults with a variety of disabilities. Coed, ages 5-99, families, seniors and single adults.

**1246 Rotary Camp**
Akron Area YMCA
4460 Rex Lake Dr
Akron, OH 44319-3430 330-644-4512
FAX: 330-644-1013
e-mail: rotarycamp@akronymca.org
www.akronymca.com

*Dan Reynolds, Dir. of Endless Possibilities*
*Dawn Housley, Dir. of First Impressions*
*Joshua Strelbicki, The Innovator*
*Kristen Dunbar, Dir. of S'more Programs*
Offers camping experiences for children and adults with disabilities. Rotary Camp is American Camping Association (ACA) accredited and provides a nurturing and enriching atmosphere where campers develop friendships, skills and memories that will last a lifetime. Coed, ages 6-17.

**1247 St. Augustine Rainbow Camp**
Disability Ministries at St. Augustine Parish
2486 W 14th St
Cleveland, OH 44113-4407 216-781-5530
FAX: 216-781-1124
e-mail: staugch@earthlink.net
www.staugustine-west14.org

*Sr. Corita Ambro, CSJ, Program Dir.*
*Terry Hogan, Dir. of Special Religious Ed*
*Mary Ellen Czelusniak, Education Specialist*
*Mary Smith, Disability Advocate*

Day camp for all children, disabled and non-disabled working together.

**1248 YMCA Outdoor Center Campbell Gard**
P.O. Box 13029
Hamilton, OH 45013
513-867-0600
877-224-9622
FAX: 513-867-0127
e-mail: camp@gmvymca.org
www.gmvymca.org

*Jim Sexstone, Exec. Dir.*
*Pete Fasano, Outdoor School Program Dir.*
*Darren Corns, Special Needs Coordinator*
*Tom Andrews, Properties & Facilities Mgr*
Camp is located in Hamilton, Ohio. Camping sessions for children with ADD, autism, developmental disabilities and blindness/visual impairment. Coed, ages 6-17 and families.

## Oklahoma

**1249 Camp Classen YMCA**
YMCA of Greater Oklahoma City
10840 Main Camp Rd
Davis, OK 73030-9405
580-369-2272
FAX: 580-369-2284
e-mail: bdoherty@ymcaokc.org
www.itsmycamp.org

*Rick Warren, Property Manager*
*Heather Doherty, Outdoor School Coordinator*
*Bradley Doherty, Director of Camping*
*Russel Gholson, Equine Director*
Camp is located in Davis, Oklahoma. Sessions for children and adults with diabetes. Coed, ages 8-17, families, seniors and single adults.

**1250 Camp Perfect Wings**
3800 N. May Avenue
Oklahoma City, OK 73112
405-942-3800
e-mail: info@bgco.org
www.bgco.org/campperfectwings

*Amanda Davis, Camp Director*
*Becka Johnson, Camp Director*
*Keith Burkhart, BGCO Family Ministry*
*Jeremy Davis, BGCO Family Ministry*
Specifically for children ages 8-17 with special needs. Campers enjoy canoeing, pool games, low ropes challenges, and crafts.

**1251 Easter Seals Oklahoma**
701 NE 13th St
Oklahoma City, OK 73104-5003
405-239-2525
FAX: 405-239-2278
e-mail: vwasinger@easterseals oklahoma.org
ok.easterseals.com/

*Paula K. Porter, President & CEO*
*Vida Wasinger, Director of Operations*
*Aundria Goree, Programs Director*
*Samantha Pascoe, Child Development Cente*
A nationally accredited, full-day program welcoming all children, including those with disabilities and those at risk of disability. The center offers developmentally appropriate learning activities and services to meet the unique needs of each child. Our Adult Day Health Center provides solutions to meet the physical, social and emotional needs of adults from the ages of 21 to 100+.

## Oregon

**1252 Camp Christmas Seal**
American Lung Association of Oregon
7420 SW Bridgeport Road
Suite 200
Tigard, OR 97224-7790
503-924-4094
FAX: 503-924-4120
e-mail: info@lung.org
www.lung.org/associations/states/oregon/

*Don Awerkamp, Ph.D., J.D., Board of Director*
*Timothy D. Byrum, MSN, CRNP, Board of Director*
*Michael V. Carstens, Board of Director*
*Mario Castro, M.D., MPH, Board of Director*
Camp is located in Sisterhood, Oregon. Sessions for children with asthma/respiratory ailments. Coed, ages 8-15.

**1253 Camp Easter Seals**
Easter Seals: Oregon
5757 SW Macadam Ave
Portland, OR 97239-3765
503-228-5108
800-556-6020
FAX: 503-228-1352
www.easterseals.com

*Donna Waller, Executive Vice President*
*Sue Wimmer, Medical Rehabilitation Manager*
Camp is located in Corbett, Oregon. Summer sessions for children and adults with a variety of disabilities. Coed, ages 6-90.

**1254 Camp Latgawa Special Needs, Inc.**
Oregon-Idaho Conference Center
13250 S Fork Little Butte Cr Rd
Eagle Point, OR 97524-5593
541-826-9699
e-mail: camplatgawa@hotmail.com
latgawa.gocamping.org/

*Eva LaBonty, Camp Director*
*Greg Clensy, Camp Director*
We are located in a beautiful, wooded area of the Rogue National Forest. Two gentle flowing creeks and towering evergreens provide a peaceful setting just 35 miles east of Medford, Oregon.

**1255 Camp Magruder**
Oregon-Idaho Conference Center
17450 Old Pacific Hwy
Rockaway Beach, OR 97136-9609
503-355-2310
FAX: 503-355-8701
e-mail: director@campmagruder.org
www.campmagruder.org

*Steve Rumage, Camp Director*
*Amy Wood, Program Services Director*
*Diana Gutzke, Reservations/ Guest Services*
*Mark Burley Manager, Burley Manager*
Camp is located in Rockaway Beach, Oregon. Sessions for children and adults with cancer and developmental disabilities. Coed, ages 9-18, families, seniors and single adults.

**1256 Camp Taloali**
Lions Club of Oregon and Washington
P.O. Box 32
Stayton, OR 97383-9619
971-239-8153
FAX: 503-769-6415
TTY:503-400-6547
e-mail: camptaloali@comcast.net
www.taloali.org

*Jeffrey Howard, Chair*
*Sylvia Hall, Vice Chair*
*George Scheler, Secretary*
*Rod Kerber, Treasurer*
Summer sessions for children with hearing impairment. Coed, ages 9-17.

1257 **Gales Creek Diabetes Camp**
Gales Creek Camp Foundation
6975 SW Sandburg Street #150
Portland, OR 97223-8136
503-968-2267
FAX: 503-443-2313
e-mail: info@galescreekcamp.org
www.galescreekcamp.org

*Cheryl Sheppard, Executive Director*
*Eric Hanson, Development Specialist*
*Joannie Kono, RN, CDE*

Camp is located in Forest Grove, Oregon. Summer sessions for children with diabetes. Coed, ages 6-16, family and pre-school family camps also available.

1258 **Meadowood Springs Speech and Hearing Camp**
Institute for Rehab., Research, & Recreation Inc
316-A SE Emigrant
P.O. Box 1025
Pendleton, OR 97801-30
541-276-2752
FAX: 541-276-7227
e-mail: info@meadowoodsprings.org
www.meadowoodsprings.org

*Michael Ashton, Executive Director*
*Kathy Hosek, Administrative Assistant*
*Cliff Story, Property Manager*
*Missy Newcomb, MS, CCC-SLP, Clinical Director*

On 143 acres in the Blue Mountains of Eastern Oregon, this camp is designed to help young people who have diagnosed clinical disorders of speech, hearing or language. A full range of activities in recreational and clinical areas is available.

1259 **Mt Hood Kiwanis Camp**
Kiwanis Club of Montavilla
10725 Sw Barbur Blvd.
Suite 50
Portland, OR 97219
971-230-2921
FAX: 503-452-0062
e-mail: Kenney@mhkc.org
www.mhkc.org

*Kaleen Deatherage, Exec. Dir.*
*Terri Hammond, Mktg/Communications Dir.*
*Jason Behunin, President*
*Dale DeVries, President-Elect*

Camp is located in Government Camp, Oregon. Summer sessions for children and adults with a variety of disabilities. Coed, ages 9-35.

1260 **Strength for the Journey**
Oregon-Idaho Conference Center
1505 SW 18th Ave
Portland, OR 97201-2524
800-593-7539
FAX: 503-228-3196
e-mail: camping@gocamping.org
getmorestrength.org/

*Rev. Lisa Jean Hoefner, Executive Director*
*Geneva Cook, Registrar*
*Susan Delaney, Camping Office Assistant*

Camp is located near Sisters, Oregon. For adults living with HIV/AIDS.

1261 **Suttle Lake Camp**
Oregon/Idaho Conference Center
29551 Suttle Lake Rd
Sisters, OR 97759-9508
541-595-6663
FAX: 503-228-3196
e-mail: suttlelake@gocamping.org
www.gbgm-umc.org/suttlelake/

*Jane Petke, Camp Director*
*Daniel Petke, Facilities Director*
*Wendy White, Food Service*
*Steven Willson, Camping Ministry Intern*

Camp is located in Sisters, Oregon. Camping sessions for children and adults with HIV. Coed, ages 6-18, families, seniors and single adults.

1262 **Upward Bound Camp for Persons With**
P.O.Box C
Stayton, OR 97383-90
503-897-2447
FAX: 503-897-4116
e-mail: upward.bound.camp@gmail.com
www.upwardboundcamp.org

Camping Christian for children and adults with a variety of disabilities. Ages 12-99, seniors and single adults. The name of the company is "Upward Bound Camp for Persons With Special Needs, Inc."

1263 **Wallowa Lake Camp**
Oregon-Idaho Conference Center
84522 Church Ln
Joseph, OR 97845
541-432-1271
e-mail: wallowa@gocamping.org
www.wallowalakecamp.org

*David Cook, Manager*
*Ingrid Cook, Manager*

Camp offers volleyball, baseball, badminton, horseshoes, crafts, nature viewing and more

1264 **YWCA Camp Westwind**
YWCA of Greater Portland
1111 SW 10th Ave
Portland, OR 97205-2496
503-294-7476
FAX: 503-794-7399
e-mail: westwind@ywca-pdx.org
www.ywcapdx.org

*Janette McMurran - Kunkel, Camp Director*
*Sarah Keplinger, Camp Westwind Office Manager*

Promotes the understanding of racism and all forms of discrimination and fosters value, respect, and enjoyment of each person's unique contribution.

## Pennsylvania

1265 **Achieva**
711 Bingham St
Pittsburgh, PA 15203-1007
412-995-5000
888-272-7229
FAX: 412-995-5001
e-mail: nmurray@achieva.info
www.achieva.info

*Marsha S. Blanco, President and CEO*
*Reid Wolfe, Senior VP*
*Gary K. Horner, Exec VP*
*Shayne Roos, VP of ACHIEVA Support*

Life-long services for people with disabilities.

1266 **Camp AIM**
South Hills YMCA
51 McMurray Road
Pittsburgh, PA 15241
412-833-5600
FAX: 412-653-7115
e-mail: campaiminfo@gmail.com
www.campaim.org

*Paulette Colonna, Camp Administrator*
*Tom DiPietro, Camp Director*
*Julie Blanc, Administrative Assistant*
*Sarah Kettell, Activities Director*

It is the goal of our program to create an environment that offers a variety of activities centered on positive recreational and social interactions that enrich the lives of our campers. Our staff and volunteers are dedicated to this endeavor.

**1267 Camp Can Do**
Easter Seals: Southeastern Pennsylvania
1161 Forty Foot Road
P.O. Box 333
Kulpsville, PA 19443- 333
215-263-7000
FAX: 215-368-1199
www.easterseals.com

*Bill Barnes, Camp Director*
*Madeline Melendez*
Camp is located in Kulpsville, Pennsylvania. Summer sessions for children and young adults with a variety of disabilities. Coed, ages 5-21

**1268 Camp Dunmoreia**
Easter Seals: Southeastern Pennsylvania
468 N Middletown Rd
Media, PA 19063-5506
610-565-2353
FAX: 610-565-5256
e-mail: recreation@easterseals-sepa.org
www.easterseals-sepa.org

*Eileen Mills, Contact*
Summer sessions for children and young adults with a variety of disabilities. Coed, ages 5-21. The name of the company is ""Camp Dumore""

**1269 Camp Joy**
3325 Swamp Creek Rd
Schwenksville, PA 19473-1518
610-754-6878
FAX: 610-754-7880
e-mail: campjoy@fast.net
www.campjoy.com

A special needs camp for kids and adults (ages 4-80+) with developmental disabilities such as: mental retardation, autism, brain injury, neurological disorder, visual and/or hearing impairments, Angelman and Down syndromes, and other developmental disabilities.

**1270 Camp Kweebec**
P.O.Box 511
Narberth, PA 19072-511
610-667-2123
FAX: 610-667-6376
e-mail: info@kweebec.com
www.kweebec.com

*Les Weiser, Director*
*Maddy Weiser, Director*
*Josh Weiser, Associate Director*
*Amy Weiser, Associate Director*
Camp is located in Schwenksville, Pennsylvania. Sessions for children and adults with diabetes. Coed, ages 6-16, families, seniors and single adults.

**1271 Camp Lee Mar**
805 Redgate Rd
Dresher, PA 19025-1432
215-658-1708
FAX: 215-658-1710
e-mail: gtour400@aol.com
www.leemar.com

*Ari Segal, Exec. Dir.*
*Lee Morrone, Dir. and Founder*
*Laura Leibowitz, Assistant Director*
*Lynsey Trohoske, Program Director*
Seven week summer camp for children and young adults with mild to moderate developmental disabilities. 5-21 years of age

**1272 Camp Make-a-Friend**
Easter Seals: Southeastern Pennsylvania
3975 Conshohocken Ave
Philadelphia, PA 19131-5426
215-879-1000
FAX: 215-879-8424
e-mail: recreation@easterseals-sepa.org
www.easterseals.com

*Dell Edwards-Burke, Camp Director*
*Betty Ingram*
Mission is to create solutions that change lives of children and adults with disabilities or other special needs and their families.

**1273 Camp Ramah in the Poconos Education, Inc.**
2100 Arch Street
Philadelphia, PA 19103
215-885-8556
FAX: 215-885-8905
e-mail: info@ramahpoconos.org
www.ramahpoconos.org

*Rabbi Todd Zeff, Director*
*Michelle Sugarman, Assistant Director*
*Sue Ansul, Ramah Day Camp Director*
*Bruce Lipton, Director of Finance & Operations*
The Camp Ramah Tikvah Family Camp is located in Lakewood, Pennsylvania. It has a week-long camp in mid-August for families who have children with special needs.

**1274 Camp Setebaid**
Setebaid Services
P.O.Box 196
Winfield, PA 17889-196
570-524-9090
e-mail: info@setebaidservices.org
www.setebaidservices.org

*Mark Moyer, Executive Director*
*Suzanne Lee, Director*
*David E. Keefer, Vice President*
*Peggy Coleman, Director*
Camping sessions for children with diabetes. Coed, ages 3-13 years. Family retreat for children with diabetes and their families.

**1275 Camp Surefoot Center**
Easter Seals: Southeastern Pennsylvania
2400 Trenton Rd
Levittown, PA 19056-1425
215-945-7200
FAX: 215-945-4073
e-mail: recreation@easterseals-sepa.org
www.easterseals.com

*Bill Barnes, Executive Director*
*Pat Vanartsdalen*
Camp is located in Levittown, Pennsylvania. Sessions for children and young adults with a variety of disabilities. Coed, ages 5-21.

**1276 Camp Wesley Woods: Northeastern Pennsylvan**
Western PA United Methodist Church
1001 Fiddlersgreen Rd
Grand Valley, PA 16420-4429
814-436-7802
FAX: 814-436-7669
e-mail: info@wesleywoods.com
www.wesleywoods.com

*Rick Frederick, Exec. Dir.*
*Marie Goodwill, Mktg Asst.*
*Andy Blystone, Prograns and Mktg Dir.*
Exceptional children's camp for children with emotional and intellectual handicaps.

**1277 Elling Camps**
1635 State Route 2036
Thompson, PA 18465-9100
570-756-2660
FAX: 570-756-3083
e-mail: info@camptioga.com
www.camptioga.com

*Ron Kuznetz, Camp Director*
*Dale Kuznetz, Camp Director*
*Mike Wagenberg, Camp Director*
*Mike Kuznetz, Camp Director*
For youth ages 6-21 with learning disabilities and accompanying difficulties. This camp allows them to learn to adjust socially in a community atmosphere. The structured camp program includes land and water sports, nature and forestry, industrial arts, construction and work programs, and arts and crafts. The name of the company is ""Camp Tioga""

**1278 Handi Camp**
Handi Vangelism Ministries International
P.O.Box 122
Akron, PA 17501-122
717-859-4777
FAX: 717-859-4505
e-mail: info@hvmi.org
www.hvmi.org

*Tim Sheetz, Exec. Dir.*
*Deb Clark, Dir. of Member Care*
*Kathy Sheetz, Exec. Secretary*
*Brian Robinson, Assistant Director*
Christian, overnight camping program for people with disabilities, ages 7-50, in Eastern PA and Southern NJ. Sponsored by Handi Vangelism Ministries International.

**1279 Innabah Camps**
United Methodist Church: Eastern Pennsylvania
712 Pughtown Rd
Spring City, PA 19475-3311
610-469-6111
FAX: 610-469-0330
e-mail: camp@innabah.org
www.innabah.org

*Christy Heflin, Dir.*
*James Yates, Mgr of Maintenance*
*Jim Heflin, Operations/Food Mgr*
*Alison Bennett, Summer Camp Registar*
Sessions for children and young adults with developmental disabilities. Ages 4-18, families and seniors.

**1280 Lions Camp Kirby**
1735 Narrows Hill Rd
Upper Black Eddy, PA 18972-9712
610-982-5731
e-mail: info@lionscampkirby.org
www.lionscampkirby.org

*Alice Breon, Camp Director*
Offers 4-week camps for deaf and hearing impaired children and their siblings in eastern Pennsylvania.

**1281 Outside In School Of Experiential**
P.O.Box 639
Greensburg, PA 15601-639
724-837-1518
FAX: 724-837-0801
e-mail: administration@outsideinschool.com
www.outsideinschool.com

*Michael C. Henkel, Executive Director*
Camp is located in Bolivar, Pennsylvania. Sessions for children with ADD and substance abuse problems. Boys 11-18 and girls 13-18.

**1282 Phelps School Summer School**
583 Sugartown Rd
Malvern, PA 19355-2800
610-644-1754
FAX: 610-644-6679
e-mail: admis@thephelpsschool.org
www.thephelpsschool.org

*Michael J. Reardon, Head of School*
*James Bruce, President*
*Gerald D. Fahey, Treasurer*
*Stephany Phelps Fahey, Secretary*
Open for grades 7-11 to make up academic deficiencies or complete studies in English, math and reading. Sports include riding, tennis and swimming. A program is also available to a limited number of international students in English as a Second Language.

**1283 Variety Club Camp & Developmental**
2950 Potshop Road
P.O.Box 609
Worcester, PA 19490-609
610-584-4366
FAX: 610-584-5586
www.varietyphila.org

*Francis Naselli, President*
*Edward Radetich, Vice President*
*Donald Faul, Treasurer*
*John H. Gilliam, Jr., Secretary*
Year-round camping and recreation facility for children with special needs and their families. Includes summer camping, aquatics, weekend retreats and other specialty programs. Coed, ages 5-21.

**1284 YMCA Camp Fitch**
The YMCA's Camp Fitch On Lake Erie
12600 Abels Rd
North Springfield, PA 16430-1014
814-922-3219
FAX: 814-922-7000
e-mail: info@campfitchymca.org
www.campfitchymca.org/

*Brian Rupe, Executive Director*
*Greg Donahue, Assistant Camp Director*
*Dann Olin, Operations Director*
*Barb Olin, Senior Program Director*
Camp is located in North Springfield, Pennsylvania. Camping sessions for children and adults with diabetes, hearing impairment, developmental disabilities, mobility limitation and speech/communication impairment. Ages 8-16, families and seniors.

## Rhode Island

**1285 Camp Mauchatea**
Rhode Island Lions Sight Foundation, Inc.
P.O. Box 284
Greenville, RI 02828
401-949-2442
e-mail: ralpheiannitelli@aol.com
www.lions4sight.org

*Ralph E. Iannitelli, Development Director*
*Jay Ward Providence, President*
*Gary W. Latz Westerly, Secretary*
*William Scot Narragansett, Treasurer*
Camp serving those who are blind/visually impaired. Campers enjoy developing and maintaining friendships with fellow campers. Some of the activities include boating and other water sports, as well as hiking and nature studies.

**1286 Camp Ruggles**
PO Box 353
Chepachet, RI 02814
401-567-8914
e-mail: campruggles@cox.net
www.ricamps.org

*Peter Swain, President*
Camp Ruggles is located in Glocester, RI, and is a summer day camp for emotionally handicapped children. The Camp offers a 6 week co-ed summer session for 60 children ages 6-12.

**1287 Canonicus Camp**
American Baptist Churches Rhode Island
54 Exeter Road
Exeter, RI 02822-503
401-294-6318
800-294-6318
FAX: 401-294-6318
e-mail: camp@canonicus.org
www.canonicus.org

*Linda Martin, Conference Coordinator*
*Tina Perry, Hospitality*
*Colleen Tolhurst, Camp Registrar*
*Melanie Towle, Summer Camp Director*

Summer sessions for children with asthma/respiratory ailments. Coed, ages 4-18.

**1288 Hasbro Children's Hospital Asthma Camp**
593 Eddy Street
Providence, RI 02903
401-444-4000
e-mail: webteam@lifespan.org.
www.hasbrochildrenshospital.org/services/asth

*Robert B. Klein, Medical Director*
*Miosotis Alsina, Director*
*Barbara Jandasek, Director*

Camp for children with asthma. Children learn about asthma and asthma management through interactive, educational and fun activities. The camp also offers activities such as swimming, canoeing and arts & crafts.

## South Carolina

**1289 Burnt Gin Camp**
SC Department of Health and Environmental Control
P.O.Box 101106
Mills-Jarrett Complex
Columbia, SC 29011
803-898-0784
FAX: 803-898-0613
e-mail: aimonemi@dhec.sc.gov
www.scdhec.gov

*Marie I Aimone, Camp Director*

A residental camp for children who have physical disabilities and/or chronic illnesses. Camper/staff ratio is 2:1. Five seven-day sessions for 7-15 year olds and one six-day sesssion for 16-19 year olds. Limited to residents of South Carolina.

**1290 Camp Adam Fisher**
P.O. Box 5226
Columbia, SC 29250
803-434-2442
e-mail: scottm14@earthlink.net
www.campadamfisher.com

*Elizabeth Todd-Heckel, Program Director*
*Scott McFarland, Camp Director*

For children with diabetes and their siblings. Campers enjoy swimming, horseback riding, tubing, basketball, volleyball and arts & crafts, while also learning how to manage their diabetes so they can live longer, healthier lives.

**1291 Camp Gravatt**
1006 Camp Gravatt Rd
Aiken, SC 29805-8730
803-648-1817
FAX: 803-648-7453
e-mail: office@bishopgravatt.org
www.bishopgravatt.org

*Lauri SoJourner Yeargin, Executive Director*
*Tammy Ayotte, Conference Center Director*
*Thomas K. Coleman, Program Director*
*Meredith Cook, Camp Director*

Project adventure includes swimming, fishing, music and art and more in which disabled campers participate. Enjoy the fun and adventure of exploring a river in a canoe in the new canoe program. Title: Gravatt Camp and Conference Center

**1292 Camp Spearhead**
Greenville County Recreation District
4806 Old Spartanburg Road
Taylors, SC 29687
864-288-6470
FAX: 864-288-6499
e-mail: randy@gcrd.org
www.campspearhead.org

*Randy Murr, Director*
*Gene Smith, Executive Director*
*Chanell Moore, Deputy Director*
*Don Shuman, Parks Director*

Camp for children with disabilites age 8 years and up. The mission of Camp Spearhead is to provide an enviroment of unconditional acceptance for children and adults with disabilities. A caring staff, creative programming,and a state-of-the-art campsite all combine to offer a safe and nurturing camp experience for every camper.

## South Dakota

**1293 Camp Friendship**
P.O. Box 1986
Rapid City, SD 57709
e-mail: campfriendshipdirector@hotmail.com
www.campfriendship.org

*Kristi Berg, Camp Director*
*Nancy Clary, Camp Historian*
*Stacie Kellogg, Assistant Director in Training*
*Kathleen Haibeck*

Held in the Black Hills of South Dakota, Camp Friendship is for indviduals with physical and developmental disabilities. Campers go fishing, swimming, have cook outs and sing-a-longs, and just have fun!

**1294 Camp Gilbert**
Sanford Children's Specialty Clinic
1305 W. 18th Street
P.O. Box 5039
Sioux Falls, SD 57117
605-328-0781
800-850-0064
e-mail: kay.schroeder@sanfordhealth.org
www.campgilbert.com

*Kay Schroeder, Pediatric Dietician*
*Nancy Hartung, Staffing/Treasurer*

For children ages 8-18 with diabetes. Campers can enjoy a week of canoeing, swimming, sing-a-longs, crafts, and games, while also attending educational programs covering nutrition, exercise and lifestyle management.

**1295 NeSoDak**
Lutherans Outdoors in South Dakota
3285 Camp Dakota Dr.
Waubay, SD 57273
605-947-4440
800-888-1464
e-mail: nesodak@losd.org
www.losd.org/nesodak/index.html

*Teri Gayer, Director*
*Rachel Nelson, Assistant Director*
*Nathan Skadsen, Program Director*

Camp is located in Waubay, South Dakota. Sessions for children with diabetes. Coed, ages 8-18.

## Tennessee

**1296 ACM Lifting Lives Music Camp**
Vanderbilt Kennedy Center
Vanderbilt University
PMB 40, 230 Appleton Place
Nashville, TN 37203-5721
615-322-8240
kc.vanderbilt.edu/site/services/page.aspx?id=

*Tracy P. Beard, Assistant Director*
*Kylie Beck, Art Director*
*Tammy Day, Program Director*

A camp for individuals with developmental disabilities where they can come to celebrate music by participating in songwriting workshops, recording sessions and live performances.

**1297 All Days Are Happy Days Summer Camp**
Boling Center
711 Jefferson Avenue
Memphis, TN 38105
901-448-6511
888-572-2249
FAX: 901-448-7097
TTY: 901-448-4677
www.uthsc.edu/bcdd/training/community/ADHDcam

*Belinda Hardy, Director*
Week long camp for children ages 6-11 years of age who have been diagnosed with ADHD. The primary goal is to educate campers and their parents about the diagnosis, treatment, and self-management of ADHD and related behaviors.

**1298 Bill Rice Ranch**
627 Bill Rice Ranch Road
Murfreesboro, TN 37128-4555
615-893-2767
800-253-7423
FAX: 615-898-0656
e-mail: info@billriceranch.org
www.billriceranch.org

*Wil Rice IV, President*
*Troy Carlson, Director*
*Nathan McConnell, Deaf Ministries Director*
Camping for hearing impaired children and youths ages 9-19.

**1299 Camp Discovery**
Tennessee Jaycees and Tennessee Jaycee Foundation
400 Camp Discovery Ln
Gainesboro, TN 38562-6161
931-268-0239
FAX: 931-268-6737
e-mail: director@jayceecamp.org
jayceecamp.org

*Dawn Hickman, PhD., Vice President of Camp Operations*
*Paul Ottinger, Camp Director*
*Chester Lowe, Camp Executive Director*
Serves children with skin conditions including: Epidermolysis Bullosa, Psoriasis, Alopecia, Vitiligo, Eczema, Scleroderma, Congential Nevus, Ehlers-Danlos, Ichthyosis, Ectodermal Dysplasia and more. The Camp is located at 400 Camp Discovery Lane in Gainsboro, TN.

**1300 Camp Koinonia**
University Of Tennessee
1914 Andy Holt Avenue
Knoxville, TN 37996-2700
865-974-1288
FAX: 865-974-8981
e-mail: ghayes1@utk.edu
www.thecampkoinonia.com

*Dr. Gene A. Hayes, President*
*Joseph L. Ortiz, Vice President*
*J.D. King, Executive Director*
Outdoor education program for children and young adults ages 7-22 who have multiple disabilities. The camp offers recreational activities such as canoeing, music and games.

**1301 Camp Okawehna**
1633 Church Street
Suite 500
Nashville, TN 37203
615-327-3061
FAX: 605-341-8814
e-mail: CampO@dciinc.org
www.dciinc.org/camp_info.php

*Andy Parker, Camp Director*
Week-long summer camp for critically ill children ages 6-18 years suffering from kidney disease. Children who have had kidney transplants as well as children on hemodialysis and peritoneal dialysis are welcome. The camp focuses on the critically ill child who needs to have fun and be in the company of other children who suffer from the same disease.

**1302 Camp Sugar Falls**
American Diabetes Association
4205 Hillsboro Road
Suite 200
Nashville, TN 37215
615-298-3066
888-342-2383
www.childrenwithdiabetes.com/camps/campsugarf

*Devin Anna Bradford*
Week long camp for children ages 6-12 who have diabetes and their siblings. Activities include education sessions, athletics and exercise.

**1303 Easter Seals Tennessee Camping Program**
Easter Seals Tennessee - State Headquarters
3011 Armory Drive
Suite 100
Nashville, TN 37204
615-292-6640
FAX: 615-251-0994
TTY:615-385-3485
www.easterseals.com

*Gay Bruner, Camp Director*
Offers a variety of services to people with disabilities.

**1304 Indian Creek Camp**
Kentucky Tennessee Conference
150 Cabin Circle Dr.
Liberty, TN 37095
615-548-4411
FAX: 615-548-4029
e-mail: info@indiancreekcamp.com
www.indiancreekcamp.com

*Michael , Director*
*Sandy , Program Director*
*Nicole , Pool Director*
*Richa , Assistant Director*
Camp is located in Liberty, Tennessee. Summer sessions for children and adults who are blind/visually impaired. Coed, ages 7-17, families and seniors.

**1305 LeBonheur Cardiac Kids Camp**
LeBonheur Children's Hospital
50 N. Dunlap
Memphis, TN 38103
901-287-6270
FAX: 901-287-4646
e-mail: cardiac@lebonheur.org
www.lebonheur.org/articles/registration-infor

*Meri Armour, M.S.N., M.B.A., Camp Director*
*Bill May, M.D., M.B.A, Camp Administrator*
*Larry Spratlin, M.B.A*
*Dave Rosenbaum*
Camp for children and young adults ages 8-16 with cardiac-related diagnoses. Children enjoy a fun-filled week at camp where they learn about their heart conditions and meet other children just like them.

## Texas

**1306 Camp CAMP**
P.O.Box 27086
San Antonio, TX 78227-86
210-671-5411
FAX: 210-671-5225
e-mail: campmail@campcamp.org
www.campcamp.org

*Brandon G. Briery, Camp Director*
*Susan Osborne, Interim Executive Director*
*Janice Bobo, Director of Development*
*Thomas Burney, CPA, Associate Camp Director*
Camping for children and young adults with a variety of disabilities. Coed, ages 5-21. Respite services throughout calendar year. Adult camp ages 22-45.

**1307 Camp John Marc**
Special Camps for Special Kids
2824 Swiss Ave
Dallas, TX 75204-5956
214-360-0056
FAX: 214-368-2003
e-mail: mail@campjohnmarc.org
campjohnmarc.org

*Vance C. Gilmore, Vice Chair*
*J. Marc Myers, Chairman*
*Bettye Slaven,, Executive Director*
*Dean A. Renkes*
Camp is located in Meridian, Texas. Year-round camping for children with a variety of disabilities. Coed, ages 6-16 and families.

**1308 Camp Summit**
17210 Campbell Road
Suite 180-W
Dallas, TX 75252-4202
972-484-8900
FAX: 972-620-1945
e-mail: camp@campsummittx.org
www.campsummittx.org

*Carla R. Weiland, President/CEO*
*Lisa Braziel, Camp Director*
*Nicole Hastad, Assistant Camp Director*
Camp is located in Argyle, Texas. Camping for children and adults with a variety of disabilities. Coed, ages 6-99.

**1309 Camp Sweeney**
Southwestern Diabetic Fund
P.O.Box 918
Gainesville, TX 76241-918
940-665-2011
FAX: 940-665-9467
e-mail: info@campsweeney.org
www.campsweeney.org
*, Executive Director*
*Ernie Fernandez*
Teaches self-care and self-reliance to children ages 7-18 with diabetes. Campers participate in such activities such as swimming, fishing, horseback riding and arts and crafts while learning about how to self manage their diabetes.

**1310 Camp for All**
Camp for All Foundation
6301 Rehburg Rd
Burton, TX 77835-5675
979-289-3752
FAX: 979-289-5046
e-mail: campsite@campforall.org
www.campforall.org

*Pat Prior Sorrells, President and CEO*
*Belinda Munsell, Development Director*
*Kurt R. Podeszwa, Camp Director*
*Penny Harp*
Fully-accessible year round camp facility is located in Burton, Texas. Camping for children and adults with a variety of disabilities. Coed, ages 5-35 and up and families.

**1311 Dallas Academy**
950 Tiffany Way
Dallas, TX 75218-2743
214-324-1481
FAX: 214-327-8537
e-mail: mail@dallas-academy.com
www.dallas-academy.com

*Jim Richardson, Vice Chair*
*Troy Sturrock, Chair*
*Forrest C. Brown, Headmaster*
*Sean Fleming*
7-week summer session for students who are having difficulty in regular school classes.

**1312 Growing Together Diabetes Camp**
1000 S. Beckham
P.O. Box 6400
Tyler, TX 75711-6400
903-596-3645
800-232-8318
etmc.org/diabetes_day_camp.htm

*Anjani Upponi, Camp Director*
*Vicki Jowell, Director*
*Dr. Stella Hecker, Medical Director*
A summer camp for youths ages 6 to 15 with Type 1 or Type 2 diabetes.

**1313 Hill School of Fort Worth**
4817 Odessa Avenue
Fort Worth, TX 76133-1640
817-923-9482
FAX: 817-923-4894
e-mail: hillschool@hillschool.org
www.hillschool.org

*Roxann Breyer, Principal*
*Audrey Boda-Davis, Executive Director*
*Herb Stephens, Athletic Director*
Provides an alternative learning environment for students having average or above-average intelligence with learning differences. Hill school is an established leader in North Texas with a 25 year history of effectively serving LD children. Beginning in 1961 as a tutorial service, Hill became a formal school in 1973. Our mission is to help those who learn differently develop skills and strategies to succeed. We do this by developing academic/study skills, and self-discipline.

**1314 Texas Lions Camp**
Lions Club Of Texas
P.O.Box 290247
Kerrville, TX 78029-247
830-896-8500
FAX: 830-896-3666
e-mail: tlc@ktc.com
www.lionscamp.com

*Stephen Mabry, Executive Director*
The primary purpose of the League shall be to provide, without charge, a camp for physically disabled, hearing/vision impaired and diabetic children from the State of Texas, regardless of race, religion, or national origin. Our goal is to create an atmosphere wherein campers will learn the can do philosophy and be allowed to achieve maximum personal growth and self-esteem. The camp welcomes boys and girls ages 7-16.

## Utah

**1315 Camp Hobe**
P.O. Box 520755
Salt Lake City, UT 84152-755
e-mail: wapitimama@camphobekids.org
www.camphobekids.org

*Chris Beckwith, Camp Director*
A special summer camp for children with cancer and thier siblings.

**1316 Camp Kostopulos**
Kostopulos Dream Foundation
4180 Emigration Canyon
Salt Lake City, UT 84108-1517
801-582-0700
FAX: 801-583-5176
e-mail: information@campk.org
www.campk.org

*John Reinschmidt, President*
*Rebecca Hill, Vice-President*
*Gary Ethington, Executive Director*
Summer camping for children and adults ages 7-65 with a variety of disabilities. Year round recreation on site and community based activities.

1317 **Camp Nah-Nah-Mah**
University Health Care Burn Camp Programs
50 N. Medical Drive
Salt Lake City, UT 84132
801-581-2121
www.uuhsc.utah.edu

*Brad Wiggins, Burn Camp Director*

For children ages 6-12 years of age that are burn survivors. Some of the activities include canoeing, rock climbing and archery.

1318 **FCYD Camp**
Foundation for Children and Youth with Diabetes
1995 W 9000 S
West Jordan, UT 84088-9345
801-566-6913
www.fcydcamp.org

*David Okubo, MD President and Treasurer*
*Elizabeth Elmer, Vice President*
*Sherrie Hardy, RD, MS, CDE*
*Nathan Gedge, Secretary*

Camping for children with diabetes. Coed, ages 1-18 and families.

1319 **Kris' Camp**
3359 Creek Road
Salt Lake City, UT 84121
801-733-0721
e-mail: info@kriscamp.org
www.kriscamp.org

*Leidy van Ispelen, Assistant Director*
*Michelle Hardy, Program Director*
*Kathy Berger, Executive Director*

For children with autism.

## Vermont

1320 **Camp Akeela**
3 New King Street
White Plains, NY 10604
866-680-4744
FAX: 866-462-2828
e-mail: info@campakeela.com
www.campakeela.com

*Eric Sasson, Dir.*
*Jaynie Goodbody, Assistant Dir.*
*Rob Glyn-Jones, Head Counselor*

Co-ed, overnight camp for children and young adults ages 9-17 who have been diagnosed with Asperger's Syndrome or a non verbal learning disability.

1321 **Camp Betsey Cox**
140 Betsey Cox Lane
Pittsford, VT 05763
802-483-6611
e-mail: info@campbetseycox.com
www.campbetseycox.com

*Lorrie Byrom, Director and Co-Owner*
*Devri Byrom, Winter Office Director*
*Mike Byron, Co-owner and assiciate director*

Camp is located in Pittsford, Vermont. Summer sessions for girls aged 9-15 with ADD.

1322 **Camp Thorpe**
680 Capen Hill Rd
Goshen, VT 05733-8446
802-247-6611
e-mail: cthorpe@sover.net
www.campthorpe.org

*Lyle Jepson, Director*
*Elizabeth Giard, Board of Trustee*
*Richard Giard, Board of Trustee*
*Ralph O. Hathaway, Board of Trustee*

Focuses on meeting the needs of each individual camper; showing each of them that they have the ability and potential. Also provides positive camping experience for children challenged with handicapping conditions.

1323 **Silver Towers Camp**
241 Lincoln Avenue
Rutland, VT 05701
802-775-9756
FAX: 180-38- 021
e-mail: silvertowers@comcast.net
www.silvertowerscamp.org

*Carolyn Ravenna, Camp Director*

Two-week residential camp for ages 6-75 who are physically or mentally challenged. Campers gain the social skills and personal enrichment they seek. Activities include swimming, horseback riding, music, sing-a-longs, dancing, nature studies and more.

## Virginia

1324 **Adventure Day Camp**
3480 Commission Ct
Lake Ridge, VA 22192-1753
703-491-1444
e-mail: office@princewilliamacademy.com
www.princewilliamacademy.com

*Dr. Samia Harris, President*

Camping for children with asthma/respiratory ailments and cancer. Coed, ages 2-13.

1325 **Camp Dickenson**
Holston Conference of United Methodist Church
801 Camp Dickson Ln
Fries, VA 24330-4348
276-744-7241
e-mail: campdickenson@centurylink.net
www.holston.org/

*Michael Snow, Manager*

Camp is located in Fries, Virginia. Camping for children and adults with developmental disabilities. Coed, ages 5-18, families, seniors and single adults.

1326 **Camp Easter Seals Virginia**
Easter Seals: Virginia
201 E Main St
Salem, VA 24153-3841
540-777-7325
800-365-1656
FAX: 540-777-2194
e-mail: info@va.eastersealsucp.com
nc.eastersealsucp.com/

*Tristan Robertson, Executive Director*
*C. L. Cochran, President & CEO*
*Joseph E. Pizzi, Jr., Board Chair*
*Gayle M. Rose, Executive Director*

Summer camp sessions for children and adults ages 5-99 with physical disabilities, cognitive disabilities and sensory impairments. Therapeutic recreation activities including swimming, fishing, sports, horseback riding, rock climbing, and more. Twenty-six-day speech therapy camp children with disabilities ages 8-16. Twelve-day Spina Bifida Self Help Skills Camp.

1327 **Camp Holiday Trails**
400 Holiday Trails Ln
Charlottesville, VA 22903-7774
434-977-3781
FAX: 434-977-8814
e-mail: campisgood@campholidaytrails.org
www.campholidaytrails.org

*Tina La Roche, Executive Director*
*Stephen Rogers, Program Director*
*Becky Green, Development Director*
*Christine Shifflett, Camp Coordinator*

Private, nonprofit camp for children with special health needs and various chronic illnesses. Residential, 2-week sessions are open June - August; camperships are available. Coed 7-17, nationwide and international. Canoeing, swimming, horseback riding, arts and crafts, drama, ropes course, etc. 24-hr. medical supervision by doctor and nursing staff. Air conditioned cabins.

**1328 Camp Virginia Jaycee**
2494 Camp Jaycee Road
P.O. Box 648
Blue Ridge, VA 24064-648
540-947-2972
800-865-0092
FAX: 540-947-2043
e-mail: info@campvajc.org
www.campvajc.org

*William Hartz, Chair*
*Kathleen King, Vice Chair*
*Lisa Parrish, Treasurer*
*Sabitha Venkatesh, Board of Director*
Summer camping for children and adults with developmental disabilities. Coed, ages 7-70. Weekend respite camps for children and adults with mental retardation.

**1329 Civitan Acres for the Disabled**
Eggleston Services
2210 Cedar Rd
Chesapeake, VA 23323-6303
757-487-6062
FAX: 757-487-4143
e-mail: info@egglestonservices.org
www.egglestonservices.org

*Paul Atkinson, President and CEO*
*Dave Wilber, Senior VP*
*Josh Shockley, Senior VP*
*Tom Redmond, VP, Mktg and Dev.*
Offers a summer camp for adult and children with disabilities. Participants can choose from day or overnight packages.

**1330 Loudoun County Special Recreation Programs**
Loudoun County Local Government
215 Depot Ct SE
Leesburg, VA 20175-3017
703-777-0343
FAX: 703-771-5354
TTY:703-711-0343
e-mail: prcs@loudoun.gov
www.loudoun.gov

*Diane Ryburn, Dir.*
*Mark Adams, Dir., Management*
*Lisa Cockrell, Acting Controller*
*Suzanne Lane, Accounting & Financial Analysis*
Offers and promotes integration opportunities for individuals with disabilities. Coordinates ADA issues and Very Special Arts and Special Olympics for Loudoun County. Summer camps, sports, socials and community trips.

**1331 Makemie Woods Camp**
Presbytery of Eastern Virginia
P.O.Box 39
Barhamsville, VA 23011-39
757-566-1496
800-566-1496
FAX: 757-566-8803
e-mail: makwoods@makwoods.org
www.makwoods.org

*Mike Burcher, Director*
*Karen Broughman, Office Manager*
*Sherri Egerton, Program Director*
*Fran Parkhurst, Food Services Manager*
Residential Christian camp that tailors each group and individual goals. Counselors serve as teachers, friends and activity leaders. For children 8-18 with diabetes.

**1332 Oakland School & Camp**
Boyd Tavern
Keswick, VA 22947
434-293-9059
FAX: 434-296-8930
e-mail: information@oaklandschool.net
www.oaklandschool.net

*Carol Williams, Director*
*Amanda Baber, Admissions Director*
*Leah Burger, Development Director*
A highly individualized program stresses improving reading ability. Subjects taught are reading, English composition, math and word analysis. Recreational activities include horseback riding, sports, swimming, tennis, crafts, archery and camping. For girls and boys, ages 8-14.

## Washington

**1333 Camp Fun in the Sun**
Inland NorthWest Health Services
P.O.Box 469
Spokane, WA 99210-469
509-232-8145
e-mail: randalll@cherspokane.org
www.campfuninthesun.org

*Tom Fritz, CEO*
*Nicole Stewart, Dir. of Mktg & Communications*
*Jerrie Heyamoto, Communication Coordinator*
*Tamitha Anderson, Communication Coordinator*
Summer camping for children with diabetes. Coed, ages 6-18.

**1334 Camp Killoqua**
Camp Fire USA
4312 Rucker Ave
Everett, WA 98203-2233
425-258-5437
FAX: 425-252-2267
e-mail: killoqua@campfireusasnohoneish.org
www.campfireusasnohomish.org

*Dave Surface, Executive Director*
*Carol Johnson, Assistant Executive Director*
*Michael Deal, Operations Director*
*Donna Fischer, Club Program & Training*
Camp is located in Stanwood, Washington. Camping for children with developmental disabilities. Coed, ages 6-17.

**1335 Camp Prime Time**
6 S. 2nd Street
Suite 815
Yakima, WA 98901
509-248-2854
FAX: 509-248-5505
e-mail: families@campprimetime.org
www.campprimetime.org

*Dick Haapala, President*
*Diane Eilmes, Executive Director*
*Shirley Thietje, Camp Manager*
*Mike Burnam, Vice President*
Prime Time serves children and adults with disabilities or have terminal or serious illnesses.

**1336 Camp Volasuca**
Volunteers of America: Western Washington
P.O. Box 839
Everett, WA 98206-839
425-259-3191
FAX: 425-258-2838
e-mail: info@voaww.org
www.voaww.org

*Phil Smith, President/CEO*
*Steve Sites, Chief Financial Officer*
*Will Raihl, Chief Advancement Officer*
*Lori Drabant, Regional Exec VP - King County*
Camp is located in Sultan, Washington. Summer sessions for children and adults with a variety of disabilities. Coed, ages 6-13, families and single adults.

1337 **Easter Seals Camp Stand by Me**
Easter Seal Society of Washington
17809 S. Vaughn Rd. KPN
P.O.Box 289
Vaughn, WA 98394-313
253-884-2722
800-678-5708
e-mail: mayer@wa.easterseals.com
www.wa.easterseals.com

*Cathy Bisaillon, President & CEO*
*Charissa Manglona, Board Secretary and VP*
*Ashley Francis, Ex Officio*
*Traci Michell, Board Treasurer*

Camp is located in Vaughn, Washington. Summer camping for adults and children with developmental disabilities and mobility limitation. Coed, ages 7-65, seniors. Respite weekends October thru May.

1338 **Northwest Kiwanis Camp**
P.O.Box 1227
Port Hadlock, WA 98339-1227
360-732-7222
e-mail: nwkc@earthlink.net
www.kiwaniscamp.com

*Sharron Sherfick, Camp Administrator*
*Katie Jackson, Program Director*
*Jean Edwards, Recreation Coordinator*
*Nadine Jonientz, Food Service Manager*

Campers range from 6-60 in age, and includes those with developmental disabilities, cerebral palsy, autism, downs syndrome, and other physical and/or mental handicaps.

1339 **YMCA Camp Orkila**
YMCA of Greater Seattle
909 4th Ave
Seattle, WA 98104-1194
203-382-5009
FAX: 203-382-4920
e-mail: dstankevich@seattleymca.org
www.seattleymca.org

*David Affolter, Senior Programs Dir.*
*Dimitri Stankevich, Camp Orkila Dir.*
*Cheryl Rau, Associate Exec. Dir.*
*Dave Bell, Overnight Camp Exec.*

Camping for children with blood disorders and diabetes, ages 8-18.

## West Virginia

1340 **Mountaineer Spina Bifida Camp**
5100 Ohio Street
South Charleston, WV 25309
304-766-0383
800-642-9704
e-mail: info@drewsday.org
drewsday.org/

*Susan Nelsen, 5K Coordinator*
*Stephanie Gregory, 5K run/walk/stroll coordinator*
*Suzie Humphreys, 5K run/walk/stroll coordinator*

Is a non profit organization which pursues education and training and focuses on activities that promote independence and those that facilitate everyday life. The objectives are to build self esteem, promote independence and enhance the development of social skills.

1341 **YMCA Camp Horseshoe**
Ohio-West Virginia YMCA
Box 138
Rr 2
Parsons, WV 26287-9408
304-478-2481
FAX: 304-478-4446
e-mail: horseshoe@hi-y.org
www.hi-y.org/

*David King, Dev. Dir.*
*Lois Nelson, Exec. Dir.*
*Alicia Ridenou, Financial Development*
*Doug Wetsch, Alumni Dir.*

Summer camping for children with cancer, ages 7-18.

## Wisconsin

1342 **Camp Firefly**
Jewish Child & Family Services
Attn: Melissa Newman
255 Revere Dr., Suite 200
Northbrook, IL 60062
FAX: 847-412-4360
www.campfireflyjcfs.com/index.html

*Audra Kaplan, Psy.D., Camp Director*
*Andrew Rosenbloom, Psy.D., Assistant Camp Director*
*Dr Rachel Riley*

Week-long camp for children with social disabilities. The camp offers all the experiences of an overnight camp that includes gaining a sense of autonomy and friendships. Staff members are there to help provide therapeutic and support assistance to help the children accomplish these goals.

1343 **Easter Seal Camp Wawbeek**
Easter Seals: Wisconsin
1450 Highway 13
Wisconsin Dells, WI 53965
608-277-8288
800-422-2324
FAX: 608-277-8333
e-mail: camp@eastersealswisconsin.com
www.camp.eastersealswisconsin.com

*Christine Fessler, CEO*
*Nanc Howard, Executive Assistant*
*Brian Schuetz, Director*
*Pam Ganser, Chief Financial Officer*

Hundreds of people with mild to severe disabilities attend Easter Seals Wisconsin camps. The camp offers adventure programs, camp sessions for other health agencies, family camp opportunities and year round respite sessions. Coed, ages 8-99.

1344 **Lutherdale Bible Camp**
Lutherdale Ministries
N7891 Us Highway 12
Elkhorn, WI 53121-2465
262-742-2352
FAX: 888-248-4551
e-mail: execdir@lutherdale.org
www.lutherdale.org

*Jeff Bluhm, Exec. Dir.*
*Kathy Dittner, Registrar*
*Charley Shirley, Dev. Dir.*
*David Box, Program Mgr/Ropes Coordinator*

Summer camping for people with developmental disabilities. Coed, ages 9-18 and families, seniors.

1345 **Phantom Lake YMCA Camp**
S110 W30240 YMCA Camp Rd
Mukwonago, WI 53149-9535
262-363-4386
FAX: 262-363-4351
e-mail: office@phantomlakeymca.org
www.phantomlakeymca.org

*Jeff Spang, CEO*
*Tony Ayala, Camp Director*

Summer camping for children with epilepsy, ages 7-15.

1346 **Timbertop Nature Adventure Camp**
YMCA Camp Glacier Hollow
1000 Division St
Stevens Point, WI 54481-2724
715-342-2980
FAX: 715-342-2987
e-mail: pmatthai@spymca.org
www.glacierhollow.com

*Pete Matthai, Camp Director*
*Kyle Beach, Summer Camp Program Directo*
For children who can benefit from an individualized program of learning in a non-competitive outdoor setting under the skilled leadership of people who understand the environment and the unique potential of these children.

1347 **Triangle Y Ranch YMCA**
YMCA Of Southern Arizona
34434 S. Y Camp Road
P.O. Box 350
Oracle, AZ 85623
520-884-0987
e-mail: camp@tucsonymca.org
www.tucsonymca.org

*Dane Woll, President and CEO*
*Kerry Dufour, V.P. Chief Dev. Officer*
*Cathy Scheirman, Chief Financial Officer*
*Deneiva Knight, Mktg and Communications Dir.*
For children and young adults ages 6-17. The camp offers nature programs, swimming, horseback riding, sports, arts & crafts.

1348 **Wisconsin Badger Camp**
11815 Munz Lane
Prairie Du Chien, WI 53821-9524
608-988-4558
FAX: 608-988-4586
e-mail: wiscbadgercamp@centurytel.net
www.badgercamp.org

*Brent Bowers, Exec. Dir.*
*Kayla Smith, Dev/Communications Dir.*
*Theresa Kaiser, Secretary/Registrar*
Wisconsin Badger Camp, established in 1966, is a summer camp that serves individuals with developmental disabilities. Badger camp offers eight one-week camps and one two-week camp for ages 3-93. One week is for ages 14-25, one week for ages 3-13 and all other weeks for ages 18 and older.

1349 **Wisconsin Lions Camp**
Wisconsin Lions Foundation
3834 County Road A
Rosholt, WI 54473-8826
715-677-4969
FAX: 715-677-3297
TTY:715-677-6999
e-mail: info@wisconsinlionscamp.com
www.wisconsinlionscamp.com

*Andrea Yenter, Camp Operations Mgr*
*Jamie Jannusch, Assistant Camp Operations Mgr*
*Ellyse Wenos, Interim Program Coordinator*
*Paula Lauer, RN, Health Care Supervisor*
Serves children who have either a visual, hearing or mild cognitive disability, as well as diabetes types I and II. Program activities include sailing, ropes course, hiking and canoe trips, environmental education, swimming, camping, canoeing, outdoor living skills and handicrafts. ACA accredited, located in central Wisconsin, near Stevens Point.

1350 **Wisconson Badger Camp**
P.O. Box 723
Platteville, WI 53818
608-348-9689
FAX: 608-348-9737
e-mail: bbowers@badgercamp.org
www.badgercamp.org

*Brent Bowers, Exec. Dir.*
*Kayla Smith, Dev/Communications Dir.*
*Theresa Kaiser, Secretary/Registrar*
Badger Camp gives individuals with developmental disabilities a chance to experience camp and enjoy themselves in an outdoor setting.

## Wyoming

1351 **Camp Hope**
3920 West 45th Street
Casper, WY 82604
307-265-5865
FAX: 307-472-5008
e-mail: camphopewy@yahoo.com
www.camphopewy.com

*Steve Johnson, Director*
*Nancy Johnson, Director*
Camp Hope is a camp for children and young adults with diabetes. Some of the activities include biking, swimming, sports and games.

1352 **Eagle View Ranch**
SOAR
184 Uphill Road
P.O. Box 584
Dubois, WY 82513
307-455-3084
FAX: 307-455-3094
e-mail: evr@soarnc.org
http://www.soarnc.org

*Becki Burnett Neidens, Director of Wyoming and California Programs*
*Jeremy Neidens, Associate Director Eagle View Ranch*
*John Willson, M.S., LRT/CTR, Executive Director*
Camp for youths with learning disabilities and attention deficit disorder. Campers enjoy a broad range of wilderness adventure experiences that help to empower them to overcome challenges, while helping them to learn how to develop problem solving skills, effective communication strategies and social skills.

# Clothing

## Dresses & Skirts

**1353 Budget Cotton/Poly Open Back Gown**
Buck & Buck
3111 27th Ave S
Seattle, WA 98144-6502
206-722-4196
800-458-0600
FAX: 800-317-2182
e-mail: info@buckandbuck.com
buckandbuck.com

*Julie Buck, Owner*
Short raglan sleeves, lace at neck and bodice over lapping snapback closure. *$14.00*

**1354 Budget Flannel Open Back Gown**
Buck & Buck
3111 27th Ave S
Seattle, WA 98144-6502
206-722-4196
800-458-0600
e-mail: info@buckandbuck.com
www.buckandbuck.com

*Julie Buck, Owner*
3/4 raglan sleeve, lace at neck and bodice. *$17.00*

**1355 Cotton/Poly House Dress**
Buck & Buck
3111 27th Ave S
Seattle, WA 98144-6502
206-722-4196
800-458-0600
e-mail: info@buckandbuck.com
buckandbuck.com

*Julie Buck, Owner*
Comes in short and long sleeves, assorted florals and plaids. *$36.00*

**1356 Dusters**
Buck & Buck
3111 27th Ave S
Seattle, WA 98144-6502
206-722-4196
800-458-0600
e-mail: info@buckandbuck.com
buckandbuck.com

*Julie Buck, Owner*
Three types: Floral, Budget Better. Snap front styles and gathered yokes, flannel $16.00-$24.00. *$36.00*

**1357 Flannel Gowns**
Buck & Buck
3111 27th Ave S
Seattle, WA 98144-6502
206-722-4196
800-458-0600
e-mail: info@buckandbuck.com
buckandbuck.com

*Julie Buck, Owner*
Comes in long or short with a deep button-front opening for ease of slipping on. Shorter long length. *$21.00*

**1358 Fleece Cape/Poncho**
Laurel Designs
Apt A
1805 Mar West St
Belvedere Tiburon, CA 94920-1962
FAX: 415-435-1451
e-mail: laureld@ncal.verio.com
www.laureldesigns.co.uk

*Janet Sawyer, Co-Owner*
*Lynn Montoya, Co-Owner*
Warm and cozy high insulated cape with hood for wheelchair users, zip front, velcro side closure, self belt. All sizes and a variety of colors. *$53.00*

**1359 Float Dress**
Buck & Buck
3111 27th Ave S
Seattle, WA 98144-6502
206-722-4196
800-458-0600
e-mail: info@buckandbuck.com
buckandbuck.com

*Julie Buck, Owner*
A safe bet for everyone from a size medium to a 3X. Gathered yoke front and back and literally yards of fabric for fullness. Comes in cotton or polyester. *$32.00*

**1360 Muu Muu**
Buck & Buck
3111 27th Ave S
Seattle, WA 98144-6502
206-722-4196
800-458-0600
e-mail: info@buckandbuck.com
buckandbuck.com

*Julie Buck, Owner*
Comes in long and short styles, assorted bright floral prints. $20.00-$22.00. *$31.00*

**1361 Polyester House Dress**
Buck & Buck
3111 27th Ave S
Seattle, WA 98144-6502
206-722-4196
800-458-0600
e-mail: info@buckandbuck.com
buckandbuck.com

*Julie Buck, Owner*
Comes in short and long sleeves, assorted florals. *$ 36.00*

## Footwear

**1362 Booties with Non-Skid Soles**
Buck & Buck
3111 27th Ave S
Seattle, WA 98144-6502
206-722-4196
800-458-0600
FAX: 800-317-2182
e-mail: info@buckandbuck.com
buckandbuck.com

*Julie Buck, Owner*
Acrylic knit or quilted cotton/poly and shearling inner. *$17.00*

**1363 Foot Snugglers**
Buck & Buck
3111 27th Ave S
Seattle, WA 98144-6502
206-722-4196
800-458-0600
FAX: 800-317-2182
e-mail: info@buckandbuck.com
buckandbuck.com

*Julie Buck, Owner*
Quilted poly/cotton outers lined with plush shearling pile, provide a thick, comfortable cushion which helps minimize the pressure points on tender areas. *$.30*

**1364 Lok-Tie Shoe Laces**
Laurel Designs
Apt A
1805 Mar West St
Belvedere Tiburon, CA 94920-1962
FAX: 415-435-1451
e-mail: laureld@ncal.verio.com

*Janet Sawyer, Co-Owner*
*Lynn Montoya, Co-Owner*
Specially designed slide locks laces in place. Can be used with one hand. Stretch laces allow maximum comfort. *$4.00*

**1365 Propet Leather Walking Shoes**
Buck & Buck
3111 27th Ave S
Seattle, WA 98144-6502
206-722-4196
800-458-0600
FAX: 800-317-2182
e-mail: info@buckandbuck.com
buckandbuck.com

*Julie Buck, Owner*
Two velcro straps, leather upper, shock-absorbing sole. *$58.00*

**1366 TRU-Mold Shoes**
42 Breckenridge St
Buffalo, NY 14213-1555
716-881-4484
800-843-6653
FAX: 716-881-0406
trumold.com

*Husain Syed, Production Manager*
Custom made, fully molded shoes, relieve pressure in sensitive areas by taking all of the weight off the painful areas.

**1367 Terrycloth Slippers**
Buck & Buck
3111 27th Ave S
Seattle, WA 98144-6502
206-722-4196
800-458-0600
FAX: 206-722-1144
e-mail: info@buckandbuck.com
buckandbuck.com

*Julie Buck, Owner*
Lined cotton/poly terrycloth upper with sewn-on, non-skid sole. *$18.00*

**1368 Velcro Booties**
Buck & Buck
3111 27th Ave S
Seattle, WA 98144-6502
206-722-4196
800-458-0600
FAX: 800-317-2182
e-mail: info@buckandbuck.com
buckandbuck.com

*Julie Buck, Owner*
The high-domed toe, and extra-wide, non-skid sole design accommodates virtually every foot related problem. *$20.00*

**1369 Washable Shoes**
Buck & Buck
3111 27th Ave S
Seattle, WA 98144-6502
206-722-4196
800-458-0600
FAX: 800-317-2182
e-mail: info@buckandbuck.com
buckandbuck.com

*Julie Buck, Owner*
Vinyl upper with velcro closure, nonskid sole. *$20.00*

## Jackets

**1370 Fleece Bed Jacket**
Buck & Buck
3111 27th Ave S
Seattle, WA 98144-6502
206-722-4196
800-458-0600
FAX: 206-722-1144
e-mail: info@buckandbuck.com
buckandbuck.com

*Julie Buck, Owner*
Full snap front opening and collar. Assorted bright colors and pastel prints. *$22.00*

**1371 Jackets**
Special Clothes
P.O.Box 333
E Harwich, MA 02645-333
508-430-2410
FAX: 508-430-2410
e-mail: specialclo@aol.com
www.special-clothes.com

*Judith Sweeney, President*
Available styles include a unique, back opening jacket designed to fit easily over contractures and for wheelchair comfort. Prices range from $72.00-$89.00.

**1372 Rain Poncho**
Laurel Designs
Apt A
1805 Mar West St
Belvedere Tiburon, CA 94920-1962
FAX: 415-435-1451
e-mail: laureld@ncal.verio.com
www.laureldesigns.com

*Janet Sawyer, Co-Owner*
*Lynn Montoya, Co-Owner*
A favorite, this rain poncho slips on in a hurry to keep you dry. All sizes and a variety of colors. *$39.00*

**1373 Wheelchair Ponchos**
Special Clothes
P.O.Box 333
E Harwich, MA 02645-333
508-430-2410
FAX: 580-430-2410
e-mail: specialclo@aol.com
www.special-clothes.com

*Judith Sweeney, President*
These ponchos are cut shorter in the back for wheelchair comfort. Prices range from $76.00-$95.00.

## Miscellaneous & Catalogs

**1374 Adaptations by Adrian**
PO Box 7
San Marcos, CA 92079-0007
888-214-8372
FAX: 760-481-7068
e-mail: adrians1@sbcglobal.net
www.adaptationsbyadrian.com
Fashions for the physically challenged child. Clothing offers Velcro closures, front pockets, concealed back openings and fashions for seated posture.

**1375 Adaptive Clothing: Adults**
Special Clothes
P.O.Box 333
E Harwich, MA 02645-333
508-430-2410
FAX: 508-430-2410
e-mail: specialclo@aol.com
www.special-clothes.com

*Judith Sweeney, President*

Special Clothes produces a catalogue of garments for adults with disabilities and/or incontinence. Offerings include: undergarments, snap-crotch tee shirts, jumpsuits, and denim travel cath. The catalogue is available without charge. Comparable to department store prices. Special Clothes produces a catalog of adaptive clothing for children in sizes from toddler through young adults. A full line of clothing is included from undergarments through wheelchair jackets and ponchos.

**1376 Adult Long Jumpsuit with Feet**
Special Clothes
P.O.Box 333
E Harwich, MA 02645-333
508-430-2410
FAX: 580-430-2410
e-mail: specialclo@aol.com
www.special-clothes.com

*Judith Sweeney, President*
A full, snap crotch for full access. For safety, feet have non-skid bottoms. 100% cotton knit. Made in USA. Also, identical in style, but are made of fleece for extra warmth. Fleece fabric is soft 100% cotton, and is available in medium blue only. Made in USA. Options on fleece jumpsuits available for additional charge. Long knit jumpsuit with feet: #A2051; long fleece jumpsuit: #A2032; long fleece jumpsuit with feet: #A2052.

**1377 Adult Short Jumpsuit**
Special Clothes
P.O.Box 333
E Harwich, MA 02645-333
508-430-2410
FAX: 508-430-2410
e-mail: specialclo@aol.com
www.special-clothes.com

*Judith Sweeney, President*
This pull-on jumpsuit provides comfort and full coverage without bulk. Wide leg ribbing ends at mid-thigh, with snaps at the crotch. We use fine quality, comfortable cotton knit. 100% cotton knit. Made in USA. Option: long sleeves - add $3.00. Colors: white, navy, teal, light blue, light pink, red, royal blue, black, khaki and juvenile print. S,M & L $43.00; XL & XXL $45.00

**1378 Bibs**
Special Clothes
P.O.Box 333
E Harwich, MA 02645-333
508-430-2410
FAX: 580-430-2410
e-mail: specialclo@aol.com
www.special-clothes.com

*Judith Sweeney, President*
A variety of bib styles are available to protect clothing inconspicuously.

**1379 Body Suits**
Special Clothes
P.O.Box 333
E Harwich, MA 02645-333
508-430-2410
FAX: 508-430-2410
e-mail: specialclo@aol.com
www.special-clothes.com

*Judith Sweeney, President*
These are one piece garments that can be used to protect skin under braces, to add warmth and to shield incisions. S,M & L $42.00; XL & XXL $44.00.

**1380 Buck and Buck Clothing**
3111 27th Ave S
Seattle, WA 98144-6502
206-722-4196
800-458-0600
FAX: 800-317-2182
e-mail: info@buckandbuck.com
buckandbuck.com

*Julie Buck, Owner*
Clothing for the disabled and elderly.
*88 pages Yearly*

**1381 Carolyn's Catalog**
3938 S Tamiami Trl
Sarasota, FL 34231-3622
941-373-9100
800-648-2266
FAX: 941-739-5503
e-mail: support@carolynscatalog.com
www.carolynscatalog.com

*John Colton, Owner*
Free, mail-order catalog of items for visually impaired people.

**1382 Cotton Stockings**
Buck & Buck
3111 27th Ave S
Seattle, WA 98144-6502
206-722-4196
800-458-0600
FAX: 206-722-1144
e-mail: info@buckandbuck.com
buckandbuck.com

*Julie Buck, Owner*
Come in regular and snug-fit, cover leg to mid-thigh and work well for swollen legs.

**1383 Easy Dressing Fashions: JC Penney**
6501 Legacy Dr
Plano, TX 75024-3612
972-431-8676
FAX: 972-431-9103

*Natalie Torre, Marketing Manager*
This is an entire collection of women's and men's fashions that are designed for easy wear, easy care and complete comfort. Plus, a selection of women's apparel with velcro brand wavelock fasteners.

**1384 Exquisite Egronomic Protective Wear**
Plum Enterprises
P.O.Box 85
Valley Forge, PA 19481-85
610-783-7377
800-321-7586
FAX: 610-783-7577
e-mail: info@plument.com
www.plument.com

*Janice Carrington, President/CEO*
Egronomic Protective Wear; ProtectaCap custom-fitting headgear has earned an unparalleled reputation for quality, safety, and comfort. ProtectaCap+Plus technologically-advanced protective headgear closes the gap between hard and soft helmets. Comes with optional ProtectaChin Guard and new sporty design. Protectahip protective undergarment is the intelligent, innovative solution to the problem of hip injuries for both men and women. Ladies' styles are covered with attractive stretch lace.

**1385 Fashion Ease**
1541 60th St
Brooklyn, NY 11219-5023
718-871-8188
800-221-8929
FAX: 718-436-2067
e-mail: fashionease.com@aol
fashionease.com

*Abraham Klein, Owner*
Adaptive apparel and footwear for people who require ease in dressing. Free catalogue.
*64 pages Yearly*

**1386 Forde's Functional Fashions**
Apt 137
8020 East Dr
North Bay Village, FL 33141-4138
305-754-4457
800-531-7705
FAX: 305-757-5447
e-mail: fashions@fordes.com
www.fordes.com

*Patricia Forde MA RN CEAC, President*

A fashion forward line of easy to wear clothing and accessories for men, women and children. Items include, sportswear, outerwear, ponchos, robes, sleepwear, dresses, wheelchair bags, walker bags and more. Hard to find specialty items for many special needs. Designs for people who use wheelchairs. Velcro closures if buttons are a problem. Fun clothing protectors too. Choose from our terrific assortment of fabrics and colors to suit all your fashion needs in simply functional style.

**1387 Headliner Hats**
Designs for Comfort
PO Box 671044
Marietta, GA 30066-2429
770-565-8246
800-443-9226
FAX: 770-565-8425
e-mail: headliner@mindspring.com

*Curt Maurer, President*
A patented cap and hairpiece combination, the Headliner is both a quick, stylish coverup and an upbeat wig alternative for women experiencing hair care problems or hair loss. Ideal for social gatherings and outdoor activities as well as for sleeping and hospital stays. *$ 25.00*

**1388 Knee Socks**
Buck & Buck
3111 27th Ave S
Seattle, WA 98144-6502
206-722-4196
800-458-0600
FAX: 800-317-2182
e-mail: info@buckandbuck.com
buckandbuck.com

*Julie Buck, Owner*
Comes in regular and large size. $3.00 - $8.00

**1389 Laurel Designs Catalog**
Laurel Designs
Apt A
1805 Mar West St
Belvedere Tiburon, CA 94920-1962
415-435-1891
FAX: 415-435-1451
e-mail: laureld@ncal.verio.com
www.laureldesigns.com

*Janet Sawyer, Owner*
*Lynn Montoya, Owner*
Clothing for wheelchair users including rain wear, panchos and fleece capes. Other items include quality carrying bags for wheelchairs, walkers, crutches, accessories, and cookbooks of four ingredients only recipes. Home remodeling video 'Building & Remodeling for Accessibility', reacher and large print dictionary.
*8 pages BiAnnual*

**1390 M&M Health Care Apparel Company**
Fashion Collection
1541 60th St
Brooklyn, NY 11219-5023
718-871-8188
800-221-8929
FAX: 718-436-2067
e-mail: info@fashionease.com
fashionease.com

*Abraham Klein, Owner*
Specialized clothing for disabled people.

**1391 Professional Fit Clothing**
Ste 1
831 N Lake St
Burbank, CA 91502-1600
818-563-1975
800-422-2348
FAX: 818-563-1834
e-mail: sales@professionalfit.com
professionalfit.com

*Kurt Rieback, Owner*
Professional fit clothing caters to homes that care for people with developmental disabilities and individuals who are physically challenged. Our clothing is fashionable, affordable and can be adapted to each person's special needs.

**1392 Spec-L Clothing Solutions**
849 Performance Drive
Stockton, CA 95206
714-427-0781
800-445-1981
FAX: 800-683-6510
e-mail: rlfortun@clothingsolutions.com
clothingsolutions.com

*Jim Lechner, Owner*
The nation's leading designer and manufacturer of assistive clothing for men and women. Free 56 page catalog available.

**1393 Special Clothes Adult Catalogue**
Special Clothes
P.O.Box 333
E Harwich, MA 02645-333
508-430-2410
FAX: 508-430-2410
e-mail: specialclo@aol.com
www.special-clothes.com

*Judith Sweeney, President*
Produces a catalogue of adaptive clothing for adults with disabilities. Offers include undergarments, casual bottoms, jumpsuits, swimwear, footwear and bibs. Prices are comparable to deparment store prices. The catalogue is free.

**1394 Special Clothes for Special Children**
Special Clothes
P.O.Box 333
E Harwich, MA 02645-333
508-430-2410
FAX: 508-430-2410
e-mail: specialclo@aol.com
www.special-clothes.com

*Judith Sweeney, President*
All special adaptations, such as velcro closures, snap crotches, bib fronts and G-tube access openings. Every item is fully washable. Offering optional features to customize each item to meet the needs of your child.

**1395 Specialty Care Shoppe**
16126 E 161st St S
Bixby, OK 74008-7325
918-366-2901
FAX: 918-366-9445
e-mail: deb@specialtycareshoppe.com
www.specialtycareshoppe.com

*K J Marshall, Owner*
Catalog of attractive, affordable clothing and accessories for adults with special needs. Includes items for edema, incontinence, alzheimers, limited mobility, and hand impairment.

**1396 Super Stretch Socks**
Buck & Buck
3111 27th Ave S
Seattle, WA 98144-6502
206-722-4196
800-458-0600
FAX: 800-317-2182
e-mail: info@buckandbuck.com
buckandbuck.com

*Julie Buck, Owner*
This sock has been improved to stretch laterally throughout the foot area as well as at the top. *$3.75*

**1397 Swimwear**
Special Clothes
P.O.Box 333
E Harwich, MA 02645-333
508-430-2410
FAX: 508-430-2410
e-mail: specialclo@aol.com
www.special-clothes.com

*Judith Sweeney, President*
Cotton lycra swimsuits are available in boys and girls styles from size toddler-teen. One piece, designed to completely cover a diaper.

**1398 Thigh-Hi Nylon Stockings**
Buck & Buck
3111 27th Ave S
Seattle, WA 98144-6502
206-722-4196
800-458-0600
FAX: 800-317-2182
e-mail: info@buckandbuck.com
buckandbuck.com

*Julie Buck, Owner*
A sheer, full length stocking. *$4.50*

**1399 Trisha's of Acton**
P.O.Box 599
Acton, MA 01720-599
978-263-9318
877-955-5551
FAX: 978-263-4555
e-mail: trishas@tiac.net
www.trishasofacton.com

*K Julie McCarthy, President*
Clothing and accessories that provide dignity, freedom of movement and independence for the physically challenged.

**1400 Waterproof Bib**
Buck & Buck
3111 27th Ave S
Seattle, WA 98144-6502
206-722-4196
800-458-0600
FAX: 800-317-2182
e-mail: info@buckandbuck.com
buckandbuck.com

*Julie Buck, Owner*
Made with 3 layers of fabric including waterproof backing, these attractive bibs will not soak through like most others, protecting clothing from stains. *$18.00*

**1401 Wishing Wells Collection**
Ste 965
11684 Ventura Blvd
Studio City, CA 91604-2699
818-840-6919
FAX: 818-760-3878
e-mail: wishingwells@dawn-wells.com
www.dawnwells.com

*Dawn Wells, Owner*
*Lorraine Parker, General Manager*
Features designs full of back overlap construction and all velcro closures clothing.

## Robes & Sleepwear

**1402 Adult Snap Front Sleeper**
Special Clothes
P.O.Box 333
E Harwich, MA 02645-333
508-430-2410
FAX: 508-430-2410
e-mail: specialclo@aol.com
www.special-clothes.com

*Judith Sweeney, President*
This soft, comfortable one piece garment is designed for easy dressing and full access. The top fastens down the front with snaps. The bottom section folds up from the back, and snaps to the waist. 100% cotton knit. Made in USA. Option, short sleeves - add $1.00. Colors: white, navy, teal, light blue, light pink, red, burgudy, royal blue and black. Sm & Med: $36.50/ 3 for $104.00; L & XL: $39.00/ 3 for $111.25; XXL: $42.00/3 for $119.75.

**1403 Creative Designs**
3704 Carlisle Ct
Modesto, CA 95356-924
209-523-3166
800-335-4852
e-mail: robes4you@aol.com
www.robes4you.com

*Barbara Arnold, Owner*
Designer of the original Change-A-Robe and the new Handi-Robe, which allows the wearer to put it on without having to stand up. Robes are designed especially for physically challenged, disabled individuals, and wheelchair users. *$69.95*

**1404 Flannel Pajamas**
Buck & Buck
3111 27th Ave S
Seattle, WA 98144-6502
206-722-4196
800-317-2182
FAX: 206-722-1144
e-mail: info@buckandbuck.com
buckandbuck.com

*Julie Buck, Owner*
*$25.00*

**1405 Fleece Robe**
Buck & Buck
3111 27th Ave S
Seattle, WA 98144-6502
206-722-4196
800-458-0600
FAX: 206-722-1144
e-mail: info@buckandbuck.com
buckandbuck.com

*Julie Buck, Owner*
All with full-length, snap-front openings, patch pockets, short and long. Short: $39.00.

**1406 His & Hers**
Wishing Wells Collection
Ste 965
11684 Ventura Blvd
Studio City, CA 91604-2699
818-840-6919
FAX: 818-760-3878
e-mail: wishingwells@dawn-wells.com
www.dawnwells.com

*Dawn Wells, Owner*
This sleep shirt is designed for him or her. *$21.99*

**1407 Nightshirts**
Buck & Buck
3111 27th Ave S
Seattle, WA 98144-6502
206-722-4196
800-458-0600
FAX: 800-317-2182
e-mail: info@buckandbuck.com
buckandbuck.com

*Julie Buck, Owner*
Come in flannel or cotton patterns and prints in sizes S/M, 4XL, 2XL/3XL *$29.00*

1408 **Open Back Nightgowns**
Buck & Buck
3111 27th Ave S
Seattle, WA 98144-6502
206-722-4196
800-458-0600
FAX: 800-317-2182
e-mail: info@buckandbuck.com
buckandbuck.com

*Julie Buck, Owner*
Come in cotton (sizes S-4X) or flannel (sizes S-3X). *$20.00*

1409 **Seersucker Shower Robe**
Buck & Buck
3111 27th Ave S
Seattle, WA 98144-6502
206-722-4196
800-458-0600
FAX: 800-317-2182
e-mail: info@buckandbuck.com
buckandbuck.com

*Julie Buck, Owner*
Totally covers a man or woman being wheeled to and from the shower or bath. A crisp, light weight shower robe. *$34.00*

1410 **Terrycloth Robes**
Buck & Buck
3111 27th Ave S
Seattle, WA 98144-6502
206-722-4196
800-458-0600
FAX: 206-722-1144
e-mail: info@buckandbuck.com
buckandbuck.com

*Julie Buck, Owner*
Two pockets, sash belts, assorted colors. *$36.00*

## Shirts & Tops

1411 **Adult Pull-On Feeding Bib**
Special Clothes
P.O.Box 333
E Harwich, MA 02645-333
508-430-2410
FAX: 508-430-2410
e-mail: specialclo@aol.com
www.special-clothes.com

*Judith Sweeney, President*
This basic bib does a great job of protecting clothing from messy food and drink spills. It is constructed of sturdy, rib knit neckband which slips on comfortably. The front pocket catches food particles and is fastened at both sides with velcro for easy cleaning. 100% nylon with neckband of 100% cotton rib. Made in USA. Colors: white or light blue. One size: 17 inches wide, & 23 inches from shoulder to bottom. *$15.00*

1412 **Avoid Eye Strain, Feel it T-Shirt**
Sense-Sations
919 Walnut St
Philadelphia, PA 19107-5237
215-627-0600
FAX: 215-922-0692
asb.org

*Patricia Johnson, CEO*
This slogan is printed in raised writing boldly across the front of our T-shirt. *$5.95*

1413 **Basic Rear Closure Sweat Top**
Buck & Buck
3111 27th Ave S
Seattle, WA 98144-6502
206-722-4196
800-458-0600
FAX: 800-317-2182
e-mail: info@buckandbuck.com
buckandbuck.com

*Julie Buck, Owner*
Top opens completely down the back for ease of dressing with snaps. *$19.00*

1414 **Cotton Full-Back Vest**
Buck & Buck
3111 27th Ave S
Seattle, WA 98144-6502
206-722-4196
800-458-0600
FAX: 800-317-2182
e-mail: info@buckandbuck.com
buckandbuck.com

*Julie Buck, Owner*
Wide shoulder straps that don't slide off shoulders. *$5.00*

1415 **Dutch Neck T-Shirt**
Buck & Buck
3111 27th Ave S
Seattle, WA 98144-6502
206-722-4196
800-458-0600
FAX: 800-317-2182
e-mail: info@buckandbuck.com
buckandbuck.com

*Julie Buck, Owner*
Stretchy neck makes it easy to get over the head. *$ 5.50*

1416 **Open Back T-Shirts**
Buck & Buck
3111 27th Ave S
Seattle, WA 98144-6502
206-722-4196
800-458-0600
FAX: 206-722-1144
e-mail: info@buckandbuck.com
buckandbuck.com

*Julie Buck, Owner*
Velcro tabs down the back. *$8.00*

1417 **Printed Rear Closure Sweat Top**
Buck & Buck
3111 27th Ave S
Seattle, WA 98144-6502
206-722-4196
800-458-0600
FAX: 800-317-2182
e-mail: info@buckandbuck.com
buckandbuck.com

*Julie Buck, Owner*
Comes in assorted colors, plain or with animal motifs and snaps all the way down the back. *$28.00*

1418 **Rear Closure Shirts**
Buck & Buck
3111 27th Ave S
Seattle, WA 98144-6502
206-722-4196
800-458-0600
FAX: 206-722-1144
e-mail: info@buckandbuck.com
buckandbuck.com

*Julie Buck, Owner*
Snaps down the back on T-shirts and dress shirts. *$ 33.00*

**1419 Rear Closure T-Shirt**
Buck & Buck
3111 27th Ave S
Seattle, WA 98144-6502
206-722-4196
800-458-0600
FAX: 800-317-2182
e-mail: info@buckandbuck.com
buckandbuck.com

*Julie Buck, Owner*
Closes down the back with velcro snaps. *$10.00*

**1420 Serape**
Laurel Designs
Apt A
1805 Mar West St
Belvedere Tiburon, CA 94920-1962
FAX: 415-435-1451
e-mail: laureld@ncal.verio.com

*Janet Sawyer, Co-Owner*
*Lynn Montoyo, Co-Owner*
This unique sleeveless thermal vest is designed for active wheelchair persons. Multi-colored, one size fits all. *$30.00*

**1421 T Shirt is Done in Braille: Read Gently**
Sense-Sations
919 Walnut St
Philadelphia, PA 19107-5237
215-829-9997
FAX: 215-922-0692
asb.org

*Patricia Johnson, CEO*
This slogan is printed in raised writing and braille dots. *$5.95*

## Slacks & Pants

**1422 Comanche Pants**
Wheelies Manufacturing
P.O.Box 97496
Winston, OR 97496
541-679-2318
FAX: 541-673-8719

*Alice King, Store Manager*
*Leslie Bozovich, Customer Service*
An innovative answer to dressing a person who cannot stand. These pants are sculptured to provide total coverage. A new freedom in dressing; easy for attendant or for self-dressing. They can be put on a seated person right in the chair with no lifting or standing. *$35.00*

**1423 Jumpsuits**
Special Clothes
P.O.Box 333
E Harwich, MA 02645-333
508-430-2410
FAX: 508-430-2410
e-mail: specialclo@aol.com
www.special-clothes.com

*Judith Sweeney, President*
Several styles of one-piece garments are available for dressing ease. Front opening styles are designed for easy access. Prices range from $32.20-$44.00. *$55.00*

**1424 Knit Pants**
Special Clothes
P.O.Box 333
E Harwich, MA 02645-333
508-430-2410
FAX: 508-430-2410
TTY:508-430-2410
e-mail: specialclo@aol.com
www.special-clothes.com

*Judith Sweeney, President*
Offers the best in comfort and convenience. Designed with a longer crotch and wider seat for a great fit. The elasticized waistband contains a hidden drawstring for size adjustments, and pockets are placed low for easy access while sitting. Order a full snap crotch (Option #1), for full access. Available in soft, 100% cotton knit. Made in USA. Colors: Light blue, teal, light pink, burgundy, navy and black. Sm & Med: $41.00; L & XL $45.00; XXL $48.00. Add full snap crotch.

**1425 Pants & Slacks**
Special Clothes
P.O.Box 333
E Harwich, MA 02645-333
508-430-2410
FAX: 508-430-2410
e-mail: specialclo@aol.com
www.special-clothes.com

*Judith Sweeney, President*
A variety of pant and skirt styles is available in sizes 2 toddler - 18 teen. These include straight leg and baggy jeans, drop front pleated dress pants, knit pants, shorts and skirted leggings. Prices range from $16.50-$44.00.

**1426 Side Velcro Slacks**
Buck & Buck
3111 27th Ave S
Seattle, WA 98144-6502
206-722-4196
800-458-0600
FAX: 800-317-2182
e-mail: info@buckandbuck.com
buckandbuck.com

*Julie Buck, Owner*
Slacks open down both sides from waist to hip with snap closures at sides. *$36.00*

**1427 Side-Zip Sweat Pants**
Buck & Buck
3111 27th Ave S
Seattle, WA 98144-6502
206-722-4196
800-458-0600
FAX: 800-317-2182
e-mail: info@buckandbuck.com
buckandbuck.com

*Julie Buck, Owner*
Out-seam zippers un-zip 22-inch zippers down both sides to enable dressing a resident with severe leg contractures. *$25.00*

**1428 Trunks**
Buck & Buck
3111 27th Ave S
Seattle, WA 98144-6502
206-722-4196
800-458-0600
FAX: 800-317-2118
e-mail: info@buckandbuck.com
buckandbuck.com

*Julie Buck, Owner*
Come in cotton or nylon, flare leg, full cut. *$5.00*

## Undergarments

**1429 Adult Absorbent Briefs**
Special Clothes
P.O.Box 333
E Harwich, MA 02645-333
508-430-2410
FAX: 508-430-2410
e-mail: specialclo@aol.com
www.special-clothes.com

*Judith Sweeney, President*
Soft, comfortable, 100% cotton knit brief is seven layers thick at the crotch. Sides of the brief are a non-bulky single layer. The waistband elastic is enclosed in a soft cotton knit casing and does not touch the skin. Comfortable cotton rib knit bands circle the leg. This brief will not replace a diaper, but provides absorbency for light incontinence. *$18.50*

**1430 Adult Lap Shoulder Bodysuit**
Special Clothes
P.O.Box 333
E Harwich, MA 02645-333
508-430-2410
FAX: 508-430-2410
TTY:508-430-2410
e-mail: specialclo@aol.com
www.special-clothes.com

Bodysuit styles fasten at the crotch with sturdy snaps to stay neatly tucked. All are made of soft, absorbent 100% cotton knit for maximum comfort. They are cut wide at the hip and seat for full coverage, and will accomodate a diaper if necessary. Soft knit rib circles the neck and leg. This cool tank style slips on easily. Deep armholes are banded with rib knit. all styles: S,M,L $42, XL,XXL $44. A choice of 12 colors.

**1431 Adult Sleeveless Bodysuit**
Special Clothes
P.O.Box 333
E Harwich, MA 02645-333
508-430-2410
FAX: 508-430-2410
e-mail: specialclo@aol.com
www.special-clothes.com

*Judith Sweeney, President*
Bodysuit styles fasten at the crotch with sturdy snaps to stay neatly tucked. All are made of soft, absorbent 100% cotton knit for maximum comfort. They are cut wide at the hip and seat for full coverage, and will accomodate a diaper if necessary. Soft knit rib circles the neck and leg. This cool tank style slips on easily. Deep armholes are banded with rib knit. All styles: S,M,L $42, XL,XXL $44. A choice of 12 colors.

**1432 Adult Swim Diaper**
Special Clothes
P.O.Box 333
E Harwich, MA 02645-333
508-430-2410
FAX: 508-430-2410
e-mail: specialclo@aol.com
www.special-clothes.com

*Judith Sweeney, President*
This pant is made of soft, silent, light-weight, impermeable fabric- waterproof and secure. It is a containment brief, designed to be used in the pool in place of cloth or disposable diapers, which can become waterlogged or disintegrate in the water. Waist and legbands should be snug for proper fit, so please consult sizing chart before ordering. Darlex with lining of 100% cotton knit. Lycra waist and legbands. Made in USA. *$40.00*

**1433 Adult Tee Shoulder Bodysuit**
Special Clothes
P.O.Box 333
E Harwich, MA 02645-333
508-430-2410
FAX: 508-430-2410
TTY:508-430-2410
e-mail: specialclo@aol.com
www.special-clothes.com

Styles fasten at the crotch with sturdy snaps to stay neatly tucked. All are made of soft, absorbent 100% cotton knit for maximum comfot. They are cut wide at the hip and seat for full coverage, and will accommodate a diaper if necessary. Soft knit rib circles the neck and leg. This bodysuit looks like a regular tee shirt, but snaps at the crotch for a neat appearance. S,M,L $42; XL,XXL $44. Choice of 12 colors.

**1434 Adult Waterproof Overpant**
Special Clothes
P.O.Box 333
E Harwich, MA 02645-333
508-430-2410
FAX: 508-430-2410
e-mail: specialclo@aol.com
www.special-clothes.com

*Judith Sweeney, President*
Overpants are made of a soft, silent, lightweight fabric which is waterproof and very secure. It is designed to be used over our Adult Absorbent Brief, or cloth diapers. It is completely latex-free and is an excellent non-allergenic substitute for rubber or vinyl pants. Waist and legbands should be snug to minimize leakage, so please consult the sizing chart before ordering. Lycra waist and legbands. Made in USA. *$40.00*

**1435 Adult Wet Wrap Swim Vest**
Special Clothes
P.O.Box 333
E Harwich, MA 02645-333
508-430-2410
FAX: 508-430-2410
e-mail: specialclo@aol.com
www.special-clothes.com

*Judith Sweeney, President*
This vest is made of neoprene - the same material used in wet suits - and it effectively insulates the torso to retain body heat. Muscles relax, enhancing the quality of recreational swimming or water therapy. The wrap design allows full freedom of movement. Made of Neoprene in the USA. Note: Vest provides warmth ony. It is not a flotation device. Wet wrap sizes: Adult small, adult medium and adult large.

**1436 Briefs**
Special Clothes
P.O.Box 333
E Harwich, MA 02645
508-430-2410
FAX: 508-430-2410
e-mail: specialclo@aol.com
www.special-clothes.com

*Judith Sweeney, President*
A variety of unique brief styles available for easy access and practicality.

**1437 Cloth Diapers**
Angel Fluff Diaper Company
P.O.Box 1131
Lewisburg, TN 37091-131
931-359-9604
800-996-2644
FAX: 931-359-8420
e-mail: custserv@angelfluff.com
www.angelfluff.com

Top quality cloth diapers.

**1438 Nylon Snip Slip**
Buck & Buck
3111 27th Ave S
Seattle, WA 98144-6502
206-722-4196
800-458-0600
FAX: 206-722-1144
e-mail: info@buckandbuck.com
buckandbuck.com

*Julie Buck, Owner*
Just snip with scissors at the appropriate hem length and it's ready to wear. *$12.00*

**1439 Nylon Stretch Bra**
Buck & Buck
3111 27th Ave S
Seattle, WA 98144-6502
206-722-4196
800-458-0600
FAX: 206-722-1144
e-mail: info@buckandbuck.com
buckandbuck.com

*Julie Buck, Owner*
Front hook closure with built-up shoulder straps. *$ 16.00*

**1440 Panties**
Buck & Buck
3111 27th Ave S
Seattle, WA 98144-6502
206-722-4196
800-458-0600
FAX: 800-317-2182
e-mail: info@buckandbuck.com
buckandbuck.com

*Julie Buck, Owner*
Come in nylon or cotton, band leg for comfort. *$5.00*

**1441 Safe and Dry-Feel and Sure-Toddler Dry**
Kleinerts
3968 194th Trl
Miami, FL 33160
305-937-0824
800-498-7051
FAX: 305-937-0825
e-mail: yourkleinerts@aol.com
hygienics.com

*Michael Brier, President*
A variety of stress incontinence disposable liners which absorb 8-10 oz. of fluid packaged in 20 and 40 counts. Also available are patented knit nylon panties in medium, large and extra large sizes. All products are priced for the mass market.

**1442 Support Plus**
5581 Hudson Industrial Parkway
PO Box 2599
Hudson, OH 44236-0099
508-359-2910
866-553-8875
FAX: 800-950-9569
www.supportplus.com

*Ed Janos, President*
Offers a selection of support undergarments, braces and shoes for the physically challenged and medical professionals.

# Computers

## Assistive Devices

**1443 Ability Research**
PO Box 1721
Minnetonka, MN 55345-721
952-939-0121
FAX: 952-227-5809
e-mail: info@abilityresearch.net
www.abilityresearch.net

*Suzanne Severson, Administrator*
Manufacturers and marketers of assistive technology equipment.

**1444 Academic Software Inc**
3504 Tates Creek Rd
Lexington, KY 40517-2601
859-552-1020
FAX: 253-799-4012
e-mail: asistaff@acsw.com
www.acsw.com

*Warren E Lacefield PhD, President*
*Penelope Ellis, Marketing Director*
*Sylvia P Lacefield, Graphic Artist*
Employs a unique, goal-oriented approach to aid individuals in identifying adaptive devices with potential to support various physical limitations. Devices are categorized in seven databases: Existence, Travel, In-situ Motion, Environmental Adaptation, Communication, and Sports & recreation. ADLS provides its users with device descriptions, pictures and lists of sources for locating products and product information.

**1445 Adaptivation**
Ste 100
2225 W 50th St
Sioux Falls, SD 57105-6536
605-335-4445
800-723-2783
FAX: 605-335-4446
e-mail: info@adaptivation.com
www.adaptivation.com

*Jonathan Eckrich, President*
Manufacturers of switches, voice output devices and enviromental controls.

**1446 Analog Switch Pad**
Academic Software
331 W 2nd St
Lexington, KY 40507-1113
859-233-2332
800-842-2357
FAX: 859-231-0725

*Warren E Lacefield PhD, President*
*Penelope Ellis, Marketing Director*
A touch-activated, force-adjustable, low-voltage DC, electronic switch designed to control battery-operated toys, environmental controls, and computer access interfaces. This device features a large activation area that is soft and compliant to the touch. Force sensitivity is adjusted by a small dial from approximately 1 ounce to 32 ounces activation pressure, applied over an area ranging from the size of a fingertip to the size of the entire switch surface.

**1447 Arkenstone: The Benetech Initiative**
480 S California Ave
Palo Alto, CA 94306-1609
650-644-3400
FAX: 650-475-1066
e-mail: hrdag@benetech.org
www.hrdag.org

*Jim Fruhterman, CEO*
*Roberta G Brosnaha, General Manager/VP*
Offers various models of ready-to-read personal computers for the disabled.

**1448 Augmentative Communication Systems (AAC)**
ZYGO-USA
48834 Kato Road
Suite 101A
Freemont, CA 94538
510-249-9660
800-234-6006
FAX: 510-770-4930
e-mail: zygo@zygo-usa.com
www.zygo-usa.com

*Lawrence Weiss, President*
Full range of AAC systems and assistive technology including computer-based systems and computer access programs and devices.

**1449 Away We Ride IntelliKeys Overlay**
Soft Touch Inc
17117 Oak Drive
Suite C
Omaha, NE 68130
402-334-8477
877-763-8868
FAX: 402-334-8478
www.softtouch.com

*Joyce Meyer, President*
Four full color preprinted overlays to use with Away We Ride. Just put them on an IntelliKeys keyboard and you are ready to go.

**1450 BIGmack Communication Aid**
AbleNet
2625 Patton Road
Roseville, MN 55113
651-294-2200
800-322-0956
FAX: 651-294-2222
e-mail: customerservice@ablenetinc.com
www.ablenetinc.com

*Jen Thalhuber, CEO*
A single message communication aid, BIGmack has 2 minutes of memory and has a 5 inches in diameter switch surface. *$86.00*

**1451 C2ILMAX**
Image Systems
Ste 300
12975 16th Ave N
Minneapolis, MN 55441-4551
952-935-1171
800-462-4370
FAX: 952-935-1386
e-mail: custserv@imagesystemscorp.com
www.imagesystemscorp.com

*Dean Scheff, President*
LCD or CRT displays designed for applications requiring a larger viewing area and high to ultrahigh resolution.

**1452 Close-Up 6.5**
Norton- Lambert Corporation
P.O.Box 4085
Santa Barbara, CA 93140-4085
805-964-6767
e-mail: sales@norton-lambert.com
www.norton-lambert.com

*Jeannie Vesely, Marketing Coordinator*
Remotely controls PC's via modem. Telecommute from your home or laptop PC to your office PC. Run applications, update spreadsheets, print documents remotely and access networks on remote PCs. Features: fast screen and file transfers, synchronize files, unattended transfers, multi-level security, transaction logs, automated installation. *$99.95*

**1453 Concepts on the Move Advanced Overlay CD**
Soft Touch Inc
17117 Oak Drive
Suite C
Omaha, NE 68130
402-334-8477
877-763-8868
FAX: 402-334-8478
e-mail: softtouch@softtouch.com
www.softtouch.com

*Joyce Myer, President*
Use this overlay CD with Concepts on the Move Advanced Preacademics. Overlays match the concepts and graphics in the program. Includes standard overlays with all the choices and SoftTouch's changeable format overlays. Print and laminate the blank templates. Then print and laminate the picture keys in all three sizes - small, medium and large. Includes Overlay Printer by IntelliTools for easy printing. *$115.00*

**1454 Concepts on the Move Basic Overlay CD**
Soft Touch Inc
17117 Oak Drive
Suite C
Omaha, NE 68130
402-334-8477
877-763-8868
FAX: 402-334-8478
e-mail: softtouch@softtouch.com
www.softtouch.com

*Joyce Meyer, President*
Use this Overlay CD with Concepts on the Move Basic Preacademics. Overlays match the conepts and graphics in the program. Includes standard overlays with all the choices and SoftTouch's changeable format overlays. Print and laminate the blank templates. Then print and laminate the picture keys in all three sizes - small, medium and large. It is easy and fast to place the images on the blank templates. *$115.00*

**1455 Darci Too**
WesTest Engineering Corporation
810 Shepard Ln
Farmington, UT 84025-3846
801-451-9191
FAX: 801-451-9393
e-mail: larryk@westest.com
westest.com

*Robert Lessmann, President*
A universal device which allows people with physical disabilities to replace the keyboard and mouse on a personal computer with a device that matches their physical capabilities. DARCI TOO works with almost any personal computer and provides access to all computer functions. *$995.00*

**1456 EZ Touch Panel**
1120 W Avenue J
Lancaster, CA 93534
661-723-6523
800-869-8521
FAX: 661-723-2114
www.words-plus.com

*Jess Dahlan, President*
*Momoko Deran, CEO*
*Walt Wolosz, Manager*
Touch screen input is the most direct and intuitive method for picture-based communication for those with the required motor skills. *$399.00*

**1457 Expanded Keyboard Emulator**
Words Plus
1220 W Avenue J
Lancaster, CA 93534-2902
661-723-6523
800-869-8521
FAX: 661-723-2114
e-mail: info@words-plus.com
www.words-plus.com

*Jeff Dalhen, President*
*Janet Aviles, Customer Service Supervisor*
*Walt Wolosz, Manager*
Provides DUAl word prediction, abbreviation expansion (macrocapability), five different methods of voice output, keyboard control, RAM-resident and the ability to run in graphics mode and access to commercial software applications.

**1458 Eyegaze Computer System**
LC Technologies Inc
10363A Democracy Lane
Fairfax, VA 22030
703-385-7133
800-393-4293
FAX: 703-385-7137
e-mail: info0309@eyegaze.com
www.eyegaze.com

*Nancy Cleveland, Medical Coordinator*
Enables people with physical disabilities to do many things with their eyes that they would otherwise do with their hands.

**1459 Fall Fun IntelliKeys Overlay**
Soft Touch
Ste 401
4300 Stine Rd
Bakersfield, CA 93313-2352
661-396-8676
877-763-8868
FAX: 661-396-8760
e-mail: softtouch@funsoftware.com
www.funsoftware.com

*Roxanne Butterfield, Marketing*
*Joyce Meyer, President*
Seven full color preprinted overlays to use with Fall Fun. Just put them on an IntelliKeys keyboard and you are ready to go.

**1460 FingerFoniks**
Words- Plus
1220 W Avenue J
Lancaster, CA 93534-2902
661-723-6523
800-869-8521
FAX: 661-723-2114
e-mail: info@words-plus.com
www.words-plus.com

*Ginger Woltosz, VP*
*Tim Ross, Manager*
*Walt Wolosz, Manager*
One-pound, hand-held, communicator incorporating synthesized and recorded speech. The user makes words and sentences by pressing sound (phoneme) keys on a membrane keyboard. *$995.00*

**1461 Five Green & Speckled Frogs IntelliKeys Overlay**
Soft Touch Inc
17117 Oak Drive
Suite C
Omaha, NE 68130
402-334-8477
877-763-8868
FAX: 402-334-8478
e-mail: softtouch@funsoftware.com
www.softtouch.com

*Joyce Meyer, President*
Seven full color preprinted overlays to use with Five Green and Speckled Frogs. Just put them on an IntelliKeys keyboard and you are ready to go. *$49.00*

**1462 GW Micro**

725 Airport North Office Park
Fort Wayne, IN 46825-6707
260-489-3671
FAX: 260-489-2608
e-mail: sales@gwmicro.com
gwmicro.com

*Dan Weirich, Sales Executive*
*Marty Hord, Sales Manager*

Computer hardware and software products for people with disabilities.

**1463 Infogrip: ErgoPOD Model 500**

1794 E Main St
Ventura, CA 93001-3411
805-652-0770
800-397-0921
FAX: 805-652-0880
e-mail: sales@infogrip.com
www.infogrip.com

*Liza Jacobs, President*
*Aaron Gaston, VP*

ErgoPOD Model 500 provides a workstation solution to computer users who work from a reclining position. Model 500 straddles a bed or recliner and can hold up to 21 inch monitors anywhere on its surface, and will securely position the monitor at angles up to 60 degrees. The adjustable keyboard mechanism and motorized height adjustment make ergonomic configuration easy - even for the most demanding cases. *$1895.00*

**1464 IntelliKeys IIe**

Intelli Tools
1720 Corporate Cir
Petaluma, CA 94954-6924
707-773-2000
800-899-6687
FAX: 707-773-2001
e-mail: info@intellitools.com
www.intellitools.com

*Caroline Van Howe, Marketing Director*
*Ed Koenit, CFO*
*Arjan Khalsa, CEO*

Card and cable to create keyboard port on Apple IIe computer to allow use of IntelliKeys alternative keyboard. *$129.95*

**1465 Jelly Bean Switch**

AbleNet
2625 Patton Road
Roseville, MN 55113-1308
651-294-2200
800-322-0956
FAX: 651-294-2259
e-mail: customerservice@ablenetinc.com
www.ablenetinc.com

*Jen Thalhuber, CEO*

A momentary touch switch made of shatterproof plastic, small and sensitive to 2-3 ounces of pressure, this switch is provided audible feedback when activated and is a compact version of the Big Red Switch. Choice of colors: red, blue, green and yellow.

**1466 KeyWiz**

Words+
Ste 109
42505 10th St W
Lancaster, CA 93534-7059
800-869-8521
FAX: 661-266-8969
www.words-plus.com

*Phil Lawrence, VP*
*Rachel Nielsen, Customer Support*

A software and hardware product designed to operate on an IBM compatible PC. The software provides word prediction, abbreviation expansion and access to commercial software applications. *$695.00*

**1467 Keyguards for IntelliKeys**

Intelli Tools
1720 Corporate Cir
Petaluma, CA 94954-6924
707-773-2000
800-899-6687
FAX: 707-773-2001
e-mail: info@intellitools.com
intellitools.com

*Beta Davis, Director Sales Operations*
*Lari Castle, Supervisor*
*Arjan Khalsa, CEO*

Acrylic keyguards for each of IntelliKeys six standard overlays. *$250.00*

**1468 Large Print Keyboard Labels**

Hooleon Corp
P.O.Box 589
Melrose, NM 88124-589
928-634-7515
800-937-1337
FAX: 928-634-4620
e-mail: sales@hooleon.com
www.hooleon.com

*Shannen Aikman, Admin Manager/Sales*
*Joan Crozier, President/Sales*

Pressure sensitive labels for computer keyboards.

**1469 LinkPower 50**

Words+
1220 W Avenue J Lancaster
Palmdale, CA 93543
661-723-6523
800-869-8521
FAX: 661-723-2114
e-mail: ifo@words-plus.com
www.words-plus.com

*Ginger Woltosz, VP*
*Tim Ross, Manager*
*Walt Wolosz, Manager*

AC-to-DC switching power converter provides a continuous, independent multi-output, multi-voltage power supply to any augcom device, laptop computer, pointing device, voice synthesizer, cellular phone, or other battery-operated device directly from a wheelchair. *$449.00*

**1470 MessageMate**

Words+ Inc
42505 10th Street W
Lancaster, CA 93534-7059
661-723-6523
800-869-8521
FAX: 661-723-2114
e-mail: info@words-plus.com
www.words-plus.com

*Jeff Dahlan, President*
*Ginger Woltosz, General Manager*

Lightweight, hand-held communicator providing high-quality analog recording capability using either direct select keyboards or 1 to 2 switch access. Price ranges from $549.00 to $999.00. *$1550.00*

**1471 Monkeys Jumping on the Bed IntelliKeys Overlay**

Soft Touch
Ste 401
4300 Stine Rd
Bakersfield, CA 93313-2352
661-396-8676
877-763-8868
FAX: 661-396-8760
e-mail: softtouch@funsoftware.com
www.funsoftware.com

*Roxanne Butterfield, Marketing*
*Joyce Meyer, President*

Seven full color preprinted overlays to use with Monkeys Jumping. Just put them on an IntelliKeys keyboard and you are ready to go.

**1472 Morse Code Equalizer**
Words+
Ste 109
42505 10th St W
Lancaster, CA 93534-7059
661-723-7723
800-869-8521
FAX: 661-723-5524
e-mail: info@words-plus.com
simulations-plus.com

*Walter S Woltosz, CEO*
*Tim Ross, Manager*
*Walt Wolosz, Manager*
Provides complete word processing and voice output communications with single or dual switch Morse code inputs. Originally designed for a blind user with only eyelid movement. The system can be used by both sighted and visually impaired persons. *$1395.00*

**1473 Mouthsticks**
Sammons Preston Rolyan
1000 Remington Blvd
Suite 210
Bolingbrook, IL 60440-5117
630-378-6000
800-323-5547
FAX: 630-378-6010
e-mail: sp@patterson-medical.com
www.pattersonmedical.com

*Sandra Brown, Customer Service Director*
Wide offering of mouthsticks featuring various functions (BK 5380, 5381, 5383, 5385, 6002, or BK 5370 series).

**1474 Old MacDonald's Farm IntelliKeys Overlay**
Soft Touch Inc
17117 Oak Drive
Suite C
Omaha, NE 68130
402-334-8477
877-763-8868
FAX: 402-334-8478
www.softtouch.com

*Joyce Meyer, President*
Extend your students' learning with more than 45 pre-made overlays that support all of the skills learned at the farm. Use with the IntelliKeys keyboard. Simply print and use. Print an extra set to make off computer activities, too. Note: Requires Overlay Maker or Overlay Printer by IntelliTools.

**1475 Perfect Solutions**
2685 Treanor Ter
Wellington, FL 33414-6460
561-790-1070
800-726-7086
FAX: 561-790-0108
e-mail: perfect@gate.net
www.perfectsolutions.com

*Andrew Kramer, President*
A computer for every student and it speaks! Wireless laptop computers starting at $299.00 are ideal for students to carry with them all day. Text-to-speech and web browsing are available. *$299.00*

**1476 Phillip Roy**
P.O.Box 130
Indian Rocks Beach, FL 33785-130
727-593-2700
800-255-9085
FAX: 727-595-2685
e-mail: info@philliproy.com
www.philliproy.com

*Ruth Bragman PhD, President*
*Phil Padol, VP*
Offers multimedia materials appropriate for use with individuals with disabilities. Programs range from preschool through the adult level. Many of the programs are high interest topics/low vocabulary, ideal for transition and employability skills. Materials are also available which focus on social and personal development. Call for a free catalog.

**1477 Rodeo IntelliKeys Overlay**
Soft Touch
Ste 401
4300 Stine Rd
Bakersfield, CA 93313-2352
661-396-8676
877-763-8868
FAX: 661-396-8760
e-mail: softtouch@funsoftware.com
www.funsoftware.com

*Roxanne Butterfield, Marketing*
*Joyce Meyer, President*
Four full color preprinted overlays to use with The Rodeo. Just put them on an IntelliKeys keyboard and you are ready to go.

**1478 SS-Access Single Switch Interface for PC'swith MS-DOS**
Academic Software
3504 Tates Creek Road
Lexington, KY 40517-2601
859-552-1020
800-842-2357
FAX: 253-799-4012
www.acsw.com

*Warren E Lacefield PhD, President*
*Penelope Ellis, Marketing Director*
A general purpose single switch hardware and software interface for DOS and the IBM and compatible PC family. It is designed to be easy to install, simple to use, and compatible with the widest possible range of computers and application software programs. SS-ACCESS! connects to one of the PC serial ports and provides a jack to connect an external switch. The DOS version of the software works by sending a user defined keystroke to the PC keyboard buffer whenever the switch is pressed. *$ 90.00*

**1479 Simplicity**
Words+
42505 10th Street W
Lancaster, CA 93534-7059
661-723-6523
800-869-8521
FAX: 661-723-2114
e-mail: info@words-plus.com
www.words-plus.com

*Jeff Dahlan, President*
*Ginger Wolosz, General Manager*
Swing-down mount for portable computers and other devices is made from high-quality aircraft aluminum. Simplicity contains very few moving parts and installs in minutes, providing a positive, secure support for computer/device in both the stored and overlap position. *$1199.00*

**1480 Slim Armstrong Mounting System**
AbleNet
2625 Patton Road
Roseville, MN 55113-1308
612-379-0956
800-322-0956
FAX: 651-294-2259
e-mail: customerservice@ablenetinc.com
www.ablenetinc.com

*Jen Thalhuber, CEO*
Slim Armstrong is a mounting system strong enough to hold up to five pounds in any position. Mix and match parts to create the system length you desire. *$188.00*

**1481 Smart Modem**
H AR C Mercantile
1111 W Ctr
Portage, MI 49024
269-324-0301
800-445-9968
FAX: 269-324-2387
e-mail: info@harc.com
harc.com

*Ron Slager, Owner*
Smart modem makes your computer accessible to a TTY. *$349.00*

**1482 SoftTouch Favorites IntelliKeys Overlay**
Soft Touch
Ste 401
4300 Stine Rd
Bakersfield, CA 93313-2352 661-396-8676
877-763-8868
FAX: 661-396-8760
e-mail: softtouch@softtouch.com
www.softtouch.com

*Roxanne Butterfield, Marketing*
*Joyce Meyer, President*
Four full color preprinted overlays to use with SoftTouch Favorites. Just put them on an IntelliKeys keyboard and you are ready to go.

**1483 Songs I Sing at Preschool IntelliKeys Overlay**
Soft Touch
1711 Oak Drive
Suite C
Omaha, NE 68130 402-334-8477
877-763-8868
FAX: 402-334-8478
www.softtouch.com

*Joyce Meyer, President*
Pre-made overlays for use with Songs I Sing at Preschool. Simply print and use with an IntelliKeys keyboard. Print an extra set to make off computer activities, too.

**1484 String Switch**
AbleNet
2808 Fairview Ave N
Roseville, MN 55113-1308 612-379-0956
800-322-0956
FAX: 651-294-2259
e-mail: customerservice@ablenetinc.com
www.ablenetinc.com

*Jen Thalhuber, CEO*
Ideal for students who have limited finger and hand mobility, as well as those with minimal strength. *$28.00*

**1485 Switch Basics IntelliKeys Overlay**
Soft Touch
17117 Oak Drive
Suite C
Omaha, NE 68130 402-334-8477
877-763-8868
FAX: 402-334-8478
www.softtouch.com

*Joyce Meyer, President*
Four preprinted overlays to use with Switch Basics. Just put them on an IntelliKeys keyboard and you're ready to go.

**1486 Symbi-Key Computer Switch Interface**
AbleNet
1081 10th Ave SE
Minneapolis, MN 55414-1312 800-322-0956
FAX: 651-294-2254
e-mail: hresources@ablenetinc.com
www.ablenetinc.com

*Cheryl Volkam, President/CEO*
The Symbi-Key can be programmed to simulate any key stroke or a series of keystrokes ( up to 5 per key) for single switch access to software programs whether or not it was designed for switch access. Works well in DOS and all versions of Windows providing access to any IBM program. *$299.00*

**1487 Teach Me Phonemics Blends Overlay CDSoftTouch Inc.**
17117 Oak Dr
Suite C
Omaha, NE 68130 402-334-8477
FAX: 402-334-8478
e-mail: softtouch@softtouch.com
wwww.softtouch.com

*Roxanne Butterfield, Marketing*
*Joyce Meyer, President*
Teach Me Phonemics Blends Overlay CD contains over 40 IntelliKeys overlays for use with Teach Me Phonemics - Blends program. Choose either 4-item or 9-item layout to match the presentation you use in the program. Print extra copies of the overlays for off computer activites, too.

**1488 Teach Me Phonemics Medial Overlay CD**
SoftTouch Incorporated
Ste C
17117 Oak Dr
Omaha, NE 68130-2193 402-330-1301
877-763-8868
FAX: 402-334-8478
e-mail: support@softtouch.com
www.softtouch.com

*Kip Fisher, Manager*
*Roxanne Butterfield, Marketing*
Teach Me Phonemics Medial Overlay CD contains over 40 IntelliKeys overlays for use with Teach Me Phonemics - Medial program. Choose either 4-item or 9-item layout to match the presentation you use in the program. Print extra copies of the overlays for off computer activites, too.

**1489 Teach Me Phonemics Overlay Series Bundle**
SoftTouch
Ste 401
4300 Stine Rd
Bakersfield, CA 93313-2352 661-396-8676
877-763-8868
FAX: 661-396-8760
e-mail: softtouch@funsoftware.com
www.softtouch.com

*Roxanne Butterfield, Marketing*
*Joyce Meyer, President*
Teach Me Phonemics Overlay Series Bundle includes one copy of each Teach Me Phonemics Overlay CD - Initial, Medial, Final and - four CD's in all.

**1490 Teach Me to Talk Overlay CD**
Soft Touch
17117 Oak Drive
Suite C
Omaha, NE 68130 402-334-8477
877-763-8868
FAX: 402-334-8478
www.softtouch.com

*Joyce Meyer, President*
For older version of Teach Me to Talk. Mac only version with red label and PC only version with yellow label. More than 48 pre-made overlays that match the activities on Teach Me to Talk. Simply print and use with an IntelliKeys keyboard. Print an extra set to make off computer activities, too.

**1491 Teach Me to Talk: USB-Overlay CD**
Soft Touch
17117 Oak Drive
Suite C
Omaha, NE 68130 402-334-8477
3 - -
FAX: 402-334-8478
www.softtouch.com

*Joyce Meyer, President*
Revised version of Teach Me to Talk Overlays for the newest version that is USB IntelliKeys compatible. This CD contains more

than 48 overlays that match the activities and updated graphics of Teach Me to Talk. Includes Overlay Printer by IntelliTools for easy printing.

**1492 Teen Tunes Plus IntelliKeys Overlay**
Soft Touch
17117 Oak Drive
Suite C
Omaha, NE 68130
402-334-8477
877-763-8868
FAX: 402-334-8478
www.softtouch.com

*Joyce Meyer, President*
Seven full color, preprinted overlays to use with Teen Tunes Plus. Just put them on an IntelliKeys keyboard and you're ready to go. *$49.00*

**1493 TouchCorders Holder**
Soft Touch
Ste 401
4300 Stine Rd
Bakersfield, CA 93313-2352
661-396-8676
877-763-8868
FAX: 661-396-8760
e-mail: support@softtouch.com
www.softtouch.com

*Roxanne Butterfield, Marketing*
*Joyce Meyer, President*
The TouchCorders Holder enables you to position up to 4 TouchCorders for sequencing, spelling, communication, story telling and more. The TouchCorders Holder holds TouchCorders snugly and keeps them in place even when you are offering multiple choices to students in a group setting. The sturdy triangular shape presents TouchCorders at a 30-degree angle for better visual and physical access.

**1494 Turtle Teasers IntelliKeys Overlay**
Soft Touch
Ste 401
4300 Stine Rd
Bakersfield, CA 93313-2352
661-396-8676
877-763-8868
FAX: 661-396-8760
e-mail: softtouch@funsoftware.com
www.funsoftware.com

*Roxanne Butterfield, Marketing*
*Joyce Meyer, President*
Seven full color preprinted overlays to use with Turtle Teasers. Just put them on the IntelliKeys keyboard and you're ready to go.

**1495 U-Control III**
Words+
42505 10th St W
Lancaster, CA 93534-7059
661-723-6523
800-869-8521
FAX: 661-723-2114
e-mail: info@word-plus.com
www.words-plus.com

*Jeff Dahlen, President*
*Ginger Wolosz, General Manager*
Works with the Words+ system (EX Keys, Morse WSKE, Scanning WSKE, Talking Screen) to provide wireless, portable control of items which are already infrared-controlled such as a TV, VCR, CD player, etc. *$499.00*

**1496 Universal Switch Mounting System**
AbleNet
2625 Patton Road
Roseville, MN 55113-1308
612-379-0956
800-322-0956
FAX: 651-294-2259
e-mail: customerservice@ablenetinc.com
www.ablenetinc.com

*Jen Thalhuber, CEO*
Mounting system that allows switch placement in any position. A single lever locks all joints securely in place. Extends to 20 1/2 inches and holds up to five pounds. A mounting system for quick and easy positioning. *$210.00*

**1497 WinSCAN: The Single Switch Interface for PC's with Windows**
Academic Software
3504 Tates Creek Rd
Lexington, KY 40517-2601
859-522-1020
FAX: 253-799-4012
e-mail: asistaff@acsw.com
www.acsw.com

*Warren E Lacefield, President*
*Penelope Ellis, Marketing Director/COO*
A general purpose single-switch control interface for Windows. It provides single-switch users independent control access to educational and productivity software, multimedia programs, and recreational activities that run under Windows 3.1 and higher versions on IBM and compatible PC's. The user can navigate through Windows; choose program icons and run programs, games, and CD's; even surf the Internet with WinSCAN and his or her adaptive switch. *$349.00*

**1498 Words+ Equalizer**
Words Plus
1220 W Avenue J
Lancaster, CA 93534-2902
661-723-6523
800-869-8521
FAX: 661-723-2114
e-mail: info@words-plus.com
www.words-plus.com

*Ginger Woltosz, VP*
*Walt Wolosz, Manager*
A hardware/software product designed to operate on an IBM compatible PC. The software provides an intelligent word prediction scheme, a calculator, music, plus the ability to draw and play games. Equalizer is a dedicated augmentative communication system designed for use by individuals with severe motor disability. *$1395.00*

**1499 Words+ IST (Infrared, Sound, Touch)**
Words+
42505 10th St W
Lancaster, CA 93534-7059
661-723-6523
800-869-8521
FAX: 661-723-2114
e-mail: info@words-plus.com
www.words-plus.com

*Jeff Dahlan, President*
*Ginger Wolosz, General Manager*
A unique switch that is activated by slight movement or faint sound. The switch provides user control when connected to a device driven by a single switch. Individuals are currently accessing a wide variety of communication and computer systems with movement using the IST switch. *$395.00*

## Braille Products

**1500 Access Systems International**
415 English Ave
Monterey, CA 93940-3810
831-373-6291
FAX: 831-375-5313

*Carmela Cantisani, Owner*
Developers of Braille printers.

**1501 Braille Blazer**
Blazie Engineering
11800 31st Ct N
St Petersburg, FL 33716-1805
727-803-8000
800-444-4443
FAX: 727-803-8001

Braille printer.

**1502 Braille Keyboard Labels**
Hooleon Corporation
P.O.Box 589
Melrose, NM 88124-589
928-634-7515
800-937-1337
FAX: 928-634-4620
e-mail: sales@hooleon.com
www.hooleon.com

*Barry Green, Sales Manager*
*Joan Crozier, President/Sales*
Also large print keyboard labels and large print with Braille.

**1503 Braille N' Speak**
Blazie Engineering
11800 31st Ct N
St Petersburg, FL 33716-1805
727-803-8000
800-444-4443
FAX: 727-803-8001

A compact, portable talking device with a seven-key braille keyboard, may be used as a talking computer terminal, a braille to print transcriber and a word processor.

**1504 Brailon Thermoform Duplicator**
American Thermoform Corporation
1758 Brackett St
La Verne, CA 91750-5855
909-593-6711
800-331-3676
FAX: 909-593-8001
e-mail: pnunnelly@americanthermoform.com
www.americanthermoform.com

*Patrick Nunnelly, VP*
*Gary Nunnelly, Owner*
This copy machine, for producing tactile images, copies any brailled or embossed original, by a vacuum forming process. This model is for the reproduction of teaching aids and mobility maps.

**1505 Computer Paper for Brailling**
Maxi Aids
42 Executive Blvd
Farmingdale, NY 11735-4710
631-752-0521
800-522-6294
FAX: 631-752-0689
TTY: 631-752-0738
e-mail: sales@maxiaids.com
maxiaids.com

*Elliot Zaretsky, President*
Specially made paper for braille printing. 1,500 sheets/case *$85.99*

**1506 Duxbury Braille Translator**
Duxbury Systems
Ste 6
270 Littleton Rd
Westford, MA 01886-3523
978-692-3000
FAX: 978-692-7912
e-mail: info@duxsys.com
duxburysystems.com

*Joe Sullivan, President*
A complete line of easy to use word processing and Braille translation software available for Windows (including 64 bit windows. Applications for anyone wanting to produce or communicate with Braille; signs, note cards, textbooks, business communications and forms, telephone bills, etc. Simple to use, FREE technical support. Free one year upgrades. DBT is for producing Braille in English, Spanish, French, Portuguese, Italian, Latin, Greek, German and 125 other languages. *$600.00*

**1507 Enabling Technologies Company**
1601 NE Braille Pl
Jensen Beach, FL 34957-5345
772-225-3687
800-777-3687
FAX: 772-225-3299
e-mail: info@brailler.com
www.brailler.com

*Tony Schenk, President*
*Kate Schenk, Product Manager Western US*
*Greg Schenk, Sales & Marketing*
Manufactures the most complete line of American made Braille embossers, including desktop or portable models capable of producing high quality single sided or interpoint Braille. Also carries a complete line of adaptive technology aids for the blind community at affordable prices.

**1508 Freedom Scientific Blind/Low Vision Group**
11800 31st Ct N
St Petersburg, FL 33716-1805
727-803-8000
800-444-4443
FAX: 727-803-8001
e-mail: info@freedomscientific.com
freedomscientific.com

*Brad Davis, VP Hardware Product Management*
*Dr Lee Hamilton, President/CEO*
Developer and manufacturer of assistive technology products for people who are blind or who have low vision. Innovative blindness products include: JAWS(r) screen reading software; the PAC Mate Omni(tm), an accessible Pocket PC; the SARA(tm) scanning and reading appliance; OpenBook(tm) scanning and reading software; FSReader(tm) DAISY player; FaceToFace(tm) deaf-blind communications solution; and PAC Mate and Focus Braille Displays. *$16.95*

**1509 Hooleon Corporation**
P.O.Box 589
Melrose, NM 88124-589
928-634-7515
800-937-1337
FAX: 928-634-4620
e-mail: sales@hooleon.com
hooleon.com

*Kim Green, Manager*
*Joan Crozier, President/Sales*
Large print and combination Braille adhesive keytop labels for computer keyboards. Helps visually impaired computer users access correct key strokes either by sight or by touch. Raised Braille meets ADA specifications and large print fills key top surface.

**1510 Infogrip: Large Print/Braille Keyboard Labels**
1899 E Main St
Ventura, CA 93001-3411
805-652-0770
800-397-0921
FAX: 805-652-0880
e-mail: sales@infogrip.com
www.infogrip.com

*Liza Jacobs, President*
Makes a standard keyboard more accessible for visually impaired individuals with large print or Braille keyboard labels. Characters on the large print labels are .5 by .25 inches, about 3 times larger than standard keyboard characters. Braille labels are available as clear labels with Braille dots or large print with Braille. Each set includes all the keys used on a standard Windows keyboard. *$29.00*

**1511 Raised Dot Computing**
Duxbury Systems Incorporated
Ste 6
270 Littleton Rd
Westford, MA 01886-3523
978-692-3000
FAX: 978-692-7912
e-mail: info@duxsys.com
duxburysystems.com

*Joe Sullivan, President*
*Peter Sullivan, VP/Software Development*
*Genevieve Sullivan, Treasurer*
*Dana Winikates, Software Engineer*
Software for the visually impaired.

**1512 Touchdown Keytop/Keyfront Kits**
Hooleon Corporation
P.O.Box 589 304 West Denby Ave
Melrose, NM 88124
928-634-7515
800-937-1337
FAX: 505-253-4299
e-mail: Sales@Hooleon.com
www.hooleon.com

*Barry Green, Sales Manager*
*Joan Crozier, President*
*Bob Crozier, Founder*
These kits enlarge the key legends of a computer and include Braille for easy recognition.

## Information Centers & Databases

**1513 ABLEDATA**
Ste 930
8630 Fenton St
Silver Spring, MD 20910-3820
301-608-8998
800-227-0216
FAX: 301-608-8958
TTY: 301-608-8912
e-mail: abledata@macrointernational.com
www.abledata.com

*Katherine Belknap, Project Director*
*David Johnson, Publications Director*
*Juanita Hardy, Information Specialist*
*David Johnson, Publications Director*
ABLEDATA is an electronic database of assistive technology and rehabilitation equipment products for children and adults with physical, cognitive and sensory disabilities. ABLEDATA staff can perform database searches or the database can be searched on the ABLEDATA website, database printouts, informed consumer guides and fact sheets are available at cost from the office or free from the website.

**1514 ATTAIN**
Division of Disability Aging & Rehab Services
Ste 1400
32 E Washington St
Indianapolis, IN 46204-3552
317-232-1147
800-528-8246
FAX: 317-486-8809
e-mail: attain@attaininc.org
www.attaininc.org

*Gary R Hand, Executive Director*
*Peter Bisbecos, Manager*
Nonprofit organization that creates system change by expanding the availability of community-based technology-related activities, outreach services, empowerment and advocacy activities through the development of a comprehensive, consumer-responsive, statewide program to serve individuals with disabilities, of all ages and all disabilities, their families, caregivers, educators and service providers. Provides training, information and referrals, system change and assessments for equipment needs.

**1515 Aloha Special Technology Access Center**
710 Green St
Honolulu, HI 96813-2119
808-523-5547
FAX: 808-536-3765
e-mail: astachi@yahoo.com
http://www.alohastac.org/

*Ali Silvert, President*
*Ms. Jacquely Brand, Founder*
Computer technology center.

**1516 Audiogram/Clinical Records Manager**
The Davis Center
19 State Route 10
Succasunna, NJ 07828- 1818
862-251-4637
FAX: 862-251-4642
e-mail: npdunn@thedaviscenter.com
http://www.thedaviscenter.com

*Dorinne.S Davis,MA, CCC-A, FAAA, President/Founder*
*Elizabeth Meade, Head Sound Therapist*
*Nancy Puckett-Dunn, Office Manager*
*Laura Durby, Part Time Sound Therapist*
Sound-based therapy-Uses sound vibration with special equipment, specific programs, modified music, and/or specific tones/beats, the need for which is identified with appropriate testing. Sound-based therapy fits under the term sound therapy so The Davis Center is considered a sound therapy center. *$414.75*

**1517 Birmingham Alliance for Technology Access Center**
Birmingham Independent Living Center
206 13th St S
Birmingham, AL 35233-1317
205-251-2223
FAX: 205-251-0605
TTY:205-251-2223
e-mail: bilc@bellsouth.net
www.birminghamilc.org

*Phil Klebine, President*
*Graham Sisson, VP*
*Daniel Kessler, Executive Director*
Computer technology center.

**1518 Bluegrass Technology Center**
409 Southland Drive
Lexington, KY 40503
859-294-4343
800-209-7767
FAX: 866-576-9625
e-mail: office@bluegrass-tech.org
bluegrass-tech.org

*Vickie Cooper, VP*
*Bruce.W. Turley, Treasurer*
*Jean Isaacs, Assistive Technology Consultant*
*Linda Gassaway, PhD, Assistive Technology Consultant*
Provides assistive technology information, consulting and training for education, health professionals, consumers and parents of

consumers. Maintains extensive lending library of assistive devices and adapted toys. Statewide training such as; AAC, how to obtain funding for assistive technology, augmentative and alternate communication, equipment implementation strategies, specific to hardware and software, etc.

**1519 CITE: Lighthouse for Central Florida**
215 E New Hampshire St
Orlando, FL 32804-6403
407-898-2483
FAX: 407-895-5255
e-mail: csacca@lcf-fl.org
lighthousecentralflorida.com

*Lee Nasehi, President/CEO*
*Donna Esbensen CPA,MBA, VP/CFO*
*Lee Van Eepoel, Director of Program Services*
*Casey Mathews, Access Technology Specialist*
CITE promotes the independence of adults and children with blindness, low vision and other disabilities through technology, education, support and advocacy.

**1520 Carolina Computer Access Center**
P.O.Box 247
Cramerton, NC 28032
704-342-3004
FAX: 704-342-1513
e-mail: bellsluth.net
ccac.ataccess.org

*Linda Schilling, Executive Director*
Nonprofit, community-based technology resource center for people with disabilities, providing information about and demonstration of the technology tools that enable individuals with disabilities to control and direct their own lives. Services and programs include: assessments, demonstrations, resource information, lending library, workshops and outreach.

**1521 Center for Accessible Technology**
3075 Adeline Street
Suite 220
Berkeley, CA 94703
510-841-3224
FAX: 510-841-7956
e-mail: info@cforat.org
cforat.org

*Dmitri Belser, Executive Director*
*Eric Smith, Associate Director*
A consumer-based technology resource and demonstration center for adults and children with disabilities, families, teachers, and professionals. The primary focus is on assistive technology for computer access. Seen by appointment only.

**1522 Center for Applied Special Technology**
Ste 3
40 Harvard Mill Sq
Wakefield, MA 01880-3208
781-245-2212
FAX: 781-245-5212
e-mail: cast@cast.org
www.cast.org/

*Ada Sullivan, President*
*Anne Meyer, Chief Of Education Design*
*David.H. Rose, Chief Education Officer*
Expands opportunities for individuals with special needs through innovative use of computers and related technology. We pursue this mission through research and product development that further universal design for learning.

**1523 Center for Assistive Technology & Inclusive Education Studies**
2000 Pennington Rd. P.O.Box 7718
Ewing, NJ 08628
609-771-3016
FAX: 609-637-5179
e-mail: caties@tcnj.edu
caties.tcnj.edu

*Amy G Dell, Executive Director*
*Tammy Cordwell, Assistive Technology Specialist*
*Jessica Castellini, Assistive Technology Specialist*
*Jennifer Holt Shah, Assistive Technology Specialist*
Computer technology center offering resource time, workshops, technology, training and evaluations.

**1524 Center on Evaluation of Assistive Technology**
National Rehabilitation Hospital
102 Irving St NW
Washington, DC 20010-2921
202-877-1000
TTY:202-726-3996
e-mail: justin.m.carter@medstar.net
www.nrhrehab.org

*Thomas J Collamore, Chairman*
*Jimmy V. Reyes, Vice Chairman*
*Edward Eckenhoff, CEO*
*Robert B. Ourisman, Treasurer*
The center develops ways of collecting, producing and distributing information to help users, prescribers and third-party payers make intelligent selections of devices.

**1525 Compuserve: Handicapped Users' Database**
5000 Arlington Centre Blvd
Columbus, OH 43220-2913
614-326-1002
FAX: 614-538-4023
webcenters.netscape.compuserve.com

This nationwide database with bulletin boards provides information for persons with disabilities and the issues and technologies that are of interest to them.

**1526 Computer & Web Resources for People With Disabilities**
Alliance for Technology Access
Ste 240
1304 Southpoint Blvd
Petaluma, CA 94954-7464
707-778-3011
FAX: 707-765-2080
TTY:707-778-3015
e-mail: atainfo@ataaccess.org
www.ataccess.org

*Sharon Hall, Manager*
A guide to maneuvering the growing world of computers, both the mainstream and the assistive technology.

*ISBN 0-897933-00-1*

**1527 Computer Access Center**
6234 W 87th St
Los Angeles, CA 90045-3902
310-338-9318
FAX: 310-338-9318
e-mail: info@cac.org
www.cac.org

*Mary Ann Glicksman, Executive Director*
*Joanne Orenski, Financial Administrator*
Computer technology center.

**1528 Computer Center for Visually Impaired People: Division of Continuing Studies**
Baruch College
1 Bernard Baruch Way
New York, NY 10010-5585 646-312-1420
FAX: 646-312-5101
e-mail: judith.gerber@baruch.cuny.edu
www.baruch.cuny.edu/ccvip

*Karen Gourgey, Director*
*Judith Gerber, Operations Manager*
*Lynette Tatum, Training Specialist*
*William Reed, Assistant Director*
Offers courses, tutors, equipment and assistance.

**1529 Computer Resources for People with Disabilities**
Hunter House Publishers, Inc
PO Box 2914 15151/2 Park Street
Alameda, CA 94501 510-865-5282
800-266-5592
FAX: 510-865-4295
e-mail: ordering@hunterhouse.com
www.hunterhouse.com

*Kiran Rana, Publisher*
Part One describes conventional and assistive technologies and gives strategies for accessing the Internet. Part Two features easy-to-use charts organized by key access concerns, and provides detailed descriptions of software, hardware, and communication aids. Part Three is a gold mine of Web resources, publications, support organizations, government programs, and technology vendors.

**1530 Computer-Enabling Drafting for People with Physical Disabilities**
County College of Morris
214 Center Grove Rd
Randolph, NJ 07869-2007 973-328-5000
888-226-8001
FAX: 973-328-5067
ccm.edu

*Edward J Yaw, President*
*Brandi Robinson, VP*
*Dianne Adams, Associate Professor*
*Vivek Agnihotri, Assistant Professor*
Since they opened in 1968, more than 40,000 graduates have passed through their halls. Many have become teachers, nurses, police officers, doctors and engineers. CCM has also been a community resource for those seeking to enhance their careers through additional education. They drafted a newsletter on Computer-Enabling Drafting for People with Physical Disabilities

**1531 Computers to Help People**
Apt 109
913 Acewood Blvd
Madison, WI 53714-3267 608-257-5917
FAX: 608-257-3480
e-mail: techorlochpi.org
www.chpi.org

*Carl Durocher, Assistive Technologies Manager*
*Johnny R Lee, Operations Manager*
*John J Boyer, Executive Director*
A center for assistive technology, assessment, consulting and training, specializing in computer access products for persons with sensory or mobility impairments. Also provides a print-to-braille service with a specialty in technical writing.

**1532 DIRLINE**
National Library of Medicine
8600 Rockville Pike
Bethesda, MD 20894 301-594-5983
888-346-3656
FAX: 301-402-1384
e-mail: custserv@nml.nih.gov
www.nlm.nih.gov/

*Dr. Donald A B. Lindberg, Director*
*Milton Corn, Deputy Director*
*Betsy Humphreys, Deputy Director*
*Todd Danielson, Office of Administration*
18,000 listings of organizations that serve as information resources, including libraries, professional associations and government agencies.

**1533 Developmental Disabilities Council**
647 Main St
Baton Rouge, LA 70801-1911 225-342-6804
800-450-8108
FAX: 225-342-1970
e-mail: sandee.winchell@la.gov
http://www.laddc.org

*Sandee Winchell, Executive Director*
*Shawn Fleming, Deputy Director*
*Derek White, Program Manager*
*Robbie Gray, Program Monitor*
The Louisiana Developmental Disabilities Council is made up of people from every region of the state who are appointed by the governor to develop and implement a five year plan to address the needs of persons with disabilities. Membership includes persons with developmental disabilities, parents, advocates, professionals, and representatives from public and private agencies.

**1534 Employment Resources Program**
330 South Grand Ave W
Springfield, IL 62704-3716 217-523-2587
800-447-4221
FAX: 217-523-0427
e-mail: scil@scil.org
scil.org

*Pete Roberts, Executive Director*
*Susanne Cooper, Program Director*
*Robin Ashton- Hale, Reintegration Coordinator*
*Kathryn Cline, Business Manager*
An information and referral service that encourages inquiries from professionals, individuals with disabilities, family members, organizations or anyone requesting information pertaining to disabilities. The staff at DRN uses both computer listings and in-house library files to provide the programs services. The DRN program is funded by a grant from the Illinois Department of Rehabilitation Services.

**1535 Functional Skills Screening Inventory**
Functional Resources
3905 Huntington Dr
Amarillo, TX 79109-4047 806-353-1114
FAX: 806-353-1114
e-mail: info@winfssi.com
www.winfssi.com

*Ed Hammer, Owner*
*Heather Becker PhD, Owner*
Assesses the individual's level of functional skills and identifies supports needed by educational, rehabilitation and residential programs serving moderately and severely disabled persons. Includes environmental assessments as well as profiles of jobs and training sites.

**1536 High Tech Center**
Sacremento State
6000 J St
Sacramento, CA 95819-2605 916-278-7915
e-mail: sswd@csus.edu
www.csus.edu/sswd/services

*Judy Dean, Co-Director*
*Melissa Repa, Co-Director*
*Janis Bradley, Staff Interpreter*
*Terry Gomez, Office Manager*
The Center offers assessment and training in adaptive hardware/software for eligible students with disabilities at Sacramento State upon referral from the Office of Services to Students with Disabilities.

**1537 Idaho Assistive Technology Project**
129 W 3rd St
Moscow, ID 83843-2268 208-885-3557
800-432-8324
FAX: 208-885-3628
e-mail: rseiler@uidaho.edu
www.idahoat.org

*Ron Seiler, Project Director*
*Sue House, Information Specialist*
A federally funded program managed by the center on disabilities and human development at the university of Idaho. The goal of the IATP is to increase the availability of assistive technology devices and services for Idahoans with disabilities. The IATP offers free trainings and technical assistance, a low-interest loan program, assistive technology assessments for children and agriculture workers, and free informational materials.

**1538 Increasing Capabilities Access Network**
26 Corporate Hill Dr
Little Rock, AR 72205-4538 501-666-8868
800-828-2799
FAX: 501-666-5319
TTY: 501-666-8868
e-mail: nfo@ar-ican.org
www.arkansas-ican.org

*Bryen Ayres, Member of Advisory Council*
*Billy Altom, Member of Advisory Council*
*Adrienne Brown, Member of Advisory Council*
*Carolyn Boyles, Member of Advisory Council*
A consumer responsive statewide systems change program promoting assistive technology for persons of all ages with disabilities. The program provides information on new and existing technology and maintains an equipment exchange free of charge. Training on assistive technology is also provided.

**1539 International Center for the Disabled**
340 E 24th St
New York, NY 10010-4019 212-585-6000
FAX: 212-585-6161
e-mail: info@icdnyc.org
www.icdnyc.org

*Jill Bowman, Manager*
*Les Halpert, CEO*
The ICD is a comprehensive outpatient rehabilitation facility, providing medical rehabilitation, behavioral health and vocational services to children and adults with a broad range of physical, communication, emotional and cognitive disabilities.

**1540 Kentucky Assistive Technology Service Network**
8412 Westport Rd
Louisville, KY 40242-3044 502-429-4484
800-327-5287
FAX: 502-429-7114
katsnet.org

*Derrick Cox, Manager*
Statewide network of four regional assistive technology centers with a central coordinating office in Louisville and two regional centers in eastern Kentucky. Network services include but are not limited to assistive technology of services, loan of assistive devices, funding information and referral, assessment and evaluations, consultations on appropriate technologies, training, and technical assistance.

**1541 Learning Independence Through Computers**
2301 Argonne Drive
Baltimore, MD 21218 410-554-9134
FAX: 410-261-2907
e-mail: info@linc.org
www.linc.org

*Theo Pinette, Executive Director*
*Jessica Robles, Volunteer Service Manager*
*Justice Creamer, Sr. Assistive Technology Specialist*
*John Walker, Project Coordinator*
V-LINC creates technological solutions to improve the independence and quality of life for individuals of all ages with disabilities in Maryland. We do this through a mix of off-the-shelf computer software and equipment, and one-of-a-kind, customized assistive technology. The name of the company is “”Providing Independence Through Technology"".

**1542 MEDLINE**
Dialog Corporation
2250 Perimeter Park Drive
Suite 300
Morrisville, NC 27560 800-334-2564
919-804-6400
FAX: 919-804-6410
www.dialog.com

*Tim Wahlberg, Genral Manager*
*Morten Nicholaisen, VP Global Sales and Account Management*
*Libby Trudell, VP Strategic Initiatives*
*Tim Hall, Director Integration and Business Operations*
Bibliographic citations to biomedical literature.

**1543 Maine CITE**
University of Maine at Augusta
46 University Dr
Augusta, ME 04330-9488 207-621-3195
FAX: 207-629-5429
TTY:877-475-4800
e-mail: iweb@mainecite.org
http://www.mainecite.org

*Robert McPhee, Member of Advisory Council*
*Deborah Gardner, Member of Advisory Council*
*Anita Dunham, Member of Advisory Council*
*Sandra Jaeger, Member of Advisory Council*
Computer technology center.

**1544 Maryland Technology Assistance Program**
Maryland Department of Disabilities
Rm T-17
2301 Argonne Dr
Baltimore, MD 21218-1628 410-554-9361
800-832-4827
FAX: 410-554-9237
TTY: 866-881-7488
e-mail: MDOD@mdod.state.md.us
www.mdtap.org

*Anne Blackfield, Executive Director*
*Tony Rice, Program Director*
*Tanya Goodman, Loan Program Assistant Director*
*Lori Markland, Director of Marketing & Program Development*
Assistive technology center. Information and referral, equipment display loans and demonstration, funding sources, alternative media, training, workshops and seminars. Rural outreach for individuals with disability in Maryland.

**1545 Minnesota STAR Program**
358 Centennial Office Building
Saint Paul, MN 55155- 1402 651-201-2640
800-627-3529
888-234-1267
FAX: 651-282-6671
e-mail: star.program@state.mn.us
www.admin.state.mn.us/assistivetechnology

*Chuck Rassbach, Program Director*
*Jennis Delisi, Program Staff*
*Jaoan Gillum, Program Staff*
*Kim Moccia, Program Staff*
STAR's mission is to help all Minnesotans with disabilities gain access to and acquire the assistive technology they eed to live, learn, work and lay. The Minnesota STAR program is federally funded by the Rehabilitation Services Administration.

**1546 Mississippi Project START**
2550 Peachtree Street
Jackson, MS 39216 601-987-4872
800-852-8328
FAX: 601-364-2349
e-mail: dyoung@mdrs.ms.gov
www.msprojectstart.org

*H.S. McMillan, Executive Director*
*Dorothy Young, Project Director*
*Kacee Mott, Administrative Assistant*
*Jason Bates, Repair Specialist*
Project START is a Tech Act project established to bring about systems change in the field of assistive technology in the State of Mississippi. Activities include providing training opportunities for consumers and service providers on subjects such as state-of-the-art AT devices, their application and funding resources; referral information on AT evaluation centers; technical assistance to AT users; establishment of an AT equipment loan program and an Information and Referral Service.

**1547 National Technology Database**
American Foundation for the Blind/ AF B Press
Ste 300
11 Penn Plz
New York, NY 10001-2006 212-502-7600
800-232-5463
FAX: 212-502-7777
e-mail: afbinfo@afb.net
afb.org

*Carl.R Augusto, President and CEO*
*Kelly Bleach, Technical Services Director, Chief Administrative Officer*
*Rick Bozeman, Finance Director, Chief Financial Officer*
*Maureen Matheson, Vice President, AFB Press and Web Programs*
This database includes resources for visually impaired persons.
*$99.00*

**1548 New Jersey Department of Labor & Workforce Development**
Office of the Commissioner
P.O.Box 110
Trenton, NJ 08625 609-292-7060
FAX: 609-633-1359
e-mail: cmycoff@dol.state.nj.us
www.state.nj.us/labor

*Frederick J. Zavaglia, Chief of Staff*
*Harold J. Wirths, Commissioner*
*Brian T. Murray, Director of Communications & Marketing*
*David Ramsay, Director*
Oversees various federal and state vocational rehabilitation services including sheltered workshops and independent living centers; adjudication of permanent disability claims filed with the Social Security Administration; oversees New Jersey's temporary disability program covering non-work related illnesses and injuries

**1549 New Mexico Technology Assistance Program**
435 Saint Michaels Drive
Ste D
Santa Fe, NM 87505-7679 505-827-8535
800-866-2253
FAX: 505-954-8608
e-mail: julie.martinez1@state.nm.us
www.nmtap.com

*Julie Martinez, Program Director*
Examines and works to eliminate barriers to obtaining assistive technology in New Mexico. Has established a statewide program for coordinating assistive technology services; is designed to assist people with disabilities to locate, secure, and maintain assistive technology.

**1550 Northern Illinois Center for Adaptive Technology**
3615 Louisiana Rd
Rockford, IL 61108 815-229-2163
e-mail: davegrass@eartlink.net
nicat.ataccess.org

*Dave Grass, President*
Computer technology center.

**1551 OCCK**
1710 W Schilling Rd
Salina, KS 67402-1160 785-827-9383
800-526-9731
FAX: 785-823-2015
e-mail: occk@occk.com
occk.com

*Carolee Miner, CEO*
Computer technology center; training center for employment and independent living for people with disabilities; family support center. Kansas AgrAbility program coordinator, Kansas equipment exchange site.

**1552 Parents, Let's Unite for Kids**
516 N 32nd St
Billings, MT 59101-6003 406-255-0540
800-222-7585
FAX: 406-255-0523
TTY: 406-657-2055
e-mail: info@pluk.org
pluk.org

*Roger Holt, Executive Director*
Computer technology center. Parents, Let's Unite for Kids offers an assistive technology lab that is open to people of all ages. The lab is a computer and assistive technology demonstration site. There is no charge for services.

**1553 Pennsylvania's Initiative on Assistive Technology**
Temple University
1755 N. 13th St
Student Center, Room 4115
Philadelphia, PA 19122-6024 800-204-7428
FAX: 215-204-6336
TTY:866-268-0579
e-mail: ATinfo@temple.edu
www.disabilities.temple.edu

*Amy S Goldman, Director*
Pennsylvania's Initiative on Assistive Technology (PIAT) offers information and referral about assistive Technology (AT), device demonstrations, and awareness-level presentations. PIAT also operates Pennsylvania's AT Lending Library, a free, state-supported program that loans AT devices to Pennsylvanians of all ages. This program allows you to try a device for a limited time to be sure it meets your needs.

**1554 Rehabilitation Engineering & Assistive Technology Society of North America (RESNA)**
Ste 1540
1700 N Moore St
Arlington, VA 22209-1903
703-524-6686
FAX: 703-524-6630
TTY:703-524-6639
e-mail: membership@resna.org
resna.org

*Nell Bailey, Executive Director*
*Jerry Weisman, President*
*Heidi Horstmann Koester, PhD, Treasurer*
*Alex Mihailidis, PhD, P.Eng, President- Elect*

Improves the potential of people with disabilities to achieve their goals through the use of technology and disability. Promotes research, development, education, advocacy and provision of technology, and by supporting the people engaged in theses activities.

**1555 Resource Center for Independent Living(RCIL)**
P.O.Box 210
Utica, NY 13503-210
315-797-4642
FAX: 315-797-4747
e-mail: burt.danovitz@rcil.com
www.rcil.com

*Burt Danovitz, Executive Director*

The RCIL aggressively advocates for and defends the rights of persons with disabilities. RCIL believes in integration adn assisting people to reach their full potential, encouraging a culture of risk-taking, creativity and innovation through our programs and services. They monitor and assess the current legal climate around rights for persons with disabilities on an ongoing bases and are committed and deliberate in speaking about the problems and obstacles faced by persons with disabilities.

**1556 SACC Assistive Technoloy Center**
P.O.Box 1325
Simi Valley, CA 93062-1325
805-582-1881
http://www.semel.ucla.edu

*Debi Schultze, CEO*

SACC connects children, adults and seniors with special needs to computers, technologies and resources. We provide information and referral, assessments, tutoring, presentations and outreach awareness.

**1557 South Dakota Department of Human Services: Computer Technology Services**
500 E Capitol Ave
Pierre, SD 57501-5007
605-773-5990
800-265-9684
FAX: 605-773-5483
TTY: 605-773-6412
e-mail: infodhs@state.sd.us
http://dhs.sd.gov

*Laurie.R Gill, Secretary*

Computer technology center.

**1558 Star Center**
1119 Old Humboldt Rd
Jackson, TN 38305-1752
731-668-3888
888-398-5619
FAX: 731-668-1666
TTY: 731-668-9664
e-mail: information@starcenter.tn.org
starcenter.tn.org

*John Borden, CEO*

Nation's largest assistive technology center dedicated to helping children and adults with disabilities achieve their goals for competitive employment, effective learning, returning to or starting school and independent living. Programs include: high-tech training, music therapy, art therapy, low vision evaluation, orientation and mobility evaluation and training, augmentative communication evaluation, vocational evaluations, assistive technology, job placement services and job skills training.

**1559 Students with Disabilities Office**
University of Texas at Austin
100 West Dean Keeton A5800
Austin, TX 78712-1100
512-471-5017
FAX: 512-471-7833
e-mail: deanofstudents@austin.utexas.edu
deanofstudents.utexas.edu/

*Dr. Audrey M Sorrells, Associate Dean of Students for Research*
*Soncia Reagins-Lilly, Ed.D, Sr. Associate VP for Student Affairs*
*Douglas Darrard, Ed.D, Senior Associate Dean of Students*
*LaToya Hill, Ph.D., Assistant Dean of Students*

**1560 TASK Team of Advocates for Special Kids**
100 W Cerritos Ave
Anaheim, CA 92805-6546
714-533-8275
866-828-8275
FAX: 714-533-2533
e-mail: task@taskca.org
taskca.org

*Marta Anchondo, Executive Director*
*Tom Bratkovich, Treasurer*
*Leana Way, Director*

Computer technology center.

**1561 Tech Connection**
35 Haddon Ave
Shrewsbury, NJ 07702-4007
732-747-5310
FAX: 732-747-1896
e-mail: info@frainc.org
www.techconnection.org

*Joanne Castellano, Director*

Offers a noncommercial center to examine and try computers, adapted equipment, alternative input devices, and a variety of software. Program of Family Resource Associates and a member of the Alliance for Technology Access (ATA), a growing national coalition of computer resource centers, professionals, technology developers and vendors, interacting with new technology to enrich the lives of people with disabilities. Tech Connection offers evaluations, for computer technology.

**1562 Tech-Able**
1451 Klondike Road, Suite D
Conyers, GA 30094
770-922-6768
FAX: 770-922-6769
e-mail: c.b.wright@techable.org
techable.org

*Cassandra Baker, Executive Director*
*Pat Hanus, Program Assistant*
*Erika Ruffin-Mosley, Assistive Technology Trainer*
*Jason Chadwell, AT & Blind / Low Vision Trainer*

Provide assistive technology to individuals with disabilities, toy-lending and software libraries, product demonstration, access to technology devices and fabrication of keyguards for keyboards. Low vision consultant on Thursdays; computer training for persons with disabilities.

**1563 Technical Aids & Assistance for the Disabled Center**
1950 W Roosevelt Rd
Chicago, IL 60608-1245
708-867-6060
800-346-2939
FAX: 312-421-3464
TTY: 312-421-3373

*Andres Hernandez, Executive Director*
*Robert Kaige, Technologist*

Provides consultation and technical advice on adaptive aids, software and hardware.

**1564 Technology Access Center of Tucson**
P.O.Box 13178
Tucson, AZ 85732-3178
520-638-2733
FAX: 520-519-7954
e-mail: tact1@qwestoffice.net
http://www.uacoe.arizona.edu/tact/

A resource center that provides assistive technology services for people with disabilities. Center personnel develop, provide and coordinate those services in communities throughout Middle Tennessee. Services are designed to assist people with disabilities to learn about, choose, acquire and use assistive technology devices. Services are offered to any child or adult with sensory, motor or cognitive disabilities, their family members, and professionals who serve them and employ them.

**1565 Technology Assistance for Special Consumers**
1856 Keats Drive
Huntsville, AL 35810
256-859-8300
FAX: 256-859-4332
e-mail: tasc@ucphuntsville.org
http://www.ucptasc.org/

*Linda Rags, Executive Director*

T.A.S.C. is a computer resource center with 10 computers, which are equipped with special adaptations for those who are blind, visually impaired, or severely physically disabled. Our staff demonstrates and trains individuals on this equipment so that they can become more independent at home, school, and work. Over 2,500 pieces of educational software are available for individuals who are learning disabled, mentally retarded or who have developmental delays.

**1566 Tidewater Center for Technology Access Special Education Annex**
1415 Laskin Rd
Virginia Beach, VA 23451
757-424-2672
FAX: 757-263-2801
e-mail: tcta@aol.com
tcta.access.org

*Pat Mc Gee, Manager*
*Myra Jessie Flint, Designee*

Nonprofit organization providing persons with disabilities access, support, and knowledge-re: technology; organization contracts for consultations, workshops and training, or conventional and assistive technologies including computers, augmented communication devices and software; resources: extensive lending library of educational software; books and videotape library; yearly individual membership and corporate membership fees; working/presentation and evaluation fees available upon request.

**1567 Vermont Assistive Technology Project: Department of Aging & Disabilities**
Agency of Human Services
103 S Main St
Waterbury, VT 05671-9800
802-241-2620
800-750-6355
FAX: 802-241-3048
TTY: 802-241-1464
e-mail: atinfo@dail.state.vt.us
http://atp.vermont.gov

*Julie L Tucker, Project Director*
*Betsy Ross, Administration*
*Dan Gilman, AT Access Specialist*

Increase the awareness and change policies to insure assistive technology is available to all Vermonters with disabilities.

**1568 Washington Technology Access Center**
3010 NE 113th St
Seattle, WA 98125-6847
425-883-4141
FAX: 425-776-3663

*Grant Lord, Founder*

The center was formed as a nonprofit organization to demonstrate how computer technology can transform limitations into opportunities for those with special needs. WTAC's mission is to increase the awareness, understanding and implementation of computer technology for persons with special needs, their friends, families, educators, rehabilitation and health professionals, public officials and employees.

**1569 Xerox Imaging Systems/Adaptive Products Department**
Personal Reader Department
9 Centennial Dr
Peabody, MA 01960-7906
978-977-2000
800-248-6550
FAX: 978-977-2409

Offers information on new services, assistive devices and technology for blind, visually impaired, learning disabled and other print disabled individuals.

## Keyboards, Mouses & Joysticks

**1570 A4 Tech (USA) Corporation**
5585 Brooks St
Montclair, CA 91763-4547
909-988-9633
e-mail: info@a4tech.com
www.a4tech.com

*Robert C*

Manufacturers of a cordless mouse, trackballs and joysticks that emulate mouse controls, flatbed scanners, modified keyboards, and other specialty mouses.

**1571 Abacus**
3150 Patterson Ave SE
Grand Rapids, MI 49512
616-698-0330
800-451-4319
FAX: 616-698-0325
e-mail: info@abacuspub.com
abacuspub.com

*Arnie Lee, President*

Designs a mouse software program that permits programs written for one computer to be run on another computer.

**1572 Ability Center of Greater Toledo**
5605 Monroe St
Sylvania, OH 43560-2793
419-885-5733
FAX: 419-882-4813
abilitycenter.org

*Tim Harrington, Executive Director*
*Dale Abell, Director of Program Development*
*Debbie Andriette, Director of Human Resources*
*Kimberley Arnett, Director of Community Operations*

Manufactures keyboard wrist supports to help prevent repetitive motion disorders.

**1573 Dreamer**
TS Micro Tech
17109 Gale Ave
City of Industry, CA 91745-1810
626-939-8998
FAX: 626-839-8516
e-mail: sales@fancard.com
fancard.com

*Steve Heung, Owner*

An intelligent, add-on function keyboard providing single-keystroke access to multiple-keystroke functions.

**1574 FlexShield Keyboard Protectors**
Hooleon Corporation
P.O.Box 589
Melrose, NM 88124-589
928-634-7515
800-937-1337
FAX: 928-634-4620
e-mail: sales@hooleon.com
www.hooleon.com

*Barry Green, Sales Manager*
*Joan Crozier, President*

Transparent keyboard protectors allowing instant recognition of keytop legends. They have a matte finish to reduce glare. Also available are large print and braille keyboard labels and large print/braille combo labels.

**1575 Infogrip: King Keyboard**
1794 E Main St
Ventura, CA 93001-3411
805-652-0770
800-397-0921
FAX: 805-652-0880
e-mail: support@infogrip.com
www.infogrip.com

*Aaron Gaston, VP*
Giant alternative keyboard that plugs directly into a computer- no special interface is required. The keys are 1.25 inches in diameter, slightly recessed, and provide both tactile and auditory feedback. The King has a built-in keyboard so that you can rest on its surface without activating keys. This keyboard allows you to control both keyboard and mouse functions, so it's great for people who have difficulty maneuvering a standard mouse. *$130.00*

**1576 Infogrip: Large Print Keyboard**
1794 E Main St
Ventura, CA 93001-3411
805-652-0770
800-397-0921
FAX: 805-652-0880
e-mail: support@infogrip.com
www.infogrip.com

*Aaron Gaston, VP*
Standard Windows keyboard with large print keys. The keyboard and its keys are the same size as a standard keyboard; however, the print has been enhanced. The characters measure .5 by .25 inches, about 3 times larger than standard keyboard characters. *$130.00*

**1577 Infogrip: OnScreen**
1794 E Main St
Ventura, CA 93001-3411
805-652-0770
800-397-0921
FAX: 805-652-0880
e-mail: support@infogrip.com
www.infogrip.com

*Aaron Gaston, VP*
OnScreen features word prediction/completion (with an editable dictionary), Key Dwell Timer (a timer that selects a key under the cursor), integrated Verbal Keys Feedback, Show and Hide Keys (turns on/off keys to prevent access and minimize confusion) a Smart Window (automatically re-positions the keyboard or panels off of the area in use). On Screen also offers edit, numeric, macro, calculator and Windows enhancement capabilities. *$200.00*

**1578 IntelliKeys**
Intelli Tools
1720 Corporate Cir
Petaluma, CA 94954-6924
707-773-2000
800-547-6747
FAX: 707-773-2001
e-mail: customerservice@cambiumtech.com
intellitools.com

*Arjan Khalsa, CEO*
Alternative, touch-sensitive keyboards; plugs into any Macintosh or Windows computer. *$395.00*

**1579 IntelliKeys USB**
Intelli Tools
1720 Corporate Cir
Petaluma, CA 94954-6924
707-773-2000
800-547-6747
FAX: 707-773-2001
e-mail: info@intellitools.com
intellitools.com

*Arjan Khalsa, CEO*
IntelliKeys alternative keyboard for USB computers and Windows 2000, Mac OSX. *$69.95*

**1580 Key Tronic KB 5153 Touch Pad Keyboard**
KeyTronic
N. 4424 Sullivan Road
Spokane Valley, WA 99216
509-928-8000
FAX: 509-927-5555
e-mail: EMSsales@keytronicems.com
keytronic.com

*Craig.D Gates, President/CEO*
*Ronald.F Klawitter, Executive Vice President of Administration and Chief Financial Officer*
*Douglas G. Burkhardt, Executive Vice President of Worldwide Operations*
*Philips S Hochberg, Vice President of Business Development*
Integrates a regular full-function keyboard, a numeric keypad with a cursor key capability and a touch pad into one unit.

**1581 Liaison Computer Work Station**
Genesis One Technologies
343 W Milltown Rd
Wooster, OH 44691-7287
330-345-8888
888-221-5032
FAX: 775-252-4834
e-mail: sales@genesis.net
www.genesisone.net

*Albert S Miller, Office Manager*
A full function computer work station for high level (C-2 to C-5) spinal cord injured users. It transparently emulates both keyboard and mouse, using rapid direct selection which commonly yields letter by letter typing rates of 15 to 20 words per minute. The user controls it via proportional IR remote control from the DU-IT controlled power wheelchair and chin or tongue/lip controller or via a desk-mounted proportional controller as a stand alone device. Full ECU features included. *$ 4685.00*

**1582 Magic Wand Keyboard**
In Touch Systems
11 Westview Rd
Spring Valley, NY 10977-1832
845-354-7431
800-332-6244
e-mail: sc@magicwandkeyboard.com
magicwandkeyboard.com

*Jerry Crouch, President*
*Susan Crouch, VP*
The magic wand keyboard allows your child to use a keyboard and mouse easily-no light beams, microphones, or sensors to wear of position. This miniature computer keyboard has zero-force keys that work with the slightest touch of a wand (hand-held of mouthstick). No strength required.

**1583 McKey Mouse**
In Touch Systems
11 Westview Rd
Spring Valley, NY 10977-1832
845-354-7431
800-332-6244
e-mail: sc@magicwandkeyboard.com
magicwandkeyboard.com

*Jerry Crouch, President*
*Susan Crouch, VP*
Microsoft compatible mouse for persons with little or no hand/arm movement; it's an option for the Magic Wand Keyboard and adds full mouse function without adding any extra devices.

**1584 PortaPower Plus**
Words+
Ste 109
42505 10th St W
Lancaster, CA 93534-7059
661-723-6523
800-869-8521
FAX: 661-723-2114
e-mail: info@words-plus.com
www.words-plus.com

Rechargeable battery pack designed to give longer life and remote usage time to laptop computers and other portable battery-operated devices and accessories. Requires a 12 volt auto adapter. *$149.00*

**1585 Step on It! Computer Control Pedals**
Suite 118
1290 Carmead Pkwy
Sunnyvale, CA 94086
408-736-6086
FAX: 408-736-6083
e-mail: bilbo@bilbo.com
www.bilbo.com

*Sergei Burkov, President*
BILBO Innovations, Inc. manufactures and sells Step On It keyboard control pedals. Ergonomic foot switches to emulate keystrokes and mouse clicks. Designed for victims of Repetitive Strain Injury (RSI), Carpal Tunnel Syndrome (CTS), handicapped and disabled. *$99.00*

**1586 Unicorn Keyboards**
Intelli Tools
1720 Corporate Cir
Petaluma, CA 94954-6924
707-773-2000
800-547-6747
FAX: 707-773-2001
e-mail: info@intellitools.com
intellitools.com

*Arjan Khalsa, CEO*
Alternative keyboards with membrane surface and large, user-defined keys. Large and small sizes are available. *$250.00*

## Scanners

**1587 Scanmaster**
Ste 17
4 Townsend W
Nashua, NH 03063-4220
603-886-3874
FAX: 603-886-1736

*Robert Labadini, CEO*
A digital color scanner for desktop scanning. It allows the user to digitalize, modify, enhance and store images in color or black and white.

**1588 Scanning WSKE**
Words+
Ste 109
42505 10th St W
Lancaster, CA 93534-7059
661-723-7723
888-266-9294
FAX: 661-723-5524
e-mail: info@simulations-plus.com
simulations-plus.com

*Walter S Woltosz, M.S., M.A.S., Chairman, President and Chief Executive Officer*
*Virginia E. Woltosz. M.B.A., Secretary - Treasurer*
*John DiBella, Vice President, Marketing and Sales*
*Momoko A. Beran, M.B.A., Chief Financial Officer*
A software and a hardware product designed to operate on an IBM compatible PC. The software provides dual word prediction, abbreviation expansion, five different methods of voice output, and access to commercial software applications.

**1589 System 2000/Versa**
Words+
Ste 109
42505 10th St W
Lancaster, CA 93534-7059
661-723-6523
800-869-8521
FAX: 661-723-2114
e-mail: info@words-plus.com
www.words-plus.com
Provides all of the strategies currently being used in AAC, from dynamic display color pictographic language, to dual-word prediction text language, in a single system.

**1590 Zygo-UsaSvc Corporation**
P.O.Box 1008
48834 Kato Road Suite 101-A
Fremont, CA 94538
510-493-0997
800-234-6006
e-mail: zygo@zygo-usa.com
www.zygo-usa.com

*Adam Weiss, Vp Sales & Marketing*
ZYGO-USA has been involved in manufacturing and distributing assistive technologies since 1974. They specialize in augmentative and alternative computer access. They offer a wide range of technology products to our clients so they can achieve a greater independence and to enhance the quality of their lives. These soloutins improve and individual's ability to learn, work, and interact with family and friends.

## Screen Enhancement

**1591 Boxlight**
Boxlight Corporation
NE 151 Highway 300 Suite A, PO Box
Belfair, WA 98528
360-464-2119
866-972-1549
e-mail: sales@boxlight.com
www.boxlight.com

*Herb Myers, CEO/Founder*
*Sloan Myers, Founder*
*Hank Nance, President*
BOXLIGHT is a global presentation solutions partner for trainers, educators and professional speakers. Solutions include projector sales, national rental service, technical support, repair, and presentation peripherals. For more information visit us online.

**1592 FDR Series of Low Vision Reading Aids**
Optelec U S
Ste C
3030 Enterprise Ct
Vista, CA 92081-8358
800-826-4200
FAX: 800-368-4111
e-mail: info@optelec.com
www.optelec.com

*Stephan Terwolbeck, President*
*Michiel van Schaik, VP*
*Janet Lennex , Director of Customer Excellence*
*Jade Arbelo , Director of Human Resources*
The Low Vision Reading Aids features; high resolution, positive and negative display, a high-quality zoom lens, versatile swivel and a 12 inch or 19 inch high-resolution monitor, color or black and white, computer compatible, or portable.

**1593 InFocus**
AI Squared
P.O.Box 669
Manchester Center, VT 05255
802-362-3612
800-859-0270
FAX: 802-362-1670
e-mail: zoomtext@alsquared.com
http://www.aisquared.com

*David Wu, CEO*
*Jost Eckhardt, VP of Engineering*
*Scott Moore, VP of Marketing*
*Shawn Warren, VP of Product Support*
A memory-resident program that magnifies text and graphics - the entire screen, a single line or a portion of the screen.

**1594 Portable Large Print Computer**
Human Ware
175 Mason Cir
Concord, CA 94520-1213
925-566-9242
800-722-3393
FAX: 925-681-4630
e-mail: us.info@humanware.com
humanware.com

*Gilles Pepin, CEO*
*Yves Boisjoli, Vice President, Business Development*
*Michel Cote, Corporate Director*
*Georges Morin, Corporate Director*
A portable large print computer which magnifies up to 64 times. It is linked to a PC and has a hand-held camera.

**1595 ZoomText**
A I Squared
P.O.Box 669
Manchester Center, VT 05255
802-362-3612
800-859-0270
FAX: 802-362-1670
e-mail: zoomtext@alsquared.com
www.aisquared.com

*David Wu, CEO*
*Jost Eckhardt, VP of Engineering*
*Scott Moore, VP of Marketing*
*Shawn Warren, VP of Product Support*
A RAM-resident program that enlarges screen characters up to eight times. It runs on IBM PC, XT, AT and PS/2.

## Speech Synthesizers

**1596 Artic Business Vision (for DOS) and Artic WinVision (for Windows 95)**
Artic Technologies
3456 Rodchester Road
Troy, MI 48083
248-588-7370
FAX: 248-588-2650
e-mail: info@artictech.com
http://www.articannex.ws/artictec.htm

*Dale McDaniel, Founder*
*Kathy Gargagliano, Founder*
A speech processor for blind computer users featuring true interactive speech with spread sheets, word processors, database managers, etc. Now available with both Windows 3.1 and Windows 95 access. *$ 495.00*

**1597 Computerized Speech Lab**
Kay Elemetrics Corporation
3 Paragon Drive
Montvalle, NJ 07645
973-628-6200
800-289-5297
FAX: 201-391-2063
kaypentax.com

*John Crump, President*
Hardware/software for the acquisition, analysis/display, playback and storage of speech signals.

**1598 Digital Voice for Talking Database**
Hy-Tek Manufacturing Company
1980 W Us Highway 30
Sugar Grove, IL 60554-9518
630-466-3900
FAX: 630-466-7678

*William Bastian, Owner*
This product adds speech to PC files. Uses include personnel identification and security, multilingual training, assembly instructions and reminders.

**1599 DynaVox Technologies Speech Communication Devices**
Dyna Vox Technologies
Ste 400
2100 Wharton St
Pittsburgh, PA 15203-1945
412-381-4883
866-396-2869
FAX: 412-381-5241
e-mail: sales@dynavoxtech.com
www.dynavoxtech.com

*Ed Donnelly, CEO*
*Michelle Heying, President and COO*
*Kenneth Misch, CFO*
*Richard Ellenson, Chief Vision Officer*
Develops and manufactures speech communication devices that help individuals who are unable to speak due to speech, language and/or learning disabilities to communicate quickly and easily.

**1600 Electronic Speech Assistance Devices**
Luminaud
8688 Tyler Blvd
Mentor, OH 44060-4348
440-255-9082
800-255-3408
FAX: 440-255-2250
e-mail: info@luminaud.com
luminaud.com

*Thomas M Lennox, President*
*Dorothy Lennox, VP*
Offers a full line of speech aids, voice amplifiers, mini-vox amplifiers, laryngectomec products.

**1601 In Cube Pro Voice Command**
Command Corporation
Ste 200
11080 Old Roswell Rd
Alpharetta, GA 30009-4779
770-360-1230
e-mail: webmaster@commandcorp.com
www.commandcorp.com

Continuous speech recognition system which can be used by people with disabilities. IN CUBE provides greatly increased capability, enhanced computer control and access. Blind and low-vision users gain voice access to the graphic user interface. Mobility-impaired people, including quadriplegics, benefit from voice window navigation and voice macro command input. Victims of various repetitive strain injuries RSI use IN CUBE to replace and eliminate repetitive keyboard and mouse operations. *$395.00*

**1602 Keywi**
Hoffmann + Krippner Inc.
200 Westpark Drive
Suite 270
Peachtree City, GA 30269
770-487-1950
FAX: 770-487-1945
www.keywi-usa.com

Membrane keyboard and membrane switch technology

**1603 Laptalker**
Automated Functions
Ste 420
7700 Leesburg Pike
Falls Church, VA 22043-2618
703-883-9797
FAX: 703-883-9798

*R Morford, Owner*
A portable talking computer that gives visually impaired people complete desk top PC compatibility.

**1604 Little Mack Communicator**
AbleNet
2625 Patton Road
Roseville, MN 55113-1308
651-294-2200
800-322-0956
FAX: 651-294-2259
e-mail: customerservice@ablenetinc.com
www.ablenetinc.com

*Jen Thalhuber, CEO*
The Little Mack Communicator has 2 minutes of memory and has an angled switch surface making it easy to see and access. The switch surface is 2 1/2 inches in diameter. Detachable mounting base makes it easy to position a single unit in a variety of locations. *$129.00*

**1605 Mega Wolf Communication Device**
Wayne County Regional Educational Service Agency
33500 Van Born Rd
Wayne, MI 48184-2474
734-334-1300
www.resa.net

*Kimberly Kaminski, Assistant Operations*
*Marlene E Davis, Administrator*
A low cost voice output communication device which is primarily intended to provide the power of speech to those individuals who are most severely challenged mentally and/or physically. The WOLF device is User programmable and uses the Texas Instruments' Touch and Tell case and touch panel; ADAMLAB electronics with synthesized (robotic) voice. For users able to point with approximately 6 ounces of pressure. *$400.00*

**1606 Phone Manager**
Consultants for Communication Technology
508 Bellevue Ter
Pittsburgh, PA 15202-1146
412-761-6062
FAX: 412-761-7336
e-mail: cct@concommtech.com
www.concommtech.com

*Kathleen H Miller Phd, Partner*
*Jaime Oliva, Partner*
Software that allows the user to dial an outgoing call directly from the computer, even with a single switch. Synthesized speech is sent through the phone line. The synthesizer then turns into a speaker phone enabling hands free, two way conversations. *$300.00*

**1607 Talking Screen**
Words+
Ste 109
42505 10th St W
Lancaster, CA 93534-7059
661-723-7723
888-266-9294
FAX: 661-723-5524
e-mail: info@simulations-plus.com
simulations-plus.com

*Walter S Woltosz, M.S., M.A.S., Chairman, President and Chief Executive Officer*
*Virginia E. Woltosz. M.B.A., Secretary - Treasurer*
*John DiBella, Vice President, Marketing and Sales*
*Momoko A. Beran, M.B.A., Chief Financial Officer*
An augmentative communication program that allows the user to select graphic symbols on the display to produce speech output. Symbols can be used either singly or in sequence as picture abbreviations. *$ 1395.00*

**1608 Turnkey Computer Systems for the Visually, Physically, and Hearing Impaired**
E VA S
39 Canal St P.O. Box 371
Westerly, RI 02891-1511
401-596-3155
800-872-3827
FAX: 401-596-3979
TTY: 401-596-3500
e-mail: contact@evas.com
evas.com

*Gerald Swerdlick, Owner*
*Jerry Swerdlick, CEO*
Offers clear speech with pleasant inflection and tonal quality as well as variable pitch, intonation and voices.

**1609 Voice-It**
V XI Corporation Incorporated
271 Locust Street
Denver, NH 03820
603-742-2888
800-742-8588
FAX: 603-742-5065
e-mail: info@vxicorp.com
www.vxicorp.com

*Michael Ferguson, President*
*Tom Manero, Chief Financial Officer*
*Phil Pane, Vice President Operations*
*Brian Cole, Vice President Engineering*
Adds voice to popular spreadsheet and word processing applications on IBM PCs and compatibles, turning spreadsheets and word processing documents into talking documents.

**1610 Window-Eyes**
G W Micro
725 Airport North Office Park
Fort Wayne, IN 46825
260-489-3671
FAX: 260-489-2608
e-mail: sales@gwmicro.com
www.gwmicro.com

*Dan Weirich, Owner/Vice President of Sales and Marketing*
*Doug Geoffray, Owner*
Provides access to available software automatically reading information important to the user while ignoring the rest. A screen reader for the windows operative system.

## Software: Math

**1611 AIMS Multimedia**
Discovery Education
8145 Holton Dr
Florence, KY 41042-3009
859-342-7200
FAX: 877-324-6830
e-mail: info@multimedia.com
www.aimsmultimedia.com

*Mike Wright, Director*
*Lynn Fassett, Administrative Assistant*
*Cindy Vogt, Human Resources Executive*
AIMS Multimedia is a leader in the production and distribution of training and educational programs for the business and K-12 communities via YHS, interactive CD-ROM, DVD and Internet streaming video.

**1612 Basic Math: Detecting Special Needs**
Allyn & Bacon
Ste 300
75 Arlington St
Boston, MA 02116-3988
617-848-7500
800-852-8024
FAX: 617-944-7273
e-mail: samplingdept@pearson.com
greenehoffman.com

Describes special mathematics needs of special learners.
*180 pages*
*ISBN 0-205116-35-3*

**1613 Campaign Math**
Mindplay
3130 N Dodge Blvd
Tucson, AZ 85716-1726
800-221-7911
e-mail: mail@mindplay.com
http://www.mindplay.com

*John.E Crowley, CEO*
*Dan Figurski, Senior Vice President of Business Development*
*Linda.M Garcia, Director of Educational Services*
*Chris Coleman, Manager of Software Development*
A complete program on the electoral process as well as a math package which teaches ratios, fractions and percentages.

**1614 Educational Activities Software**
5600 W 83rd Street
Suite 300, 8200
Bloomington, MN 55437
866-243-8464
FAX: 239-225-9299
e-mail: jwest@orchardlng.com
www.ea-software.com

*Jan West, Sales Director*
Comprehensive MATH SKILLS software tutorials teach concepts ranging from rounding and tables to measuring area. MAC/WIN compatible. *$369.00*
*Per Unit*

**1615 Fraction Factory**
Queue
80 Hathaway Drive
Stratford, CT 06615
800-232-2224
FAX: 800-775-2729
e-mail: jdk@queueinc.com
www.queueinc.com

*Anna Christopoulos, General Manager*
*Peter Uhrynowski, Comptroller*
*Steve Pernett, Director of Printing and Graphics*
*Ann Pleszko, Shipping Manager*
In 1980, Jonathan Kantrowitz started Queue, Inc. as an educational software company. After twenty thriving years publishing and distributing high-quality software to educators, Queue began transitioning from software to workbooks, focusing on state-specific test preparation.

**1616 Information & Referral Services**
Information + Referral Services
2590 N. Alvernon Way
Tucson, AZ 85712
520-323-1708
FAX: 520-325-8841
e-mail: inform@azinfo.org
www.azinfo.org

*Patti Caldwell, Executive Director*
*Chuck Palm, Treasurer*
*Ben Rensvold, Vice President*
*Tom DeSollar, President*
Provides information about health and human services for people in Arizona over the telephone. Information specialists help callers clarify their needs, and provide referrals to the appropriate service agency.

**1617 King's Rule**
WINGS for Learning
1600 Green Hills Rd
Scotts Valley, CA 95066-4981
831-426-2228
FAX: 831-464-3600

*Ani Stocks, Owner*
A software mathematical problem solving game. Students discover mathematical rules as they work their way through a castle and generate and test a working hypothesis by asking questions.

**1618 Learning About Numbers**
C&C Software
5713 Kentford Cir
Wichita, KS 67220-3131
316-683-6056
800-752-2086

*Carol Clark, President*
Three programs use the power of computer graphics to provide young children with a variety of experiences in working with numbers. *$50.00*

**1619 Math Rabbit**
Learning Company
Ste 1900
100 Pine St
San Francisco, CA 94111-5205
415-659-2000
800-825-4420
FAX: 415-659-2020
e-mail: thelearningco@hmhpub.com
http://www.thelearningcompany.com

*Barry O'Callaghan, CEO*
Teaches early math concepts by matching objects to numbers, then adding and subtracting up to 18.

**1620 Math for Everyday Living**
Educational Activities Software
5600 W 83rd Street
Suite 300, 8200
Bloomington, MN 55437
866-243-8464
FAX: 239-225-9299
e-mail: jwest@orchardlng.com
www.ea-software.com

*Jan West, Sales Director*
Real life math skills are taught with this tutorial and practice software program. Examples include Paying for a Meal (addition and subtraction), Working with Sales Slips (multiplication), Unit Pricing (division), Sales Tax (percent), Earning with Overtime (fractions) plus more. Software: CD-ROM, Windows, MAC, and DOS. *$159.00*

**1621 Math for Successful Living**
Siboney Learning Group
5600 W 83rd Street
Suite 300, 8200
Bloomington, MN 55437
866-243-8464
FAX: 239-225-9299
e-mail: jwest@orchardlng.com
www.ea-software.com

*Jan West, Sales Director*
These programs include managing a checking account, budgeting, shopping strategies and buying on credit.

**1622 Piece of Cake Math**
Queue Inc
80 Hathaway Drive
Stratford, CT 06615
800-232-2224
FAX: 800-775-2729
e-mail: jdk@queueinc.com
qworkbooks.com

*Anna Christopoulos, General Manager*
*Peter Uhrynowski, Comptroller*
*Steve Pernett, Director of Printing and Graphics*
*Ann Pleszko, Shipping Manager*
In 1980, Jonathan Kantrowitz started Queue, Inc. as an educational software company. After twenty thriving years publishing and distributing high-quality software to educators, Queue began transitioning from software to workbooks, focusing on state-specific test preparation.

**1623 Puzzle Tanks**
WINGS for Learning
1600 Green Hills Rd
Scotts Valley, CA 95066-4981
831-426-2228
FAX: 831-464-3600

*Ani Stocks, Owner*
A mathematical problem solving game that involves multi-step problems.

**1624 Right Turn**
WINGS for Learning
1600 Green Hills Rd
Scotts Valley, CA 95066-4981
831-426-2228
FAX: 831-464-3600

*Ani Stocks, Owner*
Requires students to predict, experiment and learn about the mathematical concepts of rotation and transformation.

**1625 RoboMath**
3130 N Dodge Blvd
Tucson, AZ 85716-1726
800-221-7911
e-mail: mail@mindplay.com
http://www.mindplay.com

*John.E Crowley, CEO*
*Dan Figurski, Senior Vice President of Business Development*
*Linda.M Garcia, Director of Educational Services*
*Chris Coleman, Manager of Software Development*
A complete program on the electoral process as well as a math package which teaches ratios, fractions and percentages.

**1626 Stickybear Math I Deluxe**
Optimum Resource
1 Mathews Drive, Suite 107
Hilton Head Island, SC 29926- 3689
843-689-8000
FAX: 843-689-8008
e-mail: info@stickybear.com
www.stickybear.com

*Richard Hefter, President*
Sharpen basic addition and subtraction skills with this captivating series of math exercises. Grades Pre-K to 2. Available in as single edition with sizing up to 30 users at a site. English/Spanish. *$59.95*

**1627 Stickybear Math II Deluxe**
Optimum Resource
1 Mathews Drive, Suite 107
Suite 107
Hilton Head Island, SC 29926-3689
843-689-8000
FAX: 843-689-8008
e-mail: info@stickybear.com
www.stickybear.com

*Richard Hefter, President*
Multiplication and division, beginning with the elementary problems and developing into the more complex problems with regrouping. Grades 2-4. Available for single user through the 30 user site package. English/Spanish. *$59.95*

**1628 Stickybear Math Splash**
Optimum Resource
1 Mathews Drive, Suite 107
Hilton Head Island, SC 29926- 3689
843-689-8000
FAX: 843-689-8008
e-mail: info@stickybear.com
www.stickybear.com

*Richard Hefter, President*
Unique multiple activities keep the learning level high while children acquire skills in addition, subtraction, multiplication and division. K-5th grade. Available as single edition up to 30 user site package. English/Spanish. *$59.95*

**1629 Stickybear Math Word Problems**
Optimum Resource
1 Mathews Drive, Suite 107
Hilton Head Island, SC 29926- 3689
843-689-8000
FAX: 843-689-8008
e-mail: info@stickybear.com
www.stickybear.com

*Richard Hefter, President*
Hundreds of different word problems make it easy for students to practice basic math skills around analyzing and solving word problems. Grades 1-5. Available as single edition up to 30 user site package. English/Spanish. *$59.95*

**1630 Stickybear Money**
Optimum Resource
1 Mathews Drive, Suite 107
Suite 107
Hilton Head Island, SC 29926-3667
843-689-8000
FAX: 843-689-8008
e-mail: info@stickybear.com
www.stickybear.com

*Chris Gintz, President*
Teaches children to recognize US coins and paper money and introduces simple counting. K to 3rd grade. Bilingual. *$59.95*

**1631 Stickybear Numbers Deluxe**
Optimum Resource
1 Mathews Drive, Suite 107
Suite 107
Hilton Head Island, SC 29926-3689
843-689-8000
FAX: 843-689-8008
e-mail: info@stickybear.com
www.stickybear.com

*Richard Hefter, President*
Counting and number recognition are as easy as 1-2-3 with this award-winning program. Teaches number recognition of numbers 0-9 and 0-30. Pre-K to 2nd grade. Available as single edition up to 30 user site package. *$59.95*

**1632 Tomorrow's Promise: Mathematics**
Compass Learning
203 Colorado Street
Austin, TX 78701
512-478-9600
800-678-1412
866-586-7387
www.compasslearning.com

*Eric Loeffel, President*
*Trey Chambers, Chief Financial Officer*
*Rebecca Tongsinoon Bristol, Vice President of Product Development*
*Ann Henson, Vice President, Curriculum & Instruction*
By integrating interdisciplinary content and real-world application of skills, this product emphasizes the practical value of fundamental math skills. It helps your students develop a problem-solving aptitude for ongoing mathematics achievement.

## Software: Miscellaneous

**1633 Adventures in Musicland**
Electronic Courseware Systems
1713 S State St
Champaign, IL 61820-7258
217-359-7099
800-832-4965
FAX: 217-359-6578
e-mail: support@ecsmedia.com
www.ecsmedia.com

*G Peters, President*
*Jodie Varner, Marketing Manager*
This unique set of music games features characters from Lewis Carroll's, Alice in Wonderland. Players learn through pictures, sounds, and animation which help develop understanding of

musical tones, composers, and musical symbols. Games include MusicMatch, Melody Mixup, Picture Perfect and Sound Concentration. *$49.95*

**1634 Ai Squared**
P.O.Box 669
Manchester Center, VT 05255-669 802-362-3612
800-859-0270
FAX: 802-362-1670
e-mail: zoomtext@aisquared.com
http://www.aisquared.com

*David Wu, CEO*
*Jost Eckhardt, VP of Engineering*
*Scott Moore, VP of Marketing*
*Shawn Warren, VP of Product Support*
Developers of software for the visually impaired.

**1635 All About You: Appropriate Special Interactions and Self-Esteem**
P CI Educational Publishing
P.O.Box 34270
San Antonio, TX 78265-4270 210-377-1999
800-594-4263
800-471-3000
FAX: 888-259-8284
e-mail: submissions@pcieducation.com
www.pcicatalog.com

*Lee Wilson, President and CEO*
*Randy Pennington, Executive VP*
*Jeff McLane, Founder*
*David Keith, Vice President of IT*
This game offers parents and game players a new line of communication when discussing various issues such as learning to be thoughtful, respecting the rights and feelings of others, how to make and keep friends and more. *$49.95*

**1636 All Star Review**
Tom Snyder Productions
Ste 6
100 Talcott Ave
Watertown, MA 02472-5703 800-342-0236
e-mail: dealer@tomsnyder.com.
tomsnyder.com

*Rick Abrams, Manager*
*Tom Synder, Founder*
This package turns group review into a baseball game for small and large groups.

**1637 Attainment Company**
I ET Resources
P.O.Box 930160
Verona, WI 53593-160 608-845-7880
800-327-4269
FAX: 608-845-8040
e-mail: info@attainmentcompany.com
attainmentcompany.com

*Don Bastian, President*
*Julie Denu, Technical Support*
*Theresa O'Connor, Office Manager*
Augmentative/alternative communication, software, videos, print and hands-on functional life skills and basic acdemics materials for developmental and cognitive disabilities.

**1638 Attention Getter**
Soft Touch
12301 Central Ave NE Ste 205
4300 Stine Rd
Blaine, MN 55434 763-755-1402
888-755-1402
FAX: 763-862-2920
e-mail: support@marblesoft.com
www.softtouch.com

*Joyce Meyer, President*
The whimsical photos morph to another photo and then to a third photo in categories. Paired with interesting sounds and music, the photo animations are so engaging that the student is motivated to activate the computer to see and hear the next one. This is a perfect vehicle to achieve goals aimed at attention getting, activating a switch or intentionally. Compatible with USB IntelliKeys keyboards.

**1639 Attention Teens**
Soft Touch
12301 Central Ave NE Ste 205
Blaine, MN 55434 763-755-1403
888-755-1403
FAX: 763-862-2921
e-mail: support@marblesoft.com
www.softtouch.com

*Joyce Meyer, President*
Attention Teens (formerly known as Loony Teens) is a program for teens with disabilities who need powerful input to get their attention. Attention Teens is a computer program to do just this. Paired with interesting sounds and music, the photo animations are so engaging that the student is motivated to activate the computer to see and hear the next one. Compatible with USB IntelliKeys keyboards.

**1640 Away We Ride**
Soft Touch
12301 Central Ave NE Ste 205
4300 Stine Rd
Blaine, MN 55434 763-755-1404
888-755-1404
FAX: 763-862-2922
e-mail: support@marblesoft.com
www.softtouch.com

*Joyce Meyer, President*
Software for children and teens. For Macintosh and PC.

**1641 Bailey's Book House**
Edmark Corporation
P.O.Box 97021
Redmond, WA 98073-9721 425-556-8400
800-691-2986
www.edmark.com

Software for children.

**1642 Battenberg & Associates**
11135 Rolling Springs Dr
Carmel, IN 46033-3629 317-843-2208

*Jan Battenberg, Owner*
Offers various software programs that develop the user's visual memory, sequencing skills, word recognition, hand-eye coordination and more.

**1643 Behavior Skills: Learning How People Should Act**
PCI Education Publishing
P.O.Box 34270
San Antonio, TX 78265-4270 210-377-1999
800-594-4263
FAX: 888-828-
www.pcieducation.com

*Jeff Clain, CEO*
*Erin Kinard, VP Product Development/Publisher*
Helps players learn what behavior is acceptable and what behavior is not acceptable in the real world. *$49.95*

**1644 Blocks in Motion**
Don Johnston
26799 W Commerce Dr
Volo, IL 60073-9675 847-740-0749
800-999-4660
FAX: 847-740-7326
e-mail: info@donjohnston.com
donjohnston.com

*Ruth Ziolkowski, President*
This unique art and motion program makes drawing, creating and animating fun and educational for all users. Based on the Piagetian Theory for motor-sensory development, this program promotes the concept that the process is as educational and as much fun as the end result. *$79.00*

**1645 CINTEX: Speak to Your Appliances**
NanoPac
Ste 302
4823 S Sheridan Rd
Tulsa, OK 74145-5717 918-665-0329
800-580-6086
FAX: 918-665-0361
TTY: 918-665-2310
e-mail: info@nanopac.com
nanopac.com

*Silvio Cianfrone, President*
CINTEX, with a voice recognition program, will control up to 256 off/on appliances, dial and answer the phone, flash for call waiting, dial from a directory, control TV's, VCR's, stereos and more - all with your voice. CINTEX2 includes the necessary hardware and voice macros which you can use to immediately control your environment. You can tailor these macros to your personal needs and add new macros. Pops-up over current application allowing instant access. $695-$2,000.

**1646 Car Builder Deluxe**
Optimum Resource
1 Mathews Drive, Suite 107
Suite 107
Hilton Head Island, SC 29926-3689 843-689-8000
FAX: 843-689-8008
e-mail: info@stickybear.com
www.stickybear.com

*Richard Hefter, President*
As design engineers, users build cars on screen, specifying chassis length, wheelbase, engine type, transmission, fuel tank size, suspension, steering, tires and brakes. All functional choices are interrelated and will affect the performance of the final design. Grades 3 & up. *$59.99*

**1647 Center for Best Practices in Early Childhood**
32 Horrabin Hall
Macomb, IL 61455 309-298-1634
FAX: 309-298-2305
e-mail: l-robinson1@wiu.edu
www.wiu.edu/thecenter/

*Linda Robinson, Assistant Director*
The Center, part of the College of Education and Human Services at Western Illinois University, provides products, training materials, and information related to best practices for educators and families of young children with disabilities.

**1648 Clock**
Compass Learning
203 Colorado St
Austin, TX 78701-3922 512-478-9600
800-678-1412
866-586-7387
www.compasslearning.com

*Eric Loeffel, President*
*Trey Chambers, Chief Financial Officer*
*Rebecca Tongsinoon Bristol, Vice President of Product Development*
*Ann Henson, Vice President, Curriculum & Instruction*
An extremely simple, easy-to-use program for children who are learning how to read the time of day from clocks and digital displays. Apple and MS-DOS and Mac available. *$39.95*

**1649 Community Skills: Learning to Function in Your Neighborhood**
Programming Concepts
P.O.Box 34270
San Antonio, TX 78265-4270 210-377-1999
800-594-4263
800-471-3000
FAX: 888-259-8284
e-mail: submissions@pcieducation.com
www.pcieducation.com

*Lee Wilson, President and CEO*
*Randy Pennington, Executive VP*
*Jeff McLane, Founder*
*David Keith, Vice President of IT*
Offers parents and educators a functional way to teach community life skills. *$49.95*

**1650 Companion Activities**
Soft Touch
12301 Central Ave NE Ste 205
4300 Stine Rd
Blaine, MN 55434 763-755-1404
888-755-1404
FAX: 763-862-2922
e-mail: support@marblesoft.com
www.softouch.com

*Joyce Meyer, President*
Print your own books, worksheets, flash cards, board games, matching games, bingo games, card games and many more. This CD offers numerous companion activities to different SoftTouch software titles. Activities range from very easy to difficult. Companion activities are great tools to reinforce learning. Use the work sheets - black and white and color - in the inclusion class for students with special needs.

**1651 Concepts on the Move Advanced Preacademics**
Soft Touch
12301 Central Ave NE Ste 205
4300 Stine Rd
Blaine, MN 55434 763-755-1404
888-755-1404
FAX: 763-862-2922
e-mail: support@marblesoft.com
www.softouch.com

*Joyce Meyer, President*
Choose from five concepts groups: categories, occupations, functions, goes with and prepositions. Use our Steps to Learning Design to choose how many concepts to present at one time and where to place each one in the scan array, on screen keyboard or IntelliKeys keyboard. Watch and listen as the concept morphs or changes and music plays. The words are also shown to reinforce emerging literacy skills. Compatible with USB IntelliKeys.

**1652 Cooking Class: Learning About Food Preparation**
Programming Concepts
P.O.Box 34270
San Antonio, TX 78265-4270
210-377-1999
800-594-4263
800-471-3000
FAX: 888-259-8284
e-mail: submissions@pcieducation.com
www.pcieducation.com

*Lee Wilson, President and CEO*
*Randy Pennington, Executive VP*
*Jeff McLane, Founder*
*David Keith, Vice President of IT*
This game offers parents and educators a new way to teach basic preparation skills. Kitchen safety and sanitation are stressed throughout the game. *$49.95*

**1653 Dilemma**
Educational Activities Software
5600 W 83rd Street
Suite 300, 8200
Bloomington, MN 55437
866-243-8464
FAX: 239-225-9299
e-mail: jwest@orchardlng.com
www.ea-software.com

*Jan West, Sales Director*
Realistic stories with a choice of different gripping endings, color graphics, a built-in dictionary and a user controlled reading rate make these computer programs compelling enough to interest all students. Comprehension and vocabulary questions follow each story. *$159.00*

**1654 Dino-Games**
Academic Software
3504 Tates Creek Road
Lexington, KY 40517-2601
859-552-1020
FAX: 253-799-4012
e-mail: asistaff@acsw.com
http://www.acsw.com/

*Warren E Lacefield PhD, President*
*Penelope Ellis, Marketing Director*
Dino-Games are single switch software programs for early switch practice. Dinosaur games provide practice in pattern recognition, cause and effect demonstration, directionality training, number concepts and problem solving. They are compatible with most popular switch interfaces and alternate keyboards. For Macintosh, IBM and compatibles. DINO-LINK is a matching game; DINO-MAZE is a series of maze games; DINO-FIND is a game of concentration; and DINO-DOT is a collection of dot-to-dot games.
*$39.95 per game*

**1655 Directions: Technology in Special Education**
DREAMMS for Kids
273 Ringwood Rd
Freeville, NY 13068-5606
607-539-9930
FAX: 607-539-9930
e-mail: janet@dreamms.org
www.dreamms.org

A CD containing all of 'Directions' past articles and information gathered from their newsletter which lists resources for assistive and adaptive computer ethnologies in the home, school and community. *$24.95*

**1656 ESI Master Resource Guide**
Educational Software Institute
4213 S 94th St
Omaha, NE 68127-1223
402-592-3300
800-955-5570
FAX: 402-592-2017
e-mail: info@edsoft.com
www.edsoft.com

*Lee Myers, President*
*Kathy Cavanaugh, Catalog Manager*
Educational Software Institute (ESI) provides a one-stop shop to purchase software titles by all of the best publishers. The ESI Master Gold Book catalog and CD-ROM represents more than 400 software publishers, with information on more than 8,000 software titles. Take the confusion out of software selection by calling ESI for all of your software needs - including competitive prices, software previews, knowledgeable assistance, and the largest selection available all in one place.
*Yearly*

**1657 EZ Keys**
Words+
Ste 109
42505 10th St W
Lancaster, CA 93534-7059
661-723-7723
888-266-9294
FAX: 661-723-5524
e-mail: info@simulations-plus.com
simulations-plus.com

*Walter S Woltosz, M.S., M.A.S., Chairman, President and Chief Executive Officer*
*Virginia E. Woltosz. M.B.A., Secretary - Treasurer*
*John DiBella, Vice President, Marketing and Sales*
*Momoko A. Beran, M.B.A., Chief Financial Officer*
A software and hardware product designed to operate on an IBM compatible PC. The software provides dual word prediction, abbreviation expansion, five different methods of voice output and access to commercial software applications. *$1395.00*

**1658 Early Games for Young Children**
Queue Incorporated
80 Hathaway Drive
Stratford, CT 06615
800-232-2224
FAX: 800-775-2729
e-mail: jdk@queueinc.com
qworkbooks.com

*Anna Christopoulos, General Manager*
*Peter Uhrynowski, Comptroller*
*Steve Pernett, Director of Printing and Graphics*
*Ann Pleszko, Shipping Manager*
Software that includes nine activities that entertain preschoolers in honing basic math and language skills.

**1659 Early Music Skills**
Electronic Courseware Systems
1713 S State St
Champaign, IL 61820-7258
217-359-7099
800-832-4965
FAX: 217-359-6578
e-mail: support@ecsmedia.com
www.ecsmedia.com

*G Peters, President*
*Jodie Varner, Marketing Manager*
A tutorial and drill program designed for the beginning music student. It covers four basic music reading skills: recognition of line and space notes; comprehension of the numbering system for the musical staff; visual and aural identification of notes moving up and down; and recognition of notes stepping and skipping up and down. *$ 39.95*

**1660 Eating Skills: Learning Basic Table Manners**
PCI Education Publishing
P.O.Box 34270
San Antonio, TX 78265-4270
210-377-1999
800-594-4263
FAX: 210-377-1121
e-mail: pciinfo@pcieducation.com
www.pcieducation.com

*Erin Kinard, VP Product Development/Publisher*
*Jeff Clain, CEO*
Offers parents and educators a functional way to teach and reinforce basic table manners. *$49.95*

**1661 Electronic Courseware Systems**
1713 S State St
Champaign, IL 61820-7258
217-359-7099
800-832-4965
FAX: 217-359-6578
e-mail: sales@ecsmedia.com
www.ecsmedia.com

*Jodie Varner, Manager*
*G Peters, President*

Offers a complete library of instructional software for music, math, science and social studies.

**1662 Fall Fun**
Soft Touch
12302 Central Ave NE Ste 205
Blaine, MN 55434
763-755-1404
888-755-1404
FAX: 763-862-2922
e-mail: support@marblesoft.com
www.softtouch.com

*Joyce Meyer, President*

Your students can begin their day with the Pledge of Allegiance, Pumpkins, Owls, and Cats. Witches adorn Five Pumpkins Sitting on the Gate. Five Fat Turkeys out smart the pilgrims with song and antics. The owl and cat have songs of their own. A variety of activities reinforce concepts such as short, tall, first, second, third, same and different. Fall Fun includes cause and effect and easy to more difficult levels. Eight songs in all.

**1663 Five Green & Speckled Frogs**
Soft Touch
12303 Central Ave NE Ste 205
Blaine, MN 55434
763-755-1404
888-755-1404
FAX: 763-862-2922
e-mail: support@marblesoft.com
www.softouch.com

*Joyce Meyer, President*

Laugh, learn and sing with Five Humorous Frogs. Activities start with cause and effect and progress to teach directionality and simple subtraction. This classic song makes learning numbers and number worlds easy. Selections can be set to 2, 3, 4, 5, or 6 on-screen choices. Two games are included. One teaches direction on a number line. If the child moves the frog in the correct direction, the frog gets a point. The other game teaches beginning subtraction.

**1664 Free and User Supported Software for the IBM PC: A Resource Guide**
McFarland & Company
960 Nc Highway 88 W
Jefferson, NC 28640-8813
336-246-4460
800-253-2187
FAX: 336-246-5018
e-mail: info@mcfarlandpub.com
www.mcfarlandpub.com

*Victor.D Lopez, Author*
*Kenneth.J Ansley, Author*

A selection of word processing, database management, spreadsheets, and graphics programs are described and evaluated. Describes how the program works and its strengths and weaknesses. Rating charts cover such aspects as ease of use, ease of learning, documentation, and general utility. *$27.50*
*224 pages Paperback*
*ISBN 0-89950 -99-0*

**1665 GoalView: Special Education and RTI Student Management Information System**
Learning Tools International
2391 Circadian Way
Santa Rosa, CA 95407-5439
707-521-3530
800-333-9954
e-mail: info@goalview.com
ltools.com

*Cathy Zier, President/CEO*
*Natalie Sipes, VP*
*Michael R. Paul, Director of IT/Senior Web Engineer*

A Web Based information system for students, educators and parents that enables accountability and achievement tracking; prepares IDEA compliant IEP's in minutes; provides over 250,000 education standards and special education goals and objectives in English and Spanish; generates Federal compliance reports; and creates IDEA GoalCard progress reports for students, schools and districts for every reporting period.

**1666 HELP**
V OR T Corporation
P.O.Box 60132
Palo Alto, CA 94306-132
650-322-8282
888-757-8678
FAX: 650-327-0747
e-mail: custserv@vort.com
vort.com

*Tom Holt, Owner*

A software version of HELP, covers over 650 skills in 6 developmental areas; cognitive, motor skills, language, gross motor, social and self-help.

**1667 Handbook of Adaptive Switches and Augmentative Communication Devices**
Academic Software
3504 Tates Creek Road
Lexington, KY 40517-2601
859-552-1020
FAX: 253-799-4012
e-mail: asistaff@acsw.com
http://www.acsw.com/

*Warren E Lacefield PhD, President/Author*
*Penelope Ellis, Marketing Director*
*Cindy L George, Author*

This second edition contains physical descriptions and laboratory test data for a variety of commercially available pressure switches and augmentative communication devices and chapters on physical interaction, seating and positioning, and control access. It is an essential tool for assistive technology professionals and therapists who make decisions concerning physical access.
*$60.00*
*300 pages Hardcover*

**1668 HandiWARE**
Microsystems Software
600 Worcester Rd
Framingham, MA 01702-5303
508-626-8511
800-828-2600
FAX: 508-879-1069
e-mail: infor@microsys.com
www.handiware.com

*Terri McGrath, Sales/Marketing*
*Bill Kilroy, Product Manager*

Adapted access software, assists persons with physical, hearing and visual impairments in accessing computers running DOS and Windows. HandiWARE is a suite of 8 software programs which provide users with screen magnification, alternate keyboard access, word prediction, augmentative communication, hands free telephone access, a visual beep. $20.00-$595.00.

**1669 How to Write for Everyday Living**
Educational Activities Software
5600 W 83rd Street
Suite 300, 8200
Bloomington, MN 55437-585
866-243-8464
FAX: 239-225-9299
e-mail: jwest@orchardlng.com
www.ea-software.com

*Jan West, Sales Director*
An individualized Life Skills WRITING Software program emphasizing the reading, writing, communication and reference skills needed for real-life tasks: preparing a resume, an employment form, a business letter and envelope, a learner's permit, a social security application and banking forms. *$159.00*

**1670 I KNOW American History**
Soft Touch
12302 Central Ave NE Ste 205
Blaine, MN 55434-2352
763-755-1404
888-755-1404
FAX: 763-862-2922
e-mail: support@marblesoft.com
www.softtouch.com

*Joyce Meyer, President*
The new I KNOW programs is the way students practice attending, choice making and turn-taking while uncovering learning puzzles. Each press reveals more of the image while the narrator reads the text on the screen. Offers three levels of language: short phrases, short sentences and longer sentences to match the student's learning level. Choose from the five topic areas: American Symbols, Westward Movement, Early Colonial Americans, Industrial Revolution and Biographies.

**1671 I KNOW American History Overlay CD**
Soft Touch
12302 Central Ave NE Ste 205
Blaine, MN 55434-2352
763-755-1404
888-755-1404
FAX: 763-862-2922
e-mail: support@marblesoft.com
www.softtouch.com

*Joyce Meyer, President*
Use this Overlay CD with I KNOW American History program. Includes standard overlays and SoftTouch's changeable overlays. Includes Overlay Printer by IntelliTools. Use Overlay Maker by IntelliTools (not included) to modify the overlays or to make additional learning materials.

**1672 Incite Learning Series**
Don Johnston
26799 W Commerce Dr
Volo, IL 60073-9675
847-740-0749
800-999-4660
FAX: 847-740-7326
e-mail: info@donjohnston.com
donjohnston.com

*Ruth Ziolkowski, President*
A collection of original short films and a thought-provoking instruction model to engage every student in the critical thinking and feeling process. This research-based program was developed around the science of how students learn best using the theory of 'anchored instruction' and 'front-loading' standards-based curriculum. *$79.00*

**1673 Innovation Management Group**
179 Niblick Rd
Ste 454
Paso Robles, CA 93446
818-701-1579
800-889-0987
FAX: 818-936-0200
e-mail: cs@imgpresents.com
www.imgpresents.com

*Jerry Hussong, VP of Marketing*
Publisher of the Assistive Technology Suite. The ultimate set of general purpose, adaptive computer access available today. Site License includes ALL computers and ALL active students and teachers at a single or multi-site location.

**1674 IntelliPics Studio 3**
Intelli Tools
1720 Corporate Cir
Petaluma, CA 94954-6924
707-773-2000
800-547-6747
FAX: 707-773-2001
e-mail: info@intellitools.com
intellitools.com

*Arjan Khalsa, CEO*
Multimedia authoring tool for both students and teachers to create activities, games, quizzes, slide shows, reports and presentations. *$395.00*

**1675 KIDS (Keyboard Introductory Development Series)**
Electronic Courseware Systems
1713 S State St
Champaign, IL 61820-7258
217-359-7099
800-832-4965
FAX: 217-359-6578
e-mail: sales@ecsmedia.com
www.ecsmedia.com

*G Peters, President*
*Jodie Varner, Marketing Manager*
A four disk series for the very young. Zoo Puppet Theater reinforces learning correct finger numbers for piano playing; Race Car Keys teaches keyboard geography by recognizing syllables or note names; Dinosaurs Lunch teaches placement of the notes on the treble staff; and Follow Me asks the student to play notes that have been presented aurally. *$49.95*

**1676 Keyboard Tutor, Music Software**
Electronic Courseware Systems
1713 S State St
Champaign, IL 61820-7258
217-359-7099
800-832-4965
FAX: 217-359-6578
e-mail: sales@ecsmedia.com
www.ecsmedia.com

*G Peters, President*
*Jodie Varner, Marketing Manager*
Presents exercises for learning elementary keyboard skills including knowledge of names of the keys, piano keys matched to notes, notes matched to piano keys, whole steps and half steps. Each lesson allows unlimited practice of the skills. The program may be used with or without a midi keyboard attached to the computer. *$39.95*

**1677 Keyboarding by Ability**
Teachers Institute for Special Education
9933 NW 45th St
Sunrise, FL 33351-4744
954-235-7940
FAX: 866-843-0765
e-mail: Support@Special-Education-Soft.com
www.special-education-soft.com

*Gary Byowitz, President*
Allows the learning disabled or dyslexic student to acquire keyboarding skills through visually cued alphabetical approach designed and tested to meet the specific learning style needs of this unique population at every grade level. Package contains: IBM software, a set of lesson plans and instructional goals; supplemental graded data input exercises. *$148.95*

1678 **Keyboarding for the Physically Handicapped**
Teachers Institute for Special Education
9933 NW 45th St
Sunrise, FL 33351-4744
954-235-7940
FAX: 866-843-0765
e-mail: Support@Special-Education-Soft.com
www.special-education-soft.com

*Jack Heller, Director/Owner*
*Gary Byowitz, President*
Custom designed touch typing programs for any student. A person needs order by the number of usable fingers on each hand (not counting the thumb), and whether or not a one finger or a head-pointer edition is wanted. Package includes IBM software; a complete set of lesson plans and instructional goals. *$149.95*

1679 **Keyboarding with One Hand**
Teachers Institute for Special Education
P.O.Box 2300
Wantagh, NY 11793-140
FAX: 516-781-4070
e-mail: jackheller@aol.com
www.users.aol.com/jackheller

*Jack Heller, Director*
This 22 lesson tutorial developed through 25 years of research, testing and teaching allows a student with one hand to acquire employable keyboarding skills using a touch system designed for the standard IBM PC keyboard. *$79.95*

1680 **LPDOS Deluxe**
Optelec U S
Ste C
3030 Enterprise Ct
Vista, CA 92081-8358
800-826-4200
FAX: 800-368-4111
e-mail: info@optelec.com
www.optelec.com

*Stephan Terwolbeck, President*
*Michiel van Schaik, VP*
*Janet Lennex , Director of Customer Excellence*
*Jade Arbelo , Director of Human Resources*
Large print software programs. *$595.00*

1681 **Large Print DOS**
Optelec U S
Ste C
3030 Enterprise Ct
Vista, CA 92081-8358
800-826-4200
FAX: 800-368-4111
e-mail: info@optelec.com
www.optelec.com

*Stephan Terwolbeck, President*
*Michiel van Schaik, VP*
*Janet Lennex , Director of Customer Excellence*
*Jade Arbelo , Director of Human Resources*

1682 **Laureate Learning Systems**
110 E Spring St
Winooski, VT 05404-1898
802-655-4755
800-562-6801
FAX: 802-655-4757
e-mail: info@llsys.com
laureatelearning.com

*Mary Wilson, Owner*
*Kathy Hollandsworth, Office Manager*
Laureate publishes award-winning talking software for children and adults with disabilities. Programs cover cause and effect, language development, cognitive processing, and reading. High-quality speech, colorful graphics and amusing animation make learning fun. Accessible with touchscreen, single switch, keyboard and mouse. No reading required. Available on a hybrid CD-ROM for Windows and Macintosh. Visit our website for more information or call for a free catalog.

1683 **Learning Company**
Ste 400
222 3rd Ave SE
Cedar Rapids, IA 52401-1542
319-395-9626
888-242-6747
FAX: 319-395-0217
e-mail: info@riverdeep.net
http://web.riverdeep.net

*Barry O'Callaghan, Executive Chairman & Chief Executive Officer*
*Tony Mulderry, Executive Vice President, Corporate Development*
*Jim*
*Jim Ruddy, Chief Revenue Officer*
*Ciara Smyth, Executive Vice President, Global Business Operations*
Software for children. For Macintosh or Windows (3.1 DOS or Windows 95, Windows 98 required). The Learning Company has been added to Riverdeep.

1684 **Little Red Hen**
Compass Learning
203 Colorado Street
Austin, TX 78701
512-478-9600
800-678-1412
866-586-7387
FAX: 619-622-7873
www.compasslearning.com

*Eric Loeffel, President*
*Trey Chambers, Chief Financial Officer*
*Rebecca Tongsinoon Bristol, Vice President of Product Development*
*Ann Henson, Vice President, Curriculum & Instruction*
Children learn about the rewards of hard work when they discover who the Little Red Hen's friends miss out on freshly baked bread. Puzzles, rhymes, story writing and other interactive exercises enhance the creative learning process. *$34.95*

1685 **Looking Good: Learning to Improve Your Appearance**
Programming Concepts
P.O.Box 34270
San Antonio, TX 78265-4270
210-377-1999
800-594-4263
800-471-3000
FAX: 888-259-8284
e-mail: submissions@pcieducation.com
www.pcieducation.com

*Janie Haugen, Program Director*
*Lee Wilson, President and CEO*
*Randy Pennington, Executive VP*
*Jeff McLane, Founder*
This game offers a creative way to discuss all areas of grooming. *$49.95*

1686 **Monkeys Jumping on the Bed**
Soft Touch
12302 Central Ave NE Ste 205
Blaine, MN 55434
763-755-1404
888-755-1404
FAX: 763-862-2922
e-mail: support@marblesoft.com
www.softouch.com

*Joyce Meyer, President*
This program combines a favorite preschool song with number and color activities. Children and adults will enjoy engaging music and delightful animation. Students with cognitive delays respond to upbeat music and interesting sounds. Large graphics help learners focus on the action. Several important concepts are presented in enjoyable activity formats. Students learn cause and effect in Let's Play and Just for Fun.

**1687 Morse Code WSKE**
Words+
Ste 109
42505 10th St W
Lancaster, CA 93534-7059
661-723-7723
888-266-9294
FAX: 661-723-5524
e-mail: info@simulations-plus.com
simulations-plus.com

*Walter S Woltosz, M.S., M.A.S., Chairman, President and Chief Executive Officer*
*Virginia E. Woltosz. M.B.A., Secretary - Treasurer*
*John DiBella, Vice President, Marketing and Sales*
*Momoko A. Beran, M.B.A., Chief Financial Officer*
A software and hardware product designed to operate on an IBM compatible PC.

**1688 Multi-Scan Single Switch Activity Center**
Academic Software
3504 Tates Creek Road
Lexington, KY 40517-2601
859-552-1020
FAX: 253-799-4012
e-mail: asistaff@acsw.com
http://www.acsw.com/

*Warren E Lacefield PhD, President*
*Penelope Ellis, Marketing Director*
A single switch activity center containing four educational games: Match, Maze, Dot-to-Dot, and Concentration, along with six graphics libraries; Dinosaurs, Sports, Animals, Independent Living, Vocations, and Cosmetology. MULTI-SCAN allows you to select a graphic library, choose games for each user, and adjust the difficulty level and other settings for each game. Other features allow you to save the game setups under each user's name and print out individual performance reports after sessions. *$154.00*

**1689 Muppet Learning Keys**
WINGS for Learning
1600 Green Hills Rd
Scotts Valley, CA 95066-4981
831-426-2228
FAX: 831-464-3600

*Ani Stocks, Owner*
Designed to introduce children to the world of the computer as they become familiar with letters, numbers and colors.

**1690 My Own Pain**
Soft Touch
12302 Central Ave NE Ste 205
Blaine, MN 55434-2352
763-755-1404
888-755-1404
FAX: 763-862-2922
e-mail: support@marblesoft.com
www.softtouch.com

*Joyce Meyer, President*
Three activities - three levels. Press the switch and the paint brush chooses the color and paints the vehicle. Music reinforces the sounds when the picture is complete. A second activity allows the student to choose the color and paint the vehicle parts any color he or she wants. The third activity is a blueprint. Print the color that matches the one in the wire drawing. Color the drawing to complete the picture.

**1691 Old MacDonald's Farm Deluxe**
Soft Touch
12302 Central Ave NE Ste 205
Blaine, MN 55434-2352
763-755-1404
888-755-1404
FAX: 763-862-2922
e-mail: support@marblesoft.com
www.softtouch.com

*Joyce Meyer, President*
Toddlers, preschoolers and early elementary students will be entertained and captivated by the six major activities and animations in the delightful program. Includes 18 real animation images or 9 cartoon like characters. The teacher or child can choose which animals they want to sing about. Some activities are designed for children within the normal population, others are designed for students with moderate and severe disabilities.

**1692 Optimum Resource Educational Software**
Optimum Resource
1 Mathews Drive, Suite 107
Suite 107
Hilton Head Island, SC 29926-3689
843-689-8000
FAX: 843-689-8008
e-mail: info@stickybear.com
www.stickybear.com

*Richard Hefter, President*
A complete topical curriculum of reading, math, keyboard skills and science programs that are age and skill specific. Programs include: Early Learning for Pre-K to 1st grade with introductions to numbers, language, shapes, and time; Language Arts from Pre-K to 12; Math for Pre-K to 12; two distinct Science programs; Tools for Educators provides Spelling and Math generators; and Bilingual programs for Pre-K through 9th grade. All are available as single user up to 30 user site packages.

**1693 Optimum Resources/Stickybear Software**
1 Mathews Drive, Suite 107
Ste 107
Hilton Head Island, SC 29926
843-689-8000
FAX: 843-689-8008
e-mail: info@stickybear.com
www.stickybear.com

*Richard Hefter, President*
Publisher of award-winning educational software for thirty years. Programs in use by millions of students nationwide. *$59.95*

**1694 Please Understand Me: Software Program and Books**
Cambridge Educational
132 West 31st Street
17th Floor
New York, NY 10001
800-322-8755
FAX: 800-678-3633
e-mail: custserv@films.com
www.cambridgeeducational.com
Promotes self-understanding while helping each student understand they are different from others. *$69.00*
*209 pages BiAnnual*
*ISBN 0-927368-56-x*

**1695 Pond**
WINGS for Learning
1600 Green Hills Rd
Scotts Valley, CA 95066-4981
831-426-2228
FAX: 831-464-3600

*Ani Stocks, Owner*
Software game that teaches pattern recognition and encourages observation, trial and error and the interpretation of data.

**1696 Print, Play & Learn #1 Old Mac's Farm**
Soft Touch Incorporated
12302 Central Ave NE Ste 205
Blaine, MN 55434
763-755-1404
888-755-1404
FAX: 763-862-2922
e-mail: support@marblesoft.com
www.softtouch.com

*Joyce Meyer, President*
Once your students have completed Old Mac's Farm, let them use the fun off-computer activities to continue learning. Over 25 activities with 250 sheets you print. Board games, dot-to-dot drawings, word puzzles, make a scene, flash cards. Concentration, sentence strips, worksheets and much more are available for teachers to expand their teaching goals. This CD is full of activities to print and use.

**1697 Print, Play & Learn #7: Sampler**
Soft Touch
12302 Central Ave NE Ste 205
Blaine, MN 55434
763-755-1404
888-755-1404
FAX: 763-862-2922
e-mail: support@marblesoft.com
www.softtouch.com

*Joyce Meyer, President*
Print, Play and Learn Sampler gives you over 200 activities organized by training, easy, medium and hard levels so you can ready to help your student advance. Activities cover a wide range of basic knowledge, including colors, shapes, numbers, letters and much, much more. Note: Requires Overlay Maker or Overlay Printer by IntelliTools and a color printer.

**1698 Puzzle Power: Sampler**
Soft Touch
12302 Central Ave NE Ste 205
Blaine, MN 55434
763-755-1404
888-755-1404
FAX: 763-862-2922
e-mail: support@marblesoft.com
www.funsoftware.com

*Joyce Meyer, President*
Puzzle Power - Sampler offers a variety of puzzles in different themes. Each theme puzzle is followed by a puzzle of one item in this category. For example, first solve a puzzle for occupations. Then, solve a puzzle that is a baker. The pictures are large, clear and easily identifiable.

**1699 Puzzle Power: Zoo & School Days**
Soft Touch
12302 Central Ave NE Ste 205
Blaine, MN 55434
763-755-1404
888-755-1404
FAX: 763-862-2922
e-mail: support@marblesoft.com
www.softtouch.com

*Joyce Meyer, President*
Here is a program for all of our students who need puzzle skills, but cannot access commercial puzzles. Puzzle Power puzzles start with just two pieces and progress to 16 pieces. The pictures are large, clear and easily identifiable. Four different activities enable all students to be successful. Automatic Placement: the student just presses the switch or keyboard to place the pieces. Magnet Mouse: all the student needs to do is move the mouse and it drops into place.

**1700 Rodeo**
Soft Touch
12302 Central Ave NE Ste 205
Blaine, MN 55434
763-755-1404
888-755-1404
FAX: 763-862-2922
e-mail: support@marblesoft.com
www.funsoftware.com

*Joyce Meyer, President*
Rodeo action and familiar tunes for teens and preteens. Four activities invite students to learn, laugh, and sing as they go to the rodeo with up to six age-peer friends. Age-appropriate graphics with surprising animations reinforce the learning. The graphics are large and colorful, the melodies familiar, and the words descriptive of the action on the screen.

**1701 Shop Til You Drop**
Soft Touch
12302 Central Ave NE Ste 205
Blaine, MN 55434
763-755-1404
888-755-1404
FAX: 763-862-2922
e-mail: support@marblesoft.com
www.softtouch.com

*Joyce Meyer, President*
Designed specifically for preteens and teens with moderate and severe disabilities, this program will become a staple for the classroom. The student goes shopping and can choose which outfits to put together. They may choose to purchase the outfit - of course, with mom's credit card. Another activity is a video arcade game about money. Shop 'Til You Drop can be adjusted from a single switch cause-and-effect program to row-and-column scanning to direct choice.

**1702 Songs I Sing at Preschool**
Soft Touch
12302 Central Ave NE Ste 205
Blaine, MN 55434
763-755-1404
888-755-1404
FAX: 763-862-2922
e-mail: support@marblesoft.com
www.funsoftware.com

*Joyce Meyer, President*
Songs I Sing at Preschool offers many options for the teacher and the student. Over the years, our software has used music because our students really respond to the sounds and rhythms of songs. Teachers select which songs to present, how many to present at one time and where to place each song on the overlay, keyboard or scan array.

**1703 Stickybear Early Learning Activities**
Optimum Resource
1 Mathews Drive, Suite 107
Suite 107
Hilton Head Island, SC 29926-3689
843-689-8000
FAX: 843-689-8008
e-mail: info@stickybear.com
www.stickybear.com

*Richard Hefter, President*
Two modes of play allow youngsters to learn through prompted direction or by the discovery method. Lively animation and sound keep attention levels high as children learn writing, counting, shapes, opposites and colors. Stickybear Early Learning Activities is bilingual, so youngsters can build skills in both English and Spanish. Pre-K to 1st grade. *$59.95*

**1704 Stickybear Kindergarden Activities**
Optimum Resource
1 Mathews Drive, Suite 107
Suite 107
Hilton Head Island, SC 29926-3689
843-689-8000
FAX: 843-689-8008
e-mail: info@stickybear.com
www.stickybear.com

*Richard Hefter, President*
This dynamic new multifaceted program covers a wide range of preschool skills that go far beyond the strictly academic. At Stickybear's house, children discover the alphabet, numbers, shapes, colors, plus - social skills, important safety messages and delightful off-screen activities that foster creativity. Over three hours of original music can be composed by a child and saved for future use. *$59.95*

**1705 Stickybear Science Fair Light**
Optimum Resource
1 Mathews Drive, Suite 107
Suite 107
Hilton Head Island, SC 29926-3689 843-689-8000
FAX: 843-689-8008
e-mail: info@stickybear.com
www.stickybear.com

*Richard Hefter, President*
The first in the new series of science-based programs Stickybear Science Fair Light presents a content rich environment which allows students in grades 7-12 to explore, experiment with and understand light and it's properties. The program presents experiments, both structured and free-form, which allow users to work with prisms, lenses, color mixing, optical illusions and more. *$59.95*

**1706 Stickybear Town Builder**
Optimum Resource
1 Mathews Drive, Suite 107
Hilton Head Island, SC 29926- 3689 843-689-8000
843-689-8008
e-mail: info@stickybear.com
www.stickybear.com

*Richard Hefter, President*
Children learn to read maps, build towns, take trips and use a compass in this simulation program. *$59.95*

**1707 Stickybear Typing**
Optimum Resource
1 Mathews Drive, Suite 107
Hilton Head Island, SC 29926- 3689 843-689-8000
FAX: 843-689-8008
e-mail: info@stickybear.com
www.stickybear.com

*Richard Hefter, President*
Sharpen typing skills with three challenging activities: Stickybear Keypress, Stickybear Thump and Stickybear Stories. Pre-K to 5th. *$59.95*

**1708 Storybook Maker Deluxe**
Compass Learning
203 Colorado Street
Austin, Te 78701 512-478-9600
800-678-1412
866-586-7387
FAX: 619-622-7873
www.compasslearning.com

*Eric Loeffel, President*
*Trey Chambers, Chief Financial Officer*
*Rebecca Tongsinoon Bristol, Vice President of Product Development*
*Ann Henson, Vice President, Curriculum & Instruction*
Using Storybook Maker Deluxe and their imaginations, students can create and publish stories filled with exciting graphics. Students can write stories and watch as the text appears in the setting they've chosen. Engaging sounds and music, plus lively animations, provide positive learning reinforcement throughout the program. *$44.95*

**1709 Super Challenger**
Electronic Courseware Systems
1713 S State St
Champaign, IL 61820-7258 217-359-7099
800-832-4965
FAX: 217-359-6578
e-mail: support@ecsmedia.com
www.ecsmedia.com

*Jodie Varner, Manager*
*G Peters, President*
An aural-visual musical game that increases the player's ability to remember a series of pitches as they are played by the computer. The game is based on a 12-note chromatic scale, a major scale, and a minor scale. Each pitch is reinforced visually with a color representation of a keyboard on the display screen. Computer/software. *$39.95*

**1710 Switch Basics**
Soft Touch
12302 Central Ave NE Ste 205
Blaine, MN 55434 763-755-1404
888-755-1404
FAX: 763-862-2922
e-mail: support@marblesoft.com
www.funsoftware.com

*Joyce Meyer, President*
Discover whimsical animations and real life pictures while learning switch operations. Intriguing and humorous, nine different programs offer a multitude of learning experiences for all ages. Program options include: cause and effect, scanning, step scanning, row and column activities for one or two players. Watch the clouds roll away revealing African animals; visit the beauty salon or barber shop; work two to sixteen piece puzzles; or add swimming fish to a huge aquarium.

**1711 Switch Interface Pro 5.0**
Don Johnston
26799 W Commerce Dr
Volo, IL 60073-9675 847-740-0749
800-999-4660
FAX: 847-740-7326
e-mail: info@donjohnston.com
donjohnston.com

*Ruth Ziolkowski, President*
Allows individuals with physical disabilities to access the computer. Five ports accommodate multiple switches and emulate everything from a single-click to a return. Consequently, individuals gain access to the widest variety of switch-accessible software available. It requires no software and can be used with both Windows and Macintosh computers. *$79.00*

**1712 Teach Me Phonemics Series Bundle**
SoftTouch
Ste 401
4300 Stine Rd
Bakersfield, CA 93313-2352 661-396-8676
877-763-8868
FAX: 661-396-8760
e-mail: support@softtouch.com
www.funsoftware.com

*Joyce Meyer, President*
*Roxanne Butterfield, Marketing*
The Teach Me Phonemics Series Bundle includes one copy of each Teach Me Phonemics program - Initial, Medial, Final and Blends - four CD's in all.

**1713 Teach Me Phonemics Super Bundle**
SoftTouch
Ste 401
4300 Stine Rd
Bakersfield, CA 93313-2352 661-396-8676
877-763-8868
FAX: 661-396-8760
e-mail: softtouch@funsoftware.com
www.funsoftware.com

*Roxanne Butterfield, Marketing*
*Joyce Meyer, President*
Teach Me Phonemics Super Bundle includes all 4 Teach Me Phonemics programs and all 4 Teach Me Phonemics overlay CD's - eight CD's in all.

**1714 Teach Me Phonemics: Blends**
SoftTouch
Ste 401
4300 Stine Rd
Bakersfield, CA 93313-2352
661-396-8676
877-763-8868
FAX: 661-396-8760
e-mail: softtouch@funsoftware.com
www.funsoftware.com

*Roxanne Butterfield, Marketing*
*Joyce Meyer, President*
Teach Me Phonemics - Blends helps students explore words and hear the initial blend sounds. It features musical interludes and movement to engage the student. Teachers select the best combination options to motivate and engage the student. Options turn off and on the fly so you can quickly make changes to keep the student engaged.

**1715 Teach Me Phonemics: Final**
SoftTouch
Ste 401
4300 Stine Rd
Bakersfield, CA 93313-2352
661-396-8676
877-763-8868
FAX: 661-396-8760
e-mail: softtouch@funsoftware.com
www.funsoftware.com

*Roxanne Butterfield*
*Joyce Meyer, President*
Teach me Phonemics - Final helps students explore words and hear the final sounds. It features musical interludes and movement to engage the student. Options turn off and on the fly so you can quickly make changes to keep the student engaged.

**1716 Teach Me Phonemics: Initial**
SoftTouch
Ste 401
4300 Stine Rd
Bakersfield, CA 93313-2352
661-396-8676
877-763-8868
FAX: 661-396-8760
e-mail: softtouch@softtouch.com
www.softtouch.com

*Roxanne Butterfield, Marketing*
*Joyce Meyer, President*
Teach Me Phonemics - Initial helps students explore the words and hear the initial sounds. It features musical interludes and movement to engage the student. Teachers select the best combination options to motivate and engage the student. Options turn off and on the fly so you can quickly make changes to keep the student engaged.

**1717 Teach Me Phonemics: Medial**
SoftTouch
Ste 401
4300 Stine Rd
Bakersfield, CA 93313-2352
661-396-8676
877-763-8868
FAX: 661-396-8760
e-mail: softtouch@softtouch.com
www.softtouch.com

*Roxanne Butterfield, Marketing*
*Joyce Meyer, President*
Teach Me Phonemics - Medial helps students explore the words and hear the medial sounds. It features musical interludes and movement to engage the student. Teachers select the best combination options to motivate and engage the student. Options turn off and on the fly so you can quickly make changes to keep the student engaged.

**1718 Teach Me to Talk**
Soft Touch
12302 Central Ave NE Ste 205
Blaine, MN 55434
763-755-1404
888-755-1404
FAX: 763-862-2922
e-mail: support@marblesoft.com
www.softtouch.com

*Joyce Meyer, President*
The first activity Teach Me to Talk is used as a springboard for the student to learn to speak the word. There are 150 real pictures. When a picture is chosen, it appears on a clear background with musical interludes, movement, written word and spoken word. It culminates by morphing to the corresponding black and white Mayer-Johnson symbol. The second activity Story Time, takes some of these nouns and puts them in four line poetry. This helps students hear the word in the midst of a sentence.

**1719 Teen Tunes Plus**
Soft Touch
12302 Central Ave NE Ste 205
Blaine, MN 55434
763-755-1404
888-755-1404
FAX: 763-862-2922
e-mail: support@marblesoft.com
www.funsoftware.com

*Joyce Meyer, President*
Introduce switch use to older students with disabilities. Large interesting graphics, a variety of musical interludes, and surprising animations are combined with calm soothing music and beautiful pictures in the software specifically designed for preteens and teens with severe cognitive delays and/or physical disabilities, and older students learning to use a switch.

**1720 There are Tyrannosaurs Trying on Pants in My Bedroom**
Compass Learning
203 Colorado St
Austin, TX 78701-3922
512-478-9600
800-678-1412
866-586-7387
FAX: 619-622-7873
www.compasslearning.com

*Eric Loeffel, President*
*Trey Chambers, Chief Financial Officer*
*Rebecca Tongsinoon Bristol, Vice President of Product Development*
*Ann Henson, / Vice President, Customer Support & Services*
In this popular story, Saturday chores turn into fun-filled frolicking when dinosaurs come for a visit. Sounds, music and animation make learning about phonics and vocabulary dyno-mite. *$34.95*

**1721 Three Billy Goats Gruff**
Compass Learning
203 Colorado St
Austin, TX 78701-3922
512-478-9600
800-678-1412
866-586-7387
FAX: 619-622-7873
www.compasslearning.com

*Eric Loeffel, President*
*Trey Chambers, Chief Financial Officer*
*Rebecca Tongsinoon Bristol, Vice President of Product Development*
*Ann Henson, Vice President, Curriculum & Instruction*
Motivating exercises and creative activities provide hours of learning fun while young students follow the adventure of The Three Billy Goats Gruff in this animated version of the timeless tale. *$ 34.95*

**1722 Three Little Pigs**
Compass Learning
203 Colorado St
Austin, TX 78701-3922
512-478-9600
800-678-1412
866-586-7387
FAX: 619-622-7873
www.compasslearning.com

*Eric Loeffel, President*
*Trey Chambers, Chief Financial Officer*
*Rebecca Tongsinoon Bristol, Vice President of Product Development*
*Ann Henson, Vice President, Curriculum & Instruction*
Help young students build reading comprehension and writing skills with this interactive version of the children's classic, The Three Little Pigs. Animated storytelling and creative activities inspire children to read, write and rhyme. *$34.95*

**1723 TouchCorders**
Soft Touch
12302 Central Ave NE Ste 205
Blaine, MN 55434
763-755-1404
888-755-1404
FAX: 763-862-2922
e-mail: support@marblesoft.com
www.funsoftware.com

*Joyce Meyer, President*
TouchCorders are the flexible and easy-to-use communicator designed by Jo Meyer and Linda Bidabe for reach classroom use. TouchCorders are sensitive to touch at every angle and give the student kinesthetic feedback. With the unique Add 'n Touch system, Jo connects the puzzles bases of 2 or more TouchCorders on the fly to present vocabulary, sequencing, story telling, social stories, concepts and other curriculum and communication opportunities.

**1724 TouchWindow Touch Screen**
Riverdeep Incorporated
Ste 1900
100 Pine St
San Francisco, CA 94111-5205
415-659-2000
800-542-4222
FAX: 415-659-2020
e-mail: info@riverdeep.net
riverdeep.net

*Barry O'Callaghan, Executive Chairman & Chief Executive Officer*
*Tony Mulderry, Executive Vice President, Corporate Development*
*Jim*
*Jim Ruddy, Chief Revenue Officer*
*Ciara Smyth, Executive Vice President, Global Business Operations*
Software for children. *$335.00*

**1725 Turtle Teasers**
Soft Touch
12302 Central Ave NE Ste 205
Blaine, MN 55434
763-755-1404
888-755-1404
FAX: 763-862-2922
e-mail: support@marblesoft.com
www.softtouch.com

*Joyce Meyer, President*
Three Games, Three Levels from Easy, Medium to Hard. The Shell Game - easy: Watch one of the three turtles get the tomato. Then watch carefully as they switch positions and pop shut. Choose incorrectly and the frog disappears until the correct one is displayed. The Pond - medium: Watch the tomato disappear somewhere in the pond scene. Tomato Dump - hard: Hit the shell and it turns into the tomato, giving a score. There are different difficulty levels to equalize all students.

**1726 Volcanoes**
Earthware Computer Services
2386 Spring Blvd
Eugene, OR 97403-1861
541-344-1862
FAX: 541-342-3416

*Kathryn Tassinari*
Simulation of volcano in which children play the role of the scientists. *$49.50*

**1727 What Was That!**
Compass Learning
203 Colorado St
Austin, TX 78701-3922
512-478-9600
800-678-1412
866-586-7387
FAX: 619-622-7873
www.compasslearning.com

*Eric Loeffel, President*
*Trey Chambers, Chief Financial Officer*
*Rebecca Tongsinoon Bristol, Vice President of Product Development*
*Ann Henson, Vice President, Curriculum & Instruction*
In this bedtime story, noises in the night send three brother bears scurrying out of bed. Thoughtful questions test young readers' comprehension, while games, voice recording, writing practice and other playful activities stimulate their creativity.

**1728 Wivik 3**
Prentke Romich Company
1022 Heyl Rd
Wooster, OH 44691-9786
330-262-1984
800-262-1984
FAX: 330-263-4829
e-mail: info@prentrom.com
prentrom.com

*David L Moffatt, President*
On-screen keyboard provides access to any application in the latest Windows operating systems. Selections are made by clicking, dwelling or switch scanning. Enhancements include word prediction and abbreviation expansion.

**1729 WordMaker**
Don Johnston
26799 W Commerce Dr
Volo, IL 60073-9675
847-740-0749
800-999-4660
FAX: 847-740-7326
e-mail: info@donjohnston.com
donjohnston.com

*Ruth Ziolkowski, President*
The computer version of Dr Patricia Cunningham's book 'Systematic Sequential Phonics They Use.' The program systematically builds spelling and word decoding skills for struggling readers and writers. *$79.00*

**1730 Write: Out Loud**
Don Johnston
26799 W Commerce Dr
Volo, IL 60073-9675
847-740-0749
800-999-4660
FAX: 847-740-7326
e-mail: info@donjohnston.com
donjohnston.com

*Ruth Ziolkowski, President*
Write: Out Loud is an easy-to-use talking word processor that uses text-to-speech and revision and editing supports to help students write more effectively, more often and with more enthusiasm as they share creative thoughts on paper. *$79.00*

**1731 You Tell Me: Learning Basic Information**
Programming Concepts
P.O.Box 34270
San Antonio, TX 78265-4270
210-377-1999
800-594-4263
800-471-3000
FAX: 888-259-8284
e-mail: submissions@pcieducation.com
www.pcieducation.com

*Lee Wilson, President and CEO*
*Randy Pennington, Executive VP*
*Jeff McLane, Founder*
*David Keith, Vice President of IT*
This game teaches and reinforces basic information all individuals need to know. Questions asked in this game help prepare people to communicate personal identification information important to community survival. *$49.95*

## Software: Professional

**1732 Acrontech International**
5500 Main St
Williamsville, NY 14221-6755
FAX: 716-854-4014
This company supplies software, audio mixers, and closed-caption televisions.

**1733 DPS with BCP**
V OR T Corporation
P.O.Box 60132
Palo Alto, CA 94306-132
650-322-8282
888-757-8678
FAX: 650-327-0747
e-mail: custserv@vort.com
vort.com

*Tom Holt, Owner*
This program uses unique DPS branching techniques to access goals and objectives.

**1734 Diagnostic Report Writer**
Parrot Software
P.O. Box 250755
West Bloomfield, MI 48322
248-788-3223
800-727-7681
FAX: 248-788-3224
e-mail: support@parrotsoftware.com
http://www.parrotsoftware.com

*Fred Weiner, Ph. D., CCC-SP, Owner*
Creates a three page single-spaced diagnostic report for a child with a communication disorder from a list of questions; sections of the report include developmental and background history, oral peripheral exam, speech and language analysis, summary and recommendations.

**1735 Discriptive Language Arts Development**
Educational Activities Software
5600 W 83rd Street
Suite 300, 8200 Tower
Bloomington, MN 55437
888-351-4199
866-243-8464
FAX: 239-225-9299
e-mail: jwest@orchardlng.com
www.ea-software.com

*Alan Stern, Manager*
This multimedia language arts development program provides instruction and application of fundamental English skills and concepts. *$395.00*

**1736 Draft: Builder**
Don Johnston
26799 W Commerce Dr
Volo, IL 60073-9675
847-740-0749
800-999-4660
FAX: 847-740-7326
e-mail: info@donjohnston.com
donjohnston.com

*Ruth Ziolkowski, President*
*Don Johnston, CEO*
*Kevin Johnston, Director of Product Design*
*Ben Johnston, Director of Marketing*
A software-based graphic organizer that breaks down the writing process into manageable chunks to structure planning, organizing, and draft-writing. *$79.00*

**1737 EZ Dot**
CAPCO Capability Corporation
Ste 200
1522 N Washington St
Spokane, WA 99201-2454
FAX: 509-535-1011
http://www.skilltran.com/about.htm, http://ww
A critical software tool used in vocational counseling, job restructuring, recruitment and placement, better utilization of workers, and safety issues. This software offers occupational data by title, code, industry, GEO, DPT, or OGA. *$295.00*

**1738 EZ Keys for Windows**
Words+
Ste 109
42505 10th St W
Lancaster, CA 93534-7059
661-723-6523
800-869-8521
FAX: 661-723-2114
e-mail: info@words-plus.com
www.words-plus.com

*Jean Dobbs, Editorial Director*
*Tim Gilmer, Editor*
*Josie Byzek, Managing Editor*
*Doug Lathrop, Senior Correspondent*
A software and hardware product designed to operate on an IBM compatible PC. The software provides dual word prediction, abbreviation expansion, five different methods of voice output and access to commercial software applications. *$1395.00*

**1739 Goals and Objectives**
JE Stewart Teaching Tools
P.O.Box 15308
Seattle, WA 98115-308
206-262-9538
FAX: 206-262-9538

*Jeff Stewart, Owner*
Goals and Objectives software helps teachers make student plans including IEP's, IPP's and IHP's. The system provides curricula for all students and programs to develop and evaluate plans, print reports and make data forms. Systems are available for Windows and Macintosh for $139.

**1740 Goals and Objectives IEP Program Curriculum Associates LLC**
P.O. Box 2001
N Billerica, MA 01862-901
978-667-8000
800-225-0248
FAX: 800-366-1158
curriculumassociates.com

*Robert Waldron, President/CEO*
*Dave Caron, Chief Financial Officer*
*Patricia Payette, Vice President, Finance*
*Renee Foster, Senior Vice President, Marketing and Product Development*
BRIGANCE CIBS-R standardized scoring conversion software, is a teacher's tool that prints goal and objective pages of the IEP. In less than two minutes per student, a teacher types student data into the computer.

**1741 Nasometer**
Kay Elemetrics Corporation
3 Paragon Drive
Montvale, NJ 07645
973-628-6200
800-289-5297
FAX: 973-628-6363
e-mail: sales@kaypentax.com
kaypentax.com

*John Crump, President*
*Steve Crump, Direct Sales*
Measures the ratio of acoustic energy for the nasal and real-time visual cueing during therapy. Used clinically in the areas of cleft palate, motor speech disorders, hearing impairment and palatal prosthetic fittings.

**1742 PSS CogRehab Software**
Psychological Software Services
6555 Carrollton Ave
Indianapolis, IN 46220-1664
317-257-9672
FAX: 317-257-9674
e-mail: nsc@neuroscience.cnter.com
www.neuroscience.cnter.com

*Odie L Bracy, Executive Director*
PSS CogRehab Software is a comprehensive and easy-to-use multimedia cognitive rehabilitation software available, for clinical and educational use with head injury, stroke LD/ADD and other brain compromises. The packages include 64 computerized therapy tasks which contain modifiable parameters that will accommodate most requirements. Exercises include attention and executive skills, multiple modalities of visuosatial and memory skills, simple, complex, problem-solving skills.
*$260 - $2500*

**1743 Parrot Easy Language Simple Anaylsis**
Parrot Software
P.O.Box 250755
W Bloomfield, MI 48322
248-788-3223
800-727-7681
FAX: 248-788-3224
e-mail: support@parrotsoftware.com
www.parrotsoftware.com

*Dr. Frederic Winer, President*
Designed for grammatical analysis of language samples. The user types and translates language samples of up to 100 utterances.

**1744 SOLO Literacy Suite**
Don Johnston
26799 W Commerce Dr
Volo, IL 60073-9675
847-740-0749
800-999-4660
FAX: 847-740-7326
e-mail: info@donjohnston.com
donjohnston.com

*Ruth Ziolkowski, President*
*Don Johnston, CEO*
*Kevin Johnston, Director of Product Design*
*Ben Johnston, Director of Marketing*
Places all of the right tools, and a wide-range of embedded learning supports, at their fingertips. SOLO includes word prediction, a text reader, graphic organizer and talking word processor, putting students in charge of their own learning and accommodations. Students of varying ages and abilities have access to, and make progress in, the general education curriculum. *$79.00*

**1745 TOVA**
Universal Attention Disorders
3321 Cerritos Avenue
Los Alamitos, CA 90720-6501
562-594-7700
800-729-2886
FAX: 800-452-6919
e-mail: info@tovatest.com
http://www.tovacompany.com

*Lawrence M. Greenberg, MD*
A computerized assessment which, in conjunction with classroom behavior ratings, is a highly effective screening tool for ADD. TOVA includes software, complete instructions, and supporting data including norms.

**1746 Visi-Pitch III**
Kayelemetrics Corporation
3 Paragon Drive
Montvale, NJ 07645
973-628-6200
800-289-5297
FAX: 973-628-6363
e-mail: sales@kaypentax.com
kaypentax.com

*John Crump, President*
*Steve Crump, Direct Sales*
Assists the speech/voice clinician in assessment and treatment tasks across an expansive range of disorders.

## Software: Reading & Language Arts

**1747 Choices, Choices 5.0**
Tom Snyder Productions
Ste 6
100 Talcott Ave
Watertown, MA 02472-5703
800-342-0236
e-mail: ask@tomsnyder.com
tomsnyder.com

*Rick Abrams, Manager*
*Bridget Dalton, Ed.D, Author*
*Peggy Healy Stearns, Ph.D., Author*
*David Dockterman, Ed.D., Author*
Teaches students to take responsibility for their behavior. Helps students develop the skills and awareness they need to make wise choices and to think through the consequences of their actions.

**1748 Co: Writer**
Don Johnston
26799 W Commerce Dr
Volo, IL 60073-9675
847-740-0749
800-999-4660
FAX: 847-740-7326
e-mail: info@donjohnston.com
donjohnston.com

*Ruth Ziolkowski, President*
*Don Johnston, CEO*
*Kevin Johnston, Director of Product Design*
*Ben Johnston, Director of Marketing*
A software-based writing assistant that uses word prediction to cut through writing barriers and improve written expression. It is intended for students who struggle to write because of difficulty with spelling, syntax, and translating thoughts into writing. As students type, Co: Writer learns the context of the sentence and accurately 'predicts' words even when spelled phonetically or inventively. *$79.00*

**1749 Community Exploration**
Compass Learning
203 Colorado St
Austin, TX 78701-3922
512-478-9600
800-678-1412
e-mail: support@compasslearning.com
www.compasslearning.com

*Trey Chambers, Chief Financial Officer*
*Eric Loeffel, Chief Executive Officer*
*Anne Henson, Vice President, Curriculum & Instruction / Vice President, Customer Su*
*Quannah Hopper, Vice President, Compass Learning Impact Teacher Academy*
An award-winning learning adventure takes students who are learning English as a second language on a field trip to the make-believe town of Cornerstone. More than 50 community locations come to life with sound and animation. While exploring

places in this typical American community where people live, work and play, students also enhance important English language skills. Offers an exciting approach for any age student who needs to improve their English language proficiency. 4-12. *$19.95*

**1750 Conversations**
Educational Activities Software
5600 W 83rd Street
Suite 300, 8200 Tower
Bloomington, MN 55437
888-351-4199
866-243-8464
FAX: 239-225-9299
e-mail: jwest@orchardlng.com
www.ea-software.com

*Alan Stern, Manager*

Using American digitized voices, CONVERSATIONS provides 14 different dialogues in which the student can participate. The topics offer learners important information about American culture and the workplace. Available for DOS. *$195.00*

**1751 Core-Reading and Vocabulary Development**
Educational Activities
P.O.Box 87
Baldwin, NY 11510
516-223-4666
800-797-3223
FAX: 516-623-9282
e-mail: learn@edact.com
edact.com

*Alfred Harris, President*
*Carol Stern, VP*

Students begin with 36 basic words and progress to more than 200. Reading and writing activities are coordinated and integrated throughout the program for more substantial permanent learning. Five units covering readability levels from pre-primer to grade three.
*Full Program*

**1752 Friday Afternoon**
203 Colorado St
Austin, TX 78701-3922
512-478-9600
800-678-1412
e-mail: support@compasslearning.com
www.compasslearning.com

*Trey Chambers, Chief Financial Officer*
*Eric Loeffel, Chief Executive Officer*
*Anne Henson, Vice President, Curriculum & Instruction / Vice President, Customer Su*
*Quannah Hopper, Vice President, Compass Learning Impact Teacher Academy*

Save hours of preparation time and dazzle your students with interesting new activities to supplement their classroom learning. With Friday afternoon, you'll produce flash cards, word puzzles, even customized bingo cards and more, all at the click of a mouse. MacIntosh diskette. *$99.95*

**1753 How to Read for Everyday Living**
Educational Activities Software
5600 W 83rd Street
Suite 300, 8200 Tower
Bloomington, MN 55437
888-351-4199
866-243-8464
FAX: 239-225-9299
e-mail: jwest@orchardlng.com
www.ea-software.com

*Alan Stern, Manager*
*Ann Edson, M.Ed., Author*
*Eunice Insel, M.S., Co-Author*

Basic vocabulary and key words are taught and, when need, retaught using alternative teaching strategies. Passages that students read help put the vocabulary into context. Each lesson is followed by crossword and other puzzles check comprehension.

**1754 Learning English: Primary**
203 Colorado St
Austin, TX 78701-3922
512-478-9600
800-678-1412
e-mail: support@compasslearning.com
www.compasslearning.com

*Trey Chambers, Chief Financial Officer*
*Eric Loeffel, Chief Executive Officer*
*Anne Henson, Vice President, Curriculum & Instruction / Vice President, Customer Su*
*Quannah Hopper, Vice President, Compass Learning Impact Teacher Academy*

Four stories and rhymes help students familiarize themselves with essential English language concepts, recognize patterns in language and associate words with objects. *$49.95*

**1755 Learning English: Rhyme Time**
Compass Learning
203 Colorado St
Austin, TX 78701-3922
512-478-9600
800-678-1412
e-mail: support@compasslearning.com
www.compasslearning.com

*Trey Chambers, Chief Financial Officer*
*Eric Loeffel, Chief Executive Officer*
*Anne Henson, Vice President, Curriculum & Instruction / Vice President, Customer Su*
*Quannah Hopper, Vice President, Compass Learning Impact Teacher Academy*

Using classic children's rhymes in an animated multimedia program, students work on language skills, vocabulary and comprehension.

**1756 Lexia I, II and III Reading Series**
Lexia Learning Systems
200 Baker Ave
Concord, MA 01742
781-259-8752
800-435-3942
FAX: 978-287-0062
e-mail: info@lexialearning.com
www.lexialearning.com

*Nick Gaehde, President and CEO*
*Joel Brown, Vice President, Sales*
*Collin Earnst, Vice President of Marketing*
*Peter Koso, Vice President of Operations*

Lexia's software helps children and adults with learning disabilities master their core reading skills. Based on the Orton Gillingham method, Lexia Early Reading, Phonics Based Reading and SOS (Strategies for Older Students) apply phonics principles to help students learn essential sound-symbol correspondence and decoding skills. The Quick Reading Tests generate detailed skill reports in only 5-8 minutes per student to provide data for further instruction. Price: $40-400 per workstation.

**1757 Memory Castle**
WINGS for Learning
1600 Green Hills Rd
Scotts Valley, CA 95066-4981
831-426-2228
FAX: 831-464-3600

*Ani Stocks, Owner*

Introduces a strategy to increase memory skills via an adventure Q198game. Set in a castle, the game requires memory, reading, spelling skills and more to win.

**1758 On a Green Bus: A UKanDu Little Book**

Don Johnston
26799 W Commerce Dr
Volo, IL 60073-9675
847-740-0749
800-999-4660
FAX: 847-740-7326
e-mail: info@donjohnston.com
donjohnston.com

*Ruth Ziolkowski, President*
*Don Johnston, CEO*
*Kevin Johnston, Director of Product Design*
*Ben Johnston, Director of Marketing*

This early literacy program that consists of several create-your-own 4-page animated stories that help build language experience on each page and then watch the page come alive with animation and sound. After completing the story, students can print it out to make a book which can be read over and over again. Because there are no wrong answers, all children can have a successful literacy experience. *$ 45.00*

**1759 Open Book**

Freedom Scientific
11800 31st Ct N
St Petersburg, FL 33716-1805
727-803-8000
800-444-4443
FAX: 727-803-8001
e-mail: info@freedomscientific.com
www.freedomscientific.com

*Lee Hamilton, President, CEO, and Chairman of the Board of Directors*
*Mike Self, Sales Representative (Alabama)*
*Joseph McDaniel, Sales Representative (Alaska and Arizona)*
*Bobby Lakey, Sales Representative (Arkansas)*

Software that reads scanned text allowed and includes other features that aid the vision-impaired. *$995.00*

**1760 Optimum Resource Software**

Ste 107
1 Mathews Dr
Hilton Head Island, SC 29926-3765
843-689-8000
FAX: 843-689-8008
e-mail: info@stickybear.com
http://www.stickybear.com

*Richard Hefter, President*

Optimum Resource publishes over 100 K-12 education curriculum software titles under its varietal brands, StickyBear, MiddleWare, High School and Tools for Teachers. Most programs are available in Bilingual English/Spanish, and are offered with options for the single user through 30 users.

**1761 Parts of Speech**

Optimum Resource
Ste 107
1 Mathews Dr
Hilton Head Island, SC 29926-3765
843-689-8000
FAX: 843-689-8008
e-mail: info@stickybear.com
www.stickybear.com

*Richard Hefter, President*

Designed to help students build grammar and vocabulary as they strengthen reading and writing ability. Grades 3 to 9. *$59.95*

**1762 Programs for Aphasia and Cognitive Disorders**

Parrot Software
P.O.Box 250755
W Bloomfield, MI 48322
248-788-3223
800-727-7681
FAX: 248-788-3224
e-mail: support@parrotsoftware.com
www.parrotsoftware.com

*Dr. Frederic Winer, President*

Over 50 different computer programs that facilitate language, memory and attention training. Programs are available for MS DOS, WINDOWS and Apple II.

**1763 Punctuation Rules**

Optimum Resource
Ste 107
1 Mathews Dr
Hilton Head Island, SC 29926-3765
843-689-8000
FAX: 843-689-8008
e-mail: info@stickybear.com
www.stickybear.com

*Richard Hefter, President*

Punctuation Rules is designed to help students improve their punctuation skills. Students work with appropriate level sentences which follow common rules of punctuation. The program covers material ranging from categories of sentences to forming possessives and allows students to gain strength in their ability to correctly use periods, commas, apostrophes, question marks, colons, hyphens, quotation marks, exclamation points and more. Grades 3-9. Bilingual. *$59.95*

**1764 Quick Reading Test, Phonics Based Reading, Reading SOS (Strategies for Older Students)**

Lexia Learning Systems
200 Baker Ave
Concord, MA 01742
781-259-8752
800-435-3942
FAX: 978-287-0062
e-mail: info@lexialearning.com
www.lexialearning.com

*Nick Gaehde, President and CEO*
*Joel Brown, Vice President, Sales*
*Collin Earnst, Vice President of Marketing*
*Peter Koso, Vice President of Operations*

Lexia's software helps children and adults with learning disabilities master their core reading skills. Based on the Orton Gillingham method, Phonics Based Reading and S.O.S. (Strategies for the Older Student) apply phonics principles to help students learn essential sound-symbol correspondence and decoding skills. The Quick Reading Tests generate detailed phonemic skills reports in only 5-8 minutes per student to provide teachers with accurate data to focus their instruction. Price: $67-$500.

**1765 Quick Talk**

Educational Activities Software
5600 W 83rd Street
Suite 300, 8200 Tower
Bloomington, MN 55437
888-351-4199
866-243-8464
FAX: 239-225-9299
e-mail: jwest@orchardlng.com
www.ea-software.com

*Alan Stern, Manager*

Students will learn and use new vocabulary immediately: high-frequency, everyday vocabulary words are introduced and used contextually using human speech, graphics and text. Voice-interactive program (MS-DOS). *$65.00*

**1766 Race the Clock**

Mindplay
Suite 400
4400 E. Broadway Blvd
Tucson, AZ 85711
520-888-1800
800-221-7911
FAX: 520-888-7904
e-mail: mail@mindplay.com
www.mindplay.com

*John E. Crowley, Chief Executive Officer*
*Dan Figurski, Senior Vice President of Business Development*
*Lisa M. Garcia, Director of Educational Services*
*Chris Coleman, Manager of Software Development*

A matching game, uses the animation capabilities to teach verbs. The player chooses a matching game from a menu.

**1767 Read: Out Loud**

Don Johnston
26799 W Commerce Dr
Volo, IL 60073-9675
847-740-0749
800-999-4660
FAX: 847-740-7326
e-mail: info@donjohnston.com
donjohnston.com

*Ruth Ziolkowski, President*
*Don Johnston, CEO*
*Kevin Johnston, Director of Product Design*
*Ben Johnston, Director of Marketing*

An accessible text reader that provides access to the curriculum. It features high-quality text to speech and study tools that help students read with comprehension. *$79.00*

**1768 Reader Rabbit**

Learning Company
Ste 1900
100 Pine St
San Francisco, CA 94111-5205
415-659-2000
800-825-4420
FAX: 415-659-2020
e-mail: thelearningco@hmhpub.com
http://www.thelearningcompany.com

*Linda K. Zecher, President and CEO*
*Eric Shuman, Chief Financial Officer*
*John K. Dragoon, Executive Vice President and Chief Marketing Officer*
*William Bayers, Executive Vice President and General Counsel*

Supports young students in building fundamental reading readiness skills in a playful, multi-sensory environment.

**1769 Reading Comprehension Series**

Optimum Resource
Ste 107
1 Mathews Dr
Hilton Head Island, SC 29926-3765
843-689-8000
FAX: 843-689-8008
e-mail: info@stickybear.com
www.stickybear.com

*Richard Hefter, President*

The Reading Comprehension Series, includes seven volumes packed with intriguing multi-level stories. Each volume will capture the interest of children ages 8-14 while teaching them crucial reading comprehension skills. These open-ended programs are versatile and easy to use, and Bilingual. *$59.95*

**1770 Simon SIO**

Don Johnston
26799 W Commerce Dr
Volo, IL 60073-9675
847-740-0749
800-999-4660
FAX: 847-740-7326
e-mail: info@donjohnston.com
donjohnston.com

*Ruth Ziolkowski, President*
*Don Johnston, CEO*
*Kevin Johnston, Director of Product Design*
*Ben Johnston, Director of Marketing*

A researched and widely field-tested phonics program for beginning readers, developed in collaboration with Dr. Ted Hasselbring of Vanderbilt University. The program uses a personal tutor to deliver individualized instruction and corrective feedback. *$79.00*

**1771 Sound Sentences**

Educational Activities Software
5600 W 83rd Street
Suite 300, 8200 Tower
Bloomington, MN 55437
888-351-4199
866-243-8464
FAX: 239-225-9299
e-mail: jwest@orchardlng.com
www.ea-software.com

*Alan Stern, Manager*
*Janet Payne, Author*

This sound-interactive program breaks away from traditional language instruction. Instead of formal concentration on verb and basic vocabulary, students meet everyday English with colloquialisms they will hear in real life situations. They reinforce their knowledge of sentence structure while acquiring the ability to communicate in daily settings. (For MAC, MS-DOS and Windows). *$65.00*

**1772 Spelling Rules**

Optimum Resource
Ste 107
1 Mathews Dr
Hilton Head Island, SC 29926-3765
843-689-8000
FAX: 843-689-8008
e-mail: info@stickybear.com
www.stickybear.com

*Richard Hefter, President*

A curriculum based, easy-to-use program that provides students with the practice they need to build strong spelling skills. Concepts discussed include plurals, compounds, i-before-e, capitalization, and more. Grades 3 to 9. Bilingual. *$59.95*

**1773 Start-to-Finish Library**

Don Johnston
26799 W Commerce Dr
Volo, IL 60073-9675
847-740-0749
800-999-4660
FAX: 847-740-7326
e-mail: info@donjohnston.com
donjohnston.com

*Ruth Ziolkowski, President*
*Don Johnston, CEO*
*Kevin Johnston, Director of Product Design*
*Ben Johnston, Director of Marketing*

Offers struggling readers a wide selection of engaging narrative chapter books written at two readability levels (2-3rd and 4-5th grade) and delivered in three media formats. Professionally-narrated audio and computer supports help scaffold reading to ensure success. *$79.00*

**1774 Start-to-Finish Literacy Starters**

Don Johnston
26799 W Commerce Dr
Volo, IL 60073-9675
847-740-0749
800-999-4660
FAX: 847-740-7326
e-mail: info@donjohnston.com
donjohnston.com

*Ruth Ziolkowski, President*
*Don Johnston, CEO*
*Kevin Johnston, Director of Product Design*
*Ben Johnston, Director of Marketing*

A reading series intended for students with multiple disabilities who are in 3-12th grade, but reading at a beginning level. Dr. Karen Erickson developed this series, which combines switch-accessible software with three types of text. *$79.00*

1775 **Stickybear Reading Comprehension**
Optimum Resource
Ste 107
1 Mathews Dr
Hilton Head Island, SC 29926-3765 843-689-8000
FAX: 843-689-8008
e-mail: info@stickybear.com
www.stickybear.com

*Richard Hefter, President*
This multi-level reading comprehension program helps children improve reading skills with 30 high-interest stories and question sets created by the Weekly Reader editors. Children learn to recognize main ideas, define sequence, using context to identify words, and more. Grades 2 to 4. Bilingual. *$59.95*

1776 **Stickybear Reading Fun Park**
Optimum Resource
Ste 107
1 Mathews Dr
Hilton Head Island, SC 29926-3765 843-689-8000
FAX: 843-689-8008
e-mail: info@stickybear.com
www.stickybear.com

*Richard Hefter, President*
Children discover and practice critical reading skills as the Stickybear family guides users through unique, action-packed activities, each with multiple levels of difficulty and skills that address both the auditory and visual needs of budding readers. Pre-K through 3rd grade. *$59.95*

1777 **Stickybear Reading Room Deluxe**
Optimum Resource
Ste 107
1 Mathews Dr
Hilton Head Island, SC 29926-3765 843-689-8000
FAX: 843-689-8008
e-mail: info@stickybear.com
www.stickybear.com

*Richard Hefter, President*
Children build vocabulary and reading comprehension skills using hundreds of word/picture sets and thousands of put-together sentence parts. K-3rd grade. Bilingual, English/Spanish. *$59.95*

1778 **Stickybear Spelling**
Optimum Resource
Ste 107
1 Mathews Dr
Hilton Head Island, SC 29926-3765 843-689-8000
FAX: 843-689-8008
e-mail: info@stickybear.com
www.stickybear.com

*Richard Hefter, President*
Children discover and practice critical spelling skills as they work with three unique action-packed activities, each with four graded levels of difficulty. The program is open-ended and teachers may add, change and modify the word lists for each individual. Stickybear Spelling contains more than 2000 recorded words. Levels may be set to allow students of different ages or abilities to compete effectively. Grades 2 through 4. *$59.95*

1779 **Tomorrow's Promise: Language Arts**
Compass Learning
13500 Evening Creek Dr N
Suite 600
San Diego, CA 92128- 8104 858-668-2586
866-475-0317
FAX: 858-408-2903
e-mail: info@bridgepointeducation.com
bridgepointeducation.com

*Andrew S. Clark, Founder, Chief Executive Officer and President*
*Rocky T. Sheng, Executive Vice President and Chief Administrative Officer*
*Jane McAuliffe, Executive Vice President and Chief Academic Officer*
*Daniel J. Devine, Executive Vice President and Chief Financial Officer*
You'll strengthen students' grammar, usage and vocabulary skills and promote higher order thinking skills with this comprehensive Language Arts curriculum. It utilizes cross-curricular, thematic instruction engaging multimedia learning exercises that encourage writing, speaking and listening proficiency. Promotes higher order thinking skills. *$279.95*

1780 **Tomorrow's Promise: Reading**
Compass Learning
203 Colorado St
Austin, TX 78701-3922 512-478-9600
800-678-1412
e-mail: support@compasslearning.com
www.compasslearning.com

*Trey Chambers, Chief Financial Officer*
*Eric Loeffel, Chief Executive Officer*
*Anne Henson, Vice President, Curriculum & Instruction / Vice President, Customer Su*
*Quannah Hopper, Vice President, Compass Learning Impact Teacher Academy*
This multimedia curriculum balances thematic, interactive exploration with core skills development, increasing your students' early reading proficiency, building a solid literacy foundation and fostering a lifelong love for reading. *$279.95*

1781 **Tomorrow's Promise: Spelling**
Compass Learning
203 Colorado St
Austin, TX 78701-3922 512-478-9600
800-678-1412
e-mail: support@compasslearning.com
www.compasslearning.com

*Trey Chambers, Chief Financial Officer*
*Eric Loeffel, Chief Executive Officer*
*Anne Henson, Vice President, Curriculum & Instruction / Vice President, Customer Su*
*Quannah Hopper, Vice President, Compass Learning Impact Teacher Academy*
Lovable characters and engaging multimedia effects put young students on a fast-track to early spelling proficiency with fourteen activities and three games. A full year's instruction on each CD includes 30 world lists per grade, in story context, or create word lists to suit your needs. This program addresses students' multiple learning styles and rewards students as they progress through each stage of spelling skill acquisition. *$99.95*

1782 **Vocabulary Development**
Optimum Resource
Ste 107
1 Mathews Dr
Hilton Head Island, SC 29926-3765 843-689-8000
FAX: 843-689-8008
e-mail: info@stickybear.com
www.stickybear.com

*Richard Hefter, President*
A featured program in the middle school series. Vocabulary Development is designed to help students increase vocabulary as they strengthen reading skills. Students relate their current

knowledge of vocabulary to the context in which they discover an unfamiliar word. Utilizing a variety of contextual aids, this program illustrates synonyms, antonyms, prefixes, suffixes, homophones, multiple meanings and context clues, allowing students to apply experience and context. *$59.95*

**1783 Whoops**
Cornucopia Software
P.O.Box 6111
Albany, CA 94706-111
510-528-7000
e-mail: supportstaff@practicemagic.com
www.practicemagic.com

*Christina Morua, Manager*
Checks spelling three ways. It checks words as they are typed, it checks an entire screen and highlights the errors and it reads ASCII text files from a disk and lists errors.

## Software: Vocational

**1784 Films Media Group**
Infobase Publishing
132 W 31st St, 17th Floor
New York, NY 10001
800-257-5126
FAX: 800-329-6687
e-mail: mgallo@infobaselearning.com
www.infobaselearning.com

*Melinda Gallo, Senior Account Executive*
Educational publisher of DVD programming for schools and libraries. *$64.86*

*ISBN 0-927368-59-5*

**1785 Functional Literacy System**
Conover Company
4 Brookwood Court
Appleton, WI 54914-8618
920-231-4667
800-933-1933
FAX: 800-933-1943
e-mail: support@conovercompany.com
www.conovercompany.com

*Terry Schmitz, Founder and Owner*
*Mike , Vice President of Operations*
*Art Janowiak, Vice President of Sales*
Assessment and skill building for basic functional literacy. This multimedia software program is adult in format and uses live action video taken in actual community settings to help learners become more capable of functioning independently. Twenty different programs are currently available. *$99.00*

**1786 Learning Activity Packets**
4 Brookwood Court
Appleton, WI 54914-8618
920-231-4667
800-933-1933
FAX: 800-933-1943
e-mail: support@conovercompany.com
www.conovercompany.com

*Terry Schmitz, Founder and Owner*
*Mike , Vice President of Operations*
*Art Janowiak, Vice President of Sales*
Demonstrates how basic academic skills relate to 30 major career areas. LAPs provide valuable diagnostics in applied academic applications and demonstrates to users the importance of academics as they relate to the workplace. Software. *$99.00*

**1787 Microcomputer Evaluation of Careers & Academics (MECA)**
Conover Company
4 Brookwood Court
Appleton, WI 54914-8618
920-231-4667
800-933-1933
FAX: 800-933-1943
e-mail: support@conovercompany.com
www.conovercompany.com

*Terry Schmitz, Founder and Owner*
*Mike , Vice President of Operations*
*Art Janowiak, Vice President of Sales*
A cost-effective, technology-based, career development system which provides users with opportunities to get their hands dirty. The MECA system utilizes work simulations and is built around common occupational clusters. Each cluster, or career area, consists of hands-on WORK SAMPLES which provide a variety of career exploration and assessment experiences, linked to LEARNING ACTIVITY PACKETS, which integrate basic academic skills into the career planning and placement process. $580-$1,070.

**1788 OASYS**
Vertek
Ste 310
12835 Bel Red Rd
Bellevue, WA 98005-2631
425-455-9921
800-220-4409
FAX: 425-454-7264
e-mail: sales@vertekinc.com
www.vertekinc.com

*Debra Callahan, Sales Representative, Northern California : North of Kern, San Luis Ob*
*Bill Chapman, Sales Representative, D.C., Maryland, Delaware*
*Beverly Duncan, Sales Representative, Florida*
*Tim Durham, Sales Representative, Georgia*
A software system that matches a person's skills and abilities to occupations and employers.

**1789 Reading in the Workplace**
Educational Activities Software
5600 W 83rd Street
Suite 300, 8200 Tower
Bloomington, MN 55437-585
888-351-4199
866-243-8464
FAX: 239-225-9299
e-mail: jwest@orchardlng.com
www.ea-software.com

*Alan Stern, Manager*
A job-based, reading software program using real-life problems and solutions to capture students' attention and improve their vocabulary and comprehension skills. Units include: automotive, clerical, health care and construction. *$295.00*

**1790 Stickybear Typing**
Optimum Resource
Ste 107
1 Mathews Dr
Hilton Head Island, SC 29926-3765
843-689-8000
FAX: 843-689-8008
e-mail: info@stickybear.com
www.stickybear.com

*Richard Hefter, President*
The award winning Stickybear Typing program allows users to sharpen typing skills and achieve keyboard mastery with three engaging and amusing multi-level activities. *$59.95*

**1791 Work-Related Vocational Assessment Systems: Computer Based**
Valpar International
P.O.Box 5767
Tucson, AZ 85703-767
262-797-0840
800-633-3321
FAX: 262-797-8488
e-mail: sales@valparint.com
www.valparint.com

*Neal Gunderson, President*
Criterion-referenced to Department of Labor standards. Evaluate academic levels for reading, spelling, math and language, interests, personalities, cognitive and physical aptitudes.

**1792 Workplace Skills: Learning How to Function on the Job**
Programming Concepts
4560 Lockhill Selma Rd.
Ste. 100
San Antonio, TX 78249- 2075
210-377-1999
800-594-4263
FAX: 888-259-8284
e-mail: lboulet@pcieducation.com
http://www.pcieducation.com

*Lee Wilson, President and CEO*
*Randy Pennington, Executive Vice President*
*Anne-Marie De Witt, Vice President, Product Development*
*Debra Covert, Vice President, Operations*
Offers parents and educators a functional means by which to discuss all aspects of finding and keeping a job. *$49.95*

## Word Processors

**1793 DARCI**
Wes Test Engineering Corporation
810 Shepard Ln
Farmington, UT 84025-3846
801-451-9191
FAX: 801-451-9393
e-mail: webmail@westest.com
westest.com

*Robert Lessmann, President*
*James Lynds*
Provides transparent access to all computer functions by replacing the computer's keyboard with a smart joystick. *$975.00*

**1794 Eye Relief Word Processing Software**
SkiSoft Publishing Corporation
P.O.Box 364
Lexington, MA 02420-4
781-863-1876
e-mail: info@skisoft.com
www.skisoft.com

*Ken Skier, President*
*Cynthia Skier, CFO*
Large-type word processing program for visually-impaired PC users. *$295.00*

**1795 IntelliTalk**
Intelli Tools
24 Prime Parkway
Natick, MA 01760
707-773-2000
800-547-6747
FAX: 707-773-2001
e-mail: customerservice@cambiumtech.com
www.intellitools.com

*Beth Davis, Director Sales Operations*
*Lori Castle, Supervisor*
*Arjan Khalsa, CEO*
Talking word-processing program available for MacIntosh, Apple IIe, IBM compatible and Windows computers. *$39.95*

**1796 Large Type**
P.O.Box T
Hewitt, NJ 07421-2088
973-853-6585
800-736-2216
FAX: 928-832-2894
e-mail: nire@theoffice.net
http://www.angelfire.com

*Don Selwyn, Vice President*
*Rev. Tom Schwanda, President & Chairman*
*Robt. Fondiller, Ph.D., P.E, Vice President*
*Everett G. Ball, Treasurer*
Display enlargement programs for visually impaired users. Consist of a variety of programs for different needs, ranging from basic to full-featured.

**1797 Pegasus LITE**
Words+
Ste 109
42505 10th St W
Lancaster, CA 93534-7059
661-723-6523
800-869-8521
FAX: 661-723-2114
e-mail: info@words-plus.com
www.words-plus.com

*Phil Lawrence, VP*
Provides all of the strategies currently being used in AAC, from dynamic display color pictographic language, to dual-word prediction text language, in a single system. *$6995.00*

**1798 Up and Running**
Intelli Tools
24 Prime Parkway
Natick, MA 01760
707-773-2000
800-547-6747
FAX: 707-773-2001
e-mail: customerservice@cambiumtech.com
www.intellitools.com

*Beth Davis, Director Sales Operations*
*Lori Castle, Supervisor*
*Arjan Khalsa, CEO*
Instantly use hundreds of popular commercial software programs with this custom collection of setups and overlays. *$69.95*

**1799 Write This Way**
Compass Learning Incorporated
203 Colorado St
Austin, TX 78701-3922
512-478-9600
800-678-1412
e-mail: support@compasslearning.com
www.compasslearning.com

*Trey Chambers, Chief Financial Officer*
*Eric Loeffel, Chief Executive Officer*
*Anne Henson, Vice President, Curriculum & Instruction / Vice President, Customer Su*
*Quannah Hopper, Vice President, Compass Learning Impact Teacher Academy*
An easy-to-use, versatile word processor designed with learning disabled or hearing-impaired individuals in mind. Apple or Mac available. *$99.95*

**1800 Write: OutLoud**
Don Johnston
26799 W Commerce Dr
Volo, IL 60073-9675
847-740-0749
800-999-4660
FAX: 847-740-7326
e-mail: info@donjohnston.com
donjohnston.com

*Ruth Ziolkowski, President*
*Don Johnston, CEO*
*Kevin Johnston, Director of Product Design*
*Ben Johnston, Director of Marketing*

The award-winning feasible and user friendly talking word processor with talking spell checker. Text-to-speech technology provides multi-sensory learning and positive reinforcements for writers of all ages and ability levels. *$99.00*

# Conferences & Shows

## General

**1801 AACRC Annual Meeting**
American Assn. of Children's Residential Centers
11700 W Lake Park Dr
Milwaukee, WI 53224-3021
877-332-2272
FAX: 877-362-2272
e-mail: info@aacrc-dc.org
www.aacrc-dc.org

*Richard Altman, MSW, ACSW, Director*
*Steven Elson, Ph.D., Director*
*Margaret Vimont, LCSW, Director*
*Andre Cooper, M.A., Director*
One-day program that addresses accreditation as it relates to current behavioral health care challenges held in Pasadena, CA.
*October*

**1802 AADB National Conference**
American Association of the Deaf-Blind
PO Box 2831
Kensington, MD 20891
301-495-4403
FAX: 301-495-4404
TTY:301-495-4402
e-mail: aadb-info@aadb.org
www.aadb.org

*Jill Gaus, President*
*Elizabeth Spiers, Support Service Provider - Chair*
*Lynn Jansen, Vice President*
*Debby Lieberman, Secretary*
A week of general meetings, workshops, tours and evening recreational activities.

**1803 AAIDD Annual Meeting**
American Association on Mental Retardation
501 3rd Street
NW Suite 200
Washington, DC 20001-1569
202-387-1968
800-424-3688
FAX: 202-387-2193
e-mail: maria@aaidd.org
www.aamr.org

*Margaret A. Nygren, EdD, Executive Director & CEO*
*Paul D. Aitken, CPA, Director, Finance & Administration*
*Ravita Maharaj, PhD, Director, Supports Intensity Scale Program*
*Lisa M. O'Hearn, MA, Director, Publications Program*
At The Crossroads: Ethics, Genetics, Leadership and self-determination, this annual meeting offers a full compliment of workshops, symposia, and multiperspective sessions that fill four days including social events.
*May/June*

**1804 AAO Annual Meeting**
American Academy Of Opthamology
655 Beach St
San Francisco, CA 94109-1336
415-561-8500
FAX: 415-561-8567
e-mail: faao@aao.org
www.faao.org

*Brad A. Wong, Executive Director*
*Betty Lucas, Director*
*Todd Lyckberg, Director of Development*
*Jenny E. Benjamin, Director*
Offers the most comprehensive program with more than 2000 scientific presentations and six subspecialty day programs
*October*

**1805 ABD Winter Conference**
American Board of Disability Analysts
Belle Meade Office Park, 4525 Hardi
Third Floor
Nashville, TN 37205-1520
615-327-2984
FAX: 615-327-9235
e-mail: americanbd@aol.com
www.americandisability.org

*Alexander Horowitz, MD, ABDA, Executive Officer Emeritus*
*Kenneth Anchor, Ph.D., ABPP, (, Administrative Offices*
*Dana Adair, MS, RN, C (ABDA, Professional Advisory Council*
*Francella W. Betancourt, MA, CRC (A, Professional Advisory Council*
Joint Conference: American Board of Disability.
*February*

**1806 ACA Annual Conference**
American Counseling Association
5999 Stevenson Ave
Alexandria, VA 22304-3304
703-823-9800
800-347-6647
FAX: 800-473-2329
e-mail: webmaster@counseling.org
counseling.org

*Richard Yep, Executive Director*
*Robin Hayes, Conference and Meeting*
*Brad Erford, President*
*Paul Nelson, Executive Director*
Promotes the development of professional counselors, advancing the counseling profession, and using the profession and practice of counseling to promote respect for human dignity and diversity.
*March/April*

**1807 ACB Annual Convention**
American Council for the Blind
2200 Wilson Boulevard
Suite 650
Arlington, VA 22201-3354
202-467-5081
800-424-8666
FAX: 703-465-5085
e-mail: info@acb.org
acb.org

*Melanie Brunson, Executive Director*
*Mitch Pomerantz, President*
*Kim Charlson, Vice President*
*Brenda Dillon, Vice President*
Offers 50-75 booths of information for the blind.
*June/July*

**1808 ADA Annual Scientific Sessions**
American Diabetes Association
1701 N Beauregard St
Alexandria, VA 22311-1742
703-549-1500
800-342-2383
FAX: 703-836-7439
e-mail: webmaster@diabetes.org
www.diabetes.org

*Larry Hausner, MBA, Chief Executive Officer*
*Shereen Arent, Executive Vice President Government Affairs & Advocacy*
*M. Vaneeda Bennett, Chief Revenue Officer*
*Greg Elfers, Chief Field Development Officer*
Trade show featuring exhibits of equipment and supplies used by professionals involved in the treatment of diabetes.

**1809 AER Annual International Conference**
Assoc. for Educ. & Rehab of the Blind/Vis. Imp.
Ste 440
1703 N Beauregard St
Alexandria, VA 22311-1744
703-671-4500
877-492-2708
FAX: 703-671-6391
e-mail: aer@aerbvi.org
www.aerbvi.org

*Lou Tutt, Executive Director*
*Ginger Croce, Director, Membership and Marketing*
*Bette Anne P Anne Preston, Director of Affiliate Affairs*
*Barbara James, Manager for Member Services*
Dedicated to rendering support and assistance to the professionals who work in all phases of education and rehabilitation of blind and visually impaired children and adults.
*July*

**1810 AG Bell Convention**
Alexander Graham Bell Association
3417 Volta Pl NW
Washington, DC 20007-2737
202-337-5220
FAX: 202-337-8314
TTY:202-337-5221
e-mail: info@agbell.org
agbell.org

*Cheryl L. Dickson, M.Ed., LSLS C, President*
*Anita Bernstein, M.Sc., Dip., Director*
*Lyn Robertson, Ph.D., President Elect*
*Lyn Robertson, Ph.D., President Elect*
Over 60 booths offering information on resources and technology for the deaf and hard of hearing.
*June*

**1811 AHEAD**
Association on Higher Education And Disability
Ste 204
107 Commerce Centre Dr
Huntersville, NC 28078- 5870
704-947-7779
FAX: 704-948-7779
e-mail: information@ahead.org
www.ahead.org

*Jean Ashmore, President*
*Scott Lissner, President-Elect*
*Michael Johnson, Treasurer*
*Stephan Hamlin-Smith, Executive Director*
AHEAD is a professional membership organization for individuals involved in the development of policy and in the provision of quality services to meet the needs of persons with disabilities involved in all areas of higher education.
*July*

**1812 APSE Conference: Revitalizing Supported Employment, Climbing to the Future**
Association for Persons in Supported Employment
416 Hungerford Dr.
Suite 418
Rockville, MD 20850
301-279-0060
FAX: 301-279-0075
e-mail: jenny@apse.org
apse.org

*David Hoff, President*
*Laura A. Owens, Ph.D., Executive Director*
*Jenny Levet, Communications/Membership Director*
*Ilycia Schwartz, Chapter Director*
A major conference on Supported Employment. The conference includes 130 sessions presented by nationally recognized leaders in the field. Conference attendees come from all 50 states, Canada and several foreign countries and include professionals in supported employment, occupational therapy, rehabilitation technology and other related fields.
*July*

**1813 ASHA Convention**
American Speech-Language-Hearing Association
2275 Research Blvd
Suite 500
Rockville, MD 20850-3289
800-638-8255
FAX: 301-296-8580
TTY:301-897-5700
e-mail: convention@asha.org
synutra.com

*Liang Zhang, Chairman of the Board and Chief Executive Officer*
*Weiguo Zhang, President and Interim Chief Financial Officer*
Exhibits by companies specializing in alternative and augmentative communication products, publishers, software and hardware companies, and hearing aid testing equipment manufacturers. Speech-Language Pathologists are professionals who identify, assess, and treat speech and language problems. Audiologists are hearing health care professionals who specialize in preventing, identifying and assessing hearing disorders as well as providing audiologic treatment including hearing aids and more.
*November*

**1814 ASIA Annual Scientific Meeting**
American Spinal Injury Association
2020 Peachtree Rd NW
Atlanta, GA 30309-1426
404-355-9772
FAX: 404-355-1826
e-mail: asia-office@shepherd.org
www.asia-spinalinjury.org

*Lesley M Hudson MA, Executive Director*
*Patricia Duncan, Administrative Coordinator*
Professional association for physicans and other health professionals working in all aspects of spinal cord injury. Also holds an annual scientific that surveys the latest advancements in the field.
*May*

**1815 American Academy for Cerebral Palsy and Developmental Medicine Annual Conference**
555 E Wells Street
Ste 1100
Milwaukee, WI 53202-3800
414-918-3014
FAX: 414-276-2146
e-mail: info@aacpdm.org
aacpdm.org

*Joseph Dutkowsky, President*
*Maureen O'Donnell, First Vice President*
*Richard Stevenson, Second Vice President*
*Gregory Liptak, Treasurer*
The Annual Meeting is a 3-day event, held in the Fall, designed to provide targeted opportunities for dissemination of information in the basic sciences, prevention, diagnosis, treatment, and technical advances as applied to persons with cerebral palsy and development disorders.
*September*

**1816 American Board of Disability Analysts Annual Conference**
Disability Analyst
Belle Meade Office Park, 4525 Hardi
Third Floor
Nashville, TN 37205-1520
615-327-2984
FAX: 615-327-9235
e-mail: americanbd@aol.com
www.americandisability.org

*Alexander Horowitz, MD, ABDA, Executive Officer Emeritus*
*Kenneth Anchor, Ph.D., ABPP, (, Administrative Offices*
*Dana Adair, MS, RN, C (ABDA, Professional Advisory Council*
*Francella W. Betancourt, MA, CRC (A, Professional Advisory Council*
Annual conference held for members to meet and discuss current events and attend seminars.

**1817 Annual Conference on Dyslexia and Related Learning Disabilities**
New York Branch International Dyslexia Association
Ste 1527
71 W 23rd St
New York, NY 10010-4197
212-691-1930
FAX: 212-633-1620
e-mail: info@everyonereading.org
nybida.org

*Jo Haines, Executive Director*
*Peter Prager, President*
*Ronald A. Wilson, Vice President*
*Judith R. Birsh, Ed.D., Second Vice President*
Provides educational support services to people concerned and affected by dyslexia and related learning disabilities.
*March*

**1818 Attention Deficit Disorders Association, Southern Region: Annual Conference**
12345 Jones Road
Suite 287-7
Houston, TX 77070-4958
281-897-0982
FAX: 281-894-6883
e-mail: addaoffice@pdq.net
www.adda-sr.org

*Pam Esser, Executive Director*
*Laura Peddicord, President*
*Opal Harris, Secretary*
*Tina Peden, Office Manager*
Mission is to: provide a resource network; to support individuals impacted by attention deficit disorders; and to advocate for the development of community resources and services that meet the educational, social, and health care needs of all individuals with ADD/ADHD.
*February*

**1819 Believable Hope Conference**
United Cerebral Palsy Association
Ste 700
1660 L St NW
Washington, DC 20036-5638
202-776-0414
800-872-5827
FAX: 202-776-0414
TTY: 202-973-7197
e-mail: info@ucp.org
www.ucpa.org

*Stephen Bennett, CEO*
National, not-for-profit self-help organization dedicated to providing information and support to individuals with cerebral palsy and other disabilities, and their families. Supports more than 160 local affiliates; these affiliates provide a variety of programs and services for affected families, including support groups. Offers several educational and support materials, including a quarterly magazine, regular newsletters, and research reports.

**1820 Blazing Toward a Cure Annual Conference**
National Parkinson Foundation
1501 NW 9th Ave
Suite 760
Miami, FL 33136-1407
305-592-9954
800-327-4545
FAX: 305-477-7379
e-mail: info@acfm-cpa.com
acfm-cpa.com

*Daniel Arty, Partner*
*Joel L. Moskowits, Partner*
*Julia Alemany, Audit Manager*
*Lester Feuer*
Purpose is to find the cause and cure for Parkinson's Disease and related neurodegenerative disorders through research, education and dissemination of current information to patients, caregivers and families.
*July/August*

**1821 Blind Childrens Center Annual Meeting**
Blind Childrens Center
4120 Marathon St
Los Angeles, CA 90029-3584
323-664-2153
800-222-3567
FAX: 323-665-3828
e-mail: Info@blindchildrenscenter.org.
blindchildrenscenter.org

*Midge Horton, Executive Director*
*Muriel Scharf, Director of Development*
*Jennifer Brown, President*
*Kristin Dark, Director*
A family-centered agency which serves children with visual impairments from birth to school-age. The center-based and home-based services help the children to acquire skills and build their independence. The Center utilizes its expertise and experience to serve families and professionals worldwide through support services, education and research.
*September*

**1822 Blinded Veterans Association National Convention**
Blinded Veterans Association
477 H St NW
Washington, DC 20001-2694
202-371-8880
800-669-7079
FAX: 202-371-8258
e-mail: bva@bva.org
bva.org

*Al Avina, Executive Director*
*Sam Huhn, National President*
*Mark Cornell, National Vice President*
*Robert Dale Stamper, National Secretary*
Conventions have a three-fold purpose, to conduct Association business, to educate blinded veterans about the resources available to them, and to provide a means whereby blinded veterans can better strengthen and help one another.
*August*

**1823 CQL Accreditation**
Council on Quality and Leadership
Ste 300
100 West Rd
Towson, MD 21204-2368
410-583-0060
FAX: 410-583-0063
e-mail: info@thecouncil.org
c-q-l.org

*James F Gardner, President and CEO*
*Holly Morrison, Vice President and Chief Operating Officer*
*Sylvia Nudler, Vice President*
*Beth Mathis, Associate Vice President, Network Development*
Prepares you for CQL Accreditation, addressing Shared Values, Basic Assurances(r), Personal Outcomes, Service Responsiveness and Commitment to Community Life.

**1824 Closing the Gap's Annual Conference**
Assist. Tech. Resources for Children & Adults
P.O.Box 68
526 Main Street
Henderson, MN 56044-68
507-248-3294
FAX: 507-248-3810
e-mail: info@closingthegap.com
www.closingthegap.com

*Dolores Hagen, Founder*
*Budd Hagen, Co-Founder*
*Connie Kneip, Vice President/General Manager*
*Megan Turek, Managing Editor/Advertising and Exhibit Sales*
Topics cover a broad spectrum of technology as it is being applied to all disabilities and age groups in education, rehabilitation, vocation and independent living. People with disabilities, special educators, rehabilitation professionals, administrators, service/care providers, personnel managers, government officials, and hardware/software developers share their experiences and insights at this significant networking experience.
*October*

**1825 Council for Exceptional Children Annual Convention and Expo**
2900 Crystal Drive
Ste 1000
Arlington, VA 22202-3557
703-620-3660
866-509-0218
888-232-7733
FAX: 703-264-9494
TTY:866-915-5000
e-mail: service@cec.sped.org
cec.sped.org

*Bruce A. Ramirez, Executive Director*
*Margaret J. McLaughlin, President*
*Christy A. Chambers, President Elect*
*James P. Heiden, Treasurer*
Works to improve the educational success of children with disabilities and/or gifts and talents.
*April*

**1826 Eye Bank Association of America Annual Meeting**
Eye Bank Association of America
Ste 1010
1015 18th St NW
Washington, DC 20036-5223
202-775-4999
FAX: 202-429-6036
e-mail: malene@restoresight.org
www.restoresight.org

*Kevin Corcoran, CAE, President / CEO*
*Molly Georgakis, Vice-President of Member Services*
*Bernie Dellario, Director of Finance*
*Jennifer DeMatteo, Director of Regulations and Standards*
A four day program, which includes a series of presentations in administrative, hospital development, scientific and technical fields that are relative to eye banking.
*June*

**1827 IDF National Conference**
Immune Deficiency Foundation
Ste 308
40 W Chesapeake Ave
Towson, MD 21204-4843
410-321-6647
800-296-4433
FAX: 410-321-9165
e-mail: idf@primaryimmune.org
www.primaryimmune.org

*Marcia Boyle, President & Founder*
*John Seymour, PhD, LMFT, Chair*
*Rebecca H. Buckley, MD, Chair, Medical Advisory Committee*
*Robert LeBien, Vice Chair*
World-renowned immunologists will share their time and expertise with families. Attendees will learn about scientific advancements in the diagnosis and treatment of these diseases and gain skills needed to manage their healthcare.
*June*

**1828 Joint Conference with ABMPP Annual Conference**
American Board of Disability Analysts
Belle Meade Office Park, 4525 Hardi
Third Floor
Nashville, TN 37205-1520
615-327-2984
FAX: 615-327-9235
e-mail: americanbd@aol.com
www.americandisability.org

*Alexander Horowitz, MD, ABDA, Executive Officer Emeritus*
*Kenneth Anchor, Ph.D., ABPP, (, Administrative Offices*
*Dana Adair, MS, RN, C (ABDA, Professional Advisory Council*
*Francella W. Betancourt, MA, CRC (A, Professional Advisory Council*
Joint Conference with ABMPP Annual Conference Charleston, South Carolina.
*May*

**1829 Lowe's Syndrome Conference**
Lowe's Syndrome Association
PO Box 864346
Plano, TX 75086-4346
972-733-1338
FAX: 612-866-3222
e-mail: info@lowesyndrome.org
www.lowesyndrome.org

*Debbie Jacobs, President*
*Jane Gallery, Treasurer*
*Fiona Fisher, Secretary*
*Christine Knight, Board Member and Director, Medical and Scientific Advisory Board*
An international conference held approximately every two years where family, friends, medical and other professionals gather to exchange ideas and information. Next Conference held in 2010.
*June*

**1830 NADD**
National Association for the Dually Diagnosed
132 Fair St
Kingston, NY 12401-4802
845-331-4336
800-331-5362
FAX: 845-331-4569
e-mail: info@thenadd.org
www.thenadd.org

*Robert Fletcher, CEO*
NADD is a non-for-profit membership organization designed to promote awareness of, and services for, individuals who have co-occuring intellectual disability and mental illness. NADD provides training, consultation services, and publishes journals and books.
*November*

**1831 NASPAC Annual Conference Association Annual Convention/Expo**
National Assoc. of Subacute and Post Acute Care
P.O.Box 65085
Washington, DC 20035-5085
202-429-2700
FAX: 202-429-2701
www.naspac.net

*Lyle Williams, President*
Totally dedicated to servicing the subacute arena and its major entities. Features 100+ booths and over 75 exhibitors.
*March*

**1832 NASW-NYS Chapter**
NASW
188 Washington Ave
Albany, NY 12210-2304
518-463-4741
800-724-6279
FAX: 518-463-6446
e-mail: info@naswnys.org
naswnys.org

*Isabel Rose, Ph.D., LMSW, President*
*Debra Fromm-Faria, LCSW, ACS, President-Elect*
*Bernadette Marson, LMSW-R, Vice President*
*Elaine Ringrette, Ph.D., LCSW, Secretary*
Workshops, keynote speakers, and presentations offered at this event will develop and enhance practice skills and knowledge in the provision of quality mental health and community services.
*March*

**1833 National Council on the Aging Conference**
Conference Department
1901 L Street, NW
4th Floor
Washington, DC 20036-3212
202-479-1200
800-424-9046
FAX: 202-479-0735
TTY: 202-479-6674
e-mail: membership@ncoa.org
http://www.ncoa.org/

*James P Firman, EdD, President and CEO*
*Jay Greenberg, ScD, Senior Vice President, Social Enterprise*
*Donna Whitt, Senior Vice President and Chief Financial Officer*
*Robert Blancato, Director*

Offers ideas and programs to increase program and administrative skills through NCOA's professional development tracks and offering of continuing education units.
*May*

**1834 National Managed Health Care Congress**
3rd Fl
71 2nd Ave
Waltham, MA 02451-1107
781-663-6000
FAX: 781-663-6422
e-mail: SMeehan@iirusa.com
www.nmhcc.com

*Megan Antonelli, Event Director*
*Shawn Meehan, Exhibit/Underwriter Sales*

Attracts nearly 7,000 delegates, thereby reinforcing its status as the nation's largest conferences for all managed care constituencies.
*April*

**1835 PWSA (USA) Conference**
Prader-Willi Alliance Of New York
PO BOX 222
Baldwinsville, NY 13027
716-276-2211
800-442-1655
FAX: 914-312-0142
e-mail: alliance@prader-willi.org
www.prader-willi.org

*Amy McDougall, President, Fulton*
*Hon. Daniel Angiolillo, President Emeritus, Director, W. Harrison*
*Dr. Jamie Bassel, Vice President, Manhattan*
*Nancy Finegold, Vice President, W. Hempstead*

Through conferences, publications, electronic communication and networking (parent-to-parent, parent-to professional, and professional-to-professional), the Prader-Willi Alliance provides a valuable resource for individuals and families sharing the same concerns.
*July*

**1836 RESNA Annual Conference**
Rehab Engineering & Assistive Tech. North America
Ste 1540
1700 N Moore St
Arlington, VA 22209-1903
703-524-6686
FAX: 703-524-6630
TTY:703-524-6639
e-mail: conference@resna.org
resna.org

*Nell Bailey, Executive Director*
*Jerry Weisman, President*
*Alex Mihailidis, PhD, P.Eng, President-Elect*
*Heidi Horstmann Koester, PhD, Treasurer*

Sponsored by a multidisciplinary association for the advancement of rehabilitation and assistive technologies, this annual conference brings together a large number of rehabilitation professionals, products and services from around the world and has something to offer for both professionals and consumers. The conference provides an informative and thought provoking forum for anyone with interests in rehabilitation technology.
*June*

**1837 Rehabilitation International**
4th Fl
25 E 21st St
New York, NY 10010-6207
212-420-1500
FAX: 212-505-0871
e-mail: ri@riglobal.org
riglobal.org

*Venus Ilagan, Manager*

RI is a global network of people with disabilities, service providers, researchers, government agencies, and advocates protecting and promoting the rights and inclusion of people with disabilities. RI has over 1,000 member organizations in all regions on the world.

**1838 Rehabilitation Technology Association Conference**
P.O.Box 1004
Institute, WV 25112-1004
304-766-4602
800-624-8284
FAX: 304-766-2689

*Betty Jo Tyler, RTA Coordinator*
*Dave Whipp, Information Manager*

RTA holds this annual conference for the rehab technology community. It also publishes a quarterly newsletter and houses the Project Enable computerized bulletin board system.
*Spring*

**1839 Source-APTA Audio Conference**
American Physical Therapy Association
1111 N Fairfax St
Alexandria, VA 22314-1488
703-684-2782
800-999-2782
FAX: 703-684-7343
TTY: 703-683-6748
e-mail: consumer@apta.org
apta.org

*Paul Rockar, Jr, PT, DPT, M, President*
*Sharon L. Dunn, PT, PhD, OCS, Vice President*
*Laurita M. Hack, PT, DPT, MBA, Ph, Secretary*
*Elmer Platz, PT, Treasurer*

The American Physical Therapy Association (APTA), a national professional organization representing more than 66,000 members, sponsors this annual conference. The goal is to foster advancements in physical therapy practice, research, and education.

**1840 TSA National Conference**
Tourette Syndrome Association
4240 Bell Blvd
Bayside, NY 11361-2874
718-224-2999
800-237-0717
FAX: 718-279-9596
e-mail: ts@tsa-usa.org
www.tsa-usa.org

*Judit Unger, President*
*Gary Frank, Executive VP*

More than 400 attendees come together for this biennial conference that includes members of the TS community and their families, educators, TS advocates, physicians, researchers, allied professionals, and TSA staff members. Attendees interact, socialize, share ideas, discuss issues of concern, learn from experts, and in many instances meet face to face for the first time.
*Spring*

**1841 Young Onset Parkinson Conference**
National Parkinson Foundation & ADPF
1501 NW 9th Ave
Miami, FL 33136-1494
305-243-6666
800-327-4545
FAX: 305-243-6073
e-mail: contact@parkinson.org
http://www.parkinson.org

*Joyce Oberdorf, President and CEO*
*Robin Boettcher, Vice President, Chapter and Community Partnerships*
*Pamela Olmo, Vice President, Finance & Administration*
*Peter Schmidt, PhD, Vice President, Programs, Chief Information Officer*
Purpose is to find the cause and cure for Parkinson's Disease and related neurodegenerative disorders through research, education and dissemination of current information to patients, care-givers and families.
*Annual*

# Construction & Architecture

## Associations

1842 **Adaptive Environments Center**
Suite 1
180-200 Portland St
Boston, MA 02114
617-695-1225
FAX: 617-482-8099
e-mail: info@HumanCenteredDesign.org
www.adaptenv.org

*Marie Trottier, Board President*
*Ana Julian, Information Specialist*
*Kathy Gips, Director of ADA Training and Technical Assistance*
*Valerie Fletcher, Executive Director*

Develops educational programs and materials on universal design, Americans with Disabilities Act, home adaptation, and more. Central Adaptive Environments publication list also available.

1843 **Building Owners and Managers Association International**
1101 15th St., NW
Suite 800
Washington, DC 20005-3999
202-408-2662
FAX: 202-326-6377
e-mail: info@boma.org
www.boma.org

*Boyd R. Zocc Zoccola, Chair & CEO*
*Joseph W. Markling, Chair-Elect*
*Richard W. Greninger, CPM, Vice Chair*
*Rebecca B. Hanner, CPM, RPA, Secretary/Treasurer*

Conducts seminars nationwide and publishes resource guidebooks for building owners and managers on ADA requirements for commercial facilities and places of public accommodation.

1844 **Mark Elmore Associates Architects**
Ste 104
42 East St
Crystal Lake, IL 60014-4400
815-455-7260
800-801-7766
FAX: 815-455-2238
e-mail: mark@elmore-architects.com
www.elmore-architects.com

*Mark A Elmore, Owner*

Architectural designs for accessible residential and commercial buildings. ADA compliance reviews.

1845 **National Conference on Building Codes and Standards**
Ste 210
505 Huntmar Park Dr
Herndon, VA 20170-5139
703-437-0100
FAX: 703-481-3596
e-mail: membership@ncsbcs.org
www.ncsbcs.org

*Debbie Becker, Administrative Assistant*
*Kevin Egilmez, Project Manager*

Serves as a forum in the interchange of information and provides technical services, education and training to our members to enhance the public's social and economic well being through safe, durable, affordable, accessible and efficient buildings.

1846 **National Council of Architectural Registration Boards (NCARB)**
Ste 700-K
1801 K St NW
Washington, DC 20006-1301
202-879-0520
FAX: 202-782-0290
e-mail: customerservice@ncarb.org
ncarb.org

*Michael J. Armstrong, Chief Executive Officer*
*Mary S. de Sousa, CAE, Vice President, Operations*
*Stephen Nutt, AIA, NCARB, CAE, Vice President, Programs*
*Erica Brown, AIA, NCARB, Director, Architect Registration Examination*

Research service in print and online information. Large collection of books and periodicals on the building/architectural environments.

1847 **Overcoming Mobility Barriers International**
1022 S 4st St
Omaha, NE 68105
402-342-5731
FAX: 402-342-5731

*Kay Neil, Executive Director*

Members are government officials, service consumers and providers, and other persons interested in removing mobility barriers for elderly, handicapped and disadvantaged persons. Advises and works in conjunction with other groups and government agencies to establish safety standards for special equipment used in retrofitting vehicles and works to retrain drivers in the use of nonconventional driving controls. Addresses such problems as possible allocation of fuel to so

1848 **Paradigm Design Group**
Paralyzed Veterans of America
801 18th St NW
Washington, DC 20006-3517
202-872-1300
800-424-8200
FAX: 202-785-4432
e-mail: info@pva.org
www.pva.org

*Bill Lawson, National President*
*Homer S. Townsend Jr., Executive Director*
*Al F. Kovach Jr., National Senior Vice Presedent*
*Craig F. Enenbach, National Treasurer*

Specialized firm providing architectural consulting services related to accessible designs. Experience includes product design and building codes and standards.

1849 **United States Access Board**
Ste 1000
1331 F St NW
Washington, DC 20004-1135
202-272-0080
800-872-2253
FAX: 202-272-0081
TTY: 800-993-2822
e-mail: info@access-board.gov
www.access-board.gov

*Dave Yanchulis, Public Affairs Specialist*

Offers information and technical assistance to the public on accessible design under the Americans with Disabilities Act and other laws. Guidance and publications are available free that address access to facilities, transit vehicles and information technology.

## Publications & Videos

**1850 Access Currents**
United States Access Board
Ste 1000
1331 F St NW
Washington, DC 20004-1111
202-272-0080
800-872-2253
FAX: 202-272-0081
TTY: 800-993-2822
e-mail: info@access-board.gov
www.access-board.gov

*Susan Brita, Chair*
*Karen L. Braitmayer, FAIA, Vice Chair*
*Regina Blye, Public Member*
*John Gunnar Box, Public Member*
Offers information and referrals on architectural accessibility for architects, designers, government agencies, building owners and consumers. A list of free publications is available on request.
*bi-monthly*

**1851 Access Equals Opportunity**
Council of B BB s Foundation
Ste 600
3033 Wilson Blvd
Arlington, VA 22201
703-276-0100
e-mail: media@cbbb.bbb.org
www.bbb.org

*Beverly Baskin, Senior VP, Chief Mission Officer*
*Genie Barton, Vice President and Director, Online Behavioral Advertising Program and*
*Rodney L. Davis, Senior VP Enterprise Programs*
*Joseph E. Dillon, VP and CFO*
These six Title III compliance guides for existing small businesses offer creative cheap and easy suggestions for complying with the public accommodations section of the ADA. Each guide is industry specific for: retail stores, car sales/service, restaurants/bars, medical offices and fun/fitness centers. They include suggestions for readily achievable removal of architectural barriers; effective communication; and guidance for nondiscriminatory policies or procedures. *$2.50*

**1852 Access House**
Northside Mental Health Center
1109 E 139th Ave
Tampa, FL 33613-3420
813-972-2289
FAX: 813-632-0933

*Cecil Woodside, Manager*
Barrier free regulations for design and construction.

**1853 Access for All**
Hospital Audiences
548 Broadway
3rd Floor
New York, NY 10012-7200
212-575-7676
FAX: 212-575-7669
e-mail: info@hostau.org
www.hospitalaudiences.org

*David Sweeny, Executive Director*
*Jane Kleinsinger, Director of Operations*
*Jill Bernard, Marketing & Outreach Manager*
*JoAnne Brockways, Chief Financial Officer*
Provides physical and program accessibility information for people with disabilities to New York City cultural institutions including theaters, museums, galleries, etc.

**1854 Accessible Home of Your Own**
Accent Books & Products
P.O.Box 700
Bloomington, IL 61702-700
309-378-2961
800-787-8444
FAX: 309-378-4420
e-mail: acmtlvng@aol.com
www.accentonliving.com

*Raymond C Cheever, Publisher*
*Betty Garee, Editor*
This guide includes 14 articles that have appeared in the magazine on the popular subject of how to make a disabled persons home more accessible. *$5.95*
*52 pages Paperback*
*ISBN 0-91570 -29-9*

**1855 Adaptable Housing: A Technical Manual for Implementing Adaptable Dwelling**
H UD U SE R
P.O.Box 23268
Washington, DC 20026-3268
202-708-3178
800-245-2691
FAX: 202-708-9981
TTY: 800-927-7589
e-mail: helpdesk@huduser.org
www.huduser.org

*Erika Poethig, Acting Assistant Secretary for Policy Development and Research*
*Sherone E. Ivey, Deputy Assistant Secretary*
*Patrick J. Tewey, Director, RB*
*Jacqueline D Buford, Director (AO), RM*
An illustrated manual describing methods for implementing adaptability in housing. *$3.00*

**1856 Adaptive Environments Center Home Assessment Form**
Ste 301
374 Congress St
Boston, MA 02210-1807
617-695-1225
FAX: 617-482-8099
e-mail: info@adaptiveenvironment.org
adaptiveenvironments.org

*Valerie Fletcher, Executive Director*
A handy checklist for evaluating a disabled person's abilities and his/her home limitations to determine what accessibility modifications will be most effective. *$5.00*

**1857 Consumer's Guide to Home Adaptation**
Adaptive Environments Center
Ste 301
374 Congress St
Boston, MA 02210-1807
617-695-1225
FAX: 617-482-8099
e-mail: info@AdaptiveEnvironments.org
adaptiveenvironments.org

*Valerie Fletcher, Executive Director*
*Ana Gomez, Coordinator Design/Communication*
*Mike DiLorenzo, Publications Coordinator*
A workbook that enables people with disabilities to plan the modifications necessary to adapt their homes. Describes how to widen doorways, lower countertops, etc. *$12.00*
*52 pages Paperback*

**1858 Design for Acessibility**
National Endowment for the Arts Office
1100 Pennsylvania Ave NW
Washington, DC 20506-1
202-682-5400
FAX: 202-682-5715
e-mail: webmgr@arts.endow.gov
arts.endow.gov

*Jamie Bennett, Chief of Staff*
*Sasha Burger, Confidential Assistant to the Chief of Staff*
*Mike Griffin, White House & Congressional Liaison*
*Kim Jefferson, Council Specialist*

A handbook for compliance with Section 504 of the Rehabilitation Act of 1973 and the Americans with Disabilities Act of 1990 including technical assistance on making arts programs accessible to staff, performers and audience.
*101 pages*
*ISBN 0-160042-83-6*

**1859 Directory of Accessible Building Products**
N AH B Research Center
400 Prince Georges Blvd
Upper Marlboro, MD 20774-8731
301-249-4000
800-638-8556
FAX: 301-430-6180
www.nahbrc.org

*Michael Luzier, CEO & President*
*Terre Belt, Vice President & Chief Operating Officer*
*Thomas Kenney, P.E, Vice President of Engineering & Research*
*Bill Ingley, Vice President & Controller*
Contains descriptions of more than 200 commercially available products designed for use by people with disabilities and age-related limitations. Paperback. *$5.00*
*104 pages Yearly*

**1860 Do-Able Renewable Home**
A AR P Fulfillment
601 E St NW
Washington, DC 20049-1
202-434-2277
888-687-2277
877-342-2277
FAX: 202-434-3443
e-mail: member@aarp.org
www.aarp.org

*A. Barry Rand, CEO*
*Hop Backus, Executive Vice President, State Operations*
*Steve Cone, Executive Vice President of Integrated Value*
*Lorraine Cortés-Vázquez, Executive Vice President, Multicultural Markets*
Describes how individuals with disabilities can modify their homes for independent living. Room-by-room modifications are accompanied by illustrations.

**1861 ECHO Housing: Recommended Construction and Installation Standards**
601 E St NW
Washington, DC 20049-1
202-434-2277
888-687-2277
877-342-2277
FAX: 202-434-3443
e-mail: member@aarp.org
www.aarp.org

*A. Barry Rand, CEO*
*Hop Backus, Executive Vice President, State Operations*
*Steve Cone, Executive Vice President of Integrated Value*
*Lorraine Cortés-Vázquez, Executive Vice President, Multicultural Markets*
Illustrated design, construction, and installation standards for temporary dwelling units for elderly people on single family residential property.

**1862 Electronic House: Enhanced Lifestyles with Electronics**
Electronic House
111 Speen Street, Suite 200
P.O. Box 989
Framingham, MA 01701-2000
508-663-1500
800-375-8015
FAX: 508-663-1599
e-mail: eheditorial@ehpub.com
electronichouse.com

*Kenneth D. Moyes, President*
*Karen Bligh, Marketing Director*
*John Brillon, Web Art Director*
*Guy Caiola, Director of Internet Operations*
Dedicated to home automation. Featuring both extravagant and affordable smart homes that can be controlled with one touch. EH covers electronic systems that give homeowners more security, entertainment, convenience, and fun. Articles cover whole house control and subsystems like residential lighting, security, home theater, energy management and telecommunications. *$23.95*
*84 pages BiMonthly*
*ISSN 0886-66 3*

**1863 Fair Housing Design Guide for Accessibility**
National Council on Multifamily Housing Industry
1201 15th & M St NW
Washington, DC 20005
202-266-8200
800-368-5242
FAX: 202-266-8400
e-mail: ggsmith@nahb.org
www.nahb.com

*Barry Rutenberg, CGP, Chairman of the Board*
*Rick Judson, CGP, First Vice Chairman of the Board*
*Kevin Kelly, Second Vice Chairman of the Board*
*Gerald M. Howard, CEO*
Specifically tailored to address the needs of architects and builders. The book includes a detailed technical analysis of the legislation's impact on multifamily design, highlights potential construction problems, and identifies possible solutions. *$29.95*

**1864 Ideas for Making Your Home Accessible**
Accent Books & Products
P.O.Box 700
Bloomington, IL 61702-700
309-378-2961
800-787-8444
FAX: 309-378-4420
e-mail: acmtlvng@aol.com
www.accentonliving.com

*Raymond C Cheever, Publisher*
*Betty Garee, Editor*
Offers over 100 pages of tips and ideas to help build or remodel a home. Includes many special devices and where to get them. *$7.50*
*94 pages Paperback*
*ISBN 0-91570 -08-6*

**1865 North Carolina Accessibility Code**
North Carolina Department of Insurance
P.O.Box 26387
Raleigh, NC 27611-6387
919-833-2110
FAX: 919-833-1801
e-mail: lwright@ncdoi.net

*Gregory Griggs, Executive VP*
Making buildings and facilities accessible to and usable by the physically handicapped. *$20.00*
*678 pages Triannually*

**1866 Removing the Barriers: Accessibility Guidelines and Specifications**
A PP A
1643 Prince St
Alexandria, VA 22314-2818
703-684-1446
FAX: 703-549-2772
e-mail: webmaster@appa.org
www.appa.org

*John F. Bernhards, Associate Vice President*
*Steve Glazner, Director of Knowledge Management*
*E. Lander Medlin, Executive VP*
*Chong-Hie Choi, Chief Financial Officer*
Offers site accessibility, building entrances, doors, interior circulation, restrooms and bathing facilities, drinking fountains and additional resources. *$45.00*
*125 pages*
*ISBN 0-91335 -59-9*

**1867 Smart Kitchen/How to Design a Comfortable, Safe & Friendly Workplace**

Ceres Press
P.O.Box 87
Woodstock, NY 12498-87
845-679-5573
FAX: 845-679-5573
e-mail: cem620@aol.com
healthyhighways.com

*David Goldbeck, Owner*

This book provides information about designing kitchens that may be helpful to people with disabilities as well as safe and energy efficient. *$16.95*

*132 pages Paperback*

**1868 United Spinal Association**

75-20 Astoria Blvd
Suite 120
East Elmhurst, NY 11370- 1177
718-803-3782
800-444-0120
FAX: 718-803-0414
e-mail: mkurtz@unitedspinal.org
www.unitedspinal.org

*Paul Tobin, President*
*Maria Kurtz, Executive Assistant*

Information on spinal cord injury and laws and regulations concerning people with disabilities, including veterans.

*Monthly*

# Education

## Aids for the Classroom

**1869 AEPS Child Progress Record: For Children Ages Three to Six**
Brookes Publishing
P.O.Box 10624
Baltimore, MD 21285-624
410-337-9580
800-638-3775
FAX: 410-337-8539
e-mail: custserv@brookespublishing.com
www.brookespublishing.com

*Paul Brooks, President*
*Melissa Behm, Executive VP*
*George Stamathis, VP and Publisher*
This chart helps monitor change by visually displaying current abilities, intervention targets, and child progress. In packages of 30. *$21.00*
*8 pages Gate-fold*
*ISBN 1-557662-51-7*

**1870 AEPS Curriculum for Three to Six Years**
Brookes Publishing
PO Box 10624
Baltimore, MD 21285-0624
410-337-9580
800-638-3775
FAX: 410-337-8539
e-mail: webmaster@brookespublishing.com
www.brookespublishing.com

*Jeff Brookes, President*
*George Stamathis, VP/Publisher*
*Diane Bricker, Editor*
*Misti Waddell, Co-Editor*
Used after the AEPS(r) Test is completed and scored, this developmentally sequenced curriculum allows professionals to match the child's IFSP/IEP goals and objectives with activity-based interventions - beginning with simple skills and moving on to more advanced skills. *$ 65.00*
*304 pages Spiral-bound*
*ISBN 1-557665-65-6*

**1871 AEPS Data Recording Forms: For Children Ages Three to Six**
Brookes Publishing
P.O.Box 10624
Baltimore, MD 21285-624
410-337-9580
800-638-3775
FAX: 410-337-8539
e-mail: custserv@brookespublishing.com
www.readplaylearn.com

*Paul Brooks, President*
These forms can be used by child development professionals on four separate occasions to pinpoint and then monitor a child's strengths and needs in the six key areas of skill development measured by the AEPS Test. Packages of 10. *$24.00*
*36 pages Saddle-stiched*
*ISBN 1-557662-49-5*

**1872 AEPS Family Interest Survey**
Brookes Publishing
P.O.Box 10624
Baltimore, MD 21285-624
410-337-9580
800-638-3775
FAX: 410-337-8539
e-mail: custserv@brookespublishing.com
www.brookespublishing.com

*Paul Brooks, President*
*Tracy Gracy, Educational Sales Manager*
This is a 30-item checklist that helps families to identify interests and concerns to address in a child's IEP/IFSP. Comes in packages of 30. *$15.00*
*8 pages Saddle-stiched*
*ISBN 1-557660-98-0*

**1873 Advanced Language Tool Kit**
School Specialty
PO Box 9031
Cambridge, MA 02139-9031
617-547-6706
800-225-5750
FAX: 888-440-2665
e-mail: support@schoolspecialty.com
eps.schoolspecialty.com

*Paula D Rome, Author*
*Jean S Osman, Co-Author*
*Rick Holden, President*
Provides an overview o the structure, organization, and sound units that are needed to develop skills for advanced reading and spelling. The kit contains a teacher's manual and 3 pack of cards, with features similar to the cards in the Language Tool Kit. *$60.00*

*ISBN 0-838885-48-9*

**1874 All Kinds of Minds**
School Specialty
PO Box 9031
Cambridge, MA 02139-9031
617-547-6706
800-225-5750
FAX: 888-440-2665
e-mail: support@schoolspecialty.com
eps.schoolspecialty.com

*Melvin D Levine, Author*
*Rick Holden, President*
A fictitious account of five different students who have learning disabilities. *$33.00*
*296 pages*
*ISBN 0-838820-90-5*

**1875 American Sign Language Handshape Cards**
T J Publishers, Distributor
Ste 206
817 Silver Spring Ave
Silver Spring, MD 20910- 4617
301-585-4440
800-999-1168
FAX: 301-585-5930
e-mail: tjpubinc@aol.com

*Angela K Thames, President*
*Jerald A Murphy, VP*
Durable flashcards illustrate basic handshapes, classifiers and the American manual alphabet. An instructional booklet describes games for differing skill levels to improve vocabulary, increase hand and eye coordination, sign recognition and usage. *$16.95*

**1876 Asthma Action Cards: Child Care Asthma/Allergy Action Card**
Asthma and Allergy Foundation of America
8201 Corporate Drive
Suite 1000
Landover, MD 20785
202-466-7643
800-727-8462
FAX: 202-466-8940
e-mail: info@aafa.org
www.aafa.org

*Tom Flanigan, Chariman*
*William Mclin, President and CEO*
*Yolanda Miller, VP and CFO*
Includes necessary information a provider needs to care for a young child who has asthma and allergies. The card includes a medication plan, a list of the child's specific signs and symptoms

that indicate the child is having trouble breathing, and steps on how to handle an emergency situation.

**1877 Asthma Action Cards: Student Asthma Action Card**

Asthma and Allergy Foundation of America
1233 20th St NW
Suite 610
Washington, DC 20036-2330
202-833-1700
800-727-8462
FAX: 202-833-2351
e-mail: info@aafa.org
www.swmlaw.com

*Bill Mc Lin, Executive Director*
*Ben C Hadden, VP Finance & Treasurer*
*Bill Lin, Executive Director*

Tool for communicating school aged children's and teen's asthma managment plan to school personnel. Includes sections for asthma triggers, daily medications, and emergency directions.

**1878 Auditech: Classroom Amplification System Focus CFM802**

P.O.Box 821105
Vicksburg, MS 39182-1105
800-229-8293
FAX: 800-221-8639
e-mail: info@auditechusa.com
www.auditechusa.com

The SOUNDFOCUS FM System is designed to cover background noise and compensate for distance. Students find it easier to focus their attention and not strain to be heard. Two speaker system. *$1052.00*

**1879 Auditech: Personal FM Educational System**

P.O.Box 821105
Vicksburg, MS 39182-1105
800-229-8293
FAX: 800-221-8639
e-mail: info@auditechusa.com
www.auditechusa.com

Personal FM Educational System is a portable system for classroom use. The teacher wears a microphone. Students use a portable receiver which works clearly and easily. For users who have a hearing problem, a switch, a necklooop telecoil coupler is available. *$679.00*

**1880 Auditory-Verbal Therapy for Parents and Professionals**

Alexander Graham Bell Association
3417 Volta Pl NW
Washington, DC 20007-2737
202-337-5220
FAX: 202-337-8314
TTY:202-337-5221
e-mail: info@agbell.org
agbell.org

*Warren Estabrooks, Author*
*Cheryl L. Dickson, M.Ed., LSLS C, President*
*Anita Bernstein, M.Sc., Dip., Director*
*Lyn Robertson, Ph.D., President Elect*

A must-have for hearing health professionals, students entering hearing health fields and parents who want to explore the theory and practices of auditory-verbal therapy. *$54.95*
*313 pages Paperback*

**1881 Barrier Free Education**

Center for Assistive Technology & Env Access
490 10th St NW
Atlanta, GA 30332-1
404-894-4960
800-726-9119
FAX: 404-894-9320
www.catea.org

*Elizabeth Bryant, Project Director*

Math and science activities pose unique accommodation challenges for students with disabilities. The Barrier Free Education resource on accessible science experiments was developed for high school chemistry and physics students with physical or visual disabilities under the National Science Foundation's Program for Persons with Disabilities.

**1882 Beginning Reasoning and Reading**

School Specialty
PO Box 9031
Cambridge, MA 02139-9031
617-547-6706
800-225-5750
FAX: 888-440-2665
e-mail: support@schoolspecialty.com
eps.schoolspecialty.com

*Joanne Carlisle, Author*
*Rick Holden, President*

This workbook develops basic language and thinking skills that build the foundation for reading comprehension. Workbook exercises reinforce reading as a critical reasoning activity. *$10.45*

*ISBN 0-838830-01-3*

**1883 Buy!**

JE Stewart Teaching Tools
P.O.Box 15308
Seattle, WA 98115-308
206-262-9538
FAX: 206-262-9538

*Jeff Stewart, Owner*

Teaches 50 words as they appear in commercial and community situations such as clinic, sale, receipt, price and cleaner. These words are functional at school, on the job and shopping. *$32.50*
*116 pages*
*ISBN 1-877866-05-9*

**1884 Catalog for Teaching Life Skills to Persons with Development Disability**

PCI Education Publishing
PO Box 34270
San Antonio, TX 78265-4270
210-377-1999
800-594-4263
FAX: 888-259-8284
www.pcieducation.com

*Lee Wilson, President/CEO*
*Erin Kinard, VP Product Development/Publisher*
*Randy Pennington, VP, Sales & Marketing*

Over 200 educational products that help individuals learn and maintain the life skills they need to succeed in an inclusive society.

**1885 Classroom GOAL: Guide for Optimizing Auditory Learning Skills**

Alexander Graham Bell Association
3417 Volta Pl NW
Washington, DC 20007-2737
202-337-5220
FAX: 202-337-8314
e-mail: info@agbell.org
www.agbell.org

*Alexander Graham, Executive Director*
*Judy Harrison, Director of Programs*
*Susan Boswell, Communications and Marketing*

This reader-friendly teacher's guide filled with tips, source materials and sample charts and plans is designed for educators who have yearned for a resource that explains how to incorporate auditory goals into academic learning for students with different degrees of hearing loss. *$34.95*
*Paperback*

**1886 Classroom Notetaker: How to Organize a Program Serving Students with Hearing Impairments**

Alexander Graham Bell Association
3417 Volta Pl NW
Washington, DC 20007-2737
202-337-5220
FAX: 202-337-8314
e-mail: info@agbell.org
www.agbell.org

*Alexander Graham, Executive Director*
*Judy Harrison, Director of Programs*
*Susan Boswell, Communications and Marketing*

This detailed manual for instructors, administrators and staff notetakers promotes classroom notetaking within long-term educational programs as absolutely vital for students who are deaf and hard of hearing from elementary school to college. *$24.95*
*127 pages Paperback*

**1887 Community Services for the Blind and Partially Sighted Store: Sight Connection**
9709 Third Ave NE
Ste 100
Seattle, WA 98115-2027
206-525-5556
800-458-4888
FAX: 206-525-0422
e-mail: support@schoolspecialty.com
www.csbps.com

*Miles Otoupal, Chair*
*Jonathan Avedovech, Vice Chair*
*David McBride, Treasurer*
*Matthew Weed, Secretary*
Over 400 products specifically designed to make life easier for people with vision loss.

**1888 Community Signs**
JE Stewart Teaching Tools
P.O.Box 15308
Seattle, WA 98115-308
206-262-9538
FAX: 206-262-9538

*Jeff Stewart, Owner*
Teaches 50 words like go, fire, rest room, men, women, danger and walk needed to successfully navigate our environment. *$ 32.50*

**1889 Comprehensive Assessment of Spoken Language (CASL)**
AGS
P.O.Box 99
Circle Pines, MN 55014-99
800-328-2560
FAX: 800-471-8457
e-mail: agsmail@agsnet.com
www.agsnet.com

*Kevin Brueggeman, President*
*Robert Zaske, Market Manager*
CASL is an individually and orally administered research-based, theory-drive oral language assessment battery for ages 3 through 21. Fifteen tests measure language processing skills - comprehension, expression, and retrieval - in four language structure categories: lexical/semantic, syntactic, supralinguistic and pragmatic. *$299.95*

**1890 Creative Arts Therapy Catalogs**
MMB Music
9051 Watson Road
Suite 161
Saint Louis, MO 63126-1019
314-531-9635
800-543-3771
FAX: 314-531-8384
e-mail: info@mmbmusic.com
www.mmbmusic.com

*Marcia Goldberg, President*
Catalogs of books, videos, recordings for the creative arts and wellness (music, art, dance, poetry, drama, therapies, photography).

**1891 Cursive Writing Skills**
School Specialty
PO Box 9031
Cambridge, MA 02139-9031
617-547-6706
800-225-5750
FAX: 888-440-2665
e-mail: support@schoolspecialty.com
eps.schoolspecialty.com

*Diana Hanbury King, Author*
*Rick Holden, President*
Boosts writing achievement through handwriting skills. Handwriting instruction helps students become fluent writers, allowing them to focus on their thoughts and ideas rather than on letter and word formation. *$12.00*

*ISBN 0-83881 -05-*

**1892 Don Johnston**
26799 W Commerce Dr
Volo, IL 60073-9675
847-740-0749
800-999-4660
FAX: 847-740-7326
e-mail: info@donjohnston.com
www.donjohnston.com

*Ruth Ziolkowski, President*
*Don Johnston, CEO*
*Kevin Johnston, Director of Product Design*
*Ben Johnston, Director of Marketing*
A provider of quality products and services that enable people with special needs to discover their potential and experience success. Products are developed for the areas of Physical Access, Augmentative Communication and for those who struggle with reading and writing.

**1893 Dyslexia Training Program**
School Specialty
PO Box 9031
Cambridge, MA 02139-9031
617-547-6706
800-225-5750
FAX: 888-440-2665
e-mail: support@schoolspecialty.com
eps.schoolspecialty.com

*Rick Holden, President*
This 2-year, cumulative series of daily 1-hour video lessons and accompanying Studet's Books and Teacher's Guides is a structured, multisensory sequence of alphabet, reading, spelling, cursive handwriting, listening, language history, and review activities. Written by the Texas Scottish Rite Hospital for Children.

**1894 Exceptional Teaching Inc**
Exceptional Teaching Inc
3994 Oleander Way
Castro Valley, CA 94546
510-889-7282
800-549-6999
FAX: 510-889-7382
e-mail: info@exceptionalteaching.com
www.exceptionalteaching.com

*Helene Holman, Owner/manager*
Providing educational products for those with special needs via catalog and online store.

**1895 Explode the Code**
School Specialty
PO Box 9031
Cambridge, MA 02139-9031
800-435-7728
800-225-5750
FAX: 888-440-2665
e-mail: support@schoolspecialty.com
eps.schoolspecialty.com

*Nancy M Hall, Author*
Helps students build the essential literacy skills needed for reading success: phonological awareness, decoding, vocabulary, comprehension, fluency and spelling. *$6.20*
*Grades K-4, 1-3*
*ISBN 0-83881 -60-*

**1896 Food!**
JE Stewart Teaching Tools
P.O.Box 15308
Seattle, WA 98115-308 206-262-9538
FAX: 206-262-9538

*Jeff Stewart, Owner*
Teaches 50 words like salt, pepper, hamburger, fruit, milk and soup, seen commonly on menus, packages and in directions used at home and at play. *$32.50*

**1897 Fun for Everyone**
AbleNet
2625 Patton Road
Roseville, MN 55113-1308 651-294-2200
800-322-0956
FAX: 651-294-2259
e-mail: customerservice@ablenetinc.com
www.ablenetinc.com

*Jen Thalhuber, CEO*
*Ann Meyer, Vice President*
*Paul Sugden, VP Finance*
*Jason Voiovich, VP Marketing*
Today, simple technology allows children and adults with disabilities to participate in leisure activities they were limited or excluded from in the past. *$20.00*

**1898 Fundamentals of Autism**
Slosson Educational Publications Inc.
538 Buffalo Road
East Aurora, NY 14052-280 716-652-0930
800-655-3840
888-756-7760
FAX: 716-655-3840
e-mail: slossonprep@gmail.com
www.slosson.com

*Steven Slosson, President*
*John Slosson, VP*
*David Slosson, VP*
The Fundamentals of Autism handbook provides a quick, user friendly, effective and accurate approach to help in identifying and developing educationally related program objectives for children diagnosed as autistic. These materials have been designed to be easily and functionally used by teachers, therapists, special education/learning disability resource specialists, psychologists and others who work with children diagnosed as autistic. *$56.00*
*72 pages*

**1899 GO-MO Articulation Cards- Second Edition**
Sage Publications
2455 Teller Road
Thousand Oaks, CA 91320 805-499-9774
800-818-7243
FAX: 800-583-2665
e-mail: info@sagepub.com
www.sagepub.com

*Blaise R Simqu, President & CEO*
*Tracey Ozmina, VP and COO*
*Chris Hickok, Senior VP and CFO*
*Stephen Barr, Managing Director*
The most popular system used for remedying defective speech articulation in children and adults. This popular card set was the first and is still the best therapy tool of its kind, as it continues to produce results and maintains the interest of students of all ages.

**1900 Gillingham Manaual**
School Specialty
PO Box 9031
Cambridge, MA 02139-9031 617-547-6706
800-225-5750
FAX: 888-440-2665
e-mail: support@schoolspecialty.com
eps.schoolspecialty.com

*Anna Gillingham, Author*
*Bessie W Stillman, Co-Author*
*Rick Holden, President*
Remedial training for children with specific disability in reading, spelling, and penmanship. The name is “"The Gillingham Manual & Materials""
*352 pages 69.95*
*ISBN 0-83880 -00-*

**1901 Guide to Teaching Phonics**
School Specialty
PO Box 9031
Cambridge, MA 02139-9031 617-547-6706
800-225-5750
FAX: 888-440-2665
e-mail: support@schoolspecialty.com
eps.schoolspecialty.com

*June Lyday Orton, Author*
*Rick Holden, President*
This flexible teacher's guide presents multisensory procedures developed in association with the late Dr. Samuel Orton. They consist of 100 phonograms for teaching phonetic elements and their sequences in words for reading, writing and spelling. Also contains coordinated Phonics Cards. *$19.25*
*96 pages*
*ISBN 0-838802-41-9*

**1902 Homemade Battery-Powered Toys**
Special Needs Project
Ste H
324 State St
Santa Barbara, CA 93101-2364 805-962-8087
800-333-6867
FAX: 805-962-5087
e-mail: books@specialneeds.com
www.specialneeds.com

*Hod Gray, Owner*
*Laraine Gray, Coordinator*
Describes how to make simple switches and educational devices for severely handicapped children. *$7.50*

**1903 Idaho Assistive Technology Project**
University of Idaho
PO Box 444061
Moscow, ID 83844-4061 208-885-6097
800-432-8324
FAX: 208-885-6145
e-mail: janicec@uidaho.edu
www.idahoat.org

*Janice Carson, Project Director*
*Sue House, Information/Referral Specialst*
A federally funded program managed by the Center on Disabilities and Human Development at the University of Idaho. The goal is to increase the availability of assistive technology devices and services for Idahoans with disabilities. *$15.00*

**1904 If It Is To Be, It Is Up To Me To Do It!**
AVKO Educational Research Foundation
3084 Willard Rd
Birch Run, MI 48415-9404
810-686-9283
866-285-6612
FAX: 810-686-1101
e-mail: webmaster@avko.org
www.avko.org

*Don McCabe, Research Director, Emeritus*
*Barry Chute, President*
*Julie Guyette, Vice President*
*Clifford Schroeder, Treasurer*
A student and tutor's text, for use on dyslexics and non-dyslexics, by parents, spouses, or friends. *$29.95*
*206 pages*
*ISBN 1-564007-42-1*

**1905 Inclusive Play People**
Educational Equity Concepts
Fl 8
100 5th Ave
New York, NY 10011-6903
212-243-1110
FAX: 212-627-0407
TTY:212-725-1803
e-mail: information@edequity.org
www.iconcapital.com

*Jacqueline Johnson, Manager*
Six sturdy multiracial wooden figures that provide a unique variety of nonstereotyped work and family roles and are inclusive of disabled and nondisabled people of various ages. For block building and dramatic play. *$25.00*

**1906 Individualized Keyboarding**
AVKO Educational Research Foundation
3084 Willard Rd
Birch Run, MI 48415-9404
810-686-9283
866-285-6612
FAX: 810-686-1101
e-mail: webmaster@avko.org
www.avko.org

*Don McCabe, Research Director, Emeritus*
*Barry Chute, President*
*Julie Guyette, Vice President*
*Clifford Schroeder, Treasurer*
Utilizes a multi-sensory approach to teach typing skills. It not only teaches typing skills, it also reinforces the reading patterns that are necessary for typing proficiency. *$14.95*
*96 pages*
*ISBN 1-654004-01-5*

**1907 Instruction of Persons with Severe Handicaps**
McGraw-Hill School Publishing
P.O. Box 182604
Columbus, OH 43272
877-833-5524
FAX: 614-759-3749
e-mail: customer.service@mcgraw-hill.com
www.mcgraw-hill.com

*Harold McGraw, President and CEO*
*Jack Callahan, Executive VP*
*John Berisford, Executive VP of HR*
A complete introduction to the status of education as it pertains to people with severe handicaps.

**1908 Keeping Ahead in School**
Educators Publishing Service
P.O.Box 9031
Cambridge, MA 2139-9031
617-547-6706
800-225-5750
FAX: 888-440-2665
e-mail: feedback@epsbooks.com
www.epsbooks.com

*Charles H Heinle, VP*
*Alexandra S Bigelow, Author*
*Gunnar Voltz, President*
This book helps students not only understand their own strengths and weaknesses but also more fully appreciate their individuality. He suggests specific ways to approach work, bypass or overcome learning disorders, and manage other struggles that may beset students in school. *$24.75*
*320 pages Paperback*
*ISBN 0-838820-69-7*

**1909 KeyMath Teach and Practice**
AGS
P.O.Box 99
Circle Pines, MN 55014-99
800-328-2560
FAX: 800-471-8457
e-mail: agsmail@agsnet.com
www.agsnet.com

*Kevin Brueggeman, President*
*Robert Zaske, Market Manager*
This set of materials provides all the tools needed to assess students' math skills...and the strategies to deal with problem areas. Three sets are available: Basic Concepts Package; Operations Package; and Applications Package. $219.95 each or $599.95 for whole set.

**1910 Lakeshore Learning Materials**
2695 E Dominguez St
Carson, CA 90895-1001
310-537-8600
800-421-5354
FAX: 800-537-5403
e-mail: lakeshore@lakeshorelearning.com
www.lakeshorelearning.com

*Bo Kaplan, President/CEO*
*Josh Kaplan, VP Merchandising*
*Mat , Vice President of Operations*
Offers books, resources, testing materials, assessment information and special education materials for the professional in the field of special education.
*190 pages*

**1911 Language Parts Catalog**
School Specialty
PO Box 9031
Cambridge, MA 02139-9031
617-547-6706
800-225-5750
FAX: 888-440-2665
e-mail: support@schoolspecialty.com
eps.schoolspecialty.com

*Melvin D Levine, Author*
*Rick Holden, President*
Offers a humorous and informative explanation of the various aspects of language and how they operate. Laid out in the form of a catalog, the book presents various parts that can help students improve their language abilities. *$12.65*

*ISBN 0-838819-80-X*

**1912 Language Tool Kit**
School Specialty
PO Box 9031
Cambridge, MA 02139-9031
617-547-6706
800-225-5750
FAX: 888-440-2665
e-mail: support@schoolspecialty.com
eps.schoolspecialty.com

*Paula D Rome, Author*
*Jean S Osman, Co-Author*
Designed for use by a teacher or parents, teaches reading and spelling to students with specific language disability. *$43.25*
*32 pages English Edition*
*ISBN 0-838885-20-3*

**1913 Language, Speech and Hearing Services in School**
American Speech-Language-Hearing Association
10801 Rockville Pike
Rockville, MD 20852-3226
301-296-5700
800-638-8255
FAX: 301-296-8580
e-mail: actioncenter@asha.org
www.asha.org

*Paul Rao, President*
*Robert Augustine, VP of Finance*
*Arlene Pietranton, Executive Director*
Professional journal for clinicians, audiologists and speech-language pathologists. *$30.00*

**1914 Learning American Sign Language**
Harris Communications
15155 Technology Dr
Eden Prairie, MN 55344-2273
952-906-1180
800-825-6758
FAX: 952-906-1099
e-mail: info@harriscomm.com
www.harriscomm.com

*Robert Harris, President*
*Kevin Horsky, Business Director*
Offers over 700 titles on ASL including books, videotapes, CDs & DVDs. Free catalog available. *$78.95*
*350 pages Video & Book*

**1915 Learning to Sign in My Neighborhood**
T J Publishers
2544 Tarpley Rd
Suite 108
Carrollton, TX 75006-2288
972-416-0800
800-999-1168
FAX: 301-585-5930
e-mail: tjpubinc@aol.com

*Angela K Thames, President*
*Jerald A Murphy, VP*
Beautifully illustrated coloring book lets children learn signs from kids just like themselves! Recommended for ages 4 and up, let children have fun while they learn signs for words typically used in day-to-day activities. *$3.50*
*32 pages Softcover*
*ISBN 0-93266 -36-1*

**1916 Literacy Program**
School Specialty
PO Box 9031
Cambridge, MA 02139-9031
617-547-6706
800-225-5750
FAX: 888-440-2665
e-mail: support@schoolspecialty.com
eps.schoolspecialty.com

*Rick Holden, President*
Written by the Texas Scottish Rite Hospital for Children. A one-year course that consists of 160 one-hour videotaped lessons accompanied by student workbooks, designed for high school students and adults who read below sixth grade level.

**1917 Literature Based Reading**
Oryx Press
4041 N Central Ave
Phoenix, AZ 85012-3330
602-265-2651
800-279-6799
FAX: 800-279-4663
Series offering children's books and activities to enrich the K-5 curriculum.

**1918 Living an Idea: Empowerment and the Evolution of an Alternative School**
Brookline Books
34 University Rd
Brookline, MA 2445-4533
617-734-6772
800-666-2665
FAX: 617-734-3952
e-mail: brbooks@yahoo.com
www.brooklinebooks.com

*William H Walters, Author*
*Esther Wilder, Co-Author*
This book is about the creation and 14 year evolution of a public alternative inner-city high school. The school lived an idea - empowerment. Students were encouraged to participate in shaping many aspects of their education, teachers were responsible for running the school, and parents invited to help govern. *$27.95*
*ISBN 0-91479 -68-9*

**1919 Low Tech Assistive Devices: A Handbook for the School Setting**
Therapro, Inc.
225 Arlington St
Framingham, MA 01702-8773
508-872-9494
800-257-5376
FAX: 508-875-2062
e-mail: info@therapro.com
www.therapro.com

*Karen Conrad, Owner*
A how-to book with step by step directions and detailed illustrations for fabrication of frequently requested low-tech assistive devices. *$45.00*
*320 pages Paperback*

**1920 MTA Readers**
Educators Publishing Service
PO Box 9031
Cambridge, MA 02139-9031
617-547-6706
800-225-5750
FAX: 888-440-2665
e-mail: support@schoolspecialty.com
www.epsbooks.com

*Rick Holden, President*
Illustrated readers for grades 1-3 that accompany the MTA Reading and Spelling Program (Multisensory Teaching Approach). Phonetic elements in a structured, but entertaining context.
*48+ pages $4.65 - $11.65*
*ISBN 0-83882 -33-3*

**1921 Making School Inclusion Work: A Guide to Everyday Practice**
Brookline Books
34 University Rd
Brookline, MA 2445-4533
617-734-6772
800-666-2665
FAX: 617-734-3952
e-mail: brbooks@yahoo.com
www.brooklinebooks.com

*William H Walters, Author*
*Esther Wilder, Co-Author*

This book tells the reader how to conduct a truly inclusive program, regardless of ethnic or racial background, economic level and physical or cognitive ability. *$24.95*
*254 pages*
*ISBN 0-914791-96-4*

**1922 Making the Writing Process Work: Strategies for Composition and Self-Regulation**
Brookline Books
34 University Rd
Brookline, MA 2445-4533 617-734-6772
800-666-2665
FAX: 617-734-3952
e-mail: brbooks@yahoo.com
www.brooklinebooks.com

*William H Walters, Author*
*Esther Wilder, Co-Author*
This book is geared toward students who have difficulty organizing their thoughts and developing their writing. The specific stategies teach students how to approach, organize, and produce a final written product.. *$24.95*
*240 pages Paperback*
*ISBN 1-571290-10-9*

**1923 Manual Alphabet Poster**
TJ Publishers
Ste 108
2544 Tarpley Rd
Carrollton, TX 75006-2288 972-416-0800
800-999-1168
FAX: 972-416-0944
e-mail: TJPubinc@aol.com
www.TJpublishers.com

*Pat O'Rourke, President*
Poster presents the manual alphabet. *$4.50*

**1924 Many Faces of Dyslexia**
40 York Rd
4th Floor
Baltimore, MD 21204-5243 410-296-0232
FAX: 410-321-5069
www.interdys.org

*Nancy Hennessy, President*
*Sandra Soper, Vice President*
*Thoman Viall, Executive Director*
Gives information on the teaching and rehabilitation techniques for people with dyslexia. *$16.50*
*Paperback*

**1925 Match-Sort-Assemble Job Cards**
Exceptional Education
P.O.Box 15308
Seattle, WA 98115-308 206-262-9538

*Jeff Stewart, Owner*
Teaches workers to use a series of symbolic cues to control their own production cycles. *$565.00*
*Class Set*

**1926 Match-Sort-Assemble Pictures**
Exceptional Education
P.O.Box 15308
Seattle, WA 98115-308 206-262-9538

*Jeff Stewart, Owner*
People with profound, severe and moderate mental retardation have immediate access with MSA Pictures. Students work with pictures (and if necessary a template) to match, sort, assemble and disassemble parts that vary in shape, length and diameter. *$426.00*
*Class Set*

**1927 Match-Sort-Assemble SCHEMATICS**
Exceptional Education
P.O.Box 15308
Seattle, WA 98115-308 206-262-9538

*Jeff Stewart, Owner*
Students with moderate and mild mental retardation and those who have completed MSA Pictures are ready for MSA Schematics. It increases abstraction and displacement of instruction from the work clearly and simply. *$495.00*
*Class Set*

**1928 Match-Sort-Assemble TOOLS**
Exceptional Education
P.O.Box 15308
Seattle, WA 98115-308 206-262-9538
FAX: 475-486-4510

*Jeff Stewart, Owner*
Students and clients learn to use the tools required for many jobs in light industry. Mastery of the production cycle with independence, endurance and the ability to learn new tasks through pictures and schematics and basic hand functions will help clients acquire and maintain employment in a competitive field. *$595.00*
*Class Set*

**1929 Meeting-in-a-Box**
Asthma and Allergy Foundation of America
1233 20th St NW
Suite 610
Washington, DC 20036-2330 202-833-1700
800-7AS-THMA
FAX: 202-833-2351
e-mail: info@aafa.org
www.swmlaw.com

*Bill Mc Lin, Executive Director*
*Bill Mclin, Executive Director*
A series of self-contained, comprehensive kits that contain all the necessary components for a successful asthma presentation.

**1930 More Food!**
JE Stewart Teaching Tools
P.O.Box 15308
Seattle, WA 98115-308 206-262-9538
FAX: 206-262-9538

*Jeff Stewart, Owner*
Teaches 50 more words found in restaurants, grocery stores, cookbooks such as pizza, carrot, tacos, oysters and pineapple. These words are functional at home, going shopping and during leisure. *$32.50*

**1931 More Work!**
J E Stewart Teaching Tools
P.O.Box 15308
Seattle, WA 98115-308 206-262-9538
FAX: 206-262-9538

*Jeff Stewart, Owner*
Teaches 50 words as they appear on parts, tools, job instructions, signs and labels, such as fill, grasp, release, lock, search, position and select. These words are functional in school and on-the-job. *$32.50*

**1932 Multisensory Teaching Approach**
Educators Publishing Service
P.O.Box 9031
Cambridge, MA 2139-9031 617-367-2700
800-225-5750
FAX: 617-547-0412
www.epsbooks.com

Comprehensive multisensory program in reading, writing, spelling, alphabet and dictionary skills for remedial and regular instruction. Based on Orton-Gillingham and Alphabetic Phonics. A

complete program organized in kits, with additional classroom materials, supplementary materials, and handwriting programs.
*$110 - $140*
*ISBN 0-83888 -10-9*

**1933 Peabody Articulation Decks**
AGS
P.O.Box 99
Circle Pines, MN 55014-99 651-287-7220
800-328-2560
FAX: 763-786-9007
e-mail: agsmail@agsnet.com
www.agsnet.com

*Keith Powel, Special Education Transition Coo*
*Robert Zaske, Marketing Manager*
Complete kit of playing-card sized PAD decks let students focus on the 18 most commonly misarticulated English consonants and blends. *$115.95*

*ISBN 0-88671 -75-4*

**1934 Phonemic Awareness in Young Children: A Classroom Curriculum**
Brookes Publishing
P.O.Box 10624
Baltimore, MD 21285-624 410-337-9580
800-638-3775
FAX: 410-337-8539
e-mail: custserv@brookespublishing.com
www.brookespublishing.com

*Clary Creighton, Exhibits Coordinator*
*Tracy Gray, Educational Sales Manager*
*Paul Brooks, Owner*
This is a supplemental, whole-class curriculum for improving pre-literacy listening skills. It contains activities that are fun, easy to use, and proven to work in any kindergarten classroom - general, bilingual, inclusive, or special education. This program takes only 15-20 minutes a day. *$24.95*
*208 pages Spiral-bound*
*ISBN 1-557663-21-1*

**1935 Phonics for Thought**
Educators Publishing Service
P.O.Box 9031
Cambridge, MA 2139-9031 617-367-2700
800-225-5750
FAX: 617-547-0412
www.epsbooks.com

*$8.00*
*Paperback*

**1936 Phonological Awareness Training for Reading**
Sage Publications
2455 Teller Road
Thousand Oaks, CA 91320 805-499-9774
800-818-7243
FAX: 800-583-2665
e-mail: info@sagepub.com
www.sagepub.com

*Blaise R Simqu, President & CEO*
*Tracey Ozmina, Executive VP*
*Chris Hickok, Executive VP and CFO*
*Stephen Barr, Managing Director*
Designed to increase the level of phonological awareness in young children. Can be taught individually or in small groups and takes about 12 to 14 weeks to complete if children are taught in short sessions three or four times a week. *$129.00*

**1937 Play!**
JE Stewart Teaching Tools
P.O.Box 15308
Seattle, WA 98115-308 206-262-9538
FAX: 206-262-9538

*Jeff Stewart, Owner*
Teaches 50 more words as they appear at recreation sites, on signs and labels and in newspapers and magazines, such as movie, visitor, ticket, gallery and zoo. These words are functional in school and at leisure. *$32.50*

**1938 Power Breathing Program**
Asthma and Allergy Foundation of America
8201 Corporate Drive
Suite 1000
Landover, MD 20785 202-466-7643
800-727-8462
FAX: 202-466-8940
e-mail: info@aafa.org
www.aafa.org

*Bill McLin, Executive Director*
Devoloped the only asthma education program specifically designed for and pre-tested with teens. Teens with asthma have special challenges. This interactive program covers everything from the basics of asthma to dealing with their asthma in social situations, in college, and on the job. Includes everything you need to present this three-four session program. *$295.00*

**1939 Primary Phonics**
School Specialty
PO Box 9031
Cambridge, MA 02139-9031 617-547-6706
800-225-5750
FAX: 888-440-2665
e-mail: support@schoolspecialty.com
eps.schoolspecialty.com

*Barbara W Makar, Author*
*Rick Holden, President*
A program of storybooks and coordinated workbooks that teaches reading for grades K-2. A structured phonetic approach. Contains 8 student workbooks, with 8 sets of 10 coordinated storybooks; consonant workbooks; initial consonant blend workbooks; picture dictionary, and coloring book.

*ISSN 0838-83 0*

**1940 Reading for Content**
School Specialty
PO Box 9031
Cambridge, MA 02139-9031 617-547-6706
800-225-5750
FAX: 888-440-2665
e-mail: support@schoolspecialty.com
eps.schoolspecialty.com

*Carol Einstein, Author*
*Rick Holden, President*
A series of 4 books designed to help students improve their reading comprehension skills. Each book contains 43 reading passages followed by 4 questions. Two questions as for a recall of main ideas, and two ask the student to draw conclusions from what they have read. *$ 11.45*
*96 pages*

**1941 Reading from Scratch**
Educators Publishing Service
P.O.Box 9031
Cambridge, MA 2139-9031 617-367-2700
800-225-5750
FAX: 617-547-0412
www.epsbooks.com

Contains multisensory reading and spelling material and oral and written lessons and exercises in syntax, grammar, and precomposition topics. Complete set.
*$6.25 - $49.30*
*ISBN 0-83888 -75-5*

**1942 Recipe for Reading**
School Specialty
PO Box 9031
Cambridge, MA 02139-9031
617-367-2700
800-435-7728
FAX: 888-440-2665
e-mail: support@schoolspecialty.com
eps.schoolspecialty.com

*Nina Traub, Author*
*Frances Bloom, Co-Author*
*Rick Holden, President*
Contains comprehensive, multisensory, phonics-based reading program presents a skill sequence and lesson structured designed for beginning, at-risk, or struggling readers.

**1943 Rewarding Speech**
Speech Bin
PO Box 1579
Appleton, WI 54912
772-770-0007
888-388-3224
FAX: 888-388-6344
e-mail: customercare@schoolspecialty.com
www.speechbin.com

*Jan J Binney, Senior Editor*
Reproducible reward certificates for children. *$12.95*
*32 pages*

**1944 SAYdee Posters**
Speech Bin
PO Box 1579
Appleton, WI 54912
772-770-0007
888-388-3224
FAX: 888-388-6344
e-mail: customercare@schoolspecialty.com
www.speechbin.com

*Jan J Binney, Senior Editor*
Colorful speech and language posters. *$20.00*
*24 pages*
*ISBN 0-93785 -47-5*

**1945 Sequential Spelling: 1-7 with 7 Student Response Books**
AVKO Educational Research Foundation
3084 Willard Rd
Birch Run, MI 48415-9404
810-686-9283
866-285-6612
FAX: 810-686-1101
e-mail: webmaster@avko.orgE
www.avko.org

*Deborah Wolf, President*
*Aaron Miller, Vice President*
Sequential Spelling uses immediate student self-correction. It builds from easier words of a word family such as all and then builds on them to teach; all, tall, stall, install, call, fall, ball, and their inflected forms such as: stalls, stalled, stalling, installing, installment. *$89.95*
*72 pages $8.95 each*
*ISBN 1-56400 -11-6*

**1946 Signing Naturally Curriculum**
Harris Communications
15155 Technology Dr
Eden Prairie, MN 55344-2273
952-906-1180
800-825-6758
FAX: 952-906-1099
e-mail: info@harriscomm.com
www.harriscomm.com

*Robert Harris, President*
*Kevin Horsky, Business Director*
A series based on the functional approach that is the most popular and widely used sign language curriculum designed for teaching American Sign Language. Book and videotape set for level 1 & 2. Teacher's curriculum is also available. *$59.95*

**1947 Small Wonder**
AGS
P.O.Box 99
Circle Pines, MN 55014-99
651-287-7220
800-328-2560
FAX: 763-786-9007
e-mail: agsmail@agsnet.com
www.agsnet.com

*Kevin Brueggeman, President*
*Robert Zaske, Marketing Manager*
This infant through toddler program offers a delightful array of activities to teach babies about themselves, others, their surroundings and the world outside. Level One - zero to 18 months; Level Two 18-36 months. Discount price of $389.95 when both levels ordered. *$229.95*

*ISBN 0-91347 -62-5*

**1948 Solving Language Difficulties**
School Specialty
PO Box 9031
Cambridge, MA 02139-9031
617-547-6706
800-225-5750
FAX: 888-440-2665
e-mail: support@schoolspecialty.com
eps.schoolspecialty.com

*Amey Steere, Author*
*Caroline Z Peck, Co-Author*
*Linda Kahn, Co-Author*
*Rick Holden, President*
This basic workbook can be used in any corrective reading program. It deals extensively with syllables, syllable division, prefixes, suffixes and accent. *$9.75*
*176 pages*
*ISBN 0-838803-26-1*

**1949 Speech Bin**
Abilitations
PO Box 1579
Appleton, WI 54912
772-770-0007
888-388-3224
FAX: 888-388-6344
e-mail: customercare@schoolspecialty.com
www.speechbin.com

*Jan J Binney, Senior Editor*
Activities, worksheets and games to encourage practice of speech and language skills. *$25.00*
*128 pages*
*ISBN 0-93785 -42-4*

**1950 Speech-Language Delights**
1965 25th Ave
Vero Beach, FL 32960-3062
772-770-0007

**1951 Spell of Words**
School Specialty
PO Box 9031
Cambridge, MA 02139-9031
617-547-6706
800-225-5750
FAX: 888-440-2665
e-mail: support@schoolspecialty.com
eps.schoolspecialty.com

*Elsie T Rak, Author*
*Rick Holden, President*
Covers syllabicataion, word building along with prefixes, phonograms, word patterns, suffixes, plurals, and possessives. *$14.70*
*128 pages Grades 7-Adult*

**1952 Spellbound**
School Specialty
PO Box 9031
Cambridge, MA 02139-9031
617-547-6706
800-225-5750
FAX: 888-440-2665
e-mail: support@schoolspecialty.com
eps.schoolspecialty.com

*Elsie T Rak, Author*
*Rick Holden, President*
This workbook begins with teaching simple, consistent rules and then moves on to those that are more difficult. By an inductive process, students use their own observations to confirm the spelling rules they learn. Each portion of the text is followed by exercises for drill and kinesthetic reinforcement. *$12.85*
*144 pages Grades 7-Adult*
*ISBN 0-838801-65-X*

**1953 Spelling Dictionary**
School Specialty
PO Box 9031
Cambridge, MA 02139-9031
617-547-6706
800-225-5750
FAX: 888-440-2665
e-mail: support@schoolspecialty.com
eps.schoolspecialty.com

*Gregory Hurray, Author*
*Rick Holden, President*
Contains the most frequently used and misspelled words for students at these grade levels. Designed to be useable and reliable, to build research and writing skills, and to help teachers promote independent learning in a classroom setting *$6.35*

*ISBN 0-838820-56-5*

**1954 Starting Over**
School Specialty
PO Box 9031
Cambridge, MA 02139-9031
617-547-6706
800-225-5750
FAX: 888-440-2665
e-mail: support@schoolspecialty.com
eps.schoolspecialty.com

*Joan Knight, Author*
*Rick Holden, President*
For students who are ready to try to learn to read again, or for those who are learning English as a second language. *$38.40*

*ISBN 0-838881-65-5*

**1955 Studio 49 Catalog**
MMB Music
9051 Watson Road
Suite 161
Saint Louis, MO 63126-1019
314-531-9635
800-543-3771
FAX: 314-531-8384
e-mail: info@mmbmusic.com
www.mmbmusic.com

*Marcia Goldberg, President*
*Michelle Greenlaw, VP*
Percussion instruments for school, therapy, church and family.

**1956 Syracuse Community-Referenced Curriculum Guide for Students with Disabilties**
Brookes Publishing
P.O.Box 10624
Baltimore, MD 21285-624
410-337-9580
800-638-3775
FAX: 410-337-8539
e-mail: custserv@brookespublishing.com
www.readplaylearn.com

*Paul Brooks, President*
Serving learners from kindergarten through age 21, this field-tested curriculum is a for professionals and parents devoted to directly preparing a student to function in the world. it examines the role of community living domains, functional academics, and embedded skills and includes practical implementation strategies and information for preparing students whose learning needs go beyond the scope of traditional academic programs.
*$54.95*
*416 pages Spiral-bound*
*ISBN 1-557660-27-1*

**1957 Teaching Individuals with Physical and Multiple Disabilities**
McGraw-Hill, School Publishing
P.O. Box 182604
Columbus, OH 43272
877-833-5524
FAX: 614-759-3749
e-mail: customer.service@mcgraw-hill.com
www.mcgraw-hill.com

*Harold McGraw, President and CEO*
*Jack Callahan, Executive VP*
*John Berisford, Executive VP of HR*
Focuses on the functional needs of the handicapped and the teaching skills of background teachers that they need to help them reach the highest possible level of self-sufficiency.
*410 pages*

**1958 Teaching Students Ways to Remember**
Brookline Books
34 University Rd
Brookline, MA 2445
617-734-6772
800-666-2665
FAX: 617-734-3952
e-mail: brbooks@yahoo.com
www.brooklinebooks.com

Teaches techniques for improving or strengthening memory.
*$21.95*

*ISBN 0-914797-67-0*

**1959 Teaching Test-Taking Skills: Helping Students Show What They Know**
Brookline Books
34 University Rd
Brookline, MA 2445-4533
617-734-6772
800-666-2665
FAX: 617-734-3952
e-mail: brbooks@yahoo.com
www.brooklinebooks.com

Test-taking skills that, when used effectively, contribute to test-wise performance and help students work productively with test materials. *$21.95*

*ISBN 0-914797-76-X*

**1960 To Teach a Dyslexic**
AVKO Educational Research Foundation
3084 Willard Rd
Birch Run, MI 48415-9404
810-686-9283
866-285-6612
FAX: 810-686-1101
e-mail: webmaster@avko.orgE
www.avko.org

*Deborah Wolf, President*
*Aaron Miller, Vice President*
A video available in DVD or video CD that shows Don McCabe working with a dyslexic teenager. The video helps teachers learn more about dyslexia and how to go about teaching a dyslexic student using the AVKO methodology and philosophy. This is a free video.
*288 pages Paperback*

**1961 Tools for Transition**
AGS
P.O.Box 99
Circle Pines, MN 55014-99
651-287-7220
800-328-2560
FAX: 763-786-9007
e-mail: agsmail@agsnet.com
www.agsnet.com

*Kevin Brueggeman, President*
*Robert Zaske, Marketing Manager*
This program prepares students with learning disabilities for postsecondary education. *$129.95*

**1962 VAK Tasks Workbook: Visual, Auditory and Kinesthetic**
Educational Tutorial Consortium
4400 S 44th St
Lincoln, NE 68516-1109
402-489-8133
FAX: 402-489-8160
e-mail: etc@altel.net
www.etc-ne.com

*T Elli Cross, Owner*
A workbook emphasizing the multisensory approach to teaching vocabulary and spelling. It is intended for middle-grade and older students working with prefixes, roots, suffixes, homonyms, and the spelling of easily confused endings. Includes spelling posters. *$7.00*
*96 pages Paperback*

**1963 Volunteer Transcribing Services**
Ste 200
205 E 3rd Ave
San Mateo, CA 94401-4028
650-357-1571
FAX: 650-632-3510

*Alanah Hoffman, Coordinator*
VTS is a nonprofit California corporation that produces large print school books for visually impaired students in grades K-12.

**1964 Wordly Wise 3000**
School Specialty
PO Box 9031
Cambridge, MA 02139-9031
617-547-6706
800-225-5750
FAX: 888-440-2665
e-mail: support@schoolspecialty.com
eps.schoolspecialty.com

*Kenneth Hodkinson, Author*
*Sandra Adams, Co-Author*
*Cheryl Dressler, Co-Author*
*Rick Holden, President*
Begins with a word list of 8-12 words, followed by clear, brief definitions and sentences that illustrate the meaning of the word. Books B and C often present more than one meaning of a word. Throughout all three books, drawings illustrate the meanings.

*ISSN 0838-84 8*

**1965 Work!**
JE Stewart Teaching Tools
P.O.Box 15308
Seattle, WA 98115-308
206-328-7664
FAX: 206-262-9538

*Jan Gleason, Executive Director*
Teaches 50 words as they appear on parts, tools, job instructions, signs, labels such as: hard hat, assembly, clamp, cut, drill, package and schedule. These words are functional in school and on-the-job. *$32.50*

**1966 Working Together & Taking Part**
A GS
P.O.Box 99
Circle Pines, MN 55014-99
651-287-7220
800-328-2560
FAX: 763-786-9007
e-mail: agsmail@agsnet.com
www.agsnet.com

*Kevin Brueggeman, President*
*Robert Zaske, Market Manager*
Two programs to build children's social skills in grades 3-6 through folk literature. Has 31 activity-rich lessons, teaching skills like: following rules, accepting differences, speaking assertively and helping others. Discount price of $279.00 when ordering both. *$149.95*

## Associations

**1967 AVKO Educational Research Foundation**
3084 Willard Rd
Birch Run, MI 48415-9404
810-686-9283
FAX: 810-686-1101
e-mail: webmaster@avko.orgE
www.avko.org

*Deborah Wolf, President*
*Aaron Miller, Vice President*
Comprised of individuals interested in helping others learn to read and spell. Develops and sells materials for teaching dyslexics or others with learning disabilities using a method involving audio, visual, kinesthetic and oral (multi-sensory) techniques.

**1968 Alliance for Parental Involvement in Education**
P.O.Box 59
East Chatham, NY 12060-59
518-392-6900
FAX: 518-392-6900
e-mail: allpie@taconic.net
www.croton.com/allpie

A nonprofit organization to encourage and assist parental involvement in education, public, private and home. Offers a newsletter, a book catolog, retreats, workshops, and a lending library.

**1969 Alternative Work Concepts**
P.O.Box 11452
Eugene, OR 97440-3652
541-345-3043
FAX: 541-345-9669
e-mail: awc@efn.com
www.alternativeworkconcepts.org

*Liz Fox, Executive Director*
To promote individualized, integrated, and meaningful employment opportunities in the community for adults with multiple disabilities; to improve the quality of life and provide continuous opportunities for personal growth for these individuals; and to assist businesses with workforce diversification.

**1970 American Council for Headache Education(ACHE)**
19 Mantua Rd
Mount Royal, NJ 8061-1006 856-423-0043
FAX: 856-423-0082
e-mail: achehq@talley.com
www.achenet.org

*Fred Sheftell, Chairman*
Nonprofit, patient-health, professional partnership dedicated to advancing the treatment and management of headaches and to raising the public awareness of headache as valid, biologically based illness.

**1971 American School Counselor Association**
American Counselling Association
1101 King St
Suite 625
Alexandria, VA 22314-2957 703-683-2722
800-306-4722
FAX: 703-683-1619
e-mail: asca@schoolcounselor.org
www.schoolcounselor.org

*Richard Wong, Executive Director*
*Kathleen Rakestraw, Director of Communications*
*Carolyn Stone, Board President*
ASCA focuses on providing professional devleopment, enhancing school counseling programs, and research effective school counseling practices. Mission is to promote excellence in professional school counseling and the development of all students.

**1972 Association on Higher Education and Disability**
107 Commerce Centre Dr
Suite 204
Huntersville, NC 28078-5870 704-947-7779
FAX: 704-948-7779
TTY:617-287-3882
e-mail: ahead@ahead.org
www.ahead.org

*Jean Ashmore, President*
*Michael Johnson, Treasurer*
*Stephan Smith, Executive Director*
Higher education for people with disabilities. A vital resource, promoting excellence through education, communication and training.

**1973 CARF International (Commission on Accreditation of Rehabilitation Facilities)**
CARF International
4891 E Grant Rd
Tucson, AZ 85712-2704 520-325-1044
888-281-6531
FAX: 520-318-1129
e-mail: info @carf.org
carf.org

*Brian J Boon, CEO*
An independent, nonprofit accreditor of human service providers in the areas of aging services, behavioral health, child and youth services, DMEPOS, employment and community services, medical rehabilitation, and opioid treatment programs.

**1974 CEC-Division for Early Childhood**
Council for Exceptional Children
27 Fort Missoula Road
Suite 2
Missoula, MT 59804 406-543-0872
888-232-7733
FAX: 406-543-0887
e-mail: dec@dec-sped.org
www.dec-sped.org

*Sarah Mulligan, Executive Director*
*Cynthia Wood, Associate Executive Director*
*Natalie Forcier, Program/Accounting Assistant*
*Marina Zaleski, Program Assistant*
Promotes policies and advances evidence-based practices that support families and enhance the optimal development of young children who have or are at risk for developmental delays and disabilities.

**1975 Council for Exceptional Children**
2900 Crystal Drive
Ste 1000
Arlington, VA 22202-3557 703-620-3660
866-509-0218
888-232-7733
FAX: 703-264-9494
TTY:866-915-5000
e-mail: service@cec.sped.org
cec.sped.org

*Bruce A. Ramirez, Executive Director*
*Margaret J. McLaughlin, President*
*Christy A. Chambers, President Elect*
*James P. Heiden, Treasurer*
The largest international professional organization dedicated to improving the educational success of individuals with disabilities and/or gifts and talents. Advocates for appropriate governmental policies, sets professional standards, provides professional development, advocates for individuals with exceptionalities, and helps professionals obtain conditions and resources necessary for effective professional practice

**1976 Division for Physical and Health Disabilities (DPHD)**
Council for Exceptional Children (CEC)
2900 Crystal Drive,
Suite 1000
Arlington, VA 22202 888-232-7733
FAX: 703-264-9494
e-mail: service@cec.sped.org
www.web.utk.edu/~dphmd/

*Linda Thomas, President of DPHMD*
*Juliet Hart, Vice President*
The DPHD is the official division of the CEC that advocates for quality education for all individuals with physical disabilities, multiple disabilities, and special health care needs served in schools, hospitals, or home settings. The goals of DPHD include: promoting the continued development adequate resources and programs; disseminating relevant and timely information on issues, instructional strategies, and research through meetings and publications; and many more services and activities.

**1977 Educational Referral Service**
Doctor Yvonne Jones and Associates
2222 Eastlake Ave E
Seattle, WA 98102-3419 206-325-2600
FAX: 206-328-9172

*Yvonne Jones*
Specializes in matching children with the learning environments that are best for them and works with families to help them identify concerns and establish priorities about their child's education.

**1978 International Association of Parents and Professionals for Safe Alternatives in Childbirth**
Box 646
Rr 4
Marble Hill, MO 63764-9418 573-238-4273
FAX: 573-238-2010
e-mail: napsac@clas.org
www.napsac.org

*Lee Stewart, Publisher*
*David Stewart, Executive Director*
Dedicated to exploring, implementing, and establishing safe, family-centered childbirth programs that meet the social and emotional needs of families as well as provide the safe, appropriate aspects of medical science.

**1979 International Childbirth Education Association**
1500 Sunday Drive
Suite 102
Raleigh, NC 27607-48
919-863-9487
800-624-4934
FAX: 919-787-4916
e-mail: info@icea.org
www.icea.org

*Denise Wheatley, President*
*Nancy Lantz, President- Elect*
*Deborah Codde, Treasuer*
*Debra Tolson, Secretary*
Offer teaching certificates, seminars, continuing education workshops, and a mail order center.

**1980 International Dyslexia Association**
40 York Road
4th Floor
Baltimore, MD 21204-5243
410-296-0232
800-222-3123
FAX: 410-321-5069
e-mail: info@interdys.org
www.interdys.org

*Guinevere Eden, President*
*Stephen Peregoy, Executive Director*
*Sandra Soper, Vice President*
IDA is a clearinghouse of scientific data and practice-based information related to dyslexia. We also provide community-based referrals and information fact sheets in response to thousands of emails, calls & letters. Our annual conference attracts thousands of researchers, clinicians, parents, teachers, psychologist, educational therapists and people with dyslexia.

**1981 International Organization for the Education of the Hearing Impaired**
Alexander Graham Bell Association
3417 Volta Pl NW
Washington, DC 20007-2737
202-337-5220
FAX: 202-337-8314
TTY:202-337-5221
e-mail: info@agbell.org
www.agbell.org

*Kathleen Treni, President*
*Meredith Knueve, Secretary Treasurer*
*Alexander Graham, Executive Director/CEO*
Professional educators of the hearing impaired make up the members of this organization which promotes the excellence in teaching the hearing impaired child.

**1982 Jewish Guild for the Blind**
15 W 65th St
New York, NY 10023-6601
212-769-6200
800-284-4422
FAX: 212-769-6266
e-mail: info@jgb.org
www.jgb.org

*Pauline Raiff, Chairman*
*Aaron Kesselman, President*
*Eileen Hanley, Senior VP*
*Barbara Klein, Director of Development*
Full service vision care agency for children, adults and elderly people who are blind or visually impaired.

**1983 Job Accommodation Network**
Office of Disability and Employment Policy
P.O.Box 6080
Morgantown, WV 26506-6080
800-232-9675
800-526-7234
FAX: 304-093-5407
TTY: 877-781-9403
e-mail: jan@jan.wvu.edu
www.jan.wvu.edu

*DJ Hendricks, Director*
International toll-free consulting service that provides information about job accommodations and the employability of people with disabilities. Also provides information regarding the Americans with Disabilities Act (ADA).

**1984 Michigan Psychological Association**
124 W Allegan St
Suite 1900
Lansing, MI 48933-1768
517-347-1885
FAX: 517-484-4442
e-mail: office@michiganpsychologicalassociation.org
www.michiganpsychologicalass ociation.org

*Judith Kovach, Executive Director*
Nonprofit organization of over 1000 psychologists, working to advance psychology as a science and a profession and to promote the public welfare by encouraging the highest professional standards, offering public education and providing a public service, and by participating in the public policy process on behalf of the profession and health care consumers.

**1985 National Association of Colleges and Employers**
62 Highland Ave
Bethlehem, PA 18017-9481
610-868-1421
800-544-5272
FAX: 610-868-0208
naceweb.org

*Vanessa Strauss, President*
*Donnie Brown, VP of Human Resources*
A national association with services for career planning, placement and recruitment professionals.

**1986 National Association of Private Special Education Centers**
Ste 1032
1522 K St NW
Washington, DC 20005-1202
202-408-3338
FAX: 202-408-3340
e-mail: napsec@aol.com
napsec.org

*Sherry Kolbe, Executive Director*
Membership directory offering information on NAPSEC member schools nationwide available.

**1987 National Center for Homeopathy**
101 S Whiting St
Alexandria, VA 22304-3418
703-548-7790
FAX: 703-548-7792
e-mail: info@homeopathic.org
nationalcenterforhomeopathy.org

*Sharon Stevenson, Executive Director*
Provides information, referral lists, online webinals to members, and an annual homeopathic conference.

**1988 National Clearinghouse for Professions**
2900 Crystal Drive
Suite 1000
Arlington, VA 22202
703-264-9454
FAX: 703-264-1637
www.cec.sped.org

*Bruce Ramirez, Executive Director*

**1989 National Council on Rehabilitation Education (NCRE)**
497 N. Clovis Ave
Suite 202 PMB # 311
Clovis, CA 93611
559-906-0787
FAX: 559-412-2550
e-mail: info@rehabeducators.org
www.rehabeducators.org

*Charles Degeneffe, President*
*Ken Hergenrather, First VP*
*Jared Schultz, Second VP*

Members include academic institutions and organizations, professional educators, researchers, and students. Assists in the documentation of the effect of education in improving services to persons with disabilities; determines the skills and training necessary for effective rehabilitation services; develops role models, standards and uniform licensure and certification requirements for rehabilitation personnel.

**1990 National Education Association of the United States**
1201 16th St NW
Washington, DC 20036-3290
202-833-4000
FAX: 202-822-7974
www.nea.org

*Dennis Van Roekel, President*
*Lily Eskelsen, Vice President*
*Rebecca Pringle, VP and Secretary*
*John Wilson, Executive Director*
Offers information to educational professionals.

**1991 National Society for Experiential Education**
19 Mantua Rd
Mount Royal, NJ 8061-1006
856-423-3427
FAX: 856-423-3420
e-mail: nsee@talley.com
www.nsee.org

*James Walters, President*
*Mary King, Vice President*
*Haley Brust, Executive Director*
National nonprofit organization which advocates experiential learning and works with college administrators and high school and college internship programs.

**1992 President's Committee for People with Intellectual Disabilities**
Administration for Children & Families
370 L Enfant Promenade SW
Washington, DC 20447-1
202-619-0634
FAX: 202-205-9519
www.acf.hhs.gov/programs/pcpid

*Sally Atwater, Executive Director*
*Dalls Rob Sweezy, Chairperson*
*MJ Karimi, Executive Director Assistant*
Prepares an annual report to the president of the United States addressing issues concerning citizens with intellectual disabilities.

**1993 Rifin Family/Daughters of Israel**
JGB Audio Library for the Blind
15 W 65th St
New York, NY 10023-6601
212-769-6200
800-284-4422
FAX: 212-769-6266
e-mail: info@JGB.org
www.JGB.org

*Pauline Raiff, Chairman*
*Aaron Kesselman, President*
*Eileen Hanley, Senior VP*

**1994 SSD (Services for Students with Disabilities)**
College Board
45 Columbus Ave
New York, NY 10023-6917
212-713-8000
866-630-9305
FAX: 212-713-8255
www.collegeboard.com

*Gaston Caperton, President*
National, nonprofit membership association dedicated to preparing, inspiring and connecting students to college and opportunity. Founded in 1900, the association is composed of more than 3,800 schools, colleges, universities and other educational organizations. Services for Students with Disabilities (SSD) provides special arrangements to minimize the possible effects of disabilities on test performance through it's Admissions Testing Program (ATP).

**1995 Target Teach**
Evans Newton
Ste 1
15941 N 77th St
Scottsdale, AZ 85260-1217
480-998-2777
800-443-0544
FAX: 480-951-2895
e-mail: info@evansnewton.com
www.target.com

*Jamie Piotti, CEO*
*Gary Davis, Director of Curriculum and Instr*
Aligns and monitors Special Education Instructional Materials to tests that are used to measure the effectiveness of Special Education Instructional Programs.

**1996 United Cerebral Palsy**
1660 L St NW
Suite 700
Washington, DC 20036-5638
202-776-0406
800-872-5827
FAX: 202-776-0414
e-mail: info@ucp.org
www.ucp.org

*Stephen Bennett, CEO*
*Bruce Fried, Chariman*
*Keith Green, Vice Chair*
Grants are awarded to institutions or organizations on behalf of a principal investigator in support of biomedical and bioengineering research in areas which have a significant relationship to cerebral palsy. While most research on central nervous system structure, function and disorder may be useful, the Foundation requires that research proposals address issues of relevance to cerebral palsy.

## Directories

**1997 BOSC: Directory of Facilities for People with Learning Disabilities**
Books on Special Children
P.O.Box 3378
Amherst, MA 1004-3378
413-256-8164
FAX: 413-256-8896
e-mail: irene@boscbooks.com
www.boscbooks.com

*Michael Young, President*
Directory of schools, independent living programs, clinics and centers, colleges and vocational programs, agencies and commercial products. Five sections in special post binder that can be updated annually. Hardcover. *$70.00*
*300+ pages Yearly*
*ISSN 0961-3888*

**1998 Complete Directory for Pediatric Disorders**
Sedgwick Press/Grey House Publishing
4919 Route 22
P.O. Box 56
Amenia, NY 12501-0056
518-789-8700
800-562-2139
FAX: 518-789-0556
e-mail: books@greyhouse.com
www.greyhouse.com

*Leslie Mackenzie, Publisher*
*Laura Mars, Editorial Director*
*Jessica Moody, Marketing Director*
*Diana Delgado, Editorial Assistant*
An annual directory for professionals, parents and caregivers. Provides valuable information on more than 200 pediatric conditions, disorders, diseases and disabilities, including informative descriptions and a wide variety of resources, from associations to publications. *$165.00*
*1000 pages Annual*
*ISBN 1-592374-30-1*

**1999 Complete Directory for People with Chronic Illness**
Sedgwick Press/Grey House Publishing
4919 Route 22
P.O. Box 56
Amenia, NY 12501-0056 518-789-8700
800-562-2139
FAX: 518-789-0556
e-mail: books@greyhouse.com
www.greyhouse.com

*Leslie Mackenzie, Publisher*
*Laura Mars, Editorial Director*
*Jessica Moody, Marketing Director*
*Diana Delgado, Editorial Assistant*

This directory is structured around the ninety most prevalent chronic illnesses. Each chronic illness chapter includes an informative description, plus a comprehensive listing of resources and support services available for people diagnosed with chronic illness and their network of supportive individuals. *$165.00*
*1000 pages Annual*
*ISBN 1-592374-15-8*

**2000 Complete Learning Disabilities Directory**
Sedgwick Press/Grey House Publishing
4919 Route 22
P.O. Box 56
Amenia, NY 12501-0056 518-789-8700
800-562-2139
FAX: 518-789-0556
e-mail: books@greyhouse.com
www.greyhouse.com

*Leslie Mackenzie, Publisher*
*Laura Mars, Editorial Director*
*Jessica Moody, Marketing Director*
*Diana Delgado, Editorial Assistant*

A comprehensive educational guide offering over 6,500 listings on associations and organizations, schools, government agencies, testing materials, camps, products, books, newsletters, legal information, classroom materials and more. Includes separate chapters on ADD and Literacy, as well as informative articles. *$150.00*
*800 pages Annual*
*ISBN 1-592375-86-3*

**2001 Complete Mental Health Directory**
Sedgwick Press/Grey House Publishing
4919 Route 22
P.O. Box 56
Amenia, NY 12501-0056 518-789-8700
800-562-2139
FAX: 518-789-0556
e-mail: books@greyhouse.com
www.greyhouse.com

*Leslie Mackenzie, Publisher*
*Laura Mars, Editorial Director*
*Jessica Moody, Marketing Director*
*Diana Delgado, Editorial Assistant*

This directory offers comprehensive information covering the field of behavioral health, with critical information for both the layman and the mental health professional. It covers, in depth, 25 specific mental disorders, and includes informative descriptions and a complete list of resources. *$165.00*
*800 pages Annual*
*ISBN 1-592375-44-8*

**2002 Directory for Exceptional Children**
Prorter Sargent
2 LAN Drive
Suite 100
Westford, MA 01886 978-692-9708
800-342-7470
FAX: 978-692-2304
e-mail: orders@portersargent.com
www.portersargent.com

*Daniel P McKeever, Senior Editor*
*Leslie A Weston, Production Manager*

Supports parents and professionals seeking the optimal educational, therapeutic or clinical environment for special-needs youth. *$75.00*
*1120 pages Triennial*
*ISBN 0-875581-50-1*

**2003 Educators Resource Directory**
Sedgwick Press/Grey House Publishing
4919 Route 22
Amenia, NY 12501 518-789-8700
800-562-2139
FAX: 845-373-6390
e-mail: books@greyhouse.com
www.greyhouse.com

*Leslie Mackenzie, Publisher*
*Laura Mars, Editorial Director*
*Jessica Moody, Marketing Director*
*Kristen Thatcher, Production Manager*

Gives education professionals immediate access to Associations and Organizations, Conferences and Trade Shows, Educational Research Centers, Employment Opportunities and Teaching Abroad, School Library Services, Scholarships, Financial Resources and much more. *$ 145.00*
*650 pages Annual*
*ISBN 1-592377-43-5*

**2004 Increasing and Decreasing Behaviors of Persons with Severe Retardation and Autism**
Research Press
PO Box 9177
Dept 12W
Champaign, IL 61826 217-352-3273
800-519-2707
FAX: 217-352-1221
e-mail: orders@researchpress.com
www.researchpress.com

*Dr Richard M Foxx, Author*

Shows how to increase desirable behaviors by using techniques such as shaping, prompting, fading, modeling, backward chaining and graduated guidance. Offers specific guidelines for arranging and managing the learning environment as well as standards for evaluating and maintaining success. *$21.95*
*230 pages*
*ISBN 0-878222-65-0*

**2005 Teaching Special Students in Mainstream**
Books on Special Children
P.O.Box 305
Congers, NY 10920-305 845-638-1236
FAX: 845-638-0847
e-mail: irene@boscbooks.com

Overview of mainstream, team of professionals managing classroom behavior, tips for teachers, social acceptance and handling of specific differences. *$33.00*
*515 pages Softcover*

## Educational Publishers

2006 **AFB Press**
American Foundation for the Blind / AFB Press
2 Penn Plz
Ste 1102
New York, NY 10121
212-502-7600
FAX: 888-545-8331
e-mail: afbinfo@afb.net
www.afb.org

*Carl R. Augusto, President and CEO*
*Maureen Matheson, Vice President*
*Sylvia Simpson, Executive Administrative Assistant*
*Kelly Bleach, Technical Services Director, Chief Administrative Officer*

Develops, publishes, and sells a wide variety of informative books, pamphlets, periodicals, and videos for students, professionals, and researchers in the blindess and visual impairment fields, for people professionally involved in making the mainstream community accessible, and for blind and visually impaired people and their families; publication and video orders.

2007 **American Counseling Association**
5999 Stevenson Ave
Alexandria, VA 22304-3304
703-823-0252
800-347-6647
FAX: 800-473-2329
e-mail: webmaster@counseling.org
www.counseling.org

*Brad Erford, President*
*Richard Yep, Executive Director*
*Brad Erford, President*
*Paul Nelson, Executive Director*

Offers tools and books for the professional.

2008 **Brookes Publishing Company**
PO Box 10624
Baltimore, MD 21285-0624
410-337-9580
800-638-3775
FAX: 410-337-8539
e-mail: webmaster@brookespublishing.com
www.brookespublishing.com

*Jeff Brookes, President*
*George Stamathis, VP/Publisher*
*Melissa A. Behm, ExecutiveVice President*
*Amy Perkins, Marketing Manager*

Publishes highly respected resources in early childhood, early intervention, inclusive and special education, developmental disabilities, learning disabilities, communication and language, behavior and mental health.

2009 **Brookline Books**
34 University Rd
Brookline, MA 02445-4533
617-734-6772
800-666-2665
FAX: 617-734-3952
e-mail: brbooks@yahoo.com
www.brooklinebooks.com

*William H Walters, Author*
*Esther Wilder, Co-Author*

Offers books for teachers and parents on law and legislation, education, integration and mainstreaming for the disabled, their families, caregivers and teachers.

2010 **Brooks/Cole Publishing Company**
511 Forest Lodge Rd
Pacific Grove, CA 93950-5040
831-373-0728
800-354-9706
FAX: 831-375-6414

Offers books in Special Education for those preparing to be special educators and for in-service professionals.

2011 **Charles C Thomas Publisher LTD**
2600 S 1st Street
Springfield, IL 62704-4730
217-789-8980
800-258-8980
FAX: 217-789-9130
e-mail: books@ccthomas.com
www.ccthomas.com

*Michael P. Thomas, President*

Publishes specialty titles and textbooks in medicine, dentistry, nursing, and veterinary medicine, as well as a complete line in the behavioral sciences, criminal justice, education, special education, and rehabilitation. Aims to accommodate the current needs for information.

2012 **ERIC Clearinghouse on Disabilities and Gifted Education**
2900 Crystal Drive
Suite 1000
Arlington, VA 22202-3557
703-264-9454
888-232-7733
FAX: 703-264-1637
www.cec.sped.org

*Bruce Ramirez, Executive Director*

2013 **Eric Clearinghouse on Disabilities and Gifted Education**
Council for Exceptional Children
2900 Crystal Drive
Suite 1000
Arlington, VA 22202-3557
703-264-9454
888-232-7733
FAX: 703-264-1637
e-mail: service@cec.sped.org
www.cec.sped.org

*Bruce Ramirez, Executive Director*

Provides information on special and gifted education. Provides referrals, offers patient networking services and provides information on current research programs. Focuses its efforts on prevention, identification, assessment, intervention and enrichment both in special settings and within mainstream communities. Offers a variety of materials including brochures and Spanish language matereials.

2014 **Gallaudet University Press**
800 Florida Ave NE
Washington, DC 20002-3695
202-651-5488
FAX: 202-651-5489
e-mail: gupress@gallaudet.edu
gupress@gallaudet.edu

*David F Armstrong, Executive Director*

Publishes scholarly trade books and journals about deaf people and their language, history, and culture for deaf people, parents of deaf children, professionals, educators and the general public. Produces spring and fall catalogs.

2015 **Greenwood Publishing Group**
88 Post Rd W
Westport, CT 6880-4208
203-226-3571
FAX: 203-222-1502
e-mail: webmaster@greenwood.com
greenwood.com

*Wayne Smith, President*
*Kirstin Olsen, Author*

ABC-CLIO and Greenwood Press are recognized as industry-leading providers of the highest-quality reference materials. These imprints offer authoritative reference scholarship and innovative coverage of history and humanities topics across the secondary and higher education curriculum. The name of the company is ""ABC-CLIO and Greenwood Press""

**2016 Grey House Publishing**
4919 Route 22
P.O. Box 56
Amenia, NY 12501-0056 518-789-8700
800-562-2139
FAX: 518-789-0556
e-mail: books@greyhouse.com
www.greyhouse.com

*Leslie Mackenzie, Publisher*
*Laura Mars, Editorial Director*
*Jessica Moody, Marketing Director*
*Diana Delgado, Editorial Assistant*
Grey House Publishing publishes directories, handbooks and reference works for public, high school and academic libraries and the business and health communities. Most titles are available as online databases.

**2017 Information from HEATH Resource Center**
National Clearinghouse on Postsecondary Education
2134 G Street, N.W.
Washington, DC 20052 202-939-9320
800-544-3284
FAX: 202-833-5696
e-mail: heath@ace.nche.edu
www.HEATH-resource-center.org
The HEATH Resource Center operates the national clearinghouse on postsecondary education for individuals with disabilities. Support from the US Department of Education enables the Center, a program of the America Council on Education, to serve as an information exchange on educational support services; adaptations; and opportunities at American campuses, vocational-technical schools, adult education programs, independent living centers, and other postsecondary training entities.

**2018 McGraw-Hill Company**
PO Box 182604
Columbus, OH 43272 877-833-5524
FAX: 614-759-3749
e-mail: customer.service@mcgraw-hill.com
www.mcgraw-hill.com

*Harold McGraw III, Chairman/President/CEO*
*Jack F. Callahan, Executive Vice President, Chief Financial Officer*
*John Berisford, Executive Vice President, Human Resources*
*Charles L. Teschner, Jr., Executive Vice President, Global Strategy*
Offers a catalog of testing resources and materials for the special educator.

**2019 National Association of School Psychologists**
4340 East West Highway
Ste 402
Bethesda, MD 20814 301-657-0270
866-311-6277
FAX: 301-657-0275
TTY: 301-657-4155
e-mail: philaz1@aol.com
www.nasponline.org

*Susan Gorin, Staff-Liaison*
*Philip Lazarus, President*
*Amy Smith, President-Elect*
*Sarah Valley-Gray, Secretary*
Represents over 22,500 school psychologists and related professionals. It serves its members and society by advancing the profession of school psychology and advocating for the rights, welfare, education and mental health of children, youth and their families.

**2020 PEAK Parent Center**
Ste 200
611 N Weber St
Colorado Springs, CO 80903-1072 719-531-9400
800-284-0251
FAX: 719-531-9452
e-mail: info@peakparent.org
www.peakparent.org

*Barbara Buswell, Executive Director*
PEAK Parent Center is a federally-designated Parent Training and Information Center (PTI). As a PTI, PEAK supports and empowers parents, providing them with information and strategies to use when advocating for their children with disabilities. PEAK works one-on-one with families and educators helping them realize new possibilities for children with disabilities by expanding knowledge of special education and offering new strategies for success.

**2021 Prufrock Press**
PO Box 8813
Waco, TX 76714-8813 254-756-3337
800-998-2208
FAX: 254-756-3339
e-mail: jmcintosh@prufrock.com
www.prufrock.com

*Joel McIntosh, Publisher & Marketing Director*
*Lacy Compton, Editor and Promotions Coordinator*
*Elizabeth Harp, Marketing Assistant*
*Cynthia Mancha, Editorial Assistant*
Publishes books, textbooks, teaching aids, journals, and magazines supporting gifted education and gifted children.

**2022 Research Press**
Dept 12W
PO Box 9177
Champaign, IL 61826 217-352-3273
800-519-2707
FAX: 217-352-1221
e-mail: orders@researchpress.com
www.researchpress.com

*Gail Adams, Author*
*Mia Sharon Adler, Author*
*Jeffrey S. Allen, Author*
*Bryce Alvord, Author*
Research Press is an independent, family-owned business founded in 1968 by Robert W. Parkinson (1920-2001). During the past 40 years, the company has earned a solid reputation for publishing practical and effective educational and mental health resources. Authors from the early years include well-known names in the field of psychology, such as B.F. Skinner, Albert Ellis, Gerald Patterson, Wesley Becker, John Gottman, Richard Foxx, Arnold Lazarus, and Joseph Cautela.

**2023 Sage Publications**
2455 Teller Road
Thousand Oaks, CA 91320-2218 805-499-0721
800-818-7243
FAX: 800-583-2665
e-mail: info@sagepub.com
www.sagepub.com

*Tracey A. Ozmina, Executive Vice President & Chief Operating Officer*
*Blaise R Simqu, President/CEO*
*Chris Hickok, Senior Vice President & Chief Financial Officer*
*Stephen Barr, Managing Director/SAGE London, President of SAGE International*
Publishes books, text books, journals, reference books, and databases mainly related to psychology, special education and speech, language and hearing.

2024 **Special Needs Project**
324 State St
Ste H
Santa Barbara, CA 93101
818-718-9900
FAX: 805-962-5087
e-mail: hgray@specialneeds.com
www.specialneeds.com

*Hod Gray, Owner*

Publishes child development textbooks, books about aspergers syndrome, autism, and other disabilities.

## State Agencies: Alabama

2025 **Alabama Department of Education: Division of Special Education Services**
50 N Ripley St
PO Box 302101
Montgomery, AL 36104
334-242-9700
FAX: 334-262-2677
e-mail: speced@alsde.edu
www.alsde.edu

*Governor Rob Bentley, President*
*Thomas R. Bice, Ed.D., Secretary and Executive Officer*
*Stephanie Bell, Vice President*
*ELLA B BELL, President Pro Tem*

Provides technical assistance to all education agencies serving Alabamas gifted children as well as children with disabilities.

2026 **Getting Ready for the Outside World(G.R.O.W.)**
Riverview School
551 Route 6A East Sandwich
Cape Cod, MA 2537-1448
508-888-0489
FAX: 508-833-7001
e-mail: admissions@riverviewschool.org
www.riverviewschool.org

*Edward Muller, Chairman*
*Janice James, Vice Chairman*
*Christopher Tolk, Treasurer*
*Deborah Cowan, Secretary*

Riverview School's G.R.O.W. Program is a unique ten month transitional prgoram (1-3 years) for young adults with complex language, learning and cognitive disabilities. This post secondary program is designed to further develop academic, vocational and independent living skills, to enable students to function as independently as possible.

## State Agencies: Alaska

2027 **Alaska Department of Education: Office of Special Education**
State of Alaska
801 West 10th Street, Suite 200
PO Box 110500
Juneau, AK 99811-0500
907-465-2800
FAX: 907-465-4156
TTY:907-465-2815
e-mail: eed.webmaster@alaska.gov
www.eed.state.ak.us

*Cynthia Curran, Division Director*

Administers special educational programs to the disabled residents of Alaska, through the Division of Teaching & Learning Support.

## State Agencies: Arkansas

2028 **Arkansas Department of Special Education**
1401 W Capitol Ave, Victory Bldg
Ste 450
Little Rock, AR 72201-2936
501-682-4221
FAX: 501-682-3456
TTY:501-682-4222
e-mail: spedsupport@arkansas.gov
arksped.k12.ar.us

*Tom Hicks, Interim Associate Director*
*Ella Albert, Management Project Analyst*
*Howie Knoff, irector*
*Tony Boaz, Director*

Provides oversight of all educational programs for children and youth with disabilities, ages 3 to 21. Provides technical assistance to all public agencies providing educational services to this population.

## State Agencies: California

2029 **California Department of Education: Special Education Division**
1430 N Street
Sacramento, CA 95814-4702
916-319-0800
FAX: 916-327-3516
e-mail: scheduler@cde.ca.gov
www.cde.ca.gov

*Michael R. Funk, Director*
*Fred Balcom, Director*
*Gordon Jackson, Director*
*Phyllis Bramson, Director*

Information and resources to serve the unique needs of persons with disabilities so that each person will meet or exceed high standards of achievement in academic and nonacademic skills.

## State Agencies: Colorado

2030 **Colorado Department of Education: Special Education Service Unit**
Colorado Department of Education
201 E Colfax Ave
Denver, CO 80203-1704
303-866-6600
FAX: 303-830-0793
e-mail: steinberg_e@cde.state.co.us
www.cde.state.co.us

*Ed Steinberg, Commissioner*

Provides consultation on materials and educational services for visually handicapped children, supervises volunteer services, transcribes textbooks for visually handicapped students.

## State Agencies: Connecticut

2031 **Connecticut Department of Education: Bureau of Special Education**
165 Capitol Avenue
Hartford, CT 06106
860-713-6543
FAX: 860-713-7014
e-mail: annelouise.thompson@ct.gov
www.sde.ct.gov

*Anne Louise Thompson, Bureau Chief*
*Lisa Spooner, Administrative Assistant*
*Regina Gaunichaux, Secretary*
*Carol Leddy, Secretary, Due Process Unit*

The State Board of Education believes each student is unique and needs an educational environment that provides for, and accommodates, his or her strengths and areas of needed improvement.

2032 **Connecticut State Board of Education and Services for the Blind**
State of Connecticut Agency
184 Windsor Ave
Windsor, CT 06095-4536 860-602-4000
800-842-4510
FAX: 860-602-4020
TTY: 860-602-4221
e-mail: brian.sigman@po.state.ct.us
www.besb.state.ct.us

*Keith Maynard, Deputy Director*
*Brian Sigman, Executive Director*
*Alan Sylvestre, Chairman*
*Eileen Akers, Director*
Provides consultation for the education of visually disabled children, provides Braille instruction, independent living skills training, vocational rehabilitation services and community outreach and advocacy.

## State Agencies: Delaware

2033 **Department of Public Instruction: Exceptional Children & Special Programs Division**
Department of Education
Ste 2
401 Federal St
Dover, DE 19901-3639 302-739-5471
FAX: 302-739-2388
www.doe.k12.de.us

*Martha Toomey, Executive Director*

## State Agencies: DC

2034 **District of Columbia Public Schools: Special Education Division**
1200 First Street, NE
Washington, DC 20002-4210 202-442-5885
202-442-5517
FAX: 202-442-5026

*Paul L Vance MD, Superintendent*
Committed to providing a continuum of services that offers students with disabilities the opportunity to actively participate in the learning environment of their neighborhood school.

2035 **National Clearinghouse on Family Support and Children's Mental Health**
Ste 800
1 Dupont Cir NW
Washington, DC 20036-1149 202-939-9320
800-544-3284
FAX: 202-833-4760
e-mail: heatah@ace.nche.edu

## State Agencies: Florida

2036 **Florida Department of Education: Bureau of Exceptional Education And Student Services**
325 W Gaines St
Turlington Building, Ste 614
Tallahassee, FL 32399-0400 850-245-0475
FAX: 850-245-9667
e-mail: Monica.Verra-Tirado@fldoe.org
www.fldoe.org/ese

*Monica Verra-Tirado, Ed.D., Bureau Chief*
*Gerard Robinson, Commissioner*
*Randy Hanna, Chancellor*
*Pam Stewart, Chancellor*
Administers programs for students with disabilities and for gifted students. Coordinates student services throughout the state and participates in multiple inter-agency efforts designed to strengthen the quality and variety of services to students with special needs.

## State Agencies: Hawaii

2037 **Hawaii Department of Education: Special Needs**
Hawaii Department of Education
3430 Leahi Ave
Honolulu, HI 96815-4246 808-941-3894
FAX: 808-941-3894

*Margaret Donovan MD, State Administrator*
Provides consultation on educational services for local schools, offers psychological testing and evaluation, maintains resource rooms in district schools and more for the blind and handicapped throughout the state.

## State Agencies: Illinois

2038 **Illinois State Board of Education: Department of Special Education**
100 N 1st St
Springfield, IL 62777 217-782-5589
FAX: 217-782-0372
www.isbe.net

*Elizabeth Hanselman, Asst Superintendent Special Ed.*
Mission is to advance the human and civil rights of people with disabilities in Illinois. Statewide advocacy organization providing self-advocacy assistance, legal services, education and public policy initiatives. Designated to implement the federal protection and advocacy system; has broad statutory power to enforce the rights of people with physical and mental disabilities, including developmental disabilities and mental illnesses.

## State Agencies: Indiana

2039 **Indiana Department of Education: Special Education Division**
Indiana Department of Education
151 West Ohio Street
Indianapolis, IN 46204-2731 317-232-0570
877-851-4106
FAX: 317-232-0589
e-mail: specialed@doe.in.gov
www.doe.in.gov/exceptional/speced/welcome.htm

*Robert A Marra, Manager*
*Tony Bennett, Chair*
Provides consultation on educational services for local schools, offers psychological testing and evaluation, maintains resource rooms in district schools and more for the blind and handicapped throughout the state.

## State Agencies: Iowa

2040 **Iowa Department of Public Instruction: Bureau of Special Education**
400 E 14th St
Des Moines, IA 50319-9000 515-457-2000
FAX: 515-242-6019
www.educateiowa.gov/

*Tom Kuehl, CEO*
*Jason Glass, Director*
*Jeff Berger, Administrative Services*

## State Agencies: Kansas

2041 **Kansas State Board of Education: Special Education Services**
120 SE 10th Ave
Topeka, KS 66612-1182 785-296-3201
800-203-9462
FAX: 785-296-7933
TTY: 785-296-6338
e-mail: contact@ksde.org
www.ksde.org

*Colleen Riley, Director*
*Patty Carter, Assitant Director*
*Kerry Haag, Assistant Director*
*Dr. Diane DeBacker, Kansas Commissioner of Education*
Provides leadership and support for exceptional learners receiving special education services throughout Kansas schools and communities.

## State Agencies: Kentucky

2042 **Kentucky Department of Education: Divisionof Exceptional Children's Services**
500 Mero St
8th Floor CPT
Frankfort, KY 40601 502-564-4970
FAX: 502-564-7749
e-mail: darlene.jesse@kde.state.ky.us
www.education.ky.gov

*Darlene Jesse, Director*
Provides consultation on educational services for local schools, offers psychological testing and evaluation, maintains resource rooms in district schools and more for the blind and handicapped throughout the state.

## State Agencies: Louisiana

2043 **Louisiana Department of Education: Office of Special Education Services**
Louisiana Department of Education
1201 North Third Street
Baton Rouge, LA 70802 225-342-0090
877-453-2721
FAX: 225-342-0193
www.doe.state.la.us

*David Elder, Manager*
*Kim Fitch, Director Human Resources*
*George Nelson, President*

## State Agencies: Massachusetts

2044 **Massachusetts Department of Education: Program Quality Assurance**
Massachusetts Department of Education
75 Pleasant Street
Malden, MA 2148-4906 781-388-3300
FAX: 617-388-3476
e-mail: boe@doe.mass.edu
www.doe.mass.edu/pqa/

*Pamela Kaufamann, Administrator*

## State Agencies: Maryland

2045 **Maryland State Department of Education: Division of Special Education**
200 W Baltimore St
9th Fl
Baltimore, MD 21201 410-767-0600
800-535-0182
FAX: 410-333-8165
e-mail: dmcmicha@msde.state.md.us
www.marylandpublicschools.org

*Nancy S Grasmick, State Supertintendent*
*Bryan Zillig, Multimedia Technical Assistant*
*James V. Foran, Assistant State Superintendent*
*Katharine Oliver, Assistant State Superintendent*
Collaborates with families, local early intervention systems, and local school systems to ensure that all children and youth with disabilities have access to appropriate services and educational opportunities to which they are entitled under federal and state laws.

## State Agencies: Michigan

2046 **Michigan Department of Education: Special Education Services**
608 W Allegan St
PO Box 30008
Lansing, MI 48909 517-373-3324
FAX: 517-373-7504
e-mail: DHS-OCS-PEP@michigan.gov
www.michigan.gov/mde

*Jacquelyn Thompson, Director*
*Kathleen N. Straus, President*
*John C. Austin, Vice President*
*Carolyn L. Curtin, Secretary*
Oversees the administrative funding of education and early intervention programs and services for young children and students with disabilities.

2047 **Services for Students with Disabilities**
University of Michigan
G664 Haven Hall
Ann Arbor, MI 48109 734-763-3000
FAX: 734-936-3947
TTY:734-615-4461
e-mail: sssegal@umich.edu
www.ssd.umich.edu

*Stuart Segal, Director*
Offers information to students of the University of Michigan and their parents.

## State Agencies: Minnesota

2048 **Community Supports for People with Disabilities (CSP)**
South Central Technical College (SCTC)
1920 Lee Blvd
North Mankato, MN 56003-2504 507-389-7200
800-722-9359
e-mail: online@southcentral.edu
www.southcentral.edu

*Christensen Tami, Executive Director*
*Keith Stover, President*
Human services program available as a physical or online program, designed for those wanting to earn a certificate, diploma or associate degree as a Direct Support Professional for use in the health and human services industries. The program comprises eight courses relating to professional services and support for people with disabilities.

2049 **Professional Development Programs**
1675 Greeley St S
Ste 101
Stillwater, MN 55082
651-439-8865
877-439-8865
FAX: 877-259-5906
e-mail: programs@pdppro.com
www.pdppro.com

*Cindy Lacosse, VP*
*Lori Lacrosse, President*
Sponsors cutting edge and popular continuing education workshops and symposia of interest to professionals who provide services to children and adults with special needs.

## State Agencies: Missouri

2050 **Missouri Department of Elementary and Secondary Education: Special Education Programs**
205 Jefferson St
PO Box 480
Jefferson City, MO 65102
573-751-5739
FAX: 573-526-4404
TTY:800-735-2966
www.dese.mo.gov

*Stephen Barr, Assistant Commissioner*
The Office of Special Education administers state and federal funds to support services for students and adults with disabilities.

## State Agencies: Mississippi

2051 **Mississippi Department of Education: Office of Special Services**
359 N West St
Jackson, MS 39201-1502
601-359-3513
FAX: 601-987-3892
www.mde.k12.ms.us

*Dr Tom Burnham, Superintendent*
Key priorities are: reading, early literacy, student achievement, teachers/teaching, leadership/principals, safe and orderly schools, parent relations/community involvement, and technology.

## State Agencies: Montana

2052 **Department of Public Health Human Services**
PO Box 4210
Helena, MT 59604-4210
406-444-5622
FAX: 406-444-1970
e-mail: hhsea@mt.gov
www.dphhs.mt.gov

*Anna Whitin Sorrell, Director*
*Bernie Jacobs, Chief Legal Counsel*
*Deb Sloat, Human Resources Office*
*Jon Ebelt, Public Information Office*
Provides consultation on educational services for local schools, offers psychological testing and evaluation, maintains resource rooms in district schools and more for the blind and handicapped throughout the state.

## State Agencies: North Carolina

2053 **North Carolina Department of Public Instruction: Exceptional Children Division**
301 N Wilmington St
Raleigh, NC 27601-1058
919-715-1565
FAX: 919-715-1569
e-mail: lharris@dpi.state.nc.us
www.ncpublicschools.org

*Mary N Watson, Director*
*June St. Clair Atkinson, Ed.D, State Superintendent*
*Dr Lillie Cox, State Superintendent*
*Dr Brock Womble, State Superintendent*
The mission is to assure that students with disabilities develop mentally, physically, emotionally, and vocationally through the provision of an appropriate individualized education in the least restrictive environment.

## State Agencies: North Dakota

2054 **North Dakota Department of Education: Special Education**
600 E Boulevard Ave
Bismarck, ND 58505-0440
701-328-2260
866-741-3519
FAX: 701-328-2461
TTY: 701-328-4920
e-mail: brutten@nd.gov
www.dpi.state.nd.us

*Robert Rutten, Director*
*Gail Schauer, Coordinated School Health, Assistant Director*
*Linda Schloer, Child Nutrition, Director*
*Frank S. Snow, Management Information Systems, Director*
Provides consultation on educational services for local schools, offers psychological testing and evaluation, maintains resource rooms in district schools and more for the blind and handicapped throughout the state.

## State Agencies: Nebraska

2055 **Nebraska Department of Education: Special Populations Office**
1200 ""N"" Street, Suite 400
PO Box 98922
Lincoln, NE 68509
402-471-2186
877-253-2603
e-mail: NDEQ.moreinfo@Nebraska.gov
nde.state.ne.us

*Rod Gangwish Shelton, Council Member*
*Douglas Anderson Aurora, Council Member*
*Mark Whitehead Lincoln, Council Member*
*Mark Czaplewski Grand Islan, Council Member*
Assists school districts in establishing and maintaining effective special education programs for children with disabilities (date of diagnosis through the school year when a child reaches 21). Major function: provide technical assistance to school districts and to parents of children with disabilities, assist programs in meeting state and federal special education regulations. Also responsible for assuring that the rights of children with disabilities and their parents are protected.

## State Agencies: New Hampshire

**2056 Institute on Disability**
University of New Hampshire
10 W Edge Drive
Ste 101
Durham, NH 03824
603-862-4320
FAX: 603-862-0555
e-mail: contact.iod@unh.edu
www.iod.unh.edu

*Linda B. Bimbo, Interim Director of Finance and Human Resources*
*Andrew Houtenville, Director of Research*
*Matthew Gianino, Director of Communications*
*Mary Schuh, Director of Development and Consumer Affairs*
Provides coherent university-based focus for the improvement of knowledge, policies, and practices related to the lives of persons with disabilities and their families.

**2057 New Hampshire Department of Education: Bureau for Special Education Services**
101 Pleasant St
Concord, NH 03301-3494
603-271-3494
FAX: 603-271-1953
e-mail: Lori.Temple@doe.nh.gov
www.education.nh.gov

*Santina Thibedeau, Administrator*
*Virginia Barry, Commissioner*
*Linda Breden, Secretary*
*Traci Biron, Secretary*
The mission of Special Education is to improve educational outcomes for children and youth with disabilities by providing and promoting leadership, technical assistance and collaboration statewide. Provides oversight and implementation of federal and state laws that ensure a free appropriate public education for all children and youth with disabilities in New Hampshire.

## State Agencies: New Jersey

**2058 New Jersey Department of Education: Office of Special Education Program**
New Jersey Department of Education
P.O.Box 500
Trenton, NJ 8625-500
609-292-8853
FAX: 609-984-8422
www.nj.gov/education/specialed/info/

*Barbara Gantwerk, Director*
*Alfred Murray, Executive Director*

## State Agencies: New Mexico

**2059 New Mexico State Department of Education**
300 Don Gaspar Ave
Santa Fe, NM 87501-2744
505-827-6508
FAX: 505-827-6696
www.sde.state.nm.us

*Bill Trant, Assistant Director*
*Judy Parks, Assistant Director*
Provides consultation on educational services for local schools, offers psychological testing and evaluation, maintains resource rooms in district schools and more for the blind and handicapped throughout the state.

## State Agencies: Nevada

**2060 Nevada Department of Education: Special Eduction Branch**
700 E Fifth St
Carson City, NV 89701-5096
775-687-9800
FAX: 775-687-9101
www.doe.nv.gov

*Nick Gakalatos, Manager*
The Office of Special Ed and School Improvement Program of the Nevada State Department of Education is responsible for management of state and federal programs providing educational opportunities for students with diverse learning needs. Included are such programs as: special education/disabled (IDEA); disadvantaged/at-risk programs (Title I/IASA); early childhood programs (Title I/ESEA); early childhood programs; migrant education; English language learners; NRS 395 student placement program.

## State Agencies: New York

**2061 New York State Education Department**
1606 One Commerce Plz
Albany, NY 12234-1
518-474-5930
FAX: 518-486-6880
e-mail: nysed@mail.gov
www.nysed.gov

*Bernard Margolis, Manager*
Provides vocational rehabilitation and educational services for eligible individuals with disabilities throughout New York State. Services include evaluation, counseling, job placement, and referral to other agencies.

## State Agencies: Ohio

**2062 Ohio Department of Education: Division of Special Education**
Ohio Department of Education
25 S Front St
Columbus, OH 43215-4183
614-995-1545
877-644-6338
FAX: 614-728-1097
TTY: 888-886-0181
www.ode.state.oh.us

*Mike Armstrong, Manager*
Provides technical assistance to educational agencies for the development and implementation of educational services to meet the needs of students with disabilities and/or those who are gifted. Provides information to parents. Administers state and federal funds allocated to educational agencies for the provision of services to students with disabilities and/or those who are gifted.

## State Agencies: Oklahoma

**2063 Oklahoma State Department of Education**
2500 N Lincoln Blvd
Oklahoma City, OK 73105-4599
405-521-3301
FAX: 405-521-6205
www.sde.state.ok.us

*Misty Kimbrough, Manager*
*Sandy Garrett, Administrator*
*Janet Barresi, State Superintendent*
Provides consultation on educational services for local schools, offers psychological testing and evaluation, maintains resource rooms in district schools and more for the blind and handicapped throughout the state.

## State Agencies: Oregon

**2064 Oregon Department of Education: Office of Special Education**
Oregon Department of Education:
255 Capitol St NE
Salem, OR 97310-1300
503-945-5600
FAX: 503-378-2897
www.dpeducation.com

*Bruce Goldberg, Manager*
*Heidi Cockrell, Executive Assistant*
*Katy Coba, Executive Director*
State agency ensuring provision of special education services to children with disabilities from birth to age 21.

## State Agencies: Pennsylvania

**2065 Pennsylvania Department of Education: Bureau of Special Education**
333 Market St
Harrisburg, PA 17126-333
717-783-6788
FAX: 717-783-6139
TTY:717-783-8445
e-mail: 00specialed@psupen.psu.edu
www.pde.state.pa.us

*Linda Rhen, Administrator*
*John Tommasini, Assistant Director*
Provides effective and efficient administration of the Commonwealth of Pennsylvania's resources dedicated to enabling school districts to maintain high standards in the delivery of special education services and programs for all exceptional students.

## State Agencies: Rhode Island

**2066 Rhode Island Department of Education: Office of Special Needs**
255 Westminster St
Providence, RI 2903
401-222-4600
FAX: 401-784-9513
www.ride.ri.gov

*Al Moscola, Manager*
*Alfred Moscola, Manager*
Provides consultation on educational services for local schools, offers psychological testing and evaluation, maintains resource rooms in district schools and more for the blind and handicapped throughout the state.

## State Agencies: South Carolina

**2067 South Carolina Assistive Technology Program (SCATP)**
Center for Disability Resources
8301 Farrow Rd
Columbia, SC 29208-3245
803-935-5263
800-915-4522
FAX: 800-935-5342
e-mail: evelyne@cdd.sc.edu
www.sc.edu/scatp

*Carol Page, Program Director*
*Mary Bechter, Program Coordinator*
SCATP is a federally funded project concerned with getting technology into th hands of people with disabilities so that they might live, work, learn and be a more independent part of the community.

**2068 South Carolina Department of Education: Office of Exceptional Children**
1429 Senate St
Suite 808
Columbia, SC 29201-3730
803-734-8224
FAX: 803-734-4824
e-mail: Sdurant@ed.sc.gov
www.scschools.com

*Susan Durant, State Director*
Provides consultation on educational services for local schools, offers psychological testing and evaluation, maintains resource rooms in district schools and more for the blind and handicapped throughout the state.

## State Agencies: South Dakota

**2069 South Dakota Department of Education & Cultural Affairs: Office of Special Education**
700 Governors Dr
Pierre, SD 57501-2291
605-773-3804
FAX: 605-773-6041

*Chelle Somsen, Manager*
*Dorothy Liegl, Manager*

## State Agencies: Tennessee

**2070 Tennessee Department of Education**
710 James Robertson Pkwy
Nashville, TN 37243-1219
615-741-2731
888-212-3162
FAX: 615-741-1791
www.state.tn.us/education

*Ruth S Letson, Manager*
*Kevin Huffman, Commissioner*
Provides consultation on educational services for local schools, offers psychological testing and evaluation, maintains resource rooms in district schools and more for the blind and handicapped throughout the state.

## State Agencies: Texas

**2071 Texas Education Agency**
1701 N Congress Ave
Austin, TX 78701-1494
512-463-8532
FAX: 512-463-8057
www.tealighthouse.org

*Shirley J Neeley, Commissioner of Education*
Provides consultation on educational services for local schools, offers psychological testing and evaluation, maintains resource rooms in district schools and more for the blind and handicapped throughout the state.

**2072 Texas Education Agency: Special Education Unit**
1701 Congress Ave
Austin, TX 78701-1402
512-463-8532
FAX: 512-463-8057
e-mail: wmccain@tmail.tea.state.tx.us
www.tdea.org

*Gene Lenz, Deputy Associate Commissioner*
*Shirley Neeley, Administrator*

**2073 Texas School of the Deaf**
1102 S Congress Ave
Austin, TX 78704-1791
512-462-5353
800-332-3873
FAX: 512-462-5424
e-mail: ercod@tsd.state.tx.us
tsd.state.tx.us

*Claire Bugen, Superintendent*
*Russell West, Residential Services Director*
*Gary Bego, Business and Operations Director*
*Brenda Fraenkel, Special Education Director*
In order to be eligible to attend TSD, a student must have a documented hearing loss, be between the of 0 to 21 years, and live in Texas. Students are not considered for residential placement until they are 5 years of age and in kindergarten.

## State Agencies: Utah

**2074 Utah State Office of Education: At-Risk and Special Education Service Unit**
Utah State Office of Education
P.O.Box 144200
Salt Lake City, UT 84114-4200
801-538-7500
FAX: 801-538-7521
e-mail: webmaster@schools.utah.gov
schools.utah.gov

*Sandra Cox, Financial Analyst*
*Mark Peterson, Director*
*Glenna Gallo, State Director of Special Education*
*Rebecca Donovan, Administrative Secretary*
Provides consultation on educational services for local schools, offers psychological testing and evaluation, maintains resource rooms in district schools and more for the blind and handicapped throughout the state.

## State Agencies: Virginia

**2075 Virginia Department of Education: Divisionof Pre & Early Adolescent Education**
Virginia Department Of Education
P.O.Box 2120
Richmond, VA 23218-2120
804-236-3631
FAX: 804-236-3635
e-mail: webmaster@doe.virginia.gov
www.pen.k12.va.us

*Thomas Broyles, Director*
*Robert Almond, Executive Assistant*
*Thomas W. Broyles, Director*
*Emma G. Henley, Administrative Assistant*
Provides consultation on educational services for local schools, offers psychological testing and evaluation, maintains resource rooms in district schools and more for the blind and handicapped throughout the state.

## State Agencies: Washington

**2076 Superintendent of Public Instruction: Special Education Section**
P.O.Box 47200
600 Washington St. S.E.
Olympia, WA 98504-7200
360-725-6000
FAX: 360-586-0247
TTY:360-664-3631
e-mail: cert@k12.wa.us
www.k12.wa.us

*Randy I. Dorn, State Superintendent of Public Instruction*
*Alan Burke, Deputy Superintendent*
*Robert Butts, Assistant Superintendent*
*Bob Harmon, Assistant Superintendent*
Provides leadership, service and support for the development and implementation of research-based curriculum to assure that all learners achieve at all levels.

## State Agencies: West Virginia

**2077 West Virginia Department of Education: Office of Special Education**
Rm 6
1900 Kanawha Blvd E
Charleston, WV 25305-1
304-558-3660
FAX: 304-558-3741
e-mail: http://wvde.state.wv.us/boe/
wvde.state.wv.us

*Liza Cordeiro, Executive Director*
*Mary Nunn, Assistant Director*
*Marshall Patton, Executive Director*
*Brenda Williams, Executive Director*
Provides consultation on educational services for local schools, offers psychological testing and evaluation, maintains resource rooms in district schools and more for the blind and handicapped throughout the state.

## State Agencies: Wyoming

**2078 Wyoming Department of Education**
2300 Capitol Ave
Hathaway Building, 2nd Floor
Cheyenne, WY 82002-0050
307-777-7690
FAX: 307-777-6234
k12.wy.us

*Gerald "'Joe Reichardt, Chairman*
*Dr. Larry McGarvin, Treasurer*
*Hugh Hageman, Board Member*
*Kathy Coon, Board Member*
Mission is to lead, model, and support continuous improvement of education for everyone in Wyoming.

## Magazines & Journals

**2079 Adapted Physical Activity Programs**
Human Kinetics
P.O.Box 5076
Champaign, IL 61825-5076
800-747-4457
FAX: 217-351-2674
e-mail: info@hkusa.com
www.humankinetics.com

*Patty Lehn, Publicity Manager*
*Lori Cooper, Marketing Manager*
*Bill Dobrik, Sales Associate*
*Dan Stebel, Sales Associate*
Human Kinetics produces a variety of resources for adapted physical education practitioners, including books on activities, a research journal and higher education references. *$24.00*
*Quarterly*
*ISSN 0736-58 9*

**2080 Advance for Providers of Post-Acute Care**
Merion Publications
2900 Horizon Drive
King of Prussia, PA 19406-956
610-278-1400
800-355-5627
FAX: 610-278-1421
e-mail: careeropportunities@merion.com
advanceweb.com

*Timothy Baum, MS, CRNP, Author*
A free magazine for providers of post-acute care.

**2081 CEC Catalog**
Council for Exceptional Children
Suite 1000
2900 Crystal Drive
Arlington, VA 22202-3557
703-264-9454
888-232-7733
FAX: 703-264-1637
TTY: 866-915-5000
e-mail: service@cec.sped.org
www.cec.sped.org

*Bruce Ramirez, Executive Director*
*Dan Ratner, Assistant Executive Director*
*Susan Simmons, Senior Director*
*Lindsay Jones, Senior Director*
Semi-annual catalog from the Council for Exceptional Children offering books, guides, materials, products and services for the special educator.
*18 pages*

**2082 Case Manager Magazine**
Elsevier Health
3251 Riverport Lane
Maryland Heights, MO 63043
314-447-8070
800-222-9570
e-mail: textbook@elsevier.com
journals.elsevierhealth.com

*Thomas Reller, Vice President Global Corporate Relations*
*Harald Boersma, Senior Manager Corporate Relations*
*Ylann Schemm, Corporate Relations Manager*
*Sacha Boucherie, Press Officer*
This national magazine is for medical case managers, social workers, counselors and home health professionals who work with people with serious injury or illness. It is a membership benefit of CMSA, the national association for case managers. *$55.00*
*84 pages BiMonthly*

**2083 Catalyst**
The Catalyst
Ste 275
1259 El Camino Real
Menlo Park, CA 94025-4208
800-647-0314
e-mail: info@thecatalyst.us
www.thecatalyst.us

*Sue Swezey, Editor*
Digest of news and information on the use of computers in special education. *$15.00*
*20 pages Quarterly*

**2084 Clinical Connection**
American Advertising Dist of Northern Virginia
708 Pendleton St
Alexandria, VA 22314-1819
703-549-5126
FAX: 703-548-5563
http://www.onlineceus.com

*Kathie Harrington, M.A., CCC, Author*
Covers speech language pathology.

**2085 College and University**
AACRAO
Ste 520
1 Dupont Cir NW
Washington, DC 20036-1148
202-293-9161
FAX: 202-872-8857
e-mail: reillym@aacrao.org
aacrao.org

*Michael Reilly, Executive Director*
*Janie Barnett, Associate Executive Director*
*Beverly Blue, Client Services, International Education Services*
*Bob Bontrager, Senior Director of AACRAO Consulting and SEM Initiatives*
Scholarly research journal. American Association of Collegiate Registrars and Admissions Offers (AACRAO) is a nonprofit, voluntary, professional, educational association of degree-granting, postsecondary institutions, government agencies, private educational organizations and education-oriented businesses in the United States and abroad. $80 per year US; $90 per year international.
*30 pages Quarterly*
*ISSN 0010-0889*

**2086 Continuing Care**
Stevens Publishing Corporation
14901 Quorum Dr,
Suite 425
Dallas, TX 75254-7507
972-687-6700
FAX: 972-687-6700
e-mail: info@1105media.com
www.stevenspublishing.com

*Neal Vitale, President & Chief Executive Officer*
*Richard Vitale, Senior Vice President & Chief Financial Officer*
*Mike Valenti, Executive Vice President*
*Jeff Klein, Non-Executive Chairman of the Board*
A national magazine for case management and discharge planning professionals published monthly except for December.
*$119.00*
*34 pages Monthly*

**2087 Counseling Psychologist**
American Psychological Association
2455 Teller Rd
Thousand Oaks, CA 91320-2218
805-499-0721
800-818-7243
FAX: 800-583-2665
e-mail: info@sagepub.com
www.sagepub.com

*Blaise R. Simqu, President & Chief Executive Officer*
*Tracey A. Ozmina, Executive Vice President & Chief Operating Officer*
*Chris Hickok, Senior Vice President & Chief Financial Officer*
*Stephen Barr, Managing Director/SAGE London, President of SAGE International*
Thematic issues in the theory, research and practice of counseling psychology. *$78.00*
*Bi-Monthly*

**2088 Counseling and Values**
American Counseling Association
5999 Stevenson Ave
Alexandria, VA 22304-3304
703-823-9800
800-347-6647
FAX: 800-473-2329
e-mail: webmaster@counseling.org
counseling.org

*Brad Erford, President*
*Richard Yep, Executive Director*
*Paul Nelson, Executive Director*
*Stacy Shaver, Executive Director*
Counseling and Values is the official journal of the Association for Spiritual, Ethical, and Religious Values in Counseling (ASERVIC), a member association of the American Counseling Association. Counseling and Values s a professional journal of theory, research, and informed opinion concerned with the relationships among psychology, philosophy, religion, social values, and counseling. *$12.00*
*TriAnnual*

**2089 Directions: Technology in Special Education**
DREAMMS for Kids
273 Ringwood Road
Freeville, NY 13068-5606
607-539-3027
FAX: 607-539-9930
e-mail: Greetings@dreamms.org
www.dreamms.org

*Janet P Hosmer, Publisher & Editor in Chief*
*Kathy S. Knight, Editor*
*Chester D. Hosmer, Jr, Technical Editor*
*Lorianne Hoenninger, Regular Contributor*
Provides technology tips to ease home instruction and use; describes and reviews adaptive educational software and hardware; reviews pertinent literature and audio and videotapes; describes adaptive and assistive technology devices; provides on-line service information for the disabled; announces upcoming educational and technology conference; and reports on new Department of Education legislation. *$14.95*
*Monthly*

**2090 Early Intervention**
Early Childhood Intervention Clearinghouse
Room 20
51 Gerty Drive
Champaign, IL 61820-7469
217-333-1386
877-275-3227
FAX: 217-244-7732
e-mail: Illinois-eic@illinois.edu
www.eiclearinghouse.org

*Susan Fowler, Director*
Features articles, conference calendar, material reviews and news concerning early childhood intervention and disability.
*4 pages Quarterly*

**2091 Exceptional Children**
Council for Exceptional Children
Suite 1000
2900 Crystal Drive
Arlington, VA 22202-3557
703-620-3660
866-509-0218
888-232-7733
FAX: 703-264-9494
TTY:866-915-5000
e-mail: service@cec.sped.org
cec.sped.org

*Margaret J. McLaughlin, President*
*Christy A. Chambers, President Elect*
*Bruce A. Ramirez, Executive Director*
*James P. Heiden, Treasurer*
Articles include research, literature surveys and position papers concerning exceptional children, special education and mainstreaming. *$58.00*
*96 pages BiMonthly*

**2092 Focus on Autism and Other Developmental Disabilities**
Sage Publications
2455 Teller Road
Thousand Oaks, CA 91320-2218
805-499-0721
800-818-7243
FAX: 800-583-2665
e-mail: info@sagepub.com
www.sagepub.com

*Sara Miller McCune, Founder, Publisher, Chairperson*
*Blaise R. Simqu, President & CEO*
*Chris Hickok, Senior Vice President & Chief Financial Officer*
*Stephen Barr, Managing Director/SAGE London, President of SAGE International*
Practical management, treatment and planning strategies; a must for persons working with individuals with autism and other developmental disabilities. *$43.00*
*64 pages Quarterly*

**2093 Focus on Exceptional Children**
Love Publishing Company
Ste 2200
9101 E Kenyon Ave
Denver, CO 80237-1854
303-221-7333
FAX: 303-221-7444
e-mail: lpc@lovepublishing.com
www.lovepublishing.com

*Steve Graham, Consulting Editor*
*Ron Nelson, Consulting Editor*
*Eva Horn, Consulting Editor*
Contains research and theory-based articles on special education topics, with an emphasis on application and intervention, of interest to teachers, professors and administrators. *$36.00*
*Monthly*

**2094 HomeCare Magazine**
Trimedia Publications
Suite 110
28th Avenue South
Birmingham, AL 35209
205-212-9402
www.homecaremag.com

*Stacy Branning, Publisher*
*Wally Evans, President and Publisher*
*George Lake, VP of Sales*
*Michelle Segrest, VP of Editorial*
The business magazine of the home medical equipment industry offering information on legislation and regulations affecting the homecare industry, monthly profiles of suppliers, operational tips, newest products in the industry, advice on sales, government regulations. *$ 65.00*
*120 pages Monthly*

**2095 I Wonder Who Else Can Help**
AARP
601 East St NW
Washington, DC 20049
202-434-3525
800-687-2277
FAX: 202-434-3443
TTY: 877-434-7598
e-mail: member@aarp.org
www.aarp.org

*Robert Romasco, President*
*Gail E. Aldrich, Chairman*
*Gretchen Dahlen, Executive Director*
*Jeannine English, President-Elect*
Contains information about crisis counseling, needs and resources, written in lay terms.

**2096 International Rehabilitation Review**
Rehabilitation International
25 E 21st St
New York, NY 10010-6207
212-420-1500
FAX: 212-505-0871
e-mail: rehabintal@aol.com
riglobal.org

*Anne Hawker, President*
*Patric Fougeyrollas, Deputy Vice President for the North America Region*
*Marca Bristo, Vice President for the North America Region*
*Martin Grabois, Treasurer*
International overview of activities and programs in vocational and medical rehabilitation, prosthesis and orthotics and special education. *$30.00*
*TriAnnual*

**2097 Intervention in School and Clinic**
Sage Publications
2455 Teller Road
Thousand Oaks, CA 91320
805-499-0721
800-818-7243
FAX: 800-583-2665
e-mail: info@sagepub.com
www.sagepub.com

*Sara Miller McCune, Founder, Publisher, Chairperson*
*Blaise R. Simqu, President & CEO*
*Tracey A. Ozmina, Executive Vice President & Chief Operating Officer*
*Dale R. Jordan, Author*
A hands-on, how-to resource for teachers and clinicians working with students for whom minor curriculum and environmental modifications are ineffective. *$35.00*
*64 pages*

**2098 Journal for Vocational Special Needs Education**
University of Wisconsin
1025 W Johnson St
Madison, WI 53706-1706
608-263-9250
FAX: 608-262-3050
e-mail: jgugerty@education.wisc.edu
www.cew.wisc.edu/jvsne/

*John Gugerty, Co-Editor*
Articles on vocational education for special needs population, including persons with physical and mental disabilities. *$16.00*

**2099 Journal of Applied School Psychology**
Haworth Press
711 Third Avenue
New York, NY 10017
212-216-7800
800-354-1420
FAX: 212-244-1563
e-mail: subscriptions@tandf.co.uk.
www.haworthpress.com

This journal disseminates the latest and the highest quality information to all professionals who provide special services in the schools and related educational settings. Haworth Press are now acquired by the Taylor & Francis Journals. *$60.00*
*BiAnnually*

**2100 Journal of Counseling & Development**
American Counseling Association
5999 Stevenson Ave
Alexandria, VA 22304-3304
703-823-0252
800-347-6647
FAX: 800-473-2329
e-mail: webmaster@counseling.org
counseling.org

*A Scott McGowan, Editor*
*Carolyn Baker, Publications Director*
*Richard Yep, President*
Publishes archival material, also publishes articles that have broad interest for a readership composed mostly of counselors and other mental health professionals who work in private practice, schools, colleges, community agencies, hospitals, and government. An appropriate outlet for articles that: critically integrate published research; examine current professional and scientific issues; report research, new techniques, innovative programs and practices; and examine ACA as an organization. *$140.00*
*128 pages Quarterly*

**2101 Journal of Emotional and Behavioral Disorders**
Sage Publications
2455 Teller Road
Thousand Oaks, CA 91320-2218
805-499-0721
800-818-7243
FAX: 800-583-2665
e-mail: info@sagepub.com
www.sagepub.com

*Sara Miller McCune, Founder, Publisher, Chairperson*
*Blaise R. Simqu, President & CEO*
*Chris Hickok, Senior Vice President & Chief Financial Officer*
*Stephen Barr, Managing Director/SAGE London, President of SAGE International*
An international, multidisciplinary journal featuring articles on research, practice and theory related to individuals with emotional and behavioral disorders and to the professionals who serve them. *$39.00*
*64 pages Quarterly*

**2102 Journal of Learning Disabilities**
Sage Publications
2455 Teller Road
Thousand Oaks, CA 91320-2218
805-499-0721
800-818-7243
FAX: 800-583-2665
e-mail: info@sagepub.com
www.sagepub.com

*Sara Miller McCune, Founder, Publisher, Chairperson*
*Blaise R. Simqu, President & CEO*
*Chris Hickok, Senior Vice President & Chief Financial Officer*
*Stephen Barr, Managing Director/SAGE London, President of SAGE International*
An international, multidisciplinary publication containing articles on practice, research and theory related to learning disabilities. Published bi-monthly. *$49.00*
*Magazine*

**2103 Journal of Motor Behavior**
Heldref Publications
Ste 800
325 Chestnut St
Philadelphia, PA 19106-2608
215-625-8900
800-354-1420
FAX: 215-625-2940
e-mail: subscribe@heldref.org
www.heldref.org

*Emilli Pawlowsky, Marketing Manager*
*Laura Rosse, Assistant Marketing Manager*
*Douglas Kirkpatrick, Publisher*
A professional journal aimed at psychologists, therapists and educators who work in the areas of motor behavior, psychology, neurophysiology, kinesiology, and biomechanics. Offers up-to-date information on the latest techniques, theories and developments concerning motor control. Titles previously published by Heldref Publications will be joining the T&F portfolio. *$77.00*
*115 pages Quarterly*

**2104 Journal of Musculoskeletal Pain**
Haworth Press
711 Third Avenue
New York, NY 10017
212-216-7800
800-354-1420
FAX: 212-244-1563
e-mail: subscriptions@tandf.co.uk.
www.haworthpress.com
William Cohen, Owner
This journal serves as a central resource for the dissemination of information about musculoskeletal pain. Haworth Press are now acquired by the Taylor & Francis Journals. *$75.00*
*110 pages Quarterly*

2105 **Journal of Postsecondary Education & Disability**
AHEAD
Ste 204
107 Commerce Centre Dr
Huntersville, NC 28078- 5870
704-947-7779
FAX: 704-948-7779
TTY:617-287-3882
e-mail: information@ahead.org
http://www.ahead.org/publications/jped

*Jean Ashmore, President*
*Stephan Hamlin-Smith, Executive Director*
*Scott Bay, Director*
*Richard Allegra, Director of Professional Development*
Provides in-depth examination of research, issues, policies and programs in postsecondary education.

2106 **Journal of Prosthetics and Orthotics**
Ste 210
330 John Carlyle St
Alexandria, VA 22314-5760
703-836-7114
FAX: 703-836-0838
e-mail: info@abcop.org
www.abcop.org

*Donald D. Virostek, President*
*Stephen B. Fletcher, Director, Clinical Resources*
*Catherine A. Carter, Executive Director*
*Heather Harris, Director, Continuing Education Programs*
Provides the latest research and clinical thinking in orthotics and prosthetics, including information on new devices, fitting techniques and patient management experiences. Each issue contains research-based information and articles reviewed and approved by a highly qualified editorial board. *$60.00*
*64 pages Quarterly*
*ISSN 1040-88 0*

2107 **Journal of Reading, Writing and Learning Disabled International**
Hemisphere Publishing Corporation
7625 Empire Dr
Florence, KY 41042-2919
800-634-7064
FAX: 800-248-4724
e-mail: orders@taylorandfrancis.com
francis
Articles on reading, writing and learning disabilities, including mainstreaming issues. *$9.00*

2108 **Journal of School Health Association**
Suite 403
4340 East West Highway
Bethesda, MD 20814
301-652-8072
FAX: 301-652-8077
e-mail: info@ashaweb.org
ashaweb.org

*Jeffrey K. Clark, President*
*Stephen Conley, Executive Director*
*Julie Greenfield, Marketing and Conferences Director*
*Beverly Samek, Chair of Advocacy*
This is a monthly journal which offers information to professionals and parents on school health. Membership dues, $95.00.

2109 **Journal of Special Education**
Sage Publications
2455 Teller Road
Thousand Oaks, CA 91320-2218
805-499-0721
800-818-7243
FAX: 800-583-2665
e-mail: info@sagepub.com
www.sagepub.com

*Sara Miller McCune, Founder, Publisher, Chairperson*
*Blaise R. Simqu, President & CEO*
*Chris Hickok, Senior Vice President & Chief Financial Officer*
*Stephen Barr, Managing Director/SAGE London, President of SAGE International*
Internationally known as the prime research journal in special education. JSE provides research articles of special education for individuals with disabilities, ranging from mild to severe. Published quarterly. *$39.00*
*Magazine*

2110 **Journal of Vocational Behavior**
Academic Press, Journals Division
www.academicpress.com/jvb
The Journal of Vocational Behavior publishes empirical and theoretical articles that expand knowledge of vocational behavior and career development across the life span. Research presented in the journal encompasses the general categories of career choice, implementation, and vocational adjustment and adaptation. The articles are also valuable for applications in counseling and career development programs in colleges and universities, business and industry, government, and the military. *$7.00*

2111 **MDA Newsmagazine**
Muscular Dystrophy Association
Ste 155
3275 W Ina Rd
Tucson, AZ 85741-2330
520-795-3434
FAX: 520-795-3989
e-mail: tusconservices@mdausa.org

*Danielle Trzyna, Manager*
Presents news related to muscular dystrophy and other neuromuscular diseases including research, personal profiles, fundraising activities and patient services.

2112 **Measurement and Evaluation in Counseling**
5999 Stevenson Ave
Alexandria, VA 22304-3304
703-823-0252
800-347-6647
FAX: 800-473-2329
e-mail: webmaster@counseling.org
www.counseling.org

*Bruce Thompson, Editor*
*Richard Yep, Executive Director*
*Brad Erford, President*
The American Counseling Association is a not-for-profit, professional and educational organization that is dedicated to the growth and enhancement of the counseling profession

2113 **Our World**
National Center for Learning Disabilities
Rm 1401
381 Park Ave S
New York, NY 10016-8829
212-545-7510
800-575-7373
888-575-7373
FAX: 212-545-9665
e-mail: help@ncld.org
ncld.org

*Mary Kalikow, Vice Chairman*
*Frederic M. Poses, Chairman*
*Margi Booth, President*
*John R. Langeler, Treasurer*
Contains features, articles, human interest news and information and information, and other practical material to benefit the millions of children and adults with learning disabilities and their families, as well as educators and other helping professionals. Magazine.
*Quarterly*

2114 **Psychiatric Staffing Crisis in Community Mental Health**
Nat l Council for Community Behavioral Healthcare
201-559-3882
800-THE-BOOK
e-mail: amilevoj@bn.com
www.barnesandnoble.com

*Andy Milevoj, Vice President, Investor Relations*

Find out some of the simple, low-cost ways you can increase workplace satisfaction among staff psychiatrists and compete successfully for their talents. *$20.00*

**2115 Readings: A Journal of Reviews and Commentary in Mental Health**
American Orthopsychiatric Association
1714 Cambridge Avenue
Sheboygan, WI 53082-1048
920-457-5051
800-558-7687
e-mail: info@americanortho.com
www.americanortho.com

*Michael Bogenschuetz, President*
*Randy Benz, Chief Executive Officer*
*Charles Achter, Assistant Controller*
*Deb Schmidt, Administrative Manager*
Reviews of recent books in mental health and allied disciplines. Includes essay reviews and brief reviews. *$25.00*
*32 pages Quarterly*

**2116 Rehab Pro**
1926 Waukegan Rd
Suite 1
Glenview, IL 60025-1770
847-657-6964
FAX: 847-657-6963
e-mail: carlw@tcag.com
www.rehabpro.org

*Carl Wangman, Executive Director*
The magazine is to promote the profession and to inform the public about the activities of the national organization, its state chapter affiliates, and the work of its special interest sections.
*38 pages BiMonthly*

**2117 Remedial and Special Education**
Sage Publications
2455 Teller Road
Thousand Oaks, CA 91320-2218
805-499-0721
800-818-7243
FAX: 800-583-2665
e-mail: info@sagepub.com
www.sagepub.com

*Sara Miller McCune, Founder, Publisher, Chairperson*
*Blaise R. Simqu, President & CEO*
*Chris Hickok, Senior Vice President & Chief Financial Officer*
*Stephen Barr, Managing Director/SAGE London, President of SAGE International*
A professional journal that bridges the gap between theory and practice. Emphasis is on topical reviews, syntheses of research, field evaluation studies and recommendations for the practice of remedial and special education. Published six times a year. *$39.00*
*64 pages*

**2118 Teaching Exceptional Children**
Council for Exceptional Children
Suite 1000
2900 Crystal Drive
Arlington, VA 22202-3557
703-620-3660
866-509-0218
888-232-7733
FAX: 703-264-9494
TTY:866-915-5000
e-mail: service@cec.sped.org
www.cec.sped.org

*Margaret J. McLaughlin, President*
*Christy A. Chambers, President Elect*
*Bruce A. Ramirez, Executive Director*
*James P. Heiden, Treasurer*
Journal designed for teachers of gifted students and students with disabilities, featuring practical methods and materials for classroom use. *$58.00*
*96 pages BiMonthly*

## Newsletters

**2119 Alert**
Association on Handicapped Student Service Program
P.O.Box 21192
Columbus, OH 43221
614-365-5216
FAX: 614-365-6718

Keeps members informed about Association activities, current legislative issues, innovative programs, and more. *$30.00*

**2120 Camp Virginia Jaycee Newsletter**
Dare Care Charity
2494 Camp Jaycee Rd
P.O. Box 648
Blue Ridge, VA 24064- 0648
540-947-2972
e-mail: info@campvajc.org
www.campvajc.org

*William Hartz, Chairman*
*Kathleen King, Vice Chair*
*Lisa Parrish, Treasurer*
Summer camping for children and adults with developmental disabilities. Coed, ages 7-70. Weekend respite camps for children and adults with mental retardation.
*8 pages quarterly*

**2121 Counseling Today**
American Counseling Association
5999 Stevenson Ave
Alexandria, VA 22304-3304
703-823-0252
800-347-6647
FAX: 800-473-2329
e-mail: webmaster@counseling.org
counseling.org

*Richard Yep, Executive Director*
*Brad Erford, President*
Aims to serve individuals active in professional counseling, in the school and university, in the workplace and the marketplace, as well as other citizens, community leaders and policy makers who appreciate the importance of the role of professional counselors in today's society.
*Monthly*

**2122 Counselor Education and Supervision**
American Counseling Association
5999 Stevenson Ave
Alexandria, VA 22304-3304
703-823-0252
800-347-6647
FAX: 800-473-2329
e-mail: webmaster@counseling.org
www.counseling.org

*Margaret L Fong, Editor*
*Richard Yep, President*
Dedicated to the growth and development of the counseling profession and those who are served. *$18.00*
*Quarterly*

**2123 Counterpoint**
National Association of State Directors of Special
10860 Hampton Rd
Fairfax Station, VA 22039-2700
703-519-3800
FAX: 703-503-8627
Newspaper designed for teachers of disabled and gifted students, featuring practical methods and materials for classroom use. *$36.00*
*Quarterly*

2124 **Disability Compliance for Higher Education**
LRP Publications
360 Hiatt Drive
Palm Beach Gardens, FL 33418-4668 561-622-6520
800-341-7874
FAX: 561-622-1375
e-mail: rfortune@lrp.com
lrp.com

*Kenneth F. Kahn, Owner and President*
*Ed Chase, Vice President*
The only newsletter that is dedicated to the exclusive coverage of disability issues that affect colleges and universities. *$195.00*
*8 pages Monthly*

2125 **Disability Resources Monthly**
Disability Resources
4 Glatter Ln
South Setauket, NY 11720-1032 631-585-0290
FAX: 631-585-0290
e-mail: pubs@disabilityresources.org
disabilityresources.org

*Avery Klauber, Executive Director*
A newsletter that monitors, reviews and reports on resources for independent living. A monthly newsletter that features short topical articles, news items and reviews of books, pamphlets, periodicals, videotapes, on-line services, organizations and other resources for and about people with disabilities. It is intended primarily for librarians, social workers, educators, rehabilitation specialists, disability advocates, ADA coordinators and other health and social service professionals. *$33.00*
*4 pages Monthly*
*ISSN 1070-72 0*

2126 **Early Childhood Reporter**
LRP Publications
747 Dresher Rd
Suite 500
Horsham, PA 19044-2247 215-784-0941
800-341-7874
FAX: 215-784-9639
www.lrp.com

*Kenneth F. Kahn, Owner and President*
*Ed Chase, Vice President*
Monthly reports with information on federal, state, and local legislation affecting the implementation of early intervention and preschool programs for children with disabilities. *$145.00*
*12-16 pages $10 shipping*

2127 **Healthline**
CV Mosby Company
1600 John F. Kennedy
Suite 1800
Philadelphia, PA 19103- 2899 215-239-3900
800-523-1649
FAX: 215-239-3990
www.mosby.com

Health and fitness information for healthcare professionals and the general public alike.
*Monthly*

2128 **Help Newsletter**
Learning Disabilities Association of Arkansas
Ste 103c
7509 Cantrell Rd
Little Rock, AR 72207-2537 501-666-8777
FAX: 501-666-8777
e-mail: info@ldaarkansas.org
www.ldaarkansas.org

*Dana Jackson, Executive Director*
*Kristen Joyner, Director Development*
Information on how to overcome obstacles and to achieve in spite of learning disabilities. *$30.00*
*8 pages Quarterly*

2129 **International Rolf Institute**
Ste 103
5055 Chaparral Ct
Boulder, CO 80301-3326 303-449-5903
800-530-8875
FAX: 303-449-5978
rolf.org

*Kevin McCoy, Chairperson*
*Diana Yourell, Executive Director*
*Jim Jones, Director of Education*
*Carah Wertheimer, Admissions Advisor*
Information, practitioner training and certification.

2130 **Learning Disabilities Consultants Newsletter**
Learning Disabilities Consultants
P.O.Box 716
Bryn Mawr, PA 19010 610-446-6126
800-869-8336
FAX: 610-446-6129
e-mail: rcooper-ldr@comcast.net

*Richard Cooper, Director*
Newsletter providing information about learning disabilities and differences. It contains both local and national news items and includes in each issue articles about various aspects of learning problems encountered in both children and adults. *$10.00*
*6 pages 5x Year*

2131 **MA Report**
National Allergy and Asthma Network
Ste 200
3554 Chain Bridge Rd
Fairfax, VA 22030-2709 703-385-4403
FAX: 703-352-4354

Offers information on medical breakthroughs, patient care, public awareness, activities and events focusing on the allergy and asthma patient. This newsletter is the only Monthly Asthma Report that a patient will need to keep fully informed with medical articles written by experts in the field. .
*Monthly*

2132 **NYALD News**
New York Association for the Learning Disabled
90 S Swan St
Albany, NY 12210-2105 518-465-6115

*Kelly Jarrard, Executive Director*
*Michael Vacek, Manager*
Newsletter offering information on the learning disabled in the New York area.
*Monthly*

2133 **O&P Almanac**
American Orthotic & Prosthetic Association
330 John Carlyle Street
Suite 200
Alexandria, VA 22314 571-431-0876
FAX: 571-431-0899
e-mail: info@aopanet.org
www.aopanet.org

*Tom DiBello, President*
*Thomas F. Kirk, President-Elect*
*Anita Liberman-Lampear, Vice President*
*Jim Weber, Treasurer*
Offers in-depth coverage on orthotics and prosthetics to current professional, government, business and reimbursement activities affecting the orthotics and prosthetics industry. *$59.00*
*80 pages Monthly*

**2134 Occupational Therapy in Health Care**
Haworth Press
711 Third Avenue
New York, NY 10017
212-216-7800
800-354-1420
FAX: 212-244-1563
e-mail: subscriptions@tandf.co.uk
www.haworthpress.com

Each issue focuses on significant practices and concerns involving occupational therapy and therapists. Haworth Press are now acquired by the Taylor & Francis Journals. *$75.00*

**2135 Ohio Coalition for the Education of Children with Disabilities**
165 W Center St
Ste 302
Marion, OH 43302-3741
740-382-5452
800-374-2806
FAX: 740-383-6421
e-mail: ocecd@ocecd.org
www.ocecd.org

*Martha Lause, Manager*
*Lee Ann Derugen, Co-Director*
*Margaret Burley, Executive Director*
*Lee Ann Derugen, Co-Director*
Forum is a newsletter reporting on educational, legislative and other developments affecting persons with disabilities.
*8 pages*

**2136 SAMHSA News**
U S Department of Health and Human Services
1 Choke Cherry Road
Rockville, MD 20857
202-690-7650
877-696-6775
www.samhsa.gov

*Pamela S. Hyde, Administrator*
*Kana Enomoto, Principal Deputy Administrator*
*Daryl Kade, Director,Office of Financial Resources*
*Tina Conners-James, Deputy Director,Office of Financial Resources*
This quarterly agency newsletter reports on information on substance abuse, mental health treatment and prevention programs of the Substance Abuse and Mental Health Services Administration.
*Quarterly*

**2137 Sibling Information Network Newsletter**
AJ Pappanikou Center
Suite 181
270 Farmington Avenue
06030, CT 06030
860-679-1500
866-623-1315
FAX: 860-679-1571
TTY: 860-679-1502
e-mail: contact.us.ucedd@uchc.edu
www.uconnucedd.org

*Mary Beth Bruder, UCEDD/LEND Director*
*Tierney Giannotti, Associate UCEDD Director*
*Gabriela Freyre-Calish, Assistant UCEDD Director*
*Kelly M. Jones, Administrative Officer*
Contains information aimed at the varying interested of our membership. Program descriptions, requests for assistance, conference announcements, literature summaries and research reports.
*$8.50*

**2138 Sibpage**
AJ Pappanikou Center
Suite 181
270 Farmington Avenue
06030, CT 06030
860-679-1500
866-623-1315
FAX: 860-679-1571
TTY: 860-679-1502
e-mail: contact.us.ucedd@uchc.edu
www.uconnucedd.org

*Mary Beth Bruder, UCEDD/LEND Director*
*Tierney Giannotti, Associate UCEDD Director*
*Gabriela Freyre-Calish, Assistant UCEDD Director*
*Kelly M. Jones, Administrative Officer*
Developed specifically for children containing games, recipes, pen pals, and articles written by siblings relating to developmental disabilities.
*4 pages*

**2139 Special Edge**
Resources in Special Education
Fl 4
1107 9th St
Sacramento, CA 95814-3616
916-492-9999
877-493-7833
FAX: 916-492-4004
e-mail: rise@wested.org

*Virigina Reynolds, President*
Provides education news, collaborative programs, amendments to the laws, tools for accommodations, resource information, a calendar of events, and more.
*BiMonthly*

**2140 Special Education Report**
LRP Publications
360 Hiatt Drive
Palm Beach Gardens, FL 33418-4668
561-622-6520
800-341-7874
FAX: 561-622-1375
e-mail: rfortune@lrp.com
lrp.com

*Kenneth F. Kahn, Owner and President*
*Ed Chase, Vice President*
Current, pertinent information about federal legislation, regulations, programs and funding for educating children with disabilities. Covers federal and state litigation on the Individuals with Disabilities Education Act and other relevant laws. Looks at innovations and research in the field. *$266.00*
*8 pages BiWeekly*
*ISSN 0194-22 5*

**2141 Topics in Early Childhood Special Education**
Sage Publications
2455 Teller Road
Thousand Oaks, CA 91320-2218
805-499-0721
800-818-7243
FAX: 800-583-2665
e-mail: info@sagepub.com
www.sagepub.com

*Sara Miller McCune, Founder, Publisher, Chairperson*
*Blaise R. Simqu, President & CEO*
*Chris Hickok, Senior Vice President & Chief Financial Officer*
*Stephen Barr, Managing Director/SAGE London, President of SAGE International*
Designed for professionals helping young children with special needs in areas such as assessment, special programs, social policies and developmental aids. *$43.00*
*Quarterly*

**2142 Treatment Review**
AIDS Treatment Data Network
2nd Floor
57 Willoughby St
Brooklyn, NY 11201
347-473-7400
800-734-7104
TTY:212-925-9560
e-mail: info@housingworks.org
www.atdn.org

*Barbara Hughes, President*
*Max Setulveda, Financing Manager*
Individual members receive treatment education, counseling, referrals and case management support. Services are available in both English and Spanish. The Treatment Review newsletter includes descriptions of approved, alternative and experimental treatments, as well as announcements of seminars and forums on treatments and clinical trials.
*Quarterly*

**2143 VIP Newsletter**
Blind Children's Fund
6761 West US 12
P.O. Box 363
Three Oaks, MI 49128
989-779-9966
FAX: 269-756-3133
e-mail: BCF@blindchildrensfund.org
www.blindchildrensfund.org

*Karla B. Kwast, Executive Director*
*Jeremy Murphy, President*
*Robert R. Storrer Jr., Vice President*
*Carrie L. Owens, Director*
Provides parents and professionals with information, materials and resources that help them successfully teach and nurture blind, visually and multi-impaired infants and preschoolers. *$10.00*

## Professional Texts

**2144 A Teacher's Guide to Isovaleric Acidemia**
150 N 18th Ave
Phoenix, AZ 85007-3232
602-542-1025
FAX: 602-542-0883
azdhs.gov

*Thomas Salow, Manager*
*Will Humble, Director*
Resource book for preschool teachers and school staff on isovaleric academia basics and classroom activities. *$2.50*

**2145 A Teacher's Guide to Methylmalonic Acidemia**
Arizona State Department of Health Services
1740 W Adams St
Phoenix, AZ 85007-2607
602-542-1020
FAX: 602-364-1150
www.azdhs.gov

*Will Humble, Director*
*Thomas Salow, Manager*
Resource book for preschool teachers and school staff on methylmalonic academia basics and classroom activities. *$2.50*

**2146 A Teacher's Guide to PKU**
Arizona Department of Health Services
1740 W Adams St
Phoenix, AZ 85007-2607
602-542-1020
FAX: 602-364-1150
www.azdhs.gov

*Will Humble, Director*
*Thomas Salow, Manager*
Resource book for preschool teachers and school staff on PKU basics, NutraSweet warning, and classroom activities. *$2.50*
*13 pages*

**2147 ADD Challenge: A Practical Guide for Teachers**
P.O.Box 9177
Champaign, IL 61826-9177
217-352-3273
800-519-2707
FAX: 217-352-1221
e-mail: orders@researchpress.com
www.researchpress.com

*Robert W. Parkinson, Founder*
*Steven B. Gordon, Author*
*Michael J. Asher, Author*
*Michael J. Asher, Author*
Research Press is an independent, family-owned business founded in 1968 by Robert W. Parkinson (1920-2001).

**2148 ADHD in the Classroom: Strategies for Teachers**
Guilford Publication
72 Spring St
New York, NY 10012-4019
212-431-9800
800-365-7006
FAX: 212-966-6708
e-mail: info@guilford.com
guilford.com

*Bob Matloff, President*
*Seymour Weingarten, Editor-in-Chief*
*Russell A. Barkley, Author*
Designed specifically to help teachers with their ADHD students, thereby providing a better learning environment for the entire class. *$95.00*

*ISBN 0-898629-85-3*

**2149 ADHD in the Schools: Assessment and Intervention Strategies**
72 Spring St
New York, NY 10012-4019
212-431-9800
800-365-7006
FAX: 212-966-6708
e-mail: info@guilford.com
www.guilford.com

*Bob Matloff, President*
*Seymour Weingarten, Editor-in-Chief*
*George J. DuPaul, Author*
*Gary Stoner, Author*
The landmark volume emphasizes the need for a team effort among parents, community-based professionals, and educators. Provides practical information for educators that is based on empirical findings. Chapters Focus on how to identify and assess students who might have ADHD, the relationship between ADHD and learning disabilities; how to develop and supplement classroom-based programs. Communication strategies to assist physicians and the need for community-based treatments *$36.00*
*269 pages Paperback*
*ISBN 0-898622-45-X*

**2150 AEPS Curriculum for Birth to Three Years**
Brookes Publishing
P.O.Box 10624
Baltimore, MD 21285-0624
410-337-9580
800-638-3775
FAX: 410-337-8539
e-mail: custserv@brookespublishing.com
readplaylearn.com
Directly linked to IEP/IFSP goals developed for a child from the AEPS test measure, the AEPS curriculum provides a complete set of learning activities to facilitate children's acquisition of functional skills. *$59.95*
*496 pages*
*ISBN 1-557660-96-4*

**2151 Access to Health Care: Number 3&4**
World Institute on Disability
Suite 280
3075 Adeline Street
Berkeley, CA 94703
510-225-6400
FAX: 510-225-0477
TTY:510-225-0478
e-mail: wid@wid.org
www.wid.org

*Susan P. Mazrui, Chairman*
*Neil Jacobson, Vice Chairman*
*Anita Shafer Aaron, Executive Director*
*Kenneth R. Chrisman, Immediate Past Chair*
These policy bulletins focus on the capacity of the private and public health insurance systems to respond to the health care needs of persons with disabilities or chronic illness. *$6.50*
*91 pages Paperback*

**2152 Activity-Based Approach to Early Intervention, 2nd Edition**
Brookes Publishing
P.O.Box 10624
Baltimore, MD 21285-0624
410-337-9580
800-638-3775
FAX: 410-337-8539
e-mail: custserv@brookespublishing.com
www.brookespublishing.com

*Paul H. Brookes, Chairman*
*Jeff Brookes, President*
*Melissa A. Behm, ExecutiveVice President*
*George Stamathis, Vice President & Publisher*
Activity-based intervention shows how to use natural and relevant events to teach infants and young children, of all abilities, effectively and efficiently. *$24.00*
*240 pages*
*ISBN 1-55766 -87-5*

**2153 Adapted Physical Education for Students with Autism**
Charles C. Thomas
2600 S 1st St
Springfield, IL 62704-4730
217-789-8980
800-258-8980
FAX: 217-789-9130
e-mail: books@ccthomas.com
ccthomas.com

*Kimberly Davis, Author*
Focuses on the physical education needs and curriculum for autistic children. Available in cloth, paperback and hardcover. *$27.95*
*142 pages Paper*
*ISBN 0-398060-85-1*

**2154 Adapting Early Childhood Curricula for Children with Special Needs**
McGraw-Hill School Publishing
P.O. Box 182604
Columbus, OH 43272
877-833-5524
FAX: 614-759-3749
e-mail: customer.service@mcgraw-hill.com
mcgraw-hill.com

*Harold McGraw III, Chairman, President and Chief Executive Officer*
*Jack F. Callahan, Jr., Executive Vice President, Chief Financial Officer*
*Douglas Peterson, President, Standard & Poor's*
*Lou Eccleston, President, McGraw-Hill Financial*
Offers information on educating the disabled.

**2155 Adapting Instruction for the Mainstream: A Sequential Approach to Teaching**
McGraw-Hill School Publishing
P.O. Box 182604
Columbus, OH 43272
877-833-5524
FAX: 614-759-3749
e-mail: customer.service@mcgraw-hill.com
mcgraw-hill.com

*Harold McGraw III, Chairman, President and Chief Executive Officer*
*Jack F. Callahan, Jr., Executive Vice President, Chief Financial Officer*
*Douglas Peterson, President, Standard & Poor's*
*Lou Eccleston, President, McGraw-Hill Financial*
This text gives both regular and special education teachers everything they need to help mildly handicapped students succeed in the mainstream.
*226 pages*

**2156 Adaptive Education Strategies Building on Diversity**
Brookes Publishing Company
P.O.Box 10624
Baltimore, MD 21285-0624
410-337-9580
800-638-3775
FAX: 410-337-8539
e-mail: custserv@brookespublishing.com
www.brookespublishing.com

*Paul H. Brookes, Chairman*
*Jeff Brookes, President*
*Melissa A. Behm, ExecutiveVice President*
*George Stamathis, Vice President & Publisher*
Based on more than two decades of systematic research, this comprehensive manual provides a road map to the effective implementation of adaptive education. *$35.00*
*304 pages Paperback*
*ISBN 1-557880-84-0*

**2157 Advanced Sign Language Vocabulary: A Resource Text for Educators**
Charles C. Thomas
2600 S 1st St
Springfield, IL 62704-4730
217-789-8980
800-258-8980
FAX: 217-789-9130
e-mail: books@ccthomas.com
www.ccthomas.com

*Elizabeth E. Wolf, Author*
*Janet R. Coleman, Author*
This book is a collection of advanced sign language vocabulary for use by educators, interpreters, parents or anyone wishing to enlarge their sign vocabulary. *$53.95*
*202 pages Spiralbound*
*ISBN 0-398057-22-2*

**2158 Advances in Cardiac and Pulmonary Rehabilitation**
Haworth Press
711 Third Avenue
New York, NY 10017
212-216-7800
800-354-1420
FAX: 212-244-1563
e-mail: subscriptions@tandf.co.uk.
www.haworthpress.com
Enhance your rehabilitation program with this authoritative volume. Haworth Press are now acquired by the Taylor & Francis Journals. *$34.95*
*74 pages Hardcover*
*ISBN 0-866869-86-3*

**2159 Aging Brain**
Taylor & Francis Group
Ste 800
325 Chestnut St
Philadelphia, PA 19106-2608
215-625-8900
800-354-1420
FAX: 215-625-2940
www.taylorandfrancisgroup.com

Elderly treatment.
*225 pages Paperback*
*ISBN 0-85066-78-0*

**2160 Aging and Disability: Crossing Network Lines**
Springer Publishing
15th Fl
11 W 42nd St
New York, NY 10036-8002
212-431-4370
877-687-7476
FAX: 212-941-7842
e-mail: marketing@springerpub.com
springerpub.com

*Theodore C. Nardin, CEO/Publisher*
*Jason Roth, VP/Marketing Director*
*Annette Imperati, Marketing/Sales Director*
*Stephanie Drew, Acquisitions Editor,Social Work and Psychology*

Michelle Putnam has set forth this volume to reflect the current research, facilitate collaboration across service networks, and encourage movement toward more effective service policies. Professional stakeholders evaluate the bridges and barriers to crossing network lines, and chapter on current websites, agencies, and coalitions provides the much needed tools to bring collaboration into practice.

**2161 Aging and Rehabilitation II**
Springer Publishing Company
15th Fl
11 W 42nd St
New York, NY 10036-8002
212-431-4370
877-687-7476
FAX: 212-941-7842
e-mail: marketing@springerpub.com
www.springerpub.com

*Anette Imperati, Marketing/Sales Director*
*Ursula Springer, President*
*Theodore C. Nardin, CEO/Publisher*
*Jason Roth, VP/Marketing Director*

Current, multidisciplinary investigations of various practice issues. Leading experts in the field use a practical perspective to provide specific comments on interventions. The scope of this work encompasses the autonomy of elderly disabled, mobility, mental health and value issues, as well as basic aspects in rehabilitation of the elderly. *$41.95*
*367 pages Hardcover*
*ISBN 0-82617-80-3*

**2162 Alphabetic Phonics Curriculum**
Educators Publishing Service
Ste 3
625 Mount Auburn St
Cambridge, MA 02138-4555
617-547-6706
800-225-5750
e-mail: Feedback.EPS@schoolspecialty.com
www.epsbooks.com

Ungraded multisensory curriculum for teaching phonics and the structure of language. Uses Orton-Gillingham approach to teach handwriting, spelling, reading, reading comprehension, and oral and written expression. program includes basic manual, workbooks, tests, teachers' guides, drill cards and all cards. *$28.15*

*ISSN 8388-42*

**2163 Alternative Educational Delivery Systems**
National Association of School Psychologists
Ste 402
4340 East West Hwy
Bethesda, MD 20814-4468
301-657-0270
866-331-NASP
FAX: 301-657-0275
TTY: 301-657-4155
e-mail: webmaster@naspweb.org
nasponline.org

*Philip Lazarus, President*
*Amy Smith, President-Elect*
*Susan Gorin, Executive Director*
*Laura Benson, Chief Operating Officer*

A book offering information to the professional on how to enhance educational options for all students.

**2164 Alternative Teaching Strategies**
Special Needs Project
Ste H
324 State St
Santa Barbara, CA 93101-2364
805-962-8087
800-333-6867
FAX: 805-962-5087
www.specialneeds.com

*Mark Darrow, Founder,The Prolotherapy Institue*

Offers help for teachers who teach behaviorally troubled students.

**2165 Antecedent Control: Innovative Approaches to Behavioral Support**
Brookes Publishing
P.O.Box 10624
Baltimore, MD 21285-0624
410-337-9585
800-638-3775
FAX: 410-337-8539
e-mail: custserv@brookespublishing.com
www.brookespublishing.com

*Paul H. Brooks, Chairman*
*Jeff Brookes, President*
*Melissa A. Behm, ExecutiveVice President*
*George Stamathis, Vice President & Publisher*

This book explains the theory and methodology of antecedent control. The treatment techniques in this book are effective for both children and adults.
*416 pages Paperback*
*ISBN 1-55766-34-3*

**2166 Anxiety-Free Kids: An Interactive Guide for Parents and Children**
Prufrock Press
PO Box 8813
Waco, TX 76714-8813
800-998-2208
FAX: 800-240-0333
e-mail: info@prufrock.com
www.prufrock.com

*Bonnie Zuvker Psy.D, Author*
*Joel McIntosh, Publisher*
*Sarah Morrison, Editor*
*Ginny Bates, Office Manager*

Offers parents strategies that help children happy and worry-free, methods that relieve a child's excessive anxieties and phobias, and tools for fostering interaction and family-oriented solutions. *$19.95*
*280 pages Paperback*
*ISBN 1-593633-43-1*

**2167 Applied Rehabilitation Counseling**

Springer Publishing Compn
15th Fl
11 W 42nd St
New York, NY 10036-8002
212-431-4370
877-687-7476
FAX: 212-941-7842
e-mail: contactus@springerpub.com
www.springerpub.com

*Sheri W. Sussman, Vice President*
*Ursula Springer, President*
*Theodore C. Nardin, CEO/Publisher*
*Jason Roth, VP/Marketing Director*

This comprehensive text describes current theories, techniques, and their applications to specific disabled populations. Perspectives on varying counseling approaches such as psychodynamic, existential, gestalt, behavioral and psychoeducational orientations are systematically outlined in an easy-to-follow format. Practical applications for counseling are emphasized with attention given to strategies, goal-setting and on-going evaluations. *$29.95*

*400 pages Softcover*
*ISBN 0-82615 -70-4*

**2168 Art-Centered Education and Therapy for Children with Disabilities**

Charles C. Thomas
2600 S 1st St
Springfield, IL 62704-4730
217-789-8980
800-258-8980
FAX: 217-789-9130
e-mail: books@ccthomas.com
ccthomas.com

*Frances E. Anderson, Author*

This book has been written to help both the regular education, and art and special education teachers, both pre- and in-service, better understand some of the issues and realities of providing education and remediation to children with disabilities. The book is also offered as model concept that has govern the author's personal and professional career of over thirty years. *$41.95*

*284 pages Paperback*
*ISBN 0-398060-06-1*

**2169 Assessing the Handicaps/Needs of Children**

Books on Special Children
P.O.Box 3378
Amherst, MA 01004-3378
413-256-8164
FAX: 413-256-8896
e-mail: irene@boscbooks.com
www.boscbooks.com

Papers on treatment, rehab and social support in assessing the needs of mentally retarded children. *$66.00*

*260 pages Hardcover*
*ISBN 0-12218 -02-0*

**2170 Assessment & Management of Mainstreamed Hearing-Impaired Children**

Sage Publications
2455 Teller Road
Thousand Oaks, CA 91320-2218
805-499-0721
800-818-7243
FAX: 800-583-2665
e-mail: info@sagepub.com
www.sagepub.com

*Sara Miller McCune, Founder, Publisher, Chairperson*
*Blaise R. Simqu, President & CEO*
*Chris Hickok, Senior Vice President & Chief Financial Officer*
*Stephen Barr, Managing Director/SAGE London, President of SAGE International*

The theoretical and practical considerations of developing appropriate programming for hearing-impaired children who are being educated in mainstream educational settings are presented in this book.

**2171 Assessment Log & Developmental Progress Charts for the Carolina Curriculum**

Brookes Publishing
P.O.Box 10624
Baltimore, MD 21285-0624
410-337-9580
800-638-3775
FAX: 410-337-8539
e-mail: custserv@brookespublishing.com
www.brookespublishing.com

*Paul H. Brookes, Chairman*
*Jeff Brookes, President*
*Melissa A. Behm, ExecutiveVice President*
*George Stamathis, Vice President & Publisher*

This 28-page booklet allows the progress of children with skills in the 12-36 month development range to be easily recorded. Available in packages of 10. *$23.00*

*28 pages Saddle-stiched*
*ISBN 1-557662-21-5*

**2172 Assessment and Remediation of Articulatoryand Phonological Disorders**

McGraw-Hill School Publishing
P.O. Box 182604
Columbus, OH 43272
877-833-5524
FAX: 614-759-3749
e-mail: customer.service@mcgraw-hill.com
mcgraw-hill.com

*Harold McGraw III, Chairman, President and Chief Executive Officer*
*Jack F. Callahan, Jr., Executive Vice President, Chief Financial Officer*
*Douglas Peterson, President, Standard & Poor's*
*Lou Eccleston, President, McGraw-Hill Financial*

Offers comprehensive coverage of articulation disorders.

**2173 Assessment in Mental Handicap: A Guide to Assessment Practices & Tests**

Brookline Books
Suite B-001
8 Trumbull Rd
Northampton, MA 01060
413-584-0184
800-666-2665
FAX: 413-584-6184
e-mail: brbooks@yahoo.com
www.brooklinebooks.com

*Esther Wilder, Co-Author*

Helps professionals understand the rationale and uses for assessment practices, and provides details of appropriate instruments within each type: adaptive behavior scales, assessment of behavioral disturbances, early development and Plagetian tests. *$20.00*

*Hardcover*
*ISBN 0-91479 -31-X*

**2174 Assessment of Children and Youth**

Longman Education/Addison Wesley
1185 Avenue of the Americas
New York, NY 10036-2601
212-997-8500
866-203-6215
TTY:800-231-5469
hess.com

*John B. Hess, Chairman of the Board and Chief Executive Officer*
*Thomas H. Kean, President, THK Consulting*
*Erin K. Macher, Assistant Treasurer*
*Randy J. Pharr, Assistant Secretary*

Introductory text for preservice and in-service special educators on assessment, based on the principle that every child is unique. Comprehensive coverage of both formal and informal assessment instruments. *$50.00*

*640 pages Paperback*
*ISBN 0-80131 -02-5*

2175 **Assessment of Individuals with Severe Disabilities**
Brookes Publishing Company
P.O.Box 10624
Baltimore, MD 21285-0624
410-337-9580
800-638-3775
FAX: 410-337-8539
e-mail: custserv@brookespublishing.com
www.brookespublishing.com

*Paul H. Brookes, Chairman*
*Jeff Brookes, President*
*Melissa A. Behm, ExecutiveVice President*
*George Stamathis, Vice President & Publisher*

This expanded text offers instructors guidelines to design a comprehensive educational assessment for individuals with severe disabilities. *$34.00*
*432 pages Paperback*
*ISBN 1-557660-67-0*

2176 **Assessment of the Technology Needs of Vending Facilitiy Managers In Tennessee**
Mississippi State University
P.O.Box 6189
Mississippi State Univers, MS 39762-6189
662-325-2001
800-675-7782
FAX: 662-325-8989
TTY: 662-325-2694
e-mail: nrtc@colled.msstate.edu
www.blind.msstate.edu/

*Jacqui Bybee, Research and Training Coordinator*
*Brenda Cavenaugh, Cavenaugh*
*Adele Crudden, Professor*
*Marty Giesen, Senior Research Scientist*

This report summarizes the results and recommendations of a survey conducted of vending facility managers throughout the state of Tennessee who participate in the Randolph-Sheppard program. *$15.00*
*39 pages Paperback*

2177 **Assessment: The Special Educator's Role**
Brookes Publishing Company
511 Forest Lodge Rd
Pacific Grove, CA 93950-0624
410-337-9580
800-638-3775
FAX: 410-337-8539
e-mail: nrtc@colled.msstate.edu
www.brookespublishing.com

*Paul H. Brooks, Chairman*
*Jeff Brookes, President*
*Melissa A. Behm, ExecutiveVice President*
*George Stamathis, Vice President & Publisher*

Aimed at students with little or no classroom experience in assessment, the book focuses on the integration of dynamic, curriculum-based and norm-referenced data for diagnostic decisions and program planning.
*580 pages Casebound*
*ISBN 0-53421 -32-1*

2178 **Asthma Management and Education**
Asthma and Allergy Foundation of America
Suite 1000
8201 Corporate Drive
Landover, MD 20785
202-466-7643
800-727-8462
e-mail: info@aafa.org
www.aafa.org

*Tom Flanagan, Jr., Chairman*
*Michele Abu Carrick, Co-Chairman*
*Christopher Cole, Immediate Past Chairman*
*Calvin Anderson, Chairman, Finance & Treasurer*

One session, two hour program developed to educate allied health professionals about up-to-date asthma care and patient education, information and materials. Includes hands on experience with peak flow meters and demonstrations of medical devices.

2179 **Aston-Patterning**
PO Box 3568
Incline Village, NV 89450-3568
775-831-8228
FAX: 775-831-8955
e-mail: office@astonkinetics.com
www.astonkinetics.com

*J Aston, Owner*
*Angelina Calafiore, Office Manager*

Integrated system of movement education, body assessment, environmental modification and fitness training.

2180 **Attention Deficit Disorder in Children**
Charles C. Thomas
2600 S 1st St
Springfield, IL 62704-4730
217-789-8980
800-258-8980
FAX: 217-789-9130
e-mail: books@ccthomas.com
www.ccthomas.com

CC Thomas has been producing a strong list of specialty titles and textbooks in the biomedical sciences since 1927.

2181 **Aural Habilitation**
Alexander Graham Bell Association
3417 Volta Pl NW
Washington, DC 20007-2737
202-337-5220
FAX: 202-337-8314
TTY:202-337-5221
e-mail: info@agbell.org
www.agbell.org

*Todd Houston, Executive Director*

This classic text for professionals, educators and parents discusses verbal learning and aural habilitation of young children with hearing losses to ensure that each child is educated in the best setting. It discusses communication, normal development of spoken language, speech audiologic assessment, hearing aids and use of residual hearing, and program designs for individualized needs, including the assessment and planning of IEPs. *$26.95*
*324 pages*

2182 **Behavior Analysis in Education: Focus on Measurably Superior Instruction**
Brookes Publishing Company
P.O.Box 10624
Baltimore, MD 21285-0624
410-337-9580
800-638-3775
FAX: 410-337-8539
e-mail: custserv@brookespublishing.com
www.brookespublishing.com

*Paul H. Brookes, Chairman*
*Jeff Brookes, President*
*Melissa A. Behm, ExecutiveVice President*
*George Stamathis, Vice President & Publisher*

Designed to disseminate measurably superior instructional strategies to those interested in advancing sound, pedagogically effective, field-tested educational practices, this book is intended for graduate-level courses and seminars in special education and/or psychology focusing on behavior analysis and instruction.
*512 pages Casebound*
*ISBN 0-53422 -60-9*

2183 **Behavior Modification**
Sage Publications
2455 Teller Rd
Thousand Oaks, CA 91320-2218
805-499-0721
800-818-7243
FAX: 800-583-2665
e-mail: info@sagepub.com
sagepub.com

*Sara Miller McCune, Founder, Publisher, Chairperson*
*Blaise R. Simqu, President & CEO*
*Chris Hickok, Senior Vice President & Chief Financial Officer*
*Stephen Barr, Managing Director/SAGE London, President of SAGE International*

Describes in detail for replication purposes assessment and modification techniques for problems in psychiatric, clinical, educational and rehabilitation settings. *$53.00*

*640 pages Quarterly*

**2184 Behavioral Disorders**

Council for Exceptional Children
Suite 1000
2900 Crystal Drive
Arlington, VA 22202-3557
703-620-3660
866-509-0218
888-232-7733
FAX: 703-264-9494
TTY:866-915-5000
e-mail: services@cec.sped.org
www.cec.sped.org

*Margaret J. McLaughlin, President*
*Christy A. Chambers, President Elect*
*Bruce A. Ramirez, Executive Director*
*James P. Heiden, Treasurer*

Provides professionals with a means to exchange information and share ideas related to research, empirically tested educational innovations and issues and concerns relevant to students with behavioral disorders. Individual, $20; Institution, $50.

*Quarterly*

**2185 Behind Special Education**

Love Publishing Company
Ste 2200
9101 E Kenyon Ave
Denver, CO 80237-1854
303-221-7333
FAX: 303-221-7444
e-mail: lpc@lovepublishing.com
www.lovepublishing.com

This new work is a critical analysis of the nature of disability, special education, school organization and reform progress. *$24.95*

*ISBN 0-89108-17-4*

**2186 Biomedical Concerns in Persons with Down's Syndrome**

Paul H Brookes Publishing Company
P.O.Box 10624
Baltimore, MD 21285-0624
410-337-9580
800-638-3775
FAX: 410-337-8539
e-mail: custserv@brookespublishing.com
www.brookespublishing.com

*Paul H. Brookes, Chairman*
*Jeff Brookes, President*
*Melissa A. Behm, ExecutiveVice President*
*George Stamathis, Vice President & Publisher*

Written by leading authorities and spanning many disciplines and specialties, this comprehensive resource provides vital information on biomedical issues concerning individuals with Down's Syndrome. *$45.00*

*336 pages Hardcover*
*ISBN 1-557660-89-1*

**2187 Breaking Barriers**

AbleNet
2625 Patton Road
Roseville, MN 55113-5423
800-322-0956
FAX: 651-294-2259
e-mail: customerservice@ablenetinc.com
www.ablenetinc.com

*Bill Sproull, Chairman*
*Jennifer Thalhuber, President*
*Cheryl Volkman, CEO*
*Paul Sugden, Former Vice President of Finance*

A practical resource for parents, caregivers, teachers and therapists. *$15.00*

**2188 Building the Healing Partnership: Parents, Professionals and Children**

Brookline Books
Suite B-001
8 Trumbull Rd
Northampton, MA 01060
413-584-0184
800-666-2665
FAX: 413-584-6184
e-mail: brbooks@yahoo.com
www.brooklinebooks.com

*Esther Wilder, Co-Author*

Successful programs understand that the disabled child's needs must be considered in the context of a family. This book was specifically written for practitioner's who must work with families but who have insufficient training in family systems assessment and intervention. It is a valuable blend of theory and practice with pointers for applying the principles. *$24.95*

*Paperback*
*ISBN 0-91479-63-8*

**2189 Career Assessment Inventories Learning Disabled**

C FK R Career Materials
P.O.Box 99
Meadow Vista, CA 95722-99
530-889-2357
800-525-5626
FAX: 800-770-0433
e-mail: requestinfo@cfkr.com
www.cfkr.com

Takes personality, ability and interest into account in pointing learning disabled students of all ages toward intelligent and realistic career choices. Contains binder with paperback teaching guide plus 50 interest inventories and 50 abilities inventories. *$50.00*

**2190 Caring for Children with Chronic Illness**

11 W 42nd St
New York, NY 10036-8002
212-431-4370
877-687-7476
FAX: 212-941-7842
e-mail: marketing@springerpub.com
www.springerpub.com

*Ursula Springer, President*
*Theodore C. Nardin, CEO/Publisher*
*Jason Roth, VP/Marketing Director*
*Annette Imperati, Marketing/Sales Director*

A critical look at the current medical, social, and psychological framework for providing care to children with chronic illnesses. Emphasizing the need to create integrated, interdisciplinary approaches, it discusses issues such as the roles of families, professionals, and institutions in providing health care, the impact of a child's illness on various family structures, financing care, the special problems of chronically ill children as they become adolescents and more. *$36.95*

*320 pages Hardcover*
*ISBN 0-82615-00-1*

**2191 Carolina Curriculum for Infants and Toddlers with Special Needs, 2nd Edition**

Brookes Publishing
P.O.Box 10624
Baltimore, MD 21285-0624
410-337-9580
800-638-3775
FAX: 410-337-8539
e-mail: custserv@brookespublishing.com
www.brookespublishing.com

*Paul H. Brookes, Chairman*
*Jeff Brookes, President*
*Melissa A. Behm, ExecutiveVice President*
*George Stamathis, Vice President & Publisher*

This book includes detailed assessment and intervention sequences, daily routine integration strategies, sensorimotor adaptations, and a sample 24-page assessment log that shows readers how to chart a child's individual progress. *$40.00*

*384 pages Spiral-bound*
*ISBN 1-55766-74-3*

**2192 Carolina Curriculum for Preschoolers with Special Needs**
Brookes Publishing
P.O.Box 10624
Baltimore, MD 21285-0624
410-337-9580
800-638-3775
FAX: 410-337-8539
e-mail: custserv@brookespublishing.com
www.brookespublishing.com

*Paul H. Brookes, Chairman*
*Jeff Brookes, President*
*Melissa A. Behm, ExecutiveVice President*
*George Stamathis, Vice President & Publisher*
This curriculum provides detailed teaching and assessment techniques, plus a sample 28-page assessment log that shows readers how to chart a child's individual progress. This guide is for children between 2 and 5 in their developmental stages who are considered at risk for developmental delay or who exhibit special needs. *$34.00*
*352 pages Spiral-bound*
*ISBN 1-55766 -32-8*

**2193 Challenge of Educating Together Deaf and Hearing Youth: Making Manistreaming Work**
Charles C. Thomas
2600 S 1st St
Springfield, IL 62704-4730
217-789-8980
800-258-8980
FAX: 217-789-9130
e-mail: books@ccthomas.com
ccthomas.com
Those who have this challenge of education: teachers, administrators, other professionals, parents, and concerned individuals will benefit from this book. Also available in cloth. *$51.35*
*198 pages Hardcover*
*ISBN 0-398063-91-5*

**2194 Challenged Scientists: Disabilities and the Triumph of Excellence**
Greenwood Publishing Group
130 Cremona Drive
Santa Barbara, CA 93117
805-968-1911
800-368-6868
FAX: 866-270-3856
e-mail: CustomerService@abc-clio.com
greenwood.com
This volume points out how the increasing need for scientists in this country can be lessened by utilizing a long overlooked pool of scientific talent in those persons who are scientifically oriented but who happen to have physical or sensory disabilities. Hardcover. $49.95-$55.00.
*208 pages*
*ISBN 0-275938-73-5*

**2195 Child Care and the ADA: A Handbook for Inclusive Programs**
Brookes Publishing
P.O.Box 10624
Baltimore, MD 21285-0624
410-337-9580
800-638-3775
FAX: 410-337-8539
e-mail: custserv@brookespublishing.com
www.brookespublishing.com

*Paul H. Brookes, Chairman*
*Jeff Brookes, President*
*Melissa A. Behm, ExecutiveVice President*
*George Stamathis, Vice President & Publisher*
This book is designed for educators and administrators in child care settings. It offers a straightforward discussion of the Americans with Disabilities Act including children with disabilities in community programs. *$25.95*
*240 pages Paperback*
*ISBN 1-55766 -85-5*

**2196 Child with Disabling Illness**
Lippincott, Williams & Wilkins
# 227
227 S 6th St
Philadelphia, PA 19106-3713
215-521-8300
800-777-2295
FAX: 301-824-7390
www.lpub.com

*$108.50*
*700 pages*

**2197 Childhood Behavior Disorders: Applied Research & Educational Practice**
Sage Publications
2455 Teller Road
Thousand Oaks, CA 91320-2218
805-499-0721
800-818-7243
FAX: 800-583-2665
e-mail: info@sagepub.com
www.sagepub.com

*Sara Miller McCune, Founder, Publisher, Chairperson*
*Blaise R. Simqu, President & CEO*
*Chris Hickok, Senior Vice President & Chief Financial Officer*
*Stephen Barr, Managing Director/SAGE London, President of SAGE International*
The only comprehensive overview of childhood behavior disorders. This book gives you the how and why for helping children with behavior disorders.

**2198 Childhood Disablity and Family Systems**
Haworth Press
711 Third Avenue
New York, NY 10017
212-216-7800
800-354-1420
FAX: 212-244-1563
e-mail: subscriptions@tandf.co.uk.
www.haworthpress.com
Focuses on what the presence of a disabled child means to a family. Those professionals involved in teaching, research, and direct care with families having disabled children will value the coverage of such topics as the contemporary context of disability, ethical issues, family effects, and care systems. Haworth Press are now acquired by the Taylor & Francis Journals. *$74.95*
*246 pages Hardcover*
*ISBN 0-866566-71-6*

**2199 Children and Youth Assisted by Medical Technology in Educational Settings, 2nd Edition**
Brookes Publishing
P.O.Box 10624
Baltimore, MD 21285-0624
410-337-9580
800-638-3775
FAX: 410-337-8539
e-mail: custserv@brookespublishing.com
www.brookespublishing.com

*Paul H. Brookes, Chairman*
*Jeff Brookes, President*
*Melissa A. Behm, ExecutiveVice President*
*George Stamathis, Vice President & Publisher*
Contains detailed daily care guidelines and emergency-response techniques, including information on working with a range of students who have the HIV infection, that rely on ventilators, that utilize tube feeding, or require catheterization. Also covers every aspect of planning for inclusive classrooms, including information on personnel training, entrance planning and transition, legal requirements, and transportation issues. *$52.00*
*432 pages Spiral-bound*
*ISBN 1-55766 -36-3*

**2200 Children's Needs Psychological Perspective**
National Association of School Psychologists
Ste 1000
8455 Colesville Rd
Silver Spring, MD 20910-3392
301-589-3300
FAX: 301-589-5175

This very popular monograph was developed with the recognition that many factors beyond the classroom and the child's own personal characteristics influence school success.
*637 pages*

**2201 Choices: A Guide to Sex Counseling for the Physically Disabled Adult**
Krieger Publishing Company
1725 Krieger Drive
Malabar, FL 32950
321-724-9542
800-724-0025
FAX: 321-951-3671
e-mail: info@krieger-publishing.com
www.krieger-publishing.com

Provides rehabilitation professionals with the basic information necessary for limited sexuality counseling of physically disabled adults. *$14.50*
*132 pages*
*ISBN 0-898749-03-4*

**2202 Choosing Options and Accommodations for Children**
Brookes Publishing
P.O.Box 10624
Baltimore, MD 21285-0624
410-337-9580
800-638-3775
FAX: 410-337-8539
e-mail: custserv@brookespublishing.com
www.brookespublishing.com

*Paul H. Brookes, Chairman*
*Jeff Brookes, President*
*Melissa A. Behm, ExecutiveVice President*
*George Stamathis, Vice President & Publisher*
Bridging the gap between the philosophy and practice of inclusive education, this important manual provides a practical assessment and planning process for the inclusion of students with disabilities in general education classrooms. *$29.00*
*192 pages*
*ISBN 1-55766 -06-5*

**2203 Cirriculum Development for Students with Mild Disabilities**
Charles C. Thomas
2600 South 1st Street
Springfield, IL 62704-4730
217-789-8980
800-258-8980
FAX: 217-789-9130
e-mail: books@ccthomas.com
www.ccthomas.com

*Carroll J. Jones, Author*
This book was designed to provide the foundation from which to write cirrocumuli that will provide academic and social skills for Individual Education Programs (IEPs). *$38.95*
*258 pages Spiral-Paper*
*ISBN 0-398070-18-2*

**2204 Classroom Success for the LD and ADHD Child**
John F Blair Publishing
1406 Plaza Dr
Winston Salem, NC 27103-1470
336-768-1374
800-222-9796
FAX: 336-768-9194
blairpub.com

*John F. Blair, Publisher*
*Suzanne H. Stevens, Author*
This book offers suggestions on teaching techniques, adapting texts, recognition of children with disabilities and testing, grading and mainstreaming the learning disabled and ADHD child. *$12.95*
*314 pages Paperback*
*ISBN 0-895871-42-4*

**2205 Clinical Alzheimer Rehabilitation**
Springer Publishing
15th Fl
11 W 42nd St
New York, NY 10036-8002
212-431-4370
877-687-7476
FAX: 212-941-7842
e-mail: marketing@springerpub.com
springerpub.com

*Theodore C. Nardin, CEO/Publisher*
*Jason Roth, VP/Marketing Director*
*Annette Imperati, Marketing/Sales Director*
*Stephanie Drew, Acquisitions Editor,Social Work and Psychology*
This comprehensive and easy-to-read guidebook contains the latest research on dementia and AD in the elderly population, including the causes and risk factors of AD, diagnosis information, and symptoms and progressions of the disease. Significant emphasis is given to the physical, mental, and verbal rehabilitation challenges of patients with AD. The authors outline specific rehabilitation goals for the physical therapist, speech-language pathologist, and general caregiver.

**2206 Clinical Management of Childhood Stuttering, 2nd Edition**
Sage Publications
2455 Teller Road
Thousand Oaks, CA 91320-2218
805-499-0721
800-818-7243
FAX: 800-583-2665
e-mail: info@sagepub.com
www.sagepub.com

*Sara Miller McCune, Founder, Publisher, Chairperson*
*Blaise R. Simqu, President & CEO*
*Chris Hickok, Senior Vice President & Chief Financial Officer*
*Stephen Barr, Managing Director/SAGE London, President of SAGE International*
Updates and integrates recent findings in childhood stuttering into a broad range of therapeutic strategies for assessing and treating the young dysfluent child. *$38.00*
*336 pages*

**2207 Cognitive Approaches to Learning Disabilities**
Sage Publications
2455 Teller Road
Thousand Oaks, CA 91320-2218
805-499-0721
800-818-7243
FAX: 800-583-2665
e-mail: info@sagepub.com
www.sagepub.com

*Sara Miller McCune, Founder, Publisher, Chairperson*
*Blaise R. Simqu, President & CEO*
*Chris Hickok, Senior Vice President & Chief Financial Officer*
*Stephen Barr, Managing Director/SAGE London, President of SAGE International*
The first to bridge the gap between cognitive psychology and information processing theory in understanding learning disabilities. *$39.00*
*495 pages Hardcover*

**2208 Cognitive Strategy Instruction That Really Improves Children's Academic Skills**
Brookline Books
Suite B-001
8 Trumbull Rd
Northampton, MA 01060
413-584-0184
800-666-2665
FAX: 413-584-6184
e-mail: brbooks@yahoo.com
www.brooklinebooks.com

*Esther Isabe Wilder, Author*
A concise and focused work that summarily presents the few procedures for teaching strategies that aid academic subject matter learning: decoding reading comprehension, vocabulary, math,

spelling and writing. Learning unrelated facts and science. Completely revised in 1995. *$27.95*
*Paperback*
*ISBN 1-571290-07-9*

**2209 Collaborating for Comprehensive Services for Young Children and Families**
Brookes Publishing Company
P.O.Box 10624
Baltimore, MD 21285-0624
410-337-9580
800-638-3775
FAX: 410-337-8539
e-mail: custserv@brookespublishing.com
www.brookespublishing.com

*Paul H. Brookes, Chairman*
*Jeff Brookes, President*
*Melissa A. Behm, ExecutiveVice President*
*George Stamathis, Vice President & Publisher*
Taking collaboration a step beyond basic implementation, this useful book shows agency and school leaders how to coordinate their efforts to stretch human services dollars while still providing quality programs. Provides the building blocks needed to establish a local interagency coordinating council. *$37.00*
*272 pages*
*ISBN 1-557661-03-0*

**2210 Collaborative Teams for Students with Severe Disabilities**
Brookes Publishing
P.O.Box 10624
Baltimore, MD 21285-0624
410-337-9580
800-638-3775
FAX: 410-337-8539
e-mail: custserv@brookespublishing.com
www.brookespublishing.com

*Paul H. Brookes, Chairman*
*Jeff Brookes, President*
*Melissa A. Behm, ExecutiveVice President*
*George Stamathis, Vice President & Publisher*
How can educators, parents and therapists work together to ensure the best possible educational experience for students with severe disabilities? This resource describes how a collaborative team can successfully create exciting learning opportunities for students, while teaching them to participate fully at home, school, work and play. *$ 30.00*
*304 pages*
*ISBN 1-55766 -88-3*

**2211 Communicating with Parents of Exceptional Children**
Love Publishing Company
Ste 2200
9101 E Kenyon Ave
Denver, CO 80237-1854
303-221-7333
FAX: 303-221-7444
e-mail: lpc@lovepublishing.com
lovepublishing.com

*Roger L. Kroth, Author*
*Denzil Denzil Edge, Author*
This book shows how teachers can facilitate parent involvement with children's education. It presents the mirror model of parent involvement, family, dynamics, how to listen actively to parents, values and perceptions, problem-solving, parent conferences and training groups. *$19.95*

*ISBN 0-89108 -67-4*

**2212 Communication & Language Acquisition: Discoveries from Atypical Development**
Brookes Publishing
P.O.Box 10624
Baltimore, MD 21285-0624
410-337-9580
800-638-3775
FAX: 410-337-8539
e-mail: custserv@brookespublishing.com
www.brookespublishing.com

*Paul H. Brookes, Chairman*
*Jeff Brookes, President*
*Melissa A. Behm, ExecutiveVice President*
*George Stamathis, Vice President & Publisher*
This text demonstrates how the study of language acquisition in children with atypical development promotes advances in basic theory. *$44.00*
*352 pages Hardcover*
*ISBN 1-557662-79-7*

**2213 Communication Skills for Working with Elders**
Springer Publishing Company
11 W 42nd St
New York, NY 10036-8002
212-431-4370
877-687-7476
FAX: 212-941-7842
e-mail: marketing@springerpub.com
www.springerpub.com

*Ursula Springer, President*
*Theodore C. Nardin, CEO/Publisher*
*Jason Roth, VP/Marketing Director*
*Annette Imperati, Marketing/Sales Director*
How aging and illness affects communication. *$17.95*
*160 pages Softcover*
*ISBN 0-82615 -20-7*

**2214 Communication Unbound**
Teachers College Press
Ste 2115
14781 Memorial Dr
Houston, TX 77079-5210
415-738-4323
FAX: 415-738-4329
e-mail: tcc.orders@aidcvt.com
www.tcp.com

Complete title is 'Communication Unbound: How Facilitated Communication is Challenging the Traditional Views of Autism and Ability/Disability'. Reveals the wonder of expression by people who have been trapped in silence and diminished by presumptions of their incompetence. *$18.95*
*240 pages Paperback*
*ISBN 0-087737-21-4*

**2215 Complete Handbook of Children's Reading Disorders: You Can Prevent or Correct LDs**
Gallery Bookshop
P.O.Box 270
Mendocino, CA 95460-270
707-937-2665
FAX: 707-937-3737
e-mail: info@gallerybookshop.com
www.gallerybooks.com

*Tony Miksak, Owner*
The complete handbook of children's reading disorders. *$34.95*
*732 pages Paperback*
*ISBN 0-80772 -83-3*

**2216 Computer Access/Computer Learning**
Special Needs Project
Ste H
324 State St
Santa Barbara, CA 93101-2364
805-962-8087
800-333-6867
FAX: 805-962-5087
www.specialneeds.com

*Mark Darrow, Founder,The Prolotherapy Institue*

A resource manual in adaptive technology and computer training. *$22.50*

**2217 Consulting Psychologists Press**

Ste. 200
1055 Joaquin Rd
Mountain View, CA 94043-1243
650-969-8901
800-624-1765
FAX: 650-969-8608
e-mail: custserv@cpp.com
www.cpp-db.com

*Carl E. Thoresen, Chairman*
*Jeffrey Hayes, President and Chief Executive Officer*
*Dalton Martin, Director*
*Calvin W Finch, Senior Vice President, Chief Financial Officer, and Treasurer*
Catalog offering job assessment software, career development reports, educational assessment information and books for the professional.

**2218 Counseling Persons with Communication Disorders and Their Families**

Sage Publications
2455 Teller Road
Thousand Oaks, CA 91320-2218
805-499-0721
800-818-7243
FAX: 800-583-2665
e-mail: info@sagepub.com
www.sagepub.com

*Sara Miller McCune, Founder, Publisher, Chairperson*
*Blaise R. Simqu, President & CEO*
*Chris Hickok, Senior Vice President & Chief Financial Officer*
*Stephen Barr, Managing Director/SAGE London, President of SAGE International*
A learning manual for speech-language pathologists and audiologists on how to deal with the emotional issues facing them in their work with clients with communication disorders and their families. *$ 29.00*
*187 pages*

**2219 Counseling in the Rehabilitation Process**

Charles C. Thomas
2600 South 1st Street
Springfield, IL 62704-4730
217-789-8980
800-258-8980
FAX: 217-789-9130
e-mail: books@ccthomas.com
www.ccthomas.com

*Gerald L. Gandy, Author*
*E. Davis Martin Jr, Author*
*Richard E. Hardy, Author*
This text provides the reader with a comprehensive overview and introduction to the field of rehabilitation counseling and services, and also has applicability in the growing field of community counseling. *$51.95*
*358 pages paper 1999*
*ISBN 0-398069-70-4*

**2220 Creating Positive Classroom Environments: Strategies for Behavior Management**

Brooks / Cole Publishing Company
511 Forest Lodge Rd
Pacific Grove, CA 93950-5040
831-373-0728
800-354-9706
FAX: 831-375-6414
e-mail: bc-info@brookscole.com
www.brookescole.com

A hands-on text that offers an approach to classroom management that encourages situation-specific decision making. Presenting research-based information on how to establish an effective behavior management system in both regular and special education settings, the book centers on ways to help students manage their own behavior, rather than on ways their behavior can be managed by teachers, peers, parents or other adults. .
*448 pages Paperbound*
*ISBN 0-53422 -54-4*

**2221 Critical Voices on Special Education: Problems & Progress Concerning the Mildly Handicapped**

State University of New York Press
Ste 305
194 Washington Ave
Albany, NY 12210-2314
518-472-5000
800-666-2211
FAX: 518-472-5038
e-mail: info@sunypress.edu
www.sunypress.edu

*James Peltz, Associate Director*
*Janice Vunk, Assistant to the Director*
*Scott B Sigmon, Editor*
Problems and progress concerning the mildly handicapped. *$24.95*
*265 pages Paperback 1990*
*ISBN 0-79140 -20-3*

**2222 Cultural Diversity, Families and the Special Education System**

Teachers College Press
1234 Amsterdam Ave
New York, NY 10027-6602
212-678-3929
800-575-6566
FAX: 212-678-4149
e-mail: tcpress@tc.columbia.edu
www.teacherscollegepress.com

*Beth Harry, Author*
This timely and thought-provoking book explores the quadruple disadvantage faced by the parents of poor, minority, handicapped children whose first language is not that of the school they attend. *$22.95*
*296 pages Paperback*
*ISBN 0-807731-19-6*

**2223 Curriculum Decision Making for Students with Severe Handicaps**

Teachers College Press
1234 Amsterdam Ave
New York, NY 10027-6602
212-678-3929
800-575-6566
FAX: 212-678-4149
e-mail: tspress@ts.columbia.edu.
www.teacherscollegepress.com

The inclusion of severely handicapped students within the scope of public education has brought about many changes for teachers in special education, this book helps the professional to distinguish which avenues are the best to take. *$17.95*
*192 pages Paperback*
*ISBN 0-807728-61-6*

**2224 Deciphering the System: A Guide for Families of Young Disabled Children**

Brookline Books
Suite B-001
8 Trumbull Rd
Northampton, MA 01060
413-584-0184
800-666-2665
FAX: 413-584-6184
e-mail: brbooks@yahoo.com
www.brooklinebooks.com

*Esther Wilder, Co-Author*
This book informs parents of disabled children (0-5) of their rights and the service system, e.g., ways to manage the cumulating information, tips on IEP and IFSP meetings and the educational assessment process, and how parents can work with multiple service providers. It includes contributions from both

parents and professionals who have experience with the service system. *$21.95*

*ISBN 0-914797-87-5*

**2225 Defining Rehabilitation Agency Types**
Mississippi State University
P.O.Box 6189
Mississippi State Univers, MS 39762-6189 662-325-2001
800-675-7782
FAX: 662-325-8989
TTY: 662-325-2694
e-mail: nrtc@colled.msstate.edu
www.blind.msstate.edu

*Jacqui Bybee, Research and Training Coordinator*
*Brenda Cavenaugh, Cavenaugh*
*Adele Crudden, Professor*
*Marty Giesen, Senior Research Scientist*
Relationships of participant selection and cost factors of service delivery across rehabilitation agency types. A national survey of state agencies for the blind was conducted to examine factors that define the characteristics of different agencies; similar programs were grouped together. Classification criteria were developed to distinguish agencies into logical groups based on line of authority, funding and operating procedures. *$10.00*
*15 pages Paperback*

**2226 Designing and Using Assistive Technology: The Human Perspective**
Brookes Publishing
P.O.Box 10624
Baltimore, MD 21285-0624 410-337-9580
800-638-3775
FAX: 410-337-8539
e-mail: custserv@brookespublishing.com
www.brookespublishing.com

*Paul H. Brookes, Chairman*
*Jeff Brookes, President*
*Melissa A. Behm, ExecutiveVice President*
*George Stamathis, Vice President & Publisher*
Presented here is a holistic perspective on how and why people choose and use AT. Features personal insights and the latest research on design and development. *$31.00*
*352 pages Paperback*
*ISBN 1-55766 -14-9*

**2227 Developing Cross-Cultural Competence:Guideto Working with Young Children & Their Families**
Brookes Publishing
P.O.Box 10624
Baltimore, MD 21285-0624 410-337-9580
800-638-3775
FAX: 410-337-8539
e-mail: custserv@brookespublishing.com
www.brookespublishing.com

*Paul H. Brookes, Chairman*
*Jeff Brookes, President*
*Melissa A. Behm, ExecutiveVice President*
*George Stamathis, Vice President & Publisher*
This enlightening book perceptively and sensitively explores cultural, ethnic, and language diversity in human services. For those who work with families whose infants and young children may have or be at risk for a disability or chronic illness. (Second Edition) *$ 32.00*
*448 pages Paperback*
*ISBN 1-55766 -31-9*

**2228 Developing Individualized Family Support Plans: A Training Manual**
Brookline Books
Suite B-001
8 Trumbull Rd
Northampton, MA 01060 413-584-0184
800-666-2665
FAX: 413-584-6184
e-mail: brbooks@yahoo.com
www.brooklinebooks.com

*Esther Wilder, Co-Author*
This manual provides in-service training coordinators, administrators, supervisors and university personnel with a compact package of functional and practical methods to train professionals about implementing family-centered individualized family support plans (IFSP'S). Also, case studies provide concrete examples to aid in learning to write IFSP's. *$24.95*

*ISBN 0-914797-69-7*

**2229 Developing Staff Competencies for Supporting People with Disabilities**
Brookes Publishing
P.O.Box 10624
Baltimore, MD 21285-0624 410-337-9580
800-638-3775
FAX: 410-337-8539
e-mail: custserv@brookespublishing.com
www.brookespublishing.com

*Paul H. Brookes, Chairman*
*Jeff Brookes, President*
*Melissa A. Behm, ExecutiveVice President*
*George Stamathis, Vice President & Publisher*
This timely second edition, now in a new easier to read format, gives service providers helpful strategies for increasing effectiveness and maintaining well-being while working in the rewarding yet challenging field of human services. *$34.00*
*480 pages Paperback*
*ISBN 1-55766 -07-3*

**2230 Development of Language**
McGraw-Hill, School Publishing
220 E Danieldale Rd
Desoto, TX 75115-2490 800-648-2970
FAX: 800-593-4418
www.mhschool.com
An organizational book based on the developmental stages of language.
*464 pages*

**2231 Developmental Disabilities of Learning**
Gallery Bookshop
P.O.Box 270
Mendocino, CA 95460-270 707-937-2665
FAX: 707-937-3737
e-mail: info@gallerybookshop.com
www.gallerybooks.com

*Tony Miksak, Owner*
Manual for professionals on developmental and learning disabilities in the growing child. *$25.00*
*224 pages Illustrated*

**2232 Developmental Disabilities: A Handbook for Occupational Therapists**
Haworth Press
711 Third Avenue
New York, NY 10017 212-216-7800
800-354-1420
FAX: 212-244-1563
e-mail: subscriptions@tandf.co.uk.
www.haworthpress.com
Provides broad coverage of the spectrum of problems confronted by patients with developmental disabilities and the many kinds of occupational therapy services these individuals need. Experts

identify exemplary institutional and community service programs for treating patients with autism, cerebral palsy, epilepsy, and mental retardation. Haworth Press are now acquired by the Taylor & Francis Journals. *$ 74.95*
*268 pages Hardcover*
*ISBN 0-866569-59-6*

**2233 Developmental Disabilities: A Handbook for Interdisciplinary Practice**
Brookline Books
Suite B-001
8 Trumbull Rd
Northampton, MA 01060 413-584-0184
800-666-2665
FAX: 413-584-6184
e-mail: brbooks@yahoo.com
www.brooklinebooks.com

*Esther Wilder, Co-Author*
Successful interdisciplinary team practice for persons with developmental disabilities that require each team member to understand and respect the contributions of the others. This handbook explains the professions most often represented on interdisciplinary teams: their natures, concerns and roles in the interdisciplinary context. *$29.95*
*256 pages*
*ISBN 1-571290-03-6*

**2234 Developmental Variation and Learning Disorders**
Educators Publishing Service
P.O.Box 9031
Cambridge, MA 02139-9031 800-435-7728
800-225-5750
e-mail: Feedback.EPS@schoolspecialty.com
www.epsbooks.com
Discusses seven major areas of development and four major areas of academic proficiency and then ties this information together by examining factors that predispose a child to dysfunction and disability, offering guidelines to assessment and management, and analyzing long-range outcomes and factors that promote resiliency for parents, educators and clinicians. *$69.00*
*640 pages Cloth*
*ISBN 0-838819-92-3*

**2235 Digest of Neurology and Psychiatry**
Institute of Living: Hartford Hospital
80 Seymour Street
Hartford, CT 06106-3309 860-545-7000
800-673-2411
FAX: 860-545-7049
e-mail: Fishe@harthosp.org
www.instituteofliving.org

*John Meehan, CEO*
*Stuart K. Markowitz, Chief Medical Officer*
*Jeffry Nestler, President, Medical Staff*
*Carol Chretien, Administrative Assistant*
Abstracts and reviews of selected current literature in psychiatry, neurology and related fields.

**2236 Disability Funding News**
8204 Fenton St
Silver Spring, MD 20910-4502 301-588-6380
800-666-6380
FAX: 301-588-6385
e-mail: info@cdpublications.com,
www.cdpublications.com

*Mike Gerecht, Publisher*

**2237 Disability and Rehabilitation**
Taylor & Francis
7625 Empire Dr
Florence, KY 41042-2919 800-634-7064
FAX: 800-248-4724
e-mail: orders@taylorandfrancis.com
www.taylorandfrancis.com

An international, multidisciplinary journal seeking to encourage a better understanding of all aspects of disability, and to promote the rehabilitation process. *$395.00*
*Monthly*
*ISSN 0963-82 8*

**2238 Divided Legacy: A History of the Schism in Medical Thought, The Bacteriological Era**
North Atlantic Books
2526 Martin Luther King Jr. Way
Berkeley, CA 94704 510-549-4270
800-337-2665
FAX: 510-549-4276
e-mail: orders@northatlanticbooks.com
www.northatlanticbooks.com

*Philip Smith, Digital Production Manager*
*Richard Grossinger, Publisher/CEO*
*Paula Morrison, Art Director*
*Erin Wiegand, Senior Editor*
Concluding volume of Coulter's history of medical philosophy, from ancient times to today. Covers the origins of bacteriology and immunology in world medicine; describes the clash between orthodox and alternative medicine.

**2239 Dual Relationships in Counseling**
5999 Stevenson Ave
Alexandria, VA 22304-3304 703-823-0252
800-347-6647
FAX: 800-473-2329
e-mail: webmaster@counseling.org
www.counseling.org

*Richard Yep, President*
Publishes archival material, also publishes articles that have broad interest for a readership composed mostly of counselors and other mental health professionals who work in private practice, schools, colleges, community agencies, hospitals, and government. An appropriate outlet for articles that: critically integrate published research; examine current professional and scientific issues; report research, new techniques, innovative programs and practices; and examine ACA as an organization.

**2240 Early Communication Skills for Children with Down Syndrome**
Woodbine House
6510 Bells Mill Rd
Bethesda, MD 20817-1636 301-897-3570
800-843-7323
FAX: 301-897-5838
e-mail: info@woodbinehouse.com
www.woodbinehouse.com

*Nancy Gray Paul, Acquisitions Editor*
*Libby Kumin, Author*
An expert shares her knowledge of speech and language development in young children with Down syndrome. Intelligibility, hearing loss, apraxia and other factors that affect communications are discussed. It also covers speech-language assessments and alternative communication options and literacy. *$19.95*
*368 pages*
*ISBN 1-890627-27-5*

**2241 Early Intervention, Implementing Child & Family Services for At-Risk Infants**
Sage Publications
2455 Teller Road
Thousand Oaks, CA 91320-2218 805-499-0721
800-818-7243
FAX: 800-583-2665
e-mail: info@sagepub.com
www.sagepub.com

*Sara Miller McCune, Founder, Publisher, Chairperson*
*Blaise R. Simqu, President & CEO*
*Chris Hickok, Senior Vice President & Chief Financial Officer*
*Stephen Barr, Managing Director/SAGE London, President of SAGE International*

New directions and recent legislation have produced a need for this guide which is designed for professionals facing the challenge of program development for disabled and at-risk infants, toddlers and their families. *$36.00*

*394 pages*

*ISBN 0-890796-21-1*

**2242 Ecology of Troubled Children**

Brookline Books Publications
Suite B-001
8 Trumbull Rd
Northampton, MA 01060
413-584-0184
800-666-2665
FAX: 413-584-6184
e-mail: brbooks@yahoo.com
www.brooklinebooks.com

*Esther Isabe Wilder, Author*

Designed for frontline mental health clinicians working with children with serious emotional disturbances; shows how to make children's' worlds more supportive by changing the places, activities and people in their lives. *$15.95*

*256 pages*

*ISBN 1-571290-57-5*

**2243 Educating Children with Disabilities: A Transdisciplinary Approach**

Brookes Publishing
P.O.Box 10624
Baltimore, MD 21285-0624
410-337-9580
800-638-3775
FAX: 410-337-8539
e-mail: custserv@brookespublishing.com
www.brookespublishing.com

*Paul H. Brookes, Chairman*
*Jeff Brookes, President*
*Melissa A. Behm, ExecutiveVice President*
*George Stamathis, Vice President & Publisher*

Widely respected textbook presents you with the strategies you need for developing an inclusive curriculum, integrating health care and educational programs and addressing needs and concerns. *$38.00*

*512 pages*

*ISBN 1-557662-46-0*

**2244 Educating Children with Multiple Disabilities: A Transdisciplinary Approach**

Brookes Publishing
P.O.Box 10624
Baltimore, MD 21285-0624
410-337-9580
800-638-3775
FAX: 410-337-8539
e-mail: custserv@brookespublishing.com
www.brookespublishing.com

*Paul H. Brookes, Chairman*
*Jeff Brookes, President*
*Melissa A. Behm, ExecutiveVice President*
*George Stamathis, Vice President & Publisher*

Emphasizing transdisciplinary cooperation between teachers, therapists, nurses and parents, this book describes a general model and specific techniques for effectively educating children with multiple disabilities. *$29.00*

*496 pages Paperback*

*ISBN 1-557662-46-0*

**2245 Educating Individuals with Disabilities**

Springer Publishing
15th Fl
11 W 42nd St
New York, NY 10036-8002
212-431-4370
877-687-7476
FAX: 212-941-7842
e-mail: marketing@springerpub.com
springerpub.com

*Theodore C. Nardin, CEO/Publisher*
*Jason Nardin, VP/Marketing Director*
*Annette Imperati, Marketing/Sales Director*
*Stephanie Drew, Acquisitions Editor,Social Work and Psychology*

Grigorenko's new book discusses how learning-disabled students are identified and assessed today, in light of the 2004 Individuals with Disabilities Education Improvement Act. Grigorenko's interdisciplinary collection is the first to comprehensively review the IDEIA 2004 Act and distill the changes professionals working with learning-disabled students face. The text takes an overarching perspective, first discussing the IDEIA in its historical, political, and legal context.

**2246 Educating Students Who Have Visual Impairments with Other Disabilities**

Brookes Publishing
P.O.Box 10624
Baltimore, MD 21285-0624
410-337-9580
800-638-3775
FAX: 410-337-8539
e-mail: custserv@brookespublishing.com
www.brookespublishing.com

*Paul H. Brookes, Chairman*
*Jeff Brookes, President*
*Melissa A. Behm, ExecutiveVice President*
*George Stamathis, Vice President & Publisher*

This introductory text provides techniques for facilitating functional learning in students with a wide range of visual impairments and multiple disabilities. With a concentration on educational needs and learning styles, the authors of this multidisciplinary volume demonstrate functional assessment and teaching adaptations that will improve students' inclusive learning experiences. *$49.95*

*552 pages Paperback*

*ISBN 1-557662-80-0*

**2247 Educating all Students in the Mainstream**

Brookes Publishing Company
P.O.Box 10624
Baltimore, MD 21285-0624
410-337-9580
800-638-3775
FAX: 410-337-8539
e-mail: custserv@brookespublishing.com
www.brookespublishng.com

*Paul H. Brookes, Chairman*
*Jeff Brookes, President*
*Melissa A. Behm, ExecutiveVice President*
*George Stamathis, Vice President & Publisher*

Incorporating the research and viewpoints of both regular and special educators, this textbook provides an effective approach for modifying, expanding, and adjusting regular education to meet the needs of all students. *$34.00*

*304 pages*

*ISBN 1-557660-22-0*

**2248 Educational Audiology for the Limited Hearing Infant and Preschooler**
Charles C. Thomas
2600 S 1st St
Springfield, IL 62704-4730
217-789-8980
800-258-8980
FAX: 217-789-9130
e-mail: books@ccthomas.com
ccthomas.com

*Donald Goldberg, Author*
*Nancy Coleffe-Schenck, Author*
*Doreen Pollack, Author*
Offers information on current concepts and practices in audio-logic screening and evaluation, development of the listening function, development of speech, development of language, the role of parents, parent education, mainstreaming of the limited-hearing child, and program modifications for the severely learning disabled child. Also includes information on auditory assessment, sensory aides, cochlear implants, acoupedics and auditory verbal programs. *$76.95*
*430 pages Paperback*
*ISBN 0-39806 -28-1*

**2249 Educational Care**
Educators Publishing Service
Ste 3
625 Mount Auburn St
Cambridge, MA 02138-4555
617-547-6706
800-225-5750
e-mail: Feedback.EPS@schoolspecialty.com
www.epsbooks.com
This book, written for both parents and teachers, is based on the view that education should be a system of care that is able to look after the specific needs of individual students. Using case studies, it analyzes various types of learning disorders and then suggests ways to help students with these problems. *$31.50*
*325 pages*
*ISBN 0-838819-87-7*

**2250 Educational Intervention for the Student**
Charles C. Thomas
2600 S 1st St
Springfield, IL 62704-4730
217-789-8980
800-258-8980
FAX: 217-789-9130
e-mail: books@ccthomas.com
www.ccthomas.com
CC Thomas has been producing a strong list of specialty titles and textbooks in the biomedical sciences since 1927.

**2251 Educational Prescriptions**
Educators Publishing Service
Ste 3
625 Mount Auburn St
Cambridge, MA 02138-4555
617-547-6706
800-225-5750
e-mail: Feedback.EPS@schoolspecialty.com
www.epsbooks.com
This book provides specific recommendations for the classroom management of students who are experiencing subtle developmental and/or learning difficulties. Intended for regular classroom teachers, specific examples of accommodations teachers can make are provided for grades 1-3 and 4-6. *$13.50*
*64 pages*
*ISBN 0-838819-90-7*

**2252 Effective Instruction for Special Education**
Sage Publications
2455 Teller Road
Thousand Oaks, CA 91320-2218
805-499-0721
800-818-7243
FAX: 800-583-2665
e-mail: info@sagepub.com
www.sagepub.com

*Sara Miller McCune, Founder, Publisher, Chairperson*
*Blaise R. Simqu, President & CEO*
*Chris Hickok, Senior Vice President & Chief Financial Officer*
*Stephen Barr, Managing Director/SAGE London, President of SAGE International*
This exciting and wide-ranging book provides special educators with effective methods for teaching students with mild and moderate learning and behavioral problems, as well as for teaching remedial students in general. *$37.00*
*419 pages Paperback*

**2253 Effectively Educating Handicapped Students**
Longman Publishing Group
9th Fl
Upper Saddle River, NJ 07458-1813
201-236-3281
FAX: 201-236-3290
www.pearsoned.com
For educators and other professionals who work with deaf and hearing impaired students in preschool and elementary programs. A developmental approach provides the foundation for several intervention methods including preparation for instruction, language, speech, audition and speechreading.
*468 pages Paperback*
*ISBN 0-801303-17-6*

**2254 Emotional Problems of Childhood and Adolescence**
McGraw-Hill School Publishing
P.O. Box 182604
Columbus, OH 43272
877-833-5524
FAX: 614-759-3749
e-mail: customer.service@mcgraw-hill.com
mcgraw-hill.com

*Harold McGraw III, Chairman, President and Chief Executive Officer*
*Jack F. Callahan, Jr., Executive Vice President, Chief Financial Officer*
*Douglas Peterson, President, Standard & Poor's*
*Lou Eccleston, President, McGraw-Hill Financial*
For future special educators, psychologists and others who work with emotionally disturbed children and adolescents.

**2255 Enabling & Empowering Families: Principles & Guidelines for Practice**
Brookline Books
Suite B-001
8 Trumbull Rd
Northampton, MA 01060
413-584-0184
800-666-2665
FAX: 413-584-6184
e-mail: brbrooks@yahoo.com
www.brooklinebooks.com

*Esther Wilder, Co-Author*
This book was written for practitioners who must work with families but who have insufficient training in family systems assessment and intervention. The authors' system enables professionals to help the family identify its needs, locate the formal and informal resources to meet these needs and develop the abilities to effectively access these resources. *$24.95*
*220 pages*
*ISBN 0-914797-59-X*

2256 **Evaluation and Educational Programming of Students with Deafblindness & Severe Disabilities**
Charles C. Thomas
2600 S 1st St
Springfield, IL 62704-4730
217-789-8980
800-258-8980
FAX: 217-789-9130
e-mail: books@ccthomas.com
ccthomas.com

*Carroll J. Jones, Author*
Subtitle: Sensorimotor Stage. This second edition offers a very complete package of information on the special education of deaf-blind students; including detailed diagnostic information to assist the instructor in evaluating the physical, social, mental status of the student, as well as the educational progress. *$50.95*
*265 pages Spiral-Paper 2001*
*ISBN 0-398072-16-2*

2257 **Evaluation and Treatment of the Psychogeriatric Patient**
Haworth Press
711 Third Avenue
New York, NY 10017
212-216-7800
800-354-1420
FAX: 212-244-1563
e-mail: subscriptions@tandf.co.uk.
www.haworthpress.com
This pertinent book assists occupational therapists and other health care providers in developing up-to-date psychogeriatric programs and understands details of treating the cognitively impaired elderly. Haworth Press are now acquired by the Taylor & Francis Journals. *$74.95*
*111 pages Hardcover*
*ISBN 1-560240-52-0*

2258 **Exceptional Children in Focus**
McGraw-Hill School Publishing
P.O. Box 182604
Columbus, OH 43272
877-833-5524
FAX: 614-759-3749
e-mail: customer.service@mcgraw-hill.com
mcgraw-hill.com

*Harold McGraw III, Chairman, President and Chief Executive Officer*
*Jack F. Callahan, Jr., Executive Vice President, Chief Financial Officer*
*Douglas Peterson, President, Standard & Poor's*
*Lou Eccleston, President, McGraw-Hill Financial*
Combines a light, personal look at the problems of special educators experiences with the basic facts of exceptionality.
*288 pages*

2259 **Exceptional Lives: Special Education in Today's Schools, 4th Edition**
Pearson Education
1 Lake St
Upper Saddle River, NJ 07458-1813
201-236-3281
FAX: 201-236-3290
www.pearsoned.com
Comprehensive coverage is built upon six guiding principles: 1) high expectations for individuals with disabilities and their educators, 2) inclusion for all students, 3) relationships and friendships as essential outcomes of collaboration, 4) positive contributions by students with disabilities, 5) the importance of choice and self-advocacy for students with disabilities, and 6) full citizenship for all students with disabilities. Emphasizes the daily lives of students and educators. *$90.00*
*592 pages*
*ISBN 0-131126-00-8*

2260 **Facilitating Self-Care Practices in the Elderly**
Haworth Press
711 Third Avenue
New York, NY 10017
212-216-7800
800-354-1420
FAX: 212-244-1563
e-mail: subscriptions@tandf.co.uk.
www.haworthpress.com
This up-to-date book is a synthesis of current knowledge from published sources and expert consultants relating to three commonly occurring problems in home health care practice: self-administration of medications, family caregiving issues, and teaching the elderly.Haworth Press are now acquired by the Taylor & Francis Journals. *$74.95*
*185 pages Hardcover*
*ISBN 1-560240-13-X*

2261 **Family-Centered Early Intervention with Infants and Toddlers**
Brookes Publishing
P.O.Box 10624
Baltimore, MD 21285-0624
410-337-9580
800-638-3775
FAX: 410-337-8539
e-mail: cutserv@brookespublishing.com
www.brookespublishing.com

*Paul H. Brookes, Chairman*
*Jeff Brookes, President*
*Melissa A. Behm, ExecutiveVice President*
*George Stamathis, Vice President & Publisher*
This informative text provides professionals with insight and practical guidelines to help fulfill the federal requirements for provision of early intervention services. *$37.00*
*368 pages Hardcover*
*ISBN 1-557661-24-3*

2262 **Feeding Children with Special Needs**
Arizona Department of Health Services
150 North 18th Avenue
Phoenix, AZ 85007-2607
602-542-1025
FAX: 602-542-0883
www.hs.state.az.us/cfhs/ons/

*Thomas Salow, Manager*
*Will Humble, Director*
Guide designed to help develop a greater awareness of the special challenges involved in the nutrition and feeding concerns for children with special health care needs, and ways to approach the issues. *$5.00*

2263 **Focal Group Psychotherapy**
New Harbinger Publications
5674 Shattuck Ave
Oakland, CA 94609-1662
510-652-0215
800-748-6273
FAX: 510-652-1613
e-mail: CUSTOMERSERVICE@NEWHARBINGER.COM
www.newharbinger.com

*Matthew McKay, Founder*
*Patrick Fanning, Co-Founder/Writer*
Guide to leading brief, theme-based groups. This book offers an extensive week-by-week description of the basic concepts and interventions for 14 theme or focal groups for: codependency, rape victims, shyness, survivors of incest, agoraphobia, survivors of toxic parents, depression, child molesters, anger control, domestic violence offenders, assertiveness, alcohol and drug abuse, eating disorders, and parent training. *$59.95*
*544 pages Cloth*
*ISBN 1-879237-18-0*

**2264 Free Hand: Enfranchising the Education of Deaf Children**
TJ Publishers
www.amazon.com

*Margaret Walworth, Author*
*Donald F. Moores, Author*
*Terrence J. O'Rourke, Author*
A select group of nationally prominent educators, linguists and researchers met at Hofstra University to consider the most vital and controversial question in education of the deaf: what role should ASL play in the classroom? Become part of that discussion with A Free Hand. *$16.95*
*204 pages Softcover*
*ISBN 0-93266 -40-X*

**2265 Functional Assessment Inventory Manual**
Stout Vocational Rehab Institute
Suite 500
655 15th St. NW
Washington, DC 20005
715-232-1411
800-538-3742
FAX: 715-232-2356
e-mail: botterbuschd@uwstout.edu

*John Collins, Librarian*
*Mark Constas, Associate Professor, Department of Education*
*Alvin Walker, Product Development Manager*
*Carl Lagoze, Senior Research Associate, Information Science*
The Functional Assessment is a systematic enumeration of a client's vocactionally relevant strengths and limitations. *$12.00*
*96 pages Paperback*
*ISBN 0-916671-53-4*

**2266 Global Perspectives on Disability: A Curriculum**
Mobility International U SA
Ste 343
132 E Broadway
Eugene, OR 97401-3155
541-343-1284
FAX: 541-343-6812
TTY:541-343-1284
e-mail: info@miusa.org
miusa.org

*Estelle Coreris-Moore, Financial Manager*
*Michele Scheib, Project Specialist*
*Susan Sygall, Co- Founder and CEO*
*Cindy Cindy Lewis, Director of Programs*
Designed for secondary and higher education instructors. Includes five lesson plans covering disability awareness, disability rights and international perspectives on disability. Available in alternative formats. *$40.00*

**2267 Glossary of Terminology for Vocational Assessment/Evaluation/Work**
Rehabilitation Resource University
University of Wisconsin-Stou
Menomonie, WI 54751
715-232-2236
FAX: 715-232-2356
e-mail: gundlachj@uwstout.edu

*Ronald Fry, Manager*
*Jennifer Gundlach Klatt, Program Assistant*
This glossary contains 254 terms and their definitions. Primary focus is on the terminology related to the practice and professionals of vocational assessment, vocational evaluation and work adjustment. *$9.50*
*40 pages Softcover*

**2268 Graduate Technological Education and the Human Experience of Disability**
Haworth Press
711 Third Avenue
New York, NY 10017
212-216-7800
800-354-1420
FAX: 212-244-1563
e-mail: subscriptions@tandf.co.uk.
www.haworthpress.com

This book examines graduate schools of theology and their limited familiarity with the study of disability - and the presence of people with disabilities in particular - on their campuses. This text offers critical research and illuminates new pathways for theologia and practice in the community of faith. It offers suggestions for incorporating disability studies into theological education and religious life.Haworth Press are now acquired by the Taylor & Francis Journals. *$34.95*
*115 pages Hardcover*
*ISBN 0-789060-08-6*

**2269 HIV Infection and Developmental Disabilities**
Brookes Publishing
P.O.Box 10624
Baltimore, MD 21285-0624
410-337-9580
800-638-3775
FAX: 410-337-8539
e-mail: cstserv@brookespublishing.com
www.brookespublishing.com

*Paul H. Brookes, Chairman*
*Jeff Brookes, President*
*Melissa A. Behm, ExecutiveVice President*
*George Stamathis, Vice President & Publisher*
A resource for service providers pinpointing the most crucial medical, legal and educational issues to control HIV infection. *$47.00*
*320 pages*
*ISBN 1-557660-83-2*

**2270 Handbook for Implementing Workshops for Siblings of Special Children**
Special Needs Project
Ste H
324 State St
Santa Barbara, CA 93101-2364
805-962-8087
800-333-6867
FAX: 805-962-5087
www.specialneeds.com

*Mark Darrow, Founder, The Prolotherapy Institue*
Based on three years of professional experience, this handbook provides guidelines and techniques for those who wish to start and conduct workshops for siblings. *$40.00*

**2271 Handbook for Speech Therapy**
Psychological & Educational Publications
P.O.Box 520
Hydesville, CA 95547
800-523-5775
FAX: 800-447-0907
e-mail: psych-edpublications@suddenlink.net
www.psych-edpublications.com

Basic handbook for beginning speech teachers, shows how speech sounds are made, what their individual characteristics are, how they relate to each other, what the most common errors are, and how to correct those errors.
*143 pages paperback*

**2272 Handbook for the Special Education Administrator**
Edwin Mellen Press
P.O. Box 450
Lewiston, NY 14092-1205
716-754-2266
FAX: 716-754-4056
e-mail: mellen@wzrd.com
www.mellenpress.com

*Arthur R. Crowell, Author*
Organization and procedures for special education. *$ 49.95*
*96 pages Hardcover*
*ISBN 0-88946 -22-9*

**2273 Handbook of Developmental Education**

Greenwood Publishing Group
130 Cremona Drive
Santa Barbara, CA 93117
805-968-1911
800-368-6868
FAX: 866-270-3856
e-mail: CustomerService@abc-clio.com
www.greenwood.com

*Wayne*

This comprehensive handbook has brought together the leading practitioners and researchers in the field of developmental education to focus on the developmental learning agenda. Hardcover.

*400 pages $65 - $75*

*ISBN 0-275932-97-4*

**2274 Handbook on Supported Education for Peoplewith Mental Illness**

Brookes Publishing
P.O.Box 10624
Baltimore, MD 21285-0624
410-337-9580
800-638-3775
FAX: 410-337-8539
e-mail: custserv@brookespublishing.com
www.brookespublishing.com

*Paul H. Brookes, Chairman*
*Jeff Brookes, President*
*Melissa A. Behm, ExecutiveVice President*
*George Stamathis, Vice President & Publisher*

Here you will find all necessary information that mental health professionals need in order to provide supported education services. There are specific suggestions on how to help people with mental illness return to or remain in college, trade school, or GED programs. Also addressed are funding and legal issues, accommodations, and specific interventions.

*208 pages Paperback*

*ISBN 1-55766 -52-1*

**2275 Head Injury Rehabilitation: Children**

Taylor & Francis
Ste G
47 Runway Dr
Levittown, PA 19057-4738
267-580-2622
FAX: 215-785-5515

Rehabilitation guide for the help of children or adolescents that have suffered brain injury.

*460 pages Cloth*

*ISBN 0-85066 -67-1*

**2276 Health Care Management in Physical Therapy**

Charles C. Thomas
2600 S 1st St
Springfield, IL 62704-4730
217-789-8980
800-258-8980
FAX: 217-789-9130
e-mail: books@ccthomas.com
www.ccthomas.com

CC Thomas has been producing a strong list of specialty titles and textbooks in the biomedical sciences since 1927.

**2277 Health Care for Students with Disabilities**

Brookes Publishing Company
P.O.Box 10624
Baltimore, MD 21285-0624
410-337-9580
800-638-3775
FAX: 410-337-8539
e-mail: custserv@brookespublishing.com
www.brookespublishing.com

*Paul H. Brookes, Chairman*
*Jeff Brookes, President*
*Melissa A. Behm, ExecutiveVice President*
*George Stamathis, Vice President & Publisher*

This practical guidebook provides detailed descriptions of the 16 health-related procedures most likely to be needed in the classroom by students with disabilities. *$25.00*

*304 pages Paperback*

*ISBN 1-557660-37-9*

**2278 Helping Learning Disabled Gifted Children**

Charles C. Thomas
2600 S 1st St
Springfield, IL 62704-4730
217-789-8980
800-258-8980
FAX: 217-789-9130
e-mail: books@ccthomas.com
ccthomas.com

*James Harry Humphrey, Author*

CC Thomas has been producing a strong list of specialty titles and textbooks in the biomedical sciences since 1927.

**2279 Helping Students Grow**

American College Testing Program
P.O.Box 168
500 ACT Drive
Iowa City, IA 52243-0168
319-337-1000
act.org

*Joseph A. Aguerrebere, Former President and CEO*
*Robert M. Berdahl, President Emeritus*
*Mark D. Musick, Chairman*
*Dixie L. Axley, Vice President*

Designed to assist counselors in using the wealth of information generated by the ACT Assessment.

**2280 Home Health Care Provider: A Guide to Essential Skills**

Springer Publishing
15th Fl
11 W 42nd St
New York, NY 10036-8002
212-431-4370
877-687-7476
FAX: 212-941-7842
e-mail: marketing@springerpub.com
springerpub.com

*Theodore C. Nardin, CEO/Publisher*
*Jason Roth, VP/Marketing Director*
*Annette Imperati, Marketing/Sales Director*
*Stephanie Drew, Acquisitions Editor,Social Work and Psychology*

This book is designed to foster quality care to home care recipients. Prieto provides information, tips, and techniques on personal care routines as well as additional responsibilities, including home safety and maintenance, meal planning, errand running, caring for couples, and making use of recreational time. The book focuses on the psycho-social needs of home care recipients, stressing the need to maintainthe house as a home, and sustaining the recipient's way of life throughout caregiving.

**2281 How to Teach Spelling/How to Spell**

Educators Publishing Service
Ste 3
625 Mount Auburn St
Cambridge, MA 02138-4555
617-547-6706
800-225-5750
e-mail: Feedback.EPS@schoolspecialty.com
www.epsbooks.com

This is a comprehensive resource manual based on the Orton-Gillingham approach to reading and spelling. It recommends what and how much to teach at each grade level at the beginning of each lesson or section. There are four student manuals that accompany this. *$22.50*

*Teachers Manual*

*ISBN 0-838818-47-1*

**2282 Human Exceptionality: Society, School, and Family**
Allyn & Bacon
Ste 300
75 Arlington St
Boston, MA 02116-3988
e-mail: ab_webmaster@abacon.com
www.ablongman.com

Examination of the definitions, classification, prevalence and characteristics of each category of exceptionality in relation to the major topics and issues of the field of special education.
*615 pages*
*ISBN 0-20528-39-0*

**2283 I Can't Hear You in the Dark: How to Lean and Teach Lipreading**
Charles C. Thomas
2600 South 1st Street
Springfield, IL 62704-4730
217-789-8980
800-258-8980
FAX: 217-789-9130
e-mail: books@ccthomas.com
www.ccthomas.com

*Betty Woerner Carter, Author*
The goal of this text is to improve communication and strengthen relationships with others. *$40.95*
*226 pages Spiral-Paper 1997*
*ISBN 0-398067-89-2*

**2284 I Heard That!**
3417 Volta Pl NW
Washington, DC 20007-2737
202-337-5220
FAX: 202-337-8314
TTY:202-337-5221
e-mail: info@agbell.org
www.agbell.org

*Todd Houston, Executive Director*
Provides a framework for teachers, clinicians and parents when writing objectives and designing activities to develop listening skills in children with hearing loss from newborn to 3 years. *$7.95*
*36 pages*

**2285 I Heard That!2**
Alexander Graham Bell Association
3417 Volta Pl NW
Washington, DC 20007-2737
202-337-5220
FAX: 202-337-8314
TTY:202-337-5221
e-mail: info@agbell.org
agbell.org

*Todd Houston, Executive Director*
Provides a framework for teachers, clinicians and parents when writing objectives and designing activities to develop listening skills in children who are deaf or hard of hearing. *$7.95*
*36 pages*

**2286 If It Is To Be, It Is Up To Us To Help!**
AVKO Educational Research Foundation
Ste W
3084 Willard Rd
Birch Run, MI 48415-9404
810-686-9283
866-285-6612
FAX: 810-686-1101
e-mail: webmaster@avko.org
avko.org

*Don Mc Cabe, Research Director*
*Barry Chute, President*
*Julie Guyette, Vice President*
*Clifford Schroeder, Treasurer*
A book of lesson plans for an Adult Community Education Course for Volunteer Tutors. Contains information on how to go about establishing such a course and how to secure cooperation from local and national organizations. Free as an e-book for Foundation members. *$ 14.95*

*ISBN 1-56400-42-1*

**2287 Images of the Disabled, Disabling Images**
Greenwood Publishing Group
130 Cremona Drive
Santa Barbara, CA 93117
805-968-1911
800-368-6868
FAX: 866-270-3856
e-mail: CustomerService@abc-clio.com
www.greenwood.com

*Robert K*
Combines an examination of the presentation of persons with disabilities in literature, film and the media with an analysis of the ways in which these images are expressed in public policy concerning the disabled. *$55.00*
*227 pages Hardcover*
*ISBN 0-275921-78-6*

**2288 Implementing Family-Centered Services in Early Intervention**
Brookline Books
Suite B-001
8 Trumbull Rd
Northampton, MA 01060
413-584-0184
800-666-2665
FAX: 413-584-6184
e-mail: brbooks@yahoo.com
www.brooklinebooks.com

This book describes a team-based decision-making workshop for implementing family-centered services in early interventions. Unlike a training curriculum, it focuses on the decisions that teams must make as they seek to become family-centered. *$19.95*
*180 pages Paperback*
*ISBN 0-91479-62-*

**2289 Including All of Us: An Early Childhood Curriculum About Disability**
Educational Equity Concepts
Fl 6
71 Fifth Avenue
New York, NY 10003
212-243-1110
FAX: 212-627-0407
e-mail: eec@fhi360.org
www.edequity.org

*Frank Schneiger, President*
*Antonia Cottrell Martin, Founder and President*
*Merle Froschl, Co-director*
*Barbara Sprung, Co-director*
The first nonsexist, multicultural, mainstreamed curriculum. Step-by-step activities incorporate disability into three curriculum areas: Same/Different (hearing impairment), Body Parts (visual impairment), and Transportation (mobility impairment). *$14.95*
*144 pages*
*ISBN 0-93162-00-4*

**2290 Including Students with Severe and Multiple Disabilites in Typical Classrooms**
Brookes Publishing
P.O.Box 10624
Baltimore, MD 21285-0624
410-337-9580
800-638-3775
FAX: 410-337-8539
e-mail: custserv@brookespublishing.com
www.brookespublishing.com

*Paul H. Brookes, Chairman*
*Jeff Brookes, President*
*Melissa A. Behm, ExecutiveVice President*
*George Stamathis, Vice President & Publisher*
This straightforward and jargon free resource gives instructors the guidance needed to educate learners who have one or more

sensory impairments in addition to cognitive and physical disabilities. *$32.95*
*224 pages Paperback*
*ISBN 1-55766-39-8*

**2291 Including Students with Special Needs: A Practical Guide for Classroom Teachers**
Allyn & Bacon
Ste 300
75 Arlington St
Boston, MA 02116-3988 e-mail: ab_webmaster@abacon.com
www.ablongman.com
Focuses on educating students with special needs in inclusive settings based on substantive admisistrative backing, support for general education teachers, and an understanding that sometimes not all needs can be met in a single location.
*544 pages*
*ISBN 0-20528-85-4*

**2292 Inclusive & Heterogeneous Schooling: Assessment, Curriculum, and Instruction**
Brookes Publishing
P.O.Box 10624
Baltimore, MD 21285-0624 410-337-9580
800-638-3775
FAX: 410-337-8539
e-mail: custserv@brookespublishing.com
www.brookespublishing.com

*Paul H. Brookes, Chairman*
*Jeff Brookes, President*
*Melissa A. Behm, ExecutiveVice President*
*George Stamathis, Vice President & Publisher*
Presents methods for successfully restructuring classrooms to enable all students, particularly those with disabilities, to flourish. Provides specific strategies for assessment, collaboration, classroom management, and age-specific instruction. *$34.95*
*448 pages Paperback*
*ISBN 1-55766-02-9*

**2293 Independent Living Approach to Disability Policy Studies**
World Institute on Disability
Suite 280
3075 Adeline Street
Berkeley, CA 94703 510-225-6400
FAX: 510-225-0477
TTY:510-225-0478
e-mail: wid@wid.org
www.wid.org

*Susan P. Mazrui, Chairman*
*Neil Jacobson, Vice Chairman*
*Anita Shafer Aaron, Executive Director*
*Kenneth R. Chrisman, Immediate Past Chair*
This collection of essays and bibliographies attempts to build a framework for understanding how the relationship between public policy, disability studies and disability policy studies will impact us in the future. *$17.50*
*240 pages Paperback*

**2294 Information & Referral Center**
Mississippi State University
P.O.Box 6189
Mississippi State Univers, MS 39762-6189 662-325-2001
800-675-7782
FAX: 662-325-8989
TTY: 662-325-2694
e-mail: nrtc@colled.msstate.edu
www.blind.msstate.edu

*Jacqui Bybee, Research and Training Coordinator*
*Brenda Cavenaugh, Cavenaugh*
*Adele Crudden, Professor*
*Marty Giesen, Senior Research Scientist*
A comprehensive website that includes information about client assistance programs, vocational rehabilitation agencies, low vision clinics and information about blindness and low vision. *$25.00*
*150 pages*

**2295 Instructional Methods for Students**
Allyn & Bacon
Ste 300
75 Arlington St
Boston, MA 02116-3988 e-mail: ab_webmaster@abacon.com
www.ablongman.com
Instructional methods for students with learning and behavior problems.
*450 pages*
*ISBN 0-205087-35-3*

**2296 Interactions: Collaboration Skills for School Professionals**
Longman Education/Addison Wesley
Ste 300
75 Arlington St
Boston, MA 02116-3988 e-mail: ab_webmaster@abacon.com
www.longman.awl.com
Shows school professionals how to develop and use the skills necessary for effective collaboration among teachers, school support staff, and parents of children with special needs. *$35.00*
*270 pages Paperback*
*ISBN 0-80131-21-2*

**2297 International Journal of Arts Medicine**
MMB Music
9051 Watson Road
Suite 161
Saint Louis, MO 63126 314-531-9635
800-543-3771
FAX: 314-531-8384
e-mail: info@mmbmusic.com
mmbmusic.com

*Norm Goldberg, Founder/chairman*
Exploration of the creative arts and healing. Presents peer-reviewed articles clearly written by educators in the creative arts, as well as internationally prominent physicians, therapists and health care professionals.

**2298 Interpreting Disability: A Qualitative Reader**
Teachers College Press
1234 Amsterdam Avenue
New York, NY 10027 212-678-3929
800-575-6566
FAX: 212-678-4149
e-mail: tcpress@tc.columbia.edu
www.tcpress.com

*Brian Ellerbeck, Executive Acquisitions Editor*
*Marie Ellen Larcada, Senior Acquisitions Editor*
*Emily Spangler, Acquisitions Editor*
*Meg Hartmann, Acquisitions Assistant*
This book offers a collection of exemplary qualitative research affecting people with disabilities and their families. Instead of focusing upon methodological details, the chapters illustrate the variety of styles and formats that interpretive research can adopt in reporting its results. *$24.95*
*328 pages Paperback*
*ISBN 0-807731-21-8*

**2299 Intervention Research in Learning Disabilities**
Gallery Bookshop
P.O.Box 270
Mendocino, CA 95460-270 707-937-2665
FAX: 707-937-3737
e-mail: info@gallerybookshop.com
www.gallerybooks.com

*Tony Miksak, Owner*
Based on the Symposium on Intervention Research, this volume presents 12 papers addressing issues in intervention research, ac-

ademic interventions, social and behavioral interventions, and postsecondary interventions. *$30.00*
*347 pages*

**2300 Introduction to Learning Disabilities**
Allyn & Bacon
Ste 300
75 Arlington St
Boston, MA 02116-3988 e-mail: ab_webmaster@abacon.com
www.pearsonhighered.com

Presents the current state of research in the area of learning disabilities, as well as intervention ideas and programs. Includes updated material on the 1997 re-authorization of IDEA (Individuals with Disabilities Education Act) and expanded coverage of ADHD and its relationship to learning disabilities. Presents the latest information on the characteristics of persons with learning disabilities, causes, and educational interventions.
*608 pages*
*ISBN 0-20529 -43-4*

**2301 Introduction to Mental Retardation**
Allyn & Bacon
Ste 300
75 Arlington St
Boston, MA 02116-3988 e-mail: ab_webmaster@abacon.com
www.pearsonhighered.com

A thorough overview of mental retardation with a level of knowledge suitable for an undergraduate or beginning graduate student.
*350 pages Casebound*
*ISBN 0-134879-27-9*

**2302 Introduction to Special Education: Teaching in an Age of Challenge, 4th Edition**
Allyn & Bacon
Ste 300
75 Arlington St
Boston, MA 02116-3988 e-mail: ab_webmaster@abacon.com
www.pearsonhighered.com

Provides an applied approach to children with disabilities through the use of specific research and suggestions to focus on how the educational practices impact the lives of children, their families, and their teachers.
*640 pages cloth*
*ISBN 0-20526 -94-4*

**2303 Introduction to the Profession of Counseling**
McGraw-Hill School Publishing
P.O. Box 182604
Columbus, OH 43272 877-833-5524
FAX: 614-759-3749
e-mail: customer.service@mcgraw-hill.com
mcgraw-hill.com

*Harold McGraw III, Chairman, President and Chief Executive Officer*
*Jack F. Callahan, Jr., Executive Vice President, Chief Financial Officer*
*Douglas Peterson, President, Standard & Poor's*
*Lou Eccleston, President, McGraw-Hill Financial*
Offers information, theories and techniques for counseling numerous cases from drug addiction to special populations.
*464 pages*

**2304 Issues and Research in Special Education**
Teachers College Press
P.O.Box 20
Williston, VT 05495-0020 800-575-6566
FAX: 802-664-7626
e-mail: tcp.orders@aidcvt.com
www.teacherscollegepress.com

Provides up-to-date research and discourse on a wide range of topics affecting professionals in the field of special education. *$38.00*
*264 pages Hardcover*
*ISBN 0-807731-95-1*

**2305 Kendall Demonstration Elementary School Curriculum Guides**
Gallaudet University Bookstore
800 Florida Ave NE
Washington, DC 20002-3695 202-651-5206
800-621-2736
FAX: 800-621-8476
TTY: 888-630-9347
e-mail: clerc.center@gallaudet.edu.
gupress.gallaudet.edu

*Dr. T Alan Hurwitz, President*
*Edward Bosso, Vice President for Administration and Finance*
*Donald Beil, Chief of Staff*
*Dr. Lynne Murray, Vice President for Development and Alumni Relations*
KDES is a day school serving students from birth through age 15, beginning with the Parent-Infant Program and ending in grade 8. Students come from the Washington, D.C., metropolitan area.

**2306 Language Arts: Detecting Special Needs**
Allyn & Bacon
Ste 300
75 Arlington St
Boston, MA 02116-3988 617-848-7500
800-852-8024
FAX: 617-944-7273
www.ablongman.com

*Bill Barke, Chairman and CEO*
*Nancy Forfyth, President*
*Thomas A. Rakes, Author*
*Kevin Stone, Vice President, National Sales Manager*
Describes special language arts needs of special learners.
*180 pages paperback*
*ISBN 0-205116-36-1*

**2307 Language Learning Practices with Deaf Children**
Sage Publications
2455 Teller Road
Thousand Oaks, CA 91320 805-499-9774
800-818-7243
FAX: 800-583-2665
e-mail: books.claim@sagepub.com
www.sagepub.com

*Sara Miller McCune, Founder, Publisher, Chairperson*
*Stephen P. Quigley, Co-Author*
*Susan Rose, Co-Author*
*Patricia L. McAnally, Co-Author*
This new edition describes the variety of language-development theories and practices used with deaf children without advocating anyone. *$38.00*
*321 pages Hardcover*

**2308 Language and Communication Disorders in Children**
McGraw-Hill School Publishn
220 E Danieldale Rd
Desoto, TX 75115-2490 972-224-4772
800-442-9685
FAX: 972-228-1982
e-mail: webmaster@mcgraw-hill.com
mcgraw-hill.com

*Harold McGraw III, Chairman, President and Chief Executive Officer*
*Jack F. Callahan, Executive Vice President, Chief Financial Officer*
*Deena K. Bernstein, Co-Author*
*Ellenmorris Tiegerman-Farber, Co-Author*
Comprehensive coverage encompassing all aspects of children's language disorders.
*512 pages*

2309 **Learning Disabilities, Literacy, and Adult Education**
Brookes Publishing
P.O.Box 10624
Baltimore, MD 21285-624 410-337-9580
800-638-3775
FAX: 410-337-8539
e-mail: pkelly@brookespublishing.com
www.brookespublishing.com

*Joyce S. Choate, Co-Author*
*Thomas A. Rakes, Co-Author*
*Paul H. Brooks, Chairman of the Board*
*Jeff Brookes, President*
This book focuses on adults with severe learning disabilities and the educators who work with them. Described are the characteristics, demographics, and educational and employment status of adults with LD and the laws that protect them in the workplace and in educational settings.
*450 pages Paperback*
*ISBN 1-55766-47-5*

2310 **Learning Disabilities: Concepts and Characteristics**
McGraw-Hill School Publishing
220 E Danieldale Rd
Desoto, TX 75115-2490 972-224-4772
800-442-9685
FAX: 972-228-1982
www.mhschool.com

*Harold McGraw III, Chairman, President and Chief Executive Officer*
*Jack F. Callahan, Executive Vice President, Chief Financial Officer*
*James A. McLoughlin, Co-Author*
*Gerald Wallace, Co-Author*
Covers the conceptual basis of learning disabilities, identification, etiology and diagnosis.
*448 pages*

2311 **Learning Disability: Social Class and the Cons of Inequality In American Education**
Greenwood Publishing Group
130 Cremona Drive
Santa Barbara, CA 93117 805-968-1911
800-368-6868
FAX: 866-270-3856
e-mail: CustomerService@abc-clio.com
greenwood.com

*James Carrier, Author*
Presents a detailed historical description of the social and educational assumptions integral to the idea of learning disability.
*167 pages $43.95 - $47.95*
*ISBN 0-313253-96-X*

2312 **Learning and Individual Differences**
National Association of School Psychologists
Ste 1000
8455 Colesville Rd
Silver Spring, MD 20910-3392 301-589-3300
FAX: 301-589-5175
e-mail: info@musictherapy.org
http://www.musictherapy.org/

*Andrea Farbman, EdD, Executive Director*
*Judy Simpson, MT-BC, Director of Government Relations*
*Jane Creagan, MME, MT-BC, Director of Professional Programs*
*E.L. Grigorenko, Editor*
A multidisciplinary journal in education.

2313 **Learning to See: American Sign Language asa Second Language**
Gallaudet University Press
800 Florida Ave NE
Washington, DC 20002-3695 202-651-5206
800-621-2736
FAX: 800-621-8476
TTY: 888-630-9347
e-mail: clerc.center@gallaudet.edu.
gupress.gallaudet.edu

*Sherman Wilcox, Co-Author*
*Phyliss Wilcox, Co-Author*
*Dr. T Alan Hurwitz, President*
*Edward Bosso, Vice President for Administration and Finance*
This important book has been updated to help teachers teach American Sign Language as a second language, including information on Deaf culture, the history and structure of ASL, teaching methods and issues facing educators. *$19.95*
*160 pages Softcover*

2314 **Let's Write Right: Teacher's Edition**
AVKO Educational Research Foundation
3084 Willard Rd
Birch Run, MI 48415-9404 810-686-9283
866-285-6612
FAX: 810-686-1101
e-mail: webmaster@avko.org
avko.org

*Don Mc Cabe, Research Director*
*Barry Chute, President*
*Julie Guyette, Vice President*
*Clifford Schroeder, Treasurer*
A manuscript and cursive writing program designed not only to teach handwriting but help with reading and spelling patterns as well. Teaches students to learn to read cursive as manuscript is being taught and ease the transition to cursive by using a D'Nealian-like script. Exercises involve phoically consistent patterns to help reinforce fluency with spelling and handwriting.
*$39.95*
*164 pages*

2315 **Library Manager's Guide to Hiring and Serving Disabled Persons**
Mc Farland & Company
960 NC Hwy 88 W
Jefferson, NC 28640 336-246-4460
800-253-2187
FAX: 336-246-5018
e-mail: infoinso@mcfarlandpub.com
www.mcfarlandpub.com

*Kieth C. Wright, Co-Author*
*Judith F. Davie, Co-Author*
Information for library staff on hiring and serving disabled persons. *$35.00*
*171 pages Illustrated*
*ISBN 0-89950-16-3*

2316 **Life-Span Approach to Nursing Care for Individuals with Developmental Disabilities**
Brookes Publishing
P.O.Box 10624
Baltimore, MD 21285 410-337-9580
800-638-3775
FAX: 410-337-8539
e-mail: pkelly@brookespublishing.com
www.brookespublishing.com

*Shirley P. Roth, Author, Editor*
*Joyce S. Morse, Editor*
*Paul H. Brooks, Chairman of the Board*
*Jeff Brookes, President*
This reference book was written by and for nurses. This guide addresses fundamental nursing issues such as health promotion, infection control, seizure management, adaptive and assistive

technology, and sexuality. Also offered are in-depth case studies, helpful charts and tables, and problem-solving strategies. *$49.95*
*464 pages Hardcover*
*ISBN 1-557661-51-0*

**2317 Mainstreaming Deaf and Hard of Hearing Students: Questions and Answers**
Gallaudet University Bookstore
800 Florida Ave NE
Washington, DC 20002-3600 202-651-5000
800-451-1073
FAX: 202-651-5489
TTY: 888-630-9347
e-mail: clerc.center@gallaudet.edu.
www.gallaudet.edu

*Donald Beil, Chief of Staff*
*Debra S. Lipkey, University Budget Director*
*Dr. T Alan Hurwitz, President*
*Edward Bosso, Vice President for Administration and Finance*
This booklet presents mainstreaming as one educational option and suggests some considerations for parents, teachers and administrators. *$6.00*
*40 pages*

**2318 Mainstreaming Exceptional Students: A Guide for Classroom Teachers**
Allyn & Bacon
Ste 300
75 Arlington St
Boston, MA 02116-3988 617-848-7500
800-852-8024
FAX: 617-944-7273
www.ablongman.com

*Bill Barke, CEO*
*Nancy Forfyth, President*
*Jane B. Schulz, Co-Author*
*C. Dale Carpenter, Co-Author*
Covers the various categories of exceptional students and discusses educational strategies and classroom management.
*464 pages paperback*
*ISBN 0-20515 -24-6*

**2319 Mainstreaming: A Practical Approach for Teachers**
McGraw-Hill School Publishing
220 E Danieldale Rd
Desoto, TX 75115-2490 972-224-4772
800-442-9685
FAX: 972-228-1982
e-mail: custserv@mcgraw-hill.com
mcgraw-hill.com

*Harold McGraw III, Chairman, President and Chief Executive Officer*
*Jack F. Callahan, Executive Vice President, Chief Financial Officer*
*John Berisford, Executive Vice President, Human Resources*
*Judy W. Wood, Editor*
Provides teachers, administrators and school psychologists with the background, techniques and strategies they need to offer appropriate services for mildly handicapped students in the mainstream classroom.

**2320 Managing Diagnostic Tool of Visual Perception**
Gallery Bookshop
P.O.Box 270
Mendocino, CA 95460 707-937-2665
FAX: 707-937-3737
e-mail: info@gallerybooks.com
www.gallerybooks.com

*Constantine Mangina, Author*
For diagnosing specific perceptual learning abilities and disabilities. *$14.00*

*ISBN 0-80580 -83-4*

**2321 Medical Rehabilitation**
Lippincott, Williams & Wilkins
# 227
227 S 6th St
Philadelphia, PA 19106-3713 215-545-5630
800-777-2295
FAX: 215-732-9988
www.lpub.com

*Cheryl Murkey, Manager*
Information for the professional on new techniques and treatments in the medical rehabilitation fields. *$80.50*
*368 pages Illustrated*
*ISBN 0-88167 -85-5*

**2322 Meeting the ADD Challenge: A Practical Guide for Teachers**
Research Press
PO Box 9177
Champaign, IL 61826-9177 217-352-3273
800-519-2707
FAX: 217-352-1221
e-mail: rp@researchpress.com
www.researchpress.com

*Dr. Michael Asher, Co-Author*
*Dr. Steven B Gordon, Co-Author*
*$24.95*

*ISBN 0-878223-45-9*

**2323 Mental & Physical Disability Law Digest**
A BA Commission on Mental and Physical Disability
9th Fl
740 15th St NW
Washington, DC 20005-1019 202-662-1570
800-285-2221
FAX: 202-442-3439
e-mail: cmpdl@abanet.org
www.abanet.org/disability

*John W. Parry, Executive Director*
*Amy L. Allbright, Director*
*Janet Jackson, Director*
*Bill Pritchard, Executive Assistant to the Director*
Provides comprehensive, summary and analysis of federal and state disability and state disability laws from mental disability law and disability discrimination law perspectives. *$60.00*
*376 pages*
*ISBN 1-590310-05-5*

**2324 Mental Health Concepts and Techniques for the Occupational Therapy Assistant**
Lippincott, Williams & Wilkins
# 227
227 S 6th St
Philadelphia, PA 19106-3713 215-521-8300
800-777-2295
FAX: 301-824-7390
www.lpub.com

*J Lippincott, CEO*
This text offers clear and easily understood explanations of the various theoretical and practiced health models. *$36.00*
*344 pages*
*ISBN 0-88167 -53-X*

**2325 Mental Health and Mental Illness**
Lippincott, Williams & Wilkins
# 227
227 S 6th St
Philadelphia, PA 19106-3713 215-592-5400
800-777-2295
FAX: 301-824-7390
www.lpub.com

*Kathy Sykes, Manager*

Concise, comprehensive and completely up to date, this book presents the most current theory in mental health nursing for the student and the new practitioner. *$28.95*
*480 pages*
*ISBN 0-39755 -73-7*

**2326 Mentally Ill Individuals**
Mainstream
Ste 830
3 Bethesda Metro Ctr
Bethesda, MD 20814-6301
301-961-9299
800-247-1380
FAX: 301-654-6714
e-mail: info@mainstreaminc.org

*Charles Moster*
Mainstreaming mentally ill individuals into the workplace. *$2.50*
*12 pages*

**2327 Midland Treatment Furniture**
Sammons Preston Rolyan
W68 n158 Evergreen Blvd
Cedarburg, WI 53012-2637
262-387-8720
800-228-3693
FAX: 262-387-8748
e-mail: CustomerSupport@PattersonMedical.com
www.sammonspreston.com
This catalog has the biggest selection of OT/PT products anywhere. Whether you deal with larger or smaller caseloads, you need treatment furniture you can count on. Midland Treatment Furniture from SPR is designed and built to stand up to the heaviest use. From tilt tables and traction packages to mat platforms and parallel bars, you'll find the complete line of Midland Treatment Furniture inside this brochure. All products are assembled from premium materials and carefully crafted.
*Free*

**2328 Multidisciplinary Assessment of Children With Learning Disabilities and Mental Retardation**
Gallery Bookshop
P.O.Box 270
Mendocino, CA 95460
707-937-2665
FAX: 707-937-3737
e-mail: info@gallerybookshop.com
www.gallerybooks.com

*David L. Wodrich, Author*
*James E. Joy, Editor*
Assessment of children with learning disabilities and mental retardation. *$24.00*
*346 pages Illustrated*
*ISBN 0-93371 -62-1*

**2329 Multisensory Teaching of Basic Language Skills: Theory and Practice**
Brookes Publishing
P.O.Box 10624
Baltimore, MD 21285
410-337-9580
800-638-3775
FAX: 410-337-8539
e-mail: pkelly@brookespublishing.com
www.brookespublishing.com

*Judith R. Birsh, Editor*
*Melissa A. Behm, Executive Vice President*
*Paul H. Brooks, Chairman of the Board*
*Jeff Brookes, President*
This book presents specific multisensory methods for helping students who are having trouble learning to read due to dyslexia or other learning disabilities. Recommended techniques are offered for teaching alphabet skills, composition, comprehension, handwriting, math, organization and study skills, phonological awareness, reading and spelling. *$59.00*
*608 pages Hardcover*
*ISBN 1-557663-49-1*

**2330 No Longer Immune: A Counselor's Guide to AIDS**
American Counceling Association
5999 Stevenson Ave
Alexandria, VA 22304-3304
703-823-9800
800-347-6647
FAX: 703-823-0252
e-mail: membership@counseling.org
counseling.org

*Richard Yep, Executive Director*
*Holly Clubb, Director, Leadership Services*
*Dr. Brad Erford, President*
*Craig D. Kain, Author*
Covers a broad range of issues such as working with specific populations, handling pre and post testing situations, coping with fear, grief and survivor guilt, struggling with spiritual issues and dealing with counter transference. *$26.95*
*295 pages*
*ISBN 1-55620 -64-1*

**2331 Occupational Therapy Across Cultural Boundaries**
Haworth Press
711 Third Avenue
New York, NY 10017
212-216-7800
800-354-1420
FAX: 212-244-1563
e-mail: subscriptions@tandf.co.uk.
http://www.taylorandfrancisgroup.com/

*Susan Cook Merrill, Author*
Examines the concept of culture from a unique perspective, that of individual occupational therapists who have worked in environments very different from those in which they were educated or had worked previously. Taylor & Francis Group acquired the Haworth Press journal and book list during 2007. Journal publications formerly published by Haworth Press are now listed on the Taylor & Francis Journals website. *$74.95*
*107 pages Hardcover*
*ISBN 1-560242-23-X*

**2332 Occupational Therapy Approaches to Traumatic Brain Injury**
Haworth Press
711 Third Avenue
New York, NY 10017
212-216-7800
800-354-1420
FAX: 212-244-1563
e-mail: subscriptions@tandf.co.uk.
http://www.taylorandfrancisgroup.com/

*Laura H Krefting, Co-Author*
*Jerry A Johnson, Co-Author*
Focuses on the disabled individual, the family, and the societal responses to the injured, this comprehensive book covers the spectrum of available services from intensive care to transitional and community living. Taylor & Francis Group acquired the Haworth Press journal and book list during 2007. Journal publications formerly published by Haworth Press are now listed on the Taylor & Francis Journals website. *$74.95*
*137 pages Hardcover*
*ISBN 1-560240-64-4*

**2333 Overcoming Dyslexia in Children, Adolescents and Adults**
Sage Publications
2455 Teller Road
Thousand Oaks, CA 91320
805-499-9774
800-818-7243
FAX: 800-583-2665
e-mail: books.claim@sagepub.com
www.sagepub.com

*Sara Miller McCune, Founder, Publisher, Chairperson*
*Blaise R Simqu, President & CEO*
*Tracey A. Ozmina, Executive Vice President & Chief Operating Officer*
*Dale R. Jordan, Author*

This book describes some forms of dyslexia in detail and then relates those problems to the social, emotional and personal development of dyslexic individuals. *$34.00*

*350 pages Paperback*

**2334 Oxford Textbook of Geriatric Medicine**
Oxford University Press
198 Madison Ave
New York, NY 10016-4308
212-726-6000
800-445-9714
FAX: 919-677-1303
e-mail: custserv.us@oup.com
www.oup.com/us

*T. Franklin Williams, Editor*
*B. Lynn Beattie, Editor*
*J-P. Michel, Editor*
*G. K. Wilcock, Editor*

This comprehensive text brings together extensive experience in clinical geriatrics with a strong scientific base in research. *$125.00*

*784 pages*

**2335 PKU for Children: Learning to Measure**
University of Washington PKU Clinic
P.O.Box 357920
University of Washington
Seattle, WA 98195-7920
206-598-1800
877-685-3015
FAX: 206-598-1915
e-mail: pku@u.washington.edu
www.depts.washington.edu/pku

*C. Ronald Scott, MD, Professor, Pediatrics, Division of Genetics and Development*
*Michael J. Bamshad, MD, Division Chief and Professor*
*Eileen Chin, BA (Acc), Division Administrator*
*Susanna Ngai, BS, Fiscal Specialist 2 - Administration*

Lesson format for parents and teachers.

**2336 Pain Centers: A Revolution in Health Care**
Lippincott Williams And Wilkins
# 227
227 S 6th St
Philadelphia, PA 19106-3713
215-521-8300
800-777-2295
FAX: 301-824-7390
www.lpub.com

*J Lippincott, CEO*
*$103.00*
*280 pages*

**2337 Parental Concerns in College Student Mental Health**
Haworth Press
711 Third Avenue
New York, NY 10017
212-216-7800
800-354-1420
FAX: 212-244-1563
e-mail: subscriptions@tandf.co.uk.
http://www.taylorandfrancisgroup.com/

*Leighton Whitaker, Author*

An instructive guide for parents and mental health professionals regarding the most important issues about psychological development in college students. Taylor & Francis Group acquired the Haworth Press journal and book list during 2007. Journal publications formerly published by Haworth Press are now listed on the Taylor & Francis Journals website. *$74.95*

*204 pages Hardcover*
*ISBN 0-866567-20-8*

**2338 Parents and Teachers**
Alexander Graham Bell Association
3417 Volta Pl NW
Washington, DC 20007-2737
202-337-5220
866-337-5220
FAX: 202-337-8314
TTY: 202-337-5221
e-mail: info@agbell.org
www.agbell.org

*Kathleen S. Treni, M.Ed., M.A., President*
*Meredith K. Knueve, Esq., Secretary-Treasurer*
*Alexander T. Graham, Executive Director/CEO*
*Corrine Altman, Director*

This excellent book offers in-depth guidance to parents and teachers whose partnership can foster language in school-aged children with hearing impairments. The first section examines roles of parents, teachers, professionals and children in language acquisition, residual hearing and audiological management, language development stages and readying children for preschool. The second portion of the book presents specific objectives and teaching strategies to use at school and at home. *$27.95*

*386 pages*

**2339 Patient and Family Education**
Springer Publishing Company
15th Fl
11 W 42nd St
New York, NY 10036-8002
212-431-4370
877-687-7476
FAX: 212-941-7842
e-mail: cs@springerpub.com
www.springerpub.com

*Dr. Ursula Springer, President*
*Ted Nardin, CEO*
*James C. Costello, Vice President, Journal Publishing*
*Diana Osborne, Production Manager*

This guide outlines the actual clinical content needed to develop, implement and maintain patient education programs. Conveniently arranged in one-hour long lesson plans, each disease or condition is organized in an easy-to-follow format. *$26.95*

*272 pages Softcover*
*ISBN 0-82615-41-7*

**2340 Person to Person: Guide for Professionals Working with the Disabled**
Paul H Brookes Publishing Company
P.O.Box 10624
Baltimore, MD 21285-624
410-337-9580
800-638-3775
FAX: 410-337-8539
e-mail: pkelly@brookespublishing.com
www.brookespublishing.com

*Lindsay Gething, Editor*
*Melissa A. Behm, Executive Vice President*
*Paul H. Brooks, Chairman of the Board*
*Jeff Brookes, President*

This second edition of an already-popular book helps professionals approach interactions with a people-first, disability second attitude. *$29.00*

*288 pages Paperback*
*ISBN 1-557661-00-6*

**2341 Personality and Emotional Disturbance**
Taylor & Francis
Ste G
47 Runway Dr
Levittown, PA 19057-4738
267-580-2622
FAX: 215-785-5515

*Richard Roberts, CEO*

The brain injured person has unique needs. Recent findings have highlighted that it is the personality, behavioral and emotional problems which most prohibit a return to work, create the greatest

burden for the long-term care and rehabilitation of physical and cognitive functions. *$72.00*
*260 pages Cloth*
*ISBN 0-85066 -71-3*

**2342 Peterson's Guide to Colleges with Programsfor Learning Disabled Students**
Special Needs Project
Ste H
324 State St
Santa Barbara, CA 93101-2364
805-962-8087
818-718-9900
FAX: 805-962-5087
e-mail: books@specialneeds.com
www.specialneeds.com

*B. B. Moose Peter, Author*
*Charles T. Mangrum, Editor*
*Stephen S. Strichart, Editor*
The most complete and accurate guide to the more than 900 colleges with programs for the learning disabled. *$19.95*
*406 pages*

**2343 Phenomenology of Depressive Illness**
Human Sciences Press
233 Spring St
New York, NY 10013-1522
212-229-2859
800-221-9369
FAX: 212-463-0742
Provides the reader with a detailed knowledge of the clinical characteristics of depressive disorders that will permit judgement of the general ability of the various theoretical models of depressive disorders. *$42.95*
*263 pages Cloth*
*ISBN 0-89885 -69-9*

**2344 Physical Disabilities and Health Impairments: An Introduction**
McGraw-Hill School Publishing
220 E Danieldale Rd
Desoto, TX 75115-2490
972-224-4772
800-442-9685
FAX: 972-228-1982
mcgraw-hill.com

*Harold McGraw III, Chairman, President and Chief Executive Officer*
*Jack F. Callahan, Executive Vice President, Chief Financial Officer*
*John Berisford, Executive Vice President, Human Resources*
*John Umbreit, Author*
A comprehensive text which presents a wealth of up-to-date medical information for teachers.

**2345 Physical Education and Sports for Exceptional Students**
McGraw-Hill Company
2460 Kerper Blvd
Dubuque, IA 52001-2224
800-338-3987
FAX: 614-755-5654
e-mail: customer.service@mcgraw-hill.com
www.mhhe.com/hper/physed

*Michael Horvat, Author*
*Harold McGraw III, Chairman, President and Chief Executive Officer*
*Jack F. Callahan, Executive Vice President, Chief Financial Officer*
*John Berisford, Executive Vice President, Human Resources*
Physical education for exceptional students and teaching students with learning and behavior exceptionalities.
*Cloth*

**2346 Physical Management of Multiple Handicaps: A Professional's Guide**
Brookes Publishing Company
P.O.Box 10624
Baltimore, MD 21285-624
410-337-9580
800-638-3775
FAX: 410-337-8539
e-mail: pkelly@brookespublishing.com
www.brookespublishing.com

*Beverly A. Fraser, Co-Author*
*Judith A. Phelps, Co-Author*
*Paul H. Brooks, Chairman of the Board*
*Robert N. Hensinger, Co-Author*
Comprehensive guide, takes a transdisciplinary approach to therapeutic/technological management of persons with multiple handicaps. *$36.00*
*352 pages Hardcover*
*ISBN 1-557660-47-6*

**2347 Physically Handicapped in Society**
Ayer Company Publishers
Ste 322
400 Bedford St
Manchester, NH 03101-1195
603-669-9307
888-267-7323
FAX: 603-669-7945
e-mail: stg@ncia.net
www.ayerpub.com

*Kathy Train, Office Manager*
*Ellie Phipps, Customer Service*
A group of 39 books. Biographies that offer studies on attitudes, sociological and psychological. Please write or call for catalog. *$965.00*
*Hardcover*
*ISBN 0-40513 -00-3*

**2348 Practicing Rehabilitation with Geriatric Clients**
Springer Publishing Company
15th Fl
11 W 42nd St
New York, NY 10036-8002
212-431-4370
877-687-7476
FAX: 212-941-7842
e-mail: cs@springerpub.com
www.springerpub.com

*Dr. Ursula Springer, President*
*Ted Nardin, CEO*
*James C. Costello, Vice President, Journal Publishing*
*J. Dermot Frengley, Author*
Physical therapy in the geriatric client, psychological and psychiatric considerations in the rehabilitation of the elderly. *$32.95*
*256 pages Hardcover*
*ISBN 0-82616 -80-5*

**2349 Pragmatic Approach**
Educators Publishing Service
3rd Floor
625 Mount Auburn St
Cambridge, MA 02138-3039
617-547-6706
800-225-5750
FAX: 617-547-0285
www.epsbooks.com
Monograph on evaluation of children's performances on Slingerland Pre-Reading Screening Procedures to Identify First Grade Academic Needs. *$6.00*
*56 pages*
*ISBN 0-838816-85-1*

**2350 Preschoolers with Special Needs: Children At-Risk, Children with Disabilities**
Allyn & Bacon
Ste 300
75 Arlington St
Boston, MA 02116-3988
617-848-7500
800-852-8024
FAX: 617-944-7273
www.ablongman.com

*Bill Barke, CEO*
*Janet W. Lerner, Co-Author*
*Barbara Lowenthal, Co-Author*
*Rosemary W. Egan, Co-Author*
Explores ways of providing preschool children with special needs and their families with a learning environment that will help them develop and learn. Emphasizes the needs of preschoolers age three to six and provides information to teachers and others who work with young children in all settings. Current models of curricula, which incorporate new features from research and practical expreiences with children who have special needs, are described and discussed. *$59.00*
*336 pages cloth*
*ISBN 0-205358-79-9*

**2351 Preventing Academic Failure**
Educators Publishing Service
3rd Floor
625 Mount Auburn St
Cambridge, MA 02138-3039
617-547-6706
800-225-5750
FAX: 617-547-0285
www.epsbooks.com
Ungraded multisensory curriculum coordinating Orton-Gillingham and Merrill Linguistic reading techniques for language disabled students. Teaches phonics, spelling and reading to reinforce the development of language skills. A separate handwriting program is available. *$42.00*
*284 pages Paperback*
*ISBN 0-838852-71-8*

**2352 Preventing School Dropouts**
Sage Publications
2455 Teller Road
Thousand Oaks, CA 91320
805-499-9774
800-818-7243
FAX: 800-583-2665
e-mail: books.claim@sagepub.com
www.sagepub.com

*Sara Miller McCune, Founder, Publisher, Chairperson*
*Blaise R Simqu, President & CEO*
*Tracey A. Ozmina, Executive Vice President & Chief Operating Officer*
*Thomas C. Lovitt, Author*
For secondary teachers, special education and regular, who have difficulty teaching youth in their classes. Presented are 120 tactics, specific instructional techniques, for helping adolescents to stay in school. Each tactic is written in a format that includes five sections. *$38.00*
*509 pages*

**2353 Prevocational Assessment**
Exceptional Education
P.O.Box 15308
Seattle, WA 98115-308
206-262-9538
FAX: 475-486-4510

*Jeff Stewart, Owner*
Use the PACG to assess your students in nine areas (attendance and endurance, learning and behavior, communication skills, social skills, grooming and eating and toileting) covering 46 specific workshop experiences. *$12.00*
*16 pages Complete Set*
*ISBN 1-87786 -23-7*

**2354 Progress Without Punishment: Approaches for Learners with Behavior Problems**
Teachers College Press
1234 Amsterdam Ave
New York, NY 10027-6602
212-678-3929
800-575-6566
FAX: 212-678-4149
e-mail: tcpress@tc.columbia.edu
www.teacherscollegepress.com

*Anne M. Donnellan, Author*
In this volume, the authors argue against the use of punishment, and instead advocate the use of alternative intervention procedures. *$17.95*
*184 pages Paperback*
*ISBN 0-807729-11-6*

**2355 Promoting Postsecondary Education for Students with Learning Disabilities**
Sage Publications
2455 Teller Road
Thousand Oaks, CA 91320
805-499-9774
800-818-7243
FAX: 800-583-2665
e-mail: books.claim@sagepub.com
www.sagepub.com

*Sara Miller McCune, Founder, Publisher, Chairperson*
*Stan F. Shaw, Co-Author*
*Joan M. McGuire, Co-Author*
*Loring Cowles Brinckerhoff, Co-Author*
Primarily designed for postsecondary service providers who are responsible for serving college students with learning disabilities. *$41.00*
*440 pages*

**2356 Psychiatric Mental Health Nursing**
Lippincott, Williams & Wilkins
# 227
227 S 6th St
Philadelphia, PA 19106-3713
215-521-8300
800-777-2295
FAX: 301-824-7390
www.lpub.com

*J Lippincott, CEO*
This text emphasizes and contrasts the roles of the generalist nurse and the psychiatric nurse specialist. *$52.00*
*1120 pages Illustrated*

**2357 Psychoeducational Assessment of Visually Impaired and Blind Students**
Sage Publications
2455 Teller Road
Thousand Oaks, CA 91320
805-499-9774
800-818-7243
FAX: 800-583-2665
e-mail: books.claim@sagepub.com
www.sagepub.com

*Sara Miller McCune, Founder, Publisher, Chairperson*
*Blaise R Simqu, President & CEO*
*Tracey A. Ozmina, Executive Vice President & Chief Operating Officer*
*Sharon Bradley-Johnson, Author*
Professional reference book that addresses the problems specific to assessment of visually impaired and blind children. Of particular value to the practitioner are the extensive reviews of available tests, including ways to adapt those not designed for use with the visually handicapped. *$29.00*
*140 pages Paperback*
*ISBN 0-890791-08-2*

**2358 Psychological and Social Impact of Illness and Disability**

Springer Publishing
15th Fl
11 W 42nd St
New York, NY 10036-8002
212-431-4370
877-687-7476
FAX: 212-941-7842
e-mail: cs@springerpub.com
springerpub.com

*Dr. Ursula Springer, President*
*Ted Nardin, CEO*
*Ph.D. Orto Arthur E. Dell, Editor*
*Paul W. Power, Editor*

The newest edition of Psychological and Social Impact of Illness and Disability continues the tradition of presenting a realistic perspective on life with disabilies and then improves upon its predecessors with the inclusion of illness as a major influence on client care needs. Further broadening the scope of this edition is the inclusion of personal perspectives and stories from those living with illness or disabilities. These stories offer a look into what it is like to cope with these issues.

**2359 Reading and Deafness**

Sage Publications
2455 Teller Road
Thousand Oaks, CA 91320
805-499-9774
800-818-7243
FAX: 800-583-2665
e-mail: books.claim@sagepub.com
www.sagepub.com

*Sara Miller McCune, Founder, Publisher, Chairperson*
*Beverly J Trezek, Co-Author*
*Peter V. Paul, Co-Author*
*Ye Wang, Co-Author*

Three areas are looked at in this book: deaf children's prereading development of real-world knowledge, cognitive abilities and linguistic skills. *$39.00*
*422 pages*

**2360 Readings on Research in Stuttering**

Longman Publishing Group
1 Penn Plaza
Suite 2222
New York, NY 10119
646-556-8401
FAX: 646-556-8415
e-mail: coffee@rothfos.com
rothfos.com

*Dan Dwyer, CEO*
*Thomas Minogue, CFO*
*Maria Tanpinco-Queyquep, Traffic Manager*
*E. Charles Healey, Author*

Collection of the key journal articles published on stuttering over the past decade, addressing trends in recent research in the field.
*231 pages Paperback*
*ISBN 0-801304-10-5*

**2361 Recreation Activities for the Elderly**

Springer Publishing Company
15th Fl
11 W 42nd St
New York, NY 10036-8002
212-431-4370
877-687-7476
FAX: 212-941-7842
e-mail: cs@springerpub.com
www.springerpub.com

*Dr. Ursula Springer, President*
*Ted Nardin, CEO*
*James C. Costello, Vice President, Journal Publishing*
*Kay Flatten, Author*

Included in this volume are simple crafts that utilize easily obtainable, inexpensive materials, hobbies focusing on collections, nature, and the arts' and games emphasizing both mental and physical activity. *$23.95*
*240 pages Softcover*
*ISBN 0-82616 -30-1*

**2362 Reference Manual for Communicative Sciences and Disorders**

Pro- Ed Publications
8700 Shoal Creek Blvd
Austin, TX 78757-6897
512-451-3246
800-897-3202
FAX: 512-451-8542
e-mail: info@proedinc.com
www.proedinc.com

*Raymond D. Kent, Author*

An indispensable guide to standards and values essential in the assessment of communication disorders. *$54.00*
*393 pages*

**2363 Rehabilitation Interventions for the Institutionalized Elderly**

Haworth Press
711 Third Avenue
New York, NY 10017
212-216-7800
800-354-1420
FAX: 212-244-1563
e-mail: subscriptions@tandf.co.uk.
http://www.taylorandfrancisgroup.com/

*Ellen D Taira, Author*

Gerontology professionals offer suggestions to enrich the quality of rehabilitation services offered to the institutionalized elderly. This volume examines up to the minute ideas, some that would have been unlikely even a few years ago, that focus exclusively on rehabilitation services for the institutionalized elderly. Taylor & Francis Group acquired the Haworth Press journal and book list during 2007. Journal publications formerly published by Haworth Press are now listed on the Taylor & Franc *$44.95*
*77 pages Hardcover*
*ISBN 0-866568-33-6*

**2364 Rehabilitation Nursing for the Neurological Patient**

Springer Publishing Company
15th Fl
11 W 42nd St
New York, NY 10036-8002
212-431-4370
877-687-7476
FAX: 212-941-7842
e-mail: cs@springerpub.com
www.springerpub.com

*Dr. Ursula Springer, President*
*Ted Nardin, CEO*
*James C. Costello, Vice President, Journal Publishing*
*Marcia Hanak, Author*

A practical new reference written especially for practicing nurses who work with neurologically disabled persons. *$ 32.95*
*240 pages*

**2365 Rehabilitation Resource Manual: VISION**

Resources for Rehabilitation
22 Bonad Rd
Winchester, MA 01890-1302
781-368-9094
FAX: 781-368-9096
e-mail: info@rfr.org
http://www.rfr.org/

*Marshall E. Flax, MS, Author*

A desk reference that enables service providers, librarians and others to make effective referrals. Includes guidelines on establishing self-help groups, information on research and service organizations, and chapters on assistive technology, for special population groups and by eye condition. *$44.95*
*Biennial*

**2366 Rehabilitation Technology**
Haworth Press
711 Third Avenue
New York, NY 10017
212-216-7800
800-354-1420
FAX: 212-244-1563
e-mail: subscriptions@tandf.co.uk.
http://www.taylorandfrancisgroup.com/

*Glenn E Hedman, Author*
Learn how the use of technological devices can enhance the lives of disabled children. Informs physical therapists, occupational therapists, and rehabilitation technologists about the devices that are available today and provides important background information on these devices. Taylor & Francis Group acquired the Haworth Press journal and book list during 2007. Journal publications formerly published by Haworth Press are now listed on the Taylor & Francis Journals website. *$74.95*
*173 pages Hardcover*
*ISBN 1-560240-33-4*

**2367 Report Writing in Assessment and Evaluation**
Stout Vocational Rehab Institute
University of Wisconsin-Stout
712 South Broadway St
Menomonie, WI 54751
715-232-1478
FAX: 715-232-2356
e-mail: giffordj@uwstout.edu
www.uwstout.edu

*Judy Gifford, Director*
*Stephen W. Thomas, Author*
*Linda Vanderloop, CFSC Office*
This examines questions of who are you writing for and what does the referral source want. Defines characteristics of good reports, common problems, writing in different settings, types of reports, getting ready to write, and writing prescriptive recommendations. *$ 17.75*
*188 pages Softcover*

**2368 Resources for Rehabilitation**
22 Bonad Rd
Winchester, MA 01890-1302
781-368-9094
FAX: 781-368-9096
e-mail: info@rfr.org
http://www.rfr.org/
Provides training and information to professionals and the public about disabilities and resources available to help. Publishes resource guides, professional publications and patient/client educational materials. Conducts custom designed training programs and workshops.

**2369 Restructuring High Schools for All Students: Taking Inclusion to the Next Level**
Brookes Publishing
P.O.Box 10624
Baltimore, MD 21285-624
410-337-9580
800-638-3775
FAX: 410-337-8539
e-mail: pkelly@brookespublishing.com
www.brookespublishing.com

*Cheryl M. Jorgensen, Author*
*Melissa A. Behm, Executive Vice President*
*Paul H. Brooks, Chairman of the Board*
*Jeff Brookes, President*
Details the process of creating an inclusive, collaborate community of learners and teachers at the secondary level. *$29.95*
*304 pages Paperback*
*ISBN 1-557663-13-0*

**2370 Restructuring for Caring and Effective Education: Administrative Guide**
Brookes Publishing
P.O.Box 10624
Baltimore, MD 21285-624
410-337-9580
800-638-3775
FAX: 410-337-8539
e-mail: pkelly@brookespublishing.com
www.brookespublishing.com

*R. A. Villa, Editor*
*J. S. Thousand, Editor*
*Paul H. Brooks, Chairman of the Board*
*W. Stainback, Editor*
In this empowering book, leading general and special education schools reform experts synthesize the major school restructuring initiatives and describe the processes and rationale for changing the organizational structure and instructional practices of schools. *$ 29.00*
*384 pages Paperback*
*ISBN 1-55766 -91-3*

**2371 Scoffolding Student Learning**
Brookline Books
8 Trumbull Rd
Suite B-001
Northampton, MA 01060
413-584-0184
800-666-2665
FAX: 413-584-6184
e-mail: brbooks@yahoo.com
www.brooklinebooks.com

*Kathleen Hogan, Co-Author*
*Michael Pres , Co-Author*
Collection of papers on the theory and practice of scoffolding-an interactive style of instructions that helps students develop more powerful thinking tools. *$21.95*
*180 pages Paperback*
*ISBN 1-571290-36-2*

**2372 Selective Nontreatment of Handicapped**
Oxford University Press
2001 Evans Rd
Cary, NC 27513-2009
919-677-0977
800-451-7556
FAX: 919-677-1303
e-mail: humanres@oup-usa.org
www.us.oup.com

*Ruth Collier, Head of Press and Information Office*
*Maria Coyle, Press Officer*
*Julia Paolitto, Press Officer*
*Robert F. Weir, Author*
Information on selective nontreatment of handicapped newborns, moral dilemmas in neonatal medicine. *$17.95*
*304 pages Paperback*

**2373 Semiotics and Dis/ability: Interogating Categories of Difference**
State University of New York Press
194 Washington Avenue
Suite 305
Albany, NY 12210-2314
518-472-5000
800-666-2211
FAX: 518-472-5038
e-mail: info@sunypress.edu
www.sunypress.edu

*James Peltz, Associate Director*
*Linda Rogers, Editor*
*Beth Blue Swadener, Editor*
Examines the ways the words disability and difference and socially and culturally constructed. *$25.95*
*265 pages Paperback 1990*
*ISBN 0-791449-06-6*

**2374 Service Coordination for Early Intervention: Parents and Friends**
Brookline Books
8 Trumbull Rd
Suite B-001
Northampton, MA 01060
413-584-0184
800-666-2665
FAX: 413-584-6184
e-mail: brbooks@yahoo.com
www.brooklinebooks.com

*Deborah D. Hatton, Co-Author*
*R. A. McWilliam, Co-Author*
*P. J. Winton, Co-Author*
This book helps administrators and professionals to structure early intervention and ongoing services so that professionals work collaboratively with parents to promote the health, well being and development of children with special needs. *$19.95*
*110 pages Paperback*
*ISBN 0-91479 -91-3*

**2375 Services for the Seriously Mentally Ill: A Survey of Mental Health Centers**
Nat'l Council for Community Behavioral Healthcare
Ste 320
12300 Twinbrook Pkwy
Rockville, MD 20852-1606
301-984-6200
FAX: 301-881-7159
www.nccbh.org

*Linda Rosenberg, CEO*
*Dale K Klatzker, Board Chair*
This ground-breaking report documents what administrators and practitioners have maintained for many years: community mental health organizations devote a significant percentage of the human and financial resources to serving the seriously mentally ill. *$30.00*

**2376 Shop Talk**
P.O.Box 9177
Champaign, IL 61826-9177
217-352-3273
800-519-2707
FAX: 217-352-1221
e-mail: rp@researchpress.com
www.researchpress.com

*Philip Roth, Author*

**2377 Signed English Schoolbook**
Gallaudet University Press
800 Florida Ave NE
Washington, DC 20002-3600
202-651-5488
800-451-1073
FAX: 202-651-5489
TTY: 888-630-9347
e-mail: clerc.center@gallaudet.edu.
gupress.gallaudet.edu

*Harry Bornstein, Co-Author*
*Karen L. Saulnier, Co-Author*
*Dr. T Alan Hurwitz, President*
*Edward Bosso, Vice President for Administration and Finance*
The Signed English Schoolbook provides vocabulary for teachers and others who serve school-age children and adolescents and covers the full range of school activities. *$13.95*
*184 pages Softcover*

**2378 Social Studies: Detecting and Correcting Special Needs**
Allyn & Bacon
Ste 300
75 Arlington St
Boston, MA 02116-3988
617-848-7500
800-852-8024
FAX: 617-944-7273
www.ablongman.com

*Harry Bornst Barke, CEO*
*Nancy Forfyth, President*
*Lana J. Smith, Co-Author*
*Dennie L. Smith, Co-Author*
Describes social studies and special needs for special learners.
*180 pages*
*ISBN 0-205121-51-9*

**2379 Social and Emotional Development of Exceptional Students: Handicapped**
Charles C. Thomas
2600 S 1st St
Springfield, IL 62704-4730
217-789-8980
800-258-8980
FAX: 217-789-9130
e-mail: books@ccthomas.com
ccthomas.com

*Michael P. Thomas, President*
*Carroll J. Jones, Author*
Sixteen years after the passage of P.L. 94-142, the dream of special educators to educate the handicapped and nonhandicapped children and youth together resulting in increased academic gains and age-appropriate school skills for handicapped children and youth has not yet materialized. This book helps eliminate an existing void by providing teachers with understandable information regarding the social and emotional development of exceptional students. Also in cloth at $41.95 (ISBN# 0-398-05781-8) *$29.95*
*218 pages Softcover*
*ISBN 0-398061-94-7*

**2380 Special Education Today**
LifeWay Christian Resources Southern Baptist Conv.
127 9th Ave N
Nashville, TN 37234
615-741-2851
800-458-2772
FAX: 615-532-9412
e-mail: specialed@lifeway.com
www.lifeway.com

*Ellen Beene, Editor*
This unique quarterly publications ministers to people with special education needs and to their families, the church, and other caregivers. It offers a variety of helps and encouragement, including: What's working in churches, Suggestions for adapting teaching techniques, inspirational stories about people who have disabilities, Parenting and family issues, Ideas for reaching, witnessing, worship, and recreation. *$4.25*
*36 pages Quarterly*

**2381 Special Education for Today**
Allyn & Bacon
Ste 300
75 Arlington St
Boston, MA 02116-3988
617-848-7500
800-852-8024
FAX: 617-944-7273
www.ablongman.com

*See search r Barke, CEO*
*Michael S. Rosenberg, Co-Author*
*David L. Westling, Co-Author*
*James McLeskey, Co-Author*

An undergraduate introduction to special education covering all major areas of exceptionality. Contains pedagogical features designed to make the book accessible to the undergraduate.
*576 pages hardcover*
*ISBN 0-138264-53-8*

**2382 Speech and the Hearing-Impaired Child**
Alexander Graham Bell Association
3417 Volta Pl NW
Washington, DC 20007-2737 202-337-5220
866-337-5220
FAX: 202-337-8314
TTY: 202-337-5221
e-mail: info@agbell.org
www.agbell.org

*Daniel Ling, Author*
*Kathleen S. Treni, M.Ed., M.A., President*
*Meredith K. Knueve, Esq., Secretary-Treasurer*
*Alexander T. Graham, Executive Director/CEO*
This textbook for professionals deals with basic theoretical issues in the acquisition of speech and the form of language (phonetics and phonology) in children with hearing losses. It provides a systematic framework to develop and evaluate speech target behaviors and their underlying subskills. *$29.95*
*402 pages Paperback*

**2383 Speech-Language Pathology and Audiology: An Introduction**
McGraw-Hill School Publishing
220 E Danieldale Rd
Desoto, TX 75115-2490 972-224-4772
800-442-9685
FAX: 972-228-1982
mcgraw-hill.com

*Harold McGraw III, Chairman, President and Chief Executive Officer*
*Jack F. Callahan, Executive Vice President, Chief Financial Officer*
*John Berisford, Executive Vice President, Human Resources*
*Franklin H. Silverman, Author*
Offers classroom-tested coverage of clinical objectives and functioning.
*301 pages*

**2384 Spinal Cord Dysfunction**
Oxford University Press
2001 Evans Rd
Cary, NC 27513-2009 919-677-0977
800-451-7556
FAX: 919-677-1303
e-mail: humanres@oup-usa.org
www.oup-usa.org

*Ruth Collier, Head of Press and Information Office*
*Maria Coyle, Press Officer*
*Julia Paolitto, Press Officer*
*L. S. Illis, Editor*
Offers information on restoration of function after spinal cord damage as seen from the point of view of identification of impaired or absent function in the nerve cells and processes which survive after the initial insult, intact but with impaired functions.
*$95.00*
*368 pages*

**2385 Strategies for Teaching Learners with Special Needs**
McGraw-Hill School Publishing
220 E Danieldale Rd
Desoto, TX 75115-2490 972-224-4772
800-442-9685
FAX: 972-228-1982
mcgraw-hill.com

*Harold McGraw III, Chairman, President and Chief Executive Officer*
*Loretta Serna, Co-Author*
*James R. Patton, Co-Author*
*Edward A. Polloway, Co-Author*
This is a text that helps special educators develop the full range of teaching competencies needed to be effective.
*560 pages*

**2386 Strategies for Teaching Students with Learning and Behavior Problems**
Allyn & Bacon
Ste 300
75 Arlington St
Boston, MA 02116-3988 617-848-7500
800-852-8024
FAX: 617-944-7273
www.ablongman.com

*Bill Barke, CEO*
*Nancy Forfyth, President*
*Sharon R. Vaughn, Co-Author*
*Candace S. Bos, Co-Author*
Provides descriptions of methods and strategies for teaching students with learning and behavior problems, managing professional roles, and collaborating with families, professionals, and paraprofessionals.
*544 pages*
*ISBN 0-205113-89-3*

**2387 Students with Acquired Brain Injury: The School's Response**
Brookes Publishing
P.O.Box 10624
Baltimore, MD 21285 410-337-9580
800-638-3775
FAX: 410-337-8539
e-mail: pkelly@brookespublishing.com
www.brookespublishing.com

*Ann Glang, Editor*
*Bonnie Todis, Editor*
*Paul H. Brooks, Chairman of the Board*
*George H. Singer, Editor*
This book is designed for school professionals and describes a range of issues that this population faces and presents proven means of addressing them in ways that benefit all students. Included topics are hospital-to-school transitions, effective assessment strategies, model programs in public schools, interventions to assist classroom teachers, and ways to involve family members in the educational program. *$29.95*
*424 pages Paperback*
*ISBN 1-55766 -85-1*

**2388 Students with Mild Disabilities in the Secondary School**
Longman Group
1185 Avenue of the Americas
New York, NY 10036-2601 212-782-3300
800-852-8024
www.ablongman.com

*William Hitchings, Co-Author*
*Michael Horvath, Co-Author*
*Bonnie Schmalle, Co-Author*
*Paul Retish, Co-Author, Editor*
Provides methods and strategies for curriculum delivery to students with mild disabilities at the secondary school level.
*2313G pages Paperback*
*ISBN 0-801301-66-1*

**2389 Supporting and Strengthening Families**
Brookline Books
8 Trumbull Rd
Suite B-001
Northampton, MA 01060 413-584-0184
800-666-2665
FAX: 413-584-6184
e-mail: brbooks@yahoo.com
www.brooklinebooks.com

*Carl J Dunst, Author*

A collection of papers addressing the theory, methods, strategies, and practices involved in adopting an empowerment and family-centered resources approach to supporting families and strengthening individual and family functioning. *$30.00*
*252 pages Paperback*
*ISBN 0-91479 -94-8*

**2390 TESTS**
Slosson Educational Publications
P.O.Box 544
East Aurora, NY 14052
716-652-0930
888-756-7766
FAX: 800-665-3840
e-mail: prep@gmail.com
www.slosson.com

*Steven W. Slosson, President*
*Dr. Georgina Moynihan, Office Personnel*
Slosson Educational Publications, Inc. offers educators an extensive selection of testing products, along with books on autism. ADED and other special needs materials. Our catalog includes 30 pages of speech-language testing and language rehabilitation products. The behavioral conduct. Special needs section includes checklist and scales on aberrant/disruptive behavior, tapes on ADD, as well as products for dyslexia and remediation of reversals.

**2391 Teacher's Guide to Including Students with Disabilities in Regular Physical Education**
Brookes Publishing
P.O.Box 10624
Baltimore, MD 21285
410-337-9580
800-638-3775
FAX: 410-337-8539
e-mail: pkelly@brookespublishing.com
www.brookespublishing.com

*Martin E. Block, Author*
*Melissa A. Behm, Executive Vice President*
*Paul H. Brooks, Chairman of the Board*
*Jeff Brookes, President*
Provides simple and creative strategies for meaningfully including children with disabilities in regular physical education programs. *$39.00*
*288 pages Paperback*
*ISBN 1-557661-56-1*

**2392 Teachers Working Together**
Brookline Books
8 Trumbull Rd
Suite B-001
Northampton, MA 01060
413-584-0184
800-666-2665
FAX: 413-584-6184
e-mail: brbooks@yahoo.com
www.brooklinebooks.com

*Carol Davis, Co-Author*
*Alice Yang, Co-Author*
This collection of papers describes collaboraborative efforts for such classroom settings as preschools, elementary, middle and high schools, for content area teaching and into the transition to work. Each chapter describes actual practice and analyzes what is required to accomplish this collaboration. *$19.95*
*Paperback*
*ISBN 1-57139 -66-4*

**2393 Teaching Adults with Learning Disabilities**
Krieger Publishing Company
1725 Krieger Drive
Malabar, FL 32902
321-724-9542
800-724-0025
FAX: 321-951-3671
e-mail: info@krieger-publishing.com
www.krieger-publishing.com

*Dale R. Jordan, Author*
*R Krieger, Owner*
Designed to teach literacy providers and classroom instructors how to recognize specific learning disability (LD) patterns and block reading, spelling, writing and arithmetic skills in students of all ages. One of the major problems faced by literary providers is keeping low-skill adults involved in basic education programs long enough to increase their literacy skills to the level of success. Shows instructors in adult education how to modify teaching strategies. *$25.50*
*160 pages*
*ISBN 0-894649-10-8*

**2394 Teaching Children With Autism in the General Classroom**
Prufrock Press
PO Box 8813
Waco, TX 76714-8813
254-756-3337
800-998-2208
FAX: 254-756-3339
e-mail: info@prufrock.com
www.prufrock.com

*Joel McIntosh, Publisher & Marketing Director*
*Vicky Spencer PhD, Author*
*Cynthia Simpson PhD, Author*
*Jennifer Robins, Senior Editor and Permissions Coordinator*
Provides an introduction to inclusionary practices that serve children with autism, giving teachers the practical advice they need to ensure each students receives the quality education he or she deserves. *$39.95*
*350 pages Paperback*
*ISBN 1-593633-64-6*

**2395 Teaching Disturbed and Disturbing Students: An Integrative Approach**
Sage Publications
2455 Teller Road
Thousand Oaks, CA 91320
805-499-9774
800-818-7243
FAX: 800-583-2665
e-mail: books.claim@sagepub.com
www.sagepub.com

*Sara Miller McCune, Founder, Publisher, Chairperson*
*Blaise R Simqu, President & CEO*
*Tracey A. Ozmina, Executive Vice President & Chief Operating Officer*
*Paul Zionts, Author*
Using an integrative approach, this text provides teachers with step-by-step details of how to implement and use the methods and theories discussed in each chapter. *$37.00*
*465 pages*

**2396 Teaching Every Child Every Day: Integrated Learning in Diverse Classrooms**
Brookline Books
8 Trumbull Rd
Suite B-001
Northampton, MA 01060
413-584-0184
800-666-2665
FAX: 413-584-6184
e-mail: brbooks@yahoo.com
www.brooklinebooks.com

*Karen R. Harris, Editor*
*Steve Graham, Editor*
*Don Deshler, Editor*
Collection of articles addressing various issues in teaching to diverse classrooms-varied in need for special educational services, English proficiency, and socioeconomic and racial backgrounds. *$19.95*
*224 pages Paperback*
*ISBN 0-57129 -40-0*

**2397 Teaching Infants and Preschoolers with Handicaps**
Mc Graw- Hill, School Publishing
220 E Danieldale Rd
Desoto, TX 75115-2490
972-224-4772
800-442-9685
FAX: 972-228-1982
mcgraw-hill.com

*Harold McGraw III, Chairman, President and Chief Executive Officer*
*Jack F. Callahan, Executive Vice President, Chief Financial Officer*
*Donald B. Bailey, Co-Author*
*Mark Wolery, Co-Author*
Builds a solid background in early childhood special education.
*380 pages*

**2398 Teaching Language-Disabled Children: A Communication/Games Intervention**
Brookline Books
8 Trumbull Rd
Suite B-001
Northampton, MA 01060
413-584-0184
800-666-2665
FAX: 413-584-6184
e-mail: brbooks@yahoo.com
www.brooklinebooks.com

*Susan Conant, Co-Author*
*Milton Budoff, Co-Author*
*Barbara Hecht, Co-Author*
Describes exactly how to play the communication games. It does not simply exhort practitioners to give topic-relevant responses and take advantage of opportunities. It provides specific teaching methods and not simply a new perspective on language remeditation. *$22.95*
*Hardcover*
*ISBN 0-91479 -38-7*

**2399 Teaching Learners with Mild Disabilities: Integrating Research and Practice**
Brooke Publishing
P.O.Box 10624
Baltimore, MD 21285-624
410-337-9580
800-638-3775
FAX: 410-337-8539
e-mail: pkelly@brookespublishing.com
www.brookespublishing.com

*Ruth Lyn Meese, Author*
*Melissa A. Behm, Executive Vice President*
*Paul H. Brooks, Chairman of the Board*
*Jeff Brookes, President*
The authors illustrate interactions among regular teachers, special education teachers and students with mild disabilities through the use of hypothetical case studies of students and teachers.
*496 pages Paperbound*
*ISBN 0-53421 -02-0*

**2400 Teaching Mathematics to Students with Learning Disabilities**
Sage Publications
2455 Teller Road
Thousand Oaks, CA 91320
805-499-9774
800-818-7243
FAX: 800-583-2665
e-mail: books.claim@sagepub.com
www.sagepub.com

*Sara Miller McCune, Founder, Publisher, Chairperson*
*Blaise R Simqu, President & CEO*
*Nancy S. Bley, Co-Author*
*Carol A. Thornton, Co-Author*
New trends in school mathematics have surfaced in the teaching world. Problem-solving, estimation and the use of computers are receiving considerably greater emphasis than in the past and these areas are included in the new text. *$38.00*
*486 pages Paperback*

**2401 Teaching Mildly and Moderately Handicapped Students**
Allyn & Bacon
Ste 300
75 Arlington St
Boston, MA 02116-3988
617-848-7500
800-852-8024
FAX: 617-944-7273
www.ablongman.com

*Bill Barke, CEO*
*Nancy Forfyth, President*
*B. R. Gearheart, Author*
*Kevin Stone, Vice President, National Sales Manager*
A cross-categorical text providing teaching ideas and techniques. Focuses on the theme of learning as a constructive process in which the learner interacts with the environment, constructing new systems of knowledge, Behavioral techniques and research are also presented.
*hardcover*
*ISBN 0-138939-00-4*

**2402 Teaching Reading to Children with Down Syndrome: A Guide for Parents and Teachers**
Woodbine House
6510 Bells Mill Rd
Bethesda, MD 20817-1636
301-897-3570
800-843-7323
FAX: 301-897-5838
www.woodbinehouse.com

*Irvin Shapell, Publisher*
*Patricia Logan Oelwein, Author*
*Beth Binns, Special Marketing Manage*
*Fran Marinaccio, Marketing Manager*
Guide includes lessons customized to meet the unique interests and learning style of each child. *$16.95*
*371 pages Paperback*
*ISBN 0-933149-55-7*

**2403 Teaching Reading to Disabled and Handicapped Learners**
Charles C. Thomas
2600 S 1st St
Springfield, IL 62704-4730
217-789-8980
800-258-8980
FAX: 217-789-9130
e-mail: books@ccthomas.com
ccthomas.com

*Michael P. Thomas, President*
*Freddie W. Litton, Co-Author*
*Harold D. Love, Co-Author*
Designed as a text for undergraduate and graduate students, it's aim is to help the many children, adolescents, and adults who encounter difficulty with reading. It guides prospective and present special education teachers in assisting and teaching handicapped learners to read. The text integrates traditional methods with newer perspectives to provide and effective reading program in special education. *$37.95*
*260 pages Paperback*
*ISBN 0-398062-48-X*

**2404 Teaching Reading to Handicapped Children**
Love Publishing Company
Ste 2200
9101 E Kenyon Ave
Denver, CO 80237-1854
303-221-7333
FAX: 303-221-7444
e-mail: lpc@lovepublishing.com
lovepublishing.com

*Charles H. Hargis, Author*

The author covers skills teaching through letter sound association, word identification, synthetic and analytic methods and others, plus testing and assessment. *$24.95*

*ISBN 0-89108 -13-5*

**2405 Teaching Self-Determination to Students with Disabilities**
Brookes Publishing
P.O.Box 10624
Baltimore, MD 21285-624 410-337-9580
800-638-3775
FAX: 410-337-8539
e-mail: pkelly@brookespublishing.com
www.brookespublishing.com

*Michael L. Wehmeyer, Co-Author*
*Martin Agran, Co-Author*
*Paul H. Brooks, Chairman of the Board*
*Carolyn Hughes, Co-Author*
Basic skills for successful transition. This teacher-friendly source will help educators prepare students with disabilities with the specific skills they need for a satisfactory, self-directed life once they leave school. *$34.95*
*384 pages Paperback*
*ISBN 1-55766 -02-5*

**2406 Teaching Students with Learning Problems**
McGraw-Hill School Publishing
220 E Danieldale Rd
Desoto, TX 75115-2490 972-224-4772
800-442-9685
FAX: 972-228-1982
mcgraw-hill.com

*Harold McGraw III, Chairman, President and Chief Executive Officer*
*Cecil D. Mercer, Co-Author*
*Ann R. Mercer, Co-Author*
*Paige C. Pullen, Co-Author*
Expanded coverage of learning strategies, generalization training, self-monitoring techniques, and techniques for increasing the time students spend on academic tasks.
*608 pages*

**2407 Teaching Students with Learning and Behavior Problems**
Sage Publications
2455 Teller Road
Thousand Oaks, CA 91320 805-499-9774
800-818-7243
FAX: 800-583-2665
e-mail: books.claim@sagepub.com
www.sagepub.com

*Sara Miller McCune, Founder, Publisher, Chairperson*
*Blaise R Simqu, President & CEO*
*Sharon R. Vaughn, Co-Author*
*Candace S. Bos, Co-Author*
*$65.00*
*444 pages Paperback*
*ISBN 0-890799-28-4*

**2408 Teaching Students with Mild and Moderate Learning Problems**
Allyn & Bacon Longman College Faculty
Ste 300
75 Arlington St
Boston, MA 02116-3988 617-367-0025
800-852-8024
FAX: 617-367-2155
www.ablongman.com

*Bill Barke, CEO*
*John Langone, Author*
*Kevin Stone, Vice President, National Sales Manager*
*Kevin Stone, Vice President, National Sales Manager*
Provides teachers with skills for assisting students with mild to moderate handicaps in making successful transitions in school and community environments.
*496 pages*
*ISBN 0-205123-62-7*

**2409 Teaching Students with Moderate/Severe Disabilities, Including Autism**
Charles C. Thomas
2600 S 1st St
Springfield, IL 62704-4730 217-789-8980
800-258-8980
FAX: 217-789-9130
e-mail: books@ccthomas.com
ccthomas.com

*Michael P. Thomas, President*
*Elva Duran, Author*
This resource and guide was written to help teachers, parents, and other caregivers provide the best educational opportunities for their students with moderate and severe disabilities. The author addresses functional language and other language intervention strategies, vocational training, community based instruction, transition and postsecondary programming, the adolescent student with autism, students with multiple disabilities, parent and family issues, and legal concerns. *$58.95*
*416 pages Paperback*
*ISBN 0-398067-01-5*

**2410 Teaching Students with Special Needs in Inclusive Settings**
Allyn & Bacon
Ste 300
75 Arlington St
Boston, MA 02116-3988 617-848-7500
800-852-8024
FAX: 617-944-7273
www.ablongman.com

*Tom E.C. Smith, Co-Author*
*Edward A. Polloway, Co-Author*
*James Patton, Co-Author*
*Carol A. Dowdy, Co-Author*
This text is intended to be a survey text providing practical guidance to general education teachers. It will help them to meet the diverse needs of students with disabilities.
*544 pages*
*ISBN 0-20527 -16-6*

**2411 Teaching Young Children to Read**
Brookline Books
8 Trumbull Rd
Suite B-001
Northampton, MA 01060 413-584-0184
800-666-2665
FAX: 413-584-6184
e-mail: brbooks@yahoo.com
www.brooklinebooks.com

*Dolores Durkin, Author*
*John P.*
Detailed instructions on teaching reading to preschoolers. Gradually develops full fluency. *$16.95*
*192 pages Paperback*
*ISBN 0-57129 -48-6*

**2412 Teaching the Bilingual Special Education Student**
Ablex Publishing Corporation
P.O.Box 811
Stamford, CT 06904-811 FAX: 201-767-6717
This book focuses on teaching those students who are bilingual, handicapped and in need of special instruction. It responds to the complex and practical issues of teaching these students in an effective way.

*ISBN 0-89391 -23-4*

**2413 Teaching the Learning Disabled Adolescent**
Love Publishing Company
9101 E Kenyon Ave
Ste 2200
Denver, CO 80237-1813
303-221-7333
FAX: 303-221-7444
e-mail: lovepublishing@compuserve.com
lovepublishing.com

*Gordon R. Alley, Author*
This book gives expert strategies and methods for teaching learning disabled adolescents how, rather than what, to learn. *$34.95*

*ISBN 0-89108 -94-5*

**2414 Teaching the Mentally Retarded Student: Curriculum, Methods, and Strategies**
Allyn & Bacon
Ste 300
75 Arlington St
Boston, MA 02116-3988
617-367-0025
800-852-8024
FAX: 617-367-2155
www.ablongman.com

*Bill Barke, CEO*
*Richard L. Luftig, Author*
*Nancy Forfyth, President*
*Kevin Stone, Vice President, National Sales Manager*
Represents a comprehensive approach to curriculum, methods and strategies for teaching the mildly mentally retarded student.
*640 pages hardcover*
*ISBN 0-205102-62-X*

**2415 Technology and Handicapped People**
Springer Publishing Company
15th Fl
11 W 42nd St
New York, NY 10036-8002
212-431-4370
877-687-7476
FAX: 212-941-7842
e-mail: cs@springerpub.com
www.springerpub.com

*Dr. Ursula Springer, President*
*Ted Nardin, CEO*
*James C. Costello, Vice President, Journal Publishing*
*Ernest W. Johnson, MD, Author*
Important information for concerned professionals about new rehabilitation techniques and treatments for handicapped people. *$29.95*
*224 pages Hardcover*
*ISBN 0-82614 -10-8*

**2416 Textbooks and the Student Who Can't Read Them: A Guide for Teaching Content**
Brookline Books
8 Trumbull Rd
Suite B-001
Northampton, MA 01060
413-584-0184
800-666-2665
FAX: 413-584-6184
e-mail: brbooks@yahoo.com
www.brooklinebooks.com
Based on a careful analysis of 10 textbook programs, the author concisely and sensibly indicate s the procedures that facilitate teachers' use of regular grade level textbooks with low-reading students. *$21.95*
*Paperback*
*ISBN 0-91479 -57-3*

**2417 The Resource Room**
State University of New York Press
194 Washington Avenue
Suite 305
Albany, NY 12210-2314
518-472-5000
800-666-2211
FAX: 518-472-5038
e-mail: info@sunypress.edu
www.sunypress.edu

*Barry Edwards McNamara, Author*
Provides teachers and administrators with helpful, practical information and explores the role of the resource room teacher as it relates to three major functions: assessment, instruction and consultation. It will also assist supervisors and administrators in evaluating their resource programs. *$28.95*
*148 pages Paperback*
*ISBN 0-887069-84-0*

**2418 There's a Hearing Impaired Child in My Class**
Gallaudet University Bookstore
800 Florida Ave NE
Washington, DC 20002-3600
202-651-5000
800-451-1073
FAX: 202-651-5489
TTY: 888-630-9347
e-mail: clerc.center@gallaudet.edu.
www.bookstore.gallaudette.edu

*Debra Nussbaum, Author*
*Dr. T Alan Hurwitz, President*
*Edward Bosso, Vice President for Administration and Finance*
*Donald Beil, Chief of Staff*
This complete package provides basic facts about deafness, practical strategies for teaching hearing impaired children, and the question-and-answer information for all students. *$16.95*
*44 pages*

**2419 Toward Effective Public School Program for Deaf Students**
Teachers College Press
525 W 120th St
New York, NY 10027-6605
212-678-3000
800-575-6566
FAX: 212-678-4149
e-mail: webcomments@tc.columbia.edu
www.tc.columbia.edu

*Mary Lynch, Manager*
*Thomas N. Kluwin, Co-Author*
*Donald F. Moores, Co-Author*
*Martha G. Gaustad, Editor*
This book translates research and data into useable recommendations and possible courses of action for organizing effective public school programs for deaf students. *$22.95*
*272 pages Paperback*
*ISBN 0-807731-59-5*

**2420 Treating Adults with Disabilities: Access and Communication**
World Institute on Disability
3075 Adeline Street
Suite 280
Berkeley, CA 94703
510-225-6400
FAX: 510-225-0477
TTY:510-225-0478
e-mail: wid@wid.org
www.wid.org

*Bryon MacDonald, Program Director*
*Thomas Foley, Deputy Director/Access to Assets Program Director*
*Marsha Saxton, PhD, Senior Researcher*
*Gabriel Many, Project Coordinator*
This training curriculum is for medical professionals who want to improve the quality of care for people with disabilities and chronic illnesses. Also covers architectural, communication, attitudinal and economic policy barriers to quality health care and

specific skills to increase good communication and rapport. *$6.50*
*63 pages Paperback*

**2421 Treating Cerebral Palsy for Clinicians by Clinicians**
Sage Publications
2455 Teller Road
Thousand Oaks, CA 91320 805-499-9774
800-818-7243
FAX: 800-583-2665
e-mail: books.claim@sagepub.com
www.sagepub.com

*Sara Miller McCune, Founder, Publisher, Chairperson*
*Blaise R Simqu, President & CEO*
*Tracey A. Ozmina, Executive Vice President & Chief Operating Officer*
*Eugene T. McDonald, Editor*
A clinical manual for professionals beginning to work with persons who have cerebral palsy. *$31.00*
*312 pages*

**2422 Treating Disordered Speech Motor Control**
Sage Publications
2455 Teller Road
Thousand Oaks, CA 91320 805-499-9774
800-818-7243
FAX: 800-583-2665
e-mail: books.claim@sagepub.com
www.sagepub.com

*Sara Miller McCune, Founder, Publisher, Chairperson*
*Blaise R Simqu, President & CEO*
*Deanie Vogel, Author*
*Michael Cannito, Editor*
This book about neuromotor disturbances of speech production is aimed at practicing professionals and advanced graduate students interested in the neuropathologies of communication. *$36.00*
*410 pages*

**2423 Treating Families of Brain Injury Survivors**
Springer Publishing Company
15th Fl
11 W 42nd St
New York, NY 10036-8002 212-431-4370
877-687-7476
FAX: 212-941-7842
e-mail: cs@springerpub.com
www.springerpub.com

*Dr. Ursula Springer, President*
*Ted Nardin, CEO*
*James C. Costello, Vice President, Journal Publishing*
*Paul Reid Sachs, Author*
Provides the mental health practitioner with a comprehensive program for helping families of head injury survivors cope with the change in their lives. Includes background on medical aspects of head injury, family structure functioning and special needs of various family members.
*220 pages*
*ISBN 0-82616 -20-1*

**2424 Understanding and Teaching Emotionally Disturbed Children & Adolescents**
Sage Publications
2455 Teller Road
Thousand Oaks, CA 91320 805-499-9774
800-818-7243
FAX: 800-583-2665
e-mail: books.claim@sagepub.com
www.sagepub.com

*Sara Miller McCune, Founder, Publisher, Chairperson*
*Blaise R Simqu, President & CEO*
*Tracey A. Ozmina, Executive Vice President & Chief Operating Officer*
*Phyllis L. Newcomer, Author*
The teacher's handbook provides information that will change misconceptions about children who are frequently labeled as emotionally disturbed. It also gives information about a wide variety of intervention methods and approaches for use in educational settings. *$41.00*
*620 pages Hardover*

**2425 Using the Dictionary of Occupational Titles in Career Decision Making**
Stout Vocational Rehab Institute
University of Wisconsin Stou
Menomonie, WI 54751 715-232-2470
FAX: 715-232-5008
e-mail: luij@uwstout.edu
www.svri.uwstout.edu

*John Lui, Contact Person*
This is a self-study manual for learning how to use the 1991 U.S. Department of Labor's Dictionary of Occupational Titles. It gives the DOT user a tool to understand the DOT and then put its information to work. Shows how to quickly obtain information about the work performed in 12,741 occupations listed and described in the DOT and the worker requirements for those occupations. *$24.00*
*142 pages Softcover*

**2426 VBS Special Education Teaching Guide**
Life Way Christian Resources Southern Baptist Conv
1 Lifeway Plz
Nashville, TN 37234-1001 615-251-2000
e-mail: specialed@lifeway.com
www.lifeway.com

*Tom Hellam, VP of Executive Communications a*
*Thom Rainer, President & CEO*
This book contains teaching plans for five bible study sessions with reproducible handouts for learners. The plans use multisensory, experiential-based learning activities designed for adults and older youth who have mental retardation. Suggestions for Bible learning, crafts, recreation, snacks and theme interpretation are included. Designed primarily for Vacation Bible School, but may be used in camp/retreat settings. *$9.95*
*56 pages Yearly*

**2427 Vermont Interdependent Services Team Approach (VISTA)**
Brookes Publishing
P.O.Box 10624
Baltimore, MD 21285-624 410-337-9580
800-638-3775
FAX: 410-337-8539
e-mail: custserv@brookespublishing.com
www.brookespublishing.com

*Paul Kelly, National Textbook Sales Manager*
*Tracy Gray, Educational Sales Manager*
*Paul Brooks, President*
A guide to coordinating educational support services. This manual enables IEP team members to fulfill the related services provisions of IDEA as they make effective support services decisions using a collaborative team approach. *$27.95*
*176 pages Spiral bound*
*ISBN 1-55766 -30-4*

**2428 When You Have a Visually Impaired Student in Your Classroom: A Guide for Teachers**
American Foundation for the Blind
2 Penn Plaza
Suite1102
New York, NY 10121 212-502-7600
800-232-5463
FAX: 888-545-8331
e-mail: afbinfo@afb.net
afb.org

*Carl Augusto, President*
This guide provides information on students' abilities and needs, resources and educational team members, federal special

education requirements, and technology materials used by students. *$9.95*
*84 pages*
*ISBN 0-891283-93-5*

**2429 Working Bibliography on Behavioral and Emotional Disorders**
Natl. Clearinghouse for Alcohol & Drug Information
1 Choke Cherry Road
Rockville, MD 20857 301-468-2600
877-SAM-SA 7
FAX: 301-468-6433
e-mail: info@health.org
www.health.org

*Lizabeth J Foster, Librarian/Info. Resource Manager*
*Pamela S. Hyde, Administrator*
NCADI is a service of the U.S. Substance Abuse and Mental Health Services Administration. As the national focal point for information on alcohol and other drugs, NCADI collects, prepares, classifies, and distributes information about alcohol, tobacco and other drugs, prevention strategies and materials, research, treatment, etc.
*40 pages*

**2430 Working Together with Children and Families: Case Studies**
Brookes Publishing Company
P.O.Box 10624
Baltimore, MD 21285-624 410-337-9580
800-638-3775
FAX: 410-337-8539
e-mail: custerv@brookespublishing.com
www.brookespublishing.com

*Paul Kelly, National Textbook Sales Manager*
*Tracy Gray, Educational Sales Manager*
*Paul Brooks, Owner*
Early interventionists will be able to bridge the gap between theory and practice with this edited collection of case studies. *$23.00*
*336 pages*
*ISBN 1-557661-23-5*

**2431 Working with Visually Impaired Young Students: A Curriculum Guide for 3 to 5 Year Olds**
Charles C. Thomas
2600 S 1st St
Springfield, IL 62704-4730 217-789-8980
800-258-8980
FAX: 217-789-9130
e-mail: books@ccthomas.com
ccthomas.com

*Michael P. Thomas, President*
*Ellen Trief, Editor*
The first step in the education process of a visually impaired child is the early identification and treatment by an eye care specialist. This book is geared to the age of birth through 3-years. Available in cloth, paperback and hardcover. *$42.95*
*194 pages Paperback*
*ISBN 0-398068-75-2*

## Testing Resources

**2432 AEPS Child Progress Report: For Children Ages Birth to Three**
Brookes Publishing
P.O.Box 10624
Baltimore, MD 21285-624 410-337-9580
800-638-3775
FAX: 410-337-8539
e-mail: custserv@brookespublishing.com
www.brookespublishing.com

*Paul Kelly, National Textbook Sales Manager*
*Tracy Gray, Educational Sales Manager*
*Paul Brooks, Owner*
This chart helps monitor change by visually displaying current abilities, intervention targets, and child progress. In packages of 30. *$18.00*
*6 pages Gate-fold*
*ISBN 1-55766 -65-0*

**2433 AEPS Data Recording Forms: For Children Ages Birth to Three**
Brookes Publishing
P.O.Box 10624
Baltimore, MD 21285-624 410-337-9580
800-638-3775
FAX: 410-337-8539
e-mail: custserv@brookespublishing.com
readplaylearn.com

*Paul Brooks, Owner*
*Melissa Behm, Executive Vice President*
These forms can be used by child development professionals on four separate occasions to pinpoint and then monitor a child's strengths and needs in the six key areas of skill development measured by the AEPS Test. Packages of 10. *$23.00*
*36 pages Saddle-stiched*
*ISBN 1-55766 -97-2*

**2434 AEPS Measurement for Birth to Three Years**
Brookes Publishing
P.O.Box 10624
Baltimore, MD 21285-624 410-337-9580
800-638-3775
FAX: 410-337-8539
e-mail: custserv@brookespublishing.com
www.brookespublishing.com

*Paul Kelly, National Textbook Sales Manager*
*Tracy Gray, Educational Sales Manager*
*Paul Brooks, Owner*
This dynamic volume explains the Assessment, Evaluation and Programming System, provides the complete AEPS Test and parallel assessment/evaluation tools for families and includes the forms and plans needed for implementation. *$39.00*
*352 pages*

**2435 AEPS Measurement for Three to Six Years**
Brookes Publishing
P.O.Box 10624
Baltimore, MD 21285-624 410-337-9580
800-638-3775
FAX: 410-337-8539
e-mail: custserv@brookespublishing.com
www.brookespublishing.com

*Paul Kelly, National Textbook Sales Manager*
*Tracy Gray, Educational Sales Manager*
*Paul Brooks, Owner*
Resources in early childhood, early intervention, inclusive and special education, developmental disabilities, learning disabilities, communication and language, behavior, and mental health. *$57.00*
*400 pages Spiral-bound*
*ISBN 1-55766 -87-1*

**2436 AIR: Assessment of Interpersonal Relations**
Sage Publications
2455 Teller Road
Thousand Oaks, CA 91320 805-499-0721
800-818-7243
FAX: 805-376-9443
e-mail: info@sagepub.com
www.sagepub.com

*Sara Miller McCune, Founder, Publisher, Chairperson*
*Blaise R Simqu, President & CEO*
A thoroughly researched and standardized clinical instrument assessing the quality of adolescents' interpersonal relationships in a hierarchical fashion, including global relationship quality and relationship quality with three domains: Family, Social and Academic. *$89.00*

**2437 ALST: Adolescent Language Screening Test**
Sage Publications
2455 Teller Road
Thousand Oaks, CA 91320 805-499-0721
800-818-7243
FAX: 805-376-9443
e-mail: info@sagepub.com
www.sagepub.com

*Sara Miller McCune, Founder, Publisher, Chairperson*
*Blaise R Simqu, President & CEO*
Provides speech/language pathologists and other interested professionals with a rapid thorough method for screening adolescents (ages 11-17). *$119.00*

**2438 Adaptive Mainstreaming: A Primer for Teachers and Principals, 3rd Edition**
Longman Publishing Group
1330 Avenue of the Americas
New York, NY 10019 212-641-2400
800-745-8489
e-mail: wendy.spiegel@pearsoned.com
www.pearson.com

*Glen Moreno, Chairman*
*Marjorie Scardino, Chief Executive Officer*
An introduction to education for handicapped and gifted students. Presents research-based rationales for teaching exceptional students in the least restrictive environment. Provides historical perspectives, offers realistic descriptions of prevailing practices in the field, and reviews trends and new directions.
*366 pages Paperback*
*ISBN 0-582285-04-6*

**2439 Ages & Stages Questionnaires**
Brookes Publishing
P.O.Box 10624
Baltimore, MD 21285-624 410-337-9580
800-638-3775
FAX: 410-337-8539
e-mail: custserv@brookespublishing.com
www.brookespublishing.com

*Paul Kelly, National Textbook Sales Manager*
*Tracy Gray, Educational Sales Manager*
*Paul Brooks, Owner*
ASQ is an economical and field-tested system for identifying whether infants and young children may require further developmental evaluation and offers a screening and tracking program that helps early intervention professionals, service coordinators, and administrators maximize financial resources while promoting the health and growth of the children they serve. Set includes 11 color-coded, reproducible questionnaires, 11 reproducible, age appropriate scoring sheets. *$135.00*

**2440 American College Testing Program**
500 Act Drive
PO Box 168
Iowa City, IA 52243-168 319-337-1000
FAX: 319-339-3021
act.org

*John Whitmore, CEO*
*Mark D Musik, President Emeritus*
An independent, nonprofit organization that provides a variety of educational services to students and their parents, to high schools and colleges, and to professional associations and government agencies.

**2441 Assessing Students with Special Needs**
Longman Publishing Group
10 Bank Street
9th Floor
White Plains, NY 10606-1933 914-993-5000
www.ablongman.com

*Joanne Dresner, President*
Step-by-step guide to informal, classroom assessment of students with special needs.
*174 pages Paperback*
*ISBN 0-801301-77-7*

**2442 Assessment Log & Developmental Progress Charts for the CCPSN**
Brookes Publishing
P.O.Box 10624
Baltimore, MD 21285-624 410-337-9580
800-638-3775
FAX: 410-337-8539
e-mail: custserv@brookespublishing.com
www.brookespublishing.com

*Paul Kelly, National Textbook Sales Manager*
*Tracy Gray, Educational Sales Manager*
*Paul Brooks, Owner*
This 28-page booklet allows readers to actually chart the ongoing progress of each preschool child. Available in packages of 10. *$22.00*
*28 pages Saddle-stiched*
*ISBN 1-55766 -39-5*

**2443 Assessment of Learners with Special Needs**
Allyn & Bacon
75 Arlinton Street
Ste 300
Boston, MA 2116-3988 617-848-7500
800-852-8024
FAX: 617-944-7273
www.ablongman.com

*Bill Barke, CEO*
*Thomas Longman, Founder*
The central goal of this book is to help teachers become sophisticated, informed test consumers in terms of choosing, using and interpreting commercially prepared tests for their special needs students.
*508 pages Casebound*
*ISBN 0-205227-33-3*

**2444 Benchmark Measures**
Educators Publishing Service
PO Box 9031
Cambridge, MA 2139 617-547-6706
800-225-5750
FAX: 888-440-2665
e-mail: feedback@epsbooks.com
www.epsbooks.com

*Charles H Heinle, VP*
*Alexandra S Bigelow, Author*
*Gunnar Voltz, President*

Ungraded test containing three sequential levels that assess alphabet and dictionary skills, reading, handwriting and spelling, and correspond to the first three schedules of the Alphabetic Phonics curriculum. The tests can be used at any level to measure a student's general knowledge of phonics. *$64.40*
*Kit*

**2445 CREVT: Comprehensive Receptive and Expressive Vocabulary Test**
Sage Publications
2455 Teller Road
Thousand Oaks, CA 91320
805-499-0721
800-818-7243
FAX: 805-376-9443
e-mail: info@sagepub.com
www.sagepub.com

*Sara Miller McCune, Founder, Publisher, Chairperson*
*Blaise R Simqu, President & CEO*
A new, innovative, efficient measure of both receptive and expressive oral vocabulary. The CREVT has two subtests and is based on the most current theories of vocabulary development, suitable for ages 4 through 17. *$174.00*
*Complete Kit*

**2446 Carolina Curriculum for Preschoolers with Special Needs**
Brookes Publishing
P.O.Box 10624
Baltimore, MD 21285-624
410-337-9580
800-638-3775
FAX: 410-337-8539
e-mail: custserv@brookespublishing.com
www.brookespublishing.com

*Paul Kelly, National Textbook Sales Manager*
*Tracy Gray, Educational Sales Manager*
*Paul Brooks, Owner*
This curriculum provides detailed teaching and assessment techniques, plus a sample 28-page Assessment Log that shows readers how to chart a child's individual progress. This guide is for children between 2 and 5 in their developmental stages who are considered at risk for developmental delay or who exhibit special needs. *$35.95*
*352 pages Spiral-bound*
*ISBN 1-557660-32-8*

**2447 DAYS: Depression and Anxiety in Youth Scale**
Sage Publications
2455 Teller Road
Thousand Oaks, CA 91320
805-499-0721
800-818-7243
FAX: 805-376-9443
e-mail: info@sagepub.com
www.sagepub.com

*Sara Miller McCune, Founder, Publisher, Chairperson*
*Blaise R Simqu, President & CEO*
A unique battery of three norm-references scales useful in identifying major depressive disorder and overanxious disorders in children and adolescents. *$129.00*
*Complete Kit*

**2448 DOCS: Developmental Observation Checklist System**
Pro- Ed Publications
8700 Shoal Creek Blvd
Austin, TX 78757-6897
512-451-3246
800-897-3202
FAX: 800-397-7633
e-mail: general@proedinc.com
www.proedinc.com

*Donald D Hammill, Owner*
*Courtney King, Marketing Coordinator*
A three-part system for the assessment of very young children with respect to general development, adjustment behavior and parent stress and support. *$124.00*

**2449 Developmental Services Center**
Therapeutic Nursery Program
4525 Lee St NE
Washington, DC 20019
202-388-3216
FAX: 202-576-8799

*Alice Anderson*
Offers assessment information and evaluation for developmentally delayed students.

**2450 Frames of Reference for the Assessment of Learning Disabilities**
Brookes Publishing
P.O.Box 10624
Baltimore, MD 21285-624
410-337-9580
800-638-3775
FAX: 410-337-8539
e-mail: custserv@brookespublishing.com
www.brookespublishing.com

*Paul Kelly, National Textbook Sales Manager*
*Tracy Gray, Educational Sales Manager*
*Paul Brooks, Owner*
New views on measurement issues. Here you'll find an in=depth look at the fundamental concerns facing those who work with children with learning disabilities - assessment and identification. *$55.00*
*672 pages Hardcover*
*ISBN 1-55766 -38-3*

**2451 How to Conduct an Assessment**
FSSI
3905 Huntington Dr
Amarillo, TX 79109-4047
806-353-1114
FAX: 806-353-1114
e-mail: info@winfssi.com
www.winfssi.com

*Ed Hammer, Owner*
The Functional Skills Screening Inventory,this behavioral checklist allows for parents and professionals to observe critical behaviors in individuals with multiple disabilities (7 years to adult years).

**2452 Inclusive & Heterogeneous Schooling: Assessment, Curriculum, and Instruction**
Brookes Publishing
P.O.Box 10624
Baltimore, MD 21285-624
410-337-9580
800-638-3775
FAX: 410-337-8539
e-mail: custserv@brookespublishing.com
www.brookespublishing.com

*Paul Kelly, National Textbook Sales Manager*
*Tracy Gray, Educational Sales Manager*
*Paul Brooks, Owner*
Presents methods for successfully restructuring classrooms to enable all students, particularly those with disabilities, to flourish. Provides specific strategies for assessment, collaboration, classroom management, and age-specific instruction. *$34.95*
*448 pages Paperback*
*ISBN 1-557662-02-9*

**2453 Infant & Toddler Convection of Fairfield: Falls Church**
Joseph Willard Health Center
3750 Old Lee Hwy
Fairfax, VA 22030-1806
703-246-7180
FAX: 703-246-7307

*Susan Sigler, Program Coordinator*
*Allan Phillips, Director Early Intervention*
Offers assessments, evaluations and educational/therapeutic infant programs for parents infants and toddlers birth to age 3.
*Sliding Scale*

**2454 K-BIT: Kaufman Brief Intelligence Test**
AGS
Ste 1000
5910 Rice Creek Pkwy
Shoreview, MN 55126-5023
651-287-7220
800-328-2560
FAX: 800-471-8457
e-mail: agsmail@agsnet.com
www.agsnet.com

*Kevin Brueggeman, President*
*Robert Zaske, Market Manager*
Quick and easy-to-use, KBIT assesses verbal and non-verbal abilities through two reliable subtests - vocabulary and matricies.
*$ 124.95*
*Ages 4-90*

**2455 K-FAST: Kaufman Functional Academic Skills Test**
AGS
Ste 1000
5910 Rice Creek Pkwy
Shoreview, MN 55126-5023
651-287-7220
800-328-2560
FAX: 800-471-8457
e-mail: agsmail@agsnet.com
www.agsnet.com

*Robert Zaske, Market Manager*
Helps assess a person's capacity to function effectively in society regarding functional reading and math skills. *$99.95*
*Ages 15-85+*

**2456 K-SEALS: Kaufman Survey of Early Academic and Language Skills**
AGS
5910 Rice Creek Pkwy
Shoreview, MN 55126-5025
651-287-7220
800-328-2560
FAX: 800-471-8457
e-mail: agsmail@agsnet.com
www.agsnet.com

*Kevin Brueggeman, President*
*Robert Zaske, Market Manager*
An individually administered test of children's of both expressive and receptive skills, pre-academic skills and articulation. K-SEALS offers reliable scores usually in less than 25 minutes. *$ 179.95*
*Ages 3-0; 6-11*

**2457 KLST-2: Kindergarten Language Screening Test Edition, 2nd Edition**
Sage Publications
2455 Teller Road
Thousand Oaks, CA 91320
805-499-9774
800-818-7243
FAX: 800-583-2665
e-mail: info@sagepub.com
www.sagepub.com

*Paul Kelly, National Textbook Sales Manager*
*Blaise R Simqu, President & CEO*
Identifies children who need further diagnostic testing to determine whether or not they have language deficits that will accelerate academic failure. *$94.00*

**2458 Kaufman Test of Educational Achievement(K-TEA)**
AGS
P.O.Box 99
Circle Pines, MN 55014-99
800-328-2560
FAX: 800-471-8457
e-mail: agsmail@agsnet.com
www.agsnet.com

*Robert Zaske, Marketing Manager*
*Kevin Brueggeman, President*
K-TEA is an individually administered diagnostic battery that measures reading, mathematics, and spelling skills. Setting the standards in achievement testing today, K-TEA Comprehensive provides the complete diagnostic information you need for educational assessment and program planning. The Brief Forum is indispensable for school and clinical psychologists, special education teachers when a quick a measure of achievement is needed.
*$249.95*

**2459 Life Centered Career Education: A Contemporary Based Approach, 4th Edition**
Council for Exceptional Children
2900 Crystal Drive
Suite1000
Arlington, VA 22202-3557
703-264-9454
888-232-7733
FAX: 703-264-1637
e-mail: president@cec.sped.org
www.cec.sped.org

*Marilyn Friend, President*
Provides a framework for building 97 functional skill competencies appropriate for preparing for adult life and special education students. *$28.00*
*175 pages*

**2460 Measure of Cognitive-Linguistic Abilities(MCLA)**
Speech Bin
PO Box 1579
Appleton, VA 54912-1579
772-770-0007
888-388-3224
FAX: 888-388-6344
e-mail: customercare@schoolspecialty.com
www.speechbin.com

*Jan J Binney, Senior Editor*
A diagnostic test of cognitive-linguistic abilities of adolescents and adults with traumatically induced brain injuries. High level. Normed. *$89.00*
*100 pages*
*ISBN 0-93785-72-*

**2461 ONLINE**
West Virginia Research and Training Center
P.O.Box 1004
Institute, WV 25112-1004
304-766-9495
800-624-8284
FAX: 304-766-2689
e-mail: info@icdi.wvu.edu
www.icdi.wvu.edu

*Clifford Lantz, President*
A quarterly newsletter offering information about hardware technology, software (commercial and home grown); applications that work and bonuses such as an exchange program for copyright-free software. *$25.00*
*Quarterly*

**2462 OWLS: Oral and Written Language Scales LC/OE & WE**
AGS
P.O.Box 99
Circle Pines, MN 55014-99
800-328-2560
FAX: 800-471-8457
e-mail: agsmail@agsnet.com
www.agsnet.com

*Kevin Brueggeman, President*
*Robert Zaske, Market Manager*
One kit provides an assessment of listening comprehension while the other assesses oral expression tasks: semantic, syntactic, pragmatic, and supralinguistic aspects of language. Written Expression may be administered individually or in small groups.
*$249.95*

**2463 PAT-3: Photo Articulation Test**
Sage Publications
2455 Teller Road
Thousand Oaks, CA 91320
805-499-9774
800-818-7243
FAX: 800-583-2665
e-mail: info@sagepub.com
www.sagepub.com

*Paul Kelly, National Textbook Sales Manager*
*Blaise R Simqu, President & CEO*
This test consists of 72 color photographs. The first 69 photos test consonants and all but one vowel and one diphthong. The remaining pictures test connected speech and the remaining vowel and diphthong. *$144.00*
*Complete Kit*

**2464 Peabody Early Experiences Kit (PEEK)**
AGS
P.O.Box 99
Circle Pines, MN 55014-99
800-328-2560
FAX: 800-471-8457
e-mail: agsmail@agsnet.com
www.agsnet.com

*Kevin Brueggeman, President*
*Robert Zaske, Market Manager*
1,000 activities and all the materials you need to build youngsters' cognitive, social and language skills. Manuals, puppets, manipulatives, picture card deck, picture mini decks and more to teach early development concepts. *$789.95*

**2465 Peabody Individual Achievement Test-Revised Normative Update (PIAT-R-NU)**
AGS
P.O.Box 99
Circle Pines, MN 55014-99
800-328-2560
FAX: 800-471-8457
e-mail: agsmail@agsnet.com
www.agsnet.com

*Kevin Brueggeman, President*
*Robert Zaske, Market Manager*
PIAT-R-NU is an efficient individual measure of academic achievement. Reading, mathematics, and spelling are assessed in a simple, non-threatening format that requires only a pointing response for most items. This multiple choice format makes the PIAT-R ideal for assessing individuals who hesitate to give a spoken response, or have limited expressive abilities. *$289.98*

**2466 Peabody Language Development Kits (PLDK)**
AGS
P.O.Box 99
Circle Pines, MN 55014-99
800-328-2560
FAX: 800-471-8457
e-mail: agsmail@agsnet.com
www.agsnet.com

*Kevin Brueggeman, President*
*Robert Zaske, Market Manager*
The main goals of the Peabody Kit language program are to stimulate overall language skills in Standard English and, for each level of the program, advance children's cognitive skills about a year. *$ 649.95*
*Level P*
*ISBN 0-88671 -25-1*

**2467 Pediatric Early Elementary (PEEX II) Examination**
Educators Publishing Service
625 Mount Auburn Street
3rd Floor
Cambridge, MA 2138- 3039
617-547-6706
800-225-5750
FAX: 888-440-2665
e-mail: feedback@epsbooks.com
www.epsbooks.com

*Charles H Heinle, VP*
*Alexandra S Bigelow, Author*
*Gunnar Voltz, President*
Assesses the second-fourth grade child's performance on thirty-two tasks in six specific areas of development: fine-motor function, language, gross-motor function, memory, visual processing, and delayed recall. At three points during the exam, the child is rated on selective attention and behavior and effect.
*$15.40 - $93*
*ISBN 0-83888 -80-6*

**2468 Pediatric Exam of Educational-PEERAMID Readiness at Middle Childhood**
Educators Publishing Service
625 Mount Auburn Street
3rd Floor
Cambridge, MA 2138- 3039
617-547-6706
800-225-5750
FAX: 888-440-2665
e-mail: feedback@epsbooks.com
www.epsbooks.com

*Charles H Heinle, VP*
*Alexandra S Bigelow, Author*
*Gunnar Voltz, President*
Assesses the 4th-10th grade child's performance on thirty-one tasks in six specific areas: minor neurological indicators, fine-motor function, language, gross-motor function, temporal-sequential organization, and visual processing. Complete set.
*$15.40 - $109*
*ISBN 0-83888 -99-3*

**2469 Pediatric Examination of Educational Readiness**
Educators Publishing Service
625 Mount Auburn Street
3rd Floor
Cambridge, MA 2139- 3039
617-547-6706
800-225-5750
FAX: 888-440-2665
e-mail: feedback@epsbooks.com
www.epsbooks.com

*Charles H Heinle, VP*
*Alexandra S Bigelow, Author*
*Gunnar Voltz, President*
Assesses the Pre-1st grade child's performance on twenty-nine tasks in six specific areas of development: orientation, gross-motor, visual-fine motor, sequential, linguistic and preacademic learning. The child is rated on ten dimensions of selective attention/activity processing efficiency and adaptation. Complete set.
*$12.85 - $86.40*
*ISBN 0-83888 -80-1*

**2470 Pediatric Extended Examination at-PEET Three**
Educators Publishing Service
625 Mount Auburn Street
3rd Floor
Cambridge, MA 2138- 3039
617-547-6706
800-225-5750
FAX: 888-440-2665
e-mail: feedback@epsbooks.com
www.epsbooks.com

*Charles H Heinle, VP*
*Alexandra S Bigelow, Author*
*Gunnar Volta, President*
Assesses the preschool-age child's performance on twenty-eight tasks in five basic areas of development: gross-motor, language,

visual-fine motor, memory, and intersensory integration. Complete set.
*$13.75 - $126*
*ISBN 0-83888 -79-4*

**2471 Pre-Reading Screening Procedures**
Educators Publishing Service
625 Mount Auburn Street
3rd Floor
Cambridge, MA 2138- 3039
617-547-6706
800-225-5750
FAX: 888-440-2665
e-mail: feedback@epsbooks.com
www.epsbooks.com

*Charles H Heinle, VP*
*Alexandra S Bigelow, Author*
*Gunnar Voltz, President*

This revised group test, for grades K-1, evaluates auditory, visual and kinesthetic strengths in order to identify children who may have some form of dyslexia or specific language disability. *$ 18.00*
*Grades K-1*
*ISBN 0-83885 -23-4*

**2472 Preparing for ACT Assessment**
American College Testing Program
500 Act Drive
PO Box 168
Iowa City, IA 52243-168
319-337-1000
FAX: 319-339-3021
act.org

*Richard L Ferguson, CEO*

Designed to help high school students ready themselves for the ACT Assessment's subject area tests, explains the purposes of the four tests, describes their content and format, provides tips and exercises to improve student's test-taking skills and includes a complete sample text with scoring key.

**2473 Psycho-Educational Assessment of Preschool Children**
National Association of School Psychologists
Ste 402
4340 East West Hwy
Bethesda, MD 20814-4468
301-657-0270
866-331-NASP
FAX: 301-657-0275
soelin.com

*Susan Gorin, Executive Director*

This is a contributed text on assessing specific skills of preschool children.
*592 pages*

**2474 RULES: Revised**
Speech Bin
PO Box 1579
Appleton, VA 54912-1579
772-770-0007
888-388-3224
FAX: 888-388-6344
e-mail: customercare@schoolspecialty.com
www.speechbin.com

*Jan J Binney, Senior Editor*

Treatment program for young children who have phonological disorders. *$43.95*
*280 pages*
*ISBN 0-93785 -51-3*

**2475 Receptive-Expressive Emergent-REEL-2 Language Test, 2nd Edition**
Sage Publications
2455 Teller Road
Thousand Oaks, CA 91320
805-499-9774
800-818-7243
FAX: 800-583-2665
e-mail: info@sagepub.com
www.sagepub.com

*Paul Kelly, National Textbook Sales Manager*
*Blaise R Simqu, President & CEO*

A revision of the popular scale used for the multidimensional analysis of emergent language. The REEL-2 is specifically designed for use with a broad range of at risk infants and toddlers in the new multidisciplinary programs developing under P.L. 99-457. *$79.00*

**2476 Slingerland Screening Tests**
Educators Publishing Service
625 Mount Auburn Street
3rd Floor
Cambridge, MA 2138- 3039
617-547-6706
800-435-7728
FAX: 888-440-2665
e-mail: feedback@epsbooks.com
www.epsbooks.com

*Charles H Heinle, VP*
*Alexandra S Bigelow, Author*
*Gunnar Voltz, President*

These tests, by Beth Slingerland, for individuals or groups of children, grades 1-6, identify children who show indications of having specific language disability in reading, handwriting, spelling or speaking. Form D evaluates personal orientation in time and space as well as the ability to express ideas in writing.
*$14.80 - $27.45*
*ISBN 0-83882 -02-2*

**2477 Special Needs Advocacy Resource Book**
Prufrock Press
PO Box 8813
Waco, TX 76714-8813
800-998-2208
FAX: 800-240-0333
e-mail: info@prufrock.com
www.prufrock.com

*Joel McIntosh, Publisher & Marketing Director*
*Rich Weinfield, Author*
*Michelle Davis, Author*

Subtitle: What You Can Do Now to Advocate for Your Exceptional Child's Education. This is a unique hadnbook that teaches parents how to work with schools to achieve optimal learning situations and accommodations for their child's needs. *$19.95*
*328 pages*
*ISBN 1-593633-09-7*

**2478 Speech Bin**
PO Box 1579
Appleton, VA 54912-1579
772-770-0007
888-388-3224
FAX: 888-388-6344
e-mail: customercare@schoolspecialty.com
www.speechbin.com

*Jan J Binney, Senior Editor*

Catalog offering test materials, assessment information, books and special education resources for speech-language pathologists, occupational and physical therapists, audiologists, and other rehabilitation professionals in schools, hospitals, clinics and private practices.

*ISSN 4773-324*

**2479 Stuttering Severity Instrument for Children and Adults**
Psychological & Educational Publications
P.O.Box 520
Hydesville, CA 95547-520 707-768-1807
800-523-5775
FAX: 800-447-0907
e-mail: psych-edpublications@cox.net
www.psych-edpublications.com

*Morrison Gardner, President*
With this tool teachers can determine whether to schedule a child for therapy or to evaluate the effects of treatment.

**2480 Taking Part: Introducing Social Skills to Young Children**
AGS
P.O.Box 99
Circle Pines, MN 55014-99 800-328-2560
FAX: 800-471-8457
e-mail: agsmail@agsnet.com
www.agsnet.com

*Kevin Brueggeman, President*
*Robert Zaske, Market Manager*
The first social skills curriculum to be linked directly to an assessment tool. More than 30 lessons correlate with the skills assessed by the Social Skills Rating System, a multirater approach to assessing prosocial and problem behaviors. *$149.95*

**2481 Test Critiques: Volumes I-X**
Sage Publications
2455 Teller Road
Thousand Oaks, CA 91320 805-499-9774
800-818-7243
FAX: 800-583-2665
e-mail: info@sagepub.com
www.sagepub.com

*Paul Kelly, National Textbook Sales Manager*
*Blaise R Simqu, President & CEO*
Provides the professional and nonprofessional with in-depth, evaluative studies of more than 800 of the most widely used of these assessment instruments. *$649.00*

**2482 Test of Early Reading Ability Deaf or Hard of Hearing**
Pro- Ed Publications
8700 Shoal Creek Blvd
Austin, TX 78757-6816 512-451-3246
800-897-3202
FAX: 800-397-7633
e-mail: general@proedinc.com
www.proedinc.com

*Donald D Hammill, Owner*
*Courtney King, Marketing Coordinator*
This adaptation of the TERA-2 for simultaneous communication of American Sign Language is the ONLY individually administered test of reading designed for children with moderate to profound sensory hearing loss. *$169.00*
*Complete Kit*

**2483 Test of Language Development: Primary**
Sage Publications
2455 Teller Road
Thousand Oaks, CA 91320 805-499-9774
800-818-7243
FAX: 800-583-2665
e-mail: info@sagepub.com
www.sagepub.com

*Paul Kelly, National Textbook Sales Manager*
*Blaise R Simqu, President & CEO*
TOLD P:2 and TOLD 1:2 are the most popular tests of spoken language used by clinicians today. They are used to identify children who have language disorders and to isolate the particular types of disorders they have. Primary Edition for ages 1-4 to 8-11: Intermediate Edition for ages 8-6 to 12-11.

**2484 Test of Mathematical Abilities, 2nd Edition**
Sage Publications
2455 Teller Road
Thousand Oaks, CA 91320 805-499-9774
800-818-7243
FAX: 800-583-2665
e-mail: info@sagepub.com
www.sagepub.com

*Paul Kelly, National Textbook Sales Manager*
*Blaise R Simqu, President & CEO*
The latest version was developed for use in grades 3 through 12. It measures math performance on the two traditional major skill areas in math as well as attitude, vocabulary and general application of math concepts in real life. *$84.00*

**2485 Test of Nonverbal Intelligence, 3rd Edition**
Sage Publications
2455 Teller Road
Thousand Oaks, CA 91320 805-499-9774
800-818-7243
FAX: 800-583-2665
e-mail: info@sagepub.com
www.sagepub.com

*Paul Kelly, National Textbook Sales Manager*
*Blaise R Simqu, President & CEO*
A language-free measure of intelligence, aptitude and reasoning. The administration of the test requires no reading, writing, speaking or listening on the part of the test subject. The items included in this test are problem-solving tasks that increase in difficulty. Each item presents a set of figures in which one or more components is missing. The test items include one or more of the characteristics of shape, position, direction, rotation, contiguity, shading, size, movement or pattern. *$229.00*
*Complete Kit*

**2486 Test of Phonological Awareness**
Sage Publications
2455 Teller Road
Thousand Oaks, CA 91320 805-499-9774
800-818-7243
FAX: 800-583-2665
e-mail: info@sagepub.com
www.sagepub.com

*Paul Kelly, National Textbook Sales Manager*
*Blaise R Simqu, President & CEO*
Measures young children's awareness of the individual sounds in words. Children who are sensitive to the phonological structure of words in oral language have a much easier time learning to read than children who are not. *$143.00*

**2487 Test of Written Spelling, 3rd Edition**
Pro- Ed Publications
8700 Shoal Creek Blvd
Austin, TX 78757-6897 512-451-3246
800-897-3202
FAX: 800-397-7633
e-mail: general@proedinc.com
www.proedinc.com

*Donald D Hammill, Owner*
*Courtney King, Marketing Coordinator*
This revised edition assesses the student's ability to spell words whose spellings are readily predictable in sound-letter patterns, words whose spellings are less predictable and both types of words considered together. *$74.00*

**2488 The Teaching of Reading: A Continuum from Kindergarten through College**
AVKO Educational Research Foundation
3084 Willard Rd
Birch Run, MI 48415-9404
810-686-9283
866-285-6612
FAX: 810-686-1101
e-mail: webmaster@avko.org
avko.org

*Don Mc Cabe, Executive Director*
A textbook for teaching teachers how to teach language arts with lessons about dyslexia, phonics, learning to write, the connection between reading and spelling, and diagnostic and prescriptive tests. Free as an e-book for Foundation members. *$49.95*
*364 pages*

**2489 Treatment and Learning Centers**
2092 Gaither Road
Suite 100
Rockville, MD 20850
301-424-5200
FAX: 301-424-8063
TTY:301-424-5203
e-mail: info@ttlc.org
www.ttlc.org

*Dr Lisa Lenhart, Tutoring/Testing Services Dir*
Diagnostic evaluations are provided on an individual basis to identify the learning differences and needs of students who may have learning disabilities, or who are struggling with the academic environment.

**2490 Woodcock Reading Mastery Tests**
Pearson
5601 Green Valley Dr
Bloomington, MN 55437-1099
800-627-7271
FAX: 800-232-1223
e-mail: pearsonassessments@pearson.com
www.pearsonassessments.com

*Christine Carlson, Product Manager*
*Doug Kubach, President & CEO*
The Woodcock Reading Mastery Tests - Revised provides an interpretive system and age range to help you assess reading skills of children and adults. Two forms, G and II, make it easy to test and retest, or you can combine the results of both forms for a more comprehensive assessment. Revised with recent updates. *$329.95*

**2491 Young Children with Special Needs: A Developmentally Appropriate Approach**
Allyn & Bacon
75 Arlington Street
Ste 300
Boston, MA 2116-3988
617-848-7500
800-852-8024
FAX: 617-944-7273
www.ablongman.com

*Bill Barke, CEO*
*Thomas Longman, Founder*
This book is designed to prepare students in making curriculum decisions in order to care for and foster the development of young children with special needs in normal early childhood settings.
*270 pages*
*ISBN 0-20518 -94-X*

## Treatment & Training

**2492 ABLE Program MCC-Longview**
500 SW Longview Rd
Lees Summit, MO 64081-2105
816-604-2366
FAX: 816-672-2719
e-mail: joan.bergstrom@mcckc.edu
mcckc.edu/ABLE

*Joan Bergstrom, Director*
*Kay Owens, Administrative Assistant*
Intensive support services program for post secondary students with neurological disabilities. The ABLE Program can be reached at http://mcckc.edu/ABLE

**2493 Academy for Guided Imagery**
30765 Pacific Coast Hwy
Ste 355
Malibu, CA 90265-3643
800-726-2070
FAX: 800-727-2070
e-mail: info@acadgi.com
www.acadgi.com

*David E Bresler, President*
The Academy aims to teach people to access and use the power of the mind/body connection for healing, and to further understanding of the imagery process in human life and development. They provide systematic training and guidance to health professionals who are interested in the use of Guided Imagery in their practice. The Academy's Imagery Store offers guided imagery CDs, DVDs and books for self-healing.

**2494 Asthma & Allergy Education for Worksite Clinicians**
Asthma and Allergy Foundation of America
8201 Corporate Drive
Suite 1000
Landover, VA 20785
202-466-7643
800-727-8462
FAX: 202-466-8940
e-mail: info@aafa.org
aafa.org

*Bill Mc Lin, President & CEO*
*Helen Taylor, Information Specialist*
Developed to teach health professionals in the worksite about asthma and allergies and ultimately improve the health of the employees who have theses de\iseases. The program gives worksite clinicians the knowledge and tools they need to give employees guidance on how to control environmental factors both in the home and in the workplace, self-manage thier asthma and/or allergies and to determaine if ti is necessary for employees to see an allergist if symptoms persist.

**2495 Asthma & Allergy Essentials for Children's Care Provider**
Asthma and Allergy Foundation of America
8201 Corporate Drive
Suite 1000
Landover, VA 20785
202-466-7643
800-727-8462
FAX: 202-466-8940
e-mail: info@aafa.org
aafa.org

*Bill Mc Lin, President & CEO*
*Helen Taylor, Information Specialist*
Course gives child care providers the tools and knowledge they need to care for children with asthma and allergies. During the interactive, three hour program, a trained health professional teaches providers how to recognize the signs and symptoms of an asthma or allergy episode, how to institute environmental control measures to prevent these episodes, and how to properly use medication and the tools for asthma management. In areas of the country serviced by AAFA's 14 chapters.

**2496 Asthma Care Training for Kids (ACT)**
Asthma and Allergy Foundation of America
8201 Corporate Drive
Suite 1000
Landover, VA 20785
202-466-7643
FAX: 202-466-8940
e-mail: info@aafa.org
www.aafa.org

*Bill Mc Lin, President & CEO*
*Helen Taylor, Information Specialist*
Interactive program for children ages seven to 12 and their families. Children and their families attend three group sessions seperately to learn their own unique styles and then come together at the end of each session to share their knowledge.

**2497 Ayurvedic Institute**
PO Box 23445
Albuquerque, NM 87292-1445
505-291-9698
800-863-7721
FAX: 505-294-7572
e-mail: registrar@ayurveds.com
ayurveda.com

*Wynn Werner, Administrator*
Directed by Dr. Vasant Lad, trains people in Ayurveda.

**2498 Harriet & Robert Heilbrunn Guild School**
JGB Audio Library for the Blind
15 W 65th St
New York, NY 10023-6601
212-769-6200
800-284-4422
FAX: 212-769-6266
e-mail: info@JGB.org
www.JGB.org

*Allen R Morse, JD, PhD, President & CEO*
*Ken Stanley, Manager*
A Jewish Guild for the blind.

**2499 Lake Michigan Academy**
West Michigan Learning Disabilities Foundation
2428 Burton St SE
Grand Rapids, MI 49546-4806
616-464-3330
FAX: 616-285-1935
e-mail: info@wmldf.org
www.wmldf.org

*Amy Barto, Executive Director*
Is a private day school for children with learning disabilities.

**2500 Mad Hatters: Theatre That Makes a World of Difference**
P.O.Box 50002
Kalamazoo, MI 49005-2
FAX: 269-385-5868

*Bobbe A Luce, Executive Director*
A nationally-known theater which has presented effective and innovative programs to more than 175,000 people in over 1,150 performances in the past 15 years. Our presentations and training programs are a proven method of changing attitudes and behaviors. The Mad Hatters is a leader in the field of sensitivity training to build community and foster the inclusion of all people in society. Fees: $500-$4000 per program, depending on topic and audience.

**2501 Ramapo Training**
Ramapo for Children
Route 52/Salisbury Turnpike
P.O. Box 266
Rhinebeck, NY 12572
845-876-8403
FAX: 845-876-8414
e-mail: office@ramapoforchildren.org
www.ramapoforchildren.org

*Adam Weiss, Chief Executive Officer*
*Bruce Kuziola, Chief Financial and Administrative Officer*
*Mike Kunin, Executive Director*
*Scott Kemp, Director of Operations*
Ramapo Training was established to provide staff training and program support for educational and recreational programs, especially those that serve children-at-risk and those with special needs.

**2502 Sandhills School**
1500 Hallbrook Dr
Columbia, SC 29209-4021
803-695-1400
FAX: 803-695-1214
e-mail: info@sandhillsschool.org
sandhillsschool.org

*Anne Vickers, Head of School*
*Erika Senneseth, Asst Head of School*
*Angela Daniel, Development Officer*
*Carmen Kennedy, Business Manager*
Exists to provide educational programs and intellectual development for average to above average students, six to 15, who learn differently and to promote the development of self-awareness, joy in learning and a vision of themselves as life-long learners.

**2503 Senior Program for Teens and Young Adults with Special Needs**
Camp J CC
6125 Montrose Rd
Rockville, MD 20852-4860
301-881-0100
FAX: 301-881-6549
e-mail: jcccamp@jccgw.org
www.jccgw.org

*Scott Cohen, President*
*Mindy Burger, Vice President for Development*
The senior Program is a transitional program for teens and young adults with mental retardation, severe learning disabilities and multiple disabilities. Socialization, recreation and independent living skills are enhanced ina fun enviroment. Activities include art, music, recreational swim and more.

**2504 The Howard School**
1192 Foster St NW
Atlanta, GA 30318-4329
404-377-7436
FAX: 404-377-0884
e-mail: admissions@howardschool.org
howardschool.org

*Marifred Cilella, Head Of School*
The Howard School educates students 5 years old through 12th grade with language learning disabilities and learning differences. Small student/teacher ratios allow for instruction that is personalized to complement the individual learning styles and to help each student understand his/her learning process. Students gain the tools and strategies needed to become independent, life-long learners.

**2505 The Vanguard School**
Valley Forge Specialized Educational Services
1777 N Valley Rd
Paoli, PA 19301
610-296-6700
FAX: 610-640-0132
e-mail: info@vanguardschool_pa.org
www.vanguardschool-pa.org

*Tim Lanshe, Director of Education*
*James Kirkpatrick, CFO*
*Peg Osborne, Admissions Director*
An Approved Private School (APS) for students aged 4-21 years with exceptionalities including autism spectrum disorder, mild emotional disturbances and/or neurological impairments.

**2506 Worthmore Academy**
3535 Kessler Boulevard East Dr
Indianapolis, IN 46220-5154
317-902-9896
877-700-6516
FAX: 317-251-6516
e-mail: bjackson@worthmoreacademy.org
www.worthmoreacademy.org

*Brenda Jackson, Director*
*Alyssa Blaire Cook, Assistant Director*

A place where children with learning disabilities receive individualized instruction to help remediate his or her condition. The most common learning disabilities we work with are Dyslexiz, A.D.D, A.D.H.D, Autism Spectrum (including Asperger's Syndrome), and communication disorders.

# Exchange Programs

## General

**2507 A Guide to International Educational Exchange**
Mobility International USA
132 E. Broadway
Suite 343
Eugene, OR 97401-2767 541-343-1284
FAX: 541-343-6812
e-mail: info@miusa.org
www.miusa.org

*Susan Sygall, CEO*
A Guide to International Educational Exchange, Community Service and Travel for People with Disabilities includes information travel and international programs, as well as personal experience stories from people with disabilities who have had successful international experiences. *$45.00*
*600 pages*
*ISBN 1-880034-24-7*

**2508 American Institute for Foreign Study**
9 W Broad St
Stamford, CT 6902-3788 203-399-5000
866-906-2437
FAX: 203-399-5590
e-mail: info@aifs.com
www.aifs.com

*William L Gertz, CEO*
Organizes cultural exchange programs throughout the world for more than 50,000 students each year and arranges insurance coverage for our own participants as well as participants of other organizations. Also provides summer travel programs overseas and in the US ranging from one week to a full academic year.

**2509 American Universities International Programs**
307 S College Ave
Fort Collins, CO 80524-2801 970-495-0084
888-730-2847
FAX: 970-495-0114
e-mail: info@auip.com
www.auip.com

*Laurie Klith, Executive Director*
Study abroad organization sending students to universities in Australia and New Zealand.

**2510 American-Scandinavian Foundation**
58 Park Ave
New York, NY 10016-3007 212-779-3587
FAX: 212-686-1157
e-mail: info@amscan.org
scandinaviahouse.org

*Edward Gallagher, President*
Promotes international understanding through educational and cultural exchange between the United States and Denmark, Finland, Iceland, Norway and Sweden.

**2511 Antioch College**
One Morgan Place
Yellow Springs, OH 45387-1635 937-319-6082
FAX: 937-319-6085
e-mail: aea@antioch-college.edu
www.antioch-college.edu

*Mark Roosevelt, President*
*Thomas Brookley, CFO & COO*
*Gariot Louima, Chief Communications Officer*
Education abroad offers numerous programs which can be included in undergraduate and graduate study programs.

**2512 Army and Air Force Exchange Services**
P.O.Box 660202
Dallas, TX 75266-202 214-312-2011
800-527-2345
FAX: 800-446-0163
TTY: 800-423-2011
www.aafes.com

*James Moore, Senior VP*
*MG Bruce Casella, Commander/CEO*
Brings a tradition of value, service, and support to its 11.5 million authorized customers at military installations in the United States, Europe and in the Pacific.

**2513 Association for International Practical Training**
10400 Little Patuxent Pkwy
Suite 250
Columbia, MD 21044-3519 410-997-2200
FAX: 410-992-3924
e-mail: aipt@aipt.org
aipt.org

*Elizabeth Chazottes, CEO*
Nonprofit organization dedicated to encouraging and facilitating the exchange of qualified individuals between the US and other countries so they may gain practical work experience and improve international understanding.

**2514 Basic Facts on Study Abroad**
International Education
809 United Nations Plz
New York, NY 10017-3503 212-883-8200
FAX: 212-984-5452
e-mail: publications@un.org
iie.org

*Allen E Goodman, CEO*
*Peggy Blumenthal, Executive Vice President*
Information book including foreign study planning, educational choices, finances and study abroad programs. *$35.00*
*30 pages*

**2515 Beaver College**
Arcadia University
450 S Easton Rd
Glenside, PA 19038-3215 215-572-2901
888-232-8379
FAX: 215-572-2174
e-mail: cea@beaver.edu
www.beaver.edu/cea

*Lorna Stern, Deputy Director*
One of the largest college-based study abroad programs in the country. Prices from $8000.00 semester to $22000.00 a year.

**2516 Buffalo State (SUNY)**
1300 Elmwood Ave
Sout 410
Buffalo, NY 14222-1095 716-878-4620
FAX: 716-878-3054
e-mail: intleduc@buffalostate.edu
www.buffalostate.edu/studyabroad

*Lee Ann Grace, Asst Dean Int'l/Exchange Program*
Provides international educational exchange opportunities for students of university age and older through its Office of International Education.

**2517 Building Bridges: Including People with Disabilities in International Programs**
Mobility International USA
132 E Broadway
Suite 343
Eugene, OR 97401-3155
541-343-1284
FAX: 541-343-6812
e-mail: info@miusa.org
miusa.org

*Susan Sygall, CEO*
*Michele Scheib, Project Specialist*
*Melissa Mitchell, Public Relations Coordinator*
Empowers people with disabilities around the world through international exhange and international development to achieve their human rights. The international exchange programs usually last two-four weeks and are held throughout the year in the US and abroad. Activities include living with homestay families, leadership seminars, disability rights workshops, cross cultural learning and teambuilding activities such as river rafting and challenging courses.

**2518 Davidson College, Office of Study Abroad**
Davidson College
P.O.Box 7171
Davidson, NC 28035-7171
704-894-2000
FAX: 704-894-2005
e-mail: kocampbell@davidson.edu
http://www3.davidson.edu/cms/x12.xml

*Carol Quillen, President*
Recognizes the value of study abroad for both the devlopment of worl understanding and the development of the student as a broadminded, objective and mature individual.

**2519 High School Students Guide to Study, Travel, and Adventure Abroad**
300 Fore Street
Portland, ME 4101
207-553-4000
FAX: 207-553-4299
e-mail: contact@ciee.org
www.ciee.org

*James P Pellow, CEO & President*
*Kenton Keith, Senior Vice President for Progra*
This guide provides high school students with all the information they need for a successful trip abroad. Included are sections to help students find out if they're ready for a trip abroad, make the necessary preparations and get the most from their experience. Over 200 programs are described including language study, summer camps, homestays, study tours and work camps. The program descriptions include information for people with disabilities.

*ISSN 0312-11*

**2520 International Christian Youth Exchange**
134 W 26th St
New York, NY 10001-6803
212-206-7307
FAX: 212-633-9085

*Ed Gragert*
Offers participants a unique experience to learn about another culture and make friends from different countries.

**2521 International Partnership for Service-Learning and Leadership**
1515 SW 5th Avenue
Suite 606
Portland, OR 97201
503-954-1812
FAX: 503-954-1881
e-mail: info@ipsl.org
ipsl.org

*Nevin Brown, President*
A not for profit educational organization incorporated in New York State serving students, colleges, universities, service agenices and related organizations around the world by fostering programs that link volunteer service to the community and academic study.

**2522 International Student Exchange Programs (I SEP)**
1655 N Fort Myer Drive
Suite 400
Arlington, VA 22209
703-504-9960
FAX: 703-243-8070
e-mail: info@isep.org
www.isep.org

*Dr. Thomas Hochstettler, Chair*
*Dr. Tony Atwater, President*
ISEP is a network of 275 post-secondary institutions in the United States and 38 other countries cooperating to provide affordable international educational experiences for a diverse student population.

**2523 International University Partnerships**
University of Pennsylvania
1011 South Dr
Indiana, PA 15705-1046
724-357-2100
FAX: 724-357-6213
iup.edu

*David Werner, President*
Offers a variety of international educational exchange programs to students who wish to study overseas.

**2524 Lake Erie College**
391 W. Washington St.
Painesville, OH 44077
440-296-1856
800-533-4996
FAX: 440-375-7005
e-mail: pr@lec.edu
www.lec.edu

*Michael Victor, President*
*Michael Keresman lll, Director*
Sends students abroad for a term or longer to develop intellectual awareness and individual maturity.

**2525 Lane Community College**
4000 E 30th Ave
Eugene, OR 97405-640
541-463-3000
FAX: 541-463-5201
e-mail: asklane@lanecc.edu
www.lanecc.edu

*Mary Spilde, President*
Lane Community Colloege offers a wide variety of instructional programs including transfer credit programs, career and technical degree and certificate programs, continuing education noncredit courses, programs in English as a Second Language and International ESL, GED programs, and customized training for local businesses.

**2526 Lions Clubs International**
300 W 22nd St
Oak Brook, IL 60523-8842
630-571-5466
FAX: 630-571-8890
e-mail: lions@lionsclub.org
www.lionsclubs.org

*Wayne A. Madden, International President*
*Barry J. Palmer, First Vice President*
*Joseph Preston, Second Vice President*
*Marvin Chambers, Second Year Directors*
Over 46,000 individual clubs in over 194 countries and geographical areas which provide community service and promote better international relations. Clubs work with local communities to provide needed and useful programs for sight, diabetes and hearing, and aid in study abroad.

**2527 Lisle**
900 County Road 269
Leander, TX 78641-1633
512-259-4404
e-mail: lisle2@io.com
www.lisle.utoledo.edu

*Barbara E Bratton, Owner*

Educational organization which works toward world peace and better quality of human life through increased understanding between persons of similar and different cultures.

**2528 National 4-H Council**
7100 Connecticut Ave
Chevy Chase, MD 20815-4934
301-961-2800
FAX: 301-961-2894
fourhcouncil.edu

*Donald Floyd, President*
*Jennifer Sirangelo, Executive Vice President*

4-H opened the door for young people to learn leadership skills and explore ways to give back. 4-H revolutionized how youth connected to practical, hands-on learning experiences while outside of the classroom.

**2529 New Directions for People with Disabilities**
5276 Hollister Avenue
Suite 207
Santa Barbara, CA 93111-3068
805-967-2841
888-967-2841
FAX: 805-964-7344
e-mail: hello@newdirectionstravel.org
newdirectionstravel.org

*Jeanne Mohlen, Director Of Operations*
*Danna Mead, Program Director*
*Dee Duncan, Executive Director*
*Kaleena Quarles, Program Manager*

Provides high quality local, national, and international travel vacations and holiday programs for people with mild to moderate developmental disabilities. Through these programs, people with disabilities are increasingly understood, appreciated and more accepted as important and contributing members of our world.

**2530 People to People International**
911 Main Street
Suite 2110
Kansas City, MO 64105-2246
816-531-4701
FAX: 816-561-7502
e-mail: ptpi@ptpi.org
www.ptpi.org

*Mary Eisenhower, CEO*
*Roseanne Rosen, Senior Vice President of Operati*
*Brian Hueben, Senior Director, Administration*
*Stacey Chance, Director, Publications*

Exchanges international understanding and friendship through educational, cultural and humantarian activities involving the exchange of ideas and experiences directly among people of different countries and diverse cultures. Is also dedicated to enhancing cross cultural communication within each communityand across communities and nations.

**2531 Rotary Youth Exchange**
Rotary International
1560 Sherman Ave
Evanston, IL 60201-4818
847-866-3000
FAX: 847-328-8554
e-mail: youthexchange@rotary.org
www.rotary.org

*Kalyan Banerjee, International President*
*Noel A Bajat, Vice President*
*Kenneth R Boyd, Director*
*Elizabeth Demaray, Director*

This worldwide organization of business and professional leaders provides humanitarian service, encourages high ethical standards in all vocations, and helps build goodwill and peace in the world. Approximately 1.2 million Rotarians belong to more than 31,000 Rotary clubs located in 167 countries for exchange opportunities.

**2532 Scandinavian Exchange**
24 Dickinson Street
Amherst, MA 1002
413-253-9737
FAX: 413-253-5282
e-mail: howery@scandinavianseminar.org
www.scandinavianseminar.org

*Jacqueline D Waldman, CEO*
*William Kaufmann, Chair*

Student exchange program founded in 1949.

**2533 Sister Cities International**
915 15th Street, NW
4th Floor
Washington, DC 20005
202-347-8630
FAX: 202-393-6524
e-mail: info@sister-cities.org
sister-cities.org

*Patrick Madden, President*
*Jim Doumas, Executive Vice President, & Inte*

A non profit citizen diplomacy network creating and strengthening partnerships between US and international communities in an effort to increase global cooperation at the municipal level, to promote cultural understnading and to stimulate economic development. Encourages local community development and volunteer action by motivating and empowering private citizens, municipal officials and business leaders to conduct long term programs of mutual benefits including exchange situations.

**2534 State University of New York**
1400 Washington Ave
Albany, NY 12222-100
518-442-3300
FAX: 518-442-5383
e-mail: ugadmissions@albany.edu
www.albany.edu

*George Philip, President*
*Alain Kaloyeros, Senior Vice President & CEO*
*Susan Phillips, Provost & VP for Academic Affai*
*James Dias, VP for Research*

Offers over 150 international educational exchange programs in 37 different countries. Broad mission of excellence in undergraduate and graduate education, research and public service engages 17,000 diverse students in nine schools and colleges across three campuses.

**2535 University of Minnesota at Crookston**
2900 University Ave
Crookston, MN 56716-5000
218-281-6510
800-862-6466
FAX: 218-281-8050
e-mail: UMCinfo@umn.edu
www.crk.umn.edu

*Charles Casey, CEO*
*Eric Kaler, President*

The University of Minnesota, Crookston (UMC) is a public, baccalaureate, coeducational institution and a coordinate campus of the University of Minnesota

**2536 University of Oregon**
5000 N Willamette Blvd
Portland, OR 97203-5798
503-943-8000
FAX: 503-725-3067
e-mail: webmaster@up.edu
up.edu

*Patricia Esley, Manager*
*Rev.E.Willia Beauchamp, President*
*James Lyons, VP University Relations*
*Jim Ravelli, VP for University Research*

Study/cultural experience is available in Tokyo and other Japanese cities as part of the Japan Studies Program at the University.

**2537 Western Washington University**
516 High St
Bellingham, WA 98225-5996
360-650-3000
FAX: 360-650-3022
www.wwu.edu

*Bruce Shepard, President*
*Paul Dunn, Senior Executive Asst. to the Pr*
*Barbara Stoneberg, Assistant to the President*
*Mary Lacher, Receptionist, President & Provis*

**2538 World Experience Teenage Exchange Program**
2440 S Hacienda Blvd
Suite 116
Hacienda Heights, CA 91745-4763
626-330-5719
800-633-6653
FAX: 626-333-4914
e-mail: info@worldexperience.org
worldexperience.org

*Kerry Gonzales, President*
*Marge Archaumbault, President*
Offers a quality and affordable program for over two decades and continues to provide students and host families a youth exchange program based on individual attention, with the help of an international network of overseas directors and USA coordinators.

**2539 World of Options**
Mobility International USA
132 E Broadway
Suite 343
Eugene, OR 97401-3155
541-343-1284
FAX: 541-343-6812
e-mail: info@miusa.org
miusa.org

*Susan Sygall, CEO*
*Cerise Roth-Vinson, COO*
*Susan Dunn, Executive Asst. to the CEO*
*Alison Eker, Project Assistant*
Empowering people with disabilities around the world through international exchange and international development to achieve their human rights. *$16.00*
*338 pages*
*ISBN 1-880034-01-8*

**2540 Youth for Understanding International Exchange**
6400 Goldsboro Road
Suite 100
Bethesda, MD 20817-5841
240-235-2100
800-833-6243
FAX: 240-352-2104
e-mail: admissions@yfu.org
yfu.org

*Rachel Andreson, Founder*
*Samantha Brizzolara, Chair*
Youth for Understanding (YFU) International Exchange, an educational, nonprofit organization, prepares young people for the opportunities and responsabilities in a changing, independent world. With YFU, students can choose a year, semester, or summer program in one or more than 35 countries worldwide. More than 200,000 young people from more than 50 nations in Asia, Europe, North and South America, Africa and the Pacific have participated in YFU exchanges.

# Foundations & Funding Resources

## Alabama

**2541 Alabama Power Foundation**
P.O. Box 2641
Birmingham, AL 35291-11
205-257-2508
800-245-2244
FAX: 205-257-1860
www.alabamapower.com/foundation

*Charles D McCrary, President & CEO*
Honoring its mission to strengthen the communities the company serves, the foundation focuses its efforts on organizations that support education, civic activities, health services, the environment and the arts. By supporting the state's educational system ¥ from pre-K to universities ¥ the foundation is investing in Alabama's future and the well-being of its residents.

**2542 Andalusia Health Services**
1208 West Bypass
PO Box 667
Andalusia, AL 36420-1213
334-222-6591
FAX: 334-222-6567
e-mail: dreeves@andalusiachamber.com
www.andalusiachamber.com

*Janna McGlamory, President*
*Debbie Marcum, Vice President*
*Ashley Eiland, Executive Vice President*
*Gail Hayes, Treasurer*
Only offers grants to the residents of Covington County in Alabama who are pursuing a degree in a medical field.

**2543 The Arc Of Alabama**
557 S Lawrence St
Montgomery, AL 36104-4611
334-262-7688
e-mail: info@thearcofalabama.com
www.thearcofalabama.com

*Thomas B. Holmes*
The Arc of Alabama, Inc. is a volunteer-based membership organization made up of individuals with intellectual (such as mental retardation, an old and outdated term seldom used anymore), developmental and other disabilities, their families, friends, interested citizens, and professionals in the disability field.

## Alaska

**2544 Arc of Alaska**
The Arc of Anchorage
2211 Arca Dr
Anchorage, AK 99508-3462
907-277-6677
800-258-2232
FAX: 907-272-2161
TTY: 907-277-0735
e-mail: info@thearcofanchorage.org
www.thearchofanchorage.com

*Rod Shipley, President*
*Dave Falsey, Vice President*
*Meredith Parham, Secretary*
*Sharon Purkis, Treasurer*
The Arc helps Alaskans who experience developmental disabilities, behavioral health concerns or deafness achieve lives of dignity and independence as valued members of our community.

**2545 Rasmuson Foundation**
301 West Northern Lights Blvd.
Suite 400
Anchorage, AK 99503-2648
907-297-2700
877-366-2700
FAX: 907-297-2770
e-mail: rasmusonfdn@rasmuson.org
www.rasmuson.org

*Diane Kaplan, President & CEO*
*Sammye Pokryfki, Senior Program Officer*
The Rasmuson Foundation invests both in individuals and well managed organizations dedicated to improving the quality of life for Alaskans.

## Arizona

**2546 Arizona Community Foundation**
2201 E Camelback Road
Suite 202
Phoenix, AZ 85016-3481
602-381-1400
800-222-8221
FAX: 602-381-1575
e-mail: sseleznow@azfoundation.org
www.azfoundation.org

*Steven Seleznow, President & CEO*
*Jim Pitofsky, Chief Strategy Officer*
*Megan Brownell, Chief Communications Officer*
The mission of the Arizona Community Foundation is to empower and align philanthropic interests with community needs and build a legacy of living.

**2547 Arizona Autism ResourcesThe Arc of Arizona**
The Arc of Arizona
PO Box 90714
Phoenix, AZ 85066
602-234-2721
800-252-9054
FAX: 602-234-5959
e-mail: thearcaz@gmail.com
www.arcarizona.org

*Ginger Pottenger, President*
*Richard Travis, Vice President*
*Sandra Malloy, Secretary*
The Arc, a national organization on mental retardaion, is committed to securing for all people with developmental disabilities the opportunity to choose and realize their goals in regard to where they live, learn, work and play.

**2548 Margaret T Morris Foundation**
P.O.Box 592
Prescott, AZ 86302-592
928-445-6633
FAX: 928-445-6633
www.archive.naccho.org

*Susan Rheem, Executive Director*

**2549 The Arizona Instructional Resource Center for Students who are Blind or Visually Impaired**
Foundation For Blind Children
1235 E. Harmont Drive
Phoenix, AZ 85020
602-678-5816
FAX: 602-678-5811
e-mail: idurre@seeitourway.org
www.seeitourway.org

*Inge Durre, Director, AIRC*
The Foundation for Blind Children contracts with the Arizona Department of Education to provide statewide media services for students between pre-kindergarten and 12th grade who have a visual impairment or are blind andEneed their instructional materials in a specialized medium such as braille, large print, or electronic files as well as adaptive equipment.

## Arkansas

**2550 Arc of Arkansas**
2004 Main St
Little Rock, AR 72206-1526
501-375-2039
FAX: 501-372-4621
e-mail: shitt@arcark.org
www.arcark.org

*Steve Hitt, Chief Executive Officer*
*Cynthia Stone, Chief Operating Officer*
*Roger Williams, Chief Financial Officer*
Serving people with disabilites and their families for over fourty years.

**2551 Winthrop Rockefeller Foundation**
225 East Markham Street
Suite 200
Little Rock, AR 72201
501-376-6854
FAX: 501-374-4797
e-mail: webfeedback@wrfoundation.org
www.wrfoundation.org

*Sherece Y. West, Ph.D, President & CEO*
*Cory Anderson, Vice President*
*Andrea M. Dobson, COO & CFO*
*Angela Kremers, Senior Associate, Education*
Mission is to improve the quality of life in Arkansas. It focuses its grantmaking efforts in three areas: education, economic development and civic affairs. Education projects funded in the past have included grants to schools that are working to involve teachers and parents in making decisions about what happens at their schools, projects that work to remove prejudice from the educational process and more. Major grants are made to support the development of new programs.

## California

**2552 Ahmanson Foundation**
9215 Wilshire Blvd
Beverly Hills, CA 90210-5538
310-278-0770
e-mail: info@theahmansonfoundation.org
www.theahmansonfoundation.org

*William Ahmanson, President*
*Karen Ahmanson Hoffman, Managing Director*
*Kristen K. O'Connor, CFO & Treasurer*
*Jennie Chin, Senior Accountant*
The Foundation primarily gives in Southern California with major emphasis in Los Angeles County. The Foundation focuses on the arts and humanities, education, mental health and support for a broad range of social welfare programs.

**2553 Alice Tweed Touhy Foundation**
205 E Carrillo Street
Suite 219
Santa Barbara, CA 93101-7186
805-962-6430

*Jeanne Mc Kay, Manager*
Rehabilitation, recreation and building funds are given to organizations only within the Santa Barbara area.

**2554 Alternating Hemiplegia of Childhood Foundation**
31250 Plymouth Road
Livonia, MI 48150
919-569-5200
e-mail: sharon@ahckids.org
www.ahckids.org

*Jeff Wuchich, President*
*Lynn Egan, Vice President*
*Vicky Platt, Secretary*
Voluntary not-for-profit organizations dedicated to promoting professional and public awareness of Alternating Hemiplegia of Childhood (AHC) and providing current information to affected individuals and their families. Supports ongoing medical research into the cause, treatment and potential cure of AHC. Disseminates information about this disorder to promote proper diagnosis and maintains a registry of families, affected children and physicians who are familiar with AHC.

**2555 Arc of California**
1225 9th Street
Suite 350
Sacramento, CA 95815
916-552-6619
800-698-6619
FAX: 916-441-3494
e-mail: arcca@arccalifornia.org
www.arccalifornia.org

*Tony Anderson, Executive Director*
*Carlos Palacios, Membership Services*
*Jordan Lindsey, Director, Public Policy*
Advocates for people with intellectual and all developmental disabilities since 1953. The ARC of California is committed to securing for all people with developmental disabilities, in partnership with thier families, legal guardians or conservators the opportunity to choose and realize their goals of where and how they learn, live, work and play.

**2556 Atkinson Foundation**
1720 S. Amphlett Blvd
Suite 100
San Mateo, CA 94402-2710
650-357-1101
FAX: 650-357-1101
e-mail: atkinfdn@aol.com
www.atkinsonfdn.org

*Elizabeth Curtis, Administrator*
The Foundation focuses and awards grants to community service and civic organizations serving the residents of San Mateo County, California through programs that benefit children, youth, seniors, the disadvantaged and those in need of rehabilitation. Grants are also made to local churches and schools, and overseas for sustainable development, health education and family planning. No grants to individuals or for research, travel, special events, annual campaigns, media and publications.

**2557 Baker Commodities Corporate Giving Program**
4020 Bandini Blvd
Los Angeles, CA 90023
323-268-2801
FAX: 323-268-5166
www.bakercommodities.com

*Jim Andreoli, President*
Baker Commodities has been one of the nation's leading providers of rendering, and grease removal services. Baker Commodities, Inc. is a completely sustainable company, recycling animal by-products and kitchen waste into valuable products that can be used to feed livestock, power vehicles, and act as a base for everyday items.

**2558 Bank of America Foundation**
315 Montgomery St
Fl 8
San Francisco, CA 94104-1803
415-622-8248
888-488-9802
FAX: 704-386-6444
www.bankamerica.com/foundation

*Ilana Orin, Manager*
The Foundation will consider grants in four categories including: Health & Human Services, which provides support to health & human service organizations primarily through grants to the United Way campaigns; Education, with the focus on preparing people to become productive employees and participating citizens; Conservation & Environment, the improvement of California communities for the benefit of their citizens; and Culture & The Arts, supporting the leading performing and visual arts groups.

**2559 Blind Babies Foundation**
1814 Franklin Street
Suite 300
Oakland, CA 94612
510-446-2229
FAX: 510-446-2262
e-mail: bbfinfo@blindbabies.org
www.blindbabies.org

*Dottie Bridge, President*
*Sharon Sacks, PhD, 1st Vice President*
*Clare Friedman, PhD, 2nd Vice President*
*Deborah Orel-Bixler, PhD, OD,, Secretary*
Founded in 1949, the foundation provides home-based early intervention services to families with young children with vision impairment in the Northern and Central regions of California.

**2560 Bothin Foundation**
1660 Bush Street
Suite 300
San Francisco, CA 94109-5308
415-561-6540
FAX: 415-561-6477
e-mail: info@pfs-llc.net
www.pfs-llc.net/bothin/index.html

*Charles Casey, President*
*Mary Gregory, Vice President*
*Eric Sloan, Senior Program Staff*
*Annie Yates, Program Officer*
The Bothin Foundation makes grants for capital, building, and equipment needs to organizations providing direct services to low-income, at risk children, youth and families, the elderly, and the disabled in San Francisco, Marin, Sonoma, and San Mateo counties.

**2561 Briggs Foundation**
1969 Lancewood Ln
Carlsbad, CA 92009-6826
760-704-6481
FAX: 760-704-6483

*Blaine A Briggs, President*
Private non-operating foundation.

**2562 Burns-Dunphy Foundation**
5 3rd Street
Suite 528
San Francisco, CA 94103-3213
415-421-6995
FAX: 415-882-7774

*Walter Gleason*
*Cressey Nakagawa*
Grants are given to promote wellness for the visually impaired, physically and mentally disabled and to promote research in these areas.

**2563 California Community Foundation**
221 S. Figueroa Street
Suite 400
Los Angeles, CA 90012
213-413-4130
FAX: 213-383-2046
e-mail: info@ccf-la.org
www.calfund.org

*Antonia Hernandez, President*
*Nichole Baker, Vice President, BD*
*Maria Blanco, Vice President, Civic Engagement*
Areas of funding priority include grants for the disabled, child welfare, rehabilitation, developmentally disabled, employment projects, research and computer projects. Giving is limited to the greater Los Angeles area.

**2564 California Endowment**
1000 N Alameda St
Los Angeles, CA 90012-1804
213-628-1001
800-449-4149
FAX: 213-703-4193
e-mail: questions@calendow.org
www.calendow.org

*Robert Ross, President & CEO*
*B. Kathlyn Mead, Executive Vice President & COO*
California Endowment's mission is to expand access to affordable, quality health care for underserved individuals and communities, and to promote fundamental improvements in the health status of all Californians.

**2565 Carrie Estelle Doheny Foundation**
707 Wilshire Boulevard
Suite 4960
Los Angeles, CA 90017-3608
213-488-1122
FAX: 213-488-1544
e-mail: doheny@dohenyfoundation.org
www.dohenyfoundation.org

*Nina Shepherd, Chief Administrative Officer*
*Peggy Morrison, Grants Administrator*
The Foundation primarily funds local, not-for-profit organizations endeavoring to advance education, medicine and religion, to improve the health and welfare of the sick, aged, incapacitated, and to aid the needy.

**2566 Coeta and Donald Barker Foundation**
P.O.Box 936
Rancho Mirage, CA 92270
760-340-1162
FAX: 760-340-1255

*Nancy Harris, President*
It is an independent organization that gives its attention to organizations that are charitable or nonprofit under the laws of the state of Oregon or California.

**2567 Crescent Porter Hale Foundation**
655 Redwood Highway
Suite 301
Mill Valley, CA 94941-3028
415-388-2333
FAX: 415-381-4799
www.crescentporterhale.org

*A.L. Ballard, President*
*E. William Swanson, Vice President*
*Robert S. Kelling, Jr., Secretary/Treasurer*
Serves organizations in the San Francisco Bay Area who are involved in the following areas of concern: education in the fields of art and music; private elementary, high school and university education; capital funding; and other worthwhile programs which can be demonstrated as serving broad community purposes, leading toward the improvement of the quality of life.

**2568 David and Lucile Packard Foundation**
300 Second Street
Los Altos, CA 94022-3632
650-948-7658
FAX: 650-948-5793
e-mail: communications@packard.org
www.packard.org

*Carol S Larson, President & CEO*
*Susan Packard Orr, Chairman*
*Julie E. Packard, Vice Chairman*
This foundation provides grants to nonprofit organizations in the following areas: conservation; population; science; children, familes, and communities; arts and organizational effectiveness; and philanthropy. It provides national and international grants and also has a special focus on the Northern California Counties.

**2569 Deutsch Foundation**
5454 Beethoven St
Los Angeles, CA 90066-7017
310-862-3000
877-340-7700
FAX: 310-862-3100
deutschinc.com

*Mike Sheldon, Manager*
Learning disabled, visually impaired, mental health, eye research, child welfare, speech and hearing impaired, physically disabled and independence projects are funded through this Foundation. Giving is limited to California.

**2570 East Bay Community Foundation**
De Domenico Building
200 Frank H Ogawa Plaza
Oakland, CA 94612-2005
510-836-3223
FAX: 510-836-7418
e-mail: operations@eastbaycf.org
www.ebcf.org

*Nicole Taylor, President & CEO*
A collection of funds created by many people, organizations and businesses, the Foundation helps those people and groups to support effective nonprofit organizations to the East Bay and beyond.

**2571 Evelyn and Walter Hans JrHaas Jr**
114 Sansome Street
Suite 600
San Francisco, CA 94104
415-856-1400
FAX: 415-856-1500
www.haasjr.org

*Ira S. Hirschfield, President*
*Jennie Lehua Watson, VP Communications*
*Michael Smith, Manager Information Services*
*Randall Miller, Senior Program Officer*
A private foundation interested in programs which assist people who are hungry, homeless, or at risk of homelessness; enable older adults to maintain independent lives in the community and support Hispanic community development in San Francisco's Mission District. The Foundation also encourages proposals for corporate social responsibility efforts within the business community.

**2572 Family Caregiver Alliance**
180 Montgomery Street
Suite 900
San Francisco, CA 94104-4240
415-434-3388
800-445-8106
FAX: 415-434-3508
e-mail: info@caregiver.org
www.caregiver.org

*William N Hancock, Owner*

**2573 Financial Aid for the Disabled and Their Families**
Reference Service Press
5000 Windplay Dr
Suite 4
El Dorado Hills, CA 95762
916-939-9620
FAX: 916-939-9626
e-mail: info@rspfunding.com
www.rspfunding.com

*Gail Schlachter, Author/Owner*
*R David Weber, Author*
This directory, which Children's Bookwatch calls invaluable describes more than 1,100 financial aid opportunities available to support persons with disabilities and members of their families. Updated ever 2 years. *$39.50*
*300 pages*
*ISBN 1-588410-31-5*

**2574 Firemans Fund Foundation**
Firemans Fund Insurance Companies
777 San Marin Dr
Novato, CA 94998
415-899-2000
800-227-1700
FAX: 415-899-3600
e-mail: customerrelations@ffic.com
www.firemansfund.com

*Lori Dickerson Fouche, President & CEO*
*Jill Paterson, Chief Financial Officer*
*Eleanor Barnard, Chief Distribution & Sales*
*Sally Narey, Chief Counsel, Corp. Secretary*
Provides discretionary grants to the disabled only in Marin and Sonoma counties in the San Francisco Bay area.

**2575 Fred Gellert Foundation**
1038 Redwood Highway
Building B, Suite 2
Mill Valley, CA 94941
415-381-7575
FAX: 415-381-8526
e-mail: patty@gellertassociates.com
www.foundationcenter.org/grantmaker/fredgell e

*Patty Oday, Administrator*
Focuses on organizations and programs serving residents of San Mateo and San Francisco and Marin counties in California, with the exception of environmentally concerned organizations.

**2576 Gallo Foundation**
P.O. Box 1130
Modesto, CA 95353-1130
209-579-3204
FAX: 209-341-3307
www.ejgallo.com

*John Gallo, Senior VP Operations*
Physically and mentally disabled, child welfare, Special Olympics, United Cerebral Palsy and Easter Seal Society are among the grants provided by this foundation.

**2577 Glaucoma Research Foundation**
251 Post Street
Suite 600
San Francisco, CA 94108-5017
415-986-3162
800-826-6693
FAX: 415-986-3763
e-mail: grf@glaucoma.org
www.glaucoma.org

*Thomas M. Brunner, President & CEO*
*Andrew L. Jackson, Director, Communications*
*Catalina San Agustin, Director, Operations*
*Nancy Graydon, Executive Director of Development*
A national organization dedicated to protecting the sight of people with glaucoma through research and education. The Foundation conducts and supports research that contributes to improved patient care and a better understanding of the disease process. Provides education, advocacy and emotional support to patients and their families.

**2578 Harden Foundation**
1636 Ercia Street
Salinas, CA 93906
831-442-3005
FAX: 831-443-1429
e-mail: joe@hardenfoundation.org
www.hardenfoundation.org

*Patricia Tynan Chapman, President*
*C. Bill Elliott, Vice President & Treasurer*
*David G. Mills, Secretary*
*Bruce C. Taylor, Director*
Founded to assist charitable organizations in the Salinas Valley.

**2579 Henry J Kaiser Family Foundation**
2400 Sand Hill Rd
Menlo Park, CA 94025-6941
650-854-9400
FAX: 650-854-4800
www.kff.org

*Drew E Altman, President & CEO*

A non-profit, private operating foundation focusing on the major health care issues facing the US, with a growing role in global health. Kaiser develops and runs its own research and communications programs, sometimes in partnership with other non-profit research organizations or major media companies.

**2580 Henry W Bull Foundation**
Santa Barbara Bank & Trust
P.O. Box 2340
Santa Barbara, CA 93120-2340
805-884-8637
FAX: 805-884-1404

*Janice Gibbons, VP/Senior Trust Officer*

Grant given to a wide range of organizations that include those which provide services for the disabled; arts, education, services for elderly and youth grants awarded two times a year. Grant size ranges from $500 to $5,000. Proposal deadlines April 1, Sept 1.

**2581 Irvine Health Foundation**
18301 Von Karman Avenue
Suite 440
Irvine, CA 92612-0120
949-253-2959
FAX: 949-253-2962
e-mail: info@ihf.org
www.ihf.org

*David G Sills, Founding Board Director, Chair*
*Timothy L. Strader, Vice Chairman*
*John C Gaffney, Treasurer*
*Gerald B Sinykin, MD, Founding & Current Board Director*

Mission is to improve the physical, mental and emotional well-being of all Orange County residents.

**2582 Joseph Drown Foundation**
1999 Avenue of the Stars
Suite 2330
Los Angeles, CA 90067-6043
310-277-4488
FAX: 310-277-4573
e-mail: staff@jdrown.org
www.jdrown.org

*Norman C Obrow, President*

Giving is focused primarily in California. No support for religious purposes or to individuals. Goal is to assist individuals in becoming successful, self-sustaining, contributing citizens.

**2583 Junior Blind of America**
5300 Angeles Vista Blvd
Los Angeles, CA 90043-1648
323-295-4555
800-352-2290
FAX: 323-296-0424
e-mail: info@juniorblind.org
www.juniorblind.org

*Miki Jordan, President & CEO*
*Jay Allen, EVP & Chief Operating Officer*
*Laura M Hardy, SVP, Development & Marketing*
*Kami Mann, SVP, Finance & CFO*

Junior Blind provides programs and services for children and adults who are blind or visually impaired and their families to achieve independence and self-esteem. Programs include; Camp Bloomfield, Visions: Adventures in Learning, Infant-Family Program, Early Childhood Program, Special Education School, Children's Residential Program, Davidson Program for Independence, and Student Transition and Enrichment Program, Vision Screening and After School enrichment.

**2584 Kenneth T and Eileen L Norris Foundation**
11 Golden Shore
Suite 450
Long Beach, CA 90802-4274
562-435-8444
FAX: 562-436-0584
e-mail: grants@ktn.org
www.norrisfoundation.org

*Lisa D Hanson, Chairman*
*Ronald R Barnes, Executive Director & Trustee*
*Walter J Zanino, Controller*
*William G Corey, Medical Advisor*

The Foundation is primarily focused on medicine and education. To a lesser extent the foundation contributes to community programs including visually impaired, autism, mentally and physically disabled, deaf and mental health in the Southern California area. Average grant size in this area is $5,000-$10,000. Grants are also given in the area of culture and youth.

**2585 Koret Foundation**
33 New Montgomery Street
Suite 1090
San Francisco, CA 94105-4526
415-882-7740
FAX: 415-882-7775
e-mail: info@koretfoundation.org
www.koretfoundation.org

*Jeffrey A. Farber, Chief Executive Officer*
*Claudia Hardin, Chief Financial Officer*
*Elaine Lai, Controller*
*Kirsten Michelwait, Communications Officer*

Koret seeks to fund outstanding examples of innovative approaches to community challenges and opportunities.

**2586 LA84 Foundation**
2141 W Adams Blvd
Los Angeles, CA 90018-2040
323-730-4600
FAX: 323-730-9637
e-mail: info@la84foundation.org
www.la84foundation.org

*Anita L. DeFrantz, President*
*Patrick Escobar, Vice President*
*Conrad R. Freund, Chief Operating Officer*
*Wayne Wilson, Vice President, Education Services*

The LA84 Foundation was established to manage Southern California's share of the surplus from the highly successful 1984 Olympic Games in Los Angeles and offers sports programs, a premier sports library and meeting facilities. The foundation currently serves two million youth in eight Southern California counties.

**2587 LJ Skaggs and Mary C Skaggs Foundation**
1221 Broadway
21st Floor
Oakland, CA 94612-1837
510-451-3300
FAX: 510-451-1527
e-mail: skaggs@fablaw.com
www.skaggs.org

*Philip M Jelley, President*
*Jayne C Davis, Vice President*
*Robert N Janopaul, Director*
*Joseph W Martin, Jr., Secretary, Treasurer*

The Foundation presently makes grants under four program categories: performing arts, social concerns, projects of historic interest and special projects.

**2588 LK Whittier Foundation**
Whittier Trust Company Foundations Office
1600 Huntington Dr
S Pasadena, CA 91030-4709 626-441-5111
FAX: 626-441-0420
e-mail: lblinkenberg@whittiertrust.com
www.whittiertrust.com

*Michael J Casey, President and CEO*
*David A. Dahl, Executive Vice President, Chief Operating Officer*
*James A. Jeffs, Executive Vice President, Chief Investment Officer*
*Harold J. Depoali, Vice President, Client Administration*

Giving is primarily offered to preselected organizations. No grants are given to individuals.

**2589 Legler Benbough Foundation**
2550 Fifth Avenue
Suite 132
San Diego, CA 92103-6622 619-235-8099
FAX: 619-235-8077
e-mail: peter@benboughfoundation.org
www.benbough.org

*Peter K. Elsworth, President*
*Thomas Cisco, Treasurer*
*Hugh C. Carter, Director*
*Thomas E. Cisco, Director*

The mission of the foundation is to improve the quality of life of the people of San Diego. The foundation focuses on three target areas for funding, one in the area of providing economic opportunity, one in the area of enhancing cultural opportunity, and one that provides focus for health, education and welfare funding.

**2590 Levi Strauss Foundation**
1155 Battery St
San Francisco, CA 94111-1264 415-501-7208
800-872-5384
FAX: 415-544-3490
www.levistrauss.com/about/foundations

*Chip Bergh, President & CEO*
*Blake Jorgensen, Executive Vice President & CFO*
*David Love, SVP & Chief Supply Chain Officer*
*Jill Nash, Chief Communications Officer*

Has a funding initiative to support organizations which provide services for people with AIDS, and/or educational programs which help prevent the further spread of the HIV virus. The Foundation will assist in the development and enhancement of such services only in those communities where Levi Strauss & Co. has plants and distribution centers.

**2591 Louis R Lurie Foundation**
555 California Street
Suite 5100
San Francisco, CA 94104-1707 415-392-2470
FAX: 415-421-8669
www.foundationcenter.org/grantmaker/lurie

*Nancy Terry, Foundation Administrator*

Visually impaired, hard-of-hearing and physically disabled in the San Francisco Bay Area and Metropolitan Chicago areas only.

**2592 Luke B Hancock Foundation**
360 Bryant St
Palo Alto, CA 94301-1409 650-321-5536
FAX: 650-321-0697

*Ruth Ramel, Director*

Has concentrated its resources over the past year on programs which provide job training and employment for at-risk youth. Consortium funding with other foundations in areas where there is unmet need; emergency and transitional funding; and selected funding for music education. .

**2593 Marin Community Foundation**
Suite 200
Novato, CA 94949-8263 415-464-2500
FAX: 415-464-2555
e-mail: info@marincf.org
www.marincf.org

*Thomas Peters, President & CEO*
*Elizabeth A Brown, Vice President for Programs*
*Alexandra Derby, VP, Philanthropic Services*
*Laura Goff, Vice President & CIO*

Mission is to encourage and apply philanthropic contributions to help improve the human condition, embrace diversity, promote a humane and democratic society, and enhance the communities quality of life, now and for future generations.

**2594 Mary A Crocker Trust**
233 Post Street
5 Hamilton Landing
San Francisco, CA 94108-5098 415-982-0138
FAX: 415-982-0141
e-mail: staff@mactrust.org
www.mactrust.org

Established in 1889, the Foundation is interested in Bay Area programs such as environment, education and community relations.

**2595 National Center on Caregiving at Family Caregiver Alliance (FCA)**
785 Market Street
Suite 750
San Francisco, CA 94103 415-434-3388
800-445-8106
FAX: 415-434-3508
e-mail: info@caregiver.org
www.caregiver.org

*Ping Hao, President*
*Claude Everhart, Vice President*
*Jeff Kumataka, Treasurer*
*Kathleen Kelly, Executive Director*

FCA offers programs at national, state and local levels to support and sustain caregivers. The National Center on Caregiving (NCC) program works to advance the development of high-quality, cost-effective policies and programs for caregivers in every state of the country. Uniting research, public policy and services, the NCC serves as a central source of information on caregiving and long term care issues for policy makers, service providers, media, funders and family caregivers.

**2596 National Foundation of Wheelchair Tennis**
940 Calle Amanecer
Suite B
San Clemente, CA 92673-6218 714-361-3663
FAX: 714-361-6603
e-mail: nfwt@aol.com
www.nfwt.org

*Bill Butler*

Founded in January of 1980, the intention of this foundation is to assist the newly physically disabled individual to realize his full potential in society by enhancing his esteem, independence productivity and physical capabilities regardless of age, sex, creed or disability extent.

**2597 Optometric Extension Program Foundation**
1921 Cernegie Avenue
Suite 3-L
Santa Ana, CA 92705-5510 949-250-8070
FAX: 949-250-8157
e-mail: rwilliams@oep.org
www.oepf.org

*Robert A. Williams, Executive Director*
*Gregory Kitchener, President*
*Paul A. Harris, Vice President*
*Robin D. Lewis, Secretary - Treasurer*

Vision care for learning disabilities and head trauma patients.

**2598 Parker Foundation**
2604-B El Camino Real
Suite 244
Carlsbad, CA 92008
760-720-0630
FAX: 760-720-1239
www.theparkerfoundation.org

*Judy McDonald, President*
*William E. Beamer, Vice President*
*Mark C. Trotter, Secretary*
*Ann Davies, Treasurer*
The assets are directed to projects which will contribute to the betterment of any aspect of the people of San Diego County, California and solely to entities which, among other things, are organized exclusively for charitable purposes and are operating in San Diego County, California.

**2599 Pasadena Foundation**
260 S. Los Robles Avenue
Suite 119
Pasadena, CA 91101- 2824
626-796-2097
FAX: 626-583-4738
e-mail: pcfstaff@pasadenacf.org
www.pasadenacf.org

*Jennifer Flemming DeVoll, Executive Director*
*Mariver Copeland, Director of Finance*
*Judy Wilson, Director of Development*
*Shawna Yetka, Donor/Grants Coordinator*
The mission of the Pasadena Foundation is to improve the quality of life for citizens of the Pasadena area through support of non-profit organizations that provide services beneficial to the community.

**2600 RC Baker Foundation**
P.O. Box 6150
Orange, CA 92863-6150
714-750-8987

*F L Scott, Manager*
Established in 1952, for general philanthropic purposes. The bulk of assistance and support has been to religious, scientific, educational institutions and youth organizations.

**2601 Ralph M Parsons Foundation**
888 West Sixth Street
Suite 700
Los Angeles, CA 90017- 2733
213-362-7600
FAX: 213-482-8878
www.rmpf.org

*Wendy Garen, President & CEO*
*Mary Kane Christian, Program Officer*
*Ricardo Lima, Grants Manager*
*Astra Anderson Galang, Chief Financial Officer*
The Foundation is concerned with the encouragement and support of projects and programs deemed beneficial to mankind in several major areas of interest such as: education; social impact; civic and cultural; health and special products. Only funds in Los Angeles County.

**2602 Robert Ellis Simon Foundation**
312 S Canyon View Drive
Los Angeles, CA 90049-3812
310-275-7335

*Joan Willens*
Mental health and visually impaired grants are the main concerns of this organization.

**2603 San Francisco Foundation**
225 Bush Street
Suite 500
San Francisco, CA 94104-4224
415-733-8500
FAX: 415-477-2783
e-mail: info@sff.org
www.sff.org

*Sandra R Hernandez, CEO*
*Nick Hodges, VP for Philanthropic Services*
*Bobbie Chapman, Director of Business Development*
*Shona Carter, Donor Relations Officer*
The Foundation's purpose is to improve life, promote greater equality of opportunity and assist those in need or at risk in the San Francisco Bay Area. The Foundation strives to protect and enhance the unique resources of the Bay Area, committed to equality of opportunity for all and the elimination of any injustice, seeks to enhance human dignity and seeks to establish mutual trust, respect and communication among the Foundation.

**2604 Santa Barbara Foundation**
1111 Chapala Street
Suite 200
Santa Barbara, CA 93101- 2780
805-963-1873
FAX: 805-966-2345
e-mail: info@sbfoundation.org
www.sbfoundation.org

*Ron Gallo, CEO*
*Guille Gil-Reynoso, Executive Special Projects Asst.*
*Jan Campbell, VP of Philanthropic Services*
*Amanda Kastelic, Donor Relations Officer*
The Foundations mission is to enrich the lives of the people of Santa Barbara County through philanthropy. The Foundation awards grants to nonprofits within the County in the areas of education, health, human services, personal development, cluture, recreation, community enhancement and environment. No support is given to individuals except through student aid.

**2605 Sidney Stern Memorial Trust**
860 Via de la Paz
PO Box 457
Pacific Palisades, CA 90272
310-459-2117

*Betty Hoffenberg, Director*
A Southern California-based foundation providing grants to non-profit organizations for various projects. The foundation gives priority to the following areas of interest: education, health and science, community service projects, youth, services to the mentally and emotionally disabled, the arts, organizations and activities serving California. The Board prefers to make contributions to organizations that use the funds directly in the furtherance of their charitable and public purposes.

**2606 Sierra Health Foundation**
1321 Garden Hwy
Sacramento, CA 95833-9754
916-922-4755
FAX: 916-922-4024
e-mail: info@sierrahealth.org
www.sierrahealth.org

*Chet Hewitt, CEO*
*Joan Kassis, Controller*
*Gil Alvarado, VP Administration / CFO*
*Amy Birthwhistle, Program Associate*
The Foundation strives to establish a collaborative relationship with its grantees, and with other funders and foundations, through an open dialogue. The Foundation approaches each grant as a partnership, with opportunities for the grantee and grantor to work cooperatively to enhance the effectiveness of the grant project.

**2607 Silicon Valley Community Foundation**
2400 West El Camino Real
Suite 300
Mountain View, CA 94040-1498
650-450-5400
FAX: 650-450-5401
e-mail: info@siliconvalleycf.org
www.siliconvalleycf.org

*Emmitt Carson, CEO*
*Eleanor Clement Glass, Chief Donor Engagement & Giving*
*Erica Wood, VP Community Leadership*
*Vera Bennett, CFO & Administrative Officer*
Serving all of San Mateo & Santa Clara counties, Silicon Valley Foundation has more than $1.5B in assets under management and 1500 philanthropic funds. The community provides grants through donor advised and corporate funds in addition to its own Community Endowment Fund. In addition, the community foundation serves as a regional center for philanthropy, providing donors simple and effective ways to give locally & globally.

**2608 Sonora Area Foundation**
362 S Stewart Street
Sonora, CA 95370-577
209-533-2596
FAX: 209-533-2412
e-mail: greg@sonora-area.org
www.sonora-area.org

*Greg Applegate, Executive Director*
*Jim Johnson, President SAF*
*Roger Francis, Vice President*
*Tricia Gardella, Secretary, Treasurer*
The Sonora Area Foundation strengthens its community through assisting donors, making grants, and providing leadership.

**2609 Stella B Gross Charitable Trust C/O Bank of The West Trust Department**
P.O. Box 1121
San Jose, CA 95108-1121
408-947-5203
e-mail: gpadilla@bankofthewest.com

*Gabe Padilla, Trust Admin*
Organization must be federal and state tax-exempt and reside within the bounds of Santa Clara County, California to be eligible.

**2610 Teichert Foundation**
3500 American River Dr
Sacramento, CA 95864-5893
916-484-3280
FAX: 916-484-6506
www.teichert.com

*Frederick Teichert, Executive Director*
Awards grants to community organizations and provides employee matching grants. Teichert Foundation expresses the companie's commitment to build and preserve a healthy and prosperous region.

**2611 WM Keck Foundation**
550 South Hope Street
Suite 2500
Los Angeles, CA 90071- 2617
213-680-3833
FAX: 213-614-0934
e-mail: info@wmkeck.org
www.wmkeck.org

*Allison Keller, Executive Director & CFO*
*Maria Pellegrini, Ph.D, Executive Director of Programs*
*Thomas Everhart, Ph.D, Senior Scientific Advisor*
*Matesh Varma, Ph.D, Senior Program Director*
Created to support accredited colleges and universities with particular emphasis on the sciences, engineering and medical research. The Foundation also maintains a Southern California Grant Program that provides support for non-profit organizations in the field of civic and community services, health care, precollegiate education and the arts.

**2612 Willam G Gilmore Foundation**
1660 Bush Street
Suite 300
San Francisco, CA 94109
415-984-0650
FAX: 415-434-3508
www.pfs-llc.net/gilmore/index.html

*William N Hancock, Owner*

## Colorado

**2613 AV Hunter Trust**
650 South Cherry Street
Suite 535
Glendale, CO 80246- 1897
303-399-5450
FAX: 303-399-5499
www.avhuntertrust.org

*Bruce K. Alexander, President*
*Allan B. Adams, Vice President*
*Mary K. Anstine, Treasurer*
*Barbara L. Howie, Executive Director*
Donated nearly $50 million to nonprofit organizations serving those who captured Mr. Hunter's attention and sparked his compassion. Trust gives aid, comfort, support, or assistance to children or aged people or indigent adults.

**2614 Adolph Coors Foundation**
4100 E. Mississippi Avenue
Suite 1850
Denver, CO 80246- 3074
303-388-1636
FAX: 303-388-1684
e-mail: generalinfo@acoorsfdn.org
www.coorsfoundation.org

*John W. Jackson, Executive Director*
*Jeanne L. Bistranin, Senior Program Officer*
*Carrie C. Tynan, Program Officer*
*Carol S. Strathman, Financial/Special Projects Coord*
Applicant organizations must be classified as 501 and must operate within the United States. The areas covered by the Foundation are health, education, youth, community services, civic and cultural and public affairs.

**2615 Arc of Colorado**
1580 Logan Street
Suite 730
Denver, CO 80203-1942
303-864-9334
800-333-7690
FAX: 303-864-9330
e-mail: mrymer@thearcofco.org
www.thearcofco.org

*Marijo Rymer, Executive Director*
A private not-for-profit, membership-based, grassroots association. The Arc of Colorado is the state office whith local units located in various areas throughout the state.

**2616 Bonfils-Stanton Foundation**
Daniels and Fisher Tower
1601 Arapahoe
Suite 500
Denver, CO 80202-2015
303-825-3774
FAX: 303-825-0802
e-mail: webinfo@bonfils-stanton.org
www.bonfils-stantonfoundation.org

*Dorothy A Horrell, President*
*Susan H. France, Vice President of Programs*
*Ann M. Hovland, CFO/Treasurer*
Grants limited to Colorado 501 (c) (3) organizations. Grants are for general, charitable philanthropic activities within the State. Major categories include education, scientific (including hospital and health services), civic and cultural, community and human services. Organizations should request foundation guidelines before submitting a proposal.

2617 **Comprecare Foundation**
P.O. Box 740610
Arvada, CO 80006-610
303-432-2808
FAX: 303-432-2808
www.comprecarefoundation.org

*Frederick G. Ihrig, Chairman of the Board*
*Milford H. Schulhof II, Vice Chairman*
*Milton W. Bollman, Secretar/Treasurer*
*M. Eugene Sherman M.D., Director*
The purpose of the Comprecare Foundation is to encourage, aid or assist specific health related programs and to make grants to support the activities of organizations which are designed to advance and promote health care education, the delivery of health care services, and the improvement of community health and welfare.

2618 **Denver Foundation**
55 Madison Street
8th Floor
Denver, CO 80206-5419
303-300-1790
FAX: 303-300-6547
e-mail: lbarrett@denverfoundation.org
www.denverfoundation.org

*David M Miller, President & CEO*
*Pamela Kenney Basey, Community Leader*
Neighbors helping neighbors, that's what the foundation is for. As Denver's only community foundation we've been accepting charitable donations since 1925. Those funds have been given back to the community in ongoing grants to nonprofit organizations - organizations that touch nearly every meaningful artistic, cultural, civic, health and human services interest of metro Denver's citizens.

2619 **El Pomar Foundation**
10 Lake Circle
Colorado Springs, CO 80906-4201
719-633-7733
800-554-7711
FAX: 719-577-5702
e-mail: grants@elpomar.org
www.elpomar.org

*William Hybl, Chairman/CEO*
*R. Thayer Tutt, Jr., President/Chief Investment*
*Dave Palenchar, COO & Trustee*
*Kyle Hybl, SVP/General Counsel*
Mission of El Pomar is to enhance, encourage and promote the current and future well being of the people of Colorado through grantmaking and community stewardship.

2620 **Helen K and Arthur E Johnson Foundation**
1700 Broadway
Suite 1100
Denver, CO 80290-1718
303-861-4127
800-232-9931
FAX: 303-861-0607
e-mail: info@johnsonfoundation.org
www.johnsonfoundation.org

*John H Alexander Jr, President*
*Cindy Willard, Senior Program Officer*
*Suzanne Bruce, Program Officer*
A nonprofit, grantmaking private foundation incorporated under the laws of the State of Colorado in 1948. The Foundation is a general purpose foundation whose grant program consists of a wide variety of creative efforts to solve problems and to enrich the quality of life. The areas of interest are: education, youth, health, community services, civic and culture and senior citizens. Grants limited to the state of Colorado.

## Connecticut

2621 **Aetna Foundation**
151 Farmington Ave
Hartford, CT 6156
860-273-6382
www.aetnahealthinsurance.com

*Marilda L Gandara, President*
The Aetna Foundation is the independent charitable and philanthropic arm of Aetna Inc. The Foundation helps build healthy communities by promoting volunteerism, forming partnerships and funding initiatives that improve the quality of life where our employees and customers live and work.

2622 **Arc of Connecticut**
43 Woodland Street
Suite 260
Hartford, CT 6105-2300
860-246-6400
FAX: 860-246-6406
e-mail: arcct@aol.com
www.arcct.com

*Leslie Simoes, Interim Executive Director*
The Arc of Connecticut is an advocacy organization committed to protecting the rights of people with intellectual, cognitive, and developmental disabilities and to promoting opportunities for their full inclusion in the life of thier communities.

2623 **Community Foundation of Southeastern Connecticut**
147 State St
New London, CT 6320-6302
860-442-3572
877-442-3572
FAX: 860-442-0584
e-mail: alice@cfsect.org
www.cfect.org

*Alice Fitzpatrick, President*
*Edward Wozniak, Chief Financial Officer*
*Allison Woods, Director of Gift Planning*
*Kip Parker, Division Director*
Provides donors with an easy and convenient way to give back to our community with joy and impact. We make grants to nonprofit organizations and support their efforts to strengthen our community.

2624 **Connecticut Mutual Life Foundation**
140 Garden St
Hartford, CT 6154
860-727-3000

*Astrida Olds, Executive Director*
Distinguished throughout its long history by unusual commitment to high principles of corporate purpose and business ethics. That commitment has been reflected not only in the firm belief that normal business functions must be carried out with a sense of responsibility beyond that required by the marketplace. Maintains an ongoing program of corporate contributions, a nationwide matching gifts plan for all employees on behalf of private and public education, skills training programs, and more.

2625 **Cornelia de Lange Syndrome Foundation**
302 West Main Street
#100
Avon, CT 6001-4331
860-676-8166
800-753-2357
FAX: 860-676-8337
e-mail: info@cdlsusa.org
www.cdlsusa.org

*Liana Fresher, Executive Director*
*Antonie Kline, MD, Medical Director*
*Marie Concklin-Malloy, Assistant Executive Director*
*Alexi Dahlstrom, Communications Coordinator*
Provides information about birth defects caused by Cornelia de Lange Syndrome.

**2626 Fidelco Guide Dog Foundation**
103 Old Iron Ore Rd
Bloomfield, CT 6002-1424
860-243-5200
FAX: 860-243-7215
e-mail: info@fidelco.org
www.fidelco.org

*Eliot D. Russman, CEO & Executive Director*
*Mary P. Craig, DVM, MBA, Director, Strategic Initiatives*
*Louise C. England, Ownership & Development*
*Stephen H. Matheson, Chairman*

The Fidelco Guide Dog Foundation, located in Bloomfield, Conn., is dedicated to providing increased freedom and independence to men and women who are blind by providing them with the highest quality guide dogs. We rely solely on the gifts and the generosity of individuals, foundations, corporations and organizations that partner with Fidelco to 'Share the Vision.'

**2627 GE Foundation**
General Electric Company
3135 Easton Tpke
Fairfield, CT 6828
203-373-3216
FAX: 203-373-3029
e-mail: gefoundation@ge.com
www.ge.com

*Jeffrey R. Immelt, CEO*
*Michael J. Cosgrove, Treasurer*
*Paul Bueker, Secretary & Controller*
*Nani Beccalli, President & CEO GE International*

Believes that our greatest national resource is the work force. If we are to successfully compete in the global arena, then we become involved in improving the education of all of our citizens. The Foundation sets examples for others to emulate helping people with their international grant program to higher education and to health care for children in developing countries.

**2628 Hartford Foundation for Public Giving**
10 Columbus Blvd
8th Floor
Hartford, CT 6106-1985
860-548-1888
FAX: 860-524-8346
e-mail: hfpg@hfpg.org
www.hfpg.org

*Linda Kelly, President*
*Deborah Battit, Research Associate*
*Donna E. Jolly, VP, Communications & Marketing*
*Maria I. Mojica, VP for Programs*

Developmentally disabled, housing, deaf, recreation and education grants.

**2629 Hartford Insurance Group**
1 Hartford Plz
Hartford, CT 6155-1708
860-547-5000
www.thehartford.com

*Liam McGee, Chairman, President & CEO*
*Greg McGreevey, EVP & Chief Investment Officer*
*Lizabeth H. Zlatkus, EVP & Chief Risk Officer*
*Alan J. Kreczko, EVP & General Counsel*

Giving is primarily in the Hartford, CT area and in communities where the company has a regional office. No support is available for political or religious purposes. Grants are given in the areas of education, health and United Way organizations.

**2630 Henry Nias Foundation**
20 Carmen Rd
Milford, CT 6460-7508
203-874-2787

*Charles D Fleischman, President*

Giving limited to NY metropolitan area. Arts, cultural programs, medical school/education, and children and youth.

**2631 Jane Coffin Childs Memorial Fund for Medical Research**
333 Cedar St, SHM
L300
New Haven, CT 6510-3206
203-785-4612
FAX: 203-785-3301
www.jccfund.org

*Dr Randy Schekman, Director*

The Fund awards fellowships to suitably qualified individuals for full time postdoctoral studies in the medical and related sciences bearing on cancer.

**2632 John H and Ethel G Nobel Charitable Trust**
Bankers Trust Company
1 Fawcett Pl
Greenwich, CT 6830-6553
203-629-7120
FAX: 203-629-7170

*Paul J Bisset, VP*

**2633 Scheuer Associates Foundation**
960 Lake Ave
Greenwich, CT 6831-3032
203-622-5002
FAX: 203-622-5002

*Thomas Scheuer, President*

**2634 Swindells Charitable Foundation Trust**
Shawmut Bank
777 Main St
Hartford, CT 6115-2303
860-000-1111
FAX: 860-240-1210

*Maggie Willard, President*

Grants made to charitable organizations or societies incorporated for the relief of sick and suffering poor children and/or the relief of sick suffering and indigent aged men and women and/or the support of public charitable hospitals. Geographic area includes Hartford, CT area primarily. Application is required, deadlines are Feb. 1 and Aug. 1.

## Delaware

**2635 Arc of Delaware**
2 S Augustine Street
Suite B
Wilmington, DE 19804-2504
302-996-9400
FAX: 302-996-0683
e-mail: eraign@arcde.org
www.thearcofdelaware.org

*Terry Reilly, President*
*Bill Seufert, Vice President*
*Ruth Lavelle, Secretary*
*Margo Johnson, Treasurer*

The Arc of Delaware is a non-profit organization of volunteers and staff who work together to improve the quality of life for people with disabilitiesand their families. We strive to include all children and adults with cognitive, intellectual and developmental disabilities in every community.

**2636 Longwood Foundation**
100 W 10th St
Suite 1109
Wilmington, DE 19801-1694
302-654-2477
FAX: 302-654-2323

*Peter Morrow, Executive Director*

Offers grants to the mentally and physically disabled - capital, program, education and housing grants in the state of Delaware.

## District of Columbia

**2637 Alexander and Margaret Stewart Trust**
Brawner Building
888 17th Street NW
Suite 1250
Washington, DC 20006-3321 202-333-1277
FAX: 202-333-3128
e-mail: aplatt@projectsinternational.com
www.projectsinternational.com

*Alexander H. Platt, Executive Vice President*
*Imtiaz T. Ladak, Managing Director & CFO*
Grants are given only to the Washington, DC area organizations providing care or treatment to cancer patients or those with childhood afflictions.

**2638 Arc of the District of Columbia**
415 Michigan Avenue, NE
Suite 400
Washington, DC 20017- 2144 202-636-2950
FAX: 202-635-7086
e-mail: arcdc@arcdc.net
www.arcdc.net

*Mary Lou Meccariello, Executive Director*
*Michael Gonzales, Chief Operating Officer*
*Ed Cabatic, Director of Finance*
*Matt Rosen, Dir. Advocacy & Public Policy*
Advocating for and providing services to persons with mental retardation. Mission is to improve the quality of life of all persons with mental retardation and their families through supports and advocacy.

**2639 Eugene and Agnes E Meyer Foundation**
The Meyer Foundation
1250 Connecticut Ave NW
Suite 800
Washington, DC 20036- 2620 202-483-8294
FAX: 202-328-6850
e-mail: meyer@meyerfdn.org
www.meyerfoundation.org

*Julie Rogers, President & CEO*
*Danielle M. Reyes, Senior Program Officer*
*Jane Robinson Ward, Grants Manager & Program Officer*
*Jennifer Burke, Business Operations Assistant*
Awards grants to projects dealing with the learning disabled, blind, mental health and vocational training in the Washington metropolitan area.

**2640 Federal Student Aid Information Center**
US Department of Education
400 Maryland Ave SW
Washington, DC 20202 202-275-5446
800-433-3243
www.ed.gov

*Arne Duncan, Secretary of Education*
*Tony Miller, Deputy Secretary*
*Martha Kanter, Under Secretary*
Answers questions about Federal student aid from students, parents and Members of Congress, as well as financial aid administrators.

**2641 GEICO Philanthropic Foundation**
1 Geico Plz
Washington, DC 20076 301-986-3000
800-841-3000
FAX: 301-986-2851
www.geico.com

*Tony M Nicely, CEO*
Hospitals, physically disabled and Special Olympics.

**2642 Giant Food Foundation**
Ste 115
8301 Professional Pl
Landover, MD 20785-2351 301-341-4100
888-469-4426
e-mail: jmiller@giantfood.com
www.giantfood.com

*Anthony Hucker, President*
*Brian Beatty, Md. Director of Marketing and External Communications*
*Stefanie Cain, Md. District Director*
*Bob Haas, Md. District Director*
Offers grants in the areas of mental health, recreation, community and cultural programs, art, and educational programs for the health and prosperity of the greater Washington area.

**2643 Jacob and Charlotte Lehrman Foundation**
1836 Columbia Rd NW
Washington, DC 20009-2002 202-328-8400
FAX: 202-338-8405
www.lehrmanfoundation.org

*Elizabeth Berry, Director*
*Robert Lehrman, Trustee*
*Samuel Lehrman, Trustee*
*Barbara Ferguson, Administrative/Program assistant*
The Jacob & Charlotte Lehrman Foundation supports and seeks to enrich Jewish life in Washington DC, Israel and around the world. It is committed to making Washington a better place for all people and supports the arts, education and undeserved children, the environment, and healthcare.

**2644 John Edward Fowler Memorial Foundation**
Ste 206
4340 East West Hwy
Bethesda, MD 20814-4467 301-654-2700
www.foundationcenter.org

*Richard H Lee, President*
*Ann Matikan, Grant Consultant*
Although not a program priority, the foundation does offer grants to the physically disabled in the Washington, DC area only.

**2645 Joseph P Kennedy Jr Foundation**
12th Fl
1133 19th St NW
Washington, DC 20036-3604 202-393-1250
FAX: 202-824-0351
e-mail: jpkf@jpkf.org
www.jpkf.org

*Rebecca Salon, President*
*Steven Eidelman, Executive Director*
Has two firm objectives: to seek the prevention of mental retardation, and to improve the way society deals with its citizens who are already mentally retarded. The Foundation uses its funds in areas where a multiplier effect can be achieved through development of innovative models for the prevention and amelioration of mental retardation, through provision of seed money that encourages new researchers, and through use of the Foundation's influence to promote public awareness.

**2646 Kiplinger Foundation**
1729 H St NW
Washington, DC 20006-3938 202-887-6400
FAX: 202-778-8976
e-mail: foundation@kiplinger.com
kiplinger.com

*Knight Kiplinger, VP*
Limited to the greater Washington, DC area, the grants focus primarily on education, social welfare, cultural activities and community programs. Matching grants to eligible secondary or higher education institutions are provided on behalf of employees and retirees of Kiplinger Washington Editors, Inc. The Foundation does not fund scholarships.

2647 **Morris and Gwendolyn Cafritz Foundation**
Ste 1400
1825 K St NW
Washington, DC 20006-1271
202-223-3100
800-544-0155
FAX: 202-296-7567
e-mail: info@cafritzfoundation.org
cafritzfoundation.org

*Calvin Cafritz, President and CEO*
*Daniel J. Callahan, Vice Chairman and Treasurer*
*Ed McGeogh, Vice President - Asset Management*
*Rohan Rodrigo, Vice President - Finance*
Grants are awarded to only 501(c)(3) organizations that are in the DC area. Grants are not awarded for capitol purposes, special events, endowments, or to individuals.

2648 **Paul and Annetta Himmelfarb Foundation**
Ste 203
4545 42nd St NW
Washington, DC 20016-4623
202-966-3796

*M Preston, Executive Director*
Primary areas of interest include health, children, human need, and Israel.

2649 **Public Welfare Foundation**
1200 U St NW
Washington, DC 20009-4443
202-965-1800
e-mail: info@publicwelfare.org
publicwelfare.org

*Mary E. McClymont, President*
*Phillipa Taylor, Chief Financial and Administrative Officer*
*Margie Robinson, Grants Manager*
*Ellen Gordon, Controller*
The foundation's funding is specifically targeted to economically disadvantaged populations. Proposals must fall within one of the following categories: criminal justice, disadvantaged elderly, disadvantaged youth, environment, health and population and reproductive health, human rights and global security, and community economic developmental and participation. Proposals should be addressed to the Review Committee.

## Florida

2650 **Able Trust**
3320 Thomasville Road
Suite 200
Tallahassee, FL 32308
850-224-4493
FAX: 850-224-4493
e-mail: info@abletrust.org
www.abletrust.org

*Susanne Homant, President*
*Guenevere Crum, Senior Vice President*
*Kathryn McManus, MA, Chief Development Director*
*Allison Chase, MS, State Director, Florida High School/High Tech*
The Able Trust is a non-profit, public/private partnership that supports non-profit vocational rehabilitation programs throughout Florida with fundraising, grant making and public awareness of disability issues.

2651 **Arc of Florida**
Ste 1
2898 Mahan Dr
Tallahassee, FL 32308-5462
850-921-0460
800-226-1155
e-mail: info@arcflorida.org
www.arcflorida.org

*Michele Poole, President*
*Greg Roe, Treasurer*
*Dick Bradley, Vice President Administration*
*Linda Bloom, Vice President Advocacy*
Promotes, for all people with mental retardation and other developmental disablilities, through education, awareness, research, advocacy and the support of families, friends and community.

2652 **BCR Foundation**
83 Mussey Rd.
Scarborough, ME 04074
207-883-8000
800-227-6111
FAX: 207-883-0100
e-mail: solutions@bcr.net
http://www.bcr.net/
Specializes on the delivery of a variety of telecommunications products and services to include digital and VoIP telephone systems, voicemail systems, computer-telephone applications, and the installation of data, voice and video cabling.

2653 **Bank of America Client Foundation**
50 Central Avenue
Suite 750
Sarasota, FL 34236-5900
941-951-4103
e-mail: maryann.l.smith@ustrust.com
http://foundationcenter.org/grantmaker/boacf/

*Maryann L. Smith, Vice President, Senior Trust Officer*
Committed to creating meaningful change in the communities we serve through our philanthropic efforts, associate volunteerism, community development activities and investing, support of arts and culture programming and environmental initiatives.

2654 **Barron Collier Jr Foundation**
2600 Golden Gate Pkwy
Naples, FL 34105-3227
239-262-2600
FAX: 239-262-1840
e-mail: ContactUs@BarronCollier.com
barroncollier.com

*Karen V. Triplett, Director of Property Management and Licensed Real Estate Broker*
*Jose Medina, Facilities Manager*
Barron Collier Companies - dedicated to the responsible development, management and stewardship of its extensive land holdings and other assets in the businesses of agriculture, real estate, and mineral management.

2655 **Camiccia-Arnautou Charitable Foundation**
Ste 402
980 N Federal Hwy
Boca Raton, FL 33432-2712
561-368-5757
FAX: 561-368-8505

*Ronda Gluck, President*

2656 **Chatlos Foundation**
P.O.Box 915048
Longwood, FL 32791-5048
407-862-5077
e-mail: info@chatlos.org
www.chatlos.org

*Bill Chatlos, Trustee*
Funds nonprofit organizations in the USA and around the globe. Funding is provided in the following areas of giving: Bible Colleges/Seminaries, Religious Causes, Medical Concerns, Liberal Arts Colleges and Social Concerns. Category of placement is determined by the organizations overall mission rather than the project under consideration. The Foundation does not make scholarship grants directly to individuals but rather to educational institutions which in turn select recipients.

2657 **Dade Community Foundation**
Ste 505
200 S Biscayne Blvd
Miami, FL 33131-2343
305-371-2711
FAX: 305-371-5342
e-mail: ruth.shack@dadecommunityfoundation.org
dadecommunityfoundation.org

*Ruth Shack, President*

The Foundation approaches all of its program activities with a focus on building the community. We conduct acticvities and support efforts that build community assets and relationships among individuals, organizations, and communities that connect people with resources and opportunities to improve their quality of life.

**2658 Dr. Jack Widrich Foundation**
400 W Rivo Alto Dr
Miami Beach, FL 33139-1262 305-673-5050

*Jack Widrich, Owner*

**2659 Edyth Bush Charitable Foundation**
Ste 100
199 E Welbourne Ave
Winter Park, FL 32789-4365 407-647-4322
888-647-4322
FAX: 407-647-7716
e-mail: dodahowski@edythbush.org
edythbush.org

*David A. Odahowski, President*
*Mary Ellen Hutcheson, Vice President and Treasurer*
*Deborah J. Hessler, Program Officer and Corporate Secretary*
*Gerald F. Hilbrich, Chairman*
Funding is resrticted to 501c3 nonprofit organizations located and operating in Orange, Osceola, Seminole and Lake Counties, Florida. Visit www.edythbush.org for a list of funding policies.

**2660 FPL Group Foundation**
700 Universe Blvd
Juno Beach, FL 33408-2657 561-694-4000
888-488-7703
FAX: 561-694-4620
e-mail: PoweringFlorida@FPL.com
http://www.fpl.com

*Maria V. Fogarty, Senior Vice President, Internal Audit & Compliance*
*James L. Robo, President and Chief Operating Officer*
*Joseph T. Kelliher, Executive Vice President, Federal Regulatory Affairs*
*Antonio Rodriguez, Executive Vice President, Power Generation Division*
The company consistently outperforms national averages for service reliability while customer bills are below the national average. A clean energy leader, FPL has one of the lowest emissions profiles and one of the leading energy efficiency programs among utilities nationwide. FPL is a subsidiary of Juno Beach, Fla.-based NextEra Energy, Inc.

**2661 Florida Rock Industries Foundation**
155 E 21st St
Jacksonville, FL 32206-2104 904-355-1781
FAX: 904-791-1810
www.flarock.com

*John D Milton Jr, President*

**2662 Frank Stanley Beveridge Foundation**
19 Homestead Park
Needham, MA 02494 800-229-9667
e-mail: administrator@beveridge.org
www.beveridge.org

*Ward Slocum Caswell, President*
*Ruth S. DuPont, Treasurer*
*Philip Caswell, Chairman and Vice President*
*Leah Beveridge Richardson, Clerk*
The mission of The Frank Stanley Beveridge Foundation, Inc. is to preserve and enhance the quality of life by embracing and perpetuating Frank Stanley Beveridge's philanthropic vision through grantmaking initiatives in support of The Stanley Park of Westfield, Inc. and programs in youth development, health, education, religion, art and environment primarily in Hampden and Hampshire Counties, Massachusetts.

**2663 Jefferson Lee Ford III Memorial Foundation**
9600 Collins Ave
Bal Harbour, FL 33154-2202 305-868-2609
FAX: 305-868-2640

*Sanford L King, Director*
*Yvonne Quatrale, President*
Disabled children, hearing and speech center. Grants are only given to tax exempt organizations, no individual grants are offered.

**2664 Jessie Ball duPont Fund**
Ste 1400
1 Independent Dr
Jacksonville, FL 32202-5011 904-353-0890
800-252-3452
FAX: 904-353-3870
e-mail: contactus@dupontfund.org
www.dupontfund.org

*Sherry P. Magill, President*
*Mark D. Constantine, Vice President for Strategy, Policy and Learning*
*Sally Howard Douglass, Director of Programs*
*Katie Ensign, Senior Program Officer*
Established under the terms of the will of the late Jessie Ball duPont. The fund is a national foundation having a special though not exclusive interest in issues affecting the South. The Fund works with the approximately 325 individual institutions to which Mrs. duPont personally contributed during the five-year period, 1960 through 1964.

**2665 Lost Tree Village Charitable Foundation**
11555 Lost Tree Way
North Palm Beach, FL 33408-2908 561-622-3780
FAX: 561-622-7558
e-mail: info@losttreefoundation.org
www.losttreefoundation.org

The Lost Tree Village Charitable Foundation is dedicated to building a stronger community and improving the quality of life for all local residents. Grants are awarded annually to local non-profit health and human service organizations providing information, expertise and assistance to those in need. Applications are only accepted from organizations located in Palm Beach and Southern Martin Counties. Visit the website for guidelines and further information.

**2666 National Parkinson Foundation**
1501 N.W. 9th Avenue / Bob Hope Roa
Miami, FL 33136-1494 305-243-6666
800-327-4545
FAX: 305-243-6073
e-mail: contact@parkinson.org
www.parkinson.org

*Joyce Oberdorf, President & CEO*
*Pamela Olmo, Vice President, Finance & Administration*
*Robin Boettcher, Vice President, Chapter and Community Partnerships*
*Peter Schmidt, PhD, Vice President, Programs, Chief Information Officer*
The mission of the NPF is to improve the quality of care for people with Parkinson's disease through research, education, and outreach.

**2667 Publix Super Markets Charities**
Publix Super Market Corporation Office
P.O.Box 407
Lakeland, FL 33802-0407 800-242-1227
publix.com

*Gino DiGrazia, Vice President of Finance*
*Maria Brous, Director of Media & Community Relations*
*Kimberly Reynolds, Media & Community Relations*
In addition to giving to thousands of local projects, Publix annually supports five organizations in companywide campaigns: Special Olympics, March of Dimes, Children's Miracle Network, United Way and Food for All

**2668 Richard W Higgins Charitable Foundation**
Marshall & Ilsley Trust of Florida
Ste 100
800 Laurel Oak Dr
Naples, FL 34108-2713
877-202-9234
applebees.com

*Ken Krei, President*
Gives primarily for medical research with geographical focus on New York and Florida.

## Georgia

**2669 Arc Of Georgia**
Ste 1675
100 Edgewood Ave NE
Atlanta, GA 30303-3068
678-733-8969
888-401-1581
FAX: 678-733-8970
e-mail: info@thearcofgeorgia.org
www.thearcofgeorgia.org/

*Torin Togut, President*
*David Glass, Vice President*
*Julie Lee, Secretary*
*Will Hudson, Treasurer*
The Arc of Georgia advocates for the rights and full participation of all children and adults with intellectual and developmental disabilities. Together with our network of members and other local Chapters, we improve systems of supports and services, connect families, inspire communities, and influence public policy.

**2670 Community Foundation for Greater Atlanta**
Ste 449
50 Hurt Plz SE
Atlanta, GA 30303-2915
404-688-5525
FAX: 404-688-3060
e-mail: info@cfgreateratlanta.org
www.atlcf.org

*Alicia Philipp, President*
*Latasha Sutherland, Executive Assistant to the President*
*Robert Smulian, Vice President of Philanthropic Services*
*Christy Eckoff, Director of Gift Planning*
The Community Foundation for Greater Atlanta is a creative, cost-effective and tax-efficient way for people to invest in our community. We help donors and their families meet their charitable goals by educating them or critical issues and by matching them with organizations that serve their interests. By working with donors and the community, we improve the quality of life for residents in our region.

**2671 Florence C and Harry L English Memorial Fund**
Sun Trust Bank Atlanta
P.O.Box 4418
Mail Code 041
Atlanta, GA 30302
404-588-8250
FAX: 404-724-3082
e-mail: raymond.king@suntrust.com
www.suntrustatlantafoundation.org

*Anil T. Cheriyan, Chief Information Officer*
*Kenneth J. Carrig, Chief Human Resources Officer*
*Rilla S. Delorier, Chief Marketing and Client Experience Officer*
*Thomas E. Freeman, Chief Risk Officer*
Grants only made to Metro Atlanta non-profit organizations; no grants to churches or individuals.

**2672 Georgia Power**
241 Ralph McGill Boulevard NE
Atlanta, GA 30308-3374
404-506-6526
888-655-5888
georgiapower.com

*W. Paul Bowers, President and CEO*
*Chief Human Owens, VP, Human Resources and Labor*
*Anthony Wilson, Executive VP, Customer Service & Operations*
*Moanica Caston, Chief Risk Officer*
Georgia Power is an investor-owned, tax-paying utility that serves 2.25 million customers in all but four of Georgia's 159 counties.

**2673 Grayson Foundation**
1701 Willa Place Drive
Kernersville, NC 2728
336-650-9914
e-mail: graysonfoundation@gmail.com
http://graysonfoundation.net/

*Donna Sherrell, Finance- Public Relations*
*Tricia Gladstone, Behavior Analyst-Finance Public Relations*
*Roger Sherrell, Information Technology-Web Manager*
*Bob Sherrell, Finance*
Grayson Foundation enhances the quality of public educationfor the students of the Grayson cluster of schools by providing funds which enrich and extend educational oppurtunities.

**2674 Harriet McDaniel Marshall Trust in Memory of Sanders McDaniel**
Sun Trust Bank Atlanta
P.O.Box 4418
Mail Code 041
Atlanta, GA 30302
404-588-8250
FAX: 404-724-3082
e-mail: raymond.king@suntrust.com
www.suntrustatlantafoundation.org

*Anil T. Cheriyan, Chief Information Officer*
*Kenneth J. Carrig, Chief Human Resources Officer*
*Rilla S. Delorier, Chief Marketing and Client Experience Officer*
*Thomas E. Freeman, Chief Risk Officer*
Grants only made to Metro Atlanta non-profit organizations, no grants to churches or individuals.

**2675 IBM Corporation**
1 New Orchard Rd
Armonk, NY 10504-1772
914-499-1900
800-426-4968
TTY:800-426-3383
ibm.com

*Samuel J Palmisano, Chairman*
*Virginia M. Rometty, President and Chief Executive Officer*
*Rodney C. Adkins, Senior Vice President*
*Michael E. Daniels, Senior Vice President and Group Executive*
Manages disability programs (which leverage IBM resources through partnerships) designed to train persons with disabilities and assist them in gaining employment. Also, disseminates information regarding products and resources for persons with disabilities with those of other companies and organizations.

**2676 John H and Wilhelmina D Harland Charitable Foundation**
Two Piedmont Center, Suite 710
3565 Piedmont Road, NE
Atlanta, GA 30305-1502
404-264-9912
FAX: 404-266-8834
e-mail: info@harlandfoundation.org
http://harlandfoundation.org/

*Jane G Hardesty, Executive Director*
*Gail G. Byers, Grants Manager*
*Margaret C. Reiser, President*
*Winifred S. Davis, Vice President and Treasurer*
The Harland Charitable Foundation was established in 1972 by John H. and Wilhelmina D. Harland to support worthy local causes in Atlanta, with a particular interest in improving the

welfare of children and youth as well as support of community services and arts and culture.

**2677 Lettie Pate Whitehead Foundation**
191 Peachtree Street NE
Suite 3540
Atlanta, GA 30303- 2951
404-522-6755
FAX: 404-522-7026
e-mail: fdns@woodruff.org
woodruff.org

*P Russell Hardin, President*
*J. Lee Tribble, Treasurer*
*Erik S. Johnson, General Counsel and Secretary*
*Elizabeth A. Smith, Grants Program Director*
Non-profit organization dedicated to the support of needy women in nine southeastern states.

**2678 Rich Foundation**
222 Summer Street
Stamford, CT 06901
203-359-2900
FAX: 203-328-7980
e-mail: info@fdrich.com
http://www.fdrich.com

A private foundation under section 509(a) of the Internal Revenue Code designed primariliy for the benefit of the residents and charitable organizations of lower Fairfield County.

**2679 SunTrust Bank, Atlanta Foundation**
Sun Trust Bank Atlanta
P.O.Box 4418
Mail Code 041
Atlanta, GA 30302
404-588-8250
FAX: 404-724-3082
e-mail: raymond.king@suntrust.com
www.suntrustatlantafoundation.org

*Anil T. Cheriyan, Chief Information Officer*
*Kenneth J. Carrig, Chief Human Resources Officer*
*Rilla S. Delorier, Chief Marketing and Client Experience Officer*
*Thomas E. Freeman, Chief Risk Officer*

## Hawaii

**2680 Arc of Hawaii**
3989 Diamond Head Rd
Honolulu, HI 96816-4413
808-737-7995
FAX: 808-732-9531
e-mail: info@thearcinhawaii.org
thearcinhawaii.org

*Thomas Huber, President*
*Lee Moriwaki, Vice President*
*Leolinda Parlin, Secretary*
*Noelle Liew, Treasurer*
The Arc is a national, grassroots organization of and for people with intellectual and related developmental disabilities. With more then 140,000 members in 1000 local and state chapters. The Arc is the largest volunteer organization devoted soley to working on behalf of people with intellectual disabilities.

**2681 Atherton Family Foundation**
827 Fort Street Mall
Honolulu, HI 96813-2817
808-566-5524
888-731-3863
FAX: 808-521-6286
e-mail: foundations@hcf-hawaii.org
www.atherton.hawaiicommunityfoundation.org

*Patricia R. Giles, Vice President*
*Judith M. Dawson, President*
*Frank C. Atherton, Vice President and Treasurer*
*Paul F. Morgan, Vice President*
Supports educational projects, programs and institutions as the highest priority, with the enterprises of a religious nature and those concerned with health and social services given careful attention. The Foundation is one of the largest private resources in the State devoted exclusively to the support of activities of a charitable nature.

**2682 GN Wilcox Trust**
Bank of Hawaii
P.O.Box 3170
Honolulu, HI 96802-3170
808-649-4945
800-272-7262
FAX: 808-538-4006
e-mail: paula.boyce@boh.com
https://www.boh.com

*Paul Boyce, AVP and Grants Administrator*
*Elaine Moniz, Trust Specialist*
*William "Bill" L. Carpenter, Senior Vice President*
*Diane W. Murakami, Senior Vice President*
Benefits the people of Hawaii by funding programs that support social services, education, culture, the arts, youth services, religion, health and rehabilitation.

**2683 Hawaii Community Foundation**
827 Fort Street Mall
Honolulu, HI 96813-2817
808-537-6333
888-731-3863
FAX: 808-521-6286
e-mail: info@hcf-hawaii.org
hawaiicommunityfoundation.org

*Kelvin Taketa, President and CEO*
*Colleen Sotomura, Director of Communications*
*Wally Chin, Vice President & Chief Financial Officer*
*Kate Lloyd, General Counsel & Vice President of Operations*
The Hawaii Community Foundation is a public, statewide, charitable services and grantmaking organization supported by donor contributions for the benefit of Hawaii's people.

**2684 McInerny Foundation Bank Of Hawaii,Corporate Trustee**
P.O.Box 3170
Honolulu, HI 96802-3170
808-538-4945
800-272-7262
FAX: 808-538-4006
e-mail: paula.boyce@boh.com
https://www.boh.com

*Paula Boyce, Avp And Grants Administrator*
*Elaine Moniz, Trust Specialist*
*William "Bill" L. Carpenter, Senior Vice President*
*Diane W. Murakami, Senior Vice President*
Although the Trust is broad-purposed, it does not make grants to churches or individuals, nor for endowments, reserve purposes, deficit financing, or for the purchase of real estate.

**2685 Sophie Russell Testamentary Trust Bank Of Hawaii**
P.O.Box 3170
Honolulu, HI 96802-3170
808-538-4944
800-272-7262
FAX: 808-538-4006
e-mail: paula.boyce@boh.com
https://www.boh.com

*Paula Boyce, Asst. Vice President*
*Elaine Moniz, Trust Specialist*
*William "Bill" L. Carpenter, Senior Vice President*
*Diane W. Murakami, Senior Vice President*
Supports qualified tax-exempt charitable organizations, in the State of Hawaii only. Offers grants to the Humane Society and institutions giving nursing care and serving the physically and mentally handicapped.

## Illinois

**2686 Alzheimer's Association**
Fl 17
225 N Michigan Ave
Chicago, IL 60601-7633
312-335-8700
800-272-3900
FAX: 312-335-5886
TTY: 312-335-5886
e-mail: info@alz.org
www.alz.org

*Harry Johns, President and CEO*
*Robert J. Egge, Vice President, Public Policy and Advocacy*
*Angela Geiger, Chief Strategy Officer*
*Richard Hovland, Chief Operations Officer*

Mission is to eliminate Alzheimer's disease through the advancement of research, to provide and enhance care and support for all affected, and to reduce the risk of dementia through the promotion of brain health.

**2687 American National Bank and Trust Company**
33 N La Salle St
Chicago, IL 60602-2650
312-661-6000
800-240-8190
FAX: 815-961-7745
https://www.amnb.com/

*Charles H. Majors, Chairman & Chief Executive Officer*
*Jeffrey V. Haley, President*
*Charles T. Canaday, Jr., Senior Vice President*
*R. Helm Dobbins, Senior Vice President*

Supports the endeavors of organizations working to meet the critical needs of the city and its surrounding communities. Success is greatly affected by the well-being of the communities the company serves, thus the foundation seeks to fulfill the social obligations both through financial funding and human resources. The Foundation funding categories include organizations and programs involved in economic development, education, community and social services, healthcare and culture and the arts.

**2688 Amerock Corporation**
P.O.Box 7018
Rockford, IL 61125-7018
815-963-9631
800-618-9559
FAX: 815-969-6029
www.amerock.com

*Robert Bailey, President*

Grants are given to organizations promoting wellness, health and rehabilitation of the visually impaired and physically disabled.

**2689 Arc of Illinois**
The Illinois Life Span Project
Ste 209
20901 S La Grange Rd
Frankfort, IL 60423-3213
815-464-1832
800-588-7002
FAX: 815-464-5292
e-mail: mike@illinoislifespan.org
http://www.thearcofil.org/

*Mike Kaminsky, Ilinois Life Span Director*
*Tony Paulauski, Executive Director*
*Shirley Perez, Family Support Network-Executive Director*
*Janet Donahue, Director of Development*

The Arc of Illinois is committed to empowering persons with disabilities to achieve full participation in community life thru informed choices.

**2690 Benjamin Benedict Green-Field Foundation**
18313 Greenleaf Ct
Tinley Park, IL 60487-2176
708-444-4241
FAX: 708-614-0496
e-mail: kathy@greenfieldfoundation.org
greenfieldfoundation.org

*Kathryn Groenendal, President*
*Colin Fisher, Chairman of the Board*
*Dan Jarke, Vice President*
*Sheldon K. Rachman, Secretary*

A privately endowed grantmaking organization trying to improve the qaulity of life for children and the elderly in the city of chicago.

**2691 Blowitz-Ridgeway Foundation**
Ste 201
1701 E Woodfield Rd
Schaumburg, IL 60173-5127
847-330-1020
FAX: 847-330-1028
e-mail: laura@blowitzridgeway.org
www.blowitzridgeway.org

*Daniel L Kline, President*
*Pierre R. LeBreton, Ph.D., Vice-President*
*Anthony M. Dean, Treasurer*
*Sandra Swantek, M.D., Secretary*

Provides limited program, capital and research grants to organizations aiding the physically and mentally disabled, and agencies serving children and youth. Grants generally limited to Illinois.

**2692 Chaddick Institute for Metropolitan Development**
Ste 9000
243 S Wabash Ave
Chicago, IL 60604-2302
312-362-5731
FAX: 312-362-5506
e-mail: chaddick@depaul.edu
http://las.depaul.edu/

*Joseph P Schwieterman PhD, Director*
*Marisa Schulz, LEED AP, Assistant Director*
*Susan Aaron, Civic Program Design*
*Brett Baden, Ph.D., Research Fellow*

Advances the principals of effective land use, transportation, and community planning. Offers planners, attorneys, developers, and entrepreneurs a forum to share expertise on difficult land-use issues through workshops, conferences, and policy studies.

**2693 Chicago Community Trust**
Ste 1400
111 E Wacker Dr
Chicago, IL 60601-4501
312-616-8000
FAX: 312-616-7955
e-mail: alla@cct.org
cct.org

*Terry Mazany, President*
*Ngoan Le, Vice President-Program*
*Jamie Phillippe, Vice President-Development and Donor Services*
*Chae Dawning, Director of HR and Administration*

A community foundation established in 1915, which receives gifts and bequests from individuals, families or organizations interested in providing through the community foundation, financial support for the charitable agencies or institutions which serve the residents of metropolitan Chicago.

**2694 Chicago Community Trust and Affiliates**
Ste 1400
111 E Wacker Dr
Chicago, IL 60601-4501
312-616-8000
FAX: 312-616-7955
TTY:312-853-0394
e-mail: alla@cct.org
cct.org

*Terry Mazany, President*
*Ngoan Le, Vice President-Program*
*Jamie Phillippe, Vice President-Development and Donor Services*
*Chae Dawning, Director of HR and Administration*
Provides critical charitable resources in the arts, community and economic development, education, health and wellness, hunger and homeless alleviation, legal services, programs for youth, the elderly, and people with disabilities, and services to assure that basic human needs are met for all members of our community.

**2695 Community Foundation of Champaign County**
307 W University Ave
Champaign, IL 61820-3411
217-359-0125
FAX: 217-352-6494
e-mail: cfcc@soltec.net
cfeci.org

*Joan M. Dixon, President & CEO*
*David Parkhill, Treasurer*
*Maureen Banks, Secretary*
*Tony Ackerman, Chair*
A network of cultural resource providers and educational organizations who collaborate in the creation, coordination, and promotion of cultural resource programs for Champaign County Schools.

**2696 Dr Scholl Foundation**
Ste 230
1033 Skokie Blvd
Northbrook, IL 60062-4109
847-559-7430
drschollfoundation.com

*Pamela Scholl, President*
The Foundation is dedicated to providing financial assistance to organizations committed to improving our world. Grants are made annually after an executive review by the staff and all the directors.

**2697 Duchossois Foundation**
Chamberlain Group
845 N Larch Ave
Elmhurst, IL 60126-1114
630-279-3600
FAX: 630-530-6091
e-mail: investments@duch.com
http://www.duch.com/

*Craig J Duchossois, CEO*
*Robert L. Fealy, President & Chief Operating Officer*
*Michael E. Flannery, Executive Vice President & Chief Financial Officer*
*Colleen M. O'Connor, Vice President & Treasurer*
Established in 1984, the foundation returns dollars to the communities supporting its facilities and employees. Within these following areas, organizations are carefully selected on the basis of community needs and the organization's value and performance. Areas aimed at include: medical research, children/youth programs and cultural institutions.

**2698 Evenston Community Foundation**
Ste 108
1007 Church St
Evanston, IL 60201-5910
847-492-0990
FAX: 847-492-0904
e-mail: info@evanstonforever.org
evanstonforever.org

*Sara Schastok, Phd., President and CEO*
*Marybeth Schroeder, Vice President for Programs*
*Jan Fischer, Chief Financial Officer*
*Jeremy R. Barrows, Director of Development and Communications*
The Foundation is a publicly supported plilanthropic organization dedicated to enriching Evanston and the lives of its people, now and in the future. The Foundation builds and manages its own and other community endowments, addresses Evanston's changing needs through grant making, and provides leadership on important community needs.

**2699 Field Foundation of Illinois**
Ste 3860
200 S Wacker Dr
Chicago, IL 60606-5848
312-831-0910
FAX: 312-831-0961
e-mail: byoung@fieldfoundation.org
fieldfoundation.org

*Aurie A. Pennick, Executive Director and Treasurer*
*Amber M. Gladney, Program Officer*
*Beatrice Young, Grants Manager/Executive Assistant*
*Kim Riordan Van Horn, Senior Program Officer*
The Field Foundation seeks to provide support for community, civic and cultural organizations in the Chicago area, enabling both new and established programs to test innovations, to expand proven strengths or to address specific, time-limited operational needs.

**2700 Francis Beidler Charitable Trust**
Ste 530
53 W Jackson Blvd
Chicago, IL 60604-3422
312-922-3792
FAX: 312-922-3799

*Francis Beidler, Owner*
Children/youth, services. Community development, business promotion, crime and violence prevention. Federated giving programs, higher education, human services and family planning.

**2701 Fred J Brunner Foundation**
9300 King St
Franklin Park, IL 60131-2114
847-678-3232
FAX: 847-678-0642
http://fjbfoundation.com/

*Fred J Brunner, CEO*
General disability grants.

**2702 George M Eisenberg Foundation for Charities**
Ste 480
2340 S Arlington Heights Rd
Arlington Heights, IL 60005-4507
847-981-0545
FAX: 847-941-0548

*James Marousis, Manager*

**2703 Grover Hermann Foundation**
233 S Wacker Dr
Chicago, IL 60606-6306
312-258-5500
FAX: 312-258-5600
e-mail: rsafer@schiffhardin.com
schiffhardin.com

*Ronald S. Safer, Managing Partner, Executive Committee Member*
Provides funds for educational, health, public policy, community and religious organizations throughout the United States. Its major interests are in higher education and health.

2704 **John D and Catherine T MacArthur Foundation**
Office of Grants Management
140 S Dearborn St
Chicago, IL 60603-5285
312-726-8000
FAX: 312-920-6258
TTY:312-920-6285
e-mail: 4answers@macfound.org
www.macfound.org

*Robert L. Gallucci, President*
*Barry Lowenkron, Vice President, International Programs*
*Joshua J. Mintz, Vice President & General Counsel*
*Marc P. Yanchura, Vice President and Chief Financial Officer*
The Foundation supports creative people and effective institutions committed to building a more just, verdant, and peaceful world. In addition, we work to defend human rights, advance global conservation, & security, make cities better places, and understand how technology is affecting children and society.

2705 **Les Turne Amyotrophic Laterial Sclerosis Foundation**
Ste 302
5550 Touhy Ave
Skokie, IL 60077-3254
847-679-3311
888-257-1107
FAX: 847-679-9109
e-mail: info@lesturnerals.org
lesturnerals.org

*Harvey Gaffen, President*
*Kenneth M. Crane, Vice President*
*Jim Derleth, Vice President*
*William N. Haarlow, PhD, Treasurer*
Voluntary health organization dedicated to raising funds for ALS research, patient services and public awareness. Provides educational materials for affected individuals and family members, health care professionals, and the general public. Program services include referrals and counseling; audio-visual aids and periodic newsletters. Offers support groups and patient networking to affected individuals, family members, and caregivers.

2706 **Little City Foundation**
1760 W Algonquin Rd
Palatine, IL 60067-4799
847-358-5510
FAX: 847-358-3291
e-mail: abechtloff@littlecity.org
www.littlecity.org

*Edward J. Hockfield, President*
*Matthew B. Schubert, Executive Vice President*
*Douglas A. Wilson, Vice President*
*Matthew B. Schubert, Treasurer*
We offer innovative and personalized programs to fully assist and empower children & adults with autism and other intellectual and developmental disabilities. With a commitment to attaining a greater quality of life for Illinois most vulnerable citizens, we actively promote choice, person-centered planning and a holistic approach to health and wellness. 'ChildBridge' services include in-home personal & family supports, clinical behavior intervention, 24/7 residential services and much more.

2707 **MAGIC Foundation for Children's Growth**
6645 North Ave
Oak Park, IL 60302-1057
708-383-0808
800-362-4423
FAX: 708-383-0899
e-mail: dianne@magicfoundation.org
www.magicfoundation.org

*Rich Buckley, Chairman*
*Ken Dickard, Vice Chairman*
*Mary Andrews, CEO and Co-Founder*
*Courtney Lance, Director*
This is a national nonprofit organization providing support and education regarding growth disorders in children and related adult disorders, including adult GHD. Dedicated to helping children whose physical growth is affected by a medical problem by assisting families of afflicted children through local support groups, public education/awareness, newsletters, specialty divisions and programs for the children.

2708 **McDonald's Corporation Contributions Program**
2111 McDonalds Dr
Oak Brook, IL 60523-5500
630-623-3000
800-244-6227
FAX: 630-623-5700
mcdonalds.com

*Don Thompson, President and Chief Executive Officer*
*Tim Fenton, Chief Operating Officer*
*Peter J. Bensen, Executive Vice President and Chief Financial Officer*
*Jose Armario, Corporate Executive Vice President Worldwide Supply Chain, Development*

2709 **Michael Reese Health Trust**
Ste 2320
150 N Wacker Dr
Chicago, IL 60606-1608
312-726-1008
e-mail: wpalmer@healthtrust.net
www.healthtrust.net

*Gregory S. Gross, EdD, President*
*Herbert S. Wander, Chairman*
*The Hon. How Carroll, Vice Chairman*
*Walter R. Nathan, Secretary*
The trust seeks to improve the health of people in Chicago's metropolitan communities through effective grantmaking in health care, health education, and health research.

2710 **National Eye Research Foundation**
Ste 207a
910 Skokie Blvd
Northbrook, IL 60062-4033
847-564-9400
800-621-2258
FAX: 847-564-0807
e-mail: info@nerf.org
subway.com

*Joel Tenner, Manager*
Dedicated to improving eye care for the public and meeting the professional needs of eye care practitioners; sponsors eye research projects on contact lens applications and eye care problems. Special study sections in such fields as orthokertology, primary eyecare, pediatrics, and through continuing education programs. Provides eye care information for the public and professionals. Educational materials including pamphlets. Program activities include education and referrals.

2711 **National Headache Foundation**
Ste 217
820 N Orleans St
Chicago, IL 60610-3498
312-274-2650
888-643-5552
FAX: 312-640-9049
e-mail: info@headaches.org
headaches.org

*Arthur H. Elkind, M.D., President*
*Vincent Martin, M.D., Vice President*
*Lee Benton, Treasurer*
*Margaret Azarian, Secretary*
Foundation exists to enhance the healthcare of headache sufferers. It is a source of help to sufferers' families, physicians who treat headache sufferers, allied healthcare professionals and to the public.

2712 **OMRON Foundation OMRON Electronics**
1 Commerce Dr
Schaumburg, IL 60173-5330
847-843-7900
800-556-6766
FAX: 847-884-1866
e-mail: omroninfo@omron.com
www.omron247.com

*Tastu Goto, CEO*

Supports local community projects through direct donations and matching employee-directed contributions.

**2713 Parkinson's Disease Foundation**
833 W Washington Blvd
Chicago, IL 60607-2331
312-733-1893
800-457-667
FAX: 312-733-1896
e-mail: info@pdf.org
www.pdf.org

*Robin Anthony Elliott, Executive Director*
*James Beck, Ph.D., Director of Research Programs*
*Valerie Holt, Research Grants Administrator-Executive Assistant*
*David Blomquist, National Programs Coordinator*
International voluntary not-for-profit organization dedicated to patient services; education of affected individuals, family members, and healthcare professionals; and promotion and support of research for Parkinson's Disease and related disorders. Offers an extensive referral service to guide affected individuals to proper diagnosis and clinical care. Provides referrals to genetic counseling and support groups; promotes patient advocacy; and offers a variety of educational and support materials
*Quarterly*

**2714 Peoria Area Community Foundation**
Ste 310
331 Fulton St
Peoria, IL 61602-1449
309-674-8730
FAX: 309-674-8754
e-mail: jim@communityfoundationci.org
www.communityfoundationci.org

*Mark Roberts, CEO*
*Chris Glynn, Chair*
*Bashir Ali, Vice Chair*
*Sandra Burke, Secretary*
Established to meet a wide variety of social, cultural, educational and other charitable needs throughout Central Illinois.

**2715 Polk Brothers Foundation**
Ste 1110
20 W Kinzie St
Chicago, IL 60654-5815
312-527-4684
FAX: 312-527-4681
e-mail: questions@polkbrosfdn.org
polkbrosfdn.org

*Sandra P. Guthman, President*
*Raymond F. Simon, Vice President*
*Gordon S. Prussian, Secretary*
*Nikki Will Stein, Executive Director*
The Polk Brothers Foundation seeks to improve the quality of life for the people of Chicago. We partner with local nonprofit organizations that work to reduce the impact of poverty and provide area residents with better access to quality education, preventive health care and basic human services.

**2716 Retirement Research Foundation**
Ste 430
8765 W Higgins Rd
Chicago, IL 60631-4170
773-714-8080
FAX: 773-714-8089
e-mail: info@rrf.org
rrf.org

*Nathaniel P. McParland, M.D., Chairman*
*Ruth Ann Watkins, Secretary*
*Downey R. Varey, Treasurer*
*Irene Frye, Executive Director*
A private philanthropy with primary interest in improving the quality of life of older persons in the United States.

**2717 Sears-Roebuck Foundation**
3333 Beverly Rd
Hoffman Estates, IL 60179
847-286-2500
800-932-3188
FAX: 800-326-0485
sears.com

*W Bruce Johnson, CEO*
Has a special interest in projects that address women, families, and diversity, but awards most of its funding to disease-specific charities and United Way in the Chicago area.

**2718 Siragusa Foundation**
Ste 2910
1 E Wacker Dr
Chicago, IL 60601-1912
312-755-0064
FAX: 312-755-0069
www.siragusa.org

*Irene S Phelps, President*
*Sharmila Rao Thakkar, Senior Program Officer*
*Kyla M. Evans, Adminstrative Assistant/ Grants Administrator*
*John E. Hicks, Jr., Chair*
The Siragusa Foundation, is a private family foundation that is committed to honoring its founder by sustaining and developing Chicago's extraordinary nonprofit resources.

**2719 Square D Foundation**
1415 S Roselle Rd
Palatine, IL 60067-7337
847-397-2600
FAX: 847-925-7500
http://www.schneider-electric.com/site/home/i

Makes donations for operating support, capital development needs, and special projects to nonprofit organizations that have been granted exemption from the Federal Income Tax. The Foundation has a strong commitment to the following areas: health and welfare, education, civic and community affairs, and culture and the arts. Support of higher education is also made for scholarships, endowments for facility and acquisition or expansion of equipment or facilities, through Matching Gift Program.

**2720 WP and HB White Foundation**
Ste 3240
540 W Frontage Rd
Northfield, IL 60093-1232
847-446-1441

*Margaret Blandford, Executive Director*
The Foundation's funds are allocated on a continuing basis within the metropolitan area of Chicago where our founder's business prospered. The Foundation helps organizations specializing in the visually impaired, mental health, youth and recreation.

**2721 Washington Square Health Foundation**
Ste 3516
875 N Michigan Ave
Chicago, IL 60611-1957
312-664-6488
FAX: 312-664-7787
e-mail: washington@wshf.org
wshf.org

*William N. Werner, MD, MPH, President*
*Howard Nochumson, Executive Director*
*Catherine Baginski, Program Officer*
Grants funds in order to promote and maintain access to adequate healthcare for all people in the Chicagoland area regardless of race, sex, creed or financial need.

**2722 Wheat Ridge Ministries**
Ste 250 E
1 Pierce Pl
Itasca, IL 60143-1253
630-766-9066
800-762-6748
FAX: 630-766-9622
e-mail: wrmail@weatridge.org
www.wheatridge.org

*Richard Herman, President*
*Brian Becker, Vice President for Ministry Programs*
*Holly Harrison Fiala, Vice President of Advancement*
*Ann Brandt, Director of Annual Giving and Advancement Services*
Weat Ridge supports more then 100 new health-related ministries each year through a variety of grant programs

## Indiana

**2723 Arc of Indiana**
Ste 800
107 N Pennsylvania St
Indianapolis, IN 46204- 2423
317-977-2375
800-382-9100
FAX: 317-977-2385
e-mail: thearc@arcind.org
arcind.org

*John Dickerson, Executive Director*
*Kim Dodson, Associate Executive Director*
*Melissa Justice, The Arc Master Trust Director*
*Brandi Davis, Assistant Trust Director*
Arc of Indiana is commited to people with cognitive and developmental disabilities realizing their goals of learning, living, working, and playing in the community.

**2724 Ball Brothers Foundation**
222 S Mulberry St
Muncie, IN 47305-2802
765-741-5500
FAX: 765-741-5518
e-mail: info@ballfdn.org
www.ballfdn.org

*Jud Fisher, President and Chief Operating Officer*
*Neil Schmottlach, Ph. D., Program Officer*
*Rich Spisak, Program Officer*
*Donna Munchel, Executive Assistant*
The Ball Brothers Foundation is dedicated to the stewardship legacy of the Ball brothers and to the pursuit of improving the quality of the Muncie, Delaware County, east Central Indiana and Indiana, through philanthropy and leadership.

**2725 Community Foundation of Boone County**
P.O.Box 92
60 E. Cedar Street
Zionsville, IN 46077
317-873-0210
FAX: 317-873-0219
e-mail: info@communityfoundationbc.org
www.communityfoundationbc.org

*Mike Caldwell, Executive Director*
*Barb Schroeder, Executive Director*
*Gabi Youran, Director of Community Relations*
*Tiffany Perdue, Scholarship Administrator*
The Community Foundation of Boone County provides pathways for connecting people who care with causes that matter for now and in the future.

**2726 John W Anderson Foundation**
402 Wall St
Valparaiso, IN 46383-2562
219-462-4611
FAX: 219-531-8954
e-mail: andersonfnd@aol.com

*Bruce Wargo, Manager*
Physically and mentally disabled, recreation and youth agencies in Northwest Indiana area.

## Iowa

**2727 Arc of Iowa**
3821 71st St
Ste A
Urbandale, IA 50322-3259
515-210-6686
800-362-2927
FAX: 515-309-0860
e-mail: casey@thearcofiowa.org
www.thearcofiowa.org

*Casey Westhoff, Executive Director*
The Arc of Iowa exists to ensure that people with intellectual disabilities and developmental disabilities receive the services, supports and opportunities necessary to fully realize their right to live, work and enjoy life in the community without discrimination.

**2728 Hall-Perrine Foundation**
Ste 803
115 3rd St SE
Cedar Rapids, IA 52401-1222
319-362-9079
FAX: 319-362-7220
hallperrine.org

*Jack Evans, President*
*William Whipple, Chairman*
*Darrel Morf, Vice President*
*Chuck Peters, Treasurer*
This foundation is dedicated tio improving the quality of life for peole in Linn County, IA by responding to the changing social, economic, and cultural needs of the community.

**2729 Mid-Iowa Health Foundation**
Ste 104
3900 Ingersoll Ave
Des Moines, IA 50312-3535
515-277-6411
FAX: 515-271-7579
e-mail: info@midiowahealth.org
www.midiowahealth.org

*Suzanne Mineck, President*
*Denise Swartz, Senior Program Officer*
Mission is to serve as a partner and catalyst for improving the health of vulnerable people in greater Des Moines.

**2730 Principal Financial Group Foundation**
711 High St
Des Moines, IA 50392
515-247-5111
800-986-3343
FAX: 515-235-5724
principalfinancialgroup.com

*Larry Zimpleman, Chairman/ President/ CEO*
*Daniel J. Houston, President - Retirement, Insurance and Financial Services*
*James P. McCaughan, President - Principal Global Investors*
*Luis Valdés, President - Principal International*
The Principal Financial Group is a leading global financial company offering businesses, individuals and industrial clients a wide range of financial products and services.

**2731 Siouxland Community Foundation**
Ste 412
505 5th St
Sioux City, IA 51101-1507
712-293-3303
FAX: 712-293-3303
e-mail: office@siouxlandcommunityfoundation.org
www.siouxlandcommunityfoundation .org

*Debbie Hubbard, Executive Director*
*Karen B. Clark, President*
*Lesley M. Bartholomew, Vice President*
*Barbara F. Orzechowski, Secretary*
The Siouxland Community Foundation strives to enhance the quality of life in the greater Siouxland tri-state area by seeking charitable gifts to build permanent endowments as charitable

capital for the community, providing a flexable vehicle to receive and distribute gifts of any size, making grants in response to community needs, and providing services that will help shape the well-being of Siouxland.

## Kansas

2732 **Arc of Kansas**
2701 SW Randolph Ave
Topeka, KS 66611-1536
785-232-0597
FAX: 785-232-3770
e-mail: info@tarcinc.org
tarcinc.org

*Eileen Doran, Executive Director*
*Jennifer Brancaccio, Case Management Director*
*Cathie Huckins, Children's Services/Assistive Technology Director*
*Sherry Lundry, Development/Public Relations Director*
Organzation works to ensure that the estimated 7.2 million Americans with intellectual and developmental disabilities have the services and supports they need to grow, develop, and live in communities across the nation.

2733 **Hutchinson Community Foundation**
P.O.Box 298
1 North Main, Suite 501
Hutchinson, KS 67504
620-663-5293
FAX: 620-663-9277
e-mail: info@hutchcf.org
www.hutchcf.org

*Aubrey Abbot Patterson, President and Executive Director*
*Terri L. Eisiminger, Vice President of Administration*
*Janet Hamilton, Community Investment Officer*
*Maria G. Kicklighter, Finance Assistant*
Connects donors to community needs and opportunities, increases philanthropy and provides community leadership.

## Kentucky

2734 **Arc of Kentucky**
706 E. Main Street
Suite A
Frankfort, KY 40601-2408
502-875-5225
800-281-1272
FAX: 502-875-5226
e-mail: arcofky@aol.com
arcofky.org

*Patty Dempsey, Executive Director*
The Arc of Kentucky works to ensure a quality of life for children and adults with intellectual and developmental disabilities to help in securing a positive future. The Arc values services and supports that enhance the quality of life through independence, friendship, choice and respect for individuals with intellectual and developmental disabilities.

## Louisiana

2735 **Arc of Louisiana**
Ste G
606 Colonial Dr
Baton Rouge, LA 70806-6535
225-383-1033
FAX: 225-383-1092
e-mail: info@thearcla.org
thearcla.org

*Dr. Laura Brackin, Executive Director*
*Kelly Serrett, Program Director*
*Dr. Duane Superneau, President*
The Arc of Louisiana advocates for and with individuals with intellectual and developmental disabilities and their families that they shall live to their fullest potential.

2736 **Baton Rouge Area Foundation**
402 N 4th St
Baton Rouge, LA 70802-5506
225-387-6126
877-387-6126
FAX: 225-387-6153
e-mail: mverma@braf.org
www.braf.org

*John G. Davies, President/ CEO*
*John Spain, Executive Vice President*
*Mukul Verma, Director of Communications*
*Dennise Reno, Art Director*
The Foundation provides grants to nonprofits to make lives better in the region. It also takes on projects, often with parters, to remake Baton Rouge.

2737 **Community Foundation of Shreveport-Bossier**
Ste 105
401 Edwards St
Shreveport, LA 71101-5551
318-221-0582
FAX: 318-221-7463
e-mail: hickman@comfoundsb.org
comfoundsb.org

*Paula Hickman, Executive Director*
*Paige Carlisle, C.P.A., Director of Finance*
*Elizabeth LaBorde, Director of Community Investment*
*Kezia L. Pigford, Director of External Relations*
Provides a variety of charitable funds and gift options to help our partners achieve their vision for a stronger, more vibrant community. By bringing together fund donors, their financial advisors and non profit agencies, the Foundation is a powerful catalyst for building charitable giving and effecting positive change in our area

## Maine

2738 **UNUM Charitable Foundation**
Maine Association of Non Profits
565 Congress St
Ste 301
Portland, ME 04101-3308
207-871-1885
FAX: 207-780-0346
e-mail: technicalassistance@nonprofitmaine.org
www.nonprofitmaine.org

*Brenda Peluso, Director of Public Policy*
*Mark Hews, Director of Programming*
*L.K. Gagnon, Operations Manager*
The Foundation encourages projects that: stimulate others in the private or public sector to participate in problem solving; advance innovative and cost-effective approaches for addressing defined, recognized needs; and demonstrate ability to obtain future project funding, if needed. The foundation generally limits its consideration of capital campaign requests to the Greater Portland, Maine area.

## Maryland

2739 **American Health Assistance Foundation**
22512 Gateway Center Dr
Clarksburg, MD 20871-2005
301-948-3244
800-437-2423
FAX: 301-258-9454
e-mail: info@ahaf.org
ahaf.org

*Stacy Pagos Haller, President / CEO*
*Donna Callison, Vice President of Development*
*Dave Marks, Vice President of Finance and Administration*
The American Health Assistance Foundation (AHAF) is a registered non-profit organization that funds research into cures for Alzheimer's disease, macular degeneration and glaucoma, and provides the public with informantion about risk factors, preventative lifestyles, availiable treatments and coping strategies.

**2740 American Occupational Therapy Foundation**
P.O.Box 31220
Bethesda, MD 20824-1220
301-652-6611
FAX: 301-656-3620
e-mail: aotf@aotf.org
aotf.org

*Charles Christiansen, Executive Director*
*Diana Ramsay, President*
AOFT provides advanced research, education and public awareness for occupational therapy, so that all people may participate fully in life regardless of their physical, social, mental or developmental circumstances.

**2741 Arc of Maryland**
Ste 205
49 Old Solomons Island Rd
Annapolis, MD 21401- 3864
410-571-9320
888-272-3449
FAX: 410-974-6021
e-mail: info@thearcmd.org
thearcmd.org

*Kathryn Fialkowski, Executive Director*
*Heather East, Director of Campaign Management*
*Judi Buehler, Finance Assistant*
*Edward Willard, ETWN Program Manager*
The Arc of Maryland works to create a world where children and adults with cognitive and developmental disabilities have and enjoy equal rights and opportunities.

**2742 Baltimore Community Foundation**
2 E Read Street
Floor 9
Baltimore, MD 21202-6903
410-332-4171
FAX: 410-837-4701
e-mail: grants@bcf.org
bcf.org

*Tom E. Wilcox, President*
*Danista Hunte, Vice President, Community Investment*
*Ralph M. Serpe, CFRE, Vice President, Development*
*Amy T. Seto, CPA, Vice President, Finance and Administration*
Makes grants in Baltimore City and Baltimore County; see website for how to apply. BCF is governed by a 30-member board of trustees, made up of a cross section of Baltimore.

**2743 Candlelighters Childhood Cancer Foundation**
P.O. Box 498
Kensington, MD 20895-0498
301-962-3520
855-858-2226
FAX: 301-962-3521
e-mail: staff@acco.org
www.acco.org

*Trevor Romain, President*
*Janine Lynne, Vice President*
*Ken Phillips, Treasurer*
*Naomi Bartley, Member*
An international organization providing information and support, and advocacy to parents of children with cancer and survivors of childhood cancer.Health and Education professionals also welcome as members.Network of local support groups. Information on disabilities related to treatment of childhood cancer. Publications. The name of the company has been changed to American Childhood Cancer Organization.

**2744 Children's Fresh Air Society Fund**
Baltimore Community Foundation
2 E Read St
Baltimore, MD 21202-2470
410-332-4171
FAX: 410-837-4701
e-mail: grants@bcf.org
bcf.org

*Tom E. Wilcox, President*
*Danista Hunte, Vice President, Community Investment*
*Ralph M. Serpe, CFRE, Vice President, Development*
*Amy T. Seto, CPA, Vice President, Finance and Administration*
Makes grants to nonprofit camps to provide tuition for disadvantaged and disabled Maryland children to attend summer camp. See website for how to apply.

**2745 Clark-Winchcole Foundation**
3 Bethesda Metro Ctr
Suite 550
Bethesda, MD 20814-5358
301-654-3607

*Laura Phillips, President*
Supported tax-exempt charitable organizations operating in the metropolitan area of Washington, DC in the following areas: deaf, higher education and physically disabled.

**2746 Columbia Foundation**
10630 Little Patuxent Parkway
Century Plaza, Suite 315
Columbia, MD 21044
410-730-7840
FAX: 410-997-6021
e-mail: info@columbiafoundation.org
columbiafoundation.org

*Beverley White Seal, President / CEO*
*Priscilla Reaver, Senior Program Officer*
*Debbie Daskaloff, Development Officer*
*April Wainwright, Office Administrator*
The Columbia Foundation serves as a catalyst for building a more caring, creative and effective community in Howard County by promoting and creating opportunities for personal and corporate philanthropy, managing endowments, anticipating and responding to community needs, and strategically granting funds.

**2747 Corporate Giving Program**
Ryland Group
11000 Broken Land Pkwy
Columbia, MD 21044
410-715-7022
800-267-0998
FAX: 410-715-7909

*Bruce N Haas, President*
Contributions of equipment, volunteers and financial support to organizations working to meet the challenges and needs of modern society.

**2748 Cystic Fibrosis Foundation**
6931 Arlington Rd
Bethesda, MD 20814-5200
301-951-4422
800-344-4823
FAX: 301-951-6378
e-mail: info@cff.org
cff.org

*Robert J Beall, CEO*
The mission of the Cystic Fibrosis Foundation, a nonprofit donor-supported organization is to assure the development of the means to cure and control cystic fibrosis and to improve the quality of life for those with the disease.

**2749 Foundation Fighting Blindness**
716b Columbia Gateway Drive
Suite 100
Columbia, MD 21046
410-423-0600
800-683-5555
FAX: 410-363-2393
TTY: 800-683-5551
e-mail: info@fightblindness.org
www.fightblindness.org

*William T. Schmidt, CEO*
*James W. Minow, Chief Development Officer*
*Stephen M. Rose, Ph.D., Chief Research Officer*
*Annette Hinkle, CPA, Chief Financial Officer*

The urgent mission is to drive the research that will provide preventions, treatments, and cures for people affected by retinitis pigmentosa, macular degeneration, Usher syndrome and the entire spectrum of retinal degenerative diseases.

**2750 George Wasserman Family Foundation**
Grossberg Company
6707 Democracy Blvd
Suite 300
Bethesda, MD 20817-1176
301-571-4977
FAX: 301-571-6250

*Helen Salud, Manager*
*Anthony Cpa, Partner*

**2751 Harry and Jeanette Weinberg Foundation**
7 Park Center Ct
Owings Mills, MD 21117-4200
410-654-8500
FAX: 410-654-4900
e-mail: rkellyjr@theweinbergfoundation.org
hjweinbergfoundation.org

*Rachel Garbow Monroe, President*
*Joel Winegarden, Vice-President, Real Estate*
*Stan Goldman, PhD, Program Director*
*Amy Gross, Program Director*

The Harry & Jeanette Weinberg Foundation, Inc. is dedicated to assisting the poor, primarily through operating and capital grants to direct service organizations located in Baltimore, Hawaii, Northeastern Pennsylvania, New York, Israel and the Former Soviet Union. These grants are focused on meeting basic needs such as shelter, nutrition, health & socialization & on enhancing an individual's ability to meet those needs. Within that focus, emphasis is placed on the elderly & Jewish community.

**2752 Miracle-Ear Children's Foundation**
5000 Cheshire Ln N
Minneapolis, MN 55446-3706
763-268-4000
800-464-8002
FAX: 763-268-4365
miracle-ear.com

Nonprofit organization that provides hearing aids to children whose families to not qualify for public assistance. Provides hearing aid fittings and follow-up care and services free of charge through Miracle-Ear Hearing Centers. Provides information on alternative communication. Offers educational materials and brochures.

**2753 National Federation of the Blind**
200 East Wells Street
At Jernigan Place
Baltimore, MD 21230-4998
410-659-9314
FAX: 410-685-5653
nfb.org

*John Berggren, Executive Director for Operation*
*John G. Paré Jr., Executive Director for Strategic Initiatives*
*Mark Riccobono, Executive Director, NFB Jernigan Institute*
*Joanne Wilson, Executive Director for Affiliate Action*

The largest consumer membership organization of the blind, founded in 1940, it has 50,000 members nationwide in 52 affiliates and over 700 local chapters. Provides public education about blindness, support services to the newly blinded, scholarships, publications about blindness, adaptive equipment for the blind, advocacy services, Newsline for the Blind, assistive technology information and Job Opportunities for the Blind.

**2754 Sjogren's Syndrome Foundation**
6707 Democracy Blvd
Suite 325
Bethesda, MD 20817-1164
301-530-4420
800-475-6473
FAX: 301-530-4415
e-mail: tms@sjogrens.org
www.sjogrens.org

*Steven Taylor, CEO*
*Sheriese Defruscio, VP Development*
*Kathy Ivory, Vice President of Field Services*
*Katherine Mo Hammitt, Vice President of Research*

Provides patients practical information and coping strategies that minimize the effects of Sjogren's syndrome. In addition, the Foundation is the clearinghouse for medical information and is the recognized national advocate for Sjogren's syndrome. *$25.00 Monthly*

## Massachusetts

**2755 Abbot and Dorothy H Stevens Foundation**
P.O. Box 111
North Andover, MA 01845
978-688-7211
FAX: 978-686-1620

*Josh Miner, Executive Director*

Established in 1953, Purpose is giving primarily to the arts, education, conservation, and health and human services.

**2756 Arc of Northern Bristol County**
141 Park St
Attleboro, MA 02703-3020
508-226-1445
888-343-3301
FAX: 508-226-1476
arcnbc.org

*Michael M. Andrade, President and CEO*
*Paul Donnelly, CEO*
*John Neill, Director of Human Resources*
*Patricia Kirby, Director of Development and Public Relations*

Mission is to strive for the right of all people with developmental disabilities to be valued as individuals, to experience choice, and to be fully included in all aspects of community life

**2757 Boston Foundation**
75 Arlington St
10th Fl
Boston, MA 02116-3992
617-338-1700
FAX: 617-338-1604
e-mail: info@tbf.org
tbf.org

*Paul S. Grogan, President & CEO*
*Stephen Chan, Chief of Staff*
*Kate Guedj, Vice President for Philanthropic and Donor Services*
*Robert Lewis, Jr., Vice President for Program*

The Foundation's grantmaking, special initiatives and civic leadership promote innovation across a broad range of compelling community issues, from educational excellence to affordable housing to workforce development and the arts.

**2758 Boston Globe Foundation**
P.O. Box 55819
Boston, MA 02205-5819
617-929-2895
e-mail: foundation@globe.com
bostonglobe.com

*Mary Jacobus, President*

The mission of the Boston Globe Foundation is to empower community-based organizations to effect real change in the ares of greatest need, where the Globe is uniquely postioned to add the most value. Priority focus areas: strengthen the reading, writing and critical thinking of young people, while fostering their inherent love of learning. Strengthen the roads that link people to culture. Strengthen the civic fabric of the city. Be responsive to the needs of our immediate community.

**2759 Bushrod H Campbell and Ada F Hall Charity Fund**
Palmer & Dodge
111 Huntington Ave
Boston, MA 02199-7610 617-239-0540
FAX: 617-227-4420

*Brenda Taylor, Foundation Administrator*
The fund's areas of interest include organizations and/or their projects supporting aid to the elderly, healthcare and population control. Medical research grants are administered through the Medical Foundation. No grants are awarded to individuals and the geographical area of support is limited to organizations located in Massachusetts within the area of Boston and Route 128.

**2760 Clipper Ship Foundation**
77 Summer St
Boston, MA 02110-1006 617-426-7080
FAX: 617-426-7087
e-mail: agm@agmconnect.org
www.agmconnect.org

*Ron Ancrum, President*
Makes grants to federally tax-qualified non-profit organizations offering human services to individuals living in Greater Boston and the cities of Lawrence and Brockton.

**2761 Community Foundation of Western Massachusetts**
P.O. Box 15769
1500 Main Street, Suite 2300
Springfield, MA 01115-5769 413-732-2858
FAX: 413-733-8565
e-mail: wmass@communityfoundation.org
www.communityfoundation.org

*Kent W Faerber, Interim President*
*William Andrews, Director of Finance and Administration*
*Caroline Deltoro, Director of Communications*
*Kristin Leutz, Vice President of Philanthropic Services*
Provides a simple way to achieve the charitable objectives of donors most effectively; supports nonprofit organizations that offer programs in the arts, education, human services, healthcare, housing, and the environment; and works to improve the quality of life in our region.

**2762 Frank R and Elizabeth Simoni Foundation**
1401 Boston Providence Tpke
Norwood, MA 02062-5053 781-762-3449
FAX: 781-769-6166

*Matthew Mac Donald, President*
*Ann Mac Donald, Secretary*
*Robert Mac Donald, Clerk*

**2763 Friendly Ice Cream Corp Contributions Program**
1855 Boston Rd
Wilbraham, MA 01095-1002 413-543-3544
800-966-9970
FAX: 413-731-4467
friendlys.com

*Ned R Lidvall, CEO*
*James M. Parrish, Executive Vice President*

**2764 Greater Worcester Community Foundation**
370 Main St
Ste 650
Worcester, MA 01608-1738 508-755-0980
FAX: 508-755-3406
e-mail: info@greaterworcester.org
greaterworcester.org

*Ann T. Lisi, President and CEO*
*Kelly A. Stimson, Director of Donor Services and Communications*
*Beckley Schowalter, Donor Services Officer and Scholarship Coordinator*
*Pamela B. Kane, Senior Program Officer*
By focusing on the entire community rather then on any specific issue, the community foundation is able to address matters of greater importance to the people of the region. The Foundation has built a permanent, flexable endowment and has distributed grants and awards to a broad range of organizations and people throughout the region.

**2765 Hyams Foundation**
50 Federal St
Fl 9
Boston, MA 02110-2241 617-426-5600
FAX: 617-426-5696
e-mail: info@hyamsfoundation.org
hyamsfoundation.org

*Elizabeth B Smith, Executive Director*
*Angela Brown, Director of Programs*
*David Moy, Program Officer*
*Maria Mulkeen, Program Officer*
Mission is to increase economic and social justice and power within low-income communities in Boston and Chelsea, Massachusetts.

**2766 Raytheon Company Contributions Program**
870 Winter St
Waltham, MA 02451-1449 781-522-3000
FAX: 781-860-2172
raytheon.com

*William H Swanson, Chairman and CEO*
*Thomas M. Culligan, Senior Vice President - Business Development*
*Keith J. Peden, Senior Vice President - Human Resources and Security*
*Jay B. Stephens, Senior Vice President - General Counsel and Secretary*
Industry leader in defense and government electronics, space, information technology, technical services, and business aviation and special mission aircraft.

**2767 TJX Foundation**
TJX Companies
770 Cochituate Rd
Framingham, MA 01701-4666 508-390-1000
FAX: 508-390-2091
tjx.com

*Carol Meyrowitz, CEO*
The purpose of the TJX Foundation's Giving Program is to support qualified, tax-exempt nonprofit organizations that provide services which promote and improve the quality of life for children, women and families in need.

**2768 The Arc of Massachusetts**
217 South St
Waltham, MA 02453-2710 781-891-6270
FAX: 781-891-6271
e-mail: arcmass@arcmass.org
www.arcmass.org

*Leo Sarkissian, Executive Director*
*Joshua Komyerox, Government Affairs Director*
*Brenda Asis, Development Director*
Quarterly newsletter for The Arc of Massachusetts is Advocate.

**2769 Vision Foundation**
8901 Strafford Cir
Knoxville, TN 37923-1500
865-357-4603
FAX: 865-690-9322
e-mail: gordon@visionfoundation.net
www.visionfoundation.net

*Gordon Adams, President*
Offers counseling, support groups, seminars and transportation for the blind providing 600 members.

## Michigan

**2770 Ann Arbor Area Community Foundation**
301 N Main St
Ste 300
Ann Arbor, MI 48104-1296
734-663-0401
FAX: 734-663-3514
e-mail: info@aaacf.org
aaacf.org

*Cheryl Elliott, President & CEO*
*Neel Hajra, Chief Operating Officer and Vice President for Community Investment*
*Jennifer Bal Hale, Development Officer*
*Christopher Lemon, Youth Council Advisor*
Interested in funding projects which will improve the quality of life for citizens of the Ann Arbor area. Eligible projects generally fall within these categories: education, culture, social service, community development, environmental awareness and health and wellness. The Foundation aims to support creative approaches to community needs and problems by making grants which will benefit the widest possible range of people.

**2771 Arc of Michigan**
State of Michigan
1325 S Washington Ave
Lansing, MI 48910-1652
517-487-5426
800-292-7851
FAX: 517-487-0303
e-mail: dhoyle@arcmi.org
arcmi.org

*Dohn Hoyle, Executive Director*
*Sherri Boyd, Director*
*Lisa Hertzer, Executive Assistant*
*Sybil Spencer, Communications Analyst*
The Arc Michigan empowers local chapters to assure that citizens with disabilities are valued and that they and their families participate fully in and contribute to the life of their community.

**2772 Berrien Community Foundation**
2900 S State St
Ste 2e
Saint Joseph, MI 49085-2467
269-983-3486
FAX: 269-983-4939
e-mail: bcf@BerrienCommunity.org
berriencommunity.org

*Nanette M. Keiser, Ed.D., President*
*Lanette M. Sanford, Finance/Program Director*
The Foundation is a union of numerous gifts, bequests and other contributions that form permanent endowments and other funds.

**2773 Blind Children's Fund**
6761 West 45-12
P.O. Box 363
Three Oaks, MI 49128
989-779-9966
FAX: 269-756-3133
e-mail: bcf@blindchildrensfund.org
www.blindchildrensfund.org

*Karla B. Kwast, Executive Director*
Provides parents and profesionsals informaion materials and resources that help them scuccesfullly teach and nurture blind, visually and multi-impaired infants and preschoolers.

**2774 Community Foundation of Monroe County**
P.O. Box 627
28 S. Macomb St.
Monroe, MI 48161-627
734-242-1976
FAX: 734-242-1234
e-mail: info@cfmonroe.org
cfmonroe.org

*Kathleen Russeau, MBA, Executive Director*
*Michele Sandiefer, Office Manager*
*Julie Rhinehart, YAC Coordinator*
*Doug Redding, Project Manager*
The mission of the Community Foundation of Monroe County is to encourage and facilitate philanthropy in Monroe County.

**2775 Cowan Slavin Foundation**
7881 Dell Rd
Saline, MI 48176-9744
734-944-1439
FAX: 734-944-3529

*David Bovee, Owner*

**2776 Daimler Chrysler**
Automobility Program
P.O. Box 5080
Troy, MI 48007-5080
800-255-9877
FAX: 855-409-0475
e-mail: rebates@chrysler.com
www.chrysleratuomobility.com

Provides a cash reimbursement to assist in reducing the cost of adaptive driving equipment and conversion aids installed on new model Daimler Chrysler LLC vehicles. Up to a maximum of $1000 on Dodge Caravan, Grand Caravan, and Chrysler Town and Country vans and up to $750 on all other vehicles.

**2777 Frank & Mollie S VanDervoort Memorial Foundation**
4646 Okemos Rd
Okemos, MI 48864-1795
517-349-7232

*Ann L Gessert, Secretary*

**2778 Fremont Area Community Foundation**
PO Box B
4424 W. 48th Street
Fremont, MI 49412-176
231-924-5350
FAX: 231-924-5391
e-mail: info@tfacf.org
tfacf.org

*Carla Roberts, President & CEO*
*Robert Jordan, Vice President of Philanthropic Services*
*Gina Van Bruggen, Vice President of Program*
*Kathy Pope, Vice President of Finance*
A local nonprofit organization serving the residence of Newaygo County. We connect the needs of the community with those who have the conviction to make a lasting impact. Our mission is to improve the quality of life for the people of Newaygo County.

**2779 Grand Rapids Foundation**
185 Oakes St SW
Grand Rapids, MI 49503-4008
616-454-1751
FAX: 616-454-6455
e-mail: grfound@grfoundation.org
grfoundation.org

*Diana R. Sieger, President*
*Roberta F. King, APR, Vice President PR & Marketing*
*Marcia Rapp, Vice President, Programs*
*Laurie Craft, Program Director*
Grand Rapids Community Foundation leads the community in making positive, sustainable change. Through our grantmaking and leadership initiatives we help foster academic achievement, build economic prosperity, achieve healthy ecosystems, encourage healthy people, support social enrichment, and create vibrant neighborhoods.

2780 **Granger Foundation**
PO Box 22187
6267 Aurelius Rd
Lansing, MI 48909-2187 517-393-1670
FAX: 517-393-1382
e-mail: elee@grangerconstruction.com
grangerconstruction.com

*Alton Granger, Chairman*
*Glenn D. Granger, President & CEO*
The primary purpose of the Granger Foundation is to enhance the quality of life within the Greater Lansing, Michigan Area. Our mission is to support Christ-centered activities. We also support efforts that enhance the lives of youth in our community.

2781 **Harvey Randall Wickes Foundation**
4800 Fashion Square Blvd
Saginaw, MI 48604-2677 989-799-1850
FAX: 989-799-3327

*James Finkbeiner*
Grants for rehabilitation.

2782 **Havirmill Foundation**
3503 Greenleaf Blvd
Ste 203
Kalamazoo, MI 49008-2580 269-375-1193
millenniumrestaurants.com

*Ken Miller, CEO, Principal Partner*
*Shelly Pastor, CFO, Partner*
*Bob Lewis, COO, Partner*
*Matthew Burian, CBDO, CPO, F&B, Partner*

2783 **Kelly Services Foundation**
999 W Big Beaver Rd
Troy, MI 48084-4716 248-244-4353
FAX: 248-244-4588
kellyservices.com

*Diana Bugariu, Manager*
*Carl Camden, Chief Executive Officer*

2784 **Kresge Foundation**
3215 W Big Beaver Rd
Troy, MI 48084-2818 248-643-9630
FAX: 248-643-0588
e-mail: info@kresge.org
kresge.org

*Rip Rapson, President and CEO*
*Amy B. Coleman, Vice President of Finance and Treasurer*
This foundation offers challenge grants for capital projects, most often for construction or renovation of buildings, but also for the purchase of major equipment and real estate. As challenge grants, they are intended to stimulate new, private gifts in the midst of an organized fund raising effort. Offers special opportunities to build capacity, both in providing enhanced facilities in which to present programs and in generating private support. Only charitable organizations may apply.

2785 **Lanting Foundation**
1575 S Shore Dr
Holland, MI 49423-4436 616-355-2740

*Arlyn Lanting, Partner*

2786 **Rollin M Gerstacker Foundation**
PO Box 1945
Midland, MI 48641-1945 989-631-6097
www.gerstackerfoundation.org

*Alan Ott, Vice President /Treasurer*
*Lisa J. Gerstacker, President*
*E. N. Brandt, Vice President /Secretary*
The Rollin M. Gerstacker Foundation was founded by Mrs. Eda U. Gerstacker in 1957, in memory of her husband. Its primary purpose is to carry on, indefinitely, financial aid to charities of all types supported by Mr. and Mrs. R.M. Gerstacker during their lifetimes. These charities are concentrated in the states of Michigan and Ohio.

2787 **Steelcase Foundation**
PO Box 1967
GH-4E
Grand Rapids, MI 49501-1967 616-246-4695
FAX: 616-475-2200
e-mail: pgebben@steelcase.com
steelcase.com

*Phyllis Gebben, Coordinator of Donations*
*James P. Hackett, President & CEO*
Established in 1951, the Foundation focuses on the areas of human service, health, education, community development, the arts and the environment - giving particular concern to people who are disadvantaged, disabled, young and elderly as they attempt to improve the quality of their lives.

## Minnesota

2788 **Arc of Minnesota**
800 Transfer Road
Suite 7A
St. Paul, MN 55114 651-523-0823
800-582-5256
e-mail: mail@arcmn.org
www.arcmn.org

*Pat Mellenthin, Executive Director*
*Steve Larson, Director of Public Policy*
*Mike Gude, Communications Manager*
Your membership in The Arc of Minnesotta benefits persons with developmental disabilities and their families as they live, learn, work and play. Please join today!

2789 **Deluxe Corporation Foundation**
Deluxe Corporation
3680 Victoria St N
Shoreview, MN 55126-2966 651-483-7111
FAX: 651-483-7270
e-mail: feedback@deluxe.com
deluxe.com

*Lee J Schram, CEO*
*Terry D. Peterson, CFO /Senior VP*
*Malcolm J. McRoberts, Senior Vice President, Small Business Services*
*John D. Filby, Senior Vice President, Financial Services*
Funds programs such as schools, museums, programs for the disadvantaged. We believe programs and services like these represent the heart and soul of our communities.

2790 **General Mills Foundation**
P.O. Box 9452
Minneapolis, MN 55440-9452 800-248-7310
FAX: 763-764-8330
e-mail: corporate.response@genmills.com
generalmills.com

*Kendall J. Powell, Chairman / CEO*
*Mark W. Addicks, Senior Vice President/ Chief Marketing Officer*
*Richard L. Best, Senior Vice President*
*Peter J. Capell, Senior Vice President*

**2791 Hugh J Andersen Foundation**
342 5th Ave N
Bayport, MN 55003-4502
651-439-1557
888-439-9508
FAX: 651-439-9480
e-mail: hjafdn@srinc.biz
www.srinc.biz

*Brad Kruse, Program Director*
Established in 1962, this fund is a nonprofit charitable corporation classified as a private foundation. The Foundation was established as a general charitable fund, but now identifies projects that build individual and community capacity to be a priority. Giving is focused primarily in the counties of Washington, Minnesota, & St, Croix, Polk and Pierce of Wl. Grants are given in the areas of human services, health, education, arts and culture, community services and the environment.

**2792 James R Thorpe Foundation**
318 W 48th St
Minneapolis, MN 55419-5418
612-822-3412
e-mail: kerrieblevins@jamesrthorpefoundation.org
www.jamesrthorpefoundation.org

*Kerrie Blevins, Foundation Manager*
*Tim Thorpe, President*
Foundation based on values of respect and compassion, and is dedicated to making the greater Minneapolis area better for all its citizens.

**2793 Jay and Rose Phillips Family Foundation**
10 SECOND STREET NE
SUITE 200
Minneapolis, MN 55413
612-623-1654
FAX: 612-623-1653
e-mail: info@phillipsfamilyfoundationmn.org
www.phillipsfnd.org

*Patrick Troska, Executive Director*
*Joel Luedtke, Senior Program Officer*
*Tracy Lamparty, Grants and Operations Manager*

**2794 Minneapolis Foundation**
80 S 8th St
Minneapolis, MN 55402-2100
612-672-3878
FAX: 612-672-3846
e-mail: email@mplsfoundation.org
www.mplsfoundation.org

*Sandra L. Vargus, President and CEO*
*Jean M. Adams, COO*
*Amy Hertel, Manager of Strategic Development, Research and Evaluation*
*Luz Maria Frias, Vice President, Community Philanthropy*
Provides a variety of charitable fund and gift options to help Minnesotans make a difference.

**2795 Ordean Foundation**
424 W Superior St
Duluth, MN 55802-1591
218-726-4785

*Steve Mangan, Executive Director*
Grants are given for a variety of purposes including: treatment and rehabilitation for persons who are chronically or temporarily mentally ill, persons whose physical capacity is impaired by injury or illness, promotes mental and physical health of the elderly, provides for youth guidance programs designed to avoid delinquency, and provides relief, aid and charity to people with no or low incomes. Grants are only offered to certain cities and townships near and around St. Louis County/Duluth.

**2796 Otto Bremer Foundation**
445 Minnesota St
Ste 2250
Saint Paul, MN 55101-2161
651-227-8036
888-291-1123
FAX: 651-312-3665
e-mail: obf@ottobremer.org
www.ottobremer.org

*Kari Suzuki, Director of Operations*
*Randi Ilyse Roth, Executive Director*
Mission is to assist people in achieving full economic, civic and social participation in and for the betterment of their communities.

**2797 Rochester Area Foundation**
400 South Broadway
Suite 300
Rochester, MN 55904
507-282-0203
FAX: 507-282-4938
e-mail: info@rochesterarea.org
rochesterarea.org

*JoAnn Stormer, President*
*Al DeBoer, Development Consultant*
The mission of the Rochester Area Foundation is to strengthen community philanthropy by promoting responsible and informed giving and to assist donors in meeting their charitable objectives.

## Mississippi

**2798 Arc of Mississippi**
7 Lakeland Cir
Ste 600
Jackson, MS 39216-5025
601-982-1180
800-717-1180
FAX: 601-982-5792
e-mail: info@arcms.org
www.arcms.org

*Matt Nalker, Executive Director*
*Don Myers, President*
*Kim Duffy, Senior Vice-President*
The Arc is Committed to securing for all people with developmental disabilities the opportunity to choose and realize their goals of where and how they learn live work and play.

## Missouri

**2799 Allen P & Josephine B Green Foundation**
1055 Broadway
Suite 130
Kansas City, MO 64105
816-627-3417
FAX: 816-268-3417
e-mail: greenfoundation@gkccf.org
www.greenfdn.org
While the Foundation makes grants in a variety of fields, in the past its major support was in the field of medical research. During a 20-year period, 1951-71, it contributed over $900,000 to research in Parkinson's and related diseases of the nervous system; $600,000 for research in pediatric neurology and lesser amounts in other areas of medical research, but the board is now trending in other directions. Grants are limited to Missouri and none are offered to individuals.

**2800 Anheuser-Busch**
1 Busch Pl
Saint Louis, MO 63118-1852
314-577-2000
800-342-5283
FAX: 314-577-2900
abcorpaffairs.com

*August A Busch Iv, President*

Supports education, helped fund health and human services organizations, provided disaster relief, and worked to preserve the environment.

**2801 Arc of the US Missouri Chapter**
PO Box 1160
Linn Creek, MO 65052
573-552-7648
e-mail: angela@arcofmissouri.org
http://www.arcofmissouri.org

chapter #42

**2802 Greater Kansas City Community Foundation & Affiliated Trusts**
1055 Broadwat St
Suite 130
Kansas City, MO 64105-1595
816-842-0944
FAX: 816-842-8079
e-mail: info@gkccf.org
gkccf.org

*Debbie Wilkerson, President/ CEO*
*Denise St. Omer, Vice President, Community Investment*

Mission is to improve the quality of life in Greater Kansas City by increasing charitable giving, connecting donors to community needs they care about, and providing leadership on critical community issues.

**2803 Greater St Louis Community Foundation**
319 N 4th St
Ste 300
Saint Louis, MO 63102-1930
314-588-8200
FAX: 314-588-8088
e-mail: dluckes@gstlcf.org
gstlcf.org

*Amelia A.J. Bond, President/ CEO*
*Dwight D. Canning, VP, Finance & Administration*
*Diane R. Drollinger, Director of Community Partnerships*

To improve the quality of life across the region by helping individuals, families and businesses make a difference through charitable giving.

**2804 H&R Block Foundation**
1 H and R Block Way
Kansas City, MO 64105-1905
816-854-4361
FAX: 816-854-8025
e-mail: foundation@hrblock.com
www.blockfoundation.org

*Henry W. Bloch, Chairman, Treasurer, and Director*
*David P. Miles, President*
*Carey Wilker Looney, Vice President and Secretary*

A charitable organization under the not-for-profit corporation law of the state of Missouri. Grants are made only to organizations which are tax exempt from Federal Income taxation and which are not classified as private foundations. Major emphasis is placed in the metropolitan areas of Kansas City, Missouri: and Columbus, Ohio. The goal is to provide proportionately significant support of relatively few activities, as opposed to minor support for a great many.

**2805 James S McDonnell Foundation**
1034 S Brentwood Blvd
Suite 1850
Saint Louis, MO 63117- 1284
314-721-1532
FAX: 314-721-7421
jsmf.org

*John T. Bruer, Ph.D., President*
*Susan M. Fitzpatrick, Ph.D., Vice President*
*Cheryl A. Washington, Grants Manager*

The Foundation supports scientific, educational, and charitable causes locally, nationally and internationally.

**2806 Lutheran Charities Foundation of St Louis**
8860 Ladue Road
Suite 200
Saint Louis, MO 63124
314-231-2244
FAX: 314-727-7688
e-mail: info@lutheranfoundation.org
www.lutheranfoundation.org

*Ann L. Vazquez, President/ CEO*

Seeks the improved care of people in the greater St. Louis metropolitan region. Lutheran Foundation of St. Louis manages the endowment established upon the sale of the Lutheran Medical Center and provides grant awards for health, human care, Lutheran congregations' community service programs, and Lutheran education.

**2807 RA Bloch Cancer Foundation**
1 H and R Block Way
Kansas City, MO 64105-1905
816-854-5050
800-433-0464
FAX: 816-854-8024
e-mail: hotline@hrblock.com
www.blochcancer.org

*Vangie Rich, Executive Director*

Provides a hotline that matches newly diagnosed cancer patients with someone who has survived the same kind of cancer. Offers free infomration, resources and support groups, and distributes lists of multidisciplinary second opinion centers. Also supplies three books at no charge: Fighting Cancer; Cancer... There's Hope; and A Guide for Cancer Supporters. All services and books are free of charge.

**2808 Victor E Speas Foundation**
10434 Indiana Ave
Kansas City, MO 64137-1532
816-868-9300
e-mail: vccmetro@crn.org
www.vcckcmetro.org

*Latricia Scott Adams, President*

VCC is a membership-based organization that brings together area volunteer managers and others interested in volunteerism for mutual support, exchange of ideas and information, and educational programs of timely interest.

## Nebraska

**2809 Arc of Nebraska**
3601 Calvert St
Suite 25
Lincoln, NE 68506-5797
402-475-4407
FAX: 402-475-0214
e-mail: info@arc-nebraska.org
www.arc-nebraska.org

*Marla Fischer-Lempke, Executive Director*

Arc of Nebraska is commited to helping children and adults with disabilities secure the oppurtunity to choose and realize their goals of where and how they learn, live, work, and play.

**2810 Cooper Foundation**
1248 O St
870 Wells Fargo Center
Lincoln, NE 68508-1493
402-476-7571
FAX: 402-476-2356
e-mail: info@cooperfoundation.org
cooperfoundation.org

*Art Thompson, President*

Serves only Nebraska with the primary interest in education, arts and humanities and the human services area.

**2811 Mosaic**
4980 S 118th St
Omaha, NE 68137-2200
402-896-9988
877-366-7242
FAX: 402-896-6111
www.mosaicinfo.org

*Linda Timmons, President / CEO*
*Cindy Schroeder, Senior VP & CFO*
*Keith Schmode, Sr VP, Mission Advancement and CEO of the MOSAIC FOUNDATION*
Headquarters for the faith-based organization providing services to people with disabilities in communities nationwide, and in conjunction with international partners. Mosaic was born of a merger of these two Lutheran organizations: Bethpage and Martin Luther Homes Society.

**2812 Slosburg Family Charitable Trust**
10040 Regency Cir
Ste 200
Omaha, NE 68114-3734
402-391-7900
FAX: 402-391-2991
richdale.com

*David Slosburg, Owner*

**2813 Union Pacific Foundation**
1400 Douglas St
Omaha, NE 68179
402-544-5000
888-870-8777
FAX: 402-501-0021
www.up.com

The Union Pacific Foundation is the philanthropic arm of the Union Pacific Corporation and Union Pacific Railroad. Union Pacific believes that the quality of life in the communities in which its employees live and work is an integral part of its own success.

## Nevada

**2814 Conrad N Hilton Foundation**
10100 Santa Monica Blvd.
Suite 1000
Los Angeles, CA 90067
310-556-4694
FAX: 310-694-9051
e-mail: cnhf@hiltonfoundation.org
hiltonfoundation.org

*Steven M. Hilton, Chairman, President & CEO*
*Patrick J. Modugno, Vice President, Administration and Chief Financial Officer*
*Randy Kim, CFA, Vice President and Chief Investment Officer*
Our grant-making style is to initiate and develop major long-term projects and then seek out the organizations to implement them. As a consequence of this proactive approach, the Foundation does not generally consider unsolicited proposals. Our major projects currently include: blindness prevention and treatment, support the work of the Catholic Sisters, drug abuse prevention among youth, support of the Conrad N. Hilton College of Hotel and Restaurant Management, and much more.

**2815 EL Wiegand Foundation**
165 W Liberty St
Suite 200
Reno, NV 89501-1955
775-333-0310
FAX: 775-333-0314

*Kristen A Avansino, President/Executive Director*

**2816 Nell J Redfield Foundation**
PO Box 61
Reno, NV 89504
775-323-1373
FAX: 775-323-4476

*Jerry Smith, Manager*

**2817 William N Pennington Foundation**
441 W Plumb Ln
Reno, NV 89509-3766
775-333-9100
FAX: 775-333-9111

*William Pennington, Owner*

## New Hampshire

**2818 Agnes M Lindsay Trust**
660 Chestnut St
Manchester, NH 03104-3550
603-669-1366
866-669-1366
FAX: 603-665-8114
e-mail: admin@lindsaytrust.org
lindsaytrust.org

*Susan E. Bouchard, Administrative Director*
Funding for health and wefare organizations, special needs, mental health, blind, deaf and cultural programs to organizations, specifically for capital needs, not operating funds, located in the New England states of Maine, Massachusetts, New Hampshire and Vermont. We highly recommend you visit our web site.

**2819 Foundation for Seacoast Health**
100 Campus Dr
Ste 1
Portsmouth, NH 03801-5892
603-422-8200
FAX: 603-422-8206
e-mail: ffsh@communitycampus.org
ffsh.org

*Debra S. Grabowski, Executive Director*
*Nancy L. Cutter, Administration Executive/ Financial Manager*
*Eligio Santana, Facility Manager*
Giving limited to Portsmouth, Rye, New Castle, Greenland, Newington, North Hampton, NH; and Kittery, Eliot, and York, ME.

## New Jersey

**2820 Arc of New Jersey**
985 Livingston Ave
N Brunswick, NJ 8902-1843
732-246-0370
FAX: 732-214-1834
e-mail: info@arcnj.org
arcnj.org

*Thomas Baffuto, Executive Director*
*Celine Fortin, Associate Executive Director*
The Arc of New Jersey is committed to enhancing the quality of life of children and adults with intellectual and developmental disabilities and their families, through advocacy, empowerment, education and prevention.

**2821 Arnold A Schwartz Foundation**
15 Mountain Blvd
Warren, NJ 7059-5611
908-757-7800
FAX: 908-757-8039
e-mail: skunzmannewjerseylaw.net

*Steven A Kunzman, President*

**2822 Campbell Soup Foundation**
1 Campbell Pl
Camden, NJ 08103-1701
800-257-8443
campbellsoup.com

*Denise Morrison, President /Chief Executive Officer*
*Anthony P. DiSilvestro, Senior Vice President - Finance*
Goal of this foundation is to match the company's assets with community needs in order to help forge solutions to community challenges. The Foundation believes that involvement at the community level can play a catalytic role in improving the quality of life. Giving is located in the areas of education, nutrition and

health, cultural and youth related programs. The major focus of the foundation is on nutrition and health related matters, and places a high priority on Camden, New Jersey areas.

**2823 Children's Hopes & Dreams Wish Fulfillment Foundation**
280 US Highway 46
Dover, NJ 07801-2084
706-482-2248
FAX: 706-482-2289
e-mail: info@chddover.org
www.helpingnow.org

Provides continual support for children and their families through the International Pen-Pal Program and the Kid's Kare Packages program. All services are free. Fulfills the last dreams of children with life threatening illnesses.

**2824 Community Foundation of New Jersey**
PO Box 338
Morristown, NJ 07963
973-267-5533
800-659-5533
FAX: 973-267-2903
e-mail: hdekker@cfnj.org
www.cfnj.org

*Hans Dekker, President*
*Nancy Hamilton, Program Officer*
The Community Foundation of New Jersey is an alliance of families, businesses, and foundations that work together to create lasting differences in lives and communities today and tomorrow.

**2825 FM Kirby Foundation**
PO Box 151
Morristown, NJ 07963-0151
973-538-4800
www.fdncenter.org/grantmaker/kirby

*S. Dillard Kirby, President and Director*
*Jefferson W Kirby, Vice President and Director*
Family foundation, grants made to a wide range of nonprofit organizations in education, health and medicine, the arts and humanities, civic and public affairs, as well as religious, welfare and youth organizations.

**2826 Fannie E Rippel Foundation**
14 Maple Avenue
Suite 200
Morristown, NJ 07960
973-540-0101
FAX: 973-540-0404
e-mail: info@rippelfoundation.org
www.rippelfoundation.org

*Laura K Landy, President/ CEO*
*Chana Fitton, CFO & Vice President, Administration*
Core purposes: research and treatment related to cancer and heart disease, the health of women and the elderly, and the quality of our nation's hospitals.

**2827 Fund for New Jersey**
One Palmer Square East
Suite 303
Princeton, NJ 08542
609-356-0421
e-mail: lmandell@fundfornj.org
fundfornj.org

*Kiki Jamieson, President*
*Leigh Gibson, Senior Program Officer*
*Laura Mandell, Office Manager*
*Brandon McKoy, Program Associate*
Our grants promote projects that share a high purpose of furthering effective democracy through a range of methods encompassing education, advocacy, public policy analysis, and community problem-solving.

**2828 Merck Company Foundation**
PO Box 100
Whitehouse Station, NJ 08889
908-423-1000
merck.com

*Kenneth C. Frazier, Chairman of the Board, President and Chief Executive Officer*
*Cuong Viet Do, Executive Vice President and Chief Strategy Officer*
Mission of the foundation is to support organizations and innovative programs in alignment with four strategic profiles: Improving access to quality health care and the appropriate use of medicines and vaccines,building capacity in the biomedical and health sciences, promoting environments that support innovation, economic growth and development in and ethical and fair context, and supporting communities where Merck employees work and live.

**2829 Nabisco Foundation**
7 Campus Dr
Parsippany, NJ 07054-4413
973-682-7096
FAX: 973-503-3018

*Henry Sandbach, Director*

**2830 Ostberg Foundation**
PO Box 1098
Alpine, NJ 07620-1098
201-569-6800
FAX: 201-767-8006

**2831 Prudential Foundation**
Prudential Financial
751 Broad St
15th Floor
Newark, NJ 07102-3714
973-802-6000
FAX: 973-802-7486
e-mail: community.resources@prudential.com
prudential.com

*John R Strangfeld, Chairman and CEO*
*Mark B. Grier, Vice Chairman*
Gives priority to national programs that further our objectives and programs serving areas where The Prudential has a substantial employee presence. Places special emphasis on the home state of New Jersey and the headquarters city, Newark.

**2832 Robert Wood Johnson Foundation**
PO Box 2361
Route 1 and College Road East
Princeton, NJ 08543-2361
609-452-8701
877-843-7953
FAX: 888-727-1966
e-mail: mail@rwjf.org
rwjf.org

*Risa Lavizzo-Mourey, President and CEO*
*Robin E. Mockenhaupt, Chief of Staff*
Our mission is to assure that all Americans have access to basic health care at reasonable cost, improve care and support for people with chronic health conditions, promote healthy communities and lifestyles and also, reduce the personal, social and economic harm caused by substance abuse.

**2833 Victoria Foundation**
31 Mulberry Street
5th Floor
Newark, NJ 07102-1397
973-792-9200
FAX: 973-792-1300
e-mail: info@victoriafoundation.org
victoriafoundation.org

*Irene Cooper-Basch, Executive Officer*
*Anne H. Jacobson, Program Officer*
Desire is to help individuals in need reach their potential remains. Provides emergency coal for needy families and treated rheumatic fever in children.

## New Mexico

**2834 Arc of New Mexico**
3655 Carlisle NE
Albuquerque, NM 87110-1644
505-883-4630
800-358-6493
FAX: 505-883-5564
e-mail: rcostales@arcnm.org
arcnm.org

*Randy Costales, Executive Director*
*Dinah Harvey, Director of Operations*
Our mission is to improve the quality of life for individuals with developmental disabilities of all ages by advocating for equal opportunities and choices in where and how they learn, live, work, play and socialize. The Arc of New Mexico promotes self-determination, healthy families, effective community support systems and partnerships.

**2835 Frost Foundation**
511 Armijo St
Suite A
Santa Fe, NM 87501-2899
505-986-0208
e-mail: info@frostfound.org
frostfound.org

*Mary Amelia Whited-Howell, President*
*Philip B. Howell, Executive Vice President*
The Frost Foundation was created to be operated excusively for educational, charitable, and religious purposes.

**2836 McCune Charitable Foundation**
345 E Alameda St
Santa Fe, NM 87501-2229
505-983-8300
FAX: 505-983-7887
e-mail: mccune@nmmccune.org
nmmccune.org

*Wendy Lewis, Executive Director*
*Norty Kalishman, M.D., Program Director*
Dedicated to enriching the health, education, environment, and cultural and spiritual life of New Mexicans.

**2837 Santa Fe Community Foundation**
PO Box 1827
501 Halona Street
Santa Fe, NM 87505
505-988-9715
FAX: 505-988-1829
e-mail: foundation@santafecf.org
santafecf.org

*Billie Blair, President*

## New York

**2838 AT&T Foundation**
24th Fl
32 Avenue of the Americas
New York, NY 10013- 2473
212-226-2216
FAX: 212-387-5097
e-mail: info@att.com
www.att.com

*Randall L Stephenson, CEO*
Committed to advancing education, strengthening communities and improving lives.

**2839 Altman Foundation**
Fl 35
521 5th Ave
New York, NY 10175-3500
212-682-0970
e-mail: info@altman.org
altmanfoundation.org

*Jane B O'Connell, President*
*Karen L. Rosa, Vice President & Executive Director*
*Jeremy Tennenbaum, CFO*
For the benefit of such charitable and educational institutions in the City of New York as said directors shall approve. Foundation grants support programs and institutions that enrich the quality of life in the city, with a particular focus on initiatives that help individuals, families and communities benefit from the services and opportunities that will enable them to achieve their full potential.

**2840 Ambrose Monell Foundation**
SUITE 301
1 Rockefeller Plz
New York, NY 10020-2002
212-586-0700
FAX: 212-245-1863
e-mail: info@monellvetlesen.org
www.monellvetlesen.org

*George Rowe Jr., President, Treasurer and Director*
*Ambrose K. Monell, Vice-President and Director*
*Eugene P. Grisanti, Vice-President and Director*
Voluntary aiding and contributing to religious, charitable, scientific, literary, and educational uses and purposes, in New York, elsewhere in the US and throughout the world.

**2841 American Chai Trust**
40th Fl
41 Madison Ave
New York, NY 10010-2202
212-889-0575
FAX: 212-743-8120
e-mail: info@perlmanandperlman.com
www.perlmanandperlman.com

**2842 American Express Foundation**
P.O. Box 981540
El Paso, TX 79998-1540
800-528-4800
TTY:800-221-9950
americanexpress.com

*Kenneth I Chenault, CEO*
Grants are awarded in the three program areas: Community Service, Cultural Heritage, and Economic Independence. Most grants are made for projects operating where the company has a major employee or market presence.

**2843 American Foundation for the Blind**
Suite 1102
11 Penn Plz
New York, NY 10001-2018
212-502-7600
200-232-5463
FAX: 212-502-7777
e-mail: afbinfo@afb.net
afb.org

*Carl Augusto, President/ CEO*
Dedicated to addressing issues of literacy, independent living, employment, and access through technology for the ten million Americans who are blind or visually impaired.

**2844 Arthur Ross Foundation**
Ste 4c
20 E 74th St
New York, NY 10021-2654
212-737-7311
FAX: 212-650-0332

*Arthur Ross, President*

**2845 Artists Fellowship**
47 5th Ave
New York, NY 10003-4303
212-255-7740
e-mail: info@artistsfellowship.org
www.artistsfellowship.org

*Babette Bloch, President*
Private, charitable foundation that assists professional fine arts and their families in times of emergency, disability, or bereavement.

**2846 Bodman Foundation**
Fl 4
767 3rd Ave
New York, NY 10017-9029
212-644-0322
FAX: 212-759-6510
e-mail: main@achelis-bodman-fnds.org
www.achelis-bodman-fnds.org

*John B. Krieger, Executive Director*
*John N. Irwin III, Chairman*
*Russell P. Pennoyer, President*
Foundation concentrates their grant programs in New York City, but foundation also makes some grants in Northern New Jersey. Funding is concentrated in six program areas: Arts & Culture, Education, Employment, Health, Public Policy and Youth and Families.

**2847 Brooklyn Home for Aged Men**
P.O.Box 280062
Brooklyn, NY 11228
718-745-1638
FAX: 718-745-0813
www.brooklynhome.org

The Brooklyn Home For Aged Men has served the community for more than one hundred years. Although originally set up as a residence for men, it later accepted women and couples as well.

**2848 Cancer Care**
275 7th Avenue
22nd Floor
New York, NY 10001-6754
212-712-8400
800-813-4673
FAX: 212-712-8495
e-mail: info@cancercare.org
www.cancercare.org

*Helen Miller, CEO*
*John Rutigliano, COO*
A national non-profit organization that provides free, professional support services to anyone affected by cancer: people with cancer, caregivers, children, loved ones, and the bereaved.

**2849 Children's Tumor Foundation**
95 Pine St
15th Floor
New York, NY 10005-3904
212-344-6633
800-323-7938
FAX: 212-747-0004
e-mail: info@ctf.org
ctf.org

*John Risner, President*
*Judi Swartout, CPA, CFO*
*John Heropoulos, Vice President*
A nonprofit 501 (c)(3) medical foundation, dedicated to improving the health and well-being of individuals and families affected by neurofibromatosis. The Foundation sponsors medical research, clinical services, public education programs and patient support services. It is the central source for up-to-date and accurate information about NF. It also assists patients and families with referrals to NF clinics and healthcare professionals specializing in NF. The goal is to find a cure for NF.

**2850 Commonwealth Fund**
1 E 75th St
New York, NY 10021-2692
212-606-3800
FAX: 212-606-3500
e-mail: info@cmwf.org
www.commonwealthfund.org

*Karen Davis, President*
*John E. Craig, Jr., Executive Vice President and Chief Operating Officer*
A private foundation with the broad charge to enhance the common good. Carries out this mandate by supporting efforts that help people live healthy and productive lives, and by assisting certain groups with serious and neglected problems. Supports independent research on health and social issues and makes grants to improve heathcare practice and policy.

**2851 Community Foundation for Greater Buffalo**
726 Exchange Street,
Suite 525
Buffalo, NY 14202
716-852-2857
FAX: 716-852-2861
e-mail: gailj@cfgb.org
cfgb.org

*Clotilde Per Dedecker, President/CEO*
Mission is connecting people, ideas, and resources to improve lives in Western New York

**2852 Community Foundation of Herkimer & Oneida Counties**
1222 State St
Utica, NY 13502-4728
315-735-8212
FAX: 315-735-9363
e-mail: info@foundationhoc.org
foundationhoc.org

*Peggy O'Shea, President/CEO*
Mission of the foundation is to improve the lives of the residents of Herkimer and Oneida Counties.

**2853 Community Foundation of the Capitol Region**
6 Tower Pl
Albany, NY 12203-3749
518-446-9638
FAX: 518-446-9708
e-mail: info@cfcr.org
cfcr.org

*Kristen Frederick, President*
Mission is to strengthen our community by attracting charitable endowments both large and small, maximizing benefits to donors, making effective gtants, and providing leadership to address community needs.

**2854 Comsearch: Broad Topics**
Foundation Center
79 5th Ave
New York, NY 10003-3034
212-620-4230
800-424-9836
FAX: 212-807-3677
e-mail: communications@foundationcenter.org
www.fdncenter.org

*Sara Engelhardt, President*
Subset publications of The Foundation Grants Index, are printouts of actual foundation grants, covering 26 key areas of grantmaking. This tool is designed for fundraisers who wish to examine grantmaking activities in a broad field of interest. *$55.00*

**2855 DE French Foundation**
Ste 503
120 Genesee St
Auburn, NY 13021-3672
315-252-3634

*Walter Lowe, Owner*

**2856 Dana Foundation**
Dana Alliance for Brain Initiatives
6th floor
505 Fifth Avenue,
New York, NY 10017 212-223-4040
FAX: 212-317-8721
e-mail: danainfo@dana.org
www.dana.org

*Edward F Rover, President /Chairman*
*Burton M. Mirsky, Vice President, Finance*
A private philanthropy with principal interests in brain science, immunology, and arts education.

**2857 David J Green Foundation**
Ste 12
599 Lexington Ave
New York, NY 10022-6030 212-317-8820
FAX: 212-371-5099
djgreene.com

*Valerie Ventolora, Manager*
*Michael Greene, Manager*
The site is under construction

**2858 Easter Seals New York**
40 W 37th St
Suite 503
New York, NY 10018-7907 212-220-2290
800-727-8785
FAX: 212-695-4807
e-mail: jmcgrath@eastersealsny.org
www.eastersealsny.org

*John W. McGrath, MPA, Senior Vice President, Organizational Development*
Offers resources and expertise that allow children and adults with disabilities to live with dignity and independence. A long standing commitment to serve those for whom no other resources exist. Statewide, provides innovative solutions that enhance the lives of people with disabilities, while heightening community awareness and acceptance.

**2859 Edna McConnel Clark Foundation**
Fl 10
415 Madison Ave
New York, NY 10017-7949 212-551-9100
FAX: 212-421-9325
e-mail: info@emcf.org
emcf.org

*Nancy Roob, President*
*Woodrow C. McCutchen, Vice President, Senior Portfolio Manager*
Helps young people, ages 9-24, from low-income backgrounds become independent, productive adults.

**2860 Edward John Noble Foundation**
Fl 19
32 E 57th St
New York, NY 10022-8562 212-759-4212
FAX: 212-888-4531

*June Noble Larkin, Owner*
*June Larkin, Owner*

**2861 Epilepsy Foundation of Long Island**
506 Stewart Ave
Garden City, NY 11530-4706 516-739-7733
888-672-7154
FAX: 516-739-1860
e-mail: jlpsky@epil.org
epil.org

*Paul Giotis, Executive Director*
Provides education, counseling and residential care to Long Island residents with epilepsy and related conditions. Site is under construction.

**2862 Episcopal Charities**
1047 Amsterdam Ave
New York, NY 10025-1747 212-316-7400
e-mail: info@dioceseny.org
dioceseny.org
Provides funding and support to a broad range of community-based human service programs throughout the Diocese of New York. These programs, sponsored by Episcopal congregations, serve disadvantaged individuals, youth and families on a non-sectarian basis.

**2863 Esther A & Joseph Klingenstein Fund**
125 Park Avenue
Suite 1700
New York, NY 10017-5529 212-492-6195
e-mail: kathleen.pomerantz@klingenstein.com
www.klingfund.org

*John Klingenstein, President*
*Kathleen Pomerantz, Vice President*
Supports young investigators engaged in basic or clinical research that may lead to a better understanding of epilepsy

**2864 Fay J Lindner Foundation**
189 Wheatley Road
Brookville, NY 11545 516-686-4440

*Terrence Ullrich, President*

**2865 Ford Foundation**
320 E 43rd St
New York, NY 10017-4890 212-573-5000
FAX: 212-351-3677
e-mail: office-of-communications@fordfoundation.org
www.fordfound.org

*Luis A Ubinas, President*
*John Colborn, Vice President for Operations*
*Marta Tellado, Vice President/Communications*
A resource for innovative people and institutions worldwide. Goals are to: strenghthen democratic values; reduce poverty and injustice; promote international cooperation; and advance human achievement. While not specific to disabilities, the Ford Foundation operates on several levels that indirectly assist and support those with disabilities through human and civil rights issues, social justice support, economic fairness and opportunity, and access to education involvements.

**2866 Fortis Foundation**
1 Chase Manhattan Plz
New York, NY 10005-1401 212-859-7029
FAX: 212-859-7010
e-mail: Investor.Relations@assurant.com
ir.assurant.com

*Melissa Kivett, Senior Vice President, Investor Relations*
*Suzanne Shepherd, Director, Investor Relations*

**2867 Foundation Center**
79 5th Ave
New York, NY 10003-3076 212-620-4230
800-424-9836
FAX: 212-807-3677
e-mail: customerservice@foundationcenter.org
foundationcenter.org

*Bradford K Smith, President*
*Maggie Morth, Communications Manager*
*Alison Alford, Marketing Coordinator*
The Foundation Center publishes Foundation Directory Online, with key facts on the US grantmakers and their grants.

**2868 Foundation Center Library Services**
Foundation Center
79 5th Ave
New York, NY 10003-3076
212-620-4230
800-424-9836
FAX: 212-807-3677
e-mail: communications@fdncenter.org
foundationcenter.org

*Bradford K Smith, President*

The Center disseminates current information on foundation and corporate giving through our national collections in New York City and Washington D.C., our field offices in San Francisco and our network of over 180 cooperating libraries in all 50 states and abroad.

**2869 Foundation for Advancement in Cancer Therapy**
P.O.Box 1242
New York, NY 10113-1242
212-741-2790
www.fact-ltd.org

*Ruth Sackman, President*

A clearinghouse for information regarding alternative cancer therapies, emphasizing nutritional and metabolic approaches.

**2870 Gebbie Foundation**
Ste 1100
111 W 2nd St
Jamestown, NY 14701-5207
716-487-1062
FAX: 716-484-6401
e-mail: info@gebbie.org
www.gebbie.org

*John C. Merino, CEO*

Giving in Chautauqua County, and secondly, in neighboring areas of western New York. Giving is offered in other areas only when the project is consonant with program objectives that cannot be developed locally.

**2871 Gladys Brooks Foundation**
Suite 208
1055 Franklin Avenue
Garden City, NY 11530
www.gladysbrooksfoundation.org

*Jessica L Rutledge, Director*

The purpose of this Foundation is to provide for the intellectual, moral and physical welfare of the people of this country by establishing and supporting nonprofit libraries, educational institutions, hospitals and clinics. The Foundation will make grants only to private, publicly supported, nonprofit, tax-exempt organizations.

**2872 Glickenhaus Foundation**
546 5th Ave
New York, NY 10036-5000
212-953-7800
e-mail: info@glickenhaus.com
glickenhaus.com

*Seth M. Glickenhaus, Senior Partner and Chief Investment Officer*

**2873 Guide Dog Foundation for the Blind**
371 E Jericho Tpke
Smithtown, NY 11787-2976
800-548-4337
FAX: 631-361-5192
e-mail: info@guidedog.org
guidedog.org

*Wells Jones, CEO*
*Laura English, CFO*

Providing mobility through the use of trained guide or service dogs to individuals who are blind or with other special needs.

**2874 Hearst Foundations**
Fl 26
300 W 57th St
New York, NY 10019-3741
212-887-6800
FAX: 212-887-6855
hearst.com

*Frank A. Bennack, Jr., CEO*

National philanthropic resources for organziations and institutions working in the fields of education, health, culture and social services. Our goal is to ensure that people of all backgrounds have the opportunity to build healthy, productive and inspiring lives.

**2875 Henry and Lucy Moses Fund**
405 Lexington Ave
New York, NY 10174-1299
212-554-7800
FAX: 212-554-7700
e-mail: klinhardt@mosessinger.com
www.mosessinger.com

*Irving Sitnick, President*

Provides legal services to many prominent industries, individuals and families in the New York City area.

**2876 Herman Goldman Foundation**
Fl 18
61 Broadway
New York, NY 10006-2708
212-797-9090
nlnfoundation.org

*Alan Nisselson, President*

A private nonoperating foundation.

**2877 Kenneth & Evelyn Lipper Foundation**
Fl 6
101 Park Ave
New York, NY 10178
212-883-6333

*Kenneth Lipper, Director*

**2878 Long Island Alzheimer's Foundation**
5 Channel Dr
Port Washington, NY 11050-2216
516-767-6856
FAX: 516-767-6864
e-mail: info@liaf.org
www.liaf.org

*Fred Jenny, Executive Director*

**2879 Louis and Anne Abrons Foundation**
First Manhattan Company
437 Madison Ave
New York, NY 10022-7001
212-756-3300
FAX: 212-832-6698
firstmanhattan.com

*David Manischewitz, CEO*

**2880 Margaret L Wendt Foundation**
Ste 277
40 Fountain Plz
Buffalo, NY 14202-2200
716-855-2146
FAX: 716-855-2149

*Robert J Kresse, Manager*

**2881 Merrill Lynch & Company Foundation**
250 Vesey St
New York, NY 10080
212-449-1000
FAX: 212-449-7969
ml.com

*Brian T Moynihan, CEO*

Ongoing support for the arts, health, human services, and civic issues. Merrill Lynch's philanthropic priority is a sustained investment in education. Q992

**2882 Metzger-Price Fund**
Ste 2300
230 Park Ave
New York, NY 10169 212-867-9500
FAX: 212-599-1759

*Isaac A Saufer, Secretary/Treasurer*

**2883 Milbank Foundation for Rehabilitation**
116 Village Boulevard
Suite 200
New York, NY 10065 609-951-2283
FAX: 609-951-2281
foundationcenter.org/grantmaker/milbank/

*Carl Helstrom, Executive Director and Assistant Treasurer*
Awarding grants from trust funds based on a competitive selection process or the preferences of the foundation managers and granters. The foundations mission is to integrate people with disabilities into all aspects of american life. Current priorities include, but are not limited to: consumer-focused initiatives that enable people with disablities to lead fulfilling,independent lives; innovative policy research and education on market-based approaches to health care and rehabilitation...

**2884 Morgan Stanley Foundation**
1585 Broadway
New York, NY 10036-8293 212-761-4000
FAX: 212-761-0086
morganstanley.com

*Michael Armstrong, President*
Our overachieving mission is threefold: build the potential of individuals and families, encourage and support our employees charitable efforts, and strengthen relationships with our communities.

**2885 Mount Sinai Medical Center**
1 Gustave L Levy Pl
New York, NY 10029-6574 212-241-3066
305-674-2777
www.msmcfoundation.org

Autism Research

**2886 National Foundation for Facial Reconstruction**
333 East 30th Street
Lobby Unit
New York, NY 10016-4974 212-263-6656
FAX: 212-263-7534
e-mail: info@nffr.org
nffr.org

*Whitney Burnett, Executive Director*
A nonprofit organization whose major purposes are to provide facilities for the treatment and assistance of individuals who are unable to afford private reconstructive surgical care, to train and educate professionals in this surgery, to encourage research in the field and to carry on public education.

**2887 National Hemophilia Foundation**
Fl 11
116 W 32nd St
New York, NY 10001-3212 212-328-3700
FAX: 212-328-3777
e-mail: webmaster@hemophilia.org
hemophilia.org

*Elvira Goody, CEO*
Dedicated to finding better treatments and cures for bleeding and clotting disorders to preventing the complications of these disorders through education, advocacy and research.

**2888 Neisloss Family Foundation**
Ste 7
1737 Veterans Hwy
Central Islip, NY 11749-1533 631-234-1600
FAX: 631-234-1066

*Stanley Neisloss, President/Owner*

**2889 New York Community Trust**
Fl 22
909 3rd Ave
New York, NY 10022-4752 212-686-0010
FAX: 212-532-8528
e-mail: info@nycommunitytrust.org
nycommunitytrust.org

*Lorie A Slutsky, President*
*Alan Holzer, CFO*
Our goal is to out charitable money to work, making grants to the city's nonprofit community and building an endowment to tackle future problems.

**2890 New York Foundation**
Fl 10
10 E 34th St
New York, NY 10016-4327 212-594-8009
nyf.org

*Maria Mottola, Executive Director*
*Kevin Ryan, Program Director*
Grants are given that involve New York City or a particular neighborhood of the city. Emphasize advocacy and community organizing. Address a critical need or disadvantaged population, particularly youth or the elderly. Are strongly identified with a particular community. Require an amount of funding to which a Foundation grant would make a substantial contribution. And can show a clear role for the Foundation's funds.

**2891 Northern New York Community Foundation**
Ste 400
120 Washington St
Watertown, NY 13601-3376 315-782-7110
FAX: 315-782-0047
e-mail: info@nnycf.org
www.nnycf.org

*Rande S. Richardson, Executive Director*
Raises, manages and administers an endowment and collection of funds for the benefit of the community

**2892 Parkinson's Disease Foundation**
1359 Broadway
Room 1509
New York, NY 10018-7867 212-923-4700
800-457-6676
FAX: 212-923-4778
e-mail: info@pdf.org
www.pdf.org

*Robin Athony Elliott, Executive Director*
The Parkinson's Disease Foundation is a leading national presence in Parkinson's disease research, education and public advocacy. We are working for the nearly one million people in the US who live with Parkinson's by funding promising scientific research to find the causes of and a cure for Parkinson's while supporting people with Parkinson's, their families and caregivers through educational programs and support services.

**2893 Reader's Digest Foundation**
Readers Digest Association
Readers Digest Rd
Pleasantville, NY 10570 914-238-1000
FAX: 914-238-4559
rd.com

*Mary G Berner, CEO*

Dedicated to creating opportunities and promoting efforts that encourage individuals to make a positive difference in their communities, and to supporting programs designed to help young people learn, grow and enrich their lives.

**2894 Research to Prevent Blindness**
Fl 21
645 Madison Ave
New York, NY 10022-1010 212-752-4333
800-621-0026
FAX: 212-688-6231
e-mail: inforequest@rpbusa.org
www.rpbusa.org

*Diane Swift, Chair*
National voluntary health foundation supported by foundations, corporations and voluntary gifts and bequests from individuals. Established to stimulate basic and applied research into the causes, prevention and treatment of blinding eye diseases.

**2895 Rita J and Stanley H Kaplan Foundation**
Rm 306
866 United Nations Plz
New York, NY 10017-1822 212-688-1047
FAX: 212-688-6907

*Stanley H Kaplan, President*
*Stanley Kaplan, President*

**2896 Robert Sterling Clark Foundation**
135 E 64th St
New York, NY 10065-7045 212-288-8900
FAX: 212-288-1033
e-mail: rscf@rsclark.org
rsclark.org

*Margaret C. Ayers, President/ CEO*
Giving primarily in New York with emphasis on advocacy, research, and public education aimed at informing New York City of state policies.

**2897 Skadden Fellowship Foundation**
4 Times Sq
New York, NY 10036-6518 212-735-3780
FAX: 212-735-2000
e-mail: info@skadden.com
www.skadden.com

*Alan C Myers, Director*
The aim of the Foundation is to give Fellows the freedom to pursue public intrest work, thus the Fellows create their own projects at public interest organizations with at least 2 lawyers on staff before they apply.

**2898 St George's Society of New York**
Rm 901
216 E 45th St
New York, NY 10017-3304 212-682-6110
FAX: 212-682-3465
e-mail: info@stgeorgessociety.org
stgeorgessociety.org

*John Shannon, Executive Director*
St George's Society provides monthly stipends to the elderly and the handicapped.

**2899 Stanley W Metcalf Foundation**
Ste 503
120 Genesee St
Auburn, NY 13021-3672 315-252-3634

*Walter Lowe, Owner*

**2900 Stonewall Community Foundation**
446 West 33rd Street
New York, NY 10001-1913 212-367-1155
FAX: 212-367-1157
e-mail: stonewall@stonewallfoundation.org
www.stonewallfoundation.org

*Paula Ettelbrick, Executive Director*
Mission is to promote the well being of lesbian, gay, bisexual, and transgender (LGBT) individuals and strengthen the LGBT community. We do this by increasing resources; targeting those resources strategically to areas of greatest need; and by serving as a catalyst and clearinghouse for ideas and solutions. Through grant-making donor-advised funds, endowment funds and charitable education, Stonewall supports LGBT organizations and helps donors realize their philanthropic goals.

**2901 Surdna Foundation**
Fl 30
330 Madison Ave
New York, NY 10017-5016 212-557-0010
e-mail: grants@surdna.org
surdna.org

*Sharon L. Alpert, Senior Director, Programs and Strategy*
The Foundation makes grants in the areas of environment, community revitalization, effective citizenry, the arts and the nonprofit sector.

**2902 Tisch Foundation**
Fl 19
655 Madison Ave
New York, NY 10065-8043 212-521-2930
FAX: 212-521-2983

*Mark J Krinsky, VP*

**2903 Van Ameringen Foundation**
509 Madison Ave
New York, NY 10022-5501 212-758-6221
FAX: 212-688-2105
e-mail: info@vanamfound.org
www.vanamfound.org

*Henry Van Ameringen, President / Treasurer*
*Eleanor Sypher, Executive Director*
From its beginning the Foundation has sought to stimulate prevention, education, and direct care in the mental health field with an emphasis on those individuals and populations having an impoverished background and few opportunities, for whom appropriate intervention would produce positive change.

**2904 Verizon Foundation**
1 Verizon Way
Basking Ridge, NJ 07920-1097 FAX: 908-630-2660
e-mail: verizonfoundation@verizon.com
www.foundation.verizon.com

*Binta Vann-Joseph, Director of Marketing Strategy*
Mission is to improve education, literacy, family safety and healthcare by supporting Verizon's commitment to deliver technology that touches life. We focus our philanthropic efforts on 3 areas: Education, Safety and Health. & Volunteerism.

**2905 Western New York Foundation**
Ste 4
11 Summer St
Buffalo, NY 14209-2256 716-839-4425
FAX: 716-N99-8883
e-mail: bgosch@wnyfoundation.org
www.wnyfoundation.org

*Beth Kinsman Gosch, Executive Director*
The Western New York Foundation makes grants in the seven counties of Western New York State: Erie, Niagra, Genesee, Wyoming, Allegany, Cattaraugus and Chautauqua

**2906 William T Grant Foundation**
18th Fl
570 Lexington Ave
New York, NY 10022-6837
212-752-0071
FAX: 212-752-1398
e-mail: info@wtgrantfdn.org
wtgrantfoundation.org

*Robert Granger, President*
*Vivian Tseng, Vice President, Program*

Purpose is to further the understanding of human behavior through research. The mission focuses on improving the lives of youth ages 8 to 25 in the United States.

## North Carolina

**2907 Arc of North Carolina**
Ste 100
4200 Six Forks Rd
Raleigh, NC 27609
919-782-4632
800-662-8706
FAX: 919-782-4634
e-mail: arcofnc@arcnc.org
www.arcnc.org

*Dave Richards, Executive Director*

Committed to securing for all people with mental retardation and other developmental disabilities the opportunity to choose and realize their goals of where and how they learn, live, work, and play.

**2908 Bob & Kay Timberlake Foundation**
1660 E Center Street Ext
Lexington, NC 27292-1309
336-243-7777
800-776-0822
FAX: 336-249-2469
bobtimberlake.com

*Daniel Timberlake, President*

**2909 Duke Endowment**
Ste 3500
100 N Tryon St
Charlotte, NC 28202-4012
704-376-0291
FAX: 704-376-9336
e-mail: info@tde.org
dukeendowment.org

*Eugene W. Cochrane Jr., President*
*Arthur E. Morehead IV, General Counsel*
*Susan L. McConnell, Director of Human Resources*
*Terri W. Honeycutt, Corporate Secretary*

Mission is to serve the people of North Carolina and South Carolina by supporting selected programs of higher education, health care, children's welfare, and spiritual life.

**2910 First Union Foundation**
301 S College St
Charlotte, NC 28288
704-383-0525
FAX: 704-374-2484

*Judy Allison, Director*

**2911 Foundation for the Carolinas**
220 N. Tryon Street
Charlotte, NC 28202
704-973-4500
800-973-7244
FAX: 704-973-4599
e-mail: mmarsicano@fftc.org
fftc.org

*Michael Marsicano, Ph.D., President & CEO*
*Laura Meyer Wellman, Executive Vice President*
*Paula J. Washam, Executive Assistant to Michael Marsicano*
*Shannon Fitzgerald, Executive Assistant to Laura Meyer Wellman*

Giving primarily to organizations serving the citizens of North and South Carolina.

**2912 Kate B Reynolds Charitable Trust**
128 Reynolda Vlg
Winston Salem, NC 27106-5123
336-397-5500
800-485-9080
FAX: 336-723-7765
e-mail: joyce@kbr.org
kbr.org

*Karen McNeil-Miller,, President*
*Christopher Spaugh, Senior Vice President*
*Sandra T. Shell, Senior Vice President, Chief Operating Officer*
*Jon S. Abramson, M.D., Chair*

Mission is to improve the quality of life and quality of health for the financially needy of North Carolina. Grants resricted to the state of North Carolina only.

**2913 Mary Reynolds Babcock Foundation**
2920 Reynolda Rd
Winston Salem, NC 27106-3016
336-748-9222
FAX: 336-777-0095
e-mail: info@mrbf.org
mrbf.org

*Katharine R. Mountcastle, President*
*Wendy Johnson, Vice President*
*Ken Mountcastle, Treasurer*
*Dee Davis, Secretary*

For 1994, this foundation is committed to an extensive educational and planning process to better understand the Southeast and to articulate the role the foundation seeks to play in the region into the twenty-first century.

**2914 Triangle Community Foundation**
Ste 1220
324 Blackwell St
Durham, NC 27701-3690
919-474-8370
FAX: 919-941-9208
e-mail: info@trianglecf.org
trianglecf.org

*Phail Wynn, Jr., Interim President and CEO*
*Lori O'Keefe, Vice President for Philanthropic Services and Chief Operating Officer*
*Ruth Peoples, Executive Assistant to the President*
*Jessica Aylor, Director of Development and Community Partnerships*

Triangle Community Foundation connects philanthropic resources with community needs, creates opportunity for enlightned change and encourages philanthropy as a way of life.

## North Dakota

**2915 Alex Stern Family Foundation**
Ste 102
4152 30th Ave S
Fargo, ND 58104-8403
701-271-0263
FAX: 701-271-0408
http://alexsternfamilyfoundation.org/

*D L Scott, Executive Director*

The Foundation supports the arts, social welfare/human services, education, youth recreation, civic projects and health issues for the benefit of the greater Fargo-Moorhead area.

**2916 Arc of North Dakota**
P.O.Box 12420
2500 DeMers Avenue
Grand Forks, ND 58208- 2420
701-772-6191
877-250-2022
FAX: 701-772-2195
e-mail: thearc@arcuv.com
www.thearcuppervalley.com

*Jennifer Wray, President*
*Peggy Johnson, First Vice President*
*Jim Berglie, Second Vice President*
*Rachel Hafner, Secretary*
Mission is to work in partnership with our constituents, members and affiliated chapters to ensure that children and adults with intellectual and developmental disabilities have the supports, benefits, and services they need, and are accepted, respected and fully included in their communities.

**2917 North Dakota Community Foundation**
309 N Mandan Street
P.O.Box 387
309 N Mandan Street, Suite 2
Bismarck, ND 58502-0387
701-222-8349
e-mail: kdvorak@ndcf.net
www.ndcf.net

*Kevin Dvorak, CFP, President & CEO*
*Amy N. Warnke, CFRE, Development Director East*
*Kara L. Geiger, Development Director West*
*Jordan J. Neufeld, CPA, Administrator & Accountant*
The mission of the North Dakota Community Foundation is to improve the quality of life for North Dakota's citizens through charitable giving and promothing philanthropy.

## Ohio

**2918 Akron Community Foundation**
345 W Cedar St
Akron, OH 44307-2407
330-376-8522
FAX: 330-376-0202
www.akroncommunityfdn.org

*John Petures, CEO*
Mission is to improve the quality of life in the Greater Akron area by building permanent endowments, and providing philanthropic leadership that enables donors to make lasting investments in the community.

**2919 Albert G and Olive H Schlink Foundation**
49 Benedict Avenue, Suite C
Norwalk, OH 44857
e-mail: curtis@hwak.com
www.schlinkfoundation.org

**2920 American Foundation Corporation**
4518 North 32nd Street
Phoenix, AZ 85018
602-955-4770
FAX: 602-955-4707
e-mail: info@americanfoundation.org
http://americanfoundation.org/corporate_foun d

*Ben L. Schaub, Founder and CEO*
The American Foundation can be your sponsor, and help your company set up a corporate foundation in a "public charity" or "support organization" format.

**2921 Arc of Ohio**
Ste 205c
1335 Dublin Rd
Columbus, OH 43215-7037
614-487-4720
800-875-2723
FAX: 614-487-4725
e-mail: info@thearcofohio.org
thearcofohio.org

*Gary Tonks, Executive Director*
*John Hannah, President*
*Connie Calhoun, Vice President*
*Josh Ebling, Treasurer*
The mission of The Arc of Ohio is to advocacte for human rights, personal dignity and community participation of individuals with mental retardation and other developmental disabilities, through legislative and social action, information and education, local chapter support and family involvement.

**2922 Bahmann Foundation**
Ste 210
8041 Hosbrook Rd
Cincinnati, OH 45236-2909
513-891-3799
FAX: 513-891-3722
e-mail: info@bahmann.org
www.bahmann.org

*John Gatch, Executive Director*
The mission of the Bahmann Foundation is to reduce isolation of low-income older adults through technology.

**2923 Cleveland Foundation**
Ste 1300
1422 Euclid Ave
Cleveland, OH 44115-2063
216-861-3810
FAX: 216-861-1729
e-mail: info@ClevelandFoundation.org
clevelandfoundation.org

*Ronald B Richard, President and Chief Executive Officer*
*Sylvia E. Perez, Chief of Staff and Manager for Governmental and International Affairs*
*Kimberly Sabo, Executive Assistant to the President and CEO*
*Charles Bolton, Chairman*
In general, grants are made in (but not restriced to) the areas of arts and culture, community development, economic development, education, environment, health and human services.

**2924 Columbus Foundation and Affiliated Organizations**
1234 E Broad St
Columbus, OH 43205-1453
614-251-4000
FAX: 614-251-4009
e-mail: info@columbusfoundation.org
columbusfoundation.org

*Doug F. Kridler, President & CEO*
*Raymond J. Biddiscombe, CPA, Senior Vice President - Finance & Administration / CFO*
*Lisa Schweitzer Courtice, P, Executive Vice President - Community Research and Grants Management*
*Tamera (Tami Durrence, Vice President - Supporting Foundations*
The Columbus Foundation offers a range of charitable fund types that can be used for individuals, families and businesses.

**2925 Eleanora CU Alms Trust**
Fifth Third Bank
Department 00864
9990 Montgomery Rd
Cincinnati, OH 45263
513-793-2200

*Robert W Laclair, President*
Giving is limited to Cincinnati, OH.

**2926 Eva L And Joseph M Bruening Foundation**
Foundation Management Services
Ste 627
1422 Euclid Ave
Cleveland, OH 44115-1952
216-621-2901
FAX: 216-621-8198
e-mail: cstarkey@fmscleaveland.com
www.fmscleveland.com

*Janet E. Narten, Founder*
*Cristin N. Slesh, President*
*Susan O. Althans, Senior Associate*
*Allison Rand, Associate*
Charitable foundation providing grants to noprofit organizations located inCuyahoga county Ohio. No grant are awarded to inviduals.

**2927 Fred & Lillian Deeks Memorial Foundation**
P.O.Box 1118
Cincinnati, OH 45201-1118
937-339-2329
FAX: 937-339-1861

**2928 GAR Foundation**
277 East Mill Street
Akron, OH 44308
330-576-2926
FAX: 330-294-5315
e-mail: info@garfdn.org
www.garfdn.org

*Christine Amer Mayer, President*
*Kirstin S. Toth, Senior Vice President*
*Candace Campbell Jackson, Consulting Program Officer*
The mission of the Foundation is to strengthen communities in our region through discerning and creative support of worthy organizations.

**2929 George Gund Foundation**
Ste 1845
45 W Prospect Ave
Cleveland, OH 44115-1008
216-241-3114
FAX: 216-241-6560
e-mail: info@gundfdn.org
gundfoundation.org

*David T. Abbott, Executive Director*
*Marcia Egbert, Senior Program Officer (human services)*
*Deena M. Epstein, Senior Program Officer (arts)*
*Ann K. Mullin, Senior Program Officer (education)*
The George Gund Foundation was established in 1952 as a private, nonprofit institution with the sole purpose of contributing to human well-being and the progress of society.

**2930 Greater Cincinnati Foundation**
200 W 4th St
Cincinnati, OH 45202-2775
513-241-2880
FAX: 513-852-6886
e-mail: info@gcfdn.org
greatercincinnatifdn.org

*Kathryn e. Merchant, President/CEO*
*Susan Soudrette, Executive Assistant*
*Elizabeth Reiter Benson, APR, Vice President for Communications & Marketing*
*Shiloh Turner, Vice President for Community Investment*
Offers a wide variety of giving tools to help people achieve their charitable goals and create lasting good work in their communities.

**2931 HCR Manor Care Foundation**
P.O.Box 10086
Toledo, OH 43699-0086
419-252-5500
FAX: 419-252-6404
e-mail: foundation@hcr-manorcare.com
hcr-manorcare.com

*Paul A Ormond, Chairman, President and Chief Executive Officer*
An independent, not-for-profit corporation that provides funding for organizations and programs that address the needs of the elderly and individuals requiring post-acute care services.

**2932 Harry C Moores Foundation**
100 S 3rd St
Columbus, OH 43215-4236
614-227-8884
bricker.com

*Mary B Cummins, Administrator*

**2933 Helen Steiner Rice Foundation**
1301 Western Ave.
Cincinnati, OH 45203
513-287-7022
800-877-2665
e-mail: hrice@cincymuseum.org
helensteinerrice.com

*Virginia J. Ruehlmann, Creative Consultant*
*Dorothy C. Lingg, Office Manager*
*Willis D. Gradison, Jr., Board of Trustee*
*Gregory Ionna, Board of Trustee*
Non-profit corporation whose purpose is to award grants to worthy charitable programs that aid the poor, the needy, and the elderly.

**2934 Herbert W Hoover Foundation**
220 Market Ave S
Canton, OH 44702-2180
330-453-5555
FAX: 330-453-5622
e-mail: contacthwh@hwhfoundation.org
www.hwhfoundation.org

*Mark Butterworth, Ohio Director*
*Lynn Davidson, Program Director*
*Elizabeth Lacey Hoover, Chair*
*Colton Hoover Chase, Member of Trust Committee*
The Herbert W Hoover Foundation will take a leadership role in funding unique opportunities that provide solutions to issues relater to the Community, Education, and the Environment.

**2935 Nationwide Foundation**
1 W Nationwide Blvd
Columbus, OH 43215-2239
614-249-7111
877-669-6877
FAX: 614-249-5721
www.nationwide.com

*Kirt A. Walker, President and COO Nationwide Financial*
*Mark A. Pizzi, President and Chief Operating Officer, Nationwide Insurance*
*Stephen S. Rasmussen, Chief Executive Officer*
*W. Kim Austen, President and Chief Operating Officer, Allied Group, Nationwide*
The Nationwide Foundation is an independent corporation funded by Nationwide Companies to help positively impact the quality of life in communities where our associates, agents and their families live and work.

**2936 Nordson Corporate Giving Program**
28601 Clemens Rd
Westlake, OH 44145-1148
440-892-1580
FAX: 440-892-9507
e-mail: kladiner@nordson.com
nordson.com

*Michael F. Hilton, President and Chief Executive Officer*
*Gregory A. Thaxton, Senior Vice President, Chief Financial Officer*
*John J. Keane, Senior Vice President, Advanced Technology Systems*
*Peter G. Lambert, Senior Vice President, Adhesive Dispensing Systems*
Nordson Corporation encourages individual financial support of nonprofit organizations, colleges, and universities

**2937 Parker-Hannifin Foundation**
6035 Parkland Blvd
Cleveland, OH 44124-4141
216-896-3000
800-272-7537
FAX: 216-896-4000
parker.com

*Donald E. Washkewicz, Chairman, Chief Executive Officer and President*
*Lee C. Banks, Executive Vice President and Operating Officer*
*Robert P. Barker, Executive Vice President, Operating Officer and President - Aerospace*
*Jon P. Marten, Executive Vice President - Finance and Administration & Chief Financia*

To be a leading worldwide manufacturer of components and systems for the builders and users of durable goods.

**2938 Reinberger Foundation**
30000 Chagrin Blvd., #300
Cleveland, OH 44124-4439
216-292-2790
FAX: 216-292-4466
e-mail: info@reinbergerfoundation.org
www.reinbergerfoundation.org

*William Reinberger, Manager*

Committed to enhancing the quality of life for individuals from all walks of life. To achieve this goal, proposals in the areas of the arts, education, healthcare, and social service are favored.

**2939 Robert Campeau Family Foundation**
7 W 7th St
Cincinnati, OH 45202-2424
513-579-7000
FAX: 513-579-7555
federated-fds.com

*Terry J Lundgren, president*

**2940 Sisler McFawn Foundation**
P.O.Box 149
Akron, OH 44309
330-849-8887
FAX: 330-996-6215

*Charlotte M Stanley, Grants Manager*

Our trust restricts giving to certain programs and types of organizations. You can see recent giving has been by referring to the list of grants approved and paid during the past year. Call foundation office to request a guidelines brochure and list.

**2941 Stark Community Foundation**
Ste 200
400 Market Ave N
Canton, OH 44702-1557
330-454-3426
FAX: 330-454-5855
e-mail: info@starkcf.org
www.starkcommunityfoundation.org

*Mark Samolczyk, President*
*Patricia Quick, Vice President*
*Carol Hawk, Director of Development*

Stark Community Foundation is dedicated to promoting the betterment of Stark County and enhancing the quality of life of all its citizens.

**2942 Stocker Foundation**
Suite C
401 Broadway
Lorain, OH 44052-1745
440-246-5719
FAX: 440-246-5720
e-mail: contact@stockerfoundation.org
stockerfoundation.org

*Patricia O'Brien, Executive Director*
*Melanie R Wilson, Office Manage*

The Stocker Foundation seeks creative ideas and projects that are catalysts for constructive change in the community through arts and culture, community needs, education, health social services and women's issues.

**2943 Toledo Community Foundation**
Ste 1300
300 Madison Ave
Toledo, OH 43604-1583
419-241-5049
FAX: 419-242-5549
e-mail: toledocf@toledocf.org
www.toledocf.org

*Keith Burwell, CEO*
*KIM CRYAN, Chief Financial Officer*
*BETSY BLUME, Accountant*

The Toledo Community Foundation is a public, charitable foundation which exists to improve the quality of life in the region.

**2944 William J and Dorothy K O'Neill Foundation**
Ste 310
30195 Chagrin Blvd
Cleveland, OH 44124-5763
216-831-4134
FAX: 216-831-3779
e-mail: oneillfdn@aol.com
www.oneillfdn.org

*Leah S Gary, President*
*William O'Neill, Owner*
*Timothy M. O'Neill, Chair*

**2945 Youngstown Foundation**
P.O.Box 1162
Youngstown, OH 44501-1162
330-744-0320
FAX: 330-744-0344
e-mail: Jan@youngstownfoundation.org
www.youngstownfoundation.org

*Jan Strasfeld, Executive Director*
*Crissi Jenkins, Program Coordinator*
*Rena Colarossi, Admin. Assistant*

Funds proposals that provide direct services to children with medically diagnosed disabilities. Grants are awarded to Ohio non-profit agencies that are qualified under the Internal Revenue Service Code 501 (c) (3) for the care of such children in the greater Youngstown Area.

## Oklahoma

**2946 Anne and Henry Zarrow Foundation**
Ste 900
401 S Boston Ave
Tulsa, OK 74103-4012
918-295-8004
FAX: 918-295-8049
e-mail: bmajor@zarrow.com
www.zarrow.com

A broad-based funding foundation. However, ares of emphasis include Jewish causes, the indignant, the disenfranchised and the homeless. The Foundation meets on a quartely basis, in the months of February, April, September and November. Proposals are due on the first day of the following months:January, April, August and October. Any proposals recieved after the due date will be held until the next quarter's meeting.

**2947 Sarkeys Foundation**
530 E Main St
Norman, OK 73071-5823
405-364-3703
FAX: 405-364-8191
e-mail: angela@sarkeys.org
sarkeys.org

*Kim Henry, Executive Director*
*linda englis weeks, Senior Program Officer*
*angella holladay, Office Manager*

Improves the quality of life in Oklahoma. Offers contributions in the areas of social services, arts and cultural programs, educational funding and health care and medical research. Funding only in agencies in the state of Oklahoma.

## Oregon

**2948 Arc of Oregon**
1745 State St
Salem, OR 97301-4342
503-581-2726
877-581-2726
FAX: 503-363-7168
e-mail: info@arcoregon.org
arcoregon.org

*Marcie Ingledue, Executive Director*
*Lisa Hawke, Manager*
Guardianship, Advocacy and Planning Services. Oregon special needs trust; information and referral.

**2949 Chiles Foundation**
1614 Mahan Center Boulevard
Suite 104
Tallahassee, Fl 32308
805-385-7800
FAX: 805-385-7808
e-mail: kchiles@lawtonchiles.org
chilesfoundation.org

*Kitty Chiles, Executive Director*
*Todd Abernethy, Chief Financial Officer*
Giving in Oregon, with emphasis on Portland, and the Pacific Northwest.

**2950 Jackson Foundation**
P.O.Box 3168
Portland, OR 97208-3168
503-275-4414
www.thejacksonfoundation.com

*Robert H Depew, President*
Purpose is to respond to the requests deemed appropriate to promote the welfare of the public of the city of Portland or the State of Oregon or both.

**2951 Leslie G Ehmann Trust**
P.O.Box 3168
Portland, OR 97208-3168
503-275-5929
800-522-9100
FAX: 503-275-4117
e-mail: william.dollan@usbank.com

*William Dolan, Trustee*

## Pennsylvania

**2952 Air Products Foundation**
7201 Hamilton Blvd
Allentown, PA 18195-9642
610-481-4911
FAX: 610-481-5900
e-mail: http://www.airproducts.com/en/contact-us.aspx
www.airproducts.com

*John E McGlade, CEO*
*Paul E. Huck, SVP*
Giving primarily in areas of company operations throughout the US.

**2953 Arc of Pennsylvania**
Ste 8
101 S 2nd St
Harrisburg, PA 17101-2535
717-234-2621
800-692-7258
FAX: 717-234-2622
e-mail: gadams@thearcpa.org
thearcpa.org

*Jean Downey, President*
*Christopher Gorton, Vice President*
The Arc's mission is to work to include all children and adults with cognitive, intellectual, and developmental disabilities in every community. We promote active citizenship and inclusion in every community.

**2954 Arcadia Foundation**
105 E Logan St
Norristown, PA 19401-3058
202-747-0876
arcadiafoundation.org

*Marilyn L Steinbright, President*

**2955 Brachial Plexus Palsy Foundation**
210 Springhaven Cir
Royersford, PA 19468-1178
e-mail: contact@brachialplexuspalsyfoundation.org
www.brachialplexuspalsyfoundation.org

Nonprofit organization dedicated to raising funds for support of families who hae children with brachial plexus injuries. Supports medical facilities that research and treat such injuries, holds fund-raising events to support further research, has support groups, and produces educational materials including a newsletter, Outreach, and brochures.

**2956 Columbia Gas of Pennsylvania Corporate Giving**
650 Washington Rd
Pittsburgh, PA 15228-2702
412-572-7104
FAX: 412-572-7140
e-mail: info@columbiaenergygroup.com
www.columbiagaspamd.com/html/

*Rosemary Martinelli, Manager Corporation*

**2957 Connelly Foundation**
Suite 1450
1 Tower Brg
West Conshohocken, PA 19428-2873
610-834-3222
FAX: 610-834-0866
e-mail: info@connellyfdn.org
connellyfdn.org

*Josephine C. Mandeville, President*
*Emily C Riley, Executive Vice President*
*Lewis W Bluemle, Senior Vice President*
Seeks to foster learning and to improve the quality of life in the Greater Philadelphia area. The Foundation supports local non-profit organizations in the fields of education, health and human services, arts and culture and civic enterprise.

**2958 Dolfinger-McMahon Foundation**
200 East Randolph St.
Chicago, IL 60601-4201
312-381-1000
aon.com

*Gregory C Case, President*

**2959 Heinz Endowments**
Howard Heinz Endowment
625 Liberty Ave
30 Dominion Tower
Pittsburgh, PA 15222-3110
412-281-5777
FAX: 412-281-5788
e-mail: bobbyvagt@heinz.org
heinz.org

*Robert F Vagt , President*
*Jack E Kime , vice president*
*Stuart Redshaw , director of human resources.*
Mission is to help our region thrive as a whole community-economically, ecologically, educationaly, and culturaly while advancing the state of knowledge and practice in the fields in which we work.

**2960 Henry L Hillman Foundation**
Suite 2000
310 Grant Street
Pittsburgh, PA 15219
412-338-3466
e-mail: foundation@hillmanfo.com
hillmanfamilyfoundations.org

*David K Roger, President*
*Lisa R Johns, Treasurer and Program Manager*
Established with a broad purpose to improve the quality of life in Pittsburgh and southwestern Pennsylvania.

**2961 Jewish Healthcare Foundation of Pittsburgh**
Ste 2400
650 Smithfield St
Pittsburgh, PA 15222-3915
412-594-2550
FAX: 412-232-6240
e-mail: info@jhf.org
jhf.org

*Karen Feinstein, President*
The mission of the JHF is to support and foster the provision of healthcare services, healthcare education, and, when appropriate, medical and scientific research, and to respond to the health-related needs of elderly, underprivileged, indigent, and undeserved persons in both the Jewish and general community throughout Western Pennsylvania. .

**2962 Juliet L Hillman Simonds Foundation**
Suite 2000
330 Grant St
Pittsburgh, PA 15219
412-281-2620
FAX: 412-338-3520
e-mail: foundation@hillmanfo.com

*Joseph Manzinger, President*
*David Rager, Program Manager*

**2963 Oberkotter Foundation**
Ste 3600
1600 Market St
Philadelphia, PA 19103-7212
215-751-2601
FAX: 215-751-2678
e-mail: orders@oraldeaf.org
oraldeafed.org

*George H Nofer, Executive Director*

**2964 PECO Energy Company Contributions Program**
Fl 7toorh
2301 Market St
Philadelphia, PA 19103-1338
215-841-4000
FAX: 215-841-6830
exceloncorp.com

*Denis P O'Brien, CEO*

**2965 PNC Bank Foundation**
249 5th Ave
Pittsburgh, PA 15222-2707
412-762-2000
FAX: 412-762-7829
e-mail: marianna.hallett@pnc.com
www.pncbank.com

*Samuel R Patterson, Senior VP*
The PNC Foundation's priority is to form partnerships with community-based nonprofit organizations within the markets PNC serves in order to enhance educational opportunities for children, particularly underserved pre-K children though our signature, PNC Grow Uo Great Program, and to promote the growth of targeted communities through economic development initiatives.

**2966 Philadelphia Foundation**
Ste 1800
1234 Market St
Philadelphia, PA 19107-3704
215-563-6417
FAX: 215-563-6882
e-mail: EOConnell@philafound.org
philafound.org

*R Andrew Swinney, President*
*Pat Meller, vice president*
*Andrea congo, executive assistant*
The Philadelphia Foundation improves our community by advancing change, leading on issues of importance, forging meaningful relationships and providing knowledge, resources and stewardship.

**2967 Pittsburgh Foundation**
Ste 250
5 Ppg Pl
Pittsburgh, PA 15222-5405
412-391-5122
FAX: 412-391-7259
e-mail: oliphantg@pghfdn.org
pittsburghfoundation.org

*Grant Oliphant, CEO*
*Jonathan Brelsford, Vice President*
*Marianne Cola, Executive Secretary*
The Pittsburgh Foundation works to improve the quality of life in the Pittsburgh region by evaluating and addressing community issues, promoting responsible philanthropy, and connecting donors to the critical needs of the community.

**2968 Shenango Valley Foundation**
7 West State Street
Suite 301
Sharon, PA 16146-2713
724-981-5882
866-901-7204
FAX: 724-983-9044
e-mail: larry@sv-foundation.org
www.sv-foundation.org

*James O'Brien, President*
*Karen Winner Sed, Vice President*
*James E Feeney , Treasurer*
*Ronald R Anderson , Secretary*
Mission is to promote the betterment of our region and enhancement of the quality of life for all of its citizens.

**2969 Staunton Farm Foundation**
Ste 210
650 Smithfield St
Pittsburgh, PA 15222-3907
412-281-8020
FAX: 412-232-3115
e-mail: office@stauntonfarm.org
stauntonfarm.org

*Joni S. Schwager, Executive Director*
*Bethany Hemingway, Program Officer,*
*Liz Veri, Office Manager,*
Dedicated to improving the lives of people who live with mental illness.

**2970 Stewart Huston Charitable Trust**
50 S 1st Ave
Coatesville, PA 19320-3418
610-384-2666
FAX: 610-384-3396
e-mail: admin@stewarthuston.org
stewarthuston.org

*Scott Huston, Executive Director*
The purpose of the Trust is to provide funds, technical assistance and collaboration on behalf of non-profit organizations engaged exclusively in religious, charitable or educational work; to extend opportunities to deserving needs persons and, in general, to promote any of the above causes.

**2971 Teleflex Foundation**
155 S Limerick Rd
Limerick, PA 19468-1603
610-948-5100
FAX: 610-948-5101
teleflex.com

*Jeffrey P Black, CEO*
The Teleflex Foundation strives to create an impact on the quality of life in Teleflex communities and build supportive relationships among our stakeholders. The Foundation places a priority on progrmas that have the commitmenet and volunteer involvement of Teleflex communities.

**2972 USX Foundation**
Ste 685
600 Grant St
Pittsburgh, PA 15219-2702
412-433-5238
FAX: 412-433-6847

*CD Mallick, General Manager*
*Patricia Funaro, Program Manager*
Giving primarily in areas of company operations located within the United States.

**2973 William B Dietrich Foundation**
Duane Morrs Llt
30 S 17th St
Philadelphia, PA 19103-4001
215-979-1000
FAX: 215-979-1020
www.duanemorrs.com

*William B Dietrich, President*

**2974 William Talbott Hillman Foundation**
523 west 37 street
New York, NY 10018-2309
212-792-2676
FAX: 212-792-2677
e-mail: info@wiliamthillman.com

*Grant Williams, Owner*

**2975 William V and Catherine A McKinney Charitable Foundation**
20 Stanwix St
Pittsburgh, PA 15222-4802
412-644-8332
FAX: 412-644-6058
verizon.com

*William M Schmidt, Senior Vice President*

## Rhode Island

**2976 Arc South County Chapter**
2 Barber Avenue
Warwick, RI 02886-3549
401-480-9355
e-mail: paul@pence.com
www.riroads.com

Developmentally disabled center/service assistance to individuals with developmental disabilities.

**2977 Arc of Blackstone Valley**
115 Manton St
Pawtucket, RI 02861-4332
401-727-0150
FAX: 401-727-0153
e-mail: contact@bvcriarc.org
www.bvcriarc.org

*Lester B Keats, President*
*Kathleen O'Neill, Vice President*
A private nonprofit organization providing residential, developmental, employment and recreational programs and services to more then 400 individuals with intellectual and related disabilities

**2978 Arc of Northern Rhode Island**
The Homestead Group Administrative Offices
68 Cumberland St
Suite 200
Woonsocket, RI 02895-3323
401-765-3700
FAX: 401-765-1124
e-mail: info@thgri.org
arcofnri.org

The mission of the Homestead Group is to help the people we support lead the lives they want and deserve

**2979 Champlin Foundations**
2000 Chapel View Boulevard
Suite 350
Cranston, RI 02920
401-944-9200
FAX: 401-944-9299
www.champlinfoundations.org

Giving in the Rhode Island area. Champlin does not give grants to individuals, only to RI tax-exempt organizations.

**2980 CranstonArc**
The Keystone Group
P.O.Box 20130
Cranston, RI 02920-942
401-941-1112
FAX: 401-383-8751
e-mail: CranstonArc.org
www.cranstonArc.org

*Thomas Kane, President & CEO*
Mission is to empower persons with differing ablilites to claim and enjoy their right to dignity and respect through their lives.

**2981 Down Syndrome Society of Rhode Island**
99 Bald Hill Rd
Cranston, RI 02920-2648
401-463-5751
FAX: 401-463-5337
TTY:800-745-5555
dssri.org

*Marilyn Blanche, board member*
The Down Syndrome Society of Rhode Island (DSSRI) is dedicated to promoting the rights, dignity and potential of all individuals with Down Syndrome through advocacy, education, public awareness, and support.

**2982 Frank Olean Center**
93 Airport Rd
Westerly, RI 02891-3420
401-315-0143
FAX: 401-315-0201
e-mail: info@oleancenter.org
oleancenter.org

*Kathy Lanni, President*
*John Turano, Vice President*
*Tony Vellucci, Executive Director*
A non-profit organization representing and providing services and supports to persons with developmental disabilities and their families throughout Southern Rhode Island and Southeastern Connecticut.

**2983 Horace A Kimball and S Ella Kimball Foundation**
23 Broad Street
Westerly, RI 02891-1879
401-348-1238
FAX: 401-364-3565
www.hkimballfoundation.org

*Thomas F Black III, President*
*Norman D. Baker, Jr., Secretary and Treasurer*
Makes grants almost exclusively to Rhode Island operatives (charities) or those benefitting Rhode Island residents and causes.

**2984 Kent County Arc**
3445 Post Rd
Warwick, RI 02886-7147
401-739-2700
FAX: 401-737-8907
e-mail: mmadden@kentcountyarc.org
www.kentcountyarc.org

*Mary Madden, CEO*
Providing individuals with disabilties meaningful opportunities throughout their communities.

**2985 Newport County Arc**
P.O.Box 4390
Middletown, RI 02842
401-846-4600
FAX: 401-849-4267

*Jack Maher, Executive Director*

**2986 Rhode Island Arc**
99 Bald Hill Rd
Cranston, RI 02920-2647
401-463-9191
FAX: 401-463-9244
e-mail: riarc@compuserve.com
riarc@compuserve.com

*Mary Lou Mc Caffray, Executive Director*

**2987 Rhode Island Foundation**
1 Union Sta
Providence, RI 02903-1758
401-274-4564
FAX: 401-331-8085
rifoundation.org

*Neil Steinberg, President & CEO*
*Lauren Paola, Executive Assistant*
*Jessica David, Vice President*
The Rhode Island Foundation works to build a better Rhode Island as a philanthropic resource, for people, communities, organizations, and programs.

## South Carolina

**2988 Arc of South Carolina**
3214 Leaphart Road
Suite C
West Columbia, SC 29169-6142
803-748-5020
FAX: 803-445-1026
e-mail: margie@arcsc.org
www.arcsc.org

*Melinda Moore, President*
*Kinsey Carlson, Vice President*
*Yolanda Gordon, Secretary*
The Arc of South Carolina advocates for and alongside people with cognitive, intellectual and developmental disabilities and their families.

**2989 Center for Disability Resources**
University of South Carolina
8301 Farrow Rd
Columbia, SC 29208-1
803-935-5231
FAX: 803-935-5059
e-mail: Joyce.Tensley@uscmed.sc.edu
www.usmc.med.edu/cdrhome

*Dr. David A. Rotholz, Director*
A University Affiliated Program which develops model programs designed to serve persons with disabilities and to train students in fields related to disabilities.

**2990 Colonial Life and Accident Insurance Company Contributions Program**
1200 Colonial Life Blvd W
Columbia, SC 29210-7670
803-798-7000
FAX: 803-731-2618

*Randall C Horn, CEO*
*Donna Northam, Plant Manager*

## Tennessee

**2991 Arc of Anderson County**
P.O.Box 4823
Oak Ridge, TN 37831-4823
865-481-0550
e-mail: arc@arcaid.org
www.arcaid.org

*Sally Browning, President*
*Dennis Eldred , Executive Director*
The Arc of Anderson County provides support and advocacy to people with cognitive, intellectual and developmental disabilities. The Arc provides support, information and training for families and caregivers of adults and children with these disabilities.

**2992 Arc of Davidson County**
111 N Wilson Blvd
Nashville, TN 37205-2411
615-248-4112
e-mail: arc@arcdc.org
arcdc.org

*Maggie Masimore, President*
*Kate Deitzer, Vice President*
*Thom Druffel, Treasurer*
Provides services to adults and children with intellectual and developmental disabilities through a contract with the Tennesee Departmant of Mental Retardation Services Medicaid Waiver Program.

**2993 Arc of Hamilton County**
4613 Brainerd Rd
Chattanooga, TN 37411-3826
423-624-6887
800-624-6887
FAX: 423-624-3974
e-mail: arcofhamilton@aol.com
www.geocities.com/localarc2001

*Shawn Ellis, Executive Director*
Provides assistance to individuals and families with mental retardation and related disabilities, in the form of advocacy, information, and support coordination

**2994 Arc of Tennessee**
Ste 100
151 Athens Way
Nashville, TN 37228-1367
615-248-5878
800-835-7077
FAX: 615-248-5879
e-mail: wrogers@thearctn.org
thearctn.org

*Walter Rogers, Executive Director*
Advocacy, information, referral and support for people with intellectual and developmental disabilities and their families.

**2995 Arc of Washington County**
110 East Mountcastle Drive
Johnson City, TN 37601-7557
423-928-9362
FAX: 423-928-7431
e-mail: kim@arcwc.org
www.arcwc.org

*Malessa Fleenor , Executive Director*
Is a non-profit organization that serves individuals with disabilities and their families. They have an independent support coordination service, as well as, early intervention, family support and respite services.

**2996 Arc of Williamson County**
Ste 151
129 W Fowlkes St
Franklin, TN 37064-3562
615-791-0042
www.thearcofwilliamsoncounty.org

*Sharon Bottorff, Executive Director*
The Arc is a family-based organization committed to securing for all people with intellectual, developmental, or other disabilities the opportunity to choose and realize their goals of where and how they live, learn, work, and play.

**2997 Arc-Diversified**
453 Gould Dr
Cookeville, TN 38506
931-432-5981
800-239-9029
FAX: 931-432-5987
www.arcdiversified.com

**2998 Benwood Foundation**
Ste 1600
736 Market St
Chattanooga, TN 37402-4812
423-267-4311
FAX: 423-267-9049
e-mail: callen@benwood.org
benwood.org

*Corinne A Allen, Executive Director*
Benwood Foundation seeks to stimulate creative and innovative efforts to build and strengthen the Chattanooga community.

**2999 Community Foundation of Greater Chattanooga**
1270 Market St
Chattanooga, TN 37402-2713
423-265-0586
FAX: 423-265-0587
e-mail: info2@cfgc.org
cfgc.org

*Peter Cooper, President*
*Rebecca Underwood, Vice President*
A non-profit organization which receives, holds, invests and distributes assets contributed by individuals and organizations for the benefit of Chattanooga, its citizens and its institutions.

**3000 Education and Auditory Research Foundation**
PO Box 330867
Nashville, TN 37203-7506
615-627-2724
800-545-4327
FAX: 615-627-2728
e-mail: info@earfoundation.org
www.earfoundation.org

*Michael Glasscock, President*
Provides the general public support services promoting the integration of the hearing and balance impaired into mainstream society; to provide practicing ear specialists continuing medical education courses and related programs specifically regarding rehabilitation and hearing preservation; to educate young people and adults about hearing preservation and early detection of hearing loss, enabling them to prevent at an early age hearing and balance disorders.

**3001 International Paper Company Foundation**
6400 Poplar Ave
Memphis, TN 38197
901-419-9000
FAX: 901-419-4439
internationalpaper.com

*John V Faraci, Chairman & CEO*
*Deano C. Orr, Executive Director; Grant Reviewer*
*Amanda E Morris, Community Relations*
The Foundation's primary focus is education-specifically environmental education, iliteracy programs for young children and minority career development opportunities for college bound youth.

**3002 Montgomery County Arc**
1825 K Street
NW, Suite 1200
Washington, DC 20006-2145
202-534-3700
800-433-5255
FAX: 202-534-3731
e-mail: info@thearc.org
www.thearc.org

*Mohan Mehra, President*
*Nancy Webster, Vice President*
Organization works to ensure that the estimated 7.2 million Americans with intellectual and developmental disabilities have the services and supports they need to grow, develop and live in communities across the nation.

## Texas

**3003 AFB Center on Vision Loss**
American Foundation for the Blind
2 Penn Plaza
Suite 1102
New York, NY 10121-4524
212-502-7600
FAX: 888-545-8331
e-mail: afbinfo@afb.net
afb.org

*Carl Augusto, President & CEO*
*Kelly Bleach, Chief Administrative Officer*
*Rick Bozeman, Chief Financial Officer*
*Paul Schroeder, Vice President, Programs & Policy*
National nonprofit organization that expands possibilities for people with vision loss.

**3004 Abell-Hangar Foundation**
P.O.Box 430
Midland, TX 79702
432-684-6655
FAX: 432-684-4474
abell-hanger.org

*David L Smith, Executive Director*
The Foundation makes grants to nonprofit organizations, which are involved in such undertakings for public welfare, including but not limited to, education, health services, human services, arts and cultural activities and community or social benefit.

**3005 Albert & Bessie Mae Kronkosky Charitable Foundation**
Ste 830
112 E Pecan St
San Antonio, TX 78205-1574
210-475-9000
888-309-9001
FAX: 210-354-2204
e-mail: kronfndn@kronkosky.org
kronkosky.org

*Palmer Moe, Managing Director*
Mission is to produce profound good that is tangible and measurable in Bandera, Bexar, Comal, and Kendall counties in Texas by implimenting the Kronkosky's charitable purposes.

**3006 Arc of Texas**
Ste 100
8001 Centre Park Dr
Austin, TX 78754-5118
512-454-6694
800-252-9729
FAX: 512-454-4956
thearcoftexas.org

*Mike Bright, Executive Director*
The Arc of Texas is the oldest and largest nonprofit, volunteer organization in the state committed to creating opportunities for people with intellectual and developmental disabilities to be included in their communities and to make the choices which affect their lives.

**3007 BA and Elinor Steinhagen Benevolent Trust**
Chase Bank of Texas
700 North St., Suite D
Beaumont, TX 77701-3928
409-832-6565
FAX: 409-832-7532
www.setxnonprofit.org

*Dean M Terrebonne, MBA, PHR, Executive Director*

**3008 Brown Foundation**
P.O.Box 130646
Houston, TX 77219
713-523-6867
FAX: 713-523-2917
e-mail: bfi@brownfoundation.org
brownfoundation.org

*Nancy Pittman, Executive Director*
The purpose of the Brown Foundation is to distribute funds for public charitable purposes, principally for support, encouragement and assistance to education, the arts and community service.

**3009 Burnett Foundation**
P.O. Box 633
Northfield, MN 55057-6881
817-877-3344
e-mail: tomburnettfamilyfoundation@msn.com
www.tomburnettfoundation.org

*V Neils Agather, Executive Director*

**3010 CH Foundation**
P.O.Box 94038
Lubbock, TX 79493-4038
806-792-0448
FAX: 806-792-7824
e-mail: ksanford@chfoundation.com
www.chfoundationlubbock.com

*Don Graf, Executive Director*
Mission of the CH foundation is to significantly improve human services and cultural and educational opportunities for the residents of the South Plain of Texas.

**3011 Cockrell Foundation**
Ste 3250
1000 Main St
Houston, TX 77002-6338
713-209-7500
e-mail: foundation@cockrell.com
www.cockrell.com

*Nancy Williams, VP*
*Ernest H. Cockrell, President*
Purpose is for giving for higher education at the University of Texas at Austin; support also for cultural programs, social services, youth services and health care. Limitations are giving in Houston, Texas and no grants are awarded to individuals.

**3012 Communities Foundation of Texas**
5500 Caruth Haven Ln
Dallas, TX 75225-8146
214-750-4222
FAX: 214-750-4210
e-mail: jsmith@cftexas.org
cftexas.org

*Brent Chrisopher, Manager*
Mission is to improve lives, we serve the community by investing wisely and making effective charitable grants.

**3013 Community Foundation of North Texas**
Ste 306
306 W 7th St
Fort Worth, TX 76102-4906
817-877-0702
FAX: 817-877-1215
cfntx.org

*Nancy E. Jones, , President*
*Rob Miller, , Director of Finance*
Community Foundation is a tax exempt organization that provides stewardship for many individual charitable funds. With its specialized services, Community Foundation of North Texas gives donors efficient charitable fund administration.

**3014 Cullen Foundation**
40th Fl
601 Jefferson St
Houston, TX 77002-7900
713-651-8837
FAX: 713-651-2374
cullenfdn.org

*Alan Stewart, Executive Director*
*Sue A Alexander, Grant administrator*
Grants are restricted to Texas-based organizations for programs in Texas, primarily in the Houston area.

**3015 Curtis & Doris K Hankamer Foundation**
Ste 530
9039 Katy Fwy
Houston, TX 77024-1656
713-461-8140

*Gregory A Herbst, Manager*

**3016 Dallas Foundation**
3963 Maple Avenue
Ste. 390
Dallas, TX 75219-4447
214-741-9898
FAX: 214-741-9848
e-mail: info@dallasfoundation.org
dallasfoundation.org

*Mary M Jalonick, President*
*Gary W. Garcia, Director*
Serves as a leader, catalyst and resource for philanthropy by providing donors with a flexible means of making gifts to charitable causes that enhance our community.

**3017 David D & Nona S Payne Foundation**
P.O.Box 174
Pampa, TX 79066
www.davidandnonapaynefoundation.com

*Vanessa G Buzzard, Director*
The David & Nona S Payne Foundation was established in August 1980. Mrs Payne established the foundation and did much of her charitable giving in honor of her late husband.

**3018 El Paso Natural Gas Foundation**
P.O.Box 2511
Houston, TX 77252-2511
713-420-2600
FAX: 713-420-5312
e-mail: foundation@elpaso.com
elpaso.com

*Douglas Foshee, CEO*
Focuses on the areas in locations where we have significant facilities or concentrated employees. Primary area of focus is Civic and Community, Education and Health and Human Services. Secondary area of focus is Arts and Culture and Environment.

**3019 Epilepsy Foundation of Southeast Texas**
8301 Professional Place
Landover, MD 20785-7608
866-330-2718
800-332-1000
FAX: 877-687-4878
e-mail: ContactUs@efa.org
www.epilepsyfoundation.org

*Donna Stahlhut, Executive Director*
The Epilepsy Foundation of Southeast Texas is a non-profit organization to improve the lives of almost 100,000 adultsand children with epilepsy in the counties of north and southeast Texas.

**3020 Epilepsy Foundation: Central and South Texas**
Ste 602
10615 Perrin Beitel Rd
San Antonio, TX 78217- 3142 210-653-5353
888-606-5353
FAX: 210-653-5355
e-mail: sindi@efcst.org
www.efcst.org

*Anna Amos, President*
*Todd Drexler, Vice President*
The Epilepsy Foundation of Central & South Texas is a voluntary health organization. We value all people with epilepsy. We commit our resources to empowering their independence and inspiring productive lives.

**3021 Harris and Eliza Kempner Fund**
P.O. Box 119
2201 Market St
Galveston, TX 77553-1529 409-765-6671
FAX: 409-765-9098
e-mail: information@kemperfund.org
kempnercapital.com

*Delynn Greene, Vice President*
Mission is to further the vision and heritage of the Kemper Family's commitment to philanthropy and sense of responsibility to society.

**3022 Hillcrest Foundation**
Bank of America
P.O.Box 830241
Dallas, TX 75283 214-209-1965

*Daniel Kelly, VP*

**3023 Hoblitzelle Foundation**
Suite 200
5556 Caruth Haven Lane
Dallas, TX 75225-8020 214-373-0462
e-mail: pharris@hoblitzelle.org
www.hoblitzelle.org

*Paul Harris, President*
*WILLIAM T SOLOMON, CHAIRMAN*
Grants made by the directors are usually focused on specific, non-recurring needs of the educational, social service, medical, cultural, and civic organizations in Texas, particularly in the Dallas area.

**3024 Houston Endowment**
Ste 6400
600 Travis St
Houston, TX 77002-3003 713-238-8100
FAX: 713-238-8101
e-mail: info@houstonendowment.org
houstonendowment.org

*Ann B Stern , President*
*Sheryl L Johns , Executive Vice President*
A private philanthropic foundation that improves life for people of the greater Houston area through its contributions to charitable organizations and educational institutions.

**3025 John G & Marie Stella Kennedy Memorial Foundation**
555 N Carancahua
Suite 1700, Tower II
Corpus Christi, TX 78401 361-887-6565
FAX: 361-887-6582
www.kenedy.org

*Judge J. A. Garcia, Jr. , President*
*Ricardo Hinojosa, Vice-President*
*Barbara Little, Secretary*
To advance and nurture activities that contribute to the foundation's core, Catholic values.

**3026 John S Dunn Research Foundation**
Ste 702
3355 W Alabama St
Houston, TX 77098-1722 713-626-0368
FAX: 713-626-3866
e-mail: jsdrf@swbell.net
johnsdunnfoundation.org

*J. Dickson Rogers, President*
*John S Dunn, Jr, Vice President*

**3027 Lola Wright Foundation**
P.O.Box 1138
Georgetown, TX 78627-1138 512-869-2574

*Sandra O Donnell, Manager*

**3028 Meadows Foundation**
3003 Swiss Ave
Dallas, TX 75204-6049 214-826-9431
800-826-9431
FAX: 21- 82- 704
e-mail: grants@mfi.org
www.mfi.org

*Linda P Evans, CEO*
*Gregory C Dowell, Vice President*
The Meadows Foundation exists to assist people and institutions of Texas improve the quality and circumstances of life for themselves and future generations.

**3029 Moody Foundation**
Ste 704
2302 Post Office St
Galveston, TX 77550-1994 e-mail: colleent@moodyf.org
moodyf.org

*Frances Moody-Dahlderg, Executive Director*
Created for the perpetual benefit of present and future generations.

**3030 Pearle Vision Foundation**
2534 Royal Ln
Dallas, TX 75229-3884 214-821-7770
www.pearlevision.com

*Leo Priolo Jr, Owner*
Organization dedicated to sight preservation through vision research and education.

**3031 San Antonio Area Foundation**
Ste 230
110 Broadway St
San Antonio, TX 78205-1974 210-225-2243
FAX: 210-225-1980
e-mail: info@saafdn.org
saafdn.org

*Dennis E. Noll, President*
*Linda Stordy, Executive Assistant*
The San Antonio Area Foundation aspires to significantly enhance the quality of life in our community by providing outstanding service to donors, producting significant asset growth, strengthning community collaboration and managing an exemplary grants program.

**3032 Shell Oil Company Foundation**
P.O.Box 2463
Houston, TX 77252-2463 281-544-7171
FAX: 713-241-3329
e-mail: info@shellfoundation.org
www.shellfoundation.org

*Robert Hummel, Plant Manager*

A not-for-profit foundation funded by donations from Shell Oil Company and other participating Shell companies and subsidiaries.

**3033 South Texas Charitable Foundation**
P.O.Box 2459
Victoria, TX 77902
512-573-4383

*Rayford L Keller, Secretary*

**3034 Sterling-Turner Foundation**
Ste 1543
815 Walker St
Houston, TX 77002-5724
713-237-1117
FAX: 713-223-4638
e-mail: jeannie.arnold@stfdn.org
www.sterlingturnerfoundation.org

Sterling Turner Foundation is a private trust which can assist any Section 501 (c) (3) organization in the state of Texas. The Foundation is not permitted to assist any individuals

**3035 TLL Temple Foundation**
109 Temple Blvd
Lufkin, TX 75901-7321
936-639-5197
e-mail: wcorley@tlltf.com

*Wayne Corley, Executive Director*

**3036 William Stamps Farish Fund**
Ste 1250
1100 Louisiana St
Houston, TX 77002-5232
713-757-7313

*Terry Ward, Manager*

## Utah

**3037 Arc of Utah**
P.O.Box 2786
Salt Lake City, UT 84110-2786
801-364-5060
800-371-3060
FAX: 801-364-6030
e-mail: gacosta@dunndunn.com
arcutah.org

*Kathy Scott, Executive Director*

The Arc of Utah advocates for and with cognitive, intellectual and developmental disabilities and their families through awareness, outreach, education, support and public policy.

**3038 Marriner S Eccles Foundation**
79 S Main St
Salt Lake City, UT 84111-1929
801-532-0934

*Shannon K Toronto*

**3039 Questar Corporation Contributions Program**
P.O.Box 45433
333 South State Street
Salt Lake City, UT 84111
801-324-5000
questarcorp.com

*Ronald W Jibson, CEO*
*R. Allan Bradley, Executive vice president,*

Focuses on promoting a healthy environment by investing in and fulfilling its corporate responsibility to support the well-being of communitites where Questar and its subsidiaries conduct business.

## Vermont

**3040 Vermont Community Foundation**
P.O.Box 30
Middlebury, VT 05753
802-388-3355
FAX: 802-388-3398
e-mail: info@vermontcf.org
www.vermontcf.org

*Stuart Comstock-Gay, President*
*Sharon D Greene, Executive Coordinator*

Helps build and manage charitable funds created by individuals, families, groups, organizations, and institutions to improve the quality of life in Vermont.

## Virginia

**3041 Arc of Virginia**
Ste 107
2025 E Main St
Richmond, VA 23223-7072
804-649-8481
FAX: 804-649-3585
e-mail: thearc@arcofva.org
www.arcofva.org

*Jamie Trosclair, Executive Director*

The Arc of Virginia advocactes for individuals with mental retardation and developmental disabilities and their families, so they may all lead productive and fulfilling lives.

**3042 Camp Foundation**
P.O.Box 813
Franklin, VA 23851
757-562-3439

*Bobby B Worrell, CEO*

**3043 Community Foundation of Richmond & Central Virginia**
Ste 110
7501 Boulder View Dr
Richmond, VA 23225-4047
804-330-7400
FAX: 804-330-5992
e-mail: info@tcfrichmond.org
tcfrichmond.org

*Darcy Oman, President*
*Bobby Thalhimer, Senior Vice President*
*Teri Lovelace, Esq., Vice President*

The Community Foundation provides effective stewardship of philanthropic assets entrusted to its care by donors who wish to enhance the quality of community life.

**3044 John Randolph Foundation**
P.O.Box 1606
Hopewell, VA 23860-1161
804-458-2239
FAX: 804-458-3754
e-mail: lsharpe@johnrandolphfoundation.org
www.johnrandolphfoundation.org

*Lisa Sharpe, Executive Director*
*M. Stephen Cates, Director*

The John Randolph Foundation is a community-based Foundation working to improve the health and quality of life for residents of Hopewell and surrounding areas through Grants and Scholarships.

**3045 Norfolk Foundation**
Suite 4500
101 W. Main Street,
Norfolk, VA 23510-2103
757-622-7951
FAX: 757-622-1751
e-mail: mbrunson@hamptonroadscf.org
www.hamptonroadscf.org

*Deborah M DiCroce , President*
*Tim McCarthy, Chief Financial Officer*
The mission of the Norfolk Foundation is to inspire philanthropy and transform the quality of life in southeastern Virginia.

**3046 Robey W Estes Family Foundation**
Robey W Estes Jr
3901 West Broad Street
Richmond, VA 23230-5612
866-378-3748
estes-express.com

*Robey W Estes Jr, President*

**3047 Virginia Beach Foundation**
Suite 4500
101 W. Main Street,
Virginia Beach, VA 23454
757-422-5249
FAX: 757-422-1849
e-mail: mbrunson@hamptonroadscf.org
www.hamptonroadscf.org

*Deborah M DiCroce , President*
*Tim McCarthy, Chief Financial Officer*
Mission is to stimulate the establishment of endowments to serve the people of Virgina Beach now and in the future. Respond to changing, emerging, community needs. Provide a vehicle and a service for donors with varied interests. Serve as a resource, broker, catalyst and leader in the community.

## Washington

**3048 Arc of Washington State**
2638 State Ave NE
Olympia, WA 98506-4880
360-357-5596
FAX: 360-357-3279
e-mail: info@arcwa.org
arcwa.org

*Sue Elliott, Executive Director*
*Cindy O'Neill,, President*
Mission is to advocacte for the rights and full participation of all people with developmental disabilities.

**3049 Ben B Cheney Foundation**
Ste A
3110 Ruston Way
Tacoma, WA 98402-5308
253-572-2442
e-mail: Info@benbcheneyfoundation.org
benbcheneyfoundation.org

*Bradbury Cheney, President*
*Piper Cheney, Vice President*
The Foundation makes grants in communities where the Cheney Lumber Company was active. The Foundation's goal is to improve the quality of life in those communities by making grants to a wide range of activities.

**3050 Community Foundation of North Central Washington**
9 South Wenatchee Ave
Wenatchee, WA 98801-3332
509-663-7716
FAX: 888-317-8314
e-mail: beth@cfncw.org
www.cfncw.org

*Beth Stipe, Executive Director*
Assists donors by helping identify their specific charitable and goals and provide grants and scholarships that help groups and people address critical issues in North Central Washington

**3051 Glaser Progress Foundation**
Suite 1080
1601 Second Avenue
Seattle, WA 98101-9223
206-728-1050
FAX: 206-728-1123
e-mail: martin@glaserfoundation.org
www.glaserfoundation.org

*Martin Collier, Executive Director*
The Glaser Prograss Foundation focuses on four program areas: measuring progress, animal advocacy, independent media and global HIV/AIDS.

**3052 Greater Tacoma Community Foundation**
Ste 1220
950 Pacific Ave
Tacoma, WA 98402-4423
253-383-5622
FAX: 253-272-8099
e-mail: info@gtcf.org
tacomafoundation.org

*Rose Lincoln, President*
Mission is fostering generosity by connecting people who care with causes that matter, forever enriching our community.

**3053 Inland Northwest Community Foundation**
Ste 302
618 W Riverside Ave
Spokane, WA 99201-5102
509-624-2606
888-267-5606
FAX: 509-624-2608
e-mail: admin@inwcf.org
www.inwcf.org

*Mark Hurtubise, President*
Serving 20 counties throughout Eastern Washington and Northern Idaho, mission is to foster vibrant and sustainable communities in the Inland Northwest.

**3054 Medina Foundation**
Ste 1300
801 2nd Ave
Seattle, WA 98104-1517
206-652-8791
FAX: 206-264-3007
e-mail: info@medinafoundation.org
www.medinafoundation.org

*Adrienne Quinn, Executive Director*
A family foundation that works to foster positive change in the Greater Puget Sound area. The Foundation strives to improve the human condition by supporting organizations that provide critical services to those in need.

**3055 Norcliffe Foundation**
Ste 1006
999 3rd Ave
Seattle, WA 98104-4001
206-682-4820
FAX: 206-682-4821
e-mail: arline@thenorcliffefoundation.com
www.thenorcliffefoundation.com

*Arline Hefferline, Manager*
Geographic area of funding limited to the Puget Sound Region in and around Seattle, Washington.

**3056 Stewardship Foundation**
1145 Broadway
Suite 1500
Tacoma, WA 98402-1278
253-620-1340
FAX: 253-572-2721
e-mail: info@stewardshipfdn.org
www.stewardshipfdn.org

*Cary Paine, Executive Director*
Christian, evangelical organizations - national or international impact.

**3057 Weyerhaeuser Company Foundation**
33663 Weyerhaeuser Way South
Federal Way, WA 98003
253-924-2345
800-525-5440
www.weyerhaeuser.com

*Daniel S Fulton, President & CEO*
*Patricia M Bedient, EVP & CFO*
*Sandy D McDade, SVP & General Counsel*
*John A Hooper, SVP, Human Resources*
Although the foundation does fund programs for disabled persons from time to time, it is not a specific priority for the foundation. Since it was formed in 1948, the foundation has given more than $81.1 million to nonprofit organizations and is one of the oldest funds for corporate philanthropy in the country. Nearly all of its contributions have been made within the communities where Weyerhaeuser employees live and work and awards approximately 600 grants annually.

## West Virginia

**3058 Bernard McDonough Foundation**
311 4th St
Parkersburg, WV 26101-5315
304-424-6280
FAX: 304-424-6281
www.mcdonoughfoundation.org

*Robert W Stephens, Ed.D., President*
*Mary Riccobene, Vice President*
Directors and officers continue the legacy of the McDonoughs by providing grants that create a healthier, more educated and culturally appreciative citizenry.

**3059 The Arc Of West Virginia**
912 Market Street
Parkersburg, WV 26101-4737
304-422-3151
e-mail: christina.smith@arcwd.org
www.thearcwv.org

chapter #54

## Wisconsin

**3060 Arc of Dunn County**
2602 Hils Court
Menomonie, WI 54751-4160
715-235-7373
FAX: 715-233-3565
e-mail: rebecca@arcofdunncounty.org
www.arcofdunncounty.org

*Rebecca Cooper, Executive Director*
*Kathy Lausted, Guardianship Director*
Advocating for the rights of citizens with disabilities.

**3061 Arc of Eau Claire**
4800 Golf Road
Suite 450
Eau Claire, WI 54701-6130
715-833-1735
FAX: 715-833-1215
e-mail: frcec@frcec.org
www.frcec.org

*Dave Swan , President*
*Jeff Sauter , Vice President*
Mission is to provide programs and services that build on family strengths through prevention, education, support and networking in collaboration with other resources in the community.

**3062 Arc of Fox Cities**
375 Winnebago Ave
Menasha, WI 54952-3444
920-735-0943
FAX: 920-725-1531
e-mail: info@arcfoxcities.com
arcfoxcities.com

*Jeff Lang, President*
Mission statement is to utilize advocacy, respect and concern to empower all people with disabilities to have the opportunity to choose and realize their goal of a full life and a secure future.

**3063 Arc of Racine County**
Ste 319
1220 Mound Ave
Racine, WI 53404-3350
262-634-6303
e-mail: sengle@thearcofracine.org
www.thearcofracine.org

*Sandy Engel, Executive Director*
The Arc of Racine's mission is to advocate for and provide information and services to improve lives.

**3064 Arc of Wisconsin Disability Association**
Ste 209
2800 Royal Ave
Monona, WI 53713-1518
608-222-8907
877-272-8400
FAX: 608-222-8908
e-mail: arcw@att.net
arc-wisconsin.org

*Jim Hoegemier, Executive Director*
The Arc-Wisconsin strives to be a major force in advocating and promoting self-determined quality of life opportunities for poeple with developmental and related disabilities and their families.

**3065 Arc-Dane County**
6602 Grand Teton Plz
Madison, WI 53719-1091
608-833-1199
FAX: 608-833-1307
e-mail: arcdane@chorus.net
arcdanecounty.org

*Paul Yochum, Executive Director*
The Arc-Dane County is a non-profit organization whose primary objective is to support children and adults with developmental disabilities and their families through advocacy to assure these individuals are offered the same opportunities and have the rights due all people. The Arc-Dane County provides numerous services through education, overall support, and legislation that assists those individuals with developmental disabilities be it within their homes, communities, or at work.

**3066 Faye McBeath Foundation**
101 W. Pleasant Street #210
Milwaukee, WI 53212-3157
414-272-2626
FAX: 414-272-6235
e-mail: info@fayemcbeath.org
www.fayemcbeath.org

*Scott Gelzer, Executive Director*
A private independent foundation providing grants to tax exempt nonprofit organizations principally the metropolitan Milwaukee area.

**3067 Helen Bader Foundation**
233 N Water St
Milwaukee, WI 53202-5761
414-224-6464
FAX: 414-224-1441
e-mail: info@hbf.org
hbf.org

*Daniel Bader, President*
Strives to be a philanthropic leader in improving the quality of life of the diverse communities in which it works. The

Foundation makes grants, convenes partners, and shares knowledge to affect emerging issues in key areas.

**3068 Johnson Controls Foundation**
5757 N Green Bay Ave
P.O. Box 591
Milwaukee, WI 53201- 4408
414-524-1200
800-333-2222
FAX: 414-524-2077
johnsoncontrols.com

*Stephen A Roell, CEO*
*Jeffrey G Augustin, Vice President*
Organized and directed to be operated for charitable purposes which include the distribution and application of financial support to soundly managed and operated organizations or causes which are fundamentally philanthropic.

**3069 Lynde and Harry Bradley Foundation**
1241 N Franklin Pl
Milwaukee, WI 53202-2901
414-291-9915
FAX: 414-291-9991
bradleyfoundation.org

*Michael Grebbe, President*
The Foundation's programs support limited, competent government; a dynamic marketplace for economic, intellectual and cultural activity; a vigorus defense at home and abroad, of American ideas and institutions; and scholarly studies and academic achievement.

**3070 Milwaukee Foundation**
Ste 210
101 W Pleasant St
Milwaukee, WI 53212-3963
414-272-5805
FAX: 414-272-6235
e-mail: info@greatermilwaukeefoundation.org
www.greatermilwaukeefoundation.org

*Ellen M Gilligan, President*
Guided by three tenets- helping donors create personal legacies of giving that last beyond their lifetimes, investing donor funds for maximum return with minimal risk, and playing a leadership role tackling the communities most challenging needs.

**3071 Northwestern Mutual Life Foundation**
720 E Wisconsin Ave
Milwaukee, WI 53202-4703
414-271-1444
www.northwesternmutual.com

*John E Schlifske , CEO*
*Gary A Poliner, President & Chief Risk Officer*

**3072 Patrick and Anna M Cudahy Fund**
1609 Sherman Ave, #207
Evanston, Il 60201
847-866-0760
FAX: 847-475-0679
cudahyfund.org

*Janet S Cudahy MD, President*
A general purpose foundation which primarily supports organizations in Wisconsin and the metropolitan Chicago area. Interests are social service, youth, and education with some giving for the arts, and other areas.

**3073 SB Waterman & E Blade Charitable Foundation**
Marshall & Ilsley Trust Company
111 E. Kilbourn Ave.,
Milwaukee, WI 53202-2980
414-287-8700
FAX: 414-765-8200
www.mitrust.com

*Thomas C Boettcher, Director*
Giving primarily to health associations. Geographical focus is Wisconsin.

## Wyoming

**3074 Arc of Natrona County**
1825 K Street, NW
Suite 1200
Washington, DC 20006
202-534-3700
800-433-5255
FAX: 202-534-3731
e-mail: info@thearc.org
www.thearc.org

*Mohan Mehra, President*
Organization works to ensure that the estimated 7.2 million Americans with intellectual and developmental disabilities have the services and supports they need to grow, develop and live in communities across the nation.

## Funding Directories

**3075 Chronicle Guide to Grants**
Ste 700
1255 23rd St NW
Washington, DC 20037-1146
202-466-1200
800-287-6072
FAX: 202-452-1033
e-mail: help@philanthropy.com
heideninc.com

*Phil Semas, Manager*
A computerized research tool, on floppy disks or a CD-ROM, for immediate use on any IBM compatible personal computer. Offers electronic listings of 10,000 grants from hundreds of foundations, with a subscription that offers 1,000 plus new listings every two months. Each listing offers grant information as well as names, addresses and phone numbers of the grant-making organizations. *$295.00*

**3076 College Student's Guide to Merit and Other No-Need Funding**
Reference Service Press
Ste 4
5000 Windplay Dr
El Dorado Hills, CA 95762-9319
916-939-9620
FAX: 916-939-9626
e-mail: info@rspfunding.com
www.rspfunding.com

*Sandy Hirsh, Editor*
More than 1,200 funding opportunities for currently-enrolled or returning college students are described in this directory. *$32.50*
*450 pages*
*ISBN 1-588410-41-2*

**3077 Community Health Funding Report**
CD Publications
8204 Fenton St
Silver Spring, MD 20910-4502
301-588-6380
800-666-6380
FAX: 301-588-6385
e-mail: subscriptions@cdpublications.com
www.cdpublications.com

*Michael Gerecht, President*
The once twice-monthly report is now web-based to allow for breaking news updates and up the the minute information about funding, including: public and private grant announcements; reports on successful health programs nationwide; interviews with grant officials; plus national news on health policy topics affecting various organizations. *$439.00*
*Web-based*

**3078 Directory of Financial Aids for Women**
Reference Service Press
Ste 4
5000 Windplay Dr
El Dorado Hills, CA 95762-9319
916-939-9620
FAX: 916-939-9626
e-mail: info@rspfunding.com
www.rspfunding.com

*Sandy Hirsh, Editor*
Funding programs listed support study, research, travel, training, career development, or innovative effort at any level; descriptions of more than 1,700 funding programs - representing billions of dollars in financial aid set aside for women; also an annotated bibliography of 60 key directories that identify even more financial aid opportunities and a set of indexes that let you search the directory by title, sponser, researching, tenability, subject, and deadline. *$45.00*
*578 pages Biennial*
*ISBN 1-588410-00-5*

**3079 Disability Funding News**
8204 Fenton St
Silver Spring, MD 20910-4502
301-588-6380
800-666-6380
FAX: 301-588-6385
e-mail: subscriptions@cdpublications.com
www.cdpublications.com

*Michael Gerecht, President*

**3080 FC Search**
Foundation Center
79 5th Ave
New York, NY 10003-3034
212-620-4230
800-424-9836
FAX: 212-807-3677
e-mail: order@foundationcenter.org
foundationcenter.org

*Bradford K Smith, President*
Provides access to the Foundation Center's comprehensive database of funders in a convenient CD-ROM format. *$1845.00*

**3081 Federal Grants & Contracts Weekly**
LRP Publications
360 Hiatt Drive
Palm Beach Gardens, FL 33418-1718
800-341-7874
FAX: 561-622-2423
e-mail: custserve@lrp.com
www.lrp.com

*Kelly Sullivan, Editor*
The latest funding announcements of federal grants for project opportunities in research, training and services. Provides profiles of key programs, tips on seeking grants, updates on legislation and regulations, budget developments and early alerts to upcoming funding opportunities. *$340.00*
*Weekly*

**3082 Financial Aid for Asian Americans**
Reference Service Press
5000 Windplay Dr
Suite 4
El Dorado Hills, CA 95762-9319
916-939-9620
FAX: 916-939-9626
e-mail: info@rspfunding.com
www.rspfunding.com

*Sandy Hirsh, Editor*
This is the source to use if you are looking for financial aid for Asian Americans; nearly 1,000 funding opportunities are described. *$35.00*
*336 pages*
*ISBN 1-588410-02-1*

**3083 Financial Aid for Hispanic Americans**
Reference Service Press
5000 Windplay Dr
Suite 4
El Dorado Hills, CA 95762-9319
916-939-9620
FAX: 916-939-9626
e-mail: info@rspfunding.com
www.rspfunding.com

*Sandy Hirsh, Editor*
Nearly 1,300 funding programs open to Americans of Mexican, Puerto Rican, Central American, or other Latin American heritage are described here. *$37.50*
*472 pages*
*ISBN 1-588410-03-X*

**3084 Financial Aid for Native Americans**
Reference Service Press
5000 Windplay Dr
Suite 4
El Dorado Hills, CA 95762-9319
916-939-9620
FAX: 916-939-9626
e-mail: info@rspfunding.com
www.rspfunding.com

*Sandy Hirsh, Editor*
Detailed information is provided on 1,500 funding opportunities open to American Indians, Native Alaskans, and Native Pacific Islanders. *$37.50*
*562 pages*
*ISBN 1-588410-04-8*

**3085 Financial Aid for Research and Creative Activities Abroad**
Reference Service Press
5000 Windplay Dr
Suite 4
El Dorado Hills, CA 95762-9319
916-939-9620
FAX: 916-939-9626
e-mail: info@rspfunding.com
www.rspfunding.com

*Sandy Hirsh, Editor*
Described here are 1,200 funding programs (scholarships, fellowships, grants, etc.) available to support research, professional, or creative activities abroad. *$45.00*
*378 pages*
*ISBN 1-588410-82-5*

**3086 Financial Aid for Veterans, Military Personnel and their Dependents**
Reference Service Press
5000 Windplay Dr
Suite 4
El Dorado Hills, CA 95762-9319
916-939-9620
FAX: 916-939-9626
e-mail: info@rspfunding.com
www.rspfunding.com

*Sandy Hirsh, Editor*
According to Reference Book Review, this directory (with its 1,100 entries) is the most comprehensive guide available on the subject. *$40.00*
*392 pages*
*ISBN 1-588410-43-9*

**3087 Financial Aid for the Disabled and Their Families**
Reference Service Press
5000 Windplay Dr
Suite 4
El Dorado Hills, CA 95762-9319
916-939-9620
FAX: 916-939-9626
e-mail: info@rspfunding.com
www.rspfunding.com

*Sandy Hirsh, Editor*
This directory, which Children's Bookwatch calls invaluable describes more than 1,100 financial aid opportunities available to

support persons with disabilities and members of their families. Updated every 2 years. *$37.50*
*508 pages Every other yr.*
*ISBN 1-588410-01-3*

**3088 Foundation & Corporate Grants Alert**
LRP Publications
360 Hiatt Drive
Palm Beach Gardens, FL 33418-1718
800-341-7874
FAX: 561-622-2423
e-mail: custserve@lrp.com
www.lrp.com

*Kelly Sullivan, Editor*
A complete guide to foundation and corporate grant opportunities for nonprofit organizations. Tracks developments and trends in funding and provides notification of changes in foundations' funding priorities. *$245.00*
*Monthly*
*ISSN 1062-46 6*

**3089 Foundation 1000**
Foundation Center
79 5th Ave
New York, NY 10003-3034
212-620-4230
800-424-9836
FAX: 212-807-3677
e-mail: order@foundationcenter.org
www.foundationcenter.org

*Jeffrey Fulkenstein, Editor*
Offers comprehensive information on the 1000 largest foundations in the US. *$195.00*

**3090 Foundation Directories**
Foundation Center
79 5th Ave
New York, NY 10003-3034
212-620-4230
800-424-9836
FAX: 212-807-3677
e-mail: order@foundationcenter.org
foundationcenter.org

*Bradford K Smith, President*
Lists key facts on the top 20,000 US foundations. *$ 125.00*

*ISBN 0-87954 -36-1*

**3091 Foundation Grants to Individuals**
Foundation Center
79 5th Ave
New York, NY 10003-3034
212-620-4230
800-424-9836
FAX: 212-807-3677
e-mail: order@foundationcenter.org
foundationcenter.org

*Bradford K Smith, President*
The only publication that provides extensive coverage of foundation funding prospects for individual grantseekers. *$40.00*
*Biennially*

**3092 From the State Capitals: Public Health**
Wakeman/Walworth
P.O.Box 7376
Alexandria, VA 22307-376
703-768-9600
FAX: 703-768-9690
e-mail: newsletters@statecapitals.com
www.statecapitals.com

*Mark Willen, Editor*
Digest of state and municipal health care financing and cost containment measures, includes medical legislation, disease control, etc. *$245.00*
*6 pages*

**3093 Grant Guides**
Foundation Center
79 5th Ave
New York, NY 10003-3034
212-620-4230
800-424-9836
FAX: 212-807-3677
e-mail: order@foundationcenter.org
foundationcenter.org

*Bradford K Smith, President*
Provides descriptions of actual foundation grants awarded in various subject fields. *$35.00*

*ISBN 0-87954 -90-6*

**3094 Guide to Funding for International and Foreign Programs**
79 5th Ave
New York, NY 10003-3034
212-620-4230
800-424-9836
FAX: 212-807-3677
e-mail: order@foundationcenter.org
foundationcenter.org

*Bradford K Smith, President*
Grantmakers featured in this guide provide funding for international relief, disaster assistance, human rights, civil liberties, community development, conferences, and education. *$190.00*

**3095 Guide to US Foundations their Trustees, Officers and Donors**
Foundation Center
79 5th Ave
New York, NY 10003-3034
212-620-4230
800-424-9836
FAX: 212-807-3677
e-mail: order@foundationcenter.org
foundationcenter.org

*Bradford K Smith, President*
Provides crucial facts on grantmaking. Each entry includes contact information, current assets, annual contributions, officers, donors and more. *$135.00*

**3096 High School Senior's Guide to Merit and Other No-Need Funding**
Reference Service Press
Ste 4
5000 Windplay Dr
El Dorado Hills, CA 95762-9319
916-939-9620
FAX: 916-939-9626
e-mail: info@rspfunding.com
www.rspfunding.com

*Sandy Hirsh, Editor*
Here's your guide to 1,100 funding programs that never look at income level when making awards to college bound high school seniors. *$29.95*
*400 pages*
*ISBN 1-588410-44-X*

**3097 How to Pay for Your Degree in Business & Related Fields**
Reference Service Press
Ste 4
5000 Windplay Dr
El Dorado Hills, CA 95762-9319
916-939-9620
FAX: 916-939-9626
e-mail: info@rspfunding.com
www.rspfunding.com

*Sandy Hirsh, Editor*
If you need funding for an undergraduate or graduate degree in business or related fields, this is the directory to use (500+ funding programs described). *$30.00*
*290 pages*
*ISBN 1-588411-45-1*

**3098 How to Pay for Your Degree in Education& Related Fields**
Reference Service Press
Ste 4
5000 Windplay Dr
El Dorado Hills, CA 95762-9319
916-939-9620
FAX: 916-939-9626
e-mail: info@rspfunding.com
www.rspfunding.com

*Sandy Hirsh, Editor*
Here's hundreds of funding opportunities available to support undergraduate and graduate students preparing for a career in education, guidance etc. *$30.00*
*250 pages*
*ISBN 1-588411-46-x*

**3099 National Directory of Corporate Giving**
Foundation Center
79 5th Ave
New York, NY 10003-3034
212-620-4230
800-424-9836
FAX: 212-807-3677
e-mail: order@foundationcenter.org
foundationcenter.org

*Bradford K Smith, President*
Offers over 2,000 corporate funders, current giving reviews and profiles of sponsoring companies. *$195.00*

**3100 Older Americans Report**
Business Publishers
2222 Sedwick Drive,
Durham, NC 27713-1995
240-514-0600
800-223-8720
FAX: 800-508-2592
e-mail: custserv@bpinews.com
www.bpinews.com

*Leonard Eiser, Publisher*
Follows all programs and funding sources in education, housing, job training, therapy, Social Security Supplemental Security Income, Medicare, Medicaid and more of importance to persons with disabilities. Also covers the latest on the Americans with Disabilities Act. Publishes a newsletter. *$327.00*

**3101 Student Guide**
US Department of Education
400 Maryland Ave SW
Washington, DC 20202
202-401-2000
800-872-5327
FAX: 202-401-0689
TTY: 800-437-0833
e-mail: customerservice@inet.ed.gov
ed.gov

*Jim Fruchterman, President*
*Andrew Friedman, CEO*
Describes the major student aid programs the US Department of Education administers and gives detailed information about program procedures.
*74 pages*

# Government Agencies

## Federal

**3102 Administration on Aging**
One Massachusetts Ave NW
Washington, DC 20001
202-401-4634
FAX: 202-357-3555
e-mail: aoainfo@aoa.hhs.gov
aoa.gov

*Kathy Greenlee, Asst Secretary*
Administers the Older Americans Act of 1965 to assist states and local communities to develop programs for older persons.

**3103 Administration on Children, Youth and Families**
370 L Enfant Promenade SW
Washington, DC 20447
202-401-4634
800-422-4453
TTY:800-787-3224
www.acf.hhs.gov

*George Sheldon, Acting Assistant Secretary*
Responsible for federal programs that promote the economic and social well-being of families, children, individuals and communities.

**3104 Administration on Developmental Disabilities**
U S Department of Health and Human Services
370 L Enfant Promenade SW
Washington, DC 20447
202-401-4634
800-422-4453
TTY:800-787-3224
www.acf.hhs.gov/programs/add

*George Sheldon, Acting Assistant Secretary*
Ensures that individuals with developmental disabilities and their families participate in the design of and have access to culturally competent services, supports, and other assistance and opportunities that promote independence, productivity, and integration and inclusion into the community.

**3105 Americans with Disabilities Act Informationn**
US Department of Justice
950 Pennsylvania Ave NW
Washington, DC 20530
800-514-0301
FAX: 202-307-1197
TTY:800-514-0383
www.ada.gov

*Gregory B. Friel , Chief*
The ADA assures that Americans with disabilities have the same opportunities as all Americans. To this end, the Justice Department produces publications and conducts programs to increase compliance of the ADA nationwide.

**3106 Civil Rights Division/Disability Rights Section**
US Department Of Justice
950 Pennsylvania Ave NW
Washington, DC 20530
202-282-8000
800-514-0301
FAX: 202-307-1197
TTY: 800-514-0383
www.ada.gov

*Gregory B. Friel , Chief*
The US Department of Justice answers questions about the American Disabilities Act (ADA) and provides free publications by mail and fax through its ADA Information Line.

**3107 Committee for Purchase from People Who Are Blind or Severely Disabled**
1421 Jefferson Davis Hwy
Jefferson Plaza 2, Ste 10800
Arlington, VA 22202-3259
703-603-7740
800-999-5963
FAX: 703-603-0655
e-mail: info@abilityone.gov
www.abilityone.gov

*Tina Ballard, Executive Director*
*J Anthony Poleo, Chairperson*
A federal agency that administers the Javits-Wagner-O'Day Program, directing federal agencies to purchase products and services from nonprofit agencies that employ people who are blind or have other severe disabilities. Provides a wide range of vocational options to individuals with severe disabilities.

**3108 Equal Opportunity Employment Commission**
131 M St NE
Washington, DC 20507
202-663-4599
800-669-4000
e-mail: info@eeoc.gov
www.eeoc.gov

*Jacgueline Berrien, Chair*
*Constance S Baker, Commissioner*
This agency is responsible for drafting and implementing the regulations of Title I of the ADA.

**3109 Federal Communications Commission**
445 12th St SW
Washington, DC 20554
888-225-5322
888-835-5322
FAX: 866-418-0232
e-mail: fccinfo@fcc.gov
fcc.gov

*David Robbins, Managing Director*
*David L Hunt J.D., Inspector General*
Enforces ADA telecommunications provisions which require that companies offering telephone service to the general public must offer telephone relay services to individuals who use text telephones or similar devices. Also enforces closed captioning rules, hearing compatibility and access to equipment and services for people with disabilities.

**3110 Health Care Financing Administration**
200 Independence Ave SW
Washington, DC 20201-4
202-690-6726
FAX: 202-690-6262

*William Roper, Administrator*
*Thomas Scully, President*
Through the Social Security administration, it administers the Medicare program under Title XVIII of the Social Security Act. Administers grants to the states for Medicaid under Title XIX of the Social Security Act for individuals who are medically indigent.

**3111 National Coalition of Federal Aviation Employees with Disabilities**
Federal Aviation Administration
6500 S Mac Authur St
Oklahoma City, OK 73169
405-954-4709
FAX: 405-954-4490
TTY:405-954-4587
www.faa.gov/acr/ncfaed.htm

*Becky Pritchett, Treasurer*
*Alan Jones, President of Aeronautical Center*
NCFAED is working on: 1) improvement of work conditions for employees; 2) expansion on National Coalition to serve all FAA employees; 3) promote equal opportunity for people with disabilities in the FAA workplace; 4) assist the FAA in its commitment to remove physical and attudinal barriers which inhibit opportunities for people with disabilities; 5) align with internal and

external organizations to attract future generations of people with disabilities to the FAA as employees.

3112 **National Council on Disability**
1331 F Street Northwest
Suite 850
Washington, DC 20004- 1138
202-272-2004
FAX: 202-272-2022
TTY:202-272-2074
www.ncd.gov

Federal agency led by 15 members appointed by the President of the United States and confirmed by the United States Senate. The overall purpose of the National Council is to promote policies, programs, practices and procedures that guarantee equal opportunities to persons with disabilities.

3113 **National Division of the Blind and Visually Impaired**
330 C St NW
Washington, DC 20001
202-205-8520

*Chester Avery, Director*
Develops methods, standards and procedures to assist state agencies in the rehabilitation of blind persons. Administers the Randolph-Sheppard Act, which assures priority for blind persons in the operation of vending facilities on federal property and serves as a program manager for the Helen Keller National Center for Youth who are deaf-blind.

3114 **National Institutes of Health: National Eye Institute**
31 Center Drive MSC 2510
Bethesda, MD 20892-3655
301-496-5248
e-mail: kcl@nei.nih.gov
www.nei.nih.gov

*Paul A Sieving MD PhD, Director*
Finances intramural and extramural research on eye diseases and vision disorders. Supports training of eye researchers.

3115 **Office of Policy**
Social Security Administration
Windosr Park Building
6401 Security Blvd
Baltimore, MD 21235
202-293-9138
800-772-1213
TTY:800-325-0778
e-mail: concepcion.mcneace@ssa.gov
www.ssa.gov/policy

*Michael J Astrue, Commissioner*
*Edward Demarco, Assitant Deputy Commissioner*
*Serge Harrison, Executive Officer*
Administers grants to the states for social services under Title XX of the Social Security Act to welfare recipients and others likely to become them.

3116 **Office of Special Education Programs: Department of Education**
400 Maryland Ave SW
Washington, DC 20202-7100
202-401-2000
800-872-5327
FAX: 202-401-0689
TTY: 800-437-0833
e-mail: customerservice@inet.ed.gov
www2.ed.gov/about/offices/list/osers/osep

*Jim Fruchterman, President*
*Andrew Friedman, CEO*
The Office of Special Education Programs (OSEP) is dedicated to improving results for infants, toddlers, children and youth with disabilities ages birth through 21 by providing leadership and financial support to assist states and local districts.

3117 **President's Committee on People with Intellecutual Disabilities**
370 L Enfant Promenade SW
Washington, DC 20447
202-619-0364
800-422-4453
TTY:800-787-3224
www.acf.hhs.gov/programs/pcpid

*George Sheldon, Acting Assistant Secretary*
Formerly the President's Committee on Mental Retardation, a federal advisory committee, estalished by the presidential executive order to adivse the President of the United States and the Secretary of the Department of Health and Human Services on issues concerning citizens with intellectual disabilities, coordinate activities between different federal agencies and assess the impact of their policies upon the lives of citizens with intellectual disabilities and their families.

3118 **Rehabilitative Services Administration**
400 Maryland Ave SW
Washington, DC 20202-7100
202-401-2000
800-872-5327
FAX: 202-401-0689
TTY: 800-437-0833
e-mail: customerservice@inet.ed.gov
www2.ed.gov

*Jim Fruchterman, President*
*Andrew Friedman, CEO*
The Rehabilitation Services Administration (RSA) oversees formula and discretionary grant programs that help individuals with physical or mental disabilities to obtain employment and live more independently through the provision of such supports as counseling, medical and psychological services, job training and other individualized services.

3119 **Social Security Administration**
5 Parks Center Court
Ste 100
Owing Mills, MD 21175
410-965-6114
800-772-1213
FAX: 410-966-2027
www.ssa.gov

*Bill Vitek, Manager*
Administers old age, survivors, and disability insurance programs under Title II of the Social Security Act. Also administers the federal income maintenance program under Title XVI of the Social Security Act. Maintains network of local/regional offices nationwide.

3120 **US Department of Education: Office of Civil Rights**
400 Maryland Ave SW
Washington, DC 20202-7100
202-401-2000
800-872-5327
FAX: 202-401-0689
TTY: 800-437-0833
e-mail: customerservice@inet.ed.gov
www2.ed/gov/about/offices/list/ocr

*Jim Fruchterman, President*
*Andrew Friedman, CEO*
Prohibits discrimination on the basis of disability in programs and activities funded by the Department of Education. Investigates complaints and provides technical assistance to individuals and entities with rights and responsibilities under Section 504.

3121 **US Department of Labor: Office of Federal Contract Programs**
200 Constitution Ave NW
Washington, DC 20210
866-487-2365
TTY:877-889-5627
www.dol.gov/ofccp

*Patricia A Shiu, Director*
Prohibits discrimination on the basis of disability and requires federal contractors and sub-contractors with contracts of $2,500

or more to take affirmative action to employ and advance individuals with disabilities.

**3122 US Department of Transportation**
1200 New Jersey Ave SE
Washington, DC 20590
202-366-4000
855-368-4200
TTY:800-877-8339
www.dot.gov

*Ray Latlood, Secretary*
Enforces ADA provisions that require nondiscrimination in public and private mass transportation systems and services.

**3123 US Office of Personnel Management**
1900 E St NW
Washington, DC 20415
202-606-1800
FAX: 202-606-0909
TTY:202-606-2532
e-mail: Informationquality@opm.gov
opm.gov

*Matthew E. Perry, CIO*
*John Berry, Director*
Establishes policies for employment of the handicapped within the federal service. Administers a merit system for the federal employment that includes recruiting, examining, training, and promoting people on the basis of knowledge and skills, regardless of sex, race, religion or other factors.

## Alabama

**3124 Alabama Council For Developmental Disabilities**
RSA Union Building
100 N Union St
PO Box 301410
Montgomery, AL 36130-1410
334-242-3973
800-232-2158
FAX: 334-242-0797
e-mail: Debra.Florea@mh.alabama.gov
www.acdd.org

*Elmyra Jones, Executive Director*
*Shungulla Moorey, Office Manager*
Serves as an advocate for Alabama's citizens with developmental disabilities and their families; to empower them with the knowledge and opportunity to make informed choices and exercise control over their own lives; and to create a climate for positive socialchange to enable them to be respected, independent and productive integrated members of society.

**3125 Alabama Department of Public Health**
RSA Tower, 201 Monroe St
PO Box 303017
Montgomery, AL 36104-3017
334-206-5300
800-ALA-1818
www.adph.org

*Kathy Vincent, Staff Assistant*
*Donald Williamson, Administrator*
Provides professional services for the improvement and protection of the public's health through disease prevention and the assurance of public health services to resident and transient populations of the state regardless of social circumstances or the ability to pay.

**3126 Alabama Department of Rehabilitation Services**
602 S Lawrence St
Montgomery, AL 36104
334-293-7500
800-441-7607
FAX: 334-293-7383
e-mail: cary.boswell@rehab.alabama.gov
www.rehab.alabama.gov

*Cary F Boswell, Commissioner*
*Jim Carden, Deputy Commissioner*
*Jim Harris Iii, Assistant Commissioner*
*Winona Nelson, Cheif Financial Officer*
To enable Alabama's children and adults with disabilities to achieve their maximum potential.

**3127 Alabama Department of Senior Services**
RSA Plaza
770 Washington Ave, Ste 570
Montgomery, AL 36130
334-242-5743
877-425-2243
FAX: 334-242-5594
e-mail: ageline@adss.state.al.us
www.adss.alabama.gov

*Irene Collins, Executive Director*

**3128 Alabama Disabilities Advocacy Program**
University of Alabama
P.O.Box 870395
Tuscaloosa, AL 35487
205-348-4928
800-826-1675
FAX: 205-348-3909
e-mail: adap@adap.ua.edu
www.adap.net

*Ellen Gillespie, Executive Director*
*Robin Lunceford, Marketing Coordinator*
*James Tucker, Associate Director*
*Rosemary Beck, Information Systems Admin*
The federally mandate statewide protection and advocacy system serving eligible individuals with disabilities in Alabama. ADAP has five program components: Protection and Advocacy for persons with developmental disabilities (PADD), Protection and Advocacy for Individuals with Mental Illness (PAIMT), Protection and Advocacy of Individual Rights (PAIR), Protection and Advocacy for Assistive Technology (PAAT) and Protection & Advocacy For Beneficiaries of Social Security (PABSS).

**3129 Alabama Division of Rehabilitation and Crippled Children**
602 S Lawrence Street
Montgomery, AL 36104
334-293-7500
800-441-7607
FAX: 334-293-7383
e-mail: sshiver@rehab.state.al.us
www.rehab.state.al.us

*Cary F Boswell, Commissioner*
*Steven Kayes, Board Member*
*Jimmie Varnado, Board Member*

**3130 Alabama Governor's Committee on Employment of Persons with Disabilities**
602 S Lawrence St
Montgomery, AL 36104
334-293-7500
800-441-7607
FAX: 334-293-7383
www.rehab.state.al.us

*Jimmie Varnado, assistant vice president*
*Cary F Boswell, commissioner*

**3131 Alabama State Department of Human Resources**
Childcare Services Division
50 Ripley St
Montgomery, AL 36130
334-242-1310
FAX: 334-353-1115
www.dhr.state.al.us

*Nancy Buckner, commissioner*
Partners with communities to promtoe family stability and provide for the safety and self-sufficiency of vulnerable Alabamians.

**3132 Client Assistance Program: Alabama**
400 S Union St
Ste 465
Montgomery, AL 36104
334-263-2749
800-288-3231
FAX: 334-230-9765
e-mail: rachel.hughes@rehab.alabama.gov
www.sacap.alabama.gov

*Rachel Hughes, Director/Advocate*

**3133 Disability Determination Service: Birmingham**
P.O.Box 830300
Birmingham, AL 35283
205-989-2100
FAX: 205-989-2295
ssa.gov

*Tommy Warren, Executive Director*
*Janet Cox, Owner*

**3134 Social Security: Mobile Disability Determination Services**
PO Box 2371
Mobile, AL 36652-2371
251-433-2820
800-292-6743
FAX: 251-436-0599
www.ssa.gov

*Tommy Warren, Executive Director*
*Jack Miller, Office Manager*

**3135 Workers Compensation Board Alabama**
649 Monroe St
Montgomery, AL 36131
334-242-2868
800-528-5166
FAX: 334-353-8262
e-mail: wc@dir.alabama.gov
www.dir.alabama.gov/wc/directory

*Scottie Spates, Director*

## Alaska

**3136 ATLA**
2217 E Tudor Rd
Ste 4
Anchorage, AK 99507-1068
907-563-2599
800-723-2852
FAX: 907-563-0699
e-mail: atla@atla.biz
www.atla.biz

*Kathy Privratsky, Executive Director*
*Mystie Rail, Commissioner*
*Margaret Cisco, AT Specialist*
Assistive Technology sales and services. ATLA is Alaska's only assistive technology resource center.

**3137 Alaska Commission on Aging**
150 Third Street
PO Box 110693
Juneau, AK 99811
907-465-3250
FAX: 970-465-1398
e-mail: hss.acoa@alaska.gov
www.hss.state.ak.us/acoa

*Denise Daniello, Executive Director*

**3138 Alaska Department of Handicapped Children**
Ste 314
1231 Gambell St
Anchorage, AK 99501-4664
907-346-1995

*Gregory Lee, CEO*

**3139 Alaska Division of Vocational Rehabilitation:**
PO Box 111149
Juneau, AK 99811-1878
907-465-2700
FAX: 907-465-2784
e-mail: dawn.duval@alaska.gov
labor.state.ak.us

*Dianne Blummer, commissioner*
*David G Stone, Deputy commissioner*
Provides comprehensive services to people with disabilities to assist in achieving an employment outcome.

**3140 Client Assistance Program: Alaska**
2900 Boniface Pkwy
Ste 100
Anchorage, AK 99504-3132
907-333-2211
800-478-0047
FAX: 907-333-1186
e-mail: akcap@alaska.com
www.home.gci.net/~alaskacap

*Pam Stratton, Executive Director*
We provide informatory referral to other programs in Alaska that are funded under the Rehabilitation Act of 1973 as amended; Individual assistance or advocacy, if an individual with disability has applied for or received services from an agency funded under the Rehabilitation Act and has concerns or questions we will work with them to help resolve their concerns with the agency.

**3141 Department Of Health& Social ServicesDivision Of Behaviorial Health**
350 Main St
Juneau, AK 99801-1149
907-465-3370
800-465-4828
FAX: 907-465-2668
www.alaska.gov

*Walter Majors, Director*
The division plans for and provides appropriate prevention, treatment and support for families impacted by mental disorders or developmental disabilities while maximizing self-determination. Community based services are provided by grantees. Inpatient services are provided in two division operated facilities.

**3142 Governor's Committee on Employment and Rehabilitation of People with Disabilities**
Division of Vocational Rehabilitation (DVR)
801 W 10 St
Ste A
Juneau, AK 99801-1878
907-465-2814
800-478-2815
FAX: 907-465-2815
e-mail: dawn.duval@alaska.gov
www.labor.state.ak.us/dvr

*Cheryl Walsh, Executive Director*
Carries on a continuing program to promote the employment and rehabilitation of citizens with disabilities in the State of Alaska. Advocates for a comprehensive statewide system for access to

assistive technology. Obtains and maintains cooperation with public and private groups and individuals in this field.

**3143 Governor's Council on Disabilities and Special Education**
201 C St
Ste 740
Anchorage, AK 99503
907-269-8990
888-269-8990
FAX: 907-269-8995
e-mail: sheryl.cobb@alaska.gov
www.hss.state.ak.us/gcdse/

*Millie Ryan, Executive Director*
*Teresa Jones, Operations Director*
*Patrick Reinhart, Project Coordinator*

**3144 Protection & Advocacy System: Alaska**
Disability Law Center of Alaska
3330 Arctic Blvd
Ste 103
Anchorage, AK 99503-4580
907-565-1002
800-478-1234
FAX: 907-565-1000
e-mail: akpa@dlcak.org
dlcak.org

*Deborah Smith, President*
*James M Shine Sr*
Deals with rights of the disabled. Works in conjunction with agencies, law offices and family members.

**3145 Protection & Advocacy for Persons with Developmental Disabilities: Alaska**
Advocacy Services of Alaska
Ste 101
615 E 82nd Ave
Anchorage, AK 99518-3100
907-222-2652
FAX: 907-677-8777
e-mail: rtessardore@dlcakelcak.org

*Greg Schomaker, Manager*

**3146 Workers Compensation Division**
Department of Labor & Workforce Development
PO Box 115512
Juneau, AK 99811-5512
907-465-2790
FAX: 907-465-2797
www.labor.state.ak.us/wc

*Clark Bishop, Commissioner*
*Trena Heikes, Division Director*

## Arizona

**3147 Arizona Department of Economic Security**
1717 W Jefferson St
Phoenix, AZ 85007-3295
602-542-4719
FAX: 602-542-5320
www.azdes.gov

*Neal Young, Director*
*Lynne Smith, Chief Exeuctive Officer*
The Department of Economic Security is a human service agency providing services in six areas: Aging and Community Services, Benefits and Medical Eligibility, Child Support Enforcement, Children and Family Services, Developmental Disabilities and Employment and Rehabilitation Services.

**3148 Arizona Department of Health Services**
150 N 18th Ave
Ste 330
Phoenix, AZ 85007-3243
602-542-1025
FAX: 602-542-0883
www.azdhs.gov

*Will Humble, Director*
The mission of Children's Rehabilitative Services is to improve the quality of life for children by providing family-centered medical treatment, rehabilitation, and related support services to enrolled individuals who have certain medical, handicapping, or potentially handicapping conditions.

**3149 Arizona Division of Aging and Adult Services**
1789 W Jefferson St
Phoenix, AZ 85007-3202
602-542-4446
FAX: 602-364-6575
www.azdes.gov

*Rex Critchfield, Manager*

**3150 Arizona Rehabilitation State Services for the Blind and Visually Impaired**
4620 N 16th St, B-106
Ste 100
Phoenix, AZ 85016-5121
602-266-9579
FAX: 602-264-7819
www.azdes.gov

*Paul Howell, Vocational Rehab Supervisor*
*Suzanne Sayre f, Rehab Counselor for Blind*
Offers clients a conservation program, eye examinations, treatments, counseling, social work, psychological testing and evaluation, professional training, computer training and more for the visually impaired. The staff includes 56 full time employees.

**3151 Developmental Disability Council: Arizona**
1717 W Jefferson St
Phoenix, AZ 85007-3202
602-542-4049
800-889-5893
FAX: 602-542-5320
e-mail: valeria.hill@mail.de.state.az.us
www.cpes.com

*David A Berns, Manager*
*Nebal Chavez, Executive Director*
*Susan Madison, Manager*
The mission of the GovernorOs Council on Developmental Disabilities is to bring together persons with disabilities representing Arizona cultural diversity and their families and other community members, to protect rights, eliminate barriers, and jointly promote equal opportunities

**3152 Governor's Council on Developmental Disabilities**
1740 W Adams
Suite 201
Phoenix, AZ 85007
602-542-8970
877-665-3176
FAX: 602-542-8978
e-mail: lclausen@azdes.gov
azgovernor.gov/DDPC/

*Larry Clausen, Executive Director*
*Shelly Adams, Executive Secretary*
The purpose of the council is to advocate for and assure that individuals with developmental disabilities and their families participate in the design of and have access to culturally competent services, supports and provides opportunities to become integrated and included in the community.

**3153 International Dyslexia Association: Arizona Branch**
PO Box 6284
Scottsdale, AZ 85261-6284
480-941-0308
e-mail: arizona.ida@gmail.com
www.dyslexia-az.org

*Linda Barr, President*
Provides free information and referral services for diagnosis and tutoring for parents, educators, physicians, and individuals with dyslexia. The voice of our membership is heard in 48 countries. Membership includes yearly journal and quarterly newsletter. Call for conference dates.

**3154 Protection & Advocacy for Persons with Disabilities: Arizona**
Arizona Center for Disability Law
5025 E Washington St
Ste 202
Phoenix, AZ 85034
602-274-6287
800-927-2260
FAX: 520-884-0992
TTY: 602-274-6287
e-mail: center@azdisabilitylaw.org
www.azdisabilitylaw.org

*Cathy Hunt, President*
*Loretta Cheeks, Vice President*
The Center provides disability-related legal information and advice to individuals who need their services and assistance. In addition to limited legal representation, their goal is to provide efficient, streamlined services to educate people with disabilities and their support on how to enforce their legal rights through self-advocacy. Guides and documents are available online by selecting Self-Advocacy Materials button on the homepage.

**3155 Social Security: Phoenix Disability Determination Services**
Social Security Admission
250 Seventh Avenue
Suite 100
Phoenix, AZ 85007
800-772-1213
TTY:800-325-0778
www.socialsecurity-disability.org/social-secu
The Social Security Administration functions as the principal agency of the United States federal government that administers Social Security, or more specifically, the federal Old-Age, Survivors, and Disability Insurance (OASDI) program. The OASDI pays retirement, disability, and survivorsO benefits to qualifying individuals.

**3156 Social Security: Tucson Disability Determination Services**
3500 N Campbell Ave
Tucson, AZ 85719-2030
520-670-5890
800-772-1213
TTY:800-325-0778
www.socialsecurity-disability.org/social-secu
The Social Security Administration functions as the principal agency of the United States federal government that administers Social Security, or more specifically, the federal Old-Age, Survivors, and Disability Insurance (OASDI) program. The OASDI pays retirement, disability, and survivorsO benefits to qualifying individuals.

## Arkansas

**3157 Arkansas Assistive Technology Projects**
Increasing Capabilities Access
26 Corporate Hill Dr
Little Rock, AR 72205-4538
501-666-8868
800-828-2799
FAX: 501-666-5319
e-mail: info@ar-ican.org
www.arkansas-ican.org

*Eddie Schmeckenbecher, Supervisor*
*Essie Hardin, Secretary*
A consumer responsive ,statewide program promoting assistive technology devices and sources for persons of all ages with all disabilities. Referral and information services provide information about devices, where to obtain them and their cost.

**3158 Arkansas Division of Aging & Adult Services**
Department of Human Services
P.O.Box 1437
Little Rock, AR 72203-1437
501-682-2441
FAX: 501-682-8155
e-mail: aging.services@arkansas.gov
www.state.ar.us/dhs/aging

*Herb Sanderson, Director*
*Coney Parker, Assistant Director*
*Sandra Barrett, Assistant Director*
*Eileen Dozier, Administrative Assistant*
The division provides services geared for adults and the elderly including supervised living, home delivered meals, adult day care, senior centers, personal care, household chores, and adult protective services.

**3159 Arkansas Division of Developmental Disabilities Services**
Donaghey Plaza
PO Box 1437
Little Rock, AR 72203-1437
501-682-1001
FAX: 501-682-8820
humanservices.arkansas.gov/ddds/Pages/default

*Charlie Green, Manager*
State agency to assist persons with developmental disabilities and their family in obtaining appropriate assistance and services.

**3160 Arkansas Division of Services for the Blind**
Department Of Health and Human Services
700 Main St
Little Rock, AR 72201-4608
501-682-5463
800-960-9270
FAX: 501-682-0366
e-mail: donnabirdwell@arkansas.gov
www.state.ar.us/dhs/dsd/newdsb/index.html

*Katy Morris, Manager*
State program which offers services in the areas of health, counseling, social work, self help and education for the visually and multihandicapped. The staff includes 4 full time and 13 part time members including mobility specialists and rehabilitation teachers.

**3161 Arkansas Governor's Developmental Disabilities Council**
5800 W 10 Street
Suite 805
Little Rock, AR 72204-1763
501-661-2589
800-462-0599
FAX: 501-661-2399
e-mail: Regina.L.Wilson@arkansas.gov
ddcouncil.org

*Regina Wilson, Executive Director*
*Brenda Mercer, Family Services Coordinator*
*Lee Russell, Information Oficer*
*Lacey Wynes, Administrative Assistant*
A federally-funded state agency established to bring the perspective of individuals with developmental disabilities and his or her family or natural support system to policy makers and make improvements to the service system.

**3162 Baptist Health Rehabilitation Institute**
Baptist Heath
9601 Interstate 630 Exit 7
Little Rock, AR 72205-7299
501-202-2000
800-991-0888
FAX: 501-202-1115
www.baptist-health.com

*Ellen Callaway, Director, Rehabilition Therapy*
*Jerry Baugh, Vice President*
*Russell Harrington, President*
Acute rehab facility serving patients with ortho, spinal cord injury, brain injury, CVA, arthritis, cardiac and generalized weakness; JCAHO and CARF accredited; 17 outpatient therapy centers throughout central Arkansas.

**3163 Children's Medical Services**
P.O.Box 1437
Little Rock, AR 72203-1437
501-682-8207
800-482-5850
FAX: 501-682-8247

*Nancy Holder, Program Director*
*Iris Fehr, Nursing Director*
*Rodney Farley, Parent Activities Coordinator*

**3164 President's Committee on People with Disabilities: Arkansas**
7th & Main St
Little Rock, AR 72203

**3165 Social Security: Arkansas Disability Determination Services**
701 S Pulaski St
Little Rock, AR 72201-3990
501-682-3030
800-772-1213
FAX: 501-682-7553
www.socialsecurity.gov

*Arthur Boutiette, COO*

## California

**3166 California Department of Aging**
1300 National Drive
Suite 200
Sacramento, CA 95834-1992
916-419-7500
FAX: 916-928-2267
TTY:800-735-2929
e-mail: webmaster@aging.ca.gov
aging.ca.gov

*Lynn Daucher, Manager*
*David Supkofl, Manager*
The Department contracts with the network of Area Agencies on Aging, who directly manage a wide array of federal and state-funded services that help older adults find employment; support older and disabled individuals to live as independently as possible in the community; promote healthy aging and community involvement; and assist family members in their vital care giving role

**3167 California Department of Handicapped Children**
714 P Street
Rm 323
Sacramento, CA 95814-6401
916-445-4171

*Maridee Gregory*
*Diana Bonta, Chief Executive Officer*

**3168 California Department of Rehabilitation**
830 K St
Sacramento, CA 95814-3510
916-445-4171
TTY:916-445-3971
e-mail: doroa.bpremo@hwl.cahwnet.gov

*Brenda Premo, Director*
*David Supkofl, Manager*
Assists people with disabilities, particularly those with severe disabilities, in obtaining and retaining meaningful employment and living independently in their communities. The department develops, purchases, provides and advocates for programs and services in vocational rehabilitation, habilitation and independent living with a priority on serving persons with all disabilities, especially those with the most severe disabilities.

**3169 California Governor's Committee on Employment of People with Disabilities**
Employment Development Department
800 Capitol Mall
Sacramento, CA 95814-4807
916-654-8055
800-695-0350
FAX: 916-654-9821
TTY: 916-654-9820
www.edd.ca.gov

*Charlie Kaplan, Staff Director*
GCEPD works to eliminate the barriers that preclude equal consideration for employment opportunities for people with disabilities. The Governor's Committee is responsible for providing leadership to increase the numbers of people with disabilities in the California workforce.

**3170 California Protection & Advocacy: (PAI) A Nonprofit Organization**
Protection and Advocacy ( PA I)
100 Howe Avenue
Ste 235n
Sacramento, CA 95825-8217
916-488-9950
800-776-5746
FAX: 916-488-9960
e-mail: legalmail@pai-ca.org
www.pai-ca.org

*Catherine Blakemore, Executive Director*
*Andrew Mudryk, Deputy Director*
*Cara Armstrong, Manager*
Advancing the human and legal rights of people with disabilities.

**3171 California State Council on Developmental Disabilities**
1507 21st Street
Suite 210
Sacramento, CA 95811-5297
916-322-8481
866-802-0514
FAX: 916-443-4957
e-mail: council@scdd.ca.gov
www.scdd.ca.gov

*Carol Risley, Executive Director*
*Tammy Eudy, Office Assistant*
*Robin Maitino, Executive Assistant*
The State Council on Developmental Disabilities (SCDD) is established by state and federal law as an independent state agency to ensure that people with developmental disabilities and their families receive the services and supports they need.

**3172 Client Assistance Program: California**
CA Health and Human Services Agency Dept of Rehab
701 Capitol Mall
Sacramento, CA 95814
916-558-5390
800-952-5544
FAX: 916-558-5391
e-mail: capinfo@dor.ca.gov
www.dor.ca.gov

*Tony P Sauer, Director*
We have a three-pronged mission to provide services and advocacy that assist people with disabilities to live independently, become employed and have equality in the communities in which they live and work.

**3173 International Dyslexia Association: Central California Branch**
4594 E Michigan Ave
Fresno, CA 93703-1556
559-251-9385
800-222-3123
FAX: 599-252-1216
e-mail: dyslexias@attbi.com
www.interdys.org

*Joy Moody, President*
Provides free information and referral services for diagnosis and tutoring for parents, educators, physicians, and individuals with dyslexia. The voice of our membership is heard in 48 countries.

Membership includes yearly journal and quarterly newsletter. Call for conference dates. Other locations also available in California.

**3174 Long Beach Department of Health and Human Services**
2525 Grand Ave
Long Beach, CA 90815-1765
562-570-4000
FAX: 562-570-4049
e-mail: info@ci.long-beach.ca.us/health
www.longbeach.gov/health/

*Ron Arias, Executive Director*
*Michael Johnson, Manager*

**3175 Los Angeles County Department of Health Services**
313 N Figueroa St
Los Angeles, CA 90012-2602
213-240-8101
800-427-8700
FAX: 213-250-4013
e-mail: webmaster@adhs.org
www.ladhs.org

*Mitchell Katz, Director*
*John Schunhoff, Chief Deputy Director*
*Allan Wrecker, CFO*
Los Angeles County Department of Health Services is one of the US's largest publicly supported health systems.The system is the main provider of health care for the area's poor and uninsured. It provides general medical and surgical care and is affiliated with the medical school at USC. The system also manages the Emergency Medical Services (EMS) Agency and the Community Health Plan HMO, a low-cost managed care plan for members of Medicaid and other state-funded programs.

**3176 Social Security: California Disability Determination Services**
3164 Garrity Way
Richmond, CA 94806-1983
800-772-1213
TTY:800-325-0778
www.ssa.gov

*Sally Keen, San Francisco Regional PDF Coord*

**3177 Social Security: Fresno Disability Determination Services**
Social Security
1052 C St
Fresno, CA 93706-3245
559-487-5391
800-772-1213
FAX: 510-970-2947
TTY: 800-325-0778
e-mail: sally.keen@ssa.gov
ssa.gov

*Sally Keen, Regional PDF Coordinator*

**3178 Social Security: Oakland Disability Determination Services**
238 11th St
Oakland, CA 94607-4490
800-772-1213
TTY:800-325-0778
www.ssa.gov

**3179 Social Security: Sacramento Disability Determination Services**
8351 Folsom Blvd
Suite A
Sacramento, CA 95826-3538
877-274-5419
800-772-1213
FAX: 916-263-5310
TTY: 916-381-9445
ssa.gov

**3180 Social Security: San Diego Disability Determination Services**
1333 Front St
San Diego, CA 92101-3603
800-772-1213
FAX: 619-278-4303
TTY:800-325-0778
e-mail: josesanbria@ssa.gov
www.ssa.gov

## Colorado

**3181 Colorado Department of Aging & Adult Services**
1575 Sherman St
10th Floor
Denver, CO 80203-1702
303-866-5700
FAX: 303-620-2696
e-mail: cdhs.communications@state.co.us
www.cdhs.state.co.us/ADRS/AAS

*Reggie Bicha, Executive Director*
A department providing services to the elderly.

**3182 Colorado Developmental Disabilities Council**
1120 Lincoln
Suite 706
Denver, CO 80203
720-941-0176
FAX: 720-941-8490
e-mail: cdppc.email@state.co.us
coddc.org

*Marcia Tewell, Manager*
The mission is to advocate in collaboration with and on behalf of people with developmental disabilities for the establishment and implementation of public policy which will further their independence, productivity and integration.

**3183 Colorado Division of Mental Health**
3520 W Oxford Ave
Denver, CO 80236-3108
303-866-7857
FAX: 303-866-7048
colorado.gov

*Keith Lagrenade, CEO*
Administration of public health program

**3184 Colorado Health Care Program for Children with Special Needs**
4300 Cherry Creek South Dr
Denver, CO 80246-1530
303-692-2000
800-886-7689
FAX: 303-839-8068
e-mail: cdphe.information@state.co.us
www.state.cdphe.co.us

*Arlene Miles, President*
*Christopher Urbina MD, Executive Director, Chief Medica*
*Rosalind Bedell, COO*
*Joni Reynolds, Public Health Program Director*
Provides information and state aid to children with disabilities.

**3185 Division of Workers' Compensation Dapartment of Labor & Employment**
633 17th Street
Suite 201
Denver, CO 80202-3660
303-318-8000
800-388-5515
888-390-7936
FAX: 303-575-8882
www.coworkforce.com/dwc/

*Ellen Golombek, Executive Director*
Infomation regarding Division Rules and procedures for Claimants, Employers, Adjusters, and parties to claim.

**3186 Eastern Colorado Services for the Disabled**
P. O. Box 1682
617 South 10th Avenue
Sterling, CO 80751-3168
970-522-7121
FAX: 970-522-1173
e-mail: peggyb@ecsdd.org
www.easterncoloradoservices.org

*Michael Erhmann, President*
*Elvin Johnson, Vice President*

Case coordination, infant stimulation, family support, residential and vocational programs.

**3187 International Dyslexia Association: Rocky Mountain Branch**
P.O.Box 461010
Glendale, CO 80246-5010
303-721-9425
800-222-3123
FAX: 303-721-9425
e-mail: ida_rmb@yahoo.com
www.dyslexia-rmbida.org

*Elenn Steinberg, President*
*Debra Coultas, Vice President*
*Sally Pistilli, Treasurer*
*Katie Johansen, Recording Secretary*

Provides free information and referral services for diagnosis and tutoring for parents, educators, physicians, and individuals with dyslexia in Utah, Colorado and Wyoming. The voice of our membership is heard in 48 countries. Membership includes yearly journal and quarterly newsletter. Call for conference dates.

**3188 Legal Center for People with Disabilities& Older People**
455 Shernan Street
Suite 130
Denver, CO 80203-4403
303-722-0300
800-288-1376
FAX: 303-722-0720
TTY: 303-722-3619
e-mail: tlcmail@thelegalcenter.org
thelegalcenter.org

*Todd Blakely, President*
*Peter Lindquist, Vice President*
*Nancy Tucker, Secretary*
*John Paul Anderson, Treasurer*

Uses the legal system to protect and promote the rights of people with disabilities and older people in Colorado through direct legal representation, advocacy, education and legislative analysis. The Legal Center is Colorado's Protection and Advocacy System. We are also the State Ombudsman for nursing homes and assisted living facilities. Call for a free publications and products list.

## Connecticut

**3189 Connecticut Board of Education and Servicefor the Blind**
184 Windsor Ave
Windsor, CT 06095-4536
860-602-4000
800-842-4510
FAX: 860-602-4020
TTY: 860-602-4221
e-mail: brian.sigman@CT.GOV
www.besb.state.ct.us

Offers rehabilitative services and information for persons with legal blindness and childrenwhonare visually impaired that are residents of Connecticut.

**3190 Connecticut Commission on Aging**
210 Capitol Ave
Hartford, CT 6106
860-240-5200
FAX: 860-240-5204
e-mail: coa@cga.ct.gov
www.cga.ct.gov/coa

*Julie Evans Starr, Executive Director*
*Robert J Norton, Communications Director*

Advocates on beha;f of elderly persons in Connecticut by regularly monitoring their status, assessing the impact of current and propsed initiatives, and conducting activities which promote the interests of these individuals and report to the Governor and the Legislature.

**3191 Connecticut Department of Children and Youth Services**
505 Hudson St
Hartford, CT 6106
860-550-6300
FAX: 860-724-2001
e-mail: Commissioner.dcf@ct.gov
www.ct.gov

*Gary Scappini, Manager*
*Bruce Douglas, Executive Director*

**3192 Connecticut Developmental Disabilities Council**
263 Farmington Avenue
Farmington, CT 6030
860-679-1561
800-653-1134
FAX: 860-679-1571
TTY: 860-679-1502
ctkasa.org

*Ed Preneta, Executive Director*

Kids As Self Advocates (KASA) is a national grassroots network that .Helps youth with special needs and their friends become self-advocatesHelps other people in the community understand what itOs like to live with special health care needs

**3193 Connecticut Office of Protection and Advocacy for Persons with Disabilities**
60 Weston Street
Suite B
Hartford, CT 06120-1551
860-297-4300
800-842-7303
FAX: 860-566-8714
TTY: 860-297-4320
e-mail: OPA-Information@po.state.ct.us
www.ct.gov/opapd

*James Mc Gaughey, Executive Director*
*Gretchen Knaff, Assistant Director*
*Linda Mizzi, Assistant Program Director*

Provides information, referrals, advocacy assistance & limited legal services to people with disabilities in the state of Connecticut whose civil rights have been violated or who are experiencing the difficulty securing relevant support services. P & A supports the development of community advocacy groups by providing training & technical assistance. P & A is responsible for investigating abuse & neglect of all individuals with intellectual disability ages 18-59.

**3194 Social Security: Hartford Area Office**
960 Main Street
2nd Floor
Hartford, CT 6103-1228
877-619-2851
800-772-1213
FAX: 860-566-1795
TTY: 860-525-4967
www.ssa.gov

*Jan Gilbert, Professional Relations Coord.*

## Delaware

**3195 Delaware Assistive Technology Initiative(DATI)**
1600 Rockland Road
PO Box 269
Wilmington, DE 19899-0269
302-651-6790
800-870-3284
FAX: 302-651-6793
TTY: 302-651-6794
e-mail: dati@asel.udel.edu
www.dati.org

*Beth Mineo, Project Director*
*Joann McCafferty, Staff Assistant*

The Delaware Assistive Technology Initiative (DATI) connects Delawareans who have disabilities with the tools they need in order to learn, work, play and participate in community life safely and independently. DATI services include: Equipment demonstration centers in each county; no-cost, short-term equipment loans that let you try before you buy; Equipment Exchange Program; AT workshops and other training sessions; advocacy for improved AT access policies and funing and several more.

**3196 Delaware Client Assistance Program**
United Cerebral Palsy Association
254 E Camden Wyoming Ave
Camden, DE 19934-1303
302-698-9336
800-640-9336
FAX: 302-698-9338
e-mail: capucp@magpage.com
www.icdri.org

*Melissa Shahan, Executive Director*
Provides advocacy services for persons involved with programs covered under the Rehabilitation Act of 1973 as amended, information and referrals on ADA, Title I.

**3197 Delaware Department of Health and Social Services**
Administration Building D HS S Campus
1901 N Dupont Hwy
New Castle, DE 19720-1160
302-255-9040
800-464-4357
FAX: 302-255-4429
e-mail: dhssinfo@state.de.us
www.dhss.delaware.gov

*Rita Landgraf, Cabinet Secretary*
Provides most of the human services available through Delaware State Government, including Medicaid, the Children's Health Insurance Program, food stamps, welfare-to-work, vaccines for children, child support enforcement, public health programs, and general services for the aging. Also for individuals with developmental and physical disabilities, visual impairements, mental illness and other vulnerable populations.

**3198 Delaware Department of Public Instructing**
P.O.Box 1402
Dover, DE 19903-1402
302-739-4686
800-433-5292
FAX: 302-739-3092

*Dr. Pascal D Forgione Jr, Superintendent*
A publicly funded, state agency that gives information about local facilities and administers supplemental funds for visually handicapped students in local schools. It also maintains special teachers of sight conservation and braille programs for both children and adults.

**3199 Delaware Developmental Disability Council**
410 Federal St
Suite 2
Dover, DE 19901-3640
302-739-2232
800-464-4357
e-mail: pat.maichle@state.de.us
www.ddc.delaware.gov

**3200 Delaware Division for the Visually Impaired**
1901 N Dupont Hwy
New Castle, DE 19720-1160
302-255-9040
FAX: 302-255-4429
e-mail: dhssinfo@state.de.us
www.dhss.delaware.gov/dvi/

*Rita Landgraf, Secretary*
*Henry Smith, Deputy Secretary*
*Betsy Deldeo, Office Manager*
State agency serving the visually impaired persons from birth, with or without other handicaps. Services offered include vocational rehabilitation, independent living, orientation and mobility, technology assessment, transition from school to work.

**3201 Delaware Industries for the Blind**
1901 N Dupont Hwy
New Castle, DE 19720-1160
302-255-9855
FAX: 302-255-4442
e-mail: awingrove@state.de.us
www.promoplace.com

*Alan Wingrove, Manager*
Delaware Industries for the Blind is a multi-faceted company that specializes in creating employment opportunities for Delaware citizens who are blind and visually impaired. DIB accomplishes this by providing quality goods and guaranteed services under contracts from Federal, State and Local Agencies and Industries.

**3202 Delaware Protection & Advocacy for Persons with Disabilities**
Arc of Delaware
144 E Market St
Georgetown, DE 19947-1411
302-856-6019
FAX: 302-856-6133
e-mail: challdover@aol.com

*Becky Allen, Executive Director*

**3203 Delaware Workers Compensation Board**
Industrial Accident Board de dept
4425 N Market St
Wilmington, DE 19802-1307
302-761-8085
FAX: 302-761-6601
www.delawareworks.com

*James Cagle, Manager*

**3204 Social Security: Wilmington Disability Determination**
U S Department of Health and Human Services
1528 S 16th Street
Wilmington, NC 28401-3908
866-964-6227
800-772-1213
FAX: 910-254-3444
TTY: 910-815-4695
www.socialsecurity.gov

*J Allen Murphy, Founder*
*Vickie O'Brien, Manager*

## District of Columbia

**3205 District of Columbia Department of Handicapped Children**
D C General Hospital
Bldg 10
1900 Massachusetts Ave SE
Washington, DC 20003- 2542
202-541-6337
FAX: 202-675-7694

*Jacqueline Mcmorris, Acting Chief*
*Nayab Ali, MD*

**3206 District of Columbia Office on Aging**
441 4th St SW
Suite 900
Washington, DC 20001-2714
202-724-5622
FAX: 202-724-4979
TTY:202-724-8925
e-mail: dcoa@dc.gov
dcoa.dc.gov

*John Thompson, Executive Director*
Serves the District of Columbia residents 60 years of age and older. Contact the Information and Assistance Unit for more information about innovative programs and services offered by the Office.

**3207 Information, Protection & Advocacy for Persons with Disabilities**
IPACHI
220 I Street, N.E.
Suite 130
Washington, DC 20002
202-547-0198
FAX: 202-547-2083
e-mail: jbrown@uls-dc.org
www.acf.hhs.gov/programs/add/states/pas.html

*Jane Brown, Executive Director*
*Ronald Tyson, Information/Referral*
Offers services and support for persons with disabilities in the Washington, DC area.

**3208 Information, Protection and Advocacy Center for Handicapped Individuals**
220 I Street, N.E.
Suite 130
Washington, DC 20002-2340
202-547-0198
FAX: 202-547-2083
e-mail: jbrown@uls-dc.org
www.acf.hhs.gov/programs/add/states/pas.html

*Jane Brown, Executive Director*
Serves all persons with disabilities in the DC, Maryland and Virginia areas offering them legal representation and advocacy, information and referrals and several publications.

**3209 International Dyslexia Association of DC**
5914 Reservoir Heights Ave
Alexandria, VA 22311-1016
703-827-9019
800-222-3123
e-mail: info@interdys.org
www.interdys.org

*Ruth R Tifford LCSW, President*
The DC Capital Area Branch, provides support for individuals with dyslexia and their families in the Washington, DC metropolitan area, including parts of Maryland, Virginia and West Virginia. Our conferences, book sales and online information resources are designed to further the understanding of dyslexia and encourage the use of systematic, multisensory teaching methods enabling children and adults to reach their educational potential.

**3210 Wage and Hour Division of the Employment Standards Administration**
US Department of Labor
200 Constitution Ave NW
Washington, DC 20210-1
202-693-5000
866-487-2365
FAX: 202-219-8822
TTY: 877-889-5627
www.dol.gov

*Hilda Solis, Secretary of Labor*
*Seth Harris, Deputy Secretary*
*Elizabeth Kim, Executive Secretariat Director*
*Betsey Stevenson, Chief Economist*
Administers regulations governing the employment of individuals with disabilities in sheltered workshops and the disabled workers industries.

**3211 Washington Hearing and Speech Society**
5255 Loughboro Rd NW
Washington, DC 20016-2633
202-537-4010
FAX: 202-243-5255
e-mail: support@dcsha.org

*Margaret Gordon, President*
*Jerome Smallwood, Vice President*
*Judyth Tinsley, Director*
Offers individuals with hearing or speech impairments, in the DC area, speech, reading classes, audiological services and new aids.

**3212 Well Mind Association of Greater Washington**
18606 New Hampshire Ave
Ashton, MD 20861-9789
301-774-6617
FAX: 301-946-1402
Holistic mental health information and publications, public lectures in the Washington D.C. area, and nationwide referrals.

**3213 Workers Compensation Board: District of Columbia**
1200 Upshur St NW
Washington, DC 20011-5626

## Florida

**3214 ARC Gateway**
3932 N 10th Ave
Pensacola, FL 32503-2807
850-434-2638
FAX: 850-438-2180
e-mail: info@arc-gateway.org
www.arc-gateway.org

*Peter Mougey, President*
*Patricia Young, Vice President*
*Lynn Erickson, Secretary*
*Donna Fassett, Executive Director*
ARC Gateway is a non-profit organization that serves children who have or are at risk of developmental disabilities as well as adults with developmental disabilitie

**3215 Advocacy Center for Persons with Disabilities**
2728 Centerview Drive
Suite 102
Tallahassee, FL 32301- 5020
850-488-9071
800-342-0823
FAX: 850-488-8640
TTY: 800-346-4127
e-mail: info@advocacy.org
advocacycenter.org

*Bob Whitley, Executive Director*
*Paige Morgan, Executive Assistant*
*Peter Schoemann, Chair*
*Catherine Piecora, Vice Chair*
Disability Rights Florida is the designated protection and advocacy system for individuals with disabilities in the State of Florida.

**3216 Assistive Technology Educational Network of Florida**
1207 S Mellonville Ave
Sanford, FL 32771-2240
800-328-3678
FAX: 407-688-4593
e-mail: diane_penn@scps.k12.fl.us
www.aten.scps.k12.fl.us

*Dee Wright, Executive Secretary*
*Diane Penn, MA, Technology Specialist*
Provides state-wide information, awareness and training for students, family members, teachers and other professionals in the area of assisted technology; a quarterly newsletter and a network of specialists (Local Assistive Technology Specialists) trained by ATEN to provide support at the district level.

**3217 Bureau Of Exceptional Education And Student Services**
325 West Gaines Street Suite 614
Tallahassee, FL 32399
850-245-0475
FAX: 850-245-0953
e-mail: Monica.Verra-Tirado@fldoe.org
www.fldoe.org

*Gerard Robinson, Education Commissioner*
Provides consultative services for the establishment and operation of school programs for visually impaired students. Provides assistance for in-service teacher training through state or regional workshops or technical assistance to individual programs.

**3218 Department of Health & Rehabilitative Services**
1317 Winewood Blvd
Building 1
Tallahassee, FL 32399-700
850-487-1111
FAX: 850-922-2993
www.dcf.state.fl.us

*David Wilkins, Secretary*
*Ramin Kouzehkanani, Deputy Secretary*
*John Bryant, Manager*
The Florida Department of Children and Families has adopted an integrated approach to programs and services as we work to help improve the lives of individuals and families.

**3219 Division of Workers Compensation**
200 East Gaines Street
Tallahassee, FL 32399-6583
850-413-4900
800-342-1741
FAX: 850-413-2950
www.fldfs.com

*Robert Kneip, PhD, Chief of Staff*
*Stephanie Iliff, Director*
*Terry Kester, Chief Information Officer*

**3220 Florida Adult Services**
1317 Winewood Blvd
Building 1
Tallahassee, FL 32399-700
850-487-1111
FAX: 850-922-2993
www.dcf.state.fl.us

*David Wilkins, Secretary*
*Ramin Kouzehkanani, Deputy Secretary*
The Florida Department of Children and Families has adopted an integrated approach to programs and services as we work to help improve the lives of individuals and families.

**3221 Florida Department of Handicapped Children**
4030 Esplanade Way
Suite 380
Tallahassee, FL 32399-7016
850-488-4257
866-273-2273
FAX: 850-245-1075
e-mail: apd_info@apd.state.fl.us
www.apd.myflorida.com

*Mike Gresham, Executive Director*
*John Bryant, Manager*
The APD works in partnership with local communities and private providers to assist people who have developmental disabilities and their families.

**3222 Florida Department of Mental Health and Rehabilitative Services**
1317 Winewood Blvd
Building 1
Tallahassee, FL 32399-700
850-487-1111
FAX: 850-922-2993
www.dcf.state.fl.us

*David Wilkins, Secretary*
*Ramin Kouzehkanani, Deputy Secretary*

**3223 Florida Developmental Disabilities Council**
124 Marriot Drive
Suite 203
Tallahassee, FL 32301-2981
850-488-4180
800-580-7801
FAX: 850-922-6702
TTY: 888-488-863
e-mail: fddc@fddc.org
fddc.org

*Debra Dowds, Executive Director*
*Mike Capp, Program Manager*
*Vanda Bowman, Staff Assistant*
To advocate and promote meaningful participation in all aspects of life for Floridians with developmental disabilities.

**3224 Florida Division of Vocational Rehabilitation**
2002 Old Saint Augustine Road
Building 1
Tallahassee, FL 32301-4862
850-245-3399
800-451-4327
FAX: 850-245-3316
TTY: 850-488-2867
e-mail: costin@vr.doe.state.fl.us
rehabworks.org

*Bill Palmer, Manager*
*Linda Parnell, Manager*
State agency serving individuals with physical or mental disabilities that interfere with them keeping or maintaining employment.

**3225 Florida's Protection and Advocacy Programs for Persons with Disabilities**
2928 Center View Drive
Suite 102
Tallahassee, FL 32301
850-488-9071
800-342-0823
FAX: 850-488-8640
TTY: 800-346-4127
www.advocacycenter.org

*Robert Whitney, Executive Director*
The Center is a non-profit organization providing protection and advocacy services in the State of Florida. The Center's mission is to advance the dignity, equality, self-determination and expressed choices of individuals with disabilities.

**3226 International Dyslexia Association: Florida Branch**
11335 SW 112 Circle Lane
South Miami, FL 33176-3896
305-431- 493
800-222-3123
FAX: 305-431-4931
e-mail: ear228@aol.com
www.interdys.org

*Guinevere Eden, President*
*Cinthia Coletti Hann, Vice President*
*Karen Dakin, Secretary*
*Ben Shifrin, Treasurer*
The Florida Branch is a non-p;rofit, scientific, educational organization committed to the study, prevention and treatment of language-based learning disabilities (dyslexia) for those in Florida and Puerto Rico. It is specifically concerned with the many children and adults with average or superior intelligence who experience difficulty in learning skills such as speaking, reading, writing, spelling and math.

**3227 Social Security Administration**
2002 Old Saint Augustine Rd
Suite B12
Tallahassee, FL 32301-4861
850-942-8978
800-772-1213
FAX: 850-942-8980
ssa.gov

*Carrie Tucker, Operations Supervisor*
*Sheila Lee, Management Support Specialist*
Administers the Title II and Title XVII disability programs. To be insured for Title II benefits, applicants must have worked in covered employment for at least five of the last ten years prior to becoming disabled. To be eligible for Title XVII disability benefits, applicants must meet an income and resource test.

**3228 Social Security: Miami Disability Determination**
Social Security
11401 W Flagler St
Miami, FL 33174-1023
305-226-0449
800-772-1213
FAX: 800-325-0778
www.ssa.gov

*Robert L Meekins, Deputy General for Executive Ope*

**3229 Social Security: Orlando Disability Determination**
Social Security
80 N Hughey Ave
Orlando, FL 32801-2231
407-648-6673
800-342-2065
TTY:407-245-7057
www.ssa.gov

*John C Massolio Jr, Founder*
*Neil Bush, President*

**3230 Social Security: Tampa Disability Determination**
Social Security Administration
P.O.Box 340572
Tampa, FL 33694-572
813-878-2906
800-772-1213
e-mail: info@dbstampabay.org
www.dbsatampabay.org

*Neil Bush, President*
*John C Massolio Jr, Founder*
The Depression and Bipolar Support Alliance Tampa Bay , is a nonprofit and all volunteer organization for individuals, family and friends of those who have been diagnosed with bipolar disorder, depression and other affective disorders.

## Georgia

**3231 ADA Technical Assistance Program**
Southeast Disability & Business Technical Assist.
1419 Mayson Street
Atlanta, GA 30324
404-541-9001
800- 94- 423
FAX: 404-541-9002
e-mail: sedbtacproject@law.syr.edu
www.sedbtac.org

*Amy Oliveras, Administrative Assistant*
*Shelley Kaplan, Director*
*Pam Williamson, Assistant Director*
One of ten regional centers funded by NIDRR, to provide information and technical assistance to assist in voluntary compliance with the Americans with Disabilities Act, and accessible education-based information technology.

**3232 Division of Birth Defects and Developmental Disabilities**
1600 Clifton Rd.
Atlanta, GA 30333
404-498-3800
800-232-4636
TTY:888-232-6348
e-mail: cdcinfo@cdc.gov
www.cdc.gov

*Thomas Frieden MD, Director*

**3233 Georgia Advocacy Office**
150 E Ponce De Leon Ave
Suite 430
Decatur, GA 30030- 2547
404-885-1234
800-537-2329
FAX: 404-378-0031
e-mail: info@thegao.org
thegao.org

*Ruby Moore, Executive Director*
*Crystal Beelner, Program Manager*
*Jennifer Puestow, Program Director*
Protection and advocacy services for Georgians with disabilities.

**3234 Georgia Client Assistance Program**
Division of Rehabilitation Services
2 Peachtree Street NW
Suite 29-250
Atlanta, GA 30303- 3141
404-656-4507
800-822-9727
FAX: 404-651-6880
dhs.georgia.gov/

*Mark Trail, Manager*
Helps eligible persons with complaints, appeals and understanding available benefits under the 1992 Rehabilitation Act Amendments and Title I of the Americans with Disabilities Act. CAP investigates complaints, mediates conflict, represents complainants in appeals, provides legal services if warranted, advocates for due process, identifies and recommends solutions to system problems, advises of benefits available under the 1992 Rehab Act Amendments and Americans with Disabilities Act.

**3235 Georgia Council On Developmental Disabilities**
2 Peachtree St N.W.
26th Floor, Suite 246
Atlanta, GA 30303-3141
404-657-2126
888-275-4233
FAX: 404-657-2132
TTY:404-657-2133
e-mail: eejacobson@dhr.state.ga.us
www.gcdd.org

*Eric Jacobson, Executive Director*
*Pat Nobbie, Depurty Director*
*Dottie Adams, Family/Individual Support Dir.*
*Valerie Meadows Suber, Public Information Director*
The Georgia Council on Developmental Disabilities collaborates with Georgia's citizens, public and private advocacy organizations and policymakers to positively influence public policies that enhance the quality of life for people with disabilities and their families. GCDD provides this through education and advocacy activities, program implementation, funding and public policy analysis and research.
*Quartlery*

**3236 Georgia Department of Aging**
2 Peachtree Street NW
Suite 29-250
Atlanta, GA 30309- 3933
404-656-4507
FAX: 404-223-2299
dhs.georgia.gov/

*Stephen Dolinger, President*
*Andrea Fuller-Ruffin, Administrator*

**3237 Georgia Department of Handicapped Children**
2600 Skyland Dr NE
Atlanta, GA 30319-3640
404-679-1625
FAX: 404-679-1630

*Ron Jackson, Manager*
*Frank Koues, Auditor*

**3238 Georgia Division of Mental Health, Developmental Disabilities & Addictive Diseases**
Two Peachtree Drive NW
24th Floor
Atlanta, GA 30303-3142
404-657-2252
FAX: 404-657-2310
e-mail: srhall1@dhr.ga.gov
mhddad.dhr.georgia.gov

*Frank Schelp MD, Commissioner*
MHDDAD provides treatment and support services to people with mental illnesses and addictive diseases, and support to people with mental retardation and related developmental disabilities. MHDDAD serves people of all ages with the most severe and likely to be long-term conditions.

**3239 Georgia State Board of Workers' Compensation**
270 Peachtree St NW
Atlanta, GA 30303-1299
404-656-3875
800-533-0682
FAX: 404-657-1767
sbwc.georgia.gov

*Stan Carter, COO*
*Thomas Risko, CFO*

**3240 International Dyslexia Association: Georgia Branch**
1951 Greystone Rd NW
Atlanta, GA 30318-2622
404-256-1232
800-222-3123
FAX: 404-256-1232
e-mail: info@idaga.org
www.interdys.org

*Guinevere Eden, President*
*Eric Tridas, President Elect*
*Suzanne Carreker PhD, CALT-QI Vice President*
*Cinthia Coletti Haan, Vice President*
The Georgi Branch was formed to increase public awareness about dyslexia in the State of Georgia. In addition, the Branch encourages teachers to train in multisensory language instruction. The Branch also provides a network for individuals with dyslexia, their families and professionals in the educational and medical fields.

**3241 Social Security: Atlanta Disability Determination**
401 W Peachtree St NW
Suite 2860
Atlanta, GA 30308-3538
800-772-1213
TTY:800-325-0778
www.socialsecurity.gov

**3242 Social Security: Decatur Disability Determination**
2853 Candler Rd
Suite 8
Decatur, GA 30034-1421
800-772-1213
TTY:800-325-0778
ssa.gov

## Hawaii

**3243 Assistive Technology Resource Centers of Hawaii**
414 Kuwilli Street
Suite 104
Honolulu, HI 96817-5362
808-532-7110
800-645-3007
FAX: 808-532-7120
TTY: 808-532-7113
e-mail: barbara@atrc.org
www.atrc.org

*Barbara Fischlowitz-Leong, Executive Director*
Provides information and referral to anyone interested in assistive technology devices and services. Operates equipment loan. Bank Provides training to consumer and professional groups including self-advocacy skills for consumers and family members. Works to ensure that schools, vocational rehabilitation agencies and health insurers provide assessments, funding and training in the use of assistive technology devices and services for their clients. Low-interest loan programs available.

**3244 Diabetes Network of East Hawaii**
1221 Kilauea Ave
Suite 70
Hilo, HI 96720-4264
808-935-1673
FAX: 808-935-6760

*Steve Fukunada, Manager*

**3245 Disability and Communication Access Board**
919 Ala Moana Blvd
Ste 101
Honolulu, HI 96814-4920
808-586-8121
FAX: 808-586-8129
e-mail: dcab@doh.hawaii.gov
hawaii.gov/health/dcab

*Francine Wai, Executive Director*
*Charlotte Townsend, Coordinator Programs/Policy Dev*
*Debbra Jackson, Planner/ADA Coordinator*
*Curtis Motoyama, Coordinator Facility Access Unit*
Provides ADA coordination for state & county government; reviews state & county construction documents to appropriate federal & state accessibility guidelines; credentials american sign language interpreters; coordinates parking for persons with disabilites; coordinates information & referral for consumers, parents and others seeking disability related information.

**3246 Hawaii Assistive Technology Training and**
414 Kuwilli Street
Suite 104
Honolulu, HI 96817-5362
808-532-7110
e-mail: barbara@atrc.org
www.atrc.org

*Barbara Fischlowitz-Leong, Executive Director*

**3247 Hawaii Department for Children With Special Needs**
Department of Health
741a Sunset Ave
Honolulu, HI 96816-2343
808-733-9055
FAX: 808-733-9068
hawaii.gov

*Patricia Heu, Manager*
*Karen Mak, Manager*

**3248 Hawaii Department of Health, Adult Mental Health Division**
P.O.Box 3378
Honolulu, HI 96801-3378
808-586-4686
FAX: 808-586-4745
www.amhd.org

**3249 Hawaii Department of Human Services**
Hawaii Department of Human Serv
1901 Bachelot St
Honolulu, HI 96817-2432
808-941-3894
FAX: 808-941-3894
hawaiianswers.com

*Linda Lingel, Governor*
*Lillian Koller, Director*
Provides services to blind and visually impaired persons in adjustment to blindness, vocational rehabilitation, low vision evaluation and assistance. Work Evaluation, operates Work Activities Center, Vending training and the Ho'opono Workshop, a sheltered workshop program for the blind and visually impaired persons.

**3250 Hawaii Disability Compensation Division Department of Labor and Industrial Relations**
Rm 211
830 Punchbowl St
Honolulu, HI 96813-5095
808-586-9200
FAX: 808-586-9219
hawaii.gov/labor

*Walter Kawamura, Administrator*
*Clyde Imada, Workers Comp Chief*
Administers Hawaii's Workers' Compensation Program.

**3251 Hawaii Disability Rights Center**
1132 Bishop Street
Suite 2102
Honolulu, HI 96813-3701
808-949-2922
800-882-1052
FAX: 808-949-2928
e-mail: info@hawaiidisabilityrights.org
hawaiidisabilityrights.org

*John Dellera, Executive Director*
*Ann Collins, Director Of Operations*

**3252 Hawaii Executive Office on Aging**
250 S Hotel Street
Suite 406
Honolulu, HI 96813-2831
808-586-0100
800-468-4644
FAX: 808-586-0185
e-mail: eoa@mail.health.state.hi.us
hawaii.gov/health/eoa

*Noemi Pendleton, Manager*
State unit on aging responsible for policy formulation, program development, planning, information dissemination, advocacy and other activities, for persons age 60 and over.

**3253 Hawaii State Council on Developmental Disabilities**
919 Ala Moana Blvd
Room 113
Honolulu, HI 96814-4920
808-586-8100
FAX: 808-586-7543
e-mail: council@hiddc.org
www.hiddc.org

*Waynette K Y Cabral, Executive Administrator*
The mission of the council is to support people with developmental disabilities to control their own destiny and determine the quality of life they desire. The Council: engages in analysis and policy development; provides training in legislative advocacy and leadership development for individuals with disabilities and their families; demonstrates new approaches to services and supports; informs policymakers about developmental disability issues; and fosters interagency collaboration.

**3254 International Dyslexia Association: Hawaii Branch**
P.O.Box 61610
Honolulu, HI 96839-1610
808-538-7007
FAX: 808-566-6837
e-mail: hida@dyslexia-hawaii.org
dyslexia-hawaii.org

*Margaret Higa, Manager*
Provides free information and referral services for diagnosis and tutoring for parents, educators, physicians, and individuals with dyslexia. The voice of our membership is heard in 48 countries. Membership includes yearly journal and quarterly newsletter. Call for conference dates.

**3255 Social Security: Honolulu Disability Determination**
Social Security
300 Ala Moana Blvd
Honolulu, HI 96850-1
808-541-3600
800-772-1213
FAX: 800-825-0778
e-mail: hivrsbd@kestrok.com
www.ssa.gov

*Neil Shim, Administrator*

**3256 State Planning Council on Developmental Disabilities**
919 Ala Moana Blvd
Suite 113
Honolulu, HI 96814-4920
808-586-8121
FAX: 808-586-8129
e-mail: tiza100w@wonder.cm.cdc.gov
hawaii.gov/health/dcab

*Francine Wai, Executive Director*
Consists of 25 Hawaii residents appointed by the governor. The council addresses the needs of the people with developmental disabilities: specifically, develops a state plan that sets the priorities for persons with developmental disabilities.

## Idaho

**3257 Idaho Commission on Aging**
3380 Americana Ter
Suite 120
Boise, ID 83720-1
208-334-3833
877-471-2777
FAX: 208-334-3033
www.idahoaging.com

*Kim Torianski, Manager*
*B*
*Cathy Hart, State Ombudsman*

**3258 Idaho Council on Developmental Disabilities**
Health and Wellfare
802 W Bannock St
Suite 308
Boise, ID 83702-5840
208-334-2178
800-544-2433
FAX: 208-334-3417
e-mail: icdd@icdd.state.id.us
www.state.id.us/icdd

*Marilyn B Sword, Manager*

**3259 Idaho Department of Handicapped Children**
Statehouse
Boise, ID 83720-1
208-334-8000

*Thomas Bruck, Chief*
*Sandy Frazier, Manager*

**3260 Idaho Disability Determinations Service**
P.O.Box 21
Boise, ID 83707-21
208-327-7333
800-626-2681
FAX: 208-327-7331
TTY: 800-377-3529
labor.idaho.gov

*Roger B Madsen, Director*
*Rogelio Valdez, Executive Director*
Under contract with the Social Security Administration, makes determinations of medical eligibility for disability benefits.

**3261 Idaho Industrial Commission**
700 S Clearwater Lane
Boise, ID 83712
208-334-6000
800-950-2110
FAX: 208-334-2321
e-mail: mholbrook@iic.idaho.gov
www.iic.idaho.gov

*Mindy Montgomery, Manager*
Free rehabilitation services to workers' who have suffered on the job injuries in Idaho. Field offices throughout the state.

**3262 Idaho Mental Health Center**
1720 N Westgate Dr
Boise, ID 83704-7164
208-334-0808
800-926-2588
FAX: 208-334-0828
healthandwelfare.idaho.gov

*Richard Armstrong, Director*
*Pat Fitzpatrick, Manager*

## Illinois

**3263 Attorney General's Office: Disability Rights Bureau & Health Care Bureau**
100 W Randolph St
Chicago, IL 60601-3218
312-814-3000
877-305-5145
FAX: 312-793-0802
TTY: 800-964-5145
illinoisattorneygeneral.gov

*Lisa Madigan, Manager*
*Raymond Throlkeld, Chief Health Care Bureau*
Information on Illinois' Comprehensive Health Insurance Plan and architectural accessibility. Enforcement of Illinois' access law and standards and other disability rights laws. Information on initiatives such as: Opening the Courthouse Doors to People with Disabilities; the abuse, neglect or financial exploitation of people with disabilities and voter accessibility. Other information and referrals.

**3264 Client Assistance Program (CAP)**
Illinois State Board of Education
100 N 1st St
1st Floor
Springfield, IL 62777-1
217-782-4321
800-641-3929
866-262-6663
FAX: 217-524-1790
TTY:217-782-1900
www.isbe.state.il.us/

*Dr. Christop Koch, State Superintendent*

**3265 Equip for Equality**
20 N Michigan Ave
Suite 300
Chicago, IL 60602-4861
312-341-0022
800-537-2632
FAX: 312-341-0295
TTY: 800-610-2779
e-mail: contactus@equipforequality.org
equipforequality.org

*Zena Naiditch, President/CEO*
*Barry C Taylor, Legal Advocacy Director*
Equip for equality is an independent, private, not-for-profit organization designated by the Governor in 1985 to implement the federally mandated Protection and Advocacy (P&A) System in Illinois. The mission of Equip for Equality is to advance the human and civil rights of children and adults with disabilities in Illinois.

**3266 Equip for Equality - Carbondale Office**
300 East Main St
Suite 18
Carbondale, IL 62901
618-457-7930
800-758-0559
FAX: 618-457-7985
TTY: 800-610-2779
e-mail: contactus@equipforequality.org
equipforequality.org

*Zena Naiditch, President/CEO*
*Barry C Taylor, Legal Advocacy Director*
Equip for equality is an independent, private, not-for-profit organization designated by the Governor in 1985 to implement the federally mandated Protection and Advocacy (P&A) System in Illinois. The mission of Equip for Equality is to advance the human and civil rights of children and adults with disabilities in Illinois.

**3267 Equip for Equality - Moline Office**
1515 Fifth Ave
Suite 420
Moline, IL 61265
309-786-6868
800-758-6869
FAX: 309-797-8710
TTY: 800-610-2779
e-mail: contactus@equipforequality.org
equipforequality.org

*Zena Naiditch, President/CEO*
*Barry C Taylor, Legal Advocacy Director*
Equip for equality is an independent, private, not-for-profit organization designated by the Governor in 1985 to implement the federally mandated Protection and Advocacy (P&A) System in Illinois. The mission of Equip for Equality is to advance the human and civil rights of children and adults with disabilities in Illinois.

**3268 Equip for Equality - Springfield Office**
235 South Fifth Street
Springfield, IL 62701
217-544-0464
800-758-0464
FAX: 217-523-0720
TTY: 800-610-2779
e-mail: contactus@equipforequality.org
equipforequality.org

*Zena Naiditch, President/CEO*
*Barry C Taylor, Legal Advocacy Director*
Equip for equality is an independent, private, not-for-profit organization designated by the Governor in 1985 to implement the federally mandated Protection and Advocacy (P&A) System in Illinois. The mission of Equip for Equality is to advance the human and civil rights of children and adults with disabilities in Illinois.

**3269 Illinois Assistive Technology Project**
1 W Old State Capitol Plz
Suite 100
Springfield, IL 62701-1200
217-522-7985
800-852-5110
FAX: 217-522-8067
TTY: 217-522-9966
e-mail: iatp@iltech.org
iltech.org

*Wilhelmina Gunther, Executive Director*
*Barbara Howell, Administration*
Directed by and for people with disabilities and their family members. As a federally mandated program, IATP strives to break down barriers and change policies that make getting and using technology difficult. IATP offers solutions to help people find what is available in products and services that will best meet their needs, where to find it, and how to get it.

**3270 Illinois Council on Developmental Disability**
State of Illinois Center
100 W Randolph St
16-100
Chicago, IL 60601-3218
312-814-2121
800-843-6154
FAX: 312-814-7441
e-mail: drs@dhs.state.il.us
www.state.il.us/agency/icdd/

*Sheila Romano, Executive Director*
*Dennis Sienko, Manager*

**3271 Illinois Department of Mental Health and Developmental Disabilities**
Suite 3b
314 E Madison
Springfield, IL 62701
217-782-6680
FAX: 217-524-3834

*Karen Perrin, Manager*
*Lori Stone, Director*

**3272 Illinois Department of Rehabilitation**
100 South Grand Avenue East
Springfield, IL 62762-1304
217-782-6680
800-843-6154
FAX: 217-524-3834
TTY: 217-557-2134
e-mail: DHS.ORS@illinois.gov
www.dhs.state.il.us/page.aspx?item=29736

*Robert Kilbury, Director*
*Timothy Martin, Manager*

**3273 Illinois Department on Aging**
One Natural Resources Way #100
Springfield, IL 62702-1271
217-785-2870
800-252-8966
FAX: 217-785-4477
TTY: 888-206-1327
e-mail: ilsenior@illinois.gov
www.state.il.us/aging

*Charles D Johnson, Executive Director*

**3274 International Dyslexia Association: Illinois Branch**
751 Roosevelt Road
Bldg 7
Glen Ellyn, IL 60137-5904
630-469-6900
800-222-3123
FAX: 630-469-6900
e-mail: info@readibida.org
www.interdys.org

*Susan Hall, President*
*Maria Leibold, Executive Director*
*Gail Oliphant, Manager*
Provides free information and referral services for diagnosis and tutoring for parents, educators, physicians, and individuals with dyslexia in Illinois and Missouri. The voice of our membership is heard in 48 countries. Membership includes yearly journal and quarterly newsletter. Call for conference dates.

**3275 Social Security: Springfield Disability Determination**
2715 W Monroe St
Springfield, IL 62704-1323
217-862-6651
800-772-1213
TTY:217-862-6681
ssa.gov

**3276 Workers Compensation Board Illinois**
100 W Randolph St
Ste 8-200
Chicago, IL 60601-3227
312-814-6611
866-352-3033
FAX: 312-814-6523
e-mail: infoquestions.wcc@illinois.gov
www.state.il.us/agency/iic/

*Dennis Ruth, Manager*

## Indiana

**3277 Indiana Client Assistance Program**
4701 Keystone Avenue
Suite 222
Indianapolis, IN 46204- 1191
317-860-2876
800-622-4845
FAX: 317-722-5564
TTY: 317-722-5555
e-mail: tgallagher@ipas.state.in.us
www.icdri.org/legal/IndianaCAP.htm

*Michael Burks, Chairman*
*Wen Lu, Secretary and Treasurer*

**3278 Indiana Developmental Disability Council**
150 West Market Street
Suite 628
Indianapolis, IN 46204-2801
317-232-7770
FAX: 317-233-3712
e-mail: gpcpd@gpcpd.org
www.acf.hhs.gov

*Mike Flores, Manager*

**3279 Indiana Protection & Advocacy Services Commission**
4701 N. Keystone Avenue
Suite 222
Indianapolis, IN 46205-1561
317-722-5555
800-622-4845
FAX: 317-722-5564
e-mail: tgallagher@ipas.in.gov
www.in.gov/ipas

*Thomas Gallagher, Executive Director*
*Milo Gray, Client & Legal Services Director*
*Gary Richter, Support Services Director*
*Karen Pedevilla, Education/Training Director*
An independent state agency established to protect and promote the rights of individuals with disabilities through empowerment and advocacy.

**3280 Indiana State Commission for the Handicapped**
P.O.Box 1964
Indianapolis, IN 46206
317-233-1292

**3281 International Dyslexia Association: Indiana Branch**
7944 Destry Place
Fisher, IN 46038
317-926-1450
800-222-3123
FAX: 317-926-1450
e-mail: gcrahen@sbcglobal.net
www.interdys.org

*Tracey Horth-Kreuger, Executive Director*
The Indiana Branch was formed to help the members of the learning disabilities community in Indiana. Promotes understanding and facilitate treatment of the Specific Language Disability (Dyslexia) in children and adults, promotes teacher training and educational intervention strategies for dyslexic students and to foster effective teaching, supports research in the field and early identification of dyslexia, serves as a clearinghouse for information and to actively disseminate knowledge.

## Iowa

**3282 Governor's Developmental Disability Council**
617 East Second Street
Des Moines, IA 50309-1831
515-281-9082
800-452-1936
FAX: 515-281-9087
e-mail: fmorris@dhs.state.ia.us
http://idaction.com/

*Becky Harker, Executive Director*
*Rik Shannon, Public Policy Manager*
*Janet Shoeman, Program Planner/Contract Manager*
*Fran Morris, Council Secretary*

The Council identifies, develops and promotes public policy and support practices through capacity building, advocacy, and systems change activities. The purpose is to ensure that people with developmental disabilities and their families are included in planning, decision making, and development of policy related to services and supports that affect their quality of life and full participation in communities of their choice.

**3283 International Dyslexia Association: Iowa Branch**
P.O.Box 11188
Cedar Rapids, IA 52410-1188
319-551-2851
800-222-3123
866-782-2930
FAX: 866-782-2930
e-mail: og-ida_tmjp@earthlink.net
www.interdys.org

*Terri Peterson, President*

The purpose of the Iowa Branch of IDA (IDA-IA) is to increase awareness of dyslexia and promote services that address the importance of diagnosis and remediation for those not meeting their reading potential. Our goal is to provide services and assistance in a way that promotes unity, support, and cooperation among those who work with these individuals so that all communities in Iowa benefit from the skills and talents of its citizens.

**3284 Iowa Child Health Specialty Clinics**
100 Hawkins Dr
Room 247 CDD
Iowa City, IA 52242-1016
319-356-1117
866-219-9119
FAX: 319-356-3715
e-mail: kathy-colbert@uiowa.edu
www.uihealthcare.com/chsc

*Jeffrey Lobas, Director*
*Brian Wilkes, Director Of Operations*

Child Health Specialty Clinics has a mission to improve the health, development, and well-being of Iowa's children and youth with special health care needs in partnership with families, service providers, and communities.

**3285 Iowa Commission of Persons with Disabilities**
Department of Human Rights
321 E 12th St
Des Moines, IA 50319-2006
515-242-6171
888-219-0471
FAX: 515-242-6119
e-mail: dhr.disabilities@dhr.state.ia.us
www.state.ia.us/dhr/pd

*Jill Fulitano-Avery, Administrator*

**3286 Iowa Compass**
Center for Disabilities and Development
100 Hawkins Dr
#S295
Iowa City, IA 52242-1011
319-353-6900
800-779-2001
FAX: 319-356-1343
TTY: 877-686-0032
e-mail: iowacompass@uiowa.edu
www.iowacompass.org/

*Jane Gay, Project Director*
*David Sorton, President*
*Mark Moser, Administrator*

A statewide program provides free information and referral about disability related services and resources: advocacy, assistive technology, community services, early intervention, education, financial support, healthcare, legal aid, residential services and transportation.
*BiMonthly*

**3287 Iowa Department for the Blind**
State Of Iowa
524 4th Street
Des Moines, IA 50309-2364
515-281-1333
800-362-2587
FAX: 515-281-1263
TTY: 515-281-1355
e-mail: contact@blind.state.ia.us
www.IDBonline.org

*Richard Sorey, Director*

Mission is to be the means for persons who are blind to obtain univeral access and full participation as citizens in whatever roles they may choose.

**3288 Iowa Department of Human Services**
1305 E Walnut St
Des Moines, IA 50319-114
515-242-6510
800-972-2017
FAX: 515-281-4597
e-mail: mfinkel@dhs.state.ia.us
www.dhs.state.ia.us

*M. Finkelstein, Compliance Officer*

Help individuals and families to achieve stable and healthy lives.

**3289 Iowa Department on Aging**
510 East 12th Street
Room 2
Des Moines, IA 50319-9025
515-725-3333
800-532-3213
www.aging.iowa.gov

*Donna K. Harvey, Director*
*Danika Welch, Executive Secretary*
*Joel Wulf, Administartor*
*Jeanne Yordi, State Long Term Care Ombudsman*

**3290 Iowa Protection & Advocacy for the Disabled**
400 East Court
Suite 300
Des Moines, IA 50309
515-278-2502
800-779-2502
FAX: 515-278-0539
e-mail: info@disabilityrightsiowa.org
ipna.org

*Sylvia Piper, Executive Director*

**3291 Social Security: Des Moines Disability Determination**
Social Security Administration
Riverpoint Office Complex
455 SW 5TH ST STE F
Des Moines, IA 50309-2115
515-284-4260
800-772-1213
FAX: 515-284-4394
TTY: 800-325-0778
ssa.gov

*Leroy Brown, Manager*

**3292 Workers Compensation Board Iowa**
1000 E Grand Ave
Des Moines, IA 50319-1020
515-281-5387
FAX: 515-281-6501
iowaworks.org

## Kansas

**3293 Beach Center on Families and Disability**
University of Kansas
1200 Sunnyside Ave
Room 3136
Lawrence, KS 66045-7600
785-864-7600
FAX: 785-864-7605
e-mail: beachcenter@ku.edu
www.beachcenter.org

*HR Turnbull, Director*
*Ann Turnbull, Co-Director*
*Robert Hemenway, CEO*
A federally funded center that conducts research and training in the factors that contribute to the successful functioning of families with members who have disabilities.

**3294 International Dyslexia Association: Kansas/West Missouri Branch**
430 E Blue Ridge Blvd
Kansas City, MO 64145-1422
816-942-6808
FAX: 816-942-6898
e-mail: info@AppliedLearningProcesses.com
appliedlearningprocesses.com

*Billie Calvery, Owner*
*Arden Murilo, VP*
IDA members in Kansas and Missouri work to establish and maintain a presence for IDA with parents, schools, and teachers in order to help individuals with dyslexia. We maintain a list of individuals in Kansas and Missouri who have specialized training and who are available for diagnosis and remediation of reading, writing, and spelling problems, information for parents, information for teachers, an annual spring conference, newsletter dealing with state and local issues.

**3295 Kansas Advocacy and Protective Services**
635 S.W. Harrison Street
Suite 100
Topeka, KS 66603-3726
785-273-9661
877-776-1541
FAX: 785-273-9414
TTY: 877-335-3725
e-mail: michelle@ksadv.org
www.drckansas.org/

*Kevin Oneslager, Owner*
*Tim Voth, Attorney*
*Michelle Rola, Director Operations*
Protection and advocacy for persons with disabilities.

**3296 Kansas Client Assistance Program**
635 SW Harrison
Suite 100
Topeka, KS 66603
785-273-9661
877-776-1541
FAX: 785-273-9414
TTY: 877-335-3725
e-mail: rocky@drckansas.org
www.icdri.org/legal/KansasCAP.htm

**3297 Kansas Commission on Disability Concerns**
900 SW Jackson
Room 100
Topeka, KS 66612-1877
785-296-1722
800-295-5232
FAX: 785-296-1795
e-mail: mgabehart@kcdcinfo.com
www.kcdcinfo.com

*Martha Gabehart, Executive Director*
*Randy Fisher, Employment/Training Liaison*
*Kerrie Bacon, Legislative Liasion*
KCDC believes that all people with disabilities are entitled to be equal citizens and partners in Kansas society. The purpose is to involve all segments of the Kansas Community through legislative advocacy, education and resource networking to ensure full and equal citizenship for all Kansans with disabilities.

**3298 Kansas Department on Aging**
503 S Kansas Ave
Topeka, KS 66603-3404
785-296-4986
800-432-3535
FAX: 785-296-0256
e-mail: wwwmail@aging.ks.us
agingkansas.org

*Kathy Greenlee, Manager*
*Barbara Conant, Public Information Officer*
Services and information for Kansas seniors, over age 60.

**3299 Kansas Developmental Disability Council**
Disability Rights Center of Kansas
1717 SW Topeka Blvd
Topeka, KS 66612-3726
785-431-7200
877-776-1541
FAX: 785-296-2608
TTY: 877-335-3725
e-mail: info@drckansas.org
www.kcdd.org/

*Jane Rhys PhD, Executive Director*
*Charline Cobbs, Senior Administrative Assistant*
To protect children and promote adult self-sufficiency.

## Kentucky

**3300 Kentucky Council on Developmental Disability**
275 E. Main St.
1E-B
Frankfort, KY 40621
502-564-5497
800-372-2973
FAX: 502-564-9523
e-mail: David.Boswell@ky.gov
www.kcdd.ky.gov

*John Burt, Manager*
Implementation of Developmental Disabilities Planning Council responsible under P.L. 101-496.

**3301 Kentucky Department for Mental Health and Mental Retardation Services**
100 Fair Oaks Lane
4E-B
Frankfort, KY 40621
502-564-4527
FAX: 502-564-5478
mhmr.ky.gov/

*John Burt, Manager*
*Deborah Anderson, Staff Assistant*
The Department for Mental Health and Mental Retardation Services contracts with fourteen regional community mental health and mental broads to provide an array of community based mental health services; operates three psychiatric hospitals and contracts with two additional hospitals; operates or contracts for 10 ICFs/MR; also operates two nursing facilities.

**3302 Kentucky Department for Mental Health:**
100 Fair Oaks Lane
4E-B
Frankfort, KY 40621
502-564-4527
FAX: 502-564-5478
mhmr.ky.gov/

**3303 Kentucky Department for the Blind**
275 East Main Street
Frankfort, KY 40601
502-782-3414
800-321-6668
FAX: 502-564-2951
TTY: 502-564-2929
e-mail: Wayne.Thompson@ky.gov
http://blind.ky.gov

*Beth Cross, Executive Director*
Provides career services and assistance to adults with severe visual handicaps who want to become productive in the home or work force. Also provides the Client Assistance Program established to provide advice, assistance and information available from rehabilitation programs to persons with handicaps.

**3304 Kentucky Office of Aging Services**
Cabinet for Health Services
275 East Main Street
Suite 1E-B
Frankfort, KY 40621
502-564-5497
FAX: 502-564-9523
e-mail: David.Boswell@ky.gov
www.kcdd.ky.gov

*Jerry Whitley, Manager*
The Kentucky Office of Aging Services is the state agency directly responsible for programs and services for people with disabilities. Efforts are made to fully integrate the service response information that considers broad familiar implications.

**3305 Kentucky Protection & Advocacy**
100 Fair Oaks Ln 3rd Fl
Frankfort, KY 40601-1108
502-564-2967
800-372-2988
FAX: 502-564-0848
e-mail: info@kypa.net
kypa.net

*Marsha Hockensmith, Executive Director*
Protection and advocacy, Kentucky's federally-mandated protection and advocacy system, protects & promotes the disability rights of individuals through free legally-based advocacy, technical assistance, and education.

**3306 Social Security: Frankfort Disability Determination**
Social Security
140 Flynn Avenue
Frankfort, KY 40601
502-875-2232
800-772-1213
866-964-1724
FAX: 502-226-4519
TTY:502-226-4519
www.ssa.gov

*Stephen Jones, Director*
*Burton Sisk, Manager*

**3307 Social Security: Louisville Disability Determination**
Social Security
601 W Broadway
Room 101
Louisville, KY 40202-2227
502-582-6690
800-772-1213
866-716-9671
TTY:502-582-5517
ssa.gov

## Louisiana

**3308 Advocacy Center**
8325 Oak Street
New Orleans, LA 70118
504-237-2337
800-960-7705
FAX: 504-522-5507
TTY: 866-935-7348
e-mail: advocacycenter@advocacyla.org
advocacyla.org

*Lois Simpson, Executive Director*
The Advocacy Center is Louisiana's protection and advocacy system. AC provides free legal services to people with disabilities in designated priority areas. In addition, AC also provides legal assistance to people residing in nursing homes in Louisiana and people over 60 in Orleans, Plaquemines and St. Tammany parishes. AC ombudsmen advocate for the rights of group home and nursing home residents. Benefits specialists help people who receive public benefits to return to work or go to work.

**3309 Louisiana Assistive Technology Access Network**
P O Box 14115
Baton Rouge, LA 70898
225-925-9500
800-270-6185
FAX: 225-925-9560
e-mail: cporciau@latan.org
www.latan.org/

*Jim Parks, President & CEO*
*Sandee Winchell, Executive Director*
An information and training resource on Assistive Technology for the State of Louisiana. LATAN operates three regional centers to provide better access for consumers.

**3310 Louisiana Center for Dyslexia and Related Learning Disorders**
P.O.Box 2050
Thibodaux, LA 70310-1
985-448-4214
FAX: 985-448-4423
e-mail: karen.chauvin@nicholls.edu
www.nicholls.edu/dyslexia

*Karen Chauvin, Director*
*Rhonda Zerinque, Administrative Secretary*
Provides free information and referral services for diagnosis and tutoring for parents, educators, physicians and individuals with dyslexia. The voice of our membership is heard in 48 countries. Membership includes yearly journal and quarterly newsletter. Call for conference dates.

**3311 Louisiana Department of Aging**
Office of Elderly Affairs
P.O.Box 629
Baton Rouge, LA 70821
225-342-9500
FAX: 225-342-5568
e-mail: elderlyaffaris@goea.la.gov
new.dhh.louisiana.gov/

*David Elder, Manager*
*Ronald Blereau, Deputy Assistant Secretary*
Serves as a focal point for Louisiana's senior citizens and administers a broad range of home and community based services through a network of 37 Area Agencies on Aging. Serve as the focal point for the development, implementation, and administration of the public policy for the state of Louisiana, and address the needs of the state's elderly citizens.

**3312 Louisiana Developmental Disability Council**
P.O.Box 3455
Baton Rouge, LA 70821-3455
225-342-6804
800-450-8108
FAX: 225-342-1970
e-mail: shawn.fleming@la.gov
www.laddc.org

*Sandee Winchell, Executive Director*

**3313 Louisiana Division of Mental Health**
P.O.Box 4049
Baton Rouge, LA 70821-4049
225-342-8552
FAX: 225-342-1984
e-mail: melanie.roberts@la.gov
new.dhh.louisiana.gov/index.cfm/directory/det

*Dr. Rochelle Head-Dunham, Director*
*William Payne, Manager*

**3314 Louisiana Learning Resources System**
2525 Wyandotte St
Baton Rouge, LA 70805-6464
225-355-6197
FAX: 225-357-3508

*Bobbie Robertson, Administrator*
Provides consultation on educational seOrvices for local schools, offers psychological testing and evaluation, maintains resource rooms in district schools and more for the blind and handicapped throughout the state.

**3315 Social Security: Baton Rouge Disability Determination**
Department of Social Services
Rm 328
755 N 3rd St
Baton Rouge, LA 70802-5233
225-342-0286
800-772-1213
FAX: 225-219-9399
e-mail: adren.wilson@dss.state.la.us
www.ssa.gov

*Shirley Williams, Director*
*Ann Williamson, Manager*

**3316 Workers Compensation Board Louisiana**
P.O.Box 94040
1001 N. 23rd Street
Baton Rouge, LA 70804-9040
225-342-3111
800-259-5154
FAX: 225-342-7960
e-mail: owd@lwc.la.gov
www.laworks.net

## Maine

**3317 Maine Assistive Technology Projects**
University of Maine at Augusta
University Hts
490 Tenth Street
Atlanta, GA 30332
404-894-4960
FAX: 404-894-9320
e-mail: catea@coa.gatech.edu
assistivetech.net

A statewide program promoting assistive technology devices and services for persons of all ages with all disabilities.

**3318 Maine Bureau of Elder and Adult Services**
11 State House Sta
Augusta, ME 04333
207-287-9200
FAX: 207-287-9229
www.maine.gov

*Diana Scully, Administrator*

**3319 Maine Department of Health and Human Services**
221 State Street
Augusta, ME 04333
207-287-3707
FAX: 207-287-3005
e-mail: brenda.harvey@maine.gov
maine.gov

*Brenda Harvey, Commissioner*
*Christopher Pierce, Deputy Commissioner, Financial Management Services*
*William Boeschenstein, Chief Operating Officer*
*Stephanie Nadeau, Director, MaineCare Service*
Provision of an array of services to people with nental illness, substance abuse issues, children with special needs and people with developmental disabilities.

**3320 Maine Developmental Disabilities Council**
295 Water Street, Ste 5
Augusta, ME 04330
207-287-4213
800-244-3990
FAX: 207-287-8001
e-mail: jbell@maineddc.org
www.maineddc.org

*Julia J Bell, Executive Director*
*Erin Howes, Office Manager*
*Rachel Dyer, Policy & Planning Specialist*
The MDDC is a partnership of people with disabilities, their families, and agencies which identifies barriers to community inclusion, self-determination, and independence, and acts to effect positive change.

**3321 Maine Division for the Blind and Visually Impaired**
2 Anthony Avenue
Augusta, ME 04333
207-624-5120
800-760-1573
FAX: 207-624-5133
TTY: 800-633-0770
e-mail: mdol@maine.gov
www.state.me.us/rehab

*Harold Lewis, Director*
*Sandra Cavanaugh, Executive Director*
Works to bring about full access to employment, independence and community integration for people with disabilities in Maine.

**3322 Maine Office of Elder Services**
State of Maine
11 State House Sta
Augusta, ME 04333
207-287-9200
800-262-2232
FAX: 207-287-9229
TTY: 800-606-0215
http://www.maine.gov/dhhs/oes

*Ricker Hamilton, Director*
*Elizabeth Gattine, Director Long Term Care*
*Romaine Turyn, Director Policy, Planning & Resource Development*
*Rick Mooers, Director Adult Protective Services*
The Office of Elder Services (OES), an Office within the Maine Department of Health and Human Services, promotes programs and services for older adults, their families and for people with disabilities.

**3323 Maine Workers' Compensation Board**
27 State House Sta
Augusta, ME 04333
207-287-3751
888-801-9087
FAX: 207-287-7198
TTY:877-832-5525
maine.gov

*Paul H Sighinolfi, Executive Director*
*Mitchell Sammons, Management Representative*
*Gary Koocher, Management Representative*
*Ron Green, Labor Representative*
The general mission of the Maine Workers' Compensation Board is to serve the employees and employers of the State fairly and expeditiously by ensuring compliance with the workers' compensation laws, ensuring the prompt delivery of benefits legally due, promoting the prevention of disputes, utilizing dispute resolution to reduce litigation and facilitating labor-management cooperation.

**3324 Social Security: Maine Disability Determination**
40 Western Ave
Augusta, ME 04330-6325
207-622-1451
800-772-1213
TTY:800-325-0778
ssa.gov

*Louis Tepin, Manager*
This office makes the ""medical determination"" about whether a consumer is disabled and, therefore, medically eligible for Social Security benefits. Legally, an individual is considered disabled if he or she is unable to do any substantial gainful work activity because of a medical condition (or conditions), that has lasted, or can be expected to last for at least 12 months, or that is expected to result in death. An individual may also be considered disabled if he or she is under the age of 18

## Maryland

**3325 Health Resources & Services Administration: State Bureau of Health**
Federal Government
5600 Fishers Ln
Rockville, MD 20857
301-443-2216
888-275-4772
e-mail: ask@hrsa.gov
http://www.hrsa.gov

*Marcia Brand, Deputy Administrator*
*Tina Cheatham, Senior Advisor*
*Mary Wakefield, Administrator*
Through appropriated funds, supports education programs, credentialing analysis, and development of human resources needed to staff the U.S. health care system.

**3326 International Dyslexia Association: Maryland Branch**
International Dyslexia Association
40 York Rd 4th floor
Baltimore, MD 21204
410-296-0232
800-222-3123
FAX: 410-321-5069
e-mail: info@interdys.org
www.interdys.org

*Eric Q. Tridas, M.D, President*
*Guinevere Eden, Immediate Past President*
*Suzanne Carreker, Ph.D., CALT, VP*
*Cinthia Coletti Haan, Vice President*
Nonprofit organization providing free information and referral services for diagnosis and tutoring for parents, educators, physicians, and individuals with dyslexia. The voice of our membership is heard in 48 countries. Membership includes yearly journal and quarterly newsletter. Call for conference dates.

**3327 Maryland Client Assistance Program Division of Rehabilitation Services**
2301 Argonne Dr
Baltimore, MD 21218-1628
410-554-9361
800-638-6243
FAX: 410-554-9362
TTY: 410-554-9360
e-mail: cap@dors.state.md.us
www.dors.state.md.us/dors/programservices/cap

*Tom Laverty, Director,Client Assistance Program*
Helps individuals with disabilities understand the rehabilitation process and receives appropriate and quality services from the Division of Rehabilitation Services and other programs and facilities providing services under the Rehabilitation Act of 1973.

**3328 Maryland Department of Aging**
State Office Building
Ste 1007
301 W Preston St
Baltimore, MD 21201-2393
877-634-6361
e-mail: drb@mail.ooa.state.md.us
www.mdoa.state.md.us/

*Dakota Burgess, Senior Information Program Manager*
*Gloria Gary Lawlah, Secretary*

**3329 Maryland Department of Handicapped Children**
Unit 50
201 W Preston St
Baltimore, MD 21201-2301
410-335-6470
http://www.msa.md.gov

*Judson Force, Director*
Children's Medical Services is a joint federal/state/local program which assists in obtaining specialized medical, surgical and related habilitative/rehabilitative evaluation and treatment services for children with special health care needs and their families. To be eligible for the program's services, an individual must be a resident of Maryland, younger than 22 years, have or be suspected of having an eligible medical condition and meet both medical and financial criteria.

**3330 Maryland Developmental Disabilities Council**
Ste 1300
217 E Redwood St
Baltimore, MD 21202-3313
410-767-3670
800-305-6441
FAX: 410-333-3686
www.md-council.org

*Brian Cox, Executive Director*
*Catherine Lyle, Deputy Director*
*Rachel London, Director, Children & Family Policy*
*Angela Castillo-Epps, Director of Communications/Policy Specialist*
A public policy organization comprised of people with disabilities and family members who are joined by state officials, service providers and other designated partners. The Council is an

independent, self-governing organization that represents the interests of people with developmental disabilities and their families.

**3331 Maryland Division of Mental Health**
2301 Argonne Dr
Baltimore, MD 21218-1628
410-243-7495
FAX: 410-333-7482

*Norma Pinette, Executive Director*

**3332 National Maternal and Child Health Bureau**
Rm 1805
5600 Fishers Ln
Rockville, MD 20852-1750
301-443-2216
888-275-4772
e-mail: ask@hrsa.gov
hrsa.gov

*Marcia Brand, Deputy Administrator*
*Tina Cheatham, Senior Advisor*
*Mary Wakefield, Administrator*
Offers information, books and pamphlets to professionals, parents and children facing health issues or disabilities.

**3333 Social Security: Baltimore Disability Determination**
711 W 40th St
Baltimore, MD 21211-2120
800-772-1213
TTY:800-325-0778
ssa.gov

This office makes the “"medical determination"" about whether a consumer is disabled and, therefore, medically eligible for Social Security benefits. Legally, an individual is considered disabled if he or she is unable to do any substantial gainful work activity because of a medical condition (or conditions), that has lasted, or can be expected to last for at least 12 months, or that is expected to result in death. An individual may also be considered disabled if he or she is under the age of 18

**3334 Workers Compensation Board Maryland**
10 E Baltimore St
Baltimore, MD 21202-1630
410-864-5100
800-492-0479
FAX: 410-333-8122
e-mail: info@wcc.state.md.us
www.wcc.state.md.us

*Karl Aumann, Chairperson*
*Mary K. Ahearn, Chief Executive Officer*
*David E. Jones, Chief Financial Officer*
*Joyce McNemar, Chief Information Officer*

## Massachusetts

**3335 Center for Public Representation**
22 Green St
Northampton, MA 01060-3708
413-586-6024
FAX: 413-586-5711
e-mail: info@cpr-ma.org
centerforpublicrep.org

*Eric Q. Tridas, M.D, President*
*Guinevere Eden, Immediate Past President*
*Suzanne Carreker, Ph.D., CALT, VP*
*Cinthia Coletti Haan, Vice President*

**3336 International Dyslexia Association of New England**
40 York Rd 4th floor
Baltimore, MD 21204
410-296-0232
800-222-3123
FAX: 410-321-5069
e-mail: info@interdys.org
www.interdys.org

*Nancy Hennessy, President*
*Guinevere Eden, Vice President*
Provides free information and referral services for diagnosis and tutoring for parents, educators, physicians, and individuals with dyslexia in Connecticut, Maine, New Hampshire, Rhode Island, and Vermont. The voice of our membership is heard in 48 countries. Membership includes yearly journal and quarterly newsletter. Call for conference dates.

**3337 Massachusetts Assistive Technology Partnership**
Children s Hospital Boston
Ste 310
1295 Boylston St
Boston, MA 02215-3407
617-355-7820
800-848-8867
FAX: 617-355-6345
e-mail: info@matp.org
www.matp.org

*Marylyn Howe, Project Director*
*Pat Hill, Training Coordinator*
A statewide program promoting assistive technology devices and services for persons with all disabilities.

**3338 Massachusetts Client Assistance Program**
Massachusetts Office on Disability
Rm 1305
1 Ashburton Pl
Boston, MA 02108-1518
617-727-7440
800-322-2020
e-mail: james.aprea@state.ma.us
www.state.ma.us

*Barbara Lybarger, Assistant Director*
*Myra Berloff, Director*
*Michael Dumont, Assistant Director*
*Jeffrey Dougan, Assistant Director*
Provides advocacy and information services.

**3339 Massachusetts Department of Mental Health**
25 Staniford St
Boston, MA 02114-2503
617-626-8000
800-221-0053
FAX: 617-727-9842
e-mail: dmhinfo@dmh.state.ma.us
http://www.mass.gov/eohhs/gov/departments/dmh

*Eileen Elias, Commissioner*
*Michele Anzaldi, Site Director*
The Massachusetts Department of Mental Health (DMH) sets the standards for the operation of mental health facilities and community residential programs and provides clinical, rehabilitative and supportive services for adults with serious mental illness, and children and adolescents with serious mental illness or serious emotional disturbance.

**3340 Massachusetts Developmental Disabilities Council**
1150 Hancock St
Quincy, MA 02169-4398
617-770-7676
FAX: 617-770-1987
TTY:617-770-9499
e-mail: adelia.deltrecco@state.ma.us
www.state.ma.us/mddc/

*Daniel Shannon, Executive Director*
Group of citizens which analyzes needs of people with severe, lifelong disabilities and works to improve public policy. MDDC produces several publications and has committees and a grants program to study and advocate for changes in the service system.

**3341 Social Security: Boston Disability Determination**
Rm 148
10 Causeway St
Boston, MA 02222-1047
800-772-1213
TTY:800-325-0778
www.socialsecurity.gov

*Michael F. Bertrand, Commissioner*

**3342 Workers Compensation Board Massachusetts**
Rm 211
1 Ashburton Pl
Boston, MA 02108-1518
617-626-7122
FAX: 617-727-1090
www.state.ma.us/dia

*Russell Gilfus, Manager*
The Massachusetts Workers' Compensation system is in place to make sure that workers are protected by insurance if they are injured on the job or contract a work-related illness. Under this system, employers are required by Massachusetts General Laws c. 152, § 25A to provide workers' compensation (WC) insurance coverage to all their employees. This insurance pays for any reasonable and necessary medical treatment related to the injury or illness and also pays partial compensation for lost wages.

## Michigan

**3343 Department of Blind Rehabilitation**
Western Michigan University
1903 W Michigan Ave
Kalamazoo, MI 49008-5200
269-387-3455
FAX: 269-387-3455
e-mail: g.dennis@wmich.edu
http://www.wmich.edu/hhs/blvs

*James Leja, Professor and Chair*
*Charles Adams, Faculty Specialist*
*Gayle Dennis, Office Coordinator*
*Jeannyne Depoian, Office Associate*
The Department of Blindness and Low Vision Studies at Western Michigan University is recognized internationally as the oldest, largest and best program of its kind. It originated in 1961 with a graduate degree in Orientation and Mobility, responding to the need for professionals to rehabilitate the many military personnel blinded during World War Two and the Korean War. Initially named the Department of Blind Rehabilitation, it prepared professionals to teach people who were blind to travel with

**3344 Michigan Association for Deaf and Hard of Hearing**
5236 Dumond Court
Suite C
Lansing, MI 48917-6001
517-487-0066
800-968-7327
FAX: 517-487-0202
TTY: 517-487-2586
e-mail: info@madhh.org
www.madhh.org

*Nancy Asher, Executive Director*
*Pat Walton, Office Manager*
MADHH is a statewide collaboration agency dedicated to improving the lives of people who are deaf and hard of hearing through leadership in education, advocacy & services. Interpreter IC print-out, assistive devices available.

**3345 Michigan Association for Deaf, and Hard of Hearing**
5236 Dumond Court
Suite C
Lansing, MI 48917-6001
517-487-0066
800-968-7327
FAX: 517-487-2586
e-mail: info@madhh.org
www.madhh.org

*Nancy Asher, Executive Director*
*Pat Walton, Office Manager*
MADHH is a statewide collaboration agency dedicated to improving the lives of people who are deaf and hard of hearing through leadership in education, advocacy and services.

**3346 Michigan Client Assistance Program**
4095 Legacy Pkwy
Lansing, MI 48911-4263
517-487-1755
800-288-5923
FAX: 517-487-0827
e-mail: molson@mpas.org
http://www.mpas.org

*Elmer Cerano, Executive Director*
The Client Assistance Program (CAP) assists people who are seeking or receiving services from Michigan Rehabilitation Services, Consumer Choice Programs, Michigan Commission for the Blind, Centers for Independent Living, and Supported Employment and Transition Programs. The CAP program is part of Michigan Protection and Advocacy Service, Inc.

**3347 Michigan Coalition for Staff Development and School Improvement**
Ste C
530 W Ionia St
Lansing, MI 48933-1062
734-513-9080
800-444-2014
FAX: 517-371-1170

**3348 Michigan Commission for the Blind - Gaylord**
Ste 102
209 W 1st St
Gaylord, MI 49735-1386
989-732-2448
800-292-4200
FAX: 989-731-3587
www.michigan.gov

*Judy Terwilliger, Manager*
The mission of the Michigan Commission for the Blind (MCB) is to provide opportunity to individuals who are blind or visually impaired to achieve employability and/or function independently in society. The MCB vision is that someday it will be said that Michigan is a great place for blind people to live, learn, work, raise a family, and enjoy life

**3349 Michigan Commission for the Blind**
Michigan Dept Of Energy, Labor & Economic Growth
P.O.Box 30652
Lansing, MI 48909-8152
517-241-8631
800-292-4200
FAX: 517-335-5140
e-mail: turneys@michigan.gov
www.michigan.gov/mcb

*Patrick Cannon, State Director*
The Michigan Commision for the blind is a state government agency that provides state and federally funded training and other services to individuals who are legally blind (blind and visually impaired). Services are provided to people of all ages throughout the state of Michigan toward the goal of employment and/or independence.

**3350 Michigan Commission for the Blind Training Center**
1541 Oakland Dr
Kalamazoo, MI 49008
269-337-3854
800-292-4200
FAX: 269-337-3872
e-mail: mossc@michigan.gov
www.michigan.gov/mcb

*Cheryl L Heibeck, Director*
*Bruce Schultz, Assistant Director*
Residential facility that provides instruction to legally blind adults in braille, computer operation and assistive technology, handwriting, cane travel, cooking, personal management, industrial arts and also crafts. During training students will develop career plans which may include work experience, internships, volunteer opprtunities and even part-time paid employment.

**3351 Michigan Commission for the Blind: Escanaba**
305 Ludington St
Escanaba, MI 49829-4029
906-786-8602
800-323-2535
FAX: 906-786-4638
michigan.gov/mcb

*Bernie Kramer, Manager*
The mission of the Michigan Commission for the Blind (MCB) is to provide opportunity to individuals who are blind or visually impaired to achieve employability and/or function independently in society. The MCB vision is that someday it will be said that Michigan is a great place for blind people to live, learn, work, raise a family, and enjoy life

**3352 Michigan Commission for the Blind: Flint**
125 E Union St
Fl 7
Flint, MI 48502-2041
810-760-2030
800-292-4200
FAX: 810-760-2032
www.dlcq.state.mi.us

*Debbie Wilson, Manager*
Vocational and Independent living skills training for individuals who are legally blind.

**3353 Michigan Commission for the Blind: Grand Rapids**
350 Ottawa Ave NW
Grand Rapids, MI 49503-2316
616-356-0180
800-292-4200
FAX: 616-356-0199
michigan.gov/mcb

*Bernie Kramer, Manager*
The mission of the Michigan Commission for the Blind (MCB) is to provide opportunity to individuals who are blind or visually impaired to achieve employability and/or function independently in society. The MCB vision is that someday it will be said that Michigan is a great place for blind people to live, learn, work, raise a family, and enjoy life

**3354 Michigan Council of the Blind and Visually Impaired (MCBVI)**
Neal Freeling
1037 Winchester Ave
Lincoln Park, MI 48146-4248
313-381-7844
888-956-2284
e-mail: info@blindmi.org
http://blindmi.org/

*Joe Sibley, President*
*John Jarzyna, VP*
*Pam Berryman, VP*
*Charis Austin, Treasurer*
MCBVI is a diverse group of very friendly people from around the state working together to improve the lives of all citizens who are blind or visually impaired.

**3355 Michigan Department of Handicapped Children**
3423 N Martin Luther King Jr Blvd
Lansing, MI 48906-2934
517-484-9312
FAX: 517-484-9836

*Alan Curtiss, President*
*Bobbie Butler, Manager*

**3356 Michigan Developmental Disabilies Council**
1033 S Washington Ave
Lansing, MI 48910-1646
517-334-6123
FAX: 517-334-7353
TTY:517-334-7354
e-mail: sharp@michigan.gov
www.michigan.gov/ddcouncil

*Vendella Collins, Executive Director*
*Andre K Robinson, Chair*
*Mitzi Allen, Administrative*
*Yasmina Bouraoui, Deputy Director*
The Michigan DD Council is a group of citizens from across the state. Its membership is made up of: people with developmental disabilities; people from families who have, among their members, people with developmental disabilities; and professionals from state and local agencies charged with assisting people with developmental disabilities.

**3357 Michigan Office of Services to the Aging**
P.O.Box 30676
Lansing, MI 48909-8176
517-373-8230
FAX: 517-373-4092
http://www.michigan.gov/miseniors/

*Rhonda Powell, Deputy Director*
State unit on aging; allocates and monitors state and federal funds for the Older American Act services: nutrition, community services, administers home and community based waiver, develops programs through Area Agencies on Aging, advocates on behalf of seniors with legislature, governor, state departments, federal government, responsible for state planning of aging services, develops formula for distribution of state and federal funds.

**3358 Michigan Protection & Advocacy Service**
4095 Legacy Pkwy
Ste 500
Lansing, MI 48911-4263
517-487-1755
800-288-5923
FAX: 517-487-0827
e-mail: molson@mpas.org
mpas.org

*Elmer Cerano, Executive Director*
People with disabilities have to deal with a wide variety of issues. TThey try to answer any questions you may have relating to disability. They have experience in the following areas: discrimination in education, employment, housing, and public places; abuse and neglect; Social Security benefits; Medicaid, Medicare and other insurance; housing; Vocational Rehabilitation; HIV/AIDS issues; and many other disability-related topics

**3359 Michigan Rehabilitation Services**
300 N. Washington Sq.
Lansing, MI 48913
517-335-4590
888-784-7328
FAX: 517-373-0059
TTY: 517-373-4035
e-mail: zimmermanng@michigan.org
www.michigan.org

*George Zimmermann, Vice President*
*Michelle Begnoche, Communications Specialist*
*Bonnie Fink, Travel Consultant Coordinator*
*David Lorenz, Public and Industry Relations Manager*
A state and federally funded program that helps persons with disabilities prepare for and fund a job that matches their interests and abilities. Assistance is also available to workers with disabilities who are having difficulty keeping a job. A person is eligible for MRS services if he or she has a disability, is unemployed and needs vocational rehabilitation services to prepare for and find a job or independent living services.

3360 **Social Security Administration**
5210 Perry Robinson Cir
Lansing, MI 48911-3878
517-393-3876
800-772-1213
FAX: 517-393-4686
TTY: 800-325-0778
e-mail: jennifer.bower@ssa.gov
ssa.gov

*Tiffany L. Flick, Executive Secretary*
*Michael J. Astrue, Commissioner*
*Carolyn W. Colvin, Deputy Commissioner*

We deliver services through a nationwide network of over 1,400 offices that include regional offices, field offices, card centers, teleservice centers, processing centers, hearing offices, the Appeals Council, and our State and territorial partners, the Disability Determination Services. We also have a presence in U.S. embassies around the globe. For the public, we are the "face of the government." The rich diversity of our employees mirrors the public we serve.

3361 **State of Michigan Workers' Compensation Agency**
PO Box 30016
Lansing, MI 48909-7516
888-396-5041
FAX: 517-322-1808
e-mail: wcinfo@michigan.gov
http://www.michigan.gov/wca/

*Kevin A. Elsenheimer, Director*
*Jack A. Nolish, Deputy Director*
*Sue Bickel, Secretary*
*Ted Day, Division Manager*

Michigan's injured workers and their employers are governed by the Workers' Disability Compensation Act. This Act was first adopted in 1912 and provides compensation to workers who suffer an injury on the job and protects employers' liability. The mission of the Workers' Compensation Agency is to efficiently administer the Act and provide prompt, courteous and impartial service to all customers.

## Minnesota

3362 **International Dyslexia Association: Minnesota Branch**
International Dyslexia Association
5021 Vernon Ave S
Minneapolis, MN 55436-2102
612-486-4242
800-222-3123
FAX: 410-321-5069
e-mail: info@ida-umb.org
www.interdys.org

*Eric Q. Tridas, M.D., President*
*Suzanne Carreker, Ph.D., CALT-, Vice President*
*Cinthia Coletti Haan, 'Vice President*
*Susan Lowell, M.A., B.C.E.T, Vice President*

UMBIDA-the Upper Midwest Branch of the International Dyslexia Association (IDA-serves the residents of Minnesota, North Dakota, South Dakota, and Winnipeg, Canada and offers: local educational conferences about dyslexia and related subjects, Orton-Gillingham training for teachers, tutors, and parents, Quarterly speaker series, member discounts on conferences, information line, and tutor referral.

3363 **Minnesota Assistive Technology Project**
STAR
358 Centennial Office Building
658 Cedar Street
Saint Paul, MN 55155-1402
651-201-2640
888-234-1267
800-627-3529
FAX: 651-282-6671
e-mail: star.program@state.mn.us
www.admin.state.mn.us/assistivetechnology

*Chuck Rassbach, Program Director*
*Nancy Stark, Executive Secretary*
*Jennie Delisi*
*Joan Gillum*

A statewide program promoting assistive technology devices and services for persons of all ages with all disabilities.

3364 **Minnesota Board on Aging**
P.O. Box 64976
Saint Paul, MN 55164-0976
651-431-2500
800-882-6262
800-333-2433
FAX: 651-297-7855
TTY:800-627-3529
e-mail: mba@sate.mn.us
www.mnaging.org

*Don Samuelson, Chair*
*Jean Wood, Executive Director*

A state unit on aging for the state of Minnesota. Funds 14 area agencies on aging throughout the state that provide services at the local level. The mission is to keep older people in the homes or places of residence for as long as possible.

3365 **Minnesota Children with Special Needs, Minnesota Department of Health**
P.O.Box 64975
Saint Paul, MN 55164-0975
651-201-5000
888-345-0823
FAX: 651-201-3655
TTY: 651-201-5797
e-mail: mcshnweb@health.state.mn.us
www.health.state.mn.us/mcshn

*Dr. Edward Ehlinger, Commissioner*
*James G. Koppel, Deputy Commissioner*
*Jeanne F. Ayers, Assistant Commissioner*
*Ellen Benavides, Assistant Commissioner*

Minnesota Children with Special Health Needs (MCSHN) provides leadership through partnerships with families and other key stakeholders to improve the access and quality of all systems impacting children and youth with special health care needs and their families.

3366 **Minnesota Department of Labor & Industry Workers Compensation Division**
443 Lafayette Rd N
Saint Paul, MN 55155-4301
651-284-5000
800-342-5354
TTY:651-297-4198
e-mail: dli.communications@state.mn.us
doli.state.mn.us

*Ken Petersom, Commissioner*
*Kris Eiden, Deputy Commisioner*
*James Honerman, Communications*
*Gail Krieg, Human Resources*

To reduce the impact of work related injuries for employees and employers. Advice is given and questions answered on the toll-free number.

**3367 Minnesota Disability Law Center**
430 1st Avenue North
Suite 300
Minneapolis, MN 55401- 1780 612-332-1441
800-292-4150
FAX: 612-334-5755
TTY: 612-332-4668
e-mail: website@mylegalaid.org
www.mndlc.org

*Mary L. Knoblauch, Chair*
*Cathy Haukedahl, Executive Director*
*Andrea Kaufman, Director of Development*
*Jeffer Ali, Director*
Provides free, civil, legal assistance to Minnesotans with disabilities on issues related to their disability.

**3368 Minnesota Governor's Council on Developmental Disabilities GCDD**
370 Centennial Office Building
658 Cedar St
Saint Paul, MN 55155-1603 651-296-4018
877-348-0505
FAX: 651-297-7200
e-mail: admin.dd@state.mn.us
www.mncdd.org

*Colleen Wieck PhD, Executive Director*
*Dan Reed, Chair*
*Anne Barnwell, Council Member*
*Stevie K. Nelson, Council Member*
The mission of the Minnesota Governor's Council on Developmental Disabilities is to provide information, education, and training to build knowledge, develop skills, and change attitudes that will lead to increased independence, productivity, self determination, integration and inclusion (IPSII) for people with developmental disabilities and their families.

**3369 Minnesota Mental Health Division**
Human Services Building
444 Lafayette Rd N
Saint Paul, MN 55155-3802 651-431-2000
800-366-5411
TTY:800-627-3529
e-mail: dhs.info@state.mn.us
www.dhs.state.mn.us/Provider/faqs/mental_heal

*Lucinda E. Jesson, Commissioner*
*Anne Barry, Deputy Commissioner*
*Dennis Benson, Chief Executive Officer*
*Patricia Carlson, Interim Chief Executive Officer*
Oversees the provision of services to people with mental illness in the state of Minnesota. Services are provided on the local level through a network of 87 county social service departments.

**3370 Minnesota Protection & Advocacy for Persons with Disabilities**
Minnesota Disability Law Center
430 1st Avenue North
Suite 300
Minneapolis, MN 55401- 1742 612-332-1441
800-292-4150
FAX: 612-334-5755
www.mnlegalservices.org/mdlc

*Pamela Hoopes, Legal Director*
OUT OF BUSSINESS

**3371 Minnesota State Council on Disability(MSCOD)**
Ste 107
121 7th Pl E
Saint Paul, MN 55101-2114 651-361-7800
800-945-8913
FAX: 651-296-5935
e-mail: council.disability@state.mn.us
www.disability.state.mn.us

*Joan Willshire, Executive Director*
*Linda Gremillion, Business Operations Manager*
*Margot Imdieke Cross, Accessibility Specialist*
*Diogo Reis, Legislative Specialist*
The MSCOD collaborates, advocates, advises and provide technical information to expand opportunities, increase the quality of life and empower all persons with disabilities. This mission is accomplished by: providing information, referral and technical assistance to thousands of individuals every year via email, letter or telephone; through trainings on a variety of disability related topics; through publications and its web site; and through its advocacy and advisory work.

**3372 Minnesota State Services for the Blind**
2200 University Avenue West
Suite 240
Saint Paul, MN 55114-1840 651-642-0500
800-652-9000
FAX: 651-649-5927
TTY: 651-642-0506
e-mail: star.program@state.mn.us
http://www.mnplan.state.mn.us/star/program.ht

*Richard Strong, Executive Director*
*Kenneth Trebelhorn, Council Member*
*Jan Bailey, Chair*
*Steve Jacobson, Council Member*
State agency serving blind and visually impaired persons with rehabilitation, information access, assistive technology, training and job placement services. Extensive older blind program.

**3373 Social Security: St. Paul Disability Determination**
5210 Perry Robinson Cir
Lansing, MI 48911-3878 517-393-3876
800-772-1213
FAX: 517-393-4686
TTY: 800-325-0778
e-mail: jennifer.bower@ssa.gov
www.ssa.gov

*Tiffany L. Flick, Executive Secretary*
*Michael J. Astrue, Commissioner*
*Carolyn W. Colvin, Deputy Commissioner*
We deliver services through a nationwide network of over 1,400 offices that include regional offices, field offices, card centers, teleservice centers, processing centers, hearing offices, the Appeals Council, and our State and territorial partners, the Disability Determination Services. We also have a presence in U.S. embassies around the globe. For the public, we are the "face of the government." The rich diversity of our employees mirrors the public we serve.

## Mississippi

**3374 International Dyslexia Association: Mississippi Branch**
1997 Atkins Rd.
Ruston, LA 71270 985-414-2575
800-222-3123
FAX: 410-321-5069
e-mail: alicehiginbotham@hotmail.com
http://www.ladyslexia.com/LaBIDA/Welcome.ht ml

*Alice Higginbotham, President*
*Maureen Landry, Vice President/Chair of Public Relations*
*Becky Clingman, Branch Council Rep*
*Dawn Amy, Director/Chair Education*

It is the mission of the Louisiana Branch to provide information and resources to parents, educators, students and the community in a way that creates a clear and positive understanding of dyslexia and related language learning needs so that every individual has the opportunity to lead a productive and fulfilling life for the benefit of society.

**3375 Mississippi Assistive Technology Division**
P.O.Box 1698
Jackson, MS 39215-1698 601-853-5160
FAX: 601-853-5158
www.mdrs.state.ms.us

*Kris Geroux, Coordinator*
*Marie Gaddis, Administrative Assistant*
A statewide program promoting assistive technology devices and services for persons of all ages with all disabilities.

**3376 Mississippi Bureau of Mental Retardation**
1101 Robert E Lee Bldg
239 North Lamar Street
Jackson, MS 39201 601-359-1288
877-240-8513
FAX: 601-359-6295
TTY: 601-359-6230
e-mail: ed.legrand@dmh.state.ms.us
www.dmh.state.ms.us

*Edwin C. Legrand, Executive Director*
*Kris Jones, Bureau Director of Quality Management, Operations and Standards*
*Glynn A. Kegley, Bureau Director of Administration*
*Diana Mikula, Bureau Director of Mental Health*
Since its inception in 1974, the Mississippi Department of Mental Health has endeavored to provide services of the highest quality through a statewide service delivery system. As one of the major state agencies in Mississippi, the Department of Mental Health provides a network of services to persons who experience problems with mental illness, alcohol and/or drug abuse/dependence, or who have intellectual and developmental disabilities. Services are provided through an array of facilities and ag

**3377 Mississippi Client Assistance Program**
Mississippi Department of Rehabilitation Services
500-G East Woodrow Wilson Drive
P.O. Box 4958
Jackson, MS 39296 601-982-7051
FAX: 601-982-1951
http://www.msdisabilities.com

*Presley Posey, Executive Director*
*Kim Inzinna, President*
*Dr. Michael Campbell, Executive Director*
*Jimmy Blackwood, Executive Director*
Advocacy program for clients/client applicants for state of MS vocational services.

**3378 Mississippi Department of Mental Health**
1101 Robert E Lee Bldg
Jackson, MS 39201 601-359-1288
877-240-8513
FAX: 601-359-6295
TTY: 601-359-6230
e-mail: ed.legrand@dmh.state.ms.us
dmh.state.ms.us

*Edwin C. Legrand, Executive Director*
*Kris Jones, Bureau Director of Quality Management, Operations and Standards*
*Glynn A. Kegley, Bureau Director of Administration*
*Diana Mikula, Bureau Director of Mental Health*
Administers Mississippi's public programs of serving persons with mental illness, mental retardation, alcohol and substance abuse problems, and alzheimer's disease and related dementia.

**3379 Mississippi Division of Aging and Adult Services**
Mississippi Department Of Human Services
750 N State St
Jackson, MS 39202-3033 601-359-4500
800-345-6347
FAX: 601-359-3664
e-mail: webspinner@mdhs.state.ms.us
www.mdhs.state.ms.us/

*Donald R. Taylor, Executive Director*
*Julia M. Todd, Director*
*Judy Collins, Director*
*Mary Scott, Director*
Protects the rights of older citizens while expanding their opportunities and access to quality services.

**3380 Mississippi State Department of Health**
Children's Medical Program
P.O.Box 1700
Jackson, MS 39215-1700 601-576-7400
866-458-4948
FAX: 601-987-5560
e-mail: web@HealthyMS.com
http://www.msdh.state.ms.us/

*Larry Clark, Director*
*Vickey Berryman, Director, Bureau of Licensure*
*Jim Craig, Director, Office of Health Protection*
*Tim Darnell, Director, MSDH Field Services*
Financial assistance to families of children with physical handicaps. Rehabilitative in nature and has as its goal the correction or reduction of physical handicaps. Eligibility determined by diagnosis and provided to children from birth to age twenty-one. Financial eligibility is determined by factors of family income, family size, estimated cost of treatment and family liabilities. Categories include, but are not limited to: orthopedic, congenital heart defects, cerebral palsy, etc.

**3381 Mississippi: Workers Compensation Commission**
1428 Lakeland Dr
Jackson, MS 39216-4718 601-987-4200
866-473-6922
FAX: 601-987-4220
e-mail: mtorres at mwcc.state.ms.us
mwcc.state.ms.us

*Liles Williams, Chairman*
*John Junkin, Commissioner*
*Debra Gibbs, Commissioner*
*Cindy Polk Wilson, Administrative Judge*
Our goal is to provide the public with useful information regarding Workers' Compensation in the state of Mississippi.

## Missouri

**3382 Institute for Human Development**
University of Missouri-Kansas City
215 W. Pershing Road
6th floor
Kansas City, MO 64108- 2639 816-235-1770
800-444-0821
FAX: 888-503-3107
TTY: 800-452-1185
e-mail: beckmanncc@umkc.edu
www.ihd.umkc.edu

*Carl Calkins, Director*
*Kay Conklin, Training Director*
*Cindy Beckmann, Assistant to the Director*
*Kathy Fuger, Director, Early Childhood and Youth Programs*
A statewide program promoting person-centered planning and services for persons of all ages with all disabilities.

**3383 Missouri Division Of Developmental Disabilities**
Missouri Department Of Mental Health
1706 E. Elm St.
P.O.Box 687
Jefferson City, MO 65102
573-751-4122
800-364-9687
FAX: 573-751-8224
e-mail: dmhmail@dmh.mo.gov
www.dmh.mo.gov

*Brent McGinty, Director*
*Keith Schafer, Director*
*Jay Nixon, Governor*
*Jan Heckemeyer, Deputy Director*

The Missouri Department of Mental Health was first established as a cabinet-level state agency by the Omnibus State Government Reorganization Act, effective July 1, 1974. State law provides three principal missions for the department: (1) the prevention of mental disorders, developmental disabilities, substance abuse, and compulsive gambling; (2) the treatment, habilitation, and rehabilitation of Missourians who have those conditions; and (3) the improvement of public understanding and attitudes.

**3384 Missouri Protection & Advocacy Services**
925 S Country Club Dr
Jefferson City, MO 65109-4510
573-893-3333
800-392-8667
FAX: 573-893-4231
TTY: 800-735-2966
e-mail: mopasjc@embarqmail.com
moadvocacy.org

*Shawn De Loyola, Executive Director*
*Linda Snider, Information Specialist*
*Connie Wright, Information Specialist*
*Julia Sanning, Information Specialist*

MO P&A potects the rights of individuals with disabilities by providing advocacy and legal services for disability related issues. As Missouri's Protection and Advocacy system, Mo P&A investigates allegations of abuse, neglect, death, and violations of rights against individuals with disabilities. Those who contact Mo P&A can receive information, referrals, advocacy services or legal counsel provided through one of nine federally-funded programs.

**3385 Missouri Rehabilitation Services for the Blind**
615 Howerton Court
P.O.Box 88
Jefferson City, MO 65103- 0088
573-522-8024
800-592-6004
FAX: 573-751-4984
e-mail: AskCD@dss.mo.gov?subject=Agency%20Contact%20I
www.dss.mo.gov/fsd/rsb/

*Mark Laird, Executive Director*
*Ronald J. Levy, Director*
*Brian Kinkade, Deputy Director*
*Jennifer Tidball, Division Director*

Offers services for the totally blind, legally blind, visually impaired, including counseling, educational, recreational, rehabilitation, computer training and professional training services.

**3386 Social Security: Jefferson City Disability Determination**
129 SCOTT STATION ROAD
Jefferson City, MO 65101-4421
877-405-9803
800-772-1213
FAX: 517-393-4686
TTY: 800-325-0778
e-mail: jennifer.bower@ssa.gov
www.ssa.gov

*Dr. Don Gann, Director*
*Tiffany L. Flick, Executive Secretary*
*Michael J. Astrue, Commissioner*
*Carolyn W. Colvin, Deputy Commissioner*

We deliver services through a nationwide network of over 1,400 offices that include regional offices, field offices, card centers, teleservice centers, processing centers, hearing offices, the Appeals Council, and our State and territorial partners, the Disability Determination Services. We also have a presence in U.S. embassies around the globe. For the public, we are the "face of the government." The rich diversity of our employees mirrors the public we serve.

**3387 Workers Compensation Board Missouri**
Department of Labor and Industrial Realtions
P.O. Box 58
Jefferson City, MO 65102-1058
573-751-4231
800-775-2667
FAX: 573-751-2012
e-mail: workerscomp@dolir.mo.gov
http://labor.mo.gov/DWC/

*DeWayne Hickey, Chief of Operations*
*Larry Rebman, Director*
*Nasreen Esmail, Chief Legal Counsel*
*Paul Rockers, LIR Manager*

The Missouri Division of Workers' Compensation administers the programs providing services to all stake holders including workers who have been injured on the job or been exposed to occupational disease arising out of and in the course of employment. The Division makes sure that an injured worker receives benefits that he/she is entitled to under the Missouri Workers' Compensation law. The Division's Administrative Law Judges have the authority to approve settlements or issue awards after a hear

## Montana

**3388 Addictive & Mental Disorders Division**
555 Fuller Ave
PO Box 202905
Helena, MT 59620-2905
406-444-3964
FAX: 406-444-4435
e-mail: lothompson@mt.gov
http://www.dphhs.mt.gov/amdd/

*Lou Thompson, Administrator*
*Joan Cassidy, Chemical Dependency Bureau Chief*
*E. Lee Simes, Medical Director*
*Deb Matteucci, Behavioral Health Program Facilitator*

The mission of the Addictive and Mental Disorders Division (AMDD) of the Montana Department of Public Health and Human Services is to implement and improve an appropriate statewide system of prevention, treatment, care, and rehabilitation for Montanans with mental disorders or addictions to drugs or alcohol.

**3389 Disability Rights Montana**
1022 Chestnut Street
Helena, MT 59601
406-449-2344
800-245-4743
FAX: 406-449-2418
TTY: 406-449-2344
e-mail: advocate@disabilityrightsmt.org
www.mtadv.org

*Bernadette Franks-Ongoy, Executive Director*
*Kelli Kaufman, Director of Finance & Administration*
*Steve Heaverlo, Director of Programs/Advocacy Specialist*
*Laurie t Danforth, Paralegal/Executive Suppor*

Protects and advocates the human and legal rights of Montanans with mental and physical disabilities while advancing dignity, equality, and self-determination. Designated federal P&A, with AT, CAP, PADD, PAIMI and PAIR programs. Advocacy and legal services for abuse, neglect, rights violations, access, discrimination in employment, accommodations and housing, and assistance with vocational rehabilitation/visual services.

**3390 MonTECH**
700 SW Higgins Ave.
Suite 250
Missoula, MT 59803
406-243-5751
877-243-5511
FAX: 406-243-4730
e-mail: montech@ruralinstitute.umt.edu
www.montech.ruralinstitute.umt.edu

*Kathleen Laurin, Program Director*
*Chris Clasby, Program Coordinator*
*Leslie Mullette*

Specialzing in Assistive Technology and oversee a variety of AT related grants and contracts. The overall goal is to develop a comprehensive, statewide system of assistive technology related assistance. Striving to ensure that all people in Montana with disabilities have equitable access to assistive technology devices and services in order to enhance their independence, productivity and quality of life.

**3391 Montana Blind & Low Vision Services**
111 N Last Chance Gulch, Suite 4C
PO Box 4210
Helena, MT 59604-4210
406-444-2590
877-296-1197
FAX: 406-444-3632
e-mail: lothompson@mt.gov
http://www.dphhs.mt.gov/vocrehab/blvs/

*Lou Thompson, Administrator*
*Joan Cassidy, Chemical Dependency Bureau Chief*
*E. Lee Simes, Medical Director*
*Deb Matteucci, Behavioral Health Program Facilitator*

Mission: promoting work and independence for Montanans with disabilities.

**3392 Montana Council on Developmental Disabilities**
2714 Billings Ave
Helena, MT 59601-9767
406-443-4332
866-443-4332
FAX: 406-443-4192
e-mail: deborah@mtcdd.or
www.mtcdd.org

*Deborah Swingley, CEO/Executive Director*
*Dee Burrell*

The Council is made up of Montanans both with and without developmental disabilities, who believe in improving the lives of Montana's citizens who have a disability. We concentrate on issues related to self-determination, education, employment, transportation, housing, recreation, health care, community inclusion and the overall quality of life of people with developmental disabilities. As a Council we are committed to both question, and action as we work to discover and promote creative ways t

**3393 Montana Department of Aging**
Room 219
Capitol Sta
Helena, MT 59620
406-444-7734
FAX: 406-444-3465

*Keith Messmer, Manager*
*Jeff Sturm, President*

**3394 Montana Department of Handicapped Children**
Cogswell Building
Helena, MT 59620
406-444-7734
FAX: 406-444-3465

*Keith Messmer, Manager*

**3395 Montana Protection & Advocacy for Persons with Disabilities**
1022 Chestnut Street
Helena, MT 59601-5019
406-449-2344
800-245-4743
FAX: 406-449-2418
TTY: 406-449-2344
e-mail: advocate@disabilityrightsmt.org
www.mtadv.org

*Susie McIntyre, President*
*Will Warberg, Sales and Marketing Manager*
*Bernadette Franks-Ongoy, Executive Director*
*Kelli Kaufman, Director of Finance & Administration*

Disability Rights Montana is the federally-mandated civil rights protection and advocacy system for Montana. We have the legal authority to represent almost any person with a disability.

**3396 Montana State Fund**
P.O.Box 4759
Helena, MT 59604-4759
406-495-5000
800-332-6102
FAX: 406-495-5020
TTY: 406-495-5030
www.montanastatefund.com

*Elizabeth Best, Chairman*

Montana State Fund is committed to the health and economic prosperity of Montana through superior service, leadership and caring individuals, working in an environment of teamwork, creativity and trust.

**3397 Social Security: Helena Disability Determination**
Ste 1600
10 W 15th St
Helena, MT 59626-9704
406-441-1270
800-772-1213
TTY:406-441-1278
www.socialsecurity.gov

*Mary E. Glenn-Croft, Deputy Commissioner*
*Theresa L. Gruber, Assistant Deputy Commissioner*
*Francis Sotaski, Associate Commissioner*
*Linda M. Dorn, Associate Commissioner*

Social Security offers online information and services to third parties who do business with them.

## Nebraska

**3398 International Dyslexia Association: Nebraska Branch**
40 York Rd.
Baltimore, MD 21204
410-296-0232
800-222-3123
FAX: 410-321-5069
e-mail: carolyn.brandle@ne-ida.com
www.interdys.org

*Eric Q. Tridas, President*
*Cinthia Coletti Haan, Vice President*
*Ben Shifrin, Treasurer*
*Gad Elbeheri, Executive Director,Centre for Child Evaluation & Teaching*

The Nebraska Branch of the International Dyslexia Association is a 501(c)(3), non-profit organization dedicated to the study and treatment of dyslexia and related learning differences. This Branch was formed in 1981 to increase public awareness of dyslexia throughout Nebraska, and to serve individuals with dyslexia and their families. The organization includes professionals in the area of learning disabilities education, counseling and medicine as well as dylexics and their families and friends.

**3399 Nebraska Advocacy Services**
Ste 600
134 S 13th St
Lincoln, NE 68508-1930
402-474-3183
800-422-6691
FAX: 402-474-3274
e-mail: info@nebraskaadvocacyservices.org
nebraskaadvocacyservices.org

*Tom Ukinski, Chairperson*
*Jill Flagel, Vice-Chairperson*
*Graciela Sharif, Secretary*
*Victoria Rasmussen, Treasurer*

Offers protection and advocacy services to people with developmental disabilities or mental illness. Direct assistance provided if issue within broad case priorities. Sliding scale fee. Information and referral at no cost.

**3400 Nebraska Client Assistance Program**
P.O.Box 94987
301 Centennial Mall South
Lincoln, NE 68509-4987
402-471-3656
800-742-7594
e-mail: victoria.rasmussen@nebraska.gov
www.cap.state.ne.us/

The Nebraska Client Assistance Program (CAP) is a free service to help you find solutions if you are having problems with Vocational Rehabilitation, Nebraska Commission for the Blind and Visually Impaired or Centers for Independent Living.

**3401 Nebraska Commission for the Blind & Visually Impaired**
Ste 100
4600 Valley Rd
Lincoln, NE 68510-4844
402-471-2891
877-809-2419
FAX: 402-471-3009
e-mail: ncbvi.commission-board@nebraska.gov.
ncbvi.state.ne.us

*Pearl Van zandt, Executive Director*
*Carlos Servan, Deputy Director*
*Bob Deaton, Deputy Director*
*Barbara Loos, Chairman*

Offers services for the totally blind, legally blind, visually impaired, mentally retarded blind and more with health, counseling, educational, recreational, rehabilitation, computer training and professional training services.

**3402 Nebraska Department of Health & Human Services of Medically Handicapped Children's Prgm**
5th Fl
301 Centennial Mall S
Lincoln, NE 68508-2529
402-471-3121
800-383-4278
FAX: 402-471-3577
e-mail: mary.gordon@nebraska.gov

*Kerry Winterer, Chief Executive Officer*
*Amy Borer, Admininstrative Assistant,Division of Children and Family Services*
*Dan Howell, CEO,Beatrice State Developmental Center*

Maternal and child health, Title V, children with special health care needs; community based, statewide programs to facilitate diagnoses and care of children with disabilities and chronic medical conditions.

**3403 Nebraska Department of Health and Human Services, Division of Aging Services**
P.O.Box 95026
Lincoln, NE 68509-5026
402-471-2115
800-942-7830
FAX: 402-471-3577
e-mail: mary.gordon@nebraska.gov
www.hhss.ne.gov

*Kerry Winterer, Chief Executive Officer*
*Amy Borer, Admininstrative Assistant,Division of Children and Family Services*
*Dan Howell, CEO,Beatrice State Developmental Center*

The Council focuses on persons who experience a severe disability that occurs before the individual attains the age of 22, which includes persons with physical disabilities, mental/behavioral health conditions and persons that are served by the current state developmental disabilities system.

**3404 Nebraska Department of Mental Health**
4545 South 86th Street
Lincoln, NE 68526-2529
402-483-6990
888-210-8064
FAX: 402-483-7045
www.nmhc-clinics.com

*Thomas I. McPherson, Technical Coordinator*
*Jill Zlomke McPherson, Executive Director*
*Lee Zlomke, Clinical Director*
*Kelly Prather, Practice Administrator*

Nebraska Mental Health Centers is a family mental health clinic for people from all walks of life. Among the many services we provide are psychological evaluations, individual and group counseling, substance abuse care, neuropsychological services, domestic violence group intervention and help for victims of domestic violence, treatment for eating disorders, an ADHD clinic, Women's Counseling and much more.

**3405 Nebraska Planning Council on Developmental Disabilities**
Department of Health and Human Services
P.O.Box 95026
Lincoln, NE 68509-5026
402-471-2115
FAX: 402-471-3577
TTY:402-471-9570
e-mail: mary.gordon@nebraska.gov
www.hhs.state.ne.us/ddplanning

*Mary Gordon, Executive Director*
*Kerry Winterer, Chief Executive Officer*
*Amy Borer, Admininstrative Assistant,Division of Children and Family Services*
*Dan Howell, CEO,Beatrice State Developmental Center*

The Council focuses on persons who experience a severe disability that occurs before the individual attains the age of 22, which includes persons with physical disabilities, mental/behavioral health conditions and persons that are served by the current state developmental disabilities system.

**3406 Nebraska Workers' Compensation Court**
State of Nebraska
P.O.Box 98908
Lincoln, NE 68509-8908
402-471-6468
800-599-5155
FAX: 402-471-8231
www.wcc.ne.gov/

*Glenn W. Morton, Administrator*
*Susan K. Davis, Public Information Manager*
*Jacqueline J Boesen, General Counsel*
*Randall Cecrle, Information Technology Manager*

It is the web site of the Nebraska Workers' Compensation Court. The court maintains this web site to enhance public access and provide general information regarding workers' compensation in Nebraska.

**3407 Social Security: Lincoln Disability Determination**
Department of Education
P.O.Box 94987
Lincoln, NE 68509-4987
402-471-2295
800-772-1213
TTY:402-471-3659
e-mail: flloyd@nde4.nde.state.ne.us
www.socialsecurity.gov

*Mary E. Glenn-Croft, Deputy Commissioner*
*Theresa L. Gruber, Assistant Deputy Commissioner*
*Francis Sotaski, Associate Commissioner*
*Linda M. Dorn, Associate Commissioner*
Social Security offers online information and services to third parties who do business with them.

## Nevada

**3408 Aging and Disability Services Division**
3416 Goni Rd
Suite D 132
Carson City, NV 89706-8008
775-687-4210
800-992-0900
FAX: 775-687-0574
e-mail: adsd@adsd.nv.gov
nvaging.net

*Mary Liveratti, Administrator*
*Tina Gerber-Winn, Deputy Administrator*
*Janet Murphy, Deputy Administrator*
Provides services for seniors in Nevada including community based care. advocacy and volunteer programs. Call write or e-mail for more information.

**3409 Nevada Assistive Technology Project**
Ste 32
3656 Research Way
Carson City, NV 89706-7932
775-687-4452
888-337-3839
FAX: 775-687-3292
www.hr.state.nv.us

*Todd Butterworth, Manager*
Serves all ages and all disabilities through partnerships with community organizations. The NATP provides training, advocacy, funding, information and referral services, a newsletter and weekly television show.

**3410 Nevada Bureau of Vocational Rehabilitation**
1370 S. Curry Street
Carson City, NV 89703
775-684-4040
FAX: 775-684-4184
TTY:775-684-8400

*Maureen Cole, Administrator*
*Melaine Mason, Deputy Administrator, Operations*
*Janice John, Deputy Administrator, Programs*
*Mechelle Merrill, Rehabilitation Chief II*
Bureau of Vocational Rehabilitation is a state and federally funded program designed to help people with disabilities become employed and to help those already employed perform more successfully through training, counseling and other support methods.

**3411 Nevada Community Enrichment Program (NCEP)**
Suite 330N
2550 University Avenue
Minnesota, MN 55114
651-645-7271
800-466-7722
FAX: 651-645-0541
TTY: 800-627-352
e-mail: info@accessiblespace.org
accessiblespace.org

*Kay Knutson, Vice Chairman*
*Maynard Bostrom, Board Member*
*Patrick C. Horan, Board Member*
*Mary Lindgren, Board Member*
Comprehensive neurological rehabilitation and life skills training.

**3412 Nevada Developmental Disability Council**
Suite 202
896 W. Nye Ln.
Carson City, NV 89703
775-687-8619
FAX: 775-684-8626
e-mail: smanning@dhhs.nv.gov
www.nevadaddcouncil.org

*Lisa Antram, Chairman*
*Santa Perez, Vice Chairman*
*Sherry Manning, Executive Director*
The mission of the Nevada Developmental Disabilities Council is to provide resources at the community level which promote equal opportunity and life choices for people with disabilities through which they may positively contribute to Nevada society.

**3413 Nevada Disability Advocacy and Law Center -Sparks/Reno Office**
Suite C, Box 3
6039 Eldora Avenue
Las Vegas, NV 89146
702-257-8150
888-349-3843
FAX: 702-257-8170
e-mail: lasvegas@ndalc.org
www.ndalc.org

*Reggie Bennettr, Secretary/Treasurer*
*Jana Spoor, President*
*John Miller, Vice President*
*Bob Bennett, Chairman*
Nevada's protection and advocacy system for the human legal and service rights of individuals with disabilities. NDALC has offices in Reno/Sparks and Las Vegas, with services provided statewide.

**3414 Nevada Division for Aging: Las Vegas**
100 Liberty Way
Dover, NH 03820
888-398-8924
libertymutual.com

*Michael J. Babcockrs, Director*
*Marian L. Heard, Director*
*Martn P. Slark, Director*
Develops, coordinates and delivers a comprehensive support service system in order for Nevada' senior citizens to lead independent, meaningful and dignified lives.

**3415 Nevada Division of Mental Health and Developmental Services**
5865 Lakeshore Road
Buford, GA 30518
770-945-4441
FAX: 678-482-1965
e-mail: info@mhds.net
mhds.com

*Keith Mixon, CEO/President*
Offers treatment, prevention, education, habitation and rehabilitation for mental disorders. Works with advocacy groups, families, agencies and the community.

**3416 Social Security: Carson City Disability Determination**
1170 Harvard Way
Reno, NV 89502-2107
775-784-5221
800-772-1213
FAX: 775-784-5501
TTY: 800-325-0778
www.socialsecurity.gov

*Mary E. Glenn-Croft, Deputy Commissioner*
*Theresa L. Gruber, Assistant Deputy Commissioner*
*Francis Sotaski, Associate Commissioner*
*Linda M. Dorn, Associate Commissioner*
Social Security offers online information and services to third parties who do business with them.

**3417 State of Nevada Client Assistance Program**
Ste E
2450 Wrondel Way
Reno, NV 89502-3767
775-688-1440
800-633-9879
FAX: 775-688-1627
TTY: 800-633-9879
e-mail: webauer@nvdetr.org
To provide information to and safegaurd rights of applicants and clients or individuals who seek services such as vocational rehabilitation or independent living from agencies which provide those services under the Rehabilitation Act, and to provide information to individuals about the employment discrimination title of the Americans with Disabilities Act.

**3418 Workers Compensation Board Nevada**
6515 E Musser St
Carson City, NV 89714
775-684-7270
FAX: 775-687-6305

## New Hampshire

**3419 New Hampshire Workers Compensation Board**
46 Donovan St
Concord, NH 03301-2624
603-225-2841
800-698-2364
FAX: 603-226-6903
www.nhprimex.org

*Ty Gagne, CEO*
*Jonathan Kipp, Operations Manager*
*Julie Converse, Director of Finance*
*Carl Weber, Director of Member Services*
Primex3 stands ready to provide our school, municipal, and county government members with the most comprehensive coverages and services available to New Hampshire local government.

**3420 New Hampshire Assistive Technology Partnership Project**
Department of Education
State of New Hampshire
Concord, NH 03824
603-862-2260
FAX: 603-228-2468

*Jan Nisbet, Director*
*Mary Schuh, Associate Director*
*Eve Fralick, Associate Director*
The goal of the New Hampshire Assistive Technology Partnership Project is to increase access to assistive technology through the creation and support of consumer driven systems for the provision of state-of-the-art assistive technology products and services for citizens with disabilities in the state of New Hampshire.OUT OFBUSINESS

**3421 New Hampshire Bureau of Developmental Services**
Department of Health and Human Services
105 Pleasant St
Concord, NH 03301-3852
603-271-5034
FAX: 603-271-5166
e-mail: mertas@dhhs.state.nh.us
www.dhhs.state.nh.us

*Matthew Ertas, Director*
*Peggy Sue Greenwood, Administrative Assistant*
Developmental Services promotes opportunities for normal life experiences for persons with developmental disabilities and aquired brain disorders in all areas of community life: employment, housing, recreation, social relationships and community association. Services and supports are organized throught a central state office and ten private nonprofit community area agencies. Family support is provided to families of children with chronic health conditions or are developmentally disabled.

**3422 New Hampshire Client Assistance Program**
57 Regional Dr
Concord, NH 03301-8518
603-271-2773
800-852-3405
FAX: 603-271-2837
e-mail: Disability@nh.gov
www.state.nh.us/disability/caphomepage.html

*Bill Hagy, Ombudsman*
*John Richards, Executive Director*
*Jillian Shedd, Accessibility Coordinator*
*Gayle Baird, Accountant*
The Commission's goal is to remove the barriers, architectural, attitudinal or programmatic, that bar persons with disabilities from participating in the mainstream of society.

**3423 New Hampshire Commission for Human Rights**
2 Chenell Dr
Concord, NH 03301-8501
603-225-3431
800-735-2964
FAX: 603-224-3766
e-mail: humanrights@nhsa.state.nh.us
www.state.nh.us

*Peggy Mc Allister, Executive Director*
Enforces New Hampshire law against discrimination in housing, employment or public accomodations. Disability discrimination is prohibited under New Hampshire law. Takes formal charges and investigates them.

**3424 New Hampshire Department of Mental Health**
State Office Park S
Concord, NH 03301
603-226-0111
FAX: 603-271-5058

*Donald Shumway, Director*
*Paul Garmon*
*Tim Rourke, Religious Leader*
OUT OF ORDER

**3425 New Hampshire Developmental Disabilities Council**
Suite 22
21 Fruit Street
Concord, NH 03301
603-271-3236
800-852-3345
800-852-3236
FAX: 603-271-1156
TTY:800-735-2964
nhddc.org

*Sue Fox, Chairman*
*Peter Fleming, Co-Vice Chairman*
*Carol Stamatakis, Executive Director*
*David Ouellette, Project Director*
Offers information, referral and support services to disabled persons. A federally funded state agency.

**3426 New Hampshire Division of Elderly and Adult Services**
Bureau of Elderly & Adult Services
129 Pleasant St
Concord, NH 03301-3852
603-271-4680
800-351-1888
FAX: 603-271-4643
e-mail: pio@dhhs.state.nh.us
www.dhhs.state.nh.us

*Nicholas A. Toumpas, Comissioner*
*Mary Maggioncaida, Administrator*

The Bureau of Elderly and Adult Services provides a variety of social and long-term supports to adults age 60 and older and to adults between the ages of 18 and 60 who have a chronic illness or disability. These services range from home care, meals on wheels, care management, transportation assistance and assisted living to nursing home care.

**3427 New Hampshire Governor's Commission on Disability**
Ste 5
57 Regional Dr
Concord, NH 03301-8518
603-271-2773
800-852-3405
FAX: 603-271-2837
e-mail: Disability@nh.gov
www.nh.gov/disability

*John Richards, Executive Director*
*Jillian Shedd, Accessibility Coordinator*
*Carol Conforti-Adams, Information and Referral Specialist*
*Gayle Baird, Accountant*

The Commission's goal is to remove the barriers, architectural, attitudinal or programmatic, that bar persons with disabilities from participating in the mainstream of socie

**3428 New Hampshire Protection & Advocacy for Persons with Disabilities**
Disabilities Rights Center, Inc
18 Low Ave
Concord, NH 03301-4971
603-228-0432
800-834-1721
FAX: 603-225-2077
TTY: 800-834-1721
e-mail: advocacy@drcnh.org
drcnh.org

*Richard Cohen, Executive Director*
*Amy Messer, Legal Director*
*Kathryn Wallenstein, Vice President*
*James Fox, Staff Attorney*

Legal services for individuals with disabilities; I & R.

**3429 Social Security: Concord Disability Determination**
Ste 100
70 Commercial St
Concord, NH 03301-5005
603-224-1939
800-772-1213
TTY:800-325-0778
www.ssa.gov

*Mary E. Glenn-Croft, Deputy Commissioner*
*Theresa L. Gruber, Assistant Deputy Commissioner*
*Francis Sotaski, Associate Commissioner*
*Linda M. Dorn, Associate Commissioner*

Social Security offers online information and services to third parties who do business with them.

**3430 Workers Compensation Board New Hampshire**
PO Box 2076
Concord, NH 03302
603-271-3176
800-272-4353
FAX: 603-271-2668
e-mail: workerscomp@labor.state.nh.us
www.labor.state.nh.us

*Kathryn J. Barger, Director, Workers' Compensation Division*
*George N. Copadis, Commissioner of Labor*
*David M. Wihby, Deputy Commissioner*

The Department of Labor monitors Employers, Workers Compensation, and Insurance Carriers to insure that they are in compliance with NH Labor laws. These laws range from minimum wage, overtime, safety issues and workers compensation.

## New Jersey

**3431 Division of Developmental Disabilities**
210 South Broad Street
Trenton, NJ 08608
609-292-9742
800-922-7233
FAX: 609-777-0187
TTY: 609-633-7106
e-mail: advocate@drnj.org
www.njpanda.org

*James W Smith Jr, Executive Director*

New Jersey's designated protection and advocacy system for poeple with disabilities and provides legal, nonlegal individual and systems advocacy.

**3432 International Dyslexia Association: New Jersey Branch**
P.O.Box 32
Long Valley, NJ 07853
908-879-1179
e-mail: riegpainting@msn.com
www.interdys.org

*Eric Q. Tridas, M.D., President*
*Suzanne Carreker, Ph.D., CALT-, Vice President*
*Cinthia Coletti Haan, Vice President*
*Susan Lowell, M.A., B.C.E.T., Vice President*

The New Jersey Branch of The International Dyslexia Association is a 501(c)(3) non-profit, scientific and educational organization which was formed to increase public awareness of dyslexia in New Jersey. We have been serving individuals with dyslexia, their families, and professionals in the field in this community for more than 25 years.

**3433 New Jersey Commission for the Blind and Visually Impaired**
153 Halsey St
Newark, NJ 7102-2807
973-648-4691
877-685-8878
FAX: 973-693-5046
e-mail: Vito.DeSantis@dhs.state.nj.us
www.state.nj.us/humanservices/cbvi

*Patricia Dunn, Manager*
*James W Smith, Jr, Acting Commissioner*
*Jose Morales, Manager*

The mission of the New Jersey Commission for the Blind and Visually Impaired is to promote and provide services in the areas of education, employment, independence and eye health through informed choice and partnership with persons who are blind or visually impaired, their families and the community. Serves Bergen, Essex, Hudson, Morris, Passaic, Sussex and Warren Counties.

**3434 New Jersey Department of Aging**
210 South Broad Street
3rd Floor
Trenton, NJ 08608
609-292-9742
800-922-7233
FAX: 609-777-0187
TTY: 609-633-7106
e-mail: advocate@drnj.org
www.drnj.org

*Ellen Catanese, Director of Administration/Advocacy*
*Joseph B. Young, Executive Director*
*Marie Davis, Executive Secretary/Office Manager*
*Lillie Lowe-Reid, CAP Coordinator/PABSS Project Director*

**3435 New Jersey Department of Health/Special Child Health Services**
New Jersey Department of Health and Senior Service
P.O.Box 360
Trenton, NJ 08625-0360
609-777-7778
FAX: 609-292-3580
e-mail: plisciotto@doh.state.nj.us
http://www.nj.gov/health/fhs/sch/

*Jennifer Velez, ESQ, Commissioner*
Provides services for New Jersey children that will prevent or reduce the effects of a developmental delay, chronic illness or behavioral disorder.

**3436 New Jersey Division of Mental Health Services**
Department Human Services
50 E State St
Trenton, NJ 8608-1715
609-777-0686
800-382-6717
FAX: 609-341-3333
www.state.nj.us/humanservices

*Jennifer Velez, ESQ, Commissioner*
Oversees the public mental health system for the state of New Jersey. Operates six regional and specialty psychiatric hospitals, and contracts with over 125 not-for-profit agencies to provide a comprehensive system of community mental health services throughout all counties in the state.

**3437 New Jersey Governor's Liaison to the Office of Disability Employment Policy**
John Fitch Plaza
Trenton, NJ 08625
609-659-9045
FAX: 609-633-9271
e-mail: cmycoff@dol.state.nj.us
www.state.nj.us/labor

*Harold J. Wriths, Commissioner*
*Frederick J. Zavaglia, Chief of Staff*
*Aaron R. Fichtner, Ph.D., Deputy Commissioner*
*Brian T. Murray, Director of Communications & Marketing*
The Division of Vocational Rehabilitation Services provides vocational rehabilitation services to prepare and place in employment eligilbe individuals with disabilities who, because of their disabling conditions, would otherwise be unable to secure and/or mantain employment

**3438 New Jersey Protection & Advocacy for Persons with Disabilities**
210 South Broad Street
3rd Floor
Trenton, NJ 08608
609-292-9742
800-922-7233
FAX: 609-777-0187
TTY: 609-633-7106
e-mail: advocate@drnj.org
www.drnj.org

*Ellen Catanese, Director of Administration/Advocacy*
*Joseph B. Young, Executive Director*
*Marie Davis, Executive Secretary/Office Manager*
*Lillie Lowe-Reid, CAP Coordinator/PABSS Project Director*

**3439 Regional ADA Technical Assistance Center**
United Cerebral Palsy Associations of New Jersey
203 Dolgen Hall
Ithaca, NY 14853
607-255-6686
800-949-4232
FAX: 607-255-2763
e-mail: northeastada@cornell.edu
http://www.northeastada.org/

*LaWanda H. Cook, Ph.D., Extension Associate/Training Specialist*
*Hannah Rudstam, Ph.D., Director of Training*
*Erin Sember-Chase, Project Coordinator and Technical Assistance Coordinator*
*Katie Steigerwalt, Project Assistant*

**3440 Social Security Administration**
6401 Security Blvd.
Baltimore, MD 21235
800-772-1213
TTY:800-325-0778
www.ssa.gov

Social Security disability is a social insurance program that workers and employers pay for with their Social Security taxes. Eligibility is based on your work history, and the amount of your benefit is based on your earnings. Social Security also has a disability program for people with limited income and resources- the Supplemental Security Income (SSI) program. For more information on these federal programs, please call our nationwide toll-free number.

## New Mexico

**3441 New Mexico Aging and Long-Term Services Department**
2550 Cerrillos Rd
Santa Fe, NM 87505-3260
505-476-4799
866-451-2901
FAX: 505-476-4836
www.nmaging.state.nm.us

*Gino Rinaldi, Deputy Secretary*
*Retta Ward, Secretary*
*Jason Sanchez, Administrative Services Division*
*Patricia Barton, IT Manager*
Information and services for seniors, people with disabilities and their families.

**3442 New Mexico Client Assistance Program**
Ste 204
1720 Louisiana Blvd NE
Albuquerque, NM 87110- 7070
505-256-3100
800-432-4682
FAX: 505-256-3184
e-mail: info@nmpanda.org
http://www.drnm.org

*Michael J. Rourke, President*
*Adam Carrasco, Vice President*
*Jonathan Toledo, Secretary Treasurer*
*Gail Falconer, Chairperson*
The mission of Disability Rights New Mexico (DRNM) is to protect, promote and expand the legal and civil rights of persons with disabilities. DRNM is an independent, private nonprofit agency operating federally mandated and other advocacy programs in pursuit of this mission.

**3443 New Mexico Commission for the Blind**
Bldg 4, Suite 100
2905 Rodeo Park Dr E
Santa Fe, NM 87505-6342
505-476-4479
888-513-7968
FAX: 505-476-4475
e-mail: greg.trapp@state.nm.us
http://www.cfb.state.nm.us/

*Helen Savoie, Commissioner*
*Arthur A. Schreiber, Chairman*
*Dallas Allen, Commissioner*
*Greg Trapp, Executive Director*
Offers services for the totally blind, legally blind, visually impaired, mentally retarded blind and more with health, counseling, educational, recreational, rehabilitation, computer training and professional training services.

**3444 New Mexico Department of Health: Children's Medical Services**
1190 S Saint Francis Dr
Santa Fe, NM 87505-4173
505-827-2613
877-890-4692
FAX: 505-827-2530
e-mail: lchristiansen@doh.state.nm
http://nmhealth.org/phd/cms.shtml

*Lynn Christiansen, LMSW, Program Manager*
*Elizabeth T. Mathews, Medical Director*
*Carla A. Ortiz, RN, BSN, Nurse Consultant*
*Susan Chacon, MSW, Coordinator*

Title V MCH Program for children with special health care needs from birth to age 21 years. Services provided include: diagnosis, medical intervention, clinics and service coordination.

**3445 New Mexico Governor's Committee on Concerns of the Handicapped**
491 Old Santa Fe Trl
Santa Fe, NM 87501-2753
505-476-0412
877-696-1470
FAX: 505-827-6328
e-mail: gcd@state.nm.us
http://www.gcd.state.nm.us/

*Jim Parker, Director*
*Anthony Cahill, Chair*
*Cory Valencia, Vice Chair*
*John Block, III, Deputy Director*

**3446 New Mexico Protection & Advocacy for Persons with Disabilities**
Ste 204
1720 Louisiana Blvd NE
Albuquerque, NM 87110- 7070
505-256-3100
800-432-4682
FAX: 505-256-3184
e-mail: info@nmpanda.org
http://www.drnm.org/

*Michael J. Rourke, President*
*Adam Carrasco, Vice President*
*Jonathan Toledo, Secretary Treasurer*
*Gail Falconer, Chairperson*

The mission of Disability Rights New Mexico (DRNM) is to protect, promote and expand the legal and civil rights of persons with disabilities. DRNM is an independent, private nonprofit agency operating federally mandated and other advocacy programs in pursuit of this mission.

**3447 New Mexico Technology Assistance Program**
435 Saint Michaels Dr
Ste D
Santa Fe, NM 87505-7679
505-827-8535
800-866-2253
FAX: 505-954-8608
TTY: 800-659-4915
e-mail: julie.martinez@state.nm.us
www.nmtap.com

*Julie Martinez, Program Director*

Examines and works to eliminate barriers to obtaining assistive technology in New Mexico. Has established a statewide program for coordinating assistive technology services; is designed to assist people with disabilities to locate, secure, and maintain assistive technology.

**3448 New Mexico Workers Compensation Administration**
P.O.Box 27198
Albuquerque, NM 87125-7198
505-841-6000
800-255-7965
FAX: 505-841-6009
http://www.workerscomp.state.nm.us/

*Ned S. Fuller, Director*
*Robert E. Doucette, Executive Deputy Director*
*Darin A. Childers, General Counsel*
*Thomas E. Dow, Executive Deputy Director*

Regulates workers' compensation in New Mexico.

**3449 Social Security: Santa Fe Disability Determination**
6401 Security Blvd.
Baltimore, MD 21235
800-772-1213
TTY:800-325-0778
www.socialsecurity.gov

**3450 Southwest Branch of the International Dyslexia Association**
International Dyslexia Association
3915 Carlisle Blvd. NE
Albuquerque, NM 87107
505-255-8234
800-222-3123
FAX: 505-262-8547
e-mail: swida@southwestida.org
southwestida.com

*Carilyn Alarid, President*
*Cathleen Tomlinson, Vice President*
*Erin Brown, Recording Secretary*
*Mary Poirier Gilroy, Corresponding Secretary*

Provides free information and referral services for diagnosis and tutoring for parents, educators, physicians, and individuals with dyslexia. The voice of our membership is heard in 48 countries. Membership includes yearly journal and quarterly newsletter. Call for conference dates.

**3451 Workers Compensation Board New Mexico**
P.O.Box 27198
Albuquerque, NM 87125-7198
505-841-6000
800-255-7965
FAX: 505-841-6009
http://www.workerscomp.state.nm.us/

*Ned S. Fuller, Director*
*Robert E. Doucette, Executive Deputy Director*
*Darin A. Childers, General Counsel*
*Thomas E. Dow, Executive Deputy Director*

Regulates workers' compensation in New Mexico.

## New York

**3452 Albany County Department for Aging and Albany Social Services**
162 Washington Ave
Albany, NY 12210-2304
518-447-7177
FAX: 518-447-7188
e-mail: aging@albanycounty.com
albanycounty.com

*Judy L. Coyne, Commissioner*
*Kathleen M. Dalton, Ph.D., Commissioner*

The Point of Entry access line provides information and assistance and comprehensive referrals, and or assessments for the elderly, adults and children with disabilities, their family, or service providers.

**3453 International Dyslexia Association of NY: Buffalo Branch**
2491 Emery Rd
South Wales, NY 14139-9408
716-687-2030
800-222-3123
e-mail: bufida@gow.org
www.interdys.org

*Timothy Madigan PhD, President*

**3454 Jawonio**
260 N Little Tor Road
New City, NY 10956-2627
845-708-2000
FAX: 845-634-7731
TTY:845-639-3521
www.jawonio.org

*Jill Warner, Executive Director & CEO*
*Marilyn Astarita, Chief Operating Officer Oversight of all Programs, Corporate Complianc*
*Diana Hess, Chief Communications Officer*
*Mark Campione, Chief Financial Officer*
A dedicated community resource providing services to more than 500 children and adults annually. Provide early intervention, day care and pre-school special ed to our children. Job training, day habilitation, recreation, medical and service coordination for adults.

**3455 Jawonio Vocational Center**
260 N Little Tor Rd
New City, NY 10956-2627
845-708-2000
FAX: 845-634-7731
TTY:845-639-3521
jawonio.org

*Jill Warner, Executive Director & CEO*
*Marilyn Astarita, Chief Operating Officer Oversight of all Programs, Corporate Complianc*
*Diana Hess, Chief Communications Officer*
*Mark Campione, Chief Financial Officer*
A dedicated community resource providing services to more than 500 children and adults annually. Provide early intervention, day care and pre-school special ed to our children. Job training, day habilitation, recreation, medical and service coordination for adults.

**3456 NYS Commission on Quality of Care & Advocacy for Persons with Disabilities**
401 State St
Schenectady, NY 12305-2300
518-388-2892
FAX: 518-388-2890
e-mail: marcelc@cqc.state.ny.us
www.cqcapd.state.ny.us

*Andrew M. Cuomo, Governor*
*Roger Bearden, Chair*
*Bruce Blower, Member*
*Patricia Okoniewski, Member*

**3457 NYSARC**
393 Delaware Ave
Delmar, NY 12054-3094
518-439-8311
800-724-2094
FAX: 518-439-1893
e-mail: info@nysarc.org
nysarc.org

*John A. Schuppenhauer, President*
*Anne Marie Lockhart, Senior Vice President*
*Marie Lockhart, Treasurer*
*Patricia Campanella, Vice President*

**3458 National Alliance on Mental Illness of New York State**
260 Washington Ave
Albany, NY 12210-1336
518-462-2000
800-950-3228
FAX: 518-462-3811
e-mail: info@naminys.org
www.naminys.org

*Sherry Grenz, President*
*Donald Capone, Executive Director*
*Sharon Clairmont, Finance & Business Office Dir.*
*Matthew Shapiro, Development/Events Coordinator*

**3459 New State Office of Mental Health Agency**
Office of Mental Health
44 Holland Ave
Albany, NY 12229
518-474-4403
800-597-8481
FAX: 518-474-2149
www.omh.state.ny.us

*Mike Hogan, Commissioner*
Promoting the mental health of all New Yorkers with a particular focus on providing hope and recovery for adults with serious mental illness and children with serious emotional disturbances.

**3460 New York Client Assistance Program**
855 Central Avenue
Suite 110
Albany, NY 12206
518-459-6422
FAX: 518-459-7847
TTY:518-459-6422
www.nls.org/caplist.htm

**3461 New York Department of Handicapped Children**
Department of Heath Education
Corning Tower
Empire State Plaza
Albany, NY 12237
518-456-0665
866-881-2809
FAX: 518-456-1126
e-mail: jcrucetti@albanycounty.com
www.health.state.ny.us

*Dr James B. Crucetti, MD, MPH, Commisioner*

**3462 New York State Commission for the Blind**
52 Washington St
Rensselaer, NY 12144-2796
518-473-7793
FAX: 518-486-7550

*Madeline Raciti, Manager*
Offers services for the totally blind, legally blind, visually impaired, mentally retarded blind and more with health, counseling, educational, recreational, rehabilitation, computer training and professional training services.

**3463 New York State Commission on Quality of Care**
401 State St
Schenectady, NY 12305-2300
518-388-2892
FAX: 518-388-2890
e-mail: marcelc@cqc.state.ny.us
www.cqc.state.ny.us

*Andrew M. Cuomo, Governor*
*Roger Bearden, Chair*
*Bruce Blower, Member*
*Patricia Okoniewski, Member*

**3464 New York State Congress of Parents and Teachers**
1 Wembley Ct
Albany, NY 12205-6258
518-452-8808
877-569-7782
FAX: 518-452-8105
e-mail: pta.office@nyspta.org
nyspta.org

*Maria Fletcher, President*
Parent Teacher Association and PTA are registered service marks of the National Congress of Parents and Teachers (National PTA). Only those groups chartered by the New York State PTA are entitled to use the name PTA. Any other use constitutes trademark infringement.

**3465 New York State Office of Advocates for Persons with Disabilities**
Ste 1001
1 Empire State Plz
Albany, NY 12223-1100
518-449-7860
800-522-4369
FAX: 518-473-6005
e-mail: oapwdinfo@oapwd.org
www.oapwd.org

*Gary O'Brien, Chair Commissioner*
Provides information and referral services; administers NYS Tech Art Project; promotes implementation of disability-related laws.

**3466 New York State Office of Mental Health**
44 Holland Ave
Albany, NY 12229-1
518-474-4403
800-597-8481
FAX: 518-474-2149
www.omh.state.ny.us

*Michael Hogan, Ph.D.*
Promoting the mental health of all New Yorkers with a particular focus on providing hope and recovery for adults with serious mental illness and children with serious emotional disturbances.

**3467 New York State TRAID Project**
New York State Commisionon Qualityof Careand Advoc
Ste 1001
1 Empire State Plz
Albany, NY 12223-1100
518-449-7860
800-522-4369
FAX: 518-473-6005
www.oatwd.org

*Cliff Sigfride, Manager*

**3468 Parent to Parent of New York State**
500 Balltown Rd
Schenectady, NY 12304-2247
518-381-4350
800-305-8817
FAX: 518-393-9607
e-mail: info@parenttoparentnys.org
parenttoparentnys.org

*Jim Costello, President*
*Linda Coull, Secretary*
*Henrietta Messier, Vice President*
*Louise Nitto, Treasurer*
Parent to Parent of NYS, which began in 1994, is a statewide not for profit organization established to support and connect families of individuals with special needs. The 13 offices, located throughout NYS, are staffed by Regional Coordinators, who are parents or close relatives of individuals with special needs.

**3469 Protection and Advocacy Agency of NY**
401 State St
Schenectady, NY 12305-2303
518-388-2892
FAX: 518-388-2890
e-mail: marcelc@cqc.state.ny.us
www.cqc.state.ny.us

*Andrew M. Cuomo, Governor*
*Roger Bearden, Chair*
*Bruce Blower, Member*
*Patricia Okoniewski, Member*

**3470 Regional Early Childhood Director Center**
One Commerce Plaza
Room 1609
Albany, NY 12234
518-474-2925
800-222-5627
e-mail: accesadm@mail.nysed.gov
www.vesid.nysed.gov

Provides information, support and referral assistance to parents and professionals who are concerned with chilren with special needs or handicapping condition between the ages of birth to five.

**3471 Schools And Services For Children With Autism Spectrum Disorders.**
Fl 5
116 E 16th St
New York, NY 10003-2164
212-677-4650
FAX: 212-254-4070
e-mail: info@resourcesnyc.org
www.resourcesnyc.org

*Rachel Howard, Executive Director*
*John Hart, Director of Program Operations*
This publication fun resource for children provides extreme coverage of services for children with autism, asbergez syndrome, and/or PDD.

**3472 Singeria/Metropolitan Parent Center**
2082 Lexington Ave.
4th Floor
New York, NY 10035
212-643-2840
866-867-9665
FAX: 212-496-5608
e-mail: intake@sinergiany.org
sinergiany.org

*Myrta Cuadra-Lash, Executive Director*

**3473 Social Security: Albany Disability Determination**
1 Clinton Ave
Albany, NY 12207
518-431-4051
800-772-1213
TTY:518-431-4050
www.ssa.gov

*Thomas A Robertson, Assistant Commissioner*

**3474 State Agency for the Blind and Visually Impaired**
52 Washington St
Rensselaer, NY 12144-2834
518-473-7793
866-871-3000
FAX: 518-486-7550
e-mail: info@ocfs.state.ny.us
www.ocfs.state.ny.us

**3475 State Education Agency Rural Representative**
89 Washington Avenue
Albany, NY 12234
518-474-3852
FAX: 518-473-2860
e-mail: RegentsOffice@mail.nysed.gov
www.nysed.gov

*Merryl H. Tisch, CHANCELLOR*
*Anthony S. Bottar, VICE CHANCELLOR*

**3476 State Mental Health Representative for Children and Youth**
44 Holland Ave
Albany, NY 12229
518-473-6328
e-mail: cocompz@omh.state.ny.us

*David Woodlock, Deputy Commissioner*

**3477 State Mental Retardation Program**
44 Holland Ave
Albany, NY 12229
518-474-6601
FAX: 518-473-1271
omr.state.ny.us

*Diana Ritter, Manager*

**3478 United We Stand of New York**
98 Moore St
Brooklyn, NY 11206-3326
718-302-4313
FAX: 718-302-4315
e-mail: uwsofny@aol.com
www.uwsony.org

*Lourdes Rivera-Putz, Executive Director*
*Lourdes Figueroa, Intake/Receptionist*
*Carmen Soltero, Outreach/Trainer*
*Martha Vizcarrondo, Family Support Associate*
Assists families with improving the quality of life for all individuals with disabilities.

**3479 University Afiliated Program/Rose F Kennedy Center**
1971
1300 Morris Park Avenue
Bronx, NY 10461
718-430-2000
e-mail: information@einstein.yu.edu
www.aecom.yu.edu/cerc

**3480 University of Rochester Medical Center**
601 Elmwood Ave
Rochester, NY 14642
585-275-8762
FAX: 585-275-3366
e-mail: phil_davidson@urmc.rochester.edu
www.urmc.rochester.edu/strong/scdd

*Brad Berk, MD, PhD, CEO*

**3481 VESID**
New York State Education Department
One Commerce Plz Room 1609
Albany, NY 12234
800-222-5627
FAX: 518-474-8802
e-mail: accesadm@mail.nysed.gov
www.acces.nysed.gov/vr/

*Dr Rebecca Cort, Deputy Commissioner*
Vocational and educational services for individuals with disabilities.

**3482 VSA Arts of New York City**
Apt 15n
1805 215th St
Bayside, NY 11360-2123
718-225-6305
FAX: 717-225-6305
e-mail: bbvsanyc@msn.com
www.vsarts.org

*Michael M. Kaiser, President*
*David M. Rubenstein, Chairman*
Provides art, educational and creative expression experiences to thousands of children, youth, and adults with disabilities who reside in the five boroughs of New York City. It provides opportunities for people with disabilities to demonstrate their accomplishments in the arts and foster increased understanding and acceptance.

**3483 Westchester Institute for Human Development**
Cedarwood Hall
Valhalla, NY 10595
914-493-8150
e-mail: wihd@wihd.org
www.wihd.org

*Ansley Bacon PhD, President/CEO*
*David O'Hara PhD, COO*
WIHD advances policies and practices that foster the healthy development and ensure the safety of all children, strengthen families and communities, and promote health and well-being among people of all ages with disabilities and special health care needs.

**3484 Workers Compensation Board New York**
328 State Street
Schenectady, NY 12305-2318
518-462-8880
877-632-4996
FAX: 518-473-1415
e-mail: general_information@wcb.ny.gov
www.wcb.state.ny.us

*Richard A. Bell, Commissioner*

## North Carolina

**3485 Developmental Disability Services Section**
Building 325n
Albemarle
Raleigh, NC 27699
919-420-7901
FAX: 919-420-7917
www.dhhs.state.nc.us/mhddsas/

*Diana Simmons, Human Resources Manager*
*Ureh N. Lekwauwa, Chief, Clinical Policy*
Makes policies and monitors public services and supports to people with mental illness, developmental disabilities and substance abuse throughout North Carolina.

**3486 International Dyslexia Association: North Carolina Branch**
40 York Rd.
4th Floor
Baltimore, MD 21204
410-296-0232
FAX: 410-321-5069
www.interdys.org

*Lee Grossman, Executive Director*
The North Carolina Branch of The International Dyslexia Association (NCIDA) is a 501 (c)(3) non-profit, scientific and organization dedicated to educating the public about the learning disability, dyslexia. The North Carolina Branch has four objectives: to increase awareness in the dyslexic and general community; to network with other learning disability groups and legislators in education;to increase membership and provide services that will strengthen members presence in their communities

**3487 North Carolina Workers Compensation Board**
4340 Mail Service Center
Raleigh, NC 27699-4340
919-833-8887
FAX: 919-715-0282
e-mail: infospec@ic.nc.gov
www.ic.nc.gov

*Julian Bunn, Owner*

**3488 North Carolina Assistive Technology Project**
Ste 101
1110 Navaho Dr
Raleigh, NC 27609-7322
919-872-2298
FAX: 919-850-2792
e-mail: ncatp@minespring.com
ncatp.org

*Ricki Cook, Project Director*
*Annette Lauber, Funding Specialist*
*Jacquelyne Gordon, Consumer Resource Specialist*
*Tony Hiatt, Executive Director*
The North Carolina Assistive Technology Project exists to create a statewide, consumer-responsive system of assistive technology services for all North Carolinians with disabilities. The project's activities impact children and adults with disabilities across all aspects of their lives.

**3489 North Carolina Children & Youth Branch**
North Carolina Publc of Health
1928 Mail Service Ctr
Raleigh, NC 27699-1900
919-839-6262
FAX: 919-733-8034
e-mail: cathy.kluttz@nemail.net
www.nchealthychilderen.com

*Lawrence J Wheeler, Manager*
*Cathy Kluttz, Unit Manager Special Service*
*Dianne Tyson, Help Line Manager*
*Ran Coble, Executive Director*

**3490 North Carolina Client Assistance Program**
2806 Mail Service Ctr
Raleigh, NC 27699-2800
919-855-3600
800-215-7227
FAX: 919-715-2456
e-mail: nccap@dhhs.nc.gov
cap.state.nc.us

*Kathy Brack, Director*
*Diane Rawdarowicz, Client Advocate*
*Sharon Wisner, Client Advocate*
A federally funded program designed to assist individuals with disabilities in understanding and using rehabilitation services. CAP serves as an integral part of the rehabilitation system by advising and informing individuals of all services and benefits available to them through programs authorized under both the Rehabilitation Act and Title 1 of the Americans with Disabilities Act.

**3491 North Carolina Developmental Disabilities**
Ste Gl103
1001 Navaho Dr
Raleigh, NC 27609-7368
919-821-2777
800-357-6916
FAX: 919-821-4778
e-mail: Holly.Riddle@ncmail.net
www.nc-ddc.org

*Caroline Valand, Executive Director*
A planning council established to assure that individuals with developmental disabilities and their families participate in the planning of and have access to culturally competent services, supports, and other assistance and opportunities that promote independence, productivity, and integration and inclusion into the community; and to promote, through systemic change, capacity building and advocacy activities, a consumer and family-centered comprehensive system.

**3492 North Carolina Division of Aging**
2101 Mail Service Ctr
Raleigh, NC 27699-2100
919-733-3983
FAX: 919-733-0443
ncdhhs.gov

*Dennis Streets, Manager*

**3493 North Carolina Industrial Commission**
4340 Mail Service Center
Raleigh, NC 27699-4340
919-854-1322
FAX: 919-854-9857
e-mail: infospec@ic.nc.gov
www.ic.nc.gov

*J Howard Bunn Jr, Chairman*
*Peg Dorer, Executive Director*

**3494 Social Security Administration**
4701 Old Wake Forest Rd
Raleigh, NC 27609-4919
877-803-6311
800-772-1213
800-325-0778
FAX: 919-790-2860
TTY:919-790-2773
e-mail: www.socialsecurity.gov
www.socialsecurity.gov

Provides information on how to obtain social security through a disability.

## North Dakota

**3495 Division of Mental Health and Substance Abuse**
Ste 1c
1237 W Divide Ave
Bismarck, ND 58501-1208
701-328-8920
800-755-2719
FAX: 701-328-8969
e-mail: dhsmhsas@nd.gov
www.nd.gov/humanservices

*Jo Anne Hoesel, Manager*
*Don Wright, Ass't. Director Substance Abuse*
The Department of Human Services' Mental Health and Substance Abuse Services Division provides leadership for the planning, development, and oversight of a system of care for children, adults, and families with severe emotional disorders, mental illness, and/or substance abuse issues.

**3496 North Dakota Workers Compensation Board**
50 E Front Ave
Bismarck, ND 58504
701-328-3800
800-777-5033
FAX: 701-329-9911
TTY: 701-328-3786
www.ndworkerscomp.com

*Brent Edison, Director*

**3497 North Dakota Client Assistance Program**
Ste 3
1237 W Divide Ave
Bismarck, ND 58501-1208
701-328-8947
800-207-6122
TTY:701-328-8968
e-mail: cap@state.nd.us
www.nd.gov/cap

*Dennis Lyon, CEO*
CAP assists clients and client applicants of North Dakota Vocational Rehabilitation services, Tribal Vocational Rehabilitation, or Independent Living services.

**3498 North Dakota Department of Human Resources**
Ste 6
1237 W Divide Ave
Bismarck, ND 58501-1208
701-328-5300
800-451-8693
FAX: 701-328-5320
e-mail: dhsaging@nd.gov
www.nd.gov

*Shane Goettle, Manager*

**3499 North Dakota Department of Human Services**
600 E Boulevard Ave
Dept 325
Bismarck, ND 58505-0250
701-328-2310
800-472-2622
FAX: 701-328-2359
e-mail: dhseo@nd.gov
www.nd.gov/dhs

*Carol K Olson, Executive Director*
Provides services that help vulnerable North Dakotans of all ages to maintain or enhance their quality of life, which may be threatened by lack of financial resources, emotional crises, disabling conditions, or an inability to protect themselves.

**3500 Protection & Advocacy Project**
1984
Ste 409
400 E Broadway Ave
Bismarck, ND 58501-4071
701-328-2950
800-472-2670
FAX: 701-328-3934
e-mail: panda@nd.gov
ndpanda.org

*Teresa Larsen, Executive Director*
The Protection and Advocacy is a state agency whose purpose is to advocate for and protect the rights of people with disabilities. The Protection and Advocacy Project has programs to serve people with developmental disabilities, mental illnesses and other types of disabilities. The projects programs and services are free to eligible individuals.

**3501 Social Security: Bismarck Disability Determination**
1680 E Capitol Ave
Bismarck, ND 58501-5603
701-250-4200
800-772-1213
TTY:701-250-4620
ssa.gov

**3502 Workers Compensation Board North Dakota**
4007 State St
Bismarck, ND 58503-689
701-328-3800
FAX: 701-328-3820

*Sandy Blunt, CEO*

## Ohio

**3503 Epilepsy Council of Greater Cincinnati**
Ste 550
895 Central Ave
Cincinnati, OH 45202-5700
513-721-2905
877-804-2241
FAX: 513-721-0799
e-mail: ecgc@fuse.net
ecgc-ohnky.net

*Kathy Stewart, Executive Director*

**3504 International Dyslexia Association: Central Ohio Branch**
40 York Rd.
4th Floor
Baltimore, MD 21204
410-296-0232
FAX: 410-321-5069
e-mail: cybdischultz@columbus.rr.com
www.interdys.org

*Lee Grossman, Executive Director*
Provides free information and referral services for diagnosis and tutoring for parents, educators, physicians, and individuals with dyslexia. The voice of our membership is heard in 48 countries. Membership includes yearly journal and quarterly newsletter. Call for conference dates. Other locations available in Ohio state.

**3505 Ohio Bureau for Children with Medical Handicaps**
Ohio Department of Health
P.O.Box 1603
Columbus, OH 43216-1603
614-466-1700
800-755-4769
FAX: 614-728-3616
e-mail: bcmh@odh.ohio.gov
www.odh.ohio.gov

*James Bryant Md, Bureau Chief*
*Alvin Jackson, MD, Director*
Provides funding for the diagnosis, treatment and coordination of services for eligible Ohio children, under age 21, with medical handicaps; conducts quality assurance activities to establish standards of care and determine unmet needs of children with handicaps and their families; collaborates with public health nurses to increase access to care; and assists families to access and use third party resources. Conducts a separate program for adults with cystic fibrosis.

**3506 Ohio Bureau of Worker's Compensation**
30 W Spring St
Columbus, OH 43215-2256
800-644-6292
FAX: 877-520-6446
TTY:800-292-4833
e-mail: ombudsperson@bwc.state.oh.us
ohiobwc.com

*Stephen Buehrer, Administrator/CEO*
*Dale Hamilton, Chief Operating Officer (COO)*
To provide a quality, customer-focused workers' compensation insurance system for Ohio's employers and employees.

**3507 Ohio Client Assistance Program**
Rm 120
30 E Broad St
Columbus, OH 43215-3414
614-466-7264
800-282-9181
FAX: 614-752-4197
TTY: 614-728-2553
www.olrs.ohio.gov

*Donald Bishop, Executive Director*

**3508 Ohio Department of Aging**
1982
50 W Broad St
Fl 9
Columbus, OH 43215-3363
614-466-5500
866-243-5678
888-243-5678
FAX: 614-466-5741
TTY:614-466-6191
www.aging.ohio.gov

*Bonnie Kantor-Burman, Director*
*John Ratliff, Public Information Officer*
The department serves and represents about 2 million Ohioans age 60 & older. They advocate for the needs of all older citizens with emphasis on improving the quality of life, helping senior citizens live active, healthy, & independent lives, & promoting positive attitudes toward aging & older people. Committed to helping the frail elderly who choose to remain at home by providing home & community based services, their goal is to promote the level of choice, independence & self-care.

**3509 Ohio Department of Mental Health**
Fl 8
30 E Broad St
Columbus, OH 43215-3414
614-466-4775
877-275-6364
FAX: 614-752-8410
e-mail: uhricks@mh.state.oh.us
mh.state.oh.us

*Michael Hogan, Director*
*Christine Vincenty, Manager*

**3510 Ohio Developmental Disabilities Council**
899 E Broad St, Ste 203
Columbus, OH 43205
614-466-5205
800-766-7426
FAX: 614-466-0298
e-mail: carla.sykes@dmr.state.oh.us
www.ddc.ohio.gov

*Carolyn Knight, Executive Director*
The Ohio Developmental Disabilities Council is one of 55 councils found in all states and territories which provides funding for systems change grant projects. The DD Council is a planning and advocacy agency that seeks to improve the lives of Ohioans with disabilities.

**3511 Ohio Developmental Disability Council (ODDC)**
899 E Broad St, Ste 203
Columbus, OH 43205
614-466-5205
800-766-7426
FAX: 614-466-0298
www.ddc.ohio.gov

*Carolyn Knight, Executive Director*

**3512 Ohio Governor's Council on People with Disabilities**
400 E Campus View Blvd
Columbus, OH 43235-4685
614-438-1200
800-282-4536
e-mail: RSC.Webmaster@rsc.state.oh.us
gcpd.ohio.gov

*Kevin Miller , Executive Director*
*Marcella Eblin, Secretary*

The Governor's Council on People with Disabilities exists to: Advise the Governor and General Assembly on statewide disability issues, promote the value of diversity, dignity and the quality of life for people with disabilities, be a catalyst to create systemic change promoting awareness of disability-related issues that will ultimately benefit all citizens of Ohio, Educate and advocate for: partnerships at the local, state and national level, promotion of equality, access and independence.

**3513 Ohio Rehabilitation Services Commission**
400 E Campus View Blvd
Columbus, OH 43235-4604
614-438-1200
800-282-4536
e-mail: RSC.Webmaster@rsc.state.oh.us
www.state.oh.us/rsc

*Kevin Miller , Executive Director*

RSC is Ohio's state agency that provides vocational rehabilitation (VR) services to help people with disabilities become employed and independent. We also offer a variety of services to Ohio businesses, resulting in quality jobs for individuals who have disabilities.

**3514 Ohio Women, Infants, & Children ProgramOhio Department of Health**
246 N High St
Columbus, OH 43215-2406
614-644-8006
FAX: 614-564-2470
odh.ohio.gov

*Michele Frizzell, Chief, Bureau of Nutrition Svcs.*

**3515 Social Security: Columbus Disability Determination**
Suite 160
90 E Washington Bridge Rd
Worthington, OH 43085
614-888-5339
800-772-1213
TTY:614-288-0226
www.socialsecurity.gov

*Jo Anne B Barnhart, Commissioner*
*Mary B Chatel, Executive Director of Disability*

## Oklahoma

**3516 Oklahoma Workers Compensation Board**
Department of Labor
3017 N. Stiles, Suite 100
Oklahoma City, OK 73105
405-521-6100
888-69 -353
FAX: 405-521-6018
www.okdol.state.ok.us

*Jim Marshall, Chief of Staff*

**3517 Oklahoma Client Assistance Program/Office of Disability Concerns**
2401 NW 23rd Street
Suite 90
Oklahoma City, OK 73107- 2431
405-521-3756
800-522-8224
FAX: 405-522-6695
www.odc.ok.gov

CAP informs and advises applicants and consumers about the vocational rehabilitation process and services available under the Federal Rehabilitation Act, including services provided by DVR and DVS. CAP staff can help you communicate concerns to the DVR/DVS and assist you with administrative, mediation, fair hearing, legal and other solutions

**3518 Oklahoma Department of Children with Disabilities**
3017 N. Stiles, Suite 100
4001 N Lincoln Blvd
Oklahoma City, OK 73105-5206
405-521-6100
888-69 -353
FAX: 405-521-6018
www.okdol.state.ok.us

*Jim Marshall, Chief of Staff*

**3519 Oklahoma Department of Human Services Aging Services Division**
25 Sigourney Street, 10th Floor
Hartford, CT 06106
405-424-5274
866-218-6621
FAX: 860-424-5301
okdhs.org

*Margaret Ger Murkette, MSW, Director*

**3520 Oklahoma Department of Mental Health & Substance Abuse Services**
P.O.Box 53277
Oklahoma City, OK 73152-3277
405-522-3908
800-522-9054
FAX: 405-522-3650
TTY: 405-522-3851
www.odmhsas.org

*Ronna Vanderslice, Ed.D., Chairperson*
*Gail Wood , Vice-Chair*

State agency providing mental helath , substance abuse and domestic violence services.

**3521 Oklahoma Department of Rehabilitation Services**
3535 NW 58th St
Suite 500
Oklahoma City, OK 73112-4824
405-951-3400
800-845-8476
FAX: 405-951-3529
e-mail: jharlan@okdrs.gov
www.okdrs.gov

*Michael O'Brien, Director*
*Jody Harlan, Public Information Administrator*
*David Ligon, Chief Of Staff*

The Oklahoma Department of Rehabilitation Services (DRS) provides assistance to Oklahomans with disabilities through vocational rehabilitation, employment, independent living, residential and outreach programs, and the determination of medical eligibility for disability benefits.

**3522 Workers Compensation Board Oklahoma**
1915 N Stiles Ave
Oklahoma City, OK 73105-4918
405-522-8600
800-522-8210
owcc.state.ok.us

*Leroy E Young, D.O. , Chairman*

## Oregon

**3523 International Dyslexia Association: Oregon Branch**
International Dyslexia Association
PO Box 2609
Portland, OR 97208-3677
503-228-4455
800-530-2234
FAX: 410-321-5609
e-mail: info@orbida.org
www.orbida.org

*Karen Brown, President*

Provides free information and referral services for diagnosis and tutoring for parents, educators, physicians, and individuals with dyslexia. The voice of our membership is heard in 48 countries. Membership includes yearly journal and quarterly newsletter. Call for conference dates.

**3524 Office of Vocational Rehabilitation Services (OVRS)**
500 Summer St NE
Salem, OR 97301-1063
503-945-5944
FAX: 503-378-2897
TTY:503-945-6214
www.oregon.gov/dhs/index.shtml

The mission of OVRS to assist Oregonians with disabilities to achieve and maintain employment and independence.

**3525 Oregon Advocacy Center**
5th Fl
620 SW 5th Ave
Portland, OR 97204-1428
503-243-2081
800-452-6094
FAX: 503-243-1738
e-mail: welcome@oradvocacy.org
oradvocacy.org

*Robert Joondeph, Executive Director*
*Barbara Herget, Operations Director*

The protection and advocacy system for Oregon.

**3526 Oregon Client Assistance Program**
Ste 500
620 SW 5th Ave
Portland, OR 97204-1420
503-243-2081
FAX: 503-243-1738
oradvocacy.org

*Robert Joondeph, Executive Director*

**3527 Oregon Commission for the Blind**
535 SE 12th Ave
Portland, OR 97214-2408
971-673-1588
888-202-5463
FAX: 503-234-7468
TTY: 971-673-1577
e-mail: ocb.mail@state.or.us
www.oregon.gov/blind

*Linda Mock, Administrator*

**3528 Oregon Department of Mental Health**
500 Summer St NE
Salem, OR 97301-1063
503-945-5944
FAX: 503-378-2897
TTY:503-945-6214
www.oregon.gov/DHS

*Bruce Goldberg, Manager*

Sets out the purpose and guides the activities of our large, complex organization. Vision is for better outcomes for clients and communities through collaboration, integration and shared responsibility.

**3529 Oregon Technology Access for Life**
3070 Lancaster Dr NE
Salem, OR 97305-1396
503-361-1201
800-677-7512
FAX: 503-725-4103
TTY: 503-361-1201
e-mail: info@accesstechnologiesinnc.com
www.accesstechnologiesinc.org

*Laurie Brooks, President*

A statewide program promoting assistive technology devices and services for persons of all ages with all disabilities.

**3530 Social Security: Salem Disability Determination**
Suite 160
90 E Washington Bridge Rd
Worthington, OH 43085-3772
614-888-5339
800-722-1213
TTY:614-288-0226
www.socialsecurity.gov

**3531 Washington County Disability, Aging and Veteran Services**
Ste 208
180 E Main St
Hillsboro, OR 97123-4054
503-640-3489
FAX: 503-693-6124
www.co.washington.or.us/aging

*Jeff Hill, Director*
*Janet Long, Support Staff*

Provides services to individuals through the Older Americans Act, state in home care services and represent, veterans in benefit claims process with Federal VA.

## Pennsylvania

**3532 International Dyslexia Association: Pennsylvania Branch**
1062 E. Lancaster Avenue, 15A
Rosemont, PA 19010-251
610-527-1548
FAX: 610-527-5011
e-mail: dyslexia@pbida.org
www.pbida.org

*Eugenie Flaherty PhD, President*
*Tracy Bowes, Office Manager*

Provides free information and referral services for diagnosis and tutoring for parents, educators, physicians, and individuals with dyslexia. The voice of membership is heard in 48 countries. Membership includes yearly journal and quarterly newsletter, and Pennsylvania newsletter; discounts to conferences and events.

**3533 Mental Health Association in Pennsysylvania**
1414 N Cameron St
Harrisburg, PA 17103-1049
717-346-0549
866-578-3659
FAX: 717-236-0192
e-mail: mfo@mhapa.org
www.mhapa.org

*Jack Boyle, President*

**3534 Pennsylvania Workers Compensation Board**
Rm 103
1171 S Cameron St
Harrisburg, PA 17104-2510
717-939-9551
FAX: 717-772-0342
dli.state.pa.us

*Joseph Brimmeier, CEO*

**3535 Pennsylvania Bureau of Blindness & VisualServices**
Department of Pennsylvania
1521 N 6th St
Harrisburg, PA 17102
717-787-3201
800-622-2842
FAX: 717-787-3210
www.dli.state.pa.us

*David Denotaris, Director*
*Jennifer Cave, Clerk Typist 3*
Offers services for the totally blind, legally blind, visually impaired, mentally retarded blind and more with health, counseling, educational, recreational, rehabilitation, computer training and professional training services.

**3536 Pennsylvania Client Assistance Program**
Ste 800
1617 John F Kennedy Blvd
Philadelphia, PA 19103-1819
215-557-7112
888-745-2357
FAX: 215-557-7602
e-mail: info@equalemployment.org
www.equalemployment.org

*Stephen Pennington, Executive Director*
*Jamie C Ray, Assistant Director*
The Pennsylvania Client Assistance Program is dedicated to ensuring that the rehabilitation system in Pennsylvania is open and responsive to your needs. CAP help is provided to you at no charge, regardless of income. CAP helps people who are seeking services from the Office of Vocational Rehabilitation, Blindness and Visual Services, Centers for Independent Living and other programs funded under federal law.

**3537 Pennsylvania Department of Aging**
5th Fl
555 Walnut St
Harrisburg, PA 17101-1925
717-787-7313
FAX: 717-783-6842
e-mail: aging@state.pa.us
www.aging.state.pa.us

*Nora Eisenhower, Manager*

**3538 Pennsylvania Department of Children with Disabilities**
P.O. Box 2675
Harrisburg, PA 17105
717-772-4131
FAX: 717-772-0323
www.pachildren.state.pa.US

**3539 Pennsylvania Developmental Disabilities Council**
569 Forum Building
Harrisburg, PA 17120
717-789-6057
877-685-4452
TTY:717-705-0819
www.paddc.org

*Graham Mulholland, Executive Director*

**3540 Pennsylvania Protection & Advocacy for Persons with Disabilities**
1414 N Cameron St
Harrisburg, PA 17103-1049
717-236-8110
800-692-7443
FAX: 717-236-0192
TTY: 877-375-7139
e-mail: ldo@drnpa.org
drnpa.org

*Mark Murphy, CEO*
Provide advocacy, information and referral for persons with disabilities and mental illness issues.

**3541 Public Interest Law Center of Philadelphia**
1709 Benjamin Franklin Parkway
Philadelphia, PA 19103-5153
215-627-7100
FAX: 215-627-3183
e-mail: general@pilcop.org
pilcop.org

*Eric J. Rothschild , Chair*
*Brian T. Feeney, Vice Chair*
A non-profit, public interest law firm with a Disabilities Project specializing in class action suits brought by individuals and organizations.

**3542 Social Security: Harrisburg Disability Determination**
Suite 160
90 E Washington Bridge Rd
Worthington, OH 17101-1925
614-888-5339
800-722-1213
TTY:614-288-0226
ssa.gov

**3543 Workers Compensation Board Pennsylvania**
Rm 103
1171 S Cameron St
Harrisburg, PA 17104-2510
717-939-9551
FAX: 717-772-0342
dli.state.pa.us

*Joseph Brimmeier, CEO*

## Rhode Island

**3544 Department of Mental Health, Retardation and Hospitals of Rhode Island**
Goverment of Rhode Isalnd
14 Harrington Rd
Cranston, RI 02920-3080
401-462-3201
FAX: 401-462-3204
www.mhrh.state.ri.us www.nhirh.ri.gov

*Ellen Nelson, Manager*
*Kathleen Spangler, Manager*
State department responsible for creating and administering systems of care for individuals with disabilities, specifically focused on mental health and mental illness; developmental disabilities, substance abuse and long term hospital care.

**3545 Rhode Island Department Health**
3 Capitol Hl
Providence, RI 02908-5097
401-222-3855
FAX: 401-222-6548
e-mail: library@doh.state.ri.us
gotasthma.com

*Mary Salerno, Manager*
*Patricia Nolan, Executive Director*
*Pamela Corcoran, Disability Health Program*

**3546 Rhode Island Department of Elderly Affairs**
35 Howard Ave
Cranston, RI 02920-3001
401-462-3000
FAX: 401-462-0503
e-mail: larry@dea.state.ri.us
www.dea.state.ri.us

*Corrine Russo, Manager*

**3547 Rhode Island Department of Mental Health**
Cottage 405 Court B
Cranston, RI 02920
401-462-2003
FAX: 401-462-2008

*Reed Cosper, Manager*
*Robert Emerson, President*

**3548 Rhode Island Developmental Disabilities Council**
Ste 515
400 Bald Hill Rd
Warwick, RI 02886-1692
401-732-3240
FAX: 401-737-3395
TTY:401-737-1238
e-mail: riddc@riddc.org
www.riddc.org

*Charles Zawacki, Chairperson, Individual & Family Advocacy Committee*
*John Susa, Chairperson, Executive Committee*
*Anne Frank, Chairperson, Individual & Family Advocacy Committee*
*Mary Okero, Executive Director*
The Rhode Island Developmental Disabilities Council works to make Rhode Island a better place for people with developmental disabilities to live, work, go to school, and be part of their community.

**3549 Rhode Island Governor's Commission on Disabilities**
John O Pastore Center
41 Cherrydale Ct
Cranston, RI 02920-3049
401-462-0100
FAX: 401-462-0106
e-mail: disabilities@gcd.state.ri.gov
http://www.warwickri.gov

*Bob Cooper, Executive Secretary*
The Commision is responsible for: coordinating compliance by state agencies with federal and state disablity right laws; approving or modifying state and local goverment agency's open meeting accessibility for persons with disabilities transition plans; assisting local boards of canvassers to ensure accessible polling places locations; aproving or rejecting requests to waive the state building code's standards for accessibility at facilities to be leased by state agencies...

**3550 Rhode Island Parent Information Network**
1210 Pontiac Avenue
Cranston, RI 02920
401-270-0101
800-464-3399
FAX: 401-270-7049
e-mail: info@ripin.org
ripin.org

*Vivian Weisman, Executive Director*
*Matthew Cox, Associate Exeutive Director*
*Dale Longworth, Secretary*
*Louis J. Simon, CPA, MST, Treasurer*
A nonprofit organization established by parents and concerned professionals providing culturally appropriate information, training and support for families and professionals designed to improve educational and life outcomes for all children. Serving the State of Rhode Island.

**3551 Rhode Island Protection & Advocacy for Persons with Disabilities**
Rhode Island Disability Law Center
275 Westminster Street
Suite 401
Providence, RI 02903- 3434
401-831-3150
800-733-5332
FAX: 401-274-5568
TTY: 401-831-5335
e-mail: info@ridlc.org
www.ridlc.org

*Raymond Bandusky, Executive Director*
Rhode Island Disability Law Center (RIDLC) provides free legal assistance to persons with disabilities. Services include individual representation to protect rights or to secure benefits and services; self-help information; educational programs; and administrative and legislative advocacy. The agency administers eight federally funded advocacy programs, each of which has its own eligibility criteria.

**3552 Rhode Island Services for the Blind and Visually Impaired**
40 Fountain St
Providence, RI 02903-1830
401-421-7005
800-752-8088
FAX: 401-421-9259
TTY: 401-277-3010
e-mail: thompson@ors.state.ri.us
www.ors.ri.gov

*Raymond A Carroll, Administrator*
*Stephen Brunero, Deputy Administrator*
Offers services for the totally blind, legally blind, visually impaired, mentally retarded blind and more with health, counseling, educational, recreational, rehabilitation, computer training and professional training services.

**3553 Services for the Blind and Visually Impaired**
40 Fountain St
Providence, RI 02903-1830
401-222-2300
FAX: 401-222-1328
www.ors.ri.gov

*Gary Wier, Deputy Administrator*
*Raymond Carroll, Administrator*
Offers services for the blind and visually impaired.

**3554 Social Security: Providence Disability Determination**
Social Security
40 Fountain Street
6th Floor
Providence, RI 02903-3246
401-222-3182
800-772-1213
FAX: 401-222-3868
TTY: 401-273-6648
e-mail: Deborah.A.Cannon@ssa.gov
www.ssa.gov

*John J Corson, Director*
*Deborah A. Cannon, Professional Relations Officer*
*Tiffany L. Flick, Executive Secretary*
*Michael J. Astrue, Commissioner*
We deliver services through a nationwide network of over 1,400 offices that include regional offices, field offices, card centers, teleservice centers, processing centers, hearing offices, the Appeals Council, and our State and territorial partners, the Disability Determination Services. We also have a presence in U.S. embassies around the globe. For the public, we are the "face of the government." The rich diversity of our employees mirrors the public we serve.

**3555 Workers Compensation Board Rhode Island**
1 Dorrance Plz
Providence, RI 02903-3973
401-458-5000
FAX: 401-222-3121
courts.ri.gov

*George E Healy Jr, Manager*
*George Healy Jr, Manager*

## South Carolina

**3556 Protection & Advocacy for People with Disabilities**
Ste 208
3710 Landmark Dr
Columbia, SC 29204-4034
803-782-0639
866-275-7273
FAX: 803-790-1946
TTY: 866-232-4525
e-mail: info@pandasc.org
protectionandadvocacy-sc.org

*Gloria Prevost, Executive Director*
*Anne Trice, Director of Administration*
*J. Ashley Twombley, Chair*
*Sherry Williams, Vice-Chair*

An independent, nonprofit organization responsible for safe guarding rights of South Carolinians with disabilities and other handicapped individuals without regard to age, income, severity of disability, sex, race, or religion.

**3557 Social Security: West Columbia Disability Determination**
P.O. Box 60
Columbia, SC 29171-0060
803-896-6400
800-772-1213
FAX: 803-822-4318
TTY: 800-325-0078
e-mail: Kenneth.Norris@ssa.gov
www.socialsecurity.gov

*Diane Hare, Medical Relations Supervisor*
*Kenneth R. Norris, Administrative Service Manager*
*Tiffany L. Flick, Executive Secretary*
*Michael J. Astrue, Commissioner*

We deliver services through a nationwide network of over 1,400 offices that include regional offices, field offices, card centers, teleservice centers, processing centers, hearing offices, the Appeals Council, and our State and territorial partners, the Disability Determination Services. We also have a presence in U.S. embassies around the globe. For the public, we are the "face of the government." The rich diversity of our employees mirrors the public we serve.

**3558 South Carolina Assistive Technology Project**
Midlands Center
8301 Farrow Road
Columbia, SC 29203
803-935-5263
800-915-4522
FAX: 803-935-5342
TTY: 803-935-5263
e-mail: jjendron@usit.net
www.sc.edu/scatp/

*Carol Page, Ph.D, CCC-SLP, A, Program Director*
*Janet Jendron, Program Coordinator*
*Mary Alice Bechtler, Program Coordinator*
*Lydia Durham, Administrative Assistant*

A statewide program promoting assistive technology devices and services for persons of all ages with all disabilities. Recently a statewide AT resource, demonstrations and equipment loan center and lab annual expo and training and workshops on a variety of disabilities and technology topics.

**3559 South Carolina Client Assistance Program**
Governor's Office oe Executive Policy & Programs
1205 Pendleton St
Columbia, SC 29201-3756
803-734-0285
800-868-0040
FAX: 803-734-0546
TTY: 803-734-1147
e-mail: : cap@oepp.sc.gov
www.govoepp.state.sc.us/cap

*Denise Barker, Executive Director*
*Cindy Popenhagen, Administrative Assistant*

The Client Assistance Program (CAP) helps citizens of the State by acting as advocates regarding services provided by the Vocational Rehabilitation Department (VR), Commission for the Blind, and all Independent Living programs and projects funded under the Rehabilitation Act of 1973. As advocates, CAP staff can investigate, negotiate, mediate, and pursue administrative, and other remedies to ensure that clients' rights are protected.

**3560 South Carolina Commission for the Blind**
1430 Confederate Avenue
P. O. Box 2467
Columbia, SC 29202-79
803-89 -731
800-922-2222
FAX: 803-898-8800
e-mail: publicinfo@sccb.sc.gov
www.sccb.state.sc.us

*James Kirby, Commissioner*
*Peter Smith, Board Member*
*Dr. Julianne Kleckley, Board Member*
*Dr. Julia Barnes, Board Member*

Offers services for the totally blind, legally blind, visually impaired, mentally retarded blind and more with health, counseling, educational, recreational, rehabilitation, computer training and professional training services.

**3561 South Carolina Department of Children with Disabilities**
2600 Bull St
Columbia, SC 29201-1708
803-434-4260

*Miroslav Cuturic, Director*
*Peter Getz, Administrator*

**3562 South Carolina Department of Mental Healthand Mental Retardation**
Administration Building
2414 Bull Streets
Columbia, SC 29202-485
803-898-8581
800-273-8255
FAX: 864-297-5130
e-mail: webmaster@scdmh.org
www.state.sc.us/dmh

*John H. Magill, State Director*
*Mark Binkley, Deputy Director*
*David Schaefer, Director*
*Eleanor Odom, Director*

The S.C. Department of Mental Health gives priority to adults, children, and their families affected by serious mental illnesses and significant emotional disorders. We are committed to eliminating stigma and promoting the philosophy of recovery, to achieving our goals in collaboration with all stakeholders, and to assuring the highest quality of culturally competent services possible.

**3563 South Carolina Developmental Disabilities Council**
Office of the Governor
Ste 450
1205 Pendleton St
Columbia, SC 29201-3756
803-734-0465
FAX: 803-734-1409
TTY:803-734-1147
e-mail: jvancleave@oepp.sc.gov
www.scddc.state.sc.us

*Valarie Bishop, Executive Director*
*Jennifer Van Cleave, Program Information Coordinator*
*Kimberly Johnson Fontanez, Grants Coord. II*
*Esther Williams, Administrative Support Specialist B*

The mission of the South Carolina Developmental Disabilities Council is to provide leadership in advocating, funding and implementing initiatives which recognize the inherent dignity of each individual, and promote independence, productivity, respect and inclusion for all persons with disabilities and their families.

**3564 Workers Compensation Board: South Carolina**
P.O.Box 1715
Columbia, SC 29202-1715
803-737-5700
FAX: 803-737-5768
www.state.sc.us/wcc

*Gary Cannon, Executive Director*
*Kim Balleutine, Admin. Assistant*

## South Dakota

**3565 Children's Special Health Services Program**
600 E Capitol Ave
Pierre, SD 57501-2536
605-773-3361
800-738-2301
FAX: 605-773-5683
e-mail: DOHcshshealthkicc@state.sd.us
www.doh.sd.gov

*Dianne Weyer, Manager*
*Barb Hemmelman, Program Manager*
Health KiCC is a program, funded through federal and state monies, that provides financial assistance for medical appointments, procedures, treatments, medications and travel reimbursement for children with certain chronic health conditions. The name is ""Health KiCC is a program""

**3566 Division of Labor and Management**
South Dakota Department of Labor
700 Governors Dr
Pierre, SD 57501-2291
605-773-3101
FAX: 605-773-6184
e-mail: jamesmarsh@state.sd.us
dol.sd.gov

*Sara Minton, Executive Director*
*Pamela S . Roberts, Secretary*
*Marcia Hultman, Deputy Secretary of Labor and Director of Workforce Services*
*Lyle Harter, Director of Administrative Services*
Our mission is to promote economic opportunity and financial security for individuals and businesses through quality, responsive and expert services; fair and equitable employment solutions; and safe and sound business practices.

**3567 Health KiCC**
South Dakota Department of Health
600 E Capitol Ave
Pierre, SD 57501-2536
605-773-3361
800-738-2301
FAX: 605-773-5683
e-mail: dohcshshealthkicc@state.sd.us
www.doh.sd.gov

*Dianne Weyer, Manager*
Health KiCC is a program, funded through federal and state monies, that provides financial assistance for medical appointments, procedures, treatments, medications and travel reimbursement for children with certain chronic health conditions.

**3568 South Dakota Advocacy Services**
221 S Central Ave
Ste. 38
Pierre, SD 57501-2479
605-224-8294
800-658-4782
FAX: 605-224-5125
e-mail: sdas@sdadvocacy.com
sdadvocacy.com

*Sandy Stocklin Hook, Partners Coordinator*
Designated protection and advocacy progam for South Dakota providing legal, administrative, mediation and other services to elgible persons with disabilities in the state.

**3569 South Dakota Department of Aging**
700 Governors Dr
Pierre, SD 57501-2291
605-773-3165
866-854-5465
FAX: 605-773-4085
e-mail: ASA@state.sd.us
www.state.sd.us/social/asa

*Marilyn Kinsman, Division Director*
*Lynne Valenti, Deputy Secretary*
*Amy Iversen-Pollreisz, Deputy Secretary*
*Kristin Kellar, Communications Director*
The Division of Adult Services and Aging (ASA) provides home and community service options to individuals 60 years of age and older and 18 years of age and older with physical disabilities, regardless of income.

**3570 South Dakota Department of Human Services Division of Community Behavioral Health**
South Dakota of Human Services
3800 East Hwy 34
Hillsview Properties Plaza
Pierre, SD 57501-5007
605-773-3123
800-265-9684
FAX: 605-773-7076
e-mail: infoMH@state.sd.us
http://dss.sd.gov/behavioralhealthservices

*Shawna Fullerton, Division Director*
South Dakota's state mental health authority.

**3571 South Dakota Developmental Disability Council**
Hillsview Plaza 3800 E Highway 34
c/o 500 East Capital Avenue
Pierre, SD 57501
605-773-5990
800-265-9684
FAX: 605-773-5483
TTY: 605-773-6412
e-mail: infodhs@state.sd.us
www.state.sd.us/dhs/ddc

*Dan Lusk, Director*
*Laurie R. Gill, Secretary*
*Carol Ruen, Assistant Director*
*Lindsay Dummer, Program Specialist II*
To assist individuals with developmental disabilities to control their own destiny and to achieve the quality of life they desire.

**3572 South Dakota Division of Rehabilitation**
700 Governors Dr
Pierre, SD 57501-2291
605-773-3101
FAX: 605-773-6184
e-mail: jamesmarsh@state.sd.us
www.sdjobs.org

*Sara Minton, Executive Director*
*Pamela S . Roberts, Secretary*
*Marcia Hultman, Deputy Secretary of Labor and Director of Workforce Services*
*Lyle Harter, Director of Administrative Services*
Offers diagnosis, evaluation and physical restoration services, counseling, social work, educational and professional training, employment and rehabilitation services for the disabled.

**3573 Workers Compensation Board: South Dakota**
700 Governors Dr
Pierre, SD 57501-2291
605-773-3101
FAX: 605-773-6184
e-mail: jamesmarsh@state.sd.us
www.sdjobs.org

*Sara Minton, Executive Director*
*Pamela S . Roberts, Secretary*
*Marcia Hultman, Deputy Secretary of Labor and Director of Workforce Services*
*Lyle Harter, Director of Administrative Services*
Our mission is to promote economic opportunity and financial security for individuals and businesses through quality, responsive and expert services; fair and equitable employment solutions; and safe and sound business practices.

## Tennessee

**3574 International Dyslexia Association: Tennessee Branch**
TTU Box 5074
Cookeville, TN 37931-2311
800-222-3123
877-836-6432
FAX: 865-693-3653
e-mail: htdainty@gmail.com.
http://www.tnida.org/

*Helen Dainty, President*
*Jean Hutchinson, Treasurer*
*Laura Graves, Secretary*
*Katrina Bryson, Membership Secretary*

The Tennessee Branch of the International Dyslexia Association (TN-IDA) was formed to increase awareness about Dyslexia in the state of Tennessee. TN-IDA supports efforts to provide information regarding appropriate language arts instruction to those involved with language-based learning differences and to encourage the identity of these individuals at-risk for such disorders as soon as possible.

**3575 Social Security: Nashville Disability Determination**
Social Security
P.O. Box 77
Nashville, TN 37202-4732
615-743-7774
800-772-1213
800-342-1117
FAX: 615-253-1840
e-mail: Betty.J.Hood@ssa.gov
ssa.gov

*Betty Hood, Professional Relations Director*
*Tom (James) Fussell, Professional Relations Supervisor*
*Rosa Gordon, Professional Relations Officer*
*Steve Christenberry, Professional Relations Officer*

We deliver services through a nationwide network of over 1,400 offices that include regional offices, field offices, card centers, teleservice centers, processing centers, hearing offices, the Appeals Council, and our State and territorial partners, the Disability Determination Services. We also have a presence in U.S. embassies around the globe. For the public, we are the "face of the government." The rich diversity of our employees mirrors the public we serve.

**3576 Tennessee Assistive Technology Projects**
Citizens Plaza State Office Buildin
400 Deaderick Stree
Nashville, TN 37243-1403
615-313-5183
800-732-5059
TTY:615-313-5695
e-mail: TN.TTAP@tn.gov
http://www.tn.gov

*Beth White, Manager*
*Julie Oden, Manager*
*Raquel Hatter, Commissioner*
*Bill Haslam, Givernor*

A statewide program promoting assistive technology devices and services for persons of all ages with all disabilities.

**3577 Tennessee Client Assistance Program**
Tennessee Protection and Advocacy
P.O.Box 121257
Nashville, TN 37212-1257
615-298-1080
800-342-1660
FAX: 615-298-2046
e-mail: gethelp@tpainc.org
www.tpainc.org

*Shirley Shea, Executive Director*
*Doris Lopez, Assistant Executive Director*

**3578 Tennessee Commission on Aging and Disability**
500 Deaderick St
8th Floor
Nashville, TN 37243-1
615-741-2056
FAX: 615-741-3309
e-mail: cindy.warf@tn.gov
www.tn.gov/comaging

*Richard M. Honn, Executive Director*
*Ryan Ellis, Aging Info. & Data Director*
*Kathy Zamata, Aging Program Director*
*Richard Presler, Fiscal Director*

**3579 Tennessee Council on Developmental Disabilities**
404 James Robertson Pkwy
Parkway Towers, Suite 130
Nashville, TN 37243
615-532-6615
FAX: 615-532-6964
e-mail: tnddc@tn.gov
www.state.tn.us/odd

*Wanda Willis, Executive Director*
*Bill Haslam, Governor*
*Alicia Cone, Coordinator, Project Research and Development*
*William Edington, Public Policy Director*

Provides leadership to ensure independence, productivity, integration and inclusion of individuals with disabilities in the community through promotion of systems change. The council works with members of the community, including public and private aencies, business, legislators and policymakers, to create a future in which; people with disabilities are full included in the community and experience no barriers related to attitudes about their disabilities as they persue their goals.

**3580 Tennessee Department of Children with Disabilities**
Rm 525
436 6th Ave N
Nashville, TN 37243-9004
615-741-9701
800-861-1935
FAX: 615-253-5216
e-mail: dcs.email@tn.gov
http://www.tn.gov

*Ruth S Letson, Manager*
*Haticile Buchanan, Manager*
*Mary Beth Franklyn, CS Program Director*
*Kristi Faulkner, Special Counsel to the Commissione*

Tennessee's children thrive in safe, healthy and stable families. Families thrive in healthy, safe and strong communities. Tennessee's citizens benefit from the best child welfare and juvenile justice agency in the country.

**3581 Tennessee Department of Mental Health**
425 5th Ave N
Nashville, TN 37243-3400
615-741-7213
800-560-5767
FAX: 615-532-6514
e-mail: oc.tdmh@tn.gov
www.state.tn.us/mental

*Doug Varney, Commissioner*
*Grant Lawrence, Director Office of Communication*
*Bob Grunow, Deputy Commissioner*
*Howard Burley, Asst Commissioner Clinical Ldrsp*

TDMH is the state's mental health and substance abuse authority. Its mission is to plan for and promote the availability of a comprehensive array of quality prevention, early intervention, treatment, habilitation, and rehabilitation services and supports based on the needs and choices of individuals and families served. Responsible for policy, and oversight, and for advocacy of the consumer within the state.

**3582 Tennessee Division of Rehabilitation**
400 Deaderick St
Nashville, TN 37243-1403
615-313-4700
800-270-1349
TTY:615-313-5695
e-mail: connie.phillips@tn.gov
http://www.tn.gov

*Patsy Matthews, Commissioner*
*Randall Beasley, Manager*
*Raquel Hatter, Commissioner*
*Bill Haslam, Givernor*
Offers rehabilitation, medical and therapeutic information and referrals to the disabled.

**3583 Workers Compensation Division Tennessee**
Dept of Labor & Workforce Development
220 French Landing Drive
1st Floor
Nashville, TN 37243- 1002
615-741-6642
800-332-2667
FAX: 615-532-1468
e-mail: wc.info@tn.gov
www.tn.gov/labor-wfd/wcomp.html

*Karla Davis, Commissioner*
*Alisa Malone, Deputy Commissioner*
*Stephanie Mitchell, General Counsel*
*Ron Jones, Administrator of Fiscal Services*
We administer the workers' compensation system and promote a better understanding of the program's benefits by informing employees and employers of their rights and responsibilities. Workers' Compenstation administers a mediation program for disputed claims, encourage workplace safety, participate in a public awareness campaign concerning fraud, and oversee an information awareness program for educating the public on laws and regulations which define workers' compensation requirements. We ensure

## Texas

**3584 Disability Policy Consortium**
Ste 171e
7800 Shoal Creek Blvd
Austin, TX 78757-1024
512-454-4816
800-252-9108
FAX: 512-323-0902
e-mail: dpctexas@advocacyinc.org
advocacyinc.org

*Mary Faithful, Executive Director*
*Roberta Rosenberg-Roque, Manager*
An independent group of statewide advocacy organizations that strives to achieve the development and full implementation of public policy that promotes and supports the rights, inclusion, integration and independence of Texans with disabilities.

**3585 Division of Special Education**
1701 Congress Ave
Austin, TX 78701-1402
512-463-9734
FAX: 512-463-9838
e-mail: teainfo@tea.state.tx.us
www.tea.state.tx.us

*Gene Lenz, Federal & State Education Policy*
*Robert Scott, Commissioner of Education*
*Lizzette Gonzalez Reynolds, Deputy Commissioner, Policy & Programs*
*Anita Givens, Associate Commissioner, Standards and Programs*
The Texas public school system is a $46 billion a year enterprise. Running a school district requires superintendents to operate one of the largest, if not the largest, business in their community. This website attempts to provide administrators with easy access to information they need to successfully carry out their duties.

**3586 Easter Seal of Greater Dallas, TX**
4443 N Josey Ln
Carrollton, TX 75010-4743
972-394-8900
800-580-4718
FAX: 972-394-6266
e-mail: wjohnson@dallas.easterseals.com
easterseals.com

*Donna Dempsey, President and Chief Executive Officer*
*Nancy Robinson, Executive Vice President & Chief Financial Officer*
*Nancy Swartz, Vice President of Development and Marketing*
*Lenee Bassham, Vice President Community Living Services*
Easter Seals has a longstanding history in our community of providing a wealth of unique programs and services for individual with a wide variety of disabilities, including Autism Spectrum Disorder, Alzheimer's disease, Down syndrome, Cerebral Palsy, Mental and Developmental Delays, and a wealth of other disabilities. We provide programs and services, education, outreach, and advocacy so that people living with disabilities can live, learn, work and play in our communities.

**3587 Easter Seals Greater NW Texas**
2100 Circle Dr
Fort Worth, TX 76119-8130
817-332-717
888-617-7171
FAX: 817-332-7601
e-mail: wjohnson@dallas.easterseals.com

*Donna Dempsey, President and Chief Executive Officer*
*Nancy Robinson, Executive Vice President & Chief Financial Officer*
*Nancy Swartz, Vice President of Development and Marketing*
*Lenee Bassham, Vice President Community Living Services*
Easter Seals has a longstanding history in our community of providing a wealth of unique programs and services for individual with a wide variety of disabilities, including Autism Spectrum Disorder, Alzheimer's disease, Down syndrome, Cerebral Palsy, Mental and Developmental Delays, and a wealth of other disabilities. We provide programs and services, education, outreach, and advocacy so that people living with disabilities can live, learn, work and play in our communities.

**3588 El Valle Community Parent Resource Center**
Ste J
530 S Texas Blvd
Weslaco, TX 78596-6262
956-969-0215
800-680-0255
FAX: 956-968-7102
e-mail: texasfiestaedu.org
www.tfepodder.org

*Robert Garza, Owner*

**3589 Grassroots Consortium**
Greenroots Consortium
6202 Belmark St
Houston, TX 77087-6324
713-643-9576
FAX: 713-643-6291
Speckids@aol.com

*Agnes A Johnson, Director*

**3590 International Dyslexia Association: Austin Branch**
P.O.Box 92604
Austin, TX 78709-2604
512-452-7658
800-222-3123
e-mail: info@interdys.org
www.interdys.org

*Sharon McMichael, President*
*Kelly O'Mullan, Vice-President*
*Regina Staffa, Treasurer*
*Alice Womack-Marsel, Recording Secretary*
The Austin Area Branch of the International Dyslexia Association is a 501(c)(3) non profit organization dedicated to promoting reading excellence for all children through early identification of

dyslexia, effective literacy education for adults and children with dyslexia, and teacher training.

**3591 NAMI Texas**
Ste 140, Fountain Park Plaza III
2800 S i H 35
Austin, TX 78704-5700
512-693-2000
800-633-3760
FAX: 512-693-8000
e-mail: namitexas@texami.org
namitexas.org

*Robin Peyson, Executive Director*
*Kelly Jeschke, Membership Coordinator/Office Manager*
*Aeren Martinez, Development Director*
*Alexis Wadsworth, Communications Director*
NAMI Texas has a variety of programs directed to mental health consumers, family members, friends, professionals, other stake holders and the community at large to address the mental health needs of Texans. NAMI Texas works to inform the public about mental illness by distributing information about mental illness through every means of communication. Interviews are produced on television, stories are featured in newspapers, brochures are distributed, referrals are provided and more.

**3592 Parent Connection**
1020 Riverwood Ct
Conroe, TX 77304-2811
936-756-8321
800-839-8876
e-mail: parentCNCT@aol.com
http://www.parentingaspergerscommunity.com/pu

*Dave Angel, Founder*
Discover the ULTIMATE collection of Parenting help and Aspergers advice that you are ever likely to need. Whatever parenting tips, tricks and techniques that you want for helping your child with Aspergers it's all here for you to access now. That's what our worldwide membership base is doing and it's helping them to understand their child with Aspergers better, become even better parents, and make their home & family life a better place to be. And to be honest wouldn't you like that too?

**3593 Parents Supporting Parents Network**
8001 Centre Park Drive
Austin, TX 78754
512-454-6694
800-252-9729
FAX: 512-454-4956
e-mail: secretary@thearcoftexas.org
www.thearcoftexas.org

*Clay Boatrigh, President*
*Carol Maxwell, Vice-President*
*Lucio Mendoza, Treasurer*
*Charlie Huber, Secretary*
Since our founding in 1950 by a group of parents of children with intellectual and developmental disabilities, The Arc at the local, state and national level has been instrumental in the creation of virtually every program, service, right, and benefit that is now available to more than half a million Texans with intellectual and developmental disabilities. Today, The Arc continues to advocate for including people with intellectual and developmental disabilities in all aspects of society.

**3594 Partners Resource Network**
Ste B
1090 Longfellow Dr
Beaumont, TX 77706-4819
409-898-4684
800-866-4726
FAX: 409-898-4869
e-mail: partnersresource@sbcglobal.net
partnerstx.org

*Janice Meyer, Executive Director*
Statewide network of three parent training and information centers.

**3595 Social Security: Austin Disability Determination**
P.O. Box 149198
Austin, TX 78714-9198
512-437-8311
800-772-1213
800-252-9627
FAX: 512-437-8595
TTY:512-916-5958
e-mail: dan.tippit@ssa.gov
www.ssa.gov

*Dan Tippit, Directorate Manager, Medical Relations*
*Brenda Bradley, Manager, Professional Relations Unit*
*Azucena Gonzalas, Professional Relations Officer, Northwest*
*Primo Molina, rofessional Relations Officer, South Central*
We deliver services through a nationwide network of over 1,400 offices that include regional offices, field offices, card centers, teleservice centers, processing centers, hearing offices, the Appeals Council, and our State and territorial partners, the Disability Determination Services. We also have a presence in U.S. embassies around the globe. For the public, we are the "face of the government." The rich diversity of our employees mirrors the public we serve.

**3596 Statewide Information at Texas School for the Deaf**
1102 S Congress Ave
Austin, TX 78704-1728
512-462-5329
FAX: 512-462-5353
e-mail: twyla.heslop@tsd.state.tx.us
www.tsd.state.tx.us

*Annette Adams, Administrative Assistant Cafeteria*
*Claire Bugen, Superintendent*
*Felix Agosto, Security Captain*
*Reagan Allen, Administrative Assistant*
Welcome to Texas School for the Deaf, a place where students who are deaf or hard of hearing including those with additional disabilities, have the opportunity to learn, grow and belong in a culture that optimizes individual potential and provides accessible language and communication across the curriculum. Our educational philosophy is grounded in the belief that all children who are deaf and hard of hearing deserve a quality language and communication-driven program that provides education tog

**3597 Texas Advocates Supporting Kids with Disabilities**
P.O.Box 162685
Austin, TX 78716-2685
512-310-2102
FAX: 512-310-2102
e-mail: ASKTASK@aol.com
www.main.org/task/

**3598 Texas Commission for the Blind**
P.O.Box 12866
Austin, TX 78711-2866
512-459-8575
800-252-5204
FAX: 512-459-0200

*Canzata Crowder, Manager*
Offers services for the totally blind, legally blind, and visually impaired, with counseling, educational, recreational, rehabilitation, computer training and professional training services.

**3599 Texas Commission for the Deaf and Hard of Hearing**
D AR S
P.O.Box 12904
Austin, TX 78711-2904
512-407-3250
FAX: 512-407-3299
TTY:512-407-3251
e-mail: david.meyers@tcdhh.state.tx.us
www.dars.state.tx.us

*David Myers, Executive Director*

**3600 Texas Council for Developmental Disabilities**
Ste 600
6201 E Oltorf St
Austin, TX 78741-7509
512-437-5432
800-262-0334
FAX: 512-437-5434
TTY: 512-437-5431
e-mail: tcdd@tcdd.state.tx.us
txddc.state.tx.us

*Roger Webb, Executive Director*
*Koren Vogel, Executive Assistant*
*Martha Cantu, Operations Director*
*Sonya Hosey, Grants Management Director*

The Texas Council for Developmental Disabilities is a 27-member board dedicated to ensuring that all Texans with developmental disabilities, about 411,479 individuals, have the opportunity to be independent, productive and valued members of their communities. The mission of the Texas Council for Developmental Disabilities is to create change so that all people with disabilities are fully included in their communities and exercise control over their own lives.

**3601 Texas Department of Human Services**
701 W 51st St
Austin, TX 78751-2312
512-472-4138
888-834-7406
FAX: 512-472-0603
TTY: 888-425-6889
e-mail: mail@dads.state.tx.us
www.dads.state.tx.us

*Bill West, Manager*
*Carlela Vogel, Vice Chair*

**3602 Texas Department of Mental Health & Mental Retardation**
P.O.Box 12668
Austin, TX 78711-2668
512-472-4138
FAX: 512-472-0603
www.mhmr.state.tx.us

*Bill West, Manager*
*Randy Fritz, Chief Operating Officer*

**3603 Texas Department on Aging**
701 W 51st St
Austin, TX 78751-2312
512-438-3011
800-252-9240
e-mail: mail@tdoa.state.tx.us
www.dadds.state.tx.us

*Adelaid Horn, Manager*
*John Willis, Director Ombudsman*
*Karl Urban, Deputy Director*

**3604 Texas Federation of Families for Children's Mental Health**
Ste 505
7701 N Lamar Blvd
Austin, TX 78752-1000
512-407-8844
866-893-3264
FAX: 512-407-8266
e-mail: info@txffcmh.org
www.txffcmh.org

*Patti Derr, Executive Director*
*Pat Calley, Chairperson*
*S Barron, Operations Director*

**3605 Texas Governor's Committee on People with Disabilities**
1100 San Jacinto Blvd
Austin, TX 78701-1935
512-463-5739
FAX: 513-463-5745
e-mail: CPD@gov.texas.gov
www.governor.state.tx.us/disabilities

*Angela English, LPC, LMFT, Executive Director*
*Erin Lawler, JD, MS, Accessibility and Disability Rights Coordinator*
*Nancy Van Loan, Executive Assistant*
*Jo Virgil, MS, Community Outreach and Information Coordinator*

The Governor's Committee on People with Disabilities is within the office of the Governor. The committee's mission is to further opportunities for persons with disabilities to enjoy full and equal access to lives of independence, productivity, and self-determination. The committee is composed of 12 members appointed by the governor and of nonvoting ex officio members. The members are appointed for staggered terms of two years. At least seven of the appointed members must be persons with disabili

**3606 Texas Protection & Advocacy Services for Disabled Persons**
Advocacy
Ste 171e
7800 Shoal Creek Blvd
Austin, TX 78757-1024
512-454-4816
800-252-9108
FAX: 512-323-0902
e-mail: dpctexas@advocacyinc.org
advocacyinc.org

*Mary Faithful, Executive Director*
*Roberta Rosenberg-Roque, Manager*

A federally funded, independent, nonprofit agency that advocates for the legal, human and service rights of persons with disabilities. Publishes 'Special Edition' newsletter, at a small fee and 'It's a Good Idea!' a parent manual for $10, plus many other handouts free of charge.

**3607 Texas Respite Resource Network**
P.O.Box 7330
San Antonio, TX 78207-330
512-228-2794
e-mail: elizabethnewhouse@srhcc.org

*Jennifer Cernoch, Director*
*Liz Newhouse, Assistant Director*

A state clearinghouse and technical assistance network for respite in Texas. TRRN identifies, initiates and improves respite options for families caring for individuals with disabilities on the local, state and national levels. TRRN provides training/technical assistance to programs/groups wanting to establish respite services.

**3608 Texas Technology Access Project**
Center for Disabilities Studies
10100 Burnet Rd
Austin, TX 78758-4445
512-232-0740
800-828-7839
FAX: 512-232-0761
TTY: 512-232-0762
e-mail: rogerlevy@austin.utexas.edu
http://techaccess.edb.utexas.edu

*Robert Levy, Program Director*
*John C. Morris, Assistive Technology Coordinator*
*Steve Thomas, Operations and External Relations*
*Darlene West, Assistive Technology Specialist*

Their mission is to increase access for people with disabilities to assistive technology that provides them more control over their immediate environments and an enhanced ability to function independently.

**3609 Texas UAP for Developmental Disabilities**
University of Texas
1 University Station
Austin, TX 78712
512-475-7348
800-828-7839
e-mail: hello@utexas.edu
www.utexas.edu

*Penny Seay, Executive Director*
*Bob Harkins, Manager*
*William Powers Jr., President*
*Steven Leslie, Executive Vice President and Provost*
Welcome to The University of Texas at Austin. Founded in 1883, UT is one of the largest and most respected universities in the nation. Ours is a diverse learning community, with students from every state and more than 100 countries. We're a university with world talent and Texas traditions. Discover more about us online and come visit our beautiful campus in person.

**3610 Texas Workers Compensation Commission**
7551 Metro Center Drive
Suite 100
Austin, TX 78744-1645
512-804-4000
FAX: 512-804-4401
e-mail: WebStaff@tdi.state.tx.us
http://www.tdi.texas.gov

*Robert Shipe, Executive Director*
*Rod Bordelon, Commissioner*
Workers' compensation is a state-regulated insurance program that pays medical bills and replaces some lost wages for employees who are injured at work or who have work-related diseases or illnesses.

**3611 United Cerebral Palsy of Texas**
National Cerebral Palsy of American
Ste 145
1016 La Posada Dr
Austin, TX 78752-3828
512-472-8696
800-798-1492
FAX: 512-472-8026
e-mail: info@ucptexas.org
ucptexas.org

*Jean Langendorf, Executive Director*
Offers a unique array of programs and services designed for one specific purpose: to ensure that people with cerebral palsy and similar disabilities have the opportunity to participate fully and equally in every aspect of our society.

## Utah

**3612 Access Utah Network**
Ste 100
155 S 300 W
Salt Lake City, UT 84101-1288
801-533-4636
800-333-8824
FAX: 801-533-3968
e-mail: access@utah.gov
accessut.org

*Mark L. Smith, Information Specialist*
Access Utah Network is Utah's prime source for information and referral for individuals with disabilities and their caregivers since 1990. Our operators can provide you with the information you need to find accessible housing, assistive technology and financial and social supports needed to live independently with a disability. Call us or explore our web site today to see how Access Utah Network can help you become more independent.

**3613 Social Security: Salt Lake City Disability Determination**
Social Security
P.O. Box 144032
Salt Lake City, UT 84111-4032
801-321-6500
800-772-1213
800-221-3493
FAX: 801-321-6599
TTY:801-524-5047
e-mail: Dave.Carlson@ssa.gov
www.ssa.gov

*Dave Carlson, Assistant Administrator/Medical Relations Officer*
*Bobbie Bennett, Professional Relations Officer*
*Tiffany L. Flick, Executive Secretary*
*Michael J. Astrue, Commissioner*
We deliver services through a nationwide network of over 1,400 offices that include regional offices, field offices, card centers, teleservice centers, processing centers, hearing offices, the Appeals Council, and our State and territorial partners, the Disability Determination Services. We also have a presence in U.S. embassies around the globe. For the public, we are the "face of the government." The rich diversity of our employees mirrors the public we serve.

**3614 Utah Assistive Technology Projects**
Utah State University
6855 Old Main Hl
Logan, UT 84322-6855
435-797-3824
800-524-5152
TTY:435-797-2355
http://www.uatpat.org/

*Martin Blair, Director, UATP*
*Alma Burgess, CReATE Program Coordinator*
*Clay Christensen, '*
*Marilyn ' Hammond, UATF Director*
A statewide program promoting assistive technology devices and services for persons of all ages with all disabilities.

**3615 Utah Client Assistance Program**
205 N 400 W
Salt Lake City, UT 84103-1125
801-363-1347
800-662-9080
FAX: 801-363-1437
www.disabilitylawcenter.org

*Barbara M. Campbell, Treasurer*
*Joshua Cannon, Board of Trustee*
*Mike Chidester, Board of Trustee*
*Bryce Fifield Ph.D, Vice President*
Since 1979, the Disability Law Center (DLC) has helped thousands of Utahns with disabilities and their families. The DLC has broad statutory powers to safeguard the human and civil rights of persons with disabilities. We provide self-advocacy assistance, legal services, disability rights education, and public policy advocacy on behalf of the more than 400,000 Utah residents with disabilities. Our services are available statewide and without regard for ability to pay.

**3616 Utah Department of Aging**
195 North 1950 West
Salt Lake City, UT 84116
801-538-3910
877-424-4640
FAX: 801-538-4395
e-mail: DAAS@utah.gov
www.hsdaas.utah.gov

*Nels Holmgren, Director*
*Michael S. Styles, Assistant Director*
*Michelle Benson, Director*
*Sarah Brenna, Director*
We administer a wide variety of home and community-based services for Utah residents who are 60 or older. Programs and services are primarily delivered by a network of 12 Area Agencies on Aging which reach all geographic areas of the state. Our goal is to provide services that allow people to remain independent.

**3617 Utah Department of Human Services: Division of Services for People with Disabilities**
Utah Department of Human Services
195 North 1950 West
Salt Lake City, UT 84116
801-538-4200
800-837-6811
FAX: 801-538-4279
e-mail: dirdhs@utah.gov
www.hsdspd.utah.gov

*Paul T. Smith, Division Director*
*Clay Hiatt, Fiscal Management*
Information and referral services for people with disabilities, including DD/MR, brain injury and physical disabilities throughout the state of Utah.

**3618 Utah Division Of Substance Abuse & MentalHealth**
Utah Department of Human Services
195 No. 1950 West
Salt Lake City, UT 84103-1550
801-538-3939
FAX: 801-538-9892
WWW.DHS.UTAH.GOV

*Lana Stohl, Executive Director*

**3619 Utah Division of Services for the Disabled**
195 North 1950 West
Salt Lake City, UT 84116
801-538-4200
800-837-6811
FAX: 801-538-4279
e-mail: dirdhs@utah.gov
www.hsdspd.utah.gov

*Paul T. Smith, Division Director*
*Clay Hiatt, Fiscal Management*
Offers services for the totally blind, legally blind, visually impaired, mentally retarded blind and more with health, counseling, educational, recreational, rehabilitation, computer training and professional training services.

**3620 Utah Governor's Council for People with Disabilities**
Ste 100
155 S 300 W
Salt Lake City, UT 84101-1288
801-533-4636
FAX: 801-533-3968
e-mail: alozano@utah.gov
www.gcpd.org/

*Mark Smith, Manager*
*Angela Allen, Administrative Secretary*

**3621 Utah Labor Commission**
P.O.Box 146630
Salt Lake City, UT 84114-6600
801-530-6800
800-222-1238
FAX: 801-530-6390
e-mail: laborcom@utah.gov
www.laborcommission.utah.gov

*Sherrie Hayashi, Commissioner and Department Director*
*Alan Hennebold, Deputy Commisioner*
*Heather Gunnarson, Director Anti-Discrimination & Labor Division*
*Louis Silva, Director Occupational Safety & Health Division*
Problems with employers not paying employees, employers not paying the minimum wage, the employment of minors and retaliation for wage complaints filed are handled by the Wage Claim Unit.

**3622 Utah Protection & Advocacy Services for Persons with Disabilities**
Disability Law Center
205 N 400 W
Salt Lake City, UT 84103-1125
801-363-1347
800-662-9080
FAX: 801-363-1437
www.disabilitylawcenter.org

*Barbara M. Campbell, Treasurer*
*Joshua Cannon, Board of Trustee*
*Mike Chidester, Board of Trustee*
*Bryce Fifield Ph.D, Vice President*
Since 1979, the Disability Law Center (DLC) has helped thousands of Utahns with disabilities and their families. The DLC has broad statutory powers to safeguard the human and civil rights of persons with disabilities. We provide self-advocacy assistance, legal services, disability rights education, and public policy advocacy on behalf of the more than 400,000 Utah residents with disabilities. Our services are available statewide and without regard for ability to pay.

## Vermont

**3623 Disability Law Project**
57 N Main St
Rutland, VT 05701-3246
800-889-2047
FAX: 802-775-0022
e-mail: nbreiden@vtlegalaid.org
vtlegalaid.org

*Nancy Breiden, Director*
*Kerry Bowen, Ombudsman*
*Rebecca Fay, Attorney*
*Meghan Roach, Attorney*
Legal services (protection and advocacy) for people with disabilities on legal issues arising from disability. Statewide. Adults and children. Employment, education, discrimination, housing, public benefits, health care.

**3624 Disability Rights Vermont**
141 Main Street
Suite 7
Montpelier, VT 05602-2916
802-229-1355
800-834-7890
FAX: 802-229-1359
TTY: 800-889-2047
e-mail: info@disabilityrightsvt.org
www.disabilityrightsvt.org

*Sarah Wendell-Launderville, President*
*David Gallagher, Vice president*
*Charlie Crocker, Treasurer*
*Michael Sabourin, Secretary*
Advocacy and legal services for people with mental illness on legal issues arising, out of disabilities. Children and adults.

**3625 Social Security: Vermont Disability Determination Services**
Ste 6
93 Pilgrim Park Rd
Waterbury, VT 05676-1729
802-241-2463
800-734-2463
800-772-1213
FAX: 802-241-2492
e-mail: Deborah.Fennell@ssa.gov
www.ssa.gov

*Trudy Lyon-Hart, Executive Director*
*Deb Fennell, Medical Relations Officer*
*Tiffany L. Flick, Executive Secretary*
*Michael J. Astrue, Commissioner*
We deliver services through a nationwide network of over 1,400 offices that include regional offices, field offices, card centers, teleservice centers, processing centers, hearing offices, the Appeals Council, and our State and territorial partners, the Disability Determination Services. We also have a presence in U.S.

embassies around the globe. For the public, we are the "face of the government." The rich diversity of our employees mirrors the public we serve.

**3626 Vermont Assistive Technology Projects**
103 S Main St
Weeks Building
Waterbury, VT 05671-2305
800-750-6355
800-750-6355
FAX: 802-871-3048
TTY: 802-241-1464
e-mail: amber.fulcher@state.vt.us
http://atp.vermont.gov/

*Amber Fulcher, Program Director*
*Sharon Alderman, Assistive Technology Reuse Coordinator*
*Emma Cobb, Assistive Technology Services Coordinator*
*Dan Gilman, ATP, Assistive Technology Access Specialists*

Increase awareness and change policies to insure assistive technology (AT) is available to all Vermonters with disabilities. Our Commitment is to enable Vermonters with disabilities to have greater independence, productivity, and confidence. To provide them with a clear and direct avenue toward integration and inclusion within the work force and community.

**3627 Vermont Client Assistance Program**
57 N Main St
Rutland, VT 05701-3246
802-775-0021
800-769-7459
www.vocrehabvermont.org/html/clientassistance

*Patrick Flood, Commissioner*

The Client Assistance Program (CAP) is an independent advocacy program to help if you are applying for or receiving services from one of the following sources: Division of Vocational Rehabilitation (VR); Vermont Center for Independent Living (VCIL); Division for the Blind and Visually Impaired (DBVI); Vermont Association of Business, Industry & Rehabilitation (VABIR); Vermont Association for the Blind and Visually Impaired (VABVI); Supported Employment Programs; Transition Programs.

**3628 Vermont Department of Aging**
103 S Main St
Weeks Building
Waterbury, VT 05671-2305
802-871-3065
FAX: 802-871-3052
TTY:802-241-3557
e-mail: AHS-DAIL-DeptWebMaster@state.vt.us
http://dail.vermont.gov/

*Susan Wehry, Commissioner*
*Marybeth McCaffrey, Director*
*Linda Henzel, Executive Staff Assistant*
*Adele Edelman, Assistant Division Director*

The Department of Disabilities, Aging, and Independent Living's (DAIL's) building at the Waterbury Office Complex was flooded during tropical storm Irene. Staff are currently working at other locations. Please click on the following link for contact information for the Waterbury DAIL staff. DAIL staff contact information

**3629 Vermont Department of Developmental and**
103 S Main St
Weeks Building
Waterbury, VT 05671-2305
802-871-3065
FAX: 802-871-3052
TTY:802-241-3557
http://dail.vermont.gov/

*Jonathan Wood, Manager*

The name of the company has been changed to ""Vermont Department of Developmental and Mental Health Services""

**3630 Vermont Department of Disabilities, Aging and Independent Living**
Aging and Disabilities
103 S Main St
Waterbury, VT 05671-9800
802-241-2401
FAX: 802-241-2325
www.dail.state.vt.us

*Susan Wehry, Commissioner*
*Camille George, Deputy Commissioner*

**3631 Vermont Department of Health: Children with Special Health Needs**
Vermont Department Of Health
108 Cherry Street
Burlington, VT 05402-70
802-863-7200
FAX: 802-865-7754
http://healthvermont.gov/

*Harry Chen, M.D., Commissioner*
*Barbara Cimaglio, Deputy Commissioner for Alcohol & Drug Abuse Programs*
*Tracy Dolan, Deputy Commissioner for Public Health*
*Dixie Henry, Esq., Senior Policy and Legal Advisor*

Multidisciplinary clinics and family support for children with chronic conditions, birth to age 21 years.

**3632 Vermont Developmental Disabilities Council**
103 S Main St
Waterbury, VT 05671-9800
082-241-2220
e-mail: vtddc@upgate1.ahs.state.vt.us
www.ahs.state.vt.us/vtddc

*Cynthia D LaWare, Secretary*

The mission of VTDDC is to facilitate connections and to promote supports that bring people with developmental disabilities into the heart of Vermont Communities.

**3633 Vermont Division for the Blind & Visually Impaired**
Agency of Human Svcs Dept Disabilities, Aging & IL
103 S Main St
Weeks Building
Waterbury, VT 5671-2304
802-871-3038
800-405-5005
888-405-5005
FAX: 802-871-3048
e-mail: DBVI-Info@state.vt.us
www.dail.state.vt.us/dbvi

*Fred Jones, Director*
*Scott Langley, Counselor*
*Wendy Edwards, Administrative Assistant*
*Paul Putnam, Rehabilitation Associate*

Offers services for the totally blind, legally blind, visually impaired, mentally retarded blind and more with health, counseling, educational, recreational, rehabilitation, computer training and professional training services.

**3634 Vermont Division of Disability & Aging Services**
103 S Main St
Weeks Building
Waterbury, VT 05671-2305
802-871-3065
FAX: 802-871-3052
TTY:802-241-3557
e-mail: AHS-DAIL-DeptWebMaster@state.vt.us
www.dail.vermont.gov

*Susan Wehry, Commissioner*
*Marybeth McCaffrey, Director*
*Linda Henzel, Executive Staff Assistant*
*Adele Edelman, Assistant Division Director*

Provides services to adults and children with developmental disabilities all to the aging.

**3635 Workers Compensation Board Vermont**
Department of Labor
5 Green Mountain Drive
PO Box 488
Montpelier, VT 05601- 0488
802-828-2286
FAX: 802-828-2195
e-mail: labor-wccomp@state.vt.us
www.state.vt.us/ladind

*Deborah Bruce, Human Resource Administrator*
*Allen Evans, Executive DirectorWorkforce Development Council*
*Annie Noonan, Commissioner*
*Erika Wolfing, Principal Assistant*
Welcome to the Vermont Department of Labor's website. VDOL's primary focus is to provide services that assist businesses, workers, and job seekers.

## Virginia

**3636 International Dyslexia Association: Virginia Branch**
804 Industrial Avenue
Suite I
Chesapeake, VA 23324
866-893-0583
800-988-8336
FAX: 804-285-1946
e-mail: info@vbida.org
www.interdys.org

*Shana Hatzopoulos, President*
*Eric Q. Tridas, M.D., IDA President*
*Suzanne Carreker, Ph.D., CALT-, IDA Vice President*
*Cinthia Coletti Haan, IDA Vice President*
The Virginia Branch of The International Dyslexia Association (VBIDA) is a 501(c)(3) non-profit, scientific and educational organization dedicated to the study and treatment of the learning disability, dyslexia. This Branch was formed to increase public awareness of dyslexia in the State of Virginia. We serve the entire state, with the exception of Northern Virginia, which is part of the DC-Capital Branch in Washington, DC. We have been serving individuals with dyslexia, their families.

**3637 Virginia Department for the Blind and Vision Impaired**
397 Azalea Ave
Richmond, VA 23227-3623
804-371-3140
800-622-2155
FAX: 804-371-3351
e-mail: Kimberley.Jennings@dbvi.virginia.gov
www.vdbvi.org

*Robert S. Dendy, Chair*
*Kimberley Jennings*
*Marc Johnson, Secretary*
*Eva F. Ampey, Board Liaison*
Offers services for the totally blind, legally blind, visually impaired, mentally retarded blind and more with health, counseling, educational, recreational, rehabilitation, computer training and professional training services.

**3638 Virginia Department of Mental Health**
P.O.Box 1797
Richmond, VA 23218-1797
80- 78- 392
FAX: 804-371-6638
e-mail: jim.stewart@dbhds.virginia.gov?subject=(E-mai
http://www.dbhds.virginia. gov/

*Jim Stewart, Commissioner*
*Olivia Garland, Deputy Commissioner*
*John Pezzoli, Assistant Commissioner of Behavioral Health Services*
*Heidi Dix, Assistant Commissioner of Developmental Services*
Available to citizens statewide, Virginia's public mental health, intellectual disability and substance abuse services system is comprised of 16 state facilities and 40 locally-run community services boards (CSBs) The CSBs and facilities serve children and adults who have or who are at risk of mental illness, serious emotional disturbance, intellectual disabilities, or substance abuse disorders.

**3639 Virginia Developmental Disability Council**
103 S Main St
Waterbury, VT 05671-9800
082-241-2220
e-mail: vtddc@upgate1.ahs.state.vt.us
www.ahs.state.vt.us/vtddc

*Cynthia D LaWare, Secretary*
The mission of VTDDC is to facilitate connections and to promote supports that bring people with developmental disabilities into the heart of Vermont Communities.

**3640 Virginia Office Protection and Advocacy for People with Disabilities**
1910 Byrd Ave, Ste 5
Richmond, VA 23230-3034
804-225-2042
800-552-3962
FAX: 804-662-7431
e-mail: general.vopa@vopa.virginia.gov
www.vopa.state.va.us

*Coleen Miller, Executive Director*
Through zealous and effective advocacy and legal representation to: protect and advance legal, human, and civil rights of persons with disabilities; combat and prevent abuse, neglect, and discrimination; and promote independence, choice, and self-determination by persons with disabilities.

**3641 Virginia Office for Protection & Advocacy**
Ste 5
1910 Byrd Ave
Richmond, VA 23230-3034
804-225-2042
800-552-3962
FAX: 80- 66- 705
e-mail: general.vopa@vopa.virginia.gov
vopa.state.va.us

*V Coleen Miller, Executive Director*
*Eric Berthiaume, Administrative Assistant*
*LaToya Blizzard, Financial Coordinator*
*Paul Buckley, Managing Attorney*
An independent state agency that helps ensure that the rights of persons with disabiltiies in the Commonwealth are protected. The mission of DRVD is to provide zealous and effective advocacy and legal representation to protect and advance legal, human and civil rights of persons with disabilities, combat and prevent abuse, neglect and discrimination, and promote independence, choice and self-determination by persons with disabilities.

**3642 Virginia Office for Protection and Advocacy**
Ste 5
1910 Byrd Ave
Richmond, VA 23230-3034
804-225-2042
800-552-3962
FAX: 80- 66- 705
e-mail: general.vopa@vopa.virginia.gov
vopa.state.va.us

*V Coleen Miller, Executive Director*
*Eric Berthiaume, Administrative Assistant*
*LaToya Blizzard, Financial Coordinator*
*Paul Buckley, Managing Attorney*
An independent state agency that helps ensure that the rights of persons with disabiltiies in the Commonwealth are protected. The mission of DRVD is to provide zealous and effective advocacy and legal representation to protect and advance legal, human and civil rights of persons with disabilities, combat and prevent abuse, neglect and discrimination, and promote independence, choice and self-determination by persons with disabilities.

**3643 Virginia's Developmental Disabilities Planning Council**
Stae Agency
9th Fl
202 N 9th St
Richmond, VA 23219-3426
804-726-1919
800-846-4464
FAX: 804-662-7662
TTY: 800-811-7893
e-mail: webmaster@drs.virginia.gov
www.vaboard.org

*Linda Redmond, Research, Policy & Program Manager*
*Heidi Lawyer, Executive Director*
*Nan Pemberton, Administrator*
*Sandra Smalls, Executive Assistant*
To create a Commonwealth that advances opportunities for independence, personal decision-making and full participation in community life for individuals with developmental disabilities.

## Washington

**3644 DSHS/Aging & Adult Disability Services Administration**
P.O.Box 45130
Olympia, WA 98504-5130
360-902-7797
800-737-0617
FAX: 360-902-7848
TTY: 800-737-7931
aasa.dshs.wa.gov

*Dan Murphy, Director*
*Bea Rector, Project Director*
*Tamarra Paradee, Executive Secretary*
*Bill Moss, Director*
The Aging and Disability Services Administration assists children and adults with developmental delays or disabilities, cognitive impairment, chronic illness and related functional disabilities to gain access to needed services and supports by managing a system of long-term care and supportive services that are high quality, cost effective, and responsive to individual needs and preferences.

**3645 Disability Rights: Washington**
315 5th Avenue South
Suite 850
Seattle, WA 98104-2691
206-324-1521
800-562-2702
FAX: 206-957-0729
TTY: 206-957-0728
e-mail: info@dr-wa.org
www.disabilityrightswa.org

*Mark Stroh, Executive Director*
WPAS is a private, non-profit right protection agency for persons with disabilities residin in Washington state. Our advocacy services include information referral, technical assistance, training, publications and systemic advocacy.

**3646 International Dyslexia Association: Washington State Branch**
P.O.Box 27435
Seattle, WA 98165
206-382-1020
800-222-3123
e-mail: info@wabida.org
www.wabita.org

*Kay Nelson, President*
*Kristie English, Vice President*
*Catherine Adams, Secretary*
*Christine Cassidy, Treasurer*
Provides free information and referral services for diagnosis and tutoring for parents, educators, physicians, and individuals with dyslexia in Arkansas, Idaho, Montana and Washington state. The voice of our membership is heard in 48 countries. Membership includes yearly journal and quarterly newsletter. Call for conference dates.

**3647 Social Security: Olympia Disability Determination**
Social Security
P.O. Box 9303-MS-45550
Olympia, WA 98507
360-664-7356
800-772-1213
800-562-6074
FAX: 360-586-0851
TTY:800-325-0778
e-mail: Jennifer.Elsen@ssa.gov
www.ssa.gov

*Jennifer Elsen, Professional Relations Manager*
*Uyen Kashani, Professional Relations Specialist*
*Ladd Wikstrom, Professional Relations Specialist*
*Scott Connors, Professional Relations Specialist*
We deliver services through a nationwide network of over 1,400 offices that include regional offices, field offices, card centers, teleservice centers, processing centers, hearing offices, the Appeals Council, and our State and territorial partners, the Disability Determination Services. We also have a presence in U.S. embassies around the globe. For the public, we are the "face of the government." The rich diversity of our employees mirrors the public we serve.

**3648 WA Department of Services for the Blind**
4565 7th Avenue SE
Lacey, WA 98503
360-725-3830
800-552-7103
FAX: 360-407-0679
e-mail: info@dsb.wa.gov
www.dsb.wa.gov

*Sue Ammeter, council chair*
*Nancy Kim*
*Veronica Baca, Council Member*
*Michael Cunningham, Council Member*
Vocational rehabilitation for the blind.

**3649 Washington Client Assistance Program**
2531 Rainier Ave S
Seattle, WA 98144-5328
206-721-5999
888-721-6072
FAX: 206-721-4537
TTY:206-721-6072
e-mail: info@washingtoncap.org
http://www.washingtoncap.org/

*Jerry Johnson, Executive Director*
*Bob Kim, rehabilitation coordinator*
Advocacy and information assistance for persons of disability seeking services through vocational rehabilitation or other program under the 1973 Rehabilitation Act as commented. We provide counseling.

**3650 Washington Department of Mental Health**
Department of Social and Health Services
P.O.Box 45330
Olympia, WA 98504-5330
360-725-3700
800-446-0259
FAX: 360-902-7691
TTY: 800-833-6384
e-mail: adsahelpdesk@dshs.wa.gov
www.dshs.wa.gov

*Chris Imhoff, DBHR Director*
*David Albert, Sr. Planner and Policy Analyst, EQA*
*Debbie Arthur, Fiscal Program Manager*
*Stephanie Atherton,, Prevention Systems Manager*
In July 2009 the DSHS Division of Alcohol and Substance Abuse and the Mental Health Division merged to become the Division of Behavioral Health and Recovery (DBHR). Through this integration, we are in a better position to both assess and treat patients with co-occurring mental health and substance use disorders. Our longer term vision calls for the fullest possible integration of behavioral health and primary care services under health reform, creating a person-centered health care home for al

**3651 Washington Developmental Disability**
Ste F
2600 Martin Way E
Olympia, WA 98506-4974 360-586-3560
800-634-4473
FAX: 360-586-2424
e-mail: Ed.Holen@ddc.wa.gov
http://www.ddc.wa.gov

*Ed Holen, Executive Director*
*Jennifer Blazian, Contracts Manager*
*Sieng Bonham, Budget & Fiscal Director*
*Brian Dahl, Support Coordinator*
Developmental Disabilities Council members are appointed by the Governor to plan comprehensive services for the State of Washington's citizens with developmental disabilities.

**3652 Washington Governor's Committee on Disability Issues & Employment**
605 Woodland Square Loop SE
Lacey, WA 98503 360-438-3168
FAX: 360-438-3208
www.gcde.org

*Toby Olson, Manager*

**3653 Washington Office of Superintendent of Public Instruction**
P.O.Box 47200
600 Washington St. S.E.
Olympia, WA 98504-7200 360-725-6000
TTY:360-644-3631
e-mail: webmaster@ospi.wednet.edu
www.k12.wa.us

*Randy Dorn, State Superintendent*
*Alan Burke, Deputy Superintendent*
*Robert Butts, Assistant Superintendent*
*Bob Harmon, Assistant Superintendent*
The Office of Superintendent of Public Instruction (OSPI) is the primary agency charged with overseeing K-12 education in Washington state. OSPI works with the state's 296 school districts to administer basic education programs and implement education reform on behalf of more than one million public school students.

**3654 Washington State Developmental Disabilities Council**
Ste F
2600 Martin Way E
Olympia, WA 98506-4974 360-586-3560
800-634-4473
FAX: 360-586-2424
e-mail: Ed.Holen@ddc.wa.gov
www.ddc.wa.gov

*Ed Holen, Executive Director*
*Jennifer Blazian, Contracts Manager*
*Sieng Bonham, Budget & Fiscal Director*
*Brian Dahl, Support Coordinator*
Developmental Disabilities Council members are appointed by the Governor to plan comprehensive services for the State of Washington's citizens with developmental disabilities.

**3655 Workers Compensation Board Washington**
State of Washington
7273 Linderson Way SW
Tumwater, WA 98501-5414 360-902-5800
800-547-8367
FAX: 360-902-5798
TTY: 360-902-5797
www.lni.wa.gov

*Judy Schurke, Director*
*Lisa Rodriguez, Executive Assistant*
*Vickie Kennedy, Special Assistant*
*Tamara Jones, Dir of Government Relations*
&I is a diverse state agency dedicated to the safety, health and security of Washington's 3.2 million workers. We help employers meet safety and health standards and we inspect workplaces when alerted to hazards. As administrators of the state's workers' compensation system, we are similar to a large insurance company, providing medical and limited wage-replacement coverage to workers who suffer job-related injuries and illness. Our rules and enforcement programs also help ensure workers are pai

## West Virginia

**3656 Bureau of Employment Programs Division of Workers' Compensation**
State of West Virginia
409 Virginia St E
Charleston, WV 25301-2531 304-357-0101
800-628-4265
FAX: 304-357-0788
e-mail: helpdesk@kanawha.us
kanawha.us

*Patricia Starkey, Manager*
*Vern Cormick, Manager*
*Michael ' Campbell, Director of IT*
*Larry McDonnell, Chief Webmaster*
Kanawha County today is an exciting technology center that is earning recognition in information technology, medical research, chemical synthesis research, and telecommunications.

**3657 Disability Determination Section**
Ste 500
500 Quarrier St
Charleston, WV 25301-2913 304-343-5055
800-772-1213
800-344-5033
FAX: 304-353-4212
e-mail: Kenneth.Lim@ssa.gov
www.ssa.gov

*Kenneth Lim, Professional Relations Officer Supervisor*
*Betty Halstead, Professional Relations Officer*
*Allyson "Sunny" Pugh, Professional Relations Officer*
*Michael J. Astrue, Commissioner*
We deliver services through a nationwide network of over 1,400 offices that include regional offices, field offices, card centers, teleservice centers, processing centers, hearing offices, the Appeals Council, and our State and territorial partners, the Disability Determination Services. We also have a presence in U.S. embassies around the globe. For the public, we are the "face of the government." The rich diversity of our employees mirrors the public we serve.

**3658 Social Security: Charleston Disability Determination**
Social Security
500 Quarrier Street
Suite 500
Charleston, WV 25301-2913 304-343-5055
800-772-1213
800-344-5033
FAX: 304-353-4212
e-mail: Kenneth.Lim@ssa.gov
www.ssa.gov

*Kenneth Lim, Professional Relations Officer Supervisor*
*Betty Halstead, Professional Relations Officer*
*Allyson Sunny Pugh, Professional Relations Officer*
*Michael J. Astrue, Commissioner*
We deliver services through a nationwide network of over 1,400 offices that include regional offices, field offices, card centers, teleservice centers, processing centers, hearing offices, the Appeals Council, and our State and territorial partners, the Disability Determination Services. We also have a presence in U.S. embassies around the globe. For the public, we are the "face of the government." The rich diversity of our employees mirrors the public we serve.

**3659 West Virginia Advocates**
4th Fl
1207 Quarrier St
Charleston, WV 25301-1826
304-346-0847
800-950-5250
FAX: 304-346-0867
e-mail: kellie.l.aikman@wv.gov
wvadvocates.org

*Clarice Hausch, Executive Director*
*Barbara Criner, Administrative Director*
*Craig Duff, System Administrator*
*Brittany Given, Administrative Assistant*
West Virginia Advocates, Inc. (WVA) is the federally mandated protection and advocacy system for people with disabilities in West Virginia. WVA is a private, nonprofit agency. Our services are confidential and free of charge.

**3660 West Virginia Client Assistance Program**
West Virginia Advocates
Rm 6
1900 Kanawha Blvd E
Charleston, WV 25305-1
304-558-3780
FAX: 304-558-4092
e-mail: vhuffman@access.k12.wv.us
legis.state.wv.us

*Clarice Hausch, Executive Director*

**3661 West Virginia Department of Aging**
1900 Kanawha Blvd. East
Charleston, WV 25305
304-558-3317
877-987-3646
FAX: 304-558-5609
e-mail: hollygrove@juno.com
http://www.wvseniorservices.gov

*Robert E. Roswall, Commissioner*
*Nel Kimble*
The information we offer is tailored to those who are seeking to locate programs and services for themselves or their loved ones and also for professionals who may be looking for up-to-date information relating to the field of aging.

**3662 West Virginia Department of Children with Disabilities**
Children with Special Health Care Needs
Rm 730
350 Capitol St
Charleston, WV 25301-1757
304-356-4519
FAX: 304-558-6646
http://www.wvdhhr.org

*Douglas M. Robinson, Deputy Commissioner*
*Michael Austin, Director*
*Gail Totten, Director*
*Melissa Rosen, CFO*
The Bureau for Public Health directs public health activities at all levels within the state to fulfill the core functions of public health: the assessment of community health status and available resources; policy development resulting in proposals to support and encourage better health; and assurance that needed services are available, accessible, and of acceptable quality.

**3663 West Virginia Department of Health**
One Davis Square
Suite 300
Charleston, WV 25301
304-558-1184
FAX: 304-558-4519
http://www.wvdhhr.org

*Douglas M. Robinson, Deputy Commissioner*
*Michael Austin, Director*
*Gail Totten, Director*
*Melissa Rosen, CFO*
The Bureau for Public Health directs public health activities at all levels within the state to fulfill the core functions of public health: the assessment of community health status and available resources; policy development resulting in proposals to support and encourage better health; and assurance that needed services are available, accessible, and of acceptable quality.

**3664 West Virginia Developmental Disabilities Council**
110 Stockton St
Charleston, WV 25387
304-558-0416
FAX: 304-558-0941
TTY:304-558-2376
e-mail: dhhrwvddc@wv.gov
http://www.ddc.wv.gov

*Clarice Hausch, Executive Director*
*Janice Holland, Associate Director*
*Karen ' Ruddle, Coordinator, Adolescent Education Office of Special Programs*
*Jane McCallister, Director*
Working to assure that West Virginians with developmental disabilities receive the services, supports, and other forms of assistance they need to exercise self-determination and achieve independence, productivity, integration, and inclusion in the community.
*6-8 pages Quarterly Newsl*

**3665 West Virginia Division of Rehabilitation Services**
107 Capitol Street
Charleston, WV 25301-2609
304-356-2060
800-642-8207
www.wvdrs.org

*Donna L. Ashworth, Acting Director*
*Kay Goodwin, Cabinet Secretary*
DRS' mission is to enable and empower individuals with disabilities to work and to live independently.

## Wisconsin

**3666 Disability Rights Wisconsin: Milwaukee Office**
Ste 3230
6737 W Washington St
Milwaukee, WI 53214-5651
414-773-4646
800-708-3034
FAX: 414-773-4647
TTY: 888-758-6049
e-mail: info@drwi.org
disabilityrightswi.org

*Tom Masseau, Executive Director*
*Linda Apple, Office Manager*
*Molly Bandt, Managing Attorney*
*Kristine Beck, Administrative Specialist*
The protection and advocacy agency for people with disabilities in Wisconsin. DRW provides guidance, advice, investigation, negotiation and in some cases legal representation to people with disabilities and their families. Local and state level systems advocacy and training are also provided.

**3667 International Dyslexia Association: Wisconsin Branch**
133 W. Ellsworth Lane Bayside
Baraboo, WI 53217
608-355-0911
800-222-3123
e-mail: wibida@gmail.com.
http://www.wibida.org/

*Cheryl Ward, President*
*Tammy Tillotson, Vice President*
*Susan Westbrook, Secretary*
*Ervin Allen Carpenter, Director*
The International Dyslexia Association actively promotes effective teaching approaches and related clinical educational intervention strategies for dyslexics. We support and encourage interdisciplinary study and research. We facilitate the exploration of the causes and early identification of dyslexia and are committed to the responsible and wide dissemination of research-based knowledge.

**3668 Social Security: Madison Field Office**
6011 Odana Rd
Madison, WI 53719-1101
866-770-2262
800-772-1213
FAX: 608-270-1021
TTY: 800-325-0778
e-mail: wi.fo.madison@ssa.gov
www.ssa.gov

**3669 West Virginia Department of Health**
One Davis Square
Suite 100 East
Charleston, WV 25301
304-558-0684
800-441-4576
FAX: 304-558-1130
e-mail: dhhrwebmaster@wv.gov
wvdhhrsecretary@wvdhhr.org

*Rocco S. Fucillo, Cabinet Secretary*
*Susan Shelton Perry, Deputy Secretary for Legal Services*
*Ellen Cannon, Privacy Officer*
*Debra Garnes, Executive Secretary*
The Department of Health and Family Services operates the federal Title V Maternal and Child Health Block Grant Program for Children with Special Health Care Needs. The program provides program monitoring, consultation and technical assistance to five regional CSHCN centers throughout Wisconsin; a Birth Defects Monitoring and Surveillance Program and a Universal Newborn Hearing Screening Program. The name is ""West Virginia Department of Health & Human""Resources

**3670 Wisconsin Board for People with Developmental Disabilities (WBPDD)**
Ste 110
201 W Washington Ave
Madison, WI 53703-2796
608-266-7826
888-332-1677
FAX: 608-267-3906
TTY:608-266-6660
e-mail: bpddhelp@wcdd.org
wcdd.org

*Jennifer Ondrejka, Manager*
*Joshua Ryf, Office Manager*
Statewide systems advocacy group for people with developmental disabilities in Wisconsin.

**3671 Wisconsin Bureau of Aging**
State Office of Wisconsin
1 West Wilson Street
Madison, WI 53703
608-266-1865
FAX: 608-267-3203
TTY:888-701-1251
e-mail: DHSwebmaster@wisconsin.gov
www.dhfs.state.wi.us/aging

*Donna Mc Dowell, Executive Director*
*Gail Schwersenska, Section Chief*
*Dennis G. Smith, Secretary*
Keeps and updates information and printed materials on senior housing directories, nursing home listings, and home care agencies.

**3672 Wisconsin Coalition for Advocacy: Madison Office**
Ste 400
16 N Carroll St
Madison, WI 53703-2762
608-267-0214
800-928-8778
FAX: 608-267-0368

*Kim Hogan, Intake Specialist*
*Mr Lynn Breedlove, Executive Director*
The protection and advocacy agency for people with disabilities in Wisconsin. WCA provides guidance, advice, investigation, negotiation and in some cases legal representation to people with disabilities and their families. Local and state level systems advocacy and training are also provided.

**3673 Wisconsin Governor's Committee for People with Disabilities**
1 West Wilson Street
Madison, WI 53703
608-266-1865
877-865-3432
FAX: 608-266-3386
TTY: 888-701-1251
e-mail: DHSwebmaster@wisconsin.gov
www.dhfs.state.wi.us

*Donna Mc Dowell, Executive Director*
*Gail Schwersenska, Section Chief*
*Dennis G. Smith, Secretary*
To advise the Governor and state agencies on problems faced by people with disabilities; to review legislation affecting people with disabilities; to promote effective operation of publicly-administered or supported programs serving people with disabilities; to promote the collection, dissemination and incorporation of adequate information about persons with disabilities for purposes of public planning at all levels of government.

**3674 Workers Compensation Board Wisconsin**
P.O.Box 7901
Room C100, 201 E. Washington Avenue
Madison, WI 53707-7901
608-266-1340
FAX: 608-267-0394

*Reggie Newson, Secretary*
*Jonathan Barry, Deputy Secretary*
*Georgia Maxwell, Executive Assistant*
*Kathleen Reed, Administrator*
The Worker's Compensation Division administers programs designed to ensure that injured workers receive required benefits from insurers or self-insured employers; encourage rehabilitation and reemployment for injured workers; and promote the reduction of work-related injuries, illnesses, and deaths.

## Wyoming

**3675 Social Security: Cheyenne Disability Determination**
Social Security
821 W Pershing Blvd
Cheyenne, WY 82002-1
307-777-7341
800-438-5788
FAX: 307-637-0247
e-mail: Jeff.Graham@ssa.gov
ssa.gov

*Vicky Johnson, Director*
*Jeffrey W. Graham, Administrator*
*James Hruby, Professional Relations Officer*
*Ree Lindgren, Disability Supervisor*
We deliver services through a nationwide network of over 1,400 offices that include regional offices, field offices, card centers, teleservice centers, processing centers, hearing offices, the Appeals Council, and our State and territorial partners, the Disability Determination Services. We also have a presence in U.S. embassies around the globe. For the public, we are the "face of the government." The rich diversity of our employees mirrors the public we serve.

**3676 WY Department of Health: Mental Health and Substance Abuse Service Division**
Suite 220
6101 Yellowstone Rd
Cheyenne, WY 82002-1
307-777-6494
800-535-4006
FAX: 307-777-5849
TTY: 307-777-5581
e-mail: wdh@state.wy.us
http://www.health.wyo.gov

*Janet Altum, Division Secretary*
*Sylvia Bagdonas, Community Services Coordinator*
*Billie Bouchard, Fiscal Support*
*Linda Briley, Executive Secretary*

State office responsible for purchase of service and program development policy.

**3677 Workers Compensation Board Wyoming**
2nd Fl
122 W 25th St
Cheyenne, WY 82001-3004
307-777-7159
FAX: 307-777-5946

**3678 Wyoming Client Assistance Program**
Protection and Advocacy System
2nd Fl
320 W 25th St
Cheyenne, WY 82001-3069
307-632-2682
877-854-5041
FAX: 307-638-0815
e-mail: wypanda@vcn.com
ap.org

*Jeanne Thobro, Manager*
*Jeanne A Thobro, Executive Director*

**3679 Wyoming Department of Aging**
State Department of Wyoming
6101 Yellowstone Rd
Cheyenne, WY 82002-1
307-777-7986
800-442-2766
FAX: 307-777-5340
e-mail: wyaging@wyo.gov
health.wyo.gov

*Beverly Morrow, Manager*
*April D. Getchius, Senior Administrator*
The Wyoming Department of Health's Aging Division is committed to providing care, ensuring safety and and promoting independent choices for Wyoming's older adults

**3680 Wyoming Developmental Disability Council**
122 W 25th St
1st. Fl. West, Herschler Building,
Cheyenne, WY 82002
307-777-7230
800-438-5791
FAX: 307-777-5690
e-mail: shannon.buller@wyo.gov
ddcouncil.state.wy.u

*Shannon Buller, Executive Director*
*Von Maul, Administrative Assistant*
*Sam Janney, Public Information Officer*
*Calob Taylor, Grants & Fiscal Coordinator*
Our purpose is to assure that individuals with developmental disabilities and their families participate in and have access to needed community services, individualized supports and other forms of assistance that promote independence, productivity, integration and inclusion in all facets of community life.

**3681 Wyoming Protection & Advocacy for Persons with Disabilities**
7344 Stockman Street
Cheyenne, WY 82009
307-632-3496
FAX: 307-638-0815
e-mail: wypanda@wypanda.com
http://wypanda.com/

*Jeanne Thobro, Executive Director*
Wyoming Protection & Advocacy System, Inc. (P&A), established in 1977, is the official non-profit corporation authorized to implement certain mandates of several federal laws. Enacted by Congress, these laws provide various protection and advocacy services.

# Independent Living Centers

## Alabama

3682 **Birdie Thornton Center**
2350 Hine Street
Athens, AL 35611
256-232-0366
FAX: 256-230-9398
www.birdiethorntoncenter.com

*Kristy Allen King, Program Director*
*Heather Mereidth, Program Professional, QMRP*
*Rabieb Clem, Senior Aid*
*Kay Green, Training Specialist*
The Birdie Thornton Center is devoted to providing care, education, and training to adults with developmental delays and disabilities.

3683 **Independent Living Center of Mobile**
5301 Moffett Rd Suite 110
Mobile, AL 36618-2926
251-460-0301
FAX: 251-341-1267
TTY:251-460-2872
e-mail: Michaeld@ilcmobile.org
ilcmobile.org

*Michael Davis, Executive Director*
*Darmita Flood, Administrative Assistant*
*Barbara Hattier, ILS/Transportation Coordinator*
*James Flora, ILS/Outreach Specialist*
Helping people with disabilities become independent.

3684 **Independent Living Resources Of Greater Birmingham: Alabaster**
Ste C
120 Plaza Cir
Alabaster, AL 35007-7034
205-685-0570
FAX: 205-251-0605
TTY:205-685-0570
e-mail: alabasterilc@bellsouth.net
www.ilrgb.org

*Daniel Kessler, Director*
The mission of this Independent Living Center is to empower people with disabilities to fully participate in the community. SITE IS UNDER CONSTRUCTION

3685 **Independent Living Resources of Greater Birmingham: Jasper**
300 Birmingham Ave
Jasper, AL 35501-3811
205-387-0159
FAX: 205-387-0162
TTY:205-387-0159
e-mail: ilcwalker@bellsouth.net
www.ilrgb.org

*Dan Kessler, Executive Director*
The purpose of this Independent Living Center is to empower people with disabilities to fully participate in the community. SITE IS UNDER CONSTRUCTION

3686 **Independent Living Resources of Greater Birmingham**
206 13th St S
Birmingham, AL 35233-1317
205-251-2223
FAX: 205-251-0605
TTY:205-251-2223
www.ilrgb.org

*Daniel G Kessler, Executive Director*
*Kay Phillips, Independent Living Specialist*
The mission of this Independent Living Center is to empower people with disabilities to fully participate in the community. SITE IS UNDER CONSTRUCTION

3687 **Montgomery Center for Independent Living**
600 S Court St
Montgomery, AL 36104-4106
334-240-2520
FAX: 334-240-6869
TTY:334-240-2520
e-mail: mcil@bellsouth.net
www.montgomerycil.org

*Scott Renner, Executive Director*
*Barbara F. Crozier, President*
*Kenneth Marshall, Vice President*
*Vickie P. FitzGerald, Secretary*
Encourgaes people with disabilities to support one another in reaching their own independent living goals.

## Alaska

3688 **Access Alaska: ADA Partners Project**
Ste 105
121 W Fireweed Ln
Anchorage, AK 99503-2044
907-248-4777
800-770-4488
888-462-1444
FAX: 907-222-5008
TTY:907-248-8799
e-mail: info@accessalaska.org
accessalaska.org

*Jim Beck, Executive Director*
*Mike O'Neill, President*
*Robert Wallis, Vice President*
*Jim Babb, Secretary*
Assisting Alaskans with disabilities to live independently in the community of their choice.

3689 **Access Alaska: Fairbanks**
526 Gaffney Rd
Suite 100
Fairbanks, AK 99701-4914
907-479-7940
800-770-7940
FAX: 907-474-4052
TTY: 907-474-8619
e-mail: info@accessalaska.org
accessalaska.org

*Kerry Turnbow, Regional Executive Director*
A local non profit agency using its resources to actively promote a society where persons with disabilities can live and work independently in the community of their choice.

3690 **Access Alaska: Mat-Su**
1075 Check St,
Suite 109
Wasilla, AK 99654-6937
907-357-2588
800-770-0228
FAX: 907-357-5585
e-mail: info@accessalaska.org
accessalaska.org

*Jim Beck, Executive Director*
*Mike O'Neill, President*
*Robert Wallis, Vice President*
*Jim Babb, Secretary*
Provides independent living services to persons with significant disabilities. Mission is to encourage and promote the total integration of persons with disabilities into the community of their choice. Services include independent living skills training, information and referral, advocacy, peer support, and at home modifications.

**3691 Alaska SILC**
Ste 206
1057 W Fireweed Ln
Anchorage, AK 99503-1760
907-263-2011
888-294-7452
FAX: 907-263-2012
e-mail: nationsa.silc@gmail.com
www.alaskasilc.org

*Andi Nations, Executive Director*

The Alaska Statewide Independent Living is committed to promoting a philosophy of consumer control, peer support, self help, self determination, equal access, and individual and systems advocacy, in order to maximize leadership, empowerment, independence, productivity, and to support full inclusion and integration of individuals with disabilities into the mainstream of American society.

**3692 Arctic Access**
P.O.Box 930
Kotzebue, AK 99752-930
907-412-0695
877-442-2393
TTY:907-442-2393
e-mail: arcticaccesskotz@gci.net
http://arcticaccesscil.org

*Roger Wright Jr, Executive Director*
*Russell Williams, Jr,, Elder & Disability Resource Coordinator*
*Audrey Aanes*

The Arctic Access Independent Living Center provides services and opportunities for elders and others with disabilities so they may remain in their village and be as active as possible with their families and commuities in the North West Arctic and Bering Straits Regions of Alaska.

**3693 Hope Community Resources**
540 W Intl Airport Rd
Anchorage, AK 99518-1105
907-561-5335
800-478-0078
FAX: 907-564-7429
e-mail: info@hopealaska.org
hopealaska.org

*Charles Brower, President*
*John Dittrich, Vice President*
*Eugene Bates, Treasure*
*Charleen McBratney, Secretary*

Provider of services to individuals who experience a disability.

**3694 Kenai Peninsula Independent Living Center**
P.O.Box 2474
Homer, AK 99603-2474
907-235-7911
800-770-7911
FAX: 907-235-6236
e-mail: ilc@xyz.net
peninsulailc.org

*Joyanna Geisler, Executive Director*

Offers peer counseling, disability education and awareness, attendant care registry and information on accessible housing.

**3695 Kenai Peninsula Independent Living Center: Seward**
P.O.Box 3523
201 Third Avenue, Suite 101Bs
Seward, AK 99664-3523
907-224-8711
FAX: 907-224-7793
e-mail: sewardilc@qci.net
www.peninsulailc.org

*Joyanna Geisler, Executive Director*

Offers peer counseling, disability, education and awareness, attendant care registry and information on accessible housing.

**3696 Keni Peninsula Independent Living Center: Central Peninsula**
47255 Princeton Avenue
Suite 8
Soldotna, AK 99669
907-262-6333
FAX: 907-260-4495
e-mail: nadine@peninsulailc.org
www.peninsulailc.org

*Joyanna Geisler, Executive Director*

Offers peer counseling, disability education and awareness, attendant care registry and information on accessible housing.

**3697 Southeast Alaska Independent Living**
3225 Hospital Drive
Suite 300
Juneau, AK 99801-7863
907-586-4920
800-478-7245
FAX: 907-586-4980
TTY: 907-523-5285
e-mail: info@sailinc.org
sailinc.org

*Joe Tompkins, Vice President*
*Paul Douglas, Treasurer*
*Jeff Irwin, Member*
*Kate Burkhart, Member*

To empower consumers with disabilities by providing services and information to support them in making choices that will positively affect their independence and productivity in society.

**3698 Southeast Alaska Independent Living: Ketchikan**
Ste 107
602 Dock St
Ketchikan, AK 99901-6574
907-225-4735
888-452-7245
FAX: 907-247-4735
e-mail: ketchikan@sailinc.org
www.sailinc.org

*Suzanne Williams, Secretary*
*Elana Rath, Member*
*Mary Gregg, Member*
*Kate Burkhart, Member*

To empower consumers with disabilities by providing services and information to support them in making choices that will positively affect their independence and productivity in society.

**3699 Southeast Alaska Independent Living: Sitka**
Ste C
514 Lake St
Sitka, AK 99835-7405
907-747-6859
888-500-7245
FAX: 907-747-6783
e-mail: sitka@sailinc.org
www.sailinc.org

*RoseMarie Duran, Member*
*Robert Purvis, President*
*Jeff Irwin, Member*
*Kate Burkhart, Member*

To empower consumers with disabilities by providing services and information to support them in making choices that will positively affect their independence and productivity in society.

## Arizona

**3700 ASSIST! to Independence**
P.O.Box 4133
Tuba City, AZ 86045-4133
928-283-6261
888-848-1449
FAX: 928-283-6284
TTY: 928-283-6672
e-mail: assist01@frontiernet.net
www.assisttoindependence.org

*Michael Blatchford, Executive Director*
*Priscilla Lane, IL Services Coordinator/Dep Dir*
A community based, American Indian owned and operated non-profit agency that was established by and for people with disabilities and chronic health conditions to help fill some of the gaps in service delivery.

**3701 Arizona Bridge to Independent Living**
Ste 200
5025 E Washington St
Phoenix, AZ 85034-7439
602-256-2245
800-280-2245
FAX: 602-254-6407
e-mail: boardofdirectors@abil.org
www.abil.org

*Phil Pangrazio, President & CEO*
*Ann Pasco, Operations Director*
*Feng Chiou, Financial Director*
*Regina Mitzel, V. P. & Chief Administrative Officer*
ABIL offers and promotes programs designed to empower people with disabilities to take personal responsibility so they may achieve or continue independent lifestyles within the community.

**3702 Arizona Bridge to Independent Living: Phoenix**
Ste D405
1229 E.Washington St.
Phoenix, AZ 85034
602-296-0551
800-280-2245
FAX: 602-256-0184
TTY: 602-296-0591
e-mail: boardofdirectors@abil.org
www.abil.org

*Phil Pangrazio, President & CEO*
*Ann Pasco, Operations Director*
*Feng Chiou, Financial Director*
*Regina Mitzel, V. P. & Chief Administrative Officer*
ABIL offers and promotes programs designed to empower people with disabilities to take personal responsibility so they may achieve or continue independent lifestyles within the community.

**3703 Arizona Bridge to Independent Living: Mesa**
Ste 10
2150 S Country Club Dr
Mesa, AZ 85210-6879
480-655-9750
800-280-2245
FAX: 480-655-9751
TTY: 480-655-9750
e-mail: boardofdirectors@abil.org
www.abil.org

*Phil Pangrazio, President & CEO*
*Ann Pasco, Operations Director*
*Feng Chiou, Financial Director*
*Regina Mitzel, V. P. & Chief Administrative Officer*
ABIL offers and promotes programs designed to empower people with disabilities to take personal responsibility so they may achieve or continue independent lifestyles within the community.

**3704 Community Outreach Program for the Deaf**
268 W Adams St
Tucson, AZ 85705-6534
520-792-1906
FAX: 520-770-8554
TTY:520-792-1906
e-mail: request@copdaz.org
copdaz.org

*Anne Levy, Executive Director*
A non-profit organization, which has been serving the needs of people in Southern Arizona who are deaf or hard of hearing.

**3705 DIRECT Center for Independence**
1023 N Tyndall Ave
Tucson, AZ 85719-4446
520-624-6452
800-342-1853
FAX: 520-792-1438
TTY: 520-624-6452
e-mail: direct@directilc.org
www.directilc.org

*Wendy Dewey, Executive Director*
*Martha Schuetz, Secretary*
A non-consumer directed, community-based advocacy organization, that promotes independent living and offers a variety of programs for all people with disabilities which encourage them to achieve their full potential and to participate in the community.

**3706 New Horizons Independent Living Center: Prescott Valley**
8085 E Manley Dr
Prescott Valley, AZ 86314-6154
928-772-1266
800-406-2377
FAX: 928-772-3808
TTY: 928-772-1266
e-mail: ltoone@newhorizonsilc.org
www.newhorizonsilc.org

*Deborah Henderson, Adminstrative Assistant*
*Liz Toone, Executive Director*
To provide services and advocacy which empower and enable people with disabilities to self-determine the goals and activities of their lives.

**3707 Services Maximizing Independent Living and Empowerment (SMILE)**
Suite 4
1931 South Arizona Ave
Yuma, AZ 85364-5721
928-329-6681
FAX: 928-329-6715
TTY:928-782-7458
e-mail: info@smile-az.org
www.smile-az.org

*Laura Duval, Executive Director*
*Brenda Howard, Finance Manager/ Admin Assistant*
*Shawnnita Miranda, Advocate/ Home modification Manager*
*Brandon Howard, Outreach Coordinator, Technology/ Data Specialist*
SMILE continually advocates for the Independent Living Philosophy, both individually and system wide. The Board and staff constantly strives to improve the system by writing letters, training staff, providing services, and creating public awareness as to the services and opportunities open to people who have disabilities.

**3708 Sterling Ranch: Residence for Special Women**
Sterling Ranch
P.O.Box 36
Skull Valley, AZ 86338-36
928-442-3289
FAX: 928-442-9272
e-mail: director@sterlingranch.info
www.sterlingranch.info

*Russell Dryer, Executive Director*
*Trent Nichel, Manager*
A nonprofit residence for women with developmental disabilities which has been in operation since 1947. As a small facility (19 residents) the orientation is personal and family-like. Offers

activities that range from gardening, quilting, academics, sign-language, crafts and a myriad of field trips and excursions. Private rooms and spacious living on 4 1/2 acres.

## Arkansas

**3709 Arkansas Independent Living Council**
11324 Arcade Drive
Suite 7
Little Rock, AR 72212
501-372-0607
800-772-0607
FAX: 501-372-0598
e-mail: arkansasilc@att.net
www.ar-ilc.org

*Katy Morris, Director*
*Cheryl ', Director*
*Brenda Stinebuck, Chair*
*Liz Adams, Vice Chair*

A non-profit organization promoting independent living for people with disabilities.

**3710 Delta Resource Center for Independent Living**
3131 West 28th Avenue
Pine Bluff, AR 71603-6249
870-535-2222
FAX: 800-824-0009
e-mail: drcilar@yahoo.com
www.ar-ilc.org

*Lynne McAllester, Director*
*Katy Morris, Director*
*Cheryl ', Director*
*Brenda Stinebuck, Chair*

Provides services, support, and advocacy which enables people with severe disabilities to live as independently as possible within their family and community.

**3711 Mainstream**
Ste 5
300 S Rodney Parham Rd
Little Rock, AR 72205-4774
501-280-0012
FAX: 501-280-9267
TTY:501-280-9262
e-mail: mainstreamlrc@earthlink.net
mainstreamilrc.com

*Rita Byers, Executive Director*
*Vincent McKinney*
*Vincent Acklin*
*Debbie Gillespie*

A non residential, consumer driven independent living resource center for persons with disabilities. Mainstream operates with conviction that people with disabilities have the right and responsibility to make choices, to control their lives and to participate fully and equally in the community.

**3712 Our Way: The Cottage Apt Homes**
10434 W 36th St
Little Rock, AR 72204-6616
501-225-5030
FAX: 501-225-5190

*Katrina Williams, Manager*
*Crystal Brown, Assistant Manager*

Advocacy and information services. One bedroom apartments for mobility impaired and elderly 62 years or older persons.
*Based on income*

**3713 Sources for Community IL Services**
1918 N Birch Ave
Fayetteville, AR 72703-2408
479-442-5600
888-284-7521
FAX: 479-442-5192
TTY: 479-251-1378
e-mail: jmather@arsources.org
www.arsources.org

*Jim Mather, Executive Director*
*Neill Williamson, President*
*Brent Williams, PhD, Vice-President*
*Burke Fanari, Secretary*

Provides services, support, and advocacy for individuals with disabilities, their families and the community.

**3714 Spa Area Independent Living Services**
80 Johnson Ferry Road, NE
Atlanta, GA 30328
404-303-7900
FAX: 404-303-7007
e-mail: info@restsearch.com
www.arsales.org

*Dejan S. Vojnovic, President*
*Joseph E. Anderson, Vice President - Real Estate*
*Bryan S. Cox, Vice President - Technology*
*Sharon D. Hendley, Administrator*

Provides services and advocacy by and for persons with all types of disabilities. The goal is to assist individuals with disabilities to achieve thier maximum potential within their families and communities.

## California

**3715 Access Center of San Diego**
Ste 131
8885 Rio San Diego Dr
San Diego, CA 92108-1625
619-293-3500
FAX: 619-293-3508
TTY:619-293-7757
e-mail: info@a2isd.org
www.a2isd.org

*Louis Frick, Executive Director*
*Deirdre DuPlessis, Director of Administration*
*Amy Kalivas, Program Manager*
*Leticia Vizcarra, Program Manager*

Access to Independence is an independent living center (ILC), a nonresidential, cross-disability, non-profit corporations that provide services to people with disabilities to help maximize their independence and fully integrate into their communities. Access to Independence is one of 391 ILCs across the country and one of 29 serving Californians. Like all ILCs, Access to Independence offers required federal and state programs and services to people of all disability types and ages at no charge.

**3716 Access to Independence**
8885 Rio San Diego Drive
#131
San Diego, CA 92108-1625
619-293-3500
FAX: 619-293-3508
TTY:619-293-7757
e-mail: info@2isd.org
www.a2isd.org

*Louis Frick, Executive Director*
*Deirdre DuPlessis, Director of Administration*
*Amy Kalivas, Program Manager*
*Leticia Vizcarra, Program Manager*

A community resource for people with disabilities to lead independent lives.

**3717 Access to Independence of Imperial Valley**
Ste D
400 Mary Ave
Calexico, CA 92231-2875 760-768-2044
FAX: 760-768-4977
TTY:760-768-0466
e-mail: info@2isd.org
www.a2sid.org

*Louis Frick, Executive Director*
*Deirdre DuPlessis, Director of Administration*
*Amy Kalivas, Program Manager*
*Leticia Vizcarra, Program Manager*
A community resource for people with disabilities to lead independent lives.

**3718 Access to Independence of North County**
209 E Broadway
Vista, CA 92084-6005 760-643-0447
FAX: 760-435-9206
www.a2sid.org

*Louis Frick, Executive Director*
A community resource for people with disabilities to lead independent lives.

**3719 Beaumont Senior Center: Community Access Center**
1310 Oak Valley Parkway
Beaumont, CA 92223-2218 951-769-8539
FAX: 951-769-1372
TTY:909-769-2794
e-mail: ilser5@ilcac.org

*Laurie Hoirup, Director*
A non profit organization; one of 29 similar programs throughout the state of California CAC is a community resource, advocate, and educator for Riverside County residents with disabilities.

**3720 California Foundation For Independent Living Centers**
1234 H Street
Suite 100
Sacramento, CA 95814-1912 916-325-1690
FAX: 916-325-1699
TTY:916-325-1695
e-mail: cfilc@cfilc.org
www.cfilc.org

*Tink Miller, Executive Director*
*Jimie Soto, Interim Director*
*Yomi Wrong, Executive Director*
*Lee Nattress, Executive Director*
Community Rehabilitation Services, Inc. (CRS) is a private, non-profit agency established in 1974 to assist persons with disabilities within the East/North East areas of Los Angeles County to enhance their options for living independently. Any person who is 18 yrs of age or more with physical, sensory, mental/emotional or developmental disabilities can work with us to become more self-sufficient. Our intake procedures provide an orientation to the staff, facilities and services at CRS.

**3721 California Foundation for Independent Living Centers**
1235 H Street
Suite 101
Sacramento, CA 95814-1913 916-325-1691
FAX: 916-325-1699
TTY:916-325-1695
e-mail: cfilc@cfilc.org
www.cfilc.org

*Tink Miller, Executive Director*
*Jimie Soto, Interim Director*
*Yomi Wrong, Executive Director*
*Lee Nattress, Executive Director*
CFILC's mission is to support independent living centers in their local communities through advocating for systems change and promoting access and integration for people with disabilities.

**3722 California State Independent Living Council (SILC)**
Ste 100
1600 K St
Sacramento, CA 95814-4010 916-445-0142
866-866-7452
FAX: 916-445-5973
TTY: 866-745-2889
e-mail: neal@calsilc.org
www.calsilc.org

*Liz Pazdral, Executive Director*
*Caroline Kuhn, Staff Services Analyst*
*Mattie Hogan-Betchik, Student Assistant*
*Elsa S. Quezada, Chair*
To maximize options for independence for persons with disabilities

**3723 Center for Independence of the Disabled**
Ste 400
1515 S El Camino Real
San Mateo, CA 94402-3062 650-645-1780
FAX: 650-645-1785
TTY:650-522-9313
e-mail: info@cidbelmont.org
http://www.cidsanmateo.org

*Brad Friedman, Co-President*
*Laura Whitsitt Hillyard, Co-President*
*Thomas J. Devine, Vice President*
*John Horgan, Secretary*
Increase the social, educational, and economic participation of persons with disabilities in San Mateo County, and to encourage, support, and provide options for self determination, equal access and freedom of choice.

**3724 Center for Independence of the Disabled- Daly City**
Ste 256
355 Gellert Blvd
Daly City, CA 94015-2675 650-991-5124
FAX: 650-757-2075
TTY:650-991-5182
e-mail: dalycity5@aol.com
www.cidbelmont.org

*Kent Mickelson, Director*
The Daly City Branch office fulfills its mission by serving disabled consumers in Brisbane, Colma, Daly City, El Granada, Half Moon Bay, Montara, Moss Beach, Pacifica, Pescadero, Princeton and South San Francisco. Our mission is to increase the social, educational, economic, social and political participants of persons with disabilities in San Mateo county, California.

**3725 Center for Independent Living**
3075 Adeline Street, Suite 100
Berkeley, CA 94703 510-841-4776
FAX: 510-841-6168
TTY:510-848-3101
e-mail: ywrong@cilberkeley.org
cilberkeley.org

*Yomi Wrong, Executive Director*
*Makr Burns, Deputy Director*
The Center for Independent Living, Inc (CIL) is a national leader in helping people with disabilities live independently and become productive members of society. Founded in 1972, CIL is a pioneer advocating for greater accessibility in communities, designing techniques in independent living and providing direct services to people with disabilities. A partial list of services includes Information and Referral, Personal Assistance Services, Independent Living Skills Training and Peer Counseling.

**3726 Center for Independent Living: East Oakland**
Ste 9a
7200 Bancroft Ave
Oakland, CA 94605-2403 510-635-4920
FAX: 510-635-4261
e-mail: cwood@cilberkeley.org

*Theo Polk, Manager*
A national leader in helping people with disabilities live independently and become productive, fully participating members of society.

**3727 Center for Independent Living: Oakland**
1904 Franklin Street
Ste 320
Oakland, CA 94612-1285 510-763-9999
FAX: 510-763-4910
TTY:510-444-1837
e-mail: info@cilberkeley.org
cilberkeley.org

*Henry Leng, President*
*Hank Stratford, Treasurer*
*Yomi Wrong, Executive Director*
*Ted Dienstfrey, Finance Committee*
A national leader in supporting disabled people in their efforts to lead independent lives.

**3728 Center for Independent Living: Tri-County**
2822 Harris Street
Eureka, CA 95503 707-445-8404
877-576-5000
FAX: 707-445-9751
TTY: 707-445-8405
e-mail: aa@tilinet.org
http://www.tilinet.org/

*Rebecca Simone, President*
*Chris Jones, Executive Director*
*Allan Bard, Information & Referral / Independent Living Specialist*
*Mary Bullwinkel, Outreach and Resource Preogram*

**3729 Center for Independent Living:Fresno**
Suite 101
3475 Wesy Shaw Ave
Fresno, CA 93711 559-221-2330
FAX: 559-276-6778
TTY:559-276-6779
e-mail: execdirector@cil-fresno.org
www.cil-fresno.org

*Bob Hand, Manager*

**3730 Center for Independent Living; Oakland**
1470 Fruitvale Ave
Oakland, CA 94601-2324 FAX: 510-261-2968
TTY:510-536-2271
e-mail: info@cilberkeley.org
cilberkeley.org

*Henry Leng, President*
*Hank Stratford, Treasurer*
*Yomi Wrong, Executive Director*
*Ted Dienstfrey, Finance Committee*
Independent living center to maximise the options for independence for persons with disabilities.

**3731 Center of Independent Living: Visalia**
Ste 7
208 W Main St
Visalia, CA 93291-6262 559-622-9276
FAX: 559-622-9638
e-mail: f_phillips@cil-fresno.org
www.cil-fresno.org

*Fran Phillips, Executive Directorram Manager*
*Renee Ezelle, Manager*

**3732 Central Coast Center for IL: San Benito**
1236 H Street
Suite 102
Sacramento, CA 95814-1914 916-325-1692
FAX: 916-325-1699
TTY:916-325-1696
e-mail: cfile@cfilc.org
www.cfilc.org

*Tink Miller, Executive Director*
*Jimie Soto, Interim Director*
*Yomi Wrong, Executive Director*
*Lee Nattress, Executive Director*
To advocate for barrier-free access and equal opportunity for people with disabilities to participate in the community life by increasing the capacity of Independent Living Centers to achieve their missions.

**3733 Central Coast Center for Independent Living**
318 Cayuga St.
Suite 208
Salinas, CA 93901-2600 831-757-2968
FAX: 831-757-5549
TTY:831-757-3949
e-mail: cccil@cccil.org
cccil.org

*Elsa Quezada, Executive Director*
CCCIL promotes the independence of people with disabilities by supporting their equal and full participation in community life. CCCIL provides advocacy, education and support to all people with disabilities, their families and the community.

**3734 Central Coast Center: Independent Living - Santa Cruz Office**
350 - 41st Avenue
Suite 101
Capitola, CA 95010-3930 831-462-8720
FAX: 831-462-8727
TTY:831-462-8729
e-mail: cccilcap@cccil.org
www.cccil.org

*Elsa Quezada, Executive Director*
CCCIL promotes the independence of people with disabilities by supporting their equal and full participation in community life. CCCIL provides advocacy, education and support to all people with disabilities, their families and the community.

**3735 Central Coast for Independent Living**
Ste 107
1111 San Felipe Rd
Hollister, CA 95023-2814 831-636-5196
FAX: 831-637-0478
TTY:831-637-6235
e-mail: cccilQ@cccil.org
www.cccil.org

*Elsa Quezada, Executive Director*
CCCIL promotes the independence of people with disabilities by supporting their equal and full particpation in community life. CCCIL provides advocacy, education and support to all people with disabilities, their families and the community.

**3736 Central Coast for Independent Living: Watsonville**
Ste Y
18 W. Beach St.
Watsonville, CA 95076-4371 831-724-2997
FAX: 831-724-2915
TTY:831-786-0915

*Elsa Quezada, Executive Director*
An advocacy and information center organized by and for people with disabilities that strives to make our communities more accessible and to empower people with disabilities with information and skills to live fulfilling lives in our communities.

**3737 Communities Actively Living Independent and Free**
2nd Fl
634 S Spring St
Los Angeles, CA 90014-3921
213-627-0477
FAX: 213-627-0535
TTY:213-623-9502
e-mail: info@calif-ilc.org
calif-ilc.org

*Lillibeth Navarro, Executive Director*
*BEN ROCKWELL, Board President*
*ALEX SAN MARTIN, Board Vice President*
*Marivic Deocampo, Administrative Assistant/Grants Support Assistant*
Envisions a culturally diverse independent living center designed to empower the Disability Community.

**3738 Community Access Center**
Ste 150
6848 Magnolia Ave
Riverside, CA 92506-2858
951-274-0358
FAX: 951-274-0833
TTY:951-274-0834
e-mail: execdir@ilcac.org
ilcac.org

*Paul Van Doren, Executive Director*
*Faustino Alvarez, Programs Director*
*Mark Dyer, President*
*Janet Newcomer, Vice President*
A non-profit organization; one of 29 similar programs throughout the state of California. CAC is a community resource, advocate, and educator for Riverside County residents with disabilities.

**3739 Community Access Center: Indio Branch**
83233 Indio Blvd
Indio, CA 92201-4748
760-347-4888
FAX: 760-347-0722
TTY:760-347-6802
e-mail: pmgr3@ilcac.org
www.ilcac.org

*Reginard Heron, Manager*
To empower persons with disabilities to control their own lives, create an accessible community and advocate to achieve complete social, economic, and political integration. We implement this vision by providing information, supportive services and independent living skills training.

**3740 Community Access Center: Perris**
371 Wilkerson Ave
Perris, CA 92570-2241
951-443-1158
FAX: 951-443-2608
TTY:951-443-1158
e-mail: spmgr@ilcac.org
www.ilcac.org
Community Access Center empowers persons with disabilities to control their own lives, create an accessible community and advocate to achieve complete social, economic, and political integration. CAC also implements this vision by providing information, suportive services and independent living skills training.

**3741 Community Rehabilitation Services**
844 E. Mission Road
Suite A & B
San Gabriel, CA 91776- 2759
323-266-0453
FAX: 626-614-1590
TTY:323-266-3016
e-mail: executivedirector@crs-ilc.org
www.crs-ilc.org

*Frances Garcia, Executive Director*
CRS is an independent living center that provides free services to persons with disabilities in the areas of advocacy, housing and independent living skills; assistive technology, employment, personal assistant services, peer counseling and information and referral.

**3742 Community Resources for Independence: Mendocino/Lake Branch**
Ste B
415 Talmage Rd
Ukiah, CA 95482-7486
707-463-8875
FAX: 707-463-8878
TTY:707-463-4498
www.cri-dove.org

*Tanner Silva, Manager*
A non-profit corporation established by a group of disabled and non-disabled individuals to advance the rights of persons with disabilities to equal justice, access, opportunity and participation in the communities.

**3743 Community Resources for Independence: Napa**
Ste 208
1040 Main St
Napa, CA 94559-2605
707-258-0270
FAX: 707-258-0275
TTY:707-257-0274
cri-dove.org

*Tyler Stanley, Manager*
*Matthew Shultz, Independent Living Advocate*
A non-profit corporation established by a group of disabled and non-disabled individuals to advance the rights of persons with disabilities to equal justice, access, opportunity and participation in the communities.

**3744 Community Resources for Independent Living: Hayward**
439 a St
Hayward, CA 94541-5013
510-881-5743
FAX: 510-881-1593
TTY:510-881-0218
e-mail: info@cril-online.org
cril-online.org

*Sheri Burns, Executive Director*
CRIL offers independent living services at no charge to persons with disabilities living in southern and eastern Alameda county. CRIL is also a resource for disability awareness education and training, advocacy and technical advice.

**3745 Community Resources for Independent Living**
Ste A100
39155 Liberty St
Fremont, CA 94538-1503
510-794-5735
e-mail: info@cril-online.org
www.cril-online.org

*Sheri Burns, Executive Director*
*Michael Galvan, PhD., Program Director*
*April Monroe, Finance Director*
*Esperanza Diaz-Alvarez, PAS Coordinator/Benefits Advocate*
Community Resources for Independent Living is a peer-based disability organization that advocates and provides resources for people with disabilities to improve lives and make communities fully accessible.

**3746 DRAIL (Disability Resource Agency for Independent Living)**
501 W Weber Ave
Ste 200-A
Stockton, CA 95203-6239
209-477-8143
FAX: 209-477-7730
TTY:209-465-5643
e-mail: barry@drail.org
www.drail.org

*Terry Gray, President*
*Bob Williams, Treasurer*
*Mona Martinez, Secretary*
*Barry Smith, Executive Director*
A non-profit corporation that is community based, consumer controlled, consumer choice, cross disability center for independent living.

**3747 Dayle McIntosh Center: Laguna Niguel**
Ste 110
24012 Calle De La Plata
Laguna Hills, CA 92653- 3632
949-460-7784
FAX: 949-855-8742
TTY:714-663-2087
www.daylemc.org

*Dayle Mc Intosh, Owner*
*Ann McClellan*
*Beverly Mastri, Benefits Advocate*
*Cheryl Hopper, Independent Living Skills Coordinator*

DMC advances empowerment and inclusion of all persons with disabilities. DMC is the largest Independent Living Center in California, and was named in memory of a young woman with a severe physical disability who worked to found the center.

**3748 Disability Resource Agency for Independent Living: Modesto**
920-12th Street
Modesto, CA 95354-543
209-521-7260
FAX: 209-521-4763
TTY:209-576-2409
e-mail: larry@drail.org
www.drail.org

*Barry Smith, Executive Director*

A non-profit corporation that is community based, consumer controlled, consumer choice, cross disability center for independent living.

**3749 Disability Services & Legal Center**
980 Hopper Ave
Santa Rosa, CA 95403-1649
707-528-2745
FAX: 707-528-9477
TTY:707-528-2151
e-mail: asbrown@sonic.net
www.disabilityserviceandlegal.org

*Adam Brown, Chairman*

A non-profit corporation established by a group of disabled and non-disabled individuals to advance the rights of persons with disabilities to equal justice, access, opportunity and participation in the communities.

**3750 Disabled Resources Center**
Ste 100
2750 E Spring St
Long Beach, CA 90806-2263
562-427-1000
FAX: 562-427-2027
TTY:562-427-1366
e-mail: info@drcinc.org
drcinc.org

*Dolores Nason, Executive Director*
*Theresa de Vera, Vice President*
*Lloyd Saposnek, President*
*Shirley Hsiao, Treasurer*

To empower people with disabilities to live independently in the community, to make their own decisions about their lives and to advocate on their own behalf.

**3751 FREED Center for Independent Living**
Ste A
117 New Mohawk Rd
Nevada City, CA 95959-3227
530-265-4444
800-655-7732
FAX: 530-265-4644
TTY: 530-265-4944
e-mail: contact-04@freed.org
freed.org

*Ana Acton, Executive Director*

To eliminate barriers to full equality for people with disabilities through programs which promote independent living.

**3752 FREED Center for Independent Living: Marysville**
508 J St
Marysville, CA 95901-5636
530-742-4476
TTY:530-742-4474
e-mail: contact-04@freed.org
freed.org

*Claudia Hallis, Manager*

To eliminate barriers to full equality for people with disabilities through programs which promote independent living.

**3753 First Step Independent Living**
1174 Nevada St
Redlands, CA 92374-2893
800-362-0312
e-mail: cvsfs@deltanet.com

Independent living center, empowers people with disabilities to become active, productive, members of the community.

**3754 Independent Living Center of Kern County**
5251 Office Park Dr
Bakersfield, CA 93309
661-325-1063
877-688-2079
FAX: 661-325-6702
TTY: 661-325-6702
e-mail: info@ilcofkerncounty.org
www.ilcofkerncounty.org

*Jimmie Soto, Executive Director*
*Valerie Guidry, Director of Finance*
*Harvey Clowers, Special Projects and AT Coordinator*
*Brandy Morgan, Systems Change Advocate*

A consumer-based consumer-directed non-profit agency assisting persons with disabilities to live independently in their community. The ILCKC presently offers a wide range of services to a growing population of persons with disabilities.

**3755 Independent Living Center of Lancaster**
Ste 102
1505 W Avenue J
Lancaster, CA 93534-2844
661-942-9726
FAX: 661-945-5690
TTY:661-723-2509
e-mail: ilcsc@ilcsc.org
www.ilcsc.org

*Taura Jacob, Manager*
*Marcy Hernandez*
*Niyanta Dave*

ILCSC is a non-profit, consumer based, non-residential agency providing a wide range of services to a growing population of people with disabilities. ILCSC is dedicated to empowering persons with disabilities to exercise indpendence-pofessionally, personally and creatively-while striving to educate the community on their needs.

**3756 Independent Living Resource Center**
Ste R
7425 El Camino Real
Atascadero, CA 93422-4656
805-464-3203
FAX: 805-462-1166
TTY:805-462-1162
e-mail: jblack@ilrc-trico.org
www.ilrc-trico.org

*Jerry Mihaic, Information and Referral bilingual English/Spanish*
*Kelly Hannula, Community Living Advocate*
*Paul Collagan, Benefits*
*Cary McGill, Assistive Technology Advocate*

To assist and encourage individuals to achieve their optimal level of self-sufficiency while eliminating the architectural, communication and attitudinal barriers which prevent them from full participation in the community.

**3757 Independent Living Resource Center: Santa Barbara**
423 W Victoria St
Santa Barbara, CA 93101-3619
805-284-9051
FAX: 805-963-1350
TTY:805-963-0595
e-mail: jblack@ilrc-trico.org
ilrc-trico.org

*Jennifer Griffin, Manager*
*Kathleen Riel, Program Manager*
*Jo Black, Executive Director*
*Petra Lowen, Community Living Advocate*

To assist and encourage individuals to achieve their optimal level of self-sufficiency while eliminating the architectural, communication and attitudinal barriers which prevent them from full participation in the community.

**3758 Independent Living Resource Center: San Francisco**
Fl 3
649 Mission St
San Francisco, CA 94105-4128
415-543-6222
FAX: 415-543-6318
TTY:415-543-6698
e-mail: info@ilrcsf.org
ilrcsf.org

*Jessie Lorenz, Executive Director*

To ensure that people with disabilities are full social and economic partners, both within their families and in a fully accessible community.

**3759 Independent Living Resource Center: Santa Maria Office**
Ste 3a
327 Plaza Dr
Santa Maria, CA 93454-6930
805-354-5948
FAX: 805-349-2416
TTY:805-925-0015
e-mail: jmorales@ilrc-trico.org
www.ilrc-trico.org

*Jennie Morales, Interpreter Registry Coordinator/Advocate*
*Paul Collagan, Community Living Advocate Benefits*
*Beth Houston, Deaf*
*Sandra Santana, Community Living Advocate/Information & Referral bilingual English/Spa*

To assist and encourage individuals to achieve their optimal level of self-sufficiency while eliminating the architectural, communication and attitudinal barriers which prevent them from full participation in the community.

**3760 Independent Living Resource Center: Ventura**
Ste 112
1802 Eastman Ave
Ventura, CA 93003-5759
805-256-1036
FAX: 805-650-9278
TTY:805-650-5993
e-mail: jmartinez@ilrc-trico.org
www.ilrc-trico.org

*Jennifer Martinez, Information and Referral*
*DeAnna Grove, Community Living Advocate*
*Carol Baizer, Benefits*
*Ken McLellan, Deaf*

An organization of, by and for persons with disabilities who reside or work in the service area. Purpose is to assist and encourage individuals to achieve their optimal level of self-sufficiency while eliminating the architectural, communication and attitudinal barriers which prevent them from full participation in the community.

**3761 Independent Living Resource of Contra Coast**
Ste 120
1850 Gateway Blvd
Concord, CA 94520-3293
925-363-7293
FAX: 925-363-7296
ilrccc.org

*Sarah BirdwelL, Board President*
*Kathy Mitsopoulos, Board Vice President*
*Teri Ruggiero, Board Secretary*
*Susan Rotchy, Executive Director*

Offers workshops, services are accessible to individuals with cognitive disabilities, physical disabilities, deaf and hard of hearing, emotional disabilities, visual impairments, learing disabilities and seniors.

**3762 Independent Living Resource of Fairfield**
470 Chadbourn Rd
Ste. B
Fairfield, CA 94534
707-435-8174
FAX: 707-435-8177
e-mail: susanr@ilrcoco-sol.org
www.ilrcoco-sol.org

*Sarah BirdwelL, Board President*
*Kathy Mitsopoulos, Board Vice President*
*Teri Ruggiero, Board Secretary*
*Susan Rotchy, Executive Director*

To empower people with disabilities to: control their own lives, provide advocacy and support for individuals with disabilities to live independently, create an accessible community free of physical and attitudinal barriers.

**3763 Independent Living Resource: Antioch**
310 W 10th St
Antioch, CA 94509-1761
925-754-0539
TTY:925-755-0934
www.ilrccc.org

*Sarah BirdwelL, Board President*
*Kathy Mitsopoulos, Board Vice President*
*Teri Ruggiero, Board Secretary*
*Susan Rotchy, Executive Director*

Non-profit organizations run and controlled by persons with disabilities. They are non-residential, community-based centers where people with disabilities can receive assistance with a variety of daily living issues and learn the skills they need to take controll of their lives from people who have had similar experiences living with a disability.

**3764 Independent Living Resource: Concord**
Ste 120
1850 Gateway Blvd
Concord, CA 94520-3293
925-363-7293
FAX: 925-363-7296
e-mail: gilc@ilrccc.org
ilrccc.org

*Bryan Balch, Executive Director*

To empower people with disabilities to: control their own lives, provide advocacy and support for individuals with disabilities to live independently, create an accessible community free of physical and attitudinized barriers. SITE IS UNDER CONSTRUCTION

**3765 Independent Living Resources (ILR)**
Bldg 2a
101 Broadway
Richmond, CA 94804-1945
510-233-7400
e-mail: info@ilrccc.org

*Marvin Dyson, Manager*

Provides services to meet the diverse needs of people who have a variety of disabilities in all age groups.

3766 **Independent Living Service Northern California: Redding Office**
Ste 128
169 Hartnell Ave
Redding, CA 96002-1849
530-242-8550
FAX: 530-241-1454
TTY:530-242-8550
e-mail: info@ilsnc.org
www.ilsnc.org

*Tracy Barker, Program Manager*
*Evan LeVang, Executive Director*
*Robin Gutzman, Resource and Referral Specialist*
*Deborah Uhl, Program Specialist*
Independent Living Services of Northern California is a private non profit organization that provides support services to help empower community members with disabilities.

3767 **Independent Living Services of Northern California**
Jennifer Roberts Building
1161 East Ave
Chico, CA 95926-1018
530-893-8527
800-464-8527
FAX: 530-893-8574
TTY: 530-893-8527
e-mail: info@ilsnc.org
ilsnc.org

*Evan Levang, Executive Director*
*Amy Myers, Service Coordinator*
*Tracy Barker, Program Manager*
*Gina Gavett, Blind Field Services Senior Specialist*
Independent Living Services of Northern California is a private, non profit organization that provides support services to help empower community members with disabilities.

3768 **Marin Center for Independent Living**
710 4th St
San Rafael, CA 94901-3213
415-459-6245
FAX: 415-459-7047
TTY:415-459-7027
marincil.org

*Herb Meyer, President*
*Dennis Foley, Vice President*
*Eli Gelardin, Executive Director*
*Susan Malardino, Deputy Director*
A non-profit organization that provides advocacy and services for seniors and persons with disabilities.

3769 **Mother Lode Independent Living Center(DRAIL: Disability Resource Agency for Independent**
Living)
Ste A
67 Linoberg St
Sonora, CA 95370-4646
209-532-0963
FAX: 209-532-1591
TTY:209-288-3309
e-mail: barry@drail.org
www.drail.org

*Terry Gray, President*
*Barry Smith, Executive Director*
*Jema Padavana, Center Coordinator*
*Mona Martinez, Secretary*
DRAIL is a non-profit, community based, consumer controlled, cross disability center for independent living.

3770 **Placer Independent Resource Services**
11768 Atwood Road
Suite 29wood Rd
Auburn, CA 95603-9074
530-885-6100
800-833-3453
FAX: 530-885-3032
TTY: 530-885-0326
e-mail: tmiller@pirs.org
pirs.org

*Susan Miller, Executive Director*
A non profit independent living center whose mission is to advocate, empower, educate and provide services for people with disabilities enabling them to control their alternatives for independent living.

3771 **Resources for Independent Living**
Ste 3
420 i St
Sacramento, CA 95814-2319
916-446-3074
FAX: 916-446-2443
e-mail: leonc@ril-sacramento.org
www.ril-sacramento.org

*Frances Gracechild, Executive Director*
*Ramona Garcia, Board Chairperson*
*Fannie Foote, Vice Chairperson*
*Joanne Bodine, Treasurer*
Promoting the socio-economic independence of persons with disabilities by providing peer-supported, consumer-directed independent living services and advocacy.

3772 **Rolling Start**
Ste 107
570 W 4th St
San Bernardino, CA 92401-1438
909-884-2129
FAX: 909-386-7446
TTY:909-884-7396
e-mail: support@rollingstart.com
rollingstart.com

*Francis Bates, Executive Director*
*Tony Chavez, Deputy Director*
*Shannon McCroskey, Resource Specialist/Independent Living Specialist*
*Jackie Greene, IL Specialist*
Empowers and educates people with disabilities to achieve the independent life of their choice.

3773 **Rolling Start: Victorville**
Suite A102
17330 Bear Valley Road
Victorville, CA 92395
760-843-7959
FAX: 760-843-7977
TTY:760-951-8175
e-mail: Patty@rollingstart.com
rollingstart.com

*Francis Bates, Executive Director*
*Tony Chavez, Deputy Director*
*Shannon McCroskey, Resource Specialist/Independent Living Specialist*
*Jackie Greene, IL Specialist*
Empowers and educates people with disabilities to achieve the independent life of their choice.

3774 **Services Center For Independent Living**
107 Spring Street
Claremont, CA 91711-549
909-621-6722
800-491-6722
FAX: 909-445-0727
TTY: 949-445-0726
e-mail: janice@scil-ilc.org.
www.scil-ilc.org

*Dr. Lee Nattress, Executive Director*
*Janice Ornelas*

Dedicated to expanding access, information and resources to help increase independence and enhance the quality of life for the East San Gabriel Valley residents with disabilities.

**3775 Silicon Valley Independent Living Center**
2202 N. First St.
San Jose, CA 95131-1115 408-894-9041
FAX: 408-894-9050
TTY:408-894-9012
e-mail: info@svilc.org
svilc.org

*Sarah Triano, Executive Director*
*Nayana Shah, Director of Finance/Administration*
*Debra Sue Stevens, Director of Development & Communications*
*Todd Teixeira, Director of Programs*
A private, consumer-driven, nonprofit corporation that offers quality services to individuals with disabilities in Silicon Valley.

**3776 Silicon Valley Independent Living Center: South County Branch**
Ste A
7800 Arroyo Cir
Gilroy, CA 95020-7346 408-846-1480
FAX: 408-842-2321
TTY:408-842-2591
e-mail: info@svilc.org
www.svilc.org

*Sarah Triano, Executive Director*
*Nayana Shah, Director of Finance/Administration*
*Debra Sue Stevens, Director of Development & Communications*
*Todd Teixeira, Director of Programs*
A private, consumer-driven, non-profit corporation that offers quality services to individuals with disabilities in Silicon Valley.

**3777 Southern California Rehabilitation Services**
Ste D
7830 Quill Dr
Downey, CA 90242-3440 562-862-6531
FAX: 562-923-5274
TTY: 562-869-093
e-mail: scrs@scrs-ilc.org
scrs-ilc.org

*Lisa Hayes, President*
*Michael Strong, Vice President*
*Carol Trees, Secretary/Treasurer*
*Chad Williams, Board Member*
Empowers persons with disabilities to achieve their personalized goals through community education and individualized services that provide the knowledge, skills, and confidence building to maximize their quality of life.

**3778 Through the Looking Glass**
3075 Adeline St.
Ste. 120
Berkeley, CA 94703 510-848-1112
800-644-2666
FAX: 510-848-4445
TTY: 510-848-1005
e-mail: tlg@lookingglass.org
www.lookingglass.org

*Stephanie Miyashiro, M.A., Board President*
*Thomas Spalding, Board Treasurer*
*Alice Nemon, D.S.W., Board Secretary*
*Karen Fessel, Ph.D., Executive Director, Autism Health Insurance Project*
To create, demonstrate and encourage non-pathological and empowering reesources and model early intervention services for families with disability issues in parent or child which integrate expertise derived from personal disability experience and disability culture.

**3779 Tri-County Independent Living Center**
2822 Harris Street
Eureka, CA 95503 707-445-8404
877-576-5000
FAX: 707-445-9751
TTY: 707-445-8405
e-mail: aa@tilinet.org
www.tilinet.org

*Chris Jones, Executive Director*
*Mari Dorenstreich, Independent Living Specialist*
*Rebecca Simone, President*
*Allan Bard, Information & Referral / Independent Living Specialist*
Promotes the philosophy of independent living, to connect individuals to services, and to create and accessible community, so that people with disabilities can have control over their lives and full access to the communities in which they live.

**3780 Westside Center for Independent Living**
12901 Venice Blvd
Los Angeles, CA 90066-3509 310-390-3611
888-851-9245
FAX: 310-390-4906
TTY: 310-398-9204
e-mail: development@wcil.org
www.wcil.org

*Aliza Barzilay, Executive Director*
*Keith Miller, Program Manager*
The Westside Center for Independent Living (WCIL) helps people living with disabilities maintain self-sufficient and productive lives through non-residential peer support services and training programs. Independent Living promotes self-determination, community living, full participation in community life and access to the same opportunities and resources available to people without disabilities.

## Colorado

**3781 Atlantis Community**
201 S Cherokee St
Denver, CO 80223-1836 303-733-7719
FAX: 303-733-6211
TTY:303-733-0047
e-mail: adaptbabs@earthlink.net
www.atlantiscommunity.net

*David Hays, Manager*
Provide direct services, and to empower people with disabilities integrating, with full and equal rights, into all parts of society including employment, affordable, accessible, housing, transportation, recreation, communication, education, and public places while exercising and exerting choice and self determination. THE SITE IS UNDER CONSTRUCTION

**3782 Center for Independence**
740 Gunnison Ave
Grand Junction, CO 81501-3222 970-241-0315
FAX: 970-245-3341
cfigj.org

*Linda Taylor, Executive Director*
The Center for Independence works to promote community solutions and to empower individuals with disabilities to live independently.

**3783 Center for People with Disabilities**
615 Main St
Longmont, CO 80501-4983
303-772-3250
FAX: 303-772-5125
TTY:303-772-3250
e-mail: info@cpwd.org
www.cpwd-ilc.org

*David Bolin, Executive Director*
*Ian Engle, Executive Director*
*Carol Thieszen-Culp*
*Howard Levett*
Provides resources, information, and advocacy to assist people with disabilities in overcoming barriers to independent living.

**3784 Center for People with Disabilities: Pueblo**
1304 Berkley Ave
Pueblo, CO 81004-3002
719-546-1271
800-659-3656
FAX: 719-546-1374
e-mail: ivaleneamidei@yahoo.com
www.du.edu/~bfox2/ilcpueblo

*Larry Williams, Executive Director*
One of the 10 centers for independent living in Colorado founded under Title VII of the Rehabilitation Act of 1973 as amended in 1978. All new centers under this Independent Living (CIL) Title of the Act received initial and ongoing grants through this new Federal Program created by the Act.

**3785 Center for People with Disabilities: Boulder**
1675 Range St
Boulder, CO 80301-2722
303-442-8662
888-929-5519
FAX: 303-442-0502
e-mail: info@cpwd.org
www.cpwd.org

*Ian Engle, Executive Director*
*David Bolin, Executive Director*
*Carol Thieszen-Culp*
*Howard Levett*
Providing resources, information and advocacy to people with disabilities. Assist people with disabilities in transitioning from nursing homes to independent living in the community. Also provide personal assistance services.

**3786 Colorado Springs Independence Center**
729 South Tejon Street
Colorado Springs, CO 80903
719-471-8181
FAX: 719-471-7829
TTY:719-471-2076
e-mail: info@csicindliving.org
www.csicindliving.org

*Vicki Skoog, Executive Director*
To empower persons with disabilities to maximize their independence within the community and to remove barriers which impact their quality of life, while encouraging them to live independently in their community.

**3787 Connections for Independent Living**
Ste E
1024 9th Ave
Greeley, CO 80631-4027
970-352-8682
800-887-5828
FAX: 970-353-8058
TTY: 970-352-8682
e-mail: pattid4z@yahoo.com

*Beth Danielson, Executive Director*
Certified IL Center, I and R advocacy, peer support, skills training, sign language interpretations, reader services, housing. Cross-disability, all ages.

**3788 Denver CIL**
Ste 100
777 Grant St
Denver, CO 80203-3501
303-837-1020
FAX: 303-837-0859

*Greg Beran, Owner*
Provides resources, information, and advocacy to assist people with disabilities in overcoming barriers to independent living.

**3789 Disability Center for Independent Living**
4821 East 38th Avenue
Denver, CO 80207-1232
303-320-1345
FAX: 303-320-1345
TTY:303-322-2330
e-mail: avillasenor.dcil@gmil.com
http://www.accil.net

*Adrian Villasenor, Executive Director*
*Bill Bass, Senior Coordinator, Cross-Cultural Specialist*
*Brent Belisle, Senior Coordinator*
*Jane Schiele, Director, Satellite Offices*
Independent living center providing quality services for people with disabilities.

**3790 Disabled Resource Services**
Ste 101
424 Pine St
Fort Collins, CO 80524-2421
970-482-2700
FAX: 970-407-7072
TTY:970-407-7060
e-mail: drs@fortnet.org
www.fortnet.org/drs

*Nancy Jackson, Executive Director*
*Marj Grell, Administrative Assistant*
*Karen Norton, O.I.B. Coordinator*
*Sharon Bottoms, Transportation/Activities Coordinator*
To empower individuals with disabilities to achieve their maximum level of independence and to gain personal dignity within society. Disabled Resource Services, as a private non-profit state certified center for independent living, is dedicated to working with individuals with all types of disabilities in Larimer County to promote their independence and equality through services which support advocacy, awareness and access to their community.

**3791 Disbled Resource Services**
640 E Eisenhower Blvd
Loveland, CO 80537-3954
970-667-0816
FAX: 970-593-6582
e-mail: drs@fortnet.org
www.fortnet.org/drs

*Don Maroney, Director*
*Nancy Jackson, Executive Director*
*Karen Norton, O.I.B. Coordinator*
*Sharon Bottoms, Transportation/Activities Coordinator*
To empower individuals with disabilities to achieve their maximum level of independence and to gain personal dignity within society.

**3792 Greeley Center for Independence**
2780 28th Ave
Greeley, CO 80634-7803
970-339-2444
800-748-1012
FAX: 970-339-0033
e-mail: gciinc@gciinc.org
http://www.gciinc.org/

*Chari Armagost, Chief Financial Officer*
*Kathleen VanSoest, Executive Director*
*Rob Rabe, Director of Outpatient Service*
*Judy Weimer, R.N., Director of Nursing*
Provides places of growth, transition and encouragement, where people with temporary and permanent disabilities can reach toward their maximum potential of personal independence and wellness.

**3793 Independent Life Center**
P.O.Box 612
Craig, CO 81626-612
970-826-0833
888-526-0833
FAX: 970-826-0832
TTY: 970-826-0833
e-mail: info@indlife.org
http://www.accil.net

*Evelyn Tileston, Executive Director*
*Jackie Lyons, Executive Director*
Provides resources, information, and advocacy to assist people with disabilities in overcoming barriers to independent living.

**3794 Pueblo Goodwill Industries**
15810 Indianola Drive
Rockville, MD 20855
240-333-5590
800-GOO-WILL
e-mail: contactus@goodwill.org
http://www.goodwill.org/

*Debi Diaz, CEO*
*Lauren Lawson-Zilai, Director of Public Relations*
*Charlene Sarmiento, Senior Specialist, Public Relations*
PGoodwill works to enhance the dignity and quality of life of individuals and families by strengthening communities, eliminating barriers to opportunity, and helping people in need reach their full potential through learning and the power of work. The name is ""Colorado Green Services Inc. ""

**3795 Southwest Center for Independence**
Ste 200
835 E 2nd Ave
Durango, CO 81301-5474
970-259-1672
866-962-2158
FAX: 970-259-0947
TTY: 970-259-1672
e-mail: director@swcidur.org
www.swcidur.org

*Martha Mason, Executive Director*
*Susan Kimbler, Chair*
*Carol Lynn Rising, Vice-President*
*Jason Armstrong, Treasurer*
Empowering individuals with disabilities and their families to achieve their maximum level of independence in work, play and other areas of life.

**3796 Southwest Center for Independence: Cortez**
PO Box 640
Cortez, CO 81321-9164
970-759-2347
866-962-2158
FAX: 970-565-7169
e-mail: director@swilc.org
http://www.swilc.org/

*Martha Mason, Executive Director*
*Jeanette Abella, Independent Living - Durango*
*Barbara Elliott, Community Transition Services*
*Tim Erickson, Low Vision Coordinator*
Empowers individuals with disabilities and their families to achieve their maximum level of independence in work, play and other areas of life.

## Connecticut

**3797 Center for Disability Rights**
Ste A
764 Campbell Ave
W Haven, CT 06516-3786
203-934-7077
FAX: 203-934-7078
TTY:203-934-7079
e-mail: info@cdr-ct.org
http://cdr-ct.org

*Marc Gallucci, Executive Director*
Resources, information, and advocacy to assist people with disabilities in overcoming barriers to independent living.

**3798 Center for Independent Living SC**
26 Palmers Hill Rd
Stamford, CT 06902-2113
203-353-8550
FAX: 203-353-1423
TTY:203-353-8550

*Dana Canevari, Director*
Provides resources, information, and advocacy to assist people with disabilities in overcoming barriers to independent living.

**3799 Chapel Haven**
1040 Whalley Ave
New Haven, CT 06515-1740
203-397-1714
FAX: 203-937-2466
e-mail: admissions@chapelhaven.org
chapelhaven.org

*Michael Storz, President*
The only combined state-accredited special education facility and independent living facility for adults with cognitive disabilities.

**3800 Disabilities Network of Eastern Connecticut**
19 Ohio Avenue
Suite 2
Norwich, CT 06360-2111
860-823-1898
FAX: 860-886-2316
e-mail: CFerry@dnec.org
dnec.org

*Cathy Ferry, Executive Director*
*Heather E. Dunn, Administrative/Data Coordinator*
*Jodi Furnia, Advocacy Supervisor*
*Brynn Hickey, Underserved Populations Vocational Advocate*
Dedicated to supporting and advancing the rights of individuals with disabilities. The goal is to creat a completely inclusive society where people live together in communities regardless of their abilities.

**3801 Disability Resource Center of Fairfield County**
Ste 210
80 Ferry Blvd
Stratford, CT 06615-6079
203-378-6977
FAX: 203-375-2748
TTY:203-378-3248
e-mail: info@drcfc.org
drcfc.org

*Anthony Lacava, Executive Director*
*Stephanie M, Assistant Directo*
*Ethel M R, President*
*Thomas D, Vice-President*
A crosss-disability resource and advocacy organization for people with disabilities that has provided unique, consumer-directed services both for individuals and for the communities of Fairfield County.

**3802 Independence Northwest Center for Independent Living**
Ste 200
1183 New Haven Rd
Naugatuck, CT 06770-5033
203-729-3299
FAX: 203-729-2839
TTY:203-729-1281
e-mail: info@independencenorthwest.org
http://www.independencenorthwest.org/

*Eileen Healy, Executive Director*
*Scott Robbins, Program Director*
*Carolyn Barbaresi, Independent Living Advocate*
*Mary Ann Cortina, Administrative Assistant*
Provides services in such areas as peer counseling, advocacy, independent living skills training and information and referral.

3803 **Independence Unlimited**
Ste D
151 New Park Ave
Hartford, CT 06106-2170 860-523-0126
FAX: 860-523-5603
e-mail: info@ctsilc.org?subject=Requesting%20Informat
http://ctsilc.org

*Daria Smith, Executive Director*
*Debbie Melaragno, Administrative Assistant*
*James Quick, President*
*Shirley Ricart, Vice President*
Center for independent living that provides skills training, peer counseling, advocacy, transition from institutions to the community and a variety of other services.

3804 **New Horizons Village**
37 Bliss Rd
Unionville, CT 06085 860-673-8893
FAX: 860-675-4369
e-mail: Michael.Shaw@NewHorizonsVillage.com
newhorizonsvillage.com

*Carolyn Fields, Administrator*
A 68 unit apartment complex designed for people who have severe physical disabilities.

## Delaware

3805 **Freedom Center for Independent Living**
400 N Broad St
Middletown, DE 19709-1089 302-376-4399
866-687-3245
FAX: 302-376-4395
TTY: 302-376-4397
e-mail: info@fcilde.org
fcilde.org

*Hersernest Cole, Executive Director*
*Lillian Evans, Independent Living Specialist*
Protects the Civil Rights and promote the empowerment of persons with disabilities and their families through our independent living philosophy.

3806 **Independent Living**
Apt 210
1800 N Broom St
Wilmington, DE 19802-3854 302-429-6693
FAX: 302-429-8031
TTY:302-429-8034

*Susan Cycyk, Executive Director*
Providing skilled support and caring guidance to adults with disabilities. Our case management services include: daily living skills training, medical coordination, transportation assistance, financial management, housing assistance, and vocational/educational planning.

3807 **Independent Resource Georgetown**
Ste 37
410 S Bedford St
Georgetown, DE 19947-1850 302-854-9330
FAX: 302-854-9408
TTY:302-854-9340
e-mail: pboyd@independentresource.org

*Larry Henderson, Director*
*Pat Boyd, Manager*
Provides independent living services to persons who experience a significant disability. Offers skills training, individually and in small groups, peer support/peer counseling and information and referral services. Strives to remove the architectural and attitudnal barriers through individual and systems advocacy.

3808 **Independent Resources: Dover**
Ste 104
32 W Loockerman St
Dover, DE 19904-7311 302-735-4599
FAX: 302-735-5623
TTY:302-735-5629
e-mail: lhenderson@independentresources.org
http://www.iri-de.org

*Deborah Justice, Office Director*
*Carolyn Miller, Secretary*
*Barty Rochester, Peer Support Coordinator*
Private, non-profit, consumer-controlled, community based organization providing services and advocacy by and for persons with all types of disabilities. Their goal is to assist individuals with disabilities to achieve their maximum potential within their families and communities.

3809 **Independent Resources: Wilmington**
Ste101
6 Denny Rd
Wilmington, DE 19809-3444 302-765-0191
FAX: 302-765-0195
TTY:302-765-0194
e-mail: fox205007@aol.com
http://www.iri-de.org

*Larry D Henderson, Executive Director*
*Phyllis Farrare, Director of Operations*
Private, non-profit, consumer-controlled, community based organization providing services and advocacy by and for persons with all types of disabilities. Their goal is to assist individuals with disabilities to achieve their maximum potential within their families and communities.

3810 **Mosaic Of De**
261 Chapman Rd.
Suite 201
Newark, DE 19702-5410 302-456-5995
877-366-7242
FAX: 302-456-5998
e-mail: info@mosaic.org
mosaicinfo.org

*Terry Olson, Executive Director*
Provides services to adults with developmental disabilities who reside in homes and apartments. Services are designed to provide them with opportunities for choices and participation in the life of their communities. Supports are geared to assist each individual in becoming more independent in activities of daily living, vocational skills, community mobility and transportation, and recreation and leisure activities.

## District of Columbia

3811 **District of Columbia Center for Independent Living**
1400 Florida Ave NE
Washington, DC 20002-5032 202-388-0033
FAX: 202-398-3018
e-mail: info@dccil.org
dccil.org

*Richard.A Simms, Executive Director*
Mission is to maximize the leadership, empowerment, independence, and productivity of individuals with disabilities, and to integrate these individuals into the mainstream of American society.

**3812 National Council on Independent Living**
5th Fl
1710 Rhode Island Ave NW
Washington, DC 20036- 3007
202-207-0334
877-525-3400
FAX: 202-207-0341
TTY: 202-207-0340
e-mail: ncil@ncil.org
www.ncil.org

*Kelly Buckland, Executive Director*
*Tim Fuchs, Operations Director*
*Jorge Pineda, Accountant*
*Denise Law, Member Services Associate*
As a membership organization, NCIL advances independent living and the rights of people with disabilities through consumer-driven advocacy.

## Florida

**3813 Ability 1st**
1300 E. Green Street
Pasadena, CA 91106
626-396-1010
877-768-4600
FAX: 626-396-1021
e-mail: info@abilityfirst.org
abilityfirst.org

*Lori.E Gangemi, President*
*Steve.S Schultz, CFO*
*Syed Kazmi, Controller*
*Joel Bronson, Director of Information Technology*
To empower persons with disabilities to live independently and participate actively in their community.

**3814 Adult Day Training**
Goodwill Industries - Suncoast
10596 Gandy Blvd N
St Petersburg, FL 33702-1422
727-523-1512
888-279-1988
FAX: 727-563-9300
TTY:727-579-1068
e-mail: gw.marketing@goodwill-suncoast.com
www.goodwill-suncoast.org

*R.Lee Waits, President and CEO*
*Deborah.A Passerini, Executive Vice President and Chief Operating Officer*
*Gary Hebert, Corporate Treasurer and Chief Financial Officer*
*James Williams, Vice President for Fund Development*
An innovative program which uses job skills to teach self-help, daily living, communication, mobility, travel, decision-making, behavioral and social skills. This focus provides concrete, transferable experiences to help prepare individuals for greater community inclusion by achieving the highest possible degree of independence in their daily life, increasing their confidence and supporting their successful transitions to less structured, self-sufficient environments.

**3815 CIL of Central Florida**
720 N Denning Dr
Winter Park, FL 32789-3020
407-623-1070
FAX: 407-623-1390
e-mail: info@cilorlando.org
cilorlando.org

*Jason Vennings, Manager*
*Allison Gould, Volunteering Department*
A private, non-profit organization dedicated to helping people with disabilities achieve their self-determined goals for independent living.

**3816 CIL of the Keys**
Ste 243
103400 Overseas Hwy
Key Largo, FL 33037-2849
305-453-3491
FAX: 305-453-3488
www.cilofthekeys.org

*Brenda K Pierce, Executive Director*
*Aleisa McGuirl, Consumer Advocate*
Offers assistance to persons with disabilities in acquiring independent living and self advocacy skills in order to obtain and maintain independence and self-sufficiency. SITE IS UNDER CONSTRUCTION

**3817 Caring and Sharing Center for Independent Living**
12552 Belcher Rd S
Largo, FL 33773-3014
727-539-7550
866-539-7550
FAX: 727-539-7588
e-mail: cascil@cascil.org
cascil.org

*Barbara Dandro, Treasurer*
*Mary Bucca, Secretary*
*Patricia Bell, Director*
*Dennis Shelt, Director*
Empowering people with disabilities. The name of the company has been changed to ""Disability Achievement Center""

**3818 Caring and Sharing Center: Pasco County**
12552 Belcher Rd S
Largo, FL 33773-3014
727-539-7550
866-539-7550
FAX: 727-539-7588
e-mail: cascil@cascil.org
www.cascil.org

*Barbara Dandro, Treasurer*
*Mary Bucca, Secretary*
*Patricia Bell, Director*
*Dennis Shelt, Director*
Empowering people with disabilities. The name of the company has been changed to ""Disability Achievement Center""

**3819 Center for Independent Living in Central Florida**
720 N Denning Dr
Winter Park, FL 32789-3095
407-623-1070
FAX: 407-623-1390
e-mail: info@cilorlando.org
cilorlando.org

*Jason Vennings, Manager*
*Allison Gould, Volunteering Department*
In partnership with the community, promotes personal right snad responsiblities among people with all disabilities.

**3820 Center for Independent Living of Broward**
Ste 102
4800 N State Road 7
Lauderdale Lakes, FL 33319- 5811
954-722-6400
888-722-6400
FAX: 954-735-1958
e-mail: cilb@cilbroward.org
www.cilbroward.org

*Craig Lilienthal, President*
*Christopher Sharp, VP*
*Shea Smith, Treasurer*
*Laurie Menekou, Secretary*
Offers assistance to people with disabilities in fulfilling the goals of independence and self-sufficiency.

**3821 Center for Independent Living of Florida Keys**
Ste 243
103400 Overseas Hwy
Key Largo, FL 33037-2849
305-453-3491
877-335-0187
FAX: 305-453-3488
TTY: 305-453-3491
e-mail: cilkeys@cilkeys.org
www.cilofthekeys.org

*Brenda K Pierce, Executive Director*
Offers assistance to persons with disabilities in acquiring independent living and self-advocacy skills in order to obtain and maintain independence and self-sufficiency. SITE IS UNDER CONSTRUCTION

**3822 Center for Independent Living of N Florida**
1823 Buford Ct
Tallahassee, FL 32308-4465
850-575-9621
FAX: 850-575-5740
e-mail: cilnf@nettally.com

*Judith Barrett, Executive Director*
Offers assistance to persons with disabilities in acquiring independent living and self-advocacy skills in order to obtain and maintain independence and self-sufficiency

**3823 Center for Independent Living of NW Florida**
3600 N Pace Blvd
Pensacola, FL 32505-4240
850-595-5566
877-245-2457
FAX: 850-595-5560
e-mail: cil-drc@cil-drc.org
cil-drc.org

*Arthur Nunamaker, President*
*Kathleen Wilks, Secretary*
*John Bouchard, Treasurer*
*Frank Cherry, Executive Director*
Provides services such as information and referral, peer counseling, housing, advocacy, training, independent living skills training, free wheelchairs, loan locker, assistive technology.

**3824 Center for Independent Living of North Central Florida**
3774 W Gulf To Lake Hwy
Lecanto, FL 34461-9214
352-527-8399
877-232-8261
FAX: 352-527-9511
www.cilncf.org

*Catherine Jackson, Manager*
Empowers people with disabilities to exert their individual rights to live as independently as possible, make personal life choices and achieve full community inclusion.

**3825 Center for Independent Living of North Central Florida**
222 SW 36th Ter
Gainesville, FL 32607-2863
352-378-7474
800-265-5724
FAX: 352-378-5582
TTY: 352-372-3443
www.cilncf.org

*William Kennedy, Executive Director*
Empowering people with disabilities to exert their individual rights to live as independently as possible, make personal life choices and achieve full community inclusion.

**3826 Center for Independent Living of S Florida**
6660 Biscayne Blvd
Miami, FL 33138-6285
305-751-8025
FAX: 305-751-8944
TTY:305-751-8891
e-mail: info@soflacil.org
soflacil.org

*Kelly Greene, Executive Director*
*Maria Rodriguez, Program Manager*
*Noel Wynter, Financial Manager*
*Marc Dubin, Director of Advocacy*
A community based non for profit, independent living center serving people of all ages with any type of disability. Services: Basic education, GED preperation, American sign language advocacy, peer support, information and referral, independent living skills training, housing assistance, transportation assistance, home modiifications, transition from nursing facility to the community assisatnace filing ADA complaints, accessibility surveys, diability awareness traing.

**3827 Center for Independent Living of SW Florida**
2321 Bruner Ln
Fort Myers, FL 33912-1904
239-277-1447
800-435-7352
FAX: 239-277-1647
www.cilfl.org

*Ronald J Muschong, Interim Executive Director*
Helping people with disabilities achieve independence and self-determination in their lives.

**3828 Coalition for Independent Living Options: Fort Pierce**
6800 Forest HIll Boulevard
West Palm Beach, FL 33412
561-966-4288
FAX: 561-641-6619
www.cilo.org

*Peter W. Ballance, Interim President*
*Charles Wenger, Interim Vice President*
*Joseph Fields Jr., Esquire, Secretary*
*Kristi Chapman, Treasurer*
Private non-profit promoting independences for people with disabilities in Palm Beach, Martin, St. Lucie & Okeechobee Counties. Services include advocacy, independent living skills & training, peer support, after school & summer programs for teens, crime victim support services, and verterans transition services.

**3829 Coalition for Independent Living Options**
6800 Forest Hill Blvd
Greenacres, FL 33413-3310
561-966-4288
FAX: 561-641-6619
www.cilo.org

*Peter W. Ballance, Interim President*
*Charles Wenger, Interim Vice President*
*Joseph Fields Jr., Esquire, Secretary*
*Kristi Chapman, Treasurer*
Private non-profit promoting independences for people with disabilities in Palm Beach, Martin, St. Lucie & Okeechobee Counties. Services include advocacy, independent living skills & training, peer support, after school & summer programs for teens, crime victim support services, and verterans transition services.

**3830 Coalition for Independent Living Options: Stuart**
Unit 104
850 NW Federal Hwy
Stuart, FL 34994-1056
772-233-4301
FAX: 772-233-4302
www.cilo.org

*Peter W. Ballance, Interim President*
*Charles Wenger, Interim Vice President*
*Joseph Fields Jr., Esquire, Secretary*
*Kristi Chapman, Treasurer*
Private non-profit promoting independences for people with disabilities in Palm Beach, Martin, St. Lucie & Okeechobee Counties. Services include advocacy, independent living skills &

training, peer support, after school & summer programs for teens, crime victim support services, and verterans transition services.

**3831 Coalition for Independent Living Options:Okeechobee**
TD Bank Building
8000 South US Hwy.
Okeechobee, FL 34972- 4160
772-878-3500
FAX: 772-878-3344
www.cilo.org

*Peter W. Ballance, Interim President*
*Charles Wenger, Interim Vice President*
*Joseph Fields Jr., Esquire, Secretary*
*Kristi Chapman, Treasurer*

Private non-profit promoting independences for people with disabilities in Palm Beach, Martin, St. Lucie & Okeechobee Counties. Services include advocacy, independent living skills & training, peer support, after school & summer programs for teens, crime victim support services, and verterans transition services.

**3832 Disability Resource Center**
625 N Highway 231
Panama City, FL 32405-4704
850-769-6890
FAX: 850-769-6891
e-mail: outreach@drcpc.org
www.drcpc.org

*Robert Cox, Executive Director*
*Becky Cadwell, Independent Living Specialist*

They are commiteed to collaborating with other disability/consumer-focused organizations in their community

**3833 Lakeland Adult Day Training**
Ste 5
3033 Drane Field Rd
Lakeland, FL 33811-3305
863-701-1351
TTY:863-701-1356
e-mail: gw.marketing@goodwill-suncoast.com
www.goodwill-suncoast.org

*R.Lee Waits, President and CEO*
*Deborah.A Passerini, Executive Vice President and Chief Operating Officer*
*Gary Hebert, Corporate Treasurer and Chief Financial Officer*
*James Williams, Vice President for Fund Development*

An innovative program which uses job skills to teach self-help, daily living, communication, mobility, travel, decision-making, behavioral and social skills. This focus provides concrete, transferable experiences to help prepare individuals for greater community inclusion by achieving the highest possible degree of independence in their daily life, increasing their confidence and supporting their successful transitions to less structured, self-sufficient environments.

**3834 Lighthouse Central Florida**
215 E New Hampshire St
Orlando, FL 32804-6403
407-898-2483
FAX: 407-895-5255
e-mail: lvaneepoel@lcf-fl.org
lighthousecentralflorida.com

*Lee Nasehi, President,CEO*
*Lee Van Eepoel, Program Service Director*
*Donna Esbensen,CPA, MBA, Vice President,Chief Financial Officer*
*Kimberley Pawling,PhD, Director of Education & Rehabilitation Services*

Promote the independence and success of people living with vision impairment.

**3835 Miami-Dade County Disability Services and Independent Living (DSAIL)**
1335 NW 14th St
Miami, FL 33125-1647
305-547-5444
FAX: 305-547-7355
e-mail: morrina@miamidade.gov
http://www.miamidade.gov/dhs/elderly_disabili

*Michael Moxam, Manager*

Offers information and referral services serving all types of disabilities with the goal of assisting the disabled acquiring independence and control over their lives. Teaches independent living skills, job readiness and placement, home health care, sensitivity training, training in ASL and Braille, counsel people with disabilities or wide range of problems.

**3836 Ocala Adult Day Training**
2920 W Silver Springs Blvd
Ocala, FL 34475-5654
352-629-0456
TTY:352-629-0874
e-mail: gw.marketing@goodwill-suncoast.com
www.goodwill-suncoast.org

*R.Lee Waits, President and CEO*
*Deborah.A Passerini, Executive Vice President and Chief Operating Officer*
*Gary Hebert, Corporate Treasurer and Chief Financial Officer*
*James Williams, Vice President for Fund Development*

An innovative program which uses job skills to teach self-help, daily living, communication, mobility, travel, decision-making, behavioral and social skills. This focus provides concrete, transferable experiences to help prepare individuals for greater community inclusion by achieving the highest possible degree of independence in their daily life, increasing their confidence and supporting their successful transitions to less structured, self-sufficient environments.

**3837 Pinellas Park Adult Day Training**
7601 Park Blvd
Pinellas Park, FL 33781-3704
727-541-6205
TTY:727-544-5835
e-mail: gw.marketing@goodwill-suncoast.com
www.goodwill-suncoast.org

*R.Lee Waits, President and CEO*
*Deborah.A Passerini, Executive Vice President and Chief Operating Officer*
*Gary Hebert, Corporate Treasurer and Chief Financial Officer*
*James Williams, Vice President for Fund Development*

An innovative program which uses job skills to teach self-help, daily living, communication, mobility, travel, decision-making, behavioral and social skills. This focus provides concrete, transferable experiences to help prepare individuals for greater community inclusion by achieving the highest possible degree of independence in their daily life, increasing their confidence and supporting their successful transitions to less structured, self-sufficient environments.

**3838 SCCIL at Titusville**
725 S Deleon Ave
Titusville, FL 32780-4115
407-268-2244
FAX: 706-724-6729
TTY:706-724-6324
e-mail: kswoil@csranet.com
www.virtualcil.net

*Gerri Martin, Executive Director*

Directory of Independent Living Centers throughout the United States.

**3839 Self Reliance**
8901 N Armenia Ave
Tampa, FL 33604-1041
813-375-3965
FAX: 813-375-3970
TTY:813-375-3972
e-mail: bruehl@self-reliance.org
www.self-reliance.org

*Brenda Ruehl, Executive Director*
*Liz Fields, Director of Finance & Operations*

A cross disability agency providing services to both children and adults with disabilities to identify and overcome barriers to independence in their lives. Self Reliance also promotes independence through empowering persons with disabilities and improving the communities in which they live.

**3840 Space Coast Center for Independent Living**
571 Haverty Court, Suite W.
Rockledge, FL 32955
321-633-6011
FAX: 321-633-6472
http://spacecoastcil.org

*Michael Lavoie, President*
*Howard Fetes, VP*
*Jason Miller, Treasurer/Secretary*
Provides overall services for individuals with al types of disabilities. Offers peer support, advocacy, skills training, accessibility surveys, support groups, transportation, specialized equipment and sign language interpreter referral services and home modifications.

**3841 Suncoast Center for Independent Living, Inc.**
3281 17th Street
Sarasota, FL 34235
941-351-9545
FAX: 941-351-9875
e-mail: Info@scil4u.org
www.scil4u.org

*Candy Partee, Chair*
*Milton Herman, Vice Chair*
*Vicke Mack, Treasurer*
*Scott Biehler, Secretary*
Helping people with disabilities live independently.

**3842 disAbility Solutions for Independent Living**
Ste 180
119 S Palmetto Ave
Daytona Beach, FL 32114-4369
386-255-1812
866-310-1039
FAX: 386-255-1814
TTY: 386-252-6222
e-mail: info@dsil.org
http://www.dsil.org/

*Julie M Shaw, Executive Director*
To maximize the leadership, empowerment, independence and productivity of individuals with disabilities, to promote and attain integration and full inclusion of individuals with disabilities in all aspects of our society; accomplished through consumer control, peer support, education, self-determination, equal access and individual and systems advocacy

## Georgia

**3843 Arms Wide Open**
3013 Rainbow Dr
Suite 1120
Decatur, GA 30034-1677
770-413-2241
FAX: 770-498-2778
e-mail: kenmorris@armswideopen.org
www.armswideopen.org

*Ken Morris, Director*
Arms Wide Open operates a durable medical equipment loan program and a life care program. The mission of Arms Wide Open is to provide support services to the aged, disabled and chronically ill for the purpose of helping them to avoid institutional placement.

**3844 Bain, Inc. Center For Independent Living**
316 W Shotwell St
Bainbridge, GA 39819-3906
229-246-0150
888-830-1530
FAX: 229-246-1715
TTY: 888-830-1530
e-mail: bain@surfsouth.com
www.baincil.org

*Virginia Harris, Executive Director*
*Malissa Thompson, Program Manager*
*Tomonia Becon, Nursing Home Transition Coordinator*
*Julie Harris, Independent Living Specialist*
A non-residential Center for Independent Living serving eleven counties throughout Southwest. BAIN is a non-profit, community based resource and advocacy center run by and for individuals with disabilities.

**3845 Disability Connections**
170 College St
Macon, GA 31201-1656
478-741-1425
800-743-2117
FAX: 478-755-1571
e-mail: dcinfo@disabilityconnections.com
disabilityconnections.com

*Jerilyn Leverett, Executive Director*
A private non-profit organization that looks to enable all people with disabilities to attain and have access to all opportunities in life.

**3846 Division of Rehabilitation Services**
Georgia Department of Labor
Ste B
410 Mall Blvd
Savannah, GA 31406-4869
912-356-2226
FAX: 912-356-2875
TTY:912-356-2940
e-mail: www.dol.state.ga.us
dol.state.ga.us

*Jody Lane, Manager*
*George Foley, Manager*
Vocational rehabilitation services.

**3847 Living Independence for Everyone (LIFE)**
5105 Paulsen Street, Suite 143-B
Savannah, GA 31405
912-920-2414
800-948-4824
FAX: 912-920-0007
e-mail: info@lifecil.com
www.lifecil.com

*John Paul Berlon, President*
*Jason Wilson, VP*
*Kim Harrison, Secretary*
*Mark Schreiber, Treasurer*
The Southeast's Regional disability resource center that offers a wide range of resources, education, and advocacy to the community to help level the playing field for people with disabilities to create a world in which everyone can fully participate.

**3848 Multiple Choices Center for Independent Living**
850 Gaines School Rd
Athens, GA 30605-3133
706-549-3131
e-mail: info@multiplechoices.us
www.multiplechoices.us

*Doug Hatch, President*
*Donald Veater, VP*
*Elllen Des Jardines, Secretary*
*William Holley, Executive Director*
To break down all barriers to inclusion by enhancing the equality of life and empowering people with disabilities through advocacy, education and training.

**3849 North District Independent Living Program**
Ste 209
311 Green St NW
Gainesville, GA 30501-3364
770-535-5930

*Sharon McCurry, Coordinator*
*Cindy Hanna, Executive Director*
Information and referral, advocacy, peer counseling, service coordination and ADA consultation.

**3850 Southwest District Independent Living Program**
P.O.Box 1606
Albany, GA 31702-1606
229-430-4170
FAX: 229-430-4466

*Bill Layton, Director*
*Diane Davis, Executive Director*
Offers peer counseling, disability education and awareness, attendant care registry, and information on accessible home for the disabled.

**3851 Statewide Independent Living Council of Georgia**
Ste 600
315 West Ponce de Leon Avenue
Decatur, GA 30030-2617
770-270-6860
888-288-9780
FAX: 770-270-5957
e-mail: shellys5@hotmail.com
silcga.org

*Shelly Simmons, President*
*Jason Wilson, Vice President*
*Dave Zilles, Treasurer*
*Barbaraann Bongiovanni, Secretary*
Founded to ensure that people with disabilities have opportunities to live as independently as possible.

**3852 Walton Options for Independent Living**
948 Walton Way
Augusta, GA 30903-519
706-724-6262
FAX: 706-724-6729
TTY:706-724-6262
e-mail: tjohnston@waltonoptions.org
www.waltonoptions.org

*Brian Mosley, Project Lead*
Services include individual and systems advocacy, peer support, skills training (including basic computer and return to work skills), information and referral services and transition from institutions back to the community.

**3853 disABILITY LINK: Rome**
755 Commerce Drive
Decatur, GA 30030
404-687-889
FAX: 404-687-8298
e-mail: info@disabilitylink.org

*Larry Brown, Director of Finance*
*Bernard Baker, Transportation Outreach Coordinator*
*Fran Durbin, Employment Coordinator*
*Hillary Elliott, Acting Executive Director*
Committed to promoting the rights of all people with disabilities. The name of the company is “”disABILITY LINK""

## Hawaii

**3854 Center For Independent Living- Kauai**
State Office Building 3060 Eiwa Str
Lihue, HI 96766-6529
808-274-3484
FAX: 808-245-3485
e-mail: kauaiddc@pixi.com
www.hiddc.org/kauai

*Humberto Blanco, Administrator*
*Teri Yamashiro, IL Specialist*
Offers peer counseling, disability education, attendant care registry, outreach services and advocacy.

**3855 Hawaii Center For Independent Living**
1055 Kinoole Street
Suite 105le St
Hilo, HI 96720-3872
808-935-3777
TTY:808-935-7888
e-mail: info@pacificil.org
http://www.cil-hawaii.org

*Gordon Fuller, Executive Director*
Provides an array of support services for people with all types of disabilities of any age.

**3856 Hawaii Center for Independent Living-Maui**
220 Imi Kala Street
Suite 103
Wailuku, HI 96793-1209
808-242-4966
866-303-4245
FAX: 808-244-6978
TTY: 808-242-4968
e-mail: mcilogg@gte.net/ clytien@pacificil.org
http://www.cil-hawaii.org/

*Clytie Nishihara, Manager*
*T Lay , Administrative Assistant*
Offers disability education and awareness, advocacy and counseling.

**3857 Hawaii Centers for Independent Living**
200 N. Vineyard Blvd Bldg. A501
Honolulu, HI 96817-3950
808-522-5400
FAX: 808-522-5427
e-mail: info@pacificil.org
http://www.cil-hawaii.org/

*Cheryl Mizusaawa, Executive Director*
*M.J. (Kimo) Keawe, COO & Executive Director*
Our staff and Board of directors are excellent advocates with the disabled community. We will connect you with resources to make your own choices for housing, employment, and personal care and to find assistive devices and technology to improve quality of life. On both the islands of Oahu and Hawaii, we have a independent living specialist who is fluent in american sign language and is well known in the deaf community. It provide statewide resources for: Peer Counseling, Outreach and Public Education.

**3858 Kauai Center for Independent Living**
4340 Nawiliwili Rd.
Lihue, HI 96766-6529
808-246-4800
FAX: 808-245-7218
e-mail: kcil@mail.aloha.net
http://www.cil-hawaii.org/

*Laurao Tobosa, Program Coordinator*
Provides a variety of support services for people with all types of disabilities.

## Idaho

**3859 American Falls Office: Living Independently for Everyone (LIFE)**
2110 Rollandet St
Idaho Falls, ID 83402-4508
208-529-8610
FAX: 208-529-6804
e-mail: deann@idlife.org
www.idlife.org

*Dean Nilson, Executive Director*
*Tina Noreen, Programs Coordinator*
Enables people with disabilities to manage their own lives, make their own choices, and give information and knowledge to assist in living with dignity and bravado.

3860 **Dawn Enterprises**
280 Cedar Street P.O.Box 388
Blackfoot, ID 83221-388
208-785-5890
FAX: 208-785-3095
www.orgsites.com/id/dawnent

*Donna Butler, Executive Director*
*Teresa Oakes, Assistant Director/Fiscal Coordinator*
To assist individuals of Southeastern Idaho with mental, physical or social disabilities in achieving independence through employment training, skill training, social development, or living enhancements up to each individual's maximum capability.

3861 **Disability Action Center NW**
505 N Main St
Moscow, ID 83843-2615
208-746-9033
800-475-0070
FAX: 208-883-0524
e-mail: moscow@dacnw.org
www.dacnw.org

*Mark Leeper, CEO*
*Krista Kramer, IL Planning Coordinator*
*Steven Corr, PAS Program Manager*
A non-profit community partnership working to promote the independence and equality of all individuals with disabilities in all aspects of society. *$45.00*

3862 **Disability Action Center NW: Coeur D'Alene**
3650 N Government Way, Suite L
Coeur D Alene, ID 83815- 4069
208-664-9896
800-854-9500
FAX: 208-666-1362
e-mail: cda@dacnw.org
www.dacnw.org

*Patrick Blum, IL Specialist*
*Selena Vasquez, PAS Program Coordinator*
*Virgil Edwards, IL Specialist*
A non-profit community partnership working to promote the independence and equality of all individuals with disabilities in all aspects of society.

3863 **Disability Action Center NW: Lewiston**
307 19th St
Suite A1
Lewiston, ID 83501-2086
208-746-9033
800-746-9033
FAX: 208-746-1004
e-mail: lewiston@dacnw.org
www.dacnw.org

*Melissa Painter, Pas Program Coordinator*
*Julie Waltermine, Independent Living Specialist*
*Vanessa Bachman, Accountant / Bookkeeper*
A non-profit community partnership working to promote the independence and equality of all individuals with disabilities in all aspects of society.

3864 **Idaho Falls Office: Living Independently for Everyone (LIFE)**
250 S. Skyline
Idaho Falls, ID 83402-3702
208-529-8610
800-631-2747
FAX: 208-232-2753
e-mail: diane@idlife.org
www.idlife.org

*Dean Nielson, Executive Director*
*Tina Noreen, Programs Coordinator*
*Mickey Palmer, Fiscal Intermediary Manager*
Enables people with disabilities to manage their own lives, make their own choices, and give information and knowledge to assist in living with dignity and bravado.

3865 **LIFE: Fort Hall**
P.O.Box 4185
Fort Hall, ID 83203
208-478-3952
e-mail: wparker@if.rmci.net
www.ilru.org

*Wnedy Parker, Director*
Enables people with disabilities to manage their own lives, make thier own choices, and give information and knowledge to assist in living with dignity and bravado.

3866 **Living Independence Network Corporation**
1878 W Overland Rd
Boise, ID 83705-3142
208-336-3335
FAX: 208-384-5037
e-mail: info@lincidaho.org
lincidaho.org

*Roger Howard, Executive Director*
A non-profit organization empowering people with disabilities to achieve their desired level of independence.

3867 **Living Independence Network Corporation: Twin Falls**
Ste C
1182 Eastland Dr North
Twin Falls, ID 83301-8972
208-733-1712
FAX: 208-733-7711
e-mail: info@lincidaho.org
www.lincidaho.org

*Melva Heinrich, Executive Director*
A non-profit organization empowering people with disabilities to achieve their desired level of independence.

3868 **Living Independence Network Corporation: Caldwell**
1609 Kimball Ave, Ste. 201
Caldwell, ID 83605-6965
208-454-5511
FAX: 208-454-5515
TTY:208-454-5511
e-mail: info@lincidaho.org
www.lincidaho.org

*Heidi Caldwell, Executive Director*
A non-profit organization empowering people with disabilities to achieve their desired level of independence.

3869 **Living Independent for Everyone (LIFE): Pocatello Office**
640 Pershing Ave
Pocatello, ID 83204-3702
208-232-2747
800-631-2747
FAX: 208-232-2753
TTY: 208-232-2747
e-mail: tracy@idlife.org
http://www.idlife.org

*Dean Nielson, Executive Director*
*Mickey Palmer, Fiscal Intermediary Manager*
Enables people with disabilities to manage thier own lives, make their own choices, and give information and knowledge to assist in living with dignity and bravado.

3870 **Living Independently for Everyone (LIFE): Blackfoot Office**
Living Independently for Everyone (LIFE): Pocate
570 W. Pacific P.O.Box 86
Blackfoot, ID 83221-86
208-785-9648
FAX: 208-785-2398
e-mail: lori@idlife.org
http://www.idlife.org

*Dean Nielson, Executive Director*
*Lori Galvan, Independent Living Advisor*
*Mickey Palmer, Fiscal Intermediary Manager*
Enable people with disabilities to manage their own lives, make their own choices, and give information and knowledge to assist in living with dignity and bravado.

**3871 Living Independently for Everyone: Burley**
Ste 7
2311 Park Ave
Burley, ID 83318-2170
208-678-7705
FAX: 208-678-7771
e-mail: hotwheels@idlife.org
www.idlife.org

*Sandra Dressel, Manager*
*Dean Nielson, Executive Director*
*Mickey Palmer, Fiscal Intermediary Manager*
Enables people with disabilities to manage their own lives, make their own choices, and give information and knowledge to assist in living with dignity and bravado.

**3872 Southwestern Idaho Housing Authority**
1108 W Finch Dr
Nampa, ID 83651-1732
208-467-7461
FAX: 208-463-1772

*David W Patten, Manager*
Offers housing for rent and section/8

## Illinois

**3873 Access Living of Metropolitan Chicago**
115 W Chicago Ave
Chicago, IL 60654-3209
312-640-2100
800-613-8549
FAX: 312-640-2101
TTY: 312-640-2102
e-mail: info@accessliving.org
accessliving.org

*Marca Bristo, CEO*
*Bhuttu Mathews, Disability Resources Coordinator*
*Gary Arnold, Public Relations Coordinator*
Established in 1980,access living is a change agent commited to fostering an incusive society that enables Chicagoans with disabilities to live fully engaged and self-directed lives. Nationally recognized as a leading force in the disability community. Access Living challenges stereotypes, protects civil rights, and champions social reform.

**3874 Center on Deafness**
3444 Dundee Rd
Northbrook, IL 60062-2258
847-559-0110
FAX: 847-559-8199
TTY:847-559-9493
e-mail: centerondeafness.org
www.centerondeafness.org

*Bonnie Simon, Executive Director*
*Donna Gomez, Residential Services/ Adult Placement*
*Rena Lovell, School Intake*
COD is dedicated to providing quality services for persons who are deaf or hard of hearing and their families, through educational, vocational, and residential services in a therapuetic, community-based environment

**3875 Community Residential Alternative**
Coleman Tri- County Services
835 W Lincoln St
Harrisburg, IL 62946-2017
618-252-3204
FAX: 618-252-0884
TTY:618-269-4211
e-mail: ctscila6@hotmail.com
http://colemantricounty.tripod.com/sep.html

*Samantha Austin, Executive Director*
Six bed group home that provides a residential alternative for the developmentally disabled adult. This program is designed to promote independence in daily living skills, economic self-sufficiency, and integration into the community.

**3876 Division of Rehabilitation Services**
Department of Human Services
400 W Lawrence Ave
Springfield, IL 62704-2625
217-782-2093
800-843-6154
FAX: 217-524-2471
e-mail: DHS.ORS@illinois.gov
www.dhs.state.il.us

*Carol Adams, President*
Provides medical, therapeutic and counseling services for the disabled, as well as employment services.

**3877 DuPage Center for Independent Living**
Bldg 8
739 Roosevelt Rd
Glen Ellyn, IL 60137-5877
630-469-2300
FAX: 630-469-2606
TTY:630-469-2300
e-mail: dcil@mcs.com
http://www.dupagecil.org/

*Leigh Ann Stephens, Executive Director*
*Lenore Varey, Business Manager*
*Monica Layman, Program Assistant*
A non residential, community based, not for profit agency wich provides advocacy and services to persons with disabilities in DuPage County.

**3878 Fite Center for Independent Living**
1230 Larkin Ave
Elgin, IL 60123-6200
847-695-5818
FAX: 847-695-5892
e-mail: info@fitecil.org
http://www.fitecil.org/

*Linda Bradford-Foster, Chairman, Board Treasurer*
*Gracia Bittner, Board Secretary*
Provides services to people with disabilities in Kane, Kendall and McHenry counties. Our non-residential agency provides independent living skills training, advocacy, systemic + individual peer counseling, information and referral and housing services. Also provides technical assistance to businesses and agencies to work with people with disabilities. Locations in Elgin and Aurora. Please call for further details.

**3879 Illinois Department of Rehab Services**
Department of Human Services
2nd Floor
400 W Laurence 100
Springfield, IL 62762-1
217-782-2093
800-843-6154
FAX: 217-524-2471
www.dhs.state.il.us

*Karen Perrin, Manager*
*Carol Adams, President*
The state's lead agency serving individuals with disabilities. DRS works in partnership with people with disabilities and their families to assist them in making informed choices to achieve full community participation through employment, education, and independent living opportunities.

**3880 Illinois Valley Center for Independent Living**
18 Gunia Dr
La Salle, IL 61301-9780
815-224-3126
800-822-3246
FAX: 815-224-3576
e-mail: ivcil@ivcil.com
ivcil.com

*Donna Joerger, Executive Director*
*Mary Fisher, President*
*John Hurst, Vice President*
A nonprofit service and advocacy organization that assists persons with disabilities in opening doors to their independence.

**3881 Illinois and Iowa Center for Independent Living**
3708 11th St P.O.Box 6156
Rock Island, IL 61231-6156
309-793-0090
877-541-2505
FAX: 309-283-0097
e-mail: iicil@iicil.com
www.iicil.com

*Liz Sherwin, Executive Director*
To create and maintain independence options for people with disabilities by advocating for civil rights, providing services, and promoting full participation of disabled individuals in all aspects of the community.

**3882 Impact Center for Independent Living**
2735 E Broadway
Alton, IL 62002-1859
618-462-1411
888-616-4261
FAX: 618-474-5309
e-mail: staff@impactcil.org
impactcil.org

*Cathy Contarino, Executive Director*
*Carla Sauerwein, Business Administrator*
*Angela Botz, Community Outreach Coordinator*
Promotes pride and respect for people with disabilities by sharing the tools that are necessary to take control of one's own life.

**3883 Jacksonville Area CIL: Havana**
220 W Main St
Havana, IL 62644-1138
309-543-6680
877-759-2187
FAX: 309-543-6711
e-mail: info@jacil.org
www.jacil.org

*Becky McGinnis, Executive Director*
*Vicky Mullis, President*
*Phil Foxworth, VP*
*Mark Arnold, Treasurer*
Committed to enabling persons with disabilities to gain effective control and director of their own lives in the home, in the workplace and in the community.

**3884 Jacksonville Area Center for Independent Living**
60 E Central Park Plz
Jacksonville, IL 62650-2071
217-245-8371
888-317-3287
FAX: 217-245-1872
TTY:217-245-8371
e-mail: info@jacil.org
www.jacil.org

*Becky Mc Ginnis, Executive Director*
Committed to enabling persons with disabilities to gain effective control and direction of their own lives in the home, in the workplace and in the community.

**3885 LIFE Center for Independent Living**
Ste 1
2201 Eastland Dr
Bloomington, IL 61704-7923
309-663-5433
888-543-3245
FAX: 309-663-7024
TTY:309-663-5433
e-mail: gail@lifecil.org
lifecil.org

*Gail Kear, Executive Director*
A community-based, not-for-profit, non-residential organization that promotes disability rights, equal access, and full community participation for persons with disabilities.

**3886 LINC-Monroe Randolph Center**
Ste 4
1514 S Main St
Red Bud, IL 62278-1382
618-282-3700
FAX: 618-282-2740
TTY:618-282-3700

*Violete Nast, Manager*

**3887 Lake County Center for Independent Living**
377 N Seymour Ave
Mundelein, IL 60060-2322
847-949-4440
FAX: 847-949-4445
TTY:847-949-0641
e-mail: lindsey@lccil.org
www.lccil.org

*Kelli Brooks, Executive Director*
*Lindsay Schultz, Information & Referral Advocate*
Lake County Center for Indepdendent Living is a disability rights organization governed and staffed by a majority of people with disabilities. LCCIL offers services and advocacy that promote a fully accessible society, which expects participation by persons with disabilities.

**3888 Life Center for Independent Living: Pontiac**
318 West Madison Street
Pontiac, IL 61764-1785
815-844-1132
FAX: 815-844-1148
e-mail: lifecil@lifecil.org
www.lifecil.org

*Dana Craig, Outreach Coordinator*
*Gail Kear, Executive Director*
*Brianne Anderson, Office Manager*
*Jill Doran, Program Director*
A community-based, not-for-profit, non-residential organization that promotes disability rights, equal access, and full community participation for persons with disabilities.

**3889 Living Independently Now Center (LINC)**
120 E a St
Belleville, IL 62220-1401
618-235-9988
FAX: 618-233-3729
TTY:618-235-9988
e-mail: info@lincinc.org
lincinc.org

*Erica Edwards, Executive Director*
Empowers persons with disabilities to live independently and to promote accessibility and inclusion in all areas.

**3890 Living Independently Now Center: Sparta**
Western Egyptian Adm. Building1820
Sparta, IL 62286-1068
618-317-4028
e-mail: info@lincinc.org
www.lincinc.org

*Linda Conley, President*
*Rebecca Ray, Vice-President*
*Lynn Jarman, Executive Director*
*Ron Tialdo, Treasurer*
Empowers persons with disabilities to live independently and to promote accessibility and inclusion in all areas.

**3891 Living Independently Now Center: Waterloo**
Western Egyptian Building
207 West
Waterloo, IL 62298-1336
618-317-4028
e-mail: info@lincinc.org
www.lincinc.org

*Linda Conley, President*
*Rebecca Ray, Vice-President*
*Lynn Jarman, Executive Director*
*Ron Tialdo, Treasurer*
Empowers persons with disabilities to live independently and to promote accessibility and inclusion in all areas.

**3892 Mosaic: Pontiac**
725 W Madison St
Pontiac, IL 61764-1621
815-842-4166
FAX: 815-842-4053
mosaicinfo.org

*Linda Timmons, President And Chief Executive Officer*
*Cindy Schroeder, Senior Vice-President And Chief Financial Officer*
*Raul Saldivar, COO*
*Keith Schmode, Senior VP*
A faith-based organization serving people with developmental disabilities.

**3893 Opportunities for Access: A Center for Independent Living**
Ste 3
4206 Williamson Pl
Mount Vernon, IL 62864-6705
618-244-9212
FAX: 618-244-9310
TTY:618-244-9575
e-mail: spud@ofacil.org
ofacil.org

*Michael Egbert, Executive Director*
Serves, trains and provides information to persons with disabilities, family members and significant others and service providers. Services include: advocacy, information and referral, peer support, skills training, volunteer programs and other related services. Services are free. A cross disability community based, non-residential, nonprofit organization serving Clay, Clinton, Edwards, Effingham, Fayette, Hamilton, Jasper, Jefferson, Marion, Wabash, Washington, Wayne and White Counties.

**3894 Options Center for Independent Living: Bourbonnais**
Ste 107
22 Heritage Dr
Bourbonnais, IL 60914-2510
815-936-0100
FAX: 815-936-0117
TTY:815-936-0132
e-mail: optionscil@optionscil.com
optionscil.com

*Barry Baron, President*
*Carol Gocken, Vice President*
*Lenda A Brasel, Independent Living Specialist*
*Dale Gerretse, Treasurer*
A non-residential, not-for-profit, community-based organization that promotes independent living for people with disabilities.

**3895 Options Center for Independent Living: Watseka**
Suite 103
103 Laird Ln
Watseka, IL 60970
815-432-1332
FAX: 815-432-1360
TTY:815-432-1361
e-mail: options@optionscil.com
www.optionscil.com

*Barry Baron, President*
*Carol Gocken, Vice President*
*Lenda A Brasel, Independent Living Specialist*
*Dale Gerretse, Treasurer*
A non-residential, not-for-profit, community-based organization that promotes independent living for people with disabilities.

**3896 PACE Center for Independent Living**
1317 E Florida Ave
Urbana, IL 61801-6007
217-344-5433
FAX: 217-344-2414
TTY:217-344-5024
e-mail: info@pacecil.org
pacecil.org

*Evelyn Brown, President*
*Fred Neubert, Vice President*
*Nancy McClellan-Hickey, Executive Director*
*Arland Stratton, Treasurer*
Promotes the full participation of people with disabilities in the rights and responsibilities of society. Provides services, which assist people with disabilities in achieving or maintaining independence.

**3897 Progress Center for Independent Living**
7521 Madison St
Forest Park, IL 60130-1407
708-209-1500
FAX: 708-209-1735
TTY:708-209-1826
e-mail: info@progresscil.org
www.progresscil.org

*Anne Gunter, Independent Living Advocate- Information and Referral*
*Kim Liddell, Independent Living Advocate - Information and Referral (South Satellit*
*Rebecca Thompson, Independent Living Advocate - The Benefits Advocacy Coordinator*
A community-based, non-profit, non-residential, service and advocacy organization operated for people with disabilities, by people with disabilities.

**3898 Progress Center for Independent Living: Blue Island**
12940 Western Ave
Blue Island, IL 60406-3766
708-388-5011
FAX: 708-388-5016
TTY:708-389-8250
e-mail: info@progresscil.org
www.progresscil.org

*Horacio Esparza, Executive Director*
*Anne Gunter, Independent Living Advocate- Information and Referral*
*Kim Liddell, Independent Living Advocate - Information and Referral (South Satellit*
A community-based, non-profit, non residential, service and advocacy organization operated for people with disabilities, by people with disabilities.

**3899 Regional Access & Mobilization Project**
202 Market St
Rockford, IL 61107-3954
815-968-7467
FAX: 815-968-7612
TTY:815-968-2401
www.rampcil.org

*Julie Bosma, Executive Director*
*Amy Morris, Development Director*
*Jackie Nieman, Human Resources & Financial Director*
*Joanne Rouse, Treasurer*
To promote an accessible society that allows and expects full participation by people with disabilities.

**3900 Regional Access & Mobilization Project: Belvidere**
Ste 103
530 S State St
Belvidere, IL 61008-3711
815-544-8404
FAX: 815-544-1896
TTY:815-544-8404
www.rampcil.org

*Becky Maggio, Boone County Services Manager*
Promote an accessible society that allows and expects full participation by people with disabilities.

**3901 Regional Access & Mobilization Project: De Kalb**
115 N First Street
Dekalb, IL 60115-3055
815-756-3202
FAX: 815-756-3556
TTY:815-756-4263
www.rampcil.org

*Heather Foulker, DeKalb County Services Manager*
Promotes an accessible society that allows and expects full partiipation by persons with disabilities.

**3902 Regional Access & Mobilization Project: Freeport**
2155 W Galena Ave
Freeport, IL 61032-3013
815-233-1128
FAX: 815-233-0743
TTY:815-233-1128
rampcil.org

*Tiffany Vondra, Stephenson County Services Manager*
*Connie Kraft, Parent Mentor*
Promotes an accessible society that allows and expects full partiipation by persons with disabilities.

**3903 Soyland Access to Independent Living(SAIL)**
2449 E Federal Dr
Decatur, IL 62526-2160
217-876-8888
800-358-8080
FAX: 217-876-7245
TTY: 217-876-8888
e-mail: jwooters@decatursail.com
www.decatursail.com

*Jeri J Wooters, Executive Director*
A community-based, non-residential Center for Independent Living whose purpose is to promote and practice independent living for all people with disabilities.

**3904 Soyland Access to Independent Living: Charleston**
757 Windsor Rd
Charleston, IL 61920-7474
217-345-7245
FAX: 217-345-7226
TTY:217-345-7245
e-mail: triplec@consolidated.net
www.decatursail.com

*Matthew Hutti, Manager*
*Jeri J Wooters, Executive Director*
A community-based, non-residential Center for Independent Living whose purpose is to promote and practice independent living for all people iwth disabilities.

**3905 Soyland Access to Independent Living: Shelbyville**
1810 W.S. 3rd ST P.O.Box 650
Shelbyville, IL 62565-650
217-774-4322
FAX: 217-774-4368
TTY:217-774-4322
e-mail: sailsel@consolidated.net
www.decatursail.com

*Jeri J Wooters, Executive Director*
*Betty Watkins, Rural Outreach Coordinator*
A community-based, non-residential Center for Independent Living whose purpose is to promote and practice independent living for all people with disabilities.

**3906 Soyland Access to Independent Living: Sullivan**
1102 W Jackson St
Sullivan, IL 61951-1067
217-728-3186
FAX: 217-728-2299
TTY:217-728-3186
e-mail: sulsail@wireless111.com
www.decatursail.com

*Lou Anne Banks, Manager*
*Jeri J Wooters, Executive Director*
*Betty Watkins, Rural Outreach Coordinator*
A community-based, non-residential Center for Independent Living whose purpose is to promote and practice independent living for all people with disabilities.

**3907 Springfield Center for Independent Living**
330 South Grand Ave W
Springfield, IL 62704-3716
217-523-4032
800-447-4221
FAX: 217-523-0427
TTY: 217-523-4032
e-mail: scil@scil.org
scil.org

*Pete Roberts, Executive Director*
*Susan Coopers, Program Director*
*Robin Ashton-Hale, Reintegration Coordinator*
*Kathryn Cline, Business Manager*
To increase opportunities for equality, integration and independence for all persons with disabilities through advocacy, services, and public education.

**3908 Stone-Hayes Center for Independent Living**
39 N Prairie St
Galesburg, IL 61401-4613
309-344-1306
888-347-4245
FAX: 309-344-1305
TTY: 309-344-1306
e-mail: stonehayes@misslink.net
stone-hayes.org

*Catherine Holland, Manager*
The purpose of INCIL is to facilitate the collaboration of all Centers for Independent Living in Illinois for promoting, through the Independent Living Movement, equal opportunities and civil rights for all persons with disaibilities.

**3909 West Central Illinois Center for Independent Living**
Ste 104
300 Maine St
Quincy, IL 62301-3922
217-223-0400
FAX: 217-223-0479
TTY:217-223-0475
e-mail: info@wcicil.org
www.wcicil.org

*Glenda Hackemack, Executive Director*
*Dale Winner, Information & Referral Coordinator*
*Dustin Gorde Director of Community, Jenny*
*Kelly Transition Co-Ordinato*
A not-for-profit advocacy center funded by state and federal grants to provide services to people with disabilities.

**3910 West Central Illinois Center for Independent Living: Macomb**
440 N Lafayette St
Macomb, IL 61455-1512
309-833-5766
FAX: 309-833-4690
TTY:217-223-0475
e-mail: info@wcicil.org
www.wcicil.org

*Glenda Hackemack, Executive Director*
*Dale Winner, Information & Referral Coordinator*
*Dustin Gorde Director of Community, Jenny*
*Kelly Transition Co-Ordinato*
A not-for-profit advocacy center funded by state and federal grants to provide services to people with disabilities.

**3911 Will Grundy Center for Independent Living**
Ste A
2415 W Jefferson St
Joliet, IL 60435-6464
815-729-0162
FAX: 815-729-3697
TTY:815-729-2085
e-mail: pamwgcil@sbcglobal.net
will-grundycil.org

*John Stanton, President*
*Val Rand, Vice President*
*Donald Cordano, Treasurer*
*Leslie Sutton, Secretary*

A cross-disability, community based organization that strives for equalityand empowerment of persons with disabilities in the Will and Grundy County areas.

## Indiana

3912 **Assistive Technology Training and Information Center (ATTIC)**
1721 Washington Ave
Vincennes, IN 47591-4823
812-886-0575
877-96A-TTIC
FAX: 812-886-1128
e-mail: inbox@atticindiana.org
www.atticindiana.org

*Patricia Stewart, Executive Director*
*Rebecca Anderson, Assistant Director*
*Mark Schmitt, Fiscal Controller*
*Jackie Evans, Independent Living Coordinator*
ATTIC provides support, information and education for individuals with disabilities and for families of children with special needs, and the professionals who assist these families. All disabilities, all ages.

3913 **DAMAR Services**
6067 Decatur Blvd.
Indianapolis, IN 46241
317-856-5201
FAX: 317-856-2333
e-mail: info@damar.org
damar.org

*Jim Dalton, President and Chief Operating Officer*
*Gregory A. Johnson, Chairman and Chief Executive Officer*
*Simone Brewer, Training Director*
*Erin Crick, Director of Educational Services*
Builds better futures for children and adults facing life's greatest developmental and behavioral challenges.

3914 **Everybody Counts Center for Independent Living**
Ste A
9111 Broadway
Merrillville, IN 46410-7097
219-769-5055
888-769-3636
FAX: 219-769-5326
TTY:219-756-3323
e-mail: info@everybodycounts.org
everybodycounts.org

*Teresa Torres, Executive Director*
*Emma Lewis Sullivan, Assistant Director*
*Mark Torres, Systems Manager*
*Jodi Hawn, Administrative Assistant*
A nonprofit corporation dedicated to the achievement of maximum independence and enhanced quality of life for persons with disabilities.

3915 **Four Rivers Resource Services**
P.O.Box 249
Linton, IN 47441-249
812-847-2231
FAX: 812-847-8836
e-mail: fourrivers@frrs.org
frrs.org

*Stephen Sacksteder, Executive Director*
*Robin Duncan, Chief Financial Officer*
*Dean Dorrell, Information Systems Director*
*Jessica Davis, Development Coordinator*
FRRS is established to enable individuals with disabilities and other challenges to attain self independence and natural interdependence, inclusion in normal life experiences and opportunities, and general life enrichment, by working in partnership with them, their families and the communities in and around Greene, Sullivan, Daviess, and Martin Counties.

3916 **Future Choices Independent Living Center**
309 N High St
Muncie, IN 47305-1618
765-741-8332
866-741-3444
FAX: 765-741-8333
futurechoices.org

*Beth Y. Quarles, President*
Provides unlimited options for minorities, youth, and Hoosiers with disabilities.

3917 **Independent Living Center of Eastern Indiana (ILCEIN)**
1818 W Main St
Richmond, IN 47374-3822
765-939-9226
877-939-9226
FAX: 765-935-2215
www.ilcein.org

*Jim McCormick, Executive Director*
*Dean Turner, Administrative Director*
*Kathy Camper, Compliance Manager*
*Michelle Satterfield, Service Coordinator*
Serving Fayette, Franklin, Henry, Decatur, Rush, Union and Wayne Counties.

3918 **Indianapolis Resource Center for Independent Living**
5302 East Washington Street
Indianapolis, IN 46219
317-926-1660
866-794-7245
FAX: 317-926-1687
e-mail: info@abilityindiana.org
ircil.org

*Melissa Madill, Executive Director*
*Erin Bullman, Development Director*
*Shannon McCauley, Administrative Assistant*
*Ross Prater, Office Administrator*
Provides services, support and information to people with disabilities to help insure equal access to all aspects of community life.

3919 **League for the Blind and Disabled**
5821 S Anthony Blvd
Fort Wayne, IN 46816-3701
260-441-0551
800-889-3443
FAX: 260-441-7760
TTY: 800-889-3443
e-mail: the-league@the-league.org
the-league.org

*David A. Nelson, CEO/President*
*Nancy Gasparini, Director Independent Living Services*
*Patrick Robinson, Administrative Assistant*
*Kevin Showalter, Youth Services Coordinator*
To provide and promote opportunities that empower people with disabilities to achieve their potential.

3920 **Martin Luther Homes of Indiana**
Mosaic
26 N Brown Ave
Terre Haute, IN 47803-1523
812-235-3399
FAX: 812-235-1590
e-mail: abean@mlhs.com
Providing a wide array of services to assist individuals and families in achieving positive life goals. Services to persons with disabilities and other special needs include community living options, training and employment options, spiritual growth and development options, training and counseling support.

3921 **Ruben Center for Independent Living**
Ste 3
4522 Indianapolis Blvd
East Chicago, IN 46312-3227
219-397-6494
FAX: 219-397-6496
TTY:219-397-6496
An independent living center providing support, information and education.

**3922 SILC, Indiana Council on Independent Living (ICOIL)**
P.O.Box 7083
Indianapolis, IN 46207-7083
317-232-1303
800-545-7763
FAX: 317-232-6478
e-mail: nancy.young@fssa.in.gov

*Nancy Young, Program Director*
*Richard Simers, SILC Chairperson*

**3923 Southern Indiana Center for Independent Living**
651 X St
Bedford, IN 47421-1943
812-277-9626
800-845-6914
FAX: 812-277-9628
sicilindiana.org

*Al Tolbert, Executive Director*
*Darlene Webster, Independent Living Center Director*
SICIL is a consumer controlled, community based, cross-disability, non-residential and not for profit organization that promotes and practices the philosophy of independent living: consumer control, peer support, self-help, self-determination, equal access, and individual and community advocacy. SICIL also promotes accesible and affordable housing, recreation and transportation.

**3924 Wabash Independent Living Center & Learning Center (WILL)**
1 Dreiser Square
Terre Haute, IN 47807
812-298-9455
877-915-9455
FAX: 812-299-9061
TTY: 877-915-9455
e-mail: info@thewillcenter.org
www.thewillcenter.org

*Peter Ciancone, Executive Director*
*Norma Bartlett, Administrative Assistant*
*Marcia Jackson, Independent Living Coordinator*
*Gloria Stamper, Independent Living Coordinator*
To empower people with disabilities to ensure that they have full and complete access to community resources to promote their independence

## Iowa

**3925 Black Hawk Center for Independent Living**
2800 Falls Ave.
P.O. Box 2275
Waterloo, IA 50701-2275
319-291-7755
888-291-7754
FAX: 319-291-7781
TTY:800-735-2942
www.blackhawkcenter.org
To create and maintain independence options by working with people with disabilities.

**3926 Central Iowa Center for Independent Living**
Ste 131
655 Walnut St
Des Moines, IA 50309-3930
515-243-1742
888-503-2287
FAX: 515-243-5385
www.centraliowacil.com

*Bob Jeppesen, Executive Director*
*Frank Strong, Associate Director*
*Crystal Toman, Office Coordinator*
*Dee Howard, Independent Living Specialist*
CICIL is a community based, non-profit, non-residential program serving persons with disabilities. CICIL assists all persons, regardless of disability in making choices about their own lives and in experiencing success in achieving independence.

**3927 Evert Conner Rights & Resources CIL**
730 S Dubuque St
Iowa City, IA 52240-4202
319-338-3870
800-982-0272
FAX: 319-354-1799
e-mail: info@ownersvoices.com
www.ownersvoices.com

*Scott Gill, Executive Director*
Provides community services like disability awareness training and classroom presentations. Individual services include independent living skills training and peer counseling. All services are custom designed to support the independence of people with disabilities in their own community.

**3928 Hope Haven**
1800 19th St
PO Box 70
Rock Valley, IA 51247-1098
712-476-2737
FAX: 712-476-3110
hopehaven.org

*David Vanningen, Executive Director*
*Calvin Helmus, Chief Operating Officer*
*Duane Obbink, Chief Financial Officer*
*Gale Van Engen, Director of Programming*
Unleashes the potential in people through work and life skills so that they may enjoy a productive life in their community.

**3929 League of Human Dignity, Center for Independent Living**
1520 Avenue M
Council Bluffs, IA 51501-1185
712-323-6863
FAX: 712-323-6811
e-mail: Cinfo@leagueofhumandignity.com
www.leagueofhumandignity.com

*Carrie England, Director*
League of Human Dignity actively promotes the full integration of individuals with disabilities into society. To this end, the League will advocate their needs and rights, and provide quality services to involve these persons in becoming and remaining independent citizens.

**3930 Martin Luther Homes of Iowa**
P.O.Box 15
Waukon, IA 52172-15
563-568-3992
FAX: 563-568-3992

*Mary Lynn ReVoir, Administrator*
*Fred Naumann III, Communications*
*Richard Wicks, Executive Director*
.

**3931 South Central Iowa Center for Independent Living**
117 1st Ave W
Oskaloosa, IA 52577-3243
641-672-1867
800-651-7911
FAX: 641-672-1867
e-mail: oskyscicil@mahaska.org

*Deb Philpot, Executive Director*
Provides services, support, information and referral to people with disabilities to help insure equal access to all aspects of community life.

**3932 Three Rivers Center for Independent Living**
900 Rebecca Avenue
Pittsburgh, PA 15221-2938
412-371-7700
800-633-4588
FAX: 412-371-9430
TTY: 412-371-6230
e-mail: sholbrook@trcil.org
trcil.myfastsite.net

*Stanley A. Holbrook, President & Executive Director*
*Erin Ryan, SR. Program Manager*
*Roxanne Huss, Director of Waiver Services*
*Charles Keenan, TRCIL Real Properties Board*

Providing a wide array of services to assist individuals and families in achieving positive life goals.

## Kansas

**3933 Advocates for Better Living For Everyone(A.B.L.E.)**
Ste C
521 Commercial St
Atchison, KS 66002
913-367-1830
888-845-2879
FAX: 913-367-1430
www.ableks.org

*Ken Gifford, President & CEO*
A not for profit agency providing services within the State of Kansas. ABLE looks to assist people with disabilities as well as any other member of the community to live an integrated, quality life with dignity, respect, and independence.

**3934 Center for Independent Living SW Kansas: Liberal**
Ste 2
1023 N Kansas Ave
Liberal, KS 67901-2655
620-624-5500
800-327-4048
FAX: 620-624-6576
TTY: 620-624-5500
www.cilswks.org

*Victor Otero, Manager*
*Crystal Tharp, Independent Living Advocate*
Dedicated to helping people achieve full participation in society.

**3935 Center for Independent Living Southwest Kansas**
P.O.Box 2090
Garden City, KS 67846-2090
620-276-1900
800-736-9443
FAX: 620-271-0200
e-mail: info@cilswks.org
cilswks.org

*Troy Horton, Executive Director*
Dedicated to helping people achieve full participation in society.

**3936 Center for Independent Living Southwest Kansas: Dodge City**
2601 Central Ave
Dodge City, KS 67801-6200
620-227-6660
800-326-1366
FAX: 620-227-8185
TTY: 620-227-6660
www.cilswks.org

*Mary Jane Sandoval, Independent Living Advocate*
Dedicated to helping people achieve full participation in society

**3937 Coalition for Independence**
4911 State Ave
Kansas City, KS 66102-1749
913-321-5140
866-201-3829
FAX: 913-321-5182
TTY: 913-321-5216
cfi-kc.org

*Clarence Smith, Executive Director*
*Laarni Sison, Executive Assistant*
*Claire Marr, Lead Independent Living Specialist*
*Shauna Garrett, Lead Accountant*
Facilitates positive and responsible independence for all people with disabilities by acting as an advocate for individuals with disabilities, providing services, and promoting accessibility and acceptance.

**3938 Cowley County Developmental Services**
P.O.Box 618
Arkansas City, KS 67005-618
620-442-5270
866-442-5270
FAX: 620-442-5623
www.ccds-cddo.org

*Bill Brooks, Executive Director*
Provides services for persons with developmental disabilities in Cowley County..

**3939 Independence**
2001 Haskell Ave
Lawrence, KS 66046-3249
785-841-0333
888-824-7277
FAX: 785-841-1094
e-mail: comment@independenceinc.org
independenceinc.org

*Edward Canda, President*
*Mary Chappell, Director*
*Boog Highberger, Treasurer*
*Brigid Jensen, Program Director*
Provides advocacy, services, and education for people with disabilities and our communities.

**3940 Independent Connection**
P.O.Box 1160
1710 W. Schilling Road
Salina, KS 67402- 1160
785-827-9383
800-526-9731
FAX: 785-823-2015
TTY: 785-827-9383
www.occk.com

*Shelia Nelson-Stout, President/CEO*
*Deanna L. Lamer, Senior Director,Human Resources*
*Tasha Suppes, Human Resources Coordinator*
Dedicated to helping people with physical or mental disabilities remove barriers to employment, independent living, and full participation in their communities.

**3941 Independent Connection: Abilene**
Suite 221
300 N. Cedar St.
Abilene, KS 67410
785-263-2208
FAX: 785-263-3795
TTY:785-263-2208
www.occk.com

*Shelia Nelson-Stout, President/CEO*
*Deanna L. Lamer, Senior Director,Human Resources*
*Tasha Suppes, Human Resources Coordinator*
Dedicated to helping people with physical or mental disabilities remove barriers to employment, independent living, and full participation in their communities.

**3942 Independent Connection: Beloit**
501 W 7th St
Beloit, KS 67420-2107
785-738-5423
FAX:785-738-3320
TTY:785-738-5423
www.occk.com

*Shelia Nelson-Stout, President/CEO*
*Deanna L. Lamer, Senior Director,Human Resources*
*Tasha Suppes, Human Resources Coordinator*
Dedicated to helping people with physical or mental disabilities remove barriers to employment, independent living, and full participation in their communities.

**3943 Independent Connection: Concordia**
1502 Lincoln St
Concordia, KS 66901-4830
785-243-1977
FAX: 785-243-4524
TTY:785-243-1977
www.occk.com

Dedicated to helping people with physical or mental disabilities remove barriers to employment, independent living, and full participation in their communities.

**3944 Independent Living Resource Center**
3033 W 2nd St N
Wichita, KS 67203-5357
316-942-6300
800-479-6861
FAX: 316-942-2078
ilrcks.org

*James Thayer, President*
*John Brennan, Vice Chairman*
*Jane Mobley, Secretary/Treasurer*
*TraceAnn Adkins, Human Resources Manager*
Empower people with disabilities to lead independent lives by providing advocacy, education and direct services. Serve people with all types of disabilities; permanent or temporary, physical disabilities, mental disabilities, and developmental disabilities.

**3945 Kansas Services for the Blind & Visually Impaired**
2601 SW East Circle Dr N
Topeka, KS 66606-2445
785-296-3738
800-547-5789
FAX: 785-291-3138
e-mail: rehab@srskansas.org
srskansas.org

*Dennis Ford, Manager*
*Michael Donnelly, Director*
Helps persons who are blind or visually to improve their quality of life. KSBVI provides people with an array of services and experiences aimed at overcoming not only the physical difficulties brought on by the loss of vision, but also the fear of change associated with vision loss. KSBVI can also help with job search and retention activities; life skills training; access to medical services; and technical assistance..

**3946 LINK: Colby**
Ste G
505 N Franklin Ave
Colby, KS 67701-2342
785-462-7600
800-736-9418
TTY:785-462-7600
www.linkinc.org

*Brian Atwell, Executive Director*
Promotes and supports the civil rights of people with disabilities and empowers them to achieve a life of independence and equality..

**3947 Living Independently in Northwest Kansas: Hays**
2401 E 13th St
Hays, KS 67601-2663
785-625-6942
800-596-5926
FAX: 785-625-2334
TTY: 785-625-6942
linkinc.org

*Brian Atwell, Executive Director*
Promotes and supports the civil rights of people with disabilities and empowers them to achieve a life of independence and equality.

**3948 Prairie IL Resource Center**
103 W 2nd St
Pratt, KS 67124-2644
620-672-9600
FAX: 620-672-9601
e-mail: info@pilr.org
www.pilr.org

*Chris Owens, Executive Director*
*Roger Frischenmeyer, Independent Living Specialist*
*Tammy Fuhr, Administrative Assistant*
*Nanette Unruh, Independent Living Counselor*
To achieve the full inclusion and acceptance of people with disabilities through education and advocacy

**3949 Prairie Independent Living Resource Center**
17th S Main St
Hutchinson, KS 67501
620-663-9920
888-715-6818
FAX: 620-663-4711
TTY:620-663-9920
e-mail: info@pilr.org
pilr.org

*Chris Owens, Executive Director*
*Roger Frischenmeyer, Independent Living Specialist*
*Tammy Fuhr, Administrative Assistant*
*Nanette Unruh, Independent Living Counselor*
To achieve the full conclusion and acceptance of people with disabilities through education and advocacy

**3950 Resource Center for Independent Living**
726 W Patterson Ave
Iola, KS 66749-8805
620-365-8144
877-944-8144
FAX: 620-365-7726
www.rcilinc.org

*Chad Wilkins, Executive Director*
Committed to working with individuals, families, and communities to promote independent living and individual choice to persons with disabilities.

**3951 Resource Center for Independent Living, Inc. (RCIL)**
P.O.Box 257/1137 Laing
Osage City, KS 66523-257
785-528-3105
800-580-7245
FAX: 785-528-3665
TTY: 785-528-3106
www.rcilinc.org

*Chad Wilkins, Executive Director*
Committed to working with individuals, families, and communities to promote independent living and individual choice to persons with disabilities. As a center for independent living in Kansas, we provide advocacy, peer counseling, information and referral, independent living skills training and deinstitutionalization. In addition to these services, we also provide HOBS payroll services and a variety of programs benefiting individuals with disabilities.

**3952 Resource Center for Independent Living: Emporia**
614 Merchant
Emporia, KS 66801-2886
620-342-1648
888-261-4024
FAX: 620-342-1821
www.rcilinc.org

*Deone Wilson, Executive Director*
*Beth Combes, Information & Outreach Coordinator*
*Amy Richardson, Targeted Case Manager*
*Trevor Larson, Office Assistant*
Committed to working with individuals, families, and communities to promote independent living and individual choice to persons with disabilities.

**3953 Resource Center for Independent Living: Arkansas City**
P.O. Box 257
1137 Laing
Osage City, KS 66523
785-528-3105
800-580-7245
FAX: 785-528-3665
TTY: 785-528-3106
www.rcilinc.org

*Deone Wilson, Executive Director*
*Tania Harrington, Director of Quality Assurance*
*Adam Burnett, Director of Core Services*
*Mike Pitts, Finance Committee Chairperson*
Committed to working with individuals, families, and communities to promote independent living and individual choice to persons with disabilities.

**3954 Resource Center for Independent Living: Burlington**
P.O. Box 257
1137 Laing
Osage City, KS 66523
785-528-3105
800-580-7245
FAX: 785-528-3665
TTY: 785-528-3106
www.rcilinc.org

*Deone Wilson, Executive Director*
*Tania Harrington, Director of Quality Assurance*
*Adam Burnett, Director of Core Services*
*Mike Pitts, Finance Committee Chairperson*
Committed to working with individuals, families, and communities to promote independent living and individual choice to persons with disabilities.

**3955 Resource Center for Independent Living: Coffeyville**
P.O. Box 257
1137 Laing
Osage City, KS 66523
785-528-3105
800-580-7245
FAX: 785-528-3665
TTY: 785-528-3106
www.rcilinc.org

*Deone Wilson, Executive Director*
*Tania Harrington, Director of Quality Assurance*
*Adam Burnett, Director of Core Services*
*Mike Pitts, Finance Committee Chairperson*
Committed to working with individuals, families, and communities to promote independent living and individual choice to persons with disabilities.

**3956 Resource Center for Independent Living: El Dorado**
615 1/2 N Main St
El Dorado, KS 67042-2027
316-322-7853
800-960-7853
FAX: 316-322-7888
www.rcilinc.org

*Macy Gaines, Independent Living Specialist*
*Doris Hammons, Targeted Case Manager*
*Shirley Mullin, Targeted Case Manager*
*Barbara Ehret, Office Assistant*
Committed to working with individuals, families, and communities to promote independent living and individual choice to persons with disabilities.

**3957 Resource Center for Independent Living: Ft Scott**
P.O. Box 257
1137 Laing
Osage City, KS 66523
785-528-3105
800-580-7245
FAX: 785-528-3665
TTY: 785-528-3106
www.rcilinc.org

*Deone Wilson, Executive Director*
*Tania Harrington, Director of Quality Assurance*
*Adam Burnett, Director of Core Services*
*Mike Pitts, Finance Committee Chairperson*
Committed to working with individuals, families, and communities to promote independent living and individual choice to persons with disabilities.

**3958 Resource Center for Independent Living: Ottawa**
233 W 23rd Street
Ottawa, KS 66067-3533
785-242-1805
800-995-1805
FAX: 785-242-1448
www.rcilinc.org

*Chad Wilkins, Executive Director*
Committed to working with individuals, families, and communities to promote independent living and individual choice to persons with disabilities.

**3959 Resource Center for Independent Living: Overland Park**
Ste 100
10200 W 75th St
Shawnee Mission, KS 66204-2242
913-362-6618
877-439-2847
FAX: 913-677-2742
www.rcilinc.org

*Chad Wilkins, Executive Director*
RCIL is committed to working with individuals, families, and communities to promote independent living and individual choice to persons with disabilities.

**3960 Resource Center for Independent Living: Topeka**
519 SW 37th St
Topeka, KS 66611-2356
785-267-1717
877-719-1717
FAX: 785-267-1711
rcilinc.org

*Rosie Cooper, Director of Independent Living Services*
*Stuart Jones, Assistive Technology Specialist*
*Mikel McCary, Assistive Technology Specialist*
*Mandy Smith, Finance Committee Chairperson*
Committed to working with individuals, families, and communities to promote independent living and individual choice to persons with disabilities.

**3961 Southeast Kansas Independent Living (SKIL)**
P.O.Box 957
1801 Main
Parsons, KS 67357-957
620-421-5502
800-688-5616
FAX: 620-421-3705
TTY: 620-421-0983
e-mail: skil@skilonline.com
www.skilonline.com

*Shari Coatney, CEO/President*
*John Kazmierksi, Chairman*
*Janet Spillman, Vice Chairman*
*Nancy Varner, Treasurer*
To empower, integrate and maximize independence for all persons with disabilities.

**3962 Southeast Kansas Independent Living: Independence**
P.O.Box 944
107 East Main
Independence, KS 67301-944
620-331-1006
866-927-1006
FAX: 620-331-1257
TTY: 620-331-1006
e-mail: skilindy@skilonline.com
www.skilonline.com

*Shari Coatney, CEO/President*
*John Kazmierksi, Chairman*
*Janet Spillman, Vice Chairman*
*Nancy Varner, Treasurer*
To empower, integrate and maximize independence for all persons with disabilities.

**3963 Southeast Kansas Independent Living: Chanute**
P.O.Box 645
106 E. Main
Chanute, KS 66720-645
620-431-0757
866-927-0757
FAX: 620-431-7274
TTY: 620-431-0757
e-mail: skilchanute@skilonline.com
www.skilonline.com

*Shari Coatney, CEO/President*
*John Kazmierksi, Chairman*
*Janet Spillman, Vice Chairman*
*Nancy Varner, Treasurer*
To empower, integrate and maximize independence for all persons with disabilities.

**3964 Southeast Kansas Independent Living: Columbus**
P.O. Box 478
125 E Maple St
Columbus, KS 66725-1801
620-429-3600
866-927-3600
FAX: 620-429-1027
e-mail: skilcolumbus@skilonline.com
skilonline.com

*Shari Coatney, CEO/President*
*John Kazmierksi, Chairman*
*Janet Spillman, Vice Chairman*
*Nancy Varner, Treasurer*
To empower, integrate and maximize independence for all persons with disabilities.

**3965 Southeast Kansas Independent Living: Fredonia**
P.O.Box 448
623 Monroe
Fredonia, KS 66736-448
620-378-4881
866-927-4881
FAX: 620-378-4851
TTY: 620-378-4881
e-mail: skilfredonia@skilonline.com
www.skilonline.com

*Shari Coatney, CEO/President*
*John Kazmierksi, Chairman*
*Janet Spillman, Vice Chairman*
*Nancy Varner, Treasurer*
To empower, integrate and maximize independence for all persons with disabilities.

**3966 Southeast Kansas Independent Living: Hays**
P.O.Box 366
1015 Centennial Blvd
Hays, KS 67601-366
785-628-8019
800-316-8019
FAX: 785-628-3116
TTY: 785-628-3128
e-mail: skilhays@skilonline.com
www.skilonline.com

*Shari Coatney, CEO/President*
*John Kazmierksi, Chairman*
*Janet Spillman, Vice Chairman*
*Nancy Varner, Treasurer*
To empower, integrate and maximize independence for all persons with disabilities.

**3967 Southeast Kansas Independent Living: Pittsburg**
P.O.Box 1706
105 W. 3rd
Pittsburg, KS 66762-1706
620-231-6780
866-927-6780
FAX: 620-231-5920
TTY: 620-231-6780
e-mail: skilpittsburg@skilonline.com
skilonline.com

*Shari Coatney, CEO/President*
*John Kazmierksi, Chairman*
*Janet Spillman, Vice Chairman*
*Nancy Varner, Treasurer*
To empower, integrate and maximize independence for all persons with disabilities.

**3968 Southeast Kansas Independent Living: Sedan**
P.O.Box 340
113 West Main,
Sedan, KS 67361-340
620-725-3990
866-906-3990
FAX: 620-725-3942
TTY: 620-725-3990
e-mail: skilsedan@skilonline.com
www.skilonline.com

*Shari Coatney, CEO/President*
*John Kazmierksi, Chairman*
*Janet Spillman, Vice Chairman*
*Nancy Varner, Treasurer*
To empower, integrate and maximize independence for all persons with disabilities.

**3969 Southeast Kansas Independent Living: Yates Center**
P.O.Box 129
119 W. Butler
Yates Center, KS 66783-129
620-625-2818
866-927-2818
FAX: 620-625-2585
e-mail: skilyc@skilonline.com
www.skilonline.com

*Shari Coatney, CEO/President*
*John Kazmierksi, Chairman*
*Janet Spillman, Vice Chairman*
*Nancy Varner, Treasurer*
To empower, integrate and maximize independence for all persons with disabilities.

**3970 The Whole Person: Nortonville**
7301 Mission Road
Suite 135
Prairie Village, KS 66208- 3006
913-262-1294
877-767-8896
FAX: 913-262-2392
e-mail: info@thewholeperson.org
www.thewholeperson.org

*David C Robinson, Executive Director*
*Brian Ellefson, President*
*Joe Marvil, Vice President*
*Venkata Vadlamani, Treasurer*
Assists people with disabilities to live independently and encourages change within the community to expand opportunities for independent living.

**3971 The Whole Person: Prairie Village**
7301 Mission Road
Suite 135
Prairie Village, KS 66208- 3006
913-262-1294
877-767-8896
FAX: 913-262-2392
e-mail: info@thewholeperson.org
www.thewholeperson.org

*David C Robinson, Executive Director*
*Brian Ellefson, President*
*Joe Marvil, Vice President*
*Venkata Vadlamani, Treasurer*
Assists people with disabilities to live independently and encourages change within the community to expand opportunities for independent living.

**3972 Three Rivers Independent Living Center**
P.O.Box 408
504 Miller Dr.
Wamego, KS 66547-0408
785-456-9915
800-555-3994
FAX: 785-456-9923
TTY: 785-456-9915
e-mail: reception@threeriversinc.org
threeriversinc.org

*Audrey Schremmer-Philips, Executive Director*
*Sandy Simmer, Finance Manager*
*Barbara Feldkamp, IL Specialist*
*Vickie Lieber, Accounting Assistant*

A nonprofit organization promoting the self reliance of individuals with disabilities through education, advocacy, training and support.

**3973 Three Rivers Independent Living Center: Clay**
P.O.Box 33
621 Court Street
Clay Center, KS 67432-0033
785-632-6117
FAX: 785-632-3105
TTY:785-632-6117
e-mail: reception@threeriversinc.org
www.threeriversinc.org

*Rose Scott, Manager*
*Audrey Schremmer-Philips, Executive Director*
*Sandy Simmer, Finance Manager*
*Vickie Lieber, Accounting Assistant*

A non-profit organization promoting the self reliance of individuals with disabilities through, education, advocacy, training and support.

**3974 Three Rivers Independent Living Center: Manhattan**
401 Houston St.
Manhattan, KS 66502
785-776-9294
800-432-2703
FAX: 785-776-9479
e-mail: reception@threeriversinc.org
www.threeriversinc.org

*Audrey Schremmer-Philips, Executive Director*
*Sandy Simmer, Finance Manager*
*Elizabeth Moore, IL Specialist*
*Vickie Lieber, Accounting Assistant*

A non profit organization promoting the self reliance of individuals with disabilities through education, advocacy, training and support.

**3975 Three Rivers Independent Living Center: Seneca**
416 Main St
Seneca, KS 66538-1926
785-336-0222
FAX: 785-336-0288
e-mail: reception@threeriversinc.org
www.threeriversinc.org

*Lynn Neihaus, Manager*
*Audrey Schremmer-Philips, Executive Director*
*Sandy Simmer, Finance Manager*
*Vickie Lieber, Accounting Assistant*

A non profit organization promoting the self reliance of individuals with disabilities through education, advocacy, training and support.

**3976 Three Rivers Independent Living Center: Topeka**
P.O.Box 4152
Topeka, KS 66604-4152
785-273-0249
FAX: 785-273-0249
e-mail: reception@threeriversinc.org
www.threeriversinc.org

*Audrey Schremmer-Philips, Executive Director*
*Sandy Simmer, Finance Manager*
*Dave Reed, Recreation Specialist*
*Vickie Lieber, Accounting Assistant*

A non profit organization promoting the self reliance of individuals with disabilities through education, advocacy, training and support.

**3977 Topeka Independent Living Resource Center**
Ste 100
501 SW Jackson St
Topeka, KS 66603-3300
785-233-4572
FAX: 785-233-1561
TTY:785-233-4572
e-mail: tilrcweb@tilrc.org
tilrc.org

*Mike Oxford, Executive Director*
*Evan Korynta, Operations Manager*
*Angie Harter, Independent Living Advocacy Staff*
*Carol Doss, Independent Living Advocacy Staff*

A civil and human rights organization that advocates for justice, equality and essential services for a fully integrated and accessible society for all people with disabilities.

**3978 Whole Person: Nortonville**
7301 Mission Road
Suite 135
Prairie Village, KS 66208- 3006
913-262-1294
877-767-8896
FAX: 913-262-2392
e-mail: info@thewholeperson.org
www.thewholeperson.org

*David C Robinson, Executive Director*
*Brian Ellefson, President*
*Joe Marvil, Vice President*
*Venkata Vadlamani, Treasurer*

Assists people with disabilities to live independently and encourages change within the community to expand opportunities for independent living.

**3979 Whole Person: Prairie Village**
7301 Mission Rd
Prairie Village, KS 66208-3006
913-262-1294
FAX: 913-262-2392
e-mail: info@thewholeperson.org
www.thewholeperson.org

*David C Robinson, Executive Director*
*Brian Ellefson, President*
*Joe Marvil, Vice President*
*Venkata Vadlamani, Treasurer*

Assists people with disabilities to live independently and encourages change within the community to expand opportunities for independent living.

**3980 Whole Person: Tonganoxie**
7301 Mission Road
Suite 135
Prairie Village, KS 66208- 3006
913-262-1294
877-767-8896
FAX: 913-262-2392
e-mail: info@thewholeperson.org
www.thewholeperson.org

*David C Robinson, Executive Director*
*Brian Ellefson, President*
*Joe Marvil, Vice President*
*Venkata Vadlamani, Treasurer*

Assists people with disabilities to live independently and encourages change within the community to expand opportunities for independent living.

## Kentucky

**3981 Center for Accessible Living**
Ste 200
305 W Broadway
Louisville, KY 40202-2121
502-589-6620
888-813-8497
FAX: 502-589-3980
TTY:502-589-6690
e-mail: info@calky.org
calky.org

*Jan Day, CEO*
*Michael Markiewicz, Chief Financial Officer*
*Jeanne M. Gallimore, Branch Director*
*Susan Tharpe, Independent Living Specialist*
To assist the individuals with disabilities who seek to live independently.

**3982 Center for Accessible Living: Murray**
Ste C
1051 N 16th St
Murray, KY 42071-8511
270-753-7676
888-261-6194
FAX: 270-753-7729
TTY:270-767-0549
e-mail: info@calky.org
www.calky.org

*Jeanne M. Gallimore, Branch Director*
*Susan Tharpe, Independent Living Specialist*
*Jan Day, CEO*
*Michael Markiewicz, Chief Financial Officer*
To assist the individuals with disabilities who seek to live independently.

**3983 Center for Independent Living: Kentucky Department for the Blind**
Independent Living Office
Rear
409 N Miles St
Elizabethtown, KY 42701-1834
270-766-5126
e-mail: buel.stalls@mail.state.ky.us

*Buel E Stalls Jr, Office Manager and IL Specialist*
*Nancy Bachuss, Manager*
Offers peer counseling, attendant care registry and other services to the community as they relate to the blind community. The Murray office is an independent living regional office which covers 20 far western counties of Kentucky..

**3984 Disability Coalition of Northern Kentucky**
Ste 219
525 W 5th St
Covington, KY 41011-1293
859-431-7668
FAX: 859-431-7688
TTY:800-648-6057
e-mail: dcnky@fuse.net

*Kitt Heeg, Executive Director*
Empowering people with disabilities through education, networking, and positive attitudes..

**3985 Disability Resource Initiative**
624 Eastwood St
Bowling Green, KY 42103-1602
270-796-5992
877-437-5045
FAX: 270-796-6630
www.dri-ky.org

*Marilyn Mitchell, Executive Director*
*Tracy Cole, Independent Living Specialist*
*Steve Burchett, IT Specialist*
*Jenny McCallister, Administrative Assistant*
One of the most important premises in Independent Living is that people with disabilities are the most knowledgable about their own needs. Because of this all of their services are designed to be consumer-driven. Within each service, Center Staff work with both participant and provider to achieve and maintain an Independent Lifestyle.

**3986 Independence Place**
Suite 1218
1093 S. Broadway
Lexington, KY 40504-1787
859-266-2807
877-266-2807
FAX: 859-335-0627
TTY: 800-648-6056
e-mail: info@independenceplaceky.org
www.independenceplaceky.org

*Pamela Roark-Glisson, Executive Director*
*Gina Wallace, Executive Administrative Coordinator*
*Bridget Boulware, Administrative Assistant*
*John W. Glisson, Newsline & Peer Services Consultant*
To assist people with disabilities to achieve their full potential for community inclusion through improving access, choice and equal opportunity.

**3987 Pathfinders for Independent Living**
105 E Mound St
Harlan, KY 40831-2355
606-573-5777
877-340-PATH
FAX: 606-573-5739
TTY: 606-573-5777
www.pahtfindersilc.org

*Sandra Goodwyn, Executive Director*
*Andrew Saylor, Director of IT (Internal) and Financial Officer*
*Stacy Marple, Director of IT (External)*
*Ron Walker, Public Affairs Specialist*
They publish a newsletter called LifeLine 4-5 times a year. Most articles are written by Sandra Goodwyn. Editor is Andrew Saylor. Serves people with disabilities to maintain as much independence as they desire

**3988 SILC Department of Vocational Rehabilitation**
209 Saint Clair St
Frankfort, KY 40601-1817
502-564-4440
800-372-7172
FAX: 502-564-6745
e-mail: sarahf.richardson@ky.gov
www.ovr.ky.org

*Sarah Richardson, SILC Liaison*
We recognize and respect the contributions of all individuals as a necessary and vital part of a productive society..

## Louisiana

**3989 New Horizons: Central Louisiana**
Ste 18
2406 Ferrand St
Monroe, LA 71201-3236
318-323-4374
800-428-5505
FAX: 318-323-5445
www.nhilc.org

A private, non-profit, non-residential, consumer-controlled, community-based organization that enables people with disabilities to live independently.

**3990 New Horizons: Northeast Louisiana**
Ste A
3400 Jackson St
Alexandria, LA 71301-4037
318-484-3596
888-361-3596
FAX: 318-484-3640
e-mail: nhilc@nhilc.org
www.nhilc.org

*Dimple Hughes, Executive Director*

A private, non-profit, non-residential, consumer controlled, community based organization that enables people with disabilities to live independently.

**3991 New Horizons: Northwest Louisiana**
Ste D
8508 Line Ave
Shreveport, LA 71106-6144
318-671-8131
877-219-7327
FAX: 318-688-7823
e-mail: nhilc@nhilc.org
nhilc.org

*Gale Dean, Manager*
A private, non-profit, non-residential, consumer-controlled, community based organization that enables people with disabilities to live independently.

**3992 Resources for Independent Living: Baton Rouge**
New Orleans Resources for Independent Living
suite 101 A
3233 South Sherwood Forest Blvd.
Baton Rouge, LA 70816
225-753-4772
877-505-2260
FAX: 225-753-4831
e-mail: contact@noril.org
www.noril.org

*Yavonka G. Archaga, Executive Director*
*Alisha S. Hammond, Assistant Director*
*Rosie Calvin, Program Manager*
*Deonne T. Bailey, Core Service Manager*
RIL provides quality services to individuals with disabilities to assist with living independent. RIL also offers services to inculde information and referral, advocacy, peer support and independent living skills training.

**3993 Resources for Independent Living: Metairie**
2001 21st Street
Kenner, LA 70065
504-522-1955
877-505-2260
FAX: 504-522-1954
e-mail: contact@noril.org
noril.org

*Yavonka G. Archaga, Executive Director*
*Alisha S. Hammond, Assistant Director*
*Rosie Calvin, Program Manager*
*Deonne T. Bailey, Core Service Manager*
RIL provides quality services to individuals with disabilities to assist with living independently. RIL also offers an array of services to include information and referral, advocacy, peer support and independent living skills training.

**3994 Southwest Louisiana Independence Center: Lake Charles**
2016 Oak Park Boulevard
Lake Charles, LA 70601-5391
337-477-7198
888-403-1062
FAX: 337-477-7198
TTY: 337-477-7198
slic.org
SILC provides Information and Referral, Advocacy, Peer Counseling and other Independent Living Services, to develop community options for persons with significant disabilities in Southwest and Central Louisiana, and to assist them in achieving and maintaining self-sufficient, productive lives.

**3995 Southwest Louisians Independence Center: Lafayette**
Ste 118
850 Kaliste Saloom Rd
Lafayette, LA 70508-4230
337-269-0027
888-516-5009
FAX: 337-233-7660
www.slic-la.org
SLIC provides Information and Referral, Advocacy, Peer Counseling and other Independent Living Services, to develop community options for persons with significant disabilities in Southwest and South Central Louisiana, and to assist them in achieving and maintaining self-sufficient, productive lives. PCA provider services

**3996 Volunteers of America of Greater New Orleans**
4152 Canal St.
New Orleans, LA 70119
504-482-2130
FAX: 504-482-1922
voagno.org

*James M. Le Blanc, President/CEO*
*Thomas J. Lee, Chairman*
*Wayne M. Baquet, Treasurer*
*Stacy E. Bonnaffons, Secretary*
Volunteers of America Greater New Orleans offers many services that aim to improve the lives of children, youth, and families.

**3997 W Troy Cole Independent Living Specialist**
Ste H
1900 Lamy Ln
Monroe, LA 71201-9200
318-323-4374

*Katherine Carnell, Manager*
.

## Maine

**3998 Alpha One: Bangar**
Suite 302
2937 SW 27th Avenue
Miami, FL 33133
305-567-9888
877-228-7321
FAX: 305-567-1317
www.alphaone.org

*John W. Walsh, President & CEO, Co-founder*
*Marcia F. Ritchie, Vice President & Chief Operating Officer*
*Marsha A. Carnes, Director of Program Evaluation*
*Robert Campbell, Communications Manager*
Committed to being a leading enterprise providing the community with information, services and products that create opportunities for people with disabilities to live independently. Provides many services including adaptive and mobility equipment selection, peer support, advocacy, information and referral services, adapted drive evaluation and training, and consumer directed personal assistance.

**3999 Alpha One: South Portland**
127 Main St
South Portland, ME 04106-2647
207-767-2189
800-640-7200
FAX: 207-799-8346
TTY: 207-767-5387
www.alphaonenow.com

*Dennis Stubbs, Chairman*
*Bob McPhee, Vice-Chairman*
*Darlene Stewart, Independent Living Specialist*
*Ketra S Crosson, Aroostook County Coordinator*
Committed to being a leading enterprise providing the community with information, services and products that create opportunities for people with disabilities to live independently. Offers adaptive equipment loan program, independent living skills instruction, adapted driver evaluation and training, information and referral services, peer support, advocacy, access design consultation, and more.

**4000 Motivational Services**
P.O.Box 229
Augusta, ME 04332-0229
207-626-3465
FAX: 207-626-3469
TTY:207-621-2542
e-mail: information@mocomaine.com.
www.mocomaine.com

*Richard M Weiss, Executive Director*
*Barb Gabri, Human Resources Director*
Improving the lives of people with disabilities through housing, employment and community support.

**4001 Shalom House**
106 Gilman St
Portland, ME 04102-3034
207-874-1080
FAX: 207-874-1077
TTY:207-842-6888
e-mail: generalmail@shalomhouseinc.org
shalomhouseinc.org

*Megan Lewis, Human Resources Manager*
*Mary Haynes-Rodgers, Executive Director*
*Kristine Lausier, Quality Assurance Administrator*
*Jane Collette, Accounting Manager*
Offers hope for adults living with severe mental illness by providing a choice of quality housing and support services that help people lead stable and fulfilling lives in the community.

## Maryland

**4002 Broadmead**
13801 York Rd
Cockeysville, MD 21030-1899
410-527-1900
877-STA-HOME
friendscare.org

*Thomas R. Mondloch, President*
*William A. Morton, Chairman*
To provide continuing care services to a diverse group of seniors in a warm, congenial community founded and operated in the spirit of the Religious Society of Friends.

**4003 Eastern Shore Center for Independent Living**
309 Sunburst Highway
Suite 9
Cambridge, MD 21613-2050
410-221-7701
800-705-7944
FAX: 410-221-7714
TTY: 410-221-4150
e-mail: escil@escil.org
www.escil.org

*Shirley Tarbox, Executive Director*
*Steven Melvin, Program Director*
*Betsy B. Jones, Executive Assistant*
*Doretha Luke, Administrative Assistant*
ESCIL provides services to people with all disabilities regardless of age, religion, gender, ethnicity, race or national origin. In addition to the core services of information and referral, skills training, peer support and advocacy, ESCIL also offers assistance with accessibility modifications, Americans with Disabilities Act education and training, housing referrals and counseling, transportation referral and information, Brailling capabilities, Personal Attendent Services referral, and more.

**4004 Freedom Center**
1560 Opossumtown Pike
Rose Hill Plaza, Unit A-20
Frederick, MD 21702-4748
301-846-7811
e-mail: advocate@thefreedomcenter-md.org
thefreedomcenter-md.org

*Jamey George, Executive Director*
*Vicki Mills, President*
*Russ Holt, Vice-President*
*Chere Goretski, Chere Goretski*
A walk in center for independent living, provides services and supports to empower individuals with disabilities to lead self-directed, independent, and productive lives in a barrier-free community.

**4005 Housing Unlimited**
Ste G1
1398 Lamberton Dr
Silver Spring, MD 20902-3435
301-592-9314
FAX: 301-592-9318
e-mail: information@housingunlimited.org
www.housingunlimited.org

*Abe Schuchman, Executive Director*
*Lisa Y. Cook, Associate Director*
*Kathy Bui, Director of Office Operations*
*Marjorie Goldman, Director of Development*
To address the housing crisis for adults with psychiatric disabilities who reside in Montgomery County, Maryland.

**4006 Independence Now**
Ste 101
12301 Old Columbia Pike
Silver Spring, MD 20904-1656
301-277-2839
FAX: 301-625-9777
e-mail: info@innow.org
innow.org

*Sarah Sorensen, Executive Director*
*Trish Foley, Director of Community Services*
*Todd Thorpe, Director of Operations*
*Eddie Snyder, Administrative Assistant*
A nonprofit organization created by people with disabilities and provides services that promote independence and the inclusion of people with disabilities in their communities.

**4007 Independence Now: Silver Spring**
Ste 101
12301 Old Columbia Pike
Silver Spring, MD 20904-1659
301-277-2839
FAX: 301-625-9777
e-mail: info@innow.org
innow.org

*Sarah Sorensen, Executive Director*
*Trish Foley, Director of Community Services*
*Todd Thorpe, Director of Operations*
*Eddie Snyder, Administrative Assistant*
A nonprofit organization created by people with disabilities that provides services that promotes independence and the inclusion of people with disabilities in their communities.

**4008 Making Choices for Independent Living**
Ste 202
1118 Light St
Baltimore, MD 21230-4152
410-234-8195
888-560-2221
e-mail: andreab@mcil-md.org
www.mcil-md.org

*Jimmie Joku Cooper, Owner*
Provides services to help empower people with disabilities to lead self-directed, independent and productive lives in the community and protect their civil rights.OUTOF ORDER.

**4009 Resources for Independence**
30 N. Mechanic Street
Cumberland, MD 21502-2705
301-784-1774
800-371-1986
FAX: 301-784-1776
www.rficil.org

*Lori Magruder, Executive Director*
*John Michaels, Assistant Director*
*Robert Cannon, Resource Developer*
*Sherry Williams, Finance Director*

Private, non-profit, consumer-controlled, community-based organization providing services and advocacy by and for persons with all type of disabilities. Their goal is to create opportunities for independence, and to assist individuals with disabilities to achieve their maximum level of independent functioning within their families and communities.

**4010 Southern Maryland Center for LIFE**
P.O.Box 657
Charlotte Hall, MD 20622-657
301-884-4498
FAX: 301-884-6099
e-mail: cflife@eartlink.net
www.somd.com

*Marie Robinson, Executive Director*
*Carrie Lanthier, Administrative Assistant*

A non-profit community based organization which provides services to disabled people who live or work in the tri-county area. Our mission is to empower people with disabilities to lead self-directed, independent, and productive lives in their community. .

## Massachusetts

**4011 Adlib**
215 North St
Pittsfield, MA 01201-4644
413-442-7047
800-232-7047
FAX: 413-443-4338
e-mail: adlib@adlibcil.org
adlibcil.org

*Joseph Sacchetti, Director*
*Michael Hinkley, President*
*Lisa Sloane, Treasurer*
*Linda Febles, Secretary*

Offers information and referral services, independent living skills training, peer counseling, individual and group advocacy services available to all people with disabilities. Access consultation provided to businesses, agencies and institutions in accordance to the Americans with Disabilities Act.

**4012 Arc of Cape Cod**
P.O.Box 428
Hyannis, MA 02601-428
508-790-3667
FAX: 508-775-5233
e-mail: info@arcofcapecod.org
www.arcofcapecod.org

Provides adults with developmental disabilities a full range of individual supports to assist them in becoming valued members of their community.

**4013 Boston Center for Independent Living**
Fl 5
60 Temple Pl
Boston, MA 02111-1301
617-338-6665
FAX: 617-338-6661
TTY:617-338-6662
e-mail: info@bostoncil.org
www.bostoncil.org

*Bill Henning, Executive Director*
*Arnold Berry, Senior IL Advocate*
*Courtland Townes, Deputy Director*
*Nassira Nicola, Director of Program Services*

A frontline civil rights organization led by people with disabilities that advocates to eliminate discrimination, isolation and segregation by providing advocacy, information and referral, peer support, skills training, and PCA services in order to enhance the independence of people with disabilities.

**4014 Cape Organization for Rights of the Disabled (CORD)**
106 Bassett Lane
Hyannis, MA 2601
508-775-8300
800-541-0282
FAX: 508-775-7022
TTY: 800-541-0282
e-mail: cordinfo@cilcapecod.org
www.cilcapecod.org

*Coreen Brinkerhoff, Executive Director*

The Cape Organization for the Rights of the Disabled (CORD) has been aggresively working since 1984 to advance the independence, productivity, and integration of people with disabilities into mainstream society. CORD is the Center for Independent Living (CIL) and is a member of the Aging and Disability Resources Consortium (ADRC) servinf Cape Cod and the Islands.

**4015 Center for Living & Working: Fitchburg**
76 Summer Street
Suite 110
Fitchburg, MA 01420-5785
978-345-1568
TTY:978-345-1568
e-mail: centerlwA@centerlw.org
www.centerlw.org

*Cindy Purcell, Board President*
*Terrence J. Briggs, Treasurer*
*Susan Bernard, Secretary*
*Jim O'Day, Advisor to CLW Board of Directors*

The Center for Living and Working is a non-profit Independent Living Center which takes its direction from persons with disabilities. The Center advocates to empower persons with disabilities to take active roles in their lives and in their community in which they live. Also provides comprehensive and innovative programs and services in order to maximize individual independence and opportunities.

**4016 Center for Living & Working: Framingham**
484 Main St
Suite 345
Worcester, MA 01608-1824
508-798-0350
FAX: 508-797-4015
TTY:508-755-1003
e-mail: opsearch@centerlw.org
www.centerlw.org

*Cindy Purcell, Board President*
*Terrence J. Briggs, Treasurer*
*Susan Bernard, Secretary*
*Jim O'Day, Advisor to CLW Board of Directors*

The Center for Living and Working is a non-profit Independent Living Center which takes its direction from persons with disabilities. The Center advocates to empower persons with disabilities to take active roles in their lives and in their community in which they live. Also provides comprehensive and innovative programs and services in order to maximize individual independence and opportunities.

**4017 Center for Living & Working: Worcester**
484 Main St
Suite 345
Worcester, MA 01608-1824
508-798-0350
FAX: 508-797-4015
TTY:508-755-1003
e-mail: opsearch@centerlw.org
centerlw.org

*Cindy Purcell, Board President*
*Terrence J. Briggs, Treasurer*
*Susan Bernard, Secretary*
*Jim O'Day, Advisor to CLW Board of Directors*

The Center for Living and Working is a non-profit Independent Living Center which takes its direction from persons with disabilities. The Center advocates to empower persons with disabilities to take active roles in their lives and in their community in which they live. Also provides comprehensive and innovative programs and services in order to maximize individual independence and opportunities.

**4018 Developmental Evaluation and Adjustment Facilities**
215 Brighton Ave
Allston, MA 02134-2013
617-254-4041
800-886-5195
FAX: 617-254-7091
e-mail: info@deafinconline.org
deafinconline.org

*Sharon L. Applegate, Executive Director*
*Thomas Keydel, President & Treasurer*
*Diana Goldfarb, Development Consultant*
*Kim Lapine, Vice President*

Encourages and empowers deaf, hard of hearing, deafblind and late-deafened individuals to lead independent and productive lives.

**4019 Independence Associates**
141 Main St
Brockton, MA 02301-4012
508-583-2166
800-649-5568
FAX: 508-583-2165
e-mail: info@iacil.org
iacil.org

*Steven Higgins, Executive Director*
*Winifred McGraw, Assistant Director and Director of Finance*
*Lea Monteiro, Secretary/Receptionist*
*Manel Desvallons, Resource Coordinator*

Provides comprehensive services which will enhance the range of acceptable options available to the consumer and improve the quality of life of persons with disabilities; to work on behalf of the objective of the disablility rights and independent living movement.

**4020 Independent Living Center of Stavros: Greenfield**
55 Federal St
Greenfield, MA 01301-2546
413-774-3001
www.stavros.org

Promoting independence and access in the communities for persons with disabilities and deaf people.

**4021 Independent Living Center of Stavros: Springfield**
210 Old Farm Rd
Amherst, MA 01002-2704
413-256-0473
800-804-1899
FAX: 413-256-0190
stavros.org

*James Kruidenier, Executive Director*

Promoting independence and access in the communities for persons with disabilities and deaf people.

**4022 Independent Living Center of the North Shore & Cape Ann**
Ste 107
27 Congress St
Salem, MA 01970-5577
978-741-0077
888-751-0077
FAX: 978-741-1133
ilcnsca.org

*Mary Margaret Moore, Executive Director*
*Shawn McDuff, Deputy Director*
*Jean Rockett, Director of Options and Transition*
*Angel Dailey, Independent Living Peer Guide*

A service and advocacy center run by and for people with disabilities that supports the struggle of people who have all types of disabilities to live independently and participate fully in community life.

**4023 MetroWest Center for Independent Living**
280 Irving St
Framingham, MA 01702-7306
508-875-7853
FAX: 508-875-8359
TTY:508-875-7853
e-mail: info@mwcil.org
mwcil.org

*Paul Spooner, Executive Director*
*Rose Quinn, Assistant Director*
*Jini Fairley, Director of Services*
*David Correia, Independent Living Coordinator*

To help individuals with disabilities become productive and contributing members of the community and to eliminate barriers within the community that impede this process.

**4024 Multi-Cultural Independent Living Center of Boston**
110 Claybourne St
Dorchester Center, MA 02124-1232
617-436-9431
FAX: 617-265-2597
TTY:617-288-2707
e-mail: admin@milcb.org
milcb.org

*Derrick Dominique, Executive Director*
*Ana Ortiz, Director of Services*
*Eleanor Slaughter, Senior IL Advocate*
*Louise Beach, Community Outreach Coordinator*

Seeks to create opportunities for people with disabilities and their families in unserved/under-served populations and cultures who reside in Boston's inner city.

**4025 Northeast Independent Living Program**
20 Ballard Rd
Lawrence, MA 01843-1018
978-687-4288
FAX: 978-689-4488
TTY:978-687-4288
e-mail: help@nilp.org
nilp.org

*June Cowen, Executive Director*
*Nanette Goodwin, Assistant Director*
*Tony Goodnough, Director of Finance*
*Jim Lyons, Director, Community Development*

A consumer controlled Independent Living Center providing Advocacy and Services to people with all disabilities in the greater Merrimack Valley who wish to live as independently as possible in the commuity.

**4026 Renaissance Clubhouse**
176 Walker St
Lowell, MA 01854-3126
978-454-7944
FAX: 978-937-7867
e-mail: renclub@channel1.com

*Elaine Walker, Executive Director*
*Pammy Sadoie, Assistant Director*

Offers daily structure, assistance wtih jobs, retirement, and housing.

**4027 Southeast Center for Independent Living**
66 Troy St
Suite 3
Fall River, MA 02720-3023
508-679-9210
FAX: 508-677-2377
TTY:508-679-9210
e-mail: scil@secil.org
secil.org

*Lisa M Pitta, Executive Director*
*Bill Boffa, Director Of Programs*
*Edith Colon, Independent Living Coordinator*
*Linda Barbosa, Independent Living Specialist*

The Philosophy of Independent Living, maintains that individuals with disabilities have the right to choose services and make decisions for themselves. This belief is the foundation and guiding principle of all of SCIL's policies and operations. SCIL provides training, information and support to help consumers achieve individual goals, experience personal growth and participate fully in community life.

**4028 Student Independent Living Experience Massachusetts Hospital School**
560 Harrison Avenue
Suite 600
Boston, MA 02118-2447
617-338-6409
800-843-5879
TTY:800-328-3202
e-mail: JurorHelp@jud.state.ma.us.
www.massjury.org

Offers young adults with disabilities an opportunity to participate in a group learning situation, where they will develop independent and transitional living skills through a residential or non-residential model.

## Michigan

**4029 Ann Arbor Center for Independent Living**
3941 Research Park Drive
Ann Arbor, MI 48104-6852
734-971-0277
FAX: 734-971-0826
www.aacil.org

*Glen Ashlock, Program Manager*
*Chris Baty, Theater Coordinator*
*Bryan Wilkinson, Director of Operations and Sales*
*Shirley Coombs, Chief Financial Officer*

AACIL assists people with disabilities and their families in living full and productive lives. AACIL assures the equality of opportunity, full participation, independent living and economic self-sufficiency of people with disabilities in the community.

**4030 Arc Michigan**
1325 S Washington Ave
Lansing, MI 48910-1652
517-487-5426
800-292-7851
FAX: 517-487-0303
arcmi.org

*Christine Lerchen, President*
*Tom Kendziorski, Vice President*
*Maggie Kolk, Secretary*
*Sherry Fernandez, Treasurer*

Exists to empower local chapters of The ARC to assure that citizens with developmental disabilities are valued and that they and their families can participate fully in and contribute to the life of their community.

**4031 Arc/Muskegon**
1145 Wesley Ave
Muskegon, MI 49442-2197
231-777-2006
FAX: 231-777-3507
e-mail: info@arcmuskegon.org
www.arcmuskegon.org

*Margaret O'Toole, Executive Director*
*Mikki Rosema, Administrative Assistant*
*Karen L. Bowne, CLS Program Coordinator*
*Tim Michalski, Director*

Offers information and referral, advocacy services and peer counseling.

**4032 Bad Axe: Blue Water Center for Independent Living**
614 N Port Crescent St
P.O. Box 29
Bad Axe, MI 48413- 1207
989-269-5421
FAX: 989-269-5422
e-mail: info@bwcil.org
www.bwcil.org

*Toni Mazure, Independent Living Specialist*
*Karen Massaro-Mundt, President*
*Chuck Wanninger, Treasurer*

A non-profit, consumer-based organization that advocates, informs and supports persons with disabilities in the community.

**4033 Bay Area Coalition for Independent Living**
Ste 17
701 S Elmwood Ave
Traverse City, MI 49684-3185
231-929-4865
FAX: 231-929-4896
e-mail: steve@bacil.org

*Steve Wade, Director*

.

**4034 Capital Area Center for Independent Living**
2812 N. Martin Luther King Jr. Blvd
Lansing, MI 48906
517-999-2760
FAX: 517-999-2767
TTY:800-649-3777
e-mail: info@cacil.org
www.cacil.org

*Ellen Weaver, Executive Director*
*Peggy Jones, Financial Manager*
*Jean Harris, Independent Living Specialist*
*Karen Kraft, Program Coordinator*

CACIL provide training, mentoring, and referrals to help people with disabilities and their families live productive lives.

**4035 Caro: Blue Water Center for Independent Living**
1184 Cleaver Rd
Caro, MI 48723-1143
989-673-3678
FAX: 989-673-3678
e-mail: info@bwcil.org
www.bwcil.org

*Alex Busch, Independent Living Specialist*
*Karen Massaro-Mundt, President*
*Chuck Wanninger, Treasurer*

A non-profit, consumer-based organization that advocates, informs and supports persons with disabilities in the community.

**4036 Center for Independent Living of Mid-Michigan**
3941 Research Park Drive
Ann Arbor, MI 48104-6832
734-971-0277
FAX: 734-971-0826
www.aacil.org

*Glen Ashlock, Program Manager*
*Chris Baty, Theater Coordinator*
*Bryan Wilkinson, Director of Operations and Sales*
*Shirley Coombs, Chief Financial Officer*

Comprised of over 51 percent of people with disabilities, and advocates for the rights of people with disabilities in the Mid-Michigan area. Call for information on disability issues or for assistance in obtaining services, within your community..

**4037 Community Connections of Southwest Michigan**
Ste 2
133 E Napier Ave
Benton Harbor, MI 49022
269-925-6422
800-578-4245
FAX: 269-925-7141
e-mail: kellis@miconnect.org
www.miconnect.org

*Kathy Ellis, Director*

An advocacy organization that teaches and empowers people with disabilities to make choices about living life to the fullest, controlling and directing their own lives and asserting their rights and responsibilites within their Berrien County communities..

**4038 Cristo Rey Handicappers Program**
1717 N High St
Lansing, MI 48906-4529
517-372-4700
FAX: 517-372-8499
e-mail: info@cristo-rey.org
www.cristo-rey.org

*Marlene M Berens, Manager*
To care for the spiritual and social needs of individuals and families by offering services that encourage self-sufficiency and recognize the dignity of the human person..

**4039 Detroit Center for Independent Living**
Suite 2
1042 Griswold
Port Huron, MI 48060
810-987-9337
FAX: 810-987-9548
e-mail: info@bwcil.org
www.bwcil.org

*Angela Hoff, Executive Director*
*Bill Ferris, Administrative Support*
*Pat Brown, Director of Services and Programs*
*Scott Shine, Employment Coordinator*
BWCIL is a consumer-based organization designed to serve persons with disabilities who have physical, psychiatric, sendory, cognitive, and multiple disabilities through the provision of advocacy, information and referral, service provision, and the promotion of needed services so to maximize the individual's optimal level of independence.

**4040 Disability Advocates of Kent County**
3600 Camelot Dr SE
Grand Rapids, MI 49546-8103
616-949-1100
FAX: 616-949-7865
e-mail: contact@dakc.us
disabilityadvocates.us

*David Bulkowski, Executive Director*
*Denise Borges, Employment Specialist*
*Kim Menninga, Access Specialist*
*Bonnie Miller, Independent Living Specialist*
Exists to advocate, assist, educate and inform on independent living options for persons with disabilities and to create a barrier-free society for all.

**4041 Disability Connection**
27 E. Clay Avenue
Muskegon, MI 49442
231-722-0088
866-322-4501
FAX: 231-722-0066
dcilmi.org

*Susan Cloutier, Executive Director*
*Joe Doyle, President*
*Peter Myers, Veteran Services Coordinator*
*Diane Russick-Rodriguez, Independent Living Specialist*
To advocate, educate, empower, and provide resources for persons with disabilities and promote accessible communities.

**4042 Disability Network Southwest Michigan**
517 E Crosstown Pkwy
Kalamazoo, MI 49001-2867
269-345-1516
FAX: 269-345-0229
www.dnswm.org

*Joel W Cooper, President*
*Karen Halsted, Associate Director*
*Roger Jones, Database Manager*
*Kristi Rudowske, Finance Director*
To educate and empower people with disabilities to create change intheir own lives, and to advocate for social change to create inclusive communities. As a center for independent living, they are part of the disability rights movement.

**4043 Disability Network of Mid-Michigan**
1705 S. Saginaw Road
Midland, MI 48640-6825
989-835-4041
800-782-4160
FAX: 989-835-8121
e-mail: info@dnmm.org
dnmm.org

*David Emmel, Executive Director*
*Steve Locke, Associate Director*
*Nancy Pococke, Director of Operations*
*Darlene Ferguson, Administrative Assistant*
To promote and encourage independence for all people with disabilities.

**4044 Disability Network of Oakland & Macomb**
16645 15 Mile Rd
Clinton Township, MI 48035-2206
586-268-4160
800-284-2457
FAX: 586-285-9942
e-mail: info@dnom.org
dnom.org

*Kellie Boyd, Executive Director*
*Michael Cadieux, Independent Living Specialist*
*Kelly McConnell, Director of Operations*
*Yolanda Pinkston, Quality Assurance Manager*
Commited to advancing personal choice, independence, and positive social change for persons with disabilities through advocacy, education and outreach.

**4045 Disability Network/Lakeshore**
426 Century Ln
Holland, MI 49423-2200
616-396-5326
800-656-5245
FAX: 616-396-3220
TTY: 616-396-5326
e-mail: info@dnlakeshore.org
dnlakeshore.org

*Todd Whiteman, Director*
*Rick Diamond, Director of Employment Services*
*Stacey Trowbridge, Program Director*
*Carrie Benchich, Information and Referral Specialist*
A cross-disability, community-based organization providing advocacy, education, and information and referral to persons with disabilities in Ottawa and Allegan counties.

**4046 Grand Traverse Area Community Living Management Corporation**
935 Barlow St
Traverse City, MI 49686-4250
231-932-9030
e-mail: mmacy@GTACLMC.com
www.gtaclmc.org

*Mary Jean Brick, Administrative Director*
We are a training home for individuals with developmental disabilities over the age of 18

**4047 Great Lakes/Macomb Rehabilitation Group**
Apt 104
4 E Alexandrine St
Detroit, MI 48201-2032
313-832-3371
FAX: 313-832-3850
e-mail: jlcil@home.msen.com

*Jeannie Meece-Brooks, Contact*
Independent living center. .

**4048 JARC**
Ste 100
30301 Northwestern Hwy
Farmington Hills, MI 48334-3277
248-538-6611
FAX: 248-538-6615
e-mail: jarc@jarc.org
jarc.org

*Richard A. Loewenstein, Chief Executive Officer*
*Christine Hench, Chief Operating Officer*
*Ronald Applebaum, President*
*Eli Scherr, Treasurer*
A nonprofit, nonsecretarian agency dedicated to enabling people with disabilities to live full, dignified lives in the community, and to providing support and advocacy for their families.

**4049 Lapeer: Blue Water Center for Independent Living**
392 W Nepessing St
Lapeer, MI 48446-2192
810-664-9098
FAX: 810-664-0937
e-mail: info@bwcil.org
www.bwcil.org

*Christine Cook, Housing Specialist*
*Karen Cook, Transition Specialist*
*Karen Massaro-Mundt, President*
A non-profit, consumer-based organization that advocates, informs and supports persons with disabilities in the community.

**4050 Livingston Center for Independent Living**
Ste 108
3075 E Grand River Ave
Howell, MI 48843-6585
517-545-9615
FAX: 517-548-1751
e-mail: dianaus1@yahoo.com

*Dan Durci, Director*
Independent living skills training and empowerment training for persons with disabilities..

**4051 Michigan Commission for the Blind: Independent Living Rehabilitation Program**
411 E Genesee Ave
Saginaw, MI 48607-1254
989-758-1765
800-292-4200
FAX: 989-758-1405
www.mfia.state.mi.us

*Debbie Wilson, Manager*
*Patrick Cannon, Agency Director*
Rehabilitation teaching, independent living skills for persons over 55 with severe vision loss.

**4052 Michigan Commission for the Blind: Detroit**
Ste 4-450
3038 W Grand Blvd
Detroit, MI 48202-6012
313-456-1646
FAX: 313-456-1645
e-mail: mcnealg@michigan.gov

*Gwen McNeal, Supervisor*
*Shawnese Laury-Johnson, Assistant East Region Manager*
Promotes the inclusion of people with legal blindness into our communities on a full and equal basis through empowerment, education, participation, and choice..

**4053 Monroe Center for Independent Living**
1285 N Telegraph Rd
Monroe, MI 48162-3368
734-242-5919
e-mail: mrawlings@aacil.org
monroecil.tripod.com

*Linda Maier, Manager*
To act as a catalyst for personal and social change through the empowerment of people with disabilities; and, to replace the perception of disability as tragic with a disability culture promoting pride, power and personal style.

**4054 Port Huron: Blue Water Center for Independent Living**
1042 Griswold St
Suite 2
Port Huron, MI 48060-5431
810-987-9337
FAX: 810-987-9548
e-mail: info@bwcil.org
bwcil.org

*Angela Hoff, Executive Director*
A non-profit, consumer-based organization that advocates, informs and supports persons with disabilities in the community.

**4055 Sandusky: Blue Water Center for Independent Living**
Ste 3
103 E Sanilac Rd
Sandusky, MI 48471-1615
810-648-2555
FAX: 810-648-2583
e-mail: info@bwcil.org
www.bwcil.org

*Lynda Freitag, Independent Living Specialist*
*Karen Massaro-Mundt, President*
*Chuck Wanninger, Treasurer*
*Ann Chapaton, Manager*
A non-profit, consumer-based organization that advocates, informs and supports persons with disabilities in the community.

**4056 Southeastern Michigan Commission for the Blind**
4450 Grandy St
Detroit, MI 48207
313-456-0334
800-292-4200
FAX: 313-456-1645
www.michigan.gov

*Patrick Cannon, Executive Director*
*Pat Bragg, Manager*
Vocational rehabilitation agency. Personal adjustment vocational assessment and training, job placement and follow-up services..

**4057 Superior Alliance for Independent Living(SAIL)**
Suite 3
1200 Wright Street
Marquette, MI 49855
906-228-5744
800-379-7245
FAX: 906-228-5573
TTY: 906-228-5744
www.upsail.com

*Amy Maes, Executive Director*
*Judy Vivian, Finance Director*
*Emily Gregorich, Independent Living Advocate*
*Sarah Peura, Associate Director*
Promotes the inclusion of people with disabilities into our communities on a full and equal basis through empowerment, education, participation and choice.

**4058 disAbility Connections**
409 Linden Ave
Jackson, MI 49203-4065
517-782-6054
FAX: 517-782-3118
www.disabilityconnect.org

*Lesia Pikaart, Executive Director*
*JoAnn Lucas, Associate Director*
*Brenda Bobon, Independent Living Counselor*
*Jim Cyphers, Independent Living Specialist*
Supporting Jackson County residents in their efforts to lead independent, fulfilling, productive lives.

## Minnesota

**4059 Accessible Space, Inc.**
2550 University Avenue West
Suite 330
Saint Paul, MN 55114-1085
651-645-7271
800-466-7722
FAX: 651-645-0541
e-mail: info@accessiblespace.org
www.accessiblespace.org

*Mark E. Hamel, Chairman*
*Kay Knutson, Vice Chairman*
*Steve Schugel, Treasurer*
*John W. Adams, Secretary*

Accessible, rent-subsidized apartments for very low-income adults with qualifying physical disabilities as well as seniors. Accessible Space, Inc., sponsors, develops and manages housing & ASI apartments are rent based on income and are located across the country.

**4060 Accessnorth CIL of Northeastern MN: Aitkin**
2104 East Sixth Avenue
Hibbing, MN 55746-1821
218-262-6675
800-390-3681
FAX: 218-262-6677
TTY: 218-262-6675
e-mail: info@accessnorth.net
www.accessnorth.net

*RoseAnn Pierce, Chairperson*
*Roberta Cich, Executive Director*
*Alice Prtine, Independent Living Program Manager*
*Anita Beckman, Independent Living Specialist*

Assists individuals to live independently, pursue meaningful goals, and have equal opportunities and choices.

**4061 Accessnorth CIL of Northeastern MN: Duluth**
118 E Superior St
Duluth, MN 55802-2155
218-625-1400
888-625-1401
FAX: 218-625-1401
e-mail: info@accessnorth.net
www.accessnorth.net

*RoseAnn Pierce, Chairperson*
*Roberta Cich, Executive Director*
*Erin Fontaine, Connections Project Coordinator*
*Sheri Cooke, Assistive Technology Specialist*

Assisting individuals with disabilities to live independently, puruse meaningful goals, and have equal opportunities and choices.

**4062 Center for Independent Living of NE Minnesota**
2104 6th Ave E
Hibbing, MN 55746-1821
218-262-6675
800-390-3681
FAX: 218-262-6677
TTY: 218-262-6675
e-mail: info@accessnorth.net
accessnorth.net

*RoseAnn Pierce, Chairperson*
*Roberta Cich, Executive Director*
*Alice Prtine, Independent Living Program Manager*
*Anita Beckman, Independent Living Specialist*

Assisting individuals with disabilities to live independently, pursue meaningful goals, and have an equal opportunities and choices

**4063 Courage Center**
3915 Golden Valley Rd
Minneapolis, MN 55422-4298
763-520-0811
888-846-8253
FAX: 763-520-0577
TTY:763-520-0245
e-mail: Information@CourageCenter.org
www.couragecenter.org

*Jan Malcolm, CEO*
*Alice Johnson, Chief Financial Officer*
*Stephen Bariteau, Chief Development Officer*
*Pamela J. Lindemoen, Executive Vice President of Operations*

A nonprofit rehabilitation and resource center that advances the lives of children and adults experiencing barriers to health and independence. Specialize in treating brain injury, spinal cord injury, stroke, chronic pain, autism and disabilities experienced since birth.

**4064 Freedom Resource Center for Independent Living: Fergus Falls**
125 W Lincoln Avenue
Suite 17
Fergus Falls, MN 56537- 2152
218-998-1799
FAX: 218-998-1798
www.freedomrc.org

*Nate Aalgaard, Executive Director*
*Angie Bosch, Office Coordinator*
*Mark Mark Bourdon Bourdon, Program Director*
*Andrea Nelson, Independent Living Advocate*

Freedom Resource Center assists people in working towards goals they establish for themselves.

**4065 Metropolitan Center for Independent Living**
Ste 16
1600 University Ave W
Saint Paul, MN 55104-3825
651-646-8342
FAX: 651-603-2006
TTY:651-603-2001
e-mail: Bob.Zimmerman@state.mn.us
wheelchairramp.org

MCIL is dedicated to the full promotion of independent living philosophy by supporting individuals with disabilities in their personal efforts to pursue self-directed lives.

**4066 Minnesota Association of Centers for Independent Living**
215 North Benton Drive
Sauk Rapids, MN 56379
320-529-9000
888-529-0743
FAX: 320-529-0747
e-mail: ilicil@independentlifestyles.org
independentlifestyles.org

*Cara Ruff, Executive Director*
*Jay Keller, Board Chairman*
*Pamela Kotzenmacher, Treasurer*
*Autumn Gould, Attorney*

A non-profit organization whose purpose is to advocate for the independent living needs of people with disabilities who are citizens of the State of Minnesota

**4067 OPTIONS**
Ste B
123 S Main St
Crookston, MN 56716-1970
218-281-5722
FAX: 218-281-5722
TTY:218-281-5722
e-mail: options3@rrv.net

*Gordie Haug, Manager*

Provides people with disabilities advocacy, information, skills training and peer mentoring relationships to help them achieve their personal goals of how and where they live their lives.

4068 **Options Interstate Resource Center for Independent Living**
318 3rd St NW
E Grand Forks, MN 56721-1887
218-773-6100
800-726-3692
FAX: 218-773-7119
TTY: 218-773-6100
e-mail: options@myoptions.info
www.macil.org/options

*Randy Sorensen, Executive Director*
Located in Minnesota, but also serves North Dakota..

4069 **Perry River Home Care**
330 High Way Pen S
Saint Cloud, MN 56304
320-255-1882
FAX: 320-255-5137

*Berna Florentine, CEO*
*Ken Figge, President*
*Courtney Salzi, Administrator*
Offers skilled nursing services RN, LPN, TV Therapy, Pediatrics, Rehabilitation Services, PT, OT, ST, Paraprofessional staff, Home Health Aides, Homemakers, Personal Care Attendents, Companions, Live-ins, Sleep overs, Respite care, Extended hours.

4070 **SMILES**
Ste 1
820 Winnebago Ave
Fairmont, MN 56031-3619
507-235-3488
FAX: 507-235-3488
www.smilescil.org

*Alan Augustin, Executive Director*
*David Cunningham, Administrative Assistant*
*Anne Murray, Education and communication Manager*
*Doug Miller, Operations Manager*
A nonprofit organization committed to providing a wide array of services that assist individuals with disabilities that live independently, pursue meaningful goals, and enjoy the same opportunities and choices as all persons.

4071 **SMILES: Mankato**
709 S. Front Street
Suite 7
Mankato, MN 56001-3887
507-345-7139
888-676-6498
FAX: 507-345-8429
e-mail: smiles@smilescil.org
smilescil.org

*Alan Augustin, Executive Director*
*Doug Miller, Operations Manager*
*Anne Murray, Community Education Manager*
A nonprofit organization committed to providing a wide array of services that assist individuals with disabilities that live independently, pursue meaningful goals, and enjoy the same oportunities and choices as all persons.

4072 **Southeastern Minnesota Center for Independent Living: Red Wing**
2200 2nd Street SW
Rochester, MN 55902
507-285-1815
888-460-1815
FAX: 507-288-8070
www.semcil.org

*Brian Koch, President*
*Becky Noble, MemberSales*
*Jay Toogood, Member Systems Advisor*
*Marie Peterson, Member Enrollment Counselor*
Non profit organization that assists people with disabilities to become independent and productive community members.

4073 **Southeastern Minnesota Center for Independent Living: Rochester**
2720 N Broadway
Rochester, MN 55906-3980
507-285-1815
888-460-1815
FAX: 507-288-8070
e-mail: semcil@semcil.org
www.semcil.org

*Vicki Dalle Molle, Executive Director*
A non profit organization that assists people with disabilities to become independent and productive community members.

4074 **Southwestern Center for Independent Living**
109 South Fifth Street
SUITE #700
Marshall, MN 56258- 1298
507-532-2221
800-422-1485
FAX: 507-532-2222
TTY: 507-532-2221
e-mail: swcil@swcil.com
www.swcil.org

*Steve Thovson, Executive Director*
SWCIl is a private, non-profit consumer controlled, non-residential, cross-disability, community-based organization providing independent living services to assist people with disabilities in obtaining and maintaining the greatest control over their lives. Services are available in southwestern Minnesota to persons of all ages, with all disability without regard to income.

4075 **Vinland Center Lake Independence**
3675 Ihduhapi Road
Loretto, MN 55357-308
763-479-3555
FAX: 763-479-2605
e-mail: vinland@vinlandcenter.org
www.vinlandcenter.org

*Duane Reynolds, Associate Director*
*Mary Roehl, Operations Director*
A Minnesota based rehabilitation center which offers services in three distinct service areas: vocational rehabilitation; inclusive community programs; and for people with cognitive disabilities, specially adapted chemical dependency treatment.

## Mississippi

4076 **Alpha Home Royal Maid Association for the Blind**
PO Drawer 30
Hazlehurst, MS 39083-30
601-894-1771
FAX: 601-894-2993
e-mail: sigworks@teclink.net

*Howard Becker, Director*
Offers attendant care registry, information on accessible housing and referrals.

4077 **Gulf Coast Independent Living Center**
18 JM Tatum Industrial Drive
Hattiesburg, MS 39401-8341
601-544-4860
FAX: 601-582-2544

*Albert Holifield, Executive Director*
Independent living center.

4078 **Jackson Independent Living Center**
300 Capers Ave
Jackson, MS 39203-2131
601-961-4140
FAX: 601-354-6678
TTY:601-351-1585

*Denea Smith, Director*
*Timothy Jackson*
Provides services to consumers with severe disabilities.

**4079 LIFE of Mississippi**
1304 Vine St
Jackson, MS 39202-3429
601-969-4009
800-748-9398
FAX: 601-969-1662
TTY: 800-748-9398
www.lifeofms.com

*Christy Dunaway, Executive Director*
*Augusta Smith, Asst. Director*
To empower people wit significant disabilities to be as independent and as fully involved in their communities as they can and want to be.

**4080 LIFE of Mississippi: Biloxi**
2030 Pass Road
Suite C
Biloxi, MS 39531
228-388-2401
FAX: 228-338-2413
www.lifeofms.com

*Terri Redding, Manager*
To empower people with significant disabilities to be as independent and as fully involved in their communities as they can and want to be.

**4081 LIFE of Mississippi: Greenwood**
502a W Park Ave
Greenwood, MS 38930-2906
662-453-9940
FAX: 662-453-9934
www.lifeofms.com

*Pamela Wraggs, Manager*
To empower people with significant disabilities to be as independent and as fully involved in their communities as they can and want to be.

**4082 LIFE of Mississippi: Hattiesburg**
710 Katie Ave
Hattiesburg, MS 39401-4377
601-583-2108
www.lifeofms.com

*Susan Hanks, Executive Director*
To empower people with significant disabilities to be as independent and as fully involved in their communities as they can and want to be.

**4083 LIFE of Mississippi: McComb**
915-A S. Locust Street
McComb, MS 39648-4817
601-684-3079
www.lifeofms.com

*Alida Moncilva, Owner*
To empower people with significant disabilities to be as independent and as fully involved in their communities as they can and want to be.

**4084 LIFE of Mississippi: Meridian**
Ste 103a
2440 N Hills St
Meridian, MS 39305-2653
601-485-7999
www.lifeofms.com

*Sharon Burt, Independent Living Specialist*
To empower people with significant disabilities to be as independent and as fully involved in their communities as they can and want to be.

**4085 LIFE of Mississippi: Oxford**
Ste 5
404 Galleria Dr
Oxford, MS 38655-4383
662-234-7010
www.lifeofms.com

*Judy Pettit, Independent Living Specialist*
To empower people with significant disabilities to be as independent and as fully involved in their communities as they can and want to be.

**4086 LIFE of Mississippi: Tupelo**
1051 Cliff Gookin Blvd
Tupelo, MS 38801-6739
662-844-6633
FAX: 662-844-6803
www.lifeofms.com

*Michael Sullivan, Regional Coordinator*
To empower people with significant disabilities to be as independent and as fully involved in their communities as they can and want to be.

## Missouri

**4087 Access II Independent Living Center**
101 Industrial Parkway
Gallatin, MO 64640-1280
660-663-2423
888-663-2423
FAX: 660-663-2517
e-mail: access@accessii.org
www.accessii.org

*Heather Swymeler, Executive Director*
*Deanna Brown, Program Director*
The mission of Access II is to remove architectural and attitudinal barriers that limit the independence of persons with disabilities, promote a positive change in attitudes about disability and persons with disabilities, and encourage greater independence for persons with disabilities within our communities. As a Center for Independent Living, Access II is comitted to the provision of a full range of independent living services.

**4088 Bootheel Area Independent Living Services**
P.O.Box 326
Kennett, MO 63857-326
573-888-0002
888-449-0949
FAX: 573-888-0708
TTY:573-888-0002
e-mail: tshaw@bails.org
www.bails.org

*Tim Shaw, Executive Director*
BAILS goal is to foster an open, barrier free society flor all people regardless of their disability. BAILS service area is predominantly rural and includes the Southeast Missouri counties of: Dunklin, New Madrid, Pemiscot and Stoddard.

**4089 Coalition for Independence: Missouri Branch Office**
3101 Broadway St
Suite #101
Kansas City, MO 64111
816-231-7166
FAX: 816-231-7899
e-mail: csmith@cfi-kc.org
www.cfi-kc.com

*Clarenece Smith, Executive Director*
Coalition For Independence (CFI) is to facilitate positive and responsible independence for all people with disabilities by acting as an advocate for individuals with disabilities, providing services, and promoting accessibility and acceptance.

**4090 Delta Center for Independent Living**
5933 S Highway 94
Suite #107
Weldon Spring, MO 63304- 5608
636-926-8761
866-727-3245
FAX: 636-447-0341
e-mail: info@dcil.org
www.dcil.org

*Nancy Murphy, Executive Director*
A non profit corporation which assists people with significant disabilities who want to live more independently.

4091 **Disability Resource Association**
420 B. South Truman Blvd
Crystal City, MO 63019-1726
636-931-7696
FAX: 636-931-4863
TTY:636-937-9016
e-mail: dra@disabilityresourcesassociation.org
www.disabilityresourceassociation .org

*Craig Henning, Executive Director*
*Nancy Pope, Assistant Director*
*Suzan Weller, Director/Resource Developer*
Independent Living Cener.

4092 **Independent Living Center of Southeast Missouri**
511 Cedar St
Poplar Bluff, MO 63901-7301
573-686-2333
888-890-2333
FAX: 573-686-0733
TTY:573-776-1178
e-mail: bruce.lynch@ilcsemo.org
www.ilcsemo.org

*Bruce Lynch, Executive Director*
*Debbie Hardin, Independent Living Director*
To make Southeast Missouri barrier free for all persons with disabilities, enabling them to live more independently, extending their rights to control and direct their own lives and empowering them to live more producitve lives.

4093 **Life Skills Foundation**
10176 Corporate Square Drive
Suite #100
Saint Louis, MO 63132-2935
314-567-7705
FAX: 314-567-6539
TTY:314-802-5299
e-mail: intake@lifeskills-stl.org
www.lifeskills-stl.org

*Wendy Sullivan, President*
*Katie Smallen, VP of Operations*
Assists people with disabilities live and work with dignity in the community.

4094 **Midland Empire Resources for Independent Living (MERIL)**
4420 S 40th St
Saint Joseph, MO 64503-2157
816-279-8558
800-637-4548
FAX: 816-279-1550
TTY: 816-279-4943
www.meril.org

*J.C. Dollar, CEO*
*Deb Powers, Chief Brand Officer*
*Fred Timberlake, Chief Financial Officer*
*Steve Bartlett, Chief Operating Officer*
Designed to promote independent living and to enhance the quality of life for persons with disabilities by empowering them to control and direct their lives.

4095 **Northeast Independent Living Services**
909 Broadway
Suite 350
Hannibal, MO 63401
573-221-8282
877-713-7900
FAX: 573-221-9445
www.neilscenter.org

*Brooke Kendrick, Executive Director*
*Tara Fortner, Finance Director*
*Rhonda Jeffries, Administrative Assistant*
*Barrnie Cooper, Independent Living Director*
To empower persons with disabilities to live as full and productive members of society.

4096 **On My Own**
428 E Highland Ave
Nevada, MO 64772-2609
417-667-7007
800-362-8852
FAX: 417-667-6262
e-mail: onmyowngundy@softnet.net
onmyowninc.com

*Jennifer Gundy, Executive Director*
A non profit independent living center.

4097 **Ozark Independent Living**
109 Aid Ave
West Plains, MO 65775-3529
417-257-0038
888-440-7500
FAX: 417-257-2380
TTY: 888-440-7500
e-mail: info@ozarkcil.com
www.ozarkcil.org

*Cindy Moore, Executive Director*
OIL?was created to provide independent living services to persons with disabilities who reside in the following counties in Missouri: Oregon Ozark, Shannon, Wright, Howell, Texas, and Douglas. OIL is non-profit, on-residential supported by grants, donations, and volunteers

4098 **Paraquad**
5240 Oakland Ave
Saint Louis, MO 63110-1436
314-289-4200
FAX: 314-289-4201
TTY:314-289-4252
e-mail: contactus@paraquad.org
www.paraquad.org

*Robert Funk, Executive Director*
Paraquad works to empower people with disabilities to increase their independence through choice and opportunity.

4099 **Places for People**
4130 Lindell Blvd
Saint Louis, MO 63108-2914
314-535-5600
FAX: 314-535-6037
e-mail: contact@placesforpeople.org
www.placesforpeople.org

*Joe Yancey, Executive Director*
Places for People provides individualized, high quality and effective services to adults with serious and persistent mental disorders to assist them in living, working and socializing responsibility to serve those individuals who rely on public funding.

4100 **RAIL**
3024 Dupont Circle
Jefferson City, MO 65109
573-526-7039
877-222-8963
888-667-2117
FAX: 573-751-1441
www.mosilc.org

*Teresa Myers, Executive Director*
*Jean Robbins, Assistant to Executive Director*
RAIL is an Independent Living Center, one of twenty-two in the State of Missouri, RAIL's Mission is to assist persons with disabilities to live as independently as they choose within the communities of their choice. RAIL offers four core services which are: Advocacy, Peer Support, Information & Referral, and Independent Living Skills Training. RAIL is a Consumer Services Directed Program vendor

**4101 SEMO Alliance for Disability Independence**
1913 Rusmar St
Cape Girardeau, MO 63703-7623
573-651-6464
800-898-7234
FAX: 573-651-6565
TTY: 573-651-6464
e-mail: miki@mail.sadi.org
www.sadi.org

*A. Wayne Wallingford Jr., President*
*Vicki Abernathy, Vice-President*
A community based, non-profit, nonresidential center for independent living that is committed to providing services to persons with disabilities to enable them to remain in their own home and community, not an institution.

**4102 Services for Independent Living**
1401 Hathman Pl
Columbia, MO 65201-5552
573-874-1646
800-766-1968
FAX: 573-874-3564
e-mail: sil@silcolumbia.org
www.silcolumbia.org

*Jim Crane, Manager*
*Leslie Anderson, Program Manager*
A non-residential, community-based center for independent living. Provides individualized and group services to persons with severe disabilities in the Mid-Missouri area; works to help people with disabilities achieve their highest potential in independent living and community life.

**4103 Southwest Center for Independent Living (S CIL)**
2864 S Nettleton Ave
Springfield, MO 65807-5970
417-886-1188
800-676-7245
FAX: 417-886-3619
TTY: 417-886-1188
e-mail: scil@swcil.org
www.swcil.org

*Gary Maddox, Executive Director*
Provides services, advocacy, and resources for people with any disability in Christian, Dallas, Greene, Lawrence, Polk, Stone, Taney and Webster Counties of Southwest Missouri.

**4104 The Whole Person**
Ste 105
3420 Broadway St
Kansas City, MO 64111-7501
816-561-0304
800-878-3037
FAX: 816-753-8163
TTY: 816-561-0304
e-mail: info@thewholeperson.org
thewholeperson.org

*David Robinson, CEO*
The Whole Person, assists people with disabilities to live independently and encourages change within the community to expand opportunities for independent living.

**4105 Tri-County Center for Independent Living**
1420 HWY 72 East
Rolla, MO 65401
573-368-5933
FAX: 573-368-5991
TTY:573-368-5933
e-mail: vevans@fidnet.com
www.tricountycenter.com

*Victoria Evans, Executive Director*
Mission is to eliminate physical and attitudinal barriers through the power of advocacy, enlightenment, and reformation.

**4106 West Central Independent Living Solutions**
610 N Ridegeview Dr
Suite B
Warrensburg, MO 64093-9323
660-422-7883
800-236-5175
FAX: 660-422-7895
TTY: 660-422-7894
e-mail: info@w-ils.org
www.w-ils.org

*Martha Fiene, Executive Director*
Works to empower people with disabilities to become more independent by providing independent living skills training, peer support, information and referral and advocacy. West Central Independent Living Solutions now has satellite offices in Sedalia, MO and Lexington.

**4107 Whole Person: Kansas City**
Ste 105
3420 Broadway St
Kansas City, MO 64111-7501
816-561-0304
800-878-3037
FAX: 816-753-8163
TTY: 816-627-2202
e-mail: info@thewholeperson.org
thewholeperson.org

*David Robinson, CEO*
Assists people with disabilities to live independently and encourages change within the community to expand opportunities for independent living.

## Montana

**4108 Living Independently for Today and Tomorrow**
3333 2nd Ave N
Suite #100
Billings, MT 59101-2033
406-259-5181
800-669-6319
FAX: 406-259-5259
TTY: 406-245-1225
e-mail: beckerb@midrivers.com
www.liftt.org

*Bobbie Becker, Executive Director*
*Martha Carstensen, Program Director*
LIFTT's Independent living program works with people with disabilities so they can live independently and have access to the community. LIFTT staff, most of whom have disabilities, serve as mentors to people as they work to achieve the goals they have set for themselves.

**4109 Montana Independent Living Project, Inc.**
34 N. Last Chance Gulch
Suite 500
Helena, MT 59601-4715
406-442-5755
800-735-6457
FAX: 406-442-1612
TTY: 406-442-5755
e-mail: bmaffit@milp.us
www.milp.us

*Bob Maffit, Executive Director*
*Connie Leveque, Independent Living Specialist*
*Kryss Kuntz, Independent Living Specialist*
*Charlene White, Financial Manager*
A not-for-profit agency that provides services that promote independence for people with disabilities.

**4110 North Central Independent Living Services**
1120 25th Ave
Black Eagle, MT 59414-1037
406-452-9834
800-823-6245
FAX: 406-453-3940
e-mail: ncils.osborn@sofast.net
www.dphhs.mt.gov

*Tom Osborn, Executive Director*
North Central Independent Living Services is located in Great Falls and provides services from Glacier County across the Hi-Line to the North Dakota border. A satellite office is set up in Glasgow.

**4111 Summit Independent Living Center: Kalipsell**
1203 Highway 2 W.
Suite #35
Kalispell, MT 59901-6020
406-257-0048
800-995-0029
TTY:406-257-0048
e-mail: flok@summitilc.org
www.summitilc.org

*Flo Kiewel, Manager*
To promote community awareness, equal access, and the independence of people with disabilities through advocacy, education, and the advancement of civil rights.

**4112 Summit Independent Living Center: Hamilton**
316 North 3rd St
Suite #113
Hamilton, MT 59840-2479
406-363-5242
800-398-9013
e-mail: jverwolf@summitilc.org
www.summitilc.org

*Joanne Berwolf, Manager*
To promote community awareness, equal access, and the independence of people with disabilities through advocacy, education, and the advancement of civil rights.

**4113 Summit Independent Living Center: Missoula**
700 SW Higgins Ave
Suite #101
Missoula, MT 59803-1489
406-728-1630
800-398-9002
FAX: 406-829-3309
e-mail: mcummerford@simmitilc.org
www.summitilc.org

*Mike Mayer, Executive Director*
To promote community awareness, equal access, and the independence of people with disabilities through advocacy, education, and the advancement of civil rights.

**4114 Summit Independent Living Center: Ronan**
111 2nd Ave SW
Ronan, MT 59864-2718
406-676-0190
800-230-6936
FAX: 406-676-0191
e-mail: gstevens@summitilc.org
www.summitilc.org

*Gary Stevens, Manager*
To promote community awareness, equal access, and the independence of people with disabilities through advocacy, education, and the advancement of civil rights.

## Nebraska

**4115 Center for Independent Living of Central Nebraska**
3204 College St
Grand Island, NE 68803-1730
308-382-9255
877-400-1004
FAX: 308-384-7832
TTY: 308-382-9255
e-mail: jthomas@cilne.org
www.cinne.org

*Joni Thomas, Executive Director*
Offers independent living skills training, peer sharing, information and referral, housing counseling and referral, accessibility and barrier removal consultation including ADA training and technical assistance, driver education and training, assistive technology services including demonstration and equipment loan, and a free lending library of adapted toys and ability switches for children with severe disabilities. Serves all disabilities and all ages.

**4116 League of Human Dignity: Lincoln**
1701 P St
Lincoln, NE 68508-1799
402-441-7871
888-508-4758
FAX: 402-441-7650
TTY:402-441-7871
e-mail: info@leagueofhumandignity.com
www.leagueofhumandignity.com

*Mike Schafer, CEO*
The mission of the League of Human Dignity is to actively promote the full integration of individuals with disabilities into society. To this end, we will advocate their needs and rights, and provide quality services to involve these persons in becoming and remaining independent citizens.

**4117 League of Human Dignity: Norfolk**
400 Elm Ave
Norfolk, NE 68701-4033
402-371-4475
800-843-5785
FAX: 402-371-4625
TTY: 402-371-4475
e-mail: ninfo@leagueofhumandignity.com
leagueofhumandignity.com

*Mike Shafer, CEO*
*Jean M. Kloppenborg, Norfolk CIL Director*
The mission of the League of Human Dignity is to actively promote the full integration of individuals with disabilities into society. To this end, we will advocate their needs and rights, and provide quality services to involve these persons in becoming and remaining independent citizens.

**4118 League of Human Dignity: Omaha**
5513 Center St
Omaha, NE 68106-3001
402-595-1256
800-843-5784
FAX: 402-595-1410
e-mail: oinfo@leagueofhumandignity.com
www.leagueofhumandignity.com

*Mike Schafer, CEO*
*Bob Gomez, Executive Director*
The mission of the League of Human Dignity is to actively promote the full integration of individuals with disabilities into society. To this end, we will advocate their needs and rights, and provide quality services to involve these persons in becoming and remaining independent citizens.

**4119 Mosaic of Axtell Bethpage Village**
P.O.Box 67
Axtell, NE 68924-67
308-743-2401
FAX: 308-743-2659
www.mosaicinfo.org/axtell
Provides services that respect the human diginity and rights of each person. An interdisciplinary team of family, staffmembers

and professional consultatns support individuals served in developing personal goals and programs, helping them to fully participate in Axtell's community life. Mosaic at Axtell offers residential and community services.

**4120 Mosaic of Beatrice**
P.O.Box 607
Beatrice, NE 68310-607
402-223-4066
FAX: 402-223-4951
e-mail: jerry.campbell@mosaicinfo.org
www.mosaicinfo.org/beatrice

*Jerry Campbell, Manager*
Provides individualized services, living options, work choices, spiritual nurture and advocacy to people with disabilities in more than 250 communities across 14 states and Great Britain through the work of 4,800 employees.

**4121 Mosiac: York**
220 W South 21st St
York, NE 68467-9316
402-362-2180
FAX: 402-362-2961
www.mosaicinfo.org

*Lisa Samson, Manager*
Providing a wide array of services to assist individuals and families in achieving positive life goals. Services to persons with disabilities and other special needs include community living options, training and employment options, spiritual growth and development options, training and counseling support.

## Nevada

**4122 Carson City Center for Independent Living**
900 Mallory Way
Carson City, NV 89701
775-841-2580

*Sandra Coyle, Owner*
Helps consumers continue to live independently in the community through a variety of individual and community services.

**4123 Northern Nevada Center for Independent Living: Fallon**
1919 Grimes St
Suite B
Fallon, NV 89406-3100
775-423-4900
800-885-3712
FAX: 775-423-1399
TTY: 775-423-4900
e-mail: nncilf@cccomm.net
www.nncil.org

*Joan Inglis, Manager*
Independent Living Center.

**4124 Rural Center for Independent Living**
1895 E Long St
Carson City, NV 89706-3214
775-841-2580
FAX: 775-841-2580
e-mail: ruralcil@yahoo.com

*Dee Dee Foremaster, Executive Director*
Advocacy, Benefit Assistance, social security assistance, peer support, housing information and home-less day drop-in center for individuals with disabilities.

**4125 Southern Nevada Center for Independent Living: North Las Vegas**
3100 E Lake Mead Blvd
North Las Vegas, NV 89030-7380
702-649-3822
800-398-0760
FAX: 702-649-5022
TTY: 702-649-3822
e-mail: sncilnv@aol.com
www.sncil.org

*Juanita Johnson, Manager*
*Rosemarie Meza, Manager*
SNCIL is committed to removing barriers preventing indpendent living by providing services designed to empower people with disabilities.

**4126 Southern Nevada Center for Independent Living: Las Vegas**
6039 Eldora Avenue
Suite H-8
Las Vegas, NV 89146-5611
702-889-4216
800-870-7003
FAX: 702-889-4574
TTY: 702-889-4216
e-mail: sncil2@aol.com
www.sncil.org

*Mary Evilsizer, Executive Director*
*Alicia Santiago, Administration Assistant*
SNCIL is committed to removing barriers preventing Independent Living by providing services designed to empower people with disabilities.

## New Hampshire

**4127 Granite State Independent Living Foundation**
76 Main St
Littleton, NH 3561-4079
603-228-9680
800-826-3700
FAX: 603-444-3128
TTY: 603-228-9680
e-mail: clyde.terry@gsil.org
www.gsil.org

*John Irwin, President*
*Ken Maillous, Second Vice President*
GSIL is a statewide non-profit that recognizes the fact that all of us will need some type of support in the course of the lives. GSIL offers tools and resources so that individuals can participate as fully as the choose in their lives, families and communities. Contact the Independent Living Foundation for referrals to living situations.

## New Jersey

**4128 Alliance Center for Independance**
Alliance for Disabled in Action
629 Amboy Ave, First Floor
Edison, NJ 08837-3579
732-738-4388
FAX: 732-738-4416
TTY:732-738-9644
e-mail: adacil@adacil.org
www.adacil.org

*Carole Tonks, Executive Director*
Alliance for Disabled in Action is a private, not-for-profit center for independent living serving people in Middlesex, Somerset and Union Counties of New Jersey. ADA's mission is to support and promote choice, self-direction and independent living in the lives of people with disabilities, with the right of individuals to inclusion in the community as the primary goal.

**4129 Assistive Technology Advocacy Center**
New Jersey Protection and Advocacy
210 S. Broad Street
Floor 3
Trenton, NJ 08608-2407
609-292-9742
800-922-7233
FAX: 609-777-0187
TTY: 609-633-7106
e-mail: advocate@drnj.org
www.drnj.org

*Joseph Young, Executive Director*
*Curtis D. Edmonds, ATAC Program Director*
Assistive Technology Advocacy Center provides assistance to personswith disabilities in helping them to obtain assistive technology devices and/or services.

**4130 Camden City Independent Living Center**
2600 Mount Ephraim Ave
Camden, NJ 8104-3236
856-966-0800
FAX: 856-966-0832
TTY:856-966-0830
e-mail: vedasmithccilc@aol.com
www.camdencityilc.org

*Veda Smith, Executive Director*
Provides services designed to empower people with disabilities. To provide services to individuals with significant disabilities. Services include information referral, advocacy, peer support, and independent living skills training. CCILC services individuals in Camden City

**4131 Center for Independent Living: Long Branch**
279 Broadway
Suite #201
Long Branch, NJ 7740-6940
732-571-4884
FAX: 732-571-4003
TTY:732-571-4878
www.moceanscil.org

*Joanne Goff, Executive Director*
*Stan Soden, Director IL Services*
Offers peer support, disability education and personal assistant services. Serving Monmouth and Ocean Counties with information and referrals, advocacy, peer support and independent living instructions.

**4132 Center for Independent Living: South Jersey**
1150 Delsea Drive
Suite #1
Westville, NJ 8093-2251
856-853-6490
800-413-3791
FAX: 856-853-1466
TTY: 856-853-7602
e-mail: cilsj@verizon.net
www.cilsj.org

*Hazel Lee-Briggs, Executive Director*
*Danuta Debicki, Program Manager*
*Terryama Davis, Independent Living Specialist*
Dedicated to providing people with disabilities in Gloucester and Camden counties the opportunity to actively participate in society, to provide freedom of choice, to work, to own a home, raise a family and in general, to participate to the fullest extent in day-to-day activities. The center provides information and referrals, advocacy, peer support, and independent living skills training.

**4133 DAWN Center for Independent Living**
30 Broad Street
Suite #5
Denville, NJ 7834-1235
973-625-1940
888-383-3296
FAX: 973-625-1942
TTY: 973-625-1932
e-mail: info@dawncil.org
www.dawncil.org

*Carmela Slivinski, Executive Director*
*Wanda Kasmedo, Program Assistant*
DAWN is the Center for Independent Living serving Morris, Sussex and Warren counties. DAWN empowers people with disabilities to strive for equality and to take control of their own lives by providing the tools that encourage independence and self-advocacy, promoting public awareness of the needs, desires and rights to individuals living with disabilities, and offering community activities that create new experiences and opportunities.

**4134 Dial: Disabled Information Awareness & Living**
2 Prospect Village Plaza
Floor 1
Clifton, NJ 7013-1918
973-470-8090
866-277-1733
FAX: 973-470-8171
TTY: 973-470-2521
e-mail: info@dial-cil.org
www.dial-cil.org

*John Petix, Executive Director*
Promotes the full inclusion of all people living with disabilities into society and encourage the consumers and the community at large to seek involvement in this self-governing organization to the fullest extent.

**4135 Family Resource Associates**
35 Haddon Ave
Shrewsbury, NJ 7702-4007
732-747-5310
FAX: 732-747-1896
e-mail: info@frainc.org
www.frainc.org

*Nancy Phalanukorn, Executive Director*
*Sue Levine, Program Administrator*
FRA is dedicated to helping children, adolescents and people of all ages with disabilities to reach their fullest potential. FRA also connects individuals to independence through modern therapies and advanced technology. FRA provides direct services to those in the greater Nonmouth/Ocean County area.

**4136 Heightened Independence and Progress: Hackensack**
131 Main St
Suite #120
Hackensack, NJ 7601-7182
201-996-9100
FAX: 201-996-9422
TTY:201-966-9424
e-mail: ber@hipcil.org
www.hipcil.org

*Eileen Goff, Executive Director*
Empowers people with disabilities to achieve independent living through outreach, advocacy and education.

**4137 Heightened Independence and Progress: Jersey City**
35 Journal Square
Suite #703
Jersey City, NJ 7306-4105
201-533-4407
FAX: 201-533-4421
TTY:201-533-4409
e-mail: hud@hipcil.org
www.hipcil.org

*Kathy Wood, Manager*
*Kathleen Wood, Branch Director*
*Marily Gonzalez, Independent Living Specialist*
Empowering People with Disabilities to Achieve Independent Living through Outreach, Advocacy, and Education.

**4138 Progressive Center for Independent Living**
1262 Whitehorse-Hamilton Square Rd
Suite 102 Bldg A
Hamilton, NJ 8690-3710
609-581-4500
877-917-4500
FAX: 609-581-4555
TTY: 609-581-4550
e-mail: info@pcil.org
www.pcil.org

*Scott Elliott, Executive Director*
*Susan Jacobsen, Independent Living Specialist*
Advocates for the rights of people with disabilities to achieve and maintain independent lifestyles. The Center has programs to assist with employment, transition from school to adult life, and emergency preparedness.

**4139 Progressive Center for Independent Living: Flemington**
Ste 410
4 Walter E Foran Blvd
Flemington, NJ 8822-4669
908-782-1055
877-376-9174
FAX: 908-782-6025
TTY: 908-782-1081
e-mail: info@pcil.org
pcil.org

*Scott Elliott, Executive Director*
*Pamela Vernon, Independent Living Manager*
Advocates for the rights of people with disabilities to achieve and maintain independent lifestyles.

**4140 Project Freedom**
223 Hutchinson Rd
Robbinsville, NJ 8691-3457
609-448-2998
FAX: 609-448-5821
e-mail: tdoherty@projectfreedom.org
www.projectfreedom.org

*Tim Doherty, Executive Director*
Dedicated to developing, supporting, and advocating opportunities for independent living persons with disabilities.

**4141 Project Freedom: Hamilton**
715 Kuser Rd
Hamilton, NJ 8619-3924
609-588-9919
FAX: 609-588-8831
e-mail: cfunk@projectfreedom.org
www.projectfreedom.org

*Cecilia Funk, Social Service Coordinator*
*Judy Wilkinson, Office Manager*
Dedicated to developing, supporting, and advocating opportunities for independent living persons with disabilities.

**4142 Project Freedom: Lawrence**
1 Freedom Blvd
Lawrence, NJ 8648-4531
609-278-0075
FAX: 609-278-1250
e-mail: jelsowiny@projectfreedom.org
www.projectfreedom.org

*Jacklene Elsowiny, Executive Director*
Dedicated to developing, supporting, and advocating opportunities for independent living persons with disabilities.

**4143 Total Living Center**
6712 Washington Ave
Egg Harbor Township, NJ 8234-1999
609-645-9547
FAX: 609-813-2318
TTY:609-645-9593
e-mail: info@tlcenter.org
www.tlcenter.org

*Jo Hudson, President*
*Cliff Anderson, Vice President*
*Cathy Shaner, Secretary*
*Julia Bonelli, Executive Director*
Total Living Center is a non-profit organization whose mission is to empower individuals with significant disabilities to maximize their potential for independence and productivity, to live as fully as possible within the community, taking responsibility for themselves, and sharing this commitment with others.

## New Mexico

**4144 Ability Center**
715 E. Idaho Ave
Building 3E
Las Cruces, NM 88001-4702
575-526-5016
800-376-4372
FAX: 575-526-1202
TTY: 505-526-5016
e-mail: freedom@theabilitycenter.org
www.theabilitycenter.org

*Vincent Montano, Executive Director*
*Cesar Rodriguez, Vice-President*
*C. Neil Gibbs, Treasurer*
The Ability Center is a private, nonresidential, nonprofit, New Mexico corporation. As a center for independent living (CIL) TACIL provides a variety of services to promote independence, self-reliance, and community integration. Our professional staff and active board of directors are dedicated to helping our consumers maintain their personal freedom at home, in the community, and throughout the state.

**4145 CASA Inc.**
P.O.Box 36916
Albuquerque, NM 87176-6916
505-298-7609
www.casaabq.com

*Francis Nye, Executive Director*
Offers peer counseling and information and referral services.

**4146 CHOICES Center for Independent Living**
200 E 4th St.
Suite #200
Roswell, NM 88201-6237
575-627-6727
800-387-4572
FAX: 575-627-6754
TTY: 505-627-6727

*Julia Calvert, Executive Director*
Offers many core services including independent living skills training, peer support, information and referral, advocacy and transition.

**4147 New Mexico Technology Assistance Program**
435 Saint Michaels Dr
Ste D
Santa Fe, NM 87505-7679
505-827-8535
800-866-2253
FAX: 505-954-8608
TTY: 800-659-4915
e-mail: awinnegar@state.nm.us
www.nmtap.com

*Julie Martinez, Program Director*
Examines and works to eliminate barriers to obtaining assistive technology in New Mexico. Has established a statewide program for coordinating assistive technology services; is designed to assist people with disabilities to locate, secure, and maintain assistive technology.

**4148 New Vistas**
1121 Alto St
Santa Fe, NM 87501-2483
505-988-3803
FAX: 505-989-8740
www.newvistas.org

*Magi Gerety, Executive Director*

Partners with and supports people with disabilities and families of children with special needs to enrich their quality of life in New Mexico.

**4149 San Juan Center for Independence**
3535 E. 30th Street
Suite #101
Farmington, NM 87402-8819
505-566-5827
877-484-4500
FAX: 505-566-5842
TTY: 505-566-5827
e-mail: sjci@sjci.org
www.sjci.org

*Patricia Ziegler, Executive Director*
*Tim Carver, CFO*
SJCI is a New Mexico private non residential, nonprofit corporation that serves people with disabilities. The purpose of SJCI is to provide a variety of community based, consumer driven service to people with disablities to promote independence, self-residence and intergration into the community.

## New York

**4150 AIM Independent Living Center: Corning**
271 E 1st St
Corning, NY 14830-2924
607-962-8225
FAX: 607-937-5125
TTY:607-962-8225
e-mail: troche@aimcil.com
www.aimcil.com

*Patricia Myers, Deputy Director Consumer Directed Personal*
*René L. Snyder, Executive Director*
*Traci Roche, Dpty Dir Consumer Srvc/Prgrm Dev*
*Noelle Gross, Director of Finance & Administration*
AIM is a non-profit organization dedicated to people with disabilities, their families, friends, the businesses that serve them and those with an interest in disabilities. The mission of AIM is to support the individuals ability to make independent, self-directing choices through education, advocacy, information and referral.

**4151 AIM Independent Living Center: Elmira**
1316 College Avenue
Elmira, NY 14901-2216
607-733-3718
FAX: 607-733-0180
TTY:607-733-7764
e-mail: troche@aimcil.com
www.aimcil.com

*Patricia Myers, Deputy Director Consumer Directed Personal*
*René L. Snyder, Executive Director*
*Traci Roche, Dpty Dir.,Csmr Svc/Program Dev*
*Noelle Gross, Director of Finance & Administration*
AIM's goal is to enable the consumer to live an independent and comfortable lifestyle in the security of their home environment so they may feel dignity and pride in their achievements while controling their own care.

**4152 ARISE**
635 James St
Syracuse, NY 13203-2661
315-472-3171
FAX: 315-472-9252
TTY:315-479-6363
e-mail: info@ariseinc.org
www.ariseinc.org

*Thomas Mc Keown, Executive Director*
*Kimberly Lipke, Director of Finance*
*Karen Lynch, Human Resources Director*
*Nancy Kronen, Director of Development and Public Relations*
Founded in 1979, ARISE's mission is to work with people of all abilities to create a fair and just community in which everyone can fully participate. As a center for independent living, ARISE is a non-profit organization run by and for individuals with disabilities. ARISE serves over 3,000 children and adults with disabilities each year through our programs and services in several broad areas including advocacy, employment, independent living/integrated recreation programs, and much more.

**4153 ARISE: Oneida**
131 Main St
Suite #107
Oneida, NY 13421-1644
315-363-4672
FAX: 315-363-4675
TTY:315-363-2364
e-mail: info@ariseinc.org
www.ariseinc.org

*James Wood, Manager*
A consumer controlled, non-profit Independent Living Center that promotes the full inclusion of people with disabilities in the community.

**4154 ARISE: Oswego**
9 Fourth Avenue
Oswego, NY 13126-1803
315-342-4088
FAX: 315-342-4107
TTY:315-342-8696
e-mail: info@ariseinc.org
www.ariseinc.org

*Tom McKeown, Executive Director*
A consumer controlled, non-profit Independent Living Center that promotes the full inclusion of people with disabilities in the community.

**4155 ARISE: Pulaski**
2 Broad St
Pulaski, NY 13142-4446
315-298-5726
FAX: 315-298-5729
e-mail: info@ariseinc.org
www.ariseinc.org

*Tom McKeown, Executive Director*
A consumer controlled, non-profit Independent Living Center that promotes the full inclusion of people with disabilities in the community.

**4156 Access to Independence of Cortland County, Inc.**
26 N Main St
Cortland, NY 13045-2198
607-753-7363
FAX: 607-756-4884
e-mail: info@aticortland.org
www.aticortland.org

*Mary E. Ewing, Executive Director*
*Chad W. Underwood, Chief Operating Officer*
Access to Independence is Cortland County's foremost disability resource. It empowers people to lead independent lives in their community and strives to open doors to full participation and access for all.

**4157 Action Toward Independence: Middletown**
130 Dolson Avenue
Suite 35
Middletown, NY 10940-6563
845-343-4284
FAX: 845-342-5269
e-mail: ati@warwick.net
actiontowardindependence.org

*Stephen McLaughlin, Executive Director*
*Joann Hargabus, Services Director, Orange Cnty.*
*Gilles Malkine, Services Director, Sullivan Cnty*
*Cheryl Babcock, Fiscal Manager*
Independent living center that serves Orange & Sullivan counties. Provides programs and services to individuals who have disabilities and to their families. These services include peer counseling, individual & systems advocacy, independent living, skills training, information and referral, benefits advisement, recreation and a drop in center. We are designed to enable people with disabilities to achieve independence, inclusion and participation in their communities..

**4158 Action Toward Independence: Monticello**
309 E Broadway
Suite A
Monticello, NY 12701-8810
845-794-4228
FAX: 845-794-4475
TTY:845-794-4228
e-mail: szecchini@atitoday.org
www.atitoday.org

*Steve McLaughlin, Executive Director*
*Joann Hargabus, Director of Services*
A not-for-profit, non residential, peer run, referral and advocacy agency for persons with disaiblities in Orange and Sullivan counties. Our services are aimed at promoting accessibility, community integration, and equal opportunity in all aspects of society for persons with all types of disabilities.

**4159 Bronx Independent Living Services**
4419 Thrid Avenue
Suite 2C
Bronx, NY 10457
718-515-2800
FAX: 718-515-2844
TTY:718-515-2803
e-mail: webmaster@bils.org
www.bils.org

*Brett Eisenberg, Executive Director*
BILS is a not-for-profit community agency serving people with all kinds of disabilities. The mission is to empower people with disabilities toward living independent lives. BILS assists individuals by providing advocacy, peer counseling, housing information, and independent living training/counseling.

**4160 Brooklyn Center for Independence of the Disabled**
27 Smith Street
Suite #200
Brooklyn, NY 11201
718-998-3000
FAX: 718-998-3743
TTY:718-998-7406
e-mail: advocate@bcid.org
www.bcid.org

*Maureen Alexander, Executive Director*
*Sandrina Kingston, Program Director*
Operated by a majority of people with disabilities, BCID is dedicated to guaranteeing the civil rights of people with disabilities. BCID exists to improve the quality of life of brooklyn residents with disabilities thgouh programs that empower them to gain greater control of their lives and achieve full and equal integration into society.

**4161 Capital District Center for Independence**
875 Central Ave
South 3
Albany, NY 12206-1342
518-459-6422
FAX: 518-459-7847
TTY:518-459-6422
e-mail: info@cdciweb.com
www.cdciweb.com

*Laurel Kelley, Executive Director*
One of 37 Independent Living Centers in New York State, the Center is a non-residential, community based organization, which primarily serves Albany and Schenetady Counties. The Center's mission is to assist people with disabilities to acquire self-advocacy skills and by teaching through example, consumers achieve greater control over the direction of their lives.

**4162 Catskill Center for Independence**
6104 State Highway 23
Oneonta, NY 13820
607-432-8000
FAX: 607-432-6907
TTY:607-432-8000
e-mail: ccfi@ccfi.us
www.ccfi.us

*Chris Zachmeyer, Executive Director*
*Christine Worden, Assistant Director*
One of 37 community-based independent living centers located throughout the state of New York. As an advocacy agency, we provide a vareity of services to people with disabilities, their friends and family members. In addition, we provide advocacy, training, and technical assistance to our community members, organizations, businesses and state and local governments in a variety of disability related areas. Serves Otsego, Delaware and Schoharie counties.

**4163 Center for Community Alternatives**
115 E Jefferson St
Suite #300
Syracuse, NY 13202-2018
315-422-5638
FAX: 315-471-4924
e-mail: mweissman@communityalternatives.org
www.communityalternatives.org

*Marsha Weissman, Executive Director*
Promotes reintegrative justice and a reduced reliance on incarceration through advocacy, services and public policy development in pursuit of civil and human rights.

**4164 Center for Independence of the Disabled of New York**
137-02A Northern Blvd
Flushing, NY 11354-4122
646-442-1520
FAX: 718-886-0428
TTY:718-886-0427
e-mail: info@cidny.org
www.cidny.org

*Susan Dooha, Executive Director*
To ensure full integration, independence and equal opportunity for all people with disabilities by removing barriers to the social, economic, cultural and civic life of the community.

**4165 Center for Independence of the Disabled of New York**
841 Broadway
Suite #301
New York, NY 10003-4708
212-674-2300
FAX: 212-254-5953
TTY:212-674-5619
e-mail: info@cidny.org
www.cidny.org

*Susan Dooha, Executive Director*
To ensure full integration, independence and equal opportunity for all people with disabilities by removing barriers to the social, economic, cultural and civic life of the community.

**4166 DD Center/St Lukes: Roosevelt Hospital Center**
St Lukes Roosevelt
1000 10th Ave
New York, NY 10019-1192
212-473-2045
FAX: 212-473-0501

*Charles Raimondo, VP*
*Farooq Chaudry, MD*
Independent living center that advocates for people with disabilities by assisting with the application process of housing, benefits, etc.

**4167 Finger Lakes Independence Center**
215 5th St
Ithaca, NY 14850-3403
607-272-2433
FAX: 607-272-0902
TTY:607-272-2433
e-mail: flic@fliconline.org
www.fliconline.org

*Lenore Schwager, Executive Director*
FLIC assists all people with disabilities, their families and friends to promote independence and make informed decisions in pursuit of their goals. The servides provided are free of charge, and services are primarily served to residents of Tompkins, Schyler counties.

**4168 Harlem Independent Living Center**
289 St. Nicholas Avenue
Suite #21
New York, NY 10027- 4805
212-222-7122
800-673-2371
FAX: 212-222-7199
e-mail: harlemilc@aol.com
www.hilc.org

*Christina Curry, Executive Director*
*Edward Randolph, Resource Specialist*
A non-profit agency that advocates for people with disabilities by assisting with the application process of housing, benefits, etc. Our services are free of charge.
*Monthly*

**4169 Independent Living**
5 Washington Ter
Newburgh, NY 12550-5383
845-565-1162
FAX: 845-565-0567
TTY:845-565-0337
e-mail: info@myindependentliving.org
www.myindependentliving.org

*Douglas J. Hovey, Executive Director*
*Anne Miller, Director of Development*
A consumer directed, cross-disability advocacy organization dedicated to enhancing quality of life for persons with disabilities.

**4170 Long Island Center for Independent Living**
3601 Hempstead Tpke
Suite #208
Levittown, NY 11756-1331
516-796-0144
FAX: 516-520-1247
TTY:516-796-0135
e-mail: licil@aol.com
www.licil.net

*Patricia Moore, Executive Director*
LICIL is committed to the empowerment of consumers with disabilities. LICIL staff functions as ambassadors to the belief that individuals with disabilities have a responsibility to take an active role in their own lives and self determined view of their futures.

**4171 Massena Center for Independent Living**
156 Center St
Massena, NY 13662-1495
315-764-9442
866-772-2482
FAX: 315-764-9442
TTY: 915-764-9464
e-mail: mindepli@twcny.rr.co,
www.milcinc.org

*Jeff Reifensnyder, Executive Director*
Provides a variety of non-residential direct services as well as educating the public through community awareness campaigns. Also seeks to address the current appropriate unmet needs of persons experiencing a disability - primarily in St Lawrence and Franklin Counties.

**4172 NYS Independent Living Council**
111 Washington Ave
Suite #101
Albany, NY 12210-2280
518-427-1060
888-469-7452
FAX: 518-427-1139
e-mail: oleanilc@yahoo.com
www.nysilc.org

*Laurel Kelley, Executive Director*
Provides support and technical assistance to 37 independent living centers-community-based organizations directed by and for people with disabilities.

**4173 Nassau County Office for the Physically Challenged**
60 Charles Lindberg Blvd
Uniondale, NY 11553-4812
516-227-7399
www.nassaucountyny.gov

*Edward P. Mangano, Executive Director*
This agency serves as the ADA compliance coordinating office for all Nassau County governmental facilities, programs and services. It also serves in an advisory capacity to local, regional and national policy-making organizations, planning committees and legislative bodies and conducts advocacy as well as direct programs and services to enhance inclusion by people with disabilities to employment, consumerism and transportation.

**4174 North Country Center for Independent Living**
80 Sharron Avenue
Plattsburgh, NY 12901-3827
518-563-9058
FAX: 518-563-0292
TTY:518-563-9058
e-mail: andrew@ncci-online.com
www.ncci-online.com

*Andrew Pulrang, Executive Director*
*Patti King, IL Planning Coordinator*
To empower people with disabilities to live more independent and productive lives, and to promote beneficial policies and community understanding of disability issues.

**4175 Northern Regional Center for Independent Living: Watertown**
210 Court St
Suite #4
Watertown, NY 13601-4546
315-785-8703
800-585-8703
FAX: 315-785-8612
TTY: 315-785-8704
e-mail: brendac@nrcil.net
www.nrcil.net

*Brenda Campany, Executive Director*
*Kathy Connor, Director Family Support Services*
A disability rights and resource center that promotes community efforts to end discrimination, segregation, and prejudice against people with disabilities.

**4176 Northern Regional Center for Independent Living: Lowville**
7632 N State St
Lowville, NY 13367-1318
315-376-8696
FAX: 315-376-3404
TTY:315-376-8696
e-mail: brendac@nrcil.net
www.nrcil.net

*Karen Boliver, Program Director*
*Brenda Campany, Executive Director*
A disability rights and resource center that promotes community efforts to end discrimination, segregation, and prejudice against people with disabilities.

**4177 Options for Independence: Auburn**
75 Genesee St
Auburn, NY 13021-3667
315-255-3447
FAX: 315-255-0836
e-mail: gguy@optionsforindependence.org
www.optionsforindependence.org

*Greg Guy, Executive Director*
*Joyce McGlynn, MSC Consulting Supervisor*
*Sara Douglass, H.O.P.E. Supervisor*
*Felicia Thompson, Benefits Advisor/Rep. Payee*
Options for Independence is an Independent Living Center which assists people with disabilities to gain opportunities, make their own decisions, pursue activities and become part of comunity life. Options provides a variety of services to all people with disabilities, their families, friends, and service providers in Cayuga and Seneca Counties.

**4178 Queens Independent Living Center**
2335 Broadway
Astoria, NY 11106-4172
718-713-4718
FAX: 718-393-8575
e-mail: contact@qilc.org
www.qilc.org

*Lilian Modu, Executive Director*
An organization dedicated to freedom and full participation in society for people with disabilities through empowerment, universal access through education and advocacy.

**4179 Regional Center for Independent Living**
497 State St
Rochester, NY 14608-1642
585-442-6470
FAX: 585-271-8558
TTY:585-442-6470
e-mail: bdarling@rcil.org
www.rcil.org

*Bruce E Darling, Executive Director*
*Diane Coleman, Director of Advocacy*
To empower people with disabilities to self-advocate, to live independently and to enhance the quality of community life.

**4180 Resource Center for Accessible Living**
727 Ulster Ave
Kingston, NY 12401-1709
845-331-0541
FAX: 845-331-2076
TTY:845-331-4527
e-mail: rcal@hvc.rr.com
www.rcal.org

*Susan J Hoger, Executive Director*
RCAL is a non-profit, community based service and advocacy run by and for people with any type of disability. RCAL is dedicated to assisting and empowering individuals, of all ages, to live independently and participate in all aspects of community life.

**4181 Resource Center for Independent Living**
347 W Main St
Amsterdam, NY 12010-2225
518-842-3561
FAX: 518-842-0905
TTY:518-842-3593
e-mail: ramon.rodriguez@rcil.com
www.rcil.ocom

*Burt Danovitz, Executive Director*
*David Lowitz, Operations Manager*
Peer counseling, advocacy, independent living skills training, information and referral services, self-advocacy training, ADA consultation, home and community based services, community education, benefits advisement and more. All programs and services are available in English and Spanish.

**4182 Rockland Independent Living Center**
873 Route 45
New City, NY 10956-2712
845-624-1366
FAX: 845-624-1369
e-mail: info@rilc.org
www.rilc.org

*George Hoehmann M.A., Executive Director*
*Monifa Peters, Administrative Assistant*
RILC serves all individuals with disabilities. We promote philosophy consumer empowerment and control. The services we provide include benefit and advisement information and referral and consumer directed personal assistants.

**4183 Southern Adirondack Independent Living**
418 Geyser Rd
Country Club Plaza
Ballston Spa, NY 12020-6002
518-584-8202
FAX: 518-584-1195
www.sail-center.org

*Karen Thayer, Executive Director*
*Anna Livingston, Assistant Director*
*Barbara Potvin, Executive Assistant*
*Michele Nicholson, Administrative Assistant*
To assist individuals with disabilities to become independent empowered self-advocates.

**4184 Southern Adirondack Independent Living Center**
71 Glenwood Ave
Queensbury, NY 12804-1728
518-792-3537
FAX: 518-792-0979
TTY:518-792-0505
www.sail-center.org

*Karen Thayer, Executive Director*
*Anna Livingston, Assistant Director*
To assist individuals with disabilities to become independent empowered self-advocates.

**4185 Southern Tier Independence Center**
135 E Frederick St
Binghamton, NY 13904-1224
607-724-2111
FAX: 607-772-3600
TTY:607-724-2111
e-mail: stic@stic-cil.org
www.stic-cil.org

*Maria Dibble, Executive Director*
*Frank Pennisi, Accessibility Services*
STIC provides assistance and services to all people with disabilities of all ages to increase their independence in all aspects of integrated community life. STIC also serves their families and friends, and businesses, agencies, and goverments to enable them to better meet the needs of people with disabilities, and finally STIC educates and influences the community in pursuit of full inclusion of people with disabilities.

**4186 Southwestern Independent Living Center**
843 N Main St
Jamestown, NY 14701-3546
716-661-3010
FAX: 716-661-3011
TTY:716-661-3012
e-mail: info@ilc-jamestown-ny.org
ilc-jamestown-ny.org

*Marie T Carrubba, Executive Director*
*Linda Rumbaugh, Independent Living Specialist*
A non-residential, private, nonprofit agency established to provide services throughout Chautauqua County that will assist individuals with disabilities in reaching maximum independence and an enriched quality of life.

**4187 Staten Island Center for Independent Living, Inc.**
470 Castleton Ave
Staten Island, NY 10301
718-720-9016
FAX: 718-720-9664
TTY:718-720-9870
e-mail: sicil@verizon.net

*Lorraine DeSantis, Executive Director*
Mission is to provide all individuals with disabilities the information, life skills training, and facilitative assistance which contributes to independence, individuality, and integration in the community and provides the skills and knowledge necessary to function in the least restrictive, personally fulfilling, most self reliant and productive manner.

**4188 Suffolk Independent Living Organization(SILO)**
3680 Rt 112
Suite #4
Coram, NY 11727
631-880-7929
FAX: 631-946-6377
TTY:631-654-8076

*Edward Ahern, Manager*
*Glenn Campbell, Co-Executive Director*
A not-for-profit organization that helps the disabled become more independent and more involved in the community by providing them with information on referrals on Housing, Education, Employment and Benefits.

**4189 Taconic Resources for Independence**
82 Washington St
Suite #214
Poughkeepsie, NY 12601-2305
845-452-3913
866-948-1094
FAX: 845-485-3196
e-mail: tri@taconicresources.org
www.taconicresources.org

*Cynthia Fiore, Executive Director*
*Patrick Muller, Program Director*
A center for independent living, benefits advisement information, and referral, advocacy, independent living skills, peer counseling, parent advocacy, sign language interpreters.

**4190 Westchester Disabled on the Move**
948 N. Broadway
Suite L1-10
Yonkers, NY 10701-1320
914-968-4717
FAX: 914-968-6137
e-mail: info@wdom.org
wdom.org

*Melvin Tanzman, Executive Director*
*Scott Smith, Program Director*
*Joe Lord, Office Manager*
WDOM empowers people with disabilities to control their own lives; advocates for civil rights and a barrier free society; encourages people with disabilities to participate in the political process; educates government, business, other entities, and a society as a whole to understand, accept, and accommodate people with disabilities; creates an environment that inspires self-respect

**4191 Westchester Independent Living Center**
200 Hamilton Avenue
Office #2
White Plains, NY 10601- 1809
914-682-3926
FAX: 914-682-8518
TTY:866-933-5390
e-mail: info@wilc.org
www.wilc.org

*Joseph Bravo, Executive Director*
A not-for-profit, community-based advocacy and resource center that serves people with all types of disabilities.

**4192 Westchester Independent Living Center: Carmel**
1961 Route 6
2nd Floor
Carmel, NY 10512-2324
845-228-7457
FAX: 845-228-7460
TTY:866-933-5390
e-mail: info@wilc.org
www.wilc.org

*Joe Bravo, Executive Director*
A non-profit, community-based advocacy and resource center that serves people with all types of disabilities.

## North Carolina

**4193 Disability Awareness Network**
609 Country Club Dr.
Suite C
Greenville, NC 27834-6210
252-353-5522
FAX: 252-353-5160
e-mail: DAWNpittco@aol.com
consolidatedmachines.com

*Jackie Hansley, Owner*
Information and referral for diabled persons; peer counseling for diabled persons; advocacy on ADA issues; independent living skills and training.

**4194 Disability Rights & Resources**
5801 Executive Center Dr.
Suite #101
Charlotte, NC 28212-8870
704-537-0550
800-755-5749
FAX: 704-566-0507
TTY: 704-537-0550
e-mail: juliasain@disability-rights.org
www.disability-rights.org

*Julia Sain, Executive Director*
*Denise Bordeman, Assistant Services Manager*
To guard the civil rights of people wtih disabilities by empowering ourselves and others to live as we choose.

**4195 Joy: A Shabazz Center for Independent Living**
235 N Greene St
Greensboro, NC 27401-2410
336-272-0501
FAX: 336-272-0575
TTY:336-272-0501
e-mail: aaron.shabazz@shabazzcenter.org
www.wangshuai.net

*Aaron Shabazz, Executive Director*
*Benita Williams, Deputy Director*
A non-profit, consumer oriented, Center for Independent Living (CIL) providing advocacy, peer counseling and peer support, independent living skills, training, information and referrals, with other related services for persons with disabilites.

**4196 Live Independently Networking Center**
P.O.Box 1135
Newton, NC 28658-1135
828-464-0331
FAX: 828-464-7375
TTY:828-464-2838
e-mail: linc@twave.net
www.linconline.org

*Donavon Kirby, Deputy Director*
Private, nonprofit, federally funded center for independent living located in Western North Carolina.

**4197 Live Independently Networking Center: Hickory**
2830 16th St NE
Apt. 17
Hickory, NC 28601-8606
828-464-0331
FAX: 828-464-7375
Private, non-profit, federally funded center for independent living

**4198 Pathways for the Future Center for Independent Living**
525 Mineral Springs Dr
Sylva, NC 28779-9077
828-631-1167
FAX: 828-631-1169
TTY:828-631-1167
e-mail: bdavis@pathwayscil.org
www.pathwayscil.org

*Barbara Davis, Executive Director*
Dedicated to increasing independence, changing attitudes, promoting equal access and building a peer support network in

western North Carolina through the use of community education, independent living services and advocacy.

**4199 Western Alliance Center for Independent Living**
30b London Rd
Asheville, NC 28803-2706
828-274-0444
FAX: 828-274-4461
e-mail: wacil@main.nc.us
westernalliance.org

*Katy Hollingsworth, Manager*
*Jerry Brewton, Independent Living Specialist*
.

**4200 Western Alliance for Independent Living**
108 New Leicester Highway
Asheville, NC 28806
828-298-1977
FAX: 828-298-0875
e-mail: khollingsworth@disabilitypartners.org
www.disabilitypartners.org

*Kathy Hollingsworth, Associate Director*
*Jerry Brewton, Independent Living Specialist*

## North Dakota

**4201 Dakota Center for Independent Living: Dickinson**
26-1st East
Suite 103
Dickinson, ND 58601-5103
701-222-3636
800-489-5013
FAX: 701-222-0511
TTY: 800489501363
e-mail: dcil@ndsupernet.com
www.dakotacil.org

*Royce Schultze, Executive Director*
*Diana Medicine Stone, Sr Independent Living Counselor*
Believes in self-determination for people with disabilities and creates the environment in which it is achieved.

**4202 Dakota Center for Independent Living: Bismarck**
3111 E Broadway Ave
Bismarck, ND 58501-5085
701-222-3636
800-489-5013
FAX: 701-222-0511
TTY: 701-222-3636
e-mail: maryr@dakotacil.org
www.dakotacil.org

*Royce Schultze, Executive Director*
*Diana Medicine Stone, Sr Independent Living Counselor*
*Mary Robinson, Program Manager*
Believes in self-determination for people with disabilities and creates the environment in which it is achieved.

**4203 Fraser**
2902 University Dr S
Fargo, ND 58103-6053
701-232-3301
FAX: 701-237-5775
e-mail: fraser@fraserltd.org
fraserltd.org

*Sandra Leyland, Executive Director*
*David A. Laske, Treasurer*
*Mark Brodshaug, Board President*
*Amy Hepper, Director of Business Operations*
Private non-profit, federally funded center for independent living

**4204 Freedom Resource Center for Independent Living: Fargo**
2701 9th Ave S
Suite H
Fargo, ND 58103-8712
701-478-0459
800-450-0459
FAX: 701-478-0510
TTY: 701-478-0459
e-mail: freedom@freedomrc.org
www.freedomrc.org

*Nate Aalgaard, Executive Director*
*Angie Bosch, Office Coordinator*
*Mark Mark Bourdon Bourdon, Program Director*
*Andrea Nelson, Independent Living Advocate*
To work toward equality and inclusion for people with disabilities through programs of empowerment, community education, and systems change.

**4205 Resource Center for Independent Living: Minot**
300 3rd Ave SW
Suite F
Minot, ND 58701-4346
701-839-4724
800-377-5114
FAX: 701-838-1677
TTY: 701-839-4724
e-mail: independencecil@independencecil.org
www.independentcil.org

*Scott Burlingame, Executive Director*
*Nancy Johnson, Independent Living Specialist*
*Dee Tischer, Direct Services Coordinator*
A resource center for independent living. Mission is to advocate for the freedom of choice for individuals with disabilities to live independently through the removal of all barriers.

## Ohio

**4206 Ability Center of Greater Toledo**
5605 Monroe St
Sylvania, OH 43560-2702
419-885-5733
866-885-5733
FAX: 419-882-4813
TTY: 419-885-5733
www.abilitycenter.org

*Tim Harrington, Executive Director*
*Dale Abell, Director of Program Development*
To assist people with disabilities to live, work and socialize within a fully accessible community.

**4207 Ability Center of Greater Toledo: Defiance**
5605 Monroe St
Sylvania, OH 43560-2702
419-885-5733
866-885-5733
FAX: 419-882-4813
TTY: 419-885-5733
www.abilitycenter.org

*Tim Harrington, Executive Director*
*Dale Abell, Director of Program Development*
To assist people with disabilities to live, work and socialize within a fully accessible community.

**4208 Ability Center of Greater Toledo: Port Clinton**
1848 East Perry Street
Suite #110
Port Clinton, OH 43452-1802
419-734-0330
877-734-0330
FAX: 419-732-6864
TTY: 419-734-0330
www.abilitycenter.org

*Tory Heilman, Rural Outreach Coordinator*
*Eryn Bauer, Information & Referral*
To assist people with disabilities to live, work and socialize within a fully accessible community.

**4209 Access Center for Independent Living**
901 S Ludlow St
Dayton, OH 45402-2614
937-341-5202
FAX: 937-341-5217
TTY:937-341-5218
e-mail: info@acils.com
www.acil.com

*Alan Cochrun, Executive Director*
*Beliza De La Cruz, Executive Assistant*
*John Dixon, Information & Referral Specialis*
Offers peer counseling, disability education and other services to the community.

**4210 Center for Independent Living Options**
2031 Auburn Avenue
Cincinnati, OH 45219-2436
513-241-2600
FAX: 513-241-1707
TTY:513-241-7170
e-mail: cilo@cilo.net.
cilo.net

*Lin Laing, Executive Director*
*Amanda Speier, Director of Programs*
*Kyle Dixon, Staff Accountant*
*Esther Wing, Administrative Assistant*
The oldest center for independent living in Ohio serving individuals with disabilities in the Greater Cincinnati/Northern Kentucky region.

**4211 Fairfield Center for Disabilities and Cerebral Palsy**
681 E 6th Ave
Lancaster, OH 43130-2602
740-653-5501
FAX: 740-653-6046
e-mail: fcdcp@sbcglobal.net
www.fcdcp.org

*David Macioci, President*
*David Welsh, Vice-President*
Adult Day Program and Transportation. The mission of the Fairfield Center for disabilities and Cerebral Palsy, Inc, is to create a better future for people with a disability by increasing and enhancing their lifestyle opportunities.

**4212 Linking Employment, Abilities and Potential**
2545 Lorain Ave.
Cleveland, OH 44113-3102
216-696-2716
FAX: 216-687-1453
www.leapinfo.org

*Melanie Hogan, Manager*
Consumer-directed to ensure a society of equal opportunity for all persons, regardless of disability.

**4213 Mid-Ohio Board for an Independent Living Environment (MOBILE)**
690 S High St
Columbus, OH 43206-1016
614-443-5936
FAX: 614-443-5954
TTY:614-443-5957
e-mail: info@mobileonline.org
www.mobileonline.org

*Beverly Rackett, Executive Director*
*Pam Bolden, Principal*
A non-profit Center for Independent Living directed by persons with disabilities. MOBILE was founded on principles that affirm the right of persons with disabilities to live their lives with a full measure of liberty and human dignity.

**4214 Ohio Statewide Independent Living Council**
670 Morrison Road
Suite 200
Gahanna, OH 43230-5324
614-892-0390
800-566-7788
FAX: 614-861-0392
www.ohiosilc.org

*Kay Grier, Executive Director*
*Eugene Iacovetta, Special Projects Coordinator*
*Mary Butler, Systems Change Coordinator*
*V. Shay Hunt, Office Clerk*
Committed to promoting a philosophy of consumer control, peer support, self-help, self-determination, equal acess, and individual and systems advocacy, in order to maximize leadership, empowerment, independence, productivity and to support full inclusion and integration of individuals with disabilities into the mainstream of American society.

**4215 Rehabilitation Service of North Central Ohio**
270 Sterkel Blvd
Mansfield, OH 44907-1508
419-756-1133
800-589-1133
FAX: 419-756-6544
e-mail: info@therehabcenter.org
www.therehabcenter.org

*Veronica L. Groff, President/CEO*
*Jonathon Reskof, Director Medical Rehab*
*Cheryl Casler, Director Vocational Rehab*
*Kelly Pack, Director Behavioral Health*
Private nonprofit organization providing coordinated, team-oriented comprehensive outpatient rehabilitation services to children and adults of all ages. Serves 8 counties in N/C Ohio. Four umbrella areas of service include medical rehabilitation services, vocational rehabilitation services, behavioral health service and drug and alcohol addiction services. Medical rehabilitation services include physical therapy, occupational therapy, speech therapy and audiology.

**4216 Samuel W Bell Home for Sightless**
3775 Muddy Creek Rd
Cincinnati, OH 45238-2055
513-241-0720
FAX: 513-241-1481
e-mail: swbellhome@fuse.net
www.samuelbell.org

*Miles L. Hoff, Executive Director*
*Holly Hoeffer, Director of Residents*
Offers a residential, independent living environment for blind and legally blind adults.

**4217 Services for Independent Living**
25100 Euclid Ave
Suite #105
Cleveland, OH 44117-2663
216-731-1529
FAX: 216-731-3083
TTY:216-731-1529
e-mail: sil@sil-oh.org
www.sil-oh.org

*Lynn Hildebrand, Executive Director*
Offers support ADA, consultation and education, advocacy, transitional education services, independent living skills training, information and referrals.

**4218 Society for Equal Access: Independent Living Center**
1458 5th St NW
New Philadelphia, OH 44663-1224
330-343-9292
888-213-4452
FAX: 330-602-7425
TTY:330-602-2557
e-mail: ilc@tusco.net
www.seailc.org

*Dianne Rennicker, Executive Director*
The Society works with individuals to become more independent. Our agency assists with peer support, advocacy, information and

referral, independent living skills and transportation. Our goal is to move those with challenges in the direction ofn independence.

## Oklahoma

4219 **Ability Resources**
823 S Detroit Ave
Suite #110
Tulsa, OK 74120-4223
918-592-1235
800-722-0886
FAX: 918-592-5651
e-mail: webadmin@ability-resources.org
www.ability-resources.org

*Carla Lawson, Executive Director*
To assist people with disabilities in attaining and maintaining their personal independence.

4220 **Green County Independent Living Resource Center**
4100 S.E. Adams Rd
Suite C-106
Bartlesville, OK 74006- 8409
918-335-1314
800-559-0567
FAX: 918-333-1814
TTY: 918-335-1314

*Vicki Haws, Executive Director*
Independent living skills training, information and referrals, advocacy, a loan library of adaptive equipment and books. Services available to all individuals with disabilities and their family members who reside in Northeastern Oklahoma.

4221 **Oklahomans for Independent Living**
601 East Carl Albert Parkway
McAlester, OK 74501-5410
918-426-6220
800-568-6821
FAX: 918-426-3245
TTY: 918-426-6263
e-mail: info@oilok.org
www.oilok.org

*Mike Ward, Executive Director*
*Leanna Amos, Independent Living Specialist*
OIL encourages individuals of all ages, with all types of disabilities to increase: personal dependence; empowerment and self determiation; and ful integration and participation in their work, community, school and home activities.

4222 **Progressive Independence**
121 N Porter Ave
Norman, OK 73071-5834
405-321-3203
800-801-3203
FAX: 405-321-7601
TTY: 405-321-2942
e-mail: heathera@progind.org
www.progind.org

*Jeff Hughes, Executive Director*
*Josh Gray, Office Manager*
Preovides four cores services of Information & Referral, Individaul& Systems Advocacy, Peer Counseling, and Skills Training; in addition, offers accessible computer lab, short term DME loans, ande benefits counseling for SSI/SSDI.

## Oregon

4223 **Central Oregon Resources for Independent Living**
20436 Clay Pigeon Ct
Bend, OR 97702
541-388-8103
FAX: 541-388-1226
TTY:541-388-8103
e-mail: coril@coril.org
www.coril.org

*Jim Lee, Executive Director*
*Mike Smith, Work Center Manager*
CORIL empowers people with disabilities to maximize their independence, productivity and inclusio in community life. CORIL envisions a society where all people have the opportunity to develop their full capabilities with independence, productivity and more meaningful involvment in local community events and activities.

4224 **Columbia Gorge Center**
2940 Thomsen Rd
Hood River, OR 97031-7433
e-mail: rrathkey@gorge.net

*Rita Radciky, Executive Director*
*C J Webb, Client Services Coordinator*
CGC assists people with disabilities or other barriers to employment or community living to: achieve control of their lives; attain competence in community and employment; an participate in satisfying lifestyles based on the same aspirations as well as citizens.

4225 **Eastern Oregon Center for Independent Living**
1021 SW 5th Ave
Ontario, OR 97914-3301
541-889-3119
866-248-8369
FAX: 541-889-4647
e-mail: eocil@eocil.org
www.eocil.org

*Kirt Toombs, Executive Director*
EOCIL is a nonprofit community based resource and advocacy center that promotes independent living and equal access for all persons with disabilities. EOCIL serves consumers in the counties of: Baker, Gilliam, Grant, harney, Malheur, Morrow, Umatilla, Union, Wallowa and Wheeler.

4226 **HASL Independent Abilities Center**
305 NE 'E' Street
Grants Pass, OR 97526
541-479-4275
800-758-4275
FAX: 541-479-7261
TTY: 541-479-3588
e-mail: haslstaff@yahoo.com
www.haslonline.org

*Randy Samuelson, Executive Director*
To promote public awareness of the special needs and legal rights of individuals with cross-disabilities; to facilitate their integration into society and provide support through advocacy, peer counseling, skills training and information and referral to encourage independence.

4227 **Independent Living Resources**
1839 NE Couch Street
Portland, OR 97232-5308
503-232-7411
FAX: 503-232-7480
TTY:503-232-8404
e-mail: info@ilr.org
www.ilr.org

*Barry Fox-Quamme, Executive Director*
*Cindy Bobzien, Executive Assistant*
*Cathy Blahut, Independent Living Coordinator*
ILR looks to promote the philosophy of Independent Living by creating opportunities, encouraging choices, advancing equal access, and furthering the level of independence for all people with disabilities

4228 **Laurel Hill Center**
2145 Centennial Plz
Eugene, OR 97401-2474
541-485-6340
FAX: 541-984-3124
TTY:541-684-6822
e-mail: info@laurel.org
www.laurel.org

*Mary Alice Johnston, PHD, Executive Director*
*Tom Fauria, President*
Provides natoinall-recognized, recovery-focused rehabilitation services in Lane County, Oregon, for people with severe and persistent mental illnesses

4229 **Progressive Options**
4909 S Coast Hwy
Suite #340
South Beach, OR 97366-9678
541-867-4335
FAX: 541-867-4336
TTY:541-574-1927
e-mail: progop541@yahoo.com
www.progressive-options.org

*Rhonda Walker, Executive Director*
Progressive Options seeks to provide free services and support to people with disabilities of all kinds to help them achieve and maintain maximum independence and self-sufficiency in Lincoln County and surrounding areas in Oregon.

4230 **SPOKES Unlimited**
415 Main St
Klamath Falls, OR 97601-6029
541-883-7547
FAX: 541-885-2469
TTY:541-883-7547
e-mail: info@spokesunlimited.org
www.spokesunlimited.org

*Wendy Howard, Executive Director*
Mission is to enhance the ability of people with disabilities to live more independently.

4231 **Umpqua Valley Disabilities Network**
736 SE Jackson Street
Roseburg, OR 97470-110
541-672-6336
FAX: 541-672-8606
TTY:541-440-2882
e-mail: uvdn@uvdn.org
www.uvdn.org

*David Fricke, Executive Director*
*Heather Vialpando, Executive Assistant*
UVDN's mission is to promote independent living and community inclusion for people with disabilities.

## Pennsylvania

4232 **Abilities in Motion**
210 N 5th St
Reading, PA 19601-3304
610-376-0010
888-376-0120
FAX: 610-376-0021
TTY: 610-228-2301
e-mail: staff@abilitiesinmotion.org
www.abilitiesinmotion.org

*Ralph Trainer, Executive Director*
*De Lores De Hart, Independent Living*
Dedicated to advancing the rights of persons with disabilities in orer to promote a full life in the community through the prevention and elimination of physical, psychological, social and attitudinal barriers which serve to deny them the rights and privileges common to the general public.

4233 **Anthracite Region Center for Independent Living**
Pennsylvania Council on Independent Living
8 West Broad St
Hazleton, PA 18201-6418
570-455-9800
800-777-9906
FAX: 570-455-1731
TTY: 570-455-9800
e-mail: dcorcoran@anthracitecil.org
www.anthracitecil.org

*Denise M. Corcoran, Executive Director*
Enables individuals with disabilities to attain their highest possible level of independence.

4234 **Brian's House**
1300 S Concord Rd
West Chester, PA 19382-8531
610-399-1175
e-mail: ekihara@brianshouse.org
brianshouse.org

*Lori Plunkett, Executive Director*
A non-profit organization that provides residential, vocational and recreational/respite programs for children and adults with intellectual and developmental disabilities.

4235 **Community Resources for Independence**
3410 W 12th St
Erie, PA 16505-3649
814-838-7222
800-530-5541
FAX: 814-838-8491
TTY: 814-838-8115
www.crinet.org

*Timothy Finegan, Executive Director*
A community based, nonprofit, nonresidential organization that offers services and assistance to enable people with disabilities to expand their options, pursue their goals, and achieve and maintain self-sufficient and producitve lives in the community.

4236 **Community Resources for Independence, Inc., Bradford**
3410 West 12th Street
Erie, PA 16505
814-838-7222
800-530-5541
FAX: 814-838-8491
TTY: 814-838-8115
crinet.org

*Mike Rapacioli, Regional Manager for Bradford & Clarion*
*Timothy J. Finegan, Executive Director*
*William Essigmann, Administrative Program Manager*
*Carl Berry, Human Resources Director*
Community Resources for Independence, Inc is committed to preserve, enhance and enrich the quality of life for all people with disabilities.

4237 **Community Resources for Independence: Lewistown**
33 East Hale Street
Suite L
Lewistown, PA 17044-2160
717-248-8011
800-309-0989
FAX: 717-248-8029
www.crinet.org

*Timothy Finegan, Executive Director*
A community based, nonprofit, nonresidential organization that offers services and assistance to enable people with disabilities to expand their options, pursue their goals, and achieve and maintain self-sufficient and producitve lives in the community.

4238 **Community Resources for Independence: Altoona**
1331 Twelth Ave
Suite #103
Altoona, PA 16601
814-994-2645
866-944-2645
FAX: 814-944-2683
www.crinet.org

*Timothy Finegan, Executive Director*

A community based, nonprofit, nonresidential organization that offers services and assistance to enable people with disabilities to expand their options, pursue their goals, and achieve and maintain self-sufficient and producitve lives in the community.

**4239 Community Resources for Independence: Clarion**
1200 Eastwood Drive
Suite #1
Clarion, PA 16214-8824
814-297-7141
800-372-0140
FAX: 814-297-7161
www.crinet.org

*Deb Camuso, Manager*
A community based, nonprofit, nonresidential organization that offers services and assistance to enable people with disabilities to expand their options, pursue their goals, and achieve and maintain self-sufficient and producitve lives in the community.

**4240 Community Resources for Independence: Clearfield**
209 E Locust St
Clearfield, PA 16830-2422
814-765-6405
866-619-6405
FAX: 814-765-1269
www.crinet.org

*Timothy Finegan, Executive Director*
A community based, nonprofit, nonresidential organization that offers services and assistance to enable people with disabilities to expand their options, pursue their goals, and achieve and maintain self-sufficient and producitve lives in the community.

**4241 Community Resources for Independence: Hermitage**
3875 East State St
Suite B
Hermitage, PA 16148-3415
724-347-4121
FAX: 724-347-5966
www.crinet.org

*Scott Jenco, Manager*
A community based, nonprofit, nonresidential organization that offers services and assistance to enable people with disabilities to expand their options, pursue their goals, and achieve and maintain self-sufficient and producitve lives in the community.

**4242 Community Resources for Independence: Lewisburg**
11 Reitz Blvd
Suite #105
Lewisburg, PA 17837-1493
570-524-4314
800-332-4135
FAX: 570-524-9236
www.crinet.org

*Bob Bartlett, Manager*
A community based, nonprofit, nonresidential organization that offers services and assistance to enable people with disabilities to expand their options, pursue their goals, and achieve and maintain self-sufficient and producitve lives in the community.

**4243 Community Resources for Independence: Oil City**
250 Elm St
Oil City, PA 16301-1413
814-677-4655
866-209-3882
FAX: 814-677-4915
www.crinet.org

*Tim Finegan, Executive Director*
A community based, nonprofit, nonresidential organization that offers services and assistance to enable people with disabilities to expand their options, pursue their goals, and achieve and maintain self-sufficient and producitve lives in the community.

**4244 Community Resources for Independence: Warren**
1003 Pennsylvania Ave W
Warren, PA 16365-1837
814-726-3404
866-579-3404
FAX: 814-726-3428
www.crinet.org

*Timothy Finegan, Executive Director*
A community based, nonprofit, nonresidential organization that offers services and assistance to enable people with disabilities to expand their options, pursue their goals, and achieve and maintain self-sufficient and producitve lives in the community.

**4245 Community Resources for Independence: Wellsboro**
38 Plaza Ln
Wellsboro, PA 16901-1766
570-724-5852
866-401-7911
FAX: 570-724-3945
www.crinet.org

*Timothy Finegan, Executive Director*
A community based, nonprofit, nonresidential organization that offers services and assistance to enable people with disabilities to expand their options, pursue their goals, and achieve and maintain self-sufficient and producitve lives in the community.

**4246 Freedom Valley Disability Center**
3607 Chapel Road
Suite B
Newtown Square, PA 19073-3602
610-353-6640
800-427-4754
FAX: 610-353-6753
TTY: 610-353-8900
fvdc.info

*Ann Cope, Executive Director*
Assists persons with disabilities in the achievement of independent living goals. Also promotes individual and community options to maximize independence for persons with disabilities. Serves people with disabilities in Chester, Delaware, and Montgomery Counties.OUT OF ORDER

**4247 Institute on Disabilities At Temple Univ.**
Temple University
1755 N. 13th St
Student Center, Rm. 4115
Philadelphia, PA 19122-6099
215-204-1356
FAX: 215-204-6336
e-mail: iod@temple.edu
www.disabilities.temple.edu

*James Earl Davis, Phd, Interim Executive Director*
*Celia Feinstein, Associate Director*
*Amy Goldman, Associate Director*
*Ann Marie White, Associate Director*
Leads by example, creating connections and promoting networks within and among communitites so that people with disabilities are recognized as integral to the fabric of community life.

**4248 Lehigh Valley Center for Independent Living**
435 Allentown Dr
Allentown, PA 18109-9121
610-770-9781
800-495-8245
FAX: 610-770-9801
TTY: 610-770-9789
e-mail: info@lvcil.org
www.lvcil.org

*Amy Beck, Executive Director*
Serves persons in Lehigh and Northampton Counties with any type of disability and/or his/her family.

**4249 Liberty Resources**
714 Market St
Suite #100
Philadelphia, PA 19106-2337
215-634-2000
888-634-2155
FAX: 215-634-6628
TTY:215-634-6630
e-mail: lrinc@libertyresources.org
www.libertyresources.org

*Thomas Earle, Executive Director*
A non-profit, consumer driven organization that advocates and promotes Independent Living for persons with disabilities.

**4250 Life and Independence for Today**
503 E Arch St
Saint Marys, PA 15857-1779
814-781-3050
800-341-5438
FAX: 814-781-1917
TTY: 814-781-3050
e-mail: lift@liftcil.org
www.liftcil.org

*Kelly Valdez, Executive Director*
*Laure Richnafsky, Independent Living Coordinator*
Offers services to enable people with disabilities to achieve new goals and broaden their horizons. It enables them to achieve and maintain self-sufficient and productive lives.

**4251 Northeastern Pennsylvania Center for Independent Living**
1142 Sanderson Ave
Suite #1
Scranton, PA 18509
570-344-7211
800-344-7211
FAX: 570-344-7218
TTY: 570-344-5275
e-mail: nepacilinfo@nepacil.org
www.nepacil.org

*Daniel Loftus, Executive Director*
Established to assist in removing barriers and expanding independent living options available to people with disabilities.

**4252 South Central Pennsylvania Center for Independence Living**
1019 Logan Blvd
Altoona, PA 16602-2434
814-949-1905
800-237-9009
FAX: 814-949-1909
TTY: 814-949-1912
e-mail: cilscpa@cilscpa.org
www.cilscpa.org

*Susan Estep, Executive Director*
The missio of the Center for Independent Living of South Central PA is to empower people with disabilities to lead independent lives in their commnuitites. The Center covers Bedford, Blair, cambria, Fulton, Huntingdon, Indiana and Somerset counties.

**4253 Three Rivers Center for Independent Living: New Castle**
1750 New Butler Road
Suite A
New Castle, PA 16101-9383
724-598-7533
800-479-2840
FAX: 724-598-7552
TTY: 724-598-7533
www.trcil.org

*Stanley A Holbrook, President*
To empower people with disabilities to enjoy self-directed, personally meaningful lives by providing outstanding consumer controlled services and by advocating for effective community college.

**4254 Three Rivers Center for Independent Livi ng: Washington**
150 W.Beau St
Suite #217
Washington, PA 15301-4425
724-222-2910
866-401-2910
FAX: 724-222-3396
e-mail: washoffice@trcil.org
www.trcil.org

*Randi Shelton, Manager*
To empower people with disabilities to enjoy self-directed, personally meaningful lives by providing outstanding consumer controlled services and by advocating for effective community college.

**4255 Three Rivers Center for Independent Livin g: Erie**
3800 W 12th St
Erie, PA 16505-3380
814-833-8997
877-833-8997
FAX: 814-833-4605
e-mail: erieoffice@trcil.org
www.trcil.org

*Anna Remberg, Manager*
To empower people with disabilities to enjoy self-directed, personally meaningful lives by providing outstanding consumer controlled services and by advocating for effective community college.

**4256 Three Rivers Center for Independent Living**
900 Rebecca Ave
Pittsburgh, PA 15221-2938
412-371-7700
800-633-4588
FAX: 412-731-0959
TTY: 412-371-6230
e-mail: cwilliams@trcil.org
www.trcil.org

*Stanley Holbrook, Manager*
To empower people with disabilities to enjoy self-directed, personally meaningful lives by providing outstanding consumer controlled services and by advocating for effective community college.

**4257 Tri-County Patriots for Independent Living**
69 E Beau St
Washington, PA 15301-4711
724-223-5115
FAX: 724-223-5119
TTY:724-228-4028
tripil.com

*Kathleen Kleinmann, Chief Executive Officer*
Brings together individuals who share common problems in equal access, education, housing, employment, attendant care, transportation, and access to technology.

**4258 Voices for Independence**
1107 Payne Ave
Erie, PA 16503-1741
814-874-0064
866-407-0064
FAX: 814-874-3497
TTY: 814-874-0064
www.vficil.org

*Shona Eakin, Executive Director*
To empower people with disabilities and promote independent living.

## Rhode Island

**4259 Blackstone Valley Center**
115 Manton St
Pawtucket, RI 2861-4396
401-727-0150
FAX: 401-727-0153
e-mail: contact@bvcriarc.org
www.bvcriarc.org

*Anna Mc Laughlin, Manager*
Committed to supporting people with developmental disabilities secure the opportunity to choose and realize their goals of where and how they live, learn, work and play

**4260 Franklin Court Assisted Living**
180 Franklin St
Bristol, RI 2809-3352
401-253-3679
FAX: 401-253-5855
e-mail: mgargano@ebcdc.org
www.ebcdc.org

*Jean Pierce, Administrator*
Offers local seniors an affordable assisted living option with first-rate services and gracious accommodations.

**4261 IN-SIGHT Independent Living**
43 Jefferson Blvd
Warwick, RI 2888-1078
401-941-3322
FAX: 401-941-3356
e-mail: insightri@gmail.com
www.in-sight.org

*Chris Butler, Executive Director*
Creating opportunities and choices for people who are blind and visually impaired

**4262 Ocean State Center for Independent Living**
1944 Warwick Ave
Warwick, RI 2889-2448
401-738-1013
866-857-1161
FAX: 401-738-1083
TTY: 401-738-1015
e-mail: oscil@oscil.org
www.oscil.org

*Lorna Ricci, Executive Director*
OSCIL is a consumer controlled, community based, nonprofit organization established to provide a range of independent living services to enhance, through self direction, the quality of life of Rhode Islander with significant disability and to promote integration into the community.

**4263 Office of Rehabilitation Services**
40 Fountain St
Suite #4B
Providence, RI 2903-1898
401-421-7005
FAX: 401-421-7016
www.ors.ri.gov

*Steve Brunero, Acting Administrator ORD*
*Ron Racine, Deputy Administrator Blind*
*John Microulis, Deputy Administrator Disability*
Their goal is to help individuals with physical and mental disabilities prepare for and obtain appropriate employment.

**4264 PARI Independent Living Center**
500 Prospect St
Pawtucket, RI 2860-6259
401-725-1966
FAX: 401-725-2104
TTY:401-725-1966
e-mail: info@pari-ilc.org
www.pari-ilc.org

*Leo Canuel, Executive Director*
*Sue Bilodau, Program Director*
Offers information and referral services, personal care attendant services, home modifications, advocacy services and peer counseling, independent living skills training, and recycled equipment.

## South Carolina

**4265 Columbia Disability Action Center**
136 Stonemark Lane
Suite #100
Columbia, SC 29210
800-681-6805
FAX: 803-779-5114
TTY:803-779-0949
www.dacsc.org

*Kimberly Tissot, Interim Executive Director*
*Sara Marin, Director of Administration*
*Diane Robinson, Independent Living Specialist*
A non-profit consumer governed Center for Independent Living. Programs and services support persons with disabilities in taking full advantage of community resources, enhancing personal opportunities, and determining the direction of their lives.

**4266 Disability Action Center**
330B Pelham Rd
Suite 102-B
Greenville, SC 29615-3116
864-235-1421
800-681-7715
FAX: 864-235-2056
TTY: 864-235-8798
e-mail: amayne@dacsc.org
www.dacsc.org

*Kat A. Tracy, Area Coordinator*
*Martha Merritt, Support Staff*
*Megan Ponce, Independent Living Specialist*
Empowering people with disabilities to reach their highest level of independence.

**4267 Graham Street Community Resources**
306 Graham St
Florence, SC 29501-4735
843-665-6674
FAX: 843-665-6674

*Faye Thompson, Manager*
Promotes independent living and empowers people with disabilities to reach their highest level of independence.

**4268 South Carolina Independent Living Council**
136 Stonemark Lane
Suite #100
Columbia, SC 29210-7318
803-217-3209
800-994-4322
FAX: 803-731-1439
TTY: 803-217-3209
e-mail: scilc@scilconline.org
www.scilconline.org

*Mike Le Fever, President*
Committed to equal opportunity, equal access, self determination, independence, and choice for all people with disabilities and pursues these goals by the means available.

**4269 Walton Options for Independent Living: North Augusta**
325 Georgia Ave
North Augusta, SC 29841-3848
803-279-9611
FAX: 803-279-9135
e-mail: tjohnston@waltonoptions.org
www.waltonoptions.org

*Cynthia Anzek, Executive Director*
Empowers persons of all ages with all types of disabilities to reach their highest level of independence, community inclusion and employment.

## South Dakota

**4270 Adjustment Training Center**
607 N 4th St
Aberdeen, SD 57401-2733
605-229-0263
FAX: 605-225-3455
www.aspiresd.org

*Jennifer Gray, Director*
*Donna Howard, Business Official*
*Arlette Keller, Special Education Director*
Offers peer counseling, attendant care registry and referrals.

**4271 Black Hills Workshop & Training Center**
Black Hills Workshop
PO Box 2104
Rapid City, SD 57709-2104
605-343-4550
FAX: 605-343-0879
TTY:800-877-1113
e-mail: mkrause@bhws.com
www.bhws.com

*Larry Meendering, Director of Vocational Services*
*Marty Krause, VP Agency Operations*
Offers job placement, housing options, case coordination, supported employment and supported living for all disability groups, as well as specialized services for brian injury victims.

**4272 Communication Service for the Deaf: Rapid City**
150 Knollwood Dr
Rapid City, SD 57701-694
605-394-6864
FAX: 605-394-6609
TTY:605-394-6864
www.c-s-d.org

*Brenda French, Manager*
*Scot Atkins, Senior VP, Human Resources*
*Kevin Barber, Senior VP Facilities/Technology*
*Robert Davila, Senior VP National Programs*
A private, nonprofit organization dedicated to providing broad-based services, ensuring public accessibility and increasing public awareness of issues affecting deaf and hard of hearing inividuals.

**4273 Native American Advocacy Program for Persons with Disabilities**
P.O.Box 527
Winner, SD 57580-527
605-842-3977
800-303-3975
FAX: 605-842-3983
TTY: 605-842-3977
e-mail: admin@sdnaap.org
www.nativeamericanadvocacy.org

*Marla Bull Bear, Executive Director*
*Shizue M LaPointe-Dutt, Office Manager*
*Chelsea Christensen, Business Manager*
*Theresa Maule, Project Manager*
The mission is to encourage a healthy organization that assists Native Americans with disabilities, by providing prevention, education and training, advocacy, support, independent living skills and referrals.

**4274 Prairie Freedom Center for Independent Living: Sioux Falls**
301 S. Garfield Ave
Suite #9
Sioux Falls, SD 57104-3100
605-367-5630
FAX: 605-367-5639
pfcil.org

*Matthew Cain, Executive Director*
Established to provide basic skills so many of us take for granted: to take care of our own needs and to make our own decisions to be independent.

**4275 Prairie Freedom Center for Independent Li ving: Madison**
Ste 102
411 SE 10th St
Madison, SD 57042-3570
605-256-5070
FAX: 605-256-5071
www.pfcil.org

*Matt Cain, Executive Director*
Established to provide basic skills so many of us take for granted: to take care of our own needs and to make our own decisions to be independent.

**4276 Prairie Freedom Center for Independent Living: Yankton**
413 West 15th St
Suite #107
Yankton, SD 57078-2800
605-668-2940
FAX: 605-668-3060
TTY:605-668-3060
e-mail: ccrisp@pfcil.org
www.pfcil.org

*Matt Cain, Executive Director*
Established to provide basic skills so many of us take for granted: to take care of our own needs and to make our own decisions to be independent.

**4277 South Dakota Assistive Technology Project: DakotaLink**
1161 Deadwood Ave N
Suite #5
Rapid City, SD 57702-382
605-394-6742
800-645-0673
FAX: 605-394-6744
e-mail: atinfo@dakotalink.net
dakotalink.tie.net

*Pat Czerny, Manager*
*Patrick Czerny, Technical Services Coordinator*
*David Scherer, Program Coordinator*
DakotaLink, the South Dakota Assistive Technology Program, provides resources and supports to individuals of all ages to ensure greater access to and acquisition of assistive technology devices and services.

**4278 Western Resources for dis-ABLED Independence**
405 E. Omaha St
Suite D
Rapid City, SD 57701-2974
605-718-1930
888-434-4943
FAX: 605-718-1933
TTY: 605-718-1930
e-mail: ann@wrdi.org
www.wrdi.org

*Ann Van Loan, Executive Director*
WRDI advocates for the rights of equal inclusion of people with disabilities in all aspects of community life. WRDI also strives to identify and promote access to existing resources and to advocate for the development of new resources, which may enable people with disabilities to live more independently.

## Tennessee

**4279 Center for Independent Living of Middle Tennessee**
955 Woodland St
Nashville, TN 37206-3753
615-292-5803
866-992-4568
FAX: 615-383-1176
TTY: 615-292-7790
e-mail: cilmt@tndisability.org
www.cil-mt.org

*Tom Hopton, Executive Director*
CILMT provides persons with disabilities opportunities to be self advocates and make their own decisions regarding living arrangements, means of transportation, employment, social and recreational activities, as well as other aspects of everyday life.

Serves Davidson, Cheatham, Wilson, Robertson, Rutherford, Sumner and Williamson Counties.

**4280 DisAbility Resource Center: Knoxville**
900 E Hill Ave
Suite #120
Knoxville, TN 37915-2567
865-637-3666
FAX: 865-637-5616
TTY:865-637-6976
e-mail: drc@drctn.org
www.drctn.org

*Lillian Burch, Executive Director*
*Nicole Craig, Service Coordinator*
*Thomas Kahler, Independent Living Specialist*
DRCTN mission is to empower people with disabilities to fully integrate and participate in the community. DRC is a community-based non-residential program of services designed to assist people with disabilities to gain independence and to assist the community in eliminating barriers of independence.

**4281 Jackson Center for Independent Living**
1981 Hollywood Drive
Jackson, TN 38305-4388
731-668-2211
FAX: 731-668-0406
TTY:731-664-3970
e-mail: jcil05-06@yahoo.com
www.j-cil.com

*Glen Barr, Executive Director*
JCIL works with people with significant disabilities and the Deaf Community in achieving their Independent Living Goals while assisting the community in eliminating barriers to Independent Living.

**4282 Memphis Center for Independent Living**
1633 Madison Ave
Memphis, TN 38104-2506
901-726-6404
FAX: 901-726-6521
TTY:901-726-6404
e-mail: mcil@mcil.org
www.mcil.org

*Deborah Cunningham, Executive Director*
*Sandi Klink, Assistant Director*
MCIL is a community based non-profit organization whose primary mission is to facilitate the full integration of persons with disabilities into all aspects of community life.

**4283 Tennessee Technology Access Program (TTAP)**
400 Deaderick St
14th Fl
Nashville, TN 37243-1403
615-313-5183
800-732-5059
FAX: 615-532-4685
TTY: 615-313-5695
e-mail: tn.ttap@state.tn.us
www.state.tn.us/humanserv/rehab/ttap.htm

*Kevin Wright, Director*
TTAP's mission is to maintain a statewide program of technology-rated assistance that is timely, comprehensive and consumer driven to ensure that all Tennesseans with disabilities have the information, services and deices that they need to make choices about where and how they spend their time as independently as possible. .

**4284 Tri-State Resource and Advocacy Corporation**
5708 Uptain Rd.
Suite 350
Chattanooga, TN 37411-5501
423-892-4774
800-868-8724
FAX: 423-892-9866
TTY: 423-892-4774
e-mail: 4trac@bellsouth.net
www.4trac.org

*Mark Woofall, Executive Director*
TRAC is dedicated to improving opportunities for individuals wuth disabilities.

## Texas

**4285 ABLE Center for Independent Living**
3415 Brentwood Drive
Odessa, TX 79762-6906
432-580-3439
e-mail: info@ablecenterpb.org
www.ablecenterpd.org

*Marilyn Hancock, Executive Director*
*Kathleen Story MA, Independent Living Specialist*
To promote independent living for people with disabilities.

**4286 Austin Resource Center for Independent Living**
825 E. Rundberg Ln
Suite E6
Austin, TX 78753-4813
512-832-6349
800-414-6327
FAX: 512-832-1869
e-mail: arcil@arcil.com
www.arcil.com

*Ronald Roacha, Executive Director*
Serving people with disabilities, their families and communities throughout Travis and surrounding counties.

**4287 Austin Resource Center: Round Rock**
525 Round Rock West
Suite A120
Round Rock, TX 78681-5020
512-828-4624
FAX: 512-828-4625
e-mail: sally@arcil.com
www.arcil.com

*Sally Decker, Manager*
Serving peole with disabilities, their families and communities throughout Travis and surrounding counties.

**4288 Austin Resource Center: San Marcos**
618 South Guadalupe St
Suite #103
San Marcos, TX 78666- 6977
512-396-5790
800-572-2973
FAX: 512-396-5794
e-mail: sanmarcos@arcil.com
www.arcil.com

*Ronald Rocha, Executive Director*
Serving people with disabilities, their families and communities throughout Travis and surounding counties.

**4289 Brazoria County Center For Independent Living**
1104 E Mullberry Street
Suite D
Angleton, TX 77515-3952
979-849-7060
888-872-7957
FAX: 979-849-8465
TTY: 979-849-7060
e-mail: bccil@neosoft.com
coalitionforbarrierfreeliving.com

*Chamane Barrow, Manager*
To promote the full inclusion, equal opportunity and participation of persons with disabilities in every aspect of community life. We believe that people with disabilities have the right to make choices affecting their lives, a right to take risks, a right to fail, and a right to succeed.

**4290 Center Serving Persons with Mental Retardation**
3550 West Dallas Rd
Houston, TX 77019
713-525-8400
FAX: 713-525-8444
www.cri-usa.org

*Jack B Manning, President*
*Brian Cohen, VP*
Provides services for more than 600 children and adults with mental retardation and other developmental disabilities. The Center also offers a wide array of programs including education, vocational training and job placement services, three different residential options representing both urban and rural living environments, special programs designed to meet the needs of older adults, and a variety of therapeutic support services.

**4291 Crockett Resource Center for Independent Living**
1020 Loop 304 East
Crockett, TX 75835-1806
936-544-2811
FAX: 936-544-7315
TTY:936-544-2811
e-mail: crcil@windstream.net
www.crockettresourcecenter.org

*Cynthia Cook, Executive Director*
Provides independent living services to cross-disability groups to increase their personal self-determination and minimize dependence on others. Maintain comprehensive information on availability of resources and provides referrals to such resources. Provides instruction to assist people with disabilities to gain skills that would empower them to live independently. Peer counseling, advocacy - both individual and community by assisting to obtain support services to make changes in society.

**4292 Houston Center for Independent Living**
6201 Bonhomme Rd
Ste 150
Houston, TX 77036
713-974-4621
FAX: 713-974-6927
TTY:713-974-2703
e-mail: hcil@neosoft.com
coalitionforbarrierfreeliving.com

*Sandra Bookman, Executive Director*
Advocacy organization created by and for people with disabilities (PWD) to empower and protect their rights. Services include but not limited to: peer support, individual and systems advocacy, independent living skills training, information and referral, disability cultural awareness, ASL classes, ADA technical assistance, computer technology training, work incentive counseling, equipment loan program.

**4293 Independent Life Styles**
P.O.Box 571874
Houston, TX 77257-1874
713-861-4266
FAX: 713-861-9846
www.independentlifestyles.org

*Peter Simmons, Director*
Offers peer counseling, advocacy and other services to the community.

**4294 Independent Living Research Utilization Project**
Institute For Rehabilitation & Research
2323 S. Sheperd Dr
Suite #100
Houston, TX 77019-7031
713-520-0232
FAX: 713-520-5785
TTY:713-520-0232
e-mail: ilru@ilru.org
www.ilru.org

*Lex Frieden, Manager*
*Laurie Redd, Executive Director*
ILRU is a national center for information, training, research and technical assistance in independent living. Its goal is to expand the body of knowledge in independent living and to improve utilization of results of research programs and demonstration projects in this field. ILRU is a program of The Institute for Rehabilitation and Research, a nationally recognized medical rehabilitation facility for persons with disabilities. TTY phone number: (713) 520-5136.

**4295 LIFE/ Run Centers for Independent Living**
4902 34th Street
Suite #5
Lubbock, TX 79410-2342
806-795-5433
FAX: 806-795-5607
TTY:806-795-5433
e-mail: wilmacrain@yahoo.com
www.liferun.org

*Michelle Crain, Executive Director*
Committed to providing individuals with disabilities the information and skills necessary to become independent and to achieve full inclusion in every aspect of their life.

**4296 Office for Students with Disabilities, University of Texas at Arlington**
P.O.Box 19510
Arlington, TX 76019-1
817-272-3364
800-735-2989
FAX: 817-272-1447
TTY: 800-735-2989
e-mail: osd@uta.edu
www.uta.edu/disability

*Dianne Hengst, Director*
Offers disability counseling and academic accomodation to UT Arlington community.

**4297 Palestine Resource Center for Independent Living**
421 Avenue a St
Palestine, TX 75801-2903
903-729-7505
888-326-5166
FAX: 903-729-7540
TTY:903-729-7505
e-mail: prcil@embarqmail.com

*Sara Minton, Executive Director*
*Susan Dorsey, Community/ Consumer Coordinator*
Provides independent living services to cross-disability groups to increase their personal self-determination and minimize dependence on others. Maintain comprehensive information on availability of resources and provides referrals to such resources. Provides instruction to assist people with disabilities to gain skills that would empower them to live independently. Peer counseling, advocacy - both individual and community by assisting to obtain support services to make changes in society.

**4298 Panhandle Action Center for Independent Living Skills**
1118 S Taylor St
Amarillo, TX 79101-4316
806-374-1400
FAX: 806-374-4550
TTY:806-374-2774
e-mail: advocacy@nts-online.net
www.panhandleilc.org

*Carl Mc Millen, Executive Director*
*Kevin Oliphant, Manager*
PILC is a non profit organization dedicated to the advancement of full participation in all aspects of life. PILC services are developed, directed, delivered, and governed primarily by individuals with disabilities.

**4299 REACH of Dallas Resource Center on Independent Living**
8625 King George Drive
Suite 210
Dallas, TX 75235-2286
214-630-4796
FAX: 214-630-6390
TTY:214-630-5995
e-mail: reachdallas@reachcils.org
reachcils.org

*Charlotte A. Stewart, Executive Director*
*Kevan Johnson, Employment Consultant*
*Janie Peachee, Administrative Assistant*
*Chris Bowman, Information Technology Specialist*
Information and referral, peer support/peer counseling, independent living skills training and advocacy assistance.

**4300 REACH of Denton Resource Center on Independent Living**
405 S. Elm St
Suite 202
Denton, TX 76201-6068
940-383-1062
FAX: 940-383-2742
e-mail: reachden@reachcils.org
www.reachcils.org

*Charlotte A. Stewart, Executive Director*
*Missy Dickenson, Assistant Director*
To provide for people with disabilities so that they are enabled to lead self-directed lives and to educate the general public about disability-related topics in order to promote a barrier free community.

**4301 REACH of Fort Worth Resource Center on Independent Living**
1205 Lake St
Fort Worth, TX 76102-4501
817-870-9082
FAX: 817-877-1622
TTY:817-870-9086
e-mail: reachftw@reachcils.org
www.reachcils.org

*Charlotte A. Stewart, Executive Director*
*Robin Lassiter, Assistant Director*
To provide services for people with disabilities so that they are enabled to lead self-directed lives and to educate the general public about disability-related topics in order to promote a barrier free community.

**4302 RISE-Resource: Information, Support and Empowerment**
755 11th Street
Suite 101
Beaumont, TX 77701-3723
409-832-2599
FAX: 409-838-4499
TTY:409-832-2599
www.risecil.org

*Jim Brocoto, Executive Director*
*Donna Hobbs, Administrative Assistant*
*Cheryl Bass, Program Director*
*Gracie Jackson, Independent Living Specialist*
A non-profit center for independent living.

**4303 SAILS**
1028 S Alamo St
San Antonio, TX 78210-1170
210-281-1878
800-474-0295
FAX: 210-281-1759
TTY: 210-281-1878
e-mail: kbrietzke@sailstx.org
www.sailstx.org

*Kitty Brietzke, Executive Director*
*Gloria Banik, Assistant Executive Director*
SAILS advocates for the rights and empowerment of people with disabilities in San Antonio; as well as surrounding areas. Services are provided to people with disabilities in the following counties: Atacosa, Bandera, Bexar, Calhoun, Comal, DeWitt, Dimmit, Edwards, Frio, Gillespie, Goliad, Gonzalez, Guadalupe, Jackson, Karnes, La Salle, Kendall, Kerr, Kinney, Lavaca, Maverick, Medina, Real, Uvalde, Val Verde, Victoria, Wilson and Zavala.

**4304 Texas Department of Assistive and Rehabilitative Services**
4800 N. Lamar Blvd
Austin, TX 78756
512-472-4138
800-628-5115
FAX: 512-472-0603
TTY: 866-581-9328
e-mail: dars.inquiries@dars.state.tx.us
www.dars.state.tx.us

*Bill West, Manager*
Provides technical assistance and other support services to the state's Independent Living Council, Independent Living Centers and Independent Living Counseling programs.

**4305 VOLAR Center for Independent Living**
1220 Golden Key Circle
El Paso, TX 79925-5823
915-591-0800
800-591-0800
FAX: 915-591-3506
TTY: 915-591-0800
e-mail: volar@volarcil.org
www.volarcil.org

*Luis Chew, Executive Director*
*Dan Monroe, Chief Fiscal Officer*
VOLAR is committed to providing independent living ervices and information and referral, and to developing community options for persons with cross disabilities to empower them to live the kind of lives they choose. VOLAR is an organization of and for people with disabilities, advocating human and civil rights, community options and empowering people to live the lives they choose. Newsletter available.

**4306 Valley Association for Independent Living (VAIL)**
P.O. Box 5035
McAllen, TX 78502-5035
956-668-8245
FAX: 956-631-7914
e-mail: wjohnston@valleyassociation.org
www.valleyassociation.org

*Woodie Johnston, Executive Director*
Offers information and referral, peer couseling, MS supprt group, independent living skills training, and advocacy, work incentives planning and assistance, transitioning people with disabilities from the nursing home into the community.

**4307 Valley Association for Independent Living: Harlingen**
1824 W. Jefferson Ave
Suite B
Harlingen, TX 78550-5247
956-428-1126
FAX: 956-428-4339
e-mail: smyers@valleyassociation.org
www.valleyassociation.org

*Soledad Myers, Manager*
Provides information and referral, peer counseling, support groups, independent living skills training, community rehab program and advocacy

## Utah

**4308 Active Re-Entry**
10 S Fairgrounds Rd
Price, UT 84501
435-637-4950
FAX: 435-637-4952
TTY:435-637-4950
e-mail: active@arecil.org
arecil.org

*Nancy Bentley, Executive Director*
Active Re-Entry is a community based program which assists individuals with disabilities to acheive or maintain self-sufficient and productive live in their own communities. Active Re-Entry is

committed to promoting the rights, dignity, and quality of life for all persons with disabilities.

**4309 Active Re-Entry: Vernal**
1472 2900 West St
Vernal, UT 84078-9727
435-789-4021
FAX: 435-789-6090
TTY:435-789-4021
www.usilc.org

*Heather Moore, President*
Active Re-Entry is a community based program which assists individuals with disabilities to achieve or maintain self-sufficient and productive lives in their own communities. We are committed to promoting the rights, dignity, and quality of life for all persons with disabilities.

**4310 Central Utah Independent Living Center**
491 N Freedom Blvd
Provo, UT 84601-2824
801-373-5044
877-421-4500
FAX: 801-373-5094
TTY: 801-373-5044
e-mail: sandra@cucil.org
www.optionsind.org

*Sandra Curcio, Executive Director*
*Jhilma Lacayo, Independent Living Specialist*
Empowers people with disabilities to reach their full potential in community settings through peer support, advocacy, and education.

**4311 OPTIONS for Independence**
Northern Utah Center for Independent Living
1095 N Main St
Logan, UT 84341-2215
435-753-5353
FAX: 435-753-5390
TTY:435-753-5353
e-mail: jbiggs@optionind.org
www.optionsind.org

*Cheryl Atwood, Executive Director*
OPTIONS for Independence, the Northern Utah Center for Independent Living serves people of all ages with all types of disabilities. OPTIONS is a nonresidential Center that provides services to individuals with disabilities to facilitate their full participation in the community and raise the understanding of disability issues and access to the community. The Independent Living philosophy is strictly adhered to: consumer control and choice being the focus.

**4312 OPTIONS for Independence: Brigham Satellite**
1080 North Main Street
Suite #105A
Brigham City, UT 84302-3379
435-723-2171
FAX: 435-723-9618
TTY:435-723-2171
e-mail: dcrockett@qwestoffice.net
www.optionsind.org

*Cheryl Atwood, Executive Director*
*Deanna Crockett, Manager*
OPTIONS is a nonresidential Independent Living Center where people with disabilities can learn skills to gain more control and independence over their lives. OPTIONS raises the vision and capability of the community at large to the point where people of all abilities will have equal access.

**4313 Red Rock Center for Independence**
515 W 300 N
Suite A
Saint George, UT 84770-4578
435-673-7501
800-649-2340
FAX: 435-673-8808
e-mail: rrci@rrci.org
www.rrci.org

*Garry Owens, Executive Director*
*Mary Light, Assistant Director*
*Mark Johnson, Independent Living Specialist*
Red Rock Center for Independence assists people with disabilities to live and participate independently.

**4314 Tri-County Independent Living Center**
P.O.Box 428
Ogden, UT 84402-428
801-612-3215
866-734-5678
FAX: 801-612-3732
TTY: 801-612-3215
www.tricountyilc.org

*Andy Curry, Executive Director*
The mission of the Tri-County ILC is to enhance independence for all people with disabilities. Serves Davis, Weber and Morgan Counties.

**4315 Utah Assistive Technology Program (UTAP) Utah State University**
6855 Old Main Hill
Logan, UT 84322-6855
435-797-3811
800-524-5152
FAX: 435-797-2355
www.uatpat.org

*Marilyn Hammond, Manager*
Provides expertise, resources, and a structure to enhance and expand AT services provided by private and public agencies in Utah. Occurs through monitoring, coordination, information dissemination, empowering individuals, the identification and removal of barriers, and expanding state resources.

**4316 Utah Independent Living Center**
3445 S Main St
Salt Lake City, UT 84115-4453
801-466-5565
800-355-2195
FAX: 801-466-2363
TTY: 801-466-5565
e-mail: uilc@xmission.com
www.uilc.org

*Debra Mair, Executive Director*
*Kim Meichle, Program Director*
*Julie Beckstead, Program Coordinator*
*Patty Trent, Fiscal Manager*
Offers information and referral services. To assist persons with disabilities achieve independence by providing services and activities which enhance independent living skillspromote the public's understanding, accomodation, and acceptance of their rights, needs and abilities.

**4317 Utah Independent Living Center: Minersville**
P.O.Box 168
Minersville, UT 84752-168
435-691-7724
e-mail: rrci@rrci.org
www.rrci.org

*Gary Owens, Executive Director*
To enhance independence for all people with disaibilities.

**4318 Utah Independent Living Center: Tooele**
48 S Main St
Tooele, UT 84074-2132
435-843-7353
FAX: 435-843-7359
TTY:435-843-7353
e-mail: uilc@trilobyte.com
www.ilru.org

*Angie Slater, Manager*
Mission is to assist persons with disabilities achieve greater independence by providing services and activities which enhance independent living skills and promote the public's understanding, accomodation, and acceptance of their rights, needs and abilities.

## Vermont

**4319 Vermont Assistive Technology Program**
Department of Aging and Independent Living
103 S Main St
Weeks Building
Waterbury, VT 5671-2305
802-241-2671
800-750-6355
FAX: 802-241-2174
TTY: 802-241-1464
e-mail: amber.fulcher@ahs.state.vt.us
www.atp.vermont.gov/tryout-centers

*Julie Tucker, Program Director*
*David Punia ATP, Information/Education Specialist*
Encompasses a state coordinating council for assistive technology issues, regional centers for demonstration, trial and technical support with computer and augmentative communication equipment and regional seating and positioning centers.

**4320 Vermont Center for Independent Living: Bennington**
532 Main St
Bennington, VT 5201-2875
802-447-0574
800-639-1522
e-mail: vcil@vcil.org
www.vcil.org

*Deborah Lisi-Baker, Executive Director*
Believes that individuals with disabilities have the right to live with dignity and with appropriate support in their own homes, fully participate in their communities, and to control and make decisions about their lives.

**4321 Vermont Center for Independent Living: Chittenden**
145 Pine Haven Shores Rd
Suite 1137A
Shelburne, VT 5482-7703
802-985-9841
TTY:802-985-9841
e-mail: vcil@vcil.org
www.vcil.com

*Deborah Lisi-Baker, Executive Director*
Believes that individuals with disabilities have the right to live with dignity and with appropriate support in their own homes, fully participate in their communities, and to control and make decisions about their lives.

**4322 Vermont Center for Independent Living: Montpelier**
11 E State St
Montpelier, VT 05602-3008
802-229-0501
800-639-1522
FAX: 802-229-0503
e-mail: vcil@vcil.org
vcil.org

*Sarah Launderville, Executive Director*
Believes that individuals with disabilities have the right to live with dignity and with appropriate support in their own homes, fully participate in their communities, and to control and make decisions about their lives.

## Virginia

**4323 Access Independence**
324 Hope Dr
Winchester, VA 22601-6800
540-662-4452
FAX: 540-662-4474
TTY:540-662-5556
e-mail: askai@accessindependence.org
www.accessindependence.org

*Donald Price, Executive Director*
*Diane Starkey, Programs Manager*
*Joan Davis, Manager Operations/Rep Payee*
Offers support services to persons with disabilities to assist in maintaining or increasing their independence and self-determination. Includes housing assistance, independent living skills training, information, referral services, assistance and representative payee and advocacy.

**4324 Appalachian Independence Center**
230 Charwood Dr
Abingdon, VA 24210-2566
276-628-2979
FAX: 276-628-4931
TTY:276-676-0920
e-mail: aicadmin@ntelos.net
aicadvocates.org

*Greg Morrell, Executive Director*
*Donna Buckland, Development Director*
*Scarlett Cox, Operations Director*
Mission is to advocate for and with people with disabilities to promote full participation in society

**4325 Blue Ridge Independent Living Center**
Ste B
1502 Williamson Rd NE
Roanoke, VA 24012-5100
540-342-1231
FAX: 540-342-9505
TTY:540-342-1231
e-mail: kmichalski@brilc.org
brilc.org

*Karen Michalski-Karn, Executive Director*
*Dana Jackson, Program Services Director*
*Lottie Diomedi, Independent Living Coordinator*
BRILC assists people with disabilities to live independently. The Center also serves the community at large by helping to create and environment that is accessible to all. BRILC offers a variety of services ranging from referrals to community resources, support services, and direct services. These include peer counseling, support groups, training and seminars, advocacy, education, support services, awareness, aid in obtaining specialized equipment, and much more.

**4326 Blue Ridge Independent Living Center: Christianburg**
210 Pepper Street S
Christiansburg, VA 24073-3571
540-381-8829
FAX: 540-381-8833
TTY:540-381-8829
e-mail: tlavinder@brilc.org
www.brilc.org

*Karen Michalski-Karney, Executive Director*
*Sara Ingram, Program Services Coordinator*
*Ava Coles, Independent Living Specialist*
Assists people with disabilities to live independently. The center also serves the community at large by helping to create an environment that is accessible to all.

**4327 Blue Ridge Independent Living Center: Low Moor**
P.O.Box 7
Low Moor, VA 24457-7
540-862-0252
FAX: 540-862-0252
TTY:540-862-0252
www.brilc.org

Assists to help people with disabilities to live independently. The center also serves the community at large by helping to create an environment that is accessible to all.

**4328 Clinch Independent Living Services**
1139C Plaza Drive
Grundy, VA 24614-6780
276-935-6088
800-597-2322
FAX: 276-935-6342
TTY: 276-935-6088
e-mail: cils@clinchindependent.org
www.cils-online.org

*Betty Bevins, Executive Director*
Nonprofit organization providing information and referral, peer counseling, advocacy and independent living skills training to persons with disabilities.

**4329 Disability Resource Center**
409 Progress St
Fredericksburg, VA 22401-3337
540-373-2559
800-648-6324
FAX: 540-373-8126
TTY: 540-373-5890
e-mail: drc@cildrc.org
www.cildrc.org

*Debe Fults, Executive Director*
Mission is to assist people with disabilities, those who support them, and the community, through information, education and resources, to achieve the highest potential and benefit of independent living.

**4330 ENDependence Center of Northern Virginia**
2300 Claredon Blvd.
Suite 3305
Arlington, VA 22201-3367
703-525-3268
866-849-3852
FAX: 703-525-3585
TTY: 703-525-3553
e-mail: info@ecnv.org
www.ecnv.org

*David V Burds, Executive Director*
ECNV is a community-based resource and advocacy enter which is managed by and for people with disabilities. ENCV promotes independent living philosophy and equal access for all persons with disabilities and, like the nearly 400 centers for independent living across the country, ECNV grew from local disability rights and self-help movements.

**4331 Equal Access Center for Independence**
4031 University Drive
Suite #301
Fairfax, VA 22030-3409
703-934-2020
TTY:703-277-7730
e-mail: drc@patriot.net

*David Sharp, Executive Director*
Provides information and referral, peer counseling, advocacy and independent living skills training to persons with disabilities.

**4332 Independence Empowerment Center**
9001 Digges Road
Suite #103
Manassas, VA 20110-4414
703-257-5400
FAX: 703-257-5043
TTY:703-257-5400
e-mail: info@ieccil.org
www.ieccil.org

*Mary D Lopez, Executive Director*
A non-profit Center for Independent Living. One of over 500 centers in the United States with roots in civil rights models of the 1960's.

**4333 Independence Resource Center**
815 Cherry Ave
Charlottesville, VA 22903-3448
434-971-9629
FAX: 434-971-8242
TTY:434-971-9629
e-mail: tvandever@ntelos.net
www.charlottesvilleirc.org

*Thomas Vandever, Executive Director*
Information and referral services.

**4334 Independent Living Center Network: Department of the Visually Handicapped**
Ste 300
1809 Staples Mill Rd
Richmond, VA 23230-3515
FAX: 804-355-9297

*Robert W Partin, Director*
*Robert Kastenbaum, Partner*
Information and referral services.

**4335 Junction Center for Independent Living**
P.O.Box 1210
Norton, VA 24273-913
276-679-5988
FAX: 276-679-6569
TTY:276-679-5988
e-mail: jcil1@junctioncenter.org
junctioncenter.org

*Dennis Horton, Executive Director*
To assist those who have significant disabilities so that they migh live independently in the least restrictive and most integrated environment possible.

**4336 Junction Center for Independent Living: Duffield**
P.O.Box 408
Duffield, VA 24244-408
276-431-1195
FAX: 276-431-1196
TTY:276-431-1195
e-mail: jcil1@junctioncenter.org
junctioncenter.org

*Dennis Horton, Executive Director*
To assist those who have significant disabilities so that they might live independently in the least restrictive and most integrated environment possbile.

**4337 Lynchburg Area Center for Independent Living**
500 Alleghany Ave
Suite #520
Lynchburg, VA 24501-2610
434-528-4971
FAX: 434-528-4976
TTY:434-528-4972
e-mail: lacil@lacil.org
www.lacil.org

*Phil Theisen, Executive Director*
LACIL is a private non-profit, non-residential consumer driven organization that promotes the efforts of persons with disabilities to live independently in the community and supports the efforts of the community to be open and accessible to all citizens.

**4338 Peidmont Independent Living Center**
Piedmont Living Center
601 S. Belvidere Street
Richmond, VA 23220
804-782-1986
800-828-1140
FAX: 877-VHD-A123
www.vhda.com

*Susan Dewey, Executive Director*
*Judson McKellar, Managing Director of Legal and Finance*
*Russ Wyatt, General Auditor*
*Tammy Neale, Chief Learning Officer*
Empowering indiviuals with disabilities to become self-sufficient and independent within their communities.

**4339 Peninsula Center for Independent Living**
2021-A Cunningham Drive
Suite #2
Hampton, VA 23666-3320
757-827-0275
FAX: 757-827-0655
TTY:757-827-8800
e-mail: rshelman@hvacil.org

*Ralph Shelman, Executive Director*
IEPCIL is a private non-profit non-residential Agency established to provide services to people with disabilities. The Centers Philosophy is that people with a disability should play a major role in deciding their future.The center provides services to people with disabilities in the cities of Hampton, Newport News, Poquoson, Williamsburg, and counties of James City, York, and Gloucester.

**4340 Piedmont Independent Living Center**
1045 Main Street
Suite #2
Danville, VA 24541-1800
434-797-2530
FAX: 434-797-2568
TTY:434-797-2530

*Clarence Dickerson, Executive Director*
*Jeanette King, ILS Coordinator/BPAD*
*Lori Penn, Office Manager*
Empowering indiviuals with disabilities to become self-sufficient and independent within their communities.

**4341 Resources for Independent Living**
4009 Fitzhugh Ave
Richmond, VA 23230-3953
804-353-6503
FAX: 804-358-5606
TTY:804-353-6583
e-mail: info@ril-va.org
www.ril-va.org

*Sandra Wagener, Executive Director*
Assisting persons who are severly disabled to live independently in the community and to encourage necessary change within the community so independent living is a possibility.

**4342 Valley Associates for Independent Living (VAIL)**
Shenandoah Valley Workforce Investment Board
P.O.Box 869
Harrisonburg, VA 22803-869
540-442-7134
FAX: 540-434-0803
TTY:800-828-1120
e-mail: svwib@valleyworkforce.com
www.valleyworkforce.com

*Marcia Du Bois, Executive Director*
*Bob Satterwhite, Executive Director*
VAIL is a not-for-profit, private Center for Independent Living providing advocacy, information and referral, independent living skills training, supported employment, and peer counseling to individuals with disabilities in our planning district.

**4343 Valley Associates for Independent Living: Lexington**
205-B South Liberty St
Harrisonburg, VA 22801-3638
540-433-6513
888-242-8245
FAX: 540-433-6313
TTY:540-438-9265
e-mail: vail@govail.org
www.govail.org

*Marcia Du Bois, Executive Director*
Promoting self-direction among people with disabilities and removing barriers to independence in the community.

**4344 Woodrow Wilson Rehabilitation Center Training Program**
P.O.Box 1500
Fishersville, VA 22939-1500
540-332-7000
800-345-9972
FAX: 540-332-7132
TTY: 800-811-7893
e-mail: WWRCInfo@wwrc.virginia.gov
www.wwrc.net

*Rick Sizemore, Executive Director*
Information & referral services. Six week Virginia residential programs and evaluation services.

## Washington

**4345 Alliance for People with Disabilities: Seattle**
1120 E. Terrace St
Suite 100
Seattle, WA 98122
206-545-7055
866-545-7055
FAX: 206-545-7059
TTY: 206-632-3456
e-mail: info@disabilitypride.org
www.disabilitypride.org

*Lucille Walls, Executive Director*
The Alliance promotes equality and choice for people with disabilities. They provide advocacy, peer support, idependent living skills training, information and referral, transition assistance for youth, civil rights legal aid, assistive technology, training and nursing home transition back into the community.

**4346 Alliance of People with Disabilities: Redmond**
East King County Office
16315 NE 87th St
Suite B-3
Redmond, WA 98052-3537
425-558-0993
800-216-3335
FAX: 425-558-4773
TTY: 425-861-4773
e-mail: infon@disabilitypride.org
www.disabilitypride.org

*Robert Blumenfeld, Manager*
*Michelle Klekota, Independent Living Program*
*Charity Ranger, Independent Living Program*
*Jeannette Murphy, Executive Director*
Services include: information and referral, independent living skills training, peer groups, disAbility law project (DLP), access reviews, health insurance advising, and systems advocacy.

**4347 Coalition of Responsible Disabled**
612 N Maple St
Spokane, WA 99201-1801
509-326-6355
877-606-2680
FAX: 509-327-2420
TTY: 509-326-6355
e-mail: contact@cordwa.info
www.cordwa.info

*Linda McClain, Executive Director*
To improve the self-determination and self-reliance of people with disabilities through systems and individual advocacy, education and independent living services.

**4348 Community Services for the Blind and Partially Sighted Store: Sight Connection**
9709 Third Ave NE
Suite #100
Seattle, WA 98115-2027
206-525-5556
800-458-4888
FAX: 206-525-0422
e-mail: csbps@csbps.com
www.csbps.com

*June Mansfield, CEO*

Over 300 practical products for living with vision loss selected by certified vision rehabilitation specialists from Community Services for the Blind and Partially Sighted. Easy-to-use online store features large print, large photos, secure transactions, and links to other vision-related resources.

**4349 DisAbility Resource Connection: Everett**
607 SE Everett Mall Way
Suite 6C
Everett, WA 98208-3210
425-347-5768
800-315-3583
FAX: 425-710-0767
TTY: 425-347-5768
e-mail: drcservices@drconline.net
www.drconline.net

*Charley Lane, Executive Director*
disAbility Resource Connection is all about living your life as you choose. The staff is committed to assisting every individual to connect to resources, connect to skills, connect to life.

**4350 Kitsap Community Resources**
845 8th St
Bremerton, WA 98337-1517
360-478-2301
FAX: 360-415-2706
e-mail: info@kcr.org
www.kcr.org

*Larry Eyer, Executive Director*
*Rick MacLennan, VP*
Kitsap Community Resources is a local, non-profit organization dedicated to helping people in need. KCR creates hope and opportunity for low-income Kitsap County Residents by providing resources that promote self-sufficiency.

**4351 Tacoma Area Coalition of Individuals with Disabilities**
6315 S 19th St
Tacoma, WA 98466-6217
253-565-9000
877-538-2243
FAX: 253-565-5578
TTY: 253-565-3486
e-mail: tacid@tacid.org
www.tacid.org

*Chris Ensor, Executive Director*
Promotes the independence of individuals with disabilities.

## West Virginia

**4352 Appalachian Center for Independent Living**
4710 Chimney Drive
Suite # C
Charleston, WV 25302-4841
304-965-0376
800-642-3003
FAX: 304-965-0377
TTY: 800-642-3003
e-mail: acil@yahoo.com
www.mtsil.org

*Larry E Paxton, Executive Director*
A resource center for persons with disabilities and their communities. Serves Kanawha, Clay, Boone and Putnam counties.

**4353 Appalachian Center for Independent Living: Spencer**
811 Madison Avenue
Suite #106
Spencer, WV 25276-1900
304-927-4080
FAX: 304-927-4330
TTY:800-642-3003
e-mail: susanacil@yahoo.com
www,mtsil.org

*Todd Ramsey, Manager*
A resource center for persons with disabilities and their communities. Serves Jackson, Roane, and Calhoun counties.

**4354 Mountain State Center for Independent Living**
329 Prince St
Beckley, WV 25801-4515
304-255-0122
FAX: 304-255-0157
TTY:304-255-0122
e-mail: aoweeks@mtstcil.org
www.mtstcil.org

*Kevin Maynus, Manager*
*Anne Weeks, Chief Executive Officer*
This office provides individual and systems advocacy, independent living skills development, information and referral, peer support, personal assistance services, housing referral and training, transportation. Serves Raleigh counties.

**4355 Mountain State Center for Independent Living**
821 Fourth Avenue
Huntington, WV 25701-1406
304-525-3324
866-687-8245
FAX: 304-525-3360
TTY: 304-525-3324
e-mail: mtstcil@mtstcil.org
www.mtstcil.org

*Ann Weeks, Executive Director*
*John Gallaher, Manager*
Services provided are: individual and systems advocacy, independent living skills development, information and referral, peer support, personal assistance services, supported employment, community integration program, housing referral and training, transportation. Serves Cabell and Wayne counties.

**4356 Northern West Virginia Center for Independent Living**
601-603 East Brockway
Suite A & B
Morgantown, WV 26501
304-296-6091
800-834-6408
FAX: 304-292-5217
e-mail: nwvcil@nwvcil.org
www.nwvcil.org

*Jan Derry, Executive Director*
NWVCIL is committed to the philosophy that all persons have equal access and unconditional value, that all individuals shall be respected for their uniqueness and shall have the right to live within the community of their choice, having equal access to participate in and contribute to that community.

## Wisconsin

**4357 Center for Independent Living of Western Wisconsin**
2920 Schneider Avenue East
Menomonie, WI 54751-2331
715-233-1070
800-228-3287
FAX: 715-233-1083
TTY: 800-228-3287
e-mail: info@cilww.com
www.cilww.com

*Tim Sheehan, Executive Director*
*Kay Sommerfeld, Assistant Director*
Advocates for the full participation in society of all persons with disabilities. Our goal is empwowering individuals to exercise choices to maintain or increase their indpendence. Our strategy is providing consumer-driven services at no cost to persons with disiabilities in Western Wisconsin

**4358 Independence First**
540 South 1st Street
Milwaukee, WI 53204-1516
414-291-7520
FAX: 414-291-7525
TTY:414-297-7520
e-mail: lschulz@independencefirst.org
www.independencefirst.org

*Lee Schulz, Executive Director*

A non-profit agency directed by, and for the benefit of, persons with disabilities, primarily serving the four county metropolitan Milwaukee area.

**4359 Independence First: West Bend**
735 S Main St
West Bend, WI 53095-3965
262-306-6717
e-mail: lschulz@independencefirst.org
www.independencefirst.org

*Lee Schulz, Executive Director*
A non-profit agency directed by, and for the benefit of, persons with disabilities, primarily serving the four county Metropolitan Milwaukee area.

**4360 Inspiration Ministries**
P.O.Box 948
Walworth, WI 53184-948
262-275-6131
FAX: 262-275-3355
e-mail: tschnake@inspirationministries.org
inspirationministries.org

*Robin Knoll, President*
*Tim Schnake, VP Resident Services*
Formerly known as Christian League for the Handicapped, Inspiration Ministries is a vibrant community of adults with disabilities engaged in living, working, leisure and faith activities designed to provide a complete living experience. The campus consists of a modern residential facility offering a range of living accomodations; a work center and resale shop; and Inspiration Center, a retreat/camping center designed to be 100% wheelchair accessible.

**4361 Mid-State Independent Living Consultants: Wausau**
415 Campus Dr
Wausau, WI 54401
715-675-7600
800-311-5044
FAX: 715-298-2335
TTY: 800-311-5044
e-mail: jkaetterhenry@milc-inc.org
www.milcinc.net

*Tom Vandehey, President*
*Becky Paulson, Independent Living Consultant*
Working for persons with disabilities towards empowerment to make informed choices.

**4362 Mid-state Independent Living Consultants: Stevens Point**
3262 Church Street
Suite #1
Stevens Point, WI 54481-5321
715-344-4210
800-382-8484
FAX: 715-344-4414
TTY: 800-382-8484
e-mail: milc@milc-inc.org
www.milcinc.net

*Jenny Fasula, Executive Director*
*Karalyn Peterson, Resource Director*
Committed to enhancing personal and community relationships, providing opportunities for growth, and helping people with varying abilities achieve their personal goals.

**4363 North Country Independent Living**
2231 Catlin Ave
Suite #16
Superior, WI 54880-5138
715-392-9118
800-924-1220
FAX: 715-392-4636
e-mail: ncil@superior-nfp.org
northcountryil.com

*John Nousaine, Executive Director*
Empowers people with disabilities.

**4364 North Country Independent Living: Ashland**
422 3rd St. W.
Suite #114
Ashland, WI 54806-1553
715-682-5676
800-499-5676
FAX: 715-682-3144
TTY: 715-682-5676
e-mail: ncilstew@superior-nfp.org
www.northcountryil.com

*John Nousaine, Director*
Empowers people with disabilities.

**4365 Options for Independent Living**
P.O.Box 11967
Green Bay, WI 54307-1967
920-490-0500
888-465-1515
FAX: 920-490-0700
TTY:920-490-0600
e-mail: info@optionsil.com
www.optionsil.com

*Thomas Diedrick, Executive Director*
A non-profit organization committed to empowering people with disabilities to lead independent and productive lives in their community through advocacy, the provision of information, education, technology and related services.

**4366 Options for Independent Living: Fox Valley**
820 West College Ave
Suite #5
Appleton, WI 54914
920-997-9999
888-465-1515
FAX: 920-997-9381
TTY:920-490-0600
e-mail: info@optionsil.com
www.optionsil.com

*John Meissner, Manager*
A non-profit organization committed to empowering people with disabilities to lead independent and productive lives in their community through advocacy, the provision of information, education, technology and related services.

**4367 Society's Assets: Elkhorn**
615 E Geneva St
Elkhorn, WI 53121-2301
262-723-8181
800-261-8181
FAX: 262-723-8184
TTY: 866-840-9763
e-mail: info@societysassets.org
www.societysassets.org

*Bruce Nelson, Director*
*Jill Vigueres, Manager*
To ensure the rights of all persons with disabilities to live and function as independently as possible in the community of their choice, through supporting individual's efforts to achieve control over their lives and become integrated into community life.

**4368 Society's Assets: Kenosha**
5727 6th Ave
Kenosha, WI 53140-4103
262-657-3999
800-317-3999
FAX: 262-657-1672
TTY: 866-840-9762
e-mail: info@societysassets.org
www.societysassets.org

*Sue Liu, Manager*
*Bruce Nelsen, Executive Director*
To ensure the rights of all persons with disabilities to live and function as independently as possible in the community of their choice, through supporting individuals efforts to achieve controll over their lives and become integrated into community life. Offers home care and independent living services.

**4369 Society's Assets: Racine**
5200 Washinton Ave
Suite #225
Racine, WI 53406-4238
262-637-9128
800-378-9128
FAX: 262-637-8646
TTY: 886-840-9761
e-mail: info@societysassets.org
www.societysassets.org

*Deb Pitsch, Administrator*
*Karen Olufs, Director Independent Living*
*Jean Rumachik, Director Home Care Services*

Society's Assets assists people with disabilities to live as independently as possible. A non-profit human services agency, Society's Assets provides information and referal, independent living skills training, peer support, advocacy, and supportive home care. Home health care is provided by SAI Home Health Care. The agency serves 5 counties in southeastern Wisconsin and also provides information about interpreters, employment, benefits, home modifications, assistive equipment and accessibility.

*Fees vary*

## Wyoming

**4370 RENEW: Gillette**
623 N Commercial Dr
Gillette, WY 82716-2555
307-686-2125
888-253-4653
FAX: 307-686-8167
www.renew-wyo.com

*Kris Blair, Manager*

Empowering persons with disabilities to enrich their lives.

**4371 RENEW: Rehabilitation Enterprises of North Eastern Wyoming**
1969 S Sheridan Ave
Sheridan, WY 82801-6108
307-672-7481
888-309-2020
FAX: 307-674-5117
e-mail: pr@renew-wyo.com
www.renew-wyo.com

*Larry Samson, CEO*

Multi-disciplinary organization dedicated to the highest possible economic and social independence for persons with disabilities. Extensive referral service, specialized employment placement, occupational therapy, psychological services, evaluation services, and coordination of external services as needed to meet client plans and objectives.

**4372 Rehabilitation Enterprises of North Eastern Wyoming: Newcastle**
35 Fairgrounds Rd
Newcastle, WY 82701-2625
307-746-4733
888-693-9245
FAX: 307-746-9701
e-mail: pr@renew-wyo.com
www.renew-wyo.com

*Dennis Birchacek, Manager*

Empowering persons with disabilities to enrich their lives.

**4373 Wyoming Services for Independent Living**
1156 S 2nd St
Lander, WY 82520-3905
307-332-4889
800-266-3061
FAX: 307-332-2491
TTY: 307-332-7582
e-mail: wsil@wyoming.com
www.wysil.org

*Carol Fontaine, Executive Director*

Committed to enhancing personal and community relationships, providing opportunities for growth, and helping people with varying abilities achieve thier personal goals.

# Law

## Associations & Referral Agencies

4374 **AIDS Legal Council of Chicago**
180 N Michigan Ave
Ste 2110
Chicago, IL 60601
312-427-8990
866-506-3038
FAX: 312-427-8419
e-mail: info@aidslegal.com
aidslegal.com

*Ann Hilton Fisher, Executive Director*
*Colleen Boraca, Attorney*
*Ruth Edwards, Senior Attorney*
*Justin Hayford, Case Manager and Paralegal*
Legal assistance for people with HIV/AIDS related issues. Greater Chicago area.

4375 **AIDSLAW of Louisiana**
3801 Canal Street
New Orleans, LA 70119
504-568-1631
800-375-5035
e-mail: info@aidslaw.org
www.aidslaw.org

*Don Paul Landry, Executive Director*
*Stacy Morris, Deputy Executive Director*
The mission of AIDSLaw is to provide excellent, specialized legal services for people living with HIV/AIDS in Louisiana, to improve their quality of life and access to health care, related to their HIV/AIDS status.
*1989*

4376 **Center for Disability and Elder Law, Inc.**
79 West Monroe Street
Suite 919
Chicago, IL 60603-4908
312-376-1880
866-519-2413
FAX: 312-376-1885
e-mail: info@cdelaw.org
www.cdelaw.org

*Michael Roth, Executive Director*
*M. Catherine Taylor, Associate Director*
*Thomas Wendt, Chief Legal Officer*
A not-for-profit, 501(c)(3) legal services organization which provids legal services to low income persons residing in Chicago and Cook County, Il., who are either elderly and/or persons with disabilities. CDEL provides legal services by matching qualified candidates with volunteer attorneys who represent them, pro bono, in a wide range of civil legal matters;and (2) through special initiatives including the Senior Center Initiative (SCI) and the Senior Tax Opportunity program (STOP).

4377 **Chicago Lawyers' Committee for Civil Rights Under Law**
100 N Lasalle Street
Suite 600
Chicago, IL 60602-2403
312-630-9744
FAX: 312-630-1127
e-mail: clccrul@clccrul.com
www.clccrul.org

*Jay Readey, Executive Director*
Promotes and protects civil rights, particularly the civil rights of poor, minority, and disadvantaged people in the social, economic, and political systems of the nation.

4378 **DNA People's Legal Services**
PO Box 306
Window Rock, AZ 86515
928-871-4151
800-789-7287
FAX: 928-871-5036
www.dnalegalservices.org

*Kathy Gallagher, Development Director*
A nonprofit legal aid organization working to protect civil rights, promote tribal sovereignty and alleviate civil legal problems for people who live in poverty in the Southwestern United States.
*1967*

4379 **Disability Rights Education and Defense Fund**
3075 Adeline Street
#210
Berkeley, CA 94703-2219
510-644-2555
800-348-4232
FAX: 510-841-8645
e-mail: info@dredf.org
dredf.org

*Sue Henderson, Executive Director*
Nonprofit organization dedicated to advancing the civil rights of individuals with disabilities through legislation, litigation, informal and formal advocacy and education and training of lawyers, advocates and clients with respect to disability issues. DREDF also provides training, advocacy, technical assistance and referrals for parents of disabled children.

4380 **Disability Rights Texas**
7800 Choal Creek Blvd
Suite 171-E
Austin, TX 78757-1024
512-454-4816
FAX: 512-323-0902
www.disabilityrightstx.org

*Mary Faithfull, Executive Director*
The federally designated legal protection and advocacy agency (P&A) for people with disabilities in Texas. Helps people with disabilities understand and exercise their rights under the law, ensuring their full and equal participation in society.

4381 **Equal Employment Advisory Council**
1501 M Street NW
Suite 400
Washington, DC 20005
202-629-5650
FAX: 202-629-5651
e-mail: info@eeac.org
www.eeac.org

*Jeffrey A Norris, President*
*Nicole McDuffie, Administrator*
Nonprofit employer association founded in 1976 to provide guidance to its member companies on understanding and complying with their EEO and affirmative action obligations.

4382 **Guardianship Services Associates**
41A South Blvd
Oak Park, IL 60302-2777
708-386-5398
FAX: 708-386-5970
e-mail: GSAoakpark@sbcglobal.net

*Robert R. Wohlgemuth, Owner*
Information and counseling on guardianship and its alternatives. Can provide direct assistance in obtaining guardianship for disabled adults in Cook County. Also provides information and direct assistance on durable powers of attorney. Can assume appointment as guardian in selected cases.

**4383 Independence Council for Economic Development**
201 N Forest Avenue
Suite 120
Independence, MO 64050-2753
816-252-5777
FAX: 816-254-1641
e-mail: tlesnak@inedc.biz
www.iced.org

*Tom Lesnak, President*
A non-profit, public/private partnership established for the purpose of supporting and enhancing the economic growth of independence.

**4384 Judge David L Bazelon Center for Mental Health Law**
1101 15th Street NW
Suite 1212
Washington, DC 20005
202-467-5730
FAX: 202-223-0409
e-mail: info@bazelon.org
www.bazelon.org

*Robert Berstein, Executive Director*
A nonprofit organization devoted to improving the lives of people with mental illnesses through changes in policy and law.

**4385 Legal Action Center**
236 Massachusetts Avenue NE
Suite 505
Washington, DC 20002-4980
202-544-5478
FAX: 202-544-5712
e-mail: lacdc@lac.org
www.lac.org

*Paul N Samuels, Director/President*
The only non-profit law and policy organization in the United States whose sole mission is to fight discrimination against people with histories of addiction, HIV/AIDS, or criminal records, and to advocate for sound public policies in these areas.

**4386 Legal Center for People with Disabilities& Older People**
455 Sherman Street
Suite 130
Denver, CO 80203
303-722-0300
FAX: 303-722-0720
e-mail: tlcmail@thelegalcenter.org
www.thelegalcenter.org

*Mary Anne Harvey, Executive Director*
*Randy Chapman, Legal Services Director*
Protects and promotes the rights of people with disabilities and older people in Colorado through direct legal representation, advocacy, education and legislative analysis.

**4387 Legislative Handbook for Parents**
NAPVI
PO Box 317
Watertown, MA 02471
617-972-7441
800-562-6265
FAX: 617-972-7444
e-mail: napvi@perkins.org
www.napvi.org

*Susan LaVenture, Executive Director*
A helpful publication for parents who make direct contact with public officials on behalf of their children. Sample letters, do's-and-dont's, and a glossary of legislative terms are some of the useful topics that are contained in this manual. *$5.50*
*24 pages Paperback*

**4388 NHeLP**
3701 Wilshire Blvd
Suite 750
Los Angeles, CA 90010
310-204-6010
FAX: 213-368-0774
e-mail: nhelp@healthlaw.org
www.healthlaw.org

*Abbi Coursolle, Staff Attorney*
*Kimberly Lewis, Managing Attorney*
A national public interest law firm that seeks to improve health care for America's working and unemployed poor, minorities, the elderly and people with disabilities. NHeLP serves legal services programs, community-based organizations, the private bar, providers and individuals who work to preserve a health care safety net for the millions of uninsured or underinsured low-income people.
*1970*

**4389 National Right to Work Legal Defense and Education Foundation**
8001 Braddock Rd, Ste 600
Springfield, VA 22160-1
703-321-8510
800-336-3600
FAX: 703-321-9319
e-mail: legal@nrtw.org
nrtw.org

*Raymond LaJeunesse, Director*
Provides free legal aid to employees whose human and civil rights are being violated by compulsory unionism abuses.

**4390 Pocket Guide to the ADA: Accessibility Guidelines for Buildings and Facilities**
Wiley Publishing
111 River St
Hoboken, NJ 07030-5774
201-748-6000
FAX: 201-748-6088
e-mail: info@wiley.com
www.wiley.com

*Evan Terry, Editor*
Helps readers understand the facilities requirements of the Americans with Disabilities Act Accessibility Guidelines. Presents the technical requirements for accessible elements and spaces in new construction, alterations and additions. *$30.00*
*198 pages Paperback*
*ISBN 0-470108-70-3*

**4391 Public Law 101-336**
US Department of Justice
950 Pennsylvania Ave NW
Washington, DC 20530-9
800-514-0301
FAX: 202-307-1197
TTY:800-514-0383
www.ada.gov

*Gregory B. Friel, Chief*
*Zita Johnson Betts, Deputy Chief*
*Sally Conway, Deputy Chief*
*James Bostrom, Deputy Chief*
Text of the Americans with Disabilities Act, as enacted on July 26, 1990.

**4392 Questions and Answers: The ADA and Hiring Police Officers**
US Department of Justice
950 Pennsylvania Ave NW
Washington, DC 20530
202-307-0663
800-574-0301
FAX: 202-307-1197
www.ada.gov

*Allison J Nichol, Chief*
Provides information on ADA requirements for interviewing and hiring police officers.
*5 pages*

4393 **REACH/Resource Centers on Independent Living**
1205 Lake St
Fort Worth, TX 76102-4501
817-870-9082
FAX: 817-877-1622
TTY:817-870-9086
e-mail: reachfwt@reachcils.org
www.reachcils.org

*Charlotte A Stewart, Executive Director*
*Miaka Palmer, Independent Living Specialist*
Providing services for people with disabilities so that they are empowered to lead self-directed lives and educating the general public on disability-related topics in order to promote a barrier-free community.

4394 **Strengthening the Roles of Independent Living Centers Through Implementing Legal Service**
Independent Living Research Utilization ILRU
Ste 1000
2323 S Shepherd Dr
Houston, TX 77019-7031
713-520-0232
FAX: 713-520-5785
TTY:713-520-0232
e-mail: ilru@ilru.org
ilru.org

*Lex Frieden, Director*
*Jacquie Brennan, Legal Specialist*
*Linda CoVan, Grant Coordinator*
*Maria Del Bosque, Project Associate*
Featuring the Disability Law Clinic at Community Resources for Independence (CRI) in Northern California.
*10 pages*

4395 **Summaries of Legal Precedents & Law Review**
Through the Looking Glass
3075 Adeline Street
Suite 120
Berkeley, CA 94703
510-848-1005
800-644-2666
FAX: 510-848-4445
e-mail: TLG@lookingglass.org
www.lookingglass.org

*Ella Callow JD, Author*
*Dan Taube JD, Co-Author*
Summarized legal precedents and law review articles relevant to marital custody and child protection situations of parents with diverse disabilities. *$25.00*
*24 pages*

4396 **TASH Connections**
1001 Connecticut Avenue NW
Suite 325
Washington, DC 20036
202-540-9020
FAX: 202-540-9019
e-mail: info@tash.org
www.tash.org

*Carol Quirk, President*
*Barbara Trader, Executive Director*
Received as a member benefit that keeps readers informed on best practices, family concerns, advocacy events and policy changes.
*Quarterly*

## Resources for the Disabled

4397 **ABDA/ABMPP Annual Conference**
American Board of Disability Analysts
4525 Harding Road
Nashville, TN 37205
615-327-2984
FAX: 615-327-9235
e-mail: americanbd@aol.com
www.americandisability.org

*Alexander E. Horowitz, Executive Officer Emeritus*
*Kenneth N. Anchor, Administrative Officer/Editor*
*Gabriel Sella, Education Coordinator*
*Lela Boggs, Business Manager*
February workshop. Workshop leader: Dr. William Tsushima.

4398 **Americans with Disabilities Act Manual**
US Department of Justice
950 Pennsylvania Ave NW
Washington, DC 20530-9
800-514-0301
FAX: 202-307-1197
TTY:800-514-0383
www.ada.gov

*Sally Conway, Director*
*Gregory B. Friel, Chief*
*Zita Johnson Betts, Deputy Chief*
*James Bostrom, Deputy Chief*
An in-depth analysis of the legal and practical implications of the ADA using non-technical language. *$20.00*

4399 **Americans with Disabilities Act: Selected Resources for Deaf**
Gallaudet University Bookstore
800 Florida Ave NE
Washington, DC 20002-3695
202-651-5271
800-621-2736
FAX: 202-651-5477
e-mail: infotech.services@gallaudet.edu
www.gallaudet.edu

*Priscilla O'Donnell, Bookstore Manager*
*Iva Williams, Bookstore Secretary*
*Elaine Vance, Human Resources Director*
*Marteal Pitts, Circulation Coordinator*
This resource identifies programs and publications specific to the ADA and deafness and also lists ADA materials and programs for people with any disability.

4400 **Approaching Equality**
T J Publishers
Ste 108
2544 Tarpley Rd
Carrollton, TX 75006-2288
972-416-0800
800-999-1168
FAX: 301-585-5930
e-mail: TJPubinc@aol.com

*Frank Bowe, Author*
Public education laws guarantee special education for all deaf children, but may find the special education system confusing, or are unsure of their rights under current laws. For anyone with an interest in education, advocacy and the deaf community, this book reviews dramatic developments in education of deaf children, youth and adults since COED's 1988 report, Toward Equality.. *$12.95*
*112 pages*
*ISBN 0-93266 -39-6*

**4401 Assessment of the Feasibility of Contracting with a Nominee Agency**

Mississippi State University
PO Drawer 6189
Mississippi State, MS 39762
662-325-2001
FAX: 662-325-8989
e-mail: rrtc@colled.msstate.edu
www.blind.msstate.edu

*Michelle Capella McDonnall, Interim Director*

Only five State Licensing Agencies currently utilize nominee agreements. This study compared the Pennsylvania BE program with four states that utilize nominee agencies and four states that do not. Results and recommendations compared state and national data from Federal FY 1991-1993. *$20.00*

*152 pages Paperback*

**4402 Bluebook: Explanation of the Contents of the ADA**

Disability Rights Education and Defense Fn
Suite 210
3075 Adeline Street
Berkeley, CA 94703
510-644-2555
800-348-4232
FAX: 510-841-8645
TTY: 510-841-8645
e-mail: info@dredf.org
dredf.org

*Susan Henderson, Executive Director*
*Arlene B. Mayerson, Directing Attorney*
*Hongyu Min, Resource Associate*
*Susan Hauser, Accounting Manager*

Written in narrative form for both professionals and lay people, DREDF's bluebook offers detailed, thorough analysis of all of the law's provisions, encompassing ADA legislative history, the statute and regulations. Available in alternative formats. *$100.00*

*214 pages*

**4403 Can America Afford to Grow Old?**

Brookings Institution
1775 Massachusetts Ave NW
Washington, DC 20036-2103
202-797-6000
FAX: 202-797-6004
e-mail: bibooks@brookings.edu
www.brookings.edu

*Henry J Aaron, Author*
*Barry P Bosworth, Author*
*Gary T Burtless, Author*

Social security laws and regulations. *$8.95*

*144 pages Paperback*
*ISBN 0-815700-43-1*

**4404 Childcare and the ADA**

Eastern Washington University
Rm 223
705 W 1st Ave
Spokane, WA 99201-3909
509-623-4200
FAX: 509-623-4230
e-mail: susan.vanmeter@mail.ewu.edu

*Nancy Ashworth, Director Child Development*
*Allen Barrom, Manager*

Provides information on how childcare providers must comply with the ADA. Eight videotapes plus an instructional manual with examples of situations and problems.. *$85.00*

*Set*

**4405 Common ADA Errors and Omissions in New Construction and Alterations**

US Department of Justice
950 Pennsylvania Ave NW
Washington, DC 20530
202-586-5000
800-574-0301
FAX: 202-307-1197
www.ada.gov

*Allison J Nichol, Chief*

Lists a sampling of common accessibility errors or omissions that have been identified through the Department of Justice's ongoing enforcement efforts.

*13 pages*

**4406 Commonly Asked Questions About Child Care Centers and the Americans with Disabilities Act**

US Department of Justice
950 Pennsylvania Ave NW
Washington, DC 20530
202-586-5000
800-574-0301
FAX: 202-307-1197
www.ada.gov

*Allison J Nichols, Chief*

Explains how the requirements of the ADA apply to Child Care Centers. Also describes some of the Department of justice's ongoing enformcement efforts in the child care area and it provides a resource list on sources of information on the ADA.

*13 pages*

**4407 Commonly Asked Questions About Title III of the ADA**

US Department of Justice
950 Pennsylvania Ave NW
Washington, DC 20530-9
800-574-0301
FAX: 202-307-1197
TTY:800-514-0383
www.ada.gov

*Sally Conway, Director*
*Gregory B. Friel, Chief*
*Zita Johnson Betts, Deputy Chief*
*James Bostrom, Deputy Chief*

A 6-page publication providing information for state and local governments about ADA requirements for ensuring that people with disabilities receive the same services and benefits as provided to others.

*on-line*

**4408 Commonly Asked Questions About the ADA and Law Enforcement**

US Department of Justice
950 Pennsylvania Ave NW
Washington, DC 20530-9
800-574-0301
FAX: 202-307-1197
TTY:800-514-0383
www.ada.gov

*Sally Conway, Director*
*Gregory B. Friel, Chief*
*Zita Johnson Betts, Deputy Chief*
*James Bostrom, Deputy Chief*

A publication explaining ADA requirements for ensuring that people with disabilities receive the same law enforcement services and protections as provided to others.

*13 pages on-line*

**4409 Complying with the Americans with Disabilis Act**
Greenwood Publishing Group
130 Cremona Drive
Santa Barbara, CA 93117
805-968-1911
800-368-6868
FAX: 866-270-3856
e-mail: CustomerService@abc-clio.com
www.greenwood.com

*Don Fresh, Author*
*Peter W Thomas, Co-Author*
A guidebook for management and people with disabilities. This unique guidebook presents a comprehensive analysis of the new Americans with Disabilities Act (ADA), the most significant federal civil rights law in almost 30 years, and its impact on over four million American businesses, state and local governments, nonprofit associations, 87 percent of American's private sector jobs, and 22.7 million working-age people with disabilities. *$117.95*
*280 pages Hardcover*
*ISBN 0-899307-14-0*

**4410 Court-Related Needs of the Elderly and Persons with Disabilities**
Mental Health Commission
2700 Martin Luther King Jr Ave SE
Washington, DC 20032- 2601
202-282-0027
FAX: 202-373-7982
This book features the ground-breaking recommendations from the national Conference on the Court-Related Needs of the Elderly and Persons with Disabilities, funded by the States Justice Institute and co-sponsored by the American Bar Association and National Judicial College. Accompanying the recommendations are detailed commentaries and extensive background research papers organized around issues.. *$20.00*
*276 pages*

**4411 Criminal Law Handbook on Psychiatric & Psychological Evidence & Testimony**
New York City Bar
42 W 44th St
New York, NY 10036-6604
212-382-6600
FAX: 212-768-8116
e-mail: phynes@nycbar.org
www.nycbar.org

*Barbara Berger Opotowsky, Executive Director*
*Alan Rothstein, General Counsel*
*Arlene Bein, Director Membership and Marketing*
*Maria Cilenti, Director Legislative Affairs*
The Criminal Law Handbook provides lawyers, judges and forensic experts with comprehensive, in-depth treatment of admissibility (and limitations on admissibility) of psychiatric and psychological evidence and testimony pertaining to key criminal mental health law standards. *$47.00*

**4412 Department of Justice ADA Mediation Program**
US Department of Justice
950 Pennsylvania Ave NW
Washington, DC 20530
800-574-0301
FAX: 202-307-1197
TTY:800-514-0383
www.ada.gov

*Allison J Nichols, Chief*
Provides an overview of the Department's Mediation Program and examples of successfully mediated cases.
*6 pages*

**4413 Dimensions of State Mental Health Policy**
Greenwood Publishing Group
130 Cremona Drive
Santa Barbara, CA 93117
805-968-1911
800-368-6868
FAX: 866-270-3856
e-mail: CustomerService@abc-clio.com
www.greenwood.com

*Christopher Hudson, Author*
*Arthur J Cox, Co-Author*
Introduces students to the emerging field of state mental health policy, its history, current policies, organizational models and required programming knowledge. *$86.95*
*320 pages Hardcover*
*ISBN 0-275932-52-7*

**4414 Disability Compliance for Higher Education**
LRP Publications
360 Hiatt Dr
Palm Beach Gardens, FL 33418
561-622-6520
FAX: 561-622-0757
e-mail: custserve@lrp.com
www.lrp.com

*Kenneth Kahn, CEO*
Gives guidance on the most difficult issues faced, such as supporting students with psychological disabilities, ensuring accessibility, understanding OCR rulings, and more. *$57.29*
*300 pages*

**4415 Disability Discrimination Law, Evidence and Testimony**
ABA Commission on Mental & Physical Disability Law
740 15th Street NW
Washington, DC 20005
202-662-1570
800-285-2221
FAX: 202-442-3439
e-mail: cmpdl@americanbar.org
www.americanbar.org

*John W Parry JD, Author*
Explains and analyzes key aspects of disability discriminiation law from several different perspectives to guide you through the myriad federal and state statutes, court cases, and regulations. *$105.00*
*694 pages Paperback*
*ISBN 1-604420-12-8*

**4416 Disability Law in the United States**
William Hein & Company
1285 Main St
Buffalo, NY 14209-1987
716-882-2600
800-828-7571
FAX: 716-883-8100
e-mail: mail@wshein.com
www.wshein.com

*Dr Bernard D Reams Jr, Author*
*Peter J McGovern, Co-Author*
*Jon S Schultz, Co-Author*
Offers thousands of pages of information on the laws and legislation affecting the disabled in the United States. Its purpose is to provide a clear and comprehensive mandate to end discrimination against individuals with disabilities and to bring disabled persons into the economic and social midstream of American Life. *$675.00*
*5750 pages*
*ISBN 0-899417-97-3*

**4417 Disability Rights Now**
Disability Rights Education and Defense Fund
Suite 210
3075 Adeline Street
Berkeley, CA 94703
510-644-2555
800-348-4232
FAX: 510-841-8645
TTY: 510-841-8645
e-mail: info@dredf.org
dredf.org

*Susan Henderson, Executive Director*
*Arlene B. Mayerson, Directing Attorney*
*Hongyu Min, Resource Associate*
*Susan Hauser, Accounting Manager*
Free quarterly publication describing the activities of the Disability Rights Education and Defense Fund, available in alternative formats.
*Quarterly*

**4418 Disability Under the Fair Employment & Housing Act: What You Should Know About the Law**
California Department of Fair Employment & Housing
2218 Kausen Drive
Suite 100
Elk Grove, CA 95758
916-478-7251
800-884-1684
FAX: 916-227-2870
e-mail: contact.center@dfeh.ca.gov
www.dfeh.ca.gov

*Phyllis W Cheng, Director*
Intended to highlight and summarize workplace disability laws enforced by the California Department of Fair Employment and Housing. It will familiarize people with the content of these laws, including recent changes and amendments to state statutes and attendent accommodation responsibilities.

**4419 Discrimination is Against the Law**
California Department of Fair Employment & Housing
2218 Kausen Drive
Suite 100
Elk Grove, CA 95758
916-478-7251
800-884-1684
FAX: 916-227-2870
e-mail: phyllis.cheng@dfeh.ca.gov
www.dfeh.ca.gov

*Phyllis Cheng, Director*
Enforces California state laws that prohibit harassment and discrimination in employment, housing, and public accomodations and that provide for pregnancy leave and family and personal leave.

**4420 Education of the Handicapped: Laws, Legislative Histories and Administrative Document**
William S Hein & Co Inc
1285 Main St
Buffalo, NY 14209-1987
716-882-2600
800-828-7571
FAX: 716-883-8100
e-mail: mail@wshein.com
www.wshein.com

*Bernard D Reams Jr, Editor*
Focuses upon Elementary and Secondary Education Act of 1965 and its amendment, Education For All Handicapped Children Act of 1975 and its amendments and acts providing services for the blind, deaf, mentally retarded, etc. *$2950.00*
*55 volumes*
*ISBN 0-899411-57-6*

**4421 ElderLawAnswers.com**
150 Chestnut Street
4th Floor, Box 15
Providence, RI 02903
617-267-9700
866-267-0947
e-mail: support@elderlawanswers.com
www.elderlawanswers.com

*Harry S Margolis, Founder/President*
*Mark Miller, Operations Director*
*Ken Coughlin, Managing Editor*
Supports seniors, their families and their attorneys in achieving their goals by providing

**4422 Employment Discrimination Based on Disability**
California Department of Fair Employment & Housing
2218 Kausen Drive
Suite 100
Elk Grove, CA 95758
916-478-7251
800-884-1684
FAX: 916-227-2870
e-mail: phyllis.cheng@dfeh.ca.gov
www.dfeh.ca.gov

*Phyllis W Cheng, Director*
Prohibits employment discrimination and harassment based on a person's disability or perceived disability. Also requires employers to reasonably accommodate individuals with mental or physical disabilities unless the employer can show that to do so would cause an undue hardship.

**4423 Employment Standards Administration Department of Labor (ESA)**
200 Constitution Ave NW
Washington, DC 20210-1
800-321-6742
TTY:877-889-5627
osha.gov

*David Michaels, Assistant Secretary*
*Jordan Barab, Deputy Assistant Secretary*
*Richard Fairfax, Deputy Assistant Secretary*
*Deborah Berkowitz, Chief of Staff*
Monitors compliance with sub-minimum wage requirements for handicapped workers in sheltered workshops, competitive industry and hospitals and institutions under Section 14 of the Fair Labor Standards Act of 1938.

**4424 Enforcing the ADA: A Status Report from the Department of Justice**
US Department of Justice
950 Pennsylvania Ave NW
Washington, DC 20530
202-307-0663
800-514-0301
FAX: 203-307-1197
www.ada.gov

*Allison J Nichol, Chief*
A brief report issued by the Justice Department each quarter providing timely information about ADA cases and settlements, building codes that meet ADA accessibility standards, and ADA technical assistance activities.

**4425 Federal Laws of the Mentally Handicapped: Laws, Legislative Histories and Admin. Documents**
William Hein & Company
1285 Main St
Buffalo, NY 14209-1987
716-882-2600
800-828-7571
FAX: 716-883-8100
e-mail: mail@wshein.com
www.wshein.com

*Bernard D Reams Jr, Editor*
Chronological compilation of all relevant federal laws dealing with the mentally handicapped along with supporting documen-

tation necessary to create a complete legislative history. *$3500.00*
*42 Volume/Set*
*ISBN 0-899411-06-1*

**4426 Formed Families: Adoption of Children with Handicaps**
Haworth Press
711 Third Avenue
New York, NY 10017
212-216-7800
800-354-1420
FAX: 212-244-1563
e-mail: subscriptions@tandf.co.uk.
www.haworthpress.com

*William Cohen, Owner*
Provides broad coverage of the issues relating to the adoption of children with handicaps. Concerned professionals can find here all the answers about clinical programs, legal issues, estimates of frequency, and important factors related to positive and negative outcomes of these adoptions. *$74.95*
*242 pages Hardcover*
*ISBN 0-866569-14-6*

**4427 Free Appropriate Public Education: The Law and Children with Disabilities**
Love Publishing Company
9101 E Kenyon Avenue
Suite 2200
Denver, CO 80237
303-221-7333
FAX: 303-221-7444
e-mail: lovepublishing@compuserve.com
www.lovepublishing.com

*H Rutherford Turnbull III, Author*
*Matthew J Stowe, Co-Author*
*Nancy E Huerta, Co-Author*
Includes the 2004 IDEA reauthorization and the proposed regulations. This up-to-the-minute resource brings you the most recent developments in legislation, case law techniques, due process, parent participation and much, much more. *$78.00*
*448 pages Hardcover*
*ISBN 0-891083-25-2*

**4428 Health Care Quality Improvement Act of 1986**
William Hein & Company
1285 Main St
Buffalo, NY 14209-1987
716-882-2600
800-828-7571
FAX: 716-883-8100
e-mail: mail@wshein.com
www.wshein.com

*Bernard D Reams Jr, Editor*
In order to encourage more stringent peer review by doctors and hospitals, and to protect reporting physicians and institutions from retaliatory lawsuits, Congress enacted The Health Care Quality Improvement Act. The Act was also intended to address the increasing incidence of medical malpractice and to prevent the ease with which incompetent practitioners moved from state to state. Hardcover. *$125.00*
*721 pages*
*ISBN 0-899416-93-4*

**4429 Housing and Transportation of the Handicapped**
William Hein & Company
1285 Main St
Buffalo, NY 14209-1987
716-882-2600
800-828-7571
FAX: 716-883-8100
e-mail: mail@wshein.com
www.wshein.com

*Bernard D Reams Jr, Editor*
National laws, recognizing the problems encountered by the handicapped in the areas of Housing and Transportation and providing assistance in an effort to surmount those problems, span more than half a century. *$1552.50*
*30000 pages 250 documents*
*ISBN 0-899412-47-5*

**4430 Human Resource Management and the Americans with Disabilities Act**
Greenwood Publishing Group
130 Cremona Drive
Santa Barbara, CA 93117
805-968-1911
800-368-6868
FAX: 866-270-3856
e-mail: CustomerService@abc-clio.com
www.greenwood.com

*John G Veres, Author*
*Ronald R Sims, Co-Author*
Concrete advice for human resource professionals on how to cope with the vague, often obscure provisions of the Americans with Disabilities Act. *$107.95*
*232 pages Hardcover*
*ISBN 0-899308-57-9*

**4431 International Handbook on Mental Health Policy**
Greenwood Publishing Group
130 Cremona Drive
Santa Barbara, CA 93117
805-968-1911
800-368-6868
FAX: 866-270-3856
e-mail: CustomerService@abc-clio.com
www.greenwood.com

The first major reference book for academics and practitioners that provides a systematic survey and analysis of mental health policies in twenty representative countries. *$179.95*
*512 pages Hardcover*
*ISBN 0-313275-67-8*

**4432 Knowing Your Rights**
A AR P Fulfillment
601 E St NW
Washington, DC 20049-1
202-434-3525
800-687-2277
FAX: 202-434-3443
TTY: 877-434-7598
e-mail: member@aarp.org
www.aarp.org

*William D. Novelli, CEO*
*Lynn Smith, Director of Human Resources*
Describes how changes in Medicare's reimbursement policies are designed to reduce health care costs and suggests steps that Medicare beneficiaries, their families and friends can take to assure that they continue to receive quality care under the Prospective Payment System.
*19 pages*

**4433 Law Center Newsletter**
Public Interest Law Center of Philadelphia
1709 Benjamin Franklin Parkway
United Way Building
Philadelphia, PA 19103
215-627-7100
FAX: 215-627-3183
e-mail: general@pilcop.org
www.pilcop.org

*Jennifer R. Clarke, Executive Director*
*Latrice Brooks, Legal Secretary*
*James Eiseman Jr., Senior Attorney*
*Taylor Goodman, Development Director*
Information on mental health, foster care and public education. Provides all updates concerning the law in these areas.

**4434 Legal Center for People with Disabilities& Older People**
Ste 130
455 Sherman St
Denver, CO 80203
303-722-0300
800-288-1376
FAX: 303-722-0720
TTY: 303-722-3619
e-mail: tlcmail@thelegalcenter.org
www.thelegalcenter.org

*Randy Chapman, Director of Legal Services*
*Mary Anne Harvey, Executive Director*
*Peter Lindquist, President*
*John R. Posthumus, Vice President*
Uses the legal system to protect and promote the rights of people with disabilities and older people in Colorado through direct legal representation, advocacy, education and legislative analysis. The Legal Center is Colorado's Protection and Advocacy System. We are also the State Ombudsman for nursing homes and assisted living facilities. Call for a free publications and products list.

**4435 Legal Right: The Guide for Deaf and Hard of Hearing People**
National Association of the Deaf
8630 Fenton Street
Suite 820
Silver Spring, MD 20910- 3819
301-587-1788
FAX: 301-587-1791
TTY:301-587-1789
www.nad.org

*Howard A. Rosenblum, Chief Executive Officer*
*Shane H. Feldman, Chief Operating Officer*
*Allison Rice, Coordinator*
*Thomas Wells, Finance Director*
This revised fifth edition is in easy-to-understand language, offering the latest state and federal statues and administrative procedures that prohibit discrimination against the deaf, hard of hearing and other physically challenged people. *$32.50*
*264 pages Paperback*
*ISBN 1-563680-00-9*

**4436 Legal Rights of Persons with Disabilities**
LRP Publications
360 Hiatt Dr
Palm Beach Gardens, FL 33418-7106
561-622-6520
800-341-7874
FAX: 561-622-0757
e-mail: custserve@lrp.com
www.lrp.com

*Kenneth Kahn, CEO*
Shows what is required, permitted and guaranteed by federal disability laws-including the ADA, Section 504 of the Rehabilitation Act and the IDEA. Explores the boundaries of accceptable behavior under disability laws and provides guidelines to help clients fulfill their legal obligations. *$365.00*
*2722 pages*

**4437 Legislative Network for Nurses**
Business Publishers
2222 Sedwick Drive
Durham, NC 27713
800-223-8720
FAX: 800-508-2592
e-mail: custserv@bpinews.com
www.bpinews.com

Provides up-to-date information on the nursing shortage, nurse training programs, AIDS and Hepatitis B, unionization, registered care technologies, compensation, child care, home health care staffing and much more. *$286.00*
*8 pages Newsl./BiMonth*

**4438 Loving Justice**
Exceptional Parent Library
P.O.Box 1807
Englewood Cliffs, NJ 7632-1207
201-947-6000
800-535-1910
FAX: 201-947-9376
e-mail: eplibrary@aol.com
www.eplibrary.com
How the Americans with Disabilities Act affects religious institutions, including congregations, hospitals, nursing homes, seminaries, universities and more.OUT OF ORDER *$10.95*

**4439 Making News: How to Get News Coverage of Disability Rights Issues**
Advocado Press
PO Box 406781
Louisville, KY 40204
888-739-1920
FAX: 502-899-9562
e-mail: contact145@avocadopress.org
www.advocadopress.org

*Tari Susan Hartman, Author*
*Mary Johnson, Co-Author*
This book gives examples and tips on how to fight back and get on the front pages, lead the newscasts and influence public debate. *$10.95*
*165 pages Paperback*
*ISBN 0-962706-43-4*

**4440 Medicare and Medicaid Patient and Program Protection Act of 1987**
William Hein & Company
1285 Main St
Buffalo, NY 14209-1987
716-882-2600
800-828-7571
FAX: 716-883-8100
e-mail: mail@wshein.com
www.wshein.com

*Bernard D Reams Jr, Editor*
Enables the HHS to protect patients and federal health care programs from censured practitioners. The Act broadens the authority of HHS to exclude practitioners from Medicare and Medicaid programs; strengthens the monetary penalities HHS may impose on violators; provides for criminal penalties in certain cases; and requires states to inform HHÆregarding sanctions against health care providers. *$195.00*
*3 Volumes*
*ISBN 0-899416-95-0*

**4441 Mental & Physical Disability Law Reporter**
American Bar Association
9th Fl
740 15th St NW
Washington, DC 20005-1019
202-662-1570
800-285-2221
FAX: 202-442-3439
e-mail: cmpdl@abanet.org
www.abanet.org

*John W Parry, Executive Director*
*Amy L. Allbright, Director*
*Janet Jackson, Director*
*Bill Pritchard, Executive Assistant to the Director*
Contains over 2,000 summanes per year of federal and state court decisions and legislation that affect persons with mental and physical disabilities. Includes bylined articles by experts in the field regarding disability law developments and trends. *$384.00*
*350+ pages BiMonthly*

**4442 Mental Disabilities and the Americans with Disabilities Act**
Greenwood Publishing Group
130 Cremona Drive
Santa Barbara, CA 93117
805-968-1911
800-368-6868
FAX: 866-270-3856
e-mail: CustomerService@abc-clio.com
www.greenwood.com

A clear, practical compliance guide, written by a psychologist, to help organizations conform to provisions on mental disabilities in the Americans with Disabilities Act. Hardcover. *$91.95*
*216 pages Hardcover*
*ISBN 0-899308-26-5*

**4443 Mental Disability Law, Evidence and Testimony**
ABA Commission on Mental & Physical Disability Law
9th Fl
740 15th St NW
Washington, DC 20005-1019
202-662-1000
800-285-2221
www.abanet.org

*Wm. T. Robinson III, President*
*Janet Jackson, Director*
*Bill Pritchard, Executive Assistant to the Director*
*Laura Banish, Special Presidential Assistant*
Provides a comprehensive analysis of federal and state statues and case law with a disability discrimination focus. *$95.00*
*491 pages Paperback*
*ISBN 1-590318-32-3*

**4444 Mental Health Law News**
Interwood Publications
3 E Interwood Pl
Cincinnati, OH 45220-1821
513-221-3715

*Frank Bardack, Marketing Director/Editor*
Mental health case law summaries - malpractice, patient rights, discrimination, alcoholism, guardianship, negligence, professional liability, commitment, drug dependency and conservatorship. *$99.00*
*6 pages Monthly Nwsltr*
*ISSN 0889-01 0*

**4445 Mental Health Law Reporter**
Business Publishers
Ste 200
2601 University Blvd W
Silver Spring, MD 20902- 1995
240-514-0600
800-274-6737
FAX: 301-587-1081
e-mail: custserv@bpinews.com
www.bpinews.com

*Leonard A Eiserer, Publisher*
*Jeremy Bond, Editor MHLR*
*Bob Grupe, Editor MHLR*
*Adam Goldstein, President*
MHLR brings you the most timely, focused and thorough information on the legal issues that concern mental health practitioners in mental health litigation. Topics include: malpractice litigation, patient-therapist confidentiality, sexual victimization of patients, the insanity defense, social security administrative case law and much more.. *$286.00*
*8 pages Monthly*

**4446 Mental and Physical Disability Law Reporter**
American Bar Association
740 15th Street NW
Washington, DC 20005-1019
202-662-1000
800-285-2221
e-mail: service@americanbar.org
www.americanbar.org

*Wm T Robinson III, President*
The only periodical that comprehensively covers civil and criminal mental disability law and disability discrimination law. *$ 324.00*
*150+ pages Bimonthly*

**4447 Mentally Disabled and the Law**
William S Hein & Company
1285 Main St
Buffalo, NY 14209-1987
716-882-2600
800-828-7571
FAX: 716-883-8100
e-mail: mail@wshein.com
www.wshein.com

*Samuel Brakel, Author*
*John Parry, Co-Author*
*Barbara A Weiner, Co-Author*
Chapters retained from 1961 and 1971 editions have been substantially rewritten. Two subjects-sterilization and sexual psychopathy-have been integrated into chapters on family law. Three new chapters on treatment rights, provider-patient relationship and rights of mentally disabled persons in the community. Sixteen new tables supplement the existing revised 41. *$92.00*
*845 pages*
*ISBN 0-910059-05-5*

**4448 Myths and Facts**
US Department of Justice
950 Pennsylvania Ave NW
Washington, DC 20530-9
202-586-5000
800-514-0301
FAX: 202-307-1197
TTY: 800-514-0383
www.ada.gov

*Gregory B. Friel, Chief*
*Zita Johnson Betts, Deputy Chief*
*Sally Conway, Deputy Chief*
*James Bostrom, Deputy Chief*
A 3-page publication dispelling some common misconceptions about the ADA's requirements and implementation.

**4449 NAD Broadcaster**
National Association of the Deaf
8630 Fenton Street
Suite 820
Silver Spring, MD 20910- 3819
301-587-1788
FAX: 301-587-1791
TTY:301-587-1789
e-mail: nad.info@nad.org
www.nad.org

*Howard A. Rosenblum, Chief Executive Officer*
*Shane H. Feldman, Chief Operating Officer*
*Donna Morris, Member and Donor Relations Specialist*
*Allison Rice, Coordinator*
National newspaper published 11 times a year by the nation's largest organization safeguarding the accessbility and civil rights of 28 million deaf and hard of hearing Americans in education, employment, health care, and telecommunications. Membership: individual $30 per year. *$7.00*

**4450 No Longer Disabled: the Federal Courts & the Politics of Social Security Disability**
Greenwood Publishing Group
130 Cremona Drive
Santa Barbara, CA 93117
805-968-1911
800-368-6868
FAX: 866-270-3856
e-mail: CustomerService@abc-clio.com
www.greenwood.com

This book is a case study of judicial policy making. It focuses on the role of adjudication in the making and refining of federal policy. *$107.95*
*208 pages Hardcover*
*ISBN 0-313254-24-9*

**4451 Nolo's Guide to Social Security Disability Getting and Keeping Your Benefits**

NOLO
950 Parker St
Berkeley, CA 94710-2524
800-955-4775
FAX: 800-645-0895
www.nolo.com

*David Morton, Author*

This guide demystifies the program and tells you everything you need to know about qualifying and applying for benefits, maintaining your benefits, and appealing the denial of a claim. *$25.49*

*512 pages paperback*

*ISBN 1-413311-04-4*

**4452 Opening the Courthouse Door: An ADA Access Guide for State Courts**

American Bar Association
740 15th Street NW
Washington, DC 20005-1019
202-662-1000
e-mail: service@americanbar.org
www.americanbar.org

*Wm T Robinson III, President*

Practical step-by-step guide walks the reader through the courthouse and court process, presenting a menu of straightforawrd access ideas to enhance communications in court, make the facility more accessbile, and nodify rules and procedures. *$12.00*

*78 pages*

**4453 PAL News**

Parent Professional Advocacy League
45 Bromfield St
Boston, MA 02108-4106
866-815-8122
FAX: 617-542-7832
e-mail: info@ppal.net
www.ppal.net

*Lisa Lambert, Executive Director*
*Deborah A. Fauntleroy, Associate Director*
*Meri Viano, Senior Regional Manager*
*Chantell Albert, Outreach Coordinator*

Parent/Professional Advocacy Leage (PPAL) is an organization that promotes a strong voice for families of children and adolescents with mental health needs. PAL advocates for supports, treatment and policies that enable families to live in their communities in an environment of stability and respect.

*Quarterly*

**4454 Power of Attorney for Health Care**

Center for Public Representation
P.O.Box 260049
Madison, WI 53726-49
608-251-4008
800-369-0388
FAX: 606-251-1263

Discusses Wisconsin law regarding medical decisions, the Cruzan case and ethical considerations in addition to legal implications and advantages of this document. Book tells how to create a personalized Power of Attorney document, including language for the special provisions portion. *$49.95*

*132 pages*

*ISBN 0-93262 -38-0*

**4455 Title II & III Regulation Amendment Regarding Detectable Warnings**

U S Department of Justice
950 Pennsylvania Ave NW
Washington, DC 20530-9
202-646-5095
800-514-0301
FAX: 202-307-1197
TTY: 800-514-0383
www.ada.gov

*Gregory B. Friel, Chief*
*Zita Johnson Betts, Deputy Chief*
*Sally Conway, Deputy Chief*
*James Bostrom, Deputy Chief*

This document suspends the requirements for detectable warnings at curb ramps, hazardous vehicular areas, and reflecting pools.

**4456 Title II Complaint Form**

US Department of Justice
950 Pennsylvania Ave NW
Washington, DC 20530
202-307-0663
800-514-0301
FAX: 202-307-1197
www.ada.gov

*Allison J Nichol, Chief*

Standard form for filing a complaint under title II of the ADA or section 504 of the Rehabilitation Act of 1973, which prohibit discrimination on the basis of disability by State and local governments and by recipients of federal financial assistance.

**4457 Title II Highlights**

US Department of Justice
950 Pennsylvania Ave NW
Washington, DC 20530
202-307-0663
800-514-0383
FAX: 202-307-1197
www.ada.gov

*Allison J Nichol, Chief*

Outline of the key requirements of the ADA for State and local governments. Provides detailed information in bullet format for quick reference.

*8 pages*

**4458 Title III Technical Assistance Manual and Supplement**

U S Department of Justice
950 Pennsylvania Ave NW
Washington, DC 20530
202-307-0663
800-574-0301
FAX: 202-307-1197
www.ada.gov

*Allison J Nichol, Chief*

Explains in lay terms what businesses and non-profit agencies must do to ensure access to their goods, services, and facilities.

*83 pages*

**4459 Toward Independence**

National Council on Disability
81 E. Main Street
Xenia, OH 45385
937-376-3996
FAX: 937-376-2046
e-mail: info@ti-inc.org
www.ti-inc.org

*Robert Archer, Executive Director*
*Sandra Baldwin, Health Services Manager*
*Maggie Bell, Finance Director*
*Cindy Dean, Program Director*

A 1986 report to the U.S. Congress on the federal laws and programs serving people with disabilities, and recommendations for legislation.

**4460 UCP Washington Wire**

United Cerebral Palsy
1660 L Street NW 700
Washington, DC 20036-1601
202-776-0406
800-872-5827
FAX: 202-776-0414
e-mail: info@ucp.org
www.ucp.org

*Stephen Bennett, President/CEO*

Publication that provides a comprehensive source of information on federal legislation, agency regulations, court decisions and other issues of interest to the disability community.

*weekly*

**4461 US Department of Health and Human Services Office for Civil Rights**
200 Independence Ave SW
Room 509F, HHH Building
Washington, DC 20201
202-619-0403
800-368-1019
TTY:800-537-7697
e-mail: ocrmail@hhs.gov
www.hhs.gov

*Georgina Verdugo, Director*
The Department's civil rights and health privacy law enforcement agency, OCR investigates complaints, enforces rights, and promulgates regulations, develops policy and provides technical assistance and public education to ensure understanding of and compliance with non-discrimination and health information privacy laws.

**4462 US Department of Labor**
200 Constitution Ave NW
Washington, DC 20210
866-487-2635
e-mail: talktosolis@dol.gov
www.dol.gov

*Hilda L Solis, Secretary of Labor*
*Seth D Harris, Deputy Secretary*
To foster, promote, and develop the welfare of the wage earners, job seekers, and retirees of the United States; improve working conditions, advance opportunities for profitable employment; and assure work-related benefits and rights.

**4463 US Department of Labor Office of Federal Contract Compliance Programs**
230 S Dearborn Street
Room 570
Chicago, IL 60604
312-596-7010
FAX: 312-596-7044
e-mail: OFCCP-MW-PreAward@dol.gov
www.dol.gov

*Melissa L Speer, Interim Regional Director*
To enforce, for the benefit of job seekers and wage earners, the contractual promise of affirmative action and equal employment opportunity required of those who do business with the Federal government.

**4464 University Legal Services AT Program**
Ste 130
220 i St NE
Washington, DC 20002-4364
202-547-4747
877-221-4638
FAX: 202-547-2083
TTY: 202-547-2657
e-mail: atpdc@uls-dc.org
dcpanda.org

*Jane Brown, Executive Director*
Designed to empower individuals with disabilities; to promote consumer involvement and advocacy, and provide information, referral and training as they relate to accessing assistive technology services and devices; and to identify and improve access to funding resources..

**4465 Washington Watch**
United Cerebral Palsy Association
Ste 700
1660 L St NW
Washington, DC 20036-5638
202-776-0406
800-872-5827
FAX: 202-776-0414
TTY: 202-973-7197
e-mail: info@ucp.org
www.ucp.org

*Ted Bertoron, Director*
Dependable, timely information on national legislative and regulatory issues affecting people with disabilities and their families.
*$25.00*
*4 pages BiWeekly*

**4466 William S Hein & Company**
1285 Main St
Buffalo, NY 14209-1987
716-882-2600
800-828-7571
FAX: 716-883-8100
e-mail: mail@wshein.com
www.wshein.com

*Kevin Marmion, President*
Offers a catalog of periodicals, publications and reprints, microforms and government publications on medical, handicapped and health law.

# Libraries & Research Centers

## Alabama

**4467 Alabama Institute for Deaf and Blind Library and Resource Center**
P.O.Box 698
205 East South Street
Talladega, AL 35160
256-761-3207
FAX: 256-761-3352
aidb.org

*Terry Graham, President*
*Paul Millard, Principal*
*Sara McConatha, Director, Elementary Department*
*Dennis Gilliam, Director, High School Department*
Book collection includes discs, cassettes, braille and large print. Also closed-circuit TV and magnifiers. Offers braille production and binding.

**4468 Alabama Radio Reading Service Network(ARRS)**
650 11th St S
Birmingham, AL 35233-1
205-934-2606
800-444-9246
FAX: 205-934-5075
wbhm.org

*Audrey Atkins, Marketing Manager*
*Mary Hendley, Development Director*
*Theresa Kidd, Office Associate*
*Michael Krall, Program Director*
Services and readings are broadcast over a subcarrier service of public radio WBHM. This is a statewide service devoted to Alabama's blind and handicapped community.

**4469 Alabama Regional Library for the Blind and Physically Handicapped**
Alabama Public Library Service
6030 Monticello Dr
Montgomery, AL 36130-1
334-213-3900
800-392-5671
FAX: 334-213-3993
e-mail: revans@apls.state.al.us
www.apls.state.al.us

*Rebecca Mitchell, Executive Director*
Recreational reading in special format for persons unable to use standard print. Reference materials offered include materials on blindness and other handicaps, films, local subjects and authors.

**4470 Houston-Love Memorial Library**
212 W Burdeshaw St
Dothan, AL 36303-4421
334-793-9767
e-mail: houstonlove@houstonlovelibrary.org
houstonlovelibrary.org

*Steve Roy, Chairman*
*Bettye Forbus, Director*
Offers magnifiers, summer reading programs and more for the blind and physically handicapped. Scanner, software, jaws for Windows.

**4471 Huntsville Subregional Library for the Blind & Physically Handicapped**
915 Monroe St SW
Huntsville, AL 35801-5007
256-532-5940
FAX: 256-532-5994
e-mail: askus@hpl.lib.al.us
www.hpl.lib.al.us

*Regina Cooper, Executive Director*
Talking books for people who are blind or disabled offering reference materials on the blind and other disabilities, large-print photocopier, thermaform duplicator and more..

**4472 Public Library Of Anniston-Calhoun County**
108 E 10th St
Anniston, AL 36201
256-237-8501
publiclibrary.cc
Reference materials on blindness, cassettes, large print books and discs.

**4473 Research for Rett Foundation**
P.O.Box 50347
Mobile, AL 36605-347
251-479-8293
800-422-7388
FAX: 251-479-8293

*Jack Tillman, CEO*
*Anna Luce, Executive Director*
National, not-for-profit, voluntary organization dedicated to raising funds for critical ongoing medical research into Rett Syndrome, hosting medical research symposia, and funding grant applications. Committed to expanding public awareness of and encouraging Rett Syndrome research within the National Institute of Child Health and Human Development. Provides a variety of educational mateials including brochures and fact sheets..

**4474 Technology Assistance for Special Consumers**
1856 Keats Drive
Huntsville, AL 35810-3859
256-859-8300
FAX: 256-859-4332
www.ucptasc.org

*Laura Parks, M.Ed., Assistive Technology Specialist*
*Julie Yockel, M.S., CCC-SLP, AAC Specialist*
*Mark Pepper, STAR Reutilization Specialist*
Provide individuals with disabilities, their families and/or advocates, and associated professionals access to assistive technology devices and services to increase independence at home, school, and work.

**4475 Tuscaloosa Subregional Library for the Blind & Physically Handicapped**
1801 Jack Warner Pkwy
Tuscaloosa, AL 35401-1027
205-345-5820
FAX: 205-752-8300
e-mail: askalibrarian@tuscaloosa-library.org
www.tuscaloosa-library.org

*Mary Elizabeth Harper, Executive Director*
*Vince Bellofatto, Public Relations*
Provide talking books to patrons who are unable to use standard print because of a visual or physical limitation. Deliver playback equipment to qualified patrons. Provides reference and referral service to this special population also.

## Alaska

**4476 Alaska State Library Talking Book Center**
Ste 125
344 W 3rd Ave
Anchorage, AK 99501-2338
907-269-6570
800-776-6566
FAX: 907-269-6580
e-mail: aslanc@alaska.gov
library.state.ak.us/dev/libdev.html

*Stephanie Schott, Library Assistant*
*Beverly Griffin, Library Assistant*
The Alaska State Library Talking Book Center is a cooperative effort between the Library of Congress National Library Service for the Blind and Physically Handicapped and the Alaska State Library to provide print handicapped Alaskans with talking book and Braille service. The Talking Book Center has 55,000 audiobooks that can be checked out to eligible Alaskans whose visual or physical handicap prevents them from reading standard print materials.

## Arizona

**4477 Arizona Braille and Talking Book LibraryArizona State Library**
1030 N 32nd St
Phoenix, AZ 85008-5108
602-255-5578
800-255-5578
FAX: 602-286-0444
e-mail: btbl@lib.az.us
lib.az.us

*Linda Montgomery, Director*
Audio and braille books and magazines, summer reading program, volunteer-produced audio books, audo described, films and more.

**4478 Books for the Blind of Arizona**
Unit A107
6120 E 5th St
Tucson, AZ 85711-2536
602-792-9153
FAX: 520-886-9839

*Betty Evans, Chairperson*
Offers large print photocopier, textbooks, recreational, career, vocational, braille books, talking books, cassettes, large print books and more for the visually impaired K-12, college students and adults..

**4479 Children's Center for Neurodevelopmental Studies**
5430 W Glenn Dr
Glendale, AZ 85301-2628
623-915-0345
FAX: 623-937-5425
e-mail: admin@ccnsaz.org
www.thechildrenscenteraz.org

*Kent Rideout, Executive Director*
*Dawna Sterner, Preschool & Education Information*
*Catherine Orsak, Therapy Information*
*Alicia Bolan, Teaching Staff*
The Center is a non-profit school and therapy center for children with autism and other developmental delays specializing in the use of sensory integration.

**4480 Flagstaff City-Coconino County Public Library**
300 W Aspen Ave
Flagstaff, AZ 86001-5304
928-779-7670
TTY:928-214-2417
www.flagstaffpubliclibrary.org
Reference materials on blindness and other handicaps, braille writer, magnifiers and large-print photocopier. Large-type books, closed captioned videos, adapters and books on tape.

**4481 Fountain Hills Lioness Braille Service**
P.O.Box 18332
Fountain Hills, AZ 85269-8332
480-837-3961

*Jean Hauck, Chairperson*
Braille and large print books on the subjects of recreation, career and vocations, religion, novels and cookbooks for the visually impaired..

**4482 Prescott Public Library**
215 E Goodwin St
Prescott, AZ 86303-3911
928-777-1500
FAX: 928-771-5829
prescottlibrary.info

*Roger Saft, Manager*
*Roger Faft, Assistant Director*
Large print, braille and audio books; magnifiers; text to voice scanner; talking book machine application; toy library for children with special needs; special needs product catalogs; home book delivery; descriptive videos; 43 point PC monitor..

**4483 Special Needs Center/Phoenix Public Library**
1221 N Central Ave
Phoenix, AZ 85004-1867
602-262-4636
TTY:602-254-8205
www.phoenixpubliclibrary.org
Offers large print books and magazines, print/braille books, and braille magazines, Descriptive video services videotapes, several video print enlargers and computer workplace for persons with disabilities.

**4484 World Research Foundation**
41 Bell Rock Plz
Sedona, AZ 86351-8804
928-284-3300
FAX: 928-284-3530
e-mail: info@wrf.org
wrf.org

*Steven A Ross, President*
*LaVerne Boeckmann, Co-Founder*
Large research library of alternative medicine; offers a computer search and printout of specific health issues for a nominal fee.

## Arkansas

**4485 Arkansas Regional Library for the Blind and Physically Handicapped**
900 West Capitol Avenue
Suite 100
Little Rock, AR 72201-3108
501-682-2053
asl.lib.ar.us/aslbph.htm

*J D Hall, Manager of BPH Services*
*Dwain Gordon, Deputy Director*
*Danny Koonce, Public Information Specialist*
*Ruth Hyatt, Manager of Extension Services*
Public library books in recorded or braille format. Popular fiction and nonfiction books for all ages, books and players are on free loan, sent to patrons by mail and may be returned postage free. Anyone who cannot see well enough to read regular print with glasses on or who has a disability that makes it difficult to hold a book or turn the pages is eligible.

**4486 Arkansas School for the Blind**
P.O.Box 668
Little Rock, AR 72203-668
501-296-1810
800-362-4451
FAX: 501-296-1831
arkansasschoolfortheblind.org

*Douglas Watson, Chairperson*
*Sharon Berry, Elementary Principal*
*Teresa Doan, Special Education Supervisor*
*William Harrison, Technology Director*
Students at the ASB receive a quality education from specially trained instructors of the Visually Impaired in all academic areas. ASB features a comprehensive Music and Art program, as well as extensive extra-curricular activities. ASB is a proud member of the Arkansas Activities Association and The North Central Association of Schools for the Blind.

**4487 Educational Services for the Visually Impaired**
2402 Wildwood Avenue
Suite 112
Sherwood, AR 72120-5085
501-835-5448
FAX: 501-835-6840
e-mail: angylnf@esvi.org
www.esvi.org

*Angyln Young, State Coordinator*
*Cindy Lester, Data Management Specialist*
*Cynthia Kelly, ESVI Office Manager*
Offers textbooks, braille books and more to the visually impaired grades K-12 in the Arizona area.

**4488 Library for the Blind and Physically Handicapped SW Region of Arkansas**
P.O.Box 668
2057 North Jackson St
Magnolia, AR 71754-668
870-234-1991
FAX: 870-234-5077
e-mail: library@cocolib.org
colcnty.lib.ar.us

*Laura Cleveland, Director*
*Dana Thornton, Assistant Director*
*Lisa Lewis, Bookkeeping*
A free library service that serves adults and children who meet the eligiblity requirements, offers free loan of cassette machine and recorded books, which meet the reading preferences of a highly diverse clientele.

**4489 Northwest Ozarks Regional Library for the Blind and Handicapped**
Fayetteville, AR 72701
479-575-2000
www.uark.edu
Offers a summer reading program, closed-circuit TV, magnifiers, braille writers and large print books.

## California

**4490 Braille Institute Library**
741 N Vermont Ave
Los Angeles, CA 90029-3594
323-663-1111
800-808-2555
FAX: 323-663-0867
e-mail: la@brailleinstitute.org
brailleinstitute.org

*Leslie E. Stocker, President*
*Sally H. Jameson, Vice President of Programs and Services*
*Peter A. Mindnich, Executive Vice President*
*Reza Rahman, Vice President of Finance/Chief Financial Officer*
Braille Institute provides an environment of hope and encouragement for people who are blind and visually impaired through integrated educational, social and recreational programs and services.

**4491 Braille Institute Santa Barbara Center**
2031 De La Vina St
Santa Barbara, CA 93105-3895
805-682-6222
800-272-4553
FAX: 805-687-6141
e-mail: sb@brailleinstitute.org
brailleinstitute.org

*Leslie E. Stocker, President*
*Sally H. Jameson, Vice President of Programs and Services*
*Peter A. Mindnich, Executive Vice President*
*Reza Rahman, Vice President of Finance/Chief Financial Officer*
Offers programs, services and information for persons with visual impairments.

**4492 Braille Institute Sight Center**
741 N Vermont Ave
Los Angeles, CA 90029-3594
323-663-1111
800-808-2555
FAX: 323-663-0867
e-mail: la@brailleinstitute.org
brailleinstitute.org

*Sally H. Jameson, Vice President of Programs and Services*
*Leslie E Stocker, President*
*Peter A. Mindnich, Executive Vice President*
*Reza Rahman, Vice President of Finance/Chief Financial Officer*
Offers help, programs, services and information to the blind and visually impaired children and adults.

**4493 Braille and Talking Book Library: California**
P.O. Box 942837
Sacramento, CA 94237-0001
916-654-0640
800-952-5666
www.btbl.ca.gov

*Stacey A. Aldrich, State Librarian*
*Debbie Newton, Bureau Chief, Administrative Services Bureau*
*Phyllis Smith, Manager, Human Resources and Business Services*
*Sharleen Finn, Budget Officer, Fiscal Services*
Free service for eligible Northern California residents.

**4494 California State Library Braille and Talking Book Library**
P.O. Box 942837
Sacramento, CA 94237-0001
916-654-0640
800-952-5666
www.btbl.ca.gov

*Stacey A. Aldrich, State Librarian*
*Debbie Newton, Bureau Chief, Administrative Services Bureau*
*Phyllis Smith, Manager, Human Resources and Business Services*
*Sharleen Finn, Budget Officer, Fiscal Services*
Provides library services to people in Northern California who are unable to read standard print books because of visual or physical disabilities. Braille and talking books, magazines, machines, catalogs and postage are provided free to qualified appicants. The service is conducted by mail.

**4495 Clearinghouse for Specialized Media and Translations**
1430 N St
Ste 3207
Sacramento, CA 95814-5901
916-445-5103
FAX: 916-323-9732
e-mail: csmt@cde.ca.gov
www.cde.ca.gov/re/pn/sm

*Jonn Paris-Salb, Manager*
Provides materials in accessible formats; aural media, braille, large print, digital talking books and electronic media access technology.

**4496 Dental Amalgam Syndrome (DAMS) Newsletter**
725-9 Tramway Ln NE
Albuquerque, NM 87122-1672
505-291-8239
FAX: 505-294-3339
Dedicated to informing the public about the potential risks of mercury in dental amalgam fillings..

**4497 Fresno County Free Library Blind and Handicapped Services**
770 N San Pablo Ave
Fresno, CA 93728-3640
559-488-3217
800-742-1011
e-mail: wendy.eisenberg@fresnolibrary.org
www.fresnolibrary.org/tblb

*Wendy Eisenberg, Manager*
*Laurel Prysiazny, County Librarian*
Magnifiers, home visits, volunteer-produced cassette books, discs and cassettes.

**4498 Glaucoma Research Foundation**
Ste 600
251 Post St
San Francisco, CA 94108-5017
415-986-3162
800-826-6693
FAX: 415-986-3763
e-mail: info@glaucoma.org
glaucoma.org

*Tom Brunner, CEO*
Clinical and laboratory studies of glaucoma. We work to prevent vision loss from glaucoma by investing in innovative research, education and support with the ultimate goal of finding a cure..

**4499 Herrick Health Sciences Library**
Alta Bates Medical Center
2001 Dwight Way
Berkeley, CA 94704-2608
510-204-4444
FAX: 510-204-4091
e-mail: sutterhealth.org
www.altabates.com

*Laurie Bagley, Librarian*
*Carol Hirsch-Butler, Administrator*
Information on rehabilitation, psychiatry and psychoanalysis.

**4500 Kuzell Institute for Arthritis and Infectious Diseases**
Medical Research Institute Of San Francisco
2200 Webster St
San Francisco, CA 94115-1821
415-923-3262
FAX: 415-441-8548

*Lowell S Young, Director*
*Edward Byrd, Owner*
One of seven units comprising the Medical Research Institute of San Francisco that offers basic and applied research in arthritis and related diseases.

**4501 New Beginnings: The Blind Children's Center**
4120 Marathon St
Los Angeles, CA 90029-3584
323-664-2153
800-222-3566
FAX: 323-665-3828
blindchildrenscenter.org

*Midge Horton, Executive Director*
*Muriel Scharf, Director of Development*
*Jennifer Brown, Board President*
*Lisa D. Hansen, Secretary*
The purpose of the Center is to turn initial fears into hope. Helps children and their families become independent by creating a climate of safety and trust. Children learn to develop self confidence and to master a wide range of skills. Services include an infant stimulation program, educational preschool, interdisciplinary assessment services, family services, correspondence program, toll free national hotline and a publication and research service.

**4502 Research & Training Center on Mental Health for Hard of Hearing Persons**
California School of Professional Psychology
Ste 140
6215 Ferris Sq
San Diego, CA 92121-3279
619-282-4443
800-HEA-R619
FAX: 800-642-0266

*Raymond J Trybus, Director*
*Thomas J Goulder, Associate Director*
Funded by the National Institute on Disability and Rehabilitation Research, this training center aims to address issues of psychological relevance to persons who are hard of hearing or late deafened (as distinct from prelingually, culturally deaf persons). Also serves as information clearinghouse on this topic.

**4503 Rosalind Russell Medical Research Center for Arthritis**
Suite 607
350 Parnassus Ave
San Francisco, CA 94117
415-476-1141
FAX: 415-476-3526
e-mail: rrac@medicine.ucsf.edu
http://www.rosalindrussellcenter.ucsf.edu/

*Ephraim P Engleman, MD, Center Director*
*David Wofsy, MD, Associate Director*
*Paula R. Gambs, Chair*
*Christine Abele, Volunteer*
Arthritis research and its probable causes.

**4504 San Francisco Public Library for the Blindand Print Handicapped**
100 Larkin St
San Francisco, CA 94102-4705
415-557-4400
FAX: 415-557-4252
TTY:415-557-4433
e-mail: webmail@sfpl.org
www.sfpl.org

*Toni Cordova, Chief of Communications, Programs and Partnerships*
*Toni Bernardi, Chief of Children & Youth Services*
*Laura Lent, Chief of Collections & Technical Services*
*Edward Melton, Chief of Branches*
Foreign-language books on cassette, children's books on cassettes and more.

**4505 San Jose State University Library**
150 E San Fernando St
San Jose, CA 95112-3580
408-808-2000
FAX: 408-924-1118
e-mail: office@wahoo.sjsu.edu
www.sjlibrary.org

*Don W Kassing, President*
*Jane Light, Library/Executive Director*
Information on physical disabilities, accessibility and learning disabilities.

## Colorado

**4506 AMC Cancer Research Center**
3401 Quebec Street
Suite 3200
Denver, CO 80207
303-233-6501
800-321-1557
FAX: 303-239-3400
e-mail: contactus@amc.org
amc.org

*Alice Norton, Executive Director & Chief Financial Officer*
*Nancy Stewart, VP of Community Relations*
*Angela DellaSalle, Senior Development Officer*
*Brianna Firestone, Communications and Marketing Manager*
Provides trained counselors who provide understanding and support for cancer patients; information and referral services; and screening programs.

**4507 Boulder Public Library**
1001 Arapahoe Ave
Boulder, CO 80302-6015
303-441-3100
e-mail: feedback@boulder.lib.co.us
www.boulder.lib.co.us

*Melinda Mattling, Manager*
*Priscilla Hudson, Manager*
Offers braille books, cassettes, talking books, large print photocopier, large print books and more for the visually impaired.

**4508 Colorado Talking Book Library**
180 Sheridan Blvd
Denver, CO 80226-8101
303-727-9277
800-685-2136
FAX: 303-727-9281
e-mail: ctbl.info@cde.state.co.us
www.myctbl.org

*Debbie Macleod, Executive Director*
Provides free library service to Coloradans of all ages who are unable to read standard print due to visual, physical or learning disabilities whether permanent or temporary. Provides audio, braille and large-print books and magazines.

4509 **National Jewish Medical & Research Center**
1400 Jackson St
Denver, CO 80206-2762
303-388-4461
877-225-5654
e-mail: allstetterw@njc.org
www.njc.org

*Russell P Bowler, MD, PhD, President/CEO*
*Nancy Hafer, Fellowship Coordinator*
The only medical center in the country whose research and patient care resources are dedicated to respiratory and immunologic diseases.

## Connecticut

4510 **Connecticut Braille Association**
107 Vanderbilt Ave
West Hartford, CT 6110-1514
860-953-4445
FAX: 860-378-0205

*Nick Martino, Owner*
Offers textbooks, cassettes, large print books, braille books and more.

4511 **Connecticut Library for the Blind and Physically Handicapped**
231 Capitol Avenue
Hartford, CT 06106-1569
860-757-6500
860-866-4478
FAX: 860-721-2056
e-mail: ctaylor@cslib.org
www.cslib.org

*Kendall F Wiggin, Librarian*
*Mollie Keller, Librarian*
*Bob Harris, Librarian*
*John Barry, Librarian*
Network library of the National Library Service for the Blind and Physically Handicapped, Library of Congress. Lends books and magazines in Braille or recorded formats along with the necessary playback equipment, free, for any Connecticut adult or child who is unable to read regular print due to a visual or physical disability. All materials are mailed to and from library patrons by postage-free mail

4512 **Connecticut State Library**
Connecticut State Government
231 Capitol Ave
Hartford, CT 06106-1569
860-757-6500
866-866-4478
FAX: 860-721-2056
e-mail: isref@cslib.org
www.cslib.org

*Kendall F Wiggin, Librarian*
*Mollie Keller, Librarian*
*Bob Harris, Librarian*
*John Barry, Librarian*
Discs, cassettes, braille, reference materials on blindness and other handicaps, closed-circuit TV and large-print photocopier.

4513 **Connecticut Tech Act Project: Connecticut Department of Social Services**
Bureau of Rehabilitations Services
25 Sigourney St
11th Floor
Hartford, CT 06106-5041
860-424-4881
800-537-2549
FAX: 860-424-4850
TTY: 860-424-4839
e-mail: arlene.lugo@ct.gov
www.cttechact.com

*Arlene Lugo, Program Director*
Single point of entry, advocacy, information and referral, peer counseling, and access to objective expert advice and consultation for people with disabilities.

4514 **Prevent Blindness Connecticut**
101 Whitney Avenue
New Haven, CT 06510
203-722-4653
800-850-2020
FAX: 203-722-4691
e-mail: info@preventblindnesstristate.org
http://tristate.preventblindness.org/

*Kathryn Garre-Ayars, President and CEO*
*Tahesha Bryan, Administrative Assistant*
*Naomi Hayner, Connecticut Program Manager*
*Maria Giarratana, Grants Manager*
The mission of Prevent Blindness Connecticut is to save sight and prevent blindness through eye screenings, education, safety activities and research.

4515 **Yale University: Vision Research Center**
310 Cedar St, LH 108
PO Box 208023
New Haven, CT 06520- 8023
203-785-2759
800-395-7949
FAX: 203-785-7303
e-mail: pamela.berkheiser@yale.edu
yalepath.org

*George Shafranov, Chairman*
*Pam Burkheiser, Manager*
Vision including studies on growth and development.

## Delaware

4516 **Delaware Assistive Technology Initiative (DATI)**
Alfred I. duPont Hospital for Children
1600 Rockland Road
PO Box 269
Wilmington, DE 19899-0269
302-651-6790
800-870-3284
FAX: 302-651-6793
TTY: 302-651-6794
e-mail: dati@asel.udel.edu
www.dati.org

*Beth Mineo Mollica, Director*
*Sonja Rathel, Project Coordinator*
The Delaware Assistive Technology Initiative (DATI) connects Delawareans who have disabilities with the tools they need in order to learn, work, play and participate in community life safely and independently. DATI services include: Equipment demonstration centers in eah county; no-cost, short-term equipment loans that let you try before you buy; Equipment Exchange Program; AT workshops and other training sessions; advocacy for improved AT access policies and funding and several more.

4517 **Delaware Library for the Blind and Physically Handicapped**
Government
121 Duke of York Street
Dover, DE 19901-7430
302-739-4748
800-282-8676
FAX: 302-739-6787
e-mail: debph@lib.de.us
http://libraries.delaware.gov/default.shtml

*Dr. Annie E. Norman, Director*
*Sonja Brown, Administrative Specialist*
*Beth-Ann Ryan, Deputy Director*
*Diann Colose, Administrative Librarian*
Books on cassette and playback equipment are provided to patrons who are unable to read regular printed books.

**4518 Elwyn Delaware**
321 E 11th St
Wilmington, DE 19801-3499
302-658-8860
FAX: 302-654-5815
e-mail: info@elwyn.org
www.elwyn.org

*Vicki Haschak, Contact*
*Kendra Johnson, Contact*
Provides work training, job placement and supported employment, and elder care services.

## District of Columbia

**4519 District of Columbia Public Library: Services for the Deaf Community**
District of Columbia Public Library
901 G St NW, Room 215
Washington, DC 20001-4531
202-727-2142
FAX: 202-727-0322
TTY:202-559-5368
e-mail: library_deaf_dc@yahoo.com
dclibrary.org

*Venetia Demson, Chief Adaptive Services*
*Janice Roseu, Library for the Deaf Community*
Offers reference services through videophone, signers for library programs, sign language classes, information about deafness, print and non-print materials for persons who have hearing disabilities. Book talks on deaf culture and American Sign Language story hours for kids, and Saturday sessions on employment-related skills are offered. Videophones for public use are available at the MLK Library.

**4520 District of Columbia Regional Library for the Blind and Physically Handicapped**
901 G St NW
Washington, DC 20001-4531
202-727-2142
FAX: 202-727-1129
TTY:202-727-2145
e-mail: lbphb_2000@yahoo.com
www.dclibrary.org

*Ginnie Cooper, Chief Librarian*
*Eric Coard, Chief Business Officer*
*Barbara Kirven, Director of Human Resources*
*Joi Mecks, Director of Communications*
Regional library/RPH is network library in the Library of Congress, National Library Services for the Blind and Physically Handicapped.

**4521 Georgetown University Center for Child and Human Development**
P.O.Box 571485
Washington, DC 20057-1485
202-687-5000
FAX: 202-687-8899
TTY:202-687-5000
e-mail: gucdc@georgetown.edu
gucchd.georgetown.edu

*Phyllis R Magrab, Phd, Director*
*John J DeGioia, President*
Established over four decades ago to improve the quality of life for all children and youth, especially those with, or at risk for, special needs and their families. Located in the nation's capital, this center both directly serves vulnerable children and their families, as well as influences local, state, national and international programs and policy.

**4522 National Institute on Disability and Rehabilitation Research**
U S Department of Education
400 Maryland Ave SW
Washington, DC 20202-1
202-401-2000
800-872-5327
FAX: 202-401-0689
TTY: 800-437-0833
e-mail: customerservice@inet.ed.gov
ed.gov

*Theresa S Shaw, COO*
*Grover J Whitehurst, Director Institute of Education*
*Margaret Spellings, CEO*
A national leader in sponsoring research. Mission is to generate, disseminate and promote new knowledge to improve the options available to disabled persons.

## Florida

**4523 Brevard County Talking Books Library**
Brevard County Libraries
308 Forrest Ave
Cocoa, FL 32922-7723
321-633-1810
FAX: 321-633-1964
TTY:321-633-1838
e-mail: kbriley@brev.org
brev.org

*Camille Johnson, Manager*
*Catherine J Schweinsburg, Library Services Director*
Subregional library for the blind and physically handicapped, assistive reading devices collection, reference materials on blindness and other handicaps, descriptive videos, CCTV, phonic ear, reading edge and LOUD-R assistive listening devices available.

**4524 Broward County Talking Book Library**
100 S Andrews Ave
Fort Lauderdale, FL 33301-1830
954-357-7444
FAX: 954-357-5548
browardlibrary.org

*Robert E. Cannon, Director*
*Carolyn Kayne, Manager*
Reference materials on blindness and other handicaps, films, closed-circuit TV, discs, cassettes and a book discussion group is offered.

**4525 Dade County Talking Book Library**
Miami Dade Public Library System
101 West Flagler Street
Miami, FL 33130
305-375-2665
800-451-9544
FAX: 305-757-8401
e-mail: talkingbooks@mdpls.org
www.mdpls.org

*Raymond Sanpiago, Executive Director*
A free Outreach Service of the Miami-Dade Public Library System. A network library, or subregional, of the National Library Service for the Blind and Physically Handicapped, Library of Congress, and of the Florida Bureau of Braille and Talking Books Library Service.

**4526 Florida Division of Blind Services**
Regional Library
101 West Flagler Street
Daytona Beach, FL 32114-2804
386-239-6000
800-226-6075
FAX: 386-239-6069
e-mail: mike-gunde@dbs.doe.state.fl.us
dbs.myflorida.com

*Mike Gunde, Manager*
*Susan Roberts, Bureau Chief*

Discs, cassettes, closed-circuit TV, large-print photocopier, films, children's books on cassettes and more.

**4527 Florida Instructional Materials Center forthe Visually Impaired (FIMC-VI)**
4210 W Bay Villa Ave
Tampa, FL 33611-1206
813-837-7826
800-282-9193
FAX: 813-837-7979
e-mail: sdalton@fimcvi.org
www.fimcvi.org

*Nick Carullo, Manager*
*Jeffrey Fitterman, Technology Specialist*
*Donna Ross, Resource Teacher*
*Kay Ratzlaff, Coordinator*
Operates a clearinghouse depository and production center for braille, large print and digital texts. Provides assistance in assessment of materials and specialized apparatus, organizes and trains volunteers for material production for the visually impaired, and provides professional development for teachers of the visually impaired. Provides electronic texts to NIMAS-eligible students in Florida.

**4528 Hillsborough County Talking Book Library Tampa-Hillsborough County Public Library**
900 N Ashley Dr
Tampa, FL 33602-3704
813-273-3652
FAX: 813-273-3707
TTY:813-273-3610
www.hcplc.org

*Joe Stines, Director of Libraries*
*Marcee Challener, Assitant Director*
*David Wullschleger, Chief of Operations*
*Linda Gillon, Manager of Staff & Administrative Support*
Serves as the reference hub and resource center for all citizens of Hillsborough County and as the flagship library of the Tampa-Hillsborough County Public Library System.

**4529 Jacksonville Public Library: Talking Books/Special Needs**
303 N Laura St
Jacksonville, FL 32202-3505
904-630-1999
FAX: 904-630-0604
e-mail: jerryr@coj.net
jpl.coj.net/lib/talkingbooks

*Barbara Gubbin, Executive Director*
Offers cassettes and digital books, reference materials on blindness and ADA issues, newsline, descriptive videos, and some assistive devices.

**4530 Lee County Library System: Talking Books Library**
13240 N Cleveland Ave
North Fort Myers, FL 33903-4855
239-479-4636
800-854-8195
FAX: 239-995-1681
TTY: 239-995-2665
e-mail: talkingbooks@leegov.com
www.lee-county.com/library

*Cynthia N Cobb, Director*
*Terri Crawford, Deputy Director*
*Debbie Parrott, Manager*
*Karen McLeish-Delgado, Librarian*
Provides free books and magazines to Lee County residents of all ages who have any disability that prevents them from reading printed material. Books are played on special players provided free by the National Library Service. Circulates low tech assistive aids and devices for temporary loan to Lee County Library card holders. Directs people to assistive technology and disability related resources.

**4531 Louis de la Parte Florida Mental Health Institute Research Library**
University of South Florida
13301 Bruce B Downs Blvd
Tampa, FL 33612-3807
813-974-4471
FAX: 813-974-7242
e-mail: library@fmhi.usf.edu
http://lib.usf.edu/fmhi/

*Ardis Hanson, Manager*
*David L Shern, Dean*
Information offered on mental illness, autism and pervasive development disabilities mental health research and archives management.

**4532 Orange County Library System: Audio-Visual Department**
101 E Central Blvd
Orlando, FL 32801-2429
407-835-7323
FAX: 407-835-7649
TTY:407-835-7641
e-mail: comments@ocls.info
www.ocls.info

*Mary Anne Hodel, Library Director and CEO*
*Debbie Moss, Assistant Director and Division Head for Technical Support*
*Bob Tessier, Comptroller*
*Craig Wilkins, Public Service Administrator*
Serves the residents of the Orange County Library District, with headquarters in downtown Orlando.

**4533 Pearlman Biomedical Research Institute**
Mt Sinai Medical Center
1600 NW 10th Ave
Miami Beach, FL 33140
305-674-2121
FAX: 305-674-2198
e-mail: william-abraham@msmc.com

*William Abraham, Director*
A 32,000 square feet facility located on the main campus of Mount Sinai. The institute consists of laboratory space, research and administrative offices. The studies conducted within the facility are primarily pre-clinical research.

**4534 Pinellas Talking Book Library for the Blind and Physically Handicapped**
1330 Cleveland St
Clearwater, FL 33755-5103
727-441-8408
FAX: 727-441-8398
TTY:727-441-3168
e-mail: contactus@pplc.us
www.pplc.us

*Mary Brown, Executive Director*
*David Saari, Facilities Manager*
*Paula Godfrey, Coordinator, Special Projects and Grant Services*
*Rosa Rodriguez, Deaf Literacy Coordinator at Safety Harbor Public Library*
The Pinellas Public Library Cooperative serves Pinellas County residents in member cities and the unincorporated county. The Cooperative Office provides cooridination of activities and funding as well as marketing services for the the member counties. The Talking Book Library servces Pinellas, Manatee, and Sarasota counties.

**4535 Talking Book Service: Mantatee County Central Library**
1301 Barcarrota Boulevard West
Bradenton, FL 34205-7522
941-748-5555
FAX: 941-751-7098
http://www.mymanatee.org

*Patricia Schubert, Manager*
Offers children's books on disc and cassette and more reference materials for the blind and physically handicapped.

**4536 Talking Books Library for the Blind and Physically Handicapped**
Palm Beach County Library
3650 Summit Blvd
West Palm Beach, FL 33406-4114 561-233-2600
888-780-4962
FAX: 561-233-2627
e-mail: webmaster@pbclibrary.org
www.pbclibrary.org

*John Callahan, Executive Director*
*Bill Rautenberg, Chair*
*Harriet Helfman, Vice Chair*
*John Callahan III, Library Director*
Established in 1967, today the County Library system serves Palm Beach County through the Main Library, 2 Regional Libraries, 11 Branch Libraries, a Bookmobile and a library annex. It continues to expand through our involvement with library networks, the Internet, and the World Wide Web.

**4537 Talking Books/Homebound Services**
Brevard County Library System
308 Forrest Ave
Cocoa, FL 32922-7723 321-635-7845
FAX: 321-633-1838
e-mail: kbriley@brev.org
www.brev.org

*Kay Briley, Librarian*
*Camille Johnson, Executive Director*
Offers reference materials on blindness and other handicaps. Subregional library for the blind and physically handicapped, assistive reading devices collection, reference materials on blindness and other handicaps; CCTV, phonic ear, reading edge and LOUD-R assistive listening devices available.

**4538 University of Miami: Bascom Palmer Eye Institute**
Department Of Ophthalmalogy
900 NW 17th St
Miami, FL 33136-1119 305-326-6000
800-329-7000
FAX: 305-326-7000
www.bascompalmer.org

*Michael Gittelman, CEO*
*Teresa Spaulding, Manager*
*Eduardo C. Alfonso, M.D., Professor and Chairman*
*Jennifer Cohen, Executive Director*
Clinical and basic research into blindness and visual impairments.

**4539 University of Miami: Mailman Center for Child Development**
1601 NW 12th Ave
Miami, FL 33136-1005 305-243-6395
FAX: 305-326-7594
e-mail: pedsinformation@med.miami.edu
pediatrics.med.miami.edu

*William Donelan, Vice President for Medical Administration and Chief Operating and Stra*
*William W. O'Neill, M.D., Executive Dean, Chief Medical Officer*
*Pascal J. Goldschmidt, M.D., SVP, Dean, CEO*
*Steven Falcone, M.D., Executive Dean*
Focuses on birth defects and children's illnesses.

**4540 West Florida Regional Library**
200 W Gregory St
Pensacola, FL 32502-4822 850-436-5060
FAX: 850-436-5039
TTY:850-436-5063
e-mail: hhudson@ci.pensacola.fl.us
wfrl.lib.fl.us

*Eugene Fischer, Executive Director*
*Helen Hudson, Outreach Librarian*
Offers children's print/braille books.

## Georgia

**4541 Athens Talking Book Center-Athens-Clarke County Regional Library**
2025 Baxter St
Athens, GA 30606-6331 706-613-3655
800-531-2063
FAX: 706-613-3660
www.clarke.public.lib.ga.us/talkingbooks/inde

*Stacey Chandler, Manager*
Discs, cassettes, large print books, reference materials on blindness, descriptive videos, films, closed-circuit TV, magnifiers, braille writer, summer reading programs, cassette books and magazines and more.

**4542 Augusta Talking Book Center**
823 Telfair Street
Augusta, GA 30901-2232 706-821-2600
FAX: 706-724-6762
TTY:706-722-1639
e-mail: talkbook@ecgrl.org
ecgrl.public.lib.ga.us

*Gary Swint, Board Of Trustee*
*Audrey Bell, Manager*
*Loran Gray, Board Of Trustee*
*Brenda Morton, Board Of Trustee*
Discs, cassettes, braille writer, films, large print books, summer reading program, magnifiers and reference materials on blindness and other handicaps.

**4543 Bainbridge Subregional Library for the Blind & Physically Handicapped**
S W Georgia Regional Library
301 S Monroe St
Bainbridge, GA 39819-4029 229-248-2680
800-795-2680
FAX: 229-248-2670
e-mail: lbph@swgrl.org
www.swgrl.org

*Susans Wittle, Manager*
*Kathy Hutchins, Supervisor*
Cassettes, large print books, summer reading programs, closed-circuit TV, magnifiers and more.

**4544 Columbus Subregional Library For The Blind And Physically Handicapped**
1120 Bradley Dr
Columbus, GA 31906-2813 706-649-0780
800-652-0782
FAX: 706-649-1914
TTY: 706-649-0974

*Dorothy Bowen, Librarian*
Braille writer, magnifiers, closed-circuit TV, large-print photocopier, cassette books and magazines, children's books on cassette, home visits and other reference materials on blindness and other handicaps.

**4545 Emory Autism Resource Center**
Emory University
1551 Shoup Ct
Decatur, GA 30033 404-727-8350
FAX: 404-727-3969
e-mail: tohannon@emory.edu
www.emory.edu/HOUSING/CLAIRMONT/autism.html

*Dr. Charles Nemeroff, Manager*
*Larry Hagan, IT Manager*
*Paul B. Pruett, MD, Director of Residency Education*
*Terri Trotter, Coordinator of Residency Education*
Offers on-line bulletin boards which are relevant to autism.

**4546 Emory University Laboratory for Ophthalmic Research**
1365b Clifton Rd NE
Atlanta, GA 30322-1013
404-778-4530
FAX: 404-778-4002
e-mail: pbennet@emory.edu
http://www.eyecenter.emory.edu/education/resi

*Henry F Edelhauser, PhD, Professor, Research (Basic Science) Section*
*Larry Hagan, IT Manager*
*Paul B. Pruett, MD, Director of Residency Education*
*Terri Trotter, Coordinator of Residency Education*
Various studies into the aspects of blindness.

**4547 Georgia Library for the Blind and Physically Handicapped**
Georgia Public Library
1150 Murphy Ave SW
Atlanta, GA 30310-3843
404-756-4619
800-248-6701
FAX: 404-756-4618
e-mail: dscott@georgialibraries.org
georgialibraries.org

*Stella Cone, Director*
*Deborah Scott, Business Manager*
*Dr. Lamar Veatch, Librarian*
Discs, cassettes, braille, films, closed-circuit TV, braille writer, large-print photocopier, cassette books and magazines.

**4548 Hall County Library: East Hall Branch and Special Needs Library**
127 Main St NW
Gainesville, GA 30501-3614
770-532-3311
FAX: 770-532-4305
TTY:770-531-2520
e-mail: info@hallcountylibrary.org
hallcountylibrary.org

*Adrian Mixson, Manager*
Summer reading programs, braille writer, magnifiers, scanners and readers, audio described videos, closed captioned videos, closed-circuit TV, large-print photocopier, cassette books and magazines, large print books, children's books on cassette, home visits and other reference materials on blindness and other handicaps.

**4549 Macon Library for the Blind and Physically Handicapped**
Washington Memorial Library
1180 Washington Ave
Macon, GA 31201-1762
478-744-0800
FAX: 478-742-3161
e-mail: jonest@bibblib.org
www.co.bibb.ga.us/library

*Thomas Jones, Director*
*Karen Monroe, Finance Officer*
*Hannah Warren, Office Manager*
*Viveca Jackson, Librarian, West Bibb Branch*
Summer reading programs, braille writer, magnifiers, closed-circuit TV, large-print photocopier, cassette books and magazines, children's books on cassette, home visits and other reference materials on blindness and other handicaps.

**4550 National Center on Birth Defects and Developmental Disabilities**
Centers for Disease Control and Prevention
1600 Clifton Rd NE
MS E-87
Atlanta, GA 30333
404-639-3311
800-232-4636
FAX: 404-498-3070
TTY: 888-232-6648
e-mail: cdcinfo@cdc.gov
www.cdc.gov/ncbddd/

*Coleen A. Boyle, PhD, MSHyg, Director*
*Chris Parker, Ph.D., Acting Deputy Director*
*Tom Bartenfeld, Ph.D., Associate Director for Public Health Practice*
*Hani Atrash, MD, MPH, Director, Division of Blood Disorders*
Promotes child development, prevents birth defects and developmental disabilities.

**4551 North Georgia Talking Book Center**
LaFayette-Walker Public Library
305 S Duke St
La Fayette, GA 30728-2936
706-638-8312
888-506-0509
888-506-0509
FAX: 706-638-4028
e-mail: cstubblefield@chrl.org
www.chrl.org

*Wendy Ellis, Manager*
*June DeLong, Library Assistant*
*Jeremy Hobbs, Library Assistant*
*Jill Trubey, Librarian*
We offer books on cassette for the visual and physically disabled induvidual, books in braille, magazines on cassette, zoom text screen magnifier, computer voice program, large-print photocopier, summer reading program, home visits na dother reference materials on blindness and other disabilities.

**4552 Oconee Regional Library**
801 Bellevue Ave
Dublin, GA 31021-4847
478-272-5710
FAX: 478-275-5381
georgialibraries.org

*Stella Cone, Director*
*Deborah Scott, Business Manager*
*Dr. Lamar Veatch, Librarian*
*Leard Daughety, Director*
Summer reading programs, braille writer, magnifiers, closed-circuit TV, large-print photocopier, cassette books and magazines, children's books on cassette, home visits and other reference materials on blindness and other handicaps.

**4553 Rome Subregional Library for the Blind and Physically Handicapped**
205 Riverside Pkwy
Rome, GA 30161-2922
706-236-4611
888-263-0769
FAX: 706-236-4631
TTY: 706-236-4618
www.floyd.public.lib.ga.us

*Diana Mills, Librarian*
*Delana Hickman, Manager*
The regional library system serves Floyd and Polk counties. System headquarters are located in Rome, Georgia, within the Rome/Floyd County Library Branch.

4554 **South Georgia Regional Library-Valdosta Talking Book Center**
300 Woodrow Wilson Dr
Valdosta, GA 31602-2532
229-333-0086
FAX: 229-333-0364
e-mail: commissioner@lowndescounty.com
sgrl.org

*Chuck Gibson, Manager*
Summer reading programs, Braille writer, magnifiers, closed-circuit TV, large print photocopier, cassette books and magazines, children's books on cassette, home visits and other reference materials on blindness and other handicaps.

4555 **Talking Book Center Brunswick-Glynn County Regional Library**
208 Gloucester St
Brunswick, GA 31520-7007
912-267-1212
FAX: 912-267-9597
e-mail: bransom@trll.org
www.trrl.org/tbc

*Betty Ransom, Librarian*
*Joe Shinnick, Executive Director*
The Three Rivers Regional Library system is named for 3 rivers that flow through all 7 counties of the library system. The Three Rivers Regional Library system serves patrons in Brantley, Camden, Charlton, Glynn, Long, McIntosh, and Wayne counties in southeast Georgia.

## Hawaii

4556 **Assistive Technology Resource Centers of Hawaii (ATRC)**
Ste 104
414 Kuwili St
Honolulu, HI 96817-5362
808-532-7110
800-645-3007
FAX: 808-532-7120
TTY: 808-532-7110
e-mail: atrc@atrc.org
www.atrc.org

*Barbara Fischlowitz-Leong, Executive Director*
*Jeff Ah Sam, Technical Assistant*
*Jodi Asato, Deputy Director*
*Steve Sullam, Director of Assistive Technology*
Provides information and training on assistive technology devices, services, and funding resources. Conducts presentations and demonstrations in the community to increase AT awareness and promote self-advocacy among people with disabilities.

4557 **Hawaii State Library for the Blind and Physically Handicapped**
874 Dillingham Blvd
Honolulu, HI 96817-4505
808-733-8444
800-559-4096
FAX: 808-733-8449
e-mail: library@hcc.hawaii.edu
honolulu.hawaii.edu/library/

*Fusako Miyashiro, Manager*
Supported by the Hawaii State Public Library System and the National Library Service for the Blind and Physically Handicapped, Library of Congress. Staff with knowledge of sign language; Special interest periodicals; Books on deafness and sign language; captioned media; Special Services: Radio Reading Service, Talking Books Reader's Club, educational and cultural programs, machine lending agency. Braille, cassette and large type. Regional and National service, quarterly newsletter.

## Idaho

4558 **Idaho Assistive Technology Project**
University of Idaho
129 W 3rd St
Moscow, ID 83843-2268
208-885-3557
800-432-8324
FAX: 208-885-3628
e-mail: rseiler@uidaho.edu
www.idahoat.org

*Ron Seiler, Project Director*
*Sue House, Information Specialist*
A federally funded program managed by the Center on Disbailities and Human Development at the University of Idaho. The goal of the IATP is to increase the availability of assistive technology devices and services for Idahoans with disabilities. The IATP offers free trainings and technical assistance, a low-interest loan program, assistive technology assessments for children and agriculture workers, and free informational materials.

4559 **Idaho Commission for Libraries: Talking Book Service**
325 W State St
Boise, ID 83702-6055
208-334-2150
800-458-3271
FAX: 208-334-4016
e-mail: talkingbooks@libraries.idaho.gov
http://libraries.idaho.gov/tbs

*Ann Joslin, Manager*
*Sue Walker, Library Consultant*
Offers audio and braille books and magazines, equipment, and accessories. All materials are mailed free to users' homes. Service is available free to all Idaho residents with a disability which limits their ability to use print materials.

## Illinois

4560 **Chicago Public Library Talking Book Center**
400 S State St
Chicago, IL 60605-1216
312-747-4300
800-757-4654
FAX: 312-747-4962
e-mail: dtaylor@chipublib.org
www.chipublib.org

*Linda Johnson Rice, President*
*Cherryl T. Thomas, Vice President, Chair, Administration and Finance Committee*
*Christopher Valenti, Secretary and Chair, Facilities Committee*
*Cristina Benitez, Vice Chair, Facilities Committee*
Summer reading programs, braille writer, closed-circuit TV, large print photocopier, cassette books and magazines, children's books on cassette, home visits and other reference materials on blindness and other handicaps. Three assistive technology centers designed and equipped for the blind and visually impaired, funded by the National Library Service for the Blind and Handicapped, a division of the Library of Congress. All services FREE!

4561 **Department of Ophthalmology and Visual Science**
1855 W Taylor St
Chicago, IL 60612-7242
312-996-7000
800-625-2013
FAX: 312-996-7770
TTY: 312-413-0123
e-mail: adriadel@uic.edu
www.uic.edu

*Paula Allen-Meares, Chancellor*
*Lon S. Kaufman, Vice Chancellor for Academic Affairs and Provost*
*Mitra Dutta, Vice Chancellor for Research*
*Barbara Henley, Vice Chancellor for Student Affairs*
Offers help, support, information and research for persons with vision problems, including Retinitis Pigmentosa.

**4562 Guild for the Blind**
Ste 1700
180 N Michigan Ave
Chicago, IL 60601-7463
312-236-8569
FAX: 312-236-8128
e-mail: info@guildfortheblind.org
guildfortheblind.org

*John Budzynski, CPA, President*
*Suzanne Miller, Ph.D., Vice President*
*Brett Christenson, Treasurer*
*Toria Emas, Secretary*
provides worship on vision rehabilitation, training on computers and other adaptive technology, career counseling, and professional development workshops and offers assistive devices for sale.

**4563 Horizons for the Blind**
125 Erick Street
A103
Crystal Lake, IL 60014-4404
815-444-8800
800-318-2000
FAX: 815-444-8830
e-mail: mail@horizons-blind.org
horizons-blind.org

*Camille Caffarelli, Executive Director*
HORIZONS for the BLIND is a nonprofit organization dedicated to providing products and services to people who are blind or visually impaired. In addition, Horizons is a leading provider of Braille transcription services to the business community; specialing in partnering with companies and nonprofits to provide billing and financial statements, newsletters, and documents in Braille, large print, and audio formats.

**4564 Illinois Early Childhood Intervention Clearinghouse**
51 Gerty Drive
Champaign, IL 61820-7469
217-333-1386
877-275-3227
FAX: 217-244-7732
e-mail: Illinois-eic@illinois.edu
www.eiclearinghouse.org

*Charlton Brandt, Manager*
*Patricia Traylor, Project Associate*
Free lending library of materials related to early childhood and disability. Books, audiovisuals and articles available. Computerized database with more than 31,000 items available to Illinois residents.

**4565 Illinois Machine Sub-Lending Agency**
607 S Greenbriar Rd
Carterville, IL 62918-1602
618-985-8375
800-455-2665
FAX: 618-985-4211
e-mail: bphdept@shawls.lib.il.us

*Loretta Broomfield, Director*
The Illinois Machine Sub-Lending Agency is a part of the Library of Congress' National Library Service for the Blind and Physically Handicapped program. Audio equipment and accessories are shipped from our location to eligible patrons who are registered for the free, mail order library service.

**4566 Illinois Regional Library for the Blind and Physically Handicapped**
1055 W Roosevelt Rd
Chicago, IL 60608-1559
312-746-9210
800-331-2351
FAX: 312-746-9192

*Shawn Thomas, Reference Librarian*
*Barbara Perkins, Acting Director*
Summer reading programs, braille writer, magnifiers, closed-circuit TV, large-print photocopier, cassette books and magazines, descriptive videos, children's books on cassette, home visits and other reference materials on blindness and other handicaps.

**4567 Mid-Illinois Talking Book Center**
600 High Point Ln
East Peoria, IL 61611-9396
309-694-9200
800-426-0709
e-mail: info@mitbc.org
www.mitbc.org

*Rose Chenoweth, Director*
*Michelle Moran, Assistant*
*Rebecca Rollings, Assistant*
*Jane Furrh, Assistant*
Providing a free library service to anyone unable to read regular print because of a visual or physical disability. There are books and magazines on tape and playback equipment; and also in Braille. Books and magazines are mailed free to and from library patrons, wherever they reside.

**4568 National Eye Research Foundation (NERF)**
Ste 207a
910 Skokie Blvd
Northbrook, IL 60062-4033
847-564-4652
800-621-2258
FAX: 847-564-0807
e-mail: info@nerf.org
http://www.nerf.org

*Joel Tenner, Manager*
Dedicated to improving eye care for the public and meeting the professional nees of eye care practitioners; sponsors eye research projects on contact lens applications and eye care problems. Special study sections in such fields as orthokertology, primary eyecare, pediatrics, and through continuing education programs. Provides eye care information for the public and professionals. Educational materials including pamphlets. Program activities include education and referrals.

**4569 National Lekotek Center**
2001 N. Clybourn
Chicago, IL 60614
773-528-5766
800-366-7529
FAX: 773-537-2922
e-mail: lekotek@lekotek.org
www.lekotek.org

*Sarah Paweni, Manager*
*Deidre Omahen, Program Director*
Toy library and play-centered programs for children with special needs and their families with branches in 17 states. Sliding fee scale. Lekotek also has a Toy Resource Helpline that provides individualized assistances in the selection of toys and play materials and general resources for families with children with disabilities.

**4570 Northwestern University Multipurpose Arthritis & Musculoskeletal Center**
303 E Chicago Ave
Chicago, IL 60611-4296
312-503-8186
FAX: 312-503-1204
e-mail: med-webteam@northwestern.edu
www.feinberg.northwestern.edu

*Cynthia Barnard, MBA, Director, Quality Strategies*
*John Vozenilek, MD, Assistant Professor*
*Eric G. Neilson, MD, Vice President for Medical Affairs*
*Sherri L. LaVela, PhD, MPH, MBA, Assistant Professor*
Conducts biomedical, educational and health services research into musculoskeletal diseases.

**4571 Skokie Accessible Library Services**
Skokie Public Library
5215 Oakton St
Skokie, IL 60077-3680
847-673-7774
FAX: 847-673-7797
TTY:847-673-8926
e-mail: tellus@skokielibrary .info
skokielibrary.info

*Carolyn Anthony, Director*
*Diana Hunter, President/President Emerita*
Library services for people with disabilities, including electronic aids, materials in special formats, programs and special services.

**4572 University of Illinois at Chicago: Lions of Illinois Eye Research Institute**
University of Illinois at Chicago
1855 West Taylor Street, m/c 648
Room 3.138
Chicago, IL 60612
312-996-6591
FAX: 312-996-7770
e-mail: eyeweb@uic.edu
www.uic.edu

*Rolanda Geddis, Manager*
*Jingtao Guo, MD*
Visual impairments and blindness research, including glaucoma studies.

**4573 Voices of Vision Talking Book Center at DuPage Library System**
127 S 1st St
Geneva, IL 60134-2771
630-208-0398
800-227-0625
FAX: 630-208-0399
e-mail: voinfo@dupagels.lib.il.us
www.vovtbc.org

*Karen L. Odean, Director*
Provides library service to persons who are unable to use standard printed material because of visual or physical disabilities. Part of the Illinois network of Talking Book Libraries. The service is free to those who are eligable. Provides books and magazines on audio-cassettes. Special playback equipment needed to use the books is also loaned. Braille books and magazines are also available. The collection includes popular books, classics and children's literature.

## Indiana

**4574 Allen County Public Library**
900 Library Plz
Fort Wayne, IN 46802-3699
260-421-1200
FAX: 260-421-1386
TTY:260-421-1302
e-mail: Genealogy@ACPL.Info
www.acpl.lib.in.us

*Jeffrey Krull, Executive Director*
*Steven Fortriede, Associate Director*
*Mark Allen, VP*
Summer reading programs, braille writer, magnifiers, closed-circuit TV, large-print photocopier, cassette books and magazines, children's books on cassette, home visits and other reference materials on blindness and other handicaps.

**4575 Bartholomew County Public Library**
536 5th St
Columbus, IN 47201-6225
812-379-1255
FAX: 812-379-1275
e-mail: library@barth.lib.in.us
barth.lib.in.us

*Beth Poor, Executive Director*
Summer reading programs, braille writer, magnifiers, closed-circuit TV, large-print photocopier, cassette books and magazines, children's books on cassette, home visits and other reference materials on blindness and other handicaps.

**4576 Elkhart Public Library for the Blind and Physicly Handicapped**
300 S 2nd St
Elkhart, IN 46516-3109
574-522-2665
800-622-4970
FAX: 574-522-2174
elkhart.lib.in.us

*Connie Jo Ozinga, Executive Director*
*Connie Ozinga, Executive Director*
Summer reading programs, braille writer, magnifiers, closed-circuit TV, large-print photocopier, cassette books and magazines, children's books on cassette, home visits and other reference materials on blindness and other handicaps.

**4577 Indiana Resource Center for Autism**
2853 E 10th St
Bloomington, IN 47408-2601
812-855-6508
800-825-4733
FAX: 812-855-9630
TTY: 812-855-9396
e-mail: prattc@indiana.edu
www.iidc.indiana.edu/irca

*Dr Cathy Pratt BCBA-D, Director*
*Scott Bellini, Assistant Director*
The Indiana Resource Center for Autism staff conduct outreach training and consultations, engage in research and develop and disseminate information focused on building the capicity of local communities, organizations, agencies and families to support children and adults across the autism spectrum in typical work, school, home and community settings. Please check our website for a complete list of publications.

**4578 Indiana University: Multipurpose Arthritis Center**
School Of Medicine, Rheumatology Division
1110 W Michigan St
Bloomington, IN 47405
317-274-4225
FAX: 317-274-7792
e-mail: dbrandt@iupui.edu
http://research.iu.edu/

*Dr. Kenneth Brandt MD, Director*
The mission of the center is to pursue major biomedical research interests relevant to the rheumatic diseases. Current areas of emphasis include; articular cartilage biology, pathogenesis of articular cartilage breakdown in osteoarthritis, causes of pain and disability in QA, the pathogenesis and treatment of various forms of amyloidosis, the pathogenesis of dermatomyositis, and immunologic and biochemical markers of cartilage breakdown and repair.

**4579 Lake County Public Library Talking Books Service**
1919 W 81st Ave
Merrillville, IN 46410-5382
219-769-3541
FAX: 219-769-0690
e-mail: webmaster@lakeco.lib.in.us
lakeco.lib.in.us

*Larry Acheff, Manager*
Large-print books, descriptive videos, braille writer, magnifiers, closed-circuit TV, large-print photocopier, cassette books and magazines, children's books on cassette, and other reference materials on blindness and other handicaps.

**4580 Special Services Division: Indiana State Library**
140 N Senate Ave
Indianapolis, IN 46204-2207
317-232-3675
800-622-4970
FAX: 317-232-3728
TTY: 317-232-7763
e-mail: delivery@statelib.lib.in.us
http://www.in.gov/isloutage/

*Roberta Brooker, Manager*
*Barbara Maxwell, State Librarian*
*C Ewick, Manager*
Circulates a collection of braille, recorded, and large print books and magazines and the special equipment needed to play the recorded materials to anyone in Indiana who cannot read regular print due to a visual or physical disability.

**4581 St. Joseph Hospital Rehabilitation Center**
700 Broadway
Fort Wayne, IN 46802-1402
260-425-3000
FAX: 260-425-3741
www.stjoehospital.com

*Kirk Ray, CEO*
*Bob Hailes, Vice President*
Information offered on rehabilitation.

**4582 Talking Books Service Evansville Vanderburgh County Public Library**
200 SE Martin Luther King Jr Blvd
Evansville, IN 47713- 1802
812-428-8200
866-645-2536
FAX: 812-428-8397
e-mail: tbs@evpl.org
www.evpl.org

*Marcia Learned Au, COO*
*Connie Davis, Vice President*
*Marcia Au, Executive Director*
*Barbara Shanks, Talking Book Manager*
The Talking Book Service of the Evansville Vanderburgh Public Library is part of a nationwide network of cooperating libraries headed by the National Library Service & a division of the Library of Congress. This free program provides library services and materials in alternative formats to person who are unable to use standard print material due to a visual or physical handicap.

## Iowa

**4583 Iowa Department for the Blind Library**
State Of Iowa
524 4th Street
Des Moines, IA 50309-2364
515-281-1333
800-362-2587
FAX: 515-281-1263
TTY: 515-281-1355
e-mail: karen.keninger@blind.state.ia.us
www.IDBonline.org

*Karen A Keninger, Director*
*Mike Hoenig, Chair*
*Steve Hagemoser, Commision Board Member*
*Peggy Elliott, Commision Board Member*
Summer reading programs, large print, disc, Braille and cassette books and magazines, descriptive videos and reference materials on blindness and other handicaps.

**4584 Iowa Registry for Congenital and Inherited Disorders**
University of Iowa
UI Research Park
100 BVC, Room W260
Iowa City, IA 52242
319-335-4107
866-274-4237
FAX: 319-335-4030
e-mail: ircid@uiowa.edu
www.public-health.uiowa.edu/ircid/

*Paul Romitti, Ph.D, Director*
The mission of the Iowa Registry for Congenital and Inherited Disorders is; maintain statewide surveillance for collecting information on selected congenital and inherited disorders in Iowa, monitor annual trends in occurrence and mortality of these disorders, provide data for research studies and educational activities for the prevention and treatment of these disorders.

**4585 Library Commission for the Blind**
State Of Iowa
524 4th Street
Des Moines, IA 50309-2364
515-281-1333
800-362-2587
FAX: 515-281-1263
TTY: 515-281-1355
e-mail: karen.keninger@blind.state.ia.us
www.blind.state.ia.us

*Karen A Keninger, Director*
Summer reading programs, Braille writer, magnifiers, closed-circuit TV, large print photocopier, cassette books and magazines, children's books on cassette and other reference materials on blindness and other handicaps.

## Kansas

**4586 Center for the Improvement of Human Functioning**
3100 N Hillside St
Wichita, KS 67219-3904
316-682-3100
FAX: 316-682-5054
e-mail: information@riordanclinic.org
www.brightspot.org

*Hugh D Riordan, President*
*Olive W Garvey, Chief Medical Officer*
Medical, research, and educational facility specializing in the treatment of chronic illness.

**4587 Central Kansas Library Systems Headquarters (CSLS)**
1409 Williams St
Great Bend, KS 67530-4020
620-792-2393
800-362-2642
FAX: 620-793-7270
e-mail: crhan@ckls.org
www.ckls.org

*Harry Williams, Administrator*
*Cathy Rhan, Special Services Dept. Head*
Summer reading programs, braille writer, magnifiers, closed-circuit TV, large-print photocopier, cassette books and magazines, children's books on cassette, home visits and other reference materials on blindness and other handicaps. Assistive technology available. Serving 17 counties in Central Kansas.

**4588 Kansas State Library**
Esu Memorial Union
Capitol Building, Room 169-W
300 SW 10th Avenue
Topeka, KS 66612-1593
785-296-3296
800-432-3919
FAX: 620-343-7124
e-mail: infodesk@library.ks.gov
kslib.info

*Christie Brandau, Manager*
*Jo Kord, Manager*

Summer reading programs, braille writer, magnifiers, closed-circuit TV, large-print photocopier, cassette books and magazines, children's books on cassette, home visits and other reference materials on blindness and other handicaps.

**4589 Kansas Talking Books Regional Library**
1200 Commercial
Box 4055
Emporia, KS 66801-4401
620-341-6280
800-362-0699
FAX: 620-343-7124
e-mail: talkingbooks@kslib.info
kslib.info

*Toni Harrell, Director*
*Christie Brandau, Manager*
*Jo Kord, Manager*
Summer reading programs, Braille writer, closed-circuit TV, large-print photocopier, cassette books and magazines, children's books on cassette, home visits and other reference materials on blindness and other handicaps.

**4590 Manhattan Public Library**
629 Poyntz Ave
Manhattan, KS 66502-6131
785-776-4741
800-432-2796
FAX: 785-776-1545
e-mail: annp@manhattan.lib.ks.us
manhattan.lib.ks.us

*Linda Knupp, Director*
*John Pecoraro, Assistant Director*
*Teri Belin, Admistrative Assistant*
*Gina Swenson, Admistrative Secretary*
Summer reading programs, Braille writer, magnifiers, closed-circuit TV, large-print photocopier, cassette books and magazines, children's books on cassette, home visits and other reference materials on blindness and other disabilities.

**4591 Northwest Kansas Library System Talking Books**
2 Washington Sq
Norton, KS 67654-1615
785-877-5148
800-432-2858
FAX: 785-877-5697
e-mail: tbook@ruraltel.net
http://www.nwkls.org/

*George Seamon, Director*
*Alice Evans, Business Manager & Acquisitions*
*David Fischer, Technology Consultant*
*Marry Boller, Consultant*
Offers books on disc and cassette. Library of Congress talking book and program for qualified individuals. Also offers descriptive videos to eligible persons.

**4592 South Central Kansas Library System**
Ste A
321 N Main St
South Hutchinson, KS 67505-1145
620-663-3211
800-234-0529
FAX: 620-663-9797
sckls.info

*Paul Hawkins, Executive Director*
*Larry Papenfuss, Director of Information Technology*
*Lee Scott, Technology Consultant*
*Lisa Sharbaugh, Technology Consultant*
Serving public, school, academic and special libraries in 12 counties since 1968, the South Central Kansas Library System (SCKLS) is the "go to" resource for innovative services, quality member awareness and assistance.

**4593 Topeka & Shawnee County Public Library Talking Books Service**
1515 SW 10th Ave
Topeka, KS 66604-1374
785-580-4400
800-432-2925
FAX: 785-580-4496
TTY: 785-580-4544
e-mail: tbooks@tscpl.lib.ks.us
www.tscpl.org

*Stephanie Hall, Manager*
Talking books is a free service that provides cassette and digital books and equipment to people who are unable to read or use standard print materials because of a visual or physical impairment. There are no fees. To apply for Talking Books you must fill out and submit an application, have it certified by the appropriate authority and return it to the library. You can find an application on our website or have one mailed out to you by contacting our office.

**4594 Wichita Public Library/Talking Book Service**
Wichita Public Library
223 S Main St
Wichita, KS 67202-3795
316-261-8500
FAX: 316-262-4540
TTY:316-262-3972
e-mail: cnazar@wichita.lib.ks.us
wichita.lib.ks.us

*Cynthia Berner-Harris, Executive Director*
*Eric J. Larson, Member of the Board*
Furnish recorded reading material (books and magazines) for visually and physically challenged citizens.

**4595 Wichita Public Library/Talking Book Service**
223 S Main St
Wichita, KS 67202-3795
316-261-8500
FAX: 316-262-4540
TTY:316-262-3972
e-mail: cnazar@wichita.lib.ks.us
wichita.lib.ks.us

*Cynthia Berner-Harris, Executive Director*
*Eric J. Larson, Member of the Board*
Furnish recorded reading material (books and magazines) for visually and physically challenged citizens.

## Kentucky

**4596 EnTech: Enabling Technologies of Kentuckiana**
Spaulding University
851 S 4th St
Louisville, KY 40203-2115
502-585-9911
800-896-8941
FAX: 502-585-7103
e-mail: info@spalding.edu
www.spalding.edu

*Laura Strickland, Manager*
*Mary Kaye Steinmietz, Outreach Coordinator*
Assistive technology resource and demonstration center, serving persons of all ages and disabilities in Kentucky and Southern Indiana. Services include: assistive technology information, demonstration, evaluation, training, technical support and short-term loan of equipment.

**4597 Kentucky Talking Book LibraryKentucky Dept. for Libraries and Archives**
P.O.Box 537
Frankfort, KY 40602-537
502-564-8300
800-372-2968
FAX: 502-564-5773
e-mail: ktbl.mail@ky.gov
www.kdla.ky.gov

*Barbara Penegor, Regional Librarian*

Provides library service to those who are physically unable to read print. Audio and braille books and magazines are available via mail or download.

**4598 Louisville Free Public Library**
301 York St
Louisville, KY 40203-2257 502-574-1611
FAX: 502-574-1666
e-mail: webteam@lfpl.org
lfpl.org

*Craig Buthod, Manager*
Summer reading programs, braille writer, magnifiers, closed-circuit TV, large-print photocopier, cassette books and magazines, children's books on cassette, home visits and other reference materials on blindness and other handicaps.

## Louisiana

**4599 Central Louisiana State Hospital Medical and Professional Library**
P.O.Box 5031
Pineville, LA 71361-5031 318-484-6200
FAX: 318-484-6501
http://wwwprd.doa.louisiana.gov/laservices/pu

*Patrick Kelly, CEO*
*Carol Gee, Manager*
Information offered on psychiatry, psychology and mental health.

**4600 Louisiana State Library**
701 N 4th St
Baton Rouge, LA 70802-5345 225-342-4913
800-543-4702
FAX: 225-219-4804
e-mail: admin@state.lib.la.us
state.lib.la.us

*Rebecca Hamilton, Assistant Secretary, State Librarian*
*Diane Brown, Deputy State Librarian*
*Beverly Dugas, Business Manager*
*Meg Placke, Associate State Librarian*
Summer reading programs, braille writer, magnifiers, closed-circuit TV, large-print photocopier, cassette books and magazines, children's books on cassette. Descriptive videoos and other reference materials on blindness and other handicaps.

**4601 Louisiana State University Genetics Section of Pediatrics**
Rm 661
533 Bolivar St
New Orleans, LA 70112-1349 504-568-6151
FAX: 504-568-8500
e-mail: genetics@lsuhsc.edu
www.medschool.lsuhsc.edu

*Steve Nelson, MD, Dean*
*Janis Letourneau, MD, Associate Dean for Faculty & Institutional Affairs*
*Cathi Fontenot, MD, Associate Dean for Alumni Affairs & Development*
*Charles Hilton, MD, Associate Dean for Academic Affairs*
Our goal is to continue building a strong department in which all of the faculty are successful in attracting funding, and committed to establishing productive programs that bring credit to the Department and to the Health Sciences Center as a whole.

**4602 State Library of Louisiana: Services for the Blind and Physically Handicapped**
701 N 4th St
Baton Rouge, LA 70802-5345 225-342-4913
800-543-4702
FAX: 225-219-4804
e-mail: sbph@state.lib.la.us
state.lib.la.us

*Rebecca Hamilton, Assistant Secretary, State Librarian*
*Diane Brown, Deputy State Librarian*
*Beverly Dugas, Business Manager*
*Meg Placke, Associate State Librarian*
Summer reading programs, braille publications, cassette books and magazines, children's books on cassette and other reference materials on blindness and other handicaps. Louisiana Hotlines - quarterly newsletter. Affiliated with National Library Service for the Blind and Physically Handicapped, Washington, DC. Louisiana Voices recording program uses volunteers to record books for the blind.

## Maine

**4603 Bangor Public Library**
145 Harlow St
Bangor, ME 04401-4900 207-947-8336
FAX: 207-945-6694
e-mail: bpill@bpl.lib.me.us
bpl.lib.me.us

*Barbara Mc Dade, Executive Director*
*Norman Minsky, President*
*Franklin E. Bragg II, MD, Vice President*
*Lee Chick, Treasurer*
Summer reading programs, braille writer, magnifiers, closed-circuit TV, large-print photocopier, cassette books and magazines, children's books on cassette, home visits and other reference materials on blindness and other handicaps.

**4604 Cary Library**
107 Main St
Houlton, ME 04730-2196 207-532-1302
FAX: 207-532-4350
e-mail: faucher!@carey.lib.me.us
cary.lib.me.us

*Linda Faucher, Librarian*
Summer reading programs, braille writer, magnifiers, closed-circuit TV, large-print photocopier, cassette books and magazines, children's books on cassette, home visits and other reference materials on blindness and other handicaps.

**4605 Lewiston Public Library**
200 Lisbon St
Lewiston, ME 04240-7234 207-513-3004
FAX: 207-784-3011
TTY:207-200-1511
e-mail: lplweb@lplonline.org
lplonline.org

*Rick Speer, Director*
*Jake Paris, Adult Services Librarian*
*David Moorhead, Children's Librarian*
*Jane Weed, Circulation Supervisor*
Summer reading programs, braille writer, magnifiers, closed-circuit T.V., large-print photocopier, cassette books and magazines, children's books on cassette, home visits and other reference materials on blindness and other handicaps.

**4606 Maine State Library**
Maine State
64 State House Sta
Augusta, ME 04333-64 207-287-5650
800-762-7106
FAX: 207-287-5624
TTY: 888-577-6690
e-mail: benitad@ursus3.ursus.maine.edu
maine.gov

*Chris Boynton, Manager*
*J Gary Nichols, State Librarian*
*Melora Norman, Manager*
Summer reading programs, cassette books and magazines, children's books on cassette, home visits and other reference materials on blindness and other handicaps.
*Newsl./BiAnnual*

**4607 New England Regional Genetics Group**
P.O.Box 920288
Needham, MA 02492-4 781-444-0126
FAX: 781-444-0127
e-mail: mfgnergg@verizon.net
www.nergg.org

*David J. Harris, MD, President*
*Erica Wellington, Secretary*
*Merrill Henderson, Treasurer*
*Lisa Demers, MS, CGC, President Elect*
New Englands primary network for collaborative exchange of genetic health information and education.

**4608 Portland Public Library**
5 Monument Sq
Portland, ME 04101-4072 207-871-1700
FAX: 207-871-1703
e-mail: reference@portland.lib.me.us
portlandlibrary.com

*Stephen J. Podgajny, Executive Director*
*Clare E. Hannan, Head of Finance and Operations*
*Linda Albert, Head of Human Resources*
*Linda Putnam, Head of Reference and Information*
Summer reading programs, magnifiers, closed-circuit T.V., large-print photocopier, cassette books and magazines, children's books on cassette, home visits and other reference materials on blindness and other handicaps.

**4609 Waterville Public Library**
73 Elm St
Waterville, ME 04901-6078 207-872-5433
FAX: 207-873-4779
e-mail: wplhelpdesk@waterville.lib.me.us
http://www.watervillelibrary.org/

*Sarah Sugden, Executive Director*
*Lee-Anne Folsom, Circulation Coordinator*
Summer reading programs, braille writer, magnifiers, closed-circuit T.V., large-print photocopier, cassette books and magazines, children's books on cassette, home visits and other reference materials on blindness and other handicaps.

## Maryland

**4610 Johns Hopkins University Dana Center for Preventive Ophthalmology**
Wilmer Ophthalmology Institute
600 N Wolfe St
Baltimore, MD 21287-5 410-955-5000
FAX: 410-955-2542
e-mail: hquigley@jhmi.edu
www.hopkinsmedicine.org/wilmer/danacenter

*Harry Quigley, Director*
Established in 1979, the Dana Center for Preventive Ophthalmology is dedicated to improving knowlege of risk factors for ocular disease and public health approaches to the prevention of these diseases and their ensuing visual impairment and blindness worldwide.

**4611 Johns Hopkins University: Asthma and Allergy Center**
5501 Hopkins Bayview Cir
Baltimore, MD 21224-6821 410-550-0545
FAX: 410-550-1733
e-mail: jhuallergy@jhmi.edu
hopkins-arthritis.org

*Lawrence Lichtenstein, Director*
Studies of allergic diseases and individuals with allergic disease, pulmonary diseases and diseases involving inflammation and immunological processes.

**4612 Maryland State Library for the Blind and Physically Handicapped**
Maryland State Department of Education
415 Park Ave
Baltimore, MD 21201-3603 410-230-2424
800-964-9209
FAX: 410-333-2095
TTY: 800-934-2541
e-mail: referenc@lbph.lib.md.us
www.lbph.lib.md.us

*Jill Lewis, Manager*
*Diana Jarvis, Administrative Specialist*
*LaTarsha Wilson, Secretary*
Provide comprehensive library services to the eligible blind and physically handicapped residents of the State of Maryland. The vision is to provide innovative and quality services to meet the needs and expectations of the patrons of Maryland.

**4613 Montgomery County Department of Public Libraries/Special Needs Library**
6400 Democracy Blvd
Bethesda, MD 20817-1638 240-777-0922
TTY:301-897-2203
http://www6.montgomerycountymd.gov/apps/libra

*Susan F Cohen, Assistant Head Librarian*
*James Montgomery, Owner*
*Joseph Eagan, Branch Manager*
Serves the library information and reading needs of people with disabilities, family members, students and service providers. Some of its services include books, periodicals, and videos on disability issues, adaptive technology, community information; the National Library for the Blind and Physically Handicapped Talking Book program; large print books; and computer room with adaptive technology.

**4614 National Epilepsy Library (NEL)**
Epilepsy Foundation
8301 Professional Pl
Landover, MD 20785-7223 866-330-2718
800-332-1000
FAX: 877-687-4878
e-mail: ContactUs@efa.org
www.epilepsyfoundation.org

*Sandy Finucane, Executive Vice President*
*Patty Dukes, Vice President Operations/Human Capital/Legal Counsel*
*Mimi Browne, Director, HRSA programs*
*Chad Hartman, Director of Major Gifts*
Contains information about epilepsy and seizure disorders and serves physicians and other health professionals. Provides in-house bibliographic database (ESDI), searches and documents delivery and interlibrary loans. Maintains the Albert and Ellen Grass Archives.

**4615 National Rehabilitation Information Center(NARIC)**
8400 Corporate Drive
Suite 500
Landover, MD 20785-2245
301-459-5900
800-346-2742
FAX: 301-459-4263
TTY: 301-459-5984
e-mail: naricinfo@heitechservices.com
www.naric.com

*Heidi W Gerding, CEO*
NARIC is a federally-funded library and information center that focuses on disability and rehabilitation information.

**4616 Red Notebook**
Friends of Libraries for Deaf Action
2930 Craiglawn Rd
Silver Spring, MD 20904-1816
301-572-5168
FAX: 301-572-5168
TTY:301-572-5168
e-mail: folda@aol.com
www.folda.net

*Alice L Hagemeyer, MLS, Founder/President*
*Merrie A. Davidson, Associate*
*Ricardo Lopez, MS, Associate*
*Joan Naturale, M.Ed, MLIS, Associate*
A binder containing fact sheets, library reprints, announcements and other printed informational materials that are related to both deaf and library issues. It is designed to help build communication among individuals and groups within the deaf community. The focus is on assisting libraries in providing cost-effective and efficient library and information services to these consumers in a unbiased fashion.

**4617 Social Security Library**
U S Social Security Administration
6401 Security Blvd
Baltimore, MD 21235-6401
800-772-1213
TTY:800-325-0778
www.socialsecurity.gov

*Bill Vitek, Manager*
*Jo B Barnhart, Chief Executive Officer*
Information on social security and disability insurance.

**4618 Warren Grant Magnuson Clinical Center**
National Institue Health
Bldg 10-Room
9000 Rockville Pike
Bethesda, MD 20892-1
301-496-2563
800-411-1222
FAX: 301-480-2984
TTY: 866-411-1010
e-mail: prpl@mail.cc.nih.gov
www.cc.nih.gov

*John I Gallin, MD, Clinical Center Director*
*Clare Hastings, PhD, RN, FAA, Chief Nurse Officer*
*Maureen E. Gormley, MPH, MA, RN, Chief Operating Officer*
*Maria D. Joyce, MBA, CPA, CFO*
Established in 1953 as the research hospital of the National Institutes of Health. Designed so that patient care facilities are close to research laboratories so new findings of basic and clinical scientists can be quickly applied to the treatment of patients. Upon referral by physicians, patients are admitted to NIH clinical studies.

## Massachusetts

**4619 Boston University Arthritis Center**
Boston University
715 Albany St
Boston, MA 02118-2526
617-638-4640
FAX: 617-638-5226
www.bumc.bu.edu

*Karen Antman, Dean & Provost, Medical School*
*Meg Aranow, Director*
*Barbara A. Cole, Associate VP for Research Admin*
*Christopher Dorney, Director*
The Arthritis Center focuses its educational, research and patient care efforts on the diagnosis and treatment of rheumatic diseases. These include the many forms of arthritis; the auto-immune diseases such as Scleroderma, Systemic Lupus, Erythematosus, Rheumatoid Arthritis; localized pain syndromes such as tendonitis, bursitis, and carpal tunnel syndrome; and metabolic bone disorders such as osteoporosis.

**4620 Boston University Center for Human Genetics**
W-4th Floor
Boston, MA 02118
617-638-7083
FAX: 617-638-7092
e-mail: amilunsk@bu.edu
www.bumc.bu.edu/hg

*Aubrey Milunsky, Co-Director*
*Jeff Milunsky, Director of Clinical Genetics*
Research and molecular diagnosis.

**4621 Boston University Robert Dawson Evans Memorial Dept. of Clinical Research**
75 East Newton St
Boston, MA 02118-2657
617-247-5019
FAX: 617-638-8728

*Norman G Levinsky, Director*
*Jack Ansel, MD*
Integral unit of the University Hospital specializing in arthritis and connective tissue studies.

**4622 Braille and Talking Book Library, Perkins School for the Blind**
175 North Beacon St
Watertown, MA 02472-2751
617-972-3434
800-852-3133
FAX: 617-926-2027
e-mail: Info@Perkins.org
www.perkins.org

*Kim Charlson, Director*
*Aubrey Webson, Director*
*Lisa A. Calise, CFO*
*Carolyn Assa, Executive Director*
The Braille and Talking Book Library loans braille and recorded reading materials and the playback equipment necessary to use them. You are eligible for services if you are unable to read print due to a disability.

**4623 Brigham and Women's Hospital: Asthma and Allergic Disease Research Center**
75 Francis St
Boston, MA 02115-6110
617-732-5500
FAX: 617-730-2858
e-mail: arc@partners.org
www.brighamandwomens.org

*Matthew H Liang, Director*
*Gary Gottlieb, President and Chief Executive Officer*
*Arthur Mombourquette, Vice President of Support Services*
*Joel T. Katz, M.D., Director*
Integral unit of the hospital focusing research attention on asthma and allergy related disorders.

**4624 Brigham and Women's Hospital: Robert B Brigham Multipurpose Arthritis Center**
Brigham and Women s Hospital
75 Francis St
Boston, MA 02115-6110
617-732-5500
FAX: 617-432-0979
www.brighamandwomens.org

*Matthew H Liang, Director*
*Gary Gottlieb, President and Chief Executive Officer*
*Arthur Mombourquette, Vice President of Support Services*
*Joel T. Katz, M.D., Director*
Research studies into arthritis and rheumatic diseases.

**4625 Caption Center**
One Guest Street
Boston, MA 02135
617-300-3600
FAX: 617-300-1020
e-mail: access@wgbh.org
www.wgbh.org/caption

*Pat McDonald, Director*
*Lauren Madden, Business Manager*
*Ian McDonald, Business Manager*
*Ira Miller, Production Manager*
Has been pioneering and delivering accessible media to disabled adults, students and their families, teachers and friends for over 30 years. Each year, the Center captions more than 10,000 hours worth of broadcast and cable programs, feature films, large-format and IMAX films, home videos, music videos, DVDs, teleconferences and CD-Roms.

**4626 Center for Interdisciplinary Research on Immunologic Diseases**
Childrens Hospital Medical Center
300 Longwood Ave
Boston, MA 02115-5724
617-355-6000
FAX: 617-355-0443
TTY:617-730-0152
e-mail: webteam@tch.harvard.edu
http://childrenshospital.org

*Dr. James Mandell, CEO*
*Sandra Fenwick, President & COO*
*Dick Argys, Senior Vice President and Chief Administrative Officer*
*Carleen Brunelli, PhD, MBA, Vice President, Research Administration*
Organizational research unit of the Children's Hospital that focuses on the causes, prevention and treatments of asthma, infections and allergies.

**4627 Harvard University Howe Laboratory of Ophthalmology**
Massachusetts Eye & Ear Infirmary
243 Charles St
Boston, MA 02114-3002
617-523-7900
FAX: 617-573-4380
TTY:617-573-5498
e-mail: richard.godfrey@schepens.harvard.edu
www.meei.harvard.edu

*John Fernandez, President and CEO*
*Javier Balloffet, Vice President Ophthalmology*
*Ken Holmes, Chief Financial Officer, MEEA*
*Melissa Paul, Chief Development Officer*
Development ophthalmology and eye research.

**4628 Laboure College Library**
2120 Dorchester Ave
Dorchester Center, MA 02124-5698
617-296-8300
FAX: 617-296-7947
e-mail: admit@laboure.edu
laboure.edu

*Andrew Callo, Manager*
Offers information on physical disabilities, independent living, peer counseling and advocacy.

**4629 Massachusetts Rehabilitation Commission**
600 Washington Street
Boston, MA 02111
617-204-3603
800-245-6543
FAX: 617-727-1354
TTY: 800-245-6543
www.mass.gov/mrc

*Elmer C Bartels, Commissioner*
*Deval L. Patrick, Governor*
*Timothy P. Murray, Lieutenant Governor*
*Thomas G. Kelley, Secretary*
Vacational Rehabilitation and Independent Living for people with disabilities.

**4630 Schepens Eye Research Institute**
20 Staniford St
Boston, MA 02114-2508
617-912-0100
FAX: 617-912-0118
e-mail: geninfo@vision.eri.harvard.edu
www.theschepens.org

*John Fernandez, President and CEO*
*Javier Balloffet, M.B.A., Vice President for Ophthalmology, MEE*
*Alan Long, Phd, Vice President for Research & Academic Affairs, MEE*
*Frances Ng, M.B.A., Director of Human Resources*
Prominent center for research on eye, vision, and blinding diseases; dedicated to research that improves the understanding, management, and prevention of eye diseases and visual deficiencies; fosters collaboration among its faculty members; trains young scientists and clinicians from around the world; promotes communication with scientists in allied fields; leader in the worldwide dispersion of basic scientific knowledge of vision.

**4631 Talking Book Library at Worcester Public Library**
3 Salem Sq
Worcester, MA 01608-2015
508-799-1730
800-762-0085
FAX: 508-799-1676
e-mail: talkbook@cwmars.org
www.worcpublib.org/talkingbook

*James Izatt, Dept Head*
Braille embosser, magnifiers, closed-circuit TV, adapted computers, cassette books and magazines, children's books on cassette, reference materials on blindness and other disabilities.

## Michigan

**4632 Artificial Language Laboratory**
Michigan State University
405 Computer Ctr
East Lansing, MI 48824-1042
517-353-5399
FAX: 517-353-4766
e-mail: artlang@pilot.msu.edu
https://www.msu.edu/

*Dr. John B Eulenberg, Phd, Director*
*Stephen R. Blosser, BSME, Technical Director*
*Shawn A. Miller, Laboratory Manager*
*Rebecca Ann Baird, Editor, Communication Outlook*
Multidisciplinary research center in the Audiology & Speech Science department, Michigan State University. Its basic research program includes speech analysis and synthesis. Applied research is carried out on computer-based systems for persons who are blind and for persons with cerebral palsy and head injury. The laboratory develops physical, cognitive and linguistic assessment technology.

**4633 Burger School for the Autistic**
31735 Maplewood St.
Garden City, MI 48135-1993
734-793-1830
FAX: 734-762-8533
garden-city.lib.mi.us

*Lawrence Marble, Library Director*
*Dan Lodge, Reference Librarian*
*Stephanie Charlefour, Youth Librarian*
Burger school for students with autism is the largest public school in the United States that specializes in the education of students with autism.

**4634 Chi Medical Library**
Ingham Regional Medical Center
401 W Greenlawn Ave
Lansing, MI 48910-2819
517-975-6000
irmc.org

*Judy Barnes, Manager*
Consumer health and patient education collection in books, videotapes, pamphlets. Open to the public.

**4635 Glaucoma Laser Trial**
Sinai Hospital of Detroit: Dept. of Opthalmology
31 Center Drive
Bethesda, MI 20892-2510
301-496-5248
e-mail: 2020@nei.nih.gov
www.nei.nih.gov/neitrials

*Paul A. Sieving, M.D., Ph.D., Director*
The purpose of the trial is to compare the safety and long-term efficacy of argon laser treatment of the trabecular meshwork with standard medical treatment for primary open-angle glaucoma.

**4636 Grand Traverse Area Library for the Blind and Physically Handicapped**
610 Woodmere Ave
Traverse City, MI 49686-3103
231-932-8500
877-931-8558
FAX: 231-932-8578
e-mail: webmaster@tadl.tcnet.org
www.tadl.org

*Metta Lansdale, Director*
*Jerry Beasley, President*
*William Fowle, Vice President*
*Thomas Kachadurian, Secretary*
The LBPH was established as a sub-regional library in 1972 and currently provides services for 783 registered individuals in 16 counties, 171 of these registrants are Grand Traverse County residents. Anyone unable to read regular printed materials because of visual or physical limitations may be eligible.

**4637 Kent District Library for the Blind and Physically Handicapped**
3350 Michael Ave SW
Wyoming, MI 49509-3420
616-784-2007
FAX: 616-336-3256
e-mail: WyomingYouthStaff@kdl.org
http://www.kdl.org

*Lori Holland, Branch Manager*
Summer reading programs, braille writer, magnifiers, large-print photocopier, cassette books and magazines, children's books on cassette, and other reference materials on blindness and other handicaps.

**4638 Library of Michigan Service for the Blind**
P.O.Box 30007
702 W. Kalamazoo St
Lansing, MI 48909-7507
517-373-5614
800-992-9012
FAX: 517-373-4480
e-mail: sbph@michigan.gov
www.michigan.gov

*Sue Chinault, Manager*
Braille writer, magnifiers, closed-circuit T.V., large-print photocopier, cassette books and magazines, children's books on cassette, and other reference materials on blindness and other handicaps.

**4639 Macomb Library for the Blind & Physically Handicapped**
40900 Romeo Plank
Clinton Township, MI 48038-1132
586-286-1580
800-649-7377
FAX: 586-286-0634
e-mail: mlbph@cmpl.org
www.libcoop.net/macspe

*Larry Neal, Library Director*
*Juliane Morian, Associate Director*
*Cathy Marshall, Circulation Manager*
*Mary Kaluzny, Head of Cataloging*
Braille writer, closed-circuit T.V., large-print books, cassette books and magazines, children's books on cassette, other reference materials on blindness and other handicaps, descriptive videos and bifokal kits. Assistive technology including JAWS, Zoomtext, OpenBook, and Duxbury.

**4640 Michigan's Assistive Technology Resource**
Physically Impaired Association of Michigan
1023 S Us Highway 27
Saint Johns, MI 48879-2423
989-224-0333
800-274-7426
FAX: 989-224-0330
e-mail: matr@edzone.net
www.cenmi.org/mits

*Jeff Diedrich, Manager*
*Maryann Jones, Coordinator*
*Barbara Warren, Information Specialist*
Provides information services, support materials, technical assistance, and training to local and intermediate school districts in michigan to increase their capacity to address the needs of students with disabilities for assistive technology.

**4641 Mideastern Michigan Library Co-op**
Ste 711
503 S Saginaw St
Flint, MI 48502-1807
810-232-7119
800-641-6639
FAX: 810-232-6639
e-mail: dhooks@mmlc.info
http://www.mmlc.info/

*Denise Hooks, Director*
*Irene Bancroft, Admin. Assistant*
*Ruth Helwig, Board Member*
*Robert Cierzniewski, Board Member*
Summer reading programs, braille writer, magnifiers, closed-circuit T.V., large-print photocopier, cassette books and magazines, children's books on cassette, home visits and other reference materials on blindness and other handicaps.

**4642 Muskegon Area District Library for the Blind and Physically Handicapped**
Ste 5
4845 Airline Rd
Muskegon, MI 49444-4503
231-737-6248
877-569-4801
FAX: 231-737-6307
TTY: 231-722-4103
e-mail: mclsm@llcoop.org
madl.org

*Stephen Dix, CEO*
*Sheila Miller, Librarian*
*Karla Bates, Assistant Director*
*Richard Schneider, Assistant Director*
Braille typewriter, magnifiers, closed-circuit TV, large-print photocopier, cassette books and magazines, children's books on cassette, home visits and other reference materials on blindness and other handicaps, The Reading Edge, and large print books.

**4643 Northland Library Cooperative**
Library Cooperative/ Library for the blind
220 W. Clinton St.
Charlevoix, MI 49720
231-855-2206
e-mail: webmaster@nlc.lib.mi.us
www.nlc.lib.mi.us

*Jennifer Dean, Director*
*Christine Johnston, Executive Director*
Summer reading programs, Braille writer, magnifiers, closed-circuit TV, large-print photocopier, cassette books and magazines, children's books on cassette and other reference materials on blindness and other handicaps.

**4644 Oakland County Library for the Visually & Physically Impaired**
1200 N Telegraph Rd
Pontiac, MI 48341-1032
248-858-5050
800-774-4542
FAX: 248-858-1153
TTY: 248-452-2247
e-mail: lvpi@.oakgov.com
www.oakgov.com/lvpi

*Dave Conklin, Manager*
The Oakland County Library for the Visually and Physically Impaired was established in 1974 to provide access to free library service for County residents who are unable to read standard printed material because of a visual impairment or physical limitation.

**4645 St. Clair County Library Special Technologies Alternative Resources (S.T.A.R.)**
210 McMorran Blvd
Port Huron, MI 48060-4014
810-982-3600
800-272-8570
FAX: 810-982-3600
TTY: 810-455-0200
e-mail: lbph@sccl.lib.mi.u
http://www.sccl.lib.mi.us/LBPH.aspx

*Arnold H. Larson, Chairperson*
*Debra A. Bevins, Trustee*
*Kathleen J. Wheelihan, Trustee*
*Helen M. Praet, Trustee*
Offers library services to the blind, deaf and blind, visually disabled, phsyically disabled, and reading disabled.

**4646 University of Michigan: Orthopaedic Research Laboratories**
1500 E. Medical Center Drive
Ann Arbor, MI 48109
734-936-6641
800-211-8181
FAX: 734-647-0003
e-mail: svaassen@umich.edu
http://www.med.umich.edu/

*Steve Goldstein, Lab Director*
*Laurence McMahon Jr MD, Contact*
Develops and studies the causes and treatments for arthritis including new devices and assistive aids.

**4647 Upper Peninsula Library for the Blind**
1615 Presque Isle Ave
Marquette, MI 49855-2811
906-228-7697
800-562-8985
FAX: 906-228-5627
TTY: 906-228-7697
e-mail: sdees@uproc.lib.mi.us
http://www.uplibraries.org/

*Suzanne Dees, Executive Director*
Summer reading programs, braille writer, magnifiers, closed-circuit T.V., large-print photocopier, cassette books and magazines, children's books on cassette, home visits and other reference materials on blindness and other handicaps.

**4648 Washtenaw County Library for the Blind & Physically Handicapped**
P.O.Box 8645
Ann Arbor, MI 48107-8645
734-222-6860
FAX: 734-222-6803
e-mail: lbpd@ewashtenaw.org
ewashtenaw.org

*Mary Udoji, Manager*
Michigan Subregional Library, Library of Congress National Library Service network. General library service for persons unable to use standard print materials for various physical reasons. Lends audio books and listening equipment, large type books, descriptive videos. Provides reference information and programs. Kurzweil scanner with components which convert standard print to Braille, large type or audio and closed circuit TV magnifier on site.

**4649 Wayne County Regional Library for the Blind**
30555 Michigan Ave
Westland, MI 48186-5310
734-727-7300
888-968-2737
FAX: 734-727-7333
TTY: 734-727-7330
e-mail: wcrlbph@wayneregional.lib.mi.us
www.wayneregional.lib.mi.us

*Vanessa Morris, Regional Librarian*
*Sue Steiger, Librarian*
*Rebecca Farmer, Student Intern*
*Mariya Webb, Student Intern*
Summer reading programs, braille writer, magnifiers, closed-circuit T.V., large-print photocopier, cassette books and magazines, children's books on cassette, and other reference materials on blindness and other handicaps.

**4650 Wayne State University: CS Mott Center for Human Genetics and Development**
275 E Hancock St
Detroit, MI 48201-1405
313-577-1485
FAX: 313-577-8554
e-mail: rsokol@med.wayne.edu
www.media.wayne.edu

*Robert Sokol, Director*
Human growth and development disorders.

## Minnesota

**4651 Century College**
3300 Century Ave N
White Bear Lake, MN 55110-1252
651-779-3300
800-228-1978
FAX: 651-779-3417
TTY: 651-773-1715
century.edu

*Lawrence Litecky, President*
*Steven Ritt, Vice President*
*Harold M. Johnson, Treasurer*
*Ralph Olsen, Jr., Secretary*

Programs of study - Orthotic Practitioner, Orthotic Technician, Prosethetic Practitioner, Prosthetic Technician. In addition, Century College offers more than 50 other programs in liberal arts, career and occupational programs.

**4652 Communication Center/Minnesota State Services for the Blind**
Services for the Blind
2200 University Avenue West
Suite 240
Saint Paul, MN 55114-1840
651-642-0500
800-652-9000
FAX: 651-649-5927
e-mail: chamilto@ssb.state.mn.us
www.mnssb.org

*Richard Strong, Executive Director*

Special library service for the blind and physically handicapped providing tape and Braille transcription of textbooks and vocational materials; Minnesota Radio Talking Book providing current newspaper, magazines and best selling books; Dial-in-News, a touch tone phone accessed newspaper service; Library of Congress cassette and phonograph talking book equipment; repair services for special audio reading equipment, with most services free to Minnesota Residents.

**4653 Duluth Public Library**
520 W Superior St
Duluth, MN 55802-1578
218-730-4200
FAX: 218-723-3822
e-mail: webmail@duluth.lib.mn.us
www.duluth.lib.mn.us

*Carla Powers, Library Manager*
*Renee Zurn, Supervisor of Digital and Outreach Services*
*Davis Ouse, Supervisor of Public Services*
*Dave Lull, Supervisor of Technical and Automation Services*

Main library computer lab contains one Sorenson Relay and accessibility computer with zoom text JAWS software.

**4654 Minnesota Library for the Blind and Physically Handicapped**
Department of Education
388 6th Ave SE
Faribault, MN 55021-6300
507-333-4828
800-722-0550
FAX: 507-333-4832
e-mail: mn.lbph@sate.mn.us
education.state.mn.us

*Catherine A. Durivage, Manager*
*Rene Perrance, Librarian*

Provides books and magazines in Braille, large print, records, and cassettes to qualified residents of Minnesota who have a visual or physical impairment, including reading disabilities due to an organic cause certified by a medical doctor, that prevents residents from reading standard print or physically handling a book. Equipment for in-house use include magnifiers, braillers, listening equipment, and CCTV. Reference collection for in-house use only on visual impairment topics.

**4655 Special U**
University of Minnesota
P.O.Box 721-Umhc
Minneapolis, MN 55455
612-625-3846
800-276-8642
FAX: 612-624-0997
e-mail: kdwb-var@umn.edu

Brings together comprehensive sources of information related to youth with chronic or disabling conditions and their families. Topics include psychosocial issues, disability awareness, developmental processes, family, sexuality, education, employment, independent living, cultural issues, gender issues, service delivery, professional issues, advocacy and legal issues, and health issues. Special focus on transition from childhood to adolesecence to adulthood.

## Mississippi

**4656 Blind and Physically Handicapped Library Services**
Mississippi Library Commission
3881 Eastwood Dr
Jackson, MS 39211-6473
601-432-4116
800-446-0892
FAX: 601-432-4476
e-mail: lbph@mlc.lib.ms.us
www.mlc.lib.ms.us

*Shellie Zeigler, BPHLS Director*

BPHLS serves as the MS Regional Library for the Library of Congress, NLS for the Blind and Physically Handicapped. Book collections include audio cassette, CDs, digital books, Braille, large print, children's 18-20 point large print, and standard print reference collection. Descriptive videos, magazines in Braille or on cassette are available, as well as equipment: adaptive workstation, Braille embosser, closed-circuit TV, magnifier, speech input/output, and more. Check for eligibility.

**4657 Mississippi Library Commission**
3881 Eastwood Dr
Jackson, MS 39211-6473
601-432-4111
800-647-7542
FAX: 601-354-4181
TTY: 601-354-6411
e-mail: mslib@mlc.lib.ms.us
http://www.mlc.lib.ms.us/index.html

*Sharman Smith, Executive Director*
*Russell Burns, Board Member*
*Curtis Sene Randolph, ILL Coordinator*
*Celia Fisher, Board Member*

Summer reading programs, braille writer, magnifiers, closed-circuit T.V., large-print photocopier, cassette books and magazines, children's books on cassette, home visits and other reference materials on blindness and other handicaps.

**4658 Mississippi Library Commission\Talking Book and Braille Services**
3881 Eastwood Dr
Jackson, MS 39211-6473
601-432-4111
800-446-0892
FAX: 601-354-4181
e-mail: mslib@mlc.lib.ms.us
http://www.mlc.lib.ms.us/index.html

*Sharman Smith, Executive Director*
*Russell Burns, Board Member*
*Curtis Sene Randolph, ILL Coordinator*
*Celia Fisher, Board Member*

Library service for the print handicapped braille, cassette and disc materials (books & periodicals) for children and adults. Large print RG production (copier & printer), braille embosser and other handicaps.

## Missouri

**4659 Assemblies of God Center for the Blind**
1445 N Boonville Ave
Springfield, MO 65802-1894
417-862-2781
FAX: 417-863-6614
e-mail: blind@ag.org
radiantlife.org

*Thomas Trask, Manager*
*Caryl Weingartner, Administrative Assistant*
Offers braille and cassette lending library, braille and cassette Sunday School materials for all ages, braille and cassette periodicals, resource assistance, and resources for blind children and children of blind parents. CHildren's braille books with tactile graphics for purchase or loan. Books in digital media for adaptive reading services.

**4660 Church of the Nazarene**
Nazarene Publishing House
P.O. Box 843116
Kansas City, MO 64184-3116
816-333-7000
800-877-0700
FAX: 800-849-9827
e-mail: it@nazarene.org
www.nazarene.org

*Eugenio R. Duarte, Board of General Superintendents*
*Jerry D. Porter, Board of General Superintendents*
*Stan A. Toler, Board of General Superintendents*
*David C. Graves, Board of General Superintendents*
Offers braille and large print books. Also offers a lending library and cassettes for the blind.

**4661 Judevine Center for Autism**
1101 Olivette Executive Pkwy
Saint Louis, MO 63132-3252
314-432-6200
FAX: 314-849-2721
e-mail: judevine@judevine.org
www.judevine.org

*Becky Blackwell, President*
Evaluations and assessments, parent and professional training programs, consultations, workshops, seminars, family support, clinical therapies, adult programs and support, residential services.

**4662 Lutheran Blind Mission**
7550 Watson Rd
Saint Louis, MO 63119-4409
314-918-0415
888-215-2455
FAX: 314-963-0738
e-mail: blind.mission@blindmission.org
www.blindmission.org

*Sherry Lambing, Manager*
*Dave Andrus, Executive Director*
*Nancy Crawford, Manager*
Offers Christian books in braille and large print books and cassettes for the blind and visually impaired, on loan, as well as Christian periodicals in braille, large print and cassette tape.

**4663 University of Missouri: Columbia Arthritis Center**
University of Missouri
1 Hospital Dr
Columbia, MO 65212-1
573-882-4141
FAX: 573-884-3996
e-mail: webeditor@missouri.edu
www.muhealth.org

*James Ross, Chief Executive Officer*
*Mitch Wasden, Chief Operating Officer*
*Anita Larsen, Chief Nurse Executive*
*Jeri Doty, Chief Planning Officer*
Research into arthritis and rheumatic diseases. One of the most comprehensive health-care networks in Missouri, our 5 hospitals and numerous clinics, all staffed by University Physicians, offer the finest primary, secondary, and tertiary health-care services. We also provide education for future health-care providers and participate in important research.

**4664 Wolfner Library for the Blind**
Secretary State Office
P.O.Box 387
Jefferson City, MO 65102-387
573-751-8720
800-392-2614
FAX: 573-526-2985
TTY: 800-347-1379
e-mail: wolfner@sos.mo.gov
www.sos.mo.gov/wolfner/

*Richard J Smith, Executive Director*
Wolfner Library provides reading material for Missouri State residents unable to read standard print due to a visual or physical disability. Book formats are recorded books on digital cartridge and cassette, braille and some childrens books in large print. Wolfner Library also lends out descriptive videos, playback equipment for the cartridges and cassettes are also on loan.

## Montana

**4665 MonTECH, Montana's Statewide Assistive Technology Program**
700 SW Higgins Ave
Suite 250
Missoula, MT 59803
406-243-5751
877-243-5511
e-mail: montech@ruralinstitute.umt.edu
montech.ruralinstitute.umt.edu

*Kathy Laurin PhD, Project Director*
*Chris Clasby MSW MATP, Project Coordinator*
*James Poelstra MA, Info Technology Specialist*
Specializing in Assistive Technology and oversee a variety of AT related grants and contracts. The overall goal is to develop a comprehensive, statewide system of assistive technology related assistance. Striving to ensure that all people in Montana with disabilities have equitable access to assistive technology devices and services in order to enhance their independence, productivity, and quality of life.

**4666 Montana State Library-Talking Book Library**
1515 E 6th Ave
P.O. Box 201800
Helena, MT 59620-1800
406-444-3115
800-332-3400
FAX: 406-444-0266
TTY: 406-444-4799
e-mail: mtbl@mt.gov
msl.mt.gov/talking_book_library

*Jennie Stapp, State Librarian*
*Stacy Bruhn, Data Technician*
*Kris Schmitz, Central Services Manager*
*Tom Marino, Web System Manager*
The Library offers FREE alternative audio and Braille reading materials for Montana citizens who cannot read standard print materials because of a visual, physical or reading handicap. Over 50,000 titles on 4-track cassette, WebBraille, Web0pac, WebBlud, summer reading programs, braille writer, magnifiers, closed-circuit T.V., large-print photocopier, cassette books and magazines, children's books on cassette, home visits and other reference materials on blindness and other handicaps.

## Nebraska

**4667 Nebraska Assistive Technology Partnership Nebraska Department of Education**
Ste C
5143 S 48th St
Lincoln, NE 68516-2261 402-471-0734
888-806-6287
888-806-6287
FAX: 402-471-6052
TTY:402-471-0734
e-mail: atp@atp.state.ne.us
nlc.nebraska.gov/tbbs/

*Steve Miller, Manager*
*Lilly Blase, Program Coordinator*
Provides statewide assistive technology and home modification services for Nebraskans of all ages and disabilities.

**4668 Nebraska Library Commission: Talking Book and Braille Service**
Talking Book and Braille Service
Ste 120
1200 N St
Lincoln, NE 68508-2020 402-471-4016
800-307-2665
FAX: 402-471-6244
TTY: 402-471-4083
e-mail: talkingbook@nlc.state.ne.us
nlc.nebraska.gov

*David Oertli, Executive Director*
*Kay Goehring, Reader Services Coordinator*
*Bill Ainsley, Audio Production Studio Manager*
*Scott Scholz, Circulation & Audio Prod. Coor.*
Summer reading programs, braille writer, magnifiers, closed-circuit T.V., large-print photocopier, audio books and magazines, children's audio books, and in braille and reference materials on blindness and other disabilities.

## Nevada

**4669 Las Vegas-Clark County Library District**
7060 W. Windmill Lane
Las Vegas, NV 89113 702-734-7323
FAX: 702-507-6187
e-mail: administration@lvccld.org.
http://www.lvccld.org/

*Jeanne Goodrich, Executive Director*
*Robb Morss, Deputy Director/COO*
*Fred James, Deputy Director/CFO*
*Danielle Patrick Milam, Director Development*
Summer reading programs, braille writer, magnifiers, closed-circuit T.V., large-print photocopier, cassette books and magazines, children's books on cassette, home visits and other reference materials on blindness and other handicaps.

**4670 Nevada State Library and Archives**
100 North Stewart Street
Carson City, NV 89701-4285 775-684-3360
800-922-2880
FAX: 775-684-3330
e-mail: ddeleon@nevadaculture.org
http://nsla.nevadaculture.org/

*Michael Fischer, Director*
*Ann Brinkmeyer, Head of Government Publications and Processing Services*
*Kathy Edwards, Government Publications Librarian*
*Sherry Glick, Library Assistant*
Summer reading programs, braille writer, magnifiers, closed-circuit T.V., large-print photocopier, cassette books and magazines, children's books on cassette, home visits and other reference materials on blindness and other handicaps.

## New Hampshire

**4671 New Hampshire State Library: Talking Book Services**
117 Pleasant St
Concord, NH 03301-3852 603-271-3429
FAX: 603-271-8370
e-mail: talking@der.nh.gov
www.nh.gov/nhsl/talking_books

*Marilyn Stevenson, Supervisor*
Regional Library for National Library Service for the Blind & Physically Handicapped offers digital and cassette books, magazines on cassette, children's books on digital and on cassette, descriptive videos, playaways, and downloadable digital audio books, and Braille services.

## New Jersey

**4672 Children's Specialized Hospital Medical Library - Parent Resource Center**
150 New Providence Rd
Mountainside, NJ 7092-2590 908-518-5806
888-244-5373
FAX: 908-233-4176
e-mail: jbrooks@childrens-specialized.org
www.childrens-specialized.org

*Amy B Mansue, President and CEO*
*David Kostinas, Chairman*
*Margaret M. Pego, Treasurer*
*Steven M. Rosenberg, Esq., Secretary*
Contains some 3,000 books, and journals specializing in nursing, pediatrics, child neurology, and rehabilitation. Also provides a Parent Resource Center, a special collection of books, videos and pamphlets designed to meet the information needs of parents and families, as well as the local community.

**4673 Christopher & Dana Reeve Foundation Resource Center**
636 Morris Turnpike
Suite 3A
Short Hills, NJ 07078-2608 973-379-2690
800-225-0292
FAX: 973-912-9433
e-mail: infospecialist@christopherreeve.org
www.paralysis.org

*Peter T. Wilderotter, President and CEO*
*Susan Howley, Executive Vice President*
A national clearinghouse for information, referral and educational materials on paralysis. Offers a free book 'Paralysis Resource Guide' in English or Spanish. Free lending library.

**4674 Eye Institute of New Jersey**
New Jersey Medical School
90 Bergen St
Newark, NJ 7103-2499 973-972-2036
FAX: 973-972-2068
e-mail: eyereplies@aol.com
www.umdnj.edu/eyeweb

*Jacinta Ogbonna, Administrative director*
*Department A*
*Tatiana Forofonova, Program Coordinator*
Ophthamology, including research into cornea, retina and neuro-ophthamalogy.

**4675 Mycoclonus Research Foundation**
Apt 17d
200 Old Palisade Rd
Fort Lee, NJ 7024-7060 201-585-0770
FAX: 201-585-0770
e-mail: research@myoclonus.com
http://www.pspinformation.com/index.html

*Mark Seiden, VP*

Supports clinical and basic research into the cause and treatment of myoclonus; four international workshops facilitated the sharing of information by physicians, scientists, and investigators active in the field, resulted in three publications; supports promising research projects, clinical neurological fellows, with special emphasis on posthypoxic myoclonus and encourages all who are interested in futhering the understanding, treatment, and cure of myoclonus.

**4676 New Jersey Center for Outreach and Services for the Autism Community (COSAC)**
Suite 530
500 Horizon drive
Robbinsville, NJ 8691-2951
609-588-8200
800-4AU-TISM
FAX: 609-588-8858
e-mail: information@autismnj.org
http://www.autismnj.org

*James A. Paone, President*
*Genare Valiant, Vice President*
*Mary Jane Weiss, Vice President*
*Kathleen Moore, Secretary*
Purpose is to assist families, individuals and agencies concerned with the welfare and education of children and adults with autism and other pervasive development disorders.

**4677 New Jersey Library for the Blind and Handicapped**
2300 Stuyvesant Ave
Trenton, NJ 8618-3226
609-530-4000
800-792-8322
FAX: 609-406-7181
TTY: 609-530-4000
e-mail: tbbc@njstatelib.org
njlbh.org

*Adam Szczepaniak, Director*
*Maria Baratta, Assistant Director*
*Information Technology*
Summer reading programs, braille writer, magnifiers, closed-circuit T.V., large-print, cassette, braille books and magazines, children's books on cassette, and other reference materials on blindness and other handicaps. Provides reading material on audio, cassette, large print and braille to eligible NJ residents.

## New Mexico

**4678 New Mexico State Library for the Blind and Physically Handicapped**
1209 Camino Carlos Rey
Santa Fe, NM 87507-4400
505-476-9770
1 -00 -56 5
FAX: 505-476-9776
TTY: 800-659-4915
e-mail: lbph@state.nm.us
http://www.nmstatelibrary.org

*Susan Bloch, President*
*Walter McWalter, Vice President*
*Paul Agriesti, Treasurer*
*Zella Kay Cox, Secretary*
Summer reading programs, braille writer, magnifiers, closed-circuit T.V., large-print photocopier, cassette books and magazines, children's books on cassette, home visits and other reference materials on blindness and other handicaps.

## New York

**4679 Andrew Heiskell Braille and Talking Book Library**
New York Public Library
40 W 20th St
New York, NY 10011-4211
212-206-5400
FAX: 212-206-5418
e-mail: ahlbph@nypl.org
talkingbooks.nypl.org

The library provides talking books and talking book players to the five boroughs of New York City, and braille books to New York City and Long Island. These items may be circulated in person or through the mail without charge to the borrower. Deposit collections may be arranged with agencies that provide service to people with visual impairments. The library also circulates large print books and materials in other formats.

**4680 Center on Human Policy: School of Education**
Syracuse University
805 S Crouse Ave
Syracuse, NY 13244-2280
315-443-3851
800-894-0826
FAX: 315-443-4338
e-mail: thechp@syr.edu
www.thechp.syr.edu

*Steven Taylor, Executive Director*
*Rachael Zubal-Ruggieri, Information Coordinator*
The Center on Human Policy is a disability policy organization concerned with ensuring the rights of people with disabilities.

**4681 DREAMMS for Kids**
190 Whispering Oaks Dr
Longs, SC 29568-6973
607-539-3027
FAX: 607-539-9930
e-mail: janet@dreamms.org
www.dreamms.org

*Janet Hosmer, Executive Director*
DREAMMS is committed to increasing the use of computers, high quality instructional technology, and assistive technologies for students with special needs in schools, homes and the workplace.

**4682 Ehrman Medical Library**
New York University Medical Center
550 1st Ave
New York, NY 10016-6402
212-263-5395
FAX: 212-263-6534
library.med.nyu.edu

*Karen Brewer, Director*
Our mission of the Fredrick L. Ehrman Library is to enhance learning, research and patient care and New York University Medical Center by effectively managing knowledge-based resources, providing client-centered information services and education, and extending access through new initiatives in information technology.

**4683 Finger Lakes Developmental Disabilities Service Office**
620 Westfall Rd
Rochester, NY 14620-4610
585-461-8500
FAX: 585-461-8764
e-mail: folwelbe@nysomr.emi.com
http://www.opwdd.ny.gov/opwdd_contacts/local_

*Mike Feeney, Director*
*Carolyn Bassett, Manager*
Information on mental retardation and developmental disabilities.

**4684 Helen Keller International**
Fl 12
352 Park Ave S
New York, NY 10010-1723
212-532-0544
877-535-5374
FAX: 212-532-6014
e-mail: info@hki.org
hki.org

*Henry C. Barkhorn III, Chairman*
*Desmond G. FitzGerald, Vice Chairman*
*Mary Crawford, Secretary*
Nonprofit international organization whose mission is to combat the causes and consequences of blindness and malnutrition.

**4685 Helen Keller National Center for Deaf - Blind Youths And Adults**
141 Middle Neck Rd
Sands Point, NY 11050-1218 516-944-8900
FAX: 516-944-7302
e-mail: hkncinfo@hknc.org
www.hknc.org

*Joseph McNulty, Executive Director*
HKNC is the only national vocational and rehabilitation program providing services exclusively to youth and adults who are deaf-blind.

**4686 Institute for Basic Research in Developmental Disabilities**
1050 Forest Hill Rd
Staten Island, NY 10314-6356 718-494-0600
FAX: 718-698-3803
opwdd.ny.gov

*W Ted Brown, Director*
*Joseph Maturi, Deputy Director*
The research component of the NYS Office for People with Developmental Disabilities (OPWDD). Consists of 7 departments and 45 laboratories thatconduct basic and clinical research in the field of developmental disabilities and mental retardation.

**4687 Institute for Visual Sciences**
221 E 71st St
New York, NY 10021-4139 212-517-0400
FAX: 212-472-0295
www.mmm.edu/

*Judson R. Shaver, Ph.D., President*
*Melissa Richman, Associate to the President for Operations*
*Wendy Malina, Executive Assistant to the President*
*Marilyn Mills, Executive Office Coordinator*
Ophthalmology with emphasis on the development of care for the eye.

**4688 JGB Cassette Library International**
15 W 65th St
New York, NY 10023-6601 212-769-7854
800-284-4422
FAX: 212-769-6266
e-mail: bemass@aol.com
http://www.jgb.org

*Jerry Bechhofer, President*
Summer reading programs, braille writer, magnifiers, closed-circuit T.V., large-print photocopier, cassette books and magazines, children's books on cassette, home visits and other reference materials on blindness and other handicaps.

**4689 Nassau Library System**
900 Jerusalem Ave
Uniondale, NY 11553-3097 516-292-8920
FAX: 516-565-0950
e-mail: outreach@nassaulibrary.org
nassaulibrary.org

*Ellen Garrison, President*
*Kathleen Seyfried, Vice President*
*Mike Turner, Treasurer*
*Joseph Carroll, Secretary*
Information about public library services in Nassau County, including services for people with disabilities and the Senior Connections volunteer project (information and referral for seniors and their families).

**4690 National Braille Association**
95 Allens Creek Road
Bldg 1 Suite 202
95 Allens creek road
Rochester, NY 14618 585-427-8260
FAX: 585-427-0263
e-mail: nbaoffice@nationalbraille.org
www.nationalbraille.org

*Dorothy Worthington, President*
*Joanna E. Venneri, Vice President*
*Whitney Gregory, Secretary*
*Betty Marshall, Treasurer*
Only national organization dedicated to the professional development of individuals who prepare and produce braille materials.

**4691 New York State Talking Book & Braille Library**
New York State Library and Education
Cultural Education Center
222 Madison Avenue
Albany, NY 12230-1 518-474-5930
800-342-3688
FAX: 518-474-5786
e-mail: tbbl@mail.nysed.gov
nysl.nysed.gov/tbbl

*Loretta Ebert, Research library director*
Lends audio and braille books and specialized playback equipment to eligible borrowers with print disabilities. Service is completely free. Serves 55 counties of upstate NY (Westchester and above). Also provides service to schools, nursing homes, and other facilities.

**4692 Postgraduate Center for Mental Health**
124 E 28th St
New York, NY 10016-8402 212-576-4150
FAX: 212-696-1679
www.dvguide.com/newyork/postgrad.html

*Marge Slobetz, Assistant Director*
*Marie Serrano, Manager*
Evaluations and psychotherapy by social workers psychologists for children, adolescents, families and couples. Neuropsychological testing and remedation for learning disabilities.

**4693 Rehabilitation Research Library**
Human Resources Center
Albertson, NY 11507 516-741-2010
FAX: 516-746-3298

*Amnon Tishler, Research Librarian*
*Susan Feifer, Manager*
Information on rehabilitation and occupational rehabilitation.

**4694 State University of New York Health Sciences Center**
P.O.Box 30032
450 Clarkson Avenue
Brooklyn, NY 11203- 2098 718-270-1000
FAX: 718-778-5397
http://www.downstate.edu/

*Meg O'Sullivan, Assistant Vice President*
*Jennifer Hayes, Staff Assistant*
Child psychiatry research programs.

**4695 Suffolk Cooperative Library System: Long Island Talking Book Library**
Long Island Talking Book Library System
P.O.Box 9000
627 North Sunrise Service Road
Bellport, NY 11713-9000
631-286-1600
866-833-1122
FAX: 631-286-1647
TTY: 631-286-4546
e-mail: lbph@suffolk.lib.ny.us
http://www.afb.org/directory.aspx?action=prof

*Valerie Louis, Administrator*
*Kevin Verbesey, Executive Director*
Offers a variety of support services to its 55 member libraries and other patrons including, an extensive talking book program, assistive technology and other services for people with disabilities.

**4696 United Spinal Association**
7520 Astoria Blvd
Suite 100
East Elmhurst, NY 11370-1177
718-803-3782
800-404-2898
FAX: 718-803-0414
e-mail: info@unitedspinal.org
www.unitedspinal.org

*Paul J. Tobin, President*
Association news and free publications on architecture and barrier-free designs, legislation and other issues affecting Americans with Disabilities.

**4697 Wallace Memorial Library**
Rochester Institute Of Technology
90 Lomb Memorial Dr
Rochester, NY 14623-5604
585-475-2562
FAX: 585-475-7007
TTY:585-475-2760
e-mail: circwml@rit.edu

*Chandra McKenzie, Director*
*William Destler, President*
*Ryan Ammerman, Administrator*
*Joseph Bellavia, Director/ Producer*
Information on physical disabilities and deafness.

**4698 Xavier Society for the Blind**
154 E 23rd St
New York, NY 10010-4595
212-473-7800
800-637-9193
http://www.xaviersocietyfortheblind.org/

*Kathleen Lynch, Executive Director*
*Chairman*
Provides spiritual and inspirational reading material to visually impaired persons in suitable format: braille, large print and cassette, throughout U.S. and Canada. Services are provided both by way of regular periodical publications sent through the mail and non-returnable; and by means of a lending library where books are returned. All services are provided free.

## North Carolina

**4699 Genova Diagnostics**
63 Zillicoa St
Asheville, NC 28801-1038
828-253-0621
800-522-4762
FAX: 828-252-9303
gdx.net

*Patrick J Hanaway, Vice president*
*Director*
Laboratory serves over 8000 primary/specialty physicians and healthcare providers, offering over 125 specialized diagnostic assessments. These innovative tests cover a wide range of physiological areas, including digestive, immune, nutritional, endocrine, and metabolic function. To date, the lab has performed over 2 million individual diagnostic tests.

**4700 North Carolina Library for the Blind and Physically Handicapped**
1841 Capital Blvd
Raleigh, NC 27635-1
919-733-4376
888-388-2460
FAX: 919-733-6910
TTY: 919-733-1462
e-mail: nclbph@ncdcr.gov
statelibrary.dcr.state.nc.us

*Francine Martin, Manager*
*Carl Ginger Rush, Secretary*
*James Benton, President*
*Dennis Thurman, Vice president*
Free loan of large print, braille, and cassette tape books and magazines and specialized playback equipment to registered eligible North Carolinians. Call for an application form. Collection contains general fiction and nonfiction titles. Registered borrowers may subscribe to receive descriptive videos for a one time fee.

**4701 Pediatric Rheumatology Clinic**
Duke Medical Center
P.O.Box 3212
Durham, NC 27715-3212
919-684-6575
FAX: 919-684-6616
e-mail: rabin001@mc.duke.edu
www.duke.edu

*Rebecca H. Buckley, Medical Director*
*Michael Duke, Owner*
Clinical and laboratory pediatric rheumatoid studies.

**4702 University of North Carolina at Chapel Hill: Neuroscience Research Building**
115 Mason Farm Road
Chapel Hill, NC 27599-7250
919-843-8536
FAX: 919-966-9605
unceye.org

*Eric Schneider, Administrator*
*Dallas Carter, Grants Manager*
*Joshua Free, Accounting Manager*
An interdepartmental research center on the campus of the UNC-Chapel Hill School of Medicine. Mission is to promote neuroscience research with specific emphasis on developmental , cellular, and disease-related processes.

## North Dakota

**4703 North Dakota State Library Talking Book Services**
Dept 250
604 E Boulevard Ave
Bismarck, ND 58505-0800
701-328-4622
800-472-2104
FAX: 701-328-2040
TTY: 800-892-8622
e-mail: statelib@snd.gov
ndsl.lib.state.nd.us

*Doris Ott, Manager*
*Hullen E. Bivins, State Lbirarian*
*Susan Hammer-Schneider, Head Disability Serves*
The Talking Books Program provides patrons with free access to cassette books and magazines. The Talking Books Program is administered by the National Library Service for the Blind and Physically Handicapped.

## Ohio

**4704 Case Western Reserve University**
10900 Euclid Ave
Cleveland, OH 44106-4901 216-368-2000
e-mail: president@case.edu
www.case.edu

*Barbara R. Snyder, President*
*Stanton L. Gerson, MD*
Programs which encompass the arts and sciences, engineering, health sciences, law, management, and social work.

**4705 Case Western Reserve University Northeast Ohio Multipurpose Arthritis Center**
11100 Euclid Ave
Cleveland, OH 44106-1716 216-844-3969
888-844-8447
www.uhhs.com

*Fred Rothstein, Executive Director*
Basic and clinical research into the causes, diagnosis and treatment of arthritis.

**4706 Cincinnati Children's Hospital Medical Center**
University Of Cincinnati Uap
3333 Burnet Ave
Cincinnati, OH 45229-3026 513-636-4200
800-344-2462
FAX: 513-636-2837
TTY: 513-636-4900
e-mail: oopes0@chmcc.org
www.cincinattichildren.org

*James Anderson, CEO*
*James M Anderson, Chief Executive Officer*
*David Schonfeld, Executive Director*
*Richard G Azizkhan, Member of the Board*
Dedicated to providing the highest level of pediatric care. As Greater Cincinnati's only pediatric hospital, Cincinnati Children's is committed to bringing the very best medical care to children in our community.

**4707 Cleveland FES Center**
11000 Cedar Ave
Cleveland, OH 44106-3056 216-231-3257
FAX: 216-231-3258
TTY:216-231-3257
e-mail: info@fesc.org
fescenter.case.edu

*Robert Kirsch, Executive Director*
*Peckham P Hunter, Director*
Research and development center on functional electrical stimulation. Houses the FES Information Center, a resource center with a library. Publications, newsletters and videotapes for persons with disabilities and others interested in electrical stimulation are offered.

**4708 Cleveland Public Library**
325 Superior Ave E
Cleveland, OH 44114-1271 216-623-2800
FAX: 216-623-2800
e-mail: info@library.cpl.org
cpl.org

*Felton Thomas, Executive Director*
*Joan Clark, Manager*
*Cindy Lombardo, Deputy Director*
Summer reading programs, braille writer, magnifiers, closed-circuit T.V., large-print photocopier, cassette books and magazines, children's books on cassette, and other reference materials on blindness and other handicaps.

**4709 Ohio Regional Library for the Blind and Physically Handicapped**
National Library Office
800 Vine St
Cincinnati, OH 45202-2009 513-369-6900
800-582-0335
FAX: 513-369-3111
TTY: 516-665-3384
e-mail: info@cincinnatilibrary.org
www.cincinnatilibrary.org

*Kimber L. Fender, Director*
Summer reading programs, braille writer, magnifiers, closed-circuit T.V., large-print photocopier, cassette books and magazines, children's books on cassette, and other reference materials on blindness and other handicaps.

**4710 State Library of Ohio: Talking Book Program**
National Library Service in Washington
Ste 100
274 E 1st Ave
Columbus, OH 43201-3692 614-644-7061
800-686-1531
FAX: 614-466-3584
e-mail: jbudler@sloma.state.oh.us
library.ohio.gov

*Jo Budler, Manager*
*Jim Buchman, Dir Patron & Catalog Services*
*Peter Bates, Deputy Director*
A machine-lending agency for the visually impaired. Provides free recorded books, and magazines to approximately 26,000 eligible blind, visually impaired, physically handicapped, and reading disabled Ohio residents.

## Oklahoma

**4711 Oklahoma Library for the Blind & Physically Handicapped**
300 NE 18th St
Oklahoma City, OK 73105-3296 405-521-3514
800-523-0288
FAX: 405-521-4582
TTY: 405-521-4672
e-mail: library@drs.state.ok.us
www.library.state.ok.us

*Paul Adams, Library Director*
*Vicky Golightly, Public Information Officer*
Braille writer, magnifiers, closed-circuit T.V., large-print photocopier, cassette books and magazines, children's books on cassette, home visits and other reference materials on blindness and other handicaps.

**4712 Oklahoma Medical Research Foundation**
825 NE 13th St
Oklahoma City, OK 73104-5097 405-271-7210
800-522-0211
FAX: 405-271-7510
e-mail: president@omrf.org
www.omrf.org

*Dr. Stephen Prescott, President*
*Mike D. ""Chip"" Morgan, Executive VP and COO*
*Adam Cohen, Senior VP and General Counsel*
*Lisa Day, VP of Business and Government Affairs*
Focuses on arthritis and muscoloskeletal disease research.

4713 **Tulsa City-County Library System: Outreach Services**
Tulsa City: County Library System
1st Fl
400 Civic Ctr
Tulsa, OK 74103-3857 918-549-7323
FAX: 918-596-2841
e-mail: os@tulsalibrary.org
tulsalibrary.org

*Susan Babbitt, Manager*
*Linda Saferite, Director*
Homebound delivery of library services for the physically disabled.

## Oregon

4714 **Oregon Health Sciences University, Elks' Children's Eye Clinic**
Casey Eye Institute
3375 SW Terwilliger Blvd
Portland, OR 97239-4146 503-494-3000
888-222-6478
FAX: 503-494-4286
e-mail: Roystere@ohsu.edu
www.ohsucasey.com

*Earl A Palmer, Director*
*Eleen Reyster, Clinic Manager*
*James Rosenbaum, Manager*
The elks children's eye clinic is the major charitable project of the Oregon State Elks association. The clinic would not be possible without the organization's dedication and commitment to providing eye care for babies and children.

4715 **Oregon Talking Book & Braille Services**
250 Winter St NE
Salem, OR 97301-3929 503-378-5389
800-452-0292
FAX: 503-585-8059
TTY: 503-378-4334
e-mail: tbabs.info@state.or.us
tbabs.org

*Mary Kay Dahlgreen, Interim State Librarian*
*Robin Speer, Fund Development Officer*
*Susan Westin, Program Manager*
*Joel Henderson, Admin Program Coordinator*
We serve the blind and physically disabled. Cassette books and magazines, Braille books-magazines, for children and adults. Descriptive videos. Audiocassette machines are provided free of charge. Call us for an application.

4716 **Talking Book & Braille Services Oregon State Library**
250 Winter St NE
Salem, OR 97301-3929 503-378-5389
800-452-0292
FAX: 503-585-8059
TTY: 503-378-4334
e-mail: tbabs.info@state.or.us
tbabs.org

*Mary Kay Dahlgreen, Interim State Librarian*
*Robin Speer, Fund Development Officer*
*Susan Westin, Program Manager*
*Joel Henderson, Admin Program Coordinator*
Braille writer, magnifiers, large-print photocopier, cassette books and magazines, children's books on cassette and braille books.

## Pennsylvania

4717 **Associated Services For The Blind & Visually Impaired**
919 Walnut St
Philadelphia, PA 19107-5237 215-627-0600
FAX: 215-922-0692
e-mail: asbinfo@asb.org
asb.org

*Patricia C. Johnson, President and CEO*
*Dolores Ferrara-Godzieba, Director*
*John Corrigan, Director*
*John Corrigan, Director*
A service of Associated Services for the Blind. 26 magazines are available on cassette through this subscription service. A magazine list can be sent, in both large print and on audio cassette.
*$18.00*

4718 **Carnegie Library of Pittsburgh Library for the Blind & Physically Handicapped**
4400 Forbes Ave
Pittsburgh, PA 15213-4007 412-622-3114
800-242-0586
FAX: 412-687-2442
e-mail: info@carnegielibrary.org
carnegielibrary.org

*Cathy Chaparro, Manager*
*Sue Murdock, Manager*
*Jane Dayton, Assistant Director*
*Jacqueline Flanagan, Executive Director*
Loans recorded books/magazines and playback equipment, large print books and described videos to western PA residents unable to use standard printed materials due to a visual, physical, or physically-based reading disability.

4719 **Free Library of Philadelphia: Library for the Blind and Physically Handicapped**
1901 Vine Street
Philadelphia, PA 19103 215-686-5322
e-mail: reardons@freelibrary.org
www.library.phila.gov

*Siobhan A. Reardon, President and Director*
*David T. Edwards, Chief Financial Officer, Foundation*
*Melissa Greenberg, Vice President of Development*
*William J. Fleming, Administrative Services Director*
Summer reading programs for children and teens. Closed-circuit T.V.for enlarging print for low vision; computers with screen readers and large print; cassette books and magazines; braille books and magazines; and descriptive videos for the blind and visually impaired. Unique and acclaimed adult education program for all disabilities. State of the art book recording facilities.

4720 **Pennsylvania College of Optometry Eye Institute**
8360 Old York Rd
Elkins Park, PA 19027-1598 215-780-1400
FAX: 215-780-1336
www.pco.edu

Since 1919 the college has led the field in education, in research, and in new approaches to vision diagnosis and correction.

4721 **Reading Rehabilitation Hospital**
Box 250
Rr 1
Reading, PA 19607 610-796-6297
FAX: 610-796-6353
http://rehab.fsnhospitals.com/USA/PA/Pottstow

*Richard Kruczek, CEO*
*Doug Mehrkam, Owner*
Information on physical disabilities, stroke, head injuries, aging and spinal cord injuries.

## Rhode Island

**4722 Office Of Library & Information Services for the Blind and Physically Handicapped**
1 Capitol Hl
4th Floor
Providence, RI 02908-5803
401-574-9300
FAX: 401-574-9320
e-mail: webmaster@olis.ri.gov
http://www.olis.ri.gov

*Howard Boksenbaum, Chief Library Officer*
*Chaichin Chen, Library Program Specialist: LORI Network Services / Web Development*
*Debbie Cullerton, Information Services Technician: Assistant to the Chief / Library Boar*
*Jeremy Cutler, Information Services Technician: LORI Network Services*
Offers information and services for the visually impaired including reference materials, braille printers, braille writers, large-print books and more.

**4723 Talking Books Plus**
Library for the Blind & Physically Handicapped
1 Capitol Hl
4th Floor
Providence, RI 02908-5803
401-574-9300
FAX: 401-574-9320
e-mail: webmaster@olis.ri.gov
http://www.olis.ri.gov

*Howard Boksenbaum, Chief Library Officer*
*Chaichin Chen, Library Program Specialist: LORI Network Services / Web Development*
*Debbie Cullerton, Information Services Technician: Assistant to the Chief / Library Boar*
*Jeremy Cutler, Information Services Technician: LORI Network Services*
Offers talking book services for the blind and physically handicapped. Collection includes reference materials, braille printer, braille writer, large-print books, adaptive computer workstations and referrals to appropriate agencies/programs for other services.

## South Carolina

**4724 Medical University of South Carolina Arthritis Clinical/Research Center**
171 Ashley Ave
Charleston, SC 29425-100
843-792-2300
800-424-MUSC
FAX: 843-792-7121
musc.edu

*Jennie Ariail, Director*
*Tom Gasque Smith, Associate Director*
*Shannon Richards-Slaughter, Assistant Professor*
*Lisa Kerr, PhD, Assistant Professor*
Offers patient care services and basic and clinical research on various types of arthritis and connective tissue diseases.

**4725 South Carolina State Library**
P.O.Box 11469
Columbia, SC 29211-1469
803-734-8026
FAX: 803-734-4757
e-mail: reference@statelibrary.sc.gov
statelibrary.sc.gov

*Deborah P. Anderson,, Administrative Coordinator*
*Flora A. DuBose, Administrative Specialist*
*David S. Goble, Director & State Librarian*
*Sandra Knowles, Director of Talking Book Services*
Summer reading programs, braille writer, magnifiers, closed-circuit T.V., large-print photocopier, cassette books and magazines, children's books on cassette, home visits and other reference materials on blindness and other handicaps.

## South Dakota

**4726 South Dakota State Library**
800 Governors Dr
Pierre, SD 57501-2294
605-773-3131
800-423-6665
FAX: 605-773-6962
TTY: 605-773-4950
e-mail: library@state.sd.us
http://library.sd.gov/

*Dan Siebersma, Manager*
*Quynn Verhelst, Senior Secretary*
*Sarah Easter, Secretary*
*Wynne Nafus Sayer, Webmaster*
Summer reading programs, braille writer, magnifiers, closed-circuit T.V., large-print photocopier, cassette books and magazines, children's books on cassette, home visits and other reference materials on blindness and other handicaps.

## Tennessee

**4727 Tennessee Library for the Blind and Physically Handicapped**
Tennessee State Library Archives
403 7th Ave N
Nashville, TN 37243-1409
615-741-3915
800-342-3308
FAX: 615-532-8856
e-mail: tlbph.tsla@tn.gov
http://www.tennessee.gov/tsla/lbph/

*Ruth Hemphill, Director*
*Ed Byrne, Assistant Director*
Provides free public library service to residents of Tennessee who are unable to read standard print due to a physical disability. Cooperating library with national network of libraries serving people with print disabilities, operating under the auspices

## Texas

**4728 Baylor College of Medicine Birth Defects Center**
6620 Main St
Houston, TX 77030-2348
713-798-1000
FAX: 832-825-3141
www.bcm.edu/obgyn/tcfs

*Frank Greenberg, Director*
One of the few centers in the world that performs fetal surgery. Provides integrated, multidisciplinary care for mothers, carrying babies with genetic or anatomic birth defects requiring therapy before or immediately after birth. This collaboration enable.

**4729 Baylor College of Medicine: Cullen Eye Institute**
Baylor College of Medicine
6565 Fannin St
Houston, TX 77030-2743
713-798-4951
888-562-3937
FAX: 713-798-1521
http://www.bcm.edu/eye/index.cfm?pmid=0

*Dan B. Jones, Professor and Chair*
*Al Vaughan, Manager*
*Michael Cassidy, Plant Manager*
Research activities focus on restoring vision and preventing blindness through a better understanding of the disease.

**4730 Brown-Heatly Library**
4900 N Lamar Blvd
Austin, TX 78751-2316
800-252-5204
800-628-5115
e-mail: dars.inquiries@dars.state.tx.us
www.dars.state.tx.us

Houses a collection of books, audio and video tapes and periodicals focusing on rehabilitation, disabilities, employment skills and practices and management for the Texas Rehabilitation Commission. Houses materials on developmental and other disabilities.

**4731 Center for Research on Women with Disabilities**
Baylor College of Medicine
Ste B
1 Baylor Plz
Houston, TX 77030-3411
713-798-5782
800-443-7693
FAX: 713-798-4688
e-mail: crowd@bcm.tmc.edu
www.bcm.edu/crowd

*Kathy Fire, Administrator*
*Margaret A. Nosek, Executive Director*
*Martha Mendez, Secretary*
*Susan Robinson-Whelen, Investigator*
Research organization dedicated to conducting research and promoting, developeing, and disseminating information to expand the life choices of women with disabilities. Conducts research and training activities on issues related to the health, independence

**4732 Christian Education for the Blind**
Suite 702
4200 S Freeway Dr
Fort Worth, TX 76115
817-920-0044
FAX: 817-920-0777
e-mail: bceb@evl.net
http://www.google.co.in/

*Rodger Dyer, Executive Director*
Offers braille and large print books and cassettes for the visually impaired.

**4733 Houston Public Library: Access Center**
1st Fl
500 McKinney St
Houston, TX 77002-5000
832-393-1313
FAX: 832-393-1474
TTY:832-393-1539
e-mail: website@hpl.lib.tx.us
houstonlibrary.org

*Rhea Brown Lawson, Director*
*Roosevelt Weeks, Deputy Director*
*Greg Simpson, Assistant Director*
Offers full library services to the visually and hearing impaired in Houston, TX at no charge. Houses unique and critical services for its users including online access to the Internet in a private and secure area.

**4734 Talking Book Program/Texas State Library**
Talking Book Program
P.O.Box 12927
Austin, TX 78711-2927
512-463-5458
800-252-9605
FAX: 512-936-0685
e-mail: tbp.services@tsl.state.tx.us
www.texastalkingbooks.org

*Ava M Smith, Director*
Provides reading materials in special formats to Texas residents who cannot read conventional printed matter because of visual or physical limitations, whether permanent or temporary. The service is free and materials are sent through the mail free. Books and magazines are available in digital cartridge, digital download, cassette, braille, and large print formats. A Disabilities Reference Center can answer questions on topics related to disabilities.

**4735 University of Texas Southwestern Medical Center/Allergy & Immunology**
5323 Harry Hines Blvd
Dallas, TX 75390-7208
214-648-3111
e-mail: philip.schoch@utsouthwestern.edu
www.utsouthwestern.edu

*Rita Koger, Director*
*Priscilla Alderman, Executive Assistant*
Mission is to improve the health care in our community, Texas, our nation, and the world through innovation and education. To educate the next generation of leaders in patient care, biomedical science and disease prevention. To conduct high-impact, intern

**4736 University of Texas at Austin Library**
1 University Sta
Austin, TX 78712-900
512-471-1655
FAX: 512-471-5784
e-mail: webform@lib.utexas.edu
finearts.utexas.edu

*Douglas Dempster, Manager*
*Sheldon Ekland-Olson, Chief Executive Officer*
Provides access to information for all users, including those with disabilities, in accordance with the overall mission of the General Libraries of the University of Texas at Austin.

## Utah

**4737 Utah State Library Division: Program for the Blind and Disabled**
250 North 1950 West,Ste A
Salt Lake City, UT 84116-7901
801-715-6789
800-662-5540
FAX: 801-715-6767
e-mail: blind@utah.gov
www.blindlibrary.utah.gov

*Donna Morris, Director*
*Lisa Nelson, Program Manager*
Summer reading programs, Braille embosser, cassette books and magazines, children's books on cassette and other reference materials on blindness and other handicaps, descriptive videos, Braille books and large print books.

## Vermont

**4738 Vermont Department of Libraries - Special Services Unit**
578 Paine Tpke N
Berlin, VT 05602
802-828-3273
800-479-1711
FAX: 802-828-2199
e-mail: lib.ssu@state.vt.us.
www.libraries.vermont.gov/ssu

*Teresa Faust, Special Services Librarian*
Regional network library pf the National Library Service for the Blind & Physically Handicapped. The SSU makes available reading material in large print and NLS talking book formats, including these special collections: children's print braille books, audio described videos and DVDs.

**4739 Vermont Department of Libraries -Special Services Unit**
578 Paine Tpke N
Berlin, VT 05602-9139
802-828-3273
800-479-1711
FAX: 802-828-2199
e-mail: lib.ssu@state.vt.us
libraries.vermont.gov/ssu

*Teresa Faust, Special Services Librarian*

## Virginia

**4740 Access Services**
Fairfax County Public Library
Ste 123
12000 Government Center Pkwy
Fairfax, VA 22035-1
703-324-7329
FAX: 703-222-3193
TTY:703-324-8365
e-mail: access@fairfaxcounty.gov
fairfaxcounty.gov

*Janice Kuch, Branch Manager*
*Beena Pandey, Volunteer Coordinator*
*Ken Plummer, Outreach Manager*
**Offers talking books, TDD access, assistive devices such as decoders for three-week loans, support groups for people who are visually impaired, adapted computer work station with braille printer and assistive listening devices.**

**4741 Alexandria Library Talking Book Service**
5005 Duke St
Alexandria, VA 22304-2903
703-746-1702
FAX: 703-519-5917
TTY:703-519-5911
e-mail: emccaffrey@alexandria.lib.va.us
alexandria.lib.va.us

*Rose T. Dawson, Director*
*Linden Renner, Deputy Director*
*Kimberly Nathaniel, Communications Officer*
**Summer reading programs, braille writer, magnifiers, closed-circuit T.V., large-print photocopier, cassette books and magazines, children's books on cassette, home visits and other reference materials on blindness and other handicaps.**

**4742 Arlington County Department of Libraries**
Arlington County Library
1015 N Quincy St
Arlington, VA 22201-4603
703-228-5990
FAX: 703-228-7720
TTY:703-228-6320
e-mail: libraries@arlingtonva.us
arlingtonva.us

*Diane Kresh, Director*
*Margaret Brown, Chief*
**Summer reading programs, braille writer, magnifiers, closed-circuit T.V., large-print photocopier, cassette books and magazines, children's books on cassette, home visits and other reference materials on blindness and other handicaps.**

**4743 Braille Circulating Library for the Blind**
2700 Stuart Ave
Richmond, VA 23220-3305
804-359-3743
FAX: 804-359-4777
http://bclministries.org

*Brian J. Barton, Executive Director*
**Offers library materials for the blind and visually impaired on a free-loan basis. Serves the entire USA and 41 foreign countries with cassette tapes, reel to reel tapes, braille books, large print books along with talking book records.**

**4744 Central Rappahannock Regional Library**
1201 Caroline St
Fredericksburg, VA 22401-3701
540-372-1144
FAX: 540-899-9867
TTY:540-371-9165
e-mail: webmaster@crrl.org
www.librarypoint.org

*Donna Cote, Executive Director*
*Alison Heartwell, Librarian*
**Offers reference materials on blindness and other disabilities.**

**4745 Council for Exceptional Children**
2900 Crystal Drive
Suite 1000
Arlington, VA 22202-3557
888-232-7733
FAX: 703-264-9494
e-mail: service@cec.sped.org
cec.sped.org

*Margaret J. McLaughin, President*
*James P. Heiden, Treasurer*
*Christy A. Chambers, President Elect*
**Members are teachers, college faculty members, administrators, supervisors and others concerned with the education and welfare of visually handicapped and blind children and youth. This is a division of the Council For Exceptional Children.**

**4746 James Branch Cabell Library**
Virginia Commonwealth University
901 Park Avenue
PO Box 842033
Richmond, VA 23284-2033
804-828-1110
866-828-2665
866-828-2665
FAX: 804-828-0151
www.library.vcu.edu

*James Branch Cabell, Founder*
*Wesley Chenault, Head*
*Yuki Hibben, Assistant Head*
*Ray Bonis, Coordinator*
**Provides individualized orientations and assistance with library research and equipment.**

**4747 Newport News Public Library System**
2400 Washington Ave
Newport News, VA 23607-4301
757-926-8000
FAX: 757-926-1365
e-mail: icieszyn@ci.newport-news.va.us
newportnewsva.com

*Fred Carroll, Chair*
*Mary Sellen, Vice Chair*
**Summer reading programs, braille writer, magnifiers, closed-circuit T.V., large-print photocopier, cassette books and magazines, children's books on cassette, home visits and other reference materials on blindness and other handicaps.**

**4748 Northern Virginia Resource Center for Deafand Hard of Hearing Persons**
Ste 130
3951 Pender Dr
Fairfax, VA 22030-6035
703-352-9056
FAX: 703-352-9058
TTY:703-352-9056
e-mail: info@nvrc.org
nvrc.org

*Gary Viall, Chair*
*Willaim Boyd, Vice Chair*
*Jim Faughnan, Treasurer*
*Alicia Henning, Secretary*
**Empowering deaf and hard of hearing individuals and their families through education, advocacy and community involvement.**

**4749 Roanoke City Public Library System**
706 S Jefferson St
Roanoke, VA 24016-5191
540-853-2473
FAX: 540-853-1781
e-mail: main.library@roanokeva.gov
www.roanokegov.com/library

*Michael L. Ramsey, President*
*Barbara Lemon, Vice President*
**Summer reading programs, braille writer, magnifiers, closed-circuit T.V., large-print photocopier, cassette books and magazines, children's books on cassette, home visits and other reference materials on blindness and other handicaps.**

4750 **Staunton Public Library Talking Book Center**
1 Churchville Ave
Staunton, VA 24401-3229
540-885-6215
800-995-6215
FAX: 540-332-3906
e-mail: talking books@ci.staunton.va.us
www.talkingbookcenter.org

*Lisa Eye, Reader Advisor*
*Deborah R. Austin, President*
*Robin Gilbert, Vice-president*
Offers free library service by circulating recorded books, magazines, and playback equipment to individuals unable to use standard print materials because of visual or physical impairment.

4751 **University of Virginia Health System General Clinical Research Group**
P.O.Box 800787
Charlottesville, VA 22908-0787
434-924-2394
FAX: 434-924-9960
e-mail: gcrc@virginia.edu
gcrc.med.virginia.edu

*Pamela Sprouse, Administrator*
*Eugene J. Barrett, Program Director*
*Mary Lee Vance, Associate Director*
Provides investigators with the specialized resources necessary to conduct advanced clinical research. The facility includes ten inpatient beds, skilled research nurses, a core assay laboratory, a metabolic kitchen, outpatient facilities, computing and st

4752 **Virginia Autism Resource Center**
4100 Price Club Blvd
Midlothian, VA 23112-3379
804-674-8888
877-667-7771
877- -
FAX: 804-276-3970
e-mail: info@varc.org
www.varc.org

*Carol Schall, Director*
*Florence McLeod, Administrative Assistant*
VARC maintains a lending library with books, tapes and DVD's. We also provide resource information to families and professionals working with individuals with autism in Virginia.

4753 **Virginia Beach Public Library Special Services Library**
936 Independence Blvd
Virginia Beach, VA 23455-6006
757-385-0150
FAX: 757-464-6741
http://www.vbgov.com/government/departments/l

*Marcy Sims, Library Director*
*David Palmer, Public Services Manager*
A public library for people with visual and physical disabilities, braille writer, magnifiers, closed-circuit T.V., large-print photocopier, cassette books and magazines, children's books on cassette, and other reference materials on blindness and other d

4754 **Virginia Chapter of the Arthtitis Foundation**
Ste 100
2201 W. Broad St
Richmond, VA 23220-3937
800-365-3811
800-456-4687
FAX: 804-359-4900
e-mail: cmogel@arthritis.org
www.arthritis.org

*Barbara Newhouse, President/CEO*
*Calaneet Balas, Chief Strategy Officer*
Provides free information, services and counseling to the public. Services include assistance in locating and accessing government and other health care programs for persons with arthritis, referral to doctors specializing in the treatment of arthritis,

4755 **Virginia State Library for the Visually and Physically Handicapped**
395 Azalea Ave
Richmond, VA 23227-3623
804-266-2477
800-552-7015
FAX: 804-266-2478
e-mail: barbara.mccarthy@dbvi.virginia.gov
virginiavoice.org

*Nicholas B Morgan, Executive Director*
*Laura Rhodes, Office Manager*
Summer reading programs, braille writer, magnifiers, closed-circuit T.V., large-print photocopier, cassette books and magazines, children's books on cassette, home visits and other reference materials on blindness and other handicaps.

## Washington

4756 **Meridian Valley Clinical Laboratory**
Ste 126
801 SW 16th St
Renton, WA 98057-2632
425-271-8689
855-405-8378
FAX: 425-271-8674
e-mail: meridian@meridianvalleylab.com
www.meridianvalleylab.com

*Jonathan V. Wright, Medical Director*
A clinical test facility dedicated to providing the most accurate and informative data for patient diagnosis and therapeutic monitoring. With our current research and up-to-date information and various aspects of clinical nutritional medicine, our methodo

4757 **Ophthalmic Research Laboratory Eye Institute/First Hill Campus**
747 Broadway
Seattle, WA 98122-4307
206-386-6000
800-833-8879
TTY:206-386-2022
www.swedish.org

*Donald G Peterson, CEO*
Color vision physiology, vision disorders and blindness research.

4758 **Washington Talking Book and Braille Library**
2021 9th Ave
Seattle, WA 98121-2783
206-615-0400
800-542-0866
FAX: 206-615-0437
TTY: 206-615-0418
e-mail: wtbbl@sos.wa.gov
wtbbl.org

*Mike Mello, Chair*
*Karen Johnson, Secretary*
Summer reading programs, braille writer, magnifiers, closed-circuit T.V., large-print photocopier, cassette books and magazines, children's books, and other reference materials on blindness and other handicaps, online catalog, reference station with assis

## West Virginia

4759 **Cabell County Public Library/Talking Book Department/Subregional Library for the Blind**
455 9th St
Huntington, WV 25701-1417
304-528-5700
FAX: 304-528-5701
e-mail: cabelllibrary@cabell.lib.wv.us
cabell.lib.wv.us

*Judy K. Rule, Director*
*Angela Straight, Assistant Director*
*Mary Lou Pratt, Adult Services Coordinator*

Summer reading programs, Braille writer, magnifiers, closed-circuit TV, cassette books and magazines, children's books on cassette reference materials on blindness and other handicaps, enlargers and Arkenstone Reader.

**4760 Division of Rehabilitation Services: Staff Library**
107 Capitol St
Charleston, WV 25301-2609
304-356-2060
800-642-8207
FAX: 304-766-4913
e-mail: carolc@mail.drs.state.wv.us
wvdrs.org

*Carol Johnson, Manager*
Specialized library with information on disabilities and the rehabilitation there of special collections: deaf and hard of hearing, visually impaired/blind, wellness center, literacy and career. The library has assistive devices such as CCTV, scanner and

**4761 Kanawha County Public Library**
123 Capitol St
Charleston, WV 25301-2686
304-343-4646
FAX: 304-348-6530
e-mail: webmaster@kanawha.lib.wv.us
kanawha.lib.wv.us

*Michael Albert, President*
*Elizabeth O. Lord, Vice President*
Summer reading programs, large print PC option, magnifiers, large type books, cassette books, and magazines, children's books on cassette, home visits and other reference materials on blindness and other handicaps

**4762 Ohio County Public Library Services for the Blind and Physically Handicapped**
52 16th St
Wheeling, WV 26003-3671
304-232-0244
FAX: 304-232-6848
e-mail: ocplweb@weirton.lib.wv.us
wheeling.weirton.lib.wv.us

*Michael Baker, Chairman*
*Jimmie McCamic, Secretary*
The Ohio Public Library exists to provide books and related materials that will assist the residents of the community in the pursuit of knowledge, information, education, research, and recreation in order to promote an enlightned citizenry and to enrich t

**4763 Talking Book Department, Parkersburg and Wood County Public Library**
3100 Emerson Ave
Parkersburg, WV 26104-2414
304-420-4587
FAX: 304-420-4589
e-mail: bhdept@park.lib.wv.us

*Lindsay Place, Talking Books Dept. Coordinator*
*Brian Raitz, Director*
Free program loaning recorded books and magazines, braille books and magazines to people who are unable to read or use standard print due to a visual or physical impairment.

**4764 West Virginia Autism Training Center**
Marshall University College Of Educational & Human
Old Main 316
Huntington, WV 25755-1
304-696-2332
800-344-5115
FAX: 304-696-2846
www.marshall.edu/coe/atc

*Barbara Becker-Cottrill, Executive Director*
Provides education, training, and treatment programs for W Virginians who have autism, pervasive developmental disorders or Asperger's disease and have formally been registered with the center.

**4765 West Virginia Library Commission**
1900 Kanawha Blvd E
Charleston, WV 25305-9
304-558-2041
800-642-9021
FAX: 304-558-2044
e-mail: web_one@wvlc.lib.wv.us
librarycommision.lib.wv.us

*Karen Goff, Secretary*
*Deborah McNeal, Personnel Officer*
*Steve Tyler, Supervisor*
Summer reading programs, braille writer, magnifiers, closed-circuit T.V., large-print photocopier, cassette books and magazines, children's books on cassette, home visits and other reference materials on blindness and other handicaps.

**4766 West Virginia School for the Blind Library**
301 E Main St
Romney, WV 26757-1828
304-822-4840
FAX: 304-822-3370
e-mail: cjohn@access.mountain.net

*Patsy Shank, Administrator*
*Cynthia Johnson, Librarian*
Summer reading programs, braille writer, magnifiers, closed-circuit T.V., large-print photocopier, cassette books and magazines, children's books on cassette, home visits and other reference materials on blindness and other handicaps.

## Wisconsin

**4767 Brown County Library**
Central Library Downtown
515 Pine Street
Green Bay, WI 54301-3743
920-448-4400
FAX: 920-448-4376
TTY:920-448-4400
e-mail: bc_library@co.brown.wi.us
www.co.brown.wi.us/library

*Terry Watermelon, President*
*Kathy Pletcher, Vice President*
*Carla Buboltz, Secretary*
*John Hickey, Financial Secretary*
Summer reading programs, braille writer, magnifiers, closed-circuit TV, large-print photocopier, cassette books and magazines, children's books on cassette, home visits and other reference materials on blindness and other handicaps.

**4768 Eye Institute of the Medical College of Wisconsin and Froedtert Clinic**
925 N 87th St
Milwaukee, WI 53226-4812
414-456-2020
FAX: 414-456-6300
e-mail: eyecare@mcw.edu
doctor.mcw.edu

*Jane D Kivlin, Director*
*Richard Schultz, MD*
A national leader as a full-service academic opthalmology program. Dedicated to the highest quality patient care, education, and vision research, the faculty and staff strive to provide state-of-the-art clinical and surgical patient care in a compassionat

**4769 Trace Research and Development Center**
2107 Ecb
Madison, WI 53706
608-262-6966
FAX: 608-262-8848
e-mail: info@trace.wisc.edu
trace.wisc.edu

*Kate Vanderheiden, Program Manager*
Research focused on how standard information and communication technology products may be designed so that more people with disabilities can use them.

**4770 Wisconsin Regional Library for the Blind& Physically Handicapped**
813 W Wells St
Milwaukee, WI 53233-1436
414-286-3045
800-242-8822
FAX: 414-286-3102
TTY: 414-286-3548
e-mail: lbph@mpl.org
dpi.state.wi.us

*Marsha J Valance, Manager*
*Meredith Wittmann, Regional Librarian*
Circulates recorded materials, playback equipment and braille materials to print-handicapped Wisconsin residents.

## Wyoming

**4771 Wyoming Services for the Visually Impaired**
Wyoming Department of Education
2300 Capitol Ave
Cheyenne, WY 82002-0050
307-777-7690
FAX: 307-777-6234
e-mail: golson@educ.state.wy.us
www.k12.wy.us/SE/svi.asp

*Gerald Reichardt, Chairman*
*Dana Mann-Tavegia, Vice-Chair*
Services for the Visually Impaired assists people of all ages who have low vision or are blind. The goal is to provide information, education, and support to individuals with low vision in order that they may lead enjoyable and productive lives with maxim

**4772 Wyoming's New Options in Technology(WYNOT) - University of Wyoming**
1000 E University Ave
Laramie, WY 82071-2000
307-766-2761
888-989-9463
FAX: 307-766-2763
TTY: 800-908-7011
e-mail: wind.uw@uwyo.edu
wind.uwyo.edu/wynot

*William MacLean Jr., Ph.D., Executive Director*
Designed to develop and implement a consumer oriented statewide system of technology-related assistance for people with disabilities of all ages.

# Media, Print

## Children & Young Adults

**4773 A Christian Approach to Overcoming Disability: A Doctor's Story**
Haworth Press
10 Alice St
Binghamton, NY 13904-1503
607-722-5857
800-429-6784
FAX: 607-722-6362
e-mail: orders@haworthpress.com
www.haworthpress.com

*S Harrington-Miller, Advertising*
*William Cohen, Owner*
This is the personal account of a Christian physician who changed her career specialty from obstetrics and gynecology when she was diagnosed with a genetic disease that would cause her to become blind. Dr. Elaine Eng offers faith-based and psychological techniques for coping with disability. *$29.95*
*174 pages Hardcover*
*ISBN 0-789022-57-5*

**4774 ABCD Newsletter Volume Reprints**
Birth Defect Research for Children
976 Lake Baldwin Lane
Suite 104
Orlando, FL 32814
407-895-0802
FAX: 407-895-0824
e-mail: staff@birthdefects.org
www.birthdefects.org

*Betty Mekdeci, Executive Director*
Offers a variety of reprints from the ABCD newsletter on birth defects
*Monthly*

**4775 AT for Infants and Toddlers with Disabilities**
Idaho Assistive Technology Project
129 W 3rd Street
Moscow, ID 83843-2268
208-885-3557
800-432-8324
FAX: 208-885-6145
e-mail: idahoat@uidaho.edu
www.idahoat.org

*Janice Carson, Project Director*
*Sue House, Information Specialist*
This handbook is designed as a guide for parents and families in Idaho who have infants and toddlers with developmental delays or disabilities. *$5.00*
*68 pages*

**4776 Assistive Technology for School Age Children**
Idaho Assistive Technology Project
129 W 3rd St
Moscow, ID 83843-2268
208-885-3559
800-432-8324
FAX: 208-885-6145
e-mail: idahoat@uidaho.edu
www.educ.uidaho.edu/idatech

*Janice Carson, Project Director*
*Sue House*
*$5.00*
*84 pages*

**4777 Birth Defect News**
Birth Defect Research for Children
976 Lake Baldwin Lane
Suite 104
Orlando, FL 32814
407-895-0802
FAX: 407-895-0824
e-mail: staff@birthdefects.org
www.birthdefects.org

*Betty Mekdeci, Executive Director*
Offers updated information on the association activities, events and updates regarding birth defects and environmental exposures.
*Monthly*

**4778 Caring for Children with Chronic Illness**
Springer Publishing Company
11 West 42nd Street
15th Floor
New York, NY 10036
212-431-4370
877-687-7476
FAX: 212-941-7842
e-mail: marketing@springerpub.com
www.springerpub.com

*Annette Imperati, Marketing/Sales Director*
*Ursula Springer, President*
A critical look at the current medical, social, and psychological framework for providing care to children with chronic illnesses. Emphasizing the need to create integrated, interdisciplinary approaches, it discusses issues such as the roles of families, professionals, and institutions in providing health care, the impact of a child's illness on various family structures, financing care, the special problems of chronically ill children as they become adolescents and more. *$36.95*
*320 pages Hardcover*
*ISBN 0-82615 -00-1*

**4779 Complete IEP Guide: How to Advocate for Your Special Ed Child**
Spina Bifida Association of America
Ste 250
4590 Macarthur Blvd NW
Washington, DC 20007-4226
202-944-3285
800-621-3141
FAX: 202-944-3295
e-mail: sbaa@sbaa.org
www.sbaa.org

*Cindy Brownstein, President/ CEO*
This all-in-one guide will help you understand special education law, identify your child's needs, prepare for meetings, develop the IEP and resolve disputes. *$28.95*

**4780 Coping with Being Physically Challenged**
Rosen Publishing Group
29 E 21st St
New York, NY 10010-6209
212-777-3017
FAX: 212-777-0277
e-mail: rosenpub@tribeca.ios.com
rosenpublishing.com

*Roger Rosen, President*
Ratto deals with strong emotions, such as general anger and depression, which affect these young adults and their families. The author shows them how to deal and cope on a day-to-day basis. *$15.95*

*ISBN 0-82391 -44-9*

**4781 Delicate Threads**
Woodbine House
6510 Bells Mill Rd
Bethesda, MD 20817-1636
301-897-3570
800-843-7323
FAX: 301-897-5838
woodbinehouse.com

*Irv Shapell, Owner*
How do friendships between children with and without disabilities develop? How do they compare to friendships between typically developing children? What happens to these friendships over time? In Delicate Threads, author Debbie staub helps to answer these questions through careful observations of friendships between seven pairs of children - each including a child with a moderate to severe disability - who are classmates in an inclusive Pacific Northwest elementary school. *$16.95*
*250 pages Paperback*
*ISBN 0-933149-90-5*

**4782 Don't Call Me Special: A First Look at Disability**
Barron's Educational Series
250 Wireless Blvd
Happaugue, NY 11788
800-645-3476
FAX: 631-494-3723
e-mail: barrons@barronseduc.com
www.barronseduc.com

*Pat Thomas, Author*
This picture book explores questions and concerns about physical disabilities in a simple and reassuring way. Youger children can find out about individual disabilities, special equipment that is available to help the disabled, and how people of all ages can deal with disabilities and live happy and full lives. *$6.26*
*32 pages Paperback*
*ISBN 0-764121-18-0*

**4783 Enabling Romance: A Guide to Love, Sex & Relationships for the Disabled**
Spina Bifida Association of America
Ste 250
4590 Macarthur Blvd NW
Washington, DC 20007-4226
202-944-3285
800-621-3141
FAX: 202-944-3295
e-mail: sbaa@sbaa.org
www.sbaa.org

*Cindy Brownstein, President/ CEO*
An uncensored, illustrated guide to intimacy and sexual expression for persons with physical disabilities. *$15.95*

**4784 For Siblings Only**
Family Resource Associates
35 Haddon Ave
Shrewsbury, NJ 07702-4007
732-747-5310
FAX: 732-747-1896
e-mail: info@frainc.org
www.frainc.org

*Sue Levine, Program Administrator*
*Nancy Phalanukorn, Executive Director*
*Rose Lloyd, Financial Operations Manager*
*Bill Sheeser, President*
A newsletter for brothers and sisters, aged 4 through 10, whose sibling has a disablilty. Includes stories, library resources, activities and discussion of feelings. $12/year for families, $20/year for professionals. *$12.00*
*12 pages Quarterly*

**4785 Helping Children Understand Disabilities**
Brookline Books
34 University Rd
Brookline, MA 02445-4533
800-666-2665
FAX: 617-734-3952
e-mail: brbooks@yahoo.com
www.brooklinebooks.com

Examines children's literature as a vehicle to help children, parents and teachers understand important issues relating to the effects of disability on children. Using the child as narrator, the author demonstrates how to use popular children's fiction to explore taboo areas and stimulate discussion by children and adults. *$10.95*
*Hardcover*
*ISBN 0-91479 -09-3*

**4786 It isn't Fair!: Siblings of Children with Disabilities**
Greenwood Publishing Group
130 Cremona Drive
Santa Barbara, CA 93117
805-968-1911
800-368-6868
FAX: 866-270-3856
e-mail: CustomerService@abc-clio.com
www.abc-clio.com

*Matt Laddin, Vice President of Marketing*
*Mike Saltzman, Director - Eastern Territories & National Accounts*
*James Lingle, International Sales & Marketing Manager Rights & Permissions*
This book presents a wide range of perspectives on the relationship of siblings to children with disabilities. These perspectives are written in the first person by parents, young adult siblings, younger siblings, and professionals.
*200 pages $39.95 - $45*
*ISBN 0-897893-32-8*

**4787 Kid Kare News**
3101 SW Sam Jackson Park Rd
Portland, OR 97239-3009
FAX: 503-241-5090
www.shrinershq.org

*Barbara Flaherty, New Patient Coordinator*
*Sonia Bouchard, Rehabilation Services Manager*
*Kerry Grindeland, Care Coordination Manager*
*Kay Weber, Public Relations*
Bi-annual publication from the Shriners Hospital for Children in Portland, Oregon. Free. Produced by the medical staff.

**4788 Kidz Korner**
Children's Hopes & Dreams Wish Foundation
280 Us Highway 46
Dover, NJ 7801-2084
706-482-2248
FAX: 706-482-2289
e-mail: chdfdover@juno.com
www.helpingnow.org

*Mariann Oswald, Manager*
*6 pages Monthly*

**4789 Laugh with Accent, #3**
Accent Books & Products
P.O.Box 700
Bloomington, IL 61702-700
309-378-2961
800-787-8444
FAX: 309-378-4420
e-mail: acmtlvng@aol.com

*Raymond C Cheever, Publisher*
*Betty Garee, Editor*
These special cartoons prove laughter is the best medicine of all. It's when the laughter stops that we become truly disabled, say readers. *$3.50*
*89 pages Paperback*
*ISBN 0-91570 -16-7*

**4790 Life Beyond the Classroom: Transition Strategies for Young People**
Brookes Publishing
P.O.Box 10624
Baltimore, MD 21285-0624
410-337-9580
800-638-3775
FAX: 410-337-8539
e-mail: custserv@brookespublishing.com
www.brookespublishing.com

*Paul H. Brooks, Chairman*
*Jeffrey D. Brookes, President*
*Melissa A. Behm, Executive Vice President*
This textbook is an essential guide to planning, designing, and implementing successful transition programs for students with disabilities. *$44.00*
*496 pages*
*ISBN 1-55766-05-7*

**4791 Life Planning Workbook**
Exceptional Parent Library
P.O.Box 1807
Englewood Cliffs, NJ 7632-1207
201-947-6000
800-535-1910
FAX: 201-947-9376
e-mail: eplibrary@aol.com
www.eplibrary.com

A hands-on guide to help parents provide for the future security and happiness of their child with a disability after their death. *$24.95*

**4792 Little Children, Big Needs**
Exceptional Parent Library
P.O.Box 1807
Englewood Cliffs, NJ 7632-1207
201-947-6000
800-535-1910
FAX: 201-947-9376
e-mail: eplibrary@aol.com
www.eplibrary.com

Contains candid interviews with fifty families of children with a wide variety of disabilities. *$12.95*

**4793 Mandy**
William Morrow & Company
1350 Avenue of the Americas
New York, NY 10019-4702
212-974-3100
FAX: 212-261-6595
www.williammorrow.com

Told from the point of view of a deaf child, this warm picture book is neither saccharine nor preachy. Mandy has never heard anyone speak or sing. It is from her close relationship with her grandmother that the small girl learns about the world through lip-reading, facial expression, gesture, touch and sign. *$14.95*
*32 pages*

**4794 Mayor of the West Side**
21st Floor
32 Court Street
Brooklyn, NY 11201
718-488-8900
800-876-1710
FAX: 718-488-8642
e-mail: info@fanlight.com
www.fanlight.com

*Ben Achtenberg, Owner*
*Anthony Sweeney, Marketing Director*
What happens when love gets in the way of letting go? As a teenager with multiple disabilities prepares for his Bar Mitzvah, his family and community consider what Mark's life will be like when they are no longer able to protect him. *$199.00*

*ISBN 1-572953-95-0*

**4795 Me, Too**
JB Lippincott
# 227
227 S 6th St
Philadelphia, PA 19106-3713
215-463-3393
800-777-2295
FAX: 215-824-7390

*Robert Scalia, Owner*
Lydia and Lornie were twins. Lydia was a bright twelve year old who vowed to spend her summer vacation teaching her retarded sister, Lornie, how to be normal.
*158 pages Hardcover*
*ISBN 0-39731 -85-X*

**4796 Miles Away and Still Caring: A Guide for Long Distance Caregivers**
AARP Fulfillment
601 E St NW
Washington, DC 20049-1
202-434-2277
800-424-3410
FAX: 202-434-3443
e-mail: member@aarp.org
www.aarp.org

*William Novelli, CEO*
This is one of the most helpful and frequently requested publications. Helps people who must coordinate the care of a loved one from a long distance.
*18 pages*

**4797 My Buddy**
Exceptional Parent Library
P.O.Box 1807
Englewood Cliffs, NJ 7632-1207
201-947-6000
800-535-1910
FAX: 201-947-9376
e-mail: eplibrary@aol.com
www.eplibrary.com

Story focuses on the friendship between a boy with a disability and his loyal golden retriever. *$5.95*
*Library Binding*
*ISBN 0-785799-24-9*

**4798 Negotiating the Special Education Maze: A Guide for Parents and Teachers**
Spina Bifida Association of America
Ste 250
4590 Macarthur Blvd NW
Washington, DC 20007-4226
202-944-3285
800-621-3141
FAX: 202-944-3295
e-mail: sbaa@sbaa.org
www.sbaa.org

*Cindy Brownstein, President/ CEO*
An excellent aid for the development of an effective special education program. *$19.00*

**4799 New Horizons Independent Living Center**
8085 E Manley Dr
Prescott Valley, AZ 86314-6154
928-772-1266
800-406-2377
FAX: 928-772-3808
TTY: 928-772-1266
e-mail: ltoone@cableone.net
www.newhorizonsilc.org

*Liz Toone, Executive Director*
*Zena Taylor, Financial Manager*
*Deborah Henderson, Administrative Assistant*
An advocacy and living center organized by and for people with disabilities, serving Apache, Coconino, Mojave, Navajo and Yavapai counties.

**4800 NoBody's Perfect....Educating Children about Disabilities**
Aquarius Health Care Videos
30 Forest Road
PO Box 249
Millis, MA 02054
508-376-1244
FAX: 508-376-1245
e-mail: lann@aquariusproductions.com
www.aquariusproductions.com

*Leslie Kussmann, President/Producer*
An upbeat, inclusion-friendly program for kids that profiles three children with disabilties. Viewers discover that accepting differences is an essential part of growing up. We learn how the kids cope and, in the process, are introduced to signing, prosthetics, and assistive technology and Braille. Videocassette, preview option is available. *$ 99.00*

**4801 On Our Own Terms: Children Living with Physical Disabilities**
Gareth Stevens Publishing
1 Readers Digest Rd
Pleasantville, NY 10570-7000
914-242-4100
FAX: 914-242-4187
www.garethstevens.com

*Lisa Herrington, Senior Managing Editor*
Meet Kicki, a three-year-old with Spina Bifida, battling to walk for the first time. Meet Annelie, nine years old, learning to walk again after a bad car accident. Face the physical challenges with her. *$13.95*
*48 pages*
*ISBN 1-555329-42-X*

**4802 Recognizing Children with Special Needs**
Aquarius Health Care Videos
P.O.Box 1159
Sherborn, MA 01770-7159
508-650-6905
FAX: 508-650-4216
e-mail: aqvideos@tiac.net
www.aquariusproductions.com
A great overview for caregivers of children on how to recognize special needs. Often-times it is the little things children do everyday to compensate for, or express, a disability that can be observed by their caregiver. All types of disabilities are addressed: emotional, physical, psychological, and chronic illness. A wonderful tool for teachers, childcare staff, and students on how to play a vital role in our children's development. Preview option available. *$125.00*
*Video*

**4803 Reflections on Growing Up Disabled**
Council for Exceptional Children
Ste 300
1110 N Glebe Rd
Arlington, VA 22201-5704
703-264-9454
FAX: 703-264-1637
www.cec.sped.org

*Bruce Ramirez, Executive Director*
Understand how it feels to be a disabled person in school by tuning in to the first-hand accounts of people who have disabilities. *$10.00*
*112 pages*

**4804 Rolling Along with Goldilocks and the Three Bears**
Spina Bifida Association of America
Ste 250
4590 Macarthur Blvd NW
Washington, DC 20007-4226
202-944-3285
800-621-3141
FAX: 202-944-3295
e-mail: sbaa@sbaa.org
www.sbaa.org

*Cindy Brownstein, President/ CEO*
The familiar fairytale with a special needs twist. Ages 3-7. *$17.00*

**4805 Sibling Forum**
Family Resource Associates
35 Haddon Ave
Shrewsbury, NJ 07702-4007
732-747-5310
FAX: 732-747-1896
e-mail: info@frainc.org
www.frainc.org

*Sue Levine, Program Administrator*
*Nancy Phalanukorn, Executive Director*
*Rose Lloyd, Financial Operations Manager*
*Bill Sheeser, President*
A newsletter for brothers and sisters, aged 10 through teen, whose sibling has a disablilty. Includes input from readers, library resources and discussion of feelings. $12/year for families, $20/year for professionals. *$12.00*
*8-12 pages Quarterly*

**4806 Sibshops: Workshops for Siblings of Children with Special Needs**
Brookes Publishing
P.O.Box 10624
Baltimore, MD 21285-0624
410-337-9580
800-638-3775
FAX: 410-337-8539
e-mail: custserv@brookespublishing.com
readplaylearn.com

*Paul H. Brooks, Chairman*
*Jeffrey D. Brookes, President*
*Melissa A. Behm, Executive Vice President*
Sibshops is a program that brings together 8-to 13-year-old brothers and sisters of children with special needs. The siblings receive support and information in a recreational setting, so they have fun while they learn. *$32.00*
*256 pages Paperback*
*ISBN 1-55766 -69-3*

**4807 Special Education Report**
Aspen Publishers
7201 McKinney Cir
Frederick, MD 21704-8356
301-698-7100
800-638-8437
FAX: 301-695-7931
e-mail: customer.service@aspenpubl.com
www.aspenpublishers.com

*Judith Ree, Manager*
Published biweekly, Special Education Report is the independent news service on law, policy and funding of programs for disabled children. *$16.00*
*8-12 pages Newsletter*

**4808 Special Format Books for Children and Youth Ages 3-19**
Cultural Education Center
Albany, NY 12230-1
518-474-5935
800-342-3688
www.nysl.nysed.gov/tbbl/index.html

*Jane Somers, Director*

**4809 Special Format Books for Children and Youth: Ages 3-19.Serving New York City/Long Islan**
476 5th Ave
New York, NY 10018-2788
212-930-0800
FAX: 212-921-2546
e-mail: pleclerc@nypl.org
nypl.org

*Paul Leclerc, CEO*
*Robert Brian, Manager*

**4810 The Comprehensive Directory: Programs and Services And Special Needs In The Metro NY Area.**
Resources for Children with Special Needs
Fl 5
116 E 16th St
New York, NY 10003-2164 212-677-4650
FAX: 212-254-4070
e-mail: info@resourcesnyc.org
www.resourcesnyc.org

*Rachel Howard, Executive Director*
*John Hart, Director of Program Operations*
The second edition of this publication from resources for children with special needs, inc. covers more than 3000 agencies providing all types of services, education, child care, after school, employment, residential, medical and health care, parenting programs and family support. provides 1500 pages of valuable and timely information. *$ 22.00*
*308 pages Yearly*
*ISBN 0-967836-57-3*

**4811 Transition Matters: from School to Independence: A Guide and Directory of Services**
Resources for Children with Special Needs
Fl 5
116 E 16th St
New York, NY 10003-2164 212-677-4650
FAX: 212-254-4070
e-mail: info@resourcesnyc.org
www.resourcesnyc.org

*Rachel Howard, Executive Director*
*John Hart, Director of Program Operations*
A guide to the need for transition planning; plus 1000 agencies and organizations that provide post secondary education, vocational services, learning options and family support to children with disabilities transitioning out of high school. *$35.00*
*496 pages*
*ISBN 0-967836-56-5*

**4812 Understanding Cub Scouts with Disabilities**
Boy Scouts of America
1325 W Walnut Hill Ln
Irving, TX 75038-3008 972-580-2000
800-323-0732
www.scouting.org

*Wayne Perry, President*
Manual on how to teach and understand boy scouts with handicaps.
*10 pages*

**4813 Views from Our Shoes**
Spina Bifida Association of America
Ste 250
4590 Macarthur Blvd NW
Washington, DC 20007-4226 202-944-3285
800-621-3141
FAX: 202-944-3295
e-mail: sbaa@sbaa.org
www.sbaa.org

*Cindy Brownstein, President/ CEO*
Siblings share what it is like to have a brother or sister with a disability. Age 9 and up. *$17.00*
*106 pages Paperback*

**4814 What About Me? Growing Up with a Developmentally Disabled Sibling**
Perseus Publishing
1094 Flex Drive
Jackson, TN 38301 800-343-4499
FAX: 800-351-5073
e-mail: celeste.winters@perseusbooks.com
www.perseusdistribution.com
Silverstein, a physician, gives a first-person account of his experiences as the older brother of an autistic sibling. Siegel, a developmental psychologist, presents discussion of family approaches to handicaps based on clinical interviews with some 1,000 families of various ethnic, social, and educational backgrounds. *$24.00*
*316 pages Paperback*
*ISBN 0-738206-30-X*

**4815 What It's Like to be Me**
Friendship Press
P.O.Box 37844
Cincinnati, OH 45222-844 513-948-8733
FAX: 513-761-3722
www.ncccusa.org

*Nancy Kennedy, Customer Service*
*Robert Bray, Manager*
This was written and illustrated entirely by children with handicapped conditions. These contributions invite the reader to set aside any pity or prejudices and listen. Black and white, and color drawings and photographs make this book visually appealing, enjoyable for all ages. *$10.95*

## Community

**4816 A Commitment to Inclusion: Outreach to Unserved/Underserved Populations**
Independent Living Research Utilization ILRU
Ste 1000
2323 S Shepherd Dr
Houston, TX 77019-7031 713-520-0232
FAX: 713-520-5785
e-mail: ilru@ilru.org
ilru.org

*Lex Frieden, Director, ILRU*
*Richard Petty, Program Director*
*Rose Shepard, Office Manager*
Carol Bradley describes Independent Living Resource Center San Francisco's community organizing/outreach approach to serving under-represented consumers. This organization successfully reaches persons with pychiatric disabilities, environmental illness/multiple chemical sensitivities, chronic fatigue immune deficiency syndrome, learning disabilities, institutionalized persons, Chinese, Latinos, deaf/hard of hearing, and lesbian/bisexual populations.
*10 pages*

**4817 California Community Care News Community Residential Care Association of CA**
Charles W Skoien Jr
P.O.Box 163270
1924 Alhambra Blvd.
Sacramento, CA 95816-9270 916-455-0723
FAX: 916-455-7201
e-mail: information@crcac.com
www.crcac.com

*Charles W Skoien Jr, Director/Lobbyist*
*Denise Johnson, Administrative Assistant*
Forum for the exchange of ideas, information and opinions among clients, families and service providers. Information regarding services and assisted living programs for the elderly, mentally ill and disabled. *$45.00*
*24 pages Monthly*

**4818 Community Recreation and People with Disabilities: Strategies for Inclusion**

Brookes Publishing
P.O.Box 10624
Baltimore, MD 21285-0624
410-337-9580
800-638-3775
FAX: 410-337-8539
e-mail: custserv@brookespublishing.com
readplaylearn.com

*Paul H. Brooks, Chairman*
*Jeffrey D. Brookes, President*
*Melissa A. Behm, Executive Vice President*

Offers creative ideas and new techniques for including people with disabilities in community recreation programs. *$39.00*
*368 pages Paperback*
*ISBN 1-55766-59-2*

**4819 Crossing the River: Creating a Conceptual Revolution in Community & Disability**

Brookline Books
34 University Rd
Brookline, MA 02445-4533
800-666-2665
FAX: 617-734-3952
e-mail: brbooks@yahoo.com
www.brooklinebooks.com

For persons with disabilities, a new conception of care is beginning to emerge-a conception seeking to embed these persons in a web of personal relationships, and to involve them in the dynamics of their community. Schwartz explores the promise, potential, and limits of this new direction. *$24.95*
*238 pages Paperback*
*ISBN 0-91479 -82-4*

**4820 Disablement in the Community**

Oxford University Press
2001 Evans Rd
Cary, NC 27513-2009
919-677-0977
800-451-7556
FAX: 919-677-1303
e-mail: jnlorders@oupjournals.org
www.oup-usa.org

This book shows how the knowledge of the epidemiology of disablement can help planners, service providers, patients and voluntary organizations choose strategies for community care. *$39.95*
*248 pages Illustrated*

**4821 Getting the Most Out of Consultation Services**

Independent Living Research Utilization I LR U
Ste 1000
2323 S Shepherd Dr
Houston, TX 77019-7031
713-520-0232
FAX: 713-520-5785
e-mail: ilru@ilru.org
ilru.org

*Lex Frieden, Director, ILRU*
*Richard Petty, Program Director*
*Rose Shepard, Office Manager*

A practical, nuts-and-bolts approach to help make working with a consultant a positive, helpful experience for independent living centers.
*10 pages*

**4822 Home and Community Care for Chronically Ill Children**

Oxford University Press
2001 Evans Rd
Cary, NC 27513-2009
919-677-0977
800-451-7556
FAX: 919-677-1303
e-mail: jnlorders@oupjournals.org
www.oup-usa.org

This book lays common ground for all who have reason and responsibility to enhance the capability of families to care for their ill children over the long term at home. *$32.95*
*192 pages*

**4823 Housing, Support, and Community**

Brookes Publishing
P.O.Box 10624
Baltimore, MD 21285-0624
410-337-9580
800-638-3775
FAX: 410-337-8539
e-mail: custserv@brookespublishing.com
readplaylearn.com

*Paul H. Brooks, Chairman*
*Jeffrey D. Brookes, President*
*Melissa A. Behm, Executive Vice President*

Choices and strategies for adults with disabilities. *$32.00*
*416 pages Paperback*
*ISBN 1-55766-90-5*

**4824 Inclusive Child Care for Infants and Toddlers: Meeting Individual and Special Needs**

Brookes Publishing
P.O.Box 10624
Baltimore, MD 21285-0624
410-337-9580
800-638-3775
FAX: 410-337-8539
e-mail: custserv@brookespublishing.com
readplaylearn.com

*Paul H. Brooks, Chairman*
*Jeffrey D. Brookes, President*
*Melissa A. Behm, Executive Vice President*

This book gives child care providers the practical guidance they need to serve infants and toddlers with and without disabilities in inclusive settings. It offers information and helpful advice on handling daily care tasks, teaching responsively, meeting individual needs, developing rapport with parents, understanding toddlers' behavior, working with IFSPs, and maintaining high standards of care. *$34.95*
*400 pages Paperback*
*ISBN 1-55766-96-7*

**4825 Independence & Transition to Community Living: The Role of Independent Living Centers**

Independent Living Research Utilization ILRU
Ste 1000
2323 S Shepherd Dr
Houston, TX 77019-7031
713-520-0232
FAX: 713-520-5785
e-mail: ilru@ilru.org
ilru.org

*Lex Frieden, Director, ILRU*
*Richard Petty, Program Director*
*Rose Shepard, Office Manager*

This publication covers important information on why we all should make assistance to people living in nursing homes a priority. Just as important, this is an excellent summary of all the facts - quality of life, health, and costs - which support deinstitutionalization.
*10 pages*

**4826 Independent Living Matters**

DisAbility Resources of Southwest Washington
Ste N
5501 NE 109th Ct
Vancouver, WA 98662-6174
360-260-2253
FAX: 360-694-6910
e-mail: ilrswwa@lqwest.net

*Jim Baker, Executive Director*
*Angela Hartford, Editor/Administrative Technician*
*Scott Anfinson, Independent Living Specialist*

To promote the philosophy of independent living by creating opportunities, encouraging choices, advancing equal access and furthering the level of independence for all people with disabilities.
*8-10 pages Quarterly*

**4827 Keys to Independence**
Coalition for Independence
1281 Eisenhower Rd
Leavenworth, KS 66048
913-250-0287
FAX: 913-250-0167
e-mail: kolson@cfikc.org
www.cfikc.org

*Kathy Cooper, Manager*
*Bi-Monthly*

**4828 National Survey Of Americans With Disabilities**
National Organization on Disability
Ste 600
910 16th St NW
Washington, DC 20006-2903
202-872-4710
FAX: 202-293-7999
e-mail: ability@nod.org
www.nod.org

*Michael Deland, President*
*Nancy Starnes, Senior Vice President*
*John Hershey, Advice/Resource Manager*
National cross-disability organization, specializing in employment and emergency preparedness.

**4829 Part Two: A Preview of Independence and Transition to Community Living**
Independent Living Research Utilization ILRU
Ste 1000
2323 S Shepherd Dr
Houston, TX 77019-7031
713-520-0232
FAX: 713-520-5785
e-mail: ilru@ilru.org
ilru.org

*Lex Frieden, Director, ILRU*
*Richard Petty, Program Director*
*Rose Shepard, Office Manager*
This publication covers important strategies for helping people leave nursing homes. It includes several important recommendations which CIL leaders and staffs will find useful in organizing transition activities.
*10 pages*

**4830 Resourceful Woman**
Rehabilitation Institute of Chicago
345 E Superior St
Chicago, IL 60611-2654
312-238-2231
FAX: 312-238-1205
TTY:312-908-8523
e-mail: hrcwd@rehabchicago.org
rehabchicago.org

*Luciano Dias, Director*
*Kristi Kirchner, MD, Medical Director*
*Linda E Miller, Domestic Violence Coordinator*
*Wayne Lerner, CEO*
Annual publication of national, not-for-profit, general health and service center providing accessible medical services for women with disabilities. Conducts research into health issues concerning disabled women and offers educational resources for healthcare professionals and women with disabilities.

**4831 Transitioning Exceptional Children and Youth Into the Community**
Haworth Press
10 Alice St
Binghamton, NY 13904-1503
607-722-5857
800-429-6784
FAX: 607-722-6362
e-mail: orders@haworthpress.com
www.haworthpress.com

*William Cohen, Owner*
Focusing on the dynamic process of mainstreaming exceptional children and youth into the community, experts examine some of the exciting technological advances made to accompany the social changes enacted over the years. *$44.95*
*202 pages Hardcover*
*ISBN 0-866567-33-X*

**4832 Transitions to Adult Life**
Books on Special Children
P.O.Box 305
Congers, NY 10920-305
845-638-1236
FAX: 845-638-0847
e-mail: irene@boscbooks.com

Transition programs that can help severely handicapped people become participating, contributing members of the community. *$ 37.00*
*385 pages Softcover*

## Employment

**4833 A Guide for People with Disabilities Seeking Employment**
US Department of Justice
950 Pennsylvania Ave NW
Washington, DC 20530-9
202-586-5000
800-574-0301
FAX: 202-307-1197
TTY: 800-514-0383
www.ada.gov

*James Bostrom, Deputy Chiefs*
*Zita Johnson Betts, Deputy Chiefs*
*Sally Conway, Deputy Chiefs*
A 2-page pamplet for people with disabilities providing a general explanation of the employment provisions of the ADA and how to file a complaint with the Equal Employment Opportunity Commission.

**4834 ADA Questions and Answers**
US Department of Justice
950 Pennsylvania Ave NW
Washington, DC 20530-9
202-586-5000
800-574-0301
FAX: 202-307-1197
TTY: 800-514-0383
www.ada.gov

*James Bostrom, Deputy Chiefs*
*Zita Johnson Betts, Deputy Chiefs*
*Sally Conway, Deputy Chiefs*
A 31-page booklet giving an overview of the ADA's requirements affecting employers, businesses, nonprofit service agencies, and state and local governments programs, including public transportation.

**4835 ANCOR Wage and Hour Handbook**
American Network of Community Options & Resources
Ste 380
1101 King St
Alexandria, VA 22314-2962
703-535-7850
FAX: 703-535-7860
e-mail: ancor@ancor.org
ancor.org

*Renee L Pietrangelo, CEO*
*Suellen Galbraith, Director Public Policy*
This useful publication contains the latest rules and interpretations from the U.S. Department of Labor relative to employment in residential support services for people with disabilities, including copies of enforcement policies and letters of interpretation. It outlines in detail when exemptions from miniimum wage and overtime rules can be applied,a nd when and how employees may be paid on a salary basis. Sample staffing patterns are provided.
*121 pages*

**4836 Ability Magazine**
Jobs Information Business Service
8941 Atlanta Ave.
Huntington Beach, CA 92646
949-854-8700
FAX: 949-548-5966
www.abilitymagazine.com

Provides an electronic classified system which allows employers to recruit qualified individuals with disabilities, and people with disabilities to locate employment opportunities.

**4837 Americans with Disabilities**
Federal Consumer Information Center
Department 513j
Pueblo, CO 81009-1
719-948-3334
888-878-3256
FAX: 719-948-9724
e-mail: catalog.pueblo@gsa.gov
www.pueblo.gsa.gov

*Alfred Pino, Manager*

Explains how civil rights of persons with disabilities are protected at work and in public places.

**4838 Americans with Disabilities Act: Questionsand Answers**
Federal Consumer Information Center
Department 513j
Pueblo, CO 81009-1
888-878-3256
FAX: 719-948-9724
e-mail: catalog.pueblo@gsa.gov
www.pueblo.gsa.gov

*Judi Mahaney, Public Affairs*

Explains how the Civil Rights of Persons with disabilities are protected at work and in public places. Free.

**4839 Career Education for Handicapped Individuals**
McGraw-Hill, School Publishing
220 E Danieldale Rd
Desoto, TX 75115-2490
972-224-4772
800-442-9685
FAX: 972-228-1982
mcgraw-hill.com

*Joseph Gavigan, President*

Based on a life-centered career education program that goes beyond elementary school level to include handicapped people of all ages.
*454 pages*

**4840 Earning a Living**
Accent Books & Products
P.O.Box 700
Bloomington, IL 61702-700
309-378-2961
800-787-8444
FAX: 309-378-4420
e-mail: acmtlvng@aol.com

*Raymond C Cheever, Publisher*
*Betty Garee, Editor*

Discusses how to prepare a person for a career, what to say in an interview, and gives examples of both home businesses and jobs away from home. Tells how to modify a worksite and how to be successful on the job. *$9.50*
*88 pages Paperback*
*ISBN 0-91570 -23-0*

**4841 Employment in the Mainstream**
Mainstream
Ste 830
3 Bethesda Metro Ctr
Bethesda, MD 20814-6301
301-961-9299
800-247-1380
FAX: 301-891-8778
e-mail: info@mainstreaminc.org
www.mainstreaminc.org

*David Pichette, Executive Director*
*Fritz Rumpel, Editor*
*Charles Moster*

Reports on issues, ideas, problems and solutions in employing persons with any kind of physical or mental disability. Quarterly magazine. *$25.00*
*32 pages*

**4842 Encyclopedia of Basic Employment and Daily Living Skills**
Phillip Roy, Inc
P.O.Box 130
Indian Rocks Beach, FL 33785-130
727-593-2700
800-255-9085
FAX: 727-595-2685
e-mail: info@philliproy.com
www.philliproy.com

*Ruth Bragman PhD, President*
*Phil Padol, Consultant*

Contains developmental skills for special education students. Contains lessons in 6 curriculum areas covering 80 objects with 541 lessons. Also includes objectives, instructional strategies, and assessment tasks. *$495.00*
*1200 pages*
*ISBN 1-568182-25-2*

**4843 Handbook of Career Planning for Special Needs Students**
Sage Publications
2455 Teller Road
Thousand Oaks, CA 91320
805-499-9774
800-818-7243
FAX: 800-583-2665
e-mail: info@sagepub.com
www.sagepub.com

*Sara Miller McCune, Founder, Publisher, Chairperson*
*Blaise R Simqu, President & CEO*

The practitioner's guide will show you how to help special needs adolescents and young adults overcome barriers to employment by identifying goals and problems, assessing interests and aptitudes, involving client families and developing communication skills. *$46.00*
*358 pages Hardcover*
*ISBN 0-890797-06-4*

**4844 Making News**
Avacado Press
P.O.Box 406781
Louisville, KY 40204
888-739-1920
FAX: 502-899-9562
e-mail: contact145@advocadopress.org
www.advocadopress.org

Book gives how-to information on influencing media coverage of disability issues. *$8.00*
*165 pages*
*ISBN 0-962706-43-4*

**4845 Making Self-Employment Work for People with Disabilities**
Brookes Publishing
P.O.Box 10624
Baltimore, MD 21285-0624
410-337-9580
800-638-3775
FAX: 410-337-8539
e-mail: custserv@brookespublishing.com
readplaylearn.com

*Paul H. Brooks, Chairman*
*Jeffrey D. Brookes, President*
*Melissa A. Behm, Executive Vice President*

Practical support for individuals with significant disabilities in starting and maintaining a small business. Covers building a business plan; pinpointing interests, strengths, and goals; and finding helpful information and support *$35.00*
*288 pages*
*ISBN 1-557666-52-0*

**4846 Making the Workplace Accessible: Guidelines, Costs and Resources**
Spina Bifida Association of America
Ste 250
4590 Macarthur Blvd NW
Washington, DC 20007-4226
202-944-3285
800-621-3141
FAX: 202-944-3295
e-mail: sbaa@sbaa.org
www.sbaa.org

*Cindy Brownstein, President/ CEO*

A 20 page reference guide on how to provide physical access to persons with disabilities in a cost effective manner. *$9.00*

**4847 People with Hearing Loss and the Workplace Guide for Employers/ADA Compliances**
Hearing Loss Association of America
Ste 1200
7910 Woodmont Ave
Bethesda, MD 20814-7022
301-657-2248
FAX: 301-913-9413
e-mail: info@hearingloss.org
www.hearingloss.org

*Brenda Battat, Executive Director*

A guide for both people with hearing loss and their employers to learn about accommodations under the law. Includes employment guidelines, resource list of manufacturers and case studies. *$15.00*
*40 pages Paperback*

**4848 Road Ahead: Transition to Adult Life for Persons with Disabilities**
Training Resource Network
PO Box 439
St. Augustine, FL 32085-0439
FAX: 904-823-3554
e-mail: info@trninc.com
www.trninc.com

Explores transition planning, assessment, instructional strategies, career development and support, social life, quality of life, supported living, and post-secondary education. *$32.95*
*223 pages*
*ISBN 1-883302-46-3*

**4849 Supported Employment for Disabled People**
Human Sciences Press
233 Spring St
New York, NY 10013-1522
877-283-3229
800-644-4831
e-mail: ainy@aveda.com
www.aveda.edu

Highlights the major features of supported employment. Contributions offer service providers in social work, education and mental health much-needed information. *$38.95*
*288 pages Cloth*
*ISBN 0-89885-46-6*

**4850 WORK**
Suite 9
64511 Via Real
Carpinteria, CA 93013
805-566-9000
FAX: 805-566-9070

*Kathy Webb, Executive Director*

Vocational and residential training and support services for adults with developmental disabilities.

## General Disabilities

**4851 A Guide to Disability Rights Law**
US Department of Justice
950 Pennsylvania Ave NW
Washington, DC 20530-9
202-514-4609
800-574-0301
FAX: 202-514-0293
TTY: 800-514-0383
usatoday.com

*James Bostrom, Deputy Chiefs*
*Zita Johnson Betts, Deputy Chiefs*
*Sally Conway, Deputy Chiefs*

A 21-page booklet providing a brief description of the ADA, the Telecommunications Act, Fair Housing Act, Air Carrier Access Act, Voting Accessibility for the Elderly and Handicapped Act, National Voter Registration Act, Civil Rights of Institutionalized Persons Act, Individuals with Disabilities in Education Act, Rehabilitation Act, Architectural Barriers Act, and the federal agencies to contact for more information.

**4852 A Practical Guide to Art Therapy Groups**
Haworth Press
10 Alice St
Binghamton, NY 13904-1503
607-722-5857
800-429-6784
FAX: 607-722-6362
e-mail: orders@haworthpress.com
www.haworthpress.com

*S Harrington-Miller, Advertising*
*William Cohen, Owner*

Unique approaches, materials, and device will inspire you to tap into your own well of creativity to design your own treatment plans. It lays out the ingredients and the skills to get the results you want. *$64.95*
*115 pages Hardcover*
*ISBN 0-789001-36-5*

**4853 A World Awaits You**
Mobility International USA
P.O.Box 10767
Eugene, OR 97440-2767
541-343-1284
FAX: 541-343-6812
e-mail: info@miusa.org
www.miusa.org

*Pamala Houston, Public Relations Coordinator*
*Tracy Scharn, Project Assstant*
*Susan Sygall, Executive Director*

Free publication from Mobility International USA.
*44 pages Yearly*

**4854 AAPD News**
American Association of People with Disabilities
Ste 503
1629 K St NW
Washington, DC 20006-1634
202-457-0046
800-840-8844
FAX: 202-457-0473
e-mail: aapd@aol.com
www.aapd-dc.org

*Anelie Bush, Editor*
*Quarterly*

**4855 ADA Guide for Small Businesses**
US Department of Justice
950 Pennsylvania Ave NW
Washington, DC 20530-9
202-586-5000
800-574-0301
FAX: 202-307-1197
TTY: 800-514-0383
www.ada.gov

*James Bostrom, Deputy Chiefs*
*Zita Johnson Betts, Deputy Chiefs*
*Sally Conway, Deputy Chiefs*
A 15-page booklet for businesses that provide goods and services to the public. This publication explains basic ADA requirements, illustrates ways to make facilities accessible, and provides information about tax credits and deductions.

**4856 ADA Guide for Small Towns**
US Department of Justice
950 Pennsylvania Ave NW
Washington, DC 20530-9
202-586-5000
800-574-0301
FAX: 202-307-1197
TTY: 800-514-0383
www.ada.gov

*James Bostrom, Deputy Chiefs*
*Zita Johnson Betts, Deputy Chiefs*
*Sally Conway, Deputy Chiefs*
A 21-page guide that presents an informal overview of some basic ADA requirements and provides cost-effective tips on how small towns can comply with the ADA.

**4857 ADA Information Services**
US Department of Justice
950 Pennsylvania Ave NW
Washington, DC 20530-9
202-586-5000
800-574-0301
FAX: 202-307-1197
TTY: 800-514-0383
www.ada.gov

*James Bostrom, Deputy Chiefs*
*Zita Johnson Betts, Deputy Chiefs*
*Sally Conway, Deputy Chiefs*
A 2-page list with the telephone numbers and internet addresses of federal agencies and other organizations that provide information and technical assistance to the public about the ADA.

**4858 ADA Pipeline**
DRTAC: Southeast ADA Center
490 10th St NW
Atlanta, GA 30318-5754
404-385-0636
800-949-4232
FAX: 404-385-0641
e-mail: sedbtacproject@law.sgr.edu
www.sedbtac.org

*Amy Oliveras, Administrative Assistant*
*Mary Morder, Alternative Format Coordinator*
*Shelley Kaplan, Director*
*Joseph Addo, Owner*
*16 pages Quarterly*

**4859 ADA Questions and Answers**
US Department of Justice
950 Pennsylvania Ave NW
Washington, DC 20530-9
202-586-5000
800-574-0301
FAX: 202-307-1197
TTY: 800-514-0383
www.ada.gov

*James Bostrom, Deputy Chiefs*
*Zita Johnson Betts, Deputy Chiefs*
*Sally Conway, Deputy Chiefs*
A 31-page booklet giving an overview of the ADA's requirements affecting employers, businesses, nonprofit service agencies, and state and local governments programs, including public transportation.

**4860 ADA Tax Incentive Packet for Business**
US Department of Justice
950 Pennsylvania Ave NW
Washington, DC 20530-9
202-586-5000
800-574-0301
FAX: 202-307-1197
TTY: 800-514-0383
www.ada.gov

*James Bostrom, Deputy Chiefs*
*Zita Johnson Betts, Deputy Chiefs*
*Sally Conway, Deputy Chiefs*
A 13-page packet of information to help businesses understand and take advantage of the tax credit and deduction available for complying with the ADA.

**4861 ADA and City Governments: Common Problems**
US Department of Justice
950 Pennsylvania Ave NW
Washington, DC 20530-9
202-586-5000
800-574-0301
FAX: 202-307-1197
TTY: 800-514-0383
www.ada.gov

*James Bostrom, Deputy Chiefs*
*Zita Johnson Betts, Deputy Chiefs*
*Sally Conway, Deputy Chiefs*
A 9-page document that contains a sampling of common problems shared by city governments of all sizes, provides examples of common deficiencies and explains how these problems affect persons with disabilities.

**4862 ADA-TA: A Technical Assistance Update from the Department of Justice**
US Department of Justice
950 Pennsylvania Ave NW
Washington, DC 20530-9
202-586-5000
800-574-0301
FAX: 202-307-1197
TTY: 800-514-0383
www.ada.gov

*James Bostrom, Deputy Chiefs*
*Zita Johnson Betts, Deputy Chiefs*
*Sally Conway, Deputy Chiefs*
A serial publication that answers Common Questions about ADA requirements and provides Design Details illustrating particular design requirements. The first edition addresses Readily Achievable Barrier Removal and Van Accessible Packing Spaces.

**4863 AEPS Family Report: For Children Ages Birth to Three**
Brookes Publishing
P.O.Box 10624
Baltimore, MD 21285-0624
410-337-9580
800-638-3775
FAX: 410-337-8539
e-mail: custserv@brookespublishing.com
www.brookespublishing.com

*Paul H. Brooks, Chairman*
*Jeffrey D. Brookes, President*
*Melissa A. Behm, Executive Vice President*
This is a 64-item questionnaire that asks parents to rank their child's abilities on specific skills. In packages of 10. *$17.00*
*20 pages Saddle-stiched*
*ISBN 1-557660-99-9*

**4864 ARC's Government Report**
Arc of the District of Columbia
817 Varnum St NE
Washington, DC 20017-2144
202-636-2950
FAX: 202-636-2996
e-mail: arcdc@arcdc.net
www.arcdc.net

Reports on government activities related to individuals with disabilities with a focus on persons with mental retardation. *$ 50.00*

**4865 ARCA Newsletter**
ARCA - Dakota County Technical College
1300 145th St E
Rosemount, MN 55068-2932 651-423-8000
800-548-5502
FAX: 651-423-7028
dctc.edu

*Ron Thomas, President*
Offers information on support groups, conventions, books, manuscripts and programs for the rehabilitation professional and the disabled.
*Monthly*

**4866 Accent on Living Magazine**
Cheever Publishing
P.O.Box 700
Bloomington, IL 61702-700 309-378-2961
800-787-8444
FAX: 309-378-4420

*Julie Cheever, Marketing Manager*
A magazine published for forty four years, serves physically disabled people, with general interest, travel, and home modification features. *$12.00*
*112 pages Quarterly*

**4867 Access Design Services: CILs as Experts**
Independent Living Research Utilization ILRU
Ste 1000
2323 S Shepherd Dr
Houston, TX 77019-7031 713-520-0232
FAX: 713-520-5785
e-mail: ilru@ilru.org
ilru.org

*Lex Frieden, Director, ILRU*
*Richard Petty, Program Director*
*Rose Shepard, Office Manager*
Featuring the Access Design Services of Alpha One in Maine, this month's Readings is another of the winners of the recent competition for innovative CIL programs.
*10 pages*

**4868 Access To Independence Inc.**
Access to Independence
3810 Milwaukee Street
Madison, WI 53714 608-242-8484
800-362-9877
FAX: 608-242-0383
TTY: 608-242-8485
e-mail: info@accesstoind.org
www.accesstoind.org

*Dee Truhn, Executive Director*
*Jason Belaungy, Assistant Director*
Independent Living Center serving people of any age and all types of disabilities in south-central Wisconsin.
*24 pages Semi-Annual*

**4869 Access for 911 and Telephone Emergency Services**
US Department of Justice
950 Pennsylvania Ave NW
Washington, DC 20530-9 202-586-5000
800-574-0301
FAX: 202-307-1197
TTY: 800-514-0383
www.ada.gov

*James Bostrom, Deputy Chiefs*
*Zita Johnson Betts, Deputy Chiefs*
*Sally Conway, Deputy Chiefs*
A 10-page publication explaining the requirements for direct, equal access to 911 for persons who use teletypewritters (TTYs).

**4870 Achieving Diversity and Independence**
Independent Living Research Utilization ILRU
Ste 1000
2323 S Shepherd Dr
Houston, TX 77019-7031 713-520-0232
FAX: 713-520-5785
e-mail: ilru@ilru.org
ilru.org

*Lex Frieden, Director, ILRU*
*Richard Petty, Program Director*
*Rose Shepard, Office Manager*
*10 pages*

**4871 Activity-Based Intervention: 2nd Edition**
Brookes Publishing
P.O.Box 10624
Baltimore, MD 21285-0624 410-337-9580
800-638-3775
FAX: 410-337-8539
e-mail: custserv@brookespublishing.com
readplaylearn.com

*Paul H. Brooks, Chairman*
*Jeffrey D. Brookes, President*
*Melissa A. Behm, Executive Vice President*
This 14 minute video illustrates how activity-based intervention can be used to turn everyday events and natural interactions into opportunities to promote learning in young children who are considered at risk for developmental delays or who have mild to significant disabilities. *$39.00*

*ISBN 1-55766 -86-3*

**4872 Ad Lib Drop-In Center: Consumer Management, Ownership and Empowerment**
Independent Living Research Utilization ILRU
Ste 1000
2323 S Shepherd Dr
Houston, TX 77019-7031 713-520-0232
FAX: 713-520-5785
e-mail: ilru@ilru.org
ilru.org

*Lex Frieden, Director, ILRU*
*Richard Petty, Program Director*
*Rose Shepard, Office Manager*
Joe describes how Ad Lib ensured consumer control in their Drop-In Center: the DIC came about because of consumer input, and consumers are involved in planning the program; members can choose to become volunteers or paid staff members. All of the staff at the DIC are consumers; and active consumer advisory board helps develop policies and programs and provides input to the Ad Lib board.
*10 pages*

**4873 Adobe News**
Santa Barbara Foundation
15 E Carrillo St
Santa Barbara, CA 93101-2706 805-963-1873
805-966-2345
FAX: 805-966-2345

*Ron Gallo, CEO*
*8 pages Bi-Annually*

**4874 Advocate**
Arc Massachusetts
217 South St
Waltham, MA 02453-2710 781-891-6270
FAX: 781-891-6271
e-mail: arcmass@arcmass.org
www.arcmass.org

*Leo Sarkissian, Executive Director*
*Judy Zacek, Associate Editor*
*Beth Rutledge, Production Coordinator/Ad*

Quarterly newsletter for The Arc of Massachusetts. *$ 20.00*
*8-12 pages Quarterly*

**4875 After School and More**
Resources for Children with Special Needs
Fl 5
116 E 16th St
New York, NY 10003-2164
212-677-4650
FAX: 212-254-4070
e-mail: info@resourcesnyc.org
www.resourcesnyc.org

*Rachel Howard, Executive Director*
*John Hart, Director of Program Operations*
More than 450 programs provide a wealth of resources for children in out-of-high school- time program. Information includes contact information, age, disability program capacity, hours, days, transportation, medication administration. *$25.00*
*240 pages*
*ISBN 0-967836-55-7*

**4876 American Herb Association Newsletter**
P.O.Box 353
Nevada City, CA 95959-353
530-265-9552
FAX: 530-274-3140
www.ahaherb.com
Information on many different herbs and herb uses. *$ 20.00*

**4877 Americans with Disabilities Act Checklist for New Lodging Facilities**
US Department of Justice
950 Pennsylvania Ave NW
Washington, DC 20530-9
202-586-5000
800-574-0301
FAX: 202-307-1197
TTY: 800-514-0383
www.ada.gov

*James Bostrom, Deputy Chiefs*
*Zita Johnson Betts, Deputy Chiefs*
*Sally Conway, Deputy Chiefs*
This 34-page checklist is a self-help survey that owners, franchisors, and managers of lodging facilities can use to identify ADA mistakes at their facilities.

**4878 Americans with Disabilities Act Handbook**
Aspen Publishers
7th Fl
76 9th Ave
New York, NY 10011-4962
212-790-2000
FAX: 212-771-0885
e-mail: customerservice@aspenpublishers.com
www.aspenpublishers.com

*Henry H Perritt Jr Esq, Author*
The Americans With Disabilities Act (ADA) Handbook provides comprehensive coverage of the ADA's employment, commercial facilities, and public accommodations provisions as well as coverage of the transportation, communication, and federal, local, and state government requirements. *$599.00*
*1671 pages 2X per year*
*ISBN 0-735531-48-X*

**4879 An Interdisciplinary Journal for the Social Study of Health, Illness and Medicine**
Sage Publications
2455 Teller Rd
Thousand Oaks, CA 91320-2218
805-499-0721
800-818-7243
FAX: 805-499-0871
hea.sagepub.com

*Alan Radley, Editor*
*Blaise Simqu, Chief Executive Officer*
*Quarterly*

**4880 Annual Report Sarkeys Foundation**
530 E Main St
Norman, OK 73071-5823
405-364-3703
FAX: 405-364-8191
e-mail: susan@sarkeys.org
sarkeys.org

*Kim Henry, Executive Director*
*Yearly*

**4881 Applied Kinesiology: Muscle Response in Diagnosis, Therapy and Preventive Medicine**
Inner Traditions
P.O.Box 388
Rochester, VT 05767-388
802-767-3174
800-246-8648
FAX: 802-767-3726
e-mail: orders@innertraditions.com
www.InnerTraditions.com

*Jessica Arsenault, Sales Associate*
*Rob Meadows, VP Sales & Marketing*
*$12.95*
*144 pages*
*ISBN 0-892813-28-8*

**4882 Arc Connection Newsletter**
Arc of Tennessee
Ste 100
151 Athens Way
Nashville, TN 37228-1367
615-248-5878
800-835-7077
FAX: 615-248-5879
e-mail: pcooper@thearctn.org
thearctn.org

*Walter Rogers, Executive Director*
*Peggy Cooper, Associate Director Operations*
The Arc of Tennessee is a nonprofit organization that offers advocacy, information, referral and support to people with intellectual or developmental disabilities and their families. This is their publication. It is free to members. *$10.00*
*12 pages Quarterly*

**4883 Aromatherapy Book: Applications and Inhalations**
North Atlantic Books
1435a 4th St
Berkeley, CA 94710
510-559-8277
FAX: 510-559-8279
e-mail: info@northatlanticbooks.com
www.northatlanticbooks.com
Considered a bible for those interested in aromatherapy. *$18.95*

*ISBN 1-556430-73-6*

**4884 Aromatherapy for Common Ailments**
Simon & Schuster
100 Front St
Delran, NJ 8075-1181
856-461-6500
800-323-7445
FAX: 856-824-2402
www.simonsays.com

*David Schaeffer, VP*
Explains aromatherapy with emphasis on medicinal uses.
*96 pages*
*ISBN 0-671731-34-3*

**4885 As I Am**
Fanlight Productions
21st Floor
32 Court Street
Brooklyn, NY 11201
718-488-8900
800-876-1710
FAX: 718-488-8642
e-mail: info@fanlight.com
www.fanlight.com

*Ben Achtenberg, Owner*
*Anthony Sweeney, Marketing Director*
Three young people with developmental disabilities speak for themselves about their lives, the problems they face and their hopes and expectations for the future. *$99.00*

*ISBN 1-572950-58-7*

**4886 Attitudes Toward Persons with Disabilities**
Springer Publishing Company
11 West 42nd Street
15th Floor
New York, NY 10036
212-431-4370
877-687-7476
FAX: 212-941-7842
e-mail: marketing@springerpub.com
www.springerpub.com

*Annette Imperati, Marketing/Sales Director*
*Ursula Springer, President*
This volume examines what is known of people's complex and multifaceted attitudes toward persons with disabilities. Divided into five areas of concern: theory, origin of attitudes, attitude measurement, attitudes of specific groups and attitude change. *$38.95*
*352 pages Hardcover*
*ISBN 0-82616 -90-1*

**4887 Authoritative Guide to Self- Help Resourcein Mental Health**
Guilford Press
72 Spring St
New York, NY 10012-4019
212-431-9800
800-365-7006
FAX: 212-966-6708
www.guilford.com

*Linda F Campbell PhD, Author*
*Thomas P Smith PsyD, Author*
*Robert Sommer PhD, Author*
*Bob Matloff, President*
Reviews and rates 600+ self-help books, autobiographies, and popular films, and evaluates hundreds of Internet sites. Addresses 28 of the most prevalent clinical disorders and life challenges- from ADHD, Alzheimer's, and anxiety disorders, to marital problems, mood disorders and weight management. Also in cloth at $45.00 (ISBN# 1-57230-506-1) *$25.00*
*377 pages Paperback*
*ISBN 1-572305-80-0*

**4888 AwareNews**
Services for Independent Living
Ste 105
25100 Euclid Ave
Cleveland, OH 44117-2663
216-731-1529
FAX: 216-731-3083
e-mail: sil@stratos.net
www.sil-oh.org

*12 pages Quarterly*

**4889 Bach Flower Therapy: Theory and Practice**
Inner Traditions
1 Park St
Rochester, VT 05767
802-767-3174
FAX: 802-767-3726
innertradition.com

*Ehud Sperling, Owner*
Contemporary study of Bach's techniques, intended for practitioners and lay readers alike. Includes lists of symptoms to facilitate diagnosis, ans aims to provide an understanding of psychosomatic elements in relation to physical complaints.

*ISBN 0-892812-39-7*

**4890 Beliefs, Values, and Principles of Self Advocacy**
Brookline Books
34 University Rd
Brookline, MA 02445-4533
800-666-2665
FAX: 617-734-3952
e-mail: brbooks@yahoo.com
www.brooklinebooks.com
Written by self-advocates around the world, they tell about the beliefs, values, and principles important to them, and the empowerment and personal growth they experience through self-advocacy. *$7.00*
*48 pages Paperback*
*ISBN 0-57129 -22-2*

**4891 Beliefs: Pathways to Health and Well Being**
Metamorphous Press
P.O.Box 10616
Portland, OR 97296-616
503-228-4972
FAX: 503-223-9117
www.metamodels.com/meta/bks/hea1.htm

*David Balding, Publisher*
Explores behavioral technologies and belief change strategies that can alter beliefs that support unhealthy habbits such as smoking, overeating, and drug use. Also covers the changing of thinking processes that create phobias and unreasonable fears, retraining the immune system to eliminate allergies and to deal optinally with cancer, AIDS, and other diseases. Includes strategies to transform unhealthy beliefs into lifelong constructs of wellness.

**4892 Bench Marks**
Govenor's Council on Developmental Disabilities
1717 W Jefferson St
Phoenix, AZ 85007-3202
602-542-4049
800-889-5893
FAX: 602-542-5320
e-mail: mward@mail.dc.state.us

*Micheal Ward, Executive Director*
*Susan Madison, Manager*
*Quarterly*

**4893 Bodie, Dolina, Smith & Hobbs, P.C.**
29 W Susquehanna Ave
Ste 110
Baltimore, MD 21204-5218
410-823-1250
888-823-1255
FAX: 443-901-0802
e-mail: chobbs@bodie-law.com
www.bodie-law.com

*Chester Hobbs, Esquire*
Law firm; provides estates, trusts and guardianship administration, estate planning, elder law, tax issues, bankruptcy, foreclosures, and real estate issues. *$25.00*
*Quarterly*

**4894 Body Reflexology: Healing at Your Fingertips**
Parker Publishing Company
Ste 2605
1501 Broadway
New York, NY 10036-5600
212-869-6350

*Hy Dubin, President*

Features step-by-step instructions of how to send healing flows of energy through the body to relieve back pain, headaches, arthritis, and other afflictions. Illustrated.
*343 pages Hardcover*
*ISBN 0-132997-36-3*

**4895 Body Silent: The Different World of the Disabled**
WW Norton & Company
324 State St
Santa Barbara, CA 93101-2362 800-333-6867
FAX: 805-962-5087
www.specialneeds.com/store/

The author's personal account of his progressive and terminal loss of muscle function caused by a spinal tumor, resulting in quadripilegia. Includes society's fears, myths, and misunderstandings about disability and the damage they inflict. *$9.95*
*256 pages*
*ISBN 0-393320-42-1*

**4896 Body of Knowledge/Hellerwork**
406 Berry St
Mount Shasta, CA 96067-2548 530-926-2500
josephheller.com

*Joseph Heller, Owner*
Information, referral directory, training and certification.

**4897 Bridge Newsletter**
Arizona Bridge to Independent Living
1229 E Washington St
Phoenix, AZ 85034-1101 602-256-2245
800-280-2245
FAX: 602-254-6407
e-mail: azbridge@abil.org
abil.org

*Phil Pangrazio, Executive Director*
*12 pages Monthly*

**4898 Bridging the Gap: A National Directory of Services for Women & Girls with Disabilities**
Educational Equity Concepts
114 E 32nd St
New York, NY 10016-5506 212-725-1803
FAX: 212-725-0947
TTY:212-725-1803
e-mail: infomration@edequity.org
www.edequity.org

*Ellen Rubin, Coordinator Disability Programs*
*Merle Froschl, Editor*
Contains a resource section of publications and videos geared specifically to women and girls with disabilities. Available in print, on cassette, and also in braille. *$24.95*

*ISBN 0-931629-16-0*

**4899 Bulletin of the Association on the Handicapped**
Assoc. on Handicapped Student Service Program
P.O.Box 21192
Columbus, OH 43221-0192 614-365-5216
FAX: 614-365-6718
Membership journal including Association news, articles and sections such as Literature in Review and Speak Out. *$16.00*

**4900 CDR Reports**
Council for Disability Rights
Ste 1540
20 N Wacker Dr
Chicago, IL 60606-2903 312-201-4800
FAX: 312-444-1977
e-mail: cdrights@interaccess.com
www.disabilityrights.org

*Jo Holzer, Executive Director/Editor*
*Bruce Moore, Employment Specialist*
*$15.00*
*8 pages Monthly*

**4901 California Financial Power of Attorney**
NOLO
950 Parker St
Berkeley, CA 94710-2524 510-549-1976
800-955-4775
FAX: 510-548-5902
www.nolo.com

*Maira Dizgalvis, Trade Customer Service Manager*
*Susan McConnell, Director Sales*
*Natasha Kaluza, Sales Assistant*
*David Rothenberg, CEO*
A plain-English book packed with forms and instructions to give a trusted person the legal authority to handle your financial affairs.
*Paperback*

**4902 Caring for America's Heroes**
Oklahoma City VA Medical Center
921 NE 13th St
Oklahoma City, OK 73104-5007 405-270-0501
FAX: 405-270-1560
www.va.gov

*Steven Gentlin, Director*
*Kathleen Fogarty, Associate Director*
*D Robert McCaffree MD, Chief of Staff*
*Tom Duchene, Plant Manager*

**4903 Center for Health Research: Eastern Washington University**
Showalter 209a
Cheney, WA 99004 509-359-2279
800-221-9369
FAX: 509-359-2778
e-mail: sharon.wilson@mail.ewu.edu
iceberg.ewu.edu
Produces eight videotapes, accompanying printed materials, and a videotaped public services announcement to serve as training and resource materials for use by daycare centers.

**4904 Center for Libraries and Educational Improvement**
400 Maryland Ave SW
Washington, DC 20202-1 202-260-2226
800-872-5327
FAX: 202-401-0689
TTY: 800-437-0833
www.ed.gov
Administers the Library Services Construction Act, which authorizes grants to the states for library services to the physically handicapped.

**4905 Centering Corporation Grief Resources**
7230 Maple Street
Omaha, NE 68134 402-553-1200
866-218-0101
FAX: 402-533-0507
e-mail: j1200@aol.com
www.centering.org

*Joy Johnson, Founder*
*Dr. Marvin Johnson, Founder*
*Janet Sieff, Executive Director*
A full catalog of all our available bereavement resources. We are a small, non-profit organization providing help to families in crisis situations.
*32 pages BiAnnually*

**4906 Centers for Disease Control and Prevention**
US Department of Health and Human Services
1600 Clifton Rd NE
Atlanta, GA 30329-4018
404-639-3311
800-311-3435
FAX: 404-498-1177
e-mail: inquiry@cdc.gov
www.cdc.gov

*Robert Delaney, Plant Manager*
Publishes an annually updated list of infectious and communicable diseases transmitted through the handling of food in accordance with Section 103 of Title I.

**4907 Child With Special Needs: Encouraging Intellectual and Emotional Growth**
Addison-Wesley Publishing Company
Ste 300
75 Arlington St
Boston, MA 02116-3988
617-848-7500
800-238-9682
FAX: 617-944-7273
www.awprofessional.com

*Bill Barke, CEO*
Covering all kinds of disabilities - including cerebral palsy, autism, retardation, ADD, and language problems - this guide offers parents specific ways of helping all special needs chidren reach their full intellectual and emotional potential. *$32.00*
*496 pages*
*ISBN 0-201407-26-4*

**4908 Chinese Herbal Medicine**
Shambhala Publications
300 Massachusetts Avenue
Boston, MA 02115
617-424-0030
FAX: 617-236-1563
e-mail: editors@shambhala.com
shambhala.com

*Richard Reoch, President*
Gives an in-depth look into herbal medicine.
*176 pages*
*ISBN 0-877733-98-8*

**4909 Christian Approach to Overcoming Disability: A Doctor's Story**
Haworth Press
10 Alice St
Binghamton, NY 13904-1503
607-722-5857
800-429-6784
FAX: 607-722-6362
e-mail: orders@haworthpress.com
www.haworthpress.com

*William Cohen, Owner*
*$29.95*
*128 pages*
*ISBN 0-789022-57-5*

**4910 Closing the Gap**
P.O.Box 68
Henderson, MN 56044-68
507-248-3294
FAX: 507-248-3810
e-mail: info@closingthegap.com
www.closingthegap.com

*Dolores Hagen, President*
*Delores Hagen, President*
Explores use of microcomputers as personal and educational tools for persons with disabilities.
*36+ pages BiMonthly*

**4911 Comprehensive Directory of Programs and Services**
Resources for Children with Special Needs
Fl 5
116 E 16th St
New York, NY 10003-2164
212-387-7091
FAX: 212-254-4070
e-mail: info@resourcesnyc.org
www.resourcesnyc.org

*Rachel Howard, Executive Director*
*John Hart, Director of Program Operations*
Published every 24-36 months. *$55.00*
*1096 pages*
*ISBN 0-976836-51-4*

**4912 Constellations**
Minnesota STAR Program
Ste 309
50 Sherburne Ave
Saint Paul, MN 55155-1402
651-296-2771
800-657-3862
FAX: 651-282-6671
e-mail: star.program@state.mn.us
www.admin.state.mn.us/assistivetechnology

*Chuck Rassbach, Executive Director*
Free quarterly publication from the Minnesota STAR Program.
*8 pages Quarterly*

**4913 Consumer Buyer's Guide for Independent Living**
American Occupational Therapy Association (AOTA)
4720 Montgomery Ln
Bethesda, MD 20814-5320
301-652-2682
800-SAY-AOTA
FAX: 301-652-7711
TTY: 800-377-8555

*Florence Clark, President*
A buyer's directory of products and publications for the general public listing suppliers' names, addresses and telephone numbers. This directory lists AOTA publications on numerous topics (back pain, Alzheimers, Carpal Tunnel Syndrome, etc.) and suppliers of equipment to assist in activities of daily living for individuals with disabilities.
*60 pages Annual*

**4914 Coping+Plus: Dimensions of Disability**
Greenwood Publishing Group
130 Cremona Drive
Santa Barbara, CA 93117
805-968-1911
800-368-6868
FAX: 866-270-3856
e-mail: CustomerService@abc-clio.com
www.abc-clio.com

*Matt Laddin, Vice President of Marketing*
*Mike Saltzman, Director - Eastern Territories & National Accounts*
*James Lingle, International Sales & Marketing Manager Rights & Permissions*
Everyone can learn new or more effective coping skills and strategies to deal with times of loss, crisis and disability. $55-$59.95
*280 pages Hardcover*
*ISBN 0-275945-44-8*

**4915 Council News**
Northern Nevada Center for Independent Living
999 Pyramid Way
Sparks, NV 89431-4471
775-353-3599
FAX: 775-353-3588
e-mail: nncil@sbcglobal.net
nncil.org

*Lisa Erquiaga, Executive Director*
*12 pages Quarterly*

**4916 Counseling in Terminal Care & Bereavement**
Brookes Publishing
P.O.Box 10624
Baltimore, MD 21285-0624
410-337-9580
800-638-3775
FAX: 410-337-8539
e-mail: custserv@brookespublishing.com
readplaylearn.com

*Paul H. Brooks, Chairman*
*Jeffrey D. Brookes, President*
*Melissa A. Behm, Executive Vice President*
Provides practical suggestions for addressing the needs of patients and family members who are anticipating or currently dealing with grief and bereavement, such as hospice care, hospitals, or at home care. *$34.00*
*210 pages Paperback*
*ISBN 1-85433 -78-7*

**4917 Creating Wholeness: Self-Healing Workbook Using Dynamic Relaxation, Images and Thoughts**
Plenum Publishing Corporation
Fl 7
233 Spring St
New York, NY 10013-1522
212-620-8000
FAX: 212-460-1575

*232 pages*
*ISBN 0-306441-72-1*

**4918 DRS Connection**
Disabled Resource Services
Ste 101
424 Pine St
Fort Collins, CO 80524-2421
970-482-2700
FAX: 970-407-7072
e-mail: drs@frii.com
www.drs@fortnet.org

*Nancy Jackson, Executive Director*
*4 pages Quaterly*

**4919 Demand Response Transportation Through a Rural ILC**
Independent Living Research Utilization ILRU
Ste 1000
2323 S Shepherd Dr
Houston, TX 77019-7031
713-520-0232
FAX: 713-520-5785
e-mail: ilru@ilru.org
ilru.org

*Lex Frieden, Director, ILRU*
*Richard Petty, Program Director*
*Rose Shepard, Office Manager*
Oklahomans for Independent Living's transportation program was selected as exemplary because they marketed it by emphasizing people with disabilities as economic constituency.
*10 pages*

**4920 Developing Organized Coalitions and Strategic Plans**
Independent Living Research Utilization ILRU
Ste 1000
2323 S Shepherd Dr
Houston, TX 77019-7031
713-520-0232
FAX: 713-520-5785
e-mail: ilru@ilru.org
ilru.org

*Lex Frieden, Director, ILRU*
*Richard Petty, Program Director*
*Rose Shepard, Office Manager*
*10 pages*

**4921 Dictionary of Congenital Malformations& Disorders**
Informa Healthcare
Fl 16
52 Vanderbilt Ave
New York, NY 10017-3846
212-520-2777
FAX: 212-661-5052
e-mail: orders@crcpress.com
www.informaworld.com

*$55.00*
*193 pages*
*ISBN 0-850705-77-1*

**4922 Dictionary of Developmental Disabilities Terminology**
Brookes Publishing
P.O.Box 10624
Baltimore, MD 21285-0624
410-337-9580
800-638-3775
FAX: 410-337-8539
e-mail: custserv@brookesopublishing.com
www.brookespublishing.com

*Paul H. Brooks, Chairman*
*Jeffrey D. Brookes, President*
*Melissa A. Behm, Executive Vice President*
With more than 3,000 easy-to-understand entries, this dictionary provides thorough explanations of terms associated with developmental disabilities and disorders. *$55.95*
*368 pages Hardcover*
*ISBN 1-557662-45-2*

**4923 Directory of Members**
American Network of Community Options & Resources
Ste 380
1101 King St
Alexandria, VA 22314-2962
703-535-7850
FAX: 703-535-7860
e-mail: ancor@ancor.org
ancor.org

*Renee L Pietrangelo, CEO*
*Suellen Galbraith, Director Public Policy*
*Renee Pietrangelo, CEO*
The Directory lists over 600 agencies that provide residential services and supports in 48 states and the District of Columbia. The listings include the name of the Executive Directors, the name, address, and phone number of the agency, describe the types of services that are provided and how many individuals receive services from that agency. *$25.00*
*189 pages*

**4924 Disability Awareness Guide**
Central Iowa Center for Independent Living
Ste 131
655 Walnut St
Des Moines, IA 50309-3930
515-243-1742
FAX: 515-243-5385
e-mail: cicil@raccoon.com
centraliowacil.com

*Bob Jeppesen, Executive Director*
*Frank Strong, Assistant Director Programs*
*Bob Jepson, Manager*
The Disability Awareness Guide contains information about our center; who we are and what we do. It also contains the telephone numbers of local and national agencies and resources available for people with disabilities.

**4925 Disability Rights Movement**
Children's Press
Sherman Tpke
Danbury, CT 6813
800-621-1115
FAX: 800-374-4329

*Elena Rockman, Marketing Manager*

Author Deborah Kent illuminates both the history of the National Disability Rights Movement and the inspiring personal stories of individuals with various disabilities. *$18.00*

*32 pages Hardcover*

*ISBN 0-53106 -32-3*

**4926 Disabled People's International Fifth World Assembly as Reported by Two US Participants**

Independent Living Research Utilization ILRU
Ste 1000
2323 S Shepherd Dr
Houston, TX 77019-7031
713-520-0232
FAX: 713-520-5785
e-mail: ilru@ilru.org
ilru.org

*Lex Frieden, Director, ILRU*
*Richard Petty, Program Director*
*Rose Shepard, Office Manager*

This report describes the international conference on independent living held in Mexico City in December 1998 as experienced by staff members from two U.S. centers. Kaye Beneke interviewed Luis Chew and Marco Antonio Coronado for this edition of Readings in Independent Living.

*10 pages*

**4927 Disabled We Stand**

Brookline Books
34 University Rd
Brookline, MA 02445-4533
800-666-2665
FAX: 617-734-3952
e-mail: brbooks@yahoo.com
www.brooklinebooks.com

This book is impassioned, often angry, but also hopeful and practical, suggesting a series of actions that will lead to constructive change. It is imbued with spirit and energy of disabled people who are determined to take their lives into their own hands. *$ 10.95*

*Paperback*

*ISBN 0-25331 -80-0*

**4928 Disabled, the Media, and the Information Age**

Greenwood Publishing Group
130 Cremona Drive
Santa Barbara, CA 93117
805-968-1911
800-368-6868
FAX: 866-270-3856
e-mail: CustomerService@abc-clio.com
www.abc-clio.com

*Matt Laddin, Vice President of Marketing*
*Mike Saltzman, Director - Eastern Territories & National Accounts*
*James Lingle, International Sales & Marketing Manager Rights & Permissions*

A short and easy-to-read overview of how disabled Americans have been portrayed by the media and how images and the role of the handicapped are changing. *$55.00*

*264 pages Hardcover*

*ISBN 0-313284-72-5*

**4929 Discovery Newsletter**

North Dakota State Library Talking Book Services
Dept 250
604 E Boulevard Ave
Bismarck, ND 58505-605
701-328-2000
800-843-9948
FAX: 701-328-2040
e-mail: sbschneider@nd.gov
ndsl.lib.state.nd.us/DisabilityServices.html

*Doris Ott, Manager*

The North Dakota State Library Disability Services produces the Doscovery Newsletter containing information on services, books, catalogs and of interest to the patron.

*6 pages Bi-Annually*

**4930 EP Resource Guide**

Exceptional Parent Library
P.O.Box 1807
Englewood Cliffs, NJ 7632-1207
201-947-6000
800-535-1910
FAX: 201-947-9376
e-mail: eplibrary@aol.com
www.eplibrary.com

Lists directories of national organizations, associations, products and services. *$9.95*

**4931 ESCIL Update Newsletter**

Eastern Shore Center for Independent Living
9 Sunburst Ctr
Cambridge, MD 21613-2057
410-221-7701
800-705-7944
FAX: 410-221-7714
e-mail: escil@comcast.net
www.escil.org

*Shirley Tarbox, Executive Director*
*Jean Reed, Administrative Assistant*
*Lisa Morgan, Director IL Services*

*6 pages Quarterly*

**4932 Easy Things to Make Things Simple: Do It Yourself Modifications for Disabled Persons**

Brookline Books
34 University Rd
Brookline, MA 02445-4533
800-666-2665
FAX: 617-734-3952
e-mail: brbooks@yahoo.com
www.brooklinebooks.com

This book aims at older adults and others with physical limitations who require adaptations for safer and easier living in the kitchen, bathroom, bedroom, yard, and garden. The adaptations can be done inexpensively, from common materials. Large print format and detailed diagrams, plus special sections with advice caregivers . *$15.95*

*160 pages Paperback*

*ISBN 1-571290-24-9*

**4933 Encyclopedia of Disability**

Sage Publications
2455 Teller Rd
Thousand Oaks, CA 91320-2218
805-499-0721
e-mail: info@sagepub.com
www.sagepub.com

*Gary L Albrecht, Editor*
*Blaise Simqu, Chief Executive Officer*

A five volume set that covers disabilities A-Z *$850.00*

*2500 pages*

*ISBN 0-761925-65-1*

**4934 EveryBody's Different: Understanding and Changing Our Reactions to Disabilities**

Brookes Publishing
P.O.Box 10624
Baltimore, MD 21285-0624
410-337-9580
800-638-3775
FAX: 410-337-8539
e-mail: custserv@brookespublishing.com
readplaylearn.com

*Paul H. Brooks, Chairman*
*Jeffrey D. Brookes, President*
*Melissa A. Behm, Executive Vice President*

This book discusses the emotions, questions, fears, and stereotypes that people without disabilities sometimes experience when they interact with people who do have disabilities. The author teaches readers to become more at ease with the concept of disability and to communicate more effectively with each other. Features activities and exercises that encourage self-examina-

tion, helping people to create more enriching personal relationships and work toward a fully inclusive society.
*Paperback*
*ISBN 1-55766-59-9*

**4935 Everybody's Guide to Homeopathic Medicines**
Jeremy P Tarcher
375 Hudson St
New York, NY 10014-3658 212-366-2000
www.us.penguingroup.com

*John Makinson, Chairman and CEO*
*Coram Williams, CFO*
Covers alternative treatments in homeopathic medicines.
*375 pages*
*ISBN 0-874778-43-3*

**4936 Everyday Social Interaction: A Program for People with Disabilities**
Brookes Publishing
P.O.Box 10624
Baltimore, MD 21285-0624 410-337-9580
800-638-3775
FAX: 410-337-8539
e-mail: custserv@brookespublishing.com
readplaylearn.com

*Paul H. Brooks, Chairman*
*Jeffrey D. Brookes, President*
*Melissa A. Behm, Executive Vice President*
This source guides teachers and human services professionals in helping people with disabilities acquire social interaction skills and develop satisfying relationships. Included is a checklist and task analyses that shows how complex skills can be broken down into major components for easy performance monitoring accompanied by tips on social courtesies, rewards, praise, and criticism. *$41.95*
*342 pages Paperback*
*ISBN 1-55766-58-4*

**4937 Family Challenges: Parenting with a Disability**
Aquarius Health Care Videos
P.O.Box 1159
Sherborn, MA 01770-7159 508-650-1616
888-440-2963
FAX: 508-650-4216
e-mail: aqvideos@tiac.net
www.aquariusproductions.com

*Lesile Kussmann, Owner*
When a parent has a disability, everyone in the family is affected. For children, these experiences may profoundly influence their lives and views of the world. In this sensitive film, you will hear about different roles that all the family members take on at varying times. *$195.00*

**4938 Force A Miracle**
Writer's Showcase Press

A testament to the inner human strength to overcome extreme adversity, to triumph and continue a worthwhile and self-rewarding life. *$14.95*
*244 pages*
*ISBN 0-595226-88-4*

**4939 Forum**
Coalition for the Education of Disabled Children
165 W Center St
Marion, OH 43302-3742 740-382-7362
800-374-2806
FAX: 740-382-3428
e-mail: oceed@gte.net
www.oceed.org

*Tracie Wilson, Manager*
*Leeann Derugen, Manager*
Forum is a newsletter reporting on legislative and other developments affecting persons with disabilities.
*Quarterly*

**4940 Foundation Fundamentals for Nonprofit Organizations**
Foundation Center
Department Ze
79 5th Ave
New York, NY 10003-3034 212-620-4230
800-424-9836
FAX: 212-807-3677
www.fdncenter.org

*Sara Engelhardt, President*
This video is designed to give fundraisers a general overview of the foundation funding process and to introduce them to the many resources available through our libraries and cooperating collections. The video gives clear, step-by-step instructions on how to build a fundraising program. *$24.00*
*Video*

**4941 Four-Ingredient Cookbook**
Laurel Designs
Apt A
1805 Mar West St
Belvedere Tiburon, CA 94920-1962 FAX: 415-435-1451
e-mail: laureld@ncal.verio.com

*Janet Sawyer, Owner*
*Lynn Montoya, Owner*
Simple, easy to follow recipes, each containing four ingredients. Particularly suited to persons with limited physical ability. Includes 400 recipes, appetizers to desserts. *$9.00*

**4942 Frequently Asked Questions About Multiple Chemical Sensitivity**
Independent Living Research Utilization ILRU
Ste 1000
2323 S Shepherd Dr
Houston, TX 77019-7031 713-520-0232
FAX: 713-520-5785
e-mail: ilru@ilru.org
ilru.org

*Lex Frieden, Director, ILRU*
*Richard Petty, Program Director*
*Rose Shepard, Office Manager*
This FAQ covers important information about multiple chemical sensitivity and environmental illness. The FAQ describes the conditions, recommends strategies for improving access, and lists resources for CILs and other organizations. As the fact sheet states, centers must set an example in assuring that all people can enter their offices.
*10 pages*

**4943 Genetic Disorders Sourcebook**
Omnigraphics
615 Griswold St
Detroit, MI 48226-3900 313-961-1340
800-234-1340
FAX: 800-875-1340
www.omnigraphics.com

*Paul Rogers, Publicity Associate*
*Georgiann Fratoni, Customer Service Manager*
Provides information on hereditary diseases and disorders. *$7800.00*
*650 pages*
*ISBN 0-789892-41-1*

**4944 Genetic Nutritioneering**
McGraw-Hill Company
2460 Kerper Blvd
Dubuque, IA 52001-2224 563-588-1451
800-338-3987
FAX: 614-755-5654
www.mhhe.com/hper/physed

*Kurt Strand, VP*
Describes how to modify the expression of genetic traits, potentially preventing heart disease, cancer, arthritis, and hormone-related problems. Features how to slow biological aging and reduce the risk of age-related diseases. *$16.95*
*288 pages*
*ISBN 0-879839-21-X*

**4945 Going to School with Facilitated Communication**
Syracuse University, School of Education
230 Huntington Hall
Syracuse, NY 13244-1 315-443-4752
FAX: 315-443-2258
e-mail: jhrusso@syr.edu
www.soe.syr.edu

*Shirley Adamczyk, Administrative Assistant*
*Rachael Gazdick, Executive Director*
A video in which students with autism and/or severe disabilities illustrate the use of facilitated communication focusing on basic principles fostering facilitated communication.
*Video*

**4946 Grief: What it is and What You Can Do**
Centering Corporation
7230 Maple Street
Omaha, NE 68134 402-553-1200
866-218-0101
FAX: 402-533-0507
e-mail: j1200@aol.com
www.centering.org

*Joy Johnson, Founder*
*Dr. Marvin Johnson, Founder*
*Janet Sieff, Executive Director*
General grief information for all grief issues. *$3.50*
*32 pages Paperback*

**4947 Guidelines on Disability**
US Department of Housing & Urban Development
451 7th St SW
Washington, DC 20410-1 202-708-1112
TTY:202-708-1455
Contains information on housing and accessibility for persons with disabilities.

**4948 Handbook of Services for the Handicapped**
Greenwood Publishing Group
130 Cremona Drive
Santa Barbara, CA 93117 805-968-1911
800-368-6868
FAX: 866-270-3856
e-mail: CustomerService@abc-clio.com
www.abc-clio.com

*Matt Laddin, Vice President of Marketing*
*Mike Saltzman, Director - Eastern Territories & National Accounts*
*James Lingle, International Sales & Marketing Manager Rights & Permissions*
A handy reference book offering information and services for disabled individuals. $59.95-$65.00.
*291 pages Hardcover*
*ISBN 0-313213-85-2*

**4949 Healing Herbs**
Rodale Press
33 E Minor St
Emmaus, PA 18098-1 610-967-5171
FAX: 610-967-8963
rodale.com

*Steve P Murphy, CEO*
Covers everything from growing the herbs to home remedies.

**4950 Helen Keller National Center for Deaf- Blind Youths And Adults**
141 Middle Neck Rd
Sands Point, NY 11050-1218 516-944-8900
FAX: 516-944-7302
e-mail: hkncinfo@hknc.org
www.hknc.org

*Joseph McNulty, Executive Director*
HKNC is the only national vacational and rehabilitation program providing services exclusively to youth and adults who are deaf-blind.

**4951 Hospice Alternative**
Harper Collins Publishers/Basic Books
10 E 53rd St
New York, NY 10022-5244 212-207-7000
800-242-7737
FAX: 212-207-7203

*Jane Friedman, CEO*
An account of the hospice experience. An innovative and humane way of caring for the terminally ill. *$8.95*
*256 pages*
*ISBN 0-46503 -61-0*

**4952 How to File a Title III Complaint**
US Department of Justice
950 Pennsylvania Ave NW
Washington, DC 20530-9 202-586-5000
800-574-0301
FAX: 202-307-1197
TTY: 800-514-0383
www.ada.gov

*James Bostrom, Deputy Chiefs*
*Zita Johnson Betts, Deputy Chiefs*
*Sally Conway, Deputy Chiefs*
This publication details the procedure for filing a complaint under Title III of the ADA.

**4953 How to Live Longer with a Disability**
Accent Books & Products
P.O.Box 700
Bloomington, IL 61702-700 309-378-2961
800-787-8444
FAX: 309-378-4420
e-mail: acmtlvng@aol.com

*Raymond C Cheever, Publisher*
*Betty Garee, Editor*
Eleven chapters to help you enjoy every aspect of your life, and live easier and happier. Includes sexuality and disability, getting more from the medical community and benefit programs. Co-authored by Robert Mauro, sociologist and Elle Becker, counselor and psychologist, both disabled. *$11.50*
*266 pages Paperback*
*ISBN 0-19570 -38-8*

**4954 Ideas for Kids on the Go**
Accent Books & Products
P.O.Box 700
Bloomington, IL 61702-700 309-378-2961
800-787-8444
FAX: 309-378-4420
e-mail: acmtlvng@aol.com

*Raymond C Cheever, Publisher*
*Betty Garee, Editor*
This guide shows kids with physical disabilities how to go for it! Lists products and where to get them, and includes tips from others for having fun and getting ahead. Ages 1-18. *$6.95*
*69 pages Paperback*
*ISBN 0-91570 -17-5*

**4955 If I Only Knew What to Say or Do**
AARP Fulfillment
601 E St NW
Washington, DC 20049-1 202-434-2277
800-424-3410
FAX: 202-434-3443
e-mail: member@aarp.org
www.aarp.org

*William Novelli, CEO*
Provides a concise discussion of how to help a friend in crisis. Learn what to say and what not to say.

**4956 If it Weren't for the Honor: I'd Rather Have Walked**
Accent Books & Products
P.O.Box 700
Bloomington, IL 61702-700 309-378-2961
800-787-8444
FAX: 309-378-4420
e-mail: acmtlvng@aol.com

*Raymond C Cheever, Publisher*
*Betty Garee, Editor*
Revealing, often humorous, highly interesting and important reading. This book offers an account told by the author who was on the scene and actually saw and participated in many events that paved the way for progress for all those with disabilities. *$14.50*
*262 pages Paperback*
*ISBN 0-91570 -41-8*

**4957 Imagery in Healing Shamanism and Modern Medicine**
Shambhala Publications
300 Massachusetts Avenue
Boston, MA 02115 617-424-0030
FAX: 617-236-1563
e-mail: editors@shambhala.com
shambhala.com

*Richard Reoch, President*
Patients use self imagery to fight sickness and pain throughout their lives. *$15.95*
*272 pages*
*ISBN 1-570629-34-x*

**4958 Independence**
Easter Seals
1219 Dunn Ave
Daytona Beach, FL 32114-2405 386-255-4568
877-255-4568
FAX: 386-258-7677
e-mail: info@eseals-vf.org
www.easterseals-volusiaflagler.org

*Penny Young, Communications Director*
*Lynn Sinnot, President*
*4-6 pages Quarterly*

**4959 Independent Living Centers and Managed Care: Results of an ILRU Study on Involvement**
Independent Living Research Utilization ILRU
Ste 1000
2323 S Shepherd Dr
Houston, TX 77019-7031 713-520-0232
FAX: 713-520-5785
e-mail: ilru@ilru.org
ilru.org

*Lex Frieden, Director, ILRU*
*Richard Petty, Program Director*
*Rose Shepard, Office Manager*
This month's Readings presents findings from an ILRU study of roles centers are taking vis-a-vis managed care. Initiated in spring 1998, we asked Drew Batavia to take the lead in conducting this study for us. We were interested in collecting data on frequency with which centers are contacted by consumers with managed care problems. This is a study that will need to be repeated periodically as our experiences with managed care evolves. Meanwhile, here are the initial findings.
*10 pages*

**4960 Independent Living Challenges the Blues**
Independent Living Research Utilization ILRU
Ste 1000
2323 S Shepherd Dr
Houston, TX 77019-7031 713-520-0232
FAX: 713-520-5785
e-mail: ilru@ilru.org
ilru.org

*Lex Frieden, Director, ILRU*
*Richard Petty, Program Director*
*Rose Shepard, Office Manager*
Patricia's article highlights the Georgia SILC's health care advocacy efforts: the Georgia legislature passed a bill enabling Georgia Bleu to convert to for-profit status without a distribution of assets to similar nonprofit corporations; the Georgia SILC joined other health care advocates in filing a class action law suit to challenge the legality of the conversion; the Georgia SILC continues advocacy efforts to involve people with disabilities in developing and monitoring health care policy.
*10 pages*

**4961 Independent Living Office**
Department of Housing & Urban Development (HUD)
451 7th St SW
Washington, DC 20410-1 202-863-2800

This office within HUD is charged with encouraging the construction of housing that is accessible to handicapped persons. The Office of Independent Living encourages modifications of apartments and other dwellings so that handicapped persons can enter without assistance.

**4962 Independent Newsletter**
Easter Seals Nebraska
638 N 109th Plz
Omaha, NE 68154-1722 402-345-2200
800-650-9880
FAX: 402-345-2500
e-mail: kginder@ne.easterseals.com
www.ne.easterseals.com

*Karen Carlson, President*
Terrific fun for campers and a much needed respite for families and care givers from the daily challenges of caring for special needs indviduals
*4 pages Quarterly*

**4963 Information Services for People with Developmental Disabilities**
Greenwood Publishing Group
130 Cremona Drive
Santa Barbara, CA 93117
805-968-1911
800-368-6868
FAX: 866-270-3856
e-mail: CustomerService@abc-clio.com
www.abc-clio.com

*Matt Laddin, Vice President of Marketing*
*Mike Saltzman, Director - Eastern Territories & National Accounts*
*James Lingle, International Sales & Marketing Manager Rights & Permissions*
Overviews the information needs of people with developmental disabilities and tells librarians how to meet them. $65.oo-$75.00.
*368 pages Hardcover*
*ISBN 0-313287-80-5*

**4964 Innovative Programs: An Example of How CILs Can Put Their Work in Context**
Culture
Ste 1000
2323 S Shepherd Dr
Houston, TX 77019-7031
713-520-0232
FAX: 713-520-5785
e-mail: ilru@ilru.org
www.ilru.org

*Lex Frieden, Director, ILRU*
*Richard Petty, Program Director*
*Rose Shepard, Office Manager*
Another winner in the innovative CIL competition- Steve Brown describes the Talking Books Program of Southeast Alaska Independent Living, discussing their efforts to record the oral history and life experiences of people with disabilities in the larger context of disability culture.
*10 pages*

**4965 Insurance Solutions: Plan Well, Live Better**
Demos Medical Publishing
15th Floor
11 West 42nd Street
New York, NY 10036
212-683-0072
800-532-8663
FAX: 212-683-0118
e-mail: info@demosmedpub.com
www.demosmedpub.com

*Matt Conmy, Sr. Director of Sales*
*Thomas Hastings, Marketing Manager*
*Paul Choi, Vice-President of Finance and Operations*
Learn how to look at various insurance options from a new perspective - including life, disability, health, and long-term care. Concrete information for dealing with potential problems in your coverage, to secure your financial future. *$24.95*
*192 pages 2002*
*ISBN 1-888799-55-2*

**4966 International Directory of Libraries for the Disabled**
KG Saur/Division of RR Bowker
121 Chanlon Rd
New Providence, NJ 7974-1541
908-286-1090
800-521-8110

*Michael Cairns, CEO*
An essential resource for improving the quality and quantity of materials available to the print-handicapped audience. Featuring talking books, braille books, large print books as well as production centers for these materials. *$46.00*
*257 pages*
*ISBN 3-59821 -81-1*

**4967 Issues in Independent Living**
Independent Living Research Utilization
Ste 1000
2323 S Shepherd Dr
Houston, TX 77019-7031
713-520-9058
FAX: 713-520-5785
ilru.org

*Lex Frieden, Manager*
*Laurie Redd, Executive Director*
This booklet is a report of the National Study Group on the Implications of Health Care Reform for Americans with Disabilities and Chronic Health Conditions.
*30 pages*

**4968 JAMA: The Journal of the American Medical Association**
American Medical Association
515 N State St
Chicago, IL 60654-4820
312-464-2551
FAX: 312-464-5909
e-mail: display@jamanetwork.com
jama.ama-assn.org

*Howard Bauchner, MD, Editor-in-Chief*
Articles cover all aspects of medical research and clinical medicine. *$66.00*

**4969 JCIL Advocate Times**
Jackson Center for Independent Living
409 Linden Ave
Jackson, MI 49203-4065
517-782-6054
FAX: 517-782-3118

*Lesia Pikaart, Executive Director*
*JoAnn Lucas, Associate Director*
*Quarterly*

**4970 Jason & Nordic Publishers, Inc.**
P.O.Box 441
Hollidaysburg, PA 16648-441
814-696-2920
FAX: 814-696-4250
e-mail: turtlbks@jasonandnordic.com
www.jasonandnordic.com

*Norma Mc Phee, Owner/Ceo*
*Norma Phee*
Turtle Books for children with disabilities present heroes who look like them, have problems like theirs, have similar doubts and feelings in non-threatening, fun stories. They are motivational, bridge the gap and promote understanding among peers and siblings. 22 children's books (grades preK-3) plus Sensitivity and Awareness Guide containing lesson plans, activities, background information keyed to the series. Disabilities include: Down syndrome, cerebral palsy, blindness, deafness and more.

**4971 Journal of Social Work in Disabilty & Rehabilitation**
Haworth Press
10 Alice St
Binghamton, NY 13904-1503
607-722-5857
800-429-6784
FAX: 607-722-6362
e-mail: orders@haworthpress.com
www.haworthpress.com

*John T Oardeck PhD, Editor*
*S Harrington-Miller, Advertising*
*William Cohen, Owner*
Presents and explores issues related to disabilities and social policy, practice, research, and theory. Reflecting the broad scope of social work in disabilty practice, this interdisciplinary journal examines vital issues aspects of the field - from innovative practice methods, legal issues, and literature reviews to program descriptions and cuttinf-edge practice research.
*Quarterly*

**4972 Just Like Everyone Else**
World Institute on Disability
Ste 100
510 16th St
Oakland, CA 94612-1520 510-763-4100
FAX: 510-763-4109
e-mail: wid@wid.org
www.wid.org

The oversize-format publication, intended for general audiences, provides perspective, inspiration and information about the Independent Living Movement and the Americans with Disabilities Act. *$5.00*
*16 pages*

**4973 Keep the Promise: Managed Care and People with Disabilities**
American Network of Community Options & Resource
Ste 380
1101 King St
Alexandria, VA 22314-2962 703-535-7850
FAX: 703-535-7860
e-mail: ancor@ancor.org
ancor.org

*Renee L Pietrangelo, CEO*
*Suellen Galbraith, Director Public Policy*
This publication presents a detailed review of the process and the lessons learned. Details a way for all stake holders to work together for a state or local system.
*119 pages $18 - $22*

**4974 Keeping Our Families Together**
Through the Looking Glass
Ste 100
2198 6th St
Berkeley, CA 94710-2212 510-848-1112
800-644-2666
FAX: 510-848-4445
e-mail: TLG@lookingglass.org
www.lookingglass.org

*Megan Kirshbaum, Executive Director*
*Tina Evoyne, Office Manager*
Report of the National Task Force on parents with disabilities and their families. Available in braille, large print or cassette. *$2.00*
*12 pages*

**4975 Learn About the ADA in Your Local Library**
US Department of Justice
950 Pennsylvania Ave NW
Washington, DC 20530-9 202-586-5000
800-574-0301
FAX: 202-307-1197
TTY: 800-514-0383
www.ada.gov

*James Bostrom, Deputy Chiefs*
*Zita Johnson Betts, Deputy Chiefs*
*Sally Conway, Deputy Chiefs*
A 10-page annotated list of 95 ADA publications and one videotape that are available in 15,000 public libraries throughout the country.

**4976 LifeLines**
Disabled & Alone/Life Services for the Handicapped
Rm 510
61 Broadway
New York, NY 10006-2734 212-532-6740
800-995-0066
FAX: 212-532-3588
e-mail: info@disabledandalone.org
www.disabledandalone.org

*Lee Ackerman, Executive Director*
Newsletter providing current and valuable information about lifetime care and planning for persons with disabilities and their families and the organizations serving them. Free upon request.
*4-10 pages BiAnnual*

**4977 Lifelong Leisure Skills and Lifestyles for Persons with Developmental Disabilities**
Brookes Publishing
P.O.Box 10624
Baltimore, MD 21285-0624 410-337-9580
800-638-3775
FAX: 410-337-8539
e-mail: custserv@brookespublishing.com
readplaylearn.com

*Paul H. Brooks, Chairman*
*Jeffrey D. Brookes, President*
*Melissa A. Behm, Executive Vice President*
This instructional manual offers ideas and detailed examples that describe how to guide individuals of all ages through popular activities using adaptations that foster skill acquisition and inclusion. Some of the concepts explored are home-school-community collaboration, choice making and the dignity of risk, and leisure skill acquisition for the life span. *$35.00*
*352 pages Paperback*
*ISBN 1-55766-47-2*

**4978 Livin'**
Lehigh Valley Center for Independent Living
435 Allentown Dr
Allentown, PA 18109-9121 610-770-9781
FAX: 610-770-9801
lvcil.org

*Amy Beck, Executive Director*
*4 pages Quarterly*

**4979 Living in a State of Stuck**
Brookline Books
34 University Rd
Brookline, MA 02445-4533 800-666-2665
FAX: 617-734-3952
e-mail: brbooks@yahoo.com
www.brooklinebooks.com

Offers explanations on how adaptive technologies affect the lives of people with disabilities. *$24.95*
*3rd ed., paper*
*ISBN 1-571290-27-3*

**4980 Living in the Community**
Independent Living Research Utilization ILRU
Ste 1000
2323 S Shepherd Dr
Houston, TX 77019-7031 713-520-0232
FAX: 713-520-5785
e-mail: ilru@ilru.org
ilru.org

*Lex Frieden, Director, ILRU*
*Richard Petty, Program Director*
*Rose Shepard, Office Manager*
James, Lori, and Jamey describe the elements of their successful program to move people out of nursing homes and into the community: providing funding for deposits, first month's rent and other neccessities, including assistive technology; providing training and the other core services before and after consumers leave the nursing home; developing relationships with housing and other service providers.
*10 pages*

**4981 Loud, Proud and Passionate**
Mobility International USA
P.O.Box 10767
132 E. Broadway, Suite 343
Eugene, OR 97401 541-343-1284
FAX: 541-343-6812
e-mail: info@miusa.org
www.miusa.org

*Susan Sygall, CEO*
*Cerise Roth-Vinson, COO*
*Cindy Lewis, Director of Programs*
A resource book for international development and women's organization about including women with disabilities in projects in the community. Informs women sith disabilities about the efforts and successes of their peers worldwide. *$30.00*

**4982 Love: Where to Find It, How to Keep It**
Accent Books & Products
P.O.Box 700
Bloomington, IL 61702-700 309-378-2961
800-787-8444
FAX: 309-378-4420
e-mail: acmtlvng@aol.com

*Raymond C Cheever, Publisher*
*Betty Garee, Editor*
Offers ideas such as how to meet other single people, avoid the wrong type; communications skills and much more for the disabled person wanting to date. *$6.95*
*104 pages Paperback*
*ISBN 0-91570-31-0*

**4983 MOOSE: A Very Special Person**
Brookline Books
34 University Rd
Brookline, MA 02445-4533 800-666-2665
FAX: 617-734-3952
e-mail: brbooks@yahoo.com
www.brooklinebooks.com

Moose, which in very human terms, teaches us that each of us is different and that we have our own unique capacity for loving, sharing, enjoying and learning. *$10.95*
*Paperback*
*ISBN 0-91479-73-5*

**4984 Mainstream Magazine**
2973 Beech St
San Diego, CA 92102-1529 619-232-2727
FAX: 619-234-3155
e-mail: editor@mainstream.mag.com
www.mainstream-mag.com

*Cyndi Jones, Executive Director*
The authoritative, national voice of people with disabilities, publishes in-depth reports on employment, education, new products and technology, legislation and disability rights advocacy, recreation and travel, disability arts and culture, plus personality profiles and challenging commentary. *$24.00*
*Monthly*

**4985 Making Changes: Family Voices on Living Disabilities**
Brookline Books
34 University Rd
Brookline, MA 02445-4533 800-666-2665
FAX: 617-734-3952
e-mail: brbooks@yahoo.com
www.brooklinebooks.com
What are the day to day impacts on the family when a disabled child is born? Or when a child who grows up without a disability becomes disabled through accident or disease? This provocative set of reports illuminates the conditions of those peoples lives, and the way they and those around them adjust to the disabilities.
*$16.95*
*216 pages Paperback*
*ISBN 0-91479-93-*

**4986 Making Informed Medical Decisions: Where to Look and How to Use What You Find**
Patient-Centered Guides
1005 Gravenstein Highway North
Sebastopol, CA 95472-3836 707-827-7000
800-998-9938
FAX: 707-824-8268
e-mail: orders@oreilly.com
www.patientcenters.com

*Tim O'Reilly, CEO*
Making Informed Medical Decisions acts like a friendly reference librarian, explaining: tips for researching for someone else; medical journal articles; statistics and risk; standard treatment options; clinical trial; making an ally of your doctor; and determining your own best course. Authors Oster, Thomas, and Joseff-a patient advocate, medical librarian, and medical doctor-also share examples and stories. *$17.95*
*280 pages Paperback*
*ISBN 1-565924-59-2*

**4987 Making Wise Decisions for Long-Term Care**
AARP Fulfillment
601 E St NW
Washington, DC 20049-1 202-434-2277
800-424-3410
FAX: 202-434-3443
e-mail: member@aarp.org
www.aarp.org

*William Novelli, CEO*
Here's a comprehensive consumer education effort in the area of long-term care.
*28 pages*

**4988 Making a Difference**
Georgia Council On Developmental Disabilities
2 Peachtree St N.W.
26th Floor, Suite 246
Atlanta, GA 30303-3141 404-657-2126
888-275-4233
FAX: 404-657-2132
TTY:404-657-2133
e-mail: eejacobson@dhr.state.ga.us
www.gcdd.org

*Eric E Jacobson, Executive Director*
*Pat Nobbie, Deputy Director*
*Dottie Adams, Family/Individual Support Dir.*
*Valerie Meadows Suber, Public Information Director*
The Georgia Council on Developmental Disabilities collaborates with Georgia's citizens, public and private advocacy organizations and policymakers to positively influence public policies that enhance the quality of life for people with disabilities and their families. GCDD provides this through education and advocacy activities, program implementation, funding and public policy analysis and research.

**4989 Making a Difference: A Wise Approach**
Easter Seals
230 W Monroe St
Chicago, IL 60606-4703 312-726-0653
FAX: 312-726-1494

*Janet D Jamieson, Communication Manager*
The town of Wise, Virginia, and its leading citizen, Virgil Craft, personify what Making a Difference is all about when a community supports implementing the provisions of the Americans with Disabilities Act. Craft, a person with a disability, has spent his life giving back to the community. The community, in turn, has supported Craft's efforts to improve the environment, education, healthcare and access for disabled persons. A must buy for companies of all sizes, clubs and organizations. *$50.00*

**4990 Managing Your Activities**
Arthritis Foundation
P.O.Box 7669
Atlanta, GA 30357-0669
404-872-7100
800-283-7800
FAX: 404-872-0457
e-mail: help@arthritis.org
arthritis.org

*John H Klippel, CEO/ President*

**4991 Managing Your Health Care**
Arthritis Foundation
P.O.Box 7669
Atlanta, GA 30357-0669
404-872-7100
800-283-7800
FAX: 404-872-0457
e-mail: help@arthritis.org
arthritis.org

*John H Klippel, CEO/ President*

**4992 Medical Aspects of Disability: A Handbook For The Rehabilitation Professional**
Springer Publishing Company
11 West 42nd Street
15th Floor
New York, NY 10036
212-431-4370
877-687-7476
FAX: 212-941-7842
e-mail: marketing@springerpub.com
www.springerpub.com

*James C. Costello, Vice President, Journal Publishing*
*Theodore C. Nardin, CEO*
*$62.92*
*744 pages*
*ISBN 0-826179-71-1*

**4993 Meeting the Needs of Employees with Disabilities**
Resources for Rehabilitation
Ste 19a
33 Bedford St
Lexington, MA 02420-4330
781-368-9094
FAX: 781-368-9096

*Susan Greenblatt*
Provides information to help people with disabilities retain or obtain employment. Information on government programs and laws, supported employment, training programs, environmental adaptations and the transition from school to work are included. Chapters on mobility impairment, vision impairment and hearing and speech impairments. *$ 47.95*
*167 pages Biennial*
*ISBN 0-92971 -13-5*

**4994 NCD Bulletin**
National Council on Disability
1331 F Street Northwest
Suite 850
Washington, DC 20004- 1138
202-272-2004
FAX: 202-272-2022

*Joan Durocher, Executive Director*
*Mark Quigley, Communications Director*
Reports on the latest issues and news affecting people with disabilities.
*2 pages Monthly*

**4995 NCDE Survival Strategies for Oversease Living for People with Disabilities**
National Clearinghouse on Disability and Exchange
P.O.Box 10767
132 E. Broadway, Suite 343
Eugene, OR 97401
541-373-1284
FAX: 541-343-6812
e-mail: info@miusa.org
www.miusa.org

*Susan Sygall, CEO*
*Cerise Roth-Vinson, COO*
*Cindy Lewis, Director of Programs*
This book will provide individuals with disabilities information, resources and guidance on pursuing international exchange opportunities. It addresses disability-related aspects of the international exchange process such as choosing a program, applying, preparing for the trip, adjusting to a new country and returning home.

**4996 NOD E-Newsletter**
National Organization on Disability
5 East 86th Street
New York, NY 10028
646-505-1191
e-mail: info@nod.org
www.nod.org

*Carol Glazer, President*
*Miranda Pax, Chief of Staff*
Monthly E-Newsletter from the National Organization on Disability. Free.
*3 pages Monthly*

**4997 National Hookup**
ISC
16 Liberty St
Larkspur, CA 94939-1520
415-924-3549
FAX: 415-927-9556
e-mail: russbo@microweb.com

*Russ Bohlke, Manager*
Newsletter published by ISC, a national organization of people with physical disabilities. *$6.00*
*12-16 pages Quarterly*

**4998 New Horizons in Sexuality**
Accent Books & Products
P.O.Box 700
Bloomington, IL 61702-700
309-378-2961
800-787-8444
FAX: 309-378-4420
e-mail: acmtlvng@aol.com

*Raymond C Cheever, Publisher*
*Betty Garee, Editor*
This manual helps both males and females progress toward a satisfying post-injury relationship. *$7.95*
*50 pages Paperback*
*ISBN 0-91570 -42-6*

**4999 New Voices: Self Advocacy By People with Disabilities**
Brookline Books
34 University Rd
Brookline, MA 02445-4533
800-666-2665
FAX: 617-734-3952
e-mail: brbooks@yahoo.com
www.brooklinebooks.com

A collection of original papers, many by self advocates, that vividly illustrate the dynamic, ever-growing self-advocacy movement - persons with disabilities speaking out and seeking better non-institutional living situations, social and political equality and decent jobs at reasonable pay. *$29.95*
*274 pages Paperback*
*ISBN 1-57129 -04-4*

**5000 North Star Community Services**
3420 University Ave
Waterloo, IA 50701-2050 319-236-0901
888-879-1365
FAX: 319-236-3701
e-mail: info@northstarcs.org
www.northstarcs.org

*Mark Witmer, Executive Director*
*Mary Wankowicz, Director of Operations*
North Star Community Services is a rehabilitative services organization with home office in Waterloo, IA and several branch offices in Northeast, Northern and Central Iowa. North Star helps indiviuals with disabilities live and work in their communities. Services include: adult day services, supported community living services, employment services, and case management/service coordination.

**5001 Nothing is Impossible: Reflections on a New Life**
Ballantine Books
1745 Broadway
New York, NY 10019 212-782-9000
www.atrandom.com

*Edward Warren, Owner*
Reeve offers a uniquely powerful message of hope on topics ranging from the controversial stem cell debate to the mind-body connection he credits with his recent physical improvements. *$6.99*
*224 pages*
*ISBN 0-345470-73-7*

**5002 Nutritional Desk Reference**
Keats Publishing
P.O.Box 876
New Canaan, CT 06840 203-966-8721
800-323-4900

**5003 Nutritional Influences on Illness:**
Third Line Press
4751 Viviana Dr
Tarzana, CA 91356-5038 818-996-0076
third-line.com

*Melvyn R Werbach, Owner*
A comprehensive summary of the world's knowledge concerning the relationship between dietary and nutrtional factors and illness. This book does not try to promote any particular school of thought. Instead of the author telling readers his opinion as to what research says, he makes it easy for them to see data for themselves and then form their own opinions.
*504 pages*
*ISBN 0-879835-31-1*

**5004 Oregon Perspectives**
Oregon Council on Developmental Disabilities
540 24th Pl NE
Salem, OR 97301-4517 503-945-9941
800-292-4154
FAX: 503-945-9947
e-mail: ocdd@ocdd.org
www.ocdd.org

*Laura Bronson, Office Manager*
*Beth Kessler, Planning & Communications Coordinator*
A quarterly publication from the Oregon Council on Developmental Disabilities.

**5005 Organ Transplants: Making the Most of Your Gift of Life**
Patient-Centered Guides
1005 Gravenstein Highway North
Sebastopol, CA 95472-3836 707-827-7000
800-998-9938
FAX: 707-824-8268
e-mail: orders@oreilly.com
www.patientcenters.com

*Linda Lamb, Editor*
*Shawnde Paull, Marketing*
*Tim O'Reilly, CEO*
Over 64,000 people in the US are awaiting an organ transplant. Although transplant surgeries are now fairly routine and can give their recipients the gift of new life, the road to getting a transplant can be long and harrowing. Living with immunosuppressive drugs and strong emotional responses can also be more challenging than families imagine. Medical journalist Robert Finn answers the concerns of these families, with the latest facts about transplantation - as well as the stories behind them. *$19.95*
*326 pages Paperback*
*ISBN 1-565926-34-X*

**5006 PEAK Parent Center**
Ste 200
611 N Weber St
Colorado Springs, CO 80903-1072 719-531-9400
800-284-0251
FAX: 719-531-9452
e-mail: info@peakparent.org
www.peakparent.org

*Barbara Buswell, Executive Director*
PEAK Parent Center is a federally-designated Parent Training and Information Center (PTI). As a PTI, PEAK supports and empowers parents, providing them with information and strategies to use when advocating for their children with disabilities. PEAK works one-on-one with families and educators helping them realize new possibilities for children with disabilities by expanding knowledge of special education and offering new strategies for success.

**5007 Parallels in Time**
MN Governor's Council on Development Disabilities
658 Cedar St
Saint Paul, MN 55155-1603 651-296-4018
877-348-0505
FAX: 651-297-7200
e-mail: admin.dd@state.mn.us
www.mncdd.org

*Colleen Wieck PhD, Executive Director*
Parallels in Time traces present attitudes and the treatment of people with disabilities, and supplements the first weekend sesion of Partners in Policymaking. This CD-ROM includes the History of the Parent Movement and the History of the Independent Living Movement, as well as personal stories of self advocates, leaders in the self advocacy movement.

**5008 Part of the Team**
Easter Seals
Ste 1800
230 W Monroe St
Chicago, IL 60606-4851 312-726-6800
FAX: 312-726-1494

*Janet D Jamieson, Communications Manager*
*James Williams Jr, Chief Executive Officer*
Designed for employers of all sizes, rehabilitation organizations and all others concerned with the employment of people with disabilities. It addresses managers' concerns and questions about supervising persons with disabilities and can be used as a discussion/team-building tool for employees with and without disabilities. The video recognizes people with disabilities as strong contenders for almost any job. *$15.00*

**5009 Partnering with Public Health: Funding& Advocacy Opportunities for CILs and SILCs**

Independent Living Research Utilization ILRU
Ste 1000
2323 S Shepherd Dr
Houston, TX 77019-7031
713-520-0232
FAX: 713-520-5785
e-mail: ilru@ilru.org
ilru.org

*Lex Frieden, Director, ILRU*
*Richard Petty, Program Director*
*Rose Shepard, Office Manager*

Laura Rauscher discusses how CILs and SCILs can use funding from the Centers for Disease Control and partnerships with public health agencies to provide innovative programs promoting the health of people with disabilities.
*10 pages*

**5010 Peer Counseling: Roles, Functions, Boundaries**

Independent Living Research Utilization ILRU
Ste 1000
2323 S Shepherd Dr
Houston, TX 77019-7031
713-520-0232
FAX: 713-520-5785
e-mail: ilru@ilru.org
ilru.org

*Lex Frieden, Director, ILRU*
*Richard Petty, Program Director*
*Rose Shepard, Office Manager*

In this article, the following points were discussed: describing peer support as counseling suggests safeguards and expectations which cannot be provided by nonprofessionals; the purpose of peer counseling is to promote the independent living philosophy and encourage consumers to embrace it; peer counseling cannot and is not intended to help individuals deal with intense emotional stress, whether it is related to their disability or to something else.
*10 pages*

**5011 Peer Mentor Volunteers: Empowering People for Change**

Independent Living Research Utilization ILRU
Ste 1000
2323 S Shepherd Dr
Houston, TX 77019-7031
713-520-0232
FAX: 713-520-5785
e-mail: ilru@ilru.org
ilru.org

*Lex Frieden, Director, ILRU*
*Richard Petty, Program Director*
*Rose Shepard, Office Manager*

Arizona Bridge to Independent Living (ABIL) in Phoenix, featured in this issue, is another winner in the innovative CIL program competition.
*10 pages*

**5012 People and Families**

New Jersey Council on Developmental Disabilities
P.O.Box 700
Trenton, NJ 08625-0700
800-792-8858
FAX: 609-292-7114
TTY:609-777-3238
e-mail: njcdd@njcdd.org
www.njcdd.org

*Alison M. Lozano, Executive Director*
*Shirla Simpson, Deputy Director*
*Jane Dunhamn, Project Manager / Diversity Coordinator*

A free magazine for people with disabilities, their families and the public about disability topics such as personal assistance, deinstitutionalization, health care and community living. Published by the New Jersey council on Developmental Disabilities, a federally funded advocacy and policy advisory body. The council has 25 members - 15 consumer/product volunteers and 10 professionals.
*48 pages Quarterly*

**5013 People with Disabilities & Abuse: Implications for Center for Independent Living**

Independent Living Research Utilization ILRU
Ste 1000
2323 S Shepherd Dr
Houston, TX 77019-7031
713-520-0232
FAX: 713-520-5785
e-mail: ilru@ilru.org
ilru.org

*Lex Frieden, Director, ILRU*
*Richard Petty, Program Director*
*Rose Shepard, Office Manager*

*10 pages*

**5014 People with Disabilities Who Challenge the System**

Brookes Publishing
P.O.Box 10624
Baltimore, MD 21285-0624
410-337-9580
800-638-3775
FAX: 410-337-8539
e-mail: custserv@brookespublishing.com
readplaylearn.com

*Paul H. Brooks, Chairman*
*Jeffrey D. Brookes, President*
*Melissa A. Behm, Executive Vice President*

Helpful forms, tables, and case studies plus an emphasis on self-determination point the way to the development of supports so that people who are deaf-blind, have severe to profound physical and cognitive disabilities, or have serious behavior problems can be fully included in the classroom, workplace, and community. *$34.00*
*464 pages Paperback*
*ISBN 1-55766 -29-0*

**5015 People's Voice**

Independence CIL
Ste F
300 3rd Ave SW
Minot, ND 58701-4346
701-839-4724
800-377-5114
FAX: 701-838-1677
e-mail: independencecil@independencecil.org
independencecil.org

*Scott Burlingame, Executive Director*
*Jill McDonald, Finance Director*

*8 pages Quarterly*

**5016 Personal Perspectives on Personal Assistance Services**

World Institute on Disability
Suite 280
3075 Adeline Street
Berkeley, CA 94703
510-225-6400
FAX: 510-225-0477
TTY:510-225-0478
e-mail: wid@wid.org
www.wid.org

*Anita Shafe Aaron, Executive Director*
*Bruce Curtis, Director of International Programs*

This collection of personal essays explores a wide range of perspectives on Personal Assistance Services. Family issues and PAS concerns for people with various different disabilities, of different ages and as members of minority groups are addressed. *$5.00*
*80 pages Paperback*

**5017 Perspectives**

National Assoc of State Directors of DD Services
113 Oronoco St
Alexandria, VA 22314-2015
703-683-4202
FAX: 703-684-1395
e-mail: dberland@nasddds.org

*Nancy Thaler, Executive Director*

Provides a concise summary of national policy developments and initiatives affecting persons with devlopmental disabilities and the programs that serve them. From bills pending before Congress, to the growth in Medicaid-funded services, to changes in federal-state Medicaid policies and the shift of responsibility from Washington to the states, keeps readers in tune with the latest national issues shaping publically funded disability services.
*$95.00*
*Monthly*

**5018 Place to Live**
Accent Books & Products
P.O.Box 700
Bloomington, IL 61702-700 309-378-2961
800-787-8444
FAX: 309-378-4420
e-mail: acmtlvng@aol.com

*Raymond C Cheever, Publisher*
*Betty Garee, Editor*
Many disabled people have found that group housing or accessible apartments are the best alternative to living in a nursing home. These articles tell about some of the alternatives people have found so they can live independently. Just one idea might be the answer for better living for you. *$4.95*
*64 pages Paperback*
*ISBN 0-91570 -30-2*

**5019 Proceedings**
AHEAD
Suite 204
107 Commerce Center Drive
Huntersville, NC 28078 704-947-7779
FAX: 704-948-7779
e-mail: information@ahead.org
www.ahead.org

*Richard Allegra, Director of Professional Development*
*Tri Do, Operations Manager*
National conferences, innovative programs, research, evaluation services, auxiliary aids, career information and other vital information.

**5020 Psychological & Social Impact of Disability**
Springer Publishing Company
11 West 42nd Street
15th Floor
New York, NY 10036 212-431-4370
877-687-7476
FAX: 212-941-7842
e-mail: marketing@springerpub.com
www.springerpub.com

*James C. Costello, Vice President, Journal Publishing*
*Theodore C. Nardin, CEO*
*$49.95*
*488 pages*
*ISBN 0-826122-13-2*

**5021 Psychology and Health**
Springer Publishing Company
11 West 42nd Street
15th Floor
New York, NY 10036 212-431-4370
877-687-7476
FAX: 212-941-7842
e-mail: marketing@springerpub.com
www.springerpub.com

*James C. Costello, Vice President, Journal Publishing*
*Theodore C. Nardin, CEO*
Content of this book spans a wide range of clinical conditions, including somatization disorders, chronic pain, migraine, anxiety and cancer. *$29.95*
*256 pages*

**5022 Psychology of Disability**
Springer Publishing Company
11 West 42nd Street,
15th Floor
New York, NY 10036-3915 212-431-4370
877-687-7476
FAX: 212-941-7842
e-mail: cs@springerpub.com
www.springerpub.com

*Theodore C Nardin, Chief Executive Officer*
*Nancy Hale, Editorial Director*
Reactions to the disabled. *$27.95*
*288 pages*
*ISBN 0-82613 -40-1*

**5023 Quality of Life for Persons with Disabilities**
Brookline Books
34 University Rd
Brookline, MA 02445-4533 800-666-2665
FAX: 617-734-3952
e-mail: brbooks@yahoo.com
www.brooklinebooks.com

Quality of life generally refers to a person's subjective experience of his or her life and focuses attention on how the individual with a disabling condition experiences the world. This book presents a comprehensive and international view of this concept as applied to a broad range of settings in which persons with disabilities live, work and play. *$35.00*
*Paperback*
*ISBN 0-91479 -92-1*

**5024 REACHing Out Newsletter**
REACH of Dallas Resource on Independent Living
8625 King George Drive
Suite 210
Dallas, TX 75235-2275 214-630-4796
FAX: 214-630-6390
TTY:214-630-5995
e-mail: reachdallas@reachcils.org
reachcils.org

Quarterly newsletter from REACH of Dallas Resource Center on Independent Living.
*16 pages Quarterly*

**5025 RTC Connection**
Research and Training Center
University of Wisconsin Stou
Menomonie, WI 54751 715-232-2236
FAX: 715-232-2251
e-mail: menz@uwstout.edu
www.rtc.uwstout.edu

*Julie Larson, Program Assistant*
Bi-annual reports on disability and rehabilitation research and policy topics.
*Newsletter*

**5026 Rehabilitation Gazette**
Gazette International Networking Institute
Ste 110
4207 Lindell Blvd
Saint Louis, MO 63108-2930 314-534-0475
FAX: 314-534-5070
e-mail: info@post-polio.org
www.post-polio.org

*Joan L Headley, Executive Director*
International journal of independent living for people with disabilities. *$12.00*
*8 pages Bi-Annually*

**5027 Relaxation: A Comprehensive Manual for Adults and Children with Special Needs**
Research Press
P.O.Box 9177
Champaign, IL 61826-9177
217-352-3273
800-519-2707
FAX: 217-352-1221
e-mail: orders@researchpress.com
www.researchpress.com

This unique contribution to the field of relaxation training presents: self relaxation techniques designed for adults, methods for teaching relaxation to adults and older children, and procedures for teaching relaxation to young children and children with developmental disabilities. The clear, concise text is supplemented by over 100 helpful illustrations. *$19.95*
*Paperback*
*ISBN 0-878221-86-8*

**5028 Resources for People with Disabilities and Chronic Conditions**
Resources for Rehabilitation
Ste 19a
33 Bedford St
Lexington, MA 02420-4330
781-890-6371
FAX: 781-861-7517

*Susan Greenblatt*
A comprehensive resource directory that helps people with disabilities and chronic conditions achieve their maximum level of independence. Chapters on spinal cord injuries, low back pain, diabetes, hearing and speech impairments, epilepsy, multiple sclerosis. Describes organizations, products and publications. *$49.95*
*215 pages Biennial*
*ISBN 0-92971 -12-7*

**5029 Role Portrayal and Stereotyping on Television**
Greenwood Publishing Group
130 Cremona Drive
Santa Barbara,, CA 93117-4208
203-226-3571
800-368-6868
805-968-1911
FAX: 866-270-3856
e-mail: customerservice@abc-clio.com
www.abc-clio.com

An annotated bibliography of studies relating to women, minorities, aging, health and handicaps.
*214 pages $55 - $59.95*
*ISBN 0-313248-55-9*

**5030 Screening in Chronic Disease**
Oxford University Press
2001 Evans Rd
Cary, NC 27513-2009
800-445-9714
877-773-4325
FAX: 919-677-1303
e-mail: custserv.us@oup.com
www.oup-usa.org

*Thomas Carty, Senior Vice President*
Early detection, or screening, is a common strategy for controlling chronic disease, but little information has been available to help determine which screening procedures are worthwhile, until this textbook. *$42.50*
*256 pages*

**5031 Sexual Adjustment**
Accent Books & Products
P.O.Box 700
Bloomington, IL 61702-700
309-378-2961
800-787-8444
FAX: 309-378-4420
e-mail: acmtlvng@aol.com

*Raymond C Cheever, Publisher*
*Betty Garee, Editor*
Essential information concerning sexual adjustment for the paraplegic male. *$4.95*
*73 pages Paperback*
*ISBN 0-19570 -00-0*

**5032 Sexuality and Disabilities: A Guide for Human Service Practitioners**
Haworth Press
6000 Broken Sound Parkway, NW
Suite 300,
Boca Raton, FL 33487-1503
561-994-0555
FAX: 561-241-7856
e-mail: orders@taylorandfrancis.com
www.tandf.co.uk

This book addresses persons with physical, sensory, intellectual and cognitive disabilities and their concerns in the areas of intimacy, family issues, sexuality and sexual functioning. *$74.95*
*159 pages Hardcover*
*ISBN 1-560243-75-9*

**5033 Sickened: The Memoir of a Muchausen by Proxy Childhood**
Bantam Books
1540 Broadway
New York, NY 10019-4039
212-782-9000
FAX: 212-572-6066
e-mail: crownpublicity@randomhouse.com
www.randomhouse.com

From early childhood, Julie Gregory was continually X-rayed, medicated, and operated on - in the vain pursuit of an illness that was created in her mother's mind. Munchausen by proxy (MBP) in which the caretaker - almost always the mother - invents or induces symptoms in her child because she craves the attention of medical professionals. *$24.95*
*256 pages Hardcover*
*ISBN 0-553803-07-7*

**5034 Socialization Games for Persons with Disabilities**
Charles C. Thomas
2600 S 1st St
Springfield, IL 62704-4730
217-789-8980
800-258-8980
FAX: 217-789-9130
e-mail: books@ccthomas.com
ccthomas.com

*Michael P. Thomas, President*
This text will assist those who want to teach severely multiple disabled students by providing information on: general principles of intervention and classroom organization; managing the behavior of students; physically managing students and using adaptive equipment; teaching eating skills; teaching toileting, dressing, and hygiene skills; teaching cognition, communication, and socialization skills; teaching independent living skills; and teaching infants and preschool students. *$38.95*
*176 pages Paperback*
*ISBN 0-398067-46-5*

**5035 Sometimes You Just Want to Feel Like a Human Being**
Brookes Publishing
P.O.Box 10624
Baltimore, MD 21285-624
410-337-9580
800-638-3775
FAX: 410-337-8539
e-mail: custserv@brookespublishing.com
readplaylearn.com

*Paul Brooks, Owner*
Case studies of empowering psychotherapy with people with disabilities. This text reveals how counseling can be beneficial to individuals with disabilities of all kinds, including autism, mental retardation, sensory impairment, cerebral palsy, or HIV infection. *$ 26.95*
*272 pages Paperback*
*ISBN 1-55766 -96-0*

**5036 South Carolina Assistive Technology Program**
University of South Carolina
Columbia, SC 29208-1
803-935-5301
800-915-4522
FAX: 803-935-5342
e-mail: carol.page@uscmed.sc.edu
www.sc.edu/scatp/

*Carol Page, Editor*
*7-8 pages Bi-annually*

**5037 Space Coast CIL News**
Space Coast Center for Independent Living
571 Haverty Court,
Suite W.
Rockledge, FL 32955-2566
321-633-6011
FAX: 321-633-6472
TTY:321-784-9008
e-mail: agrau@bellsouth.net
spacecoastcil.org

*Michael Lavoie, President*
*Howard Fetes, Vice-President*
Non-profit organization that provides services which enable people with disabilities to live as independently as possible.
*12 pages Quarterly*

**5038 Special Needs Trust Handbook**
Aspen Publishers
7th Fl
76 9th Ave
New York, NY 10011-4962
301-644-3599
800-638-8437
e-mail: customerservice@aspenpublishers.com
www.aspenpublishers.com

The Special Needs Trusts Handbook is the single-volume, comprehensive resource that provides information on how to handle the complex requirements of drafting and administering trusts for clients who are mentally or physically disabled, or who wish to provide for others with disabilities. *$245.00*
*900 pages*
*ISBN 0-735572-88-7*

**5039 Special Siblings: Growing Up With Someone with A Disability**
Brookes Publishing
P.O.Box 10624
Baltimore, MD 21285-624
410-337-9580
800-638-3775
FAX: 410-337-8539
e-mail: custserv@brookespublishing.com
readplaylearn.com

*Paul Brooks, Owner*
The author reveals what she experienced as the sister of a man with cerebral palsy and mental retardation - and shares what others have learned about being and having a special sibling. Weaving a lifetime of memories and reflections with relevant research and interviews with more than 100 other siblings and experts, McHugh explores a spectrum of feelings - from anger and guilt to love and pride - and helps readers understand the issues siblings may encounter. *$21.95*
*256 pages Paperback*
*ISBN 1-557666-07-5*

**5040 TERI**
251 Airport Rd.
Oceanside, CA 92058-1321
760-721-1706
teriinc.org

*Cheryl Kilmer, Executive Director*
A private, nonprofit corporation which has been developing and operating programs for individuals with developmental disabilities since 1980. Offers staff training videos, staff training tools and technique manuals.

**5041 To Live with Grace and Dignity**
World Institute on Disability
3075 Adeline Street
Suite 280
Oakland, CA 94703-1520
510-225-6400
FAX: 510-225-0477
TTY:510-225-0478
e-mail: wid@wid.org
www.wid.org

This unique book combines photographs and essays to allow the reader to enter some of the real day to day relationships that develop between individuals with disabilities and their personal assistants. Looking at and listening to what these relationships are all about is what motivated and inspired this book, says author Lydia Gans. The individuals included in this book represent a wide range of ages, disabilities and cultural backgrounds. *$26.00*
*72 pages Paperback*

**5042 Touch/Ability Connects People with Disabilities & Alternative Health Care Pract.**
Independent Living Research Utilization ILRU
Ste 1000
2323 S Shepherd Dr
Houston, TX 77019-7031
713-520-0232
FAX: 713-520-5785
e-mail: ilru@ilru.org
ilru.org

*Lex Frieden , Director*
*Laurie Gerke Redd, Administrative Director*
The people at DIRECT center for Independence and Touch/Ability in Tuscon, Arizona, have collaborated to develop a wellness program that makes alternative health care choices available to people with disabilities. The Touch/Ability Wellness program was selected as one of last year's winners in the Innovative CILs competition because of this outcome of increased options open to people with disabilities.
*10 pages*

**5043 US Role in International Disability Activities: A History**
World Institute on Disability
3075 Adeline Street
Suite 280
Oakland, CA 94703-1520
510-225-6400
FAX: 510-225-0477
TTY:510-225-0478
e-mail: wid@wid.org
www.wid.org

This study was undertaken to present an initial introduction to US involvement in the field of international rehabilitation and disability. *$12.00*
*169 pages Paperback*

**5044 Understanding and Accommodating Physical Disabilities: Desk Reference**
Greenwood Publishing Group
130 Cremona Drive
Santa Barbara,, CA 93117-4208
203-226-3571
800-368-6868
805-968-1911
FAX: 866-270-3856
e-mail: customerservice@abc-clio.com
www.abc-clio.com

Medical conditions that qualify as disabilities under the American's with Disabilities Act are explained in non-medical terminology. Hardcover.
*200 pages $52.95 - $55*
*ISBN 0-899308-14-7*

**5045 Vestibular Disorders Association**
Vestibular Disorders Association
P.O.Box 13305
Portland, OR 97213-305
503-229-7705
800-837-8428
FAX: 503-229-8064
e-mail: info@vestibular.org
www.vestibular.org

*Lisa Haven, Executive Director*
Many books and short publications about inner ear, (vestibular) disorders, dizziness, balance problems, and vertigo.Contents of each newsletter, onthe level,includes up-to-date information on topics such as diagnosis,treatment,research,and coping strategies related to vesticular disorders. *$15.00*

*ISBN 0-963261-15-0*

**5046 Visions & Values**
Idaho Council on Developmental Disabilities
650 W. State St., Room 100
P. O. Box 83720
Boise, ID 83720-5840
208-332-1824
800-544-2433
FAX: 208-334-2307
www.state.id.us/icdd

A quarterly publication from the Idaho Council on Developmental Disabilities.

**5047 Weiner's Herbal**
Quantum Books
4 Cambridge Ctr
Cambridge, MA 02142-1406
617-494-5042
FAX: 617-577-7282
e-mail: orders@quantumbk.com
www.quantumbooks.com

*William Szabo, Owner*
A-Z index covering all aspects of herbs.
*Paperback*
*ISBN 0-812825-86-1*

**5048 When the Brain Goes Wrong**
Fanlight Productions
32 Court Street, 21st Floor
Brooklyn, NY 11201-1731
718-488-8900
800-876-1710
FAX: 718-488-8642
e-mail: info@fanlight.com
www.fanlight.com

*Ben Achtenberg, Owner*
*Nicole Johnson, Publicity Coordinator*
*Anthony Sweeney, Marketing Director*
An extraordinary and provocative series of seven short films which profile individuals with a range of brian dysfunctions. The seven brief segments focus on schizophrenia, manic depression, epilepsy, head injury, headaches and addiction. In addition to the personal stories, the segments include interviews with physicians who speak briefly about what is known about the disorders and treatment. #131 *$245.00*

*ISBN 1-572951-31-1*

**5049 Women with Physical Disabilities: Achieving & Maintaining Health & Well-Being**
Spina Bifida Association of America
Ste 250
4590 Macarthur Blvd NW
Washington, DC 20007-4226
202-944-3285
800-621-3141
FAX: 202-944-3295
e-mail: sbaa@sbaa.org
www.sbaa.org

*Cindy Brownstein, CEO*
*Carmen J Head , Director*
Introduces the critical concept of womens health in the context of physical disabilities. *$42.00*

**5050 Work in the Context of Disability Culture**
Independent Living Research Utilization ILRU
Ste 1000
2323 S Shepherd Dr
Houston, TX 77019-7031
713-520-0232
FAX: 713-520-5785
e-mail: ilru@ilru.org
ilru.org

*Lex Frieden , Director*
*Laurie Gerke Redd, Administrative Director*
Another winner in the innovative CIL competition-Steve Brown describes the Talking Books Program of Southeast Alaska Independent Living, discussing their efforts to record the oral history and life experiences of people with disabilities in the larger context of the disability culture.
*10 pages*

## Parenting: General

**5051 AEPS Family Report: For Children Ages Three to Six**
Brookes Publishing
P.O.Box 10624
Baltimore, MD 21285-624
410-337-9580
800-638-3775
FAX: 410-337-8539
e-mail: custserv@brookespublishing.com
readplaylearn.com

*Paul Brooks, Owner*
This is a 64-item questionnaire that asks parents to rank their child's abilities on specific skills. In packages of 10 paperback. *$23.00*
*28 pages Saddle-stiched*
*ISBN 1-557662-50-9*

**5052 AT for Parents with Disabilities**
Idaho Assistive Technology Project
129 W 3rd St
Moscow, ID 83843-2268
208-885-3559
800-432-8324
FAX: 20- 88- 614
e-mail: idahoat@uidaho.edu
www.educ.uidaho.edu/idatech

*$5.00*
*80 pages*

**5053 Adapted Physical Activity Programs**
Human Kinetics
P.O.Box 5076
Champaign, IL 61825-5076
800-747-4457
FAX: 217-351-1549
e-mail: info@hkusa.com
www.humankinetics.com
Human Kinetics produces a variety of resources for adapted physical education practitioners, including books on activities, a research journal and higher education references. *$24.00*
*Quarterly*
*ISSN 0736-58 9*

**5054 All of Us: Talking Together, Sex Educationfor People with Developmental Disabilities**
Aquarius Health Care Videos
30 Forest Road
P.O. Box 249
Millis, MA 02054-7159
508-376-1244
FAX: 508-376-1245
e-mail: aqvideos@tiac.net
www.aquariusproductions.com

*Lesile Kussmann, President*
*Joyce Farmer, Assistant Director*

For parents, caregivers and young people with developmental disabilities often feel isolated and unsure when approaching sex education with their children. In this video, parents of children with developmental disabilities share their difficulties in talking to their children about the social/sexual arena. Real life conversations between parents and their children demonstrate their discomfort, concerns, thoughts and hopes. *$195.00*

*Video*

**5055 Baby Book for the Developmentally Challenged Child**
Exceptional Parent Library
P.O.Box 1807
Englewood Cliffs, NJ 7632-1207
201-947-6000
800-535-1910
FAX: 201-947-9376
e-mail: eplibrary@aol.com
www.eplibrary.com

This baby book is for parents to write milestones for their developmentally challenged child. It incorporates the usual baby book features with very special sections covering any special needs child. *$25.00*

*48 pages Hardcover*

**5056 Babyface: A Story of Heart and Bones**
Spina Bifida Association of America
Ste 250
4590 Macarthur Blvd NW
Washington, DC 20007-4226
202-944-3285
800-621-3141
FAX: 202-944-3295
e-mail: sbaa@sbaa.org
www.sbaa.org

*Cindy Brownstein, CEO*
*Carmen J Head , Director*

A must read for families that seek insight into coping with a chronic condition. Many useful resources provided. *$32.90*

**5057 Backyards and Butterflies**
Brookline Books
34 University Rd
Brookline, MA 02445-4533
800-666-2665
FAX: 617-734-3952
e-mail: brbooks@yahoo.com
www.brooklinebooks.com

Backyards And Butterflies: Ways to Include Children with Disabilities In Out Door Activites is an illustrated book with dozens of imaginative ways parents can include children with physical disabilities in outdoor activities. Offers clear concise, how-to directions for constructing homemaode toys, utensils, and other items that can be enjoyed outside safely and comfortably *$14.95*

*72 pages Paperback*
*ISBN 1-57129-11-7*

**5058 Books on Special Children**
BOSC
P.O.Box 305
Congers, NY 10920-305
845-638-1236
FAX: 845-638-0847
e-mail: irene@boscbooks.com
www.boscbooks.com

*Irene Slovak, Owner*

Distributes books by mail to professionals and parents of handicapped children. The BOSC Directory contains facilities for people with learning disabilities (all disabilities, published annually)

*300+ pages Hardcover*
*ISBN O-G61386-08-8*

**5059 Brothers, Sisters, and Special Needs**
Brookes Publishing
P.O.Box 10624
Baltimore, MD 21285-624
410-337-9580
800-638-3775
FAX: 410-337-8539
e-mail: custserv@brookespublishing.com
readplaylearn.com

*Paul Brooks, Owner*

Information and activities for helping young siblings of children with chronic illnesses and developmental disabilities. *$30.00*

*224 pages Paperback*
*ISBN 1-55766-43-3*

**5060 Building the Healing Partnership: Parents, Professionals and Children**
Brookline Books
34 University Rd
Brookline, MA 02445-4533
800-666-2665
FAX: 617-734-3952
e-mail: brbooks@yahoo.com
www.brooklinebooks.com

Successful programs understand that the disabled child's needs must be considered in the context of a family. This book was specifically written for practitioner's who must work with families but who have insufficient training in family systems assessment and intervention. It is a valuable blend of theory and practice with pointers for applying the principles. *$24.95*

*Paperback*
*ISBN 0-91479-63-8*

**5061 Children with Disabilities**
Brookes Publishing
P.O.Box 10624
Baltimore, MD 21285-624
410-337-9580
800-638-3775
FAX: 410-337-8539
e-mail: custserv@brookespublishing.com
www.brookespublishing.com

*Mark L Batshaw MD, Editor*
*Paul Brooks, Owner*

Extensive coverage of genetics, heredity, pre- and postnatal development, specific disabilities, family roles, and intervention. Features chapters on substance abuse, HIV and AIDS, Down syndrome, fragile X syndrome, behavior management, transitions to adulthood, and health care in the 21st century. Also reveals the causes of many conditions that can lead to developmental disabilities. *$69.95*

*912 pages Hardcover*
*ISBN 1-557665-81-8*

**5062 Conditional Love: Parents' Attitudes Toward Handicapped Children**
Greenwood Publishing Group
130 Cremona Drive
Santa Barbara,, CA 93117-4208
203-226-3571
800-368-6868
805-968-1911
FAX: 866-270-3856
e-mail: customerservice@abc-clio.com
www.abc-clio.com

Offers parents information on understanding disabled children and mainstreaming them into their normal family life. *$49.95*

*312 pages*
*ISBN 0-89789-24-7*

**5063 Coordinacion De Servicios Centrado En La Familia**
Brookline Books
34 University Rd
Brookline, MA 02445-4533
800-666-2665
FAX: 617-734-3952
e-mail: brbooks@yahoo.com
www.brooklinebooks.com

This book, translated into Spanish from the English original, is designed to orient and educate parents about issues of service

coordination, to assist families in caring for an infant or toddler with developmental delays or disabilities. *$7.00*
*34 pages Paperback*
*ISBN 0-91479 -90-5*

**5064 Developing Personal Safety Skills in Children with Disabilities**
Brookes Publishing
P.O.Box 10624
Baltimore, MD 21285-624
410-337-9580
800-638-3775
FAX: 410-337-8539
e-mail: custserv@brookespublishing.com
readplaylearn.com

*Paul Brooks, Owner*
A guide for teachers, parents, and caregivers, this volume explores the issue of personal safety for children with disabilities and offers strategies for empowering and protecting them at home and in school. Recognizing that children with disabilities are vulnerable to abuse, this work explores why children with disabilities need personal safety skills, offers, curriculum ideas and exercises, and advocates the development of self-esteem and assertiveness so that children can protect themselves. *$34.00*
*220 pages Paperback*
*ISBN 1-557661-84-7*

**5065 Developmental Disabilities in Infancy and Childhood**
Brookes Publishing
P.O.Box 10624
Baltimore, MD 21285-624
410-767-6100
800-638-3775
FAX: 410-767-5850
e-mail: custserv@brookespublishing.com
readplaylearn.com

*Paul Brooks, Owner*
This two volume set explores advances in assessment and treatment, retains a clinical focus, and incorporates recent developments in research and theory. Can be purchased individually or as a set (Vol. 1: Neurodevelopmental Diagnosis and Treatment Vol. 2: The Spectrum of Developmental Disabilities). *$210.00*
*Hardcover*
*ISBN 1-55766O-CA-P*

**5066 Dictionary of Developmental Disabilities Terminology**
Brookes Publishing
P.O.Box 10624
Baltimore, MD 21285-624
410-337-9580
800-638-3775
FAX: 410-337-8539
e-mail: custserv@brookespublishing.com
readplaylearn.com

*Paul Brooks, Owner*
Answers thousands of questions for medical or human services professionals, parents or advocates of children with disabilities, or students preparing for their careers. Provides thorough explanations of the most common terms associated with disabilities. *$ 55.95*
*368 pages Hardcover*
*ISBN 1-557662-45-2*

**5067 Encyclopedia of Genetic Disorders & Birth Defects**
Facts on File
Fl 17
132 W 31st St
New York, NY 10001-3406
800-322-8755
FAX: 800-678-3633
e-mail: custserv@factsonfile.com
www.factsonfile.com

*Mark Donnell, President*
Layperson-accessible entries on genetic terminology and genetically-influenced conditions. *$71.50*
*474 pages*
*ISBN 0-816038-09-0*

**5068 Exceptional Parent Magazine**
Psy-Ed Corporation
416 Main Street
Johnstown, PA 15901-2032
814-361-3860
877-372-7368
FAX: 814-361-3861
e-mail: cmellott@eparent.com
www.eparent.com

*Vanessa Ira, Sales Manager*
Magazine that provides information, support, ideas, encouragement, and outreach for parents and families of children with disabilities and the professionals who work with them. *$39.95*
*85 pages Monthly*

**5069 Face of Inclusion**
Special Needs Project
Ste H
324 State St
Santa Barbara, CA 93101-2364
805-962-8087
800-333-6867
FAX: 805-962-5087
e-mail: eplibrary@aol.com
www.eplibrary.com

*Hod Gray, Owner*
A unique and moving parents' perspective of inclusion for administrators, teachers, and parents of children with disabilities. *$99.00*

**5070 Families Magazine**
New Jersey Developmental Disabilities Council
P.O.Box 700
Trenton, NJ 8625-700
609-292-3745
800-792-8858
FAX: 609-292-7114
TTY: 609-777-3238
e-mail: njcdd@njcdd.org
www.njddc.org

*Alison M. Lozano, Ph.D, EXECUTIVE DIRECTOR*
*Shirla Simpson, DEPUTY DIRECTOR*
Quarterly magazine for people with disabilities, their families and the public, features family profiles, news, columns and the New Jersey Family support councils newsletter.
*Quarterly*

**5071 Families, Illness & Disability**
Through the Looking Glass
3075 Adeline St
Ste. 120
Berkeley, CA 94703-2212
510-848-1112
800-644-2666
FAX: 510-848-4445
TTY: 510-848-1005
e-mail: tlg@lookingglass.org
www.lookingglass.org

*Maureen Block, J.D., Co-Founder,*
*Karen Fessel, Ph.D., Executive Director*
*$35.00*
*320 pages*

**5072 Family Interventions Throughout Disability**
Springer Publishing Company
11 West 42nd Street,
15th Floor
New York, NY 10036-3915
212-431-4370
877-687-7476
FAX: 212-941-7842
e-mail: cs@springerpub.com
www.springerpub.com

*Theodore C Nardin, Chief Executive Officer*
*Nancy Hale, Editorial Director*

Family attitudes throughout chronic illness and disability. *$31.95*
*320 pages*
*ISBN 0-82615 -80-4*

**5073 Family-Centered Service Coordination: A Manual for Parents**
Brookline Books
34 University Rd
Brookline, MA 02445-4533
800-666-2665
FAX: 617-734-3952
e-mail: brbooks@yahoo.com
www.brooklinebooks.com

A manual designed to orient and educate parents about issues of service coordination, to assist families in caring for an infant or toddler with developmental delays or disabilities. *$7.00*
*34 pages Paperback*
*ISBN 0-91479 -90-5*

**5074 Handbook About Care in the Home**
AARP Fulfillment
601 E St NW
Washington, DC 20049-1
202-434-2277
888-687-2277
TTY:877-434-7598
e-mail: member@aarp.org
www.aarp.org

Offers valuable information for the disabled.
*24 pages*

**5075 LifeLines**
Disabled & Alone/Life Services for the Handicapped
Rm 510
61 Broadway
New York, NY 10006-2734
212-532-6740
800-995-0066
FAX: 212-532-3588
e-mail: info@disabledandalone.org
www.disabledandalone.org

*Leslie D. Park, Chairman*
*Rex L Davidson, Vice President*
Disabled and Alone is a national, nonprofit organization whose sole purpose is to assure the well being of disabled individuals, particularly those whose families have died and have engaged Disabled and Alone to provide advocacy and oversight for the lifetime of their disabled children. This newsletter provides information about 'future planning' for a person with a disability.
*8-16 pages Bi-annual*

**5076 Loving & Letting Go**
Centering Corporation
7230 Maple Street
Omaha, NE 68134-5064
402-553-1200
866-218-0101
FAX: 402-533-0507
e-mail: j1200@aol.com
www.centering.org

*Joy Johnson, Founder*
*Dr. Marvin Johnson, co-Founder*
For parents who decide to turn away from aggressive medical intervention for their critically ill newborn. *$5.95*
*48 pages Paperback*

**5077 Mobility Training for People with Disabilities**
Charles C. Thomas
2600 S 1st St
Springfield, IL 62704-4730
217-789-8980
800-258-8980
FAX: 217-789-9130
e-mail: books@ccthomas.com
www.ccthomas.com

*Michael P. Thomas, President*

**5078 Mother to Be**
Through the Looking Glass
3075 Adeline St
Ste. 120
Berkeley, CA 94703-2212
510-848-1112
800-644-2666
FAX: 510-848-4445
TTY: 510-848-1005
e-mail: tlg@lookingglass.org
www.lookingglass.org

*Maureen Block, J.D., Co-Founder,*
*Karen Fessel, Ph.D., Executive Director*
Guide to pregnancy and birth for women with disabilities. *$34.00*
*410 pages*

**5079 New Language of Toys: Teaching Communication Skills to Children with Special Needs**
Spina Bifida Association of America
Ste 250
4590 Macarthur Blvd NW
Washington, DC 20007-4226
202-944-3285
800-621-3141
FAX: 202-944-3295
e-mail: sbaa@sbaa.org
www.sbaa.org

*Cindy Brownstein, CEO*
*Carmen J Head , Director*
A guide for parents and teachers and a reader-friendly resource guide that provides a wealth of information on how play activities affect a child's language development and where to get the toys and materials to use in these activities. *$19.00*

**5080 NewsLine**
Federation for Children with Special Needs
45 Bromfield Street
10th Floor
Boston, MA 02108
866-815-8122
FAX: 617-542-7832
e-mail: info@ppal.net
www.ppal.net

*Lisa Lambert, Executive Director*
*Deborah A. Fauntleroy, MSW, Associate Director*
Offers information for parents and families on resources, medical updates, activities, fund-raising events and association news for their disabled children.
*Quarterly*

**5081 On the Road to Autonomy: Promoting Self- Competence in Children & Youth with Disabilities**
Brookes Publishing
P.O.Box 10624
Baltimore, MD 21285-624
410-337-9580
800-638-3775
FAX: 410-337-8539
e-mail: custserv@brookespublishing.com
readplaylearn.com

*Paul Brooks, Owner*
This book provides detailed conceptual, practical, and personal information regarding the promotion of self-esteem, self-determination, and coping skills among children and youth with and without disabilities. *$48.00*
*432 pages Paperback*
*ISBN 1-55766 -35-5*

**5082 Pain Erasure**
M Evans and Company
216 E 49th St
New York, NY 10017-1546
212-979-0880
FAX: 212-486-4544

*Mary Evans, Owner*

This book explains Bonnie Prudden's method for pain relief using myotherapy, a method hailed by doctors and patients.

*ISBN 0-345331-02-8*

**5083 Parent Centers and Independent Living Centers: Collectively We're Stronger**
Independent Living Research Utilization ILRU
Ste 1000
2323 S Shepherd Dr
Houston, TX 77019-7031
713-520-0232
FAX: 713-520-5785
e-mail: ilru@ilru.org
ilru.org

*Lex Frieden , Director*
*Laurie Gerke Redd, Administrative Director*
This article describes several examples of effective working relationships of PTIs and CILs. The examples highlight how parent and consumer organizations have identified complimentary strengths and formed partnerships to better support children with disabilities and their families. These partnerships can also be a very important way of involving youth in the disability movement so they may become leaders of tomorrow.
*10 pages*

**5084 Parent-Child Interaction and Developmental Disabilities**
Greenwood Publishing Group
130 Cremona Drive
Santa Barbara,, CA 93117
800-368-6868
805-968-1911
FAX: 866-270-3856
e-mail: customerservice@abc-clio.com
www.abc-clio.com

This volume brings together the original papers by international scholars and practitioners on the question of the effects of parent interaction with developmentally disabled children. $65.00-$69.50.
*395 pages Hardcover*
*ISBN 0-275928-35-7*

**5085 Parenting**
Accent Books & Products
P.O.Box 700
Bloomington, IL 61702-700
309-378-2961
800-787-8444
FAX: 309-378-4420
e-mail: acmtlvng@aol.com

*Raymond C Cheever, Publisher*
*Betty Garee, Editor*
Experienced parents (who are disabled) discuss: raising children from infant to teens, balancing career and motherhood, discipline methods and more when both parents are disabled. *$7.95*
*83 pages*
*ISBN 0-91570 -26-4*

**5086 Parenting with a Disability**
Through the Looking Glass
3075 Adeline St
Ste. 120
Berkeley, CA 94703-2212
510-848-1112
800-644-2666
FAX: 510-848-4445
TTY: 510-848-1005
e-mail: tlg@lookingglass.org
www.lookingglass.org

*Maureen Block, J.D., Co-Founder,*
*Karen Fessel, Ph.D., Executive Director*
International newsletter. Available in braille, large print or cassette.
*3 per year*

**5087 Perspectives on a Parent Movement**
Brookline Books
34 University Rd
Brookline, MA 02445-4533
800-666-2665
FAX: 617-734-3952
e-mail: brbooks@yahoo.com
www.brooklinebooks.com

This book captures Rosemary Dybwad's truly innovative wisdom and pioneering for people with intellectual limitations in these previously unpublished essays and speeches. *$17.95*
*Paperback*
*ISBN 0-91479 -74-3*

**5088 Sexuality and the Developmentally Handicapped**
Edwin Mellen Press
P.O.Box 450
Lewiston, NY 14092-450
716-754-2266
FAX: 716-754-4056
mellenpress.com

*Herbert Richardson, Owner*
Presents the knowledge, attitudes, and skills pertinent to responding to the sexual problems of developmentally handicapped persons, their families and communities. Details fully documented cases, issues concerning the law, and resource materials available. *$89.95*
*245 pages Hardcover*
*ISBN 0-88946 -32-5*

**5089 Shattered Dreams-Lonely Choices: Birth Parents of Babies with Disabilities**
Greenwood Publishing Group
130 Cremona Drive
Santa Barbara,, CA 93117-4208
203-226-3571
800-368-6868
805-968-1911
FAX: 866-270-3856
e-mail: customerservice@abc-clio.com
www.abc-clio.com

Written by a mother who, without warning, gave birth to a boy with Down Syndrome, this book is meant to help parents through the initial shock and the realization that they are not able to care for their child. $29.95-$35.00. *$29.95*
*208 pages Hardcover*
*ISBN 0-897892-86-0*

**5090 Since Owen, A Parent-to-Parent Guide for Care of the Disabled Child**
Special Needs Project
Ste H
324 State St
Santa Barbara, CA 93101-2364
805-962-8087
800-333-6867
FAX: 805-962-5087
www.specialneeds.com

*Hod Gray, Owner*
Against the background of his experience as the parent of a severely disabled young man, Callahan writes conscientiously to other parents. *$16.95*
*486 pages*

**5091 Sleep Better! A Guide to Improving Sleep for Children with Special Needs**
Brookes Publishing
P.O.Box 10624
Baltimore, MD 21285-624
410-337-9580
800-638-3775
FAX: 410-337-8539
e-mail: custserv@brookespublishing.com
readplaylearn.com

*Paul Brooks, Owner*
This book offers step-by-step, how to instructions for helping children with disabilities get the rest they need. For problems ranging from bedtime tantrums to night waking, parents and caregivers will find a variety of widely tested and easy-to-implement

techniques that have already helped hundreds of children with special needs. *$21.95*
*288 pages Paperback*
*ISBN 1-55766 -15-7*

**5092 Something's Wrong with My Child!**
Charles C. Thomas
2600 S 1st Street
Springfield, IL 62704-4730
217-789-8980
800-258-8980
FAX: 217-789-9130
e-mail: books@ccthomas.com
www.ccthomas.com

*Michael P. Thomas, President*
This text provides professionals and parents with the opportunity to gain insights into a family that has benefited positively and constructively from the presence of a member with a disability. The author presents a compilation of easy-to-read material that's based on real-life experiences. *$39.95*
*234 pages Paperback 1998*
*ISBN 0-398068-99-8*

**5093 Sometimes I Get All Scribbly**
Exceptional Parent Library
P.O.Box 1807
Englewood Cliffs, NJ 7632-1207
201-947-6000
800-535-1910
FAX: 201-947-9376
e-mail: eplibrary@aol.com
www.eplibrary.com

Clinical, educational and emotional information from the point of view of a parent. *$16.00*

**5094 Son-Rise: The Miracle Continues**
2080 S Undermountain Rd
Sheffield, MA 01257-9643
413-229-2100
877-766-7473
FAX: 413-229-3202
e-mail: sonrise@option.org
www.son-rise.org

*Barry Neil Kaufman, Owner*
Documents Raun Kaufman's astonishing development from a lifeless, autistic, retarded child into a highly verbal, lovable youngster with no traces of his former condition. Details Raun's extraordinary progress from the age of four into young adulthood, also shares moving accounts of five families that successfully used the Son-Rise Program to reach their own special children.
*372 pages*
*ISBN 0-915811-53-7*

**5095 Special Kids Need Special Parents: A Resource for Parents of Children With Special Needs**
Berkley Publishing Group
375 Hudson Street
New York,, NY 10014
212-366-2372
FAX: 212-366-2933
e-mail: ecommerce@us.penguingroup.com
www.us.penguingroup.com

The author, herself the parent of a child with special needs, draws on interviews with health care professionals, nationally recognized authorities, and other partens to give readers the answers, advice, and comfort they crave. *$13.95*
*319 pages Paperback*
*ISBN 0-425176-62-2*

**5096 Special Parent, Special Child**
Exceptional Parent Library
P.O.Box 1807
Englewood Cliffs, NJ 7632-1207
201-947-6000
800-535-1910
FAX: 201-947-9376
e-mail: eplibrary@aol.com
www.eplibrary.com

Offers information for facing the challenges of being a special parent. *$21.95*
*Hardcover*

**5097 Strategies for Working with Families of Young Children with Disabilities**
Brookes Publishing
P.O.Box 10624
Baltimore, MD 21285-624
410-337-9580
800-638-3775
FAX: 410-337-8539
e-mail: custserv@brookespublishing.com
readplaylearn.com

*Paul Brooks, Owner*
This text offers useful techniques for collaborating with and supporting families whose youngest members either have a disability or are at risk for developing a disability. The authors address specific issues such as cultural diversity, transitions to new programs, and disagreements between families and professionals. *$33.00*
*272 pages Paperback*
*ISBN 1-55766 -57-6*

**5098 That's My Child**
Exceptional Parent Library
P.O.Box 1807
Englewood Cliffs, NJ 7632-1207
201-947-6000
800-535-1910
FAX: 201-947-9376
e-mail: eplibrary@aol.com
www.eplibrary.com

Offers information to help parent successfully navigate the maze of resources and services available for children with special needs. *$12.95*

**5099 They Don't Come with Manuals**
Fanlight Productions
32 Court Street, 21st Floor
Brooklyn, NY 11201-1731
718-488-8900
800-876-1710
FAX: 718-488-8642
e-mail: info@fanlight.com
www.fanlight.com

*Ben Achtenberg, Owner*
*Anthony Sweeney, Marketing Director*
*Nicole Johnson, Publicity Coordinator*
The parents and adoptive parents in this video speak candidly of their day to day experiences caring for children with physical and mental disabilities. *$145.00*

**5100 They're Just Kids**
Aquarius Health Care Videos
30 Forest Road
P.O. Box 249
Millis, MA 02054-7159
508-376-1244
FAX: 508-376-1245
e-mail: aqvideos@tiac.net
www.aquariusproductions.com

*Lesile Kussmann, President*
*Joyce Farmer, Assistant Director*
The importance and value of inclusion, excellent for anyone working with kids with disabilities. The documentary explores the advantages of the inclusion of disabled children in the classroom, cub scouts and other extracurricular activities. *$99.00*
*Video*

**5101 To a Different Drumbeat**
Alliance for Parental Involvement in Education
P.O.Box 59
East Chatham, NY 12060-59
518-392-6900
FAX: 518-392-6900
Parents of special needs children contributed to this book. *$16.95*

**5102 Uncommon Fathers**
Woodbine House
6510 Bells Mill Rd
Bethesda, MD 20817-1636
301-897-3570
800-843-7323
e-mail: info@woodbinehouse.com
woodbinehouse.com

*Irv Shapell, Owner*

Nineteen fathers talk about the life-altering experience of having a child with special needs and offer a welcome, seldom-heard perspective on raising kids with disabilities, including autism, cerebral palsy, and Down syndrome. Uncommon Fathers is the first book for fathers by fathers, but it is also helpful to partners, family, friends, and service providers. *$14.95*

*206 pages Paperback*
*ISBN 0-933149-68-9*

**5103 We Can Speak for Ourselves: Self Advocacy by Mentally Handicapped People**
Brookline Books
34 University Rd
Brookline, MA 02445-4533
800-666-2665
FAX: 617-734-3952
e-mail: brbooks@yahoo.com
www.brooklinebooks.com

Practical advice and support for parents, group resident workers, and others interested in fostering self-advocacy for people with developmental disabilities. *$10.00*

*246 pages Paperback*
*ISBN 0-25336 -65-9*

**5104 You May Be Able to Adopt**
Through the Looking Glass
3075 Adeline St
Ste. 120
Berkeley, CA 94703-2212
510-848-1112
800-644-2666
FAX: 510-848-4445
TTY: 510-848-1005
e-mail: tlg@lookingglass.org
www.lookingglass.org

*Maureen Block, J.D., Co-Founder,*
*Karen Fessel, Ph.D., Executive Director*

A guide to the adoption process for prospective mothers with disabilities and their partners. Available in braille, large print or cassette. *$10.00*

*112 pages*

**5105 You Will Dream New Dreams**
Kensington Publishing
119 West 40th Street
New York, NY 10018
800-221-2647
www.kensingtonbooks.com

A parent's support group in print. The shared narratives come from those with newly diagnosed children, adult disabled children, and everything in between. *$13.00*

*278 pages Paperback*
*ISBN 1-575665-60-3*

**5106 Your Child Has a Disability: A Complete Sourcebook of Daily and Medical Care**
Brookes Publishing
P.O.Box 10624
Baltimore, MD 21285-624
410-337-9580
800-638-3775
FAX: 410-337-8539
e-mail: custserv@brookesopublishing.com
readplaylearn.com

*Paul Brooks, Owner*

Offers expert advice on a wide range of issues-from finding the right doctor and investigating the medical aspects of a child's condition to learning care techniques and fulfilling education requirements. *$24.95*

*368 pages Paperback*
*ISBN 1-557663-74-2*

## Parenting: Specific Disabilities

**5107 Cancer Clinical Trials: Experimental Treatments and How They Can Help You**
Patient-Centered Guides
1005 Gravenstein Hwy N
Sebastopol, CA 95472-3836
707-827-7019
800-889-8969
FAX: 707-824-8268
e-mail: orders@oreilly.com
www.patientcenters.com

*Tim O'Reilly, CEO*

Most cancer patients face treatment options that are less than ideal, whether because of a risk of recurrence or side effects. Finally, however, basic research on cell biology is leading to promising new treatments. If you are not evaluating potential experimental treatments alongside the standard treatment protocols, you aren't considering all the facts you need. Cancer Clinical Trials guide you through understanding your options and finding and considering experimental treatments. *$14.95*

*222 pages Paperback*
*ISBN 1-565925-66-1*

**5108 Children with Acquired Brain Injury: Education and Supporting Families**
Brookes Publishing
P.O.Box 10624
Baltimore, MD 21285-624
410-337-9580
800-638-3775
FAX: 410-337-8539
e-mail: custserv@brookespublishing.com
www.brookespublishing.com

*Ann Glang PhD, Editor*
*Janet M Williams MSW, Editor*
*Paul Brooks, Owner*
*$28.95*
*288 pages Paperback*
*ISBN 1-557662-33-9*

**5109 Children with Autism**
Woodbine House
6510 Bells Mill Rd
Bethesda, MD 20817-1636
301-897-3570
800-843-7323
e-mail: info@woodbinehouse.com
woodbinehouse.com

*Irv Shapell, Owner*

Recommended as the first book parents should read, this volume offers information and a complete introduction to autism, while easing the family's fears and concerns as they adjust and cope with their child's disorder. *$17.95*

*368 pages Paperback*
*ISBN 0-933149-16-6*

**5110 Final Report: Adapting Through the Looking Glass**
Through the Looking Glass
3075 Adeline St
Ste. 120
Berkeley, CA 94703-2212
510-848-1112
800-644-2666
FAX: 510-848-4445
TTY: 510-848-1005
e-mail: tlg@lookingglass.org
www.lookingglass.org

*Maureen Block, J.D., Co-Founder,*
*Karen Fessel, Ph.D., Executive Director*

Adapting Through the Looking Glass intervention model for deaf parents and their children. Available in braille, large print or cassette. *$2.00*
*24 pages*

**5111 Final Report: Challenges and Strategies of Disabled Parents: Findings from a Survey**
Through the Looking Glass
3075 Adeline St
Ste. 120
Berkeley, CA 94703-2212
510-848-1112
800-644-2666
FAX: 510-848-4445
TTY: 510-848-1005
e-mail: tlg@lookingglass.org
www.lookingglass.org

*Maureen Block, J.D., Co-Founder,*
*Karen Fessel, Ph.D., Executive Director*
Available in braille, large print or cassette. *$25.00*
*24 pages*

**5112 Negotiating the Special Education Maze: A Guide for Parents and Teachers**
Spina Bifida Association of America
Ste 250
4590 Macarthur Blvd NW
Washington, DC 20007-4226
202-944-3285
800-621-3141
FAX: 202-944-3295
e-mail: sbaa@sbaa.org
www.sbaa.org

*Cindy Brownstein, CEO*
*Carmen J Head , Director*
An excellent aid for the development of an effective special education program. *$19.00*

**5113 Pervasive Developmental Disorders; Findinga Diagnosis and Getting Help**
Patient-Centered Guides
1005 Gravenstein Hwy N
Sebastopol, CA 95472-3836
707-827-7019
800-889-8969
FAX: 707-824-8268
e-mail: orders@oreilly.com
www.patientcenters.com

*Tim O'Reilly, CEO*
This unique book encompassess both the practical aspects as well as ther personal stories and emotional facets of living with PDD-NOS, the most common pervasive developmental disorder. Parents of an undiagnosed child may suspect many things, from autism to servere allergies. Pervasive Developmental Disorders is for parents (or newly diagnosed adults) who struggle with this neurological condition that profoundly impacts the life of child and family. *$24.95*
*580 pages Paperback*
*ISBN 1-565925-30-0*

**5114 Raising Kids with Special Needs**
Aquarius Health Care Videos
30 Forest Road
P.O. Box 249
Millis, MA 02054-7159
508-376-1244
FAX: 508-376-1245
e-mail: aqvideos@tiac.net
www.aquariusproductions.com

*Lesile Kussmann, President*
*Joyce Farmer, Assistant Director*
An intimate look into the lives of parents of three kids with very different disabilities. The objective of this video is an understanding of paprenting a child with special nees. This outstanding program looks at safety concerns, issues of anger and grief, the importance of a support network and other important issues. Ultimately, this is a narrative about raising and educating a child with disabilities. Preview option is available. *$89.00*
*Video*

**5115 Your Child in the Hospital: A Practical Guide for Parents**
Patient-Centered Guides
1005 Gravenstein Hwy N
Sebastopol, CA 95472-3836
707-827-7019
800-889-8969
FAX: 707-824-8268
e-mail: orders@oreilly.com
www.patientcenters.com

*Linda O'Reilly, CEO*
This book offers advice from dozens of veteran parents on how to cope with a child's hospitalization, relieving anxious parents so they can help dispel their child's fears and concerns. Parents will find easy-to-read tips on preparing their child, handling procedures without trauma, and preventing insurance snafus. The second edition features a journal to help open communication and give the child a measure of control over the experience. *$11.95*
*166 pages Paperback*
*ISBN 1-565925-73-4*

## Parenting: School

**5116 Allergy and Asthma Network Mothers of Asthmatics**
8201 Greensboro Drive
Suite 300
McLean, VA 22102-4343
800-878-4403
FAX: 703-288-5271
e-mail: mgieminiani@aanma.org
www.breatherville.org

*Nancy Sander, President*
*Marcela Gieminiani, Director of Administration and Programs*
*Brenda Silvi Torma, Project Manager*
Practical, medical,information for school patients, physicians, caregivers and families. *$7.00*

**5117 Carolina Curriculum for Infants and Toddlers with Special Needs**
Brookes Publishing
P.O.Box 10624
Baltimore, MD 21285-624
410-337-9580
800-638-3775
FAX: 410-337-8539
e-mail: custserv@brookespublishing.com
readplaylearn.com

*Paul Brooks, Owner*
This book includes detailed assessment and intervention sequences, daily routine integration strategies, sensorimotor adaptations, and a sample 24-page Assessment Log that shows readers how to chart a child's individual progress. *$41.95*
*384 pages Spiral-bound*
*ISBN 1-557660-74-3*

**5118 Choosing Outcomes and Accommodations for Children (COACH)**
Brookes Publishing
P.O.Box 10624
Baltimore, MD 21285-624
410-337-9580
800-638-3775
FAX: 410-337-8539
e-mail: custserv@brookespublishing.com
readplaylearn.com

*Paul Brooks, Owner*
A guide to educational planning for students with disabilities, second edition. Focuses on life outcomes such as social relationships and participation in typical home, school, and community activities. *$37.95*
*400 pages Spiral bound*
*ISBN 1-55766 -23-8*

**5119 Complete IEP Guide: How to Advocate for Your Special Ed Child**
Spina Bifida Association of America
Ste 250
4590 Macarthur Blvd NW
Washington, DC 20007-4226
202-944-3285
800-621-3141
FAX: 202-944-3295
e-mail: sbaa@sbaa.org
www.sbaa.org

*Cindy Brownstein, CEO*
*Carmen J Head , Director*
This all-in-one guide will help you understand special education law, identify your child's needs, prepare for meetings, develop the IEP and resolve disputes. *$28.95*

**5120 Exceptional Student in the Regular Classroom**
McGraw-Hill, School Publishing
P.O. Box 182604
Columbus, OH 43272-2490
877-833-5524
FAX: 614-759-3749
e-mail: customer.service@mcgraw-hill.com
mcgraw-hill.com

*Louise Raymond, Vice President*
Offers good, solid information through a practical understandable presentation unencumbered by specialized jargon. Covers topics associated with special learners.
*480 pages*

**5121 Negotiating the Special Education Maze: A Guide for Parents and Teachers**
Spina Bifida Association of America
Ste 250
4590 Macarthur Blvd NW
Washington, DC 20007-4226
202-944-3285
800-621-3141
FAX: 202-944-3295
e-mail: sbaa@sbaa.org
www.sbaa.org

*Cindy Brownstein, CEO*
*Carmen J Head , Director*
An excellent aid for the development of an effective special education program. *$19.00*

**5122 Parent Teacher Packet**
Spina Bifida Association of America
Ste 250
4590 Macarthur Blvd NW
Washington, DC 20007-4226
202-944-3285
800-621-3141
FAX: 202-944-3295
e-mail: sbaa@sbaa.org
www.sbaa.org

*Cindy Brownstein, CEO*
*Carmen J Head , Director*
Includes educational material, learning disabilities literature, children's book, social development and the person with spina bifida and one copy of each fact sheet. *$14.00*

**5123 Study Power: Study Skills to Improve Your Learning and Your Grades: A Workbook**
Brookline Books
34 University Rd
Brookline, MA 02445-4533
800-666-2665
FAX: 617-734-3952
e-mail: brbooks@yahoo.com
www.brooklinebooks.com

The techniques in the easy-to-use, self-teaching manual have yielded remarkable success for students from elementary to medical school, at all levels of intelligence and achievement. Key skills covered include: listening, note taking, concentration, summarizing, reading comprehension, memorization, test taking, preparing papers and reports, time management, and more. These abilities are vital to success throughout every stage of learning; the benefits will last a lifetime. *$15.95*
*Paperback*
*ISBN 1-57129 -46-X*

## Parenting: Spiritual

**5124 A Miracle to Believe In**
Option Indigo Press
2080 S Undermountain Rd
Sheffield, MA 01257-9643
413-229-8727
800-562-7171
FAX: 413-229-8727
e-mail: happiness@option.org
www.optionindigo.com

A group of people from all walks of life come together and are transformed as they reach out, under the direction of the Kaufmans, to help a little boy the medical world has given up as hopeless. This heartwarming journey of loving a child back to life will inspire and presents a compelling new way to deal with life's traumas and difficulties. *$7.99*
*379 pages Paperback*
*ISBN 0-44920 -08-2*

**5125 After the Tears**
Centering Corporation
7230 Maple Street
Omaha, NE 68134-5064
402-553-1200
866-218-0101
FAX: 402-533-0507
e-mail: j1200@aol.com
www.centering.org

*Joy Johnson, Founder*
*Dr. Marvin Johnson, co-Founder*
Offers talk, articles on raising a child with a disability. This one book combines feelings and emotions of parents on the subject of raising their disabled child. *$11.00*
*87 pages Paperback*
*ISBN 0-15602 -00-6*

**5126 Before and After Zachariah**
Special Needs Project
Ste H
324 State St
Santa Barbara, CA 93101-2364
805-962-8087
800-333-6867
FAX: 805-962-5087
www.specialneeds.com

*Hod Gray, Owner*
This intimate chronicle of one family's life with a severely brain damaged child is recently back in print. *$7.95*
*241 pages*

**5127 Bethy and the Mouse: A Father Remembers His Children with Disabilities**
Brookline Books
34 University Rd
Brookline, MA 02445-4533
800-666-2665
FAX: 617-734-3952
e-mail: brbooks@yahoo.com
www.brooklinebooks.com

A moving collection of poetry, photographs, and prose following a father's experiences with two disabled children-one with Down Syndrome and one with an underdeveloped brain. *$16.95*
*184 pages Paperback*
*ISBN 0-57129 -35-4*

**5128 Disabled God: Toward a Liberatory Theologyof Disability**
Abingdon Press
201 8th Ave S
Nashville, TN 37203-3919
615-749-6000
800-251-3320
FAX: 800-836-7802
www.abingdon.org

*Dr. Rex Matthews, Senior Editor*
*Neil Alexander, President*

Draws on themes of the disability rights movement to identify people with disabilities as members of a socially disadvantaged minority group rather than as individuals who need to adjust. Highlights the history of people with disabilities in the church and society. *$ 13.95*
*27 pages Paperback*
*ISBN 0-68710 -01-2*

**5129 Dying and Disabled Children: Dealing with Loss and Grief**
Haworth Press
6000 Broken Sound Parkway, NW
Suite 300,
Boca Raton, FL 33487-1503
561-994-0555
FAX: 561-241-7856
e-mail: orders@taylorandfrancis.com
www.tandf.co.uk

In this sensitive and compassionate look at terminally ill and disabled children, professionals from the medical community examine the stresses faced by their parents and siblings. They address the crucial element of communication in dealing with a child's serious illness. Ethical decision making, learning to recognize the child's suffering, and talking to children about death are honestly and clearly discussed. *$ 59.95*
*153 pages Hardcover*
*ISBN 0-866567-59-3*

**5130 In Time and with Love: Caring for the Special Needs Infant and Toddler**
Newmarket Press
18 E 48th St
New York, NY 10017-1014
212-832-3575
FAX: 212-832-3629
e-mail: sales@newmarketpress.com
newmarketpress.com

*Esther Margolis, President*
*Heidi Sachner, Associate Publisher/Sales/Mktg*

For families and caregivers of preteen and handicapped children in their first three years - more than one hundred tips for adjusting and coping. *$15.95*
*208 pages*
*ISBN 1-557044-45-7*

**5131 Journal of Religion, Disability & Health**
Haworth Press
6000 Broken Sound Parkway, NW
Suite 300,
Boca Raton, FL 33487-1503
561-994-0555
FAX: 561-241-7856
e-mail: orders@taylorandfrancis.com
www.tandf.co.uk

This journal aims to inform religious professionals about developments in the field of disability and rehabilitation in order to facilitate greater contributions on the part of pastors, religious educators and pastoral counselors. *$60.00*
*Quarterly*

**5132 Nobody's Perfect: Living and Growing with Children Who Have Special Needs**
Brookes Publishing
P.O.Box 10624
Baltimore, MD 21285-624
410-337-9580
800-638-3775
FAX: 410-337-8539
e-mail: custserv@brookespublishing.com
readplaylearn.com

*Paul Brooks, Owner*

This book offers parents who have children with special needs a new and positive perspective on the challenges of family life. This book guides parents through the process of adaptation, describing specific strategies for success in balancing one's own life, developing a parenting partnership, and interacting with children, friends, relatives, professionals, and others. *$21.00*
*352 pages Paperback*
*ISBN 1-55766 -43-X*

**5133 Special Education Teacher Packet**
LifeWay Christian Resources Southern Baptist Conv.
One LifeWay Plaza
Nashville, TN 37234-2
615-741-2851
800-458-2772
FAX: 615-532-9412
www.lifeway.com

*Ellen Beene, Editor*
*Wade Stapleton, Manager*

Resources to help teachers who lead Sunday School classes for adults and older youth with mental retardation. Includes teaching plans, posters, and one copy of Special Education Bible Study. *$10.00*
*Quarterly*

**5134 Special Kind of Parenting**
La Leche League International
957 N. Plum Grove Road
Schaumburg, IL 60173-4079
847-519-7730
800-525-3243
FAX: 847-969-0460
e-mail: LLLI@llli.org
www.lalecheleague.org

Disabled children have special needs which challenge their parents' emotional and physical resources. This book guides parents through the problems and helps them discover their disabled child as an individual. The author covers both facts and feelings about handicaps, parents' reactions to the initial diagnosis, the grieving process, and effects on the marriage and the rest of the family. They also provide suggestions for choosing the programs and professionals best suited. *$7.50*
*172 pages Softcover*
*ISBN 0-912500-27-1*

**5135 That All May Worship**
Exceptional Parent Library
P.O.Box 1807
Englewood Cliffs, NJ 7632-1207
201-947-6000
800-535-1910
FAX: 201-947-9376
e-mail: mailto:eplibrary@aol.com
www.eplibrary.com

An interfaith handbook to assist congregations in welcoming people with disabilities to promote acceptance and full participation. *$10.00*

**5136 Why Mine?**
Centering Corporation
7230 Maple Street
Omaha, NE 68134-5064
402-553-1200
866-218-0101
FAX: 402-533-0507
e-mail: j1200@aol.com
www.centering.org

*Joy Johnson, Founder*
*Dr. Marvin Johnson, co-Founder*

Offers quotes from parents all across the country on their fears, feelings, marriage, the ill child and other children. *$3.25*
*32 pages Paperback*

**5137 Worst Loss: How Families Heal from the Death of a Child**
Exceptional Parent Library
P.O.Box 1807
Englewood Cliffs, NJ 7632-1207
201-947-6000
800-535-1910
FAX: 201-947-9376
e-mail: mailto:eplibrary@aol.com
www.eplibrary.com

Combines anecdotal case histories and the latest research to help bereaved parents cope with the loss of a child, offering practical and comforting advice on how to overcome the disabling symptoms of grief. *$25.00*

*ISBN 0-805032-41-X*

## Professional

**5138 American Journal of Physical Medicine**
Lippincott, Williams & Wilkins
P.O.Box 1551
Hagerstown, MD 21741-1551
800-638-3030
FAX: 301-824-7390
www.lww.com

Journal of the Association of Academic Psychiatrists. Articles covering research and clinical studies and applications of new equipment, procedures and therapeutic advances. *$45.00*

**5139 American Journal of Psychiatry**
American Psychiatric Publishing
Ste 1825
1000 Wilson Blvd
Arlington, VA 22209-3924
703-907-7322
800-368-5777
FAX: 703-907-1091
psychiatryonline.org

*Nancy Frey, Executive Director*
*James Scully, Manager*

Peer-reviewed articles focus on developments in biological psychiatry as well as on treatment innovations and forensic, ethical, economic, and social topics. *$56.00*
*Monthly*

**5140 American Journal of Public Health**
American Public Health Association
1555 Wilson Blvd
Suite 530
Arlington, VA 22209-2605
703-243-2443
866-243-2443
FAX: 703-243-3390
e-mail: comments@msmail.apha.org
www.apna.org

*Nicholas Croce, Jr., MS , Executive Director*
*Patricia L. Black, PhD(c), RN, Associate Executive Director*

Association journal containing professional articles and sections such as Notes from the Field and Association News. Single copies are $15.00. $50.00 per year for special consumer membership.
*Monthly*
*ISSN 0090-00 6*

**5141 American Rehabilitation**
Rehabilitation Services Administration
400 Maryland Ave, SW
Washington, DC 20202-1
202-401-2000
800-872-5327
TTY:800-437-0833
www.ed.gov

*Kiran Ahuja, Executive Director*

Covers medical, social and employment aspects of vocational rehabilitation. *$15.00*
*40 pages Quarterly*

**5142 Art Therapy**
American Art Therapy Association
225 North Fairfax Street
Alexandria, VA 22314-3302
703-548-5860
888-290-0878
FAX: 703-783-8468
e-mail: info@arttherapy.org
www.americanarttherapyassociation.org

*Mercedes ter Maat, PhD, President*
*Charlotte Boston, MA, ATR , Secretary*

Publishes articles on the uses of art in the education, enrichment, development and treatment of disabled people. *$10.00*
*76+ pages Quarterly*
*ISSN 0742-16 6*

**5143 Brown University Long Term Care Advisor**
Manisses Communications Group
208 Governor St
Providence, RI 02906-3246
401-831-6020
800-333-7771
FAX: 401-861-6370
e-mail: manisses@manisses.com
www.manisses.com

*Fraser Lang, Publisher*

Contains practical reports for health care professionals working in long-term care facilities. Published monthly. *$329.00*
*8 pages Newsletter*
*ISSN 1088-92 8*

**5144 CAREERS & the disABLED Magazine**
Equal Opportunity Publications
Ste 425
445 Broadhollow Rd
Melville, NY 11747-3615
631-421-9421
FAX: 631-421-1352
e-mail: info@eop.com
eop.com

*John R. Miller, Chairman & Chief Executive Officer*
*James Schneider, Editorial Director*

A career magazine for professional career seekers who have disabilities. Profiles disabled people who have achieved successful careers. Features a career section in Braille, career guide. *$10.00*
*64 pages 3X*

**5145 Clinician's Practical Guide to Attention-Deficit/Hyperactivity Disorder**
Brookes Publishing
P.O.Box 10624
Baltimore, MD 21285-624
410-337-9580
800-638-3775
FAX: 410-337-8539
readplaylearn.com

*Paul Brooks, Owner*

Quick reference volume with comprehensive data on psychoeducational and neuropsychological assessment, related symptoms, drug and counseling therapies and critical issues. *$39.95*
*368 pages*
*ISBN 1-557663-58-0*

**5146 Counseling Parents of Children with Chronic Illness or Disability**

Brookes Publishing
P.O.Box 10624
Baltimore, MD 21285-624
410-337-9580
800-638-3775
FAX: 410-337-8539
e-mail: custserv@brookespublishing.com
readplaylearn.com

*Paul Brooks, Owner*
*$23.00*
*144 pages Paperback*
*ISBN 1-85433 -91-8*

**5147 Cystic Fibrosis: Medical Care**

Lippincott, Williams & Wilkins
# 227
227 S 6th St
Philadelphia, PA 19106-3713
215-521-8300
800-777-2295
FAX: 301-824-7390
www.lpub.com

*J Lippincott, CEO*
A guide to the medical community to the principles and practices of cystic fibrosis care. After chapters on the molecular and cellular bases of CF and its diagnosis, they cover the major organ systems affected by CF and deal with surgery for CF patients, transplantation (lung and liver), hospitalization, and terminal care. Also included are chapters on special populations, exercise, and laboratory testing. *$ 47.95*
*365 pages*
*ISBN 0-781717-98-1*

**5148 Disability Analysis Handbook**

American Board of Disability Analysts
4525 Harding Road
Nashville, TN 37205-1520
615-327-2978
FAX: 615-327-9235
e-mail: americanbd@aol.com
www.americandisability.org

*Alexander Horowitz, MD, ABDA, Executive Officer Emeritus*
*Kenneth Anchor, President*
Official newsletter of the American Board of Disability Analysts; features Healthnews Headlines, Meeting Calendar, Application Packet and much more. Free to members; $20 per year for non-members. *$60.00*
*396 pages*
*ISBN 0-787226-70-x*

**5149 Ethical Conflicts in Management of Home Care**

Springer Publishing Company
11 West 42nd Street,
15th Floor
New York, NY 10036-3915
212-431-4370
877-687-7476
FAX: 212-941-7842
e-mail: cs@springerpub.com
www.springerpub.com

*Theodore C Nardin, Chief Executive Officer*
*Nancy Hale, Editorial Director*
Offers answers to the questions what is case management and why does it raise ethical issues. *$29.95*
*288 pages*

**5150 Families in Recovery**

Brookes Publishing
P.O.Box 10624
Baltimore, MD 21285-624
410-337-9580
800-638-3775
FAX: 410-337-8539
e-mail: custserv@brookespublishing.com
readplaylearn.com

*Paul Brooks, Owner*
This book teaches professionals how to use each families strengths to promote recovery. The authors demonstrate effective, family-focused intervention techniques developed in their combined 35 years of practice. Motivational techniques and stress reducers for counselors are also provided. *$34.00*
*352 pages Paperback*
*ISBN 1-55766 -64-9*

**5151 Journal of Children's Communication Development**

CEC Div for Childrens' Communication Development
1920 Association Dr
Reston, VA 20191-1500
703-620-3660
FAX: 703-312-9193

*Alexander Brice, Editor*
Contains scholarly articles pertaining to the many aspects of communication disorders in children, encompassing speech, language, hearing and learning disabilities. *$16.00*
*2x Year*

**5152 NHIF Newsletter**

National Head Injury Foundation
1776 Massachusetts Ave NW
Washington, DC 20036-1904
202-452-1999
800-444-6443
FAX: 202-296-7365
e-mail: worldwatch@worldwatch.org
worldwatch.org

*Robert Engelman, President*
*Tom Crain, Managing Director*
Contains news and articles for families and professionals concerned with head injury. *$25.00*

**5153 National Clearinghouse of Rehabilitation Training Materials**

6524 Old Main Hill
Logan, UT 84322
866-821-5355
FAX: 435-797-7537
e-mail: ncrtm@usu.edu
www.nchrtm.okstate.edu

*Michael Millington, Ph.D, Director*
*Jennifer Robinson, Office Assistant*
Newsletter produced quarterly to provide information and opportunities to learn more about related fields.
*Quarterly*

**5154 Partners in Everyday Communicative Exchanges**

Brookes Publishing
P.O.Box 10624
Baltimore, MD 21285-624
410-337-9580
800-638-3775
FAX: 410-337-8539
e-mail: custserv@brookespublishing.com
readplaylearn.com

*Paul Brooks, Owner*
A Guide to Promoting Intervention Involving people with Severe Intellectual Disability. This book helps improve communication with people with severe disabilities using practical forms, numerous examples, and illustrative case studies. *$43.00*
*192 pages Paperback*
*ISBN 1-55766 -41-X*

**5155 Professional Report**
National Rehabilitation Association (NRA)
633 S Washington St
Alexandria, VA 22314-4109
703-836-0850
800-813-6080
FAX: 703-836-0848
TTY: 703-836-0849
e-mail: info@nationalrehab.org
www.nationalrehab.org

*Beverlee Stafford, Executive Director*
*Sandra Mulliner , Administrative Assistant*
Association newsletter containing news, programs and information of interest to the Association and its members.

**5156 Provider Magazine**
American Health Care Association
1201 L St NW
Washington, DC 20005-4024
202-842-4444
800-321-0343
FAX: 202-842-3860
ncal.org

Magazine for long-term healthcare professionals. *$ 48.00*
*72 pages Monthly*
*ISSN 0888-03 2*

**5157 Public Health Reports**
Oxford Journals
Room 1855
Jfk Federal Building
Boston, MA 02203
513-636-0257
FAX: 617-565-4260
e-mail: robert.rinsky@chmcc.org
phr.oupjournals.org

*Robert Rinsky PhD, Editor*
Scholarly articles on issues that relate to public health and the healthcare system. *$13.00*
*BiMonthly*

**5158 Public Health/State Capitols**
Wakeman/Walworth
300 N Washington St
Alexandria, VA 22314-2530
703-768-9600
800-876-2545
FAX: 703-768-9690
e-mail: newsletters@statecapitals.com
www.statecapitals.com

*Keyes Walworth, Publisher*
*Christine Ryan, Editor*
Digest of state and municipal health care financing and legislation, including disease control, medicaid, AIDS, abortion, substance abuse programs, cancer prevention such as smoking restrictions, mental health and disability programs, regulation of hospitals & nursing homes, food safety, medical policies, health insurance for children, home regulation, managerial care, public health issues, pest control, and water quality. Issued weekly-52 issues/year. *$245.00*
*10 pages*

**5159 Sexuality and Disability**
Human Sciences Press
233 Spring St
New York, NY 10013-1522
212-460-1500
800-221-9369
FAX: 212-647-1898
www.springer.com

*Rudiger Gebauer, President*
A journal devoted to the psychological and medical aspects of sexuality in rehabilitation and community settings. The journal features original scholarly articles that address the psychological and medical aspects of sexuality in the field of rehabilitation, case studies, clinical practice reports, and guidelines for clinical practice. Plenum Publishers is now part of Kluner Academic Publishers. Journal fulfillment in the NYC office as before for HSP and Plenum Journals. *$160.00*
*64 pages Quarterly*
*ISSN 0146-10 4*

**5160 Sociopolitical Aspects of Disabilities**
Charles C. Thomas
2600 S 1st Street
Springfield, IL 62704-4730
217-789-8980
800-258-8980
FAX: 217-789-9130
e-mail: books@ccthomas.com
www.ccthomas.com

*Michael P. Thomas, President*
Provides understanding of the social and political histories of people with disabilities in the United States. This understanding is pivotal in working with persons with disabilities, to provide background and perspective on current policies and attitudes. *$41.95*
*324 pages Paperback*
*ISBN 0-398072-40-7*

**5161 Starting and Sustaining Genetic Support Groups**
Johns Hopkins University Press
2715 North Charles Street
Baltimore, MD 21218
410-516-6900
FAX: 410-516-6968

Guide to the establishment and maintenance of genetic support groups for individuals with genetic disorders and their families. For therapists and group leaders. Discusses practical matters including finding a leader, fund-raising, organizing peer support training programs. *$21.95*
*152 pages*
*ISBN 0-801852-64-1*

**5162 Substance Abuse and Physical Disability**
Haworth Press
6000 Broken Sound Parkway, NW
Suite 300,
Boca Raton, FL 33487-1503
561-994-0555
FAX: 561-241-7856
e-mail: orders@taylorandfrancis.com
www.tandf.co.uk

This book offers information on alcohol and drug abuse being a contributing factor in traumatic and disabling injuries. *$ 74.95*
*289 pages Hardcover*
*ISBN 1-560242-89-2*

**5163 TeamRehab Report**
516 Montgomery St.
Decorah, IA 52101-8987
563-382-4770
800-543-4116
FAX: 563-382-4785

*Meghan Scheidel, Accounts Manager*
A magazine for rehab professionals who prescribe, purchase or recommend assistive technology and related services for clients who are permanently disabled. *$24.00*
*48 pages Monthly*

**5164 What Psychotherapists Should Know about Disabilty**
Through the Looking Glass
3075 Adeline St
Ste. 120
Berkeley, CA 94703-2212
510-848-1112
800-644-2666
FAX: 510-848-4445
TTY: 510-848-1005
e-mail: tlg@lookingglass.org
www.lookingglass.org

*Maureen Block, J.D., Co-Founder,*
*Karen Fessel, Ph.D., Executive Director*
*$24.00*
*368 pages*

**5165 Women with Visible & Invisible Disabilitiees: Multiple Intersections, Issues, Therapies**
Haworth Press
6000 Broken Sound Parkway, NW
Suite 300,
Boca Raton, FL 33487-1503 561-994-0555
FAX: 561-241-7856
e-mail: orders@taylorandfrancis.com
www.tandf.co.uk

Addesses the issues faced by women with disabilities, examines the social construction of disability, and makes suggestions for the development and modification of culturally relevant therapy to meet the needs fo disabled women. *$69.95*
*418 pages Hardcover*
*ISBN 0-789019-36-1*

## Specific Disabilities

**5166 Applying Concepts and Data from the NHIS Child Disability Supplements**
HRSA Information Center
P.O.Box 2910
Merrifield, VA 22116-2910 888-275-4772
FAX: 703-821-2098
TTY:877-489-4772
e-mail: ask@hrsa.gov
www.ask.hrsa.gov

*Tony Louis, Project Officer*
*HT Ireys, Author*
Assists State public health programs in meeting the accountability mandates of Title V of the Social Security Act.

**5167 Dental Care Considerations of Disadvantaged and Special Care Populations**
HRSA Information Center
P.O.Box 2910
Merrifield, VA 22116-2910 888-275-4772
FAX: 703-821-2098
TTY:877-489-4772
e-mail: ask@hrsa.gov
www.ask.hrsa.gov

*Tony Louis, Project Officer*
*HT Ireys, Author*
These conference proceedings present a list of recommendations for HRSA's Bureau of Health Professions on how to modify Title VII and VIII programs to better meet the dental needs of disadvantaged and special care populations. It include tables and figures.

**5168 HIV/AIDS in the Deaf and Hard of Hearing**
HRSA Information Center
P.O.Box 2910
Merrifield, VA 22116-2910 888-275-4772
FAX: 703-821-2098
TTY:877-489-4772
e-mail: ask@hrsa.gov
www.ask.hrsa.gov

*Tony Louis, Project Officer*
*HT Ireys, Author*
Details the prevalence of HIV disease among deaf and hard of hearing in the United States. It defines deaf and hard the of hearing. It discusses the lack of HIV information among the deaf and hard of hearing population and barriers to care. It includes the HRSA Care ACTION Calendar of Events.

**5169 The Patterns of English Spelling**
AVKO Educational Research Foundation
Ste W
3084 Willard Rd
Birch Run, MI 48415-9404 810-686-9283
866-285-6612
FAX: 810-686-1101
e-mail: webmaster@avko.org
avko.org

*Don Mc Cabe, Executive Director*
*Barry Chute, President*
A 10-volume reference book with all of the words in the English language organized by word family, including CV structures, advanced patters, prefixes, and rimes. Each volume may also be purchased individually. Free as an E-book for Foundation members.
*$359.90*
*1635 pages*

## Vocations

**5170 Ability**
George J DePontis
Unit 18, Gatwick Metro Centre
Balcombe Road
Horley, RH 33137-788 www.ability.com
Features articles on living, working, playing and entertainment for the disabled. *$12.00*

**5171 Case Management in the Vocational**
Berkeley Planning Associates
P.O. Box 68
Osceola, IA 50213-5012 641-342-4598
888-342-6019
FAX: 641-342-3411
e-mail: c.oppedal@yourohs.com
www.yourohs.com

*Connie Oppedal, President*
Journal examining the effectiveness of case management services in the context of vocational rehabilitation for persons with psychiatric disabilities.

**5172 Demystifying Job Development: Field-Based Approaches to Job Development for the Disabled**
Training Resource Network
PO Box 439
St. Augustine, FL 32085 FAX: 904-823-3554
e-mail: info@trninc.com
www.trninc.com
A guide to successful placement of individuals with severe disabilities in quality jobs in the community. *$29.95*
*105 pages*
*ISBN 1-883302-37-4*

**5173 Economics, Industry and Disability**
Paul H Brookes Publishing Company
P.O.Box 10624
Baltimore, MD 21285-624 410-337-9580
800-638-3775
FAX: 410-337-8539
readplaylearn.com

*Paul Brooks, Owner*
An analysis of the movement toward nonsheltered employment, this book addresses the expanding opportunities, future challenges and economic changes surrounding efforts to ensure the development of positive and constructive employment for persons with disabilities. *$42.00*
*Hardcover*

**5174 Hiring Idahoans with Disabilities**
Idaho Assistive Technology Project
129 W 3rd Street
Moscow, ID 83843-2268
208-885-3559
800-432-8324
FAX: 20- 88- 614
e-mail: idahoat@uidaho.edu
www.educ.uidaho.edu/idatech

**5175 Life Beyond the Classroom: Transition Strategies for Young People with Disabilities**
Paul H Brookes Publishing Company
P.O.Box 10624
Baltimore, MD 21285-624
410-337-9580
800-638-3775
FAX: 410-337-8539
e-mail: custserv@brokespublishing.com
readplaylearn.com

*Paul Brooks, Owner*
Specialists in a variety of disciplines use creative and practical techniques to ensure careful transition planning, to build young people's confidence and competence in work skills, and to foster support from businesses and community organizations for training and employment programs. *$64.95*
*543 pages*
*ISBN 1-557664-76-5*

**5176 Mentally Retarded Individuals**
Mainstream
Ste 830
3 Bethesda Metro Ctr
Bethesda, MD 20814-6301
301-961-9299
800-247-1380
FAX: 301-654-6714
e-mail: info@mainstreaminc.org

*Charles Moster*
Mainstreaming mentally retarded individuals into the workplace. *$2.50*
*12 pages*

**5177 OT Practice**
American Occupational Therapy Association
Ste 301
164 Rollins Ave
Rockville, MD 20852-4038
301-762-8055
800-877-1383
FAX: 301-652-7711

*Jeanette Bair, Executive Director*
Offers information on conferences, books, resources, materials and information and referral services for persons with disabilities.

**5178 Options**
Anixter Center
2001 N. Clybourn
Chicago, IL 60614-4062
773-973-7900
FAX: 773-973-5268
e-mail: AskAnixter@Anixter.org
anixter.org

*Kevin Limbeck, Ceo*
Anixter Center's quarterly publication. Free.
*Quarterly*

**5179 Preparation and Employment of Students**
Paul H Brookes Publishing Company
P.O.Box 10624
Baltimore, MD 21285-624
410-337-9580
800-638-3775
FAX: 410-337-8539
readplaylearn.com

*Paul Brooks, Owner*
A practical guide on vocational training and employment issues for persons with severe multiple and physical disabilities. *$ 213.00*
*224 pages Paper*

**5180 Teaching Chemistry to Students with Disabilities**
American Chemical Society
1155 16th St NW
Washington, DC 20036-4839
202-872-4570
800-227-5558
FAX: 202-872-4574
TTY: 202-872-6355
e-mail: cwd@acs.org
membership.acs.org

*Elizabeth Zubritsky, Manager*
*James M Landis, CWD Chair*
*Anne Swanson, Editor*
*Madeleine Jacobs, Editor*
Promotes the full involvement of individuals with physical and learning disabilities in educational and career opportunities in the chemical and allied sciences. CWD members lead the American Chemical Society's efforts to help: individuals with disabilities who seek education or employment in chemical and allied sciences; employers and educators of persons with disabilities; other committees, offices and members of ACS who are interested in the full involvement of persons with disabilities.
*148 pages*
*ISBN 0-841238-16-2*

**5181 Transition from School to Work**
Paul H Brookes Publishing Company
P.O.Box 10624
Baltimore, MD 21285-624
410-337-9580
800-638-3775
FAX: 410-337-8539
readplaylearn.com

*Paul Brooks, Owner*
A hands-on guide to planning and implementing successful transition programs for adolescents with disabilities. *$25.00*
*336 pages Paper*

**5182 Transition from School to Work for Personswith Disabilities**
Longman Publishing Group
9th Fl
10 Bank St
White Plains, NY 10606-1933
914-993-5000
FAX: 914-421-5598

*Joanne Dresner, President*
Examines the multidimensional process needed to effectively prepare persons with disabilities for life beyond school and addresses the key issues in the transition process.
*251 pages Paper*
*ISBN 0-801302-28-5*

## Pamphlets

**5183 A Guide for People with Disabilities Seeking Employment**
US Department of Justice
950 Pennsylvania Ave NW
Washington, DC 20530-9
800-574-0301
FAX: 202-307-1197
TTY:800-514-0383
www.ada.gov

*Gregory B. Friel , Chief*
A 2-page pamplet for people with disabilities providing a general explanation of the employment provisions of the ADA and how to file a complaint with the Equal Employment Opportunity Commission.

**5184 ADA Business Brief: Restriping Parking Lots**
US Department of Justice
950 Pennsylvania Ave NW
Washington, DC 20530-9
800-574-0301
FAX: 202-307-1197
TTY:800-514-0383
www.ada.gov

*Gregory B. Friel , Chief*
A 2-page illustrated design guide explaining the number of accessible parking spaces that are required and the restriping requirements for accessible parking spaces for cars and vans.

**5185 ADA Business Brief: Service Animals**
US Department of Justice
950 Pennsylvania Ave NW
Washington, DC 20530-9
800-574-0301
FAX: 202-307-1197
TTY:800-514-0383
www.ada.gov

*Gregory B. Friel , Chief*
A 1-page publication summarizing the ADA rules on service animals.

**5186 Accessible Stadiums**
US Department of Justice
950 Pennsylvania Ave NW
Washington, DC 20530-9
800-574-0301
FAX: 202-307-1197
TTY:800-514-0383
www.ada.gov

*Gregory B. Friel , Chief*
A 4-page publication highlighting features that must be accessible in new stadiums including line of sight for wheelchair seating locations.

**5187 Arthritis in Children and La Artritis Infantojuvenil**
American Juvenile Arthritis Organization
P.O.Box 7669
Atlanta, GA 30357-669
404-872-7100
800-283-7800
e-mail: help@arthritis.org
arthritis.org

*John H Klippel, CEO*
A medical information booklet about juvenile rheumatoid arthritis. This booklet is written for parents or other adults and includes details about different forms of JRA, medications, therapies and coping issues.

**5188 Assistance at Self-Serve Gas Stations**
US Department of Justice
950 Pennsylvania Ave NW
Washington, DC 20530-9
800-574-0301
FAX: 202-307-1197
TTY:800-514-0383
www.ada.gov

*Gregory B. Friel , Chief*
A 1-page document providing guidance on the ADA and refueling assistance for customers with disabilities at self-serve gas stations.

**5189 Attention Deficit-Hyperactivity Disorder: Is it a Learning Disability?**
Georgetown University, School of Medicine
3800 Reservoir Rd NW
Washington, DC 20007-2113
202-298-6775

*Joy Drass, President*
Offers information on learning disabilities and related disorders.

**5190 BVA Bulletin**
Blinded Veterans Association
477 H St NW
Washington, DC 20001-2617
202-371-8880
800-669-7079
FAX: 202-371-8258
e-mail: bva@bva.org
bva.org

*Samuel Huhn, President*
*Mark Cornell, Vice President*
*Bi-Monthly*

**5191 Blind and Vision-Impaired Individuals**
Mainstream
1030 5th St NE
Washington, DC 20002-3534
202-898-1400
e-mail: info@mainstreaminc.org
Mainstreaming blind individuals into the workplace. *$ 2.50*
*12 pages*

**5192 Cataracts**
National Eye Institute
Drive MSC 2510
31 Center Dr
Bethesda, MD 20892-1
301-496-5248
FAX: 301-402-1065
e-mail: 2020@nei.nih.gov
www.nei.nih.gov

*Paul A. Sieving, M.D., Ph.D., Director*
A cataract is a clouding of the lens in the eye that affects vision. Most cataracts are related to aging. Cataracts are very common in older people. By age 80, more than half of all Americans either have a cataract or have had cataract surgery.

**5193 Common ADA Problems at Newly Constructed Lodging Facilities**
US Department of Justice
950 Pennsylvania Ave NW
Washington, DC 20530-9
800-574-0301
FAX: 202-307-1197
TTY:800-514-0383
www.ada.gov

*Gregory B. Friel , Chief*
This 11-page document lists a sampling of common accessibility problems at newly constructed lodging facilities that have been identified through the Department of Justice's ongoing enforcement efforts.

**5194 Commonly Asked Questions About Service Animals in Places of Business**
US Department of Justice
950 Pennsylvania Ave NW
Washington, DC 20530-9
800-574-0301
FAX: 202-307-1197
TTY:800-514-0383
www.ada.gov

*Gregory B. Friel , Chief*
A 3-page publication providing information about service animals and ADA requirements.

**5195 Connect Information Service**
150 S Progress Ave
Harrisburg, PA 17109-4624
717-657-5113
800-692-7288

Pamphlet offering information on child development, special education programs, resources for parents and local contact persons.

**5196 Easy Access Housing**
Easter Seals
PO Box 355
Wellington , 6140-4851 404-499-1064
e-mail: enquiries@atareira.org.nz
www.atareira.org.nz

Booklet with a checklist for finding homes that are already accessible or structurally adaptable to accommodate changes in physical abilities and needs. Includes suggestions for solving common accessibility problems such as narrow doors, high thresholds and round knob fixtures.
*12 pages*

**5197 Facts: Books for Blind and Physically Handicapped Individuals**
Nat'l Lib Svc/Blind And Physically Handicapped
1291 Taylor St NW
Washington, DC 20011-2 202-707-5100
FAX: 202-707-0712
TTY:202-707-0744
e-mail: nls@loc.gov
www.loc.gov/nls

*Karen Keninger , Director*
Administers a national library service that provides braille and recorded books and magazines free on loan to anyone who cannot read standard print because of visual or physical disabilities.
*Annual*

**5198 Heart to Heart**
Blind Children's Center
4120 Marathon St
Los Angeles, CA 90029-3505 323-664-2153
FAX: 323-665-3828
e-mail: info@blindchildrenscenter.org
blindchildrenscenter.org

*Midge Horton, Executive Director*
*Lena French, Director of Finance*
Parents of blind and partially sighted children talk about their feelings. *$10.00*
*12 pages*

**5199 How to Find More About Your Child's Birth Defect or Disability**
Birth Defect Research for Children
BDRC
976 Lake Baldwin Lane, Suite 104,
Orlando, FL 32814-3753 407-895-0802
e-mail: staff@birthdefects.org
www.birthdefects.org

*Betty Mekdeci, Executive Director/Manager*
An informational fact sheet that encourages parents who have a child with a birth defect or disability to become the expert on the child's disability with some suggestions on how to educate themselves.

**5200 Individuals with Arthritis**
Mainstream
1030 5th St NE
Washington, DC 20002-3534 202-898-1400
e-mail: info@mainstreaminc.org

Mainstreaming individuals with arthritis into the workplace.
*$2.50*
*12 pages*

**5201 Learning to Play**
Blind Children's Center
4120 Marathon St
Los Angeles, CA 90029-3505 323-664-2153
FAX: 323-665-3828
e-mail: info@blindchildrenscenter.org
blindchildrenscenter.org

*Midge Horton, Executive Director*
*Lena French, Director of Finance*
Discusses how to present play activities to the visually impaired preschool child. *$10.00*
*12 pages*

**5202 Marfan Syndrome Fact Sheet**
1275 Mamaroneck Ave
White Plains, NY 10605-5201 914-997-4488
FAX: 914-428-8203
www.marchofdimes.com

**5203 Marriage & Disability**
Accent Books & Products
P.O.Box 700
Bloomington, IL 61702-700 309-378-2961
800-787-8444
FAX: 309-378-4420
e-mail: acmtlvng@aol.com

*Raymond C Cheever, Publisher*
*Betty Garee, Editor*
This guide can help you make the right decision and it can help smooth the way to a happier life. *$7.95*
*Paperback*
*ISBN 0-91570-34-5*

**5204 Medical Herbalism**
Bergner Communications
P.O.Box 20512
Boulder, CO 80308-3512 303-541-9552
e-mail: bergner@concentric.com
www.medherb.com

*Paul Bergner, Editor*
Newsletter written by physicians and published six times a year.

**5205 Midtown Sweep: Grassroots Advocacy at its Best**
Independent Living Research Utilization ILRU
Ste 1000
2323 S Shepherd Dr
Houston, TX 77019-7031 713-520-0232
FAX: 713-520-5785
e-mail: ilru@ilru.org
ilru.org

*Lex Frieden , Director*
*Laurie Gerke Redd, Administrative Director*
Josie, Janetta, and Linda describe the steps their center's advocacy group have taken to ensure enforcement of the ADA: target one neighborhood; survey and collect information on businesses that are inaccessible; send letters offering to work with the businesses to help them become accessible and providing information on tax incentives; file lawsuits against businesses that do not respond; involve the media.
*10 pages*

**5206 Move With Me**
Blind Children's Center
4120 Marathon St
Los Angeles, CA 90029-3505 323-664-2153
FAX: 323-665-3828
e-mail: info@blindchildrenscenter.org
blindchildrenscenter.org

*Midge Horton, Executive Director*
*Lena French, Director of Finance*
A parent's guide to movement development for visually impaired babies. *$10.00*
*12 pages*

**5207 Newsletter of PA's AT Lending Library**
1755 N 13th Street,
Student Center, Room 411S
Philadelphia, PA 19122-6005
215-204-1356
FAX: 21- 20- 633
TTY:215-204-1805
e-mail: iod@temple.edu
disabilities.temple.edu

*Celia Feinstein, Co-Executive Director*
*Ann Marie White, Associate Director*

**5208 Reaching, Crawling, Walking....Let's Get Moving**
Blind Children's Center
4120 Marathon St
Los Angeles, CA 90029-3505
323-664-2153
FAX: 323-665-3828
e-mail: info@blindchildrenscenter.org
blindchildrenscenter.org

*Midge Horton, Executive Director*
*Lena French, Director of Finance*
Orientation and mobility for preschool children who are visually imapired. *$10.00*
*24 pages*

**5209 Selecting a Program**
Blind Children's Center
4120 Marathon St
Los Angeles, CA 90029-3505
323-664-2153
FAX: 323-665-3828
e-mail: info@blindchildrenscenter.org
blindchildrenscenter.org

*Midge Horton, Executive Director*
*Lena French, Director of Finance*
A guide for parents of infants and preschoolers with visual impairments. *$10.00*
*28 pages*

**5210 Standing On My Own Two Feet**
Blind Children's Center
4120 Marathon St
Los Angeles, CA 90029-3505
323-664-2153
FAX: 323-665-3828
e-mail: info@blindchildrenscenter.org
blindchildrenscenter.org

*Midge Horton, Executive Director*
*Lena French, Director of Finance*
A step-by-step guide to designing and constructing simple, individually tailored, adaptive mobility devices for preschool-age children who are visually impaired. *$10.00*
*36 pages*

**5211 Talk to Me**
Blind Children's Center
4120 Marathon St
Los Angeles, CA 90029-3505
323-664-2153
FAX: 323-665-3828
e-mail: info@blindchildrenscenter.org
blindchildrenscenter.org

*Midge Horton, Executive Director*
*Lena French, Director of Finance*
A language guide for parents of deaf children. *$10.00*
*11 pages*

**5212 Talk to Me II**
Blind Children's Center
4120 Marathon St
Los Angeles, CA 90029-3505
323-664-2153
FAX: 323-665-3828
e-mail: info@blindchildrenscenter.org
blindchildrenscenter.org

*Midge Horton, Executive Director*
*Lena French, Director of Finance*
A sequel to Talk To Me, available in English and Spanish. *$10.00*
*15 pages*

**5213 Teaching Social Skills to Youngsters with Disabilities**
Federation for Children with Special Needs
45 Bromfield Street
10th Floor
Boston, MA 02108
617-542-7860
866-815-8122
FAX: 617-542-7832
e-mail: info@ppal.net
www.ppal.net

*Lisa Lambert, Executive Director*
*Deborah A. Fauntleroy, MSW, Associate Director*
Explains the importance of instruction and training to learn appropriate social behavior.

**5214 Understanding**
Easter Seals
Ste 1800
230 W Monroe St
Chicago, IL 60606-4851
312-726-6800
FAX: 312-726-1494

*Janet D Jamieson, Communications Manager*
*James Williams Jr, Chief Executive Officer*
A brochure series for use in patient, family and public education programs and in career recruitment and counseling.
*10 Brochures*

**5215 Without Sight and Sound**
Helen Keller National Center
141 Middle Neck Rd
Sands Point, NY 11050-1218
516-944-8900
FAX: 516-944-7302
TTY:516-944-8637
e-mail: hkncinfo@hknc.org
www.hknc.org

Pamphlet offering facts, causes, types and descriptions of deaf-blindness.

# Media, Electronic

## Audio/Visual

**5216 A Place for MeEducational Productions**
Educational Productions
9000 SW Gemini Dr
Beaverton, OR 97008-7151
503-644-7000
800-950-4949
FAX: 503-350-7000
e-mail: custserve@edpro.com
www.edpro.com

*Diane Trister Dodge, Founder/President/Lead Author*
*Arnitra Duckett, VP, Sales & Strategic Marketing*
In this video, parents discuss the issues they face in planning for their child's future. This program is designed to stimulate discussion of these issues and help increase awareness of the options available in your local community.

**5217 Able to LaughFanlight Productions/Icarus Films**
Fanlight Productions
32 Court St 21st Floor
#2107
Brooklyn, NY 11201-4421
718-488-8900
800-876-1710
FAX: 718-488-8642
e-mail: info@fanlight.com
www.fanlight.com

*Jonathan Miller, President*
*Patricio Guzman, Director*
*Meredith Miller, Sales Manager*
*Anthony Sweeney, Acquisitions*
An exploration of the world of disability as interpreted by six professional comedians who happen to be disabled. It is also about the awkward ways disabled and able-bodied people relate to one another. *$199.00*

*ISBN 1-572951-05-2*

**5218 Acting BlindFanlight Productions/Icarus Films**
Fanlight Productions
32 Court St 21st Floor
#2107
Brooklyn, NY 11201-4421
718-488-8900
800-876-1710
FAX: 718-488-8642
e-mail: info@fanlight.com
www.fanlight.com

*Jonathan Miller, President*
*Patricio Guzman, Director*
*Meredith Miller, Sales Manager*
*Anthony Sweeney, Acquisitions*
Takes audiences behind the scenes as a company of non-professional actors rehearse a play about life without sight. The performers have no problem imagining themselves in these roles: they are blind themselves. *$229.00*

**5219 Adaptive Baby Care Equipment Video and Book Through the Looking Glass**
Through the Looking Glass
Ste 120
3075 Adeline St
Berkeley, CA 94703-2577
510-848-1112
800-644-2666
FAX: 510-848-4445
TTY: 510-848-1005
e-mail: TLG@lookingglass.org
www.lookingglass.org

*Megan Kirshbaum, Executive Director*
*Paul Preston, Assoc. Dir*
Includes Adaptive Baby care Equipment: Guide Lines; Prototypes and Resources, plus a twelve minute video. Available in braille, large print or cassette. *$79.00*

**5220 All About Attention Deficit Disorders, Revised**
Parent Magic
800 Roosevelt Rd
B-309
Glen Ellyn, IL 60137-5839
317-595-9072
800-442-4453
FAX: 317-595-9075
e-mail: custcare@parentmagic.com
www.parentmagic.com

*Nancy Roe, Administrator/Exec Admin*
*Thomas Phelan, Owner/President/CEO*
A psychologist and expert on ADD outlines the symptoms, diagnosis and treatment of this neurological disorder. Video ($49.95 - 2 parts) and audio cassette ($24.95). Also in DVD format (1 disk-$39.93).

**5221 AutismAquarius Health Care Media**
Aquarius Health Care Media
P.O.Box 249
30 Forest Rd
Millis, MA 2054-1511
508-376-1244
FAX: 508-376-1245
e-mail: aqvideos@tiac.net
www.aquariusproductions.com

*Lesile Kussmann, Owner/President/Producer*
*Kathy Newkirk, Director*
*Jane Hutchinson, Assoc. Director*
This video takes you into the lives of autistic people and their families to understand more about autism. What defines autism and how can we help those living with the disability? Children, teens, and adults are also profiled and we begin to see the varying levels of development and new technology to help these people communicate. Preview Available. *$149.00*
*Video*

**5222 Basic Course in American Sign Language(B100) Harris Communications, Inc.**
Harris Communications
15155 Technology Dr
Eden Prairie, MN 55344-2273
952-906-1180
800-825-6758
FAX: 952-906-1099
TTY: 800-825-9187
e-mail: info@harriscomm.com
harriscomm.com

*Robert Harris, Owner*
*Kevin Horsky, Business Director*
*Randall Moore, Manager*
This series of four one-hour tapes is designed to illustrate the various exercises and dialogues in the text. *$39.95*
*Video*

**5223 Beginning ASL Video CourseHarris Communications, Inc.**
Harris Communications
15155 Technology Dr
Eden Prairie, MN 55344-2273
952-906-1180
800-825-6758
FAX: 952-906-1099
TTY: 800-825-9187
e-mail: info@harriscomm.com
harriscomm.com

*Robert Harris, Owner*
*Kevin Horsky, Business Director*
*Randall Moore, Manager*
You'll watch a family teach you to learn American Sign Language during funny and touching family situations. A total of 15 tapes in the course. *$599.40*
*Video*

**5224 BlindnessLandmark Media, Inc.**
Landmark Media
3450 Slade Run Dr
Falls Church, VA 22042-3940
703-241-2030
800-342-4336
FAX: 703-536-9540
e-mail: info@landmarkmedia.com
landmarkmedia.com

*Michael Hartogs, President*
*Joan Hartogs, Vice President*
*Peter Hartogs, Vice President*
*Richard Hartogs, Vice President*
Cataracts are the most common cause of blindness in the 42 million people worldwide defined as blind. 90% live in developing countries. Cataracts are the most common cause but now can be treated cheaply and safely. *$250.00*
*Video*

**5225 Braille Documents**
Metrolina Association for the Blind
704 Louise Ave
Charlotte, NC 28204-2128
704-372-3870
800-926-5466
FAX: 704-372-3872
mabnc.org

*Robert Scheffel, President*
This production shop creates Braille and large-print documents.

**5226 Bringing Out the Best**
P.O.Box 9177
Dept. 11W
Champaign, IL 61826-9177
217-352-3273
800-519-2707
FAX: 217-352-1221
e-mail: orders@researchpress.com
www.researchpress.com

*David Parkinson, Chairman*
*Russell Pence, President*
*Gail Salyards, Dir. Of Marketing/President*

**5227 Business as UsualFanlight Productions/Icarus Films**
Fanlight Productions
32 Court St 21st Floor
#2107
Brooklyn, NY 11201-4421
718-488-8900
800-876-1710
FAX: 718-488-8642
e-mail: info@fanlight.com
www.fanlight.com

*Jonathan Miller, President*
*Patricio Guzman, Director*
*Meredith Miller, Sales Manager*
*Anthony Sweeney, Acquisitions*
An enlightening documentary, brings a unique international perspective to this struggle. This film examines five innovative programs which create opportunities for people with mental and physical disabilities to own and operate their own businesses. *$145.00*

**5228 Buying Time: The Media Role in Health CareFanlight Productions/Icarus Films**
Fanlight Productions
32 Court St 21st Floor
#2107
Brooklyn, NY 11201-4421
718-488-8900
800-876-1710
FAX: 718-488-8642
e-mail: info@fanlight.com
www.fanlight.com

*Jonathan Miller, President*
*Patricio Guzman, Director*
*Meredith Miller, Sales Manager*
*Anthony Sweeney, Acquisitions*
This video program is a thoughtful and disturbing examination in the role of the media in determining the allocation of health care resources. This program is a powerful tool on ethics, policy, journalism, sociology, medicine and nursing as well as for professional workshops, and continuing education programs. *$99.00*

**5229 Caring for Persons with Developmental Disabilities**
P.O.Box 9177
Dept. 11W
Champaign, IL 61826-9177
217-352-3273
800-519-2707
FAX: 217-352-1221
www.researchpress.com

*David Parkinson, Chairman*
*Russell Pence, President*
*Gail Salyards, Dir. Of Marketing/President*

**5230 Clockworks**
Learning Corporation of America
6493 Kaiser Dr
Fremont, CA 94555-3610
510-490-7311

*Oonchia Chia, Owner*
Scotty, who has Down Syndrome, is fascinated by clocks. This film follows him on his adventures of employment in the clock shop.
*Film*

**5231 Close Encounters of the Disabling Kind**
Mainstream
Ste 204
6930 Carroll Ave
Takoma Park, MD 20912-4468
301-891-8777
FAX: 301-891-8778
e-mail: info@mainstreaminc.org
www.mainstreaminc.org

*Lillie Harrison, Information Programs Clerk*
*Fritz Rumpel, Editor*
A training video that provides a hiring manager with information on how to learn the basics of disability etiquette and, by the end of the video, seems much better prepared and willing to interview qualified individuals with disabilities. Includes trainer and trainee guides. *$99.95*
*Video*

**5232 Deaf Children Signers**
Harris Communications
15155 Technology Dr
Eden Prairie, MN 55344-2273
952-906-1180
800-825-6758
FAX: 952-906-1099
TTY: 800-825-9187
e-mail: info@harriscomm.com
www.harriscomm.com

*Robert Harris, Owner*
*Kevin Horsky, Business Director*
*Randall Moore, Manager*
This three-part collection of children signers is great for children, teachers, parents and interpreters. *$39.95*
*Video*

**5233 Deaf Culture Series**
Harris Communicatin
15155 Technology Dr
Eden Prairie, MN 55344-2273
952-906-1180
800-825-6758
FAX: 952-906-1099
TTY: 800-825-9187
e-mail: info@harriscomm.com
www.harriscomm.com

*Robert Harris, Owner*
*Kevin Horsky, Business Director*
*Randall Moore, Manager*

Each video in this five-part series features a topic dealing with the unique culture of deaf people. It is an excellent resource for deaf studies programs, Interpreter Preparation programs and Sign Language programs. *$49.95*
*Video*

**5234 Deaf Mosaic**
Harris Communications
15155 Technology Dr
Eden Prairie, MN 55344-2273
952-906-1180
800-825-6758
FAX: 952-906-1099
TTY: 800-825-9187
e-mail: info@harriscomm.com
www.harriscomm.com

*Robert Harris, Owner*
*Kevin Horsky, Business Director*
*Randall Moore, Manager*
A national magazine show produced monthly by Gallaudet University, this show has been awarded nine Emmys. As the only nation-wide program about the deaf community, these videotapes are the best of the best from the shows programs. *$29.95*
*Video*

**5235 Do You Hear That?**
Alexander Graham Bell Association
3417 Volta Pl NW
Washington, DC 20007-2737
202-337-5220
FAX: 202-337-8314
e-mail: info@agbell.org
www.agbell.org

*Todd Houston, Executive Director*
This video shows auditory-verbal therapy sessions of a therapist working individually with 11 children who range in age from 7 months to 7 years old and have hearing aids or cochlear implants.
*Video*

**5236 Doing Things Together**
Britannica Film Company
345 4th St
San Francisco, CA 94107-1206
415-928-8466
FAX: 415-928-5027

*Dave Bekowich, Owner*
Steve went with his parents to an amusement park. He met another boy named Martin who at first was shocked by Steve's prosthetic hand.
*Film*

**5237 Emerging Leaders**
Mobility International USA
P.O.Box 10767
Eugene, OR 97440-2767
541-343-1284
FAX: 541-343-6812
e-mail: info@miusa.org
www.miusa.org

*Susan Sygall, CEO/Founder*
*Susan Dunn, Exec. Asst./Project Specialist*
*Jena Price, Manager*
Looks at the emergence of people with disabilities as leaders in the world community this video discusses the value of internation exchange programs in fostering leadership skills. Available in English, Spanish and Russian. *$49.00*
*Video*

**5238 Face FirstFanlight Productions/Icarus Films**
Fanlight Productions
32 Court St 21st Floor
#2107
Brooklyn, NY 11201-4421
718-488-8900
800-876-1710
FAX: 718-488-8642
e-mail: info@fanlight.com
www.fanlight.com

*Jonathan Miller, President*
*Patricio Guzman, Director*
*Meredith Miller, Sales Manager*
*Anthony Sweeney, Acquisitions*
In this documentary, the stories told reflect the reality faced by all those who are seen as different. Despite their difficult experiences, the survival of the profiled individuals affords comic relief &, by adulthood, they possess unusual strengths that shape their careers in pediatrics, disability care, public speaking, and journalism. *$ 195.00*

**5239 Family-Guided Activity-Based Intervention for Toddlers & Infants**
Brookes Publishing
P.O.Box 10624
Baltimore, MD 21285-624
410-337-9580
800-638-3775
FAX: 410-337-8539
e-mail: custserv@brookespublishing.com
www.readplaylearn.com

*Paul Brooks, Owner*
Early childhood professionals will be able to teach parents and other caregivers how to use daily routines and activities to help young children with special needs gain vital skills. Included on the video are activity-based teaching methods that enhance children's development, accommodate families' daily schedules, address children's IFSP goals, and promote family interactions. *$37.00*
*20 Minutes*
*ISBN 1-55766-19-3*

**5240 Filmakers Library**
124 E 40th St
New York, NY 10016-1798
212-808-4980
FAX: 212-808-4983
e-mail: info@filmakers.com
www.filmakers.com

*Sue Oscar, Co-President*
*Linda Gottesman, Co-President*
*Andrea Traubner, Dir., Broadcast Sales*
A distributor of educational, award-winning videotapes and films on issues relating to disabilities for educators, counsellors and organizations. The films and tapes are available for rental or sale to institutions, schools, hospitals and organizations. Among the topics covered in the videotapes are autism, schizophrenia, and physical disabilties.

**5241 Filmakers Library: An Imprint Of AlexanderStreet Press**
124 E 40th St
New York, NY 10016-1798
212-808-4980
FAX: 212-808-4983
e-mail: info@filmakers.com
filmakers.com

*Sue Oscar, Co-President*
A distributor of educational, award-winning videotapes and films on issues relating to disabilities for educators, counsellors and organizations. The films and tapes are available for rental or sale to institutions, schools, hospitals and organizations. Among the topics covered in the videotapes are autism, schizophrenia, and physical disabilties.
*$100 - $300*

**5242 Films & Videos on Aging and Sensory Change**
Lighthouse International
111 E 59th St
New York, NY 10022-1202
212-821-9200
800-829-0500
FAX: 212-821-9706
e-mail: info@lighthouse.org

*Joanna Mellor, VP Information Services*
*Tara Cortes, President*
An annotated list of over 80 films and videos dealing with age-related sensory change, divided into sections on vision impairment, hearing impairment, and multiple sensory impairments. *$5.00*

**5243 Heart to HeartBlind Childrens Center, Inc**
Blind Children's Center
4120 Marathon St
Los Angeles, CA 90029-3584
323-664-2153
800-222-3567
FAX: 323-665-3828
e-mail: info@blindchildrenscenter.org
www.blindchildrenscenter.org

*Midge Horton, Executive Director*
*Marion Ruth, Owner*
*Ina Zec, President*
*Lena French, Finance Executive*
Parents of blind and partially sighted children talk about their feelings. *$35.00*
*Video*

**5244 Helping HandsFanlight Productions/Icarus Films**
Fanlight Productions
32 Court St 21st Floor
#2107
Brooklyn, NY 11201-4421
718-488-8900
800-876-1710
FAX: 718-488-8642
e-mail: info@fanlight.com
www.fanlight.com

*Jonathan Miller, President*
*Patricio Guzman, Director*
*Meredith Miller, Sales Manager*
*Anthony Sweeney, Acquisitions*
The ADA mandates equal access and opportunity for the 43 million people with disabilities in the United States. These individuals may have limited speech, sight or mobility; a developmental disability; or a medical condition which limits some life activities. Many, however, are ready, willing and very able to join the workforce. This video demonstrates that many modifications or adaptations can be made simply by using ingenuity or common sense - such as keeping the aisles clear, etc. *$145.00*
*37 Minutes*

**5245 Home is in the Heart: Accommodating Peoplewith Disabilities in the Homestay Experience**
Mobility International USA
132 E. Broadway
Suite 343
Eugene, OR 97440-2767
541-343-1284
FAX: 541-343-6812
e-mail: info@miusa.org
www.miusa.org

*Susan Sygall, CEO/Founder*
*Susan Dunn, Exec. Asst./Project Specialist*
*Jena Price, Manager*
Provides information and ideas for exchange organizations. Discusses how to recruit homestay families, meet accessibility needs and accommodate international participants with disabilities. *$49.00*
*Video*

**5246 How Difficult Can This Be ? (Fat City)Rick Lavoie**
CACLD
PO Box 210
Barnstable, MA 2630-210
508-362-1052
e-mail: contact@ricklavoie.com
www.ricklavoie.com

*Rick Lavoie, Film Maker*
This informative and entertaining video allows the viewer to see the world through the eyes of a learning disabled child. It features a unique workshop attended by teacher, psychologists, social workers, parents, siblings and a student with LD They participate in a series of classroom activiteis which cause frustration, anxiety and tension; emotions all too familiar to a student with a learning disability.

**5247 How We PlayFanlight Productions/Icarus Films**
Fanlight Productions
32 Court St 21st Floor
#2107
Brooklyn, NY 11201-4421
718-488-8900
800-876-1710
FAX: 617-469-3379
e-mail: info@fanlight.com
www.fanlight.com

*Jonathan Miller, President*
*Patricio Guzman, Director*
*Meredith Miller, Sales Manager*
*Anthony Sweeney, Acquisitions*
Though most of the people in this new, short documentary are in wheelchairs, and one is blind, they are anything but handicapped. Playing tennis, snorkeling, whitewater canoeing, practicing karate - they are living proof that a disability can be a challenge, not an obstacle. *$99.00*

**5248 I'm Not DisabledLandmark Media, Inc.**
Landmark Media
3450 Slade Run Dr
Falls Church, VA 22042-3940
703-241-2030
800-342-4336
FAX: 703-536-9540
e-mail: info@landmarkmedia.com
www.landmarkmedia.com

*Michael Hartogs, President*
*Joan Hartogs, Vice President*
*Peter Hartogs, Vice President*
*Richard Hartogs, Vice President*
Young people talk about their disabilities and the importance of sports in their lives. The afflictions range from blindness and missing limbs to paralysis. Through physical education and therapy they enjoy freedom of movement and participate in sports such as tennis, basketball, kayaking, skiing, and swimming. *$195.00*
*Video*

**5249 Imagery Procedures for People with Special Needs**
Research Press
P.O.Box 9177
Dept. 11W
Champaign, IL 61826-9177
217-352-3273
800-519-2707
FAX: 217-352-1221
e-mail: rp@researchpress.com
www.researchpress.com

*David Parkinson, Chairman*
*Russell Pence, President*
*Gail Salyards, Dir. Of Marketing/President*
This video features numerous training sessions in which clinicians are shown leading individuals through imagery scenes that focus on controlling specific behaviors. *$195.00*
*32 Minutes*

**5250 Include Us**
Exceptional Parent Library
P.O.Box 1807
Englewood Cliffs, NJ 7632-1207 201-947-6000
800-535-1910
FAX: 201-947-9376
e-mail: eplibrary@aol.com
www.eplibrary.com

First children's video to feature a proportionate number of children with disabilities. Inclusion works via eight songs. *$19.95*

**5251 Intensive Early Intervention and Beyond**
P.O.Box 9177
Dept. 11W
Champaign, IL 61826-9177 217-352-3273
800-519-2707
FAX: 217-352-1221
www.researchpress.com

*David Parkinson, Chairman*
*Russell Pence, President*
*Gail Salyards, Dir. Of Marketing/President*

**5252 Invisible Children**
Learning Corporation of America
6493 Kaiser Dr
Fremont, CA 94555-3610 510-490-7311

*Oonchia Chia, Owner*

Renaldo was blind, Mandy was deaf, and Mark had Cerebral Palsy and used a wheelchair. These child-size puppet characters interacted with non-handicapped puppets.
*Film*

**5253 Look Who's LaughingAquarius Health Care Media**
Aquarius Health Care Videos
P.O. Box 249
30 Forest Rd
Millis, MA 2054-1511 508-376-1244
FAX: 508-376-1245
e-mail: aqvideos@tiac.net
www.aquariusproductions.com

*Lesile Kussmann, Owner/President/Producer*
*Kathy Newkirk, Director*
*Jane Hutchinson, Assoc. Director*

This video is packed with laugh-out-loud comedic moments, but is also full of intelligent and inspiring messages. Look Who's Laughing introduces viewers to some of today's funniest comedians - who just happen to be physically disabled. We hear them talk openly and honestly about their limitations as well as their abilities and talents. Helpful for those who work with the disabled and motivational to both the disabled and able-bodied. Preview option available. *$95.00*
*Video*

**5254 My Body is Not Who I AmAquarius Health Care Media**
Aquarius Health Care Videos
P.O. Box 249
30 Forest Rd
Millis, MA 2054-1511 508-376-1244
FAX: 508-376-1245
e-mail: aqvideos@tiac.net
www.aquariusproductions.com

*Lesile Kussmann, Owner/President/Producer*
*Kathy Newkirk, Director*
*Jane Hutchinson, Assoc. Director*

This thought-provoking video introduces viewers to people who openly discuss the struggles and triumphs they have experienced living in a body that is physically disabled. They talk honestly about the social stigma of their disability and the problems they face in terms of mobility, health care and family relationships, as well as the challenges of emotional and sexual intimacy. Preview option available. *$195.00*
*Video*

**5255 My CountryAquarius Health Care Media**
Aquarius Health Care Videos
P.O. Box 249
30 Forest Rd
Millis, MA 2054-1511 508-376-1244
FAX: 508-376-1245
e-mail: aqvideos@tiac.net
www.aquariusproductions.com

*Lesile Kussmann, Owner/President/Producer*
*Kathy Newkirk, Director*
*Jane Hutchinson, Assoc. Director*

By telling the stories of three people with disabilities and their struggle for equal rights under the law, this film draws a powerful parallel between the efforts of disability rights activists and the civil rights struggle of the 1960s. Great for disability awareness programs, and for discussions of disability rights issues. Should be part of every college curriculum on disabilities. Awarded Best of Show Superfest 98. Preview option available. *$195.00*
*Video*

**5256 No BarriersAquarius Health Care Media**
Aquarius Health Care Videos
P.O. Box 249
30 Forest Rd
Millis, MA 2054-1511 508-376-1244
FAX: 508-376-1245
e-mail: aqvideos@tiac.net
www.aquariusproductions.com

*Lesile Kussmann, Owner/President/Producer*
*Kathy Newkirk, Director*
*Jane Hutchinson, Assoc. Director*

Everyone faces the world with different abilities and disabilities. But everyone has at least one goal in common...to break through their own barriers says Mark Wellman. Mark, a paraplegic, knows this well. No Barriers takes us into Mark's world where he defies the odds for most able bodied individuals by climbing Yosemite's Half Dome and El Capitan. This video is more than inspiring and fun to watch...it helps one make that paradigm shift from can't do to can do! Preview option available *$90.00*
*Video*

**5257 On The SpectrumFanlight Productions/Icarus Films**
Fanlight Productions
32 Court St 21st Floor
#2107
Brooklyn, NY 11201-4421 718-488-8900
800-876-1710
FAX: 718-488-8642
e-mail: info@fanlight.com
www.fanlight.com

*Jonathan Miller, President*
*Patricio Guzman, Director*
*Meredith Miller, Sales Manager*
*Anthony Sweeney, Acquisitions*

Adults living with Asperger syndrome describe the ways AS has affected their lives, their work and their relationships. They discuss learning to cope with the disorder and the comfort and reinforcement of participating with others 'like them' in an Asperger's support group. 53 min. *$199.00*

**5258 Open for Business**
Disability Rights Education and Defense Fund
2212 6th St
Berkeley, CA 94710-2219 510-644-2555
800-348-4232
FAX: 510-841-8645
e-mail: info@dredf.org
dredf.org

*Sue Henderson, Executive Director*

An award-winning film that depicts the disability and business communities working together in one small town to remove architectural barriers, when readily achievable, as required by the Americans with Disabilities Act. Package includes 15 and 30 minute closed-captioned versions and 15 to 30 minute versions with audio description. *$179.00*

**5259 Open to the PublicAquarius Health Care Media**
Aquarius Health Care Videos
P.O. Box 249
30 Forest Rd
Millis, MA 2054-1511
508-376-1244
FAX: 508-376-1245
e-mail: aqvideos@tiac.net
www.aquariusproductions.com

*Lesile Kussmann, Owner/President/Producer*
*Kathy Newkirk, Director*
*Jane Hutchinson, Assoc. Director*
Provides an overview of the Americans with Disabilities Act as it applies to state and local governments. The ADA doesn't provide recommendations for solving common problems, but this film could provide enough information for governments to solve some common problems without turning to high-priced consultants. Preview option available. *$125.00*
*Video*

**5260 Our Own RoadAquarius Health Care Media**
Aquarius Health Care Videos
P.O. Box 249
30 Forest Rd
Millis, MA 2054-1511
508-376-1244
FAX: 508-376-1245
e-mail: aqvideos@tiac.net
www.aquariusproductions.com

*Lesile Kussmann, Owner/President/Producer*
*Kathy Newkirk, Director*
*Jane Hutchinson, Assoc. Director*
This video shows the disabled helping other people who are disabled and portrays the sense of pride they get from helping others. This multicultural program features many different healing techniques, and teaches the importance of helping those who are disabled become independent and productive. *$99.00*

**5261 Outsider: The Life and Art of Judith ScottFanlight Productions/Icarus Films**
Fanlight Productions
32 Court St 21st Floor
#2107
Brooklyn, NY 11201-4421
718-488-8900
800-876-1710
FAX: 718-488-8642
e-mail: info@fanlight.com
www.fanlight.com

*Jonathan Miller, President*
*Patricio Guzman, Director*
*Meredith Miller, Sales Manager*
*Anthony Sweeney, Acquisitions*
Judith Scoot has Down Syndrome, is deaf, and does not speak. Yet after 35 years of institutionalization, with the help of a sister who never gave up on her, she emerged to create a series of sculptures that have fascinated and mystified art experts and collectors around the world. 26 minutes. *$199.00*

**5262 Passion for JusticeFanlight Productions/Icarus Films**
Fanlight Productions
32 Court St 21st Floor
#2107
Brooklyn, NY 11201-4421
718-488-8900
800-876-1710
FAX: 718-488-8642
e-mail: info@fanlight.com
www.fanlight.com

*Jonathan Miller, President*
*Patricio Guzman, Director*
*Meredith Miller, Sales Manager*
*Anthony Sweeney, Acquisitions*
An engaging portrait of Bob Perske, the author of Unequal Justice and a crusader for the rights of people with developmental disabilities. The tape focuses on cases in which people with developmental disabilities have been convicted of crimes they didn't commit. The tape asks challenging questions about society's responsibility to this population, and about ways to protect their rights to equality and justice. *$99.00*
*29 Minutes*

**5263 Phoenix DanceFanlight Productions/Icarus Films**
Fanlight Productions
32 Court St 21st Floor
#2107
Brooklyn, NY 11201-4421
718-488-8900
800-876-1710
FAX: 718-488-8642
e-mail: info@fanlight.com
www.fanlight.com

*Jonathan Miller, President*
*Patricio Guzman, Director*
*Meredith Miller, Sales Manager*
*Anthony Sweeney, Acquisitions*
Reowned dancer Homer Avila lost his right leg and most of his hip to cancer. Following the creation of a pas de deux choreographed by Alonzo King, Phoenix Dance takes us on a journey of transformation and healing, challenging our expectations of what it means to be 'disabled.' Includes both 16 and 22 minute versions. *$199.00*

**5264 Pool Exercise ProgramArthritis Water Exercise / Arthritis Foundation**
Arthritis Foundation Distribution Center
P.O. Box 932915
Atlanta, GA 31193-2915
440-872-7100
800-283-7800
FAX: 404-872-0457
e-mail: aforders@arthritis.org
www.arthritis.org

*John Klippel, President/CEO*
This video features water exercises that will help you increase and maintain joint flexibility, strengthen and tone muscles, and increase endurance. All exercises are performed in water at chest level. No swimming skills are necessary. *$19.50*

**5265 Potty Learning for Children who Experience Delay**
Exceptional Parent Library
P.O.Box 1807
Englewood Cliffs, NJ 7632-1207
201-947-6000
800-535-1910
FAX: 201-947-9376
e-mail: eplibrary@aol.com
www.eplibrary.com

This video presents a unique developmental approach to supporting the child in learning independence in the management of bathroom skills. *$39.95*

**5266 Pushin' ForwardFanlight Productions/Icarus Films**
Fanlight Productions
32 Court St 21st Floor
#2107
Brooklyn, NY 11201-4421
718-488-8900
800-876-1710
FAX: 718-488-8642
e-mail: info@fanlight.com
www.fanlight.com

*Jonathan Miller, President*
*Patricio Guzman, Director*
*Meredith Miller, Sales Manager*
*Anthony Sweeney, Acquisitions*
Growing up poor and Latino, James Lilly was a gang member and drug dealer until, at fifteen, he was shot in the back and paralyzed. Today, he shares his story with inner city kids, and tells them about one thing that helped him move on; wheelchair racing. In Pushin' Forward he takes on the world's longest wheelchair race, from Fairbanks to Anchorage, Alaska, in six days! 39 minutes. *$229.00*

**5267 Relaxation Techniques for People with Special Needs**
Research Press
P.O.Box 9177
Dept. 11W
Champaign, IL 61826-9177 217-352-3273
800-519-2707
FAX: 217-352-1221
e-mail: rp@researchpress.com
www.researchpress.com

*David Parkinson, Chairman*
*Russell Pence, President*
*Gail Salyards, Dir. Of Marketing/President*
The developers discuss and demonstrate how to use special relaxation procedures with children and adolescents who have developmental disabilities. They emphasize the need for students to learn relaxation as a means of coping with stress and developing self-control. During the scenes of Dr June Groden conducting relaxation training, viewers will see how to correctly use the training procedures, how to use reinforcement during training and how to use guided imagery. 23 minutes. Includes book. *$195.00*
*Video*

**5268 Right at HomeAquarius Health Care Media**
Aquarius Health Care Videos
P.O. Box 249
30 Forest Rd
Millis, MA 2054 508-376-1244
FAX: 508-376-1245
e-mail: aqvideos@tiac.net
www.aquariusproductions.com

*Lesile Kussmann, Owner/President/Producer*
*Kathy Newkirk, Director*
*Jane Hutchinson, Assoc. Director*
Shows simple solutions for complying with the Fair Hoiusing Act amendments. Emphasizes low-cost, practical solutions, and working with people with disabilities to find the best applicable solution. Ideal for people with disabilities and their families, as well as housing providers, university courses, and disability awareness organizations. Preview option is available. *$99.00*
*Video*

**5269 Seat-A-Robics**
P.O.Box 630064
Little Neck, NY 11363-64 718-631-4007

*Daria Alinovi, President*
Offers a variety of safe, affordable and medically approved video exercise programs that are listed in our video chapter. In addition the company offers two resources. The first Healthy Eating & Facts For Kids is geared specifically to health professionals and educators that work with disabled children ($39.95). The second is a recreational resource guide that stimulates children to be creative and get involved. It keeps them actively engaged while having fun and getting fit ($29.95).

**5270 Shining Bright: Head Start Inclusion**
Brookes Publishing
P.O.Box 10624
Baltimore, MD 21285-624 410-337-9580
800-638-3775
FAX: 410-337-8539
e-mail: custserv@brookespublishing.com
readplaylearn.com

*Paul Brooks, Owner*
This documentary depicts the collaborative efforts of a Head Start and a local education agency to include children with severe disabilities in a Head Start program. This video addresses issues such as support for children with severe health impairments, benefits of participating in Head Start, ability of teachers with a general education background to serve children with severe disabilities, and staff relations. Includes a 28-page saddle-stitched booklet. *$45.00*
*23 Minutes*
*ISBN 1-55766 -95-9*

**5271 Small DifferencesAquarius Health Care Media**
Aquarius Health Care Videos
P.O. Box 249
30 Forest Rd
Millis, MA 2054-1511 508-376-1244
FAX: 508-376-1245
e-mail: aqvideos@tiac.net
www.aquariusproductions.com

*Lesile Kussmann, Owner/President/Producer*
*Kathy Newkirk, Director*
*Jane Hutchinson, Assoc. Director*
What happens when you give children with and without disabilities a camera and ask them to produce a video about disabilities? The result is an uplifting, award-winning disability video that both children and adults can relate to. The kids interviewed adults and children with physical and sensory disabilities. A top-quality production that increases understanding and awareness. Winner, Columbus International Film & Video Festival. Winner, National Education Media Network. Preview option availabe *$110.00*
*Video*

**5272 Someday's ChildEducational Productions**
Educational Productions
9000 SW Gemini Dr
Beaverton, OR 97008-7151 503-644-7000
800-950-4949
FAX: 503-350-7000
e-mail: custserv@edpro.com
www.edpro.com

*Diane Trister Dodge, Founder/President/Lead Author*
*Arnitra Duckett, VP, Sales & Strategic Marketing*
This video focuses on three families' search for help and information for their children with disabilities.

**5273 Sound & FuryAquarius Health Care Media**
Aquarius Health Care Videos
P.O. Box 249
30 Forest Rd
Millis, MA 2054-1511 508-376-1244
FAX: 508-376-1245
e-mail: aqvideos@tiac.net
www.aquariusproductions.com

*Lesile Kussmann, Owner/President/Producer*
*Kathy Newkirk, Director*
*Jane Hutchinson, Assoc. Director*
This film takes viewers inside the seldom seen world of the deaf to witness a painful family struggle over a controversial medical technology called the cochlear implant. Some of the family members celebrate the implant as a long overdue cure for deafness while others fear it will destroy their language and way of life. This documentary explores this seemingly irreconcilable conflict as it illuminates the ongoing struggle for identity among deaf people today. *$195.00*
*Video*

**5274 Special Children/Special Solutions**
Option Indigo Press
2080 S Undermountain Rd
Sheffield, MA 1257-9643 413-229-8727
800-714-2779
FAX: 413-229-8727
e-mail: indigo@option.org
www.optionindigo.com

*Barry Kaufmans, Owner/Founder/Author*
*Samahria Kaufmans, Owner/Founder*
This four-tape audio series presents concrete, down-to-earth, no-nonsense alternatives which are full of love and acceptance for the special child while being wholly supportive of parents, professionals and helpers who want to reach out. The accepting (nonjudgmental) attitude presented is the basis of all Samahria's work and is the foundation for the nurturing teaching process that has encouraged and helped parents, children and others to accomplish more than most would have believed. *$55.00*
*Audio*

**5275 Technology for the DisabledLandmark Media, Inc.**
Landmark Media
3450 Slade Run Dr
Falls Church, VA 22042-3940
703-241-2030
800-342-4336
FAX: 703-536-9540
e-mail: info@landmarkmedia.com
landmarkmedia.com

*Michael Hartogs, President*
*Joan Hartogs, Vice President*
*Peter Hartogs, Vice President*
*Richard Hartogs, Vice President*
Physically disabled people cope with the frustrations of a body they cannot control. The computer age has made many disabled more self-reliant; armless feed themselves, the blind read newspapers and the voiceless speak through marvelous technological breakthroughs. *$195.00*
*Video*

**5276 The Boy InsideFanlight Productions/Icarus Films**
Fanlight Productions
32 Court St 21st Floor
#2107
Brooklyn, NY 11201-4421
718-488-8900
800-876-1710
FAX: 718-488-8642
e-mail: info@fanlight.com
www.fanlight.com

*Jonathan Miller, President*
*Patricio Guzman, Director*
*Meredith Miller, Sales Manager*
*Anthony Sweeney, Acquisitions*
The harrowing story of the filmmaker's son Adam, a 12-year-old with Asperger Syndrome, during a tumultuous year in the life of their family. AS makes Adam's life in seventh grade a minefield, where he finds himself isolated and bullied. As he struggles to find a place for himself, his troubles escalate, both at school and at home.

**5277 Three R's for Special Education: Rights, Resources, Results**
Brookes Publishing
P.O.Box 10624
Baltimore, MD 21285-624
410-337-9580
800-638-3775
FAX: 410-337-8539
e-mail: custserv@brookespublishing.com
readplaylearn.com

*Paul Brooks, Owner*
This is a guide for parents, and a tool for educators. Through this video parents learn how to work through the steps of the special education system and work toward securing the best education and services for their children. Reviews the laws to protect children with disabilities in easy to understand language. Also provides a list of national organizations that can offer resources, information and advice to parents. *$49.95*
*50 Minutes*
*ISBN 0-96461 -80-7*

**5278 Tools for StudentsAquarius Health Care Media**
Aquarius Health Care Videos
P.O. Box 249
30 Forest Rd
Millis, MA 2054-1511
508-376-1244
FAX: 508-376-1245
e-mail: aqvideos@tiac.net
www.aquariusproductions.com

*Lesile Kussmann, Owner/President/Producer*
*Kathy Newkirk, Director*
*Jane Hutchinson, Assoc. Director*
Provides a series of 26 fun occupational therapy sensory processing activities. Designed as an in-home, in-workshop, and in-class exercise leader with students. Activities include: Strenghten the muscles necessary for normal activities, provide the muscles necessary to enhance alertness and concentration, increase the ability to use good posture, help social skills and fitting in and increase coordination; concludes with emphasis on team collaboration between the student, teacher, and parents. *$99.00*
*Video*

**5279 Training Module: Adaptive Baby Care Equipment Through the Looking Glass**
Through the Looking Glass
Ste 120
3075 Adeline St
Berkeley, CA 94703-2577
510-848-1112
800-644-2666
FAX: 510-848-4445
TTY: 510-848-1005
e-mail: TLG@lookingglass.org
www.lookingglass.org

*Megan Kirshbaum, Executive Director*
*Paul Preston, Assoc. Dir*
Curriculum for OT programs includes Adaptive Baby Care Equipment Video and Book. *$250.00*

**5280 Video Guide to Disability AwarenessAquarius Health Care Media**
Aquarius Health Care Videos
P.O. Box 249
30 Forest Rd
Millis, MA 2054-1511
508-376-1244
FAX: 508-376-1245
e-mail: aqvideos@tiac.net
www.aquariusproductions.com

*Lesile Kussmann, Owner/President/Producer*
*Kathy Newkirk, Director*
*Jane Hutchinson, Assoc. Director*
President Clinton opens and concludes this informative video about disability awareness. A series of candid interviews with people who have a wide range of disabilities provide personal insights into the issues surrounding visual, hearing, physical and mental disabilities. Video comes with written reference guide and is also available with open or closed captioning. Preview option available. *$195.00*
*Video*

**5281 Video Intensive Parenting**
Systems Unlimited/LIFE Skills
1556 S 1st Ave
Iowa City, IA 52240-6007
319-356-5412

*Ginny Kirschling, Public Information Specialist*
*Geoffrey Lauer, Program Director*
*Bill Gorman, President*
Parents who have children with special needs share their reactions to their child's diagnosis and how they have learned to cope with their feelings. *$69.95*

**5282 Vital Signs: Crip Culture Talks BackFanlight Productions/Icarus Films**
Fanlight Productions
32 Court St 21st Floor
#2107
Brooklyn, NY 11201-4421
718-488-8900
800-876-1710
FAX: 718-488-8642
e-mail: info@fanlight.com
www.fanlight.com

*Jonathan Miller, President*
*Patricio Guzman, Director*
*Meredith Miller, Sales Manager*
*Anthony Sweeney, Acquisitions*
This edgy, raw video documentary explores the politics of disability through the performances, debates and late-night conversations of artists at a recent national conference of disabilities and the art's. Vital Signs conveys the intensity, variety and vitality of disability culture today. *$225.00*
*Video*

5283 **What About Me?Educational Productions**
Educational Productions
9000 SW Gemini Dr
Beaverton, OR 97008-7151
503-644-7000
800-950-4949
FAX: 503-350-7000
e-mail: custserve@edpro.com
www.edpro.com

*Diane Trister Dodge, Founder/President/Lead Author*
*Arnitra Duckett, VP, Sales & Strategic Marketing*
This video focuses on two siblings of children with disabilities. The siblings (Brian and Julie) share their perspectives, their worries, concerns and victories about living with a sibling with a disability.

5284 **When Billy Broke His Head...and OtherFanlight Productions/Icarus Films**
Fanlight Productions
32 Court St 21st Floor
#2107
Brooklyn, NY 11201-4421
718-488-8900
800-876-1710
FAX: 718-488-8642
e-mail: info@fanlight.com
www.fanlight.com

*Jonathan Miller, President*
*Patricio Guzman, Director*
*Meredith Miller, Sales Manager*
*Anthony Sweeney, Acquisitions*
When Billy Golfus, an award-winning journalist, became brain damaged as the result of a motor scooter accident, he joined the ranks of the 43 million Americans with disabilities, this country's largest and most invisible minority. He helped create this video, which blends humor with politics and individual experience with a chorus of voices, to explain what it is really like to live with a disability in America. #136 *$195.00*

*ISBN 1-57295 -36-2*

5285 **When I Grow Up**
Britannica Film Company
345 4th St
San Francisco, CA 94107-1206
415-928-8466
FAX: 415-928-5027

*Dave Bekowich, Owner*
At a costume party each child was to come as what they wanted to be when they grew up. Some of the children had handicaps, and they talked about why their handicaps would not prevent them from fulfilling their desires.
*Film*

5286 **When Parents Can't Fix ItFanlight Productions/Icarus Films**
Fanlight Productions
32 Court St 21st Floor
#2107
Brooklyn, NY 11201-4421
718-488-8900
800-876-1710
FAX: 718-488-8642
e-mail: info@fanlight.com
www.fanlight.com

*Jonathan Miller, President*
*Patricio Guzman, Director*
*Meredith Miller, Sales Manager*
*Anthony Sweeney, Acquisitions*
This documentary looks at the lives of five families who are raising children with disabilities - the problems they face, how they have learned to cope, and the rewards and stresses of adapting to their child's condition. It explores the medical complexities and financial pressures families encounter, the emotional and physical toll on parents and siblings, and the dangers of child abuse in this population. It offers a very realistic look at different family strengths and coping styles.
*58 Min. DVD/VHS*
*ISBN 1-572958-76-6*

5287 **White Cane and WheelsFanlight Productions/Icarus Films**
Fanlight Productions
32 Court St 21st Floor
#2107
Brooklyn, NY 11201-4421
718-488-8900
800-876-1710
FAX: 718-488-8642
e-mail: info@fanlight.com
www.fanlight.com

*Jonathan Miller, President*
*Patricio Guzman, Director*
*Meredith Miller, Sales Manager*
*Anthony Sweeney, Acquisitions*
Carmen and Steve once dreamed of lives on stage and screen, but their plans were cut short by her blindness and his muscular dystrophy. This program is a funny and touching exploration of a relationship filled with frustration, but held together with patience, stubborness, forgiveness, and love. 26 minutes. *$169.00*

5288 **Why My Child**
800-313-ABDC
www.birthdefects.org
A 9 1/2 minute video that explores the feelings every parent has when their child is born with a birth defect. Emmy-award-winning producer, Karen Dorsett, has created a compelling video that begins with the parents' question, why my child? Follows through to concerns about links between birth defects and environmental exposures to drugs, pesticides, dioxin, radiation, hazardous wastes, etc. *$25.00*

## Web Sites

5289 **AbleApparelAffordable Adaptive Clothing and Accessories**
2121 Hillside Ave
New Hyde Park, NY 11040-2712
516-873-6552
FAX: 516-248-7308
e-mail: sales@abledata.com
www.ableapparel.com

*Mary Ann Tenaglia, Partner*
*Marie Harmon, Partner*
*Donna Lo Monica, Partner/Designer*
Quality products to achieve independence in performing daily living activities.

5290 **Abledata**
8630 Fenton Street
Suite 930
Silver Spring, MD 20910- 3820
301-608-8998
800-227-0216
FAX: 301-608-8958
TTY: 301-608-8912
e-mail: abledata@macrointernational.com
www.abledata.com

*Katherine Belknap, Project Director*
*Steve Lowe, Project Director*
*David Johnson, Publications Director*
*Juanita Hardy, Information Specialist*
Premier source for information on assistive technology.

5291 **Academy for Educational Development**
1825 Connecticut Ave., NW
Suite 800
Washington, DC 20009-5721
202-884-8000
e-mail: web@aed.org
www.aed.org

*Rebecca Logan, CEO/President*

Committed to addressing human development needs in the United States and throughout the world.

**5292 Access Unlimited**
570 Hance Rd
Binghamton, NY 13903-5700 607-669-4822
800-849-2143
FAX: 607-669-4595
www.accessunlimited.com

*Thomas Egan, President/Owner*
*Tom 'TC' Cole, National Sales Manager*
Adaptive transportation and mobility equipment for people with disabilities.

**5293 Ai Squared**
130 Taconic Business Park
Manchester Center, VT 5255-9752 802-362-3612
800-859-0270
FAX: 802-362-1670
e-mail: Sales@aisquared.com
www.aisquared.com

*David Wu, CEO*
*Jost Eckhardt, VP of Engineering*
*Doug Hacker, VP of Business Development*
*Scott Moore, VP of Marketing*
Leaders in low vision software.

**5294 Alternatives in Education for the Hearing Impaired (AEHI)**
9300 Capitol Drive
Wheeling, IL 60090-7207 847-850-5490
FAX: 847-850-5493
e-mail: info@agbms.org
www.aehi.org

*Debbie Blackburn, Founder/Business, Reading & Spec*
*Carol Martorano, Educational Director*
AEHI is a program of the Alexander Graham Bell Montessori School in Mt. Prospect, IL, that fosters literacy and empowers people with hearing impairments to achieve their full potential through unique educational options.

**5295 American Academy of Audiology**
11730 Plaza America Dr
Suite 300
Reston, VA 20190-4748 800-222-2336
FAX: 703-790-8631
e-mail: info@audiology.org
www.audiology.org

*Cheryl Kreider Carey, Executive Director*
*Edward Sullivan, Deputy Executive Director*

**5296 American Association of People with Disabilities**
1629 K Street NW
Suite 950
Washington, DC 20006-1675 202-457-0046
800-840-8844
FAX: 202-457-0473
www.aapd.com

*Helena Berger, Executive VP & COO*
*Mark Perriello, President/CEO*
*Michael Murray, Director of Programs*
Non-profit, non-partisan, cross-disability, national membership organization whose goals are unity, leadership and impact. AAPD's mission is to advance the economic and political power of all people with disabilities.

**5297 American Botanical Council**
PO Box 144345
Austin, TX 78714-4345 512-926-4900
800-373-7105
FAX: 512-926-2345
e-mail: abc@herbalgram.org
www.herbalgram.org

*Mark Blumenthal, Founder/Executive Director*
*Lucy Bruno, Executive Assistant*
*A. Toby Bernal, Gardener*
Conducts research and provides education on the safe, responsible and scientific uses of medicine herbs to the public, healthcare professionals, government, industry, and the media.

**5298 American College of Rheumatology, Researchand Education Foundation**
2200 Lake Boulevard NE
Atlanta, GA 30319-5310 404-633-3777
FAX: 404-633-1870
e-mail: acr@rheumatology.org
www.rheumatology.org

*Mark Andrejeski, Executive Vice President*
*David Haag, ARHP Executive Director*
*Steve Echard, REF Executive Director*
Arthritis afflictsone in every seven Americans. Your gift supports research, investigates the causes, improves treatment and works toward the prevention and cure of arthritis.

**5299 American Liver Foundation**
39 Broadway
Suite 2700
New York, NY 10006-3054 212-668-1000
FAX: 212-483-8179
www.liverfoundation.org

*Newton Guerin, COO/Interim CEO*
*Rebecca Frank, Executive Vice President*
Is the only national voluntary health organization dedicated to preventing, treating, and curing hepatitis and other liver and gall bladder diseases through research and education.

**5300 American Mobility: Personal Mobility Solutions**
60 Island St
Lawrence, MA 1840-1835 978-794-3030
www.americanmobility.com

*David Lacroix, President*
Source of Pride Scooters, Jazzy Power Chairs, personal mobility vehicles, and lift and recline chairs.

**5301 American Speech-Language and Hearing Association**
2200 Research Blvd
Rockville, MD 20850-3289 301-296-3289
800-638-8255
FAX: 301-296-8580
TTY: 301-296-5650
e-mail: actioncenter@asha.org
www.asha.org

*Paul Rao, President*
Exhibits by companies specializing in alternative and augmentative communications products, publishers, software and hardware compinies, and hearing aid testing equipment manufacturers.

**5302 Americans with Disabilities Act: ADA Home Page**
800-514-0301
TTY:800-514-0383
www.ada.gov
Provides facts on the Americans with Disabilities Act and other information relating to disability rights.

**5303 Appliance 411**
www.appliance411.com

A guide to remodeling and appliances for people with disabilities.

**5304 Arc of the United States**
1660 L Street, NW
Suite 301
Washington, DC 20036-5689
202-534-3700
800-433-5255
FAX: 202-534-3731
e-mail: info@thearc.org
www.thearc.org

*Laurie Ertz, Director*
*Leigh Ann Davis, Project & Information Specialist*
*Kate Hull, Project Specialist*
National organization of and for people with mental retardation anad thier families.

**5305 Association for the Cure of Cancer of the Prostate (CaP CURE)-Prostate Cancer Foundation**
1250 Fourth St
#360
Santa Monica, CA 90401-1444
310-570-4700
800-757-2873
FAX: 310-570-4701
e-mail: info@pcf.org
www.pcf.org

*Mike Milken, Founder/Chairman*
*Jonathon Simons, MD, President/CEO*
*Stuart Holden, Medical Director*
CURE is a nonprofit public charity that is dedicated to supporting prostate cancer research and hastening the conversion of research into cures or controls.

**5306 Asthma and Allergy Foundation of America**
8201 Corporate Drive
Suite 1000
Landover, MD 20785-2266
800-727-8462
e-mail: info@aafa.org
www.aafa.org

*Michael Breshgold, Sales Manager*
*Liana Burns, Programs Assistant*
Supports research to cure asthma and allergies and helps sufferers through patient education, practical advice, and a nationwide chapter and support group network.

**5307 Audiology Foundation of America**
3067 Sullivan St
West Lafayette, IN 47906-1261
480-219-6124
e-mail: jcapel@atsu.edu
www.audfound.org

*Susan Paarlberg, Executive Director*
*Tracy Harding, Marketing & Publicity Specialist*
*Becky White, Executive Assistant*
Commited to fostering the education and training of audiologists to meet the needs of the public, especially those with impaired hearing.

**5308 Auditory-Verbal InternationalAG Bell**
3417 Volta Place, NW
Washington, DC 20007-2737
202-204-4700
FAX: 202-337-8314
e-mail: academy@agbell.org
www.agbell.org

*Anita Bernstein, Director*
*Kathleen Treni, President of the Association*
*Cheryl Dickson, President*
Focus on education, guidance, advocacy, family support and the rigorous application of techniques to promote optimal acquision of spoken language

**5309 Cancer Immunology Research Foundation(CIRF) Cancer Research Institute National Headquar**
Concern Foundation
One Exchang Plaza, 55 Broadway
Suite 1802
New York, NY 10006-3724
212-688-7515
800-992-2623
FAX: 212-832-9376
www.cancerresearch.org

*Jill O'Donnell, CEO & Director of Scientific Aff*
Immunology research will discover why the immune system fails and cancer develops. Herein lies the cure for cancer, AIDS, and other autoimmune diseases.

**5310 Cancer Immunotherapy and Gene Therapy**
www.skcc.org

**5311 Cancer Research Institute**
One Exchang Plaza, 55 Broadway
Suite 1802
New York, NY 10006-3724
212-688-7515
800-992-2623
FAX: 212-832-9376
www.cancerresearch.org

*Jill O'Donnell, CEO & Director of Scientific Aff*
A vital force in the advancement of new immune-based approaches to cancer treatment, control and prevention.

**5312 Center on the Social & Emotional Foundations for Early Learning (CSEFEL)**
Vanderbilt University 110 Magnolia
Box 328 GPC
Nashville, TN 37203
615-322-8150
FAX: 615-343-1570
e-mail: ml.hemmeter@vanderbilt.edu
www.csefel.vanderbilt.edu

*Mary-Louise Hemmeter, Principal Investigator*
The center will: focus on promoting the social and emotional developmental of children as a means of preventing challenging behaviors; collaborate with existing T/TA providers for the purpose of ensuring the implementation and sustainability of practices at the local level; provide ongoing identification of training needs and preferred delivery formats of local programs and T/TA providers; disseminate evidence-based practices.

**5313 Damon Runyon Cancer Research Foundation**
Walter Winchell Foundation
One Exchange Plaza, 55 Broadway
Suite 302
New York, NY 10006-3720
212-455-0500
877-722-6237
e-mail: info@damonrunyon.org
www.damonrunyon.org

*Lorraine Egan, Executive Director*
*Andrea Ciminello, Director of Alliance Development*
*Clare Cahill, Administrative Director*
Goal is to cure cancer. 100% of your gift funds research. With 49 Runyon-Winchell scientists who have won Nobel Prizes, chances are good.

**5314 Disability Net**
www.bargione.co.uk/disabled.htm
The internet resource for disabled people that offers the latest news and events.

**5315 Disability Rights Activist**
www.disrights.org
Provides information to enable anyone intersted in the rights of disabled people to work for those rights.

**5316 Disability and Medical Resources Mall**
www.icdri.org/Medical/disabilitymall.hmt

Online directory committed to featuring information on disability and medical products, resources and services, with over 2,500 links including over 400 companies for one-stop shopping convenence.

**5317 DisabilityResources.org**
www.disabilityresources.org
Provides information on disability-related material on the Web.

**5318 Discover Technology**
713-885-1519
e-mail: dtinc8888@hotmail.com
www.discovertechnology.com

*Amantha Cole, Founder*
Provides links to websites that are specifically geared toward persons with disabilities who have special interest in adaptive technology.

**5319 Dynamic Living**
95 West Dudleytown Rd
Bloomfield, CT 6002-1315
860-683-4442
888-940-0605
FAX: 860-243-1910
e-mail: info@dynamic-living.com
www.dynamic-living.com

*Andrea Tannenbaum, Owner*
Kitchen products, bathroom helpers, and unique daily living products that provide a convienient, comfortable, and safe environment for people with disabilities.

**5320 ElderLawAnswers.com**
150 Chesnut St
4th Floor, Box #15
Providence, RI 2903
866-267-0947
e-mail: support@elderlawanswers.com
www.elderlawanswers.com

*Harry S. Margolis, Founder/President*
*Ken Coughlin, Editor*
*Mark Miller, Director of Operations*
Provides information about legal issues facing senior citizens and a searchable directory of attorneys.

**5321 Exploring Autism: A Look at the Genetics of Autism**
Box 3445 DUMC
Durham, NC 27710
FAX: 919-684-0952
e-mail: info@exploringautism.org
www.exploringautism.org

*Chantelle Wolpert, Project Director*
Dedicated to helping families who are living with the challenges of autism stay informed about the exciting breakthroughs involving the genetics of autism. Report and explain new genetic research findings. Explain genetic principles as they relate to autism, provide the latest research news, and seek your imput.

**5322 Foundation Fighting Blindness**
7168 Columbia Gateway Dr
Suite 100
Columbia, MD 21046- 3256
410-423-0600
800-683-5555
TTY:800-683-5551
e-mail: info@fightblindness.org
www.blindness.org

*Susan Brumley, Sr. National Director*
Largest voluntary, non-government sponsor to cure retinitis pigmentosa (RP), macular degeneration and related inherited disorders-leading causes of blindness and deaf-blindness.

**5323 Freedom Scientific**
11830 31st Court North
St. Petersburg, FL 33716-1805
727-803-8000
800-444-4443
FAX: 727-803-8001
e-mail: info@freedomscientific.com
www.freedomscientific.com

*Lee Hamilton, President/CEO/Chairman*
Assistive technology for blind and visually impaired computer users.

**5324 Gallaudet University Press**
800 Florida Ave, NE
Washington, DC 20002-3695
202-651-5488
FAX: 202-651-5489
e-mail: gupress@gallaudet.edu
www.gupress.gallaudet.edu
Source for titles on deafness and deaf related subjects.

**5325 Glaucoma Research Foundation**
251 Post Street
Suite 600
San Francisco, CA 94108-5017
415-986-3162
800-826-6693
e-mail: question@glaucoma.org
www.glaucoma.org

*Thomas Brunner, President/CEO*
*Andrew Jackson, Director of Communications*
*Catalina San Agustin, Director of Operations*
Protecting both sight and independence for those with glaucoma, by providing improved treatments and education today and by leading research towards a cure for tomarrow.

**5326 Helen Beebe Speech and Hearing Center**
www.helenbeebe.org
At the Beebe Center our mission is to help hearing-impaired children to listen and talk.

**5327 Herb Research Foundation**
5589 Arapahoe Ave
Suite 205
Boulder, CO 80303-8115
303-449-2265
www.herbs.org

*Rob McCaleb, President*
*John Lowe, Director of Research*
Research and public education on the health benefits of medicinal plants. Dedicated to world health through the informed use of herbs.

**5328 Hypokalemic Periodic Paralysis Resource Page**
155 West 68th St
Suite 1732
New York, NY 10023-5830
407-339-9499
www.periodicparalysis.org

*Jacob Levitt, President/Medical Director*
*Linda Feld, Secretary*
Provides understandable information on HKPP, dynamia linkage to several additional sources of helpful information on the Internet, and offers several online networking opportunities.

**5329 Innovation Management Group**
179 Niblick Road
#454
Paso Robles, CA 93446-4845
818-701-1579
800-889-0987
FAX: 877-464-7763
e-mail: cs@imgpresents.com
www.imgpresents.com

US and international onscreen keyboards, Word Prediction, Switch Scanning, Hover and Dwell, Joystick emulation, and Magnification software programs.

5330 **Interstitial Cystitis Association**
100 Park Ave
Suite 108-A
Rockville, MD 20850-2651
800-435-7422
FAX: 301-610-5308
e-mail: icamail@ichelp.org
www.ichelp.org

*Barbara Gordon, Executive Director*
*Marilynn Schreibstein, CFO*
Providing information, support and assistance to the patients of Interstitial Cystitis, a highly debilitating bladder disease. We'll find a cure by funding and encouraging research.

5331 **LD OnLineWETA Public Television**
2775 S. Quincy Street
Arlington, VA 22206-2269
FAX: 703-998-2060
e-mail: ldonline@weta.org
www.ldonline.org

*Noel Gunther, Executive Director*
*Christian Lindstrom, Director*
*Shalini Anand, Senior Mangager*
The interactive guide to learning disabilities for parents, teachers, and children.

5332 **Lyme Disease Foundation**
PO Box 332
Tolland, CT 6084-332
860-870-0070
FAX: 860-870-0080
e-mail: info@lyme.org
www.lyme.org

*Karen Forschuer, Chairman*
*Thomas Forschuer, Executive Director*
Provides critical information about tick-borne disease prevention, improves healthcare and funds research for solutions. 500,000 children, adults, and professionals assisted 25 countries.

5333 **Mainstream Online Magazine of the Able-Disabled**
www.mainstream-mag.com

*Cyndi Jones, Publisher*
*William G. Stothers, Editor*
The leading news, advocacy and lifestyle magazine for people with disabilities.

5334 **Microsoft Accessibility Technology for Everyone**
One Microsoft Way
Redmond, WA 98052-6399
425-882-8080
800-642-7676
FAX: 425-936-7329
TTY: 800-892-5234
www.microsoft.com/enable

*William Gates III, Chairman*
*Steven Ballmer, CEO/Director*
Information about accessibility features and options included in Microsoft products.

5335 **MossRehab ResourceNet**
1200 West Tabor Road
Philadelphia, PA 19141-3099
215-456-9900
800-225-5567
e-mail: kennedyd@einstein.edu
www.mossresourcenet.org

*John Whyte, Owner*
*Ruth Lefton, COO*
*Anthony Allonardo, Director of Technology*
Accessible travel, disability fact sheets, ADA, newsgroups, search tools.

5336 **Multiple Sclerosis National Research Institute**
11350 SW Village Parkway
Port St. Lucie, FL 34987-2352
858-597-3872
866-676-7400
FAX: 858-597-3804
e-mail: info@ms-research.org
www.ms-research.org

*Robin Offord, Chairman*
*Richard Houghten, President/CEO*
*Karen Douthitt, VP & Corporate Secretary*
Conducts research for the development of a vaccine to halt progression of mutiple sclerosis. Initial patient trials show promising results. Help us find a cure soon.

5337 **National Alliance of the Disabled(NAOTD)**
e-mail: turtle@dnaco.net
www.naotd.wheelboat.com

*Victoria Brown, President*
*Tracy Mankins, Vice President*
*Walton Dutcher, Executive Director/Operations*
Premier source for information on assistive technology.

5338 **National Association for Visually Handicapped Lighthouse International**
111 E 59th St
New York, NY 10022-1202
212-821-9200
800-829-0500
FAX: 212-821-9707
TTY: 212-821-9713
e-mail: info@lighthouse.org
www.lighthouse.org/navh

*Mark Ackermann, President/CEO*
*Jonathan Wainwright, VP & Secretary*
Works with millions of people worldwide in dealing with the difficulties of vision impairment.

5339 **National Brain Tumor FoundationNational Brain Tumor Society**
124 Watertown Street
Suite 2D
Watertown, MA 2472-2599
617-924-9997
800-770-8287
FAX: 617-928-9998
e-mail: info@braintumor.org
www.braintumor.org

*N. Paul TonThat, Executive Director*
*George Gellert, Chief Medical Officer/Director o*
An organization serving people whose lives are affected by brain tumors. The organization is dedicated to promoting a cure for brain tumors, improving the quality of life and giving hope to the brain tumor community by funding meaningful research and providing patient resources, timely information and education.

5340 **National Business & Disability Council**
201 I.U. Willets Road
Albertson, NY 11507-1516
516-465-1516
e-mail: jtowles@abilitiesonline.org
www.business-disability.com

*Jennifer Towles*
Works toward furthering the intersts of business and people with disabilities.

5341 **National Organization on Disability**
5 East 86th Street
New York, NY 10028-538
646-505-1191
e-mail: info@nod.org
www.nod.org

*Carol Glazer, President*
*Richard Stark, VP/Director*
*Ginna Baker, Development & Communications*

Promotes full and equal participation of America's 54 million men, women, and children with disabilities in all aspects of life.

**5342 National Rehabilitation Information Center**
8201 Corporate Drive
Suite 600
Landover, MD 20785-2266
301-459-5900
800-346-2742
FAX: 301-459-4263
TTY: 301-459-5984
e-mail: naricinfo@heitechservice.com
www.naric.com

*Mark Odum, Director*
Serves both professionals and the general public intersted in disability and rehabilitation.

**5343 National Women's Health Resource Center**
157 Broad Street
Suite 106
Red Bank, NJ 7701-2029
877-986-9472
FAX: 732-530-3347
e-mail: info@healthywomen.org
www.healthywomen.org

*Elizabeth Battaglino Cahill, Executive Director*
*Marisa Bushee, Director of Marketing & Communic*
Provides information for women with disabilities, health professionals, researchers, and caretakers.

**5344 NeuroControl Corporation**
8333 Rockside Rd
Valley View, OH 44125-6134
216-912-0101
800-378-6955
FAX: 216-912-0129
e-mail: skrebs@neurocontrol.com
www.neurocontrol.com

Helps people with spinal cord injuries lead more independent lives.

**5345 Newsletter of PA's AT Lending Library**
Temple University Institute on Disabilities
1601 N Broad Street
Suite 610
Philadelphia, PA 19122- 6024
215-204-3301
800-204-7428
FAX: 215-204-9371
TTY: 866-268-0579
e-mail: atlend@temple.edu
www.disabilities.temple.edu/atlend

*Amy Goldman, Project Director*
Newsletter from the Assistive Technology Lending Library in Pennsylvania. It is produced quarterly, is free of charge, and is available online only.
*4-8 pages Quarterly*

**5346 Office of Juvenile Justice and Delinquency Prevention**
810 Seventh St NW
Washington, DC 20531-3718
202-307-5911
www.childrenwithdisabilities.ncjrs.org

*Jeff Slowikowski, Acting Administrator*
*Marilynn Roberts, Deputy Administrator for Program*
Offers information and resources to disabled children, their families and service providers. This site is part of a joint effort by several federal agencies to promote a national agenda for children and foster positve youth development, and will provide informatin on learning disabilities, debilitating conditions and physical disabilities. It will include the latest research, programs and events designed specifically for children with disabilities.

**5347 Osteogenesis Imperfecta Foundation**
804 W. Diamond Ave.
Suite 210
Gaithersburg, MD 20878- 1414
301-947-0083
800-981-2663
FAX: 301-947-0456
e-mail: bonelink@oif.org
www.oif.org

*Mary Beth Huber, Director of Program Services*
Strives to improve the quality of life for indivduals with this brittle bone disorder through research, education, awareness, and mutual support.

**5348 Quantum Technologies**
17872 Cartwright Road
Irvine, CA 92614-6217
949-399-4500
FAX: 949-399-4600
www.qtww.com

*Dale Rasmussen, Chairman*
*Alan Niedzwieck, President/CEO/Director*
Provides access to information and tools for independence to serve the visually impaired and those with a learning disability.

**5349 Regional Resource Centers Program**
202-884-8215
www.rrfcnetwork.org

The Regional Resource Centers Program provides service to all states as well as the Pacific jurisdictions, the Virgin Islands, and Puerto Rico. The six regional program centers are funded by the federal Office of Special Education Programs (OSEP) to assist state education agencies in the systemic improvement of education programs, practices, and policies that affect children and youth with disabilities.

**5350 Research!America**
1101 King Street
Suite 520
Alexandria, VA 22314-2960
703-739-2577
800-366-2873
FAX: 703-739-2372
e-mail: info@researchamerica.org
www.researchamerica.org

*Mary Woolley, President*
*Barbara Love, Executive Assitant to the Presid*
Builds active public support for more government and private-industry research to find treatments and cures for both physical and mental disorders.

**5351 Skin and Dental Dysfunction Foundation**
410 E. Main Street
Mascoutah, IL 62258-2229
618-566-2020
FAX: 618-566-4718
e-mail: info@nfed.org
www.nfed.org

*Carol Ange, Director of Development*
*Mary Fete, Director of Research & Treatment*
Children left toothless from Ectodermal Dysplasia are provided dentures, support services and education. Established by National Foundation for Ectodermal Dysplasias which searches for a cure.

**5352 Social Security Online**
6401 Security Blvd
Windsor Park Bldg.
Baltimore, MD 21235-1
800-772-1213
TTY:800-325-0778
www.ssa.gov

*Michael Astrue, Commissioner of Social Security*
Official website of the Social Security Administration.

**5353 Special Clothes for Children**
PO Box 333
E. Harwich, MA 2645-333
508-430-2410
FAX: 508-430-2410
TTY:508-430-2410
e-mail: specialclo@aol.com
www.special-clothes.com

*Judi*
A catalog of adaptive clothing for children with disabilities - helping boys and girls with special needs meet the world with pride and confidence since 1987.

**5354 V Foundation for Cancer Research**
106 Towerview Court
Cary, NC 27513-3595
919-380-9505
800-454-6698
e-mail: info@jimmyv.org
www.jimmyv.org

*Joyce Aschenbrenner, VP of Special Projects*
*Sherrie Mazur, Director of Marketing & Communic*
*Jefferson Parker, VP of Operations*
*Nick Valvano, CEO*
Named for basketball coach and broadcaster, Jim Valvano. The V Foundation funds critical stage research conducted by young researchers at NCI approved cancer research facilities.

**5355 ValueOptions**
240 Corporate Blvd.
Norfolk, VA 23502-4900
757-459-5100
www.valueoptions.com

*Heyward Donigan, President/CEO*
Serves over 22 million people in behavioral healthcare through publicaly funded, federal, and commercial contracts.

**5356 Wardrobe Wagon: The Special Needs Clothing Store**
258B Route 46 E
Fairfield, NJ 7004-2324
973-244-2414
800-992-2737
e-mail: info@wardrobewagon.com
www.wardrobewagon.com

*E Oppenberg, President*
*Bonnie Oppenberg*
*Jerome Oppenberg, Owner*
Wearing apparel for individuals with special clothing needs.

**5357 We Magazine**
130 William St
New York, NY 10038
646-769-2722
FAX: 212-375-6266
TTY:212-375-6235
e-mail: sales@wemedia.com
www.icdri.org/NEWS/WEMedia.htm
Lifestyle magazine for people with disabilities.

**5358 We Media**
1610 Washington Plaza North
Reston, VA 20190-4303
703-880-2659
e-mail: help@wemedia.com
www.wemedia.com

*Andrew Nachison, Founder*
*Dale Peskin, Founder*
Online network for people with disabilities.

**5359 WebABLE**
www.hisoftware.com/press/webable.html
Provides disability-related internet resources.

**5360 WheelchairNet**
6425 Penn Ave
Suite 401 BAKSQ
Philadelphia, PA 15206
412-624-6279
e-mail: ruffing@pitt.edu
www.wheelchairnet.org

*Joseph Ruffing, Communications Specialist*
A virtual community of people who care about wheelchairs.

**5361 World Association of Persons with Disabilities**
2441 N Sterling Ave
302W
Oklahoma, OK 73127-2009
405-672-4440
e-mail: t.mecke@wapd.org
www.wapd.org

*Thomas Mecke, President*
*Lynne Walls, Business Executive*
Dedicated to improving the quality of life for those with disabilities.

**5362 disAbility Information and Resources**
e-mail: jlubin@eskimo.com
www.makoa.org

*Jim Lubin, Creator/Owner*
Offers dozens of links to sites with information, services and products for the disabled.

# Toys & Games

## General

**5363 Age Appropriate Puzzles**
7756 Winding Way
Fair Oaks, CA 95628-5735
916-961-3507
FAX: 916-961-0765
e-mail: miltcher@spcglobal.net

*Cheryl Meyers, President*
These unique puzzles teach numerous concepts: picture, name, color and shape recognition. Each of the two themes (holidays, and clothing) comes with self-adhesive stickers that name each picture in English, Hmong, Russian, Spanish and Vietnamese. A notch at each puzzle piece makes grasping and lifting the pieces easy to use., They are designed for children from 18 months and up. Special needs children, preschool through high school would also benefit. *$9.95*

**5364 All-Turn-It Spinner**
AbleNet, Inc.
2625 Patton Road
Roseville, MN 55113-1308
651-294-2200
800-322-0956
FAX: 651-294-2222
e-mail: customerservice@ablenetinc.com
www.ablenetinc.com

*Jennifer Thalhuber, CEO*
*Cheryl Volkman, Co-founder*
The All-Turn-It Spinner is a random spinner that comes with a dice overlay allowing user's to participate in any commercially-available game that require dice. Activate the spinner with its built-in switch or connect an external switch. Overlays are interchangeable with AbleNet designed spinner games or create your own overlay. A great inclusion tool!. *$89.00*

**5365 Anthony Brothers Manufacturing**
Convert-O-Bike
9 Capper Drive
Dailey Industrial Park,
Pacific,, MO 63069-5196
636-257-0533
800-346-6313
FAX: 636-257-5473
www.angelesstore.com

Manufacture wheeled toys and goods for disabled children.

**5366 Automatic Card Shuffler**
Maxi Aids
42 Executive Blvd
Farmingdale, NY 11735-4710
631-752-0521
800-522-6294
FAX: 631-752-0689
TTY: 800-281-3555
e-mail: sales@maxiaids.com
www.maxiaids.com

Simple to use, perfect for the player with limited hand dexterity. *$14.95*

**5367 Backgammon Set: Deluxe**
Maxi Aids
42 Executive Blvd
Farmingdale, NY 11735-4710
631-752-0521
800-522-6294
FAX: 631-752-0689
TTY: 800-281-3555
e-mail: sales@maxiaids.com
www.maxiaids.com

Completely factual with a felt board, raised white dividers and white braille dice for the blind and visually impaired. *$29.95*

**5368 Board Games: Snakes and Ladders**
Maxi Aids
42 Executive Blvd
Farmingdale, NY 11735-4710
631-752-0521
800-522-6294
FAX: 631-752-0689
TTY: 800-281-3555
e-mail: sales@maxiaids.com
www.maxiaids.com

A dice game for 2 to 6 players. This children's game is also fun for the whole family. Offers recreation, competition and eye/hand coordination skills. *$34.95*

**5369 Board Games: Solitaire**
Maxi Aids
42 Executive Blvd
Farmingdale, NY 11735-4710
631-752-0521
800-522-6294
FAX: 631-752-0689
TTY: 800-281-3555
e-mail: sales@maxiaids.com
www.maxiaids.com

This popular solo board game lends itself to a number of less well-known variations. The board is accompanied by brightly colored pieces that are reversible for the visually impaired player. *$30.95*

**5370 Braille Playing Cards: Plastic**
Maxi Aids
42 Executive Blvd
Farmingdale, NY 11735-4710
631-752-0521
800-522-6294
FAX: 631-752-0689
TTY: 800-281-3555
e-mail: sales@maxiaids.com
www.maxiaids.com

Playing cards that offer regular print and braille on plastic cards for the blind or visually impaired player. *$9.95*

**5371 Braille: Bingo Cards, Boards and Call Numbers**
Maxi Aids
42 Executive Blvd
Farmingdale, NY 11735-4710
631-752-0521
800-522-6294
FAX: 631-752-0689
TTY: 631-752-0738
e-mail: sales@maxiaids.com
www.maxiaids.com
Bingo products for the visually impaired. Cards, boards and call numbers offer regular print and braille. *$4.99*

**5372 Braille: Rook Cards**
Maxi Aids
42 Executive Blvd
Farmingdale, NY 11735-4710
631-752-0521
800-522-6294
FAX: 631-752-0689
TTY: 631-752-0738
e-mail: sales@maxiaids.com
www.maxiaids.com

This set of cards for Rook, the popular bidding card game with 23 variations, has regular size print and braille print for the blind/visually impaired player. *$13.75*

**5373 Card Holder Deluxe**
Maxi Aids
42 Executive Blvd
Farmingdale, NY 11735-4710
631-752-0521
800-522-6294
FAX: 631-752-0689
TTY: 631-752-0738
e-mail: sales@maxiaids.com
www.maxiaids.com
A handsome-looking card holder takes the struggle out of holding playing cards in weak or arthritic hands. The two clear plastic tiers hold up to 18 cards. The wooden base has a non-skid bottom to prevent slipping, and is also great for holding recipe cards. *$19.75*

**5374 Cards: Musical**
Sense-Sations
919 Walnut St
Philadelphia, PA 19107-5237
215-627-0600
FAX: 215-922-0692
asb.org

*Patricia Johnson, CEO*

These cards, for all occasions, play music when they are opened, for the visually impaired and blind persons. *$2.50*

**5375 Cards: UNO**
Maxi Aids
42 Executive Blvd
Farmingdale, NY 11735-4710
631-752-0521
800-522-6294
FAX: 631-752-0689
TTY: 631-752-0738
e-mail: sales@maxiaids.com
www.maxiaids.com

Traditional card game in braille for the blind player recreation. *$10.95*

**5376 Checker Set: Deluxe**
Maxi Aids
42 Executive Blvd
Farmingdale, NY 11735-4710
631-752-0521
800-522-6294
FAX: 631-752-0689
TTY: 631-752-0738
e-mail: sales@maxiaids.com
www.maxiaids.com

A wooden board with sunken playing squares. The squares have drilled holes for inserting the checker, offering help with eye/hand coordination for the physically challenged. *$25.95*

**5377 Chess Set: Deluxe**
Maxi Aids
42 Executive Blvd
Farmingdale, NY 11735-4710
631-752-0521
800-522-6294
FAX: 631-752-0689
TTY: 631-752-0738
e-mail: sales@maxiaids.com
www.maxiaids.com

Made out of wood material. Boards have raised dark squares and all squares have drilled holes for inserting pegged chessmen, for the physically challenged player with poor eye/hand coordination. *$43.95*

**5378 Dice: Jumbo Size**
New Vision Store
919 Walnut St
Philadelphia, PA 19107-5237
215-629-2990
www.thenewvisionstore.com

The large white and black dice are over-sized and have grooved dots to indicate the numbers, for easy reading for the visually handicapped. *$4.95*

**5379 Early Learning 1**
MarbleSoft
12301 Central Ave NE
Blaine, MN 55434-4902
763-755-1402
888-755-1402
FAX: 763-755-1402
e-mail: mail@marblesoft.com
www.marblesoft.com

*Vicki Larson, Manager*

Early learning 2.1 includes four activities that teach prereading skills. Single and dual-switch scanning are built in and special prompts allow blind students to use all levels of difficulty. Includes Matching Colors, Learning Shapes, Counting Numbers and Letter Match. Runs on Windows 98 or later and MAC OS 9 or OSX (classic not required). *$70.00*

**5380 Enabling Devices**
385 Warburton Ave
Hastings on Hudson, NY 10706-2837
914-478-7030
800-832-8697
FAX: 914-479-1369
e-mail: info@enablingdevices.com
www.enablingdevices.com

*Elizabeth Bell, Marketing Manager*
*Karen O'Connor, Vice President Operations*
*Steven Kanor, Owner*

For more than 25 years, Enabling Devices has been dedicated to providing affordable learning and assistive devices for the physically challenged. Products include augmentative communicators, adapted toys, capability switches, training and sensory devices and activity centers. Call for a free catalog.

**5381 Hands-Free Controller**
Nintendo
P.O.Box 957
Redmond, WA 98073-957
800-255-3700
www.nintendo.com

*Yoshio Tsuboike, Editor-in-Chief*

Nintendo controller for the physically disabled.

**5382 Let's Count Braille and Tactile Numbers Poster**
Maxi Aids
42 Executive Blvd
Farmingdale, NY 11735-4710
631-752-0521
800-522-6294
FAX: 631-752-0689
TTY: 631-752-0738
e-mail: sales@maxiaids.com
www.maxiaids.com

Cognitive skills and motor stimulation. *$34.95*

**5383 National Lekotek Center**
3204 W Armitage Ave
Chicago, IL 60647-3716
773-528-5766
800-366-PLAY
FAX: 773-276-8644
TTY: 800-573-4446
e-mail: lekotek@lekotek.org
www.lekotek.org

*Sarah Paweni, Manager*
*Clarice Brown, Programs/Training Asst Director*

Maximizes the development of children with special needs through play. Supports families through nationwide family play centers, toy lending libraries and computer play programs. Publishes six-page newsletter three times per year.

**5384 New Language of Toys: Teaching Communication Skills to Children with Special Needs**
Spina Bifida Association of America
Ste 250
4590 Macarthur Blvd NW
Washington, DC 20007-4226
202-944-3285
800-621-3141
FAX: 202-944-3295
e-mail: sbaa@sbaa.org
www.sbaa.org

*Cindy Brownstein, CEO*

A guide for parents and teachers and a reader-friendly resource guide that provides a wealth of information on how play activities affect a child's language development and where to get the toys and materials to use in these activities. *$19.00*

**5385 Puzzle Games: Cooking, Eating, Community and Grooming**

PCI
P.O.Box 34270
San Antonio, TX 78265-4270
210-670-3866
800-594-4263
FAX: 218-210-3771
www.pci.edu.com

*Janie Haugen, Program Director*
*Jeff McLane, President/CEO*
*Rebecca Phillips, Executive Director*

Each game has 63 pieces which are 2 inches in size. The completed full color puzzle is 19 inch x 15 inch. Step 1 - Work the puzzle. Step 2 - Match picture or word cards to the correct space on the puzzle. These puzzles teach basic life skills. *$19.95*

**5386 Single Switch Games**

MarbleSoft
12301 Central Ave NE
Blaine, MN 55434-4902
763-755-1402
888-755-1402
FAX: 763-755-1402
e-mail: mail@marblesoft.com
www.marblesoft.com

*Vicki Larson, Manager*

Theres alot of educational software for single switch users, but how about something that's just fun? We've taken some games similar to the ones you enjoyed as a kid and made them work just right for single switch users. Includes Single Switch Maze, A Frog's Life, Switching Lanes, Switch Invaders, Slingshot Gallery and Scurry. Runs on Windows 98 or later and MAC OS9 or OSX (classic not required) *$60.00*

**5387 Single Switch Latch and Timer**

AbleNet
1081 10th Ave SE
Minneapolis, MN 55414-1312
800-322-0956
FAX: 612-379-9143
e-mail: customerservice@ablenetinc.com
www.ablenetinc.com

A Single Switch Latch and Timer allows a user to activate a battery-operated toy or appliance in the latch, timed seconds and timed minutes modes of control. Choose for one user and one device at a time. *$63.00*

**5388 Socialization Games for Persons with Disabilities**

Charles C. Thomas
2600 S 1st St
Springfield, IL 62704-4730
217-789-8980
800-258-8980
FAX: 217-789-9130
e-mail: books@ccthomas.com
ccthomas.com

*Michael P. Thomas, President*
*Nevalyn Nevil, Author*
*Marna Beatty, Author*
*David Moxley, Author*

This text will assist those who want to teach severely multiple disabled students by providing information on: general principles of intervention and classroom organization; managing the behavior of students; physically managing students and using adaptive equipment; teaching eating skills; teaching toileting, dressing, and hygiene skills; teaching cognition, communication, and socialization skills; teaching independent living skills; and teaching infants and preschool students. *$38.95*

*176 pages Paperback*
*ISBN 0-398067-46-5*

**5389 Take a Chance**

Speech Bin
1965 25th Ave
Vero Beach, FL 32960-3062
772-770-0007
800-477-3324
FAX: 772-770-0006
e-mail: info@speechbin.com
www.speechbin.com

*Jan J Binney, Senior Editor*

Card game for practice of commonly misarticulated speech sounds. *$18.75*

*16 pages Book & Cards*
*ISBN 0-93785 -46-7*

**5390 Tic Tac Toe**

Maxi Aids
42 Executive Blvd
Farmingdale, NY 11735-4710
631-752-0521
800-522-6294
FAX: 631-752-0689
TTY: 631-752-0738
e-mail: sales@maxiaids.com
www.maxiaids.com

Several versions including tactile large peg and jumbo foam floor tile. *$5.95*

**5391 Turnabout Game**

Maxi Aids
42 Executive Blvd
Farmingdale, NY 11735-4710
631-752-0521
800-522-6294
FAX: 631-752-0689
TTY: 631-752-0738
e-mail: sales@maxiaids.com
www.maxiaids.com

A game of strategy for two, with large playing pieces and a bright gameboard for the visually impaired player. *$7.70*

# Travel & Transportation

## Newsletters & Books

**5392 A Guide for the Wheelchair Traveler**
Access for Disabled Americans
301 Village Square
Orinda, CA 94563-2317 925-254-1499
FAX: 925-254-6167
e-mail: psmither@aol.com
www.accessfordisabled.com

*Neal Smither, President*
*Patricia Smither, Editor/Secretary*
All you need to know when traveling in a wheelchair. *$30.00*
*165 pages Paperback*
*ISBN 1-928616-00-3*

**5393 A World Awaits You**
Mobility International U SA
Ste 343
132 E Broadway
Eugene, OR 97401-3155 541-343-1284
FAX: 541-343-6812
e-mail: info@miusa.org
www.miusa.org

*Susan Sygall, Executive Director*
A journal of success stories and tips of people with disabilities participating in international exchange programs.
*40 pages Yearly*

**5394 Access Travel: Airports**
Consumer Information Center
Department 575a
Pueblo, CO 81009-1 719-948-3334
e-mail: catalog.pueblo@gsa.gov

*Michael Clark, Public Affairs*
*Alfred Pino, Manager*
Tips and suggestions for easier travel for persons with disabilities and the elderly. Lists designs, facilities, and services at 553 airport terminals worldwide.

**5395 Architectural Barriers Action League**
P.O.Box 57088
Tucson, AZ 85732-7088 520-628-8118

*Martin Floerchinger, Owner*
Offers guides to accessible hotels and motels across the country.

**5396 Directory of Accessible Van Rentals(no longer being published)**
Disability Bookshop
P.O.Box 129
Vancouver, WA 98666-129 360-694-2462
www.allaboutdisabledtravel.com
Designed to help people with disabilities locate rental vans that are accessible throughout the U.S. *$9.95*
*30+ pages*
*ISBN 0-93326 -09-9*

**5397 Directory of Travel Agencies for the Disabled**
Twin Peaks Press
P.O.Box 129
Vancouver, WA 98666-129 206-694-2462
800-637-2256
e-mail: twinpeak@pacifier.com

*David Lynch, Director*
Directory lists more than 360 travel agents specializing in arrangements for people with disabilities. Handbook provides information about accessibility. *$19.95*
*40 pages Paperback*
*ISBN 0-93326 -04-8*

**5398 Elderly Guide to Budget Travel/Europe**
Pilot Books
P.O.Box 2102
Greenport, NY 11944-893 631-477-1094
FAX: 631-661-4379
Includes a list of over 250 inexpensive hotels in prime tourist areas. Covers special needs of senior citizens including inexpensive accommodations and fares. *$3.95*

**5399 Ideas for Easy Travel**
Accent Books & Products
P.O.Box 700
Bloomington, IL 61702-700 309-378-2961
800-787-8444
FAX: 309-378-4420
e-mail: acmtlvng@aol.com

*Raymond C Cheever, Publisher*
*Betty Garee, Editor*
Ideal for helping the new traveler get started having fun. Points out favorite accessible high-spots as reported by two travel experts (one is disabled), and offers basic ideas to help wherever you go. *$3.25*
*55 pages Paperback*
*ISBN 0-91570 -36-1*

**5400 Sports n' Spokes Magazine**
Paralyzed Veterans of America
801 18th St NW
Washington, DC 20006-3517 202-872-1300
800-424-8200
888-888-2201
FAX: 202-785-4432
e-mail: info@pva.org
www.pva.org

*Randy Pleva, President*
*Tom Wheaton, Senior VP*
*Gene A Crayton, National VP*
*Randy Pleza, President*
Publication of the PVA, a congressionally chartered veterans service organization, with unique expertise on a wide variety of issues involving the special needs of our members- veterans of the armed forces who have experienced spinal cord injury or dysfunction.

**5401 Survival Strategies for Going Abroad, A Guide for People with Disabilites**
132 E. Broadway St.
Suite #343
Eugene, OR 97401-3155 541-343-1284
FAX: 541-343-6812
e-mail: info@miusa.org
www.miusa.org

*Susan Sygall, Executive Director*
*Melissa Mitchell, Public Relations*
*$16.95*
*225 pages*

**5402 Travel Information Service/Moss Rehab Hospital**
Moss Rehabilitation Hospital
1200 W Tabor Rd
Philadelphia, PA 19141-3099 215-456-9900
800-225-5667
e-mail: staff@mossresourcenet.org
www.mossresourcenet.org

*Joan Appel, Manager*
*Alberto Esquenazi, Plant Manager*

Offers information and resources, to telephone callers only, for persons with special traveling/accessibility needs.

**5403 United States Department of the Interior National Park Service**
Superintendent of Documents
1849 C St NW
Washington, DC 20240-1
202-208-3100
FAX: 202-619-7302
e-mail: webteam@ios.doi.gov
www.doi.gov

*Mainella, Director*
*Gale Norton, Chief Executive Officer*
Offers an informational packet containing books, guides and tours for the disabled and elderly.

**5404 Wheelin Around**
Wheelers Accessible Van Rentals
6614 W Sweetwater Ave
Glendale, AZ 85304-1040
602-776-8830
800-456-1371
FAX: 623-412-9920
e-mail: info@WheelersVanRentals.com
www.WheelersVanRentals.com

*Tammy Smith, President*
*Ron Smith, Corporate Treasurer*

**5405 Where to Stay USA**
Council On International Educational Exchange
633 3rd Ave
New York, NY 10017-6706
212-822-2600
888-COU-NCIL
FAX: 212-822-2649

*Priscilla Tovey, Information Services*
A guide to low-cost lodging throughout the United States including information on whether the establishment is accessible. *$ 15.95*
*250 pages*
*ISBN 0-67179 -49-5*

## Associations & Programs

**5406 Access America**
Northern Cartographic
4050 Williston Rd
South Burlington, VT 5403-6062
802-860-2886
FAX: 802-865-4912

*Cynthia Belliveau, President*
Offers information on 36 national parks, providing detailed information on accessibility.

**5407 Access Yosemite National Park**
Special Needs Project
324 State Street
Santa Barbara, CA 93101-2364
805-962-8087
800-333-6867
e-mail: books@specialneeds.com
www.specialneeds.com

*Hod Gray, Owner*
Represents unprecedented combinations of intensive information survey data with high quality cartography. *$7.95*
*31 pages*

**5408 American Hotel and Lodging Foundation**
1201 New York Ave NW
Suite #600
Washington, DC 20005- 3931
202-289-3100
FAX: 202-289-3199
e-mail: comments@ahlaonline.org
www.ahla.com

*Joseph Mc Inerney, President*
Will disseminate information, develop and conduct a series of seminars for the hotel and motel industry at state-level association conferences, and develop and distribute an ADA Compliance handbook for use by the lodging industry.

**5409 Amtrak**
50 Massachusetts Ave NE
Washington, DC 20002-4214
202-000-1111
800-872-7245
FAX: 202-906-4564
TTY: 202-906-2500
e-mail: access@w0.amtrak.com
www.amtrak.com

*Alexander Kummant, President*
Amtrak is committed to making travel for passengers with disabilities more accessible. Anyone interested should contact Amtrak's Special Services Desk at 1-800-USA-RAIL at least 24 hours in advance to arrange for special assistance. The type of equipment and accessibility vary from train to train and station to station.

**5410 Easter Seals Project ACTION**
1425 K St NW
Suite #200
Washington, DC 20005-3508
202-347-3066
800-659-6428
FAX: 202-737-7914
TTY: 202-347-7385
e-mail: project_action@easterseals.com
www.easternseals.com

*Joseph Romer, VP*
A national technical assistance program designed to improve access to transportation services for people with disabilities and assist transit providers in implementing the Americans with Disabilities Act. Publishes quarterly newsletter.

**5411 General Motors Mobility Program for Persons with Disabilities**
GM Mobility Program
PO Box 5053
Troy, MI 48007
800-323-9935
www.gmmobility.com

*Frederick A Henderson, CEO*
GM Mobility Program provides up to $1000 reimbursement toward mobility adaptations for drivers or passengers and/or vehicle alerting devices for drivers who are deaf or hard of hearing. Provided on eligible new Chevrolet, Pontiac, Oldsmobile, Buick, Cadillac, and GMC vehicles. Complete GMC financing available. GM Mobility also offers free resource information, including list of area adaptive equipment installers, plus free resource video.

**5412 Kenny Foundation**
21700 Northwestern Hwy
Suite #730
Southfield, MI 48075- 4930
810-552-0202
800-237-3422
e-mail: comnet@uwcs.org

*Susan Burstein, Executive Director*
Provides education, advocacy & direct services to people with mobility impairments throughout Michigan. Services include Equipment Connection, a database, available online, that connects buyers & sellers of used adaptive equipment; Attitudes is a disability awareness program for 1st & 2nd graders; Information & Referral services; and Accessbility, a program that uses

volunteer labor and donated materials to buid ramps for people who can't afford them.

**5413 MedEscort International**
P.O.Box 8766
Allentown, PA 18105-8766
610-791-3111
800-255-7182
FAX: 610-791-9189
e-mail: serice@medescort.com
medescort.com

*Craig Poliner, President*
MedEscort International was founded over a decade ago with these basic principles and philosophies as its foundation. MedEscort has served the health care community, throughout the world, and has strived to perfect the techniques of moving patients from one place to another. Our medical staff includes registered nurses, respiratory therapists, paramedics, and physicians. MedEscort has developed comprehensive, individual aeromedical services to meet each patient's needs with a personal touch.

**5414 Melwood Access Adventures**
9035 Ironsides Rd
Nanjemoy, MD 20662-3432
301-870-3226
FAX: 301-870-2620
e-mail: accessadventures@melwood.com
www.melwood.org

*Heidi Aldous, Executive Director*
*Ron Hanley, VP Contract Services*
A year round recreation facility that serves mentally and physically disabled individuals, offers a variety of vacations, outdoor recreation, travel and respite care.

**5415 Nantahala Outdoor Center**
13077 Highway 19 W
Bryson City, NC 28713-9165
828-488-2175
888-905-7238
FAX: 828-488-2498
e-mail: rafting@noc.com
www.noc.com

*Sutton Bacon, CEO*
Nantahala Outdoor Center, the leader in outdoor recreation and education for more than 30 years, strongly encourages and supports participants with disabilities. We offer whitewater rafting adventures on six rivers in the Southeast for all skill and thrill levels for groups, also kayak and canoe adaptive instruction. NOC will tailor a whitewater program to your skill and ability level, modify the gear, and pace instruction for you. We also offer a Ropes Challenge Course and team building program

**5416 Open Road**
102 Brook Ln
Boulder Creek, CA 95006-9320
510-222-6662
FAX: 831-338-3210
www.campingunlimited.com

*Teresa Tucker, Manager*
Arts, Music, Sports, and Field Trips for disabled individuals.
*2 pages Monthly*

**5417 Paralysis Society of America**
Paralyzed Veterans of America
801 18th St NW
Washington, DC 20006-3517
202-872-1300
800-424-8200
FAX: 202-785-4432
TTY: 202-973-8422
e-mail: info@pva.org
www.pva.org

*Randy Pleva, President*
A national organization whose members are people with spinal cord injury or disease, their family members and caregivers, health-care professionals, and others with an interest in the disciplines of spinal cord medicine and paralsis. One year membership includes NewsWheels, a quarterly newsletter.

**5418 Shilo Inns & Resorts**
11600 SW Shilo Ln
Portland, OR 97225-5995
503-641-6565
800-222-2244
FAX: 503-643-1445
e-mail: franchiseinfo@shiloinns.com
www.shiloinns.com

*Ivan Mc Affee, VP*
Shilo Inns offers affordable excellence with special assist rooms at many of our locations throughout the western United States. These rooms include larger sized bathrooms equipped with assistance railings and wheelchair access. Special assist dogs are welcome free of charge ar most Shilo Inns. Call 1-800-222-2244 for details or make reservations or check out www.shiloinns.com

**5419 Travelers Aid Society**
1612 K St. NW
Suite #206
Washington, DC 20006-2849
202-546-1127
FAX: 202-546-9112
e-mail: info@travelersaid.org
www.travelersaid.org

*Raymond M Flynt, CEO*
Provides crisis intervention and casework services, limited financial assistance, protective travel assistance and information and referrals for travelers, transients and newcomers.

**5420 US Airways/America West Airlines**
4000 E Sky Harbor Blvd
Phoenix, AZ 85034-3802
480-693-0800
800-327-7810
FAX: 480-693-3702
www.usairways.org

*Douglas Parker, CEO*
This airline trains employees to make sure that passengers with disabilities enjoy convenient, safe and comfortable travel.

**5421 US Servas**
1125 16th Street
Suite # 201
Arcata, CA 95521-5585
707-825-1714
FAX: 707-825-1762
e-mail: info@usservas.org
www.usservas.org

*Judy Sears, Administrator*
International network that links travelers with hosts in 130+ countries with the hope of building world peace through understanding and friendship.
*Quarterly*

**5422 Westin Hotels and Resorts**
1111 Westchester Ave
White Plains, NY 10604-3525
914-640-8100
FAX: 914-640-8310
www.starwoodhotels.com

*Sue A Brush, Senior VP*
Westin Hotels include special parking stalls, wheelchair ramps, wide doors, wheelchairs, braille elevator buttons, recreational facilities for people with disabilities, restaurants and restrooms.

**5423 Wheelers Accessible Van Rentals**
6614 W Sweetwater Ave
Glendale, AZ 85304-1040
602-418-5076
800-456-1371
FAX: 623-412-9920
e-mail: info@wheelersvanrentals.com
www.wheelersvanrentals.com

*Tammy Smith, President*

Rental wheelchairs and scooter accessible vans. Technically advanced engineering features bring a world of independence to the user. Locations throughout the U.S. call 800-456-1371 to make reservations at any of our locations nationwide.

**5424 Wilderness Inquiry**
808 14th Ave SE
Minneapolis, MN 55414-1516
612-676-9400
800-728-0179
FAX: 612-676-9401
TTY: 612-676-9475
e-mail: info@wildernessinquiry.org
www.wildernessinquiry.org

*Jenni O Link, Manager*
Allows people of all ages and abilities to share the adventure of wilderness travel. This nonprofit organization was formed in 1978 and conducts tours to some of the most beautiful and remote parts of the world.

## Tours

**5425 AccessToThePlanet**
Accessible Journeys
35 W Sellers Ave
Ridley Park, PA 19078-2113
610-521-0339
800-846-4537
FAX: 610-521-6959
e-mail: sales@disabilitytravel.com
www.accessiblejourneys.com

*Howard Mc Coy, Owner*
All newsletters are concise and about travel with slow walkers, wheelchair travelers, their families and their friends.
*Monthly*

**5426 Accessible Journeys**
35 W Sellers Ave
Ridley Park, PA 19078-2113
610-521-0339
800-846-4537
FAX: 610-521-6959
e-mail: sales@accessiblejourneys.com
www.accessiblejourneys.com

*Howard Mc Coy, Owner*
Tour operator for slow walker and wheelchair travelers their families and their friends offering tours to culturally intriguing destinations like Europe, Canada, Alaksa, Great Britain and Hawaii.

**5427 American The Beautiful; National Parks & Federal Recreation Lands**
National Parks Service
1849 C St NW
Washington, DC 20240-1
202-208-6843
888-275-8747
FAX: 202-219-0910
e-mail: webteam@ios.doi.gov
www.nps.gov

*Mary A Bomar, CEO*
A free lifetime passport to federally operated parks, monuments, historic sites, recreation areas and wildlife refuges for persons who are blind or permanently disabled.

**5428 Anglo California Travel Service**
4250 Williams Rd
San Jose, CA 95129-3344
408-257-2257
FAX: 408-257-2664
www.acts4travel.com

*Audrey Cooper, President*
Plans for one and two week accessible tours.

**5429 Cunard Line**
6100 Blue Lagoon Dr
#400
Miami, FL 33126-2079
305-463-3000
800-528-6273
FAX: 305-463-3010
www.cunard.com

*Pamela C Conover, CEO*
Cunard Line, one of the world's most recognized brand names with a classic British heritage, operated by Cunard Line Limited, has provided the ultimate in deluxe ocean travel experience for the past 158 years. The fleet consists of famed liner Queen Elizabeth 2 and the Caronia, a classic ship formerly identified as Vistafjord. The Cunard Line brand, the epitome of British essence, focuses on recalling the golden age of sea travel for those who missed the first.

**5430 Dell Rapids Sportsmens Club**
P.O.Box 126
Dell Rapids, SD 57022-126
605-332-3387
FAX: 605-428-5502
e-mail: billybuckww@sio.midco.net
www.sdshootingsports.org

*Lowell Berehns, President*
Offers leage shooting for trap, as well as shooting on individual basis for archery, trap and pistol.

**5431 Diabetic Cruise Desk**
Hartford Holiday Travel
P.O.Box 536
Williston Park, NY 11596-536
516-746-6670
800-828-4813
FAX: 516-746-6690
e-mail: info@hartfordholidays.com
www.hartfordholidays.com

*Les Kertes, President*
Offers a seven-day cruise to Alaska for people with diabetes. Includes seminars on diabetes, self management, planning, special guidance for exercise classes and individual dietary advice.

**5432 Dialysis at Sea Cruises**
2504 Merchant Ave
Odessa, FL 33556-3468
727-518-7311
800-544-7604
FAX: 727-372-7396
e-mail: info@dialysisatsea.com
www.dialysisatsea.com

*Steve Debroux, Owner*
Been in the business of providing travel opportunities for persons on hemodialysis and CAPD since 1977. Handle all aspects of their travel and medical requirements. Not Sold Through Travel Agents! Make all reservations and coordinates the total set-up and operation of an onboard ship mobile dialysis clinic. Cruises run from seven days to three weeks and have departures from cities around the world on a variety of cruise lines.

**5433 Directions Unlimited Acccessible Tours**
Empress Travel
720 N. Bedford Rd
Bedford Hills, NY 10507-1508
914-241-1700
800-533-5343
FAX: 914-241-0243

*Lois Bonanni, Director*
*Charles Digiacomo, Manager*
Arrange vacations throughout the world for all disabilities including accessible cruises, African safari, rafting and scuba diving, European and Caribbean vacations.

**5434 Environmental Traveling Companions**
Fort Mason Center
Bldg. C
San Francisco, CA 94123
415-474-7662
FAX: 415-474-3919
e-mail: info@etctrips.org
www.etctrips.org

*Diane Poslosky, Executive Director*
Aids travelers regardless of physical or financial limitations to experience the beauty and challenge of the wilderness.

**5435 Flying Wheels Travel**
P.O.Box 382
Owatonna, MN 55060-382
507-451-5005
877-451-5006
FAX: 507-451-1685
e-mail: barbaraj@flyingwheelstravel.com
www.flyingwheelstravel.com

*Barbara Jacobson, Owner*
Arranges worldwide custom independent travel and cruises for the physically challenged.

**5436 Guide Service of Washington**
734 15th St NW
Suite # 701
Washington, DC 20005-1023
202-628-2842
FAX: 202-638-2812
e-mail: sales@dctourguides.com
www.dctourguides

*Neil Amrine, President*
A guide service offering tours of Washington DC and vicinity.

**5437 Guided Tour for Persons 17 & Over with Developmental and Physical Challenges**
7900 Old York Rd
Suite 111-B
Elkins Park, PA 19027-2310
215-782-1370
800-783-5841
FAX: 215-635-2637
e-mail: gtour400@aol.com
www.guidedtours.com

*Irwin Segal, Owner*
Offers unique travel and vacation programs for individuals with mild to moderate developmental disabilities. We publish a free Rates & Dates brochure twice a year.

**5438 Hostelling North America**
Hostelling International
8401 Colesville Road
Suite #600
Silver Spring, MD 20910-6339
301-495-1240
FAX: 301-495-6697
e-mail: hostels@hiusa.org
www.hiusa.org

*Demetria Trent, Manager*
Hostels are very inexpensive accommodations for travelers of all ages. They provide dorm-style sleeping rooms with separate quarters for males and females, fully equipped self-service kitchens, dining areas and common rooms for relaxing and socializing. HI-AYH has hostels in major cities, in national and state parks, near beaches and in the mountains. Send for a copy of Hostelling North America, a directory of hostels in U.S. and Canada, which lists hostels that are handicap accessible. *$ 3.00*
*400 pages Yearly*

**5439 Kayak and Rafting Expeditions**
17921 Us Highway 285
Nathrop, CO 81236-9701
719-539-6851
800-824-3795
FAX: 719-539-3378
e-mail: info@dvorakexpeditions.com
dvorakexpeditions.com

*Bill Dvorak, Owner*
This organization does river trips for people who are deaf, visually impaired, physically or mentally disabled. Rafting trips with groups and families and whitewater instruction.

**5440 New Courier Travel**
532 Duane St
Glen Ellyn, IL 60137-4695
630-469-0511
888-777-4453
FAX: 630-469-7390
www.travelcourierinc.com

*Fred Mueller, Owner*
Offers specialized assistance for independent travel or tours for persons with disabilities including cruises and travel in the USA and abroad. Fee charged for out-of-state clients, long-distance calls and clients who have free air.

**5441 New Directions Travel**
5276 Hollister Avenue
#207
Santa Barbara, CA 93111-3068
805-967-2841
888-967-2841
FAX: 805-964-7344
e-mail: info@newdirectionstravel.com
www.newdirectionstravel.com

*Dee Duncan, Executive Director*
A non-profit organization providing high quality local, national, and international travel vacations and holiday programs for people with mild to moderate developmental disabilities. Each year New Directions serves over 600 teenagers, adults and seniors who have brain impairments such as mild to moderate developmental disabilities, mental retardation, cerebral palsy , Down Syndrome and autism.

**5442 Norwegian Cruise Line**
7665 Corporate Center Drive
Miami, FL 33126-1201
305-436-4000
866-234-7350
FAX: 305-436-4117
www.ncl.com

*Colin Veitch, President*
Has accessible cabins but urges mobility impaired passengers to travel in the same cabin with a person who is not mobility impaired. Cruise fares vary.

**5443 ROW Adventures**
P.O. Box 579
Coeur D Alene, ID 83816
208-765-0841
800-451-6034
FAX: 208-667-6506
e-mail: info@rowadventures.com
rowadventures.com

*Peter Grubb, Owner*
Offers one to six day rafting trips to physically disadvantaged people. Designs custom itineraries, or trips with a special focus for small groups. For those with special dietary needs, they prepare special meals. So come ride the rapids and enjoy life. They also offer canoe trips aboard 34' voyager canoes along the trail of Lewis and Clark on Montana's upper Missouri River. Free brochure upon request.

5444 **Sundial Special Vacations**
750 Marine Dr.
Suite 100
Astoria, OR 97103
503-325-4536
800-547-9198
FAX: 503-325-4536
e-mail: pat@sundial-travel.com
www.sundialtour.com

*Terry Conner, VP*
Provides special vacations for developmentally disabled persons. Provides quality vacations for persons with developmental disabilities. Ratio is 1 for 7 or 1 for 5 depending on tour. Only two people to a room. Exciting destinations. 3 to 4 star properties. Great fun.

5445 **Ventures Travel**
6350 Indian Chief Rd
Eden Prairie, MN 55346-1619
952-852-0107
866-692-7400
FAX: 952-852-0123
e-mail: vt@venturestravel.org
www.venturestravel.org

*Georgann Ramsey, Manager*
A limited liability company is a service of Friendship Ventures-a nonprofit organization that has been enriching the lives of people with mental retardation and related developmental disabilities since 1985. Contact us to learn about our other programs, employment information, volunteer openings or donor opportunities.

5446 **Wheelchair Getaways**
P.O.Box 1098
Mukilteo, WA 98275-1098
425-353-8213
800-536-5518
FAX: 425-355-6159
e-mail: info@wheelchairgetaways.com
www.wheelchairgetaways.com

*Edward Van Artsdalen, Director*
Wheelchair Getaways, the largest wheelchair/scooter accessible van rental company in the US, has 50 franchise locations serving major cities and airports throughout the continental US and Hawaii. Rentals by the day, week, month or longer. Delivery/pickup available.

## Vehicle Rentals

5447 **ABC Union, ACE, ANLV, Vegas Western Cab**
5010 S Valley View Blvd
Las Vegas, NV 89118-1705
702-736-8383
FAX: 702-736-8813
www.lasvegas.net

*Phyllis Frias, President*
*Charles Frias, President*
Taxi service in Las Vegas that uses vans with wheelchair lifts at regular taxi rates.

5448 **Avis Rent A Car**
379 Parsippany Road
Parsippany, NJ 7054-5111
973-428-3900
e-mail: access@avis.com
www.avis.com

*F Robert Salerno, President*
Avis Access is a program of Avis Rent A Car that provides a full range of complementary products and services to drivers and passengers with physical disabilities. Renters can simply call the designated Avis Access Reservation line (888-TRY-HARDER) at 24 hours in advance. Products or services include transfer boards, hand controls, swivel seats, and more.

5449 **Consulting & Engineering for the Handicapped (CEH)**
4457 63rd Cir
Pinellas Park, FL 33781-5981
727-522-0364
866-244-1150
FAX: 727-522-9024
e-mail: ceh@liftsandramps.com
www.liftsandramps.com

*Al Crisp, Owner*
*Brenda Crisp, Owner*
New vans, used vans, specializing in quad conversions, all types of handicap equipment. Celebrating 33 years in business. Hand controls, lifts & ramps, porch lifts, hand-crank bikes.

5450 **Mobile Care**
6201 Riverdale Rd
Suite 101
Riverdale, MD 20737-2174
301-277-7371
FAX: 301-699-1865
e-mail: jaklimo@aol.com

*Maurice Naccache, Manager*
Specializing in non-emergency wheelchair service for the elderly and physically challenged.

5451 **National Car Rental System**
600 Terminal Drive
Fort Lauderdale, FL 33315-3618
954-359-3020
877-222-9058
888-826-6890
FAX: 954-359-8313
www.nationalcar.com

*William Decker, Manager*
Accommodates special requests subject to availability. Offers hand controls, bench seats, extra mirrors and vans with lifts at many major locations.

5452 **Northwest Limousine Service**
9950 Lawrence Ave
#314
Schiller Park, IL 60176-1216
847-698-0000
800-376-5466
e-mail: chiohare@aol.com
www.oharelimousine.com

*Sam Malas, Manager*
Offers wheelchair accessible mini vans, sedans, stretch and super stretch limousines for hourly or daily rental.

5453 **Over the Rainbow Disabled Travel Services& Wheelers Accessible Van Rentals**
186 Mehani Cir
Kihei, HI 96753-8072
808-879-5521
800-303-3750
FAX: 808-871-7533

*David McKown, VP*
Offers the disabled traveler Hawaii airport arrangements and ticketing accessible accommodations, hotels and condos including roll-in showers, Wheelers' Accessible Van Rentals on Maui and Honolulu or cars with hand controls, personal care attendants, medical or recreational equipment rentals and activities such as: helicopter rides, luau's, whalewatching, boating and more. Airfare varies from departure points and time of the year.

5454 **Public Technology**
US Department of Transportation
1301 Pennsylvania Ave NW
Washington, DC 20004
202-626-2400
FAX: 202-626-2498

*J Rutter, CEO*
One of a series of reports concerned with improving transportation for elderly and disabled persons.
*28 pages*

**5455 Rehabiliation Engineering Center for Personal Licensed Transportation**
University Of Virginia School Of Engineering
P.O.Box 400246
Charlottesville, VA 22904-4246 434-924-3072

*Tom Connors, VP*
*Mitch Rosen, Director*

**5456 Wheelchair Getaways Wheelchair/Scooter Accessible Van Rentals**
4443 Dixie Highway
Louisville, KY 40216-2864 502-363-4646
800-458-1115
FAX: 502-363-9756
e-mail: corporate@wheelchairgetaways.com
www.wheelchairgetaways.com

*Rebecca Heim, Manager*
*Moon Ko, Owner*
Rents wheelchair/scooter accessible vans by the day, week, month or longer and offers delivery to major airports and other convenient locations in more than 200 cities in 42 states and Puerto Rico. Also offers full size and mini vans with automatic lifts and ramps. Some vans are equipped with hand controls, six-way power seats and remote controls for powered door operation and lifts.

**5457 WheelersMarauatha Baptist Church**
9120 N 95th Avenue
Peoria, AZ 85345-2501 623-937-7866
800-456-1371
FAX: 623-934-3971

*Greg Iehl, Religious Leader, Pastor*
*Gene Noel, Assn't Pastor*
Offers delivery to airports in 29 states and Washington, D.C. In about 40 cities, Wheelers works directly with Avis Rent-a-Car. Wheelers offers a variety of van configurations with capacity for up to three wheelchairs, automatic ramps or lifts and nylon tie-downs, hand controls or other modifications.

**5458 Wheelers Accessible Van Rentals**
6614 W Sweetwater Ave
Glendale, AZ 85304-1040 602-418-5076
800-456-1371
FAX: 623-412-9920
e-mail: info@wheelersvanrentals.com
www.wheelersvanrentals.com

*Tammy Smith, President*
*Ron Smith, Corporate Treasurer*

# Veteran Services

## National Administrations

**5459 DAV National Service Headquarters**
807 Maine Ave SW
Washington, DC 20024-2410
202-554-3501
FAX: 202-554-3581
e-mail: feedback@davmail.org
www.dav.org

*David Gorman, Executive Director*
*David W Gorman, Executive Director*
Serves America's disabled veterans and their families. Direct services include legislative advocacy; professional counseling about compensation, pension, educational and job training programs and VA health care; and assistance in applying for those entitlements.

**5460 Department of Medicine and Surgery Veterans Administration**
810 Vermont Ave NW
Washington, DC 20420
202-273-8504
FAX: 202-273-9108
www.va.gov

*Gerald McDonald MD, Senior Consultant*
Provides hospital and outpatient treatment as well as nursing home care for eligible veterans in Veterans Administration facilities. Services elsewhere provided on a contract basis in the United States and its territories. Provides non-vocational inpatient residential rehabilitation services to eligible legally blinded veterans of the armed forces of the United States.

**5461 Department of Veterans Affairs Regional Office - Vocational Rehab Division**
380 Westminster St
Providence, RI 2903-3246
401-222-2488
800-827-1000
FAX: 401-254-1340
e-mail: dhs.state.ri.us/dhs/dvetsff.htm
www.va.gov

*Gerald E Allen, Counseling Officer*
Vocational rehabilitation is a program of services administered by the Department of Veterans Affairs for service members and veterans with service-connected physical or mental disabilities. If persons are compensibly disabled and are found in need of rehabilitation services because they have an employment handicap, this program can prepare them for a suitable job; get and keep that job; assist persons to become fully productive and independent.

**5462 Department of Veterans Benefits**
810 Vermont Ave NW
Washington, DC 20420
202-273-6763
800-827-1000
FAX: 202-275-3689
www.va.gov

*Daniel L Cooper, Manager*
*Joseph Thompson, Manager*
Furnishes compensation and pensions for disability and death to veterans and their dependents. Provides vocational rehabilitation services, including counseling, training, assistance and more towards employment, to blinded veterans disabled as a result of service in the armed forces during World War II, Korea and the Vietnam era; also provides rehabilitation services to certain peace-time veterans.

**5463 Disabled American Veterans**
P.O.Box 14301
Cincinnati, OH 45250-301
859-441-7300
877-426-2838
FAX: 859-441-1416
www.dav.org

*Chuck Lambert, Manager*
Advises veterans of their rights and employers of their obligations, under the Rehabilitation Act, the Americans with Disabilities Act, and legislation governing the employment and training of Vietnam era veterans with disabilities.

**5464 Federal Benefits for Veterans and Dependents**
Government Printing Office
810 Vermont Ave NW
Washington, DC 20420
202-273-6763
800-827-1000
FAX: 202-275-3689
www.vba.va.gov

*Daniel L Cooper, Manager*
Offers information on benefits for veterans and their families.
*93 pages*
*ISBN 0-16048 -58-*

**5465 Hospitalized Veterans Writing Project**
5920 Nall Ave #101
Shawnee Mission, KS 66202-3456
913-432-1214
FAX: 913-432-1214
e-mail: veteransvoices@sbcglobal.net
www.veteransvoices.org

*Priscilla Chansky, Administrator*
Individuals and organizations united to encourage VA veterans to write for pleasure and rehabilitation. Maintains speakers' bureau and audio tape version for the blind in Cooperation with Ku Audio. Bestows numerous monetary awards including article; book review; cartoon and drawing; light verse; poetry and short story.
*$15.00*
*64 pages Magazine*
*ISSN 0504-07 9*

**5466 US Department of Veterans Affairs National Headquarters**
1120 Vermont Ave NW
Washington, DC 20420-2
202-273-5400
800-827-1000
e-mail: washingtondc.query@vba.va.gov
www.va.gov

*Togo D West Jr, Secretary Veterans Affairs*
*Hershel W Gober, Deputy Secretary Vet. Affairs*
*R Nicholson, CEO*
Administers the laws providing benefits and other services to veterans, their dependents, and their beneficiaries. Acts as their principal advocate in ensuring that they recieve medical care, benefits, social support, and lasting memorials promoting the health, welfare, and dignity of all veterans in recognition of their service to this nation. As the DVA heads into the 21st century, they will strive to meet the needs of the Nation's veterans today and tomorrow. Publishes a monthly magazine.
*80 pages*

**5467 US Veteran's Affairs**
810 Vermont Ave NW
Washington, DC 20420-2
202-273-5400
800-827-1000
www.va.gov

*Robert H Roswell, Manager*
*Michael J Kussman, Deputy Under Secretary For Healt*
Provides a wide range of services for those who have been in the military and their dependents, as well as offering information on driver assessment and education programs.

## Alabama

**5468 Alabama VA Regional Office**
Veterans Benefits Administration, U S Dept. of V A
345 Perry Hill Rd
Montgomery, AL 36109-4551
800-827-1000
FAX: 334-213-3565
e-mail: montgomery.query@vba.va.gov
www.va.gov

*Joe Morris, Val Representative*
*William Rumph, Val Representative*

**5469 Alabama Veterans Facility**
809 Green Springs Hwy
Homewood, AL 35209-4917
205-916-2700
www.birmingham.va.gov

*Robert B Herndon, Manager*

Veterans medical clinic offering disabled veterans medical treatments.

**5470 Birmingham VA Medical Center**
Veterans Health Administration U S Dept. of V A
700 South 19th Street
Birmingham, AL 35233-1927
205-933-8101
800-827-1000
e-mail: g.vhacss@forum.va.gov
www.birmingham.va.gov

*Kurt C Bachmann, Director of Palliative Care*

**5471 Central Alabama Veterans Healthcare System**
Veterans Health Administration, US Dept. of VA
215 Perry Hill Rd
Montgomery, AL 36109-3798
334-272-4670
800-214-8387
e-mail: g.vhacss@forum.va.gov
www.centralalabama.va.gov

*Kenneth Ruyle, Executive Director*

**5472 Tuscaloosa VA Medical Center**
Veterans Health Administration, U S Dept. of V A
3701 Loop Rd
Tuscaloosa, AL 35404-5015
205-554-2000
888-269-3405
FAX: 205-554-2845
www.tuscaloosa.va.gov

*Todd Hooper, Director*
*John Goldman, Executive Director*

## Alaska

**5473 Anchorage Regional Office**
Veterans Benefits Administration, U S Dept. of V A
1201 North Muldoon Rd
Anchorage, AK 99504
800-827-1000
e-mail: anchorage.query@vba.va.gov
www.va.gov

*Claude M Kicklighter, Chief Staff*
*Alex Spector, Executive Director*

**5474 DAV Department of Alaska**
2925 Debarr Rd
Room 3101
Anchorage, AK 99508-2983
907-257-4803
FAX: 907-258-9828
www.davmembersportal.org

*Walter Crary, Treasurer*
*Robert Boles, Sr. Vice President*

## Arizona

**5475 Carl T Hayden VA Medical Center**
Veterans Health Administration, U S Dept. of V A
650 E Indian School Rd
Phoenix, AZ 85012-1839
602-277-5551
800-554-7174
FAX: 602-222-6472
e-mail: g.vhacss@forum.va.gov
www.phoenix.va.gov

*D Gregg Gordon, President*
*Marva Greene, Vice President*
*John Fears, CEO*

**5476 Northern Arizona VA Health Center**
Veterans Health Administration, US Dept. of VA
500 Hwy 89N
Prescott, AZ 86313-5001
928-445-4860
800-949-1005
FAX: 928-768-6076
e-mail: g.vhacss@forum.va.gov
www.prescott.va.gov

*Deborah Thompson, Manager*

**5477 Southern Arizona VA Healthcare System**
Veterans Health Administration, U S Dept. of V A
3601 S 6th Ave
Tucson, AZ 85723
520-792-1450
800-470-8262
FAX: 520-629-1818
e-mail: g.vhacss@forum.va.gov
www.tucsan.va.gov

*Michael T Ammann, State Director*
*Jerry Colye, Manager*

## Arkansas

**5478 Eugene J Towbin Healthcare Center**
Veterans Health Administration, U S Dept. of V A
2200 Fort Roots Dr
North Little Rock, AR 72114-1706
501-257-1000
800-827-1000
FAX: 501-257-1779
e-mail: g.vhacss@forum.va.gov
www.littlerock.va.gov

**5479 Fayetteville VA Medical Center**
Veterans Health Administration, US Dept. of VA
1100 N College Ave
Fayetteville, AR 72703-1944
479-443-4301
800-691-8387
e-mail: g.vhacss@forum.va.gov
www.fayettevillear.va.gov

**5480 John L McClellan Memorial Hospital**
Veterans Health Administration, US Dept. of VA
4300 W 7th St
Little Rock, AR 72205-5446
501-257-1000
800-827-1000
e-mail: g.vhacss@forum.va.gov
www.littlerock.va.gov

*Michael Winn, Executive Director*

**5481 North Little Rock Regional Office**
Veterans Benefits Administration, U S Dept. of V A
2200 Fort Roots Drive
Building 65
N Little Rock, AR 72114-1756
501-370-3820
800-827-1000
FAX: 501-370-3829
e-mail: littlerock.query@vba.va.gov
www.va.gov

*David Fletcher, Manager*
*Doyle Batey, Deputy Director*

## California

**5482 Jerry L Pettis Memorial VA Medical Center**
Veterans Health Administration, U S Dept. of V A
11201 Benton St
Loma Linda, CA 92357-1000
909-825-7084
800-741-8387
e-mail: g.vhacss@forum.va.gov
www.lomalinda.va.gov

*James D Anholm, Director*
*Dean Stordahl, President*

**5483 Long Beach VA Medical Center**
Veterans Health Administration, U S Dept. of V A
5901 E 7th St
Long Beach, CA 90822-5201
562-826-8000
800-827-1000
888-769-8387
e-mail: g.vhacss@forum.va.gov
www.longbeach.va.gov

*Stephen B Davis, Director*
*Eric Yamaura, Director*
*Melinda Pettersen, Executive Director*

**5484 Los Angeles Regional Office**
Veterans Benefits Administration, U S Dept. of V A
11000 Wilshire Blvd
Los Angeles, CA 90024-3602
800-827-1000
e-mail: losangeles.query@vba.va.gov
www.va.gov

*Karl Lorenz, Work Group Leader*

**5485 Martinez Center for Rehab & Extended Care**
Veterans Health Administration, U S Dept. of V A
150 Muir Rd
Martinez, CA 94553-4668
925-372-2000
800-382-8387
e-mail: g.vhacss@forum.va.gov
www.va.gov

*John H Simms, Director*

**5486 Oakland VA Regional Office**
Veterans Benefits Administration U S Dept. of V A
1301 Clay Street
12th Floor
Oakland, CA 94612-5217
800-827-1000
e-mail: oakland.query@vba.va.gov
www.benefits.va.gov/oakland

*Geri Spearman, Director*

**5487 Rehabilitation Research and Development Center**
Department of Veteran s Affairs
3801 Miranda Ave
Palo Alto, CA 94304-1207
650-493-5000
FAX: 650-493-4919
e-mail: jaffe@roses.stanford.edu
www.rehad.research.va.gov

*Loretta V Barrow, Administrator*
*Louis Fajardo, MD*
*David L Jaffe MS, Research Biomedical Engineer*

The VA Center of Excellence on Mobility in Palo Alto, CA is dedicated to developing innovative clinical treatments and assistive devices for veterans with physical disabilities to increase their independence and improve their quality of life. The clinical emphasis of the center is to improve mobility, either ambulation or manipulation, in individuals with neurologic impairments or orthopaedic impairments. We do not publish any printed books, journals or periodicals.

**5488 Sacramento Medical Center**
Veterans Health Administration U S Department of V
10535 Hospital Way
Mather, CA 95655-4200
916-843-7000
800-382-8387
e-mail: g.vhacss@forum.va.gov
www.northerncalifornia.va.gov

*Gail Crimmins-Wiggins, Director*

**5489 San Diego VA Regional Office**
Veterans Benefits Administration, U S Dept. of V A
8810 Rio San Diego Dr
San Diego, CA 92108-1698
858-552-8585
800-827-1000
FAX: 858-552-7436
e-mail: oakland.query@vba.va.gov
www.vba.va.gov/ro/sandiego

*Janet M Peyton, Administrative Officer*

**5490 VA Central California Health Care Syste**
Veterans Health Administration, U S Dept. of V A
2615 E Clinton Ave
Fresno, CA 93703-2223
559-225-6100
888-826-2838
FAX: 559-268-6911
e-mail: g.vhacss@forum.va.gov
www.fresno.va.gov

*Sukhvir S Atwal, Director*
*Susan Shyshka, Associate Director*
*Alan Perry, Executive Director*

**5491 VA Greater Los Angeles Healthcare System**
Veterans Health Administration U S Deptartment of
11301 Wilshire Blvd
Los Angeles, CA 90073-1003
310-478-3711
800-827-1000
FAX: 310-268-4848
e-mail: g.vhacss@forum.va.gov
www.losangeles.va.gov

*Irene Bratti, CEO*

**5492 VA Northern California Healthcare System**
Veterans Health Administration, U S Dept. of V A
150 Muir Rd
Martinez, CA 94553-4668
925-372-2000
800-382-8387
e-mail: g.vhacss@forum.va.gov
www.northerncalifornia.va.gov

*Lawrence Sander, Director*

5493 **VA San Diego Healthcare System**
Veterans Health Administration, U S Dept. of V A
3350 La Jolla Village Dr
San Diego, CA 92161
858-552-8585
800-331-8387
e-mail: g.vhacss@forum.va.gov
www.sandiego.va.gov

*Imawati Budihardjo, Secretary Veterans Affairs*
*Claude M Kicklighter, Chief of Staff*

## Colorado

5494 **Boulder Vet Center**
2336 Canyon Blvd
Suite 103
Boulder, CO 80302
303-440-7306
FAX: 303-449-3907
www.va.gov

*Michael L Holliday, Manager*
Offers trauma and readjustment from military and civilian life counseling and assistance with disability claims, military benefits and employment are provided.

5495 **Colorado/Wyoming VA Medical Center**
Veterans Benefits Administration U S Dept. of V A
155 Van Gordon St
Suite 395
Lakewood, CO 80225
303-914-2680
800-827-1000
e-mail: denver.query@vba.va.gov
www.denver.va.gov

*Forest Farley Jr, Medical Center Director*
*Thomas E Bowen, Chief of Staff*

5496 **Denver VA Medical Center**
Veterans Health Administration, U S Dept. of V A
1055 Clermont St
#6A138
Denver, CO 80220-3808
303-393-2869
888-336-8262
e-mail: g.vhacss@forum.va.gov
www.denver.va.gov

*Lynnette Roth, Executive Director*

5497 **Grand Junction VA Medical Center**
Veterans Health Administration
2121 North Ave
Grand Junction, CO 81501-6428
970-242-0731
866-206-6415
FAX: 970-244-1300
e-mail: g.vhacss@forum.va.gov
www.grandjunction.va.gov

*Claude M Kicklighter, Chief of Staff*
*Michael Murphy, Manager*

## Connecticut

5498 **Hartford Regional Office**
Veterans Benefits Administration U S Department of
555 Willard Ave
Newington, CT 6111-2631
860-666-6951
800-827-1000
e-mail: hartford.query@vba.va.gov
www.connecticut.va.gov

*Jeanette A Chirico Post, Network Director*

5499 **Hartford Vet Center**
25 Elm St
Suite A
Rocky Hill, CT 6067-2305
860-563-8800
FAX: 860-563-8805
e-mail: donna.hryb@med.va.gov
www.va.gov

*Donna Hryb LCSW, Team Leader*
*Urania Petit BA, Office Manager*
A U.S. Department of Veterans Affairs counseling center offering counseling to Vietnam era and combat veterans. Sexual trauma/harassment counseling, medical screening and benefit referral is available to all veterans.

5500 **VA Connecticut Healthcare System: Newington Division**
Veterans Health Administration U S Department. of
555 Willard Ave
Newington, CT 6111-2631
860-666-6951
800-827-1000
FAX: 860-667-6764
e-mail: g.vhacss@forum.va.gov
www.connecticut.va.gov

*Shutish Patel, Providence Director*
The mission of VA Connecticut Healthcare Systems is to fulfill a nation's commitment to its veterans by providing quality healthcare, promoting health through prevention and maintaining excellence in teaching and research. Provides primary, secondary and tertiary care in medicine, geriatrics, neurology, psychiatry and surgery with an operating capacity of 211 hospital beds.

5501 **VA Connecticut Healthcare System: West Haven**
Veterans Health Administration, U S Dept. of V A
950 Campbell Ave
West Haven, CT 6516-2770
203-932-5711
800-827-1000
FAX: 203-937-3868
e-mail: g.vhacss@forum.va.gov
www.connecticut.va.gov

*Charles A Morgan Iii, Secretary Veteran Affairs*
*Claude Kicklighter, Chief of Staff*
*Roger Johnson, Administrator*

## Delaware

5502 **Delaware VA Regional Office**
Veterans Benefits Administration U S Dept. of V A
1601 Kirkwood Hwy
Wilmington, DE 19805-4917
302-994-2511
800-827-1000
e-mail: wilmington.query@vba.va.gov
www.wilmington.va.gov

*Martin F Konwinski, Research/Development Coordinator*
*Dexter Dix, Executive Director*

5503 **Wilmington VA Medical**
Veterans Health Administration, US Dept. of VA
1601 Kirkwood Hwy
Wilmington, DE 19805-4917
302-994-2511
800-461-8262
FAX: 302-633-5516
e-mail: g.vhacss@forum.va.gov
www.wilmington.va.gov

*Dexter Dix, Executive Director*

5504 **Wilmington Vet Center**
1601 Kirkwood Hwy
Wilmington, DE 19805-4917
302-994-2511
800-461-8262
FAX: 302-633-5250
www.wilmington.va.gov

*Mark A Kaufki EdD, Team Leader*
Veterans counseling program offering individual counseling services, advocacy services and group counseling. The focus is the counseling of all veterans coping with the aftermath of war, sexual abuse/harassment in the military and all veterans of the Vietnam era. The center also has an active outreach program to seek veterans needing services. Hours of operation are between 8:00 AM - 4:30 PM, Monday - Friday and other times by appointment only. Services are free.

## District of Columbia

5505 **Disabled American Veterans, National Service & Legislative Headquarters**
807 Maine Ave SW
Washington, DC 20024-2410
202-554-3501
FAX: 202-554-3581
dav.org

*David Gorman, Executive Director*
*Paul W Jackson, Vice Chairman*

5506 **PVA Sports and Recreation Program**
Paralyzed Veterans of America
801 18th St NW
Washington, DC 20006-3517
202-872-1300
800-424-8200
FAX: 202-785-4432
e-mail: info@pva.org
www.pva.org

*Randy Pleva, President*
*Randy Pleza, President*

5507 **VA Medical Center, Washington DC**
50 Irving St NW
Washington, DC 20422-1
202-745-8000
800-827-1000
888-553-0242
www.washingtondc.va.gov

*David J West, Associate Medical Center*
*Ross D Fletcher, Chief of Staff*
Acute general and specialized services in medicine, surgery, neurology, and psychiatry.

5508 **Washington DC VA Medical Center**
Veterans Health Administration, U S Dept. of V A
50 Irving St NW
Washington, DC 20422-1
202-745-8000
800-827-1000
FAX: 202-754-8530
e-mail: g.vhacss@forum.va.gov
www.washingtondc.va.gov

*James R Nicholson, Secretary of Veterans Affairs*
*Claude M Kicklighter, Chief of Staff*
*Bina Lakhanpal, MD*

## Florida

5509 **Bay Pines VA Medical Center**
Veterans Health Administration, U S Dept. of V A
10000 Bay Pines Blvd
P.O. Box 5005
Bay Pines, FL 33744
727-398-6661
800-827-1000
888-820-0230
e-mail: g.vhacss@forum.va.gov
www.baypines.va.gov

*Jeffery J Abraham, Medical Director*
*Kaye Green, Assistant Medical Director*
*Smith Jenkins, CEO*

5510 **Gainesville Division, North Florida/South Georgia Veterans Healthcare System**
Veterans Health Administration, U S Dept. of V A
1601 SW Archer Rd
Gainesville, FL 32608-1611
352-376-1611
800-324-8387
FAX: 352-379-7445
e-mail: g.vhacss@forum.va.gov
www.northflorida.va.gov/northflorida

*Claude M Kicklighter, Chief of Staff*
*Frederick Malphurs, Chief Executive Officer*

5511 **James A Haley VA Medical Center**
Veterans Health Administration, U S Dept. of V A
13000 Bruce B Downs Blvd
#T72
Tampa, FL 33612-4745
813-972-7662
800-827-1000
888-811-0107
e-mail: g.vhacss@forum.va.gov
www.tampa.va.gov

*M Stephen Farber, Secretary of Veterans Affairs*
*Claude M Kicklighter, Chief of Staff*
*Edgar Bueno, MD*

5512 **Miami VA Medical Center**
Veterans Health Administration, U S Dept. of V A
1201 NW 16th St #B822
Miami, FL 33125-1693
305-324-4455
800-827-1000
888-276-1785
FAX: 305-575-3266
e-mail: g.vhacss@forum.va.gov
www.miami.va.gov

*Stephen Luckus, CEO*

5513 **St. Petersburg Regional Office**
Veterans Benefits Administration, U S Dept. of V A
9500 Bay Pines Blvd
St Petersburg, FL 33708
727-319-7492
800-827-1000
e-mail: stpete.query@vba.va.gov
www.va.gov

*Warren McPherson, Executive Director*

5514 **West Palm Beach VA Medical Center**
Veterans Health Administration, U S Dept. of V A
7305 N Military Trl
West Palm Beach, FL 33410-7417
561-422-8262
800-972-8262
FAX: 561-882-6707
e-mail: g.vhacss@forum.va.gov
www.westpalmbeach.va.gov

*Claude M Kicklighter, Chief of Staff*
*Andre Desgroseillers, MD*

## Georgia

**5515 Atlanta Regional Office**
Veterans Benefits Administration, U S Dept. of V A
Atlanta, GA 30308-1210
404-463-3100
800-827-1000
FAX: 404-463-3105
e-mail: atlanta.query@vba.va.gov
www.va.gov

*Chick Krautler, Executive Director*

**5516 Atlanta VA Medical Center**
Veterans Health Administration, U S Dept. of V A
1670 Clairmont Rd
Decatur, GA 30033-4004
404-321-6111
800-827-1000
FAX: 404-728-7734
e-mail: g.vhacss@forum.va.gov
www.atlanta.va.gov

*Octavian Ioachimescu, Secretary of Veterans Affairs*
*Claude M Kicklighter, Chief of Staff*
*Thomas Cappello, CEO*

**5517 Augusta VA Medical Center**
Veterans Health Administration, U S Dept. of V A
1 Freedom Way
Augusta, GA 30904-6258
706-733-0188
800-827-1000
FAX: 706-731-7227
e-mail: g.vhacss@forum.va.gov
www.agusta.va.gov

*R James Nicholson, Secretary of Veterans Affairs*
*Claude Kicklighter, Chief of Staff*
*James Trustley III, CEO*

**5518 Carl Vinson VA Medical Center**
Veterans Health Administration, U S Dept. of V A
1826 Veterans Blvd
Dublin, GA 31021-3699
478-272-1210
FAX: 478-277-2717
e-mail: dana.doles@med.va.gov
www.dublin.va.gov

*Sailaja Bandi, Chief of Staff*
*Richard Fry, Chief Executive Officer*

**5519 Southeastern Paralyzed Veterans of America(PVA)**
4010 Deans Bridge Rd
U.S. Highway 1
Hephzibah, GA 30815-5616
706-796-6301
800-292-9335
FAX: 706-796-0363
e-mail: paravet@comcast.net
www.southeasternpva.com

*David Vaughn, President*
*Janice Weatherford, Executive Director*
*Homer Cole, Vice President*
*Alphonso Evans Jr, Secretary*
Works to maximize the quality of life for its members and all people with SCI/D as a leading adovocate for healthcare, SCI/D research and education, veteran's benefits, and rights, accessibility and the removal of architectural barriers, sports programs, and disability rights.

## Hawaii

**5520 Hawaii Veterans Centers**
Hilo Vet Center
70 Lanihuli St
Hilo, HI 96720-2067
808-969-3833
FAX: 808-969-2025
www.va.gov

*Felipe Usales, Director*
*Steven R Reeves, RCS4B Regional Manager*
Veterans medical clinic offering disabled veterans medical treatments, readjustment and PTSD counseling to combat veterans

**5521 Honolulu VBA Regional Office**
Veterans Benefits Administration, U S Dept. of V A
300 Ala Monana Blvd
Honolulu, HI 96850-1
808-566-1412
800-827-1000
e-mail: honolulu.query@vba.va.gov
www.vba.va.gov/ro/honolulu

*Claude M Kicklighter, Chief of Staff*
*Alan Furuno, Manager*

**5522 Pacific Islands Health Care System**
Veterans Health Administration, US Dept. of VA
459 Patterson Rd
Honolulu, HI 96819-1522
808-433-0600
800-827-1000
FAX: 808-433-0390
e-mail: g.vhacss@forum.va.gov
www.hawaii.va.gov

## Idaho

**5523 Boise Regional Office**
Veterans Benefits Administration, U S Dept. of V A
444 W. Fort Street
Boise, ID 83702-4531
800-827-1000
e-mail: boise.query@vba.va.gov
www.va.gov

*Jim Vance, Director*
*Pat Teague, Service Officer*
*Tom Ressler, Manager*

**5524 Boise VA Medical Center**
Veterans Health Administration, U S Dept. of V A
500 W Fort St
Boise, ID 83702-4531
208-422-1000
800-827-1000
FAX: 208-422-1326
e-mail: g.vhacss@forum.va.gov
www.boise.va.gov

*Jennifer T Shalz, Chief of Staff*

## Illinois

**5525 Edward Hines Jr Hospital**
Veterans Health Administration, U S Dept. of V A
5000 South 5th Avenue
Hines, IL 60141
708-202-8387
800-827-1000
FAX: 708-202-2684
e-mail: g.vhacss@forum.va.gov
www.hines.va.gov

*Franco Laghi, Administrative Officer*

5526 **Marion VA Medical Center**
Veterans Health Administration U S Department of V
2401 W Main St
Marion, IL 62959-1188
618-997-5311
800-827-1000
e-mail: g.vhacss@forum.va.gov
www.marion.va.gov

5527 **North Chicago VA Medical Center**
Veterans Health Administration, U S Dept. of V A
3001 North Green Bay Rd
North Chicago, IL 60064-3048
847-688-1900
800-827-1000
e-mail: g.vhacss@forum.va.gov
www.va.gov

*Lorraine Roth, Chief of Staff*
*John Avramidis, MD*

5528 **VA Illiana Health Care System**
Veterans Health Administration, U S Dept. of V A
1900 E Main St
Danville, IL 61832-5198
217-554-3000
800-320-8387
FAX: 217-554-4552
e-mail: g.vhacss@forum.va.gov
www.danville.va.gov

*Betsy Sleath, Chairman*

## Indiana

5529 **Indianapolis Regional Office**
Veterans Benefits Administration U S Department of
575 N Pennsylvania St
Indianapolis, IN 46204-1563
317-226-7860
800-827-1000
e-mail: indianapolis.query@vba.va.gov
www.benefits.va.gov/indianapolis

5530 **Richard L Roudebush VA Medical Center**
Veterans Health Administration, U S Dept. of V A
1481 W 10th St
Indianapolis, IN 46202-2803
317-554-0000
800-827-1000
FAX: 317-554-0127
e-mail: g.vhacss@forum.va.gov
www.indianapolis.va.gov

*Claude M Kicklighter, Chief of Staff*
*Becky Hall, Manager*

5531 **VA North Indiana Health Care System: Fort Wayne Campus**
Veterans Health Administration, U S Dept. of V A
2121 Lake Ave
Fort Wayne, IN 46805-5100
260-426-5431
800-360-8387
e-mail: g.vhacss@forum.va.gov
www.northernindiana.va.gov

*J Akhtar, Director*
*Cathi Spivey-Paul, Executive Director*

5532 **VA Northern Indiana Health Care System: Marion Campus**
Veterans Health Administration, U S Dept. of V A
1700 E 38th St
Marion, IN 46953-4568
765-674-3321
800-360-8387
e-mail: g.vhacss@forum.va.gov
www.northernindiana.va.gov

*Claude M Kicklighter, Chief of Staff*
*Cathi Spivey-Paul, Executive Director*

## Iowa

5533 **Des Moines VA Medical Center**
Veterans Health Administration, U S Dept. of V A
3600 30th St
Des Moines, IA 50310-5753
515-699-5999
800-827-1000
FAX: 515-699-5862
e-mail: g.vhacss@forum.va.gov
www.centraliowa.va.gov

*Claudia M Kicklighter, Chief of Staff*

5534 **Des Moines VA Regional Office**
Veterans Benefits Administration, U S Dept. of V A
210 Walnut Street
Des Moines, IA 50309-2115
515-323-7580
800-827-1000
e-mail: leander@vba.va.gov
www.va.gov

*Rich Anderson, Service Director*

5535 **Iowa City VA Medical Center**
Veterans Health Administration, U S Dept. of V A
601 Highway 6 West
Iowa City, IA 52240-2202
319-338-0581
866-687-7382
FAX: 319-339-7171
e-mail: g.vhacss@forum.va.gov
www.iowacity.va.gov

*Kirt A Sickels, Public Affairs Officer*
*Gary Wilkinson, Administrator*
Tertiary care facility, affiliated teaching hospital, and research center seving an aging veteran populatiaon in eastern Iowa and western Illinois. Satellite clinics are located in Bettendord, Dubuque, and Waterloo, Iowa and in Quincy and Galesburg, Illinois.

5536 **Knoxville VA Medical Center**
Veterans Health Administration, U S Dept. of V A
1515 W Pleasant St
Knoxville, IA 50138-3399
641-842-3101
800-816-8878
FAX: 641-828-5124
e-mail: g.vhacss@forum.va.gov
www.centraliowa.va.gov

*Claudia M Kicklighter*

5537 **VA Central Iowa Health Care System**
3600 30th St
Des Moines, IA 50310-5753
515-699-5999
800-294-8387
FAX: 515-699-5862
www.centraliowa.va.gov

*Kirby D Amonson, Executive Program Manager*
*Donald Cooper, Executive Director*
Fulfilling the promise is our primary mission.

## Kansas

5538 **Colmery-O'Neil VA Medical Center**
Veterans Health Administration, U S Dept. of V A
2200 SW Gage Blvd
Topeka, KS 66622
785-350-3111
800-574-8387
e-mail: g.vhacss@forum.va.gov
www.topeka.va.gov

*Jerry L Calhoun, Chairman*

**5539 Dwight D Eisenhower VA Medical Center**
Veterans Health Administration, U S Dept. of V A
4101 4th Street Trafficway
Leavenworth, KS 66048-5014
913-682-2000
800-952-8387
e-mail: g.vhacss@forum.va.gov
www.leavenworth.va.gov

*Donald L Courtney, Research/Development Coordinator*
*Deborah Fulk, Administrative Officer*
*Arnulfo Sulit, MD*

**5540 Kansas VA Regional Office**
Veterans Benefits Administration, U S Dept. of V A
5500 E Kellogg Dr
Wichita, KS 67218-1607
800-827-1000
e-mail: wichita.query@vba.va.gov
www.benefits.va.gov/wichita

*Edgar L Tucker, Medical Center Director*

**5541 Robert J Dole VA Medical Center**
Veterans Health Administration, U S Dept. of V A
5500 E Kellogg Dr
Wichita, KS 67218-1607
316-685-2221
888-827-6881
FAX: 316-651-3666
e-mail: g.vhacss@forum.va.gov
www.wichita.va.gov

*Sardar Bahadur, Exectuve Director*

For over 70 years, the Dole VA Medical and Regional office center has been honored to serve Kansas area veterans. The center provides a full range of primary and specialty acute and extended care services to veterans in 59 counties of Kansas. Special emphasis programs include substance abuse, post traumatic stress disorder (PTSD), women's health, spinal cord injury, visual impairment, prosthetic and sensory aids, and homeless services.

## Kentucky

**5542 Lexington VA Medical Center**
Veterans Health Administration, U S Dept. of V A
1101 Veterans Dr
Lexington, KY 40502-2235
859-233-4511
800-352-4000
e-mail: g.vhacss@forum.va.gov
www.lexington.va.gov

**5543 Louisville VA Medical Center**
Veterans Health Administration, U S Dept. of V A
800 Zorn Ave
Louisville, KY 40206-1433
502-287-4000
800-376-8387
e-mail: g.vhacss@forum.va.gov
www.louisville.va.gov

*Leslie Beavers, Director*

**5544 Louisville VA Regional Office**
Veterans Benefits Administration, U S Dept. of V A
800 Zorn Avenue
Louisville, KY 40206-1433
502-287-4000
800-376-8387
e-mail: louisville.query@vba.va.gov
www.louisville.va.gov

*Gene Brainer, Regional Officer*

## Louisiana

**5545 Alexandria VA Medical Center**
Department of Veterans Affairs
2495 Shreveport Highway
Pineville, LA 71360-9004
318-473-0010
800-375-8387
FAX: 318-483-5029
e-mail: g.vhacss@forum.va.gov
www.alexandria.va.gov

*Hollis Reed, Chief of Staff*
*Barbara C Watkins, Medical Center Director*
*Evelyn Caliste, EEO Program Manager*

**5546 New Orleans VA Medical Center**
Veterans Health Administration, U S Dept. of V A
1601 Perdido St
New Orleans, LA 70112-1262
504-412-3700
800-935-8387
FAX: 504-589-5210
e-mail: Stacie.Rivera@med.va.gov
www.neworleans.va.gov

*John D Church Jr, Medical Director/President*
*Fernando Rivera, Association Medical Center Direc*
*Sam Lucero, Special Assistant to Director*
*Stacie M Rivera, Public Affairs Officer*

A teaching hospital, providing a full range of patient care services, with state-of-the-art technology as well as education and research. Comprehensive health care is provided through primary care, tetiary care, and long-term care in areas of medicine, surgery, psychiatry, physical medicine and rehabilitation, neurology, oncology, dentistry, geriatrics, and extended care.

**5547 Shreveport VA Medical Center**
Veterans Health Administration, U S Dept. of V A
510 E Stoner Ave
Shreveport, LA 71101-4295
318-221-8411
800-827-1000
www.shreveport.va.gov

*Dorothy Jarzabak, Manager*
*Ali R Mansouri, Acting Acos/R&D*
*Gracie Specks, CEO*

## Maine

**5548 Maine VA Regional Office**
Veterans Benefits Administration, U S Dept. of V A
1 VA Center
Augusta, ME 4330-6719
207-623-8411
877-421-8263
e-mail: togus.query@vba.va.gov
www.va.gov

*Dale Demers, Director*
*Scott Karczewski, Manager*

**5549 Togus VA Medical Center**
Veterans Health Administration, U S Dept. of V A
1 VA Center
Augusta, ME 4330-6796
207-623-8411
877-421-8263
FAX: 207-623-5792
e-mail: g.vhacss@forum.va.gov
www.togus.va.gov

*John H Sims Jr, Executive Director*
*John Sims, Executive Director*

## Maryland

**5550 Baltimore Regional Office**
Veterans Benefits Administration, U S Dept. of V A
31 Hopkins Plz
Baltimore, MD 21201-2825 800-827-1000
e-mail: baltimore.query@vba.va.gov
www.va.gov

*Jerry L Calhoun*

**5551 Baltimore VA Medical Center**
Veterans Health Administration, U S Dept. of V A
10 N Greene St
Baltimore, MD 21201-1524 410-605-7000
800-463-6295
FAX: 410-605-7901
e-mail: g.vhacss@forum.va.gov
www.maryland.va.gov

*Katheleen Z Andrews, Administrative Officer*
*Peggy Wess, Research Contact*
*Dennis Smith, Executive Director*

**5552 Fort Howard VA Medical Center**
Veterans Health Administration, U S Dept. of V A
9600 N Point Rd
Fort Howard, MD 21052-3050 410-477-1800
800-351-8387
FAX: 410-477-7177
e-mail: md.veterans@erols.com
www.mdva.state.md.us

*Thomas Hutchins, Secretary*

**5553 Maryland Veterans Centers**
10 N Greene St
Baltimore, MD 21201-1524 410-605-7000
800-463-6295
FAX: 410-605-7901
www.maryland.va.gov

*J Y Jacks, Manager*
*Dennis H Smith, Executive Director*
Veterans medical clinic offering disabled veterans medical treatments.

**5554 Perry Point VA Medical Center**
Veterans Health Administration, U S Dept. of V A
Circle Drive
Perry Point, MD 21902 410-642-2411
800-949-1003
FAX: 410-642-1165
e-mail: g.vhacss@forum.va.gov
www.maryland.va.gov

*Dennis Smith, Executive Director*
*Allice Krupski, Assistant Director of Operations*

**5555 VA Maryland Health Care System**
10 N Greene St
Baltimore, MD 21201-1524 410-605-7000
800-463-6295
FAX: 410-605-7900
www.maryland.va.gov

*Christopher Bever, Director*
*Bruce Kaup, MD*
A dynamic and exciting health care organization that is dedicated to providing quality, compassionate and accessible care and service to Maryland's veterans. As a part of one of the largest health care systems in the United States, the VAMHCS has a reputation as a leader in veterans' health care, reserch and education. Provides comprehensive service to veterans including medical, surgical, rehabilitative, nurological and mental health care on both an inpatient and outpatient basis.

## Massachusetts

**5556 Boston VA Regional Office**
Veterans Benefits Administration, U S Dept. of V A
15 New Sudbury Street JFK Bldg
Boston, MA 2203-9928 617-232-9500
800-827-1000
e-mail: boston.query@vba.va.gov
www.boston.va.gov

*Liza Catucci, Administrative Officer*
*Michael Lawson, President*

**5557 Edith Nourse Rogers Memorial Veterans Hospital**
Veterans Health Administration U S Deptartment of
200 Springs Rd Bldg #23
Bedford, MA 1730-1114 781-687-2000
800-827-1000
FAX: 781-687-3536
e-mail: g.vhacss@forum.va.gov
www.bedford.va.gov

*Michael Mayo-Smith, Manager*

**5558 Northampton VA Medical Center**
Veterans Health Administration, U S Dept. of V A
421 N Main St
Leeds, MA 1062 413-584-4040
800-827-1000
e-mail: g.vhacss@forum.va.gov
www.northhampton.va.gov

*Richard Woloss, Manager*

**5559 VA Boston Healthcare System: Brockton Division**
Veterans Health Administration, U S Dept. of V A
940 Belmont St
Brockton, MA 2301-5596 508-583-4500
800-865-3384
FAX: 617-323-7700
e-mail: g.vhacss@forum.va.gov
www.boston.va.gov

*Tom Kelly, Commissioner*
*Richard Spicer, Director of Operations*
*Christine Croteau, Manager*

**5560 VA Boston Healthcare System: Jamaica Plain Campus**
Veterans Health Administration, U S Dept. of V A
150 S Huntington Ave
Boston, MA 2130-4817 617-232-9500
800-865-3384
FAX: 617-278-4549
e-mail: g.vhacss@forum.va.gov
www.boston.va.gov

*Nancy E Naguib, Research Compliance Officer*
*Geraldine McGlynn, Director*
*Michael Lawson, President*

**5561 VA Boston Healthcare System: West Roxbury Division**
Veterans Health Administration, U S Dept. of V A
1400 VFW Pkwy
West Roxbury, MA 2132-4927 617-323-7700
800-865-3384
e-mail: g.vhacss@forum.va.gov
www.boston.va.gov

*Susan A Mac Kenzie, Associate Director*

## Michigan

**5562 Aleda E Lutz VA Medical Center**
Veterans Health Administration, U S Dept. of V A
1500 Weiss St
Saginaw, MI 48602-5251
989-497-2500
800-827-1000
FAX: 989-791-2428
e-mail: g.vhacss@forum.va.gov
www.saginaw.va.gov

*Emily Houle, Research Contact*
*Menahem Lender, Research/Development Coordinator*
*Robert Sabin, Executive Director*

**5563 Battle Creek VA Medical Center**
Veterans Health Administration, U S Dept. of V A
5500 Armstrong Rd
Battle Creek, MI 49037-7314
269-966-5600
800-827-1000
888-214-1247
FAX: 269-966-5483
e-mail: g.vhacss@forum.va.gov
www.battlecreek.va.gov

*Ronald W Kelley, Research/Development Coordinator*
*Elinor J Pettee, Research/Development Coordinator*
*Alice Wood, Manager*

**5564 Iron Mountain VA Medical Center**
Veterans Health Administration, U S Dept. of V A
325 East H Street
Iron Mountain, MI 49801-4760
906-774-3300
800-827-1000
FAX: 906-779-3114
e-mail: g.vhacss@forum.va.gov
www.ironmountain.va.gov

*C L Holmes MD, Chief Of Staff*
*Janice Boss, Administrator*

**5565 John D Dingell VA Medical Center**
Veterans Health Administration, U S Dept. of V A
4646 John R St
Detroit, MI 48201-1916
313-576-1000
800-827-1000
FAX: 313-576-1112
e-mail: g.vhacss@forum.va.gov
www.detroit.va.gov

*Waseem Ullah, Administrative Officer*

**5566 Michigan VA Regional Office**
Veterans Benefits Administration, U S Dept. of V A
Rm 1400
477 Michigan Ave
Detroit, MI 48226-1217
800-827-1000
e-mail: detroit.query@vba.va.gov
www.benefits.va.gov/detroit

*Keith Thompson, Director*
*Dennis W Paradowski, Assistant Director*

**5567 VA Ann Arbor Healthcare System**
Veterans Health Administration, U S Dept. of V A
2215 Fuller Rd
Ann Arbor, MI 48105-2303
734-769-7100
FAX: 734-761-7870
e-mail: g.vhacss@forum.va.gov
www.annarbor.va.gov

*Rodney A Hayward, Director*
*Susan A Zuk, Administrative Officer*
*James Roseborough, Executive Director*
Accepting eligible veterans.

**5568 Vet Center Readjustment Counseling Service**
1940 Eastern Ave SE
Grand Rapids, MI 49507-2771
616-285-5795
FAX: 616-285-5898
www.va.gov

*William Busby, Executive Director*
*Branden K Lyon, Counselor*
*Lynn Hall, Clinical Coordinator*
Providing a broad range of counseling outreach and referral services to eligible veterans in order to help make readjustments to cilvilian life.

## Minnesota

**5569 Minneapolis VA Medical Center**
Veterans Health Administration, U S Dept. of V A
1 Veterans Dr
Minneapolis, MN 55417-2399
612-725-2158
866-414-5058
FAX: 612-725-2049
e-mail: g.vhacss@forum.va.gov
www.minneapolis.va.gov

*Hanna E Bloomfield, Director*
*Dana M Chesness, Project Coordinator*

**5570 St. Cloud VA Medical Center**
Veterans Health Administration, U S Dept. of V A
4801 Veterans Dr
Saint Cloud, MN 56303-2015
320-252-1670
800-827-1000
FAX: 320-255-6472
e-mail: g.vhacss@forum.va.gov
www.stcloud.va.gov

*Lucinda M Marty, Research/Development Coordinator*

**5571 St. Paul Regional Office**
Veterans Benefits Administration, U S Dept. of V A
1 Federal Dr
Fort Snelling, MN 55111-4080
800-827-1000
e-mail: stpaul.query@vba.va.gov
www.benefits.va.gov/stpaul

*Vincent Crawford, Director*

**5572 Vet Center**
405 E Superior St. #160
Duluth, MN 55802-2240
218-722-8654
FAX: 218-723-8212
www.vetcenter.va.gov

*Cynthia Macaulay MEd, Counselor*
*Rob Evanson, Counselor*
*Debbie Burt, Office Manager*
Counseling, social services and benefits assistance for combat veterans and those sexually traumatized in the military.

## Mississippi

**5573 Biloxi/Gulfport VA Medical Center**
Veterans Health Administration, U S Dept. of V A
400 Veterans Ave
Biloxi, MS 39531-2410
228-523-5000
800-296-8872
FAX: 228-563-2898
e-mail: g.vhacss@forum.va.gov
www.biloxi.va.gov

*Kimberly Morgan, Administrative Officer*

**5574 Jackson Regional Office**
Veterans Benefits Administration, U S Dept. of V A
1600 E Woodrow Wilson Ave
Jackson, MS 39216-5100
601-364-7000
800-827-1000
FAX: 601-364-7007
e-mail: jackson.query@vba.va.gov
www.benefits.va.gov/jackson

*Neil Anthony Mcphie, Chairman*
*Barbara Sapin, Vice Chairman*

## Missouri

**5575 Harry S Truman Memorial Veterans' Hospital**
Veterans Health Administration, U S Dept. of V A
800 Hospital Dr
Columbia, MO 65201-5275
573-814-6000
800-827-1000
FAX: 573-814-6551
e-mail: g.vhacss@forum.va.gov
www.columbiamo.va.gov

*Larry L Propp, Executive Director*
*Lawrence Propp, Administrative Officer*

**5576 John J Pershing VA Medical Center**
Veterans Health Administration, U S Dept. of V A
1500 N Westwood Blvd
Poplar Bluff, MO 63901-3318
573-778-4786
800-827-1000
FAX: 573-778-4156
e-mail: g.vhacss@forum.va.gov
www.popularbluff.va.gov

*Ginny Sartini, Research/Development Coordinator*
*Linda Haga, Research Contact*

**5577 Kansas City VA Medical Center**
Veterans Health Administration, U S Dept. of V A
4801 E Linwood Blvd
Kansas City, MO 64128-2226
816-861-4700
800-827-1000
e-mail: g.vhacss@forum.va.gov
www.kansascity.va.gov

*Kenneth Grasing, Research/Development*
*Ram Sharma, Administrative Officer*
*Kent Hill, Executive Director*

The Kansas City VA Medical Center is a modern, well-equipped teriary care inpatient and outpatient center. As the third largest teaching hospital in the metropolitan area, it maintains educational affiliations with the University of Kansas School of Medicine.

**5578 St. Louis Regional Office**
Veterans Benefits Administration, U S Dept. of V A
400 S 18th St
Saint Louis, MO 63103-2265
800-827-1000
e-mail: stlouis.query@vba.va.gov
www.stlouis.va.gov

**5579 St. Louis VA Medical Center**
Veterans Health Administration, U S Dept. of V A
915 N Grand Blvd
Saint Louis, MO 63106-1621
314-589-6333
800-827-1000
FAX: 314-289-7009
e-mail: g.vhacss@forum.va.gov
www.stlouis.va.gov

*Dolores Minor, Administrative Officer*

## Montana

**5580 Montana VA Regional Office**
3633 Veterans Drive
Fort Harrison, MT 59636-188
406-442-7310
800-827-1000
www.va.gov

**5581 V A Montana Healthcare System**
U S Dept. of V A
P.O.Box 1500
Fort Harrison, MT 59636-1500
406-442-6410
877-468-8387
FAX: 406-447-7916
e-mail: ftharrison.query@vba.va.gov
www.montana.va.gov

*Susan Epstein, Pateint Representative*

This is a complete, medically reliable dictionary of congenital malformations and disorders. As the authors explain, 'Down syndrome is the only common congenital disorder, the other defects and disorders are rare or very rare, some having been reported fewer than 20 times worlwide.' This dictionary covers them all. Examples: Aagenaes syndrome, Acrocallosal syndrome, and Acrodysostosis

**5582 VA Montana Healthcare System**
Veterans Health Administration, U S Dept. of V A
1892 William St
Fort Harrison, MT 59636
406-447-7945
800-827-1000
FAX: 406-447-7965
e-mail: g.vhacss@forum.va.gov
www.montana.va.gov

*Joseph Underkofel, Executive Director*
*Gregory Johnson, MD*

**5583 Vet Center**
Readjusment Counciling Service Western Mountain Re
2795 Enterprise Ave., Suite 1
Billings, MT 59102-3238
406-657-6071
FAX: 406-657-6603
www.va.gov

*Bob Phillips, Manager*
*Luanne Anderson, Office Manager*
*Barry Osgard MS, Counselor*

Readjustment counseling service for counseling veterans who are having difficulty adjusting from military service especially those diagnosed with PTSD.

## Nebraska

**5584 Grand Island VA Medical System**
Veterans Health Administration, U S Dept. of V A
2201 N Broadwell Ave
Grand Island, NE 68803-2153
308-382-3660
800-827-1000
e-mail: g.vhacss@forum.va.gov
www.nebraska.va.gov/visitors/grand_island.asp

*John Hilbert, Executive Director*
*Daniel L Parker, Deputy Director*

**5585 Lincoln Regional Office**
Veterans Benefits Administration, U S Dept. of V A
3800 Village Dr.
Lincoln, NE 68501-4103
402-471-4444
800-827-1000
FAX: 402-479-5124
e-mail: lincoln.query@vba.va.gov
www.veteranprograms.com

*Bill Gibson, CEO*
*Daniel Parker, Deputy Director*

**5586 Lincoln VA Medical Center**
Veterans Health Administration, U S Dept. of V A
600 S 70th St
Lincoln, NE 68510-2451
402-489-3802
800-827-1000
FAX: 402-486-7860
e-mail: g.vhacss@forum.va.gov
www.nebraska.va.gov/visitors/lincoln.asp

*Ryon L Adams, Research/Development Coordinator*

**5587 VA Nebraska-Western Iowa Health Care System**
Veterans Health Administration, U S Dept. of V A
4101 Woolworth Ave
Omaha, NE 68105-1850
402-449-0610
800-451-5796
FAX: 402-449-0684
www.nebraska.va.gov

*Doug Corum, Manager*
*Rowen Zetterman, Chief of Staff*

## Nevada

**5588 Las Vegas Veterans Center**
1919 S. Jones, Suite A
Las Vegas, NV 89146-905
702-251-7873
FAX: 702-388-6664
www.lasvegas.va.gov

*Daryl Harding, Resident Counselor LCSW*
*Matt Watson, Team Leader MSW*
Veterans clinical counseling center for veterans and their dependent individual and group counseling, marital and family counseling, alcohol and drug assessment referral or treatment. Community education and consultation, employment counseling.

**5589 Reno Regional Office**
Veterans Benefits Administration U S Deptartment o
1000 Locust St
Reno, NV 89502-2597
775-328-1486
800-827-1000
FAX: 775-328-1447
e-mail: reno.query@vba.va.gov
www.reno.va.gov

*Joseph E Dardillo, Administrative Officer*

**5590 VA Sierra Nevada Healthcare System**
Veterans Health Administration, U S Dept. of V A
1000 Locust St
Reno, NV 89502-2597
775-786-7200
888-838-6256
FAX: 775-328-1816
e-mail: https://iris.custhelp.com
www.reno.va.gov

*Carmela Cipollina, Acting Aces/Research/Development*
*Angela Fisher, Manager*

**5591 VA Southern Nevada Healthcare System**
Veterans Health Administration, U S Dept. of V A
901 Rancho Ln
Las Vegas, NV 89106-3836
702-636-3000
800-827-1000
FAX: 707-636-3027
e-mail: g.vhacss@forum.va.gov
www.lasvegas.va.gov

*Chuck Fulkerson, Executive Director*
*Steve Long, Deputy Director*

## New Hampshire

**5592 Manchester Regional Office**
Veterans Benefits Administration, U S Dept. of V A
275 Chestnut St
Manchester, NH 3101-2411
800-827-1000
e-mail: manchester.query@vba.va.gov
www.va.gov

*Jerry Beale, Director*

**5593 Manchester VA Medical Center**
Veterans Health Administration, U S Dept. of V A
718 Smyth Rd
Manchester, NH 3104-7007
603-624-4366
800-892-8384
e-mail: g.vhacss@forum.va.gov
www.va.gov

*Marc Levenson, Executive Director*

**5594 New Hampshire Veterans Centers**
103 Liberty St
Manchester, NH 3104-3118
603-668-7060
800-562-3127
FAX: 603-666-7404
www.va.gov

*Caryl Ahern, Manager*
*Paulette Landry, Office Manager*
Veterans clinic offering combat veterans outpatient counseling

## New Jersey

**5595 Disabled American Veterans: Ocean County**
P.O.Box 1806
Toms River, NJ 8754-1806
732-929-0907
e-mail: bvenga@thecore.com
community.nj.com/cc/dav24

*Mary Bencivenga, Contact*

**5596 East Orange Campus of the VA New Jersey Healthcare System**
385 Tremont Ave
East Orange, NJ 07018-1023
973-676-1000
FAX: 973-676-4226
www.va.gov

*Kenneth Mizrach, CEO*

**5597 Lyons Campus of the VA New Jersey Healthcare System**
Veterans Health Administration, U S Dept. of V A
151 Knollcroft Rd
Lyons, NJ 7939-5001
908-647-0180
800-827-1000
FAX: 908-647-3452
e-mail: g.vhacss@forum.va.gov
www.newjersey.va.gov

*James J Farsetta, Director*
*Donna Henderson, Coordinator*

**5598 Newark Regional Office**
Veterans Benefits Administration, U S Dept. of V A
20 Washington Pl
Newark, NJ 7102-3174
800-827-1000
e-mail: newark.query@vba.va.gov
www.va.gov

*Stephen G Abel, Deputy Commissioner for Veterans*

## New Mexico

**5599 New Mexico State Veterans' Home**
992 South Broadway
Truth or Consequences, NM 87901-927
575-894-4200
800-964-3976
FAX: 575-894-4270
www.nmveteranshome.org/index/shtml

*Lori S Montgomery, Administrator*
*Carol B Wilson, Admission Coordinator*
Veterans medical clinic offering disabled veterans medical treatments.

**5600 New Mexico VA Healthcare System**
Veterans Health Administration, US Dept. of VA
1501 San Pedro Dr SE
Albuquerque, NM 87108-5154
505-265-1711
800-465-8262
FAX: 505-256-2855
e-mail: g.vhacss@forum.va.gov
www.va.gov

*Norman Brownel, Executive Director*

## New York

**5601 Albany VA Medical Center: Samuel S Stratton**
Veterans Health Administration, U S Dept. of V A
113 Holland Ave
Albany, NY 12208-3410
518-626-5000
800-233-4810
888-838-7890
FAX: 518-626-5500
e-mail: g.vhacss@forum.va.gov
www.va.gov

*Donald W Stuart, Associate Director (Interim)*
*Linda W Weiss, Director*
*Laurdes Irzarry, Chief of Staff*
*Deborah Spath, Associate Director for Patient/N*

**5602 Albany Vet Center**
Ste 2
17 Computer Dr W
Albany, NY 12205-1618
518-458-7998
FAX: 518-458-8613

*Lloyd Mc Omber, Owner*
*Melodie Krahula, Team Leader*
Provides readjustment counseling for combat veterans and also provides benefits and job counseling for all veterans.

**5603 Bath VA Medical Center**
Veterans Health Administration U S Deptartment of
76 Veterans Avenue
Bath, NY 14810
607-664-4000
800-827-1000
888-823-9659
FAX: 607-664-4000
e-mail: g.vhacss@forum.va.gov
www.va.gov

*David B Krueger, Acting Medical Center Director*
*Felipe Diaz, Chief of Staff*
*Shirley A Pikula, Associate Director for Patient/N*

**5604 Bronx VA Medical Center**
Veterans Health Administration, U S Dept. of V A
130 W Kingsbridge Rd
Bronx, NY 10468-9938
718-584-9000
800-877-6976
FAX: 718-733-1223
e-mail: g.vhacss@forum.va.gov
www.va.gov

*MaryAnn P Musumeci, Director*
*Vincent F Immiti, Associate Director*
*Erik Langhoff, Chief of Staff*
*Kathleen M Capitulo, Associate Director for Patient C*

**5605 Brooklyn Campus of the VA NY Harbor Healthcare System**
Veterans Health Administration, U S Dept. of V A
800 Poly Place
Brooklyn, NY 11209-7104
718-836-6600
800-827-1000
e-mail: g.vhacss@forum.va.gov
www.va.gov

*Martina A Parauda, Director*
*Veronica J Foy, Associate Director, Facilities &*
*Michael S Simberkoff, Executive Chief of Staff*
*Elizabeth H Weinshel, Deputy Chief of Staff*

**5606 Buffalo Regional OfficeDepartment of Veterans Affairs**
Veterans Benefits Administration
130 South Elmwood Avenue
Buffalo, NY 14202-2465
716-852-3028
800-827-1000
www.va.gov

**5607 Canandiagua VA Medical Center**
Veterans Health Administration, U S Dept. of V A
400 Fort Hill Ave
Canandaigua, NY 14424-1159
585-394-2000
800-204-1442
e-mail: g.vhacss@forum.va.gov
www.va.gov

*Craig S Howard, Medical Center Director*
*Margaret Owens, Associate Director*
*Dr. Robert B Babcock, Chief of Staff*
*Patricia Hryzak Lind, Associate Director for Patient/N*

**5608 Castle Point Campus of the VA Hudson Valley Healthcare System**
Veterans Health Administration, U S Dept. of V A
Route 9D
Castle Point, NY 12511
845-831-2000
800-827-1000
FAX: 845-838-5193
e-mail: g.vhacss@forum.va.gov
www.va.gov

*Gerald F Culliton, Director*

**5609 New York City Campus of the VA NY Harbor Healthcare System**
Veterans Health Administration, U S Dept. of V A
423 E 23rd St
New York, NY 10010-5011
212-686-7500
800-827-1000
FAX: 718-567-4082
e-mail: g.vhacss@forum.va.gov
www.va.gov

*Camille R Varacchi, Administrative Officer*

**5610 New York Regional Office**
Veterans Benefits Administration, U S Dept. of V A
245 W Houston St
New York, NY 10014-4805
212-714-0699
800-827-1000
FAX: 212-807-4042
e-mail: newyork.query@vba.va.gov
www.va.gov

*Ronna Brown, President*

**5611 Northport VA Medical Center**
Veterans Health Administration, U S Dept. of V A
79 Middleville Rd
Northport, NY 11768-2296
631-261-4400
800-827-1000
FAX: 631-266-6710
e-mail: g.vhacss@forum.va.gov
www.va.gov

*Philip C Moschitta, Medical Center Director*
*Rosie A Chatman, Associate Director for Patient &*
*Maria Favale, Associate Director*
*Edward Mack, Chief of Staff*

**5612 Syracuse VA Medical Center**
Veterans Health Administration, U S Dept. of V A
800 Irving Ave
Syracuse, NY 13210-2716
315-425-4400
800-792-4334
888-838-7890
e-mail: g.vhacss@forum.va.gov
www.va.gov

*James Cody, VA Medical Center Director*
*Michael Swartz, Associate Medical Center Directo*
*William H Marx, Chief of Staff*
*Nancy Schmid, Associate Director for Patient/N*

**5613 Torah Alliance of Families of Kids with Disabilities**
T AF KI D
1433 Coney Island Ave
Brooklyn, NY 11230-4119
718-252-2236
FAX: 718-252-2216
e-mail: tafkid@worldnet.att.net
www.tafkid.org

*Juby Shapiro, Manager*
Serves over 1k families whose children have a variety of disabilities and special needs. Many of these families are large families in the low socioeconomic level. Offers monthly meetings, guest lectures, parent matching, information of new developments in software, technology and techniques, sibling support groups, pen pal lists, audio and video library, alternative medicine and nutrition information and education on legal awareness and rights of disabled citizens.

**5614 VA Hudson Valley Health Care System**
Veterans Health Administration, U S Department of
2094 Albany Post Road
Montrose, NY 10548-1454
914-737-4400
FAX: 845-788-4244
www.va.gov

*James J Farsette, Network Director*
*Michael Sabo, Executive Director*

**5615 VA Western NY Healthcare System, Batavia**
Veterans Health Administration, U S Dept. of V A
222 Richmond Ave
Batavia, NY 14020-1227
585-297-1000
800-827-1000
e-mail: g.vhacss@forum.va.gov
www.va.gov

*William F Feeley, Medical Center Director*
*Miguel Rainstein, Chief of Staff*
*Jason C Petti, Associate Medical Center Directo*
*Royce Calhoun, Assistant Director*

**5616 VA Western NY Healthcare System, Buffalo**
Veterans Health Administration, U S Dept. of V A
3495 Bailey Ave
Buffalo, NY 14215-1129
716-834-9200
800-532-8387
www.va.gov

*William F Feeley, Medical Center Director*
*Miguel Rainstein, Chief of Staff*
*Jason C Petti, Associate Medical Center Directo*
*Royce Calhoun, Assistant Director*

## North Carolina

**5617 Asheville VA Medical CenterCharles George**
Veterans Health Administration, U S Dept. of V A
1100 Tunnel Rd
Asheville, NC 28805-2043
828-298-7911
800-932-6408
FAX: 828-299-2502
e-mail: g.vhacss@forum.va.gov
www.va.gov

*Joseph Schimansky, Executive Director*
*Brian Peek, R&D Coordinator*

**5618 Charlotte Vet Center**
2114 Ben Craig Drive
Charlotte, NC 28262-2350
704-549-8025
FAX: 704-549-8261
www.va.gov

*Loretta Deaton, Team Leader*
*Cynthia Algra, Office Manager*
*Billy Moore, Counselor*
*Melissa L Saunders, Counsilor*
Preadjustment Counseling for Combat Veterans with Post Traumatic Stress Disorder (PTSD).

**5619 Durham VA Medical Center**
Veterans Health Administration, U S Dept. of V A
508 Fulton St
Durham, NC 27705-3875
919-286-0411
800-827-1000
888-878-6890
FAX: 919-286-5944
e-mail: leola.jenkins@med.va.gov
www.va.gov

*Ralph T Gigliotti, Director*
*Rudy A Klopfer, Associate Director*
*John D Shelburne, Chief of Staff*
*Kathryn Ward-Presson, Associate Director for Nursing P*

5620 **Fayetteville VA Medical Center**
Veterans Health Administration, U S Dept. of V A
2300 Ramsey St
Fayetteville, NC 28301-3856
910-488-2120
800-771-6106
FAX: 910-822-7926
e-mail: g.vhacss@forum.va.gov
www.va.gov

*Elizabeth Goolsby, Director*
*James Galkowski, Associate Director, Operations*
*Jesse Howard III, Acting Chief of Staff*
*Joyce Alexander-Hines, Associate Director, Patient Care*

5621 **WG Hefner VA Medical CenterSalisbury**
Vet Health Administration U S Department of VA
1601 Brenner Ave
Salisbury, NC 28144-2515
704-638-9000
800-469-8252
FAX: 704-638-3395
e-mail: g.vhacss@forum.va.gov
www.va.gov

*Paul M Russo, Director*
*Anthony L Dawson, Associate Medical Center Directo*
*Randy D Readling, Chief of Staff (Interim)*
*Sarah D Williams, Associate Director for Patient C*

5622 **Winston-Salem Regional Office**
Veterans Benefits Administration, U S Dept. of V A
251 N Main St
Winston-Salem, NC 27155-2
336-768-5560
800-827-1000
FAX: 336-768-7295
TTY: 800-829-4833
e-mail: winsalem.query@vba.va.gov
www.va.gov

*Glenn Cobb, Executive VP*

## North Dakota

5623 **Fargo VA Medical Center**
Veterans Health Administration, U S Dept. of V A
2101 North Elm
Fargo, ND 58102-2417
701-232-3241
800-410-9723
FAX: 701-239-7166
e-mail: g.vhacss@forum.va.gov
www.va.gov

*Michael J Murphy, Healthcare Center Director*
*Dale DeKrey, Associate Director for Operation*
*J Brian Hancock, Chief of Staff*
*Julie Bruhn, Associate Director for Patient C*

5624 **North Dakota VA Regional OfficeFargo Regional Office**
Veterans Benefits Administration, U S Dept. of V A
2101 Elm St N
Fargo, ND 58102-2417
701-451-4690
800-827-1000
FAX: 701-451-4690
e-mail: fargo.query@vba.va.gov
www.va.gov

*Thomas Santoro, Director Research Department*

## Ohio

5625 **Chillicothe VA Medical Center**
Veterans Health Administration, U S Dept. of V A
17273 State Route 104
Chillicothe, OH 45601-9718
740-773-1141
800-358-8262
888-838-6446
FAX: 740-772-7023
e-mail: g.vhacss@forum.va.gov
www.va.gov

*Jeffery T Gering, Medical Center Director*
*Keith Sullivan, Associate Medical Center Directo*
*Deborah M Meesig, Chief of Staff*
*Ruth Yerardi, Associate Director for Patient C*

5626 **Cincinnati VA Medical Center**
Veterans Health Administration, U S Dept. of V A
3200 Vine St
Cincinnati, OH 45220-2213
513-861-3100
800-827-1000
888-267-7873
FAX: 513-475-6500
e-mail: g.vhacss@forum.va.gov
www.va.gov

*Linda Smith, Director*
*David Ninneman, Associate Director*
*Sydney Steinberg, Chief of Staff*

5627 **Cleveland Regional Office**
Veterans Benefits Administration, U S Dept. of V A
1240 E 9th St
Cleveland, OH 44199-2068
800-827-1000
FAX: 216-522-8262
e-mail: cleveland.query@vba.va.gov
www.va.gov

*P Hunter Peckham, Director*
*Robert Ruff, Assistant Director*
*William Bunkley, Minority Veterans Program Coordi*

5628 **Dayton VA Medical Center**
Veterans Health Administration U S Department of V
4100 W 3rd St
Dayton, OH 45428-9000
937-268-6511
800-368-8262
888-838-6446
FAX: 937-262-2170
e-mail: g.vhacss@forum.va.gov
www.va.gov

*William D Montague, Acting Director*
*Terry E Taylor, Associate Director*
*William Germann, Acting Chief of Staff*
*Anna Jones, Associate Director, Patient Care*

5629 **Louis Stokes VA Medical CenterWade Park Campus**
Veterans Health Administration, U S Dept. of V A
10701 East Blvd
Cleveland, OH 44106-1702
216-791-3800
800-827-1000
888-838-6446
FAX: 440-838-6017
e-mail: g.vhacss@forum.va.gov
www.va.gov

*Susan M Fuehrer, Medical Center Director*
*Darwin Goodspeed, Associate Medical Center Directo*
*Susan Nelson, Deputy Medical Center Director*
*Dr. Murray D Altose, Chief of Staff*

## Oklahoma

**5630 Jack C. Montgomery VA Medical Center**
Veterans Benefits Administration, U S Dept. of V A
1011 Honor Heights Dr
Muskogee, OK 74401-1318
918-577-3000
800-827-1000
e-mail: muskogee.query@vba.va.gov
www.va.gov

*Alef Nancy Graham, Manager*

**5631 Jack C. Montomery VA Medical Center**
1011 Honor Heights Dr
Muskogee, OK 74401-1318
918-577-3000
800-827-1000
e-mail: muskogee.query@vba.va.gov
www.va.gov

*Brian A Hawkins, Director*
*Bryan C Matthews, Associate Director*
*Karen H Gribbin, Chief of Staff*
*Bonnie R Pierce, Associate Director for Patient C*

**5632 Oklahoma City VA Medical Center**
Veterans Health Administration, U S Dept. of V A
921 NE 13th St
Oklahoma City, OK 73104-5007
405-456-1000
800-827-1000
FAX: 405-270-1560
www.va.gov

*David P Wood, Director*
*Anne Kreutzer, Associate Director*
*Mark Huycke, Chief of Staff*
*Donna DeLise, Associate Director for Patient C*

**5633 Oklahoma Veterans Centers Vet Center**
3033 N Walnut Ave
Ste W101
Oklahoma City, OK 73105-2833
405-270-5184
FAX: 405-270-5125

*Peter Sharp, Manager*
*Steve Kenzie, Owner*
PTSP counseling for all combat Veterans and victims of sexual trauma/sexual harassment.

## Oregon

**5634 Oregon Health Sciences University**
3181 SW Sam Jackson Park Rd
Portland, OR 97239-3098
503-494-8311
ohsu.edu

*Joe Robertson, President*
*James Morgan, Executive Director*
Offers services for the totally blind, legally blind, visually impaired, mentally retarded blind and more with health, counseling, educational, recreational, rehabilitation, computer training and professional training services.

**5635 Portland Regional Office**
Veterans Benefits Administration, U S Dept. of V A
100 SW Main St, Floor 2
Portland, OR 97204-2802
503-373-2388
800-827-1000
e-mail: portland.query@vba.va.gov
www.va.gov

**5636 Portland VA Medical Center**
Veterans Health Administration, U S Dept. of V A
3710 SW U.S. Veterans Hospital Rd.
Portland, OR 97239-2964
503-220-8262
800-949-1004
FAX: 503-273-5319
e-mail: g.vhacss@forum.va.gov
www.va.gov

*John E Patrick, Director*
*David Stockwell, Deputy Director of Administratio*
*Tom Anderson, Chief of Staff*
*Kathleen M Chapman, Deputy Director for Patient Care*

**5637 Roseburg VA Medical Center**
Veterans Health Administration, U S Dept. of V A
913 NW Garden Valley Blvd
Roseburg, OR 97470-6523
541-440-1000
800-549-8387
FAX: 541-440-1225
e-mail: g.vhacss@forum.va.gov
www.va.gov

*Jim Willis, Director*
*Mark Traines, MD*

**5638 Southern Oregon Rehabilitation Center & Clinics**
Veterans Health Administration, U S Dept. of V A
8495 Crater Lake Hwy
White City, OR 97470
541-826-2111
800-809-8725
FAX: 541-830-3500
e-mail: g.vhacss@forum.va.gov
www.va.gov

*George Andries, Executive Director*

## Pennsylvania

**5639 Butler VA Medical Center**
Veterans Health Administration, U S Dept. of V A
325 New Castle Rd
Butler, PA 16001-2418
724-282-7171
800-362-8262
FAX: 724-282-7640
e-mail: g.vhacss@forum.va.gov
www.va.gov

*Patricia Nealon, Director*
*Richard W Cotter, Associate Director*
*Sharon Parson, Nurse Executive*
*Timothy Burke, Chief of Staff*

**5640 Coatesville VA Medical Center**
Veterans Health Administration, U S Dept. of V A
1400 Blackhorse Hill Rd
Coatesville, PA 19320-2040
610-384-7711
800-290-6172
888-558-3812
e-mail: g.vhacss@forum.va.gov
www.va.gov

*Gary Devansky, Director*
*James F Tischler, Chief of Staff*
*Rosemary Wharton, Associate Director Patient Care*
*Robin Aube-Warren, Associate Director*

**5641 Erie VA Medical Center**
Veterans Health Administration, U S Dept. of V A
135 E 38th Street Blvd
Erie, PA 16504-1559
814-868-8661
800-274-8387
888-860-2124
FAX: 814-860-2425
e-mail: g.vhacss@forum.va.gov
www.va.gov

*Michael Adelman, Medical Center Director*
*Melissa Sundin, Associate Medical Center Directo*
*Dr. Anthony Behm, Chief of Staff*
*Dorene Sommers, Associate Director for Patient C*

**5642 James E Van Zandt VA Medical Center**
Veterans Health Administration, U S Dept. of V A
2907 Pleasant Valley Blvd
Altoona, PA 16602-4377
814-943-8164
800-827-1000
FAX: 814-940-7898
e-mail: g.vhacss@forum.va.gov
www.va.gov

*Cecil B Hengeveld, Director*
*Gerald Williams, Executive Director*

**5643 Lebanon VA Medical Center**
Veterans Health Administration, U S Dept. of V A
1700 S Lincoln Ave
Lebanon, PA 17042-7597
717-272-6621
800-409-8771
FAX: 717-228-5907
e-mail: g.vhacss@forum.va.gov
www.va.gov

*Robert (Bob) Callahan Jr., Director*
*William H Mills, Associate Director*
*Kanan Chatterjee, Chief of Staff*
*Margaret G Wilson, Associate Director for Patient C*

**5644 Pennsylvania Veterans Centers**
Veterans Health Administration, U S Department of
1000 State St
Ste 2
Erie, PA 16501
717-861-8901
800-478-8
FAX: 717-861-8589
www.va.gov

*Cecil B Hengeveld, Deputy Adjustant General*
Veterans medical clinic offering disabled veterans medical treatments.

**5645 Philadelphia Regional Office and Insurance Center**
Veterans Benefits Administration, U S Dept. of V A
5000 Wissahickon Ave
Philadelphia, PA 19144-4867
215-336-3003
800-827-1000
FAX: 215-336-5542
e-mail: phillyro.query@vba.va.gov
www.va.gov

*Sonny Dicrecchio, Executive Director*

**5646 Philadelphia VA Medical Center**
Veterans Health Administration, U S Dept. of V A
3900 Woodland Avenue
Philadelphia, PA 19104
215-823-5800
800-949-1001
e-mail: g.vhacss@forum.va.gov
www.va.gov

*Joseph M Dalpiaz, Director*
*Ralph Schapira, Chief of Staff*
*Margaret O'Shea Caplan, Associate Director for Finance*
*Patricia O'Kane, Acting Associate Director for Cl*

**5647 Pittsburgh Regional Office**
Veterans Benefits Administration U S Deparment of
1000 Liberty Avenue
Pittsburgh, PA 15222
412-688-6100
800-827-1000
FAX: 412-688-6121
e-mail: pittsburgh.query@vba.va.gov
www.va.gov

*Micahel E Moreland*

**5648 VA Pittsburgh Healthcare System, University Drive Division**
Veterans Health Administration, U S Dept. of V A
University Dr
Pittsburgh, PA 15240-2400
412-688-6000
800-827-1000
FAX: 412-688-6901
e-mail: g.vhacss@forum.va.gov
www.va.gov

*Timothy Mar Carlos, CEO*

**5649 VA Pittsburgh Healthcare System, Highland Drive Division**
Veterans Health Administration, U S Dept. of V A
7180 Highland Dr
Pittsburgh, PA 15206-1206
412-688-6000
800-827-1000
FAX: 412-365-4213
e-mail: g.vhacss@forum.va.gov
www.va.gov

*Kristin Best, Deputy Adjutant General*
*Roger Sutton, MD*

**5650 Wilkes-Barre VA Medical Center**
Veterans Health Administration, U S Dept. of V A
1111 E End Blvd
Wilkes Barre, PA 18711-30
570-824-3521
800-827-1000
FAX: 570-821-7278
e-mail: g.vhacss@forum.va.gov
www.va.gov

*William H Mills, Director (Interim)*
*Douglas V Paxton Sr., Associate Director*
*Mirza Z Ali, Chief of Staff*
*Linda Stout, Associate Director for Nursing S*

## Rhode Island

**5651 Providence Regional Office**
Veterans Benefits Administration, U S Dept. of V A
380 Westminster St
Providence, RI 2903-3246
401-462-0324
800-827-1000
FAX: 401-254-2320
e-mail: providence.query@vba.va.gov
www.va.gov

*Daniel Evangelista, Acting Associate Director*

**5652 Providence VA Medical Center**
Veterans Health Administration, U S Dept. of V A
830 Chalkstone Ave
Providence, RI 2908-4799
401-273-7100
FAX: 401-457-3360
e-mail: g.vhacss@forum.va.gov
www.va.gov

*Vincent W Ng, Medical Center Director*
*William J Burney, Medical Center Associate Directo*
*Gregory M Gillette, Medical Center Chief of Staff*
*Deborah A Clickner, Medical Center Associate Directo*

## South Carolina

**5653 Columbia Regional Office**
Veterans Benefits Administration, U S Dept. of V A
6437 Garners Ferry Rd
Columbia, SC 29209-2401
803-401-1094
800-827-1000
e-mail: columbia.query@vba.va.gov
www.va.gov

*Jimmie Ruff, Executive Director*

**5654 Ralph H Johnson VA Medical Center**
Veterans Health Administration, U S Dept. of V A
109 Bee St
Charleston, SC 29401-5703
843-577-5011
800-827-1000
888-878-6884
FAX: 843-876-5384
e-mail: g.vhacss@forum.va.gov
www.va.gov

*Carolyn L Adams, Director*
*Scott Isaacks, Associate Director*
*Florence N Hutchinson, Chief of Staff*
*Mary C Fraggos, Associate Director for Patient/N*

**5655 William Jennings Bryan Dorn VA Medical Center**
Veterans Health Administration U S Department of V
6439 Garners Ferry Rd
Columbia, SC 29209-1638
803-776-4000
800-293-8262
FAX: 803-695-6739
e-mail: g.vhacss@forum.va.gov
www.va.gov

*Rebecca J Stackhouse, Acting Medical Center Director*
*Jon Zivony, Acting Medical Center Associate*
*Alfred Boykin, Chief of Staff*
*Ruth Mustard, Director for Patient Care/Nursin*

## South Dakota

**5656 Royal C Johnson Veterans Memorial Medical Center**
Veterans Health Administration, U S Dept. of VA
2501 W. 22nd St
Sioux Falls, SD 57105-5046
605-336-3230
800-316-8387
FAX: 605-333-6878
e-mail: g.vhacss@forum.va.gov
www.va.gov

*Patrick J Kelly, Director*
*Sara Ackert, Associate Director*
*Victor Waters, Chief of Staff*
*Barbara Teal, Associate Director, Patient Care*

**5657 Sioux Falls Regional Office**
Veterans Benefits Administration, U S Dept. of V A
2501 W. 22nd St
Sioux Falls, SD 57117-5046
605-773-3269
800-827-1000
FAX: 605-333-5316
e-mail: siouxfalls.query@vba.va.gov
www.va.gov

## Tennessee

**5658 Alvin C York VA Medical Center**
Veterans Health Administration, U S Dept. of V A
3400 Lebanon Pike
Murfreesboro, TN 37129-1237
615-867-6000
800-76 -093
FAX: 615-867-5768
e-mail: g.vhacss@forum.va.gov
www.va.gov

*Juan Morales, Medical System Director*
*Janice Cobb, Associate Director, Nursing Serv*
*Emma Metcalf, Chief Operating Officer*

**5659 Memphis VA Medical Center**
Veterans Health Administration, U S Dept. of V A
1030 Jefferson Ave
Memphis, TN 38104-2127
901-523-8990
800-636-8262
e-mail: g.vhacss@forum.va.gov
www.va.gov

*Jay Robinson III, Associate Medical Center Directo*
*Douglas D Southall, Assistant Medical Center Directo*
*Margarethe Hagemann, Chief of Staff*
*Marilyn Kerkhoff, Interim Associate Medical Center*

**5660 Mountain Home VA Medical CenterJames H Quillen VA Medical Center**
Veterans Health Administration, US Dept. of VA
Corner of Lamont & Veterans Way
Mountain Home, TN 37684
423-926-1171
800-827-1000
e-mail: g.vhacss@forum.va.gov
www.va.gov

*Charlene S Ehret, Medical Center Director*
*Jimmy H McGlawn, Associate Director*
*David R Reagan, Chief of Staff*
*Linda M McConnell, Associate Director, Patient/Nurs*

**5661 Nasheville Regional Office**
Veterans Benefits Administration, U S Dept. of V A
110 9th Ave S
Nashville, TN 37203-3817
800-827-1000
e-mail: nashville.query@vba.va.gov
www.va.gov

*Michael R Walsh, Administrative Officer*
*Donald H Rubin, Research/Development Coordinator*

**5662 Nashville VA Medical Center**
Veterans Health Administration, US Dept. of VA
1310 24th Ave S
Nashville, TN 37212-2637
615-327-4751
800-228-4973
FAX: 615-321-6350
e-mail: g.vhacss@forum.va.gov
www.va.gov

*Juan Morales, Medical System Director*
*Michael A Doukas, Chief of Staff*
*Gary D Trende, Associate Director, Nursing Serv*
*Gary D Trende, Chief Operating Officer*

## Texas

**5663 Amarillo VA Healthcare System**
Veterans Health Administration, U S Dept. of V A
6010 Amarillo Blvd West
Amarillo, TX 79106-1991
806-355-9703
800-687-8262
FAX: 806-354-7869
e-mail: g.vhacss@forum.va.gov
www.va.gov

*David Welch, Director*
*Lance Robinson, Associate Director*
*Grace Stringfelow, Chief of Staff*
*Louise Anderson, Executive/Chief, Nursing Service*

**5664 Amarillo Vet Center**
Department of Veterans Affairs
3414 Olsen Blvd
Suite E
Amarillo, TX 79109-3072
806-351-1104
FAX: 806-351-1104
www.va.gov

*Pedro Garcia Jr., Team Leader*
*Simon Camarillo, Counsilor*
*William C Santer, Family Therapist*
*Cathy L Williams, Office Manager*

Provides individual, group and family counseling to veterans who served in combat theaters of World War II and Korea, veterans of the Vietnam Era, and veterans of conflicts zones in Lebanon, Grenada, Panama, the Persian Guld and Somalia.

**5665 El Paso VA Healthcare Center**
Veterans Health Administration, U S Dept. of V A
5001 N Piedras
El Paso, TX 79930-4210
915-564-6100
800-672-3782
FAX: 915-564-7920
e-mail: g.vhacss@forum.va.gov
www.va.gov

*Joan M Ricard, Director*
*Perry Danner, Associate Director*
*Homer LeMar, Interim Chief of Staff*
*Timothy McMurry, Associate Director, Patient Care*

**5666 Houston Regional Office**
Veterans Benefits Administration, U S Dept. of V A
6900 Almeda Rd
Houston, TX 77030-4200
713-791-1414
800-827-1000
e-mail: houston.query@vba.va.gov
www.va.gov

*Cecil Aultman, Executive Director*
*Edgar Tucker, Chief Executive Officer*

**5667 Michael E. Debakey VA Medical Center**
Veterans Health Administration, U S Dept. of V A
2002 Holcombe Blvd
Houston, TX 77030-4211
713-791-1414
800-553-2278
e-mail: g.vhacss@forum.va.gov
www.va.gov

*Adam C Walmus, Director*
*J Kalavar, Chief of Staff*
*Francisco Vazquez, Associate Director*
*Thelma Grey-Becknell, Associate Director for Patient C*

**5668 South Texas Veterans Healthcare System**
Veterans Health Administration, U S Dept. of V A
7400 Merton Minter
San Antonio, TX 78229-4404
210-617-5300
800-827-1000
888-686-6350
e-mail: g.vhacss@forum.va.gov
www.va.gov

*Tuhin Chaudhuri, Director*
*Charles Sepich, Chief Executive Officer*

**5669 VA North Texas Health Veterans Affairs Care System: Dallas VA Medical Center**
Veterans Health Administration, U S Dept. of V A
4500 S Lancaster Rd
Dallas, TX 75216-7167
214-742-8387
800-849-3597
FAX: 214-857-1171
www.va.gov

*Mark Doskocil, Acting Director*
*Shirley Bealer, Associate Director*
*Clark R Gregg, Chief of Staff*
*Eric D Jacobsen, Assistant Director*

Health care system which serves veterans with medical care and rehabilitation services including spinal cord injury center. For VA benefit inquiries contact 1-800-827-1000. This system has locations in Bonham, Dallas, and Fort Worth.

**5670 Waco Regional Office**
Veterans Benefits Administration, U S Dept. of V A
701 Clay Ave
Waco, TX 76799-1
800-827-1000
TTY:800-829-4833
e-mail: waco.query@vba.va.gov
www.va.gov

*Keith Young, Research/Development Coordinator*

**5671 West Texas VA Healthcare System**
Veterans Health Administration, U S Dept. of V A
300 Veterans Blvd
Big Spring, TX 79720-5566
432-263-7361
800-472-1365
FAX: 915-264-4834
e-mail: g.vhacss@forum.va.gov
www.va.gov

*Daniel L Marsh, Director*
*Windia Wilbert, Associate Director*

## Utah

**5672 Utah Division of Veterans Affairs**
Utah Division of Veterans Affairs
550 Foothill Blvd
Ste 202
Salt Lake City, UT 84113-1106
801-582-1565
800-894-9497
FAX: 801-326-2369
e-mail: tandrews@utah.gov
www.veterans.utah.gov/

*David J Peifer, Director*
*Todd Andrews, Assistant to the Director*
*Lavonne Willis, Manager*

5673 **VA Salt Lake City Healthcare System**
Veterans Health Administration, U S Dept. of V A
500 Foothill Drive
Salt Lake City, UT 84148-1
801-582-1565
800-613-4012
FAX: 801-584-1289
www.va.gov

*Steven W Young, Director*
*Warren E Hill, Associate Director*
*Ronald J Gebhart, Chief of Staff*
*Shella Stovall, Associate Director, Patient Care*

## Vermont

5674 **Vermont VA Regional Office Center**
Veterans Benefits Administration U S Department V
215 N Main St
White River Junction, VT 5009-1
802-296-6339
800-827-1000
FAX: 802-290-6354
e-mail: whiteriver.query@vba.va.gov
www.va.gov

*Laura Miraldi, Executive Director*

5675 **Vermont Veterans Centers**
359 Dorset St
South Burlington, VT 5403-6210
802-862-1806
FAX: 802-865-3319
www.va.gov

*Fred Forehand, Team Leader*
*William Newkirk, Counsilor*
*George Troutman, Counsilor*
*Tamara R Thompson, Family Therapist*

Veterans medical clinic offering disabled veterans medical treatments.

## Virginia

5676 **Hampton VA Medical Center**
Veterans Health Administration, U S Dept. of V A
100 Emancipation Dr
Hampton, VA 23667-1
757-722-9961
800-827-1000
FAX: 757-728-3135
e-mail: mike.eisenberg@med.va.gov
www.va.gov

*Deanne M Seekins, Medical Center Director*
*Benita K Stoddard, Associate Director for Operation*
*G. Arul, Chief of Staff*
*Shedale Tindall, Associate Director for Patient C*

5677 **Hunter Holmes McGuire VA Medical Center**
Veterans Health Administration, U S Dept. of V A
1201 Broad Rock Blvd
Richmond, VA 23249-1
804-675-5000
800-784-8381
FAX: 804-675-5236
e-mail: g.vhacss@forum.va.gov
www.va.gov

*Charles E Sepich, Director*
*David P Budinger, Associate Director*
*Julie Beales, Interim Chief of Staff*
*Rita A Duval, Associate Director for Patient C*

5678 **Roanoke Regional Office**
Veterans Benefits Administration, U S Dept. of V A
116 North Jefferson St
Roanoke, VA 24016-1906
540-362-1999
800-827-1000
FAX: 540-563-4838
e-mail: anne.atkins@vdvs.viginia.gov
www.va.gov

*Roger Bohm, Executive*
*Bert Boyd, COO/Executive Director*

5679 **Salem VA Medical Center**
Veterans Health Administration, U S Dept. of V A
1970 Roanoke Blvd
Salem, VA 24153-6478
540-982-2463
800-827-1000
888-982-2463
FAX: 540-983-1096
e-mail: g.vhacss@forum.va.gov
www.va.gov

*Miguel H LaPuz, Director*
*Carol S Bogedain, Associate Director*
*Maureen McCarthy, Chief of Staff*
*Pearl Washington, Nurse Executive*

5680 **Virginia Department of Veterans Services**
270 Franklin Rd SW
Roanoke, VA 24011-2204
540-857-7102
FAX: 540-857-6437
e-mail: pmigrand131@worldnet.att.net
dvs.virginia.gov

*Colbert Boyd, Manager*

## Washington

5681 **Jonathan M Wainwright Memorial VA Medical Center**
Veterans Health Administration, U S Dept. of V A
77 Wainwright Dr
Walla Walla, WA 99362-3975
509-525-5200
888-687-8863
FAX: 509-946-3062
www.va.gov

*Michael W Parnicky, R and D Coordinator*

5682 **Seattle Regional Office**
Veterans Benefits Administration U S Department of
915 2nd Ave
Seattle, WA 98174-1060
206-762-1010
800-827-1000
e-mail: seattle.query@vba.va.gov
www.va.gov

*Va Ad Harabanim, Executive Director*
*Timothy Williams, Chief Executive Officer*

5683 **Spokane VA Medical Center**
Veterans Health Administration, U S Dept. of V A
4815 N Assembly St
Spokane, WA 99205-6185
509-434-7000
800-325-7940
FAX: 509-434-7119
e-mail: g.vhacss@forum.va.gov
www.va.gov

*Alan Prentiss, Chief of Staff*
*Dirk Minatre, Coordinator*
*Joseph Manley, Executive Director*

**5684 VA Puget Sound Health Care System**
Veterans Health Administration, U S Dept. of V A
1660 S Columbian Way
Seattle, WA 98108-1532
206-762-1010
800-329-8387
e-mail: g.vhacss@forum.va.gov
www.va.gov

*David Elizalde, Director*
*DeAnn Lestenkof, Deputy Director*
*Sherri Bauch, Assistant Director*
*William Campbell, Chief of Staff*

## West Virginia

**5685 Huntington Regional Office**
Veterans Benefits Administration, U S Dept. of V A
640 4th Ave
Huntington, WV 25701-1340
304-525-5131
800-827-1000
FAX: 304-399-9344
e-mail: huntington.query@vba.va.gov
www.va.gov

*Mark Bugher, President*

**5686 Huntington VA Medical Center**
Veterans Health Administration, U S Dept. of V A
1540 Spring Valley Dr
Huntington, WV 25704-9300
304-429-6755
800-827-8244
FAX: 304-429-6713
www.va.gov

*Edward H Seiler, Director*
*Suzanne Jene, Associate Director*
*Jeffery B Breaux, Chief of Staff*
*Catherine J Locher, Associate Director for Nursing S*

**5687 Louis A Johnson VA Medical Center**
Veterans Health Administration, U S Dept. of V A
1 Medical Center Drive
Clarksburg, WV 26301-4155
304-623-3461
800-733-0512
FAX: 304-626-7048
e-mail: g.vhacss@forum.va.gov
www.va.gov

*William E Cox, Director*
*Jeffrey A Beiler II, Associate Director*
*Glenn R Snider, Chief of Staff*
*Theresa J White, Nurse Executive*

**5688 Martinsburg VA Medical Center**
Veterans Health Administration, U S Dept. of V A
510 Butler Avenue
Martinsburg, WV 25404-9990
304-263-0811
800-817-3807
FAX: 304-262-7433
e-mail: g.vhacss@forum.va.gov
www.va.gov

*Ann R Brown, Director*
*Timothy J Cooke, Associate Medical Center Directo*
*Jonathan E Fierer, Chief of Staff*
*Susan George, Nursing Programs and Education*

**5689 US Department Veterans Affairs Beckley Vet Center**
1000 Jonstown Road
Beckley, WV 25801-4301
304-252-8220
FAX: 304-254-8711
www.va.gov

*Melody Friend, Director*
Vet Center services includes individual and group readjustment counseling, referral for benefits assistance, liason with community agencies, marital and family counseling, substance abuse counseling, job counseling and referral, sexual trauma counseling, and community education.

## Wisconsin

**5690 Clement J Zablocki VA Medical Center**
Veterans Health Administration U S Department of V
5000 W National Ave
Milwaukee, WI 53295-1
414-384-2000
888-827-1000
888-469-6614
FAX: 414-382-5319
www.va.gov

*Robert H Beller, Director*
*Michael D Erdmann, Chief of Staff*
*Judith A Murphy, Associate Director for Patient/N*

**5691 Tomah VA Medical Center**
Veterans Health Administration, U S Dept. of V A
500 E Veterans St
Tomah, WI 54660-3105
608-372-3971
800-872-8662
FAX: 608-372-1224
e-mail: g.vhacss@forum.va.gov
www.va.gov

*David J Houlihan, Acting Medical Center Director*
*Sandra Gregar, Associate Director*
*Katherine J Pica, Acting Chief of Staff*
*Lynda Everson, Acting Associate Director for Pa*

**5692 William S Middleton Memorial VA Hospital Center**
Veterans Health Administration, U S Dept. of V A
2500 Overlook Ter
Madison, WI 53705-2254
608-256-1901
800-827-1000
888-256-1901
FAX: 608-280-7244
e-mail: g.vhacss@forum.va.gov
www.va.gov

*Nathan Geraths, Executive Director*

**5693 Wisconsin VA Regional Office**
Veterans Benefits Administration, U S Dept. of V A
5000 W National Ave
Milwaukee, WI 53295-1
414-384-2000
800-827-1000
FAX: 414-382-5374
e-mail: milwaukee.query@vba.va.gov
www.va.gov

*Philip L Cook, Executive Director*
*Neil S Mandel, Research/Development Coordinator*
*Glen Grippen, CEO*

## Wyoming

**5694 Casper Vet Center**
1030 N. Poplar Suite B
Casper, WY 82601-2665
307-261-5355
FAX: 307-261-5439
www.vetcenter.va.gov

*James Whipps, Office Manager*
Vet Center offering re-adjustment counseling for combat veterans.

5695 **Cheyenne VA Medical Center**
Veterans Health Administration, U S Dept. of V A
2360 E Pershing Blvd
Cheyenne, WY 82001-5356
307-778-7550
800-827-1000
888-483-9127
FAX: 307-778-7531
e-mail: g.vhacss@forum.va.gov
www.va.gov

*Cynthia McCormack, Medical Center Director*
*Elizabeth Lowery, Associate Director*
*Jerry Zang, Chief of Staff*
*Polly Baird, Associate Director for Patient C*

5696 **Sheridan VA Medical Center**
Veterans Health Administration, U S Dept. of V A
1898 Fort Rd
Sheridan, WY 82801-8320
307-672-3473
800-827-1000
FAX: 307-672-1639
e-mail: g.vhacss@forum.va.gov
www.va.gov

*Debra L Hirschman, Director*
*Michele Beach, Director*
*Wendell Robison, Chief of Staff*
*Jane Votaw, Nurse Executive*

5697 **Wyoming/Colorado VA Regional Office**
Veterans Benefits Administration, U S Dept. of V A
155 Van Gordon St
Lakewood, CO 80228-1709
303-894-7474
800-827-1000
FAX: 303-894-7442
e-mail: denver.query@vba.va.gov
www.va.gov

*E William Belz, Director*

# Vocational & Employment

## Alabama

**5698 Coffee County Training Center**
P.O.Box 311343
Enterprise, AL 36331-1343
334-393-1732
FAX: 334-347-0252

*Vickie Florence, Manager*
Clients 21 years and up receive training in Independent Living Skills, Self-Care, Language Skills, Learning, Self-Direction and Economic Self-Sufficiency. Transportation is also provided to clients of the center.

**5699 Easter Seal: Opportunity Center**
6300 McClellan Blvd
Anniston, AL 36206
256-820-9960
FAX: 256-820-9592
www.opportunity-center.com

*Mike Almaroad, Administrator*
*Barbara Bradley, Vocational Instructor*
*Lisa Fincher, Employment Specialist*
A nationally accredited non-profit organization providing vocational evaluation/assessment, paid work training, and employment services for people with disabilities in Calhoun, Cleburne, Clay, Talladega, Coosa and Randolph counties.

**5700 Easter Seals: Achievement Center**
Easter Seals of Alabama
510 W Thomason Circle
Opelika, AL 36801-5499
334-745-3501
FAX: 334-749-5808
e-mail: info@achievement-center.org
www.achievement-center.org

*Furrel Bailey, Administrator*
*Star Wray, Program Coordinator*
Provides vocational development and extended employment programs for physically, mentally, and developmentally disabled individuals and to non-disabled persons who are culturally, socially, or economically disadvantaged.

**5701 Employment Service Division: Alabama**
Department of Industrial Relations
649 Monroe St
Montgomery, AL 36131-1
334-242-8990
FAX: 334-242-3960
e-mail: director@dir.alabama.us
www.dir.alabama.gov

*Tom Surtees, Director Of Industrial Relations*
*Robert Brantley, Director Of Employment Services*

**5702 Lakeshore Rehabilitation Facility**
3830 Ridgeway Drive
PO Box 59127
Birmingham, AL 35259
331-293-7500
800-441-7609
FAX: 334-293-7371
www.rehab.state.al.us
Agency with several vocational and employment programs for rehabilitation.

**5703 Montezuma Day Treatment**
402 Academy Dr
Andalusia, AL 36420
334-222-8411
FAX: 334-427-1832

*Michelle Mc Lendon, Administrator*
*W Underwood, Executive Director*
Individuals served in this program must be at least 21 years of age and have a primary diagnosis of mental retardation. Clients receive training in independent living skills, learning, self-direction and economic self-sufficiency. Special Olympic activities are also emphasized.

**5704 Thomasville Rehabilitation Center**
P.O.Box 1006
Thomasville, AL 36784-1006
334-636-5421
800-335-3237
FAX: 334-636-5421
www.rehab.state.al.us
Offers work adjustment, evaluation and job rediness skills for people with disabilities.

**5705 Vocational Rehabilitation Service Opelika**
520 W Thomason Circle
Opelika, AL 36801
334-749-1259
800-671-6835
FAX: 334-749-8753
www.rehab.state.al.us
Available through any of the 21 VRS offices statewide, services can include educational services, vocational assessment, evaluation and counseling, job training, assistive technology, orientation and mobility training and job placement.

**5706 Vocational Rehabilitation Service: Scottsboro**
203 S Market Street
PO Box 296
Scottsboro, AL 35768-0296
256-574-5813
800-418-8823
FAX: 256-574-6033
www.rehab.state.al.us
Availiable through any of the 21 VRS offices statewide, services can include educational services, vocational assesment, evaluation and counseling, job training, assistive technology, orientation and mobility training and job placement.

**5707 Vocational Rehabilitation Service: Dothan**
795 Ross Clark Circle NE
Dothan, AL 36303
334-699-8600
800-275-0132
FAX: 334-792-1783
www.rehab.state.al.us
Availiable through any of the 21 VRS offices statewide, services can include educational services, vocational assesment, evaluation and counseling, job training, assistive technology, orientation and mobility training, and job placement.

**5708 Vocational Rehabilitation Service: Gadsden**
1100 George Wallace Drive
Gadsden, AL 35903-6501
256-547-6974
800-671-6839
FAX: 256-543-1784
www.rehab.state.al.us
Availiable through any of the 21 VRS offices statewide, services can include educational services, vocational assesment, evaluation and counseling, job training, assistive technology, orientation and mobility training, and job placement.

**5709 Vocational Rehabilitation Service: Homewood**
236 Goodwin Crest Drive
Birmingham, AL 35209
205-290-4400
800-671-6837
FAX: 205-290-0486
www.rehab.state.al.us
Availiable through any of the 21 VRS offices statewide, services can include educational services, vocational assesment, evaluation and counseling, job training, assistive technology, orientation and mobility training, and job placement.

**5710 Vocational Rehabilitation Service: Huntsville**
3000 Johnson Rd SW
Huntsville, AL 35805-5847
256-650-1700
800-671-6840
FAX: 256-650-1795
www.rehab.state.al.us

Available through any of the 21 VRS offices statewide, services can include educational services, vocational assesment, evaluation and counseling, job training, assistive technology, orientation and mobility training, and job placement.

**5711 Vocational Rehabilitation Service: Jackson**
1401 Forest Ave
PO Box 1005
Jackson, AL 36545
251-246-5708
800-671-6836
FAX: 251-246-5224
www.rehab.state.al.us

Available through any of the 21 VRS offices statewide, services can include educational services, vocational assesment, evaluation and counseling, job training, assistive technology, orientation and mobility training, and job placement.

**5712 Vocational Rehabilitation Service: Jasper**
301 N Walston Bridge Road
Suite 116
Jasper, AL 35504
205-221-7840
800-671-6841
FAX: 205-221-1062
www.rehab.state.al.us

Available through any of the 21 VRS offices statewide, services can include educational services, vocational assesment, evaluation and counseling, job training, assistive technology, orientation and mobility training, and job placement.

**5713 Vocational Rehabilitation Service: Mobile**
2419 Gordon Smith Drive
Mobile, AL 36617
251-479-8611
800-671-6842
FAX: 251-478-2197
www.rehab.state.al.us

Available through any of the 21 VRS offices statewide, services can include educational services, vocational assesment, evaluation and counseling, job training, assistive technology, orientation and mobility training, and job placement.

**5714 Vocational Rehabilitation Service: Muscle Shoals**
1450 E Avalon Ave
Muscle Shoals, AL 35661
256-381-1110
800-275-0166
FAX: 256-389-3149
www.rehab.state.al.us

Available through any of the 21 VRS offices statewide, services can include educational services, vocational assessment, evaluation and counseling, job training, assistive technology, orientation and mobility training and job placement.

**5715 Vocational Rehabilitation Service: Selma**
2906 Citizens Pkwy
Selma, AL 36701-3915
334-872-8422
888-761-5995
FAX: 334-877-3796
www.rehab.state.al.us

*Richard Weishaupt, Manager*

Available through any of the 21 VRS offices statewide, services can include educational services, vocational assesment, evaluation and counseling, job training, assistive technology, orientation and mobility training, and job placement.

**5716 Vocational Rehabilitation Service: Talladega**
4 Medical Office Park
Talladega, AL 35160
256-362-1300
800-441-7592
FAX: 256-362-6387
www.rehab.state.al.us

Availiable through any of the 21 VRS offices statewide, services can include educational services, vocational assesment, evaluation and counseling, job training, assistive technology, orientation and mobility training, and job placement.

**5717 Vocational Rehabilitation Service: Troy**
1109 Troy Plaza Street
Troy, AL 36081
334-566-2491
800-441-7608
FAX: 334-566-9415
www.rehab.state.al.us

Available through any of the 21 VRS offices statewide, services can include educational services, vocational assessment, evaluation and counseling, job training, assistive technology, orientation and mobility training, and job placement.

**5718 Vocational Rehabilitation Service: Tuscaloosa**
1305 James I Harrison Jr Parkway E
Tuscaloosa, AL 35405
205-554-1300
800-331-5562
FAX: 205-554-1369
www.rehab.state.al.us

Available through any of the 21 VRS offices statewide, services can include educational services, vocational assessment, evaluation and counseling, job training, assistive technology, orientation and mobility training, and job placement.

**5719 Vocational Rehabilitation Services: Andalusa**
1082 Village Square Drive
Suite 1
Andalusia, AL 36420
334-222-4114
800-671-6833
FAX: 334-427-1216
www.rehab.state.al.us

Available through any of the 21 VRS offices statewide, services can include educational services, vocational assessment, evaluation and counseling, job training, assistive technology, orientation and mobility training, and job placement.

**5720 Vocational Rehabilitation Services: Anniston**
1105 Woodstock Ave
Anniston, AL 36207
256-238-9300
800-671-6834
FAX: 256-231-4852
www.rehab.state.al.us

Available through any of the 21 VRS offices statewide, services can include educational services, vocational assessment, evaluation and counseling, job training, assistive technology, orientation and mobility training, and job placement.

**5721 Vocational and Rehabilitation Service Columbiana**
Community Services Building
P.O.Box 856
Columbiana, AL 35051-856
205-755-8114
FAX: 205-669-0605
www.rehab.state.al.us

Available through any of the 21 VRS offices statewide, services can include educational services, vocational assessment, evaluation and counseling, job training, assistive technology, orientation and mobility training, and job placement.

**5722 Vocational and Rehabilitation Service: Decatur**
621 Cherry St NE
Decatur, AL 35601
256-353-2754
800-671-6838
FAX: 256-351-2476
www.rehab.state.al.us

Available through any of the 21 VRS offices statewide, services can include educational services, vocational assessment, evaluation and counseling, job training, assistive technology, orientation and mobility training and job placement.

**5723 Vocational and Rehabilitation Services: Montgomery**
602 S Lawrence St
Montgomery, AL 36104
334-293-7500
800-441-7578
FAX: 334-293-7372
www.rehab.state.al.us

Available through any of the 21 VRS offices statewide, services can include educational services, vocational assessment, evaluation and counseling, job training, assistive technology, orientation and mobility training and job placement.

**5724 Wiregrass Rehabilitation Center**
795 Ross Clark Circle
Dothan, AL 36303
800-395-7044
FAX: 216-521-9460
e-mail: jls@wrcjobs.com
www.wrcjobs.com

*Dr Jack Sasser, Administrator*
*Dave Coleman, Employment Services Coordinator*

Trains individuals to become employable and assists them in finding jobs withing their communities. Also assists individuals who have difficulty maintaining employment, those who are on forms of public assistance such as welfare and those who are employable and underemployed.

**5725 Workshops Inc.**
4244 3rd Ave S
Birmingham, AL 35222-2008
205-592-9683
888-805-9683
FAX: 205-592-9687
e-mail: email@workshopsinc.org
www.workshopsinc.org

*Susan Crow, Executive Director*
*Kirsten Beauchamp, Director of Programs*

Provides vocational training, sheltered employment and other support services to people with disabilities in central Alabama.

## Alaska

**5726 Alaska Division of Vocational Rehabilitation**
Department of Labor & Workforce Development
801 W 10th Street
Suite A
Juneau, AK 99801
907-465-2814
800-478-2815
FAX: 907-465-2815
TTY: 800-478-2815
www.labor.state.ak.us/dvr

*Cheryl Walsh, Director*

Assist individuals with disabilities to obtain and maintain employment.

**5727 Anchorage Job Training Center**
235 E 8th Ave
Anchorage, AK 99501-3615
907-277-0693
FAX: 907-334-2286
www.ci.anchorage.ak.us

Provides vocational training.

**5728 Fair Employment Practice Agency**
Alaska State Commission for Human Rights
Ste 204
800 a St
Anchorage, AK 99501-7500
907-274-4692
800-478-4692
FAX: 907-278-8588
www.gov.state.ak.us/aschr/aschr.htm

*Paula Haley, Executive Director*

## Arizona

**5729 Downtown Neighborhood Learning Center**
1001 W Jefferson St
Phoenix, AZ 85007-2913
602-254-6524
800-869-8521
FAX: 602-256-2524
e-mail: dnlc@swlink.net
www.swlink.net

*Scott Ritchey, Manager*
*Mattie Johnson, Receptionist*
*Peg Osinski, El Mirage Learning Lab*

Adult education agency providing basic skills, GED, ESOL, life skills, computer skills, resume assistance and career testing.

**5730 Fair Employment Practice Agency: Arizona**
Arizona Civil Rights Division
1275 W Washington St
Phoenix, AZ 85007-2926
602-542-5025
800-352-8431
FAX: 602-542-4085
www.azag.gov

*Virginia Gonzales, Director*
*Bruna Pedrini, Manager*

Provides legal advice to most state agencies. The office also investigates and prosecutes consumer fraud, white collar crime, organized crime, public corruption, and civil rights.

**5731 JOBS Administration Job Opportunities & Basic Skills**
1717 W Jefferson St
Phoenix, AZ 85007-3202
602-542-9596
FAX: 602-542-5171

*Gretchen Evans, Program Administrator*

Assist applicants and recipients of temporary assistance to needy families to obtain job training and employment that will lead to economic independence.

**5732 TETRA Services**
Beacon Group SW Inc
2222 N 24th Street
Phoenix, AZ 85008
602-685-9703
FAX: 602-244-2435
e-mail: lrusay@thebeacongroup.org
www.tetraservices.org

Provides employment services development and supportive services to individuals with disabilities and other barriers to employment.

**5733 Vocational and Rehabilitation Agency Rehabilitation Services Administrations**
Division of Employment & Rehabilitation Services
1789 W Jefferson St
Phoenix, AZ 85007-3202
602-604-8835
800-563-1221
800-563-1221
FAX: 602-604-8901
TTY:602-542-6049
e-mail: tazrsa@azdes.gov
azdes.gov/rsa

*Michelle Nitschke, Manager*
*Katharine Levandowsky, Administrator*
*Moises Gallegos, Manager*

This program serves individuals with disabilities seeking jobs and job training.

**5734 Yavapai Regional Medical Center-West**
1003 Willow Creek Rd
Prescott, AZ 86301-1668
928-445-2700
877-843-9762
FAX: 928-445-0994
yrmc.org

*Tim Barnett, CEO*

Widely recognized for the quality and success of the physical, occupational, and speech therapy programs it offers. Provides a wide range of programs and services that enable our patients to reach their maximum level of function and independence- and enjoy the highest possible quality of life.

## Arkansas

**5735 Arkansas Employment Service Agency and Job Training Program**
Arkansas Employment Security Department
P.O.Box 2981
Little Rock, AR 72203-2981
501-682-2033
FAX: 501-682-2273
www.arkansas.gov/esd

*Artee Williams, Manager*
Wide range of services including employment services, unemployment insurance, and labor market information.

**5736 Easter Seal Work Center**
11801 Fairview Rd
Little Rock, AR 72212-2406
501-221-1063
FAX: 501-227-7180
e-mail: mail@ar.easterseals.com
www.ar.easterseals.com

*Lauren Zilk, Administrator*
Mission is to provide exceptional services to ensure that all people with disabilities or special needs have equal opportunities to live,learn work and play in their communities.

**5737 VCT/A Job Retention Skill Training Program**
Arkasas Rehab Services
P.O.Box 1358
Hot Springs, AR 71902-1358
501-624-4411
FAX: 501-624-0019

*Barbara Lewis, Administrator*
*Mae Robinson, Assistant Administrator*
A training program designed for use in rehabilitation and educational settings. Using a social skill training strategy, VCT helps participants learn how to solve on-the-job problems and cope with common supervisory demands.

**5738 Vocational and Rehabilitation Agency Division of Services for the Blind**
700 Main St
Little Rock, AR 72201-4608
501-686-9433
800-960-9270
FAX: 501-686-9418
TTY: 501-682-0093
e-mail: jim.hudson@mail.state.ar.us
www.state.ar.us

*Lyndel Lybarger, Field Adminstrator*
*James Hudson, Executive Director*

**5739 Vocational and Rehabilitation Agency for Persons Who Are Visually Impaired**
Arkansas Department of Human Services
P.O.Box 3237
Little Rock, AR 72203-3237
501-686-9433
800-960-9270
FAX: 501-686-9418
TTY: 501-324-9271
e-mail: arkblind@edu.gte.net

*James C Hudson, Executive Director*
Furnishes a wide variety of services to help people with disabilities return to work.

## California

**5740 ABLE Industries**
8127 Avenue 304
Visalia, CA 93291
559-651-8150
888-813-2253
FAX: 559-651-0357
www.ableindustries.org

*Wende-Leigh Ayers, Executive Director*
Committed to improving the lives of people with disabilities by creating opportunities to maximize their independence.

**5741 ARC-Adult Vocational Program**
1500 Howard St
San Francisco, CA 94103-2525
415-255-7200
FAX: 415-255-9488
e-mail: info@thearcsanfrancisco.org
www.thearcsanfrancisco.org

*Timothy Hornbecker, Executive Director*
Job placement programs, remunerative work services and work adjustment training programs.

**5742 AbilityFirst**
1300 E Green Street
Pasadena, CA 91106
626-396-1010
877-768-4600
FAX: 626-396-1021
e-mail: info@abilityfirst.org
www.abilityfirst.org

*Lori E Gangemi, President*
Provides programs and services to help children and adults with physical and developmental disabilities reach their full potential throughout their lives. Offers a broad range of employment, recreational and socialization programs and operate 12 accessible residential housing complexes.

**5743 Achievement House & NCI Affiliates**
496 Linne Road
Paso Robles, CA 93446
805-238-6630
FAX: 805-239-9073
www.achievementhouse.org

Provides vocational opportunities for individuals with special needs that respect personal choice and diversity and reflect individualized goals that support enhanced independence, personal responsibility and self-esteem.

**5744 Bakersfield ARC**
2240 S Union Ave
Bakersfield, CA 93307-4158
661-834-2272
FAX: 661-834-1694
e-mail: lplank@barc-inc.org
www.barc-inc.org

*Jim Baldwin, President/CEO*
A non-profit organization that has been providing essential job training, employment and support services for the developmentally disabled and their families.
*1949*

**5745 California Department of Fair Employment& Housing**
2218 Kauden Drive
Suite 100
Elk Grove, CA 95758
916-478-7251
e-mail: contact.center@dfeh.ca.gov
www.dfeh.ca.gov

*Phyllis W Cheng, Director*
*Annmarie Billotti Esq, Chief Deputy Director*
To protect Californians from employment, housing and public accomodation discrimination, and hate violence.

**5746 Career Connection Transition Program**
Whittier Union High School District
9401 Painter Ave
Whittier, CA 90605-2729 562-698-8121
FAX: 562-693-4414
e-mail: Richard.Rosenberg@wuhsd.k12.ca.us
www.wuhsd.k12.ca.us

*Richard L Rosenberg PhD, Vocational Coordinator*
*Bonnie Bolton, Transition Department Head*
Job placement programs, remunerative work services and work adjustment training programs. Transition services.

**5747 Career Development Program (CDP)**
260 W Grand Ave
Escondido, CA 92025-2604 760-738-0277
FAX: 760-741-9452

*Richard Brady MD*
*Wendy Hope, Supported Employment*
*Jill Hennessy, Independent Living*
Work hardening and disciplinary programs.

**5748 Colton-Redlands-Yucaipa Regional Occupational Programs**
PO Box 8640
Redlands, CA 92374-2896 909-793-3115
FAX: 909-793-6901
www.cryrop.org

*Stephanie Houston, Superintendent*
*Sandra Moritensen, Manager Student Services*
Provides quality hands-on training programs in over 40 high demand career fields to assist high school students and adults in acquiring marketable job skills. Works in cooperation with local high schools, adult education colleges, and employers providing a collaborative team of academic and ROP occupational teachers who integrate academic and vocational competencies to provide sequenced paths within career majors. Support services, career guidance and services are provided to disabled people.

**5749 Community Outpatient Rehabilitation Center**
2823 Fresno Street
Fresno, CA 93721 559-459-6000
FAX: 559-459-1004
e-mail: complaint@jointcommission.org
www.communitymedical.org

*Tim A. Joslin, Chief Executive Officer*
*Thomas Utecht, M.D., Senior Vice President*
*Craig S. Castro, Senior Vice President*
*Vicki Anderson, Vice President, Managed Care*
Physical, occupational and speech therapy, neuropsychology services available for orthopedic and neurological diagnosis. Lymphedema program.

**5750 Desert Haven Enterprises**
43437 Copeland Circle
PO Box 2110
Lancaster, CA 93535 661-948-8402
FAX: 661-948-1080
e-mail: kmiller@desrthaven.org
www.deserthaven.org

*Jenni Moran, Executive Director*
*Kathleen Miller, Program Services Director*
A private, nonprofit organization dedicated to developing, enhancing, and promotingthe capabilities of persons with mental retardation and other developmental disabilities.

**5751 ESS Work Center**
858 Stanton Rd
Burlingame, CA 94010-1404 650-697-2642
FAX: 650-697-2405

*Ed Mentzer, Owner*
Work adjustment and remunerative work programs.

**5752 Employment Service: California**
Employment Development Department
800 Capitol Mall
Sacramento, CA 95814-4807 916-653-0707

Provides job listings and unemployment listings for all.

**5753 Feather River Industries**
1811 Kusel Rd
Oroville, CA 95966-9528 530-534-1112
FAX: 530-534-3137
www.featherriverindustries.com

*Randy Guild, Rehabilitation Counselor*
*Ed Turner, Production Coordinator*
Vocational training for persons with developmental disabilities provided through wood products fabrication and assembly tasks. Instructor to trainer rating ranging from 1 to 12, 1 to 8, 1 to 6, and 1 to 4 depending on individual needs and complexity of tasks. THE SITE IS UNDER CONSTRUCTION

**5754 Fit to Work**
Ste 401
3581 Palmer Dr
Cameron Park, CA 95682-8238 530-676-4122
FAX: 530-676-9114

*Helen Cheng*
Provides remunerative work.

**5755 Fresno City College: Disabled Students Programs and Services**
Fresno City College
1101 E University Ave
Fresno, CA 93741-1 559-442-4600
FAX: 559-489-2281
e-mail: janice.emerzian@fresnocitycollege.edu
fresnocitycollege.edu

*Dr Janice Emerzian Ed D, District Director*
*Tony Cantu, President*
*Ginna Bearden, Director of TRIO Programs*
*Cris Monahan Bremer, Director of Marketing and Communications*
This program offers programs and services to students with physical, learning and/or psychological disabilities beyond those provided by conventional Fresno City College Programs and enables students to successfully pursue their individual educational, vocational and personal goals.

**5756 Heartland Opportunity Center**
323 N E Street
Madera, CA 93638 559-674-8828
FAX: 559-674-8857
e-mail: kanderson@heartlandopportunity.com
www.heartlandopportunity.com

*Kristy Anderson, CEO*
Provides employment, job placement, vocational and life skills training to adults with mental, physical and/or emotional disabilities in order to help them reach their personal and vocational goals.

**5757 Hollister Workshop**
Hope Rehabilitation Services
Ste 7
2300 Technology Pkwy
Hollister, CA 95023-2536 831-637-8283
FAX: 831-637-8726

*Kristi Alarid, Executive Director*
Work adjustment and remunerative work programs.

**5758 Job Training Program Liaison: California**
Employment Development Department
800 Capitol Mall
Sacramento, CA 95814-4807
916-654-8210
800-300-5616
FAX: 916-657-5294
edd.ca.gov

*Patrick Henning, Manager*
Provides information on filing an Unemployment Insurance or Disability Insurance claim, on-line job and resume bank which boasts thousands of job openings.

**5759 King's Rehabilitation Center**
494 E Hanford-Armona Road
Hanford, CA 93232
559-583-5051
FAX: 559-582-1182
www.kingsrehab.com

*Robert Knudseon, President*
*Steve Mendoza, Executive Director*
To enhance the lives of adults with disabilities by providing day program services, vocational training and employment opportunities to assist such persons to attain their full potential.

**5760 Morongo Basin Work Activity Center**
74325 Joe Davis Dr
Twentynine Palms, CA 92277
760-366-8474

*Sheree Fraser*
Job placement programs, remunerative work services and work adjustment training programs.

**5761 Mother Lode Rehabilitation Enterprises**
399 Placerville Dr
Placerville, CA 95667
530-622-4848
FAX: 530-622-0204
www.morerehab.org

A private, non-profit organization dedicated to supporting persons with disabilities. MORE was established by a group of parents, educators, rehabilitation professionals and concerned citizens and first began serving adults with disabilities in 1973.

**5762 Napa Valley PSI Inc.**
P.O.Box 600
Napa, CA 94559-600
707-255-0177
FAX: 707-255-0802
e-mail: admin@napavalleypsi.org
http://www.napavalleypsi.org

*Tim Cooney, President*
*Jamie Watson, Vice President*
*Joel Momsen, Secretary & Treasurer*
*Worthy Brooks, Directors*
Work adjustment, work training and educational services for developmentally disabled adults. Emphasis is on manufacture of quality wood products, primarily wooden office furniture.

**5763 Oakland Work Activity Area**
6315 San Leandro St
Oakland, CA 94621-3727
510-639-9350

*Greg Whalley*
*Dennis Scharssenberg, Manager*
Job placement programs, remunerative work services and work adjustment training programs.

**5764 Opportunities for the Handicapped**
3340 Marysville Blvd
Sacramento, CA 95838-4567
916-925-3522

*Kathy Dodd*
Work adjustment and remunerative work programs.

**5765 Orange County ARC**
225 W Carl Karcher Way
Anaheim, CA 92801
714-744-5301
FAX: 714-744-5312
e-mail: jhearn2001@yahoo.com
ocarc.net

*Joyce Hearn, CEO*
To provide quality care, training and services to our intellectually/developmentally disabled clients.

**5766 PRIDE Industries**
10030 Foothills Blvd
Roseville, CA 95747-7102
916-788-2100
800-550-6005
FAX: 800-888-0447
e-mail: info@prideindustries.com
http://www.prideindustries.com

*Michael Ziegler, CEO*
*Tim Yamauchi, Executive Vice President and Chief Financial Officer*
*John Vaughan, Senior Vice President, Manufacturing & Logistics Services*
*Pete Berghuis, Senior Vice President, Integrated Facilities Services*
Vocational rehabilitation and employment services creating jobs for people with disabilites; services include career counseling, vocational assessment, work adjustment, work services, job seeking skills, job development, job placement, on-the-job support (coaching), mentoring, independent living skills, transition services and case management.

**5767 Parents and Friends, Inc**
350 Cypress St
PO Box 656
Fort Bragg, CA 95437
707-964-4692
FAX: 707-964-8536
e-mail: rmoon@parentsandfriends.org
www.parentsandfriends.org

*Rick Moon, Executive Director*
Serves people with developmental disabilities.

**5768 PathPoint**
315 W Haley Street
Suite 102
Santa Barbara, CA 93101
805-966-3310
e-mail: info@pathpoint.org
www.pathpoint.org

*Cynthia S Burton, President/CEO*
To provide comprehensive training and support serviceds that empower people with disabilities of disadvantages to live and work as valued members of the community.

**5769 People Services, Inc**
4195 Lakeshore Blvd
Lakeport, CA 95453
707-263-3811
FAX: 707-263-0552
e-mail: idumont@nctac.com
www.peopleservices.org

*Ilene Dumont, Executive Director*
To serve as the local community agency, providing the delivery of quality services for people with disabilities.

**5770 Pomona Valley Workshop**
4650 Brooks St
Montclair, CA 91763
909-624-3555
FAX: 909-624-5675
e-mail: karen@pvwonline.org
www.pvwonline.org

*Karen Jones, Executive Director*
To assist adults with disabilities reach their potential in vocationsl and socialization skills in order tthat they may achieve their highest level of employment and community integration.

**5771 Porterville Sheltered Workshop**
187 W Olive Ave
Porterville, CA 93257-3449
559-784-1399
FAX: 559-781-5651
e-mail: info@pswrehab.com
http://www.portervilleshelteredworkshop.com/

*Steve Tree, Executive Director*
Work adjustment and remunerative work programs. Mission is to assist disabled individuals achieve a more independent and productive life.

**5772 Project Independence**
3505 Cadillac Ave
Suite O-103
Costa Mesa, CA 92626
714-549-3464
877-444-0144
FAX: 714-549-3559
e-mail: info@proindependence.org
www.proindependence.org

*Debra Marsteller, Executive Director*
Promote civil rights for people with developmental disabilities through services which expand independence and choice.

**5773 Sacramento Vocational Services**
6950 21st Ave
Sacramento, CA 95820
916-381-1300
FAX: 916-381-9026
e-mail: info@inallianceinc.com
inallianceinc.com

Committed to providing services that contribute to the independence of adults with developments disabilities and acquired brain injury. Services focus on job placement, employment training and the facilitation of supports necessary for integrated employment and community living.

**5774 San Francisco Vocational Services**
Ste 600
814 Mission St
San Francisco, CA 94103-3025
415-512-9500
FAX: 415-512-9507
e-mail: sfvs@sfvocational.org
rsnc-centers.org

*Gina Chenoweth, Executive Director*
*Jeffrey Faircloth, Manager Case Management*
Comprehensive vocational rehabilitation center offering vocational evaluation, rehabilitative counseling, business office training, work experience, and job placement.

**5775 Shasta County Opportunity Center**
1265 Redwood Blvd
Redding, CA 96003-1965
530-225-5781
FAX: 530-225-5751
e-mail: oppcenter_info@co.shasta.ca.us
www.co.shasta.ca.us

*Del Lockwood, Manager*
*Leonard Moty, 2012 Chairman*
*David A. Kehoe, Board of Supervisor*
*Glenn Hawes, Board of Supervisor*
An employment training program for people with disabilities in Shasta County. These individuals perform paid work in a number of different work environments and at the same time learn the skills necessary to obtain competetive employment in the local community.

**5776 Social Vocational Services**
Ste A104
350 Crenshaw Blvd
Torrance, CA 90503-1725
310-783-0633
FAX: 310-783-0636
e-mail: nto@svsinc.org
socvoc.org

*Sabrina Silva, Manager*
*Dan Strohm, Manager*
The leading provider of services for people with developmental disabilities in the state of California

**5777 South Bay Vocational Center**
1526 240th St
Harbor City, CA 90710
310-784-2032
FAX: 310-539-6342
e-mail: corey@sbvc1.com
www.sbvc1.com

*Corey Sylve, President/CEO*
*Clare Grey, Vice President/COO*
A not-for-profit organization that has been providing excellent vocational programs and services for individuals with disabilities.

**5778 Tri-County Independent Living Center**
2822 Harris Street
Eureka, CA 95503
707-445-8404
877-576-5000
FAX: 707-445-9751
e-mail: aa@tilinet.org
http://www.tilinet.org

*Chris Jones, Executive Director*
*Allan Bard, Information & Referral / Independent Living Specialist*
*Mary Bullwinkel, Bullwinkel*
*Cindy Calderon, Systems Change Advocate*
To provide programs, services and information for people with disabilities living in Humboldt, Del Norte and Trinity Counties in northern California in an effort to allow choices for individuals to optimize their independence.

**5779 Unyeway**
Ste E
2330 Main St
Ramona, CA 92065-2595
760-789-5960
FAX: 760-789-8156
http://www.unyeway.com

*Kim Metli, Executive Director*
*Lisa Oertling, President*
*Dr. Richard Ferguson, Vice President/Audit Committee Chair*
*Pearl Aiello, Director*
Job placement programs, remunerative work services and work adjustment training programs.

**5780 V-Bar Enterprises**
720 Gordon Cir
Suisun City, CA 94585
707-864-1334

*Lu Brunet*
Job placement programs, remunerative work services and work adjustment training programs.

**5781 Valley Light Industries**
5360 Irwindale Avenue
Irwaindale, CA 91706
626-332-2100
e-mail: info@valleylightindustries.org
valleylightind.org

To recognize the unique capacities and fulfill the dreams of those individuals to whom we provide services.

**5782 Visalia Workshop**
2544 E Valley Oaks Dr
Visalia, CA 93292-6711
559-734-1964

*Hortensia Venegas*
Work hardening and disciplinary programs.

**5783 Westside Opportunity Workshop**
9503 Jefferson Blvd
Culver City, CA 90232-2917
310-836-4262
FAX: 310-825-0676
e-mail: ayokota@mednet.ucla.edu
http://www.semel.ucla.edu

*Peter Whybrow, Director*
*Fawzy Fawzy, Associate Director*
*Mark Wheeler, Media Relations*
*Alan Han, Director of Development*
Job placement programs, remunerative work services and work adjustment training programs.

**5784 Work Training Center**
2255 Fair Street
Chico, CA 95928
530-343-7994
FAX: 530-343-4619
e-mail: carlo@ewtc.org
www.wtcinc.org

*Carl Ochsner, Executive Director*
*Brett Barker, Vocational Services Director*
*Deb Royat, Rehabilitation Services Director*
A nonprofit organization providing services to people with disabilities.

**5785 Work Training Center for the Handicapped**
2255 Fair St
Chico, CA 95928-6747
530-343-7994
FAX: 530-343-4619
www.wtcinc.org

*Lee Laney, Manager*
A non-profit organization governed by a local Board of Directors, we are dedicated to meeting the training, vocational, and recreational needs of local adults with disabilities.

## Colorado

**5786 Blue Peaks Developmental Services**
703 4th Street
Alamosa, CO 81101-2638
719-589-5135
FAX: 719-589-0680
e-mail: info@bluepeaks.org
http://www.bluepeaks.org

*John Kreiner, Director*
*Randall P. Johnson, Human Resources/Staff Development Director*
*Brooke Hayden, Residential Director*
*George Garcia, Operations Director*
Provides remunerative work.

**5787 Cheyenne Village**
6275 Lehman Drive
Colorado Springs, CO 80918
719-592-0200
FAX: 719-548-9947
e-mail: info@cheyennevillage.org
www.cheyennevillage.org

*Ann M Turner, Executive Director*
Serves adults with developmental disabilities such as Autism, Down syndrome, Cerebral Palsy, and Mental Retardation in El Paso, Teller and Park Counties.

**5788 Colorado Civil Rights Divsion**
1560 Broadway
Suite 1050
Denver, CO 80202
303-894-2997
800-262-4845
FAX: 303-894-7830
www.dora.state.co.us

*Steven Chavez, Director*
Embraces the Department's mission of consumer protection and works to protect individuals from discrimination in employment, housing and at places of public accommodation through enforcement and outreach consistent with the Colorado Civil Rights Laws.

**5789 Colorado Employment Service**
Department of Labor and Employment
Ste 900
600 Grant St
Denver, CO 80203-3528
303-320-5733
FAX: 303-320-1338

*Clara Capano, Manager*
Job placement programs, remunerative work services and work adjustment training programs.

**5790 Developmental Training Services**
1401 Oak Creek Grade Rd
Canon City, CO 81212
719-275-1616
FAX: 719-275-4619

*Roger Jensen, CEO*
*Linda Davis, Administrator*
Residential and employment programs for adults with developmental disabilities.

**5791 Dynamic Dimensions**
567th 18 Street
Burlington, CO 80807
719-346-5367
FAX: 719-346-6010

*Cheryl Reese, Executive Director*
Vocational, evaluation and assessment, training and placement for most disabilities. Group homes and day programs for the developmentally disabled.

**5792 Gray Street Workcenter**
5685 Gray St
Arvada, CO 80002-2821
720-544-8100
FAX: 303-467-2793
http://services.ddrcco.com

*Tammy Drumright, Manager*
Residental and employment programs for adults with developmental disabilities.

**5793 Hope Center**
3400 Elizabeth St
Denver, CO 80205-4801
303-388-4801
FAX: 303-388-0249
e-mail: gghope@qwestoffice.net
www.hopecenterinc.org

*Gerie Grimes, Executive Director*
Provides educational and vocational opportunities for special-needs and at-risk children and adults from 2 1/2 to adulthood.

**5794 Imagine: Innovative Resources for Cognitive & Physical Challenges**
1400 Dixon St
Lafayette, CO 80026-2790
303-665-7789
FAX: 303-665-2648
e-mail: caroline@imaginecolorado.org
www.imaginecolorado.org

*Mark Emery, Executive Director*
*Judy James-Anderson, Behavioral Health Services Dir*
Provides support services to more than 2,600 people of all ages with developmental delays and cognitive disabilities including autism, cerebral palsy and Down syndrome.

**5795 Las Animas County Rehabilitation Center**
P.O.Box 781
Trinidad, CO 81082-781
719-846-3388
FAX: 719-846-4543
www.scdds.com

*Duane Roy, Executive Director*

Job placement programs, remunerative work services and work adjustment training programs. THE SITE IS UNDER CONSTRUCTION

**5796 NORESCO Workshop**
903 E Burlington Ave
Fort Morgan, CO 80701-3637
970-867-5702

*Ramona Proctor, Executive Director*
*Nancy Study, Manager*
Provides remunerative work.

**5797 Regional Assessment and Training Center**
3520 W Oxford Ave
Denver, CO 80236-3108
303-866-7253

*Russell Porter, Executive Director*
Work adjustment and renumerative work programs.

**5798 Sedgwick County Workshop**
113 Elm St
Julesburg, CO 80737-1634
970-474-2446

*Maria Contreras, Manager*
Provides remunerative work.

**5799 Vocational and Rehabilitation Agency**
Unit B
2211 W Evans Ave
Denver, CO 80223-3855
303-866-2500
FAX: 303-866-3419
TTY:303-866-3980
e-mail: diana.huerta@state.co.us
www.cdhs.state.co.us

*Diana Huerta, Director*
Purpose is to assist eligible individuals with disabilities to become productive members of the Colorado workforce and to live independently.

**5800 Yuma County Workshop**
710 E 2nd Ave
Yuma, CO 80759
970-848-3011

*Robert Stephens*
*Andrea Anderson, Manager*
Provides remunerative work.

## Connecticut

**5801 Abilities Without Boundaries**
615 W Johnson Avenue
Cheshire, CT 06410
203-272-5607
FAX: 203-272-4284
e-mail: cconway@abilitieswithoutboundaries.org
www.abilitieswithoutboundaries.or g

*Charlie Conway, Executive Director*
Formerly known as Cheshire Occupational & Career Opportunities (COCO), provides opportunities in the community through employment and social experiences for people with developmental disabilities.

**5802 Allied Community Services**
Three Pearson Way
Enfield, CT 06082
860-741-3701
FAX: 860-741-6870
www.alliedgroup.org

*Dean M Wern, President/CEO*
Provides individuals with disabilities or other challenges the opportunity to live and enjoy a productive, independent, and fulfilling life

**5803 Area Cooperative Educational Services(ACES)**
350 State St
North Haven, CT 06473
203-498-6800
www.aces.org

*Craig W Edmondson EdD, Executive Director*
Exists to improve public education through high quality, cost effective programs and services.

**5804 CW Resources**
200 Myrtle Street
New Britain, CT 06053
860-229-7700
FAX: 860-229-6847
www.cwresources.org

*Ronald H Buccilli, President*
Formerly Constructive Workshops, provides meaningful vocational services and employment opportunities to persons with disabilities.

**5805 Central Connecticut Association For Retarted Citizens**
950 Slater Rd
New Britain, CT 06053-1658
860-229-6665
FAX: 860-826-6883
www.ccarc.com

*Anne Ruwet, CEO*
Offers services for individuals with mental retardation and a spectrum of other disabilities, including blindness, hearing impairment, aphasia and autism.

**5806 Community Enterprises**
441 Pleasant Street
Northampton, MA 01060
413-584-1460
www.communityenterprises.com

*Dick Venne, President/CEO*
Support self-determination for individuals with disabilities and/or other challenges to actively live, learn, and work in the community.

**5807 Connecticut Governor's Committee on Employment of People With Disabilities**
200 Folly Brook Blvd
Wethersfield, CT 06109-1153
860-263-6067
FAX: 860-263-6039
e-mail: dol.webhelp@ct.gov
http://www.ctdol.state.ct.us

*Dennis Murphy, Acting Commissioner*
*Dannel P. Malloy, Governor*
Work adjustment and remunerative work programs.

**5808 Fotheringhay Farms**
84 Waterhole Rd
Colchester, CT 06415-2323
860-267-4463
FAX: 860-267-7628
http://caringcommunityct.org

*Wesley Martins, Executive Director*
Job placement programs, remunerative work services and work adjustment training programs. THE SITE IS UNDER CONSTRUCTION

**5809 George Hegyi Industrial Training Center**
5 Coon Hollow Rd
Derby, CT 06418-1149
203-735-8727
FAX: 203-735-2204
e-mail: bob.wood@snet.net
http://www.varcainc.com

*Joan Bucci, Executive Director*
*Robert Wood, President*
*Cecelia Staiano-Hayes, Program Manager*
*Jean Cota*
Work adjustment and remunerative work programs.

**5810 Kennedy Center**
2440 Reservoir Ave
Trumbull, CT 06611-4757
203-365-8522
FAX: 203-365-8533
e-mail: info@kennedyctr.org
www.thekennedycenterinc.org

*Martin Schwartz, CEO*
*Stuart Gordon, Vice President of Finance*
*Lynn Pellegrino, Vice President of HR*
*Marie Farina, HR Generalist*
Provides vocational rehabilitation, job training and job placement services to 1,000 adults with disabilities including mental retardation, traumatic brain injury, psychiatric disabilities and more. Residential services, well integrated within the community, serve 97 individuals on a daily basis. Children's programs provide support to 85 children age birth to three, in addition to after hours and recreation programs to appromxately 100 school age children. Staff size is presently 450 employees.

**5811 Quaezar**
Ste 8
2480 Black Rock Tpke
Fairfield, CT 06825-2406
203-339-3476
FAX: 203-377-6144
sterlinglp.com

*William J Sedarweck, President*
Agency for adult mentally retarded/autistic people providing residential care in a group home or apartment setting. Also provides placement in community employment.

**5812 Valley Memorial Health Center**
435 E Main St
Ansonia, CT 6401-1964
203-736-2601
FAX: 203-736-2641
e-mail: info@bghealth.org
www.bghealth.org

*Marilyn Cormack, CEO*
Provides innovative, exceptional behavioral health care through quality services and programs that focus on, and respect the consumer.

**5813 Vocational and Rehabilitation Agency**
184 Windsor Ave
Windsor, CT 06095-4536
860-602-4000
800-842-4510
FAX: 860-602-4020
TTY: 860-602-4221
e-mail: brian.sigman@CT.GOV
http://www.ct.gov/besb/site/default.asp

*Keith Maynard, Deputy Director*
*Brian Sigman, Executive Director*
*Alan Sylvestre, Chairman*
Mission is to provide quality educational and rehabilitative services to all people who are legally blind or deaf/blind and children who are visually impaired at no cost to our clients or their families.

**5814 Vocational and Rehabilitation Agency: State Department of Social Services**
Department of Social Services
25 Sigourney St
Hartford, CT 6106-5041
860-424-4844
800-537-2549
FAX: 860-424-4850
TTY: 860-424-4839
e-mail: brs.dss@po.state.ct.us
www.ct.gov/brs

*Amy L Porter, Director*
*Roderick L Bremby, Commissioner*
Provides a broad range of services to the elderly, disabled, families, and individuals who need assistance in maintaining or achieving their full potential for self-direction, self-reliance and independent living.

## Delaware

**5815 Delaware Division of Vocational Rehabilitation**
Delaware Department of Labor
4425 N Market Street
Wilmington, DE 19802
302-761-8275
www.delawareworks.com

*John McMahon, Secretary of Labor*
The state's public program that helps people with physical and mental disabilities obtain or retain employment. Also, and Independent Living Program helps people with disabilities function in the community. DVR's commitment is to help people with disabilities increase independence through employment.

**5816 Delaware Fair Employment Practice Agency**
Delaware Department of Labor
Ste 6
820 N French St
Wilmington, DE 19801-3509
302-577-8278
FAX: 302-577-6561
e-mail: delarts@state.de.us
artsdel.org

*Karen Gimbutas, VP*
*Paul Weagraff, Director*
*Susan Salkin, Deputy Director*
*Dana Wise, Administrative Specialist*
Provides opportunities and resources to eligible individuals with disabilities leading to success in employment and independent living.

**5817 Delaware Job Training Program Liaison**
Division of Employment & Training
P.O.Box 9828
Wilmington, DE 19809-828
302-761-8085

*Harold Stafford, Manager*
Work adjustment and remunerative work programs. Also offers career guidance, supported employment, work readiness and job placement.

**5818 Service Source**
3030 Bowers St
Wilmington, DE 19802
302-762-0300
800-738-1733
FAX: 302-762-8797
www.servicesource.org

*Janet Samuelson, President/CEO*
Provides exceptional services to individuals with disabilities through innovative and valued employment, training, habilitiation, housing and support services.

## District of Columbia

**5819 District of Columbia Department of Employment Services**
4058 Minnesota Avenue NE
Washington, DC 20019
202-724-7000
FAX: 202-673-6993
e-mail: does@dc.gov
does.dc.gov

To foster economic development and growth in the District of Columbia by providing workforce training, bringing together job seekers and employers, compensating unemployed and injured workers and promoting safe and healthy workplaces.

**5820 District of Columbia Dept. of Employment Services: Office of Workforce Development**
4058 Minnesota Avenue, NE
Washington, DC 20019
202-724-7000
877-319-7346
FAX:202-673-6993
TTY: 202-673-6994
e-mail: does@dc.gov
www.does.dc.gov

*Diana C Johnson, Public Information Officer*
*Marianna Lourenco, Specialist/ADA Coordinator*

To foster economic development and growth in the District of Columbia by providing workforce training, bringing together job seekers and employers, compensating unemployed and injured workers and promoting safe and healthy workplaces.

**5821 District of Columbia Fair Employment Practice Agencies**
D C Office of Human Rights
Ste 570n
441 4th St NW
Washington, DC 20001-2714
202-727-3400
FAX: 202-347-8922
TTY:202-727-3400
e-mail: oag@dc.gov
http://oag.dc.gov

*Elizabeth Noel, Executive Director*
*Irvin B. Nathan, Attorney General*
*Ariel B. Levinson-Waldman, Senior Counsel to the Attorney General*
*Victor Bonett, Legislative Director FOIA Officer*

Investigations and discrimination complaints.

**5822 Goodwill of Greater Washington**
2200 South Dakota Ave NE
Washington, DC 20018-1622
202-636-4225
888-817-4323
FAX: 202-526-3994
e-mail: info@dcgoodwill.org
dcgoodwill.org

*Catherine Meloy, CEO*
*Brendan Hurley, Vice President Marketing & Communication*
*Judy Sklar, Regional Director Retail Operations*
*Colleen Paletta, Vice President Workforce Development*

Offers vocational training, job training, sheltered employment and work experience.

**5823 Green Door**
1221 Taylor Street, NW
Washington, DC 20011-3063
202-464-9200
FAX: 202-464-5730
e-mail: info@greendoor.org
www.greendoor.org

*Judith Johnson, Executive Director*
*Brenda Randall, Assistant Director*
*Timothy J. Sawina, President and CEO*

Green Door is a community program which prepares people with a severe and persistent mental illness to live and work independently. Since 1976, Green Door has provided comprehensive services to mentally ill people, including housing, job training, job placement, education, homeless outreach, case management, support for people with substance abuse problems, family support,and specialized help for people who have had repeated hospitalizations.

**5824 Operation Job Match**
National Multiple Sclerosis Society
Ste 750
1800 M St NW
Washington, DC 20036-5802
202-887-0136
FAX: 202-296-3425
e-mail: swnissen@aol.com
operationjobmatch.org

*Steven Nissen, Manager*
*Jeanne Angulo, Executive Director*

Job readiness program for individuals with adult-onset physical disabilities.

**5825 Rehabilitation Services Administration**
10th Fl
810 1st St NE
Washington, DC 20002-4227
202-442-8663
FAX: 202-442-8742
e-mail: dds@dc.gov
rsa.dhs.dc.gov

*Elizabeth Parker, Administrator*
*Mark D. Back, FOIA Officer*
*Laura L. Nuss, Director, Department on Disability Services*

State Rehabilitation Agency providing services to eligible persons with disabilities.

**5826 WAVE Work, Achievement, Value, & Education**
Ste 500
525 School St SW
Washington, DC 20024-2762
202-484-0103
800-274-2005
FAX: 202-488-7595
e-mail: wave4kids@aol.com
www.waveinc.org

*Larry Brown, President*
*J Taylor, Senior Vice President*

Job placement programs, remunerative work services and work adjustment training programs for 18 and 21 years of age in many cities across the country including Drop-Out Recovery Programs and Drop-Out Prevention Programs. Programs also available for youth ages 12-18. Youth Professionals Development and Training and key aspects of WAVE services, as well.

## Florida

**5827 Abilities of Florida: An Affiliate of Service Source**
2735 Whitney Rd
Clearwater, FL 33760-1610
727-538-7370
FAX: 727-538-7387
e-mail: abilities@ourpeoplework.org
servicesource.org

*Janet Samuelson, President & CEO*
*Mark Hall, Executive Vice President, Corporate Developmen*
*David Hodge, Executive Vice President & Chief Financial Officer*
*Bruce Patterson, Executive Vice President & Chief Operating Officer*

Provides a full range of employment services including work evaulation, training, job coaching, job placement, advocacy and education. Also provides housing assistance and specialized to adults with cystic fibrosis.

**5828 Career Assessment & Planning Services**
Goodwill Industries - Suncoast Incorporated
10596 Gandy Blvd N
St Petersburg, FL 33702-1422
727-523-1512
888-279-1988
FAX: 727-563-9300
TTY: 727-579-1068
e-mail: gw.marketing@goodwillhisuncoast.com
www.goodwill-suncoast.org

*R. Lee Waits, President and CEO*
*Deborah A. Passerini, Executive Vice President and Chief Operating Officer*
*Gary Hebert, Corporate Treasurer and Chief Financial Officer*
*Lee C. Zeh, Corporate Secretary and Vice President for Board Development*
Career assessment and planning services help determine how prepared an individual is for employment, training, or future education. It is a comprehensive assessment that can predict current and future employment and potential adjustment factors for physically, emotionally or developmentally disabled persons who may be unemployed or underemployed.

**5829 Choices to Work Program**
Goodwill Industries-Suncoast
10596 Gandy Blvd N
St Petersburg, FL 33702-1422
727-523-1512
888-279-1988
FAX: 727-563-9300
TTY: 727-579-1068
e-mail: gw.marketing@goodwill-suncoast.com
goodwill-suncoast.org

*R. Lee Waits, President and CEO*
*Deborah A. Passerini, Executive Vice President and Chief Operating Officer*
*Gary Hebert, Corporate Treasurer and Chief Financial Officer*
*Lee C. Zeh, Corporate Secretary and Vice President for Board Development*
Assisting individuals currently eligible for Workman's Compensation, this program allows those recovering from injury on the job to prepare to return to independent employment, either through increasing ability and confidence in using adaptive behaviors and/or equipment to return to related employment, or adjusting to a more compatible employment environment.

**5830 Florida Division of Vocational Rehabilitation**
Bldg A
2002 Old Saint Augustine Rd
Tallahassee, FL 32301-4862
850-245-3399
800-451-4327
FAX: 850-245-3316
TTY: 866-515-3692
e-mail: ombudsman@vr.fldoe.org
rehabworks.org

*Bill Palmer, Manager*
*Debra Thompson, Florida Rehabilitation Council Chair*
*Roy Cosgrove, Administrator*
*Andrea Schwendinger, Government Analyst*
Rehabilitation services are important when a physical or mental handicap interferes with your ability to work. Our purpose is to help prepare for, and return to, gainful employment.

**5831 Florida Fair Employment Practice Agency**
Florida Commission on Human Relations
Ste 100
2009 Apalachee Pkwy
Tallahassee, FL 32301-4830
850-488-7082
800-342-8170
FAX: 850-488-5291
TTY: 800-955-1339
e-mail: fchrinfo!fchr.myflorida.com
http://fchr.state.fl.us

*Michelle Wilson, Executive Director*
*Gilbert Singer, Chairman*
*Mario Valle, Vice Chairman*
*Gayle Cannon, Commissioner*
The Commission is the state agency charged with enforcing the state's civil rights laws and serves as a resource on human relations for the people of Florida.

**5832 Goodwill Industries-Suncoast Adult Day Training**
10596 Gandy Blvd N
St Petersburg, FL 33702-1422
727-523-1512
888-279-1988
FAX: 727-563-9300
e-mail: gw.marketing@goodwill-suncoast.com
goodwill-suncoast.org

*Lee Waits, President*
Goodwill's adult day training programs enable people with developmental disabilities to set and achieve personal goals within a work-like setting. Participants work at various jobs throughout Goodwill and engage in a variety of activities that will allow them to become more self-sufficients.

**5833 Goodwill Industries-Suncoast Inc. Adult Day Training**
Ste 5
3033 Drane Field Rd
Lakeland, FL 33811-3305
863-701-1351
888-279-1988
FAX: 727-563-9300
TTY: 863-701-135
e-mail: gw.marketing@goodwill-suncoast.com
www.goodwill-suncoast.org

*R. Lee Waits, President and CEO*
*Deborah A. Passerini, Executive Vice President and Chief Operating Officer*
*Gary Hebert, Corporate Treasurer and Chief Financial Officer*
*Lee C. Zeh, Corporate Secretary and Vice President for Board Development*
Goodwill's adult day training programs enable people with developmental disabilities to set and achieve personal goals within a work-like setting. Participants work at various jobs throughout Goodwill and engage in a variety of activities that will allow them to become more self-sufficients.

**5834 Goodwill Industries-Suncoast Inc. Adult Day Training**
7601 Park Blvd
Pinellas Park, FL 33781-3704
727-541-6205
888-279-1988
FAX: 727-563-9300
TTY: 727-544-5835
e-mail: gw.marketing@goodwill-suncoast.com
www.goodwill-suncoast.org

*R. Lee Waits, President and CEO*
*Deborah A. Passerini, Executive Vice President and Chief Operating Officer*
*Gary Hebert, Corporate Treasurer and Chief Financial Officer*
*Lee C. Zeh, Corporate Secretary and Vice President for Board Development*
Goodwill's adult day training programs enable people with developmental disabilities to set and achieve personal goals within a work-like setting. Participants work at various jobs throughout Goodwill and engage in a variety of activities that will allow them to become more self-sufficients.

**5835 Goodwill Industries-Suncoast Non-Residential Supports And Services Program**
10596 Gandy Blvd N
St Petersburg, FL 33702-1422
727-523-1512
FAX: 727-563-9300
TTY:727-579-1068
e-mail: gw.marketing@goodwill-suncoast.com
goodwill-suncoast.org

*Lee Waits, President*
*Jean-Marie Moore, Director Of Operations*
Goodwill's adult day training programs enable people with developmental disabilities to set and achieve personal goals within a work-like setting. Participants earn paychecks working at various jobs throughout Goodwill and engage in a variety of activities that will allow them to become more self-sufficients.

**5836 Goodwill Industries-Suncoast Supported Living**
10596 Gandy Blvd N
St Petersburg, FL 33702-1422
727-523-1512
888-279-1988
FAX: 727-563-9300
TTY: 727-579-1068
e-mail: gw.marketing@goodwill-suncoast.com
goodwill-suncoast.org

*R. Lee Waits, President and CEO*
*Deborah A. Passerini, Executive Vice President and Chief Operating Officer*
*Gary Hebert, Corporate Treasurer and Chief Financial Officer*
*Lee C. Zeh, Corporate Secretary and Vice President for Board Development*
Goodwill's supported living program helps people with developmental disabilities expand their skills so they can lead increasingly independentlives. Individuals receive training and assistance with daily living activities while living in the community. Additional support includes assistance with legal issues, adocacy, community resources, banking, safety procedures, self-medication, household management, meal preparation, interpersonal relationships and parenting training.

**5837 Goodwill Industries-Suncoast,Adult Day Training**
2920 W Silver Springs Blvd
Ocala, FL 34475-5654
352- 62- 045
888-279-1988
FAX: 727-563-9300
TTY: 352-629-0874
e-mail: gw.marketing@goodwill-suncoast.com
goodwill-suncoast.org

*R. Lee Waits, President and CEO*
*Deborah A. Passerini, Executive Vice President and Chief Operating Officer*
*Gary Hebert, Corporate Treasurer and Chief Financial Officer*
*Lee C. Zeh, Corporate Secretary and Vice President for Board Development*
Goodwill's adult day training programs enable people with developmental disabilities to set and achieve personal goals within a work-like setting. Participants work at various jobs throughout Goodwill and engage in a variety of activities that will allow them to become more self-sufficients.

**5838 Goodwill Temporary Staffing**
Goodwill Industries- Suncoast
10596 Gandy Blvd N
St Petersburg, FL 33702-1422
727-577-6411
888-279-1988
FAX: 727-576-1314
e-mail: gw.marketing@goodwill-suncoast.com
goodwill-suncoast.org

*R. Lee Waits, President and CEO*
*Deborah A. Passerini, Executive Vice President and Chief Operating Officer*
*Gary Hebert, Corporate Treasurer and Chief Financial Officer*
*Lee C. Zeh, Corporate Secretary and Vice President for Board Development*
Provides employment links from potential employees, both disabled and non-disabled alike to employers with immediate employment opportunities seeking qualified candidates. Pre-screening on all applicants include: Employment history, personal references, law enforcement background checks and substance screening.

**5839 Impact: Ocala Vocational Services**
Goodwill Industries- Suncoast
10596 Gandy Blvd N
St Petersburg, FL 33702-1422
727-523-1512
888-279-1988
FAX: 727-563-9300
e-mail: gw.marketing@goodwill-suncoast.com
goodwill-suncoast.org

*R. Lee Waits, President and CEO*
*Deborah A. Passerini, Executive Vice President and Chief Operating Officer*
*Gary Hebert, Corporate Treasurer and Chief Financial Officer*
*Lee C. Zeh, Corporate Secretary and Vice President for Board Development*
Designed to enable individuals with disabilities to work in integrated settings in the community, receiving wages and benefits matching those of non-handicapped workers.

**5840 JobWorks NISH Food Service**
Goodwill Industries- Suncoast
10596 Gandy Blvd N
St Petersburg, FL 33702-1422
727-523-1512
888-279-1988
FAX: 727-563-9300
e-mail: gw.marketing@goodwill-suncoast.com
goodwill-suncoast.org

*R. Lee Waits, President and CEO*
*Deborah A. Passerini, Executive Vice President and Chief Operating Officer*
*Gary Hebert, Corporate Treasurer and Chief Financial Officer*
*Lee C. Zeh, Corporate Secretary and Vice President for Board Development*
An enclave style (or group) supported employment program designed to give consumers additional supports that allow and encourage increasingly independent employment opportunities within a food services environment.

**5841 JobWorks NISH Postal Service**
Goodwill Industries - Suncoast
10596 Gandy Blvd N
St Petersburg, FL 33702-1422
727-523-1512
888-279-1988
FAX: 727-563-9300
e-mail: gw.marketing@goodwill-suncoast.com
goodwill-suncoast.org

*R. Lee Waits, President and CEO*
*Deborah A. Passerini, Executive Vice President and Chief Operating Officer*
*Gary Hebert, Corporate Treasurer and Chief Financial Officer*
*Lee C. Zeh, Corporate Secretary and Vice President for Board Development*
An enclave style (or group) supported employment program designed to give consumers additional supports that allow and encourage increasingly independent employment opportunities within a mailroom environment.

**5842 Lighthouse Central Florida**
215 E New Hampshire St
Orlando, FL 32804-6403
407-898-2483
888-898-2483
FAX: 407-895-5255
e-mail: lvaneepoel@lcf-fl.org
lighthousecentralflorida.com

*Lee Nasehi, Executive Director*
*Lee Van Eepoel, Program Service Director*
*Donna Esbensen, Vice President, Chief Financial Officer*
*Kimberly Pawling, Director of Education & Rehabilitation Services*

Lighthouse Central Florida (LCF) is the only non-profit organization offering comprehensive, professional, vision rehabilitation services to Central Floridians of all ages with low vision or blindness.

**5843 MAClown Vocational Rehabilitation Workshop**
6390 NE 2nd Ave
Miami, FL 33138-6036 305-759-0212

*Sabrina Shelton, Manager*
Provides remunerative work.

**5844 One-Stop Service**
Goodwill Industries- Suncoast
10596 Gandy Blvd N
St Petersburg, FL 33702-1422 727-523-1512
888-279-1988
FAX: 727-563-9300
e-mail: gw.marketing@goodwill-suncoast.com
goodwill-suncoast.org

*R. Lee Waits, President and CEO*
*Deborah A. Passerini, Executive Vice President and Chief Operating Officer*
*Gary Hebert, Corporate Treasurer and Chief Financial Officer*
*Lee C. Zeh, Corporate Secretary and Vice President for Board Development*
Provides universal job search and placement related services are available to any person entering the service center. Each One-Stop Services Center provides on-site representation from a variety of employment-related service providers. All One-Stops host and/or facilitate local employment fairs and provides access to computerized job-postings.

**5845 Palm Beach Habilitation Center**
4522 S Congress Ave
Lake Worth, FL 33461-4797 561-965-8500
FAX: 561- 43- 881
e-mail: postman@pbhab.com
pbhab.com

*Jeffrey Chapman, CEO*
*David Lin, VP of Programs & Services*
*Roxanne Jacobs, Director of Developmen*
*Tina Philips, President/CEO*
Providing work evaluation, work adjustment, job placement, employment, residential and retirement services for mentally, emotionally and physically disabled adults.

**5846 Primrose Supported Employment Programs**
2733 S Ferncreek Ave
Orlando, FL 32806-5538 407-898-7201
FAX: 407-898-2120
www.primrosecenter.org

*Mary Vanburen, Executive Director*
*Leslie North, Chairman*
*Helen Galloway, Board Director*
*Faye Scott-Evans, Board Director*
Mission is to transform the lives of people with developmental disabilities by providing opportunities to achieve their fullest potential.

**5847 Quest**
500 E Colonial Dr
Orlando, FL 32803-4504 407-218-4300
888-807-8378
FAX: 407-218-4301
e-mail: contact@questinc.org
questinc.org

*Katie Porta, President*
*Michelle Bellamy, Vice President*
*Rob Cage, Director*
*Karenne Levy, Vice President Tampa Region*
Quest has built communities where people with disabilities have achieved their goals for nearly 50 years. Through a variety of residential and employment options, behavioral therapy, therapeutic day programs, charter schools and even a recreational summer camp, Quest serves more than 1000 individuals each day in the Orlando and Tampa areas.

**5848 Quest - Tampa Area**
1404 Tech Blvd
Tampa, FL 33619 813-630-4710
888-807-8378
FAX: 813-635-9614
e-mail: contact@questinc.org
www.questinc.org

*Katie Porta, President*
*Michelle Bellamy, Vice President*
*Rob Cage, Director*
*Karenne Levy, Vice President Tampa Region*
Quest has built communities where people with disabilities have achieved their goals for nearly 50 years. Through a variety of residential and employment options, behavioral therapy, therapeutic day programs, charter schools and even a recreational summer camp, Quest serves more than 1000 individuals each day in the Orlando and Tampa areas.

**5849 SCARC, Inc Evaluation, Training + Emploment Center**
213 W McCollum Ave
Bushnell, FL 33513-5916 352-793-5156
FAX: 352-793-6545
e-mail: marshaperkins@embargmail.com
http://scarcinc.com

*Marsha Perkins, Administrator*
Training and employment program for adults with disabilities. SCARC offers vocational evaluation, training, work services, transportation, supported independent living and community based training.

**5850 Seagull Industries for the Disabled**
3879 Byron Dr
West Palm Beach, FL 33404-3311 561-842-5814
FAX: 561-881-3554
e-mail: main@seagull.org
www.seagull.org

*Fred Eisinger, Executive Director*
*Linda Moore, Assistant Executive Director, Seagull Academy Principal*
*Joyce Hambrick, Director of Program Services*
*Ellen Hoffacker, Director of Finance*
Dedicated to improving the quality of life of mentally, physically and emotionally challenged adults in Palm Beach County, Florida through advocacy and the provision of a variety of social service, vocational training and residential programs designed to encourage self reliance and independence.

**5851 Supported Employment Program**
Goodwill Industries - Suncoast
10596 Gandy Blvd N
St Petersburg, FL 33702-1422 727-523-1512
888-279-1988
FAX: 727-563-9300
e-mail: gw.marketing@goodwill-suncoast.com
www.goodwill-suncoast.org

*R. Lee Waits, President and CEO*
*Deborah A. Passerini, Executive Vice President and Chief Operating Officer*
*Gary Hebert, Corporate Treasurer and Chief Financial Officer*
*Lee C. Zeh, Corporate Secretary and Vice President for Board Development*
Goodwill's supported employment program enables people with developmental disabilities to work in the community, earning wages and benefits marching those of non-disabled workers. Participants receive intensive on-the-job training at job sites that have been carefully chosen for their suitability. A support facilitator provides follow-up job coaching to ensure success. Serving people in Pinellas, Hillsborough and Pasco counties.

**5852 The Able Trust**
3320 Thomasville Road
Suite 200
Tallahassee, FL 32308
850-224-4493
888-838-2253
888-838-2253
FAX: 850-224-4496
TTY:850-224-4493
e-mail: info@abletrust.org
www.abletrust.org

*Susanne Homant, President & CEO*
*Guenevere Crum, Senior Vice President*
*Ray Ford, Assistant Director of Communications & Events*
*Jessica Taylor, Assistant to the President & CEO*
Provides grant funds for employment-related programs for non-profit agencies in Florida. Assists families, individuals and agencies through educational conferences, and youth training programs. Provides businesses free resources for hiring people with disabilities.

**5853 Vocational and Rehabilitation Agency Department of Education**
Bldg A
2002 Old Saint Augustine Rd
Tallahassee, FL 32301-4862
850-245-3399
800-451-4327
FAX: 850-245-3316
TTY: 850-488-0867
e-mail: speaker@vr.fldoe.org
rehabworks.org

*Bill Palmer, Manager*
Work adjustment and remunerative work programs.

**5854 Vocational and Rehabilitation Agency: Division of Blind Services**
2551 W Executive Center Cir
Tallahassee, FL 32301-5010
850-488-6210
800-342-1828
FAX: 850-245-3316
e-mail: craig_kiser@dbe.doe.state.fl.us
www.state.fl.us/dbs

*Bill Palmer, Manager*
Mission is to ensure blind and visually impaired Floridians have the tools, support, and opportunity to achieve success.

**5855 Work Exploration Center**
3000 N West 83rd Street i 40
Gainesville, FL 32606
352-395-5265
FAX: 352-395-5271
admin.sfcc.edu

*Karla Wooten, Coordinator*
The Work Exploration Center embraces a holistic approach to Comprehensive Vocational Evaluation and Community Employment services, encouraging individual understanding, hope and growth for a productive and fulfilling future.

## Georgia

**5856 Employment and Training Division, Region B**
Goodwill Industries of North Georgia
1123 Progress Rd
Ellijay, GA 30540-5504
706-276-4722
888-514-8112
FAX: 706-276-4732
e-mail: vti@ellijay.com

*Linda Rau, Director Programs/Services*
Employment training, assessment and job placement for people who have disabilities and/or are disadvantaged. Serving 15 counties in Northern Georgia.

**5857 Fair Housing and Equal Employment**
Georgia Commission on Equal Opportunity
2 Martin Luther King Jr Dr SE
Atlanta, GA 30334-9000
404-656-1736
800-473-6736
FAX: 404-656-4399
e-mail: gceo@gceo.state.ga.us
www.gceo.state.ga.us

*Judith A Harris, Fair Housing Division Manager*
*Stephanie Randolph, Intake Coordinator/Housing*
*Abdul Khadeem, Equal Employment Division Man.*
*Gordon Joyner, Exec Director/Administrator*
To investigate housing and employment discrimination in the state of Georgia.

**5858 Griffin Area Resource Center Griffin Community Workshop Division**
931 Hamilton Boulevard
Griffin, GA 30224
770-228-9919
FAX: 770-228-9920
e-mail: griffincomwrkshp@aol.com
http://www.gscunitedway.org

*Cary Grubbs, Executive Director*
*Charles Cary Grubbs, Garc Executive Director*
*William Wilson, President*
*Rodney Shurman, Vice-President*
A CARF (The Rehabilitation Accreditation Commission) accredited Employment and Community Support organization providing daily services to participants with disabilities from 16 years of age and up in a 5 county area.

**5859 IBM National Support Center**
Special Needs Systems
P.O.Box 2150
Atlanta, GA 30301
404-577-7995
800-426-2133
FAX: 561-982-6059
Serves to help health care leaders, agency directors, policy makers, employers, educators, public officials and individuals learn how computers can enhance the quality of life for the disabled person in the school, home and workplace. Also provide information and resource guides on disabilities affecting hearing, learning, speech and language, mobility and vision.

**5860 Kelley Diversified**
P.O.Box 967
Athens, GA 30603-967
706-549-4398
FAX: 706-549-4479

*Mary Patton, Executive Director*
*Sherry Burns, Rehabilitation Services Director*
*Jenny Taylor, Business Operations Manager*
*Patricia Horne, Bookkeeper*
Work adjustment and remunerative work programs.

**5861 New Ventures**
306 Fort Dr
Lagrange, GA 30240-5900
706-882-7723
FAX: 706-882-5401
e-mail: customersvc@newventures.org
newventures.org

*Dave Miller, CEO*
*Kelly Anderson, Quality Director*
*Jay Fager, Director of Finance*
*Doug Roberts, Production Manager*
A rehabilitation and work training facility for individuals with barriers to employability. The program utilizes community based industrial work of varying levels of difficulty. A return to work conditioning program for the industrially injured is offered which features: first-day contact, workers compensation rehabilitation team management, and light-duty work conditioning. A training stipend is paid to defray costs associated with training.

## Hawaii

**5862 Assets School**
1 Ohana Nui Way
Honolulu, HI 96818-4497
808-423-1356
FAX: 808-422-1920
e-mail: info@assets-school.net
assets-school.net

*John F. Morton, Chairman*
*Kristi L. Maynard, Vice Chairman*
*Robert W. Wo, Secretary*
*Russell J. Lau, Treasurer*
ASSETS is an independent school for gifted and or dyslexic children that provides an individualized, integrated learning enviroment. ASSETS' enviroment empowers these children to maximize their potential and to find their place as lifelong learners in school and society.

**5863 Hawaii Fair Employment Practice Agency**
Rm 411
830 Punchbowl St
Honolulu, HI 96813-5080
808-586-8636
800-586-8800
FAX: 808-586-8655
TTY: 808-586-8692
e-mail: DLIR.HCRC.INFOR@hawaii.gov
http://hawaii.gov/labor/hcrc

*Michael O Yamamoto*
HCRC enforces state laws prohibiting discrimination in employment.

**5864 Hawaii Vocational Rehabilitation Division**
1901 Bachelot St.
Honolulu, HI 96817
808-586-9744
FAX: 808-586-9755
TTY:808-586-9744
e-mail: info@hawaiivr.org
hawaiivr.org

*JONATHAN Chun, Chair*
*JOE CORDOVA, Administrator*
*SUSAN FOARD, ASSIST. ADMINISTRATOR*
*KATIE KEIM, STAFF SPECIALISTS*
Mission is our committed staff strive, day-in day-out, to provide timely efficient and effective programs, services and benefits, for the purpose of achieving the outcome of empowering those who are the most vulnerable in our state to expand thier capacity for self sufficiency , self-determination, independence, healthy choices, quality of life and personal dignity.

**5865 Lanakila Rehabilitation Center**
1809 Bachelot St
Honolulu, HI 96817-2430
808-531-0555
FAX: 808-533-7264
e-mail: cr@lanakilapacific.org
www.lanakilahawaii.org

*Marian Tsuji, President*
*Wayne Fujishige, Vice President*
*Dwayne MASUTANI, Director Budget & Finance*
*Rachael Young, Director Human Resources*
Lanakila is a private nonprofit organization whose mission is to provide services and supports that assist individuals with physical, mental, or age-related challenges to live as independently as possible within our community. A broad range of services are offered which include meal/senior services, community based adult day programming for individuals with disabilities, work training opportunities, and extended/supported employment for individuals with special needs.

**5866 Vocational and Rehabilitation Agency**
P.O.Box 339
Honolulu, HI 96809-339
808-586-5162
FAX: 808-586-5765
e-mail: nshim@dhs.state.hi.us

*Albert Perez, Manager*
Work adjustment and remunerative work programs.

**5867 Wahiawa Family**
330 Walker Ave
Wahiawa, HI 96786-1883
808-621-7407

*Leslie Chinna*
Work adjustment and remunerative work programs.

## Idaho

**5868 Idaho Employment Service and Job Training Program Liaison**
Idaho Department of Employment
317 W Main St
Boise, ID 83735-1
208-334-6300
FAX: 208-334-6455
e-mail: www@labor.idaho.gov
http://labor.idaho.gov

*Roger Madsen, Manager*
*C.L Butch Otter, Governor*
*Roger B. Madson, Director*
Work adjustment and remunerative work programs.

**5869 Idaho Fair Employment Practice Agency**
Idaho Human Rights Commission
P.O.Box 83720
Boise, ID 83720-3
208-334-2873
FAX: 208-334-2664
www2.state.id.us/ihrc/ihrchome.htm

*David Rogers, Administrator*
Mission is to admininster state and federal anti-discrimination laws in Idaho in a manner that is fair, accurate, and timely; and to work towards ensuring that all people withink the state are treated with dignity and respect in their places of employment, housing, education, and public accomodations.

**5870 Idaho Governor's Committee on Employment of People with Disabilities**
317 W Main St
Boise, ID 83735-1
Work adjustment and remunerative work programs.

**5871 Idaho Vocational Rehabilitation Agency**
Ste 101
10200 W Emerald St
Boise, ID 83704-8780
208-327-7411
FAX: 208-327-7417
TTY:208-327-7040
e-mail: darrell.quist@vr.idaho.gov
vr.idaho.gov

*Darrell Quist, Manager*
*Janet Thaldorf, Supervisor*
Vocational Rehabilitation assists many individuals with disabilities to go to work. With VR assistance, these individuals have overcome numerous obstacles and disability related barriers to achieve employment.

**5872 Vocational and Rehabilitation Agency**
Idaho Commission for the Blind & Visually Impaired
341 W Washington St
PO Box 83720
Boise, ID 83720-0012
208-334-3220
800-542-8688
FAX: 208-334-2963
e-mail: aroan@icbvi.state.id.us
icbvi.state.id.us

*Angela Roan, Manager*
*Raelene Thomas, Management Assistant*
*Bruce Christopherson, Rehabilitation Services Chief*
*Dana Ard, Vocational Rehabilitation Counselor for the Blind, Sr*
Vocational rehabilitation, independent living training, medical intervention, adaptive technology and devices and employer advocacy.

## Illinois

**5873 Ada S McKinley Vocational Services**
1359 W Washington Blvd
Chicago, IL 60607-4577
312-554-0600
FAX: 312-554-0292
TTY:312-697-9794
e-mail: info@adasmckinley.org
adasmckinley.org

*George Jones, Jr., Executive Director*
*Marion G. Sleet, Chief Operating Officer*
*Hans J. Schuster, Chief Financial Officer*
*Kathleen D. Chappell, Chief Development Officer*
Mission is to serve those who, because of disabilities or other limiting conditions, need help in finding and pursuing paths leading to healthy, productive, and fulfilling lives.

**5874 Anixter Center**
2001 N. Clybourn Ave.
3rd Floor
Chicago, IL 60614
773-973-7900
FAX: 773-973-5268
TTY:773-973-2180
e-mail: AskAnixter@anixter.org
anixter.org

*Francisco Cisneros, Ph.D., President and CEO*
*Hillary A. Ebach, Executive Vice President*
*Lauren K. Hill, Managing Director*
*Dan Sabol, Vice President and Business Development Officer*
A Chicago-based human services agency that assists people with disabilities to live and work successfully in the community. Anixter Center provides vocational training, employment services, residences, special education, prevention programs, community services and health care. In addition, Anixter Center offers Illinois' only substance abuse treatment programs specifically for people with disabilities including Addiction Recovery of the Deaf.

**5875 C-4 Work Center**
4740 N Clark S
Chicago, IL 60640
773-769-0205
www.c4chicago.org

*Eileen Durkin, President and CEO*
*Bruce Seitzer, LCPC, Chief Clinical Officer*
*John Troy, MBA, CPA, Chief Administrative Officer*
*Danielle Byron, MS, Chief Information Officer*
Aftercare, case finding, information and referrals, vocational training and work activities offered to mentally ill persons.

**5876 Clearbrook**
1835 W Central Rd
Arlington Heights, IL 60005-2410
847-870-7711
FAX: 847-870-7741
TTY:847-870-2239
e-mail: info@clearbrook.org
www.clearbrook.org

*Carl M La Mell, President*
*Tracy Martin, Admissions Director*
*Bernie Andersen, Assistant to the President*
*Rosa Baez-Lopez, Vice President of Human Resources*
Offers educational, employment and residential services to the developmentally disabled children and adults.

**5877 Cornerstone Services**
777 Joyce Rd
Joliet, IL 60436-1876
815-727-6666
FAX: 815-723-1177
e-mail: jhogan@cornerstoneservices.org
cornerstoneservices.org

*James A Hogan, CEO*
*Susan Murphy, Coordinator Public Relations*
Cornerstone Services provides progressive, comprehensive services for people with disabilities, promoting choice, dignity and the opportunity to live and work in the community. Established in 1969, the agency provides developmental, vocational, employment, residential and behavioral health services at various community-based locations. The nonprofit social service agency helps approximately 750 people each day.

**5878 Fulton County Rehab Center**
500 N Main St
Canton, IL 61520-1844
309-647-6510
FAX: 309-647-3040

*Rex Lewis, Executive Director*
Residential rehab center with health care incidental; manufactures wood pallets and skids; job training and vocational rehabilitation services.

**5879 Glenkirk**
3504 Commercial Ave
Northbrook, IL 60062-1863
847-272-5111
FAX: 847-272-7350
e-mail: info@glenkirk.org
glenkirk.org

*Allan G. Spector, CEO*
Helps infants, children and adults with developmental disabilities reach higher levels of independence. A non-profit organization serving people in north and northwest Chicago suburbs. Glenkirk's residential, vocational, educational and support programs include services which provide individual evaluation, therapeutic treatment and training.

**5880 Illinois Employment Service**
Department of Employment Security
Fl 4
401 S State St
Chicago, IL 60605-1293
312-793-4880
800-247-4984
www.state.il.us/agency/
Work adjustment and remunerative work programs.

**5881 Jewish Vocational Services**
216 West Jackson Blvd.
Suite 700
Chicago, IL 60606-4602
312-673-3400
FAX: 312-553-5544
e-mail: jvschgo@jvschicago.org
http://jvschicago.org/

*Elaine Saphi Fox, President*
*Alan S. Crane, Vice President*
*Marc Jacobs, Vice President*
*Barry S. Maram, Secretary*

Occupational training and job placement for handicapped persons of all religions.

**5882 JoDavies Workshop**
P.O.Box 6087
Galena, IL 61036-6087
815-777-2211
FAX: 815-777-3386
e-mail: jdwi@jdwi.org
www.jdwi.org

*William Wubben, Treasurer*
*Tim Zueger, Chairperson*
*Dale Gereau, Plant Manager*
Intake and referral, early intervention for children only, vocational evaluation and work adjustment training services offered.

**5883 Kennedy Job Training Center**
7361 S Meade Ave
Bedford Park, IL 60638-6122
708-594-7155
FAX: 708-594-7156
e-mail: info@stcolettail.org.
http://www.stcolettail.org

*Robin Mertes, Placement Manager*
*Kandy Stamer, QMRP/Intake Coordinator*
*Bob Loquercio, Board of Director*
*Wayne A. Kottmeyer, Executive Director*
Offers vocational evaluation, vocational training work adjustment training, and job placement services for developmentally disabled and hearing impaired persons.

**5884 Knox County Council for Developmental Disabilities**
2015 Windish Dr
Galesburg, IL 61401-9774
309-343-0480
FAX: 309-343-6937
e-mail: mcrittenden@kccdd.com
kccdd.com

*Mary Crittenden, Executive Director*
*Pam Green, Director of Operations*
*Jeff Gomer, Director of Finance*
*Lynndel Messmore, Director of Rehabilitation*
Developmental training, vocational evaluation, work adjustment training, extended training, placement, supported employment.

**5885 Kreider Services**
500 Anchor Road
Dixon, IL 61021-366
815-288-6691
FAX: 815-288-1636
TTY:815-288-5931
e-mail: info@kreiderservices.org?subject=Kreider%20Se
kreiderservices.org

*Dr. Richard Piller, President*
*Dr. Vernon Brickley, Vice President*
*Cheryl Ebens, Director*
*Mike Hickey, Director*
Offers day service programs, vocational training programs, job placement, supported employment, respite care, residential and family support for ages birth to three years.

**5886 Lambs Farm**
14245 W Rockland Rd
Libertyville, IL 60048-9745
847-362-4636
FAX: 847-362-9688
e-mail: info@lambsfarm.org
lambsfarm.org

*Dianne Yaconetti, President & CEO*
*Kathy Buresch, Director, Operations, Marketing and Communications*
*Nikki Bonamarte, Director, Development*
*Jose Martinez, Director, Quality Assurance*
Person-centered, comprehensive program of residential, vocational and social support service for adults with developmental disabilities.

**5887 Land of Lincoln Goodwill Industries**
815 N. 11th Street
Springfield, IL 62702
217-789-0400
FAX: 217-789-0540
e-mail: info@llgi.org
www.llgi.org

*Sharon Durbin, CEO and President*
*Valerie Ausmus, VP of Finance*
*Deborah Clark, VP of Retail Operations*
*Kim Wonnell, VP of Human Resources*
Empowers people with special needs to become self-sufficient through the power od work.

**5888 Orchard Village**
7670 Marmora Ave
Skokie, IL 60077-2628
847-967-1800
FAX: 847-967-9543
e-mail: info@orchardvillage.org
www.orchardvillage.org

*Joy Decker, President & CEO*
*Sally Ruecking, Vice President, Development*
*Allison Stark, Vice President, Programs*
*Jennifer Burgess, Director, Residential Services*
Vocational program and counseling, respite services and community living group homes for the disabled and cognitively impaired. Orchard village also operates a private hope school especially devoted to teaching young adults independent living and skills necessary to flourish in the community.

**5889 President's Committee on Employment of Employment of the Disabled**
623 E Adams St
Springfield, IL 62701-1614
217-782-2093
800-ASK-DORI
FAX: 217-524-2471
TTY: 217-782-5734

*Carol Adams, President*
Work adjustment and remunerative work programs.

**5890 Sertoma Centre**
4343 W 123rd St
Alsip, IL 60803-1807
708-371-9700
FAX: 708-371-9747
e-mail: info@sertomacentre.org
sertomacentre.org

*Gus Vanden Brink, Executive Director*
*Paula Phillips, Assistant Director*
A nationally accredited, not-for-profit agency that provides services to students and adults with developmental disabilities and mental illness. MIssion is to provide opportunities that empower individuals with disabilities to achieve success.

**5891 Shore Training Center**
Shore Community Services
4232 Dempster Street
Skokie, IL 60076
847-982-2030
FAX: 847-982-2039
TTY:847-581-0076
e-mail: shorecom@sbcglobal.net
shoreinc.org

*Debora Braun, Executive Director*
*Nadia Diab, Director of Residential Services*
*Debbie Shulruf, Director of SHORE Lois Lloyd Center*
*Lisa Wright, Director, SHORE Joseph Koenig, Sr. Training Center*
Mission is to improve the quality of life for citizens with developmental disabilities through community based services providing education/training.

**5892 Skills Inc.**
1122 5th Ave
Moline, IL 61265-1233
309-797-3586
FAX: 309-797-4914
skills-inc.org

*Twila Robinson, President*
Accredited through the Commission on Accreditation of Rehabilitation Facilities; offers job training partnership act and vocational evaluation services offered.

**5893 Thresholds AMISS**
12145 Western Ave
Blue Island, IL 60406-1387
708-597-7997
FAX: 708-597-8073

*Julia Rupp, Executive Director*
*Camille Rucks, Team Leader*
Services offered include psychosocial, vocational and residential programs for ages 18 or older with a primary diagnosis of mental illness. Facility is wheelchair accessible.

**5894 Vocational and Rehabilitation Agency**
207 Staehouse
Springfield, IL 62706-1
217-782-0244
800-843-6154
FAX: 217-524-6262
TTY: 888-261-3336
e-mail: ITTF.Web@illinois.gov
www.state.il.us

*Pat Quinn, Governor*
Provides work adjustment and remunerative skills.

**5895 Washington County Vocational Workshop**
781 E Holzhauer Dr
Nashville, IL 62263-2055
618-327-4461
FAX: 618-327-4477

*Keith Curran, Executive Director*
Provides job training and related services and vocational rehabilitation services.

**5896 Westside Parents Work Activity Center**
3765 W Ogden Ave
Chicago, IL 60623
773-522-1200

Offers developmental training programs providing basic skills in self care for multiply and physically handicapped persons.

## Indiana

**5897 ADEC Resources for Independence**
19670 State Road 120
Bristol, IN 46507-9162
574-848-7451
877-342-8954
FAX: 574-848-5917
e-mail: shivelyp@adecinc.com
adecinc.com

*Paula Shively, President & CEO*
*Donna Belusar, CFO*
*Sally Russell, Vice President*
*Joe Blocher, Vice President of Human Relations*
Serves Elkhart County and surrounding area.

**5898 ARC of Allen County**
4919 Coldwater Rd
Fort Wayne, IN 46825-5532
260-456-4534
800-234-7811
FAX: 260-745-5200
e-mail: delbrecht@esarc.org
www.easterseals.com

*Bill Martin, Chairperson*
*Larry Graham, Senior Vice Chairperson*
*Donna Elbrecht, President*
*Susan Klug, Chief Operating Officer*
Primary list of services includes: community living services, production and work training services, residential services, 24 hour medicaid waiver services, employment services, child care center, adult day services, and recreation.

**5899 Arc Bridges**
2650 W 35th Ave
Gary, IN 46408-1416
219-884-1138
FAX: 219-980-7315
www.thearcnwindiana.com

*Brian Davis, Contact*
*Kris Prohl, Executive Director*
Mission is to improve the welfare of people with intellectual and development disabilities and their families.

**5900 BI-County Services**
425 E Harrison Rd
Bluffton, IN 46714-9013
260-824-1253
FAX: 260-824-1892
e-mail: info@adifferentlight.com
www.bi-countyservices.com

*John Whicker, President*
Serves Wells and Adam Counties. Infant services, Medicaid waivers, music therapy, ICF, MR, group homes, sheltered employment, pay program and supported employment services available.

**5901 Balance Centers of America**
2538 Patricia St
Portage, IN 46368-2630
219-736-2930

*Jane Labar, Contact*
Offers developmental training programs providing basic skills in self care for physically handicapped persons.

**5902 Bridge Pointe Services & Goodwill of Southern Indiana, Inc**
Goodwill International
1329 Applegate Ln
P.O. Box 2488
Clarksville, IN 47131- 2488
812-283-7908
800-660-3355
FAX: 812-283-6248
e-mail: comments@goodwillsi.org
http://www.goodwillsi.org/

*Candice C. Barksdale, Chief Executive Director*
*Joel Henderson, PHR, Vice President of Human Resources*
*Bonnie Davis, Vice President of Donated Goods/Retail*
*Michelle Dayvault, Vice President of Development and Marketing*
Career assesment, job readiness and placement, office skills training. Pediatric family support services. Childrens Academy, a developmental preschool.

**5903 Carey Services**
2724 S Carey St
Marion, IN 46953-3515
765-668-8961
FAX: 765-664-6747
www.careyservices.com

*Bonnie Smith, Human Resources Manager*
*Mark R. Draves, Chief Executive Officer*
*Gary Hendricks, Corporate Compliance*
*David Sprowl, Intake Coordinator*

The mission of Carey Services is to create pathways towards self-sufficiency with personal satisfaction.

**5904 Evansville Association for the Blind**
500 North 2nd Avenue
Evansville, IN 47710-2355
812-422-1181
FAX: 812-424-3154
e-mail: eabcdc@evansville.net
http://www.evansvilleblind.org/

*Karla Horrell, Executive Director*
*Daniel Dana, President*
*Larry Arp, Vice President*
*Pam Doerter, Vice President*
An community rehabilitation facility untilizing individual goals to assist persons with disabilities achieve or maintain potenial

**5905 Four Rivers Resource Services**
P.O.Box 249
Linton, IN 47441-249
812-847-2231
FAX: 812-847-8836
e-mail: fourrivers@frrs.org
frrs.org

*Kenton Barnes, President*
*Mary Lou Chapman, Vice-President*
*Ray Hart, Treasurer*
*Kathy Pennington, Secretary*
Employment, community living, connections, follow-along, early intervention, preschool, healthy families, child care resource and referral and child care voucher program, impact, and transpotation services.

**5906 Gateway Services/JCARC**
P.O.Box 216
Franklin, IN 46131-216
317-738-5500
888-494-8069
FAX: 317-738-5522

*Karen Luehmann, Executive Director*
Utilizes individual goals to assist persons with disabilities achieve or maintain potential.

**5907 Goodwill Industries of Central Indiana**
1635 W Michigan St
Indianapolis, IN 46222-3852
317-524-4313
FAX: 317-524-4336
TTY:317-524-4309
e-mail: goodwill@goodwillindy.org
goodwillindy.org

*Jim Mc Clelland, President & CEO*
*Nicki Washburn, Disability Services Coordinator*
Goodwill is in the business of helping people find jobs and provides programs and services for people who want to work. Goodwill is a community resource committed to deploying our assets and leveraging our resources with those of others in the community to create more opportunities for people who need assistance to improve their ability to earn a living.

**5908 Indiana Civil Rights Commission**
100 North Senate Avenue
Suite N103
Indianapolis, IN 46204-2208
317-232-2600
800-628-2909
FAX: 317-232-6580
TTY: 800-743-3333
e-mail: info@icrc.in.gov
www.in.gov/icrc

*Jamal Smith, Executive Director*
Works to develop public policies that ensure equal opportunity in education to all.

**5909 Indiana Employment Services and Job Training Program Liaison**
10 N Senate Ave
Indianapolis, IN 46204-2201
317-232-6702
FAX: 317-233-5499
Offers developmental training programs providing basic skills in self care for physically handicapped persons.

**5910 Michigan Resources**
4315 E Michigan Blvd
Michigan City, IN 46360-3151
219-874-4288
FAX: 219-874-2689
TTY:219-873-2245
e-mail: michiana@michianaresources.org
michianaresources.org

*Nancy J Matela, Board Member*
*Linda Hough, Chairperson*
*Matthew Hollander, Treasurer*
*Andie Wolfinsohn, Secretary*
Vocational training center for persons 16 and older with disabilities.

**5911 New Hope Services**
725 Wall St
Jeffersonville, IN 47130-3616
812-288-8248
800-237-6604
FAX: 812-288-1206
e-mail: info@newhopeservices.org
newhopeservices.org

*' Bosley, President and CEO*
*John Broady, Vice President and CFO*
*Bonnie Long, Vice President, CAO*
*Jody Kitch, VP Director of Social Services*
Mission is to provide hope through services which are responsive to individual needs.

**5912 New Horizons Rehabilitation**
P.O.Box 98
237 Six Pine Ranch Road
Batesville, IN 47006-98
812-934-4528
FAX: 812-934-2522
e-mail: mdausch@newhorizons-rehab.org
www.nhrehab.org

*Marie Dausch, Executive Director*
Serves Ripley, Franklin, Ohio, Switzerland Dearborn, and Decatur. Provides training and services to adults with mental/physical disabilities and infants birth to age 3 with developmental delays or conditions of risk which could result in a developmental delay.

**5913 Noble Of Indiana**
Noble, Inc.
7701 E 21st St
Indianapolis, IN 46219-2406
317-375-2700
FAX: 317-375-2719
e-mail: rita.davis@nobleofindiana.org
www.nobleofindiana.org

*Julia Huffman, President & CEO*
*Rita Davis, Director, Community Relations*
*Julie Brown, Director of Human Resources*
*Jeanine Coleman, Director of Community Living*
Since 1953, Noble of Indiana has been dedicated to its mission: to create opportunities for people with developmental disabilities to live meaningful lives.

**5914 Office of State Coordinator of Vocational Education for Students with Disability**
Rm 212
10 N Senate Ave
Indianapolis, IN 46204-2201
317-232-1829
800-891-6499
e-mail: tfields@dwd.state.in.us
www.state.in.us/dwd/techd

*Scott B. Sanders, Commissioner*
*Randy Gillespie, Chief Financial Officer*
*Jeff Gill, General Counsel*
*Michelle Marshel, Deputy Commissioner of Communication, Customer Service and Governmenta*
Manages and impliments innovative employment programs, unemployment insurance systems, and facilitates regional economic growth initiatives for Indiana.

**5915 Putnam County Comprehensive Services**
630 Tennessee St
Greencastle, IN 46135-2102
765-653-9763
877-653-9763
FAX: 765-653-3646
e-mail: rehab@pccsinc.org
www.pccsinc.org

*Chuck Schroeder, CEO*
*Laura Gordon, Adult Services Director*
*Teresa Human, Community Living Director*
*Josi Blunton, Residential Director*
A not-for-profit organization serving individuals with disabilities and similar characteristics in Indiana. Their mission is to provide services to individuals with disabilities in order for them to reach their optimum potential in attitudes, habits, and skills through training and integration, making them contributing members of their community, and to promote community awareness and acceptance of people with different abilities.

**5916 Southern Indiana Resource Solutions**
1579 S Folsomville Rd
Boonville, IN 47601-9465
812-897-4840
FAX: 812-897-0123
e-mail: kelly@sirs.org
www.sirs.org

*Kelly Mitchell, CEO/President*
*Don Critchlow, Chairperson*
*Larry Oathout, Vice-Chairperson*
*Jeff Hagedorn, Board Member*
Adult services including jobs, community connections, and residential, childrens services, including service coordination and all therapies.

**5917 Sycamore Rehabilitation Services**
1001 Sycamore Ln
Danville, IN 46122-1474
317-745-4715
888-573-0817
FAX: 317-745-8271
e-mail: info@sycamoreservices.com
sycamoreservices.com

*Ralph Dunkin, President*
*Paul McManus, Vice President*
*Steve Patterson, Treasurer*
*Terry Kessinger, Secretary*
Provides individuals training and services for persons with disabilities that enhance independence in all areas of life.

**5918 Vocational and Rehabilitation Agency**
P.O.Box 7083
Indianapolis, IN 46207-7083
317-232-1401
800-545-7763
FAX: 317-232-6478
e-mail: peter.bispecos@sssa.in.gov
www.ssa.in.gov

*Mike Hedden, Executive Director*
Vocational training center for persons with disabilities.

**5919 Wabash/Employability Center**
Suite 2
S C6395 Earl Ave
Lafayette, IN 47903
765-447-0300
FAX: 765-447-6456
http://www.nbdc.com

*Bill Carmichael, Contact*
Serves Tippecanoe County.

## Iowa

**5920 ACT Assessment Test Preparation Reference Manual**
American College Testing Program
P.O.Box 168
500 ACT Drive
Iowa City, IA 52243-168
319-337-1000
FAX: 319-339-3021
act.org

*Jon Whitmore, CEO*
*Janet E. Godwin, Chief of Staff and Chief Accountability Officer*
*Jon L. Erickson, President, Education Division*
*Martin L. Scaglione, President, Workforce Development Division*
This reference manual was developed as a resource for high school teachers and counselors in assisting students with test preparation.

**5921 Franklin County Work Activity Center**
20 5th St NW
Hampton, IA 50441-1908
641-456-2532
FAX: 641-456-4682
www.accessincorportated.org

*Harry Jacoby, Executive Director*
*Jim Koenen, Owner*
Nonprofit organization providing residential and vocational services in Franklin and Hardin counties in the state of Iowa. Residential Services include RCF/MR services, Supported Community Living Services and Community Supervised Apartment Living Arrangement Services. Vocational Services include Work Services and Supported Employment Services. Accredited by the Commission on Accreditation of rehabilitation Facilities since 1984, and serves individuals with a wide range of needs.

**5922 Innovative Industries**
405 E Madison St
Winterset, IA 50273-2402
515-462-2926
FAX: 515-462-2870
e-mail: winnind@ishsi.com

*Duane Nelson, Program Manager*

**5923 Iowa Civil Rights Commission**
400 E 14th St
Des Moines, IA 50319-201
515-281-4121
800-457-4416
FAX: 515-242-5840
e-mail: don.grove@iowa.gov
www.state.ia.us/government/crc

*Ralph Rosenberg, Executive Director*
*Ron Pothast, Acting Executive Director*
*Corlis Moody, Executive Director*
*Beth Townsend, Executive Director*
A neutral, fact-finding administrative agency that enforces the 'Iowa Civi Rights Act of 1965,' Iowa's anti-discrimination law. The commission doesn not provide legal representation. The commission's vision is a state free of discrimination.

**5924 Iowa Employment Service**
1000 E Grand Ave
Suite 140
Des Moines, IA 50309
515-282-5823
FAX: 515-288-2184
e-mail: fering@iowacareerconnection.com
www.iowacareerconnection.com

*L.M. (Al) Fering, SPHR, FLMI, President*
*Miles Morrow, CPC*
Specializes in accounting and human resources talent aquisition in the Upper-Midwest.

**5925 Iowa Job Training Program Liaison**
Iowa Department of Economic Development
200 E Grand Ave
Des Moines, IA 50309-1856
515-725-3000
FAX: 515-725-3010
e-mail: info@iowa.gov
iowalifechanging.com

*David Lyons, President*
*Debi Durham, Director*
*Kathy Anderson, Director, Communications Team*
*Jody Benz, Director, Iowa Commission on Volunteer Service*
To engender and promote economic development policies and practices which stimulate and sustain Iowa's economic growth and climate and that integrate efforts across public and private sectors.

**5926 Iowa Valley Community College**
3702 S Center St
Marshalltown, IA 50158-4783
641-752-4643
800-284-4823
FAX: 641-752-5909
e-mail: ivinfo@iavalley.edu
http://www.iavalley.edu/

*Dr. Chris Wynes, Chancellor*
*Robin Anctil, Director of Marketing*
*Dr. Lisa Breja, Institutional Researcher/AQIP Liaison*
*Nate Chua, MCC Director of Retention & Learning Services*
Offers two levels of specialized vocational preparatory programming for adults with disabilities. The Career Development Center serves dependent adults. The goal of the program is to maintain or improve skills to enable persons served to enter sheltered or supported employment. The IRP/CBVT programs are non-credit specialized vocational programs for independent adults served by Vocational Rehabilitation and our programs. The goals are for competitive placements in jobs. CARF accredited.

**5927 Iowa Vocational Rehabilitation Services**
510 E 12th St
Jessie Parker Building
Des Moines, IA 50319-0240
515-281-4211
FAX: 515-281-7645
TTY:515-281-4211
e-mail: Victoria.Carrington@iowa.gov
www.ivrs.iowa.gov

*David Mitchell, Administrator*
*Matthew Coulter, Chief Financial Officer*
*Kenda Jochimsen, Bureau Chief*
*Charlie Levine, Assistant Bureau Chief*
The mission is to work for and with individuals who have disabilities to achieve their employment, independence and economic goals.

**5928 New Focus**
102 W Washington St
Centerville, IA 52544-1550
641-437-1722
FAX: 641-437-1028

*Peggy Oden, Executive Director*
Provides vocational services for adults with disabilities. Includes work activity, supported employment and supported community living.

**5929 Second Time Around**
110 W Jackson St
Centerville, IA 52544-1709
641-437-7355

*Monica Blizeck, Manager*
*Debbie Steen, Store Supervisor*
*Deana Edwards, Manager*
Work training site for adults with disabilities.

## Kansas

**5930 Clay Center Adult Training Center**
701 4th St
Clay Center, KS 67432-2903
785-632-6811
FAX: 785-632-5371

*Michael Spielman, Manager*
Work training site for adults with disabilities.

**5931 Kansas Fair Employment Practice Agency**
Rm 851s
900 SW Jackson St
Topeka, KS 66612-1220
785-296-3206
FAX: 785-296-0589
www.state.ks.us/public/khrc

*Mostafa Kamal, Manager*

**5932 Kansas Vocational Rehabilitation Agency**
300 SW Oakley Ave
Topeka, KS 66606-1995
785-232-2777
FAX: 785-267-0263
TTY:913-296-7029
e-mail: jac@srkspo.wpo.state.ks.us
www.srskansas.org/rehab

*Joyce Cussimanio, Director*
Helps people with disabilities achieve employment and self-sufficiency. Also links employers with qualified and productive individuals to meet thier work force needs.

## Kentucky

**5933 Kentucky Committee on Employment of Peoplewith Disabilities**
2nd Fl
275 E Main St
Frankfort, KY 40601-2321
502-564-7456
FAX: 502-564-7459
e-mail: VivianL.Bettis@ky.gov
www.oet.ky.gov

*Greg Higgins, Manager*
*Tom Bowell, Manager*
*Shane Smith, Manager*
*Terri Bradshaw, Communications Director*
Provides qualified people for jobs, quality jobs for people, temporary financial support for the unemployed, comprehensive labor market information, and preserve the integrity and viability of the Unemployment Insurance Trust Fund.

**5934 Kentucky Department for Employment Serviceand Job Training Program Liaison**
275 E Main Street 2-W
Frankfort, KY 40621-1
502-564-5331
FAX: 502-564-7452
e-mail: VivianL.Bettis@ky.gov
http://www.oet.ky.gov

*Gina Oney, Assistant Director*
*Linda Prewitt, Acting Division Director/ Assistant Director*
*Linda Pierce, Compliance Support Branch Manager*
*Gregory Higgins, Acting Unemployment Insurance Division Director*
Provides qualified people for jobs, quality jobs for people, temporary financial support for the unemployed.

**5935 Kentucky Department for the Blind**
275 East Main Street
Frankfort, KY 40621
502-782-3414
800-321-6668
FAX: 502-564-2951
TTY: 502-564-2929
e-mail: JenniferN.Wright@ky.gov
www.blind.ky.gov

*Christopher Smith, Executive Director*
*Michelle McElmurray, Executive Assistant*
*Allison Jessee, Director of Consumer Services*
*Cora McNabb, VR Administrator, Training and HRD*
Provides career services and assistance to adults with severe visual handicaps who want to become productive in the home or work force. Also provides the Client Assistance Program established to provide advice, assistance and information available from rehabilitation programs to persons with handicaps.

**5936 Kentucky Office for the Blind**
275 East Main Street
Frankfort, KY 40621
502-782-3414
800-321-6668
FAX: 502-564-2951
TTY: 502-564-2929
e-mail: JenniferN.Wright@ky.gov
blind.ky.gov

*Christopher Smith, Executive Director*
*Michelle McElmurray, Executive Assistant*
*Allison Jessee, Director of Consumer Services*
*Cora McNabb, VR Administrator, Training and HRD*
Our mission is to provide opportunities for employment and independence to individuals with visual impairments.

**5937 Kentucky Vocational Rehabilitation Agency**
275 East Main Street
Frankfort, KY 40621
502-564-4400
800-372-7172
FAX: 502-564-6745
e-mail: WFD.VOCREHAB@ky.gov
http://ovr.ky.gov

*Dr. David Beach, Executive Director*
*Holly Hendricks, Assistant Director of Program Services*
*Jason Jones, Director of Community Relations*
*Mindy Yates, Administrative Services Branch Manager*
Assists eligible individuals with disabilities achieve their employment goals.

**5938 Pioneer Vocational/Industrial Services**
150 Corporate Dr
P.O Box 1396
Danville, KY 40423-1396
859-236-8413
800-527-4198
FAX: 859-238-7115
TTY: 859-236-1251
e-mail: pioneer@pioneerservices.org
pioneerservices.org

*Ron Zimmerman, Chief Executive Officer/Executive Director*
*David Benedict, Industrial Services Manager*
*Kathy East, Services Director*
*Beverly Sleet, Administrative Services Director*
Mission is to provide vocational development and extended employment programs to people who are disabled and or disadvantaged to assist them in obtaining employment and maximizing independent living skills.

**5939 Work Enhancement Center of Western Kentucky**
803 Poplar St
Murray, KY 42071-2432
270-762-1100
FAX: 502-767-3600

*Steve Passmore, Director*
*John O'Shaughnessy, Chief Executive Officer*
The center has been established in order to service industry in the three state area surrounding Kentucky. This service includes job/skill evaluation, job design consultation, pre-employment employee evaluations and economic evaluation.

## Louisiana

**5940 Community Opportunities of East Ascension**
1121 E Ascension Complex Blvd
Gonzales, LA 70737
225-621-2000
FAX: 225-621-2022
http://coea.homestead.com

*Mark Thomas, Director*
Committed to affording individuals the opportunities that reflect and support choices, dignity, individuality, self-determination, community, coherency and commen sense. Programs incloude Respite, Personal Care Attendant, Support Living, Support Environment, Adult Day Training, and Elderly/Adult Waiver Services.

**5941 Louisiana Employment Service and Job Training Program Liaison**
1001 N 23rd St
Baton Rouge, LA 70802-3338
225-342-6451
800-259-5154
FAX: 225-342-0209
e-mail: owd@lwc.la.gov
http://www.laworks.net

*Curt Eysink, Executive Directo*
*Carey Foy, Deputy Executive Director*
*Jay Augustine, Executive Counsel*
*Renee Ellender Roberie, Chief Financial Officer*
Provides services for job seekers and job training programs.

**5942 Louisiana Vocational Rehabilitation Agency**
3500 Canal St
New Orleans, LA 70119-6109
504-304-7243
800-737-2963
FAX: 504-483-4777
www.dss.state.la.us/departments/lrs

*James Gaston, Manager*
*Ed Barras, Manager*
Offers individuals with disabilities a wide range of services designed to provide them with skills, resources, attitudes, and expectations needed to compete in the interview process, get the job, keep the job, and develop a lifetime career.

**5943 St. James Association for Retarded Citizens**
29150 Health Unit St
Vacherie, LA 70090-4221
225-265-2181
FAX: 225-265-7427

*Judy Bastian, Manager*
A private sheltered work program for mentally retarded and developmentally disabled adults.

**5944 Westbank Sheltered Workshop**
1728 Hermosa St
New Orleans, LA 70114-5924
504-362-1311

A private non-residential facility serving severely disabled individuals referred through Louisiana Rehabilitation Services.

## Maine

**5945 Addison Point Specialized Services**
P.O.Box 207
Addison, ME 04606
207-483-6500
FAX: 207-483-2817

*Paula Chartrand, Owner*
Provides services to individuals who are deaf/blind, mentally retarded, autistic, behaviorally challenged and/or dual diagnosed. Training services to place these individuals in community employment.

**5946 Bangor Veteran Center: Veterans Outreach Center**
Veteran's Administration
368 Harlow St
Bangor, ME 04491
207-947-3391
FAX: 207-941-8195
e-mail: Patricia.Albert-Dehetre@va.gov
http://www.maine.va.gov

*Joseph A Degrasse, Team Leader*
*Robert L Daisey LCSW, Clinical Coordinator*
*Eric K. Shinseki, Secretary*
*W. Scott Gould, Deputy Secretary*
Readjustment counseling services for veterans of Vietnam, Vietnam Era, Persian Gulf, Panama, Grenada, Lebanon, Somalia, WWII and Korean conflicts, as well as Iraq, Afganistan, and military sexual trauma.

**5947 Creative Work Systems**
619 Brighton Ave
Portland, ME 04102
207-879-1140
FAX: 207-879-1146
e-mail: kraye@creativeworks.com
creativeworksystems.com

*Susan Percy, Executive Director*
Provides residential, day habilitation and supported emploment in Central and Southern Maine.

**5948 Maine Department Of Labor**
45 Commerce Drive
Augusta, ME 04330
207-623-7900
FAX: 207-287-3042
e-mail: mdol@maine.gov
www.state.me.us/labor

*Patrick Fleming, Executive*
*Robert J. Winglas, Commissioner*
Provides a wide range of services such as employment, labor market information, rehabilitation/disability and others.

**5949 Maine Governor's Committee on Employment of the Disabled**
35 Anthony Ave
Augusta, ME 04330-7880
207-624-5335
800-794-1110
FAX: 207-624-5302

Offers supported employment programs and vocational education.

**5950 Maine Human Rights Commission**
Maine Human Rights Commission
51 State House Sta
Augusta, ME 04333-51
207-624-6290
FAX: 207-624-8729
e-mail: Amy.Sneirson@maine.gov
www.maine.gov/mhrc

*Amy Sneirson, Executive Director*
*John P. Gause, Commission Counsel*
*Barbara Lelli, Chief Investigator*
*Jill Duson, Compliance Manager*
State agency with the responsibility of enforcing Maine's anti-discrimination laws. The commission investigates complaints of unlawful discrimination in employment, housing, education, access to public accommodations, extension of credit and offensive names.

**5951 Northeast Occupational Exchange**
29 Franklin St.
Bangor, ME 04401-3857
207-942-3685
800-857-0500
FAX: 207-561-4725
TTY: 207-992-2298
www.noemaine.org

*Charles O Tingley, Executive Director*
A fully licensed, comprehensive mental health and substance abuse treatment and rehabilitation facility.

**5952 Vocational and Rehabilitation Agency**
Division for the Blind and Visually Impaired
55 State House Sta
Augusta, ME 04333-55
207-623-7981
888-457-8883
FAX: 207-624-5980
TTY: 800-794-1110
e-mail: jobbank.careercenter@maine.gov
www.mainecareercenter.com

*Jill Busond, Bureau Director*
The Maine CareerCenter provides a variety of employment and training services at no charge for Maine workers and businesses. Whether you are looking to improve your job qualifications, explore a different profession, find a new career or hire an employee, the CareerCenter can help.

## Maryland

**5953 Ardmore Developmental Center**
3000 Lottsford Vista Rd
Bowie, MD 20721-4001
301-577-2575
FAX: 301-306-9799
e-mail: info@admoreenterprises.org
www.ardmoreenterprises.org

*Patrick L. Carter, President*
*Eileen Baker, First Vice-President*
*Marilynn Riley, Secretary*
*Daphne Pallozzi, Chief Executive Officer*
Offers supported employment programs and vocational education for persons who are mentally retarded as well as residential services and Emergency Respite Care.

**5954 Job Opportunities for the Blind**
National Federation of the Blind
200 East Wells Street
Baltimore, MD 21230-4914
410-659-9315
FAX: 410-685-5653
e-mail: nfb@iamdigex.net
www.nfb.org

*Marc Mauer, President*
*John Berggren, Executive Director for Operations*
*John G. Paré Jr., Executive Director for Strategic Initiatives*
*Mark Riccobono, Executive Director, NFB Jernigan Institute*

This free service allows individuals touch-tone telephone access to the thousands of jobs listed in America's Job Bank, and internet service run by the Department of Labor. Any person registered with either a state rehabilitation agency or a state employment service can search across the country for jobs by either type of work or location.

**5955 Mainstream**
Ste 830
3 Bethesda Metro Ctr
Bethesda, MD 20814-6301
301-961-9299
FAX: 301-891-8778
e-mail: mainstrm@aol.com
investigativerisk.com

*Patricia M Jackson, Executive Director*
*Charles Moster*

Nonprofit organization dedicated to improving competitive employment opportunities for persons with disabilities. Provides specialized services and acts as a bridge that links service providers, employers and persons with disabilties. Provides training, educational publications, and videos on disablityemployment issues. Educationa materials include a magazine, brochures, and audio-visual aids.

**5956 Maryland Employment Services and Job Training Program Liaison**
Rm 600
1100 N Eutaw St
Baltimore, MD 21201-2201
410-767-2173
e-mail: det@dllr.state.md.us
http://www.dllr.state.md.us

*Maria Simms, '*
*Maureen O'Connor, Communications and Media Relations*
*Jill Porter, Director of Legislative Services*
*Kathleen Spencer, Human Resources*

Provides job development and placement and services

**5957 Maryland Fair Employment Practice Agency**
9th Fl
6 Saint Paul St
Baltimore, MD 21202-6806
410-767-8600
800-637-6247
FAX: 410-333-1841
TTY: 410-333-1737
e-mail: nbell@mccr.state.md.us
www.mchr.state.md.us

*Adrienne Jones, Executive Director*
*James Neil Bell, Deputy Director*
*Glendora Hughes, General Counsel*
*Benny F. Short, Assistant Director*

Mission is to ensure equal opportunity to all through the enforcement of Maryland's laws against discrimination in employment, housing, and public accomodations; to provide educational and outreach services related to the provisions of this law: and to promote and improve human relations in Maryland.

**5958 Maryland State Department of Education**
Division of Rehabilitation Services ( DI RS)
200 West Baltimore Street
Baltimore, MD 21218-1628
410-767-0600
866-772-8922
FAX: 410-554-9412
TTY: 410-333-6442
http://www.marylandpublicschools.org

*Robert Burns, Manager*

The Vocational Rehabilitation Program delivers to eligible individuals with physical and/or mental disabilities to enable them to become employed. The Independent Living Program's goal is to assist people in remaining in their homes and communities. The Division operates the Maryland Rehabilitation Center, a comprehensive evaluation and training center that has dormitory space. There are field offices located statewide with counselors to advise and manage the provision of services offered.

**5959 PWI Profile**
Projects W Industry Goodwill Industries of America
9200 Wisconsin Ave
Bethesda, MD 20814
Newsletter on employment of persons with disabilities.

**5960 Project LINK**
Mainstream
Ste 700
3 Bethesda Metro Ctr
Bethesda, MD 20814-6301
301-215-9100
800-247-1380
FAX: 301-891-8778
e-mail: info@cosmoscorp.com
cosmoscorp.com

*Charles Moster*

Provides job development and placement in services to dislocated workers with disabilities in the Washington, DC and Dallas, TX areas.

**5961 Treatment and Learning Centers (TLC)**
2092 Gaither Road
Suite 100
Rockville, MD 20850
301-424-5200
FAX: 301-424-8063
TTY:301-424-5203
www.ttlc.org

*Dr Patricia Ritter, Executive Director*
*Suellyn Sherwood, Operations Director*
*Rhona Schwartz, High School Program Director*
*Janet Graves-Wright, Outpatient Services Director*

A non-profit organization that specializes in educational, therapeutic and vocational services for invididuals with special needs. Programs include speech-language and occupational therapy, psycho-educational testing, tutoring, audiology, employment opportunities and the Katherine Thomas School for students with moderate to severe language and learning disabilities and/or high-functioning autism.
*Preschool-12*

## Massachusetts

**5962 Department Of Workforce Development**
State of Massachusetts
Rm 2112
1 Ashburton Pl
Boston, MA 02108-1518
617-626-7100
800-439-0183
TTY:800-439-2370
e-mail: Dhurley@detma.org
www.massworkforce.org

*Suzanne M. Bump, Secretary*
*Deval L. Patrick, Governor*
*Timothy P. Murray, Lt. Governor*

Serves as the Governor's principal advisory board on workforce development.

**5963 Gateway Arts Center: Studio, Craft Store& Gallery**
Vinsen Corporation
60-62 Harvard St
Brookline, MA 02445-7993
617-734-1577
FAX: 617-734-3199
e-mail: gateway@vinfen.org
www.gatewayarts.org

*Rae Edelson, Executive Director*
*Ted Lampe, Program Director*
*Mona Thaler, Marketing Director*
*Stephen DeFronzo, Artistic Director*
Award winning, nationally recoginized Arts based rehabilitation service with over 100 talented adults with disabilities.

**5964 Massachusetts Fair Employment Practice Agency**
Rm 601
1 Ashburton Pl
Boston, MA 02108-1524
617-994-6000
FAX: 617-720-6053
TTY:617-994-6196
e-mail: Barbara.Green@massmail.state.ma.us
www.state.ma.us/mcad

*Julian T. Tynes, Chairman*
*Sunila Thomas George, Commissioner*
*Jamie R. Williamson, Commissioner*
*Joel Berner, Esq., Chief of Enforcement*
The commission works to eliminate discrimination on a variety of bases and areas, and strives to advance the civil rights of the people of commonwealth through law enforcement, outreach and training.

**5965 Massachusetts Governor's Commission on Employment of Disabled Persons**
3rd Fl
19 Staniford St
Boston, MA 02114-2502
617-864-2000

*Theodore Schipani, Owner*
State vocational rehabilitation agency.

**5966 Vocational Rehabilitation Agency**
27 Wormwood St
Boston, MA 02210-1616
617-204-3600
800-245-6543
FAX: 617-727-1354
TTY: 800-764-0200
e-mail: elmer.bartels@mrc.state.ma.us
http://www.mass.gov

*Charles Carr, Commissioner of Rehabilitation*
*Kasper M. Goshgarian, Deputy Commissioner*
*Debra Kamen, Assistant Commissioner, Community Living Services*
*Barbara Kinney, Assistant Commissioner, Disability Determination Services*
Provides residential, day habilitation and supported employment

**5967 Vocational and Rehabilitation Agency Massachusetts Commission for the Blind**
48 Boyle St
Boston, MA 02116-4718
617-727-5550
800-245-6544
FAX: 617-727-1355
TTY: 800-764-0201
e-mail: Ronald.Gallagher@MassMail.State.MA.US
http://www.mass.gov

*Charles Carr, Commissioner of Rehabilitation*
*Kasper M. Goshgarian, Deputy Commissioner*
*Debra Kamen, Assistant Commissioner, Community Living Services*
*Barbara Kinney, Assistant Commissioner, Disability Determination Services*
Provides residentail, habilitation, and supported employment

**5968 Work Inc.**
25 Beach Street
Dorchester, MA 02122
617-691-1500
FAX: 617-691-1595
workinc.org

*Jim Cassetta, CEO*
Mission is all individuals have the ability to grow, the right to make choices and to participate in community life. It is the mission of WORK inc. to join with others in creating the conditions under which all persons with disablilities will experience.

## Michigan

**5969 Department Of Human Services**
P.O.Box 30037
Lansing, MI 48909-8152
517-887-9400
800-292-4200
FAX: 517-335-5140
TTY: 5173734025
e-mail: kreinerc@state.mi.us
www.michigan.gov.dhs

*Maura D. Corrigan, Director*
*Duane Berger, Chief Deputy Director/Chief Operating Officer*
*Terrence Beurer, Director, Field Operations*
*Susan Kangas, Deputy Director, Financial Services*
The DHS is Michigan's public assistance, child and family welfare agency. DHS directs the operations of public assistance and service programs through a network of over 100 county department of human service offices around the state.

**5970 Lamplighter's Work Center**
1320 W State St
Cheboygan, MI 49721-1402
231-627-4319

*Robert Spinella, Executive Director*
Offers small business conseling and training to individuals with disabilities

**5971 Michigan Department of Civil Rights**
Ste 3-600
3054 W Grand Blvd
Detroit, MI 48202-6054
313-456-3700
800-482-3604
FAX: 313-456-3791
TTY: 877-878-8464
e-mail: MDCR-INFO@michigan.gov
www.michigan.gov

*Daniel H. Krichbaum, Director*
Investigates and resolves discrimination complaints and works to prevent discrimination through educational programs that promote voluntary compliance with civil rights laws

**5972 Michigan Employment Service**
7310 Woodward Ave
Detroit, MI 48202-3165
313-872-1885
888-605-6722
FAX: 313-876-5760
www.michigan.gov/mdcd

*Jaye N. Porter, Director, Michigan Rehabilitation Services*
Job development and placement in services to dislocated workers with disabilities

**5973 Michigan Rehabilitation Services: Dept ofLabor & Regulatory Affairs**
PO Box 30010
Lansing, MI 48909-7510
517-373-3390
800-605-6722
FAX: 517-335-7277
TTY: 888-605-6722
e-mail: porterj3@michigan.gov
www.michigan.gov/mrs

*Jaye N Porter, Director*
*Laurie Eggers, Administrative Assistant*
State vocational rehabilitation agency.

**5974 Small Business Development Center**
Ann Arbor Center for Independent Living
2568 Packard St
Ann Arbor, MI 48104-6832
734-971-5112
FAX: 313-971-0826

*Roseanne Herzog, Director*
*Phil Zepeda, Manager*
Offers small business counseling and training to individuals with disabilities in the state of Michigan.

## Minnesota

**5975 Jewish Vocational Service of Jewish Familyand Children's Services**
401 N 3rd St
Suite 605
Minneapolis, MN 55401-1388
612-692-8920
FAX: 612-692-8921
e-mail: jfcs@jfcsmpls.org
http://www.jfcsmpls.org

*Larry Greenbaum, Executive Director*
The mission of JVS is to be a recognized leader in delivering employment, training, and career development services that positively impact individuals of all backgrounds, business and society. The name of the company is ""Jewish Family and Children's Service of Minneapolis""

**5976 Minnesota Department of Employment and Economic Development - Vocational Rehab Services**
332 Minnesota St
1st National Bank Bldg #E-200
Saint Paul, MN 55101-1314
651-259-7366
800-328-9095
FAX: 651-297-5159
TTY: 800657397373
e-mail: kim.peck@state.mn.us
deed.state.mn.us

*Kim Peck, Director*
Service for people with disabilities who need skills to prepare for work, or to find and keep a job.

**5977 Minnesota Employment Practice Agency**
Minnesota Dept. Of Human Rights
Freeman Building
625 Robert Street North
Saint Paul, MN 55155
651-539-1100
800-657-3740
FAX: 651-296-9042
TTY: 651-296-1283
e-mail: Info.MDHR@state.mn.us
humanrights.state.mn.us

*Kevin Lindsey, Commissioner*
*Denise Romero-Zasada, Executive Assistant to the Commissioner*
*Ytmar Santiago, Deputy Commisioner*
*Gregory Torrence, Assistant Commisioner*
Mission and vision is to make Minnesota discrimination free.

**5978 PWI Forum**
Multi Resource Centers
1900 Chicago Ave
Minneapolis, MN 55404-1903
612-752-8138

Newsletter for business, community and government leaders. Focuses on employment of persons with disabilities.

**5979 Vocational and Rehabilitation Agency**
2200 University Avenue West
Suite 240
Saint Paul, MN 55114
651-642-0500
800-652-9000
FAX: 651-649-5927
TTY: 612-642-0506
e-mail: info@ngwmail.des.state.mn.us
www.mnssb.org

*Richard Strong, Executive Director*
People seeking work, businesses seeking employees, students, and those looking for a first job or returning to the workforce, will find services to meet their needs.

## Mississippi

**5980 Allied Enterprises of Tupelo**
Ability Works Incorporated
2701 C R 402
Corinth, MS 38834
662-287-1461
FAX: 662-287-1463
mdrs.state.ms.us

*Michael Byrd, Manager*
Vocational evaluation, work adjustment and job placement of disabled persons in a rehabilitation workshop.

**5981 Mississippi Department of Rehabilitation Services**
P.O.Box 1698
Jackson, MS 39215-1698
601-853-5100
800-443-1000
FAX: 601-359-1695
TTY: 800-443-1000
e-mail: bmcmillan@mdrs.state.ms.us
http://www.mdrs.state.ms.us/

*H.S. "Butch" McMillan, Executive Director*
*Shelia Browning, Deputy Director*
*Chris Howard, Deputy Director*
*Richard Sorey, Director*
Offers low vision aids and appliances, counseling, social work, educational and professional training, residential services, recreational services, computer training and employment opportunities for the handicapped.

**5982 Mississippi Employment Secutity Commission**
P.O.Box 1699
1235 Echelon Parkway
Jackson, MS 39215-1699
601-321-6000
FAX: 601-961-7405
e-mail: comments@mdes.ms.gov.
www.mdes.ms.gov

*Mark Henry, Executive Director*
*Phil Bryant, Governor*
A federally funded state agency. The programs of MDES, under direction of the governor of Mississippi, report to the federal government.

**5983 Worksight**
Mississippi State University
P.O.Box 6189
Mississippi State, MS 39762-6189 662-325-2001
800-675-7782
FAX: 662-325-8989
TTY: 662-325-2694
e-mail: nrtc@colled.msstate.edu
www.blind.msstate.edu

*Michele Capella McDonnall, Research Professor and Interim Director*
*Jacqui Bybee, Research and Training Coordinator*
*Stephanie Hall, Business Manager*
*Angela Shelton, Coordinator of Instructional Materials*
Discusses news, activities, research projects and training programs of the Center.

## Missouri

**5984 Missouri Commission on Human Rights**
3315 W Truman Blvd
Jefferson City, MO 65109-6805 573-751-3325
877-781-4236
FAX: 573-751-2905
e-mail: mchr@labor.mo.gov
http://www.labor.mo.gov

*Alisa Warren, Executive Director*
*Tracey Allan, Intake Officer*
The Missouri Commission on Human Rights enforces the state's anti-discrimination law that prohibits discrimination in housing, employment and places of public accommodations. It prohibits discrimination due to race, color, religion, national origin, ancestry, sex, disability, age and familial status. Complaints must be filed within 180 days of the alleged discrimination. If discrimination is found after investigation, the Commission can hold hearings to enforce the law.

**5985 Missouri Governor's Council on Disability**
P.O.Box 1668
301 West High Street, Room 840
Jefferson City, MO 65102-1668 573-751-2600
800-877-8249
FAX: 573-526-4109
TTY: 573-751-2600
e-mail: gcd@oa.mo.gov
www.gcd.oa.mo.gov

*Douglas E. Nelson, Acting Commissioner*
*James Trout, Acting Chair and Council Members*
*Linda Baker, Executive Director Governor's Council on Disability*
*Dawn Evans, Disability Program Specialist*
Advocate training, civil rights, community education services, community resource referral, conferences, consumer education, disability awareness program, educational information and resources, information and education services, information and referral, newsletter, policy issues and services, publications, resource directory, seminars, technical assistance, training and seminars.

**5986 Missouri Job Training Program Liaison**
221 Metro Dr
Jefferson City, MO 65109-4412 573-634-2321

*Joe Jerkins, Manager*
Services for individuals with disabilities who want to become employed.

**5987 Missouri Vocational Rehabilitation Agency**
3024 Dupont Cir
Jefferson Cty, MO 65109-6188 573-751-3251
877-222-8963
FAX: 573-751-1441
TTY: 573-751-0881
e-mail: info@vr.dese.mo.gov
www.vr.dese.mo.gov

*Jeanne Loyd, Assistant Commissioner*
*Michelle Scherer, Administrator*
A team of decicated individuals working for the continuous improvement of education and services for all citizens.

**5988 WX: Work Capacities**
Suite 103
17331 E 40th Hwy
Independence, MO 64055 816-478-2333
FAX: 816-478-2335

*Chris Walters, Manager*
*Mike Heinz, Manager*
Services for individuals with disabilities who want to become employed.

## Montana

**5989 Montana Fair Employment Practice Agency**
USF&G Building
1625 11th Avenue
Helena, MT 59601-4600 406-444-2884
800-542-0807
FAX: 406-444-2978
TTY: 406-444-9696
e-mail: kcobos@mt.gov
http://erd.dli.mt.gov

*Marieke Chief, Bureau Chief*
*Kathleen Hel , Case Manager*
Advocate training, civil rights, community education services, community resource referral and conferences

**5990 Montana Governor's Committee on Employment of Disabled People**
P.O.Box 200127
Helena, MT 59620-127 406-444-3794
800-243-4091
FAX: 406-444-0544
Services for individuals with disabilities who want to become employed. Services are free to those who qualify.

## Nebraska

**5991 Nebraska Employment Services**
Department of Labor
550 S 16th St
Lincoln, NE 68508-2601 402-471-9000

Services for individuals with disabilities who want to become employed. Services are free to those who qualify.

**5992 Nebraska Fair Employment Practice Agency**
301 Centennial Mall S
Lincoln, NE 68509-4394 402-471-2024
800-642-6112
FAX: 402-471-4059
www.nol.org/home/neoc

*Kristen Yates, Chairperson*
*Royce Jeffries, Vice-Chairman*
*Ms.Barbara Albers, Executive Director*
he Nebraska Equal Opportunity Commission is a neutral administrative agency created by statute in 1965 to enforce the public policy of the state against discrimination. The principal function of

the NEOC is to receive, investigate and pass upon charges of unlawful discrimination occurring anywhere within the State of Nebraska in the areas of Employment, Housing, and Public Accommodations.

**5993 Nebraska Vocational Rehabilitation Agency**
301 Centennial Mall S
Lincoln, NE 68508-2529 402-471-3644
877-637-3422
FAX: 402-471-0788
e-mail: vr_stateoffice@vocrehab.state.ne.us
vocrehab.state.ne.us

*Cheryl Ferree, Manager*
*Rod Armstrong, Vice President of Strategic Partnerships*
*Mitch Arnolds, President*
*Amanda Jedlicka, Executive Director*
Services for individuals with disabilities who want to become employed. Services are free to those who qualify.

## Nevada

**5994 Nevada Equal Rights CommissionDepartment Of Employment,Training & Rehabilitation**
555 E. Washington Ave.
Suite 4000
Las Vegas, NV 89101- 6512 702-486-7161
FAX: 702-486-7054
http://detr.state.nv.us/nerc

**5995 Nevada Governor's Committee on Employment of Persons with Disabilities**
Ste A108
4600 Kietzke Ln
Reno, NV 89502-5062 775-688-1111
FAX: 775-688-1113
Services for individuals with disabilities who want to become employed.

**5996 Vocational and Rehabilitation Agency**
State of Nevada
Ste 502
505 E King St
Carson City, NV 89701-3705 775-684-4070
FAX: 775-684-4186
e-mail: mryasmer@nvdetr.org
detr.state.nv.us

*Frank Woodbeck, Director*
*Dennis Perea, Deputy Director*
*Renee Olson, Administrator for the Employment Security Division*
*William Anderson, Chief Economist for the Research and Analysis Bureau*

## New Hampshire

**5997 Fit for Work at Exeter Hospital**
5 Alumni Dr
Exeter, NH 03833-2160 603-778-7311
FAX: 603-580-6592
http://www.exeterhospital.com

*Kevin Calahan, President*
Staffed by a team of allied health professionals, our outpatient rehabilitation program offers functional restoration, work therapy, diagnostic testing and physical therapy.

**5998 New Hampshire Employment Security**
32 S Main St
Concord, NH 03301-4857 603-224-3311
800-852-3400
FAX: 603-228-4010
TTY: 800-735-2964
e-mail: webmaster@nhes.state.nh.us
www.nh.gov/nhes

*Tara Reardon, Commissioner*
*Darrell Gates, Deputy Commissioner*
*Zandy L. Dezonie, Administrative Assistant*
Operates a free public employment service and provides assisted and self directed employment and career related services and labor market information for employers and the general public.

**5999 New Hampshire Fair Employment Practice Agency**
2 Chenell Dr Unit 2
Concord, NH 03301-8501 603-271-2767
FAX: 603-271-6339
e-mail: humanrights@nhsa.state.nh.us
www.nh.gov/hrc

*Joni N. Esperian, Esquire, Executive Director*
Established for the purpose of eliminating discrimination in employment, public accomodations and the sale or rental of housing or commercial property.

**6000 New Hampshire Job Training Program Liaison**
64 Old Suncook Rd
Concord, NH 03301-7317 603-228-3349

Services for individuals with disabilities who want to become employed.

**6001 Vocational and Rehabilitation Agency**
Department of Education
101 Pleasant St
Concord, NH 03301-3852 603-271-3494
FAX: 603-271-7095
TTY:603-271-3471
www.ed.state.nh.us

*Paul K Leather, Manager*
Offers services for the totally blind, legally blind, visually impaired, mentally retarded blind and more with health, counseling, educational, recreational, rehabilitation, computer training and professional training services.

## New Jersey

**6002 ARC of Gloucester County**
1555 Gateway Blvd
West Deptford, NJ 08096-1018 856-629-9061
FAX: 856-848-7753
e-mail: webmaster@thearcgloucester.org
www.thearcgloucester.org

*Robert.H Weir, President*
*Charles Funk, VP*
*Ethel Lucas, Board Member*
*Ralph Sundy, Board Member*
Non-profit organization serving people with intellectual and related developmental disabilities and their families through education, advocacy and direct services.

6003 **ARC of Mercer County**
180 Ewingville Rd
Ewing, NJ 08638-2425
609-406-0181
FAX: 609-406-9258
e-mail: arc@arcmercer.org
www.arcmercer.org

*Geoffrey Morris, President*
*Charles Funk, VP*
*Ethel Lucas, Board Member*
*Ralph Sundy, Board Member*

Committed to securing for all people with disabilities mental retardation and developmental disabilities the opportunity to choose and realize their goals.

6004 **ARC of Monmouth**
1158 Wayside Rd
Tinton Falls, NJ 7712-3148
732-493-1919
FAX: 732-493-3604
e-mail: info@arcofmonmouth.org
www.arcofmonmouth.org

*Neil Fleischman, President*
*Roger Trendowski, VP*
*Francine Catanese, VP*
*Richard Harter, Treasurer*

A non-profit organization providing services and supports for individuals who have cognitive and developmental disabilities and for their families.

6005 **Abilities Center of New Jersey**
1208 Delsea Dr
Westville, NJ 08093-2227
856-848-1025
FAX: 856-848-8429
e-mail: info@abilities2work.com
abilities4work.com

*Susan Spies Perron, President/CEO*
*Sharon Kneubuehl, VP*
*Karen Weitzman, Director of Finance and Adminidtrative Support*
*Bill Urie, Director of Operations*

A non-profit organization dedicated to developing employment opportunities for people with disabilities or other disadvantages through education, training and job placement. The nme of the company is ""Abilities Center of Southern New Jersey""

6006 **Abilities of Northwest New Jersey**
264 Rte 31
Washington, NJ 07882
908-689-1118
abilities-nw.com

*a.B Wildermuth, CEO*

Private not-for-profit community rehabilitation program providing vocational training and employment services since 1974 to the disabled and disad vantaged population.

6007 **Alliance for Disabled in Action New Jersey**
629 Amboy Ave
Edison, NJ 8837-3579
732-738-4388
FAX: 732-738-4416
TTY:732-738-9644
e-mail: adacil@adacil.org
adacil.org

*Ethan Ellis, Executive Director*

A private not-for-profit center for independence living. A dynamic membership organization run by people with disabilities for people with disabilities.

6008 **Alternatives for Growth: New Jersey**
16-00 208 S
Fair Lawn, NJ 07410
201-797-8330
FAX: 201-797-3586
e-mail: experts@afg-lca.com

*Donna Flannery, Contact*

Serves all New Jersey.

6009 **Arc of Bergen and Passaic Counties**
223 Moore St
Hackensack, NJ 7601-7402
201-343-0322
FAX: 201-343-0401
e-mail: arc@arcbp.com
arcbergenpassaic.org

*Kathy Walsh, President/CEO*
*Alice Siegel, Senior VP*
*Olga Podolsky, Director of Family Support Services*
*Anne Gallucci, Vocational Services Director*

Serving persons with disabilities and their families in Bergen and Passaic Counties, NJ.

6010 **Career Opportunity Development of New Jersey**
901 Atlantic Ave
Egg Harbor City, NJ 08215-1810
609-965-6871
FAX: 609-965-3099
njcodi.org

*Linda Carney, President*
*Joe Cella, Vice Chairperson*
*Ernie Huggard, Board Chairperson*
*Robin Hackney, Secretary*

Serves Bergen and Passaic Counties. Provides services to individuals with varying forms of physical, mental and economic disabilities and disadvantages. Provides services to more than 1,000 unduplicated consumers annually.

6011 **Center for Educational Advancement New Jersey**
11 Minneakoning Rd
Flemington, NJ 08822-5726
908-782-1480
FAX: 908-782-5370
e-mail: jkunz@ceaemployment.com
ceaemployment.com

*Michael Skoczek, President*
*Robbie Lombardi, Secretary*
*Paul Mahoney, Treasurer*
*Nancy Vargas, Employee Relations*

Serves Somerset and Hunterdon Counties. Skills training in office technology and food service. Job placement and job coaching services are available. Employer Network for Ticket to Work.

6012 **Cerebral Palsy Association of Middlesex County**
10 Oak Dr
Edison, NJ 08837-2313
732-549-6187
800-852-7897
FAX: 732-549-0629
e-mail: Info@cpamc.org
cpamc.org

*Dominic Ursino, President*
*Robert Ferrara, Executive Director*
*Rob Gross, MBA, Controller*
*Debra Gilbert, M.S.I.L.R, Director of Human Resources*

Dedicated to the provision of comprehensive, superior, multi-faceted programs of service to individuals with developmental and related disabilities

6013 **Easter Seal Society of New Jersey Highlands Workshop**
Easter Seals
133 Main St
Franklin, NJ 7416-1542
973-827-9066
FAX: 973-827-3828
e-mail: pskipp@nj.easterseals.com
www.nj.easterseals.com

*Peggy Skipp, Manager*

Enabling indidividuals with special needs or disabilities and their families to learn, live, work and play in their communities with equality, dignity and independence.

**6014 Easter Seal of Ocean County**
25 Kennedy Blvd., Suite 600
East Brunswick, NJ 08816
732-257-6662
FAX: 732-257-7373
http://nj.easterseals.com

*Brian.J Fitzgerald, President/CEO*
Helping people and families with disabilities and special needs live, work, and play in their communities with equality, dignity and independence.

**6015 Easter Seals New Jersey**
25 Kennedy Blvd, Suite 600
E Brunswick, NJ 8816-2035
732-257-6662
FAX: 732-613-9127
www.eastersealsnj.org

*Brian Fitzgerald, CEO*
*Cheryl Young, CFO*
*Helen Drobnis, VP Corporate Affairs*
To enable individuals with disabilities or special needs and their families to live, work and play in their communities with equality, dignity, and independence.

**6016 Eden Acres Administrative Services**
1 Eden Way
Princeton, NJ 08540-5711
609-987-0099
FAX: 609-734-0069

*Tom Mc Cool, President*
Provides services for the disabilitated.

**6017 Edison Sheltered Workshop**
328 Plainfield Ave
Edison, NJ 08817-3117
732-985-8834
FAX: 732-985-2216
e-mail: info@eswnj.org
http://www.eswnj.org

*Veronica Valez, Executive Director*
*Robert.A Ellymer, President*
*John.J. Hogan, VP*
*Pat Colletto, Treasurer*
Serves Middlesex County. Vocational training and job placement services.

**6018 First Occupational Center of New Jersey**
391 Lakeside Ave
Orange, NJ 07050-2809
973-674-6266
800-894-6265
FAX: 973-672-0065
e-mail: ocnj@idt.net
ocnj.org

*Rocco Meola, CEO*
*Tanya M. Edghill, VP Of Program Services*
A private, nonprofit multi-service community rehabilitation program. Services are offered to all people, such as developmentally disabled, visually impaired, hearing impaired and welfare recipients. Services include vocational evaluation and training, respite care, basic and remedial education and job placement and community support services. SITE IS UNDER CONSTRUCTION

**6019 Goodwill Industries of Southern New Jersey**
2835 Route 73 S
Maple Shade, NJ 08052-1620
856-439-0200
FAX: 856-439-0843
e-mail: esmith@goodwillnj.org
goodwillnj.org

*Mark B Boyd, President and CEO*
*Michael Shaw, Chief Operating Officer*
*Stephen Castro, Chief Financial Officer*
*Deb Eckenhoff, Director of Business Development*
A non profit, community-based organization governed by a volunteer bard of trustees.

**6020 Hausmann Industries**
130 Union St
Northvale, NJ 7647-2290
201-767-0255
888-428-7626
FAX: 201-767-1369
e-mail: info@hausmann.com
hausmann.com

*David Hausmann, CEO*
*George Batchelor, Director Sales & Marketing*
*Michelle Riley, Mail order Sales*
*Julie Skoda, Sales and Marketing Adminitrator*
Wheelchair acessible exam tables, treatment tables and mat platforms.

**6021 Jersey Cape Diagnostic Training & Opportunity Center**
152 Crest Haven Rd
Cape May Court House, NJ 08210-1651
609-465-4117
FAX: 609-465-3899

*George J Plewa, Executive Director*
*George Plewa, Executive Director*
Serves Cape May County. Employment training services. A vocational rehabilitation center that serves individuals with disabilities, the disabled, and the handicapped or others having barriers to work.

**6022 New Jersey Commission for the Blind and Visually Impaired**
Department of Human Services
P.O.Box 47017
Newark, NJ 07101-8004
973-648-3333
877-685-8878
FAX: 973-648-3388
e-mail: Vito.DeSantis@cbvi.nj.us
www.cbvi.nj.gov

*Vito J Desantis, Executive Director*
*Bernice Davis, Executive Assistant*
Offers services for the totally blind, legally blind, visually impaired, deaf blind and more with eye health, counseling, educational, rehabilitation, computer training and vocational services.

**6023 New Jersey Employment Service and Job Training Program Services**
Department of Labor
Trenton, NJ 08625
609-292-1040

*Roland Machold, Manager*
Services for individuals with disabilities who want to become employed.

**6024 Occupational Center of Hudson County**
68-70 Tuers Avenue
Jersey City, NJ 07306
201-434-3303
FAX: 201-434-3660
e-mail: info@hudsoncommunity.org
http://www.hudsoncommunity.org

*Christine Remler, Executive Director*
Services for individuals with disabilities who want to become employed.

**6025 Occupational Center of Union County**
301 Cox St
Roselle, NJ 07203-1797
908-241-7200
FAX: 908-241-2025
e-mail: ocuc@OCUCNJ.com
www.occupationalcenter.org

*Michele Ford, VP*
Provides vocational rehabilitation and mental health services, along with transition from school to work.

**6026 Occupational Training Center of Burlington County**
130 Hancock Ln
Westampton, NJ 08060-4408
609-267-6677
otcbc.org

*Joseph S Bender, CEO*
Mission is to assist individuals with disabilities in reaching their maximum potential.

**6027 Occupational Training Center of Camden County, New Jersey**
520 Market St
Camden, NJ 08102-1300
866-226-3362
FAX: 856-767-1378
e-mail: freeholders@camdencounty.com
www.camdencounty.com

*Matt Treihart, President*
Serves Camden County.

**6028 Pathways to Independence, Inc.**
60 Kingsland Ave
Kearny, NJ 7032-3305
201-997-6155
FAX: 201-997-7070
e-mail: PTI450@aol.com
pathwaystoindependencenj.org

*Alvin Cox, Executive Director*
*Tessa Farrell, Program Director*
*Marie Yakabofski, Financial Director*
*Lisa M. Johnson, Qualilty Assurance Director*
Pre-vocational and vocational programming for people with disabilities. Specializing in Developmental Disabilities, Learning Disabilities and Mental Health issues. Serving over 100 people in Hudson, South Bergen, Passaic and East Essex counties. CARF accredited.

**6029 Somerset Training and Employment Program**
36 4th St
Somerville, NJ 08876-3206
732-846-2734

*Laurie Falka, Executive Director*
*Courtney Throckmorton, Owner*
Services for individuals with disabilities who want to become employed.

**6030 St. John of God Community Services Vocational Rehabilitation**
1145 Delsea Dr
Westville, NJ 8093-2252
856-848-4700
FAX: 856-848-3965
www.stjohnofgod.org

*Dr. Jerome Knast, Manager*
Serves Gloucester and Camden Counties providing exemplary special education, vocational and habilitative services to residents of southern New Jersey since 1967.

**6031 The ARC of Hunterdon County**
1465 Route 31 South
Suite 23
Annandale, NJ 08801-3127
908-730-7827
FAX: 908-730-7726
e-mail: jeff@archunterdon.org
archunterdon.org

*Jeffrey Mattison, Executive Director*
*Colleen Dennis, Deputy Executive Director*
*Gail Stepka, Executive Assistant*
our mission is to support, training and opportunities to individuals with intellectual & developmental disabilities to achieve the greatest degree of independence and productivity to become contributing, responsible, and proud members of society.

**6032 United Cerebral Palsy Associations of New Jersey**
Ste 1
1005 Whitehead Road Ext
Ewing, NJ 08638-2424
609-882-4182
888-322-1918
FAX: 609-882-4054
TTY: 609-882-0620
cpofnj.org

*Matthew P. Jacobs, President*
*Warren Kelemen, Vice President*
*Elizabeth R. Faircloth, Secretary*
*Jim Bartolomei,CPA, Treasurer*
Dedicated to changing lives and bringing independence to people with all types of disabilities.

**6033 Vocational and Rehabilitation Agency**
P.O.Box 398
Trenton, NJ 08625
609-659-3045
FAX: 609-292-8347
TTY:609-292-2919
e-mail: tjennings@dol.state.nj.us
http://lwd.dol.state.nj.us

*Brian Fitzgibbons, Manager*
*Frederick J. Zavaglia, Chief of Staff*
*Harold J. Wirths, Commissioner*
Programs and services for people with disabilities.

**6034 West Essex Rehab Center**
83 Walnut St
Montclair, NJ 07042-4088
973-744-7733
FAX: 973-744-3744

*Eugene Sefanelli, Executive Director*
*Shannon Williams, Contact*
*Eugene Stefanelli, Executive Director*
Services and programs for individuals with disabilities who want to become employed.

## New Mexico

**6035 Adelante Development Center**
3900 Osuna Rd Ne
Albuquerque, NM 87109
505-449-4021
FAX: 505-341-2001
goadelante.org

*Mike Kivitz, President*
Serves Albuquerque and Belen.

**6036 Goodwill Industries of New Mexico**
5000 San Mateo Blvd NE
Albuquerque, NM 87109-2499
505-881-6401
866-376-0182
FAX: 505-884-3157
goodwillnm.org

*Mary Best, President/CEO*
*Michael P. Keoghan, Chief Operating Officer*
*Roberta Valesquez, Finance Director*
*Ricky Sanchez, Facilities Logistics Director*
Serves Albuquerque, Santa Fe and Rio Rancho.

**6037 New Mexico Employment Services and Job Training Liaison**
P.O.Box 1928
Albuquerque, NM 87103-1928
505-898-3599
FAX: 505-827-6812
e-mail: djones2@state.nm.us
http://www.dws.state.nm.us

*Reese Suliten, Director*
*Celina Bussey, Secretary*
The name of the company has changed to ""New Mexico Department of Workforce Solutions"". Provides employment to improve economic progress.

**6038 RCI**
1111 Menaul Blvd NE
Albuquerque, NM 87107-1614
505-255-5501
FAX: 505-255-9971
e-mail: infoLifeROOTSnm.org
http://www.liferootsnm.org

*Kathleen Cates, President/CEO*
*Gwendolyn Kiwanuka, Director of Adult Services*
*Bruce Haynes, Director of Finance*
*David Griffis, Director of Contracts*

Serves Bernalillo County. Mission is to improve the abilities, interests, and choices of children and adults with physical, developmental or behavioral challenges toward achieving their highest levels of self-sufficiency. The name of the company has changed to ""LifeROOTS"".

**6039 Tohatchi Area of Opportunity & Services**
100 Manuelita Drive, P.O.Box 49
Tohatchi, NM 87325
505-733-2027
FAX: 505-733-2161
e-mail: patkeptner@yahoo.com
http://taos-inc.org

*Patrick Keptner, CEO*
*Carol Charles, Administrative Assistant*
*Judith Woodie, Accounting Clerk*
*Melinda Golden, Program Manager*

Serves McKinley County, San Jose County and the Havanjo Nation.

**6040 Vocational Rehabilitation Agency**
Ste D
435 Saint Michaels Dr
Santa Fe, NM 87505-7679
505-954-8500
800-224-7005
FAX: 505-954-8562
TTY: 877-954-8583
e-mail: dvris@state.nm.us
www.dvrgetsjobs.com

*Gary Beene, Manager*

Purpose is to help people with disabilities achieve a suitable employment outcome.

**6041 Vocational and Rehabilitation Agency**
Bldg 4
2905 Rodeo Park Dr E
Santa Fe, NM 87505-6342
505-827-4479
888-513-7968
e-mail: greg.trapp@state.nm.us
www.state.nm.us/cftb

*Greg Trapp, Executive Director*
*James Salas, Deputy Director*
*Adelmo Vigil, Deputy Director-IL/OB*
*Catherine Cross-Maple, Manager*

The Commission for the Blind provides vocational rehabilitation and independent living services designed to enable persons who are blind to become more participating and contributing members of society. Blind people lead normal lives, have families, raise children, participate in community activities, and work in a wide range of jobs. They are secretaries, lawyers, teachers, engineers, machinists, scientists, supervisors and business owners. The real challenge is to educate blind people about th

## New York

**6042 JOBS VI and SAGE**
P ES CO International
21 Paulding St
Pleasantville, NY 10570-3108
914-769-4266
800-431-2016
FAX: 914-769-2970
e-mail: pesco@pesco.org
www.pesco.org

*Joseph Kass, President*

A computerized matching system matching people to occupations, training, local jobs, local employers and giving job outlooks for the year 2005. Computerized Sage is online computerized testing with the ability for system to read all questions, and job descriptions. Manual Sage is a hands on-computer scored test battery with various adaptation. Braille, large print, bi-lingual and special devices.

**6043 Just One Break (JOBS)**
6th Floor
570 Seventh Aveune
New York, NY 10018
212-785-7300
FAX: 212-785-4513
TTY:212-785-4515
e-mail: jobs@justonebreak.com
www.justonebreak.com

*Orin Lehman, Founder*
*John D Kemp, President*
*Angela Burgess, Board of Director*
*C.Jeffrey Knittel, Board of Director*

A not-for-profit organization that is dedicated to supporting and increasing the employment of people with disabilities.

**6044 New York State Department of Labor**
Building 12
State Office Campus
Albany, NY 12240
518-457-9000
888-469-7365
TTY:800-662-1220
e-mail: nysdol@labor.state.ny.us
www.labor.state.ny.us

*James J Mcgowan, Commissioner*
*Fredda Peritz, Employment Service Division Dire*
*Thomas Malone, Unemployment Insur Div Dir*

The missin of the New York State Department of Labor is to help New York work by preparing individuals for the jobs of today and tomorrow. Provides direct job search and counseling services to job seekers, and can refer people who have disabilities for training opportunities. Provides unemployment insurance for those out of work through no fault of their own.

**6045 Rational Effectiveness Training Systems**
IRET Corporate Services Division
45 E 65th St
New York, NY 10065-6508
212-535-0822
FAX: 212-249-3582

*Michael Broder, Owner*

Offers advanced training for employee assistance professionals, full service outpatient counseling, consulting services and on-site workshops for the disabled.

**6046 Special Education and Vocational Rehabilitation Agency: New York**
Room 1606
1 Commerce Plz
Albany, NY 12234
518-474-3852
800-222-5627
e-mail: accesadm@mail.nysed.gov
www.vesid.nysed.gov

*Richard Mills, Manager*

Mission is to promote educational equity and excellence for students with disabilitites while ensuring that they receive the rights and protection to which they are entitled.

## North Carolina

**6047 Division Of Workforce Development**
NC Department Of Commerce
313 Chapanoke Road
Suite 120
Raleigh, NC 27603
919-329-5230
800-562-6333
FAX: 919-662-4770
http://www.nccommerce.com

*Sherry Allen, Accountant*
*Delores Amogida, Program Assistant V*
*Barbara Barner, Business & Technology Application Technician*
*Robbin Broome, Training Manager*
Offers vocational assessment and training, adult developmental activities.

**6048 Iredell Vocational Workshop**
200 Clanton Rd
Charlotte, NC 28217-1446
704-944-5100
www.lifespanservices.org

*John Cervantes, Secretary*
*Davan Cloninger, President & CEO*
*Robert L. Mendenhall, Vice chairman*
*Jeff Hay, Chairperson*
Mission of lifespan is to transform the lives of children and adults with developmental disabilities by providing education, employment, and enrichment programs that promote inclusion, choice, family supports, and other best practices.

**6049 North Carolina Division of Services for the Blind**
Department of Health and Human Services
2601 Mail Service Ctr
Raleigh, NC 27699-2600
919-733-9822
866-222-1546
FAX: 919-733-9769
TTY: 919-733-9700
e-mail: eddie.weaver@dhhs.nc.gov
www.dhhs.state.nc.us/dsb

*Eddie Weaver, Director*
*Carla Parker, Executive Assistant*
*Mary Flanagan, Assistant Director*
*Marvin Gilmore, LAN Administrator*
Since 1935, the mission of the North Carolina Division of Services for the Blind has been to enable people who are blind or visually impaired to reach their goals of independence and employment.

**6050 Rowan County Vocational Workshop**
2728 Old Concord Rd
Salisbury, NC 28146-1338
704-633-6223
FAX: 704-633-6224

*Carl Rapsher, Executive Director*
Offers vocational assessment and training, adult developmental activities.

**6051 Rutherford Vocational Workshop**
200 Fairground Rd
Spindale, NC 28160
828-286-4352
FAX: 828-287-3295
rutherfordlifeservices.com

*Amanda Freeman, Staff*
*Christy Beddinfield, Staff*
Offers vocational assessment and training, adult developmental activities.

**6052 Transylvania Vocational Services**
11 Mountain Industrial Dr P.O. Draw
Brevard, NC 28712-6723
828-884-3195
e-mail: info@tvsinc.org
tvsinc.org

*Nancy Stricker, Executive Director*
A private non-profit corporation with the mission to provide skills development, career opportunities and related services in a supportive environment for people with barriers to employment.

**6053 Vocational and Rehabilitation Agency**
2801 Mail Service Ctr
Raleigh, NC 27699-2800
919-855-3500
800-689-9090
FAX: 919-733-7968
TTY: 919-733-9700
e-mail: dvr.WebInfoRequest@dhhs.nc.gov
http://www.ncdhhs.gov

*Albert Delia, Acting Secretary*
*Beth Melcher, PhD, Chief Deputy Secretary for Health Services*
*Maria. F Spaulding, Deputy Secretary for Long-Term Care and Family Services*
*Steven Cline, DDS, Assistant Secretary for Health Information Technology*
Mission statement is to promote employment and independence for people with disabilities through customer partnership and community leadership.

**6054 Vocational and Rehabilitation Agency: Department of Health and Human Services**
2801 Mail Service Ctr
Raleigh, NC 27699-2800
919-855-3500
800-689-9090
FAX: 919-733-7968
TTY: 919-733-5924
e-mail: dvr.WebInfoRequest@dhhs.nc.gov
dvr.dhhs.state.nc.us

*Albert Delia, Acting Secretary*
*Beth Melcher, PhD, Chief Deputy Secretary for Health Services*
*Maria. F Spaulding, Deputy Secretary for Long-Term Care and Family Services*
*Steven Cline, DDS, Assistant Secretary for Health Information Technology*
Mission statement is to promote employment and independence for people with disabilities through customer partnership and community leadership.

**6055 Webster Enterprises Inc.**
P.O.Box 220
Webster, NC 28788-220
828-586-8981
800-978-2681
FAX: 828-586-8125
websterenterprises.org

*Gene Robinson, Executive Director*
A community based employment and training program for people with disabilities. A full service program which includes a youth transitional program for life beyond high school, job coaching, vocational assessment and job placement.

**6056 Western Regional Vocational Rehabilitation Facility Clifford File, Jr.**
P.O.Box 1443
Morganton, NC 28655
828-433-2423
dvr.dhhs.state.nc.us

*Connie Barnette, Facility Director*
Vocational Evaluation, Work Adjustment, Job Placement, On-site Work Services Program. Serves most disability groups including CMI, DD, Deaf and Physically impaired. The name of the company is “"NC Division of Vocational Rehabilitation Services, Western Regional Facility"".

## North Dakota

**6057 North Dakota Department of Labor, Human Rights Division**
Dept 406
600 E Boulevard Ave
Bismarck, ND 58505-0340
701-328-2660
800-582-8032
800-366-6888
FAX: 701-328-2031
e-mail: humanrights@nd.gov
www.nd.gov

*Mark Nelson, Manager*
*Kathy Kulesa, Human Rights Director*
*Robin Bosch, Business Manager*
*Peg Haug, Compliance Investigator*
Through a work-sharing agreement with the Equal Employment Opportunity Commission (EEOC), the North Dakota Department of Labor's Human Rights Division enforces the Americans with Disabilities Act (ADA) as related to employment discrimination.

**6058 North Dakota Employment Service and Job Training Program Liaison**
Job Service North Dakota
1601 E. Century Avenue
Bismarck, ND 58502-1537
701-258-6353

*Leslie Weiss, Manager*
Offers vocational assessment and training, adult developmental activities.

**6059 North Dakota Vocational Rehabilitation Agency**
Suite 1b
Prairie Hills Plaza 1237 W D
Bismarck, ND 58501
701-328-8950
800-756-2745
FAX: 701-328-8969
e-mail: rcusack@nd.gov
http://www.nd.gov

*Russ Cusack, State Director*
*Cheryl Wescott, Chief of Field Services*
*Harley Engelman, Business Relations/Marketing Director*
*Robin Throlson, Planning and Evaluation Administrator*
Offers services for the totally blind, legally blind, visually impaired, mentally retarded blind and more with health, counseling, educational, recreational, rehabilitation, computer training and professional training services.

## Ohio

**6060 Cornucopia**
18120 Sloane Ave
Lakewood, OH 44107-3108
216-521-4600
FAX: 216-521-9460
e-mail: Ronda.mohammad@cornucopia-inc.org
www.cornucopia-inc.org

*Ronda Saleem-Mohammad, Executive Director*
Provides work adjustment training for people with and developmental disabilities in a unique community based setting; Nature's Bin, a natural fresh foods market. Consumers learn through participation in retail operations in produce, grocery, bakery, deli, maintenance and customer service areas. Retail revenues help offset the cost of the program. Job search skills training and placement assistance available to program graduates.

**6061 Great Oaks Joint Vocational School**
3254 E Kemper Rd
Cincinnati, OH 45241-1581
513-771-8840
800-441-6257
http://www.greatoaks.com/

*Harold Carr, Medical Director*
*Deb Graw, Manager*
*Jim Perdue, Chair*
*Sue Steele, Vice Chair*
Offers vocational assessment and training, adult developmental activities.

**6062 Hearth Day Treatment and Vocational Services**
8301 Detroit Ave
Cleveland, OH 44102-1805
216-281-2660

*Don Cook, Manager*
Hearth offers time-limited, paid work adjustment experiences to consumers with mental illness. The goal of Hearth Programs is to prepare the consumer for success in the competitive workforce.

**6063 Highland Unlimited Business Enterprises of CRI**
1322 E McMillan St
Cincinnati, OH 45206-2223
513-861-6688
FAX: 513-354-7115
e-mail: ddutton@cricincy.com
gcbhs.com

*Tony Datillo, CEO*
*Debbie Dutton Lambert, Director Employment Programs*
Offers vocational assessment and training, adult developmental activities.

**6064 Ohio Civil Rights Commission**
Rhodes State Office Tower
Columbus, OH 43215- 3414
614-466-5928
TTY:614-753-2391
http://crc.ohio.gov

*Leonard Hubert, Chairman*
*Eddie Harrell, Jr, Commissioner*
*Rashmi Yajnik, Commissioner*
*Stephanie Mercado, Commissioner*
Primary function is to enforce state laws against discrimination.

**6065 Ohio Commission On Minority Health**
77 S High St
18th Fl
Columbus, OH 43215-6108
614-466-4000
FAX: 614-752-9049
e-mail: minhealth@mih.ohio.gov
www.mih.ohio.gov

*Angela C Dawson, Executive Director*
*Tawanda Boyd-Williams, Executive Assistant*
*Bounthanh Phommasathit, Program Coordinator*
*Venita O'Bannon, Fiscal Specialist*
Offers vocational assessment and training, adult developmental activities.

**6066 Vocational and Rehabilitation Agency**
400 E Campus View Blvd
Columbus, OH 43235-4685
614-438-1255
800-282-4536
FAX: 614-438-1257
TTY: 614-438-1334
e-mail: john.connellyu@rsc.state.oh.us
www.state.oh.us

*John M Connelly, Executive Director*
*Rose Reed, Manager*
State agency that provides vocational rehabilitation services to help people with disabilities become employed and independent.

## Oklahoma

**6067 Oklahoma Department of Rehabilitation Services**
Ste 500
3535 NW 58th St
Oklahoma City, OK 73112-4824
405-424-4932
800-845-8476
FAX: 405-951-3529
e-mail: jharlan@okdrs.gov
www.okrehab.org

*Michael O'Brien, Director*
*Jody Harlan, Public Information Administrator*
The Oklahoma Department of Rehabilitation Services (DRS) provides assistance to Oklahomans with disabilities through vocational rehabilitation, employment, independent living, residential and outreach programs, and the determination of medical eligibility for disability benefits.

**6068 Oklahoma Employment Services and Job Training Program Liaison**
2401 N Lincoln Blvd
Oklahoma City, OK 73105-4409
405-557-7103
FAX: 405-557-5368
TTY:800-722-0353
http://www.ok.gov

As the primary agency dedicated to disability services in Oklahoma, we offer a wide range of programs for many individuals each year.

**6069 Oklahoma Governor's Committee on Employment of People with Disabilities**
Ste 90
2401 NW 23rd St
Oklahoma City, OK 73107-2431
405-521-3756
800-522-8224
FAX: 405-522-6695
www.odc.ok.gov

*Steve Stokes, Executive Director*
Mission is to promote the employment of people with disabilities. The vision of the committee is to facilitate partnerships with commitment to full, high quality employment of people with disabilities.

## Oregon

**6070 Bend Work Activity Center**
P.O. Box 430 835 E Hwy 126
Redmond, OR 97756
541-548-2611
FAX: 541-548-9573
e-mail: info@ofco.org
www.ofco.org

*James Booth, Chairperson*
*Bill Schertzinger, Vice Chairperson*
*Cam Chambers, Manager*
*Darrel Wilson, Executive Director*
Offers vocational assessment and training, adult developmental activities and programs.

**6071 Oregon Fair Employment Practice Agency**
Oregon Bureau of Labor & Industry
Ste 1070
800 NE Oregon St
Portland, OR 97232-2180
503-731-4873
FAX: 503-731-4069
www.boli.state.or.us/civil

Agency that provides sevices to ensure fair practices are used in hiring people with disabilities.

**6072 State of Oregon Office of Vocational Rehabilitation Service**
Ste 500
3165 10th St
Baker City, OR 97814-1480
541-524-1800
800-578-9990
FAX: 541-523-5667
e-mail: wendy.m.wall@state.or.us
www.oregon.gov/dhs/vr

*Wendy Wall, Voc Rehab Counselor*
*Allan McCandless, Voc Rehab Counselor*
Offers vocational assessments and training, adult developmental activities, and helps remove disability related barriers to employment.

**6073 Vocational and Rehabilitation Agency**
500 Summer St NE
Salem, OR 97301-1063
503-945-5880
877-277-0513
FAX: 503-947-5010
e-mail: vr.info@state.or.us
www.oregon.gov/dhs/vr/index.shtml

*Stephanie Taylor, Administrator*
Offers vocational assessments and training, adult developmental activities and programs.

**6074 Vocational and Rehabilitation Agency: Oregon Commission for the Blind**
535 SE 12th Ave
Portland, OR 97214-2408
971-673-1588
888-202-5463
FAX: 503-234-7468
e-mail: ocbmail@state.or.us
http://cms.oregon.egov.com

*Linda Mock, Administrator*
*Frank Armstrong, Representative*
*Pat MacDonell, Director*
*Jodi.C Roth, Chair*
A resource for visually impaired Oregonians, as well as their families, friends, and employers. Nationally recognized programs and staff that make a difference in people's lives every day.

## Pennsylvania

**6075 ACLD/An Association for Children and Adults with Learning Disabilities: Greater Pittsburgh**
4900 Girard Rd
Pittsburgh, PA 15227-1440
412-881-2253
e-mail: info@acldonline.org
acldonline.org

*Thomas Fogarty, Administrator*
*Kathleen Donahoe, Director ACLD Tillotson School*
*Jackie Lulich, Director Business Services*
Dedicated to helping children, adolescents, and adults with Specific Learning Disabilities and related disorders succeed in school, employment and life.

**6076 Office of Vocational Rehabilitation**
7th and Forester St
Harrisburg, PA 17120-1
717-787-4746
FAX: 717-783-5221
www.dli.state.pa.us

*Barry Brandt, Rehabilitation Specialist*
Information in vocational counseling and the governor's committee on Employment of People with Disabilities. Also serves persons with disabilities that present a substantial handicap to employment and independence. Services are provided when there is a reasonable expectation that employment is possible as a result of those services.

**6077 Pennsylvania Employment Services and Job Training**
P A Department of Labor and Industry
Room 1700
7th and Forster St
Harrisburg, PA 17120-1 717-787-2500
FAX: 717-772-8284
www.dli.state.pa.us

*Edward G Rendell, Manager*
*Stephen Schmerin, Manager*
Administers benefits to unemployed individuals, oversees the administration of worker's compensation benefits to individuals with job related injuries, and provides vocational rehabilitation to individuals with disabilities.

**6078 Pennsylvania Governor's Committee on Employment of Disabled Persons**
7th and Forster Sts
Harrisburg, PA 17120-1 717-787-5279
FAX: 717-783-5221
www.dli.state.pa.us/landi/cwp
Mission is to assist with disabilities to secure and maintain employment and independence.

**6079 Pennsylvania Human Relations Commission Agency**
Ste 300
301 Chestnut St
Harrisburg, PA 17101-2529 717-787-4410
FAX: 717-772-4340
e-mail: phrc@pa.gov
phrc.state.pa.us

*JoAnn. L Edwards, Executive Director*
*Gerald.S Robinson, Chairman*
*Tom Corbett, Governor*
Mission is to administer and enforce the PHRAct and the PFEOA of the Commonwealth of Pennsylvania for the identification and elimination of discrimination and the providing of equal opportunity for all persons.

**6080 US Healthworks**
1114 Commons Blvd
Reading, PA 19605-3333 610-926-0960
FAX: 610-926-6225
www.ushealthworks.com

*Beverly Shaeff, Manager*
*Stephanie Makovsky, Sales Consultant*
Offers employers comprehensive occupational health services and state-of-the-art physical and occupational therapy. Staff works as a team to produce the best possible patient care while delivering cost savings through workers compensation disability management programs.

**6081 Vocational and Rehabilitation Agency**
1521 N 6th St
Harrisburg, PA 17102-1100 717-787-5244
800-442-6351
FAX: 717-783-5221
TTY: 717-787-5244
e-mail: ovr@dli.state.pa.us
dli.state.pa.us

*William Gannon, Manager*
*Thomas Washic, Manager*
Mission is to assist with disabilities, to secure and maintain employment and independence.

**6082 Vocational and Rehabilitation Agency: Department of Labor and Industry**
909 Green St
Harrisburg, PA 17102-2913 717-236-6211
800-622-2842
FAX: 717-236-3390
TTY: 717-787-6176
e-mail: cboone@state.pa.us

*Thomas Carlock, CEO*
Mission is to assist people with disabilities, to serve and maintain employment and independence.

## Rhode Island

**6083 Goodwill Industries of RI**
100 Houghton St
Providence, RI 02904-1013 401-861-2080
FAX: 401-454-0889
TTY:401-331-2830
www.goodwillri.org

*Jeff Machado, CEO*
*Justine Beatini, Transitional Resource Specialist*
*Shirl Berger, Employee Development & Program Director*
*Daniel Burgess, Finance Director*
The mission of Goodwill Industries of Rhode Island is to provide training, education and other services which result in employment and expanded opportunities for people with disabilities and other barriers to employment in order to enhance their capacity for independent living, increased quality of life and work.

**6084 Groden Center**
86 Mount Hope Ave
Providence, RI 02906-1648 401-274-6310
grodencenter.org

*Helen Morcos, CEO*
*Jane I Carlson, Ph.D., BCBA, VP Day & Residential Programs*
*Cooper Woodard, Ph.D., VP Clinical Services*
*Peggy Stocker, Admissions Coordinator*
The Groden Center is a school and residential treatment center in Rhode Island enhancing the lives of children and youth with autism, behavioral disorders, and developmental disabilities by providing early autism intervention services, an early childhood education program as well as providing functional and social development instruction to school-age children with learning disabilities.

**6085 Newport County Chapter of Retarded Citizens**
P.O.Box 4390
Middletown, RI 02842 401-846-0340
mahercenter.org

*John Maher, Executive Director*
*Daniel J Oakley, VP*
*Barbara Burns, Secretary*
*Walter Jachna, Chairman*
Vocational training and job placement services.

**6086 Office of Rehabilitation Services**
40 Fountain St
Providence, RI 02903-1898 401-421-7005
FAX: 401-222-3574
e-mail: garyw@ors.ri.gov
ors.ri.gov

*Ron Racine, Deputy Administrator*
*Steve Brunero, Acting Deputy Administrator-ORS*
*John Microulis, Deputy Administrator-Disability*
Their goal is to help individuals with physical and mental disabilities prepare for and obtain appropriate employment.

6087 **Vocational and Rehabilitation Agency: Department of Human Services**
RI Services for the Blind and Visually Impaired
40 Fountain St
Providence, RI 02903-1830
401-421-7005
FAX: 401-222-3574
e-mail: garyw@ors.ri.gov
ors.ri.gov

*Ron Racine, Deputy Administrator*
*Steve Brunero, Acting Deputy Administrator-ORS*
*John Microulis, Deputy Administrator-Disability*
Their goal is to help individuals with physical and mental disabilities prepare for and obtain appropriate employment.

## South Carolina

6088 **South Carolina Employment Security Commission South Carolina Center**
P.O.Box 567
Columbia, SC 29201
803-777-2400
800-436-8190
e-mail: jobs@sces.org
www.sces.org

*Camille Fallow, Disability Program Navigator*
*Regina Ratterros, Program Coordinator/State Office*
Public agency taht offers job search assistance. Unemployment Benefits and WIA program. Also offered is Disability Program Navigator who helps persons with disabilities to find needed resources

6089 **South Carolina Governor's Committee on Employment of the Handicapped**
1330 Boston St
Columbia, SC 29203
803-896-1208
FAX: 803-896-1224

*Gayle Brazell, Executive Director*
Goal is to help individuals with physical and mental disabilities prepare for and obtain appropriate employment.

6090 **South Carolina Vocational Rehabilitation Department**
P.O.Box 15
West Columbia, SC 29171-15
803-896-6833
800-832-7526
e-mail: info@scvrd.state.sc.us
www.scvrd.net

*Larry C Bryant, Commissioner*
*Barbara G Hollis, Executive Director*
*Dr. Roxzanne Breland, Vice Chair*
*Derle A Lowder Sr., Agency Board Chairman*
The SCVRD's mission is to enable eligible South Carolinians with disabilities to prepare for, achieve and maintain competitive employment.

6091 **Vocational and Rehabilitation Agency: Commission for the Blind**
Vocational and Rehabilitation Agency
P.O.Box 79
Columbia, SC 29202-79
803-737-5682
800-922-2222
FAX: 803-898-8852
e-mail: publicinfo@sccb.sc.gov

*Zertie Johnson, Manager*
Goal is to help individuals with physical and mental disabilities prepare for and obtain appropriate employment.

## South Dakota

6092 **South Dakota Governor's Advisory Committeeon Employment of the Disabled**
700 Governors Dr
Pierre, SD 57501-2291
605-773-3101
FAX: 605-773-6184
http://dlr.sd.gov

*Patrick Keating, Manager*
*Pamela S Roberts, Secretary*
Goal is to help individuals with physical and mental disabilities prepare for and obtain appropriate employment.

6093 **South Dakota State Vocational Rehabilitation**
Department of Human Services
3800 E Highway 34 Hillview Plz
Pierre, SD 57501
605-773-3195
FAX: 605-773-5483
e-mail: eric.weiss@state.sd.us
www.state.sd.us

*Jeff Pierce, Manager*
*Bernie Grimme, Assistant Director, DRS*
*Grady Kickul, Director*
South Dakota State Vocational Rehabilitation consists of two agencies; Rehab Services and service to the Blind and Visually Impaired. There mission is the same to provide individualized rehabilitation services that result in optimal employment and independent living outcomes for individuals with disabilities.

6094 **South Dakota Workforce Investment Act Training Programs**
700 Governors Dr
Pierre, SD 57501-2291
605-773-5017
800-952-3216
FAX: 605-773-6184
www.sdjobs.org

*Michael Ryan, Administrator*
*Patrick Keating, Manager*
Mission is to enhance the South Dakota workforce by providing business with employment-related solutions and helping people with job placement and career transition services

6095 **Vocational and Rehabilitation Agency: Division of Services to the Blind/Visually Impaired**
3800 E Highway 34 Hillview Plz
Pierre, SD 57501
605-773-3195
FAX: 605-773-5483
e-mail: gaye.mattke@state.sd.us
www.state.sd.us

*Kim Crossam, Manager*
To provide individualized rehabilitation services that result in optimal employment and independent living outcomes for people with disabilities.

## Tennessee

6096 **Division of Rehabilitative Services**
Tennessee Department Human Services
400 Deaderick Street
15th Floor
Nashville, TN 37243-1403
615-313-4700
FAX: 615-741-4165
e-mail: mandy.johnson@tn.gov
www.state.tn.us/humanserv/rehabilitation.htm

*Raquel Hatter, Commisioner*

**6097 Tennessee Department of Labor: Job Training Program Liaison**
501 Union St
Nashville, TN 37219-1712
615-741-2330
FAX: 615-741-1791

*Ruth S Letson, Manager*
Goal is to help individuals with physical and mental disabilities prepare for and obtain appropriate employment.

**6098 Tennessee Fair Employment Practice Agency**
Human Rights Commission
Suite 400
530 Church St
Nashville, TN 37243-1
615-741-5825
www.state.tn.us/humanrights

*Tricia Crawford, Manager*
An independent state agency charged with preventing and eradicating discrimination in employment, public accomodations, and housing.

## Texas

**6099 C-CAD Center of United Cerebral Palsy of Metropolitan Dallas**
8802 Harry Hines Blvd.
Dallas, TX 75235
800-999-1898
e-mail: info@ucpdallas.org
www.ucpdallas.org

Offers a wide range of technology opportunities for persons with all types of disabilities, their families and the professionals who serve them. Services include assesments, traiing, technology access showroom, and workshops for rehabilitation and educational personnel.

**6100 Handbook of Career Planning for Students with Special Needs**
Pro- Ed Publications
8700 Shoal Creek Blvd
Austin, TX 78757-6816
512-451-3246
800-897-3202
FAX: 512-451-8542
e-mail: general@proedinc.com
www.proedinc.com

*Donald D Hammill, Owner*
*Courtney King, Marketing Coordinator*
*Thomas F. Harrington, Editor*
The practitioner's guide will show you how to help special needs adolescents and young adults overcome barriers to employment by identifying goals and problems, assessing interests and aptitudes, involving client families and developing communication skills. *$42.00*
*358 pages*

**6101 Texas Employment Services and Job Training Program Liaison**
Texas Workforce Commission
101 E 15th St
Austin, TX 78778-1442
512-475-2571
866-938-4444
TTY:700-735-2989
http://www.twc.state.tx.us

*Larry Temple, Executive Director*
*Lasha Lenzy, Division Director*
*Reagan Miller, Division Director*
*Tom McCarty, Division Director*
State government agency charged with overseeing and providing workforce development services to employers and job seekers of Texas. Offers career development information, job search resources, training programs, and, as appropriate, unemployment benefits.

**6102 Vocational and Rehabilitation Agency: State Rehabilitation Commission**
Vocational and Rehabilitation Agency
4800 N Lamar Blvd
Austin, TX 78756-3106
512-383-7000
800-628-5115
FAX: 512-926-1503
TTY: 800-628-5115
e-mail: dars.inquiries@dars.state.tx.us
www.dars.state.tx.us

*Marilyn Hancock, Executive Director*
*Michelle Crain, Executive Director*
Helps people with disabilities prepare for, find and keep jobs. Work related services are individualized and may include counseling, training, medical treatment, assistive devices, jon placement assistance and other services.

## Utah

**6103 Utah Employment Services**
P.O. Box 45249
Salt Lake City, UT 84145-0249
801-526-9675
FAX: 801-526-9211
e-mail: dwscontactus@utah.gov

*Kristen, Cox*
*Executive Di*
To help individuals prepare and obtain appropriate employment.

**6104 Utah Governor's Committee on Employment ofthe Handicapped**
1595 W 500 S
Salt Lake City, UT 84104-5238
801-538-4200
800-837-6811
FAX: 801-538-4279
e-mail: dspd@utah.gov
chiltonshelby.org

*George Kelner, Executive Director*
Promotes opportunities and provide support for persons with disabilities to lead self-determined lives.

**6105 Utah Veterans Centers**
Ste 105
750 N Freedom Blvd
Provo, UT 84601-1686
801-377-1117
800-246-1197
FAX: 801-377-0227
www.military.com/benefits/veteran-benefits

*Dennis Stevens, Executive Director*
*Brent Price, Manager*
Readjustment counseling services to veterans.

**6106 Utah Vocational Rehabilitation Agency**
Utah State Office of Rehabilitation
P.O.Box 144200
Salt Lake City, UT 84114-4200
801-538-7530
800-473-7530
FAX: 801-538-7522
e-mail: duchida@utah.gov
usor.utah.gov

*Donald R Uchida, Executive Director*
*Heidi Kubbe, Executive Assistant*
*Jennifer Smart, Training Coordinator*
*Coy Jackson, Program Specialist*
Vocational Rehabilitation Services for individuals with disabilities. To assist individuals with disabilities to prepare for and obtain employment and increase their independence.

**6107 Vocational and Rehabilitation Agency: Division of Services for the Blind/Visually Imp.**
Ste B
250 N 1950 W
Salt Lake City, UT 84116-7902
801-323-4343
800-284-1823
FAX: 801-323-4396
e-mail: wgibson@utah.gov
utah.gov

*Willam G Gibson, Executive Director*
*Cheryl Ritchie, Administrative Secretary*
*LuWana Martin, Network Specialist*
*Sharon Pipkin, Office Specialist*
Mission is to assist individuals who are blind or visually impaired to obtain employment or increase their independence.

## Vermont

**6108 State of Vermont Department of Disabilities, Aging and Independent Living**
Agency of Human Services
103 S Main St
Weeks IC
Waterbury, VT 05671-2304
802-241-2210
888-405-5005
FAX: 802-241-2128
e-mail: Info@ahs.state.vt.us
www.ahs.state.vt.us/dbvi

*Fred Jones, Director*
*Wendy Edwards, Administrative Assistant*
Mission is to support the efforts of Vermonters who ar blind and visually impaired to achieve or sustain their economic independence, self reliance, and social integration to a level consistent with thier interests, abilities and informed choices.

**6109 Vermont Employment Services and Job Training**
5 Green Mountain Drive P.O.Box 488
Montpelier, VT 05601
802-828-4000
FAX: 802-828-4022
TTY:802-828-4203
e-mail: tdouse@labor.state.vt.us
www.labor.vermont.gov

*Annie Noonan, Commissioner*
*Deborah Bruce, Human Resource Administrator*
*Richard Gray, State Director*
*Tracy Phillips, Director, Unemployment Insurance and Wages*
The primary focus is to help support the efforts to make Vermont a more competitive place to do business and create good jobs.

**6110 Vermont Governor's Committee on Employmentof People with Disabilities**
103 S Main St
Waterbury, VT 05671-9800
802-241-6757
866-879-6757
FAX: 802-241-3359
e-mail: melita@gcepd.org.
www.vocrehabvermont.org

*Diane Dalmasse, Manager*
*Melita DeBeliss, Staff*
Committed to facilitating successful, long-term relationships between employers and people with disabilities in Vermont.

## Virginia

**6111 Alexandria Community Y Head Start**
418 S Washington St
Alexandria, VA 22314-3673
703-549-0111

*Tammy.L Mann, Ph.D, President and CEO*
*Raj Kapur, Chief Financial Officer*
*Karla Kelley, Senior Director of Out-of-School-Time Programs*
*Joy Vithespongse Trejo, MA, Senior Director, Early Childhood Programs and Family Services*
Offers social services, on-the-job-training for parents, play therapy, physical therapy, speech therapy and any other specialized services.

**6112 Department Of Rehabilitative Services**
9960 Mayland Dr Suite 200
Richmond, VA 23233
804-367-4700
FAX: 804-527-4523
e-mail: Jay.Windsor@ssa.gov
vadrs.org

*Jay Windsor, Windsor*
*Contact Pers*
Helps people with disabilities get ready for,find, and keep a job.

**6113 Didlake**
8641 Breeden Ave
Manassas, VA 20110-8431
703-361-4195
866-361-4195
FAX: 703-369-7141
www.didlake.com

*Rex Parr, CEO*
*John S Craig, VP Rehabilitation Services*
*Alice Jones, Treasurer*
*Dora Brooks, Secretary*
Offers situational assessments, work training, employment and job placement services to people with disabilities.

**6114 Learning Services: Shenandoah**
9524 Fairview Ave
Manassas, VA 20110-5829
703-335-9771
FAX: 703-335-1064

*Peter Patrick, Administrator*
Postacute rehabilitation program.

**6115 NISH**
8401 Old Courthouse Rd
Vienna, VA 22182-3820
571-226-4660
FAX: 703-849-8916
nish.org

*E. Robert Chamberlin, President and CEO*
*Dennis.A Fields, Chief Operating Officer*
*Elizabeth W. Goodman, Chief Financial Officer*
*Paul W. Plattner, Vice President of Operations*
A nonprofit agency desigated by the Committee for Purchase from People Who Are Blind or Severely Disabled to provide technical assistance to rehabilitation programs interested in obtaining federal contracts under Public Law 92-28, the Javits-Wagner-O'Day Act. NISH's primary objective is to assist community rehabilitation programs in providing jobs for people with severe disabilities.

**6116 Richmond Research Training Center**
P.O.Box 842011
Richmond, VA 23284-2011
804-828-1222

*Paul Wehman MD, Director*
*Dolores Taylor, Executive Director*
Research and training center report on the supported employment of persons with developmental and other disabilities.

**6117 ServiceSource**
Ste 175
6295 Edsall Rd
Alexandria, VA 22312-2670
703-461-6000
800-244-0817
FAX: 703-461-3906
www.ourpeoplework.org

*Janet Samuelson, President*
*Edie Castner, Assistant Director*
Provides training, job placement and employment services in private sector and government contract employment. SITE IS UNDER CONSTRUCTION

**6118 Sheltered Occupational Center of Virginia**
750 23rd St S
Arlington, VA 22202-2452
703-521-4441
FAX: 703-521-3443
socent.org

*Linda Chandler, CEO*
*Hayley Gefell, Chief Business Development Officer*
*Marshall Henson, Chief Operating Officer*
*Donnell Karimah, Chief Administrative Officer*
Assists, empowers and supports people with disabilities to achieve employment, independence and integration in the workplace and community. Our services include: printing, copying, hand work, mail shop, fulfillment and distribution. Th name of the ccompany has been changed to “"Linden Resources"”

**6119 Vocational and Rehabilitation Agency: Department for the Blind/Visually Impaired**
397 Azalea Ave
Richmond, VA 23227-3623
804-371-3353
FAX: 804-371-3154
e-mail: Kimberley.Jennings@dbvi.virginia.gov
www.vdbvi.org

*Raymond Hopkins, Commissioner*
*James A Taylor, Chief Deputy*
*Kimberley Jennings, Contact Person*
DBVI envisions a world in which blind, vision impaired and deafblind people can access all that society has to offer and can, in turn, contribute to the greater community. We believe this is achievable.

## Washington

**6120 Career Connections**
P.O.Box 141806
Spokane Valley, WA 99214-1806
509-928-0423
866-404-5867
FAX: 509-928-0441
e-mail: carconn@mindspring.com
www.peoplelinking.com

*Susan Warwick, Executive Director*
*Teresa Antosyn, Program Coordinator*
*Dan Moody, CFO*
*Sadie Takila, Production Manager*
Offers structured work sites at several locations. Production work at various skill levels, with training as needed.

**6121 Department of Services for the Blind National Business & Disability Council**
Department of Services for the Blind
P.O.Box 40933
Olympia, WA 98504-933
360-725-3830
FAX: 360-407-0679
e-mail: info@dsb.wa.gov
www.dsb.wa.gov

*Louana Durand, Executive Director*
A state rehabilitation agency that offers assistance to persons who are blind or visually impaired. Also provides various services for employers interested in accomodating or hiring workers with vision loss.

**6122 Division of Developmental Disabilities: Department of Social & Health Services**
P.O.Box 45310
Olympia, WA 98504-5310
800-737-0617
e-mail: dddcoreception@dshs.wa.gov
www1.dshs.wa.gov

*Robin Arnold-Williams, Secretary*
*Colleen Cawston, Senior Director*
*Steve Lowe, Senior Director*
*Tracy Guerin, Chief of Staff*
The Division of Developmental Disabilities offers persons with developmental disabilities quality supports and services that are individual/family driven, stable and flexible, satisfying to the person and their family, and able to meet individual needs.

**6123 SL Start and Associates**
25 W Nora Ave
Spokane, WA 99205-4800
509-328-2740
888-355-7155
FAX: 509-326-9207
e-mail: info@slstart.com
slstart.com

*Stephen L Start, Owner*
A diversified and innovative human and health services company focused on a wide range of social, employment and long-term services.

**6124 School of Piano Technology for the Blind**
2510 E Evergreen Blvd
Vancouver, WA 98661-4323
360-693-1511
FAX: 360-693-6891
e-mail: info@pianotuningschool.org
pianotuningschool.org

*Len Leger, Executive Director*
*Jeff Lane, CEO*
*Donald L.Mitchell, Director of Instructional Operations*
*Les Fitzpatrick, Technician/Instructor*
Teaches piano tuning and repair to blind and visually impaired menand women, leading to employment and/or self-employment in the piano service industry. Licensed by Washington State and accredited by the Accrediting Commission of Career Schools and Colleges of Technology (ACCSCT). 20-month course.

**6125 Vocational and Rehabilitation Agency: Division of Vocational Rehabilitation**
Department of Social and Health
P.O.Box 45340
Olympia, WA 98504-5340
360-704-3560
800-637-5627
FAX: 360-570-6941
TTY: 360-438-8000
e-mail: krulik@dshs.wa.gov
www1.dshs.wa.gov/dvr

*Patrick Raines, Manager*
*Andres , Director*
Mission is to empower individuals with disabilities to achieve a greater quality of life by obtaining and maintaining employment.

## West Virginia

**6126 West Virginia Division of Rehabilitation Services**
P.O.Box 50890
Charleston, WV 25305-890
304-356-2371
800-642-8207
FAX: 304-766-4905
TTY: 304-766-4809
www.wvdrs.org

*Deborah Lovely, Director*
*Donna Ashworth, Assistant Director*
DRS specializes in helping people with disabilities who want to find a job or maintain current employment. Rehabilitation counselors at more than 30 field offices help with applications. Once eligibility is determined, counselors & clients work as a team to develop a plan to meet the individuals employment goal. Services may include work-related counseling/guidance, evaluation/assessment, job development & placement assistance, vocational training, college assistance & assistive technology.

**6127 West Virginia Employment Services and Job Training Programs Liaison**
112 California Ave
Charleston, WV 25305-12
304-558-2660
FAX: 304-558-1343
http://workforcewv.org

*Valerie Comer, Director*
*Allan Galloway, Manager*
Workforce West Virginia, a division of the Department of Commerce, effectively coordinates all availiable state and federal resources by orchestrating the efforts of state agencies and local organizations.

**6128 West Virginia Vocational Rehabilitation**
P.O.Box 1004
Institute, WV 25112-1004
304-342-9952
www.wvdrs.org

*Earl Wolfe, Director*
Offers services for the totally blind, legally blind, visually impaired, mentally retarded blind and more with health, counseling, educational, recreational, rehabilitation, computer training and professional training services.

## Wisconsin

**6129 Vocational and Rehabilitation: State of Wisconsin**
201 E Washington Ave
Madison, WI 53702-1
608-266-0050
800-442-3477
FAX: 608-266-3131
TTY: 888-877-5939
e-mail: dvr@dwd.wisconsin.gov
www.dwd.state.wi.us/dvr

*Tamara Monsees, Office Manager/Admin. Support*
Offers vocational rehabilitation services for the totally blind, legally blind, visually impaired, mentally retarded blind and more with health, counseling, educational, rehabilitation, computer training and professional training services, and displaced worker.

## Wyoming

**6130 Division of Vocational Rehabilitation of Wyoming**
Wyoming Department of Workforce Services
1100 Herschler Buiding
Cheyenne, WY 82002-1
307-777-7364
wyomingworkforce.org/how/vr.aspx

*Jim Mcintosh, Administrator*
*Kathy Emmones, Director Workforce Services*
Provides only those services which are necessary for eligible individuals to reach the employment goal agreed to in the Individualized Plan for Employment.

**6131 Vocational Rehabilitation, Division of Department of Workforce Services**
Suite 1e
1160 Herschler Building
Cheyenne, WY 82002-1
307-777-7364
FAX: 307-777-5939
TTY:307-777-7386
e-mail: jmcint@state.wy.us
www.wyomingworkforce.org

*Jim McIntosh, Administrator*
Provides only those services which are necessary for eligible individuals to reach the employment goal agreed to in the individualized plan for employment.

**6132 Wyoming Department of Employment Unemployment Insurance**
P.O.Box 2760
Casper, WY 82602-2760
307-235-3679
FAX: 307-235-3688
doe.state.wy.us

*Randy Hopper, Manager*
A combined state/federally funded agency of the state of Wyoming, headed by a Department Director who is appointed by the Governor.

**6133 Wyoming Governor's Committee on Employment of the Handicapped**
Room 1126
1st Floor East Wing
Cheyenne, WY 82002-1
307-777-7230
FAX: 307-777-5690
e-mail: workforceservices@state.wy.us
http://wydoe.state.wy.us/ur/gcepd.asp

*Brenda Oswald, Manager*
Assists, empowers and supports people with disabilities to achieve employment, independence and intergration in the workplace and community.

# Rehabilitation Facilities, Acute

## Alabama

**6134 HealthSouth Rehabilitation Hospital of North Alabama**
107 Governors Dr SW
Huntsville, AL 35801-4326
256-535-2300
FAX: 256-428-2608
www.healthsouth.com

*Doug Beverley, CEO*
*Holly Ray, PHR, HR Director*
*Will Craig, Director of Marketing Operations*
A comprehensive 50 bed rehabilitation hospital serving the need of patients in the North Alabama area. Guides patients with physically disabling conditions along an individualized treatment pathway so they can reach their highest level of physical, social and emotional well-being. A wide range of medical and theraputic services are delivered by qualified and experienced professionals.

**6135 Lakeshore Rehabilitation Hospital**
3800 Ridgeway Dr
Birmingham, AL 35209-5599
205-868-2290
FAX: 205-868-2029
healthsouth.com

*Terry Brown, Administrator*
*Barbie Reedy, Contact*
A 100 bed facility whos key services is physical rehabilitation. Also specialized services (inpatient) infection isolation room. In addition, also has outpatient physical rehabilitation and sports medicine. Patient family support services include patient representative, transportation for elderly/handicapped and patient support groups. Imaging services(diagnostic & theraputic) include ct scanner, diagnostic diagnostic radioisotope facility, MRI, and ultrasound.

**6136 Mobile Infirmary Medical Center: Rotary Rehabilitation Division**
5 Mobile Infirmary Cir
Mobile, AL 36607-3513
251-435-2400
800-826-2085
FAX: 251-435-3403
e-mail: resource@mobileinfirmary.org
www.mobileinfirmary.org

*Joe Stough, VP*
Our vision is to appreciably enhance in a proactive manner the healthcare status and related quality of life of the residents and communities we serve.

**6137 More Than Just a Job**
Institute On Disability/UCED
10 West Edge Drive
Suite 101
Durham, NH 03824
603-862-4320
FAX: 603-862-0555

Narrative case studies and interviews with persons with disabilities, their employers, families and experts in the field. *$20.00*

**6138 Rocky Mountain Resource & Training Institute**
3630 Sinton Road
Suite 103
Colorado Springs, CO 80907- 5072
719-444-0268
800-949-4262
FAX: 719-444-0269
TTY: 800-949-4232
www.adainformation.org

*Jana Copeland, Principal Investigator*
*Patrick Going, Senior Advisor*
Serves people with disabilities and provides training to the agencies that assist them. Facilitates disabled individuals' transition from school to adult life; provides information and resources concerning assistive technology, devices, and services; promotes and ensures compliance with the federal Americans with Disabilities Act (ADA) and other legislation promoting the rights and inclusion of people with disabilities; promotes supported employment, strategic planning and development.

## Arkansas

**6139 Central Arkansas Rehab Hospital**
2201 Wildwood Ave
Sherwood, AR 72120-5074
501-834-1800
FAX: 501-834-2227
www.stvincentrehabhospital.com

*Lee Frazier, MPH, Dr, CEO*
*Dr. Sean Foley, Medical Director*
*Debbie Taylor, Director of Marketing Operations*
*Stacy Sawyer, Director Of Therapy Operations*
A nonprofit hospital licensed for 69 acute care beds with all private rooms. Opened in 1999the hospital offers a full range of outpatient diagnostic services, including MRI,CT,PET along with surgical procedures, cardiology, neurology, neurosurgery, othopedic, rehab and a 24 hour emergency department staffed with board certified emergency room physicians. Includes an outpatient surgery center, rehabilitation hospital, senior health program, diabetic program and physician offices.

**6140 HealthSouth Rehabilitation Hospital**
1401 South J St
Fort Smith, AR 72901-5158
479-785-3300
FAX: 479-785-8599
healthsouth.com

*Juli Stec, CEO*
Provides physical rehabilitation as its key services. Also provides other services such as end-of-life services, pain management and an infection isolation room.

**6141 Northwest Arkansas Rehabilitation Hospital**
153 E Monte Painter Dr
Fayetteville, AR 72703-4002
479-444-2233
FAX: 479-444-2390
www.healthsouthfayetteville.com

*Marty Hurlbut, Medical Director*
*Denise Wilson, Director Of Clinical Services*
A 60-bed acute medical rehabilitation hospital that offers comprehensive inpatient and outpatient rehabilitation services.

**6142 Rebsamen Rehabilitation Center**
P.O.Box 159
Jacksonville, AR 72078-159
501-985-7000
FAX: 501-985-7384
www.rebsamenmedicalcenter.com

*Mack McAlister, Chairperson*
*Murice Green, Vice Chairman*
*Tommy Swaim, Secretary*
Mission is to provide personal healthcare for your family. Vision is to develop a family of caregivers to become your community hospital. A 113 bed acute care facility operated by a volunteer Board of Directors made up of community leaders. Rebsamen Medical Center is accredited by the Joint Commission on Accredidation of Healthcare Organizations as well as the Arkansas Department of Health. Through JCAHO we voluntary sumbit to evaluations of our compliance with nationwide hospital standards.

## Arizona

**6143 Barrow Neurological Institute Rehab Center**
350 W Thomas Rd
Phoenix, AZ 85013-4409
602-406-3000
FAX: 602-406-4104
www.stjosephs-phx.org

*Jackie Aragon, VP Care Management*
*Linda Hunt, President*
Dedicated resources to delivering compassionate, high-quality, affordable health services; serving and advocating for our sisters and brothers who are poor and disenfranchised; and partnering with others in the community to improve the quality of life. Our vision:a growing and diversified health care ministry distinguished by excellent quality and committed to expanding access to those in need.

**6144 HealthSouth Sports Medicine Center**
5111 N Scottsdale Rd
Ste 100
Scottsdale, AZ 85250-7076
480-990-1379
FAX: 480-423-8458
e-mail: chamine@wiley@healthsouth.com
www.healthsouth.com

*Troy Meiners, Manager*
An out patient facility specialising in sports medicine and treatment of sports injuries.

**6145 Healthsouth Rehab Institute of Tucson**
2650 N Wyatt Dr
Tucson, AZ 85712-6108
520-325-1300
800-333-8628
FAX: 520-327-4045
www.rehabinstituteoftucson.com

*Lee Sanford, Plant Manager*
*Jon Larson, Medical Director*
An accredited member of the Joint Commission On Accreditation of Health Care Organizaions (JCAHO) An 80 bed facility specializing in rehabilitation

**6146 Scottsdale Healthcare**
9630 E Shea Blvd
Scottsdale, AZ 85260-6285
480-551-5400
FAX: 480-551-5401
www.shc.org

*Thomas Sadvary, CEO*
A 343 bed full-service hospital providing medical/surgical, critical care, obstetrics, pediatrics, surgery, cardiovascular, and oncology services, as well as the Sleep Disorder Center. All patient rooms are private. Emergency department is a level II Trauma Center. The Radiology Department offers state-of-the-art diagnostic equipment, including MRI, PET/CT scanning, nuclear medicine and ultrasound. Also located are the Piper Surgery Center, Cancer Center, and several medical office plazas.

**6147 St. Joseph Hospital and Medical Center**
350 W Thomas Rd
Phoenix, AZ 85013-4496
602-406-3000
FAX: 602-406-4190
www.mha.chw.edu/index.asp

*Linda Hunt, President*
Rehabilitation programs offered by the clinic assists clients with rehabilitation health needs in the comfort of their own home. The home care rehabilitation team of professionals focuses on correcting deficiencies in self-care, mobility skills and communication. Services offered include physical therapy, occupational therapy, speech pathology, rehabilitative nursing and restorative nursing assistants.

## California

**6148 Bakersfield Regional Rehabilitation Hospital**
5001 Commerce Dr
Bakersfield, CA 93309-648
661-323-5500
800-288-9829
FAX: 661-633-5254
www.healthsouthbakersfield.com

*Chris Yoon, Medical Director*
*Sandra Hegland, Chief Executive Officer*
A specialty hospital that treats an array of physical disabilities. It has 60 beds and offers physical rehabilitation services including support groups and education classes on illnesses such as arthritis, asthma and strokes. No surgery facilities on site.

**6149 Brotman Medical Center: RehabCare Unit**
3828 Delmas Ter
Culver City, CA 90232-2713
310-836-7000
FAX: 310-202-4141
e-mail: info@brotmanmed.com
www.brotmanmedicalcenter.com

*Howard Levine, CEO*
The mission of Brotman Medical Center is to deliver innovative, quality health care to our patients and their families in an environment of compassion, respect, patient saftey, education, and fiscal responsibility.

**6150 Casa Colinas Centers for Rehabilitation**
255 E Bonita Ave
Pomona, CA 91767-1923
909-596-7733
800-926-5462
FAX: 909-593-0153
e-mail: rehab@casacolina.org
casacolina.org

*Felice Loverso, CEO/President*
Casa Colina will provide individuals the opportunity to maximize their medical recovery and rehabilitation potential efficiently in an environment that recognizes their uniqueness, dignity and self esteem. The vision is to strategically reposition themselves at the forefront of the post-acute continuum by becoming the center of excellence in the provision of services to persons who can benefit from rehabilitation care.

**6151 Community Hospital of Los Gatos Rehabilitation Services**
815 Pollard Rd
Los Gatos, CA 95032-1400
408-378-6131
FAX: 408-866-4003
communityhospitallosgatos.com

*Ned Borgstrom, CEO*
Rehabilitation Services provide individualized treatment programs for inpatient/outpatient care. The team is supervised by a Physiatrist and may include Nurses, Physical Therapists, Occupational Therapists, Speech/Language Therapists, Psychologists, Case Managers, Dietitians, Respiratory Therapists, Recreation Therapists and/or Prosthetists/Orthotists.

**6152 Garfield Medical Center**
525 N Garfield Ave
Monterey Park, CA 91754-1205
626-573-2222
FAX: 626-571-8972
garfieldmedicalcenter.com

*Philip Cohen, CEO*
Provides quality care to all citizens of all ages. We are foreward looking to meet the changing health care needs of Forsyth and the surrounding area. At the same time, we are a stable organization that is financially sound. We involve all of our medical staff through good communication. We support them by trying to meet their professional needs in training, equipment and services. We emphasize good communication with all county citizens who support us financially and through the use of services

**6153 Grossmont Hospital Rehabilition Center**
5555 Grossmont Center
La Mesa, CA 91942
619-740-6000
800-827-4277
FAX: 619-644-4159
sharp.com

*Michael Murphy, President/CEO*
*Daniel Gross, EVP*
It is our mission to improve the health of those we serve with a commitment to excellence in all that we do. Our goal is to offer quality care and programs that set community standards, exceed patients' expectations and are provided in a caring, convenient, cost-effective and accessible manner.

**6154 Health South Tustin Rehabilitation Hospita**
14851 Yorba St
Tustin, CA 92780-2925
714-832-9200
FAX: 714-508-4550
www.healthsouth.com

*Sandra Yule, CEO*

**6155 Holy Cross Comprehensive Rehabilitation Center**
15031 Rinaldi St
Mission Hills, CA 91345-1207
818-365-8051
888-432-5464
FAX: 818-898-4472
www.providence.org

*Larry Bowe, CEO*
*Derek Berz, COO*
Known for providing exceptional treatment through its Cancer Centers, Heart Center, Orthopedics, Neurosciences and Rehabilitation Services, as well as Woman's and Children's Services. As a 254-bed, not-for-profit facility, Providence offers a full continuum of health services, from outpatient to inpatient to home health care. Providence operates one of the only round-the-clock trauma centers in the San Fernando Valley and surrounding communities.

**6156 Job Hunting Tips for the So-Called Handicapped**
Special Needs Project
324 State St
Ste H
Santa Barbara, CA 93101-2364
805-962-8087
800-333-6867
FAX: 805-962-5087
www.specialneeds.com

*Hod Gray, Owner*
This nifty booklet from the guru of job hunting himself is sincere, useful and brief. *$4.95*

**6157 Kentfield Rehabilitation Hospital & Outpatient Center**
1125 Sir Francis Drake Blvd
Kentfield, CA 94904-1418
415-456-9680
FAX: 415-485-3622
kentfieldrehab.com

*Deborah Doherty, MD*
Provides specialized inpatient and outpatient programs. We provide quality services that are patient centered and family-oriented. Under the medical direction of board-certified hospitalists and other physician specialists, our decicated interdisciplinary teams provide a coordinated, comprehensive treatment approach to a wide range of neurological, orthopedic, pulmonary and complex medical problems.

**6158 Laurel Grove Hospital: Rehab Care Unit**
19933 Lake Chabot Rd
Castro Valley, CA 94546-4093
510-537-1234
FAX: 510-727-2778
e-mail: nissims@sutterhealth.org
edenmedcenter.org

*Gregg Tekawa, Finance Executive*
*Ronnie Bayduza, Administrator*
*Rose Corcoran RN, VP*
The mission of Eden Medical Center is carried out by our Board of Directors, employees, physicians and volunteers who are committed to providing our patients and their families with the highest quality medical care and customer service. Creating standards of excellence to ensure quality and value for our patients. Maintaining a financially sound organization through effective clinical and administrative support. Encouraging a culture that supports employees and physicians in development.

**6159 Lodi Memorial Hospital West**
Lodi Memorial Hospital
975 S Fairmont Ave
Lodi, CA 95240
209-334-3411
800-876-6750
FAX: 209-333-7131
e-mail: lmh@lodihealth.org
lodihealth.org

*Joseph Harrington, President*
*Ron Kreutner, Vice President And CFO*
*Judy Begley RN, MSN, Chief Nursing Officer*
Our vision is to provide a system of health-care services which is clinically effective, quality driven and community focused in an environment that supports and encourages excellence. In partnership with our medical staff, we will assume accountability for the health of our community, be responsible for illness and injury prevention and provide care for the ill and injured. We will measure our success on quality outcomes and customer satisfaction.

**6160 Long Beach Memorial Medical Center Memorial Rehabilitation Hospital**
2801 Atlantic Ave
Long Beach, CA 90806-1701
562-933-2000
FAX: 562-933-9018
www.memorialcare.org

*Nissar Syed, Administrator*
*Barry Arbuckle, President*
The hospital offers rehabilitation after catastrophic injury of disabling disease to give patients the opportunity for maximum recovery. The Hospital offers many of the area's finest rehabilitation specialists and most advanced technology, making it one of Southern California's most respected rehabilitation centers.

**6161 North Coast Rehabilitation Center**
151 Sotoyome St
Santa Rosa, CA 95405-4869
707-543-2500
FAX: 707-525-8413
www.santarosamemorial.org

*Joyce Cavagnaro, Admissions*
Combines state-of-the-art medicine, compassionate care, and the widest array of resources to enhance your health and promote healthy communities. Dedicated to continually introducing new programs and services that help you live life to the fullest.

**6162 Northridge Hospital Medical Center**
18300 Roscoe Blvd
Northridge, CA 91328
818-885-8500
FAX: 818-885-5435
www.northridgehospital.org

*Mike Wall, CEO*
dedicating resources to delivering compassionate, high-quality, affordable health services; serving and advocating for our sisters and brothers who are poor and disinfranchised; and partnering with others in the community to improve the quality of life.

**6163 PEERS Program**
8912 W Olympic Blvd
Beverly Hills, CA 90211-3514
310-553-4833
FAX: 310-553-4833

*Paul Berns, Medical Director*
Offers a new approach for wheelchair users. PEERS uses a combination of modern physical therapy, the DOUGLAS Reciprocating Gait System and when necessary, functional electrical stimulation to assist selected individuals to walk with recently patented specially made lightweight braces.

**6164 PIRS Hotsheet**
Placer Independent Resource Services
11768 Atwood Rd
Ste 29
Auburn, CA 95603
530-885-6100
800-833-8453
FAX: 530-885-3032
TTY: 530-885-0326
e-mail: tmiller@pirs.org
pirs.org

*Susan Miller, Executive Director*
*Harry Powell, President*
*Paul Opper, Vice President*
*Dawn Davidson, Secretary*
Monthly newletter to customers and other constituents.
*6 pages Monthly*

**6165 Providence Holy Cross Medical Center**
Providence Health System
15031 Rinaldi St
Mission Hills, CA 91345-1285
818-365-8051
818-898-4603
FAX: 818-365-4472
www.providence.org

*Kerry Carmody, CEO*
Physicains and nurses are among the best and are recoginzed nationally for clinical excellence. We are committed to improving your health and wellness as you journey through life. Our services span beyond the latest advancements in medical procedures, equipment and medication to also include education and wellness services-all provided with compassion and respect. We help our patients understand and use some of the healthiest tools at their disposal, including nutrition & excercise.

**6166 Queen of Angels/Hollywood Presbyterian Medical Center**
1300 N Vermont Ave
Los Angeles, CA 90027-6005
213-413-3000
FAX: 213-413-3500
e-mail: info@hollywoodpresbyterian.com
www.hollywoodpresbyterian.com

*Kathy Wong, Manager*
A 434 bed acute-care facility that has been caring for the Hollywood community and surrounding areas since 1924. The hospital is committed to serving local multicultural communities with quality medical and nursing care. With more then 500 physicians representing virtually every speciality. Ready to serve your medical needs and those of your loved ones and strive to distinguish itself as a leading healthcare provider, recognized for providing quality, innovative care in a compassionate manner.

**6167 Queen of the Valley Hospital**
1000 Trancas St
Napa, CA 94558-2941
707-252-4411
FAX: 707-257-4032
queenofthevalley.com

*Walt Mickens, President*
*Vincent Morgese, Vice President*
For more then 40 years, Queen of the Valley Hospital has been the premiere medical facility in the Napa Valley. Our long history of providing high quality and caring service is founded on 4 core values:Dignity, Service, Excellence and Justice. These central principals inspire us to reach out to those in need and to help heal the whole person-mind, body and spirit.They are the driving force behind our mission to improve the health and quality of life of people in the community we serve.

**6168 Rancho Los Amigos National Rehabilitation Center**
7601 Imperial Hwy
Downey, CA 90242-3496
562-401-7111
877-726-2461
888-RAN-CHO
FAX: 562-401-6690
e-mail: webmaster@rancho.org
www.rancho.org

*Valerie Orange, CEO*
*Chris Thomas, Public Relations Director*
Internationally renowned in the field of medical rehabilitation, consistently ranked in the top Rehabilitation Hospitals in the United States by U.S. News and World Report. It is one of the largest comprehensive rehabilitaion centers in the United States. Licensed for 395 beds, providing service through over 20 centers of excellence.

**6169 San Joaquin Valley Rehabilitation Hospital**
7173 N Sharon Ave
Fresno, CA 93720-3329
559-436-3600
FAX: 559-436-3606
e-mail: jpage@svjrehab.com
sjvrehab.com

*Edward Palacios, CEO*
Complete comprehensive rehabilitation services from acute rehab, outpatient and community fitness services.

**6170 Santa Clara Valley Medical Center**
County of Santa Clara
751 S Bascom Ave
San Jose, CA 95128-2699
408-885-5000
www.scvmed.org

*Susan Murphy, Director*
The mission of the medical center is to provide high-quality, cost-effective medical care to all residence of Santa Clara County regardless of their ability to pay. Make availiable a wide range of inpatient, outpatient, emergency services within resource constraints. Maintain an environment within which the needs of our patients are paramount and where patients, their families and all our visitors are treated in a compassionate, supportive, friendly, and dignified manner.

**6171 Scripps Memorial Hospital at La Jolla**
9888 Genesee Ave
La Jolla, CA 92037-1205
858-626-6150
800-727-4777
FAX: 858-626-6122
www.scrippshealth.org/locations.asp?id=4

*Sean A Deitch, President/CEO*
*Gary Fybel, Executive Director/Administrator*
One of the county's 6 designated trauma centers, offers a wide range of clinical and surgical services including 24-hour emergency services; intensive care; interventional cardiology and radiology; radiation oncology; cardiothoracic and orthopedic services; neurology; ophthalmology; and mental health and psychology services.

**6172 South Coast Medical Center**
12 Mason
Ste A
Irvine, CA 92618-2733
714-669-4446
FAX: 714-669-4448
e-mail: info@southcoastmedcenter.com
www.southcoastmedcenter.com

*Leigh Erin Connealy, Manager*
*Bruce Christian, President*
A 208 bed acute care hospital. Services include maternity, surgical, subacute care, psychiatric program, eating disorder treatment, chemical dependency treatment, radiology, ICU/CCU,

comprehensive rehabilitation services, bariatric surgery and movement disorders program..

**6173 St. Joseph Rehabilitation Center**
St. Joseph Health System
2200 Harrison Ave
Eureka, CA 95501-3215
707-441-4414
FAX: 707-441-4429
www.stjosepheureka.org

Mission is to provide physical rehabilitation services in a positive patient-centered environment. This promotes restoration of maximum functional abilities and allows for a dignified quality of life experience. As a staff we are guided by our core values of Dignity, Excellence, Service, and Justice.

**6174 St. Jude Brain Injury Network**
St. Jude Hospital
130 W Bastanchury Rd
Fullerton, CA 92835-1058
714-446-5626
866-785-8332
FAX: 714-447-0987
e-mail: bin_tbi@yahoo.com
www.tbioc.org

*Jana Gable, Program Coordinator*
*David Bogdan, Service Coordinator*
*Lina Marroquin, Servicer Coordinator*

Provides comprehensive planning, program referral, assists with funding possibilities, and interagency coordination of services. Areas of emphasis include day treatment, vocational and housing options, and the requirements are adults who have suffered a brain injury from an external force.

**6175 St. Jude Medical Center**
101 E Valencia Mesa Dr
Fullerton, CA 92835-3809
714-871-3280
800-627-8106
FAX: 714-992-3029
stjudemedicalcenter.org

*Robert Fraschetti, President*

A 331 bed full-service regional medical center that serves as a major referral hospital attracting rehabilitation patients throughout southern California for over twenty years.

**6176 St. Mary Medical Center**
1050 Linden Ave
Long Beach, CA 90813-3393
562-491-9000
FAX: 562-491-9053
www.smmc.com

*Chris Desicco, CEO*

A 556-bed hospital owned by the Sisters of Charity of the Incarnate World Healthcare Systems, one of the nation's largest Catholic healthcare networks. Services include a trauma unit, a comprehensive Cancer Care Center, complete older adult services, a Low Vision Center, a Rehabilitation Institute, an outpatient Surgi/Center and the only kidney transplant program in Long Beach. St. Mary's is a teaching hospital affiliated with the UCLA School of Medicine.

**6177 Sunnyside Nursing Center**
22617 S Vermont Ave
Torrance, CA 90502-2595
310-320-4130
FAX: 310-212-3232

*Shane Dahl, Administrator*
*Manny Cordero, Director of Nursing*

Skilled nursing care facility; residential care facility; intermediate care facility; specialty hospital.

**6178 UCLA Medical Center: Department of Anesthesiology, Acute Pain Services**
U CL A Medical Center
Suite 225
1245 16th Street Medical Plz
Santa Monica, CA 90404
310-794-1841
FAX: 310-794-1511
e-mail: access@mednet.ucla.edu
www.medcnt.ucla.edu

*Michael Ferrante, Clinical Director*

A 337-bed acute-care medical center, has been serving the healthcare needs of West Los Angeles and Santa Monica since 1926. Highly regarded for its primary and specialty care, the medical center features many outstanding clinical programs, including its women's and children's services, emergency services, and family medicine programs.

## Colorado

**6179 Children's Hospital Rehabilitation Center**
University of Colorado Health Sciences Center
1056 E 19th Ave
Denver, CO 80218-1007
303-861-8888
800-624-6553
e-mail: webmaster@tchden.org
chipteam.org

*Lou Blankenship, CEO*
*Michael J Farrell, Chief Operating Officer*
*Helen Martinez, Manager*

Private not-for-profit pediatric healthcare network, the hospital is 100 percent dedicated to caring for kids of all ages and stages of growth. That dedication is evident in more then 1000 pediatric specialists and more then 2400 employees. It is also our continual dedication that has placed us at the forefront of research in childhood disease with several nationally and internationally recognized medical programs.

**6180 Craig Hospital**
3425 S Clarkson St
Englewood, CO 80113-2899
303-789-8000
FAX: 303-789-8214
e-mail: khosack@craighospital.org
www.craighospital.org

*Michael Fordyce, President*
*Thomas Balazy, Medical Director*

A 93-bed, private, not-for-profit, free-standing, acute care and rehabilitation hospital that provides a comprehensive system of inpatient and outpatient medical care, rehabilitation, neurosurgical rehabilitative care, an equipment company, and long-term follow up services. Nearly half of Craig's patients come from outside of Colorado, and in 2004 the hospital treated patients from 47 states and several foreign countries. Provides housing for out-of-state families and outpatiients.

**6181 HealthSouth Rehabilitation Hospital of Colorado Springs**
HealthSouth Corporation
325 S Parkside Dr
Colorado Springs, CO 80910-3134
719-630-8000
FAX: 719-520-0387
healthsouth.com

*Steve Schaefer, CEO*

A 56 bed rehabilitation hospital, its key services are: cardiology department, physical rehabilitation, and orthopedics department. Accrediddted to the Joint Commission on Accreditation of Health Care Organizations (JCAHO)

**6182 Mapleton Center**
P.O.Box 9130
Boulder, CO 80301-9130
303-441-0493
FAX: 303-441-0536
e-mail: pr@bch.org
www.bch.org

*David Gehant, President/CEO*

Comprehensive inpatient and outpatient rehabilitation services for all age groups. Treatment provided by interdisciplinary teams and staff physicians. CARF accredited in brain injury rehabilitation, pediatric rehabilitation, pain management, work hardening and inpatient rehabilitation.

**6183 Mediplex Rehab: Denver**
Vibra Health Care
8451 Pearl St
Thornton, CO 80229-4804
303-288-3000
FAX: 303-496-1120
www.northvalleyrehab.com

*Walter Sacckett, CEO*

Encompasses the broadest mix of professional talent, the finest technology and a total commitment by our people to deliver the highest quality care today, and well into the future. The services can be divided into 4 main categories: long term Acute Care and rehab. Skilled nursing facility and residential ventilator program. Outpatient services and pain management. Adult and Geriatric inpatient psychiatric services.

## Connecticut

**6184 Mariner Health Care: Connecticut**
23 Liberty Way
Niantic, CT 06357
860-739-4007
FAX: 860-701-2202

## District of Columbia

**6185 National Rehabilitation Hospital**
102 Irving St NW
Washington, DC 20010-2949
301-877-1000
FAX: 202-877-7318
www.nrhrehab.org

*Edward Healton, Medical Director*
*Robert Bunning, Associate Medical Director*

A private facility dedicated solely to medical rehabilitation. The hospital offers intensive inpatient programs and full-service outpatient programs.

## Florida

**6186 Florida Hospital Rehabilitation Center**
601 E Rollins St
Orlando, FL 32803-1248
407-303-1527
FAX: 407-303-7566
e-mail: fh.web@flhosp.org
www.flhosp.org

*Rex Alleyne, President*

Florida Hospital Orlando uses the latest technology to treat over 32,000 inpatients and 53,600 outpatients annually. This 881-bed, acute-carecommunity hospital also serves as a major tertiary facility for much of the Southeast, the Caribbean and South America

**6187 HealthSouth Regional Rehab Center/Florida**
20601 Old Cutler Rd
Miami, FL 33189-2441
305-251-3800
FAX: 305-259-0498
www.healthsouth.com

*Murray Rolnick, Medical Director*
*Elizabeth Izquierdo, Chief Executive Officer*

HealthSouth Rehabilitation Hospital of Miami is a member of the HealthSouth Corporation, the nation's largest healthcare services provider. The hospital is accredited by the Joint Commission on Accreditation of Healthcare Organizations (JCAHO) and Commission on Accreditaion of Rehabilitation Facilities (CARF). Services offered include dietary services, occupational therapy, and respitory care.

**6188 HealthSouth Rehab Hospital: Largo**
901 Clearwater Largo Rd N
Largo, FL 33770-4121
727-586-2999
FAX: 727-588-3404
www.healthsouthlargo.com

*Elaine Ebaugh, CEO*
*Linda Russo, Director, Therapies*

A specialty hospital devoted to providing comprehensive medical rehabilitation services. The hospital is licensed as a Comprehensive Medical Rehabilitation Hospital by the state of Florida, and accredited by the Joint Commission on Accreditation of Healthcare Organizations (JCAHO). HealthSouth of Largo is the only free standing Rehabilitation Hospital in the Tampa Bay region, and serves patients of all ages. Provides inpatient medical rehabilitation services as well as outpatient programs.

**6189 HealthSouth Sports Medicine & Rehabilitation Center**
3280 Ponce De Leon Blvd
Coral Gables, FL 33134-7252
305-444-0909
FAX: 305-444-5760
www.healthsouth.com

*Jay Greeney, President*
*Ray Jaffet, Administrator*

Provides specialized medical and therapeutic services designated to help physically disabled individuals reach their optimum level of independence and function by providing inpatient and outpatient comprehensive medical rehabilitation services.

**6190 HealthSouth Sports Medicine and Rehabilitation Center**
2141 South Highway A1A Alt
Jupiter, FL 33477
561-743-8890
FAX: 561-743-8795

*Diane Reiley, Manager*

Outpatient orthopedic and sports medicine/physical therapy.

**6191 HealthSouth Treasure Coast Rehabilitation Hospital**
Health South Corporation of Alabama
1600 37th St
Vero Beach, FL 32960-4863
772-778-2100
FAX: 772-567-7041
www.healthsouthtreasurecoast.com

*Jimmy Lockhart, Medical Director*

HealthSouth Treasure Coast Rehabilitation Hospital is a 90-bed inpatient comprehensive rehabilitation hospital serving Indian River, St. Lucie, Martin and Okeechobee counties. Outpatient services are available at the hospital and at four other clinics. Therapies include physical, occupational, speech and psychology services.

**6192 Manatee Springs Care & Rehabilitation Center**
5627 9th St E
Bradenton, FL 34203-6105
941-753-8941
FAX: 941-739-4409
e-mail: info@manateespringsrehab.com
www.manateespringsrehab.com

*Donna Steiermann, Administrator*

Skilled rehabilitation facility specializing in PT, OT, speech therapy, aquatic therapy and an indoor pool. Piped oxygen bed for specialized respiratory care. Compassionate end of life care. Some Medicare, private insurance, and Medicaid.

**6193 Perry Health Facility**
207 Marshall Dr
Perry, FL 32347-1897 850-584-6334
FAX: 850-838-1801

*Rebkah Hatch, Administrator*
Full rehabilitation team available, Physiatrist, DOR, Psychiatrist, Psychologist, RD, Geriatric Nursing, PT/OT/ST/RT, Orthotiet/Prosthetist. Provider for PPO's & HMO's as well as medicare, private insurance and medicare/medicaid.

**6194 Pinecrest Rehabilitation Hospital and Outpatient Centers**
Tenet South Florida
5352 Linton Blvd
Delray Beach, FL 33484-6514 561-498-4440
800-283-8326
FAX: 561-495-3103
www.pinecrestrehab.com

*Mark Bryan, CEO*
Pinecrest Rehabilitation Hospital is a 90 bed, accredited hospital and is comprised of a Specialty Unit, a Neuro Trauma Unit and Joint Replacement Unit. Additional services at Pincrest include six outpatient rehab centers throughout Palm Beach County. The Outpatient Centers each focus on various specialties such as orthopedic and neurological rehab, pain management, cardiac and pulmonary rehab, occupational medicine, Hearing Institute, dizziness and balance and wellness.

**6195 Rehabilitation Institute of Sarasota**
3251 Proctor Rd
Sarasota, FL 34231-8538 941-921-8796
FAX: 941-922-6228

*Stacy Shepherd, Director Clinical Services*
a 75-bed hospital that offers individualized medical and theraputic services tailored to patients and clinics for those affected with stroke, multiple sclerosis, Parkinson's, muscular dystrophy and Lou Gehrig's disease (ALS)

**6196 Sea Pines Rehabilitation Hospital**
101 E Florida Ave
Melbourne, FL 32901-8398 321-984-4633
FAX: 321-727-7440
e-mail: ellen.lyons-olski@healthsouth.com
www.healthsouthseapines.com

*Stuart Miller, Medical Director*
*Donna Bohdal, Director of Therapy Operations*
*Denise McGrath, Administrator*
A 90-bed facility specializing in rehabilitation of brain and spinal injuries.

**6197 Shriners Hospitals for Children: Tampa**
12502 Pine Dr
Tampa, FL 33612-9411 813-972-2250
813-281-0300
FAX: 813-975-7125
www.shrinershq.org/hospitals/tampa

*Alice Landford, CEO*
*Dennis Grogan, Chief of Staff*
Recognizing that the family plays a vital role in a child's ability to overcome an illness or injury, Shriners Hospitals helps the family provide the support the child needs by involving the family in all aspects of the child's care and recovery. The purpose of all Shriners Hospitals for Children is to provide care to children with orthopedic problems and burn injuries to help them lead fuller, more productive lives.

**6198 South Miami Hospital**
6200 SW 73rd St
South Miami, FL 33143-4679 786-662-4000
FAX: 786-662-5302
www.baptisthealth.net

*Javier Hernandez-Lich, CEO*
The mission is to improve the health and well-being of individuals, and to promote the sanctity and preservation of life, in the communities we serve. We are committed to maintaining the highest standards of clinical and service excellence, rooted in utmost integrity and moral practice.

**6199 St. Anne's Nursing Center**
11855 Quail Roost Dr
Miami, FL 33177-3956 305-252-4000
FAX: 305-969-6752
www.catholichealthservices.org

*Tony Farinella, Executive Director*
*Francisco Cruz, Medical Director*
*Julia Shillingford, Director of Nursing*
Provides spacious, comfortable accommodations with ample recreational areas in a beautifully landscaped setting.

**6200 St. Anthony's Hospital**
1200 7th Ave N
St Petersburg, FL 33705-1388 727-825-1100
www.stanthonys.com

*William Ulbricht, President*
A not-for-profit, 395-bed hospital established in 1931. St. Anthony's is dedicated to improving the health of the community through community-owned health care that sets the standard for high-quality, compassionate care.

**6201 St. Anthony's Rehabilitation Hospital**
3487 NW 35th Ave
Lauderdale Lakes, FL 33311-1107 954-485-4023
954-739-6233
www.catholichealthservices.org

*Linda Motte, Hospital Administrator*
*Kathy Torbertsonn, Dir. Rehab.*

**6202 St. Catherine's Rehabilitation Hospital and Villa Maria Nursing Center**
1050 NE 125th St
North Miami, FL 33161-5805 305-357-1735
305-891-3361
www.catholichealthservices.org

*Virginia Irving, Hospital Administrator*
*Jim Reiss, Executive Director*
*Greg Hartley, Director Rehab*
St. Catherine's Rehabilitation Hospital is a CARF accredited, 60 bed facility offering inpatient and outpatient rehabilitation and medical clinics; including physical, occupational, and speech therapy, neurology, neurodiagnostics, wound care, and hyperbaric medicine. Villa Maria Nursing center is a JCAHO accredited, 212 bed skilled nursing center providing short term nursing and rehabilitation , as well as long term care.

**6203 St. John's Nursing Center**
3075 NW 35th Ave
Lauderdale Lakes, FL 33311-1107 954-739-6233
FAX: 954-733-9579
www.catholichealthservices.org

*George Azar, Executive Director*

**6204 Successful Job Accommodation Strategies**
LRP Publications
36- Hiatt Dr
Palm Beach Gardens, FL 33418
561-622-6520
800-341-7874
FAX: 561-622-0757
e-mail: custserve@lrp.com
www.lrp.com

*Honora McDowell, Product Group Manager*
*Kenneth Kahn, Chief Executive Officer*
This monthly newsletter provides you with quick tips, new accommodation ideas and innovative workplace solutions. You learn the outcomes of the latest cases involving workplace accommodations. *$ 140.00*
*12 pages Monthly*

**6205 Tampa General Rehabilitation Center**
P.O.Box 1289
Tampa, FL 33601-1289
813-844-7700
FAX: 813-844-1477
e-mail: jstone@tgh.org
tgh.org

*Ron Hytoff, President/CEO*
*Devanand Mangar MD, Vice Chief of Staff*
*Thomas L. Bernasek MD, Chief of Staff*
Offers a full range of inpatient and outpatient programs all aimed at helping patients achieve their full potentials. JCAHO and CARF accredited and V.R. designated center. A wide range of inpatient and outpatient programs are available such as Brain and Spinal Cord Injury Programs, Comprehensive Medical Rehabilitation, Pain Management, Cardiac Rehab, Pediatric Therapy Service, Sleep Disorders, Epilepsy, and Wheelchair Seating.Hosts the Florida Alliance for Assistive Services and Technolgy.

**6206 University of Miami: Jackson Memorial Rehabilitation Center**
University of Miami
1611 NW 12th Ave
Miami, FL 33136-1005
305-585-6970
FAX: 305-585-6092
e-mail: info@jhsmiami.org
www.jhsmiami.org

*Michael Butler, Chief Medical Officer*
An accredited, non-profit, tertiary care hospital and the major teaching facility for the University of Miami School of Medicine. With more then 1,550 beds, Jackson Memorial is a referral center, a magnet for medical research, and home to the Ryder Trauma Center- the only adult and pediatric level 1 trauma center in Miami-Dade County.

**6207 Winter Park Memorial Hospital**
Florida Hospital
200 N Lakemont Ave
Winter Park, FL 32792-3273
407-646-7000
FAX: 407-646-7639
e-mail: healthcare@winterparkhospital.com
www.winterparkhospital.com

*Ken Bradley, CEO*
Offers Acute Rehabilitation.

## Georgia

**6208 Candler General Hospital: Rehabilitation Unit**
5353 Reynolds St
Savannah, GA 31405-6015
912-819-6176
FAX: 912-819-8829

*Paul Hinchey, President/CEO*
Special Physical Therapy Services at Candler Outpatient Center: Aquatic therapy, pediatric services, outpaitient neurological rehabilitation program, woman's health therapy, orthotics, and spine specialty

**6209 Children's Healthcare of Atlanta at Egleston**
1405 Clifton Rd NE
Atlanta, GA 30322-1060
404-785-6499
FAX: 404-315-2158
www.choa.org

*Donna Hyland, President/CEO*
Rehabilitation Center at Egleston accepts children from birth to age 18 with acute or chronic problems. The length of rehab stay varies for each child according to the determined program of care. The center offers inpatient, outpatient & day rehab programs for comprehensive evaluation & treatment. The program emphasizes the development of the child's abilities & concentrates on helping the family & child compensate for any long-term disabilities. Short term stays require one or two weeks.

**6210 Cobb Hospital and Medical Center: Rehab Care Center**
3950 Austell Rd
Austell, GA 30106-1121
770-732-4000
e-mail: generalinfo@wellstar.org
www.wellstar.org

*Larry Haldeman, Executive VP*
To deliver world class healthcare we equip our healthcare facilities and employees with the best technology, resources and education availiable. To deliver world class healthcare we keep seeking ways to improve the way we deliver care knowing each day holds more miracles, more life, more chances, more compassion, and more opportunities.

**6211 HealthSouth Central Georgia Rehabilitation Hospital**
3351 Northside Dr
Macon, GA 31210-2587
478-471-3500
FAX: 478-471-6536
www.centralgarehab.com

HealthSouth Central Georgia rehabilitation hospital is a 55 bed comprehensive medical rehabilitation hospital meeting the medical patients and famloity members in Central Georgia.

**6212 Specialty Hospital**
Floyd Healthcare Resources
304 Turner McCall Blvd SW
Rome, GA 30165-5621
706-509-5000
FAX: 706-802-4175
e-mail: contactus@floyd.org
www.floyd.org

*Kurt Stuenkel, CEO*
*Dee Russell, Chief Medical Officer*
Our mission is to be responsive to the communities we serve with a comprehensive and technologically advanced heal care system commited to the delivery of care that is characterized by continually improving quality, accessability, affordability and personal dignity.

## Hawaii

**6213 Shriners Hospital for Children: Honolulu**
1310 Punahou St
Honolulu, HI 96826-1099
808-941-4466
888-888-6314
FAX: 808-942-8573
www.shrinershospitalsforchildren.org

*Keith Gardner, EVP*
*Peter Armstrong, VP, Medical Affairs*
One of 22 hospitals across North America that provide excellent, no-cost medical care to children with orthopedic problems and burn industries.

## Idaho

**6214 Pocatello Regional Medical Center**
777 Hospital Way
Pocatello, ID 83201-2797
208-234-6154
FAX: 208-239-3719
e-mail: robbieo@portmed.org
www.portmed.org

*Norman Stephens, CEO*
Pocatello Regional Medical Center offers 24-hour emergency care, specialized heart services, a dialysis center, a full service rehabilitation unit including transition care, and the Woman's Center For Health including obstetrics.

## Illinois

**6215 Builders of Skills**
515 Busse Hwy
Park Ridge, IL 60068-3154
847-318-0870
FAX: 847-292-0873
e-mail: avenues@avenuesonline.org
www.avenuestoindependence.org

*Robert Okazaki, Executive Director*
Residential setting for hearing-impaired, developmentally disabled adults who are assisted with daily living skills.

**6216 Center for Learning**
National-Louis University
2840 Sheridan Rd
Evanston, IL 60201-1730
847-256-5150
FAX: 845-256-1057
e-mail: kadamle@nl.edu

*Jerry Dachs, Manager*
Psycho-educational evaluations for children, adolescents, and adults. Individualized remedial academic programs, individual counseling

**6217 DBTAC-Great Lakes ADA Center**
1640 W Roosevelt Rd
Rm 405
Chicago, IL 60608-1316
312-413-1407
800-949-4232
FAX: 312-413-1856
e-mail: gldbtac@uic.edu
www.adagreatlakes.org

*Robin Jones, Project Director*
*Glenn Fujiura, PhD, Director of Research and Co-Investigator*
*Claudia Diaz, Associate Project Director*
*Peter Berg, Project Coordinator for Technical Assistance and Employer Outreach*
Provides training, technical assistance and consultation on the rights and resposibilities of indiviualsand entities covered by the ADA. Toll free number for technical assistance and materials provided electronically or via mail at no cost.

**6218 Institute of Physical Medicine and Rehabilitation**
6501 N Sheridan Rd
Peoria, IL 61614-2932
309-692-8110
800-957-4767
FAX: 309-692-8673
e-mail: foundation@ipmr.org
ipmr.org

*Lisa Snyder, Medical Director*
Comprehensive CARF accredited programs in outpatient medical rehabilitation services. Eight outpatient locations, specialty programs include adult day services, driving evaluations, balance and visual rehabilitation board certified physiatrists.

**6219 LaRabida Children's Hospital and Research Center**
E 65th At Lake Michigan
Chicago, IL 60649
773-363-6700
FAX: 773-363-9554
e-mail: pr@larabida.org
www.larabida.org

*Brenda Wolf, President/CEO*
Dedicated to excellence in caring for children with chronic illness, disabilitiesm or who have been abused, allowing them to achieve their fullest potential through expertise and innovation within the health care and academic communities.

**6220 Marianjoy Rehabilitation Hospital and Clinics**
26W171 Roosevelt Rd
Wheaton, IL 60187-6078
630-909-8000
800-462-2366
FAX: 630-909-8001
e-mail: dlebloch@marianjoy.org
www.marianjoy.org

*Kathleen Yosko, President/CEO*
*Noel Rao, VP, Medical Affairs*
Goal at Marianjoy Rehabilitation Hospital is to help you and your family return to the lifestyle you enjoyed before your illness or injury. To meet this goal, we provide you with a dedicated team of experienced professionals to assist you every step of the way.

**6221 Rush Copley Medical Center-Rehab Neuro Physical Unit**
2000 Ogden Ave
Aurora, IL 60504-7222
630-978-6200
866-426-7539
FAX: 630-898-4565
e-mail: clord@rsh.net
www.rushcopley.com

*Barry Finn, CEO*
*Mary Shilkaitis, VP, Patient Care Services*
The mission of the medical center and the medical staff is to work together to serve your healthcare needs through excellence in education, technology and a caring touch. Rush-Copley Medical Center will be the leading healthcare provider of the greater Fox Valley area. At Rush-Copley we pride ourselves on providing everyone with extrodinary service.

## Indiana

**6222 ATTAIN**
U S Department of Education/ NI DR R
Ste 1400
32 E Washington St
Indianapolis, IN 46204-3552
317-534-0236
800-528-8246

*Gary Hand, Executive Director*
The mission of Attain is to create solutions that enable people with functional limitations to live, learn, work and play in the community of their choice. All will have access to assistive devices. We will do this in partnership with people with functional limitations, families and members of the community through training, system change, services and support, research, dissemination and consumer advocacy.

**6223 About Special Kids**
7275 N. Shadeland Avenue
Suite 1
Indianapolis, IN 46250-2879
317-257-8683
800-964-4746
FAX: 317-251-7488
e-mail: FamilyNetw@aboutspecialkids.org
www.aboutspecialkids.org

*Joe Brubaker, Executive Director*
*Jane Scott, Director Of Information*
*Nancy Stone, Project Director*

A Parent to Parent organization that works throughout the state of Indiana to answer questions and provide support, information and resources. We are parents and family members of children with special needs and we help other families and professionals understand the various systems that are encountered related to special needs. Our central office is where parents from the entire state can access information, resources and support.

**6224 Clark Memorial Hospital: RehabCare Unit**
1220 Missouri Ave
Jeffersonville, IN 47130-3743
812-282-6631
FAX: 812-283-2656
clarkmemorial.org

*Martin Padgett, CEO*
The mission of Clark Memorial Hospital is to provide superior health services to the people and communities we serve. The vision of Clark Memorial Hospital is to be the best community health care provider in the United States. We value each individual and work together to explore new ways to improve the quality of life of all. We persue excellence in all we do. We treat all individuals with the same compassion, dignity, and privacy that we want in ourselves.

**6225 Developmental Disabilities Planning Council**
Ste 628
150 W Market St
Indianapolis, IN 46204-2855
317-232-7770
FAX: 317-233-3712
e-mail: gpcpd@gpcpd.org
www.state.in.us/gpcpd

*Suellen Jackson-Boner, Executive Director*
*Christine Dahlberg, Associate Director*
*Paul Shankland, Grants Manager*
*Betty Jones, Secretary*
The mission of the Indiana Governor's Council is to promote public policy which leads to the independence, productivity and inclusion of people with disabilities in all aspects of society. This mission is accomplished through planning, evaluation, collaboration, education, research and advocacy. The Council is consumer-driven and is charged with determining how the service delivery system in both the public and private sectors can be most responsible to the people with disabilities.

**6226 Easter Seals Wayne/Union Counties**
P.O.Box 86
Centerville, IN 47330-86
765-855-2482
FAX: 756-855-2482
e-mail: eastersealswu@comcast.net
eastersealswu.tripod.com

*Kathy Stephen, Treasurer*
*Vickey Allen, President*
*Leslie Mayl Whitney, Secretary*
Helps people discover nature and much more at camps equipped to offer physcial, social and emotional support and fun for campers with physical and/or developmental disabilities.

**6227 IN-SOURCE**
Indiana Resource Center for Families with Special
1703 S Ironwood Dr
South Bend, IN 46613-3414
574-234-7101
800-332-4433
FAX: 574-234-7279
e-mail: insource@insource.org
insource.org

*Richard Burden, Executive Director*
*Scott Carson, Assistant Director*
*Dory Lawrence, Project Director*
*Sally Hamburg, Project Director*
The mission of IN*SOURCE is to provide parents, families and service providers in Indiana the information and training necessary to assure effective educational programs and appropriate services for children and young adults with disabilities.

**6228 Indiana Congress of Parent and Teachers**
2525 N Shadeland Ave
Ste D4
Indianapolis, IN 46219-1770
317-357-5881
FAX: 317-357-3751
e-mail: info@indianapta.org
www.indianapta.org

*Barry Jones, President*
The mission of the Indiana PTA is three-fold: to support and speak on behalf of children and youth in the schools, community and before governmental agencies and other organizations that make decisions affecting children; to assist parents in developing the skills they need to raise and protect their children; and, to encorage parent and community involvement in the public schools of this state and nation.

**6229 Indiana Protection and Advocacy Services Commission**
4701 N Keystone Ave
Ste 222
Indianapolis, IN 46205-1561
317-722-5555
800-838-1131
FAX: 317-722-5564
e-mail: kpedevilla@ipas.state.in.us
www.in.gov/ipas

*Karen Pedevilla, Education and Training Director*
IPAS was created in 1977 by state law to protect and advocate the rights of people with disabilities and its Indiana's federally designated Protection (P&A) system and client assist program. It is an independent state agency, with receives no state funding and is independent from all service providers, as required by federal and state law.

**6230 Kokomo Rehabilitation Hospital**
829 N Dixon Rd
Kokomo, IN 46901-7709
765-452-6700
FAX: 765-452-7470

*Brenda Harry, Admissions Director*
a 60 bed facility specializing in rehabilitation services to the people of Indiana.

**6231 Memorial Regional Rehabilitation Center**
615 N Michigan St
South Bend, IN 46601-1033
574-647-7312
www.qualityoflife.org
20-bed CARF accredited inpatient rehabilitation, outpatient orthopedic clinic and work performance program, head injury clinic. Outpatient neuro rehab and a driver education and training program are provided.

**6232 Methodist Hospital Rehabilitation Institute**
8701 Broadway
Merrillville, IN 46410-7035
219-738-5500
FAX: 219-755-0448
methodisthospitals.org

*Ian McFadden, President/CEO*
*Michael Davenport, VP Medical Affairs*
The Mission of Methodist Hospitals is to provide compassionate, quality health service to all those in need. Our vision is to provide the best place for employees to work, the best place for patients to receive care and the best place for physicians to practice medicine.

**6233 NAMI Indiana**
P.O.Box 22697
Indianapolis, IN 46222-697
317-925-9399
800-677-6442
FAX: 317-925-9398
e-mail: nami-in@nami.org
www.nami.org

*Teresa Hatten, President*
*Harriet Rosen, Executive Director*

NAMI Indiana is a non-profit grassroots organization dedicated to improving the lives of people afflicted by serious and persistant mental illness. We are dedicated to helping families through a network of support, education, advocacy, and promotion of research. NAMI's goal is to help establish a system of care that provides community based services for persons with serious mental illness, as well as support for them and their families.

**6234 Parkview Regional Rehabilitation Center**
2200 Randallia Dr
Fort Wayne, IN 46805-4638
260-373-4280
888-480-5151
FAX: 260-373-4288
www.parkview.com

*Sheryl Scott, Executive Director*
Provides a full range of inpatient, theraputic services and programs for patients as young as 3 years of age to the very elderly. Our accute care rehabilitation center, is well equipped to care for patients with neurological and orthopedic injuries and diseases.

**6235 Programs for Children with Disabilities: Ages 3 through 5**
Indiana Department of Education
151 W Ohio St
Indianapolis, IN 46204-1905
317-232-0570
877-851-4106
FAX: 317-232-0589
e-mail: specialed@doe.in.gov
www.doe.in.gov/exceptional

*Heather Neal, Chief of Staff*
The division provides leadership and state-level support for public school gifted and talented (grades K-12) programs and for students with disabilities from ages 3-21. The division ensures that Indiana, in its compliance with the federal Individuals With Disabilities Education Act, through monitoring of special education programs, oversight of community and residential programs, provision of mediation and due process rights, and sound fiscal management.

**6236 Programs for Children with Special Health Care Needs**
Indiana State Department of Health
2 N Meridian St
Indianapolis, IN 46204-3021
317-233-1325
e-mail: wgettelf@isdh.state.in.us
www.in.gov/isdh/

*Sean Keefer, Chief of Staff*
The Children's Special Health Care Services (CSHCS) program provides financial assistance for needed medical treatment to children with serious and chronic medical conditions to reduce complications and promote maximum quality of life.

**6237 Programs for Infants and Toddlers with Disabilities: Ages Birth through 2**
402 W Washington St
Indianapolis, IN 46204-2773
317-232-1144
800-441-7837
e-mail: firststepsweb@fssa.state.in.us

A family-centered, locally-based, coordinated system that provides early intervention services to infants and young children with disabilities or who are developmentally vulnerable. First Steps brings together families and professionals from education, health and social service agencies. By coordinating locally availiable services, First Steps is working to give Indiana's children and their families the widest possible array of early intervention resources.

**6238 Riley Child Development Center**
705 Riley Hospital Drive
Rm 5837
Indianapolis, IN 46202-5128
317-944-8167
FAX: 317-944-9760
e-mail: info@child-dev.com
child-dev.com

*Cristy James, Communication Coordinator*
Riley Hospital for Children is Indiana's only comprehensive children's hospital, with pediatric specialists in evry field of medicine and surgery. Riley is committed to providing the highest quality health care to children in a compassionate, family-centered environment. Riley is a national leader in cutting edge research and medical education, ensuring health care excellence for children for generations to come. Riley provides medical care to all children, regardless of family's ability to pay.

**6239 St. Anthony Memorial Hospital: Rehab Unit**
301 W Homer St
Michigan City, IN 46360-4358
219-879-8511
FAX: 219-877-1409
www.saintanthonymemorial.org

*Joseph Allegreti, Board of Directors*
*Calvin Bellamy, Board of Directors*
Saint Anthony Memorial is an acute care hospital located in Michigan City, primary serving La Porte and Porter Counties in Indiana as well as Berrien County Michigan.

**6240 State Division of Vocational Rehabilitation**
P.O.Box 7083
Indianapolis, IN 46207-7083
317-233-4454
800-545-7763
FAX: 317-233-4693
e-mail: martin@fssa.state.in.us
www.state.in.us/fssa

*Megan Ornellas, Chief of Staff*
*Susie Howard, Deputy Chief of Staff*

**6241 VSA Indiana**
Harrison Center for the Arts
1505 N Delaware St
Indianapolis, IN 46202-4466
317-974-4123
FAX: 317-974-4124
e-mail: abear@vsai.org
www.vsai.org

*Gayle Holtman, President*
*Amy Bear, Vice President*
For over 25 years VSA arts of Indiana has led the movement to make the arts accessable to people with disabilitites. VSA arts of Indiana offers a variety of opportunities for people with disabilities of all ages to engage the power of the arts as a means of education, creative self-expression, and personal and professional growth. As a result, VSA promotes change in public perceptions and raises public awareness, and advocates for increased accessability in providing art experiences for all.

## Iowa

**6242 Younker Rehabilitation Center of Iowa Methodist Medical Center**
1200 Pleasant St
Des Moines, IA 50309-1406
515-241-6741
FAX: 515-241-5137
www.ihs.org

*Bill Leaver, President*
*Kevin Vermeer, EVP*
Iowa Health System is the state's first and largest integrated healthcare system. We are physicians, hospitals, civic leaders and local volunteers committed to providing the highest possible quality and the lowest possible cost. We serve over 70 communities in Iowa, Western Illinois, and Eastern Nebraska.

## Kansas

**6243 Kansas Rehabilitation Hospital**
1504 SW 8th Ave
Topeka, KS 66606-2714
785-235-6600
FAX: 785-232-8545
www.kansasrehabhospital.com

*Mark LeNeave, CEO*
*Mindy Mitchell, Chief Nursing Officer*
A free standing physical rehabilitation hospital located in Topeka Kansas. Designated to provide a barrier-free access to all treatment and patient service areas. This 79-bed facility offers a total rehabilitation environment in a warm, caring setting that encourages patient, family and staff interaction.

**6244 Mid-America Rehabilitation Hospital HealthSouth**
Health South Corporation
5701 W 110th St
Overland Park, KS 66211-2503
913-491-2400
FAX: 913-491-1097
e-mail: tiffany.kiehl@healthsouth.com
www.midamericarehabhospital.com

*Kristen De Hart, CEO*
*Tiffany Kiehl, Director Marketing/Operations*
*Paul Matlack, Director Therapy Operations*
*Damon Parker, Chief Nursing Officer*
97 bed Acute Rehab hospital offering full continuum from in-patient, day treatment and outpatient services for individuals with physical limitations due to CVA, TBI, SCI, other traumas, joint replacement, etc.

## Kentucky

**6245 Cardinal Hill Rehabilitation Hospital**
2050 Versailles Rd
Lexington, KY 40504-1499
859-254-5701
800-233-3260
FAX: 859-231-1365
e-mail: webmaster@cardinalhill.org
www.cardinalhill.org

*Kerry Gillihan, CEO*
CARF-accredited rehab center provides comprehensive inpatient and outpatient services in two locations to people with physical and cognitive disabilities. We provide diagnosis-specific programs to 100 inpatients, outpatient clinics, outpatient therapies, pain management and therapeutic pool services. The Pediatric Center serves children from birth to age 18 years of age.

**6246 HealthSouth Rehabilitation of Louisville**
1227 Goss Ave
Louisville, KY 40217-1287
502-636-1200
FAX: 502-636-0351
www.healthsouth.com

*Tim Nichol, Manager*
*Regina Durbin, Administrator*

**6247 Lakeview Rehabilitation Hospital**
134 Heartland Dr
Elizabethtown, KY 42701-2778
270-769-4734
FAX: 270-769-6870
www.healthsouthlakeview.com

*Lori Jarboes, CEO*
*Chris Koford, Medical Director*
40-beds, comprehensive physical rehabilitation.

**6248 Shriners Hospitals for Children, Lexington**
1900 Richmond Rd
Lexington, KY 40502-1204
859-266-2101
800-444-8314
FAX: 859-268-5636
www.shrinershq.org/hospitals/lexington

*Tony Lewgood, CEO*
A 50-bed, pediatric orthopedic hospital providing FREE, expert orthopedic medical care to children and adolescents in Kentucky, Tennessee, West Virginia, Ohio, and Indiana.

## Louisiana

**6249 HealthSouth Specialty Hospital Of North Louisiana**
1401 Ezelle St
Ruston, LA 71270-7218
318-251-3126
800-548-9157
FAX: 318-251-1594
e-mail: mark.rice@lifecare-hospitals.com
www.lifecare-hospitals.com

*Mark Rice, CEO*
A 90-bed specialty hospital offering both inpatient and outpatient services. Acute long term care.

**6250 Our Lady of Lourdes Rehabilitation Center**
4801 Ambassador Caffery Pkwy
Lafayette, LA 70508
337-289-2000
FAX: 318-289-2681
e-mail: info@lourdes.net
www.lourdes.net

*William Barrow, CEO*
Our Lady of Lourdes outpatient physical medicine and rehabilitation department is compprised of a multi-disciplinary team of physical therapists, oppcuptational therapists and speech languare pathologists.

**6251 Rehabilitation Center of Lake Charles Memorial Hospital**
1701 Oak Park Blvd
Lake Charles, LA 70601-8911
337-494-3000
FAX: 337-494-2656
e-mail: webmaster@lcmh.com
www.lcmh.com

*Dale Shearer, Director*
*Larry Graham, President/CEO*
*Christopher Thompson, MD, Medical Staff President*
*Bryan Barootes, MD, Medical Staff President - Elect*
Rehabilitation center offering intensive physical, occupational, speech, neuropsychology, recreational therapies along with rehabilitation nursing.

**6252 Shriners Hospital for Children-Shreveport**
3100 Samford Ave
Shreveport, LA 71103-4239
318-222-5704
FAX: 318-424-7610
www.shrinershc.org

*Richard McCall, Chief of Staff*
*Phillip Gates, Assistant Chief*
An interdisciplinary approach is used in patient care programs to ensure comprehensive care for each patient. The staff includes orthopaedists, pediatricians, nurses, therapists, social workers, child life specialists, and more. The Shreveport Hospital is equipped and staffed to provide care for virtually all pediatric orthopaedic problems, with the exception of acute trauma.

**6253 South Louisiana Rehabilitation Hospital**
715 W Worthy St
Gonzales, LA 70737-3844
225-647-8277
FAX: 225-647-2446
e-mail: sober@powerhouseprograms.com
www.powerhouseprograms.com

*Cody Gautreux, Executive Director*
*Tonja Randolph, President*
Power House Programs is a male only facility for the treatment of Chemical Dependency/Dual Diagnosis, located in Gonzales, Louisiana. Applicants must have participated in a primary treatment program for substance abuse prior to acceptance. Our program is divided into 3 phases and is staffed by Board Certified Social Workers and Board Certified Substance Abuse Counselors. We provide individual, group and family therapy; plus 12 step meetings in a community setting.

**6254 St. Frances Cabrini Hospital: Rehab Unit**
St Frances Cabrini Hospital
3330 Masonic Dr
Alexandria, LA 71301-3899
318-487-1122
FAX: 318-448-6822
www.cabrini.org

*Curman Gaines, Chairperson*
*Dallas Hixson, Vice Chairperson*
CHRISTUS St. Frances Cabrini Hospital is a 265-bed facility located in Alexandria, Louisiana. Employing approximately 1,400 Associates and with a staff of neary 320 physicians, CHRISTUS St. Frances Cabrini Hospital offers a comprehensive array of services providing the highest quality patient care in a compassionate setting.

**6255 St. Patrick Hospital: Rehab Unit**
524 Doctor Michael Debakey Dr
Lake Charles, LA 70601-5725
337-436-2511
888-722-9355
FAX: 337-430-4284
www.christusstpatrick.org

*Ellen Jones, CEO*
Committed to providing care and service of the highest quality for children and adults, and to ensuring that the basic human rights of expression, decision making and personal dignity are preseved. We are also committed to treating our patients with respect, understanding and Christian love. We realize that this committment involves much more then attending to your medical needs.

**6256 Thibodaux Regional Medical Center**
602 N Acadia Rd
Thibodaux, LA 70301-4847
985-447-5500
800-822-8442
FAX: 985-449-4600
e-mail: info@thibodaux.com
www.thibodaux.com

*Greg Stock, CEO*
*Jacob Giardina, Chairman*
Mission is to provide the highest quality, most cost effective health care services possible to the people of Thibodaux and surrounding areas. The vision is to be the regional medical center of choice for health care services in the southeast Louisiana by recognizing the value of physicians and employees, committing to quality improvement, partnering with other health care providers, and remaining financially viable in a competitive environment.

## Maine

**6257 Brewer Rehab and Living Center**
74 Parkway S
Brewer, ME 04412-1697
207-989-7300
FAX: 207-989-4240
www.brewerrehab.com

*Janet Hope, Executive Director*
Brewer Rehab and Living Center accomodates 106 residents. We are located in Brewer, Maine. We have a 24-hour nursing staff and experienced dedicated on-site physical therapists, occupational therapists and speech language pathologists. We have a specialized inpatient program for individuals with brain injury resulting from a traumatic injury or neurological event such as a stroke. We also have a specialized care unit for individuals with Alzheimer's disease and other dementias.

**6258 New England Rehabilitation Hospital of Portland**
335 Brighton Ave
Portland, ME 04102-2363
207-775-4000
FAX: 207-879-8168
e-mail: jaye.sewall@healthsouth.com
www.nerhp.org

*Elissa Charbonneau, Medical Director*
*Amy Morse, CEO*
Mission is to provide individuals with guidance, education, support, and motivation while helping them achieve maximum independence and function. Our professionals work with the patient and family through a team approach, to establish and implement an individualized rehabilitation plan designed to meet specific patient goals.

## Maryland

**6259 Mt. Washington Pediatric Hospital**
1708 W Rogers Ave
Baltimore, MD 21209-4596
410-578-5216
FAX: 410-466-1715
www.mwph.org

*Sheldon Stein, President*
*Richard Katz, VP, Medical Affairs*
Provides inpatient, outpatient and day programs for infants and children with rehabilitation and/or complex medical needs. We are dedicated to maximizing the rehabilitation and development of our patients through the delivery of interdisciplinary services and programs and providing every resource availiable to enable our patients to attain the highest quality of life within their families and their communities.

## Massachusetts

**6260 New Bedford Rehabilitation Hospital**
4499 Acushnet Ave
New Bedford, MA 02745-4707
508-995-6900
FAX: 508-998-8131
www.newbedfordrehab.com

New Bedford Rehabilitation Hospital provides safe, high-quality, cost-effective medical and rehabilitation care to our patients and their families with the goal of improving quality of life and maximizing function.

**6261 New England Rehabilitation Hospital: Massachusetts**
2 Rehabilitation Way
Woburn, MA 01801-6098
781-939-3286
FAX: 781-933-9257
healthsouth.com

*Deniz Ozel, Medical Director*
A 168-bed comprehensive inpatient rehabilitation hospital, which includes 2 off-campus satellite units. Offers an array of

area outpatient rehabilitation centers. New England Rehabilitation Hospital remains committed to a personal caring approach. The vision is to provide the communities with a complete continuum of acute rehabilitative programs and services.

**6262 Shriners Burns Hospital: Boston**
51 Blossom St
Boston, MA 02114-2623
617-722-3000
800-255-1916
FAX: 617-523-1684
www.shrinershq.org/hospitals/boston

*Thomas D'Esmond, Administrator*
*Ronald Tompkins, Chief of Staff*
Provides treatment for children to their 18th birthday with acute, fresh burns, plastic reconstructive surgery for patients with healed burns, severe scarring and facial deformity. Some non-burn conditions such as Scalded Skin Syndrome, Cleft Lip, Cleft Palate and purpura fulminians are also treated. Call the Hospital for information. All medical treatment is without cost to the patient, parents, or any third party.

**6263 Shriners Hospital Springfield Unit Springfield Unit for Crippled Children**
516 Carew St
Springfield, MA 01104-2330
413-787-2000
800-237-5055
FAX: 413-787-2009
www.shrinershq.org/hospitals/springfiled

*David M Drvaric, Chief of Staff*
*Mark Niederpruem, Administrator*
Shriners Hospital for Children is fully equipped and staffed to provide care for pediatric orthopaedic conditions and disorders.

## Michigan

**6264 Covenant Healthcare Rehabilitation Program**
515 N Michigan Ave
Saginaw, MI 48602-4316
989-583-2930
FAX: 989-583-2843
www.covenanthealthcare.com

*Spence Maidlow, President*
*Juli Martin, Program Director*
Offers a broad spectrum of programs and services ranging from obstetrics, neonatal and pediatric care, to acute care including cardiology, oncology, surgery and many other services on the leading edge of medicine. All our programs and services exemplify our commitment to providing quality, compassionate care. As a medical facility with more then 700 beds, and a complete range of medical services, Covenant stands ready to meet the healthcare needs of the 15 counties in Michigan we serve.

**6265 Farmington Health Care Center**
34225 Grand River Ave
Farmington, MI 48335-3440
248-477-7373
FAX: 248-477-2888
www.farmingtonhealthcarecenter.com

*Brian Garavaglia, Administrator*
Skilled nursing facility specializing in ventilator dependent residents.

**6266 Flint Osteopathic Hospital: RehabCare Unit**
3921 Beecher Rd
Flint, MI 48532-3602
810-762-4682
FAX: 810-762-2153

*Susan Malone, Program Manager*
*Joy Finkenbiner, Executive Director*

**6267 Integrated Health Services of Michigan at Clarkston**
4800 Clintonville Rd
Clarkston, MI 48346-4297
248-674-0903
FAX: 248-674-3359

*Carol Doll, Admissions Director*
*Margaret Canny, Administrator*

**6268 St. John Hospital: North Shore**
Ascension Health
26755 Ballard St
Harrison Township, MI 48045-2419
586-465-5501
FAX: 586-466-5352
www.stjohn.org

*David Sessions, CEO*
A 96-bed specialty hospital that provides comprehensive physical medicine and rehabilitation, along with a wide range of medical and surgical services. St. John North Shores Hospital also provides emergency and urgent care, extensive outpatient rehabilitation services, and most ancillary diagnostic services.

## Minnesota

**6269 Sister Kenny Institute**
800 E 28th St
Minneapolis, MN 55407-3798
612-863-4200
866-880-3550
FAX: 612-863-5698
e-mail: sisterkenny@allina.com
www.allina.com/ahs/ski.nsf

*Helen Kettner, Nurse-Liaison*
Sister Kenny Rehabilitation Institute can meet your needs with any short-or long-term condition or disability. Sister Kenny specializes in providing individualized patient programs grounded in the most innovative services to give you the hope and tools you need to achieve your personal best.

## Missouri

**6270 Columbia Regional Hospital: RehabCare Unit**
404 N Keene St
Columbia, MO 65201-6698
573-882-2501
FAX: 573-449-7588
www.uhealth.org

*James Ross, CEO*
*Anita Larsen, COO*
A medical and physical rehabilitation program serving patients throughout Mid-Missouri with functional deficits due to neurologic, orthopaedic or other medical conditions.

**6271 Jewish Hospital of St. Louis: Department of Rehabilitation**
1 Barnes Jewish Hospital Plz
Saint Louis, MO 63110-1003
314-747-3000
866-867-3627
FAX: 314-454-5277
www.barnesjewish.org

*Richard Liedweg, President*
*Mark Krieger, VP/CFO*
We take exceptional care of people by providing world-class healthcare, delivering care in a compassionate, respectful and responsive way. By advancing medical knowledge and continously improving our practices. By educating current and future generations of healthcare professionals.

**6272 St. Mary's Regional Rehabilitation Center**
201 NW R D Mize Rd
Blue Springs, MO 64014-2513
816-228-5900
FAX: 816-655-5348
www.carondelethealth.org

*Fleury Yelvington, President/CEO*
*Amy McKay, Executive Director of Nursing*
A 143-bed inpatient physical rehabilitation unit offering PT, OT, ST, recreational therapy, psychiatry and all other ancillary services of a full-service hospital. Specialize in orthopedic and neurologic disabilities.

**6273 Three Rivers Health Care**
2620 N Westwood Blvd
Poplar Bluff, MO 63901-3396
573-785-7721
800-582-9533
FAX: 573-686-5388
e-mail: info@pbrmc.hma-corp.com
www.poplarbluffregional.com

*Greg Carda, CEO*
*Austin Tinsley, Chief Medical Officer*
Poplar Bluff Regional Medical Center is a regional medical center with 2 hospital campuses and more then 100 active physicians. The 423-bed facility is the largest medical center in Southeast Missouri and is located in ButlerCounty. With outreach clinics in Bloomfield, Dexter, Malden, Piedmont, and Puxico, Poplar Bluff Regional Medical Center is committed to serving its 6 county region.

## Montana

**6274 St. Vincent Hospital and Health Center**
1233 N 30th St
Billings, MT 59101-165
406-657-7000
FAX: 406-657-8817
www.svhhc.org

*Jason Barker, CEO*
*Michael Schweitzer, VP, Medical Affairs*
Vision is to be recognized for our vitality, best in class performance and providing easy access to compassionate and trust-worthy healthcare. The healthcare we offer is based on community need. We strive to improve the health status of the community, with a special concern for the poor and those who have limited access to healthcare.

## Nebraska

**6275 Madonna Rehabilitation Hospital**
5401 South St
Lincoln, NE 68506-2150
402-489-7102
800-676-5448
FAX: 402-483-9406
e-mail: info@madonna.org
www.madonna.org

*Marsha Lommel, CEO*
Provides a complete range of inpatient and outpatient rehabilitation for patients of all ages and abilities. Through highly specialized programs and services, Madona offers individualized treatment and support to help every patient.

## Nevada

**6276 University Medical Center**
1800 W Charleston Blvd
Las Vegas, NV 89102-2386
702-383-2000
FAX: 702-383-2536
e-mail: feedback@umcsn.com
www.umcsn.com

*Brian Brannman, CEO*
*Vicky Huber, Chief Nursing Officer*
Vision is to become the model community healthcare provider and hospital of choice. To provide leadership that ensures safe, high quality, accessable, comprehensive healthcare to the community and visitors while ensuring financial viablilty and social responsiveness.

## New Hampshire

**6277 Head Injury Treatment Program at Dover**
307 Plaza Dr
Dover, NH 03820-2455
603-742-2676
FAX: 603-749-5375
www.doverrehab.com

*Sue Mills, Program Rep*
*Jill Bosa, Administrator*
A provider of postacute services in the greater New Hampshire Seacost area. We accomodate 112 residents and are licensed by the state of New Hampshire. We employ nearly 150 licensed nurses, therapists, and other healthcare professionals, who strive to provide quality care. The goal of our patient service model is to bridge the gap between hospitalization and home so that recovery and physical functioning are maximized and hospital re-admission is minimized.

**6278 Lakeview NeuroRehabilitation Center**
244 Highwatch Road
Effingham, NH 03882
603-539-7451
800-473-4221
FAX: 603-539-8815
www.lakeviewsystem.com

*Sheri Capurso, Administrator*
*Christopher Slover, CEO*
Residential treatment center serving individuals with neurologic/behavioral disorders. Lakeview serves both children and adults in functionally based program environment. Transistional programs in various group homes also available to clients as they progress in their treatment.

**6279 Northeast Rehabilitation Hospital**
70 Butler St
Salem, NH 03079-3974
603-893-2900
800-825-7292
FAX: 603-893-1638
e-mail: webmaster@northeastrehab.com
www.northeastrehab.com

*John Prochilo, CEO*
NRHN is an organization characterized by the positive and proactive commitment to the delivery of customer centered care. Our employees exemplify our organizational commitment to providing quality rehabilitation services throughout the continuum. NRHN will be prudent with all resources and will take individual and collective responsibility for fiscal health. NRHN will remain a model by which other rehabilitation and post acute networks seek to emulate.

**6280 St. Joseph Hospital Rehabilitation**
172 Kinsley St
Nashua, NH 03060-3688
603-595-3636
800-210-9000
FAX: 603-595-3635
stjosephhospital.com

*Judy Grilli, Medical Staff Officer*
A comprehensive healthcare system that serves the Greater Nashua area, western New Hampshire and Northern Massachusetts. Our hospital is licensed for 208 beds and includes a Level 2 Trauma Center. In addition to the hospital, St. Joseph Healthcare system also includes a satellite emergency center in Milford, 5 family medical centers, a large network of primary care and specialty physician practices.

## New Jersey

**6281 Betty Bacharach Rehabilitation Hospital**
61 W Jimmie Leeds Rd
Pomona, NJ 08240-9102
609-652-7000
FAX: 609-748-3586
e-mail: email@bacharach.org
www.bacharach.org

*Craig Anmuth, Medical Director*
*Ross Berlin, Medical Director*
Therapists, nurses and other specialists, led by physiatrists - doctors specially trained in the medical practice of physical medicine and rehabilitation.

**6282 Children's Specialized Hospital**
150 New Providence Rd
Mountainside, NJ 07092-2590
908-518-5806
888-344-5373
FAX: 908-233-4176
e-mail: jbrooks@childrens-specialized.org
www.childrens-specialized.org

*Amy Mansue, CEO*
*Jeannie Brooks, Director*
New Jersey's largest comprehensive pediatric rehabilitation hospital, treats children and adolescents from birth through 21 years of age. Programs include spinal dysfunction, brain injury, respiratory, burn, Day Hospital, early intervention, preschool, and cognitive rehabilitation. Locations in Fairwood, Roselle Park, Newark, Toms River and Hamilton

**6283 HealthSouth Rehabilitation Hospital**
14 Hospital Dr
Toms River, NJ 08755-6402
732-244-3100
FAX: 732-244-7790
www.rehabnj.com/tomsriver/

*Patty Ostaszewski, CEO*
*Joseph Stillo, Medical Director*
A comprehensive 131-bed medical rehabilitation hospital dedicated to treating individuals with a variety of physical disabilities resulting from injury and illness. We serve all of New Jersey, Manhattan, and Philiadelphia. Accredited by the Joint Commission on Accreditation of Healthcare Organizations (JCAHO). The mission of the hospital is to get people back to work, to play, to living.

**6284 JFK Johnson Rehab Institute**
65 James St
Edison, NJ 08820-3947
732-321-7070
FAX: 732-321-0994
e-mail: jfkjri@solarishs.org
www.njrehab.org

*Krishna Urs, Physician*
*David Brown, Physician*
The mission of the JFK Johnson Rehabilitation Institute is to provide quality rehabilitation that will assist adults and children living with disabilities to obtain optimal function and independence within an accepting community. The vision is to be the benchmark for the delivery of quality, caring rehabilitative services within a seamless continuum of care.

**6285 Kessler Institute for Rehabilitation, Welkind Facility**
201 Pleasant Hill Rd
Chester, NJ 07930-2141
973-252-6300
FAX: 973-252-6343
e-mail: jkment@kessler-rehab.com
kessler-rehab.com

*Sue Kida, CEO*
*Sam Bayoumy, Director of Rehabilitation*
Set in the rolling hills of Morris County, this 72 bed facility provides specialized services to brain injury patients, including our unique Cognitive Redmediation Program, as well as a full range of stroke, amputee and orthopedic services. Kessler's team of dedicated rehabilitation professionals, including physicians, nurses and therapists, work with each patient to build physical strength, optimize movement, maximize independence, increase cognitive skills and address any other issues.

**6286 Mediplex Rehab: Camden**
1 Cooper Plz
Camden, NJ 08103-1461
856-342-2000
FAX: 856-342-7979
www.cooperhealth.org/content/locationsCamden

*Celeste Johnson, Administrator*
Cooper University Hospital is the leading provider of comprehensive health services, medical education and clinical research in Southern New Jersey and the Delaware Valley. With over 550 physicians in over 75 specialties, Cooper is uniquely equipped to provide an almost unlimited number of medical services. The hospital is committed to excellence in medical education, patient care, and research. Offers training programs to medical students, residents, and nurses in a variety of specialties.

## New Mexico

**6287 HealthSouth Rehabilitation Center: New Mexico**
7000 Jefferson St NE
Albuquerque, NM 87109-4357
505-344-9478
800-293-7226
FAX: 505-345-6722
www.healthsouthnewmexico.com

*Sylvia Kelly, CEO*
*Veronica Gadomski, Chief Nursing Officer*
*Lisa Brower, Director of Therapy Operations*
Serving our community since 1988, and committed to offering the care and support you need to achieve the most complete recovery possible. We will develop and individualized treatment plan based on the needs and goals identified by you, your family and our rehabilitation team. Then we will use that plan as a guide, working together to help you reach the highest level of physical, social and emotional well-being.

**6288 St. Joseph Rehabilitation Hospital and Outpatient Center**
Ardence
505 Elm St NE
Albuquerque, NM 87102-2500
505-727-4700
FAX: 505-727-4793
www.sjhs.org

*Janelle Raborn, Administrator/CEO*
*Sherrie Peterson, Director*
A member of the four hospital, St. Joseph healthcare system, this facility provides inpatient and outpatient care for those requiring physical medicine and rehabilitation. Specialty programs include brain injury, stroke, spinal cord, orthopedics, occupational and physical therapies, clinical psychology, speech/language pathology, hand clinic and functional capacity evaluations. The only facility in New Mexico accredited in four areas by the commission on accreditation of rehab facilities.

## New York

**6289 Burke Rehabilitation Hospital**
785 Mamaroneck Ave
White Plains, NY 10605-2523
914-597-2500
888-99B-URKE
FAX: 914-946-0866
e-mail: web@burke.org
www.burke.org

*John Ryan, Executive Director*
*Brett Langley, Physician*
A 150 bed rehabilitation hospital providing both in and out patient physical rehabilitation to people with stroke, spinal cord injury, head injury, pulmonary, cardiac, amputee, orthopedic arthritis and other related diagnoses.

**6290 Occupational Therapy Strategies and Adaptations for Independent Daily Living**
Haworth Press
10 Alice St
Binghamton, NY 13904-1503
607-722-5857
800-429-6784
FAX: 607-722-6362
e-mail: orders@haworthpress.com
www.haworthpress.com

This contains clinical expertise of some fourteen authors or author teams addressing the issue of occupational therapy to assist in independent daily living. Also available as hardcover. *$74.95*
*186 pages Softcover*
*ISBN 0-866563-50-4*

**6291 Rusk Institute of Rehabilitation Medicine**
400 E 34th St
New York, NY 10016-4901
212-263-6028
FAX: 212-263-8510
www.med.nyu.edu/rusk

*Steven Flanagan, Chairman*
Operates under the auspices of the Dept. Of Rehabilitation Medicine of New York University School of Medicine, one of the nations foremost medical schools. The relationship between Rusk and other clinical and research units within the medical center contributes to an environment which provides the optimal rehabilitation setting for patients.

**6292 Silvercrest Center for Nursing & Rehabilitation**
144-45 87th Ave
Briarwood, NY 11435-3109
718-480-4000
800-645-9806
FAX: 718-658-2367
e-mail: admissions@silvercrest.org
www.silvercrest.org

*Andrea Gibbon, Clinical Care Coordinator*
*Penny Blakely, Unit Manager*
The Silvercrest Center for Nursing and Rehabilitation has earned a wide-spread reputatiopn for combing the best in clinical care with the best in nursing care and for making available to its communities the broadest menu of services to ease a patients' path to recovery from hospital to home. The Center is for the treatment of medically complex patients beginning their recovery, for the rehabilitation of patients who need restorative therapy before going home and much more.

**6293 Vocational Rehabilitation and Employment**
Books on Special Children
P.O.Box 305
Congers, NY 10920-305
845-638-1236
FAX: 845-638-0847

Defines kinds of work, expectations, goals and programs. Contributions in general issues of supported employment, training and management and community based programs. *$47.00*
*372 pages Hardcover*

## North Carolina

**6294 Horizon Rehabilitation Center**
Trans Health Incorporated
3100 Erwin Rd
Durham, NC 27705-4505
919-383-1546
800-541-7750
FAX: 919-383-0862
A 125-bed rehabilitation, subacute and long term care facility. HRC is JCAHO and CARF accredited with a physician-directed rehabilitation program, internal case management and a therapy department composed of physical, occupational, speech, recreational and respiratory therapists - pulmonary rehabilitation/ventilator unit.

**6295 Integrated Health Services of Durham**
Duke University Medical Center
3100 Erwin Rd
Durham, NC 27705-4505
919-383-1546
FAX: 919-383-0862

*Aaron Lony, Administrator*

**6296 Learning Services Corporation**
Corporate Office
10 Speen St
Ste 4
Framingham, MA 01701-4661
508-626-3671
888-419-9955
FAX: 919-419-9966
www.learningservices.com

*Susan Snow, Director of Admissions*
A licensed postacute rehabilitation program for adults who have an acquired brain injury. Individuals who are enrolled in the program participate in active, intensive rehabilitation carried out by a team of neuropsychology, speech/language therapy, physical therapy, occupational therapy, vocational services, family services and life skills training. Services include residential rehabilitation, home based treatment, day treatment, subacute rehabilitation and supported living.

## Ohio

**6297 Columbus Rehab & Subactute**
44 S Souder Ave
Columbus, OH 43222-1539
614-228-5900
FAX: 614-228-3989
e-mail: columbusrehab@extendicare.com
www.columbusrehabskillednursing.com

*Kelly Fligor, Administrator*
Postacute rehabilitation program.

**6298 Great Lakes Regional Rehabilitation Center**
3700 Kolbe Rd
Lorain, OH 44053-1611
440-960-3470
FAX: 440-960-4636

*Julie Jones, Manager*
Provides excellent, innovative and comprehensive rehabilitation programs to people in our community. Committed to a better quality of life for all individuals, the Rehabilitation Center has grown to become a regional resource for individuals needing all types of rehabilitation services.

**6299 HCR Health Care Services**
1 Seagate
Toledo, OH 43604-1541
419-321-5470
800-736-4427
FAX: 419-252-5543
harborfund.net
Specialty transitional care and intensive rehabilitation services. Specialized services are focused on patients with catastrophic conditions or whose length of stay at an acute care or

rehabilitation hospital can be dramatically reduced by transferring to a subacute level of care.

**6300 Heather Hill Rehabilitation Hospital**
Heather Hill
12340 Bass Lake Rd
Chardon, OH 44024-8327
440-285-4040
800-423-2972
FAX: 440-285-0946
e-mail: info@heatherhill.org

*Ed Davis, Operations*
*Donald Goddard, Chief Medical Officer*
Individualized treatment programs for adults and adolescents can participate in and benefit from three-plus hours a day of active therapy.

**6301 Parma Community General Hospital Acute Rehabilitation Center**
7007 Powers Blvd
Parma, OH 44129-5437
440-743-3000
FAX: 440-843-4387
www.parmahospital.org

*Louis Ripepi, Director*
*JoAnn Mason, Secretary*
The mission of this CARF accredited unit is to provide the most comprehensive, cost-effective, acute rehabilitation program possible in order for every patient and family to adjust to his/her disability and to achieve the maximum potential of independent functioning when returning to community living.

**6302 Rehabilitation Institute of Ohio at Miami Valley Hospital**
1 Wyoming St
Dayton, OH 45409-2722
937-208-2063
www.miamivalleyhospital.com

*Vanessa Sandarusi, Executive Director*
A regional center designed for the treatment of those with disabling conditions. RIO offers physcial, occupational, speech, recreational and pool therapies, as well as the use of a transitional apartment to perpare patients for a return to independent living.

**6303 Shriners Burn Institute: Cincinnati Unit**
Shriners Hospitals for Children Cincinnati
3229 Burnet Ave
Cincinnati, OH 45229-3095
513-872-6000
800-875-8580
FAX: 513-872-6999
www.shrinershq.org

*Richard Kagan, Chief of Staff*
*Petra Warner, Assistant Chief of Staff*
All the attention and resources are focused on just one kind of patient-the burn-injured child. Shriners combine excellent clinical skill, compassionate care, and innovative research, providing comprehensive pediatric burn care and reconstructive rehabilitation to achieve the best possible outcome for a child that has suffered a burn injury. There is never a charge to the patient or family for any of the medical care or services provided by the Shriners Hospitals throughout North America.

**6304 St. Francis Health Care Centre**
401 N Broadway St
Green Springs, OH 44836-9653
419-639-2626
800-248-2552
FAX: 419-639-6225
e-mail: hr@sfhcc.org
www.sfhcc.org

*Kim Eicher, CEO*
*Jane Holmer, Admissions Coordinator*
Provides compassionate care for the elderly and physically challenged. We are a healthcare ministry under the sponsorship of the Franciscan Sisters of Our Lady of Perpetual Help. As a Catholic facility. we respectfully offer those we serve, care hope and dignity in a joyful and compassionate manner.

**6305 St. Rita's Medical Center Rehabilitation Services**
730 W Market St
Lima, OH 45801-4602
419-227-3361
800-232-7762
FAX: 419-226-9750
www.ehealthconnection.com

*James Reber, CEO*
The St. Rita's Inpatient Acute Care Rehabilitation service provides individualized service to you or your family member 7 days a week, wherever you might stay in the hospital. Acute rehabilitation care includes physical, occupational, and speech therapy services. Our goal is to make you as independent as possible before your discarge to home or, when necessary to extended services in other parts of the hospital.

**6306 University of Cincinnati Hospital**
Health Alliance
234 Goodman St
Cincinnati, OH 45219-2316
513-584-2873
FAX: 513-584-7712
www.universityhospitalcincinnati.com

*James Kingsbury, President/CEO*
University Hospital has an international reputation, bringing thousands of people, from the region and around the world to Cincinnati to receive care from world renowned physicians in state-of-the-art medical facilities.

**6307 Upper Valley Medical/Rehab Services**
3130 N County Road 25a
Troy, OH 45373-1309
937-440-7626
FAX: 937-440-7337
e-mail: info@uvmc.com
www.uvmc.com

*Rafay Atiq, Director Rehab Services*
A not-for-profit health care system serving the health care needs of Miami County and the surrounding area. The health care system features a state-of-the-art acute care hospital which opened in 1998. Comprehensive inpatient and outpatient services are provided with a full compliment of diagnostic and treatment services and behavioral health care programs.

## Oklahoma

**6308 Hilcrest Medical Center: Kaiser Rehab Center**
1125 S Trenton Ave
Tulsa, OK 74120-5498
918-579-7100
FAX: 918-579-7110
www.hillcrest.com/kaiser

*Perri Craven, Medical Director*
Kaiser Rehabilitation Center offers a wide range of services to help people regain functionality and independence after a debilitating injury or illness. Our approach to rehabilitation is a team approach, bringing the expertise of physicians, therapists, nurses and other health professionals together with patient family to achieve the best possible outcome. Each patient is given an individualized treatment plan that stimulates and challenges them to achieve their maximum potential.

**6309 Jane Phillips Medical Center**
Jane Phillips Medical Center
3500 E Frank Phillips Blvd
Bartlesville, OK 74006-2464
918-333-7200
FAX: 918-331-1360
e-mail: webmaster@jpmc.org
www.jpmc.org

*David Stire, CEO*
*Mike Moore, CFO*
Jane Phillips Health System is sponsored by St. John Health System. This partnership helps our patients by ensuing access to the most sophisticated levels of care availiable in this area. It offers a wide range of services, including general medicine, surgery,

cardiopulmonary care, maternal and infant care, cancer treatment, geriatric care, orthopedics, and physical medicine.

**6310 Jim Thorpe Rehabilitation Center at Southwest Medical Center**
Southwest Medical Center
4219 South Western
Oklahoma City, OK 73109
405-644-5200
800-677-1238
FAX: 405-644-5384
www.integris-health.com

*Al Moorad, Medical Director*
Provides inpatient rehabilitation for people with head injuries, spinal cord injuries, orthopedic conditions, pain management, neurological diseases, strokes and a variety of diagnoses that stop individuals from being able to take care of themselves independently. Services available include medical direction, physical therapy, social work, occupational therapy, speech therapy, recreational therapy, and aftercare follow-up.

**6311 Mercy Memorial Health Center-Rehab Center**
1011 14th Ave NW
Ardmore, OK 73401-1828
580-223-5400
800-572-1182
FAX: 580-220-6463
www.mercy.net

*Jan Shores, Manager*
A full service tertiary hospital with 176 licensed beds, 913 co-workers and 100 physicians. Four primary care clinics

**6312 St. Anthony Hospital: Rehabilitation Unit**
St. Anthony Hospital
1000 N Lee Ave
Oklahoma City, OK 73102-1036
405-272-7000
800-851-0888
FAX: 405-272-7075
e-mail: st_anthony@ssmhc.com
www.saintsok.com

*Joe Hodges, President*
18 spacious private rooms, each with bathroom, and furnishings designed with patient safety in mind. Horticulture room where patients can work with plants and flowers as part of their rehabilitation. And a residential-style training apartment with fully equipped kitchen, bathroom, and bedroom to make the patient feel more at home.

**6313 Valir Health**
700 NW 7th St
Oklahoma City, OK 73102-1212
405-236-3131
888-898-2080
FAX: 405-553-1153
e-mail: info@valir.com
www.valir.com

*Dirk O'Hara, Principal*
*Tonya Purvine, Corporate Compliance Officer*
Inpatient Rehab Facility including all therapy services serving people who have been injured and had an illness resulting in a decreased level of independence.

## Oregon

**6314 Shriners Hospitals for Children: Portland**
3101 SW Sam Jackson Park Rd
Portland, OR 97239-3095
503-241-5090
800-237-5055
FAX: 503-221-3701
www.shrinershospitalforchildren.org

*Michael Aiona, Chief of Staff*
Pediatric orthopedic and plastic surgery; inpatient and outpatient services. No charge for any services provided at the Hospital. Diagnosis, rehabilitation, surgery, sports and recreation for ages 0-18 for people with physical disabilities involving bones, muscles or joints or in need of plastic surgery for burn scars or cleft lip/palate.

## Pennsylvania

**6315 Allied Services John Heinz Institute of Rehabilitation Medicine**
150 Mundy St
Wilkes Barre, PA 18702-6830
570-826-3900
FAX: 570-826-3898
e-mail: tpugh@allied-services.org
www.allied-services.org

*William Conaboy, CEO*
*Gregory Basting, VP Medical Affairs*
John Heinz Rehab is one of the foremost providers of rehabilitation in the country. Under the supervision of board-certified psychiatrists, a team of highly qualified professionals provides a broad range of specialized services and therapies for inpatients, with speacialized programs in the areas of brain injury, injured worker recovery and pediatrics. John Heinz Rehab is the only CARF accredited program in northeastern Pennsylvania for treatment of brain injury rehabilitation.

**6316 Allied Services Rehabilitation Hospital**
475 Morgan Hwy
Scranton, PA 18508-2656
570-348-2211
FAX: 570-348-2223
www.allied-services.org

*William Conaboy, CEO*
*Jackie Fletcher Brozena, SVP/COO*
We are committed to the people of our commuinity, to help them overcome challenges and reach their greatest potential by providing quality care, people-oriented services and comfort. Our approach is a hands-on, people-oriented style which places the physical and emotional needs of those in our care at the center of all we do. Whether in our rehabilitation hospitals, our skilled nursing facilities, or mental health/mental retardation program, we strive to help people reach their potential.

**6317 Brighten Place**
131 North Main St
Chalfont, PA 18914-245
215-997-7746
FAX: 215-997-2517
e-mail: brightenplace@enter.net
www.brightenplace.org

*William Koffros, CEO*
A residential brain injury program with the mission to encourage growth and foster independence on an individual level for each resident. We are CARF accredited and provide additional services which include a day program and respite care.

**6318 Chestnut Hill Rehabilitation Hospital**
8601 Stenton Ave
Wyndmoor, PA 19038-8395
215-233-6200
FAX: 215-233-6879
www.chestnuthillrehab.com

*Cammi Lubking, Administrator*
Chestnut Hill Rehab Hospital is dedicated to meeting patients' physical, emotional, social, and vocational goals. Through innovative programs, sophisticated equipment, and support by specially trained staff members committed to the progress of every patient, Chestnut Hill achieves results.

**6319 Doylestown Hospital Rehabilitation Center**
595 W State St
Doylestown, PA 18901-2597
215-345-2200
FAX: 215-345-2512
www.dh.org

*Richard Reif, CEO*
*Gloria Peterson, Inpatient Rehab Services*

The mission of Doylestown Hospital is to provide a responsive healing environment for patients and their families, and to improve the quality of life for all members of our community. We combine the creative energies of Medical Staff, Board, Associates and Volunteers to make Doylestown Hospital a place where each patient and family feels healed and whole, even when disease cannot be cured.

**6320 Health Care Solutions**
500 Abbott Dr
Ste B
Broomall, PA 19008-4301 610-544-6023
800-451-1671
FAX: 610-544-6035
www.lincare.com

*John Byrnes, CEO*
*Shawn Schabel, President/COO*
Develops unique containment programs, offers equipment set-up, patient instruction, patient assessment and equipment usage. Offers clinical services that include oxygen systems, ventilators, aerosol therapy, suction equipment, T.E.N.S. programs, compression pumps, custom orthotics, enteral feeding.

**6321 HealthSouth Harmarville Rehabilitation Hospital**
P.O.Box 11460
Pittsburgh, PA 15238-460 412-828-1300
877-937-7342
FAX: 412-828-7705
www.healthsouthharmarville.com

*Ken Anthony, CEO*
A 202-bed facility providing inpatient and outpatient physical medicine and rehabilitation to adults and adolescents in Pennsylvania, West Virginia, Ohio and Maryland.

**6322 HealthSouth Nittany Valley Rehabilitation Hospital**
Health South of Nittany Valley
550 W College Ave
Pleasant Gap, PA 16823-7401 814-359-5621
800-842-6026
FAX: 814-359-5898
www.nittanyvalleyrehab.com

*Richard Allatt, Medical Director*
*Susan Hartman, CEO*
*Sara Godwin, CNO*
*Ann Foster, Therapy Operations Director*
Comprehensive inpatient and outpatient facilities. Treatment for symptoms relating to: stroke, head injury, pulmonary disease, orthopedic conditions, neurological disorders, cardiac illnesses and spinal cord injuries. Healthsouth Nittany Valley Rehabilitation Hospital is a part of Healthsouth's national network of more than 2,000 facilities in 50 states.

**6323 HealthSouth Rehab Hospital Of Erie**
143 E 2nd St
Erie, PA 16507-1501 814-878-1200
800-234-4574
FAX: 814-878-1399
www.healthsoutherie.com

*Douglas Grisier, Medical Director*
*Shelly Mayes, Director of Therapy Operations*
An acute inpatient rehabilitation hospital that was founded in 1986. HealthSouth Erie is one of the only rehabilitation hospitals in the country to hold a triple-certification by the Joint Commission in the areas of Brain Injury, Stroke and Parkinson's disease Rehabilitation.

**6324 HealthSouth Rehabilitation Hospital of Altoona**
2005 Valley View Blvd
Altoona, PA 16602-4548 814-944-3535
800-873-4220
FAX: 814-944-6160
www.healthsouthaltoona.com

*Scott Filler, Administrator*
*Paul Sutton, Director Of Clinical Services*
Inpatient and outpatient physical rehabilitation programs and services.

**6325 Healthsouth Rehabilitation Hospital of Greater Pittsburgh**
2380 McGinley Rd
Monroeville, PA 15146-4400 412-856-2400
FAX: 412-856-9320
www.lifecare-hospitals.com

*Mary Lee Dadey, Administrator*
Rehabilitation and long-term acute care hospital that treats brain injury, stroke, multiple sclerosis, Parkinson's disease, back and spinal cord injuries, cancer, pulmonary disease, cardiac disease, traumatic and work injuries.

**6326 Healthsouth Rehabilitation Hospital of Mechanicsburg**
175 Lancaster Blvd
Mechanicsburg, PA 17055-3562 717-691-3831
800-933-3831
FAX: 717-697-6524
e-mail: annette.bates@healthsouth.com
www.healthsouthpa.com

*Mark Freeburn, CEO*
*Elizabeth Bebe, Chief Nursing Officer*
*Annette Bates, Director of Marketing*
HealthSouth provides comprehensive rehabilitation and recovery services to patients with stroke, brain injury, hip fracture, medically complex, pulmonary, wound, spinal cord injury, amputation, and other neuro-muscular, and orthopedic impairments. Our primary goal is to provide individualized treatment programs to people requiring physical rehabilitation and medical recovery in order to help patients get back to work, to play, to living.

**6327 Healthsouth Rehabilitation Hospital of York**
1850 Normandie Dr
York, PA 17408-1552 717-767-6941
FAX: 717-767-8776
www.healthsouthyork.com

*Steven Alwine, CEO*
*Bruce Sicilia, Medical Director*
A 120-bed rehabilitation hospital dedicated to providing advanced, comprehensive services to patients who have suffered head injury, spinal cord injury, stroke, burns, amputation, chronic pain and other neurological and musculoskeletal disorders. HRH of York provides outpatient services in seven locations. Healthsouth is located in York, Pennsylvania, approximately 50 miles north of Baltimore and 25 miles south of Harrisburg.

**6328 Magee Rehabilitation Hospital**
1513 Race St
Philadelphia, PA 19102-1177 215-587-3000
800-966-2433
FAX: 215-568-3736
e-mail: hskoczen@mageerehab.org
www.mageerehab.org

*Jack Carroll, CEO*
A not-for-profit health organization which is the home to the nation's first brain injury rehabilitation program to be accredited by the Commission on the Accreditation of Rehabilitation Facilities (CARF) and is one of 14 federally designated Regional Spinal Cord Injury Centers. Our staff and management are committed to restoring the highest level of independence possible to individuals with disabilities.

**6329 Moss Rehabilitation Hospital**
1200 W Tabor Rd
Philadelphia, PA 19141-3099
215-456-9900
FAX: 215-456-9646
www.einstein.edu/yourhealth/physicalrehab

*Alberto Esquenazi, Plant Manager*

The Philadelphia region's major resource for medical rehabilitation since 1959. This 152 bed facility offers comprehensive care to people with broad ranges of conditions, diagnostic laboratories and a multidisciplinary team of rehabilitation professionals.

**6330 Shriners Hospitals for Children, Philadelphia**
Shrinners Hospitals for Children
3551 N Broad St
Philadelphia, PA 19140-4105
215-430-4000
800-281-4051
FAX: 215-430-4126
www.shrinershq.org

*Ernest Perilli, Administrator*
*Randal Betz, Chief of Staff*
*Richard Gallier, Chairman of the Board*

The Shriners Hospital in Philadelphia is a 59-bed pediatric orthopaedic hospital providing a complete range of specialized medical and rehabilitation services at no charge to children with orthopaedic problems or spinal injuries. The hospital is one of 22 Shriners Hospitals for Children throughout North america. In addition to treating children with routine and complex orthopaedic problems, the Philadelphia Hospital provides a comprehensive and individualized rehabilitation program.

**6331 Shriners Hospitals for Children, Erie**
1645 W 8th St
Erie, PA 16505-5007
814-875-8700
FAX: 814-875-8756
www.shrinershq.org

*John Lubahn, Chief of Staff*
*Charles Walczak, Administrator*

The Shriners Hospitals for Children, Erie, is a 30-bed pediatric orthopaedic hospital providing comprehensive orthopaedic care to children at no charge. The hospital is one of 22 Shriners Hospitals throughout North America. The Erie Hospital accepts and treats children with routine and complex orthopaedic and neuromuscular problems, utilizing the latest treatments and technology available in pediatric orthopaedics, resulting in early ambulation and reduced length of stay.

**6332 Shriners Hospitals, Philadelphia Unit, for Crippled Children**
3551 N Broad St
Philadelphia, PA 19140-4105
215-430-4000
FAX: 215-430-4079
www.shrinershq.org/hospitals/philadelphia

*Randal Betz, Chief of Staff*
*Ernest Perilli, Administrator*

Provides comprehensive medical, surgical and rehabilitative care for children with orthopaedic conditions and spinal cord injuries. All services are provided at no charge. The hospital is one of 22 located throughout North America. In addition to treating children with routine and complex orthopaedic problems, the Philadelphia hospital provides a comprehensive and individualized rehabilitation program for children and adolescents who have sustained a traumatic injury to their spine.

## South Carolina

**6333 Colleton Regional Hospital: RehabCare Unit**
501 Robertson Blvd
Walterboro, SC 29488-5714
843-782-2000
FAX: 843-549-7562
www.colletonmedical.com

*Mitchell Mongel, CEO*

Colleton Medical Center's 8-bed physical and mental rehabilitation department is the oldest in the Lowcountry and has been serving the community for nearly 20 years. Strives to provide patient-centered care in a family atmosphere. The team includes nurses, physical therapists, occupational therapists, speech therapists, and nutritionists. The typical patient requires rehabilitation following a stroke, spinal injury, close head injury, and orthopedic rehabilitation.

**6334 HealthSouth Rehab Hospital: South Carolina**
2935 Colonial Dr
Columbia, SC 29203-6811
803-254-7777
FAX: 803-414-1414
www.healthsouthcolumbia.com

*James Rogers, CEO*
*Lydia Carpenter, Director of Therapy Operations*

Offers a wide range of specialized medical and therapeutic services designed to help physically disabled individuals reach their optimum level of function and independence.

**6335 Shriners Hospitals for Children, Greenville**
950 W Faris Rd
Greenville, SC 29605-4255
864-271-3444
866-459-0013
FAX: 864-271-4471
www.shrinershq.org/hospitals/greenville

*Randall Romberger, Administrator*
*Peter Stasikelis, Chief of Staff*

A 50-bed pediatric orthopaedic hospital providing comprehensive orthopaedic care to children at no charge to their families. The hospital is one of 22 Shriners Hospitals throughout North America. The hospital accepts and treats children with routine and complex orthopaedic problems, utilizing the latest tretments and technology availiable in pediatric orthopaedics, resulting in early ambulatory and reduced length of stay.

## Tennessee

**6336 Health South Cane Creek Rehabilitation Center**
Health South Corporation
180 Mount Pelia Rd
Martin, TN 38237-3812
731-587-4231
FAX: 731-588-1454
e-mail: dayle.unger@healthsouth.com

*Eric Garrard, CEO*
*William Eason, Medical Director*

Offers a wide variety of programs and services for patients in need of acute rehabilitation. Programs and services are availiable through inpatient and outpaitent. Thereapy services availiable are physical, occupational, speech, and respiratory.

**6337 HealthSouth Chattanooga Rehabilitation Hospital**
2412 McCallie Ave
Chattanooga, TN 37404-3398
423-697-9129
800-763-5189
FAX: 423-697-9124
www.healthsouthchattanooga.com

*Scott Rowe, CEO*
*Amjad Munir, Medical Director*
*Karen Jonakin, Director Clinical Services*

Offers orthopaedic rehabilitation, stroke rehabilitation, amputee rehabilitation, brain injury program, pain management, ventilator weaning, carpal tunnel screening, low intensity program, oncology program, aquatic therapy, day treatment, burn program and outpatient services.

**6338 HealthSouth Rehabilitation Cntr/Tennessee**
1282 Union Ave
Memphis, TN 38104-3414
901-722-2000
FAX: 901-729-5171
healthsouthmemphis.com

*Tracy Willis, CEO*
*Toni Wackerfuss, Director of Therapy Operation*
An 80-bed acute medical rehabilitation hospital that offers comprehensive inpatient and outpatient rehabilitation services.

**6339 James H And Cecile C Quillen Rehabilitation Hospital**
2511 Wesley St
Johnson City, TN 37601-1723
423-952-1700
800-235-1994
FAX: 423-283-0906
www.msha.com

*Tammy Bishop, Manager*
A 60-bed, freestanding comprehensive medical rehabilitation hospital. Full range of outpatient and day treatment, 14-bed traumatic brain injury unit, in ground therapeutic pool, transitional living apartment, outdoor ambulation course. All inpatient and outpatient programs utilize an interdisciplinary team approach designed to improve a patient's physical and cognitive functioning.

**6340 Nashville Rehabilitation Hospital**
610 Gallatin Ave
Nashville, TN 37206-3225
615-650-2600
800-227-3108
FAX: 615-650-2562
www.nrhcares.com

*Alan Miller, CEO*
*Marc Miller, President*
A free-standing physical rehabilitation facility offering services to patients on an inpatient and outpatient basis. Programs include CVA, orthopedic, neuromuscular, traumatic brain injury, spinal cord injury, general rehabilitation and Bridges - geriatric psychiatric unit. Intra-disciplinary team approach is utilized to assist patients in obtaining their maximum fuctional level.

**6341 Patricia Neal Rehab Center : Ft. Sanders Regional Medical Center**
Covenant Health
1901 W Clinch Ave
Knoxville, TN 37916-2307
865-541-1605
800-728-6325
FAX: 865-541-2247
www.patneal.org

*J.E. Henry, Co-Chair*
*David Kugley, Co-Chair*
A CARF accredited 73-bed facility, it offers a comprehensive team approach to care. Physical, occupational, recreational, behavioral medicine and speech language therapists work with physiatrists to develop individual plans of care designed to return patients to a normal lifestyle as quickly as possible. In addition, rehabilitation nurses collaborate with specialists to teach self-care techniques and provide education to help patients reach optimal functionality.

**6342 Rehabilitation Center Baptist Hospital**
137 E Blount Ave
Suite 6-B
Knoxville, TN 37920-1643
865-632-5520

Primary focus: Mix of mental health and substance abuse services.

**6343 Rehabilitation Center at McFarland Hospital**
University Medical Center
500 Park Ave
Lebanon, TN 37087-3721
615-449-0500
FAX: 615-453-7405
www.universitymedicalcenter.com

*Saad Ehtisham, CEO*
An Acute Inpatient Rehab, located on the hospital's second floor. The center has 26 patient rooms, three therapy treatment rooms, a patient dining area, and an 'activities of daily living' area which includes a kitchen/laundry area and a patient apartment, for those individuals who will be returning home.

**6344 St. Mary's Medical Center: RehabCare Center**
900 E Oak Hill Ave
Knoxville, TN 37917-4505
865-545-7962
FAX: 865-545-8133
mercy.com

*Jeffrey Ashin, President*
Committed to providing individualized and flexable treatment programs designed for individuals who have been disabled by an injury or illness. The primary mission of the RehabCare Center is to help patients achieve basic skills that may allow independent living and working.

**6345 Sumner Regional Medical Center**
555 Hartsville Pike
Gallatin, TN 37066-2400
615-328-8888
FAX: 615-328-3903
www.mysumnermedical.com

*Mary Jo Lewis, CEO*
*William Mize, Administrator*
Inpatient general rehabilitation programs for orthopedic injury, joint replacements, head injury, arthritis, general weakness and cardio/pulmonary diseases.

## Texas

**6346 Bayshore Medical Center: Rehab**
4000 Spencer Hwy
Pasadena, TX 77504-1202
713-359-2000
FAX: 713-359-1283
www.bayshoremedical.com

*Jeffrey Holland, CEO*
*Jeanna Barnard, COO*
A 373-bed facility, providing the award-winning care for which we have been nationally recogiznized. Members are here to care for the physical and emotional well-being of those who arrive at Bayshore Medical Center often frightned, in pain and perhaps even alone. We offer patients solace and security through constant communication and compassionate listening in the midst of their medical emergencies and surgical or diagnostic procedures. Kindness, empathy & quality are triats that patients trust.

**6347 Cecil R Bomhr Rehabilitation Center of Nacogdoches Memorial Hospital**
1204 N Mound St
Nacogdoches, TX 75961-4027
936-564-4611
FAX: 936-564-4616
e-mail: info@nacmem.org
nmh.org

*Dean Harrison, President/CEO*
*Peter McCanna, EVP*
*Dennis Murphy, COO*
The goal of Nacogdoches Memorial Hospital's rehabilitation services is to assist patients in attaining their highest potential activity level for independent daily living, thereby reducing the number of necessary hospitalizations. Keeping folks healthy and in their homes lowers healthcare costs for all of us.

**6348 Covenant Health Systems Owens White Outpatient Rehab Center**
4010 22nd St
Lubbock, TX 79410-1116
806-725-0000
FAX: 806-723-6009
www.covenanthealth.org

*Walt Cathey, Manager*
A comprehensive rehabilitation program designed to help patients attain their maximum level of independence following a debilitating stroke, illness or injury. Our fully accredited program features outpatient physical, occupational and speech language therapies, as well as certified athletic trainers and a certified strength and conditioning specialist.

**6349 Gonzales Warm Springs Rehabilitation Hospital**
200 Memorial Dr
Luling, TX 78648-3213
830-875-8400
FAX: 830-875-5029
www.warmsprings.org

*Anthony Misitano, President/CEO*
*Vonnie Cromwell, Operations Manager*
Statewide not-for-profit system of inpatient and outpatient rehabilitation speciality centers. Throughout the communities we serve, the Warm Springs Rehabilitation System offers hope and acts as a catalyst for achieving an optimal quality of life by providing comprehensive physical and/or cogenitive care. Investing resources in educational and recreational programs. Supporting research efforts.

**6350 Harris Methodist Fort Worth Hospital Mabee Rehabilitation Center**
1301 Pennsylvania Ave
Fort Worth, TX 76104-2122
817-878-5500
866-847-7342
FAX: 814-250-6846
www.texashealth.org

*Douglas Hawthorne, CEO/President*
*Joan Clark, Chief Nursing Officer*
Professionals at the Harris Methodist Fort Worth Hospital's Mabee Rehabilitation Center work closely with each patient to develop a specialzed treatment plan for personal achievement. The center offers highly trained clinical staff members and spacious facilities An incredibly wide range of treatment programs and educational services are provided for both inpatient and outpatient needs.

**6351 HealthSouth Plano Rehabilitation Hospital**
2800 W 15th St
Plano, TX 75075-7526
972-612-9000
FAX: 972-423-4293
www.healthsouth.com

*Jennifer Brewer, CEO*
*Omar Colon, Chief Medical Officer*
A 62-bed medical reahabilitation facility serving inpatient and out patient needs in the Northern Dallas area. The team coordinate all aspects of the patient's rehabilitation to maximize results. The overall effort is directed by board-certified physical medicine and rehabilitation physicians who specialize in medical rehabilitation. Whatever the cause of the disability, our services can benefit patients who have functional limitations in such areas as mobility, communication and self care.

**6352 HealthSouth Rehab Hospital Of Arlington**
3200 Matlock Rd
Arlington, TX 76015-2911
817-468-4000
FAX: 817-468-3055
healthsouth.com

*Rizwan Shah, Medical Director*
*Kathy Dickerson, Controller*
A modern 65-bed hospital dedicated to providng inpatient programs in a general rehabilitation setting for persons recovering for a disabling injury or illness. As part of our continuum of care, we also offer outpatient therapy, a day program, and individual therapy services. Our goal is to help our patients resume a productive and more meaningful life through appropriate rehabilitative care and restorative nursing in a wellness-oriented environment that promotes healing and functional recovery.

**6353 HealthSouth Rehab Hospital Of Austin**
1215 Red River St
Austin, TX 78701-1921
512-479-3551
FAX: 512-479-3765
www.healthsouthaustin.com

*Duke Saldiver, CEO*
*Corey Helm Swartz, Director of Therapy Operations*
A comprehensive 83 bed medical rehabilitation hospital serving the needs of patients in the Central Texas area. The mission is to promote recovery for persons with disabling conditions by providing individualized treatment so they can reach the highest level of physical, social and emotional well-being.

**6354 HealthSouth Rehabilitation Center of Humble Texas**
18902 S Memorial Dr
Humble, TX 77338
281-319-9541
FAX: 281-446-5616
www.healthsouthhumble.com

*Angie Simmons, CEO*
*Mikael Simpson, Director of Therapy Operations*
Offers comprehensive rehabilitation services for patients with diverse diagnoses. Rehabilitation can be defined as multidisciplinary therapy designed to increase patient's overall functioning to a level that meets or exceeds where the patient was prior to illness or injury or to maximize current level of ability. The benefits of these services to patients and their families is invaluable.

**6355 HealthSouth Rehabilitation Hospital**
6701 Oakmont Blvd
Fort Worth, TX 76132-2957
817-370-4700
FAX: 817-370-4977
www.healthsouthcityview.com

*Deborah Hopps, CEO*
*Mark Bussell, Medical Director*
A 62-bed acute medical rehabilitation hospital that offers comprehensive inpatient and outpatient rehabilitation services.

**6356 HealthSouth Rehabilitation Hospital of Beaumont**
3340 Plaza 10 Dr
Beaumont, TX 77707-2551
409-839-3333
FAX: 409-835-0898
www.healthsouthbeaumont.com

*Sam Coco, Director of Therapy Operations*
*HJ Gaspard, CEO*
A state of the art freestanding 61-bed comprehensive physical rehabilitation hospital. The hospital is specifically designed to meet the needs of individuals and their families who have experienced a disabling injury or illness or are recovering from a surgery. An experienced team of physicians, nurses, therapists, treat conditions and other disorders.

**6357 HealthSouth Rehabilitation Institute Of San Antonio (RIOSA)**
9119 Cinnamon Hill
San Antonio, TX 78240-5401
210-691-0737
FAX: 210-558-1297
www.hsriosa.com

*Scott Butcher, CEO*
*Richard Senelick, Medical Director*
HealthSouth Rehabilitation Institute of San Antonio is the largest free-standing physical rehabilitation hospital in San Antonio and is proud to enter our 11th year of delivering quality, comprehensive medical rehabilitation in a pristine environment. HealthSouth annually serves over 1,500 inpatients and more then 20,000 outpatient visits from throughout San Antonio and Mexico. 108-bed hospital has more then 300 personell on staff providing extensive experience.

**6358 Hillcrest Baptist Medical Center: Rehab Care Unit**
3000 Herring Ave
Waco, TX 76708-3239 254-202-2000
FAX: 254-202-8975
e-mail: info@hillcrest.net
www.hillcrest.net

*Fred Walters, President*
*Jon Ellis, Secretary*
A fully accredited 393-bed acute care facility in Waco including a Level II Trauma Center, Hillcrest Family Health Center, a network of family medicine clinics; and many key services. Hillcrest is a ministry of Texas Baptists and is one of 7 health care institutions affiliated with the Baptist General Convention of Texas.

**6359 Institute for Rehabilitation & Research**
1333 Moursund St
Houston, TX 77030-3405 713-942-6159
800-447-3422
FAX: 713-942-5289
e-mail: tirr.referrals@memorialhermann.org
www.memorialhermann.org

*Jeffrey Berliner, Physician*
*Michelle Pu, Physician*
A national center for information, training, research, and technical assistance in independent living. The goal is to extend the body of knowledge in independent living and to improve the utilization of results of research programs and demonstration projects in this field. It has developed a variety of strategies for collecting, synthesizing, and disseminating information related to the field of independent living.

**6360 Midland Memorial Hospital & Medical Center**
2200 W Illinois Ave
Midland, TX 79701-6499 432-685-1111
800-833-2916
e-mail: russell.meyers@midland-memorial.com
midland-memorial.com

*Russell Meyers, CEO*
*Jay Reynolds, Board Member*
The Occupational and Physical Therapy Center is a specialzed outpatient clinic. The clinic provides a wide variety of rehabilitation services designed to adequately assist you in returning back to your normal duties. Our highly trained professionals are here to help you with all your rehabilitation needs.

**6361 Navarro Regional Hospital: RehabCare Unit**
Navarro Hospital
3201 W State Highway 22
Corsicana, TX 75110-2469 903-654-6800
FAX: 903-654-6955
www.navarrohospital.com

*Xavier Villarreal, CEO*
*Glenda Teri, Chief Nursing Officer*
The rehab unit is located on the 4th floor and is designed for individuals who require intense rehab for an injury or disease process where the goal would be to return home. Our team is committed to helping individuals return to the highest level of functioning. Our team consists of physicians, nurses, physical therapist, occupational therapist, speech therapist, social workers, dieticians and other professionals as needed.

**6362 Rebound: Northeast Methodist Hospital**
12412 Judson Rd
Live Oak, TX 78233-3255 210-757-7000
FAX: 210-757-5072
www.nemh.sahealth.com

*Joe Hernandez, Manager*
Methodist Healthcare provides quality, comprehensive rehabilitation services for children and adults. Working as a team, rehabilitation professionals help patients define and achieve individual goals in restoring function and productivity.

**6363 Rio Vista Rehabilitation Hospital**
1740 Curie Dr
El Paso, TX 79902-2900 915-544-8336
800-999-8392
FAX: 915-544-4838

*Gene Miller, Administrator*

**6364 San Antonio Warm Springs Rehabilitation Hospital**
5101 Medical Dr
San Antonio, TX 78229-4801 210-595-2380
FAX: 210-614-0649
www.warmsprings.org

*Kurt Meyer, SVP Operations*
*Rick Marek, VP Post Acute Medical*
A statewide not-for-profit system of inpatient and outpatient rehabilitation specialty centers. Warm Springs Rehabilitation System offers hope and acts as a catalyst for achieving an optimal quality of life by providing comprehensive physical and/or cognitive rehabilitative care. Invensting resources in educational and recreational programs. Supporting research efforts.

**6365 Shannon Medical Center: RehabCare Unit**
120 E Harris Ave
San Angelo, TX 76903-5904 325-653-6741
FAX: 325-657-5706
www.shannonhealth.com

*Bryan Horner, CEO*
*Irv Zeitler, VP Medical Affairs*
Committed to improving the health of our community, using the latest technologies available in the spirit of caring and integrity. Strives to create an environment committed to the values of accountability, service, pride, integrity, respect and excellence. We foster growth toward the highest quality care and customer service and strive for excellent financial performance. We hire and develop the best people to accomplish these tasks.

**6366 Shriners Burn Institute: Galveston Unit**
815 Market St
Galveston, TX 77550-2720 409-770-6731
FAX: 409-770-6919
www.totalburncare.com

*David Herndon, Chief Of Staff*
Providing expert, orthopaedic and burn care to children under 18 regardless of ability to pay.

**6367 Shriners Hospitals for Children, Houston**
6977 Main St
Houston, TX 77030-3701 713-797-1616
800-853-1240
FAX: 713-797-1029
www.shrinershq.org

*David Ferrell, Administrator*
*Douglas Barnes, Chief of Staff*
Shriners Hospitals provides at no charge quality pediatric orthopedic serivces to children ages newborn to 18 years old. These services include both outpatient and inpatient needs. Specialties include cerebrel palsy, spina bifida, scoliosis, hand, hip and feet problems. An application is required and may be completed by phone.

**6368 South Arlington Medical Center: Rehab Care Unit**
3301 Matlock Rd
Arlington, TX 76015-2908 817-472-4906
FAX: 817-472-4878
e-mail: mca@hcahealthcare.com
www.medicaclcenterarlington.com

*Patrice Oliver, Manaager*
Above all else, we are committed to the care and improvement of human life. In recognition of this committment, we strive to deliver high-quality, cost-effective healthcare in the communities we serve.

**6369 South Texas Rehabilitation Hospital**
Ernest Health
425 E Alton Gloor Blvd
Brownsville, TX 78526-3361
956-554-6000
FAX: 956-350-6150
e-mail: askus@earnesthealth.com
www.strh.ernesthealth.com

*Christopher Wilson, Medical Director*
*Jessie Eason, CEO*
*Mary Valdez, Director of Marketing*
STRH was designed for the provision of specialized rehabilitative care, in the only freestanding acute rehabilitation hospital serving Brownsville and the Rio Grande Valley. The hospital provides rehabilitative services for patients with functional deficits as a result of debilitating illnesses or injuries.

**6370 St. David's Rehabilitation Center**
St. David s Medical Center
98 San Jacinto Blvd
Ste 1800
Austin, TX 78701-4237
512-544-5100
FAX: 512-482-4125
www.stdavids.com

*Anisa Godinez, Medical Director*
Mission is to provide exceptional care to every patient every day with a spirit of warmth, friendliness and personal pride. Values are integrity, compassion, accountability, respect and excellence.

**6371 Texas NeuroRehab Center**
1106 W Dittmar Rd
Austin, TX 78745-6328
512-444-4835
800-252-5151
FAX: 512-462-6749
www.texasneurorehab.com

*Alison Crawford Sinsky, Inpatient and Outpatient Manager*
*Ed Varando, Occupational Therapy Manager*
Internationally recognized provider in brain injury/neurobehavioral treatment for children, adolescents, and adults with complex medical, physical and/or behavioral issues. Medical rehabilitation, neurobehavioral, and neuropsychiatric programs combine traditional therapies with education, vocational, substance abuse, and sensory integration services.

**6372 Texas Specialty Hospital at Dallas**
7955 Harry Hines Blvd
Dallas, TX 75235-3305
214-637-0000

*Robin Burns, CEO*
66 beds offering active/acute rehabilitation, brain injury day treatment, cognitive rehabilitation, complex care, extended rehabilitation and short term evaluation.

**6373 Touchstone Neurorecovery Center**
Nexus Health Systems
9297 Wahrenberger Rd
Conroe, TX 77304-2441
936-788-7770
800-414-4824
FAX: 936-788-7785
e-mail: tncinfo@nhsltd.com
www.touchstoneneuro.com

*Cindy Mostaffa, CEO*
*John Cassidy, Executive Medical Director*
*Nelson Valena, Director of Rehabilitation*
Provides leading edge neurobehavioral rehabilitation. Develops and provides state-of-the-art transitional, residential and vocational rehabilitation services for indivduals with traumatic brain injuries, and other long term ilnesses.

**6374 Valley Regional Medical Center: RehabCare Unit**
100A E Alton Gloor Blvd
Brownsville, TX 78526-3328
956-350-7000
FAX: 956-350-7111
www.valleyregionalmedicalcenter.com

*David Handley, CEO*
*Jose De Luna, Chief of Staff*

## Utah

**6375 HealthSouth Rehab Hospital Of Utah**
8074 S 1300 E
Sandy, UT 84094-743
801-565-6666
FAX: 801-565-6576
www.healthsouthutah.com

*Phil Eaton, CEO*
*William McNutt, Director of Therapy Operations*
A full spectrum of services, including inpatient, outpatient, day hospital and home health. Holistic patient care, education and community assimilation are the hallmarks of our programs, and evidence of our leadership in the field of rehabilitation. Working together as a team, we are able to tailor the needs of our patients and provide the highest quality services. We believe that education and involvement of family and friends, will assist them in maintaining independence after discharge.

**6376 LDS Hospital Rehabilitation Center**
8th Ave & C Street
Salt Lake City, UT 84143-0001
801-408-1100
800-527-1118
FAX: 801-408-5610
e-mail: contactus@intermountainmail.org
www.intermountainhealthcare.org

*Lizz Daley, Administrator*
Located within a Trauma I Center, this facility provides comprehensive inpatient and outpatient rehabilitation to people with physical disabilities. CARF/JCAHO accredited. Low cost family housing is available and Medicaid/Medicare is accepted.

**6377 Primary Children's Medical Center**
100 Mario Capecchi Dr
Salt Lake City, UT 84113-1100
801-662-1000
FAX: 801-588-2318
www.ihc.com

*Kevin Jones, Manager*
*Scott Parker, President*
Primary Children's Medical Center is the pediatric center serving 5 states in the Intermountain West Utah, Idaho, Wyoming, Nevada and Montana. The 235-bed facility is equipped and staffed to treat children with complex illness and injury. PCMC is owned by Intermountain Healthcare, a non-profit health care system. In addition, it is affiliated with the Dept. of Pediatrics, University of Utah, integrating pediatric programs. The hospital is designed to meet the needs of children & their families.

**6378 Shriners Hospitals for Children: Intermountain**
Fairfax Road at Virginia St
Salt Lake City, UT 84103
801-536-3500
800-313-3745
FAX: 801-536-3782
www.shrinershq.org

*Kevin Martin, Administrator*
*Jacques D'Astous, Chief of Staff*
One of nineteen hospitals in North America specializing in pediatric orthopedics (plus four hospitals providing pediatric burn treatment). This hospital serves the Intermountain region. All services provided in the hospital are at no cost to family, insurance company, nor state/federal agency regardless of ability to pay.

**6379 Stewart Rehabilitation Center: McKay Dee Hospital**
4401 Harrison Blvd
Ogden, UT 84403-3195 801-387-2080
FAX: 801-387-7720
e-mail: contactus@intermountainmail.org
www.intermountainhealthcare.org

*Corey Anden, Nurse Coordinator*
*Judy Grover, Manager*
With 10 affiliated clinics, McKay-Dee serves northern Utah, and portions of southeast Idaho and western Wyoming. A part of Intermountain Healthcare's system of 21 hospitals, McKay-Dee Hospital Center offers nationally ranked programs such as the Heart & Vascular Institute, the Newborn ICU and a new Cancer Treatment Center.

**6380 University Healthcare-Rehabilitation Center**
50 N Medical Dr
Salt Lake City, UT 84132-1 801-587-3422
FAX: 801-581-2111
www.healthcare.utah.edu/rehab/

*David Entwistle, Administrator*
*Trish Jensen, Program Coordinator*
Provides quality, comprehensive, rehabilitation services to persons with complex rehabilitation needs, including spinal cord injuries, head trauma, stroke, and other disabling conditions. Rehabilitation Services has been serving physicians, their patients, and the community since 1965. Rehabilitation Services has been an established leader in comprehensive inpatient, outpatient and home/community rehabilitation programs. Accredited by CARF and JCAHO.

## Vermont

**6381 Vermont Achievement Center**
88 Park St
Rutland, VT 05701-4715 802-775-2395
FAX: 802-773-9656
e-mail: kmcshane@vac-rutland.com
www.vac-rutland.com

*Kiki Mc Shane, CEO*
*Rebecca Wisell, Administrator*
Vermont Achievement Center is recognized as a catalyst in building a community where all people are capable of change. Individuals flourish because they are nutured, valued and treated with respect. Education is empowering. The family is the primary influence in a person's life. Children belong in a family. Families are enhanced by support of the community. Children and family services are flexible and responsive to changing needs.

## Virginia

**6382 Inova Mount Vernon Hospital Rehabilitation Program**
Inova Rehabilitation Center
2501 Parkers Ln
Alexandria, VA 22306-3209 703-664-7000
800-554-7342
FAX: 703-664-7423
www.inova.com

*Barbara Doyle, CEO*
Inova Rehabilitation Center at Inova Mount Vernon Hospital provides comprehensive inpatient and outpatient programs for patients with brain injuries, stroke and spinal cord, neurological and orthopedic injuries.

**6383 Kluge Children's Rehabilitation Center**
University of Virginia
2270 Ivy Rd
Charlottesville, VA 22903-4977 434-924-5161
800-627-8596
FAX: 434-924-5559
www.healthsystem.virginia.edu

*Janet Allaire, Administrator*
*Richard Stevenson, Research Director*
The Kluge Childrens's Rehabilitation Center (KCRC) is a place dedicated to serving children with special needs. Children between the ages of birth and 21 come to the KCRC from all over Virginia, the United States, and even overseas for many reasons. Some need specific therapy or rehabilitation after injuries, accidents, or surgery. Others have chronic illness such as diabetes, and cystic fibrosis. Many families come to find out why their child is experiencing behavior problems.

## Washington

**6384 Good Samaritan Healthcare Physical Medicine and Rehabilitation**
Good Samaritan Hospital
407 14th Ave SE
Puyallup, WA 98372-3770 253-697-2065
FAX: 253-697-5157
e-mail: info@goodsamhealth.org
www.multicare.org

*Glenn Kassman, President*
*Vince Schmitz, CFO*
Good Samaritan is part of the Multi-Care Health System, a non-for-profit medical system serving the growing populations of Pierce and King Counties in the greater Puget Sound region of Washington. Our medical staff includes 1,600 of the regions most respected primary care physicians and specialists.

**6385 Northwest Hospital Center for Medical Rehabilitation**
1550 N 115th St
Seattle, WA 98133-8401 206-364-0500
FAX: 206-368-1399
www.nwhospital.org

*C W Schneider, CEO*
*Peter Evans, Chairman*
Provides complete medical and surgical services in both inpatient and outpatient settings. Services across multiple specialties include: 24hr emergency services, critical care, cardiac care, stroke program, cancer care, childbirth center, rehabilitation center, diagnostic imaging and education and wellness services. Mission is to raise the long-term health status of our community by providing personalized, quality care with compassion dignity, and respect.

**6386 Providence Medical Center**
500 17th Ave
Seattle, WA 98122-5711 206-000-1111
FAX: 206-320-3387
www.swedish.org

Swedish offers a complete continuum of rehabilitation services, from acute inpatient care to extensive outpatient therapies, to meet virtually every rehabilitative need for patients of all ages. Nearly 7,000 patients turn to Swedish for these services every year. Through our multidisciplinary team of physical and occupational therapists and speech-language pathologists, Swedish provides the reassurance of a high level of clinical expertise in comfortable, state-of-the-art facilities.

**6387 Providence Rehabilitation Services**
Providence Rehabilitation Services
1321 Colby Ave
Everett, WA 98201-1665
425-261-3825
FAX: 425-261-3823
www.providence.org

*Jim Phillips, Manager*
*Leslie Baumgarten, Manager*
Continuum of care available: Acute Care, Inpatient Rehabilitation Unit, Transitional Care, Outpatient therapies, and In-home services.

**6388 Shriners Hospitals for Children: Spokane**
Shriners Hospitals
911 W 5th Ave
Spokane, WA 99204-2901
509-455-7844
FAX: 509-623-0474
www.shrinershq.org/hospitals/spokane

*Gene Raynaud, Administrator*
*Glen Baird, Assistant Chief of Staff*
*Paul Caskey, Chief of Staff*
Provides pediatric orthopedic services plus burn scar revision to children birth to 18. All services at no charge to the family.

## West Virginia

**6389 HealthSouth Mountain View Regional Rehab Hospital**
1160 Van Voorhis Rd
Morgantown, WV 26505-3437
304-598-1100
800-388-2451
FAX: 304-598-1103
e-mail: healthsouthmountainview.com
www.healthsouth.com

*Vicki Demers, CEO*
A 96-bed inpatient accute rehabilitation hospital. Outpatient services, physical, occupational and speech therapy, and interior therapy pool. Programs include neuro/stroke, brain injury, spinal cord injury and pediatric.

**6390 HealthSouth Western Hills Regional Rehab Hospital**
3 Western Hills Dr
Parkersburg, WV 26105-8122
304-420-1392
FAX: 304-420-1374
www.healthsouthwesternhills.com

*Kalapala Rao, Medical Director*
*Elizabeth Halkett, Director of Clinical Services*
A 40-bed medical rehabilitation hospital serving inpatient and outpatient needs in the western West Virginia area. Our hospital is accredited by the Joint Commission on Accreditation of Healthcare Organizations (JCAHO) Our mission is to guide patients whtih physically disabling conditions along an individualized treatment pathway so they can reach the highest level of physical, social and emotional well-being. We strive to provide the highest quality care for you and your family.

## Wisconsin

**6391 Extendicare Health Services, Inc.**
111 W Michigan St
Milwaukee, WI 53203-2903
414-908-8000
800-395-5000
FAX: 414-908-8059
extendicare.com

*Timothy Lukenda, CEO*
*Douglas Harris, SVP*
*David Pearce, Vice President, General Counsel*

**6392 St. Catherine's Hospital**
9555 76th St
Kenosha, WI 53140
262-577-8000
FAX: 262-653-5795
www.uhsi.org

*Vicki Lewis, Manager*
Committed to living out the healing ministries of the Judeo-Christian faiths by providing exceptional and compassionate healthcare service that promotes the dignity and well-being of the people we serve.

**6393 St. Joseph Hospital**
611 Saint Joseph Ave
Marshfield, WI 54449-1898
715-387-1713
FAX: 715-389-3939
e-mail: sjhweb@stjosephs-marshfield.org
www.ministryhealth.org

*Michael Schmidt, CEO*
*Catherine Olson, Director*
A values-driven healthcare delivery network of aligned hospitals, clinics, long-term care facilities, home care agencies, dialysis centers and many other programs and services in Wisconsin and Minnesota.

## Wyoming

**6394 Spalding Rehabilitation Hospital at Memorial Hospital of Laramie**
2301 House Ave
Ste 300
Cheyenne, WY 82001-3748
307-635-4141
www.imgwy.com

*Maria Rodenbaugh, Physician*
*John Hartman, Physician*

# Rehabilitation Facilities, Post-Acute

## Alabama

6395 **Alabama Department of Rehabilitation Services**
602 S Lawrence St
Montgomery, AL 36104-4787 334-293-7500
800-441-7607
FAX: 334-293-7383
rehab.state.al.us

*Cary Boswell, Manager*
State agency which provides services and assistance to Alabama's children and adults with disabilities.

6396 **Alabama Goodwill Industries**
2350 Green Springs Hwy S
Birmingham, AL 35205-6834 205-323-6331
FAX: 205-324-9059
goodwill.org

*Jim Gibbons, CEO*
The mission of Goodwill is to provide rehabilitation services, training, employment, and opportunities for personal growth to the disabled/disadvantaged.

6397 **Briarcliff Nursing Home & Rehab Facility**
3201 N. Ware Road
McAllen, TX 78501 956-631-5542
http://www.briarcliffnursingcenter.com

Postacute rehabilitation program.

6398 **Butler Adult Training Center**
680 Hardscramble Rd
Greenville, AL 36037-3615 334-382-2353
FAX: 334-382-9518
http://www.scamhc.org

*Diane Baugher, CPA, MBA, Executive Director*
Clients 21 years of age and older who are mentally retarded. School age clients are also served at the center and must also be mentally retarded. Clients receive training in Independent Living Skills, Self-Care, Language Skills, Learning, Self Direction and Economic Self-Sufficiency. The clients also participate in Special Olympics activities.

6399 **Cheaha Mental Health**
P.O.Box 1248
Sylacauga, AL 35150-1248 256-245-1340
FAX: 256-245-1343

*Cynthia L. Atkinson, Executive Director*
*Dr.Garry Grayon, Medical Director*
*Steve Persons, Human Resources Coordinator*
*Karen McKinney, Clinical Director of Mental Health Services*
Offers mental health rehabilitation, respite care, residential facilities and more for the mentally disabled. Serves Talladega, Coosa, Clay and Randolph counties.

6400 **Children's Rehabilitation Service**
602 S. Lawrence St.
Montgomery, AL 36104 334-293-7500
800-441-7607
FAX: 334-293-7383
www.rehab.state.al.us/home/services/crs/main

*Steve Shivers, Manager*
Statewide organization of skilled professionals providng quality medical, rehabilitative, coordination and support services for children with special health care needs and their families.

6401 **Chilton-Shelby Mental Health Center/ The Mitchell Center**
67 Highway 67
Calera, AL 35040 205-668-1327
FAX: 205-668-2443
chiltonshelby.org

*Melodie D. Crawford, CEO*
*Jamie Herren, CFO*
*Kathryn T. Crouthers, COO*
*Mary Pat Davidson, MA, Intellectual Disabilities Division Director*
Offers mental health rehabilitation services and more for the recovery of mentally disabled adults. Serves Chilton and Shelby counties.

6402 **EL Darden Rehabilitation Center**
1001 E Broad Street
Suite C
Gadsden, AL 35903-2400 256-547-5751
FAX: 256-547-5761
e-mail: darden@dardenrehab.org
dardenrehab.org

*Brent McCoy, Executive Director*
*Greg Johnson, Financial/Operations Manager*
*Sam Bishop, Information Systems and Workshop Manager*
*Lisa Wilson, Executive Assistant*
Work adjustment and job placement programs. Serves the counties of Etawah, Marshall, Dekalb, Clair and Cherokee.

6403 **Easter Seals Central Alabama**
2125 E South Blvd
Montgomery, AL 36116-2409 334-288-0240
FAX: 334-288-7171
e-mail: easterseals@worldnet.att.net
www.eastersealsca.or

*Debbie Lynn, Executive Director*
*Ed Collier, Programs Manager*
*Sharis LeMay, CNA Instructor*
*Frankie Thomas, Senior Employment Program*
A private, nonprofit organization offering services audiology, physical, occupational, lymphedemia and speech therapy, psychological counseling, vocational evaluation and assessment, person, social and work adjustment training, GED preparation, computer service training, job placement and follow-up, and special learning disabilities service and supported employment service.

6404 **Easter Seals West Alabama**
1110 Dr Edward Hillard Dr
Tuscaloosa, AL 35401-7446 205-759-1211
800-726-1216
FAX: 205-349-1162
e-mail: eswa@easterseaslswestal.org
eastersealswestal.org

*Ronny Johnston, Administrator*
*Dusty Beam, Administrative Assistant*
*Gwen Stewart, Business Office*
*Jennifer Goode Davis, Director of Community Relations*
Leading organization in helping children and adults with disabilities to live with equality, dignity and independence. Rehabilitation services are provided in two divisions: outpatient rehabilitation division (physical therapy, occupational therapy, speech therapy, hearing evaluation, sell and service hearind aids) and vocational division (vocational evaulation and vocational development). Services are rendered regardless of age, race, sex, color, creed, national origin, veteran's status.

6405 **Geer Adult Training Center**
P.O.Box 419
Carrollton, AL 35447-419 205-367-8032
FAX: 205-367-8032

*Yvonne Williams, Program Coordinator*

**6406 Goodwill Easter Seals of the Gulf Coast**
2448 Gordon Smith Dr
Mobile, AL 36617-2319 251-471-1581
800-411-0068
FAX: 251-476-4303
e-mail: info@al.easterseals.com
alabama.easterseals.com

*Frank Harkins, President*
*Stephanie Constantine, VP Marketing*
*John Ives, Chairman*
*Tommy Hester, Treasurer*
Vocational, medical, pre-school education, day care, recreation and other support services.

**6407 Indian Rivers**
2209 9th Street
Tuscaloosa, AL 35401 205-391-3131
FAX: 205-391-3135
http://www.irmhc.org

Services are available to adults who have serious mental illness resulting in personal, family or work-related problems. Counseling may take place in either individual or group settings, identification, evaluation and treatment services are available to persons who experience problems related to alcohol and drug abuse and counseling services are available for children and adolescents who have a severe emotional disturbance causing discipline problems at home and school.

**6408 MARC Enterprises**
2424 Gordon Smith Dr
Mobile, AL 36617-2397 251-479-7409
FAX: 251-473-7649
e-mail: jzoghby@mobilearc.org
mobilearc.org

*Jeff Zoghby, Executive Director*
*Lindsay Hutchinson, PR & Development Director*
Serving the mentally retarded of Mobile County both locally and through its state and national affiliations. Their united efforts through this voluntary association assure the availability of services and provide the opportunity for achievement.

**6409 North Central Alabama Mental Retardation Authority**
1602 Church Street SE
P.O. Box 2091
Decatur, AL 35602-597 256-350-1458
FAX: 256-350-1485
http://www.cddnca.org

*Earl Brightwell, Executive Director*
NCA, MRA, Inc. functions as an entrance to the service delivery system for the Alabama Department of Mental Health and Mental Retardation and is responsible for planning, development, implementation of programs, sanction, monitoring, referral, and case management for persons with mental retardation/developmental disabilities in Morgan, Lawrence and Limestone Counties. The name of the company has been changed to ""The Centers for the Developmentally Disabled, North Central Alabama, Inc.""

**6410 Northwest Alabama Easter Seals Children's Clinic Rehabilitation Center**
1450 Avalon Ave
Muscle Shoals, AL 35661-3110 256-391-1110
FAX: 256-314-5101
e-mail: info@al.easterseals.com
www.alabama.easter-seals.org

*Robert H Nelson, Administrator*
*John Ives, Chairman*
*Tommy Hester, Treasurer*
Easter Seals has been helping individuals with disabilities and special needs, and their families live better lives for more then 80 years. From child development centers to physical rehabilitation and job training for people with disabilities, Easter Seals offers a variety of services to help people with disabilities address lif's challenges and achieve personal goals.

**6411 Southeastern Blind Rehabilitation Center**
Department of Veterans Affairs Medical Center
700 19th St S
Birmingham, AL 35233-1927 205-933-8101
FAX: 205-933-4484
e-mail: george.sands@med.va.gov
www1.va.gov/blindrehab

*Frank D Wilkes, Director*
*Y Parris, Administrator*
*Eric K. Shinseki, Secretary*
The Center is a 32-bed inpatient blind rehabilitation program which serves the southeastern region. The majority of client services are for basic adjustment and management to sight loss. Basic services include: low vision, orientation and mobility, manual skills, ADL and communications. Training on electronic mobility aids and adapted computers is also available on a restricted basis. The program maintains graduate education affiliations and an active applied research program.

**6412 Tennessee Valley Rehabilitation**
P.O.Box 1926
Decatur, AL 35602-1926 256-350-2041
866-350-2041
FAX: 256-350-2806
www.tvrcdecatur.com

*Kathy Cagle, Executive Director*
*Bill Grissim, Vice President*
Mission is to help persons with disabilities gain and maintain employment in the competitive market. The mission is accomplished by providing quality services for individuals. Being attuned to the needs of each individual served. Respecting the rights of individuals served. Promoting the welfare and dignity of each individual served at all times. Not showing partiality to individuals based on race, color, national origin, gender and religion. OU OF BUSINESS

**6413 The ARC of Jefferson County**
215 21st Ave S
Birmingham, AL 35205-6801 205-323-6383
FAX: 205-323-0085
www.arcofjeff.org

*William Hoehle, Executive Director*
*Phiip Richards, President*
The ARC has four primary components. The HOPE Program provides early intervention therapy services to developmentally delayed infants and toddlers up to the age of three years. The ARC also provides services to adults ages 21 and over with intellectual disabilities. Adult services provides education, pre-vocational screening, and socialization skills training. Employment services provides vocational training, a sheltered workshop, off-site job skills training, job coach services and more.

**6414 UAB Eye Care**
University Of Alabama At Birmingham
1716 University Blvd
Birmingham, AL 35294-1 205-975-2020
FAX: 205-934-6755
www.main.uab.edu/eyecare

*RW Nowakowski, Dean*
*Dr. Marsha Snow, Chief, Low Vision Patient Care*
*Brittney Bolen, Optometric Technician*
*Joseph Fleming, D.D., Chief Of Staff*
Complete eye services, including low vision services and materials.

**6415 Vaughn-Blumberg Services**
2715 Flynn Road P.O.Box 8646
Dothan, AL 36304-646
334-793-3102
FAX: 334-793-7740
http://vaughnblumbergservices.com

*Ed Dorsey, Executive Director*
*Linda Cunningham, Director of HR*
*Billy McCarthy, Director of Finance*
*Karen Amos, Director of Nursing*

Child early intervention services for the mentally handicapped adult including diagnosis and evaluation and physical, speech, and occupational therapies. They also offer counseling, day training,employment assistance and residental homes.

**6416 West Central Alabama Easter Seals Rehabilitation Center**
2906 Citizens Pkwy
Selma, AL 36701-3915
334-872-8421
800-801-4776
FAX: 334-872-3907
e-mail: wcarcdw@tomnet.com
www.al.easter-seals.org

*David White, Administrator*
*John Ives, Chairman*
*Tommy Hester, Treasurer*

Vocational evaluation, job development, employment development, job coaching, counseling, medical services, audiology, pre-school development programs.

## Alaska

**6417 Alaska Center for the Blind and Visually Impaired**
3903 Taft Dr
Anchorage, AK 99517-3069
907-248-7770
800-770-7517
FAX: 907-248-7517
e-mail: info@alaskabvi.org
www.alaskabvi.org

*CB Brady, President*
*Dennis P. Cimmings, Vice President*
*Christina Y. Dobbins, Treasurer*
*Karla Jutzi, Executive Director*

Services to help the adult residential or community-based student become independent and self-sufficient by offering independent travel, Braille reading and writing, use of assiative technology such as talking computers, manual skills and personal, as well as home management. There is a special program for those 55 years of age and older who are experiencing a vision loss and another program for rural Alaska Native youth who are visually impaired.

**6418 Alaska Veterans Facility**
Ste 115
4201 Tudor Centre Dr
Anchorage, AK 99508-5914
907-563-6966
FAX: 907-561-7183

*Bob Erwin, Manager*
*Robert Nelson, Counselor*

Veterans medical clinic offering disabled veterans medical treatments.

## Arizona

**6419 Arizona Center for the Blind and Visually Impaired**
3100 E Roosevelt St
Phoenix, AZ 85008-5036
602-273-7411
FAX: 602-273-7410
e-mail: jlamay@acbvi.org
acbvi.org

*James La May, CEO*
*Frank Vance, Director*
*Steven Walker, Chair*
*Christine Boisen, Secretary*

A private, nonprofit organization that provides comprehensive rehabilitation services and more for the blind and visually handicapped. The staff includes 20 instructional and adminstrative professionals.

**6420 Arizona Industries for the Blind**
Ste 130
515 N 51st Ave
Phoenix, AZ 85043-2711
602-771-9100
FAX: 602-484-0442
www.azdes.gov/aib

*Tim Adams, Manager*

Offers rehabilitation services, vocational/pre-vocational evaluation and training, work adjustment, job development and employment and training opportunties for individuals who are blind.

**6421 Banner Good Samaritan Medical Center**
1111 E McDowell Rd
Phoenix, AZ 85006-2666
602-239-2000
FAX: 602-239-5868
www.bannerhealth.com

*Peter Fine, CEO*
*Lorraine Hudspeth, Controller*
*Letty Cerpa, Senior Accountant*
*Larry Mann, IT Manager*

Nearly 1,700 physicians representing more than 50 specialties work with Banner Good Samaritan staff to care for more then 36,000 inpatients a year. Houses more then 650 licensed patient care beds. A teaching hospital that trains more then 220 physicians annually and a premier medical center in Arizona and the Southwest. Provides a comprehensive foundation of major programs and an equally impressive offering of highly specialized programs not availiable in most hospitals.

**6422 Beacon Foundation for the Mentally Retarded**
308 W. Glenn St.
Tucson, AZ 85703
520-622-4874
e-mail: sking@beacongroup.org
http://beacongroup.org

*Steven R King, President*
*Chuck Tiller, Vice President Rehabilitation Services*
*Greg Natvig, Vice President of Business Operations*
*Michelle Kroeger, CFO*

Committed to effectively assisting adults with disabilities to maximize their personal, social, vocational and educational skills in order to attain a successful and meaningful independence within the Tucson community.

**6423 Carondelet Brain Injury Programs and Services (Bridges Now)**
350 N Wilmot Rd
Tucson, AZ 85711-2602
520-873-3761
FAX: 520-873-3743
e-mail: comments@carondelet.org
carondelet.org

*Daisy M Jenkins, Executive VP, Chief HR/Administrative Officer*
*James K Beckmann, Chief Executive Officer*
*Alan Strauss, Executive VP, Finance and Chief Financial Officer*
*Christen Castellano, MBA, Executive Vice President and Chief Strategy Officer*

Comprehensive outpatient rehabilitation program. PT, OT, ST, Psychology and Rehab Counseling Services.

**6424 Desert Life Rehabilitation & Care Center**
1919 W Medical St
Tucson, AZ 85704-1133
520-297-8311
FAX: 520-544-0930
www.desertlifercc.com

*Amad Nazifi, Executive Director*
Accomodates 240 residents. Provides skilled and intermediate nursing with occupational, physical, speech and respiratory therapy services. Offers special programs including an Alzheimer's Unit and a Young Adult program

**6425 Freestone Rehabilitation Center**
10617 E Oasis Dr
Apache Junction, AZ 85220
480-986-1531
FAX: 480-986-1538

*Randy Gray, Executive Director*
*Cherie Vance, Manager*

**6426 HealthSouth Valley Of The Sun Rehabilitation Hospital**
13460 N 67th Ave
Glendale, AZ 85304-1000
623-878-8800
FAX: 623-878-5254
healthsouth.com

*Beth Bacher, Manager*
A 60-bed free-standing hospital that offers acute physical rehabilitation, outpatient therapy services and day hospital treatment. Works in cooperation with local, regional and national managed care organizations and other sources to maximise patient recovery while conserving financial resources.

**6427 Institute for Human Development**
Northern Arizona University
912 Riordan Rd. P.O.Box 5630
Flagstaff, AZ 86011-5630
928-523-4791
FAX: 928-523-9127
e-mail: ihd@nau.edu
www.nau.edu/ihd

*Levi Esguerra, Director*
*Lisa Andrew, Advisory Commitee*
*Lynn Black, Advisory Commitee*
*Maria Bravo, Advisory Commitee*
The Institute values and supports the independence, productivity and inclusion of Arizona's citizens with disabilities. Based on the values and beliefs, the Institute conducts training, research and services that further these goals.

**6428 John C Lincoln Hospital North Mountain**
250 E Dunlap Ave
Phoenix, AZ 85020-2871
602-943-2381
FAX: 602-944-8062
e-mail: webmaster@jcl.com
www.jcl.com/content/northmountain/default.htm

*Rhonda Forsyth, President and CEO*
*Bruce Pearson, FACHE, Senior Vice President & Chief Executive Officer*
*Maggi Griffin, RN, MS, Vice President & Network Chief Nursing Officer*
Mission is to assist each person entrusted to our care to enjoy the fullest gift of health possible, and work with others to build a community where a helping hand is available for our most vulnerable members.

**6429 La Frontera Center**
504 W 29th St
Tucson, AZ 85713-3394
520-884-9920
FAX: 520-792-0654
www.lafronteraaz.org

*Daniel Ranieri, CEO & President*
*Lois Bloom, Board Chair*
*Kathy Wells, VP & COO*
*Michael Prudence, CFO*
A nonprofit community-based behavioral health agency that has been helping southern Arizona children, adults, and families since 1968.

**6430 Manor Care Nursing and Rehab Center: Tucson**
3705 N Swan Rd
Tucson, AZ 85718-6939
520-299-7088
FAX: 520-529-0038
www.hcr-manorcare.com

*Clifton J. Porter II, Vice President - Government Relations*
*Martin Allen, Vice President*
A leading provider of short-term post-acute medical care and rehabilitation and long-term skilled nursing care. High quality medical care is provided through registered (RN) and licensed practical (LPN) nurses and certified nursing assistants (CNA) in concert with physical , occupational and speech rehabilitation therapists. Our more then 275 skilled nursing centers are Medicare-and Medicaid-certified.

**6431 Nova Care**
Ste 102
1010 E McDowell Rd
Phoenix, AZ 85006-2607
602-256-7232
FAX: 602-256-7292
novacare.com

*Scott Lusted, General Manager*
*Brian Beal, Market Manager*
NovaCare Rehabilitation's highly respected clinical team provides preventative and rehabilitative services that maximize functionality and promote well-being. NovaCare Rehabilitation also provides physical therapy and athletic training services to more then 20 professional sports teams and 300 universities, colleges, and highschools thoughout the nation.

**6432 Perry Rehabilitation Center**
3146 E Windsor Ave
Phoenix, AZ 85008-1199
602-956-0400
FAX: 602-957-7610
e-mail: perrycenter@qwest.net
www.azafh.com

*Diana Casillas, Human Resources Director*
*Jim Musick, President*
Provides services for people with disabilities, cognitive disabilities including residential services, day treatment, job training and job placement.

**6433 Phoenix Veterans Center**
Ste 100
141 E Palm Ln
Phoenix, AZ 85004-1554
602-379-4769
FAX: 602-379-4130

*Ken Benckwitz, Manager*
Veterans medical clinic offering disabled veterans medical treatments.

**6434 Progress Valley: Phoenix**
AZ 85254-6106
480-922-9427
FAX: 602-274-5473
e-mail: mailto:recovery@progressvalley.org
progressvalley.org

*Susanne Lambert, Executive Director*
*Jennifer White, Director of Programs*
*Cathie Scott, Sober Housing Manager*
*Kristine Peltier, Finance Director*
Residential aftercare for alcoholism and chemical dependency. Certified chemical dependency counselors provide individual treatment.

**6435 Rehabilitation Services Administration**
2
1789 W Jefferson St
Phoenix, AZ 85007-3202
602-542-3332
800-563-1221
FAX: 602-542-3778
TTY: 602-542-6049
e-mail: azrsa@azdes.gov
azdes.gov/rsa

*Katharine Levandowsky, Administrator*
Provides a variety of specialized services to assist in removing barriers to employment and/or independent living for individuals with physical or mental disabilities. RSA offers 3 major service programs and several specialized programs/services.

**6436 Southern Arizona Association For The Visually Impaired**
3767 E Grant Rd
Tucson, AZ 85716-2935
520-795-1331
FAX: 520-795-1336
e-mail: reception@saavi.us
www.saavi.us

*Michael Gordon, Executive Director*
*Amy Murillo, Associate Director*
*Carol Lopez, Finance Director*
Offers health services, counseling, social work, home and personal management, computer training, low vision aids and more for the visually handicapped 18 years or older.

**6437 Toyei Industries**
P.O.Box 55
Ganado, AZ 86505-55
928-736-2417
888-45T-OYEI
FAX: 928-736-2495

*Anthony Lincoln, CEO*
Serves the needs of developmentally disabled and the severely mentally impaired adult citizens of the Navajo Nation and other Indian Nations. Staff of 60+ serves the needs of all the Navajo adults. Services include day treatment programs, and residential and group home services.

**6438 Yuma Center for the Visually Impaired**
113 W George St
Yuma, AZ 85364-6580
928-726-1310
FAX: 928-783-3261

*Calvin Roberts, Executive Director*
A private nonprofit agency offering services for totally blind and legally blind children and adults in the Arizona area.

## Arkansas

**6439 Arkansas Lighthouse for the Blind**
P.O.Box 192666
6818 Murray St.
Little Rock, AR 72219- 2666
501-562-2222
FAX: 501-568-5275
e-mail: info@arkansaslighthouse.org
arkansaslighthouse.org

*Bill Johnson, CEO*
*Danny Novielli, COO*
*John McAtee, CFO*
Manufacturer of textiles, apparel and paper products and employs blind and legally blind individuals.

**6440 Beverly Enterprises Network**
1200 S Waldron Rd
Fort Smith, AR 72903-2629
479-201-2000
800-666-9996
FAX: 479-452-5131

*Randy Churchey, CEO*
Offers a progressive approach to subacute care. The goal of this organization is to assist injured and disabled individuals regain the level of independence to which they have been accustomed. Provides support and training programs, patient and family services and specialty programs for patients.

**6441 Easter Seals: Arkansas**
3920 Woodland Heights Rd
Little Rock, AR 72212-2495
501-227-3600
877-533-3700
FAX: 501-227-4021
TTY: 501-227-3686
e-mail: lrogers@ar.easterseals.com
www.eastersealsar.com

*Sharon Moone-Jochums, President/ CEO*
*Linda Rogers, VP Programs*
Their mission is to provide exceptional services to ensure that all people with disabilities or special needs have equal opportunities to live, learn, work and play in their communitites.

**6442 HealthSouth Rehabilitation Hospital Of Fort Smith**
1401 South J. Street
Fort Smith, AR 72901-5158
479-785-8595
FAX: 479-785-8599
healthsouth.com

*Ryan Cassedy, CEO*
*Cygnet Schroeder, Medical Director*
*Donna Beallis, Director of Medical Management*
*Janette Daniels, Director of Human Resources*
A free-standing 80-bed comprehensive physical medicine and rehabilitation hospital offering inpatient and outpatient services. Provides specialized medical and therapy services, designed to assist physically challenged persons to reach their highest level of independent function.

**6443 Lions World Services for the Blind**
2811 Fair Park Blvd
Little Rock, AR 72204-5044
501-664-7100
800-248-0734
FAX: 501-664-2743
e-mail: training@lwsb.org
lwsb.org

*Larry Dickerson, President/ CEO*
*Tony Woodell, COO*
*Bill Smith, Director of Development*
*Melanie Jones, Marketing Director*
Offers services in the areas of health education, recreation, rehabilitation, counseling, employment, computer training and more for all legally blind residents of the U.S. The staff includes 56 full time employees.

**6444 Little Rock Vet Center #0713**
Department of Veterans Affairs of Washington DC
Ste A
201 W Broadway St
North Little Rock, AR 72114-5505
501-324-6395
FAX: 501-324-6928
www.hud.gov/offices/cpd/about/hudvet/state/ar

Vet Center provides PTSD counseling to veterans of a combat zone. No medical care provided.

**6445 Timber Ridge Ranch NeuroRestorative Services**
4500 W Commerce Dr
North Little Rock, AR 72116
501-758-8799
800-743-6802
FAX: 501-758-8778
e-mail: neuroinfo@thementornetwork.com
www.neurorestorative.com

*Bill Duffy, COO*
*Michael E. Hofmeister, Vice President of Operations*
*Sean Byrne, CFO*
*Roger P. Carrillo, Vice President of Business Development*

Comprehensive, individualized services from a transdisciplinary team of licensed professionals assist clients along a course to greater independence. A separate team is dedicated to the needs of children, adolescents, and their families. A clinical team may include professionals from the disciplines of: behavior analysis, neuropsychology, physiatry, psychology, speech-language pathology, occupational therapy, physical therapy, social work, couseling, education, nursing, and case management.

## California

**6446 ARC Fresno-Kelso Activity Center**
4567 N Marty Ave
Fresno, CA 93722-7810
559-226-6268
FAX: 559-226-6269
arcfresno.org

*Lori Ramirez, Executive Director*
*Catherine Wooliever, Director of Human Resources*
*Bruce Nieman, Director of Program Services*

The Arc Fresno is a private, non-profit 501(c)(3) organization who was founded in 1953. They provide services and supports for over 550 individuals with developmental disabilities throughout Fresno County. They currently offer eight (8) programs, and do so with the help of 145 employees.

**6447 ARC Of San-Diego-South Bay**
1280 Nolan Ave
Chula Vista, CA 91911-3738
619-427-7524
FAX: 619-427-4657
e-mail: info@arc-sd.com
www.arc-sd.com/locations

*Terri Thorn, Director*
*Steve Hojsan, Arc Enterprises Director*
*Michael Bruce, Workshop Manager*

Provides remunerative work.

**6448 ARC Of Southeast Los Angeles-Southeast Industries**
9501 Washburn Rd
Downey, CA 90242-2913
562-803-1556
FAX: 562-803-4080
e-mail: sales@arcselac.org
www.arcselac.org/

Provides an offisite extension of your production and warehouse facility. We have reliable and highly trained personnel to meet your needs, including pick-up and delivery service with prompt turn-around times. We offer assembly and packaging at competitive rates while maintaining the highest standards.

**6449 ARC: VC Community Connections West**
5103 Walker Street
Ventura, CA 93003-2705
805-650-8611
FAX: 805-644-7308
www.arcvc.org

*Robert Hogan, President*
*Gene West, First Vice President*

Caring and experienced staff is dedicated to serving participants with a variety of physical, mental and social disabilities who require a higher level of support and supervision. Using a person-centered planning approach, Arc Ventura County promotes self-directed services for all clients and families served. Adult development centers serve individuals with physical and mental disabilities, as well as people with challenging behaviors, who require assistance with basic skills such as self care.

**6450 ARC: VC Ventura**
5104 Walker Street
Ventura, CA 93003-2705
806-650-8611
FAX: 806-644-7308
www.arcvc.org

*Robert Hogan, President*
*Gene West, First Vice President*

Arc Ventura County is a private, nonprofit organization that provides educational, vocational and residential services for people with developmental disabilities. Informed decisions, positive changes, and integration in the community are fundamental principals in all programs. As evidence of our programming excellence, Arc Ventura County has been accredited by CARF (The Rehabilitation Accreditation Commission.

**6451 AbilityFirst**
1300 E Green St
Pasadena, CA 91106-2606
626-396-1010
877-768-4600
FAX: 626-396-1021
e-mail: info@abilityfirst.org
www.abilityfirst.org

*Lori Gangemi, President/ CEO*
*Steven Schultz, CFO*

AbilityFirst serves children and adults with special needs through 24 locations in Southern California.

**6452 Accentcare**
17855 North Dallas Pkwy
Dallas, TX 75287-2468
800-834-3059
e-mail: info@accentcare.com
accentcare.com

*Mark Pacala, Chairman of the Board and CEO (interim)*
*Vincent E. Cook, EVP and Chief Financial Officer*
*Melvin Warriner, SVP and Chief Culture Officer*
*Mel Deutsch, General Counsel*

Postacute rehabilitation program: home care aides follow through with rehabilitation instructions given by physical, occupational and speech therapists. Other home care services are available, serving special needs for Alzheimer's, blind, brain injury, MS, ostomies, parkinsonism, spinal injury and stroke.

**6453 Anaheim Veterans Center**
859, South Harbor Blvd
Anaheim, CA 92805-4680
714-776-0161
800-225-8387
FAX: 714-776-8904
www.longbeach.va.gov/visitors/vet_center.asp

Veterans medical clinic offering disabled veterans medical treatments.

**6454 Association for Retarded Citizens: Alameda County**
575 Independent Rd
Oakland, CA 94621-3721
510-639-4680
FAX: 510-639-4684

*Ram Sirck, Director*

Offers the Right Track program in which selected workers are grouped together on a contract basis to maximize work productivity. Provides a full benefit package, as well as a permanent supervisor. A worker is matched to a job of at least 20 hours per week and then trained by the staff of The Right Track.

**6455 Azure Acres Recovery Center**
2264 Green Hill Rd
Sebastopol, CA 95472-9034
877-762-3735
FAX: 707-823-8972
e-mail: info@azureacres.com
azureacres.com

*Shannon Clay, Executive Director*
*Irenne Magoulas, Clinical Director*
Offers rehabilitation services and residential care for the person with an alcohol or drug abuse related problems.

**6456 Back in the Saddle**
6037 Eastwood Ave
Rancho Cucamonga, CA 91737-2813
760-240-3217
FAX: 760-240-3274
www.thesaddle.com

*Richard Smith PhD, Owner*
*Erika Reed, Co-Director*
A long term community residential facility for head injured adults. House parents live on-site; and oversee a variety of programs which are individually designed and might include classes in community college, placement in a workshop or on a workstation, volunteer positions and home skills assignments. Recreational outing range from horseback riding to weekend camping. Apartment programs available as set-up. Price: $2800-$3000 per month.

**6457 Ballard Rehabilitation Hospital**
1760 W 16th St
San Bernardino, CA 92411-1150
909-473-1200
800-761-1226
FAX: 909-473-1276
www.ballardrehab.com

*Edward C. Palacios, RN,MPH, Administrator*
*Mary Hunt, Chief Operating Officer*
*Patty Meinhardt, Director Marketing/Admissions*
Ballard Rehab Hospital is a free standing specialty hospital and provides the complete continuum of acute rehabilitation and outpatient rehabilitation, dedicated to providing rehab care to adults and children. The following inpatient and outpatient programs are available: CNA (Stroke) Rehab; Spinal Cord Injury Rehab; Brain Injury Rehab; Pain Management Rehab; Bariatric program, pulmonary program, injured Worker Programs; and Post Amputation Rehab.

**6458 Bayview Nursing and Rehabilitation**
516 Willow St
Alameda, CA 94501-6132
510-521-5600
FAX: 510-865-9035
http://www.bayviewnursing.com/

*Richard S Espinoza, Administrator*
Offers a full range of medical services to meet the individual needs of our residents, including short-term rehabilitative services and long termed skilled care. Working with the resident's physician, our staff-including medical specialists, nurses, nutritionists, dietitians, and social workers-establishes a comprehensive treatment plan intended to restore you or your loved one to the highest practicable potential.

**6459 Belden Center**
606 Humboldt St
Santa Rosa, CA 95404-4219
707-579-2735
FAX: 707-579-4145

*Casey Harding, Owner*
*Pamela Fadden, Owner*
Postacute rehabilitation program.

**6460 Blind Babies Foundation**
Suite 300
1814 Franklin St
Oakland, CA 94612-3487
510-446-2229
FAX: 510-446-2262
e-mail: bbfinfo@blindbabies.org
blindbabies.org
Mission: when an infant or pre school child is identified as blind or visually impaired, provides family-centered services to support the child's optimal development and access to the world.

**6461 Brotman Medical Center: RehabCare Unit**
Brotman Medical Center
3828 Delmas Ter
Culver City, CA 90232-2713
310-836-7000
800-677-1238
FAX: 310-202-4105
e-mail: info@brotmanmed.com
phvc.com

*Jennifer Cortez, Program Manager*
Culver City is centrally located within the city of Los Angeles. These are two programs offering inpatient rehabilitation. The acute rehab program is designed for patients who need physical rehabilitation due to injury or medical disability. This program requires patients to participate in 3 hours therapy per day. The sub-acute program is designed especially for patients who need rehab but cannot tolerate the intensity of the acute rehab program..

**6462 Build Rehabilitation Industries**
12432 Foothill Blvd
Sylmar, CA 91342
818-898-0020
FAX: 818-898-1949
buildindustries.com
Comprehensive C.A.R.F. Accredited vocational rehabilitation services for adults with disabilities or other barriers to employment. Programs include: Sheltered Workshops, Work Evaluation, Work Hardening and Adjustment, Supported Employment, Job Placement, Independent Living Skills, Behavior Management, Adult Development Center, On-the-Job Training, and One-Stop Workforce Development Career Center.

**6463 California Elwyn**
18325 Mount Baldy Cir
Fountain Valley, CA 92708-6115
714-557-6313
FAX: 714-963-2961
e-mail: info@elwyn.org
elwyn.org

*Sandra S. Cornelius, President of Elwyn*
*Daniel M. Reardon, Senior Vice President and Chief Financial Officer*
*Stan H. Retif, Vice President for Development and Communications*
*Richard T. Smith, Vice President for Information Technology*
Provides opportunities for people challenged by physical and mental disabilities who are 18 or older. California Elwyn develops an Individual Rehabilitation Plan for all consumers. Contract work, shrinkwrap, janitorial are just some of the types of jobs done. Supported Employment Services are available and over 100 consumers currently are employed. Funded by the State Department of Rehabilitation and Vocational Rehabilitation.

**6464 California Eye Institute**
1360 E Herndon Ave
Fresno, CA 93720-3326
559-449-5000
www.samc.com

*Nancy Hollingsworth, President and CEO*
*Mark Bateman, Chief Operating Officer*
*Stephen Soldo, Chief Medical Officer*
*Christine Sarrico, Chief Financial Officer*
A private, nonprofit agency offering services such as health, educational, recreational, rehabilitation and employment counseling to the totally blind, legally blind and visually impaired. The staff includes two full time workers.

**6465 Camp Recovery Center**
3192 Glen Canyon Rd
Scotts Valley, CA 95066-4916
877-557-6237
camprecovery.com

*James Bailey, Executive Director*
*Tim Sinnott, Clinical Director*
*Zoe R., Case Manager*
*Jeff Geiger, Clinical Tech Director*

A free-standing social model recovery center for chemical dependency located on 25 wooded acres in the Santa Cruz Mountains. The services include: medical detoxification, complete medical evaluation, psychiatric evaluation and counseling, psychological testing, individual counseling and more. Helps the recovery from chemical dependency in a easier, warm and caring environment.

**6466 Campobello Chemical Dependency Recovery Center**
3250 Guerneville Rd
Santa Rosa, CA 95401-4030
707-579-4066
800-805-1833
FAX: 707-579-1603
campobello.org

Our mission is to provide primary treatment, education, ongoing support and family services for clients seeking a more rewarding, chemically free lifestyle. Our primary goals are: to improve understanding/acceptance of the disease model of addiction. To improve self esteem. To reduce family, job and legal problems. To improve physical/emotional health. To enhance coping and problem solving strategies for recovery.

**6467 Casa Colina Centers for Rehabilitation**
P.O.Box 6001
255 East Bonita Avenue
Pomona, CA 91769- 6001
909-596-7733
866-724-4127
FAX: 909-593-0153
TTY: 909-596-3646
casacolina.org

*Steve Norin, Chairman*
*Felice L Loverso, CEO/President*
*Chandrahas Agarwal, Medical Director*
*Rohinder Sandhu, Chief Of Medical Staff*

Casa Colina, has pioneered effective programs to create opportunity for health, productivity and self-esteem for persons with disability since 1936. Through medical rehabilitation, transitional living, residential, community, and prevention and wellness programs. Casa Colina serves more than 7,000 persons annually. Casa Colina, a non-profit organization, offers a unique spectrum of opportunities, achievement and results to patients and their families.

**6468 Casa Colina Padua Village**
P.O.Box 6001
255 East Bonita Avenue
Pomona, CA 91769- 6001
909-596-7733
866-724-4127
FAX: 909-593-0153
TTY: 909-596-3646
casacolina.org

*Steve Norin, Chairman*
*Chandrahas Agarwal, Medical Director*
*Felice L Loverso, CEO/President*
*Rohinder Sandhu, Chief Of Medical Staff*

Long term residential services for adults with developmental disability. Residences include Malmquist House, Woodbend House, and Hillsdale House, all located in Claremont, California.

**6469 Casa Colina Residential Services: Rancho Pino Verde**
Casa Colina Center for Rehabilitation
11981 Midway Ave
Lucerne Valley, CA 92356-7517
760-248-6245
www.casacolina.org

*Steve Norin, Chairman*
*Stephen W. Graeber, Vice Chairman*
*Felice L. Loverso, President*
*Rohinder Sandhu, Chief Of Medical Staff*

Long term residential services in rural environment for adults with brain injury.

**6470 Casa Colina Transitional Living Center**
255 E Bonita Ave
Pomona, CA 91767-1923
909-596-7733
866-724-4127
FAX: 909-593-0153
TTY: 909-596-3646
casacolina.org

*Steve Norin, Chairman*
*Felice L Loverso, CEO/President*
*Chandrahas Agarwal, Medical Director*
*Rohinder Sandhu, Chief Of Medical Staff*

Postacute rehabilitation program.

**6471 Casa Colina Transitional Living Center: Pomona**
P.O.Box 6001
255 East Bonita Avenue
Pomona, CA 91769- 6001
909-596-7733
866-724-4127
FAX: 909-593-0153
TTY: 909-596-3646
casacolina.org

*Steve Norin, Chairman*
*Felice L Loverso, CEO/President*
*Chandrahas Agarwal, Medical Director*
*Rohinder Sandhu, Chief Of Medical Staff*

Post acute short term residential program for persons with brain injury. In a home-like setting, therapy promotes successful re-entry to home and community living.

**6472 Cedars of Marin**
P.O.Box 947
Ross, CA 94957-947
415-454-5310
FAX: 415-454-0573
e-mail: lauren@thecedarsofmarin.org
thecedarsofmarin.org

*Martin Williamson, Administrator*
*Lauren Sockler, Project Manager*
*Chuck Greene, Executive Director*

The Cedars of Marin has provided residential and day programs for adults with developmental disabilities for over 91 years. Our award-winning programs help our clients to live creative, productive, joyous lives.

**6473 Center for Neuro Skills**
2658 Mount Vernon Ave
Bakersfield, CA 93306-2988
661-872-3408
800-922-4994
FAX: 661-872-5150
e-mail: skatomski@neuroskills.com
neuroskills.com

*Mark J Ashley, President/CEO and Co-Founder*

A comprehensive, post-acute, community based head-injury rehabilitation program serving over 100 clients per year. Since 1980, CNS has effectively treated the entire spectrum of head-injured clients, including those with severe behavioral disorders, cognitive/perceptual impairments, speech/language problems, physical disabilities and post-concussion syndrome.

**6474 Center for the Partially Sighted**
Suite 150
6101 W. Centinela Ave.
Culver City, CA 90230
310-988-1970
FAX: 310-988-1980
e-mail: info@low-vision.org
low-vision.org

*La Donna Ringering, President/CEO*
*Pam Thompson, Director of Psychological Services*
*Phyllis Amaral, Clinical Director*
*Laura Valencia, Psychosocial Services Coordinator*

Services for partially sighted and legally blind people include low vision evaluations, the design and prescription of low vision devices and adaptive technology, as well as counseling and rehabilitation training (independent living skills and orientation/mobility training). Special programs include children's program, diabetes and vision loss program, Technology demonstrations. Store carries low vision aids. Catalog available.

**6475 Central Coast Neurobehavioral Center OPTIONS**
P.O.Box 877
Morro Bay, CA 93443-877
805-772-6066
FAX: 805-772-6067
e-mail: info@optionsccnbc.org
www.optionsccnbc.org

*Michael Mamot, CEO*
*Ole von Frausing-Borch, COO*

Serves adults with developmental disabilities, traumatic head injuries, or other neurological impairments. OPTIONS operates two transitional living centers, eight licensed residential facilities, two licensed community integration day programs and a licensed short term stabilization center. Services offered include: supported and independent living services, group and individual vocational services, neuropsychological assessment, occupational therapy, cognitive therapy, speech therapy and more.

**6476 Cerebral Palsy: North County Center**
Ste 209
8525 Gibbs Dr
San Diego, CA 92123-1758
858-571-7803
FAX: 858-571-0919
www.ucpsd.org

*David Carucci, Executive Director*
*Mary Krieger, Associate Executive Director*
*Bruce Neufeld, Chief Financial Officer*
*Sophia Williams, Director of Human Resources*

The mission of UCP San Diego County is to advance the independence, productivity and full citizenship of people affected by cerebral palsy and other disabilities. By making solid steps, UCP can build a better community for all in the process.

**6477 Children's Hospital Central California Rehabilitation Center**
9300 Valley Childrens Pl
Madera, CA 93636-8762
559-353-3000
www.valleychildrens.org

*Todd Suntrapak, President & Chief Executive Officer*
*David Christensen, MD, Vice President Medical Affairs & Chief Medical Officer*
*Beverly Hayden-Pugh, Vice President & Chief Nursing Officer*
*Kirk Larson, Vice President & Chief Information Officer*

A 297-bed pediatric medical center on a 50-acre campus. We now have more then 500 doctors practicing in over 40 pediatric subspecialties with clinics and services throughout the state.

**6478 Children's Hospital Los Angeles Rehabilitation Program**
4650 W Sunset Blvd
Los Angeles, CA 90027-6062
323-660-2450
888-631-2452
e-mail: webmaster@chla.usc.edu
www.childrenshospitalla.org

*Richard D. Cordova, President and Chief Executive Officer*
*Rodney B. Hanners, Senior Vice President and Chief Operating Officer*
*Henri R. Ford, M.D., Lawrence L.*
*Foust, J.D., , Senior Vice President and General Counsel*

Designated as a Level I Pediatric Trauma Canter by the Los Angeles County EMS Agency, the hospital treats more then 1,500 pediatric trauma patients per year. Performs more then 13,900 pediatric surgeries a year, including more complex surgical procedures then any other hospital in Southern California

**6479 Children's Therapy Center**
Ste 120
770 Paseo Camarillo
Camarillo, CA 93010-6092
805-383-1501
FAX: 805-383-1504
e-mail: ctcinc@isle.net

*Beth Maulhardt, Owner*

Provides individual occupational therapy, speech/language therapy, family/child consulting, education services and physical therapy consultation for children. Evaluations and treatment are on an individual basis and special emphasis is placed on a multidisciplinary approach with information sharing, and often team treatment.

**6480 Clausen House**
88 Vernon St
Oakland, CA 94610-4217
510-839-0050
e-mail: info@clausenhouse.org
clausenhouse.org

*Deborah Levy, Interim Executive Director*
*Jessica S. Derrick, Director of Development*
*Stan Nicholson, Director of Human Resources*
*Jaynette Underhill, Director of Program Services*

Residential, supported employment, independent and supported living, adult education, and social recreation activities. Serving the developmentally disabled since 1967.

**6481 Community Gatepath**
1764 Marco Polo Way
Burlingame, CA 94010-4503
650-259-8544
e-mail: helpmychild@gatepath.com
communitygatepath.com

*Sheryl Young, Chief Executive Officer*
*Malyka Chop, Chief Financial Officer*
*Toby Mumford, Strategic Advisor*
*Anne Jarchow, Director of Special Projects*

Popular center and Peninsula Care merged into a new organization named Community Gatepath. Driving forces behind the merger were to be able to provide expanded and/or better services to indidviduals throughout San Mateo County, using the best practices of both organizations.

**6482 Community Hospital and Rehabilitation Center of Los Gatos-Saratoga**
815 Pollard Rd
Los Gatos, CA 95032-1438
408-378-6131
FAX: 408-866-4003
communityhospitallosgatos.com

*Gary Honts, CEO*

Offers rehabilitation services, inpatient and outpatient care, physical therapy, occupational therapy and more for the physically challenged adult. We have a commitment to health care excellence. It is in this commitment that we have dedicated ourselves to provide personal and professional service to our patients. Our goal is to work closely with staff, physicians and the community to attain shared goals and positive changes, now and in the future..

**6483 Contra Costa ARC**
1340 Arnold Dr
Suite 127
Martinez, CA 94553-4189
925-370-1818
FAX: 925-370-2048
e-mail: feedback@arcofcc.org
www.ContraCostaARC.com

*Christine Imrie, Executive Director*
*Diana Jorgensen, Program Coordinator*
A private nonprofit membership-based organization dedicated to enhancing the quality of life of individuals with mental retardation and other developmental disabilities.

**6484 Corona Regional Medical Center- Rehabiltation Center**
730 Magnolia Ave
Corona, CA 92879-3117
951-736-7200
FAX: 951-736-7276

*Diane Mc Donald, Manager*
*John Calderone, Chief Executive Officer*
Offers inpatient and outpatient rehabilitation services. The Center consists of an acute rehab unit, a subacute rehab unit containing modules for long-term ventilator care, respiratory rehab, coma intervention and orthopedics. In addition to inpatient therapies, the Center's outpatient programs include sports and industrial medicine.OUTOFBUSINESS.

**6485 Critical Air Medicine**
Montgomery Field
4141 Kearny Villa Rd
San Diego, CA 92123-1705
858-514-6060
800-247-8326
FAX: 619-571-0835
Offers emergency medical care by air medical transport carriers. These carriers are fully equipped with medical equipment and supplies for cardiovascular emergencies, respiratory supplies, orthopedic supplies and medications..

**6486 Crutcher's Serenity House**
P.O.Box D
Deer Park, CA 94576-504
877-274-4968
FAX: 707-963-2309
e-mail: crutchersh@earthlink.net
www.crutcherssh.com

*Robert Crutcher, Owner/CEO*
*Lu Crutcher, Executive Director*
A privately owned and operated facility that introduces to residents a new lifestyle free of all chemicals, and a new awareness of their total being. The length of the program is four weeks and is within five minutes of an acute care hospital. The Center is licensed for 19 beds, male and female located in a home-like setting with an emphasis on maintaining a family atmosphere.

**6487 Daniel Freeman Rehabilitation Centers**
333 N Prairie Ave
Inglewood, CA 90301-4501
310-674-7050
FAX: 310-674-3886

*H Arndt, Associate Administrator*
Comprehensive rehabilitation services which address needs and issues of the physically diabled and their families. We offer accute input rehabilitation, outpatient and short term skilled nursing rehabilitaion. Specialty areas include: brain injury, stroke, spinal chord injury, chronic pain, arthritis..

**6488 Delano Regional Medical Center**
1401 Garces Hwy
Delano, CA 93215-3690
661-725-4800
e-mail: info@drmc.com
drmc.com

*Bahram Ghaffari, Executive Director*
*Jeremy Klemm, HealthStream Regional Director*
*Robert A. Frist, HealthStream CEO*
Delano Regional Medical Center (DRMC) is proud to be known throughout California & beyond as an innovative regional hospital, deeply rooted in the local communities and committed to providing an exceptional patient experience. A non-profit acute-care facility serving a region of 10 rural central Californiatowns. With over 100 physicians on our active medical staff and additional courtesy or consulting physicians, patients are assured of receiving high-quality care in multiple specialties.

**6489 Desert Regional Medical Center**
1156 N Indian Canyon Dr
Palm Springs, CA 92262
760-323-6511
800-491-4990
www.desertmedctr.com

*Karolee Sowle, CEO*
*Tracey Cowles, Physician Relations Manager*
*Jeanne Stanton, Administrator /Secretary*
*Lee Bledsoe, Physician Relations Manager*
Our dedicated physicians and caregivers provide a broad array of quality programs and services, including comprehensive cancer care, women's health services, heart care, surgical weight loss reduction and orthopedics.

**6490 Devereux Santa Barbara**
P.O.Box 6784
Santa Barbara, CA 93160-6784
805-968-2525
FAX: 805-968-3247
e-mail: amcniff@devereux.org
www.devereux.org

*David Dennis, Executive Director*
*Amy Evans, Executive Administrator*
*Janis Johnson, Public Relations Coordinator*
*Alan Purucker, Clinical Case Manager*
Serves ages 8-88, who have developmental disabilities, emotional disturbances, neurological impairments, brain injuries, schizophrenia, autism, and dual diagnosis. The Center has a licensed capacity of 188 served in a continuum of services including residential, vocational, educational and more.

**6491 Division of Physical Medicine and Rehabilitation**
San Joaquin General Hospital
500 W Hospital Rd
French Camp, CA 95231-9693
209-468-6820
FAX: 209-468-6281
e-mail: pmradministration@sjgh.hs.co.san-joaquin.ca.u
www.sjphysicalmedicine.com
Offers rehabilitation services, inpatient and outpatient care, speech therapy, physical therapy, occupational therapy and more for the physically challenged individual.

**6492 Dr. Karen H Chao Developmental Optometry Karen H. Chao. O.D.**
Ste A
121 S Del Mar Ave
San Gabriel, CA 91776-1345
626-287-0401
FAX: 626-287-1457
e-mail: drkhchao@yahoo.com

*Karen Chao, Owner*
*Karen Chao OD, Owner*
Developmental optometrist specializing in the testing and treatment of vision problems and the enhancement of visual performance. Performs visual perceptual testing and training for children and adults. Undetected vision problems interfere with the ability to achieve and are highly correlated with learning difficulties and developmental problems. Provides the opportunity to overcome vision and visual-perceptual dysfunctions..

**6493 Early Childhood Services**
Desert Area Resources and Training
201 E Ridgecrest Blvd
Ridgecrest, CA 93555-3919
760-375-3045
FAX: 760-375-1288
e-mail: dart@dartontarget.org
dartontarget.org

*Virginia Deangelis, CEO*
*Cris Bridges, Chief of Client Services*
*Bob Beecroft, Chief Operations Officer*
*Jeannie Luke, Human Resources Director/Risk Manager*
Provides early intervention services to children who have disabilities or are experiencing delays in development. Provides developmental activities to promote the attainment of developmental milestones so that each child may reach his/her maximum potential. The program also provides therapeutic and educational intervention and offers support and guidance to families.

**6494 East Los Angeles Doctors Hospital**
4060 Whittier Blvd
Los Angeles, CA 90023-2596
323-268-5514
www.elalax.com

*Hector Hernandez, Chief Executive Officer*
*Kamlesh Dhawan, Chief Of Staff*
*Michael Austerlitz, Vice-Chief Of Staff*
*Horacio Fleischman, Secretary Treasurer*
Postacute rehabilitation program.

**6495 Easter Seals Disability Svcs: Bay Area**
Ste 1800
230 W Monroe St
Chicago, IL 60606-4851
312-726-6200
800-221-6827
FAX: 312-726-1494
e-mail: info@easterseals.com
www.bayarea.easterseals.com
Creates solutions that change the lives of children and adults with disabilities and special needs; and provides support to family members. Through innovative services, Easter Seals Bay Area promotes equality and dignity, providing opportunities for independence, integration, and enhanced health and wellness.

**6496 Easter Seals Superior California**
Sacramento Center & Regional Offices
3205 Hurley Way
Sacramento, CA 95864-3853
916-485-6711
888-877-3257
FAX: 916-485-2653
www.superiorca.easterseals.com

*Gary T. Kasai, President/CEO*
*Kathie Wright, Program Director*
*Terry Colborn, VP Programs/Government Affairs*
*Joanne Budge, Chief Financial Officer*
Provides outpatient rehabilitation services including day training programs for adults with disabilities and traumatic brain injuries, warm water therapy, non-public agency services to children including pediatric OT and PT services, work training/employment services, medical equipment loans, early intervention services for infants and toddlers. Serving the counties of Alpine, Calaveras, El Dorado, Sacramento, San Joaquin, Sutter, Tuolumne, Yolo, Yuba, Amador, Stanislaus, Nevada and Placer, CA.

**6497 Exceed: A Division of Valley Resource Center**
P.O.Box 1773
Perris, CA 92572-1773
951-657-0609
800-423-1227
FAX: 909-657-2277
e-mail: vrctwohip@aol.com
www.exceed-aws.com

*Pattie Robert, Business Development Specialist*
*Mary Morse, Marketing Director*
*Kathy Cooke, Manager*
Our vision is an environment where each client is valued as an individual and is provided the opportunity to reach his/her maximum potential. Our mission is to provide service and advocacy, which creates choices and opportunities, for adults with disabilities to reach their maximum potential..

**6498 Eye Medical Center of Fresno**
Eye Medical Center
1122 S St
Fresno, CA 93721-1498
559-486-5000
emcfresno.com
A private, nonprofit agency offering services such as health, educational, recreational, rehabilitation, employment and counseling to the totally blind, legally blind and visually impaired. The staff includes hundreds of full time workers.

**6499 Fontana Rehabilitation Workshop**
Industrial Support Systems
8333 Almeria Ave
Fontana, CA 92335-3283
909-428-3883
800-755-4755
FAX: 909-428-3835
e-mail: ceo@industrialsupport.org
www.industrial-support.org

*Carole Holt, Executive Director*
*Antonio Diaz, Owner*
The Fontana Rehabilitation Workshop, Inc., through its business divisions is committed to maintaining a stable environment wherein people with disabilities are provided with those services and supports that enable them to overcome barriers to employment and empower them to maximize their employment potential.

**6500 Foothill Vocational Opportunities**
789 N Fair Oaks Ave
Pasadena, CA 91103-3045
626-449-0218
FAX: 626-449-0218
e-mail: info@foothillvoc.org
foothillvoc.org
Foothill Vocational Opportunities maximizes the personal and economic potential of disabled individuals by creating meaningful employment opportunities. Foothill provides our clients and thier families with the tools they need to live fuller, richer lives, bringing a sense of inclusion and dignity to a chronically marginalized and underdeserved group of people.

**6501 Fred Finch Youth Center**
3800 Coolidge Ave
Oakland, CA 94602-3399
510-482-2244
FAX: 510-530-2047
e-mail: barbarabautista@fredfinch.org
fredfinch.org

*Vonza Thompson, President/CEO*
*Kathie Jacobson, COO*
*Ed Hsu, CFO*
*Sue Guy, Chief Human Resource Officer*
Seeks to provide a continum of high quality programs for the care and treatment of children, youth, young adults and their families, whose changing needs can best be met by a variety of mental health and social services. The goal is for clients to be professionally served in the least restricitive environment appropriate to their needs so that they may function at their highest potential.

**6502 Gateway Center of Monterey County**
850 Congress Ave
Pacific Grove, CA 93950-4898
831-372-8002
FAX: 831-372-2411
e-mail: info@gatewaycenter.org
gatewaycenter.org

*Stephanie Lyon, Executive Director*
*Mike Price, Chief Financial Officer*
*Desiree Boller, Accounting Assistant*
*Heidy Welch, Human Resources*
Our mission is to be a caring and stimulating environment for the Developmentally Disabled where all people can achieve their individual goals safely and with dignity. Our goal is to continue our

programs and to find new and innovative ways of assisting the developmentally disabled to live in our community in surroundings compatable with their ability to live and work at the highest level possible.

**6503 Gateway Industries: Castroville**
712 Hawthorne Street
Monterey, CA 93940
831-655-8710
888-473-3744
FAX: 83- 64- 653
e-mail: sales@redshift.com
www.redshift.com

Located in the Sand City Industrial Park, it provides vocational training and employment to developmentally disabled adults so they can achieve their vocational potential while also providing quality services to bussiness along the Central Coast. The sheltered work environment assists the employees by increasing their income, improving their work skills and habits, and enabling them to participate in the community.

**6504 Gilroy Workshop**
8855 Murray Ave
Gilroy, CA 95020-3629
408-842-0334
FAX: 408-842-6770

*Kristi Alarid, Manager*
*Sally French, Manager*
Work adjustment and remunerative work programs..

**6505 Glendale Adventist Medical Center**
1509 Wilson Ter
Glendale, CA 91206-4098
818-409-8000
FAX: 818-546-5609
www.glendaleadventist.com/services/rehab

*Kevin Roberts, President/CEO*
*Warren Tetz, Vice President and COO*
*Kelly Turner, Vice President and CFO*
*Judy Blair, Vice President and CNO*
Rehabilitative team is made up of physician specialists, as well as professional and certified staff nurses, thereapists and others who meet regularly to ensure tht each patients progress is carefully planned and closely monitored.

**6506 Glendale Memorial Hospital and Health Center Rehabilitation Unit**
Glendale Memorial Hospital and Health Center
1420 S Central Ave
Glendale, CA 91204-2508
818-502-1900
FAX: 818-409-7688
www.glendalememorialhospital.org

*Catherine M. Pelley, President*
Offers rehabilitation services, occupational therapy, physical therapy, residential services and more for the disabled.

**6507 Goleta Valley Cottage Hospital**
Cottage Health System
351 S Patterson Ave
Santa Barbara, CA 93111-2496
805-967-3411
FAX: 805-681-6437
e-mail: cverkiak@cottagehealthsystem.org
www.sbch.org

*Ronald C. Wreft, President & CEO*
*Rosemary Bray, Clinical Manager*
*Diana Gray Miller, Administrator*
*Betty Jane Petrich, Manager*
A 122-bed acute care hospital was founded in 1966 to serve the growing community of Goleta Valley. Today, we admit more then 2,000 patients a year, see more then 17,000 emergency visits, and welcome nearly 400 newborns to our designated 'Baby Friendly' Birth Center each year. We are also recognized for our Level IV trauma designation. We take great pride in fulfilling our goal of providing each patient with comfortable, personalized care.

**6508 HealthSouth Tustin Rehabilitation Hospital**
Health South Corporation
14851 Yorba St
Tustin, CA 92780-2925
714-832-9200
healthsouth.com

*Diana Hanyak, Chief Executive Officer*
*Rodric Bell, Medical Director*
*Lindsey Barrett, Director of Case Management*
*John Bowie, Director, Pharmacy*
HealthSouth Tustin Rehabilitation Hospital is part of the HealthSouth Corporation, the nation's largest provider of rehabilitative healthcare services, we are the only facility of its kind in Orange County. Fully accredited by the Joint Commission on Accreditation of Healthcare Organizations (JACHO) we provide inpatient and outpatient care designed to meed individual needs of patients and their families.

**6509 Hi-Desert Medical Center**
6601 White Feather Rd
Joshua Tree, CA 92252-760
760-366-3711
hdmc.org

*Lionel Chadwick, Chief Executive Officer*
*Tom Duda, Chief Financial Officer*
*Judy Austin, Chief Operating Officer & Chief Nursing Officer*
*Barbara Staresinic, Director, Human Resources*
Postacute rehabilitation program.

**6510 Home of the Guiding Hands**
Ste 200
1825 Gillespie Way
El Cajon, CA 92020-0501
619-938-2850
FAX: 619-938-3055
e-mail: info@guidinghands.org
guidinghands.org

*Susan Havens, President*
*Joan Stein, Vice President*
*Michael Harris, Treasurer*
*Mark Klaus, Executive Director*
The mission of Home og the Guiding Hands is to provide quality services, training and advocacy for people with developmental disabilities, their families, and others who will benefit.

**6511 Hospital of the Good Samaritan Acute Rehabilitation Unit**
1225 Wilshire Blvd
Los Angeles, CA 90017-1901
213-977-2121
800-366-8338
FAX: 213-482-2770
e-mail: info@goodsam.org
goodsam.org

*Andrew B Leeka, President and CEO*
*Charles T. Munger, Chairman*
Physicians, researchers and staff are united by a common mission: to foster growth into one of the most comprehensive medical centers in the West. Services offered include: cardiology and cardiovascular services, neurosciences, movement disorders and Parkinsons disorder, wound care center and transfusion-medicine and surgery center.

**6512 Innovative Rehabilitation Services**
Hacienda La Puente Unified School District
14101 E. Nelson Avenue
La Puente, CA 91746
626-934-2920
FAX: 626-934-2900
e-mail: info@hlpusd.k12.ca.us
www.hlpusd.k12.ca.us

*Matthew Smith, Site Administrator*
*George Stransky, Counselor*
*Crystal Ontiveros, Counselor*
Provides innovative student-centered learning opportunities and support services to a diverse population that enable individuals to achieve thier goals as lifelong learners, productive workers and effective communicators.

**6513 Janus of Santa Cruz**
Ste 150
200 7th Ave
Santa Cruz, CA 95062-4669
831-462-1060
866-526-8772
janussc.org

*Rod Libbey, Executive Director*
*Bill Morris, Medical Director*
*Margie Storms, Clinical Director*
*Chris Storms, Intake Manager*
A private not-for-profit corporation, licensed by the state of California. The Janus Clinic has a 3 year accreditation by the Council on Accreditation for Health Care Facilities.

**6514 John Muir Medical Center Rehabilitation Services, Therapy Center**
1601 Ygnacio Valley Rd
Walnut Creek, CA 94598-3122
925-939-3000
FAX: 925-308-8944
www.jmmdhs.com

*Jane A. Willemsen, President and CEO*
*Helen Doughty, Librarian*
A 324-bed acute care facility that is designated as the only trauma center for Contra Costa County and portions of Solano County. Recognized as one of the region's premier healthcare providers, areas of specialty include high-and low-risk obstetrics, orthopedics, neurosciences, cardiac care and cancer care. The campus is accredited by the Joint Commission on Accreditation of Healthcare Organizations (JCAHO), a national surveyor of quality patient care.

**6515 Kindred Hospital-La Mirada**
14900 E. Imperial Hwy
La Mirada, CA 90638-2172
562-944-1900
FAX: 562-906-3455
TTY:800-735-2922
www.kindredlamirada.com

*April Myers, Administrator*
*Adam Darvish, Executive Director*
Committed to the delivery of high quality care in a cost-effective manner to enable us to become 'a model of excellence' in Long-Term Acute Care. Committed to treat our patients and families with dignity and respect, in the same manner we would want to be treated.

**6516 King's View Work Experience Center- Atwater**
100 Airpark Rd
P.O. Box 774
Atwater, CA 95301-0774
209-357-0321
FAX: 209-357-0398
www.kingsview.org

*Leon Hoover, Chief Executive Officer*
*Stephen Reclusado, Chief Financial Officer*
*Sue Essman, Director of Human Resources*
*Jeff Gorski, Director of Business Development*
The primary mission of the Kings View Work Experience Center (KVWEC) is to serve people who have developmental disabilities. We believe in the dignity and worth of each person and in their right to rehabilitation, education and community integration. It is Kings View's aim to provide quality services to people who need assistance in the development of social, vocational and independent living skills.

**6517 LaPalma Intercommunity Hospital**
7901 Walker St
La Palma, CA 90623-1764
714-670-7400
e-mail: ssalas@primehealthcare.com
www.lapalmaintercommunityhospital.com

*Virg Narbutas, Regional CEO*
*Sami Shoukair, Chief Medical Officer*
*Helene Saad, Chief of Staff*
*Marlene Pritchard, Community Member*
Lapalma Intercommunity Hospital endeavors to provide comprehensive, quality healthcare in a convenient, compassionate and cost effective manner. Lapalma is consistenty at the forefront of evolving national healthcare reform. Our organization provides an innovative and integrated healthcare delivery system. We remain ever cognizant of our patient's needs and desires for high quality affordable healthcare.

**6518 Learning Services of Northern California**
10855 De Bruin Way
Gilroy, CA 95020-9315
408-848-4379
888-419-9955
FAX: 866-491-7396
www.learningservices.com

*Kayree Shreeve, Administrator*
*Jill Winegardner, Regional Program Director*
Located on 10 acres of ranchland in rural Santa Clara Valley, our Gilroy Program offers treatment, structure, and support in a spacious, campus-based living environment. Sharing living residences are complimented by a treatment and recreation facility for individuals who require intensive support.

**6519 Learning Services: Morgan Hill**
10855 De Bruin Way
Gilroy, CA 95020-9315
408-848-4379
888-419-9955
FAX: 866-491-7396
www.learningservices.com

*Jill Winegardner, Regional Program Director*
*Kayree Shreeve, Administrator*
Located in the quaint rural town within walking distance from the old main street of Morgan Hill. Our Morgan Hill program offers the convenience and amenities of small-town living within the supportive community of Morgan Hill.

**6520 Learning Services: Supported Living Programs**
10855 De Bruin Way
Gilroy, CA 95020-9315
408-848-4379
888-419-9955
FAX: 866-491-7396
www.learningservices.com

*Jill Winegardner, Regional Program Director*
*Kayree Shreeve, Administrator*
We offer a variety of diverse and stimulating environments for people with different needs, capabilities and personal goals. Within comfortable, homelike, age-appropriate settings we provide the structure and support necessary to ensure the richest possible quality of life. Program offered in both Northern and Southern facilities of California

**6521 Leon S Peters Rehabilitation Center**
2823 Fresno St
Fresno, CA 93721-1324
559-459-6000
www.communitymedical.org/crmc.htm

*Susan Abundis, Chairwoman*
*Ralph P. Garcia, Secretary*
*Jack Chubb, CEO*
Community's flagship hospital that offers world class specialized critical care with the area's only stroke unit with 24-hour vascular neurology and neurosurgery coverage and a team of specially trained stroke nurses. The world's first G4 CyberKnife. The table Mountain Rancheraia Level 1 Trauma Center. The Leon S. Peters burn center. The region's only perinatology program for high rish pregnancies and deliveries. The Da-Vinci robotic surgical system, and 3 helicopeter landing pads.

**6522 Lion's Blind Center of Diablo Valley, Inc. Lions Center For The Visually Impaired**
175 Alvarado Ave
Pittsburg, CA 94565-4862 925-432-3013
800-750-3937
FAX: 925-432-7014
e-mail: edward.329@comcast.net

*Edward Schroth, Executive Director*
*Peggy Nichols, Executive Director*
A private, nonprofit agency offering services such as health, educational, recreational, rehabilitation, employment and counseling to the totally blind, legally blind and visually impaired. The staff includes two full time workers..

**6523 Lion's Blind Center of Oakland**
2115 Broadway
Oakland, CA 94609-2698 510-450-1580
FAX: 510-654-3603
e-mail: info@lbcenter.org
lbcenter.org

*Michelle Taylor Lagunas, Executive Director/ CEO*
*Christina Easiley, Administrative Manager*
*Scott Blanks, Director of Rehabilitation Services*
*Danette Davis, rientation & Mobility Instructor*
A private nonprofit organization offering services for the totally blind, legally blind, deaf-blind and multihandicapped blind. Services include: professional training, rehabilitation, education, counseling, social work, self help and more. The staff includes 12 full time and 1 part time worker.

**6524 Living Skills Center for the Visually Impaired**
2430 Road 20
San Pablo, CA 94806-5005 510-234-4984
FAX: 510-234-4986
e-mail: info@hcblind.org
www.hcblind.org

*Patricia Williams, Executive Director*
*Patricia Maffei, Program Director*
*Ronald Hideshima, Adaptive Technology Instructor*
*Katie Mazza, Orientation and Mobility Instructor*
A private, nonprofit agency offering services such as independent living skills training, recreational, employment and accessible technology training to the totally blind, legally blind and visually impaired. The staff includes six full time teachers.

**6525 Loma Linda University Orthopedic and Rehabilitation Institute**
25333 Barton Rd
Loma Linda, CA 92354-3123 909-558-6000
FAX: 909-558-0308
www.llu.edu/lluhc/rehabilitation

*Ruthita Fike, CEO*
Offers a full range of clinical programs for both inpatients and outpatient. The specific diagnosis leading to patient admission includes stroke, spinal cord injury, traumatic or anoxic brain damage, amputation, post neurosurgery, chronic neurological disease, Guillain-Barre syndrome, arthritis, multiple trauma or other complex orthopedic problems. The facilities and professional services are comprehensive and ensure that the best care is provided to pediatric and adult patients..

**6526 Manor Care Health Services- Citrus Heights**
7807 Uplands Way
Citrus Heights, CA 95610-7500 916-967-2929
FAX: 916-965-8439
hcr-manorcare.com

*Steven M. Cavanaugh, Chief Financial Officer*
*Paul A. Ormond, Chairman, President and Chief Executive Officer*
The nations leader in skilled nursing and rehabilitation care. Our facility has been serving the Sacramento area for more then 12 years. We are known for our beautiful decor, outstanding rehabilitation staff and loving nursing care. We offer short term rehabilitation, long term skilled nursing care, respite care and post hospital surgical care.

**6527 Manor Care Health Services- Palm Desert**
74350 Country Club Dr
Palm Desert, CA 92260-1608 760-341-0261
FAX: 760-779-1563
hcr-manorcare.com

*Steven M. Cavanaugh, Chief Financial Officer*
*Paul A. Ormond, Chairman, President and Chief Executive Officer*
Centrally located in the Coachella Valley, specializing in skilled nursing whith an emphasis on rehabilitation, post surgery recovery, hospice, alzheimer's care and long term care. In addition, we offer 2 unique service options for the discriminating consumer. Our Arcadia unit offers a specialized Alzheimer's care program in a dedicated secure wing. ManorCare offers rehabilitation services including physical, occupational and speech therapies for those recovering from illness injury or surgery.

**6528 Manor Care Health Services-Fountain Valley**
11680 Warner Ave
Fountain Valley, CA 92708-2513 714-241-9800
FAX: 714-966-1654
hcr-manorcare.com

*Steven M. Cavanaugh, Chief Financial Officer*
*Paul A. Ormond, Chairman, President and Chief Executive Officer*
Provides 24-hour skilled nursing, rehabilitative therapies and specialized Alzheimer's care. Our in-house therapists provide physical, occupational and speech therapies in our rehabilitation area. Our team is goal oriented and focuses on producing positive outcomes for those recovering from illness, injury or surgery. Our respite care program provides a full range of services for a few days, a week or even a season.

**6529 Manor Care Health Services-Hemet**
1717 W Stetson Ave
Hemet, CA 92545-6882
951-925-9171
FAX: 951-925-8186
hcr-manorcare.com

*Steven M. Cavanaugh, Chief Financial Officer*
*Paul A. Ormond, Chairman, President and Chief Executive Officer*
Provides skilled nursing, Rehabilitation services, and specialized Alzheimer's care. In addition we offer short term respite stays for family caregivers that simply need a break from the stress of daily care. Our Arcadia unit staff is specially trained in the care of residents with Alzheimer's disease. The secured unit is designed to provide a soothing and homelike environment while enhancing each resident's remaining abilities.

**6530 Manor Care Health Services-Sunnyvale**
1150 Tilton Dr
Sunnyvale, CA 94087-2440 408-735-7200
FAX: 408-736-8629
hcr-manorcare.com

*Steven M. Cavanaugh, Chief Financial Officer*
*Paul A. Ormond, Chairman, President and Chief Executive Officer*
Our in-house therapists provide physical, occupational and speech therapies in our rehabilitation area. Our team is goal oriented and focuses on producing positive outcomes for those recovering from illness, injury or surgery. Our skilled nursing staff works with our therapy department and dietary department to provide positive wound care programs for patients requiring skin management care.

**6531 Manor Care Health Services-Walnut Creek**
1226 Rossmoor Pkwy
Walnut Creek, CA 94595-2538
925-975-5000
FAX: 925-937-1132
hcr-manorcare.com

*Steven M. Cavanaugh, Chief Financial Officer*
*Paul A. Ormond, Chairman, President and Chief Executive Officer*
Provides luxurious long term care and rehabilitation services. In house therapists provide, physical, occupational and speech

therapies in our rehabilitation area. Our team is goal oriented and focuses on producing positive outcomes for those recovering from illness, injury or surgery. Our years of combined management experience add value to our resident's quality of life.

**6532 Maynord's Chemical Dependency Recovery Centers**
19325 Cherokee Road
Tuolumne, CA 95379-1657
209-928-3737
800-228-8208
FAX: 209-928-1152
maynords.com

*James Berry, Director*

Maynord's Recovery Centers has always been dedicated to the recovery of good people whose lives are being destroyed by alcohol and drugs. Since 1978, Maynord's residential program has helped thousands of people put their lives back together after addiction has taken its toll. Today, Maynord's offers a treatment system over much of the San Joaquin Valley and the San Francisco Bay Area.

**6533 Maynord's Ranch for Men**
19325 Cherokee Road
Tuolumne, CA 95379-1657
209-928-3737
800-228-8208
FAX: 209-928-1152
www.maynords.com

Provides treatment for chemical dependency problems to men. The treatment addresses their recovery through a comprehensive plan created for their individual needs. Also offers a program for women called the Meadows.

**6534 Meadowbrook Manor**
431 West Remington Boulevard
Bolingbrook, IL 60440
630-759-1112
FAX: 630-759-6925
www.meadowbrookmanor.com

Postacute rehabilitation program.

**6535 Meadowview Manor**
41 Crestview Terrace
Bridgeport, WV 26330
304-842-7101
FAX: 304-842-7104
e-mail: info@meadowviewmanor.com
www.meadowviewmanor.com

Provides treatment designed for women that is directed at every important facet of their lives - mentally, physically and spiritually. Clients receive a variety of treatment approaches to facilitate their recovery and a comprehensive treatment plan is created for their individual needs. Issues relating to the cause of addictions are addressed in lectures, one-on-one counseling sessions, group therapy and re entry groups. Also offers a male treatment programs called Maynord's Ranch.

**6536 Memorial Hospital of Gardenia**
1145 W Redondo Beach Blvd
Gardena, CA 90247-3528
310-532-4200
800-782-2288

Postacute rehabilitation program..

**6537 Mercy Medical Group**
Mercy Hospital
3000 Q Street
Sacramento, CA 95816
916-733-3333
www.mymercymedicalgroup.org

Located near the Old Rosevill Hospital. There are several primary care physicians, including Family Practice, Internal Medicine and Pediatrics at this location. Specialty services include Diagnostic Imaging, Laboratory and Mental Health Services.

**6538 Napa County Mental Health Department**
Bldg D
2344 Old Sonoma Rd
Napa, CA 94559-3708
707-253-6188
www.countyofnapa.org

Work hardening and disciplinary programs.

**6539 Napa Valley Support Systems**
Ste 202
650 Imperial Way
Napa, CA 94559-1344
707-253-7490
FAX: 707-253-0115
napavalleysupportservices.org

*Beth Kahiga, Executive Director*
*Heather Jump, Administrative Manager*
*Katy Vanzant, Program Director*
*Emmy Lesko, Program Supervisor*

Work hardening and disciplinary programs.

**6540 North Valley Services**
1040 Washington
Red Bluff, CA 96080-4509
530-527-0407
FAX: 530-527-7091
www.northvalleyservices.org

Provides vocational rehabilitation services, such as job counseling, job training, and work experience, to unemployed and underemployed persons, persons with disabilities.

**6541 Northridge Hospital Medical Center Rehabiltation Medicine**
18300 Roscoe Blvd
Northridge, CA 91328-4167
818-885-8500
FAX: 818-701-7367
www.northridgehospital.org

*Mike L. Wall, President*
*Thomas L. Hedge, Medical Director*
*Joel S. Rosen, Associate Medical Director*
*Alex L. Lin, Managing Director*

A full service, comprehensive rehabilitation program suited to treat patients of all ages who have suffered catastrophic or debilitating injury or illness. The goal of the program is to deliver exceptional patient care to maximise each individual's skills and independence.

**6542 Northridge Hospital Medical Center: Centerfor Rehabilitation Medicine**
18300 Roscoe Blvd
Northridge, CA 91328-4167
818-885-8500
FAX: 818-701-7367
www.northridgehospital.com

*Mike L. Wall, President*
*Thomas L. Hedge, Medical Director*
*Joel S. Rosen, Associate Medical Director*
*Alex L. Lin, Managing Director*

Committed to serving the health needs of our communities with particular attention to the needs of the poor, the disadvantaged, and vulneralbe, and the comfort of the suffering and dying. Catholic Healthcare West has a commitment to quality-quality healthcare services and the promotion of optimal quality of life for all of life.

**6543 Old Adobe Developmental Services**
1301 Rand Street
Suite A
Petaluma, CA 94954-5697
707-763-9807
FAX: 707-763-7708
e-mail: webmaster@oadsinc.org
www.oadsinc.org

*Elizabeth Clary, Executive Director*
*Marie Padgett, Controller*

The mission of Old Adobe to provide opportunities for individuals with developmental challenges to reach thier fullest potentials. Our job at OADS is to find ways for these individuals to find full expression in all parts of their lives. We have a partnership with the Adult Education Department of the Petaluma School District in providing services to persons with developmental challenges. We are funded by the Dept. of Rehabilitation and the Dept. Of Developmental services.

**6544 Old Adobe Developmental Services-Rohnert Park Services (Behavioral)**
5401 Snyder Ln.
Rohnert Park, CA 94928-3124
707-584-5859
FAX: 707-664-8057
www.oadsinc.org

*Elizabeth Clary, Executive Director*
*Helen Gunderson, Administrative Assistant*
The program services are designed to assist individuals who demonstrate basic work skills, to develop social skills and work habits necessary to succeed in supported or competitive employment. Most often individual program services involve working with the client to replace those behavioral excesses that have been a barrier to vocational placement.

**6545 PRIDE Industries**
10030 Foothills Blvd
Roseville, CA 95747-7102
916-788-2100
800-550-6005
FAX: 800-888-0447
e-mail: info@prideindustries.com
prideindustries.com

*Michael Ziegler, President & CEO*
*Bob Selvester, Vice Chair*
*Mike Snegg, Treasurer*
*Tim Yamauchi, Executive Vice President and Chief Financial Officer*
To provide opportunities through employment, training, evaluation and placement maximizing community access, independence and quality of life for people with barriers to employment.

**6546 Pacific Hospital Of Long Beach-Neuro Care Unit**
2776 Pacific Ave
Long Beach, CA 90806-2613
562-997-2000
e-mail: webmaster@phlb.org
www.phlb.org

*Michael D. Drobot, CEO*
*Clark Todd, President*
*Teri Plemmons, Administrative Assistant*
Our mission is to heal with compassion and to perform with distinction. Our vision: to improve the hospital's orthopedic and Spine Center of Excellence. Achieve exceptional financial performance to enhance hospital services. Improve the vertically integrated ancillary, outpatient and inpatient surgery system. Develop a professionally challenging work environment that reflects an agile, peak performance culture.

**6547 Paradise Vally Hospital-South Bay Rehabilitation Center**
2400 E 4th St
National City, CA 91950-2026
619-470-4321
paradisevalleyhospital.org

*Luis Leon, Chief Executive Officer*
*Neerav Jadeja, Administrator*
*Janet Caceres, Chief Financial Officer*
*Gemma Rama-Banaag, Chief Nursing Officer*
South Bay Rehabilitation Center, offers a complete range of treatment for patients with physical disabilities. Our specialized inpatient and outpatient programs are designed to meet each person's individual needs or injuries, with the goal of restoring as much independence as possible and significantly improving their lives.

**6548 Parents and Friends**
350 Cypress St
Fort Bragg, CA 95437-5408
707-964-4940
e-mail: moon@parentsandfriends.org
parentsandfriends.org

*Rick Moon, Executive Director*
*Jessica Dickey, Administrative Assistant*
*Terry Hinkle, Manager,Coastal Support Services*
*Kathy Connell, Bookkeeper*
Parents and Friends provides opportunities for persons with developmental challenges and similar needs to participate fully in our community.

**6549 People Services**
4195 Lakeshore Blvd
Lakeport, CA 95453-6411
707-263-3810
e-mail: idumont@nctac.com
peopleservices.org
Providing an array of services for adults with developmental disabilities and other people with disabilities. Services include supported employment, work services, supported living, personal, social and community training, transportation, specialized individual services and much more.

**6550 Petaluma Recycling Center**
Old Adobe Developmental Services
315 2nd St
Petaluma, CA 94952-4230
707-763-4761
FAX: 707-763-4921
e-mail: davide@oadsinc.org
www.oadsinc.org/petarecycle

*Elizabeth Clary, Executive Director*
Began in 1974; has been one of the major employers of persons with developmental challenges for 26 years; is the primary recycling facility in the growing city of 52,000; accepts over 20 different kinds of recyclables; employs 20-25 persons a day.

**6551 Pomerado Rehabilitation Outpatient Service**
15615 Pomerado Rd
Poway, CA 92064-2405
858-485-6511
FAX: 858-613-4248

*Bob Blake, Director Rehab Services*
*Jonathan Pee, Manager*
A 107-bed acute care hospital. In addition to a round-the-clock Emergency Department, Pomerado offers the area's finest outpaitent surgery center and general medical/surgical services. Pomerado Hospital also is home to a world-class Birth Center and a Level II NICU. Fully JCAHO-accredidted, Pomerado is well-known for offering only private rooms, each with a scenic view of the North Countryside, which enhances the healing atmosphere..

**6552 Pride Industries: Grass Valley**
12451 Loma Rica Dr
Grass Valley, CA 95945-9059
530-477-1832
800-550-6005
FAX: 530-477-8038
e-mail: info@prideindustries.com
prideindustries.com

*Michael Ziegler, President & CEO*
*Bob Selvester, Vice Chair*
*Mike Snegg, Treasurer*
*Tim Yamauchi, Executive Vice President and Chief Financial Officer*
Work adjustment and remunerative work programs. We offer an adult day program as well.

**6553 Rancho Adult Day Care Center**
Rancho Los Amigos Medical Center
7601 Imperial Hwy
Downey, CA 90242-3456
562-401-7111
FAX: 562-401-7991
TTY:562-401-8450
e-mail: radscenter@aol.com
www,rancho.org/ser_adultday

*Valerie Orange, CEO*
*Margaret L Campbell, Research Director*
Provides personal care, social services and a therapeutic program to older adults in order to improve their quality of life. Offers a Clinical Gerontology Service, an Alzheimer's Disease Diagnostic and Treatment Center and a Geriatric Assessment and Rehabilitation Unit..

**6554 Regional Center for Rehabilitation**
2288 Auburn Blvd
Sacramento, CA 95821-1618
916-421-4167
FAX: 916-925-1586

Postacute rehabilitation program..

**6555 Rehabilitation Institute of Santa Barbara**
2415 De La Vina St
Santa Barbara, CA 93105-3819
805-569-8999
FAX: 805-687-3707
risb.org

*Ralph Pollock, President*
*Scott Silic MBA, Vice President Of Operations*
*Cheryl Ellis MD, MHA, VP Medical Services*

A regional rehabilitation system with an acute care hospital at the center, the Institute provides specialized inpatient and outpatient programs for brain injury, spinal cord injury, stroke, work-related injury, chronic pain, orthopedic problems and more. Offers a 46-bed acute-care rehabilitation hospital, a free-standing outpatient center, the brain injury continuum, chronic pain program..

**6556 Rehabilitation Institute of Southern California**
1800 E La Veta Ave
Orange, CA 92866-2902
714-633-7400
FAX: 714-633-4586
e-mail: adults@rio-rehab.com
rio-rehab.com

*Praim S. Singh, Executive Director*
*Carol Reese, Executive Assistant*
*Grace Lee, Administrative Assistant*
*Dana Patton, Personnel Officer*

Outpatient rehabilitation serving physically and disabled children and adults. Child development programs, adult day care for disabled seniors, child care for disabled and non-disabled children, outpatient therapy, aquatics, adult day healthcare, independent living, vocational services, social services, and housing.

**6557 Rubicon Programs**
2500 Bissell Ave
Richmond, CA 94804-1815
510-235-1516
FAX: 510-235-2025
e-mail: rubicon@rubiconpgms.org
www.rubiconprograms.org

*Rob Hope, Director of Economic Empowerment*
*Jane Fischberg, President and Executive Director*
*David Samuels MBA CPA, CFO*
*Kelly Dunn, General Counsel and Director of Legal Services*

Rubicon Programs Inc. helps people and communities build assets to achieve greater independence. Since 1973, Rubicon has built and operated affordable housing and provided employment, job training, mental health, and other supportive services to individuals who have disabilities, are homeless, or are otherwise economically disadvantaged.

**6558 San Bernardino Valley Lighthouse for the Blind**
762 N Sierra Way
San Bernardino, CA 92410-4438
909-884-3121
FAX: 909-884-2965

*Robert Mc Bay, Executive Director*
*Sandra Wood, Administrative Assistant*

Provides training in independent living skills - cooking, mobility and orientation, sewing, Braille and typing. Also, we have classes in macrame, ceramics and basket weaving. Weekly support group and Bible study..

**6559 Santa Clara Valley Blind Center, Inc.**
101 N Bascom Ave
San Jose, CA 95128-1805
408-295-4016
FAX: 408-295-1398
e-mail: info@visionbeyondsight.org
visionbeyondsight.org

*Daniel Steve Mahan, Ceo*
*Judy Arvidson, Coo*

SCVBC's mission is to increase the confidence, independence, and quality of life of the blind and visually impaired through educational, recreational, and rehabilitative programs.

**6560 Scripps Memorial Hospital: Pain Center**
9888 Genesee Ave
La Jolla, CA 92037-1205
858-626-4123
www.scrippshealth.org

*Gary G. Fybel, Chief Executive, Senior Vice President*
*A. Brent Eastman, Chief Medical Officer & Corporate Sr. Vice President*

Offers both inpatient and outpatient programs including: physical activity management, individual pain management, group therapy, medication adjustment, pain control classes, occupational therapy, biofeedback training, family counseling, vocational and leisure counseling and recreational therapy.

**6561 Sharp Coronado Hospital**
250 Prospect Pl
Coronado, CA 92118-1999
619-522-3600
sharp.com

*Marcia Hall, CEO*
*Mark Tamsen, Chairman*
*Tom Smisek, Vice Chairman*
*Dan Gensler, Secretary*

Providing medical and surgical care, intensive care, sub-acute and long-term care, rehabilitation therapies and emergency services in a peaceful setting is part of our live+heal+grow philosophy. We are one of the county's few community-owned hospitals and are proud of our history of providing convenient , award-winning heath care to Coronado and San Diego.

**6562 Shriners Hospitals For Children-Northern California**
2900 Rocky Point Dr.
Tampa, Fl 33607
813-281-0300
e-mail: patientreferrals@shrinenet.org
www.shrinershq.org/hospitals

*John McCabe, Executive Vice President*

The only hospital in the Shriners system that houses facilities for treatment of all 3 Shriner specialties -spinal cord injuries, orthopaedic, and burns. The hospital features 80 patient beds, 9 parent apartments, 5 state-of-the-art operating rooms, a high-tech Motion Analysis lab, and an entire floor devoted to research.

**6563 Shriners Hospitals for Children: Los Angeles**
2900 Rocky Point Dr.
Tampa, Fl 33607
813-281-0300
e-mail: patientreferrals@shrinenet.org
www.shrinershq.org

*John McCabe, Executive Vice President*

Shriners Hospitals for Children: Los Angeles, treats children under age 18 with burn scars, orthopedic conditions, cleft lip and palate and limb deficiencies at no cost to the patient or their families.

**6564 Society for the Blind**
1238 S Street
Sacramento, CA 95818-3256
916-452-8271
FAX: 916-492-2483
e-mail: frontdesk@societyfortheblind.org
societyfortheblind.org

*William Carter, President*
*Bryce McAnally, Vice President*
*Gary M. Orr, Secretary*
*Dawn Cornelius, Treasurer/CFO*

A private, local nonprofit organization providing blind and visually impaired people with the training supplies and support they need to live independent, productive and fulfilled lives with limited vision. Services include the Low Vision Clinic, Braille classes, computer training, support groups, living skills instruction, mobility training and the Products for Independence Store.

**6565 Solutions at Santa Barbara: Transitional Living Center**
1135 N Patterson Ave
Santa Barbara, CA 93111-1113 805-683-1995
FAX: 805-683-4793
winwaysrehab.com

*Sue Hannigan, Director*
Postacute rehabilitation program. Short-term transitional living program for individuals with traumatic brain injury, stroke, aneurysm and other neurological disorders.

**6566 St. John's Pleasant Valley Hospital Neuro Care Unit**
2309 Antonio Ave
Camarillo, CA 93010-1414 805-389-5800
shw.org

*Jerry Conway, President*
*Maureen M. Malone, Administrator*
*Raye Burkhardt, Vice President and Chief Nursing Officer*
Houses 82 acute-care beds, a 99-bed extended care unit, and the only hyperbaric medicine unit in Ventura County. Employ's 1,800 people and count 250 active medical staff.

**6567 St. John's Regional Medica Center- Industrial Therapy Center**
1600 N Rose Ave
Oxnard, CA 93030-3723 805-988-2850
www.stjohnshealth.org

*Gudrun Moll, Vice President and Chief Nursing Officer*
A non-profit health care facility offering multi-disciplinary programs for pain management and work hardening, as well as physical and occupational therapy.

**6568 Sub-Acute Saratoga Hospital**
13425 Sousa Ln
Saratoga, CA 95070-4663 408-378-8875
FAX: 408-378-7419
subacutesaratoga.com

*Michael Zarcone, President & CEO*
*Paul Quintana, Medical Director*
*Milton Wheeler, NHA Administrator*
*Bob Opp, Director of Nursing*
Dedicated to the fulfillment of human needs, desires, and wishes in illness and in health. The cohesiveness of caring in a family community of staff, patients, and their loved ones. The celebration of each unique life through their therapeutic journey, while preserving their individual spirit. The achievement of advanced medical expertise, knowledge, and skill given with the human touch of caring toward the ultimate goal: enhancing the healing process from acute illness to the joy of going home.

**6569 Synergos Neurological Center: Hayward**
27200 Calaroga Ave
Hayward, CA 94545-4383 510-264-4000
FAX: 510-264-4007
strosehospital.org

*Mak Nakayama, Interim President and Chief Executive Officer*
*John Davini, Director, Human Resources*
*Pamela A. Russo, Executive Director, Foundation & Marketing*
*Tracey Talley, Interim Chief Financial Officer*
Postacute rehabilitation program.

**6570 Synergos Neurological Center: Mission Hills**
27200 Calaroga Ave
Hayward, CA 94545-4383 510-264-4000
FAX: 510-264-4007
www.strosehospital.org

*Mak Nakayama, Interim President and Chief Executive Officer*
*John Davini, Director, Human Resources*
*Pamela A. Russo, Executive Director, Foundation & Marketing*
*Tracey Talley, Interim Chief Financial Officer*
For over 30 years, St. Rose Hospital Rehabilitation Services Department has helped thousands of patients recover from illness and injury through the help of our specially trained therapists. These therapists have been trained in specific rehabilitative areas such as physical, occupational, and speech therapies.

**6571 Temple Community Hospital**
235 N Hoover St
Los Angeles, CA 90004-3672 213-382-7252
FAX: 213-382-7252
e-mail: info@templecommunityhospital.com
templecommunityhospital.com

The mission of Temple Community Hospital is to improve the quality of health in our community and to provide necessary hospital services for those individuals requiring such care.

**6572 The ARC Of San Diego-ARROW Center**
3030 Market Street
San Diego, CA 92102-3297 619-685-1175
FAX: 619-234-3759
arc-sd.com

*David W. Schneider, President & CEO*
*Melanie McCoy, Area Director*
*Matt Mouer, Director*
*Anthony J. DeSalis, Executive Vice President & COO*
The ARC of San Diego will be the premier provider of services to persons with disabilities. Arc-SD will be an advocate for diversity of opportunities, enhancing individual life choices as a member of the community. Our values: Everyone will be be treated equally, without prejudice and with respect. Will provide Quality Services and Supports with a well trained and caring staff. State of the art equipment and methods. A willingness to innovate and collaborate.

**6573 The ARC Of San Diego-East County Training Center**
1374 E Lexington Ave
El Cajon, CA 92019-2312 619-444-9417
FAX: 619-234-3759
arc-sd.com

*Dwight Stratton, Chairman*
*Monica Peralta, Area Director*
*Jerry Wechsler, 1st Vice Chairman*
*Gerald Hansen, Secretary/Treasurer*
Work adjustment and remunerative work programs.

**6574 The ARC Of San Diego-Rex Industries**
9575 Aero Dr
San Diego, CA 92123-1803 760-471-0250
800-748-5575
FAX: 858-715-3788

*Gary Luce, Operations Manager*
Offers many different programs including: North County Parent/Infant Program which is an educational program for children, birth to three years who are showing delays in development or who are at risk for developmental delays. The Adult Development Center is a program for adults, eighteen and over, with a developmental disability in the severe to profound range. The program focuses on self-help, communication, daily living and pre-vocational skills. Other programs are available..

**6575 Tunnell Center for Rehab**
1359 Pine St
San Francisco, CA 94109-4807 415-673-8405
kindredhealthcare.com

*Mary R., Activities Assistant*
*Kristen W., Health and Rehabilitation Center Executive Director*
The Tunnell Center for Rehabilitation and Healthcare accomodates 178 residents. We are dedicated to short-term complex medical and rehabilitative care. Using a holistic care management approach we work with residents who have suffered debilitating injury or illness, and who need comprehensive nursing and rehabilitation services to achieve their highest practicable level of functional ability and independence.

**6576 Ukiah Valley Association for Habilitation**
Ukiah, CA 95482-689
707-468-8824
FAX: 707-468-9149
TTY:800-735-2929
www.uvah.org

*Pamela Jensen, Executive Director*
*Kris Vipond, Business Manager*
*Janeen Saunders, Director*
*Connie Diamond, Employment Training Specialist*
Work adjustment and suppoted employment and social and community services.

**6577 Valley Center for the Blind**
2491 W Shaw Avenue
Suite 124
Fresno, CA 93711-3331
559-222-4088
FAX: 559-222-4844
e-mail: info@valleycenterblind.org
www.valleycenterblind.org

*Bud Breslin, Executive Director*
*Millie Marshall, Marriage Family Therapist*
*Saramarie Katich, Office Mngr/Program Director*
*Connie Parrick, Secretary*
A private, nonprofit organization that offers educational, health, recreational and professional training services to the totally blind, legally blind or severely visually impaired.

**6578 Villa Esperanza Services**
2060 East Villa Street
Pasadena, CA 91107
626-449-2919
FAX: 626-449-2850
www.villaesperanzaservices.org

*Vicky Castillo, CFO*
*Kelly White, Chief Executive Officer*
*Aaron Kitzman, MA, MFT, Vice President Adult Programs*
*Gioia Pastre, Vice President of Development & Public Relation*
Serving disabled infants to seniors in a school, adult day program, adult work program and residences and adult day health care program and care management program.

**6579 Village Square Nursing And Rehabilitation Center**
Kindred Healthcare, Inc.
1586 W San Marcos Blvd
San Marcos, CA 92078-4019
760-471-2986
www.villagesquarerehab.com
Accomodates 118 residents offering spacious private and semi-private rooms. We are Medicare and Medi-Cal certified and contracted with most managed care insurance groups.

**6580 Vista Center for the Blind & Visually Impaired**
2470 El Camino Real, Ste 107
Palo Alto, CA 94306-1715
650-858-0202
800-660-2009
FAX: 650-858-0214
e-mail: info@vistacenter.org
www.vistacenter.org

*Pam Brandin, Executive Director*
*Meg Faville, Administrative Services Manager*
Private nonprofit agency that serves the visually impaired in the San Mateo, Santa Clara, San Benito and Santa Cruz Counties with offices in Palo Alto and Santa Cruz. Offers Low Vision Evaluations, mobility training, daily living skills training, social services, counseling, support groups, computer training, other rehabilitation services, and a store.

**6581 Winways at Orange County**
7732 E Santiago Canyon Rd
Orange, CA 92869-1829
714-771-5276
FAX: 714-771-1452
winwaysrehab.com

*Pamela Kauss, Director*
The program offers clients highly personalized, comprehensive programs to meet the needs of individuals with traumatic brain injury, stroke, tumors, aneurysm, post concussive syndrome or other neurological disorders. Winways also has a special program that provides services to Spanish speaking clients, called Contigo Adelante with materials in Spanish, and Spanish speaking interpreters to assist in the therapy process.

## Colorado

**6582 Capron Rehabilitation Center**
Penrose Hospital/ St. Francis Healthcare System
2222 N Nevada Ave
Colorado Springs, CO 80907-6819
719-776-5000
penrosestfrancis.org

*Margaret Sabin, President & CEO*
*Nate Olson, Chief Executive Officer*
*Jameson Smith, Chief Operating Officer & Executive Vice President*
*Jeff Oram-Smith, Chief Medical Officer*
Southern Colorado's most complete inpatient and outpatient rehabilitation center.

**6583 Cerebral Palsy of Colorado**
801 Yosemite St.
Denver, CO 80230
303-691-9339
FAX: 303-691-0846
www.cpco.org

*Judith I Ham, CEO*
*James Reuter, Chairman of the Board*
*Penfield Tate, Vice Chairman*
*Kathy Higgins, Treasurer*
Provides services for children birth-5 years, employment services for adults, information and referral, donation pickup and cell phone/ink cartridge recycling services.

**6584 Cherry Hills Health Care Center**
Kindred
3575 S Washington St
Englewood, CO 80110-3807
303-789-2265
www.cherryhillshc.com
Accomodates 92 residents. We serve Medicare, Medicaid, managed-care and private pay clients. Our 2 story facility has a home-like environment with a dining room and a day room one each floor. Our short-term rehab unit was designed for patients who have been in the hospital and need continued intensive nursing care or rehabilitation before returning home.

**6585 Community Hospital Back and Conditioning Clinic**
1060 Orchard Ave
Grand Junction, CO 81501-2997
970-243-3400
800-621-0926
FAX: 970-856-6510

*Amy Hibberd, Executive Director*
*David Scherman, Manager*
Post-accute rehabilitation program .

**6586 Laradon Hall Society for Exceptional Children and Adults**
5100 Lincoln St
Denver, CO 80216-2056
303-296-2400
866-381-2163
FAX: 303-296-4012
laradon.org

*Frank Lucero, Executive Director*
*Annie Green, Deputy Director*
*Corey Kala, Director Financial Management and Information Technology*
*Paul Durack, Director of General Services*
Laradon provides educational, vocational and residential services to children and adults with developmental disabilities and other special needs. Laradon was founded in 1948. It is among the largest and most comprehensive service providers in Colorado.

**6587 Learning Services: Bear Creek**
7201 W Hampden Ave
Lakewood, CO 80227-5305
303-989-6660
888-419-9955
e-mail: lengland@learningservices.com
learningservices.com

*Susan Snow, Director of Admissions*
Supported living program for persons with acquired brain injury.

**6588 MOSAIC In Colorado SpringsMOSAIC**
888 W. Garden of the Gods Road
Ste 100
Colorado Springs, CO 80907-6251
719-380-0451
FAX: 719-380-7055
e-mail: mosaic_cosprings@mosaicinfo.org
www.mosaicincoloradosprings.org

*Tom Maltais, Executive Director*
Mosaic in Colorado Springs provides a variety of services to assist adults and families in achieving positive goals. Services to persons with intellectual disabilities include community living options, vocational training and supported employment, spiritual growth and personal development options, and day programs habilitation and community participation.

**6589 Manor Care Nursing and Rehabilitation Center: Boulder**
Manor Care Ohio
2800 Palo Pkwy
Boulder, CO 80301-1540
303-440-9100
FAX: 303-440-9251
www.hcrmanorcare.com

*Steven M. Cavanaugh, Chief Financial Officer*
*Paul A. Ormond, Chairman, President and Chief Executive Officer*
150 bed center offers a full spectrum of nursing care and rehabilitation. This includes our Arcadia Special Care Unit for Alzheimer's patients. Specialized unit for post acute skilled nursing care. Physical and massage therapies. And a 48 bed upscale Heritage unit offering additional amenities and furnishings.

**6590 Manor Care Nursing: Denver**
290 S Monaco Pkwy
Denver, CO 80224-1105
303-355-2525
FAX: 303-333-6960
www.hcrmanorcare.com

*Steven M. Cavanaugh, Chief Financial Officer*
*Paul A. Ormond, Chairman, President and Chief Executive Officer*
Our center has delveloped a reputation for its luxurious environment, comprehensive rehabilitation service and focus on quality care. A wide range of individual and group activities and many gracious amenities create the finest combination of elegance and professional skilled nursing care. Arcadia, our special care unit for persons with Alzheimer's disease and related memory impairments, promotes independence and preserves dignity within a safe and secure environment.

**6591 Mediplex of Colorado**
8451 Pearl St
Thornton, CO 80229-4804
303-288-3000
FAX: 303-286-5136
e-mail: info@vhdenver.com
www.northvalleyrehab.com

*Dianne Chartier, Chief Executive Officer*
Our programs and services help each patient along the road to recovery toward our ultimate aim; the greatest possible restoration of the individual's self-esteem, ability to set goals, and self-sufficiency. Also offer specialized acute inpatient rehabilitative services, including special programs in Trauma Rehabilitation.

**6592 Platte River Industries**
490 Bryant St
Denver, CO 80204-4808
303-825-0041
FAX: 303-825-0564
e-mail: pri01_lil@attglobal.net

*Bob Smith, Executive Director*
Postacute rehabilitation facility and program..

**6593 Pueblo Diversified Industries**
2828 Granada Blvd
Pueblo, CO 81005-3198
800-466-8393
FAX: 719-564-3407
e-mail: pdihs@qwest.net
www.pdipueblo.net

*Karen K Lillie, President & CEO*
*Robin Forbes, Director Human Services*
*Tom Drolshagen, Chief Operating Officer*
*Tom Denslow, Manager, Human Resources*
A place where people can turn limitations into opportunities. People can experience the independence, pride and self worth of securing and maintaining a job.

**6594 SHALOM Denver**
2498 W 2nd Ave
Denver, CO 80223-1007
303-623-0251
FAX: 303-620-9584
shalomdenver.com

*Arnie Kover, Disability and Employment Services Director*
*Sara Leeper, Coordinator of Client Services*
*Vicky Brittain, Mailing Business Manager*
*Bari Belinsky, Work Services Manager*
SHALOM Denver provides employment, training, and job placement opportunities to people with disabilities, resettled immigrants, and people moving from welfare to work.

**6595 SPIN Early Childhood Care & Education Cntr**
1333 Elm Ave
Canon City, CO 81212-4431
719-275-0550
www.starpointco.com/spin

*Diane Trujillo, Manager*
SPIN center is a fully inclusive non-discriminating community early childhood program, offering a variety of schedule choices for families. The philosophy of the SPIN program is to promote each child's growth and development. Special attention is given to cognitive, physical, speech language and social-emotional growth. Staff is specifically trained to facilitate and prepare environments that promote exploration, key experiences, creativity and self-expression..

**6596 Schaefer Enterprises**
500 26th St
Greeley, CO 80631-8427
970-353-0662
FAX: 970-353-2779
e-mail: schaefenterprises@comcast.net
schaeferenterprises.com

*Valorie Randall, Executive Director*
*Alex Witt, Executive Assistant*
*Veronica Griego, Production Director*
Schaefer Enterprises, Inc., located in Greely, Colorado, is a vaulable community resource that has been fulfilling the outsourcing needs of businesses in Weld County and outlying areas since 1952.

**6597 Spalding Rehab Hospital West Unit**
150 Spring St
Morrison, CO 80465
303-697-4334
FAX: 303-697-0570

Postacute rehabilitation program.OUT SO BUSINESS.

## Connecticut

**6598 ACES/ACCESS Inclusion Program**
60 United Dr
North Haven, CT 06473-3218
203-234-1334
FAX: 203-234-1369
e-mail: conukwugha@aces.k12.ct.us
www.aces.k12.ct.us

*Cheryl Saloom, Director*
Provides a person centered planning approach for integrated employment, volunteer community based opportunities for adults who have developmental disabilities..

**6599 Apria Healthcare**
26220 Enterprise Court
Lake Forest, CA 92630-1015
800-277-4288
e-mail: Patient_Satisfaction@Apria.com
www.apria.com

*Lisa M. Getson, Executive Vice President, Government Relations and Corporate Complianc*
*Peter Reynolds, Chief Accounting Officer and Controller*
*Daniel E. Greenleaf, Chief Executive Officer, Coram Specialty Infusion Services*
*Dena R. Parker, Chief Financial Officer*
Provides a broad range of high quality and cost effective specialty infusion therapies and related services to patients in their homes throughout the Northeastern United States. Offer home infusion antibiotic therapy, quality pharmacy services, skilled nursing services and related support services.

**6600 Arc Of Meriden-Wallingford, Inc.**
200 Research Parkway
Meriden, CT 06450
203-237-9975
FAX: 203-639-0946
e-mail: info@mwsinc.net
www.mwsinc.org

*Pamela Fields, Executive Director*
*Barry Sheftel, Board President*
*Robert Fitzgerald, Financial Director*
*Diane Morra, Director of Program Services*
A membership agency that provides comprehensive, full-service, community-based opportunities for people with disabilities. Guided by over 120 community members and an active Board of Directors, the Arc always has its focus on improving the lives of people with disabilities. The Arc of Meriden-Wallingford offers advocacy and assistance to our members along with advocating for the rights and choices of people with disabilities in our community.

**6601 Arc of the Farmington Valley**
P.O.Box 1099
225 Commerce Dr
Canton, CT 06019-1099
860-693-6662
FAX: 860-693-8662
e-mail: rcipolla@favarh.org
favarh.org

*Stephen E. Morris, Business Relations Manager*
Serving over 300 mentally retarded adults through a comprehensive program of residential and support services. These include three group homes, three apartments, competitive and supported employment options, a day program for mentally retarded seniors, community experience day services for severe and profoundly disabled adults, recreation and leisure services, advocacy, transportation, case management, in-home respite and other support services.

**6602 Connecticut Subacute Corporation**
19 Tuttle Pl
Middletown, CT 06457-1881
860-347-6300
FAX: 860-347-2446
www.cpl-usa.com

*Evan K Lyle, Managed Care Director*
*Cheri Kauset, Corporate Rep.*
Specializes in subacute medical and rehabilitation programming. The strength of our system is in its' ability to service a broad range of clinical and psychosocial needs which enable each individual to attain his/her optimal potential. Programming includes neurological and orthopedic rehabilitation, post-surgical and wound care management, intravenous therapy, pulmonary rehabilitation including ventilator services, and long term care..

**6603 Datahr Rehabilitation Institute**
4 Berkshire Blvd
Bethel, CT 06801-1001
203-775-4700
888-8DA-TAHR
FAX: 203-775-4688
abilitybeyonddisability.com

*Thomas Fanning, CEO*
Providers of comprehensive rehabilitation services with a history of nearly 5 decades of service. This institute is recognized as a leading resource in meeting the needs of those disabled by illness, injury or developmental disorders in Connecticut and New York. A team of rehabilitation and health care professionals offering career development, residential services, supported employment, volunteer services, occupational therapy, day activities and more.OUT OF ORDER.

**6604 Eastern Blind Rehabilitation Center**
810 Vermont Avenue
Washington, DC 20420
202-461-7600
800-273-8255
www1.va.gov/blindrehab

*Eric K. Shinseki, Secretary of Veterans Affairs*
*W. Scott Gould, Deputy Secretary of Veterans Affairs*
*John R. Gingrich, Chief of Staff*
*Will A. Gunn, General Counsel*
Provides residential rehabilitation services to eligible legally blind veterans in the Northeast and Middle Atlantic portions of the country. Referral applications by Veterans Administration Medical Centers and Outpatient Clinics in the geographical area served by the Blind Rehabilitation Center.

**6605 FAVRAH Senior Adult Enrichment Program**
23 W Avon Rd
Avon, CT 06001
860-674-8839
FAX: 860-676-0275

*Nancy Ralston, Manager*
Provides remunerative work. Post acute rehabilitation programs and facility.

**6606 Gaylord Hospital**
P.O.Box 400
Wallingford, CT 06492-7048
203-284-2800
866-429-5673
FAX: 203-284-2894
TTY: 203-284-2700
e-mail: lcrispino@gaylord.org
www.gaylord.org

*James Cullen, President*
Works to restore ability and build courage. Offers rehabilitation care with one goal in mind: to help patients return to their homes, communities and jobs.

**6607 Hockanum Greenhouse**
Hockanum Industry
290 Middle Tpke
Storrs Mansfield, CT 06268-2908
860-429-6697
FAX: 860-429-7496
hockanumindustries.org

*Christopher Campbell, Manager*
*Beth Chaty, Director*
*Betsy Treiber, Director*
A non profit agency that strives to provide gainful employment, training, support and retirement services for developmentally disabled individuals through the dignity of work, community interaction and structured activities..

**6608 Kuhn Employment Oppurtunities**
P.O.Box 941
Meriden, CT 06450
203-235-2583
860-347-5843
www.kuhngroup.org

*Robert L Stephens, Executive Director*
*Beth Fisher, Director of Programs*
*Jerry Brennan, Director of Finance and Administration*
*Erin Gasparini, Senior Program Manager*
Kuhn is committed to developing quality skill enhancement programs which provide meaningful employment for persons with disabilities so that they will become independentm gain self-esteem, and be accepted by the community. Our vision is that all individuals have the ability to fully participate in the community through work. Kuhn believes that all participants have a right to integrated community employment.

**6609 Norwalk Hospital Section Of Physical Medicine And Rehabilitation**
34 Maple Street
Norwalk, CT 06856
203-852-2000
FAX: 800-789-4584
e-mail: marketing@norwalkhealth.org
www.norwalkhosp.org

*Daniel DeBarba, President and CEO*
*Thomas Ayoub, Chief of Medical Staff*
*Paul Gagne, Assistant Chief of Medical Staff*
*Mark Gudis, Managing Director*
A 25 bed inpatient Rehabilitation Unit. This CARF and JCAHO accredidted rehab unit is located on the 8th floor of Norwalk Hospital. The focus of the rehab unit is to restore lost function and assist patients in returning to the community. Who have recently experienced a life changing medical event. The progam is tailored to meet individual therapy needs and address activities of daily living. Family and caregiver participation in the program is welcomed and encouraged.

**6610 Rehabilitation Associates, Inc.**
1931 Black Rock Tpke
Fairfield, CT 06825-3506
203-384-8681
FAX: 203-384-0956
e-mail: info@rehabassocinc.com
www.rehabilitationassociatesinc.com

*Carol Landsman, Director*
A comprehensive outpatient rehabilitation facility offering physical therapy, occupational therapy, speech-language pathology, clinical social work services and nutritional services to all age groups. Facility locations in Fairfield, Stratford, Milford, Shelton and Westport.

**6611 Reliance House**
40 Broadway
Norwich, CT 06360-5702
860-887-6536
FAX: 860-885-1970
reliancehouse.org

*David Burnett, Executive Director*
*Carrie Dyer, Chief Operating Officer*
*Linda Smith, CFO*
*Kerry Lee, Clinical Director*
A residential vocational and recreational support network. An active and productive clubhouse where people with mental illness can gain skills, strength and self-esteem.

**6612 Yale New Haven Health System-Bridgeport Hospital**
789 Howard Avenue
New Haven, CT 06519
203-384-3000
www.yalenewhavenhealth.org

*Marna P. Borgstrom, President and CEO*
*Richard D'Aquila, Executive Vice President*
*Peter N. Herbert, MD, Senior VP, Medical Affairs*
*Kevin Myatt, Senior VP of Human Resources*
Medical services are provided by physicians who are specialists in physical medicine and rehabilitation. The physical therapy department provides a variety of services and utilizes sophisticated modalities to restore and reinforce physical abilities.

## Delaware

**6613 Alfred I DuPont Hospital for Children**
Division of Rehabilitation
P.O.Box 269
Wilmington, DE 19899-269
302-651-4000
888-533-3543
FAX: 302-651-4055
e-mail: infodupont@nemours.org
www.nemours.org

The hospital is a division of Nemours, which operates one of the nations largest subspecialty group practices devoted to pediatric patient care, teaching, and research. A 180-bed hospital that offers all the specialties of pediatric medicine, surgery, and dentistry in a spacious, comfortable, and family focused facility.

**6614 Community Systems Inc.**
Suite 301
2 Penns Way
New Castle, DE 19720
302-325-1500
FAX: 302-325-1505
e-mail: info@csi-del.org
communitysystems.org

*David Paige, Executive Director*
A 4 state family of non-profit, tax exempt corporations whose mission is helping persons with disabilities to find happiness in their own homes, in their personal relationships, and as contributing members of their community.

**6615 DDDS/Georgetown Center**
5 Academy St
Georgetown, DE 19947-1915
302-856-5366
FAX: 302-856-5305
dhss.delaware.gov/dhss

Mission is to improve the quality of life for Delaware's citizens by promoting health and well-being, fostering self-sufficiency, and protecting vulnerable operations. The vision statement is that together we provide quality services as we create a better future for the people of Delaware.

**6616 Delaware Association for the Blind**
2915 Newport Gap Pike
Landis Lodge Building
Wilmington, DE 19808
302-998-5913
888-777-3925
FAX: 302-994-1805
e-mail: contact@dabdel.org
dabdel.org

*Sharon Sutlic, Executive Director*
*Lynn Davis, Administrative Assistant*
*Judy Engelgau, Activities Program Director*
*Caryn Robertson, Recording Services Program Director*
A private, nonprofit organization that offers adjustment to blindness counseling, recreation activities, summer camps and financial assistance for the legally blind. The staff includes five full

time, nine part time and twelve seasonal. Operates a store selling items for the blind.

**6617 Delaware Veterans Center**
1601 Kirkwood Hwy
Wilmington, DE 19805-4917
302-994-2511
800-461-8262
FAX: 302-633-5591
www1.va.gov/directory/guide

A 60-bed hospital and 60-bed NHCU, both accredited by the Joint Commission on Accreditation of Healthcare Organizations with a VBA Regional Office and 2 Vet Centers (one on campus) offering veterans the unique opportunity to obtain heathcare, benefits services, and Readjustment Counseling at one location. The center provides a wide spectrum of primary and tertiary acute and extended care inpatient and outpatient activities an an academic setting..

**6618 Easter Seals Delaware & Maryland's Eastern Shore**
61 Corporate Cir
New Castle, DE 19720-2439
302-324-4444
800-677-3800
FAX: 302-324-4441
TTY: 302-324-4442
easterseals.com

*Sandy Tuttle, President*
Provides exceptional services to ensure that all people with disabilities or special needs and their families have equal opportunities to live, learn, work and play in their communities.

**6619 Edgemoor Day Program**
500 Duncan Rd
Wilmington, DE 19809-2369
302-762-1391
FAX: 302-762-1652
e-mail: eec@dca.net
ecc-de.org

*Scott Borino, Executive Director*
*Carol Koyste, Manager, Finance & Administration*
*Brandon Furrowh, Director, Recreation & Youth Programs*
*Avani Patel, Administrative Assistant*
Our mission is providing affordable and accessible services which help improve the quality of life for community members of all ages through a broad range of educational, recreational, self-enrichment, and family support services. ECC is a not-for-profit, community-based, multi-service agency located just north of Wilmington. We provide a broad range of educational, recreational, self-enrichment, and family support services.

**6620 Elwyn Delaware**
321 E 11th St
Wilmington, DE 19801-3422
302-658-8860
FAX: 302-654-5815
e-mail: info@elwyn.org
www.elwyn.org

*Sandra S. Cornelius, President of Elwyn*
*Daniel M. Reardon, Senior Vice President and Chief Financial Officer*
*Stan H. Retif, Vice President for Development and Communications*
*Richard T. Smith, Vice President for Information Technology*
A non-profit human services organization recognized nationally and internationally as experts in the education and care of individuals with special challenges and disadvantages. Today Elwyn is a leading provider of services for people with special needs of all ages.

**6621 First State Senior Center**
291a N Rehoboth Blvd
Milford, DE 19963-1303
302-422-1510
www.dhss.delaware.gov

Improves the quality of life for Delaware's citizens by promoting health and well-being, fostering self-sufficiency, and protecting vulnerable populations.

**6622 Woodside Day Program**
941 Walnut Shade Rd
Dover, DE 19901-7765
302-739-4494
FAX: 302-697-4490

*Connie Grace, Supervisor*
*Joyce Oliver, Manager*

## District of Columbia

**6623 Barbara Chambers Children's Center**
1470 Irving St NW
Washington, DC 20010-2804
202-387-6755
FAX: 202-319-9066
e-mail: bcchildrencenter@erols.com
barbarachambers.org

*Barbara Chambers, Founder*
Mission is to provide comprehensive, quality child care services to the community at large, by offering a variety of opportunities for childrens's intellectual, emotional, social and physical development in a clean, safe, and nurturing environment. Our philosophy is to provide a supportive environment in which children can be children..allowing each child to learn at his/her pace and most of all allowing the child to learn through his/her daily play.

**6624 District of Columbia General Hospital Physical Medicine & Rehab Services**
Room 1358
19th and Mass Ave
Washington, DC 20003
202-727-6055
FAX: 202-675-7819

*Dr. Maribel Bieberach, Chairperson PM&R*
*Dr. Raman Kapur, Staff Physiatrist*
Offers comprehensive physical medicine and rehabilitation services including in and outpatient consultations and electrodiagnostic testing; in and outpatient physical and occupational therapy; inpatient recreational therapy, and a multidisciplinary prosthetic clinic which meets once a month..

**6625 George Washington University Medical Center**
George Washington University Medical Center
2150 Pennsylvania Ave NW
Washington, DC 20037-3201
202-741-3560
FAX: 202-741-3183
www.gwdocs.com

Offers an Ambulatory Physical Therapy/Sports Medicine Center, a Medical Center Prosthetics/Orthotics Clinic and a Speech and Hearing Center to persons in the District of Columbia, Virginia and Maryland.

**6626 HSC Pediatric Center, The**
1731 Bunker Hill Rd NE
Washington, DC 20017-3026
202-466-8483
800-226-4444
FAX: 202-467-0978
e-mail: nburch@hospsc.org
www.hfscsite.org

*Debbie Zients, CEO*
*Dr Murry M Pollack, VP, Medical Affairs*
Provides the highest quality rehabilitative and transitional care for infants, children, adolescents, and young adults with special health care needs and their families in a supportive environment that respects their needs, strengths, vslues and priorities..

**6627 Howard University Child Development Center**
1911 5th St NW
Washington, DC 20001-2314
202-797-8134
FAX: 202-986-6580

*Connie Siler, Manager*
Offers children with developmental problems diagnosis, treatment, evaluation and follow along visits..

**6628 Psychiatric Institute of Washington**
4228 Wisconsin Ave NW
Washington, DC 20016-2138
202-885-5600
800-369-2273
FAX: 202-885-5614
e-mail: ceo@piw-dc.com
psychinstitute.com

*Ken Courage, CEO*
*Carol Desjuns, VP/Chief Operations Officer*
*Howard Hoffman, Executive Medical Director*
*Charles J. Baumgardner, Executive VP/Chief Financial Officer*

Psychiatric intensive care, crisis intervention, adult day treatment, drug treatment and other services to children and adults who have psychiatric and chemical dependency problems.

**6629 Spina Bifida Program of DC Children's Hospital**
Department of Physical Medicine and Rehabilitation
111 Michigan Ave NW
Washington, DC 20010-2916
202-476-5000
FAX: 202-476-2270
www.cnmc.org

*Kurt Newman, President and Chief Executive Officer*
*Mark Batshaw, Nurse PractitonerExecutive Vice President and Chief Academic Officer*
*Jacqueline Bowens, Executive Vice President and Chief Government and External Affairs Off*
*Mary Anne Hilliard, Chief Risk Counsel*

Offers neurosurgery, orthopedics,physical medicine, social work, urology and nursing. Mission is to improve health outcomes for children regionally, nationally, and internationally. Be a leader in creating innovative solutions to pediatric healthcare problems. Excel in Care, Advocacy, Research, and Education to meet the unique needs of children, adolescents and their families.

## Florida

**6630 Bayfront Rehabilitation Center**
Bayfront Medical Center
701 6th St S
St Petersburg, FL 33701-4814
727-823-1234
www.bayfront.org

*Sue Brody, President and CEO*
*Bob Thornton, Executive VP & CFO*
*Eric Feder, Executive VP & COO*
*David Weiland, VP of Medical Affairs*

Bayfront Medical Center has an Inpatient Rehabilitation Hospital and two outpatient rehabilitation clinics that each provide progressive, comprehensive, individualized treatment. Specialized care in Physiatry (physical medicine), rehab nursing, occupational therapy, speech language pathology, recreational therapy, patient/family services and psychology is tailored to each patient from admission to community and/or school reintegration.

**6631 Brain Injury Rehabilitation Center Dr. P. Phillips Hospital**
Brain Injury Rehabilitation Center Dr. P. Phillips
9400 Turkey Lake Rd
Orlando, FL 32819-8001
407-351-8580
www.drpphillipshospital.org

*Shannon Elswick, President*
*Linda Chapin, Chairman*
*Mark Swanson, Chief Quality Officer*
*John Hillenmeyer, CEO Emeritus, Orlando Health*

Dedicated to restoring brain injured patients with rehabilitation potential to their highest level of functioning. This is accomplished through an interdisciplinary team demonstrating personal responsibility to the patient, their family and each other.

**6632 Brooks Memorial Hospital Rehabilitation Center**
3599 University Blvd. South
Jacksonville, FL 32207-6215
904-858-7600
FAX: 904-858-7619
e-mail: louise.spierre@brookshealth.org
www.brooksrehab.org

*Douglas Baer, Chief Executive Officer/ President*
*Holly Morris, Director, Brooks Rehabilitation Clinical Research Center Research*
*Louise Spierre, Medical Director*
*Floris Singletary, Research Manager, Clinical Research Center*

An entire care facility featuring five day inpatient evaluation, pre-operative evaluation programs, five week pain management program, referral criteria and treatment goals, therapy services, psychological services and more to the physically challenged.

**6633 Center for Pain Control and Rehabilitation**
Ste 607
2780 Cleveland Ave
Fort Myers, FL 33901-5858
239-337-4332

*Mary Bonnette, Owner*

.

**6634 Comprehensive Rehabilitation Center at Lee Memorial Hospital**
2776 Cleveland Ave
Fort Myers, FL 33901-5864
239-332-1111
leememorial.org

*James R. Nathan, Chief Executive Officer System President*
*Larry Antonucci, Chief Operating Officer*
*Jon Cecil, Chief Human Resources Officer*
*Mike German, Chief Financial Officer*

Lee Memorial hospital has achieved national recognition as one of the top 100 hospitals for stroke, orthopedics, and Intensive Care Unit (ICU) It is a 367 bed hospital that provides 24-hour emergency and trauma care, inpatient rehabilitation, orthopedics, neuroscience, trauma, cancer, diabetes, digestive, general surgery, urology, endocrinology, gastroenterology, opthamology, and many others.

**6635 Comprehensive Rehabilitation Center of Naples Community Hospital**
350 7th Street North
Naples, FL 34102
239-436-5000
FAX: 239-436-5250
www.nchmd.org

*Allen S. Weiss, CEO*
*Mariann MacDonald, Chairman*
*Thomas Gazdic, Chairman/Treasurer*
*John Lewis, Secretary*

Offers rehabilitation services, inpatient and outpatient care at 5 locations in the county and more for the benefit of the disabled.

**6636 Conklin Center for the Blind**
405 White St
Daytona Beach, FL 32114-2999
386-258-3441
FAX: 386-258-1155
e-mail: info@conklincenter.org
www.conklincenter.org

*Robert T Kelly, Executive Director*

Serves adults who are blind and who are challenged by one or more additional disabling conditions. The Center offers functional skills training and employment services, including supported employment. Serves blind infants, toddlers and their families through a community based program.

**6637 Davis Center for Rehabilitation Baptist Hospital of Miami**
8900 N Kendall Dr
Miami, FL 33176-2118 786-596-1960
e-mail: corporatepr@baptisthealth.net
www.baptisthealth.net/bhs

*Brian E. Keeley, President and Chief Executive Officer*
*Calvin Babcock, Chairman*
A full-service, nonprofit community hospital providing a full range of inpatient and outpatient rehabilitation services. The overall commitment to excellence has extended to this specialized field. Access to medical expertise and services ensures that the best in medical resources are available should an unforeseen medical problem arise.

**6638 Division of Blind Services**
1320 Executive Center Drive
Room 201, Atkins Blvd.
Tallahassee, FL 32399-6511 850-245-0370
800-672-7038
FAX: 850-245-0386
e-mail: ana.saint-ford@dbs.fldoe.org
dbs.myflorida.com

*Ana Saint-Fort, Administrator*
*Antoinette Williams, B. Chief*
*Joyce Hildreth, Director*
*Ellen McCarron, Deputy Director*
Serves the totally blind, legally blind, visually impaired, deaf-blind, learning disabled, mentally retarded and other multiply handicapped by offering health, counseling, educational, recreational and computer training services.

**6639 Easter Seals Broward County**
2880 W. Oakland Park Blvd
Suite 227
Fort Lauderdale, FL 33311 954-497-2910
FAX: 954-497-2911
www.broward.easterseals.com
ESBC provides direct services to children and adults with physical, neurological and communications disabilities and their families.

**6640 Easter Seals South Florida**
1475 NW 14th Avenue
Miami, FL 33125-1616 305-325-0470
FAX: 305-325-0578
e-mail: info@southflorida.easterseals.com
www.southflorida.easterseals.com

*Luanne Welch, President*
Provides services to children and adults with or without disabilities and other special needs. Through our services, we also give support to their families.

**6641 Easter Seals Southwest Flordia**
Sarasota, FL 34243-2001 941-812-8692
themeadowscup.com
Easter Seals Sothwest Florida creates solutions that change lives for children, adults and their families through high quality therapeutic, educational and supportive services.

**6642 Easter Seals: Volusia and Flagler Counties, FL**
Easter Seals National
1219 Dunn Ave
Daytona Beach, FL 32114-2405 386-255-4568
877-255-4568
FAX: 386-258-7677
e-mail: info@eseals-vf.org
easterseals.com
Provides early intervention services: inclusive pre-school, aquatherapy and sensory processing therapy, OT, PT, ST and parenting programs, audiology services, equipment loan program, assistive technology information and referral. Residential summer camp and respite.

**6643 Florida CORF**
Columbia Medical Center: Peninsula
www.memorial-health.com

*John Feore, Executive VP*
*Sandra Trovato, Executive Director*
Offers Medicare authorized therapy programs for seniors, disabled and others who need rehabilitation. CORF can provide coordinated and extended services in the home after a hospital stay, or when physical status changes. Patients who are treated at CORF, include amputations, arthritis, chronic/acute pain, depression/anxiety, nerve injury, sports injury, stroke and swallowing problems.

**6644 Florida Community College at Jacksonville/ Services for Students with Disabilities**
501 State St W
Jacksonville, FL 32202-4086 904-633-8100
fscj.edu

*Steven R. Wallace, President*
*James E. McCollum, Chairman*
*Patti Williams, Project Coordinator*
*Shirley Hendley, Administrative Assistant II*
Florida Community College provides educational support services through the Auxiliary Aids Program within the Office of Services for Students With Disabilities.

**6645 Florida Institute Of Rehabilitation Education (FIRE)**
3071 Highland Oaks Terrace
Tallahassee, FL 32301-4876 850-942-3658
888-827-6033
FAX: 850-942-4518
e-mail: info@lighthousebigbend.org
www.firesight.org

*Barbara Ross, Executive Director*
*Evelyn Worley, Assistant Director*
*Wayne Warner, Vocational Program Director*
*Alex Crawford, Independent Living Specialist*
Provides independent living and vocational rehabilitation services to Florida residents who are legally blind. Services include instruction in orientation and mobility, accessible technology, daily living skills and employability skills. Information, referral and counseling services are also offered. All services are provided without charge.

**6646 Florida Institute for Neurologic Rehabilitation, Inc**
P.O.Box 1348
1962 Vandolah Road
Wauchula, FL 33873-1348 863-773-2857
800-697-5390
FAX: 863-773-0867
finr.net

*Abigail Ashe, NHA, Administrator*
*Stephanie Ortiz, RN, Director of Nursing*
*Bennie Colbert, Program Director*
*Lisa Applequist, RN, Director of Nursing*
A residential rehabilitation facility providing a therapeutic environment in which children, adolescents and adults who have survived head-injury can develop the independence and skills necessary to re-enter the community.

**6647 Fort Lauderdale Veterans Medical Center**
713 NE 3rd Ave
Fort Lauderdale, FL 33304-2619 954-356-7926
FAX: 954-356-7609

*Robert White, Executive Director*
Veterans medical clinic offering disabled veterans medical treatments.

**6648 Halifax Hospital Medical Center Eye Clinic Professional Center**
303 N Clyde Morris Blvd
Daytona Beach, FL 32114 386-254-4000
www.halifax.org

*Jeff Feasel, President and CEO*
*David Davidson, General Counsel*
*Wanda Gerson, Chief Nursing Officer*
*Eric Peburn, Chief Financial Officer*
Offers services for the totally blind, legally blind, visually impaired, mentally retarded blind and more with health, counseling, educational, recreational, rehabilitation, computer training and professional training services.

**6649 HealthQuest Subacute and Rehabilitation Programs**
Regenta Park
8700 a C Skinner Pkwy
Jacksonville, FL 32256-836 FAX: 904-641-7896
HealthQuest offers four centers within the state of Florida offering exceptional staff, comfortable surroundings and individually designed, closely monitored programs dedicated to enabling patients to achieve their goals. Each location offers a progressive and cost effective alternative to in-hospital subacute and rehabilitative care. Centers are offered in Jacksonville, Winter Park, Sarasota and Sunrise..

**6650 HealthSouth Emeral Coast Sports & Rehabilitation Center**
1710 Lisenby Ave
Panama City, FL 32405-3730 850-784-4878
FAX: 850-769-7566

*Tony Bennett, CEO*
*Michelle Miller, Manager*
Outpatient sports medicine and rehabilitation center providing physical therapy, occupational therapy, industrial rehab, work hardening/work simulation, worksite and ergonomic analysis, FCE's, work assessment and pre-employment goals of returning the clients back to work, and returning to all recreational, sports and functional activities safely..

**6651 HealthSouth Rehabilitation Hospital of Tallahassee**
Healthsouth Corporation
1675 Riggins Rd
Tallahassee, FL 32308-5315 850-656-4800
www.healthsouthtallahassee.com

*Heath Phillips, Chief Executive Officer*
*Robert Robert Rowland, Medical Director*
*Tom Abbruscato, Controller*
*Deborah Baird, Director of Quality and Risk Management*
North Florida's sole acute rehabilitation hospital between Jacksonville \, Panama City, and Gainesville. With 250 employees providing a full continuum of care form its 70 bed facility, the hospital is accredited by JCAHO, CARF and state designated and certified by Vocational Rehabilitation for traumatic brain injury, as well as a wide variety of other diagnoses. With the addition of our outpatients, the facility has served the greater community by touching the lives of over 50,000 patients.

**6652 HealthSouth Rehabilitation Hospital Of Miami**
20601 Old Cutler Rd
Miami, FL 33189-2441 305-251-3800
www.healthsouthmiami.com

*Elizabeth Izquierdo, Chief Executive Officer*
*Angelo Appio, Director of Marketing Operations*
*Reyna M. Hernandez, Chief Financial Officer*
*Paige Keil, Director of Quality and Risk Management*
A comprehensive source of medical rehabilitation services for Pinellas County, Florida area residents, their families and their physicians. Offers the people of Florida all the clinical, technical and professional resources of the nation's leading provider of comprehensive rehabilitation care.

**6653 HealthSouth Rehabilitation Hospital of Sarasota**
Health South Corporation in Burmingham Alabama
6400 Edgelake Dr
Sarasota, FL 34240-8813 941-921-8600
866-330-5822
www.healthsouthsarasota.com

*Marcus Braz, Chief Executive Officer*
*Alexander DeJesus, Medical Director*
*Nancy Arnold, Director of Marketing Operations*
*Brenda Benner, Director of Human Resources*
HealthSouth Rehabilitation Hospital of Sarasota is a 96-bed inpatient rehabilitation hospital that offers comprehensive inpatient rehabilitation services designed to return patients to leading active and independent lives.

**6654 HealthSouth Sea Pines Rehabilitation Hospital**
Sea Pines Rehabilitation Hospital
101 E Florida Ave
Melbourne, FL 32901-8398 321-984-4600
FAX: 321-952-6532
www.healthsouthseapines.com

*Stuart Miller, Medical Director*
*Denise McGrath, Chief Executive Officer*
*Donna Anderson, Director of Human Resources*
*Jerry Bishop, Director of Quality and Risk Management*
Designed to return patients to leading active, independent lives, HealthSouth Sea Pines Rehabilitation Hospital is a 90-bed rehabilitation hospital that provides a higher level of comprehensive rehabilitation services.

**6655 Holy Cross Hospital**
Catholic Southwest
4725 N Federal Hwy
Fort Lauderdale, FL 33308-4668 954-771-8000
www.holy-cross.com

*Patrick Taylor, President & Chief Executive Officer*
*Luisa Gutman, Senior Vice President & Chief Operating Officer*
*Linda Wilford, Senior Vice President & Chief Financial Officer*
*Kenneth Homer, Chief Medical Officer & Medical Director*
Holy Cross Hospital in Fort Lauderdale is a full-service, non-profit Catholic hospital, sponsored by the Sisters of Mercy. Holy Cross is a US News & World Report 'Best Hospital' and HealthGrades Distinguished Hospital for Clinical Excellence, 2004 and 2005

**6656 Lee Memorial Hospital**
2776 Cleveland Ave
Fort Myers, FL 33901-5855 239-343-2000
www.leememorial.org

*James R. Nathan, Chief Executive Officer System President*
*Larry Antonucci, Chief Operating Officer*
*Jon Cecil, Chief Human Resources Officer*
*Mike German, Chief Financial Officer*
Offers a complete inpatient program of intensive rehabilitation designed to restore a patient to a more independent level of functioning. The comprehensive care includes medical rehabilitation and training for spinal cord injury, brain injury, stroke and neurological disorders.

**6657 Lighthouse for the Blind of Palm Beach**
1710 E Tiffany Dr
West Palm Beach, FL 33407-3224 561-586-5600
FAX: 561- 84- 802
lighthousepalmbeaches.org

*Marvin A. Tanck, President and CEO*
*John R. Banister, Vice Chairman*
*David B. Cano, MD*
*April L. Jasper, OD*
A private, non-profit rehabilitation and education agency in its 55th year of service. Offers programs to assist persons who areblind or visually impaired, an on-site Industrial Center, a technology training center, an Aids and appliances Store, special equipment grant programs, outreach services for children and

adults, Early Intervention and Preschool Services, and a variety of support groups. These programs provide services and education for blind children and their parents.

**6658 Lighthouse for the Visually Impaired and Blind**
8610 Galen Wilson Blvd
Port Richey, FL 34668-5974
727-815-0303
FAX: 727-815-0203
www.lvib.org

*Sylvia Stinson-Perez, Executive Director*
*Laurel Brown, Independent Living Program Manager*
*Melissa M. Suess, Orientation and Mobility Instructor*
*Peter James, Business Development Specialist*

The Lighthouse offers services for visually impaired or blind adults and children ages 0-5 years old. Counseling, educational services, recreational services, rehabilitation, computer training and support groups.

**6659 MacDonald Training Center**
5420 W Cypress St
Tampa, FL 33607-1706
813-870-1300
FAX: 813-872-6010
TTY:813-873-7631
e-mail: jfreyvogel@macdonaldcenter.org
macdonaldcenter.org

*Jim Freyvogel, President/CEO*
*Judith DeStasio, CFO*
*Debi Hamilton, Director of Services*
*Joe Donato, COO*

A private, non-profit, community-based human services organization serving adults with disabilities (since 1953). Persons are provided the opportunity to achieve their highest potential through the Center's various programs that include day training, employment, community living and various support services.

**6660 Medicenter of Tampa**
4411 N Habana Ave
Tampa, FL 33614-7211
813-872-2771
FAX: 813-871-2831

*Dan Davis, President*

Postacute rehabilitation program. A 174 bed non-profit facility with postacute reahbilitation programs..

**6661 Miami Heart Institute Adams Building**
4300 Alton Rd
Miami Beach, FL 33140-2997
305-674-2121
www.msmc.com

*Steven D. Sonenreich, President/CEO*

The mission is to provide high quality health care to our diverse community enhanced through teaching, research, charity care and financial responsibility.

**6662 Miami Lighthouse for the Blind**
601 SW 8th Ave
Miami, FL 33130-3200
305-856-2288
FAX: 305-285-6967
e-mail: info@miamilighthouse.com
miamilighthouse.org

*Virginia A. Jacko, President & Chief Executive Officer*
*Sharon Caughill, Special Projects Manager Center of Excellence*
*Jeannie Reinoso, Executive Assistant*
*Heidy Farinas, Development Database Manager*

Offers services for the legally blind and severely visually impaired (including those who are developmentally delayed) of all ages in the areas of counseling and educational, recreational, rehabilitation, computer and vocational training services.

**6663 Mount Sinai Medical Center Rehabilitation Unit**
4300 Alton Rd
Miami Beach, FL 33140-2997
305-674-2121
www.msmc.com

*Steven D. Sonenreich, President/CEO*

A comprehensive inpatient and outpatient rehabilitation programs have been helping patients recover for more then 20 years. Fully customized treatment plans based on the needs of each patient is 1 reason why our services are among the best in South Florida. Our team approach takes into account the medical, physical, psychological, social, spiritual, cultural and economic needs of patients and their families.

**6664 Neurobehavioral Medicine Center**
Ste 1
4821 Us Highway 19
New Port Richey, FL 34652-4259
727-849-2005
FAX: 727-849-2087

*Otsenre Matos, Medical Director*
*Gerard Taylor PhD, Counseling/Stress Management*
*Donna Taylor RN, Manager*
*Joyce Park Matos ARNP, Clinical Specialist*

A multidisciplinary outpatient program for the evaluation and treatment of chronic pain. Consultation services for hospitalized patients are also provided upon request. Comprehensive treatment of individuals with closed traumatic brain injuries..

**6665 North Broward Rehab Unit**
North Broward Medical Center
201 E Sample Rd
Deerfield Beach, FL 33064-3596
954-941-8300
www.browardhealth.org

*Douglas Ford, Chiefs of Staff*
*Pauline Grant, Chief Executive Officer*

CARF accredited, 30-bed inpatient rehabilitation unit treating adults with brain injuries, spinal cord injuries, stroke, orthopedic and neurologic injuries.

**6666 Northwest Medical Center**
Health Care Corporation of America
2801 N State Road 7
Margate, FL 33063-5727
954-974-4000
866-256-7720
northwestmed.com

*Dianne Goldenberg, CEO*

Above all else, we are committed to the care and improvement of human life. In recognition of this commitment, we strive to deliver high quality, cost effective healthcare in the communities we serve. We recognize and affirm the unique and intrinsic work of each individual. We treat all those we serve with compassion and kindness. We act with absolute honesty, integrity, and fairness in the way we conduct our business and the way we live our lives.

**6667 Pain Institute of Tampa**
4178 N Armenia Ave
Tampa, FL 33607-6429
813-875-5913
www.barsahealth.com

*John E Barsa, Founder*

Offers a comprehensive and multidisciplinary approach to pain controll and management. Most services are provided on-site but other services may require you to be referred elswhere. We will monitor and coordinate your care in a manner to provide optimal recovery potential.

**6668 Pain Treatment Center, Baptist Hospital of Miami**
8900 N Kendall Dr
Miami, FL 33176-2118
786-596-1960
e-mail: corporatepr@baptisthealth.net
www.baptisthealth.net

*Brian E. Keeley, President and Chief Executive Officer*
*Calvin Babcock, Chairman*
Since 1960, Baptist Hospital of Miami has been one of the most respected medical centers in South Florida. The hospitals full range of medical and technological services is the natural choice for a growing number of people throughout the world.

**6669 Pine Castle**
4911 Spring Park Rd
Jacksonville, FL 32207-7496
904-733-2650
FAX: 904-733-2681
e-mail: info@pinecastle.org
pinecastle.org

*Jonathan May, Executive Director*
*Randall Duncan, Associate Executive Director*
*Leigh Griffin, Director of Finance*
*DuVal Malone, Development Director*
Provides remunerative work, training, community employment and community living options for adults with developmental disabilities.

**6670 Polk County Association for Handicapped Citizens**
1038 Sunshine Dr E
Lakeland, FL 33801-6338
863-858-2252
FAX: 863-665-2330
e-mail: sbaloghweb@pcahc.org
www.pcahc.org

*Kecia Howell, Owner*
*Anthony J. Senzamici Jr., 1st Vice Chairman*
*Carol N. Asbill, 2nd Vice Chairman*
A private non-profit organization that provides an adult day training program to people with developmental disabilities and is under the direction of a volunteer board of directors. The primary goal for our services is to provide people with knowledge and practical experience to be independent adults so they can become contributing members of their community..

**6671 Quest**
500 E Colonial Dr
Orlando, FL 32853-4504
407-218-4300
888-807-8378
FAX: 407-218-4301
questinc.org

*Katie Porta, President*
*Lynn Larson, Admissions Coordinator*
*Janet Ginn, Director Development*
*Phil Nahajewski, Vice President Finance*
Quest has built communities where people with disabilities have achieved their goals for nearly 50 years. Through a variety of residential and employment options, behavioral therapy, therapeutic day programs, charter schools and even a recreational summer camp, Quest serves more than 1000 individuals each day in the Orlando and Tampa areas.

**6672 Quest - Tampa Area**
1404 Tech Blvd
Tampa, FL 33619
813-630-4710
888-807-8378
FAX: 813-635-9614
e-mail: contact@questinc.org
www.questinc.org

*David Canora, Chair*
*Greg Rhodeghier, Vice-Chair*
*Ruth Bresnick, Secretary*
Quest has built communities where people with disabilities have achieved their goals for nearly 50 years. Through a variety of residential and employment options, behavioral therapy, therapeutic day programs, charter schools and even a recreational summer

**6673 Rehabilitation Center for Children and Adults**
300 Royal Palm Way
Palm Beach, FL 33480-4305
561-655-7266
FAX: 561-655-3269
e-mail: info@rcca.org
rcca.org

*John C. Whelton, Chairman*
*Jacob L. Lochner, Co-Chairman*
*Christopher Adams, MD*
A private, nonprofit organization whose purpose is to improve physical function, independence and communication of people with physical disabilities. Any child or adult with a physical or speech disability is eligible for services.

**6674 Renaissance Center**
3599 University Blvd
Suite 604
Jacksonville, FL 32216- 9249
904-399-0905
FAX: 904-743-5109
http://www.obiplasticsurgery.com/index.php

*Lewis Obi, MD*

**6675 Rosomoff Comprehensive Pain Center, The**
5200 NE 2nd Ave
Miami, FL 33137-2706
305-532-7246
FAX: 305-534-3974
e-mail: painrelief@rosomoffpaincenter.com
www.rosomoffpaincenter.com

*Elsayed Abdel-Moty, Director*
*Hubert Rossomoff, Owner*
A state-of-the-art Center of Excellence offering inpatient, outpatient, outpatient rehabilitation services and seniors programs. The Center became an internationally renowned model for the evaluation and treatment of all persons seeking pain relief.

**6676 Sarasota Memorial Hospital/Comprehensive Rehabilitation Unit**
1700 S Tamiami Trl
Sarasota, FL 34239-3509
941-917-9000
FAX: 941-917-2211
www.smh.com

*Gwen M Mackenzie, CEO*
*David Verinder, Chief Operating Officer*
*William Woeltjen, Chief Financial Officer*
The goal of the 34-bed Comprehensive Rehabilitation Unit (CRU) is to increase patient functional independence, adjust to illness or disability and successfully return to the community. The unit is dedicated to patients who have experienced conditions such

**6677 Strive Physical Therapy Centers**
2620 SE Maricamp RD
Ocala, FL 34471-4517
352-732-8868
FAX: 352-732-8890
www.striverehab.com

*R W Shutes, Owner*
*Johanna Solbato, Administrator*
Certified as an Outpatient Rehabilitation Agency, providing a comprehensive approach to patient evaluation and treatment. Our objective is to return our patients back to a productive life as quickly as possible and safely as possible.

**6678 Sunbridge Care and Rehabilitation**
5627 9th St E
Bradenton, FL 34203-6105
941-753-8941
FAX: 941-753-7576
http://www.sunbridgehealthcare.com/

*Joyce Frey, Manager*
A comprehensive medical rehabilitation facility that is committed to helping individuals with disabilities improve their quality

of life. This is a 120-bed facility offering a full range of acute and sub-acute inpatient programs as well as community-based

**6679 Tampa Bay Academy**
12012 Boyette Rd
Riverview, FL 33569-5631
813-677-6700
800-678-3838
FAX: 813-671-3145
e-mail: info@tampayfcs,com
http://www.tampahope.org/

*Renee Scott, Chair*
*Amy McClure, Vice-Chair*
*Titania Lamb, Executive Director*

A psychiatric residential treatment center and partial hospitalization program for ages 7 to 17.

**6680 Tampa General Rehabilitation Center**
P.O.Box 1289
Tampa, FL 33606-1289
813-844-7719
FAX: 813-844-1477
e-mail: jstone@tgh.org
tgh.org

*Ron Hytoff, President & CEO*
*Thomas L. Bernasek, Chief Of Staff*
*David A. Straz, Chairman of the Board*

Offers a full range of programs all aimed at helping patients achieve their full potentials. It is one of three centers in the state that provides Driver Training and Evaluation Programs for persons with disabilities, and also an Assisted Reproduction Pro

**6681 Tampa Lighthouse for the Blind**
1106 W Platt St
Tampa, FL 33606-2142
813-251-2407
FAX: 813-254-4305
e-mail: tlh@templelighthouse.org
tampalighthouse.org

*Clifford E Olstrom, Executive Director*

Offers services for the totally blind, legally blind, visually impaired, mentally retarded blind and more with health, counseling, educational, recreational, rehabilitation, computer training and professional training services.

**6682 Upper Pinellas Association for Retarded Citizens**
Ste 249
1501 N Belcher Rd
Clearwater, FL 33765-1300
727-797-3330
FAX: 727-799-4632
e-mail: info@uparc.com
www.uparc.com

*Karen Crown, Executive Director*

Offers services to more than 500 persons with mental retardation and other developmental disabilities. Services include two early intervention pre-schools, physical, speech and occupational therapies, homebound education and family support for children, b

**6683 Visually Impaired Persons of Southwest Florida**
35 W Mariana Ave
North Fort Myers, FL 33903-5515
239-997-7797
FAX: 239-997-8462
e-mail: mmcgrael@vipcenter.org
vipcenter.org

*Doug Fowler, Executive Director*
*Margaret Ruhe Lincoln, Director of operations*

Provides training in independent living skills, orientation and mobility, counseling, computer and other communication skills, family support groups, peer counseling, socialization and a low vision clinic. Second location in Charlotte County. Phone: 941-6

**6684 West Florida Hospital: The Rehabilitation Institute**
8383 N Davis Hwy
Pensacola, FL 32514-6039
850-494-6100
800-342-1123
FAX: 850-494-4881
www.westfloridahospital.com

*Roman S Bautista, President/CEO*
*Carol Saxton, Senior VP Patient Care Services*

A 58-bed comprehensive rehabilitation facility offering inpatient and outpatient services. JCAHO and CARF accredited and a State designed head and spinal cord injury center. CARF accredited programs include: comprehensive inpatient rehab, spinal cord inju

**6685 West Gables Health Care Center**
2525 SW 75th Ave
Miami, FL 33155-2800
305-265-6800
FAX: 888-453-1928
http://www.westgablesrehabhospital.com/

*Mark Carrosco, Administrator*
*Charlotte Raymor, Chief Executive Officer*

Services provide by West Gables Health Center: activities services are provided onsite to residents. Clinical laboratory services are provided, dental, dietary, housekeeping, mental health services, nursing services, occupational therapy, pharmacy, physic

**6686 Willough at Naples**
9001 Tamiami Trl E
Naples, FL 34113-3397
239-775-4500
800-722-0100
FAX: 239-793-0534
e-mail: info@thewilloughatnaples.com
thewilloughatnaples.com

*James O'Shea, President*

A licensed psychiatric hospital in Southwest Florida which provides quality management and treatment for eating disorders and chemical dependency in adults.

## Georgia

**6687 Annandale at Suwanee**
3500 Annandale Ln
Suwanee, GA 30024-2150
770-945-8381
FAX: 770-945-8693
e-mail: administration@annandale.org
annandale.org

*Adam Pomeranz, Chief Executive Officer*
*Melissa Burton, Chief Financial Officer*
*Tammy Severino, Chief Development Officer*

Private nonprofit residential facility for adults with developmental disabilities. Located on 124 acres just north of Atlanta. Annandale provides full program and 24 hour residential services, pay program services, respite care and skilled nursing services.

**6688 Atlanta Institute of Medicine and Rehabilitation**
Ste E
2911 Piedmont Rd NE
Atlanta, GA 30305-2782
404-365-0160
FAX: 404-365-0751
e-mail: contact@atlantaimr.com
www.atlantaimr.com

*Lawrence E Eppelbaum, Founder*
*Galina Vayner, MD*

One of the most famous medical centers in the state of Georgia. The Institute employs more then 40 highly qualified medical professionals and fully equipped with the latest medical equipment. It has gathered recognition and respect from the people of Atla

**6689 Bobby Dodd Institute (BDI)**
2120 Marietta Blvd NW
Atlanta, GA 30318-2122
678-365-0071
FAX: 678-365-0098
e-mail: wmcmillan@bdi-atl.org
bobbydodd.org

*Don Chapman, CEO*
*David Turner, Director Finance*
*Barbara Massey, VP Operations/Marketing*
BDI annually serves approximately 400 clients in Atlanta, GA. BDI works primarily with people with developmental disabilities such as autism, down syndrome or mental retardation, but includes clients with physical or acquired disabilities. Client age va

**6690 Cave Spring Rehabilitation Center**
Georgia Department of Labor
7 Georgia Ave
Cave Spring, GA 30124-2718
706-777-1770
FAX: 706-777-2366
e-mail: russell.fleming@dol.state.ga.us

*Joe Holcombe, Director*
*David Stevenson, Assistant Director*

**6691 Center for Assistive Technology and Environmental Access**
490 10th St
Atlanta, GA 30332-0156
404-894-4960
800-726-9119
FAX: 404-894-9320
e-mail: catea@coa.gatech.edu
www.catea.org

*Carrie Bruce, Research Scientist*
*Charlie Drummond, Administrative Assistant*
The Center for Assistive Technology and Environmental Access (CATEA) promotes maximum function, activity and access of persons with disabilities through the use of technology. The foci of the Center includes the development, evaluation and utilization of

**6692 Center for the Visually Impaired**
739 W Peachtree St NW
Atlanta, GA 30308-1137
404-875-9011
FAX: 404-607-0062
e-mail: info@cviatlanta.org
cviga.org

*Susan Hoy, Chair*
*Susan B. Green, President*
*Bill Woolf, Senior Vice President*
Offers services to people of all ages who are blind or visually impaired with training in orientation and mobility, computer technology, activities of daily living, communication skills and employment readiness. Aso offers two children's programs, a comm

**6693 Devereux Georgia Treatment Network**
1291 Stanley Road
Kennesaw, GA 30152-8688
770-427-0147
800-342-3357
FAX: 770-427-4030
e-mail: cfrost@devereux.org
www.devereuxga.org

*Helena T. Devereux, Founder*
*Robert Q. Kreider, President & CEO*
Serves ages 10 to 17, males and females with a capacity for up to 187. Serves moderate to severe emotional, behavioral and/or learning disabilities. A specialized psychiatric hospital/intensive residential treatment program for below average to superior i

**6694 Easter Seals East Georgia**
1500 Wrightsboro Road
Augusta, GA 30904-2441
706-667-9695
866-667-9695
FAX: 706-667-8831
e-mail: sthomas@esega.org
www.ga-ea.easter-seals.org

*Sheila H. Thomas, CEO*
*Patrick Clayton, Chairman*
Easter Seals East Georgia assists people with disabilities and other special needs to maximize opportunities for employment, independence and full inclusion into society.

**6695 Georgia Industries for the Blind**
700 Faceville Highway
Bainbridge, GA 39819-218
229-248-2666
FAX: 229-248-2669
http://www.vocrehabga.org/gib/

*James Hughes, Executive Director*
Offers services for the totally blind, legally blind, visually impaired, mentally retarded blind and more with health, counseling, educational, recreational, rehabilitation, computer training and professional training services.

**6696 Hillhaven Rehabilitation**
26 Tower Rd NE
Marietta, GA 30060-6947
770-422-8913
800-526-5782
FAX: 770-425-2085

*Leslie Ann Marie Parrish, Case Manager*
*Valerie Hamilton, Administrator*
Routine skilled and subacute medical and rehabilitation care including physical therapy, occupational therapy, speech pathology and therapeutic recreation. Programs include stroke and head injury rehab; orthopedic rehab; complex IV therapy; woundcare; can.

**6697 In-Home Medical Care**
Care Master Medical Services
240 Odell Rd
Griffin, GA 30224-4787
770-227-1264
800-542-8889
FAX: 770-412-0014
e-mail: caremaster@accesunited.com
caremastermedical.com

*Nancy Frederick, VP*
*Eddie Grogan, Chief Executive Officer*
Offers the devoted attention of a professional nurse, the use of I.V. therapies, pain management and provision of medical equipment and supplies right where the patient wants to be.

**6698 Learning Services: Harris House Program**
3914 Sable Dr
Stone Mountain, GA 30083-4446
404-298-0144
888-419-9955
FAX: 404-294-3629
learningservices.com

*Linda Latimer, Manager*
Situated in the small, historic district of Stone Mountain, just outside of Atlanta, this 6 bed program is designed to encourage independence while providing appropriate support for each individuals needs. Community-based productive activities are customi

**6699 Pain Control & Rehabilitation Institute of Georgia**
Ste 120
2784 N Decatur Rd
Decatur, GA 30033-5993
404-297-1400
FAX: 404-297-1427

*Shulim Spektor, CEO*
*Anna Britman, Office Manager*

Provides pain management for chronic and acute pain resulted from injuries, diseases of muscles and nerve, Reflex Sympathetic Dystrophy, perform disabilities and impairment ratings.

**6700 Savannah Association for the Blind**
214 Drayton St
Savannah, GA 31401-4021
912-236-4473
FAX: 912-234-4156
www.sabinc.org

*Gregory Hodges, President*
*Lee Mundell, Treasurer*
*Lula Baker, Secretary*
Offers services for the totally blind, legally blind, visually impaired, mentally retarded blind and more with health, counseling, educational, recreational, rehabilitation, computer training and professional training services.

**6701 Shepherd Center for Treatment of Spinal Injuries**
2020 Peachtree Rd NW
Atlanta, GA 30309-1465
404-352-2020
FAX: 404-350-7479
e-mail: webmaster@shepherd.org
www.shepherd.org

*Gary R. Ulicny, President & CEO*
*David F. Apple, MD*
Dedicated exclusively to the care of patients with spinal cord injuries and other paralyzing spinal disorders. It serves predominately residents of Georgia and neighboring states as one of the only 14 hospitals designated by the U.S. Department of Educati

**6702 Transitional Hospitals Corporation**
Ste 1000
7000 Central Pkwy NE
Atlanta, GA 30328-4592
770-821-5328
800-683-6868
FAX: 770-913-0015
csins.com

*Dean Rustin, Owner*
A national network of intensive care hospitals providing care for patients who suffer from a chronic illness and/or catastrophic accident. The mission is founded on providing quality health care to patients who require highly skilled nursing care and acce.

**6703 Walton Rehabilitation Health System**
1355 Independence Dr
Augusta, GA 30901-1037
706-724-7746
866-492-5866
FAX: 706-724-5752
e-mail: postmaster@wrh.org
wrh.org

*Dennis Skelley, CEO*
A 58-bed comprehensive physical rehabilitation hospital offering inpatient and outpatient services. Services offered include: stroke recovery, orthopedic injury, pediatrics, head injury, pain management for chronic pain syndrome, TMJ/Craniofacial pain and

## Hawaii

**6704 Rehabilitation Hospital of the Pacific**
226 N Kuakini St
Honolulu, HI 96817-2498
808-531-3511
FAX: 808-566-3411
e-mail: rehabfoundation@rehabhospital.org
www.rehabhospital.org

*John Komeiji, Chair*
*Dennis Teranishi, Vice Chair*
*Cherylee Chang, MD*
The only acute care medical rehabilitation organization serving both Hawaii and the Pacific. For over 52 years, the hospital and its 7 outpatient clinics on Oahu, and Maui and Hawaii have been dedicated to providing comprehensive, cost effective rehabilit

## Idaho

**6705 Ashton Memorial Nursing Home and Chemical Dependency Center**
700 N 2nd
Ashton, ID 83420
208-652-7461
FAX: 208-652-7595
e-mail: ashmem@frtel.com
ashtonmemorial.com

*Sheila Kellogg, Administrator*

**6706 Easter Seals-Goodwill Northern Rocky Mountains**
Easter Seals National
1465 S Vinnell Way
Boise, ID 83709-1659
208-378-9924
800-374-1910
FAX: 208-378-9965
www.easterseals.org

*Duncan Hawthorn, Chair*
*Doug Ackhurst, Vice-Chair*
Provides services for children and adults with disabilities and other special needs, and support to their families

**6707 Idaho Elks Rehabilitation Hospital**
600 N Robbins Rd
Boise, ID 83702
208-489-4444
FAX: 208-344-8883
idahoelksrehab.org

*Joseph P. Caroselli, CEO*
*Doug Lewis, Chief Financial Officer*
*Mellisa Honsinger, Chief Operating Officer*
A nonprofit hospital serving Idaho and the Pacific Northwest. All inpatient and outpatient programs and services are supervised by the hospital's full-time medical directors whose specialty is physical rehabilitative medicine. Services include: occupation

**6708 Portneuf Medical Center Rehabilitation**
651 Memorial Dr
Pocatello, ID 83201-4004
208-239-1836
FAX: 208-239-1838
e-mail: charlesa@portmed.org
www.portmed.org

*Mark Buckalew, Chairman*
*Michael Nosacka, MD*
*Norman Stephens, CEO*
*John Abreu, Vice President*
Provides compassionate, quality health care services needed by the people of eastern Idaho in collaboration with other providers and community resources.

## Illinois

**6709 Advocate Christ Hospital and Medical Center**
4440 W 95th St
Oak Lawn, IL 60453-2600
708-684-8000
FAX: 708-684-4440
advocatehealth.com

*Jim Skogsbergh, CEO*
*Bill Santulli, COO*
*Kate K, Director*
A 665-bed, not-for-profit teaching, research and referral medical center in Oak Lawn, Illinois. It also is home to the Advocate Hope Childrens's Hospital, one of the most comprehensive providers of pediatric care in the state. The medical center is a lead

**6710 Advocate Christ Medical Center & Advocate Hope Children's Hospital**
4440 W 95th St
Oak Lawn, IL 60453-2600
708-684-8000
800-323-8622
FAX: 708-684-4440
www.advocatehealth.com/christ

*Kenneth Lukhard, CEO*
*Darcie Brazel, Market Chief Nurse Executive*
*Jan McCrea, Rehab Services Director*
*William Adair MD, Medical Director/Rehab Services*
The largest fully integrated not-for-profit health care delivery system in metropolitan Chicago and is recognized as one of the top 10 systems in the country. The mission of Advocate Health Care is to serve the health needs of individuals, families and co

**6711 Advocate Illinois Masonic Medical Center**
836 W Wellington Ave
Chicago, IL 60657-5147
773-975-1600
www.advocatehealth.com/masonic

*Jim Skogsbergh, CEO*
*Ajay V. Maker, MD*
Consultation, education, family counseling, parent training in behavior modification techniques offered to developmentally disabled adults.

**6712 Alexian Brothers Medical Center**
800 Biesterfield Rd
Elk Grove Village, IL 60007-3396
847-437-5500
e-mail: AlexianBrothersMedicalCenter @alexian.net
www.alexian.org

*John Werrbach, President/CEO*
A threefold mission: Works toward maximizing physical function, enhance independent social skills and optimize communication skills consistent with an individual's ability. The Center helps those disabled by accident or illness achieve a new personal best

**6713 Back in the Saddle Hippotherapy Program**
Corcoran Physical Therapy
4200 W Peterson Ave
Chicago, IL 60646-6074
312-286-2266
847-604-4145
FAX: 847-673-8895
e-mail: info@hippotherapychicago.com

*Julie Naughton, Program Coordinator*
*Maureen Corcoran, Physical Therapist*
*Tom Corcoran, Owner*
A direct medical treatment used by licensed physical therapists who have a strong treatment background in posture and movement, neuromotor function and sensory processing. The benefits of Hippotherapy are available to individuals with just about any disab

**6714 Barbara Olson Center of Hope**
3206 N Central Ave
Rockford, IL 61101-1797
815-964-9275
FAX: 815-964-9607
e-mail: wdovenport@b-olsoncenterofhope.org
b-olsoncenterofhope.org

*Carm Herman, Manager*
*Nancy Flanagan, President of the Board*
*Susan Nagy, Accoutant*
We provide vocational employment, educational and social opportunities for adults with developmental disabilities.

**6715 Bartolucci Center, The- ILC Enterprises**
6415 Stanley Ave
Berwyn, IL 60402-3130
708-788-0511
FAX: 708-788-0831
http://www.pillarscommunity.org

*John C. Neylon, Chairman*
*John Shustitzky, President & CEO*
*Margie Thomas Morris, Vice Chair*
*Joanne Klonoski, Secretary*
A nonprofit tax exempt private social service agency serving suburban Chicago offering day treatment and vocational counseling to individuals who encountered a pattern of job loss due to emotional problems.

**6716 Baxter Healthcare Corporation**
1 Baxter Pkwy
Deerfield, IL 60015-4633
847-948-4770
800-422-9837
FAX: 847-948-3642
baxter.com

*Robert L Parkinson Jr, CEO*
*Gail D Fosler, Executive VP/Chief Economist*
*Robert Parkinson Jr, CEO*
Baxter International Inc. is a global healthcare company that, through its subsidiaries assists healthcare professionals and their patients with treatment of complex medical conditions including hemophelia, immune disorders, kidney disease, cancer, trauma and other conditions. Baxter applies its expertise in medical devices, pharmaceuticals, and biotechnology to make a meaningful difference in patient's lives.

**6717 Beacon Therapeutic Diagnostic and Treatment Center**
10650 S Longwood Dr
Chicago, IL 60643-2617
773-881-1005
FAX: 773-881-1164
www.beacon-diabetic.org

*Susan Reyha-Guerrero, President & CEO*
*Cheryl Thompson, Deputy CEO*
*Paul Morley, Chief Operating Officer*
Offers community day treatment, education, diagnostic services, family counseling, learning disabled, speech and hearing and psychiatric services.

**6718 Blind Service Association**
Ste 1050
17 N State St
Chicago, IL 60602-3510
312-236-0808
http://blindserviceassociation.org

*Ann Lousin, President*
*Linda Schwartz, Executive Vice President*
*Arthur M. Shapiro, Secretary*
Offers services for the totally blind, legally blind and visually impaired with reading and recording low vision network, social services, referrals and support groups.

**6719 Brandecker Rehabilitation Center**
9455 S Hoyne Ave
Chicago, IL 60643-6316
773-233-1799
FAX: 773-239-6229
e-mail: mstroube@eastersealschicago.org
www.eastersealschicago.org

*F. Timothy Muri, President & CEO*
We offer early intervention services for infants and toddlers with developmental delays and disabilities. Our outpatient Medical Rehabilitation Program offers direct therapy services for children from age birth-16.

**6720 Brentwood Subacute Healthcare Center**
T HI Brentwood
5400 W 87th St
Burbank, IL 60459-2913
708-423-1200
800-430-0098
FAX: 708-423-8405
www.thicare.com

*Audrey Protrowski, Director Business Development*
*Jill Sattersield, Administrator*
*John Walton, CEO*
Seeks to help patients and their families through what can be a very emotional decision-making process. We provide guidance and consultation on everything from how to properly choose the facility to providing resources that help you cope with the nature of the decision itself.

**6721 Caremark Healthcare Services**
2211 Sanders Rd
Northbrook, IL 60062-6128
847-559-4700
800-423-1411
FAX: 847-559-3905
e-mail: phu@caremark.com
www.caremark.com

*Larry J. Merlo, President & CEO*
*Mark Cosby, Executive Vice President*
An 80-service-center network providing services anywhere in the U.S. Offers 24 hour access to nursing and pharmacy services, case management resource centers, HIV/AIDS services, women's health services, transplant care services, nutrition support services

**6722 Centegra Northern Illinois Medical Center**
4201 W Medical Center Dr
McHenry, IL 60050-8499
815-344-5000
877-236-8347
FAX: 815-759-8062
www.centegra.org

*Michael S. Eesley, CEO*
*Jason Sciarro, President*
*Robert M. Rosenberger, Executive Vice President*
*Ted Lorenc, MD*
Providing rehabilitation services in Lake and McHenry Counties, the Rehabilitation Unit is a complete living environment for up to 15 patients after a debilitating illness of trauma. Various locations offering a multitude of services: PT, OT, speech, HT,

**6723 Center for Comprehensive Services**
Mentor Network
P.O.Box 2825
Carbondale, IL 62902-2825
618-457-4008
800-582-4227
FAX: 618-457-5372
e-mail: dayna.foreman@thementornetwork.com
mentorabi.com

*Bill Duffy, Chief Operating Officer*
*Michael E. Hofmeister, Vice President*
*Sean Byrne, Chief Financial Officer*
Post-acute rehabilitation services for adults and adolescents with acquired brain injuries. Residential, day-treatment and out-patient services tailored to individual needs.

**6724 Center for Rehabilitation at Rush Presbyterian: Johnston R Bowman Health Center**
1653 W Congress Pkwy
Chicago, IL 60612-3833
312-942-5000
FAX: 312-942-3601
e-mail: teri_sommerfeld@rush.edu
www.rush.edu

*Larry J. Goodman, CEO*
A 613-bed hospital serving adults and children, the John R. Bowman Health Center and Rush University is home to one of the first medical colleges in the Midwest and one of the nation's top-ranked nursing colleges, as well as graduate programs in allied he

**6725 Center for Spine, Sports & Occupational Rehabilitation**
345 E Superior St
Chicago, IL 60611-2654
312-238-7767
800-354-7342
FAX: 312-238-7709
e-mail: webmaster@ric.org
www.rehabchicago.org

*Joanne C. Smith, President & CEO*
*Edward B. Case, Executive Vice President*
*M. Jude Reyes, Chair*
Offers evaluation and treatment of patients with acute and subacute musculoskeletal and sports injuries. RIC offers different levels of care, including inpatient, day rehabilitation, and outpatients services, according to the special needs of each patient

**6726 Children's Home and Aid Society of Illinois**
Fl 14
125 S Wacker Dr
Chicago, IL 60606-4448
312-424-0200
e-mail: contact@chasi.org
http://www.childrenshomeandaid.org

*Nancy B Ronquillo, President/CEO*
*Michael J. Shaver, Executive Vice President*
*Elizabeth Connelly, Chairman*
*Paul Wood, Vice Chairman*
Private state-wide. Multi-service, racially integrated staff and client populations. Provides educational, placement and community services for children-at-risk and their families. Advocacy, consultation and follow-up services provided according to our ph

**6727 Clinton County Rehabilitation Center**
1665 N 4th St
Breese, IL 62230-1791
618-526-8800
FAX: 618-526-2021
e-mail: info@commlink.org
commlink.org

*John L. Lengerman, President*
*Brag G. Beck, Vice President*
*Michael A. Nettemeier, Treasurer*
Provides Adult Day Programs (developmental training, work training, job readiness and job placements); Residentail Programs (CILA Intermittent Care, CILA 24 hour care); Infant Programs (early interventions, early head start); Community Services (specializ

**6728 Continucare, A Service of the Rehab Institute of Chicago**
West Suburban Hospital Medical Center
3 Erie Ct
Oak Park, IL 60302-2519
708-383-6200
800-354-7342
FAX: 312-908-1369
www.westsuburbanmedicalcenter.research.org

*Heidi Asbury MD*
We respond to the needs of the whole person: body, mind and spirit. We foster a climate of care, hospitality and a spirit of community. We develop systems and structures that attend to the needs of those at risk of discrimination because of age, gender, lifestyle, ethnic background, religious beliefs or socioeconomic status.

**6729 Delta Center**
1400 Commercial Ave
Cairo, IL 62914-1978
618-734-2665
800-471-7213
FAX: 618-734-1999
e-mail: delta1@midwest.net
deltacenter.org

*Lisa Tolbert, Executive Director*
*Lisa Tholbert, Assistant Executive Director*

The Delta Center is a non-profit mental health center, substance abuse counseling facility, and also provides various community services to Alexander and Pulaski County, Illinois. The purpose and mission is to promote, encourage, foster and engage exclusi

**6730 Division of Rehabilitation-Education Services, University of Illinois**
Beckwith Hall
201 E. John Street
Champaign, IL 61820- 6901 217-333-4603
FAX: 217-333-0248
e-mail: disability@uiuc.edu
www.disability.ui.uc.edu

*Ann Fredricksen, Disability Specialist*
*Jon Gunderson, Coordinator*
*Pat Malik, Director*
*Dennis Cable, Accountant*

Offers services for the totally blind, legally blind, visually impaired, mentally retarded blind and more with health, counseling, educational, recreational, rehabilitation, computer training and professional training services.

**6731 Easter Seals**
Easter Seals Joliet Region
233 South Wacker Drive
Suite 2400
Chicago, IL 60606-5272 312-726-6200
800-221-6827
FAX: 312-726-1494
www.easterseals.com

*Stephen F. Rossman, Chairman*
*Richard F. Vincent, Treasurer*
*Alison A. Coady, Secretary*

Services for children and adults with disabilities and their families. Pediatric outpatient medical rehabilitation, inclusive childcare, fostercare, residential homes, clinics.

**6732 Easter Seals DuPage And The Fox Valley Region**
830 S Addison Ave
Villa Park, IL 60181-2877 630-620-4436
FAX: 630-620-1148
www.easterseals.com

*Theresa Forthofer, President & CEO*
*Diana Dixon, Admissions Coordinator*

The mission of Easter Seals DuPage & the Fox Valley Region is to enable infants, children & adults with disabilities to achieve maximum independence and to provide support to the families who love and care for them. Key services include: physical, occupational, speech-language, nutrition and assistive technology therapies and audiology services for all ages.

**6733 Easter Seals Gilchrist-Marchman Rehab Center**
1001 West Roosevelt Road
Chicago, IL 60608-5332 312-412-7402
FAX: 312-939-0283
e-mail: Mcancel@eastersealschicago.org
http://chicago.easterseals.com

*Morayma Cancel, Interim Manager*

Provides comprehensive services for individuals with disabilities or other special needs and their families to improve quality of life and maximize independence.

**6734 Easter Seals Jayne Shover Center**
799 S McLean Blvd
Elgin, IL 60123-6704 847-742-3264
FAX: 847-742-9436
e-mail: il-ja.easter-seals.org
www.il-js.easter-seals.org

*Theresa Forthofer, President & CEO*
*Sara Cohen, Vice President*
*Kelly N. Taira, Treasurer*
*Karen Janousek, Secretary*

A free-standing, comprehensive outpatient rehabilitation center serving children and adults with physical and developmental disabilities.

**6735 El Valor Corporation**
Early Intervention Program
1850 W 21st St
Chicago, IL 60608-2799 312-666-4511
FAX: 312-666-6677
e-mail: info@elvalor.net
http://www.elvalor.org/

*Vincent A. Allocco, President*
*Clara A. Lopez, Vice President*
*Rey B. Gonzalez, Chairman*
*Maria Esther Lopez, Director*

Mission is to challenge people with disabilities. It is a center for people with disabilities and their families and serves Chicago and surrounding areas, providing services in English and Spanish to individuals whose lives would be drastically impoverish

**6736 Elgin Training Center**
Association For Individual Development Elgin Area
1135 Bowes Road
Elgin, IL 60123-1321 847-931-6200
FAX: 847-888-6079
www.the-association.org

*Lynn O'Shea, Executive Director*
*Michael Rosenfeld, Marketing & Communications Coor.*

Day training services to develop work habits and attitudes while providing training in small product assembly, sorting, packaging, collating, & material handling. Instruction also offered in job related knowledge & in personal, social and independent living skills. There is also an on-site specialized Autism Program. Additionally, residential programs (group homes & apartments) are also available for people with developmental disabilities.

**6737 Family Counseling Center**
PO Box 759
Golconda, IL 62938 618-683-2461
FAX: 618-683-2066
e-mail: fccgolconda@shawneelink.com
//fccinconline.org

*Larry Mizell, Executive Director*
*Connie Duncan, Director*
*Nora Beth Hacker, Financial Director*

Provides counseling, developmental training, evaluations, assisted living services, referrals, psychosocial rehabilitation, and a variety of work services.

**6738 Family Matters**
A RC Community Support Systems
1901 S. 4th St
Ste 209
Effingham, IL 62401-4123 217-347-5428
866-436-7842
FAX: 217-347-5119
e-mail: deinhorn@arc-css.org
www.fmptic.org

*Debbie Einhorn, Director Family Support*
*Nancy Mader, Project Coordinator*
*Barbara Utz, Vice President*

Parent Training and Information Center and family support programs for families of children who have disabilities from the ages of birth through 21. Services include: Parent support and training, school advocacy, home visits, information and referral, pa

**6739 Five Star Industries**
P.O.Box 60
1308 Wells Street Road
Du Quoin, IL 62832-60
618-542-5421
FAX: 618-542-5556
e-mail: fivestarinc@5starind.com
5starind.com

*Susan Engelhardt, Executive Director*
Incorporated as a private, non-profit corporation under the laws of the State of Illinois, is an equal opportunity employer and provides equal opportunity in compliance with the Civil Rights Act of 1964 and all other appropriate laws, rules and regulation

**6740 HSI Austin Center For Development**
1819 S Kedzie Ave
Chicago, IL 60623-2623
773-854-1676
FAX: 773-854-8300
Provides an educational program designed to enhance academic, behavioral and social performance of children 4-14 years of age experiencing emotional disorders that result in exclusion from the public school setting.

**6741 Hyde Park-Woodlawn**
950 E 61st St
Chicago, IL 60637-2623
773-324-0280
FAX: 773-324-0285
e-mail: jvshp@jvschicago.org

*Clarissa Williams, Manager*

**6742 Illinois Center for Autism**
548 S Ruby Ln
Fairview Heights, IL 62208-2614
618-398-7500
FAX: 618-394-9869
e-mail: info@illinoiscenterforautism.org
illinoiscenterforautism.org

*Susan Szekely, Executive Director*
A community-based mental health/educational treatment center dedicated to serving autistic clients.

**6743 Julius and Betty Levinson Center**
332 Harrison St
Oak Park, IL 60304-1557
708-383-8887
FAX: 708-383-9025
e-mail: info@ucp.net.org
www.ucp.org

*Paul J, Dulle, President & CEO*
*Peggy Childs, Vice President*
Houses one of its three adult developmental training programs for substantially physically disabled men and women.

**6744 Lake County Health Department**
18 N. County St
Waukegan, IL 60085
847-377-2000
FAX: 847-336-1517
www.co.lake.il.us

*David Stolman, Chairman*
*Stevenson Mountsier, Vice Chairman*
*Barry Burton, Administrator*
Includes counseling, crisis intervention, emergency management, psychotherapy and chemotherapy management for individuals and families.

**6745 Little Friends, Inc.**
140 N Wright St
Naperville, IL 60540-4799
630-355-6533
FAX: 630-355-3176
e-mail: chamilton@lilfriends.com
www.littlefriendsinc.com

*Mike Krol, Chairman*
*Tom Falcone, Vice Chairman*
*John Miller, Treasurer*
*Kathy West, Secretary*
Little Friends has been serving children and adults with autism and other developmental disabilities for over 40 years. Based in Naperville, Little Friends operates three schools, vocational training programs, community-based residential services and the

**6746 MAP Training Center**
7th and Mc Kinley St
Karnak, IL 62956
618-634-9401
FAX: 618-634-9090

*Larry Earnhart, President*
*Cindy Earnhart, Community Liaison*
Training, employment, residential and support services, targeted for adults with developmental disabilities.

**6747 Macon Resources**
P.O.Box 2760
2121 Hubbard Ave.
Decatur, IL 62524-2760
217-875-1910
FAX: 217-875-8899
TTY:217-875-8898
e-mail: jpatterson@maconresources.org
maconresources.org

*Mike Boliek, President*
*Tom Hill, Vice President*
*Molly Smalley, Secretary*
*Chris Funk, Treasurer*
The purpose is to provide a comprehensive array of habilitative/rehabilitative training programs and support services to assist individuals and/or family units of an individual with a developmental disability, mental illness, or other handicapping conditi

**6748 Mary Bryant Home for the Blind**
2960 Stanton St
Springfield, IL 62703-4385
217-529-1611
888-529-1611
FAX: 217-529-6975
e-mail: mbha@marybryanthome.org
marybryanthome.org

*Jerry Curry, Executive Director*
*Sue Lederbrand, Store Manager*
*Bobbi Hickey, Office Manager*
Supportive living facility for blind or visually impaired adults over the age of 22. A supportive living facility remodeled to foster the move to increased independence for residents. The new apartment style housing combined with personal care and other a

**6749 Northern Illinois Special Recreation Association (NISRA)**
285 Memorial Drive
Crystal Lake, IL 60014-3650
815-459-0737
FAX: 815-459-0388
e-mail: info@nisra.org
www.nisra.org

*Brian Shahinian, Executive Director*
Leisure and recreation services to those with disabilities who are unable to participate successfully in park district and city recreation programs.

**6750 Oak Forest Hospital of Cook County**
15900 Cicero Ave
Oak Forest, IL 60452
708-687-7200
FAX: 708-687-7979
TTY:708-687-4794
http://www.cchil.org

*Robert Weinstein, Department Chair*
*Suja Mathew, Associate Chair*
A 654 bed health care center devoted to the diagnosis, rehabilitation and long-term care of adults suffering from chronic illnesses, diseases and physical impairments.

**6751 PARC**
P.O.Box 3418
Peoria, IL 61612-3418
309-691-3800
FAX: 309-689-3613
e-mail: rricketts@arcpeoria.org
parcway.org

*Pamela Creager, Chair*
*Mary Carlson, Vice Chair*
*Mark Windsor Photo, Treasurer*
Serves all ages that are diagnosed with mental retardation and other developmental and physical disabilities. Programs include early intervention, family support, respite care, vocational training, supported employment, adult day programs and residential

**6752 Peoria Area Blind People's Center**
2905 W Garden St
Peoria, IL 61605-1316
309-637-3693
FAX: 309-494-9656
http://peoriablindcenter.org

*Carol Warren, President*
*Cora Quinn, Vice President*
*Prasad Parupalli, Treasurer*
Offers services for the totally blind, legally blind, visually impaired, mentally retarded blind and more with health, counseling, educational, recreational, rehabilitation, computer training and professional training services.

**6753 Pioneer Center of McHenry County**
4001 W Dayton St
McHenry, IL 60050-8379
815-344-1230
FAX: 815-344-3815
e-mail: info@pioneercenter.org
www.pioneercenter.org

*Lorraine Kopczynski, CEO*
*Michael Moushey, Chairman of the Board*
*Dan Haligus, VP Programs*
Pioneer Center is the largest social service agency in McHenry County delivering direct services to more than 2,500 individuals annually. The organization also provides education and outreach to schools and community organizations reaching over 10,000 additional individuals. Pioneer Center delivers community-based services in the areas of:McHenery County PADS, Youth Service Bureau, Autism Services, Developmental Disabilities, Mental Illness, Traumatic Brain Injury and VOICE Sexual Assault.

**6754 Prosthetics and Orthotics Center in Blue Island**
2310 York St
Blue Island, IL 60406-2411
708-597-2611
800-354-7342
FAX: 800-908-1932
www.rehabchicago.org/about/blue_island.php
Provides orthotic and prosthetic fittings and follow-up services to adults and children in the south suburbs of Chicago.

**6755 RB King Counseling Center**
2300 N Edward St
Decatur, IL 62526-4163
217-877-8121
FAX: 217-875-0966

*Gordon Cross MD*
Offers outpatient, individual, group, divorce and meditation, family and re-adjustment counseling.

**6756 REHAB Products and Services**
3715 N Vermilion St
Danville, IL 61832-1130
217-446-1146
FAX: 217-446-1191
e-mail: rehab@soltec.net
workse.org

*Frank L. Brunacci, CEO*
*Crystal Meece, Vice President*
*Carolyn Warner, Production Manager*
janitorial, lawn care, distribution services.

**6757 RIC Northshore**
Rehabilitation Institute of Chicago
345 E Superior St
Chicago, IL 60611-2654
312-238-1000
800-354-7342
e-mail: webmaster@ric.org
www.rehabchicago.org

*Joanne C. Smith, President/CEO*
*Edward B. Case, Vice President*
Provides rehabilitation for sports-related injuries, musculoskeletal conditions, neurological conditions, stroke, arthritis, amputation, burns, and general deconditioning.

**6758 RIC Prosthetics and Orthotics Center**
Rehabilitation Institute of Chicago
Ste 101
1055 175th St
Homewood, IL 60430-4615
312-238-1000
FAX: 708-957-8353
e-mail: webmaster@rehabchicago.org
ric.org

*Don Mc Govern, Cpo*
*George Du, Cp*
Offers almost all the prosthetics and orthotics services provided at RIC's main hospital in downtown Chicago, including consultations, fittings and training.

**6759 RIC Windermere House**
5548 S Hyde Park Blvd
Chicago, IL 60637-1909
773-256-5050
800-354-7342
FAX: 773-256-5060
www.rehabchicago.org

*Meghan Scalise, Manager*
Evaluation, therapeutic services and patient education are offered in the areas of arthritis, multiple sclerosis, musculoskeletal conditions, orthopedics, stroke, spinal cord injury, brain injury and sports medicine.

**6760 Ray Graham Association for People with Disabilities**
901 Warrenville Road
Suite 500
Lisle, IL 60532-1038
630-620-2222
FAX: 630-628-2350
TTY:630-628-2352
e-mail: cathyfickerterill@yahoo.com
ray-graham.org

*Marry Rozzolo Mann, Chairperson*
*Michael Komoli, Vice Chairperson*
*Lou Leonardi, Secretary*
Provides developmental services at 15 sites to infants, children and adults with disabilities. Services range from 1 hr/wk respite to full-time residential.

**6761 Reach Rehabilitation Program: Americana Healthcare**
9401 S Kostner Ave
Oak Lawn, IL 60453-2697
708-423-1505
FAX: 708-423-3822

*Jean M Roche, Owner*
Postacute rehabilitation program.

**6762 Rehabilitation Achievement Center**
345 E Superior St
Chicago, IL 60611-4805
773-792-7948

*Richard Green, Program Director*
*Mary Helen Ekstam, Director Clinical Relations*
Rehabilitation Institute of Chicago (RIC) has aquired the assets of the Rehabilitation Achievement Center (RAC) On Tuesday, August 5, 2003 RIC, took over the leadership, management and operation of RAC's 3 day rehabilitation centers.

**6763 Rehabilitation Institute of Chicago: Alexian Brothers Medical Center**
800 Biesterfield Rd
Elk Grove Village, IL 60007-3361
847-631-5500
800-354-7342
FAX: 847-631-5663
TTY: 847-956-5116
www.alexian.org

*Janice Jastrowski, Manager*
A 32-bed rehabilitation unit under the medical direction and supervision of the Rehabilitation Institute of Chicago.

**6764 Riverside Medical Center**
Mental Health Unit
350 N Wall St
Kankakee, IL 60901-2991
815-933-1671
FAX: 815-935-8160
e-mail: rhuber@rsh.net
riversidehealthcare.org

*Phillip Kambic, CEO*
*Bill W. Douglas, Vice President*
Offers recreation, parenting therapy, emergency services, psychological testing and inpatient treatment programs. Riverside is nationally recognized for its specialty programs in heart care, obstetrics, trauma, oncology, rehabilitation, geriatrics, occupa

**6765 Robert Young Mental Health Center Division of Trinity Regional Haelth System**
Trinity Health Foundation
2701 17th St
Rock Island, IL 61201-5351
309-779-2800
800-322-1431
FAX: 309-779-2027
www.trinityqc.com

*Rick Seidler, President & CEO*
*Greg Pagliuzza, CFO*
Services include comprehensive inpatient rehabilitation, chronic pain management programs, outpatient medical rehabilitation, work hardening programs, vocational evaluation, alcohol and other drug dependency rehabilitation programs, Burn Center, and menta

**6766 Sampson-Katz Center**
2020 W Devon Ave
Chicago, IL 60659-2104
773-761-9000
FAX: 773-764-3131
TTY:773-761-6672
e-mail: jvsskc@jvschicago.org
www.jvschicago.org

*Tobey Andre, President*

**6767 Shelby County Community Services**
160 N Main
Suite 350
Memphis, TN 38103-650
901-222-2300
FAX: 912-222-2090
http://www.shelbycountytn.gov

*Dottie Jones, Director*
Primary focus is substance abuse treatment.

**6768 Streator Unlimited**
305 N Sterling St
Streator, IL 61364-2369
815-673-5574
FAX: 815-673-1714
e-mail: contact@streatorunlimited.org
www.streatorunlimited.org

*Jeffrey Dean, Executive Director*
*Lynn Fukar, Director of Day Services*
*Julie Caestens, Director Residential Services*
Vocational and personal skills training, residential services, client and family support, supported and computerized employment. Serves adults with intellectual disabilities with the goal of enabling them to reach their fullest potential, live as independ

**6769 Swedish Covenant Hospital Rehabilitation Services**
5145 N California Ave
Chicago, IL 60625-3661
773-878-8200
FAX: 773-561-0490
e-mail: ask_us@schosp.org
www.schosp.org

*Mark Newton, President & CEO*
Provides acute rehabilitation services, subacute care and outpatient services for many types of disabling injuries and conditions, including amputation, arthritis, brain injury, general deconditioning, multiple sclerosis, musculoskeletal injuries, stroke,

**6770 TCRC Sight Center**
21310 Route 9
Tremont, IL 61568-2558
309-347-7148
FAX: 309-925-4241
e-mail: info@tcrcorg.com
www.tcrcorg.com

*Jamie Durdel, President & CEO*
*Molly Anderson, Vice President*
Offers services for persons who are totally blind, legally blind, partially sighted or visually impaired along with other disabilities. Have support group, rehabilitation classes, orientation and mobility services, counseling services, low vision clinic,

**6771 Tazewell County Resource Center**
Box 12
Rr 1
Tremont, IL 61568
309-347-7148
FAX: 309-925-4241
e-mail: info@tcrcorg.com
http://www.tcrcorg.com

*Jamie Durdel, President & CEO*
*Molly Anderson, Vice President*
A private, nonprofit agency providing programs for the special needs of infants, adults, children and their families residing in Tazewell County. Services offered include: birth-three infant/parent program, adult day care services, family support, residen

**6772 Thresholds Bridge Deaf North Program**
Thresholds Psychiatric Rehabilitation Centers
4814 N California Ave
Chicago, IL 60625-3624
773-989-8568
FAX: 773-989-1075
e-mail: herminio@thresholds.org
www.thresholds.org

*Michael Szkatulski, President*
*Gregory Hedges, Vice President*
A private, nonprofit psychosocial rehabilitation center that serves the deaf mental health consumers at the highest risk of hospitalization, those with serious and persistent mental illness. The program provides residential case management services focuse

**6773 Thresholds South Suburbs**
12145 Western Ave
Blue Island, IL 60406-1387
708-597-8073
FAX: 708-597-8053
www.thresholds.org

*Natalie Marsh, Program Director*
Services offered include psychosocial, vocational and residential programs for ages 18 or older with a primary diagnosis of mental illness. Facility is wheelchair accessible.

**6774 Trumbull Park**
10530 S Oglesby Ave
Chicago, IL 60617-6140
773-375-7022
FAX: 773-375-5528

*Gregory Terry, Director*
*Diana Moore, Site Supervisor*
*Ada McKinley, Manager*
Offers consultation, education, general counseling, recreation, self-help and social services for children and adults.

**6775 University of Illinois Medical Center**
1740 W Taylor St
Chicago, IL 60612-7232
312-355-4000
FAX: 312-996-7770
http://hospital.uillinois.edu/

*Rajiv Pai, Chief*
*Marilyn Plomann, Manager*
Offers services for the totally blind, legally blind, visually impaired, mentally retarded blind and more with health, counseling, educational, recreational, rehabilitation, computer training and professional training services.

**6776 VanMatre Rehabilitation Center**
950 S Mulford Rd
Rockford, IL 61108-4274
815-381-8500
866-754-3347
FAX: 815-484-9953
e-mail: webcontentcoordinator@rhsnet.org
http://www.rockfordhealthsystem.org

*Ken Bowman, CEO*
*Scott Craig, Medical Director*
A CARF-accredited comprehensive rehabilitation center based within the Rockford Memorial Hospital providing inpatient and outpatient services for physically and cognitively challenged persons with debilitating illness and injuries.

**6777 Warren Achievement Center**
1220 E 2nd Ave
Monmouth, IL 61462-2404
309-734-3131
FAX: 309-734-7114
e-mail: info@warrenachievement.com
warrenachievement.com

*Michael Lewis, President*
*Jim Kesse, Vice President*
For developmentally disabled children and adults. Parent-infant education programs are for parents of infants with disabilities or developmental delays; Children's Group Homes which serve children on a fulltime basis and can serve additional children on a

## Indiana

**6778 Ball Memorial Hospital**
2401 W University Ave
Muncie, IN 47303-3499
765-747-3111
FAX: 765-747-3313
http://iuhealth.org/ball-memorial/

*Mike Haley, CEO*
Offers rehabilitation services, occupational therapy, physical therapy and more for the physically challenged child or adult.

**6779 Community Health Network**
1500 N Ritter Ave
Indianapolis, IN 46219-3027
317-355-4275
800-775-7775
FAX: 317-351-7723
www.ecommunity.com

*Keith Thompson, Manager*
*Anita Harden, President*
A leading not-for-profit health system offering convenient access to expert physicians, advanced treatments and leading edge technology, all focused on getting patients well and back to their lives. With caring compassion, Community's 5 hospitals and 70 + sites of care continually strive to improve the health and well being of those individuals in central Indiana who entrust care to us.

**6780 Crossroads Industrial Services**
8320 E 33rd St
Indianapolis, IN 46226
317-897-7320
FAX: 317-897-9763
e-mail: info@crossroadsindustrialservices.com
www.crossroadsindustrialservices. com

*Anne Shupe, Finance Executive*
*Curtiss Quirin, CEO*
Assisting customers with short-term, seasonal, and long-term outsourcing needs. Many consider Crossroads an extension of their company

**6781 Department of Veterans Affairs Vet Center #418**
302 W. Washington St
Room E120
Indianapolis, IN 46204- 2738
317-232-3910
FAX: 317-232-7721
e-mail: vcen418@evansville.net
www.in.gov/veteran/sso/fac

*Charles T. Applegate, Director*
Provides readjustment counseling to combat veterans. Onsite assistance for employment problems, vocational rehabilitation and sexual trauma counsel.

**6782 Frasier Rehabilitation Center Division of Clark Memorial Hospital**
2201 Greentree N
Clarksville, IN 47129-8957
812-218-6590
FAX: 812-218-6597
http://www.jhsmh.org/Frazier-Rehab-Institute-

*Catherine Lucas Spalding, Administrator*
Designed to help patients in their adjustment to a physically limiting condition, both psychologically and physically, by helping to maximize each patient's abilities so he or she can function as independently as possible. The program treats patients whos

**6783 HealthSouth Deaconess Rehabilitation Hospital**
4100 Covert Ave
Evansville, IN 47714-5559
812-476-9983
800-677-3422
FAX: 812-476-4270
healthsouth.com

*Barbara Butler, President*
*Tina Densley, Opperations Director*
*Brett Hirt, Director, Therapy Operations*
*Trish Draeger, Chief Nursing Officer*
An 80-bed JCAHO accredited freestanding hospital specializing in comprehensive medical rehabilitation for Brain Injury, Spinal Cord Injury, Orthopedic, Pulmonary, Cardiac, Oncology and disabilities and general disabilities.

**6784 Healthwin Specialized Care**
20531 Darden Rd
South Bend, IN 46637-2999
574-272-0100
FAX: 574-277-3233
e-mail: contact@healthwin.org
healthwin.org

*Connie McCahill, President*
*Lauren Davis, Vice President*
*John Cergnul, Treasurer*
No other facility in the area has a homelike environment like ours. Its simply part of our culture. Rehabilitation therapy that includes physical, occupational, speech, respiratory and a full time in-house therapist. Other services include a wound special

**6785 Memorial Regional Rehabilitation Center**
615 N Michigan St
South Bend, IN 46601-1033
574-647-7312
877-282-0964
20-bed CARF accredited inpatient rehabilitation, outpatient orthopedic clinic and work performance program, head injury clinic. Outpatient neuro rehab and a driver education and training program are provided.

**6786 Saint Joseph Regional Medical Center- South Bend**
837 E. Cedar Street
Suite 350
South Bend, IN 46617-2814
574-237-7377
FAX: 574-237-7312
e-mail: thefoundation@sjrmc.com
sjmed.com

*Albert Gutierrez, President & CEO*
*Steven Gable, Vice President*
*Janice Dunn, CFO*
Continuum of rehabilitation services offered. Included are: acute rehabilitation, a 26 bed CARF accredited comprehensive inpatient unit, a CARF certified inpatient brain injury program, a CARF outpatient day treatment brain injury program, comprehensive o

## Iowa

**6787 Crossroads of Western Iowa**
1 Crossroads Pl
Missouri Valley, IA 51555-6069
712-642-4114
FAX: 712-642-4115
e-mail: info@cwiowa.org
explorecrossroads.com

*Brent Dillinger, CEO*
*Pat Kocour, President*
*Steven Van Riper, Vice President*
*Darci Tierney, Secretary*
CWI provides services in Missouri Valley, Onawa and Council Bluffs, Iowa. An array of services for people with mental illness, mental retardation and brain injury are provided in each location.

**6788 Des Moines Division-VA Central Iowa Health Care System**
3600 30th St
Des Moines, IA 50310-5753
515-699-5999
800-294-8387
FAX: 515-699-5862
http://www.centraliowa.va.gov

*Donald Cooper, Director*
*Fredrick Bahls, Chief Of Staff*
*Christine Gregory, Associate Director*
VA Cental Iowa Health Care System is the result of the 1997 merger of the Des Moines and Knoxville, Iowa, VA Medical Centers. This integrated healthcare system brings 2 previously separate organizational structures, located 40 miles apart, into one cohesi

**6789 Easter Seals Iowa**
Easter Seals National
PO Box 4002
Des Moines, IA 50333-4002
515-289-1933
FAX: 515-289-1281
TTY:515-289-4069
e-mail: infi@eastersealsia.org
http://ia.easterseals.com

*Sherri Nielsen, President & CEO*
Easter Seals is a leading nonprofit provider of services to Iowans with disabilities. Services include vocational and employment training, camping recreation and respite services, craft training and sales, home and farm adaptations, transportation, schola

**6790 Genesis Regional Rehabilitation Center**
Genesis Health System
1227 E.Rusholme St
Davenport, IA 52803-3396
563-421-1000
FAX: 563-421-3499
genesishealth.com

*Doug Cropper, President & CEO*
*Kenneth Croken, Vice President*
Serves persons of all ages experiencing a disability, whether acquired at birth or following a serious interdisciplinary service. Rehabilitation programs include acute rehabilitation; adult rehabilitation, pediatric rehabilitation, outpatient orthopaedics

**6791 Homelink**
Van G Miller & Associates
1111 W S Marnan Drive
Waterloo, IA 50701-2817
319-235-7173
800-482-1993
FAX: 319-235-7822
http://www.vgmhomelink.com/

*Dave Kazynski, President*
*Rick Hibben, Coordinator*
A national network of home medical equipment, respiratory therapy, rehabilitation and infusion therapy service providers with over 2,500 locations serving all fifty states.

**6792 Iowa Central Industries**
127 Avenue M
Fort Dodge, IA 50501-5797
515-576-2126
FAX: 515-576-2251
http://www.bloglines.com/company/3495669/post

*Tom Eckman, Executive Director*
Services include evaluation and training in pre-vocational and vocational skills, personal behavior management, cognitive skills, communication skills, self-care skills and social skills. Services arranged include: independent living training, medical ser

6793 **Life Skills Laundry Division**
1510 Industrial Rd SW
Le Mars, IA 51031-3009
712-546-4785
FAX: 712-546-4985

*Don Nore, Executive Director*

6794 **MIW**
909 S 14th Ave
Marshalltown, IA 50158-3610
641-752-3697
FAX: 641-752-1614

*Rich Byers, President/CEO*
Vocational services for adults with disabilities. Includes organizational employment services, supported employment, job placement.

6795 **Mercy Dubuque Physical Rehabilitation Unit**
250 Mercy Dr
Dubuque, IA 52001-7320
563-589-8000
FAX: 563-589-8162
www.mercydubuque.com

*Russel M. Knight, CEO*
Provides services which open the door to improved communication, offering the opportunity to enrich the quality of life. Mercy offers many other branches of services including, rehabilitation services for children, pulmonary rehabilitation program, servic

6796 **Mercy Medical Center-Pain Services**
1111 6th Ave
Des Moines, IA 50314-2611
515-247-3121
FAX: 515-248-8867
www.mercydesmoines.org/services/painservices

*Dana L. Simon, MD*
*Dave Vellinga, President & CEO*
*Steven Kukla, Vice President*
An outpatient program dedicated to helping people with chronic pain live more productive, satisfying lives. The program is not designed for conditions that are surgically curable, but rather approaches the problem using a comprehensive, holistic treatment

6797 **Nishna Productions-Shenandoah Work Center**
P.O.Box 70
Shenandoah, IA 51601-70
712-246-1242
FAX: 712-246-1243
e-mail: nci@nishna.org
nishna.org

*Mary Rolf, President*
Shelter, workshop and job training for the disabled. Some of the services we provide are Work Activity, Adult Day Activity Program, Personal & Social Adjustment, Residential Services, Home & Community Based Services & Employment Resources.

6798 **Northstar Community Services**
3420 University Ave
Waterloo, IA 50701-2050
319-236-0901
888-879-1365
FAX: 319-236-3701
e-mail: info@northstarcs.org
www.northstarcs.org

*Mark Witmar, Executive Director*
*Mary Wankowicz, Director of operations*
*Patty Holcomb, Assistant Director*
Provides adult day services, employment services and supported community living so people with disabilities can live and work in the community. Populations served include, but are not limited to: senior adults with age-related disabilities, youth with dis

6799 **Options of Linn County**
935 2nd street
SW
Cedar Rapids, IA 52404-3100
319-892-5000
FAX: 319-892-5849
e-mail: optons@linncounty.org
linncounty.org

*Joel D. Miller, Auditor*
*Sharon Gonzalez, Treasurer*
Options of Lynn County works with community businesses in providing employment services to adults with disabilities. Options is a publicly operated service provider within the Linn County Community Services department. Options serves over 350 people annua

6800 **RISE**
106 Rainbow Dr
Elkader, IA 52043-9075
563-245-1868
FAX: 563-245-2859

*Ed Josten, Manager*

6801 **Ragtime Industries**
116 N 2nd St
Albia, IA 52531-1624
641-932-7813
FAX: 641-932-7814
e-mail: ragtime@cknet.net
www.ragtimeind.com

*Lisa Glenn, Executive Director*
A work-oriented rehabilitation organization which provides training for mentally and physically disabled adults in Monroe County. A variety of programs which help to develop each person's individual potential are offered so that the person may live as nor

6802 **Sunshine Services**
1106 East 9th St
Spencer, IA 51301-225
712-262-7805
FAX: 712-262-8369

*Ann Vandehar, Executive Director*

6803 **Tenco Industries**
710 Gateway Dr
Ottumwa, IA 52501-2204
641-682-8114
FAX: 641-684-4223
e-mail: clogan@tenco.org
www.tenco.org

*Carol Logan, Acting Executive Director*
*Denny Baum, Director Of Vocational Services*
To advocate and provide opportunities for people with disabilities, or conditions that limit their abilities, to develop and maintain the skills necessary for personal dignity and independence in all areas of life. Provide a wide array of services to individuals with disabilities. By looking at each person as individuals, we are able to work with them to maximize their skills. Residentials services, including HCBS and CSALA are also provided in all communities.

## Kansas

6804 **Arrowhead West**
1100 E Wyatt Earp Blvd
Dodge City, KS 67801-5337
620-227-8803
FAX: 620-227-8812
e-mail: web@arrowheadwest.org
www.arrowheadwest.org

*Kelly Mason, Chairperson*
*Michael Stein, Vice Chairperson*
*Lori Pendergast, President*
*Anita Allard, Treasurer*

Services and programs offered include: developmental and therapy services for children birth to age 3. Adult center-based work services and community integrated employment options; adult life skills and retirement programs; adult residential services incl

**6805 Big Lakes Developmental Center**
1416 Hayes Dr
Manhattan, KS 66502-5066
785-776-9201
FAX: 785-776-9830
e-mail: biglakes@biglakes.org
biglakes.org

*Lori Feldkamp, President*
*Shawn Funk, Community Education Director*
A private nonprofit Community Developmental Disability Organization (CDDO) serving individuals with developmental disabilities in Riley, Geary, Clay and Pottawatome counties in Kansas. Big lakes is supported by county mill levy and federal and state fundi

**6806 Developmental Services of Northwest Kansas**
Ste 10
2703 Hall St
Hays, KS 67601-1964
785-625-5678
800-637-2229
FAX: 785-625-8204
e-mail: comments@notes1.dsnwk.org
dsnwk.org

*Jerry Michaud, President*
*Ruth Lang, Administrative Assistant*
A private nonprofit organization serving both children and adults with disabilities. Offers services to children ages birth to three years, youth and adults through a network of community-based and outreach programs and inter-agency agreements with other

**6807 ENVISION**
2301 S Water St
Wichita, KS 67213-4819
316-267-2244
FAX: 316-267-4312
e-mail: envision@envisionus.com
www.envisionus.com

*Frank D. Clepper, President*
*Kent Wilson, CFO*
*Kathy Cox, Vice President*
*Buddy Sell, COO*
Provides jobs, job training and vision rehabilitation services to people who are blind or low vision. A private not-for-profit agency uniquely combining employment opportunitites with rehabilitation services and public education.

**6808 Heartspring**
8700 E 29th St N
Wichita, KS 67226-2169
316-634-8700
800-835-1043
FAX: 316-634-0555
e-mail: kgrover@heartspring.org
www.heartspring.org

*Gary Singleton, CEO*
*Paul Faber, VP Of Operations*
*Katie Grover, Director Of Marketing*
Heartspring provides outpatient therapies, evaluations and consultations for children with special needs through Heartspring Pediatric Services. The Heartspring School is a residential and day school for children ages 5-21 with multiple disabilities. Children with autism and their families receive resources through the Heartspring CARE program. The Heartspring Hearing Center provides services to individuals of all ages.

**6809 Indian Creek Nursing Center**
6515 W 103rd St
Overland Park, KS 66212-1798
913-633-7000
FAX: 913-642-3982

*Randy Sutterfield, Administrator*
Postacute rehabilitation program. A 120-bed nursing home facility.

**6810 Johnson County Developmental Supports**
10501 Lackman Rd
Lenexa, KS 66219-1223
913-826-2626
FAX: 913-492-5171
e-mail: info@jocogov.org
jcds.org

*Dale Chaffin, Chairman*
*Michael Lally, Vice Chair*
*Scott Tschudy, Treasurer*
*Jessica Dain, Secretary*
JCDS is the community Developmental Disability Organization for Johnson County, Kansas. Provides supports in the form of direct services to people on a daily basis. Through a person-centered process and within availiable resources services are shaped to f

**6811 Ketch Industries**
1006 E Waterman St
Wichita, KS 67211-1525
316-383-8700
800-766-3777
FAX: 316-383-8715
e-mail: webmaster@ketch.org
ketch.org

*Fred Badders, Chairman*
*Carla Bienhoff, Chairman*
*Loren Anthony, Secretary*
*Dan Crug, Treasurer*
The mission of Ketch is to promote independence for persons with disabilities through innovative learning experiences that support individuals choices for working, living and playing in their community.

**6812 Lakemary Center**
100 Lakemary Dr
Paola, KS 66071-1855
913-557-4000
FAX: 913-557-4910
lakemaryctr.org

*William Craig, President*
*Paul Sokoloff, Chair*
*Gayle Richardson, Vice Chair*
*Lydia Marien, Secretary*
A private, not-for-profit day and residential training facility which provides for the assessment, education, training, therapy and social development of children and adults, moderate and severe mental retardation. The Center is based 28 miles southwest o

**6813 Northview Developmental Services**
700 E 14th St
Newton, KS 67117-5702
316-283-5170
FAX: 316-283-5196
e-mail: nds@northviewdsi.com
http://northviewdev.mennonite.net/

*Mary Holloway, CEO*
The mission is to provide quality supportive and coordinating services to persons with developmental disabilities, assisting them to grow as they integrate into the community. Further, our mission is to improve the quality of their lives by providing acce

## Kentucky

**6814 Cardinal Hill Rehabilitation Hospital**
Cadinal Hill Medical Center
2050 Versailles Rd
Lexington, KY 40504-1499
859-254-5701
800-233-3260
FAX: 859-231-1365
www.cardinalhill.org

*Gary R. Payne, CEO*

Provides occupational health services, therapy services and urgent medical treatment of injured workers.

**6815 Frazier Rehab Institute**
220 Abraham Flexner Way
Louisville, KY 40202-1887 502-582-7400
FAX: 502-582-7477
www.frazierrehab.org

*Jamie Ochsner, Manager*
*Steve Ahr, VP Frazier Rehab/Neurscience*
Frazier Rehab Institute is a regional healthcare system dedicated entirely to rehabilitation. Through an expansive network of inpatient and outpatient facilites in Kentucky and southern Indiana, Frazier offers a wide array of services based on one common

**6816 HealthSouth Northern Kentucky Rehabilitation Hospital**
201 Medical Village Dr
Edgewood, KY 41017-3407 859-341-2044
800-860-6004
FAX: 859-341-2813
healthsouth.com

*Richard Evans, CEO*
*Mary Pfeffer, Director Therapy Operations*
*Regina Soloria, Director Nursing*
*Kathleen Geers, Director Marketing*
Offers all types of inpatient and outpatient rehabilitation services such as occupational therapy, physical therapy, speech therapy. Respiratory therpay, Psychology, Aquatics, Case Managemenet/Social Work and Nutritional Services.

**6817 King's Daughter's Medical Center's Rehab Unit/Work Hardening Program**
2201 Lexington Ave
Ashland, KY 41101-2843 606-408-4000
888-377-5362
FAX: 606-327-7542
e-mail: info@kdmc.net
www.kdmc.com

*Fred Jackson, CEO*
*Cathy Cooper-Weidner, Vice President*
Offers a 27-bed, inpatient rehabilitation services unit treating physical disabilities related to accident or illness. The program provides an interdisciplinary inpatient program designed to restore the individual to the highest level of independence. It

**6818 LifeSkills Industries**
380 Suwannee Trail St
Bowling Green, KY 42103-6499 270-901-5000
FAX: 270-782-0058
e-mail: sbell@lifeskills.com
lifeskills.com

*Alice Simpson, CEO*
LifeSkills will be the reliable advocate, dependable safety net and provider of choice, for high quality, accessable services and supports for the citizens of south-central Kentucky whos lives are affected by mental illness, developmental disablilities or

**6819 Low Vision Services of Kentucky**
120 N. Eagle Creek Drive
Suite 501
Lexington, KY 40509- 1827 859-264-2916
800-627-2020
FAX: 859-977-1136
e-mail: jvanarsdall@retinaky.com
www.lowvisionky.com

*Regina Callihan-May, O.D.*
*Jeanne Van Arsdall, Co-ordinator*
*Maryanne Inman, Practice Administrator*
Offers educational, recreational and rehabilitational services and devices for the visually impaired, legally blind, totally blind.

**6820 Muhlenberg County Opportunity Center**
615 Oppurtunity Way
Greenville, KY 42345-1416 270-338-5970
FAX: 270-338-5977
muhlon.com

*Chuck Hammonds, Manager*
*Charles Hamonds, Director*
Post-acute rehabilitation facility with programs including a workshop with hand packaging of manufactured goods.

**6821 New Vision Enterprises**
1900 Brownsboro Rd
Louisville, KY 40206-2102 502-893-0211
800-405-9135
FAX: 502-893-3885

*Larry Sherman, Plant Manager*
Offers employment training and services for the blind and legally blind.

**6822 Park DuValle Community Health Center, Inc.**
3015 Wilson Ave
Louisville, KY 40211-1969 502-774-4401
FAX: 502-775-6195
e-mail: rjones@pdchc.org
www.pdchc.org

*Richard K Jones, President*
*John Howard MD, Medical Director*
*Dave Gerwig, CFO*
*Ann Hagan, Administrator*
Offers services for the totally blind, legally blind, visually impaired, mentally retarded blind and more with health, counseling, educational, recreational, rehabilitation, computer training and professional training services.

## Louisiana

**6823 Alliance House**
427 S Foster Drive
Baton Rouge, LA 70806-2723 225-987-0013
FAX: 225-346-0857

A non-residential facility serving male and female chronically mentally ill. Services include: social service, vocational evaluation, pre-vocational training and job placement.

**6824 Assumption Activity Center**
4201 Highway 1
Napoleonville, LA 70390-8628 985-369-2907
FAX: 985-369-2657
e-mail: arcoa.catbl.net

*Warren Gonzales, Manager*
A community work center providing prevocational training and extended employment for adults with disabilities. Services include: social services, work activities, specialized training and supported employment.

**6825 Bancroft Rehabilitation Living Centers**
3434 Canal St
New Orleans, LA 70119-6208 504-482-3075
FAX: 504-483-2135
www.bancroftneurohealth.org

*Dr. Robert Voogt, Owner*
*Toni Pergolin, President & CEO*
*Cynthia Boyer, Executive Director*
Mission is to nurture abilities and independence of people with neurological challenges by providing a broad spectrum of advanced therapeutic and educational programs and by fostering the development of best practices in the field through research and pro

**6826 Caddo-Bossier Association for Retarded Citizens**
4103 Lakeshore Dr
Shreveport, LA 71109-1998
318-636-0258
FAX: 318-221-4262

*Janet Parker, Director*
A community operated workshop for male and female mentally retarded individuals. It provides work evaluation and transitional and extended employment.

**6827 Deaf Action Center Of Greater New Orleans**
Catholic Charities
1000 Howard Ave
Suite 200
New Orleans, LA 70113-1903
504-523-3755
FAX: 504-523-2789
TTY:504-615-4944
e-mail: ccano@ccano.org
www.ccano.org

*Gordon R. Wadge, President & CEO*
*Susan R. Johnson, Chairwoman*
This community service and resource center serves deaf, deaf-blind, hard of hearing and speech-impaired persons in the greater New Orleans area regardless of age, religion, race or secondary disability. DAC provides interpreting services, equipment distri

**6828 Donaldsville Association for Retarded Citizens**
1030 Clay St
Donaldsonville, LA 70346-3518
225-473-4516
FAX: 225-473-4517
e-mail: daarc@eatel.net

*Marlene Domingue, Executive Director*
A private, nonprofit sheltered work program working with the mentally retarded and developmentally disabled adults.

**6829 East Jefferson General Hospital Rehab Center**
4200 Houma Blvd
Metairie, LA 70006-2996
504-454-4000
www.ejgh.org

*Mark J, Peters, President & CEO*
*Judy Brown, Vice President*
*Raymond DeCorte, Chief Medical Officer*
Provides the highest quality, compassionate healthcare to the people we serve. East Jefferson General Hospital will be the region's healthcare leader providing the highest quality care through innovation and collaboration with our team members, medical st

**6830 Family Service Society**
Ste 201
2515 Canal St
New Orleans, LA 70119-6489
504-822-0800
FAX: 504-822-0831
http://www.fsgno.org

*Ronald Mc Clain, CEO*
*Jim B. Hubbard, Vice President*
*Rebecca Garside, Director*
Offers services for the totally blind, legally blind, visually impaired, mentally retarded blind and more with health, counseling, educational, recreational, rehabilitation, computer training and professional training services.

**6831 Foundation Industries**
9995 Highway 64
Zachary, LA 70791
225-654-6288
FAX: 225-654-3988

*Jim Lambert-Oswald, President*
*Jim Oswald, General Manager*
A private, nonprofit sheltered workshop providing extended employment and work activities for the mentally retarded and developmentally disabled clients. Objectives are to build work skills through supervision, develop social interaction and manifest basi.

**6832 Handi-Works Productions**
2700 Lee St
Alexandria, LA 71301-4358
318-442-3377
FAX: 318-473-0858
This is a nonprofit workshop for male and female clients who have vocational handicapping conditions. All types of handicapped persons are served in this non-residential workshop.

**6833 HealthSouth Rehabilitation Hospital Of Baton Rouge**
8595 United Plaza Blvd
Baton Rouge, LA 70809-2251
225-927-0567
800-264-0567
FAX: 225-928-0317
healthsouth.com

*Jacque Shadle, CEO*
*Derrick Landreneau, Director of Nursing services*
Dedicated to one field of medicine - physical rehabilitation medicine - and are committed to one goal, helping patients achieve the highest level of functioning possible after a debilitating injury or illness.

**6834 Iberville Association for Retarded Citizens**
24615 J.Gerald Berret Blvd
Plaquemine, LA 70764-201
225-687-4062
FAX: 225-687-3272
e-mail: arci@eatel.net

*Paul Rhorer, Executive Director*
A private sheltered work program operating out of one facility and providing transitional, extended employment and work activities for mentally and developmentally ill adults.

**6835 Lighthouse for the Blind in New Orleans**
123 State St
New Orleans, LA 70118-5793
504-899-4501
888-792-0163
FAX: 504-895-4162
lhb.org

*Katy Casbarian, Chair*
*Adrienne Casbarian, Vice Chair*
Offers services for the totally blind, legally blind, visually impaired, mentally retarded blind and more with health, counseling, educational, recreational, rehabilitation, computer training and professional training services.

**6836 Louisiana Center for the Blind**
101 S Trenton St
Ruston, LA 71270-4431
318-251-2891
800-234-4166
FAX: 318-251-0109
e-mail: pallen@lcb-ruston.com
lcb-ruston.com

*Pam Allen, Executive Director*
*Neita Ghrigsby, Office Manager*
A new kind of orientation and training center for blind persons. The center is privately operated and provides quality instruction in the skills of blindness. Offers employment assistance, computer literacy training, summer training and employment project

**6837 Louisiana State University Eye Center**
Lousiana State University
3700 St.
Charles Avenue
New Orleans, LA 70115-2272
504-412-1200
FAX: 504-412-1315
www.lsuhsc.edu

*Jayne S. Weiss, Director*
*Kelli McMichael, Manager*
The LSU Eye Center is part of the LSU Medical Center complex in downtown New Orleans. It is in the LSU-Lions Building at

2020 Gravier Street between South Bolivar and South Prieur streets. The Center provides expert eye care at every level, from routine e

**6838 New Orleans Speech and Hearing Center**
1636 Toledano St
New Orleans, LA 70115-4598 504-897-2606
FAX: 504-891-6048
noshc.org

*Josh Marino, President*
*Mary Beth Green, Vice President*
*Alan Ganucheau, Treasurer*
*Kindall James, Secretary*
This non-residential facility serves male and female clients for purposes of evaluating speech and hearing problems and providing speech therapy, hearing aids and other assistive technology for speech and hearing.

**6839 Port City Enterprises**
836 N 7th St.
Port Allen, LA 70767-113 225-344-1142
877-344-1142
FAX: 225-344-1192
http://www.portcityenterprises.org

*William Kleinpeter, President*
*Mark Graffeo, Vice President*
*L.J. Treuil, Secretary*
*Philip Bourgoyne*
Offers supported employment, sheltered work and supervised programs for the mentally retarded, ages 22 and over.

**6840 Rehabilitation Center at Thibodeaux Regional**
Rehab Care
602 N Acadia Rd
Thibodaux, LA 70301-4847 985-493-4731
800-822-8442
FAX: 985-449-4600
e-mail: infoA@thibodaux.com
www.thibodaux.com/rehabilitation.html

*Jan Torres, Program Manager*
*Rose Pipes, Clinical Coordinator*
Designed to help patients in their adjustment to a physically limiting condition, both physically and psychologically, by helping to maximize each patients abilities so he or she can function as independently as possible.

**6841 St. Patrick RehabCare Unit**
RehabCare
524 Doctor Michael Debakey Dr
Lake Charles, LA 70601-5725 337-491-7590
888-722-9355
FAX: 337-491-7157
www.stpatrichospital.org/serv_rehab_main.htm

*Larry A Hauskins, Manager*
*Ruth Thornton, Admissions*
A comprehensive physical and cognitive rehabilitation program designed to help individuals who have experienced a disabling injury or illness. The goal of the Rehabilitation Center is to ensure an optimum level of recovery in a cost-effective way for each

**6842 Touro Rehabilitation CenterLCMC (Louisiana Children's Medical Center)**
1401 Foucher St
New Orleans, LA 70115-3515 504-897-8345
FAX: 504-897-8393
e-mail: info@touro.com
www.touro.com

*Jeanette Ray, VP of Rehab and Post Acute Srv*
*Janet Clark, Director of Inpatient Service*
*Marylee Pontillas, Director of Outpatient Rehab Srv*
*James Montgomery, CEO*
Located in New Orleans' Garden District, Touro Rehabilitation is a comprehensive rehabilitation facility dedicated to the restoration of function and independence for individuals with disabilities. The scope of rehabilitation services is broad, with 3 CARF accreditations for Brain Injury, Spinal Cord Injury and General Rehabilitation. TRC opened in 1984 and offers 69 rehab beds. TRC is part of Touro Infirmary which has a proud 150 year history as a nonprofit teaching hospital.

**6843 Training, Resource & Assistive-Technology**
P.O.Box 1051
New Orleans, LA 70148-1 504-280-5700
FAX: 504-280-5707
e-mail: ggaglian@uno.edu
www.uno.edu/trac

*Ken Zangla, Director*
*Naomi Moore, Assistant Director*
*Connie Lanier, Coordinator*
Provides quality services to persons with disabilities, rehabilitation professionals, educators and employers. Built a solid reputation for its innovative training programs and community outreach efforts. The Center is recognized as a valuable resource st

## Maine

**6844 Charlotte White Center**
572 Bangor Rd
Dover Foxcroft, ME 04426-3373 207-564-2426
888-440-4158
FAX: 207-564-2404
e-mail: info@charlottewhite.org
charlottewhitecenter.com

*Richard M. Brown, CEO*
*Charles G. Clemons, COO*
*Dale Shaw, CFO*
*Mary Louis McEwen, President*
A nonprofit agency, devoted to assisting adults and children with mental retardation, mental health, physical handicaps, and elder age related issues. With headquarters in Dover-Foxcroft Maine, the agency provides multiple levels of social services, inclu

**6845 Iris Network for the Blind**
189 Park Ave
Portland, ME 04102-2909 207-774-6273
FAX: 207-774-0679
e-mail: ashah@theiris.org
theiris.org

*James E. Phipps, Executive Director*
*Aparna Shah, Executive Assistant*
*Tom Fortier, Manager*
A statewide resource and catalyst for people who are visually impaired or blind so they can attain their determined level of independence and integration into the community.

**6846 Roger Randall Center**
45 School St
Houlton, ME 04730-2010 207-532-4068
FAX: 207-532-7334
www.cla-maine.org

*Tom Moakler, CEO*
*Lloyd Chase, Vice President*
*Rob Faulkner, Treasurer*
The Roger Randall Cneter is one of five Day Habilitation Programs adminsitered by Community Living Association, a private, non-profit agency. These programs may provide a supportive environment that allows the individual to achieve their maximum growth po

**6847 Sebasticook Farms-Great Bay Foundation**
P.O.Box 65
Saint Albans, ME 04971 207-487-4399
FAX: 207-938-5670
e-mail: tad@tdstelme.net
www.greatbayfoundation.org

*Tom Davis, Executive Director*
*Pam Erskin, Program Coordinator*
Provides residential, educational and vocational services to adults who are developmentally disabled in order to maximize independent living and to provide assistance in obtaining an earned income.

**6848 Social Learning Center**
80 Strawberry Avenue
Lewiston, ME 04240-3363 207-783-4672
877-208-6134
FAX: 207-783-4673
http://www.oslc.org/

*Debbie Beam, Manager*
Post accute rehabilitation program.

## Maryland

**6849 Blind Industries and Services of Maryland**
3345 Washington Blvd
Baltimore, MD 21227-1602 410-737-2600
888-322-4567
FAX: 410-737-2665
bism.org

*Fredrick J. Puente, President*
*Donald J. Morris, Chairperson*
*Walter A. Brown, Vice Chairperson*
*James R. Berens, Treasurer*
Offers a comprehensive residential rehabilitation training program for people who are blind. Areas of instruction: braille, cane travel, independent living, computer, adjustment and blindness seminars.

**6850 Center for Neuro-Rehabilitation**
2340238 N Cary St
Annapolis, MD 21223 410-263-1704
410-462-4711
e-mail: cnrnhq@erols.com

*Jeanne Fryer*
*Laurent Pierre-Philippe*
Provide community-based inpatient and outpatient acute rehabilitation, vocational services and long-term care. Specializing in treating complex neurological conditions including spinal cord injuries, multiple sclerosis, strokes, and other brain injuries resulting from trauma, anoxia, tumors, genetic malformations and other related conditions. Locations in Annapolis, Bethesda, Frederick, Towson, MD and Fairfax, Va. CNR is licensed, a Medicare provider and CARF accredited.

**6851 Child Find/Early Childhood Disabilities Unit Montgomery County Public Schools**
Ste A4
10731 Saint Margarets Way
Kensington, MD 20895- 2831 301-929-2224
FAX: 301-929-2223

*Julie Bader, Supervisor*
Offers free developmental screening for children ages 3 years until eligible for kindergarten, evaluation and placement services.

**6852 Greater Baltimore Medical Center**
6701 N Charles St
Baltimore, MD 21204-6881 443-849-2000
800-597-9142
FAX: 443-849-2631
www.gbmc.org/medicine/hoover

*John B. Chessare, President & CEO*
*Harold J. Tucker, Chief Of Staff*
*Eric L. Melchoir, Vice President*
Offers services for the visually impaired and blind with low vision exams. Rehabilitation teaching and orientation and mobility in the home or workplace. Also offers a bimonthly newsletter for $12/yr for Hoover patients and monthly share group.

**6853 Greenery Extended Care Center: Baltimore**
1300 S Ellwood Ave
Baltimore, MD 21224-4900 410-342-6644
FAX: 410-327-3949

*Shane Duffy, Administrator*
150 beds offering complex care treatment, extended rehabilitation and neurological restorative care. OUT OG BUSINESS

**6854 James Lawrence Kernan Hospital**
2200 Kernan Dr
Baltimore, MD 21207-6697 410-285-6566
888-453-7626
FAX: 410-448-6854
www.kernan.org

*Michael Jablonover, President & CEO*
*John P. Straumanis, Vice President*
*Gaylene Adamczyk, Director*
Kernan reigns as Maryland's origional orthopaedic hospital with a staff which consists of a support team of orthopaedic physician assistants and dedicated nurses in the Post Anesthesia Care Unit and on the Medical/Surgical Unit, guaranteeing the highest q

**6855 Levindale Hebrew Geriatric Center**
2434 W Belvedere Ave
Baltimore, MD 21215-5267 410-466-8700
FAX: 410-601-2700
www.lifebridgehealth.org

*Jason A. Blavatt, Chair*
*David Uhlfelder, Vice Chair*
*Edward L. Morris, Treasurer*
*Sharon Caplan, Secretary*
a 292-licensed bed facility, which includes 172-comprehensive care beds, 20 subacute beds, and a 26-bed dementia care unit. Levindale's 120-bed specialty hospital consists of 20 gerospychiatric beds, 80 complex medical beds, some with ventilator capacity

**6856 Meridan Medical Center For Subacute Care**
770 York Rd
Towson, MD 21204 410-821-5500
FAX: 410-821-6735

*Yvette Caldwell, Administrator*
Patients receive around-the-clock professional nursing care; physical and occupational, speech and respiratory therapists also assist patients. Each patient's individualized plan of care is reviewed and updated as patient needs change. Careful discharge p.

**6857 Rehabilitation Opportunities**
5100 Philadelphia Way
Lanham, MD 20706-4412 301-731-4242
FAX: 301-731-4191
roiworks.org

*Tom Purcell, President*
*Bruce Shapiro, Vice President*
*David Fierst, Secretary*
*Henry Neloms, Treasurer*

Organization offering day programs, evaluation, work adjustments and sheltered workshops for persons who are mentally retarded or developmentally disabled.

**6858 Rosewood Center**

410-951-5000
888-300-7071
FAX: 410-581-6157
www.dhmh.state.md.us/dda/rosewood

*Leslie Smith, Program Director*
*James Anzalone, Director*
Rosewood Center is a State residential Center that supports adults with mental retardation from the central Maryland region. Rosewood will provide comprehensive supports to Maryland citizens with developmental disabilities and their families in a setting .

**6859 TLC: Treatment and Learning Centers**
2092 Gaither Road
Suite 100
Rockville, MD 20850-3316
301-424-5200
FAX: 301-424-8063
e-mail: dpaton@ttlc.org
www.ttlc.org

*Patricia Ritter, Executive Director*
*Cathleen Burgess, Director*
*Suellyn Sherwood, CFO*
Provides audiological evaluations, testing and hearing aids, physical and occupational therapy and evaluation; speech-language evaluation and therapy, psycho-educational testing and tutoring services for learning disabled students, head injury services an

**6860 Workforce and Technology Center**
Division of Rehabilitation Services
2301 Argonne Dr
Baltimore, MD 21218-1628
410-554-9442
888-554-0334
FAX: 410-554-9112
www.dors.state.md.us

*Dan Frye, Chairperson*
*Josie Thomas, Vice Chairperson*
Is one of nine state operated comprehensive rehabilitation facilities in the country providing a wide range of services to individuals with disabilities. The Maryland Division of Rehabilitation Services operates the Workforce and Technology Program. Avail

## Massachusetts

**6861 Baroco Corporation**
Ste 204
489 Whitney Ave
Holyoke, MA 01040-2711
413-534-9978
FAX: 413-585-9019
www.baroco.com

*Richard Barnard, President/Owner*
*Suzanne Darby, Executive Administrator*
*Julia McLaughlin, Executive Administrator*
Provides training and therapeutic support for its recipients with developmental disabilities in order to aid them in securing and maintaining placement in a less-restrictive setting.

**6862 Berkshire Meadows**
160 Gould Street
Suite 300
Needham, MA 02494-2300
781-559-4900
FAX: 413-528-0293
e-mail: berkshiremeadows@jri.org
berkshiremeadows.org

*Andy Pond, President*
*Gregory Canfield, Vice President*
*Deborah Reuman, CFO*
*Stephen H. Webster, Executive Advisor*
Private, non profit school for children, adolescents, young adults who are severely, developmentally disabled. approved special education learning center, work site program and foster care. Physical therapy, speech and language development, behavioral pro *$8200.00*

**6863 Blueberry Hill Healthcare**
75 Brimbal Ave
Beverly, MA 01915-6009
978-927-2020
FAX: 978-922-4643
www.blueberryhillrehab.com

*Ralph Epstein, Medical Director*
Accomodates 146 residents. We are centrally located close to Route 128 and Route 1A in Beverly Massachusetts. We offer short-term rehab care, long term care and Alzheimer's Special Care Programs. Our interdisciplinary team designs individual care plans fo

**6864 Boston University Hospital Vision Rehabilitation Services**
732 Harrison Ave
Boston, MA 02118-2371
617-638-7869
FAX: 617-638-7769
http://www.bmc.org/rehab.htm

*Simona Manasian, Medical Director*
Offers services for the totally blind, legally blind, visually impaired, mentally retarded blind and more with health, counseling, educational, recreational, rehabilitation, computer training and professional training services.

**6865 Burbank Rehabilitation Center**
275 Nichols Rd
Fitchburg, MA 01420-1919
978-343-5000
FAX: 978-343-5342
www.umassmemorial.org

*Patrick Muldoon, President & CEO*
*Paul D'Onfro, Chair*
*John Clementi, Vice Chair*
The largest community hospital and regional referral center in the area. Offers the most extensive high quality, cost-effective healthcare services in the region. The hospital provides outstanding hospital-based services such as case management of high ri

**6866 CPB/WGBH National Center for Access Media**
W GB H Educational Foundation
One Guest Street
Boston, MA 02135
617-300-3400
FAX: 617-300-1035
TTY:617-300-2489
e-mail: ncam@wgbh.org
www.wgbh.org/ncam

*Larry Goldberg, Director*
*Marcia Brooks, Project Director*
Dedicated to the issues of media and information technology for people with disabilities in their homes, schools, workplaces, and communities. NCAM's mission is to expand access to present and future media for people with disabilities; explore how existin

**6867 Carroll Center for the Blind**
770 Centre St
Newton, MA 02458-2597
617-969-6200
800-852-3131
FAX: 617-969-6204
e-mail: joe.abely@carroll.org
www.carroll.org

*Joseph Abely, President*
*Arthur O'Neill, Vice President*
Offers services for the totally blind, legally blind, visually impaired, mentally retarded blind and more with health, counseling, educational, in dependent living, tronell skills, computer traing, recreational, rehabilitation, computer training and professional training services.

**6868 Center for Psychiatric Rehabilitation**
Boston University
940 Commonwealth Ave
West
Boston, MA 02215-1203
617-353-3549
FAX: 617-353-7700
e-mail: psyrehab@bu.edu
www.bu.edu/cpr

*Kim T. Mueser, Executive Director*
*Carol Crawford, Director of operations*
*Jake Briggs, Staff Assistant*
*Elizabeth Brennan, Coordinator*
The mission of the Center is to increase knowledge, to train treatment personnel, to develop effective rehabilitation programs and to assist in organizing both personnel and programs into efficient and coordinated service delivery systems for people with

**6869 Clark House Nursing Center At Foxhill Village**
Kindred Healthcare
30 Longwood Dr
Westwood, MA 02090-1132
781-326-5652
FAX: 781-326-4034
http://www.clarkhousefhv.com/

*Chris Wasel, Administrator*
Clark House At Fox Hill Village accomodates 70 residents. We are part of the Fox Hill Village Assisted Living and Retirement Center campus. Clark House Nursing center has been named a recipient of a 2005 step II quality Award from the American Health Care

**6870 College Internship Program at the Berkshire Center**
18 Park St
Lee, MA 01238-1702
413-243-2576
FAX: 413-243-3351
e-mail: admissions@berkshirecenter.org
berkshirecenter.org

*Lucy Gosselin, Program Director*
*Laina Hubbard, Admissions Coordinator*
*Charles D. Houff, Head Therapist*
A highly individualized postsecondary program for learning disabled young adults 18-30. Provides job placement services and follow-ups; college support; money management and social skills. Residential students share an apartment and have their own room. T

**6871 Eagle Pond Rehabilitation and Living Center**
P.O.Box 208
South Dennis, MA 02660-3445
508-385-6034
FAX: 508-385-7064
www.eaglepond.com

*Paul Marchwat, Executive Director*
*Ellen Reil, Marketing Director*
Eagle Pond accomodates 142 residents. Medicare and Medicaid certified as well as being accredited by the Joint Comission (formerly (JCAHO) which enables us to contract with many insurance companies.

**6872 FOR Community Services**
75 Litwin Ln
Chicopee, MA 01020-4817
413-592-6142
FAX: 413-598-0478
e-mail: ggolash1@aol.com

*Gina Golash, Executive Director*
Providing a world of meaning for individuals with developmental disabilities throughout Western Massachusetts since 1967.

**6873 Fairlawn Rehabilitation Hospital**
189 May St
Worcester, MA 01602-4399
508-791-6351
FAX: 508- 83- 127
www.fairlawnrehab.org

*Dave Richer, CEO*
*Peter Bagley, Medical Director*
*Matthew Akulonis, Director Of Support Operations*
Offers comprehensive rehabilitation on both an inpatient and outpatient basis. Specialty programs include: head injury, spinal cord injury, young/senior stroke, oncology, geriatrics and orthopedics.

**6874 Greenery Extended Care Center: Worcester**
59 Acton St
Worcester, MA 01604-4899
508-791-3147
800-633-0887
FAX: 508-753-6267
wingatehealthcare.com

*Scott Schuster, Founder & President*
*Brian Callahan, CFO*
*Michael Benjamin, Vice President*
*Trent Guthrie, Senior Director*
173 beds offering complex care, extended rehabilitation and neurobehavioral intervention. Offering life care homes and Nursing home services. Specialties include life events and physical care, long term and home health care, and nursing homes and nursing

**6875 Greenery Rehabilitation & Skilled Nursing Center**
P.O.Box 1330
Middleboro, MA 02346-4330
508-947-9295
FAX: 508-947-7974

201 beds offering programs of active/acute rehabilitation, cognitive rehabilitation, respiratory care and short-term evaluations..

**6876 Harrington House Nursing And Rehabilitation Center**
160 Main St
Walpole, MA 02081-4037
508-660-3080
FAX: 508-660-1634
http://www.harringtonrehab.com/

*Joseph Haron, Medical Director*
Accomodates 90 residents. Our state-of-the-art center offers post-accute services including rehabilitation and medical management. Our center also provides a long term care program including hospice services.

**6877 HealthSouth Rehabilitation Hospital Of Western Massachusetts**
14 Chestnut Pl
Ludlow, MA 01056-3478
413-589-7581
FAX: 413-547-2738
www.healthsouthrehab.org

*Scott Keen, CEO*
*Adnan Dahdul, Medical Director*
*Deborah Cabanas, Chief Nursing Officer*
*Victoria Healy, Controller*
A 53-bed acute Rehabilitation Hospital. The facility has been operating for 14 years and has provided rehabilitative care to patients and families in the greater Springfield area with an outstanding reputation for attention to detail and compassion. Becau

**6878 Holiday Inn Boxborough Woods**
242 Adams Pl
Boxborough, MA 01719-1735 978-263-8701
800-465-4329
FAX: 978-263-0518
e-mail: box_sales@fine-hotels.com
www.holiday-inn.com

*Kevin Murray, Manager*
*Marcel Girard, Manager*
*Nancy Ellen Hurley, Chief Marketing Officer*
Located on 35 acres of wooded countryside just off I-495 at exit #28. Minutes from the Mass Turnpike, Route 2, 290 and 9. Conference center located on main level with 30,000 square feet of meeting space. Guest rooms feature two-line telephones, voice mail
*$129 - $159*

**6879 Lifeworks Employment Services**
1400 Providence Highway
Suite 2300
Norwood, MA 02062- 4551 781-769-3298
FAX: 781-551-0045
e-mail: able@lifeworksma.org
www.lifeworksma.org

*Dan Burke, President & CEO*
*Chris Page, Vice President*
*Brenda Calder, CFO*
*Mary Hagen, Controller*
Providing homes, jobs, education and supportive living for people with developmental disabilities.

**6880 Massachusetts Eye and Ear Infirmary & Vision Rehabilitation Center**
243 Charles St
Boston, MA 02114-3002 617-523-7900
FAX: 617-573-4178
TTY:617-523-5498
www.meei.harvard.edu

*John Fernandaz, President & CEO*
*Javier Balloffet, Vice President*
*Wycliffe Grousbeck, Chairman*
*Jonathan Uhrig, Treasurer*
Visual rehabilitation encompasses a low vision rehabilitation evaluation, occupational therapy evaluation (with home visit if necessary), and social service evaluation.

**6881 New England Center for Children**
33 Turnpike Rd
Southborough, MA 01772-2108 508-481-1015
FAX: 508-485-3421
e-mail: cwelch@necc.org
necc.org

*Lisel Macenka, Chair*
*James C. Burling, Vice Chair*
*L.Vincent Strully, President*
*Michael F. Downey, Treasurer*
A comprehensive year-round program for students with autism and PDD who require a highly specialized educational and behavior management program. Students are from all over the country and receive intensive, positive, behavioral counseling and social skil

**6882 New England Eye Center, Tufts Medical Center**
Vision Rehabilitation Service
800 Washington St
Boston, MA 02111-1533 617-636-4600
800-231-3316
FAX: 617-636-4866
e-mail: eli@vision.eri.harvard.edu
www.neec.com

*Harry P. Selker, Principal Investigator*
*Anastassios Pittas, Program Director*
*Tamsin A. Knox, Associate Director*
*June S. Wasser, Executive Director*
Offers services for the legally blind, visually impaired, mentally retarded blind and more with health, counseling, educational, recreational, rehabilitation, computer training and professional training services.

**6883 New Medico Rehabilitation and Skilled Nursing Center at Lewis Bay**
89 Lewis Bay Rd
Hyannis, MA 02601-5207 508-775-7601
FAX: 508-790-4239

*Edmund Steinle, Executive Director*
Post acute rehabilitation services.

**6884 Protestant Guild Learning Center**
411 Waverley Oaks Rd
Waltham, MA 02452-8449 781-893-6000
FAX: 781-893-1171
e-mail: admin@protestantguild.org
protestantguild.org

*Kim Fulton Marchand, President*
*Eric H. Rosenberger, Vice President*
*Thomas P. Corcoran, Treasurer*
*Linda E. Croteau, Clerk*
Offers services for the diagnostically disabled children and adolescents with ages 6-22 years with health, counseling, educational, recreational, rehabilitation, computer training and professional training services.

**6885 Shaughnessy-Kaplan Rehabilitation Hospital**
Dove Ave
Salem, MA 01970 978-745-9003
FAX: 978-740-4730
e-mail: skrhinfo@partners.org
www.shaughnessy-kaplan.org

*Anthony Sciola, CEO*
A 160-bed private, non-profit hospital. We have been providing care for residents of greater North Shore communities since 1975. Shaughnessy has 120 long-term care hospital beds and a 40-bed transitional care unit sometimes referred to as a skilled nursin

**6886 Son-Rise Program**
2080 S Undermountain Rd
Sheffield, MA 01257-9643 413-229-2100
877-766-7473
FAX: 413-229-3202
e-mail: correspondence@option.org
www.autismtreatmentcenter.org

*Barry Neil Kaufman, Co Founder*
*Samahria Lyte Kaufman, Co Founder*
THe Son-Rise Program is a powerful, effective and totally unique treatment for children and adults challengedby Autism, Autuism Spectrum Disorders, Pervasive Developmental Disorder (PDD), Asperger's Syndrome and other developmental difficulties.

**6887 Southern Worcester County Rehabilitation Inc. D/B/A Life-Skills, Inc.**
44 Morris St
Webster, MA 01570-1812
508-943-0700
FAX: 508-949-6129
e-mail: life-skills@lifeskillsinc.org
www.life-skillsinc.org

*J Thomas Amick, Executive Director*

Life-Skills, Inc. assists mentally and developmentally challenged adults with meeting their individual needs, and empowering them to take full advantage of meaningful opportunities in their communities. We provide residential, employment, transportation, behavior, and theraputic day habilitation services to 350 adults in MA. We operate thrift & consignment stores, a small cafe, an ice cream shop, mini golf & arcade center, vending and greenhouse businesses, bank courier service, and others.

**6888 Vinfen Corporation**
950 Cambridge St
Cambridge, MA 02141-1001
617-441-1800
877-284-6336
FAX: 617-441-1858
TTY: 617-225-2000
e-mail: info@vinfen.org
www.vinfen.org

*Bruce L. Bird, Ph.D., CEO/ President*
*Elizabeth K. Glaser, COO*

A private, nonprofit company, Vinfen Corporation is the largest human services provider in Massachusetts. Vinfen offers clinical, educational, residential and support services to individuals of all ages with mental illness and or mental retardation, who also may have another disability (e.g. substance abuse, homelessness, AIDS). The company also trains professionals in the mental health field and helps consumers to learn to live in community-based settings at the highest levels.

**6889 Visiting Nurse Association of North Shore**
5 Federal St
Danvers, MA 01923-3687
978-777-6100
800-728-1862
FAX: 978-777-0308
www.vnacarenetwork.org

*Mary Ann O'Connor, CEO/ President*
*Joanne M. Kramer, CFO / Vice President of Finance*

Home health services including nurses, physical, occupational and speech therapy, home health aides and more. Special programs include nutrition counseling, IV care, pediatric therapy, HIV/AIDS services and wound management. Provides services 7 days a week, 365 days a year and we accept Medicare, Medicaid and most HMO's and health insurers.

**6890 Weldon Center for Rehabilitation**
233 Carew St
Springfield, MA 01104-2377
413-748-6800
FAX: 413-748-6806
mercycares.com

*Barbara Haswell, Manager*

One of the most vital, necessary health resources in the region by helping thousands of people toward restored health and independence. A comprehensive, integrated, non-profit facility offering inpatient, outpatient, day rehabilitation and pediatric services on one site.

**6891 Youville Hospital & Rehab Center**
1575 Cambridge St
Cambridge, MA 02138-4398
617-876-4344
FAX: 617-547-5501
http://www.youville.org/

Meets the long and short term health care and rehabilitation needs of patients who are physically disabled and chronically ill. Strives to develop and maintain health as a human right on physical, social, vocational and spiritual levels. The ultimate goal of the hospital is to treat and assist each individual patient in reaching his or her optimal level of living. Services include: stroke, brain injury, spinal cord trauma, orthopedic disabilities and more.

## Michigan

**6892 Botsford Center For Rehabilitation & Health Improvement-Redford**
26905 Grand River Ave
Redford, MI 48240-1602
313-387-3800
877-442-7900
FAX: 313-387-3838
e-mail: info@botsfordsystem.org
www.botsfordsystem.org

*John Darin, Manager*

A 20 bed inpatient physical rehabilitation unit, servicing individuals who have experienced a stroke, amputation, orthopedic fracture, or other neurological impairment.

**6893 Chelsea Community Hospital Rehabilitation Unit**
775 S Main St
Chelsea, MI 48118-1383
734-593-6000
FAX: 734-475-4191
cch.org

*Nancy K. Graebner, CEO/ President*
*Jim Birchler, CFO/ Vice President for Finance*

A private, non-profit, acute care facility that combines the best of small town values with national standards of healthcare excellance. The hospital has a 19-bed acute care inpatient rehabilitation unit with comprehensive outpatient programs, including a coordinated brain injury program.

**6894 Clare Branch**
790 Industrial Dr
Clare, MI 48617-9224
989-386-7707
888-773-7664
FAX: 989-386-2199
e-mail: mail@mmionline.com
www.mmionline.org

*Cris Zeigler, Executive Director*

MMI will strive to be the premier provider of person-centered services to people with barriers to employment. We will connect individuals with community resources that provide mutual benefit to them and to the community. MMI will be known for excellence in service provision, ethical business practices, a quality work environment, and for providing services that enhance the dignity and value of the people we serve.

**6895 Clarkston Spec Healthcare Center**
4800 Clintonville Rd
Clarkston, MI 48346-4297
800-454-5909
fundltc.com

*Margaret Canny, Administrator*

120 beds offering active/acute rehabilitation, complex care, day treatment, extended rehabilitation, neurobehavioral intervention and short-term evaluation.

**6896 DMC Health Care Center-Novi**
42005 W 12 Mile Rd
Novi, MI 48377-3113
248-347-8294
FAX: 248-347-4578
www.dmc.org

*Jolanta Malinowski, Intake Coordinator*
*James Cole, Executive Director*

The Detroit Medical Center's record of service has provided medical excellence throughout the history of the Metropolitan Detroit area. From the founding of the Children's Hospital in 1886, to the creation of the first mechanical heart at Harpers Hospital 50 years ago, to our compassion for the underdeserved, our legacy of caring is unmatched.

**6897 Eight CAP, Inc. Head Start**
904 Oak Dr
Greenville, MI 48838-9277
616-754-2660
FAX: 616-754-9310
http://www.eightcap.net/SitePages/Home.aspx

*Ralph Loeschner, Executive Director*
*Nancy Secor, Contact*
Post accute rehabilitation programs.

**6898 Greater Detroit Agency for the Blind and Visually Impaired**
16625 Grand River Ave
Detroit, MI 48227-1419
313-272-3900
FAX: 313-272-6893
e-mail: Information@gdabvi.org
gdabvi.org

*Victor A. Arbulu, MBA, Managing Director*
Offers services for seniors 60 and over who are legally blind. Also provides eye health information, counseling, education and rehabilitation services.

**6899 Hope Network Rehabilitation Services**
Hope Network
1490 E Beltline Ave SE
Grand Rapids, MI 49506-4336
616-940-0040
FAX: 616-940-8151
e-mail: jbaker@hopenetwork.org
hopenetwork.org

*Margaret Kroese, Vice President/Executive Director*
An office of Hope Network, one of the largest, private, nonprofit organizations of its kind in Michigan. The purpose is to assist people with brain injuries and/or physical disabilities in achieving an optimal level of self-determination, dignity, and independence as they develop and attain goals to overcome environmental barriers and mobilize adaptive skills.

**6900 Lakeland Center**
26900 Franklin Rd
Southfield, MI 48033-5312
248-350-8070
FAX: 248-350-8078
e-mail: peggys@thelakelandcenter.net
thelakelandcenter.net

*Irving Shapiro, CEO*
*Santhosh Madhavan, Director Physical Medicine*
*Gary Yashinsky, Associate Medical Director*
Subacute rehabilitation program directed toward those with severe neurologic diagnoses, ie: TBI, cerebral aneurysm, anoxic encephalopathy, CVA and cerebral hemorrhage, orthopedic injuries, and spinal cord injury. Subacute rehabilitation is provided for those who recover slowly and require individualized treatment plans. Residential program available as well.

**6901 Mary Free Bed Rehabilitation Hospital**
235 Wealthy St SE
Grand Rapids, MI 49503-5247
800-528-8989
FAX: 616-454-3939
e-mail: info@maryfreebed.com
maryfreebed.com

*Kent Riddle, CEO*
*John Butzer, MD, Medical Director*
*Randy DeNeff, Vice President of Finance*
Founded more than 100 years ago, Mary Free Bed Rehabilitation Hospital is and 80-bed, not-for-profit, acute rehabilitation center. Its mission is to restore hope and freedom through rehabilitation to people with disabilities. Mary Free Bed offers comprehensive inpatient and outpatient rehabilitationfor children and adults using an interdisciplinary approach. Also available are numerous specialty programs designed to increase the quality of life and independence of people with disabilities.

**6902 Michigan Career And Technical Institute**
11611 Pine Lake Rd
Plainwell, MI 49080-9225
269-664-4461
877-901-7360
FAX: 269-664-5850

*Dennis Hart, Executive Director*
A residential vocational training center for adults with physical, mental or emotional disabilities.

**6903 Michigan Commission for the Blind Training Center**
1541 Oakland Dr
Kalamazoo, MI 49008
269-337-3848
800-292-4200
FAX: 269-337-3872
e-mail: mossc@michigan.gov
www.mcb1.org

*Christine Boone, Director*
*Bruce Schultz, Assistant Director*
Residential facility that provides instruction to legally blind adults in braille, computer operation and assistive technology, handwriting, cane travel, cooking, personal management, industrial arts and also crafts. During training students will develop career plans which may include work experience, internships, volunteer opprtunities and even part-time paid employment.

**6904 Mid-Michigan Industries**
2426 Parkway Dr
Mt Pleasant, MI 48858-4723
989-773-6918
888-773-7664
888-773-7664
FAX: 989-773-1317
e-mail: mail@mmionline.com
mmionline.com

*Alan Schilling, President*
*Andrea Christopher, Director Admissions*
*Linda Wagner, Branch Director*
*Sheri Alexander, Director of Community Employment*
Providing jobs and training for persons with barriers to employment. Services include vocational evaluation, job placement, supported employment, work services, prevocational training and case management

**6905 New Medico Community Re-Entry Service**
216 St Marys Lake Rd
Battle Creek, MI 49017-9710
FAX: 269-962-2241

*James Rekshan, Executive Director*

**6906 Sanilac County Community Mental Health**
171 Dawson St
Sandusky, MI 48471-1062
810-648-0330
888-225-4447
888-225-4447
FAX: 810-648-0319
e-mail: deanr@sanilacmentalhealth.org
sanilacmentalhealth.org

*Roger Dean, Executive Director*
Post-acute rehabilitation facility and programs.

**6907 Special Tree Rehabilitation System**
600 Stephenson Highway
Troy, MI 48083-1110
248-616-0950
800-649-5011
FAX: 248-616-0957
e-mail: info@specialtree.com
www.specialtree.com

*Joseph Richart, CEO*
Special Tree exists to provide hope, encouragement, and expertise for people who have experienced life-altering changes. Our team approach to rehabilitation, custom designed for each person's needs and goals, offers these individuals the best opportunity for healing and recovery.

**6908 Thumb Industries**
1263 Sand Beach Rd
Bad Axe, MI 48413-8817
989-269-9229
FAX: 989-269-2587
http://www.thumbindustries.com/

*Rhonda Wisenbaugh, Executive Director*
Provides job training and employment for disabled persons. Vocational rehabilitation agency, manufactures household furnishings, direct mail advertising service.

**6909 Visually Impaired Center**
1422 W Court St
Flint, MI 48503-5008
810-767-4014
FAX: 810-767-0020
e-mail: info@vicflint.org
www.vicflint.org

Committed to developing resources and collaborative programs as well as providing services that enable independent life for people with vision loss. Services include: Information and referals, assessments of needs, peer support groups, training by a Rehabilitation teacher of the blind and visually impaired, independent living skills, computer skills, training by an Orientation and Mobility Specialist, safe traveling skills, Diabetes management/education.
*a pages*

**6910 Welcome Homes Retirement Community for the Visually Impaired**
1953 Monroe Ave NW
Grand Rapids, MI 49505-6242
616-447-7837
888-939-9292
888-939-9292
FAX: 616-447-9891
e-mail: info@welcomehomes.org

*Beth Lucksted, Manager*
Offers services for the totally blind, legally blind, visually impaired, mentally retarded blind and more with health, counseling, educational, recreational, rehabilitation, computer training and professional training services.

**6911 William H Honor Rehabilitation Center Henry Ford Wyanclotte Hospital**
Henry Ford Health System
2333 Biddle Ave
Wyandotte, MI 48192-4668
734-246-6000
FAX: 734-246-6926
www.henryfordwyandotte.com

*Denise Dailing, Administration Leader/rehabilita*
*James Sexton, Chief Executive Officer*
*Henry Ford, Owner*
Henry Ford Wyandotte Hospital offers an array of educational programs, health screenings, and support groups. The hospital is CARF accredited and has a CARF certified stroke specialty unit.

## Minnesota

**6912 Industries: Cambridge**
601 Cleveland St S
Cambridge, MN 55008-1752
763-689-5434
FAX: 763-552-1281
e-mail: aarmstrong@industriesinc.org
www.industriesinc.org

*Denise Johnson, Co-Executive Director- Programs and Services*
*Michelle Thomas, Sales/Marketing Director*
*Kris McNally, Co-Executive Director- Finance and Human Resources*
Nonprofit organization that does vocational assessment and training for people with disabilities.

**6913 Industries: Mora**
500 Walnut St S
Mora, MN 55051-1936
320-679-2354
FAX: 320-679-2355
e-mail: djohnson@industriesinc.org
industriesinc.org

*Kris Mc Nally, Manager*
*Julie Kettner, Development Director*
Nonprofit organization that does vocational assessment and training for people with disabilities.

**6914 Shriners Hospitals for Children: Twin Cities**
2025 E River Pkwy
Minneapolis, MN 55414-3696
612-596-6100
888-293-2832
888-293-2832
FAX: 612-339-5954
www.shrinershospitalsforchildren.org

*Charles Lobeck, Administrator*
*Dr Kenneth Guidera MD, Chief of Staff*
Shriners Hospital for Children-Twin Cities offers quality orthopedic medical care regardless of the patients' ability to pay. Shriners Hospitals provide inpatient and outpatient services, surgery, casts, braces, artificial limbs, x-rays and physical and occupational therapy to any child under the age of 18 who may benefit from treatment.

**6915 Vision Loss Resources**
1936 Lyndale Ave S
Minneapolis, MN 55403-3101
612-871-2222
FAX: 612-872-0189
TTY:612-382-8422
e-mail: info@vlrw.org
visionlossresources.org

*Kate Grathwol, PhD., Executive Director*
Offers services for the totally blind, legally blind, visually impaired, and more with health, counseling, educational, recreational, rehabilitation, computer training and professional training services.

## Mississippi

**6916 Addie McBryde Rehabilitation Center for the Blind**
PO Box 5314
Jackson, MS 39296-5314
601-364-2700
800-443-1000
FAX: 601-364-2677
e-mail: kbrown@mdrs.ms.us
www.mdrs.state.ms.us/client/addie_2.asp

*H. S. McMillan, Executive Director*
*Shelia Browning, Deputy Director Non-Vocational Programs*
Offers services for the totally blind, legally blind, visually impaired, mentally retarded blind and more with health, counseling, educational, recreational, rehabilitation, computer training services and orientation and mobility.

**6917 Mississippi Methodist Rehabilitation Center**
1350 E Woodrow Wilson Ave
Jackson, MS 39216-5198
601-981-2611
800-223-6672
FAX: 601-364-3571
www.mmrcrehab.org

*Mark A. Adams, President/ CEO*
Rebuild lives that have been broken by disabilities and impairments from serious illness or severe injury. The challenge is to help patients regain abilities, restore function and movement, and renew emotionally. It features personal rehabilitation treatment plans administered by specialized teams of health care professionals through a variety of outpatient programs, treatments and other services.

## Missouri

**6918 Alpine North Nursing and Rehabilitation Center**
4700 NW Cliff View Dr
Kansas City, MO 64150-1237
816-741-5105
FAX: 816-746-1301

*Mike Stacks, Executive Director*
*Bob Richard, Administrator*
Postacute rehabilitation program.

**6919 Christian Hospital Northeast**
11133 Dunn Rd
Saint Louis, MO 63136-6119
314-653-5000
877-747-9355
FAX: 314-653-4130
christianhospital.org

*John Katsianis, Vice President Finance*
*Ron McMullen, President*
A non-profit organization, a 493 bed acute care facility on 28 acres. Christian Hospital has more then 600 physicians on staff and a diverse workforce of more then 2,5000 health-care professionals who are dedicated to providing the absolute best care with the latest technology and medical advances.

**6920 Integrated Health Services of St. Louis at Gravois**
10954 Kennerly Rd
Saint Louis, MO 63128-2018
314-843-4242
FAX: 314-843-4031

*Lisa Niehaus, Administrator*
Subacute, skilled and intermediate care; ventilator/tracheostomy management program; wound management program and complex rehabilitation program.

**6921 Metropolitan Employment & Rehabilitation Service**
M ER S Goodwill
1727 Locust St
Saint Louis, MO 63103-1703
314-241-3464
FAX: 314-241-9348
e-mail: info@mersgoodwill.org
www.mersgoodwill.org

*Lewis C. Chartock, Ph.D., President/ CEO*
*Dawayne Barnett, CFO*
Vocational rehabilitation, primarily with the disabled, skills training and placement services.

**6922 Missouri Easter Seal Society: Southeast Region**
233 South Wacker Drive
Suite 2400
Chicago, IL 60606
312-726-6200
800-221-6827
FAX: 312-726-1494
easterseals.com

The mission of the Easter Seal Society is to work with individuals, their families and the community to enhance the independence and quality of life for persons with disabilities.

**6923 Poplar Bluff RehabCare Program**
Lucy Lee Hospital
2620 N Westwood Blvd
Poplar Bluff, MO 63901-3396
573-785-7721
FAX: 573-686-5987

*Jim Martin, Program Manager*
*Chris Murray, Care Coordinator*
*Darlene Hill, Care Admissions Coordinator*
Provides physical medicine and rehabilitation to individuals with a physically limiting condition. The program is designed to help individuals function as independently as possible by maximizing their strength and abilities.

**6924 Shriners Hospitals for Children St. Louis**
2001 S Lindbergh Blvd
Saint Louis, MO 63131-3504
314-432-3600
800-850-2960
FAX: 314-432-2930
www.shrinershq.org/hospitals/st.louis

*John O'Shaughnessy, Administrator*
*Tammy M Dugan, Director Community Relations*
*Alice Woodruff, Executive Assistant*
Medical care is provided free of charge for children 18 and under with orthopaedic conditions.

**6925 St. Louis Society for the Blind and Visually Impaired**
8770 Manchester Rd
Saint Louis, MO 63144-2724
314-960-9000
FAX: 314-968-9003
e-mail: socscrv@slsbvi.org
www.slsbvi.org

Offers vision rehabilitation services for the totally blind, legally blind, visually impaired, including counseling, educational, recreational, rehabilitation, computer training and professional training services. Low vision aids and appliance available through low vision clinic by appointment.

**6926 Truman Medical Center Low Vision Rehabilitation Program**
Eye Foundation of Kansas City
2300 Holmes St.
Kansas City, MO 64108
816-404-1780
FAX: 816-404-1786
www.umkc-efkc.org

*Nelson R. Sabates, M.D., Chairman*
Our program is designed to maximize daily tasks for a person with low vision. We are able to evaluate a person's home and provide recommendations as needed.

**6927 Truman Neurological Center**
15600 Woods Chapel Rd
Kansas City, MO 64139-1354
816-373-5060
FAX: 816-373-5787
e-mail: info@tnccommunity.com
tnccommunity.com

*James Landrum, Executive Director*
*Ann Johnson, Finance Director*
A licensed habilitation center established for the purpose of assisting persons with developmental disabilities and/or mental retardation. The minimum age is 18. Residential care is provided in four group homes in the community licensed by the DMH and CARF accredited.

## Montana

**6928 Benefis Healthcare**
1101 26th St S
Great Falls, MT 59405-5104
406-455-5000
FAX: 406-455-2110
e-mail: benefis@benefis.org
www.benefis.org

*John Goodnow, CEO*
*Laura Goldhahn-Konen, President*
*Steve Ballock, CFO*
Benefis Healthcare is a not-for-profit community asses governed by a 15-member local board of directors. Benefis is locally owned and controlled. Benefis is a Level II trauma center- one of only 4 in the state and 107 in the country.

6929 **Disability Services Division of Montana**
Department of Public Health
Helena, MT 59604 406-444-7734
FAX: 406-444-3465
e-mail: dphhs@mt.gov
www.dphhs.state.mt.us/dsd

*Keith Messmer, Manager*
*Sandi Gory, Administrative Assistant*
*Janice Frisch, Chief Management Operations*
Responsible for coordinating, developing and implementing comprehensive programs to assist Montanans with disabilities with activities of daily living, community base services and coordinated programs of habilitation, rehabilitation and independent living.

## Nebraska

6930 **Las Vegas Healthcare And Rehabilitation Center**
680 South Fourth Street
Louisville, KY 40202 502-596-7300
TTY:800-545-0749
e-mail: web_administrator@kindredhealthcare.com
kindredhealthcare.com

*Paul J. Diaz, President/ CEO*
Accomodates 79 residents. Serving the community for approximately 40 years. Located in close proximity to local hospitals and surrounded by medical complexes, out center offers both short-term rehabilitation and long term.care.

6931 **Sierra Pain Institute**
265 Golden Ln
Reno, NV 89502-1205 775-323-7092
FAX: 775-323-5259

*Lyle Smith, Owner*
The program consists of a medically supervised outpatient program managed by an interdisciplinary team with input from specialties of Pain Medicine, Physical Therapy and Occupational Science. The format insures that each patient receives the full range of behavioral techniques in a well-integrated, individually tailored therapeutic regimen.

## New Hampshire

6932 **Crotched Mountain Adult Brain Injury Center**
Crotched Mountain Foundation
1 Verney Dr
Greenfield, NH 03047-5000 603-547-3311
800-966-2672
FAX: 603-547-3232
e-mail: admissions@crotchedmountain.org
www.crotchedmountain.org

*Donald Shumway, President*
Adult Brain Injury Center provides sub-acute rehabilitative services and individualized care to survivors of acquired (including traumatic) brain injury. Ambulatory and non-ambulatory adults are served. Ages range from 18-59, the staff to client ratio is 3:1 and services are provided by experienced interdisciplinary clinical and therapeutic teams. Crotched Mountain is a licensed Special Hospital providing 24 hour medical coverage and skilled nursing. Clients reside in semi-private rooms w/superv

6933 **Department of Physical Medicine and Rehabilitation**
Exeter Hospital
5 Alumni Dr
Exeter, NH 03833-2128 603-778-7311
FAX: 603-580-6592
www.foreveryday.com

*Kevin Calahan, President*
Offers patient treatment, committed to enhancing the lives of individuals with short and long term physically disabling conditions.

6934 **Farnum Rehabilitation Center**
580 Court St
Keene, NH 03431-1718 603-354-6630
FAX: 603-355-2078

*Susan Loughrey, Program Director*
*Judy Bell, Manager*
Offers rehabilitation services, occupational therapy, physical therapy and more for the physically challenged individual.

6935 **Hackett Hill Nursing Center and Integrated Care**
191 Hackett Hill Rd
Manchester, NH 03102-8993 603-668-8161
FAX: 603-622-2584

*Daniele Peckham, Administrator*
*Brett Lennerton, Administrator*
A 68-bed certified nursing home.Postacute rehabilitation program.

6936 **New Hampshire Rehabilitation and Sports Medicine**
Catholic Medical Center
Ste 201
769 S Main St
Manchester, NH 03102-5166 603-647-1899
800-437-9666
FAX: 603-668-5348

*Stuart Draper, Owner*
*Victor Carbone, Manager*
A specialized facility for comprehensive rehabilitation for individuals who have been injured or have a disability.

6937 **New Medico, Highwatch Rehabilitation Center**
Highwatch Rd
Center Ossipee, NH 03814 FAX: 603-539-8888

*William Burke, Executive Director*
Post-acute rehabilitation service.

6938 **Northern New Hampshire Mental Health and Developmental Services**
87 Washington St
Conway, NH 03818-6044 603-447-3347
FAX: 603-447-8893
www.nnhmhds.org

*Dennis Mackay, CEO*
Provides mental health and developmental services to northern New Hampshire, including early intervention, elderly services, residential program, outpatient services, employee assistance programs, inpatient services, etc.

6939 **The Mental Health Center: Riverside Courtyard**
3 Twelfth St
Berlin, NH 03570-3860 603-752-7404
FAX: 603-752-5194

*Eileen Theriault, Manager*
A center to help people that have mental disabilities.

## New Jersey

6940 **All Garden State Physical Therapy**
44 Ridge Road
North Arlington, NJ 07031 201-998-6300
FAX: 201-998-6344
http://gardenstatept.com/index.html

Post-acute rehabilitation program.

**6941 Bancroft**
PO Box 20
Haddonfield, NJ 08033-1284
856-429-0010
800-774-5516
FAX: 856-429-1613
e-mail: inquiry@bancroft.org
www.bancroft.org

*Toni Pergolin, CEO*
*Kathy Ross, Vice President*
*Julie Walsh, Director of Public Relations*
Private, not-for-profit organization serving people with disabilities since 1883. Based in Haddonfield, New Jersey, help more than 1000 children and adults with autism, developmental disabilities, brain injuries, and other neurological impairments. Operates more than 140 sites throughout the U.S. and abroad.

**6942 Daughters of Miriam Center/The Gallen Institute**
155 Hazel St
Clifton, NJ 07011-3423
973-772-3700
FAX: 973-253-5389
e-mail: administration@daughtersofmiriamcenter.org
www.daughtersofmiriamcenter.o rg

*Fred Feinstein, Executive Director*
Dedicated to providing the highest quality care, the Center has far exceeded a stereotypical nursing home by offering a continuum of care environment, making us a leader in Jewish eldercare.

**6943 Devereux Center in New Jersey**
Bldg 4
286 Mantua Grove Rd
West Deptford, NJ 08096
856-599-6400
FAX: 856-423-8916
www.devereux.org

*Robert Q. Kreider, President*
*Carol Poirier, Admissions Assistant*
Serves emotionally disturbed females, ages 5-21, who have affective disorders, bi-polar disorders, adjustment reactions, behavioral disorders, specific developmental disorders, identity disorders, attention deficit disorders, schizoid disorders, anxiety disorders, enuresis, runaway behavior, substance abuse, in remission and personality disturbances. The center offers 95-100 full-time staff including, teachers, administrators, counselors, therapists, recreation staff and support services.

**6944 Ladacain Network**
Schroth School & Technical Education Center
1701 Kneeley Blvd
Wanamassa, NJ 07712-7622
732-493-5900
FAX: 732-493-5980
ladacin.org

*Patricia Carlesimo, Executive Director*
Provides an array of services and programs specifically for children and adults with developmental and physical disabilities. Services include approved Department of Education school programs; adult education and training; vocational training, personal care assistance services, in-home and Saturday respite; child care programs, housing opportunities, and more.

**6945 Lourdes Regional Rehabilitation Center**
Our Lady of Lourdes Medical Center
1600 Haddon Ave
Camden, NJ 08103-3101
856-757-3864
856-757-3500
FAX: 856-968-2511
e-mail: info@lourdesnet.org
www.lourdesnet.org

*Alexander J. Hatala, President*
The only comprehensive rehabilitation facility located within an acute care hospital in Southern New Jersey. Patients benefit from the proximity to the full range of state of the art medical and surgical services should the need arise.

**6946 Mt. Carmel Guild**
1160 Raymond Blvd
Newark, NJ 07102-4168
973-596-4100
FAX: 973-639-6583

*Anita Holland, Manager*
Offers services for the totally blind, legally blind, visually impaired, mentally retarded blind and more with health, counseling, educational, recreational, rehabilitation, computer training and professional training services.

**6947 Pediatric Rehabilitation Department, JFK Medical Center**
65 James St
Edison, NJ 08820-3947
732-321-7362
732-321-7000
FAX: 732-548-7751
www.jfkmc.org

*Raymond Fredericks, President*
Comprehensive interdisciplinary, family focused outpatient pediatric rehabilitation services including evaluation and individual and group treatment programs for children birth-21.

**6948 REACH Rehabilitation Program: Leader Nursing and Rehabilitation Center**
550 Jessup Rd
West Deptford, NJ 08066-1921
856-848-9551

*Karen Fattore, Case Manager*
*Anthony Stenson, Administrator*
Postacute rehabilitation program.

**6949 REACH Rehabilitation and Catastrophic Long-Term Care**
1180 Us Highway 22
Mountainside, NJ 07092-2810
908-654-0020
FAX: 908-654-8661

*Allen Swanson, Manager*
*Archie Ordana, Manager*
Postacute rehabilitation program.

**6950 Rehabilitation Specialists**
18-01 Pollitt Drive
Ste 1A
Fair Lawn, NJ 07410-2815
201-478-4200
800-441-7488
FAX: 201-478-4201
e-mail: pres@rehab-specialist.com
www.rehab-specialist.com

*Virgilio Caraballo, President/CEO*
Rehabilitation Specialists, founded in 1983, is a quality, cost effective community re-entry center treating individuals with acquired brain injury. A non clinical environment based in the community is utilized that offers professional services enabling participants to learn skills they need to return to a productive life. Both our Day and Residential programming emphases focus on Functional Life Skills, Work Skills and Learning Skills. Each participant's program is tailored to meet their needs.

**6951 Somerset Valley Rehabilitation and Nursing Center**
Care-One
11300 Cornell Park Drive
Suite 360
Cincinnati, OH 45242
513-469-7222
FAX: 513-469-7230
e-mail: info@healthbridge.org
healthbridge.org

*Trudi Matthews, Director of Policy and Public Relations*
Subacute rehabilitation program, long term care, respite care..

6952 **Summit Ridge Center**
20 Summit St
West Orange, NJ 07052-1501
973-736-2000
FAX: 973-736-2764
genesishcc.com

Offers rehabilitation services, occupational therapy, physical therapy and more for the physically challenged. A 152-bed nursing home.

## New Mexico

6953 **SJR Rehabilitation Hospital**
525 S Schwartz Ave
Farmington, NM 87401-5955
505-609-2625
FAX: 505-327-6562
www.sjrrh.com

*Ena M Niemand, Executive Director*
*Sue Clay, Program Director*
*Jill Morgan, Nursing Director*
Uses a team of professionals to provide a comprehensive rehabilitation program. Accomplishing the best possible physical and cognitive improvement is the aim of the following treatment members: nurses, physical therapists, physicians, speech and occupational therapists, therapeutic recreation specialist. Providing inpatient and out patient services.

6954 **Southwest Communication Resource**
P.O.Box 788
Bernalillo, NM 87004-788
505-867-3396
FAX: 505-867-3398
e-mail: info@abrazosnm.org
swcr.org

Services for infants, children and adults with developmental disabilities in Sandoval County New Mexico.

## New York

6955 **Aspire of Western New York**
2356 N Forest Rd
Getzville, NY 14068-1224
716-838-0047
FAX: 716-894-8257
e-mail: info@aspirewny.org
aspirewny.org

*Thomas A. Sy, Executive Director*
*Janet Hansen, Associate Executive Director*
Provides comprehensive services to individuals with disabilities from infancy through adulthood. Also serves people with all types of developmental disabilities as well as providing clinical services to persons with other types of disabilities such as: spinal cord injury, head trauma and others. Aspire employs 1500 people.

6956 **Bronx Continuing Treatment Day Program**
1527 Southern Blvd
Bronx, NY 10460-5619
718-893-1414
FAX: 718-893-0707

*Mary Jane Purcell, Manager*
Post-acute rehabilitation program.

6957 **Brooklyn Bureau of Community Service**
285 Schermerhorn St
Brooklyn, NY 11217-1098
718-310-5600
FAX: 718-855-1517
e-mail: info@bbcs.org
bbcs.org

*Marla Simpson, Executive Director*
*Anthony B. Edwards, MBA, CCF, MFM, CFO*
Offers independent living skills, counseling, work readiness, vocational trianing, job placement and job follow-up services to individuals with disabilities (to include individuals with psychiatric, physical, and developmental disabilities). Special programs to move disabled welfare recipients from welfare to work. Publishes a bi-annual newsletter.

6958 **Buffalo Hearing and Speech Center**
50 E North St
Buffalo, NY 14203-1002
716-885-8318
FAX: 716-885-4229
askbhsc.org

*Joseph J. Cozzo, President/ CEO*
Assists individuals with speech, language and/or hearing impairments to achieve maximum communication potential.

6959 **Cora Hoffman Center Day Program**
2324 Forest Ave
Staten Island, NY 10303-1506
718-447-8205
FAX: 718-815-2182

*Kevin Kenney, Manager*
Post-acute rehabilitation program specializing in Cerebral Palsy. Part of the Cerebral Palsey Association of New York State.

6960 **Elmhurst Hospital Center**
7901 Broadway
Elmhurst, NY 11373-1368
718-334-4000
www.nyc.gov/html/hhc/ehc/html/home/home.shtml

*Chris D Constantino, Executive Director*
Hospital is comprised of 525 beds and is a Level I Trauma Center, and Emergency Heart Care Stattion and a 911 recieving hospital. It is the premiere health care organization for key areas such as Surgery, Cardiology, Women's health, Pediatrics, Rehabilitation Medicine, Renal and Mental Health Services.

6961 **Federation Employment And Guidance Service(F-E-G-S)**
315 Hudson St
New York, NY 10013-1086
212-366-8400
FAX: 212-366-8441
e-mail: info@fegs.org
www.fegs.org

*Gail Magaliff, CEO*
*Ira Machowsky, Executive Vice President*
*Angela R. Falcone, CFO*
The largest and most diversified private, not-for-profit health related and human service organization in the United States. With operations in over 258 facilities, residences, and off-site locations, F-E-G-S has served more then 2 million people since its inception.

6962 **Flushing Hospital**
4500 Parsons Blvd
Flushing, NY 11355-2205
718-670-5000
FAX: 718-670-3082
flushinghospital.org

*Robert V. Levine, Executive Vice President and COO*
*Bruce J. Flanz, President/ CEO*
*Mounir Doss, Executive Vice President/CFO*
Offers services for the totally blind, legally blind, visually impaired, mentally retarded blind and more with health, counseling, educational, recreational, rehabilitation, computer training and professional training services.

6963 **Gateway Community Industries Inc.,**
1 Amy Kay Pkwy
Kingston, NY 12401-6444
845-331-1261
800-454-9395
FAX: 845-331-4920
e-mail: info@gatewayindustries.org
gatewayindustries.org

*Francoise C. Gunefsky, President/ CEO*
*Eva Graham, CFO*
Gateway Community Industries, Inc., founded in 1957, is one of the leading independent not-for-profit vocational rehabilitation

and training centers for people with mental and/or physical disabilities. The agency provides comprehensive services in vocational evaluation, job training, job placement, vocational work center employment, supported employment, psychiatric rehabilitation, continuing day treatment, and residential habilitation/rehabilitation.

**6964 Henkind Eye Institute Division of Montefiore Hospital**
3400 Bainbridge Ave
Bronx, NY 10467-2404
718-741-2426
www.montefiore.org

*Philip O. Ozuah, MD, PhD, Executive Vice President/ COO*
*Steven M. Safyer, MD, President/ CEO*
Offers services for the totally blind, legally blind, visually impaired, mentally retarded blind and more with health, counseling, educational, recreational, rehabilitation, computer training and professional training services. Low vision services offered.

**6965 Industries for the Blind of New York State**
296 Washington Avenue Ext
Albany, NY 12203-6314
518-456-8671
800-421-9010
FAX: 518-456-3587
ibnys.org

*Richard Healey, CEO*
Offers services for the totally blind, legally blind, visually impaired, mentally retarded blind and more with health, counseling, educational, recreational, rehabilitation, computer training and professional training services.

**6966 Inpatient Pain Rehabilitation Program**
301 E 17th St
New York, NY 10003-3804
212-598-6745
FAX: 212-598-6468
http://www.med.nyu.edu/

*William Pinter Phd, Administrative Director*
The Inpatient Rehabilitation Program, established in 1983 specializes in the treatment of chronic pain. Our inpatient program is one of the oldest and well established pain programs in the country. It is the only interdisciplinary inpatient pain program in the tri-state area and one of only 20 pain programs in the entire US to have CARF accreditation. Upon completion of an extensive evaluation, patients are admitted for an 18-day inpatient stay.

**6967 Koicheff Health Care Center**
2324 Forest Ave
Staten Island, NY 10303-1506
718-447-0200
FAX: 718-981-1431

*Paul Castello, Clinic Director*
Post-accute rehabilitation programs.

**6968 New York-Presbyterian Hospital**
622 W 168th St
New York, NY 10032-3796
212-305-4600
FAX: 212-305-1017
www.nyp.org

*Steven J. Corwin, MD, CEO*
*Robert E. Kelly, MD, President*
New York Presbyterian Hospital is internationally recognized for its outstanding comprehensive services. Its medical, surgical, and emergency care services provide each patient with the highest possible level of care. In addition, as part of the Hospital's commitment to the total well-being of each patient, it offers a range of specialized services, as well as special healthcare programs for neighboring communities.

**6969 Norman Marcus Pain Institute**
30 E 40th St
Ste 1100
New York, NY 10016
212-532-7999
FAX: 212-532-5957
e-mail: support@nmpi.com
backpainusa.com

*Norman J Marcus, Medical Director*
We focus on muscles as the cause of most common pains, i.e. back, neck, shoulders, and headaches. We make specific muscle diagnoses and have specific treatments that in many cases will eliminate the need for surgery or relieve the pain. Patients diagnosed with herniated disc, spinal stenosis, rotator cuff tear, impingement syndrome, sciatica, fibromyalgia and headache will generally find relief.

**6970 Pain Alleviation Center**
Comprehensive Pain Management Associates
125 S Service Rd
Jericho, NY 11753-1038
516-997-7246
FAX: 516-997-7281
www.paincenter.com

*Alex Weingarten, Director*
*Phillip Fyman, Director*
*Marisa French, Manager*
One of the first pain clinics to gain national accreditation from the Commission on Accreditation of Rehabilitation Facilities. This is due largely to a patient-centered program based on the latest research.

**6971 Pathfinder Village**
3 Chenango Rd
Edmeston, NY 13335-2314
607-965-8377
FAX: 607-965-8655
e-mail: info@pathfindervillage.org
www.pathfindervillage.org

*Paul Landers, CEO*
Pathfinder Village is a warm, friendly community in the rolling hills of Central New York. Here children and adults with Down Syndrome gain independence, build lasting friendships, become partners in the world and take in all that life has to offer.

**6972 Pilot Industries: Ellenville**
845-331-4300
48 Canal St
Ellenville, NY 12428-1327
845-647-7711
FAX: 845-647-7711

*Peter Pierri, Executive Director*
*Betty Marks, Plant Manager*
Post-accute rehabilitation services.

**6973 Skills Unlimited**
405 Locust Ave
Oakdale, NY 11769-1695
631-567-3320
FAX: 631-567-3285
e-mail: info@skillsunlimited.org
skillsunlimited.org

*Richard Kassnove, Executive Director*
Our basic goals is to offer persons with disabilities the opportunity to explore and develop their full vocational potential. Our programs are unique in that by offering comprehensive services, individuals are able to deal with many different issues that could potentially affect their vocational success. Any individual that has an impairment that interferes with their ability to work is entitles to the services that we offer.

## North Carolina

**6974 Center for Vision Rehabilitation**
Academy Eye Associates
3115 Academy Rd
Durham, NC 27707-2652
919-493-7456
800-942-1499
FAX: 919-493-1718
e-mail: henry.greene@academyeye.com
academyeye.com

*Henry A Greene, Owner*
Vision rehabilitation and low-vision care for the visually impaired, post-stroke, head trauma and for neuro-oncology vision complications.

**6975 Diversified Opportunities**
1010 Herring Ave E
Wilson, NC 27893-3311
252-291-0378
FAX: 252-291-1402
www.diversifiedopportunities.com

*Cindy Dixon, Executive Director*
Vocational rehabilitation agency, better outcomes, lower cost, guaranteed performance standards.

**6976 Forsyth Medical Center**
3333 Silas Creek Pkwy
Winston Salem, NC 27103-3090
336-718-5000
FAX: 336-718-9250
www.forsythmedicalcenter.org

*Olayinka D Akinola, Director*
Provides care that is state-of-the-art and second to none, both because of advanced treatments availiable through our clinical research and technology to the academic excellence-and caring nature-of our doctors and nurses.

**6977 Industries of the Blind**
920 W Lee St
Greensboro, NC 27403-2803
336-274-1591
800-909-7086
FAX: 336-544-3739
e-mail: customerservice@iob-gso.com
industriesoftheblind.com

*David LoPresti, President*
Offers services for the totally blind, legally blind, visually impaired, mentally retarded blind and more with health, counseling, educational, recreational, rehabilitation, computer training and professional training services.

**6978 Johnston County Industries**
1100 East Preston Street
Selma, NC 27576-3162
919-743-8700
FAX: 919-965-8023
jcindustries.com

JCI is an entrepreneurial not-for-profit corporation dedicated to empowering people with disabilities or disadvantages to succeed through training and employment

**6979 Learning Services: Carolina**
707 Morehead Ave
Durham, NC 27707-1319
919-688-4444
FAX: 919-419-9966
learningservices.com

Located in an historic neighborhood in the heart of Durham, this campus-style setting offers easy access to resources at 3 outstanding facilities: Duke University, The University of North Carolina at Chapel Hill, and Research Triangle Park. This program provides a range of services and activities that draw upon the many resources available in the community.

**6980 LifeSpan**
200 Clanton Road
Charlotte, NC 28217
704-944-5100
lifespanservices.org

*Davan Cloninger, President & CEO*
Provide vocational and enrichment program for adults with developmental disabilities.

**6981 Lions Club Industries for the Blind**
4500 Emperor Blvd.
Durham, NC 27703
919-596-8277
800-526-1562
FAX: 919-598-1179
e-mail: inquire@buylci.com
http://www.lcibsc.com/

*Bill Hudson, President*
Offers services for the totally blind, legally blind, visually impaired, mentally retarded blind and more with health, counseling, educational, recreational, rehabilitation, computer training and professional training services.

**6982 Lions Services Inc.**
5 Penn Plaza
New York, NY 10001
21- 62- 210
e-mail: lsisale@aol.com
www.thomasnet.com

*Jimmy R Cranford, President*
*Jimmy Cranford, President*
Offers services for the totally blind, legally blind, visually impaired, mentally retarded blind and more with health, counseling, educational, recreational, rehabilitation, computer training and professional training services.

**6983 Regional Rehabilitation Center Pitt County Memorial Hospital**
2100 Stantonsburg Rd
Greenville, NC 27834-2818
252-847-4448
FAX: 252-816-7552
e-mail: mdixon@pcmh.com
www.uhseast.com/rehab

*Martha M Dixon, VP General Services*
An accredited, comprehensive rehabilitation center-part of a statewide network- and we're the largest such facility in eastern North Carolina. Our service area covers 29 counties, and we offer a complete array of rehabilitation services for patients of all ages. Because the Regional Rehabilitation Center is associated with both Pitt County Memorial Hospital And the Brody School of Medicine at East Carolina University, patients have access to a full range of state of the art medical services.

**6984 Rehab Home Care**
2660 Yonkers Rd
Raleigh, NC 27604-3384
800-447-8692
FAX: 919-831-2211

*Alan Silver, CEO*
*Janis Hansen, Chief Operating Officer*
A Medicare/Medicaid certified, state-licensed home health agency with emphasis on rehabilitation.

**6985 Thoms Rehabilitation Hospital**
Thoms Rehabilitation Hospital
68 Sweeten Creek Rd
Asheville, NC 28803-2318
828-277-4800
FAX: 828-277-4812
www.carepartners.org

*Tracy Buchanan, President & CEO*
*Gary Bowers, COO*
Freestanding physical rehabilitation hospital, founded 1938 - 100 beds, including 90 acute and 10 transitional - JCAHO accredited.

**6986 Winston-Salem Industries for the Blind**
7730 N Point Blvd
Winston Salem, NC 27106-3310
336-759-0551
800-242-7726
FAX: 336-759-0990
e-mail: info@wsifb.com
www.wsifb.com

*Daniel Boucher, Executive Chairman*
Offers services for the totally blind, legally blind, visually impaired, mentally retarded blind and more with health, counseling, educational, recreational, rehabilitation, computer training and professional training services.

## Ohio

**6987 Bellefaire Jewish Children's Bureau**
22001 Fairmount Blvd
Shaker Heights, OH 44118-4819
216-932-2800
800-879-2522
FAX: 216-932-6704
e-mail: info@bellefairejcb.org
www.bellefairejcb.org

*Adam Jacobs, CEO*
*Adam G. Jacobs PhD, Executive Vice President*
Residential treatment for ages 12 to 17 1/2 at time of admission offering individualized psychotherapy, special education, and group living for severaly emotionally disturbed children and adolescents. Also offers a variety of other programs including specialized and therapuetic foster care, partial hospitilization, outpatient counseling, home-based intensive counseling and adoption services.

**6988 Christ Hospital Rehabilitation Unit**
2139 Auburn Ave
Cincinnati, OH 45219-2906
513-585-2737
FAX: 513-585-4353
wwwchristhospitalcincinnati.com

*Regina Hartman, Manager*
Patients of this 555-bed, not-for-profit acute care facility receive personalized health care provided by trained specialists using the most sophisticated medical technology available, including state-of-the-art intensive care units, surgical facilities, cardiac catheterization labs, three new electrophysiology labs, and the tristates first positron emission tomography (PET) scanning capabilities.

**6989 Cleveland Society for the Blind**
Cleveland Sight Center
P.O.Box 1988
1909 East 101st Street
Cleveland, OH 44106-8696
216-861-5627
FAX: 216-696-2582
e-mail: jcarey@clevelandsightcenter.org
www.clevelandsightcenter.org

Social, rehabilitation, education and support services for blind and visually impaired children and adults, early intervention program for children birth to age 6, low vision clinic, aid and appliance shop, Braille and taping transcription, training for rehabilitation, orientation, mobility and computer access, employment services and job placement, recreation program, resident camping, talking books, radio reading services, food service training and snack bar employment. Free screening.

**6990 Columbus Speech and Hearing Center**
510 E North Broadway St
Columbus, OH 43214-4114
614-263-5151
FAX: 614-263-5365
columbusspeech.org

*Dawn Gleason, Au.D., President/ CEO*
*Karen Deeter, Director of Operations*
Serves persons who have speech-language and hearing challenges. Provides vocational rehabilitation services for individuals who are deaf, hard-of-hearing or deaf-blind.

**6991 CommuniCare of Clifton Nursing and Rehabilitation Center**
Communi Care Health Services
4700 Ashwood Drive
Suite 200
Cincinnati, OH 4524
513-281-2464
FAX: 513-281-2559
communicarehealth.com

*Stephen L. Rosedale, Founder/ CEO*
A long term care facility which specializes in rehabilitation. Offers a full range of rehabilitative services including physical therapy, occupational therapy and speech therapy.

**6992 Doctors Hospital**
5100 W Broad St
Columbus, OH 43228-1672
614-544-1000
800-837-7555
FAX: 614-544-1844
www.ohiohealth.com/homedoctors

*David Blom, President/ CEO*
*Michael Bernstein, Senior Vice President and Chief Strategy Officer*
We believe our first responsibility is to the patients we serve. We respect the physical, emotional and spiritual needs of our patients and find that compassion is essential to fostering healing and wholeness.

**6993 Dodd Hall at the Ohio State University Hospitals**
410 W 10th Ave
Columbus, OH 43210-1240
614-293-3300
800-293-5123
www.medicalcenter.osu.edu

*Steven G. Gabbe, MD, Senior Vice President / CEO*
*Larry Anstine, CEO*
Dodd Hall is a full service medical rehabilitation hospital offering comprehensive inpatient and outpatient rehabilitation.

**6994 Easter Seal Society of Mahoning**
National Easter Seals Chicago
233 South Wacker Drive
Suite 2400
Chicago, IL 60606
312-726-6200
800-221-6827
FAX: 312-726-1494
www.mtc.easterseals.com

Outpatient medical rehabilitation - physical therapy, speech therapy, occupational therapy, warm-water therapy and adult day services.

**6995 Four Oaks Center**
623 Dayton Xenia Rd
Xenia, OH 45385-2605
937-562-6779
FAX: 937-562-7539
www.greenedd.org

*Margaret Conrad, Director*
*Jill A. LaRock, Director*
Starts children on the road to discovery by providing a learning environment rich in opportunities and encouragement. The program was designed to give children with delays or disabilities, or those at-risk the extra help needed to develop fully. Any child under the age of six who exhibits developmental delays, handicapping conditions, or is considered at risk may qualify to participate.

**6996 Genesis Healthcare System**
Rehabilitation Services
800 Forest Ave
Zanesville, OH 43701-2881
740-454-5461
800-322-4762
FAX: 740-455-7527
e-mail: llynn@genesishcs.org
www.genesishcs.org

*Matt Perry, President/ CEO*
*Paul Masterson, CFO*
*Richard Helsper, COO*
A CARF and JACHO accredited 19-bed rehabilitation facility located within Genesis Healthcare System, a 732 bed, non-profit hospital system, located in Zanesville, Ohio. Freestanding outpatient services, including work hardening, pain management, vocational services, audiology, lymphedema, vestibular rehab, off-the-road driving evals, aquatic therpay, womens health and sports enhancement.

**6997 George A Martin Center**
3603 Washington Ave
Cincinnati, OH 45229-2009
513-221-1017
FAX: 513-221-3817

*Karen Doggett, Executive Director*
Offers services for the totally blind, legally blind, visually impaired, mentally retarded blind and more with health, counseling, educational, recreational, rehabilitation, computer training and professional training services.

**6998 Grady Memorial Hospital**
561 W Central Ave
Delaware, OH 43015-1489
740-615-1000
800-487-1115
FAX: 740-368-5114
ohiohealth.com

*Bruce Hagen, Regional Executive and President, Dublin Methodist Hospital and Grady*
As a progressive healthcare leader, Grady Memorial Hospital is committed to excellence while providing the Deleware community with comprehensive quality service delivered with compassionate, personal care. Our membership in Ohio's largest healthcare system, Ohio Health, enables us to improve access to a broader range of healthcare services, enhance development of new programs and services, and provide a complete continuum of care for patients in the deleware area.

**6999 Hamilton Adult Center**
3400 Symmes Rd
Hamilton, OH 45015-1359
513-867-5970
FAX: 513-874-2977

*Donald Musnuff, Executive Director*

**7000 Holzer Clinic**
90 Jackson Pike
Gallipolis, OH 45631-1562
740-446-5411
FAX: 740-446-5532
e-mail: info@holzer.org
www.holzerclinic.com

*T. Wayne Munro, MD, CEO*
Serves medical needs of patients in an 8 county area, including counties in Ohio and West Virginia.

**7001 Holzer Clinic Sycamore**
Holzer Medical Center
4th Avenue & Sycamore St
Gallipolis, OH 45631
740-446-5244
FAX: 740-446-5448
e-mail: info@holzer.org
www.holzer.org

*T. Wayne Munro, MD, CEO*
Offers an individualized quality comprehensive rehabilitation program for people with disabilities by an interdisciplinary team including physical therapy, occupational, speech, nursing and social services to restore the patient to the highest degree of rehab outcomes attainable.

**7002 IKRON Institute for Rehabilitative and Psychological Services**
2347 Vine St
Cincinnati, OH 45219-1745
513-621-1117
FAX: 513-621-2350
e-mail: ikron@ikron.org
ikron.org

*Randy Strunk, MA, LPCC-S, Executive Director*
*Ken Carbonell, BBA, Fiscal Director*
*Melissa Harmeling, MA, PCC-S, Program Director*
An accredited mental health facility and a certified rehabilitation center. Through a variety of creative treatment and rehabilitation services, IKRON assists adults with mental health and/or substance abuse problems to attain greater independence, to lead lives of sobriety, to obtain competitive work and live more satisfying lives. IKRON places a strong emphasis on respect and support for persons with problems of adjustment. Special contracts to persons desiring job placement.

**7003 Integrated Health Services at Waterford Commons**
955 Garden Lake Pkwy
Toledo, OH 43614-2777
419-382-2200
FAX: 419-381-8508

*Nicole Giesige, Executive Director*
A subacute and rehabilitation program specializing in ventilator weaning and management, I.V. therapeutics and pain management, wound management and subacute rehabilitation.

**7004 Lester H Higgins Adult Center**
3041 Cleveland Ave SW
Canton, OH 44707-3625
330-484-4814
FAX: 330-484-9416
http://www.theworkshopsinc.com/

*Margalie Belazaire, Manager*
*Ed Allar, Manager*
Post-accute rehabilitation service

**7005 Live Oaks Career Development Campus**
5936 Buckwheat Rd
Milford, OH 45150
513-575-1906
FAX: 513-575-0805

*Harold Carr MD, Superintendent*
*Robin White, President/CEO*
*Jim Dixon, Principal*
Post-accute rehabilitation facility and services.

**7006 Metro Health: St. Luke's Medical Center Pain Management Program**
2500 Metrohealth Dr
Cleveland, OH 44109-1900
216-778-7800
www.metrohealth.org

*Mark Moran, President*
CARF accredited comprehensive multidisciplinary pain management program.

**7007 MetroHealth Medical Center**
2500 Metrohealth Dr
Cleveland, OH 44109-1900
216-778-7800
www.metrohealth.org

*Mark Moran, President*
Located on the near west side of Cleveland, is a leader in trauma, emergency, and critical care; women's and childrens's services, including high risk obstetrical care and neonatal intensive care; comprehensive medical and surgical subspecialties.

**7008 Middletown Regional Hospital: Inpatient Rehabilitation Unit**
105 McKnight Dr
Middletown, OH 45044-4838
513-422-1401
800-338-4057
FAX: 513-422-1520
www.middletownhospital.org

*C N Reddy, Owner*
*Douglas McNeill, Chief Executive Officer*
Our mission is to serve and help people, improving the status of their health and the quality of thier lives. Our vision is to be the premier integrated delivery system in Southwest Ohio. Our Values are quality, respect, service and teamwork

**7009 Newark Healthcare Center**
680 South Fourth Street
Louisville, KY 40202
502-596-7300
TTY:800-545-0749
e-mail: web_administrator@kindredhealthcare.com
kindredhealthcare.com

*Paul J. Diaz, President/ CEO*
Accomodates 300 residents. We are located in the heart of Newark, Ohio. Newark Healthcare is a 2004 recipient of the American Health Care Association's Quality Award.

**7010 Parma Community General Hospital Acute Rehabilitation Center**
7007 Powers Blvd
Parma, OH 44129-5495
440-743-3000
FAX: 440-843-4387
www.parmahospital.org

*Terrence G. Deis, President*
*Barry L. Franklin, CPA, Executive Vice President/ CFO*
The mission of this CARF accredited unit is to provide the most comprehensive, cost-effective, acute rehabilitation program possible in order for every patient and family to adjust to his/her disability and to achieve the maximum potential of independent functioning when returning to community living.

**7011 Peter A Towne Physical Therapy Center**
Ste 10
447 Nilles Rd
Fairfield, OH 45014-2626
513-829-7726
FAX: 513-829-7726
www.townept.com/fairfield

*Debbie Wilkerson, Office Manager*
Outpatient, private practice physical and occupational therapy. Three other offices in Hamilton, Monroe and West Chester.

**7012 Philomatheon Society of the Blind**
2701 Tuscarawas St W
Canton, OH 44708-4638
330-453-9157
http://my.raex.com/~philo/

*Shirley Beckner, President*
Offers services for the totally blind, legally blind, visually impaired, mentally retarded blind and more with health, counseling, educational, recreational, rehabilitation, computer training and professional training services.

**7013 Providence Hospital Work**
2270 Banning Rd
Cincinnati, OH 45239-6621
513-591-5600
FAX: 513-591-5604

*Kay Brogle, Executive Director*
Post-acute rehabilitation services.

**7014 Six County, Inc.**
2845 Bell St
Zanesville, OH 43701-1794
740-454-9766
800-344-5818
FAX: 740-588-6452
e-mail: info@sixcounty.org
www.sixcounty.org

*John A Creek, President*
*Tim Llewellyn, Senior VP/Community Intervention*
*Robert Santos, Ex Vp & Coo*
*Mary Denoble, Vp Qip*
Six County, Inc., is a private, not-for-profit corporation under contract with the Mental Health and Recovery Services Board. Six County, Inc., provides comprehensive community mental health services to people of all ages in each of the six Southeastern Ohio counties served: Coshocton, Guernsey, Morgan, Muskingum, Noble, and Perry. SCI's counseling centers provide a full range of services including outpatient counseling; diagnostic assessment, referrals, and psychological testing.

**7015 Society for Rehabilitation**
9290 Lake Shore Blvd
Mentor, OH 44060-1664
440-352-8993
800-344-3159
FAX: 440-352-6632
e-mail: info@societyhelps.org
www.societyhelps.org

*Richard Kessler, Executive Director*
Vision is to provide individuals with comprehensive services to improve their quality of life. Our mission is to meet the needs of individuals and their families by delivering a wide range of affordable accessible and personalized services, providing treatment by a team of highly qualified, caring professionals. Collaborating with other agencies to meet community needs.

**7016 Southeast Ohio Sight Center**
425 E. Alvarado Street
Suite E
Fallbrook, CA 92028
800-677-4180
www.charityadvantage.com

Offers services for the blind and visually impaired to include functional low vision evaluations, community rehabilitation trading, counseling, educational, recreational, rehabilitation and vocational services.

**7017 St. Francis Rehabilitation Hospital**
401 N Broadway St
Green Springs, OH 44836-9638
419-639-2626
800-248-2552
FAX: 419-639-6225
www.sfhcc.org

*Kim Eicher, CEO*
*Dan Schwanke, Chief Executive Officer*
Program offers specialized treatment for patients who have suffered a head injury, spinal cord injury, or stroke, or who have an orthopedic injury. The Head Injury Program provides a continuum of care from coma stimulation through transitional living. Their physicians, nurses, counselors and therapists are dedicated to helping our patients develop the motivation, strength and skills needed to overcome or adapt to their disability.

**7018 TAC Enterprises**
2160 Old Selma Rd
Springfield, OH 45505-4600
937-525-7400
http://www.tacind.com/

*Clifford Meyer, CEO*
TAC Enterprises provides employment opportunities for individuals to develop marketable skills by completing contract work in partnership with other industries. Work and self-help skills, social adjustment, and a variety of daily living experiences are offered to the workers by our specialized staff.

## Oklahoma

**7019 Dean A McGee Eye Institute**
608 Stanton L Young Blvd
Oklahoma City, OK 73104-5065
405-271-6060
800-787-9012
www.dmei.org

*Gregory L. Skuta, M.D., President/CEO*
*Matthew D. Brown, Executive Vice President*
*Lana G. Ivy, Vice President of Development*

Offers services for the totally blind, legally blind, visually impaired, mentally retarded blind and more with health, counseling, educational, recreational, rehabilitation, computer training and professional training services.

**7020 Jane Phillips Medical Center**
Rehab Care
3500 E Frank Phillips Blvd
Bartlesville, OK 74006-2464
918-333-7200
FAX: 918-333-7801
e-mail: webmaster@jpmc.org
www.sjmc.org

*David Stire, CEO*
*Evan O Zorn, Executive Vice President*
*James Carver, MD*

Comprehensive inpatient rehabilitation services are provided to patients with orthopedic, neurologic, and other medical conditions of recent onset or regression, who have experienced a loss of function in activities of daily living, mobility, cognition and communication.

**7021 McAlester Regional Health Center RehabCare Unit**
1 E Clark Bass Blvd
McAlester, OK 74501-4255
918-426-1800
FAX: 918-421-6832
e-mail: nbrinlee@mrhcok.com
www.mrhcok.com

*David Keith, President/ CEO*

A 19-bed inpatient physical rehabilitation unit serving the Southeast Oklahoma area. Offers physical therapy, occupational therapy, social work, speech and psychological services in an interdisciplinary framework.

**7022 Oklahoma League for the Blind**
501 N Douglas Ave
Oklahoma City, OK 73106-5085
405-232-4644
FAX: 405-236-5438
e-mail: info@olb.org
olb.org

*Lauren White, CEO*
*Carol Campbell, Executive Assistant*
*Bob Allen, President*

Offers services for the blind and visually impaired, counseling, educational, recreational, rehabilitation, computer training and professional training services.

**7023 Valley View Regional Hospital-RehabCare Unit**
430 N Monte Vista St
Ada, OK 74820-4657
580-332-2323
FAX: 580-421-1395
e-mail: valleyview@wrh.com
www.valleyviewregional.org

*W. Kent Rogers, President/ CEO*

Comprehensive physical medicine and rehabilitation services designed to help patients in their adjustment to a physically limiting condition.

## Oregon

**7024 Garten Services**
3334 Industrial Way NE
Salem, OR 97301-59
503-581-4472
FAX: 503-581-4497
e-mail: garten@garten.org
garten.org

*Tim Rocak, CEO*
*Pamela Best, CFO*

Garten's mission is to support people with disabilities in their effort to contribute to the community through employment, career, and retirement opportunities. Our actions increase society's awareness of human potential. Garten's vision is to be recognized as an organization positively demonstrating to the community that people with disabilities can be contributing and valued employees of a thriving business.

**7025 Legacy Emanuel Rehabilitation Center**
3025 N Vancouver Ave
Portland, OR 97227-1542
503-413-6931
FAX: 503-413-1501
www.legacyhealth.org

*Gary Guidetta, Executive Director*
*Gail Weisgerber, Manager*

A non-profit tax-exempt corporation that includes 5 full-service hospitals and a children's hospital. The Legacy system provides an integrated network of healthcare services, including acute and critical care, inpatient and outpatient treatment, community health education and a variety of specialty services.

**7026 Oakcrest Care Center**
2933 Center St NE
Salem, OR 97301-4527
503-585-5850
FAX: 503-585-8781

Postacute rehabilitation program.

**7027 Oakhill-Senior Program**
1190 Oakhill Ave SE
Salem, OR 97302-3496
503-364-9086
FAX: 503-365-2879

*Jan Dillon, Senior Services Manager*

Garten Senior Services provides an adult day service program to seniors with and without developmental disabilities. The program will provide community opportunities, college classes and a wide variety of leisure activities in group and individual settings.

**7028 Pacific Spine and Pain Center**
1801 Highway 99 N
Ashland, OR 97520-9152
541-488-2255
866-482-5515
FAX: 541-482-2433

*Janel R Guyette, Manager*

**7029 Vision Northwest**
9225 SW Hall Blvd
Portland, OR 97223-6794
503-684-8389
800-448-2232
FAX: 503-684-9359
e-mail: marthaz@visionnw.com
visionnw.com

*Evelyn Maizels, Executive Director*

Offers services for the totally blind, legally blind, visually impaired, mentally retarded blind and more with health, counseling, educational, recreational, rehabilitation, computer training and professional training services.

**7030 Willamette Valley Rehabilitation Center**
1853 W Airway Rd
Lebanon, OR 97355-1233
541-258-8121
FAX: 541-451-1762
wvrc.org

*Martin Baughman, Executive Director*
Provides the best professional vocational services to those adults in the community who, by virtue of their physical or mental limitations, are negatively impacted by their ability to attain or maintain employment.

## Pennsylvania

**7031 Alpine Nursing and Rehabilitation Center of Hershey**
Pennstate
405 Martin Ter
State College, PA 16803-3426
814-865-1710
FAX: 814-863-9423
e-mail: geron@psu.edu
geron.psu.edu

*Melissa A Hardy, Director*
*Anna Shuey, Administrative Assistant*
Postacute rehabilitation program.

**7032 Alpine Ridge and Brandywood**
600 Boot Rd
Downingtown, PA 19335-3408
610-873-4900
FAX: 610-430-0567
devereux.org

*MaryAnn Fullam, Director*

**7033 Amity Lodge**
Devereux Foundation
600 Boot Rd
Downingtown, PA 19335-3408
610-873-4900
800-345-1292
FAX: 610-524-3000
devereux.org

*Kim Nash, Director*
*Sam Ewing, Owner*
Offers residents a continuum of services ranging from minimal care and supervision to total physical and medical care.

**7034 Beechwood Rehabilitation Services A Community Integrated Brain Injury Program**
469 E Maple Ave
Langhorne, PA 19047-1600
215-750-4299
800-782-3299
FAX: 215-750-4327
e-mail: dcerra-tyl@wood.org
beechwoodrehab.com

*Thomas Felicetti, President*
Services include residential, day treatment and community based support services. Individuals with brain injury are served. The facility is Care Accredited.

**7035 Beneto Center**
Devereux Foundation
2012 Renaissance Blvd
King of Prussia, PA 19406-3408
610-542-3000
800-345-1292
FAX: 610-542-3141
www.devereux.org

*Walkern Grono, Executive Director*
Offers a continuum of services for residents requiring services ranging from minimal care and supervision to total physical and medical care.

**7036 Blind & Vision Rehabilitation Services Of Pittsburgh**
1800 West St
Homestead, PA 15120-2578
412-368-4400
800-706-5050
FAX: 412-368-4090
pghvis.org

*Stephen S Barrett, President*
*Linda Hill, Manager*
Offers services for the totally blind, legally blind, visually impaired, mentally retarded blind and more with health, counseling, educational, recreational, rehabilitation, computer training and professional training services.

**7037 Bradford Regional Medical Center**
116 Interstate Pkwy
Bradford, PA 16701-1036
814-368-4143
FAX: 814-368-4130
brmc.com

*Marek Dzionara, Owner*
*Andrew Lehman, Executive Director*
Offers rehabilitation services to individuals with an alcohol or drug related problem.

**7038 Bryn Mawr Rehabilitation Hospital**
414 Paoli Pike
Malvern, PA 19355-3311
610-251-5400
888-734-2241
888-734-2241
FAX: 610-647-3648
www.brynmawrrehab.org

*Donna M. Phillips, President*
We are dedicated to serving individuals and their families whose lives can be enhanced through physical or cognitive rehabilitation. We continually strive for excellence by providing care and services which are valued by those we serve and by contributing to the community through education, research and prevention of disability.

**7039 Daman Villa**
Devereux Foundation
600 Boot Rd
Downingtown, PA 19335-3408
610-873-4900
800-345-1292
FAX: 610-430-0567
www.devereux.org

*Robert Kreider, President & CEO*
*Sam Ewing, Owner*
Offers residents a continuum of services ranging from minimal care and supervision to total physical and medical care.

**7040 Devereux**
444 Devereux Dr
Villanova, PA 19085-1932
610-520-3000
800-345-1292
FAX: 610-542-3100
e-mail: knash@devereux.org
devereux.org

*Robert Q Kreider, CEO*
*Robert Kreider, Chief Executive Officer*
Nationwide network of residential, day, and community-based services for children and adults who have special emotional and/or developmental needs.

**7041 Devereux Pennsylvania**
390 E. Boot Road
Westchester, PA 19380
610-431-8100
866-532-2212
FAX: 610-430-0567
www.devereux.org

*Melanie Beidler, Executive Director*
*Steve Silverman, Admissions Director*
*Kelly McCool, Admissions Manager*

Provides a continuum of mental health services (acute, residential, wrap-around, educational) for children and adults with developmental disabilities. Active treatment is offered in a safe and therapeutic environment which allows on-going assessment and individual growth that will enhance the quality of life for each of its residents. Special education schools also offer educatioin services. $165-$469 per day.

**7042 Devereux's Kanner**
890 E Boot Rd
West Chester, PA 19380
610-431-8100
FAX: 610-431-8105
devereux.org

*Susan Smith, Executive Director*

**7043 Fox Subacute Center**
2644 Bristol Rd
Warrington, PA 18976-1404
800-782-2288
e-mail: WebAdmin@rehabcare.com
subacute.com

*James Foulke, CEO*
*Vic Costenko, COO*
*Walter Dunsmore, CFO*
Fox subacute recognizes the great need for alternative programs for today's medically compromised patients. Fox has developed Models of Care and offers subacute programs fore the management of ventilator-dependent patients. We recognize that the best road to recovery for these patients is an environment with special care in an alternative setting. We believe that setting should be outside the hospital, in facilities where the focus is on the management of individual patients.

**7044 Fox Subacute at Clara Burke**
251 Stenton Ave
Plymouth Meeting, PA 19462-1220
610-828-2272
800-424-7201
FAX: 610-828-7939
e-mail: admissions@foxsubacute.com
www.foxsubacute.com

*Ann Marie Mims, Administrator*
*Amy Swartley, Admissions*
*Terri Herd, Marketing Director*
Postacute rehabilitation program, for ventilator patients.

**7045 Good Samaritan Health System**
P.O.Box 1281
4th & Walnut Streets
Lebanon, PA 17042-1281
717-270-7500
gshleb.org

*Robin Weiler, Manager*
*Frederick Davis, VP Clinical Services*
Offers services for the totally blind, legally blind, visually impaired, mentally retarded blind and more with health, counseling, educational, recreational, rehabilitation, computer training and professional training services.

**7046 Good Samaritan Hospital-Health System Center**
Good Samaritan Hospital
4th & Walnut Sts
P.O.Box 1281
Lebanon, PA 17042-1281
717-270-7500
www.gshleb.org

*June Nafziger-Eberl, Manager*
*Stuart Hartman, Medical Director*
Comprehensive inpatient rehab unit for adults regarding general physical rehabilitation. Specific programs include orthopedic, neurological, stroke, amputee, etc.

**7047 Kanner Center**
Devereax Foundation
2012 Renaissance Blvd
King of Prussia, PA 19406
610-542-3000
866-532-2212
FAX: 610-542-3141
e-mail: kanner@devereux.org
www.devereux.org

*Susan Smith, Executive Director*
A private nonprofit nationwide network of treatment services for individuals of all ages with emotional and/or developmental disabilities.

**7048 Pediatric Center at Plymouth Meeting Integrated Health Services**
491 Allendale Rd
King of Prussia, PA 19406-1426
610-265-9290
800-220-7337

*Fran Currick, Manager*
Subacute programs such as intensive respiratory care, stressing ventilator dependent children, pre and post transplant care, total parenteral nutrition, IV therapy, intensive/behavioral oral feeding programs. Provides extensive discharge planning including teaching or review for all the above programs with an emphasis on development and accessing community resources.

**7049 Penn State Milton S. Hershey Medical Center College Of Medicine**
500 University Dr
Hershey, PA 17033-2360
717-531-6955
800-243-1455
FAX: 717-531-4558
pennstatecancerinstitute.com

*Harold L Paz, CEO*
a non-sectarian, not-for-profit community hospital whose purpose is to provide high quality acute, rehabilitative and preventive health services for the entire community, regardless of creed, race, nationality, or ability to pay.

**7050 Pennsylvania Pain Rehabilitation Center**
Ste 2
252 W Swamp Rd
Doylestown, PA 18901-2465
215-230-9707
FAX: 215-348-5106

*Kenneth Lefkowitz, Manager*
Post acute rehabilitation facility and programs.

**7051 The Rehabilitation & Nursing Center at Greater Pittsburgh**
890 Weatherwood Ln
Greensburg, PA 15601-5777
724-837-8076
FAX: 724-837-7456
e-mail: cstepien@greaterpittsburghrnc.com
healthbridgelive.reflexions.net

*Nancy Flenner, Administrator*
*Marsha Echard, Admissions Coordinator*
*Craig Stepien, Admissions Director*
Subacute care, ventilator and pulmonary managment, comprehensive rehabilitation.

## Rhode Island

**7052 In-Sight**
43 Jefferson Blvd
Warwick, RI 02888-6400
401-941-3322
FAX: 401-941-3356
e-mail: cbutler@in-sight.org
in-sight.org

*Chris Butler, Executive Director*

Offers services for the totally blind, legally blind, visually impaired, mentally retarded blind and more with health, counseling, educational, recreational, rehabilitation, computer training and professional training services.

**7053 Vanderbilt Rehabilitation Center**
Newport Hospital
Friendship St
Newport, RI 02840
401-845-1845
FAX: 401-845-1087
lifespan.org/newport/services.vrp

*Arthur Sampson, President/CEO*
*Todd Cipriani, VP Professional/Support Services*
The Vanderbilt Rehabilitation Center at Newport Hospital has been providing comprehensive rehabilitation sercices for more than 40 years and is known throughout the region for its unique programs and high-quality, patient focused care.

## South Carolina

**7054 Association for the Blind**
1071 Morrison Dr
Charleston, SC 29403-3117
843-723-6915
FAX: 843-577-4312
e-mail: aftb@aerolina.com

*Cornelia Pelzer, Executive Director*
Offers services for people who are blind, or are visually impaired with health, counseling, educational, recreational, rehabilitation, computer training and professional training services.

**7055 Hitchcock Rehabilitation Center**
690 Medical Park Dr
Aiken, SC 29801-6348
803-648-8344
800-207-6924
FAX: 803-649-4639
e-mail: mail@hitchcockhealthcare.org
http://www.hitchcockhealthcare.org/index.ht ml

*Karen Bowlen, Administrator*
*Dan Hillman, Case Manager*
*Carrie Morgan, Finance Director*
Comprehensive outpatient rehabilitation for adults, children, geriatrics, pediatric therapy, special needs preschool, sports medicine, home health and hospice.

**7056 The Mentor Network**
3200 Devine St
Columbia, SC 29205-1891
803-799-9025
800-297-8043
FAX: 803-931-8959
thementornetwork.com

*Lynn Epps, Executive Director*
Mentor provides a full network of individually tailored services for people with development disabilities and their families. Individuals may be served in their homes, shared living home, or in a host home.

## Tennessee

**7057 Humana Hospital: Morristown RehabCare**
726 McFarland St
Morristown, TN 37814-3989
423-586-2930
FAX: 423-587-4417

*James Perry, Program Director*
Designed to help patients in their adjustment to a physically limiting condition by helping to maximize each patient's abilities so he or she can function as independently as possible.

**7058 Opportunity East Rehabilitation Services for the Blind**
758 W Morris Blvd
Morristown, TN 37813-2136
423-586-3922
800-278-6274
FAX: 423-586-1479
e-mail: bandit75@charter.net
volblind.org

*Fred Overbay, CEO*
*Vic Mende, Director Rehabilitation Services*
Offers services for the totally blind, legally blind, visually impaired, mentally retarded blind and more with health, counseling, educational, recreational, rehabilitation, computer training and professional training services.

**7059 Patrick Rehab Wellness Center**
Lincoln County Health System
106 Medical Center Blvd
Fayetteville, TN 37334-2684
931-433-0273
FAX: 931-433-0378
www.ichealthsystem.com

*Gloria Meadows, Administrator*
*Jim Stewart, Principal*
Provides rehabilitation services of physical, occupational, and speech therapy. Also, wellness memberships are available to the public.

**7060 PharmaThera**
1785 Nonconnah Blvd
Memphis, TN 38132-2104
901-348-8100
800-767-6714
FAX: 901-348-8270
Offers 10 locations serving patients throughout the southern United States, each with an in-house, expertly trained staff. All locations use the latest technologies and techniques in infusion care to provide a broad range of individualized home infusion therapies.

**7061 Siskin Hospital For Physical Rehabilitation**
1 Siskin Plz
Chattanooga, TN 37403-1306
423-634-1200
e-mail: info@siskinrehab.org
siskinrehab.org

*Bob Main, CEO*
*Robert P. Main, President*
Dedicated exclusively to physical rehabilitation and offers specialized treatment programs in brain injury, amputation, stroke, spinal cord injury, orthopedics, and major multiple trauma. The hospital also provides treatment for neurological disorders and loss of muscle strength and controll following illness or surgery.

**7062 St. Mary's RehabCare Center**
900 E Oak Hill Ave
Knoxville, TN 37917-4556
865-545-7962
FAX: 865-545-8133

*Debbie Keeton, Director*
*Beth Greco, Executive Director*
Provides comprehensive rehabilitation services for patients experiencing CVA, head trauma, orthopedic conditions, spinal cord injury or neurological impairment.

## Texas

**7063 Baylor Institute for Rehabilitation**
909 N Washington Ave
Dallas, TX 75246-1520
214-820-9300
888-7BA-YLOR
FAX: 214-841-2679

*Jon Skinner, President*
*Luci Neumann, President*
A 92-bed specialty hospital offering comprehensive rehabilitation services for persons with spinal cord injury, traumatic brain

injury, stroke, amputation, and other orthopedic and neurological disorders.

**7064 CORE Health Care**
E&J Health Care
Building B
400 Highway 290
Dripping Springs, TX 78620
512-894-0801
866-683-1007
FAX: 512-858-4627
e-mail: info@corehealth.com
corehealth.com

*Eric Makowski, CEO*
*Kristi Jones, Marketing/Admissions Director*
*George Yesian, Admissions Coordinator*
*Bethany Bounas, Admissions Coordinator*
Post acute and transitional rehabilitation, long-term care, community re-entry, for brain injury and complex psychiatric disorders.

**7065 Center for Neuro Skills**
1320 W Walnut Hill Ln
Irving, TX 75038-3007
972-580-8500
800-544-5448
FAX: 972-255-3162
e-mail: cns@neuroskills.com
neuroskills.com

*John Schultz, Administrator*
Centre for Neuro Skills (CNS) seeks to provide medical rehabilitation programs, lifecare programs, advocacy, and research for people with brain injury in order to achieve a maximum quality of life.

**7066 Dallas Services**
4242 Office Pkwy
Dallas, TX 75204-3629
214-828-9900
FAX: 214-828-9901
dallasservices.org

*Jim Gibson, Executive Director*
*Nicole Sonders, Managerof Resource Development*
Offers four programs:1) an early education for children(6weeks-6yrs)with and without special needs.2)low vision clinic-provides low cost eye examsand glasses to low-income families as well as assistance to individuals who vision problems which cannot be corrected with glasses/surgery.3)mesquite day school- an early head start program for infants and toddlers of low-income families.4)special needs advocacy and inclusion program that offers families of special need children guidance and education.

**7067 Devereux Texas Treatment Network Adult Community**
PO Box 2666
120 David Wade Drive
Victoria, TX 77902-2666
361-575-8271
800-383-5000
FAX: 361-575-6520
devereux.org

*Fred Williams, Administrator*
*April Krus, Admissions Coordinator*
Provides a permanent home for individuals with chronic psychiatric and/or developmental disabilities who require long term or lifelong care, support or a transitional home for individuals who progress to a less structured setting. Located on a beautiful 400+ acre campus in sunny south Texas, the primary focus is to offer, in keeping with the philosophies of least restrictive alternatives and normalization, active treatment which will facilitate growth.

**7068 El Paso Lighthouse for the Blind**
200 Washington St
El Paso, TX 79905-3897
915-532-4495
FAX: 915-532-6338
www.lighthouse-elpaso.com

*Harry Tyler, Executive Director*
*John McCain, Vice President*
*Lola Dawkins, Secretary*
Enables people of all ages to embody blindness and vision impairment through training, rehabilitation, employment opportunity, advocacy and research. Provides access to opportunities and quality of life so that the blind and visually impaired can reach their fullest potential for self-sufficiency and independence.

**7069 Harris Methodist Fort Worth/Mabee Rehabilitation Center**
1301 Pennsylvania Ave
Fort Worth, TX 76104-2122
817-878-5500
FAX: 817-882-2753
www.texashealth.org

*Louise Baldwin, President*
*Peggyo Ehrlich, Rehab Manager*
*Karen Mallett, Executive Director*
A hospital based inpatient rehab program and outpatient day programs in chronic pain management, work hardening and brain injury transitional services.

**7070 HealthSouth Hospital Of Houston**
17506 Red Oak Dr
Houston, TX 77090-1248
281-580-1212
FAX: 281-580-6714
healthsouth.com

*Jerome Lengel, Executive Officer*
*Dewitt Hilton, Owner*
Offers an individualized approach to the process of rehabilitation for severely injured or disabled individuals. The process begins with a pre-admissions assessment of each referred patient. The Center combines state-of-the-art technology and equipment with multi-disciplinary therapy and education in a cheerful, secure environment.

**7071 Heights Hospital Rehab Unit**
1917 Ashland St
Houston, TX 77008-3994
713-861-6161
FAX: 713-802-8660
selectmedicalcorp.com

*Theresa Davis, CEO*
This program is designed to assist patients with physical disabilities achieve their maximum functional abilities.

**7072 Hillcrest Baptist Medical Center**
100 Hillcrest Medical Blvd
Waco, TX 76712
254-202-2000
FAX: 254-202-5105
www.hillcrest.net

*Anne Hott Kimberly, Program Director*
*Ann Gammel, Nurse Manager*
*Debbie Meurer, Manager*
Designed to assist patients in adjustment to a physically limiting condition, utilizing interdisciplinary strategies to maximize each patient's ability and capability.

**7073 Institute for Rehabilitation & Research**
1333 Moursund St
Houston, TX 77030-3405
713-799-5000
800-447-3422
FAX: 713-797-5289
www.tirr.org

*John Kajander, CEO*
*Jean Herzog, President*
A national center for information, training, research, and technical assistance in independent living. The goal is to extend the

body of knowledge in independent living and to improve the utilization of results of research programs and demonstration projects in this field. It has developed a variety of strategies for collecting, synthesizing, and disseminating information related to the field of independent living.

**7074 Integrated Health Services of Amarillo**
5601 Plum Creek Dr
Amarillo, TX 79124-1801
806-351-1000
FAX: 806-355-9650
www.medcenter.org

*Mary Bearden, Chairman*
Provides acute, post acute, residential and outpatient health care services. IHS of Amarillo is a 153-bed facility with 120 beds licensed by The Texas Department of Health and Human Services, and is accredited by JCAHO. We serve urban and rural populations of over 500,000, drawing from a 5-state region.

**7075 Lighthouse of Houston**
3602 W Dallas St
Houston, TX 77019-1704
713-527-9561
FAX: 713-284-8451
e-mail: houstonlighthouse@houstonlighthouse.org
houstonlighthouse.org

*Gibson DuTerroil, President*
*Shelagh Moran, VP/COO*
*Chelean Zander, VP Community Programs*
Serves the blind, visually impaired, deaf-blind and multihandicapped blind. Provides workshops, vocational training and placement, low vision clinic, orientation and mobility, housing, Braille, volunteer services, senior center, visual aid sales, counseling and support, diabetic education and day health activity services and day summer camp, Summer Transition for Youth.

**7076 Mainland Center Hospital RehabCare Unit**
6801 Emmett F Lowry Expy
Texas City, TX 77591-2500
409-938-5000
FAX: 409-938-5501
www.mainlandmedical.com

*Michael Ehrat, CEO*
The RehabCare program is designed and staffed to assist functionally impaired patients improve to their maximum potential. The opportunities for improvement and adjustments are provided in a pleasant, supportive inpatient environment by therapists from the occupational, physical, recreational and speech therapy disciplines.

**7077 North Texas Rehabilitation Center**
1005 Midwestern Pkwy
Wichita Falls, TX 76302-2211
940-322-0771
FAX: 940-766-4943
ntrehab.org

*Mike Castles, President/ CEO*
Provides outpatient rehabilitation services to maximize independence or promote development to children and adults with disabilities. Programs include: physical, occupational, speech therapy, closed head injury, infant/child development, support groups, aquatics and wellness program and a child achievement program.

**7078 South Texas Lighthouse for the Blind**
4421 Agnes St
Corpus Christi, TX 78405-3321
361-883-6553
888-255-8011
FAX: 361-883-1041
e-mail: Customer.service@stlb.net
www.stlb.net

*Regis Barber, President*
*Nicky Ooi, Chief Operations Officer*
*Alana Manrow, Public Affairs Director*
Their mission is to Employ, Educate and Empower their neighbors who are blind and visually impaired. They offer job opportunities in manufacturing, retail and administration, as well as orientation and mobility and adaptive technology training.

**7079 Texas Specialty Hospital at Dallas**
7955 Harry Hines Blvd
Dallas, TX 75235-3305
214-637-0000
FAX: 214-637-6512
thicare.com

*Robin Burns, CEO*
*Cathy Campbell, Chief Executive Officer*
66 beds offering active/acute rehabilitation, brain injury day treatment, cognitive rehabilitation, complex care, extended rehabilitation and short term evaluation.

**7080 Transitional Learning Center at Gavelston and Lubbock**
1528 Post Office St
Galveston, TX 77550
409-762-6661
FAX: 409-763-3930
www.tlcrehab.org

*Brent Masel, MD, President and Medical Director*
Specializes solely in post-acute brain injury. A nationally known pioneer in the field and a not for profit with a three fold mission: treatment, research and education. Offers 6 hours of therapy a day from licensed/certified staff, on site physician and nursing services and long-term living for brian injured adults at Tideway on Gavelston Island. Accredited by CARF.
*1982*

**7081 Treemont Nursing And Rehabilitation Center**
5550 Harvest Hill Rd
Dallas, TX 75230-1684
972-661-1862
FAX: 972-788-1543
e-mail: moreinfo@treemonthealthcare.com
http://www.treemonthealthcare.com/index. php

*Bob Barker, Administrator*
Postacute rehabilitation program.

**7082 West Texas Lighthouse for the Blind**
2001 Austin St
San Angelo, TX 76903-8796
325-653-4231
FAX: 325-657-9367
e-mail: customerservice@lighthousefortheblind.org
www.lighthousefortheblind.org

*David Wells, Executive Director*
*Stephen Horton, Operations Manager*
Offers services for the totally blind, legally blind, visually impaired, mentally retarded blind and more with health, counseling, educational, recreational, rehabilitation, computer training and professional training services.

## Utah

**7083 Quincy Rehabilitation Institute of Holy Cross Hospital**
1050 E South Temple
Salt Lake City, UT 84102-1507
801-350-8140
FAX: 801-350-4791

*Dave Jenson, President*
Postacute rehabilitation program.

**7084 Wasatch Vision Clinic**
849 E 400 S
Salt Lake City, UT 84102-2928
801-328-2020
FAX: 801-363-2201
e-mail: email@wasatchvision.com
www.wasatchvision.com

*Craig Cutler, Owner*
*Camron Bateman OD, Doctor*
Postacute rehabilitation program.

## Vermont

**7085 Rutland Mental Health Services**
78 S Main St
Rutland, VT 05701-4594
802-775-2381
FAX: 802-775-4020
rmhsccn.org

*Dan Quinn, President/ CEO*
A private, non-profit comprehensive community mental health center. It provides services to individuals and families for mental health and substance abuse related problems and also to persons who are mentally retarded.

## Virginia

**7086 Bay Pine-Virginia Beach**
680 South Fourth Street
Louisville, KY 40202
502-596-7300
TTY:800-545-0749
e-mail: web_administrator@kindredhealthcare.com
kindredhealthcare.com

*Paul J. Diaz, President/ CEO*
Postacute rehabilitation program.

**7087 Carilion Rehabilitation: New River Valley**
P.O.Box 5
Radford, VA 24143-5
540-731-2992
800-422-8482
FAX: 540-731-2011
e-mail: info@carilion.com
www.carilion.com

*Nancy Howell Agee, President/ CEO*
CARF-accredited pain management program, work hardening program and comprehensive outpatient therapy clinic, massage therapy, outpatient programs and more. Program emphasis is on interdisiplinary behavioral rehab based pain management and functional restoration in conjunction with medical treatment. Work hardening is a transdisciplinary work simulation program taylored to the individual. Comprehensive outpatient program is multi-disciplinary with emphasis on manual treatment.

**7088 Faith Mission Home**
3540 Mission Home Ln
Free Union, VA 22940-1505
434-985-2294
FAX: 434-985-7633
www.beachyam.org

*Paul Beiler, Manager*
*Reuben Yoder, Director*
A Christian residential center that serves 60 mentally retarded children, including individuals with Down Syndrome, Cerebral palsy and other similar conditions. Children may be admitted from the time they are ambulatory until they reach 15 years of age. He or she may stay as long as it is in the child's best interests. The training program stresses the following areas: self-care, social, academic, vocational, crafts, speech and physical development.

**7089 ManorCare Health Services-Arlington**
550 S Carlin Springs Rd
Arlington, VA 22204-1022
703-379-7200
FAX: 703-578-5524
e-mail: arlington@hcr-manorcare.com
hcr-manorcare.com

*Marcia K Jarrell, Administrator*
*Ric Birch, Marketing Director*
ManorCare-Arlington offers residents a full Continuum of Care in a caring environment. ManorCare's wide range of services includes subacute medical and rehabilitation programs for short term patients transitioning from hospital to home and Skilled Nursing Care.

**7090 Pines Residential Treatment Center**
825 Crawford Pkwy
Portsmouth, VA 23704-2301
757-393-0061
FAX: 757-393-1029

*Lenard J Lexier, Medical Director*
*Judy Kemp, Admissions Director*
A 310-bed residential treatment center in Portsmouth Virginia, providing a therapeutic environment for severely emotionally disturbed children and youth. Five unique programs meet behavioral, educational and emotional needs of males and females, five to twenty-two years of age. Multi-disciplinary teams devise individual service plans to enhance strengths and reverse self-defeating behavior. A highly effective positive reinforcement program with a proven track record.

**7091 Resurrection Children's Center**
2280 N Beauregard St
Alexandria, VA 22311-2200
703-998-0888
FAX: 703-820-2912
e-mail: office@welcometoresurrection.org
www.welcometoresurrection.org

*Jane McCabe, Parish Administrator*
*Deena Jaworski, Director of Music*
Offers children ages 2-5 with varying disabilities academic education, parent education, opportunities including classes, workshops, support groups and individual counseling.

**7092 Roanoke Memorial Hospital**
Carilion Health System
P.O.Box 13367
Roanoke, VA 24033-3367
540-772-1736
800-422-8482
FAX: 540-981-8233
e-mail: direct@carilion.com
www.carilion.com

*Nancy Howell Agee, President/ CEO*
Carilion Health System exists to improve the health of the communities it serves. The vision is to assure accessible, affordable, high quality healthcare that meets the needs of the community. Motivate and educate individuals to improve their health. Champion community initiatives to reduce health risk

**7093 Southside Virginia Training Center**
P.O.Box 4030
Petersburg, VA 23803-30
804-524-7000
FAX: 804-524-7228
www.svtc.dmhmrsas.virginia.gov

*Bob Kaufman, Director, Administrative Services*
Offers residential, vocational, occupational, physical, and speech therapies.

**7094 Woodrow Wilson Rehabilitation Center**
P.O.Box 1500
Fishersville, VA 22939-1500
540-332-7000
800-345-9972
FAX: 540-332-7132
e-mail: colemawl@wwrc.state.va.lls
www.wwrc.net

*Rick Sizemore, Executive Director*
Comprehensive residential rehabilitation center offering complete medical and vocational rehabilitation services including: vocation evaluation, vocational training, transition from school to work, occupational therapy, physical therapy, speech, language and audiology, assistive technology, rehabilitation engineering, counseling/case management, behavioral health services, nursing and physician services, etc.

## Washington

**7095 Arden Rehabilitation And Healthcare Center**
680 South Fourth Street
Louisville, KY 40202
502-596-7300
TTY:800-545-0749
e-mail: web_administrator@kindredhealthcare.com
kindredhealthcare.com

*Paul J. Diaz, President/ CEO*
Arden can accomodate 90 residents- post-acute/rehabilitation patients as well as long term residents. Medicare certified, the center also takes most managed healthcare insurance plans, as well as VA, respite and hospice patients.

**7096 Bellingham Care Center**
680 South Fourth Street
Louisville, KY 40202
502-596-7300
TTY:800-545-0749
e-mail: web_administrator@kindredhealthcare.com
kindredhealthcare.com

*Paul J. Diaz, President/ CEO*
Postacute rehabilitation program.

**7097 Division of Vocational Rehabilitation Department of Social and Health Services**
P.O.Box 45130
Olympia, WA 98504-5130
360-704-3560
800-737-0617
FAX: 360-570-6941
e-mail: krulik@dshs.wa.gov
www1.dshs.wa.gov/dvr

*Patrick Raines, Manager*
*Lynnea Ruttledge, Manager*
Information on computers, supported employment, marketing rehabilitation facilities and transition.

**7098 First Hill Care Center**
1334 Terry Ave
Seattle, WA 98101
206-624-0188
FAX: 206-624-0188

Postacute rehabilitation program.

**7099 Harborview Medical Center, Low Vision Aid Clinic**
Harborview Medical Center
325 9th Ave
Seattle, WA 98104-2420
206-731-3335
www.uwmedicine.org

*Kate Freidembach, Manager*
*Susan Worden, Manager*
Offers services for the totally blind, legally blind, visually impaired, mentally retarded blind and more with health, counseling, educational, recreational, rehabilitation, computer training and professional training services.

**7100 Integrated Health Services of Seattle**
820 NW 95th St
Seattle, WA 98117-2207
206-783-7649
FAX: 206-781-1448

*Jerry Harvey, Administrator*
*Marlette Basada, Director Nursing*
*Flavia Lagrange, Director Admissions*
Postacute rehabilitation program. IHS provides 24 hour subacute and long-term care. We can handle vent/trach/hemo andritoneal dialysis and provide a full scope of rehabilitation services.

**7101 Lakeside Milam Recovery Centers (LMRC)**
3315 S. 23rd Street
Ste 102
Tacoma, WA 98405
253-272-2242
800-231-4303
FAX: 253-272-0171
e-mail: help@lakesidemilam.com
www.lakesidemilam.com

*Michael Kinder, Administrator*
LMRC was established in 1983 with a single mission, to help victims and families recover from the pain of drug/alcohol addiction. Enlightned by the work of Dr. James Milam in the 1960's and 70's, the founders of LMRC created a treatment system based on a bedrock set of principals.

**7102 Lakewood Health Care Center**
11411 Bridgeport Way SW
Lakewood, WA 98499-3047
253-581-9002
FAX: 253-581-7016
e-mail: HSDED0168@kindredhealthcare.com?subject=Websi
www.lakewoodhc.com

*Gwynn Rucker, Executive Director*
*Patty Wood, Administrator*
*Linda Doll, Social Services*
*Dr. Mian , Medical Director*
Accomodates 80 residents. We offer 24 hour skilled nursing services, long-term care and rehab services which include Physical, Occupational and Speech Therapy.

**7103 Manor Care Health Services-Tacoma**
5601 S Orchard St
Tacoma, WA 98409-1371
253-474-8421
FAX: 253-471-8857
www.hcr-manorcare.com

*Tina Irwin, Administrator*
124-bed skilled nursing and rehabilitation center provides services for those seeking long term Skilled Nursing Care, short term subacute care, hospice services, Alzheimer's and respite care. Our Acadia Wing, a specialized Alzheimer's care unit, provides specialized programming and trained staff that truly makes us the leader in Alzheimers Services.

**7104 ManorCare Health Services-Lynnwood**
3701 188th St SW
Lynnwood, WA 98037-7626
425-775-9222
FAX: 425-712-3685
hcr-manorcare.com

*Liza Loyet, Administrator*
Our in-house therapists provide physical, occupational and speech therapies in our state-of-the-art therapy gym. Our team is goal oriented and focuses on producing positive outcomes for those recovering from illness, injury or surgery.

**7105 ManorCare Health Services-Spokane**
6025 N Assembly St
Spokane, WA 99205-7674
509-326-8282
FAX: 509-326-4790
www.hcrmanorcare.com

*Cheri Kubu, Administrator*
*Sandra Hayes, Administrator*
Provides skilled nursing and respite stays for those needing a break from care giving. We specialize in Rehabilitation Services provided by our in-house occupational, physical and speech therapists.

**7106 Northwest Continuum Care Center**
Kindred Health Care
128 Old Beacon Hill Dr
Longview, WA 98632-5859
360-423-4060
FAX: 360-636-0958
e-mail: HSDED0127@kindredhealthcare.com?subject=Websi
www.nwcontinuum.com

*Steve M. Ross, Executive Director*
*Tami Wilson, Director of Nursing*
*Mary R., Activities Assistant*
*Kristen W., Health and Rehabilitation Center Executive Director*
Accomodates 69 residents. Employs the Angel Care Program designed to address any special needs that may arise during a resident's stay in our facility. The program focuses extra attention on residents and, in some cases, family members. The goal is to meet the special needs of the people we provide care to every day.

**7107 Park Manor Convalescent Center**
1710 Plaza Way
Walla Walla, WA 99362-4362
509-529-4218
FAX: 509-522-1729
e-mail: egines@ensigngroup.net
www.parkmanorcare.com

*Jed Gines, Administrator*
*Krista Maiuri, Directr Of Nursing*
*Sonya Taylor, Director of Rehabilitation*
*Mike Henckel, Admissions & Marketing Director*
Residents of Park Manor enjoy a range of activities, developed to meet their needs, inculding excercise programs, social and recreational activities, arts and crafts, shopping trips and other excursions. We also offer religious services.

**7108 Queen Anne Health Care**
Queen Anne Health Care
2717 Dexter Ave N
Seattle, WA 98109-1914
206-284-7012
FAX: 206-283-3936
e-mail: HSDED0462@kindredhealthcare.com?subject=Websi
www.queenannehealthcare.co m

*Heather Eacker, Executive Director*
*Mary R., Activities Assistant*
*Kristen W., Health and Rehabilitation Center Executive Director*
*Becky D., Activity Director*
Our goal is to provide quality, compassionate care. Our cozy building accomodates 120 residents. We offer semi private rooms with space to add items from home for a special personalized touch

**7109 Rainier Vista Care Center**
920 12th Ave SE
Puyallup, WA 98372-4920
253-841-3422
FAX: 253-848-3937
e-mail: HSDED0165@kindredhealthcare.com?subject=Websi
www.rainiervistacc.com

*Linda Larson, Administrator*
*Nancy L. Erckenbrack, Executive Director*
*Kristen W., Health and Rehabilitation Center Executive Director*
*Becky D., Activity Director*
Accomodates 120 residents. We are certified for Medicare and Medicaid and we offer a continuum of healthcare services from short-term or outpatient rehabilitation to long-term care. We offer semi-private and private rooms as well as rehabilitation and hospice suites. Rainier Vista Care Center is a 2005 recipient of the American Health Care Association Quality Award.

**7110 Rehabilitation Enterprises of Washington**
430 E Lauridsen Blvd
Port Angeles, WA 98362-7978
360-452-9789
FAX: 360-452-9700

*Brett White, President*
REW is the professional trade association representing community rehabilitation programs before government and other publics. These organizations provide a wide array of employment and training services for people with disabilities. The goal is to assist member organizations to provide the highest quality rehabilitative and employment services to their customers.

**7111 Seattle Medical and Rehabilitation Center**
Evergreen Healthcare
12040 NE 128th St
Kirkland, WA 98034-3013
425-899-1000
877-601-2271
TTY:425-899-2007
e-mail: comment@evergreenhealthcare.org
evergreenhealthcare.org

*Terrence Pheifer, MD, Immediate Past Presiden*
*Scott Burks, MD, Medical Staff Vice President*
*Jeffrey Roh, MD, Credentials Chair*
*Jack Handley, MD, Medical Staff President*
103 beds offering subacute rehabilitation, complex care, subacute treatment and short-term evaluation. Pulmonary unit offering long and short term care for ventilator dependent patients.

**7112 Slingerland Institute for Literacy**
Educators Publishing Service
12729 Northup Way
Suite 1
Bellevue, WA 98005
425-453-1190
FAX: 425-635-7762
e-mail: mail@slingerland.org
www.slingerland.org

*Bonnie Meyer, Executive Director*
*Elyce Newton, Program Support*
A nonprofit public corporation founded in 1977 to carry on the work of Beth H. Slingerland in providing classroom teachers with the techniques, knowledge and understanding necessary for identifying and teaching children with Specific Language Disability. The main objective is to educate teachers in successful methods of identifying, diagnosing and instructing children and adults with SLD and to promote literacy through reading, writing and oral expression.

**7113 Timberland Opportunities Association**
400 W Curtis St
Aberdeen, WA 98520-7698
360-533-5823
FAX: 360-533-5848
e-mail: jimeddy@techline.com
www.users.olynet.com/timberlandopp

*Jim Eddy, Executive Director*
Provides training and employment for disabled people.

**7114 Vancouver Health and Rehabilitation Center**
400 E 33rd St
Vancouver, WA 98663-2238
360-696-2561
FAX: 360-696-9275
e-mail: HSDED0180@kindredhealthcare.com?subject=Websi
www.vancouverhealthcare.co m

*Jody Wigen, Human Resources*
*Joe Joy, Executive Director*
*Kristen W., Health and Rehabilitation Center Executive Director*
*Becky D., Activity Director*
Postacute rehabilitation program.

## Wisconsin

**7115 Colonial Manor Medical And Rehabilitation Center**
1010 E Wausau Ave
Wausau, WI 54403-3101
715-842-2028
FAX: 715-848-0510
e-mail: HSDED0766@kindredhealthcare.com?subject=Websi
www.colonialmanormrc.com

*Ericca Ylitalo, Administrator*
*Shelley Solberg, Executive Director*

Colonial Manor Medical and Rehabilitation Center is part of the Kindred Community and is located in Wausau, Wisconsin. The corporate headquarters are based in Louisville Kentucky. Our facility accomodates 150 residents.

**7116 Waushers Industries**
210 E Chicago Rd
Wautoma, WI 54982-6932
920-787-4696
FAX: 920-787-4698

*Richard King, Human Resources*
Provides various programming for individuals with disabilities in waushara county.

**7117 Woodstock Health and Rehabilitation Center**
3415 Sheridan Rd
Kenosha, WI 53140-1924
262-657-6175
FAX: 262-657-5756
e-mail: HSDED0776@kindredhealthcare.com?subject=Websi
www.woodstockhealth.com

*Debra Lamb, Administrator*
*Darlene Einerson, Executive Director*
*Kristen W., Health and Rehabilitation Center Executive Director*
*Becky D., Activity Director*
Offers a full range of medical services to meet the individual needs of our residents, including short term rehabilitative services and long-tern skilled care.

# Rehabilitation Facilities, Sub-Acute

## Alabama

**7118 Rehabilitation & Healthcare Center Of Birmingham**
2728 10th Ave S
Birmingham, AL 35205-1202
205-933-7010
FAX: 205-933-8720

*Jimmie Thompson, Administrator*
Rehabilitation and Healthcare Center of Birmingham is conveniently located on Birmingham's beautiful and historic Southside. We accomodate 114 residents and we are Medicare and Medicaid certified. Saint Vincent's Hospital, University of Alabama in Birmingham Hospital, and Baptist Medical Center Montclair are either within walking distance or just minutes away. We have caring professionals who strive to meet the needs of our residents.

## Alaska

**7119 Fairbanks Memorial Hospital/Denali Center**
1650 Cowles St
Fairbanks, AK 99701-5998
907-452-8181
FAX: 907-458-5324
www.bannerhealth.com/locations/alaska

*Mike Powers, CEO*
Offers the following rehabilitation services: Physical Therapy, Occupational Therapy, Speech Therapy, Sub-Acute Rehab.

## Arizona

**7120 Desert Life Rehabilitation & Care Center**
Kindred Healthcare
1919 W Medical St
Tucson, AZ 85704-1133
520-297-8311
FAX: 520-544-0930
www.desertlifercc.com

*Amad Nazifi, Executive Director*
*Jane Olmstead, Director of Nursing*
Accomodates 240 residents. We provide skilled and intermediate nursing with occupational, physical, speech and respiratory therapy services. We offer special programs including an Alzheimer's Unit and a Young Adult Program, and are located in beautiful Southern Arizona where there is plenty of sunshine, mountains and desert views. Desert Life is a 2005 recipient of the American Health Care Association Quality Award.

**7121 Hacienda Rehabilitation and Care Center**
660 S Coronado Dr
Sierra Vista, AZ 85635-3386
520-459-4900
FAX: 520-458-4082
www.haciendarcc.com

*Monica Vandivort, Medical Director*
Accomodates 100 residents. We are located in Sierra Vista, near Kartchner Caverns, Fort Huachuca, Coronado National Forest and historic Tombstone. Serving the medical needs of the community since 1983, we strive to provide care with quality, compassion and integrity.

**7122 Kachina Point Health Care & Rehabilitation Center**
505 Jacks Canyon Rd
Sedona, AZ 86351-7856
928-284-1000
FAX: 928-284-0626
www.kachinapointrehab.com

*Michael Amadei, Medical Director*
Accomodates 120 residents. We have met the healthcare needs of the community since 1984. Kachina Point is a 2004 recipient of the American Health Care Association's Quality Award.

**7123 Mayo Clinic Scottsdale**
13400 E Shea Blvd
Scottsdale, AZ 85259-5499
480-301-8000
FAX: 480-301-4391
www.mayoclinic.org/arizona
Mayo clinic is a not-for-profit medical practice dedicated to the diagnosis and treatment of virtually every type of complex illness. Mayo clinic staff members work together to meet your needs. You will see as many doctors, specialists, and other health care professionals as needed to provide comprehensive diagnosis, understandable answers and effective treatment.

**7124 Sonoran Rehabilitation and Care Center**
Kindred
4202 N 20th Ave
Phoenix, AZ 85015-5101
602-264-3824
FAX: 602-279-6234

*Jeffrey Barrett, Executive Director*
Offers the following rehabilitation services: Respiratory Therapy, Physical Therapy, Speech Therapy, Occupational Therapy, Restorative Therapy, Sub-Acute Rehabilitation, Wound Care.

**7125 Valley Health Care and Rehabilitation Center**
Kindred Health Care Center
5545 E Lee St
Tucson, AZ 85712-4205
520-296-2306
FAX: 520-296-4072
www.valleyhcr.com

*Dale Pelton, Executive Director*
*Sandra Lewis, Administrator*
Offers the following rehabilitation services: Physical Therapy, Occupational Therapy, Speech Therapy, Sub-Acute Rehab.

## California

**7126 Alamitos-Belmont Rehab Hospital**
3901 E 4th St
Long Beach, CA 90814-1699
562-434-8421
FAX: 562-433-6732
www.alamitosbelmont.com

*Jonathan Sloey, Administrator*
Offers the following rehabilitation services: Speech Therapy, Occupational Therapy, Physical Therapy, Sub-Acute Rehab.

**7127 Bay View Nursing and Rehabilitation Center**
Kindred Health Care
516 Willow St
Alameda, CA 94501-6132
510-521-5600
FAX: 510-865-9035
www.kindredhealthcare.com

*Richard S Espinoza, Administrator*
*Say Silva, Assistant Executive Director*
Accomodates 180 residents. Bay View is a 2004 recipient of the American Health Care Association's Quality Award. We provide short-term rehabilitative care, traditional long-term skilled care and Alzheimer's/dementia special care. Our combination of clinical skill and comprehensive rehabilitation services enables us to care for a variety of complex medical conditions.

**7128 Foothill Nursing and Rehab Center**
401 W Ada Ave
Glendora, CA 91741-4241
626-335-9810
FAX: 626-963-0720
www.foothillsnursing.com

*Arnie Shafer, Executive Director*
*Marianne Schultz, Administrator*

Offers the following rehabilitation services: Physical Therapy, Occupational Therapy, Speech Therapy, In and Out Patient Rehab.

**7129 Long Beach Memorial Medical Center Memorial Rehabilitation Hospital**
2801 Atlantic Ave
Long Beach, CA 90806-1701
562-933-2000
www.memorialcare.org/long_beach

*Barry Arbuckle, President/CEO*
The hospital offers rehabilitation after catastrophic injury of disabling disease to give patients the opportunity for maximum recovery. The Hospital offers many of the area's finest rehabilitation specialists and most advanced technology, making it one of Southern California's most respected rehabilitation centers.

**7130 Mercy Medical Center Mt. Shasta**
914 Pine St
Mount Shasta, CA 96067-2143
530-926-6111
FAX: 530-926-0517
www.mercy.org

*Kenneth Platou, President*
*Morris Eagleman, VP Patient Care Services*
Mercy Medical Center is committed to furthering the healing ministry of Jesus, and to provide high-quality, affordable healthcare to the communities we serve.

**7131 Northridge Hospital Medical Center**
18300 Roscoe Blvd
Northridge, CA 91325-4167
818-885-8500
www.northridgehospital.org

*Michael Wall, CEO*
Offers the following rehabilitation services: Physical Therapy, Occupational Therapy, Speech Therapy, Sub-Acute Rehab. As a member of the Catholic Heathcare West Northridge Hospital Medical Center is committed to serving the health needs of our communities with particular attention to the needs of the poor, the disadvantaged and vulnerable, and the comfort of the suffering and dying.

**7132 Riverside Community Hospital**
4445 Magnolia Ave
Riverside, CA 92501
951-788-3000
FAX: 909-788-3616
rchc.org

*Jaime Wesolowski, President/CEO*
At Riverside Community Hospital, we are able to provide the healthcare services that you and your family will need through the many stages of your life. Services like Emergency/Trauma, Labor and Delivery, Cardiac Care, Orthopedics and Transplant are among our many Centers of Excellence.

**7133 Saint Jude Medical Center**
101 E Valencia Mesa Dr
Fullerton, CA 92835-3809
714-871-3280
800-870-7537
FAX: 714-992-3029
www.stjudemedicalcenter.org

*April De Cou, Wellness Educator*
*Jane Wang, Wellness Programs Supervisor*
Offers the following rehabilitation services: Out-patient Rehab, Sub-Acute Rehab, Occupational Therapy, Physical Therapy, Speech and Audiology Therapy, Pain Management Program.

**7134 South Coast Medical Center**
12 Mason
Ste A
Irvine, CA 92618-2733
714-669-4446
FAX: 714-669-4448
e-mail: info@southcoastmedcenter.com
www.southcoastmedcenter.com

*Leigh Erin Connealy, Manager*
*Bruce Christian, President*
Offers the following services: physical therapy, occupational therapy, speech therapy, cardica rehabilitation, incontinence program, sub-acute rehabilitation.

**7135 Valley Garden Health Care and Rehabilitation Center**
1517 Knickerbocker Dr
Stockton, CA 95210-3119
209-957-4539
FAX: 209-957-5831
www.valleygardenshealth.com

*Timothy Coats, Medical Director*
Accomodates 120 residents. Our center provides short-term nursing and rehabilitative care as well as traditional long-term skilled care. Our combination of clinical skill and comprehensive rehabilitation services enables us to care for a variety of complex medical conditions. Rehabilitative therapies are provided as needed by physical, occupational and speech therapists.

## Colorado

**7136 Boulder Community Hospital Mapleton Center**
P.O.Box 9019
Boulder, CO 80301-9019
303-440-2273
e-mail: pr@bch.org
www.bch.org

*David Gehant, President*
*Rich Lopez, Chairman*
Offers comprehensive rehabilitation services for individuals of all ages on both an inpatient and outpatient basis. Specialty programs include brain injury, chronic pain management, and pediatric rehabilitation.

**7137 Fairacres Manor**
1700 18th Ave
Greeley, CO 80631-5152
970-353-3370
FAX: 970-353-9347
fairacresmanor.com

*Kathleen Mekelburg, Administrator*
*Marla Trujillo, Director of Nursing*
Offers the following rehabilitation services: Physical Therapy, Occupational Therapy, Speech Therapy, Restorative Therapy, Skilled Nursing, and Sub-Acute Rehabilitation.

**7138 Rowan Community**
4601 E Asbury Cir
Denver, CO 80222-4722
303-757-1228
FAX: 303-759-3390
e-mail: tgleisner@pinonmgt.com
pinonmgt.com

*Jeff Jerebker, President/CEO*
*Bruce Odenthal, VP Operations*
Sixty bed skilled nursing facility in southwest Denver, serving younger residents with multiple sclerosis traumatic brain injury, chronic mental illness, 24 hour care need behavior.

## Connecticut

**7139 Hamilton Rehabilitation and Healthcare Center**
89 Viets St
New London, CT 6320-3355
860-447-1471
FAX: 860-439-0107

*Steve Roizen, Executive Director*
Offers the following rehabilitation services: Sub-Acute, Occupational Therapy, Speech Therapy, Physical Therapy.

**7140 Hospital For Special Care (HSC)**
2150 Corbin Ave
New Britain, CT 6053-2298
860-223-2761
FAX: 860-827-4849
e-mail: info@hfsc.org
www.hfsc.org

*John Votto, CEO*
HSC is a private, not-for-profit 200-bed rehabilitation long-term acute and chronic care hospital, widely-known and respected for its expertise in physical rehabilitation, respiratory care, and medically-complex pediatrics. Special programs for spinal cord injuries, pulmonary rehabilitation, acquired brain injuries, stroke, ventilator management and geriatrics, make HSC an important regional resource for patients with special healthcare needs.

**7141 Masonic Healthcare Center**
MasoniCare Corporation
22 Masonic Ave
Wallingford, CT 6492-3048
203-679-5900
877-424-3537
FAX: 203-679-6459
e-mail: info@masonicare.org
www.masonicare.org

*William Piper, President*
*Arthur Santilli, President*
The states leading provider of healthcare and retirement living communities for seniors. We are not-for-profit and have more then 100 years of experience behind us. We're recognized for the quality, compassionate care and steadfast support we provide to our residents and patients.

**7142 Stamford Hospital**
30 Shelburne Rd
Stamford, CT 6902-3628
203-276-1000
FAX: 203-325-7905
e-mail: info@stamhealth.org
www.stamfordhospital.org

*Brian Grissler, President/CEO*
*Kathy Silard, EVP*
A not-for-profit, community teaching hospital that has been serving Stamford and surrounding communities for more then 100 years. We have 305 inpatient beds in medicine, surgery, obstetrics/gynecology, psychiatry, and medical and surgical critical care units and maintain an educational partnership with Columbia University College of Physicians and Surgeons for its teaching program in the internal medicine, family practice, obstetrics/gynecology and surgery

**7143 Windsor Rehabilitation and Healthcare Center**
581 Poquonock Ave
Windsor, CT 6095-2202
860-688-7211
FAX: 860-688-6715
www.windsorrehab.com

*Jeffrey Robbins, Medical Director*
Accomodates 116 residents. We offer private and semi-private rooms with access to private telephones and cable television. Our goal is to be a comprehensive, leading care center viewed by our community as an excellent resource for patients, families, and professionals.

## Delaware

**7144 Arbors at New Castle**
32 Buena Vista Dr
New Castle, DE 19720-4660
302-328-2580
FAX: 302-328-2036
e-mail: leighweber@extendicare.com
www.extendedcare.com

*Annette Moore, Administrator*
A subacute and rehabilitation center offering skilled medical services, infusion therapies, cardiac recovery services, renal disease services, cancer services and digestive disease services. Skilled rehabilitation services include physical therapy, occupational therapy and speech therapy. Also provides case management and discharge planning, general nursing and restorative care and respite care.

## Florida

**7145 Avon Oaks Skilled Care Nursing Facility**
37800 French Creek Rd
Avon, OH 44011-1763
440-934-5204
800-589-5204
www.avonoaks.net

*Joan Reidy, Administrator*
*Itri Eren, Physician Supervisor*
Oaks at Avon provides a full range of skilled nursing services including infusion therapy, enteral therapy, wound care, tracheotomy care, and portable diagnostics.

**7146 Boca Raton Rehabilitation Center**
755 Meadows Rd
Boca Raton, FL 33486-2384
561-391-5200
FAX: 561-391-0685

*Stanley Mucinic, Administrator*
*Tracey Dougherty, Administrator*
Offers the following rehabilitation services: Occupational Therapy, Speech Therapy, Physical Therapy, Sub-Acute Rehabilitation

**7147 Cape Coral Hospital**
636 Del Prado Blvd
Cape Coral, FL 33990
239-424-2000
FAX: 239-574-1935
www.leememorial.org

*James Nathan, CEO*
*Scott Kashman, Administrator*
We are a progressive, financially sound health care provider with more then 8,000 employees, 3000 volunteers and auxilians, and 1,200 physicians on staff, and 1,600 licensed beds. The System is a member of Voluntary Hospitals of America, Florida Partnership

**7148 Evergreen Woods Health and Rehabilitation Center**
7045 Evergreen Woods Trl
Spring Hill, FL 34608-1306
352-596-8371
FAX: 352-596-8032

*Janet Hanciles, Administrator*
Offers the following rehabilitation services: Sub-Acute rehabilitation, Occupational therapy, Speech pathology therapy, Physical therapy.

**7149 Healthcare and Rehabilitation Center of Sanford**
950 S Mellonville Ave
Sanford, FL 32771-2237
407-322-8566
FAX: 407-322-8183
seniorhealthmanagement.com

*Kate Hilgar, Administrator*
*Vicky Smith, Director Admissions*

Offers the following rehabilitation services: Sub-Acute rehab, Stroke rehab, Cardiac rehab, Orthopedic rehab, Occupational therapy, Speech therapy, Physical therapy for long term care.

**7150 Highland Pines Rehabilitation Center**
1111 S Highland Ave
Clearwater, FL 33756-4432
727-446-0581
FAX: 727-442-9425

*Paula Anthony, Administrator*
Offers the following rehabilitation services: Sub-Acute rehabilitation, Occupational Therapy, Speech Therapy, Physical Therapy.

**7151 Jupiter Medical Center-Pavilion**
1210 S Old Dixie Hwy
Jupiter, FL 33458-7205
561-747-2234
FAX: 561-744-4467
e-mail: pr@jupitermed.com
www.jupitermed.com

*Jack Waterman, Chief of Staff*
*Steven Seeley, Chief Nursing Oficer*
Offers the following rehabilitation services: Sub-Acute Rehabilitation, Occupational Therapy, Speech Therapy, Physical Therapy.

**7152 North Broward Medical Center**
201 E Sample Rd
Deerfield Beach, FL 33064-4441
954-941-8300
FAX: 954-941-4233
www.browardhealth.org

*Pauline Grant, CEO*
*Douglas Ford, Chief of Staff*
Offers the following rehabilitation services: Sub-Acute rehabilitation, Physical Therapy, Occupational Therapy, Speech Therapy, Respiratory Therapy.

**7153 Pompano Rehabilitation and Nursing Center**
Senior Health Care Management
51 W Sample Rd
Pompano Beach, FL 33064-3542
954-942-5530
FAX: 954-942-0941

*Jeff Nusbusn, Administrator*
Offers the following rehabilitation services: Sub-Acute Rehabilitation, Physical Therapy, Occupational Therapy, Speech Therapy

**7154 Rehabilitation Center of Palm Beach**
300 Royal Palm Way
Palm Beach, FL 33480-4385
561-655-7266
FAX: 561-655-3269
e-mail: info@rcca.org
www.rcca.org

*Ellen O'Bannon, Manager*
*Pamela Henderson, Executive Director*
Offers the following rehabilitation services: Sub-Acute Rehabilitation, Physical Therapy, Occupational Therapy, Speech Therapy

**7155 Rehabilitation and Healthcare Center of Tampa**
4411 N Habana Ave
Tampa, FL 33614-7211
813-872-2771
FAX: 813-871-2831

*Raul Sierra, Medical Director*
Offers the following rehabilitation services: Sub-Acute Rehabilitation, Physical Therapy, Occupational Therapy, Speech Therapy, Respiratory Therapy.

**7156 Shands Rehab Hospital**
4101 NW 89th Blvd
Gainesville, FL 32606-3813
352-265-5497
FAX: 352-265-5420
www.shands.org

*Tim Goldfarb, CEO*
Offers the following rehabilitation services: Sub-acute rehabilitation, traumatic brain injury, spinal cord injury, stroke, degenerative neurological conditions, amputations, burns, organ transplantation.

**7157 St. Anthony's Hospital**
1200 7th Ave N
St Petersburg, FL 33705-1388
727-825-1100
www.stanthonys.com

*William Ulbricht, President*
*Ron Colaguori, VP Operations*
Offers the following rehabilitation services: Sub-Acute rehabilitation, Occupational Therapy, Speech/Language Pathology services, Physical Therapy.

**7158 Winkler Court**
3250 Winkler Avenue Ext
Fort Myers, FL 33916-9414
239-939-4993
FAX: 239-939-1743

*Michael Collier, Medical Director*
*Michael Stens, Medical Director*
Offers the following rehabilitation services: Sub-Acute Rehabilitation, Physical Therapy, Speech Therapy, Occupational Therapy.

**7159 Winter Park Memorial Hospital**
Florida Hospital
200 N Lakemont Ave
Winter Park, FL 32792-3273
407-646-7517
FAX: 407-646-7639
e-mail: healthcare@winterparkhospital.com
www.winterparkhospital.com

*Ken Bradley, CEO*
Offers the following rehabilitation services: Sub-Acute Rehabilitation, Occupational Therapy, Speech Pathology, Physical Therapy.

## Georgia

**7160 Athena Rehab of Clayton**
2055 Rex Rd
Lake City, GA 30260-3944
404-361-5144
FAX: 404-363-6366

*Reginald Washington, Administrator*
Offers the following rehabilitation services: Sub-Acute rehabilitation, Occupational therapy, Speech therapy, Physical therapy, Restorative care.

**7161 Lafayette Nursing and Rehabilitation Center**
110 Brandywine Blvd
Fayetteville, GA 30214-1500
770-461-2928
FAX: 770-461-8507
www.lafayetterehab.com

*Wendy Goza, Medical Director*
Lafayette Nursing and Rehab Center accomodates 179 residents. We are Medicare certified and our center also features a 25-bed postacute rehab unit and a 24-bed dementia unit. We have RN's LPN's and CNA's 24 hours a day. We also have physician services availiable seven days a week.

7162 **Savannah Rehabilitation and Nursing Center**
815 E 63rd St
Savannah, GA 31405-4499
912-352-8615
FAX: 912-355-4642
www.savannahrehab.com

*Sandra Casper, Executive Director*
Offers the following rehabilitation services: Sub-Acute rehabilitation, Physical Therapy, Occupational Therapy, Speech Therapy

7163 **Specialty Hospital**
P.O.Box 1566
Rome, GA 30162-1566
706-509-4100
FAX: 706-509-4159
www.thespecialtyhospital.com

A 34-bed acute long-term care hospital located in Rome, Georgia, designed for those patients who require treatment for extended periods of time. The patients of The Specialty Hospital are those who do not need the medical resources of a general hospital but whose conditions are too severe for a lower level of care. Patients are admitted to TSH through physician and case manager referrals.

7164 **Walton Rehabilitation Health System**
1355 Independence Dr
Augusta, GA 30901-1037
706-724-7746
866-492-5866
FAX: 706-724-5752
e-mail: postmaster@wrh.org
www.wrh.org

*Dennis Skelley, CEO*
Has Centers of Excellence in Stroke Brain Injury, Complex Orthopedics, Spinal Cord Injury and Pain Management. 58-bed nonprofit facility.

7165 **Warner Robins Rehabilitation and Nursing Center**
1601 Elberta Rd
Warner Robins, GA 31093-1393
478-922-2241
FAX: 478-328-1984
wwww.warnerrobinsrehabilitation.com

*Laura Fergason, Administrator*
Offers the following rehabilitation services: Sub-Acute rehabilitation, Physical Therapy, Occupational Therapy, Speech Therapy.

## Hawaii

7166 **Aloha Nursing and Rehab Center**
45-545 Kamehameha Hwy
Kaneohe, HI 96744-1943
808-247-2220
FAX: 808-235-3676
e-mail: info@alohanursing.com
alohanursing.com

*Charles Harris, Executive Director*
*Amy Lee, Administrator*
Our unique nursing care facility is nestled in the picturesque town of Kaneohe, Oahu, amid the towering Koolau Mountains and the panoramic vistas of Kaneohe Bay. In this tranquil setting, our 141-bed facility offers both long and short term care to residents who meet intermediate or skilled level of care criteria.

## Idaho

7167 **Boise Health And Rehabilitation Center**
1001 S Hilton St
Boise, ID 83705-1925
208-345-4464
FAX: 208-345-2998
www.boiserehab.com

*Jason Ludwig, Medical Director*
*Aaron Moorhouse, Medical Director*
*Debbie Mills, Executive Director*
Offers the following rehabilitation services: Sub-acute rehabilitation, occupational therapy, speech therapy, physical therapy.

7168 **Eastern Idaho Regional Medical Center**
3100 Channing Way
Idaho Falls, ID 83404-7533
208-529-6111
FAX: 208-529-7021
www.eirmc.com

*Doug Crabtree, CEO*
*Sandee Moore, COO*
The largest medical facility in the region, Eastern Idaho Regional Medical Center (EIRMC) is a modern, JCAHO-accrediated, full-service hospital. EIRMC serves as the region's healthcare hub, offering specialty services including open-heart surgery, leading-edge cancer treatment, trauma, neurosurgery, intensive care for adults and infants, and a helicopeter service.

7169 **Lewiston Rehabilitation and Care Center**
3315 8th St
Lewiston, ID 83501-4966
208-743-9543
FAX: 208-746-8662
www.lewistonrehab.com

*Debbie Freeze, Administrator*
Lewiston Rehabilitation and Care Center has years of experience providing diversified healthcare services. We have our own staff of physical, occupational and speech therapists. Our therapy gym and rehab kitchen are a lovely atmosphere in which to work toward your therapy goals. We are an Eden Alternative Certified facility.

7170 **Mountain Valley Care and Rehabilitation Center**
P.O.Box 689
Kellogg, ID 83837-689
208-784-1283
FAX: 208-784-0151
www.mountainvalleycare.com

*Maryruth Butler, Executive Director*
Mountain Valley Care and Rehabilitation Center accomodates 68 residents. We are conveniently located in the heart of Kellogg Idaho. We strive to offer quality care and superior customer service in a home-like environment. Upon admission, you or your loved one is looked after by an assigned staff member. We call this our 'Angel Care' program. Our rehabilitation program focuses on meething the individual needs of the resident so you or your loved one can see how they are going to progress.

7171 **River's Edge Rehabilitation and Healthcare**
Kindred Healthcare
714 N Butte Ave
Emmett, ID 83617-2799
208-365-4425
FAX: 208-365-6989
e-mail: jshields@ensigngroup.net
www.riversedgerehab.com

*Janis Shields, Executive Director*
*Steve Balle, Director of Rehabilitation*
Emmett Rehab & healthcare accomodates 95 residents. We are located in Emmett, Idaho, a rural community located an easy 30 minute drive from Boise. Emmett Rehab &Æhealthcare has served the area for more then 40 years by providing healthcare for residents of Gem County.

## Illinois

**7172 Chevy Chase Nursing and Rehabilitation Center**
3400 S Indiana Ave
Chicago, IL 60616-3841
312-842-5000
FAX: 312-842-3790

*Tony Prather, Administrator*
Our approach to care is multidisciplinary; our medical staff members work together as a team in a proactive fashion, challenging residents each and every day, in order to motivate them to rehabilitate and achieve their ultimate potential.

**7173 Glenview Terrace Nursing Center**
1511 Greenwood Rd
Glenview, IL 60026-1597
847-729-9090
FAX: 847-729-9135
www.glenviewterrace.com

*Ian Crook, Administrator*
Comfortable private and semi-private rooms and suites. A stylish day spa. Private dining in lavish surroundings to spend a special occasion. And, of course, compassionate skilled nursing, rehabilitative, Alzheimer's and respite care that's unsurpassed in the Chicago area.

**7174 Halsted Terrace Nursing Center**
10935 S Halsted St
Chicago, IL 60628-3189
773-928-2000
FAX: 773-928-9154

*Ted O'Brien, Administrator*
Offers the following rehabilitation services: Sub-acute rehabilitation, physical therapy, occupational therapy, speech therapy, cardiac rehabilitation.

**7175 Harmony Nursing and Rehabilitation Center**
3919 W Foster Ave
Chicago, IL 60625-6056
773-588-9500
FAX: 773-588-9533
www.harmonychicago.com

*John Sianghio, Administrator*
Offers a friendly healthcare experience. You'll find compassionate experts who provide short-term rehabilitation and therapy, wound care, Alzheimer's and memory loss care, long-term nursing care and more.

**7176 Imperial**
1366 W Fullerton Ave
Chicago, IL 60614-2199
773-525-3905
FAX: 773-935-0036

*David Hartman, Administrator*
Offers the following rehabilitation services: Sub-acute rehabilitation, physical therapy, occupational therapy, speech therapy.

**7177 Jackson Square Nursing and Rehabilitation Center**
5130 W Jackson Blvd
Chicago, IL 60644-4332
773-921-8000
FAX: 773-287-9302
www.jacksonsquarecare.com

*Farhat Sharif, Administrator*
Offers the following rehabilitation services: Sub-acute rehabilitation, physical therapy, occupational therapy, speech therapy.

**7178 Renaissance at 87th Street**
2940 W 87th St
Chicago, IL 60652-3832
773-434-8787
FAX: 773-434-8717
www.renaissanceat87.com

*Juli Foy, Administrator*
Offers the following rehabilitation services: Sub-acute rehabilitation, occupational therapy, physical therapy, speech therapy.

**7179 Renaissance at Hillside**
4600 Frontage Rd
Hillside, IL 60162-1761
708-544-9933
FAX: 708-544-9966
www.renaissanceathillside.com

*John Stare, Administrator*
Offers the following rehabilitation services: Sub-acute rehabilitation, physical therapy, occupational therapy, speech therapy.

**7180 Renaissance at Midway**
4437 S Cicero Ave
Chicago, IL 60632-4333
773-884-0484
FAX: 773-884-0485
www.renaissanceatmidway.com

*Mark Berger, Executive Director*
Offers extensive rehabilitation services, designed to aggressively assist individuals to return to thier prior levels of functioning after suffering unexpected truamas such as strokes or bone fractures. In addition, the Renaissance provides Physician Directed Complex Medical Services, Respiratory Care, Cardiac Care, Pain Management, IV therapies, and Wound Care.

**7181 Renaissance at South Shore**
2425 E 71st St
Chicago, IL 60649-2612
773-721-5000
FAX: 773-721-6850
www.rensouthshore.com

*Dave Schechter, Administrator*
Offers the following rehabilitation services: Sub-acute rehabilitation, physical therapy, occupational therapy, speech therapy.

**7182 Schwab Rehabilitation Hospital**
Mt. Sinai
1401 S California Ave
Chicago, IL 60608-1858
773-522-2010
e-mail: schwabinquiries@sini.org
www.sinai.org/rehabilitation/

*Suzan Rayner, Medical Director*
*Lisa Thornton, Medical Staff President*
Treats medically stable patients who require nursing and medical care that cannot be supplied at home, in an outpatient facility or in a nursing home. Treats stroke patients, amputees, individuals with brain injuries, burns, diabets and spinal cord injuries.

## Indiana

**7183 Angel River Health and Rehabilitation**
5233 Rosebud Ln
Newburgh, IN 47630-9283
812-473-4761
FAX: 812-473-5190
www.angelriverhc.com

*Kay Congleton, Executive Director*
Offers the following rehabilitation services: Sub-acute rehabilitation, speech therapy, occupational therapy, physical therapy.

**7184 Chalet Village Health and Rehabilitation Center**
Magnolia Health Systems
1065 Parkway St
Berne, IN 46711-2366
260-589-2127
FAX: 260-589-3521
e-mail: mwolfe@chalet-village.net
www.chalet-village.net

*Vicki Shepherd, Administrator*
Offers the following rehabilitation services: Sub-acute rehabilitation, physical therapy, occupational therapy, speech therapy, respiratory therapy.

**7185 Columbus Health and Rehabilitation Center**
2100 Midway St
Columbus, IN 47201-3722
812-372-8447
FAX: 812-375-5117
www.columbushrc.com

*Scott Tenbroeck, Executive Director*
*William Lustig, Medical Director*
Accomodates 235 residents. We offer a continuum of healthcare services. Our center also provides a Special Care Alzheimer's Unit. We are licensed by the Stat of Indiana and are Medicare and Medicaid approved provider. We are proud to offer a friendly home-like atmosphere while providing comprehensive healthcare services. These services include short-term medical and rehabilitation treatment, which is designed to address the individual needs of our residents and patients.

**7186 Harrison Health and Rehabilitation Centre**
150 Beechmont Dr NE
Corydon, IN 47112-1717
812-738-0550
FAX: 812-738-6273
www.harrisonrehab.com

*Inez Voyles, Executive Director*
*Bruce Burton, Medical Director*
Offers the following rehabilitation services: Sub-Acute rehabilitation, speech therapy, physical therapy, occupational therapy.

**7187 Indian Creek Health and Rehabilitation Center**
240 Beechmont Dr NE
Corydon, IN 47112-1718
812-738-8127
877-380-7211
FAX: 812-738-2917
www.indiancreekhrc.com

*Bonnie Fallin, Executive Director*
140 bed facility offering the following rehabilitation services: Sub-Acute rehabilitation, Physical therapy, Occupational Therapy, Speech Therapy, pain management, Wound rehabilitation. Short and long term skilled nursing care certified for Medicare, Medicaid, Private Pay and Private Insurance. Hospice and respite care rated #1 in clinical care in southern Indiana district for 2002.

**7188 Meadowvale Health and Rehabilitation Center**
Kindred Health Care
1529 Lancaster St
Bluffton, IN 46714-1507
260-824-4320
800-743-3333
FAX: 260-824-4689
www.meadowvalerehab.com

*David Mlodecki, Executive Director*
*Yadagiri Jonna, Medical Director*
Offers the following rehabilitation services: Sub-acute rehabilitation, physical therapy, occupational therapy, speech therapy.

**7189 Muncie Health Care and Rehabilitation**
4301 N Walnut St
Muncie, IN 47303-1190
765-282-0053
800-743-3333
FAX: 765-282-3290
e-mail: HSDED0406@kindredhealthcare.com?subject=Websi
http://www.muncierehab.com /

*Dee Harrold, Executive Director*
*Dr. Jeffery Hiltz, Medical Director*
Offers the following rehabilitation services: Sub-Acute rehabilitation, physical therapy, occupational therapy, speech therapy.

**7190 Rehabilitation Hospital of Indiana**
4141 Shore Dr
Indianapolis, IN 46254-2607
317-329-2000
FAX: 317-329-2104
www.rhin.com

*Sidney Norton, CEO*
*Sharyl Border, Executive Director*
Offers the following rehabilitation services: Sub-acute rehabilitation, brain injury, spinal cord injury programs.

**7191 Sellersburg Health and Rehabilitation Centre**
7823 Old State Road 60
Sellersburg, IN 47172-1858
812-246-4272
FAX: 812-246-8160
www.sellersburgrehab.com

*Dave Powell, Administrator*
*Chris Hansen, Executive Director*
Sellersburg is a modern healthcare center conveniently located on the edge of the community. Our center accomodates 110 residents and includes a rehabilitative program with a goal of returning residents home as quickly as possible. Sellersburg is a 2006 recipient of the American Health Care Association Quality Award.

**7192 Westpark Rehabilitation Center**
1316 N Tibbs Ave
Indianapolis, IN 46222-3024
317-634-8330
FAX: 317-263-9442
www.westparkhealthcare.com

*Dave Mc Carroll, Owner*
Offers the following rehabilitation services: Sub-acute rehabilitation, occupational therapy, physical therapy, speech therapy, respiratory therapy.

**7193 Westview Nursing and Rehabilitation Center**
1510 Clinic Dr
Bedford, IN 47421-3530
812-279-4494
FAX: 812-275-8313

*Sholin Montgomery, Executive Director*
*Mike Spencer, Executive Director*
Offers the following rehabilitation services: Sub-acute rehabilitation, physical therapy, occupational therapy, speech therapy.

**7194 Windsor Estates Health and Rehab Center**
429 W Lincoln Rd
Kokomo, IN 46902-3508
765-453-5600
FAX: 765-455-0110
www.windsorestateshrc.com

*Brenda Alfrey, Administrator*
We offer a full range of medical services to meet the individual needs of our residents, physician, our staff-including medical specialists, nurses, nutritionists, dietitians, and social workers-establishes a comprehensive treatment plan intended to restore you or your loved one to the highest practicable potential.

## Iowa

**7195 Madison County Rehab Services**
Madison County Hospital
300 W Hutchings St
Winterset, IA 50273-2109
515-462-2373
FAX: 515-462-4492

*Marcia Harris, CEO*
*Panndee Stebbins, Director*
Offers the following rehabilitation services: Sub-acute rehabilitation, occupational therapy, physical therapy, speech therapy, home health rehab, wellness programs.

**7196 Mercy Subacute Care**
603 E 12th St
Des Moines, IA 50309-5515
515-247-4400
FAX: 515-643-0945

*Bonnie Mc Coy, Manager*
*Pam Nelson, Intake Coordinator*
Offers the following rehabilitation services: Sub-acute rehabilitation, physical therapy, speech therapy, occupational therapy.

## Kentucky

7197 **Danville Centre for Health and Rehabilitation**
642 N 3rd St
Danville, KY 40422-1125 859-236-3972
FAX: 859-236-0703
www.danvillecentre.com

*Robert Hollins, Executive Director*
Offers the following rehabilitation services: Sub-acute rehabilitation, physical therapy, occupational therapy, speech therapy.

7198 **Fountain Circle Health & Rehabilitation**
Kindred Healthcare
200 Glenway Rd
Winchester, KY 40391 859-744-1800
FAX: 859-744-0285
www.fountaincircle.com

*William Whited, Executive Director*
*Kathryn Jones, Medical Director*
Offers the following rehabilitation services: Sub-acute rehabilitation, speech therapy, physical therapy, occupational therapy.

7199 **Lexington Center for Health and Rehabilitation**
353 Waller Ave
Lexington, KY 40504-2974 859-252-3558
FAX: 859-233-0192

*Karole Ward, Administrator*
Offers the following rehabilitation services: Sub-acute rehabilitation, speech therapy, occupational therapy, physical therapy.

7200 **Paducah Centre For Health and Rehabilitation**
Wellsouth Health Systems
501 N 3rd St
Paducah, KY 42001-749 270-444-9661
FAX: 270-443-9407

*Terri Humes, Administrator*
Offers the following rehabilitation services: subacute rehabilitation, speech therapy, occupational therapy, physical therapy.

7201 **Pathways Brain Injury Program**
4200 Browns Ln
Louisville, KY 40220-1523 502-459-8900
FAX: 502-459-5026
www.hcr-manorcare.com

*Pam Pearson, Manager*
Offers the following rehabilitation services: Sub-acute rehabilitation, speech therapy, occupational therapy, physical therapy, recreational therapy.

## Louisiana

7202 **Guest House of Slidell Sub-Acute and Rehab Center**
1051 Robert Blvd
Slidell, LA 70458-2011 985-643-5630
800-303-9872
FAX: 985-649-6065

*Brandy Wheat, Administrator*
116 bed healthcare center offering the following subacute services within the skilled nursing setting: physical, occupational, and speech therapies, infusion therapy, respiratory care, wound care, neurological rehabilitation, cardiac reconditioning, pain management, post surgical recovery, orthopedic rehabilitation.

7203 **Irving Place Rehabilitation and Nursing Center**
1736 Irving Pl
Shreveport, LA 71101-4606 318-631-9121
FAX: 318-222-2095

*Webster Johnson, Administrator*
Offers the following rehabilitation services: sub-acute rehabilitation, speech therapy, occupational therapy, physical therapy

## Maine

7204 **Augusta Rehabilitation Center**
188 Eastern Ave
Augusta, ME 04330-5928 207-622-3121
800-457-1220
FAX: 207-623-7666
www.augustarehabcenter.com

*Malcolm Dean, Executive Director*
Accomodates 72 residents. Augusta Rehabilitation Center offers a continuum of healthcare services including respite, short-term rehabilitation and long-term care. We are proud to have a dedicated team of veteran healthcare professionals on hand. This group establishes a plan of care upon admission that includes the resident and family. Our goal is to care for the medical, psychosocial, and emotional needs of your loved one, addressing all aspects of his or her care and well being.

7205 **Brentwood Rehabilitation and Nursing Center**
370 Portland St
Yarmouth, ME 04096-8101 207-846-9021
800-457-1220
FAX: 207-846-1497
www.brentwoodrnc.com

*Daniel Burns, Executive Director*
*Daniel Pierce, Medical Director*
Brentwood accomodates 82 residents. We are located at 370 Portland Street in Yarmouth, Maine. We strive to meet the healthcare needs of the greater Yarmouth community, including Portland and Brunswick, which are located within 10 miles of the center. In addition to Brentwood's rehabilitation and skilled nursing services, we also offer Alzheimer's specialty care in a comfortable setting.

7206 **Den-Mar Rehabilitation and Nursing Center**
44 South St
Rockport, MA 01966-1800 978-546-6311
800-439-2370
FAX: 978-546-9185
www.denmarrnc.com

*Christine Marek, Executive Director*
Den-Mar nursing and Rehab center accomodates 80 residents. We provide skilled nursing and rehabilitation services as well as long term care. We are certified for Medicare and Medicaid as well as many insurance carriers. We offer semi-private and private rooms, with many common areas for socializing.

7207 **Eastside Rehabilitation and Living Center**
516 Mount Hope Ave
Bangor, ME 04401-4215 207-947-6131
800-457-1220
FAX: 207-942-0884
www.eastsiderehab.com

*Hope Boyd, Executive Director*
Accomodates 67 residents. We offer short-term rehabilitation, complex medical care, skilled nursing services, respite, and traditional long-term care. We specialize in the treatment of respiratory or breathing diseases and/or disorders. Utilizing a team approach, we develop individualized plans of care for each patient or resident with a goal of restoring health and function to the fullest extent possible.

7208 **Kennebunk Nursing & Rehabilitation Center**
158 Ross Rd
Kennebunk, ME 04043-6557
207-985-7141
800-457-1220
FAX: 207-985-0961
www.kennebunknursing.com

*Laurie McFarren, Executive Director*
Kennebunk Nursing and Rehabilitation Center accomodates 76 residents. We offer short-term rehabilitation, complex medical care, skilled nursing services, traditional long-term care, and adult day care. Utilizing an interdisciplinary approach, we develop individualized plans of care for each resident.

7209 **Norway Rehabilitation and Living Center**
29 Marion Ave
Norway, ME 04268-5601
207-743-7075
800-457-1220
FAX: 207-743-9269
e-mail: info@norwayresidentialcare.com
www.norwayresidentialcare.com

*Carolyn Farley, Administrator*
Norway Rehabilitation and Living center accomodates 70 residents. We offer short-term rehabilitation, complex medical care, skilled nursing services and long-term care, plus a residential care unit for a more independent resident population. A compassionate staff dedicated to serving the physical and emotional needs of patients strives to provide high quality treatment. Utilizing an interdisciplinary team approach, we develop individualized plans of care for each patient.

7210 **Shore Village Rehabilitation & Nursing Center**
201 Camden St
Rockland, ME 04841-2534
207-596-6423
800-457-1220
FAX: 207-596-7235

*Phyllis Nickerson, Administrator*
Shore Village accomodates 60 residents and is located in the mid-coast region of the state of Maine. We have a cozy size and a primary goal for the staff is to ensure a home-like atmosphere for all the residents. Shore Village provides skilled nursing and rehabilitation, respite care, and long term care. The facility is dually certified for Medicare and Medicaid and accepts many commercial insurance plans.

## Maryland

7211 **Greater Baltimore Medical Center**
6701 N Charles St
Baltimore, MD 21204-6881
443-849-2000
FAX: 443-849-3024
www.gbmc.org

*Laurence M Merlis, CEO*
GBMC includes Greater Baltimore Medical Center (GBMC), Central Maryland's leading community hospital; Hospice of Baltimore, which provides comfort and care to patients with life-limiting illnesses; and the GBMC Foundation, which supports the GBMC mission by managing fundraising efforts. The 292-bed Medical Center, located on a beautiful suburban campus serves nearly 22,000 inpatients annually as well as providing some 50,000 emergency room visits.

## Massachusetts

7212 **Bolton Manor Nursing Home**
400 Bolton St
Marlborough, MA 01752-3912
508-481-6123
800-439-2370
FAX: 508-481-6130
www.boltonmanor.com

*Michele Ricard, Medical Director*
*Thomas Sullivan, Executive Director*
Bolton Manor accomodates 157 residents. We are located in Marlboro, Massachusetts. We provide medical management and long-term care through comprehensive skilled and post-acute nursing services. We also provide physical, occupational, and speech therapy services from an onsite dedicated staff of therapists. The facility is Joint Commission (formerly JCAHO) accredited and has an excellent survey history with the State Department of Public Health.

7213 **Brigham Manor Nursing and Rehabilitation Center**
77 High St
Newburyport, MA 01950-3071
978-462-4221
800-439-2370
FAX: 978-463-3297
www.brighammanor.com

*Stephen Cynewski, Executive Director*
Brigham Manor accomodates 64 residents. We are a Medicare-certified facility offering private, semi-private and multi-bed suites. Our bright, formal dining room, with French doors that open to a shaded courtyard, provides a warm atmosphere for entertaining family and friends. Each resident's personal tastes and medical needs are considered in the planning of our weekly menus.

7214 **Country Gardens Skilled Nursing and Rehabilitation Center**
2045 Grand Army Hwy
Swansea, MA 02777-3997
508-379-9700
800-439-2370
FAX: 508-379-0723
www.cntrygrdns.com

*Sandy Sarza, Executive Director*
Country Gardens Skilled Nursing and Rehabilitation Center accomodates 86 residents. We are located in a beautiful rural setting conveniently located about 15 minutes east of Providence and 10 minutes west of Fall River. We have provided healthcare service to the greater Swansea area for over 34 years.

7215 **Country Manor Rehabilitation and Nursing Center**
180 Low St
Newburyport, MA 01950-3519
978-465-5361
800-439-2370
FAX: 978-463-9366
www.countryrehab.com

*Stephen Doyle, Executive Director*
Country Rehabilitation and Nursing Center accomodates 123 residents. We are located in the quaint seaport town of Newburyport, Massachusetts. We provide medical management and long-term care through comprehensive skilled and intermediate nursing services. We also provide physical, occupational, and speech therapy services from an onsite dedicated staff of therapists. The center offers an Alzheimer's special care unit with staff trained in dimentia care and dementia specific programs.

7216 **Franklin Skilled Nursing and Rehabilitation Center**
130 Chestnut St
Franklin, MA 02038-3903
508-528-4600
800-439-2370
FAX: 508-528-7976
www.franklinskilled.com

*Paula Topijan, Executive Director*
Franklin Skilled Nursing and Rehabilitation Center accomodates 82 residents. Each program and department is designed and

operated to give you quality care. From our compassionate nursing staff to our helpful and friendly housekeepers, we strive to lend a listning ear, a gentle hug, and a thoroughly trained, competent staff member to assist you and your family members. We understand the necessity of working together to make our center feel a bit more like home, and we appreciate suggestions.

7217 **Great Barrington Rehabilitation and Nursing Center**
148 Maple Ave
Great Barrington, MA 01230-1906
413-528-3320
800-439-2370
FAX: 413-528-2302
www.greatbarringtonrnc.com

*William Kittler, Executive Director*
*Andrew Potler, Medical Director*
Great Barrington Rehabilitation and Nursing Center accomodates 106 residents. As part of a national network of long-term healthcare centers, we have the expertise and resources to provide care appropriate to the individual needs of each and every one of our residents. We provide personal care with minimal daily living assistance to the most skilled treatment for medically complex patients.

7218 **Ledgewood Rehabilitation and Skilled Nursing Center**
87 Herrick St
Beverly, MA 01915-2773
978-921-1392
800-439-2370
FAX: 978-927-8627
www.ledgewoodrehab.com

*Frank Silvia, Executive Director*
Ledgewood accomodates 123 residents. We are located on the campus of Beverly Hospital, with acute care services close by. The leadership and staff at Ledgewood continue to strive for excellence through thier ongoing performance inprovement mentality. We are proud that our facility has achieved outstanding survey results including eight deficiency-free Department of Public Health Surveys and a score of 96 on the 2002 Joint Commission survey.

7219 **Leo P La Chance Center for Rehabilitation and Nursing**
59 Eastwood Cir
Gardner, MA 01440-3901
978-632-8776
FAX: 978-632-5048
e-mail: souellet@legendcenter.com
www.lachancecenter.com

*Mark Alinger, Administrator*
A privately owned facility, combines the best of medical technology with the ultimate in healing, compassionate rehabilitation and nursing care. Our goal is to help each client reach that ultimate goal of living life to the fullest.

7220 **Oakwood Rehabilitation and Nursing Center**
11 Pontiac Ave
Webster, MA 01570-1629
508-943-3889
800-439-2370
FAX: 508-949-6125
www.oakwoodrehab.com

*Melissa Christian, Executive Director*
Oakwood Rehabilitation and Nursing Center accomodates 81 residents. We offer 24-hour skilled nursing, inpatient rehabilitation, respite care, and hospice services. Our center has been successfully serving the greater Webster, Massachusetts, community for 35 years. We have a dedicated and caring staff and our common goal is to promote recovery and enhance quality of live whether your needs are short or long term.

7221 **Walden Rehabilitation and Nursing Center**
785 Main St
Concord, MA 01742-3310
978-369-6889
800-439-2370
FAX: 978-369-8392
www.waldenrehab.com

*Sharon Spittle, Executive Director*
Walden Rehabilitation and Nursing Center accomodates 123 residents. We are located in the quaint town of Concord, Massachusetts, across the street from Emerson Hospital and a short drive from the town center. Walden provides medical management and long-term care through comprehensive skilled and intermediate nursing services. We also provide physical, occupational, and speech therapy services from an onsite dedicated staff of therapists.

## Michigan

7222 **Boulder Park Terrace**
14676 W Upright St
Charlevoix, MI 49720-1201
231-547-1005
FAX: 231-547-1039
www.northernhealth.org

*Reezie DeVet, President/CEO*
*Mary-Anne Ponti, COO*
A partnership formed with Charlevoix Area Hospital, Boulder Park Terrace is a long-term care facility and Sub-acute Rehabilitation Center located in Chalrevoix near the shores of Lake Michigan. The Sub-acute Rehabilitation Center was created as a transition between an acute care hospital and home. Patients enter into the program to increase their strength, endurance and over-all functioning before returning home.

## Minnesota

7223 **Park Health And Rehabilitation Center**
4415 W 36 1/2 St
St Louis Park, MN 55416-4890
952-927-9717
FAX: 952-927-7687
www.extendicare.com

*Jennifer Kuhn, Administrator*
93-bed facility that offers a full continuum of services and care focused around each individual in today's ever-changing healthcare environment.

## Missouri

7224 **Barnes-Jewish Hospital Washington University Medical Center**
1 Barnes Jewish Hospital Plz
Saint Louis, MO 63110-1003
314-747-3000
866-867-3627
FAX: 314-362-8877
www.barnesjewish.org

*Richard Liekweg, President*
*John Lynch, Chief Medical Officer*
Barnes-Jewish Hospital at Washington University Medical Center is the largest hospital in Missouri and the largest private employer in the St. Louis region. An affiliated teaching hospital of Washington University School of Medicine, Barnes-Jewish Hospital has a 1,700 member medical staff with many who are recognized in the 'Best Doctors in America.'

## Montana

7225 **Parkview Acres Care and Rehabilitation Center**
200 N Oregon St
Dillon, MT 59725-3699
406-683-5105
866-253-4090
FAX: 406-683-6388
www.parkviewacres.com

*Claire Miller, Executive Director*

We are Medicare and Medicaid certified skilled nursing facility which accomodates 108 residents serving scenic Dillon and surrounding Montana communities.

## Nebraska

**7226 Homestead Healthcare and Rehabilitation Center**
4735 S 54th St
Lincoln, NE 68516-1335
402-488-0977
800-833-0920
FAX: 402-488-4507
www.homesteadrehab.com

*Matt Romshek, Executive Director*
*James Murray, Administrator*
Homestead Healthcare and Rehabilitation Center is one of the area's oldest providers of skilled nursing and rehabilitation services. We are a 163-bed skilled nursing and rehabilitation center nestled in a lovely, quiet established neighborhood in South Lincoln.

**7227 Madonna Rehabilitation Hospital**
5401 South St
Lincoln, NE 68506-2150
402-489-7102
FAX: 402-486-5448
e-mail: info@madonna.org
www.madonna.org

*Marsha Lommel, CEO*
*Tom Stalder, VP Medical Affairs*
Patients who need only one or two types of therapy for a specific condition are served in the subacute program. Patients who have a diagnosis suggesting a positive course of recovery are typical for the subacute level of care.

**7228 Mary Lanning Memorial Hospital**
715 N Saint Joseph Ave
Hastings, NE 68901-4497
402-463-4521
866-460-5884
e-mail: tanderson@mlmh.org
www.mlmh.org

*Bradley Neet, CEO*
*Joe Davis, VP Medical Affairs*
Mary Lanning Memorial Hospital, A regional health system, is committed to a tradition of excellence through leadership in the provision of quality medical services and health education for the people of Central Nebraska. Our mission is achieved through a dedicated, caring staff, using advanced technology within a healthy and pleasant environment, in a cost effective manner.

## Nevada

**7229 Las Vegas Healthcare and Rehabilitation Center**
2832 S Maryland Pkwy
Las Vegas, NV 89109-1502
702-735-5848
800-326-6888
FAX: 702-735-6218
wwww.lasvegaskindred.com

*Randall Fuller, Executive Director*
Las Vegas Healthcare accomodates 79 residents. We have been serving the community for approximately 40 years. Located in close proximity to local hospitals and surrounded by medical complexes, our center offers both short-term rehabilitation and long-term care.

## New Hampshire

**7230 Dover Rehabilitation and Living Center**
307 Plaza Dr
Dover, NH 03820-2455
603-742-2676
800-735-2964
FAX: 603-749-5375
www.doverrehab.com

*Daniel Estee, Executive Director*
Dover Rehab is a provider of postacute services in the greater New Hampshire Seacost area. We accomodate 112 residents and are licensed by the state of New Hampshire. We employ nearly 150 licensed nurses, therapists and other healthcare professionals, who strive to provide quality care. The goal of our patient service model is to bridge the gap between hospitalization and home so that recovery and physical functioning are maximized and hospital readmission is minimized.

**7231 Northeast Rehabilitation Clinic**
70 Butler St
Salem, NH 03079-3925
603-893-2900
800-825-7292
FAX: 603-893-1638
e-mail: webmaster@northeastrehab.com
northeastrehab.com

*John Prochilo, CEO*
Subacute rehabilitation at NRH was designed for people who have experienced an acutely disabling orthopedic, medical, or neurologic condition but who either do not require or are unable to participate in a full acute inpatient program. Impairment groups pertinent to this level of care include brain injury, spinal cord injury (traumatic/non-traumatic), stroke, orthopedic injury, amputation, and neurologic disorder.

## New Jersey

**7232 Atlantic Coast Rehabilitation & Healthcare Center**
485 River Ave
Lakewood, NJ 8701-4720
732-364-7100
FAX: 732-364-2442
e-mail: abby@atlanticcoastrehab.com
atlanticcoastrehab.com

*Simon Shain, Administrator*
*Sharon Sckbower, Director of Nursing*
Offers the following rehabilitation services: Sub-acute rehab, physical therapy, occupational therapy, speech therapy.

**7233 Crestwood Nursing & Rehabilitation Center**
101 Whippany Rd
Whippany, NJ 7981-1407
973-887-0311
FAX: 973-887-8355

*Carol Shepard, Administrator*
Sub-acute rehabilitation facility.

**7234 Lakeview Subacute Care Center**
130 Terhune Dr
Wayne, NJ 7470-7104
973-839-4500
FAX: 973-839-2729
e-mail: info@lakeviewsubacute.com
www.lakeviewsubacute.com

*Richard Grosso, Director*
*Susan R Ahlers, Director of Admission*
*Kerry Iamurri, Director of Rehab*
Offers physical therapy, occupational therapy, speech therapy, recreational therapy, respiratory therapy, aqua therapy. 68-bed subacute unit.

**7235 Merwick Rehabilitation and Sub-Acute Care**
79 Bayard Ln
Princeton, NJ 8540-3045 609-497-3000
FAX: 609-497-3024

*Ryan Wismer, Administrator*
76-bed skilled nursing and residential center as well as a separate 17-bed comprehensive rehabilitation center. Offers rehabilitation, physiatry, occupational therapy, respite care, speech/hearing therapy, sub-acute care.

**7236 Seacrest Village Nursing Center**
1001 Center St
Little Egg Harbor Twp, NJ 8087-1364 609-296-9292
FAX: 609-296-0508
e-mail: info@seacrestvillagenj.com
seacrestvillagenj.com

*Brian T Holloway, Administrator*
Seacrest Village Nursing and Rehabilitation Center has specialized in quality rehabilitation, transitional and restorative care for more then a decade and is a perfect alternative for bridging the gap between hospital and home.

**7237 St. Lawrence Rehabilitation Center**
2381 Lawrenceville Rd
Lawrenceville, NJ 8648-2098 609-896-9500
FAX: 609-895-0242
e-mail: epiechota@slrc.org
www.slrc.org

*Charles Terry, Medical Director*
St. Lawrence Rehabilitation Center, a non-profit facility sponsored by the Roman Catholic Diocese of Trenton, is committed to maximizing the quality of human life by providing comprehensive physical rehabilitation and related programs to meet the healthcare needs of our communities.

**7238 Summit Ridge Center Genesis Eldercare**
20 Summit St
West Orange, NJ 7052-1501 973-736-2000
800-699-1520
FAX: 973-736-2764
e-mail: info@genesishcc.com
www.genesishcc.com

*Chad Murin, Administrator*
*Elizabeth Martin, Customer Relations Manager*
Skilled nursing facility with a total of 152 beds. 40 bed sub-acute unit and 24 bed secure dementia unit. Able to care for a wide variety of rehab and medical cases from orthopedics to TPN and tracheostomies.

## New York

**7239 Beth Abraham Health Services**
612 Allerton Ave
Bronx, NY 10467-7495 718-519-5901
888-238-4223
FAX: 718-547-1366
e-mail: info@bethabe.org
bethabe.org

*Michael Fassler, CEO*
*Paul Rosenfeld, SVP/COO*
*Ira Green, VP Finance*
Offers the following rehabilitation services: Sub-Acute rehabilitation, brain injury rehabilitation, pain management, post-operative recovery. Home visits and a network of community-based programs help patients and their families with a successful transition home.

**7240 Central Island Healthcare**
825 Old Country Rd
Plainview, NY 11803-4913 516-433-0600
FAX: 516-868-7251
www.centralislandhealthcare.net

*Michael Ostreicher, Administrator*
Serving the community for over 33 years, Central Island Healthcare is Long Island's largest and most active sub-acute care provider. We offer comprehensive programs focused on restoring our patients to their maximum potential and returning home. Central Island's 202-bed facility provides top notch professionals and the latest in rehabilitation and therapeutic equipment in a beautiful and comfortable setting.

**7241 Clove Lakes Health Care and Rehabilitation Center**
25 Fanning St
Staten Island, NY 10314-5307 718-289-7900
FAX: 718-761-8701
e-mail: webmaster@clovelakes.com
www.clovelakes.com

*Helene Demisay, CEO*
CLove Lakes provides a full range of services to individuals who are in need of skilled nursing, therapeutic and/or rehabilitation care. Our success in providing compassionate quality care is evidenced by the excellent reputation we enjoy in our areas of specialization.

**7242 Dr. William O Benenson Rehabilitation Pavilion**
36-17 Parsons Blvd
Flushing, NY 11354-5931 718-961-4300
FAX: 718-939-5032
www.flushingmanors.com

*Richard Sherman, Administrator*
*Esther Benenson, Executive Director*
The Dr. William O Benson Reahbilitation Pavilion is a subacute short-term rehabilitation center committed to the excellence of elevated health care for our patients. Through the use of the most comprehensive and specialized services available, our staff of dedicated professionals are devoted to putting patients back to the road to full recovery 24 hours a day.

**7243 Flushing Manor Nursing and Rehab**
35-15 Parsons Blvd
Flushing, NY 11354-4297 718-961-3500
FAX: 718-461-1784
www.flushingmanors.com

*Jordan Kaufman, Administrator*
*Esther Benenson, Executive Director*
*Ion Oltean, Medical Director*
At the Flusing Manor Nursing and Rehabilitation, we stress the importance of family involvement because it is the true source of strength and stability in ones life...a tie that brings us all together as a team, enhancing the quality of life of the patients in our care.

**7244 Glengariff Health Care Center**
141 Dosoris Ln
Glen Cove, NY 11542 516-676-1100
FAX: 516-759-0216
e-mail: info@glenhaven.org
www.glenhaven.org

*Jean Campo, Director Admissions*
*Michael Miness, President*
Licensed skilled nursing and subacute medical and rehabilitation facility.

**7245 Haym Salomon Home for The Aged**
2340 Cropsey Ave
Brooklyn, NY 11214-5706 718-266-4063
FAX: 718-372-4781

*Chain Lipschitz, Administrator*
Religious nonmedical health care institution.

**7246 Kings Harbor Multicare Center**
2000 E Gun Hill Rd
Bronx, NY 10469-6016
718-320-0400
FAX: 718-320-0557
e-mail: info@kingsharbor.com
www.kingsharbor.com

*Morris Tenenbaum, Owner*
*Octavio Marin, Vice President*
Kings Harbor Multicare Center provides long-term and short-term skilled nursing care for more then 700 residents. Kings Harbor is located in the Pelham Gardens neighborhood of Northeast Bronx, easily accessible to major highways and near public transportation. A 3 building campus facility with surrounding gardens ensures that residents with similar capabilities are grouped together.

**7247 Northwoods of Cortland**
28 Kellogg Rd
Cortland, NY 13045-3155
607-753-9631
FAX: 607-756-2968
www.northwoodshealth.net

*Lawrence Mennig, Administrator*
Subacute rehabilitation facility.

**7248 Port Jefferson Health Care Facility**
141 Dosoris Lane
Glen Cove, NY 11542
631-676-1100
FAX: 631-759-0216
e-mail: info@glenhaven.org
www.glengariffcare.com

*Ellen Harte, Administrator*
Subacute medical and rehabilitative care and long term residential skilled nursing care.

**7249 Rehab Institute at Florence Nightingale Health Center**
1760 3rd Ave
New York, NY 10029-6810
212-410-8760
800-786-8968
FAX: 212-410-8792
e-mail: info@rehabinstitute.org

Sub-acute rehabilitation facility.

**7250 Schnurmacher Center for Rehabilitation and Nursing**
Beth Abraham of Family Health Services
12 Tibbits Ave
White Plains, NY 10606-2438
914-287-7200
888-238-4223
FAX: 914-428-1824
e-mail: info@schnurmacher.org
www.schnurmacher.org

*Linda Murray, Executive Director*
*Thomas Camisa, Medical Director*
*Iryn Obaldo Fontanosa, Director of Rehabilitation*
The environment at Schnurmacher is tailored to the needs of patients who require medical and nursing services but who do not need the complexity of services associated with an acute-care hospital. And Schnurmacher Subacute Medical patients are out of bed more quickly and as often as possible, which helps them maintain functional status while recovery progresses.

**7251 South Shore Healthcare**
275 W Merrick Rd
Freeport, NY 11520-3346
516-623-4000
FAX: 516-223-4599
www.northshorelij.com

*Cathie Doyle, Administrator*
*Daniel Raj, Director of Sub-acute*
Serving the community for over 45 years, South Shore Healthcare is Long Island's first sub-acute care provider. We offer comprehensive programs focused on restoring our patients to their maximum potential and returning home. Our facility offers top notch professionals and the latest in rehabilitation and therapeutic equipment in a beautiful and comfortable setting.

**7252 St. Camillus Health and Rehabilitation Center**
813 Fay Rd
Syracuse, NY 13219-3009
315-488-2951
FAX: 315-488-3255
e-mail: info@st-camillus.org
www.st-camillus.org

*Aileen Balitz, President*
Since our founding in 1969, St. Camillus' mission has been to provide high-quality services and facilities emphasizing the rehabilitation of individuals to their maximum potential. The importance of the human spirit drives all we do. We are dedicated to caring for life and helping individuals achieve their highest possible level of independence.

## North Carolina

**7253 Chapel Hill Rehabilitation and Healthcare Center**
1602 E Franklin St
Chapel Hill, NC 27514-2892
919-967-1418
800-735-8262
FAX: 919-918-3811
www.chapelhillhc.com

*Turner Prichett, Executive Director*
Chapel Hill Rehabilitation and Healthcare Center accomodates 120 residents. We are located in downtown Chapel Hill on Franklin Street and we provide roud the clock nursing care 365 days a year. Intensive rehabilitation services are administered by our licensed speech, occupational and physical therapists. Our staff is trained to care for medically complex patients such as those requiring intensive wound care, dialysis, and artificial nutrition.

**7254 Cypress Pointe Rehabilitation and Healthcare Center**
2006 S 16th St
Wilmington, NC 28401-6613
910-763-6271
800-735-8262
FAX: 910-251-9803
kindredhealthcare.com

*Cheryl Smith, Executive Director*
*George Sylvestri, Medical Director*
Cypress Pointe offers comprehensive physical, occupational, speech and respiratory therapy services. Following a physician's referral, patients are evaluated to determine their needs. Recommendations are then made for the appropriate interventions and rehabilitation. If therapy is required, a personalized care plan is developed.

**7255 Pettigrew Rehabilitation and Healthcare Center**
1551 W Pettigrew St
Durham, NC 27705
919-286-0751
800-735-8262
FAX: 919-286-5992
www.pettigrewghc.com

*La'Ticia Beatty, Executive Director*
Pettigrew Rehabilitation and Healthcare Center accomodates 107 residents. Our healthcare center is certified by Medicare and Medicaid. We have experienced staff members who care for our residents. We strive to improve the quality of life our residents experience as a result of the services they receive from our nursing and therapy departments.

**7256 Raleigh Rehabilitation and Healthcare Center**
616 Wade Ave
Raleigh, NC 27605-1237
919-828-6251
800-735-8262
FAX: 919-828-3294
www.raleighrehabhc.com

*Steven Jones, Administrator*

Raleigh Rehabilitation and Healthcare Center accomodates 172 residents. We provide short-term rehabilitation-including, physical, occupational, and speech therapies-as well as long-term nursing services. We specialize in neurological disorders, complex diabetes treatment, amputation recovery and pain management. We welcome short stays (respite care). Transportation services are availiable for physician appointments and dialysis treatments.

**7257 Rehabilitation and Healthcare Center of Almanace**
779 Woody Dr
Graham, NC 27253-3812
336-227-8498
800-735-8262
FAX: 336-228-7413
www.almanacehc.com

*C Gordon Smith, President*
Our center houses ambulatory as well as bedfast residents and our goal is to offer quality nursing and rehabilitation care at a reasonable price. We are approved by the State Board of Health and employ only trained personnel to cater to resident needs. Our staff is supervised by licensed RN's and there is a physician on call 24 hours a day.

**7258 Rehabilitation and Healthcare Center of Monroe**
1212 E Sunset Dr
Monroe, NC 28112-4318
704-283-8548
800-735-8262
FAX: 704-283-4664
www.monroehc.com

*Judy Olson, Administrator*
We accomodate 159 residents and are certified for Medicare and Medicaid. We specialize in short-term rehabilitation as well as long-term care. Our therapists, wound nurse and dietician work closely to administer wound care. We hav 2 dialysis centers within a 10-block radius and gladly accpet their patients. We have an on-staff medical director as well as a psychiatrist.

**7259 Winston-Salem Rehabilitation and Healthcare Center**
1900 W 1st St
Winston Salem, NC 27104-4220
336-724-2821
800-735-8262
FAX: 336-725-8314

*Tom Bauer, Administrator*
We accommodate 230 residents and we have approximately 250 employees. Our staffing ratio averages 1 licensed nurse for every 20 residents and 1 Certified Nursing Assistant for every 10 residents. We offer a wide range of services including but not limited to respiratory care, tracheotomy care and gastric tube feeding and we also feature an in house licensed therapy program.

## Ohio

**7260 Arbors East Subacute and Rehabilitation Center**
5500 E Broad St
Columbus, OH 43213-1476
614-501-1622
FAX: 614-575-9101
e-mail: arborseast@extendicare.com
www.arborseastskillednursing.com

Subacute rehabilitation facility.

**7261 Arbors at Canton Subacute And Rehabilitation Center**
2714 13th St NW
Canton, OH 44708-3121
330-456-2842
FAX: 330-456-5343
www.laurelsofcanton.com

*Amy McDermand, Director of Marketing*
*Beth Jones, Director of Physical Therapy*
*Jennifer Fess, Administrator*
Subacute rehabilitation programs and facility.

**7262 Arbors at Dayton**
320 Albany St
Dayton, OH 45408-1402
937-496-6200
FAX: 937-496-1990
www.extendicare.com

*Dave Maxwell, Administrator*
*Carlisa Pedalino, Administrator*
Subacute rehabilitation facility with with 106 certified beds. Rehabilitation programs.

**7263 Arbors at Marietta**
400 N 7th St
Marietta, OH 45750-2024
740-373-3597
FAX: 740-373-3915
www.extendicarehealth.com

*Joan Florence, Director of Nursing*
*Kenneth Leopold, Medical Director*
Subacute rehabilitation services and facility.

**7264 Arbors at Milford**
5900 Meadow Creek Dr
Milford, OH 45150-5641
513-248-1655
FAX: 513-248-7340
e-mail: milford@extendicare.com
www.extendicareus.com/milford

*Mark Ostendorf, Administrator*
A nursing center hospital in search of giving the joy and fulfillment to the elderly.

**7265 Arbors at Sylvania**
7120 Port Sylvania Dr
Toledo, OH 43617-1158
419-841-2200
FAX: 419-841-2822
e-mail: sylvania@extendicare.com
www.extendicareus.com/sylvania

*Sheril Flowers, Administrator*
*Graig Hopple, Medical Director*
Subacute rehabilitation programs and facility.

**7266 Arbors at Toledo Subacute and Rehab Centre**
2920 Cherry St
Toledo, OH 43608-1716
419-242-7458
FAX: 419-242-6514
www.extendicare.com

*Jill Schlievert, Administrator*
Subacute rehabilitation services and facility.

**7267 Bridgepark Center for Rehabilitation and Nursing Services**
145 Olive St
Akron, OH 44310-3236
330-762-0901
800-750-0750
FAX: 330-762-0905
www.bridgeparkrehab.net

*Joseph Burick, Medical Director*
A skilled nursing and rehabilitation center located in Akron, Ohio, across the street from St. Thomas Hospital with a beautiful view of the Akron skyline. Access to Interstate 77 and State Route 8 is just minutes away. Our entire staff is committed to providing caring, customer-focused skilled nursing and rehabilitation. For your convenience, we accept Medicare, Medicaid and most managed care and private insurance.

**7268 Broadview Multi-Care Center**
5520 Broadview Rd
Parma, OH 44134-1605
216-749-4010
FAX: 216-778-6860
e-mail: info@broadviewmulticare.com
www.broadviewmulticare.com

*Harold Shachter, Owner*
*Mike Flank, VP*

Broadview Multi-Care Center's Comprehensive Medical Rehabilitation Program has been developed to maximize the functional, psychological and social capabilities of its residents, using a Transdisciplinary Approach. Our multidisciplinary team asses each resident and individualizes a plan to attain the highest practicable functioning of each person under our care.

**7269 Caprice Care Center**
9184 Market St
North Lima, OH 44452-9558
330-965-6358
FAX: 330-726-6097
e-mail: capriceadm@chcccompanies.com
www.chcccompanies.com/CapriceMain

*Lori Crowl, Owner*
A 106-bed skilled nursing, subacute and rehabilitation facility. Our goal is to provide comfortable living to all who are in our care. Caprice Health Care Center is a contemporary Medicare and Medicaid approved facility specializing in short-term rehabilitation services. The inpatient/outpatient rehab department includes physical, occupational, speech therapies, indoor aquatic therapy pool, as well as complimentary van transportation for outpatient services.

**7270 Cleveland Clinic**
9500 Euclid Ave
Cleveland, OH 44195-2
216-444-2200
800-801-2273
FAX: 216-444-7021
www.ccf.com

*Gene Altus, Executive Director*
*Delos M. Cosgrove, MD, Chief Executive Officer, President, Director*
*Joseph F. Hahn, MD, Chief of Staff, Vice Chairman of the Board of Governors, Director*
*David Bronson, MD, Chief Executive Officer, Cleveland Clinic Regional Hospitals*
A not-for-profit, multispecialty academic medical center that integrates clinical and hospital care with research and education. Cleveland clinic was founded in 1921 by 4 renowned physicians with a vision of providing outstanding patient care based upon the principals of cooperation, compassion and innovation. Today, Cleveland Clinic is one of the largest and most respected hospitals in the country.

**7271 Columbus Rehabilitation And Subacute Institute**
44 S Souder Ave
Columbus, OH 43222-1539
614-228-5900
FAX: 614-228-3989
e-mail: columbusrehab@extendicare.com?subject=CRSI%20
www.extendicareus.com

*Kelly Fligor, Administrator*
Subacute rehabilitation programs and facility.

**7272 LakeMed Nursing and Rehabilitation Center**
70 Normandy Dr
Painesville, OH 44077-1616
440-357-1311
800-750-0750
FAX: 440-352-9977
e-mail: HSDED1229@kindredhealthcare.com?subject=Websi
www.lakemednursing.com

*Connie Eyman, Administrator*
*Vesta Jones, Executive Director*
Our goal is to provide you with quality care and we are known for our successful short-term rehab and care of the clinically complex. We also offer respite services to give caregivers a rest, and hospice services through our local hospice care provider. Our interdisciplinary team works together as they strive to deliver quality care and responsive service to our residents.

**7273 Oregon Nursing And Rehabilitation Center**
904 Isaac Streets Dr
Oregon, OH 43616-3204
419-691-2483
FAX: 419-697-5401

*Mark Rogers, Administrator*
Subacute rehabilitation facility and services.

**7274 Sunset View Castle Nursing Homes Castle Nursing Homes**
434 N Washington St
Millersburg, OH 44654-1188
330-674-0015
FAX: 330-763-2238
e-mail: info@castlenursinghomes.com
www.castlenursinghomes.com

*Becky Snyder, Admissions Coordinator*
*Kathy Edwards, Admissions And Marketing*
310 licensed, certified beds. Subacute rehabilitation facility and programs.

## Oregon

**7275 Care Center East Health & Specialty Care Center**
Expendicare
11325 NE Weidler St
Portland, OR 97220-1950
503-253-1181
FAX: 503-253-1871
e-mail: carecentereast@extendicare.com?subject=Care%2
www.extendicareus.com

*Glydon Kimbrough, Administrator*
Subacute rehabilitation facility and programs

**7276 Medford Rehabilitation and Healthcare Center**
Kindred Healthcare
625 Stevens St
Medford, OR 97504-6719
541-779-3551
800-735-1232
FAX: 541-779-3658
e-mail: HSDED0453@kindredhealthcare.com?subject=Websi
www.medfordrehab.com

*Grant Gloor, Administrator*
*Dane Reeves, Executive Director*
*Kristen W., Health and Rehabilitation Center Executive Director*
*Becky D., Activity Director*
We strive to provide quality, compassionate care. Our cozy building accomodates 110 residents. Our smaller size creates an inviting and homelike environment. We offer semi-private rooms with space to add items from home for a special personalized touch.

## Pennsylvania

**7277 Dresher Hill Health and Rehabilitation Center**
1390 Camp Hill Rd
Dresher, PA 19034-2805
215-643-0600
FAX: 215-641-0628
e-mail: dresherhill@extendicare.com?subject=Dresher%2
www.dresherhillskillednurs ing.com

*Earl Kimble, Administrator*
Subacute rehabilitation facility and programs: physical/speech.

**7278 Good Shepherd Rehabilitation**
850 S 5th St
Allentown, PA 18103-3295
610-776-3586
888-447-3422
FAX: 610-776-8336
e-mail: info@goodshepherdrehab.org
goodshepherdrehab.org

*Sally Gammon, President & CEO*
*Mike Bonner, MBA, Vice President, Neurosciences*
*Daniel C. Confalone, FHFMA, Senior Vice President, Finance & Chief Financial Officer*
*Joe Hess, MSA, NHA, Administrator, Good Shepherd Home-Bethlehem*

A world class rehabilitation network, Good Shepherd provides comprehensive inpatient and outpatient services throughout Pennsylvania's Lehigh Valley. Founded in 1908, Good Shepherd has steadily expanded over last 95 years. Good Shepherd is one of the most comprehensive rehabilitation institutes in the worlld.

**7279 Statesman Health and Rehabilitation Center**
2629 Trenton Rd
Levittown, PA 19056-1428
215-943-7777
FAX: 215-943-1240
e-mail: statesman@extendicare.com?subject=Statesman%2
www.statesmanskillednursin g.com

*Jamie Tanner, Administrator*

Subacute rehabilitation facility and programs.

**7280 UPMC Braddock**
400 Holland Ave
Braddock, PA 15104-1598
412-351-0131
FAX: 412-636-5398
upmc.com

*Mark Sevco, Administrator*
*Rodney Jones, Vice President*

With a team of more then 43,000 employees, UPMC serves the health needs of more then 4 million people each year, improving lives in western Pennsylvania-and beyond-through redefined models of health care delivery and superb clinical outcomes.

**7281 UPMC McKeesport**
Presby
1500 5th Ave
McKeesport, PA 15132-2422
412-664-2000
1 8-0 5-3 UP
FAX: 412-664-2309
e-mail: fisherpj@upmc.edu
http://mckeesport.upmc.com

*Ronald H Ott, CEO*

Offers 56 beds for patients who need skilled nursing care. Offers ongoing rehabilitation and educational programs to patients with cardiac, neurologic, and orthopaedic diagnosis.

**7282 UPMC Passavant**
9100 Babcock Blvd
Pittsburgh, PA 15237-5842
412-367-6700
800-533-8762
e-mail: gloordc@ph.upmc.edu
http://passavant.upmc.com

*William Kristan, Dir Inpatient Physical Therapy*
*Teresa Petrick, Chief Executive Officer*

Patients who have had an acute illness, injury, or exacerbation of a disease and no longer need the intensity of services in the acute care setting, but still require some complex medical care or supervision and rehabilitation services, may be appropriate to be transferred into the Subacute Unit.

## Rhode Island

**7283 Kindred Heights Nursing & Rehabilitation Center**
Kindred Healthcare
100 Wampanoag Trl
Riverside, RI 02915-3736
401-438-4275
800-745-6575
FAX: 401-438-8093
www.kindredheights.com

*Sandra Sarza, Manager*
*Jean Aubin, Director*

Kindred Heights Nursing and Rehabilitation Center accomodates 58 residents and serves the needs of elders in the greater East Bay and Providence area. We are conveniently located on Wampanoag Trail in East Providence. Kindred Heights provides skilled nursing, short-term rehab and long-term care in a family environment, but we are large enough to manage the complex nursing and rehab care needs our residents may have.

**7284 Oak Hill Nursing and Rehabilitation Center**
Kindered Health Care
544 Pleasant St
Pawtucket, RI 02860-5776
401-725-8888
800-745-6575
FAX: 401-723-5720
e-mail: HSDED1231@kindredhealthcare.com?subject=Websi
www.oakhillrehab.com

*Scott M. Sandborn, Executive Director*
*Heidi Capela, Director Nursing*
*Amybeth Almeida, Director Admissions*
*Aman Nanda, Medical Director*

Accomodates 143 residents. Throughout our 40 year history, Oak Hill has developed a reputation as one of the finest healthcare centers in Rhode Island. Our center consists of 3 separate units. A 34-bed post-acute unit provides care to the medically complex and those in need of extensive rehabilitative services. A 20-bed Alzheimer's Special Care Unit provides a unique style of care utilizing habilitative therapy in comfortable, home-like surroundings.

**7285 Southern New England Rehab Center**
200 High Service Avenue
North Providence, RI 02904
401-456-3801
888-456-4501
FAX: 401-456-3784
snerc.com

*Vivian Hagstrom, Manager*

The Center's skilled staff of over 100 professionals provides a full range of coordinated rehabilitative care. Our clinical expertise and compassion make a big difference as we develop first-rate plans of care for the unique needs of each patient. Our medical staff is comprised of physicians board-certified in rehabilitation medicine and internal medicine.

## South Carolina

**7286 Tuomey Healthcare System**
129 N Washington St
Sumter, SC 29150-4949
803-774-9000
FAX: 803-774-8737
www.tuomey.com

*R Jay Cox, CEO*

Here to anticipte the needs of the communities we serve, responding with proactive healthcare initiatives, providing expert rehabilitative services and delivering life-saving acute care.

## Tennessee

**7287 Camden Healthcare and Rehabilitation Center**
197 Hospital Dr
Camden, TN 38320-1617
731-584-3500
FAX: 731-584-2753
kindredhealthcare.com

*Mark Walker, Administrator*
Subacute rehabilitation products and services, nursing and life care homes.

**7288 Centennial Medical Center Tri Star Health System**
2300 Patterson St
Nashville, TN 37203-1538
615-342-1000
800-242-5662
FAX: 615-342-1045
e-mail: Laurel.Haskamp@HCAHealthcare.com
www.centennialmedicalcenter.com

*Thomas L Herron, President/Chief Executive Officer*
Above all else we are committed to the care and improvement of human life by caring for those we serve with integrity, compassion, a positive attitude, respect and exceptional quality.

**7289 Cordova Rehabilitation and Nursing Center**
955 N Germantown Pkwy
Cordova, TN 38018-6215
901-754-1393
800-848-0299
FAX: 901-754-3332
www.cordovahealthcare.com

*John Palmer, Administrator*
*Renee Tutor, Executive Director*
Our professional staff can help you make an informed decision. Upon admission, our interdisciplinary team develops a comprehensive care plan to meet not only physical and rehabilitative goals, but also social and emotional needs. We understand the importance of family and resident involvement and encourage participation in the development of a personalized plan of care.

**7290 Erlanger Medical Center Baronness Campus**
975 E 3rd St
Chattanooga, TN 37403-2147
423-778-7000
FAX: 423-778-7615
e-mail: Mickey.milita@erlanger.org
www.erlanger.org

*Charlesetta Woodard-Thompson, CEO*
*Ronald A. Loving, Chair*
*James D. Hutcherson, Vice Chair*
*Kim H. White, Secretary*
Our mission is to improve the health of the people we touch. Our vision is to be recognized locally, regionally, and and nationally, as a premiere healthcare system.

**7291 Huntington Health and Rehabilitation Center**
635 High St
Huntingdon, TN 38344-1703
731-986-8943
FAX: 731-986-3188
e-mail: w.summers@huntingdonhealth.com
huntingdonhealth.com

*Heidi Hawkins, Administrator*
*Windi Summers, Admissions Director*
Subacute rehabilitation facility and programs.

**7292 Madison Healthcare and Rehabilitation Center**
431 Larkin Springs Rd
Madison, TN 37115-5005
615-865-8520
800-848-0299
FAX: 615-868-4455
kindredhealthcare.com

*Phyllis Cherry, Executive Director*
Madison Healthcare and Rehabilitation Center accomodates 102 residents. We are certified for Medicare and located near 2 major hospitals in the Madison area. We provide inpatient and outpatient therapies with a concentration on inpatient treatments. We have a proven success rate- we discharge approximately one third of our patients home or to an increased level of care (IE assisted living).

**7293 Mariner Health of Nashville**
3939 Hillsboro Cir
Nashville, TN 37215-2708
615-297-2100
FAX: 615-297-2197

*David Reeves, Administrator*
*Amy Artrip, Director of Nursing*
Religious nonmedical health care institution. 150-bed subacute rehabilitation facility

**7294 Pine Meadows Healthcare and Rehabilitation Center**
700 Nuckolls Rd
Bolivar, TN 38008-1531
731-658-4707
FAX: 731-658-4769
e-mail: s.mckeen@pinemeadowshc.com
www.pinemeadowshc.com

*Larry Shrader, Administrator*
*Sharon McKeen, Admissions Director*
Our goal is to take care of your loved ones. Our professional team works with skilled hands, is directed by creative minds and is guided by compassionate hearts. Upon your admission, our interdisciplinary team develops a comprehensive care plan designed with a goal of meeting not only physical and rehabilitative objectives, but also social and emotional needs. We understand the importance of family and resident involvement and encourage participation in the development of a plan of care.

**7295 Primacy Healthcare and Rehabilitation Center**
Kindred Health Care
6025 Primacy Pkwy
Memphis, TN 38119-5763
901-767-1040
800-848-0299
FAX: 901-685-7362
e-mail: HSDED0822@kindredhealthcare.com?subject=Websi
www.primacyrehab.com

*Donnie Dubert, Executive Director*
*Dr. Mark Hammond, Medical Director*
*Kristen W., Health and Rehabilitation Center Executive Director*
*Becky D., Activity Director*
Upon a resident's admission, our interdisciplinary team develops a comprehensive care plan with a goal of meeting not only physical and rehabilitative objectives but also social and emotional needs. We understand the importance of family and resident involvement and encourage participation in the development of a personalized plan of care.

**7296 Ripley Healthcare and Rehabilitation Center**
118 Halliburton St
Ripley, TN 38063-2011
731-635-5180
FAX: 731-635-0663
e-mail: j.hodge@ripleyhc.com
www.ripleyhc.com

*Johnny Rea, Executive Director*
*Brandon Whiteside, Executive Director*
*Jan Hodge, Admissions Directo*
*Jennifer Pitts, Administrator*
Upon admission, our interdisciplinary team develops a comprehensive care plan to meet not only physical and rehabilitative goals, but also social and emotional needs. We understand the importance of family and resident involvement and encourage participation in the development of a personalized care plan. Our goal is to take care of your loved ones.

**7297 Shelby Pines Rehabilitation and Healthcare Center**
3909 Covington Pike
Memphis, TN 38135-2281
901-377-1011
FAX: 901-377-0032

*Rene Tutor, Executive Director*
Subacute rehabiltation facility and programs.

**7298 Siskin Hospital for Physical Rehabilitation**
1 Siskin Plz
Chattanooga, TN 37403-1306
423-634-1200
FAX: 423-634-4538
TTY:423-634-1201
e-mail: info@siskinrehab.org
siskinrehab.org

*Robert Main, CEO*
*Lindsay Wyatt, Media Coordinator, Marketing Communications*
Dedicated exclusively to physical rehabilitation and offers specialized treatment programs in brain injury, amputation, stroke, spinal cord injury, orthopeadics, and major multiple trauma.

## Texas

**7299 North Hills Hospital**
4401 Booth Calloway Rd
North Richland Hills, TX 76180-7399
817-255-1000
FAX: 817-255-1991
northhillshospital.com

*Randy Moresi, CEO*
North Hills Hospital's services include a wide range of cardiovascular services, surgical services, emergency services, radiology, a rehabilitation unit, a senior health center, therapy services, and women's services.

**7300 Valley Regional Medical Center**
100 E Alton Gloor Blvd
Brownsville, TX 78526-3328
956-350-7000
FAX: 956-350-7111
valleyregionalmedicalcenter.com

*David Handley, CEO*
*Francisco Javier Del Castillo, MD*
*Subramaniam Anandasivam, MD*
*Christopher Olson, MD*
Above all else, we are committed to the care and improvement of human life. In recognition of this committment, we strive to deliver high quality, cost effective healthcare in the communities we serve. In persuit of our mission, we recognize and affirm the unique and intrinsic worth of each individual. We treat all those we serve with compassion and kindness. We act with absolute honesty and integrity and fairness in the way we conduct our business and the way we live our lives.

## Utah

**7301 Crosslands Rehabilitation and Healthcare Center**
575 E 11000 S
Sandy, UT 84070-5326
801-571-7600
800-346-4128
FAX: 801-571-4875
e-mail: HSDED0230@kindredhealthcare.com?subject=Websi
www.crosslandsrehab.com

*John Williams, Executive Director*
*Lyle Black, Manager*
Crossroads Rehabilitation and Healthcare accomodates 120 residents. We are fully Medicare and Medicaid certified. We are proud of our reputation for providing quality, compassionate care. Services availiable include in-house physical, occupational and speech therapies, as well as 24-hour licensed nursing staff coverage. We offer therapeutic recreation, in-house social services and registered dietician services, among many other professional services.

**7302 Federal Heights Rehabilitation and Nursing Center**
Kindred Health Care
41 South Ninth East
Salt Lake City, UT 84102-1306
801-532-3539
800-346-4128
FAX: 801-328-3926
e-mail: HSDED0655@kindredhealthcare.com?subject=Websi
www.federalheightsrehab.co m

*Pete Zeigler, Executive Director*
*Dr. Charles Canfield, Medical Director*
Federal Heights accomodates 120 residents. We are located near three major hospitals in the Salt Lake Valley. We specialize in providing nursing services for complex medical and rehabilitation conditions. Our discharge planning works jointly with the family and resident in determining the future needs and goals upon discharge.

**7303 St. George Care and Rehabilitation Center**
Kindred Health Care Publications
1032 E 100 S
Saint George, UT 84770-3005
435-628-0488
800-346-4128
FAX: 435-628-7362
e-mail: HSDED0247@kindredhealthcare.com?subject=Websi
www.stgeorgecare.com

*John Larson, Plant Manager*
*Erin Hammon, Director of Nursing*
*Derrick Glum, Executive Director*
St. George Care and Rehabilitation accomodates 95 residents. We offer a 4,000 square foot rehabilitation gym with an indoor therapy pool for inpatient and outpatient services. Therapy is provided to meet specific needs seven days a week. There is a dietitian on staff for individualized nutritional needs. We offer an Alzheimer's unit with specialized staff. We provide compassionate health services including physicians, nurses, physical therapists, and occupational therapist and licensed aides.

**7304 St. Mark's Hospital**
1200 E 3900 S
Salt Lake City, UT 84124-1390
801-268-7111
FAX: 801-270-3489
www.stmarkshospital.com

*Steve B. Bateman, CEO*
Above all else we are committed to the care and improvement of human life. In recognition of this commitment, we strive to deliver high quality, cost effective healthcare in the communities we serve. We define quality as 'caring people with the commitment to a continuous process of improvement in the services provided, that will better enable the hospital to meet or exceed our customer's needs and expectations.

**7305 Wasatch Valley Rehabilitation**
Kindred Healthcare
2200 E 3300 S
Salt Lake City, UT 84109-2635
801-486-2096
800-346-4128
FAX: 801-484-3443
kindredhealthcare.com

*Alex Stevenson, Executive Director*
*Ric Toomer, Executive Director*
Wasatch Valley accomodates 110 residents. We are licensed for Medicare and Medicaid and we are conveniently located in the heart of Salt Lake City with easy access from I-15 and I-215. We are known by the area hospitals as a specialist in wound care and for the care we provide to those with complex medical conditions.

## Virginia

**7306 Nansemond Pointe Rehabilitation and Healthcare Center**
200 Constance Rd
Suffolk, VA 23434-4960
757-539-8744
800-828-1140
FAX: 757-539-6128
e-mail: HSDED0825@kindredhealthcare.com?subject=Websi
www.nansemondhc.com

*Mel Epelle, Executive Director*
*Mary R, Activities Assistant*
*Kristen W., Health and Rehabilitation Center Executive Director*
*Becky D., Activity Director*
Nansemond Pointe Rehabilitation and Healthcare Center accomodates 160 residents in private and semi-private rooms. We have been serving the needs of Suffolk, Virginia and the surrounding areas for over 38 years. We offer an entire continuum of care from assisted living apartments to skilled nursing to long-term care. Our licensed therapists, working with our dedicated nursing staff, share a common goal- to help our residents improve their level of recovery and independence.

**7307 Rehabilitation and Research Center Virginia Commonwealth University**
1250 East Marshall Street
Richmond, VA 23298-661
804-828-9000
FAX: 804-828-5074
e-mail: beagle@hsc.vcu.edu
www.rrc.pmr.vcu.edu

*Michael Rao, Ph.D., VCU President & VCUHS President, VCUHS Authority Board Chair*
*Sheldon M. Retchin, M.D., VP Health Sciences & CEO, VCUHS*
*John Duval, Chief Executive Officer MCV Hospitals, VCUHS*
*Dominic J. Puleo, Executive VP Finance and CFO, VCUHS*
The Rehabilitation and Research Center is a collaborative effort between the Department of Physical Medicine and Rehabilitation and the Medical College of Virginia Hospitals. The goals of the Rehabilitation and Research Center at the Medical College of Virginia Hospitals (MCVH) are to provide highly-skilled, interdisciplinary, inpatient rehabilitative care to adults with complex needs; to be an advocate and educator for patients and people with disabilities.

**7308 Warren Memorial Hospital**
1000 N Shenandoah Ave
Front Royal, VA 22630-3598
540-636-0300
FAX: 540-636-0258
e-mail: complaint@jointcommission.org
www.valleyhealthlink.com

*Patrick B. Nolan, CEO*
*Mark H. Merrill, President & Chief Executive Officer*
*Craig Lewis, Senior Vice President & Chief Financial Officer*
*Joan Roscoe, Vice President of Information Systems & Chief Information Officer*
A nonprofit organization of health care providers, Valley Health offers a full spectrum of services in acute care, rehabilitation and extended care facilities, and outpatient and community settings to help the people of the region manage their health and enjoy a high quality of life. Valley Health has the resources to diagnose, treat and help patients manage virtually any medical problem that may be encountered.

**7309 Winchester Rehabilitation Center**
333 W Cork St
Winchester, VA 22601-3870
540-536-5115
800-382-0772
FAX: 540-536-1122
e-mail: wwilliam@valleyhealthlink.com
www.valleyhealthlink.com

*Patrick B. Nolan, CEO*
*Mark H. Merrill, President & Chief Executive Officer*
*Craig Lewis, Senior Vice President & Chief Financial Officer*
*Joan Roscoe, Vice President of Information Systems & Chief Information Officer*
Offers the following rehabilitation services: Sub-Acute inpatient rehabilitation, Speech therapy, Physical therapy, Occupational therapy, Disability evaluations. 30-bed inpatient center.

## Washington

**7310 Aldercrest Health and Rehabilitation Center**
21400 72nd Ave W
Edmonds, WA 98026-7702
425-775-1961
FAX: 425-771-0116

*Rick Milsow, Administrator*
Subacute rehabilitation facility and programs.

**7311 Arden Rehabilitation and Healthcare Center**
16357 Aurora Ave N
Seattle, WA 98133-5651
206-542-3103
800-833-6384
FAX: 206-542-7192
e-mail: HSDED0114@kindredhealthcare.com?subject=Websi
www.ardenrehab.com

*Matthew Preston, Administrator*
*Ann Zell, Executive Director*
*Kristen W., Health and Rehabilitation Center Executive Director*
*Becky D., Activity Director*
Arden Rehabilitation has been an integral part of the Shoreline community since 1953. It is a one-level building set on mature grounds with several beautiful courtyards for the residents to enjoy. Arden can accomodate 90 residents-post acute/rehabilitation patients as well as long-term residents. Medicare certified, the center also takes most managed healthcare insurance plans, as well as VA, respite and hospice patients. Arden is well known for its rehabilitative and nursing care and wound care

**7312 Bellingham Health Care and Rehabilitation Services**
1200 Birchwood Ave
Bellingham, WA 98225-1302
360-734-9295
800-833-6384
FAX: 360-671-4368
e-mail: HSDED0158@kindredhealthcare.com?subject=Websi
www.bellinghamhc.com

*Melissa Nelson, Executive Director*
*Dr. Richard McClenahan, Medical Director*
*Kristen W., Health and Rehabilitation Center Executive Director*
*Becky D., Activity Director*
At Bellingham Health Care and Rehab, we strive to provide quality, compassionate care. Our cozy building accomodates 84 residents. Our smaller size creates an inviting and homelike environment for your loved one. We offer semi-private rooms with space to add items from home for a special personalized touch. Provides meals served restaurant style in our dinning room overlooking our beautiful grounds.

**7313 Bremerton Convalescent and Rehabilitation Center**
2701 Clare Ave
Bremerton, WA 98310-3313
360-377-3951
FAX: 360-377-5443

*Stephanie Bonanzino, Administrator*
Subacute rehabilitation facility and programs.

**7314 Edmonds Rehabilitation & Healthcare Centerer**
Kindred Healthcare
21008 76th Ave W
Edmonds, WA 98026-7104
425-778-0107
800-833-6384
FAX: 425-776-9532
www.edmondsrehab.com

*Jane Davis, Executive Director*

At Edmonds Rehabilitation and Healthcare, we strive to provide quality, compassionate care. Our center accomodates 91 residents. Our smaller size creates an inviting and homelike environment. We offer semi-private rooms with space to add items from home for a special personalized touch. Edmonds Rehabilitation and Healthcare provides delicious meals served restaurant style in our dinning room.

**7315 Heritage Health and Rehabilitation Center**
Kindred Health Care
3605 Y St
Vancouver, WA 98663-2647
360-693-5839
800-833-6384
FAX: 360-693-3991
www.heritagerehab.com

*Michael Moses, Executive Director*
*Su Patchett, Director of Nursing*

Heritage Health & Rehabilitation Center is the smallest free-standing healthcare center in southwest Washington with accomodations of 49, enabling more personal care and a more home-like environment. Heritage has licensed nursing staff, restorative aides, and certified nurses assistants, trained and experienced in providing Alzheimer's care, end of life/hospice care, psychiatric care, rehabilitative care, and respite care.

**7316 North Auburn Rehabilitation And Health Center**
2830 i St NE
Auburn, WA 98002-2410
253-854-4142
800-395-5000
FAX: 253-735-5159
extendicare.com

*Allyson Jenkins, Administrator*

Subacute rehabilitation facility and programs.

**7317 Northwoods Lodge**
2321 NW Schold Pl
Silverdale, WA 98383-9504
360-698-3930
FAX: 360-692-2169
e-mail: mhalverson@encorecommunities.com
www.encorecommunities.com

*Leslie Krueger, Owner*
*Debbie Griffin, Director of Rehab Services*

Provides you with a full-range of services from weekly housekeeping and laudry services, to grounds keeping and maintenance. Our monthy fee inculdes utilities and hot, delicious, nutritious meals served table side every day. We offer transportation services, full-time activities directors, and numerous amenities to add to your comfort and enjoyment.

**7318 Pacific Specialty & Rehabilitation Center r**
1015 N Garrison Rd
Vancouver, WA 98664-1313
360-694-7501
FAX: 360-694-8148
www.pacificskillednursing.com

*Rebecca Pruett, Administrator*

Subacute rehabilitation facility and programs.

**7319 Puget Sound Healthcare Center**
4001 Capitol Mall Dr SW
Olympia, WA 98502-8657
360-754-9792
FAX: 360-754-2455
e-mail: pugetsound@extendicare.com?subject=Puget%20So
www.pugetsoundskillednursi ng.com

*Sheila Oberg, Administrator*

Our goal is to provide excellence in patient care, veteran's benefits and customer satisfaction. We have reformed our department internally and are striving for high quality, prompt and seamless service to veterans. Our department employees continue to offer their dedication and commitment to help veterans get the services they have earned.

**7320 Vancouver Health & Rhabilitation Center**
400 E 33rd St
Vancouver, WA 98663-2238
360-696-2561
800-833-6384
FAX: 360-696-9275
e-mail: HSDED0180@kindredhealthcare.com?subject=Websi
http://www.vancouverhealth care.com

*Jody Wigen, Human Resources*
*Joe Joy, Executive Director*
*Kristen W., Health and Rehabilitation Center Executive Director*
*Becky D., Activity Director*

At Vancouver Health and Rehab Center we strive to provide quality, compassionate care. Our cozy building accomodates 98 residents. Our smaller size creates an inviting and homelike environment. We offer semi-private rooms with space to add items from home for a special personalized touch. Provides delicious meals served restaurant style in our dining room.

## West Virginia

**7321 War Memorial Hospital**
1 Healthy Way
Berkeley Springs, WV 25411-1743
304-258-1234
FAX: 304-258-5618
www.valleyhealthlink.com/War

*Neil R. McLaughlin, President*
*Christine Lowman, Vice President and CFO*
*Gerald Béchamps, M.D., Vice President of Medical Affairs*
*Gena Swisher, Vice President of Nursing*

Offers physical therapy, occupational therapy, speech therapy, social services, and patient/family education for individuals who have experienced a recent physical disability due to disease, dysfunction, or general debilitation. Helps patients to maximize their abilities through activities of daily living, mobility, self-medication, and self-care and restore their ability to return to their previous lifestyle.

## Wisconsin

**7322 Cedar Spring Health and Rehabilitation Center**
N27w5707 Lincoln Blvd
Cedarburg, WI 53012-2852
262-376-7676
FAX: 262-375-8161

*Mary Wirth, Executive Director*

Subacute rehabilitation facility and programs.

**7323 Clearview-Brain Injury Center**
198 Home Rd
Juneau, WI 53039-1401
920-386-3400
877-386-3400
FAX: 920-386-3800
e-mail: lbertagnoli@co.dodge.wi.us
co.dodge.wi.us/clearview

*Jane E. Hooper, Administrator*
*Jacqueline Kuhl, Household Coordinator*
*Laura Bertagnoli*
*Kathy Lorenz, AFH Manager*

A 30-bed, state certified, subacute neuro-rehabilitation program in Juneau, WI. We are located just 45 minutes northeast of Madison WI and 10 minutes east of Beaver Dam, WI. We are the first and longest standing of only 2 community re-entry programs in the state of Wisconsin providing subacute neuro-rehabilitation to teens and adults who have experienced a brain injury.

**7324 Colonial Manor Medical and Rehabilitation Center**
1010 E Wausau Ave
Wausau, WI 54403-3101 715-842-2028
800-947-6644
FAX: 715-848-0510
e-mail: HSDED0766@kindredhealthcare.com?subject=Websi
www.colonialmanormrc.com

*Ericca Ylitalo, Administrator*
*Shelley Solberg, Executive Director*
*Kristen W., Health and Rehabilitation Center Executive Director*
*Becky D., Activity Director*
Colonial Manor Medical and Rehabilitation Center is part of the Kindred Community and is located in Wausau, Wisconsin. The corporate headquarters are based in Louisville Kentucky. Our facility accomodates 150 residents.

**7325 Eastview Medical and Rehabilitation Center**
729 Park St
Antigo, WI 54409-2745 715-623-2356
800-947-6644
FAX: 715-623-6345
e-mail: HSDED0765@kindredhealthcare.com?subject=Websi
www.eastviewmedrehab.com

*Wanda Hose, Administrator*
*Wanda Hose, Executive Director*
*Kristen W., Health and Rehabilitation Center Executive Director*
*Becky D., Activity Director*
Eastview Medical Center and Rehabilitation Center accomodates 165 residents. We are Medicare and Medicaid certified, as well as being Joint Commission accredited. Our 'TEAM' approach means specially trained staff work around the clock to assist in meeting rehabilitative goals established by our team of professionals. We encourage family involvement in our rehabilitative process. The support of loved ones is a major key to a speedy recovery.

**7326 Hospitality Nursing Rehabilitation Center**
8633 32nd Ave
Kenosha, WI 53142-5187 262-694-8300
FAX: 262-694-3622
e-mail: hospitality@extendicare.com?subject=Hospitali
http://www.hospitalityskil lednursing.com/

*Marla Benson, Administrator*
*LaRae Nelson, President*
*Lisa Behling, Secretary*
*Scott Miller, Treasurer*
Subacute rehabilitation facility and programs.

**7327 Kennedy Park Medical Rehabilitation Center**
Kindred Healthcare
6001 Alderson St
Schofield, WI 54476-3614 715-359-4257
800-947-6644
FAX: 715-355-4867
e-mail: HSDED0771@kindredhealthcare.com?subject=Websi
www.kpmrc.com

*Judy Kowalski, Manager*
*Jim Torgerson, Executive Director*
*Kristen W., Health and Rehabilitation Center Executive Director*
*Becky D., Activity Director*
Kennedy Park Medical & Rehabilitation Center accomodates 154 residents. We are located in Schofield, WI. At Kennedy Park, we specialize in dementia care, with our Reflections and Passages Units. Short-term rehabilitation and sub-acute care are provided in a setting conducive to meeting the individual needs of our residents and patients. We also provide general nursing care for persons with long-term care needs.

**7328 Middleton Village Nursing & Rehabilitation**
Kindred
6201 Elmwood Ave
Middleton, WI 53562-3319 608-831-8300
800-947-6644
FAX: 608-831-4253
e-mail: HSDED1216@kindredhealthcare.com?subject=Websi
www.middletonvillage.com

*Nicholas Stamatas, Manager*
*Ashley Ostrowski, Executive Director*
*Kristen W., Health and Rehabilitation Center Executive Director*
*Becky D., Activity Director*
Middleton Village accomodates 97 residents. We specialize in post-surgical and post-acute rehabilitation and long-term care services.

**7329 Mount Carmel Health & Rehabilitation Center**
5700 W Layton Ave
Milwaukee, WI 53220-4099 414-281-7200
FAX: 414-281-4620
e-mail: HSDED0774@kindredhealthcare.com?subject=Websi
http://www.milwaukeemtcarm el.com

*Mike Berry, Administrator*
*Darrin Hull, Executive Director*
*Kristen W., Health and Rehabilitation Center Executive Director*
*Becky D., Activity Director*
Subacute rehabilitation facility and programs. The name of the company is ""Kindred Transitional Care and Rehabilitation - Milwaukee""

**7330 Mount Carmel Medical and Rehabilitation Center**
677 E State St
Burlington, WI 53105-1639 262-763-9531
800-947-6644
FAX: 262-763-7579
kindredhealthcare.com

*Randy Nitschke, Administrator*
*Jeanne Piccioni, Executive Director*
Mount Carmel Medical and Rehabilitation Center accomodates 155 residents. We are located in Burlington Wisconsin. Mount Carmel Medical and Rehabilitation center is a 2005 recipient of the American Health Care Association Quality Award.

**7331 North Ridge Medical and Rehabilitation Center**
1445 N 7th St
Manitowoc, WI 54220-2011 920-682-0314
800-947-6644
FAX: 920-682-0553
www.nmrc.com

*Jane Conway, Interim ED*
North Ridge Medical and Rehabiliation Center accomodates 110 residents. We have been serving the Manitowoc, Wisconsin area for over 25 years. Our goal is to provide services in a warm, homey environment. Many of our staff in all departments have a long history with North Ridge and have worked here for more then 20 years. We also take pride in the fact that we have all in-house staff. Our therapy team is availiable to provide physical, occupational and speech therapy 7 days a week.

**7332 Oshkosh Medical and Rehabilitation Center**
1580 Bowen St
Oshkosh, WI 54901 920-426-5520
FAX: 920-426-5252

*Tom Wagner, President*
Subacute rehabilitation facility and programs.

7333 **San Luis Medical and Rehabilitation Center**
2305 San Luis Pl
Green Bay, WI 54304-5211
920-494-5231
800-947-6644
FAX: 920-494-1958
e-mail: HSDED0289@kindredhealthcare.com?subject=Websi
www.sanluismedrehab.com

*Heather Dreier, Administrator*
*Tim Dietzen, Executive Director*
*Dr. John T. Warren, Medical Director*
*Kristen W., Health and Rehabilitation Center Executive Director*

San Luis Medical and Rehabilitation Center accomodates 126 residents. We are located in Green bay, WI. At San Luis, we strive to meet the needs of our residents and we specialize in dementia care, with our Reflections Unit. Our goal is to provide short-term rehabilitation and sub-acute care in a setting conducive to assisting the needs of our residents.

7334 **Strawberry Lane Nursing & Rehabilitation Center**
130 Strawberry Lane
Wisconsin Rapids, WI 54494-2156
715-424-1600
FAX: 715-424-4817
www.strawberrylanenursing.com

*Mary Schweitzer, Administrator*

Skilled nursing facility that provides both long term and short term care. Offer Alzheimer's and Dementia care units, as well as Hospice Care. Medicare and Medicaid certified.

## Wyoming

7335 **Mountain Towers Healthcare & Rehabilitation Center**
3128 Boxelder Dr
Cheyenne, WY 82001-5808
307-634-7901
800-877-9975
FAX: 307-634-7910
e-mail: HSDED0441@kindredhealthcare.com?subject=Websi
www.mttowersrehab.com

*Dan Stackis, Administrator*
*Toni Wyenn, Director of Nursing*
*Daniel G. Stackis, Executive Director*
*Dr. Kent Britton, Medical Director*

Mountain Towers Healthcare and Rehabilitation Center accomodates 170 residents, including a 16-bed acute secure unit. We offer a full range of nursing and medical care to meet individual needs. We have a full staff to meet the needs of our residents.

7336 **South Central Wyoming Healthcare and Rehabilitation**
Kindred Healthcare
542 16th St
Rawlins, WY 82301-5241
307-324-2759
800-877-9975
FAX: 307-324-7579
e-mail: HSDED0481@kindredhealthcare.com?subject=Websi
www.scwhr.com

*Chris Tanner, Executive Director*
*Anthony Janusz, Administrator*
*Kristen W., Health and Rehabilitation Center Executive Director*
*Becky D., Activity Director*

South Central Wyoming Healthcare and Rehabilitation accomodates 52 residents. We are located in Rawlings, in south central Wyoming. We are Medicare and Medicaid certified by the State of Wyoming. We strive to provide quality personal services, long-term care or short-term rehabilitation to our residents in a comfortable home-like environment.

7337 **Wind River Healthcare and Rehabilitation Center**
Kindred Health Care
1002 Forest Dr
Riverton, WY 82501-2918
307-856-9471
800-877-9975
FAX: 307-856-1665
e-mail: HSDED0482@kindredhealthcare.com?subject=Websi
www.windriverhealthcare.co m

*Jo Ann Aldrich, Executive Director*
*Amelia Asay, Business Office Manager*
*Kristen W., Health and Rehabilitation Center Executive Director*
*Becky D., Activity Director*

Offers a full range of medical services to meet the individual needs of our residents, including short-term rehabilitative services and long-term skilled care. Working with the residents physician, our staff-including medical specialists, nurses, nutritionists, dietitians and social workers-establishes a comprehensive treatment plan intended to restore you or your loved one to the highest practicable potential.

# Aging

## Associations

**7338 Aging Services of California**
1315 I St
Ste 100
Sacramento, CA 95814-2915
916-392-5111
FAX: 916-428-4250
e-mail: aburnsjohnson@aging.org
aging.org

*Joanne Handy, President/CEO*
*Linda McGuire, Director of Operations*
*Rick Taylor, Director of Communications*
*Cassie Bangerter, Controller*

The California Association of Homes and Services for the Aging (CAHSA) is the primary statewide association for not-for-profit organizations providing health care, housing and community services to older adults.

**7339 Aging Services of Michigan**
6512 Centurion Drive
Suite 380
Lansing, MI 48917
517-323-3687
FAX: 517-323-4569
e-mail: david@agingMI.org
www.agingmi.org

*David Herbel, President & CEO*
*Deanna Ludlow Mitchell, Senior Vice President for Performance and Education*
*Sheri Deisler, CMP, Vice President of Business Development*
*Stephanie Shooks Winslow, Vice President for Government Strategy*

Aging Services of Michigan represents and promotes the common interests of its members through leadership, advocacy, education and other services in order to enhance members' ability to serve their constituencies.

**7340 Aging Services of South Carolina**
2711 Middleburg Dr
Ste 309A
Columbia, SC 29204-2413
803-988-0005
FAX: 803-988-1017
e-mail: vmoody@agingservices.org
www.agingservices.org

*Vickie Moody, President/CEO*

Aging Services of South Carolina represents not-for-profit organizations dedicated to providing high-quality health care, housing and services to the seniors of South Carolina.

**7341 Aging Services of Washington**
1495 Wilmington Driv
Ste 340
Dupont, WA 98327-8773
253-964-8870
FAX: 253-964-8876
e-mail: info@leadingagewa.org
www.agingwa.org

*Deb Murphy, CEO*
*Heather Skinner, COO*

Washington Association of Housing and Services for the Aging (WASHA) is the state association serving primarily not-for-profit organizations dedicated to providing quality housing, health, community and related services to older persons.

**7342 Aging in America**
1000 Pelham Pkwy South
Bronx, NY 10461-1198
718-824-4004
877-244-6469
FAX: 718-824-4242
e-mail: admissiondept@aiamsh.org
www.aginginamerica.org

*William T Smith, President/CEO*

Research and services organization for professionals in gerontology. Objectives are: to produce, implement and share effective and affordable programs and services that improve the quality of life for the elderly community; to better prepare professionals and students interested in or currently involved with, aging and the aged. Conducts research projects, educational and training seminars, and in-service curricula for long-term and acute care facilities.

**7343 American Association of Homes and Servicesfor the Aging**
2519 Connecticut Ave NW
Washington, DC 20008-1520
202-783-2242
FAX: 202-783-2255
e-mail: info@LeadingAge.org
aahsa.org

*William L Minnix Jr, President/CEO*
*Katrinka Smith Sloan, Chief Operating Officer and Senior Vice President*
*Robyn I. Stone, Senior Vice President of Research*
*Cheryl Phillips, Senior Vice President, Public Policy and Advocacy*

The American Association of Homes and Services for the Aging (AAHS) represents not-for-profit organizations dedicated to providing high-quality health care, housing and services to the nation's elderly. AAHSA organizations serve more than one million older persons af all income levels, creeds and races.

**7344 American Association of Retired Persons**
601 E St NW
Washington, DC 20049-2
800-687-2277
TTY:877-434-7589
e-mail: member@aarp.org
www.aarp.org

*A Barry Rand, President/CEO*
*Hop ', Executive Vice President, State Operations.*
*Steve Cone, Executive Vice President of Integrated Value and Strategy*
*Lorraine Cortés-Vázquez, Executive Vice President, Multicultural Markets and Engagement*

A nonprofit membership organization of persons 50 and older dedicated to addressing their needs and interests.

**7345 Arizona Association of Homes and Housing for the Aging**
3877 N 7th St
Ste 240
Phoenix, AZ 85014
602-230-0026
FAX: 602-230-0563
e-mail: azaha@azaha.org
www.azaha.org

*Genny Rose, Executive Director*
*Jon Scott Williams, Chair*

The Arizona Association of Homes and Houses for the Aging is a not-for-profit trade association representing more than 100 facilities dedicated to providing quality health care, housing and services to over 12,000 elderly Arizona citizens. AzAHA is the only association in Arizona representing the full continuum of long term care, housing and services including: retirement communities, HUD subsidized senior housing, assisted living and nursing facilities.

**7346 Association of Ohio Philanthropic Homes, Housing and Services for the Aging**
855 S Wall St
Columbus, OH 43206-1921
614-444-2882
FAX: 614-444-2974
e-mail: info@aopha.org
aopha.org

*John Alfano, CEO*
Founded in 1937, AOPHA, the advocate of not-for-profit services for older Ohioans, is a statewide nonprofit trade association representing over 335 not-for-profit senior housing apartments, home and community-based service providers, assisted living facilities, nursing homes and continuing care retirement communities (CCRCs).

**7347 Children of Aging Parents**
PO Box 167
Richboro, PA 18954-167
215-945-6900
800-227-7294
FAX: 215-945-8720
e-mail: info@caps4caregivers.org
www.caps4caregivers.org

*Karen Rosenberg, Director*
A national clearinghouse for caregivers of the elderly. It provides information and referral, educational programs and materials and caregiver support groups. CAPS also produces a quarterly newsletter which is available through the organization. Individuals: $25.00. Organizational/Professional: $100.00.

**7348 Colorado Association of Homes and Services for the Aging**
303 E. 17th Ave.
Suite 502
Denver, CO 80203-1160
303-837-8834
FAX: 303-837-8836
e-mail: Jennifer@LeadingAgeColorado.org
www.cahsa.org

*Laura Landwirth, Executive Director*
*Michael Meehan, Secretary*
*Dan Stenersen, Treasurer*
*Jennifer Stone, Member Services Manager*
The American Association of Homes and Services for the Aging (AAHS) represents nonprofit organizations dedicated to providing high quality health care, housing and services to the nation's elderly. AAHSA organizations serve more than one million older persons af all income levels, creeds and races.

**7349 Connecticut Association of Not-for-Profit Providers for the Aging**
1340 Worthington Rdg
Berlin, CT 6037-3208
860-828-2903
FAX: 860-828-8694
e-mail: leadingagect@leadingagect.org

*Mag Morelli, President*
*Nurka Carrero, Office Manager*
*Andrea Bellofiore, Director of Member Programs & Services*
*Beth Ricker, Finance Manager & Membership Director*
CANPFA promotes a vision of the world in which every community offers an integrated and coordinated continuum of high quality, affordable health care, housing and community based services. CANPFA members are all mission-driven, not-for-profits. Not-for-profits focus on caring and providing services for their residents and clients. They re-invest their income into their facilities, resident programs and staff development. They are rooted in their communities.

**7350 Georgia Association of Homes and Services for the Aging**
1440 Dutch Valley PL NE
STE 120
Atlanta, GA 30324-5367
404-872-9191
FAX: 404-872-1737
e-mail: selahi@leadingagega.org
centerforpositiveaging.org

*Walter Coffey, President & C.E.O.*
*Susan Watkins, Dir. of Member Services*
*Jacque Thornton, Sr. Vice President*
The Georgia Association of Homes and Services for the Aging (GAHSA) is an affiliated partner of the American Association of Homes and Services of the Aging (AASHA), which represents over 5,600 nonprofit facilities, over one million older adults in the United States and maintains an impressive staff of 80 professionals at its headquarters in Washington, D.C.

**7351 Gulf States Association of Homes and Services for the Aging**
PO Box 1748
Marrero, LA 70073-1748
504-442-0483
FAX: 504-689-3982
e-mail: kcontrenchis@gulfstatesahsa.org
gulfstatesahsa.org

*Karen Contrenchis, President*
*Cindy Ladnier, Chair*
*Dennis Adams, Vice-Chair*
*Scott Crabtree, Secretary/Treasurer*
Along term care system which offers accessable, affordable, high-quality and innovative healthcare, housing and comminuty services. Provides value to the the senior population and their families through personal and professional commitment, in a compassionate manner, supported by benevolence and integrity. Socially resposible and accountable for promoting excellence in long-term care and support services.

**7352 Indiana Association of Homes and Services for the Aging**
PO Box 68829
Indianapolis, IN 46268-0829
317-733-2380
FAX: 317-733-2385
e-mail: jimleich@LeadingAgeIndiana.org
iahsa.com

*Jim Leich, President*
*Susan Darwent, Vice President of Operations*
*Kathy Johnson, RN, WCC, Vice President of Clinical & Regulatory Services*
*Emilie Perkins, Director of Special Events and Training*
Indiana Association of Homes and Services for the Aging (IAHSA) members are non-profit organizations, providing hgh quality health care, services and housing for over 25,000 seniors in Indiana.

**7353 Iowa Association of Homes and Services forthe Aging**
1701 48th St
Ste 203
West Des Moines, IA 50266-6723
515-440-4630
888-440-4630
FAX: 515-440-4631
e-mail: info@leadingageiowa.org
www.ageiowa.org

*Dana Petrowsky, President/CEO*
*Bill Nutty, Director of Government Relations & Member Services*
*Kathy Strang, Director of Professional Development*
*Dawn Balder, Event Coordinator/Administrative Assistant*
IAHSA inspires leadership and benevolence in its members through networking education, information and advocacy.

**7354 Kentucky Association of Homes and Services for the Aging**
2501 Nelson Miller Pkwy
Suite 200
Louisville, KY 40223- 2221 502-992-4380
FAX: 502-992-4390
e-mail: info@leadingageky.org
kahsa.com

*Timothy Veno, President*
Founded in 1977, the association represents not-for-profit community, church, proprietary and govt. sponsored health care facilities, retirement communities, assisted living, housing and service programs for the elderly and disabled. The mission of the (KAHSA)is to provide services to the members that will enchance the quality of life of those they serve.

**7355 Life Services Network of Illinois**
1001 Warrenville Rd
Ste 150
Lisle, IL 60532 630-325-6170
FAX: 630-325-0749
e-mail: info@lsni.org
www.lsni.org

*Christopher Laxton, President*
*Betty Morrell, Office Manager*
*Jean Elliott, Associate Vice President*
*Kelly Hohman, Executive Assistant*
For nearly 75 years, Life Services Network of Illinois, a statewide trade association, has represented providers of the complete contiuum of services for older adults, including nursing facilities, assisted living, senior housing and home and community based services. Our success as an association is founded in our commitment to helping our members overcome obstacles while identifying future opportunities for their success.

**7356 LifeSpan Network: Maryland**
10280 Old Columbia Road
Suite 220
Columbia, MD 21046- 2382 410-381-1176
FAX: 410-381-0240
e-mail: www.lifespan-network.org
www.mantha.org

*Isabella Firth, President*
Senior care provider association representing more than 300 senior care provider organizations in Maryland and the District of Columbia. Lifespan members include non-profit and proprietary independent living, continuing care retirement communities, nursing facilities, subsidized senior housing and community and hospital based services. Also provide education, advocacy and products and services, as well as networking for our members.

**7357 Massachusetts Aging Services Association**
180 Wells Ave
Ste 105
Newton, MA 02459-3328 617-244-2999
FAX: 617-244-2995
e-mail: office@LeadingAgeMA.org
www.massaging.org

*Elissa Sherman, President*
*Sue Pouliot, Director of Education and Events*
*Don Powell, Director of Member Services*
*Lisa Miano, Officer Manager*
The Massachusetts Aging Services Association (MassAging) is the only Massachusetts membership association representing the full continuum of not-for-profit providers of aging services. MassAging works to achieve a system of healthy, affordable, and ethical aging services for older persons in Massachusetts. MassAging is proudly affiliated with the American Association of Homes and Services for the Aging (AAHSA), a national associaton of not-for-profit homes and services for he aging.

**7358 Missouri Association of Homes for the Aging**
3412 Knipp Dr
Ste 102
Jefferson City, MO 65109 573-635-6244
FAX: 573-635-6618
e-mail: diana@moaha.org
www.moaha.org

*Denise Clemonds, CEO*
*Diana Love*
*Patricia Hubbs*
Founded in 1969 and devoted to furthering the interests of the continuum of long term care, including skilled nursing facilities, health related facilities, residential care facilities, independent housing facilities, HUD facilities and other community based services.

**7359 National Association of Area Agencies on Aging**
1730 Rhode Island Ave NW
Ste 1200
Washington, DC 20036- 3109 202-872-0888
FAX: 202-872-0057
e-mail: smarkwood@n4a.org
n4a.org

*Sandra Markwood, CEO*
*Nick Beamer, President*
*Joseph Ruby, 1st Vice President*
*Jaklyn DeVore, 2nd Vice President*
National Association of the Area Agencies on Aging is the umbrella organization for the 655 area agencies on aging. Advocates on behalf of the local aging agencies to ensure that needed resources and support services are available to older Americans. The fundamental mission of the AAAs and Title VI programs is to provide services which make it possible for older individuals to remain in their home, thereby preserving their independence and dignity.

**7360 National Association of Counties**
25 Massachusetts Ave NW, Ste 500
Washington, DC 20001-1430 202-393-6226
888-407-6226
888-407-6226
FAX: 202-393-2630
naco.org

*Larry Naake, CEO*
NACO represents elected officials and aging administrators who are interested in providing quality programs to their older constituents. NACO members work with Congress, the Administration on Aging, and other federal agencies to ensure that the nationa maintains an effective and efficient safety net of services for the elderly and their families.

**7361 National Association of Nutrition and Aging Services Programs**
1612 K St NW
Ste 400
Washington, DC 20006-2829 202-682-6899
FAX: 202-223-2099
e-mail: pcarlson@nanasp.com
www.nanasp.org

*Robert Blancato, Executive Director*
*Shannon Donahue, Associate*
*Pamela (Pam) Carlson, Membership & Education*
*Scott Carlson, Finance & Operations*
A national membership organization for persons across the country working to provide older adults healthful food and nutrition through community-based services.

**7362 National Association of State Units on Aging**
1201 15th St NW
Ste 350
Washington, DC 20005-2842
202-898-2578
FAX: 202-898-2583
e-mail: info@nasuad.org
www.nasuad.org

*Martha Roherty, Executive Director*
*Lance Robertson, President*
*Gloria Lawlah, Vice President*
*James Bulot, Secretary*

A non-profit association representing the nation's 56 officially designated state and territorial agencies on aging. The mission of the Association is to advance social, health, and economic policies responsive to the needs of a diverse aging population and to enhance the capacity of its membershup to promote the rights, dignity and independence of, and expand opportunities and resources for, current and future generations of older persons, adults with disabilities and their families.

**7363 National Council on Aging**
1901 L St NW
4th Fl
Washington, DC 20036-3540
202-479-1200
FAX: 202-479-0735
TTY:202-479-6674
e-mail: membership@ncoa.org
www.ncoa.org

*James P Firman, EdD, President/CEO*
*Jay Robertson, Senior Vice President*
*Richard Birkel, PhD, MPA, Acting Senior Vice President, Center for Healthy Aging and Director, S*
*Nora Dowd Eisenhower, JD, Acting Senior Vice President, Economic Security and Director, National*

A non-profit organization with a national network of more than 14,000 organizations and leaders. Our members include senior centers, area agencies on aging, adult day service centers, faith-based service organizations, senior housing facilities, employment services, consumer groups, and leaders from academia, business and labor. Our programs help older people remain healthy and independent, find jobs, increase access to benefits programs, and discover meaningful ways to contribute to society.

**7364 National Hispanic Council on Aging**
734 15th St NW
Ste 1050
Washington, DC 20005-1038
202-347-9733
FAX: 202-347-9735
e-mail: nhcoa@nhcoa.org
www.nhcoa.org

*Yanira Cruz, DrPH, President/CEO*
*Eric Rodriguez, Director*
*Bárbara Robles, PhD, Director*
*John Feather, M.A., PhD, Director*

NHCOA focuses on the following program priorities: health promotion and disease prevention, financial security and civic engagement, policy, leadership development, education and housing. Its policy priorities include addressing health disparities, promoting economic security, ensuring availability of affordable and elder accessible housing, and building stronger and more cohesive communities through provision of technical support and financial assistance to community-based organizations.

**7365 National Indian Council on Aging**
10501 Montgomery Blvd NE
Ste 210
Albuquerque, NM 87111- 3851
505-292-2001
FAX: 505-292-1922
e-mail: info@nicoa.org
www.nicoa.org

*Randella Bluehoose, Executive Director*
*Dorinda Fox, SCSEP Director*
*Jonnie Gilbert, Finance Director*
*Darrell Begay, Arizona Central Employment Specialist*

A non-profit organization, was founded by members of the National Tribal Chairmen's Association that called for a national organization to advocate for improved, comprehensive health and social services to American Indian and Alaska Native Elders.

**7366 National Senior Citizens Law Center**
1444 Eye Street
NW Suite 1100
Washington, DC 20005-6547
202-289-6976
FAX: 202-289-7224
e-mail: nsclc@nsclc.org
www.nsclc.org

*Paul Nathanson, Executive Director*
*Kevin Prindiville, Deputy Director*
*Noris Weiss Malvey, Development Director*
*Scott Parkin, Communications Director*

The National Senior Citizens Law Center advocates before the courts, Congress and federal agencies to promote the independence and well-being of low-income elderly and disabled Americans.

**7367 Nebraska Association of Homes and Services for the Aging**
900 North 90th Street
#940
Omaha, NE 68114
402-990-2346
e-mail: kaminskij@leadingagene.org
www.nebahsa.org

*Julie Kaminski, Executive Director*

Serves the needs of the Nebraska's not-for-profit facilities and services for our state's elderly with representation and advocacy, educational and professional development, shared services and programs, and statewide leadership.

**7368 New Jersey Association of Homes and Services for the Aging**
13 Roszel Rd
Ste C200
Princeton, NJ 08540-6211
609-452-1161
FAX: 609-452-2907
e-mail: mkent@leadingagenj.org
http://www.leadingagenj.org/

*Michele M. Kent, President/CEO*
*Amy S. Greenbaum, Director of Professional Development*
*Darlene Arden, Administrative Assistant*
*Diane Borgstrom, Bookkeeper*

The New Jersey Association of Homes and Services for the Aging (NJAHSA) is the statewide association of not-for-profit organizations which are dedicated to providing and enhancing quality of life services to the diverse aging population. The Association encourages cooperaton with communities and ther entities, both public and private, interested in aging.

**7369 New York Association of Homes and Services for the Aging**
13 British American Blvd
Suite 2
Latham, NY 12110-1431
518-867-8383
e-mail: info@leadingageny.org
www.nyahsa.org

*James W. Clyne Jr., President/CEO*
*Dan Heim, Executive VP*
*Denise Mitchell Alper, Executive VP*
*Nancy Caban, Executive Assistant*

NYAHSA is a statewide organization of socially responsible, community-benefit organizations dedicated to providing high quality health care, housing, and community services to the elderly and people with special needs.

**7370 North Carolina Association of Non-Profit Homes for the Aging**
100 Carolina Meadows
Chapel Hill, NC 27517
919-571-8333
FAX: 919-571-1297
e-mail: info@leadingagenc.org
www.ncanpha.org

*Tom Akins, President/CEO*
*Leslie Roseboro, Vice President*
*Anne Moffat, Chair*
*Kevin McLeod, Chair Elect*

The North Carolina Association of Non-Profit Homes for the Aging (NCANPHA) is the state association of not-for-profit providers dedicated to providing quality health care, housing, health, community and related services to the elderly.

**7371 Northern New England Association of Homes and Services for the Aging**
PO Box 339
New Gretna, NJ 08224-0339
603-391-9881
FAX: 603-391-9881
e-mail: rgoedtel@leadingagemenh.org
http://www.agingservicesmenh.org/

*Kathryn Callnan, Director*
*Maureen Carland, Director*
*Bonnie Cohen, Director*
*Timothy Martin, Director*

NNEAHSA's mission is to promote the interests of its not-for-profit members in Maine, New Hampshire, and Vermont which provide healthy, affordable and ethical long-term care to our older citizens through education, advocacy, representation and collaboration.

**7372 Oklahoma Association of Homes and Services for the Aging**
PO Box 1383
El Reno, OK 73036-1383
405-640-8040
e-mail: info@leadingageok.org
www.okahsa.org

*Mary Brinkley, Executive Director*
*Jessica Pfau, President*
*Lindsay Fick, Secretary*
*Jim O'Brien, Treasurer*

The Oklahoma Association of Homes and Services for the Aging is the Oklahoma state association of not-for-profit organizations dedicated to establishing the highest standards of excellence for services to the aging in Oklanhoma. OKAHSA's purpose is to be supportive of each member organization's quest for excellence.

**7373 Oregon Alliance of Senior and Health Services**
7340 SW Hunziker St
Ste 104
Tigard, OR 97223-2303
503-684-3788
FAX: 503-624-0870
e-mail: info@leadingageoregon.org
oashs.org

*Ruth Gulyas, Executive Director*
*Margaret Cervenka, Deputy Director*
*Karen Nichols, Manager of Membership Services and Resident Programs*
*Denise Wetzel, Administrative Coordinator and Bookkeeper*

The Oregon Alliance of Senior & Health Services is the state association of not-for-profit, mission-directed organizations dedicated to providing quality housing, health, community and related services to the elderly and disabled.

**7374 Pennsylvania Association of Nonprofit Senior Services**
1100 Bent Creek Blvd
Mechanicsburg, PA 17050-1872
717-763-5724
800-545-2270
FAX: 717-763-1057
e-mail: info@leadingagepa.org
www.panpha.org

*Ronald L Barth, President/CEO*
*Jennifer Chornak, Executive Assistant*
*Heidi Geist, Communications Manager*
*Beth Greenberg, Regulatory Affairs & Research Manager*

PANPHA represents over 320 nonprofit providers of long-term care and housing services for 65,000 elderly residents across Pennsylvania. The Association is committed to helping its members provide quality care efficiently and effectively for the individuals and families they serve. In the age of impersonal care, PANPHA members put people before profits.

**7375 Quality Healthcare Foundation of Wyoming**
6909 Foxglove Drive
Cheyenne, WY 82009
307-287-4594
800-773-2273
FAX: 307-638-8472
e-mail: steve@qhcf.org
www.qhcf.org

*Steve Bahmer, Executive Director*
*Eric Boley, President*
*Sandy Ward, Vice President*
*Jill Hult, Secretary/Treasurer*

The American Association of Homes and Services for the Aging (AAHS) represents not-for-profit organizations dedicated to providing high-quality health care, housing and services to the nation's elderly. AAHSA organizations serve more than one million older persons af all income levels, creeds and races.

**7376 Rhode Island Association of Facilities and Services for the Aging**
225 Chapman St
2nd Floor
Providence, RI 02905-4533
401-490-7612
866-883-1631
FAX: 401-490-7614
TTY: 401-383-6578
e-mail: info@leadingageri.org
www.riafsa.org

*James P Nyberg, Director*
*Cindy Conant-Arp, President*
*Matt Trimble, Vice-President*
*Sandra Cullen, Treasurer*

RIAFSA was formally organized in 1989 as an associaton of non-profit facilities and services primarily for the elderly. RIAFSA members include senior housing, assisted living, nursing homes and home and community based services.

**7377 Tennessee Association of Homes and Services for the Aging**
500 Interstate Blvd S
Ste 325
Nashville, TN 37210-4634
615-256-8240
FAX: 615-242-4803
e-mail: webmaster@tha.com
www.tha.com

*Craig Becker, President*
*Mary Layne Van Cleave, Executive Vice President, Chief Operating Officer*
*Tammy Kemp, Senior Executive Assistant*
*Donna Owen, Senior Executive Assistant*

TNAHSA is an association of faclities and professionals providing quality housing, health, community and related services for the elderly. TNAHSA represents and promotes the common interest of its members through leadership, advocacy, education, communication and other services in order to enhance members' ability to serve their constituencies.

**7378 Texas Association of Homes and Services for the Aging**
2205 Hancock Dr
Austin, TX 78756-2508
512-467-2242
FAX: 512-467-2275
e-mail: info@leadingagetexas.org
www.tahsa.org

*George Linial, President/CEO*
*David Thomason, Senior VP of Advocacy & Public Policy*
*Crystal Laza, Director of Operations & Membership Services*
*Claire Morris, Director of Education*
The American Association of Homes and Services for the Aging (AAHS) represents not-for-profit organizations dedicated to providing high-quality health care, housing and services to the nation's elderly. AAHSA organizations serve more than one million older persons af all income levels, creeds and races.

**7379 Wisconsin Association of Homes and Services for the Aging**
204 S Hamilton St
Madison, WI 53703-3212
608-255-7060
FAX: 608-255-7064
e-mail: info@LeadingAgeWI.org
wahsa.org

*John Sauer, President/CEO*
*Pam Walker, Executive Secretary*
*Sarah Paterson, Member Services Assistant*
*Janice Mashak, Vice President of Member Services & Innovation*
The Wisconsin Association of Homes and Services for the Aging (WAHSA) is a statewide membership organization of not-for-profit corporations principally serving the elderly and disabled.

## Print: Books

**7380 Activities in Action**
Routledge
270 Madison Ave
Fl 4 #4
New York, NY 10016-0601
212-695-6599
800-634-7064
FAX: 212-563-2269
e-mail: www.routledgementalhealth.com/contact/
www.routledgementalhealth.com

*Jeffrey Lim, Director*
*Francis Chua, Manager*
*Tamaryn Anderson, Marketing Manager*
An invaluable resource which serves as a catalyst for professional and personal growth and provides a national forum on geriatric and activity issues. *$30.00*
*116 pages Hardcover*
*ISBN 1-560241-32-4*

**7381 Activities with Developmentally Disabled Elderly and Older Adults**
Routledge
270 Madison Ave
Fl 4 #4
New York, NY 10016-601
212-695-6599
800-637-7064
FAX: 212-563-2269
e-mail: www.routledgementalhealth.com/contact/
www.routledgementalhealth.com

*Jeffrey Lim, Director*
*Francis Chua, Manager*
*Tamaryn Anderson, Marketing Manager*
Learn how to effectively plan and deliver activities for a growing number of older people with developmental disabilities. It aims to stimulate interest and continued support for recreation program development and implementation among developmental disability and aging service systems. *$42.00*
*164 pages Hardcover*
*ISBN 1-560241-74-4*

**7382 Aging and Developmental Disability: Current Research, Programming, and Practice**
Routledge
270 Madison Ave
Fl 4 #4
New York, NY 10016-601
212-695-6599
800-634-7064
FAX: 212-563-2269
e-mail: www.routledgementalhealth.com/contact/
www.routledgementalhealth.com

*Joy Hammel, Author*
*Susan Nochajski, Co-Author*
Explores research findings and their implications for practice in relation to normative and disability-related aging experiences and issues. It discusses the effectiveness of specific intervention targeted toward aging adults with developmental disabilities such as Down's Syndrome, cerebral palsy, autism, and epilepsy, and offers suggestions for practice and future research in this area. *$48.00*
*112 pages Hardcover*
*ISBN 0-789010-39-1*

**7383 Aging and Family Therapy: Practitioner Perspectives on Golden Pond**
Routledge
270 Madison Ave
Fl 4 #4
New York, NY 10016-601
212-695-6599
800-634-7064
FAX: 212-563-2269
e-mail: www.routledgementalhealth.com/contact/
www.routledgementalhealth.com

*George Hughston, Author*
*Victor Christopherson, Co-Author*
*Marilyn Bojean, Co-Author*
Here are creative strategies for use in therapy with older adults and their families. This significant new book provides practitioners with information, insight, reference tools, and other sources that will contribute to more effective intervention with the elderly and their families. *$48.00*
*260 pages Hardcover*
*ISBN 0-866567-78-7*

**7384 Aging in Stride**
IllumínAge Communications Partners
2200 1st Ave South
Suite 400
Seattle, WA 98134-1408
206-269-6363
888-620-8816
FAX: 206-269-6350
e-mail: www.cobaltgroup.com/contact/
www.cobaltgroup.com

*Dennis Kenny, Owner*
*Elizabeth N Oettinger, Co-Author*
*Dennis E Kenny JD, Co-Author*
Guide to aging, the special needs of older adults, and the demands of providing care and support. Experts explain potential conflicts, planning opportunities and strategies for success. Six guides. *$24.95*
*Paperback*

**7385 Aging in the Designed Environment**
Routledge
270 Madison Ave
Fl 4 #4
New York, NY 10016-601
212-216-7800
800-634-7064
FAX: 212-563-2269
www.routledgementalhealth.com

*Margaret Christenson, Author*
*Ellen D Taira, Co-Author*

The key sourcebook for physical and occupational therapists developing and implementing environmental designs for the aging. *$30.00*
*146 pages Hardcover*
*ISBN 1-560240-31-0*

**7386 Aging with a Disability**
Special Needs Project
1405 Anderson Lane
Santa Barbara, CA 93111-2946
805-962-8087
800-333-6867
FAX: 805-962-5087
www.specialneeds.com

*Hod Gray, Owner*
*Laura Mosqueda, Co-Author*
This unique and recent book discusses the role of family, financial resources and the American health care system in the life of aging adults with developmental disabilities. *$24.95*
*328 pages Paperback*

**7387 Assistive Technology and Older Adults**
121 West Sweet Ave
Moscow, ID 83843
208-885-6097
800-432-8324
FAX: 208-885-6145
e-mail: sueh@uidaho.edu
www.educ.uidaho.edu/idatech

*Ron Seiler, Project Director*
The Idaho Assistive Technology Project (IATP) is a federally funded program administered by the Center on Disabilities and Human Development at the University of Idaho. IATPO's goal is to increase the availability of assistive technology devices and services for older persons and Idahoians with disabilities.

**7388 Caring for Those You Love: A Guide to Compassionate Care for the Aged**
Horizon Publishers & Distributors
191 N 650 E
Bountiful, UT 84010-3628
801-295-9451
866-818-6277
FAX: 801-298-1305
www.duanescrowther.com

*Duane S. Crowther, Author/President*
*Jean Crowther, Vice President/Sec*
*David Crowther, Vice President*
This book is a practical guide to coping with special problems of the aged and infirm, and examines the many challenges of caring for the elderly on a personal and family level. *$12.98*
*108 pages*
*ISBN 0-882902-70-9*

**7389 Chronically Disabled Elderly in Society**
Greenwood Publishing Group
88 Post Rd W
Westport, CT 06880-4208
203-226-3571
800-225-5800
FAX: 877-231-6980
e-mail: customer-service@greenwood.com
www.greenwood.com

*Merna J Alpert, Author*
*Lisa Scott, President*
*Herman Bruggink, CEO*
This timely work increases awareness of and knowledge about problems of societal living among the chronically disabled elderly, with implications for policy makers, educational institutions, advocacy groups, families and individuals. *$76.95*
*160 pages Hardcover*
*ISBN 0-313291-09-8*

**7390 Coping and Caring: Living with Alzheimer's Disease**
AARP Fulfillment
601 E St NW
Washington, DC 20049-2
800-687-2277
TTY:877-434-7589
e-mail: member@aarp.org
www.aarp.org

*Charles Leroux, Author*
*Hop ', Executive Vice President, State Operations.*
*Steve Cone, Executive Vice President of Integrated Value and Strategy*
*Lorraine Cortés-Vázquez, Executive Vice President, Multicultural Markets and Engagement*
Addresses the questions: What is Alzheimer's? How does the disease progress? How long does it last? How can families cope?
*24 pages*

**7391 Elder Abuse and Mistreatment**
Routledge
270 Madison Ave
Fl 4 #4
New York, NY 10016-601
212-695-6599
800-634-7064
FAX: 212-563-2269
e-mail: www.routledgementalhealth.com/contact/
www.routledgementalhealth.com

*Joanna Mellor, Author*
*Patricia Brownell, Co-Author*
Practice, policy and laws for abuse on the aging. *$ 120.00*
*284 pages Paperback*
*ISBN 0-789030-22-1*

**7392 Explore Your Options**
Kansas Department on Aging
503 S Kansas Ave
New England Building
Topeka, KS 66603- 3404
785-296-4986
800-432-3535
FAX: 785-296-0256
TTY: 785-291-3167
e-mail: www.agingkansas.org/kdoa/contact.htm
www.agingKansas.org

*Maria Russo, President*
This book will help you through the maze of services available to Kansas seniors. It is designed to help you take an active role in making decisions that affect your health care and living situation.

**7393 Falling in Old Age**
Springer Publishing Company
11 W 42nd St
Fl 15 #15
New York, NY 10036-8002
212-431-4370
877-687-7476
FAX: 212-941-7842
e-mail: cs@springerpub.com
www.springerjournals.com

*Ursula Springer, President*
*Ted Nardin, CEO*
*Edie Lambiase, CFO*
Presented are practical techniques for the prevention of falls and for determining and correcting the causes. *$60.00*
*412 pages Hardcover*
*ISBN 0-826152-91-6*

**7394 Family Intervention Guide to Mental Illness**
New Harbinger Publications
5674 Shattuck Ave
Oakland, CA 94609-1662 510-652-0215
800-748-6273
FAX: 510-652-5472
e-mail: customerservice@newharbinger.com
www.newharbinger.com

*Matthew McKay, Owner*
*Kim T Mueser, Co-Author*
*Kirk Johnson, CFO*
*Bodie Morey, Co-Author*
This book helps readers understand, identify, and assist family members or close loved ones who suffer from the early signs of mental illness. It offers nine fundamental techniques for recognizing, managing, and recovering from mental illness. *$17.95*
*240 pages*
*ISBN 1-572245-06-8*

**7395 Handbook of Assistive Devices for the Handicapped Elderly**
Routledge
270 Madison Ave
Fl 4 #4
New York, NY 10016-601 212-695-6599
800-634-7064
FAX: 212-563-2269
www.routledgementalhealth.com

*Joseph A Breuer, Author*
*Jeffrey Lin, Director*
*Francis Chua, Manager*
*Tamaryn Anderson, Marketing Manager*
Concise yet comprehensive reference of assistive devices for handicapped elders. *$42.00*
*77 pages Hardcover*
*ISBN 0-866561-52-5*

**7396 Handbook on Ethnicity, Aging and Mental Health**
Greenwood Publishing Group
88 Post Rd W
Westport, CT 6880-4208 203-226-3571
800-225-5800
FAX: 877-231-6980
e-mail: customer-service@greenwood.com
www.greenwood.com

*Deborah K Padgett, Author*
*Lisa Scott, President*
*Herman Bruggink, CEO*
State-of-the-art reference by leading experts and first book-length appraisal of research, practices and policies concerning mental health needs of the ethnic elderly in America. *$141.95*
*376 pages Hardcover*
*ISBN 0-313282-04-8*

**7397 Health Care of the Aged: Needs, Policies, and Services**
Routledge
270 Madison Ave
Fl 4 #4
New York, NY 10016-601 212-695-6599
800-634-7064
FAX: 212-563-2269
www.routledgementalhealth.com

*Abraham Monk, Author*
*Jeffrey Lim, Director*
*Francis Chua, Manager*
*Tamaryn Anderson, Marketing Manager*
Focusing on the need for developing new service delivery models for the aged, this book examines fiscal, political, and social criteria influencing this challenge of the 1990's. The aged are caught in the sweeping changes currently occurring in the financing, organizing and delivery of human health care services. *$36.00*
*800 pages Hardcover*
*ISBN 1-560240-65-5*

**7398 Health Promotion and Disease Prevention in Clinical Practice**
Lippincott, Williams & Wilkins
530 Walnut St
Philadelphia, PA 19106-3603 215-521-8300
800-638-3030
FAX: 215-521-8902
e-mail: customerservice@lww.com.
www.lww.com

*Karl Durst, Manager*
*Steven Jonas MD MPH MS FNYAS, Co-Author*
*Evonne Kaplan-Liss, Co-Author*
*Rick Perry, CEO*
Professional directory offering information on health care and rehabilitation for the elderly. *$52.95*
*218 pages Softcover*
*ISBN 0-781775-99-1*

**7399 Life Planning for Adults with Developmental Disabilities**
New Harbinger Publications
5674 Shattuck Ave
Oakland, CA 94609-1662 510-652-0215
800-748-6273
FAX: 510-652-5472
e-mail: customerservice@newharbinger.com
www.newharbinger.com

*Matthew McKay, Publisher*
*Kirk Johnson, CFO*
A much-needed resource for parents, family, and caregivers of adults with developmental disabilities like downs syndrome, fragile x, and autism, this book offers resources and planning tools for helping developmentally disabled adults build skills in employment, education, relationships, independant living, and finances. *$19.95*
*208 pages*
*ISBN 1-572244-51-1*

**7400 Long-Term Care: How to Plan and Pay for It**
NOLO
950 Parker St
Berkeley, CA 94710-2524 510-549-1976
800-728-3555
FAX: 800-645-0895
www.nolo.com

*Joseph L Matthews, Author*
*Ralph Warner, Chariman/CEO*
*Ann Heron, COO*
*Bob Dubow, CFO*
This book helps you choose a nursing home, or find a viable alternative. Covers how to get the most out of Medicare and other benefit programs.
*384 pages Paperback*
*ISBN 1-413305-21-0*

**7401 Mentally Impaired Elderly: Strategies and Interventions to Maintain Function**
Routledge
270 Madison Ave
Fl 4 #4
New York, NY 10016-601 212-695-6599
800-634-7064
FAX: 212-653-2269
www.routledgementalhealth.com

*Ellen D Taira, Author*
*Jeffrey Lim, Director*
*Francis Chua, Manager*
*Tamaryn Anderson, Marketing Manager*
Provides effective support and sensitive care for the most vulnerable segment of the elderly population, those with mental impairment. *$34.00*
*171 pages Hardcover*
*ISBN 1-560241-68-3*

7402 **Mirrored Lives: Aging Children and Elderly Parents**
Praeger Publishers
88 Post Rd W
Westport, CT 06880-4208
203-226-3571
800-225-5800
FAX: 877-231-6980
e-mail: customer-service@greenwood.com
www.greenwood.com

*Tom Koch, Author*
*Lisa Scott, President*
*Herman Bruggink, CEO*
Discusses geriatric decline connected to nonterminal illness in old age. Koch takes a sensitive but thorough look at the declining years of his father. *$117.95*
*240 pages Hardcover*
*ISBN 0-275936-71-6*

7403 **Physical & Mental Issues in Aging Sourcebook**
Omnigraphics
155 W Congree St
Suite 200 #200
Detroit, MI 48226-3261
313-961-1340
800-234-1340
FAX: 313-961-1383
e-mail: info@omnigraphics.com
www.omnigraphics.com

*Jennifer Swanson, Editor*
*Frederic Ruffner, Chairman*
*Kay Gill, Vice President*
*Laurie Harris, Manager*
Basic information about maintaining health through the post-reproductive years. Includes stats, recommendations for lifestyle modifications, a glossary and resrouce information *$84.00*
*660 pages Hard cover*
*ISBN 0-780802-33-9*

7404 **Prescriptions for Independence: Working with Older People Who are Visually Impaired**
American Foundation for the Blind/AFB Press
11 Penn Plz
Suite 300 #300
New York, NY 10001-2006
212-502-7600
800-232-3044
FAX: 212-502-7777
e-mail: afborder@abdintl.com
www.afb.org

*Carl Augusto, President*
*Gerda Groff, Co-Author*
*Richard Obnen, Chairman Of The Board*
*Alan Lindroth, Principal*
Easy-to-read manual on how older visually impaired persons can pursue their interests and activities in community residences, senior centers, long-term care facilities and other community settings. Paperback.
*99 pages Paperback*
*ISBN 0-891282-44-0*

7405 **Sharing the Burden**
Brookings Institution
1775 Massachusetts Ave NW
Washington, DC 20036-2188
202-797-6000
FAX: 202-797-6004
www.brookings.edu

*Joshua N Weiner, Author*
*Laurel Hixon Illston, Co-Author*
*Raymond J Hanley, Co-Author*
*Strobe Talbott, President*
Financial information for the elderly. *$42.95*
*342 pages Cloth*
*ISBN 0-815793-78-2*

7406 **Social Security, Medicare, and Government Pensions**
NOLO
950 Parker St
Berkeley, CA 94710-2524
510-549-1976
800-728-3555
FAX: 800-645-0895
www.nolo.com

*Joseph L Matthews, Author*
*Dorothy Matthews Berman, Co-Author*
*Ralph Warner, Chairman/CEO*
*Ann Heron, COO*
A plain-speaking guide explaining the ins and outs of the Social Security system; retirement, disability and benefits for dependents and survivors. *$24.95*
*480 pages Paperback*
*ISBN 1-413307-53-5*

7407 **Successful Models of Community Long Term Care Services for the Elderly**
Routledge
270 Madison Ave
Fl 4 #4
New York, NY 10016-601
212-695-6599
800-637-7064
FAX: 212-563-2269
www.routledgementalhealth.com

*Eloise Killeffer, Author*
*Ruth Bennett, Co-Author*
*Jeffrey Lim, Director*
*Francis Chua, Manager*
Experienced practitioners provide examples of successful community-based long term care service programs for the elderly. *$ 72.00*
*174 pages Hardcover*
*ISBN 0-866569-87-3*

7408 **Therapeutic Activities with Persons Disabled by Alzheimer's Disease**
Sage Publications
804 Anacapa Stree
Sanat Barbara, CA 93101-2212
805-899-8620
e-mail: info@sagepub.com
www.sagepub.com

*Sara Miller McCune, Founder, Publisher, Chairperson*
*Blaise Simqu, CEO*
*Tracey Ozmina, COO*
*Stephen Barr, Managing Director*
A program of functional skills for activities of daily living. Hardcover. *$86.00*
*432 pages*
*ISBN 0-834211-62-9*

7409 **Visually Impaired Seniors as Senior Companions: A Reference Guide**
American Foundation for the Blind/AFB Press
11 Penn Plz
Suite 300 #300
New York, NY 10001-2006
212-502-7600
800-232-3044
FAX: 212-502-7777
e-mail: afborders@abdintl.com
www.afb.org

*Carl Augusto, President*
*Alan Lindroth, Principal*
*Richard Obnen, Chairman Of The Board*
*Michael Gilliam, Vice Chairman*
This useful guide describes the Senior Companion Program that is intended to broaden opportunities for older persons with disabilities. Appendix includes training materials, evaluation forms, recruitment and public relations information. *$15.00*
*108 pages Paperback*
*ISBN 0-891282-38-6*

**7410 Work, Health and Income Among the Elderly**
Brookings Institution
1775 Massachusetts Ave NW
Washington, DC 20036-2188
202-797-6000
FAX: 202-797-6004
www.brookings.edu

*Gary Burtless, Author*
*Strobe Talbott, President*
*Steven Bennett, Vice President/COO*
*Stewart Uretsky, Vice President/CFO*
Employment, health and financial information for the elderly.
*$26.95*
*276 pages Cloth*
*ISBN 0-815711-76-6*

## Print: Journals

**7411 Gerontology: Abstracts in Social Gerontology**
National Council on the Aging
1901 L St NW
4th Floor
Washington, DC 20036-3506
202-479-1200
FAX: 202-479-0735
TTY:202-479-6674
e-mail: info@ncoa.org
www.ncoa.org

*Austin Han, Manager*
*James Firman, President/CEO*
*Donna Whitt, SVP/CFO*
Detailed abstracts are provided for recent major journal articles, books, reports and other materials on many facets of aging, including: adult education, demography, family relations, institutional care and work attitudes. Item No. AB100; Journals $114.00; Member Discount: $94.00.
*Quarterly*

**7412 Physical & Occupational Therapy in Geriatrics**
Taylor & Francis Group, LLC
325 Chestnut Street
Suite 800 #800
Philadelphia, PA 19106-2608
215-625-8900
800-354-1420
FAX: 215-625-2940
e-mail: haworthpress@taylorandfrancis.com
www.haworthpress.com

*Ellen Dunleavey Taira, Editor*
*Barbara Pucher, CFO*
Focuses on current practices and emerging issues in the care of the older client, including long-term care in institutional and community settings, crisis intervention, and innovative programming; the entire range of problems experienced by the elderly; and the current skills needed for working with older clients.
*$99.00*
*Quarterly*

## Print: Magazines

**7413 AARP Magazine**
American Association of Retired Persons
601 E St NW
Washington, DC 20049-3
202-434-7700
888-687-2277
FAX: 202-434-7710
aarp.org

*Barry Rand, CEO*
*Philip Zarlengo, Chairman*
*Gail Aldrich, Vice Chairman*
A nonprofit membership organization of persons 50 and older dedicated to addressing their needs and interests.

## Print: Newsletters

**7414 Aging & Vision News**
Lighthouse International
111 E 59th St
New York, NY 10022-1202
212-821-9216
800-829-0500
FAX: 212-821-9707
e-mail: info@lighthouse.org
www.lightfair.com

*Laurie A Silbersweig, Editorial Director*
Intended for professionals engaged in research, education or service delivery in the field of vision and aging.
*6-12 pages Newsletter*

**7415 Aging News Alert**
C D Publications
8204 Fenton St
Silver Spring, MD 20910-4502
301-588-6380
800-666-6380
FAX: 301-588-6385
e-mail: subscription@cdpublications.com
www.cdpublications.com/seniors/ana

*Michael Gerecht, President*
*Ash Gerecht, Co-Owner*
Reports on successful senior programs, funding opportunities, and federal actions that effect the elderly. Available in 6, 12 or 24 month subscriptions online and online/print combinations.
*$192.00*
*8 pages Monthly*

**7416 Aging and Vision News**
Lighthouse International
111 E 59th St
New York, NY 10022-1202
212-821-9216
800-829-0500
FAX: 212-821-9707
TTY: 212-821-9713
e-mail: info@lighthouse.org
www.lighthouse.org

*Robert Rosenberg, Editor*
*Newsletter*

**7417 Enabling News**
Access II Independent Living Centers
101 Industrial Parkway
Gallatin, MO 64640-1280
660-663-2423
888-663-2423
FAX: 660-663-2517
e-mail: access@accessii.org
accessii.org

*Debra Hawman, Executive Director*
*Gary Matticks, Owner*
*Debra Hawman, Executive Director*
*8 pages Quarterly*

**7418 Part B News**
DecisionHealth
9737 Washingtonian Blvd
Gaithersburg, MD 20878-7337
301-287-2700
877-602-3835
FAX: 301-287-2535
www.decisionhealth.com

*Scott Kraft, Editor*
*Steve Greenberg, President*
*Tonya Nevin, Vice President Of Publishing*
*Sean Weiss, Vice President, Prof. Services*
Washington news and practical strategies for maximizing Medicare Part B. *$519.00*
*Yearly*

**7419 Social Security Bulletin**
US Social Security Administration
500 E Street SW
Suite 829 #829
Washington, DC 20254-0002
202-358-6066
800-772-1213
FAX: 202-282-7219
www.ssa.gov/policy

*Karyn Tucker, Managing Editor*
*Richard Balkus, Assoc. Comm. Office Of Dis*
Reports on results of research and analysis pertinent to the Social Security and SSI programs. *$16.00*
*Monthly*

## Non Print: Newsletters

**7420 AGRAM**
Assoc of Ohio Philanthropic Homes, Housing/Service
855 S Wall St
Columbus, OH 43206-1921
614-444-2882
FAX: 614-444-2974
e-mail: info@aopha.org
www.aopha.org

*John Alfano, CEO*
*Tim White, Executive Director*
*P Alfano, President/CEO*
*Weekly*

**7421 Aging News Alert**
C D Publications
8204 Fenton Street
Silver Spring, MD 20910-4502
301-588-6380
800-666-6380
FAX: 301-588-6385
e-mail: subscription@cdpublications.com
www.cdpublications.com

*Ash Gerecht, Co-Owner*
*Sharon Livermore, Businesss Manager*
Reports on successful senior programs, funding opportunities, and federal actions that effect the elderly. Available in 6, 12 or 24 month subscriptions online and online/print combinations. *$192.00*
*8 pages Monthly*

**7422 CAHSA Connecting**
Colorado Assoc of Homes and Services for the Aging
Ste 610
1888 Sherman St
Denver, CO 80203-1160
303-837-8834
FAX: 303-837-8836
www.leadingagecolorado.org

*Laura Landwirth, Executive Director*
Publishes timely information on legislation, regulation, news of interest to senior housing, nursing home and aging services providers, and association activties.

**7423 CANPFA-Line**
CT Assoc of Not-for-Profit Providers of the Aging
1340 Wilmington Rdg
Berlin, CT 6037
860-828-2903
FAX: 860-828-8694
e-mail: leadingagect@leadingagect.org
www.leadingagect.org

*Mag Morelli, President*
*Ñurka Carrero, Office Manager*
*Andrea Bellofiore, Director of Member Programs & Services*
*Beth Ricker, Finance Manager & Membership Director*
LeadingAge Connecticut promotes and advocates for a vision of the world in which every community offers an integrated and coordinated continuum of high quality, affordable health care, housing and community based services. Founded in 1961, LeadingAge Connecticut is Connecticut's leading membership association of not-for-profit and Quality First aging services organizations. Our 130+ provider members and 57 business affiliate members serve over 16,000 older adults every day.
*Bi-Monthly*

**7424 Capitol Focus**
Colorado Assoc of Homes and Services for the Aging
Ste 610
1888 Sherman St
Denver, CO 80203-1160
303-837-8834
FAX: 303-837-8836
www.leadingagecolorado.org

*Laura Landwirth, Executive Director*
During the legislative session, keeps members up-to-date on legislation on CAHSA's advocacy efforts.

**7425 Capsule**
Children of Aging Parents
P.O.Box 167
Richboro, PA 18954-167
215-945-6900
800-227-7294
FAX: 215-945-8720
e-mail: info@caps4caregivers.org
www.caps4caregivers.org

*Karen Rosenberg, Director*
An informative newsletter for caregivers.
*Quarterly*

**7426 CommuniquŠ**
Iowa Association of Homes & Services for the Aging
1701 48th Street
Suite 203 #203
West Des Moines, IA 50266-6723
515-440-4630
888-440-4630
FAX: 515-440-4631
e-mail: iahsa@ageiowa.org
www.ageiowa.org

*Dana Petrowsky, President*
*Kirstie Oliver, Vice President*
*Bill Nutty, Director*
Provides up to date aging services information.
*Bi-weekly*

**7427 Elder Visions Newsletter**
National Indian Council on Aging
10501 Montgomery Blvd NE
Albuquerque, NM 87111-3832
505-292-2001
FAX: 505-292-1922
www.nicoa.org

*Traci Mc Clellan, Executive Director*
*James Delacruz, Chairman Of The Board*
*Phyllis Antone, Director*
Provides information on issues affecting American Indian and Alaska Native Elders.
*Quarterly*

**7428 Innovations**
National Council on Aging
1901 L Street NW
4th Floor
Washington, DC 20036-3506
202-479-1200
FAX: 202-479-0735
TTY:202-479-6674
e-mail: info@ncoa.org
www.ncoa.org

*Austin Han, Manager*
*James Firman, President/CEO*
*Donna Whitt, SVP/CFO*
*Nancy Whitelaw, SVP/Director*

Explores significant developments in the field of aging, keeping individuals informed on a broad range of topics.
*Quarterly*

**7429 NASUA News**
National Association of State Units on Aging
1201 15th Street NW
Suite 350 #350
Washington, DC 20005-2842
202-898-2578
FAX: 202-898-2583
e-mail: info@nasua.org
www.nasua.org

*Martha Roherty, Executive Director*
*Mike Hann, Executive Director*
*Clarence Brown, Executive Director*
*Monthly*

**7430 NCOA Week**
National Council on Aging
1901 L Street NW
4th Floor
Washington, DC 20036-3540
202-479-1200
FAX: 202-479-0735
TTY:202-479-6674
e-mail: info@ncoa.org
www.ncoa.org

*James P Firman, President/CEO*
*Donna Whitt, SVP/CFO*
*Nancy Whitelaw, SVP/Director*
Contains valuable information on public policy, regulatory news, aging-field research, funding, NCOA activities and more.
*Weekly*

**7431 NNEAHSA**
Northn New England Assoc of Homes & Svcs for Aging
P.O.Box 1428
Standish, ME 04084-1428
207-773-4822
FAX: 207-773-0101
e-mail: sderingis@nneahsa.org
www.agingservicesmenh.org

*Sheila Deringis, Editor*
Providing healthy, affordable and ethical long-term care to older citizens throughout Maine, New Hampshire and Vermont.

**7432 NSCLC Washington Weekly**
National Senior Citizens Law Center
1444 Eye St NW
Suite 1100 #1100
Washington, DC 20005- 6547
202-289-6976
FAX: 202-289-7224
e-mail: nscls@nsclc.org
www.nsclc.org

*Paul Nathanson, Executive Director*
*Edward King, Executive Director*
*Edward Spurgeon, Executive Director*
Provides the latest case information, administration and congressional developments of importance for the elderly.

**7433 Quality First**
American Assoc of Homes and Services for the Aging
2519 Connecticut Ave NW
Washington, DC 20008-1520
202-783-2242
FAX: 202-783-2255
www.leadingage.org

*William L Minnix Jr, President*
Features helpful tips for marketing services and earning the public's trust through the web site.
*Quarterly*

**7434 Senior Focus**
National Council on Aging
1901 L Street
4th Floor
Washington, DC 20036-3540
202-479-1200
FAX: 202-479-0735
TTY:202-479-6674
e-mail: info@ncoa.org
www.ncoa.org

*Austin Han, Manager*
*James Firman, President/CEO*
*Donna Whit, SVP/CFO*
*Nancy Whitelaw, SVP/Director*
Contains health, financial, lifestyle tips written for seniors
*Quarterly*

## Support Groups

**7435 Area Agency on Aging of Southwest Arkansas**
600 East Columbia Street #11
Magnolia, AR 71753
870-234-7410
800-272-2127
FAX: 870-234-6804
e-mail: inref@magnolia-net.com
agewithdignity.com

*Janet Morrison, Executive Director*
Family Caregiver Support Program is a new program that provides support to family caregivers of any age providing care for an older family member.

**7436 Area Agency on Aging: Region One**
1366 E Thomas Rd
Suite 108 #108
Phoenix, AZ 85014-5739
602-264-2255
888-783-7500
FAX: 602-230-9132
aaaphx.org

*Mary Lynn Kasunic, President*
*Jeannine Berg, Vice Chairman*
*Bobbie Garland, Vice Chairman*
*Richard Peitzmeier, Vice Chairman*
Promotes and provides essential services to enhance the quality of life in a dicerse and changing society. We meet this challenge through advocacy, coordination, building alliances, and promoting public awareness guided by integrity, vision, and caregiver support groups.

**7437 High Country Council of Governments Area Agency on Aging**
468 New Market Blvd
Boone, NC 28607-1820
828-265-5434
FAX: 828-265-5439
e-mail: breece@regiond.org
www.regiond.org

*Gary D Blevins, Chairman*
*Robert Johnson, Vice Chairman*
*Brenda Lyerly, Secretary*
*Danny McIntosh, Treasurer*
We serve to facilitate and support the development of programs to address the needs of older adults and to support investment in their talents and interests.

**7438 Institute on Aging**
3575 Geary Blvd
San Francisco, CA 94118-3212
415-750-4180
877-750-4111
FAX: 415-750-4179
e-mail: info@ioaging.org
www.ioaging.org

*David Werdegar, President*
*Barbara Schraeger, Vice-Chairman*
*Cheryl Jackson, COO*
Support Services for Elders (SSE) provides care coordination, household management, personal support, bookkeeping, and other assistance to help protect your financial affairs.

**7439 Land-of-Sky Regional Council Area Agency on Aging**
339 New Leicester Hwy #140
Asheville, NC 28806-2087
828-251-6622
FAX: 828-251-6353
e-mail: joeconnolly@landofsky.org
www.gettingaround-wnc.com

*Joe Mc Kinney, Manager*
*Terry Albrecht, Program Director*
*Joan Tuttle, Director*
Is the designated regional organization to meet the needs of persons over 60 in Buncombe, Henderson, Madison, and Transylvania counties, by the North Carolina Division of Aging and Adult Services.

**7440 Lumber River Council of Governments Area Agency on Aging**
30 Cj Walker Rd
Pembroke, NC 28372-7340
910-618-5533
FAX: 910-618-5576
e-mail: aco@mail.lrcog.dst.nc.us
www.lcrog.dst.nc.us

*James Perry, Executive Director*
The Family Caregiver Support Program was created to assist family members, neighbors, and friends who help care for a person over the age of 60, or minor grandchildren being reared by a grandparent over 60.

**7441 Mid-Carolina Area Agency on Aging**
130 Gillespie Street
3rd Floor, Post Office Drawer 1510
Fayetteville, NC 28302-1510
910-323-4191
FAX: 910-323-9330
e-mail: gdye@mccog.org
www.mccog.org

*James Caldwell, COG Executive Director*
*Tami Wohlrab Smale, Executive Secretary*
We serve to facilitate and support the development of programs to address the needs of older adults and to support investment in their talents and interests.

**7442 Piedmont Triad Council of Governments Area Agency on Aging**
2216 W Meadowview Rd #201
Greensboro, NC 27407-3406
336-294-4950
FAX: 336-632-0457
e-mail: acalhoun@ptcog.org
www.ptcog.org

*Randall Billings, Executive Director*
*Larry Beck, Chairman*
*Linda Massey, Chairman*
*Sherrill Shaw, Vice Chairman*
Responsible for planning, developing, implementing, and coordinating aging services for seven counties in the Piedmont Triad (Alamance, Caswell, Davidson, Guilford, Montgomery, Randolph, and Rockingham) and their 185,00 residents age 60 and older.

**7443 Southwestern Commission Area Agency on Aging**
125 Bonnie Ln
Sylva, NC 28779-8552
828-586-4091
FAX: 828-586-3129
e-mail: mary@regiona.org
www.regiona.org

*Cecil L Groves, President*
*Bill Gibson, Executive Director*
Our mission is to assure that every older person in Region A has the opportunity to live life to the fullest in the least restrictive setting possible.

**7444 Tompkins County Office for the Aging**
320 North Tioga St
Ithaca, NY 14850-4299
607-274-5482
FAX: 607-274-5495
e-mail: lholmes@tompkins-co.org
www.tompkins-co.org

*Lisa Holmes, Executive Director*
*Danielle Conte, Aging Services Planner*
*Robert Slocum, Principal Accountant*
Provides information and referral, counseling, support groups and training opportunities for caregivers of elderly relatives and friends or other adults with disabilities.

**7445 Triangle J Council of Governments Area Agency on Aging**
P.O.Box 12276
Research Triangle Park, NC 27709-2276
919-549-0551
FAX: 919-549-9390
e-mail: ejones@tjcog.org
tjcog.dst.nc.us

*Dee Freeman, President*
*Kirby Bowers, Executive Director*
*Renee Boyette, Asst To Executive Director*
*Matt Day, Regional Planning*
We serve to facilitate and support the development of programs to address the needs of older adults and to support investment in their talents and interests.

**7446 University of California Memory and Aging Center**
350 Parnassus Ave
Suite 905
San Francisco, CA 94143-1207
415-476-6880
FAX: 415-476-4800
www.memory.ucsf.edu

*Bruce L Miller, Director*
*Mary Koestler, Project Administrator*
Provides support for patients and families affected by neurodegenerative diseases. In addition to our established support groups, we continue to develop new support groups.

**7447 Upper Coastal Plain Council of Governments Area Agency on Aging**
P.O.Box 9
Wilson, NC 27894-9
252-234-5952
FAX: 252-234-5971
e-mail: helen.page@ucpcog.org
www.ucpcog.org

*Greg Godard, Executive Director*
*Helen Page, Aging Programs Specialist*
Provides a comprehensive and coordinated system for delivering services to senior adults and their caregivers. This accomplished through planning, advocacy, funding and service development.

# Blind & Deaf

## Associations

**7448 American Association of the Deaf-Blind**
8630 Fenton Street
Suite 121
Silver Spring, MD 20910- 3803
301-495-4403
FAX: 301-495-4404
TTY:301-495-4402
e-mail: aadb-info@aadb.org
www.aadb.org

*Jamie Pope, Executive Director*
*Elizabeth Spiers, Information Services Director*
Provides a support service provider (SSP) program, a technology program, information and referral, outreach and education, organizational amd individual memberships and national conferences.
*Membership dues*

**7449 American Society for Deaf Children**
800 Florida Ave NE
Washington, DC 20002-3695
800-942-2732
FAX: 410-795-0965
e-mail: asdc@deafchildren.org
www.deafchildren.org

*Jodee Crace, President*
Supports and educates families of deaf and hard of hearing children and advocates for high quality programs and services.

**7450 Arena Stage**
11101 Sixth St
Washington, DC 20024
202-554-9066
FAX: 202-488-4056
TTY:202-484-0247
e-mail: arena@arenastage.org
www.arenastage.org

*David E. Shiffrin, Chair*
*Edgar Dobie, Managing Director*
*Molly Smith, Artistic Director*
*Michele G. Berman, Vice Chair*
A pioneer in providing access to theater for people with disabilities and the birthplace of Audio Description. Offers infrared assistive listening devices (both loop and headset), program books in Braille, large print and wheelchair accessible seating with adjacent companion seating. Audio cassette format available upon request. Sign Interpretation and Audio Description are offered at selected performances. Cafe menus and shop lists in Braille. Wheelchair-accessible with lifts and ramps.

**7451 Association of Late-Deafened Adults**
8038 Macintosh Ln
Suite 2
Rockford, IL 61107-5300
815-332-1515
866-402-2532
e-mail: info@alda.org
www.alda.org

*Linda Drattell, President*
*Matt Ferrara, Region I Director*
*Marsha Kopp, Region II Directo*
*Dave Litman, Region III Director*
Supports the empowerment of late-deafened people.

**7452 Canadian Deafblind Association (CDBA) National Office**
2000 Appleby Line
Suite 421
Burlington, ON L7L-7H7
866-229-5832
FAX: 902-737-1114
e-mail: info@cdbanational.com
www.cdbanational.com

*Carolyn Monaco, President*
*Suzanne McConnell, VP Administration*
*Sara-Lee Salterio, VP Special Projects*
*Don Koreen, Director*
The mission of the Canadian Deafblind Association's National organization is to promote and enhance the well-being of people who are deafblind through: advocacy, the development and dissemination of information, and the provision of support to our chapters, members, and community partners.

**7453 Foundation Fighting Blindness**
716B Columbia Gateway Drive
Suite 100
Columbia, MD 21046
410-423-0600
800-683-5555
FAX: 410-363-2393
TTY: 800-683-5551
e-mail: info@fightblindeness.org
www.fightblindness.org

*William T. Schmidt, CEO*
*James W. Minow, Chief Development Officer*
*Stephen M. Rose, Ph.D., Chief Research Officer*
*Annette Hinkle, CPA, Chief Financial Officer*
the urgent mission is to drive the research that will provide preventions, treatments, and cures for people affected by retinitis pigmentosa, macular degeneration, Usher syndrome and the entire spectrum of retinal degenerative diseases.

**7454 Hearing Loss Association of America**
7910 Woodmont Ave
Ste 1200
Bethesda, MD 20814-7022
301-657-2248
FAX: 301-913-9413
TTY:301-657-2248
hearingloss.org

*Brenda Battat, Executive Director*
*Barbara Kelley, Dep Exec Dir, Editor-In-Chief*
*Nancy Macklin, Director of Events & Marketing*
*Lise Hamlin, Director of Public Policy*
The mission of the Hearing Loss Association of America is to open the world of communication to people with hearing loss through information, education, advocacy and support.

**7455 Helen Keller National Center for Deaf- Blind Youths And Adults**
141 Middle Neck Rd
Sands Point, NY 11050-1218
516-944-8900
FAX: 516-944-7302
TTY:516-944-8637
e-mail: hkncinfo@hknc.org
hknc.org

*Joseph McNulty, Executive Director*
Enables each person who is deaf/blind to live and work in his or her community of choice.

**7456 Idaho Commission for the Blind and Visually Impaired**
PO Box 83720
341 W. Washington St.
Boise, ID 83720-0012
208-334-3220
800-542-8688
FAX: 208-334-2963
e-mail: ajones@icbvi.idaho.gov
www.icbvi.state.id.us

*Angela Jones, Administrator*
*Raelene Thomas, Management Assistant*
*Bruce Christopherson, Rehabilitation Services Chief*
*Dana Ard, Vocational Rehabilitation Counselor for the Blind*
Empowers persons who are blind or visually impaired by providing vocational rehabilitation training, skills training and educational opportunities to achieve self fulfillment through quality employment and independent living; to serve as a resource to families and employers and to expand public awareness regarding the potential of all persons who are blind or visually impaired.

**7457 International Hearing Society**
16880 Middlebelt Rd
Ste 4
Livonia, MI 48154-3374
734-522-7200
FAX: 734-522-0200
e-mail: bdemicoli@ihsinfo.org
www.ihsinfo.org

*Kathleen Mennillo MBA, Executive Director*
*Bernadette "Bennie" Demicoli, Member Services Coordinator*
*Sandra den Boer, Communications Specialist*
*Marlene Deuby, Continuing Education Specialist*
IHS members are engaged in the practice of testing human hearing and selecting, fitting and dispensing hearing instruments.

**7458 Lilac Services for the Blind**
1212 N Howard St
Spokane, WA 99201-2410
509-328-9116
800-422-7893
FAX: 509-328-8965
e-mail: info@lilacblind.org
www.lilacblind.org

*Cheryl Martin, Executive Director*
*Mathew Plank, Marketing Director*
*Peggy Swanson, Office Manager*
*Debbie Bowcutt, Rehabilitation Teacher & Low Vision Specialist*
Lilac Services for the Blind provides independent living instruction, adaptive aids, counseling, low-vision evaluations, support groups, Braille transcription services, and much more for 14 counties in the inland Northwest.

**7459 National Consortium on Deaf-Blindness**
345 Monmouth Ave N
Monmouth, OR 97361-1329
800-438-9376
FAX: 503-838-8150
TTY:800-854-7013
e-mail: dblink@tr.wou.edu
www.nationaldb.org

*D. Jay Gense, Director*
*Kathy McNulty, Associate Director*
*Joe Mcnulty, Co-Principal Investigator*
*Amy Parker, ED. D, Associate Director*
Promotes academic achievement and results for children and youth who are deaf-blind, through technical assistanve, model demonstration, and information dissemination activities that are supported by evidence-based practices. Information about deaf-blindness is available free of charge through the Consortium's information services branch, DB-Link.

**7460 National Family Association for Deaf-Blind**
141 Middle Neck Rd
Sands Point, NY 11050-1218
516-944-8900
800-255-0411
FAX: 516-883-9060
TTY: 516-944-8637
e-mail: NFADB@aol.com
www.nfadb.org

*Susan Green, President*
*Janette Peracchio, Vice President*
*Cynthia Jackson-Glenn, Treasurer*
*Paddi Davies, Secretary*
NFADB exists to empower the voices of families of individuals who are deaf-blind and advocate for their unique ideas.

**7461 National Federation of the Blind**
200 E Wells St
Baltimore, MD 21230-4998
410-659-9314
FAX: 410-685-5653
e-mail: pmaurer@nfb.org
nfb.org

*Marc Maurer, President*
*Fredric Schroeder, First Vice President*
*Ron Brown, Second Vice President*
*James Gashel, Secretary*
The largest membership organization of blind people in the nation, with chapters in every state and approximately 50,000 individual members. It seeks to integrate the blind into society on the basis of equality with the sighted so that the blind are seen as normal, participating citizens. Has 700 local chapters.

**7462 National Information Center for Children and Youth with Disabilities (NICHCY)**
1825 Connecticut Ave
Ste 700
Washington, DC 20009
202-884-8200
800-695-0285
FAX: 202-884-8441
e-mail: nichcy@aed.org
www.nichcy.org

*Suzanne Ripley, Manager*
Provides fact sheets, state resource sheets and general information to assist parents, educators, caregivers, advocates and others in helping children and youth with disabilities participate as fully as possible in their communities.

**7463 National Information Clearinghouse on Children who are Deaf-Blind**
National Consortium on Deaf-Blindness
345 Monmouth Ave N
Monmouth, OR 97361-1329
503-838-8391
877-877-1593
FAX: 503-838-8150
TTY: 503-838-8000
e-mail: triweb@wou.edu
www.tr.wou.edu

*Dr. Ella Taylor, Director*
*Nancy Ganson, Assistant to the Director*
*Mike Stewart, Grants Management Office*
*Cindi Mafit, Grants Management Office*
Collects, organizes, and disseminates information related to children and youth of ages 0 to 21 who are deaf-blind and connects consumers of deaf-blind information to the appropriate resources. Publishes a number of topical papers and publishes Deaf-Blind Perspective.

**7464 Ultratec**
450 Science Dr
Madison, WI 53711-1166
608-238-5400
800-482-2424
FAX: 608-238-3008
TTY: 800-482-2424
ultratec.com

*Jackie Morgan, Marketing Director*
Ultratec works to make telephone access more convenient and reliable for people with hearing loss.

## Camps

**7465 Florida Lions Camp**
Lions of Multiple District 35
2819 Tiger Lake Road
Lake Wales, FL 33898-9582
863-696-1948
FAX: 863-696-2398
e-mail: bjcage@hotmail.com
www.lionscampfl.org

*Barbara Cage, Executive Director*
*Liz Cage, Program Director*
*Carissa Moen, Bookkeeping/Registrar*
One-week sessions June-August for youths and adults with visual impairments and other challenging disabilities. Coed, ages 5 and up. A variety of traditional summer camp activities which include: swimming, canoeing, fishing, hiking, camping out and cooking over a fire, games, arts & crafts, singing & dancing, hay-wagon rides, challenge course and much more. Activities are adapted to the age and ability of each camper to ensure maximum participation, safety and fun.

**7466 Florida School for the Deaf and Blind**
207 San Marco Ave
St Augustine, FL 32084-2799
904-827-2200
800-344-3732
FAX: 904-827-2325
e-mail: info@fsdb.k12.fl.us
www.fsdb.k12.fl.us

*Dr. Jeanne Glidden Prickett, EdD, Shelter Administrator*
*Debbie Schuler, Administrator of Instructional Services*
*Cindy Day, Executive Director of Parent Services*
*Terri Wiseman, Administrator of Business Services*
Statewide public boarding school for eligible students who are deaf/hard-of-hearing or blind/visually impaired. FSDB serves children who are pre-k through high school.

## Print: Books

**7467 Communicating with People Who Have Trouble Hearing & Seeing: A Primer**
National Association for Visually Handicapped
Fl 6
22 W 21st St
New York, NY 10010-6943
212-255-2804
FAX: 212-727-2931
www.lighthouse.org

*Roger O Goldman, Chairman Of The Board*
Line drawings that depict problems for those with both deficiencies. *$2.00*

**7468 Helen and Teacher: The Story of Helen & Anne Sullivan Macy**
American Foundation for the Blind/AFB Press
11 Penn Plz
Suite 300 #300
New York, NY 10001-2006
212-502-7600
800-232-5463
FAX: 212-502-7777
e-mail: afbinf@afb.net
www.afb.org

*Carl Augusto, President*
*Richard Obnen, Chairman Of The Board*
*Michael Gilliam, Vice Chairman*
*Alan Lindroth, Principal*
A pictorial biography emphasizing Hellen Keller's accomplishments in public life over a period of more than 60 years. Traces Anne Sullivan's early years and her meeting with Helen Keller, and goes on to recount the joint events of their lives. A definitive biography. $29.95.
*Paperback*
*ISBN 0-891282-89-0*

**7469 Independence Without Sight and Sound: Suggestions for Practitioners**
American Foundation for the Blind/AFB Press
11 Penn Plz
Suite 300 #300
New York, NY 10001-2006
212-502-7600
800-232-8463
FAX: 212-502-7777
e-mail: afbinfo@afb.net
www.afb.org

*Carl Augusto, President*
*Richard Obnen, Chairman Of The Board*
*Michael Gilliam, Vice Chairman*
*Alan Lindroth, Principal*
This practical guidebook covers the essential aspects of communicating and working with deaf-blind persons. Includes useful information on how to talk with deaf-blind people, and adapt orientation and mobility techniques for deaf-blind travelers. *$39.95*
*193 pages Paperback*
*ISBN 0-891282-46-7*

**7470 Reclaiming Independence: Staying in the Drivers Seat When You Are no Longer Drive.**
American Printing House for the Blind
1839 Frankfort Ave
Louisville, KY 40206-3148
502-895-2405
800-223-1839
FAX: 502-899-2274
e-mail: info@aph.org
www.aph.org

*Tuck Tinsley, President*
*Joseph Paradis, Chairman*
*Kathleen Huebner, Vice Chairman*
*Jane Thompson, Executive Director*
Useful for both individuals and professionals, this video/resource guide will help you successfuly use rehabilitation and transportation resources. *$60.00*

**7471 Verbal View of the Web & Net**
American Printing House for the Blind
1839 Frankfort Ave
Louisville, KY 40206-3148
502-895-2405
800-223-1839
FAX: 502-899-2274
e-mail: info@aph.org
www.aph.org

*Tuck Tinsley, President*
*Joseph Paradis, Chairman*
*Kathleen Huebner, Vice Chairman*
*Jane Thompson, Executive Director*

One of a series of Verbal View titles, Verbal View of the Net & Web explains how to access information on the internet and teaches accessability features of Internet Explorer. *$50.00*

## Print: Magazines

7472 **Braille Montior**
National Federation of the Blind Senior Division
200 E Wells St
Baltimore, MD 21230-4914
410-659-9314
FAX: 410-685-5653
e-mail: nfb@nfb.org
www.nfb.org

*Barbara Pierce, Editor*
The Braille Monitor is the leading publication of the National Federation of the Blind. It covers the events and activities of the NFB and addresses the many issues and concerns of the blind.
*11 times a year*

7473 **Deaf-Blind American**
American Association of the Deaf-Blind (AADB)
8630 Fenton Street
Suite 121
Silver Spring, MD 20910- 3803
301-495-4403
FAX: 301-495-4404
e-mail: aadb-info@aadb.org
www.aadb.org

*Jamie Pope, Executive Director*
*Elizabeth Spiers, Information Services Director*
*Timothy Jackson, President*
We are a consumer membership organization of, by and for people who have dual vision and hearing loss. Services we provide include an information clearinghouse on deaf blindness, a quarterly magazine (The Deaf Blind American), a newsletter, AADB news, a task force to improve interpreting for deaf-blind people, a listen for members, a partnership with the American Red Cross, and national conferences. *$5.00*
*Quartlery*

7474 **Hearing Loss Magazine**
HearingLoss Association of America
Ste 1200
7910 Woodmont Ave
Bethesda, MD 20814-7022
301-657-2248
FAX: 301-913-9413
www.hearingloss.org

*Brenda Battat, Executive Director*
*Barbara Kelley, Deputy Executive Director/EIC*
*Lisa Hamlin, Director Of Public Policy*
Provides readers with the latest information on products, services, research, and technology in the hearing healthcare field.
*Bi-Monthly*

7475 **Hearing Professional Magazine**
International Hearing Society
Ste 4
16880 Middlebelt Rd
Livonia, MI 48154-3374
734-522-7200
FAX: 734-522-0200
e-mail: knacarato@ihsinfo.org
www.ihsinfo.org

*Scott Beall, Treasurer Director*
*Alan Lowell, President*
*Kathleen Mennillo, Executive Director*
Provides authoritative technical and business information that will help hearing aid specialists serve the hearing impaired.

## Print: Newsletters

7476 **Deaf-Blind Perspective**
National Consortium on Deaf-Blindness
345 Monmouth Ave
Monmouth, OR 97361
503-838-8391
800-438-9376
FAX: 503-838-8150
TTY: 800-854-7013
e-mail: dbp@wou.edu
www.tr.wou.edu/dblink

*John Reiman PhD, Director*
*Peggy Malloy, Managing Editor*
A free publication with articles, essays, and announcements about topics related to people who are deaf-blind. The primary focus is on the education of children and youth with deaf-blindness. Published two times a year (Spring and Fall) by the national consortium on Deaf-blindness at the Teaching Research Institute at Western Oregon University.

7477 **InFocus**
716B Columbia Gateway Drive
Suite 100
Columbia, MD 21046
410-568-0150
800-683-5555
FAX: 410-363-2393
TTY: 800-683-5551
e-mail: info@fightblindeness.org
www.blindness.org

*William Schmidt, CEO*
Presents articles on coping, research updates, and Foundation news.
*3x/year*

7478 **News from Advocates for Deaf-Blind**
National Family Association for Deaf-Blind
141 Middle Neck Rd
Sands Point, NY 11050-1218
516-944-8900
800-225-0411
FAX: 516-883-9060
TTY: 516-944-8637
e-mail: NFADB@aol.com
www.NFADB.org

*Susan Green, President*
*Janette Peracchio, Vice President*
*Cynthia Jackson-Glenn, Treasurer*
*Paddi Davies, Secretary*
A membership organization which provide resources, education, advocacy, referrals and support for families with children who are deaf-blind; professionals in the field; and individuals who are deaf-blind.
*20 pages TriAnnual*

## Non Print: Newsletters

7479 **AADB E-News**
American Association of the Deaf-Blind
8630 Fenton Street
Suite 121
Silver Spring, MD 20910- 3803
301-495-4403
FAX: 301-495-4404
e-mail: aadb-info@aadb.org
www.aadb.org

*Jamie McNamara-Pope, Executive Director*
*Timothy Jackson, President*
*Michael Reese, Treasurer*
Contains information about the latest events occurring within AADB and in the deaf-blind community.

**7480 ALDA Newsletter**
ALDA
8038 Macintosh Ln
Suite 2
Rockford, IL 61107-5336
815-332-1515
866-402-2532
FAX: 877-907-1738
e-mail: info@alda.org
www.alda.org

*Nancy Kingsleyy, Editor-in-Chief*
*Eileen Hollywood, Managing Editor*
Articles, stories and poems by and about late-deafened adults.

**7481 Beam**
1850 W Roosevelt Rd
Chicago, IL 60608-1298
312-666-1331
FAX: 312-243-8539
TTY:312-666-8874
www.chicagolighthouse.org

*James Kesteloot, President*
*Terrence Longo, Assistant Director*
Quarterly newsletter of the organization offering progressive programs for the blind, visually impaired, deaf-blind and multi-disabled children and adults, including vocational programs, computer and office skills training, job placement, independent living skills, orientation and mobility training, counseling and a low vision clinic.

**7482 Endeavor**
American Society for Deaf Children
3820 Hartzdale Dr
Camp Hill, PA 17011-7809
717-703-0073
866-895-4206
FAX: 717-909-5599
e-mail: endeavoreditor@aol.com
www.deafchildren.org

*Robert B Wells, Editor*
*Tami Hossler, Editor*
ASDC's qurterly publication featuring committee reports, stories, and fun.
*Quarterly*

**7483 HKNC Newsletter**
Helen Keller National Center
141 Middle Neck Rd
Sands Point, NY 11050-1218
516-944-8900
FAX: 516-944-7302
TTY:516-944-8637
e-mail: hkncinfo@hknc.org
www.hknc.org

*Joseph McNulty, Executive Director*
Highlights recent activities at the national center.

**7484 NAT-CENT**
Helen Keller National Center
141 Middle Neck Rd
Sands Point, NY 11050-1218
516-944-8900
FAX: 516-944-7302
TTY:516-944-8637
e-mail: hkncinfo@hknc.org
www.hknc.org

*Joseph McNulty, Executive Director*
Contains articles on legislation, services, aids and devices, human interest and issues related to deaf-blindness.

## Non Print: Software

**7485 Braille + Mobile Manager**
American Printing House for the Blind
1839 Frankfort Ave
Louisville, KY 40206-3148
502-895-2405
800-223-1839
FAX: 502-899-2274
e-mail: info@aph.org
aph.org

*Tuck Tinsley, President*
*Joseph Paradis, Chairman*
*Kathleen Huebner, Vice Chairman*
*Jane Thompson, Executive Director*
Use it like a hand-held PDA or like a laptop. *$1395.00*

**7486 MaximEyes**
American Printing House for the Blind
1839 Frankfort Ave
Louisville, KY 40206-3148
502-895-2405
800-223-1839
FAX: 502-899-2274
e-mail: info@aph.org
aph.org

*Tuck Tinsley, President*
*Joseph Paradis, Chairman*
*Kathleen Huebner, Vice Chairman*
*Jane Thompson, Executive Director*
MaximEyes is a plug-in for Internet Explorer that adds a toolbar that allows you to controll the size of website text and images. *$59.95*

## Non Print: Video

**7487 Getting in Touch**
2612 N Mattis Ave
Champaign, IL 61826-1053
217-352-3273
FAX: 217-352-1221
www.researchpress.com

*Russell Pence, President*
*David Parkinson, Chairman*
*Cynthia Martin, Principal*
*Ann Parkinson, Principal*

**7488 Journey**
Landmark Media
3450 Slade Run Dr
Falls Church, VA 22042-3940
703-241-2030
800-342-4336
FAX: 703-536-9540
e-mail: info@landmarkmedia.com
landmarkmedia.com

*Michael Hartogs, President*
*Richard Hartogs, VP Acquisitions*
*Peter Hartogs, VP New Business & Development*
*Eric Miller, Sales Representative*
A moving portrayal of the extraordinary journey to Japan of 74-year-old Billie Sinclair, who is deaf, blind and mute. He funds his travels by weaving and selling baskets. In Japan he rides a roller coaster, tries judo and visits a deaf and blind acupuncturist. He demonstrates how it is possible to communicate by touch alone. *$195.00*
*Video*

## Support Groups

**7489 Aurora of Central New York**
518 James Street
Suite 100 #100
Syracuse, NY 13203-2094
315-422-7263
FAX: 315-422-4792
TTY:315-422-9746
e-mail: auroracny@auroracny.org
aurorаofcny.org

*Debra Chaiken, Executive Director*
*Michael O'Connor, President*
*Anne Costa, Director/Program Development*
*Cindy Sicherman, Finance Executive*

**Professional counseling services to assist individuals and their families deal with the trauma of hearing or vision loss.**

# Cognitive

## Associations

**7490 ARC**
1660 L Street NW
Suite 301
Washington, DC 20036
202-534-3700
800-433-5255
FAX: 202-534-3731
e-mail: info@thearc.org
www.thearc.org

*Mohan Mehra, President*
*Nancy Webster, Vice President*
*Ronald Brown, Treasurer*

The ARC promotes and protects the rights of people with intellectual and developmental disabilities and actively supports their inclusion and participation in the community throughout their lifetimes.

**7491 Autism Research Institute**
4182 Adams Ave
San Diego, CA 92116-2536
619-281-7165
866-366-3361
FAX: 619-563-6840
e-mail: matt@autism.com
www.autismresearchinstitute.com

*Steve Edelson Ph.D., Executive Director*
*Rosemary King, President*

Conducts research on the causes, diagnosis, and treatment of autism and publishes a quarterly newsletter that reviews worldwide research. Literature on causes and treatment available. Refers patients and families to health care professionals and clinics. Request publication list and sample newsletter, Autism Research Review International.

**7492 Autism Services Center**
929 4th Ave
Second Floor
Huntington, WV 25701-1408
304-525-8014
FAX: 304-525-8026
e-mail: candy@autismwv.org
autismservicescenter.org

*Jimmie Beirne, CEO*

Provides developmental disabilities services with a specialty in autism. Services include case management, residential, personal care, assessments and evaluations, supported employment, independent living and family support.

**7493 Autism Treatment Center of America**
2080 S Undermountain Rd
Sheffield, MA 01257-9643
413-229-2100
877-766-7473
FAX: 413-229-3202
e-mail: correspondence@option.org
www.son-rise.org

*Barry Kausman, Co-Founder/ Co-Originator/ Senior Teacher/Trainer*
*Samahria Lyte Kaufman, Co-Founder/ Co-Originator/ Senior Teacher/Trainer*
*Bryn Hogan, ATCA Senior Staff*
*William Hogan, ATCA Senior Staff*

Since 1983, the Autism Treatment Center of America has provided innovative training programs for parents and professionals caring for children challenged by Autism, Autism Spectrum Disorders, Pervasive Developmental Disorders (PDD) and other development difficulties. The Son-Rise Program teaches a specific yet comprehensive system of treatment and education designed to help families and caregivers enable their children to dramatically improve in all areas of learning.

**7494 Beck Institute for Cognitive Therapy and Research**
1 Belmont Ave
Ste 700
Bala Cynwyd, PA 19004-1610
610-664-3020
FAX: 610-709-5336
e-mail: info@beckinstitute.org
www.beckinstitute.org

*Aaron T Beck, President Emeritus*
*Judith S Beck PhD, President*
*Deborah Beck Busis, LSW, Diet Program Coordinator*
*Norman Cotterell, PhD, Senior Therapist and Clinical Coordinator*

Serves as a critically important training ground for cognitive therapists/cognitive behavior therapists.

**7495 Best Buddies**
1243 Islington Ave
Ste 907
Toronto, ON M8X-1Y9
416-531-0003
888-779-0061
FAX: 416-531-0325
e-mail: info@bestbuddies.ca
www.bestbuddies.ca

*Steven Pinnock, Executive Director*
*Emily Bolyea-Kyere, Director of Program and Special Events*
*Amy Lynn Taylor, Program Manager*
*Gemma ', Program Manager*

Our program gives people with intellectual disabilities the chance to have experiences which most people take for granted.

**7496 Brain Injury Association of America**
1608 Spring Hill Rd
Ste 110
Vienna, VA 22182
703-761-0750
FAX: 703-761-0755
e-mail: sconnors@biausa.org
www.biausa.org

*Susan H Connors, President/CEO*
*Mary S. Ritter, Executive VP/COO*
*Marianna Abashian, Director of Professional Services*
*Gregory Ayotte, Director of Consumer Services*

Creates a better future through brain injury prevention, research, education and advocacy.

**7497 Brain Injury Association of New York State**
10 Colvin Ave
Albany, NY 12206-1242
518-459-7911
800-228-8201
FAX: 518-482-5285
e-mail: President@bianys.org
bianys.org

*Judith Avner, Executive Director*
*Marie Cavallo, Ph.D., President*
*Debbie Berenda, Director of Finance & Administration*
*Renee Bullis, Family Services Program Assistant*

(BIANYS) is a statewide non-profit membership organization that advocates on behalf of individuals with brain injury and their families, and promotes prevention. Established in 1982, BIANYS provides education, advocac, and community support services that lead to improved outcomes for children and adults with brain injuries and their families. BIANYS also offers chapters and support groups throughout the state, prevention programs, mentoring programs, speakers bureau and publications library.

**7498 Brain Injury Association of Texas**
316 W 12th St
Ste 405
Austin, TX 78701-1845
512-326-1212
800-392-0040
FAX: 512-478-3370
e-mail: info@biatx.org
www.biatx.org

*Jane Boutte, President*
*Marc Lenahan, Vice President*
*Erin Garrison, Administrative Director*
*San Marcos, Secretary*

The Brain Injury Association of Texas is an organization which arose from the mutual frustration and sense of helplessness experienced by families in their search for appropriate facilities and support to return loved ones who had sustained brain injuries to maximum functioning potential. It was organized in 1982 as the Texas Head Injury Association by a group of family members and health care professionals in an effort to meet the needs of the survivors of brain injury.

**7499 Center Academy At Pinellas Park**
6710 86th Ave North
Pinellas Park, FL 33782-4502
727-541-5716
FAX: 727-544-8186
e-mail: NickiMaddalena@centeracademy.com
www.centeracademy.com

*Andrew P. Hicks, Ph.D., Chief Executive Officer and Clinical Director*
*Eric V. Larson, Ph. D., President and Chief Operating Officer*
*Steven Hicks, Vice President, Operations*
*Lisa Hartmann, Director of Education*

Since 1968, Center Academy has been specifically designed for the learning disabled child and other children with difficulties in concentration, social skills, impulsivity, distractibility and study strategies. Programs offered include: academic day school and 5 week remedial summer program. 11 locations throughout Florida.

**7500 Dynamic Learning Center**
PO Box 112
Ben Lomond, CA 95005
831-336-3457
FAX: 503-738-9546
e-mail: teresanlp@aol.com
www.nlpu.com

*Robert B Dilts, President*
*Teresa Epstein, Coordinator*

The vision of NLP (neuro-lingusitic programming)University is to create a context in which professionals of different backgrounds can develop fundamental and advanced NLP skills for applications relevant to their profession. The mission of NLP University is to provide the organizational structure through which the necessary guidance, training, culture, and community support can be brought to the people who are interested in exploring the global potential of Systemic NLP.

**7501 Focus Alternative Learning Center**
PO Box 452
Canton, CT 6019-452
860-693-8809
FAX: 860-693-0141
e-mail: info@focus-alternative.org
www.focus-alternative.org

*Donna Swanson, Executive Director*
*Fred Evans, Associate Director*

A private non profit, licensed clinical and learning center specialized in the treatment of creatively wired and socially challenged kids. We treat kids on the autism spectrum who suffer from high anxiety, experience processing difficulties and learning problems.

**7502 Life Development Institute**
18001 N 79th Ave
Ste E71
Glendale, AZ 85308-8396
866-736-7811
FAX: 623-773-2788
e-mail: info@life-development-inst,org
www.life-development-inst.org

*Robert Crawford, CEO*
*Veronica Lieb (Crawford), President*
*Justin Coller, Manager of Marketing*
*Elissa C. Levine M.C., LPC, Director of Program Services*

Serves older adolescents and adults with learning disabilities, ADD and related disorders. The purpose of the training is to enable program participants to pursue responsible independent living, enhance academic/workplace literacy skills and facilitate placement in educational/employment opportunities, commensurate with individual capabilities. Includes a stand alone, regionally accredited 2-year college.

**7503 NLP Comprehensive**
PO Box 648
Indian Hills, CO 80454-0348
303-987-2224
800-233-1657
FAX: 303-987-2228
e-mail: learn@nlpco.com
www.nlpco.com

*Tom Dotz, President*
*Sharon DeBault, Director of Community Relations*
*Jamie Reaser, PhD, Director of Professional Relations*
*Christian Miller, Publishing Manager*

NLP, or Neuro-Linguistic Programming, is the science of how the brain codes learning and experience. This coding affects all communication and behavior. NLP Comprehensive helps individuals and businesses make the fullest use of their talents and resources. We teach the thought processes and communication strategies of exceptional performers through workshops, books, and tapes.

**7504 National Alliance on Mental Illness(NAMI)**
3803 N Fairfax Drive
Ste 100
Arlington, VA 22203
703-524-7600
800-950-6264
888-999-6264
FAX: 703-524-9094
TTY:703-516-7227
e-mail: mfitzpatrick@nami.org
nami.org

*Kevin B. Sullivan, President*
*Keris Jän Myrick, Ph.Dc., First Vice President*
*Henry Acosta, M.A., M.S.W.,, Second Vice President*
*Ralph E. Nelson, Jr., M.D., Treasurer*

NAMI is a nonprofit, grassroots, self-help, support and advocacy organization of consumers, families, and friends of people with severe mental illnesses, such as schizophrenia, schizoaffective disorder, bipolar disorder, major depressive disorder, obsessive-compulsive disorder, panic and other severe anxiety disorders, autism and pervasive developmental disorders, attention deficit/hyperactivity disorder, and other severe and persistent mental illnesses that affect the brain.

**7505 National Association for Down Syndrome**
PO Box 206
Wilmette, IL 60091-206
630-325-9112
FAX: 847-723-3138
e-mail: info@nads.org
www.nads.org

*Patrick Crawford, First Vice President*
*Deanne Medina, Second Vice President*
*Jackie Rotondi, President*
*Michael Walther, Treasurer*

Works for a strong network of support systems within their own organization and with medical, educational and school service professionals who work with children and adults with Down Syndrome. NADS serves the Chicago Metropolitan area.

**7506 National Association of Cognitive-Behavioral Therapists**
PO Box 2195
Weirton, WV 26062-1395
304-723-3982
800-853-1135
FAX: 304-723-3982
e-mail: nacbt@nacbt.org?subject=General%20Message%20t
www.nacbt.org

*Aldo R Pucci, President*
*Paul A. Hauck, Ph.D., Director*
*Michael R. Edelstein, Ph.D., Director*
*Bill Borcherdt, ACSW, BCD, Director*
Dedicated exclusively to supporting, promoting, teaching, and developing cognitive-behavioral therapy.

**7507 National Down Syndrome Congress**
30 Mansell Court
Suite 108
Roswell, GA 30076
770-604-9500
800-232-6372
FAX: 770-604-9898
e-mail: info@ndsccenter.org
ndsccenter.org

*David Tolleson, Executive Director*
*Thea Grimaldo, Office Administrator*
*John Kupris, Development Director*
*Sue Joe, Affiliate Relations Director*
Provides information, advocacy and support concerning all aspects of life for individuals with Down syndrome. A world with equal rights and opportunitites for people with Down syndrome. It is the purpose of the NDSC to create a national climate in which all people will recognize and embrace the value and dignity of people with Down syndrome. That purpose is enhanced by the commitment of the NDSC to promote the accessability to a full range of opportunities that meet the needs of the individual.

**7508 National Down Syndrome Society**
666 Broadway
New York, NY 10012-2317
212-460-9330
800-221-4602
FAX: 212-979-2873
e-mail: info@ndss.org
ndss.org

*Jon Colman, President*
*Patricia Baker, Program Manager*
*Madeline Alemar, Development Associate*
*Chris Burke, Goodwill Ambassador/Administrative Assistant*
Not-for-profit organization increases public awareness about Down syndrome and works to discover its underlying causes through research, education and advocacy. Distributes timely and informative materials, encourages and supports the activities of local parent support groups, sponsors sonferences and scientific symposia and undertakes major advocacy efforts-all to increase awareness and acceptance of people with Down syndrome.

**7509 National Institute on Deafness and Other Communication Disorder**
Federal Government
31 Center Dr
MSC 2320
Bethesda, MD 20892-2320
301-496-7243
800-241-1044
FAX: 301-402-0018
e-mail: wengerj@nidcd.nih.gov
www.nidcd.nih.gov

*James F Battey Jr. Dr., Director*
*Timothy J. Wheeles, Executive Officer and Chief*
*Chris Clements, Program Advisor*
*Chad Wysong, Deputy Executive Officer*
The National Institute on Deafness and Other Communication Disorders (NIDCD) one of the National Institude of Health, supports and conducts research and research training on the normal and disordered processes of hearing, balance smell, taste, voice, speech and language.

**7510 Oak Leyden Developmental Services**
411 Chicago Ave
Oak Park, IL 60302
708-524-1050
FAX: 708-524-2469
e-mail: batkinson@oak-leyden.org
www.oak-leyden.org

*Bob Atkinson, President/CEO*
*Ken Cheatham, Division Chief of Facilities, Maintenance, & Vehicles*
*Nancy Thomas, Director of Human Resources*
*Mary Taylor, Vice President of Finance*
The mission of Oak-Leyden Developmental Services is to help people with developmental disabilities meet life's challenges and reach their highest potential. Our mission is to achieved through the following programs: Early Intervention Program, Vocational Evaluation, Developmental Training Program, Supported Employment Program, Community Integrated Living Arrangements and Multi-disciplinary Clinic.

**7511 St. John Valley Associates**
291 Newberry Dr
Madawaska, ME 04756-1219
207-728-7197
FAX: 207-728-7550

*Megan Gendreau, Executive Director*
A nonprofit association with the mission of empowering adult citizens with mental retardation to dignify themselves. Three broad-based programs and services (Independence Plus, Job Involvements, People Now) are designed to allow each individual to upgrade learning skills, assert rights, increase independence and accept new responsibilities. *$75.00*

**7512 TEACCH**
University of North Carolina at Chapel Hill
100 Renee Lynne Ct
Carrboro, NC 27510
919-966-2174
FAX: 919-966-4127
e-mail: teacch@unc.edu
www.teacch.com

*Dr. Laura Klinger, Director*
*Rebecca Mabe, Assistant Director of Business*
*Walter Kelly, Business Officer*
*Mark Klinger, Director of Research*
Focus on the person with autism and the development of a program around this person's skills, interests and needs.

## Camps

**7513 Adventure Learning Center at Eagle Village**
4507 170th Ave
Hersey, MI 49639-8785
231-832-1424
800-748-0061
FAX: 231-832-1468
e-mail: alcinfo@eaglevillage.org
www.eaglevillage.org/alcabout.html

*Cathey Prudhomme, President/CEO*
*Scott Cherry, Community Services Director*
*James McCain, CAO/CFO*
Offers a variety of fun camp experiences with a low staff-to-camper ratio and exciting, challenging activities. This program accepts youth, ages 5-17, who are high risk or special needs - behavioral problems, emotionally unstable or Attention Deficit. The camping experience includes canoeing, hiking, swimming and high adventure activities. Half-week, one-week, and two-week sessions June-August. Coed.

**7514 CNS Camp New Connections**
Mclean Hospital Child/Adolescent Program
115 Mill St
Mailstop115
Belmont, MA 02478-1064
617-855-2000
800-333-0338
FAX: 617-855-2833
e-mail: mcleaninfo@mclean.harvard.edu
www.mclean.harvard.edu/patient/child/cnc.p hp

*Roya Ostovar PhD, Center Director*
*Scott L. Rauch, MD., President and Psychiatrist in Chief*
*Joseph Gold MD, Clinical Director*
*Cynthia Kaplan, CAP Administrative Director*

Four-week summer day camp for children ages 7-17 who have pervasive developmental disorders, Asperger's Syndrome, autism spectrum disorders and non-verbal learning disabilities. The camp is designed to help children develop social skills through fun activities including: communication games, swimming, field trips, drama, and arts and crafts. *$4500.00*

**7515 Camp Baker**
Greater Richmond ARC
7600 Beach Rd
Chesterfield, VA 23838-6513
804-748-4789
FAX: 804-796-6880
e-mail: campbaker@RichmondARC.org
richmondarc.org

*Charles Sutherland, Executive Director*
*Thom Horsey, Chairman*

An organization created by families, for families that has grown to provide a continuum of programs and services for individuals with developmental disablities acroos the lifespan, helping each person achieve his or her potential and improving the quality of life for everyone in the community.

**7516 Camp Betsey Cox**
140 Betsey Cox Ln
Pittsford, VT 05763-9456
802-483-6611
e-mail: info@campbetseycox.com
www.campbetseycox.com

*Lorrie Byrom, Camp Director*
*Devri Byrom, Winter Office Director*
*Mike Byrom, Camp Director*

Camp Betsey Cox is a summer camp with an educational mindset. Betsey Cox is a perfect setting to give children the chance to completely make their own choices in the course of the day. For many campers, this is the beggining of learning how to make intelligent and informed choices in life.

**7517 Camp Buckskin**
P.O.Box 389
Ely, MN 55731-389
218-365-2121
FAX: 218-365-2880
e-mail: info@campbuckskin.com
www.campbuckskin.com

*Thomas R Bauer CCD, Camp Director*
*Mary Bauer, Co-Director*
*Jared Griffin, Program Director*

Camp is located in Ely, Minnesota. Buckskin assists LD, AD/HD, Asperger's, and adopted individuals to realize and develop the potentials and abilities which they possess. Teaches a combination of traditional camp, academic activities and social skills so the campers experience success in many areas. Ages 6-18.

**7518 Camp Horizons**
P.O.Box 323
South Windham, CT 6266-323
860-456-1032
FAX: 860-456-4721
e-mail: scott.lambeck@camphorizons.org
www.camphorizons.org

*Neil Rothstein, Owner*
*Michelle Heimall, Director Health/Camper Svcs*
*Jill McCarthy, Assistant Director Staff Svcs*
*Alan Pressman, Director*

Bordering Lake Probus, the facilities at the camp are equipped to accomodate a wide range of activities and programs for campers with developmental disabilities, or other challenging emotional and social needs. There is a 5:1 camper-counselor ratio with a schedule of three programs in the morning and four in the afternoon.

**7519 Camp Huntington**
P.O.Box 37
High Falls, NY 12440-37
845-687-7840
866-514-5281
FAX: 845-853-1172
e-mail: dfalk@camphuntington.com
www.camphuntington.com

*Daniel Falk, Executive Director*
*Bruria Bodek-Falk, Executive Director, Emeritus*
*Stacy Kane Greenzeig, Visiting Prgm Supervisor Spec Ed*

A co-ed residential summer camp specifically designed to focus on Adaptive and Therapeutic Recreation. Campers include those with learning and developmental disabilities, ADD/HD, Autism Spectrum Disorders, Asperger's, PDD, and other special needs. Three programs are offered that focus on: recreation and social skills; independence; and participation.

**7520 Camp Nissokone**
YMCA Camping Services
7300 Hickory Ridge Rd
Holly, MI 48442-8929
248-887-4533
FAX: 248-887-5203
e-mail: office@ycampingservices.org
www.ymcadetroit.org

*Doug Grimm, Vice President Camping Services*
*David Marks, Director*

A six week summer resident camp program for boys and girls whose learning and behavior styles have made successful participation in the traditional camp program difficult. All camp activities have a special emphasis on building self-esteem and peer relationships. Strong in waterfront, nature, campcrafts and a special arts program.

**7521 Camp Northwood**
132 State Route 365
Remsen, NY 13438-5700
315-831-3621
FAX: 315-831-5867
e-mail: northwoodprograms@hotmail.com
www.nwood.com

*Gordon Felt, Camp Director*
*Donna Felt, International Counselor*

Summer sessions for children with ADD. Coed, ages 8-18.

**7522 Camp Nuhop**
404 Hillcrest Dr
Ashland, OH 44805-4152
419-289-2227
FAX: 419-289-2227
e-mail: info@campnuhop.org
www.campnuhop.org

*Trevor Dunlap, CEO*
*Jim Machin, Director of Facilities and Maintenance*
*Terri Ru Lon, Secretary and camp registrar*
*Terri Pringle, Director of Dining Services*

A summer residential program for any youngster from 6 to 18 with a learning disability, behavior disorder or Attention Deficit Disorder. 84 campers and 41 staff members live on site in groups of to seven campers to every three counselors. Activities focus on positive self-concept and behaviors and teaches children to learn how to find their strengths, abilities and talents from a positive, yet realistic viewpoint.

**7523 Camp Ramapo**
Route 52 Salisbury Turnpike
P.O.Box 266
Rt. 52 / Salisbury Turnpike
Rhinebeck, NY 12572-266
845-876-8403
FAX: 845-876-8414
e-mail: office@ramapoforchildren.org
ramapoforchildren.org

*Mike Kunin, Executive Director*
*Jennifer Buri da Cunha, Associate Executive Director*
*Scott Kemp, Director of Operations*
*Adam Weiss, Chief Executive Officer*
Ramapo's specific focus is adventure-based, experiential learning programs that promote positive character values in children and teens with special needs.

**7524 Camp Royall**
Autism Society of North Carolina
250 Bill Ash Road
Moncure, NC 27559-1345
919-542-1033
e-mail: sgage@autismsociety-nc.org
www.autismsociety-nc.org

*Sara Gage, Program Director*
*David Yell, Property Director*
*Darryl R. Marsch, Secretary*
*Elizabeth Phillippi, Treasurer*
The best source in North Carolina for connecting people who live with autism (and those who care about them) with resources, support, advocacy and informantion tailored to thier unique needs.

**7525 Camp Ruggles**
PO Box 353
Chepachet, RI 02814
401-567-8914
e-mail: campruggles@cox.net
www.ricamps.org

*Mr. Edward M Queenan, President*
*Jim Field, Camp Director*
*Mr. Robert Tyler, Treasurer*
*Ms. Nan Levine, Director*
Camp Ruggles is located in Glocester, RI, and is a summer day camp for emotionally handicapped children. The Camp offers a 6 week co-ed summer session for 60 children ages 6-12.

**7526 Camp Sisol**
Jewish Community Center of Greater Rochester/JCC
1200 Edgewood Ave
Rochester, NY 14618-5408
585-461-2000
FAX: 585-461-0805
e-mail: rrosner@jccrochester.org
www.jccrochester.org

*Leslie Berkowitz, Executive Director*
*Dan Irving, Children's Programs/Camp Sisol Director*
*Bill Blodgett, Facilities Director*
*Tamara Cohen, Associate Executive Director, Development, Marketing and Membership*
Camp is located in Honeoye Falls, New York. Summer sessions for children with autism. Coed, ages 5-16.

**7527 Camp World Light**
Florida Baptist Convention
1230 Hendricks Ave
Jacksonville, FL 32207-8619
904-396-2351
800-226-8584
FAX: 904-396-6470
www.campworldlight.com

*Anne Wilson, Camp Director*
*Delicia Garland, Ministry Assistant to Director*
Camp is located in Marianna, Florida. One-week sessions June-July for girls with ADD. Ages 3-12. Activities include arts/crafts, challenge/rope courses, clowning, community service, dance, drama, drawing/painting, leadership development, performing arts and sailing.

**7528 Camp-A-Lot And Leisure Express (PALS Program)**
Arc of San Diego
3030 Market Street
San Diego, CA 92102
619-685-1175
FAX: 619-234-3759
e-mail: pals@arc-sd.com
www.arc-sd.com

*Lin Taylor, Camp Director*
*David W Schneider, President/CEO*
*Anthony J Desalis, Esq, Executive Vice President*
*Rich Coppa, Vice President Of Infrastructure*
Offers one-week sessions for children and adults with attention deficit disorder, autism, mobility limitation and developmental disabilities.

**7529 Carroll School Summer Programs**
25 Baker Bridge Rd
Lincoln, MA 01773-3199
781-259-8342
FAX: 781-259-8842
e-mail: info@carrollscholl.org
carrollschool.org

*Steve Wilkins, Head of School*
*Brooke Ablon, Treasurer*
*Linda Anderson-Snow, Registrar*
*Eileen Archambault, Technology Specialist*
Academic and recreational programs designed to improve learning skills and build self-confidence. The school is a tutorial program for students not achieving their potential due to poor skills in reading, writing and math. The summer camp complements the summer school offering outdoor activities in a supportive, non-competitive environment.

**7530 Casowasco Camp, Conference and Retreat Center**
158 Casowasco Dr
Moravia, NY 13118-3498
315-364-8756
FAX: 315-364-7636
e-mail: info@casowasco.org
www.casowasco.org

*Mike Huber, Executive Director*
*Shelby Wilson, Program Dorector*
*Joan Newlon, Executive Assistant*
*Shelley Sherboneau, Coordinating Registrar*
Camp is located in Moravia, New York. Summer sessions for children with ADD. Coed, ages 6-18 and families.

**7531 Center Academy at Pinellas Park**
6710 86th Ave North
Pinellas Park, FL 33782-4502
727-541-5716
FAX: 727-544-8186
e-mail: infopp@centeracademy.com
www.centeracademy.com

*Patricia Lambert, Principal*
*Mack R Hicks PhD, Founder/Chairman of the Board*
*Andrew P Hicks PhD, CEO/Clinical Director*
*Lisa Hartmann, Director Education*
Specifically designed for the learning disabled child and other children with difficulties in concentration, strategy, social skills, impulsivity, distractibility and study strategies. Programs offered include: attention training, visual-motor remediation, socialization skills training, relaxation training, horseback riding and more. The day camp meets weekdays from 9-3 for 3,4 or 5 week sessions.

**7532 Council for Extended Care of Mentally Retarded Citizens**
11140 So. Towne Square
Ste. 101
Saint Louis, MO 63123
314-845-3900
FAX: 314-845-3901
e-mail: info@sunnyhillinc.org
cecstl.org

*Derrick Good, Chairman of the Board*
*Wes Burns, Vice Chairman*
*Vicky James, President/CEO*
*Sean King, Secretary*
Services are provided to adults and children with developmental disabilities. Supported living arrangements are located in St. Louis city, St. Louis county and St. Charles County. Group home and camp services are located in Dittmer, MO. Travel program also available.

**7533 Dallas Academy**
950 Tiffany Way
Dallas, TX 75218-2743
214-324-1481
FAX: 214-327-8537
e-mail: mail@dallas-academy.com
www.dallas-academy.com

*Jim Richardson, M.S., QMRP, Headmaster*
*Ms. Melanie Ferguson, Head of Lower School*
*Ms. Elizabet Murski, Principal, Upper School*
*Troy Sturrock, Chair*
7-week summer session for students who are having difficulty in regular school classes.

**7534 Eagle Hill School: Summer Program**
242 Old Petersham Road
P.O. Box 116
Hardwick, MA 01037- 0116
413-477-6000
FAX: 413-477-6837
e-mail: admission@ehs1.org
www.ehs1.org

*Peter J. Mc Donald, Headmaster*
*Marilyn Waller, President*
*Alden Bianchi, Vice President*
*Arthur Langhaus, Treasurer*
For children ages 9-19 with specific learning (dis)abilities and/or Attention Deficit Disorder, this summer program is designed to remediate academic and social deficits while maintaining progress achieved during the school year. Electives and sports activities are combined with the academic courses to address the needs of the whole person in a camp-like atmosphere.

**7535 Easter Seals Oklahoma**
701 NE 13th St
Oklahoma City, OK 73104-5003
405-239-2525
FAX: 405-239-2278
e-mail: sbusch@eastersealsoklahoma.org
www.eastersealsoklahoma.org

*Paula K. Porter, CEO*
*Vida Wasinger, Director of Operations*
*Aundria Goree, Programs Director*
*Samantha Pascoe, Child Development Center*
Adult day health center, and child development center.

**7536 Englishton Park Academic Remediation**
Englishton Park Presbyterian
P.O.Box 228
Lexington, IN 47138-228
812-889-2046
e-mail: ThomasLisaBarnett@etczone.com
www.englishtonpark.org

*Lisa Barnett, Director*
*Thomas Barnett, Co-Director*
Camp is located in Lexington, Indiana. Two-week sessions for children with ADD. Boys and girls, ages 7-12.

**7537 Florida Sheriffs Caruth Camp**
Florida Sheriffs Youth Ranches
14770 SE U.S. Hwy 19
Ingllis, FL 34449
352-447-2259
800-765-3797
FAX: 352-447-0400
e-mail: rbouchard@youthranches.org
www.youthranches.org

*Roger Bouchard, President*
*Bill Frye, Vice President of Programs*
*Janet Bass, Vice President of Operations*
*Alison Evans, Vice President of Donor Relations*
Camp is located in Inglis, Florida. One-week sessions for children with ADD. Coed, ages 10-15.

**7538 Gow School Summer Programs**
2491 Emery Road
P.O. Box 85
South Wales, NY 14139-0085
716-652-3450
FAX: 716-652-3457
e-mail: webmaster@gow.org
www.gow.org

*Gayle Hutton, Director of Development*
*Robert Garcia, Director of Admissions*
*Eric Bray, Summer Program Director*
*Rosemary Shields, CPA, Director of Finance*
Co-ed summer programs for students ages 8-16 with dyslexia or similar learning disabilities offer a balanced blend of morning academics, afternoon/evening traditional camp activities and weekend overnights. The primary purpose of these programs is to provide a positive experience while balancing these three elements. Committed to the creation of a positive and enjoyable experience for each participant by defining and merging the goals of the camp and the school, with those of camper students.

**7539 Hill School of Fort Worth**
4817 Odessa Ave
Fort Worth, TX 76133-1640
817-923-9482
FAX: 817-923-4894
e-mail: hillschool@hillschool.org
www.hillschool.org

*Roxann Breyer, Principal*
*Audrey Boda-Davis, Executive Director*
*Janet Smith, Account & Records Manager*
*Kathy Edwards, Principal, Grapevine campus*
Provides an alternative learning environment for students having average or above-average intelligence with learning differences. Hill school is an established leader in North Texas with a 25 year history of effectively serving LD children. Beginning in 1961 as a tutorial service, Hill became a formal school in 1973. Our mission is to help those who learn differently develop skills and strategies to succeed. We do this by developing academic/study skills, and self-discipline.

**7540 Indian Acres Camp for Boys**
1712 Main St
Fryeburg, ME 04037-4327
207-935-2300
FAX: 954-349-7812
e-mail: geoff@indianacres.com
www.indianacres.com

*Michael Burness, Assistant Director*
*Mary Beth ""Bert"" Wiig, Head Counselor, Camp Forest Acres*
*Lisa Newman, Director*
*Geoff Newman, Director*
Camp is located in Fryeburg, Florida. Four and seven-week sessions June-August for boys with ADD ages 7-16.

**7541 Lab School of Washington**
4759 Reservoir Rd NW
Washington, DC 20007-1921
200-965-6600
e-mail: labschool@webmail.org
www.labschool.org

*Katherine Schantz, Head of School*
*Diana Meltzer, Associate Head of School*
*Laurelle Sheedy McCready, Associate Head of School for Finance and Operations*
*Susan Feeley, Director of Admissions*

The Lab School six week summer session includes individualized reading, spelling, writing, study skills and math programs. A multisensory approach addresses the needs of bright learning disabled children. Related services such as speech/language therapy and occupational therapy are integrated into the curriculum. Elementary/Intermediate; Junior High/High School.

**7542 Lions Den Outdoor Learning Center**
600 Kiwanis Dr
Eureka, MO 63025-2212
636-938-5245
FAX: 636-938-5289
e-mail: info@wymancenter.org
www.wymancenter.org

*David Hilliard, President*

Varied programs for mentally retarded children, ages 6 and up, includes daily living, socialization and language skills. Sports, tent camping, crafts, and nature study are also offered. Sliding scale tuition for 2 weeks.

**7543 Maplebrook School**
5142 Route 22
Amenia, NY 12501-5357
845-373-9511
FAX: 845-373-7029
e-mail: admin@maplebrookschool.org
www.maplebrookschool.org

*Paul Scherer, Administrator*
*Donna Konkolics, Head Of School*

A coeductional boarding school which offers a six week camp for children with learning differences and ADD.

**7544 Marvelwood Summer**
Marvelwood School
476 Skiff Mountain Road
P.O. Box 3001
Kent, CT 06757- 3001
860-927-0047
FAX: 860-927-0021
e-mail: summerschool@marvelwood.org
www.marvelwood.org

*Alfred C Brooks, President*
*Arthur F Goodearl, Jr, Head Of School*

The emphasis in this summer program is on diagnosis and remediation of individual reading, spelling, writing, mathematics and study problems. Offered to ages 12-16.

**7545 New Horisons Summer Day Camp**
YMCA
13821 Newport Avenue
Suite 200
Tustin, CA 92780-7803
714-549-9622
FAX: 714-838-5976
www.ymcaoc.org

*Jeff Black, Director*
*Tom Reyes, Director*
*Christian Buell, Director*
*John Rochford, Director*

One-week sessions for children with ADD and speech/communication impairment. Coed, ages 5-14.

**7546 New Jersey YMHA/YWHA Camps Milford**
21 Plymouth St
Fairfield, NJ 07004-1686
973-575-3333
800-776-5657
FAX: 973-575-4188
e-mail: info@njycamps.org
www.njycamps.org

*Leonard Robinson, President*
*Bruce Nussman, President*

Camp is located in Milford, Pennsylvania. Summer sessions for children with ADD. Coed, ages 6-17 and families.

**7547 Oakland School & Camp**
Boyd Tavern
Keswick, VA 22947
434-293-9059
FAX: 434-296-8930
e-mail: information@oaklandschool.net
www.oaklandschool.net

*Carol Williams, School Director*
*Amanda Baber, Admissions Director*

A highly individualized program stresses improving reading ability. Subjects taught are reading, English composition, math and word analysis. Recreational activities include horseback riding, sports, swimming, tennis, crafts, archery and camping. For girls and boys, ages 8-14.

**7548 Outside In School Of Experiential Education, Inc.**
P.O.Box 639
Greensburg, PA 15601-639
724-837-1518
FAX: 724-837-0801
e-mail: administration@outsideinschool.com
www.outsideinschool.com

*Michael C. Henkel, Executive Director*

Camp is located in Bolivar, Pennsylvania. Sessions for children with ADD and substance abuse problems. Boys 11-18 and girls 13-18.

**7549 Phelps School Summer School**
583 Sugartown Rd
Malvern, PA 19355-2800
610-644-1754
FAX: 610-644-6679
e-mail: admis@thephelpsschool.org
www.thephelpsschool.org

*Christopher Chirieleison, Principal*
*Daniel E. Knopp, Head of School*
*Amy Anderson, Director of College Counseling*
*Janessa Davis, Director of Student Services*

Open for grades 7-11 to make up academic deficiencies or complete studies in English, math and reading. Sports include riding, tennis and swimming. A program is also available to a limited number of international students in English as a Second Language.

**7550 Quest Camp**
2355 San Ramon Valley Blvd.
Suite 208
San Ramon, CA 94583-1763
925-743-2900
FAX: 925-820-9761
e-mail: questcamps@mac.com
www.questcamps.com

*Robert Field, Founder/Executive Director*
*Debra Forrester-Field, M.A., Administrative Director*
*Aimee Coonerty-Femiano, Director*
*Jodie Knott , Ph.D., Director*

Camp is located in Alamo, California. Day camp offering three to eight-week sessions including psychological treatment for children with ADD and other mild to moderate psychological disorders. Coed, ages 6-15.

7551 **Raven Rock Lutheran Camp**
17912 Harbaugh Valley Road
P.O.Box 136
Sabillasville, MD 21780-136
410-303-2108
800-321-5824
e-mail: ravenrock@innernet.net

*Brenda Minnich, Executive Director*
Christ-centered program for youth and mentally retarded adults.

7552 **Rimland Services for Autistic Citizens**
1265 Hartrey Ave
Evanston, IL 60202-1056
847-328-4090
877-395-6937
FAX: 847-328-8364
e-mail: pwatson@rimland.org
www.rimland.org

*Pamela Watson, CEO*
*Dave Work, Assoc Executive Director Program*
*Brendy Sims, Chief Operating Officer*
*Terrance Wimberly, Associate Executive Director of Client Services*
An accessible camp facility that can be utilized by groups for day use or overnight camping experiences. Six winterized cabins, a meeting facility, indoor pool, full food service, and an excellent staff are available. Educational programs can be arranged or you can utilize the facility to manage your own programs.

7553 **Rolling Hills Country Day Camp**
P.O.Box 172
Marlboro, NJ 07746
732-308-0405
FAX: 732-780-4726
e-mail: info@rollinghillsdaycamp.com
www.rollinghillsdaycamp.com

*Billy Breitner, Director*
Summer sessions for children with ADD. Coed, ages 3-12.

7554 **SOAR Summer Adventures**
NC Base Camp
P.O.Box 388
226 SOAR Lane
Balsam, NC 28707-0388
828-456-3435
FAX: 828-456-3449
e-mail: admissions@soarnc.org
www.soarnc.org

*Jonathan Jones, Executive Director*
*Catey Terry, CFO*
*Laura Pate, Director of North Carolina Programs*
*Joe Geier, Director of the Academy at SOAR*
A nonprofit adventure program working with disadvantaged youth diagnosed with learning disabilities in an outdoor, challenge based environment. Focuses on esteem building and social skills development through rock climbing, backpacking, whitewater rafting, mountaineering, sailing, snorkeling, and much more. Offers two week, one month, and semester programs available. SOAR programs utilize North Carolina, Florida, Colorado, American Southwest, Alaska, and Jamaica as program areas.

7555 **Sherman Lake YMCA Outdoor Center**
6225 N 39th St
Augusta, MI 49012-9722
269-731-3000
FAX: 269-731-3020
e-mail: shermanlakeymca@ymcasl.org
www.shermanlakeymca.org

*Luke Austenfeld, Executive Director*
*Kathy Simpson, Business Manager*
*Lorrie Syverson, Director of Camping, Education & Retreat Services*
*Mark VanDaff, Facility Manager*
Summer camping sessions for campers with ADD and spina bifida. Coed, ages 6-15 and families, seniors.

7556 **Squirrel Hollow Summer Camp**
The Bedford School
5665 Milam Rd
Fairburn, GA 30213-2851
770-774-8001
FAX: 770-774-8005
e-mail: bbox@thebedfordschool.org
www.thebedfordschool.org

*Betsy Box, Executive Director*
*Jeff James, Headmaster/Athletic Director./MS Mat*
*Allisom DaY, Asst. Headmaster/MS Admin./ MS English*
*Susan Blake, Art/After-School Care Coordinator*
A remedial summer program for children with academic needs held on the campus of The Bedford School in Fairburn, Georgia. It is a five week day camp held from June 19 to July 21 and serves ages 6-16. For mor information contact Betsy Box at (770) 774-8001.

7557 **Summit Camp**
322 Route 46 West
Suite 210
Parsippany, NJ 07054
973-732-3230
800-323-9908
FAX: 973-732-3226
e-mail: info@summitcamp.com
www.summitcamp.com

*Mayer Stiskin, Owner*
*Eugene Bell, Senior Director*
*Debs Hugill, Head Counselor/Program Director*
*Maryann Santora, Clinical Social Worker & Admissions Director*
Camp is located in Honesdale, Pennsylvania. Summer sessions for children with ADD. Coed, ages 8-17.

7558 **Sunnyhill Adventure Center**
Council for Extended Care
6555 Sunlit Way
Dittmer, MO 63023-3306
636-274-9044
314-781-4950
FAX: 636-285-1305
e-mail: dropin4fun@aol.com
sunnyhilladventures.org

*Victoria James, President/CEO*
*Jessica Erfling, Vice President of Operations*
*Donald Mitchell, Director of ISLA*
*Rob Darroch, Director of Sunnyhill Adventures*
Camp is located in Dittmer, Missouri. Summer sessions for campers with developmental disabilities and autism. Coed, ages 8-99. Sunnyhill Adventures is program that offers campers fun, exciting, educational experiences in a beautiful outdoor setting. Our residential summer camp combines traditional camping activities plus specially selected and adapted events to meet the needs of each camper group.

7559 **Talisman Summer Camp**
64 Gap Creek Rd
Zirconia, NC 28790-8791
828-697-6249
855-588-8254
e-mail: info@talismancamps.com
www.talismancamps.com

*Linda Tatsapaugh, Executive Director*
*Amy Allen, Admission Counselor*
*Doug Smathers, Summer Camps Director*
Camp is located in Black Mountain, North Carolina. Offers a program of hiking, rafting, climbing, and caving for learning disabled ADD/ADHD and autistic young people. Coed, ages 9-18.

**7560 Timbertop Nature Adventure Camp**
YMCA Camp Glacier Hollow
1000 Division St
Stevens Point, WI 54481-2724 715-342-2980
FAX: 715-342-2987
e-mail: pmatthai@spymca.org
www.glacierhollow.com

*Dave Morgan, Executive Director*
*Pete Matthai, Camp Director*
*Kyle Beach, Summer Camp Program Director*
For children who can benefit from an individualized program of learning in a non-competitive outdoor setting under the skilled leadership of people who understand the environment and the unique potential of these children.

**7561 Triangle Y Ranch YMCA**
YMCA of Southern Arizona
34434 S. Y Camp Road
P.O. Box 350
Oracle, AZ 85623 520-884-0987
FAX: 520-523-6418
e-mail: camp@tucsonymca.org
www.tucsonymca.org

*Dane Woll, President and CEO*
*Kerry Dufour, V.P. Chief Development Officer*
*Cathy Scheirman, Chief Financial Officer*
*Deneiva Knight, Administration and Communications Director*
Summer camp programs for children and young adults ages 6-17. Camp offers horseback riding, sports, story telling, arts & crafts, swimming, archery and nature programs.

**7562 Wendell Johnson Speech And Hearing Clinic**
University Of Iowa
250 Hawkins Dr
Iowa City, IA 52242-1025 319-335-8736
FAX: 319-335-8851
e-mail: dorothy-albright@uiowa.edu
www.uiowa.edu

*Dorothy Albright, Department Administration*
*Lauren Eldridge, Undergraduate Academic Programs*
*Mary Jo Yotty, Graduate Programs*
*Lauren Eldridge, Clinic Appointments*
The clinic offers assessment and remediation for communication disorders in adults and children. The clinic also offers a Intensive Summer Residential Clinic for school age children needing intervention services because of speech, language, hearing and/or reading problems.

## Print: Books

**7563 A Miracle to Believe In**
Option Indigo Press
2080 S Undermountain Rd
Sheffield, MA 01257-9643 413-229-8727
800-714-2779
FAX: 413-229-8727
e-mail: indigo@bcn.net
www.optionindigo.com

*Barry Neil Kaufman, Author*
A group of people from all walks of life come together and are transformed as they reach out, under the direction of the Kaufmans, to help a little boy the medical world had given up as hopeless. This heartwarming journey of loving a child back to life will not only inspire you, the reader, but presents a compelling new way to deal with life's traumas and difficulties.
*379 pages*
*ISBN 0-449201-08-2*

**7564 ADD: Helping Your Child**
Warner Books
1271 Avenue of the Americas
New York, NY 10020-1300 212-522-7200
FAX: 212-522-7989

*Barbara Smalley, Author*
*Bruce Paonessa, Vice President*
*Elizabeth Nunuz, Manager*
The definitive guide to helping children with AD/HD *$ 12.95*
*224 pages Paperback*
*ISBN 0-446670-13-8*

**7565 ADHD Book of Lists: A Practical Guide for Helping Children and Teens with ADDs**
Jossey-Bass
111 River St
Hoboken, NJ 7030-5773 201-748-6000
FAX: 201-748-6008
e-mail: info@wiley.com
www.wiley.com

*Sandra F Rief, Author*
Information about Attention Deficit/Hyperactivity Disorder including strategies, supports, and interventions that have been found to be the most effective. For teachers, parents, and counselors. *$29.95*
*320 pages*
*ISBN 0-787965-91-X*

**7566 ADHD in the Schools: Assessment and Intervention Strategies**
Guilford Press
72 Spring St
New York, NY 10012-4019 212-431-9800
800-365-7006
FAX: 212-966-6708
e-mail: info@guilford.com
www.guilford.com

*George J DuPaul, Author*
*Gary Stoner, Co-Author*
This landmark volume emphasizes the need for a team effort among parents, community-based professionals, and educators. Provides practical information for educators that is based on empirical findings. Chapters focus on: how to identify and assess students who might have ADHD; the relationship between ADHD and learning disabilities; how to develop and implement classroom-based programs; communication strategies to assist physicians; and the need for community-based treatments. *$ 36.00*
*269 pages Hardcover*
*ISBN 0-898622-45-X*

**7567 ADHD with Comorbid Disorders: Clinical Assessment and Management**
Guilford Press
72 Spring St
New York, NY 10012-4019 212-431-9800
800-365-7006
FAX: 212-966-6708
e-mail: info@guilford.com
www.guilford.com

*Steven R Pliszka, MD, Author*
*Caryn Leigh Carlson, Co-Author*
*James M Swanson, Co-Author*
*$44.00*
*Cloth*
*ISBN 1-572304-78-2*

**7568 AT for Individuals with Cognitive Impairment**
Idaho Assistive Technology Project
121 West Sweet Ave
Moscow, ID 83843
208-885-6097
800-432-8324
FAX: 208-885-6145
e-mail: sueh@uidaho.edu
www.idahoat.org

*Ron Seiler, Project Director*

**7569 Adolescents with Down Syndrome: Toward a More Fulfilling Life**
Brookes Publishing
P.O.Box 10624
Baltimore, MD 21285-624
410-337-9580
800-638-3775
FAX: 410-337-8539
e-mail: custserv@brookespublishing.com
www.brookespublishing.com

*Maria Sustrova, Author*
*Lauren Smith, Western Region Sales Representative*
*Jeannine Blimline, Central Region Sales Representative*
*Kevin Warg, Northeastern Region Sales Representative; AEPS(r) Specialist*
Written for health care professionals, psychologists, other developmental disabilities practitioners, educators, and parents, it covers biomedical concerns; behavioral, psychological, and psychiatric challenges; and education, employment, recreation, community, and legal concerns. *$35.95*
*416 pages Paperback*
*ISBN 1-55766-81-9*

**7570 Adult ADD: The Complete Handbook: Everything You Need to Know About How to Cope with ADD**
Prima Publishing
P.O.Box 1260
Rocklin, CA 95677-1260
916-787-7000
800-632-8676
FAX: 916-787-7001

*David B Sudderth, Author*
In simple and friendly terms, the authors offer help to those leading frustrating lives. They provide coping mechanisms, both psychological and an up-to-date guide to the latest technology *$14.95*
*272 pages*
*ISBN 0-761507-96-5*

**7571 All About Attention Deficit Disorders, Revised**
Parent Magic
800 Roosevelt Rd
Glen Ellyn, IL 60137-5839
317-595-9072
800-442-4453
FAX: 317-595-9075
www.parentmagic.com

*Thomas Phelan, Owner*
A psychologist and expert on ADD outlines the symptoms, diagnosis and treatment of this neurological disorder. *$12.95*
*248 pages Paperback*
*ISBN 1-889140-11-2*

**7572 Attention Deficit Disorder**
Sage Publications
2455 Teller Road
Thousand Oaks, CA 91320
800-818-7243
FAX: 800-583-2665
e-mail: info@sagepub.com
www.sagepub.com

*Sara Miller McCune, Founder, Publisher, Chairperson*
*Blaise R Simqu, President & CEO*
A book providing helpful suggestions for both home and classroom management of students with attention deficit disorder.

**7573 Attention Deficit Disorder and Learning Disabilities**
Books on Special Children
P.O.Box 305
Congers, NY 10920-305
845-638-1236
FAX: 845-638-0847
e-mail: irene@boscbooks.com

*Barbara Ingersoll, Author*
Introduces ADD and learning disabilities. This is an easy reading book. Gives definitions and discusses some effective and controverial medication, dietary, biofeedback, cognitive therapy, and many more issues. *$15.95*
*246 pages Softcover*
*ISBN 0-385469-31-4*

**7574 Attention Deficit Disorder in Adults Workbook**
Taylor Publishing Company
1550 W Mockingbird Ln
Dallas, TX 75235-5007
214-637-2800
800-677-2800
FAX: 214-819-8220
e-mail: sw_support@balfour.com
www.taylorpub.com

*Don Percenti, CEO*
We're BalfourTaylor Yearbooks, and we help thousands of schools and community organizations produce exceptional yearbooks each year. Whatever type of school or organization yours is - from elementary to university to civic or military organizations - we have a publishing solution to fit your needs. We'll also see to it that you receive unmatched help and personal service throughout the process. Balfour is the on-campus brand of American Achievement Corporation (AAC). *$17.99*
*192 pages Paperback*
*ISBN 0-878338-50-0*

**7575 Attention Deficit Disorder: A Different Perception**
Underwood Books
P.O.Box 1919
Nevada City, CA 95959-1919
800-788-3123
www.underwoodbooks.com

*Thorn Hartmann, Author*
Supports theory linking ADD to the genetic makeup of men and women who hunted for their food in prehestoric times. Also links second hand smoke to disruptive behavior. *$9.95*
*180 pages Paperback*
*ISBN 0-887331-56-4*

**7576 Attention Deficit Disorders: Assessment & Teaching**
Brooks/Cole Publishing Company
10650 Toebben Drive
Independence, KY 41051
859-525-2230
FAX: 859-282-5700
www.brookscole.com

*Janet W Lerner, Author*
A handy resource that offers teachers, school psychologists, councelors, social workers, administrators, and parents practical advice for working with children who have attention deficit disorders. *$18.95*
*258 pages Paperback*
*ISBN 0-534250-44-0*

**7577 Attention-Deficit Hyperactivity Disorder: Symptoms and Suggestons for Treatment**

Slosson Educational Publications Inc.
P.O.Box 280
East Aurora, NY 14052-280 716-652-0930
888-756-7766
FAX: 800-655-3840
e-mail: slossonprep@gmail.com
www.slosson.com

*Thomas W Phelan, Author*
*Steven Slosson, President*
*John Slosson, Vice President*
*David Slossan, Vice President*

An exhaustive review of current research and decades of experience as practicing school-based professionals, as well as being a parent of an ADHD child, have culminated in this brief, to-the-point, and yet informed ADHD package which has recieved tremendous reviews. Well-grounded answers and suggestions which would facillitate behavior, learning, social-emotional functioning, and other factors in preschool and adolesence are discussed. Answers most commonly asked questions about ADHD/ADD. *$60.00*

*61 pages*

**7578 Attention-Deficit/Hyperactivity Disorder, What Every Parent Wants to Know**

Brookes Publishing
P.O.Box 10624
Baltimore, MD 21285-624 410-337-9580
800-638-3775
FAX: 410-337-8539
e-mail: custserv@brookespublishing.com
www.brookespublishing.com

*David L Wodrich, Author*
*Lauren Smith, Western Region Sales Representative*
*Jeannine Blimline, Central Region Sales Representative*
*Kevin Warg, Northeastern Region Sales Representative; AEPS(r) Specialist*

New easy-to-understand, non-technical edition helps teachers and parents get accessible answers to their ADHD. *$21.95*

*304 pages Paperback*
*ISBN 1-557663-98-X*

**7579 Augmenting Basic Communciation in Natural Contexts**

Brookes Publishing
P.O.Box 10624
Baltimore, MD 21285-624 410-337-9580
800-638-3775
FAX: 410-337-8539
e-mail: custserv@brookespublishing.com
www.brookespublishing.com

*Jeanne M Johnson, Author*
*Lauren Smith, Western Region Sales Representative*
*Jeannine Blimline, Central Region Sales Representative*
*Kevin Warg, Northeastern Region Sales Representative; AEPS(r) Specialist*

Here you will find the techniques needed to establish a basic communication system for people of all ages with cognitive disabilities or motor sensory impairments. *$41.95*

*304 pages Paperback*
*ISBN 1-55766 -43-6*

**7580 Autism 24/7: A Family Guide to Learning at Home & in the Community**

Autism Society of North Carolina Bookstore
Ste 230
505 Oberlin Rd
Raleigh, NC 27605-1345 919-743-0204
800-442-2762
FAX: 919-743-0208
e-mail: jchampion@autismsociety-nc.org
www.autismsociety-nc.org

*David Lax, Manager*
*Martina Ballen, Chair*
*Beverly Moore, Vice Chair*
*Elizabeth Phillippi, Secretary*

Parents are encouraged to focus on skill sets and behaviors that most negatively affect family functioning, and replacing these behaviors with acceptable alternatives. *$19.95*

**7581 Autism Handbook: Understanding & Treating Autism & Prevention Development**

Oxford University Press
2001 Evans Rd
Cary, NC 27513-2009 919-677-0977
800-451-7556
FAX: 919-677-1303
www.oup-usa.org

*Thomas Carty, Senior Vice President*
*Simon Li, Regional Director*
*Adam Glazer, Director*
*Thomas McCarty, Manager/VP Operations*

*$25.00*
*320 pages*
*ISBN 0-195076-67-2*

**7582 Autism and Learning**

Taylor & Francis
37-41 Mortimer St
London, 1 171-405-5606
FAX: 171-831-4840
www.taylorandfrancis.com

*Rita Jordan, Author*
*Stuart Powell, Co-Author*

This book is about how a cognitive perception on the way in which individuals with autism think and learn may be applied to particular curriculum areas.

*160 pages Paperback*
*ISBN 1-853464-21-X*

**7583 Autism in Adolescents and Adults**

Springer Publishing
11 W 42nd St
Floor 15 #15
New York, NY 10036-8002 212-431-4370
FAX: 212-460-1575
e-mail: service-ny@springer.com
www.springerjournals.com

*Eric Schopler, Editor*
*$63.00*
*456 pages*
*ISBN 0-306410-57-5*

**7584 Autism...Nature, Diagnosis and Treatment**

Autism Society of North Carolina Bookstore
505 Oberlin Road
Suite 230
Raleigh, NC 27605-1345 919-743-0204
800-442-2762
FAX: 919-743-0208
e-mail: jchampion@autismsociety-nc.com
www.autismbookstore.com

*David Lax, Manager*

Covers perspectives, issues, neurobiological issues and new directions in diagnosis and treatment. *$49.00*

**7585 Autism: Explaining the Enigma**
Wiley Publishers
111 River St
Suite 2000
Hoboken, NJ 7030-5773
201-748-6000
FAX: 201-748-6088
e-mail: info@wiley.com
www.wiley.com

*Uta Firth, Author*
Explains the nature of autism. *$27.95*

**7586 Autism: From Tragedy to Triumph**
Branden Books
Po Box 812094
Wellesley, MA 02482
617-734-2045
FAX: 781-790-1056
www.brandenbooks.com

*Carol Johnson, Author*
*Julia Crowder, Co-Author*
A new book that deals with the Lovaas method and includes a foreward by Dr. Ivar Lovaas. The book is broken down into two parts - the long road to diagnosis and then treatment. *$12.95*

**7587 Autism: Identification, Education and Treatment**
Routledge
270 Madison Ave
Floor 4 #4
New York, NY 10016-0601
212-695-6599
FAX: 212-563-2269
www.routledge.com

*Dianne Zager, Editor*
*Jeffrey Lin, Director*
*Francis Chua, Manager*
*Tamaryn Anderson, Marketing Manager*
Chapters include medical treatments, early intervention and communication development in autism. *$36.00*

*ISBN 0-805820-44-7*

**7588 Autism: The Facts**
Oxford University Press
2001 Evans Rd
Cary, NC 27513-2010
919-677-0977
800-451-7556
FAX: 919-677-1303
www.oup-usa.org

*Simon Cohen, Author*
*Patrick Bolton, Co-Author*
*$22.50*
*128 pages*
*ISBN 0-192623-27-3*

**7589 Autistic Adults at Bittersweet Farms**
Routledge
270 Madison Ave
Floor 4 #4
New York, NY 10016-0601
212-695-6599
FAX: 212-563-2269
www.routledge.com

*Norman Giddan PhD, Author*
*Jane Giddan MA, Co-Author*
*Jefferey Lin, Director*
*Francis Chua, Manager*
A touching view of an inspirational residential care program for autistic adolescents and adults. Also available in softcover. *$94.95*
*Hardcover*
*ISBN 1-560240-42-3*

**7590 Be Quiet, Marina!**
Star Bright Books
30-19 48th Ave
Long Island City, NY 11101-3419
718-784-9112
FAX: 718-784-9012
e-mail: orders@starbrightbooks.com
www.starbrightbooks.com

*Kirsten Debear, Author*
A noisy little girl with cerebral palsy and a quiet little girl with Down Syndrome learn to play together and eventually become best friends. *$16.95*
*40 pages Hardcover*
*ISBN 1-887734-79-1*

**7591 Breakthroughs: How to Reach Students with Autism**
Aquarius Health Care Media
30 Forest Road
PO Box 249
Millis, MA 02054
508-376-1244
FAX: 508-376-1245
e-mail: aqvideos@tiac.net
www.aquariusproductions.com

*Leslie Krussman, President/Producer*
*Joseph Wellington, Distribution Coordinator*
*Anne Baker, Billing & Accounting*
*Jane Hutchinson, Associate Director William Patterson University*
A hands-on, how-to program for reaching students with autism, featuring Karen Sewell, Autism Society of America's teacher of the year. Here Sewell demonstrates the successful techniques she's developed over a 20-year career. A separate 250 page manual ($59) is also available which covers math, reading, fine motor, self help, social adaptive, vocational and self help skills as well as providing numerous plan reproducibles and an exhaustive listing of equipment and materials resources. Video. *$99.00*

**7592 Bus Girl: Selected Poems**
Brookline Books
34 University Rd
Brookline, MA 02445-4533
617-734-6772
800-666-2665
FAX: 617-734-3952
e-mail: brbooks@yahoo.com
www.brooklinebooks.com

*Gretchen Josephson, Author*
*Lula O Lubchenco, Editor*
Poems written over several decades by a young woman with Down Syndrome. *$14.95*
*144 pages Paperback*
*ISBN 1-57129-41-9*

**7593 Change Your Brain, Change Your Life: The Breakthrough Program for Conquering Depression**
Three Rivers Press
3rd Floor
175 Broadway
New York, NY 10019
212-782-9000
FAX: 212-940-7860
www.randomhouse.com

*Daniel G Amen MD, Author*
Clinical neuroscientist and psychiatrist Amen uses nuclear brain imaging to diagnose and treat behavioral problems. He explains how the brain works, what happens when things go wrong, and how to optimize brain function. Five sections of the brain are discussed, and case studies clearly illustrate possible problems. *$15.00*
*352 pages*
*ISBN 0-812929-98-5*

**7594 Child and Adolescent Therapy: Cognitive-Behavioral Procedures, Third Edition**

Guilford Press
72 Spring St
New York, NY 10012-4019
212-431-9800
800-365-7006
FAX: 212-966-6708
e-mail: info@guilford.com
www.guilford.com

*Chris Jennison, Publisher Emeritus, Education*
*Seymour Weingarten, Editor-in-Chief*
*Jody Falco, Managing Editor: Periodicals*
*Natalie Graham, Editor: School Psychology, Literacy*

Incorporating significant developments in treatment procedures, theory and clinical research, new chapters in this second edition examine the current status of empirically supported interventions and developmental issues specific to work with adolescents. *$45.00*

*432 pages Cloth*
*ISBN 1-572305-56-8*

**7595 Children with Mental Retardation**

Woodbine House
6510 Bells Mill Rd
Bethesda, MD 20817-1636
301-897-3570
800-843-7323
FAX: 301-897-5838
e-mail: info@woodbinehouse.com
www.woodbinehouse.com

*Irv Shapell, Owner*

A book for parents of children with mild to moderate mental retardation, whether or not they have a diagnosed syndrome or condition. It provides a complete and compassionate introduction to their child's medical, therapeutic, and educational needs, and discusses the emotional impact on the family. New parents can rely on Children with Mental Retardation to provide that solid foundation and confidence they need to help their child reach his or her highest potential. *$14.95*

*437 pages Paperback*
*ISBN 0-933149-39-5*

**7596 Cognitive Behavioral Therapy for Adult Asperger Syndrome**

Autism Society of North Carolina Bookstore
Ste 230
505 Oberlin Rd
Raleigh, NC 27605-1345
919-743-0204
800-442-2762
FAX: 919-743-0208
e-mail: jchampion@autismsociety-nc.org
www.autismbookstore.com

*David Lax, Manager*

Text is prepared with case studies and examples from the author's own experiences working as a cognitive-behavioral therapist specializing in adults and adolescents with dual diagnosis, autism spectrum disorders, mood disorders, and anxiety disorders.

**7597 Communication Development in Children with Down Syndrome**

Brookes Publishing
P.O.Box 10624
Baltimore, MD 21285-624
410-337-9580
800-638-3775
FAX: 410-337-8539
e-mail: custserv@brookespublishing.com
www.brookespublishing.com

*Libby Kumin, Author*
*Lauren Smith, Western Region Sales Representative*
*Jeannine Blimline, Central Region Sales Representative*
*Kevin Warg, Northeastern Region Sales Representative; AEPS(r) Specialist*

This book offers an extensive, detailed explanation of communication development in children with Down syndrome relative to their advancing cognitive skills. It introduces a critical framework for assessing and treating hearing, speech, and language problems and provides explicit intervention methods and tested clinical protocols.

*Paperback*
*ISBN 1-55766 -50-5*

**7598 Comprehensive Guide to ADD in Adults: Research, Diagnosis & Treatment**

ADD Warehouse
Ste 102
300 NW 70th Ave
Plantation, FL 33317-2360
954-792-8100
800-233-9273
FAX: 954-792-8545
e-mail: websales@addwarehouse.com
www.addwarehouse.com

*Harvey C Parker, Owner*

The first to provide broad coverage of the burgeoning field. Written for professionals who diagnose and treat adults with ADD, it provides information from psychologists and physicians on the most current research and treatment issues *$50.95*

*426 pages*
*ISBN 0-876307-60-8*

**7599 Concentration Cockpit: Explaining Attention Deficits**

Educators Publishing Service
P.O.Box 9031
Cambridge, MA 02139-9031
617-367-2700
800-225-5750
FAX: 617-547-0412
e-mail: CustomerService.EPS@schoolspecialty.com
www.epsbooks.com

*Melvin D Levine, Author*

This eight-page pamphlet explains the administration of The Concentration Cockpit, a newly revised poster that helps children with attention deficits gain insight into their problems and monitor their progress in grappling with these problems. *$64.50*

*ISBN 0-838820-59-X*

**7600 Coping with ADD/ADHD**

Rosen Publishing Group
29 E 21st St
New York, NY 10010-6209
212-420-1600
800-237-9932
FAX: 888-436-4643
e-mail: rosenpub@tribeca.ios.com
www.rosenpublishing.com

*Jaydene Morrison, Author*

At least 3.5 million American youngsters suffer from attention deficit disorder. This book defines the syndrome and provides specific information about treatment and counseling. *$16.95*

*ISBN 0-823920-70-4*

**7601 Count Us In**

Exceptional Parent Library
P.O.Box 1807
Englewood Cliffs, NJ 7632-1207
201-947-6000
800-535-1910
FAX: 201-947-9376
e-mail: eplibrary@aol.com
www.eplibrary.com

*Jason Kingsley, Author*
*Mitchell Levitz, Co-Author*

Offers information on growing up with Downs Syndrome. *$9.95*

**7602 Culture and the Restructuring of Community Mental Health**
Greenwood Publishing Group
130 Cremona Drive
Santa Barbara, CA 93117
80- 96- 191
800-368-6868
FAX: 866-270-3856
e-mail: CustomerService@abc-clio.com
www.greenwood.com

*William A Vega, Author*
*John W Murphy, Co-Author*
Examines treatment, organizational planning and research issues and offers a critique of the theoretical and programmatic aspects of providing mental health services to traditionally underserved populations. $45.00-$52.95. *$95.00*
*168 pages Hardcover*
*ISBN 0-313268-87-8*

**7603 Difficult Child**
Bantam Books
1745 Broadway
New York, NY 10019
212-782-9000
FAX: 212-302-7985
e-mail: BBDPublicity@randomhouse.com
www.randomhouse.com/bantamdell

*Stanley Turecki, Author*
*Leslie Tonner, Co-Author*
The classic and definitive work on parenting hard-to-raise children with new sections on ADHD and the latest medications for childhood disorders. *$15.95*
*302 pages Paperback*
*ISBN 0-553380-36-2*

**7604 Disability Culture Perspective on Early Intervention**
Through the Looking Glass
3075 Adeline Street
Suite 120
Berkeley, CA 94703-2212
510-848-1112
800-644-2666
FAX: 510-848-4445
e-mail: TLG@lookingglass.org
www.lookingglass.org

*Megan Kirshbaum PhD, Author*
For parents with physical or cognitive disabilities and their families. Available in braille, large print or cassette. *$2.00*
*12 pages*

**7605 Down Syndrome**
Aquarius Health Care Media
30 Forest Road
Po Box 249
Millis, MA 02054-1066
508-376-1244
888-440-2963
FAX: 508-376-1245
e-mail: aqvideos@tiac.net
www.aquariusproductions.com

*Lesile Kussmann, Owner*
This is an excellent video for families who have just had a baby with Down Syndrome as well as professionals in the field of genetics and nursing. Through honest and open discussion, parents of children with Down Syndrome express the feelings and concerns they had during the early years of their child's life. Preview option available. *$150.00*
*Video*

**7606 Driven to Distraction**
Simon & Schuster/Touchstone Publishing
Fl 11
1230 Avenue of the Americas
New York, NY 10020- 1513
212-698-7000
FAX: 212-698-7009
www.simonsays.com

*Edward M Hallowell, MD, Author*
*John J Ratey, MD, Co-Author*
A practical book discussing adult as well as child attention deficit disorder (ADD). Non-technical, realistic and optimistic, it is an informative how-to manual for parents and consumers. *$23.00*

**7607 Dyslexia over the Lifespan**
Educators Publishing Service
P.O.Box 9031
Cambridge, MA 02139-9031
617-367-2700
800-225-5750
FAX: 617-547-0412
e-mail: eps@schoolspecialty.com
www.epsbooks.com

*Margaret B Rawston, Author*
Discusses the educational and career development of 56 dyslexic boys from a private school that was one of the first to have a program to detect and treat developmental language disabilities. *$ 18.00*
*224 pages*
*ISBN 0-838816-70-3*

**7608 Embracing the Monster: Overcoming the Challenges of Hidden Disabilities**
Paul H Brookes Publishing Company
P.O.Box 10624
Baltimore, MD 21285-624
410-337-9580
800-638-3775
FAX: 410-337-8539
e-mail: custserv@brokespublishing.com
www.brookespublishing.com

*Veronica Crawford M.A., Author*
*Larry B Silver, MD, Foreword/Commentary*
The author shares her experience of living with LD, ADHD and bipolar disorder to give readers an awareness of the challenges of living with hidden disabilities and what can be done to help *$24.95*
*272 pages paperback*
*ISBN 1-557665-22-2*

**7609 Encounters with Autistic States**
Jason Aronson
400 Keystone Industrial Park
Dunmore, PA 18512-1507
800-782-0015
FAX: 201-840-7242

*Theodore Mitrani, Author*
This book explores and explands the work of the late Frances Tustin, which was devoted to the psychoanalytic understanding of the bewildering elemental world of the autistic child. *$50.00*
*448 pages Hardcover*
*ISBN 0-765700-62-*

**7610 Equal Treatment for People With Mental Retardation: Having and Raising Children**
Harvard University Press
79 Garden St
Cambridge, MA 2138-1423
617-495-1000
800-405-1619
FAX: 617-495-5898
www.hup.harvard.edu

*William Sisler, President*
*Valerie A Sanchez, Co-Author*
*Martha A Field, co-Author*

A Harvard law professor and civil liberties practitioner provide a comprehensive examination of the reproductive and parental rights of mentally retarded citizens. *$19.95*

*464 pages Paperback*

*ISBN 0-674006-97-6*

**7611 Families of Adults With Autism: Stories & Advice For the Next Generation**

Autism Society of North Carolina Bookstore
Ste 230
505 Oberlin Rd
Raleigh, NC 27605-1345
919-743-0204
800-442-2762
FAX: 919-743-0208
e-mail: tsheriff@autismsociety-nc.org
www.autismbookstore.com

*Tracey Sheriff, Chief Executive Officer*
*Paul Wendler, Chief Financial Officer*
*David Laxton, Director of Communications*
*Kristy White, Director of Development*

This book's unique point of view is that of a parent who's been there and done that and is now willing to tell the reader what it was like. *$19.95*

**7612 Family Therapy for ADHD: Treating Children, Adolescents and Adults**

Guilford Press
72 Spring St
New York, NY 10012-4019
800-365-7006
www.guilford.com

*Craig A Everett, Author*
*Sandra Volgy Everett, Co-Author*

Presents an innovative approach to assesing and treating ADHD in the family context. *$29.00*

*Paperback*

*ISBN 1-572304-38-3*

**7613 Fighting for Darla: Challenges for Family Care & Professional Responsibility**

Teachers College Press
1234 Amsterdam Ave
New York, NY 10027-6602
212-678-3929
FAX: 212-678-4149
e-mail: tcpress@tc.columbia.edu

*Mary Lynch, Manager*
*Susan M Klein, Co-Author*
*Samuel Guskin, Co-Author*

Follows the story of Darla, a pregnant adolescent with autism. *$18.95*

*161 pages*

*ISBN 0-807733-56-3*

**7614 Fragile Success**

Brookes Publishing
P.O.Box 10624
Baltimore, MD 21285-624
410-337-9580
800-638-3775
FAX: 410-337-8539
www.brookespublishing.com

*Virginia Walker Sperry, Author*

A book about the lives of autistic children, whom the author has followed from their early years at the Elizabeth Ives School in New Haven, CT, through to adulthood. *$27.50*

*ISBN 1-557664-58-7*

**7615 Getting Our Heads Together**

Thoms Rehabilitation Hospital
68 Sweeten Creek Rd
Asheville, NC 28803-2318
828-274-2400
FAX: 828-274-9452

*Kathi Petersen, Director Planning/Communication*
*Edgardo Diez MD, Medical Director Brain Injury*
*Kathy Price, Director Admissions*
*Chat Norvell, CEO*

A handbook for families of head injured patients - available in Spanish as well as English. *$4.00*

*40 pages Paperback*

**7616 Getting a Grip on ADD: A Kid's Guide to Understanding & Coping with ADD**

Educational Media Corporation
P.O.Box 21311
4256 Central Ave
Minneapolis, MN 55421-311
763-781-0088
800-966-3382
FAX: 763-781-7753
e-mail: emedia@educationalmedia.com
educationalmedia.com

*Kim Frank Ed.S., Author*
*Susan Smith-Rex Ed.D., Co-Author*

Free catalog of resources.

*64 pages Yearly*

**7617 Getting the Best for Your Child with Autism**

Autism Society of North Carolina Bookstore
Ste 230
505 Oberlin Rd
Raleigh, NC 27605-1345
919-743-0204
800-442-2762
FAX: 919-743-0208
e-mail: tsheriff@autismsociety-nc.org
www.autismbookstore.com

*Tracey Sheriff, Chief Executive Officer*
*Paul Wendler, Chief Financial Officer*
*David Laxton, Director of Communications*
*Kristy White, Director of Development*

This treatment guide helps parents navigate the complex and overwhelming world of Autism. *$16.95*

**7618 Group Activity for Adults with Brain Injury**

Sage Publications
2455 Teller Road
Thousand Oaks, CA 91320
805-499-9774
800-818-7243
FAX: 800-583-2665
e-mail: info@sagepub.com
www.sagepub.com

*Sara Miller McCune, Founder, Publisher, Chairperson*
*Blaise R Simqu, President & CEO*
*Tracey A. Ozmina, Executive Vice President & Chief Operating Officer*
*Chris Hickok, Senior Vice President & Chief Financial Officer*

This manual addresses attention, memory, reasoning, and language skills in group settings. *$53.00*

**7619 Guide to Successful Employment for Individuals with Autism**

Brookes Publishing
P.O.Box 10624
Baltimore, MD 21285-624
410-337-9580
800-638-3775
FAX: 410-337-8539
e-mail: custserv@brookespublishing.com
www.brookespublishing.com

*Marcia Daltow Smith, Author*
*Ronald G Belcher, Co-Author*
*Patricia D Juhrs, Co-Author*
*Lauren Smith, Western Region Sales Representative*

Describing all aspects of job placement, this book details strategies for assessing workers, networking for job opportunities, and tailoring job supports to each individual. Also illustrates how to help individuals with autism become productive workers, and with detailed descriptions of specific jobs help provide ideas for employment. *$ 32.95*

*336 pages Paperback*

*ISBN 1-55766-71-5*

**7620 Handbook of Autism and Pervasive Developmental Disorders**

Autism Society of North Carolina Bookstore
Ste 230
505 Oberlin Rd
Raleigh, NC 27605-1345 919-743-0204
800-442-2762
FAX: 919-743-0208
e-mail: books@autismsociety-nc.org
www.autismbookstore.com

*David Lax, Manager*

A list of contributors address such topics as characteristics of autistic syndromes and interventions. *$125.00*

**7621 Helping People with Autism Manage Their Behavior**

Indiana Resource Center For Autism
2853 E 10th St
Bloomington, IN 47408-2696 812-855-6508
FAX: 812-855-9630
e-mail: prattc@indiana.edu
www.iidc.indiana.edu

*David Mank, Executive Director*
*Scott Bellini, Assistant Director*

Covers the broad topic of helping people with autism manage their behavior. *$7.00*

**7622 Helping Your Child with Attention-Deficit Hyperactivity Disorder**

Learning Disabilities Association of America
4156 Library Rd
Pittsburgh, PA 15234-1349 412-341-1515
FAX: 412-344-0224
e-mail: info@ldaamerica.org
www.ldaamerica.org

*Patricia H. Latham, President*
*Ernie Florence, First Vice President*
*Ed Schlitt, Treasurer*
*Sharon Bloechle, Secretary*

LDA is the largest non-profit volunteer organization advocating for individuals with learning disabilities

**7623 Helping Your Hyperactive: Attention Deficit Child**

Crown Publishing Company (Random House)
1745 Broadway
New York, NY 10019-4305 212-782-9000
800-632-8676
FAX: 212-572-6066
e-mail: websupportlife@primapub.com
www.randomhouse.com/crown

*John Taylor, Author*

*$19.95*

*ISBN 1-559584-23-8*

**7624 Hidden Child: The Linwood Method for Reaching the Autistic Child**

Woodbine House
6510 Bells Mill Rd
Bethesda, MD 20817-1636 301-897-3570
800-843-7323
FAX: 301-897-5838
e-mail: info@woodbinehouse.com
www.woodbinehouse.com

*Irv Shapell, Owner*
*Sabine Oishi, Co-Author*

Chronicle of the Linwood Children's Center's successful treatment program for autistic children. *$17.95*

*286 pages Paperback*

*ISBN 0-933149-06-9*

**7625 How To Reach and Teach Children and Teens with Dyslexia**

Jossey-Bass
111 River St
Hoboken, NJ 7030-5773 201-748-6000
FAX: 201-748-6008
e-mail: info@wiley.com
www.wiley.com

*Cynthia M Stowe, Author*

This practical resource gives educators at all levels essential information, techniques, and tolls for understanding dyslexia and adapting teaching methods in all subject areas to meet the learning style, social, and emotional needs of students who have dyslexia. *$ 22.95*

*340 pages*

*ISBN 0-130320-18-8*

**7626 How to Own and Operate an Attention Deficit Disorder**

Learning Disabilities Association of America
4156 Library Rd
Pittsburgh, PA 15234-1349 412-341-1515
FAX: 412-344-0224
e-mail: info@ldaamerica.org
www.ldaamerica.org

*Debra Maxey, Author*
*Patricia H. Latham, President*
*Ernie Florence, First Vice President*
*Ed Schlitt, Treasurer*

Clear, informative and sensitive introduction to ADHD. Packed with practical things to do at home and school, from a professional and mother of a son with ADHD. *$8.95*

*43 pages*

**7627 Hyperactive Child, Adolescent, and Adult: ADD Through the Lifespan**

Oxford University Press
198 Madison Ave
New York, NY 10016-4308 212-726-6000
www.us.oup.com/us

*Paul H Wender, Author*

Comprehensive general review. Update on previous research by the author, offering a basic text. Published by Connecticut Association for Children & Adults with Learning Disabilities (CACLD). *$8.75*

*162 pages*

*ISBN 0-195113-49-7*

**7628 Hyperactivity, Attention Deficits, and School Failure: Better Ways**

Learning Disabilities Association of America
4156 Library Rd
Pittsburgh, PA 15234-1349 412-341-1515
FAX: 412-344-0224
e-mail: info@ldaamerica.org
www.ldaamerica.org

*Patricia H. Latham, President*
*Ernie Florence, First Vice President*
*Ed Schlitt, Treasurer*
*Sharon Bloechle, Secretary*

LDA is the largest non-profit volunteer organization advocating for individuals with learning disabilities

**7629 In Search of Wings: A Journey Back from Traumatic Brain Injury**

Lash & Associates Publishing/Training
100 Boardwalk Drive, Suite 150
Youngsville, NC 27596 919-556-0300
FAX: 919-556-0900
e-mail: orders@lapublishing.com
www.lapublishing.com

*Beverly Bryant, Author*
*Bob Cluett, CEO*
*Marilyn Lash, President*
*Nick Vidal, Director of IT*

The true story of one woman coping with traumatic brain injury after a car accident that affected her cognitive skills and memory *$14.95*
*233 pages*
*ISBN 1-882332-00-8*

**7630 In Their Own Way**

Alliance for Parental Involvement in Education
375 Hudson Street
New York, NY 10014 212-366-2000
e-mail: ecommerce@us.penguingroup.com
http://us.penguingroup.com

*Thomas Armstrong, Author*
*John Makinson, Chairman and Chief Executive*
*Coram Williams, CFO*
*David Shanks, CEO*

For the parents whose children are not thriving in school, Armstrong offers insight into individual learning styles. *$11.95*

**7631 Increasing and Decreasing Behaviors of Persons with Severe Retardation and Autism**

Research Press
P.O.Box 9177
Champaign, IL 61826-9177 217-352-3273
800-519-2707
FAX: 217-352-1221
e-mail: rp@researchpress.com
www.researchpress.com

*Dennis Wiziecki, Marketing*
*Richard M Fox, Author*

These well-organized manuals are written for teachers, aides and persons responsible for designing or evaluating behavioral programs. Offers specific guidelines for arranging and managing the learning environment as well as standards for evaluating and maintaining success. In Volume Two of this series, chapters address more restrictive procedures including physical restraing, punishment, time-out and overcorrection. Set of two volumes. *$39.50*
*230 pages Paperback*
*ISBN 0-878222-63-4*

**7632 Jumpin' Johnny Get Back to Work, A Child's Guide to ADHD/Hyperactivity**

Ste 15-5
25 Van Zant St
Norwalk, CT 6855-1729 203-838-5010
FAX: 203-866-6108
e-mail: CACLD@optonline.net
www.CACLD.org

*Beryl Kaufman, Executive Director*

Written primarily for elementary age youngsters with ADHD to help them understand their disability. Also valuable as an educational tool for parents, siblings, friends and classmates. Includes two pages on medication. *$12.50*
*24 pages*

**7633 Keys to Parenting a Child with Attention Deficit Disorder**

Barron's Educational Series
250 Wireless Blvd
Hauppauge, NY 11788-3924 631-434-3311
800-645-3476
FAX: 631-434-3723
e-mail: barrons@barronseduc.com
barronseduc.com

*Manuel H Barron, CEO*
*Francine McNamara MSW CSW, Co/Author*

This book shows how to work with the child's school, effectively manage the child's behavior and act as the child's advocate. *$6.95*
*160 pages Paperback*
*ISBN 0-812014-59-6*

**7634 Keys to Parenting a Child with Downs Syndrome**

Barron's Educational Series
250 Wireless Blvd
Hauppauge, NY 11788-3924 631-434-3311
800-645-3476
FAX: 631-434-3723
e-mail: barrons@barronseduc.com
barronseduc.com

*Manuel H Barron, CEO*
*Lucy Guarino*

Down Syndrome poses many challenges for children and their families. This book prepares parents and guardians to raise a child with Down Syndrome by discussing adjustment, advocacy, health and behavior, education and planning for greater independence. *$5.95*
*160 pages Paperback*
*ISBN 0-812014-58-8*

**7635 Keys to Parenting the Child with Autism**

Barron's Educational Series
250 Wireless Blvd
Hauppauge, NY 11788-3924 631-434-3311
800-645-3476
FAX: 631-434-3723
e-mail: barrons@barronseduc.com
barronseduc.com

*Manuel H Barron, CEO*

Parents of children with autism will find a solid balance between home and practical information in this book. It explains what autism is and how it is diagnosed, then advises parents on how to adjust to their child and give the best care. *$6.95*
*208 pages Paperback*
*ISBN 0-812016-79-3*

**7636 LD Child and the ADHD Child: Ways Parents & Professionals Can Help**
1406 Plaza Dr
Winston Salem, NC 27103-1470
336-768-1374
800-222-9796
FAX: 336-768-9194
e-mail: southern@blairpub.com
www.blairpub.com

*Carolyn Sakowski, President*
*Susan H Stevens, Author*
Book about learning disabilities available to parents. Stevens cuts through the jargon and complex theories which usually characterize books on the subject to present effective and practical techniques that parents can employ to help their child succeed at home and at school. New edition adds information about ADHD children. *$12.95*
*201 pages Paperback*
*ISBN 0-895871-42-4*

**7637 Labeling the Mentally Retarded**
University of California Press
2120 Berkeley Way
Berkeley, CA 94704-1012
510-642-4247
FAX: 510-643-7127
www.ucpress.edu

*Lynne Whity, Executive Director*
*Jane R Mercer, Author*
Clinical and social system perspectives on mental retardation. *$12.95*
*333 pages Paper*

**7638 Let Community Employment be the Goal for Individuals with Autism**
Indiana Resource Center For Autism
2853 E 10th St
Bloomington, IN 47408-2601
812-855-9396
800-825-4733
FAX: 812-855-9630
e-mail: prattc@indiana.edu
www.iidc.indiana.edu

*David Mank, Executive Director*
*Scott Bellini, Assistant Director*
A guide designed for people who are responsible for preparing individuals with autism to enter the work force. *$7.00*

**7639 Making the Writing Process Work**
Brookline Books
34 University Rd
Brookline, MA 02445-4533
617-734-6772
800-666-2665
FAX: 617-734-3952
e-mail: brbooks@yahoo.com
www.brooklinebooks.com

*Karen R Harris, Author*
*Steve Graham, Co-Author*
Making the Writing Process Work: Strategies for Composition and Self-Regulation is geared toward students who have difficulty organizing their thoughts and developing their writing. The specific strategies teach students how to approach, organize, and produce a final written product. *$24.95*
*240 pages Paperback*
*ISBN 1-57129 -10-9*

**7640 Management of Autistic Behavior**
Sage Publications
2455 Teller Road
Thousand Oaks, CA 91320
805-499-9774
800-818-7243
FAX: 800-583-2665
e-mail: info@sagepub.com
www.sagepub.com

*Sara Miller McCune, Founder, Publisher, Chairperson*
*Blaise R Simqu, President & CEO*
*Tracey A. Ozmina, Executive Vice President & Chief Operating Officer*
*Stephen Barr, Managing Director*
This excellent reference is a comprehensive and practical book that tells what works best with specific problems. *$41.00*
*450 pages*

**7641 Management of Children and Adolescents with AD-HD**
Learning Disabilities Association of America
4156 Library Rd
Pittsburgh, PA 15234-1349
412-341-1515
FAX: 412-344-0224
e-mail: info@ldaamerica.org
www.ldaamerica.org

*Patricia H. Latham, President*
*Ernie Florence, First Vice President*
*Ed Schlitt, Treasurer*
*Sharon Bloechle, Secretary*
LDA is the largest non-profit volunteer organization advocating for individuals with learning disabilities

**7642 Managing Attention Deficit Hyperactivity in Children: A Guide for Practitioners**
John Wiley & Sons Inc
111 River St
Hoboken, NJ 07030-5774
201-748-6000
800-825-7550
FAX: 201-748-6088
e-mail: info@wiley.com
www.wiley.com

*Warren J Baker, President*
*Michael Goldstein, Co-Author*
*Matthe S Kissner, CEO*
Offers information about human personality, structure and dynamics, assessment and adjustment. *$27.50*
*214 pages Hardcover*
*ISBN 0-471121-58-9*

**7643 Mental Retardation**
McGraw-Hill, School Publishing
220 E Danieldale Rd
Desoto, TX 75115-2490
972-224-1111
mcgraw-hill.com

*Harold McGraw III, Chairman, President and CEO*
*Jack F. Callahan, Executive Vice President, Chief Financial Officer*
*John Berisford, Executive Vice President, Human Resources*
*D. Edward (Ted) Smyth, Executive Vice President, Corporate Affairs*
Combines significant findings from the most current research, focusing on a unique relationship between the special educator and the learner with mental retardation.
*656 pages Casebound*

**7644 Mental Retardation: A Life-Cycle Approach**
Pearson Publishing
200 Old Tappan Rd
Old Tappan, NJ 07675-7033
201-785-2721
800-922-0579
FAX: 201-797-2993
www.pearsonhighered.com

*Clifford J Drew, Author*
*Michael L Hardman, Co/Author*

This text considers the needs of the retarded individual at every stage of life.
*512 pages*

**7645 Neurobiology of Autism**
Johns Hopkins University Press
2715 N Charles St
Baltimore, MD 21218-4363 410-516-6900
FAX: 410-516-6968
www.press.jhu.edu

*William Brody, President*
*Thomas L Kemper, Co-Author*
*Margaret L Bauman, M.D., Co-Author*
*Thomas L Kemper, M.D., Co-Author*
This book discusses recent advances in scientific research that point to a neurobiological basis for autism and examines the clinical implications of this research. *$28.00*
*272 pages*
*ISBN 0-801880-47-5*

**7646 Out of the Fog: Treatment Options and Coping Strategies for ADD**
Hyperion
114 Fifth Avenue
New York, NY 10011 212-456-0133
FAX: 212-456-0176
www.hyperionbooks.com

*Robert Miller, President*
*Suzanne Levert, Co-Author*
Discusses the recent recognition of attention deficit disorder as a problem that is not outgrown in adolescence, and cogently summarizes the stumbling blocks this affliction creates in the pursuit of a career or attainment of a healthy family life *$14.95*
*300 pages*
*ISBN 0-786880-87-2*

**7647 Overcoming Dyslexia**
Vintage-Random House
3rd Fl
1745 Broadway
New York, NY 10019-4305 212-782-9000
FAX: 212-302-7985
www.randomhouse.com/vintage

*Markus Dohle, CEO*
*Sally Shawitz, M.D., Author*
Yale neuroscientist Shaywitz demystifies the roots of dyslexia (a neurologically based reading difficulty affecting one in five children) and offers parents and educators hope that children with reading problems can be helped. *$15.00*
*432 pages*
*ISBN 0-679781-59-5*

**7648 Parent Survival Manual**
Springer Publishing Company
11 West 42nd Street
15th Floor
New York, NY 10036-8002 212-750-3383
877-687-7476
FAX: 212-941-7842
www.springerpub.com

*Ursula Springer, President*
*Ted Nardin, CEO*
*Edie Lambiase, CFO*
A guide to crises resolution in autism and related developmental disorders. *$39.95*

**7649 Parent's Guide to Down Syndrome: Toward a Brighter Future**
Brookes Publishing
P.O.Box 10624
Baltimore, MD 21285-0624 410-337-9580
800-638-3775
FAX: 410-337-8539
e-mail: custserv@brookespublishing.com
www.brookespublishing.com

*Siegfried Pueschel MD PhD, Author*
Highlights developmental stages and shows the advances that improve a child's quality of life. Includes discussions on easing the transition from home to school and choosing integration and curricular priorities, as well as guidelines for confronting adolescent and adult issues such as social and sexual needs and independent living and vocational options. *$21.95*
*352 pages*
*ISBN 1-557664-52-8*

**7650 Parenting Attention Deficit Disordered Teens**
CACLD
25 Van Zant Street
Norwalk, CT 06855-1729 203-838-5010
FAX: 203-866-6108
e-mail: CACLD@optonline.net
cacld.org

*Beryl Kaufman, Executive Director*
Detailed outline of the various problems of adolescents with ADHD. Published by Connecticut Association for Children & Adults with Learning Disabilities (CACLD). *$3.25*
*14 pages*

**7651 Parents Helping Parents: A Directory of Support Groups for ADD**
Novartis Pharmaceuticals Division
59 State Route 10
East Hanover, NJ 7936-1005 862-778-7500
800-742-2422

*Paulo Costa, CEO*

**7652 Please Don't Say Hello**
Human Sciences Press
233 Spring St
New York, NY 10013-1522 212-229-2859
800-221-9369
FAX: 212-463-0742
http://isbndb.com

*Carl Baker, Author*
Paul and his family moved into a new neighborhood. Paul's brother was autistic. The children thought that Eddie was retarded until they learned that there were skills that he could do better than they could. *$10.95*
*47 pages Paperback*
*ISBN 0-89885 -99-8*

**7653 Preventable Brain Damage**
Springer Publishing Company
536 Broadway
New York, NY 10012-3915 212-431-4370
877-687-7476
FAX: 212-941-7842
e-mail: marketing@springerpub.com
www.springerpub.com

*Donald L Templer, Author*
*Lawrence C Hartlage, Co-Author*
*Ursula Springer, President*
*Ted Nardin, CEO*
Offers information on brain injuries from motor vehicle accidents, contact sports and injuries of children. *$35.95*
*256 pages*

**7654 Reading, Writing and Speech Problems in Children**
International Dyslexia Association
Po Box 233
Brooklandville, MD 21022
410-296-0232
800-509-4980
FAX: 800-509-4980
e-mail: info@idamd.org
www.interdys.org

*Samuel Orton, Author*
*Steve Peregay, Executive Director*
*Kristin Penczek, Director Of Conferences*
*Kristi Bauman, Director Of Development*
A tribute to the man who more than any other aroused the attention of the scientific community and who provided the sound educational principles on which much teaching of dyslexics today is based. *$27.00*

*ISBN 0-89079 -79-1*

**7655 Reality of Dyslexia**
Brookline Books
34 University Rd
Brookline, MA 02445-4533
617-734-6772
800-666-2665
FAX: 617-734-3952
e-mail: brbooks@yahoo.com
www.brooklinebooks.com

*John Osmond, Author*
An informative and sensitive study of living with dyslexia which affects one in 25. He introduces the reader to the subject by sharing the difficulties of his dyslexic son. He then uses the personal accounts of other children and adult dyslexics, even entire dyslexic families, to illuminate the problems they encounter. *$14.95*
*150 pages Paperback*
*ISBN 1-57129 -17-6*

**7656 Relationship Development Intervention with Young Children**
Jessica Kingsley Publishers
116 Pentonville Rd
London, 19
207-833-2307
FAX: 207-837-2917
www.jkp.com

*Steven E Gustein, Author*
*Rachelle Sheely, Co-Author*
Social and emotional development activities for Asperger Syndrome, Autism, PDD and NLD. Comprehensive set of activities emphasizes foundation skills for younger children between the ages of two and eight. Covers skills such as social referencing, regulating behvior, conversational reciprocity, and synchronized actions. For use in therapeutic settings as well as schools and parents. *$22.95*
*256 pages*
*ISBN 1-843107-14-7*

**7657 Retarded Isn't Stupid, Mom!**
Brookes Publishing
P.O.Box 10624
Baltimore, MD 21285-624
410-337-9580
800-638-3775
FAX: 410-337-8539
e-mail: custserv@brookespublishing.com
www.pbrookescom/store/books/kaufman-3785

*Sandra Z Kaufman, Author*
Sandra Kaufman reveals the feelings of denial, guilt, frustration and eventual acceptance that resulted in a determination to help her daughter, Nicole, live an independent life. This edition, revised on the 10th anniversary of the book's original publication, adds a progress report that updates readers on Nicole's adult years and reflects on the revolutionary changes in society's attitudes toward people with disabilities since Nicole's birth. *$22.95*
*272 pages Paperback*
*ISBN 1-557663-78-5*

**7658 Rethinking Attention Deficit Disorder**
Brookline Books
34 University Rd
Brookline, MA 02445-4533
617-734-6772
800-666-2665
FAX: 617-734-3952
e-mail: brbooks@yahoo.com
www.brooklinebooks.com

*Miriam Cherkes-Julkowski, Author*
In contrast to the common focus on behavioral symptoms of attention disorders, this book emphasizes internal factors that make attention regulation difficult. In-depth discussions of social, emotional, and academic consequences and appropriate interventions are provided. *$27.95*
*250 pages Paperback*
*ISBN 1-571290-30-7*

**7659 Riddle of Autism: A Psychological Analysis**
Jason Aronson
Ste 200
4501 Forbes Blvd
Lanham, MD 20706-4346
301-459-3366
800-782-0015
FAX: 301-429-5746
www.rowmanlittlefield.com

*Jason Aronson, Author*
*James Lyons, President/CEO*
*Stanley Plotnick, Chairman*
Dr. Victor examines the myths that cloud an understanding of this disorder and describes the meanings of its specific behavioral symptoms. *$30.00*
*356 pages Paperback*
*ISBN 1-568215-73-8*

**7660 SCATBI: Scales Of Cognitive Ability for Traumatic Brain Injury**
Sage Publications
2455 Teller Road
Thousand Oaks, CA 91320
805-499-9774
800-818-7243
FAX: 800-583-2665
e-mail: info@sagepub.com
www.sagepub.com

*Sara Miller McCune, Founder, Publisher, Chairperson*
*Blaise R Simqu, President & CEO*
*Tracey A. Ozmina, Executive Vice President & Chief Operating Officer*
*Stephen Barr, Managing Director*
Assesses cognitive and linguistic abilities of adolescent and adult parents with head injuries. *$287.00*

**7661 Schools for Children with Autism Spectrum Disorders**
Resources for Children with Special Needs Inc
116 E 16th St
Fl 5 #5
New York, NY 10003-2164
212-677-4650
FAX: 212-254-4070
e-mail: info@resourcesnyc.org
www.resourcesnyc.org

*Rachel Howard, Executive Director*
*Edie Novicki, Director Of Finance*
Published every 24-36 months. *$20.00*
*160 pages*
*ISBN 0-967836-53-0*

**7662 Sex Education: Issues for the Person with Autism**
Indiana Resource Center For Autism
2853 E 10th St
Bloomington, IN 47408-2601 812-855-9396
800-825-4733
FAX: 812-855-9630
e-mail: prattc@indiana.edu
www.iidc.indiana.edu

*David Mank, Executive Director*
*Scott Bellini, Assistant Director*
Discusses issues of sexuality and provides methods of instruction for people with autism. *$4.00*

**7663 Son-Rise: The Miracle Continues**
2080 S Undermountain Rd
Sheffield, MA 01257-9643 413-229-2100
800-562-7171
FAX: 413-229-3202
e-mail: sonrise@option.org
www.autismtreatmentcenter.org

*Barry Neil Kaufman, Owner*
*Samahria Lyte Kaufman, Co-Founder*
*Bryn Hogan, Executive Director*
*William Hogan, Executive Director of Programs*
Part One is the astonishing record of Raun Kaufman's development from an autistic and retarded child into a loving, brilliant youngster who shows no traces of his former condition. Part Two follows Raun's development after the age of four, teaching the limitless possibilities of the Son-Rise Program. Part Three shares moving accounts of five other ordinary families who became extraordinary when they used the Son-Rise Program to reach their own unreachable children. *$12.95*
*343 pages*
*ISBN 0-915811-53-7*

**7664 Soon Will Come the Light**
Future Horizons Inc
721 W Abram St
Arlington, TX 76013-6995 817-277-0727
800-479-0727
FAX: 817-277-2270
www.fhautism.com

*Wayne Gilpin, Owner*
*Jennifer Gilpin, Vice President*
*Annette Vick, Manager*
Offers new perspectives on the perplexing disability of autism. *$19.95*

**7665 Successful Job Search Strategies for the Disabled: Understanding the ADA**
Wiley Publishing
605 3rd Ave
New York, NY 10158-180 212-850-6000
FAX: 212-850-6088
www.wiley.com

*Jeffrey G Allen, Author*
Following a concise overview of the Americans with Disabilities Act (ADA), covers such topics as job identification, self-assessment, job leads, resumes, disability disclosure, interviewing, and accommodating specific disabilities. Includes dozen of relevant and instructive situation analyses, case examples, and answers to commonly asked questions. *$165.00*
*229 pages*

**7666 Taking Charge of ADHD Complete Authoritative Guide for Parents**
Guilford Press
72 Spring St
New York, NY 10012-4019 212-431-9800
800-365-7006
FAX: 212-966-6708
e-mail: info@guilford.com
www.guilford.com

*Russell A Barkley, Author*
Revised and updated to incorporate the most current information on ADHD and its treatment. Provides parents with the knowledge, guidance and confidence they need to ensure that their child receives the best care possible. Also in cloth at $40.00 (ISBN# 1-57230-600-9 *$18.95*
*331 pages Paperback*
*ISBN 1-572305-60-1*

**7667 Teaching Children with Autism: Strategies for Initiating Positive Interactions**
Brookes Publishing
P.O.Box 10624
Baltimore, MD 21285-624 410-337-9580
800-638-3775
FAX: 410-337-8539
e-mail: custserv@brookespublishing.com
www.brookespublishing.com

*Robert L Kroegel, Author*
*Lynn Kern Kroegel, Co-Author*
*Lauren Smith, Western Region Sales Representative*
*Jeannine Blimline, Central Region Sales Representative*
Stategies for initiating positive interactions and improving learning opportunities. This guide begins with an overview of characteristics and long-term strategies and proceeds through discussions that detail specific techniques for normalizing environments, reducing disruptive behavior, improving language and social skills, and enhancing generalization. *$32.95*
*256 pages Paperback*
*ISBN 1-55766 -80-4*

**7668 Teaching and Mainstreaming Autistic Children**
Love Publishing Company
Ste 2200
9101 E Kenyon Ave
Denver, CO 80237-1854 303-221-7333
FAX: 303-221-7444
e-mail: lpc@lovepublishing.com
www.lovepublishing.com

*Stan Love, Owner*
*Peter Knoblock, Author*
Dr. Knoblock advocates a highly organized, structured environment for autistic children, with teachers and parents working together. His premise is that the learning and social needs of autistic children must be analyzed and a daily program designed with interventions that respond to this functional analysis of their behavior. *$24.95*

*ISBN 0-89108 -11-9*

**7669 Techniques for Aphasia Rehab: (TARGET) Generating Effective Treatment**
Speech Bin
1965 25th Ave
Vero Beach, FL 32960-3062 772-770-0007
800-477-3324
FAX: 772-770-0006
www.speechbin.com

*Mary Jo Santo Pietro, Co-Author*
*Robert Goldfarb, Co-Author*
TARGET is the kind of resource aphasia clinicians beg for. A practical resource that answers not only the what and how questions of treatment, but also the why. It describes dozens of treatment methods and gives you practical exercises and activities to

implement each technique. It shows you how to treat all components of the disability, language disorder, overall impairment, communication problems, and the needs of the person with aphasia. *$45.00*
*384 pages*
*ISBN 0-93785 -50-5*

**7670 Teenagers with ADD**
Woodbine House
6510 Bells Mill Rd
Bethesda, MD 20817-1636 301-897-3570
800-843-7323
FAX: 301-897-5838
www.woodbinehouse.com

*Irv Shapell, Owner*
*Chris A Ziegler Dendy, M.S., Author*
This best selling guide to understanding and coping with teenagers with attention deficit disorder (ADD) provides complete coverage of the special issues and challenges faced by these teens. Based on current diagnostic criteria and the latest literature and research in the field, the book discusses diagnosis, medical treatment, family and school life, intervention, advocacy, legal rights, and options after high school. Parents find strategies for dealing with their teen's difficult behaviors. *$18.95*
*370 pages Paperback*
*ISBN 0-933149-69-7*

**7671 Traumatic Brain Injury: Cognitive & Communication Disorders**
Federal Government
31 Center Drive Msc2320
Bethesda, MD 20892-1 800-241-1044
FAX: 301-402-0018
e-mail: nidcdinfo@nidcd.nih.gov
http://www.nidcd.nih.gov

*Dr. James F. Battey, M.D., Ph.D., Director*
*Timothy J. Wheeles, Executive Officer and Chief*
*Chad Wysong, Deputy Executive Officer*
*Chris Clements, Program Advisor*
Explains what is traumatic brain injury, who suffer from head trauma, what are the cognitive and communication problems that result from traumatic brain injury, how cognitive and communication probles assessed and how they are treated, and what research is being done for the cognitive and communication prblems caused by traumatic brain injury.

**7672 Understanding Down Syndrome: An Introduction for Parents**
Brookline Books
34 University Rd
Brookline, MA 02445-4533 617-734-6772
800-666-2665
FAX: 617-734-3952
e-mail: brbooks@yahoo.com
www.brooklinebooks.com

*Cliff Cunningham, Author*
Using positive and readable language, this book helps parents understand Down Syndrome. Medical details are explained in lay terms, and advice is given on working with professionals, obtaining services, and treatment techniques that help the child. Cunningham alerts families to potential problems, the prospects for the child in schooling and the passage to adulthood. Revised 1996. *$14.95*
*Softcover*
*ISBN 1-57129 -09-5*

**7673 Valley News Dispatch**
New York Families For Autistic Children
95-16 Pitkin Avenue
Ozone Park, NY 11417-2834 718-641-3441
FAX: 718-641-2228
e-mail: help@nyfac.org
www.nyfac.org

*Andrew Baumann, CEO*
Education, recreation and support services for families and children with developmental disabilities.

**7674 Verbal Behavior Approach: How to Teach Children with Autism & Related Disorders**
Autism Society of North Carolina Bookstore
Ste 230
505 Oberlin Rd
Raleigh, NC 27605-1345 919-743-0204
800-442-2762
FAX: 919-743-0208
e-mail: books@autismsociety-nc.org
www.autismbookstore.com

*David Lax, Manager*
Provides full descriptions of how to teach the verbal operants that make up expressive languate which include: manding, tacting, echoing and intraverbal skills. *$19.95*

**7675 Without Reason: A Family Copes with two Generations of Autism**
Books on Special Children
721 W Abram St
Arlington, TX 76013-6995 817-277-0727
800-489-0727
FAX: 817-277-2270
www.futurehorizons-autism.com

*Wayne Tilton, President*
The author discovers his son has autism. He delves into problems of the autistic person and explains reasons for their actions. *$20.95*
*292 pages Hardcover*

**7676 Women with Attention Deficit Disorder: Embracing Disorganization at Home and Work**
Underwood-Miller
708 Westover Dr
Lancaster, PA 17601-1242
Addresses the millions of withdrawn little girls and chronically overwhelmed women with ADD who go undiagnosed because they don't fit the stereotypical notion of people with ADD. *$11.95*
*288 pages*
*ISBN 1-887424-05-9*

**7677 You Mean I'm Not Lazy, Stupid or Crazy?!: A Self-Help Book for Adults with ADD**
Simon & Schuster
1230 Avenue Of The Americas
11th Floor
New York, NY 10020-1513 212-698-7000
FAX: 212-698-7099
www.simonsays.com

*Kate Kelly, Author*
*Peggy Ramundo, Co-Author*
Practical advice on controlling adult ADD, a straightforward guide explains how to get along in groups, become organized, improve memory, and pursue professional help. *$15.00*
*464 pages*
*ISBN 0-684815-31-1*

**7678 You and Your ADD Child**
Nelson Publications
1 Gateway Plz
Port Chester, NY 10573-4674 914-481-5490
FAX: 914-937-8950

*Paul Warren MD, Author*
*Jody Capehart M.Ed., Co-Author*
*$12.99*
*252 pages Paperback*
*ISBN 0-785278-95-8*

## Print: Journals

**7679 American Journal on Mental Retardation**
American Association on Mental Retardation
501 3rd Street NW
Suite 200
Washington, DC 20001
202-387-1968
800-424-3688
FAX: 202-387-2193
e-mail: aamr@access.digex.net
www.aamr.org

*Leonard Abbeduto, Editor*
Articles cover biological, behavioral, and educational research: theory papers; and reviews of research literature on specific aspects of mental retardation. *$142.00*
*112 pages BiMonthly*

**7680 Annals of Dyslexia**
International Dyslexia Association
40 York Road
Suite 400
Baltimore, MD 21204-5243
410-296-0232
800-ABC-D123
FAX: 410-321-5069
www.interdys.org

*Lee Grossman, Executive Director*
*Kristin Penczek, Director Of Conferences*
*Kristi Bauman, Director Of Development*
*Anna Reuter, Director of Field Services*
IDA is a clearinghouse of scientific data and practice-based information related to dyslexia. Provides community-based referrals and information fact sheets in response to thousands of emails, calls & letters. Our annual conference attracts thousands of outstanding researchers, clinicians, parents, teachers, psychologists, educational therapists and people with dyslexia. *$15.00*
*Paper*

**7681 Journal of Cognitive Rehabilitation**
Neuroscience Publishers
6555 Carrollton Ave
Indianapolis, IN 46220-1664
317-257-9672
FAX: 317-257-9674
e-mail: nsc@neuroscience.cnter.com
neuroscience.cnter.com

*Odie L Bracy, Executive Director*
Publication for therapists, family and patient, designed to provide information relevant to the rehabilitation of impairment resulting from brain injury. *$50.00*
*36-48 pages Quarterly*

## Print: Magazines

**7682 AWARE**
National Fibromyalgia Association
Ste 300
2121 S Towne Centre Pl
Anaheim, CA 92806-6124
714-921-0150
FAX: 714-921-6920
www.fmaware.org

*Lynne Matallana, President*
*Mark Dobrilovic, Board of Director*
*John Fry, PhD, Board of Director*
*Michael Seffinger, DO, FAAFP, Board of Director*
Magazine published three times a year with membership only.

**7683 Attention**
Children & Adults with ADHD
8181 Professional Place
Suite 150
Landover, MD 20785- 2264
301-306-7070
800-233-4050
FAX: 301-306-7090
www.chadd.org

*Bryan Goodman, Director*
A bi-monthly publication from CHADD. Free with membership.
*Bi-monthly*

## Print: Newsletters

**7684 ADHD Report**
Guilford Press
72 Spring St
New York, NY 10012-4019
212-431-9800
800-365-7006
FAX: 212-966-6708
e-mail: info@guilford.com
www.guilford.com

*Russell A Barkley PhD, Editor*
Presents the most up-to-date information on the evaluation, diagnosis and management of ADHD in children, adolescents and adults. This important newsletter is an invaluable resource for all professionals interested in ADHD. *$49.95*
*16 pages BiMonthly*
*ISSN 1065-8025*

**7685 Arc Connection Newsletter**
Arc of Tennessee
151 Athens Way
Suite 100
Nashville, TN 37228-1367
615-248-5878
800-835-7077
FAX: 615-248-5879
e-mail: info@thearctn.org
thearctn.org

*Carrie Hobbs Guiden, Executive Director*
*Steve Jacobs, Assistant Executive Director*
*Peggy Cooper, Membership, Chapter and Communications Manager*
*Nicole Davidson, Business Manager*
Quarterly publication from the ARC of Tennessee. *$ 10.00*
*12 pages Quarterly*

**7686 Autism Research Review International**
Autism Research Institute
4182 Adams Ave
San Diego, CA 92116-2599
619-281-7165
FAX: 619-563-6840
e-mail: br@autismresearchinstitute.com
autism.com

*Steve Edelson, Executive Director*
The Autism Research Institute has pubished this quarterly newsletter, Autism Research Review International (ARRI), since 1987. The ARRI has received worldwide praise for it's thoroughness and objectivity in reporting the current developments in biomedical and educational research. The latest findings are gleaned from a computer search of the 25,000 scientific and medical articles published every week. *$18.00*
*8 pages Quarterly*

**7687 Chadder**
Children & Adults with Attention Deficit Disorder
8181 Professional Place - Suite 150
Landover, MD 2078
301-306-7070
FAX: 301-306-7090
www.chadd.org

*Michael Garza, EdD, Secretary*
*Steven Peer, President*
*Ruth Hughes, CEO*
*Susan Buningh, Executive Editor*
Quarterly newsletter
*Quarterly*

**7688 Down Syndrome News**
National Down Syndrome Congress
Ste 102
1370 Center Dr
Atlanta, GA 30338-4132
770-604-9500
800-232-6372
FAX: 770-604-9898
e-mail: info@ndsccenter.org
www.ndsccenter.org

*George Capone, Director*
*David Tolleson, Executive Director*
*Thea Grimaldo, Office Administrator*
Must become a member to receive the newsletter.

**7689 Farmington Valley ARC**
225 Commerce Dr
Canton, CT 06019-1099
860-693-6662
FAX: 860-693-8662
favarh.org

*Diane Brown, President*
*Stephen Morris, Executive Director*
The official newsletter containing information, new ideas, progress and more on the Farmington Valley Association for Retarded and Handicapped Citizens.

**7690 Imagine!**
Imagine!
1400 Dixon St
Lafayette, CO 80026-2790
303-665-7789
FAX: 303-665-2648
e-mail: gstebick@imaginecolorado.org
imaginecolorado.org

*John Taylor, President*
*Mark Emery, Executive Director*
*John Nevins, CFO*
*Susan LaHoda, Foundation Executive Director*
For people of all ages with cognitive, developmental, physical & health related needs, so they may live lives of independence & quality in their homes and communities.
*12-16 pages quarterly*

**7691 Pure Facts**
Feingold Association of the US
37 Shell Road
2nd Floor
Rocky Point, NY 11778
631-369-9340
800-321-3287
FAX: 631-369-2988
e-mail: fausmem@yahoo.com
www.feingold.org

*Debbie Lehner, Manager*
Relationship between foods, food additives and behavior/learning problems, including Attention Deficit Disorder (ADD) and hyperactivity. *$38.00*
*10+ pages Monthly*

## Non Print: Newsletters

**7692 Arc Light**
Arc of Arizona
5610 S Central Ave
Phoenix, AZ 85040-3090
602-268-6101
800-252-9054
FAX: 602-268-7483
e-mail: thearcaz@gmail.com
www.arcofarizona.org

*Cindy Waymire, Editor*
For people with intellectual and developmental disabilities.
*Quarterly*

**7693 BIATX Newsletter**
Brain Injury Association of Texas
316 W 12th Street
Suite 405 #405
Austin, TX 78701-1845
512-326-1212
800-392-0040
FAX: 512-478-3370
e-mail: info@biatx.org
www.biatx.org

*Judith Abner, Director*
*Margaret Struchen, President*
*Donna Kuhlmann, Chairman*
A online quarterly e-newsletter, as well as news and updates on the Brain Injury Association of Texas.

**7694 BIAWV Newsletter**
Brain Injury Association of America
P.O.Box 574
Institute, WV 25112-0574
304-766-4892
800-356-6443
FAX: 304-766-4940
e-mail: biawv@aol.com
www.bia.usa.org/wvirginia

*Peggy Brown, Director*
*Mike Davis, President*

**7695 Best Buddies Times**
Best Buddies Times
Suite 907
416-531-0003
888-779-0061
FAX: 416-531-0325
e-mail: info@bestbuddies.ca
www.bestbuddies.ca

*Steven Pinnock, Director*
*Emily Bolyea-Kyere, Regional Program Manager*
Bi-annual newsletter.

**7696 Cognitive Therapy Today**
Beck Institute for Cognitive Therapy & Research
One Belmont Avenue
Suite 700
Bala Cynwyd, PA 19004-1610
610-664-3020
FAX: 610-709-5336
e-mail: beckinstitute@beckinstitute.org
www.beckinstitute.org

*Judith S Beck, Director*
*Aaron T Beck, President*

**7697 Focus Times Newsletter**
Focus Alternative Learning Center
P.O.Box 452
126 Dowd Avenue
Canton, CT 06019-0452
860-693-8809
FAX: 860-693-0141
e-mail: info@focus-alternative.org
www.focus-alternative.org

*Donna Swanson, Executive Director*
Monthly online newsletter.

**7698 NAMI Advocate**
National Alliance on Mental Illness
3803 N Fairfax Dr
Suite 100
Arlington, VA 22203-3080
703-524-7600
FAX: 703-524-9094
www.nami.org

*Suzanne Vogel-Scibilia, President*
A quarterly online magazine.

**7699 NLP News**
NLP Comprehensive
P.O.Box 648
Indian Hills, CO 80454-648
303-987-2224
800-233-1657
FAX: 303-987-2228
e-mail: learn@nlpco.com
www.nlpco.com

*Christian Miller, Editor*
*Tom Dotz, President*
*Tom Hoobyar, Director Of Planning*
*Sharon DeBault, Director Of Community Relations*
An online e-newsletter.

**7700 REACH**
TEACCH
100 Renee Lynn Ct
Chapel Hill, NC 27599-1
919-966-2174
FAX: 919-966-4127
e-mail: teacch@unc.edu
www.teacch.com

*Dr. Laura Klinger, Director*
*Walter Kelly, Business Officer*
*Rebecca Mabe, Assistant Director of Business*
*Mark Klinger, Director of Research*
Free online newsletter.

**7701 Weekly Wisdom**
Autism Treatment Center of America
2080 S Undermountain Rd
Sheffield, MA 01257-9643
413-229-8727
877-766-7473
FAX: 413-229-3202
www.son-rise.org

*Barry Kausman, Owner*
Weekly Wisdom is available through a free email subscription.

## Non Print: Software

**7702 Cogrehab**
Life Science Associates
1 Fenimore Rd
Bayport, NY 11705-2115
631-472-2111
FAX: 631-472-8146
e-mail: lifesciassoc@pipeline.com
www.lifesciassoc.home.pipeline.com

*Joann Mandriota, President*

Divided into six groups for diagnosis and treatment of attention, memory and perceptual disorders to be used by and under the guidance of a professional. $95.-$1,950

## Non Print: Video

**7703 ADD, Stepping Out of the Dark**
Child Development Media
Ste 286
5632 Van Nuys Blvd
Van Nuys, CA 91401-4602
818-994-0933
800-405-8942
FAX: 818-989-7826
e-mail: info@childdevelopmentmedia.com
www.childdevelopmentmedia.com

*Margie Wagner, Owner*
A powerful, effective video, ideal for health professionals, educators and parents providing a visual montage designed to promote an understanding and awareness of attention deficit disorder. Based on actual accounts of those who have ADD, including a neurologist, an office worker, and parents of children with ADD. The DVD allows the viewer to feel the frustration and lack of attention that ADD brings to many. *$52.95*
*Video*

**7704 ADHD in Adults**
Guilford Press
72 Spring St
New York, NY 10012-4019
212-431-9800
800-365-7006
FAX: 212-966-6708
e-mail: info@guilford.com
www.guilford.com

*Russell A Barkley, Editor*
This program integrates information on ADHD with the actual experiences of four adults who suffer from the disorder. Representing a range of professions, from a lawyer to a mother working at home, each candidly discusses the impact of ADHD on his or her daily life. These interviews are augmented by comments from family members and other clinicians who treat adults with ADHD. *$99.00*
*DVD 1906*
*ISBN 0-898629-86-1*

**7705 ADHD: What Can We Do?**
Guilford Press
72 Spring St
New York, NY 10012-4019
212-431-9800
800-365-7006
FAX: 212-966-6708
e-mail: info@guilford.com
www.gulford.com

*Russell A Barkley, Editor*
A video program that introduces teachers and parents to a variety of the most effective technologies for managing ADHD in the classroom, at home, and on family outings. *$99.00*
*DVD 1906*
*ISBN 0-898629-72-1*

**7706 ADHD: What Do We Know?**
Guilford Press
72 Spring St
New York, NY 10012-4019
212-431-9800
800-365-7006
FAX: 212-966-6708
e-mail: info@guilford.com
guilford.com

*Bob Matloff, President*
*Russell A Barkley, Editor*
An introduction for teachers and special education practitioners, school psychologists and parents of ADHD children. Topics outlined in this video include the causes and prevalence of ADHD,

ways children with ADHD behave, other conditions that may accompany ADHD and long-term prospects for children with ADHD. *$99.00*
*DVD 1906*
*ISBN 0-898629-71-3*

**7707 Around the Clock: Parenting the Delayed AD HD Child**
Guilford Press
72 Spring St
New York, NY 10012-4019
212-431-9800
800-365-7006
FAX: 212-966-6708
e-mail: info@guilford.com

*Joan F Goodman, Editor*
*Susan Hoban, Editor*
This videotape provides both professionals and parents a helpful look at how the difficulties facing parents of ADHD children can be handled. Video. *$150.00*
*VHS 1994*
*ISBN 0-898629-68-3*

**7708 Attention Deficit Disorder: Adults**
Aquarius Health Care Media
30 Forest Road
Po Box 249
Millis, MA 02054
508-376-1244
888-440-2963
FAX: 508-376-1245
e-mail: aqvideos@tiac.net
www.aquariusproductions.com

*Lesile Kussmann, President/Owner*
*Joseph Wellington, Distribution Coordinator*
*Anne Baker, Billing & Accounting*
Adults with ADD talk about how the disorder that went undiagnosed for so many years has affected their choice of spouses and work, and what they have found to help them. Biofeedback, which is growing as a treatment, is explained and demonstrated by its founder, Dr. Joel Lubar. Medical treatments like antidepressants and stimulants are also discussed, along with behavioral changes that can help the person with ADD and his or her spouse and family. *$149.00*
*Video*

**7709 Attention Deficit Disorder: Children**
Aquarius Health Care Media
30 Forest Rd
Po Box 249
Millisrn, MA 02054-7159
508-376-1244
888-440-2963
FAX: 508-376-1245
e-mail: aqvideos@tiac.net
www.aquariusproductions.com

*Lesile Kussmann, President/Owner*
Everyone has been impulsive or easily distracted for different periods of time, so these symptoms that are hallmarks of Attention Deficit Disorder (ADD) have also led to criticism that too many people are being diagnosed with this biochemical brain disorder. This program examines who is being diagnosed, and what treatments are working. An innovative private school specializing in alternative education is profiled, and tips on structuring the school and home environment are included. *$149.00*
*Video*

**7710 Autism: A World Apart**
Fanlight Productions C/O Icarus Films
32 Court Street
Brooklyn, NY 11201-1731
718-488-8900
800-876-1710
FAX: 718-488-8642
e-mail: info@fanlight.com
www.fanlight.com

*Ben Achtenberg, Owner*
*Nicole Johnson, Publicity Coordinator*
*Anthony Sweeney, Marketing Director*
In this documentary, three families show us what the textbooks and studies cannot: what it's like to live with autism day after day; to raise and love children who may be withdrawn and violent and unable to make personal connections with their families. 29 minutes. *$195.00*
*VHS/DVD 1988*
*ISBN 1-572950-39-0*

**7711 Autism: the Unfolding Mystery**
Aquarius Health Care Media
30 Forest Road
Po Box 249
Millis, MA 02054
508-376-1244
FAX: 508-376-1245
e-mail: lkussmann@aquariusproductions.com
www.aquariusproductions.com

*Lesile Kussmann, Owner*
Explore what it means to be autistic, how you can recognize the signs of autism in your child, and hear about new treatments and programs to help children learn to deal with the disorder. *$145.00*
*DVD 1905*

**7712 Biology Concepts Through Discovery**
Educational Activities Software
5600 W 83rd Street
Suite 300, 8200
Bloomington, MN 5543
866-243-8464
FAX: 239-225-8464
e-mail: achieve@ea-software.com
http://www.ea-software.com

*Alan Stern, Editor*
These videos, available in English and Spanish versions, encourage learning by presenting interactive problem solving in an effective VISUAL/AUDITORY style. *$89.00*
*Video*

**7713 Concentration Video**
Learning disAbilities Resources
6 E Eagle Road
Havertown, PA 19083
610-446-6126
800-869-8336
FAX: 610-525-8337
e-mail: rcooper-ldr@comcast.net
An instructional video which provides a perspective about attention problems, possible causes and solutions. *$19.95*
*Video*

**7714 Educating Inattentive Children**
ADD Warehouse
300 Northwest 70th Avenue
Suite 102
Plantation, FL 33317-2360
954-792-8100
800-233-9273
FAX: 954-792-8545
e-mail: websales@addwarehouse.com
www.addwarehouse.com

*Harvey C Parker, Owner*
Ideal for in-service to regular and special educators concerning the problems inattentive, elementarty and secondary students experience. *$49.00*
*Video*

**7715 Getting Started with Facilitated Communication**
Facilitated Communication Institute, Syracuse Univ
230 Huntington Hal
Syracuse, NY 13244-1
315-443-4752
FAX: 315-443-2258
http://thefci.syr.edu

*Annegret Schubert, Director*
Describes in detail how to help individuals with autism and/or severe communication difficulties to get started with facilitated communication.
*Video*

**7716 Getting Together: A Head Start/School District Collaboration**

Brookes Publishing
P.O.Box 10624
Baltimore, MD 21285-624 410-337-9580
800-638-3775
FAX: 410-337-8539
e-mail: custserv@brookespublishing.com
www.brookespublishing.com

*David P Lindeman, Producer*
*Lauren Smith, Western Region Sales Representative*
*Jeannine Blimline, Central Region Sales Representative*

This video describes how to include children with disabilities in the Head Start classrooms. Addresses such issues as leadership, staff support, and policy development. Comes with a 24-page saddle-stitched booklet. *$34.95*

*Video*
*ISBN 1-55766 -97-5*

**7717 How to Cope with ADHD: Diagnosis, Treatment & Myths**

Aquarius Health Care Media
30 Forest Road
Po Box 249
Millis, MA 02054 508-376-1244
FAX: 508-376-1245
e-mail: lkussmann@aquariusproductions.com
www.aquariusproductions.com

*Lesile Kussmann, President/Owner*

Learn how ADHD is diagnosed, clear up some of the myths, explain the treatmens that are availiable, and give you tips on how you can help your child at home. *$145.00*

*DVD 1905*

**7718 I Just Want My Little Boy Back**

Autism Treatment Center Of America
2080 S Undermountain Rd
Sheffield, MA 01257-9643 413-229-2100
800-714-2779
FAX: 413-229-8931
e-mail: happiness@option.org
www.option.org

*Barry Neil Kaufman, Founder*
*Samahria Lyte Kaufman, Founder*

A great video for parents and professionals caring for children with special needs. Join one British family and their autistic son before, during and after their journey to America to attend The Son-Rise Program at The Autism Treatment Center of America. This informative, inspirational and deeply moving story not only captures the joy, tears, challenges and triumps of this amazing little boy and his family, but also serves as a powerful introduction to the attitude and principles of the program. *$25.00*

**7719 It's Just Attention Disorder**

Western Psychological Services
625 Alaska Avenue
Torrance, CA 90503-5124 424-201-8800
800-648-8857
FAX: 424-201-6950
e-mail: customerservice@wpspublish.com
wpspublish.com

*Gregg Gillmar, VP*

This ground-breaking videotape takes the critical first steps in treating attention-deficit disorder: it enlists the inattentive or hyperactive child as an active participant in his or her treatment. *$99.50*

*Video*

**7720 Understanding ADHD**

Aquarius Health Care Videos
30 Forest Road
Po Box
Millis, MA 02054 508-376-1244
FAX: 508-376-1245
e-mail: aqvideos@tiac.net
www.aquariusproductions.com

*Leslie Kussmann, President/Owner*

A look at some of the controversies surrounding Attention Deficit Hyperactivity Disorder. This video shows how the disorder is diagnosed and presents strategies for living with a child with the disorder. Diverse and candid opinions from teachers, social workers, a behavior specialist, a pediatrician and a parent with ADHD twins. Recommended for child development students, social workers, and caregivers. Preview option available. *$120.00*

*Video*

**7721 Understanding Attention Deficit Disorder**

CACLD
25 Van Zant Street
Norwalk, CT 6855-1713 203-838-5010
FAX: 203-866-6108
e-mail: CACLD@optonline.net
www.CACLD.org

*Beryl Kaufman, Executive Director*
*Helen Bosch, President*

A video in an interview format for parents and professionals providing the history, symptoms, methods of diagnosis and three approaches used to ease the effects of attention deficit disorder. Publishéd by Connecticut Association for Children & Adults with Learning Disabilities (CACLD). *$20.00*

*45 Minutes VHS*

**7722 Understanding Autism**

Fanlight Productions C/O Icarus Films
32 Court Street
Brooklyn, NY 11201 718-488-8900
800-876-1710
FAX: 718-488-8642
e-mail: info@fanlight.com
www.fanlight.com

*Ben Achtenberg, Owner*
*Susan Newman, Editor*

Parents of children with autism discuss the nature and symptoms of this lifelong disability and outline a treatment program based on behavior modification principles. 19 minutes *$199.00*

*VHS/DVD 1993*
*ISBN 1-572951-00-1*

**7723 We're Not Stupid**

Media Projects Inc
5215 Homer St
Dallas, TX 75206-6623 214-826-3863
FAX: 214-826-3919
e-mail: mail@mediaprojects.org
www.mediaprojects.org

*Fonya Naomi Mondell, Producer*

We're Not Stupid is an insightful and very personal video that gives a voice to people who are struggling with learning disabilities. It was made by filmmaker Fonya Naomi Mondell, who is also living with learning differences. The filmmaker camptures the personal stories of young people from all walks of life who discuss what it's like to live with Attention Deficit Disorder and Dyslexia. Their comments are open, honest and direct, and their determination to manage their condition shines through. *$125.00*

*Video*

**7724 Why Won't My Child Pay Attention?**
ADD Warehouse
300 Northwest 70th Avenue
Suite 102
Plantation, FL 33317-2360
954-792-8100
800-233-9273
FAX: 954-792-8545
www.addwarehouse.com

*Sam Goldstein, Ph.D, Author*
*Michael Goldstein, M.D., Co-Author*
Practical and reassuring videotape, noted child psychologist tells parents about two of the most common and complex problems of childhood: inattention and hyperactivity. *$49.50*
*224 pages Hardcover 1992*
*ISBN 0-471530-77-8*

## Support Groups

**7725 Autism Society of America**
4340 East-West Highway
Suite 350
Bethesda, MD 20814
301-657-0881
800-328-8476
FAX: 301-657-0869
e-mail: info@autism-society.org
www.autism-society.org

*Scott Badesch, President/CEO*
*Jennifer Repella, VP Programs*
*Ling Thompson, CFO*
*Robin Gurley, Associate Director*
ASA is the largest and oldest grassroots organization within the autism community, with more than 200 chapters and over 20,000 members and supporters nationwide. ASA is the leading source of education, information and referral about autism and has been the leader in advocacy and legislative initiatives for more than three decades.

**7726 National Autism Hotline**
Autism Services Center
929 4th Ave
Second Floor
Huntington, WV 25701-1408
304-525-8014
FAX: 304-525-8026
www.autismservicecenter.com

*Mike Grady, CEO*
*Jimmie Beirne, COO*
*Nathel Lewis, ASC Training Coordinator*
Service agency for individuals with autism and developmental disabilities, and their families. Assists families and agencies attempting to meet the needs of individuals with autism and other developmental disabilities. Makes available technical assistance in designing treatment programs and more. The hotline provides informational packets to callers and assists via telephone when possible.

**7727 National Health Information Center**
Office Of Disease Prevention And Health Promotion
P.O.Box 1133
Washington, DC 20013-1133
301-565-4167
800-336-4797
301-468-7394
FAX: 301-984-4256
e-mail: info@nhic.org
www.health.gov/nhic

*Jessica Rowden, Sec Dept. Health Human Services*
*William Corr, J.D., Deputy Secretary*
National health information center provides information referral and support. NHIC links consumers and health professionals to organizations that are best able to provide reliable health information.

# Dexterity

## Associations

7728 **American Amputee Foundation, Inc.**
PO Box 94227
North Little Rock, AR 72190
501-835-9290
FAX: 501-835-9292
e-mail: info@americanamputee.org
www.americanamputee.org

*Catherine J Walden LSW MPA CLCP, Executive Director*
Serves primarily as a national information clearinghouse and referral center assisting mainly amputees and their families. AAF researches and gathers information including studies, product information, services, self-help publications and review articles written within the field. AAF has helped with claims, justification letters to payers, testimony and life care planning. Free information packet for phone or letter inquiries.

7729 **American Board for Certification in Orthotics & Prosthetics And Pedorthics, Inc.**
330 John Carlyle Street
Suite 210
Alexandria, VA 22314- 5760
703-836-7114
FAX: 703-836-0838
e-mail: info@abcop.org
www.abcop.org

*Catherine Carter, Executive Director*
*Heather Harris, Director, Continuing Ed. Program*
*Stephen B. Fletcher, CPO/LPO*
*Chrissy Heckenberg, Director, Facility Accreditation*
The American Board for Certification in Orthotics and Prosthetics (ABC) is the national certifying and accrediting body for the orthotic and prosthetic professions. The public requires and deserves assurance that the persons providing orthotic and prosthetic services and care are qualified to provide the appropriate services, and it was on this basis that the ABC was established as a credentialing organization.

7730 **American Stroke Association**
American Heart Association
7272 Greenville Ave
Dallas, TX 75231-4596
800-242-8721
888-478-7653
FAX: 214-706-5231
e-mail: strokeconnection@heart.org
www.stokeassociation.org/STROKEORG/

*Ralph L Sacco MS, President*
Fifty-five state affiliates monitoring local chapters offering educational materials, seminars, conferences and transportation for members nationwide. Maintains a listing of over 1,000 stroke support groups across the nation for referral to stroke survivors, their families, caregivers and interested professionals.

7731 **Epilepsy Foundation**
8301 Professional Place
Landover, MD 20785-7223
301-459-3700
800-332-1000
FAX: 301-577-2684
e-mail: ContactUs@efa.org
www.epilepsyfoundation.org

*Eric Harkgis, President/CEO*
The Epilepsy Foundation is the national voluntary agency solely dedicated to the welfare of the 2.7 million people with epilepsy in the U.S. and their families. The organization works to ensure that people with seizures are able to participate in all life experiences; and to prevent, control and cure epilepsy through research, education, advocacy and services.

7732 **National Amputation Foundation**
40 Church St
Malverne, NY 11565-1735
516-887-3600
FAX: 516-887-3667
e-mail: amps76@aol.com
www.nationalamputation.org

*John Devine, President*
*William Sturges, 1st Vice President*
*Al Pennacchia, 2nd Vice President*
*Doanld A. Sioss, Executive Secretary*
Information & resources for amputees. Scholarship programs for college students with major limb amputation. Free donated durable medical equipment open to anyone in need locally-as items need to be picked up.
*Quarterly*

7733 **National Commission on Orthotic and Prosthetic Education**
330 John Carlyle Street
Suite 210
Alexandria, VA 22314- 5760
703-836-7114
FAX: 703-836-0838
e-mail: info@ncope.org
www.ncope.org

*Robin C Seabrook, Executive Director*
*Jonathan D. Day, CPO*
The mission of NCOPE is to be recognized authority for the development and accreditation of O&P education and residency standards leading to competent patient care in the changing healthcare environment.

7734 **National Institute of Neurological Disorde Disorders & Stroke**
PO Box 5801
Bethesda, MD 20824-5801
301-496-5751
800-352-9424
FAX: 301-402-2186
www.ninds.nih.gov

*Samahria Lyt Landis, Executive Director*
*Walter J Koroshetz MD, Deputy Director*
*Caroline Lewis, Executive Officer*
*Alfred W. Gordon, Ph.D., Associate Director for Special Programs in Diversity*
The mission of the National Institute of Neurological Disorders and Stroke is to reduce the burden of neurological disease.

7735 **National Stroke Association**
9707 E Easter Ln
Centennial, CO 80112-3754
303-649-9299
800-787-6537
FAX: 303-649-1328
e-mail: info@stroke.org
www.stroke.org

*James Baranski, CEO*
*Carol Griffin, Development Manager*
*Teran Nash, Customer Relations*
The only national health organization solely committed to stroke prevention, treatment, rehabilitation and community reintegration. Provides packaged training programs, on-site assistance, physician, patient and family education materials to acute and rehab hospitals. Develops workshops; operates the Stroke Information & Referral Center and produces professional publications such as Stroke: Clinical Updates and the Journal of Stroke and Cerebrovascular Diseases.

7736 **World Chiropractic Alliance**
2950 N Dobson Rd
Ste 3
Chandler, AZ 85224-1819
480-786-9235
800-347-1011
FAX: 480-732-9313
e-mail: comments@worldchiropracticalliance.org
www.worldchiropracticalliance.org

*Terry A Rondberg, Founder/CEO*
*Richard Barwell, President*
Dedicated to protecting and strengthening chiropractic around the world. Serving as a watchdog and advocacy organization, we place our emphasis on education and political action.

## Print: Books

7737 **Carpal Tunnel Syndrome**
Arthritis Foundation
P.O.Box 7669
Atlanta, GA 30357-0669
404-872-7100
800-283-7800
FAX: 404-872-0457
e-mail: help@arthritis.org
www.arthritis.org

*John H Klippel, President/CEO*
*David E. Shuey, Chairman Of The Board*
*Daniel T. McGowan, Vice Chair*
*Frank Kelly Jr., Vice Chair And Secretary*
Offers an introduction to Carpal Tunnel, causes, symptoms, diagnosis and resources.

7738 **Don't Feel Sorry for Paul**
Harper Collins Publishing
1350 Avenue of the Americas
New York, NY 10019-4702
212-246-2058
FAX: 212-261-6895
www.harpercollins.com

*Bernard Wolf, Author*
*Ann Ledden, Vice President*
*Lorna Metzler, Manager*
Paul is seven but was born with deformities of both hands and feet. Paul must wear a prosthesis on both feet so that he can walk. He has a third prosthesis for his right hand. The third prosthesis has a pair of hooks Paul uses as fingers.
*94 pages Hardcover*
*ISBN 0-39731 -88-0*

7739 **Functional Restoration of Adults and Children with Upper Extremity Amputation**
Demos Medical Publishing
11 West 42nd Street
15th Floor
New York, NY 10036-8804
212-683-0072
800-532-8663
FAX: 212-683-0118
e-mail: orderdep@demospub.com
www.demosmedpub.com

*Robert Meier III, Author*
*Diane Atkins, OTR, Co-Author*
Provides a comprehensive reference to the surgery, prosthetic fitting, and rehabilitation of individuals sustaining an arm amputation. Covers the recent advancements in prosthetics and rehabilitation. *$165.00*
*384 pages*
*ISBN 1-888799-73-0*

## Print: Magazines

7740 **ABC Mark of Merit Newsletter**
Amer Board for Cert in Otthotics & Prosthetics
330 John Carlyle St
Suite 210
Alexandria, VA 22314-5760
703-836-7114
FAX: 703-836-0838
e-mail: info@abcop.org
www.abcop.org

*Bruce Raizdeh, President*
*Catherine Carter, Executive Director*
*Heather Harris, Director Continuing Ed. Programs*
*Stephen B. Fletcher, CPO/LPO*
An online bi-monthly newsletter.

7741 **Active Living Magazine**
American Amputee Foundation
P.O.Box 94227
North Little Rock, AR 72190
501-835-9290
FAX: 501-835-9292
e-mail: info@americanamputee.org
www.americanamputee.org

*Catherine J Walden, Executive Director*
A print magazine published four times a year.

7742 **Stroke Connection Magazine**
American Heart Association
7272 Greenville Ave
Dallas, TX 75231-5129
214-373-6300
888-478-7653
FAX: 214-706-5231
www.strokeassociation.org

*John Caswell, Editor*
*Debra Lockwood, Chairman*
*Nancy Brown, CEO*
*Ralph Sacco, President/Director*
Free magazine for stroke survivors and their family caregivers.

## Print: Newsletters

7743 **NINDS Notes**
Ntn'l Institute of Neurological Disorders & Stroke
P.O.Box 5801
Bethesda, MD 20824-5801
301-496-5751
800-352-9424
www.ninds.nih.org

*Samahria Lyt Landis, Executive Director*
*Walter J Koroshetz MD, Deputy Director*
*Caroline Lewis, Executive Officer*
*Alfred W. Gordon, Ph.D., Associate Director for Special Programs in Diversity*
A print newsletter published three times a year.

## Non Print: Newsletters

7744 **Advocacy Pulse**
American Stroke Association
7272 Greenville Ave
Dallas, TX 75231-5129
214-373-6300
888-478-7653
FAX: 214-706-5231
www.strokeassociation.org

*Ralph Sacco, President/Director*
*Debra Lockwood, Chairman*
*Nancy Brown, CEO*

**7745 Noteworthy Newsletter**
Ntn'l Comm on Orthotic & Prosthetic Education
330 John Carlyle Street
Suite 210
Alexandria, VA 22314- 5760
703-836-7114
FAX: 703-836-0838
e-mail: info@ncope.org
www.ncope.org

*Robin C Seabrook, Editor*
*Jonathan D. Day, Chair*
*Miguel Mojica, CPO*
An online newsletter.

**7746 Stroke Smart Magazine**
National Stroke Association
Ste B
9707 E Easter Ln
Centennial, CO 80112-3754
303-649-9299
800-878-6537
FAX: 303-649-1328
e-mail: info@stroke.org
www.stroke.org

*James Baranski, CEO*
Stroke Smart magazine is published bi-monthly by the National Stroke Association. With a circulation of 40,000 plys, Stroke Smart reaches more than 100,000 stroke survivors, caregivers and doctors across the United States, providing critical information in the areas of prevention, recovery, research, and rehabilitation.

# Hearing

## Associations

**7747 Academy of Rehabilitative Audiology**
PO Box 2323
Albany, NY 12220-0323
952-920-0484
FAX: 952-920-6098
e-mail: ARA@audrehab.org
www.audrehab.org

*Carol Cokely, Ph.D., President*
*Jan Moore, Ph.D, Treasurer*
*Sarah Ferguson, Ph.D, Secretary*
*Sheila Pratt, Ph.D., JARA Editor*

Provides professional education, research and interest in programs for hearing handicapped persons. The primary purpose of the ARA¦is to promote excellence in hearing care through the provision of comprehensive rehabilitative and habilitative services.

**7748 Alexander Graham Bell Association for the Deaf and Hard of Hearing**
3417 Volta Pl NW
Washington, DC 20007-2737
202-337-5220
FAX: 202-337-8314
TTY:202-337-5221
e-mail: info@agbell.org
agbell.org

*Donald M. Goldberg, Ph.D, President*
*Alexander T. Graham, Executive Director/CEO*
*Joni Alberg, Ph.D, Director*
*Corrine Altman, Director*

The Alexander Graham Bell Association for the Deaf and Hard of Hearing (AG Bell) is the world's oldest and largest membership organization promoting the use of spoken language by children and adults who are hearing impaired. Members include parents of children with hearing loss, adults who are deaf or hard of hearing, educators, audiologists, speech-language pathologists, physicians and other professionals in fields related to hearing loss and deafness.

**7749 American Association of People with Disabilities**
2013 H Street, NW, 5th Floor
Ste 950
Washington, DC 20006
202-457-0046
800-840-8844
FAX: 866-536-4461
www.aapd.com

*Mark Perriello, President/CEO*
*Helena Berger, COO*
*Adam Abosedra, Executive Assistant*
*Zach Baldwin, Development Associate*

Dedicated to ensuring economic self-sufficiency and political empowerment for more than 50 million Americans with disabilities.

**7750 American Society for Deaf Children**
800 Florida Ave NE
Ste 2047
Washington, DC 20002-3695
800-942-2732
866-895-4206
FAX: 410-795-0965
e-mail: ascd@deafchildren.org
www.deafchildren.org

*Beth S Benedict PhD, President*

Supports and educates families of deaf and hard of hearing children and advocates for high quality programs and services.

**7751 American Speech-Language-Hearing Association**
2200 Research Blvd
Rockville, MD 20850-3289
301-296-5700
800-638-8255
FAX: 301-296-8255
e-mail: actioncenter@asha.org
www.asha.org

*Shelly S. Chabon, PhD, President*
*Patricia A. Prelock, PhD, President-Elect*
*Jaynee A. Handelsman, PhD, Vice President for Audiology Practice*
*Karen I. Kirk, PhD, Vice President for Science and Research*

Provides information for both the general public and physicians in an easy-to-access manner, on speech, hearing and language disorders. Exhibits by companies specializing in alternative and augmentative communications products, publishers, software and hardware companies, and hearing aid testing equipment manufacturers.

**7752 American Tinnitus Association**
PO Box 5
Portland, OR 97207-5
503-248-9985
800-634-8978
FAX: 503-248-0024
e-mail: tinnitus@ata.org
www.ata.org

*Michael Manusevec, Executive Director*
*Wes Breazeale, Development Director*
*Jennifer Born, Director of Public Affairs*
*Wes Breazeale, Development Director*

The American Tinnitus Association (ATA) is the national champion of tinnitus awareness, prevention, and treatment. Under its guiding principles-Education, Advocacy, Research and Support-the ATA offers prevention programs in schools, urges governmental and private organizations to support hearing conservation, funds the nation's brightest researchers, and facilitates self-help groups around the country.

**7753 Association of Late-Deafened Adults**
8038 Macintosh Ln
Rockford, IL 61107-5336
815-332-1515
866-402-2532
e-mail: info@alda.org
www.alda.org

*Bernie Palmer, President*
*Brenda Estes, Member*
*Richard Bundy, Engineer*

Provides resources, information, and advocacy of the needs of deafened adults. Publishes ALDA News.

**7754 Better Hearing Institute**
1444 I St NW
Ste 700 #700
Washington, DC 20005-6542
202-449-1100
800-327-9355
FAX: 202-216-9646
e-mail: mail@betterhearing.org
www.betterhearing.org

*Charles Gross, Chairman Director*
*Norm Crosby, Chairman*
*Shari Lewis, Chairman*

The BHI is a not-for-profit corporation that educates the public about the neglected problem of hearing loss and what can be done about it. Founded in 1973 we are working to erase the stigma and end the embarassment that prevents millions of people from seeking help for hearing loss and show the negative consequences of untreated hearing loss for millions of Americans. And to promote treatment and demonstrate that this is a national problem that can be solved.

**7755 Center for Hearing and Communication**
50 Broadway
Fl 6 #6
New York, NY 10004-3810
917-305-7700
FAX: 917-305-7888
TTY:917-305-7999
e-mail: info@chchearing.org
www.chchearing.org

*Laurie Hanin PhD CCC-A, Executive Director*
*Jim Rosenthal, CEO*
*Ronald Nurnberg, Managing Partner*
National diagnostic rehabilitation, human services agency founded in 1910. Offers comprehensive services for infants, children and adults with hearing loss regardless of age or mode of communication. Clinical programs iclude Tinnitus Center and Cochlear Implant evaluation, consultation, auditory training. LHH also offers extensive public education programs, advocacy, support and publications.

**7756 Communication Service for the Deaf**
3520 Gateway Lane
Sioux Falls, SD 57106
866-246-5759
FAX: 605-362-2806
TTY:605-367-5761
www.c-s-d.org
Since 1975, CSD has provided a variety of services to deaf and hard of hearing individuals. From relay services to community interpreting, advocacy to education, CSD promotes self-actualization, professional growth, independence and greater access for our consumers across the country.

**7757 Conference of Educational Administrators of Schools and Programs for the Deaf**
PO Box 1778
St Augustine, FL 32085-1778
904-810-5200
866-697-8805
FAX: 904-810-5525
e-mail: nationaloffice@ceasd.org
www.ceasd.org

*Joseph Finnegan, Executive Director*
*Ronald Stern, President*
*Nancy Hlibok Amann, Secretary*
*Peter L. Bailey, Treasurer*
CEASD provides an opportunity for professional educators to work together for the improvement of schools and educational programs for individuals who are deaf or hard of hearing. The organization brings together a rich composite of resources and reaches out to both enhance educational programs and influence educational policy makers.

**7758 Council of American Instructors of the Deaf (CAID)**
P.O.Box 377
Bedford, TX 76095-377
817-354-8414
FAX: 817-354-8414
e-mail: caid@swbell.net
www.caid.org

*Keith Mousley, President*
*Helen Lovato, Office Manager*
The mission of CAID is to establish and bring together State and Regional organizations of teachers of students who are deaf and hard of hearing and support personnel for the purpose of promoting quality education.

**7759 Deaf REACH**
3521 12th St NE
Washington, DC 20017-2545
202-832-6681
FAX: 202-832-8454
e-mail: info@deaf-reach.org
deaf-reach.org

*Teresa Arcari, Secretary*
*Annette Reichman, President*
*Jonathan Tomar, Vice-President*
*Emilia A. Chukwuma, Treasurer*
The psychosocial rehabilitation approach, ulitzed by all Deaf-REACH programs, provides the solid foundation to member's success. Participants are activly involved in establishing the format and level of highly individualized service delivery that they receive. The concept, which has achieved national acclaim, involves teaching members necessary life skills, thus minimizing the need for assistance from a service professional. This is part of what distinguishes the approach at Deaf-REACH.

**7760 Deafness Research Foundation**
363 Seventh Avenue, 10th Floor
New York, NY 10001-3904
212-257-6140
866-454-3924
FAX: 212-257-6139
TTY: 888-435-6104
e-mail: info@hearinghealthfoundation.org
www.drf.org

*Andrea Boidman, Executive Director*
*Doug Olson, Development Director*
*Leticia Bido, Associate, Development and Operations*
*Sarah Stickney, Development Coordinator*
Founded in 1958, the Deafness Research Foundation is the leading source of private funding for basic and clinical research in the hearing science. The DRF is committed to making lifelong hearing health a national priority by funding research and implementing education projects in both the government and private sectors.

**7761 Dogs for the Deaf**
10175 Wheeler Rd
Central Point, OR 97502-9360
541-826-9220
800-990-3647
FAX: 541-826-6696
TTY: 541-826-9220
e-mail: info@dogsforthedeaf.org
dogsforthedeaf.org

*Robin Dickson, CEO*
*Pam Slater, Development Director*
*Vaughn Maurice, Genral Manager*
Rescues dogs from shelters and professionally trains them for people with special needs such as: deafness, autism for children, seniors, stroke victims, cerebral palsy, etc.

**7762 Ear Foundation**
1817 Patterson St
Nashville, TN 37203-2110
615-329-7849
800-545-4327
FAX: 615-329-7935
e-mail: info@earfoundation.org
www.earfoundation.org

*Suzanne Wyatt, Executive Director*
National, nonprofit organization committed to integrating the hearing and balance impaired into the mainstream of society through public awareness and medical education. Also administers The Meniere's Network, a national network of patient support groups providing people with the opportunity to share experiences and coping strategies.

**7763 Georgiana Institute**
736 Harmony Street
New Orleans, LA 70115
203-994-8215
e-mail: georgianainstitute@snet.net
www.georgianainstitute.org

*Annabel Stehli, President*
The information source for Auditory Integration Training (AIT)/Digital Auditory Aerobics (DAA).

**7764 HEAR Center**
301 E Del Mar Blvd
Pasadena, CA 91101-2714
626-796-2016
FAX: 626-796-2320
e-mail: info@hearcenter.org
hearcenter.org

*Ellen Simon, Executive Director*
*Deborah Lorino, Office Manager*
*Berenice Castro, Accounting Supervisor*
*Maline Medina, Accounts Receivable/Billing Clerk*

Auditory and verbal program designed to help hearing impaired children, infants and adults lead normal and productive lives. Seeks to develop auditory techniques to aid people who have communication problems due to deafness. Offers diagnostic evaluations for speech and hearing. Individual auditory, verbal training and speech-language therapy.

**7765 Hearing Education and Awareness for Rockers**
1405 Lyon St
San Francisco, CA 94115-2914
415-409-3277
FAX: 415-409-5683
e-mail: hear@hearnet.com
www.hearnet.com

*Kathy Peck, Executive Director*

Dedicated to the prevention of hearing loss among musicians and music fans.

**7766 Hearing Loss Association of America**
7910 Woodmont Ave
Ste 1200
Bethesda, MD 20814-7022
301-657-2248
FAX: 301-913-9413
TTY:301-657-2248
hearingloss.org

*Brenda Battat, Executive Director*
*Barbara Kelley, Dep Exec Dir, Editor-In-Chief*
*Nancy Macklin, Director of Events & Marketing*
*Lisa Hamlin, Director of Public Policy*

The mission of the Hearing Loss Association of America is to open the world of communication to people with hearing loss through information, education, advocacy and support.

**7767 Hearing, Speech and Deafness Center (HSDC)**
1625 19th Ave
Seattle, WA 98122-2848
206-323-5770
888-222-5036
FAX: 206-328-6871
TTY: 206-388-1275
e-mail: hsdc@hsdc.org
www.hsdc.org

*Susie Burdick, Executive Director*
*Steve Atkins, President*

Our mission is to enrich lives of all adults and children who experience hearing loss, speech and language impairments or who are deaf, by providing professional services and by promoting community awareness and accessibility.

**7768 House Ear Institute**
2100 W 3rd St
Los Angeles, CA 90057-1944
213-483-4431
800-388-8612
FAX: 213-484-8789
e-mail: info@hei.org
www.hei.org

*Jim Boswell, CEO*
*John.W House, M.D, President*
*Daniel. M Graham, Executive Vice President Development, Marketing, & Communications*
*Neil Segil, Ph.D, Executive Vice President Research*

Offers pediatric hearing tests, otologic and audiologic evaluation and treatment, rehabilitation, hearing aid dispensing, and cochlear implant services. Outreach programs focus on families with hearing impaired children.

**7769 International Catholic Deaf Association**
7202 Buchanan St
Landover Hills, MD 20784-2236
301-429-0697
FAX: 301-429-0698
e-mail: homeoffice@icda-us.org
icda-us.org

*Jean Cox, President*
*Kate Slosar, Vice President*
*T.K Hill, Secretary*
*James Kelly, Treasurer*

An organization of Catholic deaf people and hearing people in the church working with the deaf in the united states of America.

**7770 International Hearing Dog**
5901 E 89th Ave
Henderson, CO 80640-8315
303-287-3277
FAX: 303-287-3425
e-mail: info@hearingdog.org
www.pawsforsilence.org

*Valerie Foss-Brugger, President*
*Robert Cooley, Field Representative/Placement Counselor*
*Kelly Hennegan, Secretary*
*Matt Bailey, Treasurer*

Trains and places Hearing dogs with deaf or hard-of-hearing persons, with or without multiple disabilities, nationwide, free of charge to the recipient.

**7771 International Hearing Society**
1688 Middlebelt Rd
Ste 4
Livonia, MI 48154-3374
734-522-7200
800-521-5247
FAX: 734-522-0200
e-mail: chelms@ihsinfo.org
ihsinfo.org

*Kathleen Mennillo, Executive Director*
*Joy Wilkins, Director of Education*
*Fran Vincent, Marketing Manager*
*Alissa Parady, Manager of Government Affairs*

The IHS is the professional association that represents Hearing Instrument Specialists worldwide. IHS members are engaged in the practice of testing human hearing and selecting, fitting and dispensing hearing instruments. Founded in 1951, the Society continues to recognize the need for promoting and maintaining the highest possible standards for its members in the best interestof the hearing impaired it serves.

**7772 League for the Hard of Hearing**
50 Broadway
6th Fl
New York, NY 10004-3810
917-305-7700
TTY:917-305-7999
www.lhh.org

*Laurie Hanin, Executive Director*
*Ellen Pfeffer Lafargue, Au.D, Director*
*Lois Kam Heymann, M.A., CCC, Director*
*Anita Stein-Meyers, Au.D, C, Assistant Director*

**7773 Lexington School for the Deaf: Center for the Deaf**
30th Avenue and 75th St
Jackson Heights, NY 11370
718-350-3300
FAX: 718-899-9846
TTY:718-350-3056
e-mail: generalinfo@lexnyc.org
www.lexnyc.org

*Regina Carroll PhD, CEO/Executive Director*
*Philip W. Bravin, President*
*Gregory Hlibok, Vice President*
*Seth Bravin, Treasurer*

Offers a comprehensive range of services to deaf, hard of hearing and speech impaired persons from infancy to elderly through its affiliate agencies: The Center for Mental Health Services; The Lexington Hearing and Speech Center, Lexington Vocational

Services, and the Lexington School for the Deaf. The Lexington Center also provides services through its research division which houses the only federally funded Rehabilitation Engineering Center.

**7774 Michigan Association for Deaf and Hard of Hearing**
5236 Dumond Court
Suite C
Lansing, MI 48917-6001 517-487-0066
800-968-7327
FAX: 517-487-0202
e-mail: info@madhh.org
www.madhh.org

*Nancy Asher, Executive Director*
*Pat Walton, Office Manager*
MADHH is a statewide collaboration agency dedicated to improving the lives of people who are deaf or hard of hearing through leadership in education, advocacy and services.

**7775 National Association of Hearing Officials**
PO Box 4999
Midlothian, VA 23112-17 www.naho.org

*Bonny M Fetch CALJ, President*
The mission of the National Association of Hearing Officials is to improve the administrative hearing process and thereby benefit hearing officials, their employing agencies, and the individuals they serve through promoting professionalism and by providing traininf, continuing education, a national forum for discussion of issues, and leadership concerning administrative harings.

**7776 National Association of Special Education Teachers**
1250 Connecticut Ave NW
Ste 200
Washington, DC 20036- 2643 202-296-7739
800-754-4421
FAX: 800-754-4421
e-mail: contactus@naset.org
www.naset.org

*Dr Roger Pierangelo, Executive Director*
*Dr. George Giuliani, Executive Director*
The mission of NASET is to render all possible support and assistanve to professionals who teach children with special needs.

**7777 National Association of the Deaf**
8630 Fenton Street
Suite 820
Silver Spring, MD 20910- 3819 301-587-1788
FAX: 301-587-1791
TTY:301-587-1789
e-mail: nadinfo@nad.org
www.nad.org

*Howard A. Rosenblum, CEO*
*Shane H. Feldman, COO*
*Marc P. Charmatz, Staff Attorney*
Nation's largest organization safeguarding the accessability and civil rights of 28 million deaf and hard of hearing Americans in education, employment, health care, and telecommunications. Focuses on grassroots advocacy and empowerment, captioned media deafness-related information and publications, legal assistance, and policy development.

**7778 National Black Association for Speech Language and Hearing**
700 McKnight Park Drive
Pittsburgh, PA 15237-1116 412-366-1177
FAX: 412-366-8804
e-mail: nbaslh@nbaslh.org
www.nbaslh.org

*Arnell Brady, Exec Board Chair*
*Carolyn Mayo, PhD, Secretary*
*Linda McCabe Smith, PhD, Treasurer*
*Rachel M. Williams, PhD, Convention Chair*
The mission of the National Black Association of Speech-Language and Hearing is to maintain a viable mechanism through which the needs of black professionals, students and individuals with communication disorders can be met.

**7779 National Black Deaf Advocates**
PO Box 32
Frankfort, KY 40602 585-475-2411
800-421-1220
FAX: 585-475-6500
e-mail: president@nbda.org
www.nbda.org

*Cory Parker, VP*
*Benro Ogunyipe, President*
*Sharon.D White, Secretary*
*Betty Henderson, Treasurer*
The Mission of the National Black Deaf Advocate is to promote the leadership development, economic and educational opportunities, social equality, and to safeguard the general health and welfare of Black deaf and hard of hearing people.

**7780 National Catholic Office of the Deaf**
7202 Buchanan St
Landover Hills, MD 20784-2299 301-577-1684
FAX: 301-577-1684
TTY:301-577-4184
e-mail: info@ncod.org
www.ncod.org

*Consuelo Martinez Wild, Executive Director*
Helps coordinate efforts of deaf or hard of hearing people who are involved in the ministry, acts as a resource center, assists bishops and pastors become available to the deaf and hard of hearing.

**7781 National Cued Speech Association**
5619 McLean Dr
Bethesda, MD 20814-1021 301-915-8009
800-459-3529
e-mail: info@cuedspeech.org
www.cuedspeech.org

*Amy Ruberl, Executive Director*
*Marah Baltzell, Executive Assistant*
*Shannon Howell , President*
Champions effective communication, language development and literacy through the use of cued speech.

**7782 National Deaf Women's Bowling Association**
9244 E Mansfield Ave
Denver, CO 80237-1915 303-771-9018
e-mail: ndwbast@gmail.com
www.ndwba.com

*Gayle Willingham, President*
*Ali Martinez, VP*
Holds world Deaf Bowling Torunament annually in July. Also holds Las Vegas Scratch Classic annually in October.

**7783 National Hearing Conservation Association**
3030 W 81st Ave
Westminster, CO 80031 303-224-9022
FAX: 303-458-0002
e-mail: nhcaoffice@hearingconservation.org
www.hearingconservation.org

*Susan Griest, President*
*Erin Erickson, Executive Director*
*Laura Kauth, President*
*Richard Stepkin, Director of Communication*
The mission of the NHCA is to prevent hearing loss due to noise and other environmental factors in all sectors of society.

7784 **National Student Speech Language Hearing Association**
2200 Research Blvd
Ste 450
Rockville, MD 20850-3289 800-498-2071
e-mail: nsslha@asha.org
www.nsslha.org

*Kachina Smith, Programs Liaison*
*Lia Byndon, Marketing*
National organization for graduate and undergraduate students interested in the study of normal and disordered human communication.

7785 **Registry of Interpreters for the Deaf**
333 Commerce St
Alexandria, VA 22314-2801 703-838-0030
FAX: 703-838-0454
TTY:7038380459
e-mail: info@rid.org
rid.org

*Clay Nettles, Executive Director*
*Elijah Sow, Office Manager*
A national membership organization representing the professionals who make communication possible between people who are deaf or hard of hearing and people who can hear. Interpreters serve as professional communicators in a vast array of settings such as: churches, schools, courtrooms, hospitals and theaters, as well as on political grandstands and television.

7786 **Spring Dell Center**
6040 Radio Station Rd
La Plata, MD 20646-3368 301-934-4561
FAX: 301-870-2439
e-mail: cynthiahayes@springdellcenter.org
www.springdellcenter.org

*Donna Retzlaff, Executive Director*
*Patsy Finch, President*
*Judy Hall, VP*
*Jean Hubbard, Secretary*
Since 1967, Spring Dell center has been, bridging the gap to enhance the lives of developmentally disabled people. Spring Dell's goal is to empower people in every aspect of their lives through the implementation of two programs, employment/vocational services and residential services including transportation. Spring Dell offers transportation door-to-door for persons with developmental disabilities, including day care programs, supportive environment, residential and any other transportation.

7787 **Starkey Hearing Foundation**
6700 Washington Ave S
Eden Prairie, MN 55344-3405 866-354-3254
FAX: 952-828-6900
e-mail: hearingfoundation@starkey.com
www.starkeyhearingfoundation.org

*Peter Lecy, President*
*Brady Forseth, Executive Director*
*Steven Sawalich, Executive Director*
*Dr.Paul Nash, Vice President*
Continues to provide over 50,000 hearing aids per year to people in the U.S. and all over the world.

7788 **Telecommunications for the Deaf and Hard of Hearing**
Ste 121
8630 Fenton St
Silver Spring, MD 20910-3822 301-589-3786
FAX: 301-589-3797
TTY:301-589-3006
e-mail: info@tdi-online.org
http://tdiforaccess.org/

*Claude L Stout, Executive Director*
*James House, Director of Public Relations*
*John Skjeveland, Business Manager*
Promoting equal access to telecommunications and media for people who are deaf, late-deafened, hard of hearing or deaf-blind through consumer education and involvement; technical assistance and consulting; applications of exisiting and emerging technologies; networking and collaboration; uniformity of standards; and national policy development and advocacy.

7789 **The Davis Center**
19 State Route 10 E
Ste 25
Succasunna, NJ 07876 862-251-4637
FAX: 862-251-4642
e-mail: npdunn@thedaviscenter.com
www.thedaviscenter.com

*Dorinne S Davis MA CCC-A FAAA, Director*
The Davis Center's Sound Therapy Programs make positive changes for children and adults with autism, ADD/ADHD, auditory processing issues, Dyslexia, learning disabilities, and other learning and wellness challenges. Our programs address issues such as phonics, spelling, writing, reading comprehension, hearing only parts of words, following directions, discriminating between sounds, sound sensitivity, behavioral responses, focus, attention, and more.

7790 **Vestibular Disorders Association**
PO Box 13305
Portland, OR 97213-305 503-229-7705
800-837-8428
FAX: 503-229-8064
e-mail: veda@vestibular.org
www.vestibular.org

*Sue Hickey, President*
*Cynthia Ryan, MBA, Executive Director*
*Kerrie Denner, Outreach Coordinator*
*Alan Butchman, Secretary*
Provides information and support for people with inner-ear vestibular disorders and the professionals who treat them, and develops awareness of the issues surrounding these disorders.

## Camps

7791 **ASD Summer Camp**
Alabama School for the Deaf
P.O.Box 698
Talladega, AL 35161-0698 256-761-3260
FAX: 256-761-3278
e-mail: Pshaw@aidb.state.al.us
www.aidb.org

*Pam Shaw, Camp Director*
*Carl Ponder, PhD, Principal*
The Alabama School for the Deaf Summer Enrichment Camp is designed especially for deaf and hard of hearing children ages 6-15. Recreation activities include swimming, skating, outdoor games, horseback riding, field trips, arts and craft. Tuition is free.

7792 **Aspen Camp School for the Deafearing**
P.O.Box 1494
Aspen, CO 81612-1494 970-923-2511
FAX: 970-923-0643
www.aspencamp.org

*Lesa Thompson, Camp Director*

7793 **Aspen Camp of the Deaf & Hard of Hearing**
PO Box 1494
Aspen, CO 81612 970-923-2511
FAX: 970-923-0643
e-mail: office@aspencamp.org
www.aspencamp.org

*Lesa Thompson, Camp Director*
Provide enriching experiential educational and recreational experiences for Deaf and Hard of Hearing individuals.

**7794 CHAMP Camp**
212 West 10th Street
Suite B-210
Indianapolis, IN 46202-5629 317-679-1860
FAX: 317-245-2291
e-mail: admin@champcamp.org
www.champcamp.org

*Dave Carter, Camp Director*
*Jennifer Kobylarz, Executive Director*
*Kristina Watkins, Program Director*
*Donna Guider, Lead Nurse*

**7795 Camp Alexander Mack**
Indiana Deaf Camps Foundation
P.O.Box 158
Milford, IN 46542-158 574-658-4831
www.campmack.org

*Phil Harden, Camp Director*
*Rex M. Miller, Executive Director*
*Galen Jay, Facility Manager*
*Norma Miller, Spiritual Director*
Our program is intentionally designed to provide campers with life changing experiences that lead to a formation of personal faith within a safe faith community.

**7796 Camp Bishopswood**
Diocese of Maine Episcopal
143 State St
Portland, ME 04101-3701 207-772-1953
800-244-6062
FAX: 207-773-0095
e-mail: georgia@bishopswood.org
www.bishopswood.org

*Georgia Koch, Director*
Camp is located in Hope, Maine. One to seven-week sessions for hearing impaired children June-August. Coed, ages 7-16.

**7797 Camp Capella**
8 Pearl Point Road
P.O. Box 552
Holden, ME 04429-552 207-843-5104
e-mail: dana@campcabella.org
www.campcapella.org

*Dana Mosher, Religious Leader*
Provides an opportunity for children with disabilities to engage in various recreational and social experiences.

**7798 Camp Chris Williams**
Lions 11 B-2 and MADHH
5236 Dumond Court
Suite C
Lansing, MI 48917-6001 586-778-4188
FAX: 586-285-1842
TTY:586-285-1842
e-mail: info@madhh.org
www.madhh.org

*Nancy Asher, Executive Director*
An exciting summer camp experience for deaf and hard of hearing youth and their siblings ages 8-14.

**7799 Camp Comeca & Retreat Center**
United Methodist Church
75670 Road 17
Conzad, NE 69130 308-784-2808
e-mail: comeca@cozadtel.net
www.campcomeca.com

*Mike Mook, Director*
Camp is located in Cozad, Nebraska. Summer sessions for campers with diabetes and hearing impairment. Coed, ages 6-19, families, seniors, single adults.

**7800 Camp Emanuel**
P.O. Box 752343
Dayton, OH 45475 937-477-5504
e-mail: crawford@campenamuel.org
www.campemanuel.org

*Douglas Lehrer, M.D., President*
*Nan Crawford, Executive Director*
*Dan Trunk, Vice President*
*Mary Foreman, Treasurer*
Camp for hearing impaired and normal hearing youth.

**7801 Camp Grizzly**
NorCal Services For Deaf & Hard Of Hearing, Inc.
4708 Roseville Road
Suite 112
North Highlands, CA 95660-5172 916-349-7500
FAX: 916-349-7580
TTY:919-349-7611
e-mail: info@nocalcenter.org
www.norcalcenter.org

*Sheri Farinah, CEO*
*Cheryl Bella, Chair*
*Yim Orsi, Secretary*
*Michael.D Wilson, Treasurer*
This camp is designed the deaf and hard of hearing youth or hearing youth with deaf or hard of hearing parent. The camp helps with social interaction, building self esteem, leadership skills while enriching the lives of the deaf and hard of hearing.

**7802 Camp Isola Bella On Twin Lakes,Salisbury, Ct.**
American School for the Deaf
139 N Main St
West Hartford, CT 06107-1264 860-570-2300
FAX: 860-570-2301
TTY:860-570-2222
e-mail: Steve.Borsotti@asd-1817.org
www.asd-1817.org

*Alyssa Pecorino, Director*
*Edward Peltier, Executive Director*
Hearing-impaired children, ages 6-19, blend educational instruction in communications with recreational activities. Qualified deaf and hearing staff members with experience in education, child care and counseling are employed at the camp.

**7803 Camp Joy**
3325 Swamp Creek Rd
Schwenksville, PA 19473-1518 610-754-6878
FAX: 610-754-7880
e-mail: campjoy@fast.net
www.campjoy.com

*Angus Murray, Camp Director*
A special needs camp for kids and adults (ages 4-80+) with developmental disabilities such as: mental retardation, autism, brain injury, neurological disorder, visual and/or hearing impairments, Angelman and Down syndromes, and other developmental disabilities.

**7804 Camp Juliena**
Georgia Council for the Hearing Impaired
4151 Memorial Drive
Suite 103B
Decatur, GA 30032-1511 404-292-5312
800-541-0710
FAX: 404-299-3642
e-mail: campjuliena@gmail.com
www.gachi.org

*Sondra Rhoades Johnson, Executive Director*
*Bonna Lenyszyn, Camp Director*
*Faithlyn Peart, Deputy Director*
*Ron Vickery, President*
A weeklong residential summer camp for youths and teens who are deaf or hard of hearing. Through challenging, team-oriented

activities, campers form lasting friendships and acquire valuable leadership, social and communication skills.

**7805 Camp Mark Seven**
Mark Seven Deaf Foundation
144 Mohawk Hotel Rd
Old Forge, NY 13420-4010 315-357-6089
FAX: 315-357-6403
e-mail: cm7campdirector@gmail.com
www.campmark7.org

*Dr. Andrew T Brinks, Executive Director*
*Chris McQuaid, Office Manager*
*AJ Hess, Deaf Programs Director*
*Jenn Legg, KODA Programs Director*
Adirondack Mountain camp for hard-of-hearing, deaf and hearing people. Coed, ages 1-99, families, seniors and single adults.

**7806 Camp Pacifica, Inc.**
California Lions Camp
P.O.Box 577663
Modesto, CA 95357-7663 209-523-9403
FAX: 209-543-9418
e-mail: webmaster@camppacifica.org
www.californialionscamp.org

*Ann Tognetti, President*
*Bob Ransom, Treasurer*
*Russ Custer, VP*
*Jill Loving, Secretary*
Camp Pacifica is a camp for special needs children ages 7-15 years old. The camp offers outdoor recreational activities, along with promoting greater independence and self confidence among the children, and provides opportunities for social interaction, and further development of social skills.

**7807 Camp Shocco for the Deaf**
AL Baptist State Board of Missions
216 North Street East
P.O. Box 602
Talladega, AL 35161- 886 256-761-1100
800-264-1225
FAX: 256-761-1270
e-mail: shoccosprings@shocco.org
www.campshocco.org

*Rev. Ricky Milford, Director Children*
*Chris MaGaha, Director Youth*
*Linnea Elliott, Assistant Director Youth*
*Chad Fleming, Director of the Camp Shocco for*
Camp Shocco gives each child and teenager attending camp the opportunity to have an unforgettable one week of fun, games, and spiritual growth. Each camper also learns essence of teamwork, while developing their own unique abilities and talents that can often be overlooked.

**7808 Camp Taloali**
Lions Club of Oregon and Washington
15934 N Santiam Hwy
P.O. Box 32
Stayton, OR 97383-9619 503-769-6415
TTY:503-769-6415
e-mail: camptaloali@comcast.net
www.taloali.org

*Rolland Hart, Executive Director*
Summer sessions for children with hearing impairment. Coed, ages 9-17.

**7809 Camp Tekoa UMC**
Western NC Conference/United Methodist Church
P.O.Box 160
Hendersonville, NC 28793-0160 828-692-6516
FAX: 828-697-3288
e-mail: director@camptekoa.org
www.camptekoa.org

*James Johnson, Executive Director*
*Mike Pruett, Program Director*
*Melisa Coates, Administrative Assistant*
*Karen Roehrer, Business Manager*
Camping for children with asthma/respiratory ailments, hearing impairment and developmental disabilities. Coed, ages 6-17.

**7810 Deaf Kid's Kamp**
Sproul Ranch, Inc.
42263 50th Street West
Suite 610
Quartz Hill, CA 93536- 3500 661-675-3323
877-399-5449
e-mail: deafkidskamp@earthlink.net
www.deafkidskamp.com

*Buffy Sproul, Executive Director*
Our purpose is to meet the needs of deaf children outside of the classroom setting. These needs, as we have defined them, would include but are not limited to: social contact with peers; contact with the culture of the Deaf Community; educational and recreational programs not available in most school settings.

**7811 Easter Seals Oklahoma**
701 NE 13th St
Oklahoma City, OK 73104-5003 405-239-2525
e-mail: sbusch@easterseals oklahoma.org
www.eastersealsoklahoma.org

*Paula Porter, CEO*
*Vida Wasinger, Director of Operations*
*Aundria Goree, Program Director*
*Mike Nunley, Treasurer*
Adult day health center, and child development center.

**7812 Father Drumgoole Connelly Summer Camp**
MIV: Mount Loretto
6581 Hylan Blvd
Staten Island, NY 10309-3830 718-317-2600
FAX: 718-317-2830
www.mountloretto.org

*Brian Landano, Camp Director*
Summer sessions for children with epilepsy, hearing impairment and developmental disabilities. Coed, ages 5-13.

**7813 Lions Camp Crescendo, Inc.**
1480 Pine Tavern Road
P.O. Box 607
Lebanon Junction, KY 40150-0607 502-833-3554
888-879-8884
FAX: 502-833-4249
e-mail: bjflannery@lions-campcrescendo.org
www.lions-campcrescendo.org

*Billie Flannery, Administrator*
*Kevin Patton, Resident Manager*
*Lion Paul Witten, Chairperson*
*Lion Cebert Gilbert, Vice-Chairperson*
The enhancement of the quality of life for youth, especially those with disabilities, through the delivery of a traditional camp experience by caring individuals and to enable others to use our camping and retreat facilities to serve the larger communities humanitarian needs.

**7814 Lions Camp Kirby**
1735 Narrows Hill Rd
Upper Black Eddy, PA 18972-9712
610-982-5731
e-mail: info@lionscampkirby.org
www.lionscampkirby.org

*Bob Hunsberger, President*
*Alice Breon, Camp Director*
Offers 4-week camps for deaf and hearing impaired children and their siblings in eastern Pennsylvania.

**7815 Lions Camp Merrick**
Lions Clubs of District 22-C
3650 Rick Hamilton Place
P.O. Box 56
Nanjemoy, MD 20662-56
301-870-5858
FAX: 301-246-9108
e-mail: CampOfficeLCM@aol.com
lionscampmerrick.org

*Heidi.A Fick, Director*
*Susanna Ruspi, Bookkeeper*
*Donna Wadsworth, Office Administrator*
*Kenny Shontere, Maintenance*
This recreational camp for special needs children offers a complete waterfront program including swimming, canoeing and fishing for ages 6-16. Designed for children who are deaf and hard of hearing, children of deaf parents, and children with diabetes. Also helps children to learn to deal with their special conditions.

**7816 Lions Wilderness Camp for Deaf Children, Inc.**
Lions Clubs of California and Nevada
P.O.Box 195
Knightsen, CA 94548-195
877-896-1598
888-613-1557
e-mail: campdirector@lionswildcamp.org
www.lionswildcamp.org

*Rachel Mix, Camp Program Director*
*William Arnold, President*
*Benjamin Fregoso, VP*
*Denise Arnold, Secretary*
A camp experience where a deaf child age 7 to 15 can learn outdoor skills and enjoy the wonder and beauty of nature to the fullest extent.

**7817 Meadowood Springs Speech and Hearing Camp**
Oregon State Elks Association
136-A SE Emigrant
P.O. Box 1025
Pendleton, OR 97801-30
541-276-2752
FAX: 541-276-7227
e-mail: info@meadowoodsprings.org
www.meadowoodsprings.org

*Michael Ashton, Executive Director*
*Kathy Hosek, Administrative Assistant*
*Patti Hall, Camp Staff Manager*
On 143 acres in the Blue Mountains of Eastern Oregon, this camp is designed to help young people who have diagnosed clinical disorders of speech, hearing or language. A full range of activities in recreational and clinical areas is available.

**7818 Ramah in the Poconos**
261 Old York Road
Suite 734
Jenkintown, PA 19046-3725
215-885-8556
FAX: 215-885-8905
e-mail: info@ramahpoconos.org
www.ramahpoconos.org

*Todd Zeff, Executive Director*
Camp is located in Lake Como, Pennsylvania. Summer sessions for children and adults with hearing impairment. Coed, ages 10-16, families and seniors.

**7819 Sandcastle Day Camp**
Children's Beach House
1800 Bay Ave
Lewes, DE 19958-1859
302-645-9184
FAX: 302-645-9467
e-mail: cterranova@cbhinc.org
www.cbhinc.org

*Richard Garrett, CEO*
*Jennifer A. Clement, Director, Delaware Center for Youth Development*
*Amanda Ryan, Director of Development*
*Steven T. Martinenza, Director of Youth Development Program*
Camp is located in Lewes, Delaware. Four-week sessions June-August for Delaware children with hearing impairment or speech/communication impairment. Coed, ages 6-12.

**7820 Sertoma Camp Endeavor**
Sertoma Camp Endeavor
P.O.Box 910
Dundee, FL 33838-0910
863-439-1300
FAX: 863-439-1300
e-mail: info@sertomacampendeavor.com
www.sertomacampendeavor.org

*Jeff Nunemaker, Executive Director*
The intergration of deaf, hard of hearing and hearing youngsters is a unique characteristic of our camping program. Both hearing, deaf and hard of hearing children have the opportunity to learn about themselves and each other in an informal and empowering setting.

**7821 Texas Lions Camp**
Lions Club of Texas
P.O.Box 290247
Kerrville, TX 78029-247
830-896-8500
FAX: 830-896-3666
e-mail: smabry@lionscamp.com
www.lionscamp.com

*Stephen Mabry, Executive Director*
The primary purpose of the League shall be to provide, without charge, a camp for physically disabled, hearing/vision impaired and diabetic children from the State of Texas, regardless of race, religion, or national origin. Our goal is to create an atmosphere wherein campers will learn the can do philosophy and be allowed to achieve maximum personal growth and self-esteem. The camp welcomes boys and girls ages 7-16.

**7822 YMCA Camp Fitch**
The YMCA's Camp Fitch on Lake Erie
12600 Abels Rd
North Springfield, PA 16430-1014
814-922-3219
FAX: 814-922-7000
e-mail: info@campfitchymca.org
www.campfitch.com

*Brian Rupe, Executive Director*
*Greg Donahue, Assistant Camp Director*
*Dann Olin, Operations Director*
*Barb Olin, Senior Program Director*
Camp is located in North Springfield, Pennsylvania. Camping sessions for children and adults with diabetes, hearing impairment, developmental disabilities, mobility limitation and speech/communication impairment. Ages 8-16, families and seniors.

**7823 YWCA Camp Westwind**
YWCA of Greater Portland
1111 SW 10th Ave
Portland, OR 97205-2496
503-294-7476
FAX: 503-721-1751
e-mail: westwiind@ywcapdx.org
http://www.ywcapdx.org

*Janette McMurran, Camp Director*
*Sarah Keplinger, Office Manager*
*Secretary*

Promotes the understanding of racism and all forms of discrimination and fosters value, respect, and enjoyment of each person's unique contribution.

**7824 Youth Leadership Camp**

National Association of the Deaf
8630 Fenton Street
Suite 820
Silver Spring, MD 20910- 3819
301-587-1788
FAX: 301-587-1791
TTY:301-587-1789
e-mail: infor@nad.org
www.nad.org

*Howard A. Rosenblum, CEO*
*Bobbies Beth Scoggin, President*
*Christopher Wagner, VP*
*Shane H Feldman, COO*

Sponsored by the National Association of the Deaf, this camp emphasizes leadership training for deaf teenagers and young adults. In addition to many recreational activities and sports, there are academic offerings and camp projects.

## Print: Books

**7825 A Basic Course in American Sign Language**

TJ Publishers
2544 Tarpley Rd
Suite 108 #108
Carrollton, TX 75006-2288
972-416-0800
800-999-1168
FAX: 972-416-0944
e-mail: customerservice@tjpublishers.com
www.tjpublishers.com

*Tom Humphries, Author*
*Carol Padden, Co-Author*
*Terrence J O'Rouke, Co-Author*
*Tanner Beach, Director*

Accompanying videotapes and textbooks will include voice translations. Hearing students can analyze sound for initial instruction, or opt to turn off the sound to sharpen visual acuity. Package includes the A Basic Course in American Sign Language text, Student Study Guide, the original four 1-hour videotapes plus the ABCASL Vocabulary Videotape. *$35.95*

*288 pages Spiral Bound*
*ISBN 0-932666-42-6*

**7826 A Basic Course in Manual Communication**

Gallaudet University Bookstore
800 Florida Ave NE
Washington, DC 20002-3600
202-651-5000
FAX: 202-651-5508
e-mail: Oluyinka.Fakunle@gallaudet.edu
www.clerccenter.gallaudet.edu

*Terrence J O'Rourke, Author*
*T. Alan Hurwitz, President*
*Paul Kelly, Vice President Adm And Finance*

Teach your students manual communication - that living, changing, growing language of signs.

*161 pages Softcover*

**7827 A Basic Vocabulary: American Sign Languagefor Parents and Children**

TJ Publishers
2544 Tarpley Rd
Suite 108 #108
Carrollton, TX 75006-2288
972-416-0800
800-999-1168
FAX: 972-416-0944
e-mail: customerservice@tjpublishers.com
www.tjpublishers.com

*Terrence J O'Rouke, Author*
*Tanner Beach, Director*

Carefully selected words and signs include those that children use every day. Alphabetically organized vocabulary incorporates developmental lists helpful to both deaf and hearing children and over 1000 clear sign language illustrations. *$9.95*

*240 pages Softcover*
*ISBN 0-932666-00-0*

**7828 A Handbook for Writing Effective Psychoeducational Reports**

Sage Publications
2455 Teller Road
Thousand Oaks, CA 91320
800-818-7243
FAX: 800-583-2665
e-mail: info@sagepub.com
www.sagepub.com

*Sara Miller McCune, Founder, Publisher, Chairperson*
*Blaise R Simqu, President & CEO*
*Tracey A. Ozmina, Executive Vice President & Chief Operating Officer*
*Stephen Barr, Managing Director*

This book includes a comprehensive presentation of issues and procedures related to the assessment of hearing-impaired students. *$27.00*

*134 pages Paperback*
*ISBN 1-416401-40-7*

**7829 A Loss for Words**

HarperCollins Publishers
10 E 53rd St
New York, NY 10022-5244
212-207-7000
FAX: 212-207-7617
www.harpercollins.com

*Lou Ann Walker, Author*

She was an interpreter for her parents at four, a virtual head of household at eight, teacher and helper for her little sisters, buffer between her family and the world. Here is a daughter's account of growing up with loving parents, both of whom are deaf. *$13.00*

*224 pages Paperback 1987*
*ISBN 0-060914-25-4*

**7830 Access for All: Integrating Deaf, Hard of Hearing and Hearing Preschoolers**

Gallaudet University Bookstore
800 Florida Ave NE
Washington, DC 20002-3600
202-651-5340
866-637-0102
e-mail: Oluyinka.Fakunle@gallaudet.edu
http://www.gallaudet.edu

*Gail Solit, Author*
*Maral Taylor, Co-Author*
*Angela Bednarczyk, Co-Author*

This exciting new 90 minute videotape and manual describes a model program for integrating deaf and hard of hearing children in early education.

*169 pages Book & Video*

**7831 Advanced Sign Language Vocabulary: A Resource Text for Educators**

Charles C. Thomas
2600 S 1st St
Springfield, IL 62704-4730
217-789-8980
800-258-8980
FAX: 217-789-9130
e-mail: books@ccthomas.com
www.ccthomas.com

*Michael P. Thomas, President*
*Elizabeth E Wolf, Co-Author*

A resource text for educators, interpreters, parents and sign language instructors. *$53.95*

*202 pages Spiral Paper*
*ISBN 0-398057-22-0*

**7832 American Sign Language Handshape Dictionary**
Gallaudet University Press
800 Florida Ave NE
Washington, DC 20002-3600
202-651-5000
FAX: 202-651-5508
e-mail: gupress@gallaudet.edu
gupress.gallaudet.edu

*Richard A Tennant, Author*
*Marianne Gluszak Brown, Co-Author*
*Valerie Nelson-Metlay, Illustrator*
*T. Alan Hurwitz, President*

More than 1,600 sign illustrations arranged by handshape for easy identification. Allows readers to look up signs they have seen without needing to know their English meaning beforehand, complemented by a complete English index cross-referenced to every sign. *$45.00*
*408 pages Hardcover*
*ISBN 1-563680-43-2*

**7833 American Sign Language Phrase Book**
TJ Publishers
2544 Tarpley Rd
Suite 108 #108
Carrollton, TX 75006-2288
972-416-0800
800-999-1168
FAX: 972-416-0944
e-mail: customerservice@tjpublishers.com
www.tjpublishers.com

*Lou Fant, Author*
*Terrence O'Rourke, Principal*
*Tanner Beach, Director*

The author provides interesting, realistic and meaningful situations. Sign language is learned through novel remarks cleverly organized around everyday topics. *$18.95*
*362 pages Softcover*
*ISBN 0-809235-00-5*

**7834 American Sign Language: A Look at Its History, Structure & Community**
TJ Publishers
2544 Tarpley Rd
Suite 108 #108
Carrollton, TX 75006-2288
972-416-0800
800-999-1168
FAX: 972-416-0944
e-mail: customerservice@tjpublishers.com
www.tjpublishers.com

*Charlotte Baker-Shenk, Author*
*Carol Padden, Co-Author*
*Terrence O'Rourke, Principal*
*Tanner Beach, Director*

Answers basic questions about American Sign Language. What is it? What is its history? Who uses it? What is the deaf community? *$4.95*
*22 pages Softcover*
*ISBN 0-93266 -01-9*

**7835 At Home Among Strangers**
Gallaudet University Press
800 Florida Ave NE
Washington, DC 20002-3600
202-651-5000
FAX: 202-651-5508
e-mail: gupress@gallaudet.edu
www.gupress.gallaudet.edu

*Jerome D Schein, Author*
*T. Alan Hurwitz, President*
*Paul Kelly, Vice President Adm And Finance*

Discusses deaf culture and its uniqueness in two sections: the first describes the deaf community - its development, structure and culture; the second explains Schein's theory of deaf community development. *$36.95*
*264 pages Paperback*
*ISBN 1-563681-41-2*

**7836 BPPV: What You Need to Know**
Vestibular Disorders Association
4035 Ne Sandy Blvd
Portland, OR 97212-5331
503-229-7705
800-837-8428
FAX: 503-229-8064
e-mail: info@vestibular.org
www.vestibular.org

*P J Haybach, Author*
*Lisa Haven, Executive Director*
*Jerry Underwood, Managing Director*
*Vincente Honrubia, Director*

The aim of this book is to present basic information about benign paroxysmal positional vertigo (BPPV) including what it is, causes, how it is diagnosed, various treatments currently in use, and strategies for coping with the symptoms associated with BPPV. *$29.95*
*207 pages Hardcover*
*ISBN 0-963261-14-2*

**7837 Ben's Story: A Deaf Child's Right to Sign**
Gallaudet University Bookstore
800 Florida Ave NE
Washington, DC 20002-3600
202-651-5340
866-637-0102
FAX: 202-398-7694
e-mail: Oluyinka.Fakunle@gallaudet.edu
http://www.gallaudet.edu

*Laura Fletcher, Manager*
*T. Alan Hurwitz, President*
*Paul Kelly, Vice President Adm. And Finance*

This is a mother's story of how she responded to the diagnosis of her son's deafness and how she struggled to have her son educated using sign language.
*267 pages Softcover*
*ISBN 0-930323-47-5*

**7838 Book of Name Signs: Naming in American Sign Language**
DawnSign Press
6130 Nancy Ridge Dr
San Diego, CA 92121-3223
858-625-0600
FAX: 858-625-2336
e-mail: info@dawnsign.com
www.dawnsign.com

*Joe Dannis, President*
*Sam Supalla, Author*

To explain how a name sign is chosen in the Deaf community, professor and researcher Sam Supalla wrote this valuable resource book. Revealing fascinating insights about the origins of ASL name signs, Supalla shows how they serve the same function as given names used in the hearing community. He also details how the history of the name sign system dates back to the early years of deaf education in America. Included for reference is a list of more than 500 name signs available for selection. *$12.95*
*120 pages Paperback 1992*
*ISBN 0-915035-30-4*

**7839 Chelsea: The Story of a Signal Dog**
Gallaudet University Bookstore
800 Florida Ave NE
Washington, DC 20002-3600
202-651-5000
FAX: 202-651-5508
e-mail: Oluyinka.Fakunle@gallaudet.edu
www.clerccenter.gallaudet.edu

*Paul Ogden, Author*
*T. Alan Hurwitz, President*
*Paul Kelly, Vice President Adm. And Finance*

This is a story of a young deaf couple and their Belgian sheepdog, who acts as their ears. It explains how these dogs are trained and paired with their new owners.
*169 pages*

**7840 Children of a Lesser God**
Gallaudet University Bookstore
800 Florida Ave NE
Washington, DC 20002-3600
202-651-5000
FAX: 202-651-5508
e-mail: Oluyinka.Fakunle@gallaudet.edu
www.clerccenter.gallaudet.edu

*Mark Medoff, Author*
*T. Alan Hurwitz, President*
*Paul Kelly, Vice President Adm. And Finance*
The movie that won the hearts of thousands. This is a story of a deaf woman who refuses to succumb to the hearing people's image of what a deaf person should be.
*91 pages Softcover*
*ISBN 0-822202-03-4*

**7841 Choices in Deafness: A Parent's Guide to Communication Options**
Woodbine House
6510 Bells Mill Rd
Bethesda, MD 20817-1636
301-897-3570
800-843-7323
FAX: 301-897-5838
e-mail: info@woodbinehouse.com
www.woodbinehouse.com

*Irv Shapell, Owner*
*Sue Schwartz, PhD., Editor*
A useful aid in choosing the appropriate communication option for a child with a hearing loss. Experts present the following communication options: Auditory-Verbal Approach, Bilingual-Bicultural Approach, Cued Speech, Oral Approach, and Total Communication. This new edition explains medical causes of hearing loss, the diagnostic process, audiological assessment, and cochlear implants. Children and parents also offer their personal experiences. *$24.95*
*400 pages Paperback*
*ISBN 1-890627-73-7*

**7842 Cochlear Implants for Kids**
Alexander Graham Bell Association
3417 Volta Pl NW
Washington, DC 20007-2737
202-337-5220
FAX: 202-337-8314
e-mail: info@agbell.org
www.agbell.org

*Warren Estabrooks MEd, Editor*
Designed to educate readers about cochlear implants, including surgery, the importance of rehabilitation and the significance of parents' and professionals' roles. *$12.49*
*404 pages Paperback*
*ISBN 0-882002-08-2*

**7843 Cognition, Education and Deafness: Directions for Research and Instruction**
Gallaudet University Press
800 Florida Ave NE
Washington, DC 20002-3600
202-651-5000
FAX: 202-651-5508
e-mail: gupress@galladuet.edu
www.gupress.galladuet.edu

*David S Martin, Editor*
*T. Alan Hurwitz, President*
*Paul Kelly, Vice President Adm. And Finance*
The work of 54 authors is gathered in this definitive collection of current research on deafness and cognition. The articles are grouped into seven sections: cognition, problem solving, thinking processes, language development, reading methodologies, measurement of potential, and intervention programs. *$50.00*
*248 pages Paperback*
*ISBN 1-563681-49-8*

**7844 College and University Programs for Deaf and Hard of Hearing Students**
Gallaudet & NTID
Gallaudet University
800 Florida Avenue NE
Washington, DC 20002
202-651-5000
800-451-8834
FAX: 202-651-5508
www.lulu.com/content/1238777

*S. Benaissa, & L. Dunning, Co-Authors*
*J. DeCaro, M. Karchmer, Co-Authors*
*J Hochgesang , Co-Author*
*T. Alan Hurwitz, President*
Compiled by Gallaudet University and the National Technical Institute for the Deaf, this publication is a guide to accessibility for deaf and hard of hearing students in American colleges and universities. Available through LuLu Publishing. *$11.50*
*240 pages Paperback*
*ISBN 9-998242-81-9*

**7845 Come Sign with Us**
Gallaudet University Press
800 Florida Ave NE
Washington, DC 20002-3600
202-651-5000
800-621-2736
FAX: 202-651-5000
TTY: 800-621-9347
e-mail: gupress@gallaudet.edu
www.gupress.gallaudet.edu

*Jan C Hafer, Author*
*Robert M Wilson, Co-Author*
*T. Alan Hurwitz, President*
*Paul Kelly, Vice President Adm. And Finance*
This fun guide for parents and educators on teaching hearing children how to sign has been thoroughly revised with completely new activities that provide contexts for practice. *$39.95*
*160 pages Paperback*
*ISBN 1-563680-51-3*

**7846 Comprehensive Reference Manual for Signers and Interpreters**
Charles C. Thomas
2600 S 1st St
Springfield, IL 62704-4730
217-789-8980
800-258-8980
FAX: 217-789-9130
e-mail: books@ccthomas.com
www.ccthomas.com

*Michael P. Thomas, President*
*Cheryl M. Hoffman, Author*
This 6th Edition contains almost seven thousand entries, including vocabulary and idioms, with cross-references and sign descriptions. *$59.95*
*404 pages Spiral Paper 1909*
*ISBN 0-398078-58-4*

**7847 Comprehensive Signed English Dictionary**
Gallaudet University Press
800 Florida Ave NE
Washington, DC 20002-3600
202-651-5000
800-621-2736
FAX: 202-651-5508
e-mail: gupress@gallaudet.edu
www.gupress.gallaudet.edu

*Harry Bornstein, Editor*
*Karen L. Saulnier, Editor*
*Lillian B. Hamilton, Editor*
*T. Paul Hurwitz, President*
This complete dictionary has over 3,100 signs, including signs reflecting lively and contemporary vocabulary. *$45.00*
*464 pages Casebound*
*ISBN 0-913580-81-3*

**7848 Conversational Sign Language II: An Intermediate Advanced Manual**

Gallaudet University Press
800 Florida Ave NE
Washington, DC 20002-3600
202-651-5000
FAX: 202-651-5508
e-mail: gupress@gallaudet.edu
www.gupress.gallaudet.edu

*William J Madsen, Author*
*T. Alan Hurwitz, President*
*Paul Kelly, Vice President Adm. And Finance*

This book presents English words and their American Sign Language equivalents. *$17.95*

*236 pages Paperback*
*ISBN 0-913580-00-7*

**7849 Deaf Empowerment: Emergence, Struggle and Rhetoric**

Gallaudet University Press
800 Florida Ave NE
Washington, DC 20002-3600
202-651-5000
FAX: 202-651-5508
e-mail: gupress@gallaudet.edu
www.gupress.gallaudet.edu

*Katherine A Jankowski, Author*
*T. Alan Hurwitz, President*
*Paul Kelly, Vice President Adm. And Finance*

The story of the Deaf social movement, from its beginnings in the mid 1800s through its growth and strengthening in the late 20th century, much of it due to rhetoric and tactics adopted from other social movements. *$49.95*

*192 pages Hardcover*
*ISBN 1-563680-61-0*

**7850 Deaf History Unveiled: Interpretations from the New Scholarship**

Gallaudet University Press
800 Florida Ave NE
Washington, DC 20002-3600
202-651-5000
FAX: 202-651-5508
e-mail: gupress@gallaudet.edu
www.gallaudet.edu

*John Vickrey Van Cleve, Editor*
*T. Alan Hurwitz, President*
*Paul Kelly, Vice President Adm. And Finance*

An all-star cast of historians explores the new themes driving Deaf History, including comparisons with other minority cultures and the social paternalism that affects deaf communities around the globe. *$36.95*

*316 pages Paperback*
*ISBN 1-563680-87-4*

**7851 Deaf Like Me**

Gallaudet University Press
800 Florida Ave NE
Washington, DC 20002-3600
202-651-5000
FAX: 202-651-5508
e-mail: gupress@gallaudet.edu
www.gupress.gallaudet.edu

*Thomas S Spradley, Author*
*James P Spradley, Co-Author*
*T. Alan Hurwitz, President*
*Paul Kelly, Vice President Adm. And Finance*

Written by the uncle and father of a deaf girl, this is an account of parents coming to terms with deafness. This paperback edition contains a special epilogue by Lynn Spradley, grown and in her twenties, as she reflects on her growing-up years with the advantage of hindsight. *$16.95*

*292 pages Paperback*
*ISBN 0-930323-11-4*

**7852 Deaf Parents and Their Hearing Children**

Through the Looking Glass
3075 Adeline St., Ste. 120
Berkeley, CA 94710-2212
510-848-1112
800-644-2666
FAX: 510-848-4445
e-mail: TLG@lookingglass.org
www.lookingglass.org

*Jenny L Singleton, Author*
*Stephanie Miyashiro, President*
*Thomas Spalding, Treasurer*
*Alice Nemon, Secretary*

The focus of this review article is on families with Deaf parents and hearing children. We provide a brief description of the Deaf community, their language, and culture; describe communication patterns and parenting issues in Deaf-parented families, examine the role of the hearing child in a Deaf family and how that experience affects their functioning in the hearing world; and discuss important considerations and resources for families, educators, and health care and service providers. *$2.00*

*8 pages*

**7853 Deaf in America: Voices from a Culture**

TJ Publishers
2544 Tarpley Rd
Suite 108 #108
Carrollton, TX 75006-2288
972-416-0800
800-999-1168
FAX: 972-416-0944
e-mail: customerservice@tjpublishers.com
www.tjpublishers.com

*Carol Padden, Author*
*Tom Humphries, Co-Author*
*Terrence O'Rourke, Principal*
*Tanner Beach, Director*

Now available in paperback, this book opens deaf culture to outsiders, inviting readers to imagine and understand a world of silence. This book shares the joy and satisfaction many people have with their lives and shows that deafness may not be the handicap most hearing people think. *$15.95*

*134 pages Softcover*
*ISBN 0-674194-24-1*

**7854 EASE Program: Emergency Access Self Evaluation**

Telecommunications for the Deaf (TDI)
Ste 604
8630 Fenton St
Silver Spring, MD 20910-3822
301-589-3786
FAX: 301-589-3797
e-mail: info@tdi-online.org
tdi-online.org

*Claude L Stout, Executive Director*
*Gloria Carter, Executive Secretary*
*James House, Public Relations Director*
*Robert McConnell, Advertising Manager*

A complete training, testing, maintenance and self evaluation program that helps emergency service providers prepare for emergency calls from TTY users and to comply with the American with Disabilities Act. *$35.00*

*48 pages*

**7855 Encyclopedia of Deafness and Hearing Disorders**

Powell's Books
1005 W Burnside St
Portland, OR 97209-3114
503-228-4651
800-873-7323
e-mail: help@powells.com
www.powells.com

*Carol Turkington, Author*

Presents the most current information on deafness and hearing disorders in an authoritative A-to-Z compendium. *$7.50*

*294 pages Hardcover*
*ISBN 0-816056-15-3*

**7856 Expressive and Receptive Fingerspelling for Hearing Adults**
Gallaudet University Bookstore
800 Florida Ave NE
Washington, DC 20002-3600
202-651-5000
FAX: 202-651-5508
e-mail: Oluyinka.Fakunle@gallaudet.edu
www.clerccenter.gallaudet.edu

*LaVera M Guillory, Author*
*T. Alan Hurwitz, President*
*Paul Kelly, Vice President Adm. And Finance*

Here is a new and meaningful way for adults to increase their comfort with fingerspelling. The system is based on the principles of phonetics rather than letters of the English alphabet.
*42 pages Softcover*
*ISBN 0-875110-55-X*

**7857 Eye-Centered: A Study of Spirituality of Deaf People**
National Catholic Office for the Deaf
7202 Buchanan St
Hyattsville, MD 20784-2236
301-577-1684
FAX: 301-577-1684
e-mail: info@ncod.org
www.ncod.org

*Bill Key, Author*
*Arvilla Rank, Executive Director*

The findings of the five-year De Sales Project conducted by The National Catholic Office for the Deaf. *$16.70*
*167 pages*

**7858 For Hearing People Only**
Harris Communications
15155 Technology Dr
Eden Prairie, MN 55344-2273
952-906-1180
800-825-6758
FAX: 952-906-1099
e-mail: info@harriscomm.com
www.harriscomm.com

*Robert Harris, Owner*
*Linda Levitan, Co-Author*
*Matthew S. Moore, Co-Author*
*Harlan Lane, Foreword*

A book that answers some of the questions hearing people ask about deaf culture. Also availible in hardcover. *$35.95*
*724 pages Paperback*
*ISBN 0-963401-63-7*

**7859 From Gesture to Language in Hearing and Deaf Children**
Gallaudet University Press
800 Florida Ave NE
Washington, DC 20002-3600
202-651-5000
800-621-2736
FAX: 202-651-5508
e-mail: gupress@galladuet.edu
www.gupress.gallaudet.edu

*Virginia Volterra, Editor*
*Carol J. Erting, Editor*

In 21 essays on communicative gesturing in the first two years of life, this vital collection demonstrates the importance of gesture in a child's transition to a linguistic system. *$45.95*
*358 pages Paperback*
*ISBN 1-563680-78-5*

**7860 From Mime to Sign Package**
TJ Publishers
2544 Tarpley Rd
Suite 108 #108
Carrollton, TX 75006-2288
972-416-0800
800-999-1168
FAX: 972-416-0944
e-mail: customerservice@tjpublishers.com
www.tjpublishers.com

*Gilbert C Eastman, Author*
*Terrence O'Rourke, Principal*
*Tanner Beach, Director*

As a drama professor, television personality, performer and storyteller, multiple Emmy winner Gil Eastman has developed a unique presentation style. *$27.95*
*183 pages Softcover*
*ISBN 0-932666-34-5*

**7861 GA and SK Etiquette**
Telecommunications for the Deaf
8630 Fenton Street
Suite 604 #604
Silver Spring, MD 20910-3822
301-589-3786
FAX: 301-589-3797
e-mail: info@tdi-online.org
www.tdi-online.org

*Claude L Stout, Executive Director*
*Keith Cagle, Co-Author*
*Roy Miller, President*
*Gloria Carter, Administrator*

Promoting equal access to telecommunications and media for people who are deaf, late-deafened, hard-of-hearing or deaf-blind through consumer education and involvement; technical assistance and consulting; applications of exisiting and emerging technologies; networking and collaboration; uniformity of standards; and national policy development and advocacy. *$11.95*
*54 pages Paperback*
*ISBN 0-961462-17-5*

**7862 Gallaudet Survival Guide to Signing**
Gallaudet University Press
800 Florida Ave NE
Washington, DC 20002-3600
202-651-5000
800-621-2736
FAX: 202-651-5508
e-mail: gupress@gallaudet.edu
www.gallaudet.edu

*Jon Mitchiner, Manager*
*Leonard G. Lane, Author*
*Jan Skrobisz, Illustrator*
*T. Alan Hurwitz, President*

Features 500 of the most frequently used signs with clear illustrations and descriptions for each one. *$9.95*
*218 pages Paperback*
*ISBN 0-930323-67-X*

**7863 Goldilocks and the Three Bears: Told in Signed English**
Gallaudet University Press
800 Florida Ave NE
Washington, DC 20002-3600
202-651-5000
800-621-2736
FAX: 202-651-5508
e-mail: gupress@gallaudet.edu
www.gupress.gallaudet.edu

*Harry Bornstein, Author*
*Karen L Saulnier, Co-Author*
*T. Alan Hurwitz, President*
*Paul Kelly, Vice President Adm. And Finance*

The classic story is told again but with a twist. Full color illustrations show the Bears, Goldilocks and the text. Includes line drawings that show the story in Signed English. *$21.95*
*48 pages Hardcover*
*ISBN 1-563680-57-2*

**7864 Hearing Impaired Children and Youth with Developmental Disabilities**
Gallaudet University Bookstore
800 Florida Ave NE
Washington, DC 20002-3600
202-651-5000
800-621-2736
FAX: 202-651-5508
e-mail: Oluyinka.Fakunle@gallaudet.edu
www.clerccenter.gallaudet.edu

*Evelyn Cherow, Editor*
*T. Alan Hurwitz, President*
*Paul Kelly, Vice President Adm. And Finance*
The insights of 24 experts help clarify relationships between hearing impairment and developmental difficulties and propose interdisciplinary cooperation as an approach to the problems created. *$29.95*
*394 pages Hardcover*
*ISBN 0-913580-97-X*

**7865 Hollywood Speaks: Deafness and the Film Entertainment Industry**
University of Illinois Press
1325 S Oak St
Champaign, IL 61820-6903
217-333-0950
FAX: 217-244-8082
e-mail: uipress@uillinois.edu
www.press.uillinois.edu

*Willis G. Regier, Director*
*John S. Schuchman, Author*
*Kathy O'Neill, Assistant To The Director*
How deafness has been treated in movies and how it provides yet another window onto social history in addition to a fresh angle from which to view Hollywood. *$27.00*
*200 pages Paperback 1999*
*ISBN 0-252068-50-8*

**7866 I Have a Sister, My Sister is Deaf**
HarperCollins Publishers
1350 Ave Of The Americas
New York, NY 10019-4702
212-246-2058
FAX: 212-207-7145
www.harpercollins.com

*Jeanne Whitehouse Peterson, Author*
*Ann Ledden, Vice President*
*Lorna Metzler, Manager*
An emphatic, affirmative look at the relationship between siblings, as a young deaf child is affectionately described by her older sister. This Coretta Scott King Honor Award winner helps young children develop an understanding that deaf children share the same interests as hearing children. *$6.99*
*32 pages Paperback 1984*
*ISBN 0-064430-59-6*

**7867 Independence Without Sight or Sound**
AFB Press
11 Penn Plz
Suite 300 #300
New York, NY 10001-2006
212-502-7600
800-232-5463
FAX: 212-502-7777
e-mail: afbinfo@afb.net
www.afb.org

*Carl Augusto, President*
*Richard Obnen, Chairman Of The Board*
*Michael Gilliam, Vice Chairman*
*James Kesteloot, CEO*
This practical guidebook covers the essential aspects of communicating and working with deaf-blind persons. Full of valuable information on subjects such as how to talk with deaf-blind people, adapt orientation and mobility techniques for deaf-blind travelers, and interact with deaf-blind individuals socially, this useful manual also contains a substantial resource section detailing sources of information and adapted equipment. *$39.95*
*193 pages Paperback*
*ISBN 0-891282-46-4*

**7868 Innovative Practices for Teaching Sign Language Interpreters**
Gallaudet University Press
800 Florida Ave NE
Washington, DC 20002-3600
202-651-5000
800-621-2736
FAX: 202-651-5508
e-mail: gupress@gallaudet.edu
www.gupress.gallaudet.edu

*Cynthia B Roy, Editor*
Six experts draw upon the new understanding of sign language interpreting as a discourse between two languages and cultures. Develops bold, original techniques for training interpreters. *$45.95*
*200 pages Hardcover*
*ISBN 1-563680-88-2*

**7869 Intermediate Conversational Sign Language**
Gallaudet University Press
800 Florida Ave NE
Washington, DC 20002-3600
202-651-5000
800-621-2736
FAX: 202-651-5508
e-mail: gupress@gallaudet.edu
www.gupress.gallaudet.edu

*Willard J Madsen, Author*
Unique approach to using American Sign Language and English in a bilingual setting. Each of the 25 lessons includes an introductory paragraph, glossed vocabulary review, translation exercises, grammatical notes, substitution drills and activities. *$31.50*
*400 pages Softcover*
*ISBN 0-913580-79-1*

**7870 Interpretation: A Sociolinguistic Model**
Sign Media
4020 Blackburn Ln
Burtonsville, MD 20866-1167
301-421-0268
FAX: 301-421-0270
e-mail: info@signmedia.com
www.signmedia.com

*Verden Ness, President*
*Dennis Cokely, Author*
This text presents a sociolinguistically sensitive model of the interpretation process. The model applies to interpretation in any two languages although this one focuses on ASL and English. *$22.95*
*199 pages*
*ISBN 0-932130-10-0*

**7871 Interpreting: An Introduction**
Registry of Interpreters for the Deaf
333 Commerce St
Alexandria, VA 22314-2801
703-838-0030
FAX: 703-838-0454
www.rid.org

*Nancy J Frishberg, Author*
*Al Pimentel, Director*
*Don Roose, Director*
*Emil Ladner, Director*
This text is written by a practicing interpreter and includes information on history, terminology, research, competence, setting and a comprehensive bibliography. *$24.95*
*249 pages Softcover*
*ISBN 0-916883-07-8*

**7872 Joy of Signing**
Gospel Publishing House
1445 N Boonville Ave
Springfield, MO 65802-1894
800-641-4310
FAX: 417-862-5881
e-mail: CustSrvReps@ag.org
www.gospelpublishing.com

*Lottie L Riekehof, Author*
This manual on signing includes illustrations, information on sign origins, practice sentences, and step-by-step descriptions of hand positions and movements. *$23.99*
*352 pages Hardcover*
*ISBN 0-882435-20-5*

**7873 Joy of Signing Puzzle Book**
Harris Communications
15155 Technology Dr
Eden Prairie, MN 55344-2273
952-906-1180
800-825-6758
FAX: 952-906-1099
e-mail: info@harriscomm.com
www.harriscomm.com

*Robert Harris, Owner*
*Lottie L Riekehof, Co-Author*
Whether you are learning sign language to communicate with a family member, co-worker, student or friend, this puzzle book makes the learning fun and interesting. *$4.50*
*57 pages Softcover*
*ISBN 0-882436-76-7*

**7874 Kid-Friendly Parenting with Deaf and Hard of Hearing Children**
Gallaudet University Press
800 Florida Ave NE
Washington, DC 20002-3600
202-651-5000
800-621-2736
FAX: 202-651-5508
e-mail: gupress@gallaudet.edu
www.gupress.gallaudet.edu

*Daria Medwid, Author*
*Denise Chapman Weston, Co-Author*
Scores of activities, parenting techniques and insights by experts, both hearing and deaf, to help parents of deaf and hard of hearing children. Activities are designed to promote better behavior and educate. *$35.95*
*320 pages Paperback*
*ISBN 1-563680-31-9*

**7875 Laurent Clerc: The Story of His Early Years**
Gallaudet University Press
800 Florida Ave NE
Washington, DC 20002-3600
202-651-5000
800-621-2736
FAX: 202-651-5508
e-mail: gupress@gallaudet.edu
www.gupress.gallaudet.edu

*Cathryn Carroll, Author*
*T. Alan Hurwitz, President*
*Paul Kelly, Vice President Adm. And Finance*
This imaginative tale recounts the youthful history of Laurent Clerc, the deaf teacher who helped Thomas Gallaudet establish schools for the deaf in the 19th century. Early experiences influenced the teaching methods Clerc developed in later life and young adults will relish identifying with the hero of this entertaining story. *$13.95*
*208 pages Paperback*
*ISBN 0-930323-23-8*

**7876 Linguistics of American Sign Language: An Introduction**
Gallaudet University Press
800 Florida Ave NE
Washington, DC 20002-3600
202-651-5000
800-621-2736
FAX: 202-651-5508
e-mail: gupress@gallaudet.edu
www.gupress.gallaudet.edu

*Clayton Valli, Author*
*Ceil Lucas, Co-Author*
*Kristin J Mulrooney, Co-Author*
*T. Alan Hurwitz, President*
An introduction to the struture of American Sign Language, featuring all the linguistic disciplines plus practice exercises. *$ 75.00*
*560 pages Hardcover*
*ISBN 1-563682-83-4*

**7877 Literacy & Your Deaf Child: What Every Parent Should Know**
Gallaudet University Press
800 Florida Ave NE
Washington, DC 20002-3600
202-651-5000
800-621-2736
FAX: 202-651-5508
e-mail: gupress@gallaudet.edu
www.gupress.gallaudet.edu

*David A Stewart, Author*
*Bryan R Clarke, Co-Author*
*T. Alan Hurwitz, President*
*Paul Kelly, Vice President Adm. And Finance*
An instructional guide specifically appropriate for parents of deaf and hard-of-hearing children who want to do everything they can to insure their hearing-impaired child learns to read and write with fluency and competence. *$24.95*
*240 pages Paperback*
*ISBN 1-563681-36-6*

**7878 Mother Father Deaf: Living Between Sound and Silence**
Harvard University Press
79 Garden St
Cambridge, MA 02138-1423
617-495-1000
800-405-1619
FAX: 617-495-5898
e-mail: contact hup@harvard.edu
www.hup.harvard.edu

*William Sisler, President*
*Paul Preston, Author*
The book explores the intimate intersection of families like his own - families which embody the conflicts and resolutions of two often opposing world views, the Deaf and the Hearing. Although I have normal hearing, both of my parents are profoundly deaf. *$19.50*
*278 pages Paperback*
*ISBN 0-674587-48-0*

**7879 My First Book of Sign**
Gallaudet University Press
800 Florida Ave NE
Washington, DC 20002-3600
202-651-5000
800-621-2736
FAX: 202-651-5508
e-mail: gupress@gallaudet.edu
www.gupress.gallaudet.edu

*Pamela J Baker, Author*
*Patricia Bellan Gillen, Illustrator*
*T. Alan Hurwitz, President*
*Paul Kelly, Vice President Adm. And Finance*
Full-color book gives alphabetically grouped signs for 150 words most frequently used by young children. *$22.95*
*80 pages Hardcover*
*ISBN 0-930323-20-3*

**7880 My Signing Book of Numbers**
Gallaudet University Press
800 Florida Ave NE
Washington, DC 20002-3600 202-651-5000
800-621-2736
FAX: 202-651-5508
e-mail: gupress@gallaudet.edu
www.gupress.gallaudet.edu

*Patricia Bellan Gillen, Author*
This full-color book helps children learn their numbers in sign language. Each two-page spread of this delightfully illustrated book has the appropriate number of things or creatures for the numbers 0 through 20. *$22.95*
*56 pages Hardcover*
*ISBN 0-930323-37-8*

**7881 Nursery Rhymes from Mother Goose**
Gallaudet University Press
800 Florida Ave NE
Washington, DC 20002-3600 202-651-5000
800-621-2736
FAX: 202-651-5508
e-mail: gupress@gallaudet.edu
www.gupress.gallaudet.edu

*Harry Bornstein, Author*
*Karen L Saulnier, Co-Author*
*Patricia Peters, Illustrator*
*Linda Tom, Illustrator*
Each complete nursery rhyme is presented in Signed English and delightfully illustrated in full color. *$21.95*
*64 pages Hardcover*
*ISBN 0-930323-99-8*

**7882 Outsiders in a Hearing World: A Sociology of Deafness**
Sage Publications
2455 Teller Rd
Thousand Oaks, CA 91320-2218 805-499-9774
800-818-7243
FAX: 805-499-0871
www.sagepub.com

*Paul C Higgins, Author*
An introduction to the social world of deaf people. The author gives a sociologists view of what it's like to be deaf. *$72.95*
*208 pages Hardcover 1980*
*ISBN 0-803914-22-3*

**7883 Perigee Visual Dictionary of Signing**
Harris Communications
15155 Technology Dr
Eden Prairie, MN 55344-2273 952-906-1180
800-825-6758
FAX: 952-906-1099
e-mail: info@harriscomm.com
www.harriscomm.com

*Robert Harris, Owner*
*Mickey Flodin, Co-Author*
*Rod R Butterworth, Co-Author*
An A-to-Z guide to American Sign Language vocabulary. *$15.26*
*450 pages Softcover*
*ISBN 0-399519-52-1*

**7884 Phone of Our Own: The Deaf Insurrection Against Ma Bell**
Gallaudet University Press
800 Florida Ave NE
Washington, DC 20002-3600 202-651-5000
800-621-2736
FAX: 202-651-5508
e-mail: gupress@gallaudet.edu
www.gupress.gallaudet.edu

*Harry G Lang, Author*
*T. Alan Hurwitz, President*
*Paul Kelly, Vice President Adm. And Finance*
A recount of the history of the teletypewriter, from the three deaf engineers who developed the acoustic coupler that made mass communication on TTY's feasible, through the deaf community's twenty-year struggle against the government and AT&T to have TTY's produced and distributed. *$36.50*
*256 pages Hardcover*
*ISBN 1-563680-90-4*

**7885 Place of Their Own: Creating the Deaf Community in America**
Gallaudet University Press
800 Florida Ave NE
Washington, DC 20002-3600 202-651-5000
800-621-2736
202-651-5508
FAX: 202-651-5489
e-mail: gupress@gallaudet.edu
www.gallaudet.edu

*John V Van Cleve, Author*
*Barry A Crouch, Co-Author*
*T. Alan Hurwitz, President*
*Paul Kelly, Vice President Adm. And Finance*
Traces development of American deaf society to show how deaf people developed a common language and sense of community. Views deafness as the distinguishing characteristic of a distinct culture. *$22.95*
*224 pages Paperback*
*ISBN 0-930323-49-1*

**7886 PreReading Strategies**
Gallaudet University Bookstore
800 Florida Ave NE
Washington, DC 20002-3600 202-651-5000
800-621-2736
FAX: 202-651-5508
e-mail: Oluyinka.Fakunle@gallaudet.edu
www.clerccenter.gallaudet.edu

*David R Schleper, Author*
*T. Alan Hurwitz, President*
*Paul Kelly, Vice President Adm. And Finance*
Here is a wealth of good advice for preparing students to understand what they read, building comprehension and enjoyment. *$ 14.95*
*65 pages*

**7887 Quad City Deaf & Hard of Hearing Youth Group: Tomorrow's Leaders for our Community**
Independent Living Research Utilization ILRU
2323 S Shepherd Dr
Houston, TX 77019-7019 713-520-9058
FAX: 713-520-5785
e-mail: ilru@ilru.org

*Lex Frieden, Director*
*Rose Sheperd, Manager*
IICIL staff see this program as a way to develop young leaders for themovement. Emphasis is given to providing oppportunities for members of the youth group to develop skills in planning and organizing activities.

**7888 Religious Signing: A Comprehensive Guide for All Faiths**
TJ Publishers
2544 Tarpley Rd
Suite 108 #108
Carrollton, TX 75006-2288 800-999-1168
FAX: 972-416-0944
e-mail: customerservice@tjpublishers.com
www.tjpublishers.com

*Elaine Costello, Author*
*Terrence O'Rourke, Principal*
*Tanner Beach, Director*
Contains over 500 religious signs for all denominations and their meanings illustrated by clear upper torso illustrations that show

movements of hand, body and face. Includes a section on signing favorite verses, prayers and blessings. *$18.95*
*219 pages Softcover*
*ISBN 0-553342-44-4*

**7889 Seeing Voices**
Vintage and Anchor Books
1745 Broadway
New York, NY 10019
212-572-2882
FAX: 212-572-6043
e-mail: vintageanchor@randomhouse.com
www.randomhouse.com

*Oliver Sacks, Author*
*Madeline McIntosh, President/Sales/Operations*
*Markus Dohle, Chairman/CEO*
*Andrew Weber, SVP Operations And Technology*
Well known for his exploration of how people respond to neurological impairments, Dr Sacks explores the world of the deaf and discovers how deaf people respond to their loss of hearing and how they develop language. A highly readable introduction to deaf people, deaf culture and American Sign Language. *$13.95*
*240 pages Softcover 2000*
*ISBN 0-375704-07-8*

**7890 Sign Language Interpreting and Interpreter Education**
Oxford University Press
2001 Evans Rd
Cary, NC 27513-2009
919-677-0977
800-445-9714
FAX: 919-677-1303
e-mail: custserv.us@oup.com
www.oup.com

*Marc Marschark, Editor*
*Rico Peterson, Editor*
*Elizabeth A Winston, Editor*
*Patricia Sapere, Contributing Editor*
Provides a coherent picture of the field as a whole, including evaluation of the extent to which current practices are supported by validating research. The first comprehensive source, suitable as both a reference book and a textbook for interpreter training programs and a variety of courses on bilingual education, psycholinguistics and translation, and cross-linguistic studies. *$65.00*
*328 pages Hardcover*
*ISBN 0-195176-94-4*

**7891 Signing for Reading Success**
Gallaudet University Press
800 Florida Ave NE
Washington, DC 20002-3600
202-651-5000
800-621-2736
FAX: 202-651-5508
e-mail: gupress@gallaudet.edu
www.gupress.gallaudet.edu

*Jan C Hafer, Author*
*Robert M Wilson, Co-Author*
*T. Alan Hurwitz, President*
*Paul Kelly, Vice President Adm. And Finance*
This booklet provides summaries of four research students on the usefulness of signing for reading achievement. *$7.95*
*24 pages Paperback*
*ISBN 0-930323-18-1*

**7892 Signing: How to Speak with Your Hands**
TJ Publishers
2544 Tarpley Rd
Suite 108 #108
Carrollton, TX 75006-2288
972-416-0800
800-999-1168
FAX: 972-972-4160
e-mail: customerservice@tjpublishers.com
www.tjpublishers.com

*Elaine Costello, Author*
*Terrence O'Rourke, Principal*
*Tanner Beach, Director*
Presents 1,200 basic signs with clear illustrations in logical topical groupings. Linguistic principles are described at the beginning of each chapter, giving insight into the rules which govern American Sign Language. *$19.95*
*248 pages Softcover*
*ISBN 0-553375-39-3*

**7893 Signs Across America**
Gallaudet University Press
800 Florida Ave NE
Washington, DC 20002-3600
202-651-5000
800-621-2736
FAX: 202-651-5508
e-mail: gupress@gallaudet.edu
www.gupress.gallaudet.edu

*Edgar H Shroyer, Author*
*Susan P Shroyer, Co-Author*
*T. Alan Hurwitz, President*
*Paul Kelly, Vice President Adm. And Finance*
A look at regional variations in ASL. Signs for selected words collected from 25 different states. More than 1,200 signs illustrated in the text. *$28.95*
*304 pages Paperback*
*ISBN 0-913580-96-1*

**7894 Signs for Me: Basic Sign Vocabulary for Children, Parents & Teachers**
TJ Publishers
2544 Tarpley Rd
Suite 108 #108
Carrollton, TX 75006-2288
972-416-0800
800-999-1168
FAX: 972-972-4160
e-mail: customerservice@tjpublishers.com
www.tjpublishers.com

*Ben Bahan, Author*
*Joe Dannis, Co-Author*
*Terrence O'Rourke, Principal*
*Tanner Beach, Director*
Sign language vocabulary for preschool and elementary school children introduces household items, animals, family members, actions, emotions, safety concerns and other concepts. *$14.95*
*112 pages Softcover*
*ISBN 0-915035-27-8*

**7895 Signs for Sexuality: A Resource Manual**
Planned Parenthood of Western Washington
2001 E Madison St
Seattle, WA 98122-2959
206-320-7605
FAX: 206-328-6810
www.plannedparenthood.org

*Marlyn Minken, Author*
*Laurie Rosen-Ritt, Co-Author*
An important book for those who want to listen to and talk with other people about feelings, loving and caring. *$40.00*
*122 pages Softcover*

**7896 Signs of the Times**
Gallaudet University Press
800 Florida Ave NE
Washington, DC 20002-3600
202-651-5000
800-621-2736
FAX: 202-651-5508
e-mail: gupress@gallaudet.edu
www.gupress.gallaudet.edu

*Edgar H Shroyer, Author*
*Susan P Shroyer, Illustrator*
*T. Alan Hurwitz, President*
*Paul Kelly, Vice President Adm. And Finance*

An excellent beginner's contact signing book that fills the gap between sign language dictionaries and American Sign Language text. Designed for use as a classroom text. *$34.95*

*448 pages Softcover*
*ISBN 0-913580-76-7*

**7897 Sing Praise Hymnal for the Deaf**
LifeWay Christian Resources
1 Lifeway Plz
MSN 146
Nashville, TN 37234-1001
615-251-2000
800-458-2772
FAX: 615-251-3899
www.lifeway.com

*Thom Rainer, President/CEO*
*Jerry Rhyne, CFO/ VP Finance And Buisness*
*Tim Vineyard, VP Technology And CIO*

Designed to be used by interpreters to the deaf, sign-language students, and deaf members of the congregation, this special combinded hymnal edition offers 234 of the most popular hymns. *$12.95*

*Hardcover 2000*
*ISBN 0-767314-09-3*

**7898 TDI National Directory & Resource Guide: Blue Book**
Telecommunications for the Deaf
8630 Fenton Street
Suite 604
Silver Spring, MD 20910- 3822
301-589-3786
FAX: 301-589-3797
e-mail: info@tdi-online.org
tdi-online.org

*Claude L Stout, Executive Director*

Promoting Equal Access to Telecommunications and Media for People who are Deaf, Late-Deafened, Hard-of-Hearing or Deaf-Blind. *$ 20.00*

*600 pages Annual*

**7899 The Mask of Benevolence: Disabling the Dea Community**
DawnSign Press
6130 Nancy Ridge Dr
San Diego, CA 92121-3223
858-625-0600
FAX: 858-625-2336
e-mail: info@dawsign.com
www.dawnsign.com

*Joe Dannis, President*
*Harlan Lane, Author*

Dr. Harlan Lane does not view deafness as a handicap but rather a different state from hearing. Deaf people are a societal minority and should be treasured, not eradicated. *$12.95*

*360 pages Paperback 1992*
*ISBN 1-581210-09-5*

**7900 The Signed English Starter**
Gallaudet University Press
800 Florida Ave NE
Washington, DC 20002-3600
202-651-5000
800-621-2736
FAX: 202-651-5508
e-mail: gupress@gallaudet.edu
www.gupress.gallaudet.edu

*Harry Bornstein, Author*
*Karen L Saulnier, Co-Author*
*T. Alan Hurwitz, President*
*Paul Kelly, Vice President Adm. And Finance*

A first course in Signed English for adults and children, the book is fully illustrated (several figures per page), and it is organized in a way that leads to rewarding learning quite rapidly. The authors of this new and exciting text believe firmly that Signed English must be made as easy as possible if it is going to be as useful (and used) as it can and should be. The book explains the rationale for the Signed English system and the conventions used to teach it. *$18.50*

*232 pages Paperback*
*ISBN 0-913580-82-1*

**7901 The Signing Family: What Every Parent Shounow About Sign Communication**
Gallaudet University Press
800 Florida Ave NE
Washington, DC 20002-3600
202-651-5000
800-621-2736
FAX: 202-651-5508
e-mail: gupress@gallaudet.edu
www.gupress.gallaudet.edu

*David A Stewart, Author*
*Barbara Luetke-Stahlman, Co-Author*
*T. Alan Hurwitz, President*
*Paul Kelly, Vice President Adm. And Finance*

This reader-friendly book shows parents how to create a set of goals around the communication needs of their deaf child. Describes in even-handed terms the major signing options available, from American Sign Language to Signed English. *$29.95*

*192 pages Paperback*
*ISBN 1-563680-69-6*

**7902 The Silent Garden**
Gallaudet University Press
800 Florida Ave NE
Washington, DC 20002-3600
202-651-5000
800-621-2736
FAX: 202-651-5508
e-mail: gupress@gallaudet.edu
www.gupress.gallaudet.edu

*Paul W Ogden, Author*
*T. Alan Hurwitz, President*
*Paul Kelly, Vice President Adm. And Finance*

The author explain the broad range of hearing loss types, from minor to profound. Parents also are advised about what type of school their child should attend and what kinds of professional help will be best for the entire family. The book describes all forms of communication, including choices in signing from American Sign Language to the various manual systems based upon English. Technological alternatives are presented also, including when and when not to consider cochler implants. *$34.95*

*304 pages*
*ISBN 1-563680-58-0*

**7903 The Week the World Heard Gallaudet**

Gallaudet University Press
800 Florida Ave NE
Washington, DC 20002-3600
202-651-5000
800-621-2736
FAX: 202-651-5508
e-mail: gupress@gallaudet.edu
www.gupress.gallaudet.edu

*Jack R Gannon, Author*
*T. Alan Hurwitz, President*
*Paul Kelly, Vice President Adm. And Finance*

This day-to-day description of the events surrounding the Deaf President Now movement at Gallaudet University includes full color and black and white photographs and interviews with people involved in the events of that week. *$49.95*

*176 pages Hardcover*
*ISBN 0-930323-54-8*

**7904 Theoretical Issues in Sign Language Research**

University of Chicago Press
1427 E 60th St
Chicago, IL 60637-2902
773-702-7733
FAX: 773-702-9756
e-mail: sales@press.uchicago.edu
www.press.uchicago.edu

*Donald A Collins, President*
*Susan D Fischer, Author*
*Patricia Siple, Co-Author*

These volumes are an outgrowth of a conference held at the University of Rochester in 1986, dealing with the four traditional core areas of phonology, morphology, syntax and semantics. *$29.95*

*348 pages Paperback 1990*
*ISBN 0-226251-52-7*

**7905 We CAN Hear and Speak**

Alexander Graham Bell Association
3417 Volta Pl NW
Washington, DC 20007-2737
202-337-5220
FAX: 202-337-8314
e-mail: info@agbell.org
www.agbell.org

*Carol Flexer PhD, Author*
*Catherine Richards MA, Co-Author*
*K Houston PhD, Executive Director*
*John Wyant, Owner*

Written by parents for families of children who are deaf or hard of hearing, this work describes auditory-verbal terminology and approaches and contains personal narratives written by parents and their children who are deaf or hard of hearing. *$6.98*

*184 pages Softcover*

**7906 What is Auditory Processing?**

Abilitations - Speech Bin
P.O.Box 922668
Norcross, GA 30010-2668
770-449-5700
800-850-8602
FAX: 770-510-7290
e-mail: info@speechbin.com
www.speechbin.com

*Susan Bell, Author*

What is Auditory Processing? It is and information-packed 16-page booklet created to explain auditory processing and it's disorders and offers practical suggestions for coping with this problem. It describes the listening process and tells how to help children with auditory processing problems. It shows what families and teachers can do to help children who have trouble remembering and understanding what they hear and offers easy-to-use activities and practical suggestions. *$ 22.69*

*16 pages Softcover*

**7907 You and Your Deaf Child: A Self-Help Guidefor Parents of Deaf and Hard of Hearing Children**

Gallaudet University Press
800 Florida Ave NE
Washington, DC 20002-3600
202-651-5000
800-621-2736
FAX: 202-651-5508
e-mail: gupress@gallaudet.edu
www.gupress.gallaudet.edu

*John W Adams, Author*
*T. Alan Hurwitz, President*
*Paul Kelly, Vice President Adm. And Finance*

The classic self-instructional guide has been completely written with more information dealing with feelings, communication and other issues. Includes worksheets and practice exercises. *$29.95*

*224 pages Paperback*
*ISBN 1-563680-60-2*

## Print: Journals

**7908 American Journal of Audiology**

American Speech-Language-Hearing Association
2200 Research Blvd
Rockville, MD 20850-3289
240-632-2081
800-638-8255
FAX: 301-296-8580
e-mail: actioncenter@asha.org
www.asha.org

*Anthony Cacace, Editor*
*Kathleen Halverson, Production Editor*
*Peter Hoffman, Production Editor*
*Michael Cannon, Production Manager*

Articles concern screening, assesment, and treatment techniques; prevention; professional issues; supervision; administration. Includes clinical forums, clinical reviews, letters to the editor, or research reports that emphasize clinical practice.

*2 x year*

**7909 Hearing Professional**

International Hearing Society
Ste 4
16880 Middlebelt Rd
Livonia, MI 48154-3374
734-522-7200
800-521-5247
FAX: 734-522-0200
e-mail: akovach@ihsinfo.org
www.ihsinfo.org

*Kathleen Mennillo, MBA, Executive Director*
*Kara Nacarato, Editor & Mgr Of Strgc. Alliances*

Provides authoritative technical and business information that will help hearing aid specialists serve the hearing impaired.

*bi-monthly*

**7910 JADARA**

ADARA National Office
12461 Stottlemeyer Rd
Myersville, MD 21773-9620
301-293-8969
FAX: 301-293-9698
e-mail: adaraorg@comcast.net
www.adara.org

*David Fledman, Editor*
*Theresa Johnson, President*
*Steve Hamerdinger*

A professional journal sharing new procedures, thoughts, and research with application to the working professional.

**7911 Journal of Speech, Language and Hearing Research**
American Speech-Language-Hearing Association
2200 Research Blvd
Rockville, MD 20850-3289
301-296-5700
800-638-8255
FAX: 301-296-8580
e-mail: actioncenter@asha.org
www.asha.org

*Robert Schlauch, Editor*
*Sue Hale, President/Director*
*Arlene Pietranton, Executive Director/Board Member*
*Robert Augustine, VP Finance And Director*
Pertains broadly to studies of the processess and disorders of hearing, language, and speech diagnosis and treatment of such disorders.

**7912 Journal of the Academy of Rehabilitative Audiology**
Academy of Rehabilitative Audiology
PO Box 2323
Albany, NY 12220-0323
952-920-0484
FAX: 952-920-6098
e-mail: ARA@audrehab.org
www.audrehab.org

*Kathleen Cienkowski, Editor*
A peer-reviewed journal published annually. *$25.00*

**7913 Sign Language Studies**
Gallaudet University Press
800 Florida Ave NE
Washington, DC 20002-3600
202-651-5000
800-621-2736
FAX: 202-651-5508
e-mail: gupress@gallaudet.edu
www.gupress.gallaudet.edu

*Ceil Lucas, Editor*
*T. Alan Hurwitz, President*
*Paul Kelly, Vice President Adm. And Finance*
Presents a unique forum for revolutionary papers on signed languages and other related disciplines, including linguistics, anthropology, semiotics, and deaf studies, history, and literature. *$ 55.00*
*Quarterly*

**7914 The Literature Journal**
Gallaudet University
800 Florida Ave NE
Washington, DC 20002-3600
202-651-5000
800-621-2736
FAX: 202-651-5508
e-mail: Oluyinka.Fakunle@gallaudet.edu
www.clerccenter.gallaudet.edu

*Charles C Welsh-Charrier, Author*
*T. Alan Hurwitz, President*
*Paul Kelly, Vice President Adm. And Finance*
This book includes extensive examples of student and teacher entries taken from actual journals of deaf high school students. *$12.95*
*44 pages Spiral Bound*

**7915 Volta Review**
Alexander Graham Bell Association
3417 Volta Pl NW
Washington, DC 20007-2778
202-337-5220
FAX: 202-337-8314
e-mail: mfelzien@agbell.org
www.agbell.org

*Jackson Roush, PhD, Editor*
*K Houston, PhD, Executive Director*
*John Wyant, Owner*
Professionally refereed journal that publishes articles and research on education, rehabilitation and communicative development of people who have hearing impairments. Also includes subscription to Volta Voices, up-to-date magazine, bimonthly. *$60.00*
*Quarterly*

## Print: Magazines

**7916 Endeavor Magazine**
American Society for Deaf Children
3820 Hartzdale Dr
Camp Hill, PA 17011-7809
717-703-0073
866-895-4206
FAX: 717-909-5599
e-mail: asdc@deafchildren.org
www.deafchildren.org

*Sherry Williams, Editor*

**7917 Hearing Health Magazine**
Deafness Research Foundation
363 Seventh Avenue
10th Floor
New York, NY 10001-3904
212-257-6140
866-454-3924
FAX: 212-257-6139
e-mail: info@drf.org
www.drf.org

*Andrea Boidman, Executive Director*
*Andrea Delbanco, Senior Editor*
*Yishane Lee, Editor*
*Julie Grant, Art Director*
Serves as a source of quality information and provides the tools and resources to help people seek treatment for and manage hearing loss. Each issue features relevant and timely information on the latest research, articles written by leading authorities in the field, news about the latest technology, and human interest stories about those living with hearing loss.

**7918 Hearing Loss Magazine**
Hearing Loss Association of America
Ste 1200
7910 Woodmont Ave
Bethesda, MD 20814-7022
301-657-2248
FAX: 301-913-9413
e-mail: info@hearingloss.org
www.hearingloss.org

*Barbara Kelley, Editor-In-Chief/Deputy Ex. Dir.*
*Cindy Dyer, Graphic Design*
Provides the latest information on products, services, research, and technology in the hearing health care field. *$35.00*
*40 pages BiMonthly*

**7919 Tinnitus Today**
American Tinnitus Association
P.O.Box 5
Portland, OR 97207-5
503-493-2550
800-634-8978
FAX: 503-248-0024
e-mail: tinnitus@ata.org
www.ata.org

*Nina Rogozen, Editor*
*Michael Malusevic, Executive Director*
The magazine contains up-to-date medical and research news, feature articles on urgent tinnitus issues, questions and answers, self-help suggestions and letters to the editor from others with tinnitus. *$35.00*
*28 pages 3 x year*

**7920 Volta Voices**
Alexander Graham Bell Association
3417 Volta Pl NW
Washington, DC 20007-2737
202-337-5220
FAX: 202-337-8314
e-mail: mfelzien@agbell.org
www.agbell.org

*Melody Felzien, Editor*
*K Houston, Executive Director*
*John Wyant, Owner*
Covers a variety of topics, including hearing aids and cochlear implants, early intervention and education, professional guidance, legislative updates and perspectives from individuals from across the United States and around the world. *$60.00*
*Bi-Monthly*

## Print: Newsletters

**7921 AAPD Newsletter**
American Association of People with Disabilities
1629 K Street NW
Suite 950 #950
Washington, DC 20006- 1634
202-457-0046
800-840-8844
www.aapd.com

*Mark Perriello, President/CEO*
*Helena Berger, COO*
*Robin Shaffert, Senior Director*
Provides latest information on a variety of national disability policies and issues.

**7922 American Annals of the Deaf**
Gallaudet University Press
800 Florida Ave NE
Washington, DC 20002-3600
202-651-5000
800-621-2736
FAX: 202-651-5508
e-mail: paul.3@osu.edu
www.gupress.gallaudet.edu

*Peter V. Paul, Editor, Literary Issues*
*T. Alan Hurwitz, President*
*Paul Kelly, Vice President Adm. And Finance*
Quarterly publication from the Conference of Educational Administrators Serving the Deaf. *$55.00*
*Quarterly*

**7923 CommuniquŠ**
Michigan Assoc for the Deaf and Hard of Hearing
5236 Dumond Court
Suite C
Lansing, MI 48917-6001
517-487-0066
800-968-7327
FAX: 517-487-0202
e-mail: info@madhh.org
www.madhh.org

*Nan Asher, Executive Director*
*Dave Coyne, NIC Program Coordinator*
A publication of Michigan Association for Deaf and Hard of Hearing.
*Quarterly*

**7924 Connect - Commmunity News**
Hearing, Speech & Deafness Center (HSDC)
1625 19th Ave
Seattle, WA 98122-2848
206-323-5770
FAX: 206-328-6871
e-mail: hsdc@hsdc.org
www.hsdc.org

*David Delmar, Editor*
Connect is the quarterly eNews of the Hearing, Speech & Deafness Center.
*8 pages Annual*

**7925 Deaf Catholic**
International Catholic Deaf Association
7202 Buchanan St
Landover Hills, MD 20784-2236
301-429-0697
FAX: 301-429-0698
e-mail: homeoffice@icda-us.org
www.icda-us.org

*Peter Noyes, Editor*
*Jean Cox, President*
*Kate Slosar, Vice President*
*T.K Hill, Secretary*
Newsletter reporting the news of the Archdiocese, Deaf Apostolate and each of the Catholic Deaf Organizations. *$20.00*
*16 pages Quarterly*

**7926 Hearing, Speech & Deafness Center (HSDC)**
1625 19th Ave
Artz Communication Center
Seattle, WA 98122-2848
206-323-5770
888-222-5036
FAX: 206-328-6871
e-mail: admin@hsdc.org
hsdc.org

*Steven Atkins, President*
*Ken Block, Chairman*
*Gordon Braun, CFO*
Newsletter with information on Center services, activities, news, helpful articles.
*10 pages Quarterly*

**7927 League Letter**
Center for Hearing and Communication
50 Broadway
6th Floor
New York, NY 10004-3810
917-305-7700
FAX: 212-635-0767
TTY:917-305-7999
e-mail: info@chchearing.org
www.lhh.org

*George Figliolia, President*
*Jim Rosenthal, CEO*
*Laurie Hanin, Executive Director*
*Ronald Nurnberg, Managing Partner*
*Quarterly*

**7928 NAHO News**
National Association of Hearing Officials
P.O.Box 4999
Midlothian, VA 23112-17
701-328-3260
e-mail: jwezelman.wezelmanlaw@midconectwork.com
www.naho.org

*Joy Wezelman, Editor*
*Janice Deshais, Editor*
National Association of Hearing Officials newsletter.

**7929 Newsletter Bulletin**
John Tracy Clinic
806 W Adams Blvd
Los Angeles, CA 90007-2505
213-748-5481
800-522-4582
FAX: 213-749-1651
e-mail: ealaniz@jtc.org
www.jtc.org

*Gaston Kent, President Director*
*Blythe Maling, Vice President Of Development*
A newsletter for our friends and families.
*8 pages Bi-annually*

7930 **On the Level**
Vestibular Disorders Association
4035 NE Sandy Blvd
Portland, OR 97212-5331
503-229-7705
800-837-8428
FAX: 503-229-8064
e-mail: veda@vestibular.org
www.vestibular.org

*Lisa Haven PhD, Executive Director*
*Jerry Underwood, Director*
*Vincente Honrubia, Director*
Contents of each issue include information about local support groups, a calendar of conferences and training opportunities for health professionals, a list of donors, and special items indexed below. *$5.00*
*12 pages Quarterly*

7931 **Paws for Silence**
International Hearing Dog
5901 E 89th Ave
Henderson, CO 80640-8315
303-287-3277
FAX: 303-287-3425
e-mail: ihdi@aol.com
ihdi.org

*Valerie Foss-Brugger, President*
*Robert Cooley, Field Representative*
*Andrea Paul, Veterinary Technician/Hd Trainer*
Publication features stories from the recipients of hearing dogs.
*4-8 pages Quarterly*

7932 **Soundings Newsletter**
American Hearing Research Foundation
8 South Michigan Avenue
Suite 1205
Chicago, IL 60603- 4539
312-726-9670
FAX: 312-726-9695
e-mail: ahrf@american-hearing.org
american-hearing.org

*Sharon Parmet, Executive Director*
Promote, conduct and furnish financial assistance for medical research into the cause, prevention and cure of deafness, impaired hearing and balance disorders; encourage the collaboration of clinical and laboratory research; encourage and improve teaching in the medical aspects of hearing problems; and disseminate the most reliable scientific knowledge to physicians, hearing professionals and the public.
*Quarterly*

7933 **Spring Dell Center Newsletter**
Spring Dell Center
6040 Radio Station Rd
La Plata, MD 20646-3368
301-870-2474
FAX: 301-870-2439
e-mail: donnaretzlaf@springdellcenter.org
www.springdellcenter.org

*Donna Retzlaff, Executive Director*
*Jody Loper, President*
*Brett Hamorsky, Vice President*
*Jeff Hubbard, Treasurer*
*Quarterly*

7934 **The ASHA Leader**
American Speech-Language-Hearing Association
2200 Research Blvd
Rockville, MD 20850-3289
240-632-2081
800-638-8255
FAX: 301-296-8580
e-mail: leader@asha.org
www.asha.org

*Susan Boswell, Editor*
*Judith Kuster, Author*
Association publication containing news, notices of events and activities and information for members on issues facing the profession of audiology and speech-language pathology. *$80.00*
*35 pages 2 x month*

## Non Print: Newsletters

7935 **Canine Listener**
Dogs for the Deaf
10175 Wheeler Rd
Central Point, OR 97502-9360
541-826-9220
800-990-3647
FAX: 541-826-6696
TTY: 541-826-9220
e-mail: info@dogsforthedeaf.org
dogsforthedeaf.org

*Robin Dickson, CEO*
*Leanne Moon, CFO*
*Vaughn Maurice, General Manager*
*Dianne Gee, Human Resources Officer, Office Manager*
Provides information on Hearing Dogs, placements, dog training, and other news about happenings at Dogs for the Deaf.
*Quarterly*

7936 **Cochlear Implants In Children: Ethics and Choices**
Gallaudet University Press
800 Florida Ave NE
Washington, DC 20002-3600
202-651-5000
800-621-2736
FAX: 202-651-5508
e-mail: gupress@gallaudet.edu
www.gupress.gallaudet.edu

*John B Christiansen, Author*
*Irene W Leigh, Co-Author*
*T. Alan Hurwitz, President*
*Paul Kelly, Vice President Adm. And Finance*
Designed to educate readers about cochlear implants, including surgery, the importance of rehabilitation and the significance of parents' and professionals' roles. *$55.00*
*340 pages Casebound*
*ISBN 1-563681-16-1*

7937 **Communique**
Michigan Association for Deaf Hard of Hearing
5236 Dumond Court
Suite C
Lansing, MI 48917-6001
517-487-0066
800-968-7327
FAX: 517-487-2586
e-mail: info@madhh.org
www.madhh.org

*Nancy Asher, Executive Director*
*Pat Walton, Office Manager*
Provides leadership through advocacy and education. The association conducts leadership training for youth, information and referral services, interpreter referral, legislative advocacy, and a variety of other services.
*4-8 pages Bi-annually*

7938 **Listner**
HEAR Center
301 E Del Mar Blvd
Pasadena, CA 91101-2714
626-796-2016
FAX: 626-796-2320
e-mail: info@hearcenter.org
hearcenter.org

*Ellen Simon, Executive Director*
*Berenice Castro, Accounting Supervisro*
*Debbie Lorino, Office Manager*
Chronicals current events, spotlights pediatric and adult clients as well as community outreach events.
*Semi-Quarterly*

**7939 NAD E-Zine**
National Association of the Deaf
8630 Fenton Street
Suite 820
Silver Spring, MD 20910- 3819
301-587-1788
FAX: 301-587-1791
TTY:301-587-1789
e-mail: nadinfo@nad.org
www.nad.org

*Bobbie Beth Scoggins, President*
*Christopher Wagner, Vice President*
Includes up-to-the-minute information about the NAD, including Board news, advocacy, outreach and community activities, as well as NAD Conference and other information.

**7940 Pinnacle Newsletter**
Academy of Rehabilitative Audiology
P.O.Box 26532
Minneapolis, MN 55426-532
952-920-0484
FAX: 952-920-6098
e-mail: ara@audrehab.org
www.audrehab.org

*John Greer Clark, Editor*
*Diana Derry, Co-Editor*
*Joseph Montano, President*
Academy of Rehabilitative Audiology newsletter.

**7941 So the World May Hear**
Starkey Hearing Foundation
6700 Washington Ave S
Eden Prairie, MN 55344-3405
952-941-6401
866-354-3254
FAX: 952-828-6944
www.sotheworldmayhear.org

*Peter Lecy, President*
*Paul Nash, Vice President*
*Jeff Papineau, Treasurer*
Starkey Hearing Foundation magazine.
*Quarterly*

**7942 Vision Magazine**
National Catholic Office of the Deaf
7202 Buchanan St
Hyattsville, MD 20784-2236
301-577-1684
FAX: 301-577-1684
www.ncod.org

*Arvilla Rank, Editor/Executive Director*
Published as a pastoral service for the deaf and hard of hearing. Provides information to members and others working in ministry. *$15.00*
*Quarterly*

## Non Print: Video

**7943 Christmas Stories**
Video Learning Library
15838 N 62nd St
Scottsdale, AZ 85254-1988
480-596-9970
800-383-8811
FAX: 480-596-9973
e-mail: info@videolearning.com
www.videolearning.com

*Jim Spencer, Owner*
Told by popular deaf story-tellers, the stories included are A Christmas Carol, Night Before Christmas, Story of the First Christmas Tree, Birth of Christ, The Great Walled City, and Little Match Girl. *$29.95*
*Video/80 Mins 1986*
*ISBN 1-882257-02-2*

**7944 Fantastic Series Videotape Set**
Gallaudet University Press
800 Florida Ave NE
Washington, DC 20002-3600
202-651-5000
800-621-2736
FAX: 202-651-5508
e-mail: gupress@gallaudet.edu
www.gupress.gallaudet.edu

*Rita Corey, Director*
*T. Alan Hurwitz, President*
*Paul Kelly, Vice President Adm. And Finance*
These videotapes offer a blend of entertainment and information to both deaf and hearing children ages 6-10. A total of eight tapes in the series. *$254.00*
*Video 8 VHS*
*ISBN 1-563680-12-2*

**7945 Fantastic: Colonial Times, Chocolate, and Cars**
Gallaudet University Press
800 Florida Ave NE
Washington, DC 20002-3600
202-651-5000
800-621-2736
FAX: 202-651-5508
e-mail: gupress@gallaudet.edu
www.gupress.gallaudet.edu

*Rita Corey, Director*
*T. Alan Hurwitz, President*
*Paul Kelly, Vice President Adm. And Finance*
Young viewers visit Colonial Williamsburg in Virginia to see various crafts. Other parts show chocolate being made, and films of old cars. *$39.95*
*Video*
*ISBN 1-563680-06-8*

**7946 Fantastic: Dogs at Work and Play**
Gallaudet University Press
800 Florida Ave NE
Washington, DC 20002-3600
202-651-5000
800-621-2736
FAX: 202-651-5508
e-mail: gupress@gallaudet.edu
www.gupress.gallaudet.edu

*Rita Corey, Director*
*T. Alan Hurwitz, President*
*Paul Kelly, Vice President Adm. And Finance*
See how dogs are trained, including Fantastic's own hearing-ear dog, police dogs, plus puppies, and dogs in space? *$39.95*
*Video*
*ISBN 1-563680-03-3*

**7947 Fantastic: Exciting People, Places and Things!**
Gallaudet University Press
800 Florida Ave NE
Washington, DC 20002-3600
202-651-5000
800-621-2736
FAX: 202-651-5508
e-mail: gupress@gallaudet.edu
www.gupress.gallaudet.edu

*Rita Corey, Director*
*T. Alan Hurwitz, President*
*Paul Kelly, Vice President Adm. And Finance*
Welcomes young viewers for a trip to a crayon factory, a jump rope tournament, and mime by actor Bernard Bragg. *$39.95*
*Video*
*ISBN 1-563680-01-7*

**7948 Fantastic: From Post Offices to Dairy Goats**
Gallaudet University Press
800 Florida Ave NE
Washington, DC 20002-3600
202-651-5000
800-621-2736
FAX: 202-651-5508
e-mail: gupress@gallaudet.edu
www.gupress.gallaudet.edu

*Rita Corey, Director*
*T. Alan Hurwitz, President*
*Paul Kelly, Vice President Adm. And Finance*
In this video children follow the route of a letter from the mailbox through the post office to its final destination. Also, they visit dairy goats and other animals. *$39.95*
*Video*
*ISBN 1-563680-05-X*

**7949 Fantastic: Imagination, Actors, and 'Deaf Way'**
Gallaudet University Press
800 Florida Ave NE
Washington, DC 20002-3600
202-651-5000
800-621-2736
202-651-5508
FAX: 202-651-5489
e-mail: gupress@gallaudet.edu
www.gupress.gallaudet.edu

*Rita Corey, Director*
*T. Alan Hurwitz, President*
*Paul Kelly, Vice President Adm. And Finance*
Deaf clowns, mimes, and actors display the wonders of imagination, along with performances at the international cultural celebration 'Deaf Way.' *$39.95*
*Video*
*ISBN 1-563680-04-1*

**7950 Fantastic: Roller Coasters, Maps, and Ice Cream!**
Gallaudet University Press
800 Florida Ave NE
Washington, DC 20002-3600
202-651-5000
800-621-2736
FAX: 202-651-5508
e-mail: gupress@gallaudet.edu
www.gupress.gallaudet.edu

*Rita Corey, Director*
*T. Alan Hurwitz, President*
*Paul Kelly, Vice President Adm. And Finance*
In this program Mike Montangino leads the way on rides at Kings Dominion, and also to see how maps are drawn, and how ice cream is made. *$39.95*
*Video*
*ISBN 1-563680-07-6*

**7951 Fantastic: Skiing, Factories, and Race Hores**
Gallaudet University Press
800 Florida Ave NE
Washington, DC 20002-3600
202-651-5000
800-621-2736
FAX: 202-651-5508
e-mail: gupress@gallaudet.edu
www.gupress.gallaudet.edu

*Rita Corey, Director*
*T. Alan Hurwitz, President*
*Paul Kelly, Vice President Adm. And Finance*
Snow Skiing starts this program, which continues in a factory where 'who-knows-what' is made. Also, young viewers learn about horse care, and also about the making of Oreos. *$39.95*
*Video*
*ISBN 1-563680-08-4*

**7952 Fantastic: Wonderful Worlds of Sports and Travel**
Gallaudet University Press
800 Florida Ave NE
Washington, DC 20002-3600
202-651-5000
800-621-2736
FAX: 202-651-5508
e-mail: gupress@gallaudet.edu
www.gupress.gallaudet.edu

*Rita Corey, Director*
*T. Alan Hurwitz, President*
*Paul Kelly, Vice President Adm. And Finance*
In this program, young viewers ride on a train, watch deaf athletes compete, and see actor Bernard Bragg perform 'The Lion and the Mouse.' *$39.95*
*Video*
*ISBN 1-563680-02-5*

**7953 Fingerspelling: Expressive and Receptive Fluency**
DawnSign Press
6130 Nancy Ridge Dr
San Diego, CA 92121-3223
858-625-0600
FAX: 858-625-2336
e-mail: info@dawnsign.com
www.dawnsign.com

*Joe Dannis, President*
*Joyce Linden Groode, Fingerspelling Teacher*
Improve your fingerspelling with this new video guide. A 24-page instructional booklet is included with fingerspelling practice suggestions. *$29.95*
*120 Minutes*
*ISBN 1-581210-46-9*

**7954 Getting Better**
Vestibular Disorders Association
4035 NE Sandy Blvd
Portland, OR 97212-5331
503-229-7705
800-837-8428
FAX: 503-229-8064
e-mail: veda@vestibular.org
www.vestibular.org

*Lisa Haven PhD, Executive Director*
*Jerry Underwood, Director*
*Vicente Honrubia, Director*
Interviews with physicians, physical therapists, psychologists, social workers, and patients on Managing Symptoms, Diagnosis & Treatment, and Cognitive/Psychological Impacts. *$24.95*
*Video*

**7955 Helping the Family Understand**
Vestibular Disorders Association
4035 NE Sandy Blvd
Portland, OR 97212-5331
503-229-7705
800-837-8428
FAX: 503-229-8064
e-mail: veda@vestibular.org
www.vestibular.org

*Lisa Haven PhD, Executive Director*
*Jerry Underwood, Director*
*Vicente Honrubia, Director*
Interviews with physicians, physical therapists, psychologists, social workers, and patients on Managing Symptoms, Diagnosis & Treatment and Cognitive/Psychological Impacts. *$24.95*
*Video*

7956 **Managing Your Symptoms**
Vestibular Disorders Association
4035 NE Sandy Blvd
Portland, OR 97212-5331
503-229-7705
800-837-8428
FAX: 503-229-8064
e-mail: veda@vestibular.org
www.vestibular.org

*Lisa Haven PhD, Executive Director*
*Jerry Underwood, Director*
*Vicente Honrubia, Director*
Interviews with physicians, physical therapists, psychologists, social workers, and patients. on Managing Symptoms, Diagnosis & Treatment, and Cognitive/Psychological Impacts. *$24.95*
*Video*

## Sports

7957 **American Hearing Impaired Hockey Association**
1143 W Lake St
Chicago, IL 60607-1618
312-226-5880
FAX: 312-829-2098
e-mail: info@ahiha.org
ahiha.org

*Stan Mikita, President*
*Cheryl Hager, General Manager*
*Helen Tovey, Registrar, USA Hockey Reg.*
Supports hockey for hearing-impaired youths.

7958 **USA Deaf Sports Federation**
102 N Krohn Pl
Sioux Falls, SD 57103-1800
605-367-5760
FAX: 605-782-8441
e-mail: homeoffice@usadeafsports.org
www.usdeafsports.org

*Jack C Lamberton, President*
*Chris Kaftan, VP Of Member Services*
*Mark Apodaca, VP Of Financial Affairs*
*William J Bowman, VP Of International Affairs*
The USA Deaf Sports Federation's purpose was to foster and regulate uniform rules of competition and provide social outlets for deaf members and their friends; serve as a parent organization for regional sports organizations; conduct annual athletic competitions; and assist in the participation of U.S. teams in international competition.

## Support Groups

7959 **Dial-a-Hearing Screening Test**
Occupational Hearing Services Inc.
300 S Chester Rd
Suite 301 #301
Swarthmore, PA 19081- 1800
610-544-7700
800-622-3277
FAX: 610-543-2802
e-mail: DAHST@aol.com

*George Biddle, President/Owner*
*James Biddle, Vice President*
*Phyllis Biddle, Treasurer*
A national telephone resource providing information about hearing impairments and deafness. Dial-A-Hearing Screening Test: national test number for free telephone hearing test: 1-800-222-EARS, MON-FRI: 9:00 AM to 5:00 PM Eastern time.

# Mobility

## Associations

**7960 American Association of Spinal Cord Injury Psychologists & Social Workers**
7520 Astoria Blvd
Jackson Heights, NY 11370-1138
718-803-3782
FAX: 718-803-0414
e-mail: info@unitedspinal.org
http://www.unitedspinal.org/donations/online-

*Paul Tobin, President and Chief Executive Officer*
*Michael B. Kinne, Secretary*
*Janeen Earwood, Treasurer*
*Lex Frieden, Chairman of the Board*
Organized and operated for scientific and educational purposes to advance and improve the psychosocial care of persons with spinal cord impairment, develop and promote education and research related to the psychosocial care of persons with spinal cord injury, recognize psychologists and social workers whose careers are devoted to the problems of spinal cord impairment.

**7961 American Back Society**
2647 International Blvd
Ste 502
Oakland, CA 94601-1537
510-536-9929
FAX: 510-536-1812
e-mail: info@americanbacksoc.org
www.americanbacksoc.org

*James W Simmons M.D. F.A.C.S., President*
*Ronald G Donelson M.D. M.S, Vice President*
*Carol McFarland, Secretary*
*Thomas E Dreisinger PhD, Treasurer*
The American Back Society was founded in Oakland, California in 1982 as a nonprofit organization dedicated to providing an interdisciplinary forum for health care professionals and scientists interested in relieving pain and diminishing impairment through proper diagnosis and treatment of patients suffering from spinal pathology.

**7962 American Stroke Association**
7272 Greenville Ave
Dallas, TX 75231-4596
800-242-8721
888-478-7653
e-mail: strokeconnection@heart.org
www.americanheart.org

*Ralph Sacco, President/Director*
*Nancy Brown, CEO*
*Debra Lockwood, Chairman*
Fifty-five state affiliates monitoring local chapters offering educational materials, seminars, conferences and transportation for members nationwide. Maintains a listing of over 1,000 stroke support groups across the nation for referral to stroke survivors, their families, caregivers and interested professionals.

**7963 Amytrophic Lateral Sclerosis Association**
27001 Agoura Rd
Ste 250
Calabasas Hills, CA 91301-5104
818-880-9007
800-782-4747
FAX: 818-880-9006
e-mail: alsinfo@alsa-national.org
alsa.org

*Janes H Gilbert, President/CEO*
*Steve Gibson, VP*
*Daniel M. Reznikov, CFO*
*Kimberly Maginnis, Chief of Care Services*
The ALS association is the only national not-for-profit health organization dedicated soley to lead the fight against ALS. The Association covers all the bases-research, patient and community services, public education, and advocacy-in providing help and hope to those facing the disease. The mission is to lead the fight to cure and treat ALS through global cutting edge research, and to empower people with Lou Gehrig's disease to live fuller lives & provide them with compassion care and support.

**7964 Arthritis Foundation**
PO Box 7669
Atlanta, GA 30357
404-872-7100
800-283-7800
FAX: 404-872-0457
e-mail: help@arthritis.org
arthritis.org

*John H Klippel, CEO*
*Cecile K Perich, Chair*
Offers information and referrals regarding educational materials and programs, fund-raising, support groups, seminars and conferences offered by 55 local chapters across the United States.

**7965 Association for Neurologically Impaired Brain Injured Children**
61-35 220th St
Oakland Gardens, NY 11364
718-423-9550
FAX: 718-423-9838
e-mail: mail@anibic.org
www.anibic.org

*Gerard Smith, Executive Director*
*John F DeBiase, Associate Executive Director*
ANIBIc is a voluntary, multi-service organization that is dedicated to serving individuals with severe learning disabilities, neurological impairments and other developmental disabilities. Services include: residential, vocational, family support services, recreation (children and adults), respite (adult), in home support services, counseling and tramatic brain injury services (adults).

**7966 Christopher & Dana Reeve Paralysis Resource Center**
636 Morris Turnpike
Suite 3A
Short Hills, NJ 07078-2608
973-467-8270
800-539-7309
FAX: 973-912-9433
e-mail: information@christopherreeve.org
www.paralysis.org

*Peter Wilderotter, President*
*Susan Howley, Executive VP*
*Maggie Goldberg, Senior Vice President, Marketing and Communications*
*Joe Canose, Senior Vice President, Quality of Life*
Our goal is to provide you with the information you need to live a healthy life, make informed decisions, and better understand paralysis, spinal cord injury and other conditions.

**7967 Epilepsy Foundation**
8301 Professional Pl
Landover, MD 20785-7223
800-332-1000
86- 33- 271
FAX: 877-687-4878
e-mail: ContactUs@efa.org
www.epilepsyfoundation.org

*Phil Gattone, President/CEO*
*Brien Smith, Chair*
*Alexandra Finucane, Executive Vice President*
*Joseph I. Sirven, MD, Chair*
The Epilepsy Foundation is the national voluntary agency solely dedicated to the welfare of the 2.7 million people with epilepsy in the U.S. and their families. The organization works to ensure that people with seizures are able to participate in all life experiences; and to prevent, control and cure epilepsy through research, education, advocacy and services.

**7968 Friends of Disabled Adults and Children**
4900 Lewis Rd
Stone Mountain, GA 30083-1104 770-491-9014
866-977-1204
e-mail: chrisbrand@fodac.org
www.fodac.org

*Chris Brand, President*
Not-for-profit organization dedicated to providing necessary services and support to physically and mobility impaired people of all ages. Provides free mobility impairment, rehabilitative, and home healthcare equipment. Provides variety of brochures and pamphlets. Community reentering program.

**7969 Head Injury Rehabilitation And Referral Service, Inc. (HIRRS)**
11 Taft Court
Suite 100
Rockville, MD 20850-4162 301-309-2228
FAX: 301-309-2278
e-mail: tbi@headinjuryrehab.org
www.hirrs.org

*Ricardo Hunter, President*
*Maggie Hunter, Director of Admissions and Quality Assurance*
*Robert Cousland, Director of Rehabilitation*
*Debbie Jones, Director of Individual Support Services and Community Supported Living*
Head Injury Rehabilitation and Referral Services, Inc. (HIRRS) is a private not-for-profit agency that provides comprehensive brain injury support including long-term living, daily programs, vocational supports and services to individuals that live in the community. The agency is located in Rockville, MD, but serves the DC Metropolitan area.

**7970 Mobility International USA**
132 E Broadway
Ste 343
Eugene, OR 97401-3155 541-343-1284
FAX: 541-343-6812
e-mail: info@miusa.org
www.miusa.org

*Susan Sygall, Executive Director*
*Alison Ecker, Project Assistant*
*Cerise Roth Vinson, Chief Operating Officer*
*Cindy Lewis, Director of Programs*
A US based national nonprofit organization dedicated to empowering people with disabilities around the world through leadership development, training and international exchange to ensure inclusion of people with disabilities in international exchange and development programs. The National Clearinghouse on Disability & Exchange, a joint project managed by MIUSA provides free information and referrals.

**7971 Multiple Sclerosis Association of America**
706 Haddonfield Rd
Cherry Hill, NJ 08002-2652 856-488-4500
800-532-7667
FAX: 856-661-9797
e-mail: webmaster@msassociation.org
msassociation.org

*Andrea L Grlese, Vice Presidentof Comm & Mrkting*
MSAA is a national non-profit organization dedicated to enriching the quality of life for evryone affected by multiple sclerosis.

**7972 National Coalition for Assistive and Rehab Technology**
161 Huxley Dr
Buffalo, NY 14226 716-839-9728
FAX: 716-839-9624
e-mail: info@ncart.us
www.ncart.us

*Don Clayback, Executive Director*
*Gary Gilberi, President*
*Doug Westerdahl , Treasurer*
The coalition's mission is to ensure proper and appropriate access to complex rehab and assistive technologies.

**7973 National Council on Independent Living**
1710 Rhode Island Ave NW
Washington, DC 20036-3007 202-207-0334
877-525-3400
FAX: 202-207-0341
TTY: 202-207-0340
www.ncil.org

*Kelly Buckland, Executive Director*
*Tim Fuchs, Operations Director*
*Jorge Pineda, Accountant*
*Denise Law, Member Services Associate*
NCIL advances independent living and the rights of people with disabilities through consumer-driven advocacy.

**7974 National Fibromyalgia Association**
2121 S Towne Centre Place
Ste 300
Anaheim, CA 92806-6124 714-921-0150
FAX: 714-921-6920
e-mail: fmaware.org
fmaware.org

*Lynne Matallana, President*
*Mark Dobrilovic, Board of Director*
*John Fry, PhD, Board of Director*
*Michael Seffinger, DO, FAAFP, Board of Director*
National Fibromyalgia Association's mission is to develop and execute programs dedicated to improving the quality of life for people with fibromyalgia.

**7975 National Mobility Equipment Dealers Association**
3327 W Bearss Ave
Tampa, FL 33618-2100 813-264-2697
866-948-8341
FAX: 813-962-8970
e-mail: info@nmeda.org
www.nmeda.org

*Dave Hubbard, CEO*
*Marilyn Myers, Administrative Assistant*
*Sam Cook, President*
*Mark DiRosa, VP*
NMEDA is a non-profit trade association of mobility equipment dealers, driver rehabilitation specialists, and other professionals dedicated to broadening the opportunities for people with disabilities to drive or be transported in vehicles modified with mobility equipment. All members work together to improve transportation options of people with disabilities.

**7976 Paralyzed Veterans of America**
801 18th St NW
Washington, DC 20006-3517 202-872-1300
800-555-9140
FAX: 202-785-4432
e-mail: info@pva.org
www.pva.org

*Bill Lawson, President*
*Homer S Townsend Jr, Executive Director*
*AL.F Kovach, Senior VP*
*Craig.F Enenbach, Treasurer*
A congressionally chartered veterans service organization, has developed a unique expertise on a wide variety of issues involving the special needs of our members- veterans of the armed forces who have experienced spinal cord injury or dysfunction.

7977 **Post-Polio Health International**
4207 Lindell Blvd
Ste 110
Saint Louis, MO 63108-2930
314-534-0475
FAX: 314-534-5070
e-mail: info@post-polio.org
www.post-polio.org

*Joan L Headley, Executive Director*
*Gayla Hoffman, Editor*
*Sheryl R. Rudy, Editor*
*Judith Raymond Fischer, MSLS, Editor*

Educates, advocates and networks the survivors of polio and the health professionals who treat them. Funds a research grant, publishes Post Polio Health (Quarterly, 12 page newsletter).

7978 **Society for Progressive Supranuclear Palsy**
30 E. Padonia Road, Suite 201
Timonium, MD 21093
800-457-4777
FAX: 410-785-7009
e-mail: info@curepsp.org
www.psp.org

*Richard Gordon Zyne DMin, President/CEO*
*Kathleen Matarazzo Speca, Vice President, Development & Donor Relations*
*Trish Caruana, MSW, Vice President, Programs & Education*
*Karin Martin, Executive Assistant*

The Society for PSP is dedicated to increasing awareness of Progressive Supranuclear Palsy, advancing research towards a cure, and providing hope, support and education for persons with PSP, their families and healthcare professionals.

7979 **Vermont Back Research Center**
1 S Prospect St
Burlington, VT 05405
802-656-3131
FAX: 802-660-9243
e-mail: learn@uvm.edu
http://www.uvm.edu

Conducts research aimed at reducing back-related disability following injury or acute pain episodes. Current research includes studies of posture, seating, vibration, materials handling, and exercise. The Center develops and tests assistive devices, and promotes employment of people with back disorders and rapid return to work after injury. The staff provides a variety of information services, including bibliographic searches and fact finding.

7980 **World Chiropractic Alliance**
2683 Via De La Valle
Suite G 629
Del Mar, CA 92014
480-786-9235
866-789-8073
FAX: 480-732-9313
e-mail: comments@worldchiropracticalliance.org
www.worldchiropracticalliance.org

*Linda Bevel, Manager*
*Terry A Rondberg DC, Founder/CEO*

Dedicated to protecting and strengthening chiropractic around the world. Serving as a watchdog and advocacy organization, we place our emphasis on education and political action.

## Camps

7981 **Autism Day Camp**
Hillcroft Services: Isanogel
7601 W Isanogel Road
Muncie, IN 47304
765-288-1073
FAX: 765-288-3101
TTY:765-288-1073
e-mail: demcintosh@bsu.edu
www.hillcroft.org

*Elizabeth Piazza, Camp Manager*
*Joan Bahlmann, Director*
*Bruce Baldwin, Director*
*Tanner Jordan, Director*

The camp is designed to improve the academic, social skills, and behaviors of children with autism spectrum disorders. The day camp is an 8-week intensive experience for children classified with autism spectrum disorders.

7982 **Camp Esperanza**
Southern California Chapter
800 W 6th Street
Suite 1250
Los Angeles, CA 90017
213-986-4700
800-954-2873
FAX: 213-954-5790
e-mail: jziegler@arthritis.org
www.arthritis.org

*Jennifer Ziegler, Camp Director*

A one-week camp in August that allows children with arthritis to participate in such activities as horseback riding, swimming, etc. in a fun-filled environment.

7983 **Camp Oakhurst**
New York Service for the Handicapped
111 Monmouth Rd
Oakhurst, NJ 7755-1514
732-531-0215
FAX: 732-531-0292
e-mail: info@campoakhurst.com
www.campoakhurst.com

*Charles Sutherland, Camp Director*

Camp is located in Oakhurst, New Jersey. Summer sessions for campers with cerebral palsy, mobility limitation and spina bifida. Coed, age 8-18.

7984 **Easter Seals Camp Stand by Me**
Easter Seal Society of Washington
P.O.Box 289
Vaughn, WA 98394-313
253-884-2722
FAX: 253-884-0200
e-mail: camp@wa.easterseals.com
www.wa.easterseals.com

*Cathy Bisaillon, President/Camp Director*
*Lindsay Anderson, Board Chair*
*Paul Thibodaux, Vice Chair*

Camp is located in Vaughn, Washington. Summer camping for adults and children with developmental disabilities and mobility limitation. Coed, ages 7-65, seniors. Respite weekends October thru May.

7985 **Summer Wheelchair Sports Camp**
University of Illinois
1207 S Oak St
Champaign, IL 61820-6901
217-333-1970
FAX: 217-333-0248
e-mail: sportscamp@uiuc.edu
www.disability.uiuc.edu

*Brian Walsh, Camp Director*

Rigorous camps designed for individuals with lower extremity physical disabilities. Camp attendees will spend an average of 8-9 hours a day, focusing on development and refinement of fitness, techniques and strategies. Strength training, nutrition and mental training sessions will also be included in all camps. The camp staff is comprised of athletic staff and faculty front, the Division of Rehabilitation Education Services and local wheelchair athletes with coaching experience.

**7986 Twin Lakes Camp**
1451 E Twin Lakes Rd
Hillsboro, IN 47949-8004
765-798-4000
e-mail: outdoors@twinlakescamp.com
www.twinlakescamp.com

*Jon Beight, Executive Director*
*Duane Bush, Guest Service*
*Dan Daily, Program Director*
*Donna Beight, Secretary*
Provides a summer camp program for special needs children and young adults. Campers suffer from a wide range of maladies including crippling accidents, Spina Bifida, epilepsy, Cerebral Palsy, Muscular Dystrophy, Quadriplegia, Paraplegia, and other disabling diseases. Campers range in age from 8 to 27.

**7987 YMCA Camp Fitch**
Youngstown YMCA
17 N Champion St
P.O. Box 1287
Youngstown, OH 44501-1636
330-744-8411
FAX: 330-744-8415
e-mail: info@campfitchymca.com
www.youngstownymca.org

*Kenneth Rudge, CEO*
Camp is located in North Springfield, Pennsylvania. Camping sessions for children and adults with diabetes, hearing impairment, developmental disabilities, mobility limitation and speech/communication impairment. Ages 8-16, families and seniors.

## Print: Books

**7988 Adapted Physical Education and Sport**
Human Kinetics, Inc.
1607 N Market Street
Champaign, IL 61820-2220
217-351-5076
800-747-4457
FAX: 217-351-1549
e-mail: info@hkusa.com
www.naspem.org

*Joseph P Winnick EdD, Author*
*Scott Kimberly, Owner*
*Rainer Martens, President/Treasurer*
*Jill Wikgren, COO*
Designed as a resource for both present and future physical education leaders, this book is an exceptional book for teaching exceptional children. It emphasizes the physical education of young people with disabilities. *$68.00*
*592 pages Hardcover*
*ISBN 0-736052-16-X*

**7989 Arthritis Bible**
Inner Traditions - Bear & Company
P.O.Box 388
Rochester, VT 05767-388
802-767-3174
800-246-8648
FAX: 802-767-3726
e-mail: customerservice@InnerTraditions.com
www.InnerTraditions.com

*Craig Weatherby, Author*
*Leonid Gordin MD, Co-Author*
A comprehensive guide to the alternative therapies and conventional treatments for Arthritic diseases including Osteoarthritis, Rheumatoid Arthritis, Gout, Fibromyalgia and more. *$16.95*
*272 pages Paperback 1999*
*ISBN 0-892818-25-5*

**7990 Arthritis Helpbook: A Tested Self Management Program for Coping with Arthritis**
Da Capo Press
Eleven Cambridge Center
Cambridge, MA 02142
617-252-5200
FAX: 617-252-5265
www.dacapopress.com

*Kate Lorig, Author*
*James Fries, Co-Author*
A self-care program for coping with arthritis that includes diet, nutrition, exercise, and mind/body techniques such as guided imagery and meditation. *$18.95*
*Paperback*
*ISBN 0-738210-38-2*

**7991 Arthritis Sourcebook**
McGraw-Hill Professional
7500 Chavenelle Rd
Dubuque, IA 52002-9655
563-584-6000
877-833-5524
FAX: 614-759-3749
e-mail: pbg.ecommerce_custserv@mcgraw-hill.com
www.mhprofessional.com

*Earl J Brewer Jr MD, Author*
*Kathy Cochran Angel, Co-Author*
A comprehensive guide to the latest information on treatments, medications, and alternative therapies for arthritis. *$ 16.95*
*272 pages Paperback*
*ISBN 0-737303-81-6*

**7992 Arthritis, What Exercises Work: Breakthrough Relief for the Rest of Your Life**
MacMillan - St. Martin's Press
175 5th Ave
New York, NY 10010-7703
646-307-5151
FAX: 212-420-9314
www.us.macmillan.com

*Dava Sorbel, Author*
*Arthur C Klein, Co-Author*
What is the most powerful arthritis treatment ever developed to help restore you to a healthy, pain-free, and vigorous life-for the rest of your life? It's exercise. Here are the right exercised for your kind of arthritis, pain-level, age, occupation, and hobbies. *$14.99*
*200 pages Paperback 1995*
*ISBN 0-312130-25-2*

**7993 Arthritis: A Take Care of Yourself Health Guide**
Da Capo Press
Eleven Cambridge Center
Cambridge, MA 02142
617-252-5200
FAX: 617-252-5265
www.dacapopress.com

*James F Fries, Author*
*Donald M Vickery, Co-Author*
In this updated book the author draws on new research to recommend exercises and new pain medications for both arthritis and fibromyalgia. *$18.95*
*Paperback 1909*
*ISBN 0-738202-25-8*

**7994 Disability and Sport**
Human Kinetics, Inc.
1607 N Market Street
Champaign, IL 61820-2220
217-351-5076
800-747-4457
FAX: 217-351-1549
e-mail: info@hkusa.com
www.naspem.org

*Karen P DePauw, Author*
*Susan J Gavron, Co-Author*
*Scott Kimberley, Owner*
*Rainer Martens, President/Treasurer*

Provides a comprehensive and practical look at the past, present, and future of disability sport. Topics covered are inclusive of youth through adult participation with in-depth coverage of the essential issues involving athletes with disabilities. This new edition has updated references and new chapter-opening outlines that assist with individual study and class discussions. *$48.00*

*408 pages Hardcover*
*ISBN 0-736046-38-0*

**7995 Fitness Programming for Physical Disabilities**
Human Kinetics, Inc.
1607 N Market Street
Champaign, IL 61820-2220
217-351-5076
800-747-4457
FAX: 217-351-1549
e-mail: info@hkusa.com
www.naspem.org

*Patricia D Miller, Editor*
*Scott Kimberley, Owner*
*Rainer Martens, President/Treasurer*
*Jill Wikgren, COO*

A book offering information for developing and conducting exercise programs for groups that included people with physical disabilities. A dozen authorities in exercise science and adapted exercise programming explain how to effectively and safely modify existing programs for individuals with physical disabilities. *$42.00*

*232 pages Paperback*
*ISBN 0-873224-34-5*

**7996 Freedom from Arthritis Through Nutrition**
Tree of Life Publications
P.O.Box 126
Joshua Tree, CA 92252-0126
760-366-2937
FAX: 760-366-2937
e-mail: office@booxr.us
www.treelifebooks.com

*Philip J Welsh DDS ND, Author*
*Bianca Leonardo ND, Co-Author*

Here you will find simple, natural, inexpensive, tested ways of coping with the various forms of arthritis, using only nutrition and other natural methods. *$24.95*

*255 pages Softcover*

**7997 Functional Electrical Stimulation for Ambulation by Paraplegics**
Krieger Publishing Company
P.O.Box 9542
Melbourne, FL 32902
321-724-9542
800-724-0025
FAX: 321-951-3671
e-mail: info@krieger-publishing.com
www.krieger-publishing.com

*Daniel Graupe, Author*
*Kate H Kohn, Co-Author*

FES is employed to enable spinal cord injury patients who are complete paraplegics to stand and ambulate without bracing. The text covers 12 years of amulation experience. *$49.50*

*210 pages Paperback 1994*
*ISBN 0-894648-45-4*

**7998 Guide to Managing Your Arthritis**
Arthritis Foundation
1330 W. Peachtree St
Atlanta, GA 30309
404-872-7100
800-283-7800
FAX: 404-872-0457
e-mail: AFOrders@pbd.com
www.arthritis.org

*Mary Anne Dunkin, Author*
*John Klippel, President/CEO*
*Cecile Perich, Chairman*
*William Brackney, Vice Chair*

Expert reviewers answer questions about basic arthritis facts, treatments, research, surgery and more. Also, specific information about six common conditions: rheumatoid arthritis, osteoarthritis, osteoporosis, fibromyalgia, lupus and gout. *$9.95*

*193 pages Paperback*
*ISBN 0-912423-28-5*

**7999 How to Deal with Back Pain and Rheumatoid Joint Pain: A Preventive and Self Treatment Manua**
Global Health Solutions
2146 Kings Garden Way
Falls Church, VA 22043-2593
703-848-2333
800-759-3999
FAX: 703-848-0028
e-mail: information@watercure.com
www.watercure.com

*Fereydoon Batmanghelidj, Author*
*Xiaopo Batmanjhelidj, President*
*Kristin Swan, Administrator*

The physiology of pain production and its direct relationship to chronic regional dehydration of some joint spaces is explained: Special movements that would create vacuum in the disc spaces and draw water and the displaced discs into the vertebral joints are demonstrated. *$14.95*

*100 pages Paperback*
*ISBN 0-962994-20-0*

**8000 Inclusive Games**
Human Kinetics
1607 N Market Street
Champaign, IL 61820-2220
217-351-5076
800-747-4457
FAX: 217-351-1549
e-mail: info@hkusa.com
www.humankinetics.com

*Susan L Kasser, Author*
*Scott Kimberley, Owner*
*Rainer Martens, President/Treasurer*
*Jill Wikgren, COO*

Features more than 50 games, helpful illustrations, and hundreds of game variations. The book shows how to adapt games so that children of every ability level can practice, play and improve their movement skills together. The game finder makes it easy to locate an appropriate game according to its name, approximate grade level, difficulty within the grade level, skills required/developed, and number of players. *$17.95*

*120 pages Paperback*
*ISBN 0-873226-39-9*

**8001 Inside The Halo and Beyond: The Anatomy of a Recovery**
WW Norton & Company
500 5th Ave
New York, NY 10110-2
212-354-5500
FAX: 212-869-0856
www.wwnorton.com

*Maxine Kumin, Author*
*W Drake McFeely, Chairman/President*
*Stephen King, VP Finance/CFO*
*Robert Weil, VP/Executive Editor*

A skilled horsewoman and lifelong athlete, poet Kumin was 73 when a riding accident left her with two broken vertebrae in her neck. Kumin survived in the face of overwhelming odds that she would be paralyzed for the rest of her life. Miraculously, however, she was walking again within weeks of the accident; now, though one hand and an arm remain partially immobilized, her life has largely resumed its normal course. Here is the journal of her first nine months of recovery. *$ 13.95*

*192 pages Softcover*

*ISBN 0-393049-00-0*

**8002 Life on Wheels: For the Active Wheelchair User**

Patient-Centered Guides
1005 Gravenstein Hwy North
Sebastopol, CA 95472-2811
707-827-7000
800-998-9938
FAX: 707-829-0104
e-mail: order@oreilly.com
www.patientcenters.com

*Gary Karp, Author*

For 1.5 million Americans, life includes a wheelchair for mobility. Life on Wheels is for people who want to take charge of their life experience. Author Gary Karp describes medical issues (paralysis, circulation, rehab, cure research); day-to-day living (exercise, skin, bowel and bladder, sexuality, home access, maintaining a wheelchair); and social issues (self-image, adjustment, friends, family, cultural attitudes, activism). *$24.95*

*565 pages Paperback 1999*

*ISBN 1-565922-53-0*

**8003 Paralysis Resource Guide**

Christopher and Dana Reeve Paralysis Resource Ctr
636 Morris Turnpike
Suite 3A
Short Hills, NJ 07078-2608
973-467-8270
800-225-0292
FAX: 973-912-9433
e-mail: information@christopherreeve.org
www.paralysis.org

*Peter Wilderotter, President*
*Susan Howley, Executive VP*
*Maggie Goldberg, Senior Vice President, Marketing and Communications*
*Joe Canose, Senior Vice President, Quality of Life*

A comprehensive information tool for people affected by paralysis and for those who care for them. English or Spanish.

*336 pages*

**8004 Primer on the Rheumatic Diseases**

Arthritis Foundation
Ste 200
2970 Peachtree Rd NW
Atlanta, GA 30305-2111
404-237-8771
800-933-7023
FAX: 404-237-8153
e-mail: AFOrders@pbd.com
www.arthritis.org

*Rob Shaw, President*
*Patience White M.D., Editor*

Written to educate medical students and family physicians, this is the authoritative guide on the rheumatic diseases. *$79.95*

*724 pages Softcover*

*ISBN 0-387356-64-8*

**8005 Sport Science Review: Adapted Physical Activity**

Human Kinetics
1607 N Market Street
Champaign, IL 61820-2220
217-351-5076
800-747-4457
FAX: 217-351-1549
e-mail: info@hkusa.com
www.naspem.org

*Rainer Martens, President/Treasurer*
*Scott Kimberley, Owner*
*Jill Wikgren, COO*

This issue of Sport Science Review examines the newly emerging academic discipline of adapted physical activity. Researchers from diverse academic backgrounds and parts of the world review the issues and controversies surrounding inclusion in physical education and sport. *$15.00*

*96 pages Paperback*

*ISBN -073602-07-9*

**8006 Still Me**

Random House
1745 Broadway
New York, NY 10019-4305
212-782-9000
www.randomhouse.com

*Christopher Reeve, Author*
*Markus Dohle, Chairman/CEO*
*Madeline McIntosh, President*
*Andrew Weber, SVP Operations*

The man who was Superman begins with his debilitating riding accident, then weaves back and forth between past and present, creating a thorough biography of Reeve's life. *$7.99*

*336 pages Paperback 1999*

*ISBN 0-345432-41-4*

**8007 When Your Student Has Arthritis**

Arthritis Foundation
Ste 200
2970 Peachtree Rd NW
Atlanta, GA 30305-2111
404-237-8771
800-933-7023
FAX: 404-237-8153
e-mail: info.ga@arthritis.org
www.afstore.org

*Rob Shaw, President*

An overview of arthritis, including juvenile rhuematoid arthritis and treatment. Also includes a school activities checklist for students, education rights, and how teachers can help.

*28 pages*

**8008 Yoga for Fibromyalgia: Move, Breathe, and Relax to Improve Your Quality of Life**

Mobility Limited
PO Box 838
Morro Bay, CA 93443-0838
805-772-3560
800-366-6038
FAX: 805-772-4717
e-mail: shsh@mobilityltd.com
www.mobilityltd.com

*Shoosh Lettick Crotzer, Director*

The first book devoted exclusively to managing the symptoms of fibromyalgia; the comprehensive program of 26 illustrated poses, breathing techniques, and guided visualization and relaxation sessions can be practiced regardless of age or experience. The Living with Fibromyalgia section discusses lifestyle concerns. *$14.95*

*128 pages 1908*

## Print: Magazines

**8009 Arthritis Today**

Arthritis Foundation
2970 Peachtree Rd NW
Atlanta, GA 30305-2192
404-237-8771
800-933-7023
FAX: 404-237-8153
e-mail: info.ga@arthritis.org
arthritis.org

*Rob Shaw, President*
*Ayana Charleston, Program and Services Director*
*Margaux Espy, Senior Development Coordinator*
*Beth Kernan, Foundation Advisor*

Magazine for patients, physicians, public authorities and others with an interest in the field of arthritis. ( Price noted paid for yearly subscription ) *$12.95*
*Bi-Monthly*

**8010 Fibromyalgia AWARE Magazine**
National Fibromyalgia Association
2121 S Towne Centre Pl
suite 30
Orange, CA 92865-6124
714-921-0150
FAX: 714-921-6920
e-mail: paird@fmaware.org
fmaware.org

*Lynne Matallana, Editor In Chief*
*Malina Anderson, CFO*
*Eroll Landy, Treasurer*
Addresses the needs and concerns of people affected by fibromyalgia and overlapping conditions. *$35.00*
*3 times a year*

**8011 New Mobility**
Leonard Media Group
415 Horsham Rd
Horsham, PA 19044-2068
215-675-9133
888-850-0344
FAX: 215-675-9376
e-mail: jeff@leonardmedia.com
www.newmobility.com

*Jeff Leonard, Owner*
The full-service, full-color lifestyle magazine for the disability community. The award-winning magazine is contemporary, witty and candid. Produced by professional journalists and visual artists, the magazine's voice is uncompromising and unsentimental, yet practical, knowing and friendly. The magazine covers issues that matter to readers: medical news, and cure research; jobs, benefits and civil rights; sports, recreation and travel; product news, technology and innovation. *$27.95*
*Monthly*

**8012 PALAESTRA: Forum of Sport, Physical Education and Recreation for Those with Disabilities**
Challenge Publications Limited
P.O.Box 508
Macomb, IL 61455-508
309-833-1902
FAX: 309-833-1902
e-mail: challpub@macomb.com
www.palaestra.com

*David P Beaver EdD, Editor*
*Martin.E Block, Editor-in-Chief*
*Julian U. Stein, Associate Editor*
The most comprehensive resource on sport, physical education and recreation for individuals with disabilities, their parents and professionals in the field of adapted physical activity. Published in cooperation with US Paralympics and AAHPERD's Adapted Physical Activity Council. Informative yet entertaining and delivers valuable insights for consumers, families and professionals in the field. Published quarterly.

**8013 PN/Paraplegia News**
PVA Publications
Ste 180
2111 E Highland Ave
Phoenix, AZ 85016-4756
602-224-0500
888-888-2201
FAX: 602-224-0507
e-mail: info@pnnews.com
www.pn-magazine.com

*Richard Hoover, Editor*
*Ann Santos, Assistant Editor*
Packed with timely information on spinal-cord-injury research, new products, legislation that impacts people with disabilities, accessible travel, computer options, car/van adaptations, news for veterans, housing, employment, health care and all issues affecting wheelers and caregivers around the world.

**8014 Spirit Magazine**
Special Olympics International
1133 19th St NW
Washington, DC 20036-3604
202-628-3630
FAX: 202-824-0200
e-mail: info@specialolympics.org
www.specialolympics.org

*Kathy Smallwood, Editor*
*Timothy P Shriver PhD, Chariman/CEO*
*J Brady Lum, President/COO*
This magazine reflects the power of Special Olympics to build bridges between people with and without intellectual disabilities and spark personal insight, compassion and gratitude for life.
*Quarterly*

**8015 Strides Magazine**
North American Riding for the Handicapped Assoc
7475 Dakin Street
suite 600 #600
Denver, CO 80221-6920
303-452-1212
800-369-7433
FAX: 303-252-4610
e-mail: narha@narha.org
www.narha.org

*Carol Nickell, CEO*
*Sheila Dietrich, Executive Director*
*William Scebbi, CEO*
This engaging magazine is a non-technical, yet accurate journal that focuses on the work of NARHA. Rider profiles, how-to articles, editorials and instructional columns seek to educate a general readership of the diverse aspects of equine facilitated therapy and activities. Each seasonal issue carries a theme.
*Quarterly*

**8016 Stroke Connection Magazine**
American Stroke Association
7272 Greenville Ave
Dallas, TX 75231-5129
214-373-6300
800-242-8721
FAX: 214-706-1191
www.strokeassociation.org

*Ralph Sacco, President/Director*
*Nancy Brown, CEO*
*Debra Lockwood, Chairman*
From in-depth information on conditions such as aphasia, central pain, high blood pressure and depression, to tips for daily living from healthcare professionals and other stroke survivors, keeps people abreast of how to cope, how to reduce the risk of stroke and how to make the most of each day.
*6 issues*

## Print: Newsletters

**8017 Arthritis Foundation Great West Region**
Arthritis Foundation
115 N.E. 100th St
Suite 350
Seattle, WA 98125
206-547-2707
800-746-1821
FAX: 206-547-2805
e-mail: tzuehl@arthritis.org
www.arthritis.org

*Scott Weaver, CEO*
Offers regional updates, information on activities and events, resources and medical research for members.
*Newsletter*

**8018 Arthritis Update**
Arthritis Foundation
Ste 319
3300 Monroe Ave
Rochester, NY 14618-4617
585-264-1480
e-mail: info.uny@arthritis.org
arthritis.org

*Melinda Merante, Executive Director*
*Patti Carter-Morrison, Community Development Coordinator*
*Jodi MacLean, Administrative Assistant*
*Cynthia Pegado, Program Manager*
Offers chapter updates, information on activities and events, resources and medical research for members.
*Newsletter*

**8019 Focus**
Arthritis Foundation
3740 Ridge Mill Dr
Hilliard, OH 43026-9231
614-876-8200
e-mail: info.coh@arthritis.org
www.arthritis.org

*Rochelle Bailey, Community Development Manager*
*Heather Schwenker, Division Vice President*
*Morgan Patten, Program Manager*
*Christy Rice, Operations Manager*
Offers chapter updates, information on activities and events, resources and medical research for members.
*Newsletter*

**8020 Joint Efforts**
Arthritis Foundation
Ste 603
657 Mission St
San Francisco, CA 94105-4120
415-356-1230
800-464-6240
FAX: 415-356-1240
e-mail: info.nca@arthritis.org
www.arthritis.org

*PJ Handeland, President*
*Deborah Jackson, Senior VP*
*Peter Grace, VP Finance and Operations*
*Erin Badillo, Executive Assistant & Special Events Coordinator*
Offers chapter updates, information on activities and events, resources and medical research for members.
*Newsletter*

**8021 Post-Polio Newsletter**
Post-Polio Health International
Ste 110
4207 Lindell Blvd
Saint Louis, MO 63108-2930
314-534-0475
FAX: 314-534-5070
e-mail: info@post-polio.org
www.post-polio.org

*Joan Headley, Executive Director*
*Gayla Hoffman, Editor*
Contains current information about the late effects of polio, updates about post-polio related and neuromuscular respiratory research, as well as articles that offer practical and useful advice by experienced survivors and health care professionals. Available with membership.
*12 pages Quarterly*

**8022 SCILIFE**
National Spinal Cord Injury Association
75-20 Astoria Blvd
Jackson Heights, NY 11370
718-803-3782
e-mail: info@spinalcord.org
www.spinalcord.org

*K.Eric Larson, Senior VP*
Filled with issue-driven articles, and news of interest to the SCI community and the larger disability community.
*Bi-monthly*

## Non Print: Newsletters

**8023 A World Awaits You**
Mobility International USA
132 E Broadway
Suite 343
Eugene, OR 97401-3155
541-343-1284
FAX: 541-343-6812
e-mail: clearinghouse@miusa.org
www.miusa.org

*Susan Sygall, Executive Director*
Includes interviews with people with disabilities who have participated in a wide range of international exchange programs.

**8024 ABS Newsletter**
American Back Society
2648 International Blvd
Suite 502
Oakland, CA 94601-1547
510-536-9929
FAX: 510-536-1812
e-mail: info@americanbacksoc.org
www.americanbacksoc.org

*Scott Haldeman, President*
*Aubrey Swartz MD, Executive Director*
Keeps subscribers current with timely topics on the diagnosis and treatment of a wide spectrum of painful and disabling conditions of the spine.

**8025 CurePSP Magazine**
Society for Progressive Supranuclear Palsy
Ste 906
11350 McCormick Rd
Hunt Valley, MD 21031-1002
410-785-7004
800-457-4777
FAX: 410-785-7009
e-mail: info@curepsp.org
www.psp.org

*Richard Gordon Dyne DMin, President*
*Janet Edmunson, Chair*
*Dan Johnson, Vice Chair*
Informs readers of findings in the area of PSP.

**8026 EpilepsyUSA Magazine**
Epilepsy Foundation of America
8301 Professional Pl
Landover, MD 20785-2237
301-459-3700
FAX: 301-577-2684
www.epilepsyfoundation.org

*Brien J Smith Md, Chair*
*Mark E Nini, Senior Vice Chair*
*Richard P Denness, President/CEO*
*Alexandra K Finucane Esq, Executive Vice President*
Reports on new developments in a wide range of fields of interest to people with epilepsy and to those who provide services to them.

**8027 Exchange**
ALS Association
27001 Agoura Rd
Suite 250
Agoura Hills, CA 91301-5105
818-340-0182
FAX: 818-880-9006
www.alsa.org

*Gary A Leo, CEO*
*Morton Charlestein, Chairman*
*Andrew Soffel, Chairman*
*Julie Sharpe, Executive Director*

Covers a broad range of subjects including stories about the lives of ALS patients, special events, research and public policy in the ALS community.
*4-6 times/year*

**8028 Fibromyalgia Online**
National Fibromyalgia Association
2121 S Towne Centre Pl
suite 300
Ornage, CA 92865-6124 714-921-0150
FAX: 714-921-6920
www.fmaware.org

*Lynne Matallana, President/Editor In Chief*
*Malina Anderson, CFO*
*Eroll Landy, Treasurer*
An educational resource for patients and healthcare professionals that brings the latest news on fibrmyalgia and overlapping conditions.
*Monthly*

**8029 MIUSA's Global Impact Newsletter**
Mobility International USA
132 E Broadway
Suite 343
Eugene, OR 97401-3155 541-343-1284
FAX: 541-343-6812
www.miusa.org

*Susan Sygall, Executive Director*
*Cindy Lewis, Director*
*Olivia Hardin, Information Services Coordinator*
Each issue features photos, alumni updates, highlights from recent activities, and new publications.
*semi-annually*

**8030 Motivator**
Multiple Sclerosis Association of America
706 Haddonfield Rd
Cherry Hill, NJ 8002-2652 856-488-4500
800-532-7667
FAX: 856-661-9797
e-mail: webmaster@msassociation.org
www.msassociation.org

*Andrea L GriesŠ, Editor*
*Susan W Courtney, Sr Writer & Creative Director*
*Amanda Bednar, Contributing Writer*
Addresses the physical, emotional, and social issues that arise with MS, and provides information and support to many of those affected by this disorder.
*48 pages Quarterly*

**8031 New York Arthritis Reporter**
New York Chapter of the Arthritis Foundation
122 East 42nd Street
New York, NY 10168-1898 212-984-8700
FAX: 212-878-5960
e-mail: info.ny@arthritis.org
www.arthritis.org

*Phyllis Geraghty, Editor*
*Ross Alfieri, President*
*Daniel T. McGowan, Chair*
Provides public access to current arthritis information and resources on important health issues.
*Quarterly*

**8032 SCI Psychosocial Process**
American Assoc of Spinal Cord Injury Psych/Soc Wor
7520 Astoria Blvd
East Elmhurst, NY 11370-1138 718-803-3782
800-404-2898
FAX: 718-803-0414
e-mail: info@unitedspinal.org
http://www.unitedspinal.org

*E Jason Mask MSW, Editor*
*Paul Tobin, President/CEO*
*Lex Frieden, Chairman of the Board*
*Michael B. Kinne, Secretary*
The purpose of this e journal is disseminating information of value to psychologists, social workers and other psychological caring for spinal cord injured persons.
*2 time a year*

## Non Print: Video

**8033 A Wheelchair for Petronilia**
Fanlight Productions C/O Icarus Films
32 Court Street
Brooklyn, NY 11201-1731 718-488-8900
800-876-1710
FAX: 718-488-8642
e-mail: info@fanlight.com
www.fanlight.com

*Ben Achtenberg, Owner*
Profiles a program, organized and run by Guatemalans with disabilities, which trains them to manufacture and repair cheap, sturdy wheelchairs designed for conditions in developing countries. 28 Minutes.
*VHS/DVD*
*ISBN 1-572953-98-5*

**8034 Beyond the Barriers**
Aquarius Health Care Videos
30 Forest Road
Po Box 249
Millis, MA 02054 508-376-1244
888-440-2963
FAX: 508-376-1245
www.aquariusproductions.com

*Mark Wellman, Director*
*Leslie Kussmann, President/Producer*
For too many years, paraplegics, amputees, quadraplegics and the blind have felt trapped by their disabilities. No more! Mark Wellman and other disabled adventurers, rock climb the desert towers of Utah, sail in British Columbia, body-board the big waves of Pipeline and Waimea Bay, scuba dive with sea lions in Mexico and hand glide the California coast. This film delivers the simple message: Don't give up, and never give in. If you can't ever lose, then you can't ever win. Preview option.
*Video/47 Mins*

**8035 Breathing Lessons: The Life and Work of Mark O'Brien**
Fanlight Productions C/O Icarus Films
32 Court Street
Brooklyn, NY 11201-1731 718-488-8900
800-876-1710
FAX: 718-488-8642
e-mail: info@fanlight.com
www.fanlight.com

*Jessica Yu, Director*
A new documentary which focuses on poet-journalist Mark O'Brien. Crippled by polio in childhood, and later forced to rely on an iron lung as a result of post-polio syndrome, for more than forty years he has fought against illness and bureaucracy in his determination to lead an independent life. *$225.00*
*Video/35 Mins 1996*
*ISBN 1-572958-41-3*

**8036 Complete Armchair Fitness**
CC-M Productions
7755 16th St NW
Washington, DC 20012-1460
202-882-7430
800-453-6280
FAX: 202-882-7432
e-mail: info@armchairfitness.com
www.armchairfitness.com

*Robert Mason, Manager*
Armchair Fitness video series. 4 DVDs: Armchair Fitness Aerobic, Armchair Fitness Gentle, Armchair Fitness Strength and Armchair Fitness Yoga. *$120.00*
*Video*

**8037 How Come You Walk Funny?**
Fanlight Productions C/O Icarus Films
32 Court Street
Brooklyn, NY 11201-1731
718-488-8900
800-876-1710
FAX: 718-488-8642
e-mail: info@fanlight.com
www.fanlight.com

*Tina Hahn, Director*
Profiles a unique experiment in reverse integration: a school where non disabled kids attend a kindergarten designed for children with physical disabilities. The kids and families tackle their differences and discover common ground through finding a way that all can play. *$ 179.00*
*Video/47 Mins 2004*
*ISBN 1-572958-84-7*

**8038 Key Changes: A Portrait of Lisa Thorson**
Fanlight Productions C/O Icarus Films
32 Court Street
Brooklyn, NY 11201-1731
718-488-8900
800-876-1710
FAX: 718-488-8642
e-mail: info@fanlight.com
www.fanlight.com

*Cindy Marshall, Director*
A documentary profiling Lisa Thorson, a gifted vocalist who uses a wheelchair. Ms. Thorson defines herself as a performer first, a person with a disability second, and this thoughtful portrait respects that distinction. Her work as a jazz singer is at the heart of the film, reflecting her philosophy that the biggest contribution that she can make to the struggle for the rights of people with disabilities is doing her art the best way she can. *$149.00*
*Video/28 Mins 1993*
*ISBN 1-572959-30-4*

**8039 Wheelchair Bowling**
American Wheelchair Bowling Association
P.O.Box 69
Clover, VA 24534-69
434-454-2269
FAX: 434-454-6276
e-mail: DLR1745@aol.com
www.awba.org

*Dick Schaaf, Author*
*Dave Roberts, Executive Secretary Treasurer*
In addition to providing historical background, it includes principles of the game from keeping score through ball drilling for the wheelchair bowler. Through profiles of wheelchair bowlers, the text covers ball delivery, spare making techniques and special equipment that can be used. *$9.95*
*96 pages*

**8040 Yoga for Arthritis**
Mobility Limited
365 Quintana Rd
Suite F2
Morro Bay, CA 93442-2000
805-772-3560
800-366-6038
FAX: 805-772-4717
e-mail: shsh@mobilityltd.com
www.mobilityltd.com

*Shoosh Crotzer, Owner/Executive Director*
A yoga-based program with five separate segments, which includes breathing and relaxation techniques, stretching and strengthening routines, and aerobic exercises. This 52-minute program can also be performed seated. Available on DVD or VHS; DVD includes Spanish version. *$19.95*
*Video*

**8041 Yoga for MS and Related Conditions**
Mobility Limited
365 Quintana Rd
Suite F2
Morro Bay, CA 93442-2000
805-772-3560
800-366-6038
FAX: 805-772-4717
e-mail: shsh@mobilityltd.com
www.mobilityltd.com

*Shoosh Crotzer, Owner/Executive Director*
A yoga-based program. Shows assisted versions of each exercise for those who require it; is available with an optional Instructional Guidebook with illustrations, alternative positions, and hints. This 48-minute program can also be performed seated. Available on DVD or VHS; DVD includes Spanish version. *$19.95*
*Video*

## Sports

**8042 Access to Sailing**
423 E Shoreline Village Drive
Long Beach, CA 90802
562-901-9999
e-mail: info@accesstosailing.org
www.accesstosailing.org

*Duncan Milne, Founder/Executive Director*
*Cliff Larson, Director*
*Gaile Oslapas, Assistant Director*
Provides therapeutic rehabilitation to disabled and disadvantaged children and adults, through interactive sailing outings.

**8043 Achilles Track Club**
42 West 38th Street
Suite 400
New York, NY 10018-6241
212-354-0300
FAX: 212-354-3978
e-mail: info@achillestrackclub.org
www.achillestrackclub.org

*Richard Traum PhD, President/Founder*
*Mary Bryant, Vice President*
*Kathleen Bateman, Director*
Organization whose goal is to guide disabled athletes into the able-bodied community.

**8044 Adaptive Sports Center**
P.O.Box 1639
Crested Butte, CO 81224-1639
970-349-2296
866-349-2296
FAX: 970-349-2077
e-mail: info@adaptivesports.org
www.adaptivesports.org

*Christopher Hensley, Executive Director*
*Chris Read, CTRS Program Director*
*Ella Fahrlander, Development Director*
*Erin English, Marketing/Communications Dir.*
Year round adaptive, adventure recreation program located at the base of Crested Butte Mountain Resort, Crested Butte ,CO. The Adaptive Sports Centers provides adaptive downhill and cross country ski lessons, ski rentals and snowboarding lessons in the winter. Offers a variety of wilderness based programs in the summer including multi-day trips into the back country, extensive cycling programs, canoeing, and white water rafting.

**8045 American Wheelchair Bowling Association**
P.O.Box 69
Clover, VA 24534-69
434-454-2269
FAX: 434-454-6276
e-mail: DLR1745@aol.com
www.awba.org

*Dave Roberts, Executive Secretary Treasurer*
A non-profit organization, composed of wheelchair bowlers, dedicated to encouraging, developing, and regulating wheelchair bowling and wheelchair bowling leagues.

**8046 Basketball School**
Alabama Institute for Deaf and Blind
205 South St E
Talladega, AL 35160-2411
256-761-3335
FAX: 256-761-3505
www.aib-aidb.com

*Terry Graham, President*
*John Mascia, Executive Director*
*Cindy Baker, Director*
We offer Class 1A champion football, basketball, volleyball, track and field, soccer and cheerleading. Our students have competed in the international Deaf-Olympics and our teams have won state and national championships in every major sport. We compete against public schools around Alabama and schools for the deaf from across the nation.

**8047 Bold Tracks**
Big Earth Publishing
1524 S Commercial Street 3N
Neenah, WI 54956
800-258-5830
FAX: 920-886-6674
e-mail: books@bigearthpublishing.com
www.bigearthpublishing.com

*Hal O'Leary, Author*
*Janet Heisz, Sales Manager*
This guide is essential for instructor and student alike. It covers skiing for the visually and hearing impaired as well as the physically and developmentally disabled. *$24.95*
*156 pages Paperback*
*ISBN 1-555661-14-4*

**8048 Chesapeake Region Accessible Boating**
P.O.Box 6564
Annapolis, MD 21401-564
410-626-0273
FAX: 410-626-6070
e-mail: info@crabsailing.org
www.crab-sailing.org

*Daniel Jarzynski, President*
*Lance Hinrichs, Vice President*
*Ernie Shineman, Treasurer*
*Loren Barnett, Secretary*
Provides opportunities for the disabled and their friends to sail the Chesapeake Bay. Day sails, lessons, organized races. Call for charter information. Sail for free on the fourth Sunday of each month, May through October.

**8049 Disabled Sports Program Center**
Disabled Sports USA Far West
P.O.Box 9780
Truckee, CA 96162-7780
530-581-4161
FAX: 530-581-3127
e-mail: info@disabledsports.net
www.dsusafw.org

*Haakon Lang-Ree, Manager*
Our Program provides ski and snowboard lessons to students of all abilities. Our PSIA certified instructors, and trained volunteers make skiing or snowboarding possible for anyone with physical, cognitive or developmental disabilities.

**8050 Disabled Sports USA**
451 Hungerford Dr
Suite 100
Rockville, MD 20850-5102
301-217-0960
FAX: 301-217-0968
e-mail: information@dusa.org
www.dsusa.org

*Kirk Bauer, Executive Director*
*Kathy Chandler, Executive Director*
*Kathy Celo, Operations*
Provides year-round sports and recreation opportunities for people with physical disabilities, veterans and non-veterans alike, such as sanctioned regional and national events in alpine and Nordic skiing, cycling, shooting swimming, table tennis, track and field, volleyball, and weightlifiting. The organization handles physical disabilities which restrict mobility, including amputations paraplegia, quadriplegia, cerebral palsy, head injury, mulitple sclerosis, muscular dystrophy, and more.

**8051 Disabled Watersports Program**
Mission Bay Aquatic Center
1001 Santa Clara Pl
San Diego, CA 92109-7228
858-488-1000
FAX: 858-488-9625
e-mail: mbac@sdsu.edu
www.missionbayaquaticcenter.com

*Glen Brandenburg, Executive Director*
*Kevin Straw, Instructional Manager*
*Kevin Waldick, Programs Manager*
*Amanda Burgess, Office Manager*
Devoted to providing accessible water sports and recreational opportunities for individuals with disabilities. Specially designed equipment makes water skiing, wake boarding, keelboat sailing, windsurfing, rowing, surfing, and kayaking possible for people with varying levels of mobility and ability.

**8052 Galvin Health and Fitness Center**
Rehabilitation Institute of Chicago
541 North Fairbanks, Mezzanine
Chicago, IL 60611-3006
312-238-5001
FAX: 312-238-5017
e-mail: sports@ric.org
http://www.ric.org

*Joanne C Smith MD MBA, President*
*Glenn Paustian, Director*
*Jill Beemer, Manager, Caring for Kids*
*Derek Daniels, Manager, Sports and Recreation*
The RIC Sports and Fitness Program offers people with physical disabilities an on-site fitness center, specialized exercise classes and services, and adult and junior competitive and recreational sports opportunities, including the recreational/social Caring for Kids program for youth ages 7-17. Most programs are provided free of charge or for a nominal fee.

**8053 Guide to Wheelchair Sports and Recreation**
Paralyzed Veterans of America
801 Eighteenth Street NW
Washington, DC 20006-3517
202-872-1300
800-424-8200
888-860-7244
FAX: 202-785-4432
e-mail: info@pva.org
www.pva.org

*Randy Pleva, President*
*Homer Toensenp, Director*
*Louis Irvin, Director*
*Kelly Noble, Director*
This guide is published to introduce and increase awareness of people with disabilities to the many sports and recreational opportunities available. It lists descriptions of adaptive sports and recreation, activity and equipment directories, and additional resources for people with disabilities.
*28 pages Booklet*

**8054 Handicapped Scuba Association International**
Handicapped Scuba Association
1104 El Prado
San Clemente, CA 92672-4637
949-498-4540
FAX: 949-498-6128
e-mail: hsa@hsascuba.com
www.hsascuba.com

*Jim Gatacre, President*
*Patricia Derk, Vice President*
A nonprofit volunteer organization dedicated to improving the physical and social well being of those with special needs through the exhilarating sport of scuba diving. An educational program for able bodied scuba instructors to learn to teach and certify people with special needs. Accessible travel opportunities.

**8055 Lakeshore Foundation**
4000 Ridgeway Dr
Birmingham, AL 35209-5563
205-313-7400
FAX: 205-313-7475
e-mail: information@lakeshore.org
www.lakeshore.org

*Jeffery Underwood, President*
*Cathy Miller, CFO*
*Beth Curry, CPO*
Promotes independence for persons with physically disabling conditions and provides opportunities to pursue active, healthy lifestyles.

**8056 National Disability Sports Alliance**
25 W Independence Way
Kingston, RI 02881-1124
401-792-7130
FAX: 401-792-7132
e-mail: info@ndsaonline.org
http://nationaldisabilitysportsalliance.webs.

*Jerry McCole, Executive Director*
Serves to present disabled athletes with the opportunity to perform in many different sports. Participants range from the beginning athlete to the elite, international caliber athlete.

**8057 National Skeet Shooting Association**
5931 Roft Rd
San Antonio, TX 78253-9261
210-688-3371
800-877-5338
FAX: 210-688-3014
e-mail: nsca@nssa-nsca.com
www.mynssa.com

*Michael Hampton, Jr., Executive Director*
*Linda Steen, NSSA Director*
*Phyllis Mills, NSSA Administrative Assistant*
Offers information on sporting clay targets for the disabled hunter.

**8058 National Sports Center for the Disabled**
P.O.Box 1290
Winter Park, CO 80482-1290
970-726-1540
FAX: 970-726-4112
e-mail: info@nscd.org
www.nscd.org

*A Fleishman, President*
*Patty Disney, CFO*
*Joe Ellis, Chairman*
Our mission is to provide quality outdoor sports and therapeutic recreation programs that positively impact the lives of people with physical, cognitive, emotional, or behavioral challenges.
*6-8 pages Quarterly*

**8059 National Wheelchair Poolplayers Association**
9757 Mount Lompoc Ct
Las Vegas, NV 89178-7511
702-250-1665
FAX: 714-486-2048
www.nwpainc.org

*Jeffrey Dolezal, President*
Works together with other groups, organizations, and tournaments to update rules to include wheelchair players.

**8060 North American Riding for the Handicapped Association**
7475 Dakin Street
Suite 600
Denver, CO 80221-6920
303-452-1212
800-369-7433
FAX: 303-252-4610
e-mail: narha@narha.org
www.narha.org

*Sheila Dietrich, Executive Director*
*William Scebbi, CEO*
Changes lives by promoting excellence in equine assisted activities. *$35.00*
*42 pages Quarterly*

**8061 Special Olympics**
1133 19th St NW
Washington, DC 20036-3604
202-393-1251
FAX: 202-715-1146
e-mail: info@specialolympics.org
www.specialolympics.org

*Timothy P Shriver PhD, Chariman/CEO*
*J Brady Lum, President/COO*
*Stephen M Carter, Lead Director/CEO/Vice Chair*
A year-round worldwide program that promotes physical fitness, sports training and athletic competition for children and adults with intellectual disabilities.

**8062 Special Olympics International**
1133 19th St NW
Washington, DC 20036-3604
202-393-1251
FAX: 202-715-1146
e-mail: info@specialolympics.org
www.specialolympics.org

*Timothy P Shriver PhD, Chariman/CEO*
*J Brady Lum, President/COO*
*Stephen M Carter, Lead Director/CEO/Vice Chair*
Provides year-round training and athletic competition in a variety of well-coached, Olympic-type sparts for persons with mental retardation. Offers opportunities to develop physical fitness, prepare for entry into school and community sports programs. Athletes express courage, experience joy and participate in gifts, skills and friendship with their families and other Special Olympics athletes. Local information can be provided by regional offices.

**8063 United Foundation for Disabled Archers**
P.O.Box 251
Glenwood, MN 56334-251
320-634-3660
e-mail: info@uffdaclub.com
www.uffdaclub.com

*Daniel James Hendricks, President*
*Russ Kalk, Vice President*
*Debbie Kalk, Treasurer*
Promotes and provides access to the sport of archery for any physically challenged person. Arranges Archery hunts throughout the United States.

**8064 Wheelchair Sports, USA**
Po Box 5266
Kendall Park, NJ 08824-5266
732-266-2634
FAX: 732-355-6500
e-mail: office@wsusa.org
www.wsusa.org

*Kelly Behlmann, Owner*
Initiates, stimulates and promotes the growth and development of wheelchair sports.

## Support Groups

**8065 Information Hotline**
Arthritis Foundation, Southeast Region Inc
2970 Peachtree Rd NW
Ste 200
Atlanta, GA 30305
404-237-8771
800-933-7023
FAX: 404-237-8153
e-mail: info.ga@arthritis.org
www.arthritis.org

*Rob Shaw, Regional VP Georgia Area*
*Ayana Charleston, Program and Services Director*
*Margaux Espy, Senior Development Coordinator*
*Beth Kernan, Foundation Advisor*
The mission of the Arthritis Foundation is to improve lives through leadership in the prevention, control and cure of arthritis and related diseases.

**8066 Kids on the Block Programs**
9385 Gerwig Lane
Suite C
Columbia, MD 21046-2893
410-290-9095
800-368-5437
FAX: 410-290-9358
e-mail: kob@kotb.com
www.kotb.com

*Aric Darroe, President*
*Jane Thuman, Vice President*
*Christina Grogan, Marketing Manager*
Features life-size puppets in educational programs that enlighten children and adults on the issues of disability awareness, medical and educational differences, and social concerns.

# Specific Disorders

## Associations

**8067 Academy of Dentistry for Persons with Disabilities**
401 N Michigan Ave
Ste 2200
Chicago, IL 60611-4245
312-527-6764
FAX: 312-673-6663
e-mail: scda@scdonline.org
www.scdonline.org

*Meghan Carey, Executive Director*
*Kate Martinez, Operations Manager*
*Maureen M. Romer, President*
*Jason Grinter, Vice President*
Special Care Dentistry (SCD) is headquartered in Chicago and has a wide ranging membership that includes: dentists, dental hygienists; dental assistants; non-dental health care providers; health program administrators; and others who share our mission. There is also a participating membership category for hospitals, agencies that serve people with special needs and other advocacy and heath care organizations.

**8068 Academy of Spinal Cord Injury Professionals**
801 18th Street NW
Washington, DC 20006
202-416-7704
FAX: 212-416-7641
www.ascipro.org

*Maurice L Jordan, Acting Executive Director*
*Brenda Finkel, Administrative Assistant*
The premier, interdisciplinary organization dedicated to advancing the care of people with spinal cord injury/dysfunction.

**8069 Acid Maltase Deficiency Association (AMDA)**
PO Box 700248
San Antonio, TX 78270-248
210-494-6144
FAX: 210-490-7161
e-mail: tianrama@aol.com
www.amda-pompe.org

*Tiffany House, President*
Offers a newletter, informational materials, networking, referrals to local resources, national advocacy efforts, and also maintains a research registry.

**8070 American Academy of Allergy, Asthma and Immunology**
555 E Wells St
Ste 1100
Milwaukee, WI 53202-3823
414-272-6071
FAX: 414-272-6070
e-mail: info@aaaai.org
aaaai.org

*Dr Mark Ballow FAAAAI, President*
Nonprofit association representing allergists, clinical immunologists, asthma specialists, allied health professionals, and others with a special interest in allergy and asthma. The AAAAI's mission is to advance the knowledge, education and practice of allergy, asthma and immunology.

**8071 American Academy of Child and Adolescent Psychiatry**
3615 Wisconsin Ave NW
Washington, DC 20016-3007
202-966-7300
FAX: 202-966-2891
e-mail: communications@aacap.org
www.aacap.org

*Laurence Lee Greenhill, President*
*William Bernet, Treasurer*
*James C. MacIntyre II, M.D., Secretary*
*Elizabeth Hughes, Asst. Director of Education & Recertification*
A 501 (C)(3) nonprofit membership organization composed of over 6,500 child and adolescent psychiatrists. Members actively research, evaluate, diagnose and treat psychiatric disorders and pride themselves on giving direction to and responding quickly to new developments in addressing the health care needs of children and their families.
*53 pages*

**8072 American Academy of Osteopathy**
3500 Depauw Blvd, Ste 1080
Indianapolis, IN 46268-1174
317-879-1881
FAX: 317-879-0563
e-mail: dfinley@academyofosteopathy.org
academyofosteopathy.org

*Diana Finley, Executive Director*
*Michael Seffinger, President*
The mission of the American Academy of Osteopathy is to teach, advocate, and research the science, art and philosophy of osteopathic medicine, emphasizing the integration of osteopathic principles, practice and manipulative treatment in patient care.

**8073 American Academy of Otolaryngology: Head and Neck Surgery**
1650 Diagonal Rd
Alexandria, VA 22314-2857
703-836-4444
TTY:703-519-1585
www.entnet.org

*David Nielson, EVP/CEO*
*Rodney P Lusk, President*
*John W. House, Secretary/Treasurer*
*Michael G. Stewart, MD, MPH, Director - Academic*
Promotes the art and science of medicine related to otolaryngology-head and neck surgery, including providing continuing medical education courses and publications.

**8074 American Academy of Physical Medicine and Rehabilitation**
9700 W Bryn Mawr Ave
Ste 200
Rosemont, IL 60018-5701
847-737-6000
FAX: 847-737-6001
e-mail: info@aapmr.org
aapmr.org

*Thomas Stautzenbach, Executive Director*
*M Elizabeth Sandel, President*
*Sherry Milligan, Website Content Editor*
*Beth Binkley, Communications Coordinator*
This national medical specialty society represents more than 6,500 physical medicine and rehabilitation physicians, whose patients include people with physical disabilities and chronic, disabling illnesses. The academy's mission is to maximize quality of life, minimize the incidence and prevalence of impairments and disability, promote societal health and enhance the understanding and development of the specialty. The organization offers information, referrals, and patient materials.

**8075 American Association For Respiratory Care**
9425 N. Macarthur Blvd.
Suite 100
Irving, TX 75063-4706
972-243-2272
FAX: 972-484-2720
e-mail: info@aarc.org
www.aarc.org

*Sam Giordano, CEO*
*Tom Kallstrom, COO*
AARC's mission is to advance the science, technology, ethics and art of respiratory care through research and education for its members and to teach the general public about pulmonary health and disease prevention.

**8076 American Association of Cardiovascular and Pulmonary Rehabilitation**
401 North Michigan Avenue
Suite 220
Chicago, IL 60611
312-321-5146
FAX: 312-673-6924
e-mail: aacvpr@aacvpr.org
www.aacvpr.org

*Jessica Eustice, Development Manager*
*Joanne Ray, Executive Director*
*Erica Naranjo, Administrative Associate*
*Abigail Lynn, Operations Manager*

The mission of American Assoication of Cardiovascular and Pulmonary Rehabilitation is to reduce morbidity, mortality, and disability from cardiovascular and pulmonary diseases through education, prevention, rehabilitation, research, and aggressive disease management.

**8077 American Brain Tumor Association**
8550 W. Bryn Mawr
Chicaog, IL 60631-4106
773-577-8750
800-886-2282
FAX: 773-577-8738
e-mail: info@abta.org
abta.org

*Elizabeth Wilson, Executive Director*

A non-profit organization founded in 1973 dedicated to the elimination of brain tumors through research and patient education services. Exists to eliminate brain tumors through research and to meet the needs of brain tumor patients and their families.

**8078 American Diabetes Association**
1701 N Beauregard St
Alexandria, VA 22311-1733
703-549-1500
800-232-3472
FAX: 703-836-7439
e-mail: askada@diabetes.org
www.diabetes.org

*Larry Hausner, CEO*

Provides diabetes research, information and advocacy. The mission of the Association is to prevent and cure diabetes and to improve the lives of all people affected by diabetes.

**8079 American Group Psychotherapy Association**
25 East 21st Street
6th Floor
New York, NY 10010-6207
212-477-2677
877-668-2472
FAX: 212-979-6627
e-mail: info@agpa.org
www.agpa.org

*Marsha Block, CEO*
*Kathleen H. Ulman, Ph.D, President*
*Anne McEneaney, Ph.D, Secretary*

AGPA serves as the national voice specific to the interests of group psychotherapy. Its 4,100 members and 31 affiliate societies provide a wealth of professional, educational and social support for group psychotherapists in the United States and around the world.

**8080 American Head and Neck Society**
11300 W Olympic Blvd
Ste 600
Los Angeles, CA 90064-1663
310-437-0559
FAX: 310-437-0585
e-mail: admin@ahnns.info
www.headandneckcancer.org

*Mark Wax, MD, President*
*Doug Girod, VP*
*Dennis.H Kraus, Secretary*
*Ehab Hanna, Treasurer*

AHNS is a professional organization, formed in 1998 to promote research and education in head and neck oncology. The website includes clinical practice guidelines, details of events, grants, and patient information. To promote and advance the knowledge of prevention, diagnosis, treatment, and rehabilitation of neoplasms and other diseases of the head and neck.

**8081 American Lung Association**
1301 Pennsylvania Ave
Ste 800
Washington, DC 20004
202-785-3355
800-586-4872
FAX: 202-452-1085
e-mail: info@lungusa.org
www.lungusa.org

*Charles Dean Connor, President/CEO*

The mission of the American Lung Association is to prevent lung disease and promote lung health.

**8082 American Psychiatric Association**
Psychiatric Services
1000 Wislon Blvd
Ste 1825
Arlington, VA 22209-3901
703-907-7300
FAX: 703-907-1085
e-mail: apa@psych.org
www.psych.org

*Dilip Jeste, MD, President*
*Margaret Cawley Dewar, Director, Association Governance*
*Ardell Lockerman, Senior Governance Specialist - Board of Trustees*

The American Psychiatric Association is a medical specialty society recognized worldwide. Its over 35,000 U.S. and international member physicians work together to ensure humane care and effective treatment for all persons with mental disorder, including mental retardation and substance-related disorders. It is the voice and conscience of modern psychiatry. Its vision is a society that has avaliable, accessible quality psychiatric diagnosis and treatment.

**8083 American SIDS Institute**
528 Raven Way
Naples, FL 34110
239-431-5425
FAX: 239-431-5536
e-mail: prevent@sids.org
www.sids.org

*Betty McEntire PhD, Executive Director*
*Marc Peterzell, Chairman*

American SIDS Institute is a national nonprofit health care organization that is dedicated to the prevention of sudden infant death and the promotion of infant health through an aggressive, comprehensive nationwide program of: research, clinical services, education and family support.

**8084 American Social Health Association**
PO Box 13827
Research Triangle Park, NC 27709-3827
919-361-8400
FAX: 919-361-8425
e-mail: info@ashastd.org
www.ashastd.org

*Lynn Barclay, President/CEO*
*Deborah Arrindell, VP Health Policy*
*H. Hunter Handsfield, MD, Secretary*
*Leandro Antonio Mena, M.D., MP, Treasurer*

The American Social Health Association is recognized by the public, patients, providers and policy makers for developing and delivering accurate, medically reliable information about STDs. Public and college health clinics across the US order ASHA educational pamphlets and books to give to clients and students. Community-based organizations depend on ASHA, too, to help communicate about risk, transmission, prevention, testing, and treatment.

**8085 American Society of Pediatric Hematology/Oncology**
4700 W Lake Ave
Glenview, IL 60025-1468
847-375-4716
FAX: 847-375-4777
e-mail: info@aspho.org
www.aspho.org

*Cynthia Porter, Executive Director*
*Holcombe Grier, President*
*Amy Sherwood, Manager*
ASPHO is multidisciplinary organization dedicated to promoting optimal care of children and adolescents with blood disorders and cancer by advancing research, education, treatment and professional practice.

**8086 American Thoracic Society**
61 Broadway
New York, NY 10006-2755
212-315-8600
FAX: 212-315-6498
e-mail: atsinfo@thoracic.org
www.thoracic.org

*Steve Crane, Executive Director*
*Dean E Schraufnagel, President*
*Monica Kraft, VP*
*Nicola Black, Associate Director*
A non-profit, international, professional and scientific society for respiratory, critical care and sleep medicine. The ATS is committed to the prevention and treatment of respiratory disease through research, education, patient care and advocacy. The long-range goal of ATS is to decrease morbidity and mortality from respiratory, critical care and sleep disorders and life threatening acute illnesses in people of all ages.

**8087 Aplastic Anemia and MDS International Foundation**
Ste 108 100 Park Ave
Rockville, MD 20850
301-279-7202
800-747-2820
FAX: 301-279-7205
e-mail: help@aamds.org
www.aamds.org

*John Huber, Executive Director*
This organization, formerly known as Aplastic Anemia Foundation of America was founded in 1983. It provides a resource directory for patient assistance, produces educational material and supports research into AA and MDS.

**8088 Behavior Therapy and Research Society**
Temple University Medical School
3420 N Broad St
Philadelphia, PA 19140-5104
215-707-3133
800-331-2839
FAX: 215-707-4086
www.medschool.temple.edu

*John Daly, Dean*
*Judith Russo, Manager*
*Larry R. Kaiser, MD, FACS, Senior Executive Vice President for the Health Sciences*
This organization promotes behavior therapy by conducting and facilitating research in behavioral interventions and providing information through consultations, conferences and publications, about the use of these methods.

**8089 Canadian Cancer Society**
55 St. Clair Avenue West.
Suite 30
Toronto, ON, Canada M4V-3B1
416-961-7223
FAX: 416-961-4189
e-mail: ccs@cancer.ca
www.cancer.ca

*Anne Vezina, President/CEO*
*Heather Chapels, Director*
*Anthony Fuchs, Director*
*Dan Demers, Director*
A national community based organization of volunteers whose mission is the eradication of cancer and the enhancement of the quality of life of people living with cancer.

**8090 Canadian Diabetes Association**
1400-522 University Avenue
Toronto, ON, Canada M5G-2R5
800-226-8464
FAX: 416-408-7015
e-mail: info@diabetes.ca
www.diabetes.ca

*Michael Cloutier, President/CEO*
*Anna Kennedy, SVP/CFO*
*Doug Macnamara, Chair*
*Maureen Clement, Board of Director*
The mission of the Canadian Diabetes Association is to promote the health of Canadians through diabetes research, education, service and advocacy.

**8091 Canadian Lung Association**
1750 Courtwood Crescent
Ottawa, ON, Canada K2C-2B5
613-569-6411
888-566-5864
FAX: 613-569-8860
e-mail: info@lung.ca
www.lung.ca

*Heather Borquez, President/CEO*
*Mark Hass, Director*
The Canadian Lung Association has been dedicated to its mission of promoting and improving lung health for all Canadians. A non-profit and volunteer-based health charity, The Lung Associatin depends on donations from the public to support lung health research, education, prevention and advocacy.

**8092 Candlelighters Childhood Cancer Foundation of Canada**
21 St Clair Ave E
Ste 801
Toronto, ON, Canada M4T-1L9
416-489-6440
800-363-1062
FAX: 416-489-9812
e-mail: info@childhoodcancer.ca
www.childhoodcancer.ca

*Megan Davidson, President/CEO*
*Gillian Hill, Manager, Donor Relations*
*Melody Khodaverdian, Manager, Donor Relations*
*Dana Stanescu, Director of Marketing & Community Programs*
A national, volunteer governed, charitable organization dedicated to improving the qualtiy of life for children with cancer and their families. We will achieve our mission through undertaking and supporting national initiatives resulting in the increased survival and wellbeing of our children, and ultimately a cure for all childhood cancers.

**8093 Cerebral Palsy Associations of New York State Annual Conference**
90 State Street
Suite 929
Albany, NY 12207-1709
518-436-0178
e-mail: AffiliateServices@cpofnys.org
www.cpofnys.org

*Susan Constantino, President & CEO*
*Michael Alvaro, Executive Vice President*
*Marie Colbert, Administrative Assistant*
*Cheryl Bradway, Administrative Assistant*
Offers 50 sessions and features many outstanding presenters in areas such as assitive technology, education, health care, clinical services, public relations and development, and finance and management.
*October*

**8094 Child Neurology Service**
Inova Fairfax Hospital For Children
8110 Gatehouse Rd
Falls Church, VA 22042
703-776-2515
FAX: 703-776-4010
e-mail: tony.raker@inova.org
www.inova.org

*Knox Singleton, CEO*
*Mark Stauder, President/COO*
*Richard Magenheimer, Chief Financial Officer*
*Loring Flint, MD, Executive Vice President and Chief Medical Officer*
Offers infants and children to age 21 with neurological problems diagnosis, consultation, recommendations for therapy and more services. We also care for adults with cerebral palsy.

**8095 Children's Hemiplegia & Stroke Association**
4101 W Green Oaks Blvd
Ste 149
Arlington, TX 76016
817-478-0861
e-mail: info437@chasa.org
www.chasa.org

*Nancy Atwood, President*
*Julie Ring, VP*
*Jana Smoot White, President*
Offering support and information to families of infants, children and young adults who have hemiplegia or hemiplegic cerebral palsy.

**8096 Diabetes Exercise & Sports Association**
310 W Liberty St
Ste 604
Louisville, KY 40202-3017
502-581-0207
800-898-4322
FAX: 502-581-0206
e-mail: desa@diabetes-exercise.org
mentalhealthamerica.net

*Doug Dressman, Executive Director*
Exists to enhance the quality of life for people with diabetes through exercise and physical fitness.

**8097 Division for Physical and Health Disabilities**
1110 N Glebe Rd
Ste 300
Arlington, VA 22201-5704
866-232-7733
FAX: 703-264-9494
TTY:866-915-5000
www.cec.sped.org

*Bruce Ramirez, Executive Director*
*Twanna Clark, Senior Executive Assistant*
*Sharon Rodriguez, Senior Executive Assistant*
Advocates for quality education for individuals with physical disabilities, multiple disabilities, and special health care needs served in schools, hospitals, or home settings. DPHD's members include classroom teachers, administrators, related service personnel, hospital/homebound teachers, and parents.

**8098 Emphysema Foundation for our Right to Service**
239 NE Highway 69
Ste D
Claycomo, MO 64119
816-452-9300
FAX: 816-413-0176
e-mail: efforts-request@home.ease.lsoft.com
www.emphysema.net

*Linda Watson, President*
*Becky Collison, Treasurer*
EFFORTS is a nonprofit organization that takes an active role in promoting research for more effective treatment and perhaps a cure for emphysema and related lung diseases. It also works to further education about the disease and provides a support mailing list for members.

**8099 Environmental Health Center: Dallas**
8345 Walnut Hill Lane
Ste 220
Dallas, TX 75231-4205
214-368-4132
FAX: 214-691-8432
e-mail: contact@ehcd.com
ehcd.com

*William J Rea, Director*
*Chris Rea, Business Manager*
Clinic providing patient care in the areas of Immunotherapy, Nutrition, Physical Therapy, Chemical Depuration, Energy Balancing, Electromagnetic Sensitivity Testing, Psychological Support Services, Family Practice Medicine and Internal Medicine.

**8100 Epilepsy Foundation**
8301 Professional Pl
Landover, MD 20785-2237
301-459-3700
800-332-1000
86- 33- 271
FAX: 877-687-4878
e-mail: ContactUs@efa.org
epilepsyfoundation.org

*Phil Gattone, President/CEO*
*Brien Smith, Chair*
*Alexandra Finucane, Executive Vice President*
*Joseph I. Sirven, MD, Chair*
The Epilepsy Foundation is the national voluntary agency solely dedicated to the welfare of the 2.7 million people with epilepsy in the U.S. and their families. The organization works to ensure that people with seizures are able to participate in all life experiences; and to prevent, control and cure epilepsy through research, education, advocacy and services.

**8101 Eunice Kennedy Shriver National Institute of Child Health and Human Development (NICHD)**
National Institutes of Health (NIH)
PO Box 3006
Rockville, MD 20847-3006
301-496-5097
800-370-2943
FAX: 866-760-5947
TTY: 888-320-6942
e-mail: nichdinformationresourcecenter@mail.nih.gov
www.nichd.nih.gov

*Alan Guttmacher, Acting Director*
*Dexter Collins, Deputy Executive Office*
The NICHD, part of the federal National Institutes of Health, conducts and supports research topics related to the health of children, adults, families, and populations, including growth and development; parenting; learning and reading; and mental retardation, autism, and developmental disabilities, and provides information on these topics.

**8102 Families of Spinal Muscular Atrophy**
925 Busse Rd
PO Box 196
Elk Grove Village, IL 60007
847-367-7620
800-886-1762
FAX: 847-367-7623
e-mail: info@fsma.org
www.fsma.org

*Kenneth Hubby, President*
*Jill Jarecki, Research Director*
*Karen O'Brien, Membership*
*Colleen McCarthy O'Toole, Family Support Director*
Families of Spinal Muscular Atrophy is the largest international organization dedicated solely to: eradicating spinal muscular atrophy (SMA) by promoting and supporting research, helping families cope with SMA through informational programs and support, and educating the public and professional community about SMA.

**8103 Health Education AIDS Liason (HEAL)**
PO Box 1103
New York, NY 10113-1103
212-873-0780
FAX: 212-873-0891
e-mail: revdocnyc@aol.com
www.healaids.com

*Michael Ellner, President*
*Tom DiFerdinando, Executive Director*
*Barnett.J Weiss, Board Member*
*Robert Giraldo, Board Member*
Nonprofit, community-based educational organization providing information, hope, and support to people who are HIV positive or living with AIDS. The men and women at HEAL are health professionals, people living with life threatening diseases, and concerned volunteers.

**8104 Herpes Resource Center**
American Social Health Association
P.O.Box 13827
Research Triangle Park, NC 27709-3827
919-361-8400
800-227-8922
FAX: 919-361-8425
e-mail: info@ashastd.org
www.ashastd.org

*Lynn Barclay, President/CEO*
*Deborah Arrindell, VP, Health Policy*
*H. Hunter Handsfield, MD, Secretary*
*Leandro Antonio Mena, M.D., MP, Treasurer*
The Herpes Resource Center (HRC) focuses on increasing education, public awareness, and support to anyone concerned about herpes. Since its formation in 1979, the HRC has helped over five million people. The work of the HRC is funded primarily through individual gifts, subscriptions and product sales, with additional support in the form of corporate contributions. Today, people continue to depend on ASHA and the HRC for educational information about herpes.

**8105 International Academy of Biological Dentistry and Medicine**
19122 Camellia Bend Circle
Ste 101
Spring, TX 77379
281-651-1745
FAX: 281-440-1258
e-mail: drdawn@drdawn.net
www.iabdm.org

*John Trowbridge, President*
*Gary Verigni, Co-Founder*
*Ed Arana, Co-Founder*
Promotes non-toxic diagnostic and therapeutic approaches in dentistry; hosts seminars on biological diagnosis and therapy.

**8106 International Academy of Oral Medicine and Toxicology**
8297 Champions Gate Blvd
Ste 193
Champions Gate, FL 33896-8387
863-420-6373
FAX: 863-419-8136
e-mail: info@iaomt.org
iaomt.org

*Maths Berlin, Advisor*
*Boyd Haley, PhD, FIAOMT, Chairman*
*Kym Smith, Executive Director*
Nonprofit organization dedicated to funding solid peer-reviewed scientific research in the area of toxic substances used in dentistry as well as providing continuing education and carefully reviewed procedures, protocols, and methodologies to reduce the risk for patients and professionals.

**8107 International Association for Cancer Victors: Northern California Chapter**
POB 745
Lakeport, CA 95158
408-834-5300
FAX: 408-264-9659
e-mail: contact@cancervictors.net
http://www.cancervictors.net

*Cecile Pollack Hoffman, Founder*
Volunteer community service organization to inform and support interested persons who want to learn more about natural, non-toxic remedies and practices.

**8108 International Association of Hygienic Physicians-IAHP**
4620 Euclid Blvd
Youngstown, OH 44512-1633
330-788-0526
FAX: 330-788-0093
e-mail: alecburton@dodo.com.au
www.iahp.net

*Alec Burton, Co-Founder*
*Mark A Huberman, Secretary/Treasurer*
Members are licensed, primary care physicians who specialize in therapeutic fasting supervision.

**8109 International Medical and Dental Hypnotherapy Association**
Box 2468
Rr 2
Laceyville, PA 18623-9417
570-869-1021
800-553-6886
FAX: 570-869-1249
http://www.imdha.com

*Robert Otto, President/CEO*
*Linda Otto, Executive Director*
*Christie Boecker, Services Coordinator*
*Diane Meislohn, Membership Online Services*
provides and encourages education programs to further the knowledge, understanding and application of hypnosis in complimentary health care; to encourage research and scientific publications in the field of hypnosis; to promote the further recognition and acceptance of hypnosis as an important tool in health care and focus for scientific research; to cooperate with other professional organizations that share mutual goals, ethics, and interests and provide professional community who use hypnosis.

**8110 International Myeloma Foundation**
12650 Riverside Dr
Ste 206
North Hollywood, CA 91607- 3421
818-487-7455
800-452-2873
FAX: 818-487-7454
e-mail: theimf@myeloma.org
www.myeloma.org

*Susie Novis, President*
*David Girard, Executive Director*
*Diane Moran, Senior Vice President, Strategic Planning*
*Jennifer Scarne, Chief Financial Officer*
Dedicated to improving the quality of life of myeloma patients while working toward prevention and a cure.

**8111 International Ozone Association**
PO Box 28873
Scottsdale, AZ 85255
480-529-3787
FAX: 480-473-9068
e-mail: infO3zone@io3a.org
www.io3a.org

The IOA is a not-for-profit educational association which performs its information-sharing functions through sponsorship of international symposia, seminars, publications, and the development of personal relationships among ozone specialists throughout the world.

**8112 International Rett Syndrome Foundation**
4600 Devitt Dr
Cincinnati, OH 45246-1104 513-847-3020
800-818-7388
FAX: 513-874-2520
e-mail: admin@rettsyndrome.org
www.rettsyndrome.org

*Stephen E Bajardi, Executive Director*
*Mary Joyce Griffin, Administrative Officer*
*Paige Nues, Family Support Director*
*Steven Kaminsky, Ph.D., Chief Science Officer*
The core mission of the IRSF is to fund research for treatments and a cure for Rett syndrome while enhancing the overall quality of life for those living with Rett syndrome by providing information, programs, and services.

**8113 Leukemia and Lymphoma Society**
1311 Mamaroneck Ave
Ste 310
White Plains, NY 10605-5228 914-949-5213
800-955-4572
FAX: 914-949-0391
e-mail: infocenter@lls.org
www.leukemia.org

*John Walter, CEO*
*Louis DeGennaro, Executive VP*
*George Omiros, CFRE, CAE, Executive Vice President of Campaign & Field Development*
*Jimmy Nangle, Chief Financial Officer*
The Leukemia and Lymphoma Society is the world's largest voluntary health organization dedicated to funding blood cancer research, education and patient services. Thier mission: cure leukemia, lymphoma, Hodgkin's disease and myeloma, and improve the quality of life of patients and their families. Since its founding in 1949, the Society has invested more then $483 million for research specifically targeting blood cancers.

**8114 Little People of America**
250 El Camino Real
Ste 201
Tustin, CA 92780 714-368-3689
888-572-2001
FAX: 714-368-3367
e-mail: info@lpaonline.org
www.lpaonline.org

*Lois Gerage-Lamb, President*
*Bill Bradford, Senior VP*
*Jon North, VP Programs*
*Joanna Campbell, Executive Director*
Assists dwarfs with their physical and developmental concerns resulting from short stature, usually no taller then 4' 10 inches. Provides medical, environmental, educational, vocational, and parental guidance, so that short-statured individuals and their families may enhance their lives and lifestyles with minimal limitations.

**8115 Lymphoma Foundation Canada**
16-1375 Southdown Rd
Mississauga, ON, Canada L5J-2Z1 905-822-5135
866-659-5556
FAX: 905-814-9152
e-mail: info@lymphoma.ca
www.lymphoma.ca

*Sue Robson, Executive Director*
*Jan Coleman, Program Coordinator*
*John Sutherland, Treasurer*
*Tanja Loeb , National Director, Programs and Operations*
We provide information on new treatments and research, as well as support patient education workshops and seminars to help people understand and manage their cancer. We support lymphoma-specific research through the creation of fellowships, as well as provide community-based resources to help people learn about and cope with their cancer.

**8116 Medic Alert Foundation International**
2323 Colorado Ave
Turlock, CA 95382-2018 209-668-3333
e-mail: customer_service@medicalert.org
www.medicalert.org

*Andrew B Wigglesworth, President/CEO*
*Shilpun Patel, CFO*
*Karen M. Lamoree, Chief Operating Officer*
*Ramesh Srinivasan, Senior Vice President of Marketing and Business Development*
Emergency medallions and bracelets containing emergency medical information and 24-hour emergency information telephone services.

**8117 Mental Health America**
2000 N Beauregard St
6th Fl
Alexandria, VA 22311 703-684-7722
800-969-6642
FAX: 703-684-5968
mentalhealthamerica.net

*David Shern, CEO*
*Dianne Felton, Senior Vice President of Operations*
*Julie Nicholson Burke, Vice President of Finance and Human Resources*
*Mike Turner, Vice President of Development*
Nonprofit organization addressing all issues related to mental health and mental illness. With more than 340 affiliates nationwide, NMHA works to improve the mental health of all Americans, especially the 54 million individuals with mental disorders, through advocacy, education, research and service.

**8118 Multiple Sclerosis Association of America**
706 Haddonfield Rd
Cherry Hill, NJ 8002-2652 856-488-4500
800-532-7667
FAX: 856-661-9797
e-mail: webmaster@msassociation.org
www.msassociation.org

*Douglas Franklin, President*
*Cindy Richman, Senior Director of Services*
A national non-profit organization dedicated to enriching the quality of life for everyone affected by multiple sclerosis. MSAA provides ongoing support and direct services to these individuals with MS and the people close to them. MSAA also serves to promote greater understanding of the needs and challenges of those who face physical obstacles.

**8119 Multiple Sclerosis Center of Oregon**
Oregon Health & Sciences University
3181 SW Sam Jackson Park Rd
Portland, OR 97239-3098 503-494-5759
FAX: 503-494-3480
www.ohsu.edu

*Joseph Robertson Jr MBA, President*
*Steven D Stadum JD, Executive VP*
OHSU's fundamental purpose is to improve the well-being of people in Oregon and beyond. As part of its multifaceted public mission, OHSU strives for excellence in education, research, clinical practice, scholarship and community service. Through its dynamic interdisciplinary environment, OHSU stimulates the spirit of inquiry, initiative and cooperation among students, faculty and staff.

**8120 Multiple Sclerosis Foundation**
6350 N Andrews Ave
Fort Lauderdale, FL 33309-2130
954-776-6805
800-225-6495
FAX: 954-938-8708
e-mail: admin@msfocus.org
www.msfocus.org

*Jules Kuperberg, Executive Director*
*Michael Austin, Vice President, Director*
*John Blackstock, Secretary Director*
*Alan Segaloff, Executive Director*

Contemporary national, nonprofit organization that provides free support services and public education for persons with Multiple Sclerosis, newsletters, toll-free phone support, information, referrals, home care, assitive technology, and support groups.

**8121 Myositis Association**
1737 King Street
Ste 600
Alexandria, VA 22314
703-299-4850
800-821-7356
FAX: 703-535-6752
e-mail: tma@myositis.org
www.myositis.org

*Bob Goldberg, Executive Director*
*Theresa Reynolds Curry, Communications Manager*
*Aisha Morrow, Operations Manager*

The Myositis Association is dedicated to finding a cure for inflammatory and other related myopathies, while serving those affected by these diseases. The aim of TMA's programs and services is to provide information, support, advocacy and research for those concerned about myositis. Support groups offer members the chance to share their feelings and discuss their concerns with people in similar situations. These groups encourage an atmosphere of communication and compassion.

**8122 National AIDS Fund**
1424 K Street, N.W., Suite 200
Washington, DC 20005-1511
202-408-4848
888-234-2437
FAX: 202-408-1818
e-mail: info@aidsfund.org
www.aidsfund.org

*Victor.A Barnes, Interim President & CEO*
*Rob Banaszak, Communications Director*
*Vignetta Charles, Ph.D., Senior Vice President*
*Alanna Adams, Program Associate*

The National AIDS Fund was founded in 1988 to reduce the incidence and impact of HIV/AIDS by promoting leadership and generating resources for effective community responses to the epidemic. Through its unique expanding network of Community Partnerships, NAF supports over 400 grassroots organizations annually which in turn provide HIV prevention, care and support services to underserved individuals and populations most impacted by HIV/AIDS including communities of color, youth and women.

**8123 National Association for Children of Alcoholics**
10920 Connecticut Avenue
Suite 100
Kensington, MD 20895-3007
301-468-0985
888-554-2627
FAX: 301-468-0987
e-mail: nacoa@nacoa.org
www.nacoa.org

*Sis Wenger, President/CEO*
*Steve Hornberger, Program Director*

National non-profit membership and affiliate organization working on behalf of children of alcohol and drug dependent parents. NACoA has publications available for the individual as well as the professional in the field.

**8124 National Association for Continence**
P.O.Box 1019
Charleston, SC 29402-1019
843-377-0900
800-252-3337
FAX: 843-377-0905
e-mail: memberservices@nafc.org
www.nafc.org

*Katherine F Jeter EdD, Founder*
*Nancy Muller, Executive Director*
*Meghan Hansen, Membership and Fund Development*

NAFC's mission is to educate the public about the causes, diagnosis, categories, treatment options and management alternatives for incontinence, voiding disfunction and related pelvic floor disorders. To network with other organizations and agencies to elevate the visibility and priority given to these areas; and to advocate on behalf of consumers who suffer from such symptoms as a result of disease or other illness.

**8125 National Association for Home Care & Hospice**
228 7th St SE
Washington, DC 20003-4306
202-547-7424
FAX: 202-547-3540
e-mail: webmaster@nahc.org
nahc.org

*Val Halamandaris, President/Executive Director*

This is a non-profit trade association representing various home care, hospice and health aid organizations. Website contains a section with information on how to choose a home care provider and a zip code driven locator for home care and hospice. Publishes monthly newsletter.

**8126 National Association for Medical Direction of Respiratory Care**
8618 Westwood Center Dr
Ste 210
Vienna, VA 22182-2222
703-752-4359
FAX: 703-752-4360
e-mail: execoffice@namdrc.org
www.namdrc.org

*Phillip Porte, Executive Director*
*Vickie Parshall, Member Services Director*

A national organization of physicians whose mission is to educate its members and address regulatory, legislative and payment issues that relate to the delivery of healthcare to patients with respiratory disorders. NAMDRC's primary mission is to improve access to quality care for patients with respiratory disease by removing regulatory and legislative barriers to appropriate treatment.

**8127 National Association for Proton Therapy**
1301 Highland Dr
Silver Spring, MD 20910-1623
301-587-6100
FAX: 301-565-0747
e-mail: lenarzt@proton-therapy.org
proton-therapy.org

*Leonard Arzt, Executive Director*

Promotes the clinical benefits of proton beam radiation therapy for cancer patients and their families. It serves as a resource center for cancer patients and their families, physicians and health care providers, academic medical centers, cancer centers, the US Centers for Medicare and Medicaid Services (CMS) and other federal health care agencies, members of Congress and staff, and the nation's news media.

**8128 National Association for the Dually Diagnosed**
132 Fair St
Kingston, NY 12401-4802
845-331-4336
800-331-5362
FAX: 845-331-4569
e-mail: info@thenadd.org
thenadd.org

*Robert Fletcher, CEO*

Promotes awareness of, and services for individuals who have co-occuring intellectual disability and mental illness. NADD provides training and consultation services.

**8129 National Association of Anorexia Nervosa and Associated Disorders**
1530 Old Skokie Rd
Highland Park, IL 60035
847-831-3438
FAX: 847-433-4632
e-mail: anadhelp@anad.org
www.anad.org

*Laura Discipio, Executive Director*

A non-profit corporation that seeks to alleviate the problems of eating disorders, especially anorexia nervosa and bulimia nervosa.

**8130 National Association of Chronic Disease Directors**
2872 Woodcock Blvd
Ste 220
Atlanta, GA 30341-4096
770-458-7400
FAX: 770-458-7401
e-mail: jrobitscher@chronicdisease.org
www.chronicdisease.org

*John Robitscher, Executive Director*
*Jillian Jacobellis, PhD, MS, President*
*David M. Vigil, MBA, Treasurer*
*Pama Joyner, Secretary*

A national public health association, founded in 1988 to link the chronic disease program directors of each state and US territory to provide a national forum for chronic disease prevention and control efforts. Since its founding, NACDD has made impressive strides in mobilizing national efforts to reduce chronic diseases and the associated risk factors.

**8131 National Association of Cognitive Behavioral Therapists**
PO Box 2195
Weirton, WV 26062-1395
304-723-3982
800-853-1135
FAX: 304-723-3982
e-mail: nacbt@nacbt.org
www.nacbt.org

*Aldo R Pucci, President*

An organization dedicated solely to the teaching and practice of cognitive-behavioral psychotherapy. The mission of the NACBT is two fold: to promote and support the teaching and practice of cognitive-behavioral psychotherapy and to support those professionals and students seeking to practice it; and to set standards for credentialing that enable the general public to be confident that they will receive quality CBT from our certified members.

**8132 National Association of Epilepsy Centers**
5775 Wayzata Blvd
Ste 200
Minneapolis, MN 55416-1227
952-525-4562
888-525-6232
FAX: 952-525-1560
e-mail: info@naec-epilepsy.org
www.naec-epilepsy.org

*David.M Labiner, President*
*Nathan.B Fountain, VP*
*Susan T. Herman, Secretary/Treasurer*

NAEC educates public and private policy makers and regulators about appropriate patient care standards, reimbusement and medical services policies. NAEC is designed to complement, not compete with, the efforts of existing scientific and charitable epilepsy organizations.

**8133 National Association of People with AIDS**
8401 Colesville Rd
Ste 505
Silver Spring, MD 20910-3349
240-247-0880
866-846-9366
FAX: 240-247-0574
e-mail: development@napwa.org
www.napwa.org

*Frank Oldham, President/CEO*
*Stephen Bailous, Executive VP*
*Matt Lesieur, Vice President for Public Policy*
*Leslie Talley, Vice President for Development*

The NAPWA believes in making a difference in the lives of our constituents. They also provide information and resources.

**8134 National Association to Advance Fat Acceptance**
PO Box 22510
Oakland, CA 94609
916-558-6880
FAX: 916-558-6881
www.naafa.org

*Jason Docherty, Chair*
*Lisa Tealer, Director of Programs & Treasurer*
*Peggy Howell , Public Relations Director*
*Phyllis Warr, Membership and Member Services Director*

A non-profit human rights organization dedicated to improving the quality of life for fat people. NAAFA works to eliminate discrimination based on body size and provide fat people with the tools for self-empowerment through public education, advocacy, and member support.

**8135 National Ataxia Foundation**
2600 Fernbrrok Ln
Ste 119
Minneapolis, MN 55447-4752
763-553-0020
FAX: 763-553-0167
e-mail: naf@ataxia.org
www.ataxia.org

*DeNiece Roach, President*
*Charlene Danielson, VP*
*Michael Parent, Executive Director*
*William P. Sweeney, Treasurer*

The National Ataxia Foundation is a nonprofit, membership-supported organization established in 1957 to help ataxia families. The Foundation is dedicated to improving the lives of persons affected by ataxia through support, education, and research.

**8136 National Autism Association**
20 Alice Agnew Drive
Attleboro Falls,, MA 02763
877-622-2884
FAX: 774-643-6331
e-mail: naa@nationalautism.org
www.nationalautismassociation.org

*Rita Shreffler, Administrator/Executive Director*
*Wendy Fournier, President*
*Ann Brasher, VP*
*Joanne Quinn, Treasurer*

The mission of the National Autism Association is to educate and empower families affected by autism and other neurological disorders, while advocating on behalf of those who cannot fight for their own rights.

**8137 National Brachial Plexus/Erb's Palsy Association**
P.O.Box 23
Larsen, WI 54947-23
920-836-2151
FAX: 920-836-5813
e-mail: info@nbpepa.org
www.nbpepa.org

*Brenda Copeland-Moore, President*
*Kris Kiesow, Treasurer*
*Cheryl Pratt, VP*
*Donna Schott, VP*

To educate, inform, and assist those affected by Brachial Plexus Palsy by offering information, contacts, resources, parent matching, and assistance developing chapters or support groups throughout the United States. National Brachial Plexus/Erb's Palsy Association, Inc. Programs include parent matching services, assistance forming chapters, or support groups, provide support to families dealing with children with diagnosis of Brachial Plexus Injury & Erb's Palsy as well as other conditions.

**8138 National Cancer Institute**
6116 Executive Blvd
Ste 300
Bethesda, MD 20892-8322
301-496-0909
800-422-6237
TTY:800-332-8615
e-mail: cancergovstaff@mail.nih.gov
www.cancer.gov

*Harold Varmos, Director*
The National Cancer Institute coordinates the National Cancer Program, which conducts and supports research, training, health information dissemination, and other programs with respect to the cause, diagnosis, prevention, and treatment of cancer, rehabilitation from cancer, and the continuing care of cancer patients and the families of cancer patients.

**8139 National Children's Leukemia Foundation**
7316 Avenue U
Brooklyn, NY 11234-6250
718-251-1222
800-448-4673
FAX: 718-251-1444
e-mail: info@leukemiafoundation.org
www.leukemiafoundation.org

*Yehuda Guttwein, President*
Provides the cure for cancer and other life-threatening diseases throughout the world, and to insure that all persons, regardless of race, religion, ethnicity, gender, socioeconomic status or country of residence, have access to life-saving medical care. The NCLF supports medical research and direct patient care programs that ease the financial, social and psychological burdens of families with a diagnosis of cancer or other serious blood disorders.

**8140 National Diabetes Information Clearinghouse**
1 Information Way
Bethesda, MD 20892-3560
800-860-8747
FAX: 703-738-4929
TTY:866-569-1162
e-mail: ndic@info.niddk.nih.gov
www.diabetes.niddk.nih.gov

*Michael T Sheppard CPA CAE, Executive Director*
An information and referral service of the National Institute of Diabetes and Digestive and Kidney Diseases, one of the National Institutes of Health. The clearinghouse responds to written inquiries, develops and distributes publications about diabetes, and provides referrals to diabetes organizations, including support groups. The NDIC maintains a database of patient and professional education materials, from which literature searches are generated.

**8141 National Digestive Diseases Information Clearinghouse**
2 Information Way
Bethesda, MD 20892-3570
800-891-5389
FAX: 703-738-4929
TTY:866-559-1162
e-mail: nddic@info.niddk.nih.gov
www.digestive.niddk.nih.gov

*Stephen P. James M.D., Executive Editor*
Information and referral service of the National Institute of Diabetes and Digestive and Kidney Diseases. A central information resource on the prevention and management of digestive diseases, the clearinghouse responds to written inquiries, develops and distributes publications about digestive diseases, provides referrals to digestive disease organizations and support groups, and maintains a database of patient and professional education materials from which literature searches are generated.

**8142 National Fibromyalgia Association**
2121 S Towne Centre Pl
Ste 300
Anaheim, CA 92806-6124
714-921-0150
FAX: 714-921-6920
e-mail: shausen@fmaware.org
www.fmaware.org

*Lynne Matallana, President*
*Mark Dobrilovic, Board of Director*
*John Fry, PhD, Board of Director*
*Michael Seffinger, DO, FAAFP, Board of Director*
National Fibromyalgia Association's mission is to develop and execute programs dedicated to improving the quality of life for people with fibromyalgia.

**8143 National Fragile X Foundation**
1615 Bonanza St. Suite 202 PO Box 3
Walnut Creek, CA 94597
925-938-9300
800-688-8765
FAX: 925-938-9315
e-mail: NATLFX@FragileX.org
www.fragilex.org

*Robert Miller, Executive Director*
*Michael Kelley, President*
*Linda Sorensen, MS, Associate Director*
*David Salomon, Communications Coordinator*
Unites the fragile X community to enrich lives through educational and emotional support, promote public and professional awareness and advance research toward improvement treatments and cure for fragile X syndrome.

**8144 National Hemophilia Foundation**
116 W 32nd St
Fl 11
New York, NY 10001-3212
212-328-3700
800-424-2634
FAX: 212-328-3777
e-mail: handi@hemophilia.org
www.hemophilia.org

*Val Bias, CEO*
*Neil Frick, VP Research*
*John Indence, Vice President for Marketing & Communications*
*Joseph J. Kleiber, Senior Vice President for Chapter Services*
The National Hemophilia Foundation is dedicated to finding better treatments and cures for bleeding and clotting disorders and to preventing the complications of these disorders through education,advocacy and research. Established in 1948, The National Hemophilia Foundation has chapters throughout the country. Its programs and initiatives are made possible through the generosity of individuals, corporations, and foundations as well as through the Centers for Disease Controll and Prevention (CDC)

**8145 National Hydrocephalus Foundation**
12413 Centralia St
Lakewood, CA 90715-1653
562-924-6666
888-857-3434
e-mail: nhf@earthlink.net
www.nhfonline.org

*Debbi Fields, Executive Director*
*Michael Fields, President*
*Jaynie Dunn, Secretary*
*Sarah Dunn, Junior Director*
Assembles and disseminates information pertaining to hydrocephalus, its treatments and outcomes. Establishes and facilitates a communication network among affected families and individuals.

**8146 National Kidney and Urologic Diseases Information Clearinghouse**
3 Information Way
Bethesda, MD 20892-3580
800-891-5390
FAX: 703-738-4929
TTY:866-569-1162
e-mail: nkudic@info.niddk.nih.org
www.kidney.niddk.nih.gov

*Mel Eagle, Manager*
*Griffin P. Rogers M.D., Director*
NKUDIC was established in 1987 to increase knowledge and understanding about diseases of the kidneys and urologic system among people with these conditions and their families, health care professionals, and the general public.

**8147 National Organization for Albinism and Hypopigmentation**
PO Box 959
E Hampstead, NH 03826-0959
603-887-2310
800-473-2310
FAX: 800-648-2310
e-mail: info@albinism.org
www.albinism.org

*Michael McGowan, Executive Director*
*Kelsey Thompson, Chair*
*Donna Appell, Vice-Chair*
*Kelsey Thompson, Secretary*
Offers information and support to people with albinism, their families and the professionals who work with them.

**8148 National Organization on Fetal Alcohol Syndrome**
1200 Eton Ct NW
Washington, DC 20007-3239
202-785-4585
800-666-6327
FAX: 202-466-6456
e-mail: information@nofas.org
www.nofas.org

*Tom Donaldson, President*
*Kathleen Tavenner Mitchell, VP*
*Brianna Montgomery, Program Manager*
*Andy Kachor, Media and Communications Coordinator*
Dedicated to eliminating birth defects caused by alcohol consumption during pregnancy and improving the qualtiy of life for those individuals and families affected.

**8149 National Service Dog Center**
Delta Society
875 124th Ave NE
Ste 101
Bellevue, WA 98005-2531
425-679-5500
FAX: 425-379-5539
e-mail: info@deltasociety.org
www.deltasociety.org

*R.Stephen Browning, President/CEO*
*Michelle Matheson, Director of Finance*
*Jill F. Bentler, Executive Assistant*
*Jayne Ryan, Therapy Animal Program Coordinator*
A service of the Delta Society, provides information about the selection, training, stewardship, and roles of service dogs; referral to service dog training programs and related resources; education to businesses and health care professionals regarding service dog issues; research assistance through a resource library and network of professional experts and advocacy on behalf of people with service dogs.

**8150 Okada Specialty Guide Dogs**
543 Esteppe Rd
Front Royal, VA 22630
540-635-3937
FAX: 352-344-0210
e-mail: okada@okadadogs.com
www.okadadogs.com

*Pat Putnam, Director*
Trains dogs to aid deaf, hearing-impaired, Alzheimer's, seizure, amnesia and residential companion guide dogs.

**8151 Ontario Cerebral Palsy Sports Association**
7-46 Antares Dr
Nepean, ON, Canada K2E-7Z1
613-723-1806
866-286-2772
FAX: 613-723-6742
www.ocpsa.on.ca

*Amanda Fader, Executive Director*
*Don Sinclair, President*
*Steven Dukovich, VP*
*Don Borsk, Treasurer*
Believes in the value of sport and that sport builds success in all aspects of life. It provides, promotes and coordinates competitive opportunities as well as encourages individual excellence through sport for athletes within the cerebral palsy family. To that end, OCPSA recruits, develops and supports athletes, coaches and volunteers.

**8152 Ontario Federation for Cerebral Palsy**
104-1630 Lawrence Avenue W
Toronto, ON, Canada M6L-1C5
416-244-9686
877-244-9686
FAX: 416-244-6543
e-mail: info@ofcp.on.ca
www.ofcp.on.ca

*Clarence Meyers, Executive Director*
*Gordana Skrba, Assistant Executive Director*
*Steve Chandler, Senior Manager*
*Syed Alam, Operations Manager*
Assisting individuals and member groups in the development and provision of services and programs including accommodation in all parts of the province of Ontario.

**8153 Overeaters Anonymous World Service Office**
PO Box 44020
Rio Rancho, NM 87174-4020
505-891-2664
FAX: 505-891-4320
e-mail: info@oa.org
www.oa.org

*Naomi Lippel, Manager*
OA is not just about weight loss, obesity or diets; it addresses physical, emotional and spiritual well-being. It is not a religious organization and does not promote any particular diet. To address weight loss, OA encourages members to develop a food plan with a health care professional and a sponsor.

**8154 People Against Cancer**
604 East Street PO Box 10
Otho, IA 50569
515-972-4444
800-662-2623
FAX: 515-972-4415
e-mail: info@PeopleAgainstCancer.net
www.peopleagainstcancer.com

*Frank Wiewel, Executive Director*
Publication of People Against Cancer, a nonprofit, grassroots, public benefit organization dedicated to 'New Directions in the War on Cancer.' We are a democratic organization of people with cancer, their loved ones and citizens working together to protect and enhance medical freedom of choice.
*8 pages*

**8155 Prader-Willi Alliance of New York**
PO Box 222
Baldwinsville, NY 13027
716-276-2211
800-442-1655
FAX: 315-320-0443
e-mail: alliance@prader-willi.org
www.prader-willi.org

*Amy McDougall, President*
*Harry Persanis, VP*
*Henry Singer, VP*
To provide information to the general public about Prader-Willi syndrome (PWS):|to promote awareness of PWS among the general public and medical professionals; to provide forms for

discussion and professional interchange on the subject of PWS. To provide assistance, information, referral, and advocacy services to families and friends of persons suffering from PWS. To encourage and support research into the causes, cure and treatment of PWS.

**8156 Prader-Willi Syndrome Association USA**
8588 Potter Park Drive
Suite 500
Sarasota, FL 34238
941-312-0400
800-926-4797
FAX: 941-312-0142
e-mail: pwsausa@pwsausa.org
www.pwsausa.org

*Craig Polhemus, Executive Director*
*Janalee Heinemannh, Dir Research & Medical Affairs*
*Dale Cooper, Interim Executive Director*
*Dottie Cooper, Interim Executive Director*
National, nonprofit public charity that works for the benefit of individuals with Prader-Willi syndrome and their families. An organization of parents and others who are making a difference in the lives of those with Prader-Willi syndrome. Dedicated to serving individuals affected by Prader-Willi syndrome (PWS) their families, and interested professionals. To provide information, education, and support services to its members.

**8157 Rasmussen's Syndrome and Hemispherectomy Support Network**
8235 Lethbridge Rd
Millersville, MD 21108-1609
410-987-5221
FAX: 410-987-521
e-mail: rssnlynn@aol.com

*Al & Lynn Miller, Founders*
National not-for-profit organization dedicated to providing information and support to individuals affected by Rasmussen's Syndrome and Hemispherectomy. Publishes a periodic newsletter and disseminates reprints of medical journal articles concerning Rasmussen's Syndrome and its treatments. Maintains a support network that provides encouragement and information to individuals affected by Rasmussen's Syndrome and their families.

**8158 Scientific Health Solutions**
1621 N Circle Dr
Colorado Springs, CO 80909-2407
719-548-1600
800-331-2303
FAX: 719-572-8081
www.tomlevymd.com/serumtest.htm

*Blanche Grube, Owner*
*Thomas Levy, President*
SHS seeks to help those who are looking to avoid new dental toxicity by offering serum biocompatibility testing to help guide the choice of replacement dental materials. Every attempt is also made to help these people find dentists who are familiar with the testing, as well as with the general concepts of dental toxicity that are addressed on TomLevyMD.com

**8159 Simon Foundation for Continence**
PO Box 815
Wilmette, IL 60091-815
847-864-3913
800-237-4666
FAX: 847-864-9758
e-mail: cbgartley@simonfoundation.org
www.simonfoundation.org

*Cheryle B Gartley, Founder/President*
*Anita Saltmarche, VP*
*Twila Yednock, Director of Special Events*
*Elizabeth LaGro, Director of Communications*
Publishes items of interest to people with bladder or bowel incontinence, including medical articles, helpful devices, publications and a pen pal list.

**8160 Simonton Cancer Center**
PO Box 6607
Malibu, CA 90264-6607
818-879-7904
800-459-3424
FAX: 310-457-0421
e-mail: simontoncancercenter@msn.com
www.simontoncenter.com

*O Carl Simonton, Founder*
*Mariusz Wirga, Medical Director*
*Karen Smith Simonton, Executive / Program Director*
*Jessica Jedvaj, BA, Administrative Assistant*
The Simonton Cancer Center offers a 'New Patient Program' for cancer patients and their support person. In these sessions, Dr. Simonton presents the refined specific information for increasing survival, decreasing tumor growth and most important, improving the quality of life of the individual.

**8161 Spina Bifida Association**
4590 Macarthur Blvd NW
Washington, DC 20007-4226
202-944-3285
800-621-3141
FAX: 202-944-3295
e-mail: sbaa@sbaa.org
www.sbaa.org

*Cindy Brownstein, President and Chief Executive Officer*
*Robin Austin, Communications Manager*
*Amanda Darnley, Director of Communications & Marketing*
*Carmen J. Head, Director, Education & Support Services*
Nonprofit organization. Mission is to promote the prevention of spina bifida and to enhance the lives of all affected. Addresses the specific needs of the spina bifida community and serves as the national representative of almost 60 chapters. Toll free 800 information and referral service. Legislative updates.

**8162 Spina Bifida and Hydrocephalus Association of Canada**
Suite 647-167 Av Lombard Avenue
Winnipeg, MB, Canada R3B- 0V3
204-925-3650
800-565-9488
FAX: 204-925-3654
e-mail: info@sbhac.ca
www.sbhac.ca

*Colleen Tablot, President/Executive Director*
*Linda Randall, VP*
*Pauline Dooley, Treasurer*
*Lorelei Fletcher, Secretary*
The Spina Bifida and Hydrocephalus Association of Canada has been working on behalf of people with spina bifida and/or hydrocephalus and their families.

**8163 Taking Control of Your Diabetes (TCOYD)**
1110 Camino Del Mar
Ste B
Del Mar, CA 92014-2649
858-755-5683
800-998-2693
FAX: 858-755-6854
e-mail: info@tcoyd.org
www.tcoyd.org

*Sandra Bourdette, Co-Founder/Executive Director*
*Steven V Edelman, Founder/Director*
*Jill Yapo, Director of Operations*
*Roz Hodgins, Director, External Affairs*
Taking Control of Your Diabetes works to educate and motivate people with diabetes to take a more active role in their condition and to provide innovative and integrative continuing diabetes education to medical professionals caring for people with diabetes.

8164 **Tourette Syndrome Association**
4240 Bell Blvd
Bayside, NY 11361-2874
718-224-2999
888-486-8738
FAX: 718-279-9596
e-mail: ts@tsa-usa.org
www.tsa-usa.org

*Judit Ungar, President*
*Kevin St. P. McNaught, Vice President, Medical and Scientific Programs*
*Gary Frank, Executive Vice President*
*Dan Rostan, Vice President, Field Services*

National, nonprofit membership organization. Mission is to identify the cause of, find the cure for, and control the effects of this disorder. A growing number of local chapters nationwide provide educational materials, seminars, conferences and support groups for over 35,000 members. Publishes brochures, flyers, educational materials and papers on treatment and research. Offers videos for purchase through a catalog of publications.

8165 **United Cerebral Palsy**
1825 K Street NW
Suite 600
Washington, DC 20006
202-776-0406
800-872-5827
FAX: 202-776-0414
e-mail: info@ucp.org
www.ucp.org

*Stephen Bennett, President/CEO*
*Marc Irlandez, Director of Technology & Life Labs*
*Tanneka Jones, Director of Finance*
*Giselle Pole, Director of Development*

National not-for-profit self-help organization dedicated to providing information and support to individuals with Cerebral Palsy and other disabilities, and their families. Supports more than 160 local affiliates; these affiliates provide a variety of programs and services for affected families, including support groups. Offers several educational and support materials, including a quarterly magazine, regular newsletters, and research reports.

8166 **United Cerebral Palsy of New York City**
80 Maiden Lane
8th Floor
New York, NY 10038
212-683-6700
800-484-3827
e-mail: info@ucpnyc.org
ucpnyc.org

*Linda B. Laul, Associate Executive Director, Program Services*
*Edward R. Matthews, CEO*
*Celia T. Solomita, Assistant Executive Director for Program Planning and Development*
*Rajesh Shah, Chief Financial Officer*

Has a more than 60 year history in the disability field and currently serves 14,000 individuals and family members through more than 75 programs. Its mission is to provide the highest quality services in health care, education, employment, housing and technology resources that support people with cerebral palsy and related disabilities in leading independent and productive lives.

8167 **Universal Institute: Rehab & Fitness Center**
15-17 Microlab Rd
Ste 101
Livingston, NJ 07039
973-992-8181
800-468-5440
FAX: 973-992-9797
www.uirehab.com

*Adam Steinberg, President*
*Lisa Lasso, VP CFO*

Universal institute is a 15,000 square foot, state of the art rehabilitation facility that specializes in neurological disorders such as brain injuries, spinal cord injury, strokes, etc. We offer PT, OT, speech patholgy, cognitive remediation, aqua therapy and EMG biofeedback.

## Camps

8168 **ADA Camp Grenada**
American Diabetes Association
Chatham Rd
Suite 210
Springfield, IL 62704
217-875-9011
FAX: 217-726-2260
e-mail: volunteerupdates@diabetes.org.
diabetes.org

*Donna Scott, Executive Director*

Camp Granada is an American Diabetes Association resident Camp located in Monticello, Illinois at the 4H Memorial Camp owned by the University of Illinois. For children with diabetes, ages 8-16. Activities include swimming, canoeing, wall climbing, tie-dying shirts, arts & crafts and fun filled evening programs.

8169 **ADA Camp Kushtaka**
American Diabetes Association
801 W. Fireweed Lane
Suite 103
Anchorage, AK 99503-1893
907-272-1424
800-342-2383
FAX: 907-272-1428
e-mail: pbell@diabetes.org
www.childrenwithdiabetes.com

*Lori Cowie, Executive Director*
*Pam Bell, Organizer*
*Katherine Swartz, Program Director*

ADA Camp Kushtaka is for children ages 7-17 with diabetes and their family (space permitting) and is located on the shores of Kenai Lake on the Kenai Peninsula in Cooper Landing. Camp is held in June and combines ongoing and informal diabetes management and education along with the fun of outdoor activities such as hiking, canoeing, crafts and swimming.

8170 **ADA Camp Needlepoint**
American Diabetes Association
5100 Gamble Dr
St Louis Park, MN 55416
763-593-5333
800-676-4065
FAX: 952-582-9000
e-mail: cholten@diabetes.org
www.diabetes.org

*Becky Barnett, Camp Director*
*Carol Holten, Coordinator*
*Jenni Hargraves, Executive Director*
*Molly Duerr, Associate Director*

Camping for children who have type 1 diabetes. Coed, ages 5-16.

8171 **ADA Camp Sunshine**
American Diabetes Association
160 Allens Creek Rd
Rochester, NY 14618-3309
585-458-3040
FAX: 585-458-3810
www.diabetescamps.org

*Danielle Humphreys, Associate Manager*
*Brian Foster, Camp Director*

The American Diabetes Association New York Area's Camp is a residential camp for children with diabetes. The program is held on the Rotary Sunshine Campus in Rush, only 15 miles from Rochester. The camp is located on 133 acres of land in a rural setting including modern year round cabins, an Olympic-sized swimming pool, nature trails, athletic fields and a fishing pond. Ages 8-16; held during July.

**8172 ADA Camp for Kids**
American Diabetes Association
2625 Pennsylvania NE
suite 225
Albuquerque, NM 87110- 3649
505-266-5716
888-342-2383
FAX: 505-268-4533
e-mail: lbrown@diabetes.org
www.diabetes.org/adacampnm

One-week camping session for children with diabetes. Coed, ages 8-13. Camp will be held at Manzano Mountain Retreat, one hour from Albuquerque, New Mexico. Please call for exact dates.

**8173 ADA Teen Adventure Camp**
American Diabetes Association
55 East Monroe
Ste. 3420
Chicago, IL 60603
312-346-1805
888-342-2383
FAX: 312-346-5342
e-mail: mejohnson@diabetes.org
www.diabetes.org/adacampteenadventure

*Sue Apsey, Program Director*
*Megan Johnson, Program Director*

Camping for teenagers with diabetes. Coed, ages 14 to 18. Camp dates are early in August. Located at the YMCA Camp Duncan in Ingleside, Illinois. Featured activities include archery and crafts, singing, outdoor movie night, and roller skating.

**8174 ADA Triangle D Camp**
American Diabetes Association
55 East Monroe
Ste. 3420
Chicago, IL 60603
312-346-1805
888-342-2383
FAX: 312-346-5342
e-mail: mejohnson@diabetes.org
www.diabetes.org/adacamptriangled

*Sue Apsey, Program Director*
*Megan Johnson, Program Director*

Triangle D Camp is a resident camp program located at the YMCA Camp Duncan in Ingleside, Illinois. Activities include swimming, row boating, canoeing, high ropes (11-13 yr. olds), climbing tower (9-10 yr. olds), Camp games, singing, archery, campfires, soccer, basketball, volleyball and diabetes education.

**8175 ASCCA**
Alabama Easter Seal Society
5278 Camp Ascca Drive
P.O. Box 21
Jacksons Gap, AL 36861-21
256-825-9226
800-843-2267
FAX: 256-825-8332
e-mail: info@campascca.org
www.campascca.org

*John Stephenson, Administrator*
*Matt Rickman, Camp Director*
*Joe Spavone, R.N., Director of Health Services*
*Allison Wetherbee, Director of Community Relations*

Camp ASCCA is for children and adults with disabilities or health impairements. Camp ASCCA strives to help these individuals achieve equality, independence and dignity in a safe environment.

**8176 Adventure Day Camp**
3480 Commission Ct
Lake Ridge, VA 22192-1753
703-491-1444
e-mail: office@princewilliamacademy.com
www.princewilliamacademy.com

*Dr. Samia Harris, President*

Camping for children with asthma/respiratory ailments and cancer. Coed, ages 2-13.

**8177 Agassiz Village**
238 Bedford St
Suite B
Lexington, MA 02420-3477
781-860-0200
FAX: 781-860-0352
e-mail: lgillis@agassizvillage.org
www.agassizvillage.org

*Allison D Burroughs, President*
*Craig Alie, Vice President*
*Warren H Burroughs, Honorary Chairman*
*Cliff Simmonds, Executive Director*

Agassiz Village offers a variety of activities for all campers, boys and girls, younger camper and teens, and programs for physically challenged children and teens. By participating in daily activities, campers build a cooperative and positive community of different races, ages, ethnic and cultural backgrounds while enhancing confidence and individuality. Camp is located in Poland, Maine. For ages 8-17.

**8178 Arizona Camp Sunrise**
American Cancer Society
4550 E. Bell Road
Suite 126
Phoenix, AZ 85032-9344
602-952-7550
800-865-1582
FAX: 602-404-1118
e-mail: barb.nicholas@cancer.org
www.azcampsunrise.org

*Barbara Nicholas, Director*
*Leigh Ansley, Manager*
*Melissa Lee, Camp Director*
*Jason Poulter, Technical Media Director*

Provides one-week summer camping sessions to children aged 8-16 who have had, or currently have, cancer. The classes range from sports and outdoor games to dance and drama, arts, crafts, and cooking. Other activities planned for the campers include horseback riding, a trip to a lake, a dance, and learning to make friendship bracelets.

**8179 Bearskin Meadow Camp**
Diabetic Youth Foundation
5167 Clayton Road
Suite F
Concord, CA 94521-3163
925-680-4994
FAX: 925-680-4863
e-mail: info@dyf.org
www.dyf.org

*Mats Wallin, Executive Director*
*Paula Gogin, Director of Development*
*Janet Kramschuster, Director of Programs*
*Jennifer Goerzen, Camp Director*

Bearskin Meadow Campis is for children, teens and their families who are affected by diabetes. Bearskin teaches skills for blook glucose checking and techniques for adjusting insulin, food choices and how to have a fun, active life while living with diabetes.

**8180 Becket Chimney Corners YMCA Camps and Outdoor Center**
748 Hamilton Rd
Becket, MA 01223-9686
413-623-8991
FAX: 413-623-5890
e-mail: cburke@bccymca.org
www.bccymca.org

*Phil Connor, CEO*
*Jim Brown, Chief Operations Officer*
*Christine Kalakay, Chief Financial Officer*
*Steve Turner, Director of Property & Maintenance*

Half-week and one-week sessions for campers with asthma/respiratory ailments. Coed, ages 3 and up, families, seniors, single adults.

**8181 Bright Horizons Summer Camp**
Sickle Cell Disease Association of Illinois
8100 S. Western Avenue
Chicago, IL 60620
773-526-5016
866-798-1097
FAX: 773-526-5012
e-mail: scdai@mgci.com
sicklecelldisease-illinois.org

*TaLana Hughes, Executive Director*
*Tamiko Brooks, Program Coordinator*
*Anquineice Brown, Outreach Coordinator*
*Alana Burke, Case Manager*

Camping for children with blood disorders, ages 7-13. The joys of learning include instruction in first aid, swimming and water safety, boating, horseback riding and bowling plus arts and crafts. In addition, there is a traditional menu of camp pleasures, like hayrides, cookouts, nature hikes and sing-a-longs.

**8182 Camp Alpine**
Alpine Alternatives
2518 E. Tudor Road
Suite 105
Anchorage, AK 99507-1105
907-561-6655
800-361-4174
FAX: 907-563-9232
e-mail: info@alpinealternatives.org

*Margaret Webber, Executive Director*

Our programs are designed to help people expand their horizons, master new skills, make new friends, and increase motor coordination. Most importantly, participants experience growth in self-confidence and independence that affects all aspects of an individual's life. Our services are open to all, regardless of type of disability or age. Activities include canoeing, hiking, swimming, outdoor games, sports, nature identification and much more.

**8183 Camp Anuenue**
2370 Nuuanu Ave
Honolulu, HI 96817-1778
808-595-7500
888-227-7107
FAX: 808-595-7502
e-mail: debra.glowik@cancer.org
www.cancer.org

*Debra Glowik, Director*

(1 week) June, children with or recovered from cancer.

**8184 Camp Birchwood**
Muscular Dystrophy Association
P.O.Box 670049
Chugiak, AK 99567-49
907-688-2734
FAX: 907-688-2734
e-mail: info@birchwoodcamp.org
www.birchwoodcamp.org

*Marie Sweezey, Camp Director*
*Stephen Sweezey, Program Director/Manager*
*Berneita Norris, Food Service Manager*
*Joyce Del Rosario, Office Manager*

A summer camp at Birchwood Camp in Chugiak, Alaska for individuals ages 6-21 who are affected by any of the 40-plus neuromuscular diseases in MDA's program. Common activities include: swimming, hockey, baseball, soccer, football, boating, horseback riding, fishing, music, cooking, arts and crafts, movies, dancing, talent shows, Harley-Davidson motorcycle sidecar or three-wheeled cycle rides, a visit from fire fighters and time for socializing and laughing.

**8185 Camp Boggy Creek**
30500 Brantley Branch Rd
Eustis, FL 32736-9596
352-483-4200
866-462-6449
FAX: 352-483-0589
e-mail: info@BoggyCreek.org
www.boggycreek.org

*June Clark, President/CEO*
*Dorcas Tomasek, Camp Director*
*Robin Brubaker, Volunteer Coordinator*
*Cindy Handley, Office Manager*

Year-round sessions for children with a variety of chronic or life-threatening illnesses including cancer, hemophila, epilepsy, heart defects, HIV, spina bifida and asthma/respiratory ailments. Coed, ages 7-16.

**8186 Camp Bon Coeur**
Bon Coeur, Inc.
P.O.Box 53765
Lafayette, LA 70505-3765
337-233-8437
FAX: 337-233-4160
e-mail: info@heartcamp.com
www.heartcamp.com

*Susannah Craig, Executive Director*
*Antonio Conner, MBA, President*
*Susan Randol, RN, MSN, Vice-President*
*Martha Wyatt, CPA, Treasurer*

Two-week sessions June-July for children with heart defects. Coed, ages 8-16.

**8187 Camp Breathe Easy**
American Lung Association
404-231-9887
e-mail: annie@camptwinlakes.org
campbreatheeasy.com

*Annie Garrett, Camp Director*

Camp Breathe Easy is a seven-day, six-night overnight camp for children, ages 7-13, with asthma who need medication and are limited in summer camping opportunities. The children learn asthma self-management techniques and coping strategies to better handle their illness. Campers swim, repel off trees, fish, canoe, play soccer, basketball and miniature golf, and participate in ceramics and arts and crafts.

**8188 Camp Carefree**
American Diabetes Association
1846 West Seventh Street
Piscataway, NJ 08850-1918
732-752-5847
e-mail: carefreecamp@aol
www.campcarefreekids.org

*Phyllis Woestemeyer, Director*

Camp is located in Wolfeboro, New Hampshire. Sessions for campers with diabetes.

**8189 Camp Carolina Trails for Children**
American Diabetes Association
Ste 336m
222 S Church St
Charlotte, NC 28202-3247
704-373-9111
800-342-2383
888-342-2383
FAX: 704-373-9113
e-mail: enivens@diabetes.org
www.childrenwithdiabetes.com

*Dianne Roth, Manager*

The American Diabetes Association Camp Carolina Trails is an exciting week of summer fun for boys and girls entering grades 4 through 11. Camp includes many sports and activities such as swimming, hiking, canoeing and arts and crafts. It is held at YMCA Camp Hanes on 400 acres next to hanging Rock State Park which is located at the base of Sauratown Mountain, just 30 minutes north of Winston-Salem, North Carolina. Camp for ages 10-17. Use address given in Virginia for more information.

**8190 Camp Catch-a-Rainbow**
American Cancer Society
2370 Nuuanu Ave
Honolulu, HI 96817-1778
808-595-7500
888-227-7107
FAX: 808-595-7502
e-mail: debra.glowik@cancer.org
www.cancer.org

*Debra Glowik, Director*

Camp Catch-a-Rainbow's programs are available completely free to any child in MI or IN who has or has had cancer, between the ages of 4 and 20, with their doctor's approval. Family Camp is reserved for those campers who have attended camp during that year's summer sessions and their families. Day, week, adult retreat, and family camp are available options.

**8191 Camp Cheerful**
Achievement Centers For Children
15000 Cheerful Ln
Strongsville, OH 44136-5420
440-238-6200
FAX: 440-238-1858
www.achievementcenters.org

*Tim Fox, Executive Director*

Sessions for campers with developmental disabilities, mobility limitation and speech/communication impairment. Coed, ages 7-99.

**8192 Camp Christmas Seal**
American Lung Association of Oregon
7420 SW Bridgeport Road
Suite 200
Tigard, OR 97224-7790
503-924-4094
FAX: 503-924-4120
e-mail: info@lungoregon.org
www.lungoregon.org

*Kathryn A. Forbes, Board Chair-Elect*
*Ross P. Lanzafame, Chairman*
*John F. Emanuel, Secretary/Treasurer*

Camp is located in Sisterhood, Oregon. Sessions for children with asthma/respiratory ailments. Coed, ages 8-15.

**8193 Camp Classen YMCA**
YMCA of Greater Oklahoma City
10840 Main Camp Rd
Davis, OK 73030-9405
580-369-2272
FAX: 580-369-2284
www.itsmycamp.org

*Bradley Doherty, Camping Director*

Camp is located in Davis, Oklahoma. Sessions for children and adults with diabetes. Coed, ages 8-17, families, seniors and single adults.

**8194 Camp Conrad-Chinnock**
Diabetic Youth Services
12045 E. Waterfront Drive
Playa Vista, CA 90094
310-751-3057
FAX: 888-800-4010
www.dys.org

*Rocky Wilson, Executive and Camp Director*
*Dale Lissy, Camp Manager*
*Ryan Martz, Program Director*
*Tom Jenkins, Chief Operating Officer*

Camp Conrad-Chinnock offers many recreational programs such as swimming, canoeing, arts & crafts to young adults and their families with diabetes. Dietary education programs and diabetes management are also available.

**8195 Camp Courage North**
Courage Center
3915 Golden Valley Rd
Golden Valley, MN 55422-4249
763-520-0811
888-846-8253
FAX: 763-520-0577
e-mail: Information@CourageCenter.org
www.couragecenter.org

*Jan Malcolm, CEO*
*Pamela J. Lindemoen, Executive Vice President of Operations*
*Stephen Bariteau, Chief Development Officer*
*Alice Johnson, Chief Financial Officer*

Courage Center Camps - Camp Courage & Camp Courage North - are part of Courage Center, a non-profit rehabilitation and resource center for people of all ages and abilities who are experiencing barriers to health & independence. For more than 50 years, Courage Center camps have served children and adults with physical disabilities and those who are deaf and hard of hearing. In 2008, more than 800 people attended a Courage Center camp session. For more information, visit our web-site.

**8196 Camp Del Corazon**
11615 Hesby St
North Hollywood, CA 91601-3620
818-754-0312
888-621-4800
FAX: 818-754-0842
e-mail: information@campdelcorazon.org
www.campdelcorazon.org

*Lisa Knight, Executive Director*
*Kevin Shannon, Medical Director & Co-founder*
*Ronya Waters, Sr. Development Director*
*Chrissie Endler, Program Director*

Active program for campers with heart disease, Camp del Corazon provides summer activities free of charge that include hiking and archery, arts and crafts, court and field games, waterfront activities and a beach barbecue.

**8197 Camp Discovery**
American Diabetes Association
5081 Gore Rd
Dorchester, ON
613-688-5930
FAX: 519-660-8992
e-mail: amanda.grassick@diabetes.ca
www.diabetescamps.org

*Amanda Grassick, Camp Manager*
*Bridget Kroner, Associate Manager*

Camp is located in Junction City, Kansas. Offers young people with diabetes a week of fun at rock springs 4-H Center. Special attention to diabetes makes Camp Discovery a safe environment for active youth while providing valuable diabetes managment education. Call the American Diabetes Association Kansas area office for more information. Coed, ages 8-17.

**8198 Camp Eden Wood**
Friendship Ventures
10509 108th St NW
Annandale, MN 55302-2912
952-852-0101
800-450-8376
FAX: 952-852-0123
e-mail: info@friendshipventures.org
friendshipventures.org

*Ed Stracke, CEO*

Camp is located in Eden Prairie, Minnesota. Offers resident camp programs for children, teenagers and adults with developmental, physical or multiple disabilities, Down Syndrome, special medical conditions, Williams Syndrome, autism and/or other conditions. Fishing, creative arts, golf, sports and other activities are available. Respite care weekend camps year round for children, teenagers and adults. Guided vacations for teens and adults with developmental disabilities or other unique needs.

**8199 Camp Floyd Rogers**
Floyd Rogers Foundation
P.O.Box 31536
Omaha, NE 68131-536
402-341-0866
FAX: 402-341-0866
www.campfloydrogers.com

*Buzz Wheeler, Camp Director*

A camp for diabetic children. Coed, ages 8-18. 100 children come to Camp Floyd Rogers each summer. They come to enjoy activities, participate in special events, engage in innovative evening programs, and they meet other children their own age with diabetes. Camp Floyd Rogers offers young people an opportunity to share some of life's adventures with others who also happen to have diabetes.

**8200 Camp Fun in the Sun**
Inland NorthWest Health Services
P.O.Box 469
Spokane, WA 99210-0469
509-232-8145
www.campfuninthesun.org

*Lisa Randall, Director*

Summer camp for children ages 8-18 whom have diabetes.

**8201 Camp Glengarra**
Girl Scouts - Foothills Council
33 Jewett Pl
Utica, NY 13501-4715
315-733-2391
FAX: 315-733-1909
e-mail: nbrown@girlscoutsfoothills.org
www.girlscoutsfoothills.org

*Natalie Brown, Executive Director*
*Karen Lubecki, Director*

Camp Glengarra is located on 500+ acres of fields and forests, about eight miles west of Camden. This Girl Scout Camp hosts a myriad of programs throughout the year as well as summer day and resident camp. Summer sessions for girls 5-17 with ADD or asthma/respiratory ailments.

**8202 Camp Glyndon**
American Diabetes Association
Ste 110
800 Wyman Park Dr
Baltimore, MD 21211-2837
410-265-0075
800-342-2383
FAX: 410-235-4048
e-mail: askada@diabetes.org
www.childrenwithdiabetes.com

*Heather Magoon, Director*

Camp is located in Nanjemoy, Maryland. One and two-week sessions July-August for children with diabetes and their families. Coed, ages 8-16.

**8203 Camp Harkness**
Arc of New London County
125 Sachem St
Norwich, CT 6360-4128
860-889-4435
FAX: 860-889-4662
TTY:860-859-5493
e-mail: info@thearcnlc.org
www.campharkness.com/Default.htm

*Tom Sullivan, President*

In 1991 a group of parents and adults with spina bifida, were brought together with the mission to educate the public about spina bifida and issues affecting people who have this disability in addition To providing support and information and promoting programs that will help people with spina bifida. Since then SBAC has worked hard to support parents, adults with spina bifida and families

**8204 Camp Hertko Hollow**
101 Locust St
Des Moines, IA 50309-1720
515-471-8523
888-437-8652
FAX: 515-288-2531
e-mail: a.wolf@camphertkohollow.com
www.camphertkohollow.com

*Ann Wolf, Executive Director*
*Vivian Murray, Camp Director*
*Deb Holwegner, Director of Development*
*Steve Roy, Legal Counsel*

Camp Hertko Hollow is a resident camp held at the Des Moines YMCA Camp site, located along the Des Moines River north of Boone, Iowa. Activities include horseback riding, swimming, canoeing, rappelling, crafts, ropes course, archery and riflery to name a few, plus special activities for different ages. Half-week and one-week sessions for children with diabetes. Coed, ages 6-16.

**8205 Camp Hickory Hill**
Central Missouri Diabetic Childrens Camp
P.O.Box 1942
Camp Hickory Hill
Columbia, MO 65205-1942
573-445-9146
e-mail: camphickoryhill@yahoo.com
www.camphickoryhill.com

*Jessica La Mantia Bernhardt, Camp Director*
*David Bernhardt, President*
*Michael Gardner MD, Medical Director*
*Frank La Mantia, Development Director*

Educates diabetic children concerning diabetes and its care. In addition to daily educational sessions on some aspects of diabetes, campers participate in swimming, sailing, arts and crafts and overnight camping. Coed, ages 8-17.

**8206 Camp Ho Mita Koda**
Diabetes Association Of Greater Cleveland
3601 South Green Road
Suite 100
Cleveland, OH 44122-5719
216-591-0800
FAX: 216-591-0320
e-mail: information@diabetespartnership.org
www.dagc.org

*Suzanne Johnson, MA, Director of I.T.*
*Julie Hewitt, MEd, Director of Camp and Youth Programs*
*Ruth Dobranic, Director of Finance*
*Melinda Carter, Development Operations Specialist*

Camp is located in Newbury, Ohio. Summer sessions for children with type 1 diabetes. Coed, ages 6-15. Type 2 diabetes, coed, ages 12-17. Bicycle adventure, coed, ages 13-19. Mini-day camp, ages 4-7, coed.

**8207 Camp Hodia**
1701 N 12th Avenue
Boise, ID 83702-2713
208-891-1023
FAX: 208-891-1023
e-mail: alan@hodia.org
www.hodia.org

*Lisa Gier, Executive Director*
*Alan Bean, MD, Director*
*Kathlynn Ireland, Director, Hodia Shooting Stars Camp*
*Vicki Cutshall, R.N., Director, Hodia Kids Camp*

Camp is located in Alturas Lake, Idaho. One-week sessions for children with diabetes. Coed, ages 8-18. Ski Camp in Sun Valley in January, ages 12-18.

**8208 Camp Honor**
Hemophilia Association
818 East Osborn Road
Suite 105
Phoenix, AZ 85014-5218
602-955-3947
888-754-7017
FAX: 602-955-1962
e-mail: cindy@hemophiliaz.org
www.hemophiliaz.org

*Steve Helms, President*
*Jessica Steed, Vice President*
*Melinda Cadena, Community Relations Manager*
*Katie Stringham, Event Coordinator*
Camp is located in Payson, Arizona at the Whispering Hope Ranch. One-week sessions for children with hemophilia or HIV and their siblings, as well as children of hemophiliacs. Coed, ages 7-17. Activities include swimming, canoeing, sports, archery and arts and crafts (to name a few fun things).

**8209 Camp Independence**
National Kidney Foundation
2951 Flowers Road South
Suite 211
Atlanta, GA 30341-5533
770-452-1539
800-633-2339
FAX: 770-452-7564
e-mail: nkfga@kidney.org
www.kidneyga.org

*Beth Irick, Division President*
*Cara McKinney, Division Director of Development*
*Andrea Sharper, Division Project Manager*
*Danielle Hall, Regional Program Director*
Camp Independence is Georgia's a overnight, week-long summer camp providing essential medical care, treatment & fun for kids with kidney disease and transplants. Camp Independence recognizes that campers are normal children but have special needs providing these children with opportunities for development & individual growth, peer support & normal life experiences. Activities include swimming, arts & crafts, fishing and horsebackriding, in addition to archery, games and sports, and ceramics.

**8210 Camp Jened**
United Cerebral Palsy Association New York
P.O.Box 483
Rock Hill, NY 12775-483
845-434-2220
FAX: 845-434-2253
www.campjened.org

*Michael Branam, Executive Director*
Camp is located in Rock Hill, New York. Sessions for adults with severe developmental and physical disabilities. Coed, ages 18-99.

**8211 Camp John Warvel**
American Diabetes Association
6145 Castleway West Drive
Suite 114
Indianapolis, IN 46250-1939
317-352-9226
888-342-2383
FAX: 317-594-0748
www.diabetes.org

*Jennifer Pferrer, Executive Director*
*Lisa Patton, Associate Director, Fundraising & Special Events*
*Janell Love, Associate Director, Corporate Development*
*Carol Dixon, Senior Manager*
Camp is located in North Webster, Indiana. Provides an enjoyable, safe and educational out-of-doors experience for children with insulin-dependent diabetes. A unique learning atmosphere for children to acquire new skills in caring for their disease. The camp experience instills confidence for the child's self-management of diabetes. Offers one-week sessions and can accommodate 200 campers, boys and girls aged 7-16.

**8212 Camp Joslin**
Barton Center for Diabetes Education
30 Ennis Road
North Oxford, MA 01537-0356
508-987-2056
FAX: 508-987-2002
e-mail: info@bartoncenter.org
www.bartoncenter.org

*Kevin Wilcoxen, Executive Director*
*Jesse Welch, Site & Facilities Director*
*Thomas Racine, Facilities Assistant*
*Brendan Duffy, Facilities Assistant*
Camp is located in Charlton, Massachusetts. For boys, ages 7-16, with diabetes. This program offers active summer sports and activities, supplemented by medical treatment and diabetes education. Coed Winter Camp and Coed Weekend Retreats are offered during the school year.

**8213 Camp Joy**
3325 Swamp Creek Rd
Schwenksville, PA 19473-1518
610-754-6878
FAX: 610-754-7880
e-mail: campjoy@fast.net
www.campjoy.com

*Robert G Griffith, President*
A special needs camp for kids and adults (ages 4-80+) with developmental disabilities such as: mental retardation, autism, brain injury, neurological disorder, visual and/or hearing impairments, Angelman and Down syndromes, and other developmental disabilities.

**8214 Camp Ko-Man-She**
American Diabetes Association
West Medical Plaza
1 Elizabeth Place, Suite 180
Dayton, OH 45408
937-220-6611
FAX: 937-224-0240
e-mail: infoSdiabetesdayton.org
www.diabetesdayton.org

*Susan Mc Govern, Executive Director*
*Janae Reynolds, Program & Event Coordinator*
*Carol Clark, President*
*Terry Fague, Secretary, Legal Advisor*
Camp is located in Bellefontaine, Ohio. Summer sessions for children with diabetes. Coed, ages 8-17. Held in July.

**8215 Camp Kweebec**
P.O.Box 511
Penn Valley, PA 19072-511
610-667-2123
FAX: 610-667-6376
e-mail: info@kweebec.com
www.kweebec.com

*Les Weiser, Owner/Director*
*Maddy Weiser, Owner/Director*
*Rachel Weiser, Associate Director, Director of Operations*
*Josh Weiser, Associate Director*
Camp is located in Schwenksville, Pennsylvania. Sessions for children and adults with diabetes. Coed, ages 6-16, families, seniors and single adults.

**8216 Camp L-Kee-Ta**
1308 Broadway Street
P.O. Box 190
West Burlington, IA 52655-190
319-752-3639
FAX: 319-753-1410
www.gseiwi.org

*Chet Scott, Camp Ranger/Site Manager*
*Val Harle, Troop Camp Director*
Camp is located in Danville, Iowa. Half-week and one-week sessions June-August for children with asthma/respiratory ailments. Girls, ages 7-18 and families.

**8217 Camp Latgawa**
Oregon-Idaho Conference Center
13250 S Fork Little Butte Creek Rd
Eagle Point, OR 97524- 5593
541-826-9699
e-mail: camplatgawa@hotmail.com
www.latgawa.gocamping.org

*Eva LaBonty, Director*

Camp Latgawa provides year round hospitality for groups up to 90 people. The bunk/dormitory style facilities are heated and have restrooms and showers either in the cabin or nearby.

**8218 Camp Libbey**
Maumee Valley Girl Scout Center
2244 Collingwood Blvd
Toledo, OH 43620-1147
419-243-8216
800-860-4516
FAX: 419-245-5357
e-mail: KelleeChancellor@girlscoutsofwesternohio.org
www.girlscoutsofwesternohio .org

*Laura Bowerman, Executive Director*
*Amelia Gibbon, Manager*
*Deb Laren, CTO/Finance Manager*

Camp for girls 7-18 with asthma/respiratory ailments, diabetes, epilepsy and muscular dystrophy is located in Defiance, Ohio.

**8219 Camp MITIOG**
Share, Inc
7615 N. Platte Purchase Drive
Suite 116
Kansas City, MO 64118
816-221-4450
877-221-4450
FAX: 816-221-1420
e-mail: midlands@midlandsmc.org
www.midlandsmc.org

*Mike Hale, President/Financial Officer*
*Pam Mathena, Adm. Assistant to MMC Financial Officer*
*Donna Fletcher, Congregational Consultant*
*Don McLaughlin, Outreach Coordinator*

Camp is located in Excelsior Springs, Missouri. One-week summer sessions for children with spina bifida. Coed, ages 6-16.

**8220 Camp Magruder**
Oregon-Idaho Conference Center
17450 Old Pacific Hwy
Rockaway Beach, OR 97136-9609
503-355-2310
FAX: 503-355-8701
e-mail: director@campmagruder.org
www.campmagruder.org

*Steve Rumage, Camp Director*
*Amy Wood, Program Services Director*
*Diana Gutzke, Reservations/ Guest Services*
*Mark Burley Manager, Maintenance Team*

Camp is located in Rockaway Beach, Oregon. Sessions for children and adults with cancer and developmental disabilities. Coed, ages 9-18, families, seniors and single adults.

**8221 Camp Nejeda**
Camp Nejeda Foundation
910 Saddlebrook Road
P.O. Box 156
Stillwater, NJ 07875- 0156
973-383-2611
FAX: 973-383-9891
e-mail: information@campnejeda.org
www.campnejeda.org

*Philip E. De Rea, Executive Director*
*Jim Daschbach, Camp Director*
*Rich Ramage, Maintenance Director*
*Jennifer Passerini, Development Director*

For children with diabetes, ages 7-15. Provides an active and safe camping experience which enables the children to learn about and understand diabetes. Activities include boating, swimming, fishing, archery, as well as camping skills.

**8222 Camp Not-A-Wheeze**
American Lung Association In Arizona
102 W McDowell Rd
Phoenix, AZ 85003-1213
602-258-7505
FAX: 202-452-1805
e-mail: info@lungoregon.org
www.lungarizona.org

*Terry Daane, Chairman*

Camp Not-A-Wheeze is designed especially for kids ages 7-14 with moderate to severe asthma and was created to provide a traditional residential camp experience and teach children how to manage their asthma.

**8223 Camp Okizu**
Okizu Foundation
16 Digital Dr
Novato, CA 94949-5755
415-382-9083
FAX: 415-382-8384
e-mail: info@okizu.org
www.okizu.org

*Suzie Randall, Executive Director/Camp Director*
*Heather Ferrier, Assistant Executive Director*
*Beth Dekker, Assistant Camp Director*
*Jeff Winfrey, Site Manager*

Camp Okizu offers a place where children struggling with a life threatening illness and thier families can come to explore and enjoy a normal life experience. The camp also provides peer support, respite, mentoring, and a variety of other programs designed to help members of families affected by childhood cancer. The camp is open from April through October

**8224 Camp Pelican**
Louisiana Lions Camp
292 L. Beauford Dr
Anacoco, LA 71403-3258
800-348-6567
FAX: 337-239-9975
e-mail: lalions@lionscamp.org
www.lionscamp.org

*Tim Matakas, President*
*Kim Breaux, Vice President*
*Tessie Guillory, Treasurer*
*Autumn Gaspard, Secretary*

Camp Pelican is an overnight residential camp for children with moderate to severe asthma or other pulmonary problems. Founded in 1977, Camp Pelican is jointly sponsored by the Louisiana Pulmonary Disease Camp Inc and the Louisiana Lions Camp. Over 100 children attend annually and participate in education, sports, arts and crafts, swimming and other camping activities. Medical staff including physicians, nurses, respiratory therapists and social workers participate in camp. Coed, ages 5-17.

**8225 Camp Rainbow**
Phoenix Childrens Hospital
1919 East Thomas Road
Phoenix, AZ 85016-7710
602-546-0157
888-908-5437
FAX: 602-546-0276
e-mail: rlyddon@phoenixchildrens.com
www.pchrainbowkids.org

*Rachael Lyddon, Camp Planning/Operations Manager*

Camp is located in Prescott, Arizona. Offers one-week sessions for children who have had, or currently have, cancer. Boys and girls ages 7-17. Camp activities include swimming, horseback riding, arts and crafts, canoeing, performing arts, archery, rollerskating, fishing, an overnight camping trip and much more! It's a week filled with laughter, new experiences and new friends.

**8226 Camp Rap-A-Hope**
2701 Airport Blvd
Mobile, AL 36606-2319 251-476-9880
FAX: 251-476-9495
e-mail: info@camprapahope.org
www.camprapahope.org

*Melissa McNichol, Executive Director*
*Roz Dorsett, Assistant Director*
*Nell Gustavson, Financial Secretary*
*West Sanders, Special Events and Public Relations*
Camp Rap-A-Hope is a one-week summer camp for children and teenagers who are battling cancer or have ever been diagnosed with cancer and are 7 to 17 years of age. It is free of charge. Camp Rap-A-Hope strives to make sure every camper gets the opportunity to develop new skills and self-confidence. Camp activities are appropriate for our campers' ages and abilities and include, but are not limited to: swimming, music, arts and crafts, archery, fishing, canoeing and horseback riding.

**8227 Camp Ronald McDonald for Good Times**
Ronald McDonald House For Charities-Southern Calif
1954 Cotner Ave
Los Angeles, CA 90025-5602. 310-268-8488
800-625-7295
FAX: 310-473-3338
www.campronaldmcdonald.org

*Brad Baillie, Facility Supervisor*
*Brian Crater, Associate Executive Director*
*Chad Edwards, Program Director*
*Eileen McDermott, Operations Manager*
Free year-round residential camping for children with cancer and their families.

**8228 Camp Sawtooth**
Oregon-Idaho Conference Center
P.O.Box 68
Fairfield, ID 83327-68 800-593-7539
e-mail: sawtooth@gocamping.org
www.gocamping.org

*David Hargreaves, Director*
Camp located 35 miles north of fairfield, centrally located for all of southern Idaho.

**8229 Camp Seale Harris**
Southeastern Diabetes Education Services
500 Chase Park South
Suite 104
Hoover, AL 35244-1869 205-402-0415
FAX: 205-402-0416
e-mail: info@southeasterndiabetes.org
www.southeasterndiabetes.org

*Rhonda McDavid, Executive Director*
*Donna Harden, Operations Manager*
*Sara Latimer, Camp Director*
*William Parkhurst, Outreach and Programs Director*
A summer residential program that is located at Camp ASCCA (Alabama's Special Camp for Children and Adults), that encourages and motivates youth to reach their full potential despite diabetes, and teaches families how to serve as the primary educators and supporters for children and adolescents living with this illness. Fpur programs are offered: Senior Camp; Junior Camp; Family Camp; and Adventure Camps.

**8230 Camp Setebaid**
Setebaid Services
PO Box 196
Winfield, PA 17889 570-524-9090
866-738-3224
FAX: 570-523-0769
e-mail: info@setebaidservices.org
www.setebaidservices.org

*Mark Moyer, President*
Camping sessions for children with diabetes. Coed, ages 3-18 years. Family retreat for children with diabetes and their families.

**8231 Camp Sioux**
American Diabetes Association
1323 23rd Street South
Suite C
Fargo, ND 58103 763-593-5333
FAX: 952-582-9000
e-mail: AskADA@diabetes.org
www.diabetescamp.org

*Sheila Chrspensen, Executive Director*
*Becky Barnett, Camp Director*
Camp Sioux, located in Park River, ND, is a week-long residential summer camp for children ages 8-14 who are living with diabetes. Programs encourage independence and self management with appropriate medical supervision to ensure the best possible experience for every camper. Nutrition activities, blood glucose monitoring, and injections/medications are integrated into the camp program.

**8232 Camp Smile-A-Mile**
P.O.Box 550155
Birmingham, AL 35255-155 205-323-8427
888-500-7920
FAX: 205-323-6220
e-mail: info@campsam.org
www.campsam.org

*Bruce N. Hooper, Executive Director*
*Jennifer B. Amundsen, Program Director*
*Melissa M. Allphin, Development Director*
*Judice A. McKenzie, Executive Assistant*
Camp Smile-A-Mile is a non-profit organization for children who have or had cancer in Alabama. Camp Smile-A-Mile's mission is to provide challenging, unforgettable recreational and educational experiences for young cancer patients from across Alabama at no cost to their families. Our purpose is to provide these children with avenues for fellowship, to help them cope with their disease, and to prepare them for life.

**8233 Camp Sunrise**
Johns Hopkins Hospital
600 North Wolfe Street
CMSC 800
Baltimore, MD 21287-5904 410-955-5311
www.campsunrisemd.org

*Sherryce Robinson, Mission Delivery Manager*
*Kira Elring, Regional Mission Director*
*Gloria Jetter, Regional Executive Director*
*Jack Shipkoski, CEO*
Week long summer camp in White Hall, MD., for children ages 6-18 who have been diagnosed with or have survived cancer. Camp sunrise also has a 'day camp' program available for children ages 4-5. Camp activities include sports & games, swimming, arts & crafts, and nature hikes.

**8234 Camp Sweeney**
Southwestern Diabetic Fund
P.O.Box 918
Gainesville, TX 76241-0918 940-665-2011
FAX: 940-665-9467
e-mail: info@campsweeney.org
www.campsweeney.org

*Ernie Fernandez, Executive Director*
Teaches self-care and self-reliance to children ages 7-18 with diabetes. Campers participate in such activities such as swimming, fishing, horseback riding and arts and crafts while learning about how to self manage their diabetes.

**8235 Camp Tall Turf**
816 Madison SE
Grand Rapids, MI 49507
616-452-7906
FAX: 616-988-4596
e-mail: info@turf.org
www.tallturf.org

*Jack Kooyman, President/CEO*
Camp is located in Walkerville, Michigan. Summer camping sessions for youth with asthma/respiratory ailments and ADD. Coed, ages 8-16.

**8236 Camp Taylor, Inc.**
5424 Pirrone Road
Salida, CA 95368-9094
209-545-4715
FAX: 209-543-1861
e-mail: kimberlie@kidsheartcamp.org
www.kidsheartcamp.org

*Kimberlie Gamino, Executive Director/Founder*
*Rollin A. Podwys, Camp Director*
*Steven Barbieri, Camp Councelor*
*Charlie Liamos, Venture Capitalist*
Camp Taylor is a place where children and young adults with heart disease and thier families can come for recreational activities and programs. The camp is open from May through September.

**8237 Camp Vacamas**
256 Macopin Rd
West Milford, NJ 07480-3718
973-838-0942
877-428-8222
e-mail: info@vacamas.org
www.vacamas.org

*Michael Friedman, Executive Director*
*Ely Connelly Newberry, Camp Director*
*Sandra I. Friedman, Associate Executive Director*
*Wilson A. Santos, Program Director*
Disadvantaged children with asthma or sickle cell anemia, ages 8-16, are offered special programs in canoeing, backpacking, camping, music and leadership training. Sliding scale tuition. Year round programs for youth at risk groups. Conference center facility open for group rentals.

**8238 Camp Waziyatah**
530 Mill Hill Rd
Waterford, ME 04088-4011
207-583-2267
FAX: 509-357-2267
e-mail: info@wazi.com
wazi.com

*Gregg Parker, Owner/Director*
*Mitch Parker, Owner/Director*
Camp is located in Waterford, Massachusetts. Three, four and seven-week sessions June-August for campers with cancer and diabetes. Coed, ages 8-15 and families, single adults.

**8239 Camp WheezeAway**
American Lung Association Of Alabama
P.O.Box 3188
Bessemer, AL 35023-188
205-933-8821
800-586-4872
FAX: 251-491-1297
e-mail: kwaters@alabamalung.org
www.alabamalung.org

*Kim Waters, Director*
Camp WheezeAway is a 5 day overnight camp for children ages 8-12 with moderate to severe asthma, and is sponsored by the American Lung Association. Children are monitered while enjoying all the normal camp activities including ropes courses, canoeing, swimming, arts & crafts, horseback riding, fishing, tubing & more and above all learn to manage their asthma.

**8240 Camps for Children & Teens with Diabetes**
Diabetes Society
1165 Lincoln Ave
Suite 300
San Jose, CA 95125-3052
408-287-3785
800-989-1165
FAX: 408-287-2701
e-mail: info@diabetessociety.org
www.diabetessociety.org/camps

*Sharon Ogbor, Executive Director*
*Thomas Smith, Director*
Since 1974, sponsors up to 20 day camps, family camps and resident camps for children 4 through 17. These camps provide an opportunity for children with diabetes to go to camp, meet other children and gain a better understanding of their diabetes. The total experience can help campers develop more confidence in their abilities to control their diabetes effectively while enjoying the traditional camp experience. Camps are located throughout CA and parts of Nevada.

**8241 Cedar Ridge Camp**
Old 4010 Routt Road
Cedar Ridge Camp
Louisville, KY 40299-4924
502-267-5848
FAX: 502-267-0116
e-mail: info@cedarridgecamp.com
www.cedarridgecamp.com

*Andrew Hartmans, Executive Director*
Half-week, one and two-week sessions for children with diabetes, developmental disabilities and muscular dystrophy. Coed, ages 6-17.

**8242 Champ Camp**
American Lung Association In Alaska
500 West International Airport Rd.
Suite A
Anchorage, AK 99518-1175
907-276-5864
800-586-4872
e-mail: kpv@aklung.org
www.aklung.org

*Ross P. Lanzafame, Chairman*
*Kathryn A. Forbes, Board Chair-Elect*
*John F. Emanuel, Secretary/Treasurer*
Champ Camp is a week long summer recreation and asthma education program at Camp Kushtaka on the beautiful shores of Kenai Lake. Campers are able to explore their skills in outdoor activities including canoeing, hiking, swimming, archery, and arts and crafts. More importantly, Champ Camp boosts self-confidence and instills a sense of responsibility. It teaches preventive measures to improve asthma management, and avoid asthmatic episodes as well as increases a camper's sense of independence.

**8243 Clara Barton Diabetes Camp**
Clara Barton for Girls with Diabetes
30 Ennis Road
North Oxford, MA 01537-0356
508-987-2056
FAX: 508-987-2002
e-mail: info@bartoncenter.org
www.bartoncenter.org

*Kevin Wilcoxen, Executive Director*
*Jesse Welch, Site & Facilities Director*
*Thomas Racine, Facilities Assistant*
*Brendan Duffy, Facilities Assistant*
Girls, ages 3-17, with diabetes participate in a well-rounded camp program with special education in diabetes, health and safety. Activities include swimming, boating, sports, dance, music and arts and crafts. Two week adventure camp for high school girls offering camping, hiking, canoeing, etc. Also a minicamp (one week) for girls 6-12. Day camps are offered in Worcester, Boston, and New York City.

**8244 Diabetes Camp**
Tanager Place
1614 W Mount Vernon Road
Mount Vernon, IA 52314
319-363-0681
FAX: 319-365-6411
e-mail: dpirrie@tanagerplace.org
www.camptanager.org

*Donald Pirrie, Camp Director*

Provides children and adolescents with Diabetes a safe and healthy environment and healthy environment to enjoy a variety of recreational activities designed for fun and fitness. The camp held each July has an on-site 24-hour physician and nursing staff. Ages 6-13.

**8245 EDI Camp**
Wyman Center
600 Kiwanis Dr
Eureka, MO 63025-2212
636-938-5245
FAX: 636-938-5289
e-mail: info@wymancenter.org
www.wymancenter.org

*David Hilliard, President*
*Theresa Mayberry, Senior Vice President*

Youngsters with diabetes learn how to care for themselves while participating in a wide variety of outdoor activities and trips. The camp, managed and financed by the American Diabetes Association Greater St. Louis Affiliate, offers camperships to children from the Greater St. Louis area, ages 7-16, but nonresidents may also apply.

**8246 Echoing Hills**
36272 County Road 79
Warsaw, OH 43844-9770
740-327-2311
800-419-6513
FAX: 740-327-6371
e-mail: info@echoinghillsvillage.org
www.echoinghillsvillage.org

*Buddy Busch, President/CEO*

Summer camp for children and adults with cerebral palsy. Coed, ages 7-70.

**8247 Edward J Madden Open Hearts Camp**
250 Monument Valley Road
Great Barrington, MA 01230
413-528-2229
e-mail: hearts@openheartscamp.org
www.openheartscamp.org

*David Zaleon, Executive Director*
*Jill Helme, Assistant Director*
*Jacqueline Reasor, Counselor*
*David Andrew*

Eight week program for children who have had and are fully recovered from open heart surgery or a heart transplant. Four two week sessions by age group. Small camp - 25 campers per session.

**8248 FCYD Camp**
Foundation for Children and Youth with Diabetes
1995 W 9000 S
West Jordan, UT 84088-9345
801-566-6913
www.fcydcamp.org

*David Okubo, President*
*Elizabeth Elmer, Vice President*
*Sherrie Hardy, Director*
*Nate Gedge, Chair*

Camping for children with diabetes. Coed, ages 1-18 and families.

**8249 Father Drumgoole Connelly Summer Camp**
MIV Mount Loretto
718-317-2803
www.mountloretto.org

*Steven Rynn, Executive Director*
*Maryann Virga, Executive Assistant*
*William D'Ambrosio, Assistant Executive Director for Operations*
*Loretta Polanish, Executive Secretary*

Summer sessions for children with epilepsy, hearing impairment and developmental disabilities. Coed, ages 5-13.

**8250 Florida Diabetes Camp**
P.O.Box 14136
Gainesville, FL 32604-2136
352-334-1321
FAX: 352-334-1326
e-mail: fccyd@floridadiabetescamp.org
www.floridadiabetescamp.org

*Gary Cornwell, Program Director*

Camp is located in Florida. One and two-week sessions June-August for children with diabetes. Coed, ages 6-18 and families. Camps throughout the year.

**8251 Friends Academy Summer Camps**
Duck Pond Rd
Locust Valley, NY 11560
516-393-4207
FAX: 516-465-1720
e-mail: camp@fa.org
www.fasummercamp.org

*Rich Mack, Camp Director*

Summer sessions for children with diabetes. Coed, ages 3-14, families.

**8252 God's Camp**
Episcopal Church of Hawaii
68-729 Farrington Hwy
Waialua, HI 96791-9314
808-637-6241
808-637-5505
FAX: 808-637-5505
e-mail: info@campmokuleia.com
www.campmokuleia.com

*Debbie Alemeda, Manager*

Episcopal Church tent camping, 5 nights, July. Church groups, family reunions, weddings, other organizations.

**8253 Growing Together Diabetes Camp**
ETMC
1000 S. Beckham
P.O. Box 6400
Tyler, TX 75701-6400
903-597-0351
800-232-8318
e-mail: info@etmc.org
www.etmc.org

*Anjani Upponi RD/CDE, Program Manager*
*Vicki Jowell, Director*
*Elmer G. Ellis, President*
*Jerry Massey, Senior Vice President*

A summer camp for youths ages 6 to 15 with Type 1 or Type 2 diabetes.

**8254 Happiness Is Camping**
2169 Grand Concourse
Bronx, NY 10453-2201
718-295-3100
FAX: 718-295-6733
e-mail: hicoffice@happinessiscamping.org
www.happinessiscamping.org

*Kurt Struver, Executive Director*
*Louis D'Agostino, President Of The Board*
*Antonio Dominiguez, Secretary*

Camp is located in Blairstown, New Jersey. Free camping sessions for children with cancer. Coed, ages 6-15. June 30 - July 31, 2008.

**8255 Hemophilia Camp**
Tanager Place
1614 W Mount Vernon Road
Mount Vernon, IA 52314
319-363-0681
FAX: 319-365-6411
e-mail: dpirrie@tanagerplace.org
www.camptanager.org

*Donald Pirrie, Camp Director*
During the six-day camp children with Hemophilia and their siblings participate in individual and group activities designed for fun and fitness. The camp held each year in mid-June has a 24-hour physician and nursing staff. Ages 5-16.

**8256 Hole in the Wall Gang Camp**
565 Ashford Center Rd
Ashford, CT 06278-1720
860-429-3444
FAX: 860-429-7295
e-mail: ashford@holeinthewallgang.org
www.holeinthewallgang.org

*Matthew Cook, Director of Camp Operations*
*Sharon Space, Medical Director*
*James H. Canton, Chief Executive Officer*
*Kevin M. Magee, Chief Financial Officer*
Low-cost eight-week sessions June-August for children with cancer and HIV. Coed, ages 7-15.

**8257 Kiwanis Camp Wyman**
Wyman Center
600 Kiwanis Dr
Eureka, MO 63025-2212
636-938-5245
FAX: 636-938-5289
e-mail: info@wymancenter.org
www.wymancenter.org

*Dave Hilliard, President/CEO*
*Kristine Ramsey, Sr. Vice President, Development*
*Tom Etzkorn, Vice President, Special Projects*
*Mindy Sharp, MBA, Sr. Vice President, Finance & Administration*
Summer sessions for youth with diabetes. Coed, ages 8-16, run in conjunction with the American Diabetes Association. Call for program description.

**8258 Makemie Woods Camp**
Presbytery of Eastern Virginia
P.O.Box 39
Barhamsville, VA 23011-39
757-566-1496
800-566-1496
FAX: 757-566-8803
e-mail: makwoods@makwoods.org
www.makwoods.org

*Mike Burcher, Director*
*Sherri Egerton, Program Director*
*Karen Broughman, Office Manager*
*Fran Parkhurst, Food Services Manager*
Residential Christian camp that tailors each group and individual goals. Counselors serve as teachers, friends and activity leaders. For children 8-18 with diabetes.

**8259 Makemie Woods Camp/Conference Retreat**
Presbytery of Eastern Virginia
P.O.Box 39
Barhamsville, VA 23011-39
757-566-1496
800-566-1496
FAX: 757-566-8803
e-mail: makwoods@makwoods.org
www.makwoods.org

*Mike Burcher, Director*
*Sherri Egerton, Program Director*
*Karen Broughman, Office Manager*
*Fran Parkhurst, Food Services Manager*
Counselors serve as teachers, friends and activity leaders. The individual is important within the small group. No camper is lost in the crowd, but is an integral partner in the group process. Residential Christian Camp and conference center. Summer camp for children 8-18 and special camp for children with diabetes.

**8260 Marist Brothers Mid-Hudson Valley Camp**
PO Box 197
Esopus, NY 12429-197
845-384-6620
e-mail: maristretreathouse@gmail.com
www.maristretreathouse.net

*Don Nugent, Property Director*
Serves special people: children who have cancer or who are HIV positive, deaf or mentally retarded.

**8261 Med-Camps of Louisiana**
102 Thomas Road
Suite 615s Rd
West Monroe, LA 71291-5550
318-329-8405
877-282-0802
FAX: 318-329-8407
e-mail: infos@medcamps.com
www.medcamps.com

*Caleb Seney, Executive Director*
Serves children with severe asthma and allergies and many more.

**8262 Mountaineer Spina Bifida Camp**
Ste 427
350 Capitol St
Charleston, WV 25301-1757
304-558-7098
800-642-9704
FAX: 304-558-2866
www2.kidscamps.com

*Nancy Dunst, Camp Director*
*Tonya Brown-Stobble, RN*
Is a non profit organization which pursues education and training and focuses on activities that promote independence and those that facilitate everyday life. The objectives are to build self esteem, promote independence and enhance the development of social skills.

**8263 Muscular Dystrophy Association Free Camp**
121 W Fireweed Ln
Suite 100
Anchorage, AK 99503-2053
907-276-2131
FAX: 907-276-0946
www.mdaalaska.com

*Sabrina Hoppas, Executive Director*
*Christin Crowder, Healthcare Services Coordinator*
*Kelli Buchanan, Administrative Assistant*
MDA Camp provides a wide range of activities for those who have limited mobility or are in wheelchairs. The camp offers may outdoor sporting activities, art's & crafts and talent shows.

**8264 NeSoDak**
Lutherans Outdoors in South Dakota
2001 S Summit Ave
Sioux Falls, SD 57197-1
605-274-5326
800-888-1464
FAX: 605-274-5024
e-mail: info@losd.org
www.losd.org

*Teri Gayer, Director*
*Layne Nelson, Executive Director*
Camp is located in Waubay, South Dakota. Sessions for children with diabetes. Coed, ages 8-18.

**8265 Northwest Kiwanis Camp**
P.O.Box 1227
Port Hadlock, WA 98339-1227
360-732-7222
e-mail: nwkc@earthlink.net
www.kiwaniscamp.com

*Sharron Sherfick, Camp Administrator*
*Katie Jackson, Program Director*
*Brandan Davidson, Counselor Advocates*
*Keri Lester, Counselor Advocates*

Campers range from 6-60 in age, and includes those with developmental disabilities, cerebral palsy, autism, downs syndrome, and other physical and/or mental handicaps.

**8266 Phantom Lake YMCA Camp**
S110 W30240 YMCA Camp Road
Mukwonago, WI 53149-9535
262-363-4386
FAX: 262-363-4351
e-mail: office@phantomlakeymca.org
www.phantomlakeymca.org

*Jeff Spang, CEO*
*Tony Ayala, Camp Director*

Summer camping for children with epilepsy, ages 7-15.

**8267 Shady Oaks Camp**
16300 Parker Road
Homer Glen, IL 60491-9749
708-301-0816
FAX: 708-301-5091
e-mail: soc16300@sbcglobal.net
shadyoakscamp.org

*Mary Pisano, Camp Treasurer*
*Scott Steele, Executive Director*

Shady Oaks Camp provides outdoor fun and recreation for children and adults with cerebral palsy and similar disabilities. Our camp is organized with the goal of providing stimulating life experiences that our campers may not have the opportunity to engage in elsewhere.

**8268 Sherman Lake YMCA Summer Camp**
Sherman Lake YMCA Outdoor Center
6225 N 39th St
Augusta, MI 49012-9722
269-731-3000
FAX: 269-731-3020
e-mail: shermanlakeymca@ymcasl.org
www.shermanlakeymca.org

*Luke Austenfeld, Executive Director*
*Kathy Simpson, Business Manager*
*Lorrie Syverson, Director of Camping, Education & Retreat Services*
*Mark VanDaff, Facility Manager*

Summer camping sessions for campers with ADD and spina bifida. Coed, ages 6-15 and families, seniors.

**8269 Strength for the Journey**
Oregon-Idaho Conference Center
1505 SW 18th Ave
Portland, OR 97201-2524
503-802-9210
800-593-7539
FAX: 503-228-3196
e-mail: camping@gocamping.org
www.gocamping.org

*Lisa Jean Hoefner, Executive Director*

Camp is located near Sisters, Oregon. For adults living with HIV/AIDS.

**8270 Summer Camp for Children with Muscular Dystrophy**
Muscular Dystrophy Association - USA
3300 E Sunrise Dr
Tucson, AZ 85718-3208
520-529-2000
800-572-1717
FAX: 520-529-5300
e-mail: mda@mdausa.org
www.mdausa.org

*Robert Ross, President*
*Michael A Blishak, Director Community Programs*
*Valerie A Cwik MD, Medical Director*

Offers a wide range of activities such as adaptive sports, swimming, fishing, archery, scavenger hunts, dances & talent shows, art's & crafts, karaoke, and campfires.

**8271 Summer Camp for Physically & Mentally Challenged Children & Adults**
Kansas Jaycees' Cerebral Palsy Foundation
P.O.Box 267
Augusta, KS 67207-267
316-775-2421
FAX: 316-775-2421
e-mail: execdirector@cpranch.org
www.cpranch.org

*Cheryl Schmeidler, Executive Director*
*Sarah Walker, Camp Director*

Our mission is to provide a program which will allow individuals to enjoy their highest level of functioning and independence, consistant with their abilities, in a summer camp setting.

**8272 Suttle Lake Camp**
Oregon/Idaho Conference Center
29551 Suttle Lake Rd
Sisters, OR 97759-9508
541-595-6663
FAX: 541-595-2818
e-mail: suttlelake@gocamping.org
www.gbgm-umc.org

*Jane Petke, Camp Director*
*Daniel Petke, Facilities Director*
*Wendy White, Food Service*
*Steven Willson, Camping Ministry Intern*

Camp is located in Sisters, Oregon. Camping sessions for children and adults with HIV. Coed, ages 6-18, families, seniors and single adults.

**8273 TSA CT Kid's Summer Event**
Tourette Syndrome Association of Connecticut (TSA)
PO Box 185883
Hamden, CT 06518
203-980-4215
e-mail: joytavo@tsact.org
www.tsact.org

*Tom Meehan, Chairman*
*Peter Tavolacci, Vice-Chairman*
*Paul Nazario, Treasurer*

TSA of Connecticut sponsors summer events for children with TS/Tourette Syndrome activities of which include minature golf in addition to an Annual Conference. The kids' program at this annual conference provides children who have TS a unique opportunity to meet other children like them who also struggle with TS. Entertainment includes puppeteers, magicians, learning karate from the experts, getting face paintings and more.

*uniqu pages*

**8274 Texas Lions Camp**
Lions Club Of Texas
P.O.Box 290247
Kerrville, TX 78029-0247
830-896-8500
FAX: 830-896-3666
www.lionscamp.com

*Stephen Mabry, Executive Director*

The primary purpose of the League shall be to provide, without charge, a camp for physically disabled, hearing/vision impaired and diabetic children from the State of Texas, regardless of race, religion, or national origin. Our goal is to create an atmosphere wherein campers will learn the can do philosophy and be allowed to achieve maximum personal growth and self-esteem. The camp welcomes boys and girls ages 7-16.

**8275 Twin Lakes Camp**
1451 E Twin Lakes Rd
Hillsboro, IN 47949-8004
765-798-4000
e-mail: outdoors@twinlakescamp.com
www.twinlakescamp.com

*Jon Beight, Executive Director*
*Dan Daily, Program Director*
*Duane Bush, Guest Service*
*Donna Beight, Secretary*

Provides a summer camp program for special needs children and young adults. Campers suffer from a wide range of maladies including crippling accidents, Spina Bifida, epilepsy, Cerebral Palsy, Muscular Dystrophy, Quadriplegia, Paraplegia, and other disabling diseases. Campers range in age from 8 to 27.

**8276 VACC Camp**
Miami Childrens Hospital
3200 W.W. 60 Ct
Suite 203
Miami, FL 33155-4076
305-662-8222
FAX: 305-663-8417
e-mail: bela.florentin@mch.com
www.vacccamp.com

*Bela Florentin, Camp Coordinator*

Free week-long overnight camp for ventilation assisted children and their families.

**8277 Wallowa Lake Camp**
Oregon-Idaho Conference Center
84522 Church Ln
Joseph, OR 97845
541-432-1271
e-mail: wallowa@gocamping.org
www.wallowalakecamp.org

*David Lovegren, Manager*
*Ingrid Lovegren, Manager*

Camp offers volleyball, badminton, horseshoes, baseball, crafts and wildlife viewing.

**8278 Wisconsin Lions Camp**
Wisconsin Lions Foundation
3834 County Road A
Rosholt, WI 54473-8826
715-677-4969
FAX: 715-677-3297
TTY:715-677-6999
e-mail: info@wisconsinlionscamp.com
wisconsinlionscamp.com

*Andrea Yenter, Camp Operations Manager*
*Jamie Jannusch, Assistant Camp Operations Manager*
*Ellyse Wenos, Interim Program Coordinator*
*Paula Lauer, RN, Health Care Supervisor*

Serves children who have either a visual, hearing or mild cognitive disability, as well as diabetes types I and II. Program activities include sailing, ropes course, hiking and canoe trips, environmental education, swimming, camping, canoeing, outdoor living skills and handicrafts. ACA accredited, located in central Wisconsin, near Stevens Point.

**8279 Y Camp**
YMCA of Greater Des Moines
1192 166th Drive
Boone, IA 50036-1720
515-432-7558
FAX: 515-432-5414
e-mail: ycamp@dmymca.org
www.y-camp.org

*David Sherry, Executive Director*
*Mike Havlik, Program Director- Environmental Education*
*BJ Murray, Program Director- Summer Camp*
*Cole Bowermaster, Program Director - Groups and Retreats*

Camp is located in Boone, Iowa. Year-round one and two-week sessions for boys and girls with cancer, diabetes, asthma, cystic fibrosis, hearing impaired and other disabilities. Coed, ages 6-16 and families.

**8280 YMCA Camp Fitch**
The YMCA Of Youngstown - Metro Office
17 N Champion St
P.O. Box 1287
Youngstown, OH 44501
330-744-8411
FAX: 330-744-8415
e-mail: info@campfitchymca.com
www.youngstownymca.org

*Kenneth L. Rudge, CEO*
*John H. Yerian Jr., President*
*William Bigelow, Secretary*
*Phillip Kocon, Treasurer*

Camp is located in North Springfield, Pennsylvania. Camping sessions for children and adults with diabetes, hearing impairment, developmental disabilities, mobility limitation and speech/communication impairment. Ages 8-16, families and seniors.

**8281 YMCA Camp Horseshoe**
Ohio-West Virginia YMCA
Po Box 239
Point Pleasant, WV 25550-9408
304-675-5899
FAX: 304-478-4446
e-mail: horseshoe@hi-y.org
www.hi-y.org

*David King, Executive Director*

Summer camping for children with cancer, ages 7-18.

**8282 YMCA Camp Ihduhapi**
Minneapolis YMCA Camping Services
3425 Ihduhapi Rd
Loretto, MN 55357-9512
763-479-1146
FAX: 612-823-2482
e-mail: info@campihduhapi.org
campihduhapi.org

*Kerry Pioske, Camp Executive*
*Josh Cobb, Overnight Camp Director*
*Devin Hanson, Day Camp Director*
*Eric Wobschall, Building Superintendent*

Camp is located in Loretto, Minnesota. Summer sessions for campers with asthma/respiratory ailments and epilepsy. Coed, ages 7-16.

**8283 YMCA Camp Kitaki**
Lincoln YMCA
570 Fallbrook Blvd.
Suite 210
Lincoln, NE 68521
402-434-9225
FAX: 402-434-9208
www.ymcalincoln.org

*Chris Klingberg, Executive Director*
*Anh Nguyen, Associate Executive Director*
*Michelle Kiddoo, Program Director - Health/Wellness*
*Jennifer Roller, Program Director - Aquatics/Youth/Teen/Family*

Camp is located in Louisville, Nebraska. Summer sessions for children with cystic fibrosis. Coed, ages 7-17 and families.

**8284 YMCA Camp Orkila**
YMCA of Greater Seattle
909 4th Ave
Seattle, WA 98104-1194
206-382-5000
FAX: 206-382-4920
e-mail: dstankevich@seattleymca.org
www.seattleymca.org

*Robert B. Gilbertson, President/CEO*
*Jane Brenneman, Human Resources*
*Sue Camou Arrant, Chief Operating Officer*
*Glenn Tsugawa, Chief Financial Officer*

Camping for children with blood disorders and diabetes, ages 8-18.

**8285 YMCA Camp Shady Brook**
YMCA of the Pikes Peak Region (PPYMCA)
316 N. Tejon Street
Colorado Springs, CO 80903-1306 719-329-7266
FAX: 719-272-7026
e-mail: campinfo@ppymca.org
www.campshadybrook.org

*Joanna Stark, Executive Director*
*Pat Soldan, Program Director*
*Patrick Casey, Facility Director*
*Michaela Eddleston, Conference & Retreat Director*
Camp is located in Sedalia, Colorado. One-week sessions for campers with HIV. Boys and girls 7-16. Also families, seniors and single adults.

**8286 YMCA Camp Weona**
YMCA of Greater Buffalo
301 Cayuga Rd
Suite 100
Buffalo, NY 14225-1912 716-565-6000
FAX: 716-565-6007
e-mail: contactus@ymcabuffaloniagra.org
www.ymcabuffaloniagara.org

*John D. Murray, President/CEO*
Camp is located in Gainesville, New York. Camping sessions for children and adults with epilepsy. Coed, ages 7-16, families and single adults. Nestled in 1,000 acres of hardwood and pine forests, Weona has miles of picturesque hiking trails, brooks, a heated outdoor pool and a world class adventure ropes course. Our indoor facilities include arts and crafts studios, environmental classrooms and a challenging rock climbing wall. It is the ideal setting for hands-on fun, adventure and learning.

**8287 YMCA Camp jewell**
YMCA of Greater Hartford
6 Prock Hill Road
P.O. Box 8
Colebrook, CT 06021 860-379-2782
888-412-2267
FAX: 860-379-8715
e-mail: camp.jewell@ghymca.org
www.ghymca.org

*Eric Tucker, Executive Director*
Camp is located in Colebrook, Connecticut. Two-week sessions for children with cancer. Coed, ages 8-16. Also families.

**8288 YMCA Camp of Maine**
305 Winthrop Center Rd
P.O. Box 446
Winthrop, ME 04364- 3543 207-395-4200
FAX: 207-395-7230
e-mail: info@maineycamp.org
www.maineycamp.org

*Barry W Costa, Executive Director*
*Larry Gardella, Camp Director*
Activities include arts and crafts, nature study, hiking, and overnight camping, dancing, and singing. Summer session dates run from June through August; for ages 8-16.

**8289 YMCA Outdoor Center Campbell Gard**
4803 Augspurger Rd
Hamilton, OH 45011-9547 513-867-0600
877-224-9622
FAX: 513-867-0127
e-mail: camp@gmvymca.org
www.ccgymca.org

*Jim Sexstone, Executive Director*
Camp is located in Hamilton, Ohio. Camping sessions for children with ADD, autism, developmental disabilities and blindness/visual impairment. Coed, ages 6-17 and families.

## Print: Books

**8290 A Woman's Guide to Living with HIV Infection**
Johns Hopkins University Press
2715 N Charles St
Baltimore, MD 21218-4319 410-516-6900
FAX: 410-516-6998
e-mail: jwehmueller@press.jhu.edu
www.press.jhu.edu

*Rebecca A Clark M.D., PhD, Author*
*Robert T Maupin Jr. M.D. FACOG, Co-Author*
*Jill Hayes Hammer PhD, Co-Author*
A resource for women with HIV that discusses coping with the diagnosis, finding a physician, recognizing symptoms, and preventing complications. Explains the latest treatment options and advice on coping with gynecologic infections. *$18.00*
*328 pages Hardback*

**8291 ABC of Asthma, Allergies & Lupus**
Global Health Solutions
2146 Kings Garden Way
Falls Church, VA 22043-2593 703-848-2333
800-759-3999
FAX: 703-848-0028
e-mail: information@watercure.com
www.watercure.com

*Fereydoon Batmanghelidj MD, Author*
*Xiaopo Batmanghelidj, President*
*Kristin Swan, Administrator*
This book introduces new approaches in preventing and treating asthma, allergies and lupus without toxic chemicals. It also offers new insight on how to prevent and treat children's asthma. *$ 17.00*
*240 pages*
*ISBN 0-962994-26-x*

**8292 AIDS Sourcebook**
Omnigraphics, Inc.
Po Box 31-1640
Detroit, MI 48231 313-961-1340
800-234-1340
FAX: 313-961-1383
www.omnigraphics.com

*Sandra J Judd, Editor*
Basic consumer health information about the Human Immunodeficiency Virus (HIV) and Acquired Immunodeficiency Syndrome (AIDS), including facts about its origins, stages, types, transmission, risk factors, and prevention, and featuring details about diagnostic testing, antiretroviral treatments, and co-occurring infections. *$ 85.00*
*600 pages 5th Edition 1911*
*ISBN 0-780811-47-8*

**8293 AIDS Sourcebook, 4th Edition**
Omnigraphics
PO Box 31-1640
Detroit, MI 48231 313-961-1340
800-234-1340
FAX: 313-961-1383
e-mail: info@omnigraphics.com
www.omnigraphics.com

*Ivy L Alexander, Editor*
Basic consumer health information about the Human Immunodeficiency Virus (HIV) and Acquired Immunodeficiency Syndrome (AIDS), featuring updated statistics and facts about risks, prevention, screening, diagnosis, treatment, side effects, and complications, including a section about the impact of HIV/AIDS on the health of women, children, and adolescents. *$84.00*
*680 pages Hard cover*
*ISBN 0-780809-97-0*

**8294 AIDS and Other Manifestations of HIV Infection**
Elsevier Inc
30 Corporate Dr
Suite 400
Burlington, MA 01803-4252
781-313-4700
800-545-2522
FAX: 800-568-5136
e-mail: usbkinfo@elsevier.com
www.elsevier.com

*Gary Wormser MD, Editor*
A comprehensive overview of the biological properties of this etiologic viral agent, its clinicopathological manifestations, the epidemiology of its infection, and present and future therapeutic options. *$249.95*
*1000 pages 2004*
*ISBN 0-127640-51-7*

**8295 AIDS in the Twenty-First Century: Disease and Globalization**
Palgrav Macmillan
175 5th Ave
New York, NY 10010-7703
888-330-8477
FAX: 800-672-2054
e-mail: customerservice@vhpsva.com
www.palgrave-usa.com

*Gabriella Georgiades, Editor*
*Alan Whiteside, Author*
*Tony Barnett, Co-Author*
The authors - exprets in the field for over 15 years - argue that it is vital to not only look at AIDS in terms of prevention and treatment, but to also consider consequences which affect households, communities, companies, governments, and countries. This is a major contribution toward understanding the global public health crisis, as well as the relationship between poverty, inequality, and infectious diseases. *$32.00*
*464 pages*
*ISBN 1-403997-68-5*

**8296 Adult Leukemia: A Comprehensive Guide for Patients and Families**
O'Reilly Media Inc
1005 Gravenstein Hwy N
Sebastopol, CA 95472-2811
707-827-7000
800-998-9938
FAX: 707-829-0104
e-mail: order@oreilly.com
www.oreilly.com

*Linda Lamb, Editor*
*Barb Lackritz, Author*
For the tens of thousands of Americans with adult leukemia, Adult Leukemia: A Comprehensive Guide for Patients and Families addresses diagnosis, medical tests, finding a good oncologist, treatments, side effects, getting emotional and other support, resources for further study, and much more. The book includes real-life stories from those who have battled leukemia themselves. *$29.95*
*536 pages Paperback*
*ISBN 0-596500-01-7*

**8297 Advanced Breast Cancer: A Guide to Living with Metastic Disease**
O'Reilly Media Inc
1005 Gravenstein Hwy N
Sebastopol, CA 95472-2811
707-827-7000
800-998-9938
FAX: 707-829-0104
e-mail: order@oreilly.com
www.oreilly.com

*Linda Lamb, Editor*
*Musa Mayer, Author*
This is the only book on breast cancer that deals honestly with the realities of living with metastic disease, yet offers hope and comfort. All aspects of facing the disease are covered, including: coping with the shock of recurrence, seeking information and making treatment decisions, communicating effectively with medical personnel finding support, and handling disease progression and end-of-life issues. A comprehensive guide, it also provides updated resources and treatment developments. *$24.95*
*532 pages Paperback 1998*
*ISBN 1-565925-22-X*

**8298 Allergies Sourcebook**
P.O.Box 311640
Detroit, MI 48231-1640
313-961-1340
FAX: 313-961-1383
www.omnigraphics.com

*Amy L Sutton, Editor*
Basic comsumer health information about the immune system and allergic disorders, including rhinitis (hay fever), sinusitis, conjunctivitis, asthma, atopic dermatitis, and anaphylaxis, and allergy triggers such as pollen, mold, dust mites, animal dander, chemicals, foods and additives, and medications; along with facts about allergy diagnosis and treatment, tips on avoiding triggers and preventing symptoms, a glossary of related terms, and directories of resources for additional help and info. *$95.00*
*608 pages 4th Edition 1911*

**8299 Allergies Sourcebook, 3rd Edition**
Omnigraphics
PO Box 31-1640
Detroit, MI 48231
313-961-1340
800-234-1340
FAX: 313-961-1383
e-mail: info@omnigraphics.com
www.omnigraphics.com

*Amy L Sutton, Editor*
Includes information on the causes of allergies, identification, treatments and statistics. *$84.00*
*588 pages Hard cover*
*ISBN 0-780809-50-5*

**8300 Alternative Approach to Allergies**
Harper Collins Publishers
10 E 53rd St
New York, NY 10022-5244
212-207-7000
FAX: 212-207-7901
e-mail: orders@harpercollins.com
www.harpercollins.com

*Theron G Randolph M.D., Author*
*Ralph W Moss PhD, Co-Author*
A comprehensive guide to staying well and allergy-free by a pioneer in the field of environmental medicine.

*ISBN 0-060916-93-1*

**8301 Alzheimer Disease Sourcebook**
Omnigraphics
Po Box 8002
Aston, PA 19014-8002
800-234-1340
FAX: 800-875-1340
e-mail: info@omnigraphics.com
www.omnigraphics.com

Basic consumer health information about alzheimer disease and otehr forms of dementia, including mild cognitive impairment, corticobasal degeneration, dementia with lewy bodies, frontotemporal dementia, huntington disease, parkinson disease, and vascular dementia; along with information about recent research on the diagnosis and prevention of alzheimer disease and genetic testing, tips for maintaining cognitive functioning, strategies for long-term planning, advice for caregivers, etc. *$95.00*
*600 pages 1911*
*ISBN 0-780811-50-8*

**8302 Alzheimer Disease Sourcebook, 4th Edition**

Omnigraphics
PO Box 31-1640
Detroit, MI 48231
610-461-3548
800-234-1340
FAX: 800-875-1340
e-mail: info@omnigraphics.com
www.omnigraphics.com

Basic consumer health information about alzheimer disease, other dementias, and related disorders, including multi-infarct dementia, dementia with lewy bodies, frontotemporal dementia (pick disease), Wernicke-Korsakoff syndrome (alcohol-related dementia), AIDS dementia complex, Huntington disease, Creutzfeldt-Jacob disease, and delirium. *$84.00*

*603 pages*

*ISBN 0-780810-01-3*

**8303 American Academy of Pediatrics Guide to Your Child's Alleriges and Asthma**

American Academy of Pediatrics
141 Northwest Point Blvd
Elk Grove Vlg, IL 60007-1098
847-228-0604
FAX: 847-434-8000
e-mail: newpubs@aap.org
www.aap.org

*Judith Palfrey, President*
*Errol Alden, Executive Director*

Consumer resource for parents who need answers and information about their children's allergies and asthma. Current advice on identifying allergies and asthma, preventing attacks, minimizing triggers, understanding medications, explaining allergies to young children, and helping children manage symptoms. *$15.00*

*191 pages*

*ISBN 0-679769-82-X*

**8304 Amyotrophic Lateral Sclerosis: A Guide for Patients and Families**

Demos Medical Publishing
15th Floor
11 West 42nd Street
New York, NY 10036
212-683-0072
800-532-8663
FAX: 212-683-0118
e-mail: info@demosmedpub.com
www.demosmedpub.com

*Richard Winters, Executive Editor*
*Beth Barry, Publisher*
*Noreen Henson, Executive Director of Demos Health*
*Reina Santana, Director of Special Sales & Rights*

This comprehensive guide covers every aspect of the management of ALS. Beginning with discussions of its clinical features of the disease, diagnosis, and an overview of symptom management, major sections deal with medical and rehabilitative management, living with ALS, managing advanced disease and end-of-life issues, and reources that can provide support and assistance. *$29.95*

*470 pages 2001*

*ISBN 1-888799-28-5*

**8305 Arthritis Sourcebook**

P.O.Box 311640
Detroit, MI 48231-1640
313-961-1340
FAX: 313-961-1383
www.omnigraphics.com

*Amy L Sutton, Editor*

**8306 Arthritis Sourcebook.**

Omnigraphics
PO Box 31-1640
Detroit, MI 48231
313-961-1340
800-234-1340
FAX: 313-961-1383
e-mail: info@omnigraphics.com
www.omnigraphics.com

*Amy L Sutton, Editor*

Basic consumer health information about osteoarthritis, rheumatoid arthritis, other rheumatic disorders, infectious forms of arthritis, and diseases with symptoms linked to arthritis, and facts about diagnosis, pain management, and surgical therapies. *$84.00*

*567 pages 2nd Edition*

*ISBN 0-780806-67-2*

**8307 Asthma Sourcebook**

P.O.Box 311640
Detroit, MI 48231-1640
313-961-1340
FAX: 313-961-1383
www.omnigraphics.com

*Karen Bellenir, Editor*

**8308 Asthma Sourcebook.**

Omnigraphics
PO Box 31-1640
Detroit, MI 48231
313-961-1340
800-234-1340
FAX: 313-961-1383
e-mail: info@omnigraphics.com
www.omnigraphics.com

*Karen Bellenir, Editor*

Provides information about asthma, including symptoms, remedies and research updates. *$84.00*

*581 pages 2nd Edition*

*ISBN 0-780808-66-9*

**8309 Asthma and Allergy Answers: A Patient Education Library**

Asthma and Allergy Foundation of America
8201 Corporate Dr
Suite 1000
Landover, MD 20785
202-466-7643
800-727-8462
FAX: 202-466-8940
e-mail: info@aafa.org
www.aafa.org

*William McLin, President/CEO*
*Yolanda Miller, Vice President/CFO*
*Charlotte Collins, J.D., Vice President Of Policy Prgrms*

A resource tool has information on more than 40 topics of interest to patients. These reproducible camera ready Answers are written in a patient friendly questions and answer format. There is space to personalize these handy patient education materials with your practice or facility information. *$50.00*

**8310 Back & Neck Sourcebook**

P.O.Box 311640
Detroit, MI 48231-1640
313-961-1340
FAX: 313-961-1383
www.omnigraphics.com

*Amy L Sutton, Editor*

**8311 Back & Neck Sourcebook.**
Omnigraphics
PO Box 31-1640
Detroit, MI 48231
313-961-1340
800-234-1340
FAX: 313-961-1383
e-mail: info@omnigraphics.com
www.omnigraphics.com

*Amy L Sutton, Editor*
Basic consumer health information about back and neck pain, spinal cord injuries, and related disorders, such as degenerative disk disease, osteoarthritis, scoliosis, sciatica, spina bifida, and spinal stenosis, and featuring facts about maintaining spinal health, self-care, rehabilitative care, chiropractic care, spinal surgeries, and complementary therapies. *$84.00*
*607 pages 2nd Edition*
*ISBN 0-780807-38-9*

**8312 Being Close**
National Jewish Health
1400 Jackson St
Denver, CO 80206-2761
303-270-2708
FAX: 303-398-1125
e-mail: allstetterw@njc.org
www.nationaljewish.org

*Michael Salem M.D., President/CEO*
*William Allstetter, Director Media/External Relation*
A booklet offering information to patients suffering from a respiratory disorder such as emphysema, asthma or tuberculosis, that discusses sexual problems and feelings.

**8313 Bittersweet Chances: A Personal Journey o f Living and Learning in the Face of Illness**
PublishAmerica
P.O.Box 151
Frederick, MD 21705-151
301-695-1707
FAX: 301-631-9073
e-mail: support@publishamerica.com
www.publishamerica.com

*Dana Selenke Broehl, Author*
Recounts Doug and Dana Broehl's journey of growth through the darkness of cystic fibrosis and the renewed hope of a double lung transplant. *$24.95*
*189 pages Softcover*
*ISBN 1-413713-24-6*

**8314 Blood and Circulatory Disorders Sourcebook**
Omnigraphics
P.O.Box 311640
Detroit, MI 48231-1640
313-961-1340
800-234-1340
FAX: 313-961-1383
e-mail: info@omnigraphics.com
www.omnigraphics.com

*Amy L Sutton, Editor*
This Sourcebook provides patients and consumers with general information and specific facts about blood and circulatory system disorders. It also offers helpful information about scientific advancements and safety procedures in blood, bone marrow, and stem cell donation and transplantation, as well as tips for improving blood and circulatory healsorders and injuries, and a directory of sources for further help and information. *$84.00*
*634 pages 2nd Edition*
*ISBN 0-780807-46-4*

**8315 Blooming Where You're Planted: Stories From The Heart**
Meeting Life's Challenges
9042 Aspen Grove Lane
Madison, WI 53717-2700
608-824-0402
FAX: 608-824-0403
e-mail: help@MeetingLifesChallenges.com
www.MeetingLifesChallenges.com

*Shelley Peterman Schwatz, Editor*
Author Shelley Peterman Schwarz takes you on her journey of self-discovery and change following her diagnosis of multiple sclerosis in 1979. Her personal stories are warm and humorous, and insightful. This 138-page book will motivate and inspire you to rise above life's challenges and live life to its fullest. *$12.95*
*138 pages 1998*
*ISBN 0-891854-01-1*

**8316 Brain Allergies: The Psychonutrient and Magnetic Connections**
McGraw-Hill
www.allergiesshop.com

*William Philpott PhD, Author*
*Dwight Keating PhD, Author*
*Linus Pauling PhD, Author*
A complete overview of the concept of brain allergies - the theory that exposure to certain foods and other substances triggers mental disorders in people so predisposed, and that such disturbances can be cured by eliminating these substances. *$16.95*

*ISBN 0-658003-98-1*

**8317 Brain Disorders Sourcebook**
P.O.Box 311640
Detroit, MI 48231-1640
313-961-1340
FAX: 313-961-1383
www.omnigraphics.com

*Sandra J Judd, Editor*

**8318 Brain Disorders Sourcebook.**
Omnigraphics
PO Box 31-1640
Detroit, MI 48231
313-961-1340
800-234-1340
FAX: 313-961-1383
e-mail: info@omnigraphics.com
www.omnigraphics.com

*Sandra J Judd, Editor*
Brain Disorders Sourcebook, Second Edition, provides readers with basic health information about acquired and traumatic brain injuries, infections and disorders. It also includes information on the brain's structure and function, treatment and rehabilitation options, reports on current research initiatives, a glossary of terms related to brain disorders and injuries, and a directory of sources for further help and information. *$84.00*
*600 pages 2nd Edition*
*ISBN 0-780807-44-0*

**8319 Breast Cancer Sourcebook**
P.O.Box 311640
Detroit, MI 48231-1640
313-961-1340
FAX: 313-961-1383
www.omnigraphics.com

*Sandra J Judd, Editor*

**8320 Breast Cancer Sourcebook.**
Omnigraphics
PO Box 31-1640
Detroit, MI 48231
313-961-1340
800-234-1340
FAX: 313-961-1383
e-mail: info@omnigraphics.com
www.omnigraphics.com

*Sandra J Judd, Editor*
Provides information on the prevention of Breast Cancer, self care, treatment options, alternative therapies and diagnostic methods. *$84.00*
*600 pages 3rd Edition*
*ISBN 0-780810-30-3*

**8321 Breathe Free**
Lotus Press
P.O.Box 325
Twin Lakes, WI 53181-325
262-889-8561
800-824-6396
FAX: 262-889-8591
e-mail: lotuspress@lotuspress.com
www.lotuspress.com

*D Gagnon, Author*
*A Morningstar, Co-Author*
A nutritional and herbal medicine self-help guide to treating a full range of respiratory conditions, including colds and flu. *$14.95*
*179 pages*
*ISBN 0-914955-07-1*

**8322 Cancer Sourcebook**
P.O.Box 311640
Detroit, MI 48231-1640
313-961-1340
FAX: 313-961-1383
www.omnigraphics.com

*Karen Bellenir, Editor*

**8323 Cancer Sourcebook for Women**
P.O.Box 311640
Detroit, MI 48231-1640
313-961-1340
FAX: 313-961-1383
www.omnigraphics.com

*Amy L Sutton, Editor*

**8324 Cancer Sourcebook for Women.**
Omnigraphics
PO Box 31-1640
Detroit, MI 48231
313-961-1340
800-234-1340
FAX: 313-961-1383
e-mail: info@omnigraphics.com
www.omnigraphics.com

*Amy L Sutton, Editor*
This Sourcebook provides patients and consumers with general information and specific facts about types of cancer that affect women. It offers basic information on cancer and the female reproductive system, as well as strategies that may help women prevent cancer. *$ 84.00*
*687 pages 5th Edition*
*ISBN 0-780808-67-6*

**8325 Cancer Sourcebook.**
Omnigraphics
PO Box 31-1640
Detroit, MI 48231
313-961-1340
800-234-1340
FAX: 313-961-1383
e-mail: info@omnigraphics.com
www.omnigraphics.com

*Karen Bellenir, Editor*
Includes information on the major forms and stages of cancer. *$84.00*
*1105 pages 5th Edition*
*ISBN 0-780809-47-5*

**8326 Cardiovascular Diseases and Disorders Sourcebook, 3rd Edition**
Omnigraphics
P.O.Box 311640
Detroit, MI 48231-1640
610-461-3548
800-234-1340
FAX: 800-875-1340
e-mail: info@omnigraphics.com
www.omnigraphics.com

Cardiovascular Diseases and Disorders Sourcebook, Third Edition, provides information about the symptoms, diagnosis, and treatment heart diseases and vascular disorders. It includes demographic and statistical data, an overview of the cardiovascular system, a discussion of risk factors and prevention techniques, a look at cardiovascular concerns specific to women, and a report on current research initiatives. *$84.00*
*687 pages Hard cover*
*ISBN 0-780807-39-6*

**8327 Childhood Cancer Survivors: A Practical Guide to Your Future**
O'Reilly Media Inc
1005 Gravenstein Hwy N
Sebastopol, CA 95472-2811
707-827-7000
800-998-9938
FAX: 707-829-0104
e-mail: order@oreilly.com
www.oreilly.com

*Linda Lamb, Editor*
*Nancy Keene, Author*
*Wendy Hobbie, Co-Author*
*Kathy Ruccione, Co-Author*
More than 250,000 people have survived childhood cancer - a cause for celebration. Authors Keene, Hobbie, and Ruccione chart the territory of long-term survivorship: relationships; overcoming employment or insurance discrimination; maximizing health; follow-up schedules; medical late effects. The stories of over sixty survivors - their challenges and triumphs - are told. Includes medical history record-keeper. *$27.95*
*464 pages Paperback 1906*
*ISBN 0-596528-51-5*

**8328 Childhood Cancer: A Parent's Guide to Solid Tumor Cancers**
O'Reilly Media Inc
1005 Gravenstein Hwy N
Sebastopol, CA 95472-2811
707-827-7019
800-889-8969
FAX: 707-824-8268
e-mail: order@oreilly.com
www.oreilly.com

Childhood Cancer: A Parent's Guide to Solid Tumor Cancers features a wealth of resources for parents of children with solid tumor cancers, plus many stories of veteran parents. Parents will encounter medical facts simply explained, practical advice to ease their daily lives, and tools to be strong advocates for their child. Includes a passport to record patient's medical history. *$29.95*
*560 pages Paperback*
*ISBN 0-596500-14-9*

**8329 Childhood Diseases and Disorders Sourcebook, 2nd Edition**
Omnigraphics
P.O.Box 311640
Detroit, MI 48231-1640
610-461-3548
800-234-1340
FAX: 800-875-1340
e-mail: info@omnigraphics.com
www.omnigraphics.com

*Sandra J Judd, Editor*

Basic consumer health information about medical problems often encountered in pre-adolescent children, including respiratory tract ailments, ear infections, sore throats, disorders of the skin and scalp, digestive and genitourinary diseases, infectious diseases, inflammatory disorders, chronic physical and developmental disorders, allergies, and more. *$84.00*

*600 pages Hard cover*

*ISBN 0-780810-31-0*

**8330 Childhood Leukemia: A Guide for Families, Friends & Caregivers**

O'Reilly Media Inc
1005 Gravenstein Hwy N
Sebastopol, CA 95472-2811
707-827-7000
800-998-9938
FAX: 707-829-0104
e-mail: order@oreilly.com
www.oreilly.com

*Linda Lamb, Editor*
*Nancy Keene, Author*

The second edition of this comprehensive guide offers detailed and precise medical information for parents that includes day-to-day practical advice on how to cope with procedures, hospitalization, family and friends, school, and social, emotional, and financial issues. It features a wealth of tools for prents and contains significant updates on treatments and procedures. *$29.95*

*528 pages 4th Edition 1910*

*ISBN 0-596500-15-7*

**8331 Children with Cerebral Palsy: A Parents' Guide**

Woodbine House
6510 Bells Mill Rd
Bethesda, MD 20817-1636
301-897-3570
800-843-7323
FAX: 301-897-5838
e-mail: info@woodbinehouse.com
www.woodbinehouse.com

*Irvin Shapell, Publisher*
*Beth Binns, Special Marketing Manager*
*Sarah Glenner, Office Receptionist;*
*Fran Marinaccio, Marketing Manager*

A classic primer for parents that provides a complete spetrum of information and compassionate advice about cerebral palsy and its effect on their child's development and education. *$18.95*

*481 pages*

*ISBN 0-933149-82-4*

**8332 Chronic Fatigue Syndrome: Your Natural Gu ide to Healing with Diet, Herbs and Other Methods**

Random House Publishing
1745 Broadway
New York, NY 10019-4305
212-216-9299
FAX: 212-940-7381
e-mail: ecustomerservice@randomhouse.com
www.randomhouse.com

*Susanna Porter, Editor*
*Michael T Murray N.D.*

Explains specific measures sufferers can take to improve stamina, mental energy, and physical abilities. *$15.00*

*208 pages*

*ISBN 1-559584-90-6*

**8333 Coffee in the Cereal: The First Year with Multiple Sclerosis**

Pathfinder Publishing
800-977-2282
e-mail: bill@pathfinderpublishing.com
www.pathfinderpublishing.com

Moorhead recounts the experience of her first year with multiple sclerosis with a vitality unique in the often gloomy world of personal medical histories. *$14.95*

*96 pages*

*ISBN 0-934793-07-7*

**8334 Colon & Rectal Cancer: A Comprehensive Guide for Patients & Families**

O'Reilly Media Inc
1005 Gravenstein Hwy N
Sebastopol, CA 95472-2811
707-827-7000
800-998-9938
FAX: 707-829-0104
e-mail: order@oreilly.com
www.oreilly.com

*Linda Lamb, Editor*
*Lorraine Johnston, Author*

The fourth most common cancer, colon and rectal cancer is diagnosed in 130,000 new cases in the United States each year. Patients and families need uo-to-date and in-depth information to participate wisely in treatment decisions (e.g., knowing what sexual and fertility issues to discuss with the doctor before surgery). This book covers coping with tests and treatment side effects, caring for ostomies, finding supportt, and other practical issues. *$24.95*

*544 pages Paperback 1999*

*ISBN 1-565926-33-1*

**8335 Colon Health: Key to a Vibrant Life**

Norwalk Press
P.O.Box 190526
Boise, ID 83719-526
928-445-5567
FAX: 928-445-5567
e-mail: info@drnormanwalker.com
www.drnormanwalker.com

*Norman Walker MD, Editor*

Includes complete glossary of terms and index of referrals.

**8336 Complementary Alternative Medicine and Multiple Sclerosis**

Demos Medical Publishing
Ste 301
11 West 42nd Street
New York, NY 10036
212-683-0072
800-532-8663
FAX: 212-683-0118
e-mail: info@demosmedpub.com
www.demosmedpub.com

*Richard Winters, Executive Editor*
*Beth Barry, Publisher*
*Noreen Henson, Executive Director of Demos Health*
*Reina Santana, Director of Special Sales & Rights*

Offers reliable information on the relevance, safety, and effectiveness of various alternative therapies that are not typically considered in discussions of MS management, yet are in widespread use. *$24.95*

*304 pages*

*ISBN 1-932603-54-9*

**8337 Conquering the Darkness: One Story of Recovering from a Brain Injury**

Paragon House
1925 Oakcrest Avenue
Suite 7
Saint Paul, MN 55113-2619
651-644-3087
800-447-3709
FAX: 800-494-0997
e-mail: paragon@paragonhouse.com
www.paragonhouse.com

*Rosemary Yokoi, Publicity Director*
*Gordon Anderson, Executive Director*
*Deborah Quinn, Author*

The course of recovery from a brain injury by a woman who lived through it. *$15.95*

*276 pages 1998*

*ISBN 1-557787-63-8*

**8338 Coping with Cerebral Palsy**
Rosen Publishing
29 E 21st St
New York, NY 10010-6209
800-237-9932
FAX: 888-436-4643
www.rosenpublishing.com

*Laura Anne Gilman, Author*
This second edition book provides parents of children and adults with cerebral palsy the answers to more than 300 questions that have been carefully researched. It represents 40 years of experience by the author and is presented in a highly readable, jargon-free manner. *$31.95*

*ISBN 0-823931-50-1*

**8339 Curing MS: How Science is Solving the Mysteries of Multiple Sclerosis**
Random House Publishing
1745 Broadway
New York, NY 10019-4305
212-785-1100
FAX: 212-572-6066
www.randomhouse.com

*Howard L Weiner M.D., Author*
Founder-director of the Multiple Sclerosis Center at Mass General Hospital discusses what ends up as a deconstruction of the last 30 years of his own and general MS research and of experience in treating patients with the puzzling disorder. Weiner summarizes what is currently known about treatments and the potential for a cure. *$14.95*
*352 pages 1905*
*ISBN 0-307236-04-8*

**8340 Cystic Fibrosis: A Guide for Patient and Family**
Lippincott Williams & Wilkins
P.O.Box 1620
Hagerstown, MD 21741-1620
301-223-2300
800-638-3030
FAX: 301-223-2400
e-mail: customerservice@lww.com
www.lww.com

*David M Orenstein MD, Author*
Text is designed specifically for patients with cystic fibrosis and their families. Explains the disease process, outlines the fundamentals of diagnosing and screening, and addresses the challenges of treatment for those living with CF. Includes new material on carrier testing, infection control, and more. *$51.50*
*448 pages 3rd Edition*
*ISBN 0-781741-52-1*

**8341 Diabetes Sourcebook**
P.O.Box 311640
Detroit, MI 48231-1640
313-961-1340
FAX: 313-961-1383
www.omnigraphics.com

*Karen Bellenir, Editor*

**8342 Diabetes Sourcebook.**
Omnigraphics
PO Box 31-1640
Detroit, MI 48231
313-961-1340
800-234-1340
FAX: 313-961-1383
e-mail: info@omnigraphics.com
www.omnigraphics.com

*Karen Bellenir, Editor*
Diabetes Sourcebook, Fourth Edition contains updated information for people seeking to understand the risk factors, complications, and management of diabetes. It discusses medical interventions, including the use of insulin and oral diabetes medications, self-monitoring of blood glucose, and complementary and alternative therapies. *$84.00*
*627 pages 4th Edition*
*ISBN 0-780810-05-1*

**8343 Digestive Diseases & Disorders Sourcebook**
Omnigraphics
P.O.Box 311640
Detroit, MI 48231-1640
610-461-3548
800-234-1340
FAX: 800-875-1340
e-mail: info@omnigraphics.com
www.omnigraphics.com

*Frederick Gale Ruffner, Founder*
*Peter Ruffner, Co-Founder*
Digestive Diseases and Disorders Sourcebook provides basic information for the layperson about common disorders of the upper and lower digestive tract. It also includes information about medications and recommendations for maintaining a healthy digestive tract in addition to a glossary of important terms and a directory of digestive diseases organizations are also provided. *$84.00*
*323 pages Hard cover*
*ISBN 0-780803-27-5*

**8344 Duchenne Muscular Dystrophy**
Oxford University Press
198 Madison Ave
New York, NY 10016-4308
212-726-6000
800-445-9714
FAX: 212-726-6443
e-mail: custserv.us@oup.com
www.us.oup.com

*William Lamsback, Editor*
*Alan Emery, Author*
*Francesco Muntoni, Co-Author*
Identification of the genetic defect responsible for Duchenne Muscular Dystrophy and isolation of the protein dystrophin have led to the development of new theories for the disease's pathogenesis. This title incorporates these advances from the field of molecular biology, and describes the resultant opportunities for screening, prenatal diagnosis, genetic counselling and management. *$135.00*
*282 pages 3rd Edition 2003*
*ISBN 0-198515-31-6*

**8345 Ear, Nose, and Throat Disorders Sourcebook**
Omnigraphics
P.O.Box 311640
Detroit, MI 48231-1640
313-961-1340
800-234-1340
FAX: 313-961-1383
e-mail: info@omnigraphics.com
www.omnigraphics.com

*Sandra J Judd, Editor*
Ear, Nose and Throat Disorders Sourcebook, Second Edition, provides consumers with updated health information on the most common disorders of the ear, nose, and throat. The book also includes descriptions of current diagnostic tests, discussion of common surgical procedures, including cosmetic surgery on the nose and ears, a glossary of related medical terms, and a directory of sources for further help and information. *$84.00*
*631 pages 2nd Edition*
*ISBN 0-780808-72-0*

**8346 Eating Disorders Sourcebook**
P.O.Box 311640
Detroit, MI 48231-1640
313-961-1340
FAX: 313-961-1383
www.omnigraphics.com

*Joyce Brennfleck Shannon, Editor*

**8347 Eating Disorders Sourcebook.**
Omnigraphics
PO Box 31-1640
Detroit, MI 48231
313-961-1340
800-234-1340
FAX: 313-961-1383
e-mail: info@omnigraphics.com
www.omnigraphics.com

*Joyce Brennfleck Shannon, Editor*
Provides general information, causes and treatments of eating disorders. *$84.00*
*557 pages 2nd Edition*
*ISBN 0-780809-48-2*

**8348 Educational Issues Among Children with Spina Bifida**
Spina Bifida Association of America
Ste 250
4590 Macarthur Blvd NW
Washington, DC 20007-4226
202-944-3285
800-621-3141
FAX: 202-944-3295
e-mail: sbaa@sbaa.org
www.sbaa.org

*Cindy Brownstein, President & CEO*
*Donald J. Lollar, Ed.D., Author*
*Sara Struwe, Chief Operating Officer & Director of Chapter Development*
*Robin Austin, Communications Manager*
Children with spina bifida/ hydrocephalus often show unique learning strengths and weaknesses that affect their schoolwork. Parents and schools need to work together to help the young people meet their physical, social, emotional, and academic goals.

**8349 Epilepsy, 199 Answers: A Doctor Responds to His Patients' Questions**
Demos Medical Publishing
Ste 301
11 West 42nd Street
New York, NY 10036
212-683-0072
800-532-8663
FAX: 212-683-0118
e-mail: info@demosmedpub.com
www.demosmedpub.com

*Andrew N. Wilner MD, FACP, FAAN, Author*
*Richard Winters, Executive Editor*
*Beth Barry, Publisher*
*Noreen Henson, Executive Director of Demos Health*
An epilepsy specialist answers questions about the causes, diagnosis, and treatments, and how to live and work with this brain disorder. Includes an epilepsy history timeline, patient health record form, resources, and a glossary. *$19.95*
*180 pages*
*ISBN 1-932603-35-2*

**8350 Epilepsy: Patient and Family Guide**
Demos Medical Publishing
Ste 301
11 West 42nd Street
New York, NY 10036
212-683-0072
800-532-8663
FAX: 212-683-0118
e-mail: info@demosmedpub.com
www.demosmedpub.com

*Orrin Devinsky, MD, Author*
*Richard Winters, Executive Editor*
*Beth Barry, Publisher*
*Noreen Henson, Executive Director of Demos Health*
A guide for adults with epilepsy and for parents of children with the disorder explains the nature and diversity of seizures, the risks and benefits of the various antiepileptic drugs, and medical and surgical therapies. *$16.95*
*408 pages*
*ISBN 1-932603-41-7*

**8351 Ethnic Diseases Sourcebook**
Omnigraphics
P.O.Box 311640
Detroit, MI 48231-1640
610-461-3548
800-234-1340
FAX: 800-875-1340
e-mail: info@omnigraphics.com
www.omnigraphics.com

*Frederick Gale Ruffner, Founder*
*Peter Ruffner, Co-Founder*
Ethnic Diseases Sourcebook provides health information about genetic and chronic diseases that affect ethnic and racial minorities in the United States. Information about mental health services, women's health, and tips for improving health are also included, along with a glossary and a list of resources for additional help and informatio methods, treatment options, and current research initiatives. *$84.00*
*648 pages Hard cover*
*ISBN 0-780803-36-7*

**8352 From Where I Sit: Making My Way with Cerebral Palsy**
Scholastic
557 Broadway
New York, NY 10012-3962
212-343-6100
FAX: 212-343-6934
e-mail: news@scholastic.com
www.scholastic.com

*Shelley Nixon, Author*
*Dick Robinson, Chairman, President and Chief Executive Officer*
*Maureen O'Connell, Executive Vice President, Chief Financial Officer and Chief Administra*
*Kyle Good, Senior Vice President, Corporate Communications and Media Relations*
An autobiographical account of a young woman explores how it feels to live with cerebral palsy while struggling to have a full life despite the challenges facing her every day. *$13.00*
*136 pages*
*ISBN 0-590395-84-X*

**8353 Genetics and Spina Bifida**
Spina Bifida Association of America
Ste 250
4590 Macarthur Blvd NW
Washington, DC 20007-4226
202-944-3285
800-621-3141
FAX: 202-944-3295
e-mail: sbaa@sbaa.org
www.sbaa.org

*Cindy Brownstein, President & CEO*
*Elizabeth C. Melvin, MS, CGC,, Editor*
*Sara Struwe, Chief Operating Officer & Director of Chapter Development*
*Robin Austin, Communications Manager*
Spina bifida is a birth defect involving incomplete formation of the spine.

**8354 Growing Up with Epilepsy: A Pratical Guide for Parents**
Demos Medical Publishing
Ste 301
11 West 42nd Street
New York, NY 10036
212-683-0072
800-532-8663
FAX: 212-683-0118
e-mail: info@demosmedpub.com
www.demosmedpub.com

*Lynn Bennett Blackburn, PhD, Author*
*Richard Winters, Executive Editor*
*Beth Barry, Publisher*
*Noreen Henson, Executive Director of Demos Health*
Developed to help parents with the uniques challenges that this disorder presents *$19.95*
*168 pages*
*ISBN 1-888799-74-9*

**8355 Guide to Living with HIV Infection: Developed at the Johns Hopkins AIDS Clinic**
Johns Hopkins Universty Press
2715 N Charles St
Baltimore, MD 21218-4319
410-516-6900
800-537-5487
FAX: 410-516-6998
e-mail: webmaster@jhupress.jhu.edu
www.press.jhu.edu

*William Brody, President*
*John G Bartlett, M.D., Author*
*Ann K Finkbeiner, Co-Author*
A handbook and reference for people living with HIV infection and their families, friends, and caregivers. *$19.95*
*408 pages 6th Edition*
*ISBN 0-801884-85-6*

**8356 Handbook of Chronic Fatigue Syndrome**
John Wiley & Sons
432 Elizabeth Ave
Somerset, NJ 8873
732-469-4400
800-225-5945
FAX: 732-302-2300
www.wiley.com

*Leonard A Jason, Editor*
*Patricia A Fennell, Editor*
*Renee R Taylor, Editor*
Discusses diagnosis and treatment as well as the history, phenomenology, symptomatology, assessment, and pediatric and community issues. Introduces phase-based therapy and nutritional approaches. *$ 110.00*
*794 pages 2003*
*ISBN 0-471415-12-1*

**8357 Handbook of Epilepsy**
Lippincott, Williams & Wilkins
Philadelphia, PA 19106-3713
215-521-8300
800-777-2295
FAX: 301-824-7390
www.lpub.com

*J Lippincott, CEO*
Pocket-sized reference provides concise, up-to-date, clinically oriented reviews of each of the major areas of diagnosis and management of epilepsy. *$42.95*
*272 pages*
*ISBN 0-781743-52-4*

**8358 Healthy Breathing**
National Jewish Health
1400 Jackson St
Denver, CO 80206-2761
303-270-2708
FAX: 303-398-1125
e-mail: allstetterw@njc.org
www.nationaljewish.org

*Michael Salem, CEO*
*William Allstetter, Director Media/External Relation*
Offers patients with lung or respiratory disorders information on exercise and healthy breathing.

**8359 Heart of the Mind**
New World Library
14 Pamaron Way
Novato, CA 94949-6215
415-884-2100
800-972-6657
FAX: 415-884-2199
www.newworldlibrary.com

Provides common NLP problems and several new techniques.
*208 pages*
*ISBN 1-577311-56-6*

**8360 Hepatitis Sourcebook**
Omnigraphics
P.O.Box 311640
Detroit, MI 48231-1640
610-461-3548
800-234-1340
FAX: 800-875-1340
e-mail: info@omnigraphics.com
www.omnigraphics.com

*Frederick Gale Ruffner, Founder*
*Peter Ruffner, Co-Founder*
Hepatitis Sourcebook provides basic consumer health information about hepatitis A, hepatitis B, hepatitis C, and other types of hepatitis, including autoimmune hepatitis, alcoholic hepatitis, nonalcoholic steatohepatitis, and toxin-induced hepatitis. It gives the facts about risk factors, prevention, transmission, screening and diagnostic methods, treatment options, and current research initiatives. *$84.00*
*570 pages Hard cover*
*ISBN 0-780807-49-5*

**8361 Hip Function & Ambulation**
Spina Bifida Association of America
Ste 250
4590 Macarthur Blvd NW
Washington, DC 20007-4226
202-944-3285
800-621-3141
FAX: 202-944-3295
e-mail: sbaa@sbaa.org
www.sbaa.org

*Cindy Brownstein, President & CEO*
*Richard E. Lindseth, MD, Author*
*Sara Struwe, Chief Operating Officer & Director of Chapter Development*
*Robin Austin, Communications Manager*
The ability to walk is important in our society, despite recent advances in wheelchair design and wheelchair accessibility. It also is a desire of children with spina bifida.

**8362 Hydrocephalus: A Guide for Patients, Families & Friends**
O'Reilly Media Inc
1005 Gravenstein Hwy N
Sebastopol, CA 95472-2811
707-827-7000
800-998-9938
FAX: 707-829-0104
e-mail: order@oreilly.com
www.oreilly.com

*Linda Lamb, Editor*
*Chuck Toporek, Author*
*Kellie Robinson, Author*
Hydrocephalus is a life-threatening condition often referred to as, water on the brain, that is treated by surgical placement of a shunt system. Hydrocephalus: A Guide for Patients, Families and Friends educates families so they can select a skilled neurosurgeon, understand treatments, participate in care, know what symptoms need attention, discover where to turn for support, keep records needed for follow-up treatments, and make wise lifestyle choices. *$19.95*
*379 pages Paperback 1999*
*ISBN 1-565924-10-X*

**8363 Hypertension Sourcebook**
Omnigraphics
P.O.Box 311640
Detroit, MI 48231-1640
610-461-3548
800-234-1340
FAX: 800-875-1340
e-mail: info@omnigraphics.com
www.omnigraphics.com

*Frederick Gale Ruffner, Founder*
*Peter Ruffner, Co-Founder*
This Sourcebook describes the known causes and risk factors associated with essential (or primary) hypertension, secondary hypertension, prehypertension, and other hypertensive disorders. The book also provides information about blood pressure

management strategies, including dietary changes, weight loss, exercise, and medications. *$ 84.00*

*588 pages Hard cover*

*ISBN 0-780806-74-0*

**8364 Immune System Disorders Sourcebook**

P.O.Box 311640
Detroit, MI 48231-1640
313-961-1340
FAX: 313-961-1383
www.omnigraphics.com

*Joyce Brennfleck Shannon, Editor*

**8365 Immune System Disorders Sourcebook.**

Omnigraphics
PO Box 31-1640
Detroit, MI 48231
313-961-1340
800-234-1340
FAX: 313-961-1383
e-mail: info@omnigraphics.com
www.omnigraphics.com

*Joyce Brennfleck Shannon, Editor*

Immune System Disorders Sourcebook provides information about inherited, acquired, and autoimmune diseases including primary immune deficiency, acquired immunodeficiency syndrome (AIDS), lupus, multiple sclerosis, type one diabetes, rheumatoid arthritis, and Graves' disease. Tips for coping with an immune disorder, caregiving, and treatments are presented along with a glossary and directory of additional resourcesories of additional resources. *$84.00*

*643 pages 2nd Edition*

*ISBN 0-780807-48-8*

**8366 Informed Touch; A Clinician's Guide To TheEvaluation Of Myofascial Disorders**

Inner Traditions/Bear And Company
One Park Street
Rochester, VT 05767
802-767-3174
800-246-8648
FAX: 802-767-3726
e-mail: orders@innertraditions.com
www.innertraditions.com

*Rob Meadows, VP Sales/Marketing*
*Jessica Arsenault, Sales Associate*
*Donna Finando, LAc, LMT, Author*
*Steven Finando, PhD, LAc, Co-Author*

A Clinician's guide to the evaluation and treatment of myofascial disorders. *$30.00*

*224 pages*

*ISBN 0-892817-40-5*

**8367 Injured Mind, Shattered Dreams: Brian's Survival from a Severe Head Injury**

Brookline Books
34 University Rd
Brookline, MA 02445-4533
617-734-6772
800-666-2665
FAX: 617-734-3952
e-mail: brbooks@yahoo.com
www.brooklinebooks.com

Brian, headed for normal adulthood, crashes his car and suffers a severe head injury. This book speaks to the issues in his recovery and the victory a family can achieve through caring advocacy and faith. *$17.95*

*Paperback*

*ISBN 0-91479 -95-6*

**8368 Interdisciplinary Clinical Assessment of Young Children with Developmental Disabilities**

Brookes Publishing
P.O.Box 10624
Baltimore, MD 21285-0624
410-337-9580
800-638-3775
FAX: 410-337-8539
www.brookespublishing.com

*Paul H. Brookes, Chairman*
*Jeffrey D. Brookes, President*
*Melissa A. Behm, Executive Vice President*
*George S. Stamathis, Vice President & Publisher*

Offers insight from veteran team members on interdisciplinary team assessments. Professionals organizing a team as well as students preparing for practice will find advice on how practitioners gather information, approach assessment, make decisions, and face the challenges of their individual fields. Includes case studies and appendix of photocopiable questionnaires for clinicians and parents. *$44.95*

*796 pages Hardcover*

*ISBN 1-557664-50-1*

**8369 Introduction to Spina Bifida**

Spina Bifida Association of America
Ste 250
4590 Macarthur Blvd NW
Washington, DC 20007-4226
202-944-3285
800-621-3141
FAX: 202-944-3295
e-mail: sbaa@sbaa.org
www.sbaa.org

*Cindy Brownstein, President & CEO*
*David McLone, MD, PhD, Co- Author*
*Joy Ito, RN, Co- Author*
*Sara Struwe, Chief Operating Officer & Director of Chapter Development*

An aid for parents, family and nonmedical people who care for a child with spina bifida. *$7.00*

**8370 It's All in Your Head: The Link Between Mercury Amalgams and Illness**

Avery Publishing Group
299 W. Houston Street
New York, NY 10014-3658
212-859-1100
FAX: 212-859-1150
e-mail: info@programexchange.com
programexchange.com

Dr. Higgins's critique of the use of mercury, a toxic element and environmental hazard, in dentistry. For those suffering mercury poisoning, the book examines a number of conventional and alternative treatments.

*208 pages*

**8371 Joslin Guide to Diabetes: A Program for Managing Your Treatment**

Joslin Diabetes Center
1 Joslin Pl
Boston, MA 02215-5306
617-732-2400
FAX: 617-732-2452
www.joslin.org

*Richard S Beaser, M.D., Author*
*Amy Campbell,Ms, RD, CDE, Co-Author*

Discusses the causes of diabetes, the role of diet and exercise, meal planning and complications. Also provide information on drawing blood, mixing and injecting insulin, special challenges, living with diabetes. *$16.95*

*352 pages Revised Edition*

**8372 Journey to Well: Learning to Live After Spinal Cord Injury**

Altarfire Publishing
1835 Oak Terrace
Newcastle, CA 95658
www.altarfire.com

*Margie Williams, Author*

The author's close-up view of what life is like during and after such an incident, including her experience with institutional medicine and insurance companies (for better and for worse), and her determined - and ultimately successful - effort to rehabilitate herself and reconstruct her life. *$15.95*
*251 pages*
*ISBN 0-965555-82-8*

**8373 Ketogenic Diet: A Treatment for Children and Others with Epilepsy**
Demos Medical Publishing
Ste 301
11 West 42nd Street
New York, NY 10036
212-683-0072
800-532-8663
FAX: 212-683-0118
e-mail: info@demosmedpub.com
www.demosmedpub.com

*John M. Freeman, MD, Co Author*
*Eric Kossoff, MD, Co Author*
*Jennifer B. Freeman, Co Author*
*Millicent T. Millicent T. Kelly, RD, Co Author*
Patient education reference on the use of the ketogenic diet to conrol epilepsy in children. *$24.95*
*328 pages Paperback*
*ISBN 1-932603-18-2*

**8374 Latex Allergy in Spina Bifida Patients**
Spina Bifida Association of America
Ste 250
4590 Macarthur Blvd NW
Washington, DC 20007-4226
202-944-3285
800-621-3141
FAX: 202-944-3295
e-mail: sbaa@sbaa.org
www.sbaa.org

*Cindy Brownstein, President & CEO*
*Elli Meeropol, RN, MS, Author*
*Sara Struwe, Chief Operating Officer & Director of Chapter Development*
*Robin Austin, Communications Manager*
The Spina Bifida Association (SBA) serves adults and children who live with the challenges of Spina Bifida.

**8375 Learning Among Children with Spina Bifida**
Spina Bifida Association of America
Ste 250
4590 Macarthur Blvd NW
Washington, DC 20007-4226
202-944-3285
800-621-3141
FAX: 202-944-3295
e-mail: sbaa@sbaa.org
www.sbaa.org

*Cindy Brownstein, President & CEO*
*Donald Lollar, EdD, Author*
*Sara Struwe, Chief Operating Officer & Director of Chapter Development*
*Robin Austin, Communications Manager*
The Spina Bifida Association (SBA) serves adults and children who live with the challenges of Spina Bifida.

**8376 Let's Talk About Having Asthma**
Rosen Publishing
29 E 21st St
New York, NY 10010-6209
212-420-1600
800-237-9932
FAX: 888-436-4643
www.rosenpublishing.com

*Marianna Johnstone, Co-Author*
*Elizabeth Weitzman, Co-Author*
*Kelly Chambers, Marketing Assistant*
Many kids suffer from asthma, which can overtake them suddenly, causing them terror as they struggle for breath. This book talks about the causes and treatments for asthma, as well as precautions sufferers should take. *$21.95*

*ISBN 0-823950-32-8*

**8377 Leukemia Sourcebook**
Omnigraphics
P.O.Box 311640
Detroit, MI 48231-1640
610-461-3548
800-234-1340
FAX: 800-875-1340
e-mail: info@omnigraphics.com
www.omnigraphics.com

*Frederick Gale Ruffner, Founder*
*Millicent T. Ruffner, Co-Founder*
This Sourcebook provides health information about adult and childhood leukemias focusing on the diagnosis and treatments for leukemia, including chemotherapy, radiation, drug therapy, and transplantation of peripheral blood stem cells or marrow. Also included are tips for nutrition, pain and fatigue control, and recognizing possible long-term and late effects of leukemia treatment, along with a glossary and directories of additional resources. *$84.00*
*564 pages Hard cover*
*ISBN 0-780806-27-6*

**8378 Life After Trauma: A Workbook for Healing**
Guilford Press
72 Spring St
New York, NY 10012-4019
212-431-9800
800-365-7006
FAX: 212-966-6708
e-mail: info@guilford.com
www.guilford.com

*Denaour Rosenbloom, Author*
*Mary Beth Williams, Co-Author*
*Barbar E Watkins, Co-Author*
*Laurie Anne Pearlman, Foreword*
A self-help book on how to deal with trauma. *$19.95*
*300 pages Paperback 1910*
*ISBN 1-606236-08-6*

**8379 Life Line**
National Hydrocephalus Foundation
12413 Centralia St
Lakewood, CA 90715-1623
562-402-3523
888-857-3434
888-260-1789
FAX: 562-924-6666
e-mail: debbifields@nhfonline.org
www.nhfonline.org

*Debbi Fields, Executive Director*
*Michael Fields, President/Treasurer*
*Jaynie Dunn, Secretary*
*Sarah Dunn, Junior Director*
National Hydrocephalus Foundation quarterly newsletter. *$35.00*
*12 pages Quarterly*

**8380 Lipomas & Lipomyelomeningocele**
Spina Bifida Association of America
Ste 250
4590 Macarthur Blvd NW
Washington, DC 20007-4226
202-944-3285
800-621-3141
FAX: 202-944-3295
e-mail: sbaa@sbaa.org
www.sbaa.org

*Cindy Brownstein, President & CEO*
*Jorge Lazareff, MD, Author*
*Sara Struwe, Chief Operating Officer & Director of Chapter Development*
*Robin Austin, Communications Manager*

The Spina Bifida Association (SBA) serves adults and children who live with the challenges of Spina Bifida.

**8381 Liver Disorders Sourcebook**
Omnigraphics
P.O.Box 311640
Detroit, MI 48231-1640
610-461-3548
800-234-1340
FAX: 800-875-1340
e-mail: info@omnigraphics.com
www.omnigraphics.com

*Frederick Gale Ruffner, Founder*
*Peter Ruffner, Co-Founder*

Liver Disorders Sourcebook contains basic consumer health information about the liver, how it works, and how to keep it healthy through diet, vaccination, and other preventive care measures. Readers will learn about the symptoms and treatment options for such diseases as hepatitis, primary biliary cirrhosis, Wilson's disease, hemochromatosis, liver failure, cancer of the liver, and disorders related to drugs and other toxins. *$84.00*

*580 pages Hard cover*
*ISBN 0-780803-83-1*

**8382 Living Beyond Multiple Sclerosis: A Woman's Guide**
Hunter House
P.O.Box 2914
Alameda, CA 94501-914
510-865-5282
800-266-5592
FAX: 510-865-4295
e-mail: ordering@hunterhouse.com
www.hunterhouse.com

*Judith Lynn Nichols, Author*
*Lily Jung, Foreword*

This collection of e-mail conversations provides anecdotal and personal information contributed by women with multiple sclerosis. *$14.95*

*256 pages*
*ISBN 0-897932-93-6*

**8383 Living Well with Asthma**
Guilford Press
72 Spring St
New York, NY 10012-4019
212-431-9800
800-365-7006
FAX: 212-966-6708
e-mail: info@guilford.com
www.guilford.com

*Cynthia L Divino, Author*
*Michael R Freedman, Co-Author*
*Samuel J Rosenberg, Co-Author*
*James D Crapo, Foreword*

A self help book for people living with Asthma. *$15.95*

*213 pages Paperback*
*ISBN 1-572300-51-4*

**8384 Living Well with Chronic Fatigue Syndrome and Fibromyalgia**
Harper Collins Publishers
10 E 53rd St
New York, NY 10022-5244
212-207-7000
FAX: 212-207-7901
e-mail: orders@harpercollins.com
www.harpercollins.com

*Mary J Shomon, Author*

A comprehensive guide to the diagnosis and treatment of chronic fatigue syndrome and fibromyalgia. *$14.95*

*416 pages 2004*
*ISBN 0-060521-25-2*

**8385 Living Well with HIV and AIDS**
Bull Publishing
P.O.Box 1377
Boulder, CO 80306-1377
800-676-2855
FAX: 303-545-6354
www.bullpub.com

*Allen L Gifford MD, Author*
*Virginia Gonzalez MPH, Co-Author*
*Daina Laurent MPH, Co-Author*
*Kate Lorig RN, Co-Author*

New drugs and drug combinations have turned HIV/AIDS into a long-term illness rather than a death sentence. Practical advice on mental adjustments and physical vigilance is outlined. *$18.95*

*245 pages 3rd Edition*
*ISBN 0-923521-52-6*

**8386 Living With Spinal Cord Injury Series**
Fanlight Productions C/O Icarus Films
32 Court Street
Brooklyn, NY 11201
718-488-8900
800-876-1710
FAX: 718-488-8642
e-mail: info@fanlight.com
www.fanlight.com

*Barry Corbet, Producer*

A series of three videos produced by an individual who has experienced spinal cord injury himself. Changes: is about the consequences of spinal cord injury and the process of rehabilitation. Outside: emphasizes the life-long aspect of rehabilitation for people with spinal cord injury. Survivors: interviews 23 men and women who have lived at least 24 years with spinal cord injury. *$210.00*

*VHS 1973*

**8387 Living with Brain Injury: A Guide for Families**
Delmar Cengage Learning
P.O.Box 6904
Florence, KY 41022-6904
800-354-9706
FAX: 800-487-8488
e-mail: esales@cengage.com
www.delmarlearning.com

*Richard C Senelick MD, Author*
*Karla Dougherty, Co-Author*

A consumer text to aid people living with brain-injured survivors, includes facts on neuroplasticity, experimental rehabilitation research, and the process of rehabilitation itself. *$19.95*

*225 pages Softcover 2001*
*ISBN 1-891525-09-3*

**8388 Living with Spina Bifida: A Guide for Families and Professionals**
University of North Carolina at Chapel Hill
116 S Boundary St
Chapel Hill, NC 27514-3808
919-966-3561
800-848-6224
FAX: 919-962-2704
e-mail: uncpress@unc.edu
www.uncpress.unc.edu

*Adrian Sandler MD, Author*

A handbook that addresses patients' biopsychosocial and developmental needs from birth through adolescence and into adulthood. Sandler's holistic approach encourages families to focus more on the child and less on the disability while providing abundant information about this condition. *$20.95*

*296 pages 2004*
*ISBN 0-807855-47-8*

**8389 Lung Cancer: Making Sense of Diagnosis, Treatment, and Options**

O'Reilly Media Inc
1005 Gravenstein Hwy N
Sebastopol, CA 95472-2811
707-827-7000
800-998-9938
FAX: 707-829-0104
e-mail: order@oreilly.com
www.oreilly.com

*Linda Lamb, Editor*
*Lorraine Johnston, Author*

Straightforward language and the words of patients and their families are the hallmarks of this book on the number one cancer killer in the US. Written by a widely respected author and patient advocate, Lung Cancer: Making Sense of Diagnosis, Treatment, & Options has been meticulously reviewed by top medical experts and physicians. Readers will find medical facts simply explained, advice to ease their daily life, and tools to be strong advocates for themselves or a family member. *$ 27.95*

*530 pages Paperback 2001*
*ISBN 0-596500-02-5*

**8390 Lung Disorders Sourcebook**

Omnigraphics
P.O.Box 311640
Detroit, MI 48231-1640
610-461-3548
800-234-1340
FAX: 800-875-1340
e-mail: info@omnigraphics.com
www.omnigraphics.com

*Dawn D Matthews, Editor*
*Frederick Gale Ruffner, Founder*
*Peter Ruffner, Co-Founder*

Lung Disorders Sourcebook offers information about specific types of lung disorders, including diagnosis, treatment, and prevention issues. The book offers advice for preventing some types lung disorder that are acquired by asbestos, radon, and other environmental exposures. *$84.00*

*657 pages Hard cover*
*ISBN 0-780803-39-8*

**8391 Lupus: Alternative Therapies That Work**

Inner Traditions
1 Park St
Rochester, VT 05767
802-767-3174
800-246-8648
FAX: 802-767-3726
e-mail: info@innertraditions.com
www.innertraditions.com

*Sharon Moore, Author*

A comprehensive guise to noninvasive, nontoxic therapies for lupus - written by a lupus survivor. *$14.95*

*256 pages 2000*
*ISBN 0-892818-89-1*

**8392 MAGIC Touch**

MAGIC Foundation for Children's Growth
6645 North Ave
Oak Park, IL 60302-1057
708-383-0808
800-362-4423
FAX: 708-383-0899
e-mail: mary@magicfoundation.org
www.magicfoundation.org

*Mary Andrews, CEO*
*Dianne Kremidas, Executive Director*
*Pam Pentaris, Office Manager*
*Jamie Harvey, Technical Education Teacher*

Provides support and education regarding growth disorders in children and related adult disorders, including adult GHD. Dedicated to helping children whose physical growth is affected be a medical problem by assisting families of afflicted children through local support groups, public education/awareness, newsletters, specialty divisions and programs for the children.

*36-40 pages Quarterly*

**8393 Management of Autistic Behavior**

Sage Publications
2455 Teller Road
Thousand Oaks, CA 91320
805-499-9774
800-818-7243
FAX: 800-583-2665
e-mail: info@sagepub.com
www.sagepub.com

*Sara Miller McCune, Founder, Publisher, Chairperson*
*Blaise R Simqu, President & CEO*
*Tracey A. Ozmina, Executive Vice President & Chief Operating Officer*
*Chris Hickok, Senior Vice President & Chief Financial Officer*

Comprehensive and practical book that tells what works best with specific problems. *$51.00*

*450 pages Paperback*
*ISBN 0-890791-96-1*

**8394 Management of Genetic Syndromes**

John Wiley & Sons
111 River St
Hoboken, NJ 7030-5773
201-748-6000
201-748-6088
e-mail: info@wiley.com
www.wiley.com

*Suzanne B Cassidy, Editor*
*Judith E Allanson, Editor*

Clinical information on 30 of the most common genetic syndromes. *$204.95*

*720 pages 3rd Edition*
*ISBN 0-470191-41-5*

**8395 Managing Post Polio: A Guide to Living Well with Post Polio**

ABI Professional Publications
P.O.Box 149
St Petersburg, FL 33731-149
727-556-0950
800-551-7776
FAX: 727-556-2560
e-mail: webmaster@vandamere.com
www.abipropub.com

*Lauro S Halstead MD, Editor*

A guide to living well and aging well with post-polio syndrome.

*256 pages*
*ISBN 1-886236-17-8*

**8396 Meniere's Disease**

Vestibular Disorders Association
P.O.Box 13305
Portland, OR 97213-305
800-837-8428
FAX: 503-229-8064
e-mail: info@vestibular.org
www.vestibular.org

*Cynthia Ryan MBA, Executive Director*
*Kerrie Denner, Outreach Coordinator*
*Fionn MacCool, Office Assistant*
*Alan Butchman, Secretary*

VEDA's website contains a wealth of information on the symptoms, diagnosis and treatment of various types of vestibular disorders. *$5.00*

**8397 Menopause without Medicine**
Hunter House
P.O.Box 2914
Alameda, CA 94501-914
510-865-5282
800-266-5592
FAX: 510-865-4295
e-mail: ordering@hunterhouse.com
www.hunterhouse.com

*Linda Ojeda PhD, Author*
Research on nutrition, exercise, and osteoporosis, including good news about the body's ability to rebuild bone later in life; describes how women can best prepare their minds and bodies for the transition of menopause, and explains how women can prevent osteoporosis and control the disturbing symptoms of hot flashes, insomnia, fatigue, and weight gain. *$18.95*
*304 pages 5th Edition*
*ISBN 0-897934-05-3*

**8398 Movement Disorders Sourcebook**
Omnigraphics
P.O.Box 311640
Detroit, MI 48231-1640
610-461-3548
800-234-1340
FAX: 800-875-1340
e-mail: info@omnigraphics.com
www.omnigraphics.com

*Amy L Sutton, Editor*
*Frederick Gale Ruffner, Founder*
*Peter Ruffner, Co-Founder*
This Sourcebook provides health information about neurological movement disorders, their symptoms, causes, diagnostic tests, and treatments. Readers will learn about Essential Tremor, Parkinson's Disease, Dystonia, and many other early-onset and adult-onset movement disorders. Information about mobility and assistive technology aids is included, along with a glossary and a listing of additional resources. *$84.00*
*600 pages Hard cover*
*ISBN 0-780810-34-1*

**8399 Multiple Sclerosis and Having a Baby**
Inner Traditions
P.O.Box 388
Rochester, VT 05767-388
802-767-3174
800-246-8648
FAX: 802-767-3726
e-mail: customerservice@innertraditions.com
www.innertraditions.com

*Judy Graham, Author*
Everything you need to know about conception, pregnancy and parenthood. *$12.95*
*160 pages 2001*
*ISBN 0-892817-88-7*

**8400 Multiple Sclerosis: 300 Tips for Making Life Easier**
Demos Medical Publishing
Ste 301
11 West 42nd Street
New York, NY 10036
212-683-0072
800-532-8663
FAX: 212-683-0118
e-mail: info@demosmedpub.com
www.demosmedpub.com

*Shelley Peterman Schwarz, Author*
*Richard Winters, Executive Editor*
*Beth Barry, Publisher*
*Noreen Henson, Executive Director of Demos Health*
This latest book in the Making Life Easier series features tip, techniques and shortcuts for conserving time and energy so you can do more of the things you want to do. These tips should help increase the number of good days you have while encouraging you to develop your own techniques for making life easier. *$16.95*
*128 pages*
*ISBN 1-932603-21-2*

**8401 Multiple Sclerosis: A Guide for Families**
Demos Medical Publishing
Ste 301
11 West 42nd Street
New York, NY 10036
212-683-0072
800-532-8663
FAX: 212-683-0118
e-mail: info@demosmedpub.com
www.demosmedpub.com

*Rosalind C. Kalb, Ph.D., Author*
*Richard Winters, Executive Editor*
*Beth Barry, Publisher*
*Noreen Henson, Executive Director of Demos Health*
Guide for living and coping with multiple sclerosis. *$24.95*
*256 pages*
*ISBN 1-932603-10-7*

**8402 Multiple Sclerosis: A Guide for the Newly Diagnosed**
Demos Medical Publishing
Ste 301
11 West 42nd Street
New York, NY 10036
212-683-0072
800-532-8663
FAX: 212-683-0118
e-mail: info@demosmedpub.com
www.demosmedpub.com

*Nancy J. Holland, RN, EdD,, Co Author*
*T. Jock Murray, MD,, Co Author*
*Stephen C. Reingold, PhD, Co Author*
*Richard Winters, Executive Editor*
A must-have title for anyone who has recently been diagnosed with MS and a good idea for family members and friends. *$ 19.95*
*256 pages*
*ISBN 1-932603-27-1*

**8403 Multiple Sclerosis: The Guide to Treatment and Management**
Demos Medical Publishing
Ste 301
11 West 42nd Street
New York, NY 10036
212-683-0072
800-532-8663
FAX: 212-683-0118
e-mail: info@demosmedpub.com
www.demosmedpub.com

*Chris H. Polman, MD, FRCP, Co Author*
*Alan J. Thompson MD, FRCP, FRC, Co Author*
*T. Jock Murray, MD,, Co Author*
*Allen C. Bowling, MD, PhD,, Co Author*
A current guide to modern therapies. *$24.95*
*216 pages*
*ISBN 1-932603-15-4*

**8404 Muscular Dystrophies**
Oxford University Press
198 Madison Ave
New York, NY 10016-4308
212-726-6000
800-451-7556
FAX: 919-677-1303
e-mail: custserv.us@oup.com
www.oup.com

*Alan E.H. Emery, Author*
Describes the opportunities for management of more than 30 types of MD through respiratory care, physiotherapy and surgical correction of contractures, and examines the potential for effec-

tive treatment utilizing the new techniques of gene and cell therapy *$ 165.00*
*330 pages*
*ISBN 0-192632-91-4*

**8405 Muscular Dystrophy in Children: A Guide for Families**
Demos Medical Publishing
Ste 301
11 West 42nd Street
New York, NY 10036
212-683-0072
800-532-8663
FAX: 212-683-0118
e-mail: info@demosmedpub.com
www.demosmedpub.com
Defines the available medical options at every stage of the disease and offers guidance even when it may seem that little or nothing can be done. Includes a glossary and suggestions for furhter reading. *$19.95*
*144 pages Paperback*
*ISBN 1-888799-33-1*

**8406 Muscular Dystrophy: The Facts**
Oxford University Press
198 Madison Ave
New York, NY 10016-4308
212-726-6000
800-451-7556
FAX: 919-677-1303
e-mail: custserv.us@oup.com
www.oup.com

*Peter Harper, Author*
A good first book for individuals and families faced with the likelihood or reality of a muscular dystrophy diagnosis. *$22.50*
*178 pages*
*ISBN 0-192632-17-5*

**8407 My House is Killing Me! The Home Guide for Families with Allergies and Asthma**
Johns Hopkins University Press
2175 N Charles St
Baltimore, MD 21218
410-516-6900
FAX: 410-516-6968
e-mail: webmaster@jhupress.jhu.edu
www.press.jhu.edu

*Jeffrey C May, Author*
*Jonathan M Samet, M.D., Foreword*
Chemical consultant May describes where and how the various parts of a residence can cause temporary or chronic illness for those with allergies or other sensitivities. *$20.95*
*352 pages*
*ISBN 0-801867-30-9*

**8408 Neuropsychiatry of Epilepsy**
Cambridge University Press
100 Brookhill Dr
West Nyack, NY 10994-2133
845-353-7500
845-353-4141
www.cambridge.org

*Michael R Trimble, Editor*
*Bettina Schmitz, Editor*
Covers the practical implications of ongoing research, and offers a diagnostic and management perspective. Topics include cognitive aspects, nonepileptic attacks, and clinical aspects. For professionals treating epileptic patients. *$104.00*
*232 pages 2nd Edition 1911*
*ISBN 0-521154-69-7*

**8409 Nick Joins In**
Spina Bifida Association of America
Ste 250
4590 Macarthur Blvd NW
Washington, DC 20007-4226
202-944-3285
800-621-3141
FAX: 202-944-3295
e-mail: sbaa@sbaa.org
www.sbaa.org

*Cindy Brownstein, President & CEO*
*Sara Struwe, Chief Operating Officer & Director of Chapter Development*
*Robin Austin, Communications Manager*
*Mickey Daguiso, Development Coordinator*
When Nick, who is in a wheelchair, enters a regular classroom for the first time, he realizes that he has much to contribute. *$17.00*

**8410 No More Allergies**
Random House
1745 Broadway
3rd Floor
New York, NY 10019-4305
212-782-9000
FAX: 212-302-7985
e-mail: ecustomerservice@randonhouse.com
www.randomhouse.com

*Markus Dohle, CEO*
*Gary Null PhD, Author*
A detailed investigation into the causes of allergies related both to food and the environment, as well as their link to other illnesses, such as asthma, arthritis, chrinic fatigue syndrome, and diabetes. Also outlines testing methods, treatments, and a diet plan to restore immune function. *$23.00*
*464 pages 1992*
*ISBN 0-679743-10-1*

**8411 No Time for Jello: One Family's Experience**
Brookline Books
34 University Rd
Brookline, MA 02445-4533
617-734-6772
800-666-2665
FAX: 617-734-3952
e-mail: brbooks@yahoo.com
www.brooklinebooks.com
One family's story of their attempts to remediate and cure the effects of a cerebral palsied condition the oldest son was born with. The Bratts traveled traditional routes, through distinguished medical centers in Boston, and nontraditional routes in a search for treatments that would help their son. *$17.95*
*Softcover*
*ISBN 0-91479-56-5*

**8412 Nocturnal Asthma**
National Jewish Health
1400 Jackson St
Denver, CO 80206-2761
303-270-2708
FAX: 303-398-1125
e-mail: allstetterw@njc.org
nationaljewish.org

*Michael Salem, CEO*
*Christine Forkner, Chief Financial Officer and Executive Vice President*
*Laszlo Pook, MBA, Chief Information Officer*
*Ron Berge, MBA, Chief Operating Officer*
Offers information to patients about how to understand and manage asthma at night.

**8413 Obesity**
Spina Bifida Association of America
Ste 250
4590 Macarthur Blvd NW
Washington, DC 20007-4226
202-944-3285
800-621-3141
FAX: 202-944-3295
e-mail: sbaa@sbaa.org
www.sbaa.org

*Cindy Brownstein, President & CEO*
*Alison Schultz RN, PNPC, Co- Author*
*Gregory S. Liptak, MD, Co- Author*
*Robin Austin, Communications Manager*
The Spina Bifida Association (SBA) serves adults and children who live with the challenges of Spina Bifida. *$8.00*

**8414 Obesity Sourcebook**
Omnigraphics
P.O.Box 311640
Detroit, MI 48231-1640
610-461-3548
800-234-1340
FAX: 800-875-1340
e-mail: info@omnigraphics.com
www.omnigraphics.com

*Frederick Gale Ruffner, Founder*
*Peter Ruffner, Co-Founder*
Discusses diseases and other problems associated with obesity. *$78.00*
*376 pages*
*ISBN 0-780803-33-6*

**8415 Occulta**
Spina Bifida Association of America
Ste 250
4590 Macarthur Blvd NW
Washington, DC 20007-4226
202-944-3285
800-621-3141
FAX: 202-944-3295
e-mail: sbaa@sbaa.org
www.sbaa.org

*Cindy Brownstein, President & CEO*
*Sara Struwe, Chief Operating Officer & Director of Chapter Development*
*Robin Austin, Communications Manager*
*Mickey Daguiso, Development Coordinator*
The Spina Bifida Association (SBA) serves adults and children who live with the challenges of Spina Bifida. *$8.00*

**8416 Official Patient's Sourcebook on Bell's Palsy**
Icon Group International
FAX: 858-635-9414
e-mail: orders@icongroupbooks.com
www.icongroupbooks.com
Provides patients with guidance on where and how to look for information covering virtually all topics related to bell's palsy (also Antoni's Palsy; facial nerve palsy; facial palsy; facial paralysis; idiopathic facial palsy; idiopathic facial paralysis), from the essentials to the most advanced areas of research. *$24.95*

*ISBN 0-597835-20-9*

**8417 Official Patient's Sourcebook on Cystic Fibrosis**
Icon Group International
FAX: 858-635-9414
e-mail: orders@icongroupbooks.com
icongroupbooks.com
For parents who have decided to make education and research an integral part of the treatment process. Although it also gives information useful to doctors, caregivers and other health professionals, it tells paretns where and how to look for information covering virtually all topics related to cystic fibrosis (also fbrocystic disease of pancreas; mucosis; mucoviscidosis; pancreatic fibrosis), from the essentials to the most advanced areas of research. *$28.95*
*356 pages*
*ISBN 0-597831-46-7*

**8418 Official Patient's Sourcebook on Muscular Dystrophy**
Icon Group International
FAX: 858-635-9414
e-mail: orders@icongroupbooks.com
icongroupbooks.com
Created for patients who have decided to make education and research an integral part of the treatment process. Although it also gives information useful to doctors, caregivers and other health professionals, it tells patients where and how to look for information covering virtually all topics related to muscular dystrophy. *$24.95*
*268 pages*
*ISBN 0-597832-10-2*

**8419 Official Patient's Sourcebook on Osteoporosis**
Icon Group International
FAX: 858-635-9414
e-mail: orders@icongroupbooks.com
icongroupbooks.com
Provides patients with guidance on where and how to look for information covering virtually all topics related to bell's palsy (also Antoni's Palsy; Facial Nerve Palsy; Facial palsy; Facial Paralysis; Idiopathic Facial Palsy; Idiopathic facial paralysis), from the essentials to the most advanced areas of research. *$34.95*

*ISBN 0-597833-04-4*

**8420 Official Patient's Sourcebook on Post-Polio Syndrome: A Revised and Updated Directory**
Icon Group International
FAX: 858-635-9414
e-mail: orders@icongroupbooks.com
icongroupbooks.com
A sourcebook created for patients who have decided to make education and Internet-based research an integral part of the treatment process. Although it gives information useful to doctors, caregivers and other health professionals, it also tells patients where and how to look for information covering virtually all topics related to post-polio syndrome, from the essentials to the most advanced areas of research. *$28.95*
*124 pages*
*ISBN 0-597835-31-4*

**8421 Official Patient's Sourcebook on Primary Pulmonary Hypertension**
Icon Group International
FAX: 858-635-9414
e-mail: orders@icongroupbooks.com
icongroupbooks.com
Provides patients with guidance on where and how to look for information covering virtually all topics related to primary pulmonary hypertension (also familial primary pulmonary hypertension; idiopathic pulmonary hypertension; primary obliterative pulmonary vascular disease; primary pulmonary vascular disease; and pulmonary hypertension), from the essentials to the most advanced areas of research. *$24.95*

*ISBN 0-597831-54-8*

**8422 Official Patient's Sourcebook on Pulmonary Fibrosis**
Icon Group International
FAX: 858-635-9414
e-mail: orders@icongroupbooks.com
icongroupbooks.com
Provides patients with guidance on where and how to look for information covering virtually all topics related to idiopathic pulmonary fibrosis (also alveolocapillary block; cryptogenic fibrosing alveolitis; diffuse fibrosing alveolitis; fibrosing alveolitis; Hamman-Rich syndrome; and idiopathic diffuse inter-

stitial pulmonary fibrosis), from the essentials to the most advanced areas of research. *$24.95*

*ISBN 0-597831-65-3*

**8423 Official Patient's Sourcebook on Scoliosis**
Icon Group International
FAX: 858-635-9414
e-mail: orders@icongroupbooks.com
icongroupbooks.com

Provides patients with guidance on where and how to look for information covering virtually all topics related to scoliosis (also Idiopathic scoliosis; Kyphoscoliosis; Paralytic scoliosis; Sciatic scoliosis), from the essentials to the most advanced areas of research. *$28.95*

*ISBN 0-597829-90-X*

**8424 Official Patient's Sourcebook on Sickle Cell Anemia**
Icon Group International
FAX: 858-635-9414
e-mail: orders@icongroupbooks.com
icongroupbooks.com

Provides patients with guidance on where and how to look for information covering virtually all topics related to sickle cell anemia (also Hb S disease; Hemoglobin S disease; Hemoglobin SS disease; sickle cell disease; sickle cell trait), from the essentials to the most advanced areas of research. *$28.95*

*ISBN 0-597831-57-2*

**8425 Official Patient's Sourcebook on Ulcerative Colitis**
Icon Group International
FAX: 858-635-9414
e-mail: orders@icongroupbooks.com
icongroupbooks.com

Provides patients with guidance on where and how to look for information covering virtually all topics related to ulcerative colitis (also Chronic Non-Specific Ulcerative Colitis; Colitis Gravis; Idiopathic Non-Specific Ulcerative Colitis; Idiopathic proctocolitis; Inflammatory bowel disease (IBD); Nonspecific ulcerative colitis), from the essentials to the most advanced areas of research. *$34.95*

*ISBN 0-597834-09-1*

**8426 One Day at a Time: Children Living with Leukemia**
Gareth Stevens Publishing
111 East 14th Street
Suite #349
New York, NY 10003
800-542-2595
FAX: 877-542-2596
e-mail: customerservice@gspub.com
www.garethstevens.com

Focus on Hanna, two years old, and 3 year old Frederick. Both diagnosed with Leukemia and follows them as they are treated for their illness. Includes such daily routines as eating breakfast, washing and playing. *$16.95*

*56 pages Hardcover*
*ISBN 1-55532 -13-6*

**8427 Options: Revolutionary Ideas in the War on Cancer**
People Against Cancer
P.O.Box 10
604 East Street
Otho, IA 50569
515-972-4444
FAX: 515-972-4415
e-mail: info@PeopleAgainstCancer.net
www.peopleagainstcancer.com

*Frank Wiewel, Executive Director/Founder*

Publication of People Against Cancer, a nonprofit, grassroots public benefit organization dedicated to 'New Directions in the War on Cancer.' We help people to find the best cancer treatment. We are a democratic organization of people with cancer, their loved ones and citizens working together to protect and enhance medical freedom of choice.

**8428 Osteoporosis Sourcebook**
Omnigraphics
P.O.Box 311640
Detroit, MI 48231-1640
313-961-1340
800-234-1340
FAX: 313-961-1383
e-mail: info@omnigraphics.com
www.omnigraphics.com

*Allan R Cook, Editor*
*Frederick Gale Ruffner, Founder*
*Peter Ruffner, Co-Founder*

Discusses causes, risk factors, treatments and traditional and non-traditional pain management issues concerning osteoporosis. *$ 84.00*

*568 pages Hard cover*
*ISBN 0-780802-39-1*

**8429 Parent's Guide to Allergies and Asthma**
Allergy & Asthma Network Mothers of Asthmatics
Ste 150
2751 Prosperity Ave
Fairfax, VA 22031-4343
703-641-9595
800-756-5525
FAX: 703-573-7794
www.parent-institute.com

*John H Wherry, Ed.D, President*

A up-to-date, easy-to-read resource offering essential information on asthma and allergies.

**8430 Partial Seizure Disorders: A Guide for Patients and Families**
O'Reilly Media Inc
1005 Gravenstein Hwy N
Sebastopol, CA 95472-2811
707-827-7000
800-998-9938
FAX: 707-829-0104
e-mail: order@oreilly.com
www.oreilly.com

*Linda Lamb, Editor*
*Mitzi Waltz, Author*

Partial Seizure Disorders helps patients and families get an accurate diagnosis of this condition, understand medications and their side effects, and learn coping skills and other adjuncts to medication. It walks readers through developmental and school issues for young children; adult issues such as employment and driving; working with an existing health plan; and getting further help through advocacy and support organizations, articles, and online resources. *$19.95*

*288 pages Paperback*
*ISBN 0-596500-03-3*

**8431 Penitent, with Roses: An HIV+ Mother Reflects**
University Press of New England
1 Court St
Lebanon, NH 03766-1358
603-448-1830
800-421-1561
FAX: 603-448-1533
www.upne.com

*Paula W Peterson, Author*

Peterson, a married, middle-class, Jewish mother, was diagnosed with full-blown AIDS four years into her marriage and 11 months after her son was born. In seven poignant autobiographical essays and a collection of letters to her uninfected, four-year-old son, the author maintains an upbeat tone and describes her unsuccessful attempts to find the source of her infection (her husband tested negative), her relationships with her doctors, and her work as an HIV activist. *$ 26.95*

*256 pages 2001*
*ISBN 1-584651-28-4*

**8432 Plan Ahead: Do What You Can**
Spina Bifida Association of America
Ste 250
4590 Macarthur Blvd NW
Washington, DC 20007-4226
202-944-3285
800-621-3141
FAX: 202-944-3295
e-mail: sbaa@sbaa.org
www.sbaa.org

*Cindy Brownstein, President & CEO*
*Sara Struwe, Chief Operating Officer & Director of Chapter Development*
*Robin Austin, Communications Manager*
*Mickey Daguiso, Development Coordinator*
Folic aciid information for women at risk for recurrence. *$15.00*

**8433 Post-Polio Syndrome: A Guide for Polio Survivors and Their Families**
Yale University Press
P.O.Box 209040
New Haven, CT 6520-9040
203-432-0960
203-432-0948
e-mail: customer.care@triliteral.org
www.yalepress.yale.edu

*Julie K Silver M.D., Author*
*Laro S Halstead, M.D., Foreword*
A guide for polio survivors, their families, and their health care providers offers expert advice on all aspects of post-polio syndrome. Based on the author's experience treating post-polio patients, Silver discusses issues of critical importance, including how to find the best medical care, deal with symptoms, sustain mobility, manage pain, approach insurance issues, and arrange a safe living environment. *$ 19.50*
*304 pages 2002*
*ISBN 0-300088-08-3*

**8434 Prader-Willi Syndrome: Development and Manifestations**
Cambridge University Press
32 Avenue of the Americas
New York, NY 10013-2473
212-924-3900
212-691-3239
www.cambridge.org

*Joyce Whittington, Author*
*Tony Holland, Co-Author*
Seeks to identify and provide the latest findings about how best to manage the complex medical, nutritional, psychological, educational, social and therapeutic needs of people with PWS. *$130.00*
*230 pages 2004*
*ISBN 0-521840-29-3*

**8435 Preventing Secondary Conditions Associated with Spina Bifida or Cerebral Palsy**
Spina Bifida Association of America
Ste 250
4590 Macarthur Blvd NW
Washington, DC 20007-4226
202-944-3285
800-621-3141
FAX: 202-944-3295
e-mail: sbaa@sbaa.org
www.sbaa.org

*Cindy Brownstein, President & CEO*
*Sara Struwe, Chief Operating Officer & Director of Chapter Development*
*Robin Austin, Communications Manager*
*Mickey Daguiso, Development Coordinator*
This report is for health professionals, parents and teachers. *$3.00*

**8436 Prostate and Urological Disorders Sourcebook**
Omnigraphics
P.O.Box 311640
Detroit, MI 48231-1640
313-961-1340
800-234-1340
FAX: 313-961-1383
e-mail: info@omnigraphics.com
www.omnigraphics.com

*Karen Bellenir, Editor*
*Frederick Gale Ruffner, Founder*
*Peter Ruffner, Co-Founder*
Prostate and Urological Disorders Sourcebook provides information about prostate cancer and other prostate problems, such as prostatitis and benign prostatic hyperplasia. A glossary of andrological terms and a directory of resources for additional help and information are also included. *$84.00*
*604 pages Hard cover*
*ISBN 0-780807-97-6*

**8437 Protecting Against Latex Allergy**
Spina Bifida Association of America
Ste 250
4590 Macarthur Blvd NW
Washington, DC 20007-4226
202-944-3285
800-621-3141
FAX: 202-944-3295
e-mail: sbaa@sbaa.org
www.sbaa.org

*Cindy Brownstein, President & CEO*
*Sara Struwe, Chief Operating Officer & Director of Chapter Development*
*Robin Austin, Communications Manager*
*Mickey Daguiso, Development Coordinator*
Because awareness and proper action may help prevent an allergic reation, learning about latex allergy is especially important for parents, health care workers and anyone who is exposed to latex regulary. *$20.00*

**8438 Questions and Answers: The ADA and Personswith HIV/AIDS**
US Department of Justice
950 Pennsylvania Ave NW
Washington, DC 20530-9
800-514-0301
TTY:800-514-0383
www.ada.gov

*Joanne Graham, Manager*
A 16-page publication explaining the requirements for employers, businesses and nonprofit agencies that serve the public, and state and local governments to avoid discriminating against persons with HIV/AIDS.

**8439 Raynaud's Phenomenon**
Arthritis Foundation
P.O.Box 7669
Atlanta, GA 30357-0669
404-872-7100
800-283-7800
FAX: 404-872-0457
arthritis.org

*John H Klippel, M.D., CEO/President*
*David E. Shuey, Executive Vice President*
*Daniel T. McGowan, Vice Chair*
*Kenneth G. Baltes, Treasurer*
The Arthritis Foundation is the largest national nonprofit organization that supports the more than 100 types of arthritis and related conditions. Founded in 1948, with headquarters in Atlanta, the Arthritis Foundation has multiple service points located throughout the country.

8440 **Reaching the Autistic Child: A Parent Training Program**
Brookline Books
34 University Rd
Brookline, MA 02445-4533
617-734-6772
800-666-2665
FAX: 617-734-3952
e-mail: brbooks@yahoo.com
www.brooklinebooks.com

Detailed case studies of social and behavioral change in autistic children and their families show parents how to implement the principles for improved socialization and behavior. *$15.95*
*Softcover*
*ISBN 1-571290-56-7*

8441 **Respiratory Disorders Sourcebook**
Omnigraphics
P.O.Box 311640
Detroit, MI 48231-1640
313-961-1340
800-234-1340
FAX: 313-961-1383
e-mail: info@omnigraphics.com
www.omnigraphics.com

*Sandra J Judd, Editor*
*Frederick Gale Ruffner, Founder*
*Peter Ruffner, Co-Founder*
Respiratory Disorders Sourcebook provides up-to-date information about infectious, inflammatory, occupational, and other types of respiratory disorders. Tips for managing chronic respiratory diseases and suggestions for ways to promote lung health are presented, and the book concludes with a glossary of related terms and a list of additional resources. *$84.00*
*638 pages Hard cover*
*ISBN 0-780810-07-5*

8442 **SPINabilities: A Young Person's Guide to Spina Bifida**
Spina Bifida Association of America
Ste 250
4590 Macarthur Blvd NW
Washington, DC 20007-4226
202-944-3285
800-621-3141
FAX: 202-944-3295
e-mail: sbaa@sbaa.org
www.sbaa.org

*Cindy Brownstein, President & CEO*
*Sonya Oppenheimer MD, Editor*
*Marlene Lutkenhoff, RN, MSN, Co-Editor*
*Sara Struwe, Chief Operating Officer & Director of Chapter Development*
A cool and practical book for young adults becoming independent. *$22.30*

8443 **Seizures and Epilepsy in Childhood: A Guide**
John Hopkins University Press
2715 N Charles St
Baltimore, MD 21218-4319
410-516-6900
800-548-1784
FAX: 410-516-6998
e-mail: webmaster@jhupress.jhu.edu
www.press.jhu.edu

*William Brody, President*
*Eileen P G Vining MD, Co-Author*
*Diana J Pillas, Co-Author*
*John M Freeman, M.D., Co-Author*
A resources for parents of a child with epilepsy. Information allows parents to have informed discussions with physician and treatment teams. Also provides information for parents to become participants in treatment plans. *$54.00*
*432 pages 3rd Edition*
*ISBN 0-801870-51-4*

8444 **Sexuality and the Person with Spina Bifida**
Spina Bifida Association of America
Ste 250
4590 Macarthur Blvd NW
Washington, DC 20007-4226
202-944-3285
800-621-3141
FAX: 202-944-3295
e-mail: sbaa@sbaa.org
www.sbaa.org

*Cindy Brownstein, President & CEO*
*Stephen Sloan, PhD, Author*
*Sara Struwe, Chief Operating Officer & Director of Chapter Development*
*Robin Austin, Communications Manager*
Dr Sloan foucuses on sexual development, sexual activity and other important issues. *$11.00*

8445 **Sinus Survival: A Self-help Guide**
Penguin Group
375 Hudson St
New York, NY 10014-3658
212-366-2372
FAX: 212-366-2933
e-mail: insidesales@penguingroup.com
us.penguingroup.com

*Robert S Ivker, Author*
Self-help manual for sufferers of bronchitis, sinusitis, allergies, and colds. *$15.95*
*336 pages Paperback 2000*
*ISBN 1-101798-02-6*

8446 **Social Development and the Person with Spina Bifida**
Spina Bifida Association of America
Ste 250
4590 Macarthur Blvd NW
Washington, DC 20007-4226
202-944-3285
800-621-3141
FAX: 202-944-3295
e-mail: sbaa@sbaa.org
www.sbaa.org

*Cindy Brownstein, President & CEO*
*Donald Lollar, EdD, Author*
*Sara Struwe, Chief Operating Officer & Director of Chapter Development*
*Robin Austin, Communications Manager*
Examines how spina bifida and hydrocephalus may influence development and learning social skills.

8447 **Solving the Puzzle of Chronic Fatigue**
Essential Science Publishing
Ste A
1216 S 1580 W
Orem, UT 84058-4906
801-224-6228
800-336-6308
FAX: 801-224-6229
e-mail: info@essentialscience.net
www.essentialsciencepublishing.com

*Michael Rosenbaum, Author*
*Murray Susser, Co-Author*
Although primarily a book about CFS, this comprehensive study also provides a detailed overview of candidiasis, including its causes and best approaches for treatment. *$14.95*
*190 pages*
*ISBN 0-943685-11-7*

8448 **Son Rise: The Miracle Continues**
New World Library
14 Pamaron Way
Novato, CA 94949-6215
415-884-2100
800-972-6657
FAX: 415-884-2199
www.newworldlibrary.com

*Barry Neil Kaufman, Author*

Documents Raun Kaufman's astonishing development from a lifeless, autistic, retarded child into a highly verbal, lovable youngster with no traces of his former condition. Details Raun's extraordinary progress from the age of four into young adulthood, also shares moving accounts of five families that successfully used the Son-Rise Program to reach their own special children. *$14.96*
*372 pages*
*ISBN 0-915811-53-7*

**8449 Steps to Independence: Teaching Everyday Skills to Children with Special Needs**
Spina Bifida Association of America
Ste 250
4590 Macarthur Blvd NW
Washington, DC 20007-4226
202-944-3285
800-621-3141
FAX: 202-944-3295
e-mail: sbaa@sbaa.org
www.sbaa.org

*Cindy Brownstein, President & CEO*
*Alan J Brightman, Co-Author*
*Bruce L. Baker, Co-Author*
*Sara Struwe, Chief Operating Officer & Director of Chapter Development*
A guide to help parents teach life skills to their disabled child. *$34.25*

**8450 Stroke Sourcebook**
P.O.Box 311640
Detroit, MI 48231-1640
313-961-1340
FAX: 313-961-1383
www.omnigraphics.com

*Amy L Sutton, Editor*
*Frederick Gale Ruffner, Founder*
*Peter Ruffner, Co-Founder*
Basic Consumer Health Information about Stroke, Including Ischemic, Hemorrhagic, and Mini Strokes, as Well as Risk Factors, Prevention Guidelines, Diagnostic Tests, Medications and Surgical Treatments, and Complications of Stroke.

**8451 Stroke Sourcebook, 2nd Edition**
Omnigraphics
PO Box 31-1640
Detroit, MI 48231
313-961-1340
800-234-1340
FAX: 313-961-1383
e-mail: info@omnigraphics.com
www.omnigraphics.com

*Amy L Sutton, Editor*
*Frederick Gale Ruffner, Founder*
*Peter Ruffner, Co-Founder*
Stroke Sourcebook, Second Edition provides updated information about stroke, its causes, risk factors, diagnosis, acute and long-term treatment, and recent innovations in poststroke care. Information on rehabilitation therapies, prevention strategies, and tips on caring for a stroke survivor is also included, along with a glossary of related terms and a directory of organizations that offer additional information to stroke survivors and their families. *$84.00*
*626 pages Hard cover*
*ISBN 0-780810-35-8*

**8452 Succeeding With Interventions For Asperger Syndrome Adolescents**
Autsim Society of North Carolina Bookstore
Ste 230
505 Oberlin Rd
Raleigh, NC 27605-1345
919-743-0204
800-442-2762
FAX: 919-743-0208
www.autismbookstore.com

*Tracey Sheriff, Chief Executive Officer*
*John Harpur, Co-Author*
*Maria Lawlor, Co-Author*
*Michael Fitzgerald, Co-Author*
This book includes a very useful outline of all the therapy sessions, which can be used as a template by a practitioner for creating their own interaction therapy intervention for adolescents.

**8453 Symptomatic Chiari Malformation**
Spina Bifida Association of America
Ste 250
4590 Macarthur Blvd NW
Washington, DC 20007-4226
202-944-3285
800-621-3141
FAX: 202-944-3295
e-mail: sbaa@sbaa.org
www.sbaa.org

*Cindy Brownstein, President & CEO*
*Jerry Oakes, MD, Author*
*Sara Struwe, Chief Operating Officer & Director of Chapter Development*
*Robin Austin, Communications Manager*
The Spina Bifida Association (SBA) serves adults and children who live with the challenges of Spina Bifida.

**8454 Taking Charge**
Spina Bifida Association of America
Ste 250
4590 Macarthur Blvd NW
Washington, DC 20007-4226
202-944-3285
800-621-3141
FAX: 202-944-3295
e-mail: sbaa@sbaa.org
www.sbaa.org

*Cindy Brownstein, President & CEO*
*Sara Struwe, Chief Operating Officer & Director of Chapter Development*
*Robin Austin, Communications Manager*
*Mickey Daguiso, Development Coordinator*
Teenagers talk about life and physical disabilities. *$7.95*

**8455 Ten Things I Learned from Bill Porter**
New World Library
14 Pamaron Way
Novato, CA 94949-6215
415-884-2100
800-972-6657
FAX: 415-884-2199
www.newworldlibrary.com

*Shelly Brady, Author*
Bill Porter worked for the Watkins Corp, selling household products door-to-door in one of Portland's worst neighborhoods. Afflicted with cerebral palsy and burdened with continual pain, Porter was determined not to live on government disability and went on to become Watkin's top-grossing salesman in Portland, the Northwest, and the US. This book was written by the woman who worked as Porter's typist and driver and later became his friend and cospeaker. *$20.00*
*192 pages*
*ISBN 1-577312-03-1*

**8456 Thyroid Disorders Sourcebook**
Omnigraphics
P.O.Box 311640
Detroit, MI 48231-1640
313-961-1340
800-234-1340
FAX: 313-961-1383
e-mail: info@omnigraphics.com
www.omnigraphics.com

*Frederick Gale Ruffner, Founder*
*Peter Ruffner, Co-Founder*
Thyroid Disorders Sourcebook provides essential information about thyroid and parathyroid function, diseases, and treatments. Also presented are symptoms, risk factors, diagnosis, treatments, thyroid effects on the body, and the impact of environmental conditions on the thyroid. *$84.00*
*573 pages Hard cover*
*ISBN 0-780807-45-7*

**8457 Tourette Syndrome: The Facts**
Oxford University Press
198 Madison Ave
New York, NY 10016-4308
212-726-6000
800-451-7556
FAX: 919-677-1303
e-mail: custserv.us@oup.com
www.oup.com

*Mary Robertson, Co-Editor*
*Andrea Cavanna, Co-Editor*
The causes of the syndrome, how it is diagnosed, and the ways in which it can be treated. *$35.00*
*122 pages*
*ISBN 0-198523-98-X*

**8458 Tourette's Syndrome: Finding Answers and Getting Help**
O'Reilly Media Inc
1005 Gravenstein Hwy N
Sebastopol, CA 95472-2811
707-827-7019
800-889-8969
FAX: 707-824-8268
e-mail: order@oreilly.com
www.oreilly.com

Tourette's Syndrome is a neurological disorder usually diagnosed in childhood and characterized by tics, physical jerks, and involuntary vocalizations. Tourette's can be a devastating disability. The good news is that it's very treatable. Tourette's Syndrome helps you secure a diagnosis, understand medical interventions, get healthcare coverage, and manage Tourette's in family life, school, community, and workplace. *$24.95*
*416 pages Paperback*
*ISBN 0-596500-07-6*

**8459 Tourette's Syndrome: Tics, Obsessions, Compulsions: Developmental Psychopathology**
John Wiley & Sons
111 River St
Hoboken, NJ 07030-5774
201-748-6000
FAX: 201-748-6088
e-mail: info@wiley.com
www.wiley.com

*James F Leckman MD, Author*
*Donald J Cohen MD, Co-Author*
*Stephen M. Smith, President and Chief Executive Officer*
*Ellis E. Cousens, Executive Vice President, Chief Financial and Operations Officer*
Contains 21 contributions compromising the work of researchers associated with the Yale Child Study Center, which has been at the forefront of research on Tourette's syndrome and associated disorders. *$85.00*
*600 pages*
*ISBN 0-471113-75-1*

**8460 Treating Epilepsy Naturally: A Guide to Alternative and Adjunct Therapies**
McGraw-Hill Company
P.O.Box 182604
Columbus, OH 43272
877-833-5524
FAX: 614-759-3749
e-mail: customer.service@mcgraw-hill.com
www.mcgraw-hill.com

*Harold McGraw III, Chairman, President and Chief Executive Officer*
*Jack F. Callahan, Executive Vice President, Chief Financial Officer*
*John Berisford, Executive Vice President, Human Resources*
*Kenneth M. Vittor, Executive Vice President and General Counsel*
Offers alternative treatments to replace and to complement traditional therapies and sound advice to find the right health practitioner. *$15.95*
*288 pages*
*ISBN 0-658013-79-3*

**8461 Understanding Asthma**
National Jewish Health
1400 Jackson St
Denver, CO 80206-2761
303-270-2708
FAX: 303-398-1125
e-mail: allstetterw@njc.org
nationaljewish.org

*Michael Salem, CEO*
*Christine Forkner, Chief Financial Officer and Executive Vice President*
*Laszlo Pook, MBA, Chief Information Officer*
*Ron Berge, MBA, Chief Operating Officer*
Offers a brief introduction to asthma and then goes into the physiology of asthma, the triggers of asthma, and diagnosis and monitoring of asthma.
*27 pages*

**8462 Understanding Asthma: The Blueprint for Breathing**
Allergy & Asthma Network Mothers of Asthmatics
Suite 300
8201 Greensboro Drive
McLean, VA 22102
703-641-9595
800-878-4403
FAX: 703-288-5271
www.aanma.org

*Nancy Sander, President and Founder*
*Marcela Gieminiani, Director of Administration and Programs*
*Brenda Silvia-Torma, Project Manager*
*Gary Fitzgerald, Managing Editor*
A layman's guide to asthma facts based on a presentation from the first national asthma patient conference.

**8463 Understanding Cystic Fibrosis**
University Press of Mississippi
3825 Ridgewood Rd
Jackson, MS 39211-6453
601-432-6205
800-737-7788
FAX: 601-432-6217
e-mail: press@ihl.state.ms.us
www.upress.state.ms.us

*Karen Hopkin PhD, Author*
*Craig Gill, Assistant Director/Editor-in-Chief*
*Anne Stascavage, Managing Editor*
*Walter Biggins, Acquiring Editor*
A reference for CF patients and their families. *$14.00*
*128 pages*
*ISBN 0-878059-67-9*

**8464 Understanding Multiple Sclerosis**
University Press of Mississippi
3825 Ridgewood Rd
Jackson, MS 39211-6453
601-432-6205
800-737-7788
FAX: 601-432-6205
e-mail: press@ihl.state.ms.us
www.upress.state.ms.us

*Melissa Stauffer, Author*
*Craig Gill, Assistant Director/Editor-in-Chief*
*Anne Stascavage, Managing Editor*
*Walter Biggins, Acquiring Editor*
Two psychologists discuss their roles with a member who has multiple sclerosis. Includes chapters on adolescents with multiple sclerosis, employment, and research. *$14.00*
*136 pages*
*ISBN 1-578068-03-7*

**8465 Urologic Care of the Child with Spina Bifida**
Spina Bifida Association of America
Ste 250
4590 Macarthur Blvd NW
Washington, DC 20007-4226
202-944-3285
800-621-3141
FAX: 202-944-3295
e-mail: sbaa@sbaa.org
www.sbaa.org

*Cindy Brownstein, President & CEO*
*David Joseph, MD, Author*
*Sara Struwe, Chief Operating Officer & Director of Chapter Development*
*Robin Austin, Communications Manager*
The Spina Bifida Association (SBA) serves adults and children who live with the challenges of Spina Bifida.

**8466 Usher Syndrome**
National Institute on Deafness & Other Communicati
31 Center Drive Msc 2320
Bethesda, MD 20892-2320
800-241-1044
FAX: 301-770-8977
TTY:800-241-1055
e-mail: nidcdinfo@nidcd.nih.gov
www.nidcd.nih.gov

*James F Battey Jr MD PhD, Director*
Explains what is Usher Syndrome, who is affected by Usher syndrome, what causes Usher syndrome, how is Usher syndrome treated, and what research is being conducted on Usher syndrome.

**8467 What Everyone Needs to Know About Asthma**
Allergy & Asthma Network Mothers of Asthmatics
Suite 300
8201 Greensboro Drive
McLean, VA 22102
703-641-9595
800-878-4403
FAX: 703-288-5271
www.aanma.org

*Nancy Sander, President and Founder*
*Marcela Gieminiani, Director of Administration and Programs*
*Brenda Silvia-Torma, Project Manager*
*Gary Fitzgerald, Managing Editor*
Offers information and facts on gaining control of asthma, asthma triggers and monitoring asthma disorders.

**8468 When the Road Turns: Inspirational Stories About People with MS**
Health Communications
3201 SW 15th St
Deerfield Beach, FL 33442-8157
954-360-0909
800-441-5569
FAX: 954-360-0034
www.hci-online.com

An inspiring collection of stories written by people living with multiple sclerosis. *$10.36*
*300 pages*
*ISBN 1-558749-07-1*

**8469 Young Person's Guide to Spina Bifida**
Spina Bifida Association of America
Ste 250
4590 Macarthur Blvd NW
Washington, DC 20007-4226
202-944-3285
800-621-3141
FAX: 202-944-3295
e-mail: sbaa@sbaa.org
www.sbaa.org

*Cindy Brownstein, President & CEO*
*Marlene Lutkenhoff, RN, MSN, Co-Editor*
*Sonya Oppenheimer, MD, Co-Editor*
*Robin Austin, Communications Manager*
Gives practical tips and suggestions for becoming independent and managing your health. *$19.00*

**8470 Your Child and Asthma**
National Jewish Health
1400 Jackson St
Denver, CO 80206-2761
303-270-2708
FAX: 303-398-1125
e-mail: allstetterw@njc.org
nationaljewish.org

*Michael Salem, CEO*
*Christine Forkner, Chief Financial Officer and Executive Vice President*
*Laszlo Pook, MBA, Chief Information Officer*
*Ron Berge, MBA, Chief Operating Officer*
A booklet offering information to parents and family about their child with asthma. Offers information on diagnosis, treatments, triggers and family concerns.

**8471 Your Cleft Affected Child**
Hunter House Inc. Publisher
P.O.Box 2914
Alameda, CA 94501-914
510-865-5282
800-266-5592
FAX: 510-865-4295
e-mail: ordering@hunterhouse.com
www.hunterhouse.com

*Carrie T Gruman Trinker, Author*
Pocket-sized consumer text covers causes of cleft palate and how it can be fixed. Includes advice on feeding, dental and speech-related issues. *$16.95*
*288 pages Paperback*
*ISBN 0-897931-85-4*

**8472 Your Guide to Bowel Cancer**
Oxford University Press
2001 Evans Rd
Cary, NC 27513-2009
919-677-0977
FAX: 919-677-1303
e-mail: custserv.us@oup.co
www.us.oup.com

Offers information and public awareness on the disease of bowel cancer. *$18.95*

*ISBN 0-340927-46-1*

## Print: Journals

**8473 AIDS: The Official Journal of the International AIDS Society**
Lippincott Williams & Wilkins
530 Walnut St
Philadelphia, PA 19106-3603
215-521-8300
FAX: 215-521-8902
e-mail: customerservice@lww.com
lww.com

*JA Levy, Co Editor*
*B. Autran, Co Editor*
*R. A Coutinho, Co Editor*
*J. P Phair, Co Editor*
The latest groundbreaking research on HIV and AIDS. *$ 433.00*
*18 per year*

**8474 American Journal of Orthopsychiatry**
American Psychological Association
750 1st St NE
Washington, DC 20002-4242
202-336-5500
800-374-2721
FAX: 202-336-5502
TTY: 202-336-6123
www.apa.org

*Nancy Felipe Russo PhD, Editor*
*Norman B. Anderson, PhD, Chief Executive Officer & Executive Vice President*
*L. Michael Honaker, PhD, Chief Operating Officer*
*Cynthia D. Belar, PhD, Executive Director, Education Directorate*
Mental health issues from multidisciplinary and interprofessionals perspectives: clinical, research and expository approaches. *$45.00*
*160 pages Quarterly*

**8475 Annals of Otology, Rhinology and Laryngology**
Annals Publishing Company
4507 Laclede Ave
Saint Louis, MO 63108-2103
314-367-4987
FAX: 314-367-4988
e-mail: manager@annals.com
www.annals.com

*Ken Cooper, President*
Original, peer-reviewed articles in the fields of otolaryngology - head and neck medicine and surgery, broncho-esophagology, audiology, speech, pathology, allery, and maxillofacial surgery. Official journal of the American Laryngological Association/American Broncho-Esophagological Association. *$170.00*
*112 pages Monthly*

**8476 Archives of Neurology**
American Medical Association
P.O.Box 10946
Chicago, IL 60610-946
773-768-6400
800-262-2350
FAX: 312-464-4184
e-mail: ama-subs@ama-assn.org
www.archneur.ama-assn.org

*Margaret Vanner, Manager*
Mission is to publish scientific information primarily important to those physicians caring for people with neurologic disorders, but also for those interested in the structure and function of the normal and diseased nervous system. *$235.00*
*198 pages Monthly*

**8477 Cleft Palate-Craniofacial Journal**
Cleft Palate Foundation
Ste 102
1504 E Franklin St
Chapel Hill, NC 27514-2820
919-933-9044
800-242-5338
FAX: 919-933-9604
e-mail: membership@acpa-cpf.org
www.cpcjournal.org

*Nancy Smythe, Executive Director*
*Lisa K Gist, Director of Family Services*
A peer revived international multidisciplinary journal dedicated to current research on the care and treatment of children born with cleft lip and palate and other craniofacial anomalies. 6 issues/year

**8478 Journal of Head Trauma Rehabilitation**
Lippincott, Williams & Wilkins
P.O.Box 1620
Hagerstown, MD 21741-1620
301-223-2300
800-638-3030
FAX: 301-223-2400
www.lww.com

*John D Corrigan PhD, ABPP, Editor*
Scholarly journal designed to provide information on clinical management and rehabilitation of the head-injured for the practicing professional. Published bimonthly. *$113.96*

## Print: Magazines

**8479 Coping with Cancer Magazine**
Media America
P.O.Box 682268
Franklin, TN 37068-2268
615-790-2400
FAX: 615-794-0179
copingmag.com

Provides knowledge, hope and inspiration, its readers include cancer patients (survivors) and their families, caregivers, healthcare teams and support group leaders. *$19.95*
*53 pages 6 x year*

**8480 CurePSP Magazine**
Society for Progressive Supranuclear Palsy
Suite 201
30 E. Padonia Road
Timonium, MD 21093
800-457-4777
866-457-4777
e-mail: info@curepsp.org
www.psp.org

*Richard Gordon Zyne, President-CEO*
*Kathleen Matarazzo Speca, Vice President, Development & Donor Relations*
*Adrienne Bantum, Staff Accountant/Research Services Administrator*
Quarterly newsletter. The society's mission is to promote and fund research into finding the cause and cure for progressive supranuclear palsy (PSP). Provides information, support and advocacy to persons diagnosed with PSP, their families and caregivers. Educates physicians and allied health professionals on PSP and how to improve patient care.

**8481 EpilepsyUSA**
Epilepsy Foundation
8301 Professional Pl
Landover, MD 20785-2237
301-459-3700
800-332-1000
FAX: 301-577-2684
e-mail: ContactUs@efa.org
epilepsyfoundation.org

*Phil Gattone, President and CEO*
*Sandy Finucane, Executive Vice President*
*Temi Aregbesola, Progam Manager*
*Mary Ann Thornton, Information Specialist*
Magazine reporting on issues of interest to people with epilepsy and their families. *$15.00*
*22 pages Bi-Monthly*

**8482 MSFOCUS Magazine**
Multiple Sclerosis Foundation
6520 North Andrews Avenue
Fort Lauderdale, FL 33309-2130
954-776-6805
888-673-6287
FAX: 954-938-8708
e-mail: support@msfocus.org
www.msfocus.org

*Jules Kuperberg, Executive Director*
*Alan Segaloff, Co- Executive Director*
*Eric Schenck, President, Director*
*Charles Eader, Vice President, Treasurer*
Contemporary national, nonprofit organization that provides free support services and public education for persons with Multiple Sclerosis, newsletters, toll-free phone support, information, referrals, home care, assitive technology and support groups.
*48 pages Quarterly*

**8483 Orthotics and Prosthetics Almanac**
American Orthotic & Prosthetics Association
Ste 200
330 John Carlyle St
Alexandria, VA 22314-5760
571-431-0876
FAX: 571-431-0899
e-mail: info@aopanet.org
www.aopanet.org

*Thomas F. Fise, JD, Executive Director*
*Don DeBolt, Chief Operating Officer*
*Lauren Anderson, Coordinator of Membership, Operations, and Meetings*
*Devon Bernard, Manager of Reimbursement*
Features articles covering current professional, patient care, government, business and National Office activities affecting the orthotics and prosthetics profession and industry. *$40.00*
*80 pages Monthly*
*ISSN 1061-46 1*

**8484 PDF News**
Parkinson's Disease Foundation
1359 Broadway
Room 1509
New York, NY 10018-7867
212-923-4700
800-457-6676
FAX: 212-923-4778
e-mail: info@pdf.org
www.pdf.org

*Robin Anthony Elliott, Executive Director*
*Yasnahia Cortorreal, Director of Administration*
*Jeff Wallerstein, Administration Controller*
*Kristin Brinkman, Administrative Assistant*
*8-12 pages Quarterly*

**8485 POZ Magazine**
Smart + Strong
462 Seventh Ave
19th Floor
New York, NY 10018
212-242-2163
FAX: 212-675-8505
e-mail: webmaster@poz.com
poz.com

*Megan Strub, Publisher*
*Regan Hofmann, Editor In-Chief*
A health title written for individuals who are HIV+, their friends and families. POZ provides the latest treatment information, investigative journalism and survivor profiles.

**8486 SCI Life**
National Spinal Cord Injury Association
Ste 302
11426 Rockville Pike
Rockville, MD 20852
301-468-3902
FAX: 301-468-3904
e-mail: info@ilcreations.com
ilcreations.com

SCI/LIFE is dedicated to the presentation of news concerning people with spinal cord injuries caused by trauma or disease.
*Quarterly/Free*

**8487 Spine**
Lippincott, Williams & Wilkins
530 Walnut St
Philadelphia, PA 19106-3603
215-521-8300
FAX: 215-521-8411
e-mail: customerservice@lww.com
lww.com

*James N Weinstein DO MSc, Editor*
Publishes original papers on theoretical issues and research concerning the spine and spinal cord injuries. *$9.00*
*26 Issues Year*

**8488 Ventilator-Assisted Living**
International Ventilator Users Network
Ste 110
4207 Lindell Blvd
Saint Louis, MO 63108-2930
314-534-0475
FAX: 314-534-5070
e-mail: info@ventusers.org
www.ventusers.org

*Joan L. Headley, Editor*
*Brian M. Tiburzi, Assistant Executive Director*
*Judith Raymond Fischer, MSLS, Information Specialist*
*Gayla Hoffman, Editor*
To enhance the lives and independence of ventilator-assisted living by promoting education, networking, and advocacy among these individuals and healthcare providers. Ventilator-Assisted Living supports Post-Polio Health International's educational, research, and advocacy efforts. Offers information about relevant events.
*Quarterly*

## Print: Newsletters

**8489 ACPOC News**
Assoc of Children's Prosthetic-Orthotic Clinics
Ste 727
6300 N River Rd
Rosemont, IL 60018-4226
847-698-1637
FAX: 847-823-0536
e-mail: acpoc@aaos.org
www.acpoc.org

*J Ivan Krajbich, MD, President*
*Jorge A Fabregas, MD, Secretary-Treasurer*
*Eugene Banziger, CPO, Newsletter Editor*
*Janet Walker, MD, Program Committee*

Quarterly publication from the Association of Children's Prosthetic/Orthotic Clinics. Included with membership.
*40 pages Quarterly*

**8490 AID Bulletin**
Project AID Resource Center
P.O. Box 5190
Kent, OH 44242-1
330-672-2672
FAX: 330-672-4724

*Alex Boros PhD, Director AID*
*J Sue Adams, Senior Counselor*
*Peter Mueller, Executive Director*
Has the latest news on upcoming conferences, literature, developments in programs and/or services for disabled persons who are substance abusers. Offers articles on their experiences, ideas and questions of others in this field which includes providers and consumers. *$7.50*

**8491 AIDS Alert**
AHC Media LLC
Bldg 6-400
3525 Piedmont Rd NE
Atlanta, GA 30305-1578
404-262-5436
800-688-2421
FAX: 404-262-5560
www.ahcpub.com

*Joy Daughtery Dickinson, Senior Managing Editor*
Source of AIDS news and advice for health care professionals. Covers up-to-the-minute developments and guidance on the entire spectrum of AIDS challenges, including treatment, education, precautions, screening, diagnosis and policy. *$499.00*
*Monthly*

**8492 Adaptive Tracks**
Adaptive Sports Center
P.O.Box 1639
Crested Butte, CO 81224-1639
970-349-2296
866-349-2296
FAX: 970-349-2077
e-mail: info@adaptivesports.org
www.adaptivesports.org

*Christopher Hensley, Executive Director*
*Chris Read, CTRS, Program Director*
*Ella Fahrlander, Development Director*
*Mike Neustedter, Marketing Director*
The Adaptive Sports Center (ASC) of Crested Butte, Colorado is a non-profit organization that provides year-round recreation activities for people with disabilities and their families. The ASC provides adaptive snowboarding downhill skiing, cross country skiing as well as backcountry trips. Summer activities include a variety of wilderness-based programs, multi-day trips into the back country, extensive cycling programs, canoeing, and white water rafting.
*6 pages Quarterly*

**8493 Arthritis Self-Management**
Rapaport Publishing, Inc.
Ste 800
150 W 22nd St
New York, NY 10011-2421
212-989-0200
FAX: 212-989-4786
e-mail: webeditor@arthritis-self-mgmt.com
arthritisselfmanagement.com

*Richard A Rapaport, President*
Arthritis Self-Management publishes practical 'how-to' information for the growing number of people with arthritis who want to know more about managing their condition. We focus on the day-to-day and long-term aspects of arthritis in a positive and upbeat style, giving our subscribers up-to-date news, facts, and advice to help them make informed decisions about their health.
*$9.97*
*BiMonthly*

**8494 Breaking Ground**
Tennessee Council on Developmental Disabilities
404 James Robertson Pkwy
Nashville, TN 37243-1
615-532-6615
FAX: 615-532-6964
e-mail: tnddc@tn.gov
www.tn.gov/cdd

*Wanda Willis, Executive Director*
*20 pages 6 x Year*

**8495 Breaking New Ground News Note**
Purdue University
225 W University St
W Lafayette, IN 47907
765-494-4600
FAX: 765-496-1356
www.breakingnewground.info

*Paul Jones, Project Manager*
*Bill Field, Project Director*
*Steve Swain, Rural Rehabilitation Specialist*
*Robert Stuthridge, Project Ergonomist*
News, practical ideas and success stories of and for farmers and other agricultural workers with physical disabilities.
*2 pages Quarterly*

**8496 Diabetes Self-Management**
Rapaport Publishing, Inc.
Ste 800
150 W 22nd St
New York, NY 10011-2421
212-989-0200
FAX: 212-989-4786
e-mail: webeditor@diabetes-self-mgmt.com
diabetesselfmanagement.com

*Richard A Rapaport, President*
Publishes practical how-to information, focusing on the day-to-day and long-term aspects of diabetes in a positive and upbeat style. Gives subscribers up-to-date news, facts and advice to help them maintain their wellness and make informed decisions regarding their health. *$9.97*
*BiMonthly*

**8497 Directions**
Families of Spinal Muscular Dystrophy
Ste 107
14047 W Petronella Dr
Libertyville, IL 60048- 9429
847-367-7620
800-886-1762
FAX: 847-367-7623
e-mail: newsletter@fsma.org
www.fsma.org

*Audrey Lewis, Manager*
*$35.00*
*60-70 pages Quarterly*

**8498 IAL News**
International Association of Laryngectomees
Ste 316
925b Peachtree St NE
Atlanta, GA 30309-3918
866-425-3678
www.larynxlink.com

*David Blevins, Editor*
*Bob Herbst, President*
*Wade Hampton, Vice President*
*Susan Reeves, Administrative Manager*
Focuses on rehabilitation and well-being of persons who have had laryngectomy surgery.

**8499 Informer**
Simon Foundation
P.O.Box 815
Wilmette, IL 60091-815
847-864-3913
800-237-4666
FAX: 847-864-9758
e-mail: cbgartley@simonfoundation.org
simonfoundation.org

*Cheryle B Gartley, President and Founder*
*Twila Yednock, Director of Special Events*
*Elizabeth LaGro, Director of Communications*
*Bridget Bean, Administrative Assistant*
Publishes items of interest to people with bladder or bowel incontinence, including medical articles, helpful devices, publications and a pen pal list. Quarterly newsletter.
*Quarterly*

**8500 Moisture Seekers**
Sjogren's Syndrome Foundation
6707 Democracy Boulevard
Suite 325
Bethesda, MD 20817
301-530-4420
800-475-6473
FAX: 301-530-4415
e-mail: tms@sjogrens.org
www.sjogrens.org

*Steven Taylor, Executive Director*
*Pat Spolyar, Director of Awareness*
*Elizabeth Trocchio, Director of Marketing*
*Cynthia Williamson, Director of Field Services*
Newsletter of the organization for lay people and professionals interested in Sjogren's Syndrome. Contains medical news, current research, and essential tips for daily living. *$25.00*
*15-16 pages Monthly*

**8501 Momentum**
National Multiple Sclerosis Society
Ste 6
421 New Karner Rd
Albany, NY 12205-3838
518-464-0850
800-344-4867
FAX: 518-464-1232
e-mail: nyr@nmss.org
www.nationalmssociety.org

*Edward A Kangas, President*
News and information on research progress, medical treatments, patient services, therapeutic claims and activities.

**8502 Options**
People Against Cancer
P.O.Box 10
604 East Street
Otho, IA 50569
515-972-4444
FAX: 515-972-4415
e-mail: info@PeopleAgainstCAncer.com
www.peopleagainstcancer.com

*Frank Wiewel, Executive Director/Founder*
Publication of People Against Cancer, a nonprofit, grassroots public benefit organization dedicated to 'New Directions in the War on Cancer.' We help people to find the best cancer treatment. We are a democratic organization of people with cancer, their loved ones and citizens working together to protect and enhance medical freedom of choice.
*8 pages Quarterly*

**8503 PDF Newsletter**
Parkinson's Disease Foundation
1359 Broadway
Room 1509
New York, NY 10018-7867
212-923-4700
800-457-6676
FAX: 212-923-4778
e-mail: info@pdf.org
www.pdf.org

*Robin Anthony Elliott, Executive Director*
*Yasnahia Cortorreal, Director of Administration*
*Jeff Wallerstein, Administration Controller*
*Kristin Brinkman, Administrative Assistant*
The Parkinson's Disease Foundation (PDF) is a leading national presence in Parkinson's disease research, education and public advocacy.
*12-16 pages Quarterly*

**8504 Parkinsons Report**
National Parkinson Foundation
1501 NW 9th Ave
Miami, FL 33136-1494
305-243-6666
800-327-4545
FAX: 305-243-6037
e-mail: contact@parkinson.org
www.parkinson.org

*Joyce Oberdorf, President and CEO*
*Michael S. Okun, National Medical Director*
*Anusha Alikhan, Marketing Manager*
*David Waugh, IT Manager*
Articles, reports and news on Parkinson's disease and the activities of the National Parkinson Foundation.
*32 pages Qarterly*

**8505 Post-Polio Health**
Post-Polio Health International
Ste 110
4207 Lindell Blvd
Saint Louis, MO 63108-2930
314-534-0475
FAX: 314-534-5070
e-mail: info@post-polio.org
www.post-polio.org

*Joan L. Headley, Executive Director*
*Brian M. Tiburzi, Assistant Executive Director*
*Gayla Hoffman, Editor*
*Judith Raymond Fischer, Information Specialist*
To enhance the lives and independence of polio survivors by promoting education, networking, and advocacy among these individuals and healthcare providers. Post-Polio Health supports Post-Polio Health International's educational, research, and advocacy efforts. Offers information about relevant events. *$30.00*
*12 pages quarterly*

**8506 Prader-Willi Alliance of New York Newsletter**
2224 Agnew Ter
The Villages, FL 32162-2284
716-276-2211
800-442-1655
FAX: 585-271-2782
e-mail: alliance@prader-willi.org
www.prader-willi.org

*Nina Roberto, Executive Director*
*Linda LeTendre, Conference Coordinator*
*Amy McDougall, President*
*Jamie Bassel, Vice President*
The Prader-Willi Foundation is a national, nonprofit public charity that works for the benefit of individuals with Prader-Willi syndrome and their families. *$20.00*
*Quarterly*

**8507 Quality Care Newsletter**
National Association for Continence
P.O.Box 1019
Charleston, SC 29402-1019
843-377-0900
800-252-3337
FAX: 843-377-0905
e-mail: memberservices@nafc.org
www.nafc.org

*Nancy Muller, Executive Director*
*Katherine F. Jeter, EbD Founder*
*Niall T.M. Galloway, Chairman*
*Ted Johnson, Vice Chaiperson*
Newsletter from NAFC. By donating $25 and becomming a Quality Care donor, you may receive our quarterly newsletter. *$25.00*
*14-16 pages Quarterly*

**8508 Rasmussen's Syndrome and Hemispherectomy Support Network Newsletter**
8235 Lethbridge Rd
Millersville, MD 21108-1609
410-987-5221
FAX: 410-987-5211
e-mail: rssnlynn@aol.com
http://www.rarediseases.org/rare-disease-info

*Al Miller, Co-Author*
*Lynn Miller, Co-Author*
National, not-for-profit organization dedicated to providing information and support to individuals affected by Rasmussen's Syndrome and hemispherectomy. Publishes a periodic newsletter and disseminates reprints of medical journal articles concerning Rasmussen's Syndrome and its treatments. Maintains a support network that provides encouragement and information to individuals affected by Rasmussen's Syndrome and their families.

**8509 SCI Psychosocial Process**
Amer Assn of Spinal Cord Injury Psych & Soc Wks
75-20 Astoria Blvd
East Elmhurst, NY 11370-1138
718-803-3782
FAX: 718-803-0414
e-mail: info@unitedspinal.org
http://www.unitedspinal.org/

*Paul Tobin, President and Chief Executive Officer*
*Lex Frieden, Chairman of the Board*
*Denise A. Mc Quade, Vice Chairman of the Board*
*Janeen Earwood, Treasurer*
Quarterly newsletter.

**8510 Special Care in Dentistry**
Blackwell Publishing
350 Main St
Malden, MA 02148-5089
781-388-0200
FAX: 781-388-8210
www.blackwellpublishing.com

*Ronald L Ettinger BDS/MDS/DDS, Editor*
*$125.00*
*48 pages BiMonthly*

**8511 TSA Newsletter**
Tourette Syndrome Association
4240 Bell Blvd
Bayside, NY 11361-2874
718-224-2999
800-237-0717
FAX: 718-279-9596
e-mail: ts@tsa-usa.org
www.tsa-usa.org

*Stephen M. McCall, President*
National non-profit membership organization whose mission is to identify the cause of, find the cure for, and control the effects of this disorder. A growing number of local chapters nationwide provide educational materials, seminars, conferences and support groups for over 35,000 members.
*Quarterly*

**8512 Tethering Cord**
Spina Bifida Association of America
Ste 250
4590 Macarthur Blvd NW
Washington, DC 20007-4226
202-944-3285
800-621-3141
FAX: 202-944-3295
e-mail: sbaa@sbaa.org
http://www.ninds.nih.gov/disorders/tethered_c

*Cindy Brownstein, CEO*
Tethered spinal cord syndrome is a neurological disorder caused by tissue attachments that limit the movement of the spinal cord within the spinal column. Attachments may occur congenitally at the base of the spinal cord (conus medullaris) or they may develop near the site of an injury to the spinal cord.

**8513 Tourette Syndrome Association Children's Newsletter**
4240 Bell Blvd
Bayside, NY 11361-2874
718-224-2999
800-237-0717
FAX: 718-279-9596
e-mail: ts@tsa-usa.org
tsa-usa.org

*Stephen M. McCall, President*
National, nonprofit membership organization. Mission is to identify the cause of, find the cure for, and control the effects of this disorder. A growing number of local chapters nationwide provide educational materials, seminars, conferences and support groups for over 35,000 members.

**8514 Voice of the Diabetic**
NFB Diabetes Action Network
200 East Wells Street
Baltimore, MD 21230-4914
410-659-9314
888-581-4741
FAX: 410-685-5653
e-mail: editor@diabetes.nfb.org
www.nfb.org

*Elizabeth Lunt, Editor*
Newsletter containing personal stories and practical guidelines by blind diabetics and medical professionals, medical news, resource column and a recipe corner. We are a support and information network for all diabetics.
*28 pages Quarterly*

## Non Print: Newsletters

**8515 Teens & Asthma**
American Lung Association
530 7th St SE
Washington, DC 20003-2768
202-546-5864
FAX: 202-546-5607
e-mail: fthompson@aladc.org
www.aladc.org

*Rolando E Bates Jr, CEO*
Tips from other teens with asthma to help those having it get on with the serious business of having fun with the rest of their lives.
*Online/Free*

## Non Print: Video

**8516 Fragile X Family**
Fanlight Productions
32 Court Street
Brooklyn, NY 11201-1731
718-488-8900
800-876-1710
FAX: 718-488-8642
e-mail: info@fanlight.com
www.fanlight.com

*Eric Kutner, Producer*
Fragile X Family takes viewers inside the lives of a developmentally disabled family who are affected by Fragile X Syndrome, an inherited chromosomal disorder which is the second most common cause of mental retardation. *$149.00*
*VHS/VIDEO*
*ISBN 1-572954-14-0*

**8517 In the Middle**
Fanlight Productions
32 Court Street
Brooklyn, NY 11201-1731
718-488-8900
800-876-1710
FAX: 718-488-8642
e-mail: info@fanlight.com
www.fanlight.com

*Ben Achtenberg, Owner*
Documents the problems and joys shared by Ryanna, who has Spina Bifida, and her parents, teachers and classmates during her first year of being mainstreamed in a Head Start Program. *$99.00*

**8518 Narcolepsy**
Fanlight Productions
32 Court Street
Brooklyn, NY 11201-1731
718-488-8900
800-876-1710
FAX: 718-488-8642
e-mail: info@fanlight.com
www.fanlight.com

*Jason Margolis, Producer*
Presents the experiences of three individuals who lives and relationships have been disrupted by narcolepsy. Rental $50/day. *$199.00*
*VHS/25 Minutes*

**8519 Twitch and Shout**
Fanlight Productions
32 Court Street
Brooklyn, NY 11201-1731
718-488-8900
800-876-1710
FAX: 718-488-8642
e-mail: info@fanlight.com
www.fanlight.com

*Laurel Chitden, Producer*
This documentary provides an intimate journey into the startling world of Tourette Syndrome (TS), a genetic disorder that can cause a bizarre range of involuntary movements, vocalizations, and compulsions. Through the eyes of a photojournalist with TS, the film introduces viewers to others who have this puzzling disorder. This is an emotionally absorbing, sometimes, unsettling, and finally uplifting program about people who must contend with a society that often sees them as crazy or bad. *$225.00*

## Sports

**8520 National Sports Center for the Disabled**
P.O.Box 1290
Winter Park, CO 80482-1290
970-726-5514
FAX: 970-726-4112
e-mail: info@nscd.org
www.nscd.org

*Becky Zimmermann, President/CEO*
*Scott Franssen, Vice President*
*Diane Eustace, Marketing Director*
*Beth Fox, Operations Director*
Innovative non-profit organization that provides year-round recreation for children and adults with disabilities. The world's largest adaptive ski program, teaching 25,000 lessons per winter at Winter Park Resort, Colorado. Also snowboarding, ski racing, showshoeing, cross-country skiing. Summer sports: rafting, sailing, camping, hiking, hand cycling, mountain biking, tandem biking, in-line skating, horseback riding, fishing, rock climbing. Sports symposium and clinics.

**8521 Rehabilitation Institute of Chicago's Virginia Wadsworth Sports Program**
541 North Fairbanks
Mezzanine
Chicago, IL 60611-2654
312-238-5001
866-999-3344
FAX: 312-238-5017
e-mail: sports@ric.org
www.ric.org

*Glenn Paustian, Director*
*Jill Beemer, Manager*
*Patrick Byrne, Instructor*
RIC's Center for Health and Fitness is a full service fitness center for individuals with disablilties and the administrative offices for RIC's Wirtz Sports Program. Eighteen different sport and recreation programs are offered free of charge. The facility is adjacent to RIC's main building and also is the location of a branch of The National Center for Physical Activity and Disability (NCPAD), a joint project operated by the University of Illinois-Chigcago.

**8522 US Paralympics**
1 Olympic Plz
Colorado Springs, CO 80909-5760
719-866-2030
FAX: 719-866-2029
e-mail: paralympicinfo@usoc.org
www.usparalympics.org

*Jessica Galli, Track & Field*
*Derek Arneaud, Soccer*
*Willie Steward, Nordic Skiing*
*Muffy Davis, Alpine Skiing*
A division of the US Olympic Committee focused on enhancing programs, funding and opportunities for persons with physical disabilities to participate in Paralymic sports.

## Support Groups

**8523 AAN's Toll-Free Hotline**
Allergy and Asthma Network Mothers of Asthmatics
8201 Greensboro Driver
Suite 300
McLean, VA 22102-4343
703-641-9595
800-878-4403
FAX: 703-288-5271
aanma.org

*Nancy Sander, President*
*Marcela Gieminiani, Director*
*Brenda Silvia-Torma, Project Manager*
*Michael Amato, Chair*

Offers answers to questions regarding allergies and asthma, provides referrals and support to assist the patient and his or her family.

**8524 Breaking New Ground Resource Center**
Purdue University
225 S University St
West Lafayette, IN 47907-2093
765-494-5088
800-825-4264
FAX: 765-496-1356
e-mail: bng@ecn.purdue.edu
www.breakingnewground.info

*Bill Field, Project Director*
*Paul Jones, Project Manager*
*Steve Swain, Rural Rehab Specialist*
*Robert Stuthridge, Project Ergonomist*

A resource center devoted to helping farmers and ranchers with physical disabilities. Resource materials and a free newsletter are available to anyone.

**8525 Camp Candlelight**
Epilepsy Foundation Arizona
Ste 310
273 Azalea Rd
Mobile, AL 36609-1970
251-432-0970
800-768-2690
FAX: 251-432-0975
e-mail: tom.walsh002@chw.edu
http://www.epilepsyfoundationalabama.org

*Frank Mitchell Garrett, Executive Director*
*Lea Valentine, Office Manager*
*Caroline Foster, Director Of Public Relations*

Camp Candlelight provides children ages 8 to 15 a unique camp experience that mixes traditional summer camp with special sessions that teach campers about their seizures and gives them resources to manage the challenges that the seizures represent. Staff includes a neurologist, several nurses and a school psychologist, in addition to traditional camp staff who are given specialized training in responding appropriately to the needs of kids with epilepsy.

**8526 Cancer Information Service**
National Cancer Institute
Suite 300
6116 Executive Blvd
Bethesda, MD 20892-8322
301-496-8531
800-422-6237
FAX: 304-402-0181
e-mail: cancergovstaff@mail.nih.gov
www.cancer.gov

*Barbara K. Rimer, Dean*
*Owen N. Witte, Director*
*Abby Sandler, Chief*
*Bruce A. Chabner, Chair*

A nationwide network of 19 regional field offices supported by the National Cancer Institute which provides accurate, up-to-date information on cancer to patients and their families, health professionals and the general public. The CIS can provide specific information in understandable language about particular types of cancer, as well as information on second opinions and the availability of clinical trials.

**8527 Clearinghouse on Disability Information: Office Special Education & Rehabilitative Service**
U S Department of Education
400 Maryland Ave SW
Washington, DC 20202-1
202-245-7549
800-872-5327
FAX: 202-245-7614
www.ed.gov

*Arne Duncan, Secretary Of Education*
*Tony Miller, Deputy Secretary*
*Martha Kanter, Under Secretary*
*Jo Anderson, Senior Advisor*

Provides information to people with disabilities or anyone requesting information, by doing research and providing documents in response to inquiries. The information provided includes areas of federal funding for disability-related programs. Information provided may be useful to disabled individuals and their families, schools and universities, teacher's and/or school administrators, and organizations who have persons with disabilities as clients.

**8528 Cornerstone Services**
777 Joyce Rd
Joliet, IL 60436-1876
815-741-7600
FAX: 815-723-1177
e-mail: jhogan@cornerstoneservices.org
cornerstoneservices.org

*Jim Hogan, President/CEO*
*Don Hospell, Vice President/COO*
*Ben Stortz, CAO*
*Bette Reed, CDO*

Cornerstone Services provides progressive, comprehensive services for people with disabilities, promoting choice, dignity and the opportunity to live and work in the community. Established in 1969, the agency provides developmental, vocational, residential and behavior health services.

**8529 Disability Network**
Ste 54
3600 S Dort Hwy
Flint, MI 48507-2054
810-742-1800
FAX: 810-742-2400
TTY:810-742-7647
e-mail: tdn@disnetwork.org
www.disnetwork.org

*Bruce Chargo, Chairman*
*Diane Brown, Treasurer*
*Zach Tomlinson, Secretary*
*Duncan Beagle, Director*

The Disability Network's mission is to realize consumer empowerment, self determination, full inclusion and participation of all people in the communities through independent living philosophy and the unequivocal implementation of the Americans with Disabilities Act

**8530 Disability and Health: National Center for Birth Defects and Developmental Disabilities**
Centers for Disease Control and Prevention
1600 Clifton Rd NE
Atlanta, GA 30333-4018
404-498-3012
800-232-4636
FAX: 404-498-3060
TTY: 888-232-6348
e-mail: cdcinfo@cdc.gov
www.cdc.gov/ncbddd/dh

*Coleen A. Boyle, Director*
*Chris Parker, Acting Deputy Director*
*Tom bartenfeld, Associate Director*

Located within the new CDC, National Center for Birth Defects and Developmental Disabilities, the Disability and Health section, operates a ralatively small program that primarily supports: data collection on the prevalence of people with disabilities & their health status and risk factors for poor health and well-being; research on measures of disability, functioning and health; health promotion intervention studies; and dissemination of health information.

**8531 Easter Seals**
233 South Wacker Drive
Suite 2400
Chicago, IL 60606-1237
312-726-6200
800-221-6827
FAX: 312-726-1494
www.easterseals.com

*Stephen F. Rossman, Chairman*
*Richard F. Vincent, Treasurer*
*Alison A. Coady, Secretary*
Easter Seals has been helping individuals with disabilities and special needs, and their families, live better lives for over 80 years. From child development centers to physical rehabilitation and job training for people with disabilities, Easter Seals offers a variety of services to help people with disabilities address life's challenges and achieve personal goals.

**8532 Epilepsy Foundation**
8301 Professional Pl
Landover, MD 20785-7223
866-330-2718
800-332-1000
FAX: 877-687-4878
e-mail: ContactUs@efa.org
epilepsyfoundation.org

*Phil Gattone, President/CEO*
*Brien Smith, Chair*
*Alexandra Finucane, President*
Offers information and referrals, support groups for dually diagnosed persons.

**8533 Family Support Project for the Developmentally Disabled**
3424 Kossuth Ave
Bronx, NY 10467-2410
718-519-5000
FAX: 718-519-4902
www.nyc.gov/html/hhc/ncbh/home.html

*William Walsh, Vice President*
*Sheldon McLeod, COO*

**8534 Head Injury Hotline**
Brain Injury Resource Center
P.O.Box 84151
Seattle, WA 98124-5451
206-621-8558
FAX: 206-329-0912
e-mail: brain@headinjury.com
www.headinjury.com

*Hugh R. MacMahon, Medical Advisor*
*Bill Levinger, Medical Director*
*Constance Miller, Founder*
Disseminates head injury information and provides referrals to facilitate adjustment to life following head injury. Organizes seminars for professionals, head injury survivors, and their families.

**8535 International Braille and Technology Center for the Blind**
National Federation of the Blind
200 East Wells Street
Baltimore, MD 21230-4914
410-659-9314
FAX: 410-685-5653
e-mail: nfb@nfb.org
nfb.org

*Marc Maurer, CEO*
World's largest and most complete evaluation and demonstration center of all assistive technology used by the blind from around the world. Includes all braille, synthetic speech, print-to-speech scanning, internet and portable devices and programs. Available for tours by appointment to blind persons, employers, technology manufacturers, teachers, parents and those working in the assistive technology field.

**8536 Lung Line Information Service**
National Jewish Health
1400 Jackson St
Denver, CO 80206-2761
877-225-5654
800-222-5864
FAX: 303-398-1125
e-mail: lungline@njhealth.org.
nationaljewish.org

*Gregory P. Downey, Executive Vice President*
*Richard J. Martin, Department Chairman*
A free information service answering questions, sending literature and giving advice to patients with immunologic or respiratory illnesses. The Line is an educational service and not a substitute for medical care. Diagnosis or suggested treatment will not be provided for a caller's specific condition.

**8537 National AIDS Hotline**
Centers for Disease Control and Prevention
1600 Clifton Rd NE
Atlanta, GA 30333-4018
404-639-3311
800-232-4636
888-232-6348
FAX: 404-498-3060
e-mail: cdcinfo@cdc.gov
www.cdc.gov

*Coleen A. Boyle, Director*
*Chris Parker, Acting Deputy Director*
*Tom bartenfeld, Associate Director*
Offers free confidential information and publications on HIV infection and AIDS.

**8538 PALS Support Groups**
Parent Professional Advocacy League
10th Fl
45 Bromfield St
Boston, MA 02108-4106
617-542-7860
866-815-8122
FAX: 617-542-7832
e-mail: info@ppal.net
ppal.net

*Lisa Lambert, Executive Director*
*Chip Wilder, Chair*
*Joanna Allison, Vice Chair*
*Anne Silver, Treasurer*
Offers emotional support to parents and families of disabled children.

**8539 PXE International**
Ste 404
4301 Connecticut Ave NW
Washington, DC 20008- 2369
202-362-9599
FAX: 202-966-8553
e-mail: info@pxe.org
www.pxe.org

*Patrick Terry, President*
*Bud Moon, Webmaster*
Provides support for individuals and families affected by psukdoxanthoma elasticum (PXE), and resources for healthcare professionals. PXE causes select elastic tissue to mineralize, and effects the skin, eyes, cardiovascular, and GI systems.

**8540 Parent Assistance Network**
Good Samaritan Hospital
P.O.Box 1990
Kearney, NE 68848-1990
308-865-7100
800-235-9905
FAX: 308-865-2924
e-mail: sheilameyer@catholichealth.net
www.gshs.org

*Randy DeFreece, President*
*Kent Barney, Chairman*
*Mary Henning, Vice Chairman*
*Julie Speirs, Secretary*

Provides information and emotional support to all parents and especially to parents of children with disabilities in the central Nebraska area. Ongoing activities include parent support group meetings, parent-to-parent networking and referrals and Respite Care provider trainings.

**8541 Post-Polio Support Group**
Adventist Hinsdale Hospital
120 N Oak St
Hinsdale, IL 60521-3829
630-856-9000
FAX: 630-856-6000
www.keepingyouwell.com

*David Crane, President*
Information and support for polio patients and their families; meets the fourth Wednesday of each month.

**8542 Prevent Child Abuse America**
288 South Wabash Avenue
10th floor
Chicago, IL 60604- 3703
312-663-3520
FAX: 312-939-8962
e-mail: mailbox@preventchildabuse.org
preventchildabuse.org

*Christopher Greeley, Chair*
*Angelo Giardino, Vice Chair*
*Nancy Nelson Warren, Secretary*
*Tom Carhart, Treasurer*
Through public education, community partnerships and support services, PCAMW helps everyone play a role in prevention. We share information on prevention stategies and effective parenting at community forums and events and advocate for polices and services that keep children safe. We operate PhoneFriend, a telephone support line for children at home without adult supervision and conduct personal safety workshops in schools, camps and libraries.

**8543 Son-Rise Program**
Option Institute
2080 S Undermountain Rd
Sheffield, MA 01257-9643
413-229-2100
877-766-7473
FAX: 413-229-3202
e-mail: correspondence@option.org
www.autismtreatmentcenter.org

*Barry Neil Kaufman, Co Founder*
*Samahria Lyte Kaufman, Co Founder*
Internationally renowned and highly effective method for working with children challenged by autism, autism spectrum disorders, PDD and all other developmental difficulties. The program teaches parents, relatives, volunteers and professionals how to design and implement a child-centered, home-based educational program. Modality comprises an innovative and comprehensive system for learning and growth with specific impact in areas including eye contact, speech and communication and more.

**8544 Special Children**
1306 Wabash Ave
Belleville, IL 62220-3370
618-234-6876
FAX: 618-234-6150
e-mail: kathleencullan@sbcglobal.net
specialchildren.net

*Kathleen Cullen, Administrator*
A nonprofit agency serving children with developmental disabilities ages birth to 6 years

**8545 Support Works**
1607 Dilworth Rd W
Charlotte, NC 28203-5213
704-331-9500
e-mail: feedback@supportworks.org
www.supportworks.org

*Joel Fisher, Manager*
SupportWorks helps people find and form support groups. An 8 page publication Power Tools, clearly walks new group leaders through steps of putting together a healthy self-help group. SupportWorks also has a telephone conference program which allows people with similar diseases or other nonprofit issues to meet by phone conference for free or at very low cost.

**8546 The Compassionate Friends**
P.O.Box 3696
Oak Brook, IL 60522-3696
630-990-0010
877-969-0010
FAX: 630-990-0246
e-mail: nationaloffice@compassionatefriends.org
compassionatefriends.org

*Patrick O'Donnell, President*
*Georgia Cockerham, Vice President*
*Nivia Vazquez, Secretary*
*Patricia Loder, Executive Director*
Peer support for bereaved parents, grandparents and siblings, offering over 600 chapters in the United States. The organization also offers a quarterly magazine, We Need Not Walk Alone, and TCF resources of brochures, DVDs, and memorial wristbands for the bereaved parent, grandparent and sibling.

**8547 Toll-Free Information Line**
Asthma and Allergy Foundation of America
8201 Corporate Drive
Suite 1000
Landover, MD 20785-2330
202-466-7643
800-727-8462
FAX: 202-466-8940
e-mail: info@aafa.org
aafa.org

*Tom Flanagan, Chair*
*Nancy Kercher, Secretary*
*William McLin, President & CEO*
*Yolanda Miller, Vice President & CFO*
The Asthma and Allergy Foundation of America (AAFA) provides practical information, community based services and support through a national network of chapters and support groups. AAFA develops health education, organizes state and national advocacy efforts and funds research to find better treatments and cures.

**8548 Visiting Nurse Association of America**
Ste 200
900 19th St NW
Washington, DC 20006-2122
202-289-1420
FAX: 202-384-1444
e-mail: vnaa@vnaa.org
vnaa.org

*Andy Carter, President & CEO*
*Lauren Chandler, Project Coordinator*
*Eileen Grande, Manager Of Education*
*Shane Boyle, Director*
The VNAA is the official national association for not-for-profit, community based home health organizations known as the Visiting Nurse Associations (VNA's). They created the profession of home health care more then 100 years ag. They have a united mission to bring compassionate, high-quality and cost-effective home care to individuals in their communities.

# Speech & Language

## Associations

**8549 American Speech-Language-Hearing Association**
2200 Research Blvd
Rockville, MD 20850-3289
301-296-5700
888-498-6699
FAX: 301-296-8590
e-mail: actioncenter@asha.org
www.asha.org

*Shelly S. Cabon, President*
*Arlene A. Pietranton, CEO*
*Carolyn W. Higdon, Vice President Of Finance*
*Patricia A. Prelock, President-Elect*
The American Speech-Language Association is the professional, scientific, and credentialing association for 135,000 members and affiliates who are speech-language pathologists, audiologists, and speech, language, and hearing scientists in the United States and internationally. ASHA provides information for the public, professionals, students, and the research community related to hearing, balance, speech, language and swallowing disorders.

**8550 Aphasia Hope Foundation**
PO Box 26304
Shawnee Mission, KS 66225
913-839-8083
e-mail: judistradinger@aphasiahope.org
www.aphasiahope.org

*Sandy Caudell, Program Diretor*
*Judi Stradinger, Executive Director*
Aphasia Hope Foundation is a nonprofit foundation with a two-fold mission: 1.to promote research into the prevention and cure of aphasia and 2. to ensure that all survivors of aphasia and their caregivers are aware of and have access to the best possible tratments.

**8551 Atlanta Aphasia Association**
1811 Windemere Drive
Atlanta, GA 30324
404-413-8299
e-mail: jlaures@gsut.edu
www.atlantaaphasia.org

*Nancy Morris, President*
*Jacqueline Laures-Gore PhD, Co-President*
*Alan Morris, Secretary/Treasurer*
The Altanta Aphasia Association has several purposes: to organize and provide resources to individuals with aphasia and those involved with aphasia at vaious levels; to educate the community about aphasia through resources, discussions and communication about research advances in stroke and aphasia; to promote socialization of those with aphasia through various functions; to provide support and training for the vocational needs of those with aphasia.

**8552 Autism Research Institute**
4182 Adams Ave
San Diego, CA 92116-2599
619-281-7165
866-366-3361
FAX: 619-563-6840
www.autism.com

*Stephen Edelson, Executive Director*
*Jane Johnson, Managing Director*
*Valerie Paradiz, Director*
*Anthony Morgali, Producer*
Conducts research on the causes, diagnosis, and treatment of autism and publishes a quarterly newsletter that reviews worldwide research. Literature on causes and treatment available. Refers patients and families to health care professionals and clinics. Request publication list and sample newsletter, Autism Research Review.

**8553 Autism Services Center**
929 4th Ave
Huntington, WV 25701-1408
304-525-8014
FAX: 304-525-8026
e-mail: candy@autismwv.org
autismservicescenter.org

*Mike Grady, CEO*
*Jimmie Beirne, COO*
Provides developmental disabilities services with a specialty in autism. Services include case management, residential, personal care, assessments and evaluations, supported employment, independent living and family support.

**8554 Autism Treatment Center of America**
2080 S Undermountain Rd
Sheffield, MA 1257-9643
413-229-2100
877-766-7473
e-mail: correspondence@option.org
http://www.autismtreatmentcenter.org/

*Barry Neil Kaufman, Co Founder*
*Samahria Lyte Kaufman, Co Founder*
Since 1983, the Autism Treatment Center of America has provided innovative training programs for parents and professionals caring for children challenged by Autism, Autism Spectrum Disorders, Pervasive Developmental Disorders (PDD) and other development difficulties. The Son-Rise Program teaches a specific yet comprehensive system of treatment and education designed to help families and caregivers enable their children to dramatically improve in all areas of learning.

**8555 Communication Help, Education, Research, Apraxia Base (CHERAB)**
PO Box 8524
PSL, FL 34952-8524
772-335-5135
www.cherab.org

*Lisa Geng, Founder, President*
The Cherab Foundation is a world-wide nonprofit organization working to improve the communication skills and education of all children with speech and language delays and disorders. Their area of emphasis is verbal and oral apraxia, severe neurologically-based speech and language disorders that hinder children's ability to speak.

**8556 Communication in Autism**
Federal Government
31 Center Drive
Bldg 1
Bethesda, MD 20892-2320
800-241-1044
TTY:800-241-1055
e-mail: nidcdinfo@nidcd.nih.gov
http://www.nih.gov/

*James M. Anderson, M.D., Ph.D., Chairperson*
*Francis S. Collins, M.D., Ph.D., Director*
*LaVarne A. Burton, M.A., Chief Executive Officer*
*Elizabeth B. Concordia, M.A.S., Executive Vice President*
The National Institute on Deafness and Other Communication Disorders (NIDCD) one of the National Institute of Health, supports and conducts research and research training on the normal and disordered processes of hearing, balance smell, taste, voice, speech and language.

**8557 Deafness and Communicative Disorders Branch of Rehab Services Administration Office**
Special Education And Rehab Services
400 Maryland Ave SW
Washington, DC 20202-1
202-245-7489
800-872-5327
FAX: 202-245-7614
TTY: 800-437-0833
e-mail: customerservice@inet.ed.gov
www.ed.gov

*Arne Duncan, Secretary Of Education*
*Tony Miller, Deputy Secretary*
*Martha Kanter, Under Secretary*
*Jo Anderson, Senior Advisor*

Promotes improved rehabilitation services for deaf and hard of hearing people and individuals with speech or language impairments. Provides technical assistance to public and private agencies and individuals.

**8558 Hearing, Speech and Deafness Center (HSDC)**
Hearing, Speech & Deafness Center (HSDC)
1625 19th Ave
Seattle, WA 98122-2848
206-323-5770
888-222-5036
FAX: 206-328-6871
TTY: 206-388-1275
e-mail: hsdc@hsdc.org
www.hsdc.org

*Isabelle Banville, Chair*
*Norman Guadagno, Vice Chair*
*Bob Leingang, Treasurer*
*Janis Jung Lee, Secretary*

Our mission is to enrich lives of all adults and children who experience hearing loss, speech and language impairments or who are deaf, by providing professional services and by promoting community awareness and accessibility.

**8559 International Fluency Association**
Northern Illinois University
Dept. of Communicative Disorders
DeKalb, IL 60115-2899
e-mail: msugarman1@aol.com
www.theifa.org

*Willie E Botterill, President*
*Amy Weiss, Secretary*
*Dorothy Ross, Treasurer*
*Herman Peters, Director*

The International Fluency Association is a not-for-profit, international, interdisciplinary organization devoted to the understanding and management of fluency disorders, and to the improvement in the quality of life for persons with fluency disorders.

**8560 Lindamood-Bell Home Learning Process**
416 Higuera Street
San Luis Obispo, CA 93401
805-541-3836
800-233-1819
FAX: 805-541-8756
www.lindamoodbell.com

*Nanci Bell, Founder/Director*
*Patricia C. Lindamood, Founder/Director*

Founded in 1986 by Nanci Bell and Patricia Lindamood, Lindamood-Bell Learning Process is dedicated to enhancing human learning. Our critically acclaimed instructional programs teach children and adults to read, spell, comprehend, and express language.

**8561 National Aphasia Association**
350 Seventh Avenue
Suite 902
New York, NY 10001
800-922-4622
e-mail: naa@aphasia.org
www.aphasia.org

*Barbara C Martin, Executive Board President*
*Ellayne Ganzfried, Executive Director*
*Amy Hsiao, Administrative Coordinator*
*Mike Adler, Member*

The National Aphasia Association is a nonprofit organization that promotes public education, research, rehabilitation and support services to assist people with aphasia and their families.

**8562 National Association of Special Education Teachers**
1250 Connecticut Ave NW
Ste 200
Washington, DC 20036- 2643
202-296-7739
800-754-4421
FAX: 800-754-4421
e-mail: contactus@naset.org
www.naset.org

*Dr Roger Pierangelo, Executive Director*
*Dr George Giuliani, Executive Director*

The mission of NASET is to render all possible support and assistanve to professionals who teach children with special needs.

**8563 National Black Association for Speech-Language and Hearing**
700 McKnight Park Drive
Pittsburgh, PA 15237
412-366-1177
FAX: 412-366-8804
e-mail: nbaslh@nbaslh.org
www.nbaslh.org

*Arnell Brady, Chair*
*Carolyn Mayo, Secretary*
*Linda McCabe Smith, Treasurer*

The mission of the National Black Association of Speech-Language and Hearing is to maintain a viable mechanism through which the needs of black professionals, students and individuals with communication disorders can be met.

**8564 National Center for Accessible Media**
WGBH Educational Foundation
1 Guest St
Boston, MA 02135-2016
617-300-3400
FAX: 617-300-1035
TTY:617-300-2489
e-mail: access@wgbh.org
www.ncam.wgbh.org

*Larry Goldberg, Director*
*Brad Botkin, Director*
*Marcia Brooks, Project Director*
*Donna Danielewski, Manager*

Aims to increase access to public mass media (television, radio, print, movies, multimedia) for unserved customers, such as disabled people or speakers of other languages.

**8565 National Cued Speech Association**
Information Service
1300 Pennsylvania Avenue
Suite 190-713
Washington, DC 20004-1021
301-915-8009
800-459-3529
FAX: 301-915-8009
TTY: 800-459-3529
e-mail: info@cuedspeech.org
www.cuedspeech.org

*Shannon Howell, President*
*Penny Hakim, Vice President*
*Marah Baltzell, Executive Assistant*
*Doug Dawson, Treasurer*

The NCSA champions effective communication, language development and literacy through the use of cued speech. The NCSA envisions that individuals communicate effectively in the languageof their family and society. Families are informed about Cued Speech along with other communication options. Their rights are respected and instruction is provided to facilitate the use of cued languages. Students achieve literacy through full access to language and education.

**8566 National Student Speech Language Hearing Association**
2200 Research Blvd
Rockville, MD 20850-3289
240-632-2081
800-498-2071
e-mail: nsslha@asha.org
www.nsslha.org

*Kaci Roger, Council Member*
*Lauren Zanfardino, Council Member*
National organization for graduate and undergraduate students interested in the study of normal and disordered human communication.

**8567 National Stuttering Association**
119 W 40th St
Fl 14
New York, NY 10018-2514
212-944-4050
800-937-8888
FAX: 212-944-8244
e-mail: info@westutter.org
www.nsastutter.org

*Tammy Flores, Executive Director*
*Jim McClure, Media Communications*
A nonprofit organization dedicated to bringing hope, dignity, support, education, and empowerment to children and adults who stutter and their families, and the professionals who serve them.

**8568 Providence Speech and Hearing Center**
1301 W Providence Ave
Orange, CA 92868-3892
714-639-4990
FAX: 714-744-3841
e-mail: pshc@pshc.org
pshc.org

*Bruce May, President*
*Richard Van Dyke, Executive Vice President*
*Casey Immel, Treasurer*
*Robbie Nicoli, Secretary*
Mission is to provide the highest quality services available in the identification, diagnosis, treatment and prevention of speech, language and hearing disorders for persons of all ages.

**8569 Scottish Rite Center for Childhood Language Disorders**
Seattle Clinic
1207 North 152nd St
Shoreline, WA 98133
206-324-6293
FAX: 206-324-3332
e-mail: hfray@ritecarewa.org
www.srccld.org

*Jacqueline Brown, Clinical Director*
Offers speech-language evaluations and treatment, hearing screening and consultations to children ages birth through adolescence. Bilingual services are also available.

**8570 Stern Center**
183 Talcott Road
Suite 101
Williston, VT 05495-9209
802-878-2332
FAX: 802-878-0230
www.sterncenter.org

*Blanche Podhajski PhD, President*
*Jane Nathan, Research Director*
*John Connell, COO*
*Edward R. Wilkens, Development Director*
The Stern Center was founded as a nonprofit learning center dedicated to helping children and adults reach their full potential. Stern Center professionals evaluate and teach all kinds of learners, including those with learning disabilities such as dyslexia or attention deficit disorders. We evaluate and teach over 1,000 children and adults each year including those with learning disabilities, dyslexia, language disorders, autism, attention deficit disorders, and learning style differences.

**8571 Stuttering Foundation of America**
1805 Moriah Woods Blvd, Suite 3
Memphis, TN 38111-749
901-761-0343
800-992-9392
FAX: 901-761-0484
e-mail: info@stutteringhelp.org
www.stutteringhelp.org

*Jane Fraser, President*
Provides resources, services, and support to those who stutter and their families, as well as support for research into the causes of stuttering.

**8572 Texas Speech-Language-Hearing Association**
918 Congress Ave
Ste 200
Austin, TX 78701-2342
512-494-1128
888-729-8742
FAX: 512-494-1129
e-mail: tsha@assnmgmt.com
http://www.txsha.org/

*Judith Keller, President*
*Larry Higdon, Director*
*Melanie McDonald, President Elect*
*Tori Gustafson, Vice President*
Mission is to encourage and promote the role of the speech-language pathologist and audiologist as a professional in the delivery of clinical services to persons with communications disorders. Encourages basic scientific study of processes of individual human communication with reference to speech, hearing and language.

**8573 The Childhood Apraxia of Speech Association**
416 Lincoln Ave
Pittsburgh, PA 15209
412-343-7102
www.apraxia-kids.org

*Mary Sturm, President*
*Sharon Gretz, Executive Director*
*Sue Freiburger, Secretary*
The mission of the Childhood Apraxia of Speech Association is to strengthen the support systems in the lives of children with apraxia, so that each child has their best opportunity to develop speech.

**8574 The Davis Center**
19 State Route 10 E
Ste 25
Succasunna, NJ 07876
862-251-4637
FAX: 862-251-4642
e-mail: info@thedaviscenter.com
www.thedaviscenter.com

*Dorinne S Davis MA CCC-A FAAA, Director*
The Davis Center's Sound Therapy Programs make positive changes for children and adults with autism, ADD/ADHD, auditory processing issues, Dyslexia, learning disabilities, and other learning and wellness challenges. Our programs address issues such as phonics, spelling, writing, reading comprehension, hearing only parts of words, following directions, discriminating between sounds, sound sensitivity, behavioral responses, focus, attention, and more.

**8575 Wendell Johnson Speech And Hearing Clinic**
University Of Iowa
250 Hawkins Dr
Iowa City, IA 52242-1025 319-335-8736
FAX: 319-335-8851
e-mail: kathy-miller@uiow.edu
www.uiow.edu

*Ruth Bentler, Professor & Department Chair*
*Dorothy Albright, Secretary*
*Kathy Miller, Clerk*
*Elizabeth Walker, Audiologist*

The clinic offers assessment and remediation for communication disorders in adults and children. The clinic also offers a Intensive Summer Residential Clinic for school age children needing intervention services because of speech, language, hearing and/or reading problems.

## Camps

**8576 CNS Camp New Connections**
Mclean Hospital Child/Adolescent Program
115 Mill St
Belmont, MA 02478-1064 617-855-2000
800-333-0338
FAX: 617-855-2833
e-mail: mcleaninfo@mclean.harvard.edu
mcleanhospital.org

*Roya Ostorar, Ph.D., Director, Center for Neurodevelopmental Services (CNS), Training and F*
*Scott L. Rauch, MD, President and Psychiatrist in Chief*
*Joseph Gold, MD, Chief Medical Officer*
*Cynthia Kaplan, Associate Clinical and Administrative Director, Child and Adolescent P*

Four-week summer day camp for children ages 7-17 who have pervasive developmental disorders, Asperger's Syndrome, autism spectrum disorders and non-verbal learning disabilities. The camp is designed to help children develop social skills through fun activities including: communication games, swimming, field trips, drama, and arts and crafts. *$4500.00*

**8577 Camp Royall**
Autism Society of North Carolina
250 Bill Ash Road
Moncure, NC 27559-1345 919-542-1033
e-mail: sgage@autismsociety-nc.org
www.autismsociety-nc.org

*Sara Gage, Program Director*
*Lesley Fraser, Assistant Program Director*

The best source in North Carolina for connecting people who live with autism (and those who care about them) with resources, support, advocacy and informantion tailored to thier unique needs.

**8578 Camp Sisol**
Jewish Community Center of Greater Rochester/JCC
1200 Edgewood Ave
Rochester, NY 14618-5408 585-461-2000
e-mail: rrosner@jccrochester.org
www.jccrochester.org

*Leslie Berkowitz, Executive Director*
*Dan Irving, Director*
*Anna Gossin, Librarian*
*Mary Ann Colamarino, Administration*

Camp is located in Honeoye Falls, New York. Summer sessions for children with autism. Coed, ages 5-16.

**8579 Childrens Beach House**
100 West 10th Street
Suite 411
Wilmington, DE 19801-1674 302-655-4288
FAX: 302-655-4216
e-mail: inquiry@cbhinc.org
www.cbhinc.org

*Richard T Garrett, Executive Director*
*Jennifer A. Clement, Director*
*Nicholas Imhoff, Manager*
*Sandy White, Case Manager*

Camp is located in Lewes, Delaware. Four-week sessions June-August for Delaware children with hearing impairment or speech/communication impairment. Coed, ages 6-12.

**8580 Easter Seals Oklahoma**
701 NE 13th St
Oklahoma City, OK 73104-5003 405-239-2525
FAX: 405-239-2278
e-mail: sbusch@eastersealsoklahoma.org
www.eastersealsoklahoma.org

*Paula Porter, CEO*
*Vida Wasinger, Director Of Operations*
*Aundria Goree, Programs Director*
*Deborah Rucker, Accountant*

Adult day health center, and child development center.

**8581 Meadowood Springs Speech and Hearing Camp**
Institute for Rehab., Research, & Recreation Inc
136-A SE Emigrant
P.O. Box 1025
Pendleton, OR 97801-30 541-276-2752
FAX: 541-276-7227
e-mail: info@meadowoodsprings.org
www.meadowoodsprings.com

*Michael Ashton, Executive Director*
*Cliff Story, Property Manager*
*Missy Newcomb, Clinical Director*
*Audrey Black, Program Director*

On 143 acres in the Blue Mountains of Eastern Oregon, this camp is designed to help young people who have diagnosed clinical disorders of speech, hearing or language. A full range of activities in recreational and clinical areas is available.

**8582 New Horizons Summer Day Camp**
YMCA
13821 Newport Avenue
Suite 200
Tustin, CA 92780-7803 714-549-9622
FAX: 714-838-5976
www.ymcaoc.org

*Jeffrey S. McBride, President/CEO*
*Mitch Markowitz, Owner*
*Ulrich Gottschling, COO*
*Tom Reyes, President*

One-week sessions for children with ADD and speech/communication impairment. Coed, ages 5-14.

**8583 Sequanota Lutheran Conference Center and Camp**
P.O. Box 245
Jennerstown, PA 15547-3235 814-629-6627
FAX: 814-629-0128
e-mail: contact@sequanota.com
www.sequanota.com

*George Mason, Executive Director*
*Ang Illar, Program Director*
*Laura Waltermire, Office Assistant*
*Mike Pluta, Maintenance Director*

Summer sessions for adults with developmental disabilities and speech/communication impairment.

**8584 Talisman Summer Camp**
64 Gap Creek Rd
Zirconia, NC 28790-8791
828-697-6313
855-588-8254
e-mail: info@talismancamps.com
www.talismancamps.com

*Linda Tatsapaugh, Executive Director*
*Amy Allen, Admissions Coordinator*
Camp is located in Black Mountain, North Carolina. Offers a program of hiking, rafting, climbing, and caving for learning disabled ADD/ADHD and autistic young people. Coed, ages 9-18.

**8585 Wendell Johnson Speech & Hearing Clinic**
University Of Iowa
250 Hawkins Dr
Iowa City, IA 52242-1025
319-335-8736
FAX: 319-335-8851
e-mail: kathy-miller@uiowa.edu
www.uiowa.edu

*Ruth Bentler, Professor & Department Chair*
*Dorothy Albright, Secretary*
*Kathy Miller, Clerk*
*Elizabeth Walker, Audiologist*
The clinic offers assessment and remediation for communication disorders in adults and children. The clinic also offers a Intensive Summer Residential Clinic for school age children needing intervention services because of speech, language, hearing and/or reading problems.

**8586 YMCA Camp Fitch**
The YMCA Of Youngstown - Metro Office
17 N Champion St
P.O. Box 1287
Youngstown, OH 44501
330-744-8411
FAX: 330-744-8415
e-mail: info@campfitchymca.org
www.youngstownymca.org

*Kenneth L. Rudge, CEO*
*John H. Yerian Jr., President*
*Thomas Flemming, Vice President*
*James B. Greene, Vice President*
Camp is located in North Springfield, Pennsylvania. Camping sessions for children and adults with diabetes, hearing impairment, developmental disabilities, mobility limitation and speech/communication impairment. Ages 8-16, families and seniors.

## Print: Books

**8587 Autism 24/7: A Family Guide to Learning at Home & in the Community**
Autism Society of North Carolina Bookstore
Ste 230
505 Oberlin Rd
Raleigh, NC 27605-1345
919-743-0204
800-442-2762
FAX: 919-743-0208
e-mail: jchampion@autismsociety-nc.org
http://www.autismsociety-nc.org/

*Andy Bondy Ph.D., Co-Author*
*Lori Frost, Co-Author*
*Tracey Sheriff, Chief Executive Officer*
*Paul Wendler, Chief Financial Officer*
Parents are encouraged to focus on skill sets and behaviors that most negatively affect family functioning, and replacing these behaviors with acceptable alternatives. *$19.95*

**8588 Autism Handbook: Understanding & Treating Autism & Prevention Development**
Oxford University Press
2001 Evans Rd
Cary, NC 27513-2009
919-677-0977
800-852-7323
FAX: 919-677-1714
e-mail: jnlorders@oupjournals.org
http://www.oup.com/us/

Oxford University Press USA is the US branch of Oxford University Press in Oxford, England (OUP UK), which is a department of Oxford University and is the oldest and largest continuously operating university press in the world. *$25.00*
*320 pages*
*ISBN 0-195076-67-2*

**8589 Autism and Learning**
Taylor & Francis
37-41 Mortimer St
London, 1
http://www.informatandm.com

*Stuart Powell, Author*
*Rita Jordan, Editor*
This book is about how a cognitive perception on the way in which individuals with autism think and learn may be applied to particular curriculum areas.
*160 pages Paperback*
*ISBN 1-853464-21-X*

**8590 Autism in Adolescents and Adults**
Springer Publishing
233 Spring St
New York, NY 10013-1522
877-283-3229
e-mail: ainy@aveda.com
http://aveda.edu/new-york

*Eric Schopler, Editor*
*Gary B. Mesibov, Editor*
This book is a great history lesson in the development of understanding about autism spectrum disorders, and is a testament to how far research and services in the field have come. This book contains lots of information about what general thinking and services used to be like, in an era when still little was understood about these disorders. *$ 63.00*
*456 pages*
*ISBN 0-306410-57-5*

**8591 Autism...Nature, Diagnosis and Treatment**
Autism Society of North Carolina Bookstore
Ste 230
505 Oberlin Rd
Raleigh, NC 27605-1345
919-743-0204
800-442-2762
FAX: 919-743-0208
e-mail: jchampion@autismsociety-nc.com
http://www.autismsociety-nc.org/

*Geraldine Dawson PhD, Editor*
*Tracey Sheriff, Chief Executive Officer*
*Paul Wendler, Chief Financial Officer*
*David Laxton, Director of Communications*
Covers perspectives, issues, neurobiological issues and new directions in diagnosis and treatment. *$49.00*

**8592 Autism: Explaining the Enigma**
Wiley Publishers
111 River St
Hoboken, NJ 7030-5773
201-748-6000
e-mail: info@wiley.com
http://as.wiley.com

*Uta Frith, Author*
*Mari J. Baker, CEO*
*Jean-Lou Chameau, President*
*Peter B. Wiley, Chairman*
Explains the nature of autism. *$27.95*

**8593 Autism: From Tragedy to Triumph**
Branden Publishing Company
17 Station St
Brookline, MA 2445-7995 617-730-5757
e-mail: branden@branden.com
http://www.yogainthevillage.com

*Carol Johnson, Co-Author*
*Julia Crowder, Co-Author*
A new book that deals with the Lovaas method and includes a foreward by Dr. Ivar Lovaas. The book is broken down into two parts - the long road to diagnosis and then treatment. *$12.95*

**8594 Autism: Identification, Education and Treatment**
Routledge
270 Madison Ave
New York, NY 10016-601 212-576-1411
http://books.google.co.in/books/about/Autism.

*Dianne Zager, Editor*
Chapters include medical treatments, early intervention and communication development in autism. *$36.00*

*ISBN 0-805820-44-7*

**8595 Autism: The Facts**
Oxford University Press
2001 Evans Rd
Cary, NC 27513-2009 919-677-0977
800-451-7556
http://www.oup.com/us/corporate/contact/?view

*Simon Baron-Cohen, Co-Author*
*Patrick Bolton, Co-Author*
*$22.50*
*128 pages*
*ISBN 0-192623-27-3*

**8596 Autistic Adults at Bittersweet Farms**
Routledge
270 Madison Ave
New York, NY 10016-601 e-mail: mtilkins@bittersweetfarms.org.
http://www.bittersweetfarms.org/

*John Ahlberg, President*
*Jan Toczynski, Secretary*
*Robert Clair, Treasurer*
A touching view of an inspirational residential care program for autistic adolescents and adults. Also available in softcover. *$94.95*
*Hardcover*
*ISBN 1-560240-42-3*

**8597 Beyond Baby Talk: From Sounds to Sentences, a Parent's Guide to Language Development**
Prima Publishing
P.O.Box 1260
Rocklin, CA 95677-1260 916-787-7000
800-632-8676
FAX: 916-787-7001
www.primapublishing.com

*Kenn Apel PhD, Co-Author*
*Julie Masterson PhD, Co-Author*
The authors discuss the best ways to help your child develop the all-important skill of communication and to recognize the signs of language development problems. OUT OF BUSINESS *$15.95*
*224 pages*
*ISBN 0-761526-47-1*

**8598 Breaking the Speech Barrier: Language Develpment Through Augmented Means**
Brookes Publishing
P.O.Box 10624
Baltimore, MD 21285-624 410-337-9580
800-638-3775
FAX: 410-337-8539
e-mail: custserv@brookespublishing.com
readplaylearn.com

*Paul Brookes, Owner*
This resource describes the creation of the System for Augmenting Language (SAL) for school-age youth with mental retardation and offers important insights into the language development of children who are not learning to communicate typically. *$39.95*
*224 pages Paperback*
*ISBN 1-557663-90-0*

**8599 Breakthroughs: How to Reach Students with Autism**
Aquarius Health Care Media
P.O.Box 1159
Sherborn, MA 1770-7159 e-mail: aqvideos@tiac.net
http://www.autismtreatmentcenter.org/contents

*Raun K. Kaufman, Author*
A hands-on, how-to program for reaching students with autism, featuring Karen Sewell, Autism Society of America's teacher of the year. Here Sewell demonstrates the successful techniques she's developed over a 20-year career. A separate 250 page manual ($59) is also available which covers math, reading, fine motor, self help, social adaptive, vocational and self help skills as well as providing numerous plan reproducibles and an exhaustive listing of equipment and materials resources. Video. *$99.00*

**8600 Childhood Speech, Language & Listening Problems**
Wiley Publishing
605 3rd Ave
New York, NY 10158-180 212-850-6000
FAX: 212-850-6088
http://books.google.co.in/books/about/Childho

*Patricia McAleer Hamaguchi*
Language pathologist Hamaguchi employs her 15 years of experience to show parents how to recognize the most common speech, language, and listening problems. *$16.95*
*224 pages Paperback*
*ISBN 0-471387-53-3*

**8601 Cognitive Behavioral Therapy for Adult Asperger Syndrome**
Autism Society of North Carolina Bookstore
Ste 230
505 Oberlin Rd
Raleigh, NC 27605-1345 919-743-0204
800-442-2762
FAX: 919-743-0208
e-mail: jchampion@autismsociety-nc.org
http://www.autismsociety-nc.org

*Tracey Sheriff, CEO*
*Paul Wendler, CFO*
*David Laxton, Director*
*Dawn Eberwein, Manager*
Text is prepared with case studies and examples from the author's own experiences working as a cognitive-behavioral therapist specializing in adults and adolescents with dual diagnosis, autism spectrum disorders, mood disorders, and anxiety disorders.

**8602 Communication Development and Disorders in African American Children**
Brookes Publishing
P.O.Box 10624
Baltimore, MD 21285-624 410-337-9580
800-638-3775
FAX: 410-337-8539
e-mail: custserv@brookespublishing.com
readplaylearn.com

*Paul Brooks, Owner*
Research, Assessment, and Intervention. This text presents research on communication disorders and language development in African American children. Also addresses multicultural aspects of service delivery and intervention and discusses issues in assessing, diagnosing, and treating communication disorders. *$39.00*
*400 pages Paperback*
*ISBN 1-55766 -53-3*

**8603 Communication Development in Children with Down Syndrome**
Brookes Publishing
P.O.Box 10624
Baltimore, MD 21285-624 410-337-9580
800-638-3775
FAX: 410-337-8539
e-mail: custserv@brookespublishing.com
readplaylearn.com

*Paul Brooks, Owner*
This book offers an extensive, detailed explanation of communication development in children with Down syndrome relative to their advancing cognitive skills. It introduces a critical framework for assessing and treating hearing, speech, and language problems and provides explicit intervention methods and tested clinical protocols.
*Paperback*
*ISBN 1-55766 -50-5*

**8604 Coping for Kids Who Stutter**
Speech Bin
W6316 Design Drive
Greenville, WI 54942 800-850-8602
FAX: 888-388-6344
e-mail: customercare@schoolspecialty.com
www.speechbin.com

*Jan J Binney, Senior Editor*
Informative book for children and adults about stuttering and how to manage it. *$15.95*
*32 pages*
*ISBN 0-93785 -43-2*

**8605 Disorders of Motor Speech: Assessment, Treatment, and Clinical Characterization**
Brookes Publishing
P.O.Box 10624
Baltimore, MD 21285-624 410-337-9580
800-638-3775
FAX: 410-337-8539
e-mail: custserv@brookespublishing.com
readplaylearn.com

*Paul Brooks, Owner*
This book provides a probing examination of normal, dysarthric, and apraxic speech. Great for speech-language pathologists, neurologists, physical or occupational therapists, and physiatrists. *$47.00*
*400 pages Hardcover*
*ISBN 1-55766 -23-1*

**8606 Employment for Individuals with Asperger Syndrome or Non-Verbal Learning Disability**
Jessica Kingsley Publishers
440 Market Street
Suite 400t St
Philadelphia, PA 19106- 2513 215-922-1161
866-416-1078
FAX: 215-922-1474
e-mail: orders@jkp.com
www.jkp.com

*Laurie Schlesinger, Vp Of Sales & Marketing*
With practical and technical advice on everything from job-hunting to interview techniques, from fitting in in the workplace to whether or not to disclose diagnosis, this book guides people with NLD or AS successfully through the employment field. *$22.95*
*272 pages*
*ISBN 1-843107-66-X*

**8607 Encounters with Autistic States**
Jason Aronson
400 Keystone Industrial Park
Dunmore, PA 18512-1507 800-782-0015
This book explores and explands the work of the late Frances Tustin, which was devoted to the psychoanalytic understanding of the bewildering elemental world of the autistic child. *$50.00*
*448 pages Hardcover*
*ISBN 0-765700-62-*

**8608 Kitten Who Couldn't Purr**
William Morrow & Company
1350 Avenue of the Americas
New York, NY 10019-4702 212-261-6500
FAX: 212-261-6925
http://www.goodreads.com/book/show/2319648.Th

*Eve Titus, Author*
Jonathan the kitten doesn't know how to purr to say thank you, so he sets off to find someone to teach him. *$12.95*
*32 pages*

**8609 Language Disabilities in Children and Adolescents**
McGraw-Hill School Publishing
220 E Danieldale Rd
Desoto, TX 75115-2490 972-224-4772
800-442-9685
FAX: 972-228-1982
mcgraw-hill.com

*Elisabeth H. Wiig, Co-Author*
*Eleanor Messing Semel, Co-Author*
A comprehensive review of research in language disabilities.

**8610 Language and the Developing Child**
International Dyslexia Association
40 York Road
Baltimore, MD 21204 410-296-0232
800-ABC-D123
FAX: 410-321-5069
www.interdys.org

*Lee Grossman, Executive Director*
*Denise Douce, Editor*
*Jill Eagan, Manager Of Membership*
This collection of papers introduces a new generation of teachers, clinicians and parents to the work of one of the key figures in the search for the causes and treatment of dyslexia. *$15.00*

**8611 Late Talker: What to Do If Your Child Isn't Talking Yet**
St Martin's Griffin
175 5th Ave
New York, NY 10010-7703 646-307-5151
888-330-8477
FAX: 212-674-6132
e-mail: customerservice@mpsvirginia.com
www.us.macmillan.com

*Marilyn C Agin, Author*
This handbook offers advice on ways to identify the warning signs of a speech disorder, information on how to get the right kind of evaluations and therapy, ways to obtain appropriate services through the school system and health insurance, at-home activities that parents can do with their child to stimulate speech, benefits of nutritional supplementation, and advice from experienced parents who've been there on what to expect and what you can do to be your child's best advocate. *$13.95*
*256 pages Paperback*
*ISBN 0-312309-24-4*

**8612 Let Community Employment be the Goal for Individuals with Autism**
Indiana Resource Center For Autism
2853 E 10th St
Bloomington, IN 47408-2696 812-855-6508
800-825-4733
FAX: 812-855-9630
e-mail: prattc@indiana.edu
www.iidc.indiana.edu/irca

*Cathy Pratt, Director*
*Scott Bellini, Assistant Director*
A guide designed for people who are responsible for preparing individuals with autism to enter the work force. *$7.00*

**8613 Lollipop Lunch**
Speech Bin-Abilitations
P.O.Box 922668
Norcross, GA 30010-2668 770-449-5700
800-850-8602
FAX: 770-510-7290
e-mail: info@speechbin.com
www.speechbin.com

*Patricia Easterly Hoon, Author*
Cleverly illustrated stories and activities for phonological and language development. *$19.95*
*128 pages*
*ISBN 0-937857-54-8*

**8614 Management of Autistic Behavior**
Sage Publications
2455 Teller Road
Thousand Oaks, CA 91320 800-818-7243
800-818-7243
FAX: 800-583-2665
e-mail: info@sagepub.com
www.sagepub.com

*Sara Miller McCune, Founder, Publisher, Chairperson*
*Blaise R Simqu, President & CEO*
*Chris Hickok, Vice President*
*Gretchen Bataille, Director*
This excellent reference is a comprehensive and practical book that tells what works best with specific problems. *$41.00*
*450 pages*

**8615 Motor Speech Disorders**
WB Saunders Company
14 Main Street
Southampton, NY 11968-2822 631-283-5050
800-523-1649
FAX: 631-283-2290
e-mail: info@saunders.com
www.wbsaunders.com

*Joseph R Duffy PhD, Author*
Professional text on rehabilitation techniques for motor speech disorders. *$74.00*
*592 pages*
*ISBN 0-323024-52-5*

**8616 Neurobiology of Autism**
Johns Hopkins University Press
2715 N Charles St
Baltimore, MD 21218-4319 410-516-6900
FAX: 410-516-6998
http://www.ncbi.nlm.nih.gov/pubmed/17919129

*Pardo CA, Co-Author*
*Ebarhat CG, Co-Author*
This book discusses recent advances in scientific research that point to a neurobiological basis for autism and examines the clinical implications of this research. *$28.00*
*272 pages*
*ISBN 0-801880-47-5*

**8617 Nonverbal Learning Disabilities at Home: A Parent's Guide**
Jessica Kingsley Publishers
400 Market Street
Suite 400t St
Philadelphia, PA 19106- 2513 215-922-1161
866-416-1078
FAX: 215-922-1474
e-mail: orders@jkp.com
www.jkp.com

*Robert Rooney, Owner*
Explores the variety of daily life problems children with NLD may face, and provides practical strategies for parents to help them cope and grow, from preschool age through their challenging adolescent years. *$19.95*
*272 pages Paperback*
*ISBN 1-853029-40-0*

**8618 Parent Survival Manual**
Springer Publishing Company
15th Fl
11 W 42nd St
New York, NY 10036-8002 212-355-1501
FAX: 212-355-7370
e-mail: christieseducation@christies.edu
http://www.christieseducation.com

*Craig Lickliter, Manager*
A guide to crises resolution in autism and related developmental disorders. *$39.95*

**8619 Perspectives: Whole Language Folio**
Gallaudet University Bookstore
800 Florida Ave NE
Washington, DC 20002-3600 202-651-5750
800-995-0550
FAX: 202-651-5744
http://www.cpcc.edu/disabilities/student-clas

*Tony Zeiss, President*
The 19 articles in this collection offer practical help to teachers seeking to emphasize whole language strategies in their classroom. *$9.95*
*64 pages*

**8620 Please Don't Say Hello**
Human Sciences Press
233 Spring St
New York, NY 10013-1522
877-283-3229
800-221-9369
e-mail: ainy@aveda.com
http://aveda.edu/new-york

*Phyllis Terri Gold, Author*
Paul and his family moved into a new neighborhood. Paul's brother was autistic. The children thought that Eddie was retarded until they learned that there were skills that he could do better than they could. *$10.95*
*47 pages Paperback*
*ISBN 0-89885 -99-8*

**8621 Promoting Communication in Infants and Young Children: 500 Ways to Succeed**
Speech Bin-Abilitations
P.O.Box 922668
Norcross, GA 30010-2668
770-449-5700
800-850-8602
FAX: 770-510-7290
e-mail: info@speechbin.com
www.speechbin.com

*Jennifer Quick, Author*
This practical reference for parents, caregivers and professional service providers how to promote communication development in infants and young children. Gives down-to-earth information and activities to help your youngest children succeed. It provides step-by-step suggestions for stimulationg children's speech and language skills. Paperback. *$14.95*

*ISBN 0-937857-72-6*

**8622 Reading, Writing and Speech Problems in Children**
International Dyslexia Association
40 York Road
Baltimore, MD 21204
410-296-0232
800-ABC-D123
FAX: 410-321-5069
www.interdys.org

*Lee Grossman, Executive Director*
*Denise Douce, Editor*
*Jill Eagan, Manager Of Membership*
A tribute to the man who more than any other aroused the attention of the scientific community and who provided the sound educational principles on which much teaching of dyslexics today is based. *$27.00*

*ISBN 0-89079 -79-1*

**8623 Relationship Development Intervention with Young Children**
Taylor & Francis Group
116 Pentonville Rd
London, N1 19
004- 20-8332
FAX: 004- 20-8372
e-mail: post@jkp.com
http://www.jkp.com/jkp/distributors.php

*Jessica Kingsley, Chairman*
*Rachelle Sheely, Co-Author*
*Dee Brigham, Director*
Social and emotional development activities for Asperger Syndrome, Autism, PDD and NLD. Comprehensive set of activities emphasizes foundation skills for younger children between the ages of two and eight. Covers skills such as social referencing, regulating behivor, conversational reciprocity, and synchronized actions. For use in therapeutic settings as well as schools and parents. *$22.95*
*256 pages*
*ISBN 1-843107-14-7*

**8624 Riddle of Autism: A Psychological Analysis**
Jason Aronson
Ste 200
4501 Forbes Blvd
Lanham, MD 20706-4346
301-459-3366
800-782-0015
FAX: 301-429-5746
http://www.nbnbooks.com

*Barbara Pierce, Commission Rep*
*Michael Sullivan, Sales*
Dr. Victor examines the myths that cloud an understanding of this disorder and describes the meanings of its specific behavioral symptoms. *$30.00*
*356 pages Paperback*
*ISBN 1-568215-73-8*

**8625 Schools for Children with Autism Spectrum Disorders**
Resources for Children with Special Needs
Fl 5
116 E 16th St
New York, NY 10003-2164
212-677-4650
FAX: 212-677-254
e-mail: info@resourcesnyc.org
resourcesnyc.org

*Ellen Miller-Wachtel, Chair*
*Owen King, President*
*Geraldine Telchin, Secretary*
Published every 24-36 months. *$20.00*
*160 pages*
*ISBN 0-967836-53-0*

**8626 Self-Therapy for the Stutterer**
Stuttering Foundation of America
Ste 603
3100 Walnut Grove Rd
Memphis, TN 38111-3543
901-452-7343
800-992-9392
FAX: 901-452-3931
e-mail: info@stutteringhelp.org.
www.stutterhelp.org

*Jane Fraser, President*
*Jean Gruss, Journalist*
*Robert M. Kurtz, Chairman & CEO*
A guide to help adults who stutter overcome the problem on their own. *$3.00*
*191 pages Paperback*
*ISBN 0-933388-32-2*

**8627 Sex Education: Issues for the Person with Autism**
Indiana Resource Center For Autism
2853 E 10th St
Bloomington, IN 47408-2696
812-855-6508
800-825-4733
FAX: 812-855-9630
e-mail: prattc@indiana.edu
www.iidc.indiana.edu/irca

*David Mank, Director*
*Harriet L. Figg, Manager*
*Becky Hudson, Secretary*
Discusses issues of sexuality and provides methods of instruction for people with autism. *$4.00*

**8628 Son-Rise: The Miracle Continues**
2080 S Undermountain Rd
Sheffield, MA 1257-9643
413-229-2100
800-562-7171
e-mail: sonrise@option.org
http://www.option.org

*Barry Neil Kaufman, Owner*
*William Hogan, Teacher*
Part One is the astonishing record of Raun Kaufman's development from an autistic and retarded child into a loving, brilliant

youngster who shows no traces of his former condition. Part Two follows Raun's development after the age of four, teaching the limitless possibilities of the Son-Rise Program. Part Three shares moving accounts of five other ordinary families who became extraordinary when they used the Son-Rise Program to reach their own unreachable children. *$12.95*
*343 pages*
*ISBN 0-915811-53-7*

**8629 Sound Connections for the Adolescent**
Speech Bin
1965 25th Ave
Vero Beach, FL 32960-3062 772-770-0007
800-477-3324
FAX: 772-770-0006
www.speechbin.com

A resource to help older elementary and secondary students understand their sound systems an how it functions. It targets skills critical for academic achievement: phonological awareness, phonemic relationships, phonemic processing, listening and memory and teaches linguistic rules they need to succeed. *$19.95*
*Paperback*

**8630 Talkable Tales**
Speech Bin-Abilitations
P.O.Box 922668
Norcross, GA 30010-2668 770-449-5700
800-850-8602
FAX: 770-510-7290
e-mail: info@speechbin.com
www.speechbin.com

*Jan J Binney, Editor*
Read-a-rebus stories and pictures targeting most consonant phonemes for K-5 children. *$25.95*
*128 pages*
*ISBN 0-93783 -44-0*

**8631 Teaching Children with Autism: Strategies for Initiating Positive Interactions**
Brookes Publishing
P.O.Box 10624
Baltimore, MD 21285-624 410-337-9585
888-337-8808
FAX: 410-337-8539
e-mail: custserv@healthpropress.com
http://www.healthpropress.com

*Melissa A. Behm, President*
*Mary Magnus, Director*
Stategies for initiating positive interactions and improving learning opportunities. This guide begins with an overview of characteristics and long-term strategies and proceeds through discussions that detail specific techniques for normalizing environments, reducing disruptive behavior, improving language and social skills, and enhancing generalization. *$32.95*
*256 pages Paperback*
*ISBN 1-55766 -80-4*

**8632 Teaching and Mainstreaming Autistic Children**
Love Publishing Company
Ste 2200
9101 E Kenyon Ave
Denver, CO 80237-1854 303-221-7333
FAX: 303-221-7444
e-mail: lpc@lovepublishing.com
http://www.lovepublishing.com/

*Peter Knoblock, Author*
Dr. Knoblock advocates a highly organized, structured environment for autistic children, with teachers and parents working together. His premise is that the learning and social needs of autistic children must be analyzed and a daily program designed with interventions that respond to this functional analysis of their behavior. *$24.95*

*ISBN 0-89108 -11-9*

**8633 Techniques for Aphasia Rehab: (TARGET) Generating Effective Treatment**
Speech Bin
1965 25th Ave
Vero Beach, FL 32960-3062 800-477-3324
www.speechbin.com
Practical treatment manual for use by aphasia clinicians. *$45.00*
*384 pages*
*ISBN 0-93785 -50-5*

**8634 Understanding & Controlling Stuttering: A Comprehensive New Approach Based on the Valsa Hyp**
National Stuttering Association
Fl 14
119 W 40th St
New York, NY 10018-2514 212-944-4050
800-937-8888
FAX: 212-944-8244
e-mail: info@westutter.org
www.nsastutter.org

*Sheryl Hunter, Chairwoman*
*Kenny Koroll, Vice Chairman*
*Bill Smith, Treasurer*
*Cathy Olish, Secretary*
Demonstrates how physical and psychological factors may interact to stimulate and perpetuate stuttering through a Valsalva-Stuttering cycle. *$25.00*
*176 pages*
*ISBN 7-929773-01-3*

**8635 Verbal Behavior Approach: How to Teach Children with Autism & Related Disorders**
Autism Society of North Carolina Bookstore
Ste 230
505 Oberlin Rd
Raleigh, NC 27605-1345 919-743-0204
800-442-2762
FAX: 919-743-0208
e-mail: jchampion@autismsociety-nc.com
http://www.autismsociety-nc.org

*Tracey Sheriff, CEO*
*Paul Wendler, CFO*
*David Laxton, Director*
*Dawn Eberwein, Manager*
Provides full descriptions of how to teach the verbal operants that make up expressive languate which include: manding, tacting, echoing and intraverbal skills. *$19.95*

**8636 Without Reason: A Family Copes with two Generations of Autism**
Books on Special Children
721 W Abram St
Arlington, TX 76013-6995 817-277-0727
800-489-0727
FAX: 817-277-2270
http://www.fhautism.com/

*R. Wayne Gilpin, President*
*Jennifer Gilpin, Vice President*
*Shelley Hines, Manager*
*Kim Fritschen, Coordinator*
The author discovers his son has autism. He delves into problems of the autistic person and explains reasons for their actions. *$20.95*
*292 pages Hardcover*

## Print: Journals

**8637 American Journal of Speech-Language Pathology**
American Speech-Language-Hearing Association
2200 Research Blvd
Rockville, MD 20850-3289 240-632-2081
800-638-8255
FAX: 301-897-7348
e-mail: info@asha.org
www.asha.org

*Kaci Roger, Council Member*
*Lauren Zanfardino, Council Member*
This is a quarterly journal of clinical practice for speech-language pathologists and language researchers. This journal will be online only beginning January 2010.

**8638 Journal of Speech, Language and Hearing Research**
American Speech-Language-Hearing Association
2200 Research Blvd
Rockville, MD 20850-3289 301-897-5700
800-638-8255
FAX: 301-897-7348
e-mail: irc@asha.org
www.asha.org

*Kaci Roger, Council Member*
*Lauren Zanfardino, Council Member*
This bimonthly journal contains basic, as well as applied research in normal and disordered communication processes. It will be available online only beginning January 2010.

**8639 Language, Speech, and Hearing Services in Schools**
International Fluency Association
Northern Illinois University
Dept. of Communicative Disorders
DeKalb, IL 60115-2899 www.theifa.org

*Willie E Botterill, President*
*Amy Weiss, Secretary*
*Dorothy Ross, Treasurer*
*Herman Peters, Director*
This is a quarterly journal focusing on research appropriate to speech-language pathologists and audiologists in schools. The journal will only be available online beginning in January 2010.

## Print: Magazines

**8640 Communication Outlook**
Artificial Language Laboratory
405 Computer Ctr
East Lansing, MI 48824-1042 517-353-0870
FAX: 517-353-4766
e-mail: artling@msu.edu
www.msu.edu

*Rebecca Baird, Editor*
Communication Outlook (CO) is an international quarterly magazine, which focuses on the techniques and technology of augmentative and alternative communication. CO provides information on technological developments for persons experiencing communication handicaps due to neurological, sensory or neuromuscular conditions. *$18.00*
*32 pages Quarterly*

## Print: Newsletters

**8641 Access Audiology**
American Speech-Language-Hearing Association
2200 Research Blvd
Rockville, MD 20850-3289 240-632-2081
e-mail: info@asha.org
www.asha.org

*Kaci Roger, Council Member*
*Lauren Zanfardino, Council Member*
Dedicated to the specific needs of all professionals interested in hearing, balance, and the field of audiology. Each issue spotlights a specific topic of interest and relevance to audiologists.

**8642 Autism Research Review International**
Autism Research Institute
4182 Adams Ave
San Diego, CA 92116-2599 619-281-7165
866-366-3361
FAX: 619-563-6840
e-mail: br@autismresearchinstitute.com
autism.com

*Stephen Edelson, Executive Director*
*Jane Johnson, Managing Director*
*Valerie Paradiz, Director*
*Anthony Morgali, Producer*
Provides clearly written summaries of articles selected from computer searches. *$18.00*
*8 pages Quarterly*

**8643 Communicologist**
Texas Speech-Language-Hearing Association
Ste 200
918 Congress Ave
Austin, TX 78701-2342 512-494-1128
888-729-8742
FAX: 512-494-1129
e-mail: tsha@assnmgmt.com
cisaustin.org

*Judith Keller, President*
*Larry Higdon, Director*
*Melanie McDonald, President Elect*
*Tori Gustafson, Vice President*
A forum for distributing current information relevant to the practices of speech-language pathology and audiology across the state. Provides TSHA membership with the latest news from the Executive Board and Task Forces, as well as information about regional associations, distinguished service providers, the TSHA Annual Convention, and committee honors and nominations. Also contains advertisements of interest to the field.

**8644 Connect**
Hearing, Speech & Deafness Center (HSDC)
1625 19th Ave
Seattle, WA 98122-2848 206-323-5770
888-222-5036
FAX: 206-328-6871
TTY: 206-388-1275
e-mail: hsdc@hsdc.org
www.hsdc.org

*Isabelle Banville, Chair*
*Norman Guadagno, Vice Chair*
*Bob Leingang, Treasurer*
*Janis Jung Lee, Secretary*
A newsletter that addresses concerns of those affected by speech and language disorders.
*8 pages Quarterly*

**8645 NSSLHA Now**
Ntn'l Student Speech Language Hearing Association
2200 Research Blvd
Rockville, MD 20850-3289
240-632-2081
800-638-8255
FAX: 301-897-7348
e-mail: nsslha@asha.org
www.asha.org

*Kaci Roger, Council Member*
*Lauren Zanfardino, Council Member*
Published three times per year.

**8646 On Cue**
National Cued Speech Association
5619 McLean Dr
Bethesda, MD 20814-1021
301-915-8009
800-459-3529
www.cuedspeech.org

*Shannon Howell, President*
*Penny Hakim, Vice President*
*Elizabeth Richardson, Secretary*
*Doug Dawson, Treasurer*
Published several times a year and mailed to members of the Association.

**8647 Stuttering & Your Child: Help For Parents**
Stuttering Foundation of America
18005 Moriah Woods Blvd
Suite 3
Memphis, TN 38117-7119
901-761-0343
800-992-9392
FAX: 901-761-0484
e-mail: info@stutteringhelp.org
www.StutteringHelp.org

*Jane Fraser, President*
The Stuttering Foundation provides resources, services and support to those who stutter and their families, as well as support research into the cause of stuttering. The Stuttering Foundation provides a referral list of speech-language pathologists and referrals to other information including research on stuttering, intensive workshops and camps. *$10.00*

**8648 Stuttering Foundation Newsletter**
Stuttering Foundation of America
P.O.Box 11749
Memphis, TN 38111-749
901-452-7343
800-992-9392
FAX: 901-452-3931
e-mail: info@stutteringhelp.org
www.stutteringhelp.org

*Jane Fraser, President*
*Jean Gruss, Journalist*
*Robert M. Kurtz, Chairman & CEO*

**8649 Voice**
Providence Speech and Hearing Association
1301 W Providence Ave
Orange, CA 92868-3808
714-639-4990
FAX: 714-744-3841
e-mail: pshc@pshc.org
www.pshc.org

*Bruce May, President*
*Richard Van Dyke, Executive Vice President*
*Casey Immel, Treasurer*
*Robbie Nicoli, Secretary*
People of all ages with speech and hearing problems by providing specialized products and services.

## Non Print: Newsletters

**8650 Access Academics & Research**
American Speech-Language-Hearing Association
2200 Research Blvd
Rockville, MD 20850-3289
240-632-2081
800-638-8255
FAX: 301-897-7348
e-mail: info@asha.org
www.asha.org

*Kaci Roger, Council Member*
*Lauren Zanfardino, Council Member*
Dedicated to the specific needs of academic and clinical faculty, PhD students and researchers. The e-newsletter was developed as part of the Focused Initiative on the PhD Shortage in Higher Education.

**8651 Access SLP Health Care**
American Speech-Language-Hearing Association
2200 Research Blvd
Rockville, MD 20850-3289
240-632-2081
800-638-8255
FAX: 301-897-7348
e-mail: info@asha.org
www.asha.org

*Kaci Roger, Council Member*
*Lauren Zanfardino, Council Member*
An e-newsletter dedicated to the specific needs of speech-language pathologists in healthcare settings. Each issue of Access SLP Health Care features recent legislative activity impacting SLPs and provides information on clinical issues, continuing education opportunities, and ASHA web-based resources.

**8652 Access Schools**
American Speech-Language-Hearing Association
2200 Research Blvd
Rockville, MD 20850-3289
240-632-2081
800-638-8255
FAX: 301-897-7348
e-mail: info@asha.org
www.asha.org

*Kaci Roger, Council Member*
*Lauren Zanfardino, Council Member*
Dedicated to the specific needs of school-based speech-language pathologists. Each Access Schools e-newsletter features recent legislative activity impacting school SLPs and provides information on clinical issues, continuing education opportunities, and ASHA web-based resources.

**8653 Stuttering**
Federal Government
31 Center Drive Msc2320
Bethesda, MD 20892-2320
301-496-7243
800-241-1044
FAX: 301-402-0018
e-mail: nidcdinfo@nidcd.nih.gov
www.nidcd.nih.gov

*James F. Battey, Director*
Describes how speech is produced, treatments for stuttering and research supported by the federal government.

## Non Print: Video

**8654 Autism: A World Apart**
Fanlight Productions
32 Court Street
Brooklyn, NY 11201-1731
718-488-8900
800-876-1710
FAX: 718-488-8642
e-mail: info@fanlight.com
www.fanlight.com

*Ben Achtenberg, Owner*
*Nicole Johnson, Publicity Coordinator*
*Anthony Sweeney, Marketing Director*
In this documentary, three families show us what the textbooks and studies cannot: what it's like to live with autism day after day; to raise and love children who may be withdrawn and violent and unable to make personal connections with their families. 29 minutes.
*VHS/DVD*
*ISBN 1-572950-39-0*

**8655 Autism: the Unfolding Mystery**
Aquarius Health Care Media
18 N Main St
Sherborn, MA 1770-1066
508-650-1616
e-mail: lkussmann@aquariusproductions.com

*Lesile Kussmann, Owner*
Explore what it means to be autistic, how you can recognize the signs of autism in your child, and hear about new treatments and programs to help children learn to deal with the disorder. *$145.00*
*DVD*

**8656 Getting Started with Facilitated Communication**
Facilitated Communication Institute, Syracuse Univ
370 Huntington Hall
Syracuse, NY 13244-1
315-443-9657
FAX: 315-443-9218
e-mail: fcstaff@syr.edu
www.thefci.syr.edu

*Annegret Schubert, Producer*
Describes in detail how to help individuals with autism and/or severe communication difficulties to get started with facilitated communication.
*Video*

**8657 I Just Want My Little Boy Back**
Autism Treatment Center Of America
2080 S Undermountain Rd
Sheffield, MA 1257-9643
413-229-2100
800-714-2779
e-mail: happiness@option.org
http://www.option.org

*Barry Neil Kaufman, Owner*
*William Hogan, Teacher*
A great video for parents and professionals caring for children with special needs. Join one British family and their autistic son before, during and after their journey to America to attend The Son-Rise Program at The Autism Treatment Center of America. This informative, inspirational and deeply moving story not only captures the joy, tears, challenges and triumps of this amazing little boy and his family, but also serves as a powerful introduction to the attitude and principles of the program. *$25.00*

**8658 Understanding Autism**
Fanlight Productions
32 Court Street
Brooklyn, NY 11201-1731
718-488-8900
800-876-1710
FAX: 718-488-8642
e-mail: info@fanlight.com
www.fanlight.com

*Ben Achtenberg, Owner*
*Nicole Johnson, Publicity Coordinator*
*Anthony Sweeney, Marketing Director*
Parents of children with autism discuss the nature and symptoms of this lifelong disability and outline a treatment program based on behavior modification principles. 19 minutes
*VHS/DVD*
*ISBN 1-572951-00-1*

## Support Groups

**8659 Autism Society of America**
4340 East West Highway, Suite 350
Bethesda, MD 20814-3067
301-657-0881
800-328-8476
FAX: 301-657-0869

*Jennifer Repella, VP Programs*
ASA is the largest and oldest grassroots organization within the autism community, with a nationwide network of chapters and over 20,000 members and supporters nationwide. ASA is the leading source of education, information and referral about autism and has been the leader in advocacy and legislative initiatives for more than four decades.

**8660 Cherab Foundation**
P.O.Box 8524
Port St Lucie, FL 34985-8524
772-335-5135
FAX: 772-337-4812
e-mail: help@cherab.org
www.cherab.org

*Marilyn Agin, MD*
*Lisa Geng, Co Author*
Helps to start, supports, and works together with other support groups and nonprofits (such as ECHO, VOICES, and Apraxia Network) that have mutual goals for helping children with apraxia and other speech disorders.

**8661 Friends: National Association of Young People who Stutter**
38 S Oyster Bay Rd
Syosset, NY 11791-5033
866-866-8335
e-mail: lcaggiano@aol.com
www.friendswhostutter.org

*Lee Caggiano, President*
A national organization created to provide a network of love and support for children and teenagers who stutter, their families, and the professionals who work with them.

**8662 National Health Information Center**
US Department of Health
P.O.Box 1133
Washington, DC 20013-1133
301-565-4167
800-336-4797
301-468-7394
FAX: 301-984-4256
e-mail: healthypeople@nhic.org
http://www.healthypeople.gov

*Jonathan Fielding, Chair*
*Shirika Kumanyika, Vice Chair*
A health information referral service that puts health professionals and consumers who have health questions in touch with those organizations that are best able to provide answers.

**8663 Speech Pathways**
Ste 403
532 Baltimore Blvd
Westminster, MD 21157-6146 410-374-0555
800-961-2724
FAX: 410-374-8620
e-mail: kim.bell@speechpathways.net
speechpathways.net

*Kimberly Bell, Owner*

We realize that parent and family support is critical to a child's success, in therapy as well as in life. We offer support at local and regional levels along with traditional speech and language services, and a wide variety of specialized pediatric programs. Our support groups/services are open to the larger community as well as to our clients.

# Visual

## Associations

**8664 ACB Government Employees**
American Council of the Blind
2200 Wilson Blvd
Ste 650
Arlington, VA 22201-3354
202-467-5081
800-424-8666
FAX: 703-465-5085
e-mail: info@acb.org
www.acb.org

*Mitch Pomerantz, President*
*Kim Charlson, Vice President*
*Marliana Lieberg, Secretary*
*Carla Ruschival, Treasurer*
Members are present, former and retired employees of federal, state and local government agencies. Concerns of the organization include recruitment, placement and advancement of blind and visually impaired employees.

**8665 ACB Radio Amateurs**
American Council of the Blind
167 Green St
Reading, MA 01867
202-467-5081
800-424-8666
FAX: 202-467-5085
e-mail: s.dresser@verizon.net
www.acbhams.org

*Steve Dresser, President*
*Mike Duke, Vice President*
*Robert Rogers, Treasurer*
ACBRA is an organization of blind and sighted licensed radio amateurs who work together to make the hobby more accessible to people who are blind

**8666 ACB Social Service Providers**
American Council of the Blind
2200 Wilson Blvd
Ste 650
Arlington, VA 22201-3354
202-467-5081
800-424-8666
FAX: 703-465-5085
e-mail: info@acb.org
www.acb.org

*Mitch Pomerantz, President*
*Kim Charlson, Vice President*
*Marliana Lieberg, Secretary*
*Carla Ruschival, Treasurer*
Blind and visually impaired social workers, social service professionals, students pursuing careers in social work and other interested persons are members of this organization. ACBSSP works to promote full participation by visually impaired social services professionals in the field of social welfare.

**8667 Achromatopsia Network**
P.O.Box 214
Berkeley, CA 94701-214
510-540-4700
FAX: 510-540-4767
e-mail: achromatopsia@cox.net
www.achromat.org

*Frances Futterman, President*
The Achromatopsia Network is a nonprofit organization for individuals concerned with acrhomatopsia. It is committed to sharing information about achromatopsia and providing resources to meet the special needs of those affected by this eye condition; helping individuals and families concerned with achromatopsia to connect with one another; and promoting awareness and educating with a special emphasis on accomplishing this goal among those who provides services to the visually impaired.

**8668 American Academy of Ophthalmology**
PO Box 7424
San Francisco, CA 94120-7424
415-561-8500
866-561-8558
FAX: 415-561-8533
e-mail: customer_service@aao.org
www.aao.org

*Randy Johnston, President*
Founded in 1896, but was incorporated as an independent organization in 1979 when the AAOO was divided into separate academies. The American Academy of Ophthalmology is the largest national membership association of Eye MDs. Eye MDs are ophthalmologists, medical doctors who provide comprehensive eye care, including medical, surgical and optical care. More than 90 percent of practicing US Eye MDs are Acadmey members, and the Academy has more than 7,000 international members.

**8669 American Action Fund for Blind Children and Adults**
1800 Johnston St
Ste 100
Baltimore, MD 21230-4914
410-659-9315
FAX: 410-685-5653
e-mail: actionfund@actionfund.org
www.actionfund.org

*Barbara Loos, President*
*Ramona Walhof, Vice President*
*Gary Mackenstandt, Secretary*
*James Omvig, Treasurer*
A service agency which specializes in providing to blind people help which is not readily available to them from government programs or other existing service systems. The services are planned especially to meet the needs of blind children, the elderly blind, and the deaf-blind.

**8670 American Council of Blind Lions**
2200 Wilson Boulevard
Suite 650
Arlington, VA 22201-3354
202-467-5081
800-424-8666
FAX: 703-465-5085
e-mail: info@acb.org
www.acb.org

*Mitch Pomerantz, President*
*Kim Charlson, First Vice President*
*Brenda Dillon, Second Vice President*
*Marlaina Lieberg, Secretary*
A wonderful combination of Lionism and visual impairment nurtures the American Council of Blind Lions. ACBL's mission is awareness and highlights the great activities of the Knights of the Blind. The goals are to assist all clubs in their understanding of issues surrounding blind and visually impaired individuals.

**8671 American Council of the Blind**
2200 Wilson Blvd
Ste 650
Arlington, VA 22201-3354
202-467-5081
800-424-8666
FAX: 703-465-5085
e-mail: info@acb.org
acb.org

*Mitch Pomerantz, President*
*Kim Charlson, Vice President*
*Marliana Lieberg, Secretary*
*Carla Ruschival, Treasurer*
A national membership organization whose members are visually impaired and fully sighted individuals who are concerned about the dignity and well-being of blind people throughout America. Formed in 1961, the Council has become the largest organization of blind people in the US with over 70 state affiliates and special interest chapters.

**8672 American Foundation for the Blind**
2 Penn Plz
Ste 1102
New York, NY 10121-2018
212-502-7600
800-232-5463
FAX: 212-502-7777
e-mail: afbinfo@afb.net
www.afb.org

*Carl Augusto, President/CEO*
*Paul Schroeder, Vice President*
*Rick Bozeman, Director*
*Scott Truax, Manager*

The organizaton to which Helen Keller devoted her life, is a national nonprofit organization whose mission is to ensure that the ten million Americans who are blind or visually impaired enjoy the same rights and opportunities as other citizens.

**8673 American Optometric Association**
243 N Lindbergh Blvd
Saint Louis, MO 63141-7881
314-991-4100
800-365-2219
FAX: 314-991-4101
e-mail: MDJones@aoa.org
aoa.org

*Ronald L Hopping, President*
*Mitchell Munson, President-Elect*
*David A. Cockrell, Vice President*
*Steven Loomis, Secretary-Treasurer*

the AOA is the acknowledged leader and recognised authority for the eye and vision care in the world. The objectives of the AOA are centered on improving the quality and availiability of eye and vision care. The AOA fulfills its missions in accordance with health care and public policy related to eye care will uniformly recognise optometrists as primary health care providers and ensure the public has acess to the full scope of optometric care.

**8674 American Printing House for the Blind**
PO Box 6085
Louisville, KY 40206-0085
502-895-2405
800-223-1839
FAX: 502-899-2284
e-mail: info@aph.org
www.aph.org

*Charles Barr, Chairman*

The world's largest nonprofit organization creating educational, workplace and independent living products and services for people who are visually impaired. Also promotes independence of the blind and visually impaired persons by providing specialized materials, products, and services needed for educationand life.

**8675 Associated Blind**
212-683-4950
FAX: 212-683-4975
e-mail: memberservices@esightcareers.net
www.tabinc.org

*Nancy O'Connell, Executive Director*

Privately funded, non-profit agency, that was founded by a group of blind individuals as an organization promoting autonomy and self-determination. The mission is to assist individuals who are blind, visualy impaired or who have physical disabilities to become self-reliant and achieve financial independence through mainstream employment.

**8676 Associated Services for the Blind**
919 Walnut St
Philadelphia, PA 19107-5287
215-627-0600
FAX: 215-922-0692
e-mail: asbinfo@asb.org
www.asb.org

*Patricia Johnson, CEO*

ASB, a non-private, non-profit organization, promotes self esteem, independence, and self-determination in people who are blind or visually impaired. ASB accomplishes this by providing support through education, training and resources, as well as through community action and public education, serving as a voice and advocate for the rights of all people who are blind or visually impaired.

**8677 Association for Education & Rehabilitationof the Blind & Visually Impaired**
1703 N Beauregard St
Ste 440
Alexandria, VA 22311-1744
703-671-4500
877-492-2708
FAX: 703-671-6391
e-mail: jgandorf@aerbvi.org
www.aerbvi.org

*Lou Tutt, Executive Director*
*Ginger Croce, Director of Memberships*
*Barbara James, Manager*

The only international organization dedicated to rendering all possible support and assistance to the professionals who work in all phases of education and rehabilitation of blind and visually impaired children and adults. Our membership is comprised of more than 4,800 professionals who provide services to people with visual impairments.

**8678 Association for Macular Diseases**
210 E 64th St
8th Fl
New York, NY 10065-7471
212-605-3719
800-622-8524
FAX: 212-605-3795
e-mail: association@retinal-research.org
macula.org

*Nikolai Stevenson, President*

The Macula Foundation, Inc., a not-for-profit organization was established in 1978 to support basic and clinical research in vitreous retinal and macular diseases, a major cause of blindness of all age groups. Since it was formed, the Foundation has distributed grants and awards of approximately 15 million dollars earmarked for important clinical and scientific research and related teaching programs. Numerous research projects have been successful as a result of the Foundation.

**8679 Blind Childrens Center**
4120 Marathon St
Los Angeles, CA 90029-3584
323-664-2153
800-222-3566
FAX: 323-665-3828
e-mail: info@blindchildrenscenter.org
blindchildrenscenter.org

*Midge Horton, Executive Director*

A family centered agency which serves children with visual impairments from birth to school-age. The center-based and home-based programs and services help the children aquire skills and build their independence. The center utilizes its expertise and experience to serve families and professionals worldwide through support services, education, and research.

**8680 Blind Information Technology Specialists**
American Council of the Blind
2200 Wilson Blvd
Ste 650
Arlington, VA 22201-3354
703-841-0048
800-424-8666
202-465-5085
FAX: 703-465-5085
e-mail: president@bits-acb.org
www.bits-acb.org

*Mitch Pomerantz, President*
*Kim Charlson, Vice President*
*Marliana Lieberg, Secretary*
*Carla Ruschival, Treasurer*

BITS is a non profit organization which fosters the career development of blind computer professionals, promotes the use of computer technology by blind persons to improve the qualtiy of their personal and professional lives, and advocate for improved information access for all visually impaired people.

**8681 Blinded Veterans Association**
477 H St NW
Washington, DC 20001-2694
202-371-8880
800-669-7079
FAX: 202-371-8258
e-mail: bva@bva.org
bva.org

*Samuel Huhn, President*
*Mark Cornell, Vice President*
*Robert Dale Stamper, Secretary*
*Roy Young, Treasurer*
BVA locates blinded veterans who need assistance, guides them through the rehabilitation process, and acts as advocates for them before Congress and the Department of Veterans Affairs in the securing of all the benefits they have earned throught their service to the nation. Promotes access to technology and the practical use of the latest research. Its Field Service Program provides encouragement and emotional support through role models, who can demonstrate that the challenges can be overcome.

**8682 Books for Blind and Physically Handicapped Individuals**
Library of Congress
1291 Taylor St NW
Washington, DC 20011
202-707-5100
888-657-7323
FAX: 202-707-0712
TTY: 202-707-0744
e-mail: nls@loc.gov
www.loc.gov/nls

*Frank Cylke, Director*
Administers a national library service that provides braille and recorded books and magazines on free loan to anyone who cannot read standard print because of visual of physical disabilities who are eligible residents of the Unites States of America citizens living abroad.

**8683 Braille Institute of America**
741 N Vermont Ave
Los Angeles, CA 90029-3594
323-663-1111
800-272-4553
FAX: 323-663-0867
e-mail: la@brailleinstitute.org
www.brailleinstitute.org

*Lester M. Sussman, Chair*
*Percy Duran, Audit*
*Richard Larson, Development*
*Harvey Strode, Finance*
Provides an environment of hope and encouragement for people who are blind and visually impaired through integrated educational, social and recreational programs and services. Provides assistance at 5 regional centers in Southern California and through 200 community outreach programs. In 2005-06, the Institute provided these services to more than 55,000 people. The Institute is operated and funded almost entirely through private individual and foundation sources.

**8684 California State Library Braille and Talking Book Library**
P.O. Box 942837
Sacramento, CA 94237-1
916-634-0640
800-952-5666
FAX: 916-654-1119
e-mail: btbl@library.ca.gov
www.btbl.ca.gov

*Mike Marlin, Director*
The State Library stands as one of California's great public research institutions with a five-fold mission:serving the needs of elected officials and state agency employees;preserving the state's cultural heritage by collecting historic materials on California and the West;assisting public libraries through financial aid and consulting services;offering special services to disadvantaged and handicapped clients;ensuring that the general public has convenient and consistent access to resources.

**8685 Canine Helpers for the Handicapped**
5699 Ridge Rd
Lockport, NY 14094-9408
716-433-4035
FAX: 716-439-0822
e-mail: chhdogs@aol.com
caninehelpers.netfirms.com

*Beverly Underwood, Executive Director*
*Laura Gates, Trainer*
A nonprofit organization devoted to custom training Assistance Dogs to assist people with disabilities to lead more independent, secure lives.

**8686 Caption Center**
125 Western Ave
Boston, MA 02134
617-300-3600
FAX: 617-300-1020
TTY:617-300-3600
e-mail: access@wgbh.org
mattapanchc.org

*Cristopher Brandon, Chair*
*Glenola Mitchell, Vice Chair*
*Dale L. Kurtz, Treasurer*
*Nelda M. Headley, Secretary*
Has been pioneering and delivering accessible media to disabled adults, students and their families, teachers and friends for over 30 years. Each year, the Center captions more than 10,000 hours worth of broadcast and cable programs, feature films, large-format and IMAX films, home videos, music videos, DVDs, teleconferences and CD-Roms.

**8687 Chicago Lighthouse for People who are Blind and Visually Impaired**
1850 W Roosevelt Rd
Chicago, IL 60608-1298
312-666-1331
FAX: 312-243-8539
TTY:312-666-8874
e-mail: support@chicagolighthouse.org
www.chicagolighthouse.org

*Bruce R. Hague, Chairman*
*Sandra C. Forsythe, Vice Chairman*
*Janet P. Szlyk, President*
*David Huber, Treasurer*
A non profit agency committed to providing the highest quality educational, clinical, vocational, and rehabilitation services for children, youth and adults who are blind or visually impaired, including deaf blind and multi disabled. Also respects personal dignity and partners with individuals to enhance independent living and self sufficiency. This agency is a leader, innovator and advocate for people who are blind or visually impaired, enhancing the quality of life for all individuals.

**8688 Clovernook Center for the Blind and Visually Impaired**
7000 Hamilton Ave
Cincinnati, OH 45231-5240
513-522-3860
888-234-7156
FAX: 513-728-3946
TTY:513-522-3860
e-mail: contact@clovernook.org
clovernook.org

*Alfred J. Tuchfarber, Chair*
*Wilbert F. Schwartz, Vice Chair*
*Mark Jackson, Treasurer*
*William H. Thorner, Secretary*
Mission is to promote independence and foster the highest quality of life for people with visual impairments, including those with additional disabilities. We provide comprehensive program services including training and support for independent living, orientation and mobility instruction, vocational training, job placement, counseling, recreation, and youth services. Meaningful employment opportunities are also provided to individuals who are blind or visually impaired.

**8689 Clovernook Printing House, The Clovernook Center for the Blind and Visually Impaired**
7000 Hamilton Ave
Cincinnati, OH 45231-5240
513-522-3860
888-234-7156
FAX: 513-728-3946
e-mail: contact@clovernook.org
clovernook.org

*Alfred J. Tuchfarber, Chair*
*Wilbert F. Schwartz, Vice Chair*
*Mark Jackson, Treasurer*
*William H. Thorner, Secretary*
Clovernook also offers Braille Transcription Services including: Literary Books, Literary Magazines, Religious Materials, Instructional Manuals, ADA Conformance Materials, Literary Textbook Materials, Menus, Braille Alphabet Cards, and Forms. In addition, our Business Operations provide meaningful employment opportunities for individuals who are blind or visually impaired, while at the same time manufacturing high-quality products for customers across the country. *$145.00*
*591 pages*
*ISBN 1-930956-48-7*

**8690 College of Optometrists in Vision Development**
215 W Garfield Rd
Ste 200
Aurora, OH 44202-7884
330-995-0718
888-268-3770
FAX: 330-995-0719
e-mail: info@covd.org
www.covd.org

*David A. Damari, President*
*Kara Heying, Vice President*
*Christine Allison, Secretary-Treasurer*
*Pamela R. Happ, Executive Director*
The College of Optometrists in Vision Development (COVD) is an international membership association of eye care professionals including optometrists, optometry students, and vision therapists. Members of COVD provide developmental vision care, vision therapy and vision rehabilitation services for children and adults.

**8691 College of Syntonic Optometry**
322 N Aurora St
Ithaca, NY 14850-4202
607-277-4749
877-559-0541
FAX: 607-277-5216
www.syntonicphototherapy.com

*Larry Wallace, President*
*Ron Wahlmeier, Admin Director*
An active and growing post-graduate educational organization. Established in 1933 its members include optometrists and other health professionals and supporters from around the world. Those who achieve a clinical level of experience and mastery are awarded the status of Fellow. Today, scientific as well as clinical verification of light's impact on health and healing and a growing public demand for functional and rehabilitative vision therapy continue to vitalise the college and its mission.

**8692 Columbia Lighthouse for the Blind**
1825 K St NW
Ste 1103
Washington, DC 20006-1261
202-454-6400
877-324-5252
FAX: 202-955-6401
e-mail: info@clb.org
www.clb.org

*Tony Cancelosi, President*
Offer programs that enable individuals who are blind or visually impaired to obtain and maintain independence at home, school, work and in the community. The programs and services include asistive technology training, career services, rehabilitation services, comprehensive low vision care and a wide range of children's programs.

**8693 Council of Families with Visual Impairments**
American Council of the Blind
1155 15th St NW
Ste 1004
Washington, DC 20005-2706
202-467-5081
800-424-8666
FAX: 202-467-5085
e-mail: cindy.vw@msn.com
www.acb.org

*Jill Gaus, President*
*Lynn Jansen, Vice President*
*Debby Lieberman, Secretary*
*Mike Reese, Treasurer*
A network of parents with blind or visually impaired children that offers support and outreach, shares experiences in parent/child relationships, exchanges educational, cultural and medical information about child development and more.

**8694 Deaf-Blind Division of the National Federation of the Blind**
200 East Wells Street
Baltimore, MD 21230-4914
410-659-9314
FAX: 410-685-5653
e-mail: nfb@nfb.org
nfb.org

*Marc Maurer, CEO*
The nation's largest and most influential membership organization of blind persons, with a two-fold purpose: to help blind persons achieve self-confidence and self respect and to act as a vehicle for collective self-expression by the blind. The NFB improves blind people's lives through advocacy, education, research, technology, and programs encouraging independence and self-confidence. It is the leading force in the blindness field today and is the voice of the nations blind.

**8695 Eye Bank Association of America**
1015 18th St NW
Ste 1010
Washington, DC 20036-5223
202-775-4999
FAX: 202-429-6036
e-mail: info@restoresight.org
www.restoresight.org

*David Korroch, Chair*
*David Glasser, Chair-Elect*
*Donna Drury, Secretary*
*Woodford Van Meter, Treasurer*
Established in 1961 by the American Academy of Ophthalmology's Committee on Eye Banks, the EBAA is a not-for-profit organization of eye banks dedicated to the restoration of sight through the promotion and advancement of eye banking. The EBAA has lead the transplantation field with the establishment of medical standards for the procurement and distribution of corneal tissue, accreditation of eye banks, and comprehensive education programs for doctors, technicians, and administrators.

**8696 Fidelco Guide Dog Foundation**
103 Vision Way
Bloomfield, CT 6002-1424
860-243-5200
FAX: 860-243-7215
e-mail: info@fidelco.org
fidelco.org

*Stephen H. Matheson, Chairman*
*John H. Gotta, Vice Chairman*
*Glynis Cassis, Secretary*
*Mary P. Craig, Treasurer*
The Fidelco Guide Dog Foundation, located in Bloomfield, Conn., is dedicated to providing increased freedom and independence to men and women who are blind by providing them with the highest quality guide dogs. We rely solely on the gifts and the generosity of individuals, foundations, corporations and organizations that partner with Fidelco to 'Share the Vision.'

**8697 Fight for Sight**
381 Park Ave S
Rm 809
New York, NY 10016-8806
212-679-6060
FAX: 212-679-4466
e-mail: info@fightforsight.com
www.fightforsight.com

*Mike Wilke, Executive Director*
*Janice Benson, Asst Director*

The mission is to support vision research, to find causes and cures for blindness, and to help save the sight of children through support of pediatric eye centers.

**8698 Guide Dog Users**
14311 Astrodome Dr
Silver Spring, MD 20906-2245
301-598-2131
866-799-8436
FAX: 301-871-7591
e-mail: treasurer@gdui.org
www.gdui.org

*Elizabeth Barnes, President*
*Jane Sheehan, Membership Inquiries*

Guide Dog Users Inc, (GDUI) an affiliate of the American Council of the Blind, is the largest guide dog consumer driven group in the world. Since 1972, members can excercise the privilege of shaping the initiatives and issues that most profoundly affect guide dog handlers. GDUI has 19 affiliate organizations throughout the US where members can personally interact and work together on local as well as global issues.

**8699 Guide Dogs for the Blind**
PO Box 151200
San Rafael, CA 94915-1200
415-499-4000
800-295-4050
FAX: 415-499-4035
e-mail: information@guidedogs.com
www.guidedogs.com

*Bob Burke, Chair*
*Paul A. Lopez, President & CEO*
*George Kerscher, Vice Chair*

A nonprofit, charitable organization with a mission to provide Guide Dogs and training in their use to visually impaired people throughout the United States and Canada.

**8700 Guiding Eyes for the Blind**
611 Granite Springs Rd
Yorktown Heights, NY 10598-3499
914-245-4024
800-942-0149
FAX: 914-245-1609
e-mail: info@guidingeyes.org
guidingeyes.org

*Bill Badger, President/CEO*
*Sue Dishart, Vice President*
*Carolyn Kihm, Director*
*Jerry Attard, Comptroller*

An internationally recognized guide dog school that is dedicated to enriching the lives of blind and visually impaired men and women by providing them with the freedom to travel safely, thereby assuring greater independence, dignity and new horizons of opportunity

**8701 Guiding Eyes for the Blind: Breeding and Placement Center**
Guiding Eyes for the Blind
611 Granite Springs Rd
Yorktown Heights, NY 10598-3499
914-245-4024
800-942-0149
FAX: 914-245-1609
e-mail: infor@guidingeyes.org
www.guidingeyes.org

*Bill Badger, President/CEO*
*Sue Dishart, Vice President*
*Carolyn Kihm, Director*
*Jerry Attard, Comptroller*

Provides the means for blind and visually impaired individuals to achieve mobility, independence and companionship through the use of our professionally bred and trained guide dogs. Each month Guiding Eyes graduates approximately 12 guide dog/student teams from all over the US, Canada, and internationally. The guide dogs, 26 day residential training program, special needs program and lifetime follow-up services are offered at no cost to the students. Also provides at home training at no cost.

**8702 Horizons for the Blind**
125 Erick Street
A103
Crystal Lake, IL 60014-4404
815-444-8800
800-318-2000
FAX: 815-444-8830
e-mail: mail@horizons-blind.org
www.horizons-blind.org

*Camille Caffarelli, Executive Director*
*Jeff T. Thorsen, Vice President*
*Maryann Bartkowski, Secretary*

HORIZONS for the BLIND is a nonprofit organization dedicated to providing products and services to people who are blind or visually impaired. In addition, Horizons is a leading provider of Braille transcription services to the business community; specialing in partnering with companies and nonprofits to provide billing and financial statements, newsletters, and documents in Braille, large print, and audio formats.

**8703 Independent Visually Impaired Enterprisers**
American Council of the Blind
1155 15th St NW
Ste 1004
Washington, DC 20005-2706
202-467-5081
800-424-8666
FAX: 202-467-5085
e-mail: info@acb.org
www.ivie-acb.org

*Jill Gaus, President*
*Lynn Jansen, Vice President*
*Debby Lieberman, Secretary*
*Mike Reese, Treasurer*

Strives to broaden vocational opportunities in business for the visually impaired. Works to improve rehabilitation facilities for all types of business enterprises and publicizes the capabilities of blind and visually impaired business persons.

**8704 Institute for Families**
4650 Sunset Blvd
Ms 111
Los Angeles, CA 90027-6062
323-361-4649
FAX: 323-665-7869
e-mail: info@instituteforfamilies.org
www.instituteforfamilies.org

*Margaret Yoshina, Executive Director*
*Jazmin Asbun, Administrative Assistant*

A non profit organization and all services are provided at no cost to families and professionals. Offers counseling and support to families facing the devastating diagnosis of visual impairment in their child and is there for every family member of the family during the many difficult days, weeks, and months of treatment.

**8705 International Association of Audio Information Services (IAAIS)**
1102 W Intl Airport Rd
Anchorage, AK 99518-1007
412-434-6023
800-280-5325
e-mail: lrk@ku.edu
www.iaais.org

*Kim Walsh, President*
*Lori Kesinger, Chair*

A volunteer driven membership organization of services that turn text into speech for people who cannot see, hold or comprehend the printed word and who may be unable to access information due to a disability or health condition. IAAIS shall encourage and support the establishment and maintenance of audio information services that provide access to printed information for individuals who cannot read conventional print because of blindess or any other visual, physical or learning disability.

**8706 Jewish Braille Institute International**
110 E 30th St
New York, NY 10016-7393
212-821-9200
800-433-1531
FAX: 212-689-3692
e-mail: library @jbilibrary.org
www.jbilibrary.org

*Dr. Ellen Isler, President*
*Israel A. Taub, Vice President*
The JBI Library provides the visually impaired, blind, physically handicapped and reading disabled of all backgrounds and ages with books, magazines and cultural programs in Audio (in 7 languages) in Large Print and Braille. Its unique programs enrich the lives of 35,000 individuals in the United States, Israel and around the world. The JBI Library is an affiliated library of the Library of Congress and all of its services and materials are free of charge to those that are eligible.

**8707 Lighthouse International**
111 E 59th St
New York, NY 10022-1202
212-821-9200
800-829-0500
FAX: 212-821-9707
TTY: 212-821-9713
e-mail: info@lighthouse.org
lighthouse.org

*Mark G Ackerman, President/CEO*
*Barbara Gyde, Vice President*
*Ralph Caprio, Director*
Founded in 1905, lighthouse international is a leading non-profit organization that helps people of all ages overcome the challenges of vision loss. Through services, education, research and advocacy, the Lighthouse enables people with low vision and blindness to enjoy safe, independent and productive lives.

**8708 Lions Clubs International**
300 W 22nd St
Oak Brook, IL 60523-8842
630-571-5466
FAX: 630-571-8890
TTY:630-571-6533
e-mail: lions@lionsclubs.org
www.lionsclubs.org

*Wayne A. Madden, President*
*Benedict Ancar, Director*
*Barry J. Palmer, Vice President*
Lions are known for their service to persons who are blind and visually impaired. The Lions ambitious Sight First Program has restored sight through cataract surgeries, prevented serious vision loss and improved eye care services for hundreds of millions of adults and children. To continue and expand this effort, Lions have launced Campaign Sight First with a goal of raising at least $150 million dollars.

**8709 Macular Degeneration Foundation**
PO Box 531313
Henderson, NV 89053-1313
888-633-3937
FAX: 702-450-2908
e-mail: liz@eyesight.org
www.eyesight.org

*Liz Trauernicht, President*
*Julie Zavala, VP/Asst Director of Operations*
*Ron Gallemore, Board Of Scientific Advisors*
*Edmund J. Alexandrovich, Founder*
The Macular Degeneration Foundation is interested in promising near-term, scientific studies designed to inhibit the progression of macular degeneration and restore a measurable amount of vision to all.

**8710 National Alliance of Blind Students NABS Liaison**
American Council of the Blind
1155 15th St NW
Ste 1004
Washington, DC 20005-2706
202-467-5081
800-424-8666
FAX: 202-467-5085
e-mail: info@acb.org
www.acb.org

*Jill Gaus, President*
*Lynn Jansen, Vice President*
*Debby Lieberman, Secretary*
*Mike Reese, Treasurer*
A student affiliate of the American Council of the Blind which is a national organization of blind and visually impaired high school and college students who believe that every blind and visually impaired student has the right to an equal and accessible education. Also encourages blind and visually impaired students to challenge their limits and reach their potential.

**8711 National Association for Parents of Children with Visual Impairments (NAPVI)**
PO Box 317
Watertown, MA 02471-317
617-972-7441
800-562-6265
FAX: 617-972-7444
e-mail: spedex.com@gmail.com
www.spedex.com/napvi

*Julie Urban, President*
*Venetia Hayden, Vice President*
*Randi Sher, Secretary*
*Kim Alfonso, Treasurer*
A non profit organization of, by and for parents committed to providing support to the parents of children who have visual impairments . Also a national organization that enables parents to find information and resources for their children who are blind or visually impaired including those with additional disabilities. NAPVI also provides leadership, support, and training to assist parents in helping children reach their potential.

**8712 National Association for Visually Handicapped (NAVH)**
Fl 6
22 W 21st St
New York, NY 10010-6943
212-889-3141
FAX: 212-727-2931
e-mail: staff@navh.org
navh.org

*Mark G Ackerman, President & CEO*
*Barbara Gyde, Vice President*
*Ralph Caprio, Director*
NAVH is unique in the services it offers to the hard of seeing(tm) worldwide and is the only non-profit organization solely dedicated to providing assistance to this population. NAVH runs senior support groups, provides individual consultations, informational materials, training in the use of visual aids, and numerous other tools to ensure that the visually impaired can remain independent and lead fulfilling lives.

**8713 National Association of Blind Educators**
National Federation of the Blind
200 East Wells St
Baltimore, MD 21230-4914
410-659-9314
FAX: 410-685-5653
e-mail: nfb@nfb.org
nfb.org

*Marc Maurer, CEO*
Membership organization of blind teachers, professors and instructors in all levels of education. Provides support and information regarding professional responsibilities, classroom techniques, national testing methods and career obstacles. Publishes The Blind Educator, national magazine specifically for blind educators.

**8714 National Association of Blind Lawyers**
National Federation of the Blind
200 East Wells Street
Baltimore, MD 21230-4914
410-659-9314
FAX: 410-685-5653
e-mail: nfb@nfb.org
nfb.org

*Marc Mauer, President*
Membership organization of blind attorneys, law students, judges and others in the law field. Provides support and information regarding employment, techniques used by the blind, advocacy, laws affecting the blind, current information about the American Bar Association and other issues for blind lawyers.

**8715 National Association of Blind Merchants**
National Federation of the Blind
1837 S.Nevada Avenue
Colorado Springs, CO 80905-4286
719-527-0488
866-543-6808
e-mail: kevanwirkey@blindmerchants.org
www.blindmerchants.org

*Kevan Worley, President*
Membership organization of blind persons employed in either self-employment work or the Randolph-Sheppard vending program. Provides information regarding rehabilitation, social security, tax and other issues which directly affect blind merchants. Serves as advocacy and support group.

**8716 National Association of Blind Secretaries and Transcribers**
National Federation of the Blind
200 East Wells St
Baltimore, MD 21230-4914
410-659-9314
FAX: 410-685-5653
e-mail: nfb@nfb.org
nfb.org

*Marc Maurer, CEO*
Membership organization of blind secretaries and transcribers at all levels, including medical and paralegal transcription, office workers, customer-service personnel and many other similar fields. Addresses issues such as technology, accomodation, career planning and job training.

**8717 National Association of Blind Students**
National Federation of the Blind
200 East Wells St
Baltimore, MD 21230-4914
410-659-9314
FAX: 410-685-5653
e-mail: nfb@nfb.org
nfb.org

*Marc Maurer, CEO*
The mission of the National Federation of the Blind is to achieve weidespread emotional acceptance and intellectual understanding that the real problem of blindness is not the loss of eyesight but the misconceptions and lack of information which exist. We do this by bringing blind people together to share success, to support each other in times of failure and to create imaginative solutions

**8718 National Association of Blind Teachers**
American Council of the Blind
1155 15th St NW
Ste 1004
Washington, DC 20005-2706
202-467-5081
800-424-8666
FAX: 202-467-5085
e-mail: info@acb.org
www.blindteachers.net

*Jill Gaus, President*
*Lynn Jansen, Vice President*
*Debby Lieberman, Secretary*
*Mike Reese, Treasurer*
Works to advance the teaching profession for blind and visually impaired people, protects the interest of teachers, presents discussions and solutions for special problems encountered by blind teachers and publishes a directory of blind teachers in the US.

**8719 National Association of Guide Dog Users**
National Federation of the Blind
1003 Papaya Dr
Tampa, FL 33619-4629
813-626-2789
800-558-8261
e-mail: info@nfb-nagdu.org
www.nfb-nagdu.org

*Marion Gwizdala, President*
Provides information and support for guide dog users and works to secure high standards in guide dog training. Addresses issues of discrimination of guide dog users and offers public education about guide dog use. Biennial newsletter available: Harness Up!

**8720 National Association to Promote the Use of Braille**
National Federation of the Blind
39481 Gallaudet Dr
Apt 127
Fremont, CA 94538
510-248-0100
877-558-6524
FAX: 818-344-7930
e-mail: mwillows@sbcglobal.net
www.nfbcal.org

*Nadine Jacobson, President*
*Robert Jaquiss, Vice President*
*Jennifer Dunnam, Secretary*
*Warren Figueiredo, Treasurer*
Dedicated to securing improved Braille instruction, increasing the number of braille materials available to the blind and providing information of braille in securing independence, education and employment for the blind.

**8721 National Braille Association**
95 Allens Creek Rd
Bldg 1 Ste 202
Rochester, NY 14618- 3252
585-427-8260
FAX: 585-427-0263
e-mail: nbaoffice@nationalbraille.org
www.nationalbraille.org

*Dorothy Worthington, President*
*Whitney Gregory-Williams, Vice President*
*Heidi Lehmann, Secretary*
*Betty Marshall, Treasurer*
The only national organization dedicated to the professional development of individuals who prepare and produce braille materials.

**8722 National Braille Press**
88 Saint Stephen St
Boston, MA 02115-4302
617-266-6160
888-965-8965
888-965-8965
FAX: 617-437-0456
e-mail: contact@nbp.org
www.nbp.org

*Brian A. Mac Donald, President*
*Diane L. Croft, Publisher*
*Kimberley Ballard, Vice President*
*Susan Challis, Controller*
The guiding purposes of National Braille Press are to promote the literacy of blind children through braille, and to provide access to information that empowers blind people to actively engage in work, family, and commuity affairs.

**8723 National Center for Vision and Child Development**
Lighthouse International
111 E 59th St
New York, NY 10022-1202
212-821-9200
800-829-0500
FAX: 212-821-9707
TTY: 212-821-9713
e-mail: info@lighthouse.org
lighthouse.org

*Mark G Ackerman, President/CEO*
*Barbara Gyde, Vice President*
*Ralph Caprio, Director*
The worldwide leader in helping people of all ages who are blind or partially sighted overcome the challenges of vision loss.

**8724 National Diabetes Action Network for the Blind**
National Federation of the Blind
1212 London Dr
Columbia, MO 65203-2012
573-875-8911
e-mail: ebryant@socket.net
www.nfb.org

*Ed Bryant, Manager*
Leading support and information organization of persons losing vision due to diabetes. Provides personal contact and resource information with other blind diabetics about non-visual techniques of independently managing diabetes, monitoring glucose levels, measuring insulin and other matters concerning diabetes. Publishes Voice of the Diabetic, the leading publication about diabetes and blindness.

**8725 National Eye Institute**
31 Center Drive
Bethesda, MD 20892-2510
301-496-5248
www.nei.nih.gov

*Paul A Sieving MD PhD, Director*
The mission of NEI is to develop public and professional education programsthat help prevent blindness, reduce visual impairment and increase awareness of services and devices that are available for people with low vision.

**8726 National Federation of the Blind**
200 E Wells St
Baltimore, MD 21230-4914
410-659-9314
FAX: 410-685-5653
e-mail: nfb@nfb.org
www.nfb.org

*Marc Maurer, CEO*
The largest membership organization of blind people in the nation, with chapters in every state and approximately 50,000 individual members. It seeks to integrate the blind into society on the basis of equality with the sighted so that the blind are seen as normal, participating citizens. Has 700 local chapters.

**8727 National Industries for the Blind**
1310 Braddock Pl
Alexandria, VA 22314-1691
703-310-0500
FAX: 703-998-8268
e-mail: info@nib.org
nib.org

*Gary J. Krump, Chairperson*
*Ronald Tascarella, Vice Chairperson*
*Kristin Graham Koehler, Secretary*
A nonprofit organization that represents over 100 associated industries serving people who are blind in thirty-six states. These agencies serve people who are blind or visually impaired and help them to reach their full potential. Services include job and family counseling, job skills training, instruction in Braille and other communication skills, children's programs and more.

**8728 National Organization of Parents of Blind Children**
National Federation of the Blind
200 East Wells St
Baltimore, MD 21230-4914
410-659-9314
FAX: 410-685-5653
e-mail: nfb@nfb.org
nfb.org

*Marc Maurer, CEO*
Support information and advocacy organization of parents of blind or visually impaired children. Addresses issues ranging from help to parents of a newborn blind infant, mobility and braille instruction, education, social and community participation, development of self confidence and other vital factors involved in growth of a blind child.

**8729 New Eyes for the Needy**
549 Millburn Avenue
P.O. Box 332
Short Hills, NJ 07078- 332
973-376-4903
FAX: 973-376-3807
e-mail: neweyesfortheneedy@verizon.net
www.neweyesfortheneedy.org

*Clelia Biamonti, President*
*Marianne Muench Busby, Vice President*
*Barbara Daney, Treasurer*
*Suzanne Escousee, Secretary*
New Eyes provides new prescription glasses for poor children and adults in the U.S. through a voucher system.

**8730 Prevent Blindness America**
211 W Wacker Drive
Ste 1700
Chicago, IL 60606
312-363-6001
800-331-2020
FAX: 312-363-6052
e-mail: info@preventblindness.org
preventblindness.org

*Hugh Parry, CEO*
*Kira Baldanado, Director*
*Sue Corbett, Manager*
*Kathy Nelson, Vice President*
The nation's leading volunteer eye health and safety organization dedicated to fighting blindness and saving sight. Also touches the lives of millions of people each year through public and professional education, advocacy, certified vision screening training, community and patient service programs and research.

**8731 Services for the Visually Impaired**
Ste 210
8720 Georgia Ave
Silver Spring, MD 20910-3614
301-589-0894
FAX: 301-589-0884
e-mail: info@clb.org
www.clb.org

*Ann Cook, Executive Director*
Provides skills and resources to DC area residents who are blind or experiencing vision loss, and are also committed to helping people regain their indepence and maintaining it.

**8732 The Seeing Eye**
10 Washington Valley Rd
Morristown, NJ 07963-0375
973-539-4425
FAX: 973-539-0922
e-mail: info@seeingeye.org
www.seeingeye.org

*James A Kutsch Jr, President & CEO*
*Peggy Gibbon, Canine Development Director*
*Robert Pudlak, CFO*
*Jean Thomas, Director Of Donor*
An organization that concentrates on its mission to enhance the independence, dignity, and self confidence of blind people through the use of seeing eye dogs. The Seeing Eye will be an organization that concentrates on its mission to enhance the

independence, dignity, and self confidence of blind people through the use of Seeing Eye dogs, and on improving its ability to fulfill this mission. We will maintain and nuture the spirit of our founders and adhere to the highest standards of respect

**8733 United States Association of Blind Athletes**
1 Olympic Plaza
Colorado Springs, CO 80909-3508 719-866-3224
FAX: 719-866-3400
e-mail: mlucas@usaba.org
www.usaba.org

*Mark Lucas, Executive Director*
*Ryan Ortiz, Assistant Executive Director*
*John Potts, Sports Director*
The mission is to increase the number and quality of grassroots through competitive, world class athletic opportunities for Americans who are blind or visually impaired. Also value the life enhancing aspects of sports and the opportunity to demonstrate the abilities of people who are blind and visually impaired.

**8734 Vermont Association for the Blind and Visually Impaired**
60 Kimball Ave
South Burlington, VT 05403 802-863-1358
800-639-5861
FAX: 802-863-1481
e-mail: general@vabvi.org
www.vabvi.org

*James Mooney, President*
*Thomas Chase, Vice President*
*Debbie Balserus, Secretary*
*Patricia Henderson, Treasurer*
Founded from assistance with the Helen Keller and the American Foundation for the Blind with the mission to enable Vermonters with vision problems, whether blindness or impairment, to achieve and maintain independence. Also promotes self advocacy, independence, and coping skills through our education programsand adult services.

**8735 Vision World Wide**
Apt 302
5707 Brockton Dr
Indianapolis, IN 46220-5481 317-254-1332
800-431-1739
FAX: 317-251-6588
e-mail: info@visionww.org
www.visionww.org

*Patricia L Prince, President*
A non profit organization dedicated to improving the lives of the vision impaired through direct interaction and indirectly through the caregiving community. Also serve both the totally blind and those with various degrees and forms of vision loss.

**8736 Visions Center on Blindness (VCB)**
111 Summit Park Rd
Spring Valley, NY 10977-1221 212-625-1616
888-245-8333
FAX: 845-354-5130
e-mail: info@visionsvcb.org
www.visionsvcb.org

*Nancy T. Jones, President*
*Richard P. Simon, Vice President*
*Burton M. Strauss, Treasurer*
*Carol Spawn Desmond, Secretary*
A non-profit agency that promotes the independence of people of all ages who are blind or visually impaired. VCB offers braille classes, computers with large print and voice output, support groups, discussions, mobility sessions, cooking classes, and home management training, as well as large-print and braille books, family services, and employment training. Services are available throughout New York City, and in Rockland and Westchester counties.

**8737 Visually Impaired Veterans of America**
American Council of the Blind
1155 15th St NW
Ste 1004
Washington, DC 20005-2706 202-467-5081
800-424-8666
FAX: 202-467-5085
e-mail: bj2kiowa@worldnet.att.net
www.acb.org

*Jill Gaus, President*
*Lynn Jansen, Vice President*
*Debby Lieberman, Secretary*
*Mike Reese, Treasurer*
Maintain, promote and foster the well bring and rehabilitation of all visually Impaired Veterans of the Armed Forces of the United States of America who are eligible to receive from the Veterans Administration; develops and encourages the practice of high standards of personal professional conduct among Visually Impaired Veterans; maintain, promote, and foster public confidence and awareness In Visually Impaired Veterans.

**8738 Washington Ear**
12061 Tech Rd
Ste B
Silver Spring, MD 20904-7826 301-681-6636
FAX: 301-625-1986
e-mail: information@washear.org
washear.org

*Neely Oplinger, Executive Director*
*Debbie Fitch, Manager*
*Rosemary Roussil, Development Officer*
A non profit organization providing reading and information services for blind, visually impaired and physically disabled people who cannot effectively read print, see plays, watch television programs and films, or view museum exhibits. Ear free services strive to substitute hearing for seeing, improving the lives of people with limited or no vision by enabling them to be well-informed, fully productive members of their families, their communities and the working world.

## Camps

**8739 Camp Barakel**
P.O.Box 159
Fairview, MI 48621-0159 989-848-2279
FAX: 989-848-2280
e-mail: info@campbarakel.org
www.campbarakel.org

*Paul Gardner, Camp Director*
Five-day Christian camp experience in mid-August for campers ages 18-55 who are physically disabled, visually impaired, upper trainable mentally impaired or educable mentally impaired, bus transportation provided from locations in Lansing, Flint and Bay City, Michigan.

**8740 Camp Challenge**
8914 Us Highway 50 East
Bedford, IN 47421-8704 812-834-5159
e-mail: info@gocampchallenge.com
www.gocampchallenge.com

*Ralph Price, Executive Director*
One and two-week sessions for campers with developmental and or physical disabilities, hearing impairment and the blind/visually impaired. Ages 6-99 and families.

**8741 Camp Lawroweld**
Northern New England Conference
228 West Side Road
Weld, ME 04285
207-585-2984
FAX: 207-585-2985
www.lawroweld.org

*Harry Sabnani, Executive Director*
Camp is located in Weld, Maine. Week sessions July for campers who are blind or visually impaired, all ages. Other camps coed, ages 9-16 and families, single adults, June - September.

**8742 Camp Lou Henry Hoover**
Girl Scouts of Washington Rock Council
201 E Grove St
Westfield, NJ 07090-5614
908-518-4400
FAX: 908-232-4508
e-mail: dhooker@gswrc.com.
www.gshnj.org

*Samantha Basek, Field Executive*
*Susan Brooks, CEO*
Camp is located in Middleville, New Jersey. Sessions for girls who are blind/visually impaired, ages 7-18.

**8743 Camp Merrick**
PO Box 56
Nanjemoy, MD 20662-56
301-870-5858
FAX: 301-246-9108
e-mail: CampOfficeLCM@aol.com
lionscampmerrick.org

*Wayne Magoon, President*
*Ray Shumaker, Vice President*
*Heather Zeolla, Secretary*
*Frank Culhane, Treasurer*
Programs offered April-January for children who are blind/visually impaired, hearing impaired or diabetic. Coed, ages 6-15.

**8744 Camp Winnekeag**
P.O. Box 1169
South Lancaster, MA 01561-1169
978-365-4551
FAX: 978-365-3838
e-mail: sneconference@sneconline.org
www.campwinnekeag.com

*Frank Tochterman, Religious Leader*
Camp is located in Ashburnham, Massachusetts. Camping sessions for blind/visually impaired children. Coed, ages 8-16.

**8745 Columbia Lighthouse for the Blind Summer Camp**
Columbia Lighthouse for the Blind
Ste 1103
1825 K St NW
Washington, DC 20006-1261
202-454-6400
877-324-5252
FAX: 202-955-6401
e-mail: info@clb.org
clb.org

*Tony Cancelosi, President*
Helps enable the blind or visually impaired to obtain and maintain independence at home, school, work and in the community. Programs and services include early intervention services, training and consultation in assistive technology, career placement services, comprehensive low vision care and a wide range of rehabilitation services. Highly acclaimed summer camp, picnics and holiday activities encourage blind and visualy impaired children to make new friends and experience the joys of childhood.

**8746 Easter Seals Oklahoma**
701 NE 13th St
Oklahoma City, OK 73104-5003
405-239-2525
FAX: 405-239-2278
e-mail: sbusch@easterse alsoklahoma.org
www.eastersealsoklahoma.org

*John P. Sullivan, Chairman*
*Jim Kern, Treasurer*
*Mike Nunley, Secretary*
*Nick Fletcher, Director*
Adult day health center, and child development center.

**8747 Enchanted Hills Camp for the Blind**
Lighthouse for the Blind
214 Van Ness Ave
San Francisco, CA 94102-4508
415-431-1481
888-400-8933
FAX: 415-863-7568
TTY:415-431-4572
e-mail: info@lighthouse-sf.org
lighthouse-sf.org

*Joshua A. Milie, President*
*Stephen Dobbs, Vice President*
*Gena Harper, Secretary*
*Joseph Chan, Treasurer*
Camp is located in Napa, California. Half-week, one and two-week sessions for blind, deaf/blind children and adults, ages 5 and up. This program offers a basic camping experience. Activities include music, art, dance, hiking and riding. Camperships are available to California residents.

**8748 Highbrook Lodge**
PO Box 1988
Cleveland, OH 44106-8696
216-791-8118
FAX: 216-791-1101
www.clevelandsightcenter.org

*Andrew L. Sikorovsky, Chair*
*Michael D. Lundin, Vice Chair*
*Gary W. Poth, Treasurer*
*Sheryl King Benford, Secretary*
Camp is located in Chardon, Ohio. Summer sessions for children, adults and familieswho are blind or have low vision. There are seven sessions held annually through June, July and August with an wide range of outdoor camp activities. Camp activities focus on gaining independent skills, mobility, orientation and self confidence in an accessable and traditional camp setting.
*220-660/session*

**8749 Indian Creek Camp**
Kentucky Tennessee Conference
P.O.Box 1088
Goodlettsville, TN 37070-1088
615-859-1391
FAX: 615-850-1931
e-mail: info@indiancreekcamp.com
www.indiancreekcamp.com

*Jerry Mahn, Director*
Camp is located in Liberty, Tennessee. Summer sessions for children and adults who are blind/visually impaired. Coed, ages 7-17, families and seniors.

**8750 Kamp A-Komp-Plish**
9035 Ironsides Rd
Nanjemoy, MD 20662-3432
301-870-3226
301-934-3590
FAX: 301-870-2620
e-mail: recreation@melwood.org
www.kampakomplish.org

*Jonathan Rondeau, Chief Program Officer*
*Bekah Carmichael, Director*
*Doria Fleisher, Associate Director*
*Marisa Cucuzella, Assistant Director*
Camp is located in Nanjemoy, Maryland. Half-week, one-week and two-week sessions for blind/visually impaired children and

those with developmental disabilities and mobility limitation. Coed, ages 8-16.

**8751 Kamp Kaleo**

46872 Willow Springs Rd
Burwell, NE 68823-8805
308-730-0333
e-mail: kampkaleo@nctc.net
www.kampkaleo.com

*Gaylene O'Brien, Administrator*
*Sandy Denton, Minister Of Faith Development*

Camp is located in Burwell, Nebraska. Summer sessions for campers who are blind/visually impaired or have developmental disabilities. Coed, ages 9-18 and families, seniors, single adults.

**8752 National Camp for Blind Children**

Christian Record Services
4444 South 52nd Street
P.O. Box 60979
Lincoln, NE 68506-0097
402-488-0981
FAX: 402-488-7582
e-mail: infochristianrecord.org
www.christianrecord.org

*Dan Jackson, Chair*
*Tom Lemon, Vice Chair*
*Larry Pitcher, Secretary*

To enrich lives of those who are blind, visually impaired or physically challenged regardless of race, creed, economic status or gender. Also encourages each camper to achieve greater self-esteem and self confidence while seeking to excel in the use of his/her physical , mental, and spiritual capacities. Provides fee Christian publications and programs for people with visual impairments.

*Monthly*

**8753 National Camps for Blind Children**

Christian Record Services
4444 S 52nd St
P.O. Box 6097
Lincoln, NE 68506-0097
402-488-0981
FAX: 402-488-7582
e-mail: info@christianrecord.org
blindcamps.com

*Dan Jackson, Chair*
*Tom Lemon, Vice Chair*
*Larry Pitcher, Secretary*

Provides free Christian publications and programs, as well as new opportunities for people with visual impairments. Free services include subscription magazines available in braille, large print and audio cassette, full-vision books combining braille and print, lending library, gift bibles and study guides in braille, large print and audio cassette, national camps for blind children and scholarship assistance for blind young people trying to obtain a college education.

**8754 Texas Lions Camp**

Lions Club Of Texas
P.O.Box 290247
Kerrville, TX 78029-0247
830-896-8500
FAX: 830-896-3666
e-mail: tlc@ktc.com
www.lionscamp.com

*Stephen Mabry, Executive Director*

The primary purpose of the League shall be to provide, without charge, a camp for physically disabled, hearing/vision impaired and diabetic children from the State of Texas, regardless of race, religion, or national origin. Our goal is to create an atmosphere wherein campers will learn the can do philosophy and be allowed to achieve maximum personal growth and self-esteem. The camp welcomes boys and girls ages 7-16.

**8755 VISIONS Vacation Camp for the Blind**

VISIONS Center on Blindness
111 Summit Park Rd
Spring Valley, NY 10977-1221
212-625-1616
888-245-8333
FAX: 845-354-5130
e-mail: cthorne@visionsvcb.org
www.visionsvcb.org

*Nancy T. Jones, President*
*Richard P. Simon, Vice President*
*Burton M. Strauss, Treasurer*
*Carol Spawn Desmond, Secretary*

Is a non profit agency that promotes the independence of people of all ages who are blind or visually imparied. Camp offers braille classes, computers with large print and voice output, support groups, discussions, mobility lessions, cooking classes, personal and home management training, large print and Braille books.

**8756 Wendell Johnson Speech And Hearing Clinic**

University Of Iowa
250 Hawkins Dr
Iowa City, IA 52242-1025
319-335-8736
FAX: 319-335-8851
e-mail: kathy-miller@uiowa.edu
www.uiowa.edu

*Ruth Bentler, Professor & Department Chair*
*Dorothy Albright, Secretary*
*Kathy Miller, Clerk*
*Elizabeth Walker, Audiologist*

The clinic offers assessment and intervention for communication disorders in adults and children as well as an audiology clinic. The clinic also offers several summer programs for children with hearing, speech, language, autism and/or reading disorders, including a summer residential program for teens who stutter.

**8757 YMCA Camp Chingachgook on Lake George**

Capital District YMCA
1872 Pilot Knob Rd
Kattskill Bay, NY 12844-1802
518-656-9462
FAX: 518-656-9362
e-mail: chingachgook@cdymca.org
www.cdymca.org

*George Painter, Executive Director*
*Billy Rankin, Senior Program Director*
*Dan Poole, Adventure Trip Director*
*Carol Lewis, Office Manager*

Sailing programs for people with disabilities. Sessions for campers who are blind/visually impaired. Coed, ages 7-16, families, seniors and single adults.

## Print: Books

**8758 AFB Directory of Services for Blind and Visually Impaired Persons in the US and Canada**

American Foundation for the Blind/AFB Press
Suite 1102
2 Penn Plz
New York, NY 10121-2018
212-502-7600
800-232-3044
FAX: 212-502-7777
e-mail: afbinfo@afb.net
http://www.afb.org/section.aspx?documentID=52

*Carl Augusto, President*
*Rick Bozeman, Director*
*Patsy Carvache, Accouting Manager*
*Priscilla Rogers, Director*

Comprehensive print resource containing more that 2,500 local, state, regional, and national services throughout the US and Canada for persons who are blind or visually impaired. *$79.95*

*624 pages Paperback/onlin*
*ISBN 0-891288-05-3*

**8759 About Children's Eyes**
National Association for Visually Handicapped
111 E 59th St
New York, NY 1002-1202
212-821-9200
800-829-0500
FAX: 212-821-9707
e-mail: info@lighthouse.org
lighthouse.org/navh

*Mark G. Ackermann, President / CEO*
How to identify the child with a visual problem. LightHouse acquired NAVH.

**8760 About Children's Vision: A Guide for Parents**
National Association for Visually Handicapped
111 E 59th St
New York, NY 1002-1202
212-821-9200
800-829-0500
FAX: 212-821-9707
e-mail: info@lighthouse.org
lighthouse.org/navh

*Mark G. Ackermann, President / CEO*
Offers a better understanding of the normal and possible abnormal development of a child's eyesight. LightHouse acquired NAVH. *$.50*

**8761 Access to Art: A Museum Directory for Blind and Visually Impaired People**
American Foundation for the Blind/AFB Press
Suite 1102
2 Penn Plaza
New York, NY 10121
212-502-7600
800-232-3044
FAX: 888-545-8331
e-mail: afborders@abdintl.com
www.afb.org

*Carl R. Augusto, President and CEO*
Details the access facilities of over 300 museums, galleries and exhibits in the United States. Also included are organizations offering art-related resources such as, art classes, competitions and traveling exhibits. *$19.95*
*144 pages Large Print*
*ISBN 0-891281-56-8*

**8762 African Americans in the Profession of Blindness Services**
Mississippi State University
P.O.Box 6189
Mississippi State, MS 39762-6189
662-325-2001
FAX: 662-325-8989
TTY:662-325-2694
www.blind.msstate.edu

*Jacqui Bybee, Research and Training Coordinator*
This study investigated the level of participation by African Americans in vocational rehab. (VR) services to persons who are visually impaired. Using surveys and interviews with all state VR directors, national census data and national RSA data, it was found nationally that African Americans are substantially under-represented in the service provider ranks, yet over-represented as clients. *$20.00*
*61 pages Paperback*

**8763 Age-Related Macular Degeneration**
National Association for Visually Handicapped
111 E 59th St
New York, NY 1002-1202
212-821-9200
800-829-0500
FAX: 212-821-9707
e-mail: info@lighthouse.org
lighthouse.org/navh

*Mark G. Ackermann, President / CEO*
A large booklet offering information and up-to-date research on Macular Degeneration. Also available in Russian. Revised in 2007. LightHouse acquired NAVH. *$5.00*

**8764 American Anals of the Deaf Reference**
800 Florida Ave NE
Washington, DC 20002-3600
202-651-5530
FAX: 202-651-5489
e-mail: gupress@gallaudet.edu
gupress.gallaudet.edu/annals

*Donald Moores, Manager*
The controlled scope of GUPress operations allows the continuance of a highly focused commitment to individual titles that has contributed significantly to its 20 years of leadership in publishing on Deaf issues. Gallaudet University Press brings unmatched experience and knowledge to the marketplace for books on and for the Deaf community, its advocates, and scholars invested in the study of deaf society.

**8765 Americans with Disabilities Act Guide for Places of Lodging: Serving Guests Who Are Blind**
US Department of Justice
950 Pennsylvania Ave NW
Washington, DC 20530-9
800-574-0301
FAX: 202-307-1197
TTY:800-514-0383
www.ada.gov

*Gregory B. Friel, Chief*
A 12-page publication explaining what hotels, motels, and other places of transient lodging can do to accommodate guests who are blind or have low vision.

**8766 Art and Science of Teaching Orientation and Mobility to Persons with Visual Impairments**
American Foundation for the Blind/AFB Press
Suite 1102
2 Penn Plaza
New York, NY 10121
212-502-7600
800-232-3044
FAX: 888-545-8331
e-mail: afborders@abdintl.com
www.afb.org

*Carl R. Augusto, President and CEO*
Comprehensive decription of the techniques of teaching orientation and mobility, presented along with considerations and strategies for sensitive and effective teaching. Hardcover. Paperback also available. *$48.00*
*200 pages*
*ISBN 0-891282-45-9*

**8767 Awareness Training**
Landmark Media
3450 Slade Run Dr
Falls Church, VA 22042-3940
703-241-2030
800-342-4336
FAX: 703-536-9540
e-mail: info@landmarkmedia.com
landmarkmedia.com

*Michael Hartogs, President*
*Peter Hartogs, VP New Business & Development*
Covers disabilities of various types - vision, hearing, speech disorders, loss of limbs, loss of mobility, or mental/emotional limitations and how to integrate such individuals into various business and educational settings. It is a 4-part series designed to identify and enable others to interact effectively with those suffering such disabilities. *$495.00*
*Set of 4*

**8768 Babycare Assistive Technology**
Through the Looking Glass
Ste. 120
3075 Adeline St.
Berkeley, CA 94703
510-848-1112
800-644-2666
FAX: 510-848-4445
TTY: 510-848-1005
e-mail: tlg@lookingglass.org
www.lookingglass.org

*Christi Tuleja, Author*
*Anitra DeMoss, Co-Author*
Available in braille, large print or cassette. Provides an overview of the baby care assistive technology work at Through The Looking Glass including a discussion of TLG's intervention model, the impact of babycare equipment and guidelines for equipment development. *$2.00*
*8 pages*

**8769 Babycare Assistive Technology for Parents with Physical Disabilties**
Through the Looking Glass
Ste. 120
3075 Adeline St.
Berkeley, CA 94703
510-848-1112
800-644-2666
FAX: 510-848-4445
TTY: 510-848-1005
e-mail: tlg@lookingglass.org
www.lookingglass.org

*Megan Kirshbaum PhD, Author*
Examines the provision of babycare equipment through the lens of ithe infant/parent relationship, the lens of the family system, and through the lens of culture. Availiable in braille, large print or cassette. *$2.00*
*7 pages*

**8770 Basic Course in American Sign Language**
TJ Publishers
Ste 108
2544 Tarpley Rd
Carrollton, TX 75006-2288
972-416-0800
800-999-1168
FAX: 972-416-0944
TTY: 301-585-4440
e-mail: TJPubinc@aol.com
www.tjpublishers.com/

*Tom Humphries, Author*
*Carol Padden, Co-Author*
*Terrance J O'Rourke, Co-Author*
Accompanying videotapes and textbooks include voice translations. Hearing students can analyze sound for initial instruction, or opt to turn off the sound to sharpen visual acuity. Package includes the Basic Course in American Sign Language text, Student Study Guide, the original four 1-hour videotapes plus the ABCASI Vocabulary videotape. *$139.95*
*280 pages*

**8771 Behavioral Vision Approaches for Persons with Physical Disabilities**
Optometric Extension Program Foundation
Ste 31
1921 Carnegie Ave
Santa Ana, CA 92705-5510
714-250-0176
e-mail: Info@depf.org
www.depf.org

*Robert Williams, Executive Director*
A discussion of the behavioral vision/neuro-motor approach to providing directions for prescriptive and therapeutic services for the visually handicapped child or adult. *$49.50*
*197 pages*

**8772 Belonging**
Dial Books
375 Hudson St
New York, NY 10014-3658
212-366-2000
FAX: 212-414-3394

*Deborah Kent, Author*
Meg attended special schools for the blind until she was ready for high school. She decided that she wanted to go to a regular high school. She and her mother practiced her walks to school and studied the layout of the building prior to school starting, but Meg was unprepared for the trip when there were 1,500 students. She adjusted quickly to the crowds and the pace of the new school.
*200 pages Hardcover*
*ISBN 0-80370 -30-1*

**8773 Berthold Lowenfeld on Blindness and Blind People**
American Foundation for the Blind/AFB Press
Suite 1102
2 Penn Plaza
New York, NY 10121
212-502-7600
800-232-3044
FAX: 888-545-8331
e-mail: afborders@abdintl.com
www.afb.org

*Carl R. Augusto, President and CEO*
These writings of the pioneering educator, author and advocate range over a forty-year period include various ground-breaking papers for the blind educator, a rememberance of Helen Keller and other essays on education, sociology and history. *$21.95*
*254 pages Paperback*
*ISBN 0-891281-01-0*

**8774 Blind and Vision-Impaired Individuals**
Mainstream
Ste 830
3 Bethesda Metro Ctr
Bethesda, MD 20814-6301
301-961-9299
800-247-1380
FAX: 301-654-6714
e-mail: info@mainstreaminc.org

*Charles Moster*
Mainstreaming blind individuals into the workplace. *$ 2.50*
*12 pages*

**8775 Blindness and Early Childhood Development Second Edition**
American Foundation for the Blind/AFB Press
Suite 1102
2 Penn Plaza
New York, NY 10121
212-502-7600
800-232-5463
FAX: 888-545-8331
e-mail: afbinfo@afb.net
afb.org

*Carl R. Augusto, President and CEO*
A review of current knowledge on motor and locomotor development, perceptual development, language and cognitive processes, and social, emotional and personality development. Paperback. *$34.95*
*384 pages*
*ISBN 0-891281-23-8*

**8776 Blindness: What it is, What it Does and How to Live with it**
American Foundation for the Blind/AFB Press
Suite 1102
2 Penn Plaza
New York, NY 10121
212-502-7600
800-232-3044
FAX: 888-545-8331
e-mail: afborders@abdintl.com
www.afb.org

*Carl R. Augusto, President and CEO*

A classic work on how blindness affects self-perception and social interaction and what can be done to restore basic skills, mobility, daily living and an appreciation of life's pleasures. *$15.95*
*396 pages Paperback*
*ISBN 0-891282-05-*

**8777 Books are Fun for Everyone**
Nat'l Lib Svc/Blind And Physically Handicapped
1291 Taylor St NW
Washington, DC 20011
202-707-5100
FAX: 202-707-0712
TTY:202-707-0744
e-mail: nls@loc.gov
www.loc.gov/nls

*Karen Keninger, Director*

**8778 Books for Blind & Physically Handicapped Individuals**
Nat'l Lib Svc/Blind And Physically Handicapped
1291 Taylor St NW
Washington, DC 20011
202-707-5100
FAX: 202-707-0712
TTY:202-707-0744
e-mail: nls@loc.gov
www.loc.gov/nls

*Karen Keninger, Director*
A free national library program of braille and recorded materials for blind and physically handicapped persons.

**8779 Books for Blind and Physically Handicapped Individuals**
Nat'l Lib Svc/Blind And Physically Handicapped
1291 Taylor St NW
Washington, DC 20011
202-707-5100
FAX: 202-707-0712
TTY:202-707-0744
e-mail: nls@loc.gov
www.loc.gov/nls

*Karen Keninger, Director*
A free national library program of braille and recorded materials for blind and physically handicapped persons is administered by the National Library Service for the Blind and Physically Handicapped Library of Congress.
*Annual*

**8780 Braille Book Bank, Music Catalog**
National Braille Association
Bldg. 1, Suite 202
95 Allens Creek Road
Rochester, NY 14618-3252
585-427-8260
FAX: 585-427-0263
e-mail: nbaoffice@nationalbraille.org
www.nationalbraille.org

*Dorothy Worthington, President*
*David Shaffer, Executive Director*
Offers hundreds of musical titles in print form, braille and on cassette.
*62 pages*

**8781 Braille: An Extraordinary Volunteer Opportunity**
Nat'l Lib Svc/Blind And Physically Handicapped
1291 Taylor St NW
Washington, DC 20011
202-707-5100
FAX: 202-707-0712
TTY:202-707-0744
e-mail: nls@loc.gov
www.loc.gov/nls

*Karen Keninger, Director*

**8782 Burns Braille Transcription Dictionary**
American Foundation for the Blind/AFB Press
Suite 1102
2 Penn Plaza
New York, NY 10121
212-502-7600
800-232-5463
FAX: 888-545-8331
e-mail: afbinfo@afb.net
afb.org

*Carl R. Augusto, President and CEO*
A handy, portable guide that is a quick reference for anyone who needs to check print-to-braille and braille-to-print meanings and symbols. Paperback. *$21.95*
*96 pages 96 pages*
*ISBN 0-891282-32-7*

**8783 Can't Your Child See? A Guide for Parents of Visually Impaired Children**
Sage Publications
2455 Teller Road
Thousand Oaks, CA 91320
800-818-7243
FAX: 800-583-2665
e-mail: info@sagepub.com
www.sagepub.com

*Sara Miller McCune, Founder, Publisher, Chairperson*
*Blaise R Simqu, President & CEO*
This second edition offers parents optimistic, practical guidelines for helping visually impaired children reach their full potential. *$26.00*
*279 pages Paperback*

**8784 Career Perspectives: Interviews with Blindand Visually Impaired Professionals**
American Foundation for the Blind/AFB Press
Suite 1102
2 Penn Plaza
New York, NY 10121
212-502-7600
800-232-5463
FAX: 888-545-8331
e-mail: afbinfo@afb.net
afb.org

*Carl R. Augusto, President and CEO*
Profiles of 20 successful archivers who describe in their own words what it takes to pursue and attain professional success in a sighted world. Available in large print, cassette and braille. *$19.95*
*96 pages*
*ISBN 0-891281-70-2*

**8785 Careers in Blindness Rehabilitation Services**
Mississippi State University
P.O.Box 6189
Mississippi State, MS 39762-6189
662-325-2001
FAX: 662-325-8989
TTY:662-325-2694
www.blind.msstate.edu

*Jacqui Bybee, Research and Training Coordinator*
In a follow-up study in a series examining the substantial under-representation of African Americans as professionals in blindness services, researchers questioned college students about their knowledge, opinions and interests in blindness services. *$15.00*
*54 pages Paperback*

**8786 Cataracts**
National Association for Visually Handicapped
111 E 59th St
New York, NY 1002-1202
212-821-9200
800-829-0500
FAX: 212-821-9707
e-mail: info@lighthouse.org
lighthouse.org/navh

*Mark G. Ackermann, President / CEO*
A booklet offering information about Cataracts, diagnosis and treatment of this common condition. LightHouse acquired NAVH. *$ 4.00*

**8787 Characteristics, Services, & Outcomes of Rehab. Consumers who are Blind/Visually Impaired**
Mississippi State University
P.O.Box 6189
Mississippi State, MS 39762-6189
662-325-2001
FAX: 662-325-8989
TTY:662-325-2694
www.blind.msstate.edu

*Jacqui Bybee, Research and Training Coordinator*
Issues regarding the efficacy of separate state agencies providing specialized vocational rehabilitation (VR) services to consumers who are blind have generated spirited discussions within the rehabilitation community throughout the history of the state-federal program. In this monograph, RRTC researches report results of their investigation of services provided to blind consumers in separate and general (combined) rehabilitation agencies. *$20.00*
*45 pages Paperback*

**8788 Childhood Glaucoma: A Reference Guide for Families**
NAPVI
P.O.Box 317
Watertown, MA 02471-317
617-972-7441
800-562-6265
FAX: 617-972-7444
e-mail: napvi@perkins.org
www.napvi.org

*Susan LaVenture, Executive Director*
A vaulable tutorial and resource covering all aspects from genetics through diagnosis, sibling relationships and more.
*36 pages*

**8789 Children with Visual Impairments: A Guide For Parents**
American Foundation for the Blind/AFB Press
105 East 22nd Street
New York, NY 10010
212-949-4800
childrensaidsociety.org

*Richard R. Buery, Jr., President & CEO*
Written by parents and professional, this book presents a comprehensive overview of the issues that are crucial to the healthy development of children with mild to severe visual impaiments. It also offers insight from parents about coping with the emotional aspects of raising a child with special needs. *$16.95*
*416 pages*
*ISBN 0-933149-36-0*

**8790 Classification of Impaired Vision**
National Association for Visually Handicapped
111 E 59th St
New York, NY 1002-1202
212-821-9200
800-829-0500
FAX: 212-821-9707
e-mail: info@lighthouse.org
lighthouse.org/navh

*Mark G. Ackermann, President / CEO*
Designed to provide a foundation for a better understanding of teaching reading, writing, and listning skills to students with visual impairments from preschool age through adult levels. LightHouse acquired NAVH. *$57.95*
*322 pages*
*ISBN 0-398066-93-2*

**8791 Communication Skills for Visually Impaired Learners**
Charles C. Thomas
2600 S 1st St
Springfield, IL 62704-4730
217-789-8980
800-258-8980
FAX: 217-789-9130
e-mail: books@ccthomas.com
ccthomas.com

*Michael P. Thomas, President*
*Randall Harley, Author*
*Mila Truan, Author*
*LaRhea Sanford, Author*
This book has been designed to provide a foundation for a better understanding of teaching reading, writing, and listening skills to students with visual impairments from preschool age through adult levels. The plan of the book incorporates the latest research findings with the practical experiences learned in the classroom.
*$57.95*
*322 pages Paperback*
*ISBN 0-398066-93-2*

**8792 Comprehensive Examination of Barriers to Employment Among Persons who are Blind or Impaire**
Mississippi State University
P.O.Box 6189
Mississippi State, MS 39762-6189
662-325-2001
FAX: 662-325-8989
TTY:662-325-2694
www.blind.msstate.edu

*Jacqui Bybee, Research and Training Coordinator*
A multi-phase research project designed to: identify barriers to employment; identify and develop innovative successful strategies to overcome these barriers; develop methods for others to utilize these strategies; disseminate this information to rehabilitation providers; replicate the use of selected strategies in other settings. *$20.00*
*90 pages Paperback*

**8793 Contrasting Characteristics of Blind and Visually Impaired Clients**
Mississippi State University
P.O.Box 6189
Mississippi State, MS 39762-6189
662-325-2001
FAX: 662-325-8989
TTY:662-325-2694
www.blind.msstate.edu

*Jacqui Bybee, Research and Training Coordinator*
This report examines cases in the National Blindness and Low Vision Employment Database to identify and profile environmental and personal characteristics of clients who are blind or visually impaired and who were achieving successful and unsuccessful retention of competitive jobs. A total of 787 cases were analyzed.
*$15.00*
*44 pages Paperback*

**8794 Dancing Cheek to Cheek**
Blind Children's Center
4120 Marathon St
Los Angeles, CA 90029-3584
323-664-2153
800-222-3567
FAX: 323-665-3828
e-mail: info@blindchildrenscenter.org
www.blindchildrenscenter.org

*Midge Horton, Executive Director*
*Pamela Lansky, Co-Author*
Beginning social, play and language interactions. *$ 10.00*
*23 pages*

**8795 Development of Social Skills by Blind and Visually Impaired Students**

American Foundation for the Blind/AFB Press
Suite 1102
2 Penn Plaza
New York, NY 10121
212-502-7600
800-232-5463
FAX: 888-545-8331
e-mail: afbinfo@afb.net
www.afb.org

*Carl R. Augusto, President and CEO*

Offers an examination of the social interactions of blind and visually impaired children in mainstreamed settings and the community that highlights the need to teach social interaction skills to children and provide them with support. Paperback. *$45.95*

*232 pages*

*ISBN 0-891282-17-4*

**8796 Diabetic Retinopathy**

National Association for Visually Handicapped
111 E 59th St
New York, NY 1002-1202
212-821-9200
800-829-0500
FAX: 212-821-9707
e-mail: info@lighthouse.org
lighthouse.org/navh

*Mark G. Ackermann, President / CEO*

A booklet offering information about Diabetic Retinopathy. LightHouse acquired NAVH.

**8797 Diversity and Visual Impairment: The Influence of Race, Gender, Religion and Ethnicity**

American Foundation for the Blind
Suite 1102
2 Penn Plaza
New York, NY 10121
212-502-7600
800-232-5463
FAX: 888-545-8331
e-mail: afbinfo@afb.net
www.afb.org

*Carl R. Augusto, President and CEO*

Cultural, social, ethnic, gender, and religious issues can influence the way an individual perceives and copes with a visual impairment. *$45.95*

*480 pages*

*ISBN 0-891283-83-8*

**8798 Do You Remember the Color Blue: The Questi Ons Children Ask About Blindness**

Viking Books
375 Hudson St
New York, NY 10014-3657
212-366-2372
FAX: 212-366-2933
www.us.penguingroup.com

*John Makinson, Chairman & CEO*

The author answers thirteen thought-provoking questions that children have asked her over the years about being blind.

*78 pages*

*ISBN 0-670880-43-4*

**8799 Don't Lose Sight of Glaucoma**

National Eye Institute
31 Center Drive
Building 31 Room 6a32
Bethesda, MD 20892-2510
301-496-5248
800-869-2020
FAX: 301-402-1065
e-mail: 2020@nei.nih.gov
www.nei.nih.gov

Publication about the risk of getting open-angle Glaucoma. Encourages regular eye exams through dialated pupils.

**8800 Early Focus: Working with Young Children Who Are Blind or Visually Impaired & Their Families**

American Foundation for the Blind/AFB Press
Suite 1102
2 Penn Plaza
New York, NY 10121
212-502-7600
800-232-5603
FAX: 888-545-8331
e-mail: afbinfo@afb.net
www.afb.org

*Carl R. Augusto, President and CEO*

Describes early intervention techniques used with blind and visually impaired children and stresses the benefits of family involvement and transdisciplinary teamwork. Paperback. *$32.95*

*176 pages*

*ISBN 0-891282-15-7*

**8801 Encyclopedia of Blindness and Vision Impairment Second Edition**

Facts on File
Fl 17
132 W 31st St
New York, NY 10001-3406
800-322-8755
FAX: 800-678-3633
e-mail: support@factsonfile.com
www.factsonfile.com

*Jill Sardenga, Author*
*Susan Shelly, Co-Author*
*Alan Shelly MD, Co-Author*
*Scott M Steidl MD, Co-Author*

Designed to provide both laymen and professionals with concise, practical information on the second most common disability in the U.S. *$65.00*

*340 pages Hardcover*

*ISBN 0-816042-80-2*

**8802 Equals in Partnership: Basic Rights for Families of Children with Blindness**

NAPVI
P.O.Box 317
Watertown, MA 02471-317
617-972-7441
800-562-6265
FAX: 617-972-7444
e-mail: napvi@perkins.org
www.napvi.org

*Susan LaVenture, Executive Director*

A comprehensive compilation of educational advocacy materials to help parents better understand the special needs of their children with visual impairments and to assist them in accessing appropriate services for their children.

**8803 Eye Research News**

Research to Prevent Blindness
Fl 21
645 Madison Ave
New York, NY 10022-1010
212-752-4333
800-621-0026
FAX: 212-688-6231
e-mail: inforequest@rpbusa.org
www.rpbusa.org

*Diane Swift, President*
*James V Romano, COO*

Yearly publication from Research to Prevent Blindness. Free.

*4 pages Yearly*

**8804 Eye and Your Vision**
National Association for Visually Handicapped
111 E 59th St
New York, NY 1002-1202
212-821-9200
800-829-0500
FAX: 212-821-9707
e-mail: info@lighthouse.org
lighthouse.org/navh

*Mark G. Ackermann, President / CEO*
A large booklet offering information, with illustrations, on the eye. Includes information on protection of eyesight, how the eye works and vision disorders. Available in Russian and Spanish also. LightHouse acquired NAVH. *$5.00*

**8805 Eye-Q Test**
National Association for Visually Handicapped
111 E 59th St
New York, NY 1002-1202
212-821-9200
800-829-0500
FAX: 212-821-9707
e-mail: info@lighthouse.org
lighthouse.org/navh

*Mark G. Ackermann, President / CEO*
Five questions and answers to assist in knowing more about vision. Also available in Spanish and Russian. LightHouse acquired NAVH.

**8806 Family Context and Disability Culture Reframing: Through the Looking Glass**
Through the Looking Glass
Ste. 120
3075 Adeline St.
Berkeley, CA 94703
510-848-1112
800-644-2666
FAX: 510-848-4445
TTY: 510-848-1005
e-mail: tlg@lookingglass.org
www.lookingglass.org

*Mega Kirshbaum, Author*
This article provides an overview of the issues and guiding perspectives underlying 'Through the Lookinglass' eighteen years of work with families. Available in braille, large print or cassette.
*$2.00*
*5 pages*

**8807 Family Guide to Vision Care (FG1)**
American Optometric Association
243 N Lindbergh Blvd
Saint Louis, MO 63141-7851
800-365-2219
aoa.org

*Barry Barresi, Executive Director*
Offers information on the early developmental years of your vision, finding a family optometrist and how to take care of your eyesight through the learning years, the working years and the mature years.

**8808 Family Guide: Growth & Development of the Partially Seeing Child**
National Association for Visually Handicapped
111 E 59th St
New York, NY 1002-1202
212-821-9200
800-829-0500
FAX: 212-821-9707
e-mail: info@lighthouse.org
lighthouse.org/navh

*Mark G. Ackermann, President / CEO*
Offers information for parents and guidelines in raising a partially seeing child. LightHouse acquired NAVH. *$.60*

**8809 Fathers: A Common Ground**
Blind Children's Center
4120 Marathon St
Los Angeles, CA 90029-3584
323-664-2153
800-222-3567
FAX: 323-665-3828
e-mail: info@blindchildrenscenter.org
www.blindchildrenscenter.org

*Midge Horton, Executive Director*
*Fernanda Schmitt PhD, Co-Author*
Exploring the concerns and roles of fathers of children with visual impairments. *$10.00*
*50 pages*

**8810 Fighting Blindness News**
Foundation Fighting Blindness
7168 Columbia Gateway Drive
Suite 100
Columbia, MD 21046
410-423-0600
800-683-5555
FAX: 410-363-2393
TTY: 800-683-5551
e-mail: info@FightBlindness.org
www.blindness.org

*William T. Schmidt, CEO*
Offers information on medical updates, donor programs, assistive devices, resources and clinical trial information for persons with visual impariments, blindness and retinal degenerative diseases.
*2x Year*

**8811 First Steps**
Blind Children's Center
4120 Marathon St
Los Angeles, CA 90029-3584
323-664-2153
800-222-3567
FAX: 323-665-3828
e-mail: info@blindchildrenscenter.org
www.blindchildrenscenter.org

*Midge Horton, Executive Director*
*Ferdinand Schmitt PhD, Co-Author*
A handbook for teaching young children who are visually impaired. Designed to assist students, professionals and parents working with children who are visually impaired. Visit our website for many publications addressing training very young children who are blind or visually impaired. *$35.00*
*203 pages*

**8812 Foundations of Orientation and Mobility**
American Foundation for the Blind/AFB Press
Suite 1102
2 Penn Plaza
New York, NY 10121
212-502-7600
800-232-5463
FAX: 888-545-8331
e-mail: afborders@abdintl.com
www.afb.org

*Carl R. Augusto, President and CEO*
This text has been updated and revised and includes current research from a variety of disciplines, an international perspective, and expanded contents on low vision, aging, multiple disabilities, accessibility, program design and adaptive technology from more that 30 eminent subject experts. *$79.95*
*775 pages*
*ISBN 0-891289-46-3*

**8813 Foundations of Rehabilitation Counseling with Persons Who Are Blind r Visually Impaired**
American Foundation for the Blind/AFB Press
Suite 1102
2 Penn Plaza
New York, NY 10121
212-502-7600
800-232-5603
FAX: 888-545-8331
e-mail: afborders@abdintl.com
www.afb.org

*Carl R. Augusto, President and CEO*
Rehabilitation professionals have long recognized that the needs of people who are blind or visually impaired are unique and requie a special knowledge and expertise to provide and corrdinate rehabilitation services. *$59.95*
*477 pages*
*ISBN 0-891289-45-3*

**8814 General Facts and Figures on Blindness**
Prevent Blindness America
Ste 1700
211 W Wacker Dr
Chicago, IL 60606-1375
312-922-8710
800-331-2020
FAX: 312-922-8713

*Hugh Parry, President*

**8815 Get a Wiggle On**
American Alliance for Health, Phys. Ed. & Dance
1900 Association Dr
Reston, VA 20191-1502
703-476-3400
FAX: 703-476-9527
e-mail: aapar@aahperd.org
aahperd.org

*E. Paul Roetert, CEO*
Gives teachers and parents practical suggestions for helping blind and visually impaired infants grow and learn like other children. *$5.00*
*80 pages*
*ISBN 0-88314 -77-2*

**8816 Gift of Sight**
RP Foundation Fighting Blindness
1401 W Mount Royal Ave
Baltimore, MD 21217-4245
410-225-9409
800-683-5555
FAX: 410-225-3936

A pamphlet offering information on the Retina Donor Program, which studies diseased, human retinal tissue in their search for a cure of retinal degenerative diseases.

**8817 Glaucoma**
Glaucoma Research Foundation
Ste 600
251 Post St
San Francisco, CA 94108-5017
415-986-3162
800-826-6693
FAX: 415-986-3763
e-mail: question@glaucoma.org
glaucoma.org

*Thomas M. Brunner, CEO*
*Nancy Graydon, Executive Director of Development*
Offers information on what glaucoma is, the causes, treatments, types of glaucoma, eye exams and prevention.

**8818 Glaucoma: The Sneak Thief of Sight**
National Association for Visually Handicapped
Fl 6
22 W 21st St
New York, NY 10010-6943
212-242-4438
FAX: 212-242-4450
e-mail: navh@navh.org
cancos.com

*Denise Green, Owner*
A pamphlet describing the disease, treatment and medications. Also available in Russian and Spanish. Revised in 1999. *$3.50*

**8819 Guidelines and Games for Teaching Efficient Braille Reading**
American Foundation for the Blind/AFB Press
Suite 1102
2 Penn Plaza
New York, NY 10121
212-502-7600
800-232-5603
FAX: 888-545-8331
e-mail: afbinfo@afb.net
www.afb.org

*Carl R. Augusto, President and CEO*
Based on research in the areas of rapid reading and precision teaching, these guidelines represent a unique adaptation of a general reading program to the needs of braille readers. Paperback. *$ 24.95*
*116 pages Paperback*
*ISBN 0-891281-05-4*

**8820 Guidelines for Comprehensive Low Vision Care**
National Association for Visually Handicapped
111 E 59th St
New York, NY 1002-1202
212-821-9200
800-829-0500
FAX: 212-821-9707
e-mail: info@lighthouse.org
lighthouse.org/navh

*Mark G. Ackermann, President / CEO*
A description of the proper method to conduct a low vision evaluation.LightHouse acquired NAVH. *$.50*

**8821 Handbook for Itinerant and Resource Teachers of Blind Students**
National Federation of the Blind
200 East Wells St
Baltimore, MD 21230-4914
410-659-9314
e-mail: nfb@iamdigex.net

*Doris Willoughby, Author*
*Sharon L Monthei, Co-Author*
The Handbook provides help to teachers, school administrators or other school personnel that have experience with blind or visually impaired students. The Handbook devotes 45 pages to Braille and how to teach Braille for parents and teachers. There are other chapters offering information on the law, physical education, fitting in socially, testing and evaluation, home economics, daily living skills and more. *$23.00*
*533 pages Softcover*
*ISBN 0-962412-20-1*

**8822 Handbook of Information for Members of the Achromatopsia Network**
P.O.Box 214
Berkeley, CA 94701-214
510-540-4700
FAX: 510-540-4767
e-mail: futterman@achromat.org
www.achromat.org

**8823 Health Care Professionals Who Are Blind or Visually Impaired**
American Foundation for the Blind
Suite 1102
2 Penn Plaza
New York, NY 10121
212-502-7600
800-232-5463
FAX: 888-545-8331
e-mail: afbinfo@afb.net
afb.org

*Carl R. Augusto, President and CEO*
This resource is essential reading for older students and young adults who are blind or visually impaired, their families, and the professionals who work with them. *$21.95*
*160 pages*
*ISBN 0-891283-88-9*

**8824 Heart to Heart**
Blind Children's Center
4120 Marathon St
Los Angeles, CA 90029-3584
323-664-2153
800-222-3567
FAX: 323-665-3828
e-mail: info@blindchildrenscenter.org
www.blindchildrenscenter.org

*Midge Horton, Executive Director*
*Dori Hayashi MA, Co-Author*
Parents of children who are blind and partially sighted talk about their feelings. *$10.00*
*12 pages*

**8825 Heartbreak of Being A Little Bit Blind**
National Association for Visually Handicapped
111 E 59th St
New York, NY 1002-1202
212-821-9200
800-829-0500
FAX: 212-821-9707
e-mail: info@lighthouse.org
lighthouse.org/navh

*Mark G. Ackermann, President / CEO*
Summary of what it means to have impaired vision; includes illustrations. LightHouse acquired NAVH.

**8826 Helen Keller National Center Newsletter**
141 Middle Neck Rd
Sands Point, NY 11050-1218
516-944-8900
800-225-0411
FAX: 516-944-7302
e-mail: development@hknc.org
www.hknc.org

*Joseph McNulty, Executive Director*
The center provides evaluation and training in vocational skills, adaptive technology and computer skills, orientation and mobility, independent living, communication, speech-language skills, creative arts, fitness and leisure activities.

**8827 Helping the Visually Impaired Child with Developmental Problems**
Teachers College Press
1234 Amsterdam Ave
New York, NY 10027-6602
212-678-3929
800-575-6566
FAX: 212-678-4149
e-mail: tcpress@tc.columbia.edu
www.teacherscollegepress.com

*Mary Lynch, Manager*
This book aims to explore the human consequences of severe visual problems combined with other handicaps. The application of child development research to educational interventions, the need for educational and rehabilitative services that serve the human and the special needs of children and their families and the promise of technology in helping to expand communicative possibilities are also discussed. *$18.95*
*216 pages Paperback*
*ISBN 0-807729-02-7*

**8828 History and Use of Braille**
American Council of the Blind
Suite 650
2200 Wilson Boulevard
Arlington, VA 22201-3354
202-467-5081
800-424-8666
FAX: 202-467-5085
e-mail: info@acb.org
acb.org

A system of touch reading and writing for blind persons in which raised dots represent the letters of the alphabet.

**8829 How to Thrive, Not Just Survive**
American Foundation for the Blind/AFB Press
Suite 1102
2 Penn Plaza
New York, NY 10121
212-502-7600
800-232-5463
FAX: 888-545-8331
e-mail: afbinfo@afb.net
www.afb.org

*Carl R. Augusto, President and CEO*
Practical, hands-on guide for parents, teachers, and everyone involved in helping children develop the skills necessary for socialization, orientations and mobility, and leisure and recreational activities. Some of the subjects covered are eating, dressing, personal hygiene, self-esteem and etiquette. *$24.95*
*104 pages Paperback*
*ISBN 0-89128 -48-7*

**8830 Hub**
SPOKES Unlimited
415 Main St
Klamath Falls, OR 97601-6029
541-883-7547
FAX: 541-885-2469
e-mail: spokes@internetcds.com
spokesunlimited.org

*Wendy Howard, Executive Director*
*Celeste Wolf, Clerical Support Specialist II*
Newsletter on rehabilitation, peer counseling, blindness, visual impairments, information and referral.

**8831 If Blindness Comes**
National Federation of the Blind
200 East Wells St
Baltimore, MD 21230-4914
410-659-9314
FAX: 410-685-5653
e-mail: nfb@iamdigex.net
www.nfb.org

*Kenneth Jerrigan, Editor*
An introduction to issues relating to vision loss and provides a positive, supportive philosophy about blindness. It is a general information book which includes answers to many common questions about blindness, information about services and programs for the blind and resource listings. Contact the Materials Center.

**8832 If Blindness Strikes Don't Strike Out**
2600 S 1st St
Springfield, IL 62704-4730
217-523-5075
FAX: 217-523-0506
www.ccthomas.com

*Bob Stork, Owner*

**8833 Imagining the Possibilities: Creative Approaches to Orientation and Mobility Instructio**

American Foundation for the Blind
Suite 1102
2 Penn Plaza
New York, NY 10121
212-502-7600
800-232-5463
FAX: 888-545-8331
e-mail: afbinfo@afb.net
afb.org

*Carl R. Augusto, President and CEO*

Innovative and varied approaches to O&M techniques and teaching and dynamic suggestions on how to analyze learning styles are just some of the important topics included. *$49.95*

*378 pages*

*ISBN 0-891283-82-X*

**8834 Increasing Literacy Levels: Final Report**

Mississippi State University
P.O.Box 6189
Mississippi State, MS 39762-6189
662-325-2001
FAX: 662-325-8989
TTY:662-325-2694
www.blind.msstate.edu

*Jacqui Bybee, Research and Training Coordinator*

This study is composed of three research projects to identify and analyze the appropriate use of and instruction in Braille, optical devices and other technologies as they relate to literacy and employment of individuals who are blind or visually impaired. *$20.00*

*148 pages Paperback*

**8835 Information Access Project**

National Federation of the Blind
200 East Wells St
Baltimore, MD 21230-4914
410-659-9314
FAX: 410-685-5653
e-mail: nfb@nfb.org
nfb.org

*Marc Maurer, President*

Assists entities covered by the ADA in finding methods for converting visually displayed information, such as flyers, brochures and pamphlets, to formats accessible to individuals who are visually impaired.

**8836 Information on Glaucoma**

Glaucoma Research Foundation
Ste 600
251 Post St
San Francisco, CA 94108-5017
415-986-3162
800-826-6693
FAX: 415-986-3763
e-mail: question@glaucoma.org
www.glaucoma.org

*Thomas M. Brunner, CEO*
*Nancy Graydon, Executive Director of Development*

**8837 Intervention Practices in the Retention of Competitive Employment**

Mississippi State University
P.O.Box 6189
Mississippi State, MS 39762-6189
662-325-2001
FAX: 662-325-8989
TTY:662-325-2694
www.blind.msstate.edu

*Jacqui Bybee, Research and Training Coordinator*

This study investigated the methods by which an individual can retain competitive employment after the onset of a significant vision loss. Interviews were conducted with 89 rehabilitation counselors across the US Strategies that contribute to successful job retention were identified as well as best rehabilitation practices in job retention. *$15.00*

*60 pages Paperback*

**8838 Know Your Eye**

American Council of the Blind
Suite 650
2200 Wilson Boulevard
Arlington, VA 22201-3354
202-467-5081
800-424-8666
FAX: 202-467-5085
e-mail: info@acb.org
acb.org

**8839 Large Print Loan Library**

National Association for Visually Handicapped
111 E 59th St
New York, NY 1002-1202
212-821-9200
800-829-0500
FAX: 212-821-9707
e-mail: info@lighthouse.org
lighthouse.org/navh

*Mark G. Ackermann, President / CEO*

A huge large print catalog of all the publications, fiction and non-fiction, cassette tapes, books-on-tape and videos available for the visually impaired from the loan library of the National Association for the Visually Handicapped. LightHouse acquired NAVH.

**8840 Large Print Loan Library Catalog**

National Association for Visually Handicapped
111 E 59th St
New York, NY 1002-1202
212-821-9200
800-829-0500
FAX: 212-821-9707
e-mail: info@lighthouse.org
lighthouse.org/navh

*Mark G. Ackermann, President / CEO*

Listing of over 7,000 commercially published and NAVH large print books available through NAVH on a loan basis. Includes a limited selection of titles available for purchase. LightHouse acquired NAVH.

**8841 Large Print Recipies for a Healthy Life**

123601 Wilshire
Los Angeles, CA 90025
310-826-8280
800-481-EYES
FAX: 310-458-8179

*Judith Caditz PhD, Author*

*$21.95*

*283 pages*

*ISBN 0-962236-82-9*

**8842 Learning to Play**

Blind Children's Center
4120 Marathon St
Los Angeles, CA 90029-3584
323-664-2153
800-222-3567
FAX: 323-665-3828
e-mail: info@blindchildrenscenter.org
www.blindchildrenscenter.org

*Midge Horton, Executive Director*

Presenting play activities to the pre-school child who is visually impaired. *$10.00*

*12 pages*

**8843 Let's Eat**
Blind Children's Center
4120 Marathon St
Los Angeles, CA 90029-3584
323-664-2153
800-222-3567
FAX: 323-665-3828
e-mail: info@blindchildrenscenter.org
www.blindchildrenscenter.org

*Midge Horton, Executive Director*
Feeding a child with visual impairment. *$10.00*
*28 pages*

**8844 Library Resources for the Blind and Physically Handicapped**
Nat'l Lib Svc/Blind And Physically Handicapped
1291 Taylor St NW
Washington, DC 20011
202-707-5100
FAX: 202-707-0712
TTY:202-707-0744
e-mail: nls@loc.gov
www.loc.gov/nls

*Karen Keninger, Director*
NLS administers a national library service that provides braille and recorded books and magazines on free loan to anyone who cannot read standard print because of visual or physical disabilities and who are eligible residents of the United States or American citizens living abroad. The directory describes the cooperating libaries. Online at www.loc.gov/reference/directories.html.
*83 pages*

**8845 Library Services for the Blind**
South Carolina State University
300 College St NE
Orangeburg, SC 29117-1
803-536-7000
FAX: 803-536-8902
e-mail: bagingu@scsu.edu
library.scsu.edu

*Mary L Small Dean, Library/Information Services*
*Andrew Hugine, President*
News and information on developments in library services for readers who are blind and physically disabled.

**8846 Lifestyles of Employed Legally Blind People**
Mississippi State University
P.O.Box 6189
Mississippi State, MS 39762-6189
662-325-2001
FAX: 662-325-8989
TTY:662-325-2694
www.blind.msstate.edu

*Jacqui Bybee, Research and Training Coordinator*
Results from a telephone survey show that visually impaired respondents are involved in a wide variety of activities with little restrictions on their range of activities. Sighted respondents tended to spend more time in child care, obtaining goods and services, attending to self-care activities and engaging in social activities, while visually impaired respondents spent more time in education and passive activities. This report is a study of expenditures and time use. *$ 10.00*
*193 pages Paperback*

**8847 Lion**
Lion's Clubs International
300 W 22nd St
Oak Brook, IL 60523-8806
630-571-5466
FAX: 630-571-8890
TTY:630-571-6533

*Peter Lynch, Executive Director*
Publication for the blind.

**8848 Living with Achromatopsia**
P.O.Box 214
Berkeley, CA 94701-214
510-540-4700
FAX: 510-540-4767
e-mail: futterman@achromat.org
www.achromat.org

*Frances Futterman, Author*
Consists entirely of comments from persons who know firsthand about living with achromatopsia.

**8849 Low Vision Questions and Answers: Definitions, Devices, Services**
American Foundation for the Blind/AFB Press
Suite 1102
2 Penn Plaza
New York, NY 10121
212-502-7600
800-232-5603
FAX: 888-545-8331
e-mail: afbinfo@afb.net
afb.org

*Carl R. Augusto, President and CEO*
What does low vision mean? What do low vision services cost? What diseases cause low vision? Answers to these and other questions are presented in a comprehensive format with accompanying photographs. $50.00/pack of 25.
*21 pages Pamphlet*
*ISBN 0-891281-96-7*

**8850 Low Vision: Reflections of the Past, Issues for the Future**
American Foundation for the Blind/AFB Press
Suite 1102
2 Penn Plaza
New York, NY 10121
212-502-7600
800-232-5463
FAX: 888-545-8331
e-mail: afbinfo@afb.net
www.afb.org

*Carl R. Augusto, President and CEO*
Background papers and a strategies section are used to identify the shifting needs of visually impaired persons and the resources that may be needed to address them. Paperback. *$34.95*
*Paperback*
*ISBN 0-891282-18-1*

**8851 Mainstreaming and the American Dream**
American Foundation for the Blind/AFB Press
Suite 1102
2 Penn Plaza
New York, NY 10121
212-502-7600
800-232-5463
FAX: 888-545-8331
e-mail: afbinfo@afb.net
www.afb.org

*Carl R. Augusto, President and CEO*
Based on in-depth interviews with parents and professionals, this research monograph presents information on the needs and aspirations of parents of blind and visually impaired children. Paperback. *$34.95*
*256 pages Paperback*
*ISBN 0-891281-91-7*

**8852 Mainstreaming the Visually Impaired Child**
NAPVI
P.O.Box 317
Watertown, MA 02471-317
617-972-7441
800-562-6265
FAX: 617-972-7444
e-mail: napvi@perkins.org
www.napvi.org

*Susan LaVenture, Executive Director*

A unique, informative guide for teachers and educational professionals that work with the visually impaired. *$10.00*
*121 pages Paper*

**8853 Making Life More Livable**
American Foundation for the Blind
Suite 1102
2 Penn Plaza
New York, NY 10121
212-502-7600
800-232-5463
FAX: 888-545-8331
e-mail: afbinfo@afb.net
www.afb.org

*Carl R. Augusto, President and CEO*
Shows how simple adaptations in the home and environment can make a big difference in the lives of blind and visually impaired older persons. The suggestions offered are numerous and specific, ranging from how to mark food cans for greater visibility to how to get out of the shower safley. Large print. *$24.95*
*128 pages*
*ISBN 0-891283-87-0*

**8854 Meeting the Needs of People with Vision Loss: Multidisciplinary Perspective**
Resources for Rehabilitation
22 Bonad Rd
Winchester, MA 01890-1302
781-368-9080
FAX: 781-368-9096
e-mail: orders@rfh.org
www.rfr.org

*Susan L Greenblatt, Editor*
Written by rehabilitation professionals, physicians, and a sociologist, this book discusses how to provide appropriate information and how to serve special populations. Chapters on the role of the family, diabetes and vision loss, special needs of children and adolescents, adults with hearing and vision loss. *$29.95*

*ISBN 0-929718-07-0*

**8855 Model Program Operation Manual: Business Enterprise Program Supervisors**
Mississippi State University
P.O.Box 6189
Mississippi State, MS 39762-6189
662-325-2001
FAX: 662-325-8989
TTY:662-325-2694
www.blind.msstate.edu

*Jacqui Bybee, Research and Training Coordinator*
This monograph serves as a Model Program Operation Manual for Business Enterprise Program Supervisors who administer Randolph-Sheppard vending facilities under the Randolph-Sheppard Act. A wide variety of topics are covered including the role of the State Committee of Blind Venders, the role and responsibilities of the Vending Facility Operator, model qualification, for potential Facility Managers, guidelines for location of vending facilities and policies for closing vending facilities. *$20.00*
*199 pages Paperback*

**8856 More Alike Than Different: Blind and Visually Impaired Children**
American Foundation for the Blind/AFB Press
Suite 1102
2 Penn Plaza
New York, NY 10121
212-502-7600
800-232-3044
FAX: 888-545-8331
e-mail: afborders@abdintl.com
www.afb.org

*Carl R. Augusto, President and CEO*
Offers photographs of blind and visually impaired children around the world learning to read and write, travel independently and performing basic living skills. Covers the most recent technological advances and demonstrates the universality of educational needs and goals. Paperback. $100.00/pack of 25.

*ISBN 0-891281-69-0*

**8857 Mothers with Visual Impairments who are Raising Young Children**
American Foundation for the Blind/AFB Press
Suite 1102
2 Penn Plaza
New York, NY 10121
212-502-7600
800-232-3044
FAX: 888-545-8331
e-mail: afbinfo@afb.net
www.afb.org

*Carl R. Augusto, President and CEO*
Available in braille, large print or cassette. *$2.00*
*16 pages*

**8858 Move With Me**
Blind Children's Center
4120 Marathon St
Los Angeles, CA 90029-3584
323-664-2153
800-222-3567
FAX: 323-665-3828
e-mail: info@blindchildrenscenter.org
www.blindchildrenscenter.org

*Midge Horton, Executive Director*
*Nancy Chernus-Mansfield MA, Co-Author*
A parent's guide to movement development for babies who are visually impaired. *$10.00*
*12 pages*

**8859 National Eye Institute**
National Institute of Health
2020 Vision Pl
Bethesda, MD 20892-1
301-496-5248
FAX: 301-402-1065
e-mail: 2020@nei.nih.gov
www.nei.nih.gov

To conduct and support research for blinding eye diseases, visual disorders, mechanisms of visual function, and the preservation of sight.

**8860 National Library Services for the Blind& Physically Handicapped**
Library of Congress
1291 Taylor St NW
Washington, DC 20011
202-707-5100
FAX: 202-707-0712
TTY:202-707-0744
e-mail: nls@loc.gov
www.loc.gov/nls

*Karen Keninger, Director*
NLS is responsible for the selection, copyright clearance, and procurement of reading materials for blind and physically handicapped individuals. Distribution of the materials and relevant biblographic information either directly or through cooperating state and local network libraries. Design, development, and procurement of sound reproduction equipment and its distribution either directly or through cooperating agencies.

**8861 Orientation and Mobility Primer for Families and Young Children**
American Foundation for the Blind/AFB Press
Suite 1102
2 Penn Plaza
New York, NY 10121
212-502-7600
800-232-5463
FAX: 888-545-8331
e-mail: afbinfo@afb.net
www.afb.org

*Carl R. Augusto, President and CEO*

Practical information for helping a child learn about his or her environment right from the start. Covers sensory training, concept development and orientation skills. Paperback. *$14.95*
*48 pages*
*ISBN 0-891281-57-6*

**8862 Out of the Corner of My Eye: Living with Vision Loss in Later Life**
American Foundation for the Blind/AFB Press
Suite 1102
2 Penn Plaza
New York, NY 10121
212-502-7600
800-232-5463
FAX: 888-545-8331
e-mail: afbinfo@fb.net
www.afb.org

*Carl R. Augusto, President and CEO*
A personal account of students' vision loss and subsequent adjustment that is full of practical advice and cheerful encouragement, told by an 87 year old retired college teacher who has maintained her independence and zest for life. Available in paperback or on audio cassette. *$23.95*
*120 pages*
*ISBN 0-891281-82-1*

**8863 Out of the Corner of My Eye: Living with Macular Degeneration**
American Foundation for the Blind/AFB Press
Suite 1102
2 Penn Plaza
New York, NY 10121
212-502-7600
800-232-5463
FAX: 888-545-8331
e-mail: afbinfo@afb.net
www.afb.org

*Carl R. Augusto, President and CEO*
A personal account of students' vision loss and subsequent adjustment that is full of practical advice and cheerful encouragement, told by an 87 year old retired college teacher who has maintained her independence and zest for life. *$29.95*
*168 pages Paperback*
*ISBN 0-891238-31-2*

**8864 Pain Erasure: the Bonnie Prudden Way**
Ballantine Books
1540 Broadway
New York, NY 10036-4039
212-751-2600
FAX: 212-572-4949

*Bonnie Prudden, Author*
Revolutionary breakthrough in pain relief involves trigger points-tender areas where muscles have been damaged from falls, childhood ailments, poor posture, and the stresses of daily life.

**8865 Patient's Guide to Visual Aids and Illumination**
National Association for Visually Handicapped
111 E 59th St
New York, NY 1002-1202
212-821-9200
800-829-0500
FAX: 212-821-9707
e-mail: info@lighthouse.org
lighthouse.org/navh

*Mark G. Ackermann, President / CEO*
A reference booklet offering information on aids for the visually impaired. LightHouse acquired NAVH. *$.75*

**8866 Pediatric Visual Diagnosis Fact Sheets**
Blind Children's Center
4120 Marathon St
Los Angeles, CA 90029-3584
323-664-2153
800-222-3567
FAX: 323-665-3828
e-mail: info@blindchildrenscenter.org
blindchildrenscenter.org

*Midge Horton, Executive Director*
Collection of fact sheets addressing commonly encountered eye conditions, diagnostic tests and materials. *$10.00*
*10 pages*

**8867 Perkins Activity and Resource Guide: A Handbook for Teachers**
Perkins School for the Blind
175 North Beacon St
Watertown, MA 02472-2751
617-972-7240
FAX: 617-972-7363
e-mail: info@perkins.org
www.perkins.org

*Kim Charlson, Director*
*Mary Jane Clark, Co-Author*
*Charlotte Cushman, Co-Author*
*Susan Edwards, Co-Author*
This is a comprehensive, two volume guide with over 1,000 pages of activities, resources and instructional strategies for teachers and parents of students with visual and multiple disabilities. *$80.00*

**8868 Personal Reader Update**
Personal Reader Department
9 Centennial Dr
Peabody, MA 01960-7906
978-977-2000
800-343-0311
FAX: 978-977-2409

Offers information on new services, assistive devices and technology for the blind.

**8869 Preschool Learning Activities for the Visually Impaired Child**
NAPVI
P.O.Box 317
Watertown, MA 02471-317
617-972-7441
800-562-6265
FAX: 617-972-7444
e-mail: napvi@perkins.org
www.napvi.org

*Susan LaVenture, Executive Director*
This guide for parents offers games and activities to keep visually impaired children active during the preschool years. *$8.00*
*91 pages Paperback*

**8870 Reaching, Crawling, Walking....Let's Get Moving**
Blind Children's Center
4120 Marathon St
Los Angeles, CA 90029-3584
323-664-2153
800-222-3567
FAX: 323-665-3828
e-mail: info@blindchildrenscenter.org
www.blindchildrenscenter.org

*Midge Horton, Executive Director*
*Sharon O'Mara Maida M.ED, Co-Author*
Orientation and mobility for preschool children who are visually imapired. *$10.00*
*24 pages*

**8871 Reading Is for Everyone**
Nat'l Lib Svc/Blind And Physically Handicapped
1291 Taylor St NW
Washington, DC 20011
202-707-5100
FAX: 202-707-0712
TTY:202-707-0744
e-mail: nls@loc.gov
www.loc.gov/nls

*Karen Keninger, Director*

**8872 Reading with Low Vision**
Nat'l Lib Svc/Blind And Physically Handicapped
1291 Taylor St NW
Washington, DC 20011
202-707-5100
FAX: 202-707-0712
TTY:202-707-0744
e-mail: nls@loc.gov
www.loc.gov/nls

*Karen Keninger, Director*

**8873 Recording for the Blind & Dyslexic**
20 Roszel Rd
Princeton, NJ 08540-6294
800-221-4792
FAX: 609-987-8116
e-mail: Custserv@LearningAlly.org
www.learningally.org/

*Andrew Friedman, President & CEO*
Provides recorded and computerized textbooks, library services and other educational resources to people who cannot effectively read standard print because of visual impairment, dyslexia or other physical disability. RFB&D is now Learning Ally.

**8874 Reference and Information Services From NLS**
Nat'l Lib Svc/Blind And Physically Handicapped
1291 Taylor St NW
Washington, DC 20011
202-707-5100
FAX: 202-707-0712
TTY:202-707-0744
e-mail: nls@loc.gov
www.loc.gov/nls

*Karen Keninger, Director*

**8875 Resource List for Persons with Low Vision**
American Council of the Blind
Suite 650
2200 Wilson Boulevard
Arlington, VA 22201-3354
202-467-5081
800-424-8666
FAX: 202-467-5085
e-mail: info@acb.org
acb.org

**8876 Rose-Colored Glasses**
Human Sciences Press
233 Spring St
New York, NY 10013-1522
212-229-2859
800-221-9369
FAX: 212-463-0742
After a vacation, Deborah was excited about going back to school. Renewing old friendships, she met a classmate who seemed stuck up. Deborah learned that Melanie was in a recent accident resulting in impaired vision. She did not wish to wear her glasses, which were rose-colored and very funny looking. With Deborah's help, Miss Davis, the teacher showed a blurry film and then had Melanie speak about her impaired vision. When Melanie began to participate in the class they accepted her. *$16.95*
*30 pages Hardcover*
*ISBN 0-87705 -08-8*

**8877 Say it with Sign**
Harris Communications
15155 Technology Dr
Eden Prairie, MN 55344-2273
800-825-6758
FAX: 952-906-1099
e-mail: info@harriscomm.com
harriscomm.com

*Robert Harris, Owner*
Contains both the serious and fun side of signing and provides the basic signs that might be needed in an emergency situation.
*$299.50*
*10-DVD set*

**8878 See A Bone**
Facts on File
Fl 17
132 W 31st St
New York, NY 10001-3406
212-967-8800
800-322-8755
FAX: 212-967-9196
e-mail: jchambers@factsonfile.com
northernleasing.com

*Mark Donnell, President*
*$65.00*
*352 pages*
*ISBN 0-816042-80-2*

**8879 See What I Feel**
Britannica Film Company
345 4th St
San Francisco, CA 94107-1206
415-928-8466
FAX: 415-928-5027

*Dave Bekowich, Owner*
A blind child tells her friends about her trip to the zoo. Each experience was explained as a blind child would experience it. A teacher's guide comes with this video.
*Film*

**8880 Selecting a Program**
Blind Children's Center
4120 Marathon St
Los Angeles, CA 90029-3584
323-664-2153
800-222-3567
FAX: 323-665-3828
e-mail: info@blindchildrenscenter.org
www.blindchildrenscenter.org

*Midge Horton, Executive Director*
*Mary Ellen McCann MA, Co-Author*
A guide for parents of infants and preschoolers with visual impairments. *$10.00*
*28 pages*

**8881 Show Me How: A Manual for Parents of Preschool Blind Children**
American Foundation for the Blind/AFB Press
Suite 1102
2 Penn Plaza
New York, NY 10121
212-502-7600
800-232-3044
FAX: 888-545-8331
e-mail: afborders@abdintl.com
www.afb.org

*Carl R. Augusto, President and CEO*
A practical guide for parents, teachers and others who help preschool children attain age-related goals. Covers issues on playing precautions, appropriate toys and facilitating relationships with playmates. Paperback. *$12.95*
*56 pages*
*ISBN 0-891281-13-4*

**8882 Sign of the Times**
Fanlight Productions
21st Floor
32 Court Street
Brooklyn, NY 11201
718-488-8900
800-876-1710
FAX: 718-488-8642
e-mail: info@fanlight.com
www.fanlight.com

*Ben Achtenberg, Owner*
Profiles a public school in the heart of Los Angeles - an American microcosm where over 300 languages are spoken, and where cultures and races collide. Fairfax High, publicized as the site of gang activity and murder, has long been a focus for bad press. But something very right is going on in this school. A Sign of the Times offers a positive example of how the American dream and American education are still alive

**8883 Special Technologies Alternative Resources**
210 McMorran Blvd
Port Huron, MI 48060-4014
810-987-7323
877-987-7323
e-mail: star@sccl.lib.mi.us
www.sccl.lib.mi.us/star.html

*Stan Arnetti, Director*
Addresses the needs of a very unique diverse group of people by offering a full range of library services for people who cannot read standard print. Provides reading material in specialized formats that permit individuals with disabilities to have access to the written word, delivering to customer's mailboxes free of charge. Talking Book Machines, recorded books and magazines, descriptive videos, large print editions and braille books and magazines.

**8884 Standing on My Own Two Feet**
Blind Children's Center
4120 Marathon St
Los Angeles, CA 90029-3584
323-664-2153
800-222-3567
FAX: 323-665-3828
e-mail: info@blindchildrenscenter.org
www.blindchildrenscenter.org

*Midge Horton, Executive Director*
A guide to constructing mobility devices for children who are visually impaired. *$10.00*
*38 pages*

**8885 Starting Points**
Blind Children's Center
4120 Marathon St
Los Angeles, CA 90029-3584
323-664-2153
800-222-3567
FAX: 323-665-3828
e-mail: info@blindchildrenscenter.org
www.blindchildrenscenter.org

*Midge Horton, Executive Director*
*Jamie Dote-Kwan PhD, Co-Author*
Basic information for the clasroom teacher of 3 to 8 year olds whose multiple disabilities include visual impairment. *$35.00*
*157 pages*
*ISBN 0-891280-61-8*

**8886 Step-By-Step Guide to Personal Management for Blind Persons**
American Foundation for the Blind/AFB Press
Suite 1102
2 Penn Plaza
New York, NY 10121
212-502-7600
800-232-3044
FAX: 888-545-8331
e-mail: afborders@abdintl.com
www.afb.org

*Carl R. Augusto, President and CEO*
A manual of techniques in the areas of hygiene, grooming, clothing, shopping and child care. *$19.95*
*136 pages Spiralbound*
*ISBN 0-891280-61-8*

**8887 Student Teaching Guide for Blind and Visually Impaired College Students**
American Foundation for the Blind/AFB Press
Suite 1102
2 Penn Plaza
New York, NY 10121
212-502-7600
800-232-3044
FAX: 888-545-8331
e-mail: afborders@abdintl.com
www.afb.org

*Carl R. Augusto, President and CEO*
A comprehensive resource designed to enable the student to enter the classroom of a university or college with confidence. Large print. *$14.95*
*52 pages*
*ISBN 0-891281-42-8*

**8888 Survey of Direct Labor Workers Who Are Blind & Employed by NIB**
Mississippi State University
P.O.Box 6189
Mississippi State, MS 39762-6189
662-325-2001
FAX: 662-325-8989
TTY:662-325-2694
www.blind.msstate.edu

*Jacqui Bybee, Research and Training Coordinator*
This report is a follow-up to surveys by National Industries for the Blind in 1983 and 1987 and summarizes the results of a national survey of approximately 500 legally blind direct labor workers. *$10.00*
*101 pages Paperback*

**8889 Talk to Me**
Blind Children's Center
4120 Marathon St
Los Angeles, CA 90029-3584
323-664-2153
800-222-3567
FAX: 323-665-3828
e-mail: info@blindchildrenscenter.org
www.blindchildrenscenter.org

*Midge Horton, Executive Director*
*Linda Kekelis MA, Co-Author*
A language guide for parents of children who are visually impaired. *$10.00*
*11 pages*

**8890 Talk to Me II**
Blind Children's Center
4120 Marathon St
Los Angeles, CA 90029-3584
323-664-2153
800-222-3567
FAX: 323-665-3828
e-mail: info@blindchildrenscenter.org
www.blindchildrenscenter.org

*Midge Horton, Executive Director*
*Dori Hayashi MA, Co-Author*
*Linda Kekelis MA, Co-Author*
a sequel to Talk to Me *$10.00*
*15 pages*

**8891 Talking Books & Reading Disabilities**
Nat'l Lib Svc/Blind And Physically Handicapped
1291 Taylor St NW
Washington, DC 20011
202-707-5100
FAX: 202-707-0712
TTY:202-707-0744
e-mail: nls@loc.gov
www.loc.gov/nls

*Karen Keninger, Director*

**8892 Talking Books for People with Physical Disabilities**
Nat'l Lib Svc/Blind And Physically Handicapped
1291 Taylor St NW
Washington, DC 20011
202-707-5100
FAX: 202-707-0712
TTY:202-707-0744
e-mail: nls@loc.gov
www.loc.gov/nls

*Karen Keninger, Director*

**8893 Teaching Orientation and Mobility in the Schools: An Instructor's Companion**
American Foundation for the Blind
Suite 1102
2 Penn Plaza
New York, NY 10121
212-502-7600
800-232-5463
FAX: 888-545-8331
e-mail: afbinfo@afb.net
www.afb.org

*Carl R. Augusto, President and CEO*

This book, with its useful forms, checklists, and tips, will help O&M instructors and teachers of visually impaired students master the arts of planning schedules, organizing equipment and work routines, working with school personnel and educational team members, and effectively providing instruction to children with diverse needs. *$ 45.95*
*176 pages*
*ISBN 0-891283-91-1*

**8894 Teaching Visually Impaired Children**
Charles C. Thomas
2600 S 1st St
Springfield, IL 62704-4730
217-789-8980
800-258-8980
FAX: 217-789-9130
e-mail: books@ccthomas.com
www.ccthomas.com

*Michael P. Thomas, President*

A comprehensive resource for the classroom teacher who is working with a visually impaired child for the first time, as well as a systematic overview of education for the specialist in visual disabilities. It approaches instructional challenges with clear explanations and practical suggestions, and it addresses common concerns of teachers in a reassuring and positive manner. Also available in cloth. *$49.95*
*352 pages Paper 2004*
*ISBN 0-398074-77-7*

**8895 Textbook Catalog**
National Braille Association
Bldg. 1, Suite 202
95 Allens Creek Road
Rochester, NY 14618-3252
585-427-8260
FAX: 585-427-0263
e-mail: nbaoffice@nationalbraille.org
www.nationalbraille.org

*Dorothy Worthington, President*
*David Shaffer, Executive Director*

Lists hundreds of scholarly, college and professional textbooks offered in large print, braille or on cassette for visually impaired readers.
*80 pages*

**8896 Three Rivers News**
Carnegie Library of Pitts. Library for the Blind
4724 Baum Blvd
Pittsburgh, PA 15213-1321
412-687-2440
800-242-0586
FAX: 412-687-2442
e-mail: clbph@clpgh.org
www.clpgh.org

*Kathleen Kappel, Executive Director*

Loans recorded books/magazines and playback equipment, large print books and described videos to western PA residents unable to use standard printed materials due to a visual, physical, or physically-based reading disability.
*12 pages Quarterly*

**8897 To Love this Life: Quotations by Helen Keller**
American Foundation for the Blind/AFB Press
Suite 1102
2 Penn Plaza
New York, NY 10121
212-502-7600
800-232-5463
FAX: 888-545-8331
e-mail: afbinfo@afb.org
www.afb.org

*Carl R. Augusto, President and CEO*

Inspirational work that offers the penetrating observations of Helen Keller, the beloved deaf-blind champion of the rights of people with disabilities. Also available on cassette at $21.95 (ISBN# 0-89128-348-X) *$21.95*
*144 pages Hardcover*
*ISBN 0-891283-47-1*

**8898 Touch the Baby: Blind & Visually Impaired Children As Patients**
American Foundation for the Blind/AFB Press
Suite 1102
2 Penn Plaza
New York, NY 10121
212-502-7600
800-232-3044
FAX: 888-545-8331
e-mail: afborders@abdintl.com
www.afb.org

*Carl R. Augusto, President and CEO*

A how-to manual for health care professionals working in hospitals, clinics and doctors' offices. Teaches the special communication and touch-related techniques needed to prevent blind and visually impaired patients from withdrawing from the healthcare workers and the outside world. $25.00/pack of 25.
*13 pages*
*ISBN 0-891281-97-5*

**8899 Transition Activity Calendar for Students with Visual Impairments**
Mississippi State University
P.O.Box 6189
Mississippi State, MS 39762-6189
662-325-2001
FAX: 662-325-8989
TTY:662-325-2694
www.blind.msstate.edu

*Jacqui Bybee, Research and Training Coordinator*

The Transition Activity Calendar guides the student with a visual disability through the maze of college preparation. Beginning in junior high school, clearly written steps are listed for each grade level. Students planning to enter college after high school graduation can check-off their accomplishments each step of the way. The calendar helps students focus on their goals while providing reminders of tasks yet to be completed. It can be used in a self-directed manner or in a group format. *$4.25*
*16 pages Paperback*

**8900 Transition to College for Students with Visual Impairments: Report**

Mississippi State University
P.O.Box 6189
Mississippi State, MS 39762-6189 662-325-2001
FAX: 662-325-8989
TTY:662-325-2694
www.blind.msstate.edu

*Jacqui Bybee, Research and Training Coordinator*

A report offering results from telephone interviews of college students with visual impairments and mail surveys of college officials which examines the transition experience of successful college students. General domains in the study include demographics, educational history, computers, specialized and adaptive equipment, resources, college preparation, problems adjusting to college and O&M skills. A literature review covers preparing for college, task timelines,and classroom, labs and tests. *$20.00*

*151 pages Paperback*

**8901 Unseen Minority: A Social History of Blindness in the United States**

American Foundation for the Blind/AFB Press
Suite 1102
2 Penn Plaza
New York, NY 10121 212-502-7600
800-232-3044
FAX: 888-545-8331
e-mail: abfinfo@abf.org
www.afb.org

*Carl R. Augusto, President and CEO*

A lively narrative, with anecdotes, that recounts how the blind overcame discrimination to gain full participation in the social, educational, economic and legislative spheres. Hardcover. *$59.95*

*573 pages Paperback*

*ISBN 0-891288-96-1*

**8902 Vision Enhancement**

UN Printing
# 122
1790 E 54th St
Indianapolis, IN 46220-3454 317-254-1332
800-431-1739
FAX: 317-251-6588
e-mail: info@visionenhancement.org
www.visionww.org

*Patricia L Price, Managing Editor*

Designed to encourage and support individuals with vision loss, family members, and caregivers. *$25.00*

*72-78 pages Quarterly*

**8903 Visual Impairment: An Overview**

American Foundation for the Blind/AFB Press
Suite 1102
2 Penn Plaza
New York, NY 10121 212-502-7600
800-232-5463
FAX: 888-545-8331
e-mail: afbinfo@afb.net
www.afb.org

*Carl R. Augusto, President and CEO*

An overall look at the most common forms of vision loss and their impact on the individual. Includes drawings as well as photographs that stimulate how people with vision loss see. Paperback. *$19.95*

*56 pages*

*ISBN 0-891281-74-0*

**8904 Visual Impairments And Learning**

Sage Publications
2455 Teller Road
Thousand Oaks, CA 91320 800-818-7243
FAX: 800-583-2665
e-mail: info@sagepub.com
www.sagepub.com

*Sara Miller McCune, Founder, Publisher, Chairperson*
*Blaise R Simqu, President & CEO*

The major focus of this new, third edition is to present a new way of thinking about individuals with visual impairment so that they are viewed as participating members of a seeing world despite their reduced visual functioning. *$40.00*

*213 pages*

*ISBN 0-890798-68-3*

**8905 Walking Alone and Marching Together**

National Federation of the Blind
200 East Wells St
Baltimore, MD 21230-4914 410-659-9314
FAX: 410-685-5653
e-mail: nfb@iamdigex.net
www.nfb.org

*Floyd Matson, Author*

The history of the organized blind movement, this book spans more than 50 years of civil rights, social issues, attitudes and experiences of the blind. Published in 1990, it has been read by thousands of blind and sighted persons and is used in colleges, libraries and programs across the country as an important tool in understanding blindness and it's impact on both personal lives and the society at large. Braille $130, 2 track or 4 track cassette $40, Print $33.00. Contact Materials Center.

**8906 What Do You Do When You See a Blind Person- and What Don't You Do?**

American Foundation for the Blind/AFB Press
Suite 1102
2 Penn Plaza
New York, NY 10121 212-502-7600
800-232-5463
FAX: 888-545-8331
e-mail: afbinfo@afb.net
afb.org

*Carl R. Augusto, President and CEO*

Examples of real-life situations that teach sighted persons how to interact effectively with blind persons. Topics covered include how to help someone across the street, how not to distract a guide dog and how to take leave of a blind person. *$25.00*

*8 pages*

*ISBN 0-891281-95-5*

**8907 What Museum Guides Need to Know: Access for the Blind and Visually Impaired**

American Foundation for the Blind/AFB Press
Suite 1102
2 Penn Plaza
New York, NY 10121 212-502-7600
800-232-3044
FAX: 888-545-8331
e-mail: afborders@abdintl.com
www.afb.org

*Carl R. Augusto, President and CEO*

Explains how blind and visually impaired museum-goers experience art and offers pointers on greeting people, asking if help is needed and teaching about a specific work of art. Contains information on access laws, resources, training guides and guidelines for preparing large print, cassette and braille materials. *$14.95*

*64 pages Paperback*

*ISBN 0-891281-58-4*

**8908 Work Sight**
Lighthouse International
111 E 59th St
New York, NY 10022-1202
212-821-9200
800-829-0500
FAX: 212-821-9706
e-mail: info@lighthouse.org
www.lighthouse.org

*Mark G. Ackermann, President / CEO*
Intended for employers and employees who have concerns about vision loss and job performance. *$25.00*

**8909 World Through Their Eyes**
Lighthouse International
111 E 59th St
New York, NY 10022-1202
212-821-9200
800-829-0500
FAX: 212-821-9706
e-mail: info@lighthouse.org
www.lighthouse.org

*Mark G. Ackermann, President / CEO*
Intended to help nursing home staff understand how residents with impaired vision perceive the world. Concrete suggestions help staff provide better care to visually impaired residents. *$25.00*

**8910 You Seem Like a Regular Kid to Me**
American Foundation for the Blind/AFB Press
Suite 1102
2 Penn Plaza
New York, NY 10121
212-502-7600
800-232-3044
FAX: 888-545-8331
e-mail: afborders@abdintl.com
www.afb.org

*Carl R. Augusto, President and CEO*
An interview with Jane, a blind child, tells other children what it's like to be blind. Jane explains how she gets around, takes care of herself, does her school work, spends her leisure time and even pays for things when she can't see money.
*16 pages*
*ISBN 0-891289-21-6*

## Print: Journals

**8911 Journal of Visual Impairment and Blindness**
Sheridan Press,
450 Fame Ave
Hanover, PA 17331-1585
717-632-3535
800-352-2210
FAX: 717-633-8929
e-mail: pubsvc@tsp.sheridan.com
www.sheridanreprints.com

*Sharon Shively, Editor*
Published in braille, regular print and on ASC II disk and cassette, this journal contains a wide variety of subjects including rehabilitation, psychology, education, legislation, medicine, technology, employment, sensory aids and childhood development as they relate to visual impairments. $130 annual individual subscription, $180 annual institutional subscription.
*64 pages Monthly*
*ISSN 0145-48 x*

## Print: Magazines

**8912 Blind Educator**
National Organization of Blind Educators
1800 Johnson St
Baltimore, MD 21230-4914
410-659-9314
FAX: 410-685-5653
e-mail: nfb@iamdigex.net
www.nfb.org

*Marc Mauer, President*
Magazine specifically for blind educators.

**8913 Braille Forum**
American Council of the Blind
Suite 650
2200 Wilson Boulevard
Arlington, VA 22201-3354
202-467-5081
800-424-8666
FAX: 202-467-5085
e-mail: info@acb.org
www.acb.org

Offered in print, braille, cassette, IBM computer disk and e-mail. $25 per format per year for companies and non-US residents.
*48 pages Magazine*

**8914 Braille Monitor**
Deaf-Blind Division of the Ntn'l Fed of the Blind
200 East Wells St
Baltimore, MD 21230-4914
410-659-9314
FAX: 410-685-5653
nfb.org

*Marc Maurer, CEO*
Covers the events and activities of the NFB and addresses the many issues and concerns of the blind. Offers a positive philosophy about blindness to both blind readers and the public at large.

**8915 Dialogue Magazine**
Blindskills Inc
P.O.Box 5181
Salem, OR 97304-181
503-581-4224
800-860-4224
FAX: 503-581-0178
e-mail: info@blindskills.com
www.blindskills.com

*Karen Lynn Thomas, Editor*
*B.T. Kimbrough, Executive Director*
Publishes quarterly magazine in braille, large-type, cassette, e-mail and disk of news items, technology and articles of special interest to visually impaired youth and adults. $40.00 for not blind/legally blind. *$28.00*
*Quarterly*

**8916 Future Reflections**
Deaf-Blind Division of the Ntn'l Fed of the Blind
200 East Wells Street
Baltimore, MD 21230-4914
410-659-9314
FAX: 410-685-5653
nfb.org

*Marc Maurer, President*
A magazine for parents and teachers of blind children.

**8917 Guide Magazine**
The Seeing Eye
P.O.Box 375
10 Washington Valley Rd.
Morristown, NJ 7963-375
973-539-4425
FAX: 973-539-0922
e-mail: info@seeingeye.org
seeingeye.org

*James A. Kutsch, Jr., Ph.D., President & CEO*

The Guide offers stories of inspiration from our graduates and news of the latest program developments.

**8918 JBI Voice**
Jewish Braille Institute of America
110 E 30th St
New York, NY 10016 212-889-2525
800-433-1531
FAX: 212-689-3692
e-mail: admin@jbilibrary.org
www.jbilibrary.org

*Israel A Taub, Vice President and CFO*
*Dr. Ellen Isler, President and CEO*
Monthly recorded magazine emphasizing Jewish current events and culture.

**8919 Jewish Braille Review**
Jewish Braille Institute of America
110 E 30th St
New York, NY 10016 212-889-2525
800-433-1531
FAX: 212-689-3692
e-mail: admin@jbilibrary.org
www.jbilibrary.org

*Israel A Taub, Vice President and CFO*
*Dr. Ellen Isler, President and CEO*
The JBI seeks the integration of Jews who are blind, visually impaired and reading disabled into the Jewish community and society in general. More than 20,000 men, women and children in 50 countries receive a broad variety of JBI services.

**8920 Merchant Messenger**
National Association of Blind Merchants
Ste D
1223 Lake Plaza Dr
Colorado Springs, CO 80906-3580 719-527-0488
FAX: 719-527-0129
e-mail: markharris1222@sbcglobal.net
www.blindmerchants.org

*Kevin Worley, President*

**8921 Musical Mainstream**
Nat'l Lib Svc/Blind And Physically Handicapped
1291 Taylor St NW
Washington, DC 20011 202-707-5100
FAX: 202-707-0712
TTY:202-707-0744
e-mail: nlsm@loc.gov
www.loc.gov/nls

*Karen Keninger, Director*
Articles selected from print music magazines.
*Quarterly*

**8922 Opportunity**
National Industries for the Blind
1310 Braddock Pl
Alexandria, VA 22314-1691 703-998-0770
FAX: 703-998-8268
www.nib.org

*James M Kesteloot, Director*
Offers information and articles on the newest technology, equipment, services and programs for blind and visually impaired persons.
*Quarterly*

**8923 Providing Services for People with Vision Loss: Multidisciplinary Perspective**
Resources for Rehabilitation
22 Bonad Rd
Winchester, MA 01890-1302 781-368-9080
FAX: 781-368-9096
e-mail: orders@rfr.org
www.rfr.org

*Susan L Greenblatt, Editor*
A collection of articles by ophthalmologists and rehabilitation professionals, including chapters on operating a low vision service, starting self-help programs, mental health services, aids and techniques that help people with vision loss. *$19.95*
*136 pages*
*ISBN 0-929718-02-0*

## Print: Newsletters

**8924 AFB News**
American Foundation for the Blind/AFB Press
Suite 1102
2 Penn Plaza
New York, NY 10121 212-502-7600
800-232-3044
FAX: 888-545-8331
e-mail: afborders@abdintl.com
www.afb.org

*Carl R. Augusto, President and CEO*
National newsletter for general readership about blindness and visual impairments featuring people, programs, services and activities.
*12 pages Quarterly*

**8925 ASB Visions Newsletter**
Associated Services for the Blind
919 Walnut St
Philadelphia, PA 19107-5237 215-627-0600
FAX: 215-922-0692
e-mail: asbinfo@asb.org
www.asb.org

*Dolores Ferrara-Godzieba, Director*
Newsletter associated services for the blind and visually impaired.

**8926 Adaptive Services Division**
District of Columbia Public Library
901G St NW, Rm 215
Washington, DC 20001-4531 202-727-2142
FAX: 202-727-0322
TTY:202-559-5368
e-mail: lbph.dcpl@dc.gov
www.dclibrary.org

*Venetia Demson, Chief, Adaptive Services*
DC Regional Library for the blind, deaf and physically handicapped. Provides adaptive technology and training programs.
*8 pages Quarterly*

**8927 Alumni News**
Guide Dogs for the Blind
P.O.Box 151200
San Rafael, CA 94915-1200 415-499-4000
800-295-4050
FAX: 415-499-4035
guidedogs.com

*Paul A. Lopez, President and CEO*
Restricted to graduates only.

8928 **Annual Report/Newsletter**
National Accreditation Council for Agencies/Blind
Rm 1004
15 E 40th St
New York, NY 10016-401 212-683-5068
FAX: 212-683-4475

*Ruth Westman, Executive Director*
Provides standards and a program of accreditation for schools and organizations which serve children and adults who are blind or vision impaired.

8929 **Association for Macular Diseases Newsletter**
8th Fl
210 E 64th St
New York, NY 10065-7471 212-605-3719
FAX: 212-605-3795
e-mail: association@retinal-research.org
macula.org

*Walter Ross, Editor-In-Chief*
Not-for-profit organization promotes education and research in this scarcely explored field. Acts as a nationwide support group for individuals and their families endeavoring to adjust to the restrictions and changes brought about by macular disease. Offers hotline, educational materials, quarterly newsletter, support groups, referrals and seminars for persons and families affected by macular disease.

8930 **Awareness**
NAPVI
P.O.Box 317
Watertown, MA 02471-317 617-972-7441
800-562-6265
FAX: 617-972-7444
e-mail: napvi@perkins.org
www.napvi.org

*Susan LaVenture, Executive Director*
Newsletter offering regional news, sports and activities, conferences, camps, legislative updates, book reviews, audio reviews, professional question and answer column and more for the visually impaired and their families.
*Quarterly*

8931 **BTBL News**
Braille and Talking Book Library
P.O. Box 942837
Sacramento, CA 94237-1 916-634-0640
800-952-5666
FAX: 916-654-1119
e-mail: btbl@library.ca.gov
www.btbl.ca.gov

*Janet Coles, Editor*
BTBL News, the quarterly newsletter of the California Braille and Talking Book Library, features articles on topics of interest to library customers, including information about new services, existing services, events, staff and more.

8932 **Canes and Trails**
Guide Dogs for the Blind
P.O.Box 151200
San Rafael, CA 94915-1200 415-499-4000
800-295-4050
FAX: 415-499-4035
guidedogs.com

*Paul A. Lopez, President and CEO*
A quarterly newsletter for orientation and mobility specialists, rehabilitation professionals, teachers, and service providers in the field of blindness and visual impairment.

8933 **Community Connection**
Guide Dogs for the Blind
P.O.Box 151200
San Rafael, CA 94915-1200 415-499-4000
800-295-4050
FAX: 415-499-4035
guidedogs.com

*Paul A. Lopez, President and CEO*
A newsletter produced for our volunteers and other friends of Guide Dogs.

8934 **DVH Quarterly**
University of Arkansas at Little Rock
2801 S University Ave
Little Rock, AR 72204-1000 501-569-3000

*Bob Brasher, Editor*
*Mary Boaz, Manager*
Offers information on upcoming events, conferences and workshops on and for visual disabilities. Book reviews, information on the newest resources and technology, educational programs, want ads and more.
*Quarterly*

8935 **Deaf-Blind Perspective**
National Consortium on Deaf-Blindness
345 Monmouth Ave
Monmouth, OR 97361 503-838-8391
800-438-9376
FAX: 503-838-8150
TTY: 800-854-7013
e-mail: dbp@wou.edu
www.tr.wou.edu

*John Reiman PhD, Editor*
*Peggy Malloy, Managing Editor*
A free publication with articles, essays, and announcements about topics related to people who are deaf-blind. Published two times a year (Spring and Fall) by the Teaching Research Institute of Western Oregon University, its purpose is to provide information and serve as a forum for discussion and sharing ideas.

8936 **Fidelco**
Fidelco Guide Dog Foundation
103 Vision Way
Bloomfield, CT 06002-1424 860-243-5200
FAX: 860-243-7215
e-mail: info@fidelco.org
fidelco.org

*Nancy R Levin, VP*
A newsletter published by Fidelco Guide Dog Foundation.

8937 **Focus**
Visually Impaired Center
1422 W Court St
Flint, MI 48503-5008 810-767-4014
FAX: 810-767-0020
www.vcflint.org

*Charles Tommasulo, Executive Director*
Newsletter offering information for the visually impaired person in the forms of legislative and law updates, ADA information, support groups, hotlines, and articles on the newest technology in the field.
*Quarterly*

**8938 Gleams Newsletter**
Glaucoma Research Foundation
Ste 600
251 Post St
San Francisco, CA 94108-5017
415-986-3162
800-826-6693
FAX: 415-986-3763
e-mail: info@glaucoma.org
auorthodontics.com

*Tom Brunner, CEO*

Offers updated medical & research information on glaucoma. Included are glaucoma treatmant and coping tips, legsilative information, professional articles and book reviews.
*6 pages Quarterly*

**8939 Guide Dog News**
Guide Dogs for the Blind
P.O.Box 151200
San Rafael, CA 94915-1200
415-499-4000
800-295-4050
FAX: 415-499-4035
guidedogs.com

*Paul A. Lopez, President and CEO*

Read about changes to our teaching techniques, our new Adult Learning Program, vet tips, and find news about our graduates.

**8940 Guideway**
Guide Dog Foundation for the Blind
371 E Main St
Smithtown, NY 11787-2906
415-499-4000
800-295-4050
FAX: 415-499-4035
www.guidedog.org

*Paul A. Lopez, President and CEO*

Offers updates and information on the foundation's activities and guide dog programs. In print form but is also available on cassette.
*Monthly*

**8941 Guild Briefs**
Catholic Guild for The Blind
Suite 1010
65 E. Wacker Place
Chicago, IL 60601
312-236-8569
FAX: 312-236-8128
e-mail: info@guildfortheblind.org
www.guildfortheblind.org

*David Tabak, Executive Director*

Monthly publication for individuals who are blind or visually impaired. It contains articles on topics such as service programs, scholarships, education, seniors, research, and government.
*12 pages monthly*

**8942 IAAIS Report**
Int'l Association of Audio Information Services
3920 Willshire Dr
Lawrence, KS 66049-3673
412-434-6023
800-280-5325
e-mail: aiblink@ak.net
www.iaais.org

*Stuart Holland, Editor*

Newsletter for persons interested in radio reading services. *$7.00*
*Quarterly*

**8943 Insight**
United States Association of Blind Athletes
1 Olympic Plaza
Colorado Springs, CO 80909
719-630-0422
FAX: 719-630-0616
e-mail: media@usaba.org
www.usaba.org

*Mark A. Lucas, MS, Executive Director*

Covers news, announcements and activities of the association.
*20 pages Quarterly*

**8944 LampLighter**
Columbia Lighthouse for the Blind
Ste 1103
1825 K St NW
Washington, DC 20006-1261
202-454-6400
FAX: 202-454-6401
e-mail: info@clb.org
clb.org

*Tony Cancelosi, President*

Dedicated to helping the blind or visually impaired population.

**8945 Library Users of America Newsletter**
American Council of the Blind
Suite 650
2200 Wilson Boulevard
Arlington, VA 22201-3354
202-467-5081
800-424-8666
FAX: 202-467-5085
e-mail: info@acb.org
www.acb.org

Published twice yearly, the newsletter contains much information about library services of particular interest to blind and visually impaired patrons, and is available in the following formats: Braille, audiocassette, large print and e-mail.

**8946 Light the Way**
Blind Children's Center
4120 Marathon St
Los Angeles, CA 90029-3584
323-664-2153
800-222-3567
FAX: 323-665-3828
e-mail: info@blindchildrenscenter.org
blindchildrenscenter.org

*Midge Horton, Executive Director*

Newsletter of the Blind Childrens Center, a family-centered agency which serves young children with visual impairments. The center-based and home-based services help the children to acquire skills and build their independence. The center utilizes its expertise and experience to serve families and professionals worldwide through support services, education and research.

**8947 Lighthouse Publication**
Chicago Lighthouse
1850 W Roosevelt Rd
Chicago, IL 60608-1200
312-666-1331
FAX: 312-243-8539
TTY:312-666-8874
e-mail: publications@chicagolighthouse.org
www.thechicagolighthouse.org

*Dr Janet Szlyk, Executive Director*

**8948 Lights On**
Fight for Sight
Ste 809
391 Park Ave S
New York, NY 10016-8806
212-679-6060
FAX: 212-679-4466
www.fightforsight.com

*Mary Prudden, Executive Director*

A newsletter published by Fight for Sight.

**8949 Long Cane News**
American Foundation for the Blind/AFB Press
Suite 1102
2 Penn Plaza
New York, NY 10121
212-502-7600
800-232-3044
FAX: 888-545-8331
e-mail: afborders@abdintl.com
www.afb.org

*Carl R. Augusto, President and CEO*
*SemiAnnual*

**8950 Magnifier**
Macular Degeneration Foundation
P.O.Box 531313
Henderson, NV 89053-1313
888-633-3937
www.eyesight.org

*Liz Trauernicht, President*
The Magnifier is the distributed without charge via email and by regular mail to those without access to the Internet. It features breaking news, clinical trails, clarifies recent reports in the media, announces new Internet resources and informs the public of important additions to the web site.

**8951 NAVH Update**
National Association of Visually Handicapped
111 E 59th St
New York, NY 1002-1202
212-821-9200
800-829-0500
FAX: 212-821-9707
e-mail: info@lighthouse.org
lighthouse.org/navh

*Mark G. Ackermann, President / CEO*
A newsletter published by the National Association of Visually Impaired. LightHouse acquired NAVH.

**8952 NBA Bulletin**
National Braille Association
Bldg. 1, Suite 202
95 Allens Creek Rd
Rochester, NY 14618-3252
585-427-8260
FAX: 585-427-0263
e-mail: nbaoffice@nationalbraille.org
www.nationalbraille.org

*David Shaffer, Executive Director*
*Dorothy Worthington, President*
Published quarterly and included int he price of the regular and student NBA membership.

**8953 NLS News**
Nat'l Lib Svc/Blind And Physically Handicapped
1291 Taylor St NW
Washington, DC 20011
202-707-5100
FAX: 202-707-0712
TTY:202-707-0744
e-mail: nls@loc.gov
www.loc.gov/nls

*Karen Keninger, Director*
Newsletter on current program developments.
*Quarterly*

**8954 NLS Newsletter**
Nat'l Lib Svc/Blind And Physically Handicapped
1291 Taylor St NW
Washington, DC 20011
202-707-5100
FAX: 202-707-0712
TTY:202-707-0744
e-mail: nls@loc.gov
www.loc.gov/nls

*Karen Keninger, Director*
Newsletter on the service's volunteer activities.
*Quarterly*

**8955 PBA News**
Prevent Blindness America
Ste 1700
211 W Wacker Dr
Chicago, IL 60606
800-331-2020
e-mail: info@preventblindness.org
www.preventblindness.org

*Hugh Parry, President & CEO*
Newsletter is filled with the information you need to protect your eyes, preserve your sight, and educate yourself about your own eye condition or that of a family member. Publication offered three times yearly.
*3 times yearly*

**8956 Planned Giving Department of Guide Dogs for the Blind**
Guide Dogs for the Blind
P.O.Box 151200
San Rafael, CA 94915-1200
415-499-4000
800-295-4050
FAX: 415-499-4035
guidedogs.com

*Paul A. Lopez, President and CEO*
A newsletter published by Guide Dogs for the Blind.

**8957 Playback**
Recording for the Blind & Dyslexic
Ste 100
3520 Executive Center Dr
Austin, TX 78731-1636
800-221-4792
FAX: 609-987-8116
e-mail: Custserv@LearningAlly.org
www.learningally.org/

*Andrew Friedman, President & CEO*
A publication dedicated to our unit's family of members, volunteers, supporters and staff. RFB&D is now Learning Ally.
*3x Year*

**8958 Quarterly Update**
National Association for Visually Handicapped
111 E 59th St
New York, NY 1002-1202
212-821-9200
800-829-0500
FAX: 212-821-9707
e-mail: info@lighthouse.org
lighthouse.org/navh

*Mark G. Ackermann, President / CEO*
Quarterly newsletter offering information on new products for the visually impaired, advances in medical treatments, new books available in the NAVH large print loan library and any new/updated booklets. Free. LightHouse acquired NAVH.

**8959 RP Messenger**
Texas Association of Retinitis Pigmentosa
P.O.Box 8388
Corpus Christi, TX 78468-8388
361-852-8515
FAX: 361-852-8515
e-mail: tarp@homebiz101.com
www.geocities.com

*Dorothy Steifel, Executive Director*
A bi-annual newsletter offering information on Retinitis Pigmentosa. *$15.00*
*BiAnnual*

**8960 SCENE**
Braille Institute
527 N Dale Ave
Anaheim, CA 92801
714-821-5000
800-272-4553
FAX: 714-527-7621
e-mail: oc@brailleinstitute.org
brailleinstitute.org

*Gene Mathiowetz, Director*
Offers information on the organization, question and answer column, articles on the newest technology and more for visually impaired persons.

**8961 STAR**
Special Technologies Alternative Resources
210 McMorran Blvd
Port Huron, MI 48060-4014
810-987-7323
877-987-7323
e-mail: star@sccl.lib.mi.us
www.sccl.lib.mi.us

*Stan Arnetti, Director*
A newsletter published by Special Technologies Alternative Resources.

**8962 Seeing Eye Guide**
The Seeing Eye
P.O.Box 375
10 Washington Valley Rd.
Morristown, NJ 7963-375
973-539-4425
FAX: 973-539-0922
e-mail: info@seeingeye.org
seeingeye.org

*James A. Kutsch, Jr., Ph.D., President & CEO*
A quarterly publication from Seeing Eye.
*Quarterly*

**8963 Shared Visions**
Vista Center for the Blind & Visually Impaired
413 Laurel St
Santa Cruz, CA 95060-4904
831-458-9766
800-705-2970
FAX: 831-426-6233
e-mail: information@vistacenter.org
doranblindcenter.org

*Pam Brandin, Executive Director*
A quarterly publication for Blind and Visually Impaired individuals from Vista Center for the Blind and Visually Impaired.

**8964 Sharing Solutions: A Newsletter for Support Groups**
Lighthouse International
111 E 59th St
New York, NY 10022-1202
212-821-9200
800-829-0500
FAX: 212-821-9707
e-mail: info@lighthouse.org
www.lighthouse.org

*Mark G. Ackermann, President / CEO*
A newsletter for members and leaders of support groups for older adults with impaired vision. The letter provides a forum for support groups members to network and share information, printed in a very large type format.

**8965 Sightings Newsletter**
Schepens Eye Research Institute
20 Staniford St
Boston, MA 02114-2508
617-912-0100
FAX: 617-912-0110
www.schepens.harvard.edu

*Michael Gilmore, Director*
Publication of prominent center for research on eye, vision, and blinding diseases; dedicated to research that improves the understanding, management, and prevention of eye diseases and visual deficiencies; fosters collaboration among its faculty members; trains young scientists and clinicians from around the world; promotes communication with scientists in allied fields; leader in the worldwide dispersion of basic scientific knowledge of vision.

**8966 Smith Kettlewell Rehabilitation Engineering Research Center**
2318 Fillmore St
San Francisco, CA 94115-1813
415-345-2000
FAX: 415-345-8455
e-mail: rerc@ski.org
ski.org/rerc

*Arthur Jampolsky, Director*
Reports on technology and devices for persons with visual impairments.

**8967 Student Advocate**
National Alliance of Blind Students NABS Liaison
Ste 1004
1155 15th St NW
Washington, DC 20005-2706
202-467-5081
800-424-8666
FAX: 202-467-5085
www.blindstudents.org

*Melanie Brunson, Executive Director*
A newsletter created by members of NABS and for any interested parties.

**8968 TBC Focus**
Chicago Public Library Talking Books Center
400 S State St
Chicago, IL 60605-1203
312-747-4300
800-757-4654
FAX: 312-747-1609
www.chipublib.org

*Karim Adib, Director*
Published quarterly by the Chicago Public Library Talking Book Center. Free of charge.
*4 pages Quarterly*

**8969 Talking Books Topics**
Nat'l Lib Svc/Blind And Physically Handicapped
1291 Taylor St NW
Washington, DC 20011
202-707-5100
FAX: 202-707-0712
TTY:202-707-0744
e-mail: nls@loc.gov
www.loc.gov/nls

*Karen Keninger, Director*
New recorded books and program news
*Bi-monthly*

**8970 Upstate Update**
New York State Talking Book & Braille Library
Empire State Plz
Albany, NY 12230-1
518-474-5935
800-342-3688
FAX: 518-486-1957
TTY: 518-474-7121
e-mail: tbbl@mail.nysed.gov
www.nysl.nysed.gov

*Peter Douglas, Editor*
Books on audio cassette, cassette players, braille books, summer reading programs, braille writer, magnifiers, closed-circuit T.V., large-print photocopier, cassette books and magazines, children's books on cassette, reference materials on blindness and other handicaps.
*4 pages Quarterly*

**8971 Visual Aids and Informational Material**
National Association for Visually Handicapped
111 E 59th St
New York, NY 1002-1202 212-821-9200
800-829-0500
FAX: 212-821-9707
e-mail: info@lighthouse.org
lighthouse.org/navh

*Mark G. Ackermann, President / CEO*
A complete listing of the visual aids NAVH carries such as magnifiers, talking clocks, large print playing cards, etc. LightHouse acquired NAVH. *$2.50*
*65 pages*

**8972 Voice**
Vermont Assn for the Blind & Visually Impaired
37 Elmwood Ave
Burlington, VT 05401-4347 802-863-1358
800-639-5861
FAX: 802-863-1481
vabvi.org

*Stephen P Pouliot, Manager*
The Voice is a newsletter published by Vermont Association for the Blind and Visually Impaired.

**8973 Voice of Vision**
GW Micro
Fort Wayne, IN 46825 260-489-3671
FAX: 260-489-2608
e-mail: sales@gwmicro.com
www.gwmicro.com

*Dan Weirich, Owner*
Offers product reviews, product announcements, tips for making systems or applications more accessible, or explanations of concepts of interest to any computer user or would-be computer user. This association newsletter is available in braille, in large print, on audio cassette and on 3.5 or 5.25 IBM format diskette.
*Quarterly*

## Non Print: Newsletters

**8974 Insight**
Eye Bank Association of America
Ste 1010
1015 18th St NW
Washington, DC 20036-5223 202-347-9882
FAX: 202-429-6036
e-mail: info@restoresight.org
www.restoresight.org

*Patricia Aiken-O'Neill Esq, President*
An electronic newsletter.

**8975 Listen Up**
Recording for the Blind & Dyslexic
20 Roszel Rd
Princeton, NJ 8540-6206 609-452-0606
866-732-3585
FAX: 609-520-7990
www.rfbd.org

*John Kelly, CEO*
RFB&D's bi-monthly electronic newsletter for members.

## Non Print: Video

**8976 Aging and Vision: Declarations of Independence**
American Foundation for the Blind/AFB Press
Suite 1102
2 Penn Plaza
New York, NY 10121 212-502-7600
800-232-3044
FAX: 888-545-8331
e-mail: afborders@abdintl.com
www.afb.org

*Carl R. Augusto, President and CEO*
A very personal look at five older people who have successfully coped with visual impairmant and continue to lead active, satisfying lives. Their stories are not only inspirational, but also provide practical, down-to-earth suggestions for adapting to vision loss later in life. 18 minute video tape. Also available in PAL, $52.95, 0-89128-276-9. *$42.95*
*VHS*
*ISBN 0-891282-20-3*

**8977 Blindness, A Family Matter**
American Foundation for the Blind/AFB Press
Suite 1102
2 Penn Plaza
New York, NY 10121 212-502-7600
800-232-3044
FAX: 888-545-8331
e-mail: afborders@abdintl.com
www.afb.org

*Carl R. Augusto, President and CEO*
A frank exploration of the effects of an individual's visual impairment on other members of the family and how those family members can play a positive role in the rehabilitation process. Features interviews with three families whose 'success stories' provide advice and encouragement, as well as interviews with newly blinded adults currently involved in a rehabilitation program. 23 minute video tape. Also available in PAL, $49.95, 0-89128-271-8. *$43.95*
*VHS*
*ISBN 0-891282-22-X*

**8978 Building Blocks: Foundations for Learning for Young Blind and Visually Impaired Children**
American Foundation for the Blind/AFB Press
Suite 1102
2 Penn Plaza
New York, NY 10121 212-502-7600
800-232-5463
FAX: 888-545-8331
e-mail: afbinfo@afb.net
www.afb.org

*Carl R. Augusto, President and CEO*
Presents the essential components of a successful early intervnetion program, including collaboration with family members, positive relationships between parents and professionals, public education, and attention to important programming components such as space exploration, braille readiness, orientation and mobility, play, cooking and music. Includes interviews with parents. Available in English or Spanish. 10 minute video tape. Also available in PAL, $33.95, 0-89128-268-8. *$26.95*
*VHS*
*ISBN 0-891282-14-9*

**8979 Choice Magazine Listening**
85 Channel Dr
Port Washington, NY 11050-2278 516-883-8280
888-724-6423
888-724-6423
FAX: 516-944-5849
e-mail: choicemag@aol.com
www.choicemagazinelistening.org

*Lois Miller, Manager*

A free audio anthology is available bi-monthly to visually impaired/physically disabled or dislexic persons nationwide. Playable on the special free 4-track cassette playback equipment which is provided by the Library of Congress through the National Library Service. Each issue features eight hours of unabridged magazine articles, short stories, poetry and media selections from over 100 sources. College level and older. Bimonthly distribution.
*Bi-Monthly*

**8980 Juggler**
Beacon Press
25 Beacon St
Boston, MA 02108-2824 617-742-2110
FAX: 617-723-3097
beacon.org

*Helen Atwan, Executive Director*
Andre was the young son of a wealthy, early Quebec fur trader. Because he was almost totally blind, he was overly protected by his family, and his movement outside his home was very limited.
*Film*

**8981 Let's Eat Video**
Blind Children's Center
4120 Marathon St
Los Angeles, CA 90029-3584 323-664-2153
800-222-3567
FAX: 323-665-3828
e-mail: info@blindchildrenscenter.org
blindchildrenscenter.org

*Midge Horton, Executive Director*
Babies and toddlers with visual impairments lack one major avenue of exploration, and this significantly infulences their awareness, perceptions, and anticipation of the food which is presented to them. *$35.00*
*VHS/DVD*

**8982 Look Out for Annie**
Lighthouse International
111 E 59th St
New York, NY 10022-1202 212-821-9200
800-829-0500
FAX: 212-821-9706
e-mail: info@lighthouse.org
www.lighthouse.org

*Mark G. Ackermann, President / CEO*
Depicts an older woman coping with her vision loss. It focuses on the emotional issues surrounding vision loss and conveys the idea that both the person with the vision disorder and their family and friends will need to make adjustments. *$25.00*
*Video*

**8983 Not Without Sight**
American Foundation for the Blind/AFB Press
P.O.Box 1020
Sewickley, PA 15143-920 412-741-1142
800-232-3044
FAX: 412-741-0609
e-mail: afborders@abdintl.com
www.afb.org

*Carl R Augusto, President/CEO*
*Tracy Charlovich, Css*
This video describes the major types of visual impairment and their causes and effects on vision, while camera simulations approximate what people with each impairmant actually see. Also demonstrates how people with low vision make the best use of the vision they have. 20 minute video tape, $49.95. *$42.95*
*VHS 17 min*
*ISBN 0-891282-27-3*

**8984 Out of Left Field**
American Foundation for the Blind/AFB Press
Suite 1102
2 Penn Plaza
New York, NY 10121 212-502-7600
800-232-5463
FAX: 888-545-8331
e-mail: afbinfo@afb.net
afb.org

*Carl R. Augusto, President and CEO*
Illustrates how youngsters who are blind or visually impaired integrated with their sighted peers in a variety of recreational and athletic activities. 17 minute video tape. Also available in PAL, $33.95, 0-89128-270-X. *$29.95*
*VHS 17 minutes*
*ISBN 0-891282-28-0*

**8985 See What I'm Saying**
Fanlight Productions
21st Floor
32 Court Street
Brooklyn, NY 11201 617-469-4999
800-937-4113
FAX: 617-469-3379
e-mail: info@fanlight.com
www.fanlight.com

*Ben Achtenberg, Owner*
The documentary follows Patricia, who is deaf and from a Spanish-speaking family, through her first year at the Kendall Demonstration Elementary School of Gallaudet University.
*VHS/DVD*

**8986 See for Yourself**
Lighthouse International
111 E 59th St
New York, NY 10022-1202 212-821-9200
800-829-0500
FAX: 212-821-9706
e-mail: info@lighthouse.org
www.lighthouse.org

*Mark G. Ackermann, President / CEO*
This video features older adults with impaired vision who have been helped by vision rehabilitation. *$50.00*

**8987 Shape Up 'n Sign**
Harris Communications
15155 Technology Dr
Eden Prairie, MN 55344-2273 952-906-1180
800-825-6758
FAX: 952-906-1099
e-mail: info@harriscomm.com

*Robert Harris, Owner*
An aerobic exercise tape introducing the basic sign language for deaf and hearing children ages six to ten. *$29.95*
*30 Minutes DVD*

**8988 Sight by Touch**
Landmark Media
3450 Slade Run Dr
Falls Church, VA 22042-3940 703-241-2030
800-342-4336
FAX: 703-536-9540
e-mail: info@landmarkmedia.com
landmarkmedia.com

*Michael Hartogs, President*
*Peter Hartogs, VP New Business & Development*
This video features the life and importance of Louis Braille. Vision-impaired performers and teachers demonstrate how Braille has benefitted their lives, and how improvements are constantly being made. *$195.00*
*Video*

**8989 Taping for the Blind**
3935 Essex Ln
Houston, TX 77027-5113
713-622-2767
FAX: 713-622-2772
e-mail: taping@hal-pc.org
www.tapingfortheblind.org

*Krista Moser, Executive Director*
An independent non profit educational organization funded by corporations, listeners and individuals, with a mission to turn sight into sound, enriching the lives of individuals with visual, physical and learning disabilities. Founded in 1967 to read materials not availiable through other sources onto standard audio cassettes in our custom recording division. In 1978, Houston Taping fFor The Blind signed on the air. Reading several dozen popular magazines and best selling books on the air.

**8990 We Can Do it Together!**
American Foundation for the Blind/AFB Press
Suite 1102
2 Penn Plaza
New York, NY 10121
212-502-7600
800-232-5463
FAX: 888-545-8331
e-mail: afbinfo@afb.net
afb.org

*Carl R. Augusto, President and CEO*
This video illustrates a transdisciplinary team orientation and mobility program for students with severe visual and multiple impairments, covering both adapted communication systems used to teach mobility skills and basic indoor mobility in the school. For mobility instructors, administrators, teachers of the visually and severely handicapped, occupational, physical and speech therapists and parents. Discussion guide included. 10 minute video tape. Also available in PAL, $33.95, 0-89128-267-X.
*$26.95*
*VHS*
*ISBN 0-891282-13-0*

## Sports

**8991 American Blind Bowling Association**
1209 Somerset Rd
Raleigh, NC 27610-1136
919-755-0700
www.americanblindbowlers.com

*James Benton, President*
Promotes blind bowling throughout the US and Canada by sanctioning blind bowling leagues and conducting a National Tournament. Current membership exceeds 2,000 people in the United States and Canada.

**8992 Basketball: Beeping Foam**
Maxi Aids
42 Executive Blvd
Farmingdale, NY 11735-4710
631-752-0521
800-522-6294
FAX: 631-752-0689
TTY: 631-752-0738
e-mail: sales@maxiaids.com
www.maxiaids.com

*Elliot Zaretsky, President*
This sound making basketball enables the visually impaired to play basketball or other games. *$29.95*

**8993 Blind Outdoor Leisure Development**
P.O.Box 6639
Snowmass Village, CO 81615-6639
970-923-7464
FAX: 970-923-7338
e-mail: possibilities@challengeaspen.com
challengeaspen.org

*Houston Cowan, CEO*
Outdoor recreation for the blind. Winter program of skiing with guides plus numerous summer programs for the visually impaired.

**8994 Challenge Golf**
otivation Media
1245 Milwaukee Ave
Glenview, IL 60025-2400
847-827-9057
FAX: 847-297-6829

*Dorothy Bauer, Coordinator*
A plain-language video, Challenge Golf is packed with information for beginners or veterans. Peter Longo covers 5 handicaps (one-arm, one-leg, in a seated position, blind, and arthritis) clearly and concisely, on how to play golf with a physical disability. In color, complete with special effects, graphs and real handicapped golfers at play. *$38.95*
*Home Edition*

**8995 US Association of Blind Athletes**
1 Olympic Plaza
Colorado Springs, CO 80909
719-630-0422
FAX: 719-630-0616
e-mail: media@usaba.org
www.usaba.org

*Mark A. Lucas, MS, Executive Director*
Provides athletic opportunities and training in competitive sports for visually impaired and blind individuals throughout the US Competitions indlcude local, regional and national events, internation events, and the Winter and Summer Paralympic Games.

**8996 United States Blind Golf Association**
3094 Shamrock St N
Tallahassee, FL 32309-2735
864-987-9688
e-mail: roger.matas@internationalblindgolf.org
www.blindgolf.com

*Phil Blackwell, President*
*Bruce Hooper, VP*
Provides blind and vision impaired gold tournaments to members.

## Support Groups

**8997 Braille Institute Orange County Center**
527 N Dale Ave
Anaheim, CA 92801
714-821-5000
800-272-4553
FAX: 714-527-7621
e-mail: oc@brailleinstitute.org
brailleinstitute.org

*Gene Mathiowetz, Director*
Offers services, publications, information and programs free of charge to blind and visually impaired persons of all ages.

**8998 Consumer and Patient Information Hotline**
Prevent Blindness America
211 W Wacker Dr
Ste 1700
Chicago, IL 60606
800-331-2020
e-mail: info@preventblindness.org
preventblindness.org

*Hugh Parry, President & CEO*
A toll-free line offering free information on a broad range of vision, eye health and safety topics including sports eye safety, diabetic retinopathy, glaucoma, cataracts, children's eye disorders and more.

**8999 Department of Ophthalmology Information Line**
Eye & Ear Infirmary
1855 W Taylor St
Chicago, IL 60612-7242
312-996-6590
FAX: 312-996-7770
e-mail: eyeweb@uic.edu
www.uic.edu

*Jospeh White, President*
Offers eye clinic and physician referrals to persons suffering from vision disorders as well as offers emergency information.

**9000 Lighthouse International Information and Resource Service**
111 E 59th St
New York, NY 10022-1202
212-821-9200
800-829-0500
FAX: 212-821-9707
e-mail: info@lighthouse.org
lighthouse.org

*Mark G. Ackermann, President / CEO*
Provides information about eye diseases, low vision, age-related vision loss, adaptive technology, optical devices, large print and braille publishers, helps people find low vision services, vision rehabilitation services, and support groups across the U.S.; offers large selection of consumer products.

**9001 National Association for Parents of Children with Visual Impairments (NAPVI)**
P.O.Box 317
Watertown, MA 02471-317
617-972-7441
800-562-6265
FAX: 617-972-7444
e-mail: napvi@perkins.org
www.napvi.org

*Susan LaVenture, Executive Director*
In 1979, a group of parents responding to their own needs founded NAPVI, the National Association for Parents of the Visually Impaired, Inc. Never before was there a self-help organization specific to the needs of families of children with visual impairments. Since that time, NAPVI has grown and helped families across the US and in other countries.

**9002 VUE: Vision Use in Employment**
Carroll Center for the Blind
770 Centre St
Newton, MA 02458-2530
617-969-6200
800-852-3131
FAX: 617-969-6204
e-mail: info@carrol.org
www.carroll.org

*Rachel Rosenbaum, President*
Provides engineering solutions plus training to help people keep jobs despite their vision loss.

**9003 Washington Connection**
American Council of the Blind
Suite 650
2200 Wilson Boulevard
Arlington, VA 22201-3354
202-467-5081
800-424-8666
FAX: 202-467-5085
e-mail: info@acb.org
acb.org
Coverage of issues affecting blind people via legislative information, participates in law-making, legislative training seminars and networking of support resources across the US.

## A

## B

## C

## D

## F

## G

## H

## I

## J



## K

## M

## N

## O

## P

## Q



## R

## S

## T

## U

## W

## X



## Y



## Z

## Alabama



## Alaska



## Arizona



## Arkansas



## BC



## California

## Colorado



## Connecticut



## Delaware



## District of Columbia

## Florida



## Georgia

## Hawaii



## Idaho



## Illinois

## Indiana



## Iowa



## Kansas

## Kentucky



## Louisiana



## MB



## Maine



## Maryland



## Massachusetts

## Michigan



## Minnesota

## Mississippi



## Missouri



## Montana



## Nebraska



## Nevada



## New Hampshire

## New Jersey



## New Mexico



## New York

## North Carolina



## North Dakota

## Rhode Island



## South Carolina



## South Dakota



## Tennessee

## Texas



## Utah



## Vermont



## Virginia

## Washington



## West Virginia



## Wisconsin



## Wyoming

## AIDS



## Accupressure



## Aging

## Alternative Therapies



## Amputation



## Amythrophic Lateral Sclerosis



## Art & Music Therapies

## Arthritis



## Asthma



## Attention Deficit Disorder

## Autism



## Behavioral Disorders



## Birth Defects



## Blind/Deaf



## Brain Injuries



## Cancer

## Cerebral Palsy



## Chiropractics



## Chronic Disabilities



## Cleft Palate



## Cognitive Disorders



## Cystic Fibrosis



## Dental Issues



## Depression



## Developmental Disabilities

## Diabetes



## Diet & Nutrition



## Down Syndrome



## Dyslexia

## Education & Counseling



## Emergency Alert



## Environmental Disorders



## Epilepsy



## Head & Neck Injuries



## Hearing Impairments

## Hemophilia



## Herbal Medicine



## Human Interaction Disabilities



## Immune Deficiencies



## Incontinence



## Language Disorders



## Learning Disabilities

## Lowe's Syndrome



## Lung Disorders



## Massage Therapy



## Mental Disabilities



## Mental Retardation

## Multiple Disabilities



## Multiple Sclerosis

## Muscular Dystrophy



## Neurological Impairments



## Obesity



## Orthopedical Disabilities



## Pain Management



## Parkinson Disease



## Pediatric Issues



## Phenylketonuria



## Physical Disabilities

### Polio



### Prader-Willi Syndrome



### Rare Disabilities



### Respiratory Disorders



### Riding Programs



### Severe Disabilites



### Sexual Abuse & Related Conditions



### Sjogren's Syndrome



### Speech Disorders

## Spina Bifida



## Spinal Cord Injuries



## Stroke



## Theater & Dance Therapies



## Tinnitus



## Tourette Syndrome



## Visual Impairments

## Women